ANNUAL REGISTER OF
GRANT SUPPORT™
A DIRECTORY OF FUNDING SOURCES

Annual Register of Grant Support™
55th Edition

Publisher
Thomas H. Hogan

Director, ITI Reference Group
Owen O'Donnell

Managing Editor
Debra James

Consulting Editor
Stephen L. Torpie

ANNUAL REGISTER OF
GRANT SUPPORT™
A DIRECTORY OF FUNDING SOURCES

55th EDITION | 2022

Published by

Information Today, Inc.
143 Old Marlton Pike
Medford, NJ 08055-8750
Phone: (609) 654-6266
Fax: (609) 654-4309
E-mail (Orders): **custserv@infotoday.com**
Web site: http://www.infotoday.com

ISSN 0066-4049
ISBN 978-1-57387-575-2
Library of Congress Catalog Card Number: 69-18307

Information Today, Inc.
143 Old Marlton Pike
Medford, NJ 08055-8750
Phone: 800-300-9868 (Customer Service)
       800-409-4929 (Editorial)
Fax: 609-654-6098
E-mail (orders): custserv@infotoday.com
Web Site: www.infotoday.com

Printed and bound in the United States of America

US $399.50

ISBN 13: 978-1-57387-575-2

39950>

9 781573 875752

Contents

PREFACE..vii

INTRODUCTION..ix

KEY TO ENTRY INFORMATION..xiv

NEW LISTINGS IN 2022 EDITION..xvii

MULTIPLE SPECIAL PURPOSE..1

HUMANITIES..99

    Architecture...125

    Arts (multiple disciplines)..131

        Performing Arts 163

        Fine Arts..169

    History..178

    Languages...203

    Literature..208

    Museums and Libraries...222

    Music...233

    Religion and Theology..248

INTERNATIONAL AFFAIRS AND AREA STUDIES....................................257

    International Studies and Research Abroad...273

    Programs for Foreign Scholars...303

    Technical Assistance and Cooperative Research...307

SPECIAL POPULATIONS..309

    African-American...329

    Native American..333

    Spanish-speaking...340

    Women..341

URBAN AND REGIONAL AFFAIRS...355

    Children and Youth...357

    Community Development and Services...371

    Crime Prevention..439

    Public Health...441

    Social Welfare..455

EDUCATION...469

    Educational Projects and Research (general)..471

    Elementary and Secondary Education..490

    Higher Education Projects and Research...495

    Scholar Aid Programs (all disciplines)..504

Continued

SCIENCES (multiple disciplines)............555

SOCIAL SCIENCES............573
   Business and Economics............588
   Communications............597
   Labor............611
   Law............612
   Political Science............617
   Sociology and Anthropology............627

PHYSICAL SCIENCES............631
   Astronomy and Aerospace Science............637
   Chemistry............641
   Earth Sciences............645
   Mathematics............651
   Physics............654

LIFE SCIENCES............657
   Agriculture, Land Resources, Rural Development............661
   Biology............670
   Environment............678
   Medicine (multiple disciplines)............691
   Allergy, Immunology, Infectious Diseases............724
   Dentistry............725
   Internal Medicine............729
      Cardiovascular and Pulmonary............733
      Metabolism, Gastroenterology, Nephrology............742
      Oncology............753
      Rheumatology............762
   Neurology............762
   Nursing............773
   Obstetrics and Gynecology............778
   Ophthalmology and Otolaryngology............780
   Osteopathy............789
   Pediatrics............790
   Pharmacology............792
   Physical Medicine and Rehabilitation............795
   Psychiatry, Psychology, Mental Health............800

TECHNOLOGY AND INDUSTRY............811
   Aeronautics and Astronautics............819
   Engineering............823
   Home Economics and Nutrition............836
   Mining and Metallurgy............840

INDEXES............843
   Entry Listing by Chapter............844
   Subject Index............845
   Organization and Program Index............861
   Geographical Index............925
   Personnel Index............939

Preface

Now in its 55th edition, the *Annual Register of Grant Support™: A Directory of Funding Sources* has achieved a deserved reputation as an authoritative standard reference source on financial support. Known and relied upon by academic scholars and researchers, *Grant Support* also responds to the needs of those in the fields of business, civic improvement, and social welfare. Recognized for its value to the individual, *Grant Support* assists hospitals, arts organizations, community service groups, medical research facilities, and other institutional applicants as well.

The 2022 edition includes details of 2,425 grant support programs of government agencies, public and private foundations, corporations, community trusts, unions, educational and professional associations, and special interest organizations. These organizations support a total of 3,845 grant programs and cover a broad spectrum of interests from academic and scientific research, project development, travel and exchange programs, and publication support to equipment and construction grants, in-service training, and competitive awards and prizes in a variety of fields. Please see the "Key to entry information" and associated definitions on pages xiv and xv. This feature illustrates a sample listing with all the data elements defined.

Grant Support attempts to be as comprehensive as possible by including the following forms of financial aid: programs that offer non-repayable financial assistance directly to the grantee or indirectly through payment to the sponsoring institution; programs that accept applicants from the United States or Canada or directly benefit the United States or Canada; study grants and fellowships aimed principally though not exclusively at the graduate or postgraduate levels; grants for construction, facilities, or project costs for education, medical research, health care, civic improvement, etc.; and programs donating consulting services in lieu of a direct monetary grant.

Funding sources are given the opportunity annually to update entry data. Staff research continues to within weeks of *Grant Support*'s publication date to assure information is as current and complete as possible and to identify new funding sources for inclusion. Essential programs for which no updated information has been returned are included, either as they appeared in the last edition, revised where possible, or compiled entirely through secondary research.

Support programs are divided into eleven major areas, further subdivided into more specific subject fields. Each entry contained in *Grant Support* has been placed in the section that reflects its principal interest. If program interests equally emphasize diverse fields, such as communications and business and economics, one full entry and a cross-reference will appear in the respective sections. Similarly, a program for minority political scientists will appear in either "Special Populations" or "Political Science," with a cross-reference in the appropriate section. However, organizations with broad support purposes or interests in three or more well-defined areas are listed in the "Multiple Special Purpose" section.

Four helpful indexes conclude the volume: Subject, Organization and Program, Geographic, and Personnel. Please note: *References in each index point to the entry number visible in the listing—not to a page number.*

In the Subject Index, each grant has been indexed in terms of the specific areas to which it may be applied (e.g., Cartography, Mathematics), the type of grant (e.g., Medical Research, Theology), and the individuals or organizations eligible for support, if limitations are specified (e.g., Religious Institutions, Women). The Organization and Program Index lists grant programs in upper/lower case and funding organizations in all upper case. Programs are also listed following the organizations that sponsor them. The Geographic Index groups grantmaking organizations according to the state or country in which they are located. In the Personnel Index, officers of the organizations, trustees, directors, and awards committee members are listed with their program entry number.

While consulting the Subject Index, should the reader wish to know in which chapter a particular entry appears, he or she may consult the Emtry Listing by Chapter Index, a one page outline that precedes the Subject Index.

The editorial staff of *Annual Register of Grant Support* strives continually to provide the professional community with the most comprehensive information on existing forms of financial aid from as wide a variety of sources as possible. The staff urges the users of this edition to inform us of any corrections or additions to existing entries and of funding sources not included, and cordially invites suggestions for improvement of future editions.

Introduction

In the United States today, the support of human services through grants, awards, fellowships, and private gifts is a multibillion-dollar enterprise. Private foundations, corporations, individuals, charitable organizations, and agencies gave an estimated $471.44 billion to charity in 2020, an increase of 5.1 percent compared with the revised estimate of $448.66 billion given in 2019, according to the Giving USA Foundation.

Of the total $471.44 billion given in 2020, $324.10 billion came from individuals and accounts for 69 percent of all estimated giving. Grants from foundations, excluding those affiliated with business enterprises, totalled $88.55 billion, an increase of 17.0 percent. Gifts received through bequests increased an estimated 10.3 percent to $41.91 billion; corporations contributed $16.88 billion, a decrease of 6.1 percent.

When total charitable giving is analyzed by recipient fields, religion received the largest share of 2020 dollars— $131.08 billion—followed by education ($71.34 billion); human services ($65.14 billion); foundations ($58.17 billion); public society benefit ($48.00 billion); health ($42.12 billion); international affairs ($25.89 billion); arts, culture, and humanities ($19.47 billion); environment and animals ($16.14 billion); and individuals ($16.22 billion).

The entries listed in this edition of *Annual Register of Grant Support*™ represent billions of dollars in financial assistance to potential grant seekers.

Part of the success in using the *Annual Register of Grant Support*™ will depend on an understanding of the various types of grantmaking entities, how they differ in their objectives and grantmaking procedures, what they look for in the grant applicant, and how they are approached. It is hoped that the following descriptions of grant supporting organizations will increase the usability of *Grant Support* to the potential grant seeker.

PRIVATE FOUNDATIONS

Probably no area of philanthropy is so misunderstood and misused as that of private foundations. According to studies, as many as 80 percent of all applications to private foundations are incorrect, inappropriate, or misdirected. While at least part of the blame for this error must be attributed to private foundations themselves, grant seekers often compound the error by tending to lump all private foundations together as if they shared a common purpose.

Not only do private foundations differ greatly from public funding sources, but there is a wide diversity among private foundations themselves. What may be an appropriate application to The Ford Foundation, for example, may be totally inappropriate to the San Francisco Foundation.

There are more than 75,000 grantmaking foundations in the United States. The reason that an approximate figure must

be used is that the federal government defines private foundations more by exclusion than by anything else. If an organization cannot qualify as a charitable, religious, educational, scientific, or governmental organization, it may be classified as a private foundation even if it has never made a grant nor intends to make one. Potential grant seekers should be aware that the mere use of the word "foundation" in the title of an organization is not evidence that the organization will make grants.

Of particular interest to the potential grant seeker is a requirement that every private foundation with assets of $5,000 or more (virtually all of them) must submit an annual report that is available for public inspection. These annual reports, printed on special Internal Revenue Service form 990-PF (Private Foundation), include the names and addresses of all principal officers of the foundation, the total assets and investments of the foundation and, most important, a complete listing of every grant made during the year of record. Users of *Grant Support* may wish to review selected 990-PFs of those foundations included in this edition in order to supplement information on current grants.

These 990-PF forms may be obtained directly from the private foundations themselves, or they may be found in over 400 Foundation Center Funding Information Network locations. To obtain a list of participating Network organizations near you, visit the Foundation Center web site at: http://fconline.foundationcenter.org.

A substantial number of private foundations publish their own annual reports, over and above the 990-PF requirement mentioned earlier. Copies of these annual reports may be obtained by writing the foundation directly.

TYPES OF FOUNDATIONS

There are certain aspects common to all private foundations in the United States. However, foundations can be broken down into five types, which will assist the grant seeker in understanding their current objectives and grant distribution patterns.

1. National Foundations

Most of the foundations listed in Grant Support are national foundations, meaning that they are not limited to any geographic area in their grant support. National foundations are usually quite large, with assets of $25 million or more. They include all the better-known foundations, such as The Ford Foundation, the Lilly Endowment, The Rockefeller Foundation, and the Carnegie Corporation of New York. Because national foundations may make grants anywhere in the country, it is important to remember that these foundations are usually more attracted to programs and proposals with national, or at least regional, implications. Most of the national foundations are staffed with professional grantmakers, publish their own annual reports, and often have well-defined philanthropic goals.

While national foundations are large enough to fund projects of almost any size—and have been known to make grants of a million dollars or more—it should be remembered that competition for these national foundation grants is extremely fierce. The Ford Foundation, for example, will receive as many as 30,000 proposals every year and will fund only about 2,000.

2. Special-Interest Foundations

Many foundations listed in this edition of *Grant Support* devote their entire grant efforts to programs within a single field of interest. These special-interest foundations, just as the national foundations, often make grants without any geographic limitations so long as the projects relate to the specific areas. Special-interest foundations range from the massive Robert Wood Johnson Foundation (health) to the Joseph P. Kennedy Foundation (mental retardation) to those supporting research on a single disease.

Some of the larger special-interest foundations employ staff whose purpose is not only to review grants but to stay abreast of information being gathered about that special field of interest. Potential grant seekers, then, should consider special-interest foundations as a potential source of information about a given subject as well as a potential source of funds.

3. Corporate Foundations

During the 1950s, many major corporations created private foundations to serve as the corporate philanthropic arm, although the Tax Reform Act of 1969 greatly slowed the increase in their number. The ExxonMobil Foundation, Inc. is an example. Readers should be alerted to the fact that while many foundations carry names of large corporations, they are not corporate foundations. The Ford Foundation, for example, is not a corporate foundation; it was created by the Ford family.

Most corporate foundations, while "independent," are very much creatures of the corporations that founded them and fund them. Corporate foundations will, therefore, often be more receptive to proposals that are in line with their corporate interest. Historically, corporate foundations more often have made grants in the fields of education, federated giving (United Way, etc.), minority enterprises, and local social services that demonstrate a benefit to the company employees as well as the community at large. Most corporate foundations will have relatively small assets in comparison with the amount of grants. This is because once the money has moved from the corporation to the corporate foundation, it can never go back to the corporation. Usually corporations will keep only enough funds in the corporate foundation to sustain the foundation's grant efforts without harming the corporate financial position.

4. Family Foundations

By far, the largest number of private foundations are family foundations. They range in assets from hundreds of millions of dollars, such as those of the several Rockefeller Foundations, to a few thousand dollars.

The grant support pattern of family foundations is very often a personal matter. Often the family foundation will be controlled entirely by family members, and even when these family members have died, the family foundation will often continue to reflect their wishes. Unlike special interest foundations, family foundations seldom have set fields of interest. Grants more probably will reflect areas of current family interest rather than any recognizable pattern of traditional philanthropy.

Most family foundations are small, and few will have staff or guidelines for submitting proposals. A vast majority of family foundations limit their grants to the city or locality in which the family resides and accumulated its wealth. Unlike national foundations, family foundations are best approached as if they were individual donors, not private foundations.

Because most family foundations are relatively small and have such a limited geographic giving pattern, few are included in *Grant Support*. These foundations should be explored, however, for modest gifts of a local nature. While the average gift of small family foundations is less than $5,000, the sheer volume of family foundations makes them an important factor in grant support.

5. Community Foundations

In a strictly legal sense, community foundations are not really foundations at all but, rather, public charities. Community foundations maintain this favored tax status by collecting money from the public and directing grants within the community for which they are named. Because community foundations are not private foundations, they have no minimum giving requirements and pay no excise taxes on their net investment income. This is partly responsible for their rapid growth during the past decade, for hundreds of foundations (including some with assets in the many millions of dollars) have given all their money to community foundations.

A number of the larger community foundations, such as The Cleveland Foundation and The New York Community Trust, are listed in *Grant Support*. It is easy to distinguish a community foundation, for it will always be named for the community it serves. The San Francisco Foundation serves San Francisco, The Chicago Community Trust serves Chicago, and so forth. Readers of *Grant Support* should bear in mind that community foundations cannot, by law, make grants outside the geographic regions they serve. The San Francisco Foundation, for example, is not likely to fund a project in Texas, regardless of the merit of the proposal.

For more information about the existence of a community foundation in a given city, readers may wish to consult the local trust bank in that city. (Information can also be obtained by writing the Council on Foundations, Inc., 2121 Crystal Drive, Suite 700, Arlington, VA 22202 or via their web site at *www.cof.org*.)

CORPORATE GIVING

Although the practice of corporations making grants and gifts to charity is now largely accepted, it was not until 1935 that the Internal Revenue Service allowed a charitable deduction for corporate gifts. In 1982, changes in the tax law enhanced the value of donations of company products, and increased the deduction of corporate contributions from 5 to 10 percent of net income. Yet while this modest federal government incentive has spurred corporate philanthropy, approximately only one-third of all corporations in the United States make corporate gifts. Corporations made the largest percentage of their donations to education over the last several years, with health and human services receiving the second largest amounts. Cultural and arts groups, civic and community activities, and various other recipients received the balance of corporate dollars. Most corporations do not have professional grant reviewers but will often have grant guidelines, specific philanthropic objectives, or well-defined procedures for grant applicants.

An important consideration when approaching corporations is to introduce a benefit, either directly to the company or indirectly through its employees, that grant support can make. A proposal for support of an alcoholism program may be received more readily if the corporation feels alcoholism is a problem among its employees.

Many corporations are willing to provide volunteer service and specific expert assistance as well as money. Corporations also make in-kind contributions, such as free printing, equipment, etc., and will sometimes match gifts made by individual employees.

FEDERATED GIVING

Grant Support lists many grant opportunities from funding sources which, though neither foundations nor corporations, provide many millions of dollars of grant support every year. These funding sources can best be described as federated giving organizations, in that a number of small organizations combine their funding efforts for maximum effect.

The largest and best known federated agency is, of course, United Way. Most United Ways, however, do not make grants so much as they support existing agencies.

There are a number of other federated agencies that do make grants. The Catholic Campaign for Human Development, which is the federated arm of the Catholic Church in America, provides millions in grant support annually. Other federated agencies include the United Negro College Fund, the United Jewish Appeal, and the American Association of University Women.

PUBLIC MONEY

Government funding is as complex and confusing as it is big, and the special terms and language of government grants make the subject seem more confusing than it really is. An understanding of the various types of grants and some of the most often used terms may help readers break through the perplexing language of government grants.

Types of Grants

The federal government makes grants in many forms, some of which allow the independent grant seeker an opportunity to be funded, and some which do not. Below are some of the most common types of government grants.

Block Grants: Sometimes called "bloc" grants, these are made from the federal government directly to states or local units of government, such as counties and municipalities. The grant most often comes to the state in a "block," and the state may spend the money as it wishes as long as the funds are being used to fulfill the basic purposes for which they were authorized. Many of the more recent federal grants under what is called "new federalism" have been block grants such as the Housing and Community Development Act money, the Comprehensive Employment and Training Act money, and funds to support programs for older Americans. Under the rules of most block grants, the state must submit an annual "state plan" to the federal government explaining how and where the funds are to be used. This state plan is public information, and potential grant seekers may wish to review it for programs under which they wish to seek grant support. One important aspect of block grants is that while the money is federal, the authority to spend it is local, and the recipients of block grant funds are allowed great flexibility in how they use the money.

Capitation Grants: Stemming from a concept of providing funds per capita of service, capitation grants are awarded based on the actual number of people served, rather than on the task to be performed. For example, an organization may be providing housing for runaway youths. This organization's annual budget is $100,000, and last year it provided housing for 1,000 youths. A capitation grant would provide $100 for each youth housed during the coming year ($100,000 divided by 1,000 youths). Capitation grants are most often used for training grants where payment is based on enrollment, rather than training outcome.

Categorical Grants: Simply stated, funds under a certain "category" must be expended within a certain field of interest, such as mental health, services for the handicapped, or maternity and child care. Although the number of categorical grants provided by the federal government has decreased in the past few years because of an increase in block grants, there are still more than 850 federal grant programs active within the federal government.

Construction Grants: Unless specifically stated, most federal grants will not provide funds for capital purposes, requiring instead that the grantee rent or lease the appropriate facility. Special construction grants, especially in the fields of health and mental health, have been made in the past for construction, renovation, and expansion. Many more important construction grant programs have been severely cut in the past few years, however, and it appears that the federal government is less enamored with this type of grant than in the past.

Demonstration Grants: Among the most common types of grants made in the human services field, demonstration grants, as opposed to basic research grants, are made to agencies in order to illustrate the effectiveness of a certain procedure or methodology, while at the same time providing a direct benefit to a group of clients. Unlike research grants, there is usually a large amount of evidence that the methodology to be demonstrated should prove effective before the grant is awarded. Often, demonstration grants are the second step of research grants, attempting to show that the success of a research grant may have greater applicability or a wider target population than originally envisioned.

Formula Grants: Not so much a type of grant as a method of determining the amount of funds to be made available, formula grants are based most often on the population, income, taxation, and special need of a given area.

The formula for grants will be written into the legislation or regulation that established the fund. The capitation grant mentioned earlier is one type of formula.

Matching Grants: Often confused with formula grants in that there is usually a "formula" for establishing the matching grant requirement, a matching grant means that the agency or individual who is receiving the grant guarantees to provide a certain portion of the total grant funds from sources other than the government. This "match" may be as small as one percent to as much as 50 percent with organizations such as the National Endowment for the Arts and National Endowment for the Humanities. Often there is a "sliding match" requirement, which means that the agency receiving the grant will provide a greater share of the total costs in the second and subsequent years of the award. Matching requirements may be for a "hard" or "soft" match. A "hard" match means that actual dollar matches must be secured, whereas a "soft" match allowed for such donated services as volunteer time and goods or equipment to be counted in lieu of "hard" dollars.

Project Grants: The grants allow the granting agency, usually a department or agency of the federal government, to determine funding based solely on the merits of the project of an individual or organization, rather than by formula requirements mentioned earlier. This is one of the most flexible types of grants in that the granting agency may have complete control in selecting the project, the grant recipient, and the amount of the award.

Research Grants: As opposed to demonstration grants and project grants, research grants are provided to test theories and hypotheses, develop or interpret new information, or revise accepted theories without the requirement that some benefit be immediately passed on to the clients. In fact the term "client" is often replaced with the term "subject" in research grants. There are two types, basic and applied. Basic research, which enjoyed great favor in the 1960s, has found funding harder to obtain lately, while applied research funds have continued to grow, especially in environmental programs.

Staffing Grants: As the phrase implies, these grants are provided for support of salaries of professional and technical staff members, plus in-service training in many cases. Most staffing grants come with a sliding match requirement.

Training Grants: These are awarded to organizations, corporations, or individuals to support the costs of training existing staff, students, or potential staff in the techniques or procedures needed to develop skills in a particular field, such as nursing, paramedical training and legal aid.

Seeking Governmental Sources

In addition to the *Annual Register of Grant Support*™, there are several places potential grant seekers can look for information about federal grants.

Catalog of Federal Domestic Assistance

The most important index for identifying federal resources can be found on *beta.SAM.gov* (formerly the *Catalog of Federal Domestic Assistance* whose web site, www.cfda.gov, has since been retired). The resources on *beta.SAM.gov* give you access to a database of all Federal programs available to state and local governments (including the District of Columbia); federally-recognized Native American tribal governments; territories (and possessions) of the United States; domestic public, quasi-public, and private profit and nonprofit organizations and institutions; specialized groups; and individuals.

Federal Register

Another valuable source is the *Federal Register*, available at *www.federalregister.gov*. Published by the Office of the Federal Register, National Archives and Records Administration (NARA), the Federal Register is the official daily publication for rules, proposed rules, and notices of Federal agencies and organizations. It includes such items as presidential orders, advisory meetings, program announcements, requests for applications and deadline dates.

Grants.gov

Grants.gov is a central storehouse for information on over 1,000 grant programs and provides access to approximately $500 billion in annual awards. The Department of Health and Human Services is the Grants.gov program's managing partner, and allows access to 26 federal grant-making agencies through the *www.grants.gov* web site.

Clearinghouses

Begun in the 1960s on a limited basis, a coordinated grant support process known as clearinghouse review was once required on hundreds of government grants.

As part of this review process, an applicant submits a brief description of the project or activity for which federal support is sought. Some clearinghouses have developed special forms for this "notification of intent," while others ask for a simple program description, along with the name and location of the applicant agency. Clearinghouses then notify the government agencies and elected officials of local governments that might be interested in the project, in order for the departments and agencies to comment.

If the clearinghouse does not identify any problems or possible conflicts, the applicant may complete and submit the proposal to the funding agency unless the clearinghouse specifies that it wants to review the completed proposal.

If there are concerns or unresolved issues, the clearinghouse may arrange a meeting between the applicant and the various departments that have expressed the concern. After any issues have been addressed, the applicant may wish to rewrite the proposal, continue discussions with the departments that are expressing concern, or submit the proposal to the funding source with the comments of the clearinghouse attached.

Key to entry information

(1) **XYZ FOUNDATION** (2) **[101]**

(3) One Central Commerce Building
Main and Division Streets
Anytown, IL 60009

(4) (312) 555-5555
Fax: (312) 555-1234
E-Mail Address: abcd@xyzfdn.edu
Web Site Address: www.xyzfdn.edu

(5) FOUNDED: 1950

(6) AREAS OF INTEREST:
Education, medical research, the
environment, youth groups, law and
social welfare.

(7) CONSULTING OR VOLUNTEER
SERVICES:
Technical assistance to community
groups, particularly to those providing
cultural activities.

(8) NAME OF PROGRAM
John Doe Project Grants Fund

(9) TYPE:
Project/Program grants. Support for a
variety of activities in the areas of
education, medical research, desert
research, atmospheric, earth, and
oceanographic sciences, youth
organizations, libraries, conservation
projects, water pollution studies, fish
and game management, preservation,
parks and recreation, environmental
studies, law, judicial education, crime
delinquency, law enforcement, relief and
social agencies, museums and historical
projects, health, hospitals, and
community improvement organizations.
Awards are not available for
endowment, contingency or reserve
purposes.

(10) YEAR PROGRAM STARTED: 1990

(11) PURPOSE:
To support endeavors for the benefit of
mankind.

(12) LEGAL BASIS:
Private foundation; tax-exempt under
statute 501(c)(3) of the Internal
Revenue Code.

(13) ELIGIBILITY: U.S. tax-exempt
nonprofit organizations with
appropriate interests are eligible to
apply. Grants are not made, however,
to organizations which distribute them
to beneficiaries of their own selection.
Priority is given to projects which are
not normally financed by public tax
funds.

(14) GEOGRAPHIC RESTRICTIONS:
United States.

(15) FINANCIAL DATA:
Grants vary in amount depending upon
the needs and nature of the request.

(16) *Amount of support per award:*
$1,000 to $500,000.

(17) *Total amount of support:*
$6,005,000 for the year ended May 31,
2020.

(18) *Matching fund requirements:* Grants
exceeding $25,000 must be matched by
an amount not less than one-third the
total amount of the grant.

(19) COOPERATIVE FUNDING PRO-
GRAMS: The Foundation prefers joint
funding whenever possible.

(20) NUMBER OF APPLICANTS MOST
RECENT YEAR: 512

(21) NUMBER OF AWARDS: 92 for the
year ended May 31, 2020.

(22) REPRESENTATIVE AWARDS:
$75,000 to Anytown Hospital, toward
facilities and equipment for its new
Community Health Center; $25,000 to
State University, for development of an
interdisciplinary studies program;
$15,000 to City Youth Center, toward
purchase of equipment for its model
reading laboratory program for youths.

(23) APPLICATION INFORMATION:
No official application forms are issued.
Interested applicants should submit an
informal proposal which briefly
includes: (1) amount requested and an
explanation of the necessity or purpose
therefore; (2) aid sought and amounts
received from other foundations and
sources (include names) during the
preceding three years; (3) aid presently
being sought from other sources (or
whether such solicitation is contem-
plated) and, if so, from whom; (4) copy
of tax-exempt letter from the U.S.
Treasury and Section 509 classification
determination; (5) latest audited balance
sheet and detailed income account and;
(6) signature and approval of the
overall head of the applicant institution
or organization. Seven copies of
application proposals and covering
letters should be submitted. Letters of
support from appropriate authorities
and/or organizations are also encouraged.

(24) *Duration:* Varies according to length
of project. Grants may be renewed if
continued support can be shown to be
beneficial and vital to project success.

(25) *Deadline:* Formal proposals and
supporting documents must be received
two months prior to board meetings,
held in June and December.

(26) PUBLICATIONS:
Annual report; application guidelines.

(27) IRS IDENTIFICATION NUMBER:
00-1234567

(28) BOARD OF TRUSTEES:
John Doe III, Chairman
Margaret Lee, Vice Chairman
Samuel Smith, Treasurer
Robert Johnson, Secretary
Arthur Boyle
Anthony Cates
Phillip Sevoy

(29) OFFICERS:
Phyllis Hartley, Executive Director
David Lisle, President
Susan Banks, Vice President
John Quincy Smith, Project Grants
Coordinator

(30) ADDRESS INQUIRIES TO:
John Quincy Smith, Project Grants
Coordinator
P.O. Box 777
Neartown, IL 60008

(31) * PLEASE NOTE:
If an applicant is unclear as to the
Foundation's current fields of interest,
an inquiry directed to it describing the
applicant's project may save the trouble
or expense of preparing and submitting
a formal application.

(1)   Grantmaking organization.

(2)   Entry number, reference corresponding to numbers used in the indexes.

(3)   Address.

(4)   Telephone and fax numbers. E-mail, Web Site addresses, and TDD numbers when available.

(5)   Date organization was founded.

(6)   Major fields of organizational interest.

(7)   Fields in which the organization donates consulting, volunteer, or similar services, if applicable; nature of the service.

(8)   Name(s) of grant program(s).

(9)   Nature of support available under the program(s), e.g., fellowships, project grants, research grants, technical assistance, etc.

(10)   Date program was established.

(11)   Objective of the grant program and/or sponsoring institution.

(12)   Organization's legal status or type (e.g., IRS ruling, state statute, corporate giving program, etc.); legal authority for expenditure of government funds, etc.

(13)   Qualifications required of the applicant individual or project and/or sponsoring institution.

(14)   Restrictions or preferences as to geographic location of the applicant individual or project and/or sponsoring institution.

(15)   Fiscal nature of the grant, including expenses to which it may be applied, restrictions on its use and non-cash benefits.

(16)   Fixed sum, average amount, or range of funds offered for each award.

(17)   Total funding available for the program or, when indicated, for all programs of a grantmaking organization, and the year in question.

(18)   Cost-sharing stipulations.

(19)   Nature of participation with other donors for project support.

(20)   Total applicants, for the most recent year statistics are available.

(21)   Total recipients, and the year in question.

(22)   Representative awards made under the program for the most recent year, including the amount, recipient, and project title or purpose of the award.

(23)   Application requirements and procedures, or references for further information.

(24)   Period for which support is provided; renewal possibilities.

(25)   Closing date(s) for application submission; award announcement date(s).

(26)   Publications that are available from the organization, e.g., annual report, application guidelines, program announcements, etc.

(27)   Internal Revenue Service tax identification number, if applicable.

(28)   Names and titles of principal personnel, e.g., Trustees, Directors, Awards Committee members, etc.

(29)   Names and titles of organization and/or program officers.

(30)   Source of further information and/or recipient of applications.

(31)   Unusual specifications or conditions concerning the program.

An asterisk (*) following an organization name indicates no or incomplete data was received from the source to update or compile the entry. The program listing is then reprinted from the last edition of *Grant Support*, revised where possible, or compiled entirely through staff research.

New listings in 2022 edition

The following is a list of foundations that are offering new grant programs. Bulleted items (•) reflect new program names for the foundation listed.

MULTIPLE SPECIAL PURPOSE
West Pharmaceutical Services, Inc., Exton, PA

HUMANITIES
Architecture
Society of Architectural Historians, Chicago, IL
- (•) Gill Family Foundation Dissertation Research Fellowship
- (•) Charles E. Peterson Fellowship of the Buildings of the United States and the Athenaeum of Philadelphia
- (•) Study Program Fellowships

Arts (multiple disciplines)
Louisiana Division of the Arts, Department of Culture, Recreation and Tourism, Baton Rouge, LA
- (•) Louisiana Project Grants

History
Cushwa Center for the Study of American Catholicism, Notre Dame, IN
- (•) The Cyprian Davis, O.S.B., Prize

INTERNATIONAL AFFAIRS AND AREA STUDIES
International studies and research abroad
Sommerhochschule - University of Vienna, Vienna, Austria
- (•) univie: winter school for Cultural Historical Studies

Villa I Tatti: The Harvard University Center for Italian Renaissance Studies, Florence, Italy
- (•) Berenson Fellowship
- (•) Fellowship in the Digital Humanities
- (•) Craig Hugh Smythe Fellowship
- (•) David and Julie Tobey Fellowship
- (•) Wallace Fellowship

SPECIAL POPULATIONS
Women
American Association of University Women, Washington, DC
- (•) Research Publication Grants in Engineering, Medicine and Science

EDUCATION
Scholar aid programs (all disciplines)
Asian American Journalists Association, Washington, DC
- (•) Vincent Chin Memorial Scholarship
- (•) CIC/Anna Chennault Scholarship
- (•) Dinah Eng Leadership Fellowship
- (•) Mary Quon Moy Ing Memorial Scholarship
- (•) Michael Kim Broadcast Fellowship
- (•) Sports Task Force/Al Young Sports Journalism Scholarship
- (•) Jimmie & Suey Fong Yee Scholarship

PHYSICAL SCIENCES
Chemistry
Canadian Society for Chemistry, Ottawa, ON Canada
- (•) Award for Research Excellence in Materials Chemistry
- (•) Environment Division Early Career Research Award
- (•) IntelliSyn Pharma Research Excellence Award

LIFE SCIENCES
Agriculture, land resources, rural development
Northeastern Loggers' Association, Inc., Old Forge, NY
- (•) William J. Cox Memorial Fund Scholarship

(continued on next page)

Biology

Virginia Society of Ornithology, Williamsburg, VA
  (•) VSO Conservation Fund

Medicine (multiple disciplines)

Canadian Blood Services, Ottawa, ON Canada
  (•) Blood Efficiency Accelerator Program

Metabolism, gastroenterology, nephrology

American Gastroenterological Association (AGA),
    Bethesda, MD
  (•) AGA-Bern Schwartz Family Fund Research Scholar
  Award in Pancreatic Cancer
  (•) Pilot Research Award in Health Disparities

Oncology

Cancer Research Institute, New York, NY
  (•) Lloyd J. Old STAR Program
  (•) Technology Impact Award

MULTIPLE SPECIAL PURPOSE

Multiple special purpose

THE ABELL FOUNDATION, INC. [1]

111 South Calvert Street
Suite 2300
Baltimore, MD 21202-6174
(410) 547-1300
Fax: (410) 539-6579
E-mail: abell@abell.org
Web Site: www.abell.org

FOUNDED: 1953

AREAS OF INTEREST:
Arts and culture, community development, education, conservation and environment, health and human services, workforce development, criminal justice and addiction.

TYPE:
Capital grants; Challenge/matching grants; Demonstration grants; Development grants; General operating grants; Matching gifts; Project/program grants; Seed money grants.

YEAR PROGRAM STARTED: 1953

PURPOSE:
To improve the quality of life in the area around Baltimore, MD.

LEGAL BASIS:
Private foundation.

ELIGIBILITY:
Individuals are not eligible for grants. Qualifying organizations must have IRS 509(a) and 501(c)(3) not-for-profit status. Religious organizations are eligible.

GEOG. RESTRICTIONS: Maryland, with a focus on Baltimore.

FINANCIAL DATA:
Amount of support per award: $500 to $1,000,000.

Total amount of support: $13,731,857 in grants approved for the year 2019.

NO. AWARDS: 223 for the year 2019.

APPLICATION INFO:
Foundation application form must be completed and submitted. Applicant organizations must provide IRS 501(c)(3) and 509(a) documentation, the most recently audited financial statement, operating budget, projected budget for each year funding is requested, a list of the board of directors as well as pertinent information regarding the program. Application needs to be preceded by a two-page letter of inquiry.

Duration: Primarily one-year grants; few multiyear awards.

Deadline: Grants will be awarded five times a year: February, April, June, August and December.

PUBLICATIONS:
Annual Report; *Abell Report*, newsletter; periodic research reports.

IRS I.D.: 52-6036106

OFFICER:
Robert C. Embry, Jr., President
Frances M. Keenan, Senior Vice President

ADDRESS INQUIRIES TO:
Robert C. Embry, Jr., President
(See address above.)

THE ABNEY FOUNDATION [2]

100 Vine Street
Anderson, SC 29621
(864) 964-9201
Fax: (864) 964-9209
E-mail: info@abneyfoundation.org
Web Site: www.abneyfoundation.org

FOUNDED: 1957

AREAS OF INTEREST:
Religious, charitable, scientific, literary or educational, including encouragement of art and music.

TYPE:
Development grants; Endowments; Project/program grants; Research grants.

YEAR PROGRAM STARTED: 1957

PURPOSE:
To make grants for innovative and creative projects and to programs which are responsive to changing community needs in the areas of education, health, social service and cultural affairs.

LEGAL BASIS:
Tax-exempt, private foundation.

ELIGIBILITY:
Applicants must be tax-exempt organizations. No grants to individuals.

GEOG. RESTRICTIONS: South Carolina.

FINANCIAL DATA:
Amount of support per award: $1,000 to $250,000.

Total amount of support: $1,855,000 for the year 2020.

NO. MOST RECENT APPLICANTS: 200.

NO. AWARDS: 41.

APPLICATION INFO:
Applicants may submit a Letter of Intent briefly describing the project before submitting a proposal in order to find out if their ideas are potentially fundable by the Foundation.

Duration: No grants on a continuing basis.

Deadline: November 15.

PUBLICATIONS:
Application guidelines.

IRS I.D.: 57-6019445

TRUSTEES AND OFFICERS:
John R. Fulp, Jr., Chairman
Dr. Lisa C. McWherter, Vice Chairman and Executive Director
Bonnie Nash, Treasurer and Secretary
Lebrena Fulp Campbell
Carl T. Edwards
John R. Fulp, III
Dr. John T. Meehan
Edd Sheriff

ADDRESS INQUIRIES TO:
Dr. Lisa C. McWherter
Vice Chairman and Executive Director
(See address above.)

ACADIA UNIVERSITY [3]

18 University Avenue
Wolfville NS B4P 2R6 Canada
(902) 585-1914
Fax: (902) 585-1096
E-mail: theresa.starratt@acadiau.ca
Web Site: www.acadiau.ca

AREAS OF INTEREST:
English, political science, sociology, biology, chemistry, computer science, geology, psychology, education, community development, mathematics, statistics and applied geomatics, and social and political thought.

NAME(S) OF PROGRAMS:
- **Acadia Graduate Scholarships/Acadia Graduate Teaching Assistantships**

TYPE:
Assistantships; Awards/prizes.

PURPOSE:
To financially support graduate students.

ELIGIBILITY:
Open to registered full-time graduate students at Acadia University. Candidates must possess a 3.0/4.3 grade point average in each of the last two years of undergraduate study in their major.

FINANCIAL DATA:
Amount of support per award: Varies depending on budget and decision of department or school.

APPLICATION INFO:
Consult the University for guidelines.
Duration: One or two years.
Deadline: February.

ADDRESS INQUIRIES TO:
Theresa Starratt, Graduate Studies Officer
(See address above.)

*SPECIAL STIPULATIONS:
Acadia Graduate Teaching Assistantship recipients should expect to undertake certain duties during the academic year (up to maximum of 12 hours per week and to a maximum of 144 hours per semester) as a condition of tenure. Specific duties will be established by agreement at the beginning of each academic year. An Acadia Graduate Scholarship does not require students to do any work.

THE ACHELIS AND BODMAN FOUNDATION [4]

420 Lexington Avenue
Suite 2803
New York, NY 10170
(212) 644-0322
E-mail: info@achelisbodman.org
Web Site: achelisbodman.org

FOUNDED: 2015

AREAS OF INTEREST:
Primarily arts and culture, education, employment, health, public policy and youth and families.

TYPE:
Challenge/matching grants; Conferences/seminars; Development grants; General operating grants; Internships; Matching gifts; Project/program grants; Research grants; Scholarships; Technical assistance; Training grants. Over 90% of the Foundation's grants fall into its six program areas.

PURPOSE:
To impact the greater New York City region and enhance the quality of life for its people, especially the disadvantaged; to advance human dignity, inspire personal achievement and foster self-reliance.

LEGAL BASIS:
Private foundation under Section 501(c)(3) of the Internal Revenue Code.

ELIGIBILITY:
Nonprofit organizations based in New York City and northern New Jersey that are tax-exempt under Section 501(c)(3) of the Internal Revenue Code and fall within the

program areas of the Foundation are welcome to submit an inquiry or proposal letter.

The Foundation generally does not make grants to nonprofit organizations outside of New York and New Jersey; annual appeals, dinner functions and fund-raising events; endowments and capital campaigns; loans and deficit financing; direct grants to individuals (such as scholarships and financial aid); individual day-care and after-school programs; housing; international projects; films and travel; projects for the elderly; small art, dance, music and theater groups; independent or public K-12 schools (except charter schools); national health and mental health organizations and; government agencies and nonprofit programs and services significantly funded or substantially reimbursed by government.

GEOG. RESTRICTIONS: Primarily New York City and northern New Jersey.

FINANCIAL DATA:
Amount of support per award: $5,000 to $300,000 for the year 2019.

Total amount of support: $5,455,000 for the year 2019.

NO. AWARDS: 131 for the year 2019.

APPLICATION INFO:
It is recommended that an organization's initial contact with the Foundation include only the following items:
(1) an inquiry or proposal letter briefly summarizing the history of the project, need, research, objectives, time period, key staff, project budget, and evaluation plan emphasizing measurable outcomes and specific program results;
(2) latest annual report;
(3) current and complete audited financial statements and;
(4) copy of the organization's IRS 501(c)(3) tax-exemption letter.
Duration: One year. Renewal does not generally follow the year of a grant.

OFFICERS:
John N. Irwin, III, Chairman
Russell P. Pennoyer, President
Tatiana Pouschine, Vice President
Horace I. Crary, Jr., Treasurer
John B. Krieger, Executive Director, Secretary and Assistant Treasurer

BOARD OF TRUSTEES:
Horace I. Crary, Jr.
Oliver Grace
John N. Irwin, III
Leslie Lenkowsky
George McCabe
Russell P. Pennoyer
Tatiana Pouschine
Magdalena Zavalia de Miguens

ADDRESS INQUIRIES TO:
John B. Krieger, Executive Director
(See address above.)

AETNA FOUNDATION, INC. [5]
151 Farmington Avenue
Hartford, CT 06156-3180
(860) 273-6382
Fax: (860) 273-4764
E-mail: aetnafoundation@aetna.com
Web Site: cvshealth.com/social-responsibility/aetna-foundation

FOUNDED: 1972

AREAS OF INTEREST:
Social determinants of health.

NAME(S) OF PROGRAMS:
● **Cultivating Healthy Communities**
● **Healthiest Cities and Counties Challenge**

TYPE:
Matching gifts; Project/program grants; Research grants.

YEAR PROGRAM STARTED: 1972

PURPOSE:
To promote wellness, health and access to high-quality health care for everyone, while supporting the communities Aetna serves.

LEGAL BASIS:
Corporate giving program.

ELIGIBILITY:
Nonprofit organizations with evidence of IRS 501(c)(3) designation of de facto tax-exempt status may apply for a grant. Complete details are available on the Foundation web site.

FINANCIAL DATA:
Amount of support per award: Varies.

APPLICATION INFO:
Unsolicited requests for funding are not accepted. Requests for proposals are posted online when opportunities are available.
Duration: Varies.
Deadline: Varies.

PUBLICATIONS:
Aetna Annual Giving Report.

IRS I.D.: 23-7241940

STAFF:
Garth N. Graham, M.D., M.P.H., President
Patti MacRae, Executive Director
Amy Aparicio Clark, Managing Director, Community Impact and Strategy
Sharon R. Ions, Corporate Relations Director
Lamond Daniels, Program Officer
Kate Lincoln, Program Officer
Cheryl A. Tourigny, Program Associate
Alan C. Eversley, Program Consultant
Juanita Galvis Rueda, Program Consultant

BOARD OF DIRECTORS:
Mark T. Bertolini
Shawn Guertin
Steven B. Kelmar
Harold Paz, M.D., M.S.

ADDRESS INQUIRIES TO:
See e-mail address above.

ALABAMA POWER FOUNDATION [6]
600 North 18th Street
Birmingham, AL 35291
(205) 257-0231
Web Site: powerofgood.com

FOUNDED: 1989

AREAS OF INTEREST:
Education, arts and culture, civic and community, health and human services, and environment.

NAME(S) OF PROGRAMS:
● **ABC Trust Community Grant**
● **Classroom Grant**
● **Elevate Grant**
● **Foundation Grants**
● **Gateway Grant**
● **Good Roots Grant**
● **Power to Play Grant**
● **Students to Stewards Program**

TYPE:
Capital grants; Challenge/matching grants; Endowments; General operating grants; Project/program grants; Scholarships; Seed money grants.

PURPOSE:
To improve the quality of life of Alabamians and to strengthen the communities in which they live.

LEGAL BASIS:
Corporate foundation.

ELIGIBILITY:
Applicant must be a 501(c)(3) tax-exempt, nonprofit Alabama organization. No grants to individuals, religious or political groups.

GEOG. RESTRICTIONS: Alabama.

FINANCIAL DATA:
Amount of support per award: ABC Trust Community Grant: Up to $500; Classroom Grant and Good Roots Grant: Up to $1,000; Elevate Grant: Up to $10,000; Foundation Grants: Varies; Gateway Grant: Up to $2,500; Students to Stewards: Up to $7,500.
Total amount of support: $12,500,000 for the year 2019.

NO. AWARDS: 1,064 for the year 2019.

APPLICATION INFO:
All grant applications are received online. Applicants will be asked for specific information about their organization. On the last page, applicants will be prompted to attach the following:
(1) actual grant request with cover letter outlining goals, objectives and specific needs addressed, including an implementation plan and timeline with an outline for any activities planned in the near future and achievements thus far (no more than four pages);
(2) project budget with an evaluation plan with specific criteria for judging the effectiveness;
(3) a copy of the program's most recent audited financial statement;
(4) a copy of the program's current operating budget and;
(5) a copy of the program's Section 501(c)(3) IRS determination letter.

Attachments must be in MS Word, MS Excel or Adobe Acrobat file formats to be accepted.
Duration: One-time funding.
Deadline: Classroom Grant: February. Elevate Grant: September 1. Foundation Grant: February, April, July and October. Gateway Grant: Late June. Good Roots Grant: May. Students to Stewards: January.

PUBLICATIONS:
Annual report; information and guidelines.

ADDRESS INQUIRIES TO:
Myla Calhoun, President
(See address above.)

ALCOA FOUNDATION [7]
201 Isabella Street
Suite 500
Pittsburgh, PA 15212-5858
E-mail: alcoafoundation@alcoa.com
Web Site: www.alcoa.com/foundation

FOUNDED: 1952

AREAS OF INTEREST:
Environment, education and workforce development.

TYPE:
Project/program grants.

YEAR PROGRAM STARTED: 1964

PURPOSE:
To promote the prevention of and resilience to climate change; to promote the restoration and preservation of biodiversity.

LEGAL BASIS:
Nonprofit foundation.

ELIGIBILITY:
Organizations and programs must meet the following basic requirements in order to be considered for funding:
(1) must serve communities where Alcoa has operating plants or offices;
(2) U.S. organizations must be classified as not-for-profit public charities and tax-exempt under Section 501(c)(3) of the U.S. Internal Revenue Code. Public educational institutions and government entities, while not classified as 501(c)(3) public charities, may be eligible for grant funds provided that funds are used for charitable purposes;
(3) non-U.S. organizations must operate as the equivalent of a U.S. 501(c)(3) public charity, public educational institution or government entity and must complete the required Equivalency Determination process and;
(4) organizations must demonstrate a commitment to diversity and nondiscrimination and sign the Alcoa Foundation inclusivity statement.

FINANCIAL DATA:
Amount of support per award: Varies.
Total amount of support: Varies.

APPLICATION INFO:
Applications are accepted on an invitation-only basis.
Duration: Varies.
Deadline: Generally July 31.

GEORGE I. ALDEN TRUST   [8]
c/o Fletcher Tilton P.C.
370 Main Street, 11th Floor
Worcester, MA 01608
(508) 459-8005
Fax: (508) 459-8305
E-mail: trustees@aldentrust.org
Web Site: www.aldentrust.org

FOUNDED: 1912

AREAS OF INTEREST:
Higher education.

TYPE:
Capital grants; Challenge/matching grants. Capital projects related to teaching and learning technology, in general, and to the sciences, in particular; some support for need-based scholarship endowment and faculty development.

YEAR PROGRAM STARTED: 1912

LEGAL BASIS:
Probate Trust.

ELIGIBILITY:
Principal focus is on independent colleges and universities with full-time traditional undergraduate enrollments of at least 1,000 students and with a total undergraduate and graduate student population (full-time equivalents) of under 5,000. Also, educationally related entities in the Worcester (MA) area and at YMCAs in Massachusetts.

GEOG. RESTRICTIONS: New Jersey, New York, Pennsylvania and the six New England states.

FINANCIAL DATA:
Total amount of support: $10,675,000 for the year 2020.
Matching fund requirements: Usually 1:2 or 1:3 (Alden Trust:matching dollars), with 18-month challenge period. The Trust only pays when the challenge is met in full. The Trust makes no interim or partial payments.

APPLICATION INFO:
Guidelines are available on the web site.
Deadline: Completed proposals received for March, June, September and December meetings must be received by the 15th of the month prior to the meeting.

IRS I.D.: 04-6023784

TRUSTEES:
Warner S. Fletcher, Chairperson
James E. Collins
Douglas Q. Meystre
Gail T. Randall

ADDRESS INQUIRIES TO:
Warner S. Fletcher, Chairperson
(See address above.)

ALLEGHENY FOUNDATION   [9]
One Oxford Centre
301 Grant Street, Suite 3900
Pittsburgh, PA 15219-6402
(412) 392-2900
Web Site: www.scaife.com

AREAS OF INTEREST:
Education, civic development and historic preservation.

TYPE:
General operating grants.

ELIGIBILITY:
Applicant must be a 501(c)(3) nonprofit organization.

GEOG. RESTRICTIONS: Western Pennsylvania.

FINANCIAL DATA:
Amount of support per award: Varies.
Total amount of support: $22,835,800 for the year 2020.

APPLICATION INFO:
Initial inquiries to the Foundation should be in letter form signed by the organization's President, or authorized representative, and have the approval of the Board of Directors. The letter should include a concise description of the specific program for which funds are requested. Additional information must include a budget for the program and for the organization, the latest audited financial statement and annual report. A copy of the organization's current ruling letter evidencing tax exemption under Section 501(c)(3) of the Internal Revenue Code is required.
Duration: Typically one year.
Deadline: The Foundation considers grants on a quarterly basis. Requests may be submitted at any time and will be acted upon as expeditiously as possible.

ADDRESS INQUIRIES TO:
Matthew A. Groll, Chairman
(See address above.)

AMCOR CARES
FOUNDATION   [10]
2200 Badger Avenue
Oshkosh, WI 54904
E-mail: kim.wetzel@amcor.com
Web Site: www.amcor.com/about/foundation

FOUNDED: 1959

AREAS OF INTEREST:
Basic needs, K-12 education and life skills, mental health, art and culture, and STEM.

NAME(S) OF PROGRAMS:
- **Community Enrichment Grant Program**
- **Community Support Grant Program**
- **Nonprofit/Educational Gift Matching Program**
- **United Way Program**

TYPE:
Capital grants; Challenge/matching grants; General operating grants; Matching gifts; Project/program grants. Grants to tax-exempt organizations in the communities in which the Amcor Flexibles North America operates in the U.S. Scholarships, matching educational and matching nonprofit gifts are for employees only.

The Amcor Scholarship Program provides financial aid to sons and daughters of AFNA employees.

The Gift Matching program gives employees an opportunity to have their personal contributions of time and money to eligible secondary schools, vocational/technical schools, colleges and universities and eligible 501(c)(3) nonprofits matched by Amcor Cares Foundation.

In the United Way program, Amcor contributes to the United Way in communities where the company has facilities.

YEAR PROGRAM STARTED: 1959

PURPOSE:
To match available funds with those public needs where the interests of the company and its employees are inseparable; to support communities where Amcor has operations in the U.S.

LEGAL BASIS:
Corporate foundation.

ELIGIBILITY:
Nonprofits and schools must be located in or serve U.S. Amcor facility communities. Grants are made to tax-exempt, U.S.-based organizations only. Priorities in grants will be given to those organizations and/or programs that will contribute the most to advancing the quality of life for all peoples in the communities in which Amcor operates. Emphasis will be on those programs that encourage the development of our human resources, education programs and, in a lesser degree, civic and art institutions that encourage participation by the general public. Special consideration will be given to those programs in which the company's employees actively participate or are directly benefited.

The Foundation will not make grants to individuals or to organizations for religious purposes or for political purposes, either for lobbying efforts or campaigns. The Foundation prefers not to make grants for educational capital funds programs, endowment purposes or to support trips or tours.

Amcor Scholarship Program is only open to the children of full-time AFNA employees.

GEOG. RESTRICTIONS: United States.

FINANCIAL DATA:
Amount of support per award: Community Enrichment Grant Program: Up to $1,000; Community Support Grant Program: $1,000 and up; All others: Varies.

Total amount of support: Approximately $2,500,000 for the year 2019.

Matching fund requirements: The Plan provides that the employee's contribution be to an eligible 501(c)(3) nonprofit or accredited educational institution and will be matched dollar-for-dollar. Under this Plan, employee volunteer hours are matched $10 per hour. Each employee has up to $2,500 per year for matching.

APPLICATION INFO:
Complete application information may be obtained online. Grant proposals need not follow a specific format, but all proposals should include:
(1) name of the organization and amount requested;
(2) brief description of the objectives for which the grant is sought;
(3) details as to how the objectives are to be attained;
(4) budget, including information about existing and other possible sources of income;
(5) officers and board members and;
(6) statement that the organization has tax-exempt status under Section 501(c)(3) of the Internal Revenue Code and that contributions to it are tax-deductible.
It is preferred that all initial inquiries be by e-mail and not by telephone or personal visits.
Duration: Varies.

PUBLICATIONS:
Application guidelines.

IRS I.D.: 41-6038616

ADDRESS INQUIRIES TO:
See e-mail address above.

*SPECIAL STIPULATIONS:
All initial inquiries should be made by e-mail.

AMERICAN PHILOSOPHICAL SOCIETY [11]
104 South Fifth Street
Philadelphia, PA 19106-3387
(215) 440-3429
E-mail: lmusumeci@amphilsoc.org
Web Site: www.amphilsoc.org/grants/franklin-research-grants

FOUNDED: 1743

AREAS OF INTEREST:
Scholarly research.

NAME(S) OF PROGRAMS:
● **Franklin Research Grants**

TYPE:
Grants-in-aid; Research grants. Postdoctoral grants toward the cost of scholarly research in all areas of knowledge except those in which support by government or corporate enterprise is more appropriate. Scholarly research covers most kinds of scholarly inquiry by individuals. It does not include journalistic or other writing for general readership; the preparation of textbooks, casebooks, anthologies, or other materials for classroom use by students; or the work of creative and performing artists.

The Society does not have fellowships or scholarships for study, nor does it give grants for travel to conferences.

YEAR PROGRAM STARTED: 1933

PURPOSE:
To support scholarly research by individual scholars.

LEGAL BASIS:
Nonprofit learned society.

ELIGIBILITY:
Applications may be made by residents of the U.S., by American citizens resident abroad and by foreign nationals. American citizens and foreign nationals employed by an American institution may apply for support to carry out work anywhere in the world. Foreign nationals not employed by an American institution may apply for funding to work in the U.S. Applicants expecting to use materials or conduct interviews in a foreign language must possess the necessary competence in the language or languages involved. Grants are never made for predoctoral study or research.

It is the Society's long-standing practice to encourage research by younger and less well-established scholars.

FINANCIAL DATA:
Grants are made payable to the applicant.

The Society offers no funds for conference support, fellowships and scholarships, maintenance work already done, or costs of publication.
Amount of support per award: Funding is offered up to a maximum of $6,000.
Total amount of support: $525,800 for the year 2019-20.

CO-OP FUNDING PROGRAMS: If an applicant receives an award for the same project from another granting insititution, the Society will consider limiting its award to costs that are not covered by the other grant.

NO. MOST RECENT APPLICANTS: 339.

NO. AWARDS: 98 for the year 2019-20.

APPLICATION INFO:
Applications are submitted through the Society's online application portal. Two letters of support are required.
Duration: One year.
Deadline: October 1 and December 3.

ADDRESS INQUIRIES TO:
Linda Musumeci
Director of Grants and Fellowships
(See address above.)

AMERICAN PHILOSOPHICAL SOCIETY [12]
The Lewis and Clark Fund
104 South Fifth Street
Philadelphia, PA 19106-3387
(215) 440-3429
E-mail: lmusumeci@amphilsoc.org
Web Site: amphilsoc.org/grants/lewis-and-clark-fund-exploration-and-field-research

FOUNDED: 1743

AREAS OF INTEREST:
Scholarly research.

NAME(S) OF PROGRAMS:
● **The Lewis and Clark Fund for Exploration and Field Research**

TYPE:
Research grants. The Lewis and Clark Fund for Exploration and Field Research (initially supported by the Stanford Ascherman/Baruch Blumberg Fund for Basic Science, established by a benefaction from the late Stanford Ascherman, M.D., of San Francisco) encourages exploratory field studies for the collection of specimens and data and to provide the imaginative stimulus that

accompanies direct observation. Applications are invited from disciplines with a large dependence on field studies, such as archeology, anthropology, biology, ecology, geography, geology, linguistics, paleontology and population genetics, but grants will not be restricted to these fields.

YEAR PROGRAM STARTED: 2005

PURPOSE:
To support scholarly research by individual scholars.

LEGAL BASIS:
Nonprofit learned society.

ELIGIBILITY:
Grants will be available to doctoral students. Postdoctoral fellows, Master's degree candidates, and undergraduates are not eligible. Applicants who have received Lewis and Clark Fund grants may reapply after an interval of two years.

The competition is open to U.S. residents wishing to carry out research anywhere in the world. Foreign applicants must either be based at a U.S. institution or plan to carry out their work in the U.S.

Funding is contingent on successful applicants demonstrating that required permits and permissions have been secured.

FINANCIAL DATA:
Amount of support per award: Up to $5,000.
Total amount of support: $255,300 for the year 2019-20.

NO. MOST RECENT APPLICANTS: 339.

NO. AWARDS: 58 for the year 2019-20.

APPLICATION INFO:
Applications must be submitted electronically through the Society's online portal. The applicant should ask his or her academic adviser to write one of the two letters of recommendation, specifying the student's qualifications to carry out the proposed work and the educational content of the trip. Budgets should be limited to travel and related expenses, including personal field equipment.

When appropriate, the applicant should provide assurances that safety measures will be taken for potentially hazardous projects. When necessary, the applicant and his or her supervisor should discuss the field training that will be provided and the provisions for experienced supervision.

Duration: Preferably one year.

Deadline: Letters of Support: November 13. Application: November 16. Notification in March, for work in May and beyond.

ADDRESS INQUIRIES TO:
Linda Musumeci
Director of Grants and Fellowships
(See address above.)

AMERICAN SCHLAFHORST FOUNDATION [13]
8801 South Boulevard
Charlotte, NC 28273
(704) 554-0800
Fax: (704) 556-1643

AREAS OF INTEREST:
Arts, children, education, health care, sciences, senior citizens and social services.

TYPE:
Capital grants; Endowments; General operating grants; Research grants; Scholarships; Seed money grants.

PURPOSE:
To improve the quality of life in the community.

LEGAL BASIS:
Corporate foundation.

ELIGIBILITY:
Grants are made to organizations that have tax-exempt status under Section 501(c)(3) of the Internal Revenue Code. No grants are made to individuals.

GEOG. RESTRICTIONS: Greater Charlotte, North Carolina.

FINANCIAL DATA:
Amount of support per award: Varies.
Total amount of support: Varies.

APPLICATION INFO:
Applicants should submit a Letter of Inquiry to the Foundation at the address above.
Duration: Varies.
Deadline: October.

ADDRESS INQUIRIES TO:
Dan Loftis, Grant Administrator
(See address above.)

AMGEN FOUNDATION, INC. [14]
One Amgen Center Drive, M/S 28-4-C
Thousand Oaks, CA 91320-1799
(805) 447-1000
E-mail: amgenfoundation@amgen.com
Web Site: www.amgen.
com/responsibility/amgen-foundation

FOUNDED: 1991

AREAS OF INTEREST:
Science education, human services and community life including arts and culture, social services and environment.

TYPE:
Challenge/matching grants; General operating grants; Grants-in-aid; Matching gifts; Project/program grants. The Foundation funds national-level science education programs.

YEAR PROGRAM STARTED: 1991

PURPOSE:
To advance excellence in science education to inspire the next generation of innovators; to invest in strengthening communities where Amgen staff members live and work.

LEGAL BASIS:
Company-sponsored foundation.

ELIGIBILITY:
The Foundation will consider grant requests from nonprofit organizations that are recognized by the IRS as tax-exempt public charities under Sections 501(c)(3) and 509(a)(1), (2) or (3) of the Internal Revenue Code, located in the U.S. and Puerto Rico. In addition, the Foundation will consider requests for funding from governmental organizations located in the U.S. where the purpose of the grant is to support a charitable, educational, scientific or literary purpose. Thus, eligible grantees may include public elementary and secondary schools, as well as public colleges and universities, public libraries and public hospitals. Successful requests will fall within both the current eligibility guidelines and funding priority areas established by the Foundation.

The Foundation has established a grantmaking partnership with United Way Worldwide (UWW) to manage donations to organizations chartered in Europe.

GEOG. RESTRICTIONS: California, Florida, Massachusetts, Puerto Rico, Rhode Island, and parts of Europe.

FINANCIAL DATA:
Amount of support per award: Varies.
Total amount of support: Varies.

APPLICATION INFO:
Letter of intent must first be submitted online.
Duration: Typically one year. Possible multiyear funding.

ADDRESS INQUIRIES TO:
Jennifer Egglin, Manager
(See address above.)

THE ANNENBERG FOUNDATION [15]
2000 Avenue of the Stars
Suite 1000 S
Los Angeles, CA 90067
(310) 209-4560
Fax: (310) 209-1631
E-mail: info@annenberg.org
requests@annenberg.org
Web Site: www.annenberg.org

FOUNDED: 1989

AREAS OF INTEREST:
Arts, culture and humanities; animal welfare; civic and community; environment; education; human health and wellness; military veterans.

TYPE:
General operating grants; Grants-in-aid; Project/program grants; Technical assistance.

PURPOSE:
To provide funding and support to nonprofit organizations in the U.S. and globally; to advance the public well-being through improved communication; to encourage the development of effective ways to share ideas and knowledge.

ELIGIBILITY:
The Foundation seeks to fund organizations that have a deep level of community involvement, are led by effective leaders and tackle challenging and timely problems. The Foundation values the following organizational attributes: visionary leadership, impact, sustainability, innovation, organizational strength, network of partnerships, plus the population being served (hence the acronym VISION).

Only organizations that have 501(c)(3) not-for-profit status are eligible.

GEOG. RESTRICTIONS: Greater Los Angeles, California area (five-county region including Los Angeles, Orange, Riverside, San Bernardino and Ventura).

FINANCIAL DATA:
Total assets of $1.6 billion for year ended December 31, 2017.
Amount of support per award: Varies.
Total amount of support: Varies.

APPLICATION INFO:
Application guidelines are available on the Foundation web site.
Duration: One year. Grants are renewable, but applicant must reapply.

APPLIED MATERIALS, INC. [16]
3050 Bowers Avenue
Mail Stop 0106
Santa Clara, CA 95052-3299
(408) 727-5555
E-mail: community_affairs@amat.com
Web Site: www.appliedmaterials.com

FOUNDED: 1967

AREAS OF INTEREST:
Arts and culture, community development, education and the environment.

NAME(S) OF PROGRAMS:
● **Applied Materials Corporate Philanthropy Program**

TYPE:
Project/program grants.

YEAR PROGRAM STARTED: 1990

PURPOSE:
To support the arts and culture, education, community development and the environment.

LEGAL BASIS:
Corporate giving program.

ELIGIBILITY:
Organizations classified as 501(c)(3) by the IRS can apply. Preference is given to areas of company operation. Individuals and religious organizations are ineligible.

FINANCIAL DATA:
Amount of support per award: Varies.
Total amount of support: Varies.

APPLICATION INFO:
Application procedures are available online.
Duration: One year. May be renewed for up to two additional years based on results.
Deadline: January 15 and June 15.

PUBLICATIONS:
Annual report; community report; guidelines.

ADDRESS INQUIRIES TO:
See e-mail address above.

*SPECIAL STIPULATIONS:
Progress is requested to be shared in writing with the Corporate Contribution Committee at least once a year.

APS CORPORATE GIVING PROGRAM [17]
Arizona Public Service Company
400 North 5th Street, 10th Floor
Phoenix, AZ 85004
(602) 250-2702
Fax: (602) 250-2113
E-mail: corporategiving@aps.com
Web Site: aps.com/corporategiving

FOUNDED: 1888

AREAS OF INTEREST:
Education, most specifically STEM engineering; community vitality; community and economic development in APS service territories.

TYPE:
Challenge/matching grants; Development grants; Project/program grants. Primary focus is on program support.

YEAR PROGRAM STARTED: 1981

PURPOSE:
To enhance the quality of life in Arizona.

LEGAL BASIS:
Corporate giving program.

ELIGIBILITY:
Applicants must be 501(c)(3) nonprofit organizations for a minimum of three years. Preference is given to organizations within the APS service territory, although there are exceptions. No funds for individuals, individual scholarships, religious, political, fraternal, legislative or lobbying efforts, travel or hotel expenses. The program will not fund any organization that discriminates.

GEOG. RESTRICTIONS: Arizona.

FINANCIAL DATA:
Amount of support per award: $2,500 to $250,000.
Total amount of support: Approximately $9,000,000 for the year 2017.

NO. AWARDS: Varies.

APPLICATION INFO:
Applications must be submitted online and will require the following documentation:
(1) 501(c)(3) IRS letter of determination;
(2) current list of board members;
(3) list of sponsorship levels (if applicable);
(4) line-item budget;
(5) list of other funders and dollar amounts and;
(6) grant evaluation form (if applicable).
Duration: One year. Renewable by reapplication.
Deadline: APS Foundation: March 1 and September 1. Corporate Funding is on a rolling basis.

PUBLICATIONS:
Community Investment Report.

IRS I.D.: 95-3735903

THE ARCA FOUNDATION   [18]
1308 19th Street, N.W.
Washington, DC 20036
(202) 822-9193
E-mail: proposals@arcafoundation.org
Web Site: www.arcafoundation.org

FOUNDED: 1952

AREAS OF INTEREST:
Wall Street reform, financial regulation, corporate accountability, and advocating for a U.S. foreign policy approach that increases peace and security.

TYPE:
General operating grants; Project/program grants.

YEAR PROGRAM STARTED: 1952

PURPOSE:
To provide funding for nonprofit organizations working on ways to engage citizens in social change, promote democracy, and reform unjust practices in public policy.

LEGAL BASIS:
Private foundation.

ELIGIBILITY:
Nonprofit organizations.

GEOG. RESTRICTIONS: United States.

FINANCIAL DATA:
Amount of support per award: $50,000.
Total amount of support: Approximately $2,500,000 annually.

NO. MOST RECENT APPLICANTS: 500.

NO. AWARDS: Approximately 60 to 70 annually.

APPLICATION INFO:
Applications must be submitted online. Applications submitted by any other method will not be considered.

The Foundation highly recommends the applicant review the instructions on using the system and online application system FAQs before beginning the application process. The Proposal FAQs outlines the information to be included in the narrative of the proposal, as well as the list of documents that the organization should be prepared to submit/upload electronically. Documents include the organization's IRS 501(c)(3) letter and Arca's Lobbying Expenditure Form. As always, the Foundation only considers full proposals and does not accept letters of inquiry.
Duration: One year, or the program period.
Deadline: February 1 or August 1 by 5 P.M., or first business day following if the first falls on a weekend.

STAFF:
Anna Lefer Kuhn, Executive Director
Stacie Posie, Grants Officer

BOARD OF DIRECTORS AND OFFICERS:
Nancy R. Bagley, President
Nicole Bagley, Vice President
Mike Lux, Treasurer
Mary E. King, Secretary
Austin Belali
Rev. Joseph Elderidge
Amaha Kassa
Janet Shenk
Margery Tabankin

ARRAS FOUNDATION   [19]
800 North White Street
Lancaster, SC 29720
(803) 286-8772
E-mail: info@arrasfoundation.org
Web Site: arrasfoundation.org

FOUNDED: 1995

AREAS OF INTEREST:
Building a healthy community.

YEAR PROGRAM STARTED: 1995

PURPOSE:
To provide community support.

LEGAL BASIS:
Private foundation.

ELIGIBILITY:
Organizations and agencies classified as 501(c)(3) by the IRS can apply. Individuals are ineligible.

GEOG. RESTRICTIONS: Fort Lawn, Great Falls and Lancaster County, South Carolina.

FINANCIAL DATA:
Amount of support per award: Varies.

NO. MOST RECENT APPLICANTS: Varies.

APPLICATION INFO:
Application guidelines are available on the Foundation web site.
Duration: Typically one year.

PUBLICATIONS:
Annual report.

IRS I.D.: 57-0355295

STAFF:
Susan W. DeVenny, President and Chief Executive Officer
Cynthia Curtis, Community Investment Officer
Karen Ormond, Grants Administrator

ADDRESS INQUIRIES TO:
Susan W. DeVenny, President and Chief Executive Officer
(See address above.)

*PLEASE NOTE:
Formerly operated under the name J. Marion Sims Foundation, Inc.

ASSISI FOUNDATION OF MEMPHIS INC.   [20]
515 Erin Drive
Memphis, TN 38117
(901) 684-1564
Fax: (901) 684-1997
E-mail: twamble@assisifoundation.org
Web Site: www.assisifoundation.org

AREAS OF INTEREST:
Education and life long learning, health and human services, social justice and ethics, and cultural enrichment and the arts.

TYPE:
Challenge/matching grants; Endowments; General operating grants; Matching gifts; Project/program grants; Research grants; Technical assistance. Capacity building.

YEAR PROGRAM STARTED: 1994

PURPOSE:
To address pressing challenges while also searching for root causes with the goal of creating community-wide transformation.

ELIGIBILITY:
Grants are made to organizations that already have tax-exempt status under Section 501(c)(3) of the Internal Revenue Code.

GEOG. RESTRICTIONS: Crittenden County, Arkansas; Desoto County, Mississippi; Fayette, Shelby and Tipton counties, Tennessee.

FINANCIAL DATA:
Amount of support per award: Varies.
Total amount of support: Varies.

APPLICATION INFO:
Grant application process and required forms are available to download from the Foundation's web site.
Duration: Varies.
Deadline: Dates are posted online.

ADDRESS INQUIRIES TO:
Dr. Jan Young, Executive Director
(See address above.)

ATHWIN FOUNDATION   [21]
Center for Organizational Development
7101 York Avenue South, Suite 306
Edina, MN 55435
(612) 616-0256
E-mail: jstormcod1@aol.com
Web Site: www.catchcod.com

FOUNDED: 1956

AREAS OF INTEREST:
Newly emerging small organizations, with a focus on rural areas.

TYPE:
Capital grants; General operating grants; Project/program grants.

YEAR PROGRAM STARTED: 1956

PURPOSE:
To provide funds for charitable, scientific, literary or educational purposes.

LEGAL BASIS:
Tax-exempt private foundation.

ELIGIBILITY:
Only tax-exempt organizations may apply. No grants are awarded to individuals.

GEOG. RESTRICTIONS: Primarily Twin Cities and greater Minnesota.

FINANCIAL DATA:
Amount of support per award: Varies.

NO. MOST RECENT APPLICANTS: 100.

NO. AWARDS: Approximately 35.

REPRESENTATIVE AWARDS:
$12,500 to Lakes Area Music Festival; $20,000 to Wildlife Rehabilitative Center; $20,000 to Camp Cantus Male Choral Group.

APPLICATION INFO:
The Foundation will initiate communication with those organizations it selects for potential funding. All organizations receiving notification will complete the application process and submit material by the date identified by the Foundation.

Potential applicants may contact the Administrator via e-mail.

Duration: Varies.

PUBLICATIONS:
Annual report.

IRS I.D.: 41-6021773

TRUSTEES:
Andrew Bean
Bruce W. Bean
Glen Bean
Mary F. Bean
Rachael Bean

ADDRESS INQUIRIES TO:
Jim Storm, Administrator
(See address above.)

ATKINSON FOUNDATION [22]

c/o Pacific Foundation Services
1660 Bush Street, Suite 300
San Francisco, CA 94019
(415) 561-6540
Web Site: www.atkinsonfdn.org
www.pfs-llc.net

FOUNDED: 1939

AREAS OF INTEREST:
Social services and education in San Mateo County, CA, as well as American private volunteer organizations.

NAME(S) OF PROGRAMS:
● **Community**
● **Education and Youth Development**

TYPE:
General operating grants; Project/program grants.

YEAR PROGRAM STARTED: 1939

PURPOSE:
To foster the efforts of individuals and families to become socially, economically and physically self-sufficient, and to increase their economic and social welfare.

LEGAL BASIS:
Private foundation.

ELIGIBILITY:
Applicants must be organizations with Internal Revenue Code 501(c)(3) status.

No loans or grants to individuals or for doctoral study or research. The Foundation does not sponsor nor contribute to one-time events or nationwide appeals from organizations and does not fund publications, films or conferences.

GEOG. RESTRICTIONS: San Mateo County, California.

FINANCIAL DATA:
Amount of support per award: Generally $5,000 to $25,000.

Total amount of support: $1,131,500 for the year 2020.

NO. AWARDS: 112 for the year 2020.

REPRESENTATIVE AWARDS:
$20,000 to Boys & Girls Club of the Coastside; $10,000 to Second Harvest of Silicon Valley; $15,000 to Ravenswood Family Health Center; $10,000 to Marine Science Institute.

APPLICATION INFO:
Application information is available on the Foundation web site.
Duration: Usually one year.
Deadline: February 1, May 1, August 1 and November 1.

IRS I.D.: 94-6075613

ATRAN FOUNDATION, INC. [23]

155 North Dean Street, Suite 3-D
Englewood, NJ 07631
(201) 569-9677
Fax: (201) 569-2290
E-mail: foundatran@gmail.com

FOUNDED: 1948

AREAS OF INTEREST:
Civic, medical, charitable and educational organizations aligned with the Foundation's principles.

TYPE:
General operating grants; Project/program grants.

YEAR PROGRAM STARTED: 1948

PURPOSE:
To support worthy civic, medical, charitable, or educational organizations that align with the founding philanthropic principles of the Foundation.

LEGAL BASIS:
Tax-exempt under Section 501(c)(3) of the Internal Revenue Code.

ELIGIBILITY:
Grants are made only to 501(c)(3) tax-exempt organizations. No grants to individuals.

GEOG. RESTRICTIONS: United States.

FINANCIAL DATA:
Amount of support per award: Varies.
Total amount of support: Varies.

NO. MOST RECENT APPLICANTS: 50.

NO. AWARDS: Approximately 35 per year.

APPLICATION INFO:
No formal application form is required. Application guidelines may be requested from the Foundation.
Duration: One year.
Deadline: September 30.

PUBLICATIONS:
Guideline for application procedure.

IRS I.D.: 13-5566548

OFFICERS:
Allison Fischer, President
Robert Kaplan, Vice President
Samuel Norich, Treasurer
Harris Atran, Secretary

ADDRESS INQUIRIES TO:
Judah Fischer, Executive Director
(See address above.)

MARY REYNOLDS BABCOCK FOUNDATION [24]

2920 Reynolda Road
Winston-Salem, NC 27106
(336) 748-9222
Fax: (336) 777-0095
E-mail: info@mrbf.org
Web Site: www.mrbf.org

FOUNDED: 1953

AREAS OF INTEREST:
Democracy and civic engagement, economic opportunity, supportive policies and institutions.

NAME(S) OF PROGRAMS:
● **Moving People and Places Out of Poverty**

TYPE:
General operating grants. Program-related investments.

YEAR PROGRAM STARTED: 2005

PURPOSE:
To help people and places move out of poverty and achieve greater social and economic justice.

LEGAL BASIS:
Private foundation.

ELIGIBILITY:
Applicants must be nonprofit tax-exempt organizations with appropriate interests, located or working in the Southeast.

GEOG. RESTRICTIONS: Southeastern United States.

FINANCIAL DATA:
Amount of support per award: Varies.

Total amount of support: Approximately $8,000,000.

Matching fund requirements: Varies.

NO. AWARDS: Varies.

APPLICATION INFO:
Applications must be submitted electronically.

Duration: One to three years depending on the grant.

Deadline: Applications are accepted on a rolling basis.

PUBLICATIONS:
Application form.

IRS I.D.: 56-0690140

BOARD OF DIRECTORS:
Jerry Gonzalez, President
Ken Mountcastle, Treasurer
Kara Mountcastle, Secretary
LaVeeda Battle
Chad Berry
Ashleigh Gardere
Micah Gilmer
Zachary Lassiter
James Mitchell
Holt Mountcastle
Kathy Mountcastle
Mary Mountcastle
Stephanie Tyree

ADDRESS INQUIRIES TO:
Network Officers
(See address above.)

BADER PHILANTHROPIES, INC. [25]

3300 North Dr. Martin Luther King Jr. Drive
Milwaukee, WI 53212
(414) 224-6464
Fax: (414) 224-1441
E-mail: baderphilanthropies@bader.org
Web Site: www.bader.org

FOUNDED: 1991

AREAS OF INTEREST:
Alzheimer's disease and dementia, workforce development, Jewish education, program-related investments, and youth development.

TYPE:
Capital grants; Challenge/matching grants; Conferences/seminars; General operating grants; Matching gifts; Project/program grants; Technical assistance; Training grants.

YEAR PROGRAM STARTED: 1991

PURPOSE:
To fund innovative projects and programs in four primary areas including Alzheimer's disease and dementia, workforce development, children and youth, and Jewish education.

LEGAL BASIS:
Family foundation.

ELIGIBILITY:
U.S. organizations must be tax-exempt under Section 501(c)(3) of the IRS or governmental entities. Grants will only be approved for foreign entities which meet specific charitable status requirements.

GEOG. RESTRICTIONS: Milwaukee, Wisconsin.

FINANCIAL DATA:
Amount of support per award: $500 to $180,000. Median is $10,000.
Total amount of support: Average $16,000,000 annually.

CO-OP FUNDING PROGRAMS: Milwaukee Area Workforce Funding Alliance.

NO. AWARDS: 558 grants awarded for the year 2019-20.

REPRESENTATIVE AWARDS:
Above the Clouds, Inc.; City Year, Inc.; Wisconsin Humane Society, Inc.

APPLICATION INFO:
Application information is available on the Foundation web site.
Duration: Varies. Renewal possible.
Deadline: Applications are accepted at any time.

IRS I.D.: 39-1710914

BOARD OF DIRECTORS:
Jere D. McGaffey, Chairman and Treasurer
Daniel J. Bader, President
David M. Bader, Vice President
Deirdre Britt, Secretary
Linda C. Bader
Michelle Berrong Bader
Margaret Foster
Adina Shapiro
Frances Wolff

ADDRESS INQUIRIES TO:
Kristen Lie, Grants Manager
(See address above.)

R.C. BAKER FOUNDATION [26]

330 Encinitas Boulevard
Suite 101
Encinitas, CA 92024-8705
(760) 632-8322

FOUNDED: 1952

AREAS OF INTEREST:
Education, health, cultural, scientific research, social services for youth and elderly, and crime prevention.

TYPE:
Capital grants; Fellowships; General operating grants; Project/program grants; Scholarships; Technical assistance; Training grants; Work-study programs.

LEGAL BASIS:
Private foundation.

ELIGIBILITY:
Applicant organizations must have IRS tax-exempt status. No grants are made to individuals, endowments or loans. No grants to capital programs of tax-supported institutions.

GEOG. RESTRICTIONS: United States.

FINANCIAL DATA:
Amount of support per award: Varies.

APPLICATION INFO:
Applications should include a description of the proposed project and goals, a recently audited financial statement, amount requested, and a list of other sources of support. In addition, the applicant should include its IRS statement of tax-exempt status. The Foundation does not grant personal interviews.
Duration: Typically, one-time grants.
Deadline: May 1 and October 1.

IRS I.D.: 95-1742283

BOARD OF TRUSTEES:
Frank L. Scott, Chairman
James Benedict
Dennis Cronin
F. Laurence Scott, Jr.

ADDRESS INQUIRIES TO:
F. Laurence Scott, Jr., Board of Trustees
(See address above.)

BALL BROTHERS FOUNDATION [27]

222 South Mulberry
Muncie, IN 47305
(765) 741-5500
Fax: (765) 741-5518
E-mail: info@ballfdn.org
Web Site: www.ballfdn.org

FOUNDED: 1926

AREAS OF INTEREST:
Education, arts, culture and humanities, human services, public/society benefit, health and environment.

TYPE:
Awards/prizes; Challenge/matching grants; General operating grants; Project/program grants; Seed money grants; Technical assistance; Training grants.

YEAR PROGRAM STARTED: 1926

PURPOSE:
To promote recreational, educational or charitable purposes within the state of Indiana.

LEGAL BASIS:
Private foundation.

ELIGIBILITY:
Indiana not-for-profit organizations or institutions are eligible to apply. No grants to individuals.

GEOG. RESTRICTIONS: Indiana.

FINANCIAL DATA:
Amount of support per award: $1,000 to $1,000,000.
Total amount of support: $8,149,935 for the year 2019.

NO. MOST RECENT APPLICANTS: 201 for the year 2019.

NO. AWARDS: 119 for the year 2019.

REPRESENTATIVE AWARDS:
$2,500 to Forward Visions, Inc.; $17,500 to Daleville Community Schools; $4,884 to Jay-Randolph Developmental Services, Inc.; $5,000 to the City of Muncie; $5,000 to Academy of Model Aeronautics.

APPLICATION INFO:
Application must include a description of the project, project staff and budget, IRS determination letter, objective of the proposal, plan of development, expected results and method of evaluation.
Duration: One year.
Deadline: February 15 and July 15.

PUBLICATIONS:
Guidelines; annual report.

IRS I.D.: 35-0882856

OFFICERS:
James A. Fisher, Chairman
Frank B. Petty, Vice Chairman
Tamara S. Phillips, Treasurer
Terry L. Walker, Secretary
Scott E. Shockley, Assistant Treasurer and Assistant Secretary

DIRECTORS:
Charles Ball
Jeff Bird
Elizabeth Bracken
William Bracken
Stephanie Duckmann
Nancy B. Keilty
Terri Matchett
Stacy McHenry
Judy Oetinger

ADDRESS INQUIRIES TO:
Donna Munchel, Program Officer and Grants Manager
(See address above.)

GEORGE AND FRANCES BALL FOUNDATION [28]

222 South Mulberry Street
Muncie, IN 47305
(765) 741-5500
Fax: (765) 741-5518
Web Site: gfballfdn.org

FOUNDED: 1937

AREAS OF INTEREST:
Education and youth, community enhancement, nature and historic preservation, wrap-around services, and arts and culture.

TYPE:
Challenge/matching grants; General operating grants; Project/program grants.

LEGAL BASIS:
Family foundation.

ELIGIBILITY:
Applicants must be 501(c)(3) organizations or institutes.

GEOG. RESTRICTIONS: East central Indiana, primarily Delaware County.

FINANCIAL DATA:
Amount of support per award: $25,000 median.
Total amount of support: $5,400,000 for the year ended December 31, 2020.
Matching fund requirements: Usually 1:1.

NO. AWARDS: 62 for the year 2020.

APPLICATION INFO:
General grant guidelines are available on the Foundation web site.
Deadline: Mid-January, early April, mid-July and early November.

STAFF:
Thomas J. Kinghorn, President and Chief Executive Officer
Tamara S. Phillips, C.P.A., Treasurer
Carol E. Seals, Assistant Treasurer
Kortney Zimmerman, Program Officer
Kelsey Harrington, Program Associate

BOARD OF DIRECTORS:
Jon H. Moll, Chairman
Ronald K. Fauquher, Vice Chairman
Ted Wiese, Secretary
Will Bracken
Ermalene M. Faulkner
Michael B. Galliher
Steven M Smith
Marianne Vorhees

ADDRESS INQUIRIES TO:
Shannon Cline, Executive Assistant
(See address above.)

BALTIMORE COMMUNITY FOUNDATION [29]
11 East Mount Royal Avenue
2nd Floor
Baltimore, MD 21202
(410) 332-4171
Fax: (410) 837-4701
E-mail: info@bcf.org
Web Site: www.bcf.org

FOUNDED: 1972

AREAS OF INTEREST:
Education and neighborhoods.

TYPE:
Scholarships. Neighborhood grants. Education grants.

YEAR PROGRAM STARTED: 1972

PURPOSE:
To work for a healthy productive Baltimore region and to provide a flexible effective way for charitable individuals, corporations and foundations to invest in those efforts.

LEGAL BASIS:
Community foundation.

ELIGIBILITY:
The Foundation welcomes grant applications from organizations in the Greater Baltimore region that are tax-exempt under Section 501(c)(3) of the Internal Revenue Code.

The Foundation will be most likely to fund programs that:
(1) address underlying causes of specific problems and seek long-term systemic solutions;
(2) are preventive rather than remedial;
(3) reach a broad segment of the community;
(4) increase individual access and opportunity;
(5) attract financial or volunteer resources or involve collaboration;
(6) build the capacity of grantee organizations and;
(7) strengthen the private, nonprofit sector.

The Foundation does not make grants for annual fund campaigns, operating support except for start-up, religious or sectarian purposes, capital campaigns, or individuals (including scholarships and fellowships).

GEOG. RESTRICTIONS: City of Baltimore and Baltimore County, Maryland.

FINANCIAL DATA:
Amount of support per award: Varies.
Total amount of support: Approximately $19,700,000 for the year 2019.

APPLICATION INFO:
Contact the Foundation for guidelines and application form.
Duration: Typically one year; multiyear grants are dependent upon funds available and is at the discretion of the board committee.
Deadline: Letters of inquiry are welcomed throughout the year. Proposal deadlines vary by grant program.

PUBLICATIONS:
The BCF Edge, newsletter; annual report.

OFFICERS:
Thomas S. Bozzuto, Chairman
Patricia P. Baum, Vice Chairman
Guy E. Flynn, Vice Chairman
Shanaysha M. Sauls, President
Josh E. Fiddler, Treasurer
Marsha Y. Reeves, Secretary

STAFF:
Shanaysha M. Sauls, President and Chief Executive Officer
Patricia Chandler, C.P.A., Vice President, Finance and Administration

BARRA FOUNDATION [30]
200 West Lancaster Avenue
Suite 202
Wayne, PA 19087-4046
(610) 964-7601
Fax: (610) 964-0155
E-mail: info@barrafoundation.org
Web Site: www.barrafoundation.org

FOUNDED: 1963

AREAS OF INTEREST:
Arts and culture, human services, education and health.

TYPE:
Project/program grants. Emergency funding; Impact investing.

PURPOSE:
To improve the lives of individuals, families and communities.

LEGAL BASIS:
Private foundation.

ELIGIBILITY:
501(c)(3) nonprofit organizations only.

GEOG. RESTRICTIONS: Philadelphia, Pennsylvania metropolitan area.

FINANCIAL DATA:
Amount of support per award: $5,000 to $300,000.
Total amount of support: Approximately $4,249,000.

NO. AWARDS: 257.

APPLICATION INFO:
Applications are accepted online only.
Duration: Varies.
Deadline: Applications accepted on a continuous basis.

PUBLICATIONS:
Policy statement.

STAFF:
Kristina L. Wahl, President
Kristi Poling, Program Director, Catalyst Fund
Linda Rich, Senior Program Officer, Learning and Network
Stephanie Mullen, Administrative Coordinator

ADDRESS INQUIRIES TO:
Kristina L. Wahl, President
(See address above.)

*SPECIAL STIPULATIONS:
No grants for environmental programs, exhibitions, publications or religious organizations.

BATTLE CREEK COMMUNITY FOUNDATION [31]
32 West Michigan Avenue
Suite 1
Battle Creek, MI 49017-3505
(269) 962-2181
Fax: (269) 962-2182
E-mail: bccf@bccfoundation.org
Web Site: www.bccfoundation.org

FOUNDED: 1974

AREAS OF INTEREST:
Education, health, and liveable communities for the greater Battle Creek area.

TYPE:
Challenge/matching grants; Conferences/seminars; Demonstration grants; Development grants; Endowments; Project/program grants; Research grants; Scholarships; Technical assistance; Training grants. Emerging needs grants.

YEAR PROGRAM STARTED: 1974

PURPOSE:
To promote philanthropic giving and the use of endowment funds; to serve as a leader in coordinating local resources to meet the current and future needs of the Battle Creek community.

LEGAL BASIS:
Community foundation.

ELIGIBILITY:
Applicants must be nonprofit organizations whose programs will benefit residents or students of the greater Battle Creek community.

No grants for general operating support, endowments, annual fund-raising programs, or projects outside of the Battle Creek area which do not benefit the local community.

General operating support is only given for arts and culture initiatives.

GEOG. RESTRICTIONS: Battle Creek, Michigan area.

FINANCIAL DATA:
Amount of support per award: Average: $10,000 to $15,000.
Total amount of support: $8,500,000.

NO. MOST RECENT APPLICANTS: Approximately 1,500.

NO. AWARDS: Approximately 165.

APPLICATION INFO:
Prospective grant applicants must attend a grantseeker orientation and should contact Foundation staff to gather information on upcoming orientations, dates/times, etc.

Duration: One year.

Deadline: Varies by program.

PUBLICATIONS:
Guidelines; annual report.

ADDRESS INQUIRIES TO:
Annette Chapman, Senior Vice President
(See address above.)

THE BAXTER INTERNATIONAL FOUNDATION   [32]
One Baxter Parkway
Deerfield, IL 60015
(847) 948-2000
E-mail: fdninfo@baxter.com
Web Site: www.baxter.com

FOUNDED: 1981

AREAS OF INTEREST:
Diabetes prevention, digital health, nutrition, and clean water initiatives.

TYPE:
Matching gifts; Project/program grants. The Foundation supports health care awards programs, including the Foster G. McGaw Prize, a $100,000 grant awarded annually to a U.S. hospital that has distinguished itself in community service, the William Graham Health Services Research Award, a $50,000 award made annually to an individual who has made significant contributions to the improved delivery of medical care through innovative health-services research, and the Episteme Award, a $15,000 award given once every two years to recognize outstanding research conducted by a nurse.

YEAR PROGRAM STARTED: 1982

PURPOSE:
To increase access to health care services for the disadvantaged; to improve the quality and cost-effectiveness of health care.

LEGAL BASIS:
Corporate foundation.

ELIGIBILITY:
Grants are made to nonprofit 501(c)(3) organizations with new or expanded programs or direct health care services proposals consistent with the Foundation's priorities. The Foundation strategically identifies specific programs that align with their lines, including geographies where Baxter employees work and live, evidence that the project is a response to a valid need and is superior to other competing projects, and evidence of the agency's capacity to accomplish its goals.

In general, the Foundation does not make grants to capital and endowment campaigns, hospitals, disease-specific organizations, educational institutions, individuals, organizations with a limited constituency such as fraternal, veterans' or religious organizations, organizations soliciting contributions for advertising space, tickets to dinners and fund-raising events and promotional materials.

FINANCIAL DATA:
Amount of support per award: Varies.

Total amount of support: Approximately $7,000,000 in Signature, Healthcare, STEM and Community Grants for the year 2020.

NO. AWARDS: More than 70 grants for the year 2020.

APPLICATION INFO:
The Foundation does not accept unsolicited grant proposals.

Duration: 12 to 36 months.

ADELAIDE BREED BAYRD FOUNDATION   [33]
350 Main Street
Box 30
Malden, MA 02148
(781) 324-1231
Fax: (781) 397-0531
E-mail: kezer@kezer.com
Web Site: bayrd.org

FOUNDED: 1927

AREAS OF INTEREST:
Community services, education and cultural projects, health-related projects and youth-related projects.

TYPE:
Capital grants; Project/program grants; Scholarships; Seed money grants.

PURPOSE:
To support organizations whose activities are centered in the Malden, MA, area, and to support organizations elsewhere, whose activities give substantial benefit to the citizens of Malden.

LEGAL BASIS:
Private foundation.

ELIGIBILITY:
Grants are made to nonprofit, 501(c)(3) organizations in the Foundation's areas of interest. Requests from individuals, endowment funds, performing arts (excepting educational projects and programs) and research will generally be excluded.

In general, the Foundation favors grants toward project services over operational expenditures.

GEOG. RESTRICTIONS: Boston area, with emphasis on Malden and vicinity.

FINANCIAL DATA:
Amount of support per award: Varies.

Total amount of support: Average $1,000,000 annually.

REPRESENTATIVE AWARDS:
$33,000 to ABBF Scholarships; $5,000 to Agassiz Village.

APPLICATION INFO:
To request a grant, applicants must submit the following documents:
(1) cover letter, including contact information, the name and address of the organization, summary of purpose, focus, goals, missions or objectives, amount of funds requested, and how the funds will be used;
(2) grant proposal;
(3) IRS 501(c)(3) letter;
(4) financial documents, which may include financial statement, budget and IRS 990 and;
(5) any additional documentation applicant believes will help further assist the Bayrd Foundation.

Duration: Typically one year. Scholarships may be renewed.

Deadline: Grants: Second Tuesday in February. Scholarships: October 15.

PUBLICATIONS:
Annual report.

IRS I.D.: 04-6051258

TRUSTEES:
C. Henry Kezer, President
Susan C. Mansur, Treasurer
Francis K. Brown, II

Richard R. Burns, Jr.
Laura L. Hodgin
Rev. Paul C. McPheeters
Robert M. Wallask
Dorothy Whittier

ADDRESS INQUIRIES TO:
C. Henry Kezer, President
(See address above.)

H.N. AND FRANCES C. BERGER FOUNDATION   [34]
P.O. Box 13390
Palm Desert, CA 92255
(760) 341-5293
Fax: (760) 341-3518
Web Site: www.hnberger.org

FOUNDED: 1961

AREAS OF INTEREST:
Arts, culture, children, education, environment, health, human services and youth.

TYPE:
Project/program grants.

PURPOSE:
To provide people with the opportunity to improve their own situations.

LEGAL BASIS:
Private family foundation.

ELIGIBILITY:
Grants are made to organizations that have tax-exempt status under Section 501(c)(3) of the Internal Revenue Code. No grants are made to individuals. Nonsectarian religious programs may apply.

GEOG. RESTRICTIONS: United States, primarily southern California.

FINANCIAL DATA:
Amount of support per award: Grants vary in amount, depending upon the needs and nature of the request.

Total amount of support: Varies.

APPLICATION INFO:
The only grant requests the Foundation will consider are those requested by Foundation trustees or staff.

Duration: Typically one year.

ADDRESS INQUIRIES TO:
Catharine N. Reed
Vice President of Charitable Programs
(See address above.)

THE GRACE AND FRANKLIN BERNSEN FOUNDATION   [35]
15 West 6th Street, Suite 1308
Tulsa, OK 74119-5407
(918) 584-4711
E-mail: info@bernsen.org
Web Site: www.bernsen.org

FOUNDED: 1968

AREAS OF INTEREST:
Arts, civic, education, medical, religious, and children.

TYPE:
Challenge/matching grants; Project/program grants.

YEAR PROGRAM STARTED: 1968

PURPOSE:
To provide grants in support of religious, charitable, scientific, literary or educational purposes, or for the prevention of cruelty to children.

LEGAL BASIS:
Private family foundation.

ELIGIBILITY:
The Foundation gives priority to applications from nonprofit organizations with clearly defined benefits, such as those for building and capital funding purposes, and other special program needs. Education programs, including those in the arts, higher education, human services and community programs, religious causes and youth programs are eligible for support.

Grants may require matching funds to be raised by the recipient.

No grants are made to elementary or secondary education institutions unless they involve programs for at-risk, handicapped or learning-disabled children. No grants are made to individuals, or for the benefit of specific individuals.

GEOG. RESTRICTIONS: Tulsa, Oklahoma area.

FINANCIAL DATA:
Amount of support per award: Average: $10,000.
Total amount of support: $1,500,000.

NO. MOST RECENT APPLICANTS: 200.

NO. AWARDS: 50 to 75.

APPLICATION INFO:
Applicants are urged to review the grant guidelines before submitting a proposal. Applications that do not conform to the required format will not be considered. The Foundation welcomes questions about the Foundation and potential applications.
Deadline: Grant applications are accepted monthly.

IRS I.D.: 23-7009414

TRUSTEES:
Melissa P. Easterling
Barbara H. Pray
Donald E. Pray
W. Bland Williamson

ADDRESS INQUIRIES TO:
David M. Zemel, Director
(See address above.)

*PLEASE NOTE:
Applicants are urged to review the grant guidelines before submitting a proposal.

BERRIEN COMMUNITY FOUNDATION   [36]
2900 South State Street
Suite 2E
St. Joseph, MI 49085
(269) 983-3486
E-mail: bcf@berriencommunity.org
Web Site: www.berriencommunity.org

FOUNDED: 1952

AREAS OF INTEREST:
Building spirit of community/arts and culture, nurturing our children, encouraging youth leadership and development.

TYPE:
Development grants; General operating grants; Project/program grants; Scholarships; Seed money grants.

PURPOSE:
To promote philanthropy, build a spirit of community and enhance the quality of life in Berrien County, MI.

ELIGIBILITY:
501(c)(3) or equivalent.

GEOG. RESTRICTIONS: Berrien County, Michigan.

FINANCIAL DATA:
Amount of support per award: Varies.
Total amount of support: $8,149,935 for the year 2019.

APPLICATION INFO:
Contact the Foundation.
Duration: Typically one year.

ADDRESS INQUIRIES TO:
Program Manager
(See address or e-mail above.)

BERWIND CORPORATION   [37]
2929 Walnut Street
Suite 900
Philadelphia, PA 19104
(215) 575-2350
(215) 575-2420
E-mail: jgreen@berwind.com
Web Site: www.berwind.com

FOUNDED: 1886

AREAS OF INTEREST:
Education and community development.

TYPE:
Matching gifts.

LEGAL BASIS:
Nonprofit 501(c)(3) philanthropic organization.

ELIGIBILITY:
Applicants must be 501(c)(3) organizations within Berwind operating areas. Matching gift program is for employees or retired employees only.

GEOG. RESTRICTIONS: Primarily Philadelphia area, Pennsylvania.

FINANCIAL DATA:
Amount of support per award: Varies.
Matching fund requirements: $50 to $10,000 for employee grants only.

APPLICATION INFO:
Contact the Corporation.
Duration: One year.
Deadline: Must receive completed form no later than 90 days from the eligible participant's gift.

ADDRESS INQUIRIES TO:
Jennifer Green, Human Resources Analyst
(See address above.)

BINC FOUNDATION   [38]
3135 South State Street
Suite 203
Ann Arbor, MI 48108
(866) 733-9064
Fax: (734) 477-2806
E-mail: info@bincfoundation.org
Web Site: www.bincfoundation.org

FOUNDED: 1996

AREAS OF INTEREST:
Book and comic book industry.

NAME(S) OF PROGRAMS:
● **Emergency Financial Assistance Grants**
● **Professional Development Scholarships**

TYPE:
Challenge/matching grants; Grants-in-aid; Scholarships. Scholarships are awarded to bookstore and comic shop employees to pursue a variety of professional development opportunities.

PURPOSE:
To assist bookstore and comic store employees across the U.S. in their greatest time of need.

LEGAL BASIS:
501(c)(3) nonprofit organization.

ELIGIBILITY:
To be eligible for a Financial Assistance Grant or scholarship, applicant must be a regular full-time or part-time owner or employee at a bricks-and-mortar bookstore or comic book shop in the U.S., Puerto Rico, the U.S. Virgin Islands or Guam, currently employed for a minimum of 90 days.

FINANCIAL DATA:
Scholarship awards may be used for fees and travel.
Amount of support per award: Emergency Financial Assistance: Varies by need; Matching Grants: Up to $2,000; Scholarships: Varies.
Total amount of support: Emergency Financial Assistance: $250,000 for the year 2019; Scholarships: $60,000 for the year 2020.

NO. AWARDS: Varies.

APPLICATION INFO:
Applications for Emergency Financial Assistance are available online under the Request Assistance menu.

Details on applying for a Binc Scholarship can be found on the Foundation's web site.
Deadline: Varies.

ADDRESS INQUIRIES TO:
See e-mail address above.

THE WILLIAM BINGHAM FOUNDATION   [39]
1375 East 9th Street, Suite 900
Cleveland, OH 44114
(216) 759-9142
E-mail: info@wbinghamfoundation.org
Web Site: wbinghamfoundation.org

FOUNDED: 1955

AREAS OF INTEREST:
Education, science, health and human services, and the arts.

TYPE:
Capital grants; Challenge/matching grants; Endowments; General operating grants; Project/program grants.

YEAR PROGRAM STARTED: 1955

PURPOSE:
To provide funding to nonprofit organizations that sponsor programs in the areas of education, science, health and human services, and the arts; to strengthen civil society and its institutions.

LEGAL BASIS:
Private family foundation.

ELIGIBILITY:
Grants are made only to public charities. Grants are not made to individuals or to organizations located outside of the U.S.

GEOG. RESTRICTIONS: United States.

FINANCIAL DATA:
Amount of support per award: Varies.
Total amount of support: $615,000 for the year 2018.

NO. AWARDS: 17 for the year 2018.

APPLICATION INFO:
The majority of grantmaking is by invitation only.

Duration: Generally one year.

IRS I.D.: 34-6513791

ADDRESS INQUIRIES TO:
Daniel L. Horn, Administrator
(See address above.)

THE BLUESCOPE FOUNDATION NORTH AMERICA   [40]
1540 Genessee Street
Kansas City, MO 64102
(816) 968-3208
Fax: (816) 627-8993
E-mail: jill.harmon@bluescope.com
Web Site: www.bluescopebuildings.com

FOUNDED: 1952

AREAS OF INTEREST:
United charities, scholarship program, aid to education, community needs, youth and civic cultural activities, hospitals and health, and minorities.

TYPE:
Capital grants; General operating grants; Matching gifts; Project/program grants; Scholarships. Scholarship program available to children of Company employees only. Matching gift program for employee contributions to eligible educational or cultural institutions.

In the area of community needs, support is given to organizations which serve broadly the communities in which the Company has employees and significant capital investment. Programs falling within this category include United Way organizations in Company plant cities, minority assistance limited to nonprofit agencies that help provide jobs or job training for the disadvantaged, foster the movement of minorities into the mainstream of economic life and enable minorities to improve their level of educational attainment, and neighborhood and nonresidential building programs utilizing the company's products.

In the area of education, grants are made to colleges and universities which supply significant numbers of employees to the Company and/or which provide opportunities for continuing education to employees, help disadvantaged students who demonstrate ability and desire to prepare for and remain in colleges and universities, have programs which have the objective of providing education to residents of Company plant locations and provide educational opportunities which advance minorities, women and individuals with disabilities.

In the area of culture, the Foundation considers programs which help broaden the cultural experience of the residents of local communities through the support of visual and performing arts organizations, demonstrate concern for excellence and innovation in the arts, and bring cultural opportunity to the economically disadvantaged.

In the area of public affairs, the Foundation helps promote strong relationships between the public and private sectors to assist in the solution to urban problems, reinforce the efforts of groups formed to gather and disseminate information that is in the general public interest, encourage community

volunteerism, and promote economic education and the merits of the free enterprise system.

YEAR PROGRAM STARTED: 1952

PURPOSE:
To provide sustained financial assistance to worthy charitable, educational, health and welfare programs in the U.S.; to enhance the quality of life in those communities where employees of BlueScope Steel reside.

LEGAL BASIS:
A nonprofit, benevolent and charitable corporation under the laws of the State of Missouri. A 501(c)(3) private foundation under IRS code.

ELIGIBILITY:
Grants are made only to nonprofit organizations located in areas where the company has facilities. Organizations must have a clear statement of purpose in the public interest, a program consistent with the organization's stated purpose, evidence of interagency cooperation to avoid duplication of services, an active and responsive governing body of volunteers holding regular meetings, evidence of professional program management and reasonable fund-raising expenses, maintenance of ethical publicity and promotion of the program that excludes exaggerated or misleading claims, and fund solicitation policies which prohibit the payment of commission or other compensation based on total funds raised or undue pressures.

Grants are not normally made to individuals, political organizations, religious organizations for sectarian purposes, pre-school, primary and secondary educational institutions, fraternal or veteran's organizations, organizations receiving United Way support for operating expenses, national health organizations, including local or regional chapters, hospitals (except those providing unique services, burn centers or children's services), tours, conferences, seminars, workshops, testimonial dinners, tables, tickets, advertisements, walk-a-thons, endowment funds, and other foundations of any type providing grants to not-for-profits or programs beyond the Foundation's stated geographic areas of interest.

GEOG. RESTRICTIONS: Rainsville, Alabama; Pine Bluff, Arkansas; Sacramento and Visalia, California; Kansas City and St. Joseph, Missouri; Greensboro, North Carolina; Annville, Pennsylvania; Jackson and Memphis, Tennessee; Kalama, Washington; and Evansville, Wisconsin.

FINANCIAL DATA:
Amount of support per award: $1,000 to $10,000.

Total amount of support: $450,000 annually.

Matching fund requirements: The minimum single gift the Foundation will match per eligible donor is $25. The maximum single gift or total of annual gifts to be matched per eligible donor for full-time employees is $2,000 per calendar year.

NO. MOST RECENT APPLICANTS: 100.

NO. AWARDS: Approximately 100, excluding matching gifts.

REPRESENTATIVE AWARDS:
$10,000 to Harvesters, Kansas City, MO; $5,000 to Genesis School, Kansas City, MO.

APPLICATION INFO:
Initial contact should be made by telephone, e-mail or letter addressed to the Foundation

Administrator or, in non-Kansas City locations, to the plant or division manager describing the need, purpose and general activities of the requesting charitable organization. The letter will be reviewed by the plant or division manager to assure compliance with the policies established by the Foundation Trustees with a recommendation and forwarded to the Foundation Administrator.

Applicants must provide evidence of compliance with eligibility requirements, plus an annual report describing program activities and supporting services including financial statements, detailed annual budget and copy of IRS not-for-profit determination.

Duration: One year.

Deadline: Announcements are made after quarterly Trustee meetings.

PUBLICATIONS:
Annual report; contributions policy; application guidelines.

IRS I.D.: 44-0663648

ADDRESS INQUIRIES TO:
Jill Harmon, Foundation Director
(See address above.)

THE BOOTH-BRICKER FUND   [41]
826 Union Street
Suite 300
New Orleans, LA 70112
(504) 581-2430
Fax: (504) 566-4785
E-mail: heather@boo-ker.com

FOUNDED: 1966

AREAS OF INTEREST:
The Fund focuses exclusively on taking advantage of the historic opportunity to reform public education in New Orleans.

TYPE:
Capital grants; Development grants; Project/program grants.

PURPOSE:
To promote, develop and foster religious, charitable, scientific, literary and educational nonprofit organizations.

ELIGIBILITY:
The Fund generally does not provide sustaining (operations and maintenance) funding. Requests are welcomed for capital needs, special projects and other one-time requirements. No grants are made to individuals or supporting organizations (i.e., a Section 501(c)(3) organization with further designation under Section 509(a)(3)).

GEOG. RESTRICTIONS: Louisiana, with priority given to the New Orleans area.

FINANCIAL DATA:
$50,850,000 in market value assets for the year ended December 31, 2018.

Amount of support per award: Varies.

Total amount of support: Charitable distributions of $2,393,000 for the year ended December 31, 2018.

NO. AWARDS: 83 for the year 2018.

APPLICATION INFO:
Applications, which should be made by letter, are considered by the board of trustees at its quarterly meetings. There are no forms or deadlines. Requests should include complete information about the applicant organization, including its history, purpose, finances, current operations, governing board

and tax status. A detailed explanation of the proposed use of the funds must be provided. Videotapes or DVDs should not be submitted.

Duration: Varies.

BOARD OF TRUSTEES:
Charles B. Mayer
Gray S. Parker
Mary Kay Parker
Nathaniel P. Phillips, Jr.
Nathaniel P. Phillips, III
Elizabeth S. Raindre
H. Hunter White, Jr.

OFFICERS:
Gray S. Parker, Chairman
Ingrid C. Laffont, Treasurer
Heather A. Travland, Secretary

ADDRESS INQUIRIES TO:
Gray S. Parker, Chairman
(See address above.)

JAMES GRAHAM BROWN FOUNDATION, INC. [42]

471 West Main Street
Suite 401
Louisville, KY 40202
(502) 896-2440
Fax: (502) 896-1774
E-mail: grants@jgbf.org
Web Site: www.jgbf.org

FOUNDED: 1954

AREAS OF INTEREST:
Education and workforce, community and economic prosperity, and quality of life.

TYPE:
General operating grants; Grants-in-aid.

YEAR PROGRAM STARTED: 1954

PURPOSE:
To establish the commonwealth as a national leader; to create a public image of Louisville and Kentucky of which we can all be proud.

LEGAL BASIS:
Private foundation.

ELIGIBILITY:
Only Kentucky organizations that have a tax-exempt designation under Section 501(c)(3) of the IRS Code can apply.

GEOG. RESTRICTIONS: Kentucky, with emphasis on Louisville.

FINANCIAL DATA:
Amount of support per award: $500 and up.
Total amount of support: Approximately $16,000,000.

NO. MOST RECENT APPLICANTS: Approximately 100.

NO. AWARDS: Approximately 50.

REPRESENTATIVE AWARDS:
$3,000,000 to Louisville Urban League for the Sports and Learning Complex;
$1,000,000 to Metro United Way for improving developmental, educational and life outcomes for Louisville citizens;
$500,000 to Gilda's Club Louisville for the Red Door Campaign in order to establish a Shared Services Group among local nonprofits with similar goals and operations to FCP.

APPLICATION INFO:
Contact the Foundation for details.
Duration: One year.
Deadline: Varies.

PUBLICATIONS:
Annual report.

ADDRESS INQUIRIES TO:
Mason Rummel, President and Chief Executive Officer
(See address above.)

THE JOE W. AND DOROTHY DORSETT BROWN FOUNDATION [43]

320 Metairie Hammond Highway
Suite 500
Metairie, LA 70005
(504) 834-3433
Fax: (504) 834-3441
E-mail: bethbuscher@thebrownfoundation.org
Web Site: www.thebrownfoundation.org

FOUNDED: 1959

AREAS OF INTEREST:
Human services; medical, health and science; education; community benefit; and conservation and environment.

TYPE:
General operating grants; Project/program grants; Research grants; Training grants.

PURPOSE:
To alleviate human suffering.

ELIGIBILITY:
Applicants must be nonprofit 501(c)(3). The Foundation favors requests for funds where funds are generally unavailable from most other sources. Within the five focus areas, the focus is primarily on relieving human suffering; secondary interest includes cultural, spiritual, educational or scientific initiatives. No grants are made to individuals.

GEOG. RESTRICTIONS: Louisiana and Mississippi. Preference is given to the greater New Orleans area and Mississippi gulf coast.

FINANCIAL DATA:
Amount of support per award: Varies.
Total amount of support: Varies.

APPLICATION INFO:
Contact the Foundation.
Duration: One year. Must reapply.
Deadline: August 30.

THE MARGARET E. BURNHAM CHARITABLE TRUST [44]

c/o H.M. Payson & Co.
P.O. Box 31
Portland, ME 04112-0031
(207) 772-3761
Fax: (207) 871-7508
E-mail: jbe@hmpayson.com
Web Site: www.margaretburnham.org

AREAS OF INTEREST:
Community/social services, medical, educational, arts and culture, and environment.

TYPE:
Grants-in-aid; Project/program grants. Annual grant dedicated to responding to the needs of the Maine communities served.

PURPOSE:
To benefit nonprofit organizations located or operating in the state of Maine.

ELIGIBILITY:
Organizations must be 501(c)(3) and must operate in and serve the state of Maine.

Individuals, private foundations under Section 509, and religious organizations are not eligible.

GEOG. RESTRICTIONS: Maine.

FINANCIAL DATA:
Amount of support per award: $1,000 to $15,000.
Total amount of support: Varies.

APPLICATION INFO:
A completed application consists of the following:
(1) certification, application, project description, and budget pages;
(2) copy of the organization's most recent 501(c)(3) IRS ruling;
(3) copy of the organization's most recent financial statement or tax return and;
(4) list of the organization's officers and directors.
Duration: One year.
Deadline: October 1.

ADDRESS INQUIRIES TO:
Thomas M. Pierce, Trustee
(See address above.)

EDYTH BUSH CHARITABLE FOUNDATION, INC. [45]

P.O. Box 1967
Winter Park, FL 32790-1967
(407) 647-4322
E-mail: grantsinfo@edythbush.org
Web Site: www.edythbush.org

FOUNDED: 1973

AREAS OF INTEREST:
Children, youth and families, education, health care, limited interest in the arts, improvement of nonprofit organizations, and human services.

TYPE:
Capital grants; Challenge/matching grants; Demonstration grants; Development grants; Matching gifts; Project/program grants; Technical assistance; Training grants. Capacity building grants.

PURPOSE:
To create innovative civic solutions to help people help themselves.

LEGAL BASIS:
Private foundation.

ELIGIBILITY:
The Foundation welcomes grant applications from nonprofit organizations that have secured their 501(c)(3) and 509(a) IRS rulings. The Foundation has elected to focus its resources within Lake, Orange, Osceola and Seminole counties, FL. The Foundation will not fund organizations that are chiefly tax-supported, nor does it fund individual scholarships, individual research (even if through an exempt or otherwise qualified educational organization), alcoholism or drug abuse programs or facilities, routine operating expenses, the pay-off of deficits or pre-existing debt, foreign organizations or foreign expenditures, travel projects or fellowships, chiefly church, sacramental, denominational or interdenominational purposes (except those outreach programs for elderly, indigents, needy, youth or homeless, regardless of belief, race, color, creed, or sex), endowment funds, advocacy organizations, or organizations that have receipts or revenues from memberships and/or contributions of less than $25,000.

GEOG. RESTRICTIONS: Lake, Orange, Osceola and Seminole counties, Florida.

FINANCIAL DATA:
Amount of support per award: Typically $5,000 to $50,000.
Total amount of support: Varies.
Matching fund requirements: Must be new or increased cash contributions or pledges. Capital projects are not funded unless matched.

APPLICATION INFO:
Applicants should review the limitations and procedures before inquiry. Eligible organization may send the Grants Manager a Letter of Inquiry stating the amount sought, purpose of the grant, and nature of the organization. Grant applications are available by invitation only.
Duration: Most grants are for one year.
Deadline: Applications are accepted year-round.

PUBLICATIONS:
Guidelines.

IRS I.D.: 23-7318041

OFFICERS:
David A. Odahowski, President and Chief Executive Officer
Mary Ellen Hutcheson, CPA, Vice President and Treasurer
Matthew W. Certo, Corporate Secretary

BOARD OF DIRECTORS:
Richard J. Walsh, Chairman
Matthew W. Certo, Vice Chairman and Corporate Secretary
Brian M. Butler
Elizabeth Dvorak
Patricia Engfer
Anne B. Kerr, Ph.D.
David A. Odahowski
John A. Riley

ADDRESS INQUIRIES TO:
Heidi Findlay, Grants Manager
(See e-mail address above.)

*PLEASE NOTE:
Inquiries must contain organization's Federal EIN and Florida's State Solicitation Registration number.

CABOT FAMILY CHARITABLE TRUST   [46]
22 Batterymarch Street
Boston, MA 02109
(617) 226-7505
Fax: (617) 451-1733
E-mail: elynch@cabotwellington.com
Web Site: www.cabotfamilytrust.org

FOUNDED: 1942

AREAS OF INTEREST:
Arts and culture, education and youth development, environment and conservation, health and human services, and for the public benefit.

TYPE:
Capital grants; General operating grants; Project/program grants. Capital campaigns.

YEAR PROGRAM STARTED: 1942

PURPOSE:
To provide funding for nonprofit organizations working in the arts, environment, youth development, education, health and human services.

LEGAL BASIS:
Charitable trust.

ELIGIBILITY:
The Trust supports only nonprofit organizations holding active 501(c)(3) status under the IRS code. The Trust does not make contributions to individuals, political organizations, religious institutions, advertising, sponsorship or fraternal organizations.

Applicants must meet the following criteria: (1) extend important services to individuals and groups not served adequately through other programs and institutions; (2) manage change by assessing community needs and developing programs to meet emerging needs; (3) promote productive cooperation and full use of resources by nonprofit organizations and community groups and; (4) test new approaches to problems or adapt solutions that have been successful elsewhere.

GEOG. RESTRICTIONS: Boston and other contiguous communities.

FINANCIAL DATA:
Assets of $48,000,000.
Amount of support per award: $5,000 to $50,000 per year.
Total amount of support: $2,000,000.

NO. MOST RECENT APPLICANTS: Approximately 280 for the year 2019.

NO. AWARDS: Approximately 80.

REPRESENTATIVE AWARDS:
$20,000 to Eliot School of Fine Arts for the Teen Bridge program, offering talented youth a chance to develop as artists and leaders; $50,000 to Boston Medical Center to support the renovation of the pediatric emergency department; $35,000 to Urban Farming Institute to support educational community programs at the new headquarters at the Fowler Clark Epstein farm.

APPLICATION INFO:
Applicants should submit a concept paper of three pages plus cover sheet and budget. Application form is available on the web site.
Duration: Usually, one year; multiyear considered.
Deadline: February 1 and September 1.

PUBLICATIONS:
Annual report.

IRS I.D.: 04-6035446

TRUSTEES:
Shoma Aditya
Frank Bradley
Laura C. Carrigan
Mary Schneider Enriquez
Greenfield Sluder
Hendrika Sluder

EXECUTIVE DIRECTOR:
Elizabeth M. Lynch

ADDRESS INQUIRIES TO:
Elizabeth M. Lynch, Executive Director
(See address above.)

THE MORRIS AND GWENDOLYN CAFRITZ FOUNDATION   [47]
1825 K Street, N.W.
Suite 1400
Washington, DC 20006
(202) 223-3100
Fax: (202) 296-7567
E-mail: info@cafritzfoundation.org
Web Site: cafritzfoundation.org

FOUNDED: 1948

AREAS OF INTEREST:
Community services, arts and humanities, education, health and the environment.

TYPE:
Challenge/matching grants; General operating grants; Project/program grants; Scholarships; Technical assistance.

YEAR PROGRAM STARTED: 1948

PURPOSE:
To build a stronger community for residents of the Washington, DC area through support of programs in arts and humanities, community services, education, health and the environment.

LEGAL BASIS:
Private foundation.

ELIGIBILITY:
Grants are made only to charitable, educational and cultural institutions exempt from taxation under the Internal Revenue Code. IRS-registered, tax-exempt, 501(c)(3) organizations with a public charity status of 509(a)(1) or 509(a)(2) only. The general policy is to concentrate grants to organizations, operating within the greater Washington metropolitan area, with projects of direct assistance to the District of Columbia and its environs. Grants are not made for capital purposes, endowments or to individuals.

GEOG. RESTRICTIONS: Montgomery and Prince George's counties in Maryland; Arlington and Fairfax counties, and the cities of Alexandria and Falls Church in Virginia; and Washington, DC.

FINANCIAL DATA:
Amount of support per award: Varies.
Total amount of support: Approximately $7,500,000.

NO. MOST RECENT APPLICANTS: Approximately 700.

NO. AWARDS: Approximately 425.

APPLICATION INFO:
To be considered for funding, an organization must submit a complete proposal, not a Letter of Inquiry (LOI). LOIs are not required. Organizations may submit a proposal for only one deadline within a 12-month period.
Duration: One year.
Deadline: November 1, March 1 and July 1.

PUBLICATIONS:
Annual report; application guidelines.

OFFICERS:
Calvin Cafritz, President and Chief Executive Officer
John E. Chapoton, Vice Chairman

STAFF:
Mardell Moffett, Executive Director
Mary Mulcahy, Associate Director
Tobi Printz-Platnick, Associate Director
Gretchen Greiner-Lott, Program Officer
Hannah Hahn, Program Officer
Sarah Hashmall, Program Officer
Debbi Lindenberg, Program Officer
Jessica Plocher, Program Officer
Mike Schwartz, Program Officer
Nailah Hart, Grants Manager
Arielle Phillips, Program Assistant
Esthanette Reid, Program Assistant

DIRECTORS:
Calvin Cafritz, Chairman of the Board
Michael F. Brewer
Jane Lipton Cafritz
John E. Chapoton
Dorothy Kosinski
Patricia McGuire
Whayne Quinn
Robert Sloan

ADVISORY BOARD:
Anthony W. Cafritz
Elliot S. Cafritz
The Hon. Constance A. Morella
Elizabeth M. Peltekian

ADDRESS INQUIRIES TO:
Mardell Moffett, Executive Director
(See address above.)

CALERES CARES CHARITABLE TRUST [48]
8300 Maryland Avenue
St. Louis, MO 63105
(314) 854-4000
Web Site: www.caleres.com

FOUNDED: 1951

AREAS OF INTEREST:
Family, healthy living/wellness, arts and culture, local community, and footwear industry.

TYPE:
Project/program grants.

YEAR PROGRAM STARTED: 1951

PURPOSE:
To help develop stronger families by providing opportunities for enrichment; to encourage individuals to live better lives through health and wellness efforts; to provide occasions for families and individuals to step feet-first into the arts and cultural opportunities in the community.

LEGAL BASIS:
Corporate contributions program.

ELIGIBILITY:
The Caleres Trust encourages 501(c)(3) tax-exempt, nonprofit organizations who meet the Trust's funding priorities to apply.

The Trust supports charitable organizations which are either strategically aligned with the Trust's mission, vision and values, focused on advancing the footwear industry or benefit the overall St. Louis community in growing and attracting new businesses and residents.

Grants are not made to individuals. In general, the Trust does not support galas, walks, golf outings, trivia nights, etc.

FINANCIAL DATA:
To date, Caleres has donated more than $30,000,000 to 501(c)(3) organizations.

APPLICATION INFO:
Applications must be submitted through the application link found on the Caleres web site. The online application requires the following attachments:
(1) current year's operating budget;
(2) list of board members and;
(3) program or project budget (if applicable). Attachments can be in Microsoft Word, Excel or Adobe PDF format. Compressed ZIP files must not be included.

Deadline: Grant proposals: March 31, June 30, September 30 and December 31.

*PLEASE NOTE:
The Caleres Cares Charitable Trust was formerly known as the Brown Shoe Company, Inc. Charitable Trust.

CAMPBELL SOUP FOUNDATION [49]
One Campbell Place
Camden, NJ 08103
(856) 342-5264
Web Site: www.campbellsoupcompany.com

FOUNDED: 1953

AREAS OF INTEREST:
Increasing access to healthy food, encouraging healthy living and nurturing Campbell neighborhoods.

NAME(S) OF PROGRAMS:
- **Dollars for Doers Fund**
- **Matching Gift Program**
- **United Way Match Program**

TYPE:
Matching gifts. Dollars for Doers Program provides financial support to nonprofit organizations where Campbell employees volunteer in Campbell communities.

Matching Gift Program supports employee's gifts to higher education and to six pre-selected nonprofit organizations whose mission closely meets the Foundation's CSR goals.

The Campbell Soup Foundation also supports 15 separate United Way campaigns hosted at Campbell and Pepperidge Farm operating facilities throughout the U.S.

YEAR PROGRAM STARTED: 1954

PURPOSE:
To provide financial support to local champions that inspire positive change in communities throughout the U.S. where Campbell Soup Company employees live and work.

LEGAL BASIS:
Tax-exempt private foundation.

ELIGIBILITY:
Grants are made to tax-exempt organizations providing service consistent with Foundation's goals. Grants are not directed at supporting individuals.

GEOG. RESTRICTIONS: United States.

FINANCIAL DATA:
Amount of support per award: Varies.
Total amount of support: Approximately $1,900,000 each fiscal year.

NO. MOST RECENT APPLICANTS: 90 grant applications for the year 2018.

NO. AWARDS: 33 grants awarded for the year 2018.

APPLICATION INFO:
Grants are offered by invitation only.
Duration: Usually one-time grants.
Deadline: Two funding cycles per year, one in the fall and one in the spring, typically four months in length. Fall cycle runs September through December and Spring cycle runs January through April.

OFFICERS:
Kim Fortunato, President
Gary Biscoll, Treasurer
Andrew Kupchik, Secretary
Stanley Polomski, Controller

TRUSTEES:
Gary Biscoll

Monica Diaz
Deb Fair
Kim Fortunato
Carrie Griesser
Richard Landers
Helen Le Du
Leah Murphy
Anthony Sanzio
Tara Smith
Scott Swanson
Emily Waldorf

ADDRESS INQUIRIES TO:
Kate Barrett, Vice President and Program Manager
(See address above.)

THE CANNON FOUNDATION, INC. [50]
52 Spring Street, N.W.
Concord, NC 28025
(704) 786-8216
Fax: (704) 782-2812
E-mail: tmarkanda@cannonfoundation.org
info@cannonfoundation.org
Web Site: www.cannonfoundation.org

FOUNDED: 1943

AREAS OF INTEREST:
Primarily health care, higher education and human services. Limited grants to arts, historical preservation and environment.

TYPE:
Capital grants.

YEAR PROGRAM STARTED: 1943

LEGAL BASIS:
Private foundation.

ELIGIBILITY:
Applicant must be 501(c)(3) nonprofit organization. No grants to individuals.

GEOG. RESTRICTIONS: North Carolina.

FINANCIAL DATA:
Amount of support per award: $5,000 to $200,000.

APPLICATION INFO:
Applications are requested through the web site. Links to the online application are sent to the applying organization's chief executive officer/executive director, not to grant writers or consultants.
Duration: One year.
Deadline: January 10, May 10 and September 10. Notification approximately 12 weeks after deadline.

STAFF:
Tina Markanda, Executive Director

ADDRESS INQUIRIES TO:
Tina Markanda, Executive Director
(See address above.)

CARNEGIE CORPORATION OF NEW YORK [51]
437 Madison Avenue
New York, NY 10022
(212) 371-3200
Fax: (212) 754-4073
E-mail: grantsinfo@carnegie.org
Web Site: www.carnegie.org/grants

FOUNDED: 1911

AREAS OF INTEREST:
Education, democracy, international peace and security, and higher education and research in Africa.

TYPE:
Conferences/seminars; Development grants;
Project/program grants; Research grants;
Seed money grants.

YEAR PROGRAM STARTED: 1911

PURPOSE:
To promote the advancement and diffusion of
knowledge and understanding.

LEGAL BASIS:
Private foundation.

ELIGIBILITY:
Grants are made primarily to academic
institutions and national or regional
organizations.

FINANCIAL DATA:
Amount of support per award:
Approximately $550,000.
Total amount of support: $151,958,937
appropriated for the year 2019.

NO. AWARDS: Varies.

APPLICATION INFO:
After a letter of inquiry has been reviewed,
applicants may be invited via e-mail to
submit a full proposal. Only full proposals
that have been invited for submission will be
considered.
Duration: Varies.

PUBLICATIONS:
Program guidelines; pamphlet; meeting and
occasional papers; *Carnegie Reporter,*
magazine; annual report.

IRS I.D.: 13-1628151

ADDRESS INQUIRIES TO:
See e-mail address above.

AMON G. CARTER FOUNDATION [52]
201 Main Street, Suite 1945
Fort Worth, TX 76102
(817) 332-2783
Fax: (817) 332-2787
E-mail: mwallace@agcf.org
Web Site: www.agcf.org

FOUNDED: 1945

AREAS OF INTEREST:
Education, arts, health and medical services,
and human and social services.

TYPE:
Capital grants; Challenge/matching grants;
Seed money grants. Program expansion.

PURPOSE:
To support arts, education, health and
medical services, programs benefiting youth
and elderly, and civic and community
endeavors that enhance quality of life.

LEGAL BASIS:
Private foundation.

ELIGIBILITY:
Applicants must be 501(c)(3) organizations.
Board focus on Fort Worth and Tarrant
County, TX.

No loans. No grants to individuals.

GEOG. RESTRICTIONS: Texas.

FINANCIAL DATA:
Amount of support per award: $1,000 to
$500,000.
Total amount of support: $32,000,000.

NO. MOST RECENT APPLICANTS: 400.

NO. AWARDS: 200.

REPRESENTATIVE AWARDS:
$500,000 to All Saints Health Foundation;
$3,000,000 to Texas Christian University;
$150,000 to University of Texas Medical
Branch; $175,000 to Communities in Schools
of Greater Tarrant County.

APPLICATION INFO:
Send brief letter request supplemented with
project budget and/or other pertinent
information in support of request.
Duration: Most grants are for one year.
Deadline: January, April and October.

PUBLICATIONS:
Grant policy and guideline statement.

OFFICERS:
John H. Robinson, Executive Vice President,
Grant Administration
Tamara Dean, Controller

BOARD OF DIRECTORS:
Robert W. Brown, M.D.
Kate L. Johnson
Mark L. Johnson
Sheila B. Johnson

ADDRESS INQUIRIES TO:
John H. Robinson
Executive Vice President
Grant Administration
P.O. Box 1036
Fort Worth, TX 76102

HAROLD K.L. CASTLE FOUNDATION [53]
1197 Auloa Road
Kailua, HI 96734-4606
(808) 263-7073
Fax: (808) 261-6918
E-mail: amatsukado@castlefoundation.org
Web Site: www.castlefoundation.org

FOUNDED: 1962

AREAS OF INTEREST:
Hawaii's public education redesign and
enhancement, Hawaii's nearshore marine
resource conservation, strengthening the
communities of Windward Oahu, and other
areas of focus when the Foundation sees a
special opportunity to make a difference with
limited resources.

TYPE:
Capital grants; Project/program grants; Seed
money grants.

PURPOSE:
To benefit the people of Hawaii.

LEGAL BASIS:
Family foundation.

ELIGIBILITY:
Nonprofit organizations serving the state of
Hawaii with Internal Revenue Code Sections
501(c)(3) and 509(a) public charity status and
public schools in Hawaii.

GEOG. RESTRICTIONS: Hawaii.

CO-OP FUNDING PROGRAMS: Hawaii Community
Stabilization Initiative.

NO. MOST RECENT APPLICANTS: 125.

NO. AWARDS: 74.

REPRESENTATIVE AWARDS:
$750,000 to Teach for America; $1,200,000
to The Nature Conservancy of Hawaii;
$1,500,000 to The Hawaii Community
Foundation.

APPLICATION INFO:
Prospective grant applicants must submit an
Online Inquiry Form, which is the first step

in requesting funds from the Foundation. The
Foundation will contact applicants within one
month to request more information, invite the
submission of a full proposal, or to inform
applicant that the Foundation will be unable
to consider a full proposal due to limited
resources and/or a mismatch with Foundation
priorities.
Duration: Program grants: Up to five years.
Deadline: Applications accepted on a rolling
basis. Capital support requests due each year
by October 1.

PUBLICATIONS:
Application guidelines; annual report.

IRS I.D.: 99-6005445

STAFF:
Terrence R. George, President and Chief
Executive Officer
Carlton K.C. Au, Vice President, Chief
Financial Officer and Treasurer
Alex Harris, Vice President of Programs
Eric Co, Senior Program Officer for Ocean
Resiliency
Ann Matsukado, Controller/Grants Manager
Susan Sumida, Corporate Secretary
Linda Mekaru, Accountant

BOARD OF DIRECTORS:
H. Mitchell D'Olier, Chairman of the Board
Dr. Claire L. Asam, Director
Dr. Kittredge A. Baldwin, Director
Corbett A.K. Kalama, Director
Dee Jay Mailer, Director
James C. McIntosh, Director
James H. McIntosh, Director
Eric K. Yeaman, Director

ADDRESS INQUIRIES TO:
Ann Matsukado, Controller/Grants Manager
(See address above.)

CENTRAL MAINE POWER COMPANY [54]
83 Edison Drive
Augusta, ME 04330
Fax: (207) 629-4737
E-mail: amy.marston@cmpco.com
Web Site: www.cmpco.com

AREAS OF INTEREST:
Education, civic, science, technology
education and economic development.

NAME(S) OF PROGRAMS:
● **Central Maine Power Company
Corporate Contributions Program**

TYPE:
Capital grants; Challenge/matching grants;
Demonstration grants; General operating
grants; Project/program grants; Research
grants.

LEGAL BASIS:
Corporation giving program.

ELIGIBILITY:
Organization must be tax-exempt under
501(c)(3) of the Internal Revenue Code,
limited to the area serviced by Central Maine
Power.

GEOG. RESTRICTIONS: Maine.

FINANCIAL DATA:
Amount of support per award: $100 to
$1,000.

NO. MOST RECENT APPLICANTS: 250.

NO. AWARDS: 50.

APPLICATION INFO:
Applicants should send a proposal letter,
which includes a specific goal and purpose
for the request.

Duration: Typically one year. Some multiyear funding.

Deadline: Applications accepted throughout the year. Grants announced monthly.

ADDRESS INQUIRIES TO:
Public Affairs
(See address above.)

*SPECIAL STIPULATIONS:
Only available to schools and nonprofits within company's service territory in Maine.

THE CHAMPLIN FOUNDATION [55]

2000 Chapel View Boulevard, Suite 350
Cranston, RI 02920
(401) 944-9200
Fax: (401) 944-9299
E-mail: office@champlinfoundation.org
Web Site: champlinfoundation.org

FOUNDED: 1932

AREAS OF INTEREST:
Conservation, environment, education, health, cultural programs, youth, social services, historic preservation, animal welfare and libraries.

TYPE:
Capital grants. Direct grants for capital needs including the purchase of equipment, real estate, renovations, construction and reduction of mortgage indebtedness.

Other grants are made only in certain circumstances.

Challenge grants are made at the Foundations' discretion.

YEAR PROGRAM STARTED: 1932

PURPOSE:
To make grants to qualified charitable organizations to promote the general well-being of humanity, with preference to Rhode Island.

LEGAL BASIS:
Tax-exempt private foundation.

ELIGIBILITY:
Only tax-exempt organizations located in Rhode Island may apply. No grants are awarded to individuals.

GEOG. RESTRICTIONS: Rhode Island.

FINANCIAL DATA:
Amount of support per award: Average: $25,000 to $65,000.

Total amount of support: Approximately $19,000,000 for the year 2019.

NO. MOST RECENT APPLICANTS: 350 to 400.

NO. AWARDS: 200 for the year 2019.

REPRESENTATIVE AWARDS:
$4,965 to RI Companion Animal Alliance to equip a new exam room at the Pets in Need Veterinary Clinic; $7,950 to Revive the Roots Foundation to bring electricity to Mowry Commons; $48,329 to Johnston Senior High School to equip a materials processing lab; $39,960 to General Nathanael Greene Homestead Association to complete construction of the educational/event barn; $63,000 to Jonnycake Center of Westerly for thrift store and receiving area renovation.

APPLICATION INFO:
The Foundation uses a web-based grant application. Guidelines and policies for submission are detailed on the Foundation web site.

Duration: No grants are awarded on a continuing basis. Applicants may apply annually.

Deadline: Capital Grants are awarded in two cycles: December 15 to January 15 and June 1 to July 1. Notification in June and November, respectively.

PUBLICATIONS:
Annual report; guidelines; Report on Open Space and Recreation Grants.

IRS I.D.: 51-0165988

ADDRESS INQUIRIES TO:
Nina Stack, Executive Director
(See address above.)

BEN B. CHENEY FOUNDATION [56]

3110 Ruston Way, Suite A
Tacoma, WA 98402
(253) 572-2442
E-mail: info@benbcheneyfoundation.org
Web Site: www.benbcheneyfoundation.org

AREAS OF INTEREST:
Charity, civic affairs, culture, education, the elderly, health, social services and youth.

TYPE:
Capital grants; Project/program grants.

PURPOSE:
To improve the quality of life in communities where the Cheney Lumber Company operated.

LEGAL BASIS:
Foundation.

ELIGIBILITY:
Applicants must be 501(c)(3) tax-exempt organizations.

GEOG. RESTRICTIONS: Tacoma and Pierce County, Washington; Medford and Jackson County, Oregon and the seven northernmost counties in California.

FINANCIAL DATA:
Amount of support per award: $1,000 to $15,000 for small grants; $16,000 to $100,000 for regular grants.

Total amount of support: $3,053,881 for the year 2020.

NO. MOST RECENT APPLICANTS: Approximately 300.

NO. AWARDS: 165 for the year 2020.

APPLICATION INFO:
Details are available on the Foundation web site. Application must be submitted electronically.

Duration: Typically one to two years. No renewals.

ADDRESS INQUIRIES TO:
Brad Cheney, Executive Director
(See address above.)

THE CHRISTENSEN FUND [57]

660 Fourth Street, No. 235
San Francisco, CA 94107
(415) 644-1600
Fax: (415) 644-1601
E-mail: info@christensenfund.org
Web Site: www.christensenfund.org

FOUNDED: 1957

AREAS OF INTEREST:
Indigenous peoples' rights; biological and cultural diversity.

NAME(S) OF PROGRAMS:
● **Kenya/East Africa**
● **Mexico/Latin America**

TYPE:
General operating grants; Project/program grants.

YEAR PROGRAM STARTED: 2004

PURPOSE:
To back the global Indigenous Peoples movement in its efforts to advance the rights and opportunities of stewards of biocultural diversity.

LEGAL BASIS:
Private, independent foundation.

ELIGIBILITY:
Must have nonprofit 501(c)(3) status or similar not-for-profit organization based either in the U.S. or another country.

FINANCIAL DATA:
Amount of support per award: $100,000 to $300,000.

Total amount of support: Approximately $10,000,000 for the year 2020.

NO. AWARDS: 60 on average.

APPLICATION INFO:
Unsolicited requests are not accepted.

Duration: Typically two years.

ADDRESS INQUIRIES TO:
See e-mail address above.

THE CLEVELAND-CLIFFS FOUNDATION [58]

200 Public Square
Suite 3300
Cleveland, OH 44114-2589
(216) 694-5700
Fax: (216) 694-4880
E-mail: clevelandcliffsfoundation_ohio@clevelandcliffs.com
Web Site: www.clevelandcliffs.com

FOUNDED: 1962

AREAS OF INTEREST:
Education and community building.

TYPE:
Capital grants; General operating grants.

PURPOSE:
To enhance the quality of life of the Company's employees and communities in which the Company operates.

ELIGIBILITY:
501(c)(3) organizations, as defined by the IRS, may apply. Request must address Cliffs Foundation funding priorities, including geographical and cause areas of interest. Organizations and their proposed programs must address specific community needs.

GEOG. RESTRICTIONS: Upper Peninsula of Michigan; northeastern Minnesota and Cleveland, Ohio.

FINANCIAL DATA:
Amount of support per award: $250 minimum.

APPLICATION INFO:
A brief project summary must be e-mailed to the regional public affairs contact listed online. Summary must be no greater than two paragraphs in length.

Duration: One year.

Deadline: Applications accepted throughout the year.

PUBLICATIONS:
Guidelines.

ADDRESS INQUIRIES TO:
Anna Ediger, Manager of
Government Relations
(See address above.)

COASTAL BEND COMMUNITY FOUNDATION   [59]
555 North Carancahua Street
Suite 900
Corpus Christi, TX 78401
(361) 882-9745
Fax: (361) 882-2865
E-mail: kselim@cbcfoundation.org
Web Site: www.cbcfoundation.org

FOUNDED: 1981

AREAS OF INTEREST:
Arts, children and youth, community
development, crime prevention, elderly,
environment, health, social welfare, education
and human services.

TYPE:
Project/program grants; Scholarships.

YEAR PROGRAM STARTED: 1981

PURPOSE:
To improve the quality of life in the Coastal
Bend area.

LEGAL BASIS:
Community foundation.

ELIGIBILITY:
Grants are made to organizations that have
tax-exempt status under Section 501(c)(3) of
the Internal Revenue Code. No grants are
made to individuals.

GEOG. RESTRICTIONS: Aransas, Bee, Jim Wells,
Kleberg, Nueces, Refugio and San Patricio
counties, Texas.

FINANCIAL DATA:
Amount of support per award: Varies.
Total amount of support: $11,079,883 for the
year 2018.
Matching fund requirements: Determined on
individual basis.

CO-OP FUNDING PROGRAMS: Coastal Bend Day
of Giving.

NO. AWARDS: Varies.

APPLICATION INFO:
Applications accepted online between May 1
and June 15. Organizations should submit
application with requested documentation by
the application deadline. Applications that do
not conform to the required format will not
be considered.
Duration: Grants must be completed by the
following September 30.
Deadline: Posted online.

PUBLICATIONS:
Annual report.

IRS I.D.: 74-2190039

ADDRESS INQUIRIES TO:
Karen W. Selim, President and
Chief Executive Officer
(See address above.)

THE COCKRELL FOUNDATION   [60]
3737 Buffalo Speedway
Suite 1100
Houston, TX 77098
(713) 209-7500
E-mail: foundation@cockrellfoundation.org
Web Site: www.cockrellfoundation.org

FOUNDED: 1957

AREAS OF INTEREST:
Education, health, culture and community.

TYPE:
Endowments; Professorships; Project/program
grants; Scholarships. Endowments,
fellowships, professorships and scholarships
at University of Texas, Cockrell School of
Engineering.

YEAR PROGRAM STARTED: 1966

PURPOSE:
To provide financial support for charitable
organizations in the Houston area in support
of education, health, civic, religious and
social services.

LEGAL BASIS:
Private foundation.

ELIGIBILITY:
Endowments, fellowships, professorships and
scholarships to the University of Texas
Cockrell School of Engineering only.

In general, the Foundation gives support for
annual and capital campaigns, building funds,
endowment funds, general purposes,
matching funds, and special projects. Grants
are made only to nonprofit, tax-exempt
organizations. To be eligible, an organization
must have a determination letter from the
IRS indicating that it is an organization
described in Section 501(c)(3) of the Internal
Revenue Code and is not a private foundation
within the meaning of Section 509(a) of the
Code.

GEOG. RESTRICTIONS: Primarily Houston, Texas.

FINANCIAL DATA:
Amount of support per award: Varies.
Total amount of support: $8,722,728 in
grants for the year 2019.

NO. AWARDS: 33 grants for the year 2018.

APPLICATION INFO:
The Foundation accepts online grant
applications only. The following materials
must be uploaded to the online application:
(1) name and address of tax-exempt
organization which will be the recipient if a
donation is made and a copy of the
exemption letter from the U.S. Treasury
Department;
(2) specific sum being requested;
(3) an Executive Summary sheet (one page)
describing the need or problem with an
explanation of how the grant money will be
used and what is hoped to be accomplished;
(4) budget for the project or program giving
the total cost;
(5) amount raised to date toward the project
or program and the souces from which it has
come, including private, religious
organizations and/or government sources and,
in particular, the total amount contributed by
the individuals on the Board of Directors;
(6) plans for raising any uncovered balance;
(7) an explanation of why it is necessary to
seek outside support;
(8) current status of the project;
(9) plans for putting continuing projects on a
self-sustaining basis and an estimate of when
this will occur;
(10) copy of the organization's current annual
budget;
(11) copy of the organization's latest
IRS-990;
(12) copy of the organization's latest audited
financials;
(13) list of the members of the Board of
Directors and;
(14) list of the officers of the organization.

Duration: One year.

IRS I.D.: 74-6076993

OFFICERS AND DIRECTORS:
Ernest H. Cockrell, President and Director
M. Nancy Williams, Executive Vice President
Sherrie J. Reinhackel, Vice President
Stacy L. White, Secretary/Treasurer
David A. Cockrell, Director
Ernest D. Cockrell, Director
Janet S. Cockrell, Director
Richard B. Curran, Director
Milton T. Graves, Director
J. Webb Jennings, III, Director
Ronald T. Nixon, Director
Laura Jennings Turner, Director

ADDRESS INQUIRIES TO:
M. Nancy Williams
Executive Vice President
(See address above.)

THE OGDEN CODMAN TRUST   [61]
c/o Rackemann, Sawyer & Brewster
160 Federal Street, 15th Floor
Boston, MA 02110-1700
(617) 951-1108
Fax: (617) 542-7437
E-mail: smonahan@rackemann.com
Web Site: www.codmantrust.org

FOUNDED: 1968

AREAS OF INTEREST:
Environment, conservation, historic
preservation, cultural, health and social
services in the town of Lincoln, MA.

TYPE:
Project/program grants. Support for special
programs.

YEAR PROGRAM STARTED: 1972

PURPOSE:
To improve the quality of life in Lincoln.

LEGAL BASIS:
Private independent foundation.

ELIGIBILITY:
Organizations must be IRS 501(c)(3)
tax-exempt.

GEOG. RESTRICTIONS: Lincoln, Massachusetts.

FINANCIAL DATA:
Amount of support per award: $2,000 to
$50,000.
Total amount of support: Approximately
$205,000 for the year 2020.
Matching fund requirements: Case-by-case
basis.

NO. MOST RECENT APPLICANTS: 14 for the year
2020.

NO. AWARDS: 11 for the year 2020.

REPRESENTATIVE AWARDS:
Town of Lincoln; Codman Community Farm;
Saint Vincent de Paul; Mass Audubon.

APPLICATION INFO:
Contact Grants Coordinator prior to
submitting an application.
Duration: Varies.
Deadline: Applications are reviewed on a
rolling basis.

PUBLICATIONS:
Application guidelines.

TRUSTEES:
Susan T. Monahan

Maura E. Murphy, Esq.
Michael F. O'Connell, Esq.

ADDRESS INQUIRIES TO:
Susan T. Monahan
Grants Coordinator and Trustee
(See e-mail address above.)

THE GEORGE W. CODRINGTON CHARITABLE FOUNDATION [62]

c/o Thompson Hine LLP
3900 Key Center, 127 Public Square
Cleveland, OH 44114-1291
(216) 566-5699
Fax: (216) 566-5800
E-mail: craig.martahus@thompsonhine.com
tommie.robertson@thompsonhine.com

FOUNDED: 1955

AREAS OF INTEREST:
Greater Cleveland area community projects, with an emphasis on contributions to diversity, equity and inclusion.

TYPE:
Capital grants; Challenge/matching grants; Endowments; General operating grants; Matching gifts. Annual grants to public charitable or educational projects.

YEAR PROGRAM STARTED: 1955

PURPOSE:
To assist, encourage and promote the well-being of mankind, regardless of race, color or creed.

LEGAL BASIS:
Private foundation.

ELIGIBILITY:
The Foundation's supportive services are limited to public charitable or educational projects. No grants are made to individuals.

GEOG. RESTRICTIONS: Cuyahoga County, Ohio and immediately adjacent areas.

FINANCIAL DATA:
Amount of support per award: $5,000 to $50,000.
Total amount of support: Varies.

NO. MOST RECENT APPLICANTS: 130.

NO. AWARDS: 55.

REPRESENTATIVE AWARDS:
$50,000 to Musical Arts Association; $10,000 to YWCA Greater Cleveland; $5,000 to Cleveland Public Theatre.

APPLICATION INFO:
Application should state fully, but briefly, the following:
(1) specific amount of the grant requested, if not less than $5,000;
(2) purpose for or use of the grant;
(3) geographic area served by the applicant;
(4) a brief history of the applicant's organization;
(5) a description of the applicant's contributions to the community, with an emphasis on contributions to diversity, equity and inclusion;
(6) budget for the current year, financial statements as of the end and for the year most recently concluded (audit, if available, should be provided) and;
(7) a listing of the applicant's officers and trustees.

Applicant must include IRS letter as evidence of the applicant's Section 501(c)(3) status.

Please provide an original plus four copies of all materials.

Duration: One year.
Deadline: Pending applications are considered at meetings of the Supervisory Board held in April, June, September and December.

IRS I.D.: 34-6507457

SUPERVISORY BOARD:
Craig R. Martahus, Esq., Chairman
William R. Seelbach, Vice Chairman
Raymond T. Sawyer, Esq., Secretary
Robyn Minter Smyers

ADDRESS INQUIRIES TO:
Tommie Robertson, Legal Secretary
E-mail:
tommie.robertson@thompsonhine.com or
Craig Martahus, Esq., Chairman
(See address above.)

THE COLEMAN FOUNDATION, INC. [63]

651 West Washington Boulevard
Suite 306
Chicago, IL 60661-2134
(312) 902-7120
Fax: (312) 902-7124
E-mail: info@colemanfoundation.org
Web Site: www.colemanfoundation.org

FOUNDED: 1951

AREAS OF INTEREST:
Entrepreneurship education, cancer care, and developmental disability services.

TYPE:
Capital grants; Challenge/matching grants; Conferences/seminars; Project/program grants. The major areas of grantmaking include:
(1) education, with a strong emphasis on entrepreneurship education (national in scope, with focus in Chicago);
(2) cancer care and treatment in the Chicago metropolitan area and;
(3) services for the disabled in the Chicago metropolitan area, with a strong emphasis on developmental disabilities.

PURPOSE:
To improve the lives of individuals in the Chicago metropolitan area.

ELIGIBILITY:
Grants are only made to IRS-certified tax-exempt nonprofit organizations, 501(c)(3) or 509(a)(1) and that are not supporting foundations. Funding is prohibited to individuals, for-profit businesses, advertising books and tickets. General solicitations and annual appeals will not be considered.

Only programs within the Foundation's region of focus will be considered.

GEOG. RESTRICTIONS: Primarily metropolitan Chicago and other select parts of the Midwest.

FINANCIAL DATA:
Amount of support per award: Varies.
Total amount of support: Varies.

NO. AWARDS: Approximately 100.

APPLICATION INFO:
All requests begin with a Letter of Inquiry submitted via Fluxx that provides an overview of the organization and the concept for which funding is sought. If the Letter of Inquiry meets the eligibility requirements, a program officer will contact the applicant to discuss the concept presented.
Duration: Typically one year.

Deadline: Letters of Inquiry are accepted on a continuing basis.

ADDRESS INQUIRIES TO:
Shelley A. Davis
President and Chief Executive Officer
(See address above.)

THE COLLINS FOUNDATION [64]

1618 S.W. First Avenue
Suite 505
Portland, OR 97201
(503) 227-7171
Fax: (503) 295-3794
E-mail: information@collinsfoundation.org
Web Site: www.collinsfoundation.org

FOUNDED: 1947

AREAS OF INTEREST:
Arts, children and youth, community welfare, education, environment, health and science, humanities, and religion.

TYPE:
Challenge/matching grants; Project/program grants. Grants made to agencies exclusively in the state of Oregon to improve, enrich and give greater expression to its religious, educational, cultural and scientific endeavors. Also, to assist in improving the quality of life in the state.

YEAR PROGRAM STARTED: 1947

PURPOSE:
To help fund programs or projects that will make life better in the community.

LEGAL BASIS:
Private, nonprofit foundation.

ELIGIBILITY:
The Foundation is organized in the state of Oregon for projects within the state. All applicant agencies must be tax-exempt, as established by the Treasury Department of the United States. No support is given to individuals.

GEOG. RESTRICTIONS: Oregon.

FINANCIAL DATA:
Amount of support per award: Varies.
Total amount of support: Approximately $10,000,000 annually.
Matching fund requirements: The Foundation looks favorably on grants which must be matched.

NO. AWARDS: 241 for the year 2019.

APPLICATION INFO:
Application information is available online.
Duration: Varies.
Deadline: Not specified. Awards are announced periodically throughout the year.

OFFICERS:
Truman W. Collins, Jr., President
Cynthia G. Addams, Chief Executive Officer

BOARD OF TRUSTEES:
Jaime Arredondo
Truman W. Collins, Jr.
Serena Cruz
Ryan Luria
Kimberlee Pierce Sheng
Cherida Collins Smith
Lee Diane Collins Vest

ADDRESS INQUIRIES TO:
Cynthia G. Addams, Chief Executive Officer
(See address above.)

COMMUNITIES FOUNDATION OF TEXAS, INC. [65]

Grants Department
5500 Caruth Haven Lane
Dallas, TX 75225
(214) 750-4222
Fax: (214) 750-4210
E-mail: eliser@cftexas.org
Web Site: www.cftexas.org

AREAS OF INTEREST:
Arts, community improvement, disaster relief, education, health, housing, religion, scientific research, social services and youth.

NAME(S) OF PROGRAMS:
- **CFT for Business**
- **Community Impact Grants**
- **Donor-Advised Grants**
- **Educate Texas**

TYPE:
Project/program grants.

YEAR PROGRAM STARTED: 1953

LEGAL BASIS:
Public charity.

ELIGIBILITY:
Organizations with IRS 501(c)(3) tax-exempt designation.

GEOG. RESTRICTIONS: Primarily Dallas, Denton, Colin, Rockwell and Tarrant counties in Texas.

FINANCIAL DATA:
Amount of support per award: Varies.
Total amount of support: Varies.

APPLICATION INFO:
Requests must be submitted using the Foundation Letter of Inquiry checklist and form, which can be downloaded from the web site above.
Duration: Varies.
Deadline: Letter of Intent: March 1, April 1 and May 1.

ADDRESS INQUIRIES TO:
Grants Processing
(See address above.)

COMMUNITY FOUNDATION FOR A GREATER RICHMOND [66]

3409 Moore Street
Richmond, VA 23230
(804) 330-7400
Fax: (804) 330-5992
E-mail: sblackwell@cfrichmond.org
info@cfrichmond.org
Web Site: www.cfrichmond.org

FOUNDED: 1968

AREAS OF INTEREST:
Community vibrancy, economic prosperity, educational success, and health and wellness.

TYPE:
Awards/prizes; Capital grants; Challenge/matching grants; Conferences/seminars; Development grants; General operating grants; Project/program grants; Research grants; Scholarships; Seed money grants; Technical assistance; Training grants. Community grants programs.

YEAR PROGRAM STARTED: 1995

PURPOSE:
To develop a healthy, thriving community.

LEGAL BASIS:
Community foundation.

ELIGIBILITY:
Proposals will be accepted from 501(c)(3) charitable organizations which serve the city of Richmond, outlying counties or the Tri-Cities.

GEOG. RESTRICTIONS: Richmond, Virginia metropolitan area and the Tri-Cities, Colonial Heights, Goochland, Hopewell and Petersburg.

FINANCIAL DATA:
Amount of support per award: Typically $10,000 to $50,000.
Total amount of support: Over $50,000,000 annually.

APPLICATION INFO:
Instructions for submitting preliminary proposals are available on the Foundation's web site.
Duration: Usually one year. Renewal possible.
Deadline: Varies.

PUBLICATIONS:
Annual report; policy and guidelines for grant requests.

IRS I.D.: 23-7009135

OFFICERS:
Pamela J. Royal, M.D., Chairperson
Austin Brockenbrough, IV, Vice Chairperson
Sherrie Armstrong, President and Chief Executive Officer
Philip H. Goodpasture, Treasurer
Kristen Hager, Secretary

ADDRESS INQUIRIES TO:
Charles Dyson, Director of Data and Customer Support
(See address above.)

COMMUNITY FOUNDATION FOR SOUTHEAST MICHIGAN [67]

333 West Fort Street
Suite 2010
Detroit, MI 48226
(313) 961-6675
Fax: (313) 961-2886
E-mail: cfsem@cfsem.org
Web Site: www.cfsem.org

FOUNDED: 1984

AREAS OF INTEREST:
Environment, health, arts and culture, education, economic development, human services and civic affairs.

TYPE:
Development grants; Endowments; Project/program grants; Seed money grants.

LEGAL BASIS:
Public Foundation.

ELIGIBILITY:
The Foundation grants to federal 501(c)(3) tax-exempt organizations, government entities, school districts and universities. No grants for buildings, equipment, religious programs, fund-raising, individuals, conferences or annual meetings.

GEOG. RESTRICTIONS: The seven counties of southeast Michigan: Livingston, Macomb, Monroe, Oakland, St. Clair, Washtenaw and Wayne.

FINANCIAL DATA:
Amount of support per award: Varies.

NO. AWARDS: 3,900 grants were awarded for the year 2018.

APPLICATION INFO:
Guidelines are available on the Foundation web site. Interested organizations should call a program officer before applying.
Duration: One year.
Deadline: Quarterly.

PUBLICATIONS:
Annual report; newsletters.

STAFF:
Mariam C. Noland, President
Karen L. Leppanen, Vice President, Finance and Administration
Sheryl G. Arb, Vice President, Marketing and Communications
Katie G. Brisson, Vice President, Programs

OFFICERS OF THE TRUSTEES:
James B. Nicholson, Chairman
Penny B. Blumenstein, Vice Chairman
David M. Hempstead, Vice Chairman
Reginald M. Turner, Vice Chairman
Michael T. Monahan, Treasurer
Mary M. Weiser, Secretary

ADDRESS INQUIRIES TO:
Mariam C. Noland, President
(See address above.)

COMMUNITY FOUNDATION OF EASTERN CONNECTICUT

68 Federal Street
New London, CT 06320
(860) 442-3572
Fax: (860) 442-0584
E-mail: jennob@cfect.org
Web Site: www.cfect.org

TYPE:
General operating grants; Project/program grants; Scholarships.

See entry 1110 for full listing.

COMMUNITY FOUNDATION OF GREATER MEMPHIS [68]

1900 Union Avenue
Memphis, TN 38104
(901) 728-4600
Fax: (901) 722-0010
E-mail: ewarren@cfgm.org
Web Site: www.cfgm.org

FOUNDED: 1969

AREAS OF INTEREST:
Grants administered for charitable purposes in metropolitan Memphis.

NAME(S) OF PROGRAMS:
- **Nonprofit Capacity Building Grants**
- **Scholarship Funds**

TYPE:
Challenge/matching grants; Project/program grants; Scholarships; Technical assistance.

YEAR PROGRAM STARTED: 1969

PURPOSE:
To provide support for the benefit of the geographic area that the Foundation serves; to strengthen the community through philanthropy.

LEGAL BASIS:
Community foundation.

ELIGIBILITY:
Applicants must be charitable and nonprofit under IRS regulations, holding a 501(c)(3) tax-exempt status. Applicants must be located in the geographic area that the Foundation serves.

GEOG. RESTRICTIONS: Eastern Arkansas, northern Mississippi and West Tennessee.

FINANCIAL DATA:
Amount of support per award: Varies.
Total amount of support: Varies.
Matching fund requirements: Stipulated with some grant awards.

NO. MOST RECENT APPLICANTS: Varies.

APPLICATION INFO:
Grant guidelines and application forms are available online.
Duration: One year.
Deadline: Varies.

PUBLICATIONS:
Newsletters; annual report.

IRS I.D.: 58-1723645

ADDRESS INQUIRIES TO:
Elizabeth Warren
Director of Grants and Initiatives
(See address above.)

COMMUNITY FOUNDATION OF THE EASTERN SHORE

1324 Belmont Avenue, Suite 401
Salisbury, MD 21804
(410) 742-9911
Fax: (410) 742-6638
E-mail: hmahler@cfes.org
Web Site: www.cfes.org

TYPE:
Awards/prizes; Challenge/matching grants; Demonstration grants; Project/program grants; Scholarships; Seed money grants; Technical assistance; Training grants.

See entry 1123 for full listing.

THE COMMUNITY FOUNDATION OF THE HOLLAND/ZEELAND AREA [69]

85 East Eighth Street
Suite 110
Holland, MI 49423
(616) 396-6590
Fax: (616) 396-3573
E-mail: info@cfhz.org
Web Site: www.cfhz.org

FOUNDED: 1951

AREAS OF INTEREST:
Education, arts and culture, recreation, community and economic development, the needs of youth and the elderly, health and human services, environment and housing.

TYPE:
Research grants; Scholarships; Technical assistance.

YEAR PROGRAM STARTED: 1951

PURPOSE:
To ensure the community thrives today, tomorrow and forever by building our community's endowment to support high-impact charitable projects, helping donors achieve their charitable goals, and leading and partnering in community-level initiatives.

LEGAL BASIS:
Corporation and public charity, 501(c)(3).

ELIGIBILITY:
Grants are made to organizations that have tax-exempt status under Section 501(c)(3) of the Internal Revenue Code or governmental agencies. No grants are made to individuals. Nonsectarian religious programs may apply.

GEOG. RESTRICTIONS: Holland and Zeeland, Michigan area only.

FINANCIAL DATA:
Amount of support per award: $500 to $75,000.
Total amount of support: Varies.

NO. MOST RECENT APPLICANTS: 521.

NO. AWARDS: 318.

APPLICATION INFO:
Grant applicants must contact the Foundation to discuss a proposal prior to submitting an application.
Scholarship applications must be completed on the Foundation web site.
Duration: One year.
Deadline: Varies.

PUBLICATIONS:
Annual report; application guidelines.

IRS I.D.: 38-6095283

STAFF:
Elizabeth Kidd, Vice President of Community Impact
Stacy Timmerman, Director of Scholarships

ADDRESS INQUIRIES TO:
Vice President of Community Impact
(See address above.)

THE COMMUNITY FOUNDATION OF WESTERN NORTH CAROLINA [70]

4 Vanderbilt Park Drive
Suite 300
Asheville, NC 28803
(828) 254-4960
Fax: (828) 251-2258
E-mail: info@cfwnc.org
Web Site: www.cfwnc.org

FOUNDED: 1978

AREAS OF INTEREST:
Food and farming, people in need, early childhood development, and natural and cultural resources.

TYPE:
Project/program grants; Scholarships.

YEAR PROGRAM STARTED: 1978

PURPOSE:
To inspire philanthropy and mobilize resources to enrich lives and communities in western North Carolina.

ELIGIBILITY:
Grants are awarded to tax-exempt organizations. Eligibility varies by program.

GEOG. RESTRICTIONS: Western North Carolina.

FINANCIAL DATA:
Amount of support per award: Varies.
Total amount of support: Approximately $20,000,000 in grants and scholarships for the fiscal year 2019.

NO. AWARDS: Varies.

APPLICATION INFO:
Application information is available on the web site.
Duration: Varies.
Deadline: Varies.

PUBLICATIONS:
Quarterly newsletter; annual report.

IRS I.D.: 56-1223384

ADDRESS INQUIRIES TO:
Diane Crisp, Grants Manager
(See address above.)

COMPTON FOUNDATION, INC. [71]

44 Montgomery Street
Floor 3
San Francisco, CA 94104
(415) 391-9001
Fax: (415) 391-9007
Web Site: www.comptonfoundation.org

FOUNDED: 1946

AREAS OF INTEREST:
Climate change, peace and national security, and reproductive rights and justice.

TYPE:
Project/program grants.

PURPOSE:
To ignite change; to support transformative leadership and courageous storytelling, inspiring action toward a peaceful, just, sustainable future.

ELIGIBILITY:
501(c)(3) nonprofit organizations in the U.S. that are working domestically may apply.
The Foundation does not support organizations that work solely in one city or state.

FINANCIAL DATA:
Amount of support per award: Varies.
Total amount of support: $1,900,000 for the year 2019.

NO. AWARDS: Varies.

APPLICATION INFO:
Proposals are by invitation only. Unsolicited proposals are not accepted.

PUBLICATIONS:
Grant Highlights (available on web site).

STAFF:
Ellen Friedman, Executive Director
Jennifer Turnage, Director of Finance
Deborah K. Daughtry, Director of Operations
Johanna Hanson, Senior Program Officer

BOARD OF DIRECTORS:
Vanessa Davenport, President
Ian Compton, Vice President
Emilie Cortes, Treasurer
Jakada Imani, Secretary

ADDRESS INQUIRIES TO:
Deborah K. Daughtry, Director of Operations
(See address above.)

THE CONNELLY FOUNDATION [72]

One Tower Bridge
100 Front Street, Suite 1450
West Conshohocken, PA 19428
(610) 834-3222
Fax: (610) 834-0866
E-mail: info@connellyfdn.org
Web Site: www.connellyfdn.org

FOUNDED: 1955

AREAS OF INTEREST:
Educational, civic and cultural institutions, health with emphasis on human services. A significant portion of funding is directed toward organizations affiliated with the Catholic Church.

TYPE:
Capital grants; General operating grants; Project/program grants.

PURPOSE:
To enhance the quality of life in the Delaware Valley.

LEGAL BASIS:
Private foundation.

ELIGIBILITY:
No grants to individuals, political or national organizations or other foundations, nor does the Foundation respond to annual appeals or general letters of solicitation. Foundation guidelines restrict funding any organization more than once during a 12-month period. Applicants who have received previous grants from the Foundation should submit final reports under separate cover.

GEOG. RESTRICTIONS: Camden, New Jersey; Bucks, Chester, Delaware and Montgomery counties and city of Philadelphia, Pennsylvania.

FINANCIAL DATA:
Amount of support per award: Varies.
Total amount of support: $15,400,000 for the year 2020.

NO. AWARDS: 497 for the year 2020.

APPLICATION INFO:
Grantseekers can submit proposals using the Foundation's online application system or by submitting hard copy through the mail.
Duration: Varies.
Deadline: Written proposals are accepted and reviewed by the Foundation throughout the year. With the exception of Foundation initiatives, there are no deadlines. Applicants receive a response within approximately three months.

PUBLICATIONS:
Application guidelines.

OFFICERS:
Thomas A. Riley, President
Emily C. Riley, Executive Vice President
Valerie Martin, Chief Financial Officer
Fran Burns, Chief Operating Officer

ADDRESS INQUIRIES TO:
Program Officer
(See address above.)

*PLEASE NOTE:
Visits to the Foundation office or contacts with its staff initiated by applicants during the proposal review process are discouraged.

CONSUMERS ENERGY FOUNDATION   [73]
One Energy Plaza, Room EP8-210
Jackson, MI 49201-2276
(517) 740-3564
(877) 501-4952
Fax: (517) 788-2281
E-mail: foundation@consumersenergy.com
Web Site: www.consumersenergy.com/community/foundation

FOUNDED: 1989

AREAS OF INTEREST:
Social welfare, education, culture and arts, community and civic affairs, and environment.

CONSULTING OR VOLUNTEER SERVICES:
Employee volunteer program.

NAME(S) OF PROGRAMS:
● **Caring for Community**
● **Volunteer Investment Program**

TYPE:
Capital grants; Challenge/matching grants; General operating grants; Matching gifts; Project/program grants; Scholarships; Seed money grants; Technical assistance. Volunteer grants.

YEAR PROGRAM STARTED: 1990

PURPOSE:
To support the charitable interest of Consumers Energy.

LEGAL BASIS:
Corporate program.

ELIGIBILITY:
501(c)(3) tax-exempt status, nonprofit organizations are eligible for support. The Foundation will not fund individuals, political, religious, labor or veteran's organizations.

Requests will be considered from organizations elsewhere for programs or projects that significantly benefit the state of Michigan.

GEOG. RESTRICTIONS: Michigan.

FINANCIAL DATA:
Amount of support per award: Typically $5,000 to $50,000.
Total amount of support: $9,700,000 for the year 2020.
Matching fund requirements: Foundation will match employee and retiree contributions to Michigan higher education, food banks, homeless shelters and community foundations. Minimum $25 and maximum $1,000 per year per employee and retiree. Retirees eligible for 50% match.

REPRESENTATIVE AWARDS:
$250,000 to Detroit Zoological Society; $100,000 to Food Bank of Eastern Michigan; $50,000 to Great Start Collaborative of Traverse Bay; $75,000 to Impression 5 Science Center; $150,000 to Michigan State University, College of Engineering.

APPLICATION INFO:
Cover letter and completed grant application required by mail only.
Duration: Varies. Renewal unlikely.

PUBLICATIONS:
Guidelines brochure.

DIRECTORS:
Patricia K. Poppe, Chairman
Brandon J. Hofmeister, President
Carolyn A. Bloodworth, Secretary and Treasurer
Jean-Francois Brossoit
Reiji P. Hayes
Catherine A. Hendrian
Venkat Dhenuvakonda Rao
Catherine Reynolds
Brian F. Rich
Garrick J. Rochow

ADDRESS INQUIRIES TO:
Carolyn A. Bloodworth
Secretary and Treasurer
(See address above.)

V.V. COOKE FOUNDATION   [74]
P.O. Box 7664
Louisville, KY 40257-0664
(502) 901-3179
E-mail: carl.vvcooke@gmail.com
Web Site: vvcooke.net

FOUNDED: 1947

AREAS OF INTEREST:
Civic affairs, education, religion and humanitarianism.

TYPE:
Capital grants; Endowments; General operating grants; Scholarships; Seed money grants.

LEGAL BASIS:
Private foundation.

ELIGIBILITY:
Grants are made to organizations that have tax-exempt status under Section 501(c)(3) and are not described in Section 509(a)(3) of the Internal Revenue Code. Grants are made for religious, educational, humanitarian and civic purposes. No grants are made to individuals.

GEOG. RESTRICTIONS: Metropolitan Louisville, Kentucky and the Commonwealth of Kentucky.

FINANCIAL DATA:
Amount of support per award: $250 to $25,000.
Total amount of support: $330,960 for the year ended August 31, 2018.

NO. MOST RECENT APPLICANTS: 87.

NO. AWARDS: 50.

REPRESENTATIVE AWARDS:
$1,000 to Lighthouse Promise; $25,000 to Baptist Healthcare Foundation.

APPLICATION INFO:
Applications should be in letter form. Applicants must:
(1) outline the organization's goals and purposes, and the intended use and amount of the grant requested;
(2) list other organizations that serve the needs addressed by this application and what distinguishes this organization and;
(3) identify the percentage of the organization's budget that is used for fund-raising and for administrative expenses.

Eight copies of the application with a single copy of the applicant's IRS 501(c)(3) letter are required.
Deadline: Mid-January, April, July and October for consideration in mid-February, May, August and November, respectively.

PUBLICATIONS:
Application guidelines.

IRS I.D.: 61-6033714

STAFF:
Carl M. Thomas, Executive Director

ADDRESS INQUIRIES TO:
Carl M. Thomas, Executive Director
(See address above.)

COOPER FOUNDATION   [75]
1248 O Street, Suite 870
Lincoln, NE 68508-1493
(402) 476-7571
E-mail: info@cooperfoundation.org
Web Site: cooperfoundation.org

FOUNDED: 1934

AREAS OF INTEREST:
Education, human services, arts and humanities, and the environment.

TYPE:
Challenge/matching grants; Demonstration grants.

PURPOSE:
To support the operations and core programs of strong, well-managed and effective nonprofit organizations located in and working in Lancaster and Lincoln counties, NE.

LEGAL BASIS:
Private foundation.

ELIGIBILITY:
Most grants are made to organizations located in and impacting residents of Lancaster and Lincoln counties, NE.

The Foundation does not fund individuals, businesses, health organizations or issues, churches, religious organizations or issues, travel, memberships, endowments, non-501(c)(3) organizations, 509(a)(3) supporting organizations, fiscal agents, or private foundations.

GEOG. RESTRICTIONS: Nebraska.

FINANCIAL DATA:
Amount of support per award: Varies.
Total amount of support: $750,000 for the year 2021.

NO. MOST RECENT APPLICANTS: 60.

NO. AWARDS: 60.

APPLICATION INFO:
The online grant process consists of two phases:
(1) invited applicants must submit a Letter of Inquiry by the deadline;
(2) Cooper Foundation staff will review the Letter of Inquiry and determine to advance it to the application state. Applicants will be notified to submit a full application.

To be invited to submit a Letter of Inquiry, submit information about your organization, project and budget to the e-mail address listed above.

Duration: One year. Must reapply annually.

Deadline: January 15, April 1, July 1 and October 1.

ADDRESS INQUIRIES TO:
Victoria Grasso, President
(See address above.)

THE MARY S. AND DAVID C. CORBIN FOUNDATION   [76]

Akron Centre Plaza
50 South Main Street, Suite 703
Akron, OH 44308-1830
(330) 762-6427
Fax: (330) 762-6428
E-mail: info@corbinfdn.org
Web Site: corbinfdn.org

FOUNDED: 1968

AREAS OF INTEREST:
Arts, culture, environment, health, housing, human services, education, youth and medical research.

TYPE:
Project grants.

PURPOSE:
To benefit charities in the Akron and Summit County, OH areas and national charities that have a presence in the Akron and Summit County areas of Ohio.

ELIGIBILITY:
Organizations classified as 501(c)(3) by the IRS can apply. The Foundation gives primary consideration to the City of Akron and Summit County, OH charitable organizations

and/or local chapters of national charities located in the Akron, Summit County area of Ohio.

The Foundation does not fund individuals, annual fund-raising campaigns, ongoing requests for general operating support, operating deficits, or organizations which in turn make grants to others. The Foundation generally does not fund endowments, faith-based or religious organizations, nor does it support schools.

GEOG. RESTRICTIONS: City of Akron and Summit County, Ohio.

FINANCIAL DATA:
Amount of support per award: $500 to $50,000.

Total amount of support: $950,400 for the year 2020.

NO. AWARDS: 74 for the year 2020.

APPLICATION INFO:
Guidelines are available on the Foundation web site. Applications must be submitted through the online application portal system.

Duration: One year.

Deadline: March 1 and September 1, for consideration in May and November respectively.

ADDRESS INQUIRIES TO:
Erika J. May, Grants Administrator
(See address above.)

MARION STEDMAN COVINGTON FOUNDATION   [77]

P.O. Box 29304
Greensboro, NC 27429-9304
(336) 282-0480
E-mail: info@mscovingtonfoundation.org
Web Site: www.mscovingtonfoundation.org

AREAS OF INTEREST:
Historic preservation.

TYPE:
Capital grants; Challenge/matching grants; Conferences/seminars; General operating grants; Project/program grants; Research grants; Seed money grants.

YEAR PROGRAM STARTED: 1986

PURPOSE:
To provide grants to nonprofit organizations operating in the area of historic preservation.

ELIGIBILITY:
Grants are made to federally tax-exempt, nonprofit organizations.

GEOG. RESTRICTIONS: Primarily North Carolina.

FINANCIAL DATA:
Amount of support per award: $10,000 average.

Total amount of support: Approximately $350,000.

NO. AWARDS: Varies.

APPLICATION INFO:
Application procedures are available on the web site.

Duration: Varies.

Deadline: August 1 and March 1. Announcements in mid-October and mid-May.

PUBLICATIONS:
Annual report; guidelines.

IRS I.D.: 56-6286555

ADDRESS INQUIRIES TO:
Alexa S. Aycock, Executive Director
(See address above.)

*PLEASE NOTE:
Challenge grants may be requested or the Foundation may designate a grant as such. In either event, there will be a specified time period in which the matching funds are to be raised.

S.H. COWELL FOUNDATION   [78]

595 Market Street, Suite 950
San Francisco, CA 94105
(415) 397-0285
Fax: (415) 986-6786
E-mail: farley@shcowell.org
Web Site: shcowell.org

FOUNDED: 1955

AREAS OF INTEREST:
Family resource centers, public education, youth development, and improving the quality of life of low-income children and families in neighborhoods that meet the Foundation's place-based criteria.

TYPE:
Capital grants; Challenge/matching grants; Project/program grants; Technical assistance; Training grants. Community building. Operating support.

YEAR PROGRAM STARTED: 1955

PURPOSE:
To improve the quality of life of children living in poverty in northern California by making grants that support and strengthen their families and the neighborhoods where they live.

LEGAL BASIS:
Independent nonprofit foundation.

ELIGIBILITY:
Organization must be tax-exempt and must submit evidence that a grant would qualify under the Tax Reform Act of 1969. Grants are restricted to organizations, projects and programs in northern California, except by invitation of the Foundation.

As a matter of policy, the Foundation typically does not make grants to hospitals for construction or research, sectarian religious groups, individuals for scholarships or financial aid.

GEOG. RESTRICTIONS: Northern and central California.

FINANCIAL DATA:
Amount of support per award: $1,000 to over $500,000.

APPLICATION INFO:
The application process is rigorous, and prospective grantees should expect to work with Cowell staff before, during, and after a formal proposal is submitted. There are five steps to the process:
(1) make sure that your project meets Foundation funding criteria;
(2) call the Foundation;
(3) if asked to do so, submit a letter of inquiry;
(4) if asked to do so, submit a full proposal. Please do not send a formal proposal unless a program officer requests one. If you are asked to submit a proposal, staff will give you a list of required information and;
(5) plan on at least one site visit.

Duration: Varies.

Deadline: The Directors meet regularly and review only those proposals recommended by staff.

STAFF:
Anu Cairo, Program Director

OFFICERS AND BOARD OF DIRECTORS:
Ann Alpers, President
Ken Doane, Executive Vice President and Chief Program Officer
Nina Washburne, Vice President, Administration
Dr. Lisa Backus
Charles E. Ellwein
Charles A. Higueras
Dr. Mikiko Huang
Scott Mosher
Lydia Tan
Kim Thompson

ADDRESS INQUIRIES TO:
Cynthia Farley, Administrative Assistant
(See e-mail address above.)

*SPECIAL STIPULATIONS:
No grants to individuals, for media projects, conferences, seminars, to sectarian organizations, hospitals or public/governmental agencies.

HENRY P. AND SUSAN C. CROWELL TRUST　　　　　[79]
102 North Cascade Avenue
Suite 300
Colorado Springs, CO 80903
(719) 645-8119
Fax: (719) 418-2695
E-mail: info@crowelltrust.org
Web Site: www.crowelltrust.org

FOUNDED: 1927

AREAS OF INTEREST:
Evangelical foreign missions.

TYPE:
General operating grants; Project/program grants.

YEAR PROGRAM STARTED: 1927

PURPOSE:
To aid evangelical Christianity by support to organizations having for their purposes its teaching, advancement and active extension at home and abroad.

LEGAL BASIS:
Private foundation.

ELIGIBILITY:
No grants to churches, individuals or for endowment funds or research. No loans.

GEOG. RESTRICTIONS: United States.

FINANCIAL DATA:
Amount of support per award: Average $35,000.
Total amount of support: $3,500,000.

NO. MOST RECENT APPLICANTS: 375.

NO. AWARDS: 100.

APPLICATION INFO:
Applicants must ensure the project fits the guidelines of the Trust by completing the online Self-Screening Aid to determine eligibility and begin the application process. If the organization and project fit the minimum requirements, applicants should proceed to the online grant management system. No proposals will be accepted in hard copy or through e-mail.
Duration: One year. May resubmit annually.

Deadline: Proposals should be submitted by February 28 for spring and July 31 for fall consideration.

PUBLICATIONS:
Application guidelines.

IRS I.D.: 36-6038028

STAFF:
Candace Sparks, Chief Executive Officer

ADDRESS INQUIRIES TO:
Angela Hunter
Assistant to the Executive Director
(See address above.)

THE CULLEN FOUNDATION [80]
2727 Allen Parkway
Suite 1050
Houston, TX 77019
(713) 651-8837
E-mail: gina@cullenfdn.org
Web Site: www.cullenfdn.org

FOUNDED: 1947

AREAS OF INTEREST:
Cultural, education, health care and public service.

TYPE:
Capital grants; Challenge/matching grants; Development grants; Endowments; Fellowships; Professorships; Project/program grants.

PURPOSE:
To provide charitable grants to cultural, educational, health care and public service organizations.

LEGAL BASIS:
Tax-exempt, private foundation.

ELIGIBILITY:
Grants are limited to the state of Texas by indenture. No grants are made to individuals or businesses.

GEOG. RESTRICTIONS: Texas, primarily Houston.

FINANCIAL DATA:
Amount of support per award: Minimum $10,000.

NO. MOST RECENT APPLICANTS: 117.

NO. AWARDS: 31 new grants.

APPLICATION INFO:
Applications are accepted online only through the link on the Foundation web site.
Duration: No grants are awarded on a continuing basis.

IRS I.D.: 76-0647361

STAFF:
Scott W. Wise, President and Treasurer
Laura Chapman, Vice President

OFFICERS AND DIRECTORS:
Wilhelmina E. Robertson, Chairman
Carla Knobloch, Vice Chairman
Meredith T. Cullen, Secretary
Isaac Arnold, III
Marvin E. Odum

ADDRESS INQUIRIES TO:
Gina McEvily, Grant Administrator
(See address above.)

*SPECIAL STIPULATIONS:
Grants are made to qualified charities in the state of Texas, primarily in the Houston area. No grants to individuals or businesses.

THE NATHAN CUMMINGS FOUNDATION, INC.　　　　[81]
120 Wall Street, 26th Floor
New York, NY 10005
(212) 787-7300
Fax: (212) 787-7377
E-mail: contact@nathancummings.org
Web Site: nathancummings.org

FOUNDED: 1949

AREAS OF INTEREST:
Inequality and climate change.

NAME(S) OF PROGRAMS:
● **Corporate and Political Accountability**
● **Inclusive Clean Economy**
● **Racial and Economic Justice**
● **Voice, Creativity and Culture**

TYPE:
General operating grants; Project/program grants.

YEAR PROGRAM STARTED: 1989

PURPOSE:
To promote democratic values and social justice, including fairness, diversity and community; to build a socially and economically just society that values and protects the ecological balance for future generations; to promote humane health care; to foster arts and culture that enrich communities.

LEGAL BASIS:
Private foundation.

ELIGIBILITY:
Applying organizations must be recognized as 501(c)(3) tax-exempt public charities, as defined by the IRS. Projects that are not recognized as tax-exempt public charities must have a fiscal sponsor.

GEOG. RESTRICTIONS: United States.

FINANCIAL DATA:
Amount of support per award: Varies.

APPLICATION INFO:
To apply for a grant, applicant must take the eligibility quiz. Those projects which align with the Foundation goals will be prompted to complete the registration process.
Duration: Varies.
Deadline: Letters of Inquiry are accepted on a rolling basis.

IRS I.D.: 23-7093201

STAFF:
Nealon DeVore, Chief of Staff
Shelly Harper, Vice President of Administration
Bob Bancroft, Vice President of Finance
Laura Campos, Director, Corporate and Political Accountability
Kristina Nieto, Director, Finance and Accounting
Lavastian Glenn, Director, Racial and Economic Justice
Isaac Luria, Director, Voice, Creativity and Culture
Janet Disla, Senior Grants Manager

ADDRESS INQUIRIES TO:
Program Associate
E-mail: gadmin@nathancummings.org

THE CUMMINS FOUNDATION, INC.　　　　　　　　　　　[82]
500 Jackson Street, MC 60633
Columbus, IN 47201
Fax: (812) 377-7897
E-mail: cummins.foundation@cummins.com
Web Site: www.cummins.com

FOUNDED: 1954

AREAS OF INTEREST:
Focus on environment, education and equality of opportunity.

TYPE:
Development grants. Incubator grants. Matching grants.

YEAR PROGRAM STARTED: 1954

PURPOSE:
To improve the quality of life in communities where Cummins has manufacturing operations and subsidiaries; to promote the Foundation's philanthropic objectives through grants in priority areas as well as projects of special interest in Columbus and subsidiary communities.

LEGAL BASIS:
Corporate foundation.

ELIGIBILITY:
Grantees must be tax-exempt organizations or institutions located in areas where Cummins has a presence. Organizations must have proof of past Cummins employee engagement.

No grants are made to individuals or for denominational religious organizations. No scholarships are granted.

FINANCIAL DATA:
Amount of support per award: Varies.
Total amount of support: Varies.

APPLICATION INFO:
The Foundation requires initial contact via e-mail.

PUBLICATIONS:
Sustainability report.

IRS I.D.: 35-6042373

ADDRESS INQUIRIES TO:
See e-mail address above.

DANIELS FUND   [83]
101 Monroe Street
Denver, CO 80206-4467
(303) 393-7220
E-mail: info@danielsfund.org
grantsinfo@danielsfund.org
Web Site: www.danielsfund.org

FOUNDED: 2000

AREAS OF INTEREST:
Daniels Fund Grants Program: Aging, amateur sports, disabilities, drug and alcohol addiction, early childhood education, K-12 education reform, ethics and integrity in education, homeless and disadvantaged, youth development.

NAME(S) OF PROGRAMS:
● **Daniels Fund Ethics Initiative**
● **Daniels Fund Grants Program**
● **Daniels Fund Scholarship Program**

TYPE:
Capital grants; General operating grants; Project/program grants; Scholarships. Daniels Fund Ethics Initiative delivers principle-based ethics education and reinforces the value of ethical business and personal conduct. The Ethics Initiative consists of a Collegiate Program, High School Program, Middle School Program, Community College Program, Elementary School Program, Law Enforcement Program, Business Program, and an online Case Bank. Each of the Ethics Initiative's components utilizes a specific

approach to reach its target audience. Funding is provided through the Daniels Fund Grants Program.

Daniels Fund Grants Program supports highly effective nonprofit organizations in Colorado, New Mexico, Utah and Wyoming.

Daniels Fund Scholarship Program consists of the Daniels Scholarship Program and the Boundless Opportunity Scholarship Program. The Daniels Scholarship Program provides a comprehensive, four-year annually-renewable college scholarship for highly motivated students to earn a Bachelor's degree that helps them build a successful career and rewarding life. Daniels Scholars are honest, respectful, self-reliant, and compassionate. They are proud Americans who value our free enterprise system and are prepared to give the world their very best shot. The scholarship applies toward the expense of attaining a Bachelor's degree at any nonprofit, accredited college or university in the U.S. The Boundless Opportunity Scholarship Program provides college scholarships for non-traditional students of all ages, awarded by select colleges and universities using funds provided by the Daniels Fund.

YEAR PROGRAM STARTED: 2000

PURPOSE:
To help excellent nonprofits achieve a high level of effectiveness and impact; to help Daniels Scholars succeed in college and ultimately become independent, successful in a rewarding career, and actively engaged in their community.

ELIGIBILITY:
Daniels Grants Program: Applying organizations must have 501(c)(3) not-for-profit status or government equivalent.

Daniels Scholarship Program: High school seniors seeking to obtain a Bachelor's degree. Applicants must meet the core values of character, leadership and service, and demonstrate financial need.

Boundless Opportunity Scholarship: Applicants must demonstrate financial need and be:
(1) an adult entering or returning to college;
(2) a GED recipient;
(3) a former foster care youth;
(4) a former juvenile justice youth or;
(5) a veteran entering or returning to college.

GEOG. RESTRICTIONS: Colorado, New Mexico, Utah and Wyoming.

FINANCIAL DATA:
Total assets of $1,600,000,000 for the year ended December 31, 2020.

Amount of support per award: Varies.
Total amount of support: $64,900,000 in grants, scholarships and ethics funding for the year ended December 31, 2020.

NO. AWARDS: Daniels Fund Grants Program and Boundless Opportunity Scholarship: Varies. Daniels Scholarship Program: Approximately 230.

APPLICATION INFO:
Online application process. Daniels Scholarship Program application process opens in September.
Duration: Grants: Typically one year. Must reapply. Daniels Scholarship Program: Four years. Boundless Opportunity Scholarship: Varies.
Deadline: Daniels Scholarship Program: November 15.

IRS I.D.: 84-1393308

ADDRESS INQUIRIES TO:
E-mail: grantsinfo@danielsfund.org

MARGARET A. DARRIN CHARITABLE TRUST   [84]
120 Columbia Turnpike
Florham Park, NJ 07932
(973) 822-2905

FOUNDED: 2015

AREAS OF INTEREST:
Arts, humanities, civic affairs, education, health, social services and women's issues.

TYPE:
General operating grants.

PURPOSE:
To utilize the power of giving to empower and transform lives of individuals facing extraordinary adverse circumstances, as well as to promote the common good.

ELIGIBILITY:
No restrictions or limitations on funding. Grants made to nonprofit 501(c)(3) organizations only.

GEOG. RESTRICTIONS: Northeastern United States.

FINANCIAL DATA:
Amount of support per award: Varies.
Total amount of support: $1,661,000 for the year 2018.

APPLICATION INFO:
Applications should take the form of a brief letter describing the charity, its background and the purpose of the contribution. Applicant must include a copy of their 501(c)(3) status.

Applicant will be notified only if approved.
Duration: One year. Must reapply for additional funding.

IRS I.D.: 47-6723443

STAFF:
Michael Hanifin, Executive Director and Trustee
Kevin J. O'Donnell, Trustee

ADDRESS INQUIRIES TO:
Charitable Contributions
(See address above.)

THE ARTHUR VINING DAVIS FOUNDATIONS   [85]
814 North Highway A1A
Suite 300
Ponte Vedra Beach, FL 32082
(904) 359-0670
E-mail: office@avdf.org
Web Site: www.avdf.org

FOUNDED: 1952

AREAS OF INTEREST:
Private higher education, public educational media, interfaith leadership and religious literacy, environmental engagement, and palliative care.

TYPE:
Project/program grants.

LEGAL BASIS:
Privately endowed foundation established by the will of Arthur Vining Davis.

ELIGIBILITY:
Grants are limited to institutions in the U.S. and its territories. Activities and functions not supported include assistance to

individuals, capital projects, scholarships, endowments, indirect costs associated with projects, voter registration drives and voter education, efforts to influence elections or legislation, and expenditures for noncharitable purposes.

GEOG. RESTRICTIONS: United States.

FINANCIAL DATA:
Amount of support per award: Varies by grant award type.

Total amount of support: Approximately $9,706,532 approved for the year 2019.

CO-OP FUNDING PROGRAMS: As a policy, the Foundations' support increased cooperation among foundations and expanded communication with the public. The staff has taken an active part in national and regional efforts in this direction.

NO. MOST RECENT APPLICANTS: 226 for the year 2019.

NO. AWARDS: 42 program grants for the year 2019.

APPLICATION INFO:
Application information is available online.
Duration: Typically one to two years.
Deadline: Letter of Intent: August 27. Full Proposal: November 12.

PUBLICATIONS:
65th Anniversary brochure.

OFFICERS:
Michael J. Murray, Ph.D., President
Timothy Michel, Chief Financial Officer
Doreen A. Gross, Chief Operating Officer

TRUSTEES:
Serena Davis Hall, Chairperson
James Cote
Christopher V. Davis
Jonathan P. Davis
Sarah H. Davis
Tamara A. Davis
Dorothy Davis Kee
William Given Kee
Haley Davis Madole

ADDRESS INQUIRIES TO:
See e-mail address above.

DELAWARE COUNTY FOUNDATION
737 Enterprise Drive
Suite A
Lewis Center, OH 43035
(614) 764-2332
Fax: (614) 764-2333
E-mail: foundation@delawarecf.org
Web Site: www.delawarecf.org

TYPE:
Project/program grants; Scholarships.

See entry 1139 for full listing.

DELUXE CORPORATION FOUNDATION   [86]
3680 Victoria Street North
Shoreview, MN 55126-2966
(651) 490-8165
E-mail: alex.goodwin@deluxe.com
deluxefoundation@deluxe.com
Web Site: deluxe.com/about/deluxe-cares

FOUNDED: 1952

AREAS OF INTEREST:
Financial literacy, community, education, entrepreneurship and empowerment.

TYPE:
Capital grants; General operating grants; Project/program grants. Volunteer match on behalf of employee volunteerism at 501(c)(3) nonprofits.

LEGAL BASIS:
Corporate foundation.

ELIGIBILITY:
Nonprofit organizations that meet the grant focus areas are encouraged to apply. The Foundation accepts grant proposals from qualifying nonprofit organizations that serve the general communities in which Deluxe facilities are located. In addition, nonprofits must:
(1) have obtained tax-exempt status under section 501(c)(3) or 509(a)(1), (2), or (3);
(2) have operated as a nonprofit for at least two years;
(3) have secured support from other corporate funders and;
(4) be located in the general community of a Deluxe facility.

GEOG. RESTRICTIONS: United States.

FINANCIAL DATA:
Amount of support per award: $5,000 to $10,000 average.

Total amount of support: Varies.

Matching fund requirements: Qualifying organizations for matching funds: Accredited educational institutions; public television and radio; professional arts; historical societies; museums.

CO-OP FUNDING PROGRAMS: United Way.

NO. MOST RECENT APPLICANTS: 255 for the year 2020.

NO. AWARDS: 27 for the year 2020.

APPLICATION INFO:
Applications are submitted online.
Duration: One year.
Deadline: Spring and fall.

BOARD OF DIRECTORS:
Barry McCarthy, President
Andrea Kroska, Vice President and Secretary
Timothy Cooper, Treasurer
Keith Bush
Garry Capers, Jr.
Jeffrey Cotter
Jane Elliott
Chris Thomas

ADDRESS INQUIRIES TO:
E-mail: deluxefoundation@deluxe.com

GERALDINE R. DODGE FOUNDATION   [87]
14 Maple Avenue, Suite 400
Morristown, NJ 07960
(973) 540-8442
Fax: (973) 540-1211
E-mail: info@grdodge.org
Web Site: www.grdodge.org

FOUNDED: 1974

AREAS OF INTEREST:
The arts, environment, education, Morris County projects, informed communities, and poetry.

TYPE:
General operating grants; Project/program grants. Grants in four key areas:
(1) Art grants enhance the cultural richness of the community in which citizens reside and contribute to New Jersey's creative economy;

(2) Educational grants provide transformational experiential educational opportunities both inside and outside of the classroom for young people who have limited access to educational excellence;
(3) Environmental grants help to achieve ecosystem resilience and sustainable community solutions and;
(4) Media grants support traditional and innovative uses of media to educate and engage the public around issues of importance to New Jersey and its citizens, as well as efforts to uncover the abuses of power by the institutions in which citizens have placed their trust.

PURPOSE:
To support and encourage those educational, cultural, social and environmental values that contribute to making our society more humane and our world more livable.

LEGAL BASIS:
Private foundation.

ELIGIBILITY:
Applicants must be nonprofit, 501(c)(3) tax-exempt organizations located in or providing benefits to the residents of the state of New Jersey. No grants in areas of higher education, health and religion. No support for capital programs, endowments, equipment purchases, scholarships, indirect costs or deficit reduction. No direct awards to individuals nor grants to conduit organizations, nor is funding made for lobbying efforts.

GEOG. RESTRICTIONS: New Jersey.

FINANCIAL DATA:
Total amount of support: Approximately $9,000,000 annually.

APPLICATION INFO:
Unsolicited requests for scholarships and grants are not accepted. New applicants should submit a one-page letter of inquiry to determine if a project falls within the Foundation's guidelines. Letters of inquiry may be submitted throughout the year, but must be received at least two weeks prior to the corresponding submission deadline. Letters of inquiry must be submitted online or e-mailed, without attachments. Following staff review of initial inquiries, applicants will be notified whether or not to submit a full proposal.

Applicants invited to apply are then required to submit an electronic copy of their proposal.

Duration: Typically 12 months.

Deadline: Arts: December 16 and March 8. Notification April and July, respectively. Education: March 8 and September 13. Notification July and December, respectively. Environment: December 16 and September 13. Notification April and December, respectively. Informed Communities: March 8. Notification in July.

PUBLICATIONS:
Application guidelines; biannual report.

IRS I.D.: 23-7406010

STAFF:
Tanuja Dehne, President and Chief Executive Officer

ADDRESS INQUIRIES TO:
Marisa Benson, Grants Manager
Tel: (973) 695-1187
E-mail: mbenson@grdodge.org

*SPECIAL STIPULATIONS:
The Foundation does not accept fax proposals or proposals sent via express mail carriers.

DOMINION ENERGY CHARITABLE FOUNDATION [88]
707 East Main Street
Richmond, VA 23219
E-mail: dominionfoundation@dominionenergy.com
Web Site: www.dominionenergy.com/foundation

FOUNDED: 1985

AREAS OF INTEREST:
Human needs, environmental stewardship, education and community vitality.

NAME(S) OF PROGRAMS:
- **ArtStars Awards**
- **Community Impact Awards**
- **COVID-19 Relief Grants**
- **Dollars for Doers Grants**
- **Environmental Education and Stewardship Grants**
- **Solar for Students Program**

TYPE:
Matching gifts; Project/program grants.

PURPOSE:
To improve the physical, social and economic well-being of the communities served by Dominion companies.

ELIGIBILITY:
Applicants must be 501(c)(3) organizations. No grants to individuals, sectarian purposes, fraternal, political, advocacy or labor organizations, religious programs of churches, or operating funds of individual United Way agencies.

GEOG. RESTRICTIONS: ArtStars Awards and Solar for Students Program: Virginia; Community Impact Awards: Ohio.

FINANCIAL DATA:
Amount of support per award: Generally $1,000 to $15,000.
Total amount of support: Approximately $22,300,000 annually.
Matching fund requirements: Must be employee or retiree of Dominion Energy.

NO. MOST RECENT APPLICANTS: 2,344.

NO. AWARDS: 1,295.

APPLICATION INFO:
Grant applications are accepted online. Before applying for a grant, it is recommended to review the Grant Guidelines and Restrictions, as well as the Frequently Asked Questions. Those organizations meeting the eligibility requirements can begin the application process by completing the eligibility quiz.
Deadline: Year-round on a calendar year, except competitive programs.

PUBLICATIONS:
Grant guidelines.

IRS I.D.: 47-2746460

OFFICER:
Hunter A. Applewhite, President

GAYLORD AND DOROTHY DONNELLEY FOUNDATION [89]
35 East Wacker Drive, Suite 2600
Chicago, IL 60601
(312) 977-2700
E-mail: info@gddf.org
Web Site: gddf.org

FOUNDED: 1952

AREAS OF INTEREST:
Artistic vitality, land conservation and collections in Chicago or the Lowcountry of South Carolina.

TYPE:
General operating grants; Project/program grants; Technical assistance.

YEAR PROGRAM STARTED: 1952

PURPOSE:
To sustain and build resilient, vital, engaged, and equitable communities in Chicago and South Carolina's Lowcountry by supporting conservation, arts, and collecting organizations.

LEGAL BASIS:
Tax-exempt, private foundation.

ELIGIBILITY:
Grants are made to tax-exempt, nonprofit 501(c)(3) organizations. Grants are not made to individuals, for community welfare, education, benefits, conferences, loans or pledges.

GEOG. RESTRICTIONS: Chicago region and South Carolina's Lowcountry.

FINANCIAL DATA:
Amount of support per award: Varies.
Total amount of support: Varies.
Matching fund requirements: Cash Reserve Challenge program in Chicago Artistic Vitality.

NO. MOST RECENT APPLICANTS: 275 for the year 2020.

NO. AWARDS: 350 for the year 2020.

APPLICATION INFO:
Proposals should be submitted in response to guidelines, if projects are applicable.
Duration: One to three years.
Deadline: March and July.

OFFICERS AND DIRECTORS:
David Farren, Executive Director
Brian Bannon, Director
Betsy Chaffin, Director
Inanna Donnelly, Director
Laura Donnelley, Director
Shawn M. Donnelley, Director
Laura Gates, Director
Rick Lowe, Director
Alex Shuford, Director
Mark Templeton, Director
Alaka Wali, Director
Trenholm Walker, Director
Mimi Wheeler, Director

ADDRESS INQUIRIES TO:
See e-mail address above.

THE DOUTY FOUNDATION [90]
P.O. Box 1437
Philadelphia, PA 19105
(215) 620-1869
E-mail: jennifer@doutyfoundation.org
Web Site: www.doutyfoundation.org

FOUNDED: 1968

AREAS OF INTEREST:
Economic and educational opportunities to disadvantaged people, especially children.

TYPE:
General operating grants; Project/program grants. Projects with social impact, innovative projects and general operations.

YEAR PROGRAM STARTED: 1969

PURPOSE:
To support programs that provide either educational opportunities for the disadvantaged or local innovative social services.

LEGAL BASIS:
Tax-exempt private foundation.

ELIGIBILITY:
Qualifying tax-exempt organizations are eligible. Grants are not made for capital expenditures, agency promotions, annual reports, renovations or to organizations with annual budgets of more than $1,000,000. Grants are not made to individuals or for religious or political purposes.

GEOG. RESTRICTIONS: Greater Philadelphia, Pennsylvania area with preference to Montgomery and Philadelphia counties.

FINANCIAL DATA:
Amount of support per award: Maximum $20,000 per year.
Total amount of support: $12,000,000 for the year 2020.

NO. AWARDS: 86 for the year 2020.

APPLICATION INFO:
Applications may be submitted online via the Foundation web site.
Duration: Three years.
Deadline: September 15.

IRS I.D.: 46-3309525

TRUSTEES:
Judith L. Bardes
Carrolle Perry Devonish
Peter Gonzales, Esq.
Thomas B. Harvey, Esq.
Nancy J. Kirby
Elbert Sampson
Ludy Soderman

STAFF:
Jennifer Leith, Executive Director

ADDRESS INQUIRIES TO:
Jennifer Leith, Executive Director
(See address above.)

*SPECIAL STIPULATIONS:
Organizations that have been funded for a six-year period may not reapply until at least two years have passed.

DOW JONES FOUNDATION [91]
1211 Avenue of the Americas, 7th Floor
New York, NY 10036
(212) 416-3202
E-mail: brad.rolston@dowjones.com

FOUNDED: 1954

AREAS OF INTEREST:
Journalism, free press, literacy and education, and diversity and inclusion.

TYPE:
General operating grants. Program support.

PURPOSE:
To support causes engaged in the promotion and protection of journalism and free press, as well as causes devoted specifically to literacy and education or diversity and inclusion.

LEGAL BASIS:
Corporate foundation.

ELIGIBILITY:
Applicant must be a U.S. 501(c)(3) organization.

FINANCIAL DATA:
Amount of support per award: Varies.

APPLICATION INFO:
All requests for Foundation support must be submitted in writing. Each request must indicate IRS tax-exemption certificate number.
Deadline: Normally, requests received will be considered by the board of directors only at their annual meeting in June for distribution in the next fiscal year.

PUBLICATIONS:
Application guidelines.

IRS I.D.: 27-1756118

STAFF:
Bradley P. Rolston, Esq., President and Director

ADDRESS INQUIRIES TO:
Bradley P. Rolston, Esq.
President and Director
(See address above.)

JOSEPH DROWN FOUNDATION   [92]
9800 Wilshire Boulevard
Suite 213
Beverly Hills, CA 90212
(310) 277-4488
E-mail: alyssa@jdrown.org
Web Site: www.jdrown.org

FOUNDED: 1953

AREAS OF INTEREST:
Education.

TYPE:
General operating grants; Project/program grants.

YEAR PROGRAM STARTED: 1953

PURPOSE:
To assist individuals in becoming successful, self-sustaining and contributing members of society.

ELIGIBILITY:
No funds to individuals, endowments, capital campaigns or building funds. The Foundation will not underwrite annual meeting or conferences. No funding for religious programs and special events.

In the area of medical research, the Foundation does not accept unsolicited requests.

GEOG. RESTRICTIONS: Los Angeles, California.

FINANCIAL DATA:
Amount of support per award: $5,000 to $50,000.
Total amount of support: Approximately $2,800,000 in grants paid for the fiscal year ended March 31, 2020.

NO. AWARDS: 83 for the year 2020.

APPLICATION INFO:
Applications are accepted online only.
Duration: One year.
Deadline: January 15, April 15, July 15 and October 15.

PUBLICATIONS:
Application guidelines.

OFFICERS AND STAFF:
Wendy Wachtell, President
Ann T. Miller, Chief Financial Officer
Alyssa Santino, Program Director

ADDRESS INQUIRIES TO:
Alyssa Santino, Program Director
(See address above.)

*SPECIAL STIPULATIONS:
In the area of medical research, the Foundation does not accept unsolicited requests.

DORIS DUKE CHARITABLE FOUNDATION   [93]
650 Fifth Avenue, 19th Floor
New York, NY 10019
(212) 974-7000
Fax: (212) 974-7590
Web Site: www.ddcf.org

FOUNDED: 1996

AREAS OF INTEREST:
Environment, performing arts, child well-being and medical research.

NAME(S) OF PROGRAMS:
- **Arts Program**
- **Child Well-being Program**
- **Environment Program**
- **Medical Research Program**

TYPE:
Grants-in-aid. The Arts Program supports performing artists with the creation and public performance of their work. The Program focuses its support on contemporary dance, jazz and theatre, and the organizations that nurture, present and produce them.

The Child Well-being Program promotes children's healthy development and protects them from abuse and neglect. The Program favors a public health approach and is especially interested in place-based, whole-community approaches that seek to engage a range of participants from various disciplines to ensure that family well-being is supported by strong communities.

The Environment Program enables communities to protect and manage wildlife habitat and create efficient built environments. The Program's awareness of climate change as the greatest emerging threat to biodiversity - and the need to aggressively mitigate it without unnecessarily sacrificing wildlife habitat - shapes the Program's grantmaking priorities.

The Medical Research Program supports the prevention, treatment and cure of human disease. The goal of the Program is to strengthen and support clinical research to help advance the translation of basic biomedical discoveries into new treatments, preventions and cures for human diseases.

YEAR PROGRAM STARTED: 1997

PURPOSE:
To improve the quality of people's lives through grants supporting the performing arts, environmental conservation, medical research and the prevention of child abuse, and through the preservation of the cultural and environmental legacy of Doris Duke's properties.

LEGAL BASIS:
Nonprofit foundation.

ELIGIBILITY:
While all Foundation programs require that grantee organizations be publicly supported 501(c)(3) tax-exempt organizations based in the U.S., each program has a customized approach to its grantmaking strategy.

FINANCIAL DATA:
Amount of support per award: $315,000 average.
Total amount of support: Approximately $76,000,000.

APPLICATION INFO:
The majority of the Foundation's grants are awarded through competitive (request-for-proposal) processes or by invitation. Open competitions and funding opportunities for grants are listed on the Foundation's web site. Foundation staff also welcome letters of inquiry from qualifying organizations.

To submit a letter of inquiry, the Foundation requests that organizations visit its web site and submit letters of inquiry through the online form. To do so, applicant will need a nonprofit tax ID as well as the title of the proposed project, a brief description of the specific project for which funding is sought, the requested funding amount, a description of how the objectives of the proposed project relate to those of the Foundation, the organization's mission and strategies, and a primary contact for the organization. Staff will respond to the letters of inquiry within two months and will notify the writer if additional information is desired.
Duration: Short-term or multiyear grants are awarded.

TRUSTEES:
William H. Wright, II, Chairperson
Anthony S. Fauci, Vice Chairperson
Afsaneh Beschloss
Mary Schmidt Campbell
Vishakha N. Desai
Clive Gillinson
Nannerl O. Keohane
Catie Marron
Marie Lynn Miranda
Angela K. Mwanza
John Talty
David S. Wilcove

STAFF:
Sam Gill, President

THE DUKE ENDOWMENT   [94]
800 East Morehead Street
Charlotte, NC 28202
(704) 376-0291
Fax: (704) 376-9336
E-mail: cperkins@tde.org
Web Site: www.dukeendowment.org

FOUNDED: 1924

AREAS OF INTEREST:
Health care in North Carolina and South Carolina; children's welfare and adoption assistance in North Carolina and South Carolina; rural United Methodist churches and retired ministers in North Carolina and four colleges: Duke, Furman and Johnson C. Smith universities and Davidson College.

TYPE:
Capital grants; General operating grants; Project/program grants.

YEAR PROGRAM STARTED: 1924

PURPOSE:
To carry out the terms of the Trust Indenture, as written by James B. Duke, by supporting four institutions in higher education, not-for-profit hospitals and children's homes in North Carolina and South Carolina, retired pastors of the United Methodist Church and programs and projects of rural United Methodist Churches in North Carolina.

LEGAL BASIS:
Charitable trust.

ELIGIBILITY:
North and South Carolina organizations and institutions with appropriate interests and activities are eligible.

GEOG. RESTRICTIONS: North Carolina and South Carolina.

FINANCIAL DATA:
Amount of support per award: Varies.
Total amount of support: $185,736,378 for the year 2019.
Matching fund requirements: Varies with grant.

NO. MOST RECENT APPLICANTS: Varies.

NO. AWARDS: Varies.

REPRESENTATIVE AWARDS:
$2,200,000 to support statewide implementation of Triple P (Positive Parenting Program) in North and South Carolina; $4,200,000 to expand a two-state initiative to increase breastfeeding rates throughout the Carolinas; $24,000,000 to Davidson College to expand the James B. Duke Scholarship Program; $5,700,000 to continue the Thriving Rural Communities initiative.

APPLICATION INFO:
Applicants must check the eligibility criteria before applying. Complete guidelines and application form are available on the web site.
Duration: Varies. All eligible beneficiaries may request continued and renewed support.
Deadline: Varies.

PUBLICATIONS:
Annual report; e-newsletter, occasional papers and reports on projects and programs.

IRS I.D.: 56-0529965

OFFICERS:
Rhett N. Mabry, President
Karen H. Rogers, Chief Financial Officer/Treasurer
K. Todd Walker, Managing Director, Investments

TRUSTEES:
Minor M. Shaw, Chairperson
Dennis M. Campbell, Ph.D., Vice Chairperson
Jean G. Spaulding, M.D., Vice Chairperson
William Barnet, III
John F.A.V. Cecil
Ravenel B. Curry, III
Pamela Davies
Harris E. DeLoach, Jr.
Constance F. Gray
J. Trent Jones
Thomas S. Kenan, III
Charles C. Lucas, III
Clarence G. Newsome
Kenneth D. Weeks, Jr., M.D.
Judy Woodruff

ADDRESS INQUIRIES TO:
Charity L. Perkins
Director of Communications
(See address above.)

DUNSPAUGH DALTON FOUNDATION [95]
1501 Venera Avenue, Suite 312
Coral Gables, FL 33146
(305) 668-4192
Fax: (305) 668-4247
E-mail: ddf@dunspaughdalton.org
Web Site: dunspaughdalton.org

AREAS OF INTEREST:
Higher, secondary, and elementary education; social services; youth; health associations and hospitals; cultural programs; and civic affairs.

TYPE:
Capital grants; General operating grants; Project/program grants.

ELIGIBILITY:
Grants are made to organizations that have tax-exempt status under Section 501(c)(3) of the Internal Revenue Code. No grants are made to individuals.

GEOG. RESTRICTIONS: Monterey County, California; Miami-Dade County, Florida; Charlotte and Mecklenburg County, North Carolina.

FINANCIAL DATA:
Amount of support per award: $5,000 average.

APPLICATION INFO:
Applicant must submit:
(1) proposal summary (not to exceed one-half page) explaining why the grant is requested, what outcomes are hoped to be achieved and how funds will be spent;
(2) narrative including background, funding requirements and evaluation (not to exceed five pages);
(3) completed Grant Application Form and;
(4) the most recent financial statements used as the basis for filing IRS Form 990.

Submit all application documents to the office listed on the Grant Application Form.
Duration: One year. Can reapply.

OFFICERS:
Alexina H. Lane, President
Robert C. Bonner, III, Vice President/Treasurer
Leslie W. Buchanan, Vice President/Secretary

ADDRESS INQUIRIES TO:
Leslie W. Buchanan, Secretary or Alexina Lane, President
(See address above.)

JESSIE BALL DUPONT FUND [96]
40 East Adams Street
Suite 300
Jacksonville, FL 32202-3302
(904) 353-0890
E-mail: info@dupontfund.org
Web Site: www.dupontfund.org

FOUNDED: 1976

AREAS OF INTEREST:
Education, religion, health and human services, arts and culture, juvenile justice, environment, housing, community and economic development, historic preservation, nonprofit capacity building and financial asset building.

TYPE:
Challenge/matching grants; General operating grants; Project/program grants; Technical assistance. Organizational capacity building.

Geared to nonprofit, religious organizations and educational institutions.

YEAR PROGRAM STARTED: 1976

PURPOSE:
To expand access and create opportunity through investing in people, organizations and communities that were important to Jessie Ball duPont.

LEGAL BASIS:
Private foundation.

ELIGIBILITY:
The Fund makes grants only to a defined universe of organizations. An organization is eligible if it received a contribution from Mrs. duPont between January 1, 1960 and December 31, 1964. Proof of eligibility is determined by examining Mrs. duPont's personal or tax records or by the applicant presenting written, verifiable evidence of having received a contribution during the eligibility period.

GEOG. RESTRICTIONS: Primarily the South, especially Delaware, Florida, and Virginia.

FINANCIAL DATA:
Amount of support per award: Feasibility Grants: Up to $5,000; Technical Assistance Grants: Up to $4,000.
Total amount of support: $6,684,936 in grants awarded for the year 2018.

NO. MOST RECENT APPLICANTS: Varies.

NO. AWARDS: Varies.

APPLICATION INFO:
Grants are made by invitation only. The trustees do not entertain unsolicited proposals.
Duration: One year.
Deadline: Trustees meet at the end of January, June and November to consider grant applications. Awards are announced immediately after the meetings.

PUBLICATIONS:
Annual report; policy briefings; *Notes from the Field.*

IRS I.D.: 59-6368632

TRUSTEES:
Rev. Eddie E. Jones, Jr., Chairperson
Anna Escobedo Cabral, Vice Chairperson
David Llewellyn, Representing Corporate Trustee, Northern Trust
Rev. Jen Bailey
Elizabeth Kiss
Marty Lanahan
Chuck Redmond

STAFF:
Mari Kuraishi, President
Katie Ensign, Vice President for Placemaking and Administration
Barbara Roole, Director of Equity
Chris Crothers, Director of Impact Investing
Mark Walker, Senior Program Officer
Marilyn Benjamin, Senior Grants Manager

*PLEASE NOTE:
Guidelines must be followed carefully when submitting proposal.

EASTERN BANK CHARITABLE FOUNDATION [97]
195 Market Street
Lynn, MA 01901
(781) 598-7595
Fax: (781) 598-7640
E-mail: n.stager@easternbank.com
Web Site: www.easternbank.com

FOUNDED: 1994

AREAS OF INTEREST:
Human services, family and children, affordable housing, health care, education, social justice, LGBTQ, disabilities, early childhood development, and workforce development.

NAME(S) OF PROGRAMS:
- **Community Grants**

TYPE:
Project/program grants.

YEAR PROGRAM STARTED: 1994

PURPOSE:
To contribute, in a meaningful way, to the health and vitality of the various communities which are served by Eastern Bank, by providing financial support to selected nonprofit organizations operating within those communities; to support organizations providing services to the underserved and neediest members of our community; to ensure all our neighbors have equal access to food, shelter, education, employment, child care and other basic human needs.

LEGAL BASIS:
Corporate foundation.

ELIGIBILITY:
Applicants must be nonprofit 501(c)(3) organizations and be located in the market area served by Eastern Bank. The Foundation does not accept applications from organizations with 509(a)(3) designation or private foundations.

GEOG. RESTRICTIONS: Eastern Massachusetts and southern and coastal New Hampshire.

FINANCIAL DATA:
Amount of support per award: Community Grants: $250 to $10,000.
Total amount of support: $9,500,000 for the year 2019.
Matching fund requirements: Full-time employees, trustees and directors: Minimum $50, maximum $1,000 per year.

NO. MOST RECENT APPLICANTS: 3,000.

NO. AWARDS: 2,000.

APPLICATION INFO:
Applications are only accepted through the online application site.
Deadline: Ongoing for requests up to $10,000.

PUBLICATIONS:
Annual report, available online.

IRS I.D.: 22-3317340

ADDRESS INQUIRIES TO:
Nancy Huntington Stager
Chief Executive Officer and President
(See address above.)

EATON CHARITABLE FUND [98]
Eaton Center
1000 Eaton Boulevard
Cleveland, OH 44122
(440) 523-4502
(440) 523-4905
Web Site: www.eaton.com

FOUNDED: 1953

AREAS OF INTEREST:
Health and human services, education, arts and culture, community improvement and neighborhood development.

TYPE:
Capital grants; Challenge/matching grants; Matching gifts; Product donations; Project/program grants. The Corporation places a priority on contributing to those organizations in which Eaton employees are personally involved and which serve their

needs. Contributions are made to health, human service, civic, arts and cultural organizations and educational institutions.

Support of capital campaigns at educational institutions is generally limited to programs of direct interest to Eaton, which prefers to invest in engineering, scientific, technological and business-related projects.

YEAR PROGRAM STARTED: 1953

PURPOSE:
To contribute to the betterment of life in communities where Eaton employees live and work; to support employee involvement and investment; to promote self-sufficiency; to sustain arts and cultural institutions; to enhance education.

LEGAL BASIS:
Corporate foundation.

ELIGIBILITY:
501(c)(3) organizations within the Corporation's areas of interest are eligible for support. Grants are not made to religious, fraternal or labor organizations; to individuals or individual endeavors; debt retirement; medical research; endowment funds; fund-raising benefits, sponsorships or other events; or annual operating budgets of United Way agencies or hospitals.

Grants are only made in communities where Eaton has operations.

FINANCIAL DATA:
Cash grants are mainly from the Charitable Fund, but also from the company.
Amount of support per award: Typically, $1,000 to $100,000. Average: $5,000 to $15,000.
Total amount of support: Approximately $8,500,000 for the year 2019.
Matching fund requirements: Donations are matched fifty cents on the dollar to most 501(c)(3) nonprofits, including arts, cultural, educational, and health and human services organizations. Religious, political and fraternal organizations are ineligible. U.S. employees are eligible to participate. Match maximum per employee per year is $5,000.

APPLICATION INFO:
Contact the nearest Eaton facility for more information on charitable grants. Each facility determines the organizations and interests they wish to support and will provide the link to the online application and more information on the application and approval processes.
Duration: Grants are typically given for one year. Multiyear commitments are usually capital grants.
Deadline: Grant requests are accepted and reviewed throughout the year.

PUBLICATIONS:
Annual report; guidelines.

STAFF:
Lisa Durst, Manager, Community Affairs

CONTRIBUTIONS COMMITTEE:
Taras Szmagala, Jr., Chairman
Revathi Advaithi
Bill Blausey
Cynthia Brabander
Ken Semelsberger
Uday Yadav

ADDRESS INQUIRIES TO:
Taras Szmagala, Jr., Senior Vice President
Public and Community Affairs
(See address above.)

EDISON INTERNATIONAL [99]
2244 Walnut Grove Avenue
Rosemead, CA 91770
(626) 302-2222
Web Site: edison.com/home/community.html

FOUNDED: 1996

AREAS OF INTEREST:
Education (science, technology, engineering, arts and math), environment, public safety and emergency preparedness, and civic engagement.

CONSULTING OR VOLUNTEER SERVICES:
Volunteer Program, Energy in Action.

NAME(S) OF PROGRAMS:
- **Corporate Contributions Program**
- **Edison Scholars Program**
- **Employee Matching Gifts Program**
- **Volunteer Program**

TYPE:
Challenge/matching grants; General operating grants; Matching gifts; Project/program grants; Scholarships. Matching gifts and employees for education only: private and public schools (K-University).

YEAR PROGRAM STARTED: 1986

PURPOSE:
To promote the economic prosperity and overall quality of life in the areas where its employees live and work by supporting numerous community initiatives and historically supporting a variety of effective educational, civic and charitable activities.

ELIGIBILITY:
Organization must have 501(c)(3) status. Primary focus on Southern California and other areas where Edison International operates.

No grants to individuals, political organizations or candidates, veterans organizations, fraternal orders, labor groups, commercial profit-making enterprises, religious or sectarian organizations or any group whose activities are not in the best interests of Edison International, its employees, shareholders, customers or the communities it serves.

FINANCIAL DATA:
Amount of support per award: Edison Scholars: $40,000 over four years.
Total amount of support: Varies.
Matching fund requirements: Equal match to $2,000 for accredited public and private educational institutions; Up to $2,000 for Energy Assistance Fund.

NO. AWARDS: Edison Scholars: 30 annually; Grants: Varies.

APPLICATION INFO:
Applications for Edison grants and sponsorships must be submitted online during Edison's funding cycles. Application links are active only during funding cycles.

PUBLICATIONS:
Annual report; contributions policy; application guidelines.

ADDRESS INQUIRIES TO:
Lisa Woon, Corporate Philanthropy
(See address above.)

EL POMAR FOUNDATION [100]
10 Lake Circle
Colorado Springs, CO 80906
(719) 633-7733
Fax: (719) 577-5702
E-mail: grants@elpomar.org
Web Site: www.elpomar.org

FOUNDED: 1937

AREAS OF INTEREST:
Arts and culture, civic and community initiatives, education, health and human services that impact the state of Colorado.

NAME(S) OF PROGRAMS:
- **American Council of Young Political Leaders**
- **Awards for Excellence**
- **El Pomar Fellowship**
- **El Pomar Internship**
- **Emerging Leaders Development**
- **Empty Stocking Fund**
- **Forum for Civic Advancement**
- **Grants Program**
- **Military Affairs**
- **Nonprofit Executive Leadership Program**
- **Penrose House Conference Center**
- **Pikes Peak Heritage Series**
- **Regional Partnerships**

TYPE:
Capital grants; General operating grants; Project/program grants.

PURPOSE:
To support general-purpose grantmaking, civic collaboration, projects of major community importance and initiatives that provide various kinds of assistance to nonprofit organizations; to provide leadership development opportunities for a range of individuals, from those just out of college to those responsible for the state's most important nonprofits; to help those least able to help themselves.

LEGAL BASIS:
Private nonprofit charitable foundation.

ELIGIBILITY:
Priority consideration will be provided to projects and organizations that have received local community and other support. The Foundation does not accept grant applications for grant support to:
(1) other foundations or nonprofits that distribute money to recipients of its own selection;
(2) endowments;
(3) organizations that practice discrimination of any kind;
(4) organizations that do not have fiscal responsibility for the proposed project;
(5) organizations that do not have an active 501(c)(3) nonprofit IRS determination letter;
(6) camps, camp programs, or other seasonal activities;
(7) religious organizations for support of religious programs;
(8) cover deficits or debt elimination;
(9) cover travel, conferences, conventions, group meetings, or seminars;
(10) influence legislation or support candidates for political office;
(11) produce videos or other media projects;
(12) fund research projects or studies and;
(13) primary or secondary schools (K-12). The Foundation will consider, on a limited basis, capital requests from nonpublicly funded secondary schools.

Capital grant requests exceeding $100,000, unless initiated by the Foundation, will not be considered.

GEOG. RESTRICTIONS: Colorado.

FINANCIAL DATA:
Amount of support per award: Capital Grants: $10,000 to $25,000; General Operating Grants and Program Grants: $2,500 to $10,000.

Total amount of support: Approximately $22,000,000 in grants and program contributions annually.

NO. MOST RECENT APPLICANTS: Over 1,700 for the year 2020.

NO. AWARDS: Over 1,500 grants approved for the year 2020.

APPLICATION INFO:
Online grant application includes a concise narrative and three years of financial documents. Fellowship and grant guidelines are available on the Foundation web site.
Duration: Typically one year.
Deadline: Proposals are accepted on a rolling basis.

PUBLICATIONS:
Annual report; application guidelines.

IRS I.D.: 84-6002373

OFFICERS:
William J. Hybl, Executive Chairman
R. Thayer Tutt, Jr., Vice Chairman and Chief Investment Officer
Kyle H. Hybl, President and Chief Executive Officer
Matt Carpenter, Executive Vice President and Chief Operating Officer
Elaine Martinez, Chief Financial Officer

TRUSTEES:
Andrea Aragon
Judy Bell
Matt Carpenter
Col. Gail Colvin, (Ret.)
Erik Estrada
Nechie Hall
Kyle H. Hybl
William J. Hybl, Jr.
Gen. Charles H. Jacoby, Jr. (Ret.)
David J. Palenchar
R. Thayer Tutt, Jr.
William R. Ward

ADDRESS INQUIRIES TO:
See e-mail address above.

ERION FOUNDATION [101]
P.O. Box 732
Loveland, CO 80539
(970) 667-4549
Fax: (970) 663-6187
E-mail: erionfoundationorg@gmail.com
Web Site: www.erionfoundation.org

FOUNDED: 1986

AREAS OF INTEREST:
Education, health, welfare, and culture.

TYPE:
Capital grants; Challenge/matching grants; Development grants.

YEAR PROGRAM STARTED: 1986

PURPOSE:
To support the Loveland, CO community.

LEGAL BASIS:
Private foundation.

ELIGIBILITY:
Eligible organizations must be IRS 501(c)(3) tax-exempt.

GEOG. RESTRICTIONS: Loveland, Colorado and the immediate surrounding area.

FINANCIAL DATA:
Amount of support per award: Varies.

APPLICATION INFO:
Organization must submit an application packet that includes the following:

(1) completed application form;
(2) a copy of the organization's 501(c)(3) designation letter and;
(3) page one of the organization's most recent IRS Form 990.

Additional information is included in the Grant Guidelines section.

The Foundation prefers that grant requests be submitted via e-mail to GrantRequest@erionfoundation.org. Organization may also submit the application and attachments online.
Duration: Varies.

ADDRESS INQUIRIES TO:
Doug Erion, President
(See address above.)

*PLEASE NOTE:
Due to numerous large capital projects, the Foundation is not currently accepting grant applications.

EVERSOURCE ENERGY FOUNDATION [102]
P.O. Box 270
Hartford, CT 06103
(888) 682-4639
E-mail: responsibleenergy@eversource.com
Web Site: www.eversource.com

FOUNDED: 1981

AREAS OF INTEREST:
Health and well-being of youth and advancement and promotion of clean energy and related technologies.

TYPE:
Challenge/matching grants; Development grants; Matching gifts; Project/program grants; Research grants; Scholarships; Technical assistance. Grants to nonprofit charitable organizations in the Foundation's service territory.

YEAR PROGRAM STARTED: 1981

PURPOSE:
To make a positive difference in the lives of Eversource customers.

LEGAL BASIS:
Corporate foundation.

ELIGIBILITY:
Applicants must be institutions and organizations with a 501(c)(3) tax-exempt designation.

The Foundation does not support personal expenses related to events, conferences or travel, corporations that do not qualify as charitable organizations as defined by the IRS Code, projects benefiting limited groups (religious, fraternal or political), private foundations or endowments, requests aimed at reducing or eliminating a pre-existing debt, golf outings, organizations located outside the Foundation areas served and whose services do not benefit Eversource customers, and advertising. Generally speaking, grants are not provided to organizations that receive direct support from United Way or other federated funds, as these umbrella agencies are supported through Eversource direct giving and employee giving campaigns.

FINANCIAL DATA:
Amount of support per award: $1,000 to $100,000. $2,500 average.

Total amount of support: $1,000,000 to $1,500,000.

Matching fund requirements: The Foundation matches dollar-for-dollar employee gifts to approved educational or cultural organizations and homeless shelters. Minimum of $100 and maximum of $2,500 in any calendar year.

APPLICATION INFO:
Applications for support must be submitted through the online application form. Requests by e-mail or other means will not be considered.

Duration: Usually one year.

Deadline: November 15.

PUBLICATIONS:
Guidelines; matching grants program brochure.

EXELON CORPORATION   [103]
Corporate Relations
10 South Dearborn Street
Chicago, IL 60603
(312) 394-4361
E-mail: steve.solomon@exeloncorp.com
Web Site: www.exeloncorp.com

FOUNDED: 1888

AREAS OF INTEREST:
Math and science, environmental education, arts and culture, neighborhood development, and environmental conservation.

NAME(S) OF PROGRAMS:
● **Corporate Giving Program**

TYPE:
General operating grants; Matching gifts; Project/program grants. Sponsorship for events.

PURPOSE:
To strengthen customer and community relations by promoting the advancement of math, science and energy education, contributing to charitable organizations that promote efficiency and renewable energy, promoting economic and community development, and contributing to organizations that promote diversity in the workplace and community.

LEGAL BASIS:
Corporate contributions program.

ELIGIBILITY:
Grants are made to institutions, organizations and agencies located in Exelon's service area (District of Columbia, northern Illinois, central Maryland and southeastern Pennsylvania). The company does not purchase ads in benefit programs. No contributions are made to religious organizations for religious purposes, political organizations, or to individuals.

GEOG. RESTRICTIONS: District of Columbia, northern Illinois, central Maryland and southeastern Pennsylvania.

FINANCIAL DATA:
Total amount of support: $51,000,000 to nonprofit organizations for the year 2018.

NO. AWARDS: Approximately 16,000.

APPLICATION INFO:
Application must be submitted online.

Duration: One year.

Deadline: Applications are reviewed on an ongoing basis.

PUBLICATIONS:
Guidelines.

STAFF:
Christopher M. Crane, President and Chief Executive Officer of Exelon Corporation

ADDRESS INQUIRIES TO:
Steve Solomon
Vice President, Corporate Relations
(See address above.)

FAIRFIELD COUNTY'S COMMUNITY FOUNDATION   [104]
40 Richards Avenue
Norwalk, CT 06854
(203) 750-3200
Fax: (203) 750-3232
E-mail: info@fccfoundation.org
Web Site: fccfoundation.org

FOUNDED: 1992

AREAS OF INTEREST:
Community development, housing, education, youth development, health and human services, and arts and culture.

NAME(S) OF PROGRAMS:
● **Competitive Grantmaking Program**

TYPE:
General operating grants; Project/program grants. Capacity building grants. Scholarships are for high school students pursuing college or postsecondary training.

YEAR PROGRAM STARTED: 1992

PURPOSE:
To promote philanthropy as a means to create change in Fairfield County, CT, focusing on innovative and collaborative solutions to critical issues impacting the community.

ELIGIBILITY:
Grants are made to organizations that have tax-exempt status under Section 501(c)(3) of the Internal Revenue Code. No grants are made to individuals.

Competitive grants are awarded to nonprofit organizations benefitting residents of Fairfield County, CT.

Discretionary grants are only made to organizations serving Fairfield County, CT.

Donor-advised grants can be awarded to nonprofits throughout the U.S. and also abroad.

FINANCIAL DATA:
Assets over $230,000,000 for the year ended June 30, 2018.

Amount of support per award: Grants vary in amount, depending upon the needs and nature of the request.

Total amount of support: Approximately $19,000,000 in grants and scholarships for fiscal year 2019.

NO. AWARDS: Varies.

APPLICATION INFO:
Application information is available on the web site.

Duration: One year. Renewal possible.

STAFF:
Juanita T. James, President and Chief Executive Officer

ADDRESS INQUIRIES TO:
Sharon Jones, Community Impact Associate
E-mail: sjones@fccfoundation.org
(See address above.)

FARGO-MOORHEAD AREA FOUNDATION   [105]
409 7th Street South
Fargo, ND 58103
(701) 234-0756
Fax: (701) 234-9724
E-mail: lexi@areafoundation.org
Web Site: www.areafoundation.org

FOUNDED: 1960

AREAS OF INTEREST:
Basic human needs, education, community building, arts, culture and creativity, and women and children.

TYPE:
Project/program grants; Scholarships.

PURPOSE:
To encourage philanthropy; to develop a permanent endowment to assess and respond to emerging and changing community needs; to provide a permanent charitable trust to donors with varied interests and giving capacities.

ELIGIBILITY:
Must be 501(c)(3) nonprofit organization.

GEOG. RESTRICTIONS: Clay County, Minnesota and Cass County, North Dakota.

FINANCIAL DATA:
Amount of support per award: Varies per award.

Total amount of support: Approximately $4,300,000 annually.

NO. MOST RECENT APPLICANTS: 85.

NO. AWARDS: Varies.

APPLICATION INFO:
Organizations applying for funds are required to use the Foundation Grant Proposal Forms available online.

Duration: One year.

ADDRESS INQUIRIES TO:
Lexi Oestreich, Program Officer
(See address above.)

FIELD FOUNDATION OF ILLINOIS   [106]
200 West Madison Street
Third Floor
Chicago, IL 60606
(312) 831-0910
Fax: (312) 831-0961
E-mail: communications@fieldfoundation.org
Web Site: www.fieldfoundation.org

FOUNDED: 1960

AREAS OF INTEREST:
Justice, art, leadership investment, and media and storytelling.

TYPE:
Capital grants; Challenge/matching grants; Conferences/seminars; General operating grants; Matching gifts; Project/program grants.

YEAR PROGRAM STARTED: 1960

PURPOSE:
To provide support to organizations serving the people of Chicago, with a focus on communities commonly divested in.

LEGAL BASIS:
Private foundation.

ELIGIBILITY:
Support is limited to programs primarily serving Chicago residents. Grants are made to nonprofit institutions. Grants are not made directly to individuals.

GEOG. RESTRICTIONS: Chicago, Illinois.

FINANCIAL DATA:
Amount of support per award:
Programs/projects: $10,000 to $50,000.
Grants to individual schools do not exceed
$20,000 a year.

Total amount of support: Approximately
$3,000,000 annually.

Matching fund requirements: Only Board of
Directors and staff can submit matching gift
applications.

NO. MOST RECENT APPLICANTS: 400.

NO. AWARDS: 110.

APPLICATION INFO:
All organizations must create an account on
the Foundation's online portal. Applicants
must submit an online Letter of Inquiry
(LOI) outlining the proposed project. All
fields must be completed for the LOI to be
considered. If invited, applicants will be
asked to submit a full application.

Duration: Programs/projects and capital
funding: One year. Possible renewal up to
three years.

Deadline: Grants are awarded three times per
year. Deadlines are listed on the Foundation
web site.

PUBLICATIONS:
Biennial reports; information brochure
(including application guidelines).

IRS I.D.: 36-6059408

ADDRESS INQUIRIES TO:
Operations/Grants Manager
(See address above.)

FIRMAN FUND [107]
1422 Euclid Avenue
Hanna Building, Suite 1150
Cleveland, OH 44115
(216) 303-8060
Fax: (216) 862-2737

FOUNDED: 1953

AREAS OF INTEREST:
Medicine, education, culture, youth, welfare,
conservation and community funds.

TYPE:
Capital grants; Endowments; General
operating grants; Project/program grants;
Research grants.

LEGAL BASIS:
Tax-exempt, private foundation.

ELIGIBILITY:
No grants are awarded to individuals. No
unsolicited requests accepted.

GEOG. RESTRICTIONS: Denver, Colorado;
Thomasville, Georgia and Cleveland, Ohio.

FINANCIAL DATA:
Amount of support per award: $1,000 to
$250,000.

Total amount of support: Approximately
$400,000.

NO. AWARDS: Approximately 25.

APPLICATION INFO:
The Fund does not accept unsolicited
requests for funds.

Duration: Grants awarded are not to be
considered on a continuing basis.

TRUSTEES:
Stephanie Firman
Pamela Murphy
Robert C. Webster, III

FIRST COMMUNITY FOUNDATION PARTNERSHIP OF PENNSYLVANIA [108]
201 West Fourth Street
Williamsport, PA 17701
(570) 321-1500
Fax: (570) 321-6434
E-mail: FCFP@fcfpartnership.org
Web Site: www.fcfpartnership.org

FOUNDED: 1916

AREAS OF INTEREST:
Arts and culture, education, recreation and
environment, health, human services,
economic and community development.

CONSULTING OR VOLUNTEER SERVICES:
Estate planning seminars, grant applicant
training.

TYPE:
Project/program grants; Scholarships.

PURPOSE:
To improve the quality of life in northcentral
Pennsylvania.

LEGAL BASIS:
Community foundation.

ELIGIBILITY:
Central and northcentral Pennsylvania
qualified 501(c)(3) organizations only.

GEOG. RESTRICTIONS: Bradford, Clinton,
Columbia, Lycoming, Montour,
Northumberland, Potter, Snyder, Sullivan,
Tioga and Union counties, Pennsylvania.

FINANCIAL DATA:
Amount of support per award: Varies.
Total amount of support: $4,350,690 for the
year ended December 31, 2020.

CO-OP FUNDING PROGRAMS: Scholarships in
combination with donor-advised, designated,
organizational endowment and unrestricted
funds.

NO. AWARDS: 659 grants and 104 scholarships
for the year 2020.

APPLICATION INFO:
Application information is available on the
web site. Application must include a copy of
the IRS tax determination letter.
Duration: Typically one year.
Deadline: Varies.

PUBLICATIONS:
Annual report; grants and loans policy;
Insights in Estate and Financial Planning;
other tax and estate planning brochures.

IRS I.D.: 24-6013117

ADDRESS INQUIRIES TO:
Betty Gilmour
Director of Grantmaking
E-mail: bettyg@fcfpartnership.org

FIRSTENERGY FOUNDATION [109]
76 South Main Street
Akron, OH 44308-1890
(330) 384-5022
Fax: (330) 245-5566
E-mail: fe_comm_involve@firstenergycorp.com
Web Site: www.firstenergycorp.
com/community/firstenergy_foundation.html

FOUNDED: 1961

AREAS OF INTEREST:
Principally education, the arts, community
improvements, professional development and
literacy, and overall health of the community.

TYPE:
Capital grants; General operating grants;
Matching gifts; Project/program grants.

PURPOSE:
To improve the vitality of our communities
and support key safety initiatives; to promote
local and regional economic development and
revitalization efforts; to support FirstEnergy
employees' community leadership and
volunteer interests; to advance an educated
workforce by supporting professional
development and literacy, and science,
technology, engineering and mathematics
(STEM) education initiatives.

LEGAL BASIS:
Corporate foundation.

ELIGIBILITY:
The Foundation supports nonprofit,
tax-exempt organizations within the
FirstEnergy operating companies' service
area including Ohio Edison, The Illuminating
Company and Toledo Edison in Ohio;
Met-Ed, Penelec, Penn Power and West Penn
Power in Pennsylvania; Jersey Central Power
and Light in New Jersey; Mon Power and
Potomac Edison in West Virginia and
Maryland; and where FirstEnergy Solutions
Corp., FirstEnergy Generation and
FirstEnergy Nuclear Operations conduct
business.

Generally, no grants are made to individuals
or for political organizations, endowment
funds, deficit financing, research, scholarships
or fellowships. No loans.

FINANCIAL DATA:
Amount of support per award: Grants vary in
amount, depending upon the needs and
nature of the request.

Matching fund requirements: Employees
only.

NO. AWARDS: Varies.

APPLICATION INFO:
The Foundation does not accept unsolicited
grant applications. Applicants are encouraged
to discuss grant inquiries with the local
management of FirstEnergy companies and
the staff of FirstEnergy's Community
Involvement Department.

ADDRESS INQUIRIES TO:
Lorna Wisham, President
(See address above.)

*SPECIAL STIPULATIONS:
Unsolicited grant applications are not
accepted.

A.J. FLETCHER FOUNDATION [110]
909 Glenwood Avenue
Raleigh, NC 27605
(919) 322-2580
Fax: (919) 322-2581
E-mail: natalie@ajf.org
contact@ajf.org
Web Site: ajf.org

AREAS OF INTEREST:
Artistic endeavors, education, elderly, infirm
and indigent, media and communication,
public recreation, and religious faith.

TYPE:
General operating grants; Project/program
grants.

PURPOSE:
To support nonprofit organizations in their endeavors to improve the quality of life in North Carolina.

ELIGIBILITY:
Eligible organizations must be IRS 501(c)(3) tax-exempt.

GEOG. RESTRICTIONS: North Carolina.

FINANCIAL DATA:
Amount of support per award: Varies.
Total amount of support: Varies.

APPLICATION INFO:
Applications for funding are by request only.
Duration: One-time to multiyear funding.
Deadline: Varies.

ADDRESS INQUIRIES TO:
Natalie Fogg, Director of Operations and Grants Administration
(See address above.)

THE FLINN FOUNDATION   [111]
1802 North Central Avenue
Phoenix, AZ 85004
(602) 744-6800
E-mail: info@flinn.org
Web Site: flinn.org

FOUNDED: 1965

AREAS OF INTEREST:
Biosciences, education, arts and culture, and civic leadership in Arizona.

NAME(S) OF PROGRAMS:
● **Arizona Center for Civic Leadership**
● **Flinn Scholars Program**

TYPE:
Demonstration grants; Fellowships; Project/program grants; Scholarships; Seed money grants. The arts and culture grants program assists Arizona's large arts and culture organizations in generating capital through creative programming and fiscal planning.

The Foundation's biosciences grant projects aim to strengthen Arizona's biosciences infrastructure and thereby improve the state's capacity to compete nationally and internationally in the biosciences economy.

The Arizona Center for Civic Leadership seeks to strengthen civic leadership in Arizona.

The Flinn Scholars Program annually awards top Arizona high school graduates full scholarship support.

YEAR PROGRAM STARTED: 1981

PURPOSE:
To improve the quality of life in Arizona to benefit future generations through support of the biosciences, arts and culture, the Flinn Scholars and civic leadership.

LEGAL BASIS:
Tax-exempt private foundation.

ELIGIBILITY:
Flinn Scholarship applicant must be a U.S. citizen or lawful permanent resident and be an Arizona resident for two full years immediately preceding entry to the university.

Grant applicants must be tax-exempt, nonprofit organizations which have qualified for exemption under Section 501(c)(3) of the IRS code and, generally, are not those classified as private foundations.

Grants are made only for charitable purposes that support organizations and activities in Arizona. The Foundation generally does not make grants to support individuals, building and equipment projects, endowment or annual fund-raising campaigns or to meet ongoing operating costs or deficits.

GEOG. RESTRICTIONS: Arizona.

FINANCIAL DATA:
Foundation assets of approximately $250,000,000.
Amount of support per award: Varies.
Total amount of support: Varies.

CO-OP FUNDING PROGRAMS: The Flinn-Brown Civic Leadership Academy, a component of the Arizona Center for Civic Leadership, is co-funded by the Thomas R. Brown Foundations.

NO. AWARDS: Flinn Scholars: Approximately 20 annually.

REPRESENTATIVE AWARDS:
$504,000 to Arizona State University for Flinn Scholarship awards; $1,500,000 to Translational Genomics Research Institute for support of three genomic-based research projects in collaboration with Arizona institutions; $100,000 to Mesa Arts Center to choose and expand programming that connects to the Center's audiences and donors under age 40.

APPLICATION INFO:
No unsolicited applications accepted. There is no standard application form, except for those proposals submitted in response to a Foundation-initiated program.
Duration: Varies.

PUBLICATIONS:
Annual report; special reports; electronic newsletters.

STAFF:
Dawn Wallace, Vice President, Arizona Center for Civic Leadership
Sara Larsen, Program Manager, Arizona Center for Civic Leadership
Danielle Underwood, Program Coordinator, Arizona Center for Civic Leadership

*SPECIAL STIPULATIONS:
No unsolicited applications accepted.

THE FORD FOUNDATION   [112]
320 East 43rd Street
New York, NY 10017
(212) 573-5000
Fax: (212) 351-3677
Web Site: www.fordfoundation.org

FOUNDED: 1936

NAME(S) OF PROGRAMS:
● **Cities and States Program**
● **Civic Engagement and Government Program**
● **Creativity and Free Expression Program**
● **Future of Work(ers) Program**
● **Gender, Racial and Ethnic Justice Program**
● **Natural Resources and Climate Change Program**
● **Technology and Society Program**

TYPE:
Conferences/seminars; Endowments; Fellowships; General operating grants; Matching gifts; Project/program grants; Research grants; Seed money grants;

Technical assistance. General purposes, publications, program-related investments, special projects, individual grants.

Cities and States Program addresses geographic disparities across the nation.

Civic Engagement and Government Program deals with the issues of expanding participation, engaging government and equitable resources.

Creativity and Free Expression Program deals with the issues of social justice storytelling and 21st century arts infrastructure.

Future of Work(ers) Program deals with the opportunity for decent work and fair reward, which is key to reducing inequality.

Gender, Racial and Ethnic Justice Program deals with the issues of freedom and dignity and rights of race, gender and ethnicity, and to recognize they are deeply connected.

Natural Resources and Climate Change Program aims to address inequality as it relates to the climate crisis.

Technology and Society Program supports the growth of technically sophisticated, diverse organizations dedicated to advancing equitable and more inclusive digital spaces and systems.

PURPOSE:
To reduce poverty and injustice and to promote democratic values, free expression and human achievement.

LEGAL BASIS:
Private foundation.

ELIGIBILITY:
Qualified institutions, individuals and communities with appropriate interests are eligible to apply. Most of the Foundation's grant funds are given to organizations. Although the Foundation also makes grants to individuals, such grants are few in number relative to demand. These are limited to research, training and other activities related to the Foundation's program interests and subject to certain limitations and procedural requirements under the U.S. Internal Revenue Code.

The Foundation does not award undergraduate scholarships or make grants for purely personal or local needs. Support for graduate fellowships is generally funneled through grants to universities and other organizations, which are responsible for the selection of recipients. Support is not normally given for routine operating costs of institutions or for religious activities. Except in rare cases, funding is not available for the construction or maintenance of buildings.

FINANCIAL DATA:
Amount of support per award: Grants vary in amount, depending upon the needs and nature of the request. Average grant to organizations: $230,000.
Total amount of support: Approximately $8,000,000 in total grants, program-related investments and Foundation-administered projects annually.

NO. MOST RECENT APPLICANTS: Approximately 40,000 grant proposals annually.

NO. AWARDS: Approximately 1,500 grants annually.

APPLICATION INFO:
Prospective applicants should, as a first step, submit a brief letter of inquiry in order to

determine whether the Foundation's present interests and funds permit consideration as a proposal.

There is no application form. Proposals should set forth objectives, the proposed program for pursuing objectives, qualifications of persons engaged in the work, a detailed budget, present means of support and status of applications to other funding sources and legal and tax status.

Duration: Varies.

Deadline: Applications are considered throughout the year.

PUBLICATIONS:
Annual report; program policy statement including application guidelines; *Ford Foundation Report*, issued quarterly.

IRS I.D.: 13-1684331

OFFICERS:
Darren Walker, President
Depelsha McGruder, Chief Operating Officer and Treasurer
Hilary Pennington, Executive Vice President of Programs
Nishka Chandrasoma, Vice President, Secretary and General Counsel
Eric W. Doppstadt, Vice President and Chief Investment Officer
Michele Moore, Vice President, Global Communications
Martin Abregu, Vice President, International Programs
Diane Samuels, Vice President, People and Culture
Maria Torres-Springer, Vice President, U.S. Programs

BOARD OF TRUSTEES:
Francisco G. Cigarroa, M.D., Chairman
Ursula Burns
Amy C. Falls
Henry Ford, III
Thomas L. Kempner, Jr.
Lourdes Lopez
Paula Moreno
Gbenga Oyebode
Ai-jen Poo
Cecile Richards
Chuck Robbins
Bryan Stevenson
Gabrielle Sulzberger

ADDRESS INQUIRIES TO:
Office of the Secretary
E-mail: secretary@fordfoundation.org

FORD MOTOR COMPANY FUND AND COMMUNITY SERVICES [113]
One American Road
Dearborn, MI 48126-2701
(888) 313-0102
E-mail: fordfund@ford.com
Web Site: www.fordfund.org

FOUNDED: 1949

AREAS OF INTEREST:
Education, community development and auto-related safety.

NAME(S) OF PROGRAMS:
● **Community Grants Program**

TYPE:
Project/program grants; Scholarships. Grants are awarded to organizations and initiatives that support the Fund's key areas of focus: education, driving safety and community development.

PURPOSE:
To support initiatives and institutions that enhance and/or improve opportunities for those who live in communities where Ford Motor Company operates.

LEGAL BASIS:
Corporate foundation.

ELIGIBILITY:
No grants are made directly to individuals. Not-for-profit organizations with 501(c)(3) tax-exempt status may apply.

GEOG. RESTRICTIONS: United States.

FINANCIAL DATA:
Amount of support per award: Varies.
Total amount of support: Varies.

APPLICATION INFO:
Organization must complete a grant application online.
Duration: Varies.
Deadline: Requests for support are accepted and reviewed throughout the year.

FREEMAN FOUNDATION [114]
c/o The Rockefeller Trust Company, N.A.
45 Rockefeller Plaza, Fifth Floor
New York, NY 10111
(212) 549-5270
Fax: (212) 549-5524
E-mail: gtsandikos@rockco.com

FOUNDED: 1993

AREAS OF INTEREST:
Asian studies, environmental conservation and preservation, and Hawaii and Vermont programs.

TYPE:
Challenge/matching grants; Exchange programs; Fellowships; General operating grants; Professorships; Project/program grants; Research grants; Scholarships; Seed money grants; Technical assistance; Training grants; Travel grants; Visiting scholars.

PURPOSE:
To support a range of charitable organizations; to strengthen the bonds of friendship between the U.S. and the countries of East Asia; to preserve and protect the forests, lands and natural resources of the U.S. for future generations; to contribute to and enhance the development of a vibrant, international free enterprise system.

ELIGIBILITY:
Eligible organizations must be IRS 501(c)(3) tax-exempt.

FINANCIAL DATA:
Foundation grants since inception now total over $885,000,000.
Amount of support per award: Generally, $5,000 to $750,000.
Total amount of support: $16,193,660 in total grants for the year 2020.

APPLICATION INFO:
Letters of Inquiry: Applicants should submit a letter describing the program and financial needs.

A grant proposal should:
(1) include a cover letter for the grant request;
(2) provide a brief history of one's organization, its mission and leadership;
(3) provide financial information for the most recent fiscal year as well as financials for the next fiscal year, if available, and;
(4) provide a list of current funding sources, including amounts.

Six sets of the proposal should be mailed. Two of the six sets should include the organization's IRS Form 990, the IRS 501(c)(3) determination letter and the most recent audit. The length of the proposal, including cover letter and project budget sheet, should not exceed six pages. Mail proposals to Mr. Graeme Freeman; President; The Freeman Foundation; 1601 East-West Road; Honolulu, HI 96848-1601.

Duration: Varies by the program. Renewal possible.

Deadline: Applications must be received at least one month prior to Trustees' meetings, which occur three times yearly.

PUBLICATIONS:
Annual report.

IRS I.D.: 13-2965090

TRUSTEES AND OFFICERS:
Graeme Freeman, President
David Stack, Trustee
George Tsandikos, Trustee

ADDRESS INQUIRIES TO:
The Rockefeller Trust Company
George S. Tsandikos, Managing Director
(See address above.)

FREEPORT-MCMORAN FOUNDATION [115]
333 North Central Avenue
Phoenix, AZ 85004
(602) 366-8116
Fax: (602) 366-7368
E-mail: foundation@fmi.com
communitydevelopment@fmi.com
Web Site: www.freeportinmycommunity.com

FOUNDED: 1953

AREAS OF INTEREST:
Education and workforce development, economic opportunity and capacity, resiliency and leadership.

NAME(S) OF PROGRAMS:
● **Matching Gifts Program**
● **Social Investment Program**

TYPE:
Matching gifts; Project/program grants. In the area of capacity, resiliency and leadership, the Foundation supports programs that engage citizens, activate community leaders, improve financial well-being, and strengthen organizational effectiveness and efficiency to steward and amplify investments.

In the area of economic opportunity, the Foundation supports programs that create diverse jobs, strengthen local businesses, ensure attainable housing, enable accessible health resources, protect land and waterways, and increase food security.

In the area of education and workforce development, the Foundation supports programs that improve academic performance, enable reskilling, up-skilling and transferable skills for jobs of the future, facilitate completion of postsecondary education, and create pathways to jobs with a living wage or better.

YEAR PROGRAM STARTED: 1932

PURPOSE:
To serve as a catalyst of positive change in the communities where the company has major facilities and update the quality of life.

LEGAL BASIS:
Corporate foundation.

ELIGIBILITY:
Nonprofit programs and organizations aligned with the core values of the company. Must be located in communities where the company has a presence.

GEOG. RESTRICTIONS: United States.

FINANCIAL DATA:
Amount of support per award: Varies.
Total amount of support: Varies.
Matching fund requirements: Minimum $25. Maximum $40,000. First $1,000 is matched 2:1; above $1,000 is matched dollar-for-dollar.

NO. MOST RECENT APPLICANTS: Varies.

NO. AWARDS: Varies.

APPLICATION INFO:
Guidelines and application are available on the Foundation web site.
Duration: Social Investment Program: One year. Renewable.
Deadline: Social Investment Program: Letter of Intent may be submitted by May 26 to be considered for funding.

OFFICERS:
Tracy Bame, President and Director of Social Responsibility and Community Development

ADDRESS INQUIRIES TO:
Social Investment Administrator
(See address above.)

FREY FOUNDATION   [116]
40 Pearl Street, N.W.
Suite 1100
Grand Rapids, MI 49503-3028
(616) 451-0303
Fax: (616) 451-8481
E-mail: contact@freyfdn.org
Web Site: freyfdn.org

FOUNDED: 1974

AREAS OF INTEREST:
Children and their families, environment, community arts, civic progress, and philanthropy.

NAME(S) OF PROGRAMS:
● **Building Community**
● **Children and Families**
● **Community Arts**
● **Environment**

TYPE:
Capital grants; Demonstration grants; Project/program grants; Seed money grants; Technical assistance. Grants are available for special one-time only or time-limited purposes, such as "start-up" or program expansion, demonstration projects, planning or other forms of technical assistance, evaluation, advocacy, and applied research. Capital is available in some program areas.

YEAR PROGRAM STARTED: 1974

PURPOSE:
To promote healthy development of children and their families, particularly infants and children under the age of six and their parents, with special attention to traditionally disadvantaged populations; to protect, preserve and improve the ecological health of natural resources; to stimulate vitality, effectiveness and growth of community-based arts; to encourage civic action to improve the livability of cities and communities; to improve the effectiveness of organized philanthropy and stimulate its growth.

LEGAL BASIS:
Private family foundation.

ELIGIBILITY:
Applicants must be public institutions and 501(c)(3) nonprofit organizations. No grants to individuals, endowment funds, debt retirement, general operating expenses, scholarships, travel, to cover routine, current or emergency expenses and/or sectarian charitable activities.

GEOG. RESTRICTIONS: Charlevoix, Emmet or Kent counties and lower western Michigan.

FINANCIAL DATA:
Amount of support per award: Varies upon nature of request.
Total amount of support: Over $5,000,000 for the year 2018.

NO. MOST RECENT APPLICANTS: 222 inquiries and 112 applicants.

NO. AWARDS: Approximately 50 to 60 per year.

APPLICATION INFO:
Applicants must submit a brief inquiry using the online system.
Duration: One to three years.
Deadline: February 15, May 15, August 15 and November 15.

PUBLICATIONS:
Annual report; *Taking Care of Civic Business*; *Charting the Course*; *Today's Winners, Tomorrow's Losers*.

STAFF:
Holly A. Johnson, President
Ken E. Long, Chief Financial and Operations Officer
Lynne J. Ferrell, Program Director
Sarah J. Hockin-Mix, Program and Accounting Associate
Bryana Hopkins, Program and Communication Associate

BOARD OF TRUSTEES:
Mary Frey Bennett, Chairperson
Ellie Frey Zagel, Vice Chairperson
David J. Frey, Jr., Treasurer
Sarah Frey, Secretary
Campbell W. Frey
Edward J. Frey, Jr.
Katrine E. Frey
Laura D. Frey

ADDRESS INQUIRIES TO:
Holly A. Johnson, President
(See address above.)

THE FROST FOUNDATION, LTD.   [117]
511 Armijo Street, Suite A
Santa Fe, NM 87501
(505) 986-0208
Fax: (505) 986-0430
E-mail: info@frostfound.org
Web Site: www.frostfound.org

FOUNDED: 1959

AREAS OF INTEREST:
Social service and humanitarian needs, the environment and education.

CONSULTING OR VOLUNTEER SERVICES:
Professional services of staff are offered for special projects.

TYPE:
Project/program grants; Research grants.

YEAR PROGRAM STARTED: 1959

PURPOSE:
To seek and assist innovative projects that will have positive impact beyond the boundaries of a single state.

LEGAL BASIS:
Tax-exempt private foundation.

ELIGIBILITY:
The Foundation encourages self-reliance, creativity and ingenuity on the part of prospective recipients.

Its efforts are directed primarily to support exemplary organizations and programs which can generate positive change beyond traditional boundaries, to encourage creativity which recognizes emerging needs, and to assist innovation which addresses current urgent problems.

Within these parameters, it provides initial impetus to exemplary organizations and programs, to operating funds, to pioneering organizations and programs which other institutions might similarly use, and to programs which have potential for wider service or educational exposure than an individual community.

The Foundation encourages collaborations, mergers and the formation of alliances among agencies within the community to reduce duplication of effort and to promote a maximum effective use of funds. The Foundation also considers requests for operating. It is prepared to review applications of human service needs, environmental and education programs in New Mexico and Louisiana from organizations which have an IRS 501(c)(3) determination.

GEOG. RESTRICTIONS: Louisiana and New Mexico.

FINANCIAL DATA:
Amount of support per award: $15,000 average.
Total amount of support: Approximately $2,000,000 annually.

NO. MOST RECENT APPLICANTS: Approximately 500.

NO. AWARDS: Approximately 65.

APPLICATION INFO:
A brief description of the institution/organization, including its mission, must be submitted along with evidence of tax-exempt status, the amount requested, a statement of the specific need(s) to be met by the project, a budget projection with the time frame expected and the qualifications of the staff members selected to serve the project. Faxed summaries are not accepted.
Duration: Typically one year. On rare occasions, because of special circumstances, applicant can reapply.
Deadline: December 1 for March Board meeting and June 1 for September Board meeting.

PUBLICATIONS:
Annual report; application guidelines.

OFFICERS:
Mary Amelia Whited-Howell, President
Philip B. Howell, Executive Vice-President
Taylor F. Moore, Secretary/Treasurer

BOARD OF DIRECTORS:
Ann Rogers Gerber
Amelia Reid Howell
Philip B. Howell
Philip Carter Howell
Taylor F. Moore
Mary Amelia Whited-Howell

ADDRESS INQUIRIES TO:
Mary Amelia Whited-Howell, President
(See address above.)

LLOYD A. FRY FOUNDATION [118]
120 South LaSalle Street
Suite 1950
Chicago, IL 60603
(312) 580-0310
Fax: (312) 580-0310
E-mail: info@fryfoundation.org
Web Site: www.fryfoundation.org

FOUNDED: 1983

AREAS OF INTEREST:
Education, arts and culture education, access to health care, and employment, with special emphasis on support of inner-city projects.

TYPE:
Project/program grants.

PURPOSE:
To address persistent problems of urban Chicago resulting from poverty, violence, ignorance and despair.

LEGAL BASIS:
Private foundation.

ELIGIBILITY:
501(c)(3).

GEOG. RESTRICTIONS: Inner-city Chicago, Illinois.

FINANCIAL DATA:
Amount of support per award: $15,000 to $50,000 average.
Total amount of support: Over $7,000,000 in grants and awards annually.

NO. MOST RECENT APPLICANTS: 355 for fiscal year 2020.

NO. AWARDS: 306 for fiscal year 2020.

APPLICATION INFO:
Application guidelines are available at the Foundation web site.
Duration: One to two years.
Deadline: Letters of Intent are accepted year-round. Proposals: March 1, June 1, September 1 and December 1.

PUBLICATIONS:
Annual report.

IRS I.D.: 36-6108775

STAFF:
Unmi Song, President
Merril Prager, Controller
Sydney Sidell, Director of Education and Arts Learning
Sabrina Greig, Program Officer, Art
Jennifer Miller-Rehfeldt, Program Officer, Employment
Brian Bragg, Program Officer, Health
Carrie Roche, Program Assistant
Jessica Thompson, Program Assistant

ADDRESS INQUIRIES TO:
Ms. Unmi Song, President
(See e-mail address above.)

GANNETT FOUNDATION [119]
7950 Jones Branch Drive
McLean, VA 22107-0150
(703) 854-3780
(703) 854-6000
E-mail: foundation@gannett.com
Web Site: www.gannettfoundation.org

FOUNDED: 1991

AREAS OF INTEREST:
Education and neighborhood improvement, economic development, youth development, community problem-solving, assistance to disadvantaged people, environmental conservation and cultural enrichment.

TYPE:
General operating grants; Matching gifts; Project/program grants.

PURPOSE:
To improve the education, health and advancement of the people who live in Gannett communities.

LEGAL BASIS:
Corporate foundation.

ELIGIBILITY:
Local organizations determined by the IRS to be tax-exempt under 501(c)(3) in communities where the Gannett Company, Inc. owns a daily newspaper.

FINANCIAL DATA:
Amount of support per award: Average $1,000 to $5,000.
Total amount of support: Approximately $4,500,000 in grants for the year 2018.
Matching fund requirements: Gifts for programs or initiatives where the primary purpose is the promotion of religious doctrine or tenets are excluded.

NO. MOST RECENT APPLICANTS: 1,000.

NO. AWARDS: 700.

APPLICATION INFO:
Application form and guidelines are available online.
Duration: One year. Renewal possible.

ADDRESS INQUIRIES TO:
Sue Madden, Director
(See address above.)

THE CARL GELLERT AND CELIA BERTA GELLERT FOUNDATION [120]
455 Hickey Boulevard
Suite 509
Daly City, CA 94015
(650) 985-2080
Fax: (650) 985-2084
E-mail: info@gellertfoundation.org
Web Site: www.gellertfoundation.org

FOUNDED: 1958

AREAS OF INTEREST:
Religious, charitable, scientific, literary or educational purposes.

TYPE:
Capital grants; Development grants; Endowments; General operating grants; Project/program grants; Scholarships; Technical assistance.

YEAR PROGRAM STARTED: 1958

LEGAL BASIS:
Private foundation.

ELIGIBILITY:
Organization must have proof of current IRS 501(c)(3) tax-exempt status and classification as a public charity under Sections 509(a)(1) and 170(b)(1)(A) of the Internal Revenue Code, or 509(a)(2), or 509(a)(3), types I or II.

The Foundation does not fund individuals or private foundations, sponsorships or fund-raising events such as dinners,

walk-a-thons, tournaments and fashion shows, or lobbying and attempts to influence legislation.

GEOG. RESTRICTIONS: Alameda, Contra Costa, Marin, Napa, San Francisco, San Mateo, Santa Clara, Solano and Sonoma, the nine counties of the Greater San Francisco Bay area, California.

FINANCIAL DATA:
Amount of support per award: Varies.
Total amount of support: $1,797,213 for the year 2020.

NO. AWARDS: 94 for the year 2020.

APPLICATION INFO:
Application information can be found at the Foundation's web site. Application must be submitted online.
Deadline: August 15, annually or following Monday if 15th falls on a weekend.

IRS I.D.: 94-6062858

DIRECTORS:
Andrew A. Cresci
Jack Fitzpatrick
Kevin Flynn
Robert J. Grassilli, Jr.
Michael J. King
J. Malcolm Visbal
Christine Whelan

ADDRESS INQUIRIES TO:
Jack Fitzpatrick, Executive Director
(See address above.)

THE FRED GELLERT FAMILY FOUNDATION [121]
1038 Redwood Highway
Building B, Suite 2
Mill Valley, CA 94941
(415) 381-7570
Fax: (415) 381-8526
E-mail: FGFamilyFoundation@gmail.com
Web Site: www.fgfamilyfoundation.com

FOUNDED: 1958

AREAS OF INTEREST:
Long-term sustainability planning, advanced and specialized education, local community support through social service organizations, and reproductive health.

TYPE:
Challenge/matching grants; Endowments; Fellowships; General operating grants; Matching gifts; Professorships; Project/program grants; Research grants; Seed money grants.

YEAR PROGRAM STARTED: 1958

PURPOSE:
To advance positive forces for social change to ensure quality of life for future generations.

LEGAL BASIS:
Private family foundation.

ELIGIBILITY:
Applicants must be 501(c)(3) organizations. No grants to individuals or for purchasing development rights or land.

GEOG. RESTRICTIONS: Primarily the Greater Bay area, Marin and San Francisco, California.

FINANCIAL DATA:
Amount of support per award: $1,000 to $20,000; Average: $5,000.
Total amount of support: Approximately $318,000 for the year 2020.

Matching fund requirements: Provide information on challenge grant.

NO. AWARDS: 57 for the year 2020.

REPRESENTATIVE AWARDS:
$5,000 to Aim High for High School; $20,000 to Green Science Policy Institute; $10,000 to NARAL Pro-Choice America Foundation; $8,000 to SupplyBank.Org; $2,000 to Youth Food Project.

APPLICATION INFO:
The Foundation does not accept unsolicited letters of inquiry or grant proposals.

Duration: Typically one year.

IRS I.D.: 94-6062859

STAFF:
Julia Gellert, Grant Manager
Landon Gellert, Grant Manager
Serena Lim, Accountant

BOARD OFFICERS:
Annette Gellert, Co-Chairperson and Trustee
Fred Gellert, Jr., Co-Chairperson and Trustee

*PLEASE NOTE:
Grant monies awarded September to November.

GENERAL SERVICE FOUNDATION   [122]
2120 University Avenue
Berkeley, CA 94704
(510) 679-3876
E-mail: info@generalservice.org
Web Site: www.generalservice.org

FOUNDED: 1946

AREAS OF INTEREST:
Racial and gender justice.

NAME(S) OF PROGRAMS:
● **Building Voice and Power**

TYPE:
General operating grants.

YEAR PROGRAM STARTED: 1946

PURPOSE:
To build a more just and sustainable world.

LEGAL BASIS:
Private foundation, tax-exempt under IRS statute 501(c)(3).

ELIGIBILITY:
Organizations must be tax-exempt under U.S. law.

In general, the Foundation does not contribute to annual campaigns, nor to capital campaigns, to individuals or for relief.

Because the Foundation's areas of concern are broad, the Board has determined guidelines within each area. All applicants are urged only to submit applications falling within the Foundation's Contribution Policy and Guidelines.

GEOG. RESTRICTIONS: United States.

FINANCIAL DATA:
Amount of support per award: New grantees: $20,000 to $35,000 annually; Renewing grantees: Up to $35,000 annually.

NO. MOST RECENT APPLICANTS: Approximately 165.

NO. AWARDS: 49 for the year 2020.

APPLICATION INFO:
The Foundation requests that applications for contributions be in line with the approved guidelines and be submitted online.

Duration: One to three years.

IRS I.D.: 36-6018535

OFFICERS:
Robin Snidow, Board Chairperson
Griff Foxley, Vice Chairperson
Peter Halby, Treasurer
Marcie J. Musser, Secretary
William M. Repplinger, Assistant Treasurer

DIRECTORS:
Eliot Estrin
Jesse Estrin
Mary Lloyd Estrin
Griff Foxley
Zoe L. Foxley
Peter Halby
Will Halby
Kierra Johnson
Marcie J. Musser
Robert W. Musser
Carmen Rojas
Robin Snidow

ADDRESS INQUIRIES TO:
Elaine Mui, Grants and Operations Manager
E-mail: elaine@generalservice.org

*PLEASE NOTE:
GSF has allocated its grants through 2020 and will not be taking on any new grants through open intake. The process will be reopened in 2021 if new funds are available.

GEORGIA-PACIFIC FOUNDATION   [123]
133 Peachtree Street, N.E.
12th Floor
Atlanta, GA 30303
(404) 652-4193
E-mail: gpfoundation@gapac.com
Web Site: www.gp.com/community

FOUNDED: 1958

AREAS OF INTEREST:
Education, environment, entrepreneurship, community enrichment and employee involvement.

TYPE:
Project/program grants; Scholarships.

PURPOSE:
To fund and support community-based programs, volunteer service projects, disaster relief and other initiatives that improve the quality of life in communities where Georgia-Pacific employees live and work.

LEGAL BASIS:
Corporate foundation.

ELIGIBILITY:
Organizations must have 501(c)(3) tax-exemption status from the IRS.

The Foundation does not support organizations that discriminate on the basis of race, color, creed, national origin or gender; private organizations; "bail-out" funds given to provide emergency assistance to organizations for general operating purposes; individuals, other than through scholarship and community service programs; political causes, candidates and legislative lobbying or advocacy efforts of any type; churches or religious denominations, religious or theological schools; general operating support for United Way member agencies; operating support for colleges and universities; fund-raising events such as raffles, telethons, walk-a-thons and auctions; and for trips and tours.

FINANCIAL DATA:
Amount of support per award: Minimum $1,000.

APPLICATION INFO:
Prospective applicants must first complete the Eligibility Quiz. If their program meets the initial criteria for funding, the applicant will be invited to submit a full proposal.

Only one copy of the proposal is required. Proposals must be sent via mail. E-mails or faxes will not be accepted.

Deadline: Charitable contribution requests are reviewed on a rolling cycle. Within 60 days of receipt of the request with the appropriate documentation, the Foundation will respond with written notification as to whether the grant is accepted.

THE GHEENS FOUNDATION, INC.   [124]
401 West Main Street
Suite 705
Louisville, KY 40202
(502) 584-4650
E-mail: barry@gheensfoundation.org
Web Site: gheensfoundation.org

FOUNDED: 1957

AREAS OF INTEREST:
Culture, education, economic/community development, health and human services.

TYPE:
Capital grants; Challenge/matching grants; Development grants; General operating grants; Project/program grants; Technical assistance.

YEAR PROGRAM STARTED: 1957

PURPOSE:
To support programs that meet the needs of society and improve the quality of life in the community.

LEGAL BASIS:
501(c)(3), private foundation.

ELIGIBILITY:
Grants are made to organizations that have tax-exempt status under Section 501(c)(3) of the Internal Revenue Code. No grants are made to individuals.

GEOG. RESTRICTIONS: Metropolitan Louisville, Kentucky.

FINANCIAL DATA:
Amount of support per award: Varies depending on the nature of the request.
Total amount of support: Approximately $6,500,000 annually.

NO. MOST RECENT APPLICANTS: 250.

NO. AWARDS: Approximately 125 per year.

APPLICATION INFO:
Application is available on the Foundation web site.
Duration: One year. May reapply.
Deadline: Prior to meetings in March, June, September and December.

ADDRESS INQUIRIES TO:
Kathy Knotts, Grants Officer
E-mail: kathy@gheensfoundation.org

HERMAN GOLDMAN FOUNDATION   [125]
14 Wall Street, 20th Floor
New York, NY 10005
(212) 461-2132
Fax: (212) 461-2223
E-mail: rbaron@hermangoldman.com

FOUNDED: 1942

AREAS OF INTEREST:
Arts, health, social justice and education.

TYPE:
General operating grants; Grants-in-aid;
Project/program grants.

YEAR PROGRAM STARTED: 1943

PURPOSE:
To benefit those in need.

LEGAL BASIS:
Private foundation.

ELIGIBILITY:
Grants for individuals are not considered. It
is not possible to respond to emergency
requests, nor to financial needs of crash
programs because of the time the Foundation
requires to study grant proposals. Applicants
must be tax-exempt organizations.

GEOG. RESTRICTIONS: Primarily, New York City
metropolitan area.

FINANCIAL DATA:
Amount of support per award: $1,000 to
$50,000.
Total amount of support: Varies.

APPLICATION INFO:
Applicants should submit one copy only of a
written proposal and/or can use the New
York-New Jersey area Common Grant
Application Form. No letter of inquiry
required. Applicants must provide IRS
tax-exempt documentation.
Duration: One year.
Deadline: Applications accepted throughout
the year.

PUBLICATIONS:
Annual report.

ADDRESS INQUIRIES TO:
Richard K. Baron, Executive Director
(See e-mail address above.)

THE GOODYEAR TIRE & RUBBER COMPANY   [126]
200 Innovation Way
Akron, OH 44316-0001
(330) 796-7977
E-mail: gyexternalinquiries@goodyear.com
Web Site: www.goodyear.com
corporate.goodyear.com/en-
US/responsibility/community/community-
support.html

FOUNDED: 1898

AREAS OF INTEREST:
Safety, health and human services, culture
and the arts, education, civic and community
improvement.

TYPE:
Project/program grants.

PURPOSE:
To promote healthy, high-functioning
communities in locations where Company
major plants and offices reside; to be a
socially aware and responsive global citizen
wherever the Company operates or does
business.

LEGAL BASIS:
Corporate contributions program.

ELIGIBILITY:
Grants are made to nonprofit, tax-exempt
organizations in communities where
Goodyear plants and headquarters offices are
located. No grants are made to individuals.

Requests are required to meet guidelines of
strategic giving based on safety by focusing
on safety programs plus at least one
additional category noted below and/or
provide volunteer opportunities for Company
associates which are appropriately aligned
with Company strategy:
(1) Civic and Community and Other: Grant
awards will depend on local needs and
customs in the communities in which the
Company operates;
(2) Culture and the Arts: Requests from
organizations and institutions serving plant
communities and selected national arts
organizations will be considered provided
they comply with the connection to safety;
(3) Education: Requests for support from
colleges, universities, and other educational
institutions serving the areas in which
Company plants and principal offices are
located must demonstrate a connection with
safety and/or must be a source of subsidized
educational opportunities for Company
associates and their families; a limited
number of private and public universities of
national or regional significance whose
programs are of special interest or those that
provide a continuing source of associates to
the Company may also receive priority and;
(4) Health and Human Services: Highest
priority is given to United Way campaigns in
communities where Company plants and
principal offices are located; organizations
receiving United Way support may not be
eligible for additional funding.

A limited number of traditional grants will be
honored at the Company's discretion.

FINANCIAL DATA:
Amount of support per award: Typically
$5,000 to $25,000.
Total amount of support: Varies.

APPLICATION INFO:
All requests for community grants must be
submitted through the online application
system. If a proposal meets specific
guidelines and strategic goals and objectives,
it will be considered for funding.
Applications that are faxed or mailed will be
returned to the organization with an invitation
to the online application system.

PUBLICATIONS:
Overview.

ADDRESS INQUIRIES TO:
Community Affairs
(See address above.)

*PLEASE NOTE:
The Company does not accept grant requests
by telephone.

GRAHAM HOLDINGS COMPANY   [127]
1300 North 17th Street
Suite 1700
Arlington, VA 22209
(703) 345-6450
E-mail: pinkie.mayfield@ghco.com
Web Site: www.ghco.com

FOUNDED: 1947

AREAS OF INTEREST:
Civic and community, health and human
services, education and cultural programs.

TYPE:
General operating grants. Employee
Matching Gifts Program.

PURPOSE:
To support communities where Graham
Holdings Company operates.

ELIGIBILITY:
Applicants must be nonprofit 501(c)(3)
organizations.

GEOG. RESTRICTIONS: Metropolitan Washington,
DC area.

FINANCIAL DATA:
Amount of support per award: Average $500
to $2,500.
Total amount of support: Varies.
Matching fund requirements: $25 minimum,
$2,000 per year/per employee maximum. 1:1
or 1:2 for schools or where employee is an
active volunteer.

REPRESENTATIVE AWARDS:
The Phillips Collection; Martha's Table;
Capital Area Food Bank; Inner City-Inner
Child; Northern Virginia Family Services.

APPLICATION INFO:
Send a short letter describing proposed
program and budget.
Duration: One year. Renewal possible.
Deadline: Proposals are accepted on an
ongoing basis.

ADDRESS INQUIRIES TO:
Pinkie Mayfield
Vice President-Corporate Affairs and
Chief Communications Officer
(See address above.)

PHILIP L. GRAHAM FUND   [128]
c/o Graham Holdings Company
1300 North 17th Street, Suite 1700
Arlington, VA 22209
(703) 345-6515
E-mail: plgfund@ghco.com
Web Site: www.plgrahamfund.org

FOUNDED: 1963

AREAS OF INTEREST:
Primarily health and human services,
education, arts and humanities, and
community endeavors in the Washington, DC
metropolitan area.

TYPE:
Capital grants.

YEAR PROGRAM STARTED: 1963

PURPOSE:
To use resources for the betterment of the
Washington, DC metropolitan area.

LEGAL BASIS:
General interest foundation.

ELIGIBILITY:
Applicants must be 501(c)(3) organizations
located in the Washington, DC metropolitan
area.

No grants to individuals, for religious or
political purposes, research, conferences,
travel, fund-raising, event sponsorships,
hospitals or publications.

GEOG. RESTRICTIONS: Primarily Washington,
DC metropolitan area.

FINANCIAL DATA:
Amount of support per award: $25,000 to
$35,000 average grant.
Total amount of support: $6,850,000 for the
year 2020.

NO. AWARDS: 239 for the year 2020.

APPLICATION INFO:
Organizations interested in applying for funding must first submit a letter of inquiry (LOI) through the online application system prior to one of the three deadlines each year.

Duration: Typically one year.

Deadline: Varies each year. Refer to web site for annual application deadlines.

IRS I.D.: 52-6051781

TRUSTEES:
Richard Bynum
Pinkie Mayfield
Carol Melamed
Laura O'Shaughnessy
Katharine Weymouth

ADDRESS INQUIRIES TO:
Eileen Daly, President
(See address above.)

*PLEASE NOTE:
Proposals accepted only through the Fund web site.

GRAND RAPIDS COMMUNITY FOUNDATION [129]
185 Oakes Street, S.W.
Grand Rapids, MI 49503
(616) 454-1751
Fax: (616) 454-6455
E-mail: grfound@grfoundation.org
Web Site: www.grfoundation.org

FOUNDED: 1922

AREAS OF INTEREST:
Education, environment, engagement, health, neighborhoods and prosperity.

NAME(S) OF PROGRAMS:
• **Access Camps**

TYPE:
Capital grants; Challenge/matching grants; Demonstration grants; Development grants; Project/program grants; Scholarships; Technical assistance.

YEAR PROGRAM STARTED: 1922

PURPOSE:
To build and manage our community's permanent endowment and lead the community to strengthen the lives of its people.

LEGAL BASIS:
Nonprofit organization established by resolution and declaration of trust. Incorporated in 1989.

ELIGIBILITY:
Applicant must have a current 501(c)(3) nonprofit designation from the IRS or be a governmental organization located in Kent County and serve local residents. No grants to individuals except through the scholarship program.

GEOG. RESTRICTIONS: Grand Rapids, Michigan and surrounding communities.

FINANCIAL DATA:
Amount of support per award: General grants vary by fund; typically $2,000 to $250,000.

Total amount of support: $13,487,488 in grants and scholarships authorized for fiscal year ended June 30, 2020.

REPRESENTATIVE AWARDS:
$10,000 to African Resource Center of West Michigan to support FutureNow!, a youth support program that focuses on ensuring participants are able to achieve academic excellence and flourish in community;

$150,000 to Michigan Justice Fund to advance effective and equitable justice policy, practices, and funding in the state of Michigan; $5,000 to Seeds of Promise for development of a community Health Information Hub to provide health education for communities of color.

APPLICATION INFO:
For the general fund, applicants fill out an online pre-application on the Foundation's web site. After committee review, applicants may be asked to submit a Full Proposal, with final grant disposition determined by the Board of Trustees.

Duration: Generally, one-time grants. Foundation will, under certain circumstances, award multiyear grants.

Deadline: Varies by Fund. No deadline for the General Fund; pre-applications are reviewed every two weeks.

PUBLICATIONS:
Annual report; quarterly newsletter.

IRS I.D.: 38-2877959

OFFICERS:
Diana R. Sieger, President
Stan Vander Roest, Chief Financial Officer
Marilyn Zack, Vice President of Development
Kate Schmid, Vice President of Program
Ashley Lee, Vice President of Strategic Communications

ADDRESS INQUIRIES TO:
Keri Jaynes, Grants Manager
(See address above.)

JOHN SIMON GUGGENHEIM MEMORIAL FOUNDATION [130]
90 Park Avenue
New York, NY 10016
(212) 687-4470
Fax: (212) 697-3248
E-mail: fellowships@gf.org
Web Site: www.gf.org

FOUNDED: 1925

AREAS OF INTEREST:
Sciences, social sciences, humanities and the creative arts.

NAME(S) OF PROGRAMS:
• **Guggenheim Fellowships**

TYPE:
Fellowships.

YEAR PROGRAM STARTED: 1925

PURPOSE:
To further the development of scholars and artists by assisting them to engage in research in any field of knowledge and creation in any of the arts.

LEGAL BASIS:
Private foundation.

ELIGIBILITY:
The Fellowships are awarded to men and women who have already demonstrated exceptional capacity for productive scholarship or exceptional creative ability in the arts.

Fellowships are awarded through two annual competitions: one open to citizens and permanent residents of the U.S. and Canada, and the other open to citizens and permanent residents of Latin America and the Caribbean. The Fellowships will be awarded by the Trustees upon nominations made by a Committee of Selection.

FINANCIAL DATA:
The amounts of the grants will be adjusted to the needs of the Fellows, considering their other resources and the purpose and scope of their plans, in accord with the Foundation's annual fellowship budget.

Amount of support per award: Varies.

Total amount of support: Approximately $9,000,000 annually.

NO. AWARDS: Approximately 180 annually.

APPLICATION INFO:
Online application is available at the Foundation web site.

Duration: Appointments must be from six to 12 months. Fellows of the Foundation, until further notice from the Board of Trustees, may no longer seek renewed assistance.

Deadline: Applications must be submitted on or before September 17 for U.S. and Canadian competition. Fellowships to be announced the following April for U.S. competition.

PUBLICATIONS:
Annual report; announcement of Fellowship competition and recipients; application guidelines.

IRS I.D.: 13-5673173

OFFICERS:
Edward Hirsch, President
Andre Bernard, Vice President and Secretary

TRUSTEES:
Dwight E. Lee, Chairman
Lawrence D. Bobo
Emery Brown
Robert A. Caro
Adele Chatfield-Taylor
Joel Conarroe
Dorothy Tapper Goldman
Edward Hirsch
William P. Kelly
Steven Lavine
Lily Lynton
Eric S. Maskin
E. Wayne Nordberg
Stacy Schiff
Eric Schwartz
Cindy Sherman
G. Gabrielle Starr
Benjamin Taylor
Sandra Wijnberg
Ellen Taaffe Zwilich

ADDRESS INQUIRIES TO:
Keith Lewis, Program Officer
Fellowships Program
(See address above.)

*PLEASE NOTE:
Latin American and Caribbean Competition has been suspended pending examination of the program. The U.S. and Canadian competition is unaffected.

THE GEORGE GUND FOUNDATION [131]
1845 Guildhall Building
45 Prospect Avenue West
Cleveland, OH 44115
(216) 241-3114
Fax: (216) 241-6560
E-mail: info@gundfdn.org
Web Site: gundfoundation.org

FOUNDED: 1952

AREAS OF INTEREST:
Climate and environmental justice, creative culture and arts, public education, thriving families and social justice, and vibrant neighborhoods and inclusive economy.

TYPE:
General operating grants; Project/program grants.

YEAR PROGRAM STARTED: 1952

PURPOSE:
To enhance the quality of life, particularly for those living in the greater Cleveland area; to solve community problems; to improve living conditions, particularly for the poor and underprivileged; to provide opportunities for all people to live constructive lives in a peaceful world.

LEGAL BASIS:
Private foundation.

ELIGIBILITY:
Grants are made only to nonprofit, tax-exempt educational and philanthropic organizations. No awards are made to individuals. Grants for operating budget support will be considered only if the need is for limited duration and will accomplish some important purpose which will strengthen the future position of the institution. Preference will be given to pilot projects, innovative programs and research which hold promise of significant benefits of broad applicability.

GEOG. RESTRICTIONS: Primarily greater Cleveland and Cuyahoga County, Ohio.

FINANCIAL DATA:
Amount of support per award: Varies.

Total amount of support: $24,936,993 for the year 2019.

NO. AWARDS: 258 grants for the year 2020.

APPLICATION INFO:
Foundation requires that all applications for grants be submitted online at the Foundation's web site. Application materials to be uploaded with application include:
(1) organizational background;
(2) project description;
(3) project budget;
(4) organizational budget;
(5) list of current trustees;
(6) most recent audited financial statements and;
(7) climate change statement.

Duration: One year.

Deadline: March 15, July 15 and November 15, for board meetings to be held in June, November and February, respectively.

PUBLICATIONS:
Annual report; Guidelines for Grant Applicants (on Foundation web site).

TRUSTEES:
Catherine Gund, Chairperson
Zachary Gund, Treasurer
Lara Gund, Secretary
Margaret Bernstein
Susanna Bien-Gund
Charlotte Buhr-Gund
Mark Joseph
Nancy Mendez
Anna Traggio

ADMINISTRATIVE STAFF:
David T. Abbott, President
Robert B. Jaquay, Associate Director
John Mitterholzer, Program Director, Climate and Environmental Justice
Jennifer Coleman, Program Director, Creative Culture and Arts
Ann K. Mullin, Program Director, Public Education

Marcia Egbert, Program Director, Thriving Families and Social Justice
Alesha Washington, Program Director, Vibrant Neighborhoods and Inclusive Economy

ADDRESS INQUIRIES TO:
David T. Abbott, President or
Cynthia Gasparro
Grants and Office Administrator
(See address above.)

HALL FAMILY FOUNDATION [132]

P.O. Box 419580
Mail Drop 323
Kansas City, MO 64141-6580
(816) 274-8516
Fax: (816) 274-8547
E-mail: hff@hallmark.com
Web Site: www.hallfamilyfoundation.org

FOUNDED: 1943

AREAS OF INTEREST:
Early and K-12th-grade education, higher education, children, youth and families, neighborhood revitalization, health, the arts, and support of community-wide efforts that seek to provide long-term solutions to high-priority local issues.

TYPE:
Capital grants; Project/program grants; Training grants.

YEAR PROGRAM STARTED: 1943

PURPOSE:
To promote the health, welfare and happiness of school-age children; to promote the advancement and diffusion of knowledge; to fund activities for the improvement of public health; to advance social welfare.

ELIGIBILITY:
Applying nonprofit organizations must be 501(c)(3) and must have been in operation for at least five years. No grants are made to individuals. Grants are made to a religious organization only if its program is of a nonsectarian nature.

GEOG. RESTRICTIONS: Usually, organizations in the greater Kansas City, Missouri area.

FINANCIAL DATA:
Amount of support per award: Varies.
Total amount of support: Varies.

APPLICATION INFO:
Prospective grant recipients should first submit a brief letter of inquiry. Those applicants whose request appears to fall within the Foundation's areas of interest and to meet its guidelines will be asked to submit a full proposal.
Duration: Two to five years, depending on the type of project.

HARDEN FOUNDATION [133]

1636 Ercia Street
Salinas, CA 93906
(831) 442-3005
Fax: (831) 443-1429
E-mail: joe@hardenfoundation.org
Web Site: www.hardenfoundation.org

FOUNDED: 1963

AREAS OF INTEREST:
Children, youth and family, senior citizens, animal welfare and the environment, agriculture, education, arts and culture, and health.

TYPE:
Capital grants; General operating grants; Project/program grants.

YEAR PROGRAM STARTED: 1963

PURPOSE:
To fund groups working in the Foundation's areas of interest.

LEGAL BASIS:
Private foundation.

ELIGIBILITY:
The Foundation does not fund schools, churches or religious activities, or individuals for endowments or fund-raising. Eligible organizations must be of a 501(c)(3), not-for-profit character.

GEOG. RESTRICTIONS: Monterey County, California.

FINANCIAL DATA:
Amount of support per award: Typically $5,000 to $100,000.
Total amount of support: $1,857,200 in grants awarded for the year 2021.

APPLICATION INFO:
Guidelines and application forms are available online.
Duration: Operating grants for start-up programs: Generally up to two years.
Deadline: March 1 and September 1.

ADDRESS INQUIRIES TO:
Joseph C. Grainger, Executive Director
(See address above.)

THE JOHN A. HARTFORD FOUNDATION, INC. [134]

55 East 59th Street, 16th Floor
New York, NY 10022
(212) 832-7788
Fax: (212) 593-4913
E-mail: mark.barreiro@johnahartford.org
Web Site: johnahartford.org

FOUNDED: 1929

AREAS OF INTEREST:
Age-friendly health systems, family caregiving, and serious illness and end of life.

TYPE:
Demonstration grants; Matching gifts; Project/program grants; Research grants; Technical assistance.

YEAR PROGRAM STARTED: 1983

PURPOSE:
To improve the care of older adults.

LEGAL BASIS:
Private foundation.

ELIGIBILITY:
Grantee organizations must be located in the U.S. and must have 501(c)(3) IRS tax-exempt designation.

The Foundation's prior grantmaking related to enhancing geriatric research and training, and integrating and improving health-related services to the elderly. Currently, the Foundation makes grants that will put geriatrics expertise to work in all health care settings by:
(1) advancing practice change and innovation;
(2) supporting team-based care through interdisciplinary education of all health care providers;
(3) supporting policies and regulations that promote better care and;

(4) developing and disseminating new, evidence-based models that deliver better, more cost-effective health care.

The Foundation awards both single and multiple-year grants. No support for general purposes, endowment funds or capital budgets.

GEOG. RESTRICTIONS: United States.

FINANCIAL DATA:
Amount of support per award: Varies.
Total amount of support: $28,949,667 in grants awarded for the year 2019.

NO. AWARDS: 21 for the year 2020.

APPLICATION INFO:
All proposals are by invitation only from one of the Foundation's program officers, the program director, or the president.
Duration: One to three years.

PUBLICATIONS:
Annual report.

TRUSTEES:
Margaret L. Wolff, Chairperson
John R. Mach, Jr., M.D., Co-Vice Chairperson
Earl A. Samson, III, Co-Vice Chairperson
John H. Allen
David Di Martino
William Donohue
Charles M. Farkas
Audrey A. McNiff
Elizabeth A. Palmer
Tripler Pell
Nirav R. Shah

STAFF:
Terry Fulmer, Ph.D., R.N., President
Marcus R. Escobedo, M.P.A., Vice President, Communications and Senior Program Officer
Eva Cheng, Vice President, Finance
Rani E. Synder, M.P.A., Vice President, Program
Mark Barreiro, Senior Grants Officer
Amy J. Berman, R.N., Senior Program Officer
Jane Carmody, Senior Program Officer
Scott Bane, Program Officer
Nancy Wexler, Program Officer
Rutuma M. Gandhi, Accounting Manager
Melida Galvez, Senior Accountant
Julianne N. McLean, Program Secretary

ADDRESS INQUIRIES TO:
Mark Barreiro, Senior Grants Officer
(See address above.)

HENDERSON FOUNDATION [135]
P.O. Box 420
Sudbury, MA 01776-0420
(978) 443-4646
Fax: (978) 443-9510
E-mail: rhenderson@sudburypines.com

FOUNDED: 1947

AREAS OF INTEREST:
Charitable, educational, religious, health, political, environmental, and community outreach.

TYPE:
General operating grants.

PURPOSE:
To continue support to general operations of those organizations now supported.

LEGAL BASIS:
Nonprofit foundation.

ELIGIBILITY:
Funding limited to public charities with a nonprofit 501(c)(3) tax-exempt status. The Foundation does not support activities for which the IRS requires grantor's responsibility and reports.

GEOG. RESTRICTIONS: United States.

FINANCIAL DATA:
Amount of support per award: Minimum $500.
Total amount of support: Varies.

NO. MOST RECENT APPLICANTS: 150.

NO. AWARDS: 100.

APPLICATION INFO:
Send letter of inquiry with documentation of nonprofit 501(c)(3) tax-exempt status.
Duration: Varies.
Deadline: December 31.

TRUSTEES:
Barclay G. Henderson
Roberta Henderson
Mrs. Joseph C. Petrone

ADDRESS INQUIRIES TO:
Roberta Henderson, Trustee
(See address above.)

B. KEITH & NORMA F. HEUERMANN FOUNDATION [136]
Whitney, Newman, Mersch, Otto and Grafton
1228 L Street
Aurora, NE 68818
(402) 694-3161

FOUNDED: 1994

AREAS OF INTEREST:
Children, the aged, the developmentally challenged, disabled, physically impaired, youth education and agriculturally related activities.

TYPE:
Capital grants; Matching gifts; Project/program grants; Research grants; Technical assistance.

YEAR PROGRAM STARTED: 1994

PURPOSE:
To support programs that meet the needs of society and improve the quality of life preferably in communities in rural Nebraska.

LEGAL BASIS:
Private foundation.

ELIGIBILITY:
Grants are made to organizations that have tax-exempt status under Section 501(c)(3) of the Internal Revenue Code. No grants are made to individuals. The Foundation does not loan funds to grant applicants.

GEOG. RESTRICTIONS: Rural areas in Nebraska.

FINANCIAL DATA:
Amount of support per award: $1,000 to $25,000.
Total amount of support: Varies.

APPLICATION INFO:
The Foundation does not have an application form. The Grant Proposal should identify a special need or project to which funds will be applied including the objectives to be attained, people or groups who will benefit, work plans or timetables for achieving the stated objectives, and any other means of support. A copy of the 501(c)(3) letter from

the IRS should accompany the application. Provide the grant applicant's federal ID number.

Grant Proposal should be limited to two pages. Supporting documents such as project budget, other resources, names of supporters, and background information about the organization may be attached to the proposal. Stapled proposals are favored over bound ones. Brevity is appreciated.

Applicants must submit five original copies of the proposal.
Duration: Proposal may be for a project which extends over several years; however, the Foundation may review and make grants only on an annual basis.
Deadline: Proposals may be submitted at any time. The Directors convene at least three times per year at meetings to be scheduled in its discretion to review requests for grants.

PUBLICATIONS:
Guidelines.

IRS I.D.: 47-0748466

ADDRESS INQUIRIES TO:
Scott D. Grafton
(See address above.)

THE WILLIAM AND FLORA HEWLETT FOUNDATION [137]
2121 Sand Hill Road
Menlo Park, CA 94025
(650) 234-4500
Fax: (650) 234-4501
E-mail: communications@hewlett.org
Web Site: hewlett.org

FOUNDED: 1966

AREAS OF INTEREST:
Education, the environment, performing arts, philanthropy, gender equity and governance, democracy, and cybersecurity.

NAME(S) OF PROGRAMS:
● **Education**
● **Environment**
● **Gender Equity and Governance**
● **Performing Arts**
● **Philanthropy**

TYPE:
Capital grants; Challenge/matching grants; Conferences/seminars; Development grants; Endowments; General operating grants; Project/program grants; Research grants; Seed money grants; Technical assistance; Training grants; Travel grants.

YEAR PROGRAM STARTED: 1966

PURPOSE:
To help people build measurably better lives.

LEGAL BASIS:
Private foundation.

ELIGIBILITY:
The Foundation does not fund individuals and generally does not fund scholarships, building construction, or unincorporated associations or groups.

Requirements vary by area of interest and are available on the Foundation web site.

FINANCIAL DATA:
Total assets of $10.8 billion as of December 31, 2019.
Amount of support per award: $436,406 average for the year 2019.
Total amount of support: $454,458,000 in grants awarded for the year ended December 31, 2019.

Matching fund requirements: Foundation matches eligible employees' contributions to qualifying organizations.

NO. AWARDS: 1,043 for the year 2019.

APPLICATION INFO:
Information may be obtained at the Foundation web site.
Duration: Generally, one to three years.
Deadline: Varies according to program.

PUBLICATIONS:
Annual report; application guidelines.

BOARD OF DIRECTORS:
Stephen C. Neal, Chairman
Larry Kramer, President
Flora Hewlett Birdzell
Mariano-Florentino Cuellar
Alecia A. DeCoudreaux
Persis S. Drell
Eric Gimon
Billy Hewlett
Patricia A. House
Koh Boon Hwee
James Manyika
Susan Meaney
Rakesh Rajani
Sarah Singh

ADDRESS INQUIRIES TO:
Vidya Krishnamurthy
Director of Communications
(See address above.)

HILLSDALE FUND, INC. [138]
600 Green Valley Road
Suite 200
Greensboro, NC 27408
(336) 574-8696

FOUNDED: 1963

TYPE:
Project/program grants.

LEGAL BASIS:
Family foundation.

ELIGIBILITY:
Must have 501(c)(3) status of Internal Revenue Code to be eligible. Grants will not be made available for indirect costs or overhead as opposed to direct funding, routine, recurring operating expenses, conferences and seminars, travel and study, or individuals for any purpose.

FINANCIAL DATA:
Amount of support per award: Varies.
Total amount of support: Approximately $1,400,000 for the year 2018.

APPLICATION INFO:
Applicants should contact the Foundation for guidelines and application form.
Duration: Varies.
Deadline: Varies. Contact Fund for specific deadlines.

ADDRESS INQUIRIES TO:
Mary Scott, Executive Director
(See address above.)

HOBLITZELLE FOUNDATION [139]
5556 Caruth Haven Lane, Suite 200
Dallas, TX 75225
(214) 373-0462
Fax: (214) 750-7412
E-mail: krobbins@hoblitzelle.org
Web Site: www.hoblitzelle.org

FOUNDED: 1942

AREAS OF INTEREST:
Education, cultural affairs, social welfare and health.

TYPE:
Capital grants; Challenge/matching grants; Matching gifts.

YEAR PROGRAM STARTED: 1942

LEGAL BASIS:
Private foundation.

ELIGIBILITY:
Educational institutions, hospitals, community agencies, youth and other welfare programs and organizations with appropriate interests are eligible.

GEOG. RESTRICTIONS: Texas, primarily Dallas.

FINANCIAL DATA:
Amount of support per award: $25,000 to $500,000.
Total amount of support: Approximately $6,500,000 annually.

NO. MOST RECENT APPLICANTS: 200.

NO. AWARDS: 70.

APPLICATION INFO:
Grant applications should be submitted online. Formal oral presentations to the Board are not allowed.
Duration: One year and multiyear.
Deadline: April 15 for May meeting, August 15 for September meeting and December 15 for January meeting. If holiday or weekend, next business day.

PUBLICATIONS:
Annual report; application guidelines.

IRS I.D.: 75-6003984

BOARD OF DIRECTORS AND OFFICERS:
John W. Dayton, Chairman
Karen L. Shuford, Vice Chairman
Katie H. Robbins, President and Chief Executive Officer
Jere W. Thompson, Jr., Treasurer
Raphael M. Anchia
Holland P. Gary
Lydia H. Novakov
Daniel K. Podolsky, M.D.
Catherine Rose

ADDRESS INQUIRIES TO:
Katie H. Robbins, President and Chief Executive Officer
(See address above.)

HOUSTON ENDOWMENT INC. [140]
600 Travis, Suite 6400
Houston, TX 77002-3000
(713) 238-8100
Fax: (713) 238-8101
E-mail: connect@houstonendowment.org
Web Site: www.houstonendowment.org

FOUNDED: 1937

AREAS OF INTEREST:
Arts, education, environment, health and human services.

TYPE:
Capital grants; General operating grants; Project/program grants. Program support. Building completion.

LEGAL BASIS:
Private foundation.

ELIGIBILITY:
Organizations exempt under Section 501(c)(3). No grants are made directly to individuals. All scholarship funds are disbursed through recipient institutions. No grants made outside the U.S.

GEOG. RESTRICTIONS: Harris County and contiguous counties (Brazoria, Chambers, Fort Bend, Galveston, Liberty, Montgomery and Waller).

FINANCIAL DATA:
Amount of support per award: Varies.
Total amount of support: $74,500,000 in total funding for the year 2018.

NO. AWARDS: Grants to over 200 organizations for the year 2018.

APPLICATION INFO:
Application must be made online. Written applications will not be considered. Scholarships are never awarded directly on the basis of personal inquiry but are administered by colleges and universities.
Duration: One year to multiyear.

PUBLICATIONS:
Annual report.

MABEL Y. HUGHES CHARITABLE TRUST [141]
Wells Fargo Wealth Management
100 North Main Street, 6th Floor
MAC-D4001-065
Winston-Salem, NC 27101
(888) 235-4351 ext. 140782
E-mail: grantadministration@wellsfargo.com
Web Site: www.wellsfargo.com/private-foundations/hughes-charitable-trust

FOUNDED: 1969

AREAS OF INTEREST:
Arts, animals, environment, humanities, religion, health, education, culture and human services in the state of Colorado, with emphasis on Denver metropolitan area.

TYPE:
General operating grants; Project/program grants.

PURPOSE:
To provide funding to nonprofit and educational institutions that address vital community needs especially, but not limited to, human services.

LEGAL BASIS:
Private tax-exempt foundation.

ELIGIBILITY:
501(c)(3) tax-exempt organizations in Colorado only may apply. No grants are awarded to individuals.

GEOG. RESTRICTIONS: Colorado.

FINANCIAL DATA:
Amount of support per award: $5,000 to $25,000.
Total amount of support: Approximately $500,000 per year.

NO. MOST RECENT APPLICANTS: Approximately 300.

NO. AWARDS: 50.

APPLICATION INFO:
Submit a brief letter describing project, why needed, population to be served, brief line-item budget, information about organization seeking funds and its accomplishments to date, starting and ending dates, plans for postgrant funding and project evaluation, and a copy of latest 501(c)(3) exemption.

Duration: No grants awarded on a continuing basis.

Deadline: March 1, July 1 and November 1.

TRUSTEES:
W.R. Alexander

ADDRESS INQUIRIES TO:
Ginger Freeman, Grant Administrator
(See address above.)

THE HYDE AND WATSON FOUNDATION [142]

31-F Mountain Boulevard
Warren, NJ 07059-5617
(908) 753-3700
Fax: (908) 753-0004
E-mail: info@hydeandwatson.org
Web Site: www.hydeandwatson.org

FOUNDED: 1983

AREAS OF INTEREST:
Broad fields include education, social services, arts, health, religion and humanities.

TYPE:
Capital grants. The Foundation supports capital projects such as hard costs related to purchase and relocation of facilities and/or building improvements, purchase of capital equipment and furnishings, and other one-time capital needs.

LEGAL BASIS:
Private.

ELIGIBILITY:
Grants are made to nonprofit organizations that have received 501(c)(3) and 509(a)(1) or 509(a)(2) status from the IRS. In general, the Foundation does not accept applications for endowment, operating support, benefit fund-raisers, annual fund appeals, or from fiscal agents.

GEOG. RESTRICTIONS: Primarily the five boroughs of New York City, and Essex, Morris and Union counties in New Jersey.

FINANCIAL DATA:
Amount of support per award: Average grant: $5,000 to $15,000.
Total amount of support: $6,032,900 for the year ended December 31, 2020.

NO. MOST RECENT APPLICANTS: 855 for the year 2020.

NO. AWARDS: 538 for the year 2020.

APPLICATION INFO:
Applicants must submit the following:
(1) a completed Grant Application Form (entered online);
(2) a brief narrative (no longer than three pages), signed by an authorized official, summarizing the background of the organization and constituency served, the purpose of the appeal, project total and amount requested, anticipated time frame for the project and how the equipment/capital improvement will benefit the organization;
(3) a project budget with line items;
(4) an operating budget for the current fiscal year;
(5) a list of corporate and foundation supporters for the most recent fiscal year;
(6) a list of the Board of Directors/Trustees and their business affiliations;
(7) an audited financial report for the most recent fiscal year. If an audit is not performed, the most recent Form 990 will be accepted;
(8) a copy of the organization's annual report (optional) and;
(9) a copy of the organization's most recent 501(c)(3) and 509(a) IRS ruling letter(s).

If one's organization is a former grantee, please note that the Foundation will not consider any future proposals from one's organization until a report is provided for any previous grants received from the Foundation. The "Grant Report Form" is available on the Foundation web site.

Because there is a finite amount of funds budgeted for each grant cycle, applicant's are strongly encouraged to submit their proposal early in the application period.

Duration: Typically one year.

Deadline: Spring grant applications are accepted between November 15 and February 15. Fall grant applications are accepted between June 15 and September 15. If the 15th falls on a weekend or holiday, the deadline will be the next business day. There is an ongoing review of proposals during the application period.

PUBLICATIONS:
Program policy statement and grant application guidelines.

IRS I.D.: 22-2425725

OFFICERS:
William V. Engel, Chairperson
John W. Holman, III, Vice-Chairperson and Assistant Treasurer
Brunilda Moriarty, President
Hans Dekker, Secretary
Thomas H. MacCowatt, Treasurer
Sarah A. Kalra, Assistant Secretary
Allison J. Pena, Assistant Secretary
Thomas W. Berry, Assistant Treasurer
Maureen T. McCutcheon, Assistant Treasurer

DIRECTORS:
Deborah J. Barker
Thomas W. Berry
Hunter W. Corbin
Hans Dekker
William V. Engel
John W. Holman, Jr.
John W. Holman, III
Anne-Marie Kim
Thomas H. MacCowatt
Brunilda Moriarty
Donald C. Mullins, Jr.

ADDRESS INQUIRIES TO:
Brunilda Moriarty, President
(See address above.)

*PLEASE NOTE:
Because there is a finite amount of funds budgeted for each grants cycle, it is strongly suggested that applicants submit proposals early in the application period.

Appeals or inquiries submitted by e-mail will not be considered.

IDAHO COMMUNITY FOUNDATION [143]

210 West State Street
Boise, ID 83702
(208) 342-3535 ext. 13
E-mail: cara@idahocf.org
Web Site: www.idahocf.org

FOUNDED: 1988

AREAS OF INTEREST:
Arts, conservation, culture, environment, education opportunities, access to service, mental and physical health, family homelessness, and basic needs.

NAME(S) OF PROGRAMS:
- **Bonner County Fund for Arts Enhancement**
- **Bonner County Human Rights Task Force Fund**
- **The F.M., Anne G., and Beverly B. Bistline Foundation Fund**
- **Forever Idaho Regional Grant Program**
- **Junior Garnier and Bud Ashford Military Veterans Fund**
- **Idaho Future Fund**
- **Ifft Foundation Fund**
- **Perc H. Shelton and Gladys A. Pospisil Shelton Foundation Advised Fund**

TYPE:
Capital grants; General operating grants; Scholarships.

YEAR PROGRAM STARTED: 1988

PURPOSE:
To enrich the quality of life throughout Idaho.

LEGAL BASIS:
Community foundation; 501(c)(3) public charity.

ELIGIBILITY:
Grants are made to organizations that are nonprofit. Nonsectarian religious programs and government entities may apply. No grants are made to individuals.

GEOG. RESTRICTIONS: Idaho.

FINANCIAL DATA:
Amount of support per award: Forever Idaho Regional Grants: Up to $25,000; Other programs: Varies.
Total amount of support: Varies.

APPLICATION INFO:
Form can be downloaded from the Foundation web site.
Duration: Typically one year.
Deadline: Varies per grant or scholarship.

IRS I.D.: 82-0425063

ADMINISTRATION:
Karen Bilowith, Chief Executive Officer
Cara Nielsen, Vice President, Philanthropy and Impact

ADDRESS INQUIRIES TO:
Cara Nielsen
Vice President, Philanthropy and Impact
(See address above.)

INDEPENDENCE FOUNDATION [144]

Offices at the Bellevue
200 South Broad Street, Suite 1101
Philadelphia, PA 19102
(215) 985-4009
Fax: (215) 985-3989
E-mail: ssherman@independencefoundation.org
Web Site: www.independencefoundation.org

FOUNDED: 1932

AREAS OF INTEREST:
Community-based care, health promotion, family planning and comprehensive health care services where issues of quality, access and cost are taken into consideration; culture, arts and legal aid and assistance to the disadvantaged; visual and performing arts.

NAME(S) OF PROGRAMS:
- **Individual Artists Fellowship/Performing and Visual Arts**
- **New Theater Works Initiative**
- **Public Interest Law Fellowships**

TYPE:
Challenge/matching grants; Fellowships; General operating grants; Project/program grants.

YEAR PROGRAM STARTED: 1993

PURPOSE:
To encourage and support health services; to have a valuable impact on the quality of health care services; to strengthen nursing education's focus on community-based care in both Philadelphia and surrounding Pennsylvania counties.

LEGAL BASIS:
Private foundation.

ELIGIBILITY:
No grants to individuals.

GEOG. RESTRICTIONS: Philadelphia and four surrounding counties of Bucks, Chester, Delaware and Montgomery.

FINANCIAL DATA:
Amount of support per award: Average: $3,000 to $10,000; Multiyear: Up to $50,000.
Matching fund requirements: Match of contributions by individual new donors or increase in contributions by current individual donors (nongovernmental/nonfoundation funds).

APPLICATION INFO:
Each year the Foundation sends out a limited number of Requests for Proposals (RFP) in each of the funding initiatives. Organizations not previously funded by the Foundation are encouraged to send a two-page Letter of Inquiry including organizational background information, amount being requested, and a description of the program/services for which the funds will be used.
Duration: Varies.
Deadline: Letters of Inquiry are accepted January 1 to January 31. Deadlines vary.

PUBLICATIONS:
Annual report; application guidelines.

IRS I.D.: 23-1352110

ADDRESS INQUIRIES TO:
Susan E. Sherman
President and Chief Executive Officer
(See address above.)

ANN JACKSON FAMILY FOUNDATION [145]

P.O. Box 5580
Santa Barbara, CA 93150-5580
(805) 969-2258
Web Site: www.annjacksonfamilyfoundation.org

FOUNDED: 1978

AREAS OF INTEREST:
Community and civic infrastructure, art, education, human services and health.

TYPE:
Capital grants; General operating grants; Project/program grants.

PURPOSE:
To enhance the community.

LEGAL BASIS:
Private foundation.

ELIGIBILITY:
Grants are made to organizations that have tax-exempt status under Section 501(c)(3) of the Internal Revenue Code. No grants are made to individuals.

GEOG. RESTRICTIONS: Primarily Santa Barbara County, California.

FINANCIAL DATA:
Amount of support per award: Typically $1,000 to $10,000 for general operating grants.
Total amount of support: Varies.

NO. AWARDS: Over 100 annually.

APPLICATION INFO:
For grants of $10,000 or more and all capital requests, the Foundation encourages applicants to use the Common Grant Application form, a link to which is available on the web site. For grants under $10,000, organizations may also put their request in the form of a one- to two-page letter which clearly states the compelling nature of the request.

If an organization has not previously been funded by the Foundation, a one-page letter of intent will be accepted.
Duration: One year, with occasional multiyear. Renewal by reapplication.

ADDRESS INQUIRIES TO:
Palmer G. Jackson, Jr., Trustee
(See address above.)

THE JACKSON FOUNDATION [146]

c/o U.S. Bank, NA
111 S.W. 5th Avenue, Suite 600
Portland, OR 97204
(503) 464-4920
E-mail: march.voyles@usbank.com
Web Site: www.thejacksonfoundation.com

FOUNDED: 1960

AREAS OF INTEREST:
Arts/performing arts, economic development, substance abuse, human services, minorities, housing, disabilities, humanities, education, environment, health, children/youth, aged and women.

TYPE:
Capital grants; Challenge/matching grants; Development grants; General operating grants; Matching gifts; Project/program grants; Research grants.

YEAR PROGRAM STARTED: 1963

PURPOSE:
To support new programs that will enhance and expand the well-being of individuals, with a focus on people in the Portland metropolitan area, by granting funds for the purpose of health and education.

LEGAL BASIS:
Private foundation.

ELIGIBILITY:
Grants are made to 501(c)(3) organizations.

GEOG. RESTRICTIONS: Oregon.

FINANCIAL DATA:
Amount of support per award: $1,000 to $50,000; average $3,370.

NO. MOST RECENT APPLICANTS: 250.

NO. AWARDS: 125.

APPLICATION INFO:
Guidelines and application forms are available online.
Duration: One year.
Deadline: March 31, June 30, September 30 and December 31.

ADDRESS INQUIRIES TO:
Trustees, Jackson Foundation
(See address or e-mail above.)

HENRY M. JACKSON FOUNDATION [147]

1200 Fifth Avenue
Suite 1450
Seattle, WA 98101
(206) 682-8565
E-mail: foundation@hmjackson.org
Web Site: hmjackson.org

FOUNDED: 1983

AREAS OF INTEREST:
International affairs, public service, environment/natural resources and human rights.

NAME(S) OF PROGRAMS:
- **Environmental and Natural Resources Management Program**
- **Human Rights Program**
- **International Affairs Education Program**
- **Public Service Program**

TYPE:
Challenge/matching grants; Conferences/seminars; Internships; Professorships; Project/program grants; Seed money grants.

YEAR PROGRAM STARTED: 1983

PURPOSE:
To advance education and public understanding of critical public policy issues in the four priority areas above.

LEGAL BASIS:
Publicly supported foundation.

ELIGIBILITY:
Grants are made to private, nonprofit, tax-exempt organizations under 501(c)(3) and public, tax-exempt entities under 170(c). No grants are made to individuals.

No grants for capital or general operating expenses.

FINANCIAL DATA:
Amount of support per award: Varies.
Total amount of support: Average: $250,000 per year.

NO. AWARDS: 10 to 15 per year.

REPRESENTATIVE AWARDS:
$35,015 to Jackson School of International Studies, Seattle, WA, to support the Ph.D. fellowship program; $35,000 to Human Rights First, New York, NY, to support the implementation of the Global Magnitsky Act by coordinating the efforts of over 80 NGOs, as well as pro bono attorneys and law school clinics, to assemble viable sanctions case files for the U.S. government; $16,000 to World Affairs Council, Seattle, WA, to provide public programming and encourage policy engagement on U.S.-Russian relations and climate security.

APPLICATION INFO:
All applicants must submit a letter of inquiry as the first step.
Duration: Varies.
Deadline: January 1, April 1, July 1 and October 1, for awards announced in March, June, September and December, respectively.

PUBLICATIONS:
Application guidelines; annual report; newsletter.

IRS I.D.: 52-1313011

OFFICERS:
Craig Gannett, President

Susan Wickwire, Vice President
Linda Mason Wilgis, Vice President
David Rostov, Treasurer
Anna Marie Laurence, Secretary
Joel C. Merkel, General Counsel

JACKSONVILLE JAGUARS FOUNDATION [148]

One TIAA Bank Field Drive
Jacksonville, FL 32202
(904) 633-5437
Fax: (904) 633-5683
Web Site: www.jaguars.com/community

FOUNDED: 1993

AREAS OF INTEREST:
Social welfare for disadvantaged youths.

TYPE:
General operating grants; Project/program
grants. Limited capital grants that target
economically and socially "at-risk" youths in
northeast Florida.

YEAR PROGRAM STARTED: 1994

PURPOSE:
To support programs benefiting economically
and socially disadvantaged youth, families
and other NFL and team charitable
initiatives.

LEGAL BASIS:
Corporation foundation.

ELIGIBILITY:
Organizations in northeast Florida that work
for disadvantaged youths on a nonsectarian
basis. Must have 501(c)(3) IRS
documentation.

No grants to individuals, schools or
single-disease organizations.

GEOG. RESTRICTIONS: Baker, Clay, Duval,
Nassau, and Saint Johns counties, Florida.

FINANCIAL DATA:
Amount of support per award: Varies.
Total amount of support: Over $1,000,000
for the year 2019.

CO-OP FUNDING PROGRAMS: Youth Anti-Obesity
Grants with Baptist Health; Teen Pregnancy
Prevention Grants with Blue Cross Blue
Shield of Florida.

NO. MOST RECENT APPLICANTS: Over 50.

NO. AWARDS: Over 50.

APPLICATION INFO:
Submit a one-page summary that includes the
specific goals, objectives, proposed activities
and results expected to the Foundation.
Duration: One year. Renewal by
reapplication.
Deadline: July and February.

ADDRESS INQUIRIES TO:
Peter Racine, Senior Vice President
(See address above.)

JOHNSON & JOHNSON FAMILY OF COMPANIES [149]

One Johnson & Johnson Plaza
New Brunswick, NJ 08933
(732) 524-0400
Web Site: www.jnj.com

FOUNDED: 1953

AREAS OF INTEREST:
Health care and education.

TYPE:
Matching gifts; Project/program grants;
Research grants. International programs,
product donation, cash grants. Emphasis on
health care, with a special interest in
maternal and child health care issues. The
Company administers major programs in
partnership with selected nonprofit
organizations. Grants largely extended
through these programs on a Request for
Proposal basis.

The Corporation conducts extensive product
giving program but only through established
partnerships with selected nonprofit
organizations. No unsolicited requests
accepted.

The Corporation also conducts large
matching gifts program in areas of higher
education, hospitals, disease-specific
organizations, cultural organizations and
prevention and treatment of substance abuse.

PURPOSE:
To make life-changing, long-term differences
in human health by targeting the world's
major health-related issues through
community-based partnerships.

ELIGIBILITY:
Grants are made to organizations with
501(c)(3) status. Grants are not made for
endowments, appeals for unrestricted funds,
tours, fund-raising galas and sporting events,
political, fraternal or athletic groups,
sectarian or religious organizations, capital
expenditures, individuals or loans. Priority is
given to activities and needs in locations
where the company has a presence in the
U.S. and Puerto Rico.

FINANCIAL DATA:
Amount of support per award: Varies.
Total amount of support: Varies.

NO. AWARDS: More than 600 grants.

APPLICATION INFO:
No unsolicited requests are accepted.

PUBLICATIONS:
Corporate Contributions report; application
guidelines, policy statement.

STAFF:
Frank Welvaert, Vice President, Global
Community Impact
Ben Davies, Executive Director, Trust EMEA
Team

ADDRESS INQUIRIES TO:
Charitable Contributions
(See address above.)

JOHNSON CONTROLS FOUNDATION [150]

5757 North Green Bay Avenue
Milwaukee, WI 53209-4408
(414) 524-2296
Web Site: www.johnsoncontrols.com

FOUNDED: 1952

AREAS OF INTEREST:
Higher education, health and social services,
civic activities, culture and arts.

TYPE:
Matching gifts; Project/program grants. The
Foundation matches the personal gifts of
employees, retirees and directors to
accredited colleges and universities,
community arts and cultural organizations
and to United Way in the aggregate from its
U.S. company units.

PURPOSE:
To be operated for charitable purposes which
include the distribution and application of
financial support to soundly managed and
operated organizations or causes which are
fundamentally philanthropic.

LEGAL BASIS:
Corporate foundation.

ELIGIBILITY:
Contributions are limited to organizations
which are exempt from taxation under the
Internal Revenue Code. Applicant must meet
one or more of the Foundation's funding
priorities and benefit communities where
Johnson Controls, Inc. has operations and
employees work and live. Special
consideration is given to those requests
which impact the Milwaukee community.

No gifts will be made to any municipal,
state, federal agency or department or to any
organization established to influence
legislation. No distribution will be made to a
private individual. No gifts will be made to
sectarian institutions or programs whose
services are limited to members of any one
religious group or whose funds are used
primarily for the propagation of a religion.
Grants are not usually given to public or
private pre-schools, elementary or secondary
institutions, but are limited to colleges and
universities.

GEOG. RESTRICTIONS: United States.

FINANCIAL DATA:
Amount of support per award: Varies.
Total amount of support: Grants of more than
$7,000,000 annually.
Matching fund requirements: $50 to $3,000
on a 1:1 basis per individual, per
organization, per year to U.S. educational
institutions, U.S. arts and cultural
organizations and U.S. civic organizations.

NO. AWARDS: Up to 40.

REPRESENTATIVE AWARDS:
$300,000 to Discovery World at Pier
Wisconsin; $19,525 to Milwaukee Symphony
Orchestra; $21,000 to Milwaukee Film;
$10,000 to the University of Wisconsin,
Madison.

APPLICATION INFO:
Grant proposals must be submitted online.
Duration: Most grants are one-time only.
Deadline: Proposals submitted after October
1 will be reviewed the following calendar
year.

ADDRESS INQUIRIES TO:
Johnson Controls Foundation
P.O. Box 591
Milwaukee, WI 53201-0591

MAGIC JOHNSON FOUNDATION [151]

9100 Wilshire Boulevard
Suite 700, East Tower
Beverly Hills, CA 90212
(310) 246-4400
Fax: (310) 786-8796
Web Site: magicjohnson.org

FOUNDED: 1991

AREAS OF INTEREST:
Youth; HIV/AIDS education, prevention and
care.

NAME(S) OF PROGRAMS:
● **Magic Johnson Foundation HIV/AIDS
Grant**

TYPE:
Project/program grants; Technical assistance.

PURPOSE:
To support organizations and programs specializing in HIV/AIDS education, prevention and care, and in the areas of education, social needs and health issues of young people.

LEGAL BASIS:
National public charity.

ELIGIBILITY:
Organizations classified as 501(c)(3) by the IRS can apply. Funding will not be considered for projects by individuals and families. Advertising or sponsorship for other funding events are not eligible to receive funds. Research grants, conferences, travel, videos and capital acquisitions are also excluded.

GEOG. RESTRICTIONS: Northern and southern California; Washington, DC; Atlanta, Georgia; Chicago, Illinois; Baltimore, Maryland; New York, New York; Cleveland, Ohio; Houston, Texas.

FINANCIAL DATA:
Amount of support per award: Grants: $5,000 to $10,000.
Total amount of support: Varies.

APPLICATION INFO:
Grants are awarded by invitation only, without exception.
Duration: Grants: One year.

PUBLICATIONS:
Annual report; grant guidelines.

ADDRESS INQUIRIES TO:
Shane Jenkins, Vice President
(See address above.)

DAISY MARQUIS JONES FOUNDATION [152]

1600 South Avenue
Suite 250
Rochester, NY 14620-3921
(585) 461-4950
E-mail: mail@dmjf.org
Web Site: www.dmjf.org

FOUNDED: 1968

AREAS OF INTEREST:
Disadvantaged children and families, access to health care, assistance to senior citizens and economic security for families.

TYPE:
Capital grants; Challenge/matching grants; Development grants; General operating grants; Matching gifts; Project/program grants.

YEAR PROGRAM STARTED: 1968

PURPOSE:
To improve the well-being of residents of Monroe and Yates counties, NY, particularly within the city of Rochester; to meet the needs of the disadvantaged, focusing on prevention; to develop children and families to their maximum potential.

LEGAL BASIS:
Not-for-profit, private foundation.

ELIGIBILITY:
Applicants must be nonprofit, tax-exempt organizations in Monroe and Yates counties, NY. The Foundation does not consider requests for aid for basic research, private

schools, the arts, or religious purposes. The Foundation does not make grants to individuals.

GEOG. RESTRICTIONS: Monroe and Yates counties, New York.

FINANCIAL DATA:
Amount of support per award: Varies.
Total amount of support: $1,902,676 in grants committed in 2018.
Matching fund requirements: Stipulated with specific programs.

NO. AWARDS: 107 grants in 2018.

REPRESENTATIVE AWARDS:
$125,000 to Center for Youth Services to support the Alternative to Out-of-School Suspension Program and New Beginnings School; $50,000 to Greater Rochester Summer Learning Association for PreK-3rd grade reading skills; $45,000 to Seneca Park Zoo Society to support the Butterfly Beltway Program; $50,000 to Lifespan of Greater Rochester to support senior citizens; $25,000 to Neighborworks Rochester to support the neighborhood revitalization program.

APPLICATION INFO:
Applicant must complete the inquiry form that is available on the Foundation web site. The Foundation will reply by e-mail.
Duration: Typically one year.

PUBLICATIONS:
Annual report.

TRUSTEES AND OFFICERS:
C. John Matteson, Interim President
Roger L. Gardner

ADDRESS INQUIRIES TO:
C. John Matteson, Interim President
(See address above.)

THE JOYCE FOUNDATION [153]

321 North Clark Street
Suite 1500
Chicago, IL 60654
(312) 782-2464
Fax: (312) 595-1350
E-mail: info@joycefdn.org
Web Site: www.joycefdn.org

FOUNDED: 1948

AREAS OF INTEREST:
Education and economic mobility, environment, gun violence prevention and justice reform, democracy, and culture.

TYPE:
Awards/prizes; Challenge/matching grants; Demonstration grants; Development grants; General operating grants; Research grants; Technical assistance.

YEAR PROGRAM STARTED: 1948

PURPOSE:
To support efforts to protect the natural environment of the Great Lakes; to reduce poverty and violence in the region; to ensure that its people have access to good schools, decent jobs, and a diverse and thriving culture; to reform the system of financing elections campaigns to ensure that public policies truly reflect public rather than private interests.

LEGAL BASIS:
Private foundation.

ELIGIBILITY:
Applicants must be tax-exempt, charitable organizations that are based or have a

program in the Midwest, which the Foundation defines as including Illinois, Indiana, Michigan, Minnesota, Ohio and Wisconsin. A limited number of environment grants are made to organizations in Canada. The Foundation generally does not support capital proposals, endowment campaigns, religious activities, commercial ventures, direct service programs or scholarships.

GEOG. RESTRICTIONS: Great Lakes region, including Illinois, Indiana, Michigan, Minnesota, Ohio and Wisconsin.

FINANCIAL DATA:
Amount of support per award: Up to $1,000,000 over three years; average grant: $250,000.
Total amount of support: $44,936,336 for the year 2020.

NO. MOST RECENT APPLICANTS: Varies.

NO. AWARDS: Varies.

REPRESENTATIVE AWARDS:
$561,000 to Little Village Environmental Justice Organization to support its efforts to ensure that Chicago's environmental justice communities are engaged in riverfront development processes, clean water advocacy, and the implementation of the Illinois Future Energy Jobs Act; $150,000 to the Community Foundation for Southeast Michigan for the Michigan Justice Fund, a funders' collaborative that seeks to make investments that help stem the flow of individuals into the criminal justice system, support the investment of public dollars to community-driven alternatives to incarceration, and ensure that those who are returning home after incarceration receive the support they need to flourish; $200,000 to the UChicago Consortium on School Research to study how rigorous course taking (dual credit, dual enrollment, and advanced placement) may shape students' college outcomes and how students' experiences of rigorous coursework may differ.

APPLICATION INFO:
Letters of inquiry must precede any formal grant proposal.
Duration: The majority of awards are for one year, although multiyear grants are also considered. Renewal of funding is primarily based on grantee's fulfillment of terms and goals of the previous grant and the program's continued advancement of Foundation priorities.
Deadline: April 7 for July, August 4 for November, and December 1 for the following April.

PUBLICATIONS:
Program and Grant Proposal Guidelines (online); newsletters; annual report.

IRS I.D.: 36-6079185

STAFF:
Ellen S. Alberding, President
Catherine B. Kearney, Vice President of Finance and Administration
Darren Reisberg, Vice President of Programs and Strategy
Nickol Hackett, Chief Investment Officer and Treasurer
Kayce Ataiyero, Managing Director of Communications
Mia Khimm, Program Director, Culture
Carrie L. Davis, Program Director, Democracy
Stephanie Banchero, Program Director, Education

Elizabeth Cisar, Program Director,
Environment
Edmund Miller, Program Director,
Environment
Nina Vinik, Program Director, Gun Violence
Prevention and Justice Reform
Sameer Gadkaree, Senior Program Officer,
Education and Economic Mobility
Tim Daly, Senior Program Officer, Gun
Violence Prevention and Justice Reform
Chibuzo Ezeigbo, Program Officer, Education
and Economic Mobility
Quintin Williams, Program Officer, Gun
Violence Prevention and Justice Reform
Lynne Wiora, Grants Manager

BOARD OF DIRECTORS:
Jose B. Alvarez, Chairman
Margot M. Rogers, Vice Chairman
Ellen S. Alberding
Chanda Smith Baker
Sally Blount
Robert G. Bottoms
Michael F. Brewer
Carlton L. Guthrie
Tracey L. Meares
Cecilia Munoz
Cristian Samper
Carter Stewart

ADDRESS INQUIRIES TO:
E-mail: applications@joycefdn.org

THE J.M. KAPLAN FUND, INC. [154]

71 West 23rd Street
9th Floor
New York, NY 10010
(212) 767-0630
Fax: (212) 767-0639
E-mail: acarabine@jmkfund.org
Web Site: www.jmkfund.org

FOUNDED: 1945

AREAS OF INTEREST:
Environment, social justice, and cultural
heritage.

NAME(S) OF PROGRAMS:
• **Discretionary Grants**
• **Environment Program Grant**
• **Furthermore Grant**
• **Heritage Conservation Grant**
• **The J.M.K. Innovation Prize**
• **Social Justice Grant**

TYPE:
General operating grants; Project/program
grants.

YEAR PROGRAM STARTED: 1945

PURPOSE:
To champion inventive giving that supports
transformative social, environmental and
cultural causes.

LEGAL BASIS:
Family foundation.

ELIGIBILITY:
No grants are made to individuals.
Unsolicited requests are not accepted.

FINANCIAL DATA:
Amount of support per award: $30,000 to
$200,000 for program grants; $2,500 to
$50,000 for discretionary grants.

NO. MOST RECENT APPLICANTS: Over 750.

APPLICATION INFO:
Application is by invitation only, except for
the J.M.K. Innovation Prize.
Duration: 12 to 24 months.

TRUSTEES:
Peter W. Davidson, Chairman
Betsy Davidson
Bradford Davidson
J. Matthew Davidson
Caio Fonseca
Isabel Fonseca
Quina Fonseca

STAFF:
Amy L. Freitag, Executive Director
William P. Falahee, Director of Finance and
Administration
Angela D. Carabine, Grants Manager
Elizabeth Barthelmes Wolff, Program
Director, Environment
Will Raynolds, Program Director, Heritage
Conservation
Justin Goldbach, Program Director, The
J.M.K. Innovation Prize
Ann Birckmayer, Administrator, Furthermore
Grants in Publishing
Jack Carlile, Information and Digital
Technology Assistant

ADDRESS INQUIRIES TO:
Angela D. Carabine, Grants Manager
(See address above.)

KATE SPADE NEW YORK FOUNDATION [155]

2 Park Avenue, 12th Floor
New York, NY 10016
(800) 519-3778
E-mail: foundation@katespade.com
Web Site: www.katespade.com

FOUNDED: 1981

AREAS OF INTEREST:
Women's programs only, specifically
economic empowerment.

TYPE:
Challenge/matching grants; General operating
grants; Matching gifts; Project/program
grants; Seed money grants; Technical
assistance.

YEAR PROGRAM STARTED: 1981

PURPOSE:
To support multidimensional programs that
transition women from underserved
communities into successful individuals that
inspire the people around them.

LEGAL BASIS:
Corporate foundation.

ELIGIBILITY:
Organizations classified as 501(c)(3) by the
IRS can apply. Individuals and religious,
political and fraternal organizations are
ineligible.

GEOG. RESTRICTIONS: Hudson County, New
Jersey and New York, New York.

FINANCIAL DATA:
Amount of support per award: $15,000 to
$120,000.
Total amount of support: Approximately
$1,000,000 annually.
Matching fund requirements: 1:1; $25
minimum and $10,000 annual total per
employee; includes arts, education, health,
human services and the environment.

REPRESENTATIVE AWARDS:
International Rescue Committee; Ghetto Film
School; Didi Hirsch Mental Health Services.

APPLICATION INFO:
Guidelines and application form are available
online.

Duration: One year. Grants are renewable.
Deadline: Applications are accepted
throughout the year.

PUBLICATIONS:
Application guidelines.

IRS I.D.: 13-3060673

ADDRESS INQUIRIES TO:
Valerie Biberaj, Director
(See address above.)

MAY GORDON LATHAM KELLENBERGER HISTORICAL FOUNDATION [156]

529 South Front Street
New Bern, NC 28562
(252) 639-3500
Fax: (252) 514-4876

FOUNDED: 1978

AREAS OF INTEREST:
Historic preservation in the city of New Bern
and Craven County, NC.

TYPE:
Project/program grants.

YEAR PROGRAM STARTED: 1978

PURPOSE:
To aid in the preservation of significant
structures in New Bern as well as to assist in
historical research and study pertaining to the
city of New Bern and Craven County, NC.

LEGAL BASIS:
Special-interest foundation.

ELIGIBILITY:
Applicants must be organizations, agencies
and institutions which are tax-exempt under
the provisions of the U.S. Internal Revenue
Code.

GEOG. RESTRICTIONS: Craven County and New
Bern, North Carolina.

FINANCIAL DATA:
Amount of support per award: Varies.
Total amount of support: Varies.

APPLICATION INFO:
Contact Foundation for application form and
guidelines.
Duration: One year. Can be renewed for one
additional year.
Deadline: June 10 and December 10.
Announcement on August 1 and February 1.

PUBLICATIONS:
Application guidelines.

OFFICERS:
John A.J. Ward, Chairperson
Dr. Kevin Cherry, Vice Chairperson
William C. Cannon, Secretary and Treasurer
Joe M. Hunt, III, Project Review Committee
Chairperson

ADDRESS INQUIRIES TO:
Laurie Bowles, Administrative Support
(See address above.)

W.K. KELLOGG FOUNDATION [157]

One Michigan Avenue East
Battle Creek, MI 49017-4012
(269) 968-1611
(269) 969-2307
Fax: (269) 968-0413
E-mail: communications@wkkf.org
Web Site: www.wkkf.org

FOUNDED: 1930

AREAS OF INTEREST:
Equitable communities, thriving children and working families.

TYPE:
Challenge/matching grants; Development grants; Endowments; Fellowships; General operating grants; Matching gifts; Project/program grants; Seed money grants. Grants for pilot projects to improve human well-being are made in the U.S., Mexico, Haiti, northeastern Brazil, and with sovereign tribes. Up to two-thirds of grantmaking falls under priority places: New Orleans, Louisiana; Michigan; Mississippi; New Mexico; Chiapas and the Yucatan Peninsula, Mexico; and in Central and South Haiti. The Foundation is committed to working in each of these priority places for at least a generation.

The Foundation encourages grant seekers to review the latest information on its web site regarding its focus areas of thriving children, working families, and equitable communities.

YEAR PROGRAM STARTED: 1930

PURPOSE:
To support children, families and communities as they strengthen and create conditions that propel vulnerable children to achieve success as individuals and as contributors to the larger community and society.

LEGAL BASIS:
Independent private foundation.

ELIGIBILITY:
To be eligible for support, applying organization or institution, as well as the purpose of the proposed project, must qualify under the regulations of the U.S. IRS. Grantees must have the financial potential to sustain the project on a continuing basis after Foundation funding is ended. The Foundation is not able to provide funding directly to individuals.

GEOG. RESTRICTIONS: Haiti, Mexico and United States, with priority in Michigan, Mississippi, New Mexico and New Orleans, Louisiana.

FINANCIAL DATA:
Total assets of $8,288,613,608 for the year ended August 31, 2020.
Amount of support per award: Varies.
Total amount of support: $251,991,614 for the year ended August 31, 2020.

NO. MOST RECENT APPLICANTS: 1,099 for fiscal year 2019-20.

NO. AWARDS: 770 new commitments for fiscal year 2019-20.

REPRESENTATIVE AWARDS:
$600,000 to ZERO TO THREE: National Center for Infants, Toddlers, and Families; $500,000 to Con Alma Health Foundation; $700,000 to Southwest Economic Solutions.

APPLICATION INFO:
The preferred method for grant submissions is the Foundation's online application. The Foundation will give prompt consideration to all preproposal submissions. The initial review may take up to three months to complete. If the proposed project falls within the Foundation's priorities and available resources, applicants may be asked to develop a more detailed proposal.
Duration: Varies.
Deadline: The Foundation accepts proposals on an ongoing basis, and staff members review them as they are received.

PUBLICATIONS:
Annual report.

BOARD OF TRUSTEES:
Celeste Clark, Chairman
Milton Chen
Roderick Gillum
Christina Hanger
Cathann Kress
Ramón Murguía
Khan Nedd
Richard Tsoumas

EXECUTIVE STAFF:
La June Montgomery Tabron, President and Chief Executive Officer
Carlos Rangel, Vice President and Chief Investment Officer
Mary B. Cohen, Vice President for Communications
Donald Williamson, Vice President for Finance and Treasurer
Ross Comstock, Vice President for Information Systems and Technology
Cindy Smith, Vice President for Integrated Services
Carla Thompson, Vice President for Program Strategy
Dianna Langenburg, Vice President for Talent and Human Resources
Alandra Washington, Vice President for Transformation and Organizational Effectiveness
Paul Martinez, Chief Leadership and Human Capital Strategist
Kathryn Krecke, General Counsel and Corporate Secretary

ADDRESS INQUIRIES TO:
See e-mail address above.

HARRIS AND ELIZA KEMPNER FUND [158]

2228 Mechanic Street
Suite 220
Galveston, TX 77550-1529
(409) 762-1603
Fax: (409) 762-5435
E-mail: information@kempnerfund.org
Web Site: www.kempnerfund.org

FOUNDED: 1946

AREAS OF INTEREST:
Arts, historic preservation, community development, education, environment, and health and human services.

NAME(S) OF PROGRAMS:
● **Matching Gifts Program**
● **Primary Grant Program**
● **Program Related Investments**

TYPE:
Capital grants; Challenge/matching grants; Conferences/seminars; Demonstration grants; Endowments; General operating grants; Matching gifts; Project/program grants; Seed money grants. Primary Grant Program provides grants to qualifying organizations in the greater Galveston, TX area in the arts and historic preservation, community development, education, environment, and health and human services.

Program Related Investments are recommended by Fund trustees for Galveston projects.

YEAR PROGRAM STARTED: 1946

PURPOSE:
To support a wide range of innovative as well as traditional programs for the enhancement of the local community.

LEGAL BASIS:
Independent private foundation.

ELIGIBILITY:
Primary Grant Program: Preferred applicants are programs/projects that benefit the greater Galveston, TX community. Seed money, operating funds, small capital needs and special projects, and partnering with other funding sources are supported. Proposals will not be considered for fund-raising benefits, direct-mail solicitations, grants to individuals, or grants to non-U.S.-based organizations.

Matching Gifts Program: Restricted to Kempner family members and trustees of the Kempner Fund.

GEOG. RESTRICTIONS: Galveston, Texas.

FINANCIAL DATA:
Amount of support per award: Grants: $1,000 to $45,000 for the year ended December 31, 2019.
Total amount of support: $1,585,808 in grants and $192,636 in matching gifts for the year ended December 31, 2019.
Matching fund requirements: Restricted to descendants of Harris and Eliza Kempner.

NO. AWARDS: 101 for the year 2020.

REPRESENTATIVE AWARDS:
$45,000 to the Grand 1894 Opera House; $10,000 to Family Service, Inc.; $20,000 to The Salvation Army Galveston County.

APPLICATION INFO:
Applicants must submit proposals through the online grant application. E-mailed or printed copies will not be accepted.
Duration: Varies.
Deadline: Health or Human Services: March 15. Arts, Community Development, Environment, Historic Preservation or Education: October 15.

IRS I.D.: 74-6042458

STAFF:
Lauren E. Scott, Executive Director

BOARD OF DIRECTORS AND OFFICERS:
Eliza Quigley, President
Emily Bray, Vice President
Randall Kempner, Treasurer
Rachel Hamilton, Secretary
Carol Bunch Davis, Ph.D.
Chandler Guttersen
Jack Kempner
S. Benjamin Shabot
Daniel K. Thorne

ADDRESS INQUIRIES TO:
See e-mail address above.

*SPECIAL STIPULATIONS:
Funding is limited to Galveston, TX area only.

JOHN F. KENNEDY LIBRARY FOUNDATION [159]

220 Morrissey Boulevard
Columbia Point
Boston, MA 02125-3313
(617) 514-1630
Fax: (617) 514-1625
E-mail: kennedy.fellowships@nara.gov
Web Site: www.jfklibrary.org/archives/research-fellowships-grants

FOUNDED: 1964

AREAS OF INTEREST:
History, political science, journalism, and other academic disciplines.

NAME(S) OF PROGRAMS:
- **Marjorie Kovler Fellowship**
- **Arthur M. Schlesinger, Jr. Fellowship**
- **Abba T. Schwartz Fellowship**
- **Theodore C. Sorensen Fellowship**

TYPE:
Fellowships. Fellowships are strictly intended to support research in the holdings of the John F. Kennedy Presidential Library.

PURPOSE:
To support scholars who need to use the archival holdings of the John F. Kennedy Presidential Library.

FINANCIAL DATA:
Amount of support per award: Kovler Fellowship and Schlesinger Fellowship: Up to $5,000; Schwartz Fellowship: Up to $3,100; Sorensen Fellowship: Up to $3,600.

NO. MOST RECENT APPLICANTS: 22.

NO. AWARDS: Varies.

APPLICATION INFO:
Applicants are encouraged to contact an archivist at the Library for information about relevant archival holdings before applying. Candidates can apply for only one fellowship per year. The Fellowship Committee will access each application with the most relevant fellowship opportunity in mind.
Deadline: Varies.

ADDRESS INQUIRIES TO:
Fellowships Coordinator
(See address above.)

JOHN F. KENNEDY PRESIDENTIAL LIBRARY   [160]
220 Morrissey Boulevard
Columbia Point
Boston, MA 02125-3313
(617) 514-1630
Fax: (617) 514-1625
E-mail: kennedy.library@nara.gov
Web Site: www.jfklibrary.org

FOUNDED: 1964

AREAS OF INTEREST:
Archival administration and library science, history, government, journalism, communications and other related disciplines.

NAME(S) OF PROGRAMS:
- **Kennedy Library Archival Internships**

TYPE:
Internships. Awarded to undergraduate and graduate students majoring in history, government, archival administration, library science, journalism, communications and related disciplines for on-site work with the archives staff at the Kennedy Library.

YEAR PROGRAM STARTED: 1970

LEGAL BASIS:
Private foundation in cooperation with a U.S. government agency.

ELIGIBILITY:
Applicants must be U.S. citizens or legal residents.

FINANCIAL DATA:
Amount of support per award: Monthly stipend of $750 for part-time interns.

NO. AWARDS: Varies according to archivists' needs and capability.

APPLICATION INFO:
Candidate must complete application form, submit a copy of current college transcript, and a letter of reference.

Duration: Varies.
Deadline: Varies.

ADDRESS INQUIRIES TO:
Internship Coordinator
(See address above.)

THE KERR FOUNDATION, INC.   [161]
12501 North May Avenue
Oklahoma City, OK 73120
(405) 749-7991
Fax: (405) 749-2877
Web Site: www.thekerrfoundation.org

FOUNDED: 1963

AREAS OF INTEREST:
Education, cultural activities, and health and human services.

TYPE:
Capital grants; General operating grants; Project/program grants.

YEAR PROGRAM STARTED: 1986

PURPOSE:
To support programs of interest to the Foundation in the areas of health, education, youth services and cultural activities.

LEGAL BASIS:
Private, charitable foundation.

ELIGIBILITY:
Application is limited to nonprofit, 501(c)(3) tax-exempt organizations. No grants to individuals.

GEOG. RESTRICTIONS: Arkansas, Colorado, Kansas, Missouri, New Mexico, Oklahoma, Texas, and Washington, D.C.

FINANCIAL DATA:
Grant-seeking organizations must first raise a specified amount in actual new dollars donations or up-to-three-year pledges. The grant will be paid upon successful raising of the funds or pledges, which must occur within one year or a mutually agreed-upon time limit.
Amount of support per award: $5,000 to $50,000.

CO-OP FUNDING PROGRAMS: All Oklahoma foundations.

NO. AWARDS: 42 for the year 2019.

APPLICATION INFO:
A letter of inquiry is required before a formal grant application can be submitted. Forms and guidelines are available online.
Duration: Most grants awarded on a one-time basis. The Foundation does not give back-to-back grants. Organizations must allow one full year before reapplying.
Deadline: June 30.

OFFICERS AND TRUSTEES:
Mrs. Robert S. Kerr, Jr., President and Chairperson
Laura D. Kerr, Vice President
Steven Kerr, Treasurer
Laura Kerr Ogle, Secretary
Cody T. Kerr

ADDRESS INQUIRIES TO:
Laura D. Kerr, Vice President
E-mail: lauradkerr@thekerrfoundation.org

GRAYCE B. KERR FUND, INC.   [162]
117 Bay Street
Easton, MD 21601
(410) 822-6652
Fax: (410) 822-4546
E-mail: office@gbkf.org
Web Site: www.gbkf.org

FOUNDED: 1986

AREAS OF INTEREST:
Education, cultural programs, and public policy research, with major emphasis on education.

TYPE:
Project/program grants. Grants to nonprofit organizations. Grants are not limited to any one specific area of interest or geographical location. Currently, the Fund's principal areas of interest include nurturing educational achievement and excellence, fostering life skills critical to self-sufficiency, and encouraging cultural growth. The Fund supports research and other activities directed toward improving the information base available to the public.

YEAR PROGRAM STARTED: 1986

PURPOSE:
To provide financial support to worthy nonprofit organizations that enhance the quality of life, significantly impact and sustain long-term change and growth in organizations and institutions.

LEGAL BASIS:
Private, charitable foundation.

ELIGIBILITY:
Applicants must be nonprofit, 501(c)(3) tax-exempt organizations. No grants to individuals.

GEOG. RESTRICTIONS: United States.

FINANCIAL DATA:
Grant minimums and maximums are not designated. Preference may be given, in some years, to large grants where a genuine impact may be accomplished.
Amount of support per award: Varies.
Total amount of support: Varies.

APPLICATION INFO:
The Foundation self-selects grantees based on the interests of the family and Trustees. Unsolicited proposals are not accepted.

PUBLICATIONS:
Annual report; application.

IRS I.D.: 73-1256124

BOARD OF TRUSTEES:
Marcy Kerr Yuknat, Chairperson
John R. Valliant, President and Trustee
David A. Yuknat, Secretary and Treasurer

ADDRESS INQUIRIES TO:
John R. Valliant, President
(See address above.)

KIMBERLY-CLARK FOUNDATION, INC.   [163]
P.O. Box 619100
Dallas, TX 75261-9100
(972) 281-1200
E-mail: kcfoundation@kcc.com
Web Site: www.kimberly-clark.com

FOUNDED: 1952

AREAS OF INTEREST:
Social welfare, medicine and health.

TYPE:
Project/program grants.

YEAR PROGRAM STARTED: 1952

PURPOSE:
To support organizations that strengthen today's families.

LEGAL BASIS:
Corporate foundation.

ELIGIBILITY:
Grants are made to tax-exempt, charitable, 501(c)(3) nonprofit organizations in communities where Kimberly-Clark has operations. There are a limited number of contributions to national organizations.

FINANCIAL DATA:
Amount of support per award: Varies.
Total amount of support: Varies.

REPRESENTATIVE AWARDS:
$1,300,000 to Boys and Girls Clubs of America; $20,000 to Susan G. Komen Foundation; $50,000 to Catalyst for Women; $200,000 to American Red Cross.

APPLICATION INFO:
Applicants are required to e-mail the Foundation before sending requests.
Duration: One to five years.

PUBLICATIONS:
Annual report.

OFFICERS:
Flavio Costa, Vice President and Treasurer
Jenny Lewis, Vice President

ADDRESS INQUIRIES TO:
Jenny Lewis, Vice President
(See address above.)

STEPHEN AND TABITHA KING FOUNDATION [164]
P.O. Box 855
Bangor, ME 04402
(207) 990-2910
Fax: (207) 990-2975
E-mail: info@stkfoundation.org
Web Site: stkfoundation.org

FOUNDED: 1986

AREAS OF INTEREST:
Arts, children/youth, health, education, libraries, recovery, women's issues, human rights, literacy, public safety, and conservation.

TYPE:
Awards/prizes; Capital grants; Challenge/matching grants; Demonstration grants; Development grants; Matching gifts; Project/program grants; Seed money grants; Training grants.

PURPOSE:
To improve the quality of life in Maine.

LEGAL BASIS:
Private family foundation.

ELIGIBILITY:
Organizations classified as 501(c)(3) by the IRS and located in Maine can apply. Grants are only awarded to nonprofit organizations operating in the state of Maine. Individuals and religious organizations are ineligible.

GEOG. RESTRICTIONS: Maine.

FINANCIAL DATA:
Amount of support per award: Grants: $500 to $50,000.
Total amount of support: Varies, dependent on investment revenue.

Matching fund requirements: Must be met through grassroots local community funding.

NO. MOST RECENT APPLICANTS: 1,200 to 1,500 annually.

NO. AWARDS: Approximately 250.

APPLICATION INFO:
Applications are submitted online.
Duration: Foundation prefers one-time grants. Multiyear commitments occasionally.
Deadline: April 15 and October 15. Decisions on grants may take as long as eight weeks.

IRS I.D.: 13-3364647

STAFF:
Stephanie Leonard, Administrator

ADDRESS INQUIRIES TO:
Stephanie Leonard, Administrator
(See address above.)

*SPECIAL STIPULATIONS:
Applicants should apply only once per year and those that receive funding should wait two full years before reapplying.

F.M. KIRBY FOUNDATION, INC. [165]
17 DeHart Street
Morristown, NJ 07963
(973) 538-4800
Fax: (973) 538-4801
E-mail: fmkf@fmkirby.com
Web Site: fmkirbyfoundation.org

FOUNDED: 1931

AREAS OF INTEREST:
General charitable support.

TYPE:
Capital grants; Challenge/matching grants; Endowments; Fellowships; General operating grants; Professorships; Project/program grants; Research grants; Scholarships. Grants usually are reflective of personal interest by one or more members of the Kirby family who are, or have been, active in the affairs of the Foundation.

YEAR PROGRAM STARTED: 1931

LEGAL BASIS:
Private foundation.

ELIGIBILITY:
Organizations must be tax-exempt under applicable provisions of the IRS code and not private foundations. No grants are made to individuals. No grants are made to public foundations which would, as a result thereof, become private foundations. No grants for fund-raising activities such as benefits, charitable dinners, sports or theater events, etc. No loans are made.

GEOG. RESTRICTIONS: Morris County, New Jersey; Adirondack Park, New York area, Raleigh-Durham, North Carolina area, and Wilkes-Barre, Pennsylvania area.

FINANCIAL DATA:
Amount of support per award: Varies.
Total amount of support: $13,775,150 for the year 2020.
Matching fund requirements: Determined on a case-by-case basis.

NO. AWARDS: 248 for the year 2020.

APPLICATION INFO:
The preferred method of initial contact is a full proposal with a cover letter. The Foundation provides no formal application

forms and sets down no specific guidelines. Proposals should include:
(1) a report on the use of previous grants if applicable;
(2) a description of the organization, its purpose and the project, if any;
(3) an indication of the budget for which financial support is requested;
(4) roster of directors and principal officers;
(5) copy of the current audited financial statement;
(6) copy of the valid IRS tax determination letter and;
(7) copy of current annual budget.
Duration: One year. Renewal possible.
Deadline: October 31. Solicitations received after deadline will be held over to following year.

PUBLICATIONS:
Application guidelines.

IRS I.D.: 51-6017929

STAFF:
Erin Clifford, Program Officer

OFFICERS AND DIRECTORS:
S. Dillard Kirby, President and Director
Justin J. Kiczek, Executive Vice President
Jefferson W. Kirby, Vice President and Director
Diana L. Kostas, Treasurer and Secretary
Alice K. Horton, Assistant Secretary and Director
Wilson M. Compton, Director
Ashley Horton Freeman, Director
Leigh Kirby Klein, Director
Sandra Brown Sherman, Director

ADDRESS INQUIRIES TO:
Justin J. Kiczek, Executive Vice President
(See e-mail address above.)

KITSAP COMMUNITY FOUNDATION
9657 Levin Road, N.W.
Suite 220
Silverdale, WA 98383
(360) 698-3622
E-mail: info@kitsapfoundation.org
Web Site: www.kitsapfoundation.org

TYPE:
General operating grants; Project/program grants; Scholarships.

See entry 1191 for full listing.

JOSIAH W. AND BESSIE H. KLINE FOUNDATION, INC. [166]
515 South 29th Street
Harrisburg, PA 17104
(717) 561-4373
Fax: (717) 561-0826
E-mail: info@kline-foundation.org
Web Site: www.kline-foundation.org

FOUNDED: 1952

AREAS OF INTEREST:
Medical, academic, benevolent, community and cultural.

NAME(S) OF PROGRAMS:
● Kline Foundation Grants

TYPE:
Project/program grants; Research grants.

YEAR PROGRAM STARTED: 1952

PURPOSE:
To aid blind or incapacitated persons or crippled children in need of financial assistance; to make grants to Pennsylvania

colleges and universities, to hospitals and institutions for crippled children or to any other benevolent or charitable institution; to make grants for scientific or medical research to be performed by scientific persons or 501(c)(3) tax-exempt, nonprofit organizations.

LEGAL BASIS:
Community foundation.

ELIGIBILITY:
Grants are made to 501(c)(3) tax-exempt, nonprofit organizations. The Foundation does not make loans and does not make grants to individuals and generally does not make grants for normal operational phases of established programs or to national organizations or religious programs.

GEOG. RESTRICTIONS: South central Pennsylvania, with emphasis on Cumberland and Dauphin counties.

FINANCIAL DATA:
Amount of support per award: $500 to $250,000.
Total amount of support: Varies.

APPLICATION INFO:
Application information is available on the web site. To be considered for Foundation aid, a copy of the Foundation's completed application form must be submitted and the following information must be fully stated:
(1) a description of the need and purpose, the qualifications of the requesting organization and the location as to where and how the support will be used;
(2) a budget for the project and any support that will be received from other sources;
(3) the amount of the request from the Foundation and the dates the funds are needed and;
(4) a copy of a letter from the IRS showing that the organization is exempt from federal income tax under Section 501(c)(3) of the Internal Revenue Code and that the organization is not a private foundation under Section 509(a).

Application may be submitted online.
Deadline: March and September. Some grants are awarded in June, while others are generally awarded after December 1 of each year.

PUBLICATIONS:
Annual report; application guidelines; application.

ADDRESS INQUIRIES TO:
John A. Obrock, C.P.A.
(See address above.)

*SPECIAL STIPULATIONS:
One grant per year per organization.

JOHN S. AND JAMES L. KNIGHT FOUNDATION   [167]
200 South Biscayne Boulevard
Suite 3300
Miami, FL 33131-2349
(305) 908-2600
Fax: (305) 908-2698
E-mail: grants@knightfoundation.org
Web Site: www.knightfoundation.org

FOUNDED: 1950

AREAS OF INTEREST:
Journalism and engaged and informed communities.

NAME(S) OF PROGRAMS:
● **Arts Program**
● **Communities Program**
● **Journalism Program**
● **Learning and Impact Program**

TYPE:
Capital grants; Challenge/matching grants; Development grants; Endowments; Matching gifts; Project/program grants; Seed money grants; Technical assistance. The Foundation promotes excellence in journalism worldwide and invests in the vitality of 26 U.S. communities.

The Foundation focuses on three areas:
(1) Innovating Media and Journalism: The Foundation aims to help sustain democracy by leading journalism to its best possible future in the 21st century;
(2) Engaging Communities: To sustain healthy communities in a democracy, the Foundation's community engagement initiatives aim to give all residents a strong sense of belonging and caring, timely access to relevant information, the ability to understand that information, and the motivation to take sustainable action on the issues that matter most to them and;
(3) Fostering the Arts: Through its national arts program, the Foundation seeks to weave the arts into the fabric of the Knight resident communities to engage and inspire their residents; the Foundation believes that the arts are a catalyst for public dialogue, and that shared cultural experiences contribute to a sense of place and communal identity.

YEAR PROGRAM STARTED: 1950

PURPOSE:
To sustain democracy in the digital age by fostering informed and engaged communities; to back transformational ideas at the intersection of media, journalism, community engagement and the arts; to advance media innovation with a wide range of initiatives; to support projects, including in the arts, that increase community engagement through the use of technology and other innovative approaches.

LEGAL BASIS:
Private non-operating foundation.

ELIGIBILITY:
A segment of the Foundation's activities focuses on 26 communities where the Knight brothers owned newspapers, with donor-advised programs in 18 and program director-led programs in the eight "resident Knight communities."

An applicant organization must have received a letter of determination from the IRS granting it 501(c)(3) tax-exempt status and stating that it is not a private foundation according to the definition in Section 509(a) of the Internal Revenue Code.

The Knight News Challenge permits for-profit entities and individuals to apply from anywhere in the world.

The Knight Community Information Challenge accepts applications from community and place-based foundations in the U.S. and its territories, as well as Mexico and Canada.

The Knight Arts Challenge accepts applications from South Florida, Detroit (MI), and Greater Philadelphia individuals, for-profit and nonprofit organizations.

FINANCIAL DATA:
Amount of support per award: Varies.
Total amount of support: $133,711,354 in grants paid for the year 2019.

NO. AWARDS: 488 new grants for the year 2019.

APPLICATION INFO:
Applicants must submit an online letter of inquiry. If the inquiry is determined to fall into Knight Foundation funding priorities, applicants are asked to submit a full proposal.
Duration: Varies per project; usually from one to five years.

PUBLICATIONS:
Evaluation and Assessment publications; Reporter Analysis evaluation articles; KnightBlog posts.

IRS I.D.: 65-0464177

STAFF:
Terese Coudreaut Curiel, Vice President/Administration
Juan Martinez, Vice President and Chief Financial Officer
Jorge Martinez, Vice President and Chief Technology Officer
Victoria Rogers, Vice President/Arts
Andrew Sherry, Vice President/Communications

TRUSTEES AND OFFICERS:
Francisco L. Borges, Chairman
Alberto Ibarguen, President and Chief Executive Officer
Christopher M. Austen
Martin Baron
Stephanie Bell-Rose
Shana L. Brown
Adriana Cisneros
William H. Considine
Susan D. Kronick
Christine Amer Mayer
Anna Spangler Nelson
Beverly Knight Olson
John Palfrey
Ray Rodriguez

ADDRESS INQUIRIES TO:
Grants Administrator
(See address above.)

MARION I. AND HENRY J. KNOTT FOUNDATION, INC. [168]
3904 Hickory Avenue
Baltimore, MD 21211
(410) 235-7068
Fax: (410) 889-2577
E-mail: knott@knottfoundation.org
Web Site: www.knottfoundation.org

FOUNDED: 1977

AREAS OF INTEREST:
Education (private and Catholic schools only), health care, human and social services, arts and humanities.

TYPE:
Challenge/matching grants; Development grants; General operating grants; Matching gifts.

YEAR PROGRAM STARTED: 1977

PURPOSE:
To further Roman Catholic activities and other charitable, cultural, educational, health care and human service activities within the meaning of Section 501(c)(3) of the Internal Revenue Code.

LEGAL BASIS:
Private family foundation.

ELIGIBILITY:
Applicants must be nonprofit, charitable organizations with evidence of tax-exemption ruling under Section 501(c)(3) of the Internal Revenue Code. No grants pertaining to

scholarships, individuals, annual giving, pro-choice causes, public education or institutions, or politically oriented activities.

The Foundation does not favor multiyear requests.

GEOG. RESTRICTIONS: Central and western Maryland, including the Archdiocese of Baltimore.

FINANCIAL DATA:
Amount of support per award: Discretionary grants: $500 to $2,500; Foundation grants: $10,000 to $100,000. Average $45,000.

Total amount of support: Approximately $2,500,000 annually.

Matching fund requirements: Specific to grantee. Usually matched within a six-month period.

NO. AWARDS: 63 for the year 2020.

APPLICATION INFO:
Details are available on the Foundation web site.

Duration: Usually one year.

Deadline: Letters of Inquiry and Financials: February, June and October. Full Proposal: March, July and November, respectively.

IRS I.D.: 52-1517876

TRUSTEES AND OFFICERS:
Mary Lindsay Gallagher, President
Daniel Gallagher
David Gallagher
Michael Gallagher
Emily Hanssen
E.B. Harris
Kelly L. Harris
Thomas Harris
Carlisle Hashim
Marion Hashim
Erin Knott
Marion I. Knott
Martin G. Knott, Sr.
Martin G. Knott, Jr.
Owen M. Knott
Teresa A. Knott
Brian McDonald
Meghan McDonald
Carroll McGill
Peter McGill
David L. Porter
Joanna O. Porter
Laurel Porter
Martin Porter
John H. Riehl, IV
Margie Riehl
Michael Riehl
Brooke Rodgers
Patrick Rodgers
Geralynn D. Smyth
John Smyth
Jamie Stodd
Erin Tielsch
Emmett Voelkel
Ryan Voelkel

ADDRESS INQUIRIES TO:
Kelly Medinger, Executive Director
(See e-mail address above.)

KNOX COUNTY FOUNDATION [169]
101 East Gambier Street
Mount Vernon, OH 43050
(740) 392-3270
E-mail: marc@knoxcf.org
Web Site: knoxcf.org

FOUNDED: 1944

AREAS OF INTEREST:
New projects in educational, charitable and civic fields.

TYPE:
Capital grants; Challenge/matching grants; Matching gifts; Project/program grants; Scholarships; Seed money grants.

YEAR PROGRAM STARTED: 1944

PURPOSE:
To improve the quality of life for the people of Mount Vernon and Knox County, OH.

LEGAL BASIS:
Nonprofit, community foundation.

ELIGIBILITY:
Grants from unrestricted funds generally limited to projects in Knox County, OH.

GEOG. RESTRICTIONS: Knox County, Ohio.

FINANCIAL DATA:
Amount of support per award: Varies.
Total amount of support: $4,000,000 annually.

APPLICATION INFO:
Application forms are available online. Personal presentations only at invitation of Distribution Committee.

PUBLICATIONS:
Annual report.

IRS I.D.: 23-7002871

BOARD OF DIRECTORS:
Richard K. Mavis, Chairman
Marsha K. Rinehart, Vice Chairman
Kurt E. Schisler, Treasurer
Kim Rose, Secretary
Jeffrey L. Boucher
Chris Cordle, Ph.D.
Kathy Daniels
Sean Decatur, Ph.D.
John D. Lambert
Jan Reynolds
Vickie A. Sant
David Stuller
Susan Sukys
Dr. Michael Sullivan
Ian C. Watson

ADDRESS INQUIRIES TO:
Marc Odenweller, Finance Director
(See address above.)

KORET FOUNDATION [170]
611 Front Street
San Francisco, CA 94111-1963
(415) 882-7740
Fax: (415) 882-7775
E-mail: koret@koretfoundation.org
Web Site: koret.org

FOUNDED: 1979

AREAS OF INTEREST:
Arts, community service and volunteerism, Jewish community services, education and employment for youth, elderly, hunger and homelessness.

TYPE:
Capital grants; General operating grants; Project/program grants; Seed money grants.

YEAR PROGRAM STARTED: 1979

PURPOSE:
To address societal challenges and strengthen Bay Area life; to invest in strategic, local solutions that help to inspire a multiplier effect, encouraging collaborative funding and developing model initiatives.

LEGAL BASIS:
Private foundation.

ELIGIBILITY:
Grant applicants must be 501(c)(3) organizations. Private foundations are not eligible to apply.

Although the majority of funding is granted to six of nine bay area counties, the Foundation will consider national and Israeli projects.

GEOG. RESTRICTIONS: Alameda, Contra Costa, Marin, San Francisco, San Mateo and Santa Clara counties, California.

FINANCIAL DATA:
Amount of support per award: Grants vary in amount, depending upon the needs and nature of the request.

APPLICATION INFO:
The Foundation considers grant requests by invitation only.
Duration: Varies.

PUBLICATIONS:
Annual report; application guidelines.

IRS I.D.: 94-1624987

OFFICERS:
Jeffrey A. Farber, Chief Executive Officer

THE KRAFT HEINZ COMPANY FOUNDATION [171]
200 East Randolph
Suite 7600
Chicago, IL 60601
Web Site: www.kraftheinzcompany.com/community-involvement.html

FOUNDED: 1951

AREAS OF INTEREST:
Eliminating global hunger.

TYPE:
Project/program grants.

YEAR PROGRAM STARTED: 1951

PURPOSE:
To eliminate global hunger through the support of organizations and initiatives dedicated to increasing food access and security; to seek sustainable solutions to hunger; to promote hunger prevention programs; to feed families in times of disaster.

LEGAL BASIS:
Corporate foundation.

ELIGIBILITY:
All organizations seeking funding must be tax-exempt under Section 501(c)(3) of the Internal Revenue Code.

The Foundation does not make grants for loans or assistance to individuals, general scholarships, fellowships, travel grants, political campaigns either local or national and/or sectarian religious purposes.

FINANCIAL DATA:
Amount of support per award: Varies.
Total amount of support: Varies.

REPRESENTATIVE AWARDS:
Extra Mile Education Foundation; Make-A-Wish Foundation of Western Pennsylvania.

APPLICATION INFO:
A written project summary may be sent including the goals of the applying organization, the specific purpose for which funds are requested, how the objective will be accomplished, to whom and where the

program will be offered and whether the project is a single project or one that requires additional phases. A letter of intent is recommended to approach the Foundation.

Duration: Mostly one year. Renewal requests are considered.

TRUSTEES:
Tammy B. Aupperle, Chairperson
Ted Bobby
Kristen Clark
Beth Eckenrode
Michael Mullen
Michael Okoroafer

ADDRESS INQUIRIES TO:
Jenece Upton, Manager
(See address above.)

THE KRESGE FOUNDATION   [172]
3215 West Big Beaver Road
Troy, MI 48084
(248) 643-9630
Fax: (248) 643-0588
E-mail: info@kresge.org
Web Site: kresge.org

FOUNDED: 1924

AREAS OF INTEREST:
Arts and culture, Detroit/community development, education, environment, and health and human services.

TYPE:
General operating grants; Project/program grants. Program-related investments.

YEAR PROGRAM STARTED: 1924

PURPOSE:
To expand opportunity for low-income people so they can gain the tools and support needed to lead self-determined lives and join the economic mainstream.

LEGAL BASIS:
Independent private foundation.

ELIGIBILITY:
Tax-exempt charitable organizations operating in the fields of higher education (including community colleges), health care and long-term care, human services, science and the environment, arts and humanities and public affairs. Governmental agencies are also eligible to apply. Full accreditation is required for higher education and hospital applicants and preferred in all other fields that offer it. Evidence of initial funding for the requested project is considered essential.

The following projects are eligible:
(1) construction of facilities;
(2) renovation of facilities;
(3) purchase of major equipment or an integrated system at a cost of at least $300,000; equipment costs may include computer software expenses, if applicable and;
(4) purchase of real estate.

Religious organizations, elementary and secondary schools, private foundations and individuals are not eligible to apply. However, accredited seminaries are eligible to apply. Also, agencies operated by religious organizations that serve secular needs may be eligible if the programs have financial and governing autonomy separate from the parent organization. They must also have space formally dedicated to their programs.

Some elementary and secondary schools may be eligible in the Foundation's Human Services category, if they predominantly serve individuals with physical and/or developmental disabilities.

FINANCIAL DATA:
Amount of support per award: Varies.
Total amount of support: $120,000,000 to $150,000,000 annually.

NO. AWARDS: 521 for the year 2019.

REPRESENTATIVE AWARDS:
$205,000 to Community Catalyst Inc.; $436,015 to Michigan Public Health Institute; $250,000 to Dorothy Day House.

APPLICATION INFO:
Grant and social investment opportunities are announced online. Only electronic application is accepted.
Duration: Varies.

PUBLICATIONS:
Annual report.

ADDRESS INQUIRIES TO:
Grants Inquiry Coordinator
(See address above.)

ALBERT AND BESSIE MAE KRONKOSKY CHARITABLE FOUNDATION   [173]
112 East Pecan, Suite 830
San Antonio, TX 78205
(210) 475-9000
Fax: (210) 354-2204
E-mail: kronfndn@kronkosky.org
Web Site: www.kronkosky.org

FOUNDED: 1991

AREAS OF INTEREST:
Elderly, youth, child abuse and neglect, persons with disabilities, culture and the arts, museums, libraries, prevention of cruelty to animals, health, parks, zoos and wildlife sanctuaries.

TYPE:
Capital grants; Challenge/matching grants; Endowments; General operating grants; Matching gifts; Project/program grants; Research grants; Seed money grants; Technical assistance; Training grants; Research contracts.

YEAR PROGRAM STARTED: 1999

PURPOSE:
To produce profound good that is tangible and measurable in Bandera, Bexar, Comal, and Kendall counties in Texas by implementing the Kronkoskys' charitable purposes.

LEGAL BASIS:
Private foundation.

ELIGIBILITY:
Corporate organizations that are exempt under Section 501(c)(3) of the Internal Revenue Code. The Foundation will not make grants to individuals or for-profit organizations. In addition, the Foundation has a geographic limitation that requires that grant funds be used in the specific counties listed below.

GEOG. RESTRICTIONS: Bandera, Bexar, Comal and Kendall counties, Texas.

FINANCIAL DATA:
Amount of support per award: $10,000 to $1,000,000 for the year 2019. Average grant: $147,000.

Total amount of support: $14,873,175 for the year 2019.

NO. MOST RECENT APPLICANTS: 186 for the year 2019.

NO. AWARDS: 101 grants for the year 2019.

APPLICATION INFO:
Letter of Inquiry may be submitted online or mailed to the address above. If the Letter of Inquiry meets requirements, it will be reviewed by Foundation's staff within 10 days of receipt. If the proposal is accepted, an application package as well as a timeline for submission of the grant proposal will be forwarded. If proposal is not accepted, notification in writing will be sent. Please note geographic requirement.
Duration: Usually one year.
Deadline: Letters of Inquiry will be accepted throughout the year and reviewed on a rolling basis.

PUBLICATIONS:
Program guidelines; annual report (online only).

IRS I.D.: 74-6385152

ADDRESS INQUIRIES TO:
Tullos Wells, Managing Director
(See address above.)

THE JEAN AND E. FLOYD KVAMME FOUNDATION
P.O. Box 2494
Saratoga, CA 95070
(408) 395-2829
Fax: (408) 354-0804

TYPE:
Capital grants; Development grants; General operating grants; Project/program grants. Medical grants are given primarily in the areas of Alzheimers, leukemia, arthritis, and spondylitis; however, grants for research in other areas are considered.

See entry 1402 for full listing.

LAIDLAW FOUNDATION   [174]
2 St. Clair Avenue East
3rd Floor
Toronto ON M4T 2T5 Canada
(416) 964-3614 ext. 301
Fax: (416) 975-1428
E-mail: voctive@laidlawfdn.org
Web Site: laidlawfdn.org

FOUNDED: 1949

AREAS OF INTEREST:
Youth engagement, youth social infrastructure and policy development.

NAME(S) OF PROGRAMS:
● **Youth Action Fund**

TYPE:
General operating grants; Project/program grants. The Youth Action Fund offers grants to grassroots initiatives working with youth who are underserved by the education system and overrepresented in the justice and child welfare systems.

YEAR PROGRAM STARTED: 1949

PURPOSE:
To tackle barriers facing young people in the justice, education and child welfare systems.

LEGAL BASIS:
Private family foundation.

ELIGIBILITY:
Initiatives must be Ontario-based, demonstrate youth leadership, and be based within the communities they are serving and/or with a proven history of working with the communities they identify. Distant programming with First Nations must be welcomed by invitation and/or in partnership with the youth and supported by their community-based allies.

GEOG. RESTRICTIONS: Ontario, Canada.

FINANCIAL DATA:
Amount of support per award: Up to $100,000 per year.
Total amount of support: Varies.

NO. AWARDS: 8 for the year 2020.

APPLICATION INFO:
E-mail info@laidlawfdn.org for information regarding this grant program.
Duration: Up to three years.
Deadline: Varies.

ADDRESS INQUIRIES TO:
Veanna Octive, Grants Manager
(See address and e-mail above.)

LAMB FOUNDATION   [175]
P.O. Box 1705
Lake Oswego, OR 97035
(503) 635-8010
E-mail: lambfdn@lambfoundation.org
Web Site: www.lambfoundation.org

FOUNDED: 1971

AREAS OF INTEREST:
Social services for youth and children, arts, and environment.

TYPE:
Challenge/matching grants; General operating grants; Project/program grants.

LEGAL BASIS:
Private foundation.

ELIGIBILITY:
Applicants must be nonprofit 501(c)(3) public charity organizations.

GEOG. RESTRICTIONS: Pacific Northwest.

FINANCIAL DATA:
Amount of support per award: Typical grants: $5,000 to $15,000.
Total amount of support: Approximately $275,000.

NO. MOST RECENT APPLICANTS: 15 for the year 2019.

NO. AWARDS: 42.

REPRESENTATIVE AWARDS:
$15,000 to Eastern Oregon Regional Arts Council, La Grande, OR, for access to the arts for rural youth; $15,000 to Pacific Rivers, Portland, OR, for the Salmon-Safe Timber Initiative; $15,000 to YouthCare, Seattle, WA, for the YouthBuild Program.

APPLICATION INFO:
The Foundation does not accept unsolicited applications. Upon invitation, application information will be sent to the prospective applicant.
Duration: One year.
Deadline: Included in application materials sent to invited applicants.

PUBLICATIONS:
Brochure.

IRS I.D.: 23-7120564

STAFF:
Debra Iguchi, Administrator

ADDRESS INQUIRIES TO:
Debra Iguchi, Administrator
(See address above.)

*PLEASE NOTE:
Prospective applicants are encouraged to contact the office or web site periodically for changes.

LAND O'LAKES
FOUNDATION   [176]
4001 Lexington Avenue North
Arden Hills, MN 55126
(651) 375-2470
E-mail: landolakesfoundation@landolakes.com
Web Site: www.landolakesinc.com/responsibility

FOUNDED: 1997

AREAS OF INTEREST:
Hunger, education and community.

CONSULTING OR VOLUNTEER SERVICES:
Group projects.

NAME(S) OF PROGRAMS:
● **California Regions Grant Program**
● **Community Grants Program**
● **Dollars for Doers Program**
● **Matching Gifts to Education Program**
● **Member Co-op Match Program**
● **Mid-Atlantic Grant Program**

TYPE:
Capital grants; Endowments; General operating grants; Matching gifts; Project/program grants. Major support is in the form of cash contributions, supplemented with food and product donations to Feeding America National Food Bank Network only.

California Regions Grant Program funds community projects in three areas of California: Orland, Tulare/Kings/Bakersfield and Ontario, initiated by Land O'Lakes dairy member-leaders.

Community Grants Program provides support through cash grants to nonprofit organizations that are working to improve communities where Land O'Lakes has a significant concentration of members or employees. Foundation's primary focus area is hunger and hunger-related issues.

Dollars for Doers Program recognizes employee and retiree volunteerism with financial contributions to 501(c)(3) nonprofit organizations based on volunteer hours.

Matching Gifts to Education Program matches gifts by full- and part-time employees, Board of Directors members and Leadership Council members to grades K-12, postsecondary education, and public radio and public television stations.

Member Co-op Match Program matches dollar-for-dollar the cash donations of member cooperatives, thus doubling the funds available for hometown projects.

Mid-Atlantic Grant Program funds community projects in Maryland, New York, Pennsylvania and Virginia, initiated by Land O'Lakes dairy member-leaders.

YEAR PROGRAM STARTED: 1981

PURPOSE:
To demonstrate a commitment to improving and enhancing the quality of life in communities where Land O'Lakes has facilities, plants, members and employees; to

invest and participate in community programs that strengthen and preserve the quality of rural life; to encourage and support employee volunteerism.

LEGAL BASIS:
Corporate foundation.

ELIGIBILITY:
Contributions are generally restricted to organizations which have been granted 501(c)(3) tax-exempt status and are working to improve communities where Land O'Lakes has a significant concentration of members or employees. Contributions are focused in the western, north central and eastern states. Of our donations, 85% will be made in rural areas and 15% in urban areas within those states.

Funds generally will not be used for lobbying, political and religious organizations, veteran, fraternal and labor organizations, fund-raising events, benefits or advertising, national groups, individuals, scholarships, private colleges and universities, disease/medical research or treatment or racing/sports sponsorships.

Matching Gift recipient organizations must be located in the U.S. and be tax-exempt under Section 501(c)(3) of the Internal Revenue Code. Eligible institutions include the following:
(1) elementary and secondary schools that are fully accredited by the Department of Education;
(2) public or private colleges, universities, junior colleges, technical/vocational institutes, community colleges and graduate professional schools with appropriate regional or professional accreditation, or tax-exempt alumni funds, foundations or associations that collect funds exclusively for the direct benefit of an eligible institution and;
(3) public radio and television stations that meet the criteria established by the Corporation for Public Broadcasting.

Organizations are eligible for only one grant per calendar year.

FINANCIAL DATA:
Amount of support per award: Varies.
Total amount of support: Approximately $13,200,000 for the year 2017.
Matching fund requirements: Cash only.

CO-OP FUNDING PROGRAMS: Through the Member Co-op Match Program, Land O'Lakes member cooperatives may request that the Foundation match their donations to local nonprofits, within the parameters of the program.

REPRESENTATIVE AWARDS:
Feeding America National Food Bank Network.

APPLICATION INFO:
Grant applications are by invitation only.
Duration: Varies.

PUBLICATIONS:
Contributions program guidelines.

IRS I.D.: 41-1864977

ADDRESS INQUIRIES TO:
Vice President
Land O'Lakes Foundation
P.O. Box 64101
St. Paul, MN 55164-0101

LAND O'LAKES FOUNDATION [177]

4001 Lexington Avenue North
Arden Hills, MN 55126
(651) 375-2470
E-mail: landolakesfoundation@landolakes.com
Web Site: www.landolakesinc.
com/responsibility

AREAS OF INTEREST:
Dairy science or dairy
manufacturing/marketing.

NAME(S) OF PROGRAMS:
● **John Brandt Memorial Scholarship Fund**

TYPE:
Scholarships. John Brandt Memorial
Scholarship Program is a $5,000 scholarship
available to graduate students pursuing
dairy-related degrees. One or two
scholarships are awarded annually to
deserving candidates who have demonstrated
exceptional commitment and aptitude toward
their field of study.

PURPOSE:
To encourage graduate study in dairy science
or dairy marketing/manufacturing.

LEGAL BASIS:
Corporate foundation.

ELIGIBILITY:
Applicants must be pursuing a program of
study leading to a Master's or Doctorate
degree in dairy cattle nutrition, genetics,
physiology or management, or the
manufacturing, processing or marketing of
milk and dairy products at one of the four
following institutions: University of
Minnesota, University of Wisconsin, Iowa
State University and South Dakota State
University. Such factors as personal
recommendations, scholastic record, planned
program of study and research and future
plans for working in the dairy industry or
closely related fields shall be considered in
making the award.

FINANCIAL DATA:
Total amount of support: Up to $25,000,
depending on need and endowment market
performance.

NO. AWARDS: Up to 2 annually.

APPLICATION INFO:
The Foundation sends out Requests for
Proposals (RFPs) to the qualifying schools to
begin the application process. Those with
recommendations should send an application
form including personal history, transcripts of
scholastic record, and a plan of study and
research to be followed in pursuit of an
advanced degree. Applications should be sent
to the Land O'Lakes Foundation, P.O. Box
64101, MS 2018, St. Paul, MN 55164-0101.

Duration: One academic year. No renewals.

Deadline: June 15.

ADDRESS INQUIRIES TO:
Land O'Lakes Foundation
P.O. Box 64101
MS 2018
St. Paul, MN 55164-0101

*SPECIAL STIPULATIONS:
Scholarships for graduate-level studies.

HERBERT AND GERTRUDE LATKIN CHARITABLE FOUNDATION [178]

1021 Anacapa Street
Santa Barbara, CA 93101
(805) 884-8638
(800) 227-6468
E-mail: premier.california@unionbank.com

FOUNDED: 1991

AREAS OF INTEREST:
Animal cruelty, child abuse, emergency
medical services, health and welfare to
elderly and needy people, scholarships to
deserving college students.

TYPE:
Project/program grants; Scholarships.

YEAR PROGRAM STARTED: 1991

PURPOSE:
To promote the health and welfare of the
elderly; to prevent cruelty to animals; to
provide emergency medical service for
persons suffering as a result of calamity or
disaster; to prevent child abuse; to provide
assistance to the needy; to provide
scholarships to college students.

LEGAL BASIS:
Private family foundation.

ELIGIBILITY:
Grants are made to organizations that have
tax-exempt status under Section 501(c)(3) of
the Internal Revenue Code. No grants are
made to individuals or religious
organizations.

GEOG. RESTRICTIONS: Santa Barbara County,
California.

FINANCIAL DATA:
Amount of support per award: Varies.
Total amount of support: $295,769 for the
year 2018.

NO. AWARDS: 54 for the year 2018.

APPLICATION INFO:
Send a letter of inquiry outlining the
organization's goal and purposes, the
intended use and amount of the grant
requested and 501(c)(3) letter.

Duration: One year. Renewal possible.

Deadline: April 1 and October 1.

IRS I.D.: 77-6070540

ADDRESS INQUIRIES TO:
Stephanie Eubanks, Trust Officer
(See address above.)

THE BLANCHE AND IRVING LAURIE FOUNDATION [179]

P.O. Box 53
Roseland, NJ 07068-5788
(973) 993-1743
Fax: (973) 993-3146

AREAS OF INTEREST:
Arts, children, needs of the elderly,
education, medical care and needs of the
Jewish community.

TYPE:
Capital grants; Project/program grants.

LEGAL BASIS:
Private foundation.

ELIGIBILITY:
Funds given for specific projects only. No
funds for general organization endowments,
nor to meet general operating expenses or
budget deficits.

GEOG. RESTRICTIONS: Social service programs:
New Jersey.

FINANCIAL DATA:
Amount of support per award: $25,000 to
$50,000.

APPLICATION INFO:
Submit seven copies of proposal including
statement of program objectives, project
budget, plans for publicizing the project,
background information about the
organization and copy of IRS tax-exemption
letter.

Duration: Varies.

Deadline: Proposals accepted year-round.

PUBLICATIONS:
Informational brochure.

BOARD OF TRUSTEES:
Laura Barron
Gene R. Korf, Esq.
Scott Korf
Richard A. Patt
Harvey Rich
Robert M. Zagoren

ADDRESS INQUIRIES TO:
Gene R. Korf, Esq., Executive Director
(See address above.)

LIBRA FOUNDATION [180]

Three Canal Plaza, Suite 500
Portland, ME 04101
(207) 879-6280
Fax: (207) 879-6281
E-mail: kathi@librafoundation.org
Web Site: www.librafoundation.org

FOUNDED: 1989

AREAS OF INTEREST:
Arts, culture and humanities, education,
environment, health, human services,
public/society benefit and religion.

TYPE:
Grants-in-aid; Project/program grants.

YEAR PROGRAM STARTED: 1989

PURPOSE:
To strive for innovative ways to enrich
Maine, empower communities, and enhance
the quality of life of all Maine citizens.

ELIGIBILITY:
Charitable nonprofit organizations whose
activities, operations, or purposes take place
only within the state of Maine. Religious
organizations are eligible. Organizations must
supply a copy of tax-exempt 501(c)(3) letter.
Grants are not made to individuals.

GEOG. RESTRICTIONS: Maine.

FINANCIAL DATA:
Amount of support per award: Up to
$25,000.
Total amount of support: Approximately
$5,300,000.

NO. MOST RECENT APPLICANTS: 317.

NO. AWARDS: 48.

APPLICATION INFO:
Applicants are asked to complete a
two-paged application in accordance with the
Foundation's guidelines, both of which may
be obtained from the Foundation web site.

Duration: One-time grant. May reapply after
expiration of one year.

Deadline: February 15, May 15, August 15
and November 15.

ADDRESS INQUIRIES TO:
Kathi Giedris, Administrative Assistant
(See address above.)

LILLY ENDOWMENT INC.   [181]

2801 North Meridian Street
Indianapolis, IN 46208
(317) 924-5471
Fax: (317) 926-4431
E-mail: cebulaj@lei.org
Web Site: www.lillyendowment.org

FOUNDED: 1937

AREAS OF INTEREST:
Community development, education and
religion.

TYPE:
Awards/prizes; Challenge/matching grants;
Conferences/seminars; Development grants;
Fellowships; General operating grants;
Matching gifts; Project/program grants;
Research grants. In the area of community
development, grantmaking focuses primarily
on enhancing the quality of life in
Indianapolis and Indiana. Grants support
human and social needs, central-city and
neighborhood revitalization, low- and
moderate-income housing, and arts and
culture in Indianapolis. On a statewide level,
grants are made through initiatives to support
community foundations and United Ways.
Nationally, Lilly Endowment provides
support on an invitational basis for
compelling other causes that are consistent
with areas of interest, such as disaster relief
and recovery efforts and programs for
veterans' affairs and their families.

In the area of education, grantmaking
revolves primarily around objectives to
enhance and increase the educational
attainment and meaningful economic
opportunities of residents in Indiana and the
overall aim of improving the quality of life
of the state's residents. Lilly Endowment
supports efforts in Indiana on an invitational
basis that promote high-quality early
childhood education, strengthen K-12
education, prepare students for education and
careers beyond high school, connect college
students and graduates with meaningful
employment opportunities in Indiana,
enhance the effectiveness of Indiana colleges
and universities to prepare their students for
successful lives and careers, and build the
state's intellectual capital. Nationally, Lilly
Endowment supports on an invitational basis
programs that expand and enhance higher
education opportunities for African
Americans, Native Americans and Latino
Americans.

In the area of religion, support for programs
that enrich the religious lives of American
Christians, mainly by supporting efforts to
call, support and educate a new generation of
talented pastors and to strengthen current
pastors in their capacities for excellence in
ministry; support for programs that seek to
help congregations be healthy communities
of faith; support for theological seminaries
and other educational and religious
institutions that share these aims; and support
for projects which strengthen the
contributions that religious ideas, practices,
values and institutions make to the common
good. In addition, through grants to major
cultural institutions and 501(c)(3) news and
media organizations, Lilly Endowment seeks
to foster public understanding about religious
and lift up in fair and accurate ways the
contributions that people of all faiths and
diverse religious communities make to our
greater civic well-being.

In the area of youth, support for
direct-service organizations in central
Indiana; support for building capacity of
intermediary organizations throughout the
state; and support for professional
development for the staff and volunteer
leadership of these organizations.

In the area of fund-raising and philanthropy,
support for programs (nationally and in
Indiana) to increase the charitable giving
among Americans; support for efforts to
create a body of reliable knowledge about
giving and fund-raising; and support for
scholarly pursuit of the subject.

YEAR PROGRAM STARTED: 1937

PURPOSE:
To support the causes of community
development, education and religion.

LEGAL BASIS:
Private foundation.

ELIGIBILITY:
Applicants must be 501(c)(3) tax-exempt
public organizations and institutions with
appropriate interests in targeted areas.
Grantmaking prohibitions generally include
loans or cash to individuals, health care
projects, mass media projects, endowments,
libraries outside Indianapolis, and general
operating support/capital campaigns for
organizations outside of Indiana.

GEOG. RESTRICTIONS: Primarily Indianapolis
and the state of Indiana.

FINANCIAL DATA:
Grants vary in amount depending on the
needs and nature of the request.
Amount of support per award: Varies.
Total amount of support: $527,700,000 in
grants paid (excluding employee incentive
matching program) for the year 2019.
Matching fund requirements: Varies.

NO. MOST RECENT APPLICANTS: 2,121
(excluding employee incentive matching
program requests) for the year 2018.

NO. AWARDS: 1,009 grants paid for the year
2019.

APPLICATION INFO:
Except for specialized programs, no official
application forms are required. Guidelines for
applicants are found on the web site. The
usual first step is a two-page letter outlining
the project and budget and a description of
the applicant organization, including a
statement of federal tax-exempt status.
Duration: One to three years; typically, one
year.
Deadline: Applications accepted on an
ongoing basis.

PUBLICATIONS:
Application guidelines; annual report.

IRS I.D.: 35-0868122

OFFICERS:
N. Clay Robbins, Chairman, President and
Chief Executive Officer
Diane M. Stenson, Vice President and
Treasurer
Ben W. Blanton, Vice President, Secretary
and General Counsel
Rob Smith, Senior Vice President for
Collaborative Strategies
Julie A. Siegler, Vice President for
Administration
Ronni Kloth, Vice President for Community
Development
Ted Maple, Vice President for Education

Jacqueline Dowd, Vice President for
Evaluation and Special Initiatives
Peter A. Buek, Vice President for
Investments
Christopher L. Coble, Vice President for
Religion

DIRECTORS:
Daniel P. Carmichael
Clarence Crane
Craig R. Dykstra
William G. Enright
Charles E. Golden
Jennett M. Hill
John C. Lechleiter
Eli Lilly, II
Mary K. Lisher
N. Clay Robbins
David N. Shane

ADDRESS INQUIRIES TO:
Program Office
(See address above.)

*SPECIAL STIPULATIONS:
Awards are made to 501(c)(3) groups only.

LINCOLN FINANCIAL
FOUNDATION   [182]

1300 South Clinton Street
Fort Wayne, IN 46802
(260) 455-3868
Fax: (260) 455-4004
E-mail: deb.washler@lfg.com
Web Site: www.lfg.com

FOUNDED: 1962

AREAS OF INTEREST:
Financial wellness, youth education, and
human services.

CONSULTING OR VOLUNTEER SERVICES:
Volunteer Involvement Program for
employees of Lincoln Financial Group.

TYPE:
Matching gifts; Project/program grants.

YEAR PROGRAM STARTED: 1962

PURPOSE:
To enhance the quality of life and help
individuals face their futures with confidence
in communities where employees work.

LEGAL BASIS:
Corporate Foundation.

ELIGIBILITY:
Applicants must be 501(c)(3) organizations.

No grants to individuals, for endowments, for
sponsorship of sporting events or for the
purchase of tickets.

GEOG. RESTRICTIONS: Phoenix, Arizona;
Hartford, Connecticut; Atlanta, Georgia; Fort
Wayne, Indiana; Boston, Massachusetts;
Omaha, Nebraska; Concord and Dover, New
Hampshire; Charlotte and Greensboro, North
Carolina; Philadelphia, Pennsylvania.

FINANCIAL DATA:
Amount of support per award: Varies.
Total amount of support: Over $10,100,000
for the year 2020.

NO. AWARDS: 376 for the year 2020.

APPLICATION INFO:
The Foundation is not accepting unsolicited
grant applications.
Deadline: Varies.

PUBLICATIONS:
Guidelines.

IRS I.D.: 35-6042099

ADDRESS INQUIRIES TO:
Program Officer
(See address above.)

THE LOATS FOUNDATION, INC.   [183]
35 East Church Street
Frederick, MD 21701
(301) 663-6361
Fax: (301) 663-7747
E-mail: hahnh0630@aol.com
helen@twinspires.org

FOUNDED: 1979

AREAS OF INTEREST:
Scholarship for Frederick County residents only and charitable organizations of Frederick County, MD.

TYPE:
Scholarships.

YEAR PROGRAM STARTED: 1979

PURPOSE:
To help residents of Frederick County, MD go on to higher education by providing financial aid.

LEGAL BASIS:
Nonprofit foundation.

ELIGIBILITY:
Applicant must be a resident of Frederick County, MD. Scholarships are distributed by colleges on a need basis.

GEOG. RESTRICTIONS: Frederick County, Maryland.

FINANCIAL DATA:
Amount of support per award: $3,000 cap.
Total amount of support: Varies.

APPLICATION INFO:
Applications for scholarships are available at all Maryland colleges and universities.
Duration: One year. Renewable on need basis.

ADDRESS INQUIRIES TO:
Helen Hahn, Secretary
(See address above.)

THE LUBRIZOL FOUNDATION   [184]
29400 Lakeland Boulevard, Mail Drop 054B
Wickliffe, OH 44092-2298
(440) 347-1797
Fax: (440) 347-1858
E-mail: karen.lerchbacher@lubrizol.com
Web Site: www.lubrizol.com

FOUNDED: 1952

AREAS OF INTEREST:
Education, health and human services, civic, cultural, environmental and youth activities.

NAME(S) OF PROGRAMS:
- **Community Connection Employee Volunteer Gift Program**
- **Matching Gift Program**

TYPE:
Capital grants; Fellowships; General operating grants; Matching gifts; Project/program grants; Scholarships. The Foundation has scholarship programs at 22 selected colleges and universities. It also matches gifts of Lubrizol employees to most charitable organizations on a dollar-for-dollar basis.

In the area of education, support is given for scholarships, fellowships and awards in selected fields of study through selected colleges and universities, with major emphasis on the study of chemistry and chemical and mechanical engineering, capital and operating grants to colleges, universities, schools, educational programs and combined educational funds.

In the area of health and human services, support is provided for combined funds, direct grants to health and human service activities.

In the area of civic and cultural, support is provided for performing arts organizations, schools of fine arts and museums.

In the area of youth activities, support is given to programs that contribute to character-building, such as those which promote good citizenship, self-reliance, an understanding of free enterprise and an appreciation of nature and the environment.

In the environmental area, support is given to parks, nature centers, conservancies and local environmental education efforts.

YEAR PROGRAM STARTED: 1952

PURPOSE:
To support educational, youth, health, human services, civic and cultural and environmental activities of a tax-exempt, charitable nature.

LEGAL BASIS:
Private, tax-exempt foundation.

ELIGIBILITY:
Grants are made to U.S. nonprofit, educational or other charitable tax-exempt organizations. Grants are not generally made to endowments, religious or political purposes or individuals.

GEOG. RESTRICTIONS: Primarily Greater Cleveland, Ohio and Houston, Texas.

FINANCIAL DATA:
Amount of support per award: Grants vary in amount, depending upon the needs and nature of the request.
Total amount of support: $2,593,648, including matching gifts, for the year 2020.
Matching fund requirements: 1:1 match; $100 minimum; $5,000 maximum, and five gifts maximum.

NO. AWARDS: 465 grants for the year 2020.

REPRESENTATIVE AWARDS:
$30,000 to Cleveland Zoological Society in support of the Zoo Education and Workforce Development Initiative; $25,000 to Vocational Guidance Services to begin production for the Cleveland Clinic during the COVID-19 pandemic; $10,000 to University Hospitals in support of the Caregivers Fund; $33,710 to the American Red Cross; $30,000 to Greater Cleveland Food Bank; $25,000 to the Great Lakes Science Center for exhibit operations.

APPLICATION INFO:
Grant proposals should include the following: (1) a cover letter that summarizes the purpose of the request signed by the executive officer of the organization; (2) a narrative of specific information related to the subject of the request; (3) current audited financial statements and a specific project budget, if applicable and; (4) documentation of the organization's Federal tax-exempt status.

Additional descriptive literature (annual report, brochures, etc.) that accurately characterizes the overall activities of the

organization is appreciated. Upon review, further information may be requested including an interview or site visit.

Applicants will receive written notification of the decision on their proposal. An organization whose request has been declined should not submit another proposal for at least 12 months after such notification.
Duration: One year, with possible renewal. Some grants are ongoing.

PUBLICATIONS:
Annual report.

IRS I.D.: 34-6500595

OFFICERS:
Eric R. Schnur, Chairman
E.A. Grove, President
J. Bryan Pitts, Treasurer
K.A. Lerchbacher, Secretary

TRUSTEES:
J.A. Edgar
E.A. Grove
K.L. Jethrow
K.A. Lerchbacher
Eric R. Schnur

ADDRESS INQUIRIES TO:
Karen A. Lerchbacher, Program Officer
(See address above.)

THE HENRY LUCE FOUNDATION, INC.   [185]
51 Madison Avenue, 30th Floor
New York, NY 10010
(212) 489-7700
Fax: (212) 581-9541
E-mail: info@hluce.org
Web Site: www.hluce.org

FOUNDED: 1936

AREAS OF INTEREST:
Interdisciplinary exploration of higher education, increased understanding between Asia and the U.S., the study of religion and theology, scholarship in American art, advancement of women in science and engineering, and environmental and public policy programs.

NAME(S) OF PROGRAMS:
- **American Art Program**
- **Asia Program**
- **Higher Education Program**
- **Clare Boothe Luce Program**
- **Luce Foundation Religion and Theology Program**
- **Luce Scholars Program**
- **Public Policy Program**

TYPE:
Fellowships; Project/program grants; Scholarships. American Art Program focuses on the American fine and decorative arts and is committed to scholarship and the overall enhancement of this field. The program is national in scope and provides support for all periods and genres of American art history.

The Clare Boothe Luce Program promotes the advancement of American women through higher education in the sciences, engineering and mathematics.

The Luce Foundation's Religion and Theology program encourages the development of leadership for religious communities through theological education, and fosters scholarship that links the academy to churches and the wider public. The program provides funding for seminary education, leadership, ecumenical and interreligious programs, and religion and the arts.

The Luce Scholars Program provides stipends and internships for young Americans to live and work in Asia each year.

PURPOSE:
To promote interdisciplinary exploration of higher education, increased understanding between Asia and the U.S., the study of religion and theology, scholarship in American art, opportunities for women in science, mathematics and engineering, and public policy programs.

ELIGIBILITY:
The Foundation does not support health care or medical projects and does not fund development assistance work overseas. It does not normally assist journalism, media and film projects or the performing arts. The Foundation does not offer funding for individuals.

FINANCIAL DATA:
Amount of support per award: Varies.
Total amount of support: Varies.

APPLICATION INFO:
The Foundation receives inquiries through its web site portal. There is an eligibility quiz to perform prior to being able to submit an inquiry. Applicants must review the program guidelines before taking the eligibility quiz. If successfully completed, the applicant will be directed to create an account. Once registration is approved, applicant may begin the inquiry process.
Duration: Varies.
Deadline: Varies.

LYNDHURST FOUNDATION [186]
517 East Fifth Street
Chattanooga, TN 37403-1826
(423) 756-0767
Fax: (423) 756-0770
E-mail: bclark@lyndhurstfoundation.org
Web Site: www.lyndhurstfoundation.org

FOUNDED: 1938

AREAS OF INTEREST:
Education, conservation, arts, culture, economy, urban design and development, neighborhood revitalization and physical health.

Enhancing the quality of Chattanooga's public gathering places in downtown and along the riverfront, plus its public schools, its diverse arts and cultural organizations and its natural environment. Beyond the city's boundaries, the Foundation wants to be involved in projects that protect and enhance the natural environment of the southern Appalachian region.

TYPE:
Matching gifts; Project/program grants. The Foundation intends to focus upon continued development of the Tennessee Riverpark, redevelopment of the Southside as a live-and-work urban neighborhood, facilitation of historic preservation, stimulation of downtown housing development, strengthening of the city's arts and cultural life, protection and enhancement of the community's natural environment, the reform of the community's public schools, the continued development of improved housing opportunities for people of modest means and innovations in social service

programs that provide genuine progress against social problems and genuine enhancement of community strengths in Chattanooga.

YEAR PROGRAM STARTED: 1978

PURPOSE:
To identify and invest in initiatives, institutions, people and programs that contribute to the long-term livability and resilience of the greater Chattanooga, TN region.

LEGAL BASIS:
Private foundation.

ELIGIBILITY:
Applicants must be 501(c)(3) organizations.

Grants are distributed primarily at the initiative of the Foundation through the cultivation of strategic partnerships with nonprofit organizations which have the demonstrated capacity and leadership to engender positive and measurable outcomes within the Foundation's declared areas of interest.

Unsolicited proposals will not be eligible for consideration.

GEOG. RESTRICTIONS: The greater Chattanooga, Tennessee region.

FINANCIAL DATA:
Amount of support per award: Varies.
Total amount of support: Grants of $4,105,222 for the year 2020.

NO. AWARDS: Varies.

REPRESENTATIVE AWARDS:
$50,000 to SoundCorps; $440,000 to Open Space Institute; $815,000 to River City Company.

APPLICATION INFO:
Potential partners will be invited to submit grant proposals that:
(1) describe the program of work to be undertaken;
(2) indicate the desired level of funding;
(3) list the results that should be achieved and;
(4) define the means by which the project outcomes will be evaluated.

The narrative section of the proposal should be limited to three pages and include the following attachments:
(1) a description of the sponsoring organization;
(2) a list of the board of directors and staff;
(3) a copy of the organization's annual budget (both income and expenditures);
(4) an estimated project budget with line items and;
(5) a copy of the organization's tax-exempt ruling from the IRS.
Duration: One year. Renewal possible for up to three years.
Deadline: Proposals are due six weeks in advance of the Foundation's quarterly board meeting dates, which typically occur in February, May, August and November. Program staff will be available to work with applicants to ensure that materials are delivered on a timely basis and in the required format.

OFFICERS:
James O. Kennedy, Chairman of the Board
Benic M. Clark, III, President/Treasurer
Dana B. Perry, Secretary

TRUSTEES:
Andrew D. Carroll

Melony Collins
Ann Coulter
Kathleen S. Hunt, M.D.
James O. Kennedy
N. Carter Newbold, IV
Dana B. Perry
Margaret W. Townsend
Aaron D. Webb, Esq.

STAFF:
Benic M. Clark, III, President/Treasurer
Macon C. Toledano, Associate Director
Kathleen Nolte, Program Director
Nena Powell, Controller

ADDRESS INQUIRIES TO:
Catherine C. Cox
(See telephone number above.)

*PLEASE NOTE:
Funding is limited to a 16-county, tri-state area surrounding Chattanooga.

M & M AREA COMMUNITY FOUNDATION
1110 10th Avenue, Suite L-1
Menominee, MI 49858
(906) 864-3599
E-mail: info@mmacf.org
Web Site: www.mmacf.org

TYPE:
Project/program grants; Scholarships.

See entry 1197 for full listing.

JOHN D. AND CATHERINE T. MACARTHUR FOUNDATION [187]
140 South Dearborn Street
Chicago, IL 60603-5285
(312) 726-8000
E-mail: 4answers@macfound.org
Web Site: www.macfound.org

FOUNDED: 1978

NAME(S) OF PROGRAMS:
● **Awards**
● **Big Bets**
● **Enduring Commitments**
● **Field Support**

TYPE:
Fellowships; General operating grants; Project/program grants. The following specific programs are found under the above general program areas:

Awards: 100 & Change; MacArthur Award for Creative & Effective Institutions; MacArthur Fellows.

Big Bets: Climate Solutions; Criminal Justice; Nuclear Challenges; On Nigeria.

Enduring Commitments: Chicago Commitment; Journalism & Media.

Field Support: Impact Investments; Philanthropy; Technology in the Public Interest.

YEAR PROGRAM STARTED: 1978

PURPOSE:
To build a more just, verdant and peaceful world.

LEGAL BASIS:
Private, independent foundation.

ELIGIBILITY:
The Foundation develops grantmaking strategies designed to meet very specific goals. Please consult the Foundation's web site regarding the grantmaking guidelines for each program.

The Foundation does not provide funding for the following:
(1) scholarships or tuition assistance for undergraduate, graduate or postgraduate studies;
(2) grants to individuals, except for Leaders for a New Chicago and the MacArthur Fellows Program, which is not open to applications or public nominations;
(3) annual fund-raising drives;
(4) paid advertisements or;
(5) political activities or attempts to influence action on specific legislation.

FINANCIAL DATA:
Amount of support per award: Varies.
Total amount of support: $311,545,446 for the year 2020.

NO. MOST RECENT APPLICANTS: Over 1,000 for the year 2020.

NO. AWARDS: 416 for the year 2020.

APPLICATION INFO:
Complete details are available on the Foundation web site.
Duration: One to five years. Renewals by reapplication.
Deadline: Varies.

PUBLICATIONS:
Annual report.

IRS I.D.: 23-7093598

ADDRESS INQUIRIES TO:
Web site: macfound.fluxx.io

*PLEASE NOTE:
The Foundation awards the majority of its grants to organizations identified by its staff. Each year it also awards grants to individuals through the MacArthur Fellows program, which does not accept applications or nominations.

MARBROOK FOUNDATION [188]
730 Second Avenue South
Suite 1400
Minneapolis, MN 55402
(612) 752-1783
Fax: (612) 752-1780
E-mail: mbrooks@marbrookfoundation.org
Web Site: www.marbrookfoundation.org

FOUNDED: 1948

AREAS OF INTEREST:
Arts, environment, immigrants and refugees, and body, mind and spirit.

TYPE:
Capital grants; General operating grants; Project/program grants.

YEAR PROGRAM STARTED: 1948

PURPOSE:
To promote the values of the Brooks Family by making grants and focusing involvement in designated charitable areas and causes that reflect those values.

LEGAL BASIS:
Tax-exempt, private foundation.

ELIGIBILITY:
The Foundation's priorities in the area of arts are projects and programs that foster cultural awareness and understanding and projects and programs that encourage cross-cultural collaboration, community integration, and inclusion.

In the area of environment, the Foundation only makes grants to 501(c)(3) charitable organizations. The Foundation does not fund

health clinics and medical treatment, food shelves or food stamp programs, conferences and events, individual college and academic scholarships or affordable housing.

In the area of immigrants and refugees, the Foundation will consider proposals for programs that provide support in the following areas:
(1) Culturally safe and conducive learning environments for children and youth. These programs may include a focus on mindfulness;
(2) Intentional intercultural learning and cross-cultural experiences;
(3) Healthy development, life-skill development, and well-being for youth and families;
(4) The development of skills for financial independence;
(5) Leadership development and empowerment in the community and;
(6) Cultural preservation.

GEOG. RESTRICTIONS: Seven county metropolitan area of Minneapolis, Minnesota.

FINANCIAL DATA:
Amount of support per award: Minimum $5,000, except Environmental Grants.
Total amount of support: $652,500 for the year 2019.

NO. AWARDS: Varies.

REPRESENTATIVE AWARDS:
$12,000 to World Savvy for empowering schools to engage immigrant learners; $10,000 to Wilderness Inquiry for introductory outdoor adventures for underserved immigrant youth; $10,000 to Minnesota Museum of American Art for an exhibit called Choice of Weapons, Honor and Glory: The Visions of Gordon Parks and Jamel Shabazz; $30,000 to Fresh Energy for public policy work toward a more equitable clean energy future.

APPLICATION INFO:
Applications must be submitted online.
Deadline: March 1 for Immigrants and Refugees. September 1 for Arts and Environment.

BOARD OF DIRECTORS:
Edward Brooks, Chairperson
Katherine Werner Brooks
Anna Gibson
Markell Hapka
Bill King
John Larsen
Tyson Lien

EXECUTIVE DIRECTOR:
Minna K. Brooks

MARIN COMMUNITY FOUNDATION [189]
5 Hamilton Landing, Suite 200
Novato, CA 94949
(415) 464-2500
Fax: (415) 464-2555
E-mail: info@marincf.org
Web Site: www.marincf.org

FOUNDED: 1986

AREAS OF INTEREST:
Education, economic opportunity, health and environment.

TYPE:
Capital grants; Challenge/matching grants; General operating grants; Project/program grants; Scholarships; Technical assistance.

YEAR PROGRAM STARTED: 1987

PURPOSE:
To encourage and apply philanthropic contributions to help improve the human condition, embrace diversity, promote a humane and democratic society, and enhance the community's quality of life, now and for future generations.

LEGAL BASIS:
Community foundation.

ELIGIBILITY:
Proposals must be consistent with the Foundation's program goals and must meet two additional requirements. First, the applicant must be a public or nonprofit organization and, second, the proposed project must be conducted in and/or benefit the residents of Marin County, CA. Projects with a regional or multi-county benefit may be funded only in proportion to the extent that they benefit the Marin County community.

Ineligible activities include for-profit purposes, basic research, the start-up of new nonprofit organizations that will unnecessarily duplicate existing programs or services or undertake services that can be more effectively provided by other organizations and grants to individuals. Other limitations specific to each program area are outlined in the funding guidelines. No grants are made to individuals.

Buck Trust grants are limited to Marin County.

GEOG. RESTRICTIONS: Grants from the Buck Trust are restricted to Marin County, California.The Foundation's donor-advised funds support efforts locally and in communities around the world.

FINANCIAL DATA:
The Foundation manages more than $2.18 billion in total assets.
Amount of support per award: Varies.
Total amount of support: Over $244,400,000 in grants annually.

NO. AWARDS: 345.

APPLICATION INFO:
The following procedures apply:
(1) The Foundation issues a Request for Proposals (RFP);
(2) If interested, a representative from a nonprofit organization can register on the Foundation's online Grant Center;
(3) The nonprofit representative can then submit an online Letter of Intent (LOI) for the RFP and;
(4) Following the Foundation's review of the LOIs, selected applicants are invited to submit a full proposal through the Grant Center.
Consult the web site address above for further details.
Duration: Varies. Renewal possible.

PUBLICATIONS:
General information brochure.

IRS I.D.: 94-3007979

OFFICERS:
Thomas Peters, Ph.D., President and Chief Executive Officer
Sid Hartman, Chief Financial and Operating Officer

BOARD OF DIRECTORS:
Mark Buell, Chairperson
Mitch Cohen
Peter Hamilton

Saul Pena
Robert J. Reynolds
Roxanne Richards
Maureen Sedonaen
Daniel Skaff
Debra Wetherby

MARRIOTT INTERNATIONAL, INC. [190]

10400 Fernwood Road
Bethesda, MD 20817
E-mail: community.engagement@marriott.com
Web Site: serve360.marriott.com

FOUNDED: 1927

AREAS OF INTEREST:
Shelter and food, environment, readiness for hotel careers, vitality of children, and embracing diversity and people with disabilities.

TYPE:
Project/program grants. Support to national and global nonprofits that address help, support readiness for jobs, diversity and inclusion, poverty alleviation, and the environment.

LEGAL BASIS:
Corporate contributions program.

ELIGIBILITY:
Grants are made to tax-exempt 501(c)(3) organizations which fulfill important community needs.

FINANCIAL DATA:
Amount of support per award: Varies.
Total amount of support: Varies.

APPLICATION INFO:
The Corporation only accepts requests online via its web site.
Duration: Varies.
Deadline: Before end of October.

PUBLICATIONS:
Application guidelines.

ROBERT R. MCCORMICK FOUNDATION [191]

205 North Michigan Avenue
Suite 4300
Chicago, IL 60601-5927
(312) 445-5000
Fax: (312) 445-5001
E-mail: info@mccormickfoundation.org
Web Site: www.mccormickfoundation.org

FOUNDED: 1955

AREAS OF INTEREST:
Community strengthening, community justice, democracy, youth media, early childhood education, and veterans affairs.

NAME(S) OF PROGRAMS:
● **Communities Program**
● **Community Justice Initiative**
● **Democracy Program**
● **Education Program**
● **Veterans Program**

TYPE:
General operating grants; Project/program grants.

YEAR PROGRAM STARTED: 1955

PURPOSE:
To foster communities of educated, informed and engaged citizens.

ELIGIBILITY:
The Foundation only makes grants to 501(c)(3) organizations that serve charitable purposes and meet the Foundation's program guidelines. Programs that advance a particular religious or sectarian purpose, partisan political or electoral activities, endowments, or individual scholarships or personal research projects are not funded.

FINANCIAL DATA:
Total amount of support: $77,000,000 in total grants approved for the year ended December 31, 2018.

NO. AWARDS: 460 total grants approved for the year ended December 31, 2018.

PUBLICATIONS:
Annual report; program brochures; conference reports.

J.M. MCDONALD FOUNDATION, INC. [192]

P.O. Box 3219
Evergreen, CO 80437-3219
(303) 674-9300
Fax: (303) 674-9216
E-mail: info@jmmcdonaldfoundation.org
Web Site: jmmcdonaldfoundation.org

FOUNDED: 1952

AREAS OF INTEREST:
Education, humanities, health, and a variety of social and human services.

TYPE:
Capital grants; Development grants; Project/program grants.

YEAR PROGRAM STARTED: 1952

LEGAL BASIS:
Private foundation.

ELIGIBILITY:
Nonprofit organizations with appropriate interests are eligible for support. Applicants must be located in the U.S. and have IRS-509A and 501(c)(3) letter. No grants are made to individuals, for projects to influence legislation or elections, or solely for conferences, seminars, workshops, travel or exhibits.

GEOG. RESTRICTIONS: Primarily upstate New York.

FINANCIAL DATA:
Amount of support per award: Grants vary in amount, depending upon the needs and nature of the request.

APPLICATION INFO:
Application for funding through online granting process is available at the Foundation web site.
Duration: One year.
Deadline: April 15 and September 15, with responses in May and October, respectively.

PUBLICATIONS:
Application guidelines.

OFFICERS AND TRUSTEES:
Donald R. McJunkin, President
Nancy J. Palmer, Vice President and Director
Janet E. Stanton, Vice President and Director
Pamela Criswell, Treasurer and Director
Dana Amundson, Secretary and Director
Scott Palmer, Director

JAMES S. MCDONNELL FOUNDATION [193]

1034 South Brentwood Boulevard
Suite 1850
St. Louis, MO 63117
(314) 721-1532
E-mail: info@jsmf.org
Web Site: www.jsmf.org

FOUNDED: 1950

AREAS OF INTEREST:
Understanding human cognition, teacher learning and teacher change in K-12 classrooms; understanding dynamic and multi-scale systems.

NAME(S) OF PROGRAMS:
● **Special Initiatives**
● **Understanding Dynamic and Multi-Scale Systems**
● **Understanding Human Cognition**

TYPE:
Fellowships; Research grants. Collaborative Activity Awards are to initiate interdisciplinary discussions on problems or issues, to help launch interdisciplinary research networks, or to fund communities of researchers dedicated to developing new methods, tools and applications of basic research.

Postdoctoral Fellowship Awards are intended to provide students in the final stages of completing a Ph.D. degree more leeway in identifying and securing postdoctoral training opportunities in dynamic and multi-scale systems.

Scholar Awards provide funding in the area of Understanding Human Cognition.

Teachers as Learners focuses on research that builds from a cognitive science perspective on teachers as learners.

YEAR PROGRAM STARTED: 2000

PURPOSE:
To encourage investigators to engage difficult problems; to support ideas and approaches departing from conventional wisdom; to fund novel or interdisciplinary proposals.

LEGAL BASIS:
Private foundation.

FINANCIAL DATA:
Amount of support per award: Collaborative Activity Awards: Varies; Postdoctoral Fellowship: $200,000; Scholar Awards: Up to $600,000, depending on award; Teachers as Learners: Maximum $2,500,000 over five years.

NO. MOST RECENT APPLICANTS: Approximately 150 for the year 2019.

NO. AWARDS: 25.

APPLICATION INFO:
Guidelines and all program applications are available on the Foundation's web site. Letters of inquiry are accepted by invitation only for collaborative fund-seekers.
Duration: Varies.
Deadline: Postdoctoral Fellowship and Teachers as Learners: Varies. There are no deadlines for Collaborative Activity Awards.

IRS I.D.: 54-2074788

OFFICERS:
Dr. Susan Fitzpatrick, President

BOARD OF DIRECTORS:
Jeanne M. Champer
Holly M. James
Alicia S. McDonnell

James S. McDonnell, III
Jeffrey M. McDonnell
John F. McDonnell
Katherine Pipoli
Marcella M. Stevens

ADDRESS INQUIRIES TO:
See e-mail address above.

MCGREGOR FUND   [194]
333 West Fort Street, Suite 2090
Detroit, MI 48226-3134
(313) 963-3495
Fax: (313) 963-3512
E-mail: heidi@mcgregorfund.org
Web Site: www.mcgregorfund.org

FOUNDED: 1925

AREAS OF INTEREST:
Basic needs, recovery and restoration, and
skill building in metropolitan Detroit.

TYPE:
General operating grants; Project/program
grants. Limited capital grants; program and
operational support.

YEAR PROGRAM STARTED: 1925

PURPOSE:
To relieve misfortunes and promote the
well-being of mankind.

LEGAL BASIS:
Tax-exempt private foundation.

ELIGIBILITY:
Tax-exempt, Internal Revenue Code 501(c)(3)
organizations in the Detroit metropolitan
area.

The Fund does not provide loan funds, make
direct grants to students for scholarships,
make grants for travel, conferences, seminars
or workshops, or make grants to individuals.

GEOG. RESTRICTIONS: Tri-county area of
Detroit, Michigan.

FINANCIAL DATA:
Amount of support per award: $30,000 to
$1,000,000.

Total amount of support: Varies.

NO. AWARDS: Approximately 80 for the year
2019.

APPLICATION INFO:
Guidelines are available on the Fund web
site.

Duration: No grants are made on a
continuing basis.

Deadline: Submit applications three months
prior to Board meeting dates in March, June,
September and December.

PUBLICATIONS:
Annual report; guidelines; application
procedures.

IRS I.D.: 38-0808800

OFFICERS AND TRUSTEES:
Richard L. Rogers, Chairman
Cynthia N. Ford, Vice Chairman
Kate Levin Markel, President and Secretary
William W. Shelden, Jr., Treasurer
Gerard M. Anderson
Joyce Jenereaux
Leslie A. Murphy
Susan Schooley, M.D.

ADDRESS INQUIRIES TO:
See e-mail address above.

THE MCLEAN
CONTRIBUTIONSHIP   [195]
230 Sugartown Road
Suite 30
Wayne, PA 19087
(610) 989-8090
Web Site: fdnweb.org/mclean

FOUNDED: 1951

AREAS OF INTEREST:
Education, environment, health and hospitals,
care of the elderly and youth development.

TYPE:
Capital grants; Endowments. The
Contributionship makes a relatively limited
number of grants for projects of long-term
benefit. Its trustees focus on capital projects:
bricks and mortar and endowment; they may
make grants in ways to encourage the
successful funding of projects.

PURPOSE:
To support understanding and preserving the
environment; to encourage compassionate
and cost-effective health care; to improve the
quality of life through education and through
support of the communities' cultural assets
usually in the form of capital projects.

LEGAL BASIS:
Private foundation.

ELIGIBILITY:
Organizations, including some religious,
classified as 501(c)(3) by the IRS can apply.
Individuals are ineligible.

The Contributionship favors projects that:
(1) stimulate a better understanding of the
natural environment, and encourage the
preservation of its important features;
(2) encourage more compassionate and
cost-effective care for the ill and aging, in an
atmosphere of dignity and self-respect and;
(3) promote education, or medical, scientific
or (on occasion) cultural developments
enhancing the quality of life.

In addition, the trustees from time to time
support projects which:
(1) motivate promising young people to
assess and develop their talents despite social
and economic obstacles and;
(2) encourage those in newspaper and related
fields to become more effective and
responsible in helping people understand
better how events in their communities and
around the world affect them.

GEOG. RESTRICTIONS: Mainly in the Greater
Philadelphia area.

FINANCIAL DATA:
Amount of support per award: $1,000 to
$150,000.

Total amount of support: $2,700,000 for the
year 2019.

NO. MOST RECENT APPLICANTS: 170 for the
year 2019.

NO. AWARDS: 117 for the year 2019.

REPRESENTATIVE AWARDS:
$12,000 to Bernardine Center, Chester, PA,
towards making essential repairs and
improvements to Bernardine Center's Food
Pantry and West Side Branch; $38,075,000 to
Eastern University, St. Davids, PA, towards
equipment for the Nursing Clinical Resource
and Simulation Center Expansion Project;
$25,000 to Kencrest Centers, Blue Bell, PA,
towards the renovation of the facility for
KenCrest Day Program for Adults with
Disabilities.

APPLICATION INFO:
The Contributionship accepts the common
grant application form of the Philanthropy
Network Greater Philadelphia. Application
should include:
(1) a letter, which describes and justifies the
project;
(2) a budget and timetable, strategy for
securing funding and latest financial
statement;
(3) interim operating statements or budgets
for future periods if appropriate;
(4) evidence of tax-exempt status and;
(5) a list of officers and directors.

Application can be submitted online
(preferred) or mailed to Sandra L. McLean,
Executive Director, at the address above.

Duration: One to three years.

Deadline: Applications must be received six
weeks prior to meeting date.

IRS I.D.: 23-6396940

TRUSTEES:
John F. Bales, Chairman
Sandra L. McLean, Executive Director and
Trustee
Otis Bullock, Jr.
Diana McLean Liefer
Wendy McLean
Stephen Holt, Advisory Trustee
Martha Morris, Advisory Trustee
Marrea D. Walker-Smith, Advisory Trustee

ADDRESS INQUIRIES TO:
Sandra L. McLean
Executive Director and Trustee
(See address above.)

*PLEASE NOTE:
No grants to individuals.

THE JOSEPH AND MERCEDES
MCMICKING
FOUNDATION   [196]
1004B O'Reilly Avenue
San Francisco, CA 94129
(415) 474-1784
Fax: (415) 474-1754
E-mail: miriam@mcmickingfoundation.org
Web Site: mcmickingfoundation.org

AREAS OF INTEREST:
Arts, computer science, education and
science.

TYPE:
Project/program grants.

PURPOSE:
To improve the quality of life for San
Francisco Bay Area residents through grants
and scholarships for the education and
welfare of children and their families.

LEGAL BASIS:
501(c)(3) nonprofit corporation.

ELIGIBILITY:
The Foundation makes grants only to
organizations that are exempt from federal
tax under Section 501(c)(3) of the Internal
Revenue Code and are not classified as
private foundations under Section 509(a) of
the Code.

The Foundation does not provide support for
grants to individuals or loans.

GEOG. RESTRICTIONS: San Francisco Bay area,
California.

FINANCIAL DATA:
Amount of support per award: Varies.

Total amount of support: $602,915 in total
grants for the year 2019.

APPLICATION INFO:
Organizations seeking information should mail a letter and application to the Executive Director. Calls of inquiry are strongly encouraged. The Foundation will not accept proposals sent by facsimile.

Complete guidelines and application form are available on the web site.

Duration: One year.

Deadline: Proposals are accepted throughout the year.

ADDRESS INQUIRIES TO:
Miriam deQuadros, Executive Director
(See address or telephone number above.)

THE MARGARET MCNAMARA EDUCATION GRANTS (MMEG) [197]
The World Bank Family Network
1818 H Street, N.W.
MSN J2-202
Washington, DC 20433
(202) 473-8751
E-mail: info@mmeg.org
Web Site: www.mmeg.org

FOUNDED: 1981

AREAS OF INTEREST:
Agriculture, architecture and urban planning, civil engineering, education, forestry, journalism, nursing, nutrition, pediatrics, public administration, public health, social sciences, social work and others.

TYPE:
Scholarships. Education grants are awarded to women from developing and middle-income countries who, upon obtainment of their degree, intend to return to or remain in their countries or other developing countries, and work to improve the lives of women and/or children.

YEAR PROGRAM STARTED: 1981

PURPOSE:
To support the education of women from developing countries and underserved communities in the U.S. who are committed to improving the lives of women and children in their home countries.

LEGAL BASIS:
501(c)(3) public charity.

ELIGIBILITY:
Applicants must meet the following eligibility criteria:
(1) be at least 25 years of age at time of application deadline;
(2) be a national of a country listed on the MMEG Country Eligibility List;
(3) be enrolled at an accredited academic institution when submitting application and plan to be enrolled for a full academic term after award of the grant by the Board and;
(4) not be related to a World Bank Group, International Monetary Fund or Inter-American Development Bank staff member or spouse.

Additional criteria vary by country.

GEOG. RESTRICTIONS: United States, Canada, South Africa and Latin America.

FINANCIAL DATA:
Amount of support per award: Up to $15,000 in U.S./Canada; $7,000 in South Africa and Latin America.

NO. AWARDS: 29 for the year 2020.

APPLICATION INFO:
Complete application information is available on the web site.

Duration: One year. Nonrenewable.

Deadline: U.S. and Canada: January 15. Latin America: August 15. South Africa: September 14.

IRS I.D.: 52-1655741

ADDRESS INQUIRIES TO:
MMEG Coordinator
(See address above.)

MEADOWS FOUNDATION, INC. [198]
Wilson Historic District
3003 Swiss Avenue
Dallas, TX 75204-6049
(214) 826-9431
(800) 826-9431
Fax: (214) 827-7042
E-mail: webgrants3003@mfi.org
Web Site: www.mfi.org

FOUNDED: 1948

AREAS OF INTEREST:
Arts and culture, civic and public affairs (including the natural environment), education, health (including mental health), and human services.

TYPE:
Awards/prizes; Capital grants; Challenge/matching grants; Demonstration grants; Development grants; Endowments; General operating grants; Matching gifts; Project/program grants; Research grants; Seed money grants; Technical assistance; Training grants; Loan forgiveness programs. Program-related investments. Support for organizations, agencies, programs and projects within the areas of the Foundation's interest. Areas of high interest: environment, mental health and public education.

YEAR PROGRAM STARTED: 1948

PURPOSE:
To assist people and institutions of Texas improve the quality and circumstances of life for themselves and future generations.

LEGAL BASIS:
Tax-exempt, private foundation.

ELIGIBILITY:
Applicants must be tax-exempt organizations, benefitting Texas. No grants are awarded to individuals. Generally, no contributions for church or seminary construction, annual fund-raising drives, out-of-state travel, or professional conferences/symposia.

GEOG. RESTRICTIONS: Texas.

FINANCIAL DATA:
Amount of support per award: $120,800 average grant for the year 2018.

Total amount of support: Approximately $35,400,000 for the year 2018.

Matching fund requirements: Stipulated with specific grants.

NO. MOST RECENT APPLICANTS: 700 to 800.

NO. AWARDS: 195 for the year 2018.

APPLICATION INFO:
Application/proposal should include:
(1) a brief history of the organization, its current focus and recent accomplishments;
(2) a copy of the latest verification of tax-exempt status from the IRS;
(3) certified audits for the last three years, current operating budget and year-to-date financial statements;
(4) statement of need for the proposed project, to include population served, and how project will address need;
(5) a list of trustees or directors, corporate officers and key staff;
(6) the specific dollar amount requested and the date payment is needed;
(7) a list of all entities asked to give financial support and their responses;
(8) project line-item budget (include income and expenses);
(9) plans to evaluate the project (include measurable, time-specific goals) and;
(10) support for the project after the grant period.

Duration: Grants are seldom awarded on a continuing basis.

Deadline: Proposals are accepted throughout the year.

PUBLICATIONS:
Annual report; guidelines.

IRS I.D.: 75-6015322

STAFF:
Charles Glover, Senior Program Officer
Michael K. McCoy, Senior Program Officer
Cindy M. Patrick, Senior Program Officer
Kathy Smith, Senior Program Officer

OFFICERS AND DIRECTORS:
Robert A. Meadows, Chairman, Board of Trustees, Director and Vice President
Linda Perryman Evans, President and Chief Executive Officer, Trustee and Director
Paula Herring, Vice President and Treasurer
Tom Gale, Vice President and Chief Investment Officer
Bruce H. Esterline, Senior Vice President for Strategic Initiatives and Grants
Deborah Fitzpatrick, Vice President for Human Resources and Administration
Milly Ritzen Crawford, Director
Eric Meadows, Trustee and Director
John Meadows, Director
Mark A. Meadows, Trustee and Director
Kimberly Morris, Director
Dawn Culbertson Peterson, Trustee and Director
George Ritzen, Director
Joel T. Williams, III, Trustee and Director
Andrew Wilson, Trustee and Director

ADDRESS INQUIRIES TO:
Bruce H. Esterline
Senior Vice President for Strategic Initiatives and Grants
(See address above.)

MEDICAL LIBRARY ASSOCIATION [199]
225 West Wacker Drive
Suite 650
Chicago, IL 60606
(312) 419-9094
E-mail: awards@mail.mlahq.org
Web Site: www.mlanet.org

FOUNDED: 1898

AREAS OF INTEREST:
Health sciences librarianship.

NAME(S) OF PROGRAMS:
• **MLA Continuing Education Grants**

TYPE:
Grants-in-aid. The Continuing Education Grants are designed to aid in the study of the theoretical, administrative and technical aspects of library and information science.

PURPOSE:
To provide professional health science librarians with the opportunity to continue their education.

ELIGIBILITY:
Candidates must be U.S. or Canadian citizens, or permanent residents who are mid-level librarians with a graduate degree in library science and a practicing health sciences librarian with at least two years of work experience at the professional level. Membership in MLA is required. In exceptional cases, consideration will be given to an outstanding candidate not meeting the above eligibility criteria.

FINANCIAL DATA:
Amount of support per award: $100 to $500.

NO. AWARDS: 1 to 2.

APPLICATION INFO:
Applicants must complete and submit an application form which is available online. Candidates should also identify a continuing education program.
Duration: One year.
Deadline: December 1.

STAFF:
Maria Lopez, Grants, Scholarships and Awards Coordinator

ADDRESS INQUIRIES TO:
Coordinator
Grants, Scholarships and Awards
(See address above.)

*PLEASE NOTE:
The award is not to support work towards a degree or certificate.

MEDTRONIC FOUNDATION [200]
710 Medtronic Parkway
Minneapolis, MN 55432-5604
(763) 505-2647
(800) 633-8766
E-mail: rs.medtronicfoundation@medtronic.com
Web Site: foundation.medtronic.com

FOUNDED: 1979

AREAS OF INTEREST:
Health.

NAME(S) OF PROGRAMS:
- **Community Education**
- **HealthRise**
- **HeartRescue**
- **Strengthening Health Systems**

TYPE:
Challenge/matching grants; General operating grants; Matching gifts; Project/program grants. Sponsorships.

YEAR PROGRAM STARTED: 1979

PURPOSE:
To expand access to health care for the underserved worldwide in supporting healthy communities where we live and give.

LEGAL BASIS:
Corporate foundation.

ELIGIBILITY:
Grants are made to 501(c)(3) tax-exempt organizations, schools or government agencies by invitation only.

FINANCIAL DATA:
Amount of support per award: Varies depending on need and nature of request.
Total amount of support: $29,300,000 for fiscal year 2019.

APPLICATION INFO:
Applications are by invitation only.
Duration: Varies.

IRS I.D.: 41-1306950

ADDRESS INQUIRIES TO:
See e-mail address above.

THE ANDREW W. MELLON FOUNDATION [201]
140 East 62nd Street
New York, NY 10065
(212) 838-8400
Fax: (212) 888-4172
E-mail: inquiries@mellon.org
Web Site: www.mellon.org

FOUNDED: 1969

AREAS OF INTEREST:
Higher education and scholarship in the humanities, scholarly communications, arts and cultural heritage, diversity, and international higher education and strategic projects.

TYPE:
Challenge/matching grants; Endowments; General operating grants; Project/program grants; Research grants. Grants on a selective basis to institutions in the Foundation's areas of interest.

PURPOSE:
To build, strengthen and sustain institutions and their core capacities, rather than be a source for narrowly defined projects.

LEGAL BASIS:
Not-for-profit corporation.

ELIGIBILITY:
Organizations and institutions with appropriate interests are eligible. The Foundation does not award fellowships or grants to individuals or make grants to primarily local organizations.

FINANCIAL DATA:
Amount of support per award: Varies.

APPLICATION INFO:
Prospective grantees should review program area guidelines before inquiring about grant support. Inquiries concerning a proposed grant should be made through the Foundation's grantee portal Fluxx, located at mellon.fluxx.io. If Foundation staff find that the proposed grant fits within the Foundation's grantmaking priorities, staff will invite a grant proposal through the portal.
Duration: Varies.

PUBLICATIONS:
Annual report.

OFFICERS:
Elizabeth Alexander, President
Michele S. Warman, Chief Operating Officer, Executive Vice President and Secretary
Mariet Westermann, Executive Vice President for Programs and Research
Scott Taylor, Financial Vice President and Chief Investment Officer

TRUSTEES:
Kathryn A. Hall, Chairperson
Elizabeth Alexander
Richard H. Brodhead
Katherine Farley
Joshua S. Friedman
Heather Gerken
Thelma Golden
Jonathan Holloway
Glenn D. Lowry

Jane L. Mendillo
Eric Mindich
Alondra Nelson
Sarah E. Thomas

ADDRESS INQUIRIES TO:
Michele S. Warman, Chief Operating Officer, Executive Vice President and Secretary
(See address above.)

*PLEASE NOTE:
The Foundation rarely funds unsolicited proposals.

MERCK FAMILY FUND [202]
P.O. Box 870245
Milton Village, MA 02187
(617) 696-3580
Fax: (617) 696-7262
E-mail: merck@merckff.org
Web Site: www.merckff.org

FOUNDED: 1954

AREAS OF INTEREST:
Protecting the natural environment, meeting human needs and addressing the root causes of problems faced by social and economically disadvantaged people.

NAME(S) OF PROGRAMS:
- **Conserving Ecologically Valuable Land**
- **Promoting a Price on Carbon**
- **Promoting Energy Efficiency**
- **Promoting Sustainable Paper Production**
- **Urban Agriculture and Youth Leadership**

TYPE:
General operating grants; Project/program grants; Seed money grants.

YEAR PROGRAM STARTED: 1993

PURPOSE:
To protect and restore vital eastern ecosystems and promote economic practices for a sustainable environment.

LEGAL BASIS:
Tax-exempt corporation.

GEOG. RESTRICTIONS: Northeastern and southeastern United States.

FINANCIAL DATA:
Amount of support per award: $10,000 to $150,000.
Total amount of support: $2,852,550 for the year 2019.

NO. MOST RECENT APPLICANTS: 109.

NO. AWARDS: 86.

APPLICATION INFO:
New requests for support should be made through the online application system rather than with a full proposal or a request for a personal meeting. Applicants will be contacted if a full proposal is warranted. Unsolicited proposals will not be acknowledged.
Duration: Grants may be from one to two years. Progress reports must be received before continuation or renewal support will be considered.
Deadline: Letter of Intent: January 10 for spring and July 10 for fall. Full Proposal: January 31 for spring and July 31 for fall.

PUBLICATIONS:
Annual report; grants list; guidelines.

IRS I.D.: 22-6063382

STAFF:
Jenny Russell, Executive Director

James Maguire, Chief Financial Officer
Ruth Goldman, Consulting Program Officer

OFFICERS AND TRUSTEES:
Oona Coy, President
Eliza Hatch, Vice President
Patience Chamberlin, Secretary
Katie Chamberlin
Nat Chamberlin
Olivia Farr
Susannah Hatch
Friedrike Merck
Wil Merck
Morgan Whitridge

ADDRESS INQUIRIES TO:
Jenny Russell, Executive Director
(See address above.)

METLIFE FOUNDATION [203]

200 Park Avenue, 6th Floor
New York, NY 10166
E-mail: metlifefoundation@metlife.com
Web Site: www.metlife.com/corporate-responsibility/metlife-foundation

FOUNDED: 1976

AREAS OF INTEREST:
Financial health and program-related investments.

CONSULTING OR VOLUNTEER SERVICES:
Employee volunteer programs.

TYPE:
Matching gifts; Project/program grants; Scholarships. Program-related investments. Grants are made in the areas of financial empowerment.

MetLife Foundation has a new global focus - financial inclusion - and it has committed $200,000,000 over a five-year period to this initiative. These grants are focused in the following three categories:
(1) Access and Knowledge: Grants to partners with the ability to reach large numbers of underserved households around the world and work with them to develop financial strategies and capabilities to improve lives;
(2) Access to Services: Partnering with experts in financial inclusion to deliver high-quality services like savings, microinsurance and credit to individuals in need and ensure they are prepared, incentivized and motivated to improve the lives of their families and communities and;
(3) Access to Insights: Sharing what the Foundation learns by gathering knowledge from its partners and the communities with which it works; the Foundation offers its insights to the financial inclusion community to help enhance the approach and advance the goals they share in common.

MetLife and the Foundation make below-market-rate investments with groups and projects working to improve communities across the country. Either directly or through relending with nonprofit intermediaries, social investments reach every major city in the nation and over 30 states. Loans support affordable housing developments with social services, organizations serving the homeless and mentally ill, health care services and community-based economic development.

YEAR PROGRAM STARTED: 1976

PURPOSE:
To advance financial inclusion, helping to build a secure future for individuals and communities around the world.

LEGAL BASIS:
The Foundation is a tax-exempt organization under Section 501(c)(3) and is classified as a private foundation as defined by Section 509(a) of the Internal Revenue Code.

ELIGIBILITY:
Applicants must be 501(c)(3) tax-exempt organizations in the Foundation's areas of interest.

No grants are made to private foundations or religious, fraternal, political, athletic, or social organizations, capital fund campaigns, local chapters of national organizations, labor groups, organizations primarily engaged in patient care or direct treatment, drug treatment centers and community health clinics, elementary and secondary schools, courtesy advertising or festival participation or individuals. Generally, no support is given for endowment funds.

FINANCIAL DATA:
Total amount of support: $39,939,177 for the year 2019.
Matching fund requirements: Employee contributions to colleges and universities.

NO. AWARDS: Varies.

APPLICATION INFO:
The Foundation does not accept unsolicited proposals.
Duration: Varies.

PUBLICATIONS:
Annual report of contributions; guidelines (available online).

BOARD OF DIRECTORS:
Michael Zarcone, Chairman
A. Dennis White, President and Chief Executive Officer
Steven Goulart, Treasurer
Michel Khalaf
Esther Lee
Martin Lippert
Susan Podlogar
Oscar Schmidt

ADDRESS INQUIRIES TO:
A. Dennis White
President and Chief Executive Officer
(See address above.)

MEYER MEMORIAL TRUST [204]

425 N.W. 10th Avenue, Suite 400
Portland, OR 97209
(503) 228-5512
E-mail: questions@mmt.org
Web Site: www.mmt.org

FOUNDED: 1978

AREAS OF INTEREST:
Education, environment, affordable housing and building community.

YEAR PROGRAM STARTED: 1982

PURPOSE:
To work with and invest in organizations, communities, ideas and efforts that contribute to a flourishing and equitable Oregon.

LEGAL BASIS:
Private, independent foundation.

ELIGIBILITY:
Applicants must:
(1) be an IRS-sanctioned tax-exempt organization;
(2) be requesting support for a program that operates in Oregon and;
(3) provide equal opportunity in leadership, staffing and service regardless of age, gender, race, ethnicity, sexual orientation, disability, national origin, political affiliation or religious belief.

GEOG. RESTRICTIONS: Oregon.

FINANCIAL DATA:
Amount of support per award: Varies.

APPLICATION INFO:
Organizations must register on the Trust's online system to complete and submit the application.
Duration: Varies.

TRUSTEES:
Toya Fick, Chairperson
April Cuprill-Comas
Janet Hamada
Mitch Hornecker
Charles Wilhoite

STAFF:
Michelle DePass, President and Chief Executive Officer
Rukaiyah Adams, Chief Investment Officer

ADDRESS INQUIRIES TO:
Phoebe O'Leary
Director of Operations
(See address above.)

*SPECIAL STIPULATIONS:
No grants given to individuals or for businesses.

ROBERT R. MEYER FOUNDATION [205]

1900 5th Avenue North, Suite 2600
Birmingham, AL 35203
(205) 264-7881
E-mail: marcie.braswell@regions.com

FOUNDED: 1942

AREAS OF INTEREST:
Arts, education, humanities, civic affairs, health and human services, and charitable work.

TYPE:
Challenge/matching grants; Matching gifts; Project/program grants; Research grants; Technical assistance; Training grants.

YEAR PROGRAM STARTED: 1942

PURPOSE:
To help in community affairs.

LEGAL BASIS:
Private foundation.

ELIGIBILITY:
Grants restricted to organizations that benefit the Birmingham, AL area, or to Birmingham, AL nonprofit organizations. No grants to individuals or corporations.

GEOG. RESTRICTIONS: Birmingham, Alabama area.

FINANCIAL DATA:
Amount of support per award: $2,500 to $200,000; Average: $30,000.
Total amount of support: Approximately $2,000,000 for the year 2018.

NO. AWARDS: Approximately 70.

APPLICATION INFO:
Call for grant guidelines and application.
Duration: One year.
Deadline: March 1 and September 1.

PUBLICATIONS:
Application form.

ADVISORY COMMITTEE:
Judge Sharon L. Blackburn
John Haley
Raymond J. Harbert, Jr.
Judge Abdul Kallon

ADDRESS INQUIRIES TO:
Marcie P. Braswell, Senior Vice President
(See address above.)

THE MIAMI FOUNDATION   [206]

40 N.W. 3rd Street
Suite 305
Miami, FL 33128
(305) 371-2711
Fax: (305) 371-5342
E-mail: info@miamifoundation.org
Web Site: www.miamifoundation.org

FOUNDED: 1967

AREAS OF INTEREST:
Arts and culture, healthy lifestyles, housing
and affordability, well-being of children and
youth, LGBTQ issues, crime
prevention/deterrence, victim assistance,
public spaces, transportation, and sea level
rise.

NAME(S) OF PROGRAMS:
● **Community Grants Program**
● **LGBTQ Community Fund**
● **Denise Moon Memorial Fund**

TYPE:
Fellowships; Project/program grants;
Scholarships; Training grants. Special
initiative grants. Community Grants are
distributed in five categories:
Access to Health and Wellness: Improve
health outcomes by connecting people to
quality health resources and education,
reducing health disparities, or tackling
contributing social determinants of health.
Economic Stability: Improve residents'
ability to meet local affordability challenges
by helping them secure affordable, stable
housing, recover from financial crisis, and/or
increase earning potential.
Inclusion of People with Diverse Abilities:
Expand opportunities for people with
disabilities to lead purposeful, productive
lives and be increasingly integrated into all
aspects of community life.
Sustainable Environment: Develop a
healthier, more livable community by
preserving our unique environment, building
resiliency amid climate change, and
expanding local awareness and stewardship.
Thriving Youth and Families: Expand
opportunities for youth to excel from early
childhood to career through high-quality
education, enrichment experiences and
personal development that build resilience, or
work that ensures their safety and stability.
This can include support for adult caregivers
so the whole family can thrive.

YEAR PROGRAM STARTED: 1967

PURPOSE:
To enhance the quality of life for all the
residents of Greater Miami.

LEGAL BASIS:
Community foundation.

ELIGIBILITY:
Applicants must be 501(c)(3) organizations
as well as some grassroots organizations.

No grants to individuals. No grants for
memberships, fund-raising events or
memorials.

GEOG. RESTRICTIONS: Miami-Dade County,
Florida.

FINANCIAL DATA:
Amount of support per award: Varies.
Total amount of support: Varies.

NO. MOST RECENT APPLICANTS: 600.

NO. AWARDS: 130.

APPLICATION INFO:
Responsive grant applications must be made
through the Foundation's online portal.
Application includes cover letter with the
purpose of the grant and the amount
requested as well as a narrative about the
applicant organization and budget.
Attachments should include board list and
current fiscal year operating budget. Slight
variations per grant program may apply.
Duration: Typically one year.
Deadline: Varies.

PUBLICATIONS:
Annual report; monthly newsletter; grant
guidelines; professional advisors guides.

IRS I.D.: 65-0350357

STAFF:
Rebecca Fishman Lipsey, President and Chief
Executive Officer
Charisse Grant, Senior Vice President and
Strategy Advisor
Julie Vives, Vice President and Chief
Operating Officer
Toby Douthwright, Vice President for
Finance and Chief Financial Officer
Lindsey Linzer, Managing Director of
Community Investments
Kamilah Wallen, Grants Administration
Manager
Valerie Crum, Programs Officer
Chelsea Clark, Programs Associate
Alex Rosales, Programs Associate

ADDRESS INQUIRIES TO:
See e-mail address above.

MICROSOFT PHILANTHROPIES   [207]

One Microsoft Way
Redmond, WA 98052-6399
(425) 882-8080
(425) 706-8185
Fax: (425) 706-7329
Web Site: www.microsoft.com/en-
us/philanthropies

FOUNDED: 1983

AREAS OF INTEREST:
Inclusive economic opportunities, protection
of fundamental rights, sustainable future, and
privacy, cybersecurity and digital safety.

NAME(S) OF PROGRAMS:
● **Employee Giving and Volunteer
Programs**
● **Product Donations Program**

TYPE:
Grants-in-aid; Matching gifts; Product
donations; Scholarships; Technical assistance.

YEAR PROGRAM STARTED: 1983

PURPOSE:
To invest in programs and partnerships that
advance digital inclusion by bringing greater
social and economic opportunity to people in
underserved populations around the world; to
support Microsoft employees taking an active
role in their community through volunteer
and matching gift programs.

LEGAL BASIS:
Corporate giving program.

ELIGIBILITY:
Cash grants are awarded to nonprofit
organizations identified by Microsoft staff.
Eligible nonprofits can benefit from the
Product Donations Program.

FINANCIAL DATA:
Matching fund requirements: Employee
donations of money and time to eligible
organizations are matched up to $15,000 per
employee per year.

APPLICATION INFO:
Microsoft does not respond to unsolicited
grant proposals or letters of inquiry.

PUBLICATIONS:
Program brochure; annual report of giving.

ADDRESS INQUIRIES TO:
Community Affairs
(See address above.)

*SPECIAL STIPULATIONS:
Proposals submitted by e-mail, fax or
telephone will not be accepted.

MID-NEBRASKA COMMUNITY FOUNDATION, INC.   [208]

121 North Dewey Street, Suite 112
North Platte, NE 69101
(308) 534-3315
Fax: (308) 534-6117
E-mail: mncf@midnebfoundation.org
Web Site: www.midnebraskafoundation.org

FOUNDED: 1978

AREAS OF INTEREST:
Arts, education, civic development,
environment, health and welfare.

TYPE:
Capital grants; Demonstration grants;
Development grants; Endowments;
Project/program grants; Scholarships.

PURPOSE:
To serve charitable people and nonprofit
causes in North Platte and the surrounding
area.

GEOG. RESTRICTIONS: Custer, Dawson, Frontier,
Hayes, Keith, Lincoln, Logan, McPherson,
and Perkins counties, Nebraska.

FINANCIAL DATA:
Amount of support per award: Varies.
Total amount of support: Average:
$1,000,000 to $1,500,000.

APPLICATION INFO:
Application form required. Initial approach
by letter or telephone.
Duration: Varies.
Deadline: April 15, July 15, October 15 and
January 15.

IRS I.D.: 47-0604965

ADDRESS INQUIRIES TO:
Eric Seacrest, Executive Director
(See address above.)

ADAH K. MILLARD CHARITABLE TRUST   [209]

Northern Trust Company
One Power Lane, 24th Floor
Oakbrook Terrace, IL 60181
(630) 932-6981
Fax: (312) 429-4181
E-mail: kwm1@ntrs.com

FOUNDED: 1976

AREAS OF INTEREST:
Youth agencies, arts, cultural programs and hospitals.

TYPE:
Capital grants; Project/program grants. Project grants in areas of the Foundation's interest.

YEAR PROGRAM STARTED: 1976

PURPOSE:
To make grants to charitable agencies in Omaha and Douglas County, NE.

LEGAL BASIS:
Tax-exempt.

ELIGIBILITY:
Tax-exempt organizations in Omaha and Douglas County, NE. No grants are awarded to individuals.

GEOG. RESTRICTIONS: Douglas County and Omaha, Nebraska.

FINANCIAL DATA:
Amount of support per award: $1,000 to $35,000.
Matching fund requirements: Stipulated with specific programs.

NO. AWARDS: 35 annually.

REPRESENTATIVE AWARDS:
Salvation Army; United Way; Nebraska Food Bank.

APPLICATION INFO:
A request should be made for guidelines to submit grant applications. Six hard copies and one e-mail copy of the application are required.
Duration: No grants are awarded on a continuing basis. May reapply after two years.
Deadline: March 20 and October 1. Announcements in May and November.

PUBLICATIONS:
Application guidelines.

IRS I.D.: 36-6629069

ADDRESS INQUIRIES TO:
Kristin Weaver, Senior Vice President
(See address above.)

MILLIPORESIGMA [210]
400 Summit Drive
Burlington, MA 01803
(781) 533-6000
Web Site: www.emdmillipore.com

FOUNDED: 1985

AREAS OF INTEREST:
Science, education (K-12), sustainability, and health care.

TYPE:
Capital grants; Challenge/matching grants; Matching gifts; Project/program grants; Research grants; Scholarships.

YEAR PROGRAM STARTED: 1985

PURPOSE:
To serve the public interest in ways that are meaningful to the company and its employees.

ELIGIBILITY:
Organizations, excluding religious and political, classified as 501(c)(3) by the IRS can apply.

FINANCIAL DATA:
Since inception, over $20,000,000 has been distributed to deserving nonprofit programs on a local and national level.

Amount of support per award: Grants: $5,000 to $10,000; Scholarships: $5,000.
Matching fund requirements: 1:1 up to $1,000 per employee per year.

NO. AWARDS: Scholarships: 2.

APPLICATION INFO:
Eligible programs may submit a copy of the 501(c)(3) certificate, tax identification number, and a letter of inquiry no more than two pages in length briefly describing the organization, the program for which funding is sought, and the amount of funding requested. Those organizations whose programs are of interest to Millipore will be invited to submit full proposals.

Millipore also accepts the Associated Grant Makers Common Proposal Form.
Duration: One year. Grants are renewable. Scholarship is renewable for an additional three years.
Deadline: Proposals are considered quarterly at Review Committee meetings.

ADDRESS INQUIRIES TO:
Director of Corporate Responsibility
(See address above.)

THE MOODY FOUNDATION [211]
2302 Post Office Street, Suite 704
Galveston, TX 77550
(409) 797-1500
Fax: (409) 763-5564
E-mail: info@moodyf.org
Web Site: www.moodyf.org

FOUNDED: 1942

AREAS OF INTEREST:
Arts and humanities, community and social services, education, health and science.

TYPE:
Capital grants; Challenge/matching grants; Endowments; Grants-in-aid; Project/program grants; Research grants; Scholarships. Capital campaigns; Equipment; Matching funds; Building/renovation; Program development and research.

YEAR PROGRAM STARTED: 1942

PURPOSE:
To assist in supporting activities that are directed toward improving the general well-being of the citizens of the state of Texas, especially Galveston.

LEGAL BASIS:
Private family foundation.

ELIGIBILITY:
Tax-exempt 501(c)(3) organizations in the state of Texas only are eligible to apply. The Foundation generally does not make grant awards for deficit financing, operational expenses of established organizations, or grants for any activities considered a taxable expenditure under the 1969 Tax Reform Act. No grants to individuals (except for one scholarship program). No loans.

GEOG. RESTRICTIONS: Texas.

FINANCIAL DATA:
Amount of support per award: Varies.
Total amount of support: Varies.

NO. AWARDS: Varies.

REPRESENTATIVE AWARDS:
$175,000 to After8ToEducate, Dallas, TX, for assistance responding to the COVID-19 crisis; $50,000 to Brighton Center, San Antonio, TX, for assistance with tuition for low-income families who have children with disabilities; $25,000 to Parenting Center, Fort Worth, TX, for assistance with child abuse prevention programs for parents, children, caregivers, grandparents and professionals.

APPLICATION INFO:
Prospective candidates should consult the Foundation's web site for an online inquiry to ascertain if appropriate to request guidelines for making application.
Duration: Generally, grants are awarded for one year at a time.

PUBLICATIONS:
Annual report; application guidelines.

IRS I.D.: 74-1403105

STAFF:
Frances Anne Moody-Dahlberg, Executive Director
Garrik Addison, Chief Financial Officer
Angela Blair, Education Director
Allan Matthews, Grants Director
Bernice C. Torregrossa, Senior Grants Officer
Gerald Smith, Senior Program Officer
Jamie Williams, Regional Grants Director, North
Emily Greer, Regional Grants Officer, Central
Erica Tovar, Scholarship Coordinator

BOARD OF TRUSTEES:
Frances Anne Moody-Dahlberg, Chairperson
Elizabeth Moody
Ross R. Moody

FOUNDERS:
Libbie Shearn Moody
W.L. Moody, Jr.

ADDRESS INQUIRIES TO:
See e-mail address above.

THE CLARENCE E. MULFORD TRUST [212]
P.O. Box 290
Fryeburg, ME 04037
(207) 935-2061
Fax: (866) 225-8160
E-mail: dhastings@hastingsmalia.com

AREAS OF INTEREST:
Animals, education, literature, religion, science and youth.

TYPE:
Project/program grants.

PURPOSE:
To support charitable organizations that are working to improve the quality of life for Maine residents.

LEGAL BASIS:
Trust fund.

ELIGIBILITY:
Grants are made to organizations that have tax-exempt status under Section 501(c)(3) of the Internal Revenue Code. No grants are made to individuals. Religious organizations may apply.

GEOG. RESTRICTIONS: Primarily Fryeburg, Maine.

FINANCIAL DATA:
Amount of support per award: $500 to $10,000.
Total amount of support: Approximately $100,000 for the year 2019.

APPLICATION INFO:
Organizations should submit IRS tax exemption letter under 501(c)(3) of the Internal Revenue Code.

Duration: One year. Renewal by
reapplication.

Deadline: January 10 and July 10.

TRUSTEES:
David R. Hastings, III
Peter G. Hastings

ADDRESS INQUIRIES TO:
David R. Hastings, III, Trustee
(See address above.)

M.J. MURDOCK CHARITABLE TRUST [213]

655 West Columbia Way
Suite 700
Vancouver, WA 98660
(360) 694-8415
E-mail: info@murdocktrust.org
Web Site: murdocktrust.org

FOUNDED: 1975

AREAS OF INTEREST:
Education, science, health, human services,
and arts and culture.

TYPE:
Capital grants; Project/program grants.
Capacity building grants; Equipment and
technology grants.

PURPOSE:
To enrich the quality of life in the Pacific
Northwest by providing grants and
enrichment programs to organizations seeking
to strengthen the region's educational,
spiritual and cultural base in creative and
sustainable ways.

LEGAL BASIS:
Private foundation.

ELIGIBILITY:
Applications for grants are considered only
from organizations which have been ruled to
be tax-exempt under Section 501(c)(3) of the
Internal Revenue Code and are not private
foundations. Primary attention is given to
applications for the support of projects and
programs conducted by qualified institutions
within five states of the Pacific Northwest,
including Alaska, Idaho, Montana, Oregon
and Washington. Priority is given to
organizations and projects which are not
primarily or normally financed by public tax
funds.

Applications are not considered for loans,
endowment, debt retirement, operational
deficits, contributions to general fund drives
or annual charitable appeals, continuation of
programs previously financed from external
sources or emergency funding.

GEOG. RESTRICTIONS: Pacific Northwest.

FINANCIAL DATA:
Amount of support per award: Varies.
Total amount of support: Varies.

NO. MOST RECENT APPLICANTS: 375.

NO. AWARDS: 477.

APPLICATION INFO:
Submit a letter of inquiry through the Trust's
Grants Portal.
Duration: Varies.
Deadline: Varies.

PUBLICATIONS:
Annual report; *Grants Proposal Guidelines*;
proposal form.

TRUSTEES:
John W. Castles

Jeffrey T. Grubb
Jeff Pinneo

OFFICERS AND STAFF:
Steven G.W. Moore, Executive Director
Mike True, Chief Financial Officer
Elmer Huh, Chief Investment Officer
Moses Lee, Senior Director, Scientific
Research and Enrichment Programs
Kimberly Thornbury, Senior Program
Director for Enrichment Initiatives
Dana L. Miller, Senior Program Director for
Grant Programs
Colby Reade, Director of Communications
Jennifer Larson-Cody, Director of
Technology and Information Management
Services
Rudy Carrasco, Program Director
Lorin Dunlop, Program Director
Pauline Fong, Program Director
John Frankin, Program Director
Jill Lemke, Program Director
Kim Newman, Program Director
Jeremy White, Program Director

ADDRESS INQUIRIES TO:
E-mail: info@murdocktrust.org

NATIONWIDE FOUNDATION [214]

One Nationwide Plaza
Mail Drop 1.2.16
Columbus, OH 43215-2220
(614) 249-4310
Fax: (866) 212-7960
E-mail: corpcit@nationwide.com
Web Site: www.nationwide.com/personal/about-
us/giving/nationwide-foundation

FOUNDED: 1959

AREAS OF INTEREST:
Health and welfare, education, culture and
the arts, and civic and community affairs.
Highest priorities are emergency and basic
needs and crisis stabilization.

TYPE:
Capital grants; Challenge/matching grants;
General operating grants; Project/program
grants.

YEAR PROGRAM STARTED: 1959

PURPOSE:
To provide financial support for qualified
tax-exempt organizations whose programs
address basic human needs.

LEGAL BASIS:
Corporate foundation.

ELIGIBILITY:
Qualified, tax-exempt organizations in
Columbus, OH and locations with a large
number of Nationwide associates are eligible.

GEOG. RESTRICTIONS: Primarily Scottsdale,
Arizona; Des Moines, Iowa and Columbus,
Ohio. Tiers One and Two funding considered
in Sacramento, California; Denver, Colorado;
Gainesville, Florida; Raleigh/Durham, North
Carolina; Harrisburg, Pennsylvania; San
Antonio, Texas; and Wausau, Wisconsin.

FINANCIAL DATA:
Total amount of support: Varies.

APPLICATION INFO:
Guidelines and application form are available
at the Foundation web site.
Duration: One year. Renewal possible.
Deadline: September 1. Announcement in
mid-March.

PUBLICATIONS:
Contributions guidelines.

ADDRESS INQUIRIES TO:
Karen H. Blickley, Vice President
(See address above.)

NEW ENGLAND BIOLABS FOUNDATION [215]

240 County Road
Ipswich, MA 01938
(978) 998-7990
E-mail: info@nebf.org
Web Site: www.nebf.org

FOUNDED: 1982

AREAS OF INTEREST:
Environmental issues: landscapes and
seascapes, and the associated biocultural
diversity, ecosystem services and foodways.

TYPE:
Grants-in-aid; Project/program grants; Seed
money grants. The Foundation prefers to help
organizations start their projects with the
understanding that once they are established,
funding from other sources will be sought.

YEAR PROGRAM STARTED: 1982

PURPOSE:
To support grassroots organizations working
with the environment.

ELIGIBILITY:
The Foundation prefers to fund grassroots
organizations and/or projects (i.e., those
conceived, developed and managed by the
community). Grassroots organizations,
emerging support groups and charitable
organizations may apply. Grants are not made
to religious organizations.

FINANCIAL DATA:
Amount of support per award: International
grants: Maximum $12,000; Local grants:
Maximum $8,000.
Total amount of support: Approximately
$500,000 annually.

NO. MOST RECENT APPLICANTS: 200.

NO. AWARDS: 70.

APPLICATION INFO:
Letters of Inquiry and Proposals should be
submitted electronically through the NEBF
online portal.
Duration: Typically one year.

ADDRESS INQUIRIES TO:
Deborah Fraize, Associate Director
(See address above.)

THE NEW YORK COMMUNITY TRUST [216]

909 Third Avenue, 22nd Floor
New York, NY 10022
(212) 686-0010
Fax: (212) 532-8528
E-mail: info@nyct-cfi.org
Web Site: www.nycommunitytrust.org

FOUNDED: 1924

AREAS OF INTEREST:
Health, behavioral health, older adults, the
blind or visually impaired, children and
youth with disabilities, people with
developmental disabilities, education, arts,
human justice, human services, jobs and
workforce development, youth development,
community development, civic affairs, the
environment, historic preservation, and
technical assistance.

TYPE:
Project/program grants; Technical assistance. The Trust is a grantmaking foundation dedicated to improving the lives of residents of New York City and its suburbs. It brings together individuals, families, foundations, and businesses to build a better community and support nonprofits that make a difference.

The competitive grants are supported by hundreds of funds. Some can be used at the Trust's discretion, while others were created for particular purposes and range from specific (helping injured, needy, classical ballet dancers) to broad (improving opportunities for poor girls and women). The Trust funds programs that promote change in policy or systems, build capacity of organizations, and expand and/or improve direct service.

The Trust seeks to promote healthy lives, expand opportunities, strengthen families, develop children and youth, and create strong, vital communities. The governing board has identified three categories of activity to carry out these objectives: Healthy Lives - The Trust helps providers deliver efficient, patient-focused, equitable, and cost-effective health and behavioral health services to all New Yorkers. Projects that develop the skills and independence of four groups of people with special needs: older adults, the blind or visually impaired, children and youth with disabilities, and people with developmental disabilities are supported. The Trust also supports biomedical research and projects for animal welfare.
Promising Futures - These grants build promising futures by helping young people prosper; providing job training and placement; making the educational and justice systems work for everyone; alleviating hunger and homelessness; improving family and child welfare services; and advancing the practice of social work.
Thriving Communities - Grants are made to groups that protect and create affordable housing, promote equity in the arts, improve civic engagement, and protect our environment. Agencies working on these issues at the neighborhood level, as well as government and nonprofit institutions developing strategies, are supported. The Trust also supports efforts to improve the functioning of nonprofits and government.

YEAR PROGRAM STARTED: 1924

PURPOSE:
To support the nonprofits that make New York City a vital and secure place to live and work.

LEGAL BASIS:
Public nonprofit community foundation.

ELIGIBILITY:
Priority is given to grant proposals from nonprofit organizations that deal with the problems of the New York metropolitan region. Preference is given to proposals that support specific programs or projects.

Grants also are available to support endowments, building fund campaigns, deficit financing, annual giving, religious purposes, financial assistance and to individual applicants.

GEOG. RESTRICTIONS: Primarily New York, New York.

FINANCIAL DATA:
Amount of support per award: $5,000 to $200,000.
Total amount of support: Competitive grants: Approximately $50,000,000 annually.

NO. MOST RECENT APPLICANTS: Varies.

NO. AWARDS: Varies.

APPLICATION INFO:
Applicants should begin by going to the Grantee Application Hub on the Trust's web site.
Duration: One year or multiyear.
Deadline: Grant applications are accepted throughout the year. Trust's Board reviews grants five times per year.

PUBLICATIONS:
Annual report; application and individual program guidelines; proposal cover sheet; newsletter.

OFFICERS:
Lorie A. Slutsky, President
Mercedes Leon, Vice President, Administration
Shawn Morehead, Vice President, Grants
Kerry McCarthy, Vice President, Philanthropic Initiatives
Carolyn M. Weiss, C.P.A., Chief Financial Officer
Tatiana Pohotsky, Chief Investment Officer
Carrie Trowbridge, General Counsel

DISTRIBUTION COMMITTEE:
Valerie Peltier, Chairman
Fernando Bohorquez, Jr.
Jamie Drake
Mali Sananikone Gaw
Obaid Z. Khan
Stephen C. Robinson
Judith O. Rubin
Jane E. Salmon, M.D.
Lorie A. Slutsky
Barron Tenny
Ann Unterberg
Jason H. Wright

THE NORCLIFFE FOUNDATION   [217]
600 University Street
Suite 2003
Seattle, WA 98101
(206) 682-4820
E-mail: info@norcliffefoundation.org
Web Site: www.norcliffefoundation.org

FOUNDED: 1952

AREAS OF INTEREST:
Human services, health care, civic and community projects, education, and arts and culture.

TYPE:
Capital grants; General operating grants; Project/program grants.

YEAR PROGRAM STARTED: 1952

PURPOSE:
To improve the quality of life for all people.

LEGAL BASIS:
Private foundation.

ELIGIBILITY:
Eligible organizations must be of IRS 501(c)(3), not-for-profit status. Projects must impact the Puget Sound region of Washington state.

Grants are not given to individuals.

GEOG. RESTRICTIONS: Puget Sound area of Washington state.

FINANCIAL DATA:
Amount of support per award: Varies.
Total amount of support: $29,400,000 for fiscal year 2020.

NO. AWARDS: Over 433 for fiscal year 2020.

APPLICATION INFO:
Application details can be found on the Foundation web site.
Duration: Varies by project. Grants are generally not renewable.
Deadline: Applications are accepted throughout the year.

ADDRESS INQUIRIES TO:
Jennifer Beatty, Director
(See address above.)

THE NORDSON CORPORATION FOUNDATION   [218]
28601 Clemens Road
Westlake, OH 44145-1148
(440) 892-1580
E-mail: crender@nordson.com
Web Site: www.nordson.com

FOUNDED: 1952

AREAS OF INTEREST:
Education, human welfare, civic, arts and culture.

CONSULTING OR VOLUNTEER SERVICES:
Corporate volunteer program.

NAME(S) OF PROGRAMS:
● **Time and Talent**

TYPE:
Capital grants; Challenge/matching grants; General operating grants; Matching gifts; Project/program grants; Technical assistance.

YEAR PROGRAM STARTED: 1988

PURPOSE:
To improve the quality of life in our communities by improving educational outcomes that enable individuals to become self-sufficient, active participants in the community.

LEGAL BASIS:
Corporate foundation.

ELIGIBILITY:
Grants are made to tax-exempt organizations, as defined in Section 501(c)(3) of the Internal Revenue Code. No grants to religious organizations.

GEOG. RESTRICTIONS: North San Diego and Santa Clara counties, California; Larimer County, Colorado; New London and Windham counties, Connecticut; Emanuel and Gwinnett counties, Georgia; Chicago, Illinois; Worcester County and the cities of Billerica, Chelmsford, Dracut, Framingham, Haverhill, Lawrence, Lowell, Marlborough and Tewksbury, Massachusetts; Minneapolis, Minnesota; Manchester, Nashua and Salem, New Hampshire; Mercer County, New Jersey; Mahoning Valley and Lorain County, Ohio; Providence County, Rhode Island; and Chippewa Valley, Wisconsin.

FINANCIAL DATA:
Amount of support per award: Varies.
Total amount of support: $12,000,000 for the year 2020.
Matching fund requirements: Foundation will match minimum contributions of $25 to a maximum of $10,000 for any calendar year.

NO. MOST RECENT APPLICANTS: Approximately 1,000 for the year 2020.

NO. AWARDS: Approximately 500 for the year 2020.

APPLICATION INFO:
Application forms are available online.
Duration: Typically one year.
Deadline: February 15, May 15, August 15 and November 15 for meetings held in January, April, July and October, respectively.

STAFF:
Cecilia Render, Executive Director
Sara Vaz, Community Relations Manager/California and Colorado
Lorie Mendoza, Community Relations Manager/Connecticut, Massachusetts, New Hampshire, New Jersey, Pennsylvania and Rhode Island
Cindy Baumgardner, Community Relations Manager/Georgia, Minnesota and Wisconsin
Joan Szczepanik, Community Relations Manager/Ohio

DIRECTORS:
Joseph Kelley
Stephen Lovass
Greg Merk
Sundaram Nagarajan
Shelly Peet
Jeff Pembroke

ADDRESS INQUIRIES TO:
Cindy Baumgardner, Tel: (770) 497-3672 (GA, MN and WI)
Lorie Mendoza, Tel: (401) 601-9583 (CT, MA, NH, NJ, PA and RI)
Cecilia H. Render, Tel: (440) 892-1580
Joan Szczepanik, Tel: (440) 414-5440 (OH)
Sara Vaz, Tel: (760) 930-7246 (CA and CO)

KENNETH T. AND EILEEN L. NORRIS FOUNDATION   [219]
11 Golden Shore, Suite 450
Long Beach, CA 90802
(562) 435-8444
Fax: (562) 436-0584
E-mail: grants@ktn.org
Web Site: norrisfoundation.org

FOUNDED: 1963

AREAS OF INTEREST:
Funding categories include medicine, education and science, youth, community and culture.

TYPE:
Capital grants; Challenge/matching grants; Endowments; General operating grants; Project/program grants; Research grants.

YEAR PROGRAM STARTED: 1963

PURPOSE:
To support programs that advance better health and intellectual enlightenment through education, cultivation of the arts, individual responsibility, freedom and dignity.

LEGAL BASIS:
Family foundation.

ELIGIBILITY:
Applicants must be nonprofit, tax-exempt organizations. The Foundation does not support individuals and/or political or religious organizations.

GEOG. RESTRICTIONS: Southern California.

FINANCIAL DATA:
Amount of support per award: Grants vary in amount, depending upon the needs and nature of the request.
Total amount of support: Varies.

APPLICATION INFO:
Applications are accepted by invitation only.
Duration: Most grants are for one year.
Deadline: Education/Science and Medical: May 1 to June 30. Decision in October; Youth: February 15 to March 31. Decision in August; Community and Cultural: December 1 to January 31. Decision in May.

PUBLICATIONS:
Biannual report.

IRS I.D.: 95-6080374

TRUSTEES AND OFFICERS:
Lisa D. Hansen, Chairman
James R. Martin
Bradley K. Norris
Brooks B. Norris
Kimberley D. Presley
Walter J. Zanino

ADDRESS INQUIRIES TO:
Walter J. Zanino, Executive Director
(See address above.)

NORTH CAROLINA COMMUNITY FOUNDATION   [220]
3737 Glenwood Avenue
Suite 460
Raleigh, NC 27612
(919) 828-4387
(800) 532-1349
Fax: (919) 827-0749
E-mail: info@nccommunityfoundation.org
Web Site: www.nccommunityfoundation.org

FOUNDED: 1988

AREAS OF INTEREST:
Arts and conservation, education, health, historical and cultural resources, preservation of environmental and social services.

TYPE:
General operating grants; Project/program grants; Scholarships.

YEAR PROGRAM STARTED: 1988

PURPOSE:
To inspire North Carolinians to make lasting and meaningful contributions to their communities.

LEGAL BASIS:
501(c)(3).

ELIGIBILITY:
Nonprofit, tax-exempt organizations. No grants are made to individuals.

GEOG. RESTRICTIONS: North Carolina.

FINANCIAL DATA:
Amount of support per award: Varies.
Total amount of support: $20,250,706 for the year 2019.

NO. AWARDS: 1,803 grants and 945 scholarships for the year 2019.

APPLICATION INFO:
Details regarding eligibility criteria, program guidelines, and application process can be found on the Foundation web site.

ADDRESS INQUIRIES TO:
Grants and Scholarships
North Carolina Community Foundation
(See address above.)

THE NORTHWEST MINNESOTA FOUNDATION
201 Third Street, N.W.
Bemidji, MN 56601
(218) 759-2057
Fax: (218) 759-2328
E-mail: info@nwmf.org
Web Site: www.nwmf.org

TYPE:
Challenge/matching grants; Demonstration grants; Project/program grants; Research grants; Scholarships; Seed money grants; Technical assistance.

See entry 1214 for full listing.

WILLIAM J. AND DOROTHY K. O'NEILL FOUNDATION   [221]
2529 Detroit Avenue
Suite 126
Cleveland, OH 44113
(216) 831-4134
Fax: (216) 378-0594
E-mail: info@oneill-foundation.org
Web Site: oneill-foundation.org

FOUNDED: 1987

AREAS OF INTEREST:
Health and well-being, educational success and homelessness.

TYPE:
General operating grants; Matching gifts; Project/program grants. Capacity building; Proactive grants; Gifts in recognition of service; Youth Philanthropy grants; Responsive grants; Special initiative grants; Rapid responsive grants. In the area of capacity building, the Foundation funds projects that create and implement strategic plans, governance and board development, leadership succession planning, planning and implementing technology systems, fund development, and communications and marketing strategies.

Matching gifts and gifts in recognition of service are directed by O'Neill Family members.

Youth Philanthropy grants are made by O'Neill Family youth.

YEAR PROGRAM STARTED: 1987

PURPOSE:
To fund programs that address root causes of family strength and family disintegration, capacity building for nonprofits and areas of interest to individual family members.

LEGAL BASIS:
Family foundation.

ELIGIBILITY:
Nonprofit organizations with IRS 501(c)(3) tax-exempt status are eligible for support. No grants to individuals or to organizations which operate wholly outside the U.S. No grants in response to annual appeal form letters.

In order to be eligible, you must have either received a grant from the Foundation already and/or be notified that you are eligible.

GEOG. RESTRICTIONS: Washington, DC; Greater Orlando, Florida; Big Island, Hawaii; Anne Arundel County and Baltimore, Maryland; New York, New York; Cuyahoga County, Ohio; Harris, Montgomery and Waller counties, Texas; and Bennington and Rutland counties, Vermont.

FINANCIAL DATA:
Amount of support per award: $5,000 to $50,000.

Total amount of support: $2,435,286 for the year 2019.

NO. AWARDS: 79 Responsive Grants for the year 2019.

REPRESENTATIVE AWARDS:
$50,000 to Teaching for Change, Washington, DC; $25,000 to Adoption Network, Cleveland, OH; $30,000 to Krist Samaritan Center, Houston, TX.

APPLICATION INFO:
Proposal, budget and activity plan must be submitted through the Foundation's grants management system.
Duration: One year.
Deadline: March 9 and July 31.

PUBLICATIONS:
Annual report; application guidelines.

IRS I.D.: 34-1560893

OFFICERS:
Leslie Perkul, President and Chief Executive Officer
David Donahey, Treasurer
Timothy M. O'Neill, Secretary

TRUSTEES:
Robert W. Donahey, Chairperson
Leslie Perkul, President and Chief Executive Officer
Laura Bower
Linda France Clifford
David Donahey
Timothy M. O'Neill
Brian Sweeney

ADDRESS INQUIRIES TO:
For DC, MD, NY and VT:
Marlene Corrado, Program Officer
E-mail: mcorrado@oneill-foundation.org

For FL, HI, OH and TX:
Kara McCullough, Grants Manager
E-mail: kmccullough@oneill-foundation.org

THE JOHN R. OISHEI FOUNDATION [222]
726 Exchange Street
Suite 510
Buffalo, NY 14210
(716) 856-9490
E-mail: info@oishei.org
Web Site: www.oishei.org

FOUNDED: 1940

AREAS OF INTEREST:
Strengthening the P-20 education continuum; enhancing options for self-sufficiency; building livable, stable neighborhoods; promoting health and improving systems; expanding the role of arts, culture and heritage in regional development.

TYPE:
Capital grants; Challenge/matching grants; General operating grants; Project/program grants; Seed money grants; Technical assistance; Training grants. Education grants.

PURPOSE:
To be a catalyst for change; to enhance the economic vitality and the quality of life for the Buffalo Niagara region through grantmaking, leadership and network building.

LEGAL BASIS:
Private foundation.

ELIGIBILITY:
An organization seeking support must be determined by the Internal Revenue Code to be tax-exempt under Section 501(c)(3). Private foundations, as defined in Section 509(a) of the Internal Revenue Code, will not be eligible for Foundation support. To receive Foundation support, an organization must be well managed, including an active board drawn from a cross section of the community. It must have a consistent record of sound fiscal management and a demonstrated track record of efficient operations and effective programming. The Foundation does not make grants to governmental institutions, agencies or projects. Organizations that rely heavily on government funding are eligible to apply, but must be able to demonstrate that a grant from the Foundation would supplement rather than supplant public funding.

GEOG. RESTRICTIONS: Erie and Niagara counties and the remaining six counties in western New York.

FINANCIAL DATA:
Amount of support per award: $1,000 to $1,000,000.

Total amount of support: Approximately $11,900,000 for the year 2019.

NO. AWARDS: 160 for the year 2019.

REPRESENTATIVE AWARDS:
$75,000 to Opportunities Collaborative for Special Needs Students, for professional development and programming; $12,500 to Buffalo Urban League, for basic human needs; $99,600 to Green Options Buffalo, for planning for Grant Street revitalization; $5,000 to Pathways for the Visually Impaired, for mental health awareness guide; $30,000 to Springville Center for the Arts, for entrance addition.

APPLICATION INFO:
Letters of Inquiry (LOIs) and applications for general funding requests must be submitted online.
Duration: One to four years.
Deadline: The Foundation accepts and processes applications throughout the year. Notification generally within three months.

PUBLICATIONS:
Community reports; annual report; grantmaking reports; research briefs.

OFFICERS:
William G. Gisel, Jr., Chairman
Maureen Hurley, Vice Chairman
Robert D. Gioia, President
Edward F. Walsh, Jr., Treasurer
Gayle L. Houck, Secretary
Jackie Reisdorf, Recording Secretary

DIRECTORS:
Donald K. Boswell
William G. Gisel, Jr.
Maureen Hurley
Glenn Jackson
Luke T. Jacobs
Yvonne Minor-Ragan, Ph.D.
Francisco M. Vasquez, Ph.D.
Melva D. Visher
Edward F. Walsh, Jr.

ADDRESS INQUIRIES TO:
Robert D. Gioia, President
(See address above.)

OMAHA COMMUNITY FOUNDATION [223]
3555 Farnam Street
Suite 222
Omaha, NE 68131
(402) 342-3458
Fax: (402) 342-3582
E-mail: info@omahafoundation.org
Web Site: www.omahafoundation.org

FOUNDED: 1982

AREAS OF INTEREST:
General philanthropy.

CONSULTING OR VOLUNTEER SERVICES:
Nonprofit Capacity Building Program.

NAME(S) OF PROGRAMS:
• **African American Unity Fund**
• **Endowment Funds of Southwest Iowa**
• **Equality Fund for LGBTQIA**
• **Fund for Omaha**
• **Futuro Latino Fund**
• **Omaha Neighborhood Grants Program**

TYPE:
Capital grants; General operating grants; Project/program grants; Technical assistance. Donors can contribute through the Omaha Community Foundation to any nonprofit agency. The OCF also has 10 discretionary grant programs.

PURPOSE:
To facilitate charitable giving and serve as a vehicle for community improvement; to improve the quality of life in Greater Omaha by supporting needs not being met in the areas of civic, cultural, health, education and social service.

LEGAL BASIS:
Public foundation.

ELIGIBILITY:
Organizations applying for grants must be tax-exempt as defined by IRS 501(c)(3) status. Except under unusual circumstances, no grants for endowments, capital campaigns, deficit financing, annual fund drives or fund-raising activities. The grant request must have the approval of the governing board of the requesting organization.

GEOG. RESTRICTIONS: Nine counties in southwestern Iowa and the greater Omaha, Nebraska area.

FINANCIAL DATA:
Amount of support per award: Up to $50,000.

Total amount of support: Varies.

NO. MOST RECENT APPLICANTS: Varies.

NO. AWARDS: Varies.

APPLICATION INFO:
Contact the Foundation for details.
Duration: Varies.
Deadline: Varies.

PUBLICATIONS:
Newsletter.

IRS I.D.: 47-0645958

ADDRESS INQUIRIES TO:
Program Manager or
Director of Community Investment
(See address above.)

ORANGE COUNTY COMMITY FOUNDATION   [224]

ORANGE COUNTY
COMMUNITY
FOUNDATION   [224]
4041 MacArthur Boulevard
Suite 510
Newport Beach, CA 92660-2503
(949) 553-4202
Fax: (949) 553-4211
E-mail: info@oc-cf.org
Web Site: www.oc-cf.org

FOUNDED: 1989

AREAS OF INTEREST:
Children and youth, family relationships,
diverse communities, music education and
performance, classical music and education,
health, environment and education.

TYPE:
Endowments; General operating grants;
Project/program grants; Scholarships. The
Foundation offers several grant programs
throughout the year in human services,
education, health, arts and culture, veterans,
citizenship, and the environment. Other
special grant competitions also occur
throughout the year.

YEAR PROGRAM STARTED: 1990

PURPOSE:
To encourage, support and facilitate
philanthropy in Orange County.

LEGAL BASIS:
Community foundation.

ELIGIBILITY:
Applicant agencies must be tax-exempt, serve
its residents, and operate without
discrimination on the basis of race, religion,
gender, sexual orientation, age, national
origin or disability.

GEOG. RESTRICTIONS: Primarily Orange County,
California.

FINANCIAL DATA:
Amount of support per award: Average grant:
$5,000 to $25,000.
Total amount of support: $58,979,000 for
fiscal year ending June 30, 2017.

CO-OP FUNDING PROGRAMS: Accelerate Change
Together Anaheim; OC Veterans Initiative; I
Heart OC Giving Day; OC Grantmakers.

APPLICATION INFO:
All applications and transcripts must be
submitted through the online application
system. Guidelines are available on the web
site.
Duration: Generally one year for unrestricted
grants. Renewal occasionally possible for
scholarships.
Deadline: Varies.

PUBLICATIONS:
Annual report; newsletters; guidelines.

IRS I.D.: 33-0378778

ADDRESS INQUIRIES TO:
Cathleen Otero, Vice President
Donor Relations and Programs
(See address above.)

THE BERNARD OSHER FOUNDATION   [225]

THE BERNARD OSHER
FOUNDATION   [225]
One Market Plaza
Spear Tower, Suite 4025
San Francisco, CA 94105
(415) 861-5587
E-mail: info@osherfoundation.org
Web Site: www.osherfoundation.org

FOUNDED: 1977

AREAS OF INTEREST:
Scholarship funding to selected colleges and
universities, integrative medicine, lifelong
learning for seasoned adults, arts and
humanities.

TYPE:
Project/program grants; Scholarships. The
Foundation provides scholarship funding
nationally to selected colleges and
universities and funds integrative medicine
centers at Harvard University, Northwestern
University, Vanderbilt University, the
University of California at San Francisco,
and the Karolinska Institute in Stockholm. It
also supports a growing network of lifelong
learning institutes for seasoned adults located
at 121 colleges and universities from Maine
to Hawaii. Arts and humanities grants are
made to nonprofit organizations principally in
the Greater San Francisco Bay Area,
specifically Alameda and San Francisco
counties, as well as the state of Maine.

YEAR PROGRAM STARTED: 1977

PURPOSE:
To provide scholarship funding nationally to
selected colleges and universities and to fund
integrative medicine centers; to support a
network of lifelong learning institutes for
seasoned adults; to support the arts and
humanities.

ELIGIBILITY:
Requests will be accepted only from
organizations which are classified by the IRS
as nonprofit and designated as IRS 501(c)(3).
Organizations seeking funds should have
experience which is relevant to the proposed
project.

The Foundation is precluded by its policies
from making direct grants to individuals.

FINANCIAL DATA:
Amount of support per award: Varies.
Total amount of support: Varies.

APPLICATION INFO:
A letter of inquiry is invited as the first step
in communicating with the Foundation.
Details can be found on the Foundation web
site.
Duration: Generally one year.

STAFF:
Mary G.F. Bitterman, President
Thomas Moffett, Chief Financial
Officer/Chief Investment Officer
David Blazevich, Senior Program Director
Eric Gillespie, Program Director
Jeanie Hirokane, Corporate Secretary and
Program Director

BOARD OF DIRECTORS:
Barbro Osher, Chairman
Bernard Osher, Founder and Treasurer
Mary G.F. Bitterman, President
David Agger
Phyllis Cook
Robert Friend
John Gallo
Laura Lauder
John Pritzker

ADDRESS INQUIRIES TO:
Jeanie Hirokane, Corporate Secretary and
Program Director
(See address above.)

PACCAR FOUNDATION   [226]

PACCAR FOUNDATION   [226]
777 106th Avenue, N.E.
Bellevue, WA 98004
(425) 468-7400
Fax: (425) 468-8216
E-mail: ken.hastings@paccar.com
Web Site: www.paccar.com

FOUNDED: 1951

AREAS OF INTEREST:
Education, science, arts and humanities.

TYPE:
Capital grants.

LEGAL BASIS:
Private foundation.

ELIGIBILITY:
No grants to individuals, political or lobbying
groups, fraternal organizations or religious
organizations for sectarian purposes.

GEOG. RESTRICTIONS: Columbus, Mississippi;
Chillicothe, Ohio; Broken Arrow, Oklahoma;
Denton, Texas; Bellevue, Kirkland, Renton,
Seattle and Skagit, Washington.

FINANCIAL DATA:
Amount of support per award: $10,000 to
$250,000.
Total amount of support: Average $5,000,000
per year.

APPLICATION INFO:
Guidelines and application procedures are
available on the Foundation web site.
Duration: One year. Must reapply for
continued funding.
Deadline: Applications accepted throughout
the year. Decisions made semiannually.

STAFF:
Ken Hastings, Vice President and General
Manager

ADDRESS INQUIRIES TO:
Ken Hastings
Vice President and General Manager
(See address above.)

PACIFIC GAS AND ELECTRIC COMPANY   [227]

PACIFIC GAS AND ELECTRIC
COMPANY   [227]
77 Beale Street
San Francisco, CA 94105
(415) 973-1150
E-mail: pmm2@pge.com
communityrelations@pge.com
Web Site: www.pge.com/giving

AREAS OF INTEREST:
Emergency preparedness and safety.

CONSULTING OR VOLUNTEER SERVICES:
Volunteer program.

TYPE:
Project/program grants; Scholarships.
Signature programs.

YEAR PROGRAM STARTED: 2001

LEGAL BASIS:
Corporate contributions program.

ELIGIBILITY:
Applicants must have tax-deductible status
from the IRS under Section 501(c)(3) or be a
unit of government (including a public
school). Contributions are not made to
individuals, for tickets for contests, raffles or
other prize-oriented activities, to religious
organizations (unless for a program offered
to the public on a nondiscriminatory basis
and without regard to the recipient's religious
affiliation), endowments, debt-reduction
campaigns, films, or to political or partisan
organizations or events.

The most successful grant applications are those that:
(1) address a demonstrated community need;
(2) link a nonprofit or government program to the Company's business goals and employee presence in the community and;
(3) can provide the grantee and the Company with recognition in the community.

GEOG. RESTRICTIONS: Northern and central California.

FINANCIAL DATA:
Amount of support per award: $1,000 to $25,000. Most grants are under $5,000.
Total amount of support: $17,500,000 in grants for the year 2019.
Matching fund requirements: 1:1 basis: $25 to $1,000 per calendar year, per employee.

NO. AWARDS: 735 grants for the year 2019.

APPLICATION INFO:
Prior to applying for a grant, applicants should contact the local PG&E representative in their project area to discuss the grant proposal. All applicants must use the online grant application. PG&E will neither accept nor process grant proposals in any other format. Please submit only a fully completed application. Incomplete applications will not be considered.
Duration: Generally one year.
Deadline: Applications are preferred before September 30 of each year.

ADDRESS INQUIRIES TO:
Pat Mora, Executive Administrator
(See address above.)

PACIFIC LIFE FOUNDATION [228]

700 Newport Center Drive
Newport Beach, CA 92660-6397
(949) 219-3214
E-mail: plfoundation@pacificlife.com
Web Site: www.pacificlifefoundation.com

FOUNDED: 1984

AREAS OF INTEREST:
Broad spectrum of social issues.

NAME(S) OF PROGRAMS:
- **Arts and Culture**
- **Civic, Community, and Environment**
- **Education**
- **Health and Human Services**

TYPE:
Capital grants; General operating grants; Matching gifts; Project/program grants. Arts and Culture: Funds nonprofit agencies that provide the public with a broad spectrum of arts and cultural initiatives (e.g., workshops, performances) to help build the public's appreciation of and participation in dance, music, and theater.

Civic, Community, and Environment: Funding is directed to a wide range of programs that enhance communities through leadership development and environmental protection, as well as fund research to learn more about marine mammals.

Education: Funds nonprofit agencies committed to providing quality educational programs for youth and adults (e.g., mentoring, tutoring, literacy) to help them excel academically and in life.

Health and Human Services: Contributions are allocated to agencies that seek to improve the quality of life of those in need, including the working poor, the homeless, and individuals with physical or developmental disabilities.

PURPOSE:
To recognize and support employees' varied interests and community involvement and, through focus programs, to identify and respond to particular community needs so that, whenever possible, funds may be channeled to those areas in which the most good can be accomplished with the funds available.

LEGAL BASIS:
Corporate foundation and corporate contributions program.

ELIGIBILITY:
Grants are made to nonprofit, tax-exempt, 501(c)(3) organizations. The Foundation does not provide support for individuals, for political parties, candidates or partisan political organizations, for labor organizations, fraternal organizations, athletic clubs or social clubs, for K-12 schools, school districts, or school foundations (contact Foundation for exceptions), for sectarian or denominational religious organizations, except for programs which are broadly promoted, available to anyone, and free from religious orientation, for fund-raising events (e.g., membership drives, luncheons/dinners, tournaments and benefits), or for advertising sponsorships.

GEOG. RESTRICTIONS: The Greater Orange County, California area and other areas, such as Omaha, Nebraska and Lynchburg, VA.

FINANCIAL DATA:
Amount of support per award: General grants: $5,000 to $15,000 for a one-year period of funding; Capital grants: $20,000 to $100,000, paid out over multiple years; Matching Gift Program for Higher Education: Up to $2,000; Matching Gift Program to Nonprofits: Up to $500.
Total amount of support: $7,000,000 in grants and $363,842 in matching gifts for the year 2018.

APPLICATION INFO:
Grant guidelines and application form are available online.
Duration: Agencies may reapply annually for funding; however, grants are made to any one agency for no more than three consecutive years. Support may again be requested after a two-year interim period.
Deadline: Submissions accepted July 15 to August 15.

PUBLICATIONS:
Annual report.

OFFICERS:
James T. Morris, Chairman and Chief Executive Officer
Carol R. Sudbeck, Vice Chairman
Tennyson S. Oyler, President
Tere Segarra, Vice President
Joshua Scott, Chief Financial Officer
Joseph J. Tortorelli, General Counsel
Jane M. Guon, Secretary
Marryn D. Santucci, Assistant Secretary
Starla C. Yamauchi, Assistant Secretary

BOARD OF DIRECTORS:
Ray Dinstel
Laurie Fitzgerald
Charles Jernigan
Lori Johnstone
David Leutenachlager
James T. Morris
Tennyson S. Oyler
Tere Segarra
Tim N. Shaheen
David Spencer
Janine C. Stallings
Carol R. Sudbeck
Brian T. Woolfolk
Christina Wu

ADDRESS INQUIRIES TO:
Tennyson S. Oyler, President
(See address above.)

THE DAVID AND LUCILE PACKARD FOUNDATION [229]

343 Second Street
Los Altos, CA 94022
(650) 948-7658
E-mail: inquiries@packard.org
Web Site: www.packard.org

FOUNDED: 1964

AREAS OF INTEREST:
Arts; children and youth, families and communities, food and shelter; conservation and sciences; organizational effectiveness; philanthropy; and Pueblo, CO.

NAME(S) OF PROGRAMS:
- **Children, Families and Communities**
- **Conservation and Science**
- **Local Grantmaking Program**
- **Reproductive Health**

TYPE:
Capital grants; Challenge/matching grants; Conferences/seminars; Demonstration grants; Development grants; Fellowships; General operating grants; Matching gifts; Project/program grants; Research grants; Scholarships; Seed money grants; Technical assistance. Grants are made to provide support in the local five-county area for organizational development, arts education and traditional performing arts, as well as for areas of wetlands preservation and restoration, marine fisheries protection and restoration.

Funds are also provided to support fellowships for 20 young professors in science and engineering.

In addition, the Foundation supports children's health programs through children, families, and communities programs, population and family planning services.

Support is given for research of the deep ocean in the Monterey, CA area and community grants in Pueblo County, CO.

YEAR PROGRAM STARTED: 1964

PURPOSE:
To support private, voluntary charities.

LEGAL BASIS:
Private foundation incorporated under California law.

ELIGIBILITY:
Applicants must be qualified tax-exempt charitable organizations. Most community-oriented grants are made to organizations that serve the people of Monterey, San Benito, San Mateo, Santa Clara and Santa Cruz counties. Requests for support of community and local activities outside of these geographical areas will rarely be considered. Grants are also made in Pueblo (CO) and for national and international programs in conservation, population, public policy and children's health. No proposals may be accepted that benefit individuals or that are for religious purposes.

APPLICATION INFO:
Contact the Foundation for guidelines.
Duration: Grants are made for one year, with occasional multiyear grants.

PUBLICATIONS:
Annual report; guideline brochures.

OFFICERS:
David Orr, Chairperson
Nancy Packard Burnett, Vice Chairperson
Julie E. Packard, Vice Chairperson
Craig Neyman, President and Chief Executive Officer
Alisa E. Mulligan, Chief Financial Officer and Controller
Chris DeCardy, Vice President and Director of Programs
Mary Anne Rodgers, General Counsel

BOARD OF TRUSTEES:
Ned Barnholt
Jason K. Burnett
Nancy Packard Burnett
Michael C. Camunez
Sierra Clark
Michael J. Klag
Dr. Stephen H. Lockhart
Jane Lubchenco
Linda A. Mason
Craig Neyman
David Orr
Katherine Orr
Susan Packard Orr
Julie E. Packard
Louise Stephens

ADDRESS INQUIRIES TO:
See e-mail address above.

THE PARKER FOUNDATION   [230]

2604-B El Camino Real
Suite 244
Carlsbad, CA 92008
(760) 720-0630
E-mail: mail@theparkerfoundation.org
Web Site: www.theparkerfoundation.org

FOUNDED: 1971

AREAS OF INTEREST:
Adult and youth services, visual and performing arts, museums and zoos, education, medical purposes, environment and community activities.

TYPE:
Capital grants; Challenge/matching grants; Matching gifts; Project/program grants. Programs and capital funding.

YEAR PROGRAM STARTED: 1971

PURPOSE:
To improve all aspects of life of the people of San Diego County, CA.

LEGAL BASIS:
Tax-exempt, independent private foundation.

ELIGIBILITY:
Applicants must be organizations operating in San Diego County, CA, qualified under IRS 501(c)(3). No grants to individuals or for support of conferences or symposia. No support provided for any project to the extent that it becomes dependent on the Foundation for continued existence.

GEOG. RESTRICTIONS: San Diego County, California.

FINANCIAL DATA:
Amount of support per award: Varies.
Total amount of support: $1,913,800 for fiscal year 2020.

NO. MOST RECENT APPLICANTS: 227 for the year 2020.

NO. AWARDS: 63 for the year 2020.

APPLICATION INFO:
Prior to submitting a proposal, an applicant should review the Application Process. Proposals may be submitted electronically through the Foundation's online process. Written proposals are also accepted.
Deadline: Dates are posted online throughout the year.

ADDRESS INQUIRIES TO:
Robbin C. Powell
Chief Administrative Officer
(See address above.)

*SPECIAL STIPULATIONS:
Limited by governing documents to San Diego County, CA.

PARKER HANNIFIN FOUNDATION   [231]

6035 Parkland Boulevard
Cleveland, OH 44124
(216) 896-3000
E-mail: parkerfoundation@parker.com
Web Site: www.parker.com

FOUNDED: 1953

AREAS OF INTEREST:
Education, disaster relief, energy and water conservation, and other charitable organizations.

TYPE:
Capital grants; Matching gifts; Project/program grants. Through the National Merit Scholarship for Parker employee children only. Matching gifts are for education.

LEGAL BASIS:
Corporate foundation.

ELIGIBILITY:
Grants are made to nonprofit organizations. Emphasis will be placed on organizations that benefit Parker employees and shareholders by improving services in communities with Parker operations and educational opportunities for current and potential employees. Organization must have a Parker sponsor.

Contributions will not be made to fraternal or labor organizations. Donations to religious organizations are limited to organizations serving the general public on a nondenominational basis, such as the Y's, Salvation Army, educational institutions, hospitals, etc.

GEOG. RESTRICTIONS: United States.

FINANCIAL DATA:
Amount of support per award: $500 minimum.
Total amount of support: Over $6,000,000 annually.

APPLICATION INFO:
Applicants should submit a proposal stating needs and what the grant will be used for, to the Parker division in their locality.
Duration: One-time award.
Deadline: June 30.

IRS I.D.: 34-6555686

THE RALPH M. PARSONS FOUNDATION   [232]

888 West 6th Street, 7th Floor
Los Angeles, CA 90017
(213) 362-7600
Web Site: www.rmpf.org

FOUNDED: 1961

AREAS OF INTEREST:
Civic and cultural, education, health, and human services.

TYPE:
Capital grants; General operating grants. Program support grants.

YEAR PROGRAM STARTED: 1978

LEGAL BASIS:
Not-for-profit corporation.

ELIGIBILITY:
Applicants must be 501(c)(3) organizations not classified under 509(a). Grants limited to organizations providing services in Los Angeles County.

No funding for mass mailings, fund-raisers, individuals, conferences, religious or political activities and/or dinners or endowments.

GEOG. RESTRICTIONS: Los Angeles County, California.

FINANCIAL DATA:
Amount of support per award: Varies.
Total amount of support: $18,500,000 for the year 2019.

NO. AWARDS: 311 for the year 2019.

REPRESENTATIVE AWARDS:
$100,000 to A Community of Friends for general support of housing with supportive services; $250,000 to Boys and Girls Club of Metro Los Angeles for general support of youth development programs; $500,000 over two years to Excellent Education Development for general support to expand and sustain the capacity of charter schools in Los Angeles County.

APPLICATION INFO:
Submit preliminary letter outlining project and amount requested. Program staff will determine whether applicant is qualified and may request additional information. Applicants are encouraged to visit the Foundation web site prior to submitting Letter of Inquiry.
Duration: Generally, one year.
Deadline: Applications are accepted on a rolling basis.

STAFF:
Wendy Garen, President and Chief Executive Officer
E. Thomas Brewer, Director, Finance and Administration
Nicole Larsen, Director, Grants Administration
Jennifer Price-Letscher, Director, Programs and Special Projects

BOARD OF DIRECTORS:
Peter J. Taylor, Chairperson
Paul G. Haaga, Jr., Vice Chairperson
Manuel A. Abascal
Karen Hill Scott
Elizabeth Lowe
Steven A. Nissen
Nina Revoyr
James A. Thomas
Gayle Wilson

ADDRESS INQUIRIES TO:
Wendy Garen
President and Chief Executive Officer
(See address above.)

AMELIA PEABODY CHARITABLE FUND [233]

185 Devonshire Street
Suite 600
Boston, MA 02110
(617) 451-6178
Web Site: apcfund.org

FOUNDED: 1984

AREAS OF INTEREST:
Medicine (human and animal), social welfare, visual arts, historic preservation and land conservation.

TYPE:
Capital grants; Challenge/matching grants. Grants to qualified nonprofit organizations existing and operating in Massachusetts.

PURPOSE:
To continue Amelia Peabody's philanthropy in perpetuity through grants.

LEGAL BASIS:
Private foundation.

ELIGIBILITY:
Eligible organizations must be IRS 501(c)(3) tax-exempt and classified as a public charity under Section 509(a)(1) or 509(a)(2) of the Internal Revenue Code.

No grants to individuals, religious organizations, education, startups, operating, administrative overhead, emergencies, scholarships, fellowships, endowments, organizations located outside of Massachusetts, or Section 509(a)(3) organizations funded principally with tax dollars.

GEOG. RESTRICTIONS: Massachusetts.

FINANCIAL DATA:
Amount of support per award: Varies per project.
Total amount of support: Approximately $8,000,000 annually.

NO. MOST RECENT APPLICANTS: Approximately 300.

NO. AWARDS: 100.

APPLICATION INFO:
All proposals are submitted online through the Fund web site.
Duration: May reapply after three years.
Deadline: April 1 and August 1.

PUBLICATIONS:
Guidelines.

IRS I.D.: 23-7364949

STAFF:
Bethany B. Kendall, Executive Director
Cheryl Gideon, Business and Grants Coordinator

ADDRESS INQUIRIES TO:
Cheryl Gideon
Business and Grants Coordinator
(See address above.)

PEACOCK FOUNDATION, INC. [234]

4000 Ponce De Leon Boulevard
Suite 450
Coral Gables, FL 33146
(305) 373-1386
E-mail: barbie@peacockfoundationinc.org
Web Site: peacockfoundationinc.org

AREAS OF INTEREST:
Elderly, children, youth, art for educational purposes, environmental education, disabilities, health and hospitals, medical research and human services.

TYPE:
General operating grants; Project/program grants. Support is provided for projects/programs and limited operating funds.

ELIGIBILITY:
Organizations classified as 501(c)(3) by the IRS can apply. Individuals are ineligible.

GEOG. RESTRICTIONS: Miami-Dade County, Florida.

FINANCIAL DATA:
Amount of support per award: Average $25,000.

NO. AWARDS: 51 for the year 2019.

APPLICATION INFO:
Applicants must initially submit letter of inquiry.
Duration: One year.

ADDRESS INQUIRIES TO:
Joelle Allen, Executive Director
(See address above.)

THE WILLIAM PENN FOUNDATION [235]

Two Logan Square, 11th Floor
100 North 18th Street
Philadelphia, PA 19103-2757
(215) 988-1830
Fax: (215) 988-1823
E-mail: grants@williampennfoundation.org
Web Site: www.williampennfoundation.org

FOUNDED: 1945

AREAS OF INTEREST:
Art, communities, culture, environment, children, youth and families.

NAME(S) OF PROGRAMS:
- **Creative Communities**
- **Great Learning**
- **Watershed Protection**

TYPE:
Capital grants; Challenge/matching grants; Demonstration grants; Development grants; General operating grants; Project/program grants; Research grants; Seed money grants; Technical assistance. Planning grants; Implementation grants.

In the areas of children, youth and families, grants are made to promote a better early care and education system, more effective and equitable education policies, networks of developmental opportunities for older youth, and improvements to the systems supporting families. The program focuses on critical transitions in the lives of children as they progress from birth, through early childhood, and into young adulthood.

In the area of environment and communities, grants are made to foster greater cross-sector collaborations that build on the assets of our region through revitalization of its urban core and protection and restoration of watersheds, with a focus on key waterways. Investments are intended to catalyze innovation and leadership in the region.

In the area of arts and culture, the Foundation provides various types of core operating support for arts groups and cultural institutions, enabling them to pursue their creative missions. Work is also funded that broadly advances the region's cultural sector. General operating grants are made only for arts funding.

YEAR PROGRAM STARTED: 1945

PURPOSE:
To improve the quality of life in the Greater Philadelphia area, particularly for its economically disadvantaged residents; to serve nonprofit organizations that help people improve their lives within a more just and caring society.

LEGAL BASIS:
Private foundation.

ELIGIBILITY:
Applicants must be organizations which are defined as tax-exempt under Section 501(c)(3) of the Internal Revenue Code and which are not private foundations. Grants may be made to religious institutions for nonsectarian purposes, to governments and national organizations in support of policy and advocacy projects.

The Foundation does not fund scholarships, fellowships, or grants to individuals; loans or investment programs; debt reduction; sectarian religious activities; housing capital projects; exempt organizations that pass funds to nonexempt groups; profit-making enterprises; nonpublic schools; programs for rehabilitation or research; programs to replace discontinued government support or national or international grants.

GEOG. RESTRICTIONS: Philadelphia area (Bucks, Chester, Delaware, Montgomery and Philadelphia counties), Pennsylvania and Camden, New Jersey.

FINANCIAL DATA:
Amount of support per award: Varies.
Total amount of support: $115,282,062 in total grants for year ended December 31, 2019.

CO-OP FUNDING PROGRAMS: The Foundation regularly joins with other foundations and institutions to fund projects.

NO. AWARDS: 256 for the year 2019.

APPLICATION INFO:
All applicants must first submit a letter of inquiry. Guidelines and inquiry form are available on the Foundation web site.

PUBLICATIONS:
Annual report.

IRS I.D.: 23-1503488

BOARD OF DIRECTORS:
Janet Haas, M.D., Chairperson
Katherine Christiano, Vice Chairperson
Christina Haas, Vice Chairperson
Lorena E. Ahumada
Andrew Haas
Leonard C. Haas
Peter Haas
Sarah Haas
Thomas Haas
Don Kimelman
Claire Lomax
Howard Meyers
Marcel Pratt
Robert Victor
Suzanne Welsh

OFFICERS AND STAFF:
Shawn McCaney, Executive Director
Bryan Ulishney, Director, Finance and Administration
Barbara Scace, Director, Grants Management

ADDRESS INQUIRIES TO:
See e-mail address above.

PEPSICO FOUNDATION [236]
700 Anderson Hill Road
Purchase, NY 10577
(914) 253-2000
Web Site: www.pepsico.
com/sustainability/philanthropy

FOUNDED: 1962

AREAS OF INTEREST:
Nutrition, water, women, and waste.

TYPE:
Capital grants.

PURPOSE:
To support programs that encourage healthy
lifestyles, improve availability of affordable
nutrition, expand access to clean water,
enhance sustainable agriculture capability,
enable job readiness, and empower women
and girls.

LEGAL BASIS:
Nonprofit under 501(c)(3).

ELIGIBILITY:
Organizations seeking a grant must be
registered and have an official tax-exemption
under Section 501(c)(3) of the Internal
Revenue Code, or the equivalent. The
Foundation does not make grants to
individuals, religious organizations or
political causes.

FINANCIAL DATA:
Amount of support per award: Varies.

APPLICATION INFO:
Submit a brief Letter of Interest. Complete
details are available on the Foundation web
site.

ADDRESS INQUIRIES TO:
Grants Manager
(See address above.)

THE CARL AND LILY PFORZHEIMER FOUNDATION, INC. [237]
122 East 42nd Street
Suite 4305
New York, NY 10168
(212) 223-6500
Fax: (212) 223-2222

FOUNDED: 1942

AREAS OF INTEREST:
Education, primarily early 19th century
English literature.

TYPE:
Grants-in-aid; Project/program grants.

PURPOSE:
To provide resources for the in-depth study
of 19th century English literature.

LEGAL BASIS:
Private foundation.

ELIGIBILITY:
Grants are awarded only to IRS 501(c)(3)
tax-exempt organizations. No grants are made
directly to individuals.

GEOG. RESTRICTIONS: Primarily United States.

FINANCIAL DATA:
Amount of support per award: Average:
$25,000 to $50,000.

APPLICATION INFO:
Organizations may submit a proposal.
Duration: Varies.

ADDRESS INQUIRIES TO:
Carl H. Pforzheimer III, President
(See address above.)

THE ALBERT PICK, JR. FUND [238]
70 East Lake Street
Suite 1120
Chicago, IL 60601
(312) 236-1192
E-mail: bettyjo@albertpickjrfund.org
Web Site: www.albertpickjrfund.org

FOUNDED: 1947

AREAS OF INTEREST:
Education, health and human services.

TYPE:
Challenge/matching grants; Demonstration
grants; Development grants; General
operating grants; Project/program grants.

YEAR PROGRAM STARTED: 1947

PURPOSE:
To offer a hand when help is needed.

LEGAL BASIS:
Private family foundation.

ELIGIBILITY:
Nonprofits with offices and separately
budgeted programs operating within the city
of Chicago.

GEOG. RESTRICTIONS: Chicago, Illinois.

FINANCIAL DATA:
Amount of support per award: $15,000 to
$35,000.

Total amount of support: Approximately
$1,330,189 for the year 2018.

NO. MOST RECENT APPLICANTS: Approximately
200.

NO. AWARDS: 80.

APPLICATION INFO:
Eligible nonprofits are requested to complete
an application form, available on the Fund
web site. Only those proposals which
completely meet the requirements outlined in
the guidelines will be reviewed.
Duration: Generally, one year.
Deadline: December 15 for the Spring
quarter, March 21 for the Summer quarter,
June 15 for Fall quarter and September 14
for Winter quarter.

PUBLICATIONS:
Guidelines; grant application form.

IRS I.D.: 36-6071402

OFFICERS AND BOARD OF DIRECTORS:
Shelly A. Davis, President
Mark A. Rosenberg, Treasurer
Rachel Lindsey, Secretary

ADDRESS INQUIRIES TO:
Betty Jo Joy, Grants Manager
(See address above.)

IRWIN ANDREW PORTER FOUNDATION [239]
3817 Thomas Avenue South
Minneapolis, MN 55410
E-mail: iapfound@gmail.com
Web Site: www.iapfoundation.org

FOUNDED: 1996

AREAS OF INTEREST:
Arts, education, environment and social
programs.

TYPE:
Challenge/matching grants; Grants-in-aid;
Project/program grants.

PURPOSE:
To fund innovative projects that foster
connections between individuals,
communities, the environment and the world
at large.

ELIGIBILITY:
The Foundation provides funding for a
variety of interest areas. The quality,
innovation, thoughtfulness and effectiveness
of a project are of more importance than the
specific interest area. However, its areas of
interest are the arts, education, environment
and social programs.

International projects should be applicable to,
and repeatable in, other regions. The
Foundation gives funding to nonprofit
organizations with U.S. IRS tax-exempt
status only. International organizations must
have a fiscal agent incorporated in the U.S.
with an appropriate U.S. IRS tax-exempt
designation.

The Foundation does not provide financial
support for:
(1) general operating expenses;
(2) capital projects;
(3) endowments;
(4) scholarships;
(5) fund-raising events or activities, social
events, goodwill advertising or marketing;
(6) lobbying, political, fraternal, athletic,
social or veterans organizations;
(7) religious programs;
(8) travel for individuals or groups;
(9) individuals or;
(10) ordinary school funding.

GEOG. RESTRICTIONS: Illinois, Iowa, Michigan,
Minnesota, North Dakota, South Dakota and
Wisconsin.

FINANCIAL DATA:
Amount of support per award: Grants: $1,000
to $30,000 annually.

Total amount of support: Approximately
$135,000 annually.

APPLICATION INFO:
Organizations are selected for an invitation to
apply from a group of secret nominators.
Duration: Generally, one year.

ADDRESS INQUIRIES TO:
Amy L. Hubbard, Chairman
(See address above.)

*PLEASE NOTE:
Foundation grantmaking is by invitation only;
unsolicited proposals will not be considered.

PPG INDUSTRIES FOUNDATION [240]
One PPG Place
Pittsburgh, PA 15272
(412) 434-2962
E-mail: foundation@ppg.com
Web Site: communities.ppg.com

FOUNDED: 1951

AREAS OF INTEREST:
Education and community sustainability.

TYPE:
Grants are provided to select organizations
and programs that advance the priority giving
areas of Education and Community
Sustainability. The PPG Foundation may be
able to provide in-kind support in the form of
product donations or employee volunteers
(mentors, guest speakers etc.) in addition to
its grants.

In the area of education, the Foundation is committed to supporting science, technology, engineering and math education programs that lead to academic and career achievement in fields such as Collision Repair Training, Color Science, Ceramic Engineering, Chemistry and Material Science. These investments help communities meet today's demands for a skilled workforce in research and development, manufacturing, information technology and other industry related professions, and develop a generation of innovators for tomorrow.

The Foundation also aims to stimulate interest and achievement in subjects related to science, technology, engineering and math as well as to help young people envision a future in a related career. In addition, limited funds are available to support initiatives designed to advance key industry and STEM-related topics central to the long-term needs of the industry.

In the area of community sustainability, the Foundation aims to strengthen local communities by supporting organizations and programs that meet critical needs, promote environmental sustainability, foster economic development and support disaster relief efforts. Priority funding within this area varies by location, based on the specific needs of PPG communities.

YEAR PROGRAM STARTED: 1951

PURPOSE:
To create brighter and more colorful communities where PPG has a presence around the world.

LEGAL BASIS:
Corporate, nonprofit foundation.

ELIGIBILITY:
All grants recipients must be nonprofit, charitable organizations tax-exempt under section 501(c)(3) of the Internal Revenue Code, if U.S.-based, or must be equivalent organizations, if outside of the U.S., with registered charitable status if available.

Funding priority is with organizations that are located in PPG or wholly-owned subsidiary locations.

FINANCIAL DATA:
Amount of support per award: Varies.

Total amount of support: $11,800,000 in support paid for the year 2019.

Matching fund requirements: Contributions by PPG employees and members of the board of directors of the company are matched on a 1:1 basis by the Foundation; $25 minimum, $10,000 maximum per year per donor.

APPLICATION INFO:
Applications are accepted on an invitation-only basis.

Duration: Varies.

Deadline: Requests for funding are accepted year-round.

BOARD OF DIRECTORS:
Michael H. McGarry, Chairman and Chief Executive Officer
Vince Morales, Senior Vice President and Chief Financial Officer
Anne M. Foulkes, Senior Vice President and General Counsel
Kevin Walling, Vice President and Chief Human Resources Officer

PRINCIPAL FINANCIAL GROUP FOUNDATION INC. [241]
711 High Street
Des Moines, IA 50392-0150
(515) 247-7227
E-mail: mcreynolds.mandi@principal.com
Web Site: www.principal.com/about-us/corporate-citizenship

FOUNDED: 1987

AREAS OF INTEREST:
Civic and community, arts and culture, higher education, K-12 education, STEM education, job readiness and job training, financial security, financial literacy, and disaster relief.

CONSULTING OR VOLUNTEER SERVICES:
The mission of the Principal Volunteer Network is to be the primary volunteer network for community service to educate and recruit employees, agents and retirees of the Principal Financial Group; thus enhancing the company's social responsibility goals and business objectives.

NAME(S) OF PROGRAMS:
● **Charitable Giving Program**

TYPE:
Capital grants; General operating grants; Project/program grants.

YEAR PROGRAM STARTED: 1987

LEGAL BASIS:
Corporate foundation.

ELIGIBILITY:
Applicants must be nonprofit IRS 501(c)(3) organizations located in communities with significant employee presence.

Grants are generally not made to athletes or athletic organizations, conference or seminar attendance, goodwill advertising, endowments or memorials, festival participation, fraternal organizations, hospital or health care facility capital fund drives, individuals, K-12 schools, libraries, partisan political organizations, private foundations, sectarian, religious or denominational organizations, social organizations, tax-supported organizations, or United Way organizations seeking funds for United Way-funded programs.

Grants to global locations are by invitation only.

GEOG. RESTRICTIONS: Folsom, California; Wilmington, Delaware; Cedar Falls, Greater Des Moines, Mason City and Waterloo, Iowa; Grand Island, Nebraska; Spokane, Washington; Appleton, Wisconsin.

FINANCIAL DATA:
Amount of support per award: $10,000 minimum.
Total amount of support: Varies.

NO. MOST RECENT APPLICANTS: 125.

NO. AWARDS: 110.

APPLICATION INFO:
Applications are submitted through the Foundation's web site. Paper or e-mail applications are no longer accepted.
Duration: One to two years, depending on funding area.
Deadline: March 15, June 15 and September 15, depending on funding area.

PUBLICATIONS:
Guidelines.

ADDRESS INQUIRIES TO:
Rachel Woodhouse, Program Manager
(See address above.)

PUBLIC WELFARE FOUNDATION, INC. [242]
1200 U Street, N.W.
Washington, DC 20009-4443
(202) 965-1800
Fax: (202) 265-8851
E-mail: info@publicwelfare.org
Web Site: www.publicwelfare.org

FOUNDED: 1947

AREAS OF INTEREST:
Criminal justice and youth justice.

NAME(S) OF PROGRAMS:
● **Criminal Justice**
● **Special Opportunities**
● **Youth Justice**

TYPE:
General operating grants; Project/program grants.

YEAR PROGRAM STARTED: 1947

PURPOSE:
To support efforts to ensure fundamental rights and opportunities for people in need; to look for carefully defined points where the Foundation's funds can make a difference in bringing about systemic changes that can improve the lives of countless people.

LEGAL BASIS:
Private foundation.

ELIGIBILITY:
Applicants' requests must adhere to the Foundation's funding guidelines.

GEOG. RESTRICTIONS: United States.

FINANCIAL DATA:
Amount of support per award: Varies.

Total amount of support: $1,372,000 for fiscal year 2018.

NO. AWARDS: 175 approved grants for fiscal year 2018.

APPLICATION INFO:
Applicants should submit letters of inquiry using the online application system. This letter should contain facts and figures about the organization, describe its mission and explain the purpose of the request, including the Program under which a grant is being requested. Applicants will be invited by e-mail to submit full proposals. The Foundation cannot consider full proposals which have not been invited.

Duration: Usually one to two years. Renewal possible.

Deadline: Varies.

IRS I.D.: 54-0597601

BOARD OF DIRECTORS AND OFFICERS:
Cliff Sloan, Chairperson
Craig Aase
Stephanie Bell-Rose
Colin Diver
David Dodson
Christopher Graham
Gumersindo Oliveros
Maria Otero
Shirley Sagawa
Kim Taylor-Thompson
Eric Washington

ADDRESS INQUIRIES TO:
Grants Management
(See address above.)

THE QUAKER CHEMICAL FOUNDATION [243]

901 East Hector Street
Conshohocken, PA 19428-2380
(610) 832-8659
Fax: (610) 832-4496
E-mail: foundation@quakerchem.com
Web Site: www.quakerchem.com

FOUNDED: 1959

AREAS OF INTEREST:
Civic and community; cultural, health and welfare; and education.

NAME(S) OF PROGRAMS:
- **Grant Program**
- **Matching Gift Program**
- **Scholarship Program**

TYPE:
Matching gifts; Project/program grants; Scholarships. The Foundation matches employee gifts to qualified educational institutions, health and welfare organizations, civic and community, and arts or cultural institutions which are operated for the benefit of the general public.

YEAR PROGRAM STARTED: 1959

PURPOSE:
To help community projects where the company has domestic operations.

LEGAL BASIS:
Corporate foundation.

ELIGIBILITY:
Applicants must be IRS 501(c)(3) tax-exempt organizations. As a general rule, the Foundation does not support national organizations, limiting its interest to those organizations that are active in the areas in which the Quaker Chemical Corporation has operations, generally located within a five-mile radius of company facilities and locations.

FINANCIAL DATA:
Amount of support per award: $1,000 to $5,000; average: $1,500.
Matching fund requirements: Minimum $25 and maximum $1,000 per employee, retiree, director or spouse thereof per fiscal year.

REPRESENTATIVE AWARDS:
Conshohocken Fellowship House; Delaware Valley Science Fairs.

APPLICATION INFO:
In addition to a completed grant application, the grant request should include the following:
(1) cover letter on the organization's stationery, providing a brief history of the organization and its objectives;
(2) description of the program or activity for which funds are being requested, including the amount of funds being requested and the benefits realized by the local community;
(3) current operating budget and latest audited financial statements;
(4) list of funding sources for the organization, including past major contributors with amounts, recent applications with results, and anticipated future funding sources;
(5) list of directors and officers and their affiliations and;
(6) copy of organization's tax-exempt ruling under Section 501(c)(3) of the Internal Revenue Code.
Duration: One year.
Deadline: April 30.

PUBLICATIONS:
Grant application guidelines.

IRS I.D.: 23-6245803

TRUSTEES:
Cindy Cetnar
James Gabriel
Paul Gorman
Jennifer Hill
Jessica Sabedra

ADDRESS INQUIRIES TO:
Quaker Chemical Foundation Secretary
(See address above.)

THE NELL J. REDFIELD FOUNDATION [244]

P.O. Box 61
Reno, NV 89504
(775) 323-1373
Fax: (775) 323-4476
E-mail: gsmith@redfieldfoundation.org

FOUNDED: 1974

AREAS OF INTEREST:
Education, health care, and care for the needy.

TYPE:
Capital grants; Challenge/matching grants; Development grants; Matching gifts; Project/program grants. Grants for higher education. Medical and social welfare for disadvantaged children and seniors.

PURPOSE:
To promote education, health care and care for the homeless poor.

LEGAL BASIS:
Nonprofit foundation.

ELIGIBILITY:
Grants are made to organizations that have tax-exempt status under Section 501(c)(3) of the Internal Revenue Code. Nonsectarian religious programs may apply. No grants are made to individuals or private foundations.

Grants are restricted to organizations in Washoe County, Nevada.

GEOG. RESTRICTIONS: Washoe County, Nevada.

FINANCIAL DATA:
Amount of support per award: Varies.
Total amount of support: Varies.

NO. MOST RECENT APPLICANTS: 125.

NO. AWARDS: 75.

APPLICATION INFO:
Initially, contact the fund with a two-page summary that includes the specific goals, objectives, proposed activities and results expected.
Duration: One year. Renewal possible.
Deadline: Quarterly during each calendar year.

ADDRESS INQUIRIES TO:
Gerald C. Smith, Director
(See address above.)

THE REEBOK FOUNDATION [245]

25 Drydock Avenue
Boston, MA 02210
(857) 443-2000

FOUNDED: 1986

AREAS OF INTEREST:
Sport and fitness.

TYPE:
General operating grants; Matching gifts.

YEAR PROGRAM STARTED: 1986

PURPOSE:
To improve health outcomes of disadvantaged women and children through increased fitness access and inspiration.

LEGAL BASIS:
Corporate foundation.

ELIGIBILITY:
Grant applicants must be nonprofit organizations that provide equal access to funding and equal opportunity, and do not discriminate based on race, religion or sex. Grants are not made to individuals, political or fraternal organizations, or for advertising in program books or medical research.

GEOG. RESTRICTIONS: United States.

FINANCIAL DATA:
Amount of support per award: Grants: Up to $15,000.
Matching fund requirements: Employees of Reebok International Ltd, its subsidiaries and divisions. Organizations must be IRS 501(c)(3). Employee contributions to qualified organizations are matched dollar-for-dollar, up to $1,500 maximum.

APPLICATION INFO:
All requests for community support must be submitted online.
Deadline: Letters of Intent are accepted March 15 to April 15. Full Application: June 1. Decision by July 1.

PUBLICATIONS:
Guidelines.

IRS I.D.: 04-3073548

THE CHARLES H. REVSON FOUNDATION [246]

55 East 59th Street
23rd Floor
New York, NY 10022
(212) 935-3340
Fax: (212) 688-0633
E-mail: info@revsonfoundation.org
Web Site: revsonfoundation.org

FOUNDED: 1956

AREAS OF INTEREST:
Urban affairs, with emphasis on New York City, education, biomedical research policy and Jewish philanthropy and education.

TYPE:
Fellowships; Project/program grants; Research grants. The Foundation supports a number of ongoing fellowship programs in public policy, biomedical research and Jewish education.

YEAR PROGRAM STARTED: 1978

PURPOSE:
To make a commitment to spread knowledge and to improve human life.

LEGAL BASIS:
Private foundation.

ELIGIBILITY:
Grants are made to nonprofit, tax-exempt organizations. The Foundation does not make grants to individuals or for endowments, local health appeals, direct-service programs, building or construction funds, or routine budgetary support.

GEOG. RESTRICTIONS: New York, New York and Israel.

FINANCIAL DATA:
Amount of support per award: Varies.

APPLICATION INFO:
The Foundation welcomes e-mails from prospective grantees. Applicant should send a very brief description of the project including the following information:
(1) organization name;
(2) name of contact, including e-mail, telephone number and mailing address;
(3) project title;
(4) project budget;
(5) amount sought and;
(6) description of project.
Do not include any attachments.

The Foundation is unable to accept inquiries by mail or telephone.
Duration: Varies.

IRS I.D.: 13-6126105

STAFF:
Julie Sandorf, President
Meredith Korn, Chief Financial and Administrative Officer
Martha King, Senior Program Officer
Elizabeth Leiman Kraiem, Senior Program Officer
Rebecca Furth, Assistant Program Officer
Karen Yu, Controller

BOARD OF DIRECTORS:
Cheryl Cohen Effron, Chairman
Stacy Dick, Treasurer
Sharon Greenberger, Secretary
Steven E. Hyman, M.D.
Rev. Phillip A. Jackson
Dr. Robert Kingston
Reynold Levy
Errol Louis
David Resnick
Charles H. Revson, Jr.
Marcia Lynn Sells
Pam Wasserstein

ADDRESS INQUIRIES TO:
See e-mail address above.

Z. SMITH REYNOLDS FOUNDATION, INC. [247]
102 West Third Street
Suite 1110
Winston-Salem, NC 27101-3940
(336) 725-7541
(800) 443-8319
Fax: (336) 725-6069
E-mail: shaheent@zsr.org
Web Site: www.zsr.org

FOUNDED: 1936

AREAS OF INTEREST:
Civic participation, collaboration, dignity and equity, fairness and justice, excellence, integrity, stewardship, and sustainability.

NAME(S) OF PROGRAMS:
• All for NC

TYPE:
Challenge/matching grants; Fellowships; General operating grants; Project/program grants; Seed money grants. Sabbatical Program. All for NC aligns with the Foundation's mission and core values through three key strategies: support a network of organizations that are working to affect change through a State-Level Systemic Change Strategy; create more connections between people, places, organizations and sectors who are working to impact the communities in which they live through a Community-Based Strategy; and remain open

to bold, unconventional or higher-risk ideas that have transformative potential through an Exploratory, Visionary Ideas Strategy.

Alongside these three main strategies, the Foundation also has expressed its commitment to augment its participation in its hometown of Winston-Salem/Forsyth County, NC; use a racial equity lens to underpin all of its work; and continue to be a learning organization.

YEAR PROGRAM STARTED: 1936

PURPOSE:
To support charitable causes within the state of North Carolina.

LEGAL BASIS:
Private foundation.

ELIGIBILITY:
North Carolina public and nonprofit private institutions and organizations are eligible. No grants are made to individuals for any purpose.

GEOG. RESTRICTIONS: North Carolina.

FINANCIAL DATA:
Total amount of support: Approximately $17,055,945 for the year ended December 31, 2018.

APPLICATION INFO:
Application information can be downloaded from the web site.
Deadline: Application deadlines are posted on the Foundation web site.

PUBLICATIONS:
Annual report (online).

IRS I.D.: 58-6038145

OFFICERS:
W. Noah Reynolds, President
Daniel G. Clodfelter, Vice President
Piper Neal Beveridge, Treasurer
Pamela Spalding, Assistant Treasurer
Maurice O. Green, Secretary
Chapel Thompson, Assistant Secretary

TRUSTEES:
Nancy R. Bagley
Piper Neal Beveridge
Anita Brown-Graham
Angela R. Bryant
Daniel G. Clodfelter
Ilana Dubester
Mary Mountcastle
Anna Warburton Munroe
David L. Neal
Jane S. Patterson
W. Noah Reynolds
Virgil L. Smith
Lloyd P. Tate, Jr.

ADDRESS INQUIRIES TO:
Maurice O. Green, Secretary
(See address above.)

THE RHODE ISLAND FOUNDATION/RHODE ISLAND COMMUNITY FOUNDATION [248]
One Union Station
Providence, RI 02903-1746
(401) 274-4564
Fax: (401) 331-8085
E-mail: info@rifoundation.org
Web Site: www.rifoundation.org

FOUNDED: 1916

AREAS OF INTEREST:
Economic security, educational success, healthy lives, arts and culture, children and families, environment, housing and human basic needs.

TYPE:
Challenge/matching grants; Conferences/seminars; Demonstration grants; Development grants; Fellowships; General operating grants; Project/program grants; Research grants; Scholarships; Technical assistance; Loan forgiveness programs. Strategy grants; Small grants; Basic human needs grants; Regional grants.

YEAR PROGRAM STARTED: 1916

PURPOSE:
To support projects that address significant community challenges, aim for lasting impact, and serve disadvantaged Rhode Islanders.

LEGAL BASIS:
Community foundation.

ELIGIBILITY:
Grants are not generally made directly to individuals. Programs must primarily benefit Rhode Island.

GEOG. RESTRICTIONS: Rhode Island.

FINANCIAL DATA:
Amount of support per award: Varies.
Total amount of support: $51,107,560 for the year 2019.

APPLICATION INFO:
Guidelines are available at the Foundation web site.

PUBLICATIONS:
Annual report; newsletter; guidelines; reports.

BOARD OF DIRECTORS:
Mary Brooks Wall, Chairman
Michael K. Allio
Jonathan D. Fain
Carrie Bridges Feliz
Ann-Marie Harrington
Meghan Hughes, Ph.D
G. Alan Kurose, MD., MBA, FACP
Tony Mendez
Theresa Moore
Peter R. Phillips
Janet Robinson
Neil D. Steinberg
James Wright

ADDRESS INQUIRIES TO:
Donna Sowden, Administrative Assistant of Grant Programs
(See address above.)

SID W. RICHARDSON FOUNDATION [249]
309 Main Street
Fort Worth, TX 76102
(817) 336-0494
E-mail: sranelle@sidrichardson.org
Web Site: www.sidrichardson.org

FOUNDED: 1947

AREAS OF INTEREST:
Education, health, human service, and the arts.

TYPE:
Capital grants; Challenge/matching grants; Development grants; General operating grants; Matching gifts; Project/program grants; Research grants.

PURPOSE:
To support organizations that serve the people of Texas.

LEGAL BASIS:
Private foundation.

ELIGIBILITY:
All funds must be limited to the state of
Texas for IRS 501(c)(3) tax-exempt
institutions and organizations or 509(a)
organizations (other than a private foundation
under the latter code). An organization also
may qualify if it falls within the terms of
Section 170(c)(1) and the contribution
requested is to be used exclusively for public
purposes. No grants are made to individuals.

GEOG. RESTRICTIONS: Texas.

FINANCIAL DATA:
Amount of support per award: $1,000 to
$5,000,000.
Matching fund requirements: Varies.

NO. MOST RECENT APPLICANTS: Approximately
500 to 600.

NO. AWARDS: Approximately 145 to 160.

REPRESENTATIVE AWARDS:
Education: $150,000 to Communities in
Schools, Fort Worth, Inc. for the program to
place counselors in public schools across
Tarrant County; Health: $75,000 to Child
Study Center for diagnostic and treatment
services for children with disabilities; Human
Services: $110,000 to Catholic Charities
Diocese of Fort Worth for the transportation
program; Cultural: $50,000 to National
Cowgirl Museum and Hall of Fame, Inc. for
operational support.

APPLICATION INFO:
Instructions are available on the Foundation
web site.
Duration: Typically one year.
Deadline: January 15.

PUBLICATIONS:
Annual report.

IRS I.D.: 75-6015828

BOARD OF DIRECTORS:
Edward P. Bass, Chairman
Lee M. Bass, Vice President
Sid R. Bass, Vice President

ADDRESS INQUIRIES TO:
Pete Geren, President
(See address above.)

ROCKEFELLER FAMILY FUND   [250]

475 Riverside Drive
Suite 900
New York, NY 10115-0066
(212) 812-4252
Fax: (212) 812-4299
E-mail: ccaddle-steele@rffund.org
Web Site: www.rffund.org

FOUNDED: 1967

NAME(S) OF PROGRAMS:
● **Economic Justice for Women**
● **Environment**
● **Institutional Accountability and
Individual Liberty**

TYPE:
Challenge/matching grants; General operating
grants. Economic Justice for Women program
seeks to improve the quality of life for
working women and their families by
advocating for equitable employment
opportunities and updated employment
standards.

Initiatives under the Environment program
are designed to enact aggressive policies at
the state and national levels to reduce carbon
emissions; highlight the risks of coal-burning
power plants and mountaintop removal
coal-mining, and sound climate science,
while exposing those who distort it.

The Institutional Accountability and
Individual Liberty program encourages the
active participation of citizens in government,
seeks to make government and private
institutions more accountable and responsive,
and supports efforts to ensure that
individuals' rights and liberties under the
Constitution are protected.

YEAR PROGRAM STARTED: 1967

PURPOSE:
To make grants to nonprofit organizations in
the areas of economic justice for women, the
environment, and institutional accountability
and individual liberty.

LEGAL BASIS:
A not-for-profit charitable corporation
existing under the New York state
not-for-profit corporation law.

ELIGIBILITY:
Tax-exempt organizations engaged in
educational and charitable activities of
national significance are eligible for support.

The Fund does not ordinarily consider
projects that pertain to a single community,
except in the rare instance where a project is
unique, strategically placed to advance a
national issue, or is likely to serve as a
national model. Grants are rarely made to
organizations which traditionally enjoy
popular support, such as universities,
museums, hospitals or endowed institutions.

The Family Fund does not make grants for
academic or scholarly research or social or
human service programs. Grants are also not
made to support individuals, scholarships,
international programs, domestic programs
dealing with international issues,
profit-making businesses, construction or
restoration projects, or to reduce an
organization's debt. Instead, support is
offered for advocacy efforts that are
action-oriented and likely to yield tangible
public policy results.

GEOG. RESTRICTIONS: United States.

FINANCIAL DATA:
Amount of support per award: $25,000 to
$75,000.
Total amount of support: Approximately
$2,500,000 annually.
Matching fund requirements: Fund will
match employee contributions.

APPLICATION INFO:
The Fund has implemented an initial online
inquiry system as part of its grantmaking
process. The initial inquiry system consists of
an eligibility quiz followed by an online
letter of inquiry. Before taking the eligibility
quiz, applicants are urged to review the
Frequently Asked Questions section, which
details the funding guidelines.
Duration: One year. Limited multiyear
funding for select projects.
Deadline: Letters of inquiry are accepted
throughout the year.

PUBLICATIONS:
Annual report.

TRUSTEES:
Miranda Kaiser, President

Alexandra Chasin, Vice President
Clare M. Pierson, Vice President
Tara Rockefeller, Vice President
Lucia Gill Case
Peter Gill Case
Michael Lambert
Rebecca Lambert
Phebe Pierson
Fran Rodgers
Tracy Toon Spencer
Naomi Waletzky
Liam Wang

ADDRESS INQUIRIES TO:
Carolyn Caddle-Steele, Grants Manager
(See address above.)

ROCKWELL FUND, INC.   [251]

770 South Post Oak Lane
Suite 525
Houston, TX 77056
(713) 629-9022
Fax: (713) 629-7702
E-mail: grantsinfo@rockfund.org
Web Site: www.rockfund.org

FOUNDED: 1931

AREAS OF INTEREST:
Education, health and housing.

NAME(S) OF PROGRAMS:
● **Capacity Building Grants**
● **Operating Funds**
● **Program/Project Support**

TYPE:
Challenge/matching grants; Development
grants; General operating grants; Matching
gifts; Project/program grants; Seed money
grants; Technical assistance. Capacity
building grants.

YEAR PROGRAM STARTED: 1949

PURPOSE:
To improve the quality of life in the greater
Houston area; to pursue change through
cooperative philanthropy.

LEGAL BASIS:
Nonprofit organization.

ELIGIBILITY:
Eligible organizations must have IRS
501(c)(3) not-for-profit status. A church or
political subdivision that is not required to
obtain a Section 501(c)(3) designation in
order to be a permitted donee of a private
foundation is also eligible. Grants are not
made to individuals. The Fund does not
provide financial support to programs or
organizations outside of its stated issue areas.

GEOG. RESTRICTIONS: Greater Houston, Texas
area.

FINANCIAL DATA:
Amount of support per award: Varies.
Total amount of support: $3,876,517 in total
grants for the year 2019.

NO. AWARDS: 45 for the year 2019.

APPLICATION INFO:
Applying organizations must have IRS Form
990 and Internal Revenue Code 501(c)(3)
documentation. Consult the web site for
application details. The Fund only accepts
electronic submission of completed
applications via e-mail. It does not accept
applications sent via fax, mail or hand
delivery.
Duration: One year. Renewable by
reapplication.
Deadline: Varies.

IRS I.D.: 74-6040258

STAFF:
R. Terry Bell, President and Chief Executive Officer
Margaret E. McConn, C.P.A., Vice President, Chief Financial Officer and Chief Investment Officer
Don A. Titcombe, M.S.S.W., Senior Program Officer
Judy A. Ahlgrim, Grants Administrator
Michelle Sealey, Controller

ADDRESS INQUIRIES TO:
Judy A. Ahlgrim, Grants Administrator
(See address above.)

ROLEX SA [252]
P.O. Box 1311
1211 Geneva 26 Switzerland
(41) 22 302 7269
(41) 22 302 2200
E-mail: rae@rolex.com
Web Site: www.rolex.org

FOUNDED: 1976

AREAS OF INTEREST:
Environment, applied technology, exploration, health and science, and cultural heritage.

NAME(S) OF PROGRAMS:
- **Rolex Awards for Enterprise Program**

TYPE:
Awards/prizes; Project/program grants. For more than 40 years, Rolex has biennially honored extraordinary individuals who possess the courage and conviction to take on major challenges. Each Rolex Award for Enterprise is given for a new or ongoing project anywhere in the world - one that deserves support for its capacity to improve lives, or protect the world's natural and cultural heritage. These projects have touched all aspects of humanity by expanding knowledge or improving life on the planet.

YEAR PROGRAM STARTED: 1976

PURPOSE:
To honor individuals who possess the courage and conviction to take on major challenges.

ELIGIBILITY:
Open to candidates over the age of 18 at the time of application.

An application may be submitted only by an individual. No institutional or collective applications are allowed. Only one application per person is allowed.

The application must be completed in English by the person who plays a leading role in the project or organization.

NO. MOST RECENT APPLICANTS: 1,500 to 2,500.

NO. AWARDS: 5.

APPLICATION INFO:
Complete application information is available on the web site.
Duration: One time per project.
Deadline: Varies.

ST. CROIX VALLEY FOUNDATION
516 Second Street, Suite 214
Hudson, WI 54016
(715) 386-9490
Fax: (715) 386-1250
E-mail: info@scvfoundation.org
Web Site: www.scvfoundation.org

TYPE:
Project/program grants; Scholarships. Environmental and humane grants.

See entry 1237 for full listing.

SALISBURY-ROWAN COMMUNITY FOUNDATION [253]
220 North Tryon Street
Charlotte, NC 28202
(704) 973-4568
E-mail: aowens@fftc.org
Web Site: www.salisbury-cf.org

FOUNDED: 1944

AREAS OF INTEREST:
Arts and culture, animal welfare, career readiness and workforce development, health care, public education K-12, higher education, environment and human services.

TYPE:
Project/program grants.

YEAR PROGRAM STARTED: 1944

PURPOSE:
To inspire philanthropy and strengthen the community by supporting initiatives that address local needs and provide quality services to donors and constituents.

LEGAL BASIS:
Community foundation.

ELIGIBILITY:
Grants are awarded to eligible organizations, including 501(c)(3) nonprofit organizations, congregations, governmental and educational institutions, for projects benefitting the residents of Salisbury and Rowan County, NC. If the organization conducting the project is not an eligible organization, a grant can be applied for under the fiscal sponsorship of an eligible organization. Priority will be given to requests for projects and programs that address a community need.

For-profit businesses are not eligible.

GEOG. RESTRICTIONS: Salisbury and Rowan County, North Carolina.

FINANCIAL DATA:
Amount of support per award: Up to $10,000. Typically, $2,500 to $8,000.

APPLICATION INFO:
Grantseekers are invited to visit the Online Grants Center at fftcgrants.communityforce.com and search for Salisbury-Rowan Community Foundation to access the online application.
Duration: One year.
Deadline: September 11.

PUBLICATIONS:
Annual report.

IRS I.D.: 56-0772117

GOVERNING BOARD:
Jewell Hoover, Chairperson
Kendall Alley
Gwin Barr
Cathy Bessant
Chantay Bouler
Marian Steele Clark
Jesse Cureton
Al de Molina
Lynn Good
Barnes Hauptfuhrer
Kelly King
Todd Mansfield

Arrington Mixon
Janice Patrick
Chris Poplin
Kevin Roche
Lynne Scott Safrit
Ruth Shaw
Fred Whitfield

ADDRESS INQUIRIES TO:
Daavonia Womack-Lee, Administrative Assistant
Foundation for the Carolinas
E-mail: dwomack-lee@fftc.org or
Alexis Owens, Assistant Vice President
(See address above.)

THE FAN FOX AND LESLIE R. SAMUELS FOUNDATION, INC. [254]
275 Madison Avenue, 31st Floor
New York, NY 10016
(212) 239-3030
Fax: (212) 239-3039
E-mail: info@samuels.org
Web Site: www.samuels.org

FOUNDED: 1959

AREAS OF INTEREST:
Performing arts, health care, and quality of life for the elderly.

NAME(S) OF PROGRAMS:
- **Healthy Aging Program**
- **Performing Arts**

TYPE:
Development grants; Project/program grants. General operating grants for performing artists only.

In the area of health care, the Foundation will consider funding direct health care and social service programs to improve quality of life for New York City elderly.

The Foundation realizes that it cannot support an organization indefinitely and expects the programs it funds to become self-supporting within a few years.

YEAR PROGRAM STARTED: 1959

PURPOSE:
To provide funding for the performing arts in New York, NY; to improve the health care and quality of life of the elderly in New York, NY.

LEGAL BASIS:
Private foundation.

ELIGIBILITY:
Grants are made to organizations that are tax-exempt under Section 501(c)(3) of the Internal Revenue Code. The Foundation does not give grants to individuals or for scholarships. General operating support is for performing arts only.

GEOG. RESTRICTIONS: New York, New York.

FINANCIAL DATA:
Amount of support per award: $5,000 to $300,000.
Total amount of support: Varies.

NO. MOST RECENT APPLICANTS: 275.

NO. AWARDS: 190.

APPLICATION INFO:
A letter (not to exceed three typewritten pages) should briefly summarize the proposal and state the amount of the grant being requested. A copy of the organization's tax exemption letter issued by the IRS, most recent audited financial report, organization brochure (if available), Board of Directors list, project budget and current contributors

list should be included. Specific guidelines on the application process can be found on the Foundation web site.

Duration: Health Care: One to two years; Performing Arts: One year.

IRS I.D.: 13-3124818

STAFF:
Alexandra Francis, Program Associate

OFFICERS AND DIRECTORS:
Joseph Mitchell, Chairman
Robert Marx, President
Julio Urbina, Vice President

ADDRESS INQUIRIES TO:
Alexandra Francis, Program Associate
(See address above.)

SAN FRANCISCO FOUNDATION   [255]

One Embarcadero Center
Suite 1400
San Francisco, CA 94111
(415) 733-8500
Fax: (415) 477-2783
E-mail: info@sff.org
Web Site: sff.org

FOUNDED: 1948

AREAS OF INTEREST:
Community health, education, arts and culture, community development, and the environment.

NAME(S) OF PROGRAMS:
• **Koshland Young Leader Awards**

TYPE:
Scholarships. The Koshland Young Leader Awards recognize the next generation of leadership in the local community. This scholarship program provides financial assistance to college-bound San Francisco public high school students from economically disadvantaged backgrounds.

YEAR PROGRAM STARTED: 1999

PURPOSE:
To promote change in the areas of community health, education, arts and culture, community development, and the environment.

LEGAL BASIS:
Community foundation.

ELIGIBILITY:
Nominee must have 3.25 cumulative or continually improving grade point average, be college-bound, and embrace a commitment to strengthening their families and communities despite facing formidable life challenges.

GEOG. RESTRICTIONS: San Francisco, California.

FINANCIAL DATA:
Award to be used for education-related expenses such as academic test fees, computers, books and supplies for classes.
Amount of support per award: $10,000.

NO. AWARDS: Up to 11 each year.

APPLICATION INFO:
There is a three-part nomination process:
(1) Teacher/counselor submits the online Teacher Nomination Form, including complete official high school transcript;
(2) Student submits online Self-Nomination Form and;
(3) Finalists will be invited to a mandatory in-person interview at the San Francisco Foundation.

Late or incomplete nominations will not be considered.

Duration: Two years.

ADDRESS INQUIRIES TO:
Ali Sirkus Brody
E-mail: abrody@sff.org

SARKEYS FOUNDATION   [256]

530 East Main Street
Norman, OK 73071
(405) 364-3703
Fax: (405) 364-8191
E-mail: sarkeys@sarkeys.org
Web Site: www.sarkeys.org

FOUNDED: 1962

AREAS OF INTEREST:
Education, health care and medical research, cultural and humanitarian programs of regional interest.

TYPE:
Capital grants; Challenge/matching grants; Development grants; Endowments; Matching gifts; Professorships; Project/program grants; Research grants; Technical assistance; Training grants.

YEAR PROGRAM STARTED: 1962

PURPOSE:
To improve the quality of life in Oklahoma.

LEGAL BASIS:
Private charitable foundation.

ELIGIBILITY:
Applicants must be 501(c)(3) organizations which are not private foundations under 509(a) of the Internal Revenue Code. Organization must be headquartered and operating within the state of Oklahoma.

GEOG. RESTRICTIONS: Oklahoma.

FINANCIAL DATA:
Amount of support per award: Varies.
Total amount of support: Approximately $3,200,000 for the year 2018.

NO. AWARDS: Approximately 125.

APPLICATION INFO:
Organizations are required to submit a Letter of Inquiry to determine whether they meet the criteria and priorities for funding. Form and instructions are posted on the Foundation web site. Letter of Inquiry and grant application must be submitted electronically.

Representatives are required to speak with a program officer for a pre-grant interview.
Duration: Varies.
Deadline: Letter of Inquiry: December 1 and June 1.

PUBLICATIONS:
Application guidelines; annual report.

BOARD MEMBERS:
Teresa B. Adwan
Elizabeth Base
Dr. John Bell
Dan Little
Joseph W. Morris
Terry W. West

ADDRESS INQUIRIES TO:
Kim Henry, Executive Director
Susan Frantz, Senior Program Officer
Linda English Weeks, Senior Program Officer
or
Natalie Carns, Program Officer
(See address above.)

*SPECIAL STIPULATIONS:
The recipient must sign an agreement outlining the terms of the award and provide reports as requested. Outside independent audit required for organizations whose assets or operating budget exceeds $500,000.

DR. SCHOLL FOUNDATION [257]

1033 Skokie Boulevard
Suite 230
Northbrook, IL 60062-4109
(847) 559-7430
E-mail: grants@drschollfoundation.com
Web Site: www.drschollfoundation.com

FOUNDED: 1947

AREAS OF INTEREST:
Private education at all levels, including elementary and secondary schools, colleges and universities, and medical and nursing institutions; general charitable programs, including grants to hospitals and programs for children, developmentally disabled and senior citizens, civic, cultural, social services, health care, economic and religious activities.

TYPE:
Project/program grants.

YEAR PROGRAM STARTED: 1947

PURPOSE:
To help support worthwhile projects and activities.

LEGAL BASIS:
Private foundation.

ELIGIBILITY:
Organization must submit copy of tax-exemption letter from the IRS identifying that the applicant is a tax-exempt organization under Internal Revenue Code 501(c)(3), but is not a private foundation under 509(a) of the Internal Revenue Code. All grant requests should be in the form of a special project or program.

GEOG. RESTRICTIONS: United States.

FINANCIAL DATA:
Amount of support per award: Average $5,000 to $25,000.
Total amount of support: Varies.

NO. MOST RECENT APPLICANTS: 1,300.

NO. AWARDS: 250.

APPLICATION INFO:
Procedures are available on the Foundation web site.
Duration: Usually one year.
Deadline: March 1. Notification in November and distribution in December.

OFFICER:
Pamela Scholl, President

ADDRESS INQUIRIES TO:
Pamela Scholl, President
(See address above.)

CHARLES AND HELEN SCHWAB FOUNDATION   [258]

201 Mission Street, Suite 1950
San Francisco, CA 94105
(415) 795-4920
Fax: (415) 795-4921
E-mail: info@schwabfoundation.org
Web Site: www.schwabfoundation.org

FOUNDED: 1987

AREAS OF INTEREST:
K-12 education reform, community needs, human services and health, and trustee grants.

NAME(S) OF PROGRAMS:
- **Foundation Initiative Grants**

TYPE:
General operating grants; Project/program grants; Technical assistance. Capacity building and human services programs.

YEAR PROGRAM STARTED: 2001

PURPOSE:
To improve education and student learning for children in the San Francisco Bay area, the state of California, and the nation more broadly.

LEGAL BASIS:
Private foundation.

ELIGIBILITY:
The Foundation supports organizations characterized by strong leadership, a compelling track record and future potential.

GEOG. RESTRICTIONS: Primarily California.

FINANCIAL DATA:
Amount of support per award: Varies.
Total amount of support: $19,805,339 in total grants for the year ended December 31, 2018.

APPLICATION INFO:
The Foundation does not accept unsolicited grant applications, grant proposals or letters of inquiry.
Duration: Varies.

PUBLICATIONS:
Foundation brochure; program reports.

IRS I.D.: 94-3374170

STAFF:
Kristi Kimball, Executive Director
Erin Gilbert, Program Officer and Administrative Director

BOARD OF DIRECTORS AND OFFICERS:
Katie Schwab Paige, Chairman and President
Matt Wilsey, Secretary

ADDRESS INQUIRIES TO:
Human Services Program
(See address above.)

THE ELLEN BROWNING SCRIPPS FOUNDATION   [259]
6121 Terryhill Drive
La Jolla, CA 92037
(858) 212-3311
Fax: (858) 459-4809
E-mail: dougdawson46@yahoo.com

FOUNDED: 1935

AREAS OF INTEREST:
Health care, medical research, education, conservation, recreation, family, youth and child welfare agencies, wildlife and animals, libraries and literacy.

TYPE:
Project/program grants; Research grants; Scholarships; Technical assistance.

YEAR PROGRAM STARTED: 1935

PURPOSE:
To provide funding for a number of social causes including medical research, health care, the arts, conservation and programs to help children.

LEGAL BASIS:
Private foundation.

ELIGIBILITY:
Applicant must be a tax-exempt, 501(c)(3) organization within San Diego County, CA.

GEOG. RESTRICTIONS: San Diego County, California.

FINANCIAL DATA:
Amount of support per award: $5,000 to $110,000.
Total amount of support: $1,200,000 for the fiscal year ended June 30, 2020.

NO. AWARDS: 42.

APPLICATION INFO:
Information is available from the Foundation.
Deadline: May 1.

ADDRESS INQUIRIES TO:
E. Douglas Dawson, Executive Director
(See address above.)

SEATTLE FOUNDATION   [260]
1601 Fifth Avenue, Suite 1900
Seattle, WA 98101
(206) 515-2131
(206) 515-2109
Fax: (206) 622-7673
E-mail: c.erickson@seattlefoundation.org
grantmaking@seattlefoundation.org
Web Site: www.seattlefoundation.org

FOUNDED: 1946

AREAS OF INTEREST:
Racial and economic equity.

NAME(S) OF PROGRAMS:
- **Center for Community Partnerships**

TYPE:
General operating grants.

YEAR PROGRAM STARTED: 1946

PURPOSE:
To improve the quality of life in the Puget Sound area.

LEGAL BASIS:
Community foundation.

ELIGIBILITY:
Organizations must be IRS 501(c)(3) tax-exempt. No grants to individuals.

GEOG. RESTRICTIONS: King County, Washington.

FINANCIAL DATA:
Amount of support per award: Average $100,000.
Total amount of support: $4,000,000.

NO. MOST RECENT APPLICANTS: 500.

NO. AWARDS: 250.

APPLICATION INFO:
Application form and guidelines are available on the web site.
Duration: Multiyear grants are awarded.
Deadline: Varies by program.

PUBLICATIONS:
Annual report; *Heart & Science Magazine.*

STAFF:
Ceil Erickson, Director, Nonprofit Relations

ADDRESS INQUIRIES TO:
Ceil Erickson
Director, Nonprofit Relations
(See address above.)

THE SEAVER INSTITUTE   [261]
12400 Wilshire Boulevard
Suite 1240
Los Angeles, CA 90025
(310) 979-0298
Fax: (310) 979-0297
E-mail: vsd@theseaverinstitute.org

FOUNDED: 1955

AREAS OF INTEREST:
Arts and the sciences.

TYPE:
Project/program grants; Research grants; Seed money grants.

YEAR PROGRAM STARTED: 1955

PURPOSE:
To provide seed money to highly regarded organizations for particular projects which offer the potential for significant advancement in their fields.

LEGAL BASIS:
Tax-exempt private foundation.

ELIGIBILITY:
Applicant must be a legally tax-exempt organization. The Institute does not support endowments, scholarships, construction, ongoing projects or deficit grants.

GEOG. RESTRICTIONS: United States.

FINANCIAL DATA:
Amount of support per award: $75,000 to $400,000.

NO. MOST RECENT APPLICANTS: 30.

NO. AWARDS: 20.

REPRESENTATIVE AWARDS:
University of Hawaii for foundation reefs; National Geographic for Timur's Garrison at Lake Issyk Kul; Massachusetts Institute of Technology for music21: a toolkit for computer-aided musicology; Sustainable Conservation for ecosystem services.

APPLICATION INFO:
A written request is required. No formal guidelines.
Duration: One year. Renewal is possible.
Deadline: Early April and early October.

PUBLICATIONS:
Official guidelines letter; annual report.

BOARD OF TRUSTEES:
Nancy Bekavac
Lynne Brickner
Jennie Dean
Kyle Dean
Nathan Dean
Victoria Seaver Dean
Robert Flick
Hilary Hill
Margaret Keene
Marie Knowles
Thomas Pfister
Martha Seaver
Barbara Wagner
Roxanne Wilson

ADDRESS INQUIRIES TO:
Victoria Seaver Dean, President
(See address above.)

SIMMONS FAMILY FOUNDATION   [262]
722 West Shepard Lane
Suite 103
Farmington, UT 84025
(801) 550-5026
E-mail: elizabeth@simmonsfoundation.org
Web Site: www.simmonsfoundation.org

FOUNDED: 1986

AREAS OF INTEREST:
Religion, community enhancement, education, art and medicine.

TYPE:
Challenge/matching grants; Development grants; General operating grants; Matching gifts; Project/program grants; Research grants; Scholarships; Seed money grants.

PURPOSE:
To foster virtues of good citizenship through religious, medical, community, art and educational purposes.

LEGAL BASIS:
Private family foundation.

ELIGIBILITY:
Grants to nonprofit organizations that are tax-exempt under Section 501(c)(3) or Section 170(c) of the Internal Revenue Code. No grants to individuals.

GEOG. RESTRICTIONS: Utah.

FINANCIAL DATA:
Amount of support per award: Varies.
Total amount of support: $875,036 for the year 2019.

NO. AWARDS: 18.

APPLICATION INFO:
E-mail a one-page letter of intent summarizing the organization and project to the address posted. Organizations will then be invited to submit a formal application. Additional information is available on the Foundation web site.
Duration: Usually one year.
Deadline: August 15.

PUBLICATIONS:
Application guidelines.

IRS I.D.: 13-3420599

ADDRESS INQUIRIES TO:
Elizabeth W. Gerner
Executive Director
(See address above.)

THE SKILLMAN FOUNDATION   [263]
100 Talon Centre Drive
Suite 100
Detroit, MI 48207
(313) 393-1185
E-mail: grants@skillman.org
Web Site: www.skillman.org

FOUNDED: 1960

AREAS OF INTEREST:
K-12 education, afterschool, and college and career pathways.

TYPE:
Project/program grants.

YEAR PROGRAM STARTED: 1960

PURPOSE:
To improve the lives of children in metropolitan Detroit by improving their homes, schools and neighborhoods.

LEGAL BASIS:
Private foundation.

ELIGIBILITY:
Foundation grantseekers and grantees must:
(1) be a nonprofit 501(c)(3) tax-exempt organization and provide its tax identification (EIN) number or be a government or public agency (city, county, state, public school district);
(2) be a publicly supported charity as defined in Section 509(a) of the Internal Revenue Code;
(3) have total revenues of at least $100,000

for its preceding fiscal year and be able to provide a copy of a current financial audit conducted by an independent certified public accountant and;
(4) in policy and practice, offer opportunity and service to all, regardless of age, race, creed, gender, religion, disability, sexual orientation and ethnicity.

Multiyear grants are awarded on a case-by-case basis in special situations and may only be submitted at the invitation of a program officer.

GEOG. RESTRICTIONS: Detroit, Michigan.

FINANCIAL DATA:
Amount of support per award: Generally $20,000 to $200,000.
Total amount of support: $17,000,000 to $18,000,000 annually.

NO. MOST RECENT APPLICANTS: Over 400.

NO. AWARDS: Typically 90 to 100.

APPLICATION INFO:
Consult the Foundation web site.
Duration: Generally one year.
Deadline: New grant inquiries should be submitted approximately two months in advance of Trustee meetings in March, June, September and December.

PUBLICATIONS:
Annual report; application guidelines.

IRS I.D.: 38-1675780

TRUSTEES:
Mary L. Kramer, Chairperson
Suzanne Shank, Vice-Chairperson
Lizabeth Ardisana
Bill Emerson
Ronald Hall, Jr.
Denise Ilitch
Soloman Kinloch
Elizabeth Morales
Jerry Norcia
Mark Reuss
Gary Torgow

OFFICERS AND STAFF:
Maria Woodruff Jordan, Vice President, Operations and Chief Financial Officer
David McGhee, Vice President, Organizational Excellence and Impact
Punita Dani Thurman, Vice President, Program and Strategy
Natalie Fotias, Director of Communications
Andrea Anderson, Director of Evaluation, Learning and Impact
Kumar Raj, Senior Program Officer, College and Career Pathways
Carmen Kennedy-Rogers, Senior Program Officer, Education
Ashley Aidenbaum, Program Officer, College and Career Pathways and Afterschool
Terry Whitfield, Program Officer, Education and Afterschool
Matthew Hoerauf, Associate Program Officer, Education
Simonne Searles, Human Resource/Operations Officer
Jessica Brown, Grants Administrator
Jessica Eiland Anders, Special Projects Manager
Lauren Hawkins, Controller

ADDRESS INQUIRIES TO:
Jessica Brown, Grants Administrator
(See address above.)

ALFRED P. SLOAN FOUNDATION   [264]
630 Fifth Avenue
Suite 2200
New York, NY 10111
(212) 649-1649
Fax: (212) 757-5117
E-mail: lin@sloan.org
grantsadmin@sloan.org
Web Site: sloan.org

FOUNDED: 1934

AREAS OF INTEREST:
Research and related programs in science and technology, education in science, technology, and economic growth.

TYPE:
Fellowships; Project/program grants; Research grants.

YEAR PROGRAM STARTED: 1934

PURPOSE:
To support imaginative and constructive approaches to problems of domestic needs and uses.

LEGAL BASIS:
Private foundation.

ELIGIBILITY:
Recognized tax-exempt educational and research institutions with appropriate interests are eligible to apply. The Foundation's activities do not extend to primary or secondary education, religion, the creative or performing arts, medical research, health care or to the humanities. Grants are not made for endowments, buildings or equipment and are very rarely made for general support or for activities outside the U.S.

GEOG. RESTRICTIONS: United States.

FINANCIAL DATA:
Amount of support per award: Varies.
Total amount of support: Approximately $80,000,000 in grants annually.

NO. AWARDS: Approximately 200 annually.

APPLICATION INFO:
A brief letter of inquiry, rather than a fully developed proposal, is an advisable first step for an applicant, conserving his or her time and allowing the Foundation to make a preliminary response as to the possibility of support.
Duration: One to three years. Extensions or renewals are possible.

PUBLICATIONS:
Annual report.

BOARD OF TRUSTEES:
Marta Tienda, Chairperson
Cynthia Barnhart
Bonnie Bassler
Francine Berman
Richard Bernstein
Adam F. Falk
Frederick Henderson
Freeman A. Hrabowski, III
Jeff Knight
Robert Litterman
James Poterba
Michael Purugganan

ADMINISTRATIVE OFFICERS AND STAFF:
Adam F. Falk, President
Leisle Lin, Senior Vice President, Finance and Operations/Treasurer
Anne McKissick, Director, Grants Management and Information Services
Lauren von Eckartsberg, Grants Coordinator

ADDRESS INQUIRIES TO:
Anne McKissick
Director, Grants Management and
Information Services
(See address above.)

A.O. SMITH FOUNDATION [265]

11270 West Park Place
Suite 170
Milwaukee, WI 53224
(414) 359-4107
E-mail: foundation@aosmith.com
Web Site: www.aosmith.com

FOUNDED: 1955

AREAS OF INTEREST:
Human services, arts and culture, education,
health, and United Way.

TYPE:
Project/program grants. Employee Education
Matching Gift to secondary, four-year
colleges and universities, junior colleges,
community colleges, graduate and
professional schools, technical and
specialized schools.

YEAR PROGRAM STARTED: 1955

PURPOSE:
To make our communities a better place to
live and work; to support education, arts and
culture, health and human services in the
communities where A.O. Smith plants are
located.

LEGAL BASIS:
Corporate foundation.

ELIGIBILITY:
Organization must be located where A.O.
Smith has operating facilities. The
Foundation does not make contributions to
politically active organizations or any other
organization whose chief purpose is to
influence legislation.

GEOG. RESTRICTIONS: United States and
Canada.

FINANCIAL DATA:
Amount of support per award: $500
minimum.
Total amount of support: $1,700,000.

NO. AWARDS: Approximately 200 annually.

APPLICATION INFO:
No specific application form is required.
Inquiries should be made on organization's
letterhead and include the following
information:
(1) the exact name and location of the
organization;
(2) a description of the organization,
including its objectives and purpose;
(3) verification of IRS 501(c)(3) tax-exempt
status;
(4) the geographic area served by the
organization;
(5) an explanation of the activity for which
support is being requested;
(6) the amount of support being requested;
(7) a description of the benefits to be
achieved and who will receive them;
(8) budget information about the
organization, including other sources of
income and;
(9) plans for reporting results.
Duration: Varies.

PUBLICATIONS:
Annual report.

ADDRESS INQUIRIES TO:
Rita Schwalbach, Foundation Manager
(See address above.)

THE ETHEL SERGEANT CLARK SMITH MEMORIAL FUND [266]

Wells Fargo Philanthropic Services
123 South Broad Street
Philadelphia, PA 19109
(888) 235-4351
E-mail: grantadministration@wellsfargo.com
Web Site: www.wellsfargo.com/private-
foundations/smith-memorial-fund-ethel-sergeant-
clark

FOUNDED: 1977

AREAS OF INTEREST:
Arts, culture, education, health and human
services, and medicine.

TYPE:
Capital grants; Challenge/matching grants;
Development grants; Project/program grants.
Grants and challenge grants to community
interest organizations in southeastern
Pennsylvania. Grants to hospitals, colleges
and schools for program and capital projects.
Grants for social services, arts/cultural events
and centers.

YEAR PROGRAM STARTED: 1977

PURPOSE:
To promote the public welfare in Delaware
County, PA.

LEGAL BASIS:
Private foundation.

ELIGIBILITY:
Organizations must be tax-exempt and not
classified as private foundations or private
operating foundations within the terms of the
Tax Reform Act of 1969. Primary emphasis
is on those serving community needs in
Delaware County, the former home of Ethel
Sergeant Clark Smith. Grants will be made
for capital projects, operating expenses and
special programs that are meaningful to the
success of the individual endeavors of the
organizations. As a general rule, requests for
funds on a long-term basis or for deficit
financing will not be considered.

GEOG. RESTRICTIONS: Southeastern
Pennsylvania.

FINANCIAL DATA:
Amount of support per award: $5,000 to
$25,000.
Total amount of support: Approximately
$540,000 annually.
Matching fund requirements: Varies.

NO. MOST RECENT APPLICANTS: Approximately
200.

NO. AWARDS: Approximately 60 annually.

APPLICATION INFO:
Application process is online only.
Duration: Three consecutive years maximum.
Deadline: March 1 and September 1.

PUBLICATIONS:
Biennial report.

IRS I.D.: 23-6648857

ADVISORY COMMITTEE:
Diane R. Bricker
Jack Holefelder
Dr. Joseph E. Pappano, Jr.
Hon. Dominic F. Pileggi
Alice Strine, Esq.

ADDRESS INQUIRIES TO:
Grant Administrator
(See address above.)

THE W.W. SMITH CHARITABLE TRUST [267]

200 Four Falls Corporate Center
Suite 300
West Conshohocken, PA 19428
(610) 397-1844
Fax: (610) 397-1680
E-mail: info@wwsmithcharitabletrust.org
Web Site: www.wwsmithcharitabletrust.org

FOUNDED: 1976

AREAS OF INTEREST:
Basic medical research protocols dealing with
cancer, AIDS and heart disease; financial aid
programs for qualified needy full-time
undergraduate students; and programs
providing shelter, food and clothing for
children and needy families with children,
and the elderly.

NAME(S) OF PROGRAMS:
● **College Scholarships**
● **Food, Clothing and Shelter**
● **Maritime Education**
● **Medical Research**

TYPE:
Project/program grants; Research grants;
Scholarships.

YEAR PROGRAM STARTED: 1978

PURPOSE:
To enhance medical excellence; to enable
children, families and the elderly to improve
their lives; to assure students of a college
education.

LEGAL BASIS:
Private foundation.

ELIGIBILITY:
Grants are limited to nonprofit organizations
within the Delaware Valley area: Bucks,
Chester, Delaware, Montgomery and
Philadelphia counties (PA), as well as the
city of Camden (NJ). Grants are made only
to tax-exempt, 501(c)(3) organizations, not
classified as private foundations or private
operating foundations within the terms of the
Tax Reform Act of 1969.

Grants will be made for programs or
organizations with proven or prudently
predictable records of performance; never
directly to individuals. Renovation projects,
special programs that deal with food,
clothing and shelter for children and the
elderly may be funded, but requests for
general operating expenses, deficit financing
and capital campaigns are not considered.

As a rule, under the Basic Needs Grants, the
further away any request is from direct
provision of literal food, clothing or shelter,
the less likely funding may be granted.

Financial aid programs are for qualified
needy full-time undergraduate students
attending MSCHE accredited colleges and
universities, as well as two-year community
colleges, technical colleges, and trade schools
located in, and serving students from the
same geographic areas defined by the
existing program for MSCHE accredited
colleges and universities.

The Trust budgets no funds to purchase
charity tables, program advertisements, golf
tournament sponsorships, organizational
memberships or analogous fund-raising
events.

GEOG. RESTRICTIONS: With few exceptions, grants are limited to organizations within Bucks, Chester, Delaware, Montgomery and Philadelphia counties, Pennsylvania and Camden, New Jersey.

FINANCIAL DATA:
Amount of support per award: $5,000 to $229,000 for fiscal year 2018-19.
Total amount of support: $8,204,708 for fiscal year 2018-19.

NO. AWARDS: 198 for the year 2018-19.

APPLICATION INFO:
Complete application information is available online. Proposals will be considered only for the following purposes:
(1) specific, basic medical research projects dealing with cancer, heart disease or AIDS;
(2) by invitation of the Trust only, accredited, four-year university and college financial aid programs for needy, worthy, full-time undergraduate students (no requests ever accepted directly from individual students) and;
(3) providing shelter, food or clothing for children age 18 or under (including needy families with dependent children) or the elderly age 60 and above.

The trustees endeavor to keep abreast of the needs and conditions in the area served by the Trust and variations from these policies may be made at their discretion.

Grants are offered by invitation only.
Duration: Scholarship and Food, Clothing and Shelter grants: One year; Medical Research grant: Typically one year.
Deadline: Heart, Cancer and AIDS Research: July 15; Food, Clothing, and Shelter: December 15 and June 15; Scholarships: April 1.

PUBLICATIONS:
Biennial report (includes application guidelines).

IRS I.D.: 23-6648841

TRUSTEES:
Louise A. Havens

ADMINISTRATORS:
Brian Jones, Grant Administrator, Food, Clothing and Shelter/Scholarships
Louise A. Havens, Grant Administrator, Medical Research
Deborah J. McKenna, Advisor

ADDRESS INQUIRIES TO:
Brian Jones, Grant Administrator
(See address above.)

*SPECIAL STIPULATIONS:
Grants only in the Philadelphia, PA area and surrounding five counties, plus the city of Camden, NJ.

THE JOHN BEN SNOW FOUNDATION, INC.   [268]
131 West Seneca Street
Suite B215
Manlius, NY 13104
(315) 471-5256
Fax: (315) 471-5256
E-mail: info@johnbensnow.org
Web Site: johnbensnow.org

FOUNDED: 1948

AREAS OF INTEREST:
Arts and culture, community initiatives, disabilities and universal access, education, environment, youth programs and historic preservation.

TYPE:
Capital grants; Challenge/matching grants; Development grants; Fellowships; Project/program grants; Scholarships; Seed money grants; Technical assistance.

YEAR PROGRAM STARTED: 1948

PURPOSE:
To grant funds for educational, cultural and humanitarian purposes.

LEGAL BASIS:
Private foundation.

ELIGIBILITY:
Applicants must be IRS 501(c)(3) organizations primarily in central and northern New York state. Grants are made to qualified organizations for educational and humanitarian purposes.

The general policy of the Board of Directors gives preference to proposals seeking one-year funding of program-related grants, matching grants, startup grants and capital grants and to reject proposals from individuals, religious organizations, government agencies, or for endowments, contingency funding, or general operating support.

GEOG. RESTRICTIONS: Central New York state, primarily Cayuga, Cortland, Madison, Onondaga and Oswego counties.

FINANCIAL DATA:
Amount of support per award: Typically $5,000 to $10,000.
Total amount of support: $262,768 in total grants approved for the year ended December 31, 2020.

NO. MOST RECENT APPLICANTS: More than 60.

NO. AWARDS: 41 for the year 2020.

REPRESENTATIVE AWARDS:
Arts and Culture: $10,000 to Schweinfurth Art Center for HVAC project: $5,000 to Red House Arts Center for access to arts-based education; Education: $10,000 to Mercy Works; Youth Programs: $5,000 to Purpose Farm, Inc. for youth mentoring session.

APPLICATION INFO:
An initial letter of inquiry must be submitted through the Foundation's online grant management system. If the proposal meets the stated guidelines and priorities of the Foundation, grant application instructions will be sent to the applicant.
Duration: One year. Renewals depend on the project.
Deadline: Letter of inquiry: No later than January 31 of the year in which the grant is requested. Grant application: April 1. Notification by July 1.

PUBLICATIONS:
Guidelines; annual report.

STAFF:
Elizabeth Snow, Grants Manager

BOARD MEMBERS:
Jonathan L. Snow, President
David H. Snow, Vice President and Treasurer
Emelie M. Williams, Secretary
Angus M. Burton
Marion Hancock Fish
Valerie MacFie
Keegan Snow

ADDRESS INQUIRIES TO:
Jonathan L. Snow, President
(See address above.)

SOUTHWEST FLORIDA COMMUNITY FOUNDATION
2031 Jackson Street
Suite 100
Fort Myers, FL 33901
(239) 274-5900
Fax: (239) 274-5930
E-mail: info@floridacommunity.com
bkelly@floridacommunity.com
Web Site: collaboratory.org

TYPE:
Demonstration grants; Project/program grants; Scholarships.

See entry 1248 for full listing.

SOWERS CLUB OF NEBRASKA FOUNDATION   [269]
1701 South 17th Street
Suite 1H
Lincoln, NE 68502
(402) 438-2244
E-mail: info@thesowersclub.com
Web Site: www.thesowersclub.com

FOUNDED: 1986

AREAS OF INTEREST:
Charity and education.

TYPE:
Project/program grants; Scholarships.

PURPOSE:
To offer assistance to organizations that serve and educate the community.

ELIGIBILITY:
Agency must have been in existence for a minimum of five years and must qualify as exempt under Section 501(c)(3) of the Internal Revenue Code. Grant requests will not be considered for individuals, promoting religious purposes or for political purposes.

GEOG. RESTRICTIONS: Nebraska.

FINANCIAL DATA:
Total amount of support: $50,000 per year.

APPLICATION INFO:
Grant request must include eight copies of the following:
(1) Letter of Determination from the IRS regarding 501(c)(3) status and;
(2) annual report or current balance sheet outlining the organization's administrative costs. All information will be treated with strict confidentiality.

All blanks on the grant request form must be completed. Do not answer a question on the request form by reference to another question, document or party.
Deadline: February 15, June 15 and September 15.

BOARD OF DIRECTORS AND OFFICERS:
Michael Fiene, President
Dick Stevenson, Vice President
Roger Zajicek, Treasurer
Robby Robinson, Secretary
Bob Flynn
Ed Packer

ADDRESS INQUIRIES TO:
Wendy Rieck, Executive Director
(See address above.)

SETH SPRAGUE EDUCATIONAL AND CHARITABLE FOUNDATION [270]

c/o Bank of America Private Bank
Mail Code TAOBEB
P.O. Box 1517
Pennington, NJ 08534
(646) 855-1011
E-mail: christine.l.odonnell@bofa.com

AREAS OF INTEREST:
Hospitals, educational institutions and social agencies.

TYPE:
Project/program grants.

ELIGIBILITY:
The Foundation makes grants to hospitals, educational institutions, social agencies and other charitable organizations. No grants to individuals.

GEOG. RESTRICTIONS: San Diego, California; Maine; Boston area, Massachusetts; and New York City, New York.

FINANCIAL DATA:
Amount of support per award: $10,000 to $20,000.
Total amount of support: $3,000,000 for the year 2019.

NO. MOST RECENT APPLICANTS: 450.

NO. AWARDS: 100.

APPLICATION INFO:
Application must be submitted online. The Foundation does not accept Letters of Inquiry.
Duration: One year.
Deadline: April 1 and September 1. Award announcement in June and December.

ADDRESS INQUIRIES TO:
Christine O'Donnell, Senior Vice President (See address and e-mail above.)

STATE STREET FOUNDATION [271]

State Street Financial Center
One Lincoln Street
Boston, MA 02111-2900
(617) 664-8720
E-mail: wyoung@statestreet.com
Web Site: www.statestreet.com/values/social-consciousness/non-profit-grants.html

FOUNDED: 1804

AREAS OF INTEREST:
Assisting disadvantaged populations in gaining the skills and educational qualifications needed to secure sustainable employment.

NAME(S) OF PROGRAMS:
● **Strategic Grantmaking Program**

TYPE:
General operating grants; Project/program grants. State Street Foundation's Strategic Grantmaking Program considers two types of grants:
(1) Project Support Grants are intended to support specific projects or programs aligned with the Program's primary investment focus. These requests may include some funds earmarked for the overhead costs associated with running a project, including staff costs.
(2) General Operating Support Grants are intended to provide general operating support for the core business functions of organizations whose missions and activities are highly aligned with the Program's primary investment focus. These grants will often help the grantee build organizational, programmatic and fund-raising capacity. Operating support is not intended to help organizations in fiscal crisis.

YEAR PROGRAM STARTED: 1977

PURPOSE:
To promote economic opportunity in communities where State Street operates.

LEGAL BASIS:
Corporate foundation.

ELIGIBILITY:
Grant applicants must be tax-exempt, 501(c)(3) organizations located in communities where State Street has a presence.

The Foundation does not make individual scholarship grants, nor does it fund research, having a preference for programs emphasizing direct delivery of services. It does not support organizations by purchasing advertisements, tables or tickets at dinners or other functions.

General Operating Support Grant applicants must have a current strategic or business plan that clearly outlines the organization's goals and presents a plan for achieving results. Operating support grants must not exceed 10 to 15% of an organization's total agency budget.

FINANCIAL DATA:
Amount of support per award: $30,000 to $100,000.
Total amount of support: $13,900,000.

NO. AWARDS: 243 for the year 2019.

APPLICATION INFO:
Grant Proposal Summary Form and instructions are available at the Foundation web site.
Duration: One year.
Deadline: Applications are accepted on a rolling basis.

PUBLICATIONS:
Contributions guidelines.

ADDRESS INQUIRIES TO:
Wayne Young, Strategic Grants Manager (See address above.)

JOHN STAUFFER CHARITABLE TRUST [272]

155 North Lake Avenue, PH
Pasadena, CA 91101
(626) 793-9400
Fax: (626) 793-5900
E-mail: dfederico@lagerlof.com

FOUNDED: 1974

AREAS OF INTEREST:
Colleges, universities and hospitals within California.

TYPE:
Capital grants; Challenge/matching grants; Endowments; Fellowships; Matching gifts; Professorships; Project/program grants; Scholarships.

YEAR PROGRAM STARTED: 1974

PURPOSE:
To support universities and colleges located in the U.S. in acquiring land, erecting buildings and other facilities, obtaining equipment, instruments, books, furnishings, and providing scholarships, fellowships and professorships; to support hospitals located in the U.S. which are organized and operated for charitable purposes in acquiring land, erecting buildings and other facilities, and obtaining equipment, instruments and furnishings.

LEGAL BASIS:
Tax-exempt private foundation founded in 1974 as a Testamentary Trust under will of John Stauffer by Order of the Superior Court of the State of California in and for the County of Los Angeles.

ELIGIBILITY:
Each university, college or hospital that receives funds from the Trust must be, at the time of the receipt of the funds:
(1) an exempt organization under Section 501(c)(3) of the Internal Revenue Code;
(2) an organization described in Section 170(c) of the Internal Revenue Code (or the corresponding provisions of any subsequent federal tax law) and;
(3) an organization meeting the qualifications of Sections 13842 and 23701(d) of the Revenue and Taxation Code of the state of California (or the corresponding provisions of any subsequent California tax law).
The organization must not be a private foundation.

Because of the Trust's finite resources, its Trustees must focus their attention on a few fields of activity and on certain priorities. The Trustees will favor:
(1) projects or programs of private nonprofit universities, colleges and hospitals within southern California;
(2) grants for facilities, educational or medical equipment, scholarships, professorships and fellowships;
(3) projects and programs that link science and medicine in education, research and treatment;
(4) projects and programs that emphasize chemistry as an integral component of education or treatment;
(5) institutions and organizations that as a matter of policy and practice maintain balanced operating budgets and avoid deficit financing and;
(6) projects and programs supported by matching funds from other donors.

GEOG. RESTRICTIONS: California, with a focus on southern California.

FINANCIAL DATA:
Amount of support per award: $100,000 to $3,000,000.
Total amount of support: Varies.

NO. MOST RECENT APPLICANTS: Approximately 200.

REPRESENTATIVE AWARDS:
$3,000,000 to Huntington Hospital; $300,000 to Claremont McKenna College; $500,000 to Stanford University; $2,500,000 to California Institute of Technology.

APPLICATION INFO:
All applications must be presented to the Trustees in writing and in digital format, with proposals clear and concise. Each application should include:
(1) a brief summary that sets forth the exact amount requested, an explanation of the need for the subject of the grant, the objectives to be achieved and the manner in which John Stauffer's name will be memorialized;
(2) full financial information, including a detailed budget for the project to be assisted by the grant;
(3) a statement indicating whether a grant for the same or similar purpose is presently

being sought from other foundations or other sources, and, if so, which ones; (4) the application's being executed by an officer of the applicant institution; (5) (preferably) accompanying letters of support from board members or authorities and/or organizations in the applicant's field and; (6) where applicable, copies of the latest exemption determination letter from the IRS and the corresponding state tax authorities in the state in which the applicant is located; the IRS determination that the applicant is not a private foundation; the latest audited balance sheet; and the latest audited statement of income and expenditures.

Duration: For large grants, up to two or more years.

PUBLICATIONS:
Application guidelines.

IRS I.D.: 23-7434707

TRUSTEES:
Timothy J. Gosney, Esq.
William F. Kruse, Esq.
Michael R. Whalen, Esq.

ADDRESS INQUIRIES TO:
John Stauffer Charitable Trust
c/o Timothy J. Gosney, Esq.
(See address above.)

*SPECIAL STIPULATIONS:
Each grantee is required to make a report on the use of the funds granted by the Trustees, including a certification that the funds have been used for the purpose(s) for which the grant was made. In addition, grantees shall comply with all reporting requirements contained in conditions of the grant, which will be set forth in writing by the Trustees. The Trustees reserve the right to require a reasonable audit of the use of grant funds conducted by their representative at the Trust's expense.

STEELCASE FOUNDATION [273]
P.O. Box 1967 GH-2E
Grand Rapids, MI 49501-1967
(616) 246-4695
E-mail: jridenou@steelcase.com
Web Site: www.steelcasefoundation.org

FOUNDED: 1951

AREAS OF INTEREST:
Education and social justice.

TYPE:
Demonstration grants; Development grants; General operating grants; Matching gifts; Project/program grants; Seed money grants. Special projects, startup, capital and capacity building.

YEAR PROGRAM STARTED: 1951

PURPOSE:
To improve the quality of life in the communities where Steelcase employees live; to empower people to reach their full potential.

LEGAL BASIS:
Corporate foundation.

ELIGIBILITY:
The Foundation makes grants to IRS-certified nonprofit organizations in areas where Steelcase manufacturing plants are located.

GEOG. RESTRICTIONS: Athens, Alabama and Grand Rapids, Michigan.

FINANCIAL DATA:
Amount of support per award: $5,000 to $250,000.
Total amount of support: $5,167,818 for the year 2019.

NO. MOST RECENT APPLICANTS: 100.

NO. AWARDS: 40.

APPLICATION INFO:
To obtain a grant application, send a Letter of Inquiry through the Foundation's online portal. The request should be on the organization's letterhead and signed by the Chief Executive Officer. Include the following items with the letter:
(1) description of organization or project;
(2) expected results of the project;
(3) amount of grant funds requested and;
(4) copy of IRS 501(c)(3) nonprofit certification.

If the proposal meets the Foundation criteria, a detailed application form will be sent to the organization.
Duration: Most grants one to three years.
Deadline: Grant requests are reviewed quarterly.

PUBLICATIONS:
Annual report; application; guidelines.

IRS I.D.: 38-6050470

TRUSTEES:
Kate Pew Wolters, Chairperson
Brian Cloyd
Mary Anne Hunting
James Keane
Craig Niemann
Cary Pew
Robert C. Pew, III
Elizabeth Welch

ADDRESS INQUIRIES TO:
Julie Ridenour, President
(See address above.)

THE WILLIAM B. STOKELY, JR. FOUNDATION [274]
620 Campbell Station Road, Station West
Suite 27
Knoxville, TN 37934
(865) 966-4878
Fax: (865) 675-5095

FOUNDED: 1951

AREAS OF INTEREST:
College and university scholarship programs and cultural, educational, religious and health service organizations.

TYPE:
General operating grants; Matching gifts; Scholarships.

YEAR PROGRAM STARTED: 1951

PURPOSE:
To provide funds for colleges and universities for scholarships.

LEGAL BASIS:
Tax-exempt private foundation.

ELIGIBILITY:
The Foundation does not extend funds to individuals but rather to colleges and universities in the form of scholarships to disburse under the guidelines of their particular program. Also considered are the needs of cultural, educational, religious (Christian) and health service organizations in areas where the Stokely family has ties. Regional priority is given to the southeastern U.S. and eastern Tennessee.

Organizations requesting funds must be approved, listed nonprofit organizations with 501(c)(3) status. All proposals must be submitted in writing for review by the Board of Directors.

GEOG. RESTRICTIONS: Southeastern United States and Eastern Tennessee.

FINANCIAL DATA:
Amount of support per award: $25 to $100,000.

APPLICATION INFO:
All proposals must be submitted in writing for review by the Board of Directors.
Duration: Varies.
Deadline: Proposals are reviewed on an ongoing basis.

IRS I.D.: 35-6016402

BOARD OF DIRECTORS:
William B. Stokely, III, President
Kay H. Stokely, Executive Vice President
Andrea White, Vice President, Treasurer and Secretary
Stacy S. Byerly
Shelley S. Przewrocki
Clayton F. Stokely
William B. Stokely, IV

ADDRESS INQUIRIES TO:
William B. Stokely, III, President
(See address above.)

ROY AND CHRISTINE STURGIS CHARITABLE AND EDUCATIONAL TRUST [275]
c/o Bank of America, N.A.
901 Main Street, 19th Floor
Dallas, TX 75202-3714
E-mail: tx.philanthropic@ustrust.com
Web Site: www.bankofamerica.com/philanthropic

FOUNDED: 1981

AREAS OF INTEREST:
Arts, culture and humanities, education, health, and human services.

TYPE:
Capital grants; Challenge/matching grants; Matching gifts; Project/program grants.

PURPOSE:
To support and promote quality educational, cultural, human services and health care programming for all people.

LEGAL BASIS:
Private foundation (charitable trust).

ELIGIBILITY:
Applicants must have a 501(c)(3) exempt status from federal income tax as determined by the IRS before applying for a grant.

Charitable organizations which receive a one-payment grant must skip a year before applying again. Charitable organizations which receive multiyear payments cannot apply again while receiving payments and must skip a year after the last payment is received.

Trustee will consider grant requests for supplements for capital improvements, special projects, medical research and equipment, grants to meet challenges, endowments, start-up funds (extraordinary review), limited general operating expenses and construction or renovation of facilities.

The Trustee may favorably consider proposals which are unique, necessary and of high priority for the charitable organizations and which do not duplicate other services which are available, proposals for which funding may not be readily available from other sources and essential projects which are sufficiently described as worthwhile, important and of a substantive nature.

The Trustee will not consider providing support for political organizations, loans, scholarships for individuals, tuition for individuals or for seminars. No grants to individuals or for mass appeals for funding.

GEOG. RESTRICTIONS: Arkansas and Dallas area in Texas.

FINANCIAL DATA:
Amount of support per award: $5,000 to $200,000 for multiyear payments. Average: $23,500.

APPLICATION INFO:
Guidelines and application forms are available on the Trust web site.
Duration: One year; occasional multiyear.
Deadline: March 1. Notification on or before June 30.

PUBLICATIONS:
Guidelines.

IRS I.D.: 75-6331832

SURDNA FOUNDATION INC. [276]

200 Madison Avenue, 25th Floor
New York, NY 10016
(212) 557-0010 ext. 237
Fax: (212) 557-0003
E-mail: grants@surdna.org
Web Site: www.surdna.org

FOUNDED: 1917

AREAS OF INTEREST:
Sustainable environments, strong local economies, and thriving cultures.

NAME(S) OF PROGRAMS:
● **The Inclusive Economies**
● **Sustainable Environments**
● **Thriving Cultures**

TYPE:
General operating grants; Project/program grants; Research grants; Technical assistance.

YEAR PROGRAM STARTED: 1917

PURPOSE:
To foster catalytic, entrepreneurial programs which offer viable solutions to difficult systemic problems.

ELIGIBILITY:
Grant applicants must be 501(c)(3) nonprofits located within the U.S.

No grants to individuals. No grants for capital support.

GEOG. RESTRICTIONS: United States.

FINANCIAL DATA:
Amount of support per award: Varies.
Total amount of support: $36,132,173 in grants authorized in fiscal year 2019.

NO. MOST RECENT APPLICANTS: Approximately 1,300 per year.

NO. AWARDS: 305 authorized in fiscal year 2019.

APPLICATION INFO:
Letters of Inquiry should be submitted on the Foundation web site. Application guidelines are available online.
Duration: One to three years. Grants are renewable.

Deadline: Letters of Inquiry are reviewed on a rolling basis.

PUBLICATIONS:
Annual report.

ADDRESS INQUIRIES TO:
See e-mail address above.

TAHOE TRUCKEE COMMUNITY FOUNDATION [277]

11071 Donner Pass Road
Truckee, CA 96161
(530) 587-1776 ext. 106
Fax: (530) 550-7985
E-mail: phyllis@ttcf.net
Web Site: www.ttcf.net

FOUNDED: 1998

AREAS OF INTEREST:
Education, environment, arts and culture, civic benefits, health, human services, youth development, recreation and animal welfare.

TYPE:
Block grants; Challenge/matching grants; General operating grants; Project/program grants; Scholarships. Capacity building.

YEAR PROGRAM STARTED: 1998

PURPOSE:
To enhance the quality of life in the Truckee Tahoe community.

ELIGIBILITY:
Grants are made to organizations that have tax-exempt status under Section 501(c)(3) of the Internal Revenue Code. No grants are made to individuals.

GEOG. RESTRICTIONS: Donner Summit, Lake Tahoe, Squaw Valley and Truckee region, California.

FINANCIAL DATA:
Amount of support per award: $5,000 to $10,000.
Total amount of support: Approximately $300,000.

NO. MOST RECENT APPLICANTS: 55 for the year 2019.

NO. AWARDS: 37 for the year 2019.

APPLICATION INFO:
Guidelines are available on the Foundation web site.
Duration: One year.
Deadline: Varies.

IRS I.D.: 68-0416404

ADMINISTRATIVE STAFF:
Phyllis McConn, Community Impact Officer

EXECUTIVE OFFICERS:
Stacy Caldwell, Chief Executive Officer

ADDRESS INQUIRIES TO:
Phyllis McConn, Community Impact Officer (See address above.)

S. MARK TAPER FOUNDATION [278]

12011 San Vicente Boulevard, Suite 400
Los Angeles, CA 90049
(310) 476-5413
E-mail: grants@smtfoundation.org
Web Site: www.smtfoundation.org

FOUNDED: 1989

AREAS OF INTEREST:
Including, but not limited to, environment, independent living for the disabled, children,

hunger, AIDS, teenage pregnancy prevention, economic revitalization, the arts, public education and civic affairs.

TYPE:
Capital grants; General operating grants; Project/program grants.

YEAR PROGRAM STARTED: 1989

PURPOSE:
To enhance the quality of people's lives.

LEGAL BASIS:
Independent foundation.

ELIGIBILITY:
No grants to individuals. Applicants must be certified tax-exempt under Section 501(c)(3) of the Internal Revenue Code.

Previously funded nonprofit organizations are not eligible for another grant until after three full cycles have elapsed following the grant cycle during which previous grant was made.

GEOG. RESTRICTIONS: Southern California, primarily Los Angeles County.

FINANCIAL DATA:
Amount of support per award: Small grants: Up to $50,000; medium grants: $50,001 to $100,000; large grants: Over $100,000.
Total amount of support: Varies.

NO. MOST RECENT APPLICANTS: 400.

NO. AWARDS: 80.

APPLICATION INFO:
Letter of Inquiry must be submitted through the online grants portal. Late submissions, incomplete letters of inquiry, hard copies or documents sent via e-mail will not be considered for review.
Duration: One year, except capital projects.
Deadline: Letters of Inquiry are accepted December through February 15. Applications are mailed in May through July. Notification in September.

PUBLICATIONS:
Letter of Inquiry Guidelines.

OFFICERS:
Janice Taper Lazarof, President

ADDRESS INQUIRIES TO:
Adrienne Wittenberg, Executive Director (See address above.)

JOHN TEMPLETON FOUNDATION [279]

300 Conshohocken State Road
Suite 500
West Conshohocken, PA 19428
(610) 941-2828
Fax: (610) 825-1730
E-mail: info@templeton.org
Web Site: www.templeton.org

FOUNDED: 1987

AREAS OF INTEREST:
Higher education, science and religion, theology, medicine, philosophy, spirituality and health, character development and free enterprise education.

TYPE:
Awards/prizes; Challenge/matching grants; Project/program grants; Research grants. Awards are financial in nature.

PURPOSE:
To promote and support relationships and progress between science and religion.

LEGAL BASIS:
Private foundation.

ELIGIBILITY:
Organizations classified as 501(c)(3) by the IRS can apply.

FINANCIAL DATA:
Amount of support per award: Varies.
Total amount of support: Varies.
Matching fund requirements: Defined on an individual grant basis.

NO. AWARDS: 139 new grants for the year 2019.

APPLICATION INFO:
Online Funding Inquiry must be submitted through the Templeton Portal.
Duration: Up to three years. In rare instances, up to five years.
Deadline: Online funding inquiry: August.

PUBLICATIONS:
Brochures; newsletter; articles.

IRS I.D.: 62-1322826

TEXAS INSTRUMENTS FOUNDATION   [280]
12500 TI Boulevard
Dallas, TX 75243
(972) 995-2011
E-mail: giving@ti.com
Web Site: www.ti.com/giving

FOUNDED: 1964

AREAS OF INTEREST:
Human services and STEM education arts.

TYPE:
Matching gifts; Project/program grants.

YEAR PROGRAM STARTED: 1965

PURPOSE:
To better the communities in which Texas Instruments operates.

LEGAL BASIS:
Nonprofit foundation.

ELIGIBILITY:
Organization must be 501(c)(3) and tax-exempt. No grants to individuals, student scholarships, good will advertising or for contributions of Texas Instruments products.

GEOG. RESTRICTIONS: Texas. STEM education arts in Dallas only.

FINANCIAL DATA:
Amount of support per award: Varies.
Total amount of support: $18,600,000 in grants and matching gifts for the year 2019.
Matching fund requirements: Up to $50,000 per employee and retiree per year for most U.S.-based nonprofits.

APPLICATION INFO:
Applications are accepted mainly by request. Funding requests should be submitted online.
Duration: Varies. Renewals possible.

PUBLICATIONS:
Guidelines.

IRS I.D.: 75-6038519

STAFF:
Andy Smith, Executive Director

3M FOUNDATION, INC.   [281]
Community Affairs
3M Center Building 225-01-S-23
St. Paul, MN 55144-1000
(651) 733-0144
Fax: (651) 737-3061
E-mail: mstroik@mmm.com
Web Site: www.3Mgives.com

FOUNDED: 1953

AREAS OF INTEREST:
Education, arts and culture, human services and environment.

TYPE:
Capital grants; General operating grants; Matching gifts; Product donations; Project/program grants. 3Mgives consists of gifts by the 3M Foundation, cash and product donations by 3M and employee/retiree volunteerism.

YEAR PROGRAM STARTED: 1953

PURPOSE:
To improve every life.

LEGAL BASIS:
Corporate contributions program.

ELIGIBILITY:
Grants are made in the program areas of interest to established, well-managed organizations which have an IRS 501(c)(3) nonprofit status, and which are located in and serving 3M communities. Essential qualities are programs with broad-based community support, a reputation for leadership and high-quality service delivery and measurable results.

The 3M Foundation will not fund organizations in non-3M communities, individuals, for-profit organizations, disease-related organizations, hospitals, (in general) individual K-12 schools, organizations with a limited constituency, such as religious, fraternal, social, veterans or military organizations, and scholarship funds or organizations.

Grants are not awarded for advocacy and lobbying efforts to influence legislation; conferences, seminars, workshops or publications of their proceedings; endowments; film/video production; fund-raising, testimonial, athletic and special events; purchase of equipment that has not been manufactured by 3M; and travel for individuals or groups.

3Mgives generally will not consider organizations or causes that do not impact 3M communities, lease, conferences, seminars, workshops, symposia, publication of proceedings and all aspects relating to conferences, fund-raising and testimonial events/dinners, grants to individual K-12 schools, including tickets, silent auctions, raffles, telethons, etc., not more than 10% of the organization's campaign goal or annual budget, whichever is smaller, programs or projects beyond three years.

FINANCIAL DATA:
Amount of support per award: Varies.
Total amount of support: $13,998,124 in grants paid for the year 2018.
Matching fund requirements: Limited to 3M employees and retirees.

NO. MOST RECENT APPLICANTS: 10,000.

NO. AWARDS: Approximately 3,000.

APPLICATION INFO:
Applications are by invitation only.
Duration: Generally one year, and not more than three years.
Deadline: Varies according to focus area.

PUBLICATIONS:
Annual report; contributions guidelines.

IRS I.D.: 41-6038262

JOHN H. AND H. NAOMI TOMFOHRDE FOUNDATION   [282]
c/o Rackemann, Sawyer & Brewster
160 Federal Street, 15th Floor
Boston, MA 02110-1700
(617) 951-1108
Fax: (617) 542-7437
E-mail: smonahan@rackemann.com
Web Site: www.cybergrants.com/tomfohrde

FOUNDED: 1996

AREAS OF INTEREST:
Cultural, social and civic betterment, community health, higher education, scientific research within the New England area with a special focus on Greater Boston.

TYPE:
Capital grants; Conferences/seminars; Matching gifts; Product donations; Project/program grants; Seed money grants; Technical assistance. The Foundation's particular focus is on supporting the work of charitable institutions, organizations and agencies in the New England area and particularly in Greater Boston, which are dedicated to the cultural, social and civic betterment of the community and particularly which foster the advancement of higher education, the classic arts, scientific research in biomedicine and the improvement of community health. Each year the trustees identify a specific funding priority.

PURPOSE:
To bring about the cultural, social and civic betterment of the community and particularly to foster the advancement of higher education, the classic arts, scientific research in biomedicine and the improvement of community health.

LEGAL BASIS:
Private, independent foundation.

ELIGIBILITY:
The Foundation supports nonprofit 501(c)(3) organizations only.

GEOG. RESTRICTIONS: New England, with a preference for Greater Boston.

FINANCIAL DATA:
Amount of support per award: $5,000 to $15,000.
Total amount of support: $250,000.
Matching fund requirements: Determined on a case-by-case basis.

NO. MOST RECENT APPLICANTS: 38.

NO. AWARDS: 19 for the year 2019.

REPRESENTATIVE AWARDS:
Julie's Family Learning Program.

APPLICATION INFO:
Applicants are required to submit a Preliminary Application-Concept Cover Letter. Only applicants whose preliminary application has been approved will be invited to submit a full proposal.

IRS I.D.: 04-3338742

TRUSTEES:
Maura E. Murphy, Esq.
Michael F. O'Connell, Esq.

STAFF:
Susan T. Monahan, Grants Coordinator

ADDRESS INQUIRIES TO:
Susan T. Monahan, Grants Coordinator
(See e-mail address above.)

*PLEASE NOTE:
Applicants should check web site annually to learn of the Foundation's current funding priority.

TOPFER FAMILY FOUNDATION [283]
3600 North Capital of Texas Highway
Building B, Suite 310
Austin, TX 78746
(512) 329-0009
(866) 897-0298
Fax: (512) 329-6462
E-mail: info@topferfoundation.org
Web Site: www.topferfoundation.org

FOUNDED: 2000

AREAS OF INTEREST:
Child abuse prevention and treatment, youth enrichment, job training and support services, children's health, and aging in place.

TYPE:
Project/program grants.

PURPOSE:
To help people connect to the tools and resources needed to build self-sufficient and fulfilling lives; to address the needs of the communities in which the Topfer family resides.

ELIGIBILITY:
Organizations must be nonprofit, classified 501(c)(3). No grants to individuals.

GEOG. RESTRICTIONS: Greater Chicago, Illinois and greater Austin, Texas metropolitan areas. In Illinois, preference is given to Cook and DuPage counties.

FINANCIAL DATA:
Amount of support per award: $2,500 to $300,000.
Total amount of support: $75,000,000.

NO. MOST RECENT APPLICANTS: 150.

NO. AWARDS: 100.

APPLICATION INFO:
Application should be submitted online.
Duration: One year. Must reapply.
Deadline: Varies.

ADDRESS INQUIRIES TO:
Melanie Cazier, Program Officer
(See address above.)

*PLEASE NOTE:
Unsolicited requests are not accepted in the greater Chicago, IL area. Must be by invitation only.

TOTAL USA FOUNDATION [284]
1201 Lousiana, Suite 1800
Houston, TX 77002
(713) 483-5000
Web Site: us.total.com

FOUNDED: 1974

AREAS OF INTEREST:
Education.

TYPE:
Development grants; Matching gifts; Project/program grants.

LEGAL BASIS:
Corporate foundation.

ELIGIBILITY:
The Foundation supports the efforts of its employees to nominate potential organizations. Requested donations are submitted and reviewed by the Board to determine if the grant will be made, which in turn will decide amount of allocation. Due diligence is required for qualification.

GEOG. RESTRICTIONS: Louisiana and Texas.

FINANCIAL DATA:
Amount of support per award: Varies.
Total amount of support: Varies.
Matching fund requirements: All gifts from Total Petrochemicals & Refining USA, Inc. full-time employees are matched to four-year educational institutions from which the donor received a degree. The minimum gift that will be matched is $25 and the maximum gift per person per calendar year is $5,000. The contribution must be a personal gift of the eligible donor and cannot include resources from other people or institutions.

NO. MOST RECENT APPLICANTS: Approximately 15.

NO. AWARDS: Varies.

APPLICATION INFO:
No form is prescribed for submitting grant applications; however, budgets and statements of financial condition will assist the Foundation in acting upon any request for funds. A categorized statement regarding the expected sources of funds, excluding individual contributors and specifically whether the organization is supported by the United Way, are also of interest. Prior to issuance of a grant, an organization will be requested to furnish documentation of its status under the Code and a statement regarding its present operation and sources of support.
Duration: Varies.

OFFICERS:
Vincent Stoquart, Chief Executive Officer
Tricia Fuller, Secretary

ADDRESS INQUIRIES TO:
Tricia Fuller, Manager, Communications
(See address above.)

THE HARRY A. AND MARGARET D. TOWSLEY FOUNDATION [285]
924 North Main Street
Ann Arbor, MI 48104
E-mail: grants@towsleyfoundation.org
Web Site: www.towsleyfoundation.org

FOUNDED: 1959

AREAS OF INTEREST:
Education, cultural arts, health and community service.

TYPE:
Capital grants; Challenge/matching grants; Endowments; General operating grants; Project/program grants; Research grants.

YEAR PROGRAM STARTED: 1959

PURPOSE:
To partner with charitable organizations to accomplish common objectives for improving the lives of people and communities.

LEGAL BASIS:
Private foundation.

ELIGIBILITY:
Effectiveness, sustainability, strategic thinking, environmental awareness, and collaboration are among the strengths encouraged in Foundation grantees.

The Foundation does not make direct grants to individuals. Grants are generally not made for conference attendance, travel, books, publications, films, tapes and other communication media. Projects or organizations that are political or seen to influence legislation are not eligible.

Educational conferences hosted by the applicant are eligible.

GEOG. RESTRICTIONS: Primarily Michigan.

FINANCIAL DATA:
Amount of support per award: $5,000 to $1,000,000.
Total amount of support: Varies.

APPLICATION INFO:
Organizations seeking aid should complete the Grant Application located on the Foundation web site. All required fields, including relevant attachments, must be completed.
Duration: Varies. Renewal possible.
Deadline: February 6, July 2 and September 5.

PUBLICATIONS:
Brochure; annual report.

IRS I.D.: 38-6091798

OFFICERS:
Lynn T. White, Chairperson
Wendell Dunbar, President
Judith D. Rumelhart, Vice President
Mary Ivers, Treasurer
Margaret E. Thompson, M.D., Secretary

ADDRESS INQUIRIES TO:
See e-mail address above.

TRUIST FOUNDATION [286]
214 Tryon Street
Charlotte, NC 28202
(404) 827-6529
E-mail: truistfoundation@truist.com
Web Site: www.truist.com/truist-foundation

FOUNDED: 2020

AREAS OF INTEREST:
Leadership development, economic mobility, thriving communities, and educational equity.

TYPE:
Matching gifts; Project/program grants. Employee matching gifts program is designed to encourage Truist employees to support educational institutions and cultural organizations.

PURPOSE:
To inspire and build better lives and communities.

LEGAL BASIS:
Corporate giving program.

ELIGIBILITY:
Grants are awarded to fiscally sound organizations that service critical needs in the community. Usually, grants will be made only to organizations with records of successful operation, without a deficit for at least one year.

The Foundation does not consider requests for general operating support, such as salaries, maintenance and debt service. Grants are not awarded to political organizations, churches, individuals, nonreligious organizations that have a written policy of discrimination based on sexual orientation and/or gender identity, or organizations that foster or encourage racial, religious, class or other prejudices.

GEOG. RESTRICTIONS: Alabama, Arkansas, Florida, Georgia, Indiana, Kentucky, Maryland, Mississippi, New Jersey, North Carolina, Ohio, Pennsylvania, South Carolina, Tennessee, Texas, Virginia, Washington, DC, and West Virginia.

FINANCIAL DATA:
Amount of support per award: Varies.
Total amount of support: Varies.
Matching fund requirements: Truist will match employee contributions to eligible educational institutions and arts/cultural enrichment programs.

APPLICATION INFO:
Application should include a list of board of directors, an annual operating budget, and a project or program budget specific to the request.
Duration: Varies. Renewal possible.
Deadline: March 31, July 31 and November 30.

PUBLICATIONS:
Guidelines.

ADDRESS INQUIRIES TO:
See e-mail address above.

*PLEASE NOTE:
Formerly known as the SunTrust Foundation.

TRUST FUNDS INCORPORATED   [287]
1104 Corporate Way
Sacramento, CA 95831-3875
(916) 395-4472

FOUNDED: 1934

AREAS OF INTEREST:
Elementary, secondary and graduate Catholic education, Catholic religious and social service organizations and programs, and religious arts.

TYPE:
General operating grants; Grants-in-aid.

YEAR PROGRAM STARTED: 1934

PURPOSE:
To support worthwhile projects and programs that share the interests of the Foundation.

LEGAL BASIS:
Private foundation.

ELIGIBILITY:
Grants are usually limited to the San Francisco Bay area. No grants to individuals. No grants for buildings or endowments, annual campaigns, or to organizations which draw substantial public support.

GEOG. RESTRICTIONS: San Francisco, California and surrounding area.

FINANCIAL DATA:
Amount of support per award: $1,000 to $20,000.

APPLICATION INFO:
Application forms provided for all grant proposals complying with guidelines. Write or call first.

PUBLICATIONS:
Applications and guidelines.

IRS I.D.: 94-6062952

DIRECTORS:
James T. Healy, President
Liz Kelley, Chief Financial Officer
John Strain, Secretary
Mary Hudler, Director
Brian O'Hearn, Director

ADDRESS INQUIRIES TO:
James T. Healy, President
(See address above.)

TULL CHARITABLE FOUNDATION, INC.   [288]
191 Peachtree Street, N.E.
Suite 3950
Atlanta, GA 30303
(404) 659-7079
Fax: (404) 659-1223
E-mail: carol@tullfoundation.org
Web Site: www.tullfoundation.org

FOUNDED: 1952

AREAS OF INTEREST:
Education, health and human services, youth development and the arts.

TYPE:
Capital grants.

YEAR PROGRAM STARTED: 1952

PURPOSE:
To respond to charitable and community needs in the Atlanta metropolitan area and in Georgia.

LEGAL BASIS:
Converted from Trust to Nonprofit Corporation of Georgia.

ELIGIBILITY:
Nonprofit 501(c)(3) organizations located within Georgia are eligible for support. Eligible projects include capital infrastructure projects critical to achieving an organization's strategic growth goals, strategic expansion initiatives to enable an organization to better achieve its mission, and organizational partnerships and mergers designed to maximize community impact. Requests for early-stage investment in new and emerging projects are sometimes considered, if a project can demonstrate impact and a viable plan for financial sustainability.

GEOG. RESTRICTIONS: Georgia, with a focus on the metro Atlanta area.

FINANCIAL DATA:
Amount of support per award: Average: $50,000.
Total amount of support: Varies.

NO. MOST RECENT APPLICANTS: 180.

NO. AWARDS: 40.

APPLICATION INFO:
Prior to receiving a full proposal, the Foundation prefers a concise letter-of-intent providing a brief description of the applicant organization, the project for which funding is being requested, the total cost of the project and the amount being requested and a copy of the organization's 501(c)(3) certification. If the Foundation determines that further consideration is to be given to the proposed project, additional information will be requested.
Duration: Typically one year.
Deadline: December 1, April 1 and August 1.

PUBLICATIONS:
Guidelines; policies.

ADDRESS INQUIRIES TO:
Gabrielle K. Sheely, Executive Director or Carol Aiken, Assistant
(See address above.)

UNION PACIFIC FOUNDATION   [289]
1400 Douglas, Stop 1560
Omaha, NE 68179
(402) 544-5600
Fax: (402) 501-0011
E-mail: upf@up.com
Web Site: www.up.com/foundation

FOUNDED: 1955

AREAS OF INTEREST:
Safety, workforce development and community spaces.

TYPE:
Capital grants; Project/program grants. Support generally for capital campaigns, building funds, equipment and materials, and renovation.

YEAR PROGRAM STARTED: 1959

PURPOSE:
To improve the quality of life in the communities served by Union Pacific and where its employees live and work.

LEGAL BASIS:
Incorporated in Utah, May 13, 1955.

ELIGIBILITY:
Organization must be a public charity, 501(c)(3) tax-exempt and located in a community served by Union Pacific.

GEOG. RESTRICTIONS: Arizona, Arkansas, California, Colorado, Idaho, Illinois, Iowa, Kansas, Louisiana, Minnesota, Missouri, Montana, Nebraska, Nevada, New Mexico, Oklahoma, Oregon, Tennessee, Texas, Utah, Washington, Wisconsin and Wyoming.

FINANCIAL DATA:
Amount of support per award: Typically, $2,500 to $25,000.
Total amount of support: Approximately $9,000,000 annually.

NO. MOST RECENT APPLICANTS: 2,100.

NO. AWARDS: 615 for fiscal year 2018.

APPLICATION INFO:
Any organization interested in receiving a Local Grant must complete a survey to determine eligibility. The Foundation will provide immediate access to those invited to submit a full grant application.
Duration: Most grants are awarded annually.
Deadline: July 31. Notification in September.

TRUSTEES:
R.S. Ferguson
L.M. Fritz
R.M. Knight, Jr.
S.D. Moore
E.F. Whited

ADDRESS INQUIRIES TO:
Ranae Keckeisen, Director
(See address above.)

*PLEASE NOTE:
Due to the Foundation undergoing a strategic plan, some of this information is subject to change.

USG FOUNDATION, INC.   [290]
550 West Adams Street
Chicago, IL 60661
(312) 436-4021
(312) 436-4000
Fax: (312) 672-4021
Web Site: www.usg.com

FOUNDED: 1978

AREAS OF INTEREST:
Community, arts and culture, health and welfare, and education.

TYPE:
Project/program grants.

YEAR PROGRAM STARTED: 1978

PURPOSE:
To provide assistance to nonprofit organizations seeking solutions to educational, social or health problems or whose work contributes to cultural enrichment.

LEGAL BASIS:
Tax-exempt, corporate foundation.

ELIGIBILITY:
Applicants must be tax-exempt 501(c)(3) organizations. The Foundation supports the creation of economic opportunity through grants to organizations that provide affordable housing/shelter, encourage self-sufficiency and assist economic development.

The Foundation does not contribute to organizations without IRS tax-exempt 501(c)(3) status, sectarian organizations having an exclusively religious nature, individuals, political parties, offices or candidates, fraternal organizations, primary or secondary schools, organizations that cannot provide adequate accounting records, procedures or courtesy advertising.

GEOG. RESTRICTIONS: Primarily Chicago, Illinois.

FINANCIAL DATA:
Amount of support per award: Varies.
Total amount of support: Varies.

APPLICATION INFO:
Grant proposals should be submitted in writing to receive consideration. Application form is available on the Foundation web site.
Duration: One year. Renewal possible upon reapplication.

PUBLICATIONS:
Guidelines.

ADDRESS INQUIRIES TO:
Margaret Clark, Assistant Secretary
(See address above.)

VERIZON FOUNDATION   [291]
One Verizon Way
Basking Ridge, NJ 07920
(866) 247-2687 (volunteers program)
Fax: (908) 630-2660
E-mail: verizon.foundation@verizon.com
Web Site: www.verizon.
com/about/responsibility/giving-and-grants

FOUNDED: 2001

AREAS OF INTEREST:
Digital inclusion, climate protection, and human prosperity.

TYPE:
Matching gifts; Project/program grants.

PURPOSE:
To address critical disparities among targeted segments in education, family, safety, health care and sustainability.

LEGAL BASIS:
Private, nonprofit organization.

ELIGIBILITY:
To be considered for an invitation, an organization must be classified as tax-exempt

under Section 501(c)(3) of the Internal Revenue Code and further classified as a public charity under Section 509(a)(1)-(3).

Proposals will also be considered from elementary and secondary schools (public and private) that are registered with the National Center for Education Statistics (NCES), providing that the grant is not for the sponsorship of a field trip.

GEOG. RESTRICTIONS: United States.

FINANCIAL DATA:
Amount of support per award: Varies.
Total amount of support: Varies.

APPLICATION INFO:
Grants applications are by invitation only.

IRS I.D.: 13-3319048

THE WALLACE
FOUNDATION   [292]
140 Broadway, 49th Floor
New York, NY 10005
(212) 251-9700
Fax: (212) 679-6990
E-mail: hdodge@wallacefoundation.org
Web Site: www.wallacefoundation.org

FOUNDED: 1965

AREAS OF INTEREST:
Education leadership, arts education, building audiences for the arts, summer and expanded learning, afterschool learning, and social and emotional learning.

TYPE:
Project/program grants; Research grants; Technical assistance; Research contracts.

YEAR PROGRAM STARTED: 2003

PURPOSE:
To foster equity and improvements in learning and enrichment for young people, and in the arts for everyone.

LEGAL BASIS:
Private foundation.

ELIGIBILITY:
Grant applicants must be 501(c)(3) tax-exempt organizations. No grants are made to individuals.

Unsolicited proposals are rarely funded.

GEOG. RESTRICTIONS: United States.

FINANCIAL DATA:
Estimated assets of $1.8 billion as of December 31, 2020.
Amount of support per award: Varies depending on needs and nature of request.
Total amount of support: $55,430,977 in grants and matching gifts for the year ended December 31, 2020.

NO. MOST RECENT APPLICANTS: 258.

NO. AWARDS: 159.

APPLICATION INFO:
Virtually all of the grants the Foundation awards are made through a competitive process. In most cases, the Foundation identifies and evaluates prospective grantees through the issuance of Requests for Proposals or other careful screening processes.
Duration: Varies.
Deadline: Varies.

IRS I.D.: 13-6183757

OFFICERS AND BOARD OF DIRECTORS:
Will Miller, President

Stacy J. Martin, Chief Financial Officer and Treasurer
Thomas Lenehan, Chief Investment Officer
Kenneth W. Austin, General Counsel and Corporate Secretary
Candace K. Beinecke
Anne Dinneen
Richard L. Kauffman
Kent McGuire
Jorge Ruiz de Velasco
Amor H. Towles
Daniel H. Weiss
Mary Beth West

*PLEASE NOTE:
Grants are rarely made to unsolicited projects, especially from local organizations.

THE WASIE FOUNDATION   [293]
230 Manitoba Avenue South
Suite 110
Wayzata, MN 55391-1612
(952) 955-8500
Fax: (952) 955-8509
Web Site: www.wasie.org

FOUNDED: 1966

AREAS OF INTEREST:
Care, treatment and research regarding schizophrenia and arthritis; children's health; and organizations providing services and programs to people living with cancer.

NAME(S) OF PROGRAMS:
● **Arthritis Grants**
● **Cancer Grants**
● **Children's Medical Health Grants**
● **Schizophrenia Grants**

TYPE:
Capital grants; Challenge/matching grants; Conferences/seminars; Development grants; General operating grants; Matching gifts; Project/program grants; Research grants. The grant program provides funding in four health areas, specifically: schizophrenia, arthritis, cancer, and children with medical problems.

YEAR PROGRAM STARTED: 1966

LEGAL BASIS:
Private foundation.

ELIGIBILITY:
Grants are made to 501(c)(3) nonprofit organizations.

GEOG. RESTRICTIONS: Minnesota, primarily the Twin Cities, and Collier and Lee counties, Florida.

FINANCIAL DATA:
Amount of support per award: Varies.
Total amount of support: $517,937 in grants paid for the year 2018.

NO. AWARDS: 31 grants paid for the year 2018.

REPRESENTATIVE AWARDS:
$75,000 to Joe DiMaggio Children's Hospital Foundation; $5,000 to Camp Odayin; $21,749 to College of St. Scholastica; $11,881 to Saint Mary's University of Minnesota; $1,595 to Rein in Sarcoma.

APPLICATION INFO:
The Foundation encourages organizations which believe they fall within their funding guidelines to initiate contact through a telephone call to one of the program staff who will gather information and assist with the proposal process.

Proposal submission is by invitation only.
Duration: One to three years. Renewal possible.

Deadline: Submissions are invited throughout the year.

STAFF:
Gregg D. Sjoquist, President and Chief Executive Officer
Dani Mathison, Chief Operating Officer
Jan Preble, Vice President of Programs

ADDRESS INQUIRIES TO:
Jan Preble
Vice President of Programs
(See address above.)

*SPECIAL STIPULATIONS:
Grant proposals are by invitation only. Inquiries open to any organization falling within funding areas and within demographic areas noted.

EDWIN S. WEBSTER FOUNDATION   [294]
c/o GMA Foundations
2 Liberty Square, Suite 500
Boston, MA 02109
(617) 399-1852
Fax: (617) 426-7087
E-mail: jmellen@gmafoundations.com
Web Site: www.gmafoundations.com
websterfoundation.grantsmanagement08.com

FOUNDED: 1948

AREAS OF INTEREST:
Charitable purposes, with emphasis on hospitals, medical research and education, youth agencies, cultural activities and programs addressing the needs of minorities.

TYPE:
Capital grants; Challenge/matching grants; Endowments; General operating grants.

YEAR PROGRAM STARTED: 1982

PURPOSE:
To work towards a better society by giving grants to organizations trying to help people with serious needs not otherwise being addressed.

LEGAL BASIS:
Nonprofit foundation.

ELIGIBILITY:
No grants are given to individuals or organizations outside the U.S. The majority of contributions are made to organizations in the New England area. It is the policy of the Foundation to support charitable organizations that are well known to the Trustees, with emphasis on hospitals, medical research, education, youth agencies, cultural activities and programs addressing the needs of minorities. Grantees must have tax-exempt status.

GEOG. RESTRICTIONS: Primarily New England.

FINANCIAL DATA:
Amount of support per award: $10,000 to $25,000. Average $15,000.
Total amount of support: $1,470,000 for the year 2018.

NO. MOST RECENT APPLICANTS: 75 to 80 per grant cycle.

NO. AWARDS: 61 for the year 2018.

APPLICATION INFO:
Proposals are submitted by using the online application form.
Duration: One year.
Deadline: For consideration at spring meeting, proposals should arrive by May 1. For consideration at the fall meeting, proposals should arrive by November 1.

PUBLICATIONS:
Guidelines.

TRUSTEES:
Henry U. Harris, III
Alexander Hiam
Suzanne Harte Sears

WEINGART FOUNDATION   [295]
700 South Flower Street
Suite 1900
Los Angeles, CA 90017
(213) 688-7799
Fax: (213) 688-1515
E-mail: info@weingartfnd.org
Web Site: www.weingartfnd.org

FOUNDED: 1951

AREAS OF INTEREST:
Human services, health, education, immigrant integration, homelessness, 2020 census, youth organizing, leadership for movement building, and capacity building.

TYPE:
General operating grants.

PURPOSE:
To support historically under-resourced individuals and communities in reaching their full potential.

ELIGIBILITY:
An organization that is certified as tax-exempt under Section 501(c)(3) of the U.S. Internal Revenue Code and is not a private foundation as defined in Section 509(a) of that Code is eligible for consideration. The Foundation does not fund Section 509(a)(3) Type III nonfunctionally integrated supporting organizations.

Grants are not made:
(1) to organizations that discriminate against certain groups or individuals in the delivery of programs and services on the basis of race, religion, national origin, gender, age, sexual orientation or disability;
(2) for elections, political candidates or political campaigns;
(3) for social or political issues outside the U.S.;
(4) to individuals;
(5) for temporary exhibits, travel, surveys, films or publishing activities;
(6) for endowment funds;
(7) for fund-raising dinners or events or;
(8) for animal welfare.

Grants generally are not approved for:
(1) research;
(2) national organizations that do not have local chapters operating in the geographic area of grant focus;
(3) religious programs or consumer interest or;
(4) feasibility studies.

GEOG. RESTRICTIONS: Southern California, with priority given to Los Angeles County and South Los Angeles.

FINANCIAL DATA:
Assets of $830,894,039 for the year ended June 30, 2019.
Amount of support per award: Varies.
Total amount of support: $39,288,493 in grants approved for the fiscal year ended June 30, 2019.
Matching fund requirements: Organization matches 1:1.

CO-OP FUNDING PROGRAMS: Nonprofit Sustainability Initiative, Home for Good.

NO. MOST RECENT APPLICANTS: 407.

NO. AWARDS: 170.

APPLICATION INFO:
Applications are accepted by invitation only.
Duration: Multiyear.
Deadline: The Foundation accepts applications throughout the year.

PUBLICATIONS:
Annual report, only available on web site.

IRS I.D.: 95-6054814

OFFICERS:
Miguel A. Santana, President and Chief Executive Officer
Tim Ortez, Vice President and Chief Financial Officer

BOARD OF DIRECTORS:
Aileen Adams, Chairman
William C. Allen
Monica C. Lozano
Miriam Muscarolas
Linda Oubre
Dr. Robert K. Ross
Miguel A. Santana
Steven L. Soboroff

HERMAN O. WEST FOUNDATION   [296]
530 Herman O. West Drive
Exton, PA 19341
(610) 594-2900
Web Site: www.westpharma.com

FOUNDED: 1972

AREAS OF INTEREST:
Cultural, health and public service needs.

TYPE:
Matching gifts; Scholarships. Emergency grants.

YEAR PROGRAM STARTED: 1972

PURPOSE:
To provide employee emergency grants, scholarship programs and employee matching gifts program.

LEGAL BASIS:
Corporate contributions program; private foundation.

ELIGIBILITY:
Employees of West Pharmaceutical Services may participate in the Employee Emergency Grants Program, Employee Matching Gifts Program and Matching Gifts Program.

Scholarships are available to children of West Pharmaceutical Services employees.

GEOG. RESTRICTIONS: United States.

FINANCIAL DATA:
Amount of support per award: $500 to $20,000.
Total amount of support: $400,000 annually.

APPLICATION INFO:
Application information is available on the Foundation web site.
Duration: Varies. Renewal possible.

PUBLICATIONS:
Application guidelines.

TRUSTEES:
Mark A. Buthman
James D. Faust
Annette Favorite

ADDRESS INQUIRIES TO:
Laura Pitt
(See address above.)

WEST PHARMACEUTICAL SERVICES, INC. [297]
530 Herman O. West Drive
Exton, PA 19341
(610) 594-2900
Web Site: www.westpharma.com

AREAS OF INTEREST:
STEM education, hospital/health care and children/disabled.

TYPE:
General operating grants.

PURPOSE:
To provide funding to nonprofit organizations in the focus areas of STEM education, hospital/health care, children/disabled in the areas and communities where West Pharmaceutical Services maintains operations.

ELIGIBILITY:
501(c)(3) organizations in the U.S. or the equivalent in other countries may apply for a grant. Eligibility includes aligning with West Pharmaceutical Services focus areas.

FINANCIAL DATA:
Amount of support per award: $500 to $10,000.
Total amount of support: $2,500,000 annually.

NO. MOST RECENT APPLICANTS: 350.

NO. AWARDS: 250.

APPLICATION INFO:
Application is available on the web site listed above under "Philanthropy" and must be submitted online. Do not mail proposals or send e-mail proposals, as they will not be considered.
Duration: Generally a one-time grant. Renewal possible.
Deadline: Grants are reviewed on a monthly basis; however, no grants will be reviewed after November 15 in any given year.

ADDRESS INQUIRIES TO:
Laura Pitt
(See address above.)

WESTERN INTERSTATE COMMISSION FOR HIGHER EDUCATION [298]
3035 Center Green Drive
Suite 200
Boulder, CO 80301
(303) 541-0270
E-mail: info-sap@wiche.edu
kspringsteen@wiche.edu
Web Site: www.wiche.edu/tuition-savings/psep

FOUNDED: 1953

AREAS OF INTEREST:
Allopathic medicine, dentistry, physical and occupational therapy, optometry, podiatry, osteopathic medicine, veterinary medicine, physician assistant and pharmacy.

NAME(S) OF PROGRAMS:
● **Professional Student Exchange Program (PSEP)**

TYPE:
Scholarships. Tuition assistance/loan for service.

YEAR PROGRAM STARTED: 1953

PURPOSE:
To provide affordable access to professional health care education.

ELIGIBILITY:
Eligibility and fields funded vary by state. Must be a resident of a state listed below.

GEOG. RESTRICTIONS: Alaska, Arizona, Colorado, Hawaii, Montana, Nevada, New Mexico, North Dakota, Utah, Wyoming and the Commonwealth of the Mariana Islands.

FINANCIAL DATA:
Amount of support per award: Varies.
Total amount of support: Varies.

NO. AWARDS: 580 for the year 2020-21.

APPLICATION INFO:
Applicants should contact their home state office to apply.
Duration: One year. Grants are renewable for course of study; subject to available funding.
Deadline: October 15 of the year prior to enrollment.

ADDRESS INQUIRIES TO:
Director of Student Access Programs
(See address above.)

*PLEASE NOTE:
Grant is for residents of one western state making applications to participating schools in another western state.

E. L. WIEGAND FOUNDATION [299]
Wiegand Center
165 West Liberty Street, Suite 200
Reno, NV 89501
(775) 333-0310 ext. 112
Fax: (775) 333-0314

FOUNDED: 1982

AREAS OF INTEREST:
Education, medical research, civic and community affairs, arts and cultural affairs, and public affairs.

TYPE:
Capital grants; Project/program grants.

YEAR PROGRAM STARTED: 1982

PURPOSE:
To support charitable organizations and Roman Catholic charitable institutions.

LEGAL BASIS:
Private charitable trust.

ELIGIBILITY:
The Foundation will consider applications from institutions that are tax-exempt under Section 501(c)(3) of the IRS, and which are not private foundations as defined in Section 509.

The review process by the Foundation will consider institutions that:
(1) are exemplary in their field;
(2) have a history of high achievement and sound management;
(3) demonstrate a stable financial condition;
(4) have the potential to be self-supporting after the stage of initial funding by the Foundation;
(5) focus on strengthening traditional values essential to the preservation of a democratic society nurtured by free market principles (in the area of public affairs) and;
(6) are developing programs and projects that have a significant impact in the area for which the grant is requested.

GEOG. RESTRICTIONS: Arizona, Hawaii, Idaho, Montana, Nevada, Oregon, Utah, Washington, and New York City/Washington, DC (public policy).

FINANCIAL DATA:
Amount of support per award: $1,000 to $500,000.
Total amount of support: $4,465,750 for the year 2019.

NO. AWARDS: 30 for the year 2019.

APPLICATION INFO:
A prospective applicant should describe the highlights of the proposal (including data regarding the organization, sources of funding, a brief description of the project or program, estimated budget and timeline) in a letter addressed to the Foundation. If, after staff consideration, it is determined that the program or project complies with the preliminary review, a prospective applicant shall receive an application for grant form which shall be assigned numerically to such applicant. The Foundation is only able to support a small percentage of the proposals it receives.
Deadline: Letters of Inquiry accepted throughout the year.

IRS I.D.: 94-2839372

ADDRESS INQUIRIES TO:
Kristen A. Avansino
President and Executive Director
Grants Program
(See address above.)

*PLEASE NOTE:
Written communications to the Foundation are preferred.

MATILDA R. WILSON FUND [300]
6th Floor at Ford Field
1901 St. Antoine Street
Detroit, MI 48226
(313) 259-7777
Fax: (313) 393-7579
E-mail: roosterveen@bodmanlaw.com

FOUNDED: 1944

AREAS OF INTEREST:
Arts, education, health and human services.

TYPE:
Capital grants; Project/program grants.

PURPOSE:
To primarily fund pre-selected organizations supported by Matilda R. Wilson during her lifetime.

ELIGIBILITY:
Applicants must be 501(c)(3) organizations. Priority is given to organizations previously supported. No grants to individuals.

GEOG. RESTRICTIONS: Primarily southeast Michigan.

FINANCIAL DATA:
Amount of support per award: $500 to $1,000,000.
Total amount of support: Varies.

NO. MOST RECENT APPLICANTS: 60.

NO. AWARDS: 39.

APPLICATION INFO:
No application form. Applicants must submit a letter outlining the need and use of funds, tax-exempt status, budget, and prior history of funding.
Duration: One year; some multiyear.

Deadline: Prior to January, April and September board meetings.

IRS I.D.: 38-6087665

STAFF:
Robin L. Oosterveen, Program Director

ADDRESS INQUIRIES TO:
Robin L. Oosterveen, Program Director
(See address above.)

*PLEASE NOTE:
Priority given to organizations that Mrs. Wilson supported during her lifetime, or with which the Fund has a long-standing commitment.

THE ROBERT W. WOODRUFF FOUNDATION   [301]
191 Peachtree Street, N.E.
Suite 3540
Atlanta, GA 30303
(404) 522-6755
Fax: (404) 522-7026
E-mail: fdns@woodruff.org
Web Site: woodruff.org

FOUNDED: 1937

AREAS OF INTEREST:
K-12th-grade and higher education; health care and health outreach; human services, particularly for children and youth; community development in metropolitan Atlanta; major Atlanta arts and cultural institutions; large-scale conservation projects; and Atlanta parks and greenspaces.

TYPE:
Capital grants; Project/program grants.

YEAR PROGRAM STARTED: 1937

PURPOSE:
To improve the quality of life in Georgia by investing in health, education, economic opportunity and the vitality of the community.

LEGAL BASIS:
Independent, private foundation with a broad charter to support charitable activities in the areas of health, education, environment, human services, arts and culture, and community development.

ELIGIBILITY:
Grants generally are limited to 501(c)(3) public charities located and operating in metropolitan Atlanta, GA, although grants are occasionally considered for significant institutions and initiatives in communities throughout Georgia. Grants are typically awarded for one-time capital or capacity needs of well-established charitable organizations with strong leadership, sustainable operations, a broad base of financial support, and proven program effectiveness.

Grants for ongoing operating support or endowments are avoided. No grants are made for individuals, loans, churches, conferences, startup organizations, debt relief, political activities, professional associations, festivals, performances, exhibits, fund-raising events or sponsorships.

GEOG. RESTRICTIONS: Georgia, with a focus on metropolitan Atlanta.

FINANCIAL DATA:
Amount of support per award:
Approximately $150,000 to $30,000,000.

Total amount of support: $155,512,047 for the year 2020.

NO. MOST RECENT APPLICANTS: Approximately 350.

NO. AWARDS: 36 for the year 2020.

REPRESENTATIVE AWARDS:
$150,000 to New American Pathways for an initiative to develop collaborative resettlement services by New American Pathways, the International Rescue Committee and Catholic Charities; $1,000,000 to Trees Atlanta for construction of a new headquarters and expansion of tree planting efforts; $2,000,000 to Atlanta Police Foundation to support a comprehensive public safety strategy to reduce crime in Atlanta; $1,500,000 to Zoo Atlanta for operating support in response to the COVID-19 pandemic.

APPLICATION INFO:
Applicants should review the eligibility requirements, grantmaking guidelines and program interests. Applicants are encouraged to submit an informal inquiry to the e-mail address listed above. Applications must be submitted through the online grant portal. Do not mail a copy of the grant request to the Foundation.

The following documents must be uploaded as a single PDF:
(1) grant request letter (on company letterhead) that briefly describes the organization and the proposed project;
(2) itemized project budget;
(3) operating budget;
(4) fund raising status report;
(5) financial statements and;
(6) board list.

Deadline: August 15 and February 1.

PUBLICATIONS:
Application guidelines.

OFFICERS:
P. Russell Hardin, President
Erik S. Johnson, Treasurer and Secretary

TRUSTEES:
E. Jenner Wood, III, Chairman
Lawrence L. Gellerstedt, III, Vice Chairman
Thomas J. Lawley, M.D.
David P. Stockert

ADDRESS INQUIRIES TO:
P. Russell Hardin, President
(See address above.)

XCEL ENERGY FOUNDATION   [302]
414 Nicollet Mall
Minneapolis, MN 55401
(612) 330-6200
E-mail: foundation@xcelenergy.com
Web Site: www.xcelenergy.com

FOUNDED: 2001

AREAS OF INTEREST:
Education, economic sustainability, environmental stewardship, and access to the arts.

TYPE:
Project/program grants. Employee/retiree matching gifts program.

YEAR PROGRAM STARTED: 2001

PURPOSE:
To help promote a desirable, healthy environment in those areas served by Xcel Energy.

ELIGIBILITY:
Applicants must be 501(c)(3) nonprofit organizations in the service area. Grants will not be made to individuals, political parties, national organizations, research programs or government agencies.

GEOG. RESTRICTIONS: Cities within Xcel Energy service areas.

FINANCIAL DATA:
Amount of support per award: $1,000 to $30,000.

Total amount of support: Grants: Approximately $4,000,000 annually; Employee matching gifts: Approximately $3,000,000 annually.

Matching fund requirements: 501(c)(3) nonprofits. Employee and retiree matching gifts program: Minimum donation $50, maximum $500.

NO. MOST RECENT APPLICANTS: 400.

NO. AWARDS: 380.

APPLICATION INFO:
Grant applications are accepted by invitation only. Organizations that are deemed eligible may be contacted by a regional corporate giving representative for further discussion.
Deadline: April 1.

STAFF:
Liz Gardner, Representative, Colorado
Jennifer Prochnow, Representative, Michigan and Wisconsin
Elisa Rasmussen, Representative, Minnesota
Terry Price, Representative, New Mexico and Texas
Tony Grindber, Representative, Fargo, North Dakota
Kathleen Aas, Representative, Minot, North Dakota
Eric Pauli, Representative, South Dakota

ADDRESS INQUIRIES TO:
Ashly Ligouri
Corporate Giving Representative
(See address above.)

HUMANITIES

Humanities (general)

AMERICAN ACADEMY IN ROME   [303]

7 East 60th Street
New York, NY 10022-1001
(212) 751-7200
Fax: (212) 751-7220
E-mail: info@aarome.org
Web Site: www.aarome.org

FOUNDED: 1894

AREAS OF INTEREST:
Arts and humanities.

NAME(S) OF PROGRAMS:
● **Rome Prize Fellowships**

TYPE:
Awards/prizes; Fellowships; Residencies.
Fellowships for independent work in
architecture, landscape architecture, design,
musical composition, visual arts, historic
preservation/conservation, literature, ancient
studies, medieval studies, renaissance and
early modern studies, and modern Italian
studies. Supported projects must be
conducted at American Academy in Rome
facilities.

YEAR PROGRAM STARTED: 1894

PURPOSE:
To support emerging artists and scholars in
the early or middle stages of their careers; to
refine and expand their professional, artistic
or scholarly aptitudes, drawing on their
colleagues' erudition and experience, as well
as on the inestimable resources of the Italian
capital of Rome, Europe and the
Mediterranean.

LEGAL BASIS:
Private, not-for-profit.

ELIGIBILITY:
Must be U.S. citizen at the time of
application. Graduate students in the
humanities may apply only for Predoctoral
Fellowships. Previous winners of the Rome
Prize are not eligible to reapply.
Undergraduate students are not eligible for
Rome Prize Fellowships.

U.S. citizens and foreign nationals who have
lived in the U.S. for three years immediately
preceding the application deadline may apply
for the NEH Postdoctoral Fellowships.

FINANCIAL DATA:
Rome Prize includes stipend, meals, a
bedroom with private bath, and a study or
studio.
Amount of support per award: Fellowships
provide stipends of $16,000 (half-term) and
$28,000 (full-term).
Total amount of support: $2,700,000.

CO-OP FUNDING PROGRAMS: National
Endowment for the Arts, National
Endowment for the Humanities, Andrew W.
Mellon Foundation and Samuel Kress
Foundation.

NO. MOST RECENT APPLICANTS: 928.

NO. AWARDS: 22.

APPLICATION INFO:
Application forms are available online.
Duration: Five and one-half months for
half-term fellowships. 11 months for
full-term fellowships. Two-year fellowships
are also available for predoctoral candidates
studying art history.
Deadline: November 1.

PUBLICATIONS:
AAR Magazine, biannually.

STAFF:
Shawn Miller, Programs Director

ADDRESS INQUIRIES TO:
Programs Department
(See address above.)

AMERICAN ANTIQUARIAN SOCIETY (AAS)   [304]

185 Salisbury Street
Worcester, MA 01609-1634
(508) 755-5221
Fax: (508) 754-9069
E-mail: nwolverton@mwa.org
Web Site: www.americanantiquarian.org

FOUNDED: 1812

AREAS OF INTEREST:
American history and culture through 1876.

NAME(S) OF PROGRAMS:
● **AAS American Society for Eighteenth Century Studies Fellowship**
● **AAS National Endowment for the Humanities Fellowships**
● **American Historical Print Collectors Fellowship**
● **Stephen Botein Fellowships**
● **The "Drawn to Art" Fellowship**
● **David Jaffee Fellowship**
● **Kate Van Winkle Keller Fellowship**
● **Linda F. and Julian L. Lapides Fellowship**
● **Jay and Deborah Last Fellowship**
● **The Legacy Fellowship**
● **Alstott Morgan Fellowship**
● **Barbara Packer Fellowship**
● **Kate B. and Hall J. Peterson Fellowships**
● **The Reese Fellowship**
● **Justin G. Schiller Fellowship**
● **Joyce A. Tracy Fellowship**

TYPE:
Conferences/seminars; Fellowships.
Fellowships provide support for residence at
the Society's library for research on any topic
supported by the collections. All awards are
for research and writing using the library's
resources.

YEAR PROGRAM STARTED: 1972

PURPOSE:
To enable scholars to come to Worcester for
an extended period to do research in the
Society's collections.

LEGAL BASIS:
AAS was incorporated by the legislature of
Massachusetts, October 24, 1812.

ELIGIBILITY:
Fellows are selected on the basis of the
applicant's scholarly qualifications, the
scholarly significance of the project, and the
appropriateness of the proposed study to the
Society's collections.

The National Endowment for the Humanities
Fellowships are intended for scholars beyond
the Doctorate, for which senior and
midcareer scholars are encouraged to apply.
Applicant must be a U.S. citizen.

Short-term fellowships are available for
scholars holding Ph.D. and for doctoral
candidates engaged in dissertation research.

FINANCIAL DATA:
Amount of support per award: Long-term
fellowships carry stipends up to $5,000 per
month. Short-term fellowships are $1,850 per
month.

Total amount of support: Varies.

APPLICATION INFO:
Application information is available online.
Duration: One month for short-term
fellowships. Four to 12 months for long-term
fellowships.
Deadline: January 15. Announcement by
March 30.

ADDRESS INQUIRIES TO:
Nan Wolverton, Director of Fellowships
(See e-mail address above.)

*SPECIAL STIPULATIONS:
Recipient must maintain regular and
continuous residence at the Society during
his or her period of tenure.

AMERICAN ANTIQUARIAN SOCIETY (AAS)   [305]

185 Salisbury Street
Worcester, MA 01609-1634
(508) 755-5221
Fax: (508) 754-9069
E-mail: nwolverton@mwa.org
Web Site: www.americanantiquarian.org

AREAS OF INTEREST:
American history, literature and culture
through 1876.

NAME(S) OF PROGRAMS:
● **AAS Fellowship for Creative and Performing Artists and Writers**

TYPE:
Fellowships. Visiting fellowship for historical
research by creative and performing artists,
writers, filmmakers and journalists.

YEAR PROGRAM STARTED: 1995

PURPOSE:
To multiply and improve ways in which an
understanding of history is communicated to
the American people.

ELIGIBILITY:
Creative and performing artists, writers,
filmmakers, journalists, and others whose
goals are to produce imaginative,
non-formulaic works dealing with pre-20th
century American history. Works are for the
general public, rather than for academic or
educational audiences.

FINANCIAL DATA:
Amount of support per award: Stipend of
$1,850.
Total amount of support: Varies.

NO. MOST RECENT APPLICANTS: 40.

NO. AWARDS: Minimum 5.

APPLICATION INFO:
Instructions are included in the online
application.
Duration: Four-week residency.
Deadline: October 5, with notification on or
about December 5.

ADDRESS INQUIRIES TO:
Nan Wolverton, Director of Fellowships
(See e-mail address above.)

AMERICAN COUNCIL OF LEARNED SOCIETIES   [306]

633 Third Avenue, 8th Floor
New York, NY 10017-6706
E-mail: fellowships@acls.org
Web Site: www.acls.org

FOUNDED: 1919

AREAS OF INTEREST:
The humanities and related social sciences.

NAME(S) OF PROGRAMS:
● **ACLS Fellowship**

TYPE:
Fellowships. Postdoctoral fellowships to support research in the humanities or research projects with a predominantly humanities-related emphasis in the social sciences.

PURPOSE:
To provide opportunities for early career, non-tenured scholars to engage in humanities research.

LEGAL BASIS:
Nonprofit.

ELIGIBILITY:
Applicants must be U.S. citizens, permanent residents or DACA recipients. Ph.D. must have been earned within the past eight years. Faculty on the tenure track and scholars without faculty appointments, as well as scholars serving as adjuncts, contingent faculty, and other non-tenured roles, are eligible to apply.

FINANCIAL DATA:
Amount of support per award: Up to $60,000. Fellows who are independent or adjunct scholars will receive an additional $3,000 in research support.
Total amount of support: Varies.

NO. AWARDS: 50 for the year 2020-21.

APPLICATION INFO:
Applications must be submitted through the ACLS Online Fellowship Application system, located at ofa.acls.org.
Duration: Fellows must devote six to 12 continuous months to full-time work on supported projects.
Deadline: September. Notification by early March.

THE AMERICAN NUMISMATIC SOCIETY   [307]
75 Varick Street, Floor 11
New York, NY 10013
(212) 571-4470 ext. 153
Fax: (212) 571-4479
E-mail: vanalfen@numismatics.org
Web Site: numismatics.org

FOUNDED: 1858

AREAS OF INTEREST:
Numismatics (coins and medals), history and archeology.

NAME(S) OF PROGRAMS:
● **The Eric P. Newman Graduate Summer Seminar**

TYPE:
Grants-in-aid. Grants for graduate students and junior faculty to attend the Society's summer seminar held at its museum in New York. The Graduate Seminar in Numismatics is an intensive program of study including lectures and conferences conducted by specialists in various fields, preparation and oral delivery of a research paper and actual contact with the coinage in the Society's collection. Curatorial staff and other experts from the U.S. and abroad will participate in the seminar.

YEAR PROGRAM STARTED: 1952

PURPOSE:
To familiarize students with numismatic methodology and scholarship; to provide a deeper understanding of the contributions made by numismatics to other fields of study.

ELIGIBILITY:
Applications are accepted from students of demonstrated competence who will have completed at least one year of graduate work in history, art history, classical studies, economics, economic history or other related fields. Applications are encouraged from junior faculty members with an advanced degree in one of these fields.

Applications are also accepted from outstanding students from foreign institutions who have completed at least one year of graduate work and are able to demonstrate fluency in English; however, no financial aid for them is offered.

FINANCIAL DATA:
Stipends are available to qualified applicants who are citizens or permanent residents of the U.S.
Amount of support per award: Varies.
Total amount of support: Varies.

CO-OP FUNDING PROGRAMS: Support of attendance at the Seminar is made possible by a generous donation from Mr. and Mrs. Eric P. Newman.

NO. MOST RECENT APPLICANTS: 50.

NO. AWARDS: Up to 8.

APPLICATION INFO:
Details are available on the Society's web site.
Duration: Seven to eight weeks, June through July.
Deadline: Usually February. Specific date is posted online.

OFFICERS:
Dr. Peter Van Alfen, Director

ADDRESS INQUIRIES TO:
Dr. Peter Van Alfen, Director
(See address above.)

AMERICAN PHILOSOPHICAL SOCIETY   [308]
c/o American Philosophical Society Library
104 South Fifth Street
Philadelphia, PA 19106-3387
(215) 440-3400
Fax: (215) 440-3423
E-mail: libfellows@amphilsoc.org
Web Site: www.amphilsoc.org/grants/fellowships

FOUNDED: 1743

AREAS OF INTEREST:
Scholarly research.

NAME(S) OF PROGRAMS:
● **The Library Resident Research Fellowships**

TYPE:
Fellowships; Grants-in-aid; Research grants. Short-term residential fellowships for conducting research in the Library's collections.

YEAR PROGRAM STARTED: 1991

PURPOSE:
To encourage research by scholars in the Library's collections.

LEGAL BASIS:
Nonprofit learned society.

ELIGIBILITY:
Open to both U.S. citizens and foreign nationals who are holders of a Ph.D. or the equivalent, Ph.D. candidates who have passed their preliminary exams and degreed independent scholars. Applicants in any relevant field of scholarship may apply.

FINANCIAL DATA:
Amount of support per award: $3,000 per month.

NO. AWARDS: 25 to 30 annually.

APPLICATION INFO:
All application materials will be submitted online. This includes:
(1) cover letter;
(2) curriculum vitae;
(3) research proposal (two pages) that outlines the status of the applicant's work and what applicant will research at the American Philosophical Society Library. Special attention must be made to specific collections that will be of use during the fellowship and;
(4) two confidential letters of reference.
Duration: One to three months, taken between June 1 and May 31.
Deadline: March 6. Notification in late April.

PUBLICATIONS:
Program announcement; list of guides to the Society's collections.

ADDRESS INQUIRIES TO:
See e-mail address above.

*SPECIAL STIPULATIONS:
Fellows are expected to be in residence during the period of their award.

AMERICAN SCHOOL OF CLASSICAL STUDIES AT ATHENS
6-8 Charlton Street
Princeton, NJ 08540-5232
(609) 683-0800
Fax: (609) 924-0578
E-mail: application@ascsa.org
Web Site: www.ascsa.edu.gr

TYPE:
Fellowships. Several Fellowships awarded by the School for the full academic year: the Samuel H. Kress Fellowship in art and architecture of antiquity, the Gorham Phillips Stevens Fellowship in the history of architecture; the Ione Mylonas Shear Fellowship in Mycenaean archaeology or Athenian architecture and/or archaeology; the Homer A. and Dorothy B. Thompson Fellowship in the study of pottery. Additionally, three Fellowships are unrestricted as to field: the Edward Capps, the Doreen Canaday Spitzer, and the Eugene Vanderpool Fellowships.

See entry 811 for full listing.

AMERICAN SCHOOL OF CLASSICAL STUDIES AT ATHENS
6-8 Charlton Street
Princeton, NJ 08540-5232
(609) 683-0800
Fax: (609) 924-0578
E-mail: application@ascsa.org
Web Site: www.ascsa.edu.gr

TYPE:
Fellowships. Fellowships for postdoctoral scholars and professionals in the humanities.

See entry 809 for full listing.

AMERICAN SCHOOL OF CLASSICAL STUDIES AT ATHENS
6-8 Charlton Street
Princeton, NJ 08540-5232
(609) 683-0800
Fax: (609) 924-0578
E-mail: application@ascsa.org
Web Site: www.ascsa.edu.gr

TYPE:
Fellowships. The M. Alison Frantz Fellowship is part of the Student Associate Program, which is open to advanced graduate students in the same fields as the Regular Academic Program (classical studies and ancient Mediterranean studies and related fields such as history of art, anthropology, prehistory, studies in postclassical Greece, etc.), who plan to pursue independent research projects and who do not wish to commit to the full Regular Academic Program.

See entry 810 for full listing.

AMERICAN SCHOOL OF CLASSICAL STUDIES AT ATHENS
6-8 Charlton Street
Princeton, NJ 08540-5232
(609) 683-0800
Fax: (609) 924-0578
E-mail: application@ascsa.org
Web Site: www.ascsa.edu.gr

TYPE:
Fellowships.

See entry 816 for full listing.

AMERICAN SCHOOL OF CLASSICAL STUDIES AT ATHENS
6-8 Charlton Street
Princeton, NJ 08540-5232
(609) 683-0800
Fax: (609) 924-0578
E-mail: application@ascsa.org
Web Site: www.ascsa.edu.gr

TYPE:
Fellowships. The Heinrich Schliemann and the John Williams White Fellowships in Archaeology are awarded based on the student's performance on the archaeology examination.

The Thomas Day Seymour Fellowship in History and Literature is awarded based on the student's combined performance on the history and literature examination.

Nine fellowships are unrestricted to field. These are the Virginia Grace, the Michael Jameson, the Philip Lockhart, the Lucy Shoe Meritt, the Fowler Merle-Smith, the Martin Ostwald, and the James Rignall Wheeler Fellowships. The Bert Hodge Hill Fellowship is unrestricted, but with a preference for a student in art history. The Emily Townsend Vermeule Fellowship is unrestricted, but with a preference for Bronze Age archaeology.

See entry 817 for full listing.

ARCHAEOLOGICAL INSTITUTE OF AMERICA [309]
44 Beacon Street
Boston, MA 02108
(857) 305-9358
Fax: (857) 233-4270
E-mail: saustin@archaeological.org
Web Site: www.archaeological.org/grants/16811

FOUNDED: 1879

AREAS OF INTEREST:
Archaeology or related fields.

NAME(S) OF PROGRAMS:
● **Elizabeth Bartman Museum Internship**

TYPE:
Internships. Established in honor of AIA Honorary President Elizabeth Bartman, this internship assists graduate students or those who have recently completed a Master's degree with the expenses associated with participating in a museum internship either in the U.S. or abroad.

PURPOSE:
To assist graduate students with expenses associated with participating in a museum internship.

ELIGIBILITY:
Applicants must have been members of the AIA for at least one year at the time of application. The recipient should remain a member until the end of the internship period. Applicants must be enrolled in a graduate program in archaeology or a related field, or have recently completed a Master's degree in archaeology or a related field.

FINANCIAL DATA:
Amount of support per award: $1,250 to $2,500.

NO. MOST RECENT APPLICANTS: 1.

NO. AWARDS: 1.

APPLICATION INFO:
Applicants must complete the online application form that asks for the following: (1) Project Proposal - The Fellowships Committee attaches the greatest importance to the summary statement of the applicant's interest in museum work and how the proposed internship will help achieve the applicant's larger goals. It is helpful to include background information outlining any past museum experience, field experience, and the reasons for pursuing museum work in general, and this internship project in particular. Proposal must include information about the internship and the anticipated length of stay. (2) Budget - An outline of anticipated expenses associated with participation in the project and a statement from the applicant indicating any other financial resources available or applied for, if any, to help cover these expenses. (3) Transcripts - Applicants must include completed undergraduate transcripts and transcripts for completed postgraduate work. Transcripts may be mailed to the attention of Samantha Austin or sent digitally to saustin@archaeological.org and; (4) Letters of Recommendation - The names and e-mails of two professors or academic advisors at the applicant's college or university who know the applicant's work and who are willing to provide letters of recommendation. These references will receive further instructions from the AIA. A recommendation from the prospective supervisor of the internship is encouraged.

Duration: Minimum eight weeks or a semester. Nonrenewable.
Deadline: April 1.

ADDRESS INQUIRIES TO:
Samantha Austin
Manager of Membership and Governance
(See address and e-mail above.)

*SPECIAL STIPULATIONS:
At the conclusion of the internship tenure, the recipient is required to submit a report on the use of the award to AIA Headquarters.

ARCHAEOLOGICAL INSTITUTE OF AMERICA [310]
44 Beacon Street
Boston, MA 02108
(857) 305-9360
Fax: (857) 233-4270
E-mail: fellowships@archaeological.org
Web Site: www.archaeological.org

FOUNDED: 1879

AREAS OF INTEREST:
Archaeological research and publication.

NAME(S) OF PROGRAMS:
● **John R. Coleman Traveling Fellowship**
● **Olivia James Traveling Fellowship**

TYPE:
Fellowships. John R. Coleman Traveling Fellowship: Awarded to be used for travel and study in Italy, the western Mediterranean, or North Africa. Applicants must be engaged in dissertation research in a U.S. graduate program.

Olivia James Traveling Fellowship: Awarded, preferably, to individuals engaged in dissertation research or to recent recipients of the Ph.D. (within five years of the application deadline) for travel and study in Greece, the Aegean Islands, Cyprus, Sicily, Southern Italy, Asia Minor or Mesopotamia to conduct a project in (most suitably) classics, sculpture, architecture, archaeology or history.

YEAR PROGRAM STARTED: 1961

PURPOSE:
John R. Coleman Traveling Fellowship: To encourage the continued study of archaeological sites; to provide funding for travel and study in Italy, the western Mediterranean or North Africa.

Olivia James Traveling Fellowship: To encourage the continued study of archaeological sites; to provide fellowships for travel and study in Greece, the Aegean Islands, Cyprus, Sicily, Southern Italy, Asia Minor or Mesopotamia.

LEGAL BASIS:
Nonprofit, scientific and educational organization.

ELIGIBILITY:
Applicants must have been AIA members in good standing for at least two consecutive years before the application deadline.

John R. Coleman Traveling Fellowship: Applicants must be members of the AIA at the time of application. The recipient should remain a member until the end of the fellowship term and subsequent submission of an abstract and/or presentation at the AIA annual meeting. Applicants must be engaged in dissertation research in a U.S. graduate program.

Olivia James Traveling Fellowship: Applicants must be U.S. citizens. Preference is given to individuals engaged in dissertation research or to recent Ph.D. recipients (within five years of application deadline). Preference is also given to projects of at least a half-year's duration. The award is for travel and study in Greece, the Aegean Islands, Cyprus, Sicily, Southern Italy, Asia Minor or Mesopotamia and is not intended to support field excavation projects. Recipients may not hold other major fellowships during the requested tenure.

FINANCIAL DATA:
Amount of support per award: John R. Coleman Traveling Fellowship: $10,000. Olivia James Traveling Fellowship: $24,000.

Total amount of support: John R. Coleman Traveling Fellowship: $10,000. Olivia James Traveling Fellowship: $24,000.

NO. MOST RECENT APPLICANTS: John R. Coleman Traveling Fellowship: 5. Olivia James Traveling Fellowship: 13.

NO. AWARDS: 1 per award.

APPLICATION INFO:
Official application materials are available August of each year on the Institute's web site. Graduate transcripts, two letters of reference and a summary statement of proposed project are required. Applications for the fellowship can be submitted electronically.
Duration: Single fellowship for work to be conducted between July 1 of the award year and the following June 30.
Deadline: November 1. Announcement by February 1.

ADDRESS INQUIRIES TO:
Laurel Nilsen Sparks
Lecture and Fellowship Coordinator
(See address above.)

ARCHAEOLOGICAL INSTITUTE OF AMERICA   [311]
44 Beacon Street
Boston, MA 02108
(857) 305-9360
Fax: (857) 233-4270
E-mail: fellowships@archaeological.org
Web Site: www.archaeological.org

FOUNDED: 1879

AREAS OF INTEREST:
Archaeological research and publication.

NAME(S) OF PROGRAMS:
• **Harriet and Leon Pomerance Fellowship**

TYPE:
Fellowships. Awarded to support a person on an individual project of a scholarly nature relating to Aegean Bronze Age Archaeology. Preference will be given to candidates whose project requires travel to the Mediterranean for the purpose stated above.

YEAR PROGRAM STARTED: 1972

PURPOSE:
To promote serious scholarly study of Aegean Bronze Age Archaeology.

LEGAL BASIS:
Nonprofit, scientific and educational organization.

ELIGIBILITY:
Applicants must be citizens or permanent residents of the U.S. or Canada, or be

actively pursuing an advanced degree at a North American college or university. Applicants must have been AIA members in good standing for at least two consecutive years before the application deadline. Previous Harriet Pomerance Fellows are not eligible.

At the conclusion of the fellowship tenure, the recipient must submit a report on the use of the stipend to the president of the Institute.

FINANCIAL DATA:
Amount of support per award: $5,000.
Total amount of support: $5,000.

NO. MOST RECENT APPLICANTS: 5.

NO. AWARDS: 1.

APPLICATION INFO:
Official application materials are available online in August of each year. Graduate transcript(s), two letters of reference, and a summary statement of proposed project are required. Applications for the fellowship can be submitted electronically.
Duration: Work to be conducted between July 1 of the award year and the following June 30.
Deadline: November 1. Announcement by February 1.

ADDRESS INQUIRIES TO:
Laurel Nilsen Sparks
Lecture and Fellowship Coordinator
(See address above.)

ARCHAEOLOGICAL INSTITUTE OF AMERICA   [312]
44 Beacon Street
Boston, MA 02108
(857) 305-9360
Fax: (857) 233-4270
E-mail: fellowships@archaeological.org
Web Site: www.archaeological.org

FOUNDED: 1879

AREAS OF INTEREST:
Archaeological research and publication.

NAME(S) OF PROGRAMS:
• **Jane C. Waldbaum Archaeological Field School Scholarship**

TYPE:
Scholarships. Award to support participation in an archaeological excavation or survey project.

YEAR PROGRAM STARTED: 2006

ELIGIBILITY:
Open to junior and senior undergraduates or first-year graduate students. Applicants cannot previously have participated in archaeological excavation and must be at least a junior at the time of application. Applicants must be enrolled in a college or university in the U.S. or Canada, but do not have to be U.S. citizens or residents.

FINANCIAL DATA:
Amount of support per award: $1,000.
Total amount of support: Varies.

NO. MOST RECENT APPLICANTS: Over 80.

NO. AWARDS: 8 for the year 2019.

APPLICATION INFO:
All applications must be submitted electronically through the AIA web site. Required materials include the application form, two letters of reference, official

transcript(s) and a letter of acceptance from the field school. All application materials must be received by the deadline.
Duration: Minimum one-month stay at the field school. Nonrenewable.
Deadline: March 1.

ADDRESS INQUIRIES TO:
Laurel Nilsen Sparks
Lecture and Fellowship Coordinator
(See address above.)

ARCHAEOLOGICAL INSTITUTE OF AMERICA   [313]
44 Beacon Street
Boston, MA 02108
(857) 305-9360
Fax: (857) 233-4270
E-mail: fellowships@archaeological.org
Web Site: www.archaeological.org

FOUNDED: 1879

AREAS OF INTEREST:
Archaeological research and publication.

NAME(S) OF PROGRAMS:
• **Anna C. and Oliver C. Colburn Fellowship**

TYPE:
Fellowships. Awarded to an applicant every other year contingent upon his or her acceptance as an incoming Associate Member or Student Associate Member of the American School of Classical Studies at Athens, Greece.

YEAR PROGRAM STARTED: 1991

PURPOSE:
To support studies at the American School of Classical Studies at Athens, Greece.

LEGAL BASIS:
Nonprofit, scientific and educational organization.

ELIGIBILITY:
Applicants must be U.S. or Canadian citizens or permanent residents, or those who are actively pursuing an advanced degree at a North American college or university, who are at the predoctoral stage or who have recently received the Ph.D. degree (within five years of the date of application). They must apply concurrently to the American School for Senior Associate Membership or Student Associate Membership. Applicants may not be Members of the American School during the year of application.

Applicants must have been AIA members in good standing for at least two consecutive years (one year for graduate students) before the application deadline.

The fellowship recipient is required to submit a report on the use of the stipend both to the President of the Archaeological Institute of America and to the Director of the American School of Classical Studies at Athens at the conclusion of the tenure of the fellowship.

FINANCIAL DATA:
Amount of support per award: $5,500.
Total amount of support: $11,000.

NO. MOST RECENT APPLICANTS: 8.

NO. AWARDS: 2.

APPLICATION INFO:
Official application materials are available on the web site. Graduate transcript(s), three letters of reference, and a summary statement of the proposed project are required. Candidates must apply concurrently to the

American School for Senior Associate Membership or Student Associate Membership.

Duration: Work to be conducted between July 1 of the award year and the following June 30.

Deadline: January 15, 2020 and every other year thereafter.

ADDRESS INQUIRIES TO:
Laurel Nilsen Sparks
Lecture and Fellowship Coordinator
(See address above.)

*SPECIAL STIPULATIONS:
After the tenure of their fellowship, all fellows are expected to submit an abstract to the Program Committee within two years, in accordance with that committee's guidelines, in order to present a paper on their research at the Institute annual meeting.

THE AUSTRALIAN NATIONAL UNIVERSITY   [314]
Humanities Research Centre
Sir Roland Wilson Building
120 McCoy Circuit
Acton A.C.T. 2601 Australia
(61) 02 6125 4357
E-mail: hrc@anu.edu.au
Web Site: hrc.cass.anu.edu.au

FOUNDED: 1973

AREAS OF INTEREST:
Any area of research in the humanities (broadly interpreted).

NAME(S) OF PROGRAMS:
● **Visiting Fellows Program**

TYPE:
Conferences/seminars; Fellowships. Visiting Fellowships are offered with a grant, without a grant or with a partial grant.

YEAR PROGRAM STARTED: 1973

PURPOSE:
To stimulate research in the humanities throughout Australia.

LEGAL BASIS:
Integral part of the Australian National University, Research School of Humanities.

ELIGIBILITY:
Applicants must have an institutional affiliation to a university or equivalent research or cultural organization, and generally have at least a higher research degree, research experience, and publications.

FINANCIAL DATA:
Visiting Fellowships provide accommodation for up to 12 weeks plus airfare.
Total amount of support: Up to $150,000 (AUD) annually.

NO. AWARDS: Approximately 20.

APPLICATION INFO:
Applications for the following year are solicited in February or March each year. Applicants should submit a completed application form, curriculum vitae, and a list of publications and/or professional activities. A one- to two-page description of the proposed project must be submitted, along with the title of the research project. Applicants need to identify and provide the Referees' Comments Form to two or three referees who will support the application. Referees should submit their confidential comments separately to the HRC's Administrator on the form provided no later than May 31.

Duration: Six to 12 weeks.
Deadline: May 31. Award announcement by June 30.

PUBLICATIONS:
Annual report; descriptive brochure; journal; application guidelines; forms and HRC bulletin.

ADDRESS INQUIRIES TO:
Head, Humanities Research Centre
Tel: (61) 02 6125 0151
(See e-mail address above.)

JOHN CARTER BROWN LIBRARY
Brown University
94 George Street
Providence, RI 02906
(401) 863-2725
Fax: (401) 863-3477
E-mail: jcb-fellowships@brown.edu
Web Site: jcblibrary.org/fellowships

TYPE:
Fellowships. The John Carter Brown Library (JCB), an independently funded institution for advanced research at Brown University, contains one of the world's premier collections of primary materials related to the discovery, exploration, and settlement of the New World to 1825, including books, maps, newspapers and other printed objects.

The Library offers both Short-term and Long-term Fellowships.

See entry 530 for full listing.

CANADIAN FEDERATION FOR THE HUMANITIES AND SOCIAL SCIENCES
141 Laurier Avenue West
Suite 200
Ottawa ON K1P 5J3 Canada
(613) 238-6112 ext. 319
Fax: (613) 238-6114
E-mail: aspp-paes@ideas-idees.ca
Web Site: www.ideas-idees.ca

TYPE:
Grants-in-aid. Grants to support the publication of scholarly books in the social sciences and humanities.

See entry 1656 for full listing.

CANADIAN INSTITUTE IN GREECE/L'INSTITUT CANADIEN EN GRECE   [315]
Wilfred Laurier University
Department of Archaeology and Heritage Studies
75 University Avenue West
Waterloo ON N2L 3C5 Canada
(519) 884-0710 ext. 4260
E-mail: sgallimore@wlu.ca
Web Site: www.cig-icg.gr

FOUNDED: 1974

AREAS OF INTEREST:
Modern Greek, classical languages and literatures, history, archaeology, history of art and music.

NAME(S) OF PROGRAMS:
● **Elizabeth Alfoldi-Rosenbaum Fellowship**
● **Neda and Franz Leipen Fellowship**

● **Homer and Dorothy Thompson Fellowship**
● **Frederick E. and Joan Winter Student Travel Bursary**

TYPE:
Fellowships; Internships; Travel grants. Intended to support the graduate work of a person who needs to study in Greece.

YEAR PROGRAM STARTED: 1974

PURPOSE:
To promote the study of classical languages and literatures, history, archaeology, history of art and music in Greece.

LEGAL BASIS:
Incorporated in Canada and Greece.

ELIGIBILITY:
Open to Canadian citizens or landed immigrants.

FINANCIAL DATA:
Amount of support per award: Fellowships: $9,000 (CAN) plus housing at the Institute; Bursaries: $2,000 (CAN).
Total amount of support: Varies each year.

NO. MOST RECENT APPLICANTS: 2 to 3.

NO. AWARDS: Bursaries: 1; Fellowships: 1.

APPLICATION INFO:
Applicants must write, enclosing a curriculum vitae and an outline of the proposed research. Applicants must also arrange for three referees to send letters to the chair of the Fellowships Committee.
Duration: Bursaries: Three months. Fellowships: Nine months.
Deadline: March 1. All fellowships are not offered every year.

PUBLICATIONS:
CIG Bulletin, semi-annually.

STAFF:
Prof. Jacques Y. Perreault, Director
Dr. Jonathan E. Tomlinson, Assistant Director

ADDRESS INQUIRIES TO:
E-mail: info@cig-icg.gr

CENTER FOR HELLENIC STUDIES   [316]
3100 Whitehaven Street, N.W.
Washington, DC 20008
(202) 745-4400
Fax: (202) 797-8650
E-mail: fellowships@chs.harvard.edu
Web Site: www.chs.harvard.edu

FOUNDED: 1961

AREAS OF INTEREST:
Postdoctoral ancient Greek studies.

TYPE:
Fellowships; Residencies; Visiting scholars. The Center offers Residential Fellowships to scholars working on various aspects of ancient Greek civilization. Eligible fields of research include archaeology, art history, epigraphy, history, literary criticism, philology, philosophy, pedagogical applications and interdisciplinary research.

YEAR PROGRAM STARTED: 1961

PURPOSE:
To encourage research in Hellenic studies.

LEGAL BASIS:
A unit of Harvard University.

ELIGIBILITY:
Investigators holding a Ph.D. degree or equivalent are eligible to apply. Professional competence in ancient Greek, as evidenced by publication, is essential.

FINANCIAL DATA:
Residential fellowships provide a stipend (maximum $18,000) plus lodging.

NO. MOST RECENT APPLICANTS: 75.

NO. AWARDS: Varies.

APPLICATION INFO:
Official application materials are available on the web site.
Duration: Support is available for a nine-month period beginning September 1 and ending May 31. Fellowships are available for varying periods (four to 16 weeks) in the spring or the fall.
Deadline: October.

PUBLICATIONS:
Application form and guidelines.

STAFF:
Gregory Nagy, Director

ADDRESS INQUIRIES TO:
Lanah Koelle
Fellowships Program Manager
(See address above.)

CENTER FOR 17TH AND 18TH CENTURY STUDIES [317]
University of California, Los Angeles
10745 Dickson Plaza, 302 Royce Hall
Los Angeles, CA 90095-1404
(310) 206-8552
Fax: (310) 206-8577
E-mail: c1718cs@humnet.ucla.edu
Web Site: www.1718.ucla.edu/research

FOUNDED: 1985

AREAS OF INTEREST:
England between 1640 and 1830 (history, language and literature, religion and theology), Oscar Wilde and the 1890s, and modern fine printing.

NAME(S) OF PROGRAMS:
● **Short-Term Research Fellowships**

TYPE:
Fellowships. Short-term (one to three months) postdoctoral fellowships for research in residence for any period of the year (July 1 through June 30) at the William Andrews Clark Memorial Library on specific subjects relevant to the collections and interests of the Library.

YEAR PROGRAM STARTED: 1985

PURPOSE:
To provide support for research in the humanities.

LEGAL BASIS:
University.

ELIGIBILITY:
Applicants must hold a Ph.D. or have equivalent academic experience.

FINANCIAL DATA:
Amount of support per award: $3,000 per month.
Total amount of support: Varies.

NO. AWARDS: 7 for the year 2020-21.

APPLICATION INFO:
Applicants must submit:
(1) a curriculum vitae (maximum of three pages, including bibliography of published

and unpublished scholarly work) and;
(2) a project proposal (maximum 1,000 words, double-spaced, including bibliography of Clark materials relevant to the project).

In addition to the information provided on the application form, applicants must arrange for three scholarly references to be submitted by e-mail directly to the fellowship coordinator at ortiz@humnet.ucla.edu.
Duration: One to three months. Nonrenewable.
Deadline: February 1 of each year.

PUBLICATIONS:
Application guidelines; brochure on the Center and Library and its holdings; biennial newsletters; proceedings of conferences.

OFFICERS:
Candis Snoddy, Assistant Director

ADDRESS INQUIRIES TO:
Myrna Ortiz, Fellowship Coordinator
(See address above.)

CENTER FOR 17TH AND 18TH CENTURY STUDIES [318]
University of California, Los Angeles
10745 Dickson Plaza, 302 Royce Hall
Los Angeles, CA 90095-1404
(310) 206-8552
Fax: (310) 206-8577
E-mail: c1718cs@humnet.ucla.edu
Web Site: www.1718.ucla.edu/research

FOUNDED: 1985

AREAS OF INTEREST:
England between 1640 and 1830 (history, language and literature, religion and theology), Oscar Wilde and the 1890s, and modern fine printing.

NAME(S) OF PROGRAMS:
● **Clark Predoctoral Fellowships**

TYPE:
Fellowships. Offered for one to three consecutive months during the period July 1 through June 30 to registered University of California doctoral candidates whose dissertation project is on a specific subject relevant to the collections and interests of the Clark Library.

YEAR PROGRAM STARTED: 1990

PURPOSE:
To provide support for research in the humanities.

LEGAL BASIS:
University.

ELIGIBILITY:
Advanced, registered University of California doctoral candidates are eligible.

GEOG. RESTRICTIONS: California.

FINANCIAL DATA:
Amount of support per award: $3,000 per month.

NO. AWARDS: 4 for the year 2020-21.

APPLICATION INFO:
Applicants must submit:
(1) a curriculum vitae (maximum of three pages, including a bibliography of published and unpublished scholarly work) and;
(2) a project proposal (maximum 1,000 words, double-spaced, including a bibliography of Clark materials relevant to the project).

In addition to the information provided on the application form, applicants must arrange for three scholarly references to be submitted by e-mail directly to the fellowship coordinator at ortiz@humnet.ucla.edu.
Duration: One to three months. Nonrenewable.
Deadline: February 1 of each year.

PUBLICATIONS:
Application guidelines; brochure on the Center and Library and its holdings; biennial newsletters; proceedings of conferences.

OFFICERS:
Candis Snoddy, Assistant Director

ADDRESS INQUIRIES TO:
Myrna Ortiz, Fellowship Coordinator
(See address above.)

CENTER FOR 17TH AND 18TH CENTURY STUDIES [319]
University of California, Los Angeles
10745 Dickson Plaza, 302 Royce Hall
Los Angeles, CA 90095-1404
(310) 206-8552
Fax: (310) 206-8577
E-mail: c1718cs@humnet.ucla.edu
Web Site: www.1718.ucla.edu/research

FOUNDED: 1985

AREAS OF INTEREST:
England between 1640 and 1750 (history, language and literature, religion and theology), Oscar Wilde and the 1890s, and modern fine printing.

NAME(S) OF PROGRAMS:
● **ASECS/Clark Library Fellowships**

TYPE:
Fellowships. Postdoctoral fellowships for research in residence for a period of one month any time from July 1 through June 30 at the William Andrews Clark Memorial Library on a project in The Restoration or 18th century.

YEAR PROGRAM STARTED: 1985

PURPOSE:
To provide support for research in the humanities.

LEGAL BASIS:
University.

ELIGIBILITY:
Candidates must:
(1) have received the Doctorate prior to appointment;
(2) be members in good standing of the American Society for Eighteenth-Century Studies and;
(3) be working on a project in The Restoration or the eighteenth century.

FINANCIAL DATA:
Amount of support per award: $3,000 for one month.

NO. AWARDS: 3 for the year 2020-21.

APPLICATION INFO:
Applicants must submit:
(1) a curriculum vitae (maximum of three pages, including a bibliography of published and unpublished scholarly work) and;
(2) a project proposal (maximum 1,000 words, double-spaced, including a bibliography of Clark materials relevant to the project).

In addition to the information provided on the application form, applicants must arrange for three scholarly references to be submitted by e-mail directly to the fellowship coordinator at ortiz@humnet.ucla.edu.

Duration: One month. Nonrenewable.

Deadline: February 1 of each year.

PUBLICATIONS:
Application guidelines; brochure on the Center and Library and its holdings; biennial newsletters; proceedings of conferences.

OFFICERS:
Candis Snoddy, Assistant Director

ADDRESS INQUIRIES TO:
Myrna Ortiz, Fellowship Coordinator
(See address above.)

CENTER FOR 17TH AND 18TH CENTURY STUDIES [320]

University of California, Los Angeles
10745 Dickson Plaza, 302 Royce Hall
Los Angeles, CA 90095-1404
(310) 206-8552
Fax: (310) 206-8577
E-mail: c1718cs@humnet.ucla.edu
Web Site: www.1718.ucla.edu/research

FOUNDED: 1985

AREAS OF INTEREST:
England between 1640 and 1830 (history, language and literature, religion and theology), Oscar Wilde and the 1890s, and modern fine printing.

NAME(S) OF PROGRAMS:
● **Ahmanson and Getty Postdoctoral Fellowships**

TYPE:
Fellowships. With the support of the Ahmanson Foundation of Los Angeles and the J. Paul Getty Trust, the UCLA Center for 17th- and 18th-Century Studies and the William Andrews Clark Memorial Library have a theme-based fellowship program to encourage the participation of junior scholars in the Center's cross-disciplinary, comparative research projects. The major theme for a given year is announced the preceding fall.

Participating fellows will be expected to make a substantive contribution to program seminars.

YEAR PROGRAM STARTED: 1992

PURPOSE:
To provide support for research in the humanities.

LEGAL BASIS:
University.

ELIGIBILITY:
Candidates must have received their Ph.D. in the last six years prior to application and be engaged in research pertaining to the theme.

FINANCIAL DATA:
Amount of support per award: Stipend of $54,540, plus paid medical benefits for scholar and dependents for the academic year.

NO. AWARDS: 2 for the year 2020-21.

APPLICATION INFO:
Applicants must submit:
(1) a curriculum vitae (maximum of three pages, including bibliography of published and unpublished scholarly work) and;
(2) a project proposal (maximum 1,000

words, double-spaced, including a bibliography of Clark materials relevant to the project).

In addition to the information provided on the application form, applicants must arrange for three scholarly references to be submitted by e-mail directly to the fellowship coordinator at ortiz@humnet.ucla.edu.

Duration: Three academic quarters. Nonrenewable.

Deadline: February 1 of each year preceding the award.

PUBLICATIONS:
Application guidelines; brochure on the Center and Library and its holdings; fellowships brochure; biennial newsletters; proceedings of conferences.

OFFICERS:
Candis Snoddy, Assistant Director

ADDRESS INQUIRIES TO:
Myrna Ortiz, Fellowship Coordinator
(See address above.)

CENTER FOR THE HUMANITIES [321]

Mellon Postdoctoral Fellowship Program
Wesleyan University
95 Pearl Street
Middletown, CT 06459-0069
(860) 685-3044
Fax: (860) 685-2171
E-mail: lludwig@wesleyan.edu
Web Site: www.wesleyan.edu/humanities

FOUNDED: 1959

AREAS OF INTEREST:
The Center aims to explore fresh and vital aspects of the humanities, to realize an interdisciplinary response to human problems and to generate new possibilities for curricular reform. In fulfilling these aims, the Center must also examine the assumptions that underlie academic disciplines and humanistic theories. It must encourage research as well as the fundamental discourse of teachers and students.

NAME(S) OF PROGRAMS:
● **Andrew W. Mellon Postdoctoral Fellowship**

TYPE:
Fellowships. The aims of the Center are reflected in its constituency which includes scholars, artists, public figures and students. Fellows range in age and achievement from undergraduates to the most eminent humanists. Departments at Wesleyan University participating in the Center include Classics, Modern Languages and Literatures, English, the College of Letters, Philosophy, History, Religion, Anthropology, Psychology and the Fine Arts.

PURPOSE:
To promote advanced study and research in the humanities, arts and qualitative social sciences; to provide scholars who have lately completed their Ph.Ds. with free time to further their own work in a cross-disciplinary setting, and to associate them with a distinguished faculty.

LEGAL BASIS:
Grant from Andrew W. Mellon Foundation to Wesleyan University.

ELIGIBILITY:
Scholars who have received their Ph.D. degree after June 2016 in any field of inquiry

in the humanities or humanistic social sciences - broadly conceived - are invited to apply.

Fellows will be expected to participate in the lectures, colloquia and discussion groups that are organized each semester around a specific theme chosen for its theoretical interest and its pertinence to crucial problems in related disciplines of the humanities, the qualitative social sciences or the arts. Additional duties of the fellows will be to teach one course and to give one public lecture.

Fellow must reside in Middletown, CT for tenure of fellowship.

FINANCIAL DATA:
Amount of support per award: $55,000.

CO-OP FUNDING PROGRAMS: Andrew W. Mellon Foundation.

NO. MOST RECENT APPLICANTS: Over 600.

NO. AWARDS: 1 to 2 each year.

APPLICATION INFO:
There is no official application form. Applications should include:
(1) a letter from the applicant, including a statement of current research interests and a brief proposal for a one-semester undergraduate course related to the Center for the Humanities theme;
(2) a full curriculum vitae;
(3) three letters of recommendation and;
(4) copies of published work, extracts from the dissertation, or drafts of work in progress (not to exceed 25 pages).

Duration: Two years.

PUBLICATIONS:
Brochure.

ADDRESS INQUIRIES TO:
Natasha Korda, Director
(See address above.)

CONNECTICUT HUMANITIES [322]

100 Riverview Center, Suite 290
292 Main Street
Middletown, CT 06457
(860) 937-6535
E-mail: swands@cthumanities.org
Web Site: cthumanities.org

FOUNDED: 1973

AREAS OF INTEREST:
Humanities in Connecticut, heritage and reading.

NAME(S) OF PROGRAMS:
● **Connecticut Humanities Fund**

TYPE:
Project/program grants. Capacity building grants.

YEAR PROGRAM STARTED: 1973

PURPOSE:
To create opportunities to think, learn and understand more about ourselves, our communities and our state.

ELIGIBILITY:
Applicants must be incorporated as private, nonprofit organizations or municipalities in Connecticut, and must regularly provide service to the public.

GEOG. RESTRICTIONS: Connecticut.

FINANCIAL DATA:
Amount of support per award: $250 to $35,000.

Total amount of support: $700,000 for the year 2019.

Matching fund requirements: All Connecticut Humanities Fund grants must be matched dollar for dollar through a combination of in-kind contributions and/or cash offered by applicants, partners, and/or third parties, i.e., grants or bequests. Funds from the State of Connecticut may not be used for matching purposes.

CO-OP FUNDING PROGRAMS: Hartford Foundation for Public Giving.

NO. MOST RECENT APPLICANTS: 142 for the year 2019.

NO. AWARDS: 76 for the year 2019.

REPRESENTATIVE AWARDS:
$20,000 to Lockwood Mathews Mansion Museum for implementing an exhibition entitled "What Is It? Technologies and Discoveries of the Victorian Era;" $13,700 to Noah Webster House to develop an electronic tablet-guided tour that combines storytelling, interpretive illustrations and new technologies to tell the story of Noah Webster's life and times.

APPLICATION INFO:
Preapplication discussion with CTH staff is required two months before submission of formal application. Specify the grant line and program category when submitting proposal.
Duration: Nine months to two years.
Deadline: For quick grants: Every other month; For grants over $5,000: November and April.

STAFF:
Scott Wands, Manager, Grants and Programs

ADDRESS INQUIRIES TO:
Scott Wands, Manager
Grants and Programs
(See address above.)

CORNELL UNIVERSITY   [323]
Society for the Humanities
A.D. White House
121 Presidents Drive
Ithaca, NY 14853-1101
(607) 255-9274
(607) 255-4086
Fax: (607) 255-1422
E-mail: humctr@cornell.edu
Web Site: societyhumanities.as.cornell.edu/fellowships

FOUNDED: 1966

AREAS OF INTEREST:
Postdoctoral fellowships in the humanities.

NAME(S) OF PROGRAMS:
• **Mellon Postdoctoral Fellowships**

TYPE:
Fellowships. Postdoctoral teaching-research fellowships in the humanities, each awarded for a two-year period. While in residence at Cornell, postdoctoral fellows hold department affiliation and have limited teaching duties and the opportunity for scholarly work.

PURPOSE:
To encourage the academic growth of promising humanists with recent Ph.D. degrees.

LEGAL BASIS:
University.

ELIGIBILITY:
Applicants who will receive the Ph.D. degree by June 30 of the beginning program year are eligible to apply. Such applicants must include a letter of confirmation.

International scholars are welcome to apply.

FINANCIAL DATA:
Fellows receive stipend while in residence.
Amount of support per award: $55,000 per year.
Total amount of support: Varies.

CO-OP FUNDING PROGRAMS: Funded by a grant from the Andrew W. Mellon Foundation.

NO. MOST RECENT APPLICANTS: 150.

NO. AWARDS: 2 per year.

APPLICATION INFO:
Application procedures are found on the web site. Application materials must be uploaded to Academic Jobs Online.

If the applicant does not have a Ph.D. in hand at the time of application, a letter of confirmation must be received from applicant's committee chair or department stating that applicant will have the Ph.D. degree before the term of the fellowship begins on August 1 of the beginning program year.
Duration: Two years.
Deadline: Varies.

ADDRESS INQUIRIES TO:
Emily Parsons, Program Manager
Mellon Postdoctoral Fellowships
(See address above.)

CORNELL UNIVERSITY   [324]
Society for the Humanities
A.D. White House
121 Presidents Drive
Ithaca, NY 14853-1101
(607) 255-9274
(607) 255-4086
Fax: (607) 255-1422
E-mail: humctr@cornell.edu
Web Site: societyhumanities.as.cornell.edu/fellowships

FOUNDED: 1966

AREAS OF INTEREST:
Humanities studies.

NAME(S) OF PROGRAMS:
• **Society for the Humanities Fellowships**

TYPE:
Fellowships. Yearly fellowships with a new focal theme each year. Fellows include scholars from other universities and members of the Cornell faculty released from regular duties. Fellows spend most of their time in research and offer one course related to their research.

YEAR PROGRAM STARTED: 1966

PURPOSE:
To support research and encourage imaginative teaching in the humanities.

LEGAL BASIS:
University.

ELIGIBILITY:
Applicants must have received the Ph.D. degree before January 1 of the year of their application. They must have one or more years of teaching experience, which may include teaching as a graduate student. Fellows should be working on topics related to the year's theme. Their approach to the humanities should be broad enough to appeal to students and scholars in several humanistic disciplines.

International scholars are welcome to apply.

FINANCIAL DATA:
Amount of support per award: $55,000 stipend.
Total amount of support: Varies.

NO. MOST RECENT APPLICANTS: 200.

NO. AWARDS: 6 to 8 each year.

APPLICATION INFO:
Application guidelines are available on the Society's web site. All application materials, including letters of recommendation, must be submitted via Academic Jobs Online.
Duration: One academic year.
Deadline: October 1 of the year prior to the beginning of the fellowship. Awards are announced by the end of December of that year of application.

PUBLICATIONS:
Brochure.

ADDRESS INQUIRIES TO:
Kina Viola, Program Coordinator
Society for the Humanities
(See address above.)

*SPECIAL STIPULATIONS:
Fellows spend their time in research and writing, participate in the weekly Fellows Seminar, and offer one seminar related to their research.

GLADYS KRIEBLE DELMAS FOUNDATION   [325]
275 Madison Avenue
Suite 2102
New York, NY 10016-1101
(212) 687-0011
Fax: (212) 687-1470
E-mail: info@delmas.org
Web Site: www.delmas.org

FOUNDED: 1976

AREAS OF INTEREST:
Humanities, research libraries, performing arts and research in the history and culture of Venice and the Veneto.

NAME(S) OF PROGRAMS:
• **Humanities Program**
• **Performing Arts Program**
• **Research Library Program**
• **Venetian Research Program**

TYPE:
Fellowships; Project/program grants; Research grants.

YEAR PROGRAM STARTED: 1977

PURPOSE:
To provide grants for research projects in Venice and the Veneto; to support performing arts organizations in New York and research libraries and humanities projects.

LEGAL BASIS:
Private foundation.

ELIGIBILITY:
For Venetian Research Program, applicants must be U.S. citizens or permanent residents at the predoctoral and postdoctoral levels. If graduate students, applicants must have fulfilled all doctoral requirements except for completion of the dissertation at the time of application.

GEOG. RESTRICTIONS: Performing Arts Grants to New York City only.

FINANCIAL DATA:
Amount of support per award: Up to $20,000.

NO. MOST RECENT APPLICANTS: 280.

NO. AWARDS: 180.

REPRESENTATIVE AWARDS:
$10,000 to Morgan Library and Museum, for Walt Whitman at 200 exhibition and public programs; $11,000 to International Foundation for Art Research, for the Catalogue Raisonne Database.

APPLICATION INFO:
Applications are submitted using the Foundation's online portal.

Duration: One year.

Deadline: Applications from organizations are accepted on a rolling basis. Fellowships: December 15.

TRUSTEES:
James S. Grub
Joseph C. Mitchell
Deirdre C. Stam

DISTRICT OF COLUMBIA COMMISSION ON THE ARTS AND HUMANITIES

200 I Street, S.E.
Suite 1400
Washington, DC 20003
(202) 724-5613
Fax: (202) 727-4135
TDD: (202) 727-3148
E-mail: heran.sereke-brhan2@dc.gov
Web Site: dcarts.dc.gov

TYPE:
Awards/prizes; Capital grants; Challenge/matching grants; Conferences/seminars; Exchange programs; Fellowships; General operating grants; Grants-in-aid; Project/program grants; Research grants; Residencies. Services provided to arts institutions and individual artists including inquiry services, technical assistance and funding.

See entry 403 for full listing.

DUMBARTON OAKS   [326]

1703 32nd Street, N.W.
Washington, DC 20007
(202) 339-6400
E-mail: FellowshipPrograms@doaks.org
Web Site: www.doaks.org

FOUNDED: 1940

AREAS OF INTEREST:
Archaeology, gardens, history, history of art, philosophy, landscape, language, literature, religion and theology.

NAME(S) OF PROGRAMS:
• **Fellowships and Project Grants in Byzantine Studies, Pre-Columbian Studies and Garden and Landscape Studies**

TYPE:
Awards/prizes; Fellowships; Internships; Project/program grants; Residencies. Residential fellowships and project support in the area of Byzantine studies (including related aspects of late Roman, early Christian, western medieval, Slavic and Near Eastern studies), Pre-Columbian studies (of Mexico, Central America and Andean South America), and Garden and Landscape studies (including garden history, landscape architecture and related disciplines).

YEAR PROGRAM STARTED: 1941

PURPOSE:
To promote research in the Humanities, with a focus on Byzantine studies, Pre-Columbian studies, and Garden and Landscape studies.

LEGAL BASIS:
Research institute affiliated with Harvard University.

ELIGIBILITY:
Fellowships are awarded on the basis of demonstrated scholarly ability and preparation of the candidate, including knowledge of the requisite languages, interest and value of the study or project and the project's relevance to the resources of Dumbarton Oaks.

Junior Fellowships are awarded to degree candidates who at the time of application have fulfilled all preliminary requirements for a Ph.D. or appropriate final degree and plan to work on a dissertation or final project at Dumbarton Oaks under the direction of a faculty member from their own university.

Fellowships are awarded to scholars who hold a Ph.D. or appropriate final degree or have established themselves in their field and wish to pursue their own research. Graduate students who expect to have a Ph.D. prior to taking up residence at Dumbarton Oaks may also apply.

Summer Fellowships are awarded to Byzantine, Pre-Columbian, or Garden and Landscape scholars on any level beyond the first year of graduate (post-Baccalaureate) study.

Project grants are available to those with a terminal degree (Ph.D.).

FINANCIAL DATA:
Fellowships and Junior Fellowships: Award includes stipend, housing (with the exception of residents from the greater Washington, DC metropolitan area), lunch on weekdays, and a health insurance contribution from Dumbarton Oaks. Travel expense reimbursement may be provided for Fellows and Junior Fellows if support cannot be obtained from other sources.

Summer Fellowships: Besides maintenance allowance, support includes housing in a Dumbarton Oaks apartment, lunch on weekdays, Dumbarton Oaks's health insurance contribution, and travel expense reimbursement if other travel support cannot be obtained. No housing allowances or dependents' allowances for families are available in the summer.

Amount of support per award: Support includes a stipend of approximately $21,000 for a Junior Fellow; $35,000 stipend for a Fellow for the full academic year.

A maintenance allowance of $300 per week for Summer Fellowships.

Project grants award up to $10,000 of support.

NO. MOST RECENT APPLICANTS: 275.

NO. AWARDS: 26 fellowships in Byzantine Garden and Landscape Studies and in Pre-Columbian Studies; 6 project grants for the year 2020-21.

APPLICATION INFO:
Applications must be submitted electronically. A brochure is available upon request to the Director's office. Additional information can be found online.

Duration: Fellowships are usually awarded for a full academic year (mid-September to mid-May); however, requests for a single

term of support (mid-September to early January or mid-January to mid-May) are also considered. Projects grants are awarded for one year, from July 1 to June 30. Summer Fellowships are awarded for periods of eight weeks, beginning early June and ending early August.

Deadline: November 1. Contact Dumbarton Oaks for detailed information.

PUBLICATIONS:
Fellowship and Project award brochure; application guidelines.

OFFICERS:
Tom Cummins, Interim Director

ADDRESS INQUIRIES TO:
E-mail specific program:
Byzantine@doaks.org
Pre-Columbian@doaks.org or
Landscape@doaks.org

*SPECIAL STIPULATIONS:
Fellowships are tenable only for full-time resident work.

DUQUESNE UNIVERSITY, DEPARTMENT OF PHILOSOPHY   [327]

600 Forbes Avenue
Pittsburgh, PA 15282
(412) 396-6500
Fax: (412) 396-5353
E-mail: selcerd@duq.edu
Web Site: www.duq.
edu/academics/schools/liberal-arts/philosophy

FOUNDED: 1878

AREAS OF INTEREST:
The Ph.D. program in the Department of Philosophy at Duquesne University emphasizes continental philosophy, i.e., phenomenology and 20th century French and German philosophy, as well as the history of philosophy.

NAME(S) OF PROGRAMS:
• **Duquesne University Graduate Assistantship**

TYPE:
Assistantships; Conferences/seminars; Exchange programs. Philosophy assistantship.

PURPOSE:
To provide a stipend to enable students to obtain a Ph.D. in philosophy.

ELIGIBILITY:
Open to holders of a Bachelor's degree in philosophy, or its equivalent, who have a grade point average of at least 3.7 and an excellent graduate record examination score. Candidates should have knowledge of a second language.

FINANCIAL DATA:
Amount of support per award: Stipend of $18,000 plus all tuition for coursework.

NO. MOST RECENT APPLICANTS: 179 for the year 2020.

NO. AWARDS: 2 Ph.D. and 11 M.A. for the year 2020.

APPLICATION INFO:
Applicants must complete an application including a statement of intent and three letters of recommendation, Graduate Record Examination scores and application form and fee, plus test of English as a Foreign Language scores.

Duration: Ph.D.: Six years; M.A.: Two years.

Deadline: Ph.D. January 15; M.A. March 1.

ADDRESS INQUIRIES TO:
Daniel Selcer, Chairperson
(See address above.)

EARTHWATCH INSTITUTE

1380 Soldiers Field Road
2nd Floor
Boston, MA 02135
(800) 776-0188
E-mail: fellowshipawards@earthwatch.org
Web Site: www.earthwatch.org/education

TYPE:
Fellowships. Teachers in grades K-12 apply
for seven- to 14-day Earthwatch expedition
fellowships that take place during the
summer. Earthwatch selects teachers from all
subject areas across the U.S. to assist
scientists on expeditions by collecting data
on climate change and sustainable resource
management. Funding for these fellowships
comes from a variety of donors, e.g.,
individuals, corporations, family foundations,
community organizations and nonprofits. On
their return from the field, these teachers
must develop a lesson or action plan that ties
their experience back to their classroom or
community.

See entry 1626 for full listing.

THE HARRY FRANK GUGGENHEIM FOUNDATION

120 West 45th Street
New York, NY 10036
(646) 428-0971
Fax: (646) 428-0981
E-mail: info@hfg.org
Web Site: www.hfg.org

TYPE:
Research grants. Support for research on the
causes or reduction of violence or aggression.

See entry 1659 for full listing.

THE GWATHMEY MEMORIAL TRUST [328]

Bank of America–Philanthropic Solutions
1800 K Street, N.W., Fifth Floor
Washington, DC 20006
(202) 442-7460
E-mail: dc.grantmaking@ustrust.com
Web Site: www.bankofamerica.
com/philanthropic

FOUNDED: 1982

AREAS OF INTEREST:
Arts, culture and humanities, education, and
human services.

TYPE:
Project/program grants.

YEAR PROGRAM STARTED: 1982

ELIGIBILITY:
Grants are made to Virginia institutions and
organizations which are tax-exempt 501(c)(3)
organizations and operate for charitable,
scientific, literary, or educational purposes.
Preference is given to specific, well-defined
projects and programs whose results can be
evaluated.

Grants are not made to private foundations,
national or community organizations, or to
individuals.

GEOG. RESTRICTIONS: Virginia.

FINANCIAL DATA:
Amount of support per award: $5,000 to
$60,000; Average: $15,000 to $20,000.

Total amount of support: Average $650,000
annually.

NO. MOST RECENT APPLICANTS: 140 to 150.

NO. AWARDS: 20 to 30.

APPLICATION INFO:
All applicants must submit a description of
the organization, evidence of the
organization's tax-exempt and private
foundation status, financial statements, and
names and affiliations of the organization's
trustees, directors, advisors and principal
staff. In addition, a concise description of the
project including the needs and anticipated
benefits to be met, detailed financial plan,
brief biographical background of the person
who will conduct or supervise the proposed
program, plans for evaluation of the project's
results, and covering letter from an official of
the organization stating that the organization
has formally approved the proposed program
are required.

Duration: One year.

Deadline: Ensuring Access to Basic Services;
Creating, Sustaining and Retaining a Viable
Workforce for Virginia; and Preserving and
Protecting the Environment: March 1.
Notification by June 30. Providing Access to
Arts, Culture and/or Humanities; Preserving
the Important History of Virginia; and
Improving Educational Outcomes for
Disadvantaged Children, Youth and/or
Adults: September 1. Notification by
December 31.

PUBLICATIONS:
Guidelines for applicants.

ADDRESS INQUIRIES TO:
Lee Parker, Senior Vice President
Philanthropic Client Manager
(See address above.)

THE HASTINGS CENTER

21 Malcolm Gordon Road
Garrison, NY 10524
(845) 424-4040
Fax: (845) 424-4545
E-mail: visitors@thehastingscenter.org
Web Site: www.thehastingscenter.org

TYPE:
Residencies; Visiting scholars. Independent
study.

See entry 1895 for full listing.

HAWAII STATE FOUNDATION ON CULTURE AND THE ARTS

250 South Hotel Street
Second Floor
Honolulu, HI 96813
(808) 586-0301
Fax: (808) 586-0308
TTY: (808) 586-0740
E-mail: jonathan.johnson@hawaii.gov
Web Site: sfca.hawaii.gov

TYPE:
Project/program grants.

See entry 412 for full listing.

THE GEORGE A. AND ELIZA GARDNER HOWARD FOUNDATION

University Hall, Room 406
Brown University
One Prospect Street
Providence, RI 02912
(401) 863-2429
Fax: (401) 863-1339
E-mail: howard_foundation@brown.edu
Web Site: www.brown.edu/howard-foundation

TYPE:
Fellowships. The Foundation awards a
limited number of fellowships each year for
independent projects in fields selected on a
rotational basis.

See entry 1453 for full listing.

HUMANITIES NEW YORK [329]

150 Broadway
Suite 1700
New York, NY 10038
(212) 233-1131
Fax: (212) 233-4607
E-mail: info@humanitiesny.org
Web Site: humanitiesny.org

FOUNDED: 1975

AREAS OF INTEREST:
Humanities, public programs and education.

NAME(S) OF PROGRAMS:
- **Action Grants**
- **Community Conversations Program**
- **Quick Grants**
- **Reading and Discussion Program**
- **Vision Grants**

TYPE:
Challenge/matching grants; Project/program
grants; Seed money grants. Action Grants
help launch public programs that use the
humanities to activate conversations within a
community. Projects that encourage
participants to reflect on their values, explore
new ideas, and connect with others across
New York state are encouraged. These grants
require matching funds to demonstrate your
community's investment in the project.

Community Conversations Program promotes
thoughtful, engaged community dialogue,
using a short text and a facilitator from the
local community.

Quick Grants encourage audiences to reflect
on their values, explore new ideas, and
engage with others in their community.

Reading and Discussion Programs are
awarded to involve community members in
ongoing discussions of books and ideas.

Vision Grants help groups brainstorm,
connect, research, strategize, and design
engaging public humanities programs.
Innovation is welcomed, and projects that use
the tools of the humanities (civic
engagement, critical inquiry, debate,
discussion, historical framing, etc.) to address
contemporary issues are encouraged.

YEAR PROGRAM STARTED: 1975

PURPOSE:
To help all New Yorkers become thoughtful
participants in our communities by promoting
critical inquiry, cultural understanding, and
civic engagement.

LEGAL BASIS:
State humanities council, nonprofit under
Internal Revenue Code 501(c)(3).

ELIGIBILITY:
Tax-exempt, nonprofit 501(c)(3) organizations in New York state.

GEOG. RESTRICTIONS: New York state.

FINANCIAL DATA:
Amount of support per award: Action Grants: Typically $1,501 to $5,000; Quick Grants: Typically $500; Vision Grants: Typically $500 to $1,500.

Total amount of support: $430,000.

Matching fund requirements: All Action Grants must be matched (at least dollar-for-dollar) with cash and/or in-kind contributions. Vision Grants do not require a match.

NO. MOST RECENT APPLICANTS: Action Grants: 268; Vision Grants: 50.

NO. AWARDS: Action Grants: 120; Vision Grants: 25.

APPLICATION INFO:
All applications are available online.

PUBLICATIONS:
Application guidelines.

IRS I.D.: 51-0152266

ADDRESS INQUIRIES TO:
Scarlett Rebman, Director of Grants
E-mail: grants@humanitiesny.org

Michael Washburn, Director of Programs
E-mail: programs@humanitiesny.org

*SPECIAL STIPULATIONS:
Grants available only to New York-based, tax-exempt organizations, but fiscal sponsorship is permitted.

HUNTINGTON LIBRARY, ART MUSEUM AND BOTANICAL GARDENS [330]
1151 Oxford Road
San Marino, CA 91108
(626) 405-2194
Fax: (626) 449-5703
E-mail: cwehrey@huntington.org
Web Site: www.huntington.org

FOUNDED: 1919

AREAS OF INTEREST:
British and American history, British and American literature, art history, and the history of science, technology and medicine.

NAME(S) OF PROGRAMS:
● **Research Awards at the Huntington Library, Art Museum and Botanical Gardens**

TYPE:
Fellowships; Travel grants; Visiting scholars. Awards support scholarship in British and American history, British and American literature, art history, and the history of science, technology and medicine.

YEAR PROGRAM STARTED: 1927

PURPOSE:
To encourage, facilitate and disseminate high-quality humanities scholarship on the basis of the Huntington Library and art collections.

LEGAL BASIS:
Private, nonprofit.

ELIGIBILITY:
Humanities scholars in the fields of history, literature and art history at the doctoral and postdoctoral level are encouraged to apply. Consideration is given to the value of the

candidate's project and the degree to which the Huntington Library collections will be used. Proposals from postgraduate students who have advanced to doctoral candidacy are particularly welcome.

FINANCIAL DATA:
Amount of support per award: Short-term fellowships: $3,500 per month; Long-term fellowships: $50,000 for the academic year.

Total amount of support: $2,100,000 for fiscal year 2020-21.

CO-OP FUNDING PROGRAMS: Caltech.

NO. MOST RECENT APPLICANTS: Short-term: 347; Long-term: 114.

NO. AWARDS: Short-term: 139; Long-term: 13.

APPLICATION INFO:
Contact the Library.
Duration: Short-term grants: One to five months. Long-term awards: Minimum of nine months.
Deadline: November 16 for commencement on September 1.

IRS I.D.: 95-1644589

OFFICERS:
Karen Lawrence, President
Janet Alberti, Vice President and Chief Financial Officer
Randy Shulman, Vice President, Advancement
Susan Turner-Lowe, Vice President, Communications and Marketing
Heather Hart, Vice President, Information Technology
Christina Nielsen, Director, Art Museum
James Folson, Director, Botanical Gardens
Elizabeth Wood, Director, Education and Public Programs
Sandra Brooke, Director, Library
Steve Hindle, Director of Research

TRUSTEES:
Loren R. Rothschild, Chairperson
Andrew F. Barth
Simon K.C. Li
Wendy Munger
Gregory A. Pieschala

ADDRESS INQUIRIES TO:
Steve Hindle, Director of Research
(See address above.)

*SPECIAL STIPULATIONS:
Recipients of all fellowships are expected to be in continuous residence at the Huntington.

THE INSTITUTE FOR ADVANCED STUDIES IN THE HUMANITIES [331]
The University of Edinburgh
2 Hope Park Square
Edinburgh EH8 9NW Scotland
(44) 0131 650 4671
E-mail: iash@ed.ac.uk
Web Site: www.iash.ed.ac.uk

FOUNDED: 1969

AREAS OF INTEREST:
Arts, humanities and social science.

CONSULTING OR VOLUNTEER SERVICES:
Institute has connections with and is within easy reach of the National Library of Scotland, the National Archives of Scotland, the Royal Museum of Scotland and the Edinburgh University Library.

NAME(S) OF PROGRAMS:
● **Visiting Research Fellowships**

TYPE:
Fellowships. Visiting Research Fellowships with the use of a private office in the Institute with all the usual research facilities. Recipients of the Fellowships are expected to play a full part in the activities of the Institute.

YEAR PROGRAM STARTED: 1970

PURPOSE:
To further advanced studies in the arts, humanities and social sciences, broadly conceived.

LEGAL BASIS:
Institution of University of Edinburgh.

ELIGIBILITY:
Applicants should be scholars of established reputation or younger scholars holding a Doctorate or offering equivalent evidence of aptitude for advanced study.

The Selection Committee will consider the academic record and the publications of all applicants, their capacity to disseminate their views effectively in public and the likelihood of completing the proposed research by task by the end of the fellowship or shortly afterwards. Students who have not completed their studies for a particular degree are not eligible.

No teaching is required of Fellows in the project, but each Fellow will be expected to make at least one public presentation of his or her research activities.

FINANCIAL DATA:
Amount of support per award: GBP 1,000 to GBP 15,000.

Total amount of support: Approximately GBP 250,000 per year.

NO. MOST RECENT APPLICANTS: 479.

NO. AWARDS: Up to 60.

APPLICATION INFO:
Apply online through the Institute web site. The Selection Committee will only consider applications accompanied by full documentation and supported by a minimum of two and a maximum of three references. It is the responsibility of each applicant to ensure that their referees submit their reports directly to Edinburgh. Candidates may like to submit a copy of an article or publication relevant to their application. The Institute will not return any documents to applicants.

Duration: Fellowships are tenable for two to 10 months. Nonrenewable.

Deadline: February 26 for midcareer and senior scholars. April 30 for postdoctoral and early-career researchers.

PUBLICATIONS:
Application guidelines.

OFFICERS:
Prof. Steve Yearley, Director

ADDRESS INQUIRIES TO:
Prof. Steve Yearley, Director
(See address above.)

*SPECIAL STIPULATIONS:
Fellows, as well as carrying out research, are required to live in or near Edinburgh and will be asked to give one seminar.

INSTITUTE FOR ADVANCED STUDY

One Einstein Drive
Princeton, NJ 08540
(609) 734-8250
Fax: (609) 951-4457
E-mail: donne@ias.edu
Web Site: www.sss.ias.edu

TYPE:
Fellowships. Postdoctoral research fellowships at the School of Social Science.

See entry 1662 for full listing.

INSTITUTE FOR HUMANE STUDIES (IHS)

3434 Washington Boulevard, MS 1C5
Arlington, VA 22201
(703) 993-4880
Fax: (703) 993-4890
E-mail: hsf@theihs.org
Web Site: theihs.org/funding/humane-studies-fellowship

TYPE:
Fellowships; Research grants. Humane Studies Fellowships cover the fields of the social sciences and humanities.

See entry 1794 for full listing.

MASS HUMANITIES   [332]

66 Bridge Street
Northampton, MA 01060-2406
(413) 584-8440
Fax: (413) 584-8454
E-mail: info@masshumanities.org
Web Site: masshumanities.org

FOUNDED: 1974

AREAS OF INTEREST:
Humanities and areas of special concern in Massachusetts, historic societies and libraries.

NAME(S) OF PROGRAMS:
● **Discussion Grants**
● **Local History Grants**
● **Project Grants**

TYPE:
Project/program grants.

PURPOSE:
To identify and develop major initiatives in areas of special interest or concern.

LEGAL BASIS:
Private, nonprofit corporation.

ELIGIBILITY:
Each grant type has its own goals and guidelines. Applicants must be nonprofit or government organizations that serve Massachusetts residents.

GEOG. RESTRICTIONS: Massachusetts.

FINANCIAL DATA:
Amount of support per award: Varies.
Total amount of support: $522,000 in grants awarded for the year 2019.
Matching fund requirements: Outright Funds must be matched equally by your organization through cost-sharing.

NO. AWARDS: 78 for the year 2019.

REPRESENTATIVE AWARDS:
$58,750 to Center for Independent Documentary, Walpole, MA, for a documentary focused on the life of a Jewish teen living in Germany in the 1930s who was gradually targeted by the Nazis and eventually escaped to Britain and then to

Massachusetts; $15,000 to Filmmakers Collaborative, Melrose, MA, for a documentary on the experience of four women from Voices From Inside, a Greenfield-based organization that facilitates writing groups for incarcerated and formerly incarcerated women; $3,500 to Barrington Stage Company, Pittsfield, MA, for a free symposium in connection with a performance of "Fall Springs," a dark musical comedy about environmental disaster.

APPLICATION INFO:
Applicants should submit the Foundation's web-based Letter of Inquiry form six weeks before final proposal deadline. Application is an online process.
Duration: Typically one year.
Deadline: Varies.

PUBLICATIONS:
Newsletter; application guidelines; brochure.

STAFF:
Brian Boyles, Executive Director
John Sieracki, Director of Development and Communications
Katherine Stevens, Director of Grants
Michelle Wilson, Associate Director of Development
Jennifer Hall-Witt, Program Officer

ALLETTA MORRIS MCBEAN CHARITABLE TRUST   [333]

78140 Calle Tampico
Suite 104
La Quinta, CA 92253
(760) 564-3000
Fax: (760) 564-3030
E-mail: mcbeanproperties@att.net
Web Site: allettamcbeancharitabletrust.org

FOUNDED: 1986

AREAS OF INTEREST:
Historic and land preservation in and around Newport, RI.

TYPE:
Capital grants; Challenge/matching grants; Endowments; Project/program grants.

YEAR PROGRAM STARTED: 1986

PURPOSE:
To enhance the quality of life in and around Newport and Aquidneck Island, RI.

LEGAL BASIS:
Private charitable trust.

ELIGIBILITY:
Applicants must be tax-exempt organizations.

GEOG. RESTRICTIONS: Aquidneck Island, Rhode Island.

FINANCIAL DATA:
Amount of support per award: $25,000 to $100,000.
Total amount of support: Approximately $3,000,000 per year.
Matching fund requirements: Varies.

NO. MOST RECENT APPLICANTS: 20 to 25.

REPRESENTATIVE AWARDS:
$50,000 to American Red Cross for Hurricane Florence disaster relief; $250,000 to Newport Performing Arts Center Task Group for continued restoration of the Newport Opera House; $56,000 to Bradley Hospital Foundation for the Outdoor Learning Program.

APPLICATION INFO:
Five formal proposals with budgets are preferred, as well as other sources of funding for project, tax-exempt status and other background material.
Deadline: February 28 and July 31.

IRS I.D.: 94-3019660

OFFICERS:
Donald C. Christ, Chairman
Walter G.D. Reed, Acting Secretary
Charlene C. Kleiner, Assistant Secretary
Dorienne Farzan
Gladys V. Szapary

ADDRESS INQUIRIES TO:
Donald C. Christ, Chairman
Charlene C. Kleiner, Assistant Secretary
(See address above.)

MICHIGAN SOCIETY OF FELLOWS   [334]

University of Michigan
0540 Rackham Building
915 East Washington Street
Ann Arbor, MI 48109-1070
(734) 763-1259
E-mail: society.of.fellows@umich.edu
Web Site: www.societyoffellows.umich.edu

FOUNDED: 1970

AREAS OF INTEREST:
All schools and colleges at the University of Michigan.

NAME(S) OF PROGRAMS:
● **Postdoctoral Fellowships in the Humanities and the Arts, Sciences and Professions**

TYPE:
Fellowships. Fellows are appointed as Assistant Professors in appropriate departments and as Postdoctoral Scholars in the Michigan Society of Fellows. They are expected to be in residence in Ann Arbor during the academic years of the fellowship, to teach for the equivalent of one academic year, to participate in the informal intellectual life of the Society, and to devote time to their independent research or artistic projects.

YEAR PROGRAM STARTED: 1970

PURPOSE:
To recognize and support academic and creative excellence in humanities and the arts, the social, physical, and life sciences, and the professions.

LEGAL BASIS:
Nonprofit, tax-exempt organization.

ELIGIBILITY:
Candidates should be near the beginning of their professional careers, but not more than three years beyond completion of their degrees. The Ph.D. degree or comparable professional or artistic degree, received prior to appointment, is required.

Applications from degree candidates and recipients of the Ph.D. from the University of Michigan will not be considered.

FINANCIAL DATA:
Amount of support per award: $60,000 annually plus health benefits for fellowships. $1,500 per year allowance toward travel and research expenses.

CO-OP FUNDING PROGRAMS: Mellon Foundation.

NO. MOST RECENT APPLICANTS: Approximately 900 annually.

NO. AWARDS: 6 each year.

APPLICATION INFO:
Only online applications will be considered. Applications will be reviewed by members of the Society of Fellows and by faculty in appropriate University of Michigan departments. Final selection of candidates will be made by the senior fellows of the Society.

Duration: Three years.

Deadline: September 24. Final selections made end of February.

PUBLICATIONS:
Application guidelines.

OFFICERS:
Susan Scott Parrish, Chairperson of Society

ADDRESS INQUIRIES TO:
See e-mail address above.

*SPECIAL STIPULATIONS:
Fellows are expected to reside in Ann Arbor during the academic years of the fellowship.

NATIONAL ENDOWMENT FOR THE HUMANITIES [335]
The Constitution Center
400 7th Street, S.W.
Washington, DC 20506
(202) 606-8424
Fax: (202) 606-8240
E-mail: communications@neh.gov
Web Site: www.neh.gov

FOUNDED: 1965

AREAS OF INTEREST:
Scholarship, research, education and public programs in the humanities. In the act that established the Endowment, the term humanities includes, but is not limited to, the study of history, philosophy, languages, linguistics, literature, archaeology, jurisprudence, the history, theory and criticism of the arts, ethics, comparative religion and those aspects of the social sciences that employ historical or philosophical approaches.

NAME(S) OF PROGRAMS:
● **Research Program**

TYPE:
Research grants. Grants provide support for collaborative research in the preparation for publication of editions, translations and other important works in the humanities and in the conduct of large or complex interpretive studies including archaeology projects and the humanities studies of science and technology. Grants also support research opportunities offered through independent research centers and scholarly organizations and international research centers.

YEAR PROGRAM STARTED: 1967

PURPOSE:
To provide funding for research and the publication of that research. The work must be in a field of interest to the National Endowment.

LEGAL BASIS:
Federal agency, established by act of Congress: The National Foundation on the Arts and Humanities Act of 1965, Public Law 89-209, as amended.

ELIGIBILITY:
Applicants can be individuals, institutions of higher education, nonprofit professional associations, scholarly societies and other nonprofit organizations.

GEOG. RESTRICTIONS: United States.

FINANCIAL DATA:
Amount of support per award: Varies.

Total amount of support: Varies.

APPLICATION INFO:
Application can be downloaded from the web site.

Duration: Varies.

Deadline: Varies.

PUBLICATIONS:
Annual report; *Grant Programs; Humanities Magazine.*

IRS I.D.: 52-1098584

ADDRESS INQUIRIES TO:
Paula Wasley
Senior Public Affairs Specialist
(See address above.)

NATIONAL ENDOWMENT FOR THE HUMANITIES [336]
The Constitution Center
400 7th Street, S.W.
Washington, DC 20506
(202) 606-8424
Fax: (202) 606-8240
E-mail: communications@neh.gov
Web Site: www.neh.gov

FOUNDED: 1965

AREAS OF INTEREST:
Scholarship, research, education and public programs in the humanities. In the act that established the Endowment, the term humanities includes, but is not limited to, the study of history, philosophy, languages, linguistics, literature, archaeology, jurisprudence, the history, theory and criticism of the arts, ethics, comparative religion and those aspects of the social sciences that employ historical or philosophical approaches.

NAME(S) OF PROGRAMS:
● **Challenge Grants Program**

TYPE:
Capital grants; Challenge/matching grants; Professorships; Residencies; Visiting scholars. The Office of Challenge Grants offers grants that "challenge" local, state and national institutions to respond to opportunities that exist in this country's humanities ecosystem.

YEAR PROGRAM STARTED: 1977

PURPOSE:
To encourage long-range financial and program planning within humanities institutions and organizations; to provide means for humanities organizations and institutions to increase levels and kinds of continuing financial support; to sustain or develop high-quality work within the humanities; to join federal with nonfederal support so that those institutions in which teaching, learning and research of the humanities occur may achieve greater financial stability.

LEGAL BASIS:
Federal agency, established by act of Congress: The National Foundation on the Arts and Humanities Act of 1965, Public Law 89-209, as amended.

ELIGIBILITY:
Nonprofit postsecondary, educational, research or cultural institutions and organizations working within the humanities are eligible for support.

GEOG. RESTRICTIONS: United States.

FINANCIAL DATA:
Amount of support per award: Maximum $750,000.

Total amount of support: Varies.

APPLICATION INFO:
Applications can be downloaded from the above web site.

Duration: Five or six years, depending on institution type.

Deadline: May 18.

PUBLICATIONS:
Annual report; *Grant Programs; Humanities Magazine.*

IRS I.D.: 52-1098584

ADDRESS INQUIRIES TO:
Paula Wasley
Senior Public Affairs Specialist
(See address above.)

NATIONAL ENDOWMENT FOR THE HUMANITIES [337]
The Constitution Center
400 7th Street, S.W.
Washington, DC 20506
(202) 606-8424
Fax: (202) 606-8240
E-mail: communications@neh.gov
Web Site: www.neh.gov

FOUNDED: 1965

AREAS OF INTEREST:
Scholarship, research, education and public programs in the humanities.

NAME(S) OF PROGRAMS:
● **Fellowships**
● **Summer Stipends**

TYPE:
Awards/prizes; Fellowships. Grants provide support for scholars to undertake full-time independent research and writing in the humanities. Grants are available for a maximum of one year and a minimum of six weeks to two months of summer study.

Grants also provide support for historically Black college and university faculty to undertake one year of full-time study leading to a doctoral degree in the humanities with preference given to those individuals who are at the dissertation stage of their work.

YEAR PROGRAM STARTED: 1967

PURPOSE:
To encourage continued research and study in the humanities discipline.

LEGAL BASIS:
Federal agency, established by act of Congress: The National Foundation on the Arts and Humanities Act of 1965, Public Law 89-209, as amended.

GEOG. RESTRICTIONS: United States.

FINANCIAL DATA:
Amount of support per award: Fellowship: $5,000 per month; Summer Stipend: Up to $6,000.

Total amount of support: Varies.

APPLICATION INFO:
Application can be downloaded from the web site.

Duration: Fellowship: Six to 12 months; Summer Stipend: Two months.

Deadline: Fellowships: April 14; Summer Stipends: Late September.

PUBLICATIONS:
Annual report; *Grant Programs*; *Humanities Magazine*.

IRS I.D.: 52-1098584

ADDRESS INQUIRIES TO:
Paula Wasley
Senior Public Affairs Specialist
(See address above.)

NATIONAL ENDOWMENT FOR THE HUMANITIES [338]
The Constitution Center
400 7th Street, S.W.
Washington, DC 20506
(202) 606-8424
Fax: (202) 606-8240
E-mail: communications@neh.gov
Web Site: www.neh.gov

FOUNDED: 1965

AREAS OF INTEREST:
Scholarship, research, education and public programs in the humanities. In the act that established the Endowment, the term humanities includes, but is not limited to, the study of history, philosophy, languages, linguistics, literature, archaeology, jurisprudence, the history, theory and criticism of the arts, ethics, comparative religion and those aspects of the social sciences that employ historical or philosophical approaches.

NAME(S) OF PROGRAMS:
• **Seminars and Institutes Program**

TYPE:
Conferences/seminars. Grants support summer seminars and national institutes in the humanities for college and school teachers. These faculty development activities are conducted at colleges and universities across the country. Lists of pending seminars and institutes are available from the program.

YEAR PROGRAM STARTED: 1983

PURPOSE:
To provide opportunities for teachers to study under the direction of a master teacher and distinguished scholar in an area of mutual interest at a college or university during the summer.

LEGAL BASIS:
Federal agency, established by act of Congress: The National Foundation on the Arts and Humanities Act of 1965, Public Law 89-209, as amended.

ELIGIBILITY:
Applicants can be individuals or institutions of higher learning.

GEOG. RESTRICTIONS: United States.

FINANCIAL DATA:
Amount of support per award: Varies.
Total amount of support: Varies.

APPLICATION INFO:
Complete application information can be found online. Participant application forms and instructions can be obtained from seminar directors at the host institutions. Those wishing to participate in seminars should submit their applications to the seminar director. Information about the program is publicized in the fall preceding the summer in question.
Duration: Seminars last one to four weeks, depending on the choice of the director.
Deadline: February 11.

PUBLICATIONS:
Annual report; *Grant Programs*; *Humanities Magazine*.

IRS I.D.: 52-1098584

ADDRESS INQUIRIES TO:
Paula Wasley
Senior Public Affairs Specialist
(See address above.)

NATIONAL ENDOWMENT FOR THE HUMANITIES [339]
The Constitution Center
400 7th Street, S.W.
Washington, DC 20506
(202) 606-8424
Fax: (202) 606-8240
E-mail: communications@neh.gov
Web Site: www.neh.gov

FOUNDED: 1965

AREAS OF INTEREST:
Scholarship, research, education and public programs in the humanities. In the act that established the Endowment, the term humanities includes, but is not limited to, the study of history, philosophy, languages, linguistics, literature, archaeology, jurisprudence, the history, theory and criticism of the arts, ethics, comparative religion and those aspects of the social sciences that employ historical or philosophical approaches.

NAME(S) OF PROGRAMS:
• **Preservation and Access**

TYPE:
Project/program grants. Support may be sought to preserve the intellectual content and aid bibliographic control of collections, to compile bibliographies, descriptive catalogs and guides to cultural holdings, to create dictionaries, encyclopedias, databases and other types of research tools and reference works and to stabilize material culture collections through the appropriate housing and storing of objects, improved environmental control and the installation of security, lighting and fire-prevention systems.

Applications may also be submitted for national and regional education and training projects, regional preservation field service programs and research and demonstration projects that are intended to enhance institutional practice and the use of technology for preservation and access.

YEAR PROGRAM STARTED: 1985

PURPOSE:
To advance study in the area indicated.

LEGAL BASIS:
Federal agency, established by act of Congress: The National Foundation on the Arts and Humanities Act of 1965, Public Law 89-209, as amended.

GEOG. RESTRICTIONS: United States.

FINANCIAL DATA:
Amount of support per award: Varies.
Total amount of support: Varies.

APPLICATION INFO:
Application can be downloaded from the web site.
Duration: Varies.
Deadline: Varies.

PUBLICATIONS:
Annual report; *Grant Programs*; *Humanities Magazine*.

IRS I.D.: 52-1098584

ADDRESS INQUIRIES TO:
Paula Wasley
Senior Public Affairs Specialist
(See address above.)

NATIONAL ENDOWMENT FOR THE HUMANITIES
The Constitution Center
400 7th Street, S.W.
Washington, DC 20506
(202) 606-8269
Fax: (202) 606-8557
E-mail: publicpgms@neh.gov
Web Site: www.neh.gov

TYPE:
Project/program grants. Public Humanities Projects grants support projects that bring the ideas and insights of the humanities to life for general audiences. Projects must engage humanities scholarship to illuminate significant themes in disciplines such as history, literature, ethics and art, or to address challenging issues in contemporary life. NEH encourages projects that involve members of the public in collaboration with humanities scholars or that invite contributions from the community in the development and delivery of humanities programming. The grant program supports a variety of forms of audience engagement: Community Conversations: This format supports one- to three-year-long series of community-wide public discussions in which diverse residents creatively address community challenges, guided by the perspectives of the humanities; Exhibitions: This format supports permanent exhibitions that will be on view for at least three years, or traveling exhibitions that will be available to public audiences in at least two venues in the U.S. (including the originating location) and; Historic Places: This format supports the interpretation of historic sites, houses, neighborhoods and regions, which might include living history presentations, guided tours, exhibitions and public programs.

See entry 1748 for full listing.

NATIONAL HUMANITIES CENTER [340]
7 T.W. Alexander Drive
Research Triangle Park, NC 27709
(919) 549-0661
Fax: (919) 990-8535
E-mail: fellowships@nationalhumanitiescenter.org
Web Site: www.nationalhumanitiescenter.org

FOUNDED: 1976

AREAS OF INTEREST:
History, literature, philosophy, classics, political theory, law, religion, anthropology, art history, folklore and other humanistic fields.

NAME(S) OF PROGRAMS:
• **National Humanities Center Fellowships**

TYPE:
Fellowships; Visiting scholars. Awards for advanced study in the humanities in residence at the Center.

YEAR PROGRAM STARTED: 1978

PURPOSE:
To support advanced study in the humanities; to encourage the exchange of ideas among humanist scholars; to enhance the influence of the humanities in the U.S.

LEGAL BASIS:
Privately incorporated nonprofit institute for advanced study.

ELIGIBILITY:
Open to scholars in the humanities. As a rule, the Center does not consider applications from candidates who have not yet completed the Doctorate. Fellowships for younger scholars are not intended for an immediate postdoctoral year but are awarded to individuals who have begun their professional careers and are undertaking research significantly beyond their dissertations.

FINANCIAL DATA:
Fellows receive travel expenses to and from the Center for themselves and their families.
Amount of support per award: Individually determined based on need.
Total amount of support: Varies.
Matching fund requirements: Stipulated with specific grants.

CO-OP FUNDING PROGRAMS: Scholars who have financial support from university or other funding agencies are welcome to apply and receive from the Center the difference between that support and their normal academic salaries.

NO. MOST RECENT APPLICANTS: 638.

NO. AWARDS: 35.

APPLICATION INFO:
Applications accepted online only.
Duration: One academic year, September through May.
Deadline: October 7. Announcement in February.

PUBLICATIONS:
Annual report; application guidelines; semiannual newsletter.

IRS I.D.: 59-1735367

OFFICERS:
Ben Vinson, III, Chairman
Joshua Ruch, Vice Chairman
Thomas Scherer, Secretary

STAFF:
Robert Newman, President and Director
Matthew Booker, Vice President for Scholarly Programs

ADDRESS INQUIRIES TO:
Lynn Miller, Information Manager
(See address above.)

THE NEWBERRY LIBRARY [341]
Newberry Institute for Research and Education
60 West Walton Street
Chicago, IL 60610
(312) 255-3666
E-mail: research@newberry.org
Web Site: www.newberry.org/fellowships

FOUNDED: 1887

AREAS OF INTEREST:
The humanities of Western Europe, England and the Americas from the late Middle Ages to the early 20th century.

NAME(S) OF PROGRAMS:
● **Newberry Short-Term Resident Fellowships for Individual Research**

TYPE:
Fellowships; Residencies. Fellowships of one month for advanced research, including doctoral dissertations, in history and the humanities. Fellowships provide access to the Newberry's collections for those who live and work beyond commuting distance from Chicago.

YEAR PROGRAM STARTED: 1942

PURPOSE:
To give scholars engaged in research in the fields listed above the opportunity to utilize the specialized collections of the Newberry Library.

LEGAL BASIS:
Private research library.

ELIGIBILITY:
Applicants must have the Ph.D. or terminal degree in their field, or have completed all requirements except the dissertation. Preference will be given to applicants from outside the greater Chicago area whose research particularly requires study at the Newberry. Applicants must live and work outside of the Chicago area.

FINANCIAL DATA:
Amount of support per award: $3,000 per month.

NO. MOST RECENT APPLICANTS: Varies.

NO. AWARDS: 5.

APPLICATION INFO:
Applications must be submitted through the online webform.
Duration: One month.
Deadline: December 15.

STAFF:
Keelin Burke, Director of Fellowships and Academic Programs

ADDRESS INQUIRIES TO:
See e-mail address above.

THE NEWBERRY LIBRARY [342]
Newberry Institute for Research and Education
60 West Walton Street
Chicago, IL 60610
(312) 255-3666
E-mail: research@newberry.org
Web Site: www.newberry.org/fellowships

FOUNDED: 1887

AREAS OF INTEREST:
Late Medieval and Renaissance studies.

NAME(S) OF PROGRAMS:
● **The Audrey Lumsden-Kouvel Fellowship**

TYPE:
Fellowships. The Audrey Lumsden-Kouvel Fellowship is for postdoctoral scholars conducting extended research in residence at the Newberry Library in the areas of late medieval and early modern history and literature.

PURPOSE:
To promote individual scholarly research.

LEGAL BASIS:
Private research library.

ELIGIBILITY:
Preference will be given to projects focusing on the Colonial Americas and Romance cultures, especially translations and topics focusing on Portuguese, Spanish, and Latin American studies. Recent recipients of Ph.Ds. are encouraged to apply.

FINANCIAL DATA:
Awardees may combine this fellowship with sabbatical or other stipendiary support.
Amount of support per award: $5,000 per month.

NO. MOST RECENT APPLICANTS: 40.

NO. AWARDS: 1 to 2.

APPLICATION INFO:
Applications must be submitted through the online webform.
Duration: Four to nine months.
Deadline: November 1. Notification in mid-February.

STAFF:
Keelin Burke, Director of Fellowships and Academic Programs

ADDRESS INQUIRIES TO:
See e-mail address above.

THE NEWBERRY LIBRARY [343]
Newberry Institute for Research and Education
60 West Walton Street
Chicago, IL 60610
(312) 255-3666
E-mail: research@newberry.org
Web Site: www.newberry.org/fellowships

FOUNDED: 1887

AREAS OF INTEREST:
The humanities of Western Europe, England and the Americas from the late Middle Ages to the early 20th century.

NAME(S) OF PROGRAMS:
● **National Endowment for the Humanities (NEH) Fellowships**

TYPE:
Fellowships; Residencies. Support for projects in any field appropriate to the Library's collections.

YEAR PROGRAM STARTED: 1975

PURPOSE:
To encourage the individual scholar's research and to deepen and enrich the opportunities for serious intellectual exchange.

LEGAL BASIS:
Private research library.

ELIGIBILITY:
Established scholars at the postdoctoral level or its equivalent may apply. Awards are open to U.S. citizens and foreign nationals who have been living in the U.S. for at least three continuous years of residence. Preference is given to applicants who have not held major fellowships for three years preceding the proposed period of residency.

Projects must be appropriate for research in the Newberry collection.

FINANCIAL DATA:
Awardees may combine grants with sabbaticals or other stipendiary support.
Amount of support per award: $5,000 per month.

NO. MOST RECENT APPLICANTS: 100.

NO. AWARDS: 4 to 6.

APPLICATION INFO:
Applications must be submitted through the online webform.
Duration: Four to nine months.
Deadline: November 1. Notification in mid-February.

STAFF:
Keelin Burke, Director of Fellowships and Academic Programs

ADDRESS INQUIRIES TO:
See e-mail address above.

THE NEWBERRY LIBRARY [344]

Newberry Institute for Research and Education
60 West Walton Street
Chicago, IL 60610
(312) 255-3666
E-mail: research@newberry.org
Web Site: www.newberry.org/fellowships

FOUNDED: 1887

AREAS OF INTEREST:
The humanities of Western Europe, England and the Americas from the late Middle Ages to the early 20th century.

NAME(S) OF PROGRAMS:
- **Arthur and Lila Weinberg Fellowship for Independent Scholars and Researchers**

TYPE:
Fellowships; Residencies. Weinberg Fellowship is for humanists working outside traditional acedemic settings. The program seeks scholars, journalists, writers, filmmakers, visual and performing artists and other humanists. Preference is given to applicants working on historical issues related to social justice or reform.

LEGAL BASIS:
Private research library.

ELIGIBILITY:
Candidates are those working in a field appropriate to the Newberry collections. Preference is given to scholars working on historical issues related to social justice or reform. Applicants must be individuals working outside of traditional academic settings who are not employed, or seeking to be employed, as full-time academic faculty.

FINANCIAL DATA:
Amount of support per award: $3,000 total stipend.

NO. MOST RECENT APPLICANTS: 10.

NO. AWARDS: 1.

APPLICATION INFO:
Applications must be submitted through the online webform.
Duration: One month.
Deadline: December 15.

STAFF:
Keelin Burke, Director of Fellowships and Academic Programs

ADDRESS INQUIRIES TO:
See e-mail address above.

THE NEWBERRY LIBRARY

Newberry Institute for Research and Education
60 West Walton Street
Chicago, IL 60610
(312) 255-3666
E-mail: research@newberry.org
Web Site: www.newberry.org/fellowships

TYPE:
Fellowships. For scholars wishing to use the Newberry's collections to study the period 1660 to 1815.

See entry 572 for full listing.

THE NEWBERRY LIBRARY [345]

Newberry Institute for Research and Education
60 West Walton Street
Chicago, IL 60610
(312) 255-3666
E-mail: research@newberry.org
Web Site: www.newberry.org/fellowships

FOUNDED: 1887

AREAS OF INTEREST:
The humanities of Western Europe, England and the Americas from the late Middle Ages to the early 20th century.

NAME(S) OF PROGRAMS:
- **Lloyd Lewis Fellowships in American History**

TYPE:
Fellowships. The Lloyd Lewis Fellowships in American History are awarded to postdoctoral scholars pursuing projects in any area of American history appropriate to the Newberry's collections.

PURPOSE:
To further research in American history.

ELIGIBILITY:
Applicants must hold a Ph.D. at the time of application and be pursuing projects in any area of American history that are applicable to the Newberry Collection.

FINANCIAL DATA:
Awardees may combine these fellowship awards with sabbatical or other stipendiary support.
Amount of support per award: Monthly stipend of $5.000.

NO. MOST RECENT APPLICANTS: Varies.

NO. AWARDS: 1 to 2.

APPLICATION INFO:
Applications must be submitted through the online webform.
Duration: Four to nine months.
Deadline: November 1. Notification in mid-February.

STAFF:
Keelin Burke, Director of Fellowships and Academic Programs

ADDRESS INQUIRIES TO:
See e-mail address above.

*PLEASE NOTE:
The Newberry's long-term fellowship grants support individual research and promote serious intellectual exchange through active participation in the Newberry's scholarly activities, including fellows' seminars and a weekly colloquium.

THE NEWBERRY LIBRARY [346]

Newberry Institute for Research and Education
60 West Walton Street
Chicago, IL 60610
(312) 255-3666
E-mail: research@newberry.org
Web Site: www.newberry.org/fellowships

FOUNDED: 1887

AREAS OF INTEREST:
The humanities of Western Europe, England and the Americas from the late Middle Ages to the early 20th century.

NAME(S) OF PROGRAMS:
- **Monticello College Foundation Fellowship for Women**

TYPE:
Fellowships. The Monticello College Foundation Fellowship for Women is intended to help a postdoctoral woman scholar at an early stage (pre-tenure) of her academic career.

PURPOSE:
To provide assistance to postdoctoral woman scholars at an early stage of their academic careers.

ELIGIBILITY:
Applicants must hold a Ph.D. at the time of application. This award is intended for a postdoctoral woman scholar at an early stage (pre-tenure) of her academic career. Preference will be given to proposals particularly concerned with the study of women.

FINANCIAL DATA:
Awardees may combine this fellowship awards with sabbatical or other stipendiary support.
Amount of support per award: Monthly stipend of $5,000.

NO. MOST RECENT APPLICANTS: Varies.

NO. AWARDS: 1 to 2.

APPLICATION INFO:
Applications must be submitted through the online webform.
Duration: Four to nine months.
Deadline: November 1. Notification in mid-February.

ADDRESS INQUIRIES TO:
See e-mail address above.

*PLEASE NOTE:
The Newberry's long-term fellowship grants support individual research and promote serious intellectual exchange through active participation in the Newberry's scholarly activities, including fellows' seminars and a weekly colloquium.

THE NEWBERRY LIBRARY [347]

Newberry Institute for Research and Education
60 West Walton Street
Chicago, IL 60610
(312) 255-3666
E-mail: research@newberry.org
Web Site: www.newberry.org/fellowships

FOUNDED: 1887

AREAS OF INTEREST:
The humanities of Western Europe, England and the Americas from the late Middle Ages to the early 20th century.

NAME(S) OF PROGRAMS:
- **Newberry Consortium of American Indian and Indigenous Studies (NCAIS) Faculty Fellowship**

TYPE:
Fellowships.

PURPOSE:
To promote research in American Indian studies.

ELIGIBILITY:
This award is intended for faculty members at institutions participating in the Consortium. Preference is given to scholars at an early career stage.

FINANCIAL DATA:
Awardees may combine these fellowship awards with sabbatical or other stipendiary support.
Amount of support per award: Monthly stipend of $5,000.

NO. MOST RECENT APPLICANTS: Varies.

NO. AWARDS: 1.

APPLICATION INFO:
Awardees must indicate in their applications how many months they intend to be in residence at the Newberry. Applications must be submitted through the online webform.
Duration: Four to nine months.
Deadline: November 1. Notification in mid-February.

ADDRESS INQUIRIES TO:
See e-mail address above.

*PLEASE NOTE:
The Newberry's long-term fellowship grants support individual research and promote serious intellectual exchange through active participation in the Newberry's scholarly activities, including fellows' seminars and a weekly colloquium.

THE NEWBERRY LIBRARY [348]
Newberry Institute for Research and Education
60 West Walton Street
Chicago, IL 60610
(312) 255-3666
E-mail: research@newberry.org
Web Site: www.newberry.org/fellowships

FOUNDED: 1887

AREAS OF INTEREST:
The humanities of Western Europe, England and the Americas from the late Middle Ages to the early 20th century.

NAME(S) OF PROGRAMS:
● **Newberry Library - Jack Miller Center Fellowships**

TYPE:
Fellowships; Residencies. Support for projects in any field appropriate to the Library's collection.

PURPOSE:
To advance scholarship in those fields of study that will contribute to a deeper understanding of America's founding principles and history and wider traditions that influenced its development.

LEGAL BASIS:
Private research library.

ELIGIBILITY:
Applicants must have the Ph.D. or terminal degree in their field, or have completed all doctoral requirements except the dissertation. Preference will be given to applicants whose research particularly requires study at the Newberry.

Applicants must live and work outside the greater Chicago area.

FINANCIAL DATA:
Amount of support per award: $3,000 per month in residence.

NO. MOST RECENT APPLICANTS: Varies.

NO. AWARDS: 2.

APPLICATION INFO:
Applications may be submitted through the online webform.
Duration: One month.
Deadline: December 15.

EXECUTIVE STAFF:
Keelin Burke, Director of Fellowships and Academic Programs

ADDRESS INQUIRIES TO:
See e-mail address above.

THE NEWBERRY LIBRARY [349]
Newberry Institute for Research and Education
60 West Walton Street
Chicago, IL 60610
(312) 255-3666
E-mail: research@newberry.org
Web Site: www.newberry.org/fellowships

FOUNDED: 1887

AREAS OF INTEREST:
The humanities of Western Europe, England and the Americas from the late Middle Ages to the early 20th century.

NAME(S) OF PROGRAMS:
● **Susan Kelly Power and Helen Hornbeck Tanner Fellowship**

TYPE:
Fellowships; Residencies. Support for projects in any field appropriate to the Library's collection.

PURPOSE:
To support Ph.D. candidates and postdoctoral scholars of American Indian heritage for one or two months of residential research in any field in the humanities using the Newberry collection.

LEGAL BASIS:
Private research library.

ELIGIBILITY:
Applicants must have the Ph.D. or be a postdoctoral scholar of American Indian heritage.

Applicants within the Chicago metropolitan area are eligible.

FINANCIAL DATA:
Amount of support per award: $3,000 per month in residence.

NO. MOST RECENT APPLICANTS: 5.

NO. AWARDS: 1.

APPLICATION INFO:
Applications must be submitted through the online webform.
Duration: One to two months of residential research.
Deadline: December 15.

EXECUTIVE STAFF:
Keelin Burke, Director of Fellowships and Academic Programs

ADDRESS INQUIRIES TO:
See e-mail address above.

THE NEWBERRY LIBRARY [350]
Newberry Institute for Research and Education
60 West Walton Street
Chicago, IL 60610
(312) 255-3666
E-mail: research@newberry.org
Web Site: www.newberry.org/fellowships

FOUNDED: 1887

AREAS OF INTEREST:
The humanities of Western Europe, England and the Americas from the late Middle Ages to the early 20th century.

NAME(S) OF PROGRAMS:
● **Society of Mayflower Descendants in the State of Illinois Fellowship**

TYPE:
Fellowships; Residencies. Support for projects related to early American or transatlantic history.

PURPOSE:
To encourage research work, especially those working in early American or transatlantic history.

LEGAL BASIS:
Private research library.

ELIGIBILITY:
Applicants must have the Ph.D. or terminal degree in their field, or have completed all doctoral requirements except the dissertation. Preference will be given to applicants whose research particularly requires study at the Newberry, and whose research work is in early American or transatlantic history.

Applicants must live and work outside the greater Chicago area.

FINANCIAL DATA:
Amount of support per award: $3,000 for one month in residence.

NO. MOST RECENT APPLICANTS: Varies.

NO. AWARDS: 2.

APPLICATION INFO:
Applications must be submitted through the online webform.
Duration: One month.
Deadline: December 15.

EXECUTIVE STAFF:
Keelin Burke, Director of Fellowships and Academic Programs

ADDRESS INQUIRIES TO:
See e-mail address above.

THE NEWBERRY LIBRARY [351]
Newberry Institute for Research and Education
60 West Walton Street
Chicago, IL 60610
(312) 255-3666
E-mail: research@newberry.org
Web Site: www.newberry.org/fellowships

FOUNDED: 1887

AREAS OF INTEREST:
The humanities of Western Europe, England and the Americas from the late Middle Ages to the early 20th century.

NAME(S) OF PROGRAMS:
● **Charles Montgomery Gray Fellowship**

TYPE:
Fellowships; Residencies. Support for projects in any field appropriate to the Library's collection.

PURPOSE:
To encourage the individual scholar's research and to deepen and enrich the opportunities for serious intellectual exchange.

LEGAL BASIS:
Private research library.

ELIGIBILITY:
Applicants must have the Ph.D. or terminal degree in their field, or have completed all doctoral requirements except the dissertation. Projects must be appropriate for research in residence, within the Newberry's collection. Preference will be given to applicants whose research particularly requires study at the Newberry. Preference may be given to those working in the early modern period or Renaissance, as well as English history, legal history or European history.

Applicants must live and work outside the greater Chicago area.

FINANCIAL DATA:
Amount of support per award: $3,000 per month of residency.

NO. MOST RECENT APPLICANTS: Varies.

NO. AWARDS: 3 to 4.

APPLICATION INFO:
Applications must be submitted through the online webform.
Duration: One month.
Deadline: December 15.

EXECUTIVE STAFF:
Keelin Burke, Director of Fellowships and Academic Programs

ADDRESS INQUIRIES TO:
See e-mail address above.

THE NEWBERRY LIBRARY [352]

Newberry Institute for Research and Education
60 West Walton Street
Chicago, IL 60610
(312) 255-3666
E-mail: research@newberry.org
Web Site: www.newberry.org/fellowships

FOUNDED: 1887

AREAS OF INTEREST:
The humanities of Western Europe, England and the Americas from the late Middle Ages to the early 20th century.

NAME(S) OF PROGRAMS:
● **Andrew W. Mellon Foundation Fellowships**

TYPE:
Fellowships; Residencies. Support for projects in any field appropriate to the Library's collection.

PURPOSE:
To encourage the individual scholar's research and to deepen and enrich the opportunities for serious intellectual exchange.

LEGAL BASIS:
Private research library.

ELIGIBILITY:
Established scholars at the postdoctoral level may apply. An established scholar, as defined by the Awards Committee, is generally someone who has at least two published articles in refereed journals or the equivalent at the time of application. Projects must be appropriate for research in residence, within the Newberry's collection. There may be preference given for scholars who live and work outside of the Chicago area.

FINANCIAL DATA:
Awardees may combine this fellowship award with sabbatical or other stipendiary support.
Amount of support per award: $5,000 per month of residency.

NO. MOST RECENT APPLICANTS: Varies.

NO. AWARDS: 1 to 2.

APPLICATION INFO:
Applications may be submitted through the online webform.
Duration: Four to nine months.
Deadline: November 1. Notification in mid-February.

EXECUTIVE STAFF:
Keelin Burke, Director of Fellowships and Academic Programs

ADDRESS INQUIRIES TO:
See e-mail address above.

THE PHI BETA KAPPA SOCIETY

1606 New Hampshire Avenue, N.W.
Washington, DC 20009
(202) 745-3287
Fax: (202) 986-1601
E-mail: awards@pbk.org
Web Site: www.pbk.org

TYPE:
Fellowships. Grant to women scholars made in alternate years for advanced research dealing with Greek language, literature, history or archaeology (odd-numbered years) or with French language or literature (even-numbered years).

See entry 986 for full listing.

THE ROYAL SOCIETY OF CANADA

Walter House
282 Somerset Street West
Ottawa ON K2P 0J6 Canada
(613) 998-9920 ext. 106
Fax: (613) 991-6996
E-mail: nominations@rsc-src.ca
Web Site: www.rsc-src.ca

TYPE:
Awards/prizes. The Yvan Allaire Medal is awarded in recognition of outstanding research in governance of public and private organizations.

The Bancroft Award is given for publication, instruction and research in the earth sciences that have conspicuously contributed to public understanding and appreciation of the subject.

The Pierre Chauveau Medal is awarded for a distinguished contribution to knowledge in the humanities.

The Sir John William Dawson Medal is awarded for important contributions of knowledge in multiple domains.

The Flavelle Medal is awarded for an outstanding contribution to biological science during the preceding 10 years or for significant additions to a previous outstanding contribution to biological science.

The Ursula Franklin Award in Gender Studies is intended to recognize significant contributions by a Canadian scholar in the humanities and social sciences to furthering our understanding of issues concerning gender.

The Jason A. Hannah Medal is awarded for an important publication in the history of medicine.

The Innis-Gérin Medal is presented for a distinguished and sustained contribution to the literature of the social sciences.

The McLaughlin Medal is awarded for important research of sustained excellence in any branch of the medical sciences.

The Willet G. Miller Medal is given for outstanding research in any branch of earth sciences.

The Lorne Pierce Medal is awarded for an achievement of special significance and conspicuous merit in imaginative or critical literature written in either English or French (critical literature dealing with Canadian subjects has priority over critical literature of equal merit that does not deal with Canadian subjects).

The Miroslaw Romanowski Medal is awarded for significant contributions to the resolution of scientific aspects of environmental problems or for important improvements to the quality of an ecosystem in all aspects - terrestrial, atmospheric and aqueous - brought about by scientific means.

The Rutherford Memorial Medals are awarded for outstanding research in any branch of physics and chemistry.

The John L. Synge Award is given to acknowledge outstanding research in any of the branches of the mathematical sciences.

The Henry Marshall Tory Medal is given for outstanding research in any branch of astronomy, chemistry, mathematics, physics or an allied science.

The J.B. Tyrrell Historical Medal is awarded for outstanding work in the history of Canada.

See entry 1646 for full listing.

THE SCHOMBURG CENTER FOR RESEARCH IN BLACK CULTURE, NEW YORK PUBLIC LIBRARY [353]

515 Malcolm X Boulevard
New York, NY 10037-1801
(212) 491-2228
E-mail: sir@nypl.org
Web Site: www.nypl.org/about/locations/schomburg/fellowships

FOUNDED: 1925

AREAS OF INTEREST:
African, African-American and Afro-Caribbean history and culture.

NAME(S) OF PROGRAMS:
● **Schomburg Scholars-in-Residence**

TYPE:
Fellowships. Awarded to scholars and professionals whose research in African diasporic studies can benefit from extended access to the Center's collections. Seminars, colloquia, forums, symposia and conferences complement the residency program.

YEAR PROGRAM STARTED: 1983

PURPOSE:
To encourage research and writing in African diasporic studies; to facilitate interaction among the participants, including fellows funded by other sources; to provide for widespread dissemination of findings through lectures, publications and the Schomburg Center Seminars.

ELIGIBILITY:
Applicants must be professionals and/or scholars in the humanities studying African diaspora and fields related to the Schomburg Center's collections and program activities, including librarianship, archives and museum administration, special collections, photographs, audiovisual materials and publications. Studies in the social sciences, the arts, science and technology, psychology, education and religion are also eligible if they utilize a humanistic approach and contribute to humanistic knowledge. Creative writing projects (works of poetry and fiction) and projects that result in a performance are not eligible.

Persons seeking support for research leading to degrees are not eligible under this program. Candidates for advanced degrees must have received the degree or completed all requirements for it by the application deadline. Foreign nationals are ineligible unless they will have resided in the U.S. for three years immediately preceding the award date of the fellowship.

FINANCIAL DATA:
Amount of support per award: Long-term Fellowship: Stipend of $35,000; Short-term Fellowship: Stipend of $3,000 per month.

CO-OP FUNDING PROGRAMS: Funding support for the program has been provided by the National Endowment for the Humanities, the Ford Foundation, the Samuel I. Newhouse Foundation, the Andrew W. Mellon Foundation, the Rockefeller Foundation, the Pitts Foundation, the Aaron Diamond Foundation, and the Irene Diamond Foundation.

NO. AWARDS: 7 Long-term and 6 Short-term for the year 2020-21.

APPLICATION INFO:
Applications are accepted electronically only.
Duration: Long-term Fellowship: Six consecutive months; Short-term Fellowship: One to three months.
Deadline: December 1.

PUBLICATIONS:
Program announcement.

STAFF:
Brent Edwards, Program Director

ADDRESS INQUIRIES TO:
Scholars-in-Residence Program
(See address or e-mail above.)

*PLEASE NOTE:
The Center will assist scholars in locating housing.

*SPECIAL STIPULATIONS:
Independent scholars and writers are welcome to apply. Fellowships may not be used to support work on a thesis or dissertation for a university degree. Fellows may not be employed or hold other major residential fellowships or grants during the period of residency.

SOCIAL SCIENCES AND HUMANITIES RESEARCH COUNCIL OF CANADA
350 Albert Street
Ottawa ON K1P 6G4 Canada
(613) 943-7777
Fax: (613) 943-1329
E-mail: fellowships@sshrc-crsh.gc.ca
Web Site: www.sshrc-crsh.gc.ca

TYPE:
Fellowships. For Canadian citizens or permanent residents of Canada, to support postdoctoral research in the humanities and social sciences.

See entry 1676 for full listing.

SOCIAL SCIENCES AND HUMANITIES RESEARCH COUNCIL OF CANADA
350 Albert Street
Ottawa ON K1P 6G4 Canada
(613) 943-7777
Fax: (613) 943-1329
E-mail: fellowships@sshrc-crsh.gc.ca
Web Site: www.sshrc-crsh.gc.ca

TYPE:
Awards/prizes; Fellowships; Scholarships. Through its Doctoral Awards program, SSHRC offers two types of funding for doctoral students:
(1) SSHRC Doctoral Fellowships and;
(2) Joseph-Armand Bombardier (JAB) Canada Graduate Scholarships (CGS) program - Doctoral Scholarships.

See entry 1675 for full listing.

SOCIAL SCIENCES AND HUMANITIES RESEARCH COUNCIL OF CANADA
350 Albert Street
Ottawa ON K1P 6G4 Canada
(613) 943-7777
Fax: (613) 943-1329
E-mail: vanier@cihr-irsc.gc.ca
Web Site: www.vanier.gc.ca

TYPE:
Awards/prizes; Fellowships; Scholarships. For doctoral students in the humanities and social sciences. Administered by the Canadian Institutes of Health Research, the Natural Sciences and Engineering Research Council and the Social Sciences Research Council.

See entry 1678 for full listing.

SOCIAL SCIENCES AND HUMANITIES RESEARCH COUNCIL OF CANADA
350 Albert Street
Ottawa ON K1P 6G4 Canada
(613) 943-7777
Fax: (613) 943-1329
E-mail: fellowships@sshrc-crsh.gc.ca
Web Site: www.sshrc-crsh.gc.ca

TYPE:
Fellowships. For Canadian citizens, permanent residents of Canada and foreign citizens to support postdoctoral research in the humanities and social sciences.

See entry 1679 for full listing.

SOCIAL SCIENCES AND HUMANITIES RESEARCH COUNCIL OF CANADA
350 Albert Street
Ottawa ON K1P 6G4 Canada
(613) 943-7777
Fax: (613) 943-1329
E-mail: fellowships@sshrc-crsh.gc.ca
Web Site: www.sshrc-crsh.gc.ca

TYPE:
Awards/prizes; Fellowships; Scholarships.

See entry 1677 for full listing.

STANFORD HUMANITIES CENTER   [354]
Stanford University
424 Santa Teresa Street
Stanford, CA 94305
(650) 724-8106
(650) 723-3052
Fax: (650) 723-1895
E-mail: shc-fellowships@stanford.edu
Web Site: shc.stanford.edu

FOUNDED: 1980

AREAS OF INTEREST:
History, literature, philosophy, classics, languages, social theory, political theory, law, religion, anthropology, art history, archeology and other areas of the humanities.

NAME(S) OF PROGRAMS:
● **External Faculty Fellowships**

TYPE:
Fellowships. Fellowships are awarded to support research projects in the humanities; creative arts projects are not eligible. The Humanities Center seeks candidates whose research is likely to contribute to intellectual exchange among a diverse group of scholars within the disciplines of the humanities. The Center is open to projects employing information technology in humanities research.

YEAR PROGRAM STARTED: 1982

PURPOSE:
To promote the humanities and humanistic study at Stanford and nationally, primarily through a research fellowship program.

LEGAL BASIS:
Private, nonprofit research center at Stanford University.

ELIGIBILITY:
Postdoctoral level research in the humanities. Applicants must be at least three years beyond receipt of their Ph.D. at the start of their fellowship year.

External Faculty Fellowships are offered only once. Former External Faculty Fellows are not eligible to reapply.

FINANCIAL DATA:
Amount of support per award: Up to $70,000, plus a moving and housing allowance of up to $40,000.

Matching fund requirements: Applicants are encouraged to seek supplementary financial support.

NO. MOST RECENT APPLICANTS: 350.

NO. AWARDS: Up to 10.

APPLICATION INFO:
Online application is required and may be obtained directly from the Humanities Center web site. Access to the system opens in August.
Duration: Academic year. Normally September 15 to June 15. No renewals.
Deadline: October. Award announcement by late March.

ADVISORY COUNCIL:
R. Lanier Anderson
William Atkins
Giovanna Ceserani
Kristin Kennedy Clark
Susan Dackerman
Andrea Davies
Fred Donner
Paula Findlen
Roland Greene
Mark Greif
Niloofar Haeri
Roberta Katz
Regina Kunzel
Linda R. Meier
Kathryn Moler
Serena Rao
Mary Anne Rothberg Rowen
Peter Seymour
Dafna Zur

ADDRESS INQUIRIES TO:
See e-mail address above.

STIFTELSEN RIKSBANKENS JUBILEUMSFOND [355]
Kungstradgardsgatan 18
111 47 Stockholm Sweden
(46) 08-50 62 64 00
E-mail: rj@rj.se
Web Site: www.rj.se

FOUNDED: 1964

AREAS OF INTEREST:
Scientific research in humanities and social sciences.

NAME(S) OF PROGRAMS:
- **Flexit**
- **Global Issues**
- **Pro Futura**
- **Research Grants**

TYPE:
Conferences/seminars; Research grants.

YEAR PROGRAM STARTED: 1965

PURPOSE:
To support and promote scientific research in humanities and social sciences.

LEGAL BASIS:
Independent, non-governmental foundation.

ELIGIBILITY:
Open to single researchers or research groups. The Foundation is interested in supporting multidisciplinary or interdisciplinary research projects in which researchers from different disciplines, faculties, localities or countries collaborate with Swedish scholars.

FINANCIAL DATA:
Amount of support per award: Average Project Grant: SEK 3,600,000; Average Program Grant: SEK 35,000,000.
Total amount of support: Approximately SEK 525,314,000 for the year 2019.

CO-OP FUNDING PROGRAMS: Occasional co-financing for large projects.

NO. MOST RECENT APPLICANTS: 619 for the year 2019.

NO. AWARDS: 40 projects for the year 2019.

APPLICATION INFO:
Applicants should first submit a short outline sketch and a publication list. If the preliminary proposal is accepted, applicants will be required to send a complete application.
Duration: Three years average for projects; six to eight years for programs.
Deadline: March.

PUBLICATIONS:
Annual report; program publications; yearbook.

STAFF:
Marika Hedin, Chief Executive Officer
Bjorn Olsson, Chief Investment Officer
Hanna Kollerstrom, Head of Communications
Elisabeth Hong, Administrative Director
AnnaLena Hallner, Research Manager, Art, Languages, and Literature
Dr. Robert Hamren, Research Manager, Economics, Law, and Political Science
Dr. Eva Stenskold, Research Manager, Humanities
Dr. Torbjorn Eng, Research Manager, Social Science
Dr. Fredrik Lundmark, Research Manager, Social Science

ADDRESS INQUIRIES TO:
Hanna Kollerstrom
Head of Communications
(See address above.)

SWANN FOUNDATION FOR CARICATURE AND CARTOON [356]
Prints and Photographs Division
Library of Congress
101 Independence Avenue, S.E.
Washington, DC 20540-4730
(202) 707-9115
Fax: (202) 707-6647
E-mail: swann@loc.gov
Web Site: www.loc.gov/rr/print/swann/swann-fellow.html

FOUNDED: 1967

AREAS OF INTEREST:
Caricature and cartoons.

NAME(S) OF PROGRAMS:
- **Swann Foundation Fellowship**

TYPE:
Conferences/seminars; Fellowships; Internships; Project/program grants; Visiting scholars. Small grants. Annual fellowship awarded to candidate for a Ph.D. or Master's degree.

YEAR PROGRAM STARTED: 1995

PURPOSE:
To support the documentation and understanding of caricature and cartoon as art.

LEGAL BASIS:
Nonprofit, federal agency.

ELIGIBILITY:
Applicant must be a candidate for an M.A. or Ph.D. degree in an accredited graduate program in a university in the U.S., Canada or Mexico and working toward the completion of a dissertation or thesis for that degree, or be engaged in postgraduate research within three years of receiving an M.A. or Ph.D. Although research must focus on caricature and cartoon, there is no limitation regarding the place or time period covered. Since the Fund encourages research in a variety of academic disciplines, there is no restriction upon the university department in which this work is being done, provided the subject pertains to caricature or cartoon art.

Individuals who are not U.S. residents, but who otherwise meet the above academic qualifications, may also apply and be considered for a fellowship, contingent upon the applicant's visa eligibility.

GEOG. RESTRICTIONS: North America.

FINANCIAL DATA:
Amount of support per award: Up to $5,000.
Total amount of support: Varies.

NO. MOST RECENT APPLICANTS: Approximately 15.

NO. AWARDS: 1.

APPLICATION INFO:
In addition to the completed application cover sheet, applicants must submit the following materials:
(1) an up-to-date resume providing information as to education, degrees received, fellowships and honors, publications, positions held, and other pertinent information;
(2) a one-page abstract (250 words maximum) that specifies how the proposed project is related to the field of caricature and cartoon and identifies specifically which library collections the applicant intends to utilize in research;

(3) a description of the proposed project (no longer than five pages) which includes accomplishments to date, a timetable for completion, an itemized budget, plans for use of specific Library of Congress collections, and other pertinent information, including plans for publication and;
(4) visual materials that support the project (no more than 10 pages).

Applications lacking any of these required components will automatically be eliminated.

Letters of recommendation from two references must be sent directly to the Swann Foundation at the address listed above.
Duration: One academic year, generally fall through following late spring.
Deadline: February 15.

STAFF:
Martha H. Kennedy, Curator, Popular and Applied Graphic Art
Helena Zinkham, Swann Fund Administrator

ADDRESS INQUIRIES TO:
Martha Kennedy
Curator, Popular and Applied Graphic Art
(See address above.)

*SPECIAL STIPULATIONS:
Must be a graduate student or a postgraduate within three years of receiving an M.A. or Ph.D. from a university in the U.S., Canada, or Mexico.

UCLA CENTER FOR MEDIEVAL AND RENAISSANCE STUDIES [357]
University of California, Los Angeles
302 Royce Hall
Box 951485
Los Angeles, CA 90095-1485
(310) 825-1880
Fax: (310) 825-0655
E-mail: cmrs@humnet.ucla.edu
Web Site: www.cmrs.ucla.edu

FOUNDED: 1963

AREAS OF INTEREST:
All aspects and disciplines related to Medieval and Renaissance studies.

NAME(S) OF PROGRAMS:
- **Ahmanson Research Fellowships for the Study of Medieval and Renaissance Books and Manuscripts**
- **CMRS Conference Travel Grants**
- **CMRS Dissertation Research Fellowship**
- **CMRS Research and Study Travel Grants**
- **The George T. and Margaret W. Romani Fellowship**
- **Lynn and Maude White Fellowship**

TYPE:
Fellowships; Research grants; Travel grants.

PURPOSE:
To promote interdisciplinary and cross-cultural studies of modern civilization in its formative period between the fourth and mid-17th centuries and to provide added research opportunities, facilities and assistance.

LEGAL BASIS:
Nonprofit university research organization.

ELIGIBILITY:
Requirements vary by program. Applicants are advised to consult the CMRS web site for specific details.

FINANCIAL DATA:
Amount of support per award: Ahmanson Research Fellowships: A stipend of $2,500 per month for fellowships lasting up to three months; CMRS Dissertation Research Fellowship: $27,000; CMRS Travel Grants: Varies; Romani Fellowship and Lynn and Maude White Fellowship: $20,000.

CO-OP FUNDING PROGRAMS: Ahmanson Research Fellowships are offered through the generosity of the Ahmanson Foundation, the UCLA Center for Medieval and Renaissance Studies (CMRS) and the UCLA Library Special Collections (LSC).

NO. MOST RECENT APPLICANTS: 26 for the year 2020-21.

NO. AWARDS: Ahmanson Research Fellowships and CMRS Travel Grants: Varies; CMRS Dissertation Research Fellowship: 1 per year; Romani Fellowship and Lynn and Maude White Fellowship: 1 every other year.

APPLICATION INFO:
Instructions vary by program. Applicants are advised to review the CMRS web site for specific details.
Duration: Ahmanson Research Fellowships: Up to three months. CMRS Dissertation Research Fellowship, Lynn and Maude White Fellowship and Romani Fellowship: One year.
Deadline: Varies by program. Applicants are advised to review the CMRS web site for specific details.

PUBLICATIONS:
Viator, annual journal; *Comitatus*, graduate journal; *Cursor Mundi*, book series.

STAFF:
Zrinka Stahuljak, Director
Karen E. Burgess, Assistant Director
Benay Furtivo, Financial Analyst
Brett Landenberger, Programmer Analyst
Allison McCann, Publications Manager
Erin Romo, Program Coordinator

ADDRESS INQUIRIES TO:
Karen E. Burgess, Assistant Director
(See address above.)

UCLA CHICANO STUDIES RESEARCH CENTER
193 Haines Hall
Box 951544
Los Angeles, CA 90095
(310) 825-2363
Fax: (310) 206-1784
E-mail: csrcinfo@chicano.ucla.edu
Web Site: www.chicano.ucla.edu
www.iac.ucla.edu

TYPE:
Fellowships; Visiting scholars.
See entry 966 for full listing.

UKRAINIAN RESEARCH INSTITUTE AT HARVARD UNIVERSITY   [358]
34 Kirkland Street
Cambridge, MA 02138
(617) 495-4053
Fax: (617) 495-8097
E-mail: huri@fas.harvard.edu
Web Site: www.huri.harvard.edu/fellowships

AREAS OF INTEREST:
Ukrainian history, literature, philology, culture, and related areas of study.

NAME(S) OF PROGRAMS:
● **Petro Jacyk Distinguished Fellowship in Ukrainian Studies**

TYPE:
Fellowships. The Jacyk Distinguished Fellowship is designed to bring senior scholars to Harvard University for focused research in Ukrainian history, literature, philology, culture, and other related areas of study in the humanities and social sciences fields. This fellowship is awarded biennially.

PURPOSE:
To further professional development in the field of Ukrainian studies.

ELIGIBILITY:
All senior scholars in the field of Ukrainian studies are eligible to apply.

FINANCIAL DATA:
Stipend covers the cost of housing, health insurance, and other living expenses. In addition to the stipend, the award provides for the cost of direct round-trip travel to Harvard University.
Amount of support per award: $5,000 per month stipend.

APPLICATION INFO:
Application is available online. Nominations may also be submitted. Individuals submitting nominations should submit a letter stating the nominees name, current position, field of study, and basis for nomination.
Duration: Five months.
Deadline: January 2022.

ADDRESS INQUIRIES TO:
Megan Duncan Smith
Programs Coordinator
(See address above.)

*SPECIAL STIPULATIONS:
Jacyk Distinguished Fellow will preside over the Petro Jacyk Seminar in Ukrainian Studies, a forum presented as part of the HURI Seminar Series in Ukrainian Studies.

UKRAINIAN RESEARCH INSTITUTE AT HARVARD UNIVERSITY   [359]
34 Kirkland Street
Cambridge, MA 02138
(617) 495-4053
Fax: (617) 495-8097
E-mail: huri@fas.harvard.edu
Web Site: www.huri.harvard.edu/fellowshiups

AREAS OF INTEREST:
Ukrainian history, literature, philology, culture, and other related areas of study.

NAME(S) OF PROGRAMS:
● **The HURI Research Fellowships in Ukrainian Studies**
● **The Jaroslaw and Nadia Mihaychuk Research Fellowships in Ukrainian Studies**

TYPE:
Fellowships.

PURPOSE:
To bring scholars from the international academic community to Harvard for focused research on projects in Ukrainian history, literature, philology, culture, and other related areas of study in the humanities and social sciences fields.

ELIGIBILITY:
Individuals who hold a doctorate in one of the above-mentioned fields of study and who have demonstrated a commitment to Ukrainian studies are eligible to apply.

Applicants who have received their Ph.D. or its academic equivalent within the past eight to 10 years are especially encouraged to apply for the HURI Research Fellowship. Those individuals who are more recent Ph.Ds. or have completed or defended their dissertation by the time they submit their application are encouraged to apply for the Mihaychuk Postdoctoral Research Fellowship.

Applicants must be eligible to receive and maintain a short-term J-1 visa to carry out research on an Institute fellowship.

FINANCIAL DATA:
Stipend covers cost of housing, health insurance, and other living expenses. In addition to the stipend, the awards provide for the cost of direct round-trip travel to Harvard University.
Amount of support per award: Stipend of $4,400 per month.

APPLICATION INFO:
Application is available online.
Duration: Three to eight months.
Deadline: January.

ADDRESS INQUIRIES TO:
The HURI Fellowships in Ukrainian Studies
Megan Duncan Smith, Programs Coordinator
(See address above.)

*SPECIAL STIPULATIONS:
Fellows are expected to participate in the scholarly life of the University during Harvard's academic year and offer a formal presentation based on original research.

VILLA I TATTI: THE HARVARD UNIVERSITY CENTER FOR ITALIAN RENAISSANCE STUDIES
Via di Vincigliata, 26
50135 Florence Italy
E-mail: fellowships@itatti.harvard.edu
Web Site: itatti.harvard.edu/warburgi-tatti-joint-fellowship

TYPE:
Fellowships. Villa I Tatti - The Harvard University Center for Italian Renaissance Studies in Florence, Italy, and the Warburg Institute School of Advanced Study at the University of London offer a joint, residential fellowship. Fellows will spend the fall term (September to December) in London and the spring term (January to June) in Florence. The fellowship is designed for early and midcareer scholars in the field of history, with preference given to advanced research projects that address the history of science and knowledge related to early modern Italy, including transnational connections between Italy and other cultures. Scholars can also apply to work on the transmission and circulation of ideas, objects, and people during the Renaissance, into and beyond the Italian peninsula, or on the historiography of the Italian Renaissance, including the rebirth of interest in the Renaissance in later periods.

See entry 866 for full listing.

VILLA I TATTI: THE HARVARD UNIVERSITY CENTER FOR ITALIAN RENAISSANCE STUDIES

Via di Vincigliata, 26
50135 Florence Italy
E-mail: fellowships@itatti.harvard.edu
Web Site: itatti.harvard.edu/i-tattimuseo-nacional-del-prado-joint-fellowship

TYPE:
Fellowships. Joint fellowship designed to support early and midcareer scholars in the field of art history.

See entry 865 for full listing.

VILLA I TATTI: THE HARVARD UNIVERSITY CENTER FOR ITALIAN RENAISSANCE STUDIES

Via di Vincigliata, 26
50135 Florence Italy
E-mail: fellowships@itatti.harvard.edu
Web Site: itatti.harvard.edu/wallace-fellowship

TYPE:
Fellowships. Wallace Fellowships are designed for scholars who explore the historiography and impact of the Italian Renaissance in the Modern Era (19th to 21st centuries).

See entry 860 for full listing.

VILLA I TATTI: THE HARVARD UNIVERSITY CENTER FOR ITALIAN RENAISSANCE STUDIES

Via di Vincigliata, 26
50135 Florence Italy
E-mail: fellowships@itatti.harvard.edu
Web Site: itatti.harvard.edu/berenson-fellowship

TYPE:
Fellowships. The Berenson Fellowship is designed for scholars who explore "Italy in the World." Projects should address the transnational dialogues between Italy and other cultures (e.g., Latin American, Mediterranean, African, Asian, etc.) during the Renaissance, broadly understood historically to include the period from the 14th to the 17th century.

See entry 861 for full listing.

VILLA I TATTI: THE HARVARD UNIVERSITY CENTER FOR ITALIAN RENAISSANCE STUDIES

Via di Vincigliata, 26
50135 Florence Italy
E-mail: fellowships@itatti.harvard.edu
Web Site: itatti.harvard.edu/fellowship-digital-humanities

TYPE:
Fellowships. Fellowship in the Digital Humanities supports the work of scholars in the humanities or social sciences, librarians, archivists, and data science professionals whose research interests or practice cut across traditional disciplinary boundaries and actively employ technology in their work. Projects can address any aspect of the Italian Renaissance, broadly understood to include the period from the 14th to the 17th century, and geographically to include translational dialogues between Italy and other cultures (e.g., Latin American, Mediterranean, African, Asian, etc.). Projects should apply digital technologies such as mapping, textual analysis, visualization, or the semantic web to topics in fields such as art and architecture, history, literature, material culture, music, philosophy, religion, and the history of science.

See entry 862 for full listing.

VILLA I TATTI: THE HARVARD UNIVERSITY CENTER FOR ITALIAN RENAISSANCE STUDIES

Via di Vincigliata, 26
50135 Florence Italy
E-mail: fellowships@itatti.harvard.edu
Web Site: itatti.harvard.edu/david-and-julie-tobey-fellowship

TYPE:
Fellowships. The David and Julie Tobey Fellowship supports research on drawings, prints, and illustrated manuscripts from the Italian Renaissance, and especially the role that these works played in the creative process, the history of taste and collecting, and questions of connoisseurship.

See entry 863 for full listing.

VILLA I TATTI: THE HARVARD UNIVERSITY CENTER FOR ITALIAN RENAISSANCE STUDIES

Via di Vincigliata, 26
50135 Florence Italy
E-mail: fellowships@itatti.harvard.edu
Web Site: itatti.harvard.edu/craig-hugh-smyth-fellowship

TYPE:
Fellowships. The Craig Hugh Smyth Fellowship is designed for curators and conservators pursuing advanced research in any aspect of the Italian Renaissance.

See entry 864 for full listing.

VILLA I TATTI: THE HARVARD UNIVERSITY CENTER FOR ITALIAN RENAISSANCE STUDIES

Via di Vincigliata, 26
50135 Florence Italy
E-mail: fellowships@itatti.harvard.edu
Web Site: itatti.harvard.edu/i-tatti-fellowship

TYPE:
Fellowships. I Tatti Fellowship supports postdoctoral research in any aspect of the Italian Renaissance, broadly understood to include the period from the 14th to the 17th century and geographically to include transnational dialogues between Italy and other cultures (e.g., Latin American, Mediterranean, African, Asian, etc.).

See entry 859 for full listing.

LEWIS WALPOLE LIBRARY   [360]

Yale University
154 Main Street
Farmington, CT 06032
(860) 677-2140
Fax: (860) 677-6369
E-mail: walpole@yale.edu
Web Site: www.library.yale.edu/walpole

FOUNDED: 1979

AREAS OF INTEREST:
18th century studies (mainly British), the study of Horace Walpole and Strawberry Hill, 18th century British satirical prints.

NAME(S) OF PROGRAMS:
* **Visiting Research Fellowship Program**

TYPE:
Conferences/seminars; Fellowships; Travel grants. 18th century studies (mainly British), including history, literature, theatre, drama, art, architecture, politics, philosophy or social history.

YEAR PROGRAM STARTED: 1979

PURPOSE:
To fund study into any aspect of British 18th century studies in the Library's collection of 18th century British prints, paintings, books and manuscripts.

ELIGIBILITY:
Applicants should normally be pursuing an advanced degree or must be engaged in postdoctoral research or equivalent research. Study is at doctoral, postdoctoral, postgraduate and research levels.

FINANCIAL DATA:
Amount of support per award: Research Fellowship: Includes round-trip travel to the Library from the fellow's home location, a per diem for days in residence at the Library, and free accommodation in the fellows' quarters on the Lewis Walpole Library campus.

Travel Grant: Includes round-trip travel to the Library from the fellow's home location and free accommodation in the fellows' quarters on the Lewis Walpole Library campus but not the per diem.

Total amount of support: Varies.

CO-OP FUNDING PROGRAMS: ASECS Library fellowship; Lewis Walpole Library/Beinecke Rare Book & Manuscript Library joint eight-week fellowship.

NO. MOST RECENT APPLICANTS: 63.

NO. AWARDS: Up to 26.

APPLICATION INFO:
Applicants must submit a curriculum vitae, a brief outline of research proposal of up to three pages and two confidential letters of recommendation.

Duration: Four-week and eight-week Visiting Research Fellowship; two-week travel grants.

Deadline: Second Monday in January.

ADDRESS INQUIRIES TO:
Nicole L. Bouché
W.S. Lewis Librarian
and Executive Director
Lewis Walpole Library
Yale University
P.O. Box 1408
Farmington, CT 06034

WOODROW WILSON INTERNATIONAL CENTER FOR SCHOLARS [361]

One Woodrow Wilson Plaza
1300 Pennsylvania Avenue, N.W.
Washington, DC 20004-3027
(202) 691-4170
Fax: (202) 691-4001
E-mail: fellowships@wilsoncenter.org
Web Site: www.wilsoncenter.org

FOUNDED: 1968

AREAS OF INTEREST:
Social sciences, humanities and public policy.

NAME(S) OF PROGRAMS:
- Fellowship Program at the Woodrow Wilson International Center for Scholars

TYPE:
Fellowships; Research grants; Residencies; Scholarships; Visiting scholars. The Center seeks to commemorate, through its residential fellowship program of advanced research, both the scholarly depth and the public concerns of Woodrow Wilson. The Center welcomes outstanding project proposals in the social sciences and humanities on global issues - topics that intersect with questions of public policy or provide the historical framework to illume policy issues of contemporary importance. The Center especially welcomes projects likely to foster communication between the world of ideas and the world of public affairs.

Projects should have relevance to the world of public policy. Fellows should be prepared to interact with policymakers in Washington and with the Center's staff working on similar areas.

Fellowships are tenable in residence only at the Woodrow Wilson International Center for Scholars. The Center will not provide support for research to be carried out elsewhere. Fellows devote their full time to research and writing.

YEAR PROGRAM STARTED: 1970

LEGAL BASIS:
Government agency.

ELIGIBILITY:
The Center seeks individuals from throughout the world with superior projects representing diverse scholarly interests in the social sciences and humanities - topics that intersect with questions of public policy.

Academic participants are normally established scholars at the postdoctoral level but cannot be currently working on a Ph.D.

For nonacademic participants, namely those from careers in government, journalism, business, diplomacy and other professions, an equivalent degree of professional achievement is required.

Criteria for selection include scholarly capabilities, promise and achievements, the importance and originality of the proposed research, and the likelihood of the applicant being able to accomplish what he or she proposes.

Applicants should have a very good command of spoken English, since the Center is designed to encourage the exchange of ideas among its Fellows.

FINANCIAL DATA:
Amount of support per award: $90,000 stipend.

Total amount of support: Approximately $1,800,000 for the year 2020-21.

NO. MOST RECENT APPLICANTS: 320.

NO. AWARDS: 15 to 20.

REPRESENTATIVE AWARDS:
David Atwill, Professor of Asian History, Pennsylvania State University, "In China's Shadow: The Ascendency of High Asia, 1900-1960;" Elizabeth Chalecki, Assistant Professor of International Relations, University of Nebraska Omaha, "Rethinking Sovereignty in a Changed Climate: The National Security Role of Commons-Based Geoengineering;" Dalia Kaye, Senior Political Scientist, RAND Corporation, "The Making of U.S. Iran Policy: The Construction of Iran as an Abnormal State and Its Consequences for American Foreign Policy."

APPLICATION INFO:
A complete application must include the following:
(1) the Fellowship Application Form;
(2) a current curriculum vitae (not to exceed three pages);
(3) a list of publications that includes exact titles, names of publishers, dates of publication and status of forthcoming publications (not to exceed three pages);
(4) a project proposal (not to exceed five single-spaced typed pages, using 12-point type);
(5) a bibliography for the project that includes primary sources and relevant secondary sources (not to exceed three pages) and;
(6) two letters of reference.

All application materials must be submitted in English.

Duration: Fellowships of usually nine months are tenable September 1 of the fellowship year.

Deadline: October 5 for receipt of applications. Decisions announced by March of the following year.

PUBLICATIONS:
Annual report; application guidelines.

OFFICERS:
Ambassador Mark Green, Director, President and Chief Executive Officer

ADDRESS INQUIRIES TO:
Kim Conner, Fellowship Specialist
(See address above.)

WINTERTHUR MUSEUM, GARDEN & LIBRARY [362]

5105 Kennett Pike
Winterthur, DE 19735
(302) 888-4876
Fax: (302) 888-4870
E-mail: croeber@winterthur.org
Web Site: www.winterthur.org

FOUNDED: 1951

AREAS OF INTEREST:
Material culture studies, social and cultural history, art history, literary studies, American studies, design history, the decorative arts, landscape architecture and design, consumer culture, and conservation studies covering global topics from the 17th to the 20th centuries.

NAME(S) OF PROGRAMS:
- Dissertation Fellowships
- Maker-Creator Fellowships
- NEH Postdoctoral Fellowship
- Postdoctoral Fellowship
- Short-term Fellowship

TYPE:
Fellowships. Long-term and short-term fellowships to be held in residence, virtually or hybrid, at Winterthur Museum, Garden & Library.

The Dissertation Fellowships are for doctoral candidates. The award is a four- to nine-month fellowship.

Maker-Creator Fellowships are one- to three-month fellowships designed for artists, writers, filmmakers, horticulturalists, craftspeople and other creative professionals who wish to examine, study and immerse themselves in Winterthur's vast collections in order to inspire creative and artistic works.

Short-term Fellowship consists of one- to three-month fellowships designed to promote research and study in topics of relevance to Winterthur's collections.

All fellowships can be residential, virtual or hybrid that involves collections based research at Winterthur.

PURPOSE:
To promote research in any humanistic field related to Winterthur's collections (museum, library, garden), work of an interdisciplinary nature and/or research with both objects and documents.

LEGAL BASIS:
Tax-exempt, public charitable organization.

ELIGIBILITY:
Applicants for a Dissertation Fellowship must have completed coursework, passed qualifying exams, and have an approved prospectus. The fellowship is open to students in departments of history, anthropology, folklore, material culture, art history, American studies, African-American history, Latinx studies, Native and Indigenous studies, historic preservation, and related fields.

Maker-Creator Fellowships are available to artists, writers, filmmakers, horticulturalists, craftspeople, and those in related fields.

Short-term Fellowships are available to academic, museum and independent scholars and to support dissertation research.

FINANCIAL DATA:
Applicants may hold sabbaticals and grants from their own institutions, but may not simultaneously hold other major residential or collections based fellowships. Housing is available in cottages on the museum grounds (full housekeeping facilities and furnished rooms).

Amount of support per award: Dissertation Fellowships: $7,000 per semester; NEH Postdoctoral Fellowship: $5,000 per month; Postdoctoral Fellowships: $16,800 over four months; Short-term Fellowships: $1,750 per month.

Total amount of support: Varies.

NO. AWARDS: Varies.

REPRESENTATIVE AWARDS:
Jennifer Van Horn, Ph.D., Associate Professor, University of Delaware, "Base Metals: The Anti-Black Interior (1700-1900);" Marina Wells, Ph.D. candidate, Boston University, "Making Men from Whales: The Visual Culture and Gender of Whaling in New England, 1814-1861;" Kelly Harris, Furniture Maker/Educator, "Windsor Chairs: Accessing the Icon;" Steffi Dippold,

Ph.D., Associate Professor, Kansas State University, "Biologies and Ethnographies of the Book: Deciphering Indigenous Artifact Languages of Early American Bookmaking;" Leslie Koren, Assistant Professor of Media Arts, Robert Morris University and Adam Castelli, Architect, CannonDesign, "Pioneering Landscapes: Marian Cruger Coffin's Life and Career."

APPLICATION INFO:
Application instructions and materials are available online at the Winterthur web site. Applicants for each fellowship should submit a three- to five-page statement of purpose, a curriculum vitae and two letters of recommendation. Supporting materials for dissertation research must include a letter from the dissertation advisor.

All materials must be submitted through the online portal. E-mail or postal submissions are not accepted.

Duration: Dissertation Fellowships: Four to nine months; Maker-Creator Fellowships and Short-term Fellowships: Two weeks to three months; Postdoctoral Fellowships: Four months.

Deadline: January 15. Announcement by April 30.

IRS I.D.: 51-0066038

STAFF:
Thomas A. Guiler, Ph.D., Assistant Professor of History and Public Humanities

ADDRESS INQUIRIES TO:
Research Fellowship Program
Academic Programs Department
E-mail: academicprograms@winterthur.org
(See address above.)

WOLF HUMANITIES
CENTER   [363]
619 Williams Hall
255 South 36th Street
Philadelphia, PA 19104-6305
(215) 746-5940
E-mail: wolfhumanities@upenn.edu
Web Site: www.wolfhumanities.upenn.edu

FOUNDED: 1999

AREAS OF INTEREST:
Humanities.

NAME(S) OF PROGRAMS:
● **Andrew W. Mellon Postdoctoral Fellowships in the Humanities**

TYPE:
Fellowships. Fellows conduct research and teach one course.

YEAR PROGRAM STARTED: 1999

PURPOSE:
To support and encourage the intellectual development of untenured scholars in the humanities.

LEGAL BASIS:
Nonprofit, non-taxable university.

ELIGIBILITY:
Candidates must have research interests that relate to the Wolf Humanities Center topic of study for the year of the fellowship. Preference is given to proposals that are interdisciplinary and to candidates who have not previously used the resources of the University of Pennsylvania and whose work would allow them to take advantage of the research strengths of the institution and to make a contribution to its intellectual life.

Research proposals are invited in all areas of humanistic studies except educational curriculum-building and performing arts.

FINANCIAL DATA:
Fellowships include health insurance and a $3,000 research fund.
Amount of support per award: $59,300.

NO. AWARDS: 4.

APPLICATION INFO:
Applications are available, commencing in May, on the web site. Applicants are expected to submit the application online, which includes a description of their proposed project, as well as recommendations.
Duration: One year in residence at University of Pennsylvania.
Deadline: October 15 of the year preceding the fellowship. Announcement in December.

STAFF:
Karen Redrob, Director
Sara Varney, Associate Director
Sarah Miliniski, Program Manager
Dru Baker, Program Coordinator

ADDRESS INQUIRIES TO:
Sara Varney, Associate Director
(See address above.)

CARTER G. WOODSON
INSTITUTE FOR
AFRICAN-AMERICAN AND
AFRICAN STUDIES   [364]
University of Virginia
McCormick Road, 108 Minor Hall
Charlottesville, VA 22903
(434) 924-3109
Fax: (434) 924-8820
E-mail: woodson@virginia.edu
Web Site: woodson.as.virginia.edu

FOUNDED: 1981

AREAS OF INTEREST:
Those disciplines of the humanities and social sciences which concern themselves with Afro-American and African Studies.

NAME(S) OF PROGRAMS:
● **African-American and African Studies Fellowships**

TYPE:
Fellowships. The Woodson Institute offers residential fellowships to predoctoral and postdoctoral scholars. These fellowships are designed to facilitate the completion of works in progress by providing scholars with unencumbered leave.

Afro-American and African Studies is considered to cover Africa, Africans and peoples of African descent in North, Central and South America and the Caribbean, past and present.

YEAR PROGRAM STARTED: 1981

PURPOSE:
To help researchers complete dissertations, books and other research projects focusing on the Black experience.

LEGAL BASIS:
University.

ELIGIBILITY:
Applicants for the predoctoral fellowships must have completed all requirements for the Ph.D. except the dissertation prior to August 1. Applicants for the postdoctoral fellowship must have been awarded their Ph.D. by the

time of application or furnish proof that it will have been received prior to July. There are no restrictions as to citizenship or current residence. Employees of the University of Virginia may not apply.

Postdoctoral applicants must have received their Ph.D. no earlier than six years prior to the application deadline.

Proposals will be judged on the basis of the significance of the proposed work, the applicant's qualifications, familiarity with existing relevant research literature, the research design of the project and the promise of completion within the award period. Preference will be given to projects whose field research is already substantially completed.

Fellowship recipients must be in residence at the University of Virginia for the duration of the award period and must agree to teach one course per year in the African-American Studies Program during the fall or spring semester. In pursuit of these goals, predoctoral fellows will become visiting graduate students attached to their respective disciplinary departments, and postdoctoral fellows will receive the status of visiting scholars in their respective fields.

FINANCIAL DATA:
Amount of support per award: Predoctoral Fellowship: $24,000 per year; Postdoctoral Fellowship: $47,500.

NO. AWARDS: 6 per year.

APPLICATION INFO:
Complete guidelines are available on the Institute web site.
Duration: Two years.
Deadline: December 1. Notification by mail early March.

PUBLICATIONS:
Program guidelines.

STAFF:
Deborah E. McDowell, Director

ADDRESS INQUIRIES TO:
Program Administrator
(See address above.)

*SPECIAL STIPULATIONS:
Fellows are required to present a formal paper to the University community at least once a year.

YALE CENTER FOR BRITISH
ART   [365]
1080 Chapel Street
New Haven, CT 06520
(203) 432-9805
Fax: (203) 432-4538
E-mail: ycba.research@yale.edu
Web Site: britishart.yale.edu/visiting-scholar-award

FOUNDED: 1977

AREAS OF INTEREST:
British art, history and literature.

NAME(S) OF PROGRAMS:
● **Visiting Scholar Awards**

TYPE:
Fellowships; Research grants; Residencies; Visiting scholars. Short-term resident fellowships for scholars of literature, history, the history of art or related fields.

YEAR PROGRAM STARTED: 1978

PURPOSE:
To allow scholars of literature, history, the history of art or related fields to study the

Center's holdings of paintings, sculpture, drawings, prints and rare books and to make use of its research facilities (photograph archive and reference library).

LEGAL BASIS:
University-affiliated museum and research center.

ELIGIBILITY:
Open to scholars engaged in predoctoral and postdoctoral or equivalent research related to British art and to museum professionals whose responsibilities and research interests include British art.

FINANCIAL DATA:
Fellowships include the cost of travel to and from New Haven and also provide accommodation and a living allowance. Recipients will be required to be in residence in New Haven during the Fellowship period.
Amount of support per award: Varies.

CO-OP FUNDING PROGRAMS: One fellowship per annum is reserved for members of the American Society for Eighteenth-Century Studies; by arrangement with the Huntington Library and the Delaware Art Museum, scholars may apply for tandem awards.

NO. MOST RECENT APPLICANTS: 22.

NO. AWARDS: Approximately 20.

REPRESENTATIVE AWARDS:
Sria Chatterjee, Ph.D. candidate, Princeton University, "Colonial Weather;" Elena Korotkikh, Assistant Curator, Department for 19th and 20th century European and American Art, State Pushkin Museum of Fine Art.

APPLICATION INFO:
Application must be submitted online. Complete application information is available on the web site.
Duration: One to four months.
Deadline: January.

PUBLICATIONS:
Brochure.

STAFF:
Courtney J. Martin, Director
Martina Droth, Deputy Director and Chief Curator
Dr. Jemma Field, Associate Director of Research

ADDRESS INQUIRIES TO:
Dr. Jemma Field
Associate Director of Research
P.O. Box 208280
New Haven, CT 06520
E-mail: jemma.field@yale.edu

*SPECIAL STIPULATIONS:
Inquiries by e-mail only.

Architecture

THE AMERICAN INSTITUTE OF ARCHITECTS [366]
1735 New York Avenue, N.W.
Washington, DC 20006-5292
(202) 626-7358
Fax: (202) 626-7399
E-mail: aah@aia.org
Web Site: www.aia.org

FOUNDED: 1952

AREAS OF INTEREST:
Health care, facility planning, design and construction, facilities management, clinical engineering, and safety and security.

NAME(S) OF PROGRAMS:
● **AIA Arthur N. Tuttle, Jr. Graduate Fellowship in Health Facility Planning and Design**

TYPE:
Fellowships; Research grants. The American Institute of Architects and the Academy of Architecture for Health sponsor this program with additional support from the Steris Corporation, which offers one or more graduate fellowships.

YEAR PROGRAM STARTED: 1952

PURPOSE:
To increase the amount of research being done in the area of health care facility design and planning.

LEGAL BASIS:
Nonprofit organization.

ELIGIBILITY:
Open to graduate and postgraduate students enrolled at an accredited school of architecture. Applicants must be citizens of Canada, Mexico or the U.S.

FINANCIAL DATA:
Amount of support per award: Typically $2,000 to $10,000.

NO. AWARDS: 4 for the year 2020.

APPLICATION INFO:
Guidelines and application forms are available on the Institute web site.
Duration: One to two years depending on proposal.
Deadline: February.

PUBLICATIONS:
Guidelines.

AMERICAN SCHOOL OF CLASSICAL STUDIES AT ATHENS
6-8 Charlton Street
Princeton, NJ 08540-5232
(609) 683-0800
Fax: (609) 924-0578
E-mail: application@ascsa.org
Web Site: www.ascsa.edu.gr

TYPE:
Fellowships.

See entry 389 for full listing.

AMERICAN SOCIETY OF INTERIOR DESIGNERS EDUCATIONAL FOUNDATION, INC. [367]
1152 15th Street, N.W.
Suite 910
Washington, DC 20005
(202) 675-4443
Fax: (202) 546-3240
E-mail: foundation@asid.org
Web Site: www.asid.org/foundation

FOUNDED: 1975

AREAS OF INTEREST:
Interior design (commercial and residential) and interior design-related industry.

NAME(S) OF PROGRAMS:
● **ASID Foundation Legacy Scholarships for Graduate Students**
● **ASID Foundation Legacy Scholarships for Undergraduates**
● **ASID Foundation Transform Grant**
● **Irene Winifred Eno Grant**
● **Joel Polsky Academic Achievement Award**
● **Joel Polsky Prize**

TYPE:
Awards/prizes; Research grants; Scholarships; Seed money grants. The ASID Foundation Legacy Scholarships for Graduate Students are awarded on the basis of academic/creative accomplishment.

The ASID Foundation Legacy Scholarships for Undergraduates are given to creatively outstanding students as demonstrated through their portfolio.

The ASID Foundation Transform Grant is a research grant to address critical gaps in industry knowledge, advance design understanding, and transform the practice of interior design for the benefit of everyone. The grant provides funding for seed/start-up projects and research projects.

Irene Winifred Eno Grant provides financial assistance to individuals or groups engaged in the creation of an educational program(s) or an interior design research project dedicated to health, safety and welfare.

The Polsky Academic Achievement Award is given annually to recognize an outstanding undergraduate or graduate student's interior design research or thesis project.

The Joel Polsky Prize recognizes outstanding academic contributions to the discipline of interior design through literature or visual communication.

PURPOSE:
To encourage excellence in the field of interior design.

LEGAL BASIS:
Nonprofit foundation.

ELIGIBILITY:
The ASID Foundation Legacy Scholarships for Graduate Students are open to students who are enrolled in or have been accepted to a graduate-level interior design program at a degree-granting institution.

The ASID Foundation Legacy Scholarships for Undergraduates are open to all students in their junior or senior year of undergraduate study and enrolled in at least a three-year program of interior design.

The ASID Foundation Transform Grant is open to graduate students, educators, researchers, interior design practitioners, institutions or other research-related groups.

The Irene Winifred Eno Grant is open to students, educators, interior design practitioners, institutions or other interior design-related groups.

The Joel Polsky Academic Achievement Award judges interior design research or doctoral and Master's thesis projects.

The Joel Polsky Prize entrants should address the needs of the public, designers and students on such topics as educational research, behavioral science, business practice, design process, theory or other technical subjects.

High school students and college freshmen are not eligible.

GEOG. RESTRICTIONS: United States.

FINANCIAL DATA:
Amount of support per award: Irene Winifred Eno Grant, Joel Polsky Academic Achievement Award and Joel Polsky Prize: $5,000; Legacy Scholarship for graduate and undergraduate students: $4,000.

APPLICATION INFO:
Complete details are available online.
Duration: One-time award.

PUBLICATIONS:
ASID ICON, magazine; application guidelines.

OFFICERS:
Valerie O'Keefe, Foundation Manager

ADDRESS INQUIRIES TO:
Valerie O'Keefe, Foundation Manager
(See address above.)

THE ARCHITECTS FOUNDATION [368]
1735 New York Avenue, N.W.
Washington, DC 20006-5292
(202) 626-7514
E-mail: scholarships@architectsfoundation.org
Web Site: www.aia.org
architectsfoundation.org

FOUNDED: 1943

AREAS OF INTEREST:
Architecture.

NAME(S) OF PROGRAMS:
 • **Architects Foundation Diversity Advancement Scholarship**

TYPE:
Scholarships. Scholarships provide the opportunity for financially disadvantaged and/or minority groups to pursue a professional degree in architecture.

YEAR PROGRAM STARTED: 1973

PURPOSE:
To provide scholarships for those who would not otherwise have the opportunity to be enrolled in professional architecture studies.

ELIGIBILITY:
Student must be a U.S. citizen, have a minimum 3.0 grade point average, and be:
(1) a high school student planning to enroll in an NAAB-accredited architecture degree program;
(2) a rising second-year college student in an NAAB-accredited architecture degree program or;
(3) a technical school or community college student who has completed high school or its equivalent and intends to transfer to an NAAB-accredited architecture program.

GEOG. RESTRICTIONS: United States.

FINANCIAL DATA:
Scholarship awards vary according to financial need. The amount of the award is determined based on the financial information and consultation with the Director of Financial Aid at the student's school.
Amount of support per award: $4,000 per year (up to $20,000 total award).

NO. MOST RECENT APPLICANTS: 891.

NO. AWARDS: 6 for the year 2020.

APPLICATION INFO:
Candidates must submit:
(1) a resume;
(2) a personal essay;
(3) two letters of recommendation;
(4) a portfolio (three to five creative works,

which do not have to be architecture-specific) and;
(5) estimated college expenses (FAFSA required).
Duration: One academic year. Renewable up to five years.
Deadline: January.

STAFF:
Marci Reed, Executive Director
Amanda Malloy, Development Manager
Vinny Mandes, Associate

ADDRESS INQUIRIES TO:
Vinny Mandes, Associate
(See address above.)

ARCHITECTURAL LEAGUE OF NEW YORK [369]
594 Broadway, Suite 607
New York, NY 10012
(212) 753-1722
Fax: (212) 486-9173
E-mail: info@archleague.org
Web Site: archleague.org

FOUNDED: 1881

AREAS OF INTEREST:
Architecture, architectural history and urban studies.

NAME(S) OF PROGRAMS:
 • **Deborah J. Norden Fund**

TYPE:
Travel grants. The Deborah J. Norden Fund, established in 1995 in memory of architect and arts administrator Deborah Norden, awards travel/study grants to students and recent graduates in the field of architecture, architectural history, and urban studies.

YEAR PROGRAM STARTED: 1995

PURPOSE:
To support genuinely independent projects that require travel.

ELIGIBILITY:
Open to full-time residents of the U.S., Canada and Mexico. Applicants need not be citizens.

While requests for support of dissertation research will be considered, they are not a priority of the fund. Preference will be given to strong proposals from applicants who have not had this sort of opportunity before.

Architectural League board members or staff members, firms or immediate family of board or staff members, and firms or immediate family of jury members are not eligible to participate.

FINANCIAL DATA:
Amount of support per award: Up to $5,000.
Total amount of support: $5,000.

NO. MOST RECENT APPLICANTS: 110.

NO. AWARDS: 2.

APPLICATION INFO:
Applicants should submit a maximum three-page proposal which succinctly describes the objectives of the grant request and how it will assist the applicant's intellectual and creative development. The grant amount requested must be specified. The submission should also include a resume of not more than two pages, project schedule, and budget for travel and other project costs. Two letters of recommendation must be requested from individuals who are knowledgeable about the applicant's ability

and project. The applicant's name and brief project title must appear on the first page of the proposal.
Deadline: Mid-April. Announcement in early June.

ADDRESS INQUIRIES TO:
E-mail: norden@archleague.org

ARCHITECTURAL LEAGUE OF NEW YORK [370]
594 Broadway, Suite 607
New York, NY 10012
(212) 753-1722
E-mail: info@archleague.org
Web Site: archleague.org

FOUNDED: 1881

AREAS OF INTEREST:
Young architects.

NAME(S) OF PROGRAMS:
 • **The League Prize for Young Architects and Designers**

TYPE:
Awards/prizes; Conferences/seminars.

YEAR PROGRAM STARTED: 1982

PURPOSE:
To recognize specific works of high quality and to encourage the exchange of ideas among young architects and designers who might otherwise not have a forum; to focus on the aesthetic, cultural, and social concerns of architecture and the allied arts; to help architects, artists, and the public enrich their understanding of the purposes and importance of the art of architecture.

ELIGIBILITY:
Entrants may submit work done independently. Entrants must be 10 years or less out of graduate or undergraduate school; students are not eligible for this competition. Work completed for fulfillment of course requirements at academic institutions is not eligible.

FINANCIAL DATA:
Amount of support per award: $2,000.

NO. MOST RECENT APPLICANTS: 100.

NO. AWARDS: 6 per year.

APPLICATION INFO:
A call for entries is issued each fall. A written statement (not to exceed 250 words) is required, which defines and considers the work under the rubric of the competition theme. Significant weight is given to how an applicant's work addresses the theme. A single portfolio, which may include several projects, must be bound and no larger than 11x14 inches. The portfolio may not contain more than 30 double-sided pages. CDs, models, slides and transparencies will not be accepted.

Each submission must include a $25 entry fee. Each entrant must submit one digital form and one hard copy form. Insert form, intact, into an unsealed envelope attached to the inside back cover of the submission. To maintain anonymity, no identification of the entrant may appear on any part of the submission, except on the entry form and return envelope.

Portfolios will be returned by mail only if a self-addressed envelope with postage is also enclosed. The Architectural League assumes no liability for original drawings. The League will take every precaution to return submissions intact, but can assume no responsibility for loss or damage. Portfolios may be discarded after six months if no return envelope is provided.

Deadline: Varies.

ADDRESS INQUIRIES TO:
Anne Rieselbach, Program Director
(See address above.)

THE COMMUNITY FOUNDATION OF LOUISVILLE, INC.
325 West Main Street, Suite 1110
Louisville, KY 40202
(502) 585-4649
Fax: (502) 587-7484
E-mail: info@cflouisville.org
Web Site: www.cflouisville.org

TYPE:
Endowments; General operating grants; Scholarships.

See entry 397 for full listing.

ENTERPRISE COMMUNITY PARTNERS   [371]
334 Boylston Street, Suite 400
Boston, MA 02116
(781) 235-2006
E-mail: rosefellowship@enterprisecommunity.org
Web Site: www.enterprisecommunity.org/rose

AREAS OF INTEREST:
Architecture and community development.

NAME(S) OF PROGRAMS:
• **Enterprise Rose Fellowship**

TYPE:
Fellowships. The Rose Fellowship partners community-engaged architects and artists with local community development organizations. Architectural fellows are designers with an accredited degree in architecture and a passion for applying their skills in a community development context. Artists are defined as socially-engaged creative practitioners, teaching artists, and culture bearers working in all disciplines.

YEAR PROGRAM STARTED: 2000

PURPOSE:
To promote architectural and community design in low-income communities and to encourage architects to become lifelong leaders in public service and community development.

ELIGIBILITY:
Applicants for architectural fellowships must have an NAAB-accredited Professional Architecture Degree (B.Arch or M.Arch) or an equivalent level of professional experience.

Applicants for the arts fellowships must demonstrate experience in applying their artistic or cultural practice in a community-engaged context. Applicant must have a minimum of either a Bachelor's degree or an equivalent level of professional experience.

Applicants must be eligible to work in the U.S. for the entire fellowship period.

GEOG. RESTRICTIONS: United States.

FINANCIAL DATA:
Fellows are placed with a host organization for a two-year period in which they receive the standard employee benefits and insurance package offered to all employees. In joining, fellows are also provided with annual fellowship retreats and networking opportunities and a professional development stipend.

Amount of support per award: $62,000 per year.

Matching fund requirements:
Community-based organizations are most often required to match the grant funds received for the fellow's stipend.

NO. MOST RECENT APPLICANTS: 150.

NO. AWARDS: 8 for the 2019-21 term.

APPLICATION INFO:
Applicant must submit:
(1) resume or curriculum vitae demonstrating relevant academic and community experience;
(2) essays and response to work plan;
(3) portfolio and;
(4) references.

In-person interview is required.
Duration: Two years.
Deadline: Midsummer.

ADDRESS INQUIRIES TO:
Mark Matel, Program Director
Enterprise Rose Fellowship
(See address above.)

THE JAMES MARSTON FITCH CHARITABLE FOUNDATION   [372]
c/o Municipal Art Society
488 Madison Avenue, Suite 1900
New York, NY 10022
(212) 252-6809
Fax: (212) 471-9987
E-mail: cpena@fitchfoundation.org
Web Site: fitchfoundation.org

FOUNDED: 1989

AREAS OF INTEREST:
Architecture, engineering, environmental planning, and historic preservation.

NAME(S) OF PROGRAMS:
• **Richard L. Blinder Award**
• **Mid-Career Fellowship**

TYPE:
Research grants. Richard L. Blinder Award was created to promote studies that explore the architecture of cultural buildings which integrate historic preservation and new construction - past, present and future; presented biennially.

Mid-Career Fellowship: This grant is the primary mission and the signature grant of this Foundation. The grants are intended to support projects of innovative original research or creative design that advance the practice of historic preservation in the U.S.

PURPOSE:
To support professionals in the field of historic preservation by providing midcareer grants to those working in preservation, landscape architecture, urban design, environmental planning, decorative arts, and architectural design and history.

ELIGIBILITY:
Richard L. Blinder Award proposal must demonstrate that it fosters architectural preservation in the U.S. Applicant must be an architect holding a professional degree or a valid license to practice architecture with at least 10 years experience in architecture,

historic preservation or related fields. Grants are awarded only to individuals, not organizations or university-sponsored research projects. Grants are not awarded for professional fees.

Mid-Career Fellowships are awarded only to individuals, not organizations. Applicants must be midcareer professionals with at least ten years experience in historic preservation or related fields, including architecture, landscape architecture, architectural conservation, urban design, environment planning, archaeology, architectural history, and the decorative arts. Applicants must be legal residents or citizens of the U.S.

GEOG. RESTRICTIONS: United States.

FINANCIAL DATA:
Amount of support per award: Up to $15,000.

NO. AWARDS: Richard Blinder Award: 1 biennially; Mid-Career Fellowship: 1 to 2.

APPLICATION INFO:
Applications must be submitted electronically in PDF format. Applicants are required to submit the following materials:
(1) cover page, including project title, primary contact person, and applicant address, telephone number and e-mail address. Also specify which award and the amount of money requested;
(2) brief description of the project (up to three pages), including how the final work product will be disseminated;
(3) detailed work schedule and project budget;
(4) curriculum vita, including professional and academic background, and past and present grants received and;
(5) two letters of support.
Duration: One year.
Deadline: Blinder Award: October 22.

ADDRESS INQUIRIES TO:
See e-mail address above.

GRAHAM FOUNDATION FOR ADVANCED STUDIES IN THE FINE ARTS   [373]
Madlener House
4 West Burton Place
Chicago, IL 60610
(312) 787-4071
E-mail: grantprograms@grahamfoundation.org
Web Site: www.grahamfoundation.org

FOUNDED: 1956

AREAS OF INTEREST:
Architecture and related spatial practices that engage a wide range of cultural, social, political, technological, environmental and aesthetic issues. The Foundation is interested in projects that investigate the contemporary condition, expand historical perspectives, or explore the future of architecture and the designed environment.

NAME(S) OF PROGRAMS:
• **Carter Manny Award**
• **Production and Presentation Grants**
• **Research and Development Grants**

TYPE:
Awards/prizes; Project/program grants; Research grants. Grants to organizations, individuals and public programs.

Carter Manny Award: To support research for academic dissertations by promising scholars who are presently candidates for a doctoral degree, and whose dissertations focus on areas traditionally supported by the Foundation. Students must be nominated by their department to apply for this Award.

Production and Presentation Grants: To assist individuals and organizations with the production-related expenses that are necessary to take a project from conceptualization to realization and public presentation. These projects may include, but are not limited to, publications, exhibitions, installations, conferences, films, new-media projects, and other public programs.

Research and Development Grants: To assist individuals with seed money for research-related expenses such as travel, documentation, materials, supplies and other development costs.

YEAR PROGRAM STARTED: 1956

PURPOSE:
To make project-based grants to individuals and organizations and to produce public programs to foster the development and exchange of diverse and challenging ideas about architecture and its role in the arts, culture and society.

LEGAL BASIS:
Private foundation.

ELIGIBILITY:
Individuals and institutions may apply. No grants for endowments, general operating expenses, capital projects, scholarship aid or for work in pursuit of an academic degree (except for the Carter Manny Award), debt or expenses incurred prior to the date of grant request.

NO. AWARDS: 124 for the year 2019.

APPLICATION INFO:
Application to the Foundation involves a two-stage process and is open submission.

Stage One/Inquiry Form: Eligible candidates interested in applying for a grant must first submit an Inquiry Form. The Inquiry Form is available on the Foundation web site with each grant cycle and must be submitted online.

Stage Two/Proposal Form: Applicants whose projects best match the Foundation's priorities and interests are invited to submit a Proposal Form and supplementary materials. Applicants not invited to submit a Proposal Form are sent a decline letter at this stage. An invitation to submit a Proposal Form does not guarantee eventual funding.

Award Decision: Funding recommendations are presented to the Board of Trustees for consideration. If a grant is awarded, applicant will be asked to sign a Grant Agreement that outlines the conditions of the award, such as annual reporting. Funding decisions at all stages of the review are based on the priority of the proposed project as related to the Foundation's mission and interests, the project's fulfillment of the Foundation's criteria for evaluation, and availability of Foundation funds.

Duration: Varies.

Deadline: February 25 for grants to organizations; September 15 for grants to individuals. Carter Manny Award: November 15.

PUBLICATIONS:
Annual report; guidelines.

OFFICERS:
Sarah Herda, Director

Carolyn T. Kelly, Grants Manager
James Pike, Grant Project Manager

ADDRESS INQUIRIES TO:
See e-mail address above.

THE LEF FOUNDATION [374]
P.O. Box 382066
Cambridge, MA 02238-2066
(617) 492-5333
E-mail: gen@lef-foundation.org
Web Site: lef-foundation.org

FOUNDED: 1985

AREAS OF INTEREST:
Nonfiction film and video.

NAME(S) OF PROGRAMS:
● **Moving Image Fund**

TYPE:
The Foundation gives grants for preproduction, production and post production of nonfiction film and video.

YEAR PROGRAM STARTED: 2002

PURPOSE:
To fund the work of independent documentary film and video artists in the region; to broaden recognition and support for the artist's work both locally and nationally.

ELIGIBILITY:
Projects must be long format, with running times of 40 minutes or more. The primary creative personnel (director and/or producer) must reside in New England. Priority will be given to smaller scale projects with budgets under $400,000.

Applicants must have a fiscal sponsor, namely a nonprofit with a 501(c)(3) designation from the federal government, that has agreed to manage the fiscal activity of the grant.

Students enrolled in degree-granting programs may not apply. Multichannel or installation work will not be considered.

Selection will be based on the following criteria:
(1) quality of cinematic form and technique;
(2) originality of filmmaker's voice, vision and point of view;
(3) resonance and power of the film's core idea or story and;
(4) feasibility of production.

GEOG. RESTRICTIONS: New England.

FINANCIAL DATA:
Amount of support per award: Early Development: $2,500; Pre-Production: $5,000; Production: $15,000; Post-Production: $25,000.

Total amount of support: $235,000 annually.

NO. AWARDS: Early Development, Pre-Production and Production: Up to 6; Post-Production: Up to 4.

APPLICATION INFO:
Application form and guidelines are available on the Foundation web site.

Duration: Varies.

Deadline: January and June.

ADDRESS INQUIRIES TO:
Genevieve Carmel, Program Officer
(See address above.)

THE PAUL MELLON CENTRE FOR STUDIES IN BRITISH ART [375]
16 Bedford Square
London WC1B 3JA England
(44) 020 7580 0311
Fax: (44) 020 7636 6730
E-mail: info@paul-mellon-centre.ac.uk
Web Site: www.paul-mellon-centre.ac.uk

FOUNDED: 1970

AREAS OF INTEREST:
British art and architectural history.

NAME(S) OF PROGRAMS:
● **Educational Programme Grants**
● **Junior Fellowships**
● **Paul Mellon Centre Rome Fellowship**
● **Mid-Career Fellowships**
● **Postdoctoral Fellowships**
● **Research Support Grants**
● **Senior Fellowships**

TYPE:
Conferences/seminars; Fellowships; Project/program grants; Research grants. Educational Programme Grants for lectures, symposia, seminars or conferences on British art or architectural history.

The Junior Fellowship is to pursue ongoing doctoral research at an American or British university.

The Paul Mellon Centre Rome Fellowship offers fellowships to scholars working on Grand Tour subjects or in the field of Anglo-Italian cultural and artistic relations.

Mid-Career Fellowships are offered for research in the field of British art and architectural history.

The Postdoctoral Fellowship works to transform doctoral research into publishable form such as a book, series of articles, or exhibition catalogues.

Research Support Grants are for expenses in pursuit of research.

The Senior Fellowship supports an established scholar in the field of British art and architectural history to complete a manuscript or book for immediate publication.

YEAR PROGRAM STARTED: 1998

PURPOSE:
To promote scholarship and publications.

LEGAL BASIS:
University-affiliated research center.

ELIGIBILITY:
Candidates for the Junior Fellowship may be of any nationality but must be enrolled in a graduate program at an American or other non-British university for study in the U.K. or at a non-American university for study in the U.S.

Candidates for Mid-Career Fellowships are academics or scholars at universities, museums, galleries or other institutions who are established in their careers and were awarded their Doctorates over six years previously. Applications are also welcome from independent and freelance scholars, and from individuals who do not hold a Doctorate. All applicants must have an established scholarly profile.

The Postdoctoral Fellowship is awarded within four years of an applicant's doctoral award. Applicants must have had their doctoral theses successfully examined.

Applicants for the Rome Fellowship should, preferably, be competent in spoken and written Italian.

FINANCIAL DATA:
Amount of support per award: Varies.

NO. MOST RECENT APPLICANTS: 202 spring applicants and 236 autumn applicants for the year 2020.

NO. AWARDS: Junior Fellowships: 8; Mid-Career Fellowships: 11; Postdoctoral Fellowships: 15; Rome Fellowship: 1; Senior Fellowships: 3.

APPLICATION INFO:
Applications are submitted through the online system at grants.paul-mellon-centre.ac.uk.
Duration: Junior Fellowship and Rome Fellowship: Three months. Mid-Career Fellowship: Four months. Postdoctoral Fellowship: Six months. Senior Fellowship: Nine months.
Deadline: September 30 for autumn grant season. January 31 for spring grant season.

ADDRESS INQUIRIES TO:
Fellowships and Grants Manager
E-mail: grants@paul-mellon-centre.ac.uk

NATIONAL SOCIETY DAUGHTERS OF THE AMERICAN REVOLUTION [376]

1776 D Street, N.W.
Washington, DC 20006-5303
(202) 879-3263
E-mail: scholarships@nsdar.org
Web Site: www.dar.org

FOUNDED: 1895

AREAS OF INTEREST
Historic preservation.

NAME(S) OF PROGRAMS:
● **DAR Centennial Scholarship**

TYPE:
Scholarships.

YEAR PROGRAM STARTED: 1985

PURPOSE:
To provide ways and means to aid students in attaining higher education.

LEGAL BASIS:
Incorporated historical society.

ELIGIBILITY:
Applicants must be enrolled in the junior or senior year of a fully accredited college or university in the U.S. and pursuing a degree in the field of historic preservation, may reside in any state, and must be a U.S. citizen.

GEOG. RESTRICTIONS: United States.

FINANCIAL DATA:
Amount of support per award: $2,500.
Total amount of support: $5,000.

NO. AWARDS: 2.

APPLICATION INFO:
Applicants must use the DAR Scholarship Committee's online submission process found on the DAR public web site. Once applicants have set up their scholarship profile, they will be able to complete the application. If necessary, applicants will be able to provide access to individuals wishing to submit confidential letters of recommendations or school transcripts.
Duration: One year. Nonrenewable.
Deadline: January 31.

PUBLICATIONS:
American Spirit, magazine.

ADDRESS INQUIRIES TO:
National Vice Chairman
E-mail: darcentennialscholarship@nsdar.org

ROTCH TRAVELLING SCHOLARSHIP IN ARCHITECTURE [377]

Boston Society of Architects
290 Congress Street, Suite 200
Boston, MA 02210
(617) 391-4000
E-mail: chart@architects.org
Web Site: architects.org/rotch-travelling-scholarship

FOUNDED: 1883

AREAS OF INTEREST:
Architecture.

NAME(S) OF PROGRAMS:
● **Rotch Travelling Scholarship**

TYPE:
Awards/prizes; Fellowships; Travel grants. Traveling Fellowships. Rotch Travelling Scholarship awards a minimum of six months of foreign travel and study in the field of architecture and allied subjects.

YEAR PROGRAM STARTED: 1883

PURPOSE:
To provide young architects with the opportunity to gain experience with other cultures; to augment the architectural education of students of architecture at the highest level of scholarship within a studio format.

LEGAL BASIS:
Private trust.

ELIGIBILITY:
Candidates must be U.S. citizens who have obtained a professional degree (B.Arch./M.Arch.) from an accredited school in the last 10 years. Candidates must have one year full-time professional experience in a Massachusetts architecture firm as of January 1 of the competition year, or have obtained an accredited degree from an accredited Massachusetts school of architecture as of January 1 of the competition year.

GEOG. RESTRICTIONS: United States.

FINANCIAL DATA:
Amount of support per award: Minimum $40,000.

APPLICATION INFO:
Official application forms are available online.
Duration: Minimum six months.
Deadline: January.

ROYAL INSTITUTE OF BRITISH ARCHITECTS [378]

RIBA Research Fund
Education Department
66 Portland Place
London W1B 1AD England
(44) 020 7307 3625
E-mail: education@riba.org
Web Site: www.architecture.com

FOUNDED: 1834

AREAS OF INTEREST:
Architecture, and the arts and sciences connected therewith, in the U.K.

NAME(S) OF PROGRAMS:
● **RIBA Research Fund**

TYPE:
Research grants. Grants to support independent research conducted by academics or practitioners in the field of architecture.

PURPOSE:
To support individuals who wish to conduct research in the field of architecture, with the anticipation that the final output will contribute towards the development of architecture as a discipline and a profession.

ELIGIBILITY:
Open to applicants interested in a wide range of subjects relevant to the advancement of architecture, and connected arts and sciences, in the U.K.

Grants from the RIBA Research Fund are for closely defined pieces of architectural research and support practice-led or academic research, but will not support course fees and subsistence costs for Ph.D./M.Phil. or Master's programmes. Grants are given only to named individuals, not organisations.

Applicants based outside the U.K. are also eligible to apply; however, the research work must in the main be undertaken within the U.K.

GEOG. RESTRICTIONS: United Kingdom.

FINANCIAL DATA:
Grants will be determined by the estimated requirements of the project.
Amount of support per award: Maximum award not to exceed GBP 10,000.

CO-OP FUNDING PROGRAMS: A candidate may have funding from other sources.

NO. AWARDS: 4 for the year 2019.

APPLICATION INFO:
Application forms are available from the RIBA web site. Only requests up to GBP 10,000 will be considered.
Duration: Up to two years.
Deadline: Varies.

OFFICER:
Alan Vallance, Chief Executive

ADDRESS INQUIRIES TO:
Gillian Harrison
E-mail: gillian.harrison@riba.org

SNAME THE SOCIETY OF NAVAL ARCHITECTS AND MARINE ENGINEERS

99 Canal Center Plaza, Suite 310
Alexandria, VA 22314
(703) 997-6701
E-mail: sname@sname.org
Web Site: www.sname.org

TYPE:
Scholarships. SNAME annually offers competitive scholarships to undergraduate and graduate students of naval architecture, marine engineering, ocean engineering, or of other fields directly related to the maritime industry.

See entry 2404 for full listing.

SOCIETY OF ARCHITECTURAL HISTORIANS [379]

1365 North Astor Street
Chicago, IL 60610-2144
(312) 573-1365
Fax: (312) 573-1141
E-mail: fellowships@sah.org
Web Site: www.sah.org

FOUNDED: 1940

AREAS OF INTEREST:
Architecture and its related arts.

NAME(S) OF PROGRAMS:
- **Sally Kress Tompkins Fellowship**

TYPE:
Fellowships; Internships; Travel grants. The Sally Kress Tompkins Fellowship, a joint program of the Society of Architectural Historians and the National Park Service's Historic American Buildings Survey, permits an architectural historian to work on a 12-week project during the summer. The Fellow will prepare a written history to become part of the permanent collection focusing on either a specific nationally significant building/site, or a broader architectural history topic. The Fellow will be stationed in the field working in conjunction with a measured drawings team, or in the Washington, DC office. The Fellow will be selected by a jury of two SAH members and one HABS representative.

PURPOSE:
To advance the knowledge and understanding of architecture, design, landscape and urbanism worldwide.

LEGAL BASIS:
Nonprofit professional organization.

ELIGIBILITY:
Applicants should be pursuing graduate studies in architectural history or other related fields. SAH membership is not required, but strongly encouraged.

FINANCIAL DATA:
Award includes SAH conference registration and up to $1,000 for travel expenses.
Amount of support per award: $12,000 stipend.

CO-OP FUNDING PROGRAMS: National Park Service's Historic American Buildings Survey (HABS).

NO. AWARDS: 1.

APPLICATION INFO:
Details are available online.
Duration: 12 weeks.
Deadline: December 31.

PUBLICATIONS:
Newsletter; *Journal of the Society of Architectural Historians.*

ADDRESS INQUIRIES TO:
Beth Eifrig, Comptroller
(See address above.)

SOCIETY OF ARCHITECTURAL HISTORIANS [380]

1365 North Astor Street
Chicago, IL 60610-2144
(312) 573-1365
Fax: (312) 573-1141
E-mail: fellowships@sah.org
Web Site: www.sah.org

FOUNDED: 1940

AREAS OF INTEREST:
Architecture and its related arts.

NAME(S) OF PROGRAMS:
- **Study Program Fellowships**

TYPE:
Fellowships; Travel grants. Study Program Fellowships are offered in conjunction with each SAH Study Day or SAH Field Seminar to allow for a graduate student or emerging professional to participate in the program. These fellowships are funded by the SAH's Scott Opler Endowment for New Scholars.

PURPOSE:
To advance knowledge and understanding of architecture, design, landscape and urbanism worldwide.

LEGAL BASIS:
Nonprofit professional organization.

ELIGIBILITY:
Open to current full-time M.A. and Ph.D. students and emerging professionals who have received an M.A. or Ph.D. between 2017 and August 2021. Current membership in SAH is not required to apply; however, fellowship recipients will be required to join SAH before attending the tour and receiving the award.

FINANCIAL DATA:
Fellowship covers the single occupancy price of the tour package. In addition, a travel stipend of up to $200 is provided for travel to and from the Study Day/Field Seminar destination.

APPLICATION INFO:
Applicants must submit the following through the online portal:
(1) a statement (in English, 300 words) that explains how this fellowship will advance the applicant's studies or interests;
(2) a curriculum vitae (five pages maximum) and;
(3) one letter of recommendation (submitted using the online recommendation form).

PUBLICATIONS:
Newsletter; *Journal of the Society of Architectural Historians.*

ADDRESS INQUIRIES TO:
Beth Eifrig, Comptroller
(See address above.)

*PLEASE NOTE:
The travel stipend portion of the award is granted on a reimbursable basis, paid after the study tour with travel receipts and a completed Travel Reimbursement Form.

*SPECIAL STIPULATIONS:
Study Program Fellowship recipients are asked to complete a report for each day of the tour, which includes a paragraph explaining how the tour contributed to the recipient's research. Within one week of the conclusion of the tour, fellowship recipients are required to upload images to SAHARA (25 for a Study Day, 50 for a domestic Field Seminar, or 100 for an international Field Seminar).

SOCIETY OF ARCHITECTURAL HISTORIANS [381]

1365 North Astor Street
Chicago, IL 60610-2144
(312) 573-1365
Fax: (312) 573-1141
E-mail: fellowships@sah.org
Web Site: www.sah.org

FOUNDED: 1940

AREAS OF INTEREST:
Architecture and its related arts.

NAME(S) OF PROGRAMS:
- **Gill Family Foundation Dissertation Research Fellowship**

TYPE:
Fellowships. Gill Family Foundation Dissertation Research Fellowship supports dissertation research in the field of architectural history and related areas including, but not limited to, the history of interiors, landscapes, urbanism, architectural theory, and architectural criticism by graduate students whose work has potential to impact discourse in the field.

PURPOSE:
To advance knowledge and understanding of architecture, design, landscape and urbanism worldwide.

LEGAL BASIS:
Nonprofit professional organization.

ELIGIBILITY:
Application is open to citizens of any country who are studying at a university in the U.S. Applicant must meet the following criteria:
(1) be admitted to candidacy for a doctoral degree in architectural history or a related field including, but not limited to, the history of interiors, landscapes, urbanism, architectural theory, and architectural criticism;
(2) be a current member of the Society of Architectural Historians and;
(3) be nominated by their department and invited to apply by the SAH.

Application and dissertation must be written in English.

A department may only nominate one applicant per year. Multiple departments at a university with qualified Ph.D. programs may each nominate a candidate.

Eligibility will be focused on projects that are original and have the potential to impact the field of architecture.

FINANCIAL DATA:
Stipend to be used for dissertation research needs and expenses, including travel, accommodations and fees.
Amount of support per award: $5,000 stipend.

APPLICATION INFO:
Applicant must be nominated by their department and invited to apply by the SAH. Applicant must submit their completed application packet to the SAH office through the online portal. All submissions must include the following and be assembled into a single PDF document in this order:
(1) a cover letter with full contact details and identification of author and the main academic advisor(s), along with advisor contact details;
(2) a dissertation abstract (150 words);
(3) a project statement that describes the project goals, the significance of the work, and its contribution to the field (1,000 words);
(4) a literature review that explains how the project fits into the existing literature or research on the topic (500 words);
(5) a work plan for research (250 words);
(6) a writing sample (10 to 15 pages) and;
(7) a curriculum vitae.

Deadline: Nominations: June 30.
Application: July 31. Notification in January.

PUBLICATIONS:
Newsletter; *Journal of the Society of Architectural Historians.*

ADDRESS INQUIRIES TO:
Beth Eifrig, Comptroller
(See address above.)

*SPECIAL STIPULATIONS:
Upon announcing the fellowship recipient, SAH will release the first payment ($2,000). At a midpoint to be determined by the recipient and SAH, the recipient will submit a blog post (500 words) about their research or the challenges/process of researching their dissertation. After review and approval of the blog post, SAH will release the second payment ($2,000). At the conclusion of the recipient's stated research timeline, the recipient will submit a written narrative and financial report summarizing the research funded by the award and how the funds were spent. The recipient will also submit a minimum of 25 images to SAH's digital image archive SAHARA. After review and approval of the report and submission to SAHARA, SAH will release the final payment ($1,000).

SOCIETY OF ARCHITECTURAL HISTORIANS   [382]
1365 North Astor Street
Chicago, IL 60610-2144
(312) 573-1365
Fax: (312) 573-1141
E-mail: fellowships@sah.org
Web Site: www.sah.org

FOUNDED: 1940

AREAS OF INTEREST:
Architecture and its related arts.

NAME(S) OF PROGRAMS:
● **Charles E. Peterson Fellowship of the Buildings of the U.S. and the Athenaeum of Philadelphia**

TYPE:
Fellowships. In a joint program with the Athenaeum of Philadelphia, the Society of Architectural Historians offers an annual fellowship to support the participation of a graduate student in the research and writing for *SAH Archipedia*, the Society's open access encyclopedia of the built environment of the U.S. This fellowship was established in honor of Charles E. Peterson, FAIA, founder of the Historic American Buildings Survey. The recipient will research some aspect of American architecture prior to 1860.

YEAR PROGRAM STARTED: 2008

PURPOSE:
To advance knowledge and understanding of architecture, design, landscape and urbanism worldwide.

LEGAL BASIS:
Nonprofit professional organization.

ELIGIBILITY:
The fellowship is intended for students currently enrolled in graduate programs in art or architectural history, architectural design, urban planning, historic preservation, landscape architecture, American studies, or related disciplines. Preference will be given to SAH members.

The successful applicant need not reside in Philadelphia, although the Athenaeum will be glad to have the fellowship recipient use its collections.

FINANCIAL DATA:
Amount of support per award: $2,500.

APPLICATION INFO:
Applicants must submit the following materials through the online portal:
(1) a cover letter discussing their research interests and professional goals;
(2) a curriculum vitae or resume;
(3) a brief writing sample (five to 10 pages) and;
(4) recommendation from an advisor or principal professor (submitted using the online recommendation form).
Deadline: December 31. Awarded by February 28.

PUBLICATIONS:
Newsletter; *Journal of the Society of Architectural Historians.*

ADDRESS INQUIRIES TO:
Beth Eifrig, Comptroller
(See address above.)

*SPECIAL STIPULATIONS:
The fellowship grant will be contingent upon the recipient's completion of the project, which is expected to require 150 hours of work.

WASHINGTON UNIVERSITY IN ST. LOUIS   [383]
Graduate School of Architecture and Urban Design
One Brookings Drive, Campus Box 1079
St. Louis, MO 63130-4899
(314) 935-4636
E-mail: treece.audrey@wustl.edu
Web Site: www.steedmanfellowship.wustl.edu

FOUNDED: 1926

AREAS OF INTEREST:
Architectural education.

NAME(S) OF PROGRAMS:
● **James Harrison Steedman Memorial Fellowship in Architecture**

TYPE:
Awards/prizes; Fellowships; Travel grants. An award made on the basis of a research proposal and portfolio that requires the recipient to travel and study abroad for six to 12 months. Not to be used towards tuition.

YEAR PROGRAM STARTED: 1926

PURPOSE:
To assist well-qualified architectural graduates to benefit by travel and study of architecture in foreign countries.

ELIGIBILITY:
Open to graduates of an accredited school of architecture, regardless of age, for a period up to eight years after the receipt of their first professional degree. Candidates must have at least one year of practical experience in the office of a practicing architect. Citizens of all countries are eligible.

FINANCIAL DATA:
Amount of support per award: $50,000 stipend for six to 12 months of travel abroad.
Total amount of support: $50,000.

NO. MOST RECENT APPLICANTS: 100.

NO. AWARDS: 1 awarded biennially.

APPLICATION INFO:
Registration forms are available online. Applications are available in August every odd year and fellowships are awarded in the spring every even year.

Duration: Six to 12 months.

PUBLICATIONS:
Application guidelines.

GOVERNING BOARD:
Patty Heyda
David Polzin
William Wischmeyer

ADDRESS INQUIRIES TO:
Audrey Treece, Programs Manager
(See address above.)

Arts (multiple disciplines)

ACADEMY FOUNDATION OF THE ACADEMY OF MOTION PICTURE ARTS AND SCIENCES
1313 North Vine Street
Los Angeles, CA 90028
(310) 247-3000
E-mail: saa@oscars.org
Web Site: www.oscars.org/SAA

TYPE:
Awards/prizes.

See entry 495 for full listing.

ALABAMA STATE COUNCIL ON THE ARTS   [384]
201 Monroe Street
Suite 110
Montgomery, AL 36104-3721
(334) 242-4076
E-mail: staff@arts.alabama.gov
Web Site: www.arts.alabama.gov

FOUNDED: 1966

AREAS OF INTEREST:
Architecture, literature, fine arts, arts in education, museums and libraries, music, and creative and performing arts.

CONSULTING OR VOLUNTEER SERVICES:
Strengthens cultural activities already in existence, assists in formation of new cultural activities, works towards improving the quality of presentations by both professional and amateur organizations and offers assistance to culturally oriented groups.

NAME(S) OF PROGRAMS:
● **Art and Cultural Facilities**
● **Arts-in-Education**
● **Community Arts Development**
● **Folk Arts**
● **Literary Art**
● **Performing Arts**
● **Visual Arts and Crafts**

TYPE:
Awards/prizes; Challenge/matching grants; Conferences/seminars; Development grants; Fellowships; General operating grants; Internships; Project/program grants; Residencies; Technical assistance. Grants to various disciplines comprising technical and financial assistance to local organizations in sponsoring activities of quality and promise in the various arts disciplines of the visual and performing arts within communities throughout Alabama.

YEAR PROGRAM STARTED: 1967

PURPOSE:
To increase interest, participation and support in the arts by supplementing local initiatives

and local funds in order to enable a greater number of quality activities to be seen or heard throughout the state.

LEGAL BASIS:
Alabama Law, Act No. 551, Regular Session 1967 and Act No. 1065, Regular Session, 1969.

ELIGIBILITY:
Applicants must be qualified organizations sponsoring arts events or programs for communities. Such groups include local arts councils, arts associations, museums, literary associations, colleges and universities, dance and theatre groups. Evidence of nonprofit status is required.

GEOG. RESTRICTIONS: Alabama.

FINANCIAL DATA:
Amount of support per award: $500 to $250,000.
Matching fund requirements: Equal amounts from other sources with exception of Artists Fellowships.

APPLICATION INFO:
Application forms can be found at the web site listed above.
Duration: One year. Renewal by reapplication.
Deadline: March 1, June 1 and September 1.

PUBLICATIONS:
Guide to Programs; *Alabama Arts*, magazine; *Touring & Presenting Guide.*

IRS I.D.: 63-6000619

EXECUTIVE COUNCIL:
James Harrison, Chairman
Dr. Henry Panion, III, Vice Chairman
Lisa Weil, Secretary

ADDRESS INQUIRIES TO:
Elliot A. Knight, Ph.D., Executive Director
(See address above.)

ALASKA STATE COUNCIL ON THE ARTS   [385]
161 Klevin Street
Suite 102
Anchorage, AK 99508-1506
(907) 269-6610
Fax: (907) 269-6601
E-mail: asca.info@alaska.gov
Web Site: arts.alaska.gov

FOUNDED: 1966

AREAS OF INTEREST:
Alaska arts and culture.

CONSULTING OR VOLUNTEER SERVICES:
Technical assistance for grantees.

TYPE:
General operating grants; Project/program grants; Residencies. Grants in 16 categories for organizations and individuals based in Alaska.

YEAR PROGRAM STARTED: 1966

PURPOSE:
To foster the development of the arts for all Alaskans through education, partnerships, grants and services.

LEGAL BASIS:
State agency.

GEOG. RESTRICTIONS: Alaska.

FINANCIAL DATA:
Amount of support per award: Varies according to program.

Matching fund requirements: All organizational grants require at least 1:1 match (cash).

APPLICATION INFO:
Specific guidelines and applications are available online.
Duration: One year.
Deadline: Varies according to program.

PUBLICATIONS:
Annual report; individual grant program guidelines.

ADDRESS INQUIRIES TO:
Executive Director
(See address above.)

THE ALLIANCE FOR YOUNG ARTISTS & WRITERS   [386]
557 Broadway
New York, NY 10012
Fax: (212) 389-3939
E-mail: info@artandwriting.org
Web Site: www.artandwriting.org

FOUNDED: 1923

AREAS OF INTEREST:
Art and writing.

NAME(S) OF PROGRAMS:
● **The Scholastic Art and Writing Awards**

TYPE:
Awards/prizes; Scholarships. The Alliance for Young Artists & Writers identifies teenagers with exceptional artistic and literary talent and brings their remarkable work to a national audience through The Scholastic Art and Writing Awards.

YEAR PROGRAM STARTED: 1923

PURPOSE:
To provide guidance and support for the next generation of artists and writers and reward outstanding achievement in the creative arts.

LEGAL BASIS:
501(c)(3) organization.

ELIGIBILITY:
Public, private, or home-school students (grades 7 to 12) in the U.S., Canada, or American schools abroad, regardless of citizenship, may submit work. Foreign exchange students who are temporarily residing in the U.S. may also participate.

FINANCIAL DATA:
Scholarship recipients are additionally eligible for school-specific, tuition scholarships at more than 50 colleges.
Amount of support per award: $1,000 to $10,000.
Total amount of support: More than $250,000 given annually through the Scholastic Awards program in awards and scholarships to top Awards recipients and their educators.

NO. AWARDS: Approximately 100.

APPLICATION INFO:
Guidelines vary by region. Contact Affiliate Partner for information.
Duration: One year.
Deadline: Varies by geographic location, approximately December 15 to January 15.

IRS I.D.: 13-3780998

ADDRESS INQUIRIES TO:
Daniel Embree, Director
National Programs
(See address above.)

AMERICA-ISRAEL CULTURAL FOUNDATION
25 West 39th Street, 8th Floor
New York, NY 10018
(212) 557-1600
Fax: (212) 557-1611
E-mail: admin@aicf.org
Web Site: www.aicf.org

TYPE:
Awards/prizes; Endowments; Fellowships; Project/program grants; Scholarships. For study in the arts of music, painting and sculpture, dance and drama, film and television, to be pursued either in Israel or in other countries.

See entry 869 for full listing.

THE AMERICAN CERAMIC SOCIETY   [387]
550 Polaris Parkway
Suite 510
Westerville, OH 43082
(614) 794-5827
(866) 721-3322
Fax: (614) 794-5817
E-mail: ynatividad@ceramics.org
Web Site: ceramics.org

FOUNDED: 1898

AREAS OF INTEREST:
Ceramic education and glass.

NAME(S) OF PROGRAMS:
● **Graduate Student Poster Contest**
● **Student Speaking Contest**
● **Undergraduate Student Poster Contest**

TYPE:
Awards/prizes.

PURPOSE:
To promote and encourage materials science and engineering studies in the discipline of glass and ceramics.

FINANCIAL DATA:
Amount of support per award: Varies.

APPLICATION INFO:
Contact the Society.
Duration: One-time awards.
Deadline: Graduate Student Poster Contest: March; Student Speaking and Undergraduate Student Poster Contests: September.

ADDRESS INQUIRIES TO:
Yolanda Natividad, Membership Engagement Manager
(See address and e-mail above.)

AMERICAN FIDELITY FOUNDATION   [388]
9000 Cameron Parkway
Oklahoma City, OK 73114
(405) 523-5008
E-mail: joella.ramsey@americanfidelity.com
Web Site: americanfidelityfoundation.org

AREAS OF INTEREST:
Education, arts, culture, health and human services, and civic and economic development.

TYPE:
Endowments; General operating grants; Research grants. Employment Matching Gifts.

ELIGIBILITY:
Organization must be tax-exempt with 501(c)(3) status. No grants to individuals.

FINANCIAL DATA:
Amount of support per award: Grants to a single charity are typically $500 to $5,000.
Total amount of support: Varies.

NO. AWARDS: 193 for the year 2020.

APPLICATION INFO:
Organizations that wish to be considered for a grant are asked to submit a letter of interest. If the Foundation chooses to pursue the project or program described, a formal application will be sent for completion to the organization within two weeks.
Duration: One year.

ADDRESS INQUIRIES TO:
Jo Ella Ramsey, Administrator
(See address above.)

AMERICAN SCHOOL OF CLASSICAL STUDIES AT ATHENS [389]
6-8 Charlton Street
Princeton, NJ 08540-5232
(609) 683-0800
Fax: (609) 924-0578
E-mail: application@ascsa.org
Web Site: www.ascsa.edu.gr

FOUNDED: 1881

AREAS OF INTEREST:
Humanities, social sciences and allied natural sciences.

NAME(S) OF PROGRAMS:
● CAORC Multi-Country Research Fellowships

TYPE:
Fellowships.

PURPOSE:
To provide support for individuals whose research has regional significance and requires travel to multiple countries, at least one of which hosts an American overseas research center such as the American School.

ELIGIBILITY:
Fellowship is limited to U.S. citizens. Open to U.S. doctoral candidates who have completed all Ph.D. requirements except the dissertation and U.S. postdoctoral scholars at all levels with research requiring travel to several countries with an American overseas research center.

School programs are generally open to qualified students and scholars at colleges or universities in the U.S. or Canada; restrictions may apply for specific fellowships and programs. The American School of Classical Studies at Athens does not discriminate on the basis of race, age, sex, sexual orientation, color, religion, ethnic origin, or disability when considering admission to any form of membership.

FINANCIAL DATA:
School fees are to be paid out of the fellowship stipend by the recipient. Fellowship does not include travel costs, housing, board, and other living expenses.
Amount of support per award: Stipend up to $11,000.

CO-OP FUNDING PROGRAMS: Fellowships for Multi-Country Research are funded by the Bureau of Educational and Cultural Affairs of the U.S. Department of State through a grant to the Council of American Overseas Research Centers.

NO. AWARDS: Approximately 8.

APPLICATION INFO:
Application guidelines are available at CAORC's web site (www.caorc.org). Upon notice from CAORC, successful applicants must immediately submit the ASCSA Visiting Associate Member application with a copy of the CAORC application online.
Duration: Doctoral and postdoctoral scholars: Minimum of 90 days.
Deadline: Late January.

STAFF:
Jenifer Neils, Director

ADDRESS INQUIRIES TO:
See e-mail address above.

*SPECIAL STIPULATIONS:
Recipients may not hold any other federally funded grant at the same time, such as a Fulbright or NEH Fellowship.

Membership application to the ASCSA must be made online on the web site at the same time one applies to any outside funding organization for work at the School.

A final report is due at the end of the award period, and the ASCSA expects that copies of all publications that result from research conducted as a Fellow of the ASCSA be contributed to the relevant library of the School.

ARIZONA COMMISSION ON THE ARTS [390]
417 West Roosevelt Street
Phoenix, AZ 85003
(602) 771-6502
Fax: (602) 256-0282
E-mail: info@azarts.gov
Web Site: www.azarts.gov

FOUNDED: 1967

AREAS OF INTEREST:
Performing arts, visual arts and literary arts.

TYPE:
Challenge/matching grants; Conferences/seminars; Development grants; General operating grants; Internships; Project/program grants; Research grants; Technical assistance. Specialized library services to artists and arts organizations. Dedicated to making quality arts opportunities available to its citizens, the Arts Commission takes a leadership role in broadening the support systems for the arts and demonstrating how the arts are integral to the vitality of our communities and citizens.

YEAR PROGRAM STARTED: 1967

PURPOSE:
To stimulate and encourage public interest in the arts; to increase opportunities for all residents of Arizona to experience the arts; to assist individual artists and arts organizations in Arizona; to stimulate support and visibility for the arts in Arizona; to foster the preservation, promotion and availability of Arizona's diverse ethnic arts; to make the arts fundamental to education.

LEGAL BASIS:
State agency.

GEOG. RESTRICTIONS: Arizona.

FINANCIAL DATA:
Amount of support per award: Varies.
Total amount of support: Varies.

APPLICATION INFO:
Call for application or access from web site.

Duration: Varies.
Deadline: Varies.

ASIAN CULTURAL COUNCIL [391]
333 West 39th Street
Suite 1502
New York, NY 10018
(212) 843-0403
Fax: (212) 843-0343
E-mail: acc@accny.org
Web Site: www.asianculturalcouncil.org

FOUNDED: 1980

AREAS OF INTEREST:
Visual and performing arts of Asia.

NAME(S) OF PROGRAMS:
● Graduate Scholarship
● Individual Fellowship Program
● New York Fellowship Program
● Organization and Project Grant
● Travel Grant

TYPE:
Fellowships; Project/program grants; Scholarships; Travel grants. Support of cultural exchange in the visual and performing arts between the U.S. and those countries of Asia extending from Afghanistan through Japan.

Graduate Scholarships support students pursuing graduate degrees in the U.S., with priority given to students who do not have access to comparable programs at home, and to those studying in fields that are underrepresented in their home country.

Individual Fellowships provide support to individuals or two collaborators undertaking self-directed research trips. Partial funding for dissertation research projects of up to one year are also available in this category.

New York Fellowships provide support to individuals who wish to participate in a fellowship program based in New York City. Fellowships may involve targeted research, but open-ended exploration is also allowed and encouraged.

Organization and Project Grants are for organizations that are facilitating a cultural exchange opportunity for individual project participants, or for collaborations involving three or more individuals.

Travel Grants provide support to individuals or two collaborators who need modest financial support for travel.

YEAR PROGRAM STARTED: 1980

PURPOSE:
To award fellowships to individuals and grants to organizations to support projects that foster exchange between Asia and the U.S.; to fund regional travel within Asia.

LEGAL BASIS:
Public foundation organized under Section 501(c)(3).

ELIGIBILITY:
Grants are open to citizens and permanent residents of the countries of Asia from Afghanistan eastward through Japan and Indonesia, and citizens and permanent residents of the U.S. Individuals pursuing projects in their home countries are not supported. Priority consideration is generally given to individuals who have not previously received funding support from the Council.

FINANCIAL DATA:
The Asian Cultural Council's grant programs
are supported by endowment income and
annual contributions from foundations,
corporations, and individuals in the U.S. and
Asia. Levels of grant activity are based on
financial resources available.

Amount of support per award: Varies.

Total amount of support: Varies.

NO. MOST RECENT APPLICANTS: 500 annually.

NO. AWARDS: 50.

APPLICATION INFO:
Grant applicants must first submit the
appropriate online Individual or Organization
Inquiry form. Applications are available
through the web site September 1 through
October 31 of each calendar year for grants
in the following year.

Duration: Graduate Scholarship: One year.
Individual Fellowship: One to six months.
New York Fellowship: Six months.
Organization and Project Grant: Varies.
Travel Grant: Up to one month.

Deadline: Fall. Check web site for exact
date.

PUBLICATIONS:
Annual report.

IRS I.D.: 13-3018822

OFFICERS:
Wendy O'Neill, Chairman
Hans Michael Jebsen, Vice Chairman
Josie Cruz Natori, Vice Chairman
John R. Witt, Treasurer
Valerie Rockefeller Wayne, Secretary

TRUSTEES:
Kazuko Aso
Ernest de Leon Escaler
Jonathan Fanton
Douglas Tong Hsu
Tonia Hsu
Julie Ann Kohn
Yi Ling Mao
Janet Nathanail
Anne Straton Pierson
Carol Rattray
Missie Rennie
Charles Rockefeller
David Rockefeller, Jr.
Susan Rockefeller
Ruby Shang
Dan Swift
Sundaram Tagore
Yoichiro Ushioda
Shannon Wu
Jenny Yu Zheng
Mercedes Zobel

ADDRESS INQUIRIES TO:
E-mail: applications@accny.org

ASTRAEA LESBIAN
FOUNDATION FOR JUSTICE
116 East 16th Street, 7th Floor
New York, NY 10003
(212) 529-8021
Fax: (212) 982-3321
E-mail: info@astraeafoundation.org
Web Site: www.astraeafoundation.org

TYPE:
Awards/prizes.

See entry 890 for full listing.

THE WILLIAM G. BAKER, JR.
MEMORIAL FUND   [392]
11 East Mount Royal Avenue
2nd Floor
Baltimore, MD 21202
(410) 332-4172 ext. 150
Fax: (410) 837-4701
E-mail: mwarlow@bcf.org
Web Site: www.bcf.org/for-grantseekers/grants

FOUNDED: 1964

AREAS OF INTEREST:
Arts and culture.

NAME(S) OF PROGRAMS:
• **Baker Artist Portfolios**

TYPE:
Technical assistance.

YEAR PROGRAM STARTED: 1964

PURPOSE:
To strengthen Baltimore's arts and culture
sector.

LEGAL BASIS:
Private, nonprofit foundation.

ELIGIBILITY:
Cultural organizations (or their fiscal agents)
serving the Baltimore area that qualify as
public charities under Section 501(c)(3) of
the Internal Revenue Code.

The fund does not normally make grants to
endowment campaigns, annual appeals, event
sponsorships, services outside the greater
Baltimore area, or art programs and projects
that use the arts as a mechanism to achieve
other ends such as community development,
health, social justice, arts education or youth
development objectives.

GEOG. RESTRICTIONS: Greater Baltimore area.

FINANCIAL DATA:
Amount of support per award: $1,500 to
$45,000.
Total amount of support: $1,231,479 for the
year 2019.

NO. AWARDS: 86 for the year 2019.

APPLICATION INFO:
Applicants must complete the online
application and evaluation chart. Data Arts
Cultural Data Profile is required.
Duration: One year.
Deadline: March, July, October and
December.

IRS I.D.: 52-6057178

GOVERNING BOARD:
Connie E. Imboden, President
Gwen Davidson
Laura L. Gamble
Steven G. Ziger

ADDRESS INQUIRIES TO:
Melissa Warlow, Director
(See address above.)

BATON ROUGE AREA
FOUNDATION   [393]
100 North Street
Suite 900
Baton Rouge, LA 70802
(225) 387-6126
E-mail: lsmyth@braf.org
Web Site: www.braf.org

AREAS OF INTEREST:
Arts, cultural programs, education,
community development, human services,
environment, scholarships, medical and
health.

TYPE:
Capital grants; Challenge/matching grants;
Conferences/seminars; Demonstration grants;
Development grants; Matching gifts;
Project/program grants; Scholarships; Seed
money grants; Technical assistance; Training
grants; Visiting scholars.

PURPOSE:
To connect philanthropists with capable
nonprofits to make sure the needs of the
community are met; to invest in and manage
pivotal projects that can change the
community.

ELIGIBILITY:
Eligible organizations must be IRS 501(c)(3)
tax-exempt.

FINANCIAL DATA:
Amount of support per award: Varies.
Total amount of support: Varies.

APPLICATION INFO:
Application details are available online. All
applications must include a copy of the IRS
tax determination letter.
Duration: One year. Must reapply for
additional funding.

ADDRESS INQUIRIES TO:
Lois A. Smyth, Director of
Donor Services
(See address above.)

CALIFORNIA ARTS
COUNCIL   [394]
1300 I Street, Suite 930
Sacramento, CA 95814
(916) 322-6555
(800) 201-6201
Fax: (916) 322-6575
E-mail: kimberly.brown@arts.ca.gov
Web Site: www.arts.ca.gov

FOUNDED: 1976

AREAS OF INTEREST:
Operating and creative support to art
organizations, artists, visual and performing
arts programs in schools and after-school
programs.

CONSULTING OR VOLUNTEER SERVICES:
Sponsor conferences and technical assistance
to art organizations.

NAME(S) OF PROGRAMS:
• **Artists in Communities**
• **Artists in Schools**
• **Arts and Accessibility**
• **Arts and Public Media**
• **Arts Education Exposure**
• **Arts Integration Training**
• **Creative California Communities**
• **Cultural Pathways**
• **JUMP StArts**
• **Local Impact**
• **Organizational Development**
• **Professional Development**
• **Reentry Through the Arts**
• **Research in the Arts**
• **State-Local Partners**
• **Statewide and Regional Networks**
• **Veterans in the Arts**
• **Youth Arts Action**

TYPE:
Challenge/matching grants; Project/program
grants.

YEAR PROGRAM STARTED: 1976

PURPOSE:
To advance California in the arts and
creativity.

LEGAL BASIS:
State arts agency, funded by state budget and other sources.

ELIGIBILITY:
To be eligible for funding, a California-based group or organization should be an incorporated nonprofit and have been in existence at least two years and be able to demonstrate fiscal and managerial responsibility. Grants are given to provide in-school and after-school arts educational activities, assistance for specific artistic services such as events, exhibitions and publications, to expand participation by segments of the public who have had limited access to cultural events, and to encourage and enhance communication among artists, organizations and the general public.

GEOG. RESTRICTIONS: California.

FINANCIAL DATA:
Amount of support per award: Varies according to program.
Total amount of support: Varies.
Matching fund requirements: Varies.

NO. MOST RECENT APPLICANTS: Approximately 1,400.

NO. AWARDS: Approximately 1,100.

APPLICATION INFO:
Contact the Council.
Duration: Six months to two years.
Deadline: Varies according to program.

PUBLICATIONS:
Guide to programs; applications; newsletters.

COUNCIL MEMBERS:
Nashormeh Lindo, Chairperson
Jaime Galli, Vice Chairperson
Larry Baza
Jodie Evans
Kathleen Gallegos
Stanlee R. Gatti
Lilia Gonzales-Chavez
Donn K. Harris
Alex Israel
Consuelo Montoya
Jonathan Moscone

ADDRESS INQUIRIES TO:
Kimberly Brown
Public Affairs Specialist
(See address above.)

CINTAS FOUNDATION [395]
8724 Sunset Drive
P.M.B. 528
Miami, FL 33173
E-mail: info@cintasfoundation.org
Web Site: www.cintasfoundation.org

FOUNDED: 1981

AREAS OF INTEREST:
Architecture and design, creative writing, music composition and the visual arts.

NAME(S) OF PROGRAMS:
● Cintas Fellowships in the Arts

TYPE:
Awards/prizes; Fellowships. Awarded to persons of Cuban citizenship or lineage residing outside Cuba for achievement of a creative nature in architecture, painting, sculpture, printmaking, music composition and literature.

PURPOSE:
To recognize outstanding creative work done by a person from Cuba or a person of Cuban descent.

LEGAL BASIS:
Private, not-for-profit agency.

ELIGIBILITY:
Applications are open to professionals in the creative arts, of Cuban citizenship or lineage, who can give evidence of their creative production by records of exhibitions, performances or (when appropriate) by published books or scores. Students wishing to pursue academic programs are not eligible for awards nor are performing artists as opposed to creative artists. Although there is no fixed age limit, the Fellowships are intended for young professionals in the arts who have completed their academic and technical training.

FINANCIAL DATA:
Amount of support per award: $20,000, paid in four equal quarterly stipends.
Total amount of support: Varies.

NO. MOST RECENT APPLICANTS: 150.

NO. AWARDS: 3 to 4 annually.

APPLICATION INFO:
Eligible candidates may request application forms and letter of reference forms from the Foundation. Applications should be in English or Spanish and should be accompanied by supporting documentation of an appropriate nature, such as published books or music scores or photographs and reproductions of paintings or sculpture.
Duration: 12 consecutive months beginning October 10.
Deadline: June 1.

COLORADO CREATIVE INDUSTRIES [396]
1600 Broadway, Suite 2500
Denver, CO 80202
(303) 892-3840
Fax: (303) 892-3848
TDD: (303) 894-2664
E-mail: oedit_creativeindustries@state.co.us
Web Site: oedit.colorado.gov/colorado-creative-industries

FOUNDED: 1967

AREAS OF INTEREST:
Visual arts, literature, performing arts, folk arts and media arts, youth-at-risk and economic benefits.

NAME(S) OF PROGRAMS:
● Arts in Society
● Colorado Creates
● Creative Career Advancement Grant

TYPE:
Project/program grants.

PURPOSE:
To promote, support and expand the creative industries to drive Colorado's economy, grow jobs and enhance the quality of life.

LEGAL BASIS:
State government agency.

ELIGIBILITY:
Colorado artists, creative small business and nonprofit tax-exempt organizations and municipalities.

GEOG. RESTRICTIONS: Colorado.

FINANCIAL DATA:
Amount of support per award: Arts in Society: $5,000 to $35,000; Career Advancement: $500 to $2,500; Colorado Creates: $4,000 to $10,000.
Total amount of support: Varies.

Matching fund requirements: Career Advancement: 1:1 cash match; Colorado Creates: Based on cash operating income. Creative Districts: 1:1 match.

NO. MOST RECENT APPLICANTS: 380.

NO. AWARDS: 300.

APPLICATION INFO:
Contact Colorado Creative Industries.
Duration: Colorado Creates: Two years on, one year off. Other programs: Generally one year.
Deadline: Colorado Creates: June.

PUBLICATIONS:
Annual report; guidelines; press releases; news clips; strategic plan.

OFFICERS:
Jared Polis, Governor
Margaret Hunt, Executive Director

ADDRESS INQUIRIES TO:
Christy Costello, Deputy Director
(See address above.)

THE COMMUNITY FOUNDATION OF LOUISVILLE, INC. [397]
325 West Main Street, Suite 1110
Louisville, KY 40202
(502) 585-4649
Fax: (502) 587-7484
E-mail: info@cflouisville.org
Web Site: www.cflouisville.org

AREAS OF INTEREST:
Visual arts, crafts, theatre, historic preservation, environment, education, religion and humanities.

TYPE:
Endowments; General operating grants; Scholarships.

PURPOSE:
To enrich the quality of life for all citizens in the Louisville area and to serve as a catalyst for promoting philanthropy within the local community.

ELIGIBILITY:
Grants are made to organizations that have tax-exempt status under Section 501(c)(3) of the Internal Revenue Code.

GEOG. RESTRICTIONS: United States.

FINANCIAL DATA:
Amount of support per award: Varies.
Total amount of support: Varies.

APPLICATION INFO:
Contact the Foundation.
Duration: One year.
Deadline: Details are available on the web site.

ADDRESS INQUIRIES TO:
For Scholarships:
Emory Williamson
E-mail: emoryw@cflouisville.org

For Grants:
Program Officer
E-mail: grants@cflouisville.org

CONGRESSIONAL BLACK CAUCUS FOUNDATION, INC.
1720 Massachusetts Avenue, N.W.
Washington, DC 20036
(202) 263-2800
Fax: (202) 263-0846
E-mail: scholarships@cbcfinc.org
Web Site: www.cbcfinc.org

TYPE:
Scholarships. CBC Spouses Performing Arts Scholarship, developed in honor of the late Curtis Mayfield, is intended to ensure that students pursuing a career in the performing arts receive the financial assistance to achieve their goals.

CBC Spouses Visual Arts Scholarship was established for students who are pursuing a career in the visual arts.

See entry 930 for full listing.

CONSEIL DES ARTS DE MONTREAL [398]
1210 East Sherbrooke Street
First Floor
Montreal QC H2L 2L9 Canada
(514) 280-3582
E-mail: nathalie.maille@montreal.ca
Web Site: www.artsmontreal.org

FOUNDED: 1956

AREAS OF INTEREST:
Visual arts, dance, theatre, music, literature, cinema, new artistic practices, video and electronic arts.

NAME(S) OF PROGRAMS:
● **Programme de tournees**
● **Programme General**

TYPE:
Awards/prizes; Development grants; Exchange programs; General operating grants; Project/program grants; Technical assistance. Grants to nonprofit professional organizations having their head offices in Montreal.

YEAR PROGRAM STARTED: 1956

PURPOSE:
To assist Montreal's artistic and cultural organizations.

LEGAL BASIS:
Regional organization.

ELIGIBILITY:
Professional, nonprofit organizations in Montreal.

GEOG. RESTRICTIONS: Montreal, Quebec.

FINANCIAL DATA:
Amount of support per award: Varies.
Total amount of support: $17,258,000 (CAN) for the year 2019.

NO. AWARDS: 581 for the year 2019.

APPLICATION INFO:
Contact the Conseil des Arts.
Duration: One fiscal year.
Deadline: Programme de tournees: September. Programme General: Varies by type of grant.

PUBLICATIONS:
Annual report.

STAFF:
Sylviane Martineau, Cultural Advisor, Dance
Marie-Michele Cron, Cultural Advisor, Digital Arts and Visual Arts
Marie-Anne Raulet, Cultural Advisor, Literature, Cinema
Claire Metras, Cultural Advisor, Music
Salome Viguier, Cultural Advisor, New Artistic Practices
Frederic Cote, Cultural Advisor, Theatre

ADDRESS INQUIRIES TO:
Cultural Advisor
(See address above.)

THE CORPORATION OF YADDO [399]
312 Union Avenue
Saratoga Springs, NY 12866
(518) 584-0746
Fax: (518) 584-1312
E-mail: cwilliams@yaddo.org
Web Site: www.yaddo.org

FOUNDED: 1900

AREAS OF INTEREST:
Literature, visual arts, music composition, filmmaking, choreography, performance art and other creative arts.

NAME(S) OF PROGRAMS:
● **Artist Residencies**

TYPE:
Residencies; Travel grants.

YEAR PROGRAM STARTED: 1926

PURPOSE:
To enable artists to work in a quiet, protected and supportive environment.

LEGAL BASIS:
A publicly supported charity.

ELIGIBILITY:
For creative artists working at a professional level in their field. Artists of all backgrounds are encouraged to apply.

FINANCIAL DATA:
No cash grants. The award covers room, board and studio costs. A small fund exists to provide limited help towards the expenses of travel or renting equipment to invited guests of any discipline who otherwise might not be able to visit.

NO. MOST RECENT APPLICANTS: Approximately 1,500 annually.

APPLICATION INFO:
Applicants should apply to the Admissions Panel that best represents the project they wish to undertake should they be invited for a residency. Applicants may apply to only one admissions panel, in one genre, at a time. Applicants with concerns about choice of panel should contact the Program Director.

All application materials, including contact information, resume, work sample, and reference letters must be submitted electronically.
Duration: Up to two months.
Deadline: January 5 and August 1.

PUBLICATIONS:
Annual report; newsletter; case statement.

IRS I.D.: 14-1343055

OFFICERS:
Peter Kayafas, Chairperson
Janice Y.K. Lee, Chairperson
Alexi Worth, Vice Chairperson
Elaina Richardson, President
Candace Weir, Treasurer
Doug Wright, Corporate Secretary
Susan Brynteson, Recording Secretary

ADDRESS INQUIRIES TO:
Christy Williams, Program Manager
(See address above.)

COSTUME SOCIETY OF AMERICA [400]
P.O. Box 852
Columbus, GA 31902-0852
(706) 615-2851
(800) 272-9447 (U.S.)
E-mail: national.office@costumesocietyamerica.com
Web Site: www.costumesocietyamerica.com

FOUNDED: 1973

AREAS OF INTEREST:
Costume, art history, research, textile and fashion design, museum studies and anthropology.

NAME(S) OF PROGRAMS:
● **Stella Blum Research Grant**
● **CSA Travel Research Grant**
● **Adele Filene Student Presenter Grant**

TYPE:
Awards/prizes; Conferences/seminars; Development grants; Fellowships; Project/program grants; Research grants; Scholarships; Travel grants. Stella Blum Research Grant is a merit award for a student researching a North American costume topic.

CSA Travel Research Grant aids in travel to collections to any library, archive, museum or site for research to further an ongoing project.

Adele Filene Student Presenter Grant assists the travel of a CSA student member to that year's CSA national symposium to present either a juried paper or poster.

YEAR PROGRAM STARTED: 1987

PURPOSE:
To advance the global understanding of all aspects of dress and appearance.

ELIGIBILITY:
Must be a Costume Society of America member for all awards.

CSA Travel Research Grant: Must be a CSA nonstudent member. Proof must be given that work on the project is already underway.

Adele Filene Student Presenter Grant: Must be currently enrolled as a student with a juried paper or poster accepted by the CSA symposium.

FINANCIAL DATA:
Amount of support per award: Stella Blum Research Grant: $3,000, plus up to $600 to present completed research at the National Symposium and one day presentation registration fee; CSA Travel Research Grant: $2,100; Adele Filene Student Presenter Grant: Up to $600, plus one day presentation registration fee.
Total amount of support: Varies.

NO. MOST RECENT APPLICANTS: 12.

NO. AWARDS: 3.

APPLICATION INFO:
Information is available under "Resources/Grants, Awards and Honors" on the Society's web site.
Duration: One year.
Deadline: Grant deadlines are posted online.

ADDRESS INQUIRIES TO:
Executive Director
(See e-mail address above.)

DELAWARE DIVISION OF THE ARTS [401]
Carvel State Office Building
820 North French Street
Wilmington, DE 19801
(302) 577-8278
Fax: (302) 577-6561
E-mail: delarts@delaware.gov
Web Site: arts.delaware.gov

FOUNDED: 1969

AREAS OF INTEREST:
Performing arts, visual arts, literature and media.

CONSULTING OR VOLUNTEER SERVICES:
Technical assistance to community groups and arts organizations.

NAME(S) OF PROGRAMS:
- **Arts in Education**
- **Arts Organizations Grants**
- **Community Based Organizations Grants**
- **Gallery Program**
- **Individual Artist Fellowships**
- **Opportunity Grants**

TYPE:
Challenge/matching grants; Conferences/seminars; Fellowships; General operating grants; Project/program grants; Residencies; Technical assistance. Grants to Delaware nonprofit, tax-exempt organizations for projects in the arts. Fellowships program for individual creative artists who reside in Delaware.

YEAR PROGRAM STARTED: 1970

PURPOSE:
To nurture and support the arts to enhance the quality of life for all Delawareans.

LEGAL BASIS:
State agency.

ELIGIBILITY:
Applicants must be nonprofit, tax-exempt organizations in the state of Delaware. Fellowship applicants are individual creative artists who reside in Delaware.

GEOG. RESTRICTIONS: Delaware.

FINANCIAL DATA:
Amount of funds available is determined by state appropriation and funding from the National Endowment for the Arts.
Amount of support per award: Variable according to program.
Total amount of support: $4,235,000 for fiscal year 2020.
Matching fund requirements: Organization grants matching requirements vary according to program.

NO. MOST RECENT APPLICANTS: 498 for fiscal year 2020.

NO. AWARDS: 253 for fiscal year 2020.

APPLICATION INFO:
Application must be submitted online.
Duration: Varies.
Deadline: March 1 for most grants. Announcement July 1 for most grants.

ADDRESS INQUIRIES TO:
Paul Weagraff, Director
(See address above.)

DEPARTMENT OF ECONOMIC AND COMMUNITY DEVELOPMENT/CONNECTICUT OFFICE OF THE ARTS [402]
450 Columbus Boulevard, 4th Floor
Hartford, CT 06103
(860) 500-2300
E-mail: elizabeth.shapiro@ct.gov
Web Site: www.cultureandtourism.org

FOUNDED: 1965

AREAS OF INTEREST:
Arts, program services, and infrastructure.

CONSULTING OR VOLUNTEER SERVICES:
Volunteer Lawyers for the Arts program.

TYPE:
Challenge/matching grants; Conferences/seminars; Endowments; Fellowships; General operating grants; Internships; Project/program grants; Technical assistance. Grants are available to Connecticut artists, arts institutions, arts organizations and nonprofit arts-sponsoring organizations for program support and technical assistance.

Project grants are available to non-arts organizations using arts or conducting arts programming, as well as schools, libraries and PTOs.

YEAR PROGRAM STARTED: 1965

PURPOSE:
To invest in the state's art-based cultural activities and infrastructure in ways that will advance the attractiveness and competitiveness of Connecticut cities, towns and villages as meaningful communities in which to live, work, learn and play.

LEGAL BASIS:
The State of Connecticut Enabling Legislation, Public Act No. 78-187 created the original Connecticut Commission on the Arts.

ELIGIBILITY:
Connecticut artists, art institutions, units of state or local government, art organizations and nonprofit arts-sponsoring associations whose principle residence is in Connecticut. Ineligible programs are those which take place out of state, student projects, fund-raising benefits, social activities, membership activities, scholarships, underwriting of past deficits or capital expenditures.

GEOG. RESTRICTIONS: Connecticut.

FINANCIAL DATA:
Amount of support per award: Varies.
Total amount of support: Varies.

CO-OP FUNDING PROGRAMS: Matching funds, Federal-state partnership and designated regional service organizations.

NO. AWARDS: 713.

APPLICATION INFO:
Specific guidelines for all grant programs may be found on the Connecticut Office of the Arts web site under "funding opportunities." Grant applications are available from the online grant portal.
Duration: Varies.
Deadline: Varies.

PUBLICATIONS:
Copyright Law; *Non-Profit Incorporation-A Guide for Artists and Organizations*; *Contract Law for Artists and Organizations*; *Culture and Tourism Newsletter*; Bi-Monthly Bulletin; *Art in Public Spaces Program Guide*; *Hot Schools Transform Education*; *Economic Impact of the Nonprofit Arts Industry in Connecticut*; *Performing Artists*, online directories.

ADDRESS INQUIRIES TO:
Rhonda Olisky, Special Projects Coordinator
E-mail: rhonda.olisky@ct.gov
(See address above.)

DISTRICT OF COLUMBIA COMMISSION ON THE ARTS AND HUMANITIES [403]
200 I Street, S.E.
Suite 1400
Washington, DC 20003
(202) 724-5613
Fax: (202) 727-4135
TDD: (202) 727-3148
E-mail: heran.sereke-brhan2@dc.gov
Web Site: dcarts.dc.gov

FOUNDED: 1968

AREAS OF INTEREST:
The arts and humanities in the District of Columbia.

NAME(S) OF PROGRAMS:
- **Art Bank Program**
- **Arts and Humanities Education Projects**
- **Arts and Humanities Fellowship Program**
- **Curatorial Grant Program**
- **East of the River Program**
- **Facilities and Buildings**
- **General Operating Support**
- **LiftOff**
- **Projects, Events and Festivals**
- **Public Art Building Communities**
- **Sister Cities Grant**
- **UPSTART Program**

TYPE:
Awards/prizes; Capital grants; Challenge/matching grants; Conferences/seminars; Exchange programs; Fellowships; General operating grants; Grants-in-aid; Project/program grants; Research grants; Residencies. Services provided to arts institutions and individual artists including inquiry services, technical assistance and funding.

YEAR PROGRAM STARTED: 1968

PURPOSE:
To administer funds to arts organizations, community organizations and individual artists to support arts endeavors within the District of Columbia.

LEGAL BASIS:
State arts agency authorized by executive order.

ELIGIBILITY:
Applicants must be artists or arts professionals (e.g., presenters, producers, and educators) aged 18 or older and residents of Washington, DC.

Organizations must be located in Washington, DC and be nonprofit IRS 501(c)(3) arts organizations within the District of Columbia at least two years prior to application in some programs and one year in most others. Organizations are also required to participate in the DC Cultural Data Project.

Grant funds cannot be used for scholarships, reserve funds, or any food/receptions. Fiscal agents are strictly prohibited.

GEOG. RESTRICTIONS: Washington, DC.

FINANCIAL DATA:
Amount of support per award: Varies by program.
Total amount of support: Varies.
Matching fund requirements: Most grants require organizations to have matching funds.

CO-OP FUNDING PROGRAMS: National Endowment for the Arts.

REPRESENTATIVE AWARDS:
$18,766 to Thomas Circle Singers for general operating support; $250,000 to Studio Theatre Inc., $35,000 to Project Create.

APPLICATION INFO:
Applications must be submitted through the online grants portal. The Commission will not accept mailed, e-mailed or hand-delivered copies of grant applications.

Duration: All expenses must be paid within the District's fiscal year of October 1 to September 30.

Deadline: Varies per grant cycle.

PUBLICATIONS:
Guide to Grants.

ADDRESS INQUIRIES TO:
Heran Sereke-Brhan, Executive Director (See address above.)

EAST TENNESSEE FOUNDATION

520 West Summit Hill Drive
Suite 1101
Knoxville, TN 37902
(865) 524-1223
(877) 524-1223
Fax: (865) 637-6039
E-mail: etf@etf.org
Web Site: www.easttennesseefoundation.org

TYPE:
Project/program grants; Scholarships; Seed money grants; Technical assistance. The Foundation is comprised of 474 philanthropic funds and nine supporting organizations.

See entry 1011 for full listing.

FENIMORE ART MUSEUM   [404]

5798 State Highway 80
Cooperstown, NY 13326
(607) 547-1416
Fax: (607) 547-1404
E-mail: publications@fenimoreart.org
Web Site: www.fenimoreartmuseum.org

FOUNDED: 1899

AREAS OF INTEREST:
New York state and culture.

NAME(S) OF PROGRAMS:
● **Henry Allen Moe Prize**

TYPE:
Awards/prizes. Prizes for published catalogues treating collections located or exhibited in New York state.

YEAR PROGRAM STARTED: 1983

PURPOSE:
To foster and recognize scholarship in art history and decorative arts studies in the form of published catalogues located or exhibited in New York state.

LEGAL BASIS:
Private.

ELIGIBILITY:
Entries should add new information to what is known about the subject and may completely document an exhibition. Only catalogues treating collections located or exhibited in New York state qualify.

FINANCIAL DATA:
Amount of support per award: $250 to $1,000.

NO. MOST RECENT APPLICANTS: Approximately 8.

NO. AWARDS: 1 for the year 2017.

APPLICATION INFO:
Entries must have been published in the previous year. Submit four copies, accompanied by a letter of transmittal stating intent to enter the contest.
Deadline: On or before February 28 for awards in the current year.

PUBLICATIONS:
New York History; Heritage Magazine.

OFFICERS AND TRUSTEES:
Jeffrey H. Pressman, M.D., Chairman of the Board
Thomas O. Putnam, Vice Chairman
Stephen M. Duff
Douglas E. Evelyn
Kathleen Flanagan
Nellie Gipson
Shelley Graham
Robert S. Hanft
Josef E. Jelinek
Charles B. Kieler
Doris Fischer Malesardi
Erna Morgan McReynolds
Anne G. Older
Ellen Tillapaugh
Richard C. Vanison

ADDRESS INQUIRIES TO:
Cynthia G. Falk
Assistant Professor of Material Culture
(See address above.)

FLORIDA DEPARTMENT OF STATE, DIVISION OF CULTURAL AFFAIRS   [405]

500 South Bronough Street
Tallahassee, FL 32399-0250
(850) 245-6470
E-mail: dcainfo@dos.myflorida.com
Web Site: dos.myflorida.com/cultural

FOUNDED: 1969

AREAS OF INTEREST:
The Division of Cultural Affairs administers the cultural grant programs of the Department of State and is responsible for planning and implementing arts programs statewide, providing technical assistance to artists and arts organizations, awarding, administering, monitoring and evaluating the grants program, disseminating arts-related information and encouraging cultural development in Florida.

CONSULTING OR VOLUNTEER SERVICES:
Facilitative services in all areas are available.

NAME(S) OF PROGRAMS:
● **Cultural Facilities Program**
● **Florida Cultural Endowment Program**
● **General Program Support Grants Program**
● **Specific Cultural Projects Grants Program**

TYPE:
Capital grants; Conferences/seminars; Endowments; Formula grants; General operating grants; Grants-in-aid; Internships; Project/program grants. Cultural facilities grants. Cash grants cover program expenses or capital improvement, depending on the program.

YEAR PROGRAM STARTED: 1969

PURPOSE:
To encourage the creation of projects that promote excellence in the arts and that strive to bring arts to a communitywide audience.

LEGAL BASIS:
State government agency.

ELIGIBILITY:
To apply for a grant, an organization must qualify as a political subdivision of a municipal, county or state government in Florida or be a not-for-profit, tax-exempt Florida corporation, meet specific budgetary and program requirements as outlined for the appropriate artistic disciplines, special programs and funding categories, match dollar-for-dollar, in most cases, the grant amount requested from the Division and meet all legal and financial requirements described in the *Guide to Cultural Programs.*

An individual artist living and working in the state of Florida may apply.

GEOG. RESTRICTIONS: Florida.

FINANCIAL DATA:
Amount of support per award: Varies depending upon grant program and specific eligibility.
Total amount of support: Varies by program.
Matching fund requirements: In most cases, grants are matched 1:1.

NO. MOST RECENT APPLICANTS: 1,067 for fiscal year 2019-20.

NO. AWARDS: 978 for the year 2019-20.

APPLICATION INFO:
Program guidelines can be downloaded from the web site.
Duration: One year or up to two years.
Deadline: June for General Program Support, Cultural Facilities and Specific Cultural Projects grants.

OFFICERS:
Sandy Shaughnessy, Director, Division of Cultural Affairs

STAFF:
Teri Abstein, Contracts and Grants Manager

ADDRESS INQUIRIES TO:
Teri Abstein
Contracts and Grants Manager or
Curtis Young
Operations and Management Consultant
(See address above.)

FORECAST PUBLIC ART   [406]

2380 Wycliff Avenue
Suite 200
St. Paul, MN 55114
(651) 641-1128
E-mail: grants@forecastpublicart.org
Web Site: www.forecastpublicart.org

FOUNDED: 1978

AREAS OF INTEREST:
Public art.

CONSULTING OR VOLUNTEER SERVICES:
Provide consulting for public artists and communities.

NAME(S) OF PROGRAMS:
● **Early-Career Artist Project Grant**
● **Early-Career Artist Research and Development Grant**
● **Mid-Career Professional Development Grant**
● **Mid-Career Project Grant**

TYPE:
Awards/prizes; Project/program grants; Research grants.

YEAR PROGRAM STARTED: 1988

PURPOSE:
To fund emerging and midcareer artists of all disciplines to develop and/or produce public art projects.

LEGAL BASIS:
Private nonprofit corporation.

ELIGIBILITY:
Open to emerging and midcareer artists of all disciplines. Applicant must be a Minnesota resident.

Mid-Career Project Grant applicants must be midcareer public artists.

GEOG. RESTRICTIONS: Minnesota.

FINANCIAL DATA:
Amount of support per award: Early-Career Artist Project Grant: $8,000; Early-Career Artist Research and Development Grant: $2,500; Mid-Career Professional Development Grant: $5,000; Mid-Career Project Grant: $10,000.

NO. MOST RECENT APPLICANTS: 50 to 100 per competition.

NO. AWARDS: Early-Career Artist Project Grant: 2; Early-Career Artist Research and Development Grant: 4; Mid-Career Professional Development Grant: 2; Mid-Career Project Grant: 5.

APPLICATION INFO:
Application information is available online.
Duration: 11 months.
Deadline: October.

PUBLICATIONS:
Forward, digital publication.

IRS I.D.: 41-1361351

STAFF:
Theresa Sweetland, Executive Director
Jen Krava, Director of Programming

ADDRESS INQUIRIES TO:
Jen Krava, Director of Programming
(See address above.)

CARL M. FREEMAN FOUNDATION [407]
31255 Americana Parkway
Selbyville, DE 19975
(302) 483-7639
Fax: (302) 483-7639
E-mail: grantsmanager@freemanfoundation.org
Web Site: www.carlfreemanfoundation.org

FOUNDED: 1960

AREAS OF INTEREST:
Facilitating, supporting and promoting innovative community-based leadership and giving.

NAME(S) OF PROGRAMS:
● FACES Grant

TYPE:
Capital grants; General operating grants.

YEAR PROGRAM STARTED: 2000

PURPOSE:
To provide funding and capacity-building support to nonprofit organizations in the communities served by the Carl M. Freeman Companies.

ELIGIBILITY:
Must be IRS-recognized 501(c)(3) tax-exempt, nonprofit organizations or public agencies serving the residents of the Companies' funding areas.

GEOG. RESTRICTIONS: Sussex County, Delaware and Montgomery County, Maryland.

FINANCIAL DATA:
Amount of support per award: $2,500, $5,000 or $10,000.
Total amount of support: $200,000 annually ($100,000 per geographic area).

APPLICATION INFO:
Guidelines are available on the web site.
Duration: Six months.
Deadline: Varies.

ADDRESS INQUIRIES TO:
Lindsay Richard, Grants Manager
(See address above.)

FREER GALLERY OF ART AND ARTHUR M. SACKLER GALLERY [408]
Smithsonian Institution, MRC 707
1050 Independence Avenue, S.W.
Washington, DC 20560
(202) 633-0401
E-mail: mirzas@si.edu
Web Site: www.freersackler.si.edu/research/fellowships-internships

FOUNDED: 1923

AREAS OF INTEREST:
Asian art, 19th and early 20th century American art.

CONSULTING OR VOLUNTEER SERVICES:
Docent tours for the public through Freer Gallery of Art and Arthur M. Sackler Gallery.

NAME(S) OF PROGRAMS:
● **The J.S. Lee Memorial Fellowship**
● **Smithsonian Institution Fellowship**
● **Anne van Biema Fellowship**

TYPE:
Awards/prizes; Fellowships; Internships; Project/program grants; Research grants; Technical assistance; Visiting scholars. The J.S. Lee Memorial Fellowship facilitates the international exchange of curatorial expertise and contributes to the professional development of Chinese art curators and academics.

Anne van Biema Fellowship is established to promote excellence in research and publication on the Japanese visual arts. One award is made each year to support a scholar at the postdoctoral level for a period of two to nine months.

YEAR PROGRAM STARTED: 1923

PURPOSE:
To advance scholarship of Asian art and 19th and early 20th century American art.

LEGAL BASIS:
U.S. government agency.

ELIGIBILITY:
Varies with each fellowship.

FINANCIAL DATA:
Amount of support per award: Varies.
Total amount of support: Varies.

CO-OP FUNDING PROGRAMS: Smithsonian Office of Fellowships and Grants, University of Michigan.

APPLICATION INFO:
For Smithsonian Fellowship, write to Office of Fellowships and Internships in the Smithsonian. For the J.S. Lee Memorial Fellowship, visit the fellowship page at www.jsleefellowship.org. Van Biema Fellowship information is available on the web site.

Duration: Varies.
Deadline: Varies.

PUBLICATIONS:
Annual report.

OFFICERS:
Chase F. Robinson, Director

ADDRESS INQUIRIES TO:
Sana Mirza
Scholarly Programs and Publications
(See address above.)

THE DAVID GEFFEN FOUNDATION
12011 San Vicente Boulevard
Suite 606
Los Angeles, CA 90049
(310) 581-5955
E-mail: ddishman@geffenco.com

TYPE:
General operating grants; Project/program grants.

See entry 1292 for full listing.

GEORGIA COUNCIL FOR THE ARTS [409]
75 Fifth Street, N.W.
Suite 1200
Atlanta, GA 30308
(404) 962-4827
E-mail: gaarts@gaarts.org
Web Site: gaarts.org

FOUNDED: 1968

AREAS OF INTEREST:
The arts.

CONSULTING OR VOLUNTEER SERVICES:
Extensive technical assistance to nonprofit arts organizations in all disciplines on matters of artistic, administrative or technical concern.

NAME(S) OF PROGRAMS:
● **Arts Education Program Grants**
● **Bridge Grant**
● **Cultural Facilities Grant**
● **Partner Grants**
● **Project Grants**
● **Vibrant Communities Grants**

TYPE:
General operating grants; Project/program grants.

YEAR PROGRAM STARTED: 1968

PURPOSE:
To cultivate the growth of Georgia communities through the arts.

LEGAL BASIS:
Government agency.

ELIGIBILITY:
Grants are made to nonprofit, tax-exempt arts organizations or units of government which are incorporated in the state of Georgia.

GEOG. RESTRICTIONS: Georgia.

FINANCIAL DATA:
Amount of support per award: $1,000 to $20,000.
Total amount of support: Over $1,000,000 for the year 2019.
Matching fund requirements: Varies.

NO. AWARDS: 132 for the year 2019.

APPLICATION INFO:
Grant applications are available online.

Duration: One year. Must reapply for additional funding.

Deadline: Varies.

PUBLICATIONS:
Application guidelines; quarterly newsletter.

ADDRESS INQUIRIES TO:
Tina Lilly, Executive Director
(See address above.)

NANCY GRAVES FOUNDATION [410]

33-20 48th Avenue, 2nd Floor
Long Island City, NY 11101
(718) 482-1100
E-mail: mail@nancygravesfoundation.org
Web Site: www.nancygravesfoundation.org

FOUNDED: 1996

AREAS OF INTEREST:
Visual arts.

NAME(S) OF PROGRAMS:
• **Nancy Graves Grant for Visual Artists**

TYPE:
Grant for nominated visual artists for work in any medium other than their own.

YEAR PROGRAM STARTED: 2000

PURPOSE:
To give assistance to individual artists; to maintain an archive of the Founder's life and work and organize exhibitions of her art.

ELIGIBILITY:
Grantees must be residents of the U.S. who have been working as artists for at least five years beyond his or her schooling. Grants will not be awarded to students. Applications will be solicited from nominated visual artists who wish to have the opportunity to master a technique, medium or discipline that is different from the one in which he or she is primarily recognized.

GEOG. RESTRICTIONS: United States.

FINANCIAL DATA:
Amount of support per award: $12,500 for the year 2020.

NO. AWARDS: 4 for the year 2020.

APPLICATION INFO:
Artist applicants must be nominated by Foundation nominators and will subsequently receive an application for consideration by a second panel of jurors.

Duration: One year.

Deadline: Varies.

STAFF:
Christina Hunter, Executive Director

ADDRESS INQUIRIES TO:
Christina Hunter, Executive Director
(See address above.)

HAMBIDGE [411]

P.O. Box 339
Rabun Gap, GA 30568
(706) 746-5718
Fax: (706) 746-9933
E-mail: center@hambidge.org
Web Site: www.hambidge.org

FOUNDED: 1934

AREAS OF INTEREST:
Artist residency program.

NAME(S) OF PROGRAMS:
• **Hambidge Residency Program Fellowships**

TYPE:
Fellowships; Residencies. The Hambidge Center awards residency fellowships to distinguished artists and scientists at its 600-acre creative sanctuary in the Blue Ridge Mountains. Fellowships apply to any field or discipline of creative work.

PURPOSE:
To provide applicants with an environment for creative work in the arts and sciences.

ELIGIBILITY:
Open to qualified applicants in all disciplines who can demonstrate seriousness, dedication and professionalism. International residents are welcome.

FINANCIAL DATA:
Each of the individuals in residence has private accommodations and studio space, and shares communal dinners prepared by an in-residence chef. Eight individuals are in residence at any given time.

Amount of support per award: Each artist receives a two-week residency with no fees, a $700 stipend, and the honor of a Distinguished Fellowship.

APPLICATION INFO:
Application information is available on the web site.

Duration: Two weeks.

Deadline: January 15, April 15 and September 15.

ADDRESS INQUIRIES TO:
Christine Jason, Operations Manager
(See e-mail address above.)

HAWAII STATE FOUNDATION ON CULTURE AND THE ARTS [412]

250 South Hotel Street
Second Floor
Honolulu, HI 96813
(808) 586-0301
Fax: (808) 586-0308
TTY: (808) 586-0740
E-mail: jonathan.johnson@hawaii.gov
Web Site: sfca.hawaii.gov

FOUNDED: 1965

AREAS OF INTEREST:
Arts education, community arts, heritage and preservation, presentation, and community arts.

NAME(S) OF PROGRAMS:
• **Biennium Grants Program**

TYPE:
Project/program grants.

YEAR PROGRAM STARTED: 1965

PURPOSE:
To promote, perpetuate, preserve, and encourage culture and the arts as central to the quality of life of the people of Hawaii.

LEGAL BASIS:
State arts agency.

ELIGIBILITY:
Hawaii Revised Statutes for organizations and individuals as defined in Section 9-11.

GEOG. RESTRICTIONS: Hawaii.

FINANCIAL DATA:
Limits on the amount of funding for any one project are established by the SFCA Board. Certain costs are not allowable for SFCA funding.

Amount of support per award: $5,000 to $15,000.

Total amount of support: $537,600 for fiscal year 2021.

Matching fund requirements: 1:1 match required.

NO. MOST RECENT APPLICANTS: 66.

NO. AWARDS: 42 for the year 2021.

APPLICATION INFO:
Applicants must complete the required application forms and attachments.

Duration: Funds are awarded on a biennial basis. No funds are awarded on a continuing basis.

Deadline: Grant applications are received and reviewed during the State budgetary process.

PUBLICATIONS:
Annual Report; application guidelines.

BOARD MEMBERS:
Susan Browne
Nalani Brun
Jane Clement
Ronald Michioka
Karen Tiller Polivka
Dr. Clyde M. Sakamoto
Lloyd Unebasami
Sherman Warner
Allison Wong

ADDRESS INQUIRIES TO:
Jonathan Johnson, Executive Director
(See address above.)

HAYSTACK MOUNTAIN SCHOOL OF CRAFTS [413]

89 Haystack School Drive
Deer Isle, ME 04627
(207) 348-2306
Fax: (207) 348-2307
E-mail: haystack@haystack-mtn.org
Web Site: www.haystack-mtn.org

FOUNDED: 1950

AREAS OF INTEREST:
Craft education and exploration in ceramics, metals, wood, fibers, graphics, glass and blacksmithing.

NAME(S) OF PROGRAMS:
• **Conferences/Seminars**
• **Exhibitions**
• **Maine Programs**
• **Open Studio Residency**
• **Summer Conference**
• **Summer Workshops**

TYPE:
Conferences/seminars; Fellowships; Residencies; Scholarships; Visiting scholars; Work-study programs. Minority scholarships; Technical Assistant and Work Study Scholarships. Awards for study in diverse craft media and workshops in six studios including ceramics, metals, wood, fibers, graphics, glass and blacksmithing.

YEAR PROGRAM STARTED: 1950

PURPOSE:
To offer professional instruction and demonstration in crafts.

LEGAL BASIS:
Nonprofit educational organization.

ELIGIBILITY:
U.S. and foreign citizens who are capable of doing graduate-level work are eligible for technical assistant scholarships. Candidates must be at least 18 years of age.

FINANCIAL DATA:
Annual scholarships cover the cost of tuition, or tuition and room and board.
Amount of support per award: $1,650.
Total amount of support: $325,000.

NO. MOST RECENT APPLICANTS: 625 (250 scholarship applicants; 375 non-scholarship applicants).

NO. AWARDS: 152 (56 work-study students; 50 technical assistants; 21 fellowships; 25 current-year scholarships).

APPLICATION INFO:
Guidelines and application form are available at the web site.
Duration: One- to two-week sessions.
Deadline: Scholarship applications: March 1; Regular applications: April 1.

PUBLICATIONS:
Catalog; newsletter; scholarly monographs; regional program brochures; eNewsletters.

IRS I.D.: 01-0243548

TRUSTEES:
Susan Haas Bralove, President
Ayumi Horie, Vice President
Laura Galaida, Treasurer

ADDRESS INQUIRIES TO:
Haystack Mountain School of Crafts
22 Church Street (November to April)
89 Haystack School Drive (May to October)
Deer Isle, ME 04627

THE MAXIMILIAN E. & MARION O. HOFFMAN FOUNDATION, INC.
970 Farmington Avenue, Suite 203
West Hartford, CT 06107
(860) 521-2949
Fax: (860) 561-5082

TYPE:
Project/program grants.

See entry 2038 for full listing.

HUTCHINSON COMMUNITY FOUNDATION   [414]
One North Main Street
Suite 501
Hutchinson, KS 67501
(620) 663-5293
E-mail: info@hutchcf.org
Web Site: hutchcf.org

FOUNDED: 1989

AREAS OF INTEREST:
Arts and culture, civic improvements, early childhood and youth development, and health and human services.

TYPE:
Project/program grants; Seed money grants.

YEAR PROGRAM STARTED: 1989

PURPOSE:
To inspire philanthropy, collaboration and innovative leadership to strengthen Reno County communities.

LEGAL BASIS:
501(c)(3) public foundation.

ELIGIBILITY:
Proposals must come from organizations that are exempt from federal income tax under Section 501(c)(3) and serve Reno County, KS. Special purpose units of government may apply for support of innovative projects.

Community groups who do not have a 501(c)(3) status may apply for grant awards if another tax-exempt organization acts as a fiscal sponsor.

Grant proposals from individuals or nonqualifying organizations will not be considered.

GEOG. RESTRICTIONS: Reno County, Kansas.

FINANCIAL DATA:
Amount of support per award: Varies.
Total amount of support: Varies.

NO. AWARDS: 45 for the year 2019-20.

APPLICATION INFO:
One copy of the applicant's current IRS determination letter Section 501(c)(3) or 509(a) is required. Contact the Foundation for application procedures.
Duration: One year. Reapplication possible.
Deadline: February 16, April 20, June 22, August 24 and October 19.

PUBLICATIONS:
Annual report; application guidelines.

OFFICERS AND STAFF:
Aubrey A. Patterson, President and Chief Executive Officer
Dell Marie Shanahan Swearer, Chief Operating Officer
Sarah Blake, Program Officer
Kari Mailloux, Director of Strategic Initiatives

ADDRESS INQUIRIES TO:
Aubrey A. Patterson, President and Chief Executive Officer
(See address above.)

IDAHO COMMISSION ON THE ARTS   [415]
9543 West Emerald Street
Suite 204
Boise, ID 83704
(208) 334-2119
Fax: (208) 334-2488
E-mail: info@arts.idaho.gov
Web Site: arts.idaho.gov

FOUNDED: 1966

AREAS OF INTEREST:
All disciplines in the arts.

CONSULTING OR VOLUNTEER SERVICES:
Technical assistance in arts management.

NAME(S) OF PROGRAMS:
- **Arts Education Projects**
- **Directory of Teaching Artists**
- **Entry Track**
- **Fellowships**
- **Public Programs in the Arts**
- **Quick Funds**
- **Traditional Arts Apprenticeship Program**
- **Writer-in-Residence Program**

TYPE:
Conferences/seminars; Fellowships; General operating grants; Project/program grants; Residencies; Technical assistance. Fellowship/apprenticeship, touring/sponsorship, immediate assistance.

YEAR PROGRAM STARTED: 1966

PURPOSE:
To develop the artistic and cultural life of Idaho.

LEGAL BASIS:
State agency.

ELIGIBILITY:
Applicants must be nonprofit, tax-exempt organizations or artists living in Idaho.

GEOG. RESTRICTIONS: Idaho.

FINANCIAL DATA:
Fiscal restrictions, non-cash benefits.
Amount of support per award: Up to $25,000.
Total amount of support: $667,000 in grants and services for fiscal year 2021.
Matching fund requirements: 50:50, cash or in-kind.

NO. MOST RECENT APPLICANTS: Approximately 300 for fiscal year 2021.

NO. AWARDS: Approximately 300 for fiscal year 2021.

APPLICATION INFO:
Applicants must register online. Application cannot be submitted until all sections are completed.
Duration: 12 months.
Deadline: Varies. Consult the Commission.

PUBLICATIONS:
Application guidelines.

IRS I.D.: 82-6000952

OFFICERS:
Steve Allred, Chairperson
Michael Faison, Executive Director and Arts Education Director
Stuart Weiser, Deputy Director
John McMahon, Artist Services Director
Juta Geurtsen, Community Development Director
Steven Hatcher, Folk and Traditional Arts Director
Jocelyn Robertson, Literature Director and Public Information Officer
Jadee Carson, Grants Manager

ADDRESS INQUIRIES TO:
Jadee Carson
Grants Manager or
Stuart Weiser
Deputy Director
(See address or telephone number above.)

INDIANA ARTS COMMISSION   [416]
100 North Senate Avenue
Room N505
Indianapolis, IN 46204
(317) 232-1278
TDD: (317) 233-3001
E-mail: GrantsAdmin@iac.in.gov
Web Site: www.in.gov/arts

FOUNDED: 1969

AREAS OF INTEREST:
The arts including crafts, dance, design, education, expansion arts, folk, literature, media, multiarts, museums, music, presenters, statewide arts service organizations, theatre and visual and local arts agencies.

CONSULTING OR VOLUNTEER SERVICES:
Consultation on a limited basis to Indiana organizations and artists.

TYPE:
Block grants; Conferences/seminars; Development grants; General operating grants; Project/program grants; Technical assistance. Arts in education; Arts organizations and services; Capacity building; Individual artist projects. Most grants are awarded through a network of regional partners which serve all 92 counties.

YEAR PROGRAM STARTED: 1969

PURPOSE:
To act as public catalyst, partner and investor that serves the citizens of Indiana by funding, encouraging, promoting and expanding all the arts.

LEGAL BASIS:
State agency.

ELIGIBILITY:
Applicants must be private tax-exempt, not-for-profit arts organizations or public agencies or individual artists. Eligible organizations without tax-exempt status should submit a fiscal year budget. IAC does not fund capital improvements, purchase of permanent equipment, costs of receptions, foods or beverages or agents fees for programs contracted through commercial agencies.

Must have impact on the state of Indiana.

GEOG. RESTRICTIONS: Indiana.

FINANCIAL DATA:
Amount of support per award: Varies.
Total amount of support: $3,600,000.
Matching fund requirements: Matching funds may include in-kind as well as cash.

NO. MOST RECENT APPLICANTS: 520.

NO. AWARDS: 410.

APPLICATION INFO:
Applicants must complete an application, grant agreement and any reporting required by the program guidelines. Program guidelines are available from the Commission. Potential applicants should contact the agency before applying.
Duration: July 1 through June 30, fiscal year.

PUBLICATIONS:
Monthy newsletters; press releases; grant/program guidelines.

IRS I.D.: 35-6000158

COMMISSION MEMBERS:
Allen C. Platt, III, Chairperson
Alberta Barker, Vice Chairperson
Anne Penny Valentine, Secretary
Lisa Abbott
Chad Bolser
Libby Chiu
Ruth Ann Cowling
Dave Haist
Greg Hull
Walter Knabe
Laurie Burns McRobbie
Jake Oakman
Kelsey Peaper
Sofia Souto
Yolanda Stemer

ADDRESS INQUIRIES TO:
Paige Sharp, Deputy Director of Programs or Miah Michaelsen, Deputy Director
(See address above.)

INTERNATIONAL DOCUMENTARY ASSOCIATION   [417]

3600 Wilshire Boulevard
Suite 1810
Los Angeles, CA 90010
(213) 232-1660
Fax: (213) 232-1669
E-mail: grants@documentary.org
Web Site: www.documentary.org

FOUNDED: 1982

AREAS OF INTEREST:
Documentary film.

NAME(S) OF PROGRAMS:
- **IDA Documentary Awards**
- **IDA/David L. Wolper Student Documentary Achievement Award**
- **Pare Lorentz Award**
- **Pare Lorentz Documentary Fund**
- **Los Angeles County Arts Commission Internships**

TYPE:
Awards/prizes; Internships. IDA Documentary Awards celebrate the best nonfiction films and programs of the year. Prize awarded in seven categories: feature, short, episodic series, curated series, short film series, limited series, and the David L. Wolper Student Documentary Award.

IDA/David L. Wolper Student Documentary Achievement Award recognizes exceptional achievement in nonfiction film and video production at the university level and brings greater public and industry awareness to the work of students in the documentary field.

The Pare Lorentz Award is awarded for films that reflect the spirit and tradition of Pare Lorentz's work. The film should demonstrate one or more of Lorentz's central concerns (the appropriate use of the natural environment, justice for all, and the illumination of pressing social problems) presented as a compelling story by skillful filmmaking.

Pare Lorentz Documentary Fund supports full-length documentary films that reflect the spirit and nature of Pare Lorentz's work, exhibiting objective research, artful storytelling, strong visual style, high production values, artistic writing and outstanding music composition, as well as skillful direction, camerawork and editing.

Los Angeles County Arts Commission Internships are offered to undergraduate students who currently reside or are enrolled in a college or university located in Los Angeles County, CA. Those interested should consult the Association web site for up-to-date details.

YEAR PROGRAM STARTED: 1984

PURPOSE:
To provide resources, create community, and defend rights and freedoms for documentary artists, activists, and journalists.

LEGAL BASIS:
501(c)(3).

ELIGIBILITY:
Varies by program or award.

FINANCIAL DATA:
Amount of support per award: IDA Enterprise Documentary Fund: $50,000 to $100,000 for Production Grant and $15,000 for Development Grant; Pare Lorentz Documentary Fund: $15,000 to $25,000.
Total amount of support: IDA Enterprise Documentary Fund: $1,000,000; Pare Lorentz Documentary Fund: $115,000 for the year 2020.

NO. MOST RECENT APPLICANTS: 943.

NO. AWARDS: IDA Enterprise Documentary Fund: 22; Pare Lorentz: 7 for the year 2020.

APPLICATION INFO:
Pare Lorentz Documentary Fund: Guidelines are available on the Association web site.
Deadline: Varies by program or award.

IRS I.D.: 95-3911227

EXECUTIVE DIRECTOR:
Simon Kilmurry

ADDRESS INQUIRIES TO:
Dana Merwin, Program Officer
(See e-mail address above.)

IOWA ARTS COUNCIL   [418]

600 East Locust Street
Des Moines, IA 50319-0290
(515) 281-4641
Fax: (515) 242-6498
E-mail: iowa.arts@iowa.gov
Web Site: www.iowaculture.gov/arts

FOUNDED: 1967

AREAS OF INTEREST:
All arts disciplines, primarily in Iowa.

CONSULTING OR VOLUNTEER SERVICES:
Technical assistance in a variety of disciplines and subject areas, including information.

NAME(S) OF PROGRAMS:
- **Arts Resources and Artists Programs**
- **Funding and Arts in Education Programs**
- **Technical Assistance and Community Development Programs**

TYPE:
Awards/prizes; Capital grants; Challenge/matching grants; Conferences/seminars; Development grants; Fellowships; General operating grants; Internships; Project/program grants; Scholarships. Seminars, technical assistance and funding. Services provided to institutions and individuals statewide.

YEAR PROGRAM STARTED: 1967

PURPOSE:
To cultivate creativity, learning and participation of the arts in Iowa.

LEGAL BASIS:
State agency established under Chapter 304A, Code of Iowa.

ELIGIBILITY:
Applicants must be nonprofit, tax-exempt 501(c)(3) organizations incorporated and located in Iowa, schools or institutions of higher education located in Iowa, units of local, county or federally recognized tribal government located in Iowa, or Iowa resident artists, age 18 or older.

GEOG. RESTRICTIONS: Iowa.

FINANCIAL DATA:
Amount of support per award: Varies.
Total amount of support: Varies by program.
Matching fund requirements: One-to-one cash or in-kind match for most grant programs.

NO. MOST RECENT APPLICANTS: 403.

NO. AWARDS: 173.

APPLICATION INFO:
Refer to the Council web site.
Duration: 12 months or less.
Deadline: May 1 annually.

PUBLICATIONS:
Online e-newsletter (bimonthly).

IRS I.D.: 42-6004812

STAFF:
Veronica O'Hern, Grants and Artist Program Manager

ADDRESS INQUIRIES TO:
Veronica O'Hern
Grants and Artist Program Manager
(See address above.)

JEROME FOUNDATION, INC. [419]

550 Vandalia Street
Suite 109
St. Paul, MN 55114
(651) 224-9431
E-mail: info@jeromefdn.org
Web Site: www.jeromefdn.org

FOUNDED: 1964

AREAS OF INTEREST:
Arts with a focus on film and video, literature, dance, music, theater and visual arts. Emphasis is on creation of new works by early career artists.

TYPE:
Fellowships; Project/program grants; Residencies.

YEAR PROGRAM STARTED: 1964

PURPOSE:
To contribute to a dynamic and evolving culture by supporting the creation, development and production of new works by early career artists.

LEGAL BASIS:
Tax-exempt, private foundation.

ELIGIBILITY:
Foundation grants are made primarily to not-for-profit arts organizations and to individual professional artists through specific programs. The Foundation accepts requests from new organizations.

The Foundation does not support capital (building and endowment) campaigns.

Foundation support is restricted to emerging artists who are legal residents of Minnesota and/or New York City, NY.

GEOG. RESTRICTIONS: Minnesota and the five boroughs of New York City, New York.

FINANCIAL DATA:
Amount of support per award: Individual artists: $38,000 average; Organizations: $36,200 average.

Total amount of support: Individual artists: $1,850,000; Organizations: Average $2,100,000 annually.

APPLICATION INFO:
Guidelines and application forms are available on the web site.
Duration: Two years.

PUBLICATIONS:
Annual report.

STAFF:
Ben Cameron, President
Eleanor Savage, Program Director
Andrea Brown, Grants and Program Administrator

DIRECTORS:
Kate Barr
Sarah Bellamy
Linda Earle
Daniel Alexander Jones
Lori Pourier
Rick Scott
Elizabeth Streb
Mark Tribe
Ryan Lee Wong

ADDRESS INQUIRIES TO:
Ben Cameron, President
(See address above.)

KENTUCKY ARTS COUNCIL [420]

1025 Capital Center Drive, 3rd Floor
Frankfort, KY 40601
(502) 892-3118
Fax: (502) 564-2839
E-mail: kyarts@ky.gov
Web Site: artscouncil.ky.gov

FOUNDED: 1966

AREAS OF INTEREST:
Arts development (visual arts, performing arts, literature and media), community development, arts-in-education and individual artists.

CONSULTING OR VOLUNTEER SERVICES:
Staff available for assistance in planning in above areas and in applying for grants.

NAME(S) OF PROGRAMS:
- **Arts First Aid**
- **Emerging Artist Award**
- **Folk and Traditional Arts Apprenticeship**
- **Kentucky Arts Partnerships**
- **Kentucky Peer Advisory Network**
- **Poetry Out Loud**
- **Showcasing the Arts**
- **Al Smith Individual Artist Fellowships**
- **Teaching Art Together**
- **TranspARTation**

TYPE:
Awards/prizes; Fellowships; General operating grants; Project/program grants; Residencies; Technical assistance. Arts development and artist support.

YEAR PROGRAM STARTED: 1966

PURPOSE:
To help sponsoring organizations and artists reach and develop new audiences or strengthen themselves artistically or managerially; to act as the funding and program coordinating organization for the arts in Kentucky.

LEGAL BASIS:
State Arts Agency of the Commonwealth of Kentucky.

ELIGIBILITY:
Nonprofit organizations incorporated in the state of Kentucky or Kentucky artists. Most grant programs require IRS tax-exempt status.

GEOG. RESTRICTIONS: Kentucky.

FINANCIAL DATA:
Amount of support per award: Emerging Artist Award: $1,000; Folk and Traditional Arts Apprenticeship: Up to $3,000; Grants: Varies; Al Smith Fellowship: $7,500.

Total amount of support: $1,708,700 for the year 2019.

Matching fund requirements: Varies by program.

NO. MOST RECENT APPLICANTS: Approximately 500.

NO. AWARDS: 187 for the year 2019.

APPLICATION INFO:
Guidelines and applications are found on the Council web site.
Duration: Grants: One fiscal year, July 1 through June 30.
Deadline: Varies.

PUBLICATIONS:
Bimonthly newsletter; annual report.

IRS I.D.: 61-0600439

OFFICERS:
Christopher Cathers, Executive Director

ADDRESS INQUIRIES TO:
Christopher Cathers, Executive Director
(See address above.)

THE LEEWAY FOUNDATION

1315 Walnut Street
Suite 832
Philadelphia, PA 19107
(215) 545-4078
Fax: (215) 545-4021
E-mail: info@leeway.org
Web Site: www.leeway.org

TYPE:
Awards/prizes; Project/program grants. Art and Change Grants provide project-based grants to fund art for social change projects.

Leeway Transformation Award is an unrestricted award (not project-based) for women and trans people demonstrating a commitment of five years or more to art for social change work.

See entry 980 for full listing.

LEHIGH VALLEY COMMUNITY FOUNDATION [421]

840 West Hamilton Street
Suite 310
Allentown, PA 18101
(610) 351-5353
Fax: (610) 351-9353
E-mail: lehighvalleyfoundation@gmail.com
Web Site: www.lehighvalleyfoundation.org

FOUNDED: 1967

AREAS OF INTEREST:
Arts and culture, community development, education, environment, health care, history and heritage, human services and science.

TYPE:
Endowments; Scholarships. Community investment grants.

YEAR PROGRAM STARTED: 1967

PURPOSE:
To promote philanthropy in order to improve the quality of life in the Foundation's region.

LEGAL BASIS:
Nonprofit, tax-exempt 501(c)(3) organization.

ELIGIBILITY:
Limited to nonprofit, tax-exempt organizations serving citizens within the geographic limits of its outreach.

GEOG. RESTRICTIONS: Lehigh and Northampton counties, Pennsylvania.

FINANCIAL DATA:
Amount of support per award: Average discretionary grant: $5,000.

Total amount of support: $6,700,000 in grants for fiscal year 2019-20.

NO. AWARDS: Approximately 600 grants annually.

APPLICATION INFO:
Application can be downloaded from the Foundation's web site. Financial sheet must be submitted with grant application.
Deadline: July 1. Notification December 15. Grants: Varies.

IRS I.D.: 23-1686634

STAFF:
Erika Riddle Petrozelli, President

ADDRESS INQUIRIES TO:
Erika Riddle Petrozelli, President
(See address above.)

THE JOHN J. LEIDY FOUNDATION

305 West Chesapeake Avenue
Suite 308
Towson, MD 21204
(410) 821-3006
Fax: (410) 821-3007
E-mail: info@leidyfoundation.org
Web Site: www.leidyfoundation.org

TYPE:
General operating grants; Project/program
grants.

See entry 1194 for full listing.

LOUISIANA DIVISION OF THE ARTS, DEPARTMENT OF CULTURE, RECREATION AND TOURISM [422]

1051 North Third Street, Room 405
Baton Rouge, LA 70802
(225) 342-8200
Fax: (225) 342-8173
E-mail: arts@crt.la.gov
Web Site: www.crt.state.la.us/cultural-development/arts

FOUNDED: 1976

AREAS OF INTEREST:
Dance, design, folklife, literature, media,
music, theater, visual arts and crafts,
arts-in-education, and arts service
organizations.

NAME(S) OF PROGRAMS:
● **Louisiana Project Grants**

TYPE:
Project/program grants. Project assistance
grants.

YEAR PROGRAM STARTED: 1977

PURPOSE:
To support established and emerging arts
organizations; to stimulate public
participation in the arts.

LEGAL BASIS:
Government agency (the official state arts
agency of Louisiana).

ELIGIBILITY:
Organizations domiciled in Louisiana are
eligible to apply for grants to support arts
activities taking place in Louisiana. Eligible
applicants generally fall into one of the
following categories: nonprofit 501(c)(3)
organizations, public or private educational
institutions, colleges or universities
sponsoring arts activities intended for
community participation (not academic,
credit-producing, or curriculum-oriented
projects), agencies of local, parish, or state
government such as state or parish libraries,
units of municipal government, parish police
juries and agencies of state government.

GEOG. RESTRICTIONS: Louisiana.

FINANCIAL DATA:
Amount of support per award: $2,500 to
$7,500, depending on region applicant
applies.
Total amount of support: $697,499.

NO. MOST RECENT APPLICANTS: Varies.

NO. AWARDS: Approximately 300.

APPLICATION INFO:
Applications are submitted through the
statewide online grant application system
located at submittable.com.
Duration: Two years (October 1 to
September 30).
Deadline: July 30.

ADDRESS INQUIRIES TO:
Grants Director
Tel: (225) 342-8175
(See e-mail address above.)

LOUISIANA DIVISION OF THE ARTS, DEPARTMENT OF CULTURE, RECREATION AND TOURISM [423]

1051 North Third Street, Room 405
Baton Rouge, LA 70802
(225) 342-8200
Fax: (225) 342-8173
E-mail: arts@crt.la.gov
Web Site: www.crt.state.la.us/cultural-development/arts

FOUNDED: 1976

AREAS OF INTEREST:
Dance, design, folklife, literature, media,
music, theater, visual arts and crafts,
arts-in-education, and arts service
organizations.

CONSULTING OR VOLUNTEER SERVICES:
Grants writing, program development,
community development, and alternate
funding sources.

TYPE:
General operating grants.

YEAR PROGRAM STARTED: 1977

PURPOSE:
To support established and emerging arts
organizations; to stimulate public
participation in the arts.

LEGAL BASIS:
Government agency (the official state arts
agency of Louisiana).

ELIGIBILITY:
Grants are offered in three levels of operating
support to nonprofit arts organizations.

GEOG. RESTRICTIONS: Louisiana.

FINANCIAL DATA:
Amount of support per award: $3,200 to
$11,000.
Total amount of support: $500,000.

NO. MOST RECENT APPLICANTS: 103.

NO. AWARDS: 86.

APPLICATION INFO:
Applications are submitted through the
statewide online grant application system
located at submittable.com.
Duration: Two years (July 1 to June 30).
Deadline: April.

ADDRESS INQUIRIES TO:
Grants Director
Tel: (225) 342-8175
(See e-mail address above.)

MACDOWELL [424]

100 High Street
Peterborough, NH 03458
(603) 924-3886
(212) 535-9690
Fax: (603) 924-9142
E-mail: admissions@macdowell.org
cbethel@macdowell.org
Web Site: www.macdowell.org

FOUNDED: 1907

AREAS OF INTEREST:
Writing, theatre, visual art, music
composition, filmmaking, architecture and
interdisciplinary art.

NAME(S) OF PROGRAMS:
● **Artist Residency Program**

TYPE:
Fellowships; Residencies; Travel grants.
Residency fellowships awarded to emerging
and established artists across a spectrum of
disciplines - architecture, film,
interdisciplinary practices, literature, music,
visual art, and theatre - to support studio
time and artistic exchange in an ideal
environment for the creative process.

YEAR PROGRAM STARTED: 1907

PURPOSE:
To nurture the arts by offering creative
individuals of the highest talent an inspiring
environment in which they can produce
enduring works of the imagination.

LEGAL BASIS:
Nonprofit corporation, certified by IRS as
falling under Code Section 509(a)(2).

ELIGIBILITY:
Artists are selected based on demonstrated
ability as evidenced by their work sample
and commitment to practice outlined in their
project proposal. Established artists as well
as emerging artists of promising talent are
encouraged to apply.

FINANCIAL DATA:
No residency fees. Fellowships cover costs of
living accommodations, all meals, and use of
an individual studio building. Travel
reimbursement and stipends are available for
artists who demonstrate need.
Amount of support per award: Stipends and
travel grants up to $2,500.
Total amount of support: $4,000,000.

NO. MOST RECENT APPLICANTS: Approximately
1,200 for the year 2020.

NO. AWARDS: Approximately 123
artists-in-residence for the year 2020.

APPLICATION INFO:
Application forms are available on the web
site. There is a $30 application fee. Work
samples must be submitted digitally with the
application. Read guidelines before applying.
Duration: Residence periods are from two
weeks to two months. No more than one
application per 24-month period.
Deadline: January 15, April 15 and
September 15.

PUBLICATIONS:
Application guidelines.

OFFICERS AND STAFF:
Nell Painter, Chairman
Andrew Senchak, President
Philip Himberg, Executive Director

ADDRESS INQUIRIES TO:
Courtney Bethel, Admissions Director
(See address above.)

MAINE ARTS COMMISSION   [425]

193 State Street
25 State House Station
Augusta, ME 04333-0025
(207) 287-2724
Fax: (207) 287-2725
TTY: (877) 887-3878
E-mail: arts.grants@maine.gov
Web Site: mainearts.maine.gov

FOUNDED: 1966

AREAS OF INTEREST:
Arts.

CONSULTING OR VOLUNTEER SERVICES:
Opportunities for artists and arts
organization.

NAME(S) OF PROGRAMS:
- **Arts and Humanities Grants**
- **Arts Learning**
- **Creative Aging Grant**
- **Cultural Planning Grant**
- **Maine Artist Fellowship**
- **Jane Morrison Film Fund**
- **Organizational Development**
- **Partnership Grant**
- **Project Grant for Artists**
- **Project Grant for Organizations**
- **Springboard Artist Grant**
- **Traditional Arts Apprenticeship**

TYPE:
Awards/prizes; Conferences/seminars;
Fellowships; General operating grants;
Matching gifts; Project/program grants;
Residencies; Technical assistance.

YEAR PROGRAM STARTED: 1966

PURPOSE:
To encourage and stimulate public interest
and participation in the cultural heritage and
cultural programs of our state; to expand the
state's cultural resources; to encourage and
assist freedom of artistic expression for the
well-being of the arts; to meet the needs and
aspirations of persons in all parts of the state.

LEGAL BASIS:
Government agency.

ELIGIBILITY:
Applicants must be nonprofit Maine arts
organizations, individual artists, schools
and/or certain units of city/state or tribal
government.

GEOG. RESTRICTIONS: Maine.

FINANCIAL DATA:
Amount of support per award: $1,500 to
$10,000; average grant $3,400.
Total amount of support: $780,800 for the
year 2020.
Matching fund requirements: 1:1, cash or
in-kind for most grants. No matching
requirement for grants to individual artists.

CO-OP FUNDING PROGRAMS: Maine Community
Foundation; Maine Humanities Council.

NO. MOST RECENT APPLICANTS: 502 for the
year 2020.

NO. AWARDS: 422 for the year 2020.

APPLICATION INFO:
Applicant may speak with a staff member
about the project before submitting an
application.

Application forms must be submitted
electronically.
Duration: Varies from 30 days to a full fiscal
year period.
Deadline: Varies for all programs.

IRS I.D.: 01-6000001

COMMISSION MEMBERS:
David Hopkins, Chairperson
Cynthia Orcutt, Vice Chairperson

EXECUTIVE DIRECTOR:
David Greenham

ADDRESS INQUIRIES TO:
Kerstin Gilg, Grants Director
E-mail: kerstin.gilg@maine.gov

ROBERT MAPPLETHORPE FOUNDATION, INC.   [426]

477 Madison Avenue, 15th Floor
New York, NY 10022-5835
(212) 755-3025
Fax: (212) 941-4764
E-mail: joree@mapplethorpe.org
info@mapplethorpe.org
Web Site: www.mapplethorpe.org

FOUNDED: 1988

AREAS OF INTEREST:
Photography as an art form; scientific study
of AIDS and AIDS-related research in order
to help find a cure, and education prevention.

NAME(S) OF PROGRAMS:
- **Photography Program**

TYPE:
Project/program grants. Funds medical
research in the fight against AIDS and HIV
infection and supports the promotion of
photography as a fine art, embracing
exhibitions, acquisitions, and publications.

YEAR PROGRAM STARTED: 1988

ELIGIBILITY:
The Foundation will not provide grants or
scholarships to individual photographers. The
Foundation will supply museums and other
public institutions by assisting in the creation
or expansion of photographic departments.

GEOG. RESTRICTIONS: United States.

FINANCIAL DATA:
Amount of support per award: Varies.
Total amount of support: Varies.

APPLICATION INFO:
There is no formal application form.
Duration: Varies.
Deadline: Proposals are accepted on a
continuing basis.

ADDRESS INQUIRIES TO:
Joree Adilman, Managing Director
(See address above.)

MARYLAND STATE ARTS COUNCIL   [427]

175 West Ostend Street
Suite E
Baltimore, MD 21230
(410) 767-6555
Fax: (410) 333-1062
TDD/TTY: (410) 333-4519
E-mail: msac.commerce@maryland.gov
Web Site: www.msac.org

FOUNDED: 1967

AREAS OF INTEREST:
Arts.

NAME(S) OF PROGRAMS:
- **Arts and Entertainment Districts General Operating Support**
- **Arts and Entertainment Districts Technical Assistance**
- **Arts in Education**
- **Community Arts Development**
- **Creativity Grant Program**
- **Grants for Organizations**
- **Individual Artist Awards**
- **Maryland Traditions**
- **Professional Development Program**
- **Public Art Program**

TYPE:
Awards/prizes; Block grants; General
operating grants; Project/program grants;
Residencies; Technical assistance. Arts
program, arts project grants. Individual artist
awards. The Council awards grants to county
arts councils in Maryland through its
Community Arts Development program.

The Arts in Education program is designed to
increase access to a range of artistic
disciplines and to assist schools in integrating
the arts into the curriculum. Projects vary in
length from one-day visits to four-week
residencies.

The Grants for Organizations Program
provides support to those who produce or
present the arts to the public.

The Maryland Traditions program is
dedicated to the identification, documentation
and presentation of Maryland traditional
artists to general audiences through public
life and educational activities.

Grant program information by type can be
found on the "Programs" page on the
Council web site.

YEAR PROGRAM STARTED: 1967

PURPOSE:
To make the arts more widely available to all
Maryland residents, to strengthen the state's
cultural institutions and to encourage the
development of resident artistic activity
throughout the state.

LEGAL BASIS:
Article 41 of the Annotated Code of
Maryland as amended, Sections 387 to 395,
inclusive.

ELIGIBILITY:
Applying organizations must be
not-for-profit, tax-exempt and incorporated in
the state of Maryland. Individuals must be 18
years of age or older and a Maryland
resident.

Funding is not provided for acquisition of
capital assets, capital improvements,
depreciation, deficits, capital debt reduction
and contributions to endowments.

GEOG. RESTRICTIONS: Maryland.

FINANCIAL DATA:
Amount of support per award: Varies by
program.
Total amount of support: Varies by program.

NO. MOST RECENT APPLICANTS: Varies.

NO. AWARDS: Varies.

APPLICATION INFO:
Guidelines and grant application forms may
be acquired by writing to the Council office.
Duration: Varies by program.
Deadline: Varies by program.

EXECUTIVE DIRECTOR:
Ken Skrzesz

ADDRESS INQUIRIES TO:
Dana Parsons, Director of Grants and
Professional Development
(See address above.)

MICHIGAN COUNCIL FOR ARTS AND CULTURAL AFFAIRS   [428]

Michigan Economic Development Corporation
300 North Washington Square
Lansing, MI 48913
(517) 241-4011
E-mail: watsona11@michigan.org
Web Site: www.michigan.gov/arts

FOUNDED: 1966

AREAS OF INTEREST:
    Arts.

NAME(S) OF PROGRAMS:
● **Arts in Education Grants**
● **Capital Improvement Grants**
● **Operational Support Grants**
● **Project Support Grants**

TYPE:
    General operating grants; Project/program
    grants.

PURPOSE:
    To develop and encourage programs and
    projects that make music, painting, literature,
    cinema, dance, sculpture, crafts, architecture
    and all the arts available to the people of
    Michigan, regardless of their age, location,
    background or economic status; to support
    activities of Michigan artists.

LEGAL BASIS:
    State agency.

ELIGIBILITY:
    Generally, grants will be awarded only for
    activities within the state of Michigan. For
    most programs, applicants should be
    Michigan-based nonprofit tax-exempt
    organizations residing in Michigan. The
    Council ordinarily does not finance an
    existing deficit, capital improvements,
    curriculum-oriented activities or permanent
    equipment.

GEOG. RESTRICTIONS: Michigan.

FINANCIAL DATA:
    Amount of support per award: Varies.
    Total amount of support: $10,700,000 for the
    year 2019.
    Matching fund requirements: Varies with
    program.

CO-OP FUNDING PROGRAMS: Re-Granting and
    Partnership programs.

NO. MOST RECENT APPLICANTS: 648.

NO. AWARDS: 530.

APPLICATION INFO:
    Applicants are required to use the Council's
    online eGrant system.
    Duration: One year, October 1 through
    September 30.
    Deadline: Primary programs: June 1. All
    other programs: Varies.

PUBLICATIONS:
    Program guidelines; factsheet.

IRS I.D.: 38-6000134

OFFICERS:
    W. Omari Rush, Chairman

STAFF:
    Alison Watson, Director

ADDRESS INQUIRIES TO:
    Alison Watson, Director
    (See address above.)

MID-AMERICA ARTS ALLIANCE   [429]

2018 Baltimore Avenue
Kansas City, MO 64108
(816) 421-1388
Fax: (816) 421-3918
E-mail: christine@maaa.org
Web Site: www.maaa.org

FOUNDED: 1972

AREAS OF INTEREST:
    All artistic disciplines.

NAME(S) OF PROGRAMS:
● **Artistic Innovations Grant Program**
● **Regional Touring Program**
● **Touring Exhibits through ExhibitsUSA**

TYPE:
    Project/program grants; Technical assistance.
    Support and project/program grants for
    community arts projects and touring
    performing arts.

YEAR PROGRAM STARTED: 1973

PURPOSE:
    To increase the access to high-quality arts
    programs and to sponsor competency.

LEGAL BASIS:
    Missouri corporation, 501(c)(3).

ELIGIBILITY:
    Nonprofit organizations presenting M-AAA
    touring programs in Arkansas, Kansas,
    Missouri, Nebraska, Oklahoma and Texas
    may apply. Visual arts exhibitors throughout
    the country may request traveling exhibits.

GEOG. RESTRICTIONS: Arkansas, Kansas,
    Missouri, Nebraska, Oklahoma and Texas.

FINANCIAL DATA:
    Amount of support per award: $500 to
    $15,000.
    Total amount of support: Varies.
    Matching fund requirements: Most grants
    require a dollar-for-dollar match.

CO-OP FUNDING PROGRAMS: State arts agencies
    of Arkansas, Kansas, Missouri, Nebraska,
    Oklahoma, Texas, corporations and
    foundations, and the National Endowment for
    the Arts.

NO. MOST RECENT APPLICANTS: Approximately
    190.

NO. AWARDS: 21.

APPLICATION INFO:
    Application information is available on the
    web site.
    Duration: Varies.
    Deadline: Varies.

PUBLICATIONS:
    Annual report; exhibit catalogs.

IRS I.D.: 23-7303693

OFFICERS:
    Todd Stein, President and Chief Executive
    Officer

ADDRESS INQUIRIES TO:
    Christine Bial, Director of Arts and
    Humanities Grant Programs
    (See address above.)

MID ATLANTIC ARTS   [430]

201 North Charles Street
Suite 401
Baltimore, MD 21201
(410) 539-6656 ext. 104
Fax: (410) 837-5517
E-mail: info@midatlanticarts.org
Web Site: www.midatlanticarts.org

FOUNDED: 1979

AREAS OF INTEREST:
    Regional arts activities crossing state lines in
    Delaware, District of Columbia, Maryland,
    New Jersey, New York, Pennsylvania,
    Virginia, West Virginia and the U.S. Virgin
    Islands; national and international funding
    through Southern Exposure and USArtists
    International.

NAME(S) OF PROGRAMS:
● **ArtsCONNECT**
● **Alan Cooper Leadership in the Arts
    Award**
● **Folk and Traditional Arts Touring
    Network**
● **Jazz Touring Network**
● **Living Legacy Jazz Award**
● **Mid Atlantic Creative Fellowships**
● **Mid Atlantic Tours**
● **Performing Arts Global Exchange**
● **Special Presenter Initiatives**
● **USArtists International**

TYPE:
    Project/program grants; Residencies.

YEAR PROGRAM STARTED: 1979

PURPOSE:
    To promote the sharing of arts resources
    among the Foundation's partner states,
    regionally, nationally and internationally.

LEGAL BASIS:
    Private, not-for-profit organization.

ELIGIBILITY:
    Individuals and organizations must be based
    in the region for most programs. Other
    requirements vary according to the specific
    program.

    ArtsCONNECT provides artist fee support to
    not-for-profit presenting networks comprised
    of at least three Mid Atlantic-based
    organizations.

    Mid Atlantic Creative Fellowships places an
    artist from each member state in residence at
    selected organizations. A different artistic
    discipline is selected each year for foundation
    support.

    Mid Atlantic Tours provide fee support for
    foundation-initiated performing arts tours.

    On Screen/In Person provides fee subsidy to
    film series host sites.

    Southern Exposure provides support to U.S.
    presenters for foundation-initiated tours of
    artists from Latin America.

    USArtists International supports U.S. music,
    dance, and theatre artists at international
    festivals and performing arts markets.

GEOG. RESTRICTIONS: Delaware, District of
    Columbia, Maryland, New Jersey, New York,
    Pennsylvania, Virginia, West Virginia and the
    United States Virgin Islands for all programs
    except Southern Exposure and USArtists
    International.

FINANCIAL DATA:
    Amount of support per award: $1,000 to
    $15,000.
    Total amount of support: $1,700,000 in direct
    grants for the year 2020.
    Matching fund requirements: Varies
    according to program.

NO. AWARDS: 364 grants for the year 2020.

APPLICATION INFO:
    Guidelines are available on the web site. The
    Foundation utilizes an electronic application
    process.

Duration: Varies.
Deadline: Varies.

PUBLICATIONS:
Guidelines; monthly e-mail newsletter; biennial report.

IRS I.D.: 52-1169382

STAFF:
Theresa M. Colvin, Executive Director

THE MILLAY COLONY FOR THE ARTS, INC. [431]
454 East Hill Road
Austerlitz, NY 12017-0003
(518) 392-3103
E-mail: residency@millaycolony.org
Web Site: www.millaycolony.org

FOUNDED: 1973

AREAS OF INTEREST:
Writing, composing, music and visual arts.

NAME(S) OF PROGRAMS:
● **Artist Residencies**

TYPE:
Residencies. The Millay Colony offers a variety of residencies from the months of April through November for visual artists, writers and composers in order to immerse themselves in creative work. The Colony accommodates a multidisciplinary group of six to seven artists each month and offers special residencies to collaborating groups of artists. It also offers free arts education programs in local schools.

YEAR PROGRAM STARTED: 1973

PURPOSE:
To provide space, studio and time for writers and composers to immerse themselves in their work.

ELIGIBILITY:
Residents are selected after undergoing an application and juried process. Juries make selections anonymously.

FINANCIAL DATA:
No cash award is made. No residency fee is required. If invited, room, studio and meals are provided at no cost.
Amount of support per award: Approximate value $4,000 per resident.

NO. MOST RECENT APPLICANTS: 1,600 for the year 2019.

NO. AWARDS: 60 for the year 2019.

APPLICATION INFO:
Online application process is available.
Duration: Approximately three and one-half weeks. Two-week residencies are available in June and September.
Deadline: October 1 for the following April through July. March 1 for the following August through November.

ADDRESS INQUIRIES TO:
Calliope Nicholas, Co-Director and Manager of Residency Programs
(See address above.)

THE MOODY FOUNDATION
2302 Post Office Street, Suite 704
Galveston, TX 77550
(409) 797-1500
Fax: (409) 763-5564
E-mail: info@moodyf.org
Web Site: www.moodyf.org

TYPE:
Capital grants; Challenge/matching grants; Endowments; Grants-in-aid; Project/program grants; Research grants; Scholarships. Capital campaigns; Equipment; Matching funds; Building/renovation; Program development and research.

See entry 211 for full listing.

MARIETTA MCNEILL MORGAN AND SAMUEL TATE MORGAN, JR. TRUST
Bank of America Private Bank
1800 K Street, N.W., Mail Code
DC1-842-05-01
Washington, DC 20006
(202) 442-7460
E-mail: dc.grantmaking@ustrust.com
Web Site: www.bankofamerica.com/grantmaking

TYPE:
Capital grants.

See entry 1347 for full listing.

WILLIAM MORRIS SOCIETY IN THE U.S. [432]
P.O. Box 53263
Washington, DC 20009
E-mail: wmsusmembership@gmail.com
mroberts@tcnj.edu
Web Site: www.morrissociety.org

FOUNDED: 1971

AREAS OF INTEREST:
The life and work of William Morris as a craftsman, designer and writer.

NAME(S) OF PROGRAMS:
● **Joseph R. Dunlap Memorial Fellowship**

TYPE:
Fellowships; Research grants; Scholarships; Travel grants; Visiting scholars; Research contracts. Supports scholarly, creative, and translation projects about William Morris and his designs, writings and other work.

YEAR PROGRAM STARTED: 1996

PURPOSE:
To support research projects that deal with any subject relating to William Morris.

LEGAL BASIS:
Society.

ELIGIBILITY:
Projects may deal with any subject - biographical, literary, historical, social, artistic, political, typographical - relating to Morris. They may be scholarly or creative, and may include translations or the preparation of educational materials. Applicants for all awards may be from any country. Applications are particularly encouraged from younger members of the Society and from those at the beginning of their careers. Recipients need not have an academic or institutional appointment and the Ph.D. is not required.

FINANCIAL DATA:
Amount of support per award: $1,000.

APPLICATION INFO:
Applicants are asked to submit a resume and a two-page description of their projects, including a timeline and an indication of where the results might be published. At least one recommendation should be sent separately. Submissions will not be accepted via e-mail.

For translation submissions, send one copy of the translation (of the published version, if relevant), with a letter of reference from someone acquainted with both languages assessing the quality of the translation. Translations should have been completed within the past five years.

For teaching materials, no letters of recommendation are needed, but enclose a cover letter describing the ways in which the materials might be (or already have been) used in learning situations.
Duration: One year.
Deadline: December 15. Announcement by January 15.

PUBLICATIONS:
Announcement.

ADDRESS INQUIRIES TO:
Michael Robertson, President
E-mail: us@morrissociety.org

NATIONAL ENDOWMENT FOR THE ARTS [433]
400 7th Street, S.W.
Washington, DC 20506
(202) 682-5400
(202) 682-5403
Fax: (202) 682-5609
E-mail: webmgr@arts.gov
Web Site: www.arts.gov/grants

FOUNDED: 1965

AREAS OF INTEREST:
National artistic accomplishments of the past, present and future.

NAME(S) OF PROGRAMS:
● **Challenge America**
● **Creative Writing Fellowships**
● **Grants for Art Projects**
● **Our Town**
● **Partnership Agreements**
● **Research Grants in the Arts**
● **Translation Projects**

TYPE:
Fellowships; Project/program grants. The National Endowment for the Arts has three grant categories: Grants for Organizations, Grants for Individuals and Partnership Agreements. Under Grants for Organizations, the Endowment funds projects only.

Challenge America: An organization grant to support projects that extend the reach of the arts to underserved populations.

Creative Writing Fellowships: An individual grant offering fellowships in fiction, poetry and creative nonfiction which enable recipients to set aside time for writing, research, travel and general career advancement.

Grants for Art Projects: An organization grant to support the creation of art that meets the highest standards of excellence, public engagement with diverse and excellent art, lifelong learning in the arts and the strengthening of communities through the arts.

Our Town: An organization grant for creative placemaking projects that contribute to the livability of communities and place the arts at their core. The Our Town program offers support for projects in two areas: Arts Engagement, Cultural Planning, and Design Projects; and Projects that Build Knowledge About Creative Placemaking.

Partnership Agreements: Operates in conjunction with state arts agencies (SAAs) and regional arts organizations (RAOs).

Research Grants in the Arts: An organization grant to support research that investigates the value and/or impact of the arts, either as individual components of the U.S. arts ecology or as they interact with each other and/or with other domains of American life.

Translation Projects: An individual grant that enables recipients to translate work from other languages into English.

YEAR PROGRAM STARTED: 1966

PURPOSE:
To support artists, art forms, art events, art education, and to conserve highly significant works of art.

LEGAL BASIS:
The National Foundation on the Arts and Humanities Act of 1965, Public Law 89-209, as amended.

ELIGIBILITY:
Contact the Endowment for details.

GEOG. RESTRICTIONS: United States, American Samoa, Guam, Puerto Rico or the United States Virgin Islands.

FINANCIAL DATA:
Amount of support per award: Challenge America: $10,000; Creative Writing Fellowships: $25,000; Grants for Art Projects: Generally $10,000 to $100,000; Our Town: $25,000 to $150,000; Research Grants in the Arts: $10,000 to $100,000; Translation Projects: $12,500 or $25,000.

Total amount of support: Varies.

Matching fund requirements: Challenge America and Grants for Art Projects: A minimum cost share/match equal to the grant amount is required. Our Town and Research Grants in the Arts are also matching grants.

APPLICATION INFO:
Contact Endowment or consult its web site.
Deadline: Varies.

ADDRESS INQUIRIES TO:
Nicki Jacobs, Grants Director
Tel: (202) 682-5546

NATIONAL YOUNGARTS FOUNDATION   [434]
2100 Biscayne Boulevard
Miami, FL 33137
(305) 377-1140
(800) 970-2787
Fax: (305) 377-1149
E-mail: info@youngarts.org
Web Site: www.youngarts.org

FOUNDED: 1981

AREAS OF INTEREST:
To identify and nurture the most accomplished young artists in the visual, literary, design and performing arts and assist them at critical junctures in their educational and professional development.

CONSULTING OR VOLUNTEER SERVICES:
Offers the names of registrants and awardees of its YoungArts® program nationally to colleges, universities and performing arts institutions which subscribe to the Foundation's Scholarship List Service (SLS).

NAME(S) OF PROGRAMS:
- **National YoungArts Week**
- **U.S. Presidential Scholars in the Arts**
- **YoungArts Los Angeles**
- **YoungArts Miami**
- **YoungArts New York**

TYPE:
Awards/prizes; Conferences/seminars; Internships. Cash grants and scholarship opportunities to young artists.

YEAR PROGRAM STARTED: 1981

PURPOSE:
To recognize and support aspiring artists in their formative years and provide career entry opportunities.

LEGAL BASIS:
Private nonprofit, 501(c)(3), operating national foundation.

ELIGIBILITY:
YoungArts applicant must be 15 to 18 years old, or a high school student in grades 10 to 12. Participants must be U.S. citizens or permanent residents.

NFAA offers a conference for high school arts educators on preparing students for college auditions.

20 U.S. Presidential Scholars in the Arts are selected exclusively from YoungArts participants by the White House Commission on Presidential Scholars.

GEOG. RESTRICTIONS: United States.

FINANCIAL DATA:
Up to 170 national finalists attend YoungArts Week in Miami, all expenses paid.

Amount of support per award: YoungArts Gold Awards: $10,000 each; YoungArts Silver Awards: $5,000; YoungArts Award: Level I, $3,000; Level II, $1,500; Level III, $1,000; Honorable Mention, $250.

Total amount of support: Approximately $800,000 annually.

CO-OP FUNDING PROGRAMS: NFAA works in partnership with other arts organizations to offer workshops, internships and residencies to students in advanced stages of their arts training.

NO. MOST RECENT APPLICANTS: YoungArts: Approximately 11,000 per year.

NO. AWARDS: Approximately 800 total awards per year; approximately 450 cash awards per year.

APPLICATION INFO:
There is a $35 registration fee per category.
Deadline: YoungArts: Early registration May 16, regular registration through October 14. Audition/portfolio materials due late October.

IRS I.D.: 59-2141837

ADDRESS INQUIRIES TO:
E-mail: apply@youngarts.org

NEBRASKA ARTS COUNCIL   [435]
1004 Farnam Street, Lower Level
Omaha, NE 68102
(402) 595-2122
Fax: (402) 595-2334
E-mail: nac.info@nebraska.gov
Web Site: artscouncil.nebraska.gov

FOUNDED: 1965

AREAS OF INTEREST:
Architecture, visual arts, artists, art organizations, literature, museums and libraries, performing arts, aged, children and youth, community and rural development and services and education.

CONSULTING OR VOLUNTEER SERVICES:
Technical (staff) services for requesting organizations who desire assistance in arts programming efforts. Developmental aspects of assistance to arts organizations and/or individuals is predominant.

NAME(S) OF PROGRAMS:
- **Accessibility Grant**
- **Artists-in-Schools/Communities Grants**
- **Arts Learning Projects**
- **Arts Project Grants**
- **Basic Support Grants**
- **Individual Artist Fellowships**
- **Mini Grants**
- **Nebraska Touring Program**
- **School Bus for the Arts Grants**

TYPE:
Fellowships; General operating grants; Matching gifts; Project/program grants. Grants to encourage growth and activity in the arts for the citizens of the state of Nebraska.

YEAR PROGRAM STARTED: 1965

PURPOSE:
To stimulate and encourage, throughout the state, the study and presentation of the visual and performing arts and public interest and participation therein; to promote the arts, cultivate resources and support excellence in artistic endeavors for all Nebraskans.

LEGAL BASIS:
Government agency under state legislation. Agency also accepts federal funds (from the National Endowment for the Arts) and private funds for purposes of its intent.

ELIGIBILITY:
Nonprofit, incorporated status is required of applying organizations. Applicant organizations must have federal tax-exempt status or proof of application for that status at the time of application. Individuals not connected with nonprofit organizations are eligible only for Individual Artist Fellowships and must be Nebraska residents. The NAC does not provide funding for capital expenditures or existing deficits.

GEOG. RESTRICTIONS: Nebraska.

FINANCIAL DATA:
Amount of support per award: Basic Support Grants: Up to $50,000; All other grants: Up to $7,500.

Total amount of support: Approximately $1,400,000.

Matching fund requirements: Must be in cash.

CO-OP FUNDING PROGRAMS: Support is provided for organizations desiring programming in the Mid-America Arts Alliance (six-state consortium consisting of Arkansas, Kansas, Missouri, Nebraska, Oklahoma and Texas).

APPLICATION INFO:
Application form is available on the web site.
Duration: One year.
Deadline: March 15 and October 1.

PUBLICATIONS:
Guide to Programs and Services; Artist Directory.

STAFF:
Jennifer Dreibelbis, Grants Data Administrator

ADDRESS INQUIRIES TO:
See e-mail address above.

*SPECIAL STIPULATIONS:
Please contact NAC prior to applying for the first time.

NEVADA ARTS COUNCIL [436]

716 North Carson Street
Suite A
Carson City, NV 89701
(775) 687-6680
Fax: (775) 687-6688
E-mail: infonvartscouncil@nevadaculture.org
Web Site: www.nvartscouncil.org

FOUNDED: 1967

AREAS OF INTEREST:
Visual, literary, performing, design and folk arts, as well as community development.

CONSULTING OR VOLUNTEER SERVICES:
Provide consulting on arts management, resources in the arts, grants workshops, community arts and professional arts needs.

NAME(S) OF PROGRAMS:
● **Artist Services Program**
● **Arts Learning Program**
● **Community Arts Development**
● **Folklife Program**
● **Grants Program**

TYPE:
Awards/prizes; Challenge/matching grants; Conferences/seminars; Development grants; Fellowships; General operating grants; Project/program grants; Residencies; Technical assistance; Training grants; Work-study programs. Grants to Nevada nonprofit groups, individual artists, public institutions and for arts in education.

YEAR PROGRAM STARTED: 1967

PURPOSE:
To enrich the cultural life of the state through leadership that preserves, supports, strengthens and makes accessible excellence in the arts to all Nevadans.

LEGAL BASIS:
Government agency.

ELIGIBILITY:
Nevada nonprofit organizations with IRS tax-exempt status and individual artists with one-year minimum residency may apply for grants. Artists may also apply for artist residencies. Fellowships require residency.

GEOG. RESTRICTIONS: Nevada.

FINANCIAL DATA:
Amount of support per award: Varies.
Total amount of support: Varies.
Matching fund requirements: Varies.

NO. MOST RECENT APPLICANTS: 700.

NO. AWARDS: 346.

APPLICATION INFO:
Applications are available on the web site.
Duration: Six months to two years.
Deadline: Varies.

IRS I.D.: 88-6000022

OFFICERS:
Gail Rappa, Chairperson
Tony Manfredi, Executive Director
Kari Ward, Administrative Services Officer

NEW ENGLAND FOUNDATION FOR THE ARTS [437]

145 Tremont Street
Seventh Floor
Boston, MA 02111-1254
(617) 951-0010
Fax: (617) 951-0016
E-mail: info@nefa.org
Web Site: www.nefa.org

FOUNDED: 1975

AREAS OF INTEREST:
Performing artists, ensembles, socially engaged art, public art, cultural diplomacy, Native American art, cultural organizations and creative economy research.

NAME(S) OF PROGRAMS:
● **Center Stage**
● **Creative City Boston**
● **Fund for the Arts**
● **National Dance Project**
● **National Theater Project**
● **New England Dance Fund**
● **New England Presenter Travel Fund**
● **New England States Touring Program**
● **New Work New England**
● **Public Art Learning Fund**

TYPE:
Awards/prizes; Development grants; Project/program grants; Travel grants. Production and touring grants; Professional development grants.

PURPOSE:
To facilitate the movement of people, ideas and resources in the arts within New England and beyond; to make vital connections between artists and audiences; to build the strength, knowledge and leadership of the region's creative sector.

LEGAL BASIS:
Public/private partnership.

FINANCIAL DATA:
Amount of support per award: Varies by program.
Total amount of support: Varies.

NO. AWARDS: 450.

APPLICATION INFO:
Contact the Foundation.
Duration: Varies.
Deadline: Varies.

NEW HAMPSHIRE STATE COUNCIL ON THE ARTS [438]

19 Pillsbury Street
Concord, NH 03301
(603) 271-2789
Fax: (603) 271-3584
TTY/TDD: (800) 735-2964
E-mail: cassandra.mason@dncr.nh.gov
Web Site: www.nh.gov/nharts

FOUNDED: 1965

AREAS OF INTEREST:
The arts in New Hampshire.

CONSULTING OR VOLUNTEER SERVICES:
Artists as Entrepreneurs Workshops, Fall Arts in Education Partnership Conference and Grants Information Services Workshops.

NAME(S) OF PROGRAMS:
● **Apprenticeships**
● **Artist Entrepreneurial Workshops**
● **Artist in Residence**
● **Artist Services**
● **Arts in Education**
● **Arts in Health Project Grants**
● **Cultural Conservation**
● **General Project Grants**
● **Operating Grants**
● **Percent for Art**
● **Public Value Partnerships**
● **Traditional Arts Apprenticeship**
● **Youth Arts Project Grants**

TYPE:
Awards/prizes; Challenge/matching grants; Conferences/seminars; Fellowships; General operating grants; Project/program grants; Residencies; Technical assistance. Grant assistance to New Hampshire organizations and individual artists.

YEAR PROGRAM STARTED: 1965

PURPOSE:
To support and promote excellence, education and community investment in the arts for people in New Hampshire.

LEGAL BASIS:
Agency of the state of New Hampshire.

ELIGIBILITY:
Organizations must be incorporated in New Hampshire. Individual artists must reside in New Hampshire for at least one year.

GEOG. RESTRICTIONS: New Hampshire.

FINANCIAL DATA:
Amount of support per award: $250 to $26,000.
Total amount of support: $593,060 for the year 2019.
Matching fund requirements: Varies.

NO. MOST RECENT APPLICANTS: Varies.

NO. AWARDS: Varies.

APPLICATION INFO:
A completed application form is required for all grants. Submissions must be made online. Support materials are required from all applicants; work sample required from individual artists. IRS tax-exempt 501(c)(3) letter is required from nonprofit organizations.
Duration: One to two years.
Deadline: Varies.

PUBLICATIONS:
E-News; E-Opps.

STAFF:
Ginnie Lupi, Director

ADDRESS INQUIRIES TO:
Cassandra Mason
Chief Grants Officer
(See address above.)

*SPECIAL STIPULATIONS:
Funding is restricted to New Hampshire artists, organizations, schools, libraries, branches of government and communities.

NEW JERSEY STATE COUNCIL ON THE ARTS [439]

P.O. Box 306
Trenton, NJ 08625-0306
(609) 292-6130
E-mail: feedback@sos.nj.gov
Web Site: www.nj.gov/state/njsca/index.html

FOUNDED: 1966

AREAS OF INTEREST:
Dance, music, opera, musical theatre, theatre, visual arts, crafts, media arts, performing arts presenters, multidisciplinary, arts education, folk arts, and literature.

NAME(S) OF PROGRAMS:
● **Artists-in-Education Residency Grant Program (AIE)**
● **Arts Education Special Initiatives (AESI)**
● **Arts Project Support (APS)**
● **Folk Arts Apprenticeships (FAA)**
● **General Operating Support (GOS)**
● **General Program Support (GPS)**
● **Individual Artist Fellowship Awards (IAFA)**

TYPE:
Fellowships; General operating grants; Internships; Project/program grants; Residencies; Technical assistance. Artists-in-Education Residency Grant Program places practicing professional artists in long-term residencies (20 days) in schools across the state. This program is carried out in partnership with Young Audiences of NJ.

Arts Project Support is awarded annually to New Jersey-based, nonprofit organizations and agencies to help support single public arts events.

Folk Arts Apprenticeships are awarded to New Jersey residents to support an apprentice learning a traditional art form from a master in their shared community.

General Operating Support Grants are awarded every three years to New Jersey-based, nonprofit arts organizations to help underwrite the expense of their total operation including their expense of producing and presenting arts events.

General Program Support Grants are awarded every three years to other New Jersey-based, nonprofit organizations, agencies, institutions or units of local government to help underwrite the expense of presenting major, ongoing arts programs.

Individual Artist Fellowship Awards are awarded to New Jersey artists in 12 different arts disciplines based solely on independent peer panel assessment of work samples submitted. The anonymous process is focused solely on artistic quality, and awards may be used to help artists produce new work and advance their careers. The program is carried out in partnership with the Mid Atlantic Arts Foundation.

YEAR PROGRAM STARTED: 1966

PURPOSE:
To improve the quality of life of New Jersey, its people and communities by helping the arts to flourish.

LEGAL BASIS:
State governmental agency.

ELIGIBILITY:
The Council awards grants on a highly competitive basis, employing standardized criteria for eligibility and evaluation published in guidelines. The Council convenes panels of independent experts in the various fields of endeavor for objective feedback and recommendations.

GEOG. RESTRICTIONS: New Jersey.

FINANCIAL DATA:
Amount of support per award: Varies each fiscal year.
Total amount of support: Varies each fiscal year.
Matching fund requirements: Fellowships are non-matching. Matching grants to organizations must be on a basis of at least 1:1, 3:1 for operating and program support grants.

NO. MOST RECENT APPLICANTS: Varies each fiscal year.

APPLICATION INFO:
Details are available on the Council web site.

STAFF:
Tammy Herman, Director of Programs and Services

ADDRESS INQUIRIES TO:
Tammy Herman, Director of Programs and Services
(See address above.)

NEW MEXICO ARTS [440]
Bataan Memorial Building
407 Galisteo Street, Suite 270
Santa Fe, NM 87501
(505) 827-6490
Fax: (505) 827-6043
E-mail: JeniceE.Gharib@state.nm.us
Web Site: www.nmarts.org

FOUNDED: 1966

AREAS OF INTEREST:
Arts.

TYPE:
General operating grants; Project/program grants. Funds are available for arts projects; arts in social service; traditional folk arts; arts learning; colleges, universities and government entities; major cultural organizations; local arts councils and service organizations; economic and entrepreneurial development; arts trails; and community arts development.

PURPOSE:
To promote the arts in New Mexico.

ELIGIBILITY:
Applicants must be a New Mexico organization, government or tribal entity. Organizations must have 501(c)(3) not-for-profit status, although they can use a fiscal agent. Religious organizations can apply for grants. No grants are made to individuals.

GEOG. RESTRICTIONS: New Mexico, with a preference for rural New Mexico.

FINANCIAL DATA:
Amount of support per award: Average: $3,000 to $9,000.
Total amount of support: Average $1,000,000 annually.
Matching fund requirements: 50% match is required; half of the match can be in-kind.

NO. MOST RECENT APPLICANTS: 183.

NO. AWARDS: 183.

APPLICATION INFO:
Application is online and available each September and must include the organization's 501(c)(3) letter from the IRS. New applicants must submit an advance review application in October.
Duration: One year; applicants must reapply for renewal each year.
Deadline: Advance review in October; final review in December. Contact organization for exact dates.

ADDRESS INQUIRIES TO:
Jenice E. Gharib, Grants Program and Policy Director
(See address or e-mail above.)

*SPECIAL STIPULATIONS:
Consult guidelines for eligible expenses and specific category eligibility requirements.

NEW YORK FOUNDATION FOR THE ARTS [441]
20 Jay Street, Suite 740
Brooklyn, NY 11201
(212) 366-6900
Fax: (212) 366-1778
E-mail: fellowships@nyfa.org
Web Site: www.nyfa.org

FOUNDED: 1971

AREAS OF INTEREST:
The arts, with a primary focus on New York state.

NAME(S) OF PROGRAMS:
● Artists' Fellowships

TYPE:
Awards/prizes; Development grants; Fellowships; Grants-in-aid. Cash awards made to individual or pairs of originating artists living and working in the state of New York for use in career development. Funds are unrestricted.

YEAR PROGRAM STARTED: 1985

PURPOSE:
To provide the time and resources for the creative mind and the artistic spirit to think, work and prosper.

ELIGIBILITY:
Applicant must be 25 years of age or older and cannot be enrolled in a degree-granting program. Applicant must be a resident of New York state for the two years prior to the deadline.

GEOG. RESTRICTIONS: New York state.

FINANCIAL DATA:
Since its inception, the program has provided over $30,000,000 in unrestricted cash grants to artists in 15 disciplines at critical stages in their creative development.
Amount of support per award: $7,000 cash awards.
Total amount of support: $661,000 for the year 2019.

NO. MOST RECENT APPLICANTS: 2,000 to 4,000 each cycle.

NO. AWARDS: 98 for the year 2019.

APPLICATION INFO:
Contact the Foundation.
Deadline: February 10, 11:59 P.M.

STAFF:
Michael L. Royce, Executive Director

NEW YORK STATE COUNCIL ON THE ARTS [442]
300 Park Avenue South, 10th Floor
New York, NY 10010
(212) 459-8800
Fax: (212) 477-1471
E-mail: public.affairs@arts.ny.gov
Web Site: www.arts.ny.gov

FOUNDED: 1960

AREAS OF INTEREST:
Public support for the arts in New York state.

CONSULTING OR VOLUNTEER SERVICES:
Technical assistance is available for eligible nonprofit arts organizations.

TYPE:
Awards/prizes; Capital grants; Challenge/matching grants; Conferences/seminars; Development grants; General operating grants; Internships; Residencies; Technical assistance. Grants are awarded to eligible New York state nonprofit organizations through 16 discipline-based funding programs: Architecture and Design; Arts Education; Dance; Electronic Media and Film; Facilities; Folk Arts; Individual Artists; Literature; Museum; Music; Presenting; Regional Economic Development; Special Arts Services; State and Local Partnerships; Theater; and Visual Arts. In addition,

NYSCA support reaches an additional 1,300 community-based organizations each year in the form of regrants, which are administered by a statewide network of Local Arts Councils through NYSCA's Decentralization program.

YEAR PROGRAM STARTED: 1960

PURPOSE:
To ensure that the role of the arts in New York's communities will continue to grow and play a more significant part in the welfare and education of New York's citizens.

LEGAL BASIS:
State agency.

ELIGIBILITY:
Grants are awarded to nonprofit organizations incorporated in New York state, Indian tribes, and units of local government. Individuals and unincorporated groups may only apply through an eligible nonprofit organization.

GEOG. RESTRICTIONS: New York state.

FINANCIAL DATA:
Amount of support per award: Varies by program.
Total amount of support: $43,800,000 for fiscal year 2020.
Matching fund requirements: Varies by program.

NO. AWARDS: 2,500 for fiscal year 2020.

APPLICATION INFO:
Applications and guidelines are available online. New applicants (except municipalities and Indian tribes) must submit proof of nonprofit status. Returning applicants who have applied in the past three years must certify that their nonprofit status remains valid.
Duration: One calendar year. Organizations may reapply each year.

PUBLICATIONS:
Program guidelines.

STAFF:
Katherine A. Nicholls, Chairperson
Mara Manus, Executive Director
Abigail Young, Director of Operations
Megan White, Deputy Director of Programs

ADDRESS INQUIRIES TO:
Office of Public and Governmental Affairs
(See address above.)

NORTH CAROLINA ARTS COUNCIL   [443]
Department of Natural and
Cultural Resources
109 East Jones Street
Raleigh, NC 27601
(919) 814-6500
Fax: (919) 715-0189
E-mail: ncarts@ncdcr.gov
tanya.mcguire@ncdcr.gov
Web Site: www.ncarts.org

FOUNDED: 1964

AREAS OF INTEREST:
Arts development throughout North Carolina.

CONSULTING OR VOLUNTEER SERVICES:
Offer consulting services to arts organizations.

NAME(S) OF PROGRAMS:
- **Artist Fellowships**
- **Arts in Education Grants**
- **Grassroots Arts Program**

- **Military and Veteran Healing Arts Grants**
- **Organizational Development**
- **Program Support**
- **Regional Artist Project Grants**
- **SmART Initiative**
- **State Arts Resources**
- **Statewide Service Organizations**

TYPE:
Challenge/matching grants; Development grants; Fellowships; General operating grants; Internships; Project/program grants; Residencies; Technical assistance. Per capita distribution of funds for arts development, general operating support, project grants, local government challenge grants, arts-in-education grants, new works grants, discipline-development grants, individual artist fellowships, fee subsidy for touring groups, consultant grants, scholarship grants and workshops.

Artist Fellowships: To support the creative development of North Carolina artists. In even years, fellowships are awarded to writers, songwriters, composers, playwrights and screenwriters. In odd years, fellowships are awarded in the areas of visual art, craft, film/video and choreography.

Arts in Education Grants: For schools and nonprofit organizations to strengthen the use of the arts in pre-K-through-12 settings.

Grassroots Arts Program: Distributes funds for arts programming, primarily through local arts councils, to all 100 North Carolina counties using a per capita-based formula.

Military and Veteran Healing Arts Grants: Grants are awarded to arts organizations that have a track record of working with military or veteran audiences.

Organizational Development: Through the New Realities Program, organizations can work with a consultant over a period of two to three years to address long-term issues, including leadership transition, restructuring, and repositioning.

Program Support: To help arts organizations broaden, deepen and diversify participation in their arts programs.

Regional Artist Project Grants: For regional consortia of local arts councils, which award project grants to artists in their regions.

SmART Initiative is a catalyst for arts-driven economic development projects across the state.

State Arts Resources: For mature arts organizations that, over time, have consistently produced strong arts programs and demonstrated strong management and financial accountability.

Statewide Service Organizations: Support is provided to organizations that provide programs and services to the arts community on a statewide or regional basis.

YEAR PROGRAM STARTED: 1967

PURPOSE:
To enrich cultural life in North Carolina by nurturing and supporting excellence in the arts and by providing opportunities for every North Carolinian to experience the arts.

LEGAL BASIS:
Agency of the state of North Carolina.

ELIGIBILITY:
Except for fellowships to individual artists who are North Carolina residents, the

Council awards grants to North Carolina agencies and organizations which qualify as tax-exempt and nonprofit under Section 501(c)(3) of the Internal Revenue Code of 1954.

GEOG. RESTRICTIONS: North Carolina.

FINANCIAL DATA:
Amount of support per award: Varies.
Total amount of support: Varies.
Matching fund requirements: When required, 1:1 cash match, except for fellowships.

APPLICATION INFO:
Application form is available online.
Duration: Typically one year.
Deadline: Organizational grant applications: March 1. Individuals: November 1.

STAFF:
Wayne Martin, Executive Director

ADDRESS INQUIRIES TO:
Tanya McGuire, Grants Manager
E-mail: tanya.mcguire@ncdcr.gov
(See address above.)

NORTH DAKOTA COUNCIL ON THE ARTS   [444]
105 North 4th Street
Bismarck, ND 58501
(701) 328-7590
E-mail: arts@nd.gov
Web Site: www.arts.nd.gov

FOUNDED: 1967

AREAS OF INTEREST:
Arts.

NAME(S) OF PROGRAMS:
- **Artists in Residence**
- **Arts in Education Collaboration Grant (AIEC)**
- **Community Arts Access**
- **Individual Artists Fellowships**
- **Institutional Support**
- **Professional Development**
- **Special Projects**
- **Traditional Arts Apprenticeships**

TYPE:
Conferences/seminars; Fellowships; General operating grants; Project/program grants; Residencies. Matching grants.

YEAR PROGRAM STARTED: 1967

PURPOSE:
To sustain, advocate and inspire growth for all North Dakota arts.

LEGAL BASIS:
North Dakota Legislative Assembly.

ELIGIBILITY:
Grants are awarded only to nonprofit organizations, schools, government subdivisions and individuals in North Dakota. Requirements vary according to program. Organizations which do not have 501(c)(3) status may be considered for funding on a case-by-case basis.

GEOG. RESTRICTIONS: North Dakota.

FINANCIAL DATA:
Amount of support per award: Varies by program.
Total amount of support: $973,547 for fiscal year 2019.
Matching fund requirements: Varies by grant.

CO-OP FUNDING PROGRAMS: Institutional Support and Arts-in-Education.

NO. MOST RECENT APPLICANTS: 245 for fiscal year 2020.

NO. AWARDS: 227 for fiscal year 2020.

APPLICATION INFO:
Details for each grant program are available on the Council's web site.
Duration: Up to one year.
Deadline: Varies.

PUBLICATIONS:
Grant guidelines; brochures; eNewsletter; cultural guide.

IRS I.D.: 45-0283965

OFFICER:
Searle Swedlund, Chairperson

ADDRESS INQUIRIES TO:
Kim Konikow, Executive Director
(See address above.)

OHIO ARTS COUNCIL   [445]
30 East Broad Street
33rd Floor
Columbus, OH 43215
(614) 728-4429
Fax: (614) 466-4494
TDD: (800) 750-0750
E-mail: dia.foley@oac.ohio.gov
Web Site: oac.ohio.gov

FOUNDED: 1965

AREAS OF INTEREST:
Arts.

CONSULTING OR VOLUNTEER SERVICES:
Staff assistance related to applications and program development.

NAME(S) OF PROGRAMS:
● **Artists with Disabilities Access**
● **Arts Access**
● **Arts Learning: Artist Express**
● **Arts Learning: Arts Partnership**
● **Arts Learning: TeachArtsOhio**
● **ArtsNEXT**
● **ArtSTART**
● **Big Yellow School Bus**
● **Building Cultural Diversity**
● **Capacity Building**
● **Individual Artist Grants and Services: Traditional Arts Apprenticeships**
● **Ohio Artists on Tour**
● **Ohio Heritage Fellowship Awards**
● **Sustainability**

TYPE:
Assistantships; Awards/prizes; Conferences/seminars; Fellowships; Formula grants; General operating grants; Internships; Project/program grants; Residencies; Technical assistance. Special projects.

YEAR PROGRAM STARTED: 1965

PURPOSE:
To fund and support quality arts experiences to strengthen Ohio communities culturally, educationally and economically.

LEGAL BASIS:
State agency.

ELIGIBILITY:
All applicants for grants must meet the following legal requirements including intending your project to be nonprofit, having the fact that every tax-exempt organization must have an Employer Identification Number, every applicant having to be an Ohio resident or Ohio-based to receive direct grant support, producing projects of high aesthetic quality and artistic merit.

No person or persons shall, on the grounds of race, color, national origin, handicap, age, sex or religion, be excluded from

participation in, be denied benefits of or be otherwise subjected to discrimination under any program, service or benefit advocated, authorized or provided by the state of Ohio.

GEOG. RESTRICTIONS: Ohio.

FINANCIAL DATA:
Amount of support per award: $200 to $400,000.
Total amount of support: $12,000,000 for fiscal year 2018.
Matching fund requirements: Generally, 1:1 cash match.

REPRESENTATIVE AWARDS:
Cleveland Orchestra, Cleveland, OH; Worthington Arts Council, Worthington, OH; Lima Symphony Orchestra, Lima, OH; Actor's Summer Theatre, Columbus, OH; Southern Ohio Museum, Portsmouth, OH.

APPLICATION INFO:
Applicants must use OAC's web-based application system to submit an application.
Duration: July 1 through June 30.
Deadline: Artists with Disabilities Access, Building Cultural Diversity and Capacity Building: June 1 and December 1; Arts Access and Arts Learning-Arts Partnership: March 1 of odd-numbered years; Arts Learning-Artist Express: Application due in six weeks prior to the date of the visit; Arts Learning-TeachArtsOhio: February 1; ArtsNEXT: March 1; ArtSTART: April 1; Individual Excellence Awards: September 1; Ohio Artists on Tour: May 15; Ohio Heritage Fellowship Awards and Traditional Arts Apprenticeships: March 15; Sustainability: February 1, 2023.

PUBLICATIONS:
Guidelines; *Arts Ohio*; *Ohio Festivals & Competitions Guide*; *Focusing the Light: The Arts and Practice of Planning*; *Appreciative Journey: A Guide to Developing International Cultural Exchange.*

IRS I.D.: 31-1334820

OFFICERS:
Donna S. Collins, Executive Director
Dan Katona, Deputy Director
Dia Foley, Investment Director

ADDRESS INQUIRIES TO:
Dan Katona, Deputy Director
(See address above.)

OKLAHOMA ARTS COUNCIL   [446]
Jim Thorpe Building, Room 640
2101 North Lincoln Boulevard
Oklahoma City, OK 73105
(405) 521-2931
Fax: (405) 521-6418
E-mail: grants@arts.ok.gov
Web Site: www.arts.ok.gov

FOUNDED: 1965

AREAS OF INTEREST:
Arts.

NAME(S) OF PROGRAMS:
● **Capitol Art Travel Subsidies**
● **Major Grant Support**
● **Organizational Support**
● **Small Grant Support**
● **Small Grant Support for Schools**

TYPE:
Project/program grants; Technical assistance. State-appropriated funds and federal funds from the National Endowment for the Arts

are disbursed to nonprofit, tax-exempt and nonreligious organizations for arts projects statewide.

YEAR PROGRAM STARTED: 1965

PURPOSE:
To further the arts in the state of Oklahoma.

LEGAL BASIS:
State agency.

ELIGIBILITY:
Nonprofit, tax-exempt and nonreligious Oklahoma organizations are eligible to apply. Funding is also provided for schools, universities, libraries as well as city, county and tribal governments.

GEOG. RESTRICTIONS: Oklahoma.

FINANCIAL DATA:
Amount of support per award: Varies.

APPLICATION INFO:
Contact the Council.
Duration: Projects receiving funding must be completed during the fiscal year.
Deadline: Capitol Art Travel Subsidies: 30 days before travel. Major Grant Support: February 15. Organizational Support: March 1. Small Grant Support and Small Grant Support for Schools: 60 days before program.

PUBLICATIONS:
Program Guidelines; general brochures.

OFFICERS:
Ann Neal, Chairperson
Amber Sharples, Executive Director

ADDRESS INQUIRIES TO:
Thomas Tran, Grants Director
(See address above.)

OREGON ARTS COMMISSION   [447]
775 Summer Street, N.E.
Suite 200
Salem, OR 97301-1280
(503) 986-0082
Fax: (503) 581-5115
E-mail: oregon.artscomm@oregon.gov
Web Site: www.oregonartscommission.org

FOUNDED: 1967

AREAS OF INTEREST:
Arts.

NAME(S) OF PROGRAMS:
● **Access Reimbursement Grants**
● **Arts Build Communities**
● **Arts Learning Grants**
● **Career Opportunity Grants**
● **Individual Artists Fellowship Grants**
● **Operating Support Grants**
● **Oregon Media Arts Fellowship**
● **Small Operating Grants**

TYPE:
Awards/prizes; Conferences/seminars; Fellowships; General operating grants; Project/program grants; Technical assistance; Training grants; Travel grants. Services provided to arts institutions statewide.

YEAR PROGRAM STARTED: 1967

PURPOSE:
To enhance the quality of life for all Oregonians through the arts by stimulating creativity, leadership and economic vitality.

LEGAL BASIS:
Agency of the state of Oregon.

ELIGIBILITY:
Grants are available to nonprofit organizations and professional, nonstudent artists.

GEOG. RESTRICTIONS: Oregon.

FINANCIAL DATA:
Amount of support per award: Varies.
Matching fund requirements: Minimum 1:1.

NO. MOST RECENT APPLICANTS: Varies.

NO. AWARDS: Varies.

APPLICATION INFO:
Detailed information is available on the web site.
Duration: One year.
Deadline: Varies.

IRS I.D.: 93-0563386

PENNSYLVANIA COUNCIL ON THE ARTS [448]
216 Finance Building
Commonwealth and North Streets
Harrisburg, PA 17120
(717) 787-6883
Fax: (717) 783-2538
E-mail: ra-arts@pa.gov
Web Site: www.arts.pa.gov

FOUNDED: 1966

AREAS OF INTEREST:
Arts.

NAME(S) OF PROGRAMS:
● **Arts Organization Grants**

TYPE:
General operating grants; Residencies.
General support grants, specific support grants, and peer-to-peer consultation.

YEAR PROGRAM STARTED: 1966

PURPOSE:
To foster the excellence, diversity and vitality of the arts in Pennsylvania; to broaden the availability and appreciation of those arts throughout the state.

LEGAL BASIS:
State agency.

ELIGIBILITY:
Incorporated nonprofit organizations located in Pennsylvania and serving residents of the state may apply.

GEOG. RESTRICTIONS: Pennsylvania.

FINANCIAL DATA:
Funding comes from state-appropriated funds and federal grants.
Total amount of support: Varies.
Matching fund requirements: Usually a dollar-for-dollar match for organizations.

APPLICATION INFO:
Contact the Council.
Duration: One year.
Deadline: Varies.

PUBLICATIONS:
Guide to Fellowship Programs; Guide to Programs and Services; Guide to the Arts-in-Education Program.

STAFF:
Karl Blischke, Executive Director
Heather Doughty, Deputy Executive Director
Jamie Dunlap, Chief of Creative Catalysts and Lifelong Learning
Amy Gabriele, Chief of Finance and Administration
Sarah Merritt, Director of Creative Communities
Dana Payne, Director of DEI Initiatives, Diverse Cultures and Heritage
Norah Johnson, Director of External Affairs and Public Awareness

ADDRESS INQUIRIES TO:
Director of Pertinent Arts Discipline
(See address above.)

PERPETUAL TRUSTEE COMPANY LTD. [449]
Level 6, 123 Pitt Street
Sydney N.S.W. 2000 Australia
(61) 1800 501 227
Fax: (61) 02 8256 1471
E-mail: philanthropy@perpetual.com.au
Web Site: www.shervingallery.com.au/portiageach

FOUNDED: 1961

AREAS OF INTEREST:
Portrait painting.

NAME(S) OF PROGRAMS:
● **Portia Geach Memorial Award**

TYPE:
Awards/prizes. Cash award for the best portrait painted from life of a man or woman distinguished in Art, Letters or the Sciences, by any female artist resident in Australia.

YEAR PROGRAM STARTED: 1965

PURPOSE:
To recognize the portrait painted from life of the highest artistic merit.

LEGAL BASIS:
Trustees of the Portia Geach Memorial Fund.

ELIGIBILITY:
Entrants must be female Australian residents who are either Australian-born, naturalized, or British-born. Entries must be the original work of the competitor. Works must have been executed entirely during the commenced year previously. Each entry must be a portrait painted from life of a man or woman distinguished in Art, Letters or the Sciences. Self-portraits are accepted. Works must be two-dimensional and must use the medium of paint.

Sculptures, photographic and video works are not eligible. There is no limit to the number of entries an artist can submit.

GEOG. RESTRICTIONS: Australia.

FINANCIAL DATA:
Amount of support per award: $30,000 (AUD) for the year 2020.

NO. AWARDS: 1.

APPLICATION INFO:
Application information will be available on the web site when the award cycle opens.

ADDRESS INQUIRIES TO:
Philanthropic Services
Portia Geach Memorial Award
(See e-mail address above.)

RAGDALE FOUNDATION [450]
1260 North Green Bay Road
Lake Forest, IL 60045
(847) 234-1063
E-mail: admissions@ragdale.org
Web Site: www.ragdale.org

FOUNDED: 1976

AREAS OF INTEREST:
Visual arts, poetry, fiction, nonfiction writing, music composition, performance art, play/screenwriting and interdisciplinary arts.

NAME(S) OF PROGRAMS:
● **Residencies at Ragdale Foundation**

TYPE:
Awards/prizes; Fellowships; Internships; Residencies. Low-cost subsidized residencies at Ragdale Foundation, an artist's community, providing a place to work undisturbed on creative projects. Some financial aid and fellowships are available upon acceptance.

YEAR PROGRAM STARTED: 1976

PURPOSE:
To provide a place for artists to work undisturbed on creative projects.

LEGAL BASIS:
Not-for-profit, tax-exempt foundation.

ELIGIBILITY:
Residents are chosen by selection committees composed of professionals in the arts. Writers, composers, visual artists and artists of other disciplines are accepted. Couples and collaborators are not accepted unless each qualifies independently.

FINANCIAL DATA:
Amount of support per award: Residencies with room and board provided. Standard fee is $630 for 18-day residencies and $875 for 25-day residencies.
Total amount of support: Varies.

NO. MOST RECENT APPLICANTS: 600.

NO. AWARDS: Approximately 200.

APPLICATION INFO:
Completed application must be submitted along with references, resume, work samples and project description. Application process is online through the Submittable portal. A $25 application fee is required. Financial aid application must be completed after acceptance.
Duration: 18 or 25 days.
Deadline: May 15.

PUBLICATIONS:
Application guidelines; two newsletters annually.

IRS I.D.: 36-2937927

OFFICER:
Barbra Schumann, President

ADDRESS INQUIRIES TO:
Amy Sinclair
Grants and Admissions Manager
(See address above.)

RHODE ISLAND STATE COUNCIL ON THE ARTS [451]
One Capitol Hill, 3rd Floor
Providence, RI 02908
(401) 222-3880
(401) 222-3882
Fax: (401) 222-3018
E-mail: todd.trebour@arts.ri.gov
Web Site: www.arts.ri.gov

FOUNDED: 1967

AREAS OF INTEREST:
Arts.

NAME(S) OF PROGRAMS:
● **Artist Initiated Skill Share**
● **Artists Open Studio Tours Grant (AOST)**
● **Arts Access Grant (AAG)**
● **Big Yellow School Bus**
● **Fellowships**
● **Folk Arts Apprenticeships and Fellowships**
● **Investments in Arts and Culture (IAC)**

- **Project Grants for Education (PGE and PGA)**
- **Project Grants for Individuals (PGI)**
- **Project Grants in Healthcare**

TYPE:
Fellowships; General operating grants; Project/program grants. Organizational support includes general operating grants and project/program grants; funding for Rhode Island nonprofit organizations doing arts programming. Individual artist support includes Fellowships, Project Grants for Individuals, and Folk Arts Apprenticeships. Educational Support includes Project Grants in Education.

YEAR PROGRAM STARTED: 1967

PURPOSE:
To support and develop increased and substantial arts opportunities for Rhode Island.

LEGAL BASIS:
Agency of the state of Rhode Island.

ELIGIBILITY:
Varies with each grant category.

GEOG. RESTRICTIONS: Rhode Island.

FINANCIAL DATA:
Amount of support per award: Varies.

Total amount of support: $1,646,882 for fiscal year 2019.

Matching fund requirements: All grants, except for individual artists, require matching funds.

CO-OP FUNDING PROGRAMS: State and local cooperative programs.

APPLICATION INFO:
Contact the specific Program Director.

Duration: Varies with program.

Deadline: April 1 and October 1.

IRS I.D.: 05-6000523

OFFICERS:
Randall Rosenbaum, Executive Director
Maggie Anderson, Program Director, Arts in Education (Education Partnerships)
Elena Calderon-Patino, Program Director, Community Arts
Mollie Flanagan, Program Director, Individual Artists
Todd Trebour, Program Director, Organizations
Molly Dickinson, Program Director, Public Art

ADDRESS INQUIRIES TO:
Elena Calderon-Patino, Program Director
Community Arts
(See address above.)
Tel: (401) 222-6996

Mollie Flanagan
Program Director, Individual Artists
(See address above.)
Tel: (401) 484-8561

Todd Trebour
Program Director, Organizations
(See address or e-mail above.)
Tel: (401) 222-3882

Maggie Anderson, Program Director
Arts in Education
(See address above.)
Tel: (401) 222-6994

SAN FRANCISCO FOUNDATION [452]
One Embarcadero Center, Suite 1400
San Francisco, CA 94111
(415) 733-8500
Fax: (415) 477-2783
E-mail: info@sff.org
Web Site: sff.org

FOUNDED: 1948

AREAS OF INTEREST:
Fine arts.

NAME(S) OF PROGRAMS:
- **Edwin Anthony and Adelaide Boudreaux Cadogan Scholarships**
- **Jack K. and Gertrude Murphy Fellowships**

TYPE:
Fellowships; Scholarships.

YEAR PROGRAM STARTED: 1986

PURPOSE:
To assist San Francisco Bay Area students in pursuing graduate academic fine arts study at various Bay Area institutions.

LEGAL BASIS:
Community foundation.

ELIGIBILITY:
Student must have completed at least one semester of graduate study as of January 31, be continuously enrolled in the same program, and be in good standing through December 31. Award recipients may be required to provide proof of continuing school enrollment through December 31.

Previous winners of Murphy or Cadogan awards are not eligible to apply.

San Francisco Art Institute students will need to provide information and a form of confirmation regarding the Arts Institution to which they will be transferring to in the fall. This institution must be in one of the following counties of the Bay Area: Alameda, Contra Costa, Marin, Napa, San Mateo, Solano, Sonoma, and the city and county of San Francisco.

GEOG. RESTRICTIONS: San Francisco Bay Area, California.

FINANCIAL DATA:
Amount of support per award: Cadogan Award: Typically $6,500 in tuition assistance, based on available funding; Murphy Award: $40,000.

NO. MOST RECENT APPLICANTS: Varies.

NO. AWARDS: Cadogan Scholarship: 16 for the year 2019; Murphy Award: 1.

APPLICATION INFO:
Apply through Submittable.
Deadline: May of each year.

ADDRESS INQUIRIES TO:
Melanie Jimenez
E-mail: mjimenez@sff.org

SAN FRANCISCO FOUNDATION [453]
One Embarcadero Center
Suite 1400
San Francisco, CA 94111
(415) 733-8500
Fax: (415) 477-2783
E-mail: info@sff.org
Web Site: sff.org

FOUNDED: 1948

AREAS OF INTEREST:
Literature, visual arts, film and video, and playwriting

NAME(S) OF PROGRAMS:
- **Art Awards**

TYPE:
Awards/prizes.

PURPOSE:
To foster individual artistic growth within the community.

LEGAL BASIS:
Community foundation.

ELIGIBILITY:
Poets, writers, sculptors, painters, filmmakers, media artists, photographers, printmakers and performing artists are eligible.

GEOG. RESTRICTIONS: Alameda, Contra Costa, Marin, San Francisco and San Mateo counties, California.

FINANCIAL DATA:
Amount of support per award: $2,000.
Total amount of support: Varies.

NO. AWARDS: Varies.

APPLICATION INFO:
Contact the Foundation.
Deadline: Varies.

ADDRESS INQUIRIES TO:
Art Awards Program
E-mail: programs@sff.org

*PLEASE NOTE:
Some art awards that are administered by the Foundation are by nomination only. They are not open application processes.

SILICON VALLEY CREATES [454]
310 South First Street
San Jose, CA 95113
(408) 998-2787 ext. 204
E-mail: alyssae@svcreates.org
Web Site: www.svcreates.org

FOUNDED: 1982

AREAS OF INTEREST:
Arts organizations, individual artists and community arts.

NAME(S) OF PROGRAMS:
- **Artist Laureates**
- **Local Arts Grants**

TYPE:
Awards/prizes; Conferences/seminars; General operating grants; Technical assistance. Laureate awards.

Artist Laureate Awards provide awards to recognize the accomplishments of individual artists.

Local Arts Grants provide general operating support to arts organizations for activities that:
(1) promote artistic excellence while reflecting the dynamic diverse and innovative character of Santa Clara County;
(2) support the professional development of small and mid-sized arts organizations;
(3) recognize and encourage nonprofessional, volunteer involvement as an essential part of the county's cultural environment and;
(4) stimulate local support, particularly at the grassroots level.

LEGAL BASIS:
Private, nonprofit arts council.

ELIGIBILITY:
Requirements vary by program.

GEOG. RESTRICTIONS: Santa Clara County,
California.

FINANCIAL DATA:
Amount of support per award: Artist
Laureates: $5,000; Local Arts Grants: $4,000
to $10,000, depending on funding level.
Total amount of support: $413,700 in Relief
and Recovery Grants for the year 2020.

NO. AWARDS: Artist Laureates: Up to 4;
Operating Grants: 82; Relief and Recovery
Grants to 29 organizations and 94 individuals
for the year 2020.

APPLICATION INFO:
Applications are submitted through the online
grant portal.
Deadline: Varies.

PUBLICATIONS:
Annual report.

IRS I.D.: 94-2825213

ADDRESS INQUIRIES TO:
Alyssa Erickson, Program Manager
(See address above.)

SMITHSONIAN INSTITUTION
Office of Fellowships and Internships
470 L'Enfant Plaza, S.W., Suite 7102
MRC 902, P.O. Box 37012
Washington, DC 20013-7012
(202) 633-7070
E-mail: siofi@si.edu
Web Site: www.smithsonianofi.com

TYPE:
Fellowships. Offered to qualified scholars for
research to be conducted in residence at the
Smithsonian in association with the staff,
using collections and research facilities.

See entry 1648 for full listing.

SOUTH CAROLINA ARTS
COMMISSION   [455]
1026 Sumter Street, Suite 200
Columbia, SC 29201
(803) 734-8696
E-mail: info@arts.sc.gov
Web Site: www.southcarolinaarts.com

FOUNDED: 1967

AREAS OF INTEREST:
Arts education, community arts development
and artist development.

NAME(S) OF PROGRAMS:
● **Arts Education**
● **Community Organizations
Grants/Programs**
● **Individual Artist Grants/Programs**

TYPE:
Awards/prizes; Fellowships; General
operating grants; Project/program grants;
Seed money grants; Technical assistance;
Training grants; Travel grants.

ELIGIBILITY:
Individuals who apply must be citizens or
residents of the U.S. Grants are awarded to
South Carolina artists, organizations and
units of government.

FINANCIAL DATA:
Amount of support per award: Varies.
Total amount of support: Varies.

APPLICATION INFO:
Consult the Commission web site.

Deadline: Varies.

SOUTH DAKOTA ARTS
COUNCIL   [456]
711 East Wells Avenue
Pierre, SD 57501-3369
(605) 773-3301
(800) 952-3625
Fax: (605) 773-5977
E-mail: sdac@state.sd.us
Web Site: artscouncil.sd.gov

FOUNDED: 1966

AREAS OF INTEREST:
Statewide arts programming in all arts
disciplines.

NAME(S) OF PROGRAMS:
● **Artist Career Development Grants**
● **Artist Collaboration Grants**
● **Artist Fellowships**
● **Artists in Schools & Communities
(AISC) Grants**
● **Arts Challenge Grants**
● **Importation of Musicians Grants**
● **Project Grants**
● **Statewide Services Grants**
● **Touring Arts**
● **Traditional Arts Apprenticeship Grants**

TYPE:
Challenge/matching grants; Fellowships;
General operating grants; Grants-in-aid;
Project/program grants; Residencies; Seed
money grants; Technical assistance; Travel
grants. Artist grants; arts challenge
grants/general operating support.

YEAR PROGRAM STARTED: 1968

PURPOSE:
To support development of the arts.

LEGAL BASIS:
State agency.

ELIGIBILITY:
Requirements vary with projects. Most grants
are available to South Dakota residents only,
with the exception of Touring Arts.

GEOG. RESTRICTIONS: South Dakota.

FINANCIAL DATA:
Amount of support per award: Generally
$500 to $5,000. Large cultural organizations:
$4,000 to $40,000.
Total amount of support: $1,360,000 for
fiscal year 2020.
Matching fund requirements: Required except
for Artist Collaboration Grants, Artist Grants
and Folk Arts Apprenticeship Grants.

NO. AWARDS: 332 grants and fellowships for
fiscal year 2020.

APPLICATION INFO:
Applications are accepted through an online
e-grant system.
Duration: Generally one fiscal year.
Renewable.
Deadline: March 1 for Organizations and
Artist Grants. September 1 for Touring Arts
and Artist in Schools & Communities.

PUBLICATIONS:
Arts Alive, newsletter; strategic long-range
plan; annual report.

STAFF:
Patrick Baker, Director
Rebecca Cruse, Deputy Director
Kate Vandel, Program Coordinator

ADDRESS INQUIRIES TO:
Patrick Baker, Director
(See address above.)

H. CHASE STONE TRUST   [457]
c/o JPMorgan
370 17th Street, Suite 3200
Denver, CO 80202
(303) 607-7810
Fax: (303) 607-7761
E-mail: julie.golden@jpmorgan.com
Web Site: www.jpmorgan.com/onlinegrants

AREAS OF INTEREST:
Primarily performing, literary and fine arts.

TYPE:
Project/program grants.

PURPOSE:
To support, sustain and develop charitable
organizations operating in the El Paso
County community.

ELIGIBILITY:
Performing, literary and fine arts
organizations serving the entire El Paso
County community are eligible to apply.
Must have 501(c)(3) not-for-profit status. No
grants to individuals.

GEOG. RESTRICTIONS: El Paso County,
Colorado.

FINANCIAL DATA:
Amount of support per award: $2,500 to
$50,000.
Total amount of support: $160,000.

NO. MOST RECENT APPLICANTS: 12.

NO. AWARDS: 10.

APPLICATION INFO:
Application and guidelines are available
online. Organization must provide current
copy of IRS determination letter showing
tax-exempt status under Section 501(c)(3)
and public charity status under Section
509(a).
Duration: One year. No renewals.
Deadline: June 30.

ADDRESS INQUIRIES TO:
Julie Golden, Trust Advisor
(See address above.)

*SPECIAL STIPULATIONS:
JPMorgan will only accept applications
submitted online.

THE FRANK M. TAIT
FOUNDATION
40 North Main Street
Suite 1530
Dayton, OH 45423
(937) 222-2401
E-mail: taitfoundation@gmail.com

TYPE:
Project/program grants.

See entry 1036 for full listing.

TENNESSEE ARTS
COMMISSION   [458]
401 Dr. Martin Luther King Jr. Boulevard
Nashville, TN 37243-0780
(615) 741-6395
Fax: (615) 741-8559
E-mail: diane.williams@tn.gov
Web Site: tnartscommission.org

FOUNDED: 1967

AREAS OF INTEREST:
All arts disciplines in Tennessee.

CONSULTING OR VOLUNTEER SERVICES:
Consultant, informational and developmental services are offered to arts groups, individual artists, museums and arts councils throughout the state.

NAME(S) OF PROGRAMS:
- **Division of Arts Programs**
- **Division of Communications, Information & Technology**

TYPE:
Conferences/seminars; Fellowships; General operating grants; Project/program grants; Residencies; Technical assistance; Training grants. Professional development. Matching grants. Arts Programs consist of grants to institutions, individuals, coordinating agencies and entities of government. Consultation information and development assistance to state arts constituency is also provided.

Grant Programs: Funds may not be used for capital improvements or for permanent equipment.

YEAR PROGRAM STARTED: 1967

PURPOSE:
To support and encourage the life and growth of the arts and craft in the state of Tennessee and preservation of the state's cultural heritage.

LEGAL BASIS:
Independent state agency.

ELIGIBILITY:
Grants categories are limited to residents, artists and organizations of Tennessee. Grants are made to individuals, nonprofit organizations and/or entities of government.

GEOG. RESTRICTIONS: Tennessee.

FINANCIAL DATA:
Amount of support per award: $200 to $100,000.

Matching fund requirements: Most grant awards require a 1:1 match.

NO. MOST RECENT APPLICANTS: 1,000.

NO. AWARDS: 850.

APPLICATION INFO:
Details are available on the web site.

Duration: One fiscal year, July to June.

Deadline: Varies.

PUBLICATIONS:
Weekly online newsletter.

COMMISSION MEMBERS:
Jan McNally, Chairperson
Jennifer Wolfe, Vice Chairperson
Amy Rhodes, Secretary
Marc Burnett
Stephanie B. Conner
Michael Dumont
Mary Kilbride
Joe D. Kilgore
Deanie Parker
Dr. Shawn Pitts
Jason Rudd
Johnnie Wheeler

ADDRESS INQUIRIES TO:
Director of Grants Management
(See address above.)

TEXAS COMMISSION ON THE ARTS   [459]

E.O. Thompson Office Building
920 Colorado, Suite 501
Austin, TX 78701
(512) 463-5535
E-mail: laura@arts.texas.gov
Web Site: www.arts.texas.gov

FOUNDED: 1965

AREAS OF INTEREST:
Operational support and project support to nonprofit Texas arts organizations for ongoing programs and/or arts education, health and human services, economic development, public safety and criminal justice, and natural resources and agriculture; performance support for civic, cultural and other nonprofit organizations.

CONSULTING OR VOLUNTEER SERVICES:
Seminars, information services, technical assistance and funding. Services provided to institutions statewide.

NAME(S) OF PROGRAMS:
- **TCA Grant Programs**

TYPE:
Block grants; Challenge/matching grants; Conferences/seminars; Exchange programs; General operating grants; Project/program grants; Residencies; Technical assistance; Training grants; Travel grants; Visiting scholars. Organizational support, project support and touring support.

YEAR PROGRAM STARTED: 1965

PURPOSE:
To advance the state economically and culturally by investing in a creative Texas.

LEGAL BASIS:
Texas Government Code, Chapter 444, Section 021.

ELIGIBILITY:
Any 501(c)(3) organization, educational institution, or form of government may apply. Presenters and producers of performing arts whose programs are designed to stimulate artistic activity and to heighten awareness of and broaden public access to the arts in rural and underserved areas of the state are eligible to apply.

Award made according to project cost, program limits, ability to meet funding criteria and available funds.

GEOG. RESTRICTIONS: Texas.

FINANCIAL DATA:
Total amount of support: $5,000,000 for the year 2019.

Matching fund requirements: Funds provided by the state through the grants process must be matched by the applicant organization. Matching funds are generally expected to be in cash.

NO. MOST RECENT APPLICANTS: 1,500.

APPLICATION INFO:
Guidelines available online. All applications submitted electronically. Contact TCA staff to obtain user ID and password.
Duration: Up to one year.
Deadline: Varies.

PUBLICATIONS:
Guide to Programs and Services.

STAFF:
Dr. Gary Gibbs, Executive Director

COMMISSION MEMBERS:
Dale W. Brock, Chairperson

Mila Gibson, Vice-Chairperson
Mary Ann Apap Heller
Theresa W. Chang
Charles C. Gaines
Adrian Guerra
Karen Partee
Sean Peyton
Marci Roberts

ADDRESS INQUIRIES TO:
Laura Wiegand
Director of Programs and Technology
(See address above.)

TWO TEN FOOTWEAR FOUNDATION

1466 Main Street
Waltham, MA 02451
(781) 736-1500
Fax: (781) 736-1554
E-mail: socialservices@twoten.org
Web Site: twoten.org

TYPE:
Scholarships. Intended for students who are interested in pursuing a career in footwear design.

See entry 1585 for full listing.

UNITARIAN UNIVERSALIST ASSOCIATION OF CONGREGATIONS   [460]

UU Funding Program
P.O. Box 301149
Jamaica Plain, MA 02130
(617) 971-9600
E-mail: uufunding@gmail.com
Web Site: uua.org/college/scholarships/stanfield

FOUNDED: 1986

AREAS OF INTEREST:
Limited to the fine arts of painting, drawing, enameling, printmaking, photography and sculpture.

NAME(S) OF PROGRAMS:
- **Stanfield and D'Orlando Art Scholarships**

TYPE:
Scholarships. Annual scholarship to be awarded to an applicant majoring in fine art, for further study in that major, at an accredited school.

YEAR PROGRAM STARTED: 1980

PURPOSE:
To aid a Unitarian Universalist student majoring in fine arts.

LEGAL BASIS:
Religious organization.

ELIGIBILITY:
Applicants must be members in good standing for at least one year before date of application or sponsored by a member of a Unitarian Universalist Congregation and must be enrolled in an accredited school. Eligible art fields include drawing, painting, sculpture, enameling, printmaking and photography.

GEOG. RESTRICTIONS: United States.

FINANCIAL DATA:
Payment is made directly to the recipient.
Amount of support per award: Average $1,000.
Total amount of support: Varies.

NO. AWARDS: Varies.

APPLICATION INFO:
Completed application form (eight pages) must be submitted with official transcripts of all institutions attended, recommendation from an educator, and recommendation from the church minister or officer.

Duration: One academic year. May reapply.

Deadline: February 15. Notification in May.

*SPECIAL STIPULATIONS:
Affiliation with Unitarian Universalist Congregation required.

UNITED ARTS COUNCIL OF RALEIGH AND WAKE COUNTY, INC.　　　　　　　　　[461]

P.O. Box 26388
Raleigh, NC 27611
(919) 839-1498 ext. 209
Fax: (919) 839-6002
E-mail: rcarlile@unitedarts.org
Web Site: www.unitedarts.org

FOUNDED: 1990

AREAS OF INTEREST:
Arts, arts education, music education, theatre arts education, humanities-community development, and teacher-preparation education.

NAME(S) OF PROGRAMS:
● **Artist Support Grants**
● **Artists-in-Schools Grants Program**
● **Program Support Grants**

TYPE:
Project/program grants; Seed money grants.

YEAR PROGRAM STARTED: 1989

PURPOSE:
To enhance and strengthen arts and arts education in Wake County, NC.

ELIGIBILITY:
Funds are available to Wake County (NC) grades K-12 schools, individual artists, arts organizations and municipalities with specific arts programming.

GEOG. RESTRICTIONS: Wake County, North Carolina.

FINANCIAL DATA:
Amount of support per award: $1,000 to $20,000.

Total amount of support: Varies.

Matching fund requirements: Required for some programs.

NO. MOST RECENT APPLICANTS: Over 300.

NO. AWARDS: Varies.

APPLICATION INFO:
Application information is available on the web site.

Duration: Varies by grant program annually.

Deadline: Varies by grant program annually.

PUBLICATIONS:
Guidelines.

IRS I.D.: 56-0770175

UNIVERSITY OF MINNESOTA

Room 113, Elmer L. Andersen Library
222 21st Avenue South
Minneapolis, MN 55455
(612) 624-4576
E-mail: asc-clrc@umn.edu
Web Site: www.lib.umn.edu/clrc

TYPE:
Research grants; Travel grants; Visiting scholars. Award to travel to Kerlan Collection, University of Minnesota, plus per diem.

See entry 650 for full listing.

UNIVERSITY OF MINNESOTA　　　　　　　　　[462]

Room 113, Elmer L. Andersen Library
222 21st Avenue South
Minneapolis, MN 55455
(612) 624-4576
E-mail: asc-clrc@umn.edu
Web Site: www.lib.umn.edu/clrc

AREAS OF INTEREST:
Research and children's literature.

NAME(S) OF PROGRAMS:
● **Marilyn Hollinshead Fellowship**

TYPE:
Travel grants. Award to travel to Kerlan Collection, University of Minnesota, as well as per diem.

PURPOSE:
To fund children's literature research with manuscripts and/or original illustrations.

FINANCIAL DATA:
Award covers travel, food or lodging.

Amount of support per award: Up to $1,500.

Total amount of support: $1,500.

NO. AWARDS: 1 per year.

APPLICATION INFO:
Electronic application acceptable by deadline.

Duration: Grants are awarded annually and are not renewable.

Deadline: January 30 of research year.

ADDRESS INQUIRIES TO:
Fellowship Committee
(See address above.)

THE UNIVERSITY OF TEXAS AT AUSTIN　　　　　　　　　[463]

The Graduate School, Main Building 101
110 Inner Campus Drive, GO400
Austin, TX 78712-1710
(512) 232-3612
E-mail: adameve@austin.utexas.edu
holly.doyel@austin.utexas.edu
Web Site: dobiepaisano.utexas.edu

AREAS OF INTEREST:
Competitive writing fellowships.

NAME(S) OF PROGRAMS:
● **The Dobie Paisano Fellowship Program**

TYPE:
Project/program grants. Provides an opportunity for creative or nonfiction writers to live and write for an extended period in an environment that offers isolation and tranquility.

Ralph A. Johnston Memorial Fellowship is aimed at writers who have demonstrated some publishing and critical success.

Jesse H. Jones Writing Fellowship is aimed at, but not limited to, writers who are early in their careers.

Both fellowships provide and require free residence at the ranch.

YEAR PROGRAM STARTED: 1967

PURPOSE:
To stimulate creative writing by making it possible for a person to work without distractions in an environment that offers isolation and tranquility.

ELIGIBILITY:
Criteria for making the awards include quality of work, character of the proposed project, and suitability of the applicant for life at Paisano, the late J. Frank Dobie's ranch near Austin, TX.

At the time of application, the applicant must meet one of the following:
(1) be a native Texan;
(2) have lived in Texas at some time for at least three years or;
(3) have published significant work with a Texas subject.

FINANCIAL DATA:
Amount of support per award: Ralph A. Johnston Memorial Fellowship: Stipend of $6,000 per month; Jesse H. Jones Writing Fellowship: Stipend of $4,200 per month.

Total amount of support: Ralph A. Johnston Memorial Fellowship: $25,000; Jesse H. Jones Writing Fellowship: $18,000.

NO. MOST RECENT APPLICANTS: Ralph A. Johnston Memorial Fellowship: 27; Jesse H. Jones Writing Fellowship: 50.

NO. AWARDS: 1 each annually.

APPLICATION INFO:
Application process begins on December 1. Application fee of $20 for one fellowship or $30 for both fellowships is required. If applying for both fellowships, include the fee with the Johnston Memorial Fellowship application and check the appropriate box at the top of the Johnston application form. Application fees are nonrefundable.

Application will be accepted online through the Submittable portal.

Duration: Ralph A. Johnston Memorial Fellowship: Four months. Jesse H. Jones Writing Fellowship: January 7 to April 30.

Deadline: January 15.

ADDRESS INQUIRIES TO:
Holly Doyel, Executive Assistant
(See address above.)

*SPECIAL STIPULATIONS:
Applicant must demonstrate ability to live in a rustic secluded rural location. Fellows must reside at Paisano Ranch.

UTAH DIVISION OF ARTS & MUSEUMS　　　　　　　　　[464]

617 East South Temple
Salt Lake City, UT 84102
(801) 236-7550
Fax: (801) 236-7556
E-mail: lalder@utah.gov
Web Site: artsandmuseums.utah.gov

FOUNDED: 1899

AREAS OF INTEREST:
Arts and museums funding in Utah.

NAME(S) OF PROGRAMS:
● **Folk Arts Grants**
● **General Operating Support for Arts, Museums and Local Arts Agencies**
● **Project Grants**

TYPE:
General operating grants; Project/program grants.

PURPOSE:
To provide funding to art organizations and museums in Utah.

LEGAL BASIS:
Government agency.

ELIGIBILITY:
Varies with each grant. Organizations must have IRS 501(c)(3) not-for-profit status or be government entities. No grants to individuals or religious organizations.

GEOG. RESTRICTIONS: Utah.

FINANCIAL DATA:
Amount of support per award: Varies.
Total amount of support: $7,300,000.
Matching fund requirements: 1:1 cash match.

NO. MOST RECENT APPLICANTS: 290.

NO. AWARDS: 270.

APPLICATION INFO:
Procedure is done online. Applying organizations must have a Charitable Solicitation Permit.
Duration: One or two years. Nonrenewable.
Deadline: Varies.

STAFF:
Laurel Cannon Alder, Grants Manager
Racquel Cornali, Grants Coordinator

ADDRESS INQUIRIES TO:
Laurel Cannon Alder
Grants Manager
(See address above.)

VCCA (VIRGINIA CENTER FOR THE CREATIVE ARTS) [465]
154 San Angelo Drive
Amherst, VA 24521
(434) 946-7236
E-mail: vcca@vcca.com
Web Site: www.vcca.com

FOUNDED: 1971

TYPE:
Fellowships; Residencies. International exchange programs. Virginia Center for the Creative Arts (VCCA) hosts over 400 visual artists, writers and composers each year. Artists, whether emerging or established, are selected by peer review on the basis of the important or innovative work they are doing in their respective fields. In residence, Fellows are provided with an individual studio, private bedroom and three prepared meals a day so they can focus exclusively on their work. While uninterrupted time is assured and participation in community events or public engagement is voluntary, the dynamic interaction among the 25 Fellows in residence together, as they share work, discuss process, and enjoy each other's company, is an important component of the creative space of VCCA. With a tradition of hospitality and welcome, VCCA schedules a diverse cohort of artists across disciplines.

YEAR PROGRAM STARTED: 1971

PURPOSE:
To provide time and space for national and international writers, visual artists, and composers of talent and promise to bring forth their finest works because the arts are vital, diversity is a strength, and creativity is essential.

LEGAL BASIS:
Nonprofit corporation.

ELIGIBILITY:
Achievement or outstanding promise within a field of art must be demonstrated.

FINANCIAL DATA:
All fellowships are for periods of residency. No cash awards are offered. Some fellowships do offer stipends.
Amount of support per award: Varies.
Total amount of support: Varies.

NO. AWARDS: Over 400.

APPLICATION INFO:
Application must include two references from professionals in the applicant's field, samples of applicant's work and a curriculum vitae. Residencies available for three composers, nine visual artists and 13 writers at any time.
Duration: Two to eight weeks.
Deadline: January 15 for fellowships running from September to December. May 15 for fellowships running from January to April. September 15 for fellowships running from May to August.

PUBLICATIONS:
Application form; annual report; newsletters.

STAFF:
Sheila Gulley Pleasants, Deputy Director

ADDRESS INQUIRIES TO:
Sheila Gulley Pleasants, Deputy Director
(See address above.)

VERMONT ARTS COUNCIL [466]
136 State Street
Montpelier, VT 05633
(802) 828-3292
E-mail: mbell@vermontartscouncil.org
Web Site: www.vermontartscouncil.org

FOUNDED: 1964

AREAS OF INTEREST:
Visual arts including painting, sculpture, drawing, printmaking, crafts, film and photography; performing arts in music, theatre and dance; literature; public art; creative placemaking; and arts in schools.

NAME(S) OF PROGRAMS:
- **Animating Infrastructure Grants**
- **Art in State Buildings Program**
- **Artist Development Grants**
- **Artists in Schools Grants**
- **Arts Impact Grants**
- **Arts Partnership Grants**
- **Creation Grants**
- **Cultural Facilities Grants**
- **Head Start Arts Integration Program**

TYPE:
Project/program grants. Professional development grants. Cultural facilities improvements. Operating support for arts organizations. Public art and creative placemaking projects. Teaching artists residencies in schools. Creation of new work by artists.

YEAR PROGRAM STARTED: 1966

PURPOSE:
To advance and preserve the arts at the center of Vermont communities.

LEGAL BASIS:
Official state arts agency and a nonprofit membership corporation.

ELIGIBILITY:
Applicants must be nonprofit organizations, agencies of town, county, state government

and/or individual artists of demonstrated ability who are residents of Vermont for at least one year.

Funding is not available for:
(1) academic tuition;
(2) activities in which artists are not appropriately compensated;
(3) construction of new facilities, renovation of existing facilities, or other capital improvements (exceptions in cases that comply with Cultural Facilities Grants);
(4) deficits and debts incurred from past activities;
(5) events that present faculty members on the campus of their own institutions;
(6) events which are predominantly religious or sectarian;
(7) events whose sponsors are not in compliance with the requirements of the Americans with Disabilities Act of 1990 and Section 504 of the Rehabilitation Act of 1973;
(8) food and beverages;
(9) for-profit organizations;
(10) fund-raising events;
(11) international travel (airline tickets);
(12) lobbying expenses;
(13) private events to which the public is not invited and;
(14) purchase of permanent equipment (exceptions in cases that comply with Cultural Facilities Grants).

GEOG. RESTRICTIONS: Vermont.

FINANCIAL DATA:
Amount of support per award: Varies according to each program.
Total amount of support: $601,614 in grant awards for the year 2020.
Matching fund requirements: Generally 1:1.

CO-OP FUNDING PROGRAMS: Cultural Facilities Grants with the state of Vermont.

NO. MOST RECENT APPLICANTS: 447.

NO. AWARDS: 141.

APPLICATION INFO:
Interested applicants can view the *Arts Council Grant Guidelines* and application online. Individual artists are required to submit samples of work.
Duration: Typically one to three years.
Deadline: Varies.

IRS I.D.: 03-0218115

ADDRESS INQUIRIES TO:
Meredith Bell, Grants and Database Administrator
(See address above.)

VETERANS OF FOREIGN WARS AUXILIARY [467]
National Headquarters
406 West 34th Street, 10th Floor
Kansas City, MO 64111
(816) 561-8655
E-mail: info@vfwauxiliary.org
Web Site: vfwauxiliary.org

AREAS OF INTEREST:
Creative art for patriotic American youth.

NAME(S) OF PROGRAMS:
- **Young American Creative Patriotic Art Awards**

TYPE:
Awards/prizes.

YEAR PROGRAM STARTED: 1979

PURPOSE:
To promote artistic creativity in patriotic American youth.

LEGAL BASIS:
Nonprofit.

ELIGIBILITY:
Students must be in grades 9 through 12 and must attend school in the same state as the sponsoring VFW Auxiliary. Home-schooled students are eligible; foreign exchange students are not. National winners of the past contests may not compete in future Young American Creative Patriotic Art Contests. Students must be no older than 18 years of age and U.S. citizens or U.S. nationals.

GEOG. RESTRICTIONS: United States.

FINANCIAL DATA:
Amount of support per award: National Scholarships: $15,000 for first place; $7,500 for second place; $3,500 for third place; $1,500 for fourth and fifth place; $500 for sixth through 10th place.

Total amount of support: $31,500.

NO. MOST RECENT APPLICANTS: More than 4,000 for the year 2020.

NO. AWARDS: 10 annually.

APPLICATION INFO:
Two-dimensional art must be on paper or canvas. Water color, pencil, pastel, charcoal, tempera, crayon, acrylic, pen-and-ink, or oil may be used.

Art work must not be framed. Canvas entries must be submitted on stretcher frames or canvas board. Other entries must be matted on white. Other color mats must not be used. In matting, heavy paper must be used to reinforce back. Mounted and floating mats may also be used. The art should be no smaller than 8 x 10-inch, but no larger than 18 x 24-inch, not including mat.

Three-dimensional art can be paper, papier-mache, pottery, clay, metal work or fabric. Pieces should be no smaller than 8 x 24-inch in any direction. Art cannot be more than five pounds in weight.

Digital art, jewelry and photography is not accepted.

Applicant must be sure to complete entry form and to attach to back of entry. Submit a typed explanation of patriotism expressed in art (150 words or less).

Deadline: Student: Participants must submit entries to a local VFW Auxiliary Scholarships Chairman by March 31. Department: VFW Auxiliary or District entries must be received by the Department Scholarships Chairman by April 15. National: Department entries in the National Contest must be received at VFW Auxiliary VFW National Headquarters by May 5.

ADDRESS INQUIRIES TO:
Director of Programs and Communications
(See address above.)

*SPECIAL STIPULATIONS:
Only the first place department winner (from each state) is eligible for the national competition.

VIRGIN ISLANDS COUNCIL ON THE ARTS [468]
5070 Norre Gade, Suite 1
St. Thomas, VI 00802-6762
(340) 774-5984
Fax: (340) 774-6206
E-mail: tasidakelch@yahoo.com
vicastt@hotmail.com
Web Site: www.vicouncilonarts.org

FOUNDED: 1966

AREAS OF INTEREST:
Fine arts, language and literature, music, creative, visual and performing arts and crafts.

NAME(S) OF PROGRAMS:
● **Expanding Opportunities for Participation in the Arts**

TYPE:
Awards/prizes; Exchange programs; General operating grants; Project/program grants; Residencies; Technical assistance; Training grants; Travel grants. Professional development artist or art teacher grants. Grants and technical assistance to individual artists, arts organizations and arts institutions in the Virgin Islands.

YEAR PROGRAM STARTED: 1966

PURPOSE:
To encourage wider participation in the arts by means of individual creative development and the strengthening of cultural organizations.

LEGAL BASIS:
Government agency.

ELIGIBILITY:
Applicants must be residents of the Virgin Islands for at least two years. Grants are made to Virgin Island-based projects or applicants.

GEOG. RESTRICTIONS: Virgin Islands.

FINANCIAL DATA:
Amount of support per award: Up to approximately $10,000. Organizations can receive a maximum of $10,000 and individuals can receive a maximum of $5,000.

Total amount of support: Depends on government, local and federal funding.

Matching fund requirements: The amount varies depending on category of grant. Usually 1:1.

NO. MOST RECENT APPLICANTS: Approximately 185 grant requests.

NO. AWARDS: Approximately 150 grants awarded.

REPRESENTATIVE AWARDS:
$10,000 to Reichhold Center for the Performing Arts.

APPLICATION INFO:
Official application information is available on the Council's web site.

Duration: One year. Renewable on reapplication and reconsideration by the Board of Directors.

Deadline: January 31 and August 31.

STAFF:
Tasida Kelch, Executive Director

ADDRESS INQUIRIES TO:
Jaria Lynch, Special Projects Coordinator
(See address above.)

VIRGINIA COMMISSION FOR THE ARTS [469]
600 East Main Street, Suite 330
Richmond, VA 23219
(804) 225-3132
Fax: (804) 225-4327
E-mail: janet.starke@vca.virginia.gov
Web Site: www.arts.virginia.gov

FOUNDED: 1968

AREAS OF INTEREST:
Arts activities including but not limited to performances, exhibitions, demonstrations, workshops, readings and other presentations or participatory experiences in the fields of crafts, dance, folk arts, literature, museum work, music, public media, theatre and visual arts, provided by artists or arts organizations located in the state of Virginia.

TYPE:
Fellowships; General operating grants; Project/program grants; Technical assistance. Touring grants; In-school, after-school residency arts programs; Arts programs for adults including aging, military and incarcerated individuals; Training programs for artists; Local government challenge grants; Arts and education grants; Cultural/arts tourism marketing program.

YEAR PROGRAM STARTED: 1968

PURPOSE:
To encourage participation and invest in the arts for all Virginians.

LEGAL BASIS:
State agency.

ELIGIBILITY:
Applicants must be nonprofit, tax-exempt organizations, schools or professional artists, government units.

GEOG. RESTRICTIONS: Virginia.

FINANCIAL DATA:
Amount of support per award: Varies.
Total amount of support: $3,973,138 for fiscal year 2020.
Matching fund requirements: Varies according to program.

NO. MOST RECENT APPLICANTS: Approximately 1,000 for fiscal year 2019.

NO. AWARDS: Approximately 750 for fiscal year 2019.

APPLICATION INFO:
Contact the Commission.
Duration: One year.
Deadline: March 1 and April 1 for most programs. Varies for other programs.

PUBLICATIONS:
Performing Arts Tour directory (online); Teaching Artist Roster (online).

IRS I.D.: 54-0843105

ADDRESS INQUIRIES TO:
Executive Director
(See address above.)

VIRGINIA MUSEUM OF FINE ARTS [470]
Art and Education Division
200 North Boulevard
Richmond, VA 23220-4007
(804) 204-2685
Fax: (804) 204-2675
E-mail: vmfafellowships@vmfa.museum
Web Site: www.vmfa.museum/programs/college/visual-arts-fellowships

FOUNDED: 1940

AREAS OF INTEREST:
Education and careers in the visual arts.

NAME(S) OF PROGRAMS:
- **Professional Fellowship Program**
- **Student Fellowship Program**

TYPE:
Awards/prizes; Fellowships. Awards for undergraduate students, graduate students and professionals in the visual arts including painting, sculpture, crafts, photography, filmmaking, video, printmaking, mixed media, new/emerging media, and drawing. Art history is for graduate students only.

YEAR PROGRAM STARTED: 1940

PURPOSE:
To aid Virginians who seek financial aid for additional education or experience in the arts.

LEGAL BASIS:
State agency administering funds from an endowment and private foundations.

ELIGIBILITY:
All Applicants: Persons must be citizens or permanent residents of the U.S. and current legal residents of Virginia. A legal resident has a valid Virginia driver's license and/or pays income taxes in Virginia and/or is a registered Virginia voter. Applicants must be able to provide verification of residency upon request.

Student Applicants: Persons must be current legal residents of Virginia, and must have been legal residents for at least 12 consecutive months prior to the application deadline. Students paying in-state tuition to an accredited Virginia college, university or school of the arts qualify as legal residents of Virginia. Students must be enrolled full-time at an accredited college, university or school of the arts for the grant period of August 2022 to May 2023. Half-year fall semester Fellowship awards will be considered on a case-by-case basis for full-time students in the final year of a degree program who plan to graduate in December 2022.

Professional Applicants: Persons must be current legal residents of Virginia, and must have been legal residents for at least 24 consecutive months prior to the application deadline. Professional applicants must not be degree-seeking students at the time of the application deadline nor during the grant period of August 2022 to May 2023.

GEOG. RESTRICTIONS: Virginia.

FINANCIAL DATA:
Amount of support per award: Professional Fellowships: $8,000; Undergraduate Fellowships: $4,000; Graduate Fellowships: $6,000.
Total amount of support: $128,000 for the year 2021-22.

NO. MOST RECENT APPLICANTS: 370 for the year 2021-22.

NO. AWARDS: 21 for the year 2021-22.

APPLICATION INFO:
A complete application includes:
(1) applicant's basic information;
(2) curriculum vitae;
(3) work samples;
(4) artistic statement (visual arts only) and;
(5) transcript (students only).
Duration: August to May. No renewals.
Deadline: 5 P.M., November 5.

STAFF:
Natasha Campbell, Fellowship Program Coordinator

ADDRESS INQUIRIES TO:
See e-mail address above.

*PLEASE NOTE:
Awards are made to applicants of highest artistic merit whose education and/or careers will benefit from financial assistance.

KURT WEILL FOUNDATION
FOR MUSIC   [471]
7 East 20th Street, 3rd Floor
New York, NY 10003-1106
(212) 505-5240
Fax: (212) 353-9663
E-mail: bsansone@kwf.org
Web Site: www.kwf.org

FOUNDED: 1962

AREAS OF INTEREST:
The study and performance of music by Kurt Weill and Marc Blitzstein.

TYPE:
Grants-in-aid; Project/program grants; Research grants. College/University Performance: Grants to colleges and universities in support of general production expenses for performances of Kurt Weill's and Marc Blitzstein's stage works; grants are available to cover musical expenses in connection with performance of complete Weill and Blitzstein concert works.

Educational Outreach: Grants are awarded to performing and educational organizations which may request funding for educational activities (workshops, symposia, scholarly conferences, lectures in connection with performances, study days, secondary and college-level educational initiatives, etc.) focusing on Kurt Weill, Lotte Lenya and/or Marc Blitzstein, including payment of speakers' honoraria and travel expenses, preparation and printing of supporting materials, etc.

Publication Assistance: Grants assist in expenses related to preparing manuscripts for publication in a recognized scholarly medium, including editing, indexing, design and reproduction fees. Not-for-profit publishing companies are encouraged to apply.

Research and Travel: Grants support research and travel expenses to locations of primary source material for applicants who are researching a topic related to Kurt Weill, Lotte Lenya and/or Marc Blitzstein.

Kurt Weill Dissertation Fellowship: Assists Ph.D. candidates in Weill-research activities.

PURPOSE:
To preserve and perpetuate the legacies of composer Kurt Weill (1900-1950) and actress-singer Lotte Lenya (1898-1981).

ELIGIBILITY:
Broadcasts: Proposals are welcome from producers and not-for-profit broadcasters to support programs that feature Kurt Weill's or Marc Blitzstein's life and/or music. A complete description of the project must be accompanied by a written commitment from the broadcaster.

College/University Performance: Stage Works - All works must be presented in their authorized versions and orchestrations.
Concert works - Grants are available to cover

musical expenses in connection with performance of complete Weill and Blitzstein concert works. Compilation properties consisting solely of Weill's or Blitzstein's songs do not qualify for support.

Educational Outreach: Performing and educational organizations may request funding for educational activities (workshops, symposia, scholarly conferences, lectures in connection with performances, study days, secondary and college-level educational initiatives, etc.) focusing on Weill, Lenya and/or Blitzstein, including payment of speakers' honoraria and travel expenses, preparation and printing of supporting materials, etc.

Professional Performance: Funding may be requested by professional opera companies, theater companies, dance companies and concert groups. All works must be presented in their authorized versions and orchestrations. Applicants must furnish evidence (recordings, reviews) of the artistic merit of the organization's previous performances. Compilation properties consisting solely of Weill's songs do not qualify for support.

Publication Assistance: Funds may be requested to assist in expenses related to preparing manuscripts for publication in a recognized scholarly medium, including editing, indexing, design and reproduction fees. Not-for-profit publishing companies are encouraged to apply. All proposals must have been subject to peer review. Normally conference proceedings are ineligible unless the essays have undergone significant revision and editing as components of a book.

Research and Travel: Applicants must be researching a topic related to Kurt Weill, Lotte Lenya and/or Marc Blitzstein.

Kurt Weill Dissertation Fellowship: Applicants must be writing their dissertation on a topic related to Kurt Weill.

Kurt Weill Mentors: Grants are awarded to aid in preparation of Weill or Blitzstein stage or concert performances, to present workshops or lectures or to participate in scholarly symposia; performing arts organizations and educational institutions may request support to engage performers, conductors, directors and scholars who have been designated "Weill Mentors" by the Kurt Weill Foundation. Such requests may be considered even when the relevant performances would not otherwise be eligible for support under the Foundation's grant program. Applicants should contact the Foundation for further information.

FINANCIAL DATA:
Amount of support per award: Varies.
Total amount of support: Varies.

NO. MOST RECENT APPLICANTS: 20.

NO. AWARDS: Varies.

APPLICATION INFO:
All applications must include the following:
(1) Application Cover Sheet and Performance Grant Fact Sheet, if applying for a performance grant, available at the Foundation web site;
(2) a detailed description of the project;
(3) information about the applicant, including relevant qualifications and past achievements; performance grant applicants should also include a DVD or audio recording of a past

performance and;

(4) a detailed and itemized budget specifying entire project expenses and income, including ticket revenue and income anticipated from other funding sources and date of determination. Applicants must notify the Foundation if other grants are awarded.

In addition, specific items are requested for each category:
Broadcasts: a complete description of the project must be accompanied by a written commitment from the broadcaster;
College/University Performance: applicants must furnish evidence (recordings, reviews) of the artistic merit of the organization's previous performances;
Educational Outreach: applications must include detailed description of the educational activities and vitae for expert participants;
Professional Performance: applicants must furnish evidence (recordings, reviews) of the artistic merit of the organization's previous performances;
Publication Assistance: all proposals must have been subject to peer review; such reviews must be submitted in support of the application, along with a copy of the manuscript;
Research and Travel: grant applicants must submit a detailed outline of the proposed project, a writing sample, and at least one letter of recommendation;
Weill Dissertation Fellowship: applicants must include a copy of the dissertation proposal, at least one writing sample, and two letters of recommendation, one of which must be from the applicant's faculty advisor.
Deadline: November 1 for the following calendar year, academic year or cultural season. Applications for support of major professional productions/festivals/exhibitions, etc., will be evaluated on a case-by-case basis without application or performance deadlines. An additional application deadline of June 1 has been established, intended primarily for college/university performance grants for productions taking place in the fall semester of the current academic year.

ADDRESS INQUIRIES TO:
Brady Sansone, Director
(See address above.)

WEST VIRGINIA DEPARTMENT OF ARTS, CULTURE AND HISTORY [472]
The Culture Center
State Capitol Complex
1900 Kanawha Boulevard East
Charleston, WV 25305-0300
(304) 558-0220
Fax: (304) 558-2779
E-mail: lance.e.schrader@wv.gov
Web Site: www.wvculture.org

FOUNDED: 1967

AREAS OF INTEREST:
Artists and arts organizations, including community development, touring, institutions, special projects and support for artists, cultural facilities purchase and rehabilitation.

CONSULTING OR VOLUNTEER SERVICES:
Consultation in a variety of fields is available.

TYPE:
Capital grants; Challenge/matching grants; General operating grants; Internships; Project/program grants; Residencies;

Technical assistance; Training grants; Travel grants. Long-range planning. Individual artists grants.

YEAR PROGRAM STARTED: 1967

PURPOSE:
To provide financial and technical assistance to further the promotion, presentation and development of the arts throughout the state of West Virginia.

LEGAL BASIS:
Government agency.

ELIGIBILITY:
Nonprofit 501(c)(3) organizations and public agencies may apply. Nonprofits must have been based in West Virginia one year prior to application. Individual artists must be residents of West Virginia one year prior to application.

GEOG. RESTRICTIONS: West Virginia.

FINANCIAL DATA:
Generally, grants cover 50% of project cost.
Amount of support per award: $125 to $100,000.
Total amount of support: Approximately $2,226,826 for the year 2021.
Matching fund requirements: Dollar-for-dollar.

NO. MOST RECENT APPLICANTS: 130.

NO. AWARDS: 97.

APPLICATION INFO:
Copies of application guidelines and application forms are available upon request to the Commission or can be found on the Division web site. Online applications are preferred.
Duration: One year. Must reapply for additional funding.
Deadline: Varies.

PUBLICATIONS:
Annual report; application guidelines; *ArtWorks,* newsletter.

STAFF:
Randall Reid-Smith, Curator

ADDRESS INQUIRIES TO:
Lance E. Schrader, Arts Director
(See address above.)

WHITAKER FOUNDATION [473]
308 North 21st Street
Suite 400
St. Louis, MO 63103
(314) 241-4352
E-mail: info@thewhitakerfoundation.org
Web Site: www.thewhitakerfoundation.org

FOUNDED: 1975

AREAS OF INTEREST:
The arts, the use of and preservation of parks.

TYPE:
Project/program grants. Project/program grants are for urban parks and the arts.

PURPOSE:
To enrich lives through the arts; to encourage the preservation and use of parks.

LEGAL BASIS:
Private foundation.

ELIGIBILITY:
Organizations must be tax-exempt 501(c)(3). Project support is preferred. No support for social events.

The Foundation does not make grants to individuals.

GEOG. RESTRICTIONS: Metropolitan area of St. Louis, Missouri.

FINANCIAL DATA:
Amount of support per award: Varies.
Total amount of support: $1,001,050 for the year 2020.

NO. AWARDS: 17 for the year 2020.

APPLICATION INFO:
Application process begins with a Letter of Inquiry, which must be submitted online. Applicants, even those previously funded, must call the Foundation in advance to discuss their intent to apply.
Duration: Varies.
Deadline: Letters of Inquiry: August 1, November 1 and February 1; Invited Proposals: December 1, March 1 and September 1, respectively.

PUBLICATIONS:
Guidelines.

ADDRESS INQUIRIES TO:
Christy Gray, Executive Director
(See address above.)

WISCONSIN ARTS BOARD [474]
201 West Washington Avenue
2nd Floor
Madison, WI 53703
(608) 266-0190
Fax: (608) 267-0380
E-mail: artsboard@wisconsin.gov
Web Site: artsboard.wisconsin.gov

FOUNDED: 1973

AREAS OF INTEREST:
All arts disciplines in Wisconsin.

CONSULTING OR VOLUNTEER SERVICES:
Workshops and individual consultations.

NAME(S) OF PROGRAMS:
- **Creation and Presentation**
- **Creative Communities**
- **Folk Arts Apprenticeship Program**
- **Wisconsin Regranting Program**

TYPE:
Challenge/matching grants; Internships; Project/program grants; Technical assistance. Inquiry services, research and funding. Services provided to institutions and individuals statewide in Wisconsin.

Creative Communities Grants include Arts in Education, Local Arts and Folk Arts.

PURPOSE:
To provide support of arts projects and activities in the state of Wisconsin.

LEGAL BASIS:
Agency of the state of Wisconsin.

ELIGIBILITY:
Applicants must be organizations located in Wisconsin, operating for three years and have 501(c)(3) tax-exempt status.

GEOG. RESTRICTIONS: Wisconsin.

FINANCIAL DATA:
Amount of support per award: $1,500 to $20,000 depending on the program.
Total amount of support: $1,259,810 for the year 2018.
Matching fund requirements: All grants must be matched.

NO. AWARDS: Varies.

APPLICATION INFO:
Application form is available online.
Duration: One year.
Deadline: Varies.

STAFF:
George Tzougros, Executive Director

ADDRESS INQUIRIES TO:
Karen Goeschko, Assistant Director
Programs and Services
(See address above.)

WOMEN IN FILM
4221 Wilshire Boulevard
Suite 130
Los Angeles, CA 90010
(323) 935-2211
Fax: (323) 935-2212
E-mail: mverdugo@wif.org
Web Site: womeninfilm.org

TYPE:
Project/program grants. Awards for
completion of films on subjects that meet the
stated guidelines of WIF on an annual basis.

See entry 994 for full listing.

WOMEN'S STUDIO WORKSHOP (WSW)   [475]
722 Binnewater Lane
Kingston, NY 12401
(845) 658-9133
E-mail: info@wsworkshop.org
Web Site: www.wsworkshop.org

FOUNDED: 1974

AREAS OF INTEREST:
Book arts.

NAME(S) OF PROGRAMS:
• **Artists' Book Residency Grants**

TYPE:
Project/program grants; Residencies.

YEAR PROGRAM STARTED: 1979

PURPOSE:
To enable artists to produce a limited edition
artists' book while in residence at the
Women's Studio Workshop.

ELIGIBILITY:
Open to artists working in printmaking or the
book arts.

FINANCIAL DATA:
Amount of support per award: $350 per
week artist stipend, up to $750 materials, up
to $250 travel costs within the continental
U.S., access to all studios, and housing.

NO. MOST RECENT APPLICANTS: Approximately
100.

NO. AWARDS: 2.

APPLICATION INFO:
Application and instructions are available
online.
Duration: Six to eight weeks. Nonrenewable.
Deadline: November 15.

ADDRESS INQUIRIES TO:
Erin Zona, Artistic Director
(See address above.)

WOMEN'S STUDIO WORKSHOP (WSW)   [476]
722 Binnewater Lane
Kingston, NY 12401
(845) 658-9133
Fax: (845) 658-9031
E-mail: info@wsworkshop.org
Web Site: www.wsworkshop.org

FOUNDED: 1974

AREAS OF INTEREST:
Art-in-education.

NAME(S) OF PROGRAMS:
• **Art-in-Education Artists' Book Residency Grant**

TYPE:
Residencies. With National Endowment for
the Arts (NEA) support, WSW awards two
eight-week residencies to artists in the book
arts. This is a residency grant.

PURPOSE:
To help grantees create new work while they
simultaneously teach young people through
the workshop's studio-based art-in-education
program.

ELIGIBILITY:
Open to artists working in printmaking or the
book arts.

FINANCIAL DATA:
Amount of support per award: $350 per
week stipend, $750 materials budget,
housing, travel costs up to $250 within the
continental U.S. and unlimited studio access.

NO. AWARDS: 2.

APPLICATION INFO:
Application and instructions are available
online.
Duration: Eight to 10 weeks.
Deadline: November 15.

ADDRESS INQUIRIES TO:
Erin Zona, Artistic Director
(See address above.)

*PLEASE NOTE:
Normally, residencies are September to
October or January to April. Specific dates
are determined by the academic calendar and
vary annually.

WOMEN'S STUDIO WORKSHOP (WSW)   [477]
722 Binnewater Lane
Kingston, NY 12401
(845) 658-9133
E-mail: info@wsworkshop.org
Web Site: www.wsworkshop.
org/residencies/studio-residency-grant

FOUNDED: 1974

AREAS OF INTEREST:
Visual artists.

NAME(S) OF PROGRAMS:
• **Studio Residency Grant**

TYPE:
Residencies.

YEAR PROGRAM STARTED: 1999

PURPOSE:
To provide artists with time and resources to
create a new body of work.

ELIGIBILITY:
Printmakers, papermakers, book artists,
ceramists, photographers or artist
collaborators can apply.

FINANCIAL DATA:
Amount of support per award: $350 per
week artist stipend, up to $500 for materials,
up to $250 for travel within the continental
U.S., plus housing and unlimited studio use.

NO. MOST RECENT APPLICANTS: Approximately
100.

NO. AWARDS: 2.

APPLICATION INFO:
All applications must be submitted through
the web site listed above. Application must
include:
(1) a current resume;
(2) a description of the project (100 to 200
words), including the studio the applicant
would prefer to work in;
(3) 10 images of recent work and;
(4) an image script, including title, medium,
dimension and date of each image.
Duration: Six to eight weeks. Nonrenewable.
Deadline: September 1.

ADDRESS INQUIRIES TO:
Erin Zona, Artistic Director
(See address above.)

THE HELENE WURLITZER FOUNDATION OF NEW MEXICO   [478]
218 Los Pandos Road
Taos, NM 87571
(575) 758-2413
Fax: (575) 758-2559
E-mail: admin@wurlitzerfoundation.org
Web Site: wurlitzerfoundation.org

FOUNDED: 1954

AREAS OF INTEREST:
Creative, not interpretive, work in visual arts
(painting, sculpture, illustration, filmmaking,
etc.), literary arts (writing, poetry, playwright,
etc.), and musical composition (classical,
contemporary, songwriting).

NAME(S) OF PROGRAMS:
• **HWF Academic Scholarship Program**
• **HWF Artist Residency Program**

TYPE:
Residencies; Scholarships. Academic
Scholarship Program awards monetary
scholarships for local high school graduates
who wish to enter college as arts majors.

Artist Residency Program awards
artist-in-residence grants for national and
international artists producing creative work
in visual arts, literary arts, and musical
composition.

YEAR PROGRAM STARTED: 1954

PURPOSE:
To encourage and stimulate creative work in
all media, including visual arts, literary arts
and musical composition.

LEGAL BASIS:
Private 501(c)(3) nonprofit, educational and
charitable organization.

ELIGIBILITY:
No restrictions are made on the basis of race,
sex, age or religious or ethnic background or
national origin.

FINANCIAL DATA:
Artist Residency Program: No direct
monetary grants are made. Residency
includes housing and utilities.
Amount of support per award: Academic
Scholarship Program: $1,000 per year.

Total amount of support: Varies.

CO-OP FUNDING PROGRAMS: Robert Chesley
Foundation.

NO. MOST RECENT APPLICANTS: Academic
Scholarship Program: Approximately 8;
Artist Residency Program: Approximately
475.

NO. AWARDS: Academic Scholarship Program:
2; Artist Residency Program: 33.

APPLICATION INFO:
Residency application information is
available on the Foundation web site. Form
may be completed online or printed and
mailed to the address above.

Duration: Academic Scholarship Program:
Up to four years; Artist Residency Program:
10 to 12 weeks, depending on the session.

Deadline: January 18.

IRS I.D.: 85-0128634

OFFICERS AND BOARD OF DIRECTORS:
Peggy Nelson, President
Bill Ebie, Vice President
Michael Knight, Treasurer
Harald Hahn, Secretary
Nicholas Knight, Executive Director
Joseph Caldwell
Diane Reyna
Janet Webb

ADDRESS INQUIRIES TO:
Nicholas Knight, Executive Director
(See address above.)

*SPECIAL STIPULATIONS:
Single occupancy only; no pets, no smoking,
no outside employment while in residence.

WYOMING ARTS COUNCIL [479]

2301 Central Avenue
Barrett Building, 2nd Floor
Cheyenne, WY 82002
(307) 214-7819
E-mail: karen.merklin@wyo.gov
Web Site: wyoarts.state.wy.us

FOUNDED: 1967

AREAS OF INTEREST:
Arts within the state of Wyoming.

NAME(S) OF PROGRAMS:
● **Arts Access Project Grants**
● **Blanchan/Doubleday Fellowships**
● **Community Support Grants**
● **Folk & Traditional Arts Mentoring
  Project Grants**
● **Pattie Layser Greater Yellowstone
  Creative Writing & Journalism
  Fellowship**
● **Literary Arts Fellowships**
● **Native Art Fellowship**
● **Performing Arts Fellowships**
● **Professional Development/Career
  Advancement Grants**
● **Visual Arts Fellowships**

TYPE:
Awards/prizes; Conferences/seminars;
Development grants; Fellowships; General
operating grants; Project/program grants;
Technical assistance. Individual fellowships
are provided in visual, literary and
performing arts to Wyoming residents.

Folk & Traditional Arts Mentoring Project
Grants are designed to support the
transmission of Wyoming's finest folk and
traditional skills through the natural process
of in-person, hands-on instruction from a
master artist to a worthy apprentice.

Pattie Layser Fellowship is a national call
open to writers and journalists and seeks to
intersect science, education, current events,
and conservation to effectively communicate
the Greater Yellowstone's natural history and
singular importance to society through
creative and exceptional writing and subject
communication.

Native Art Fellowship is an unrestricted
award of merit, based on the artist's
portfolio, honoring the work of Native artists
based within Wyoming. Artists working
across any artistic discipline or medium
(visual, literary, performing, folk and
traditional, etc.) may apply. This fellowship
is designed to raise the profiles of the highly
talented Native artists in Wyoming and
celebrate their artistry. Recipients will be
given support to find a venue to showcase
their work.

YEAR PROGRAM STARTED: 1967

PURPOSE:
To assist artistic programs of outstanding
quality that serve the needs of Wyoming
citizens, further public interest in the state's
cultural heritage and resources and encourage
artistic expression, essential for the
well-being of the arts.

LEGAL BASIS:
Agency of the state of Wyoming.

ELIGIBILITY:
Grants are provided to 501(c)(3) nonprofit
organizations, educational institutions and
governmental entities within the state,
including arts centers, museums, symphonies,
schools, dance workshops, theatre and local
arts councils. Individual artists may apply for
the Blanche/Doubleday Fellowships, Folk &
Traditional Arts Mentoring Project Grants,
Native Art Fellowship, and Professional
Development/Career Advancement Grants.

GEOG. RESTRICTIONS: Wyoming.

FINANCIAL DATA:
Amount of support per award: Varies.

Total amount of support: Varies.

Matching fund requirements: A one-to-one
cash match is required on some grants.

NO. MOST RECENT APPLICANTS: More than 200.

NO. AWARDS: Over 200 grants are awarded each
year.

APPLICATION INFO:
Apply online for most grant programs.

Duration: One fiscal year (July 1 to the
following June 30).

Deadline: Varies.

PUBLICATIONS:
Newsletter.

STAFF:
Michael Lange, Executive Director
Rachel Clifton, Assistant Director
Karen Merklin, Grants Manager
Mary Billiter, Art Education Specialist
Taylor Craig, Creative Arts Specialist
Josh Chrysler, Folklorist and Health and
Wellness Specialist
Brittany Perez, Public Outreach and Events
Coordinator

ADDRESS INQUIRIES TO:
Karen Merklin, Grants Manager
(See address above.)

Performing arts

ACADEMY FOUNDATION OF THE ACADEMY OF MOTION PICTURE ARTS AND SCIENCES   [480]

1313 North Vine Street
Los Angeles, CA 90028
(310) 247-3010
Fax: (310) 247-3794
E-mail: nicholl@oscars.org
Web Site: www.oscars.org/nicholl

FOUNDED: 1927

AREAS OF INTEREST:
Motion picture arts and sciences.

NAME(S) OF PROGRAMS:
● **The Academy Nicholl Fellowships in
  Screenwriting**

TYPE:
Awards/prizes; Fellowships. Awards provide
a portion of living expenses for one year for
promising new writers so that they may
concentrate during that period on writing for
the screen.

YEAR PROGRAM STARTED: 1985

PURPOSE:
To foster the development of the art of
motion picture screenwriting.

LEGAL BASIS:
Nonpublic foundation.

ELIGIBILITY:
Applicants may not have earned more than
$25,000 or any other consideration as a
screenwriter for theatrical films or television
or sold or optioned screen or television rights
to any original story, treatment, outline
screenplay or teleplay.

FINANCIAL DATA:
Amount of support per award: Up to $35,000
per year.

NO. MOST RECENT APPLICANTS: 7,831 for the
year 2020.

NO. AWARDS: Up to 5 fellowships each year.

APPLICATION INFO:
Applicants must submit one copy of an
original screenplay in PDF format, no shorter
than 70 pages, and no longer than 160 pages
in length, written in screenplay format
standard to the U.S. motion picture industry.
Submissions must have been written
originally in English; translations will not be
accepted. Submissions must be the original
work of the applicant and may not be based,
in whole or in part, on any other person's or
persons' fictional or nonfictional material,
published or unpublished, produced or
unproduced. Sequels utilizing characters or
storylines from produced motion pictures,
television shows or published fiction are not
eligible. Nor are adaptations eligible, unless
the source material is solely the entrant's
original work.

Applicants must also fill out an application
form via an online account, completed in its
entirety and pay a nonrefundable entry fee.
This fee will be applied against judging and
administrative costs. Applications and
screenplays are accepted online only.
Submitted materials will not be returned.

Duration: One year, commencing around the
first week of November.

Deadline: Uploaded by 11:59 P.M., May 3.
Announcement in late October.

PUBLICATIONS:
Guidelines.

ADDRESS INQUIRIES TO:
Academy Nicholl Fellowships
(See address above.)

*PLEASE NOTE:
Each fellowship is payable quarterly for one year. The first payment will be made at the start of the fellowship year. The second, third, fourth and final payments will be made subject to satisfactory progress of the recipient's work, as judged by the Academy's Nicholl Fellowship Committee. The Academy reserves the right to grant no awards if, in the opinion of the Academy Nicholl Fellowship Committee, no application is of sufficient merit.

*SPECIAL STIPULATIONS:
Academy Nicholl Fellowships may not be held concurrently with other fellowships. During the fellowship year, Academy Nicholl Fellows are expected to complete an original screenplay approximately 90 to 120 pages in length.

AMERICAN DANCE FESTIVAL   [481]
Box 90772
Durham, NC 27708-0772
(919) 684-6402
Fax: (919) 684-5459
E-mail: adf@americandancefestival.org
Web Site: www.americandancefestival.org

NAME(S) OF PROGRAMS:
- Tuition Scholarships

TYPE:
Scholarships.

PURPOSE:
To offer assistance to promising students.

ELIGIBILITY:
Open to promising students who have a high level of technical ability, creative potential and who have experience in either performing and/or choreography.

GEOG. RESTRICTIONS: Primarily United States.

FINANCIAL DATA:
Amount of support per award: $200 to full tuition.
Total amount of support: Varies.

NO. MOST RECENT APPLICANTS: 420.

NO. AWARDS: 194.

APPLICATION INFO:
Student must complete the online application and submit the $50 application fee. Each program has different scholarship process requirements. Details can be found on the American Dance Festival web site.
Duration: Five-and-a-half weeks.
Deadline: Scholarships: April 1.

ADDRESS INQUIRIES TO:
School Staff Administration
E-mail: school@americandancefestival.org

AMERICAN SOCIETY FOR THEATRE RESEARCH (ASTR)   [482]
P.O. Box 922
Santa Cruz, CA 95061
(628) 222-4088
Fax: (651) 290-2266
E-mail: info@astr.org
Web Site: www.astr.org

FOUNDED: 1956

AREAS OF INTEREST:
Theatre studies (history, criticism, theory), performance studies, and dance studies.

NAME(S) OF PROGRAMS:
- The ASTR Collaborative Research Award
- ATHE-ASTR Award for Excellence in Digital Scholarship
- Biennial Sally Banes Publication Prize
- Oscar G. Brockett Essay Prize
- Cambridge University Press Prize
- Helen Krich Chinoy Dissertation Research Fellowships
- Co-sponsored Events Awards
- Selma Jeanne Cohen Conference Presentation Award
- Distinguished Scholar Award
- Grants for Researchers with Heavy Teaching Loads
- Barnard Hewitt Award
- Errol Hill Award
- Gerald Kahan Scholar's Prize
- David Keller Travel Grants
- Thomas F. Marshall Graduate Student Awards
- Brooks McNamara Publishing Subvention
- Research Fellowships
- Targeted Research Areas Grants

TYPE:
Awards/prizes; Conferences/seminars; Development grants; Exchange programs; Fellowships; Research grants; Scholarships; Seed money grants; Travel grants; Visiting scholars. The ASTR Collaborative Research Award aims to foster the exchange of research across different academic and community contexts within the U.S. or between U.S. scholars/artists and those abroad. It also aims to foster long-term relationships benefiting faculty who work in different types of institutional environments and to foster the exchange of research in subject areas underrepresented in U.S. theatre scholarship, pedagogy, and performance practice.

ATHE-ASTR Award for Excellence in Digital Scholarship is awarded each year to an individual or team that demonstrates innovation and rigor in the use of electronic/digital media for the purpose of producing or disseminating knowledge about theatre and performance.

Biennial Sally Banes Publication Prize is presented in even-numbered years for the publication (book or essay) that best explores the intersections of theatre and dance/movement in the previous two calendar years.

Oscar G. Brockett Essay Prize is jointly awarded by the Society and the Oscar G. Brockett Center for Theatre History and Criticism at the University of Texas - Austin for the best essay published in English in a refereed scholarly journal or volume published by a scholarly press. The essay can relate to any subject in theatre research, broadly construed.

The Cambridge University Press Prize is given for a Society conference plenary paper written by a first-time plenary presenter.

Helen Krich Chinoy Dissertation Research Fellowships assist Ph.D. candidates with travel to national and international collections to conduct research connected with their dissertations.

Co-sponsored Events Awards assist with events that fulfill ASTR's purpose through collaboration with other organizations and institutions and increase the visibility of the work of both ASTR and the award recipient within a wider professional context.

Selma Jeanne Cohen Conference Presentation Award goes to a scholar to participate in a plenary or working session at the ASTR conference. The presentation must explore the intersections of theatre and dance/movement.

Distinguished Scholar Award is given each year to a scholar whose body of work has made a significant contribution to the field of theatre, dance, opera, and/or performance studies.

Grants for Researchers with Heavy Teaching Loads promote scholarly and practical exchange among theatre researchers by providing opportunities to faculty at institutions with heavy teaching loads and limited support for scholarship.

The Barnard Hewitt Award for Outstanding Research in Theatre History is awarded each year to the best book in "theatre history or cognate disciplines" published during the previous calendar year. The Department of Theatre at the University of Illinois, Urbana-Champaign, provides the monetary prize.

Errol Hill Award is given in recognition of outstanding scholarship in African American theatre, drama, and/or performance studies. The book or article must be published during the previous calendar year.

Gerald Kahan Scholar's Prize is awarded for the best essay written by a junior scholar and published in English in a refereed scholarly journal on any subject in theatre research, broadly construed.

David Keller Travel Grants encourage untenured scholars with terminal degrees to become active members of the Society by helping them to meet the expenses of attending the ASTR annual meeting in November.

Thomas F. Marshall Graduate Student Awards encourage active student membership in the Society by helping to meet the expenses of attending the ASTR annual meeting.

Brooks McNamara Publishing Subvention supports the costs of securing rights to reproduce illustrations for publication, costs of acquiring illustrations, and/or the costs of reproducing illustrations in conjunction with a book under contract for publication. (Electronic publications will also be considered.)

Research Fellowships underwrite some expenses associated with projects in the field of theatre and/or performance studies.

Targeted Research Areas Grants support specific projects in areas currently underrepresented. Such areas include, but are not limited to, pre-1900 research; Asian, African, Latin American, and Middle Eastern theatre, dance and performance. Translations of important theatre documents, including plays, are also considered.

YEAR PROGRAM STARTED: 1976

LEGAL BASIS:
Nonprofit learned society.

ELIGIBILITY:

The ASTR Collaborative Research Award: At least one participant from a host institution must be a current ASTR member.

ATHE-ASTR Award for Excellence in Digital Scholarship: The principal investigator should be a member of either ATHE or ASTR, but co-principal investigators need not all be members for the project to be considered.

Biennial Sally Banes Publication Prize: Any independent, tenured or untenured scholar; eligible books and articles must have been published in the previous two calendar years.

Oscar G. Brockett Essay Prize: Author must have been a member of ASTR for at least three years and be at least seven years beyond the Ph.D. Essays must have been published in the previous calendar year and may not have appeared elsewhere previously.

Cambridge University Press Prize: ASTR conference plenary paper written by a first-time plenary presenter.

Helen Krich Chinoy Dissertation Research Fellowships: Ph.D. candidates who have passed their qualifying exams within the last two years (or will have passed their qualifying exams by June of the current year) and have begun working on their dissertations. The project must be part of the dissertation research.

Co-sponsored Events Awards: Applications may come from individuals, institutions or a combination, to support events of regional, national or international significance in the form of conferences, colloquia, symposia, summits, etc. Events must foster scholarship on theatre and performance.

Selma Jeanne Cohen Conference Presentation Award: Tenured, untenured and contingent faculty, independent scholars and graduate students are eligible to apply.

Distinguished Scholar Award: Nominations are accepted from ASTR members and previous recipients of the award. In addition to contributions made to theatre, dance, opera and/or performance studies, involvement in ASTR is also a criterion of the award.

Grants for Researchers with Heavy Teaching Loads: Any full-time or contingent instructor at the college level, with a terminal degree and a heavy teaching load or the equivalent load based on heavy production and/or service obligations.

Barnard Hewitt Award: Eligible books must have been published in the previous calendar year. They must be written by a scholar or scholars residing in the Americas, or by a scholar or scholars located outside the Americas but writing on an American topic. Plays, edited collections and anthologies are not eligible for this prize.

Errol Hill Award: The book or article must have been published in the previous calendar year. Authors may nominate their own works; nominations from publishers and editors are also accepted.

Gerald Kahan Scholar's Prize: The author must be untenured and within seven years of the Doctorate, or must be enrolled in a doctoral program, at the time the essay is published.

David Keller Travel Grants: Any untenured scholars with terminal degrees, including independent scholars and tenure-track and adjunct faculty.

Thomas F. Marshall Graduate Student Awards: Any student majoring in theatre/performance studies in any academic department at any level of higher education.

Brooks McNamara Publishing Subvention: Any scholar holding a terminal degree and who has been a member of ASTR for at least three years. Applicant must hold a book contract to qualify. Preference is given to junior scholars.

Research Fellowships: Anyone who holds a terminal degree and has been a member of the Society for at least three years is eligible to apply.

Targeted Research Areas Grants: Any independent, tenured or untenured scholar who is currently a member of the Society and holds a terminal degree, or any graduate student who is applying in support of a project that is not directly related to her/his dissertation.

FINANCIAL DATA:
Amount of support per award: Varies.
Total amount of support: Varies.

NO. MOST RECENT APPLICANTS: Varies.

NO. AWARDS: 21 for the year 2020.

APPLICATION INFO:
Application information is available on the web site, under "Awards."
Duration: Varies.
Deadline: Varies.

ADDRESS INQUIRIES TO:
Vice President for Awards
(See address above.)

ARTS MIDWEST [483]
2908 Hennepin Avenue, Suite 200
Minneapolis, MN 55408-1954
(612) 341-0755
E-mail: christy@artsmidwest.org
Web Site: www.artsmidwest.org

FOUNDED: 1985

AREAS OF INTEREST:
Performing arts booking conference and performing arts grants to presenting organizations.

NAME(S) OF PROGRAMS:
- **Arts Midwest Conference**
- **GIG Fund**

TYPE:
Conferences/seminars. Performing arts grants.

YEAR PROGRAM STARTED: 1985

PURPOSE:
To connect people throughout the Midwest and the world to meaningful arts opportunities, sharing creativity, knowledge, and understanding across boundaries.

LEGAL BASIS:
Nonprofit.

ELIGIBILITY:
Nonprofit performing arts presenters within our nine-state region.

GEOG. RESTRICTIONS: Illinois, Indiana, Iowa, Michigan, Minnesota, North Dakota, Ohio, South Dakota and Wisconsin.

FINANCIAL DATA:
Amount of support per award: $2,500.
Total amount of support: Varies.

NO. AWARDS: Approximately 150 annually.

APPLICATION INFO:
Application information is available online.
Duration: Varies.

THE BANFF CENTRE [484]
107 Tunnel Mountain Drive
Banff AB T1L 1H5 Canada
(403) 762-6180
Fax: (403) 762-6345
E-mail: registrars_office@banffcentre.ca
Web Site: www.banffcentre.ca/programs

FOUNDED: 1933

AREAS OF INTEREST:
Performing arts, literary, visual and new media arts.

TYPE:
Conferences/seminars; Residencies; Scholarships. Practicum.

PURPOSE:
To provide financial assistance to deserving artists for a residency at The Banff Centre.

ELIGIBILITY:
Open to advanced students who have been accepted for a program at The Banff Centre.

FINANCIAL DATA:
Amount of support per award: Varies.
Total amount of support: Varies depending on program.

APPLICATION INFO:
Application information can be accessed online. Applicants must submit a completed application form, accompanied by requested documentation.
Duration: Varies.
Deadline: Varies per program.

ADDRESS INQUIRIES TO:
E-mail: admissions@banffcentre.ca

CAPEZIO/BALLET MAKERS DANCE FOUNDATION, INC. [485]
One Campus Road
Totowa, NJ 07512
(973) 595-9000
(973) 653-2001
Fax: (973) 595-9120
Web Site: www.capezio.com

FOUNDED: 1952

AREAS OF INTEREST:
National, state and some local dance profession service organizations. Annual Capezio Dance Award in recognition of significant contribution to the art form.

NAME(S) OF PROGRAMS:
- **Capezio Dance Award**
- **Grants Program**

TYPE:
Awards/prizes; Development grants; General operating grants; Project/program grants. Grants to national, state and some local dance service organizations such as dance alliances, dance festivals and other organizations having a major impact on the field.

Capezio Dance Award is given annually by the Trustees to an individual, company or organization that brings respect, stature and distinction to dance in America.

YEAR PROGRAM STARTED: 1952

PURPOSE:
   To create a greater awareness and
   appreciation of dance as an art form and
   support efforts which service and increase
   interest in the dance field.

LEGAL BASIS:
   Private tax-exempt, corporate foundation.

ELIGIBILITY:
   National, state and local organizations that
   provide essential services to the dance field
   may apply. Organization must have 501(c)(3)
   status. No support for individual dancers,
   companies or schools.

GEOG. RESTRICTIONS: United States.

FINANCIAL DATA:
   Amount of support per award: $1,000 to
   $10,000.
   Total amount of support: $50,000 to
   $100,000.

NO. MOST RECENT APPLICANTS: 200.

NO. AWARDS: 50 to 70.

APPLICATION INFO:
   Guidelines are available on the Foundation
   web site.
   Duration: No limitations.
   Deadline: April 1.

PUBLICATIONS:
   Brochure of guidelines and criteria; listing of
   grantees and Capezio Award winners.

IRS I.D.: 13-6161198

*PLEASE NOTE:
   Does not fund individuals, schools, colleges
   or universities, films or media or dance
   companies.

CHOPIN FOUNDATION OF THE U.S.
1440 79th Street Causeway, Suite 117
Miami, FL 33141
(305) 868-0624
Fax: (305) 865-5150
E-mail: info@chopin.org
Web Site: www.chopin.org

TYPE:
   Scholarships. Scholarship program supporting
   young American pianists, 14 to 17 years of
   age.

See entry 697 for full listing.

MARTHA GRAHAM SCHOOL OF CONTEMPORARY DANCE, INC.   [486]
55 Bethune Street, 11th Floor
New York, NY 10014
(212) 229-9200
Fax: (212) 202-7831
E-mail: school@marthagraham.org
jpatten@marthagraham.org
Web Site: marthagraham.edu

FOUNDED: 1926

AREAS OF INTEREST:
   Training professional dancers.

NAME(S) OF PROGRAMS:
   ● **Advanced Studies Certificate**
   ● **Graham 2 Company**
   ● **Independent Program**
   ● **Summer Intensive**
   ● **Teacher Training Program**
   ● **Teens@Graham Young Artists
      Program**

   ● **Two-Year Certificate Program**
   ● **Winter Intensive**

TYPE:
   Conferences/seminars; General operating
   grants; Internships; Matching gifts;
   Project/program grants; Research grants;
   Residencies; Scholarships; Work-study
   programs. Awards for class tuition.

   Scholarship students work at the school.

YEAR PROGRAM STARTED: 1966

PURPOSE:
   To provide help to the most promising dance
   students who are studying at the Martha
   Graham School.

LEGAL BASIS:
   Nonprofit private school.

ELIGIBILITY:
   Scholarships are available on a limited merit
   and need-based system. Scholarships are
   offered for Graham 2 Company members and
   understudies in the form of School
   Assistantships and through
   faculty-determined Program Director
   Scholarships. Scholarships require regular
   attendance.

   Proficiency in dancing with special
   proficiency in the Martha Graham Technique
   is required. On-site scholarship auditions.

FINANCIAL DATA:
   Amount of support per award: Graham 2:
   $1,750 per semester; Graham 2 Understudy
   and School Assistantships: $1,250 per
   semester; Program Director Scholarships:
   Varies.
   Total amount of support: Varies.

NO. MOST RECENT APPLICANTS: 200.

NO. AWARDS: 24.

APPLICATION INFO:
   Students are automatically considered as part
   of their program audition and application
   submission.
   Duration: Normally awarded on a 12-month
   basis, on the basis of competition.
   Deadline: Rolling admissions and
   international applicants: July 1.

IRS I.D.: 13-1834089

STAFF:
   LaRue Allen, Executive Director
   Jennifer Patten, Head of School
   Tami Alesson, Dean of Student and
   Government Affairs
   Janet Eilber, Artistic Director

ADDRESS INQUIRIES TO:
   Jennifer Patten, Head of School
   (See address above.)

JACOB'S PILLOW, INC.   [487]
358 George Carter Road
Becket, MA 01223
(413) 243-9919
Fax: (413) 243-4744
E-mail: info@jacobspillow.org
Web Site: www.jacobspillow.org

FOUNDED: 1932

AREAS OF INTEREST:
   Nurturing and sustaining artistic creation,
   presentation, education and preservation as
   well as engaging and deepening public
   appreciation and support for dance.

NAME(S) OF PROGRAMS:
   ● **The School at Jacob's Pillow**

TYPE:
   Assistantships; Awards/prizes; Exchange
   programs; Fellowships; Residencies;
   Scholarships; Training grants; Visiting
   scholars. The School at Jacob's Pillow, one
   of the most prestigious and sought-after
   professional advancement training centers in
   the world, has four intensive programs:
   Ballet, Cultural Traditions, Contemporary and
   Musical Theatre Dance, all including
   awards/prizes/scholarships.

   There are creative development residencies
   available.

PURPOSE:
   To provide professional development training
   to advanced dancers in summer dance
   programs.

ELIGIBILITY:
   Open to U.S. and foreign nationals who are
   16 years of age or older and complete
   application requirements for the program(s)
   selected.

FINANCIAL DATA:
   The School at Jacob's Pillow provides
   scholarships applicable toward tuition, room
   and board.
   Amount of support per award: Varies.
   Total amount of support: Varies.

NO. MOST RECENT APPLICANTS: 3,500.

NO. AWARDS: 100 per year.

APPLICATION INFO:
   All dancers wishing to be considered for
   acceptance in The School's Summer
   Intensive Programs should follow their
   program-specific instructions and upload all
   required materials and videos to complete the
   online program application. To pre-register
   for a Master Class or Workshop, a program
   application must be submitted.
   Duration: One to three weeks.
   Deadline: Varies by program.

ADDRESS INQUIRIES TO:
   E-mail: school@jacobspillow.org

JACOB'S PILLOW, INC.   [488]
358 George Carter Road
Becket, MA 01223
(413) 243-9919
Fax: (413) 243-4714
E-mail: info@jacobspillow.org
internprogram@jacobspillow.org
Web Site: www.jacobspillow.org

AREAS OF INTEREST:
   Nurturing and sustaining artistic creation,
   presentation, education and preservation, as
   well as engaging and deepening public
   appreciation and support for dance.

NAME(S) OF PROGRAMS:
- **The Intern Program at Jacob's Pillow**

TYPE:
Internships. The Intern Program at Jacob's Pillow supports training in arts administration and technical theater production.

PURPOSE:
To provide real work projects and responsibilities that build practical experience and develop professional skills.

ELIGIBILITY:
Interested and engaged college students looking for professional advancement opportunities in arts administration may apply.

FINANCIAL DATA:
Amount of support per award: $1,500 stipend.

NO. MOST RECENT APPLICANTS: Approximately 311.

NO. AWARDS: Approximately 100.

APPLICATION INFO:
Online application form requires a cover letter explaining applicant's wish to intern at Jacob's Pillow, their qualifications and interests for the position(s) indicated on the application form, and their goals and expectations for the internship. A resume, two references, support materials, if requested, and a letter of recommendation are also required.
Duration: Up to three months.
Deadline: Late January.

ADDRESS INQUIRIES TO:
E-mail: internprogram@jacobspillow.org

NATIONAL OPERA ASSOCIATION, INC.
100 Baits Drive
Ann Arbor, MI 48109
(734) 615-3784
E-mail: ksevert@noa.org
Web Site: www.noa.org

TYPE:
Awards/prizes. Cash prizes awarded to Artist Division winners and Scholarship Division winners. Also scholarships to AIMS, awarded in both divisions. Productions of winning operas in Chamber Opera Competition will be scheduled for annual convention.

See entry 717 for full listing.

NEW DRAMATISTS [489]
424 West 44th Street
New York, NY 10036
(212) 757-6960
Fax: (646) 390-8705
E-mail: newdramatists@newdramatists.org
Web Site: www.newdramatists.org

FOUNDED: 1949

AREAS OF INTEREST:
Service organization for resident member playwrights. Work with resident member writers on new plays, providing them with workshops, readings and staged readings. Involves directors, actors and dramaturges, among other artists, in writer-led development work programming.

TYPE:
Awards/prizes; Internships; Residencies. Resident playwrights are selected by an admissions panel which consists of current resident playwrights, alumni playwrights, and other theatre professionals. The panel changes completely from year to year.

YEAR PROGRAM STARTED: 1949

PURPOSE:
To provide playwrights with the tools and freedom to make lasting contributions to the theatre.

LEGAL BASIS:
Not-for-profit corporation.

ELIGIBILITY:
Open to U.S. citizens.

GEOG. RESTRICTIONS: United States.

NO. MOST RECENT APPLICANTS: 522 for the year 2018-19.

NO. AWARDS: 5 to 8 residencies per year.

APPLICATION INFO:
Information is available online.
Deadline: Varies.

PUBLICATIONS:
Application guidelines; brochure.

OFFICERS:
David C. Rosenzweig, Chairman
Abbie Van Nostrand, President

NEW MUSIC USA
40 Wall Street, 6th Floor
New York, NY 10005
(212) 645-6949
Fax: (646) 490-0998
E-mail: info@newmusicusa.org
Web Site: www.newmusicusa.org

TYPE:
Awards/prizes; General operating grants; Project/program grants; Residencies. Amplifying Voices is a five-year residency and commissioning program that places composers of color with mid-sized orchestras to encourage collaboration and collective action toward equitable representing of artists of color in the contemporary classical canon.

New Music Capacity Building Program is a two-year program offering financial support and professional development opportunities for small- to medium-sized New York City based music groups and venues.

New Music Creator Development Fund offers project-specific funding to individual music creators.

Organizational Development Fund offers grants to nonprofit organizations, performance groups, dance organizations, festivals, presenters, and venues to support their new music programming.

Reel Change provides funding and mentorship for midcareer composers working on film projects currently in production.

See entry 720 for full listing.

PEN AMERICA [490]
588 Broadway, Suite 303
New York, NY 10012
(212) 334-1660 ext. 4813
Fax: (212) 334-2181
E-mail: awards@pen.org
Web Site: pen.org

FOUNDED: 1922

AREAS OF INTEREST:
American theater.

NAME(S) OF PROGRAMS:
- **PEN/Laura Pels International Foundation for Theater Award - Mid-Career Playwright**

TYPE:
Awards/prizes. Honors a midcareer playwright whose literary achievements are vividly apparent.

PURPOSE:
To honor the accomplishments of American playwrights.

ELIGIBILITY:
Candidates must be playwrights writing in English who have had a professional production of at least two full-length works mounted in a theater of at least 299 seats and contracted specifically for either limited or open runs. Authors who have written only one-acts or books for musicals, or who have only translated the works of others for English-language audiences, will not be considered.

Candidates must be American citizens.

Candidates may be nominated by writers, playwrights, or members of the theater community. One need not be a PEN member to submit a nomination.

The works of writers produced by regional theaters across the U.S. will be given consideration equal to work produced in major metropolitan centers.

FINANCIAL DATA:
Amount of support per award: $10,000.
Total amount of support: $10,000.

NO. AWARDS: 1 annually.

APPLICATION INFO:
Any playwright, writer or member of the theater community may submit a nomination.
Deadline: August 1.

ADDRESS INQUIRIES TO:
See e-mail address above.

PEW FELLOWSHIPS AT THE PEW CENTER FOR ARTS & HERITAGE
1608 Walnut Street, 18th Floor
Philadelphia, PA 19103
(267) 350-4920
Fax: (267) 350-4997
E-mail: mfranklin@pewcenterarts.org
Web Site: www.pewcenterarts.org

TYPE:
Fellowships. Opportunities for contemporary artists in the Philadelphia five-county area to concentrate on the development and creation of art. Fellowships to support artists at critical junctures in any stage of their career development. Fellows will be expected to participate annually in at least three meetings with other fellowship recipients.

See entry 513 for full listing.

PRINCESS GRACE FOUNDATION-USA [491]
150 East 58th Street, 25th Floor
New York, NY 10155
(212) 317-1470
E-mail: grants@pgfusa.org
Web Site: www.pgfusa.org

FOUNDED: 1982

AREAS OF INTEREST:
Theater, dance, choreography, film and playwriting.

NAME(S) OF PROGRAMS:
- **Princess Grace Awards**

TYPE:
Awards/prizes; Fellowships; Scholarships. Dedicated to identifying and assisting emerging artists in theater, dance and film through grants.

YEAR PROGRAM STARTED: 1984

PURPOSE:
To identify and assist emerging artists in the fields of dance, theater and film within the U.S.

LEGAL BASIS:
Not-for-profit, tax-exempt, publicly supported charity.

ELIGIBILITY:
Must be a U.S. citizen or permanent resident.

GEOG. RESTRICTIONS: United States.

FINANCIAL DATA:
Amount of support per award: Theater, Animation, Dance and Film Awards: $7,500 to $30,000 average; Playwrighting Award: $7,500; Choreography Awards: $10,000.
Total amount of support: More than $13,000,000 since inception.

NO. MOST RECENT APPLICANTS: Theater, animation, dance, choreography and film: 250; Playwrighting: 600.

NO. AWARDS: Over 800 since inception.

APPLICATION INFO:
All applicants, except playwrights, must be nominated by a school department chair/dean or company artistic director. The nominating organization must be a registered 501(c)(3). Detailed information is available online.
Duration: September 1 to August 31.
Deadline: Must be postmarked by March 31 for theater and playwriting; April 30 for animation, dance and choreography; June 1 for film.

PUBLICATIONS:
Fact sheet; mission statement; press releases; newsletter.

IRS I.D.: 23-2218331

OFFICERS:
Hon. John F. Lehman, Chairman
Robert O. Marx, Vice Chairman
Brisa Trinchero, Chief Executive Officer

ADDRESS INQUIRIES TO:
Diana Kemppainen, Program Director
(See address above.)

FOREST ROBERTS THEATRE [492]
Northern Michigan University
1401 Presque Isle Avenue
Marquette, MI 49855-5364
(906) 227-2082
Fax: (906) 227-2567
E-mail: newplays@nmu.edu
wdigneit@nmu.edu
Web Site: www.nmu.edu/forestrobertstheatre

FOUNDED: 1977

AREAS OF INTEREST:
Performing arts and playwriting.

NAME(S) OF PROGRAMS:
- **Mildred and Albert Panowski Playwriting Award**

TYPE:
Awards/prizes.

YEAR PROGRAM STARTED: 1977

PURPOSE:
To encourage and stimulate artistic growth among educational and professional playwrights; to provide students with the creative opportunity to produce an original work on the university stage.

LEGAL BASIS:
Tax-exempt, nonprofit.

ELIGIBILITY:
There is a broad theme selected each year for the competition that entries for that year must adhere to. There is no restriction to style. The competition is open to any playwright, but only one play per playwright may be entered per biennium. Entries must be original, full-length plays or musicals.

One-act plays and works previously entered in playwriting competitions sponsored by Northern Michigan University are ineligible.

FINANCIAL DATA:
The award will include a spring or summer workshop reading of the play and fully mounted production in the subsequent production season, and a trip to Marquette to act as Artist-in-Residence during the reading of the play and dress rehearsals leading to opening night of the show. Room and board will be provided. Conducting informal seminars and workshops will be a part of this residency. A professional dramaturge will respond to the script and work with the playwright and director.
Amount of support per award: $2,000.

NO. MOST RECENT APPLICANTS: 430.

NO. AWARDS: Generally 1 award in even-numbered years.

REPRESENTATIVE AWARDS:
Kate Danley for "Building Madness."

APPLICATION INFO:
The contest has a different theme for each cycle. Applications are to be submitted online.
Duration: One year. Renewal possibilities on a biennial basis.
Deadline: Entries accepted in odd-numbered years only. Entries must be received on or before December 1 to be considered for the current theme. Winner will be announced within six months after the December 1 deadline.

PUBLICATIONS:
Brochure.

ADDRESS INQUIRIES TO:
Playwriting Coordinator
E-mail: wdigneit@nmu.edu

THE SHUBERT FOUNDATION, INC. [493]
234 West 44th Street
New York, NY 10036
(212) 944-3777
Fax: (212) 944-3767
E-mail: grants@shubertfoundation.org
Web Site: www.shubertfoundation.org

FOUNDED: 1945

AREAS OF INTEREST:
Arts-related organizations, dance, education and theatre.

TYPE:
General operating grants.

YEAR PROGRAM STARTED: 1945

PURPOSE:
To sustain and advance the live performing arts, in particular the American theatre and secondarily dance.

LEGAL BASIS:
Private foundation.

ELIGIBILITY:
The Foundation supports not-for-profit theatre and dance companies, as well as some arts-related organizations that assist in the development of the theatre. Applicants must be nonprofit organizations with Internal Revenue Code 501(c)(3) status. Organizations must submit audited financial statements. No grants to individuals.

GEOG. RESTRICTIONS: United States.

FINANCIAL DATA:
All grants cover general operating support only.
Amount of support per award: $10,000 to $325,000.
Total amount of support: $32,100,000 for the year 2021.

NO. AWARDS: 575 for the year 2021.

REPRESENTATIVE AWARDS:
$25,000 to La Jolla Playhouse, La Jolla, CA; $250,000 to Manhattan Theatre Club; $120,000 to Signature Theatre, Arlington, VA.

APPLICATION INFO:
Grant requests must be submitted on the Foundation's Grant Portal. Organizations that have fully audited financial statements with an annual budget under $150,000 should contact the Foundation before making a formal application. Applications cannot be requested or submitted via e-mail.
Duration: One year. Renewal only with reapplication.
Deadline: December 2 for theatre category; October 15 for dance and other categories. Announcement in May each year.

PUBLICATIONS:
Annual report with application guidelines.

OFFICERS:
Robert E. Wankel, Chairman of the Board
Diana Phillips, President
Wyche Fowler, Jr.
Pamela Newkirk
Richard J. Poccia
Lee J. Seidler
Stuart Subotnick

ADDRESS INQUIRIES TO:
Vicki Reiss, Executive Director
(See address above.)

WAGNER COLLEGE [494]
Wagner College Theater
One Campus Road
Staten Island, NY 10301
(718) 390-3223
E-mail: diane.catalano@wagner.edu
Web Site: wagner.edu/theatre/stanley-drama

FOUNDED: 1957

AREAS OF INTEREST:
Playwriting.

NAME(S) OF PROGRAMS:
- **Stanley Drama Award**

TYPE:
Awards/prizes; Project/program grants. Annual award for the best play or musical submitted to the competition.

YEAR PROGRAM STARTED: 1957

PURPOSE:
To call attention to and encourage new playwrights.

LEGAL BASIS:
University.

ELIGIBILITY:
The Award is offered for an original full-length play, musical or one-act play sequence that has not been professionally produced or received trade book publication. Writers of musicals are urged to submit music on tape or CD.

The Stanley Award competition will consider only one submission per playwright. Plays entered previously in the competition may not be resubmitted. Former Stanley Award winners are not eligible to compete.

FINANCIAL DATA:
Amount of support per award: $2,000.

NO. MOST RECENT APPLICANTS: 100.

NO. AWARDS: 3 (1 winner, 2 finalists).

APPLICATION INFO:
Applications may be obtained by sending a self-addressed, stamped envelope to the address above or on the web site. All scripts must be accompanied by a completed application. A reading fee of $30 must accompany the manuscript.
Deadline: October 31. Announcement the following March.

PUBLICATIONS:
Application guidelines.

ADDRESS INQUIRIES TO:
Diane Catalano
Stanley Drama Award
(See address above.)

*SPECIAL STIPULATIONS:
Previous winners are ineligible.

THE LOREN L. ZACHARY SOCIETY FOR THE PERFORMING ARTS
2250 Gloaming Way
Beverly Hills, CA 90210-1717
(310) 276-2731
Fax: (310) 275-8245
E-mail: infoz@zacharysociety.org
Web Site: www.zacharysociety.org

TYPE:
Awards/prizes.

See entry 733 for full listing.

Fine arts

ACADEMY FOUNDATION OF THE ACADEMY OF MOTION PICTURE ARTS AND SCIENCES   [495]
1313 North Vine Street
Los Angeles, CA 90028
(310) 247-3000
E-mail: saa@oscars.org
Web Site: www.oscars.org/SAA

AREAS OF INTEREST:
Filmmakers.

NAME(S) OF PROGRAMS:
● **Student Academy Awards Competition**

TYPE:
Awards/prizes.

PURPOSE:
To recognize outstanding achievements in student filmmaking; to support and encourage filmmakers with no previous professional experience who are enrolled in accredited colleges and universities.

ELIGIBILITY:
To be eligible, the filmmaker must be a full-time student at an accredited U.S. college, university, film school or art school. The film must have been made in a teacher-student relationship within the curricular structure of that institution. The film must be in one of the following categories: Alternative, Animated, Documentary and Narrative.

FINANCIAL DATA:
Amount of support per award: $5,000 Gold Award, $3,000 Silver Award, and $2,000 Bronze Award.
Total amount of support: $50,000.

NO. MOST RECENT APPLICANTS: 1,473.

NO. AWARDS: Up to 17.

APPLICATION INFO:
Nominees are selected by Academy members.
Duration: Program launches approximately March 15 and concludes by the end of October.
Deadline: June 1.

ADDRESS INQUIRIES TO:
Shawn Guthrie
Director, Student Academy Awards and Grants
(See address above.)

AMERICAN ORIENTAL SOCIETY   [496]
Hatcher Graduate Library
University of Michigan
Ann Arbor, MI 48109-1190
(734) 747-4760
E-mail: jrodgers@umich.edu
Web Site: www.americanorientalsociety.org

FOUNDED: 1842

AREAS OF INTEREST:
Archaeology, fine arts, history, philosophy, language, literature, religion and theology.

NAME(S) OF PROGRAMS:
● **Louise Wallace Hackney Fellowship**

TYPE:
Fellowships. Fellowship for the study of Chinese art with special relation to painting.

YEAR PROGRAM STARTED: 1946

PURPOSE:
To encourage basic research in the languages and literatures of Asia.

LEGAL BASIS:
Nonprofit.

ELIGIBILITY:
Graduate students who have successfully completed at least three years of Chinese language study at a recognized university and have some knowledge or training in art. Students must have completed all requirements for the Ph.D. except research, travel and the written dissertation. Applicants should have the sponsorship of recognized scholars in the fields of Chinese language and culture.

U.S. citizenship is required.

GEOG. RESTRICTIONS: United States.

FINANCIAL DATA:
Amount of support per award: $8,000.
Total amount of support: $8,000 annually.

NO. MOST RECENT APPLICANTS: Approximately 3.

NO. AWARDS: 1 annually.

APPLICATION INFO:
Applicants should submit the following materials in duplicate:
(1) a transcript of their undergraduate and graduate course work;
(2) a statement of personal finances;
(3) a three- or four-page summary of the proposed project to be undertaken during the year of the fellowship award, appended with a financial statement explaining expenses involved in this study and;
(4) no less than three letters of recommendation.

Any scholarly papers or published materials in the area of Chinese painting are welcome along with the other application materials.
Duration: 12 months, July to June. Renewals of appointment are possible but not usually considered.
Deadline: Applications should be submitted no later than March 1. Announcement in May.

PUBLICATIONS:
Application guidelines.

DIRECTORS AND OFFICERS:
Jonathan Rodgers, Secretary and Treasurer
Stephanie W. Jamison, Editor

ADDRESS INQUIRIES TO:
Jonathan Rodgers, Secretary and Treasurer
(See address above.)

BRUCEBO FINE ART SCHOLARSHIP FOUNDATION   [497]
Concordia University
1455 De Maisonneuve Boulevard West
Montreal QC H3G 1M8 Canada
(514) 848-2424 ext. 4600
E-mail: fineartsresearch@concordia.ca
Web Site: www.bruceboscholarships.ca
www.concordia.ca/finearts

FOUNDED: 1971

AREAS OF INTEREST:
Promotion of fine arts; Canada-Sweden relationships; artist residencies.

CONSULTING OR VOLUNTEER SERVICES:
Evaluation Committee members provide free services.

NAME(S) OF PROGRAMS:
● **W.B. Bruce European Fine Art Travel Scholarship**
● **Brucebo Fine Art Summer Residency Scholarship**

TYPE:
Development grants; Research grants; Residencies; Scholarships; Travel grants. Grant principally in the fields of fine arts, visual art and design. Grant is either for stay at the Brucebo Studio on the Island of Hanseatic Gotland, Sweden, in the Baltic Sea, for three months during the summer annually, or for undertaking a European Fine Art Travel-Study journey.

YEAR PROGRAM STARTED: 1971

PURPOSE:
To support talented Canadian fine arts graduated students and fine arts practitioners, B.F.A. or M.F.A. persons, in the emerging years of their respective careers.

LEGAL BASIS:
Private.

ELIGIBILITY:
Scholarships are granted through competitions, based on academic merit, to full-time students pursing a Master's or doctorate degree in the Faculty of Fine Arts at Concordia University nearing the completion of their degrees. Degree holders include those with a research-creation studio-based practice, including M.A., M.F.A, M.Des., as well as the M.A./Ph.D. Individualized Program and the Interdisciplinary Ph.D. Program, with a primary supervisor in the Faculty of Fine Arts. Performance-based art practices are not eligible for consideration unless they are undertaken within the context of contemporary visual arts practices and form a minority of the applicant's practice.

Scholarships are open to Canadian citizens and permanent residents only.

GEOG. RESTRICTIONS: Europe, with specific reference to the Nordic countries and Baltic Rim (coastal corridor).

FINANCIAL DATA:
Amount of support per award: Travel Scholarship: Approximately $4,500 (CAN); Summer Residency Scholarship: $7,500 (CAN).
Total amount of support: $12,500 (CAN).

NO. MOST RECENT APPLICANTS: Approximately 70.

NO. AWARDS: 1 per award.

APPLICATION INFO:
Application form and guidelines can be found on the Faculty of Arts web site.
Duration: Three months. Nonrenewable.
Deadline: January 31.

PUBLICATIONS:
Research reports.

ADDRESS INQUIRIES TO:
Research Coordinator
Faculty of Studio Arts
Concordia University
(See address and e-mail above.)

*SPECIAL STIPULATIONS:
Canadian citizens and permanent residents only. Recipient submits a report on his or her activities engaged in after return to Canada.

THE CENTER FOR PHOTOGRAPHY AT WOODSTOCK   [498]
59 Tinker Street
Woodstock, NY 12498
(845) 679-9957
E-mail: info@cpw.org
Web Site: www.cpw.org

FOUNDED: 1977

AREAS OF INTEREST:
Photography.

NAME(S) OF PROGRAMS:
● **Art Administration Interns**
● **Woodstock A-I-R**

TYPE:
Project/program grants; Residencies; Work-study programs. Woodstock A-I-R is a residency program for artists of color working in the photographic arts.

PURPOSE:
To support artists working in photography and related media and engaging their audiences through opportunities in which creation, discovery and learning are made possible.

LEGAL BASIS:
Not-for-profit arts and educational organization.

FINANCIAL DATA:
Amount of support per award: Varies.

CO-OP FUNDING PROGRAMS: The Center receives funds from the National Endowment for the Arts and the New York State Council on the Arts and has received grants from IBM and the New York Council for the Humanities, The Avery Foundation, Eastman Kodak, Canon, U.S.A. and Andy Warhol Foundation.

NO. AWARDS: Art Administration Interns: Up to 4 seasonally; Woodstock A-I-R: 9.

APPLICATION INFO:
Application information can be found on the web site.

IRS I.D.: 14-1592639

OFFICERS:
Hannah Frieser, Executive Director

ADDRESS INQUIRIES TO:
See e-mail address above.

DALLAS MUSEUM OF ART [499]
1717 North Harwood
Dallas, TX 75201
(214) 922-1334
Fax: (214) 922-1354
E-mail: a2a@dma.org
Web Site: dma.org/about/awards-artists

FOUNDED: 1903

AREAS OF INTEREST:
Contemporary art.

NAME(S) OF PROGRAMS:
● **Clare Hart DeGolyer Memorial Fund**

TYPE:
Awards/prizes.

YEAR PROGRAM STARTED: 1980

PURPOSE:
To support younger, emerging visual artists who reside in the southwestern part of the U.S.

LEGAL BASIS:
Nonprofit, tax-exempt arts organization.

ELIGIBILITY:
Applicants must be between 15 and 25 years of age, have lived in the southwestern part of the U.S. (Arizona, Colorado, New Mexico, Oklahoma and Texas) for the past three years and currently reside there.

Grants are not available for college or art school tuition.

GEOG. RESTRICTIONS: Arizona, Colorado, New Mexico, Oklahoma and Texas.

FINANCIAL DATA:
Amount of support per award: Maximum $1,500.

NO. MOST RECENT APPLICANTS: 25.

NO. AWARDS: 3 to 5.

APPLICATION INFO:
Applications must be submitted via the online form.
Deadline: January 31. Notification by March or April.

PUBLICATIONS:
Bimonthly *DMAgenda*; permanent collection and exhibition catalogues.

ADDRESS INQUIRIES TO:
Awards to Artists
(See address above.)

DALLAS MUSEUM OF ART [500]
1717 North Harwood
Dallas, TX 75201
(214) 922-1334
Fax: (214) 922-1354
E-mail: a2a@dma.org
Web Site: dma.org/about/awards-artists

FOUNDED: 1903

AREAS OF INTEREST:
Contemporary art.

NAME(S) OF PROGRAMS:
● **Arch and Anne Giles Kimbrough Fund**

TYPE:
Awards/prizes. Direct grants to artists.

YEAR PROGRAM STARTED: 1980

PURPOSE:
To support younger, emerging visual artists in Texas.

LEGAL BASIS:
Nonprofit, tax-exempt arts organization.

ELIGIBILITY:
Applicants must be under 30 years of age, have lived in Texas for the past three years and currently reside there.

GEOG. RESTRICTIONS: Texas.

FINANCIAL DATA:
Amount of support per award: Maximum $3,500.

NO. MOST RECENT APPLICANTS: 35.

NO. AWARDS: 3 to 5.

APPLICATION INFO:
Applications must be submitted via the online form.
Deadline: January 31. Notification by March or April.

PUBLICATIONS:
Bimonthly *DMAgenda*; permanent collection and exhibition catalogues.

ADDRESS INQUIRIES TO:
Awards to Artists
(See address above.)

DALLAS MUSEUM OF ART [501]
1717 North Harwood
Dallas, TX 75201
(214) 922-1334
Fax: (214) 720-0862
E-mail: a2a@dma.org
Web Site: dma.org/about/awards-artists

FOUNDED: 1903

AREAS OF INTEREST:
Art. Collections include contemporary art, Pre-Columbian, Asian, African, American and European painting and sculpture, decorative arts and textiles.

NAME(S) OF PROGRAMS:
● **Otis and Velma Davis Dozier Travel Grant**

TYPE:
Awards/prizes; Travel grants.

YEAR PROGRAM STARTED: 1990

PURPOSE:
To recognize exceptional talent in professional artists who wish to expand their artistic horizons through domestic or foreign travel.

LEGAL BASIS:
Nonprofit, tax-exempt arts organization.

ELIGIBILITY:
Artists eligible for the grant must be practicing professionals, be 30 years of age or older, have lived in Texas for the past three years and be currently living in Texas. Financial need will be given consideration but will not be the determining factor in making the awards.

GEOG. RESTRICTIONS: Texas.

FINANCIAL DATA:
Amount of support per award: Varies.
Total amount of support: Varies.

NO. MOST RECENT APPLICANTS: 40 annually.

NO. AWARDS: 1 or 2.

APPLICATION INFO:
Applications must be submitted via the online form.
Deadline: January 31. Notification by March or April.

PUBLICATIONS:
Bimonthly *DMAgenda*; permanent collection and exhibition catalogues.

ADDRESS INQUIRIES TO:
Awards to Artists
(See address above.)

FINE ARTS WORK CENTER IN PROVINCETOWN   [502]
24 Pearl Street
Provincetown, MA 02657
(508) 487-9960
Fax: (508) 487-8873
E-mail: info@fawc.org
sblood@fawc.org
Web Site: www.fawc.org

FOUNDED: 1968

AREAS OF INTEREST:
Visual arts and creative writing.

NAME(S) OF PROGRAMS:
● **Visual Arts Fellowship**
● **Writing Fellowship**

TYPE:
Fellowships; Residencies.

YEAR PROGRAM STARTED: 1968

PURPOSE:
To offer opportunities to emerging artists and writers.

LEGAL BASIS:
Nonprofit corporation.

ELIGIBILITY:
Fellowships are offered to selected writers and visual artists. Applicants must be in the emerging phase of their careers and must demonstrate significant talent and commitment.

Applicants must be individuals (visual artists and creative writers) who have spent time working on their own and have created a considerable body of work which can be presented in the form of slides or manuscript.

FINANCIAL DATA:
In addition to the stipend, fellows are provided with an apartment and studio in Provincetown, MA, and have the support of a resident staff. Each residency includes private living and/or working studio in Provincetown, MA.
Amount of support per award: Stipend of $1,000 per month and $1,000 at departure.
Total amount of support: $160,000.

NO. MOST RECENT APPLICANTS: 1,400.

NO. AWARDS: 20.

APPLICATION INFO:
Applicants must apply through the online portal. Application fee is $45.
Duration: Seven months, October 1 to April 30.
Deadline: Writers: December 1. Visual Arts: February 1. Announcement by May 15.

PUBLICATIONS:
Shankpainter, online literary magazine.

OFFICERS OF THE TRUSTEES:
Carol Warshawsky, Chairperson
Lynne Kortenhaus, President
Major Jackson, Vice President
Duane Slick, Vice President
Rich Companik, Treasurer

ADDRESS INQUIRIES TO:
Susan Blood, Grant Writer
(See address above.)

*SPECIAL STIPULATIONS:
Fellowships are reserved for emerging writers and visual artists.

J. PAUL GETTY TRUST, GETTY FOUNDATION   [503]
1200 Getty Center Drive
Suite 800
Los Angeles, CA 90049-1685
(310) 440-7320
Fax: (310) 440-7703
E-mail: gettyfoundation@getty.edu
Web Site: www.getty.edu/foundation

FOUNDED: 1984

AREAS OF INTEREST:
Strengthening art history as a global discipline, promoting the interdisciplinary practice of conservation, increasing access to museums and archival collections, and developing current and future professionals and leaders.

TYPE:
Conferences/seminars; Fellowships; Internships; Project/program grants; Research grants; Training grants.

YEAR PROGRAM STARTED: 1984

PURPOSE:
To advance the understanding and preservation of the visual arts locally and throughout the world.

ELIGIBILITY:
Requirements vary according to grant category. Individuals at the undergraduate and graduate level may be eligible to apply for internships. Eligibility for all other grant categories is limited to nonprofit organizations.

Generally, grants are not made for operating or endowment purposes, for construction or maintenance of buildings or for acquisition of works of art.

FINANCIAL DATA:
Amount of support per award: Varies.
Total amount of support: $9,700,000 for the year 2020.

NO. MOST RECENT APPLICANTS: Approximately 800 for fiscal year 2020.

NO. AWARDS: 191 for the year 2020.

REPRESENTATIVE AWARDS:
$240,000 to Center for Advanced Study, Sofia, Bulgaria, for the research seminars "The Construction of Knowledge in Archaeology and Art History in Southeastern Europe;" $180,000 to Universidad del Desarrollo, Santiago, Chile, for preparation of a conservation management plan for Brother Martin Correa and Gabriel Guarda OSB's Monasterio Benedictino de la Santisma Trinidad de las Condes; $120,000 to Association of Print Scholars Inc., New York, NY, for a series of workshops on printmaking.

APPLICATION INFO:
Funding priorities and application information are available on the Foundation web site.
Duration: Typically one to three years, depending upon the grant category.
Deadline: Varies.

PUBLICATIONS:
Annual report of J. Paul Getty Trust.

IRS I.D.: 95-1790021

OFFICERS:
Joan Weinstein, Director
Anne Helmreich, Associate Director
Katie Underwood, Assistant Director, Communications

ADDRESS INQUIRIES TO:
The Getty Foundation
(See address above.)

ADOLPH AND ESTHER GOTTLIEB FOUNDATION, INC.   [504]
380 West Broadway
New York, NY 10012
(212) 226-0581
Fax: (212) 274-1476
E-mail: mjoseph@gottliebfoundation.org
Web Site: www.gottliebfoundation.org

FOUNDED: 1976

AREAS OF INTEREST:
Visual artists.

NAME(S) OF PROGRAMS:
● **Emergency Grant Program**
● **Individual Support Program**

TYPE:
Grants-in-aid. Emergency Grant Program provides cash award to mature creative painters, sculptors and printmakers who are experiencing financial hardship resulting from a current or recent emergency.

Individual Support Program was designed to encourage those artists who have dedicated their lives to developing their art, regardless of their level of commercial success.

YEAR PROGRAM STARTED: 1984

PURPOSE:
To provide interim financial assistance to qualified artists during times of emergencies (such as fire, flood, medical or other unexpected, catastrophic events), or to provide financial assistance as an encouragement to artists who have dedicated their lives to developing their art.

LEGAL BASIS:
Nonprofit corporation.

ELIGIBILITY:
Program descriptions and requirements are posted online.

FINANCIAL DATA:
Amount of support per award: Emergency Grant Program: Maximum $15,000; typical amount is $5,000. Individual Support Program: $25,000.
Total amount of support: Varies.

NO. MOST RECENT APPLICANTS: Individual Support Program: 475.

NO. AWARDS: Individual Support Program: 20.

APPLICATION INFO:
Emergency Grant Program: Application forms are available online.

Individual Support Program: Application forms are available online in early September.

Deadline: Emergency Grant Program: Available throughout the year, as budget permits. Individual Support Program: February 26.

PUBLICATIONS:
Information brochure.

BOARD OF DIRECTORS:
Sanford Hirsch, Executive Director
Charlotta Kotik
Robert Mangold
Brooke Rapaport
Franklin Sirmans
Lily Wei

ADDRESS INQUIRIES TO:
Melissa Joseph, Grants Manager
(See address above.)

*SPECIAL STIPULATIONS:
The Emergency Grant Program is to assist individuals in emergency situations only.

THE ELIZABETH GREENSHIELDS FOUNDATION   [505]
1814 Sherbrooke Street West
Montreal QC H3H 1E4 Canada
E-mail: info@greenshieldsfoundation.ca
Web Site: www.
elizabethgreenshieldsfoundation.org

FOUNDED: 1955

AREAS OF INTEREST:
Painting, drawing, printmaking and sculpture.

NAME(S) OF PROGRAMS:
● **The Elizabeth Greenshields Foundation Grant**

TYPE:
Grants for artists.

YEAR PROGRAM STARTED: 1955

PURPOSE:
To provide financial assistance, by way of grants, to young artists who are pursuing their studies or are in the early or developmental stage of their career, are working in a representational style of painting, drawing, sculpture or printmaking, and demonstrate the determination and talent to pursue a lifetime career in their art practice.

LEGAL BASIS:
Charitable foundation.

ELIGIBILITY:
Applicants must be pursuing their studies or be in the early or development stage of their

career and demonstrate the determination and talent to pursue a lifetime career in their art practice. Only those applicants who work in a representational style of painting, drawing, sculpture or printmaking will be considered. No other artistic activities or disciplines are funded. In particular, illustration, graphic design, photography, animation, video art, film, digital art, crafts, decorative arts, any work that uses a photograph or digital image as the principal medium or that is produced using computer software or graphics, and any work or activity that falls primarily into any of the foregoing categories, are not eligible for a grant. The Foundation does not provide funding for the pursuit of abstract or non-objective art.

Applicants must be at least 18 years of age and no older than 41 years of age.

The Foundation has no geographic, citizenship or residency requirements.

Applicants must be individuals applying on their own behalf. Artistic groups, collectives and organizations are not eligible.

FINANCIAL DATA:
Amount of support per award: First grants are in the amount of $15,000 (CAN) each. Subsequent grants are in the amount of $18,000 (CAN) each (maximum of three grants per artist). The Foundation reserves the right to award grants in other amounts and to disburse funds in whole or in part, as it deems advisable. Grants are made directly to the beneficiaries, not through other organizations.

APPLICATION INFO:
Candidates may only access the application by creating an account and completing an eligibility questionnaire on the Foundation's web site. Applications must be completed and submitted online. Applications submitted in any other manner, including e-mail, mail or otherwise, will not be accepted.

The material and documents required to apply include:
(1) government issued photo identification and proof of citizenship, current address and date of birth;
(2) images of six representative works (no more or less) produced in the last two years. These must be original works produced by the applicant alone;
(3) if the applicant is applying to further his or her art education or training, proof of acceptance or enrollment from the institution where he or she intends to study or train;
(4) a description of the proposed work, project or course of study or training that the applicant intends to undertake with a grant from the Foundation;
(5) a brief artist statement relating to the applicant's previous and current work;
(6) a budget for the proposed work, project, or course of study or training described in the applicant's Artistic Proposal and;
(7) a letter of reference from a teacher or professor, an artist or curator who is familiar with both the applicant and the applicant's work and is able to support his or her application.

All documents and materials (including the letter of reference) must be submitted in English or French.

Duration: Award winners may reapply for another grant one year after a grant was awarded. Applicants who were not awarded a grant may reapply two years from the last decision.

Deadline: The Foundation welcomes applications throughout the year. However, in order to allow for proper response time, it is strongly recommended that applicants file their applications six months prior to the date on which funds are required.

PUBLICATIONS:
Application guidelines.

ADDRESS INQUIRIES TO:
Applications Coordinator
(See address above.)

*PLEASE NOTE:
The Elizabeth Greenshields Foundation grant is one of the most prestigious grants available to emerging figurative artists, as well as one of the most substantial. It is one of the longest standing, with an illustrious history of recipients spanning more than half a century. It is also unique in its scope, in that it is available to students and artists around the world. To date, the Foundation has provided financial assistance to more than 1,900 students and artists in 40 countries.

SAMUEL H. KRESS FOUNDATION   [506]
174 East 80th Street
New York, NY 10075
(212) 861-4993
E-mail: lisa.schermerhorn@kressfoundation.org
Web Site: www.kressfoundation.org
www.kressfoundation.fluxx.io (grant portal)

FOUNDED: 1929

AREAS OF INTEREST:
Art history, art conservation and art interpretation in museums.

NAME(S) OF PROGRAMS:
● **Conservation Fellowships**
● **Conservation Grant Program**
● **Digital Art History Grant Program**
● **History of Art Grant Program**
● **History of Art: Institutional Fellowships**
● **Interpretive Fellowships at Art Museums**

TYPE:
Fellowships; Research grants; Travel grants. Grants: Competitive grants only awarded to nonprofit institutions. The grant programs support scholarly projects that promote the appreciation, interpretation, preservation, study and teaching of European art from antiquity to the early 19th century.

Fellowships: Competitive fellowships are awarded to art historians and art conservators in the final stages of their preparation for professional careers, as well as to students of art history and related fields who are interested in art museum education and curating.

YEAR PROGRAM STARTED: 1963

PURPOSE:
To advance the history, conservation and enjoyment of European art, architecture and archaeology from antiquity to the pre-modern era.

LEGAL BASIS:
Private foundation.

ELIGIBILITY:
Contact the Foundation for specific eligibility and application requirements for each grant and fellowship program.

FINANCIAL DATA:
Amount of support per award: Varies.
Total amount of support: Varies.

NO. MOST RECENT APPLICANTS: Approximately 500 in fiscal year 2019.

NO. AWARDS: Approximately 200 to 250 annually.

APPLICATION INFO:
Fellowship and grant applications must be submitted via the online grantmaking portal.

The first step in the application process for all grant programs is the submission of a Letter of Inquiry via the Foundation's online grantmaking portal. Institutions invited to apply for a grant will be notified via e-mail within seven business days of the LOI submission deadline.

Duration: Varies.

Deadline: Fellowships: Conservation Fellowships: January 22. Institutional Fellowships: November 30. Interpretive Fellowships: April 1.

Grant LOIs: March 1, September 1 and December 1 for Conservation Grants and History of Art Grants; March 1 and September 1 for Digital Art History Grants.

PUBLICATIONS:
Annual Report.

IRS I.D.: 13-1624176

STAFF:
Wyman Meere, Program Administrator

OFFICERS AND TRUSTEES:
Carmela Vircillo Franklin, Chairman
Max Marmor, President
Elizabeth Eveillard
William Higgins
Ken Lee
Robert B. Loper
Theodore V. H. Mayer
Nina Scherago
Daniel H. Weiss

ADDRESS INQUIRIES TO:
Lisa W. Schermerhorn, Deputy Director
(See address above.)

*SPECIAL STIPULATIONS:
No applications accepted via fax or e-mail.

LIGHT WORK   [507]
316 Waverly Avenue
Syracuse, NY 13210
(315) 443-1300
E-mail: info@lightwork.org
Web Site: www.lightwork.org

FOUNDED: 1972

AREAS OF INTEREST:
Photography.

CONSULTING OR VOLUNTEER SERVICES:
All aspects of visual arts and programs for artists.

NAME(S) OF PROGRAMS:
● **Light Work Artist-in-Residence Program**
● **Light Work Grants in Photography**

TYPE:
Project/program grants; Residencies; Visiting scholars. Artist-in-Residence, exhibitions, publications, sponsored projects, lectures and regrants.

Light Work Artist-in-Residence Program supports international artists.

Light Work Grants in Photography support regional artists near Syracuse, NY.

YEAR PROGRAM STARTED: 1973

PURPOSE:
To support artists in photography.

LEGAL BASIS:
Not-for-profit organization.

ELIGIBILITY:
Light Work Artist-in-Residence Program: Applicants must be working in photography or image-based media. Students are ineligible to apply.

Light Work Grants in Photography: Applicant must reside within an approximate 50-mile radius of Syracuse, NY.

GEOG. RESTRICTIONS: Light Work Grants in Photography: Central New York.

FINANCIAL DATA:
Amount of support per award: Light Work Artist-in-Residence Program: $5,000 stipend; Light Work Grants in Photography: $3,000.
Total amount of support: Varies.

NO. MOST RECENT APPLICANTS: 900 to 1,000.

NO. AWARDS: Light Work Artist-in-Residence Program: 12 to 15; Light Work Grants in Photography: 3.

APPLICATION INFO:
Applicants are encouraged to use the online application process.

Duration: One month.

Deadline: Light Work Artist-in-Residence Program: July 1. Light Work Grants in Photography: April 1.

STAFF:
Jeff Hoone, Executive Director

ADDRESS INQUIRIES TO:
Jeff Hoone, Executive Director
(See address above.)

*PLEASE NOTE:
Housing is provided for residencies.

THE ROBERTO LONGHI FOUNDATION FOR THE STUDY OF THE HISTORY OF ART   [508]
Via Benedetto Fortini, 30
50125 Florence Italy
(39) 055 6580794
Fax: (39) 055 6580794
E-mail: longhi@fondazionelonghi.it
Web Site: www.fondazionelonghi.it

FOUNDED: 1971

AREAS OF INTEREST:
Italian and European art from the 13th to the 18th centuries.

NAME(S) OF PROGRAMS:
● **Art History Fellowships in Florence**

TYPE:
Fellowships.

PURPOSE:
To promote and further the study of art history by keeping Roberto Longhi's cultural legacy and methods alive.

LEGAL BASIS:
Private foundation.

ELIGIBILITY:
Open to Italian citizens who possess a degree from an Italian university with a thesis in the history of art, and to non-Italian citizens who have graduated in the history of art at an accredited university or an institution of equal standing. Applicants must have a good knowledge of Italian, and elementary knowledge of English and/or French.

Students who have reached their 32nd birthday before the application deadline are not eligible.

Designed for those who want to seriously dedicate themselves to research in the history of art.

FINANCIAL DATA:
Amount of support per award: EUR 5,400 (paid in monthly installments over a period of nine months).

APPLICATION INFO:
Applications should be addressed to the Secretariat of the Foundation and sent in PDF format by certified e-mail to the address fondazionelonghi@legalmail.it. Application should include the candidate's biographical data (place and date of birth, domicile, citizenship), a transcript of the candidate's undergraduate and graduate records, a copy of the degree thesis (if available) and other original works, published or unpublished, a "curriculum studiorum," also indicating the knowledge of foreign languages spoken and written, letters of reference from at least two persons of academic standing who are acquainted with the candidate's work, the subject of the research that the candidate is interested in pursuing within the range of the history of art and two passport photographs.

Duration: Nine months beginning in October.

Deadline: June 20.

PUBLICATIONS:
Proporzioni, art review.

OFFICERS:
Mina Gregori, Chairman and President

MARYLAND INSTITUTE COLLEGE OF ART   [509]
Office of Graduate Admission
131 North Avenue
Baltimore, MD 21201
(410) 225-2256
Fax: (410) 225-5275
E-mail: graduate@mica.edu
Web Site: www.mica.edu

FOUNDED: 1826

AREAS OF INTEREST:
Fine arts, design and art education.

NAME(S) OF PROGRAMS:
● **Business of Art and Design (MPS)**
● **Filmmaking (MFA)**
● **LeRoy E. Hoffberger School of Painting (MFA)**
● **MA Graphic Design**
● **MA Illustration**
● **MA Social Design**
● **Master of Arts in Teaching**
● **MBA/MA in Design Leadership**
● **MFA Community Arts**
● **MFA Curatorial Practice**
● **MFA Illustration Practice**
● **MFA in Graphic Design**
● **Mt. Royal School of Art (MFA)**
● **MPS in Information Visualization**
● **Photographic and Electronic Media (MFA)**
● **Rinehart School of Sculpture (MFA)**
● **Studio Art (Low-residency MFA)**
● **UX Design (MPS)**

TYPE:
Awards/prizes; Challenge/matching grants; Conferences/seminars; Fellowships; Internships; Research grants; Residencies;

Scholarships; Travel grants; Visiting scholars. Teaching internships. Post-Baccalaureate Program awards certificates in fine arts.

YEAR PROGRAM STARTED: 1896

LEGAL BASIS:
Nonprofit institution.

ELIGIBILITY:
Bachelor's degree is required.

FINANCIAL DATA:
Amount of support per award: Varies.
Total amount of support: Varies.

NO. MOST RECENT APPLICANTS: 1,100.

NO. AWARDS: 225.

APPLICATION INFO:
Candidates apply for all programs online through mica.slideroom.com or mica.edu/gradprograms.
Duration: One to two years.
Deadline: January 3. Announcement April 1.

ADDRESS INQUIRIES TO:
Christopher Harring
Associate Vice President of Graduate Admission
E-mail: charring@mica.edu

THE PAUL MELLON CENTRE FOR STUDIES IN BRITISH ART

16 Bedford Square
London WC1B 3JA England
(44) 020 7580 0311
Fax: (44) 020 7636 6730
E-mail: info@paul-mellon-centre.ac.uk
Web Site: www.paul-mellon-centre.ac.uk

TYPE:
Conferences/seminars; Fellowships; Project/program grants; Research grants. Educational Programme Grants for lectures, symposia, seminars or conferences on British art or architectural history.

The Junior Fellowship is to pursue ongoing doctoral research at an American or British university.

The Paul Mellon Centre Rome Fellowship offers fellowships to scholars working on Grand Tour subjects or in the field of Anglo-Italian cultural and artistic relations.

Mid-Career Fellowships are offered for research in the field of British art and architectural history.

The Postdoctoral Fellowship works to transform doctoral research into publishable form such as a book, series of articles, or exhibition catalogues.

Research Support Grants are for expenses in pursuit of research.

The Senior Fellowship supports an established scholar in the field of British art and architectural history to complete a manuscript or book for immediate publication.

See entry 375 for full listing.

THE METROPOLITAN MUSEUM OF ART   [510]

1000 Fifth Avenue
New York, NY 10028-0198
(212) 570-3710
E-mail: collegeprograms@metmuseum.org
Web Site: www.metmuseum.org

FOUNDED: 1870

AREAS OF INTEREST:
Internships in art museums.

TYPE:
Internships. Internships for graduate and undergraduate students.

YEAR PROGRAM STARTED: 1972

PURPOSE:
To provide pre-career training and experience for students and graduates in art museums.

ELIGIBILITY:
Many projects require strong preparation in the history of art. Applicants of diverse backgrounds and disciplines are encouraged to apply.

FINANCIAL DATA:
Amount of support per award: Varies by program.
Total amount of support: Varies.

NO. AWARDS: 42.

APPLICATION INFO:
Applications must be completed through the Museum's online portal. No hard copies will be accepted.
Duration: Up to 12 months.
Deadline: Varies.

ADDRESS INQUIRIES TO:
Internship Programs
(See address and e-mail above.)

THE METROPOLITAN MUSEUM OF ART   [511]

1000 Fifth Avenue
New York, NY 10028-0198
(212) 650-2763
E-mail: academic.programs@metmuseum.org
Web Site: www.metmuseum.org

AREAS OF INTEREST:
All fields related to art history and visual culture.

NAME(S) OF PROGRAMS:
● **History of Art and Visual Culture Fellowships**

TYPE:
Fellowships. Fellowship awards to Ph.D. candidates, postdoctoral researchers, and senior scholars studying art history and/or conducting research in a field pertaining to the Met's collections.

YEAR PROGRAM STARTED: 1974

PURPOSE:
To promote research in the fine arts.

ELIGIBILITY:
Applicants should have received the Doctorate, have completed substantial work toward it, or be mature scholars of demonstrated ability.

FINANCIAL DATA:
Amount of support per award: $52,000 stipend for senior fellows for one year, $42,000 for predoctoral fellows, and up to an additional $6,000 for travel and miscellaneous expenses.

APPLICATION INFO:
Applications must be completed through the online portal. No hard copies will be accepted.
Duration: Normally, a fellow will be in residence at The Metropolitan Museum of Art for a maximum of one year. Shorter terms are available for senior fellows.

Deadline: Application and required letters of recommendation must be received by the first Friday in November. Announcement of awards will be made by late March.

STAFF:
Marcie Karp, Senior Managing Educator, Academic and Professional Programs, Education Department

ADDRESS INQUIRIES TO:
See e-mail address above.

MUSEUM OF EARLY SOUTHERN DECORATIVE ARTS (MESDA)   [512]

924 South Main Street
Winston-Salem, NC 27101-5335
(336) 721-7369
Fax: (336) 721-7367
Web Site: mesda.org

FOUNDED: 1965

AREAS OF INTEREST:
Decorative arts of the South before 1860.

NAME(S) OF PROGRAMS:
● **Horton Fellowship**

TYPE:
Fellowships.

YEAR PROGRAM STARTED: 1976

PURPOSE:
To combine the study of history and objects in a museum context.

LEGAL BASIS:
Nonprofit.

ELIGIBILITY:
Graduate student status or present employment in museum-related professions required.

FINANCIAL DATA:
Covers up to full tuition for three credit hours.
Amount of support per award: $5,000 maximum.
Total amount of support: $35,000 for the year 2021.

NO. MOST RECENT APPLICANTS: Approximately 20 per year.

NO. AWARDS: Up to 8 per year.

APPLICATION INFO:
Applicant must submit a completed application form and letters of recommendation.
Duration: Four weeks.
Deadline: February 15. Notification March 1.

IRS I.D.: 56-0587289

STAFF:
Daniel Ackermann, Curator of MESDA Collections

ADDRESS INQUIRIES TO:
MESDA Summer Institute
(See address above.)

PEW FELLOWSHIPS AT THE PEW CENTER FOR ARTS & HERITAGE   [513]

1608 Walnut Street, 18th Floor
Philadelphia, PA 19103
(267) 350-4920
Fax: (267) 350-4997
E-mail: mfranklin@pewcenterarts.org
Web Site: www.pewcenterarts.org

FOUNDED: 1991

AREAS OF INTEREST:

Fellowships are awarded for various art forms, including Choreography, Craft Arts, Folk and Traditional Arts, Literature (Fiction, Literary Non-Fiction and Poetry), Media Arts, Music Composition, Painting, Performance Art, Playwriting, Works on Paper and Visual Arts 3-D.

TYPE:

Fellowships. Opportunities for contemporary artists in the Philadelphia five-county area to concentrate on the development and creation of art. Fellowships to support artists at critical junctures in any stage of their career development. Fellows will be expected to participate annually in at least three meetings with other fellowship recipients.

YEAR PROGRAM STARTED: 1991

PURPOSE:

To provide financial support directly to artists so that they will have the opportunity to dedicate themselves wholly to the development of their artwork; to provide such support at a critical juncture in an artist's career, when a concentration on artistic development and exploration is most likely to contribute to personal and professional growth.

ELIGIBILITY:

Artists are nominated and invited to apply for the fellowship. Candidates must be residents of Bucks, Chester, Delaware, Montgomery or Philadelphia counties, PA, for two years or longer. Matriculated students, full or part-time, or immediate family members of a panelist for the year applied or of Pew Fellowships staff are not eligible.

There is no restriction as to citizenship.

GEOG. RESTRICTIONS: Bucks, Chester, Delaware, Montgomery and Philadelphia counties, Pennsylvania.

FINANCIAL DATA:

Fellowship funds are awarded in installments. Funds may be used to support costs such as equipment, materials, assistants, training and travel. The specific use of grant funds will be up to the recipient artist.

Amount of support per award: $75,000.

CO-OP FUNDING PROGRAMS: Program funded by the Pew Charitable Trusts.

NO. MOST RECENT APPLICANTS: Varies.

NO. AWARDS: Up to 12 each year.

APPLICATION INFO:

Application by nomination only.

The application procedure involves a panel review by artists and arts professionals. The first level of review is discipline-based; the second level of review is interdisciplinary; the final selection of candidates is based on the applicant's accomplishments or promise in his or her discipline, and the degree to which the fellowship will address a critical juncture in the artist's career and/or artistic development.

Duration: Up to two years.

STAFF:

Melissa Franklin, Director, Pew Fellowships

ADDRESS INQUIRIES TO:

Melissa Franklin
Director, Pew Fellowships
(See e-mail address above.)

THE POLLOCK-KRASNER FOUNDATION, INC.   [514]

863 Park Avenue
New York, NY 10075
(212) 517-5400
Fax: (212) 288-2836
E-mail: grants@pkf.org
Web Site: www.pkf.org

FOUNDED: 1985

AREAS OF INTEREST:

Visual arts.

TYPE:

Grants-in-aid. Grants to individual visual artists for personal and professional needs.

YEAR PROGRAM STARTED: 1985

PURPOSE:

To aid internationally working artists who have embarked on professional careers.

LEGAL BASIS:

Private foundation.

ELIGIBILITY:

Grants are made to painters, sculptors and artists who work on paper, including printmakers who have taken up art as a professional career. The Foundation will not accept applications from commercial artists, photographers, video artists, filmmakers, craft-makers or any artist whose work primarily falls into these categories. It does not make grants to students nor fund academic study.

The Foundation does not make grants to pay for past debts, legal fees, the purchase of real estate, moves to other cities or to pay for the costs of installations, commissions or projects ordered by others. With very few exceptions, the Foundation will not fund travel expenses.

FINANCIAL DATA:

Amount of support per award: The size of the grant is determined by the individual circumstances of the artist.

Total amount of support: Varies.

APPLICATION INFO:

Artists are required to submit a cover letter, a curriculum vitae, artist statement (optional), an application, and 10 images of current work. Applications are to be submitted online.

Duration: One year.

Deadline: Grants are awarded throughout the year.

PUBLICATIONS:

Biannual report; application guidelines.

STAFF:

Caroline Black, Program Director
Beth Cochems, Grants Manager

ROSWELL ARTIST-IN-RESIDENCE PROGRAM   [515]

409 East College Boulevard
Roswell, NM 88201
(575) 623-5600
E-mail: larrybob@rair.org
Web Site: www.rair.org

FOUNDED: 1967

AREAS OF INTEREST:

Studio-based, fine-art residencies.

TYPE:

Residencies. Roswell Artist-in-Residence Program is for artists who work in drawing, painting, sculpture, photography, printmaking, video and other fine art media.

YEAR PROGRAM STARTED: 1967

PURPOSE:

To provide time for artists to focus on their work, without distractions or interruptions.

FINANCIAL DATA:

Amount of support per award: $800 per month, plus housing, studio and utilities and $100 per dependent.

Matching fund requirements: Artists cover telephone service, food, art materials and transportation.

NO. MOST RECENT APPLICANTS: Approximately 270 average.

NO. AWARDS: Approximately 6 each year.

APPLICATION INFO:

Application information is available on the web site.

Duration: One year.

Deadline: Varies from year to year.

IRS I.D.: 33-0999247

STAFF:

Larry Bob Phillips, Director
Nancy Fleming, Museum Director

ADDRESS INQUIRIES TO:

Roswell Artist-in-Residence Program
(See e-mail address above.)

SAN DIEGO ART INSTITUTE   [516]

1439 El Prado
House of Charm, Balboa Park
San Diego, CA 92101
(619) 236-0011
E-mail: info@sandiego-art.org
Web Site: www.sandiego-art.org

FOUNDED: 1941

AREAS OF INTEREST:

Contemporary art.

NAME(S) OF PROGRAMS:

● **Matthew J. Mahoney Artist-in-Residence Program**

TYPE:

Conferences/seminars; Internships. Annual lectures, discussions and workshops.

YEAR PROGRAM STARTED: 2015

PURPOSE:

To advance contemporary art through exhibition, outreach and education.

LEGAL BASIS:

501(c)(3) nonprofit arts organization.

ELIGIBILITY:

Artists and curators working in all media and any stages of their career are welcome to apply for an approximate three-month residency.

FINANCIAL DATA:

Awards include monetary compensation.

Amount of support per award: Varies.

Total amount of support: Varies.

NO. AWARDS: Varies.

APPLICATION INFO:

Open to all media. Open calls for exhibition opportunities.

Duration: Approximately three months.

IRS I.D.: 95-1816068

SCHOOL OF THE MUSEUM OF FINE ARTS AT TUFTS UNIVERSITY, BOSTON [517]

230 The Fenway
Boston, MA 02115
(617) 627-0047
E-mail: kaitlyn.clark@tufts.edu
Web Site: smfa.tufts.edu

FOUNDED: 1876

AREAS OF INTEREST:
Contemporary visual art.

NAME(S) OF PROGRAMS:
• **Traveling Fellowship Award**

TYPE:
Fellowships. Awarded for travel and study abroad.

YEAR PROGRAM STARTED: 1899

PURPOSE:
To further the professional development of the artist recipients.

LEGAL BASIS:
A part of the Museum of Fine Arts, a nonprofit Massachusetts corporation.

ELIGIBILITY:
Applicants must be alumni of the School of the Museum of Fine Arts.

FINANCIAL DATA:
Amount of support per award: Up to $10,000.

Total amount of support: Approximately $100,000 annually.

NO. MOST RECENT APPLICANTS: 135.

NO. AWARDS: Up to 10.

APPLICATION INFO:
Proposed plan of travel and study, including itinerary, must be submitted with a presentation of art work.

Duration: Varies according to proposal. Normally not more than one year. Nonrenewable.

Deadline: August 5. Announcement in September or October.

ADDRESS INQUIRIES TO:
Kaitlyn Clark, SMFA Exhibitions and Public Programs
(See address above.)

SKOWHEGAN SCHOOL OF PAINTING AND SCULPTURE [518]

136 West 22nd Street
New York, NY 10011
(212) 529-0505
Fax: (212) 473-1342
E-mail: mail@skowheganart.org
Web Site: www.skowheganart.org

FOUNDED: 1946

AREAS OF INTEREST:
All visual arts.

TYPE:
Scholarships; Travel grants.

YEAR PROGRAM STARTED: 1946

PURPOSE:
To bring together a gifted and diverse group of individuals who have demonstrated a commitment to art-making and inquiry to create the most stimulating environment possible for a concentrated period of artistic creation, interaction and growth.

LEGAL BASIS:
Not-for-profit educational institution.

ELIGIBILITY:
Based on need. Candidate must be at least 21 years old.

FINANCIAL DATA:
Scholarships cover room, board and tuition.

Amount of support per award: Varies.

NO. MOST RECENT APPLICANTS: Approximately 2,000.

NO. AWARDS: 65.

APPLICATION INFO:
Application information is available online.

Duration: Nine-week summer program, mid-June to mid-August.

ADDRESS INQUIRIES TO:
Sarah Workneh, Co-Director
(See address above.)

W. EUGENE SMITH MEMORIAL FUND [519]

79 Essex Street
New York, NY 10002
(212) 857-0001
E-mail: info@smithfund.org
Web Site: www.smithfund.org

FOUNDED: 1979

AREAS OF INTEREST:
Photography.

NAME(S) OF PROGRAMS:
• **W. Eugene Smith Grant in Humanistic Photography**

TYPE:
Project/program grants.

PURPOSE:
To support a photographer working on a project in the humanistic tradition of W. Eugene Smith, in order to pursue the work.

ELIGIBILITY:
Open to outstanding photographers of any nationality.

FINANCIAL DATA:
Amount of support per award: $10,000.

Total amount of support: $50,000 for the year 2020.

NO. MOST RECENT APPLICANTS: Approximately 200 annually.

NO. AWARDS: 5 for the year 2020.

APPLICATION INFO:
Initial application is online only. Applicants should include a written proposal, biography and curriculum vitae, and up to 40 images. Entry fee of $50 is required.

Duration: One year.

Deadline: April 30.

*SPECIAL STIPULATIONS:
Grant recipients agree to give to the W. Eugene Smith Memorial Fund, Inc., as an unrestricted gift, 12 digital images and 12 prints of work completed as part of the project proposed, within 18 months of the award and shall become part of the Legacy Collection.

THE JOHN F. AND ANNA LEE STACEY SCHOLARSHIP FUND [520]

c/o National Cowboy and Western Heritage Museum
1700 N.E. 63rd Street
Oklahoma City, OK 73111
(405) 478-2250
Fax: (405) 478-4714
E-mail: registrar@nationalcowboymuseum.org
Web Site: nationalcowboymuseum.org

FOUNDED: 1955

AREAS OF INTEREST:
Drawing and painting in the conservative mode.

TYPE:
Awards/prizes. Cash awards to be used to further the development of young painters in the classical conservative tradition.

YEAR PROGRAM STARTED: 1975

PURPOSE:
To foster a high standard in the study of form, color, drawing, painting, design and technique, as these are expressed in modes showing patent affinity with the classical tradition of western culture.

LEGAL BASIS:
Nonprofit.

ELIGIBILITY:
Open to U.S. citizens between 18 and 35 years of age. Only those who are skilled and devoted to the painting or drawing of classical or conservative tradition of western culture should apply.

GEOG. RESTRICTIONS: United States.

FINANCIAL DATA:
Amount of support per award: $500 to $5,000.

Total amount of support: Varies.

NO. MOST RECENT APPLICANTS: More than 350.

NO. AWARDS: 3 to 5.

APPLICATION INFO:
Guidelines and application are posted online by November 1 for the following year. All applicants will be required to upload images to the Fund's FTP site. Not more than six images of their work (clearly labeled with name, title, dimensions, medium and date of execution of the work) in the following categories: painting from life, drawing from the figure (nude), composition, landscape and others.

Application forms must accompany all submissions.

Duration: One year.

Deadline: Entries need to be uploaded by February 1 of each year.

PUBLICATIONS:
Guidelines.

STAFF:
Melissa Owens, Registrar and Exhibits Coordinator

ADDRESS INQUIRIES TO:
E-mail:
scholarship@nationalcowboymuseum.org

STUDIO ARTS COLLEGE INTERNATIONAL (SACI)   [521]
Palazzo dei Cartelloni
Via Sant' Antonino 11
50123 Florence Italy
(212) 248-7225
Fax: (212) 248-7222
E-mail: admissions@saci-florence.edu
Web Site: www.saci-florence.edu

FOUNDED: 1975

AREAS OF INTEREST:
Studio art, art history, art conservation,
Italian language and culture.

NAME(S) OF PROGRAMS:
- **Fall/Spring/Summer Study Abroad**
- **MA in Art History**
- **MFA in Studio Art**
- **Post Baccalaureate Certificate Program in Conservation**

TYPE:
Awards/prizes; Scholarships.
Fall/Spring/Summer Study Abroad:
Undergraduate and graduate visiting students
may attend for a term or more. SACI offers a
wide variety of both traditional and
cutting-edge studio art and design courses as
well as classes in art history covering
medieval and contemporary art. For
conservation students, there is the unique
opportunity to participate hands-on in the
conservation of historic works in Florence.
Studio Art courses include Fresco Painting,
Serigraphy, Printmaking, Photography, Digital
Multimedia, Video, Jewelry Making, Batik,
Book Making, Sculpture, Ceramics, and
many more.

MFA in Studio Art is a two-year program in
which students work in a creative
environment of rigorous critical and technical
inquiry utilizing the unique artistic and
cultural resources of Florence to prepare for
careers as artists and college instructors.
Students pursue a curriculum integrating
practical and critical skills that encourages
individual innovation, creative collaboration,
mentorships and instruction from SACI's
outstanding faculty.

Post Baccalaureate Certificate Program in
Conservation is a one-year program of
intensive graduate study. The study program
includes graduate seminars, reviews, field
trips, lecture series and exhibitions.

YEAR PROGRAM STARTED: 1975

PURPOSE:
To prepare students to succeed in the
competitive art world.

ELIGIBILITY:
Selection is based on academic/artistic merit
as well as financial need.

FINANCIAL DATA:
Amount of support per award: Varies.

NO. MOST RECENT APPLICANTS: 120.

NO. AWARDS: 100.

APPLICATION INFO:
Application information is available on the
web site.
Duration: One semester to full year.
Deadline: Fall: March 15. Spring: October
15. Summer: March 1.

ADDRESS INQUIRIES TO:
Studio Arts College International (SACI)
454 West 19th Street
New York, NY 10011
(See e-mail address above.)

UNIVERSITY OF ILLINOIS AT URBANA-CHAMPAIGN   [522]
College of Fine and Applied Arts
608 East Lorado Taft Drive, Suite 100
Champaign, IL 61820
(217) 333-1661
(217) 333-1660
E-mail: faa@illinois.edu
Web Site: www.faa.illinois.edu/alumni-
friends/kate-neal-kinley-memorial-fellowship

FOUNDED: 1931

AREAS OF INTEREST:
Art, architecture, dance, landscape
architecture, music, theatre, and urban and
regional planning.

NAME(S) OF PROGRAMS:
- **Kate Neal Kinley Memorial Fellowship**

TYPE:
Fellowships. Awarded for advanced study in
the fine arts in the U.S. or abroad, in an
approved educational institution, with an
approved private teacher or in independent
study.

Three major Fellowships will be awarded:
(1) one in any field of music;
(2) one in architectural design and history, art
and design, theatre, dance, or instrumental or
vocal music and;
(3) one in art, architecture, dance, landscape
architecture, theatre, or urban and regional
planning.

YEAR PROGRAM STARTED: 1931

PURPOSE:
To help defray expenses of advanced study of
the fine and applied arts in America or
abroad.

Provides a meaningful opportunity for
students to enhance their professional status,
aid their pursuit of an advanced degree, or
finance a special project within the field.

ELIGIBILITY:
Open to graduates of the College of Fine and
Applied Arts of the University of Illinois at
Urbana-Champaign and to graduates of
similar institutions of equal educational
standing whose principal or major studies
have been in the fields of art, architecture,
dance, landscape architecture, music, theatre,
and urban and regional planning.

Although there is no age limitation for
applicants, other factors being equal,
preference will be given to applicants who
have not reached their 25th birthday.

Fellowships will be awarded upon the basis
of unusual promise in the fine arts as attested
by:
(1) high attainment in the applicant's major
field of study as evidenced by academic
marks and quality of work submitted or
performed;
(2) high attainment in related cultural fields
as evidenced by academic marks;
(3) the character, merit and suitability of the
program proposed by the applicant and;
(4) excellence of personality, seriousness of
purpose and good moral character.

FINANCIAL DATA:
The fellowships are to be used by the
recipients toward defraying the expenses of
advanced study in America or abroad.
Amount of support per award: Major
fellowships: Up to $20,000 in any field of
music, up to $20,000 in architectural design
and history, art and design, theatre, dance, or
instrumental or vocal music, and up to

$9,000 in art, architecture, dance, landscape
architecture, theatre, or urban and regional
planning.

CO-OP FUNDING PROGRAMS: Funded partially by
the John Robert Gregg Fund at Community
Funds, Inc. and the New York Community
Trust.

NO. AWARDS: 3 major fellowships, plus up to 3
additional fellowships of lesser amounts,
depending upon committee recommendations.

APPLICATION INFO:
Application form and guidelines are available
online.
Duration: Tenable for one academic year.
Deadline: December 1.

ADDRESS INQUIRIES TO:
Kate Neal Kinley
Memorial Fellowship Committee
(See e-mail address above.)

UNIVERSITY OF SOUTHERN CALIFORNIA, GAYLE GARNER ROSKI SCHOOL OF ART AND DESIGN   [523]
Watt Hall 104
850 West 37th Street
Los Angeles, CA 90089-0292
(213) 740-9153
Fax: (213) 740-8938
E-mail: roski@usc.edu
Web Site: roski.usc.edu

FOUNDED: 1883

AREAS OF INTEREST:
Art and design.

NAME(S) OF PROGRAMS:
- **Macomber Travel Grant**

TYPE:
Travel grants. Selected through a competitive
process, the prize will support proposed
projects involving research-based travel, the
production of new art work, and a public
presentation of the new work.

YEAR PROGRAM STARTED: 1960

PURPOSE:
To educate artists.

LEGAL BASIS:
Private university.

ELIGIBILITY:
Undergraduate applicants must be third-year
Roski majors who will begin their senior
year in the fall following the award. Graduate
applicants must be current first-year Roski
M.F.A and M.A. students. The awardee must
be in good academic standing at the time of
the award and remain in good standing
throughout the culminating year. The awardee
must be without prior or pending issues of
conduct.

FINANCIAL DATA:
Amount of support per award: Up to $7,500.

NO. MOST RECENT APPLICANTS: 5.

NO. AWARDS: Maximum 4.

APPLICATION INFO:
Applications must be submitted on
SlideRoom. Application must include a
proposal, itinerary, and budget of expenses
for travel related to the research,
development, production, and presentation of
an independent art project.
Duration: One year.

Deadline: March 29.

ADDRESS INQUIRIES TO:
Antonio Bartolome
Student Services Manager
(See address above.)

History

AGRICULTURAL HISTORY SOCIETY [524]
Mount Royal University
Department of Humanities
4825 Mount Royal Gate, S.W.
Calgary AB T3E 6K6 Canada
(403) 440-8796
E-mail: aghistorysociety@gmail.com
Web Site: www.aghistorysociety.org

FOUNDED: 1919

AREAS OF INTEREST:
Agricultural and rural history.

NAME(S) OF PROGRAMS:
• **Everett E. Edwards Awards in Agricultural History**
• **Gilbert C. Fite Dissertation Award**
• **Wayne D. Rasmussen Award**
• **Theodore Saloutos Book Award**
• **Henry A. Wallace Award**

TYPE:
Awards/prizes. The Everett E. Edwards Award is presented to the graduate student who submits the best manuscript on any aspect of agricultural history and rural studies during the current calendar year.

The Gilbert C. Fite Dissertation Award will be presented to the author of the best dissertation on any aspect of agricultural history completed during the current calendar year.

The Wayne D. Rasmussen Award is given to the author of the best article on agricultural history published by a journal other than *Agricultural History* during the current calendar year.

The Theodore Saloutos Book Award is presented to the author of a book on any aspect of agricultural history in the U.S. within the current year, broadly interpreted.

The Henry A. Wallace Award is presented to the author of a book on any aspect of agricultural history outside of the U.S. within the current year, broadly interpreted.

PURPOSE:
To promote research and publication in the field of agricultural and rural history.

FINANCIAL DATA:
Amount of support per award: Edwards Award: Honorarium of $200 and publication in *Agricultural History*; Fite Dissertation Award: Honorarium of $300 and a certificate; Rasmussen Award: Honorarium of $200 for the author and certificates for the author and publisher; Saloutos Book Award: $500 to the author.

APPLICATION INFO:
Contact the Society for details.
Deadline: January 15.

PUBLICATIONS:
Agricultural History.

AMERICAN ANTIQUARIAN SOCIETY (AAS)
185 Salisbury Street
Worcester, MA 01609-1634
(508) 755-5221
Fax: (508) 754-9069
E-mail: nwolverton@mwa.org
Web Site: www.americanantiquarian.org

TYPE:
Fellowships. Visiting fellowship for historical research by creative and performing artists, writers, filmmakers and journalists.

See entry 305 for full listing.

AMERICAN ANTIQUARIAN SOCIETY (AAS)
185 Salisbury Street
Worcester, MA 01609-1634
(508) 755-5221
Fax: (508) 754-9069
E-mail: nwolverton@mwa.org
Web Site: www.americanantiquarian.org

TYPE:
Conferences/seminars; Fellowships. Fellowships provide support for residence at the Society's library for research on any topic supported by the collections. All awards are for research and writing using the library's resources.

See entry 304 for full listing.

AMERICAN CATHOLIC HISTORICAL ASSOCIATION [525]
Mount St. Mary's University
16300 Old Emmitsburg Road
Emmitsburg, MD 21727
(301) 447-5799
E-mail: acha@achahistory.org
Web Site: achahistory.org

FOUNDED: 1919

AREAS OF INTEREST:
The history of Catholicism from antiquity to the present.

NAME(S) OF PROGRAMS:
• **The Howard R. Marraro Prize**

TYPE:
Awards/prizes. This Prize is given annually to the author of a book that is judged by a committee of experts to be the most distinguished work dealing with Italian history or Italo-American history or relations that has been published in a preceding 12-month period. It is named in memory of Howard A. Marraro (1879-1972), professor, Columbia University and the author of more than a dozen books on Italian literature, history and culture.

YEAR PROGRAM STARTED: 1973

PURPOSE:
To stimulate interest in the history of Catholicism among young scholars.

LEGAL BASIS:
An endowed fund owned by the Association.

ELIGIBILITY:
To be entered in the competition, a work must be of book length, in English, already published and must deal with Italian history or Italian-American history or relations. To be eligible for the prize, an author must be a citizen or resident of the U.S. or Canada. The work must have an imprint of the previous year.

FINANCIAL DATA:
Amount of support per award: $1,500.

NO. AWARDS: 1 per annum.

APPLICATION INFO:
Nominators must complete the online Data Collection Form. One copy of each entry must be sent to each of the three committee members.
Deadline: May 15.

ADDRESS INQUIRIES TO:
Prize Administrator
E-mail: awards@historians.org

AMERICAN CATHOLIC HISTORICAL ASSOCIATION
Mount St. Mary's University
16300 Old Emmitsburg Road
Emmitsburg, MD 21727
(301) 447-5799
E-mail: acha@achahistory.org
Web Site: achahistory.org

TYPE:
Awards/prizes; Challenge/matching grants; Conferences/seminars; Travel grants. A prize awarded annually to the author whose article, dealing with the history of the Catholic Church, is the first of his or her professional career and is judged to be the best of those in that category accepted for publication in any given year by the editors of the *Catholic Historical Review*.

See entry 736 for full listing.

AMERICAN CATHOLIC HISTORICAL ASSOCIATION
Mount St. Mary's University
16300 Old Emmitsburg Road
Emmitsburg, MD 21727
(301) 447-5799
E-mail: acha@achahistory.org
Web Site: achahistory.org

TYPE:
Awards/prizes. This Prize is given annually to the author of a book, published during a preceding 12-month period, which is judged by a committee of experts to have made the most original and distinguished contribution to knowledge of the history of the Catholic Church.

See entry 737 for full listing.

AMERICAN CATHOLIC HISTORICAL ASSOCIATION
Mount St. Mary's University
16300 Old Emmitsburg Road
Emmitsburg, MD 21727
(301) 447-5799
E-mail: acha@achahistory.org
Web Site: achahistory.org

TYPE:
Awards/prizes; Challenge/matching grants; Conferences/seminars; Research grants; Travel grants. John Tracy Ellis Dissertation Award memorializes the scholarship and teaching of Monsignor Ellis (1905-1992) and is awarded to a doctoral student in the field of Catholic Studies with a promising, but not-yet-completed dissertation.

Presidential Graduate Travel Grant was created in 2010 by the Association from donations from former presidents. This cash grant is awarded to a graduate student presenting at the Annual Meeting to assist with travel expenses.

Summer Research and Writing Grant is awarded to an ACHA member who is a graduate student or contingent faculty member to support writing or travel expenses.

See entry 738 for full listing.

THE AMERICAN HISTORICAL ASSOCIATION   [526]
400 A Street, S.E.
Washington, DC 20003
(202) 544-2422
E-mail: awards@historians.org
Web Site: www.historians.org

FOUNDED: 1884

AREAS OF INTEREST:
Promotion of historical studies, the collection and preservation of historical manuscripts and the dissemination of historical research.

NAME(S) OF PROGRAMS:
- **The Herbert Baxter Adams Prize**
- **The George Louis Beer Prize**
- **The Jerry Bentley Prize**
- **The Albert J. Beveridge Award**
- **The Albert J. Beveridge Grant**
- **The James Henry Breasted Prize**
- **The John H. Dunning Prize in United States History**
- **The John K. Fairbank Prize in East Asian History**
- **The Herbert Feis Award**
- **The Morris D. Forkosch Prize**
- **The Leo Gershoy Award**
- **The Clarence H. Haring Prize**
- **J. Franklin Jameson Award**
- **The Friedrich Katz Prize**
- **The Joan Kelly Memorial Prize in Women's History**
- **Martin A. Klein Prize in African History**
- **Michael Kraus Research Grant**
- **The Waldo G. Leland Prize**
- **Littleton-Griswold Grant**
- **The Littleton-Griswold Prize in American Law and Society**
- **The J. Russell Major Prize**
- **The Helen and Howard R. Marraro Prize in Italian History**
- **The George L. Mosse Prize**
- **The John E. O'Connor Film Award**
- **The James A. Rawley Prize in Atlantic History**
- **John F. Richards Prize in South Asian History**
- **The Dorothy Rosenberg Prize**
- **Bernadotte E. Schmitt Grant**
- **The Wesley-Logan Prize**

TYPE:
Awards/prizes; Fellowships; Research grants. Prizes and awards for distinguished scholarly publications written in English on historical subjects as follows:

Herbert Baxter Adams Prize: Awarded annually for a distinguished book by an American author in the field of European history.

Beer Prize: Awarded annually for the best work on European international history by a U.S. citizen.

Bentley Prize: Awarded annually for the best book in the field of world history.

Beveridge Award: Awarded annually for the best book in English on the history of the U.S., Canada, or Latin America from 1492 to the present.

Beveridge Grant: Given for research pertaining to the Western Hemisphere.

Breasted Prize: Awarded annually for an outstanding book in English in any field of history prior to 1000 A.D.

Dunning Prize: For a book on any subject relating to American history. Awarded biennially in odd years.

Fairbank Prize: Awarded annually for an outstanding book on the history of China proper, Vietnam, Chinese Central Asia, Mongolia, Manchuria, Korea or Japan since the year 1800.

Feis Award: Awarded for distinguished contributions to public history.

Forkosch Prize: Awarded annually in recognition of the best book in English in the field of British, British Imperial or British Commonwealth History.

Gershoy Prize: Awarded annually for an outstanding work published in English on any aspect of the fields of 17th and 18th century western European history.

Haring Prize: For a Latin American who, in the opinion of the committee, has published the most outstanding book on Latin American history during the preceding five years. Awarded every five years.

J. Franklin Jameson Award: Given for outstanding achievement in the editing of historical sources.

Friedrich Katz Prize: Awarded annually for the best book in Latin American and Caribbean history.

Kelly Memorial Prize: Awarded annually for the best work in women's history and/or feminist theory.

Martin A. Klein Prize: Awarded in the study of African history.

Michael Kraus Research Grant: Awarded for the study of colonial American history.

Leland Prize: Offered every five years for the outstanding reference tool in the field of history, i.e., bibliographies, indexes, encyclopedias and other scholarly apparatus.

Littleton-Griswold Grant: Awarded in U.S. legal history and law and society, broadly defined.

Littleton-Griswold Prize: Awarded annually for the best book in any subject on the history of American law and society, broadly defined.

J. Russell Major Prize: Awarded annually for the best work in English on any aspect of French history.

Marraro Prize: Awarded annually for the best work on any epoch of Italian history or Italian-American relations.

George L. Mosse Prize: Awarded annually for an outstanding major work of extraordinary scholarly distinction, creativity, and originality in the intellectual and cultural history of Europe since the Renaissance.

John E. O'Connor Film Award: Awarded annually to recognize outstanding interpretations of history through the medium of film.

James A. Rawley Prize in Atlantic History: Awarded annually in recognition of outstanding historical writing that explores aspects of integration of Atlantic worlds before the 20th century.

John F. Richards Prize in South Asian History: Awarded annually for the most distinguished work of scholarship on South Asian history published in English.

Dorothy Rosenberg Prize: Book prize for the Jewish Diaspora Community.

Bernadette Schmitt Grant: Given for research of Europe, Asia and Africa.

Wesley-Logan Prize: Awarded annually for an outstanding book on African diaspora history.

PURPOSE:
To promote and honor good historical writing and scholarship.

LEGAL BASIS:
Nonprofit association.

ELIGIBILITY:
Applicant must be a member to apply for grants. Preference will be given to Ph.D. candidates and postgraduates.

FINANCIAL DATA:
Amount of support per award: Varies.

NO. AWARDS: 1 in each program on the yearly basis.

PUBLICATIONS:
Annual report; *American Historical Review*; *Perspectives in History*.

OFFICERS:
Jacqueline Jones, President
James R. Grossman, Executive Director

ADDRESS INQUIRIES TO:
AHA Awards Team
(See address above.)

THE AMERICAN HISTORICAL ASSOCIATION   [527]
400 A Street, S.E.
Washington, DC 20003
(202) 544-2422
E-mail: awards@historians.org
Web Site: www.historians.org

FOUNDED: 1884

AREAS OF INTEREST:
Scholarly research.

NAME(S) OF PROGRAMS:
- **The J. Franklin Jameson Fellowship**

TYPE:
Fellowships. Award in American history offered annually by the Library of Congress and the American Historical Association.

YEAR PROGRAM STARTED: 1977

PURPOSE:
To support significant scholarly research in the collections of the Library of Congress by scholars at an early stage in their careers in history.

LEGAL BASIS:
Nonprofit association.

ELIGIBILITY:
At the time of application, applicants must hold the Ph.D. degree or equivalent, must have received this degree within the past seven years and must not have published or had accepted for publication a book-length historical work. The fellowship will not be awarded to complete a doctoral dissertation.

The applicant's project in American history must be one for which the general and special collections of the Library of Congress offer unique research support. Applicants should include a statement substantiating this relationship.

Before the conclusion of the fellowship, the Jameson fellow will summarize the results of his or her research at a professional gathering arranged by the American Historical Association and the Library of Congress. Jameson fellows are not required to complete their project during the tenure of the fellowship, nor need they necessarily have published the results as a discrete work.

The American Historical Association encourages nontenured faculty, public historians, independent scholars and two-year faculty to apply.

FINANCIAL DATA:
Amount of support per award: $5,000 stipend.

NO. MOST RECENT APPLICANTS: 5 to 10 annually.

NO. AWARDS: 1 annually.

APPLICATION INFO:
Letter of application should include a vitae, statement concerning the proposed project and its relationship to Library of Congress holdings, tentative schedule for tenure of the fellowship and three letters of recommendation by persons qualified to judge the project and the applicant's fitness to undertake it.
Duration: Two to three months in full-time residency in Washington, DC.
Deadline: April 1. Award announced in June.

PUBLICATIONS:
Annual report.

OFFICERS:
Jacqueline Jones, President
James R. Grossman, Executive Director

ADDRESS INQUIRIES TO:
AHA Awards Team
(See address above.)

THE AMERICAN HISTORICAL ASSOCIATION   [528]
400 A Street, S.E.
Washington, DC 20003
(202) 544-2422
E-mail: awards@historians.org
Web Site: www.historians.org

FOUNDED: 1884

AREAS OF INTEREST:
Scholarly research.

NAME(S) OF PROGRAMS:
● **Fellowship in Aerospace History**

TYPE:
Fellowships. The Association annually funds at least one fellow for a period of six to nine months, to undertake a proposed research project related to aerospace history. The Fellowship is supported by the National Aeronautics and Space Administration (NASA).

YEAR PROGRAM STARTED: 1986

PURPOSE:
To provide a fellow with an opportunity to engage in significant and sustained advanced research in all aspects of the history of aerospace from the earliest human interest in flight to the present, including cultural and intellectual history, economic history, history of law and public policy and the history of science, engineering and management.

LEGAL BASIS:
Nonprofit association.

ELIGIBILITY:
Applicant must possess a Doctorate degree in history or in a closely related field or be enrolled as a student, having completed all course work, in a doctoral degree-granting program. Preference is given to applicants in the early stages of their careers.

Stipends may be awarded only to U.S. citizens or permanent residents.

FINANCIAL DATA:
Amount of support per award: $21,250 stipend for a six- to nine-month fellowship, including travel expenses.

NO. AWARDS: 2.

APPLICATION INFO:
Applicants must complete an application form, available online, and offer a specific and detailed research proposal that will be the basis of the fellow's research during the term.
Duration: Six to nine months.
Deadline: April 1.

PUBLICATIONS:
Annual report.

OFFICERS:
Jacqueline Jones, President
James R. Grossman, Executive Director

ADDRESS INQUIRIES TO:
AHA Awards Team
(See address above.)

*SPECIAL STIPULATIONS:
Funds may not be used to support tuition or fees. A fellow may not hold other major fellowships or grants during the fellowship term, except sabbatical and supplemental grants from their own institutions and small grants from other sources for specific research expenses. Sources of anticipated support must be listed in the application form.

AMERICAN INSTITUTE OF THE HISTORY OF PHARMACY
University of Wisconsin School of Pharmacy
Rennebohm Hall
777 Highland Avenue
Madison, WI 53705-2222
(608) 262-5378
E-mail: aihp@aihp.org
Web Site: www.aihp.org

TYPE:
Grants-in-aid; Research grants.

See entry 2290 for full listing.

BERKSHIRE CONFERENCE OF WOMEN HISTORIANS   [529]
Penn State Brandywine
Vairo Library, 124
25 Yearsley Mill Road
Media, PA 19063
(610) 892-1464
E-mail: secretary@berksconference.org
Web Site: www.berksconference.org

FOUNDED: 1930

AREAS OF INTEREST:
Women's history.

TYPE:
Awards/prizes. The Berkshire Conference of Women Historians awards two annual book and article prizes in the following categories:

A first book that deals substantially with the history of women, gender, and/or sexuality;
A first book in any field of history that does not focus on the history of women, gender, and/or sexuality;
An article in the fields of the history of women, gender, and/or sexuality and;
An article in any field of history other than the history of women, gender, and/or sexuality.

YEAR PROGRAM STARTED: 1972

PURPOSE:
To promote historical scholarship by women.

ELIGIBILITY:
Eligibility is limited to books and articles published in the prior calendar year by any female historian or historian who identifies as a woman and is normally resident in North America.

FINANCIAL DATA:
Amount of support per award: $1,000 for each book prize; $500 for each article prize.
Total amount of support: $3,000.

NO. MOST RECENT APPLICANTS: 150.

NO. AWARDS: 1 award in each category per year.

APPLICATION INFO:
Detailed guidelines are available on the Conference web site.
Deadline: Article Prize: January 15. Book Prize: February 15.

ADDRESS INQUIRIES TO:
Julie A. Gallagher, Secretary
(See e-mail address above.)

JOHN CARTER BROWN LIBRARY   [530]
Brown University
94 George Street
Providence, RI 02906
(401) 863-2725
Fax: (401) 863-3477
E-mail: jcb-fellowships@brown.edu
Web Site: jcblibrary.org/fellowships

FOUNDED: 1846

AREAS OF INTEREST:
Historical studies pertaining to the Age of Exploration, Latin American history before 1830, North American history to approximately 1800, European impressions of America, New World travel, exploration and colonization. Also, Indian language, cartography, West Indies and Caribbean studies, maritime, slave trade, and the Jewish Experience in the colonial Americas, North and South.

NAME(S) OF PROGRAMS:
● **The John Carter Brown Library Research Fellowships**

TYPE:
Fellowships. The John Carter Brown Library (JCB), an independently funded institution for advanced research at Brown University, contains one of the world's premier collections of primary materials related to the discovery, exploration, and settlement of the New World to 1825, including books, maps, newspapers and other printed objects.

The Library offers both Short-term and Long-term Fellowships.

YEAR PROGRAM STARTED: 1981

PURPOSE:
To promote scholarly research at the library.

LEGAL BASIS:
Independently funded and administered library and research center.

ELIGIBILITY:
Fellowships and grants are reserved exclusively for scholars whose work is centered on colonial history of the Americas, North and South, including all aspects of European, African, and Native American engagements in global and comparative contexts.

Short-term fellowships are open to individuals who are engaged in pre- and postdoctoral, or independent research, regardless of nationality.

Fellowships funded by the NEH are only available to citizens of the U.S., or to those applicants residing in the U.S. for the three years preceding application. Applicants of all nationalities, however, will be considered for long-term fellowships.

FINANCIAL DATA:
Amount of support per award: Short-term Fellowships: $2,100 per month; Long-term Fellowships: $5,000 per month.
Total amount of support: Varies.

NO. AWARDS: Approximately 40 annually.

APPLICATION INFO:
Applicants must submit:
(1) a narrative description of the proposed project, including an explanation of its historiographical significance, progress to date on the project, identification of specific materials to be consulted at the Library, and plan for work to be completed while in residence;
(2) current curriculum vitae;
(3) a complete application form and;
(4) two letters of recommendation to support their proposed project.

Applicants may submit proposals in English, French, Portuguese or Spanish, although English is generally preferred by the Committee.

Duration: Short-term Fellowships: Two to four months; Long-term Fellowships: Five to 10 months.
Deadline: December 15.

PUBLICATIONS:
Application guidelines.

ADDRESS INQUIRIES TO:
See e-mail address above.

*PLEASE NOTE:
Recipients of all Fellowships must relocate to Providence and be in continuous residence at the John Carter Brown Library for the entire term of the award. Rooms are available for rent at Fiering House, the JCB Fellows' residence, a beautifully restored 1869 house just four blocks from the Library. Those living within commuting distance of the Library (approximately 45 miles distant) are ordinarily not eligible for JCB Fellowships.

CANADIAN INSTITUTE OF UKRAINIAN STUDIES [531]
University of Alberta
4-30 Pembina Hall
Edmonton AB T6G 2H8 Canada
(780) 492-2972
E-mail: cius@ualberta.ca
Web Site: www.cius.ca

FOUNDED: 1976

AREAS OF INTEREST:
Studies in history, literature, language, education, social sciences, library sciences and women's studies.

NAME(S) OF PROGRAMS:
● **The Helen Darcovich Memorial Doctoral Fellowship**
● **Neporany Doctoral Fellowship**
● **Research Grants**

TYPE:
Fellowships; Research grants; Scholarships. The Helen Darcovich Memorial Doctoral Fellowship is awarded annually to a student writing a dissertation on a Ukrainian or Ukrainian-Canadian topic in education, history, humanities, social sciences, law or library sciences.

The Neporany Doctoral Fellowship, offered by the Canadian Foundation for Ukrainian Studies, is awarded to one ore more doctoral students specializing on Ukraine in political science, economics, and related fields.

Research Grants are awarded in support of projects that have scholarly value, well-defined work plans, and modest budgets.

PURPOSE:
To foster, develop, and support Ukrainian studies in Canada and internationally.

ELIGIBILITY:
The Helen Darcovich Memorial Doctoral Fellowship: Because funding is for dissertation work only, all other degree requirements must be completed by the time the award is taken up. Applications will be judged on a points system based on the dissertation proposal, letters of reference, writing sample, academic grades, and publishing record. Canadian citizens and permanent residents of Canada, who may hold the fellowship at any institution of higher learning, and foreign students enrolled at the University of Alberta, will receive extra points.

Neporany Doctoral Fellowship is offered to doctoral students specializing on Ukraine in political science, economics, and related fields (social sciences and political, economic, and social history). Preference will be given to students completing their dissertations as well as to students at Canadian universities or Canadian citizens and residents.

FINANCIAL DATA:
Amount of support per award: Helen Darcovich Memorial Doctoral Fellowship: Up to $12,500 (CAN); Neporany Doctoral Fellowship: $5,000 to $20,000 (CAN).
Total amount of support: Varies.

NO. MOST RECENT APPLICANTS: Varies.

NO. AWARDS: Helen Darcovich Memorial Doctoral Fellowship: 3; Neporany Doctoral Fellowship: 1 or more; Research grants: 26 for the year 2020-21.

APPLICATION INFO:
Research grant applicants should read the Research Grant Application Guide prior to filling out the application form.
Duration: Varies.
Deadline: March 1.

ADDRESS INQUIRIES TO:
Serge Cipko, Assistant Director of Research (See address above.)

COLLEGE OF PHYSICIANS OF PHILADELPHIA [532]
Francis Clark Wood Institute
for the History of Medicine
19 South 22nd Street
Philadelphia, PA 19103-3097
(215) 399-2301
Fax: (215) 569-0356
E-mail: travelgrants@collegeofphysicians.org
Web Site: www.collegeofphysicians.
org/library/wood-institute

FOUNDED: 1787

AREAS OF INTEREST:
The history of medicine.

NAME(S) OF PROGRAMS:
● **Wood Institute Travel Grants**

TYPE:
Travel grants; Visiting scholars. This program allows scholars to conduct short-term research in the College's Library and/or Mutter Museum.

YEAR PROGRAM STARTED: 1983

PURPOSE:
To encourage the study and appreciation of medicine in the broader historical and social context in response to current health care issues and public and professional interests.

LEGAL BASIS:
501(c)(3) not-for-profit educational institution.

ELIGIBILITY:
Applicants must reside more than 75 miles from Philadelphia to be eligible. Grants are available to scholars and bona fide researchers.

FINANCIAL DATA:
Amount of support per award: Up to $1,500.
Total amount of support: Up to $1,500.

NO. MOST RECENT APPLICANTS: 15.

NO. AWARDS: Varies.

APPLICATION INFO:
Applicants should submit:
(1) one-page statement of the research project and the applicability of the College's resources;
(2) curriculum vitae (not to exceed three pages in length);
(3) budget estimate of travel and lodging needs; and
(4) one letter of reference (to be sent directly from the source to the College).

Electronic applications are strongly encouraged.
Duration: One to two weeks.
Deadline: Applications are accepted on a rolling basis until annual funding is depleted.

ADDRESS INQUIRIES TO:
Director, Wood Institute for the
History of Medicine
Travel Grants
(See address above.)

COLUMBIA UNIVERSITY [533]
517 Butler Library
535 West 114th Street
New York, NY 10027
(212) 854-2247
Fax: (212) 854-4972
E-mail: annthornton@columbia.edu
Web Site: library.columbia.
edu/about/awards/bancroft.html

FOUNDED: 1754

NAME(S) OF PROGRAMS:
● **Bancroft Prizes**

TYPE:
Awards/prizes. Prizes of equal rank to be awarded to the authors of distinguished works in either or both American History, including biography and diplomacy.

YEAR PROGRAM STARTED: 1948

PURPOSE:
To honor the authors of books of distinguished merit and distinction, upon the subject of American history in its broadest sense.

LEGAL BASIS:
University.

ELIGIBILITY:
Awards are made for books first published in the previous calendar year. The competition is open to all persons whether connected with Columbia University or not, and whether citizens of the U.S. or any other country.

The word "American" is interpreted to include all the Americas, North, Central and South; however, the award is confined to works originally written in English or of which there is a published translation in English. Volumes of papers, letters and speeches of famous Americans, unless edited by the author himself, are not eligible. Autobiography comes within the terms of the prize, but books reporting on recent personal experiences of Americans, within a limited area both in time and geography, are not considered eligible.

Previous winners are eligible for an award in a later year.

FINANCIAL DATA:
Amount of support per award: $10,000.
Total amount of support: $20,000 to $30,000 annually.

NO. MOST RECENT APPLICANTS: 230.

NO. AWARDS: 2.

APPLICATION INFO:
Works submitted in competition may be sent to the Bancroft Prize Committee at the address above. It is requested that four copies be furnished, three for jury members and one for the Libraries of Columbia University. A letter should accompany the books so that acknowledgement may be made.
Deadline: Works may be submitted after June 1 and before November 1. Page-proof copy may be submitted after November 1 provided the work will be published after that date and before December 31 of the year preceding the award.

ADDRESS INQUIRIES TO:
Bancroft Prize Committee
(See address above.)

THE COORDINATING COUNCIL FOR WOMEN IN HISTORY, INC.
3118 Chaucer Drive
Charlotte, NC 28210
(773) 960-2092
E-mail: execdir@theccwh.org
Web Site: www.theccwh.org

TYPE:
Awards/prizes. The Catherine Prelinger Award is given to a scholar, with a Ph.D. or ABD, whose career has not followed a traditional academic path through secondary and higher education and whose work has contributed to women in the historical profession.

See entry 975 for full listing.

THE COORDINATING COUNCIL FOR WOMEN IN HISTORY, INC.   [534]
3118 Chaucer Drive
Charlotte, NC 28210
(773) 960-2092
E-mail: execdir@theccwh.org
Web Site: www.theccwh.org

AREAS OF INTEREST:
Women's history.

NAME(S) OF PROGRAMS:
● **CCWH/Berkshire Conference of Women Historians Graduate Student Fellowship**
● **Nupur Chaudhuri First Article Prize**
● **Carol Gold Best Article Award**
● **Ida B. Wells Graduate Student Fellowship**

TYPE:
Awards/prizes; Fellowships.

PURPOSE:
To support the exploration of the diverse experiences and histories of all women; to educate men and women on the status of women in the historical profession; to promote research and interpretation in areas of women's history.

ELIGIBILITY:
CCWH/Berkshire Conference of Women Historians Graduate Student Fellowship: Applicant must be a graduate student completing a dissertation in a history department.

Nupur Chaudhuri First Article Prize: Applicant must be a CCWH member whose first article is published in a refereed journal.

Carol Gold Best Article Award: Applicant must have received the rank of Associate Professor at the time of publication and must be a current member of the CCWH.

Ida B. Wells Graduate Student Fellowship: Applicant must be an ABD graduate student working on a historical dissertation, not necessarily in a history department. Applicants in interdisciplinary areas such as women's studies or ethnic studies are particularly welcome.

FINANCIAL DATA:
Funds are issued in U.S. dollars only.
Amount of support per award: CCWH/Berkshire Conference, Nupur Chaudhuri Prize and Wells Fellowships: $1,000; Carol Gold Best Article Award: $500.

APPLICATION INFO:
Applications are available on the Council web site.
Deadline: May 15.

ADDRESS INQUIRIES TO:
Elizabeth Everton, Ph.D., Executive Director
(See e-mail address above.)

CUSHWA CENTER FOR THE STUDY OF AMERICAN CATHOLICISM   [535]
407 Geddes Hall
University of Notre Dame
Notre Dame, IN 46556
(574) 631-5441
E-mail: cushwa@nd.edu
Web Site: cushwa.nd.edu

NAME(S) OF PROGRAMS:
● **Hibernian Research Award**

TYPE:
Research grants; Travel grants. The Hibernian Research Award is offered to further the scholarly study of Irish America by scholars of any academic discipline engaged in a research project studying the Irish experience in the U.S.

PURPOSE:
To promote the scholarly study of the Irish in the U.S.

ELIGIBILITY:
Awards are made to scholars in any academic discipline.

FINANCIAL DATA:
Amount of support per award: Maximum $2,000.
Total amount of support: Varies.

NO. AWARDS: 2 to 3.

APPLICATION INFO:
Applicant must submit the following documents via e-mail:
(1) completed application form;
(2) current curriculum vitae, including a representative list of applicant's publications and;
(3) a brief description of the research project (maximum 1,000 words).
Deadline: December 31. Applicants will be notified in March.

STAFF:
Kathleen Sprows Cummings, Director
MaDonna Noak, Administrative Coordinator

ADDRESS INQUIRIES TO:
MaDonna Noak, Administrative Coordinator
(See address above.)

CUSHWA CENTER FOR THE STUDY OF AMERICAN CATHOLICISM   [536]
407 Geddes Hall
University of Notre Dame
Notre Dame, IN 46556
(574) 631-5441
E-mail: cushwa@nd.edu
Web Site: cushwa.nd.edu

FOUNDED: 1980

AREAS OF INTEREST:
Catholicism in the U.S.

NAME(S) OF PROGRAMS:
● **Research Travel Grants**

TYPE:
Travel grants. Research Travel Grants support projects that require substantial use of the collection of the library and/or the archives of the University of Notre Dame and help to defray travel and lodging costs.

YEAR PROGRAM STARTED: 1980

PURPOSE:
To make it possible for scholars to make use of the Notre Dame archives.

LEGAL BASIS:
University.

ELIGIBILITY:
Grants are made to scholars in any academic discipline.

FINANCIAL DATA:
Amount of support per award: Up to $2,000. Assistance at finding affordable accommodations is available.
Total amount of support: Varies.

NO. AWARDS: 8 to 12.

APPLICATION INFO:
Applicant must submit the following
documents via e-mail:
(1) completed application form;
(2) current curriculum vitae;
(3) 1,000-word description of the project to
be undertaken at the center and;
(4) proposed budget estimating travel,
lodging and research expenses.
Duration: Varies.
Deadline: December 31. Applicants will be
notified in March.

STAFF:
Kathleen Sprows Cummings, Director
MaDonna Noak, Administrative Coordinator

ADDRESS INQUIRIES TO:
MaDonna Noak, Administrative Coordinator
(See address above.)

CUSHWA CENTER FOR THE STUDY OF AMERICAN CATHOLICISM [537]

407 Geddes Hall
University of Notre Dame
Notre Dame, IN 46556
(574) 631-5441
E-mail: cushwa@nd.edu
Web Site: cushwa.nd.edu

FOUNDED: 2012

AREAS OF INTEREST:
Catholicism in the U.S.

NAME(S) OF PROGRAMS:
● **Peter R. D'Agostino Research Travel
Grant**

TYPE:
Travel grants. Offered in conjunction with
Italian Studies at Notre Dame, the Peter R.
D'Agostino Research Travel Grant supports
research in Roman archives for a significant
publication project on U.S. Catholic history.

YEAR PROGRAM STARTED: 2012

PURPOSE:
To facilitate the study of the American past
from an international perspective.

LEGAL BASIS:
University.

FINANCIAL DATA:
Amount of support per award: Maximum
$5,000.
Total amount of support: Varies.

NO. AWARDS: 1.

APPLICATION INFO:
Applicant must submit the following
documents via e-mail:
(1) completed application form;
(2) current curriculum vitae, including a
representative list of applicant's publications;
(3) a brief description of the research project
(maximum 1,000 words) and;
(4) a detailed budget including travel, lodging
and research expenses, and noting
cost-sharing with any other potential sources
of funding.
Duration: Varies.
Deadline: December 31. Applicants will be
notified by March.

STAFF:
Kathleen Sprows Cummings, Director
MaDonna Noak, Administrative Coordinator

ADDRESS INQUIRIES TO:
MaDonna Noak, Administrative Coordinator
(See address above.)

CUSHWA CENTER FOR THE STUDY OF AMERICAN CATHOLICISM [538]

407 Geddes Hall
University of Notre Dame
Notre Dame, IN 46556
(574) 631-5441
E-mail: cushwa@nd.edu
Web Site: cushwa.nd.edu

FOUNDED: 1980

AREAS OF INTEREST:
Catholicism in the U.S.

NAME(S) OF PROGRAMS:
● **Mother Theodore Guerin Research
Travel Grant**

TYPE:
Travel grants. The Mother Theodore Guerin
Research Travel Grant supports scholars who
seek to move Catholic women to the
forefront of historical narratives.

PURPOSE:
To make it possible for scholars to make use
of the Notre Dame archives.

LEGAL BASIS:
University.

ELIGIBILITY:
Grants are made to scholars in any academic
discipline whose projects seek to feature
Catholic women more predominantly in
stories of the past.

FINANCIAL DATA:
Amount of support per award: Up to $1,500.
Total amount of support: Varies.

NO. AWARDS: 4 to 5.

APPLICATION INFO:
Applicant must submit the following
documents via e-mail:
(1) completed application form;
(2) current curriculum vitae;
(3) 1,000-word description of the project,
including research plan detailing any research
repositories or oral history subjects applicant
plans to visit and any advance contact
between applicant and relevant archivists or
others and;
(4) proposed budget estimating travel,
lodging and research expenses.
Duration: Varies.
Deadline: December 31. Applicants will be
notified in March.

STAFF:
Kathleen Sprows Cummings, Director
MaDonna Noak, Administrative Coordinator

ADDRESS INQUIRIES TO:
MaDonna Noak, Administrative Coordinator
(See address above.)

CUSHWA CENTER FOR THE STUDY OF AMERICAN CATHOLICISM [539]

407 Geddes Hall
University of Notre Dame
Notre Dame, IN 46556
(574) 631-5441
E-mail: cushwa@nd.edu
Web Site: cushwa.nd.edu

FOUNDED: 1980

AREAS OF INTEREST:
Catholicism in the U.S.

NAME(S) OF PROGRAMS:
● **The Cyprian Davis, O.S.B., Prize**

TYPE:
Awards/prizes. In partnership with the
American Catholic Historical Association, the
Cushwa Center has established the Cyprian
Davis, O.S.B., Prize recognizing works in
progress that promise to make significant
contributions to the study of the Black
Catholic experience.

PURPOSE:
To promote the scholarly study of the Black
Catholic experience.

ELIGIBILITY:
Scholars in any academic discipline may
apply.

FINANCIAL DATA:
Amount of support per award: $1,000 and
invitation to attend the annual meeting of the
American Catholic Historical Association.

NO. AWARDS: 1.

APPLICATION INFO:
Applicants must e-mail the following
documents:
(1) completed application form;
(2) current curriculum vitae and;
(3) a brief description of the research project
(maximum 1,000 words), including plans for
publication.
Deadline: December 1. Notification in
March.

STAFF:
Kathleen Sprows Cummings, Director
MaDonna Noak, Administrative Coordinator

ADDRESS INQUIRIES TO:
MaDonna Noak, Administrative Coordinator
(See address above.)

SHELBY CULLOM DAVIS CENTER FOR HISTORICAL STUDIES [540]

Princeton University
129 Dickinson Hall
Princeton, NJ 08544-1017
(609) 258-4997
Fax: (609) 258-5326
E-mail: jhoule@princeton.edu
Web Site: history.princeton.edu

FOUNDED: 1968

AREAS OF INTEREST:
Historical research.

TYPE:
Fellowships.

YEAR PROGRAM STARTED: 1969

LEGAL BASIS:
Center is part of a Charitable Educational
Institution.

ELIGIBILITY:
Candidates must have a Ph.D. degree.
Fellowships are awarded on the strength of
the candidate's research projects, the
relationship of those projects to the Center's
theme, the candidate's previous scholarly
work, and the candidate's ability to contribute
to the intellectual life and intellectual
exchange of the Center.

Princeton faculty members are not eligible.

Applicants who are non-U.S. nationals or
who are members of traditionally
underrepresented groups are encouraged to
apply.

FINANCIAL DATA:
Fellowship includes salary plus research expenses.
Amount of support per award: Varies.
Total amount of support: Varies.

NO. AWARDS: 8 for the year 2020-21.

APPLICATION INFO:
Applicants must apply online and submit the following:
(1) cover letter;
(2) curriculum vitae;
(3) research proposal, preceded by a one paragraph abstract and;
(4) contact information for three references.
Duration: One semester or one academic year. Nonrenewable.
Deadline: December 1. Notification in early March.

ADDRESS INQUIRIES TO:
Jennifer Goldman, Manager
(See address above.)

THE DIRKSEN CONGRESSIONAL CENTER

2815 Broadway
Pekin, IL 61554
(309) 347-7113
E-mail: twhite@dirksencenter.org
Web Site: www.dirksencongressionalcenter.org

TYPE:
Research grants; Seed money grants; Travel grants. Financial awards to individuals conducting research about the U.S. Congress and its leaders.

See entry 1787 for full listing.

FENIMORE ART MUSEUM

5798 State Highway 80
Cooperstown, NY 13326
(607) 547-1416
Fax: (607) 547-1404
E-mail: publications@fenimoreart.org
Web Site: www.fenimoreartmuseum.org

TYPE:
Awards/prizes. Prizes for published catalogues treating collections located or exhibited in New York state.

See entry 404 for full listing.

FENIMORE ART MUSEUM   [541]

5798 State Highway 80
Cooperstown, NY 13326
(607) 547-1416
Fax: (607) 547-1404
E-mail: publications@fenimoreart.org
Web Site: www.fenimoreartmuseum.org

FOUNDED: 1899

AREAS OF INTEREST:
The history of New York state.

NAME(S) OF PROGRAMS:
● **The Dixon Ryan Fox Manuscript Prize of the Fenimore Art Museum**

TYPE:
Awards/prizes. Annual cash prize and publication assistance.

YEAR PROGRAM STARTED: 1973

PURPOSE:
To award the best unpublished, book-length monograph dealing with the history of New York state, as judged by an editorial committee.

LEGAL BASIS:
Private nonprofit association.

ELIGIBILITY:
Manuscripts may deal with any aspect of New York state history. Biographies of individuals whose careers illuminate aspects of the history of the state are also eligible, as are manuscripts dealing with such cultural matters as literature and the arts, provided that in such cases the methodology used is historical. Works of fiction are not eligible.

FINANCIAL DATA:
Amount of support per award: $3,000.
Total amount of support: $3,000.

NO. MOST RECENT APPLICANTS: 5 for the year 2017.

NO. AWARDS: 1 annually.

APPLICATION INFO:
Manuscripts must be typed, double-spaced, with at least one-inch margins. Please send two copies. Clear, readable photocopies or computer printouts are acceptable.
Duration: One-time award. Nonrenewable.
Deadline: March 1. Announcement by July 30 annually.

PUBLICATIONS:
Application guidelines.

OFFICERS AND TRUSTEES:
Jeffrey H. Pressman, M.D., Chairman of the Board
Thomas O. Putnam, Vice Chairman
Douglas E. Evelyn
Kathleen Flanagan
Nellie Gipson
Shelley Graham
Robert S. Hanft
Josef E. Jelinek
Charles B. Kieler
Doris Fischer Malesardi
Erna Morgan McReynolds
Anne G. Older
Ellen Tillapaugh
Richard C. Vanison

ADDRESS INQUIRIES TO:
Ashley Werner
Executive Assistant to the President
E-mail: a.werner@fenimore.org

GERMAN HISTORICAL INSTITUTE   [542]

1607 New Hampshire Avenue, N.W.
Washington, DC 20009-2562
(202) 387-3355
E-mail: fellowships@ghi-dc.org
Web Site: www.ghi-dc.org

FOUNDED: 1987

AREAS OF INTEREST:
German and European history, transatlantic studies and comparative studies in economic, social, cultural and political history.

NAME(S) OF PROGRAMS:
● **Doctoral and Postdoctoral Fellowships**

TYPE:
Fellowships. The Institute awards short-term fellowships to German and American doctoral students as well as postdoctoral scholars/Habilitanden in the fields of German and European history, the history of German-American relations, and the role of Germany and the U.S. in international relations.

YEAR PROGRAM STARTED: 1989

PURPOSE:
To support research programme for doctoral students and postdoctoral scholars in the fields of German and European history, the history of German-American relations, the role of Germany and the U.S. in international relations.

ELIGIBILITY:
Applicants should be based at or recent graduates of a North American or European university or research institute.

FINANCIAL DATA:
Amount of support per award: Monthly stipend of EUR 2,000 for doctoral students and EUR 3,400 for postdoctoral scholars.

NO. MOST RECENT APPLICANTS: 100 annually.

NO. AWARDS: 20 to 25 annually.

APPLICATION INFO:
Applications should include cover letter, curriculum vitae, proof of academic degree (or transcripts), project description (no more than 2,000 words), research schedule for the fellowship period, and at least one letter of reference. Although applicants may write in either English or German, it is recommended that they use the language in which they are most proficient.
Duration: One to five months, but can be extended one month.
Deadline: April 1 and October 1 annually.

ADDRESS INQUIRIES TO:
Bryan Hart, Program Officer
(See address above.)

HAGLEY MUSEUM AND LIBRARY   [543]

Hagley Library
298 Buck Road
Wilmington, DE 19807
(302) 658-2400 ext. 243
E-mail: clockman@hagley.org
Web Site: www.hagley.org

FOUNDED: 1953

AREAS OF INTEREST:
American business, economic and labor history and the history of technology and science.

NAME(S) OF PROGRAMS:
● **Henry Belin du Pont Dissertation Fellowship in Business, Technology, and Society**
● **Henry Belin du Pont Research Grants**
● **Hagley Exploratory Research Grant**

TYPE:
Fellowships; Research grants; Travel grants; Visiting scholars. Grants to support short-term research in the imprint, manuscript, pictorial and artifact collections of the Hagley Museum and Library.

The Henry Belin du Pont Dissertation Fellowship in Business, Technology, and Society supports research and writing by candidates for doctoral degrees. Projects should demonstrate superior intellectual quality and make substantial use of Hagley's collections.

Henry Belin du Pont Research Grants support research in the collections of the museum and library.

Hagley Exploratory Research Grant supports a one-week visit by scholars who believe that their project will benefit from Hagley research collections, but need the opportunity to explore them on-site to determine if a Henry Belin du Pont research grant application is warranted.

YEAR PROGRAM STARTED: 1962

PURPOSE:
To encourage and support research in the collections.

LEGAL BASIS:
Nonprofit educational institution.

ELIGIBILITY:
Degree candidates and advanced scholars working in Hagley's areas of collecting and research interest are invited to apply. Applications should include research proposals specifying the collections or materials to be studied. Residential award, not a scholarship for college or graduate school.

Hagley Exploratory Research Grant: Priority will be given to junior scholars with innovative projects that seek to expand on existing scholarships.

FINANCIAL DATA:
Amount of support per award: Hagley Exploratory Research Grant: Stipend of $400; Henry Belin du Pont Dissertation Fellowship: Up to $6,500; Henry Belin du Pont Research Grants: $400 per week for recipients residing more than 50 miles from Hagley, and $200 per week for those within 50 miles; International Research: $500 plus travel and on-site housing.
Total amount of support: Approximately $27,100.

NO. MOST RECENT APPLICANTS: 56.

NO. AWARDS: 40.

APPLICATION INFO:
Application forms and guidelines are available online.
Duration: Hagley Exploratory Research Grant: One week; Henry Belin du Pont Dissertation Fellowship: Up to four months; Henry Belin du Pont Research Grants: Up to eight weeks.
Deadline: Hagley Exploratory Research Grant and Henry Belin du Pont Research Grants: March 31, June 30 and October 31; Henry Belin du Pont Dissertation Fellowship in Business, Technology, and Society: November 15.

PUBLICATIONS:
Guides to Collection; application; guidelines.

STAFF:
Jill McKenzie, Executive Director
Roger Horowitz, Center Director
Carol Ressler Lockman, Center Manager

RESEARCH STAFF:
Erik Rau, Director of Library
Max Moeller, Curator, Published Collections
Kevin Martin, Andrew W. Mellon Curator of Audiovisual Collections

ADDRESS INQUIRIES TO:
Carol Ressler Lockman, Center Manager
(See address above.)

THE HISTORIC NEW ORLEANS COLLECTION   [544]
410 Chartres Street
New Orleans, LA 70130
(504) 523-4662
Fax: (504) 293-8162
E-mail: wrc@hnoc.org
Web Site: www.hnoc.org

FOUNDED: 1966

AREAS OF INTEREST:
Louisiana history and recognition of published book-length research in the field.

NAME(S) OF PROGRAMS:
- **Kemper and Leila Williams Prize in Louisiana History**

TYPE:
Awards/prizes.

YEAR PROGRAM STARTED: 1974

PURPOSE:
To encourage excellence in the writing and publishing of Louisiana history.

LEGAL BASIS:
Nonprofit foundation.

ELIGIBILITY:
Published books are eligible, but only in the year of their publication or completion.

FINANCIAL DATA:
Amount of support per award: $1,500.
Total amount of support: $1,500.

NO. MOST RECENT APPLICANTS: 22.

NO. AWARDS: 1.

APPLICATION INFO:
Application forms are available on the web site. Four copies of each entry must be submitted.
Deadline: January 15 for works published the previous calendar year. Announcement in March.

PUBLICATIONS:
Application guidelines.

STAFF:
Daniel Hammer, President and Chief Executive Officer

BOARD OF DIRECTORS:
Drew Jardine, Chairperson
John Kallenborn, Vice Chairperson
Hilton S. Bell
Bonnie Boyd
Charles Lapeyre
E. Alexandra Stafford
Lisa H. Wilson

ADDRESS INQUIRIES TO:
Chairperson
Williams Prize Committee
(See address above.)

THE HISTORIC NEW ORLEANS COLLECTION   [545]
410 Chartres Street
New Orleans, LA 70130
(504) 598-7183
Fax: (504) 598-7168
E-mail: wrc@hnoc.org
Web Site: www.hnoc.org/research/prizes-and-fellowships

FOUNDED: 1966

AREAS OF INTEREST:
Louisiana history and support of research in the field.

NAME(S) OF PROGRAMS:
- **The Dianne Woest Fellowship in the Arts and Humanities**

TYPE:
Fellowships.

YEAR PROGRAM STARTED: 2005

PURPOSE:
To encourage research using The Historic New Orleans Collection, as well as other research facilities in the greater New Orleans area.

ELIGIBILITY:
Open to doctoral candidates, academic and museum professionals and independent scholars. U.S. citizenship not required, but applicants should be fluent in English.

Fellows will be expected to:
(1) present a public lecture during their term of residence and;
(2) acknowledge The Collection in any published work drawing on fellowship research.

FINANCIAL DATA:
Amount of support per award: Maximum $4,000 stipend.
Total amount of support: Varies.

NO. MOST RECENT APPLICANTS: 32.

NO. AWARDS: 1 to 3.

APPLICATION INFO:
Information may be obtained by e-mailing Jason Wiese, Chief Curator, at jason.wiese@hnoc.org.
Duration: One to three months.
Deadline: November 15. Announcement February 1. Research to begin on or after April 1.

ADDRESS INQUIRIES TO:
Jason Wiese, Chief Curator
(See address above.)

*SPECIAL STIPULATIONS:
Fellows may select their period of residence, but all research must commence and conclude during the specified fiscal year April 1 to March 31.

HISTORY COLORADO STATE HISTORICAL FUND   [546]
1200 Broadway
Denver, CO 80203
(303) 866-3493
Fax: (303) 866-2041
E-mail: hc_shs@state.co.us
Web Site: www.historycolorado.org/state-historical-fund

FOUNDED: 1990

AREAS OF INTEREST:
Historic preservation.

TYPE:
Project/program grants. Grants for historic preservation projects.

The State Historical Fund was created by the 1990 constitutional amendment allowing limited gaming in the towns of Cripple Creek, Central City and Black Hawk. The amendment directs that a portion of the gaming tax revenues be used for historic preservation throughout the state.

YEAR PROGRAM STARTED: 1990

PURPOSE:
To promote historic preservation throughout the state of Colorado.

ELIGIBILITY:
Criteria vary for different types of grants. Funds are distributed through a competitive process, and all projects must demonstrate strong public benefit and community support. The Fund assists in a wide variety of preservation projects, including restoration and rehabilitation of historic buildings, architectural assessments, archaeological

excavations, designation and interpretation of historic places, preservation planning studies, and education and training programs.

Organizations have to have 501(c)(3) not-for-profit status. Religious organizations may apply, but no grants are given to individuals.

Historic preservation projects in the state of Colorado only.

GEOG. RESTRICTIONS: Colorado.

FINANCIAL DATA:
Amount of support per award: Mini-grants: Up to $35,000. Full grants: Up to approximately $200,000.

APPLICATION INFO:
Contact the History Colorado office and use the application on its web site. Colorado Substitute W9 Form for documentation required.
Duration: Varies; grantees can reapply for new projects.
Deadline: April 1 and October 1.

ADDRESS INQUIRIES TO:
Megan Eflin, Outreach Coordinator
(See address above.)

HISTORY OF SCIENCE SOCIETY [547]
440 Geddes Hall
University of Notre Dame
Notre Dame, IN 46556
(574) 631-1194
E-mail: info@hssonline.org
Web Site: www.hssonline.org

FOUNDED: 1924

AREAS OF INTEREST:
History of science and its cultural influences.

NAME(S) OF PROGRAMS:
• **Derek Price/Rod Webster Prize**

TYPE:
Awards/prizes. Prize for the best scholarly article published in *Isis* during the past three years.

YEAR PROGRAM STARTED: 1979

PURPOSE:
To acknowledge the best scholarly work to appear in *Isis*.

LEGAL BASIS:
Nonprofit 501(c)(3).

ELIGIBILITY:
Applicant must have published an article in *Isis*.

FINANCIAL DATA:
Amount of support per award: $1,000.

NO. AWARDS: 1 per year.

APPLICATION INFO:
All eligible articles are automatically nominated for this prize.
Deadline: April 1.

PUBLICATIONS:
Syllabus samplers, Topical Essays for Teachers, Non-Western Science.

ADDRESS INQUIRIES TO:
Robert J. Malone, Executive Director
(See address above.)

HISTORY OF SCIENCE SOCIETY [548]
440 Geddes Hall
University of Notre Dame
Notre Dame, IN 46556
(574) 631-1194
E-mail: info@hssonline.org
Web Site: www.hssonline.org

FOUNDED: 1924

AREAS OF INTEREST:
History of science, women in science and science service.

NAME(S) OF PROGRAMS:
• **Watson Davis and Helen Miles Davis Prize**
• **Joseph H. Hazen Education Prize**
• **Suzanne J. Levinson Prize**
• **Philip J. Pauly Prize**
• **Pfizer Prize**
• **Ronald Rainger Prize**
• **Nathan Reingold Prize**
• **Margaret W. Rossiter History of Women in Science Prize**

TYPE:
Awards/prizes. The Davis Prize honors books in the history of science directed to a wide public and was established through a long-term pledge from Miles and Audrey Davis.

The Joseph H. Hazen Education Prize recognizes excellence in teaching in the history of science.

The Levinson Prize is awarded in even-numbered years to an outstanding book in the life sciences and natural history.

The Philip J. Pauly Prize is awarded to the best first book on the history of science in the Americas.

The Pfizer Prize honors the best English-language work related to the history of science published in the preceding three years.

The Ronald Rainger Prize is awarded for early career work in the history of earth and environmental sciences.

The Nathan Reingold Prize is given for an original essay in the history of science and its cultural influences.

The Margaret W. Rossiter History of Women in Science Prize honors an outstanding book, or in even-numbered years an article, published in the preceding four years.

YEAR PROGRAM STARTED: 1955

PURPOSE:
To recognize and reward distinguished writing in the field of the history of science.

LEGAL BASIS:
Nonprofit.

ELIGIBILITY:
For the Davis Prize, books should be introductory in assuming no previous knowledge of the subject and be directed to audiences of beginning students and general readers. Books should introduce an entire field, a chronological period, a national tradition or the work of a noteworthy individual. Multi-authored or edited books are eligible, whereas unrevised reprints of previously published works are ineligible.

For the History of Women in Science Prize, books may take a biographical, institutional, theoretical or other approach. Include in the topic, "Women in Science," discussions of women's activities in science, analyses of

past scientific practices that deal explicitly with gender and investigations regarding women as viewed by scientists. These may relate to medicine, technology and the social sciences as well as the natural sciences.

The Levinson Prize is open to all books in the life sciences and natural history published in the four years prior to the award year.

For the Philip J. Pauly Prize, the book must have been published within the last three calendar years.

The Pfizer Prize is open to all books published in English. The quality of the work is the overriding criterion.

The Ronald Rainger Prize is open to single, specific works, such as an article, exhibition, or interactive resource, whose primary topic is the history of the earth and environmental sciences broadly construed. Works in languages other than English must be accompanied by an English translation.

The Reingold Prize is open to graduate students at any International college. Essays dealing with medical subjects are not accepted, though papers dealing with the relations between medicine and the natural sciences are welcome. Essay must be no more than 8,000 words in length and thoroughly documented.

FINANCIAL DATA:
Amount of support per award: Davis, Hazen, Levinson and Rossiter History of Women in Science Awards: $1,000; Pfizer Prize: $2,500; Reingold Prize: $500 award, $500 in travel expenses.

APPLICATION INFO:
Contact the Society for details.
Deadline: Reingold Prize: June 1: All others: April 1.

PUBLICATIONS:
Newsletter.

OFFICERS:
Bernard Lightman, President
Jan Golinski, Vice President
Gwen Kay, Treasurer
Luis Campos, Secretary
Alexandria Hui, Editor
Matthew Lavine, Editor

ADDRESS INQUIRIES TO:
Robert J. Malone, Executive Director
(See address above.)

*PLEASE NOTE:
Society does not give grants, scholarships or fellowships.

HOOVER PRESIDENTIAL FOUNDATION
P.O. Box 696
West Branch, IA 52358
(319) 643-5327
Fax: (319) 643-2391
E-mail: info@hooverpf.org
Web Site: www.hooverpresidentialfoundation.org

TYPE:
Research grants; Travel grants. Money is only available for travel to the Hoover Presidential Library in West Branch, IA. The program seeks to encourage scholarly use of the holdings of the Herbert Hoover Presidential Library. It is specifically intended to promote the study of subjects of interest and concern to Herbert Hoover, Lou

Henry Hoover, their associates and other public figures as reflected in the Library's 150 manuscript collections.

See entry 1793 for full listing.

IEEE HISTORY CENTER [549]
445 Hoes Lane
Piscataway, NJ 08854
(732) 562-5468
Fax: (732) 562-6020
E-mail: ieee-history@ieee.org
Web Site: www.ieee.org/history_center

FOUNDED: 1884

AREAS OF INTEREST:
History of technology and sociology of technology.

NAME(S) OF PROGRAMS:
- **IEEE Fellowship in the History of Electrical and Computing Technology**
- **The Elizabeth and Emerson Pugh Young Scholar in Residence at the IEEE History Center**

TYPE:
Fellowships; Internships. Fellowship in the History of Electrical and Computing Technology: Award for one year of full-time doctoral or postdoctoral work in the history of electrical engineering and technology at a college or university of recognized standing.

The Elizabeth and Emerson Pugh Young Scholar in Residence: Two-month internship for graduate research.

YEAR PROGRAM STARTED: 1980

ELIGIBILITY:
Fellowship in the History of Electrical and Computing Technology: Individuals doing graduate or postgraduate work in the history of electrical technology.

The Elizabeth and Emerson Pugh Young Scholar in Residence: Scholars at the beginning of their career studying the history of electrical technology and computing.

FINANCIAL DATA:
Total amount of support: Fellowship in the History of Electrical and Computing Technology: $25,000 annually; The Elizabeth and Emerson Pugh Young Scholar in Residence: $5,000.

NO. MOST RECENT APPLICANTS: 14.

NO. AWARDS: 1 Fellowship and 1 Internship annually.

APPLICATION INFO:
Identification and description of a research project of value is an important part of the application procedure. Further information is available upon request to the Institute.
Duration: Fellowship in the History of Electrical and Computing Technology: One academic year; The Elizabeth and Emerson Pugh Young Scholar in Residence: Two months.
Deadline: Fellowship in the History of Electrical and Computing Technology: February 1; The Elizabeth and Emerson Pugh Young Scholar in Residence: March 1.

PUBLICATIONS:
Newsletter.

ADDRESS INQUIRIES TO:
Director, IEEE History Center
(See address above.)

THE INTERCOLLEGIATE STUDIES INSTITUTE
3901 Centerville Road
Wilmington, DE 19807
(302) 652-4600
Fax: (302) 652-6112
E-mail: jdavenport@isi.org
Web Site: isi.org/fellowships

TYPE:
Awards/prizes; Fellowships; Scholarships. The Weaver Fellowship is granted to students who intend to use their advanced degree to teach.

See entry 1795 for full listing.

ISTITUTO ITALIANO PER GLI STUDI STORICI [550]
Via Benedetto Croce, 12
80134 Naples Italy
(39) 081 5517159
(39) 081 5512390
Fax: (39) 081 5514813
E-mail: info@iiss.it
Web Site: www.iiss.it

FOUNDED: 1947

AREAS OF INTEREST:
Institute for the study of history, philosophy and literature.

NAME(S) OF PROGRAMS:
- **Federico II Scholarship**
- **Istituto italiano per gli studi storici Scholarships for Graduate Students and Young Postdocs**

TYPE:
Awards/prizes; Conferences/seminars; Research grants; Scholarships. Awards for historical, literature and philosophical studies at the Istituto Italiano per gli Studi Storici in Naples.

Federico II Scholarship: Funded by the Universita di Napoli Federico II for graduates from Italian universities with medieval studies final dissertation.

YEAR PROGRAM STARTED: 1947

PURPOSE:
To promote historical, philosophical and literature research.

LEGAL BASIS:
Private institution.

ELIGIBILITY:
These annual scholarships are offered to young graduates and young postdoctorates, both Italian and non-Italian, in the disciplines of history, philosophy and literature. Applicants must have presented their final university dissertation before the final application date and must be less than 32 years of age.

Applications will not be accepted from candidates who:
(1) already received a scholarship from the Istituto in past years;
(2) will receive payment from another type of activity;
(3) will have their Ph.D. course funded by other institutions or;
(4) hold a scholarship from other institutions for the same year.

Italian language competence is required.

FINANCIAL DATA:
The scholarship will be paid to the successful candidates in 12 monthly installments starting from November of the year of application.

Amount of support per award: Scholarships: EUR 9,700 for Campania Region; EUR 12,000 for students residing outside of Campania; Federico II Scholarship: EUR 10,300.

Total amount of support: Approximately EUR 140,300 for the year 2020-21.

NO. MOST RECENT APPLICANTS: 200.

NO. AWARDS: 1 Federico II Scholarship; 10 Scholarships for Graduate Students and Young Postdocs for the year 2020-21.

APPLICATION INFO:
Application form must be sent duly filled in and signed, together with the following documents:
(1) copy of the identity card or passport;
(2) curriculum studiorum, including linguistic competences (Italian is mandatory);
(3) degree or Ph.D. certificate showing marks for individual exams and/or overall evaluation;
(4) copy of the graduation or Ph.D. dissertation and a maximum of five published or draft research publications, both in hard copy and digital file (in case of e-mail submission, only digital version is required);
(5) abstract (maximum 10 pages) of the graduation or Ph.D. dissertation and;
(6) research project (maximum five pages) including aims, timing, materials, and other institutions where the research can be carried out.

Applications which do not completely satisfy the above conditions will not be considered.
Duration: Twelve months (November to May for courses and June to November for research). The scholarship can be renewed for a second year.
Deadline: Application materials must be received no later than the deadline published on the IISS web site. (Postal dates will not be accepted.)

PUBLICATIONS:
Annali dell'Istituto Italiano per gli studi storici; series of monographs; series of historical, philosophical and literary texts; lectures; essays; inventories.

DIRECTORS:
Roberto Giordano, Chief Executive Officer
Prof. Natalino Irti, President

ADMINISTRATIVE OFFICERS:
Dr. Marta Herling, Secretary-General

ADDRESS INQUIRIES TO:
Dr. Marta Herling, General Secretary
(See address above.)

*SPECIAL STIPULATIONS:
Fellows must carry out their research project and attend lessons until the end of the academic year.

From November to May, fellows must reside in Naples in order to follow the courses and seminars organized by the Institute. In the five months that follow, they can carry out their research at another institution, either in Italy or abroad. They must make a first report about their research activities by June 30 and a final one by October 31.

The Institute reserves the right to withdraw funding should fellows prove themselves to be seriously inadequate.

ITALIAN AMERICAN STUDIES ASSOCIATION [551]

The Calandra Institute
25 West 43rd Street, 17th Floor
New York, NY 10036
(212) 642-2094
E-mail: webmaster@italianamericanstudies.net
Web Site: www.italianamericanstudies.net

FOUNDED: 1966

AREAS OF INTEREST:
Encouragement of Italian-American studies, collection, preservation, study and popularization of materials that illuminate the Italian-American experience in the U.S. and Canada.

CONSULTING OR VOLUNTEER SERVICES:
Sponsors an annual national conference, resource depositories and maintains an information network.

NAME(S) OF PROGRAMS:
● **IASA Memorial Fellowship**

TYPE:
Fellowships.

YEAR PROGRAM STARTED: 1970

PURPOSE:
To promote understanding of the Italian experience in America.

LEGAL BASIS:
Nonprofit, tax-exempt organization.

ELIGIBILITY:
Graduate students in any discipline whose work focuses on Italian American culture are eligible and encouraged to apply. Student must be in good standing in their own home institution's graduate program (i.e., fully enrolled, degree-seeking, completing work in a timely manner, and no academic probation). Prior candidates are especially encouraged to resubmit previously non-funded applications. Qualifications, seniority, and quality of application will be considered in decision making.

FINANCIAL DATA:
Amount of support per award: $1,000.
Total amount of support: $1,000.

NO. AWARDS: 1.

APPLICATION INFO:
Guidelines are available online.
Duration: One year.
Deadline: September.

PUBLICATIONS:
Annual Proceedings.

OFFICERS:
Alan J. Gravano, President

ADDRESS INQUIRIES TO:
Dr. Ryan Calabretta-Sajder
(See address above.)

THE LYNDON BAINES JOHNSON FOUNDATION

2313 Red River Street
Austin, TX 78705-5702
(512) 721-0263
E-mail: grants@lbjfoundation.org
Web Site: www.lbjlibrary.org

TYPE:
Fellowships; Research grants.

See entry 1797 for full listing.

KENTUCKY HISTORICAL SOCIETY [552]

100 West Broadway
Frankfort, KY 40601
(502) 564-1792
E-mail: khsfellowship@ky.gov
Web Site: history.ky.gov

FOUNDED: 1836

AREAS OF INTEREST:
Historical research, publishing, and public history.

NAME(S) OF PROGRAMS:
● **Scholarly Research Fellowship Program**

TYPE:
Fellowships; Research grants; Travel grants. Scholarly Research Fellowship Program encourages and promotes advanced research on all aspects of Kentucky-related local, regional, national and transnational history.

PURPOSE:
To assist - through these fellowships - researchers with travel and living expenses while using the Kentucky Historical Society research collections.

ELIGIBILITY:
These short-term fellowships are intended to support serious scholarly work. They enable individuals to pursue advanced study and research in the collections of the Kentucky Historical Society. Applications are welcome from independent scholars, as well as from college and university professors, graduate students, and scholars working in other related disciplines.

FINANCIAL DATA:
Amount of support per award: Typically $500 (for one week) to up to $2,000 (for four weeks).

APPLICATION INFO:
Applications are available on the Kentucky Historical Society web site. All applications are peer-reviewed by a panel of leading historians.
Deadline: October 1 and March 1.

ADDRESS INQUIRIES TO:
Dr. Daniel Birge
Coordinator, Research Fellowship Program
E-mail: daniel.burge@ky.gov

LIBRARY COMPANY OF PHILADELPHIA [553]

1314 Locust Street
Philadelphia, PA 19107
(215) 546-3181
Fax: (215) 546-5167
E-mail: jgreen@librarycompany.org
Web Site: www.librarycompany.org

FOUNDED: 1731

AREAS OF INTEREST:
American studies.

NAME(S) OF PROGRAMS:
● **Albert M. Greenfield Foundation Dissertation Fellowships**
● **NEH Postdoctoral Fellowships**
● **Program in African-American History**
● **Program in Early American Economy and Society**
● **Research Fellowships in American History and Culture**

TYPE:
Fellowships. Albert M. Greenfield Foundation Dissertation Fellowship: Supports

dissertation research in residence at the Library Company on any subject relevant to its collections.

Program in African-American History: Its Mellon Scholars Fellowship Program offers postdoctoral, dissertation and short-term fellowships to support scholarly work in African-American history from the 17th through the 19th centuries.

Program in Early American Economy and Society: Pre-1860 American economic and business history.

Research Fellowships in American History and Culture: 18th and 19th Century American social and cultural history.

YEAR PROGRAM STARTED: 1988

PURPOSE:
To promote early American historic studies.

ELIGIBILITY:
Both the short-term and long-term Fellowships support postdoctoral and dissertation research. Both also require that the project proposal demonstrate that the Library Company has a primary source central to the research topic. NEH fellows must be U.S. citizens or residents at least three years.

FINANCIAL DATA:
Amount of support per award: Long-term: $20,000 to $50,000; Short-term: $2,000.
Total amount of support: Approximately $170,000 annually.

CO-OP FUNDING PROGRAMS: The short-term fellowships are jointly sponsored with the Historical Society of Pennsylvania.

NO. MOST RECENT APPLICANTS: 200.

NO. AWARDS: Long-term: 11; Short-term: 44.

APPLICATION INFO:
For the short-term fellowships, applicants must complete the required electronic cover sheet and submit one portable document format (PDF) containing a resume and a two- to four-page description of the proposed research. One letter of recommendation should arrive under separate cover in PDF format as well. E-mail materials to fellowships@librarycompany.org.
Duration: Short-term: One month; Long-term: Three to nine months.
Deadline: Program and Research Fellowships: March 1; Long-term Postdoctoral Fellowships: November 1.

ADDRESS INQUIRIES TO:
Will Fenton, Director of Research and Public Programs
(See address above.)

JAMES MADISON MEMORIAL FELLOWSHIP FOUNDATION [554]

1613 Duke Street
Alexandria, VA 22314
(800) 525-6928
Fax: (703) 838-2180 (VA); (507) 931-8924 (MN)
E-mail: madison@scholarshipamerica.org
Web Site: www.jamesmadison.gov

FOUNDED: 1986

AREAS OF INTEREST:
The roots, principles, framing and development of the U.S. Constitution.

NAME(S) OF PROGRAMS:
● **James Madison Fellowship Program**

TYPE:
Fellowships. The Foundation awards fellowships to college seniors and college graduates without teaching experience (Junior Fellows) and to experienced secondary school teachers in grades seven-12 (Senior Fellows) who will normally enroll respectively in full- and part-time graduate study leading to one of the following Master's degrees: Master's degree in American history or political science, a degree of Master of Arts in Teaching in history or political science, or a related Master's degree in education that permits a concentration in American history, American government or civics.

YEAR PROGRAM STARTED: 1992

PURPOSE:
To support the graduate study of the roots, principles, framing and development of the U.S. Constitution.

LEGAL BASIS:
Foundation.

ELIGIBILITY:
Each fellowship recipient must take at least 12 semester hours or their equivalent in topics directly related to the framing and history of the U.S. Constitution.

A James Madison Fellow must be a U.S. citizen or U.S. national, qualify for study toward one of the qualifying Master's degrees indicated and agree to teach full-time in a secondary school for no less than one year for each full academic year of study under a fellowship.

A Senior Fellow must be a full-time teacher of American history, American government, or civics in grades seven through 12 during the previous year and be under contract or prospective contract to teach full-time as a secondary school teacher of the same subjects for the upcoming academic year.

A Junior Fellow must possess a Bachelor's degree or plan to receive a Bachelor's degree no later than August 31 of the year of application.

GEOG. RESTRICTIONS: United States and its territories.

FINANCIAL DATA:
Amount of support per award: Up to $24,000 for each award.

NO. MOST RECENT APPLICANTS: 250 for the year 2018.

NO. AWARDS: 1 per state per year, as funding permits.

APPLICATION INFO:
Applicant must register online to complete the application process.

Duration: Up to five years for Senior Fellows. Up to two years for Junior Fellows.

Deadline: March 1, annually.

ADDRESS INQUIRIES TO:
James Madison Fellowship Program
One Scholarship Way
St. Peter, MN 56082

*SPECIAL STIPULATIONS:
No funding for Ph.D. programs.

JACOB RADER MARCUS CENTER OF THE AMERICAN JEWISH ARCHIVES
3101 Clifton Avenue
Cincinnati, OH 45220-2408
(513) 221-1875
Fax: (513) 221-7812
E-mail: lfrankel@huc.edu
Web Site: www.americanjewisharchives.org

TYPE:
Fellowships. The Marcus Center's Fellowship Program provides recipients with month-long fellowships for research and writing at The Jacob Rader Marcus Center of the American Jewish Archives. Fellowship stipends will be sufficient to cover transportation and living expenses while in residence.

See entry 747 for full listing.

THE MASSACHUSETTS HISTORICAL SOCIETY   [555]
1154 Boylston Street
Boston, MA 02215
(617) 536-1608
Fax: (617) 859-0074
E-mail: research_programs@masshist.org
Web Site: www.masshist.org

FOUNDED: 1791

AREAS OF INTEREST:
Civil War history, Massachusetts, New England, and U.S. history.

NAME(S) OF PROGRAMS:
● **Suzanne and Caleb Loring Fellowship**

TYPE:
Fellowships. Fellowship funds research on the Civil War, its origins, and consequences, for projects that use the resources at the Massachusetts Historical Society and the Boston Athenaeum. Research must be conducted for at least four weeks at each of the two participating institutions.

YEAR PROGRAM STARTED: 2008

PURPOSE:
To support scholarship on the history of Massachusetts and the nation; to encourage projects that draw on the Civil War resources of the participating organizations.

ELIGIBILITY:
Open to independent scholars, advanced graduate students and holders of a Ph.D. or equivalent. Applicants must be U.S. citizens or already hold the J-1 visa or equivalent documents that will allow them to accept the stipend.

FINANCIAL DATA:
Amount of support per award: $4,000.

NO. AWARDS: 1.

APPLICATION INFO:
Applicants must submit the following materials online:
(1) cover letter;
(2) current curriculum vitae;
(3) project proposal, approximately 1,000 words in length, which includes a description of the project, a statement explaining the historiographical significance of the project, and an indication of the specific Massachusetts Historical Society and Boston Athenaeum collections the applicant wishes to consult and;
(4) for those not holding a Ph.D., a letter of recommendation from a faculty member familiar with the student's work and with the project being proposed.

Duration: Minimum of 20 days at each of the two institutions, for a total of 40 days.

Deadline: Applications must be submitted by 11:59 P.M. on February 15.

ADDRESS INQUIRIES TO:
E-mail: fellowships@masshist.org

THE MASSACHUSETTS HISTORICAL SOCIETY   [556]
1154 Boylston Street
Boston, MA 02215-3695
(617) 536-1608
(617) 646-0588
Fax: (617) 859-0074
E-mail: education@masshist.org
Web Site: www.masshist.org

FOUNDED: 1791

AREAS OF INTEREST:
Massachusetts, New England and U.S. history.

NAME(S) OF PROGRAMS:
● **Kass Teacher Fellowships at MHS**
● **Swensrud Teacher Fellowships at MHS**

TYPE:
Fellowships. Kass and Swensrud Teacher Fellowships are offered to public and/or parochial schoolteachers and library media specialists for on-site research at the Society.

YEAR PROGRAM STARTED: 2001

PURPOSE:
To support four weeks of research at the Society for the creation of a curriculum unit.

ELIGIBILITY:
Applications are welcome from any K-12 teacher or library media specialist who has a serious interest in using the collections at the MHS to prepare primary-source-based curricula, supported by documents and visual aids, in the fields of American history, world history or English/language arts.

The fellowship process is competitive. Awards are made on the strength of:
(1) project design;
(2) the plan for using the Society collections;
(3) the creativity of the proposed classroom activities;
(4) usability in other classrooms and;
(5) recommendations.

Open to U.S. residents only.

GEOG. RESTRICTIONS: United States.

FINANCIAL DATA:
Amount of support per award: Kass Teacher Fellowships: Stipend of $2,000; Swensrud Teacher Fellowships: Stipend of $4,000.

NO. MOST RECENT APPLICANTS: Kass Teacher Fellowships: 15; Swensrud Teacher Fellowships: 35.

NO. AWARDS: Kass Teacher Fellowships: Minimum of 1; Swensrud Teacher Fellowships: Minimum of 3.

APPLICATION INFO:
Application information is available on the web site.

Duration: Four weeks.

Deadline: February.

ADDRESS INQUIRIES TO:
Kate Melchior
Assistant Director of Education
Center for the Teaching of History
Tel: (617) 646-0588
(See address above.)

THE MASSACHUSETTS HISTORICAL SOCIETY   [557]

1154 Boylston Street
Boston, MA 02215
(617) 536-1608
Fax: (617) 859-0074
E-mail: research_programs@masshist.org
Web Site: www.masshist.org

FOUNDED: 1791

AREAS OF INTEREST:
Massachusetts, New England and U.S. history.

NAME(S) OF PROGRAMS:
● **Short-Term Research Fellowship**

TYPE:
Fellowships. Research fellowship to use the Society's collection to complete a major project.

YEAR PROGRAM STARTED: 1983

PURPOSE:
To support scholarship on the history of Massachusetts and the nation.

ELIGIBILITY:
Must be U.S. citizens or foreign nationals holding appropriate U.S. government status. Open to independent scholars, advanced graduate students, and holders of a Ph.D. or equivalent.

FINANCIAL DATA:
Amount of support per award: Stipend of $2,000.

NO. AWARDS: Approximately 20.

APPLICATION INFO:
Applicants must submit the following materials online:
(1) cover letter;
(2) current curriculum vitae;
(3) project proposal, approximately 1,000 words in length, which includes a description of the project, a statement explaining the historiographical significance of the project, and an indication of the specific MHS collections the applicant wishes to consult and;
(4) for applicants not holding a Ph.D., a letter of recommendation from a faculty member familiar with the student's work and with the project being proposed.
Duration: Minimum of 20 days.
Deadline: Applications must be submitted by 11:59 P.M. on March 1.

ADDRESS INQUIRIES TO:
E-mail: fellowships@masshist.org

THE MASSACHUSETTS HISTORICAL SOCIETY   [558]

1154 Boylston Street
Boston, MA 02215
(617) 536-1608
Fax: (617) 859-0074
E-mail: research_programs@masshist.org
Web Site: www.masshist.org

FOUNDED: 1791

AREAS OF INTEREST:
Massachusetts, New England and U.S. history.

NAME(S) OF PROGRAMS:
● **Long-Term Research Fellowship**

TYPE:
Fellowships. Research fellowship to use the Society's collection to complete a major project.

YEAR PROGRAM STARTED: 1983

PURPOSE:
To support scholarship on the history of Massachusetts and the nation.

ELIGIBILITY:
Applicants must be U.S. citizens or foreign nationals who have lived in the U.S. for at least three years prior to the application deadline. Applicants must have completed their professional training. Fellowship is not available to graduate students. Awards committee will pay special attention both to the quality of proposed projects and to their relationship to the Society's collections. Preference will be given to candidates who have not held a long-term grant during the preceding three years.

FINANCIAL DATA:
There is an allowance for professional expenses.
Amount of support per award: $5,000 per month stipend with up to $500 per month housing allowance.

NO. AWARDS: 4 for the year 2020.

APPLICATION INFO:
Applicants must submit the following materials online:
(1) cover letter;
(2) current curriculum vitae;
(3) project proposal, approximately 1,000 words in length, which includes a description of the project, a statement explaining the historiographical significance of the project, and an indication of the specific MHS collections the applicant wishes to consult;
(4) Certification for Participants form and;
(5) two letters of recommendation.
Duration: Four to 12 months of continuous tenure.
Deadline: January 15, 11:59 P.M.

ADDRESS INQUIRIES TO:
E-mail: fellowships@masshist.org

THE MEDIEVAL ACADEMY OF AMERICA   [559]

6 Beacon Street
Suite 500
Boston, MA 02108
(617) 491-1622
Fax: (617) 492-3303
E-mail: info@themedievalacademy.org
Web Site: www.medievalacademy.org

FOUNDED: 1925

AREAS OF INTEREST:
Any aspect of medieval studies, 500 to 1500 A.D.

NAME(S) OF PROGRAMS:
● **Birgit Baldwin Fellowship**
● **John Nicholas Brown Prize**
● **Van Courtlandt Elliott Prize**
● **Medieval Academy Dissertation Grants**
● **Schallek Awards**
● **Schallek Fellowship**

TYPE:
Awards/prizes; Fellowships; Research grants. Cash prizes for publications of material on medieval topics.

Birgit Baldwin Fellowship supports a graduate student studying in a North American university researching and writing a significant dissertation for a Ph.D. on any subject in French medieval history. Research must be in archives and libraries of France.

The Brown Prize is awarded annually to a first book or monograph on a medieval topic.

The Elliott Prize is awarded annually for a first published article in the medieval field, judged by the selection committee to be of outstanding quality.

Medieval Academy Dissertation Grants support advanced graduate students who are writing Ph.D. dissertations on medieval topics.

Schallek Awards support graduate students conducting doctoral research in any relevant discipline dealing with late-Medieval Britain (*circa* 1350-1500).

Schallek Fellowship supports Ph.D. dissertation research in any relevant discipline dealing with late-Medieval Britain (*circa* 1350-1500).

YEAR PROGRAM STARTED: 1940

PURPOSE:
To promote publication on medieval topics.

LEGAL BASIS:
Nonprofit corporation.

GEOG. RESTRICTIONS: North America.

FINANCIAL DATA:
Medieval Academy Dissertation Grants and Schallek Awards: These programs help defray research expenses such as the cost of travel to research collections and the cost of photographs, photocopies, microfilms and other research materials. The cost of books or equipment (e.g., computers) is not included.
Amount of support per award: Birgit Baldwin Fellowship: $20,000; Brown Prize: $1,000; Elliott Prize: $500; Medieval Academy Dissertation Grants and Schallek Awards: $2,000; Schallek Fellowship: $30,000.

NO. MOST RECENT APPLICANTS: 30.

NO. AWARDS: Medieval Academy Dissertation Grants: 10. Schallek Awards: 5. Other programs: 1 each annually.

APPLICATION INFO:
All submissions must be made online.
Duration: Fellowships: One year. Baldwin Fellowship is renewable for a second year.
Deadline: Baldwin: November 15. Schallek Fellowships and Brown Prize: October 15. Announcement in April. Medieval Academy Dissertation Grants and Schallek Awards: February 15.

ADDRESS INQUIRIES TO:
Sheryl Mullane-Corvi
Assistant to the Executive Director
(See address above.)

MOUNT VERNON HOTEL MUSEUM & GARDEN   [560]

421 East 61st Street
New York, NY 10065
(212) 838-6878
E-mail: t.daly@mvhm.org
Web Site: www.mvhm.org

AREAS OF INTEREST:
American social history, material culture, historic preservation and museum education.

NAME(S) OF PROGRAMS:
● **William Randolph Hearst Foundation Fellowship**

TYPE:
Fellowships. Provides fellowships to graduate or undergraduate students who are interested in American social history, material culture, historic preservation and museum education.

YEAR PROGRAM STARTED: 1984

PURPOSE:
To promote the study of American history.

ELIGIBILITY:
Applicants must currently be enrolled in a college, university or graduate program.

FINANCIAL DATA:
Amount of support per award: $2,750.
Total amount of support: $5,500.

CO-OP FUNDING PROGRAMS: Fellowship is funded by the William Randolph Hearst Foundation.

NO. AWARDS: 2.

APPLICATION INFO:
Students must submit the completed application form, a short essay explaining the applicant's interest in the fellowship, resume and two letters of recommendation e-mailed directly from the individuals writing the recommendations. Applications are available on the web site.
Duration: Nine weeks in June and July.
Deadline: Approximately March.

ADDRESS INQUIRIES TO:
Terri Daly, Director
(See address above.)

NANTUCKET HISTORICAL ASSOCIATION   [561]
P.O. Box 1016
Nantucket, MA 02554-1016
(508) 228-1894
E-mail: aholmes@nha.org
Web Site: www.nha.org/research/research-library/verney-fellowship

AREAS OF INTEREST:
History.

NAME(S) OF PROGRAMS:
● **E. Geoffrey and Elizabeth Thayer Verney Fellowship**

TYPE:
Fellowships; Residencies. The Verney Fellowship, which is a residency program to pursue historical research pertaining to Nantucket, MA, encourages research in the collections of the Nantucket Historical Association Research Library. The Association is the principal repository of Nantucket history, with extensive archives, collections of historic properties, and art and artifacts that broadly illustrate Nantucket's past.

YEAR PROGRAM STARTED: 1999

PURPOSE:
To enhance the public's knowledge and understanding of the heritage of Nantucket, MA.

ELIGIBILITY:
Open to graduate students, independent scholars and academics in any field to conduct research in the collections of the Association.

FINANCIAL DATA:
Amount of support per award: $300 per week stipend; housing will be provided. Travel is reimbursed up to $600.
Total amount of support: Up to $1,500.

NO. MOST RECENT APPLICANTS: 6.

NO. AWARDS: 2 for the year 2020.

APPLICATION INFO:
Applicants must e-mail a full description of the proposed project, a curriculum vitae, the names of three references, and an estimate of anticipated time and duration of stay to Amelia Holmes, Director of Collections and Research Services, at the e-mail address listed above.
Duration: Up to three weeks.
Deadline: January 31.

ADDRESS INQUIRIES TO:
Amelia Holmes, Director of Collections and Research Services
(See e-mail address above.)

*PLEASE NOTE:
The Verney Fellow resides in the Thomas Macy House, a historic property owned by the Association, for up to a three-week period.

*SPECIAL STIPULATIONS:
NHA Visiting Research Scholars are expected to produce an article suitable for publication in *Historic Nantucket*, the NHA's biannual journal, and to deliver a public lecture on the subject of their research. Projects resulting in the publication of a book, article, conference paper, or other media, are looked upon favorably.

NATIONAL HISTORICAL PUBLICATIONS AND RECORDS COMMISSION   [562]
National Archives and Records Administration
700 Pennsylvania Avenue, N.W., Room 114
Washington, DC 20408-0001
(202) 357-5010
Fax: (202) 357-5914
E-mail: nhprc@nara.gov
Web Site: www.archives.gov/nhprc

FOUNDED: 1934

AREAS OF INTEREST:
Archives and historical document collections relating to American history.

TYPE:
Project/program grants; Training grants. Technical assistance to state government archives. Grants to support the collection, preservation, digitization, arrangement, description, editing and publishing of documentary source material relating to the history of the U.S., the papers of American leaders and documents treating major subjects and events in American history.

YEAR PROGRAM STARTED: 1964

PURPOSE:
To promote the preservation and use of historical records important for an understanding and appreciation of the history of the U.S.

LEGAL BASIS:
44 U.S.C. 2501-2506.

ELIGIBILITY:
Tribal, state and local government agencies, nonprofit organizations and institutions.

GEOG. RESTRICTIONS: United States and its territories.

FINANCIAL DATA:
Amount of support per award: Average $100,000.
Total amount of support: $6,500,000 for the year 2020.

Matching fund requirements: Generally, 1:1.

NO. MOST RECENT APPLICANTS: 81 for fiscal year 2020.

NO. AWARDS: 53 for fiscal year 2020.

REPRESENTATIVE AWARDS:
$160,000 to the Massachusetts Historical Society to edit *The Papers of John Adams*; $83,636 to the State Archives of North Carolina to provide access to North Carolina's early legal records from 1665 to 1806.

APPLICATION INFO:
All applications must be submitted through Grants.gov.
Duration: Up to three years, depending on the individual project.
Deadline: Varies by program.

PUBLICATIONS:
Newsletter and special reports.

ADDRESS INQUIRIES TO:
See e-mail address above.

NATIONAL SOCIETY DAUGHTERS OF THE AMERICAN REVOLUTION   [563]
1776 D Street, N.W.
Washington, DC 20006-5303
(202) 879-3263
E-mail: scholarships@nsdar.org
Web Site: www.dar.org

FOUNDED: 1895

AREAS OF INTEREST:
American history.

NAME(S) OF PROGRAMS:
● **Dr. Aura-Lee A. and James Hobbs Pittenger American History Scholarship**

TYPE:
Scholarships. The American History Scholarship is awarded to graduating high school students in the upper one-fifth of the class or home schooled who will have a concentrated study of a minimum of 24 credit hours in American History and American Government.

PURPOSE:
To provide ways and means to help students to attain higher education; to perpetuate the memory and spirit of men and women who achieved American independence by acquisition and protection of historical spots and erection of monuments; to carry out injunction of Washington in his farewell address to American people; to maintain institutions of American Freedom; to aid liberty.

LEGAL BASIS:
Incorporated historical society.

ELIGIBILITY:
Scholarships are awarded without regard to race, religion, sex or national origin. All four-year, or more, scholarships must be for consecutive years and are renewable only upon review and approval of annual transcript. Candidates must be U.S. citizens and must attend an accredited college or university in the U.S. No affiliation or relationship to DAR is required for qualification. Awards are judged on the basis of academic excellence, commitment to field of study, as required, and financial need.

GEOG. RESTRICTIONS: United States.

FINANCIAL DATA:
Amount of support per award: $2,000 per year for maximum of $8,000.
Total amount of support: Varies.

NO. AWARDS: Varies.

APPLICATION INFO:
Applicants must use the DAR Scholarship Committee's online submission process found on the DAR public web site. Once applicants have set up their scholarship profile, they will be able to complete the application. If necessary, applicants will be able to provide access to individuals wishing to submit confidential letters of recommendations or school transcripts.
Duration: One academic year. Renewable for up to four years upon annual transcript review and approval.
Deadline: January 31.

PUBLICATIONS:
American Spirit, magazine.

ADDRESS INQUIRIES TO:
National Vice Chairman
E-mail:
pittengeramerhistoryscholarship@nsdar.org

NATIONAL TRUST FOR HISTORIC PRESERVATION [564]

2600 Virginia Avenue, N.W.
Suite 1100
Washington, DC 20037
(202) 588-6277
E-mail: grants@savingplaces.org
Web Site: forum.savingplaces.org/build/funding

FOUNDED: 1949

AREAS OF INTEREST:
To encourage public participation in the preservation of sites, buildings and objects significant in American history and culture.

NAME(S) OF PROGRAMS:
• **National Trust Preservation Funds (NTPF)**

TYPE:
Challenge/matching grants; Project/program grants; Seed money grants; Technical assistance; Training grants. Education program curricula. Project grants to support consultants with professional expertise in areas such as architecture, law, planning, economics, archeology and graphic design. Conferences that address subjects of particular importance to historic preservation also are funded. In addition, grants are made for curriculum development in preservation education directed at select audiences.

YEAR PROGRAM STARTED: 1979

PURPOSE:
To increase the flow of information and ideas in the field of preservation by helping stimulate public discussion, enabling local groups to gain the technical expertise needed for particular projects, introducing students to preservation concepts and crafts and encouraging participation by the private sector in preservation.

LEGAL BASIS:
Nonprofit corporation.

ELIGIBILITY:
Organizational Forum members or Main Street America members of the National Trust are eligible to apply for funding from the National Trust Preservation Funds. Additionally, applicant must be a public agency, 501(c)(3) or other nonprofit organization to be considered. Applicants that have received previous National Trust financial assistance are eligible provided that all grant requirements are current. No more than three grants will be awarded in any two-year period to a single grantee. Only one grant will be awarded for a particular project phase.

Activities eligible for National Trust Preservation Funds grants include hiring consultants to undertake preservation planning or design projects, obtaining professional advice to strengthen management capabilities, sponsoring preservation conferences, designing and implementing innovative preservation education programs targeted to a specific audience and undertaking other planning activities that will lead to implementation of a specific preservation project.

Grants can be used for professional consultant services, preservation education programs and conferences and rehabilitation feasibility studies. Projects, programs and conferences are not funded retroactively.

Bricks-and-mortar construction projects and the funding of ongoing staff positions are not eligible activities. In addition, historic resource surveys to create inventories or to list resources on local, state or national registers are generally not eligible for funding.

GEOG. RESTRICTIONS: United States and its territories.

FINANCIAL DATA:
Amount of support per award: $2,500 to $5,000.
Total amount of support: $1,800,000 for fiscal year 2017.
Matching fund requirements: Each grantee must match the funds on at least a dollar-for-dollar basis using cash contributions.

NO. AWARDS: 174 grants for fiscal year 2017.

APPLICATION INFO:
Guidelines and application forms may be found on the web site. Applications must be completed and submitted online by the appropriate deadline. Incomplete applications will not be considered.
Duration: Usually a one-time award.
Deadline: Applicants should contact the National Trust Grants Office to obtain information regarding application deadlines.

IRS I.D.: 53-0210807

ADDRESS INQUIRIES TO:
Grants Coordinator
National Trust Preservation Funds
(See address above.)

NEW ENGLAND REGIONAL FELLOWSHIP CONSORTIUM [565]

1154 Boylston Street
Boston, MA 02215
(617) 646-0577
Fax: (617) 859-0074
E-mail: kmorris@masshist.org
Web Site: www.masshist.org

FOUNDED: 1791

AREAS OF INTEREST:
Massachusetts, New England and U.S. history.

TYPE:
Fellowships. Research fellowship to use the resources at a minimum of three different participating institutions.

YEAR PROGRAM STARTED: 1999

PURPOSE:
To encourage projects that draw on the resources of the participating organizations.

ELIGIBILITY:
Open to individuals with a serious need to use the collections and facilities of the participating organizations.

Fellows must work at each of at least three chosen organizations for at least two weeks.

FINANCIAL DATA:
Amount of support per award: Stipend of $5,000 for a minimum of eight weeks of research at participating institutions.

NO. MOST RECENT APPLICANTS: Approximately 100.

NO. AWARDS: Approximately 25.

APPLICATION INFO:
Guidelines and fellowship applications are available on the New England Regional Fellowship Consortium (NERFC) web site. (The Massachusetts Historical Society web site provides a link to it.)
Duration: Minimum of eight weeks.
Deadline: February 1.

ADDRESS INQUIRIES TO:
Katy Morris, Research Coordinator
(See address above.)

NEW JERSEY HISTORIC TRUST [566]

101 South Broad Street
Trenton, NJ 08608-2401
(609) 984-0473
Fax: (609) 984-7590
E-mail: njht@dca.nj.gov
Web Site: www.njht.org

FOUNDED: 1967

AREAS OF INTEREST:
Historic preservation.

NAME(S) OF PROGRAMS:
• **Discover New Jersey History License Plate Fund for Heritage Tourism**
• **Preserve New Jersey Historic Preservation Fund for Planning Grants**

TYPE:
Challenge/matching grants. Planning grants. Discover New Jersey History grant program provides funding for heritage tourism.

Preserve New Jersey Historic Preservation Fund provides funding for the preservation planning of historic properties.

YEAR PROGRAM STARTED: 2013

PURPOSE:
To develop and promote visitor-ready sites as heritage tourism destinations.

LEGAL BASIS:
Public Law 2016-12. New Jersey Administrative Code 5:101-1.1.

ELIGIBILITY:
Applicants must be state, county or municipal governments or nonprofit organizations.

GEOG. RESTRICTIONS: New Jersey.

FINANCIAL DATA:
Amount of support per award: Discover New Jersey History License Plate Fund: Up to $5,000; Preserve New Jersey Historic Preservation Fund: Up to $50,000.

Total amount of support: Varies.

Matching fund requirements: Preserve New Jersey Historic Preservation Fund Planning Grants require a three-to-one match.

NO. MOST RECENT APPLICANTS: 30.

NO. AWARDS: Varies.

REPRESENTATIVE AWARDS:
$3,000 to First Presbyterian Church of Elizabeth for development of Historic Burial Groups Visitor App.

APPLICATION INFO:
Guidelines are available on the Trust web site.

Duration: Varies.

Deadline: Varies.

PUBLICATIONS:
Annual report; program announcement; *Economic Impact of Historic Preservation in New Jersey* (1997), funding resources for history; *Economic and Fiscal Impacts of Heritage Tourism in New Jersey*; *Keeping the Past Present: The New Jersey Historic Trust, 1967-2013.*

IRS I.D.: 22-3113979

STAFF:
Dorothy Guzzo, Executive Director

ADDRESS INQUIRIES TO:
See e-mail address above.

NEW JERSEY HISTORIC TRUST [567]
101 South Broad Street
Trenton, NJ 08608-2401
(609) 984-0473
Fax: (609) 984-7590
E-mail: njht@dca.nj.gov
Web Site: www.njht.org

FOUNDED: 1967

AREAS OF INTEREST:
Capital preservation of historic properties.

NAME(S) OF PROGRAMS:
● **Emergency Loans**
● **Preserve New Jersey Historic Preservation Fund for Capital Projects**

TYPE:
Capital grants. Loans. Emergency loans may be used for emergency repair or stabilization, planning or research necessary to preserve an endangered property, limited rehabilitation, restoration or improvement, acquisition of a historic property or the purchase of an option to acquire a historic property.

YEAR PROGRAM STARTED: 1990

PURPOSE:
To provide emergency funding for capital preservation projects of historic properties.

LEGAL BASIS:
Government-approved program. Statutory Citation: P.L. 1967, c. 124.

ELIGIBILITY:
Applicants must be nonprofit, tax-exempt organizations or agencies of county or municipal governments. All properties must be listed or eligible for listing in the State and National Registers of Historic Places. For

all requests other than acquisition, applicants must demonstrate control of the property through a deed or a valid lease.

GEOG. RESTRICTIONS: New Jersey.

FINANCIAL DATA:
Awards are short-term low-interest loans.
Amount of support per award: $1,000 to $10,000 for emergency loan; Up to $750,000 for a capital project.

Total amount of support: Varies.

Matching fund requirements: Matching funds for loans are encouraged but not required for emergency loans. Capital projects up to $150,000 require a three-to-one match; capital projects up to $750,000 require a one-to-one match.

NO. MOST RECENT APPLICANTS: 64.

NO. AWARDS: Varies.

REPRESENTATIVE AWARDS:
$10,000 to Newark Museum for stabilization of skylight in historic Polhemus House.

APPLICATION INFO:
A nonrefundable application fee of $25 must be submitted with each application. Applicants must consult with Trust staff before making application for these funds.

Duration: Varies.

Deadline: Early spring.

PUBLICATIONS:
Program announcement.

IRS I.D.: 21-6000928

STAFF:
Dorothy Guzzo, Executive Director

ADDRESS INQUIRIES TO:
See e-mail address above.

NEW JERSEY HISTORICAL COMMISSION [568]
New Jersey Department of State
33 West State Street, Fourth Floor
Trenton, NJ 08625-0305
(609) 292-6062
Fax: (609) 633-8168
E-mail: shawn.crisafulli@sos.nj.gov
Web Site: www.history.nj.gov

FOUNDED: 1969

AREAS OF INTEREST:
New Jersey history.

NAME(S) OF PROGRAMS:
● **General Operating Support Grants**

TYPE:
General operating grants. Provide general assistance to historical organizations, museums, historic sites, archives, libraries and similar organizations with collections or programming relating to the history of New Jersey.

YEAR PROGRAM STARTED: 2000

PURPOSE:
To provide operating support for New Jersey history organizations.

LEGAL BASIS:
Agency within the Department of State, State of New Jersey.

ELIGIBILITY:
To be eligible to apply for a General Operating Support Grant, an organization must:
(1) have an annual budget of at least $100,000 in non-state history funds;

(2) document that 25% of its audience (both virtual and actual) comes from beyond a 20-mile radius from its headquarters location;
(3) be a not-for-profit corporation or government (municipal or county) agency, commission or other organization;
(4) be based in New Jersey;
(5) be governed by a board responsible for the programs and policies of the organization;
(6) have a clearly stated mission of service to the promotion, preservation, research, interpretation or public presentation of New Jersey history;
(7) have a two-year track record of providing programs and services to the public that fulfill that mission and;
(8) be in good standing with the New Jersey Historical Commission.

GEOG. RESTRICTIONS: New Jersey.

FINANCIAL DATA:
Amount of support per award: Applicants may apply for grants of up to 33% of the non-state operating income from the last completed fiscal year and current projected year.

Matching fund requirements: Ratio of 3:1 (grantee: Commission).

NO. AWARDS: Approximately 40 for the year 2020.

APPLICATION INFO:
The Commission offers assistance to applicants in the technical aspects of completing the application. Applicants may visit the Commission web site or call Commission staff at the telephone number listed above.

Duration: Three-year funding cycle.

PUBLICATIONS:
Application guidelines.

ADMINISTRATION:
Shawn Crisafulli, Chief Grants Officer

ADDRESS INQUIRIES TO:
Shawn Crisafulli
Chief Grants Officer
P.O. Box 305
Trenton, NJ 08625-0305

*PLEASE NOTE:
The General Operating Support program is a three-year cycle. Applications for fiscal year round 2023 will be accepted in 2022.

*SPECIAL STIPULATIONS:
All funding is based on state appropriations.

NEW JERSEY HISTORICAL COMMISSION [569]
New Jersey Department of State
33 West State Street
Trenton, NJ 08625-0305
(609) 292-6062
Fax: (609) 633-8168
E-mail: sara.cureton@sos.nj.gov
Web Site: www.history.nj.gov

FOUNDED: 1969

AREAS OF INTEREST:
New Jersey history.

NAME(S) OF PROGRAMS:
● **Alfred E. Driscoll Dissertation Prize**
● **Richard P. McCormick Prize for Scholarly Publication**

TYPE:
Awards/prizes. The Driscoll Dissertation Prize is awarded in even years to the author of an outstanding doctoral dissertation on any topic on New Jersey history.

The McCormick Prize is awarded in odd years for an outstanding scholarly work on any aspect of New Jersey history.

YEAR PROGRAM STARTED: 1981

PURPOSE:
To stimulate the study and public knowledge of the history of New Jersey.

LEGAL BASIS:
Agency within the Department of State, State of New Jersey.

ELIGIBILITY:
Driscoll Prize: Doctoral dissertations in New Jersey history are eligible.

McCormick Prize: Scholarly books published in the preceding two years are eligible.

FINANCIAL DATA:
Amount of support per award: $1,000 for each prize.

NO. AWARDS: Driscoll and McCormick Prizes alternate; each year the Historical Commission may award either 1 Driscoll Prize or 1 McCormick Prize.

APPLICATION INFO:
Guidelines and application forms are available on the web site.
Duration: One-time award. Not renewable.
Deadline: Driscoll (2020) and McCormick (2021) Prizes: March.

PUBLICATIONS:
Annual report; application guidelines.

ADMINISTRATION:
Sara R. Cureton, Director, New Jersey Historical Commission

ADDRESS INQUIRIES TO:
For the Driscoll Prize:
Niquole Primiani, Chief Programs Officer

For the McCormick Prize:
Sara Cureton, Director, Grants Program
(See address above.)

NEW JERSEY HISTORICAL COMMISSION [570]
New Jersey Department of State
33 West State Street, Fourth Floor
Trenton, NJ 08625-0305
(609) 292-6062
Fax: (609) 633-8168
E-mail: shawn.crisafulli@sos.nj.gov
Web Site: www.history.nj.gov

FOUNDED: 1967

AREAS OF INTEREST:
New Jersey history.

NAME(S) OF PROGRAMS:
● **Project Grants**

TYPE:
Project/program grants. Funding for expenses of specific projects relating to New Jersey history. Examples of successful projects include conservation of historical materials (manuscripts, books, costumes, historical visuals), editorial and publication projects, educational initiatives, exhibitions, media (films, radio, videotape, digital media), public programs, and research (including archaeological projects, fellowships, oral history, and national and New Jersey registers of historic places nominations).

YEAR PROGRAM STARTED: 1975

PURPOSE:
To engage diverse audiences in the active exploration, enjoyment, interpretation, understanding and preservation of New Jersey history.

LEGAL BASIS:
Agency within the New Jersey Department of State.

ELIGIBILITY:
Grants are available for both individuals and organizations. There are general standards of eligibility, as well as specific requirements for programs. Organizations must have an annual budget of at least $100,000 in non-state history funds and must document that 25% of its audience (both virtual and actual) comes from beyond a 20-mile radius from its headquarters location.

FINANCIAL DATA:
Amount of support per award: Projects: $1 to $15,000.
Matching fund requirements: Organizations with annual operating budgets of at least $500,000 are expected to show a match equal to 50% of the grant request. The match need not be all in cash; it may include donated services.

NO. AWARDS: Approximately 20 for the year 2020.

APPLICATION INFO:
Applicants must submit a Declaration of Intent online prior to submitting an application.
Deadline: Declaration of Intent and Application: Typically early spring.

PUBLICATIONS:
Application guidelines.

ADMINISTRATION:
Shawn Crisafulli, Chief Grants Officer

ADDRESS INQUIRIES TO:
Shawn Crisafulli
Chief Grants Officer
P.O. Box 305
Trenton, NJ 08625-0305

NEW YORK LANDMARKS CONSERVANCY [571]
One Whitehall Street, 21st Floor
New York, NY 10004-2127
(212) 995-5260
Fax: (212) 995-5268
E-mail: info@nylandmarks.org
Web Site: www.nylandmarks.org

FOUNDED: 1973

AREAS OF INTEREST:
Historic preservation and restoration of buildings.

NAME(S) OF PROGRAMS:
● **Historic Properties Fund**
● **Non-Profit Technical Assistance Grants Program**
● **Sacred Sites Program**
● **Technical Services Program**

TYPE:
Project/program grants.

PURPOSE:
To provide financial and technical services to nonprofit housing corporations, community development organizations, social service agencies, homesteading groups, religious institutions and mutual housing associations.

LEGAL BASIS:
501(c)(3) not-for-profit.

ELIGIBILITY:
Eligible organizations must be IRS 501(c)(3) tax-exempt.

GEOG. RESTRICTIONS: New York.

FINANCIAL DATA:
Amount of support per award: Varies.
Total amount of support: Varies.

APPLICATION INFO:
Prospective applicants should first contact the Conservancy.
Duration: Varies.
Deadline: Varies.

IRS I.D.: 23-7181785

ADDRESS INQUIRIES TO:
Peg Breen, President
(See telephone or e-mail address above.)

THE NEWBERRY LIBRARY [572]
Newberry Institute for Research and Education
60 West Walton Street
Chicago, IL 60610
(312) 255-3666
E-mail: research@newberry.org
Web Site: www.newberry.org/fellowships

FOUNDED: 1887

AREAS OF INTEREST:
The humanities of Western Europe, England and the Americas from the late Middle Ages to the early 20th century.

NAME(S) OF PROGRAMS:
● **American Society for Eighteenth-Century Studies (ASECS) Fellowships**

TYPE:
Fellowships. For scholars wishing to use the Newberry's collections to study the period 1660 to 1815.

PURPOSE:
To help provide access to Newberry resources for people who live beyond commuting distance.

LEGAL BASIS:
Private research library.

ELIGIBILITY:
Applicants must have received their Ph.D. or equivalent degree, or be a Ph.D. candidate at dissertation level.

Applicants must be members of the ASECS at the time of award.

Applicants must live outside the Chicago area.

FINANCIAL DATA:
Amount of support per award: $3,000 per month.

NO. MOST RECENT APPLICANTS: 15.

NO. AWARDS: 1 per year.

APPLICATION INFO:
Applications must be submitted through the online webform.
Duration: One month.
Deadline: December 15.

STAFF:
Keelin Burke, Director of Fellowships and Academic Programs

ADDRESS INQUIRIES TO:
See e-mail address above.

OMOHUNDRO INSTITUTE OF EARLY AMERICAN HISTORY AND CULTURE [573]

400 Landrum Drive, Ground Floor
Swem Library
Williamsburg, VA 23185
(757) 221-1114
Fax: (757) 221-1047
E-mail: oieahc@wm.edu
Web Site: oieahc.wm.edu/fellowship

FOUNDED: 1943

AREAS OF INTEREST:
Research leading to book publication on any area of early American studies.

NAME(S) OF PROGRAMS:
- **Omohundro Institute-NEH Postdoctoral Fellowship**

TYPE:
Fellowships. The Omohundro Institute of Early American History and Culture, located on the campus of The College of William and Mary, annually offers one postdoctoral fellowship to a promising young scholar in any area of early American studies whose dissertation shows potential for making a significant book-length contribution to scholarship.

Fellows have the opportunity of teaching at the College of William and Mary with a concurrent appointment as visiting assistant professor in the appropriate department.

YEAR PROGRAM STARTED: 1945

LEGAL BASIS:
Independent, nonprofit research institution.

ELIGIBILITY:
Fellows must have successfully defended their dissertation and completed all requirements for the Doctorate by the time they begin the fellowship and may not have previously published a book or have a book under contract. Foreign nationals who have been in continuous residence in the U.S. for the three years immediately preceding the date of application are eligible to apply.

FINANCIAL DATA:
Amount of support per award: $50,400 per year stipend.

CO-OP FUNDING PROGRAMS: The fellowships are supported by the Omohundro Institute and the National Endowment for the Humanities.

NO. AWARDS: 1 annually.

APPLICATION INFO:
Applicants should apply via the Institute web site.

Duration: Two years.

Deadline: November 1 for the term beginning the following July 1.

PUBLICATIONS:
William and Mary Quarterly, scholarly journal; *Uncommon Sense,* newsletter; books.

STAFF:
Karin A. Wulf, Executive Director

ADDRESS INQUIRIES TO:
Karin A. Wulf, Executive Director
(See e-mail address above.)

*SPECIAL STIPULATIONS:
The Institute holds first rights to publishing the resulting book manuscript.

OMOHUNDRO INSTITUTE OF EARLY AMERICAN HISTORY AND CULTURE [574]

400 Landrum Drive, Ground Floor
Swem Library
Williamsburg, VA 23185
(757) 221-1114
Fax: (757) 221-1047
E-mail: oieahc@wm.edu
Web Site: oieahc.wm.edu/fellowship

FOUNDED: 1943

AREAS OF INTEREST:
Promoting the study of early American history and culture.

NAME(S) OF PROGRAMS:
- **Georgian Papers Programme Fellowships**
- **Jamestown Rediscovery-Omohundro Institute (JR-OI) Short-Term Visiting Fellowship**

TYPE:
Fellowships. Georgian Papers Programme Fellowships: With support from the Lapidus Initiative, the Omohundro Institute has entered into an international partnership that will provide opportunities for scholars to do research in the historically rich trove of Georgian materials housed at the Royal Archives in Windsor Castle's Round Tower. The Georgian Papers Programme is a five-year project that by 2020 will create an open online archive and library of approximately 350,000 digitized items from the Georgian monarchs.

Jamestown Rediscovery-Omohundro Institute (JR-OI) Short-Term Visiting Fellowship: Fellows in this program will make use of the College of William and Mary's Swem Library and collections at Historic Jamestowne as well as other resources in the Historic Triangle and Richmond region. This fellowship will also provide the opportunity to experience the Omohundro Institute's editorial expertise and intellectual community of early Americanists.

LEGAL BASIS:
Independent, nonprofit research institution.

ELIGIBILITY:
Georgian Papers Programme Fellowships: Open to scholars - from advanced graduate students to senior scholars; restricted to U.S. or U.K. citizens. Successful applicants will be required to undergo a security clearance before beginning work at Windsor Castle.

JR-OI Short-Term Visiting Fellowship: Open to scholars - from advanced graduate students to senior scholars. Scholars with strong interests in colonial history, historical archaeology, Atlantic history, Native American history, African American studies, early Jamestown, the Chesapeake, and material culture, 1500-1720, are encouraged to apply.

FINANCIAL DATA:
Amount of support per award: Georgian Papers Programme Fellowships: $2,500 stipend with up to $1,500 in additional support for travel. JR-OI Short-Term Visiting Fellowship: Stipend of $2,500.

CO-OP FUNDING PROGRAMS: JR-OI Short-Term Visiting Fellowship: This program is offered in conjunction with the Jamestown Rediscovery Foundation.

NO. AWARDS: Georgian Papers Programme Fellowships: Up to 8 annually. JR-OI Short-Term Visiting Fellowship: Up to 4 annually.

APPLICATION INFO:
Georgian Papers Programme Fellowships: Applicants need to submit a letter of application (including a description of the proposed project and its potential match with the collections), a curriculum vitae and two letters of recommendation. The letter and curriculum vitae should be uploaded via the Institute web site (above). Recommenders should e-mail letters directly to the e-mail address listed above.

JR-OI Short-Term Visiting Fellowship: Applicants need to submit an electronic file with a brief project description (1,000 words maximum) and a curriculum vitae via the Institute web site. In addition, two letters of recommendation should be sent directly to the Institute via the e-mail address above.

Duration: One month.

Deadline: March 1 and November 1.

ADDRESS INQUIRIES TO:
Omohundro Institute of Early American History and Culture
(See e-mail address above.)

OMOHUNDRO INSTITUTE OF EARLY AMERICAN HISTORY AND CULTURE [575]

400 Landrum Drive, Ground Floor
Swem Library
Williamsburg, VA 23185
(757) 221-1114
Fax: (757) 221-1047
E-mail: oieahc@wm.edu
Web Site: oieahc.wm.edu/fellowship

FOUNDED: 1943

AREAS OF INTEREST:
Graduate student research related to Early American and transatlantic print culture.

NAME(S) OF PROGRAMS:
- **Lapidus-OI Fellowship**

TYPE:
Fellowships. The Lapidus-OI Fellowship is offered annually to support advanced graduate student research related to Early American and transatlantic print culture, including authorship, production, circulation and reception.

LEGAL BASIS:
Independent, nonprofit research institution.

FINANCIAL DATA:
Amount of support per award: $1,000.

CO-OP FUNDING PROGRAMS: Fellowships are made possible through the generous support of Sid Lapidus.

NO. AWARDS: Up to 8 annually.

APPLICATION INFO:
Applicants must submit an electronic file with a 500-word description of their dissertation project, a curriculum vitae, and a one-paragraph research agenda.

Deadline: November 1.

STAFF:
Karin A. Wulf, Executive Director

ADDRESS INQUIRIES TO:
Fellowship Program
(See e-mail address above.)

*SPECIAL STIPULATIONS:
Fellowship recipients must provide a one-page report of their progress no more than 12 months after notification of their award.

PHI ALPHA THETA HISTORY HONOR SOCIETY   [576]

University of South Florida
4202 East Fowler Avenue, SOC107
Tampa, FL 33620-8100
(800) 394-8195
(813) 974-8212
Fax: (813) 974-8215
E-mail: info@phialphatheta.org
Web Site: phialphatheta.org

FOUNDED: 1921

AREAS OF INTEREST:
  History.

NAME(S) OF PROGRAMS:
  • Member's Best First Book Award
  • Member's Best Subsequent Book Award

TYPE:
  Awards/prizes. Awards for the best books published by members of Phi Alpha Theta, one for his or her first book, one for subsequent books (second, third, etc.), published in the field of history.

PURPOSE:
  To encourage the publication of distinctive books in history.

LEGAL BASIS:
  Nonprofit, 501(c)(3).

ELIGIBILITY:
  Books to be judged must be published from August 1 of the previous year to June 30 of the following (award) year to be eligible for that year's award. Awards restricted to society members.

FINANCIAL DATA:
  Amount of support per award: $1,000 each.
  Total amount of support: $2,000.

NO. MOST RECENT APPLICANTS: 4.

NO. AWARDS: 2 for the year 2020.

APPLICATION INFO:
  Six copies of each book and a completed application must be forwarded to the Society's Book Award Committee at the address above.
  Deadline: July 1 of the award year.

OFFICERS:
  Wendy M. Tunstall, Executive Director

ADDRESS INQUIRIES TO:
  Wendy M. Tunstall, Executive Director
  (See address above.)

PHI ALPHA THETA HISTORY HONOR SOCIETY   [577]

University of South Florida
4202 East Fowler Avenue, SOC107
Tampa, FL 33620-8100
(800) 394-8195
(813) 974-8212
Fax: (813) 974-8215
E-mail: info@phialphatheta.org
Web Site: phialphatheta.org

FOUNDED: 1921

AREAS OF INTEREST:
  History.

NAME(S) OF PROGRAMS:
  • Gordon Morris Bakken Scholarship in Western History
  • Thomas S. Morgan Memorial Scholarship
  • William E. Parrish Scholarship

  • Graydon A. Tunstall Undergraduate Student Scholarship
  • A.F. Zimmerman Scholarship

TYPE:
  Awards/prizes; Scholarships. The Gordon Morris Bakken Scholarship in Western History is awarded to a graduate student in history researching the Trans-Mississippi West.

  The Thomas S. Morgan, William E. Parrish and A.F. Zimmerman Scholarships are given to student members entering graduate school for the first time for work leading to a Master's degree in history.

  The Graydon A. Tunstall Undergraduate Student Scholarship is given to exceptional junior-year students majoring in Modern European History (1815 to present).

PURPOSE:
  To promote the study of history at the graduate level.

LEGAL BASIS:
  Nonprofit, 501(c)(3).

ELIGIBILITY:
  Applicants must be initiated members of the Phi Alpha Theta History Honor Society. Applicant must not be enrolled in an online degree program.

  For the Morgan, Parrish and Zimmerman Scholarships, members must be entering graduate school for the first time in the fall of the award year and must be pursuing a Master's degree in History. Students currently enrolled in a graduate program are not eligible to apply.

  For the Graydon A. Tunstall Undergraduate Student Scholarship, students must be entering the fall semester of their senior year and majoring in Modern European History (1815 to the present).

FINANCIAL DATA:
  Amount of support per award: Bakken Scholarship: $500; Morgan, Parrish and Tunstall Scholarships: $1,000 each; Zimmerman Scholarship: $1,250. In some years, there may be two additional awards of $850 each for Doctoral Scholarships.
  Total amount of support: Varies.

NO. MOST RECENT APPLICANTS: 20.

NO. AWARDS: Graduate: 4; Undergraduate: 1.

APPLICATION INFO:
  Consult the Society web site.
  Duration: One year.
  Deadline: Applications must be received on or before March 1.

OFFICERS:
  Wendy M. Tunstall, Executive Director

ADDRESS INQUIRIES TO:
  Wendy M. Tunstall, Executive Director
  (See address above.)

*SPECIAL STIPULATIONS:
  Applicants must be members of Phi Alpha Theta.

PHI ALPHA THETA HISTORY HONOR SOCIETY   [578]

University of South Florida
4202 East Fowler Avenue, SOC107
Tampa, FL 33620-8100
(800) 394-8195
(813) 974-8212
Fax: (813) 974-8215
E-mail: info@phialphatheta.org
Web Site: phialphatheta.org

FOUNDED: 1921

AREAS OF INTEREST:
  History.

NAME(S) OF PROGRAMS:
  • The Nels Andrew Cleven Founder's Paper Prize Awards
  • Dr. George P. Hammond Paper Prize
  • Dr. Lynn W. Turner Paper Prize

TYPE:
  Awards/prizes. The George P. Hammond Prize award is for the best paper by a graduate student member of the Society.

  The Dr. Lynn W. Turner Prize is awarded for the best paper by an undergraduate student member of the Society.

  The four Founder's Paper Prizes are awarded to two graduate and two undergraduate student members of the Society.

PURPOSE:
  To promote historical research.

LEGAL BASIS:
  501(c)(3).

ELIGIBILITY:
  All students must be initiated members.

FINANCIAL DATA:
  Amount of support per award: Founder's Awards: $400; Hammond Prize and Turner Award: $500 each.

NO. MOST RECENT APPLICANTS: 20.

NO. AWARDS: 6.

APPLICATION INFO:
  Essay should combine original historical research on significant subjects, based on source material and manuscripts if possible, with good English composition and superior style. Papers should not exceed 25 typewritten double-spaced pages in length, excluding bibliography. Entries received that do not comply with these guidelines will be disqualified.

  Title page of the paper must include the applicant's name, mailing address, telephone number and e-mail address, as well as the college/university, graduate or undergraduate status and year at which he or she joined Phi Alpha Theta.

  Entrants must submit five copies of each manuscript and a letter of recommendation from either the Faculty Advisor or History Department Chair indicating the applicant's chapter affiliation and whether the individual is a graduate or an undergraduate student. Send to:
  Christopher M. Kennedy, Ph.D.
  Office of the Provost
  Francis Marion University
  P.O. Box 100547
  Florence, SC 29502-0547
  E-mail: ckennedy@fmarion.edu
  Deadline: July 1.

OFFICERS:
  Wendy M. Tunstall, Executive Director

ADDRESS INQUIRIES TO:
  Wendy M. Tunstall, Executive Director
  (See address above.)

PONTIFICAL INSTITUTE OF MEDIAEVAL STUDIES   [579]

59 Queen's Park Crescent East
Toronto ON M5S 2C4 Canada
(416) 926-7142
Fax: (416) 926-7292
E-mail: allan.smith@utoronto.ca
Web Site: www.pims.ca

FOUNDED: 1929

AREAS OF INTEREST:
Medieval studies.

NAME(S) OF PROGRAMS:
● **Mellon Postdoctoral Fellowships**

TYPE:
Fellowships.

YEAR PROGRAM STARTED: 1998

PURPOSE:
To develop a candidate's personal research in
the context of the Institute's mission.

ELIGIBILITY:
Open to scholars engaged in medieval
studies. Level of study is postdoctoral.

FINANCIAL DATA:
Amount of support per award:
Approximately $40,000 (CAN).
Total amount of support: Approximately
$160,000 (CAN).

NO. MOST RECENT APPLICANTS: 26 for the year
2020.

NO. AWARDS: Up to 4.

APPLICATION INFO:
Application must include official
confirmation that the Ph.D. has been
examined and that its award has been
approved by the appropriate authority.
Duration: One year.
Deadline: February 1.

ADDRESS INQUIRIES TO:
Cynthia Watson, Institute Secretary and
Executive Assistant to the Praeses
E-mail: cynthia.watson@utoronto.ca

ROCK ISLAND ARSENAL
MUSEUM   [580]
Rock Island Arsenal Historical Society
R. Maguire Scholarship Committee
One Rock Island Arsenal
Rock Island, IL 61299-5000
(309) 782-5021
Fax: (309) 782-3598
E-mail: contact@arsenalhistoricalsociety.org
rhist37@gmail.com
Web Site: www.arsenalhistoricalsociety.org

AREAS OF INTEREST:
Postgraduate, Master's or Doctorate studies
in history and museum study.

NAME(S) OF PROGRAMS:
● **Richard C. Maguire Scholarship**

TYPE:
Scholarships.

PURPOSE:
To provide financial support to a student
working for a Master's or Doctorate degree
in the fields of history, archaeology or
museum study.

ELIGIBILITY:
Applicants must be U.S. citizens. Grants will
be awarded on an objective and
nondiscriminatory basis without regard to
age, sex, race, religion or affiliation. Level of
study is postdoctoral and postgraduate.

GEOG. RESTRICTIONS: United States.

FINANCIAL DATA:
Amount of support per award: $1,000.
Total amount of support: $1,000.

NO. MOST RECENT APPLICANTS: 1 to 3.

NO. AWARDS: 1 annually.

APPLICATION INFO:
Application is available on the Museum web
site or can be obtained by writing to the
Museum. Applicant must enclose a
self-addressed, stamped envelope.
Duration: One year.
Deadline: May 15.

ADDRESS INQUIRIES TO:
E-mail: contact@arsenalhistoricalsociety.org

ROCKEFELLER ARCHIVE
CENTER   [581]
15 Dayton Avenue
Sleepy Hollow, NY 10591
(914) 366-6309
Fax: (914) 366-6017
E-mail: archive@rockarch.org
Web Site: www.rockarch.org

FOUNDED: 1974

AREAS OF INTEREST:
Preservation of and research in the records of
The Rockefeller University, the Rockefeller
Foundation, the Rockefeller Brothers Fund,
the Rockefeller family, the Ford Foundation,
the Commonwealth Fund, the Social Science
Research Council, the Asian Cultural
Council, and other foundations, cultural
organizations, research institutions and
associated organizations and individuals
which include major concentrations in
philanthropy, education, history of medicine,
science, public health, the arts, agriculture,
social sciences, urban affairs and public
policy.

CONSULTING OR VOLUNTEER SERVICES:
Reports on holdings and their relevance to
research topics and provides assistance to
visiting scholars.

NAME(S) OF PROGRAMS:
● **Research Stipend Program at the
Rockefeller Archive Center**

TYPE:
Grants-in-aid. Grants-in-Aid to individual
scholars to defray costs of travel and
accommodation expenses while doing
research at the Rockefeller Archive Center in
the Center's collections.

YEAR PROGRAM STARTED: 1977

PURPOSE:
To foster, promote and support research by
serious scholars in the collections located at
the Rockefeller Archive Center, which
includes the records of the Rockefeller
Family and their far-reaching philanthropic
endeavors, such as the Rockefeller
University, Rockefeller Foundation, and
Rockefeller Brothers Fund.

LEGAL BASIS:
Nonprofit and educational.

ELIGIBILITY:
Grants will be made on a competitive basis
to applicants from any discipline, usually
graduate students or postdoctoral scholars,
who are engaged in research that requires use
of the collections at the Center.

FINANCIAL DATA:
Grants are for receipted, approved expenses.
Expenses are reimbursed after the completion
of the research visit.
Amount of support per award: Up to $5,000.
Total amount of support: $140,000 annually.

NO. MOST RECENT APPLICANTS: 95 for the year
2019.

NO. AWARDS: 59 for the year 2019.

APPLICATION INFO:
Two letters supporting the research stipend
application are required.
Duration: Applications for second- and
third-year support will be considered, but
preference is given to new applicants.
Deadline: November 1. Announcement of
awards at the beginning of March.

PUBLICATIONS:
*Research Reports OnLine from the
Rockefeller Archive Center;* guides to
manuscripts and photograph collections;
surveys of holdings on specific subjects.

OFFICERS AND STAFF:
Jack Meyers, President
Bob Clark, Director of Archives
Barbara Shubinski, Director, Research and
Education

ADDRESS INQUIRIES TO:
Norine Hochman, Executive Assistant
(See address above.)

FRANKLIN D. ROOSEVELT
LIBRARY AND MUSEUM   [582]
4079 Albany Post Road
Hyde Park, NY 12538
(845) 486-7770
E-mail: grants.fdr@nara.gov
Web Site: fdrlibrary.org/research-grants

FOUNDED: 1941

AREAS OF INTEREST:
Archives, museum, education and public
programs relating to the life and times of
Franklin and Eleanor Roosevelt.

NAME(S) OF PROGRAMS:
● **Roosevelt Institute Research Grants**

TYPE:
Grants-in-aid; Research grants. The Roosevelt
Institute - the Library's nonprofit partner -
supports a program of small grants-in-aid, in
support of research on the "Roosevelt years"
or clearly related subjects.

PURPOSE:
To foster research and education on the life
and times of Franklin and Eleanor Roosevelt.

ELIGIBILITY:
The grants program is particularly designed
to encourage younger scholars to expand the
knowledge and understanding of the
Roosevelt period. The Roosevelt Institute
Grants Committee makes its decision on
whether or not to provide a grant based on
the merits of each research topic and its
potential contribution to scholarship.

FINANCIAL DATA:
Funds are awarded for the sole purpose of
helping to defray living, travel and related
expenses incurred while conducting research
at the Roosevelt Library.
Amount of support per award: Up to $2,500.

NO. AWARDS: Determined based on the merit of
the applications.

APPLICATION INFO:
Application instructions are found on the
Library web site. Applicants are required to
submit to the grants administrator an original
grant application and one copy detailing the
nature and scope of their research project, the
names and institutions of three references and
a budget outlining the amount needed for
travel, lodging and any other research
expenses. Each application is evaluated by
the Library's archival staff to ascertain that

there is material at the Library appropriate for the research topic, approximately how long such research might be expected to take, and per diem.

Duration: Use of the grants is to occur within a year of the grant announcement letter.

Deadline: November 15. Grants are awarded at the beginning of each year.

ADDRESS INQUIRIES TO:
See e-mail address above.

*SPECIAL STIPULATIONS:
Letters are sent to all applicants informing them of the Roosevelt Institute Grants Committee's decision on whether or not to grant funding. Grantees are informed that the use of their grants is to occur within a year of their letter. Grantees will receive their award when they arrive for research at the Library.

SANTA BARBARA MISSION ARCHIVE-LIBRARY   [583]
2201 Laguna Street
Santa Barbara, CA 93105
(805) 682-4713 ext. 152
E-mail: research@sbmal.org
Web Site: www.sbmal.org

FOUNDED: 1786

AREAS OF INTEREST:
Preservation, cataloging and public history.

NAME(S) OF PROGRAMS:
● **Geiger Memorial Internship**

TYPE:
Internships; Residencies.

YEAR PROGRAM STARTED: 1978

PURPOSE:
To support an opportunity to gain experience working in an archive.

ELIGIBILITY:
Consideration will be given to graduate and undergraduate students furthering their studies or a career in public history, art history, library and information technology, archive management or museum studies.

FINANCIAL DATA:
Amount of support per award: $2,500 stipend.

NO. AWARDS: 1 annually.

APPLICATION INFO:
Application information is available online.
Duration: Eight weeks during the summer.
Deadline: Summer.

ADDRESS INQUIRIES TO:
Bryan Stevenson, Collections and Programs Manager
E-mail: bryanstevenson@sbmal.org

SMITHSONIAN NATIONAL AIR AND SPACE MUSEUM
601 Independence Avenue, S.W.
Room 3762, MRC 305
Washington, DC 20560
(202) 633-2214
Fax: (202) 633-1957
E-mail: staplesa@si.edu
Web Site: airandspace.si.edu/support/get-involved/internships

TYPE:
Internships. Full-time interns work 40 hours per week from approximately the first week in June until the second week in August.

See entry 2373 for full listing.

SOCIETY FOR FRENCH HISTORICAL STUDIES   [584]
Colorado College, Department of History
Palmer Hall, No. 215D
14 East Cache La Poudre Street
Colorado Springs, CO 80903
E-mail: bragan@coloradocollege.edu
Web Site: www.
societyforfrenchhistoricalstudies.net

FOUNDED: 1955

AREAS OF INTEREST:
French history.

NAME(S) OF PROGRAMS:
● **The Gilbert Chinard Prize**
● **Natalie Zemon Davis Graduate Student Award**
● **Marjorie M. and Lancelot L. Farrar Memorial Awards**
● **The Institut Francais d'America Fund Research Fellowships**
● **The William Koren, Jr. Prize**
● **The David H. Pinkney Prize**
● **Research Travel Award**

TYPE:
Awards/prizes. The Chinard Prize is for a recent book on historical relations between France and the Americas.

Davis Graduate Student Award is given for the best paper presented by a graduate student at the Society's annual meeting.

Farrar Award is for dissertation research.

The Institut Francais d'America Fund Research Fellowships are for research in France for a period of at least one month.

The Koren Prize is for a recent journal article written on French history.

The Pinkney Prize is for a recent book written on French history.

Research Travel Award is for recent recipients of Doctorates (awarded jointly with Western Society for French History).

YEAR PROGRAM STARTED: 1955

PURPOSE:
To further the study of French history in the U.S. and Canada.

ELIGIBILITY:
Gilbert Chinard Prize: Historical studies of any area or period are acceptable.

Marjorie M. and Lancelot L. Farrar Awards: Must be a doctoral student in French history at a North American university.

The Institut Francais d'America Research Fellowships: Candidate should be working on their Ph.D. dissertation or should have received their Ph.D. no longer than three years before the application deadline.

William Koren, Jr. Prize: Must be a North American scholar who published an article on any era of French History in an American, European or Canadian journal.

David Pinkney Prize: Must be a citizen of the U.S. or Canada or an author with a full-time appointment at a U.S. or Canadian college or university. Books on any aspect and period of French history will be considered.

Research Travel Award: Granted to an outstanding American or Canadian scholar who has received the Doctorate in History in the five-year period prior to the award.

FINANCIAL DATA:
Amount of support per award: Chinard and Koren Prize: $1,000; Farrar Awards: $5,000 each; Institut Francais d'America Fund Research Fellowships: Up to $11,500; Pinkney Prize: $1,500; Research Travel Award: $2,000.

NO. AWARDS: Chinard Prize, Davis Graduate Student Award, Koren Prize, Pinkney Prize and Research Travel Award: 1; Farrar Awards and Institut Francais d'America Fund Research Fellowships: 2.

APPLICATION INFO:
Application information is available on the web site.
Deadline: Chinard, Koren and Pinkney Prize: January 1; Davis Graduate Student Award: September 15; Farrar Memorial Awards and Research Travel Award: January 15; Institut Francais d'America Fellowships: February 15.

ADDRESS INQUIRIES TO:
Bryant T. Ragan, Executive Director (See address above.)

THE SOCIETY OF AMERICAN HISTORIANS   [585]
Columbia University
Graduate School of Journalism
2950 Broadway
New York, NY 10027
(212) 854-6495
E-mail: amhistsociety@columbia.edu
Web Site: sah.columbia.edu

FOUNDED: 1939

AREAS OF INTEREST:
American history and biography.

NAME(S) OF PROGRAMS:
● **Tony Horwitz Prize**
● **Allan Nevins Dissertation Prize**
● **Francis Parkman Prize**
● **SAH Prize for Historical Fiction**

TYPE:
Awards/prizes. Tony Horwitz Prize: Supported by The Cedars Foundation, this prize honors distinguished work in American history of wide appeal and enduring public significance.

Allan Nevins Dissertation Prize: Annual award for the best written doctoral dissertation on an American subject completed in the previous year.

Francis Parkman Prize: Annual award for the best nonfiction book in American history published the previous calendar year that is distinguished for its literary merit.

SAH Prize for Historical Fiction: Biennial award in odd-numbered years for a book of historical fiction on an American subject that makes a significant contribution to historical understanding, portrays authentically the people and events of the historical past, and displays skills in narrative construction and prose style published within the previous two calendar years.

YEAR PROGRAM STARTED: 1960

PURPOSE:
To encourage literary distinction in the writing of history and biography.

LEGAL BASIS:
Nonprofit.

ELIGIBILITY:
Allan Nevins Dissertation Prize: Eligible dissertation must have been defended or the Ph.D. received in the previous calendar year; dissertations must be nominated and submitted by the student's program chair or dissertation sponsor.

FINANCIAL DATA:
Amount of support per award: Horwitz Prize: $5,000; Nevins, Parkman and SAH Prize: $2,000 per prize.

NO. AWARDS: Tony Horwitz, Allan Nevins Dissertation and Francis Parkman Prizes: 1; SAH Prize for Historical Fiction: 1 biennially in odd-numbered years.

APPLICATION INFO:
Application information and guidelines are available online.
Deadline: Allan Nevins Dissertation Prize: December 31 annually. Francis Parkman Prize: December 1 annually. SAH Prize for Historical Fiction: December 1, 2020.

OFFICERS:
Megan Marshall, President
Andie Tucher, Executive Secretary

ADDRESS INQUIRIES TO:
See e-mail address above.

THE SONS OF THE REPUBLIC OF TEXAS [586]
SRT Office
1717 Eighth Street, Suite 12
Bay City, TX 77414
(979) 245-6644
Fax: (979) 244-3819
E-mail: aa-srt@son-rep-texas.net
Web Site: www.srttexas.org

FOUNDED: 1893

AREAS OF INTEREST:
Spanish colonial period of Texas history.

NAME(S) OF PROGRAMS:
● **Presidio La Bahia Award**

TYPE:
Awards/prizes. Presidio La Bahia Award is intended to promote suitable preservation of relics, appropriate dissemination of data, and research into Texas heritage, with particular emphasis on the Spanish colonial period.

PURPOSE:
To encourage literary effort and research about historical events and personalities during the days of the Spanish colonial period of Texas history, and to stimulate interest in this period.

ELIGIBILITY:
Open to all persons interested in the Spanish colonial influence on Texas culture.

Research writings have proved in the past to be the most successful type of entry. However, careful consideration will be given to other literary forms, as well as to art, architecture, and archaeological discovery.

FINANCIAL DATA:
Amount of support per award: First place: a minimum of $1,200 for the best published book. At its discretion, the organization may award a second-place book prize. There is a separate category with a prize for the best published paper, article published in a periodical, or project of a nonliterary nature.
Total amount of support: A total of $2,000 is available annually for winning participants in the competition at the discretion of the judges.

NO. AWARDS: 1 for the year 2019.

APPLICATION INFO:
Applicants must submit four copies of published writings to the office. Galley proofs are not acceptable.
Deadline: Entries are accepted from June 1 to September 30.

ADDRESS INQUIRIES TO:
Janet Knox, Office Manager
The Sons of the Republic of Texas
(See address above.)

THE SONS OF THE REPUBLIC OF TEXAS [587]
SRT Office
1717 Eighth Street, Suite 12
Bay City, TX 77414
(979) 245-6644
Fax: (979) 244-3819
E-mail: aa-srt@son-rep-texas.net
Web Site: www.srttexas.org

FOUNDED: 1893

AREAS OF INTEREST:
Republic of Texas (1836-1846).

NAME(S) OF PROGRAMS:
● **Summerfield G. Roberts Award**

TYPE:
Awards/prizes. Cash award to the author of a work of creative writing on the Republic of Texas.

PURPOSE:
To encourage literary effort and research about historical events and personalities during the days of the Republic of Texas (1836-1846), and to stimulate interest in this period.

LEGAL BASIS:
Nonprofit organization.

ELIGIBILITY:
The competition is open to all writers everywhere; they need not reside in Texas nor must the publishers be in Texas. Manuscripts may be either fiction or nonfiction, poems, essays, plays, short stories, novels, or biographies.

FINANCIAL DATA:
Amount of support per award: $2,500.
Total amount of support: $2,500 annually.

NO. AWARDS: 1 annually.

APPLICATION INFO:
Manuscripts must be written or published during the calendar year for which the award is given. The title page must have the contestant's full name, address and telephone number. Five copies of each entry must be mailed to the General Office of The Sons of the Republic of Texas at the address above. No copies will be returned.
Duration: One-time award.
Deadline: Postmarked no later than January 15 of the year following the qualifying year of the award.

ADDRESS INQUIRIES TO:
Janet Knox, Office Manager
The Sons of the Republic of Texas
(See address above.)

THE SUMMERLEE FOUNDATION
5556 Caruth Haven Lane
Dallas, TX 75225
(214) 363-9000
Fax: (214) 363-1941
E-mail: info@summerlee.org
Web Site: www.summerlee.org

TYPE:
Project/program grants; Research grants; Technical assistance.
See entry 1254 for full listing.

HARRY S. TRUMAN LIBRARY INSTITUTE
5151 Troost Avenue
Suite 300
Kansas City, MO 64110
(816) 400-1216
Fax: (816) 400-1213
E-mail: lisa.sullivan@trumanlibraryinstitute.org
Web Site: www.trumanlibraryinstitute.org

TYPE:
Awards/prizes; Fellowships; Grants-in-aid; Research grants; Travel grants. The Dissertation Year Fellowships are given to encourage historical scholarship of the public career of Harry S. Truman or the Truman era. Support is given annually to one or two graduate students who have completed the dissertation research and are in the writing stage. Preference will be given to projects based on extensive research at the Truman Library. Successful applicants will be expected to deposit one copy of their completed dissertation, or any publication resulting therefrom, with the Truman Library.

Research Grants are intended to enable graduate students as well as postdoctoral scholars to come to the Library for one to three weeks to use its archival facilities.

The Scholar's Award is given every other year, even-numbered years only, to a scholar engaged in a study of either the public career of Harry S. Truman or some aspect of the history of the Truman administration or of the U.S. during that administration. The scholar's work must be based on extensive research at the Truman Library and must be designed to result in the publication of a book-length manuscript. One copy of such book (and/or any other publication resulting from work done under this award) shall be deposited by the author with the Harry S. Truman Library.

The Harry S. Truman Book Award is given in even years for the best book dealing with some aspect of history of the U.S. between April 12, 1945 and January 20, 1953 or with the public career of Harry S. Truman.
See entry 1809 for full listing.

U.S. ARMY CENTER OF MILITARY HISTORY [588]
Dissertation Fellowship Committee
Collins Hall, Building 35
102 Fourth Avenue, Fort Lesley J. McNair
Washington, DC 20319-5060
(202) 685-2305
Fax: (202) 685-2077
E-mail: usarmy.mcnair.cmh.mbx.dissfellow@mail.mil
Web Site: www.history.army.mil/index.html

FOUNDED: 1942

AREAS OF INTEREST:
History of warfare on land, with special emphasis on the history of the U.S. Army.

NAME(S) OF PROGRAMS:
● **Dissertation Year Fellowships**

TYPE:
Fellowships. The Center offers two Dissertation Fellowships each year and sometimes awards a third fellowship to exceptional dissertations on museum-related topics. The Center will consider dissertations on the history of land warfare; preference is given to topics on the history of the U.S. Army.

YEAR PROGRAM STARTED: 1970

PURPOSE:
To encourage scholarship in military history.

LEGAL BASIS:
Government agency.

ELIGIBILITY:
Applicants must be civilian citizens or nationals of the U.S. that have demonstrated ability and special aptitude for advanced training and study in military history, be enrolled in a recognized graduate school and have successfully completed by September of the year of the award all requirements for the Ph.D. except the dissertation.

FINANCIAL DATA:
Amount of support per award: Stipend of $10,000.
Total amount of support: Up to $30,000.

NO. MOST RECENT APPLICANTS: 11 for the year 2017-18.

NO. AWARDS: Up to 3 annually.

REPRESENTATIVE AWARDS:
"Bickering Brass: Defense Unification, Interservice Rivalry, and the Pacific War;" "The Killing Spirit: American War Criminals and Military Justice, 1942-1945."

APPLICATION INFO:
Applicants must submit by mail the following materials:
(1) completed, typed application form;
(2) proposed research plan and reasons for interest in this topic (not to exceed 10 double-spaced, typed pages);
(3) letter of recommendation from dissertation director confirming dissertation proposal has been accepted by the committee;
(4) two other letters of recommendation;
(5) a writing sample of approximately 25 double-spaced, typed pages (e.g., seminar paper, published scholarly article, excerpt from M.A. thesis or Ph.D. dissertation) and;
(6) transcripts from all undergraduate and graduate schools attended.
Duration: One year.
Deadline: January 15. Announcement April 1.

ADDRESS INQUIRIES TO:
Dr. Jeffrey Seiken
CMH Dissertation Fellowship Committee
(See address above.)

U.S. ARMY HERITAGE AND EDUCATION CENTER   [589]
950 Soldiers Drive
Carlisle, PA 17013-5021
(717) 245-3803
E-mail: usarmy.carlisle.awc.mbx.ahec-ves@mail.mil
Web Site: ahec.armywarcollege.edu/ridgway.cfm

FOUNDED: 1967

AREAS OF INTEREST:
Military history with emphasis on the U.S. Army.

NAME(S) OF PROGRAMS:
● **General and Mrs. Matthew B. Ridgway Military History Research Grant**

TYPE:
Research grants; Travel grants. Research and travel fellowships to cover expenses incurred while conducting individual research in USAMHI holdings. These grants may not be used to cover costs for travel to and research at other institutions.

YEAR PROGRAM STARTED: 1977

PURPOSE:
To stimulate utilization of holdings of the Institute in preparation of scholarly, mature publications in military history (theses, dissertations or books).

LEGAL BASIS:
U.S. Department of the Army.

ELIGIBILITY:
Applicants must be actively engaged in the study of military history, to include research as part of a Masters or Doctorate program in military history (or a related field) or research toward a book, monograph, or scholarly article.

FINANCIAL DATA:
Amount of support per award: Up to $2,500.
Total amount of support: Varies.

NO. MOST RECENT APPLICANTS: 19 for the year 2019.

NO. AWARDS: 9 for the year 2019.

APPLICATION INFO:
Electronic submissions only.
Duration: Two to three years.
Deadline: Applications are due to the committee by December 31. Final announcement of recipients by March.

ADDRESS INQUIRIES TO:
Ridgway Research Grants
(See address above.)

*SPECIAL STIPULATIONS:
Must do research in U.S. Army Military History Institute holdings.

UNITED STATES HOLOCAUST MEMORIAL MUSEUM - JACK, JOSEPH AND MORTON MANDEL CENTER FOR ADVANCED HOLOCAUST STUDIES   [590]
100 Raoul Wallenberg Place, S.W.
Washington, DC 20024-2126
E-mail: vscholars@ushmm.org
Web Site: www.ushmm.org/research/opportunities-for-academics

FOUNDED: 1993

AREAS OF INTEREST:
Holocaust and genocide studies.

NAME(S) OF PROGRAMS:
● **Visiting Scholars Program**

TYPE:
Exchange programs; Fellowships. The Jack, Joseph and Morton Mandel Center for Advanced Holocaust Studies awards several types of fellowships to support significant research and writing about the Holocaust and related topics. A fellowship at the Mandel

Center not only provides time to research and access to world-renowned archives, but also an extensive network of people and institutions. Visiting scholars at the Mandel Center have access to more than 120 million pages of Holocaust-related archival documents; library resources in more than 60 languages; hundreds of thousands of oral history, film, photo, art, artifacts and memoir collections; the Database of Holocaust Survivor and Victim Names; more than 200 million images from the ITS Digital Archive; plus more. Applications from all disciplines are welcome.

YEAR PROGRAM STARTED: 1994

PURPOSE:
To support scholarship and publication in the field of Holocaust studies; to promote the growth of Holocaust studies at universities; to seek to foster strong relationships between American and international scholars; to organize programs to ensure the ongoing training of future generations of scholars specializing in the Holocaust.

ELIGIBILITY:
Fellowships are awarded to candidates working on their dissertations (ABD), postdoctoral researchers, and senior scholars. Immediate postdoctorals and faculty between appointments will also be considered.

FINANCIAL DATA:
Amount of support per award: Up to $5,000 monthly.
Total amount of support: Varies.

NO. MOST RECENT APPLICANTS: 94.

NO. AWARDS: Approximately 20 to 25.

APPLICATION INFO:
Details are available on the web site listed above.
Duration: Two to eight months.
Deadline: Typically, November of each year.

PUBLICATIONS:
Program announcement.

ADDRESS INQUIRIES TO:
Visiting Scholars Program
(See address above.)

THE UNIVERSITY OF DELAWARE-HAGLEY GRADUATE PROGRAM   [591]
Department of History, John Munroe Hall
University of Delaware
Newark, DE 19716
(302) 831-8226
Fax: (302) 831-1538
E-mail: dianec@udel.edu
Web Site: www.udel.edu/hagley
www.history.udel.edu

FOUNDED: 1954

AREAS OF INTEREST:
Technology, business, consumption, and environment.

TYPE:
Assistantships; Fellowships. The University of Delaware, in association with the Hagley Museum, sponsors a premier graduate resident program for the study of technology, business, consumption, and work in industrial and post-industrial societies leading to a Master of Arts or Ph.D. in History. Students have access to faculty with international reputations in American, European and non-Western history, and benefit from strong

interdisciplinary ties to museum studies and material culture programs, as well as the Hagley Museum and Library.

YEAR PROGRAM STARTED: 1954

PURPOSE:
To prepare students planning careers as college teachers and as professionals in museums and historical agencies.

LEGAL BASIS:
Not-for-profit organization classified by IRS as 501(c)(3) organization.

ELIGIBILITY:
All Hagley Scholars are required to complete 30 credits (ten classes). Some of these classes must be selected to fulfill History Department requirements. Hagley Scholars also must take two "Hagley courses" which reflect student and faculty interests. These are offered every semester. Ph.D. students take a written comprehensive examination and write a dissertation. A thesis is optional for M.A. students.

FINANCIAL DATA:
All Hagley Scholars receive a stipend and tuition remission. M.A. students are supported for two years. Ph.D. students receive five years of funding. In exchange, Scholars work as teaching assistants during half the semesters in which they are funded. Hagley Scholars also receive an allowance of $600 a year for travel and research expenses. The Program and the History Department also have additional funds which can be used to support internships and Ph.D. research.

NO. MOST RECENT APPLICANTS: Varies.

NO. AWARDS: Varies.

APPLICATION INFO:
Interested applicants should complete the online application for the UD History Graduate Program. Applicant should clearly indicate on the top of the personal statement that he or she wishes to be considered for the Hagley Program.
Duration: Two years for Master's students; Five years for Ph.D. students.
Deadline: January 5.

ADDRESS INQUIRIES TO:
Diane Clark, Academic Support Coordinator (See address above.)

*SPECIAL STIPULATIONS:
This is a resident graduate program.

UNIVERSITY OF DELAWARE, DEPARTMENT OF HISTORY [592]

46 West Delaware Avenue
Newark, DE 19716
(302) 831-8226
Fax: (302) 831-1538
E-mail: dianec@udel.edu
Web Site: www.udel.edu
www.history.udel.edu

AREAS OF INTEREST:
Professional training in historical studies.

NAME(S) OF PROGRAMS:
● **E. Lyman Stewart Fellowship and Assistantship**

TYPE:
Assistantships. Residential program in history.

PURPOSE:
To provide a program of graduate study leading to an M.A. or Ph.D. degree for

students who plan careers as museum professionals, historical agency administrators or seek careers in college teaching and public history.

ELIGIBILITY:
Open to U.S. residents.

FINANCIAL DATA:
Amount of support per award: M.A. students receive $20,000, plus tuition; Ph.D. students receive $25,000, plus tuition.
Total amount of support: Varies.

NO. MOST RECENT APPLICANTS: Varies.

NO. AWARDS: Varies.

APPLICATION INFO:
Applications must be submitted online using the University of Delaware application form and include transcripts, Graduate Record Examination scores, TOEFL scores (where applicable), plus three letters of recommendation and a writing sample.
Duration: Two to five years.
Deadline: January 5.

ADDRESS INQUIRIES TO:
Diane Clark, Academic Support Coordinator (See address above.)

WISCONSIN HISTORICAL SOCIETY PRESS [593]

816 State Street
Madison, WI 53706-1482
(608) 264-6582
E-mail: whspress@wisconsinhistory.org
Web Site: www.wisconsinhistory.org/whspress

FOUNDED: 1846

AREAS OF INTEREST:
Wisconsin history and culture.

NAME(S) OF PROGRAMS:
● **D.C. Everest Fellowship**
● **Amy Louise Hunter Fellowship**
● **Alice E. Smith Fellowship**

TYPE:
Fellowships; Research grants. Fellowships awarded for research and writing for publication in book form by the Society press on Wisconsin history topics.

YEAR PROGRAM STARTED: 2000

PURPOSE:
To promote research and writing on Wisconsin history topics.

LEGAL BASIS:
Agency of the state of Wisconsin.

ELIGIBILITY:
Fellowships are awarded to individuals. Organizations are not eligible to apply.

FINANCIAL DATA:
Amount of support per award: $1,000 to $2,000.

NO. AWARDS: 1 per award.

APPLICATION INFO:
Application must include a cover sheet, resume and completed book proposal.
Duration: One-time award.

PUBLICATIONS:
Program announcement.

YIVO INSTITUTE FOR JEWISH RESEARCH [594]

15 West 16th Street, 3rd Floor
New York, NY 10011-6301
(917) 606-8290
Fax: (212) 292-1892
E-mail: bkaplan@yivo.cjh.org
Web Site: yivo.org

FOUNDED: 1925

AREAS OF INTEREST:
Yiddish, East European and American Jewish history and culture.

NAME(S) OF PROGRAMS:
● **Fellowship in American Jewish Studies**

TYPE:
Fellowships. The Rose and Isidore Drench Memorial Fellowship and the Dora and Mayer Tendler Endowed Fellowship in Jewish Studies are dedicated to doctoral or postdoctoral research in American Jewish history, with special consideration given to scholars working on some aspect of the Jewish labor movement. This Fellowship is for research at the YIVO Library and Archives.

YEAR PROGRAM STARTED: 1990

PURPOSE:
To further research of American Jewish history, based on resources from the YIVO Library and Archives.

LEGAL BASIS:
Tax-exempt 501(c)(3) organization.

ELIGIBILITY:
Applicants must be working in American Jewish history with special consideration toward the Jewish Labor Movement. The research must be conducted at YIVO in New York City.

FINANCIAL DATA:
Amount of support per award: Combined stipend of $5,000
Total amount of support: $5,000.

NO. AWARDS: 1.

APPLICATION INFO:
Application materials should be sent by regular mail, fax or e-mail to:
Chairperson, Fellowship Committee
YIVO Institute for Jewish Research.

Applicants should include the following materials:
(1) curriculum vitae, including all contact information and detailing education, publications, other scholarly activity (papers presented, etc.), teaching and other relevant work experience, knowledge of relevant languages, honors, awards and fellowships, etc.;
(2) research proposal of no more than four pages, including aims for research during the period of fellowship; whether the proposed work is part of a larger project, such as a dissertation, book, etc.; how the resources of YIVO will contribute to the work and;
(3) two letters of support, which discuss the importance of the applicant's work for the relevant field, as well as the applicant's ability to carry out the proposed work.

Applicants may apply for only one fellowship.
Duration: Three months.
Deadline: January 15.

PUBLICATIONS:
Yedies: News from YIVO.

BOARD OF DIRECTORS:
Ruth Levine, Chairman
Irena Pletka, Vice Chairman
Edward Blank
Martin Flumenbaum
Emil Kleinhaus
Dr. Chava Lapin
Leo Melamed
Jacob Morowitz
Eliza New
Ilya Prizel
John Richmond
Harry Wagner

ADDRESS INQUIRIES TO:
Ben Kaplan, Director of Education
Max Weinreich Center for
Advanced Jewish Studies
(See address above.)

*PLEASE NOTE:
Each fellowship requires up to three months'
research stay and at least one public lecture
by the holder.

YIVO INSTITUTE FOR JEWISH RESEARCH [595]
15 West 16th Street, 3rd Floor
New York, NY 10011-6301
(917) 606-8290
Fax: (212) 292-1892
E-mail: bkaplan@yivo.cjh.org
Web Site: www.yivo.org

FOUNDED: 1925

AREAS OF INTEREST:
Yiddish, East European and American Jewish
history and culture.

NAME(S) OF PROGRAMS:
● **Fellowship in East European Arts, Music, and Theater**
● **Fellowship in East European Jewish Literature**

TYPE:
Fellowships. Fellowship in East European
Arts, Music, and Theater is designed to assist
an undergraduate, graduate or postgraduate
researcher in the fields of Eastern European
Jewish arts, music and theater.

Fellowship in East European Jewish
Literature is designed to assist an
undergraduate, graduate or postgraduate
researcher in Eastern European Jewish
literature.

The stipend is intended to defray expenses
connected with research in YIVO's music, art
and theater collections and library.

YEAR PROGRAM STARTED: 1994

PURPOSE:
To further research in Yiddish Studies, based
on resources from the YIVO Library and
Archives.

LEGAL BASIS:
Tax-exempt 501(c)(3) organization.

FINANCIAL DATA:
Amount of support per award: Fellowship in
East European Arts, Music, and Theater:
Stipend of $5,000; Fellowship in East
European Jewish Literature: Stipend of
$4,000.

NO. AWARDS: 1 per award.

APPLICATION INFO:
Application materials should be sent by
regular mail, fax or e-mail to:
Chairperson, Fellowship Committee
YIVO Institute for Jewish Research.

Applicants should include the following
materials:
(1) curriculum vitae, including all contact
information and detailing education;
publications; other scholarly activity (papers
presented, etc.); teaching and other relevant
work experience; knowledge of relevant
languages; honors, awards and fellowships,
etc.;
(2) research proposal of no more than four
pages, including aims for research during the
period of fellowship; whether the proposed
work is part of a larger project, such as a
dissertation, book, etc.; how the resources of
YIVO will contribute to the work and;
(3) two letters of support, which discuss the
importance of the applicant's work for the
relevant field, as well as the applicant's
ability to carry out the proposed work.

Applicants may apply for one fellowship
only.
Duration: Two to three months.
Deadline: January 15.

PUBLICATIONS:
Yedies: News from YIVO.

BOARD OF DIRECTORS:
Ruth Levine, Chairman
Irena Pletka, Vice Chairman
Edward Blank
Martin Flumenbaum
Emil Kleinhaus
Dr. Chava Lapin
Leo Melamed
Jacob Morowitz
Eliza New
Ilya Prizel
John Richmond
Harry Wagner

ADDRESS INQUIRIES TO:
Ben Kaplan, Director of Education
Max Weinreich Center for
Advanced Jewish Studies
(See address above.)

*PLEASE NOTE:
Each fellowship requires up to three months'
research stay and at least one public lecture
by the holder.

YIVO INSTITUTE FOR JEWISH RESEARCH [596]
15 West 16th Street, 3rd Floor
New York, NY 10011-6301
(212) 294-6139
Fax: (212) 292-1892
E-mail: eportnoy@yivo.cjh.org
Web Site: www.yivo.org

FOUNDED: 1925

AREAS OF INTEREST:
Eastern European Jewish studies.

NAME(S) OF PROGRAMS:
● **Fellowship in Baltic Jewish Studies**
● **Fellowship in East European Jewish Studies**
● **Fellowship in Polish Jewish Studies**

TYPE:
Fellowships. Fellowship in Baltic Jewish
Studies supports original doctoral or
postdoctoral research in the field of
Lithuanian Jewish history at the YIVO
Library and Archives or travel for Ph.D.
dissertation research in archives and libraries
of the Baltic states.

Fellowship in East European Jewish Studies
supports doctoral or postdoctoral research in
the field of East European Jewish studies.
Research is to be conducted at the YIVO
Library and Archives.

Fellowship in Polish Jewish Studies supports
doctoral or postdoctoral research on
Polish-Jewish history in the modern period,
particularly Jewish-Polish relations, including
the Holocaust period, and Jewish
contributions to Polish literature and culture.
This Fellowship is for research at the YIVO
Library and Archives.

PURPOSE:
To advance Eastern European Jewish studies.

FINANCIAL DATA:
Amount of support per award: Fellowship in
Baltic Jewish Studies and Fellowship in
Polish Jewish Studies: $4,000; Fellowship in
East European Jewish Studies: $15,000.

NO. AWARDS: 1 per award.

APPLICATION INFO:
Applications should include a curriculum
vitae, a research proposal (four-page
maximum), and two letters of support.
Duration: Varies.
Deadline: January 1.

ADDRESS INQUIRIES TO:
Dr. Eddy Portnoy, Senior Researcher
Max Weinreich Center
(See address above.)

*PLEASE NOTE:
Fellows are usually expected to spend four to
six weeks in residence and are required to
give one public lecture.

*SPECIAL STIPULATIONS:
Applicants may apply for one fellowship
only.

YIVO INSTITUTE FOR JEWISH RESEARCH [597]
15 West 16th Street, 3rd Floor
New York, NY 10011-6301
(212) 294-6139
Fax: (212) 292-1892
E-mail: eportnoy@yivo.cjh.org
Web Site: www.yivo.org

FOUNDED: 1925

AREAS OF INTEREST:
Eastern European Jewish studies.

NAME(S) OF PROGRAMS:
● **The Dina Abramowicz Emerging Scholar Fellowship**
● **The Workmen's Circle/Dr. Emanuel Patt Visiting Professorship**

TYPE:
Fellowships; Visiting scholars. The Dina
Abramowicz Emerging Scholar Fellowship is
intended for postdoctoral research on a topic
in Eastern European Jewish studies. The
work should lead to a significant scholarly
publication and may encompass the revision
of a doctoral dissertation. The Fellowship
carries a stipend for the holder to conduct
research at the YIVO Library and Archives.

The Workmen's Circle/Dr. Emanuel Patt
Visiting Professorship in Eastern European
Jewish Studies, established by the Van
Cortlandt Workmen's Circle Community
House, is designed to support postdoctoral
research at the YIVO Library and Archives.

PURPOSE:
To advance Eastern European Jewish studies.

FINANCIAL DATA:
Amount of support per award: Abramowicz Fellowships: $3,000; Workmen's Circle: $5,000.

APPLICATION INFO:
Applications should include a cover letter indicating one choice of fellowship, a curriculum vitae, a research proposal (four-page maximum), and two letters of support.
Duration: Abramowicz Fellowship: Two to three months; Workmen's Circle/Patt Professorship: Three months.
Deadline: January 1.

ADDRESS INQUIRIES TO:
Dr. Eddy Portnoy, Senior Researcher
Max Weinreich Center
(See address above.)

*PLEASE NOTE:
Fellows are usually expected to spend four to six weeks in residence and are required to give one public lecture.

*SPECIAL STIPULATIONS:
Applicants may apply for one fellowship only.

Languages

THE AMERICAN CLASSICAL LEAGUE [598]
860 N.W. Washington Boulevard
Suite A
Hamilton, OH 45013
(513) 529-7741
Fax: (513) 529-7742
E-mail: littles@aclclassics.org
Web Site: www.aclclassics.org

FOUNDED: 1919

AREAS OF INTEREST:
Latin and Classical Studies of ancient Rome and Greece.

CONSULTING OR VOLUNTEER SERVICES:
Placement service for teachers of Latin.

TYPE:
Grants-in-aid; Scholarships.

YEAR PROGRAM STARTED: 1975

PURPOSE:
To assist teachers of Latin and Greek further their educational background.

LEGAL BASIS:
Nonprofit.

ELIGIBILITY:
Applicant must be a member of American Classical League for the preceding three years and current year and teaching Latin or Greek courses.

FINANCIAL DATA:
Amount of support per award: Maximum $2,000 per individual.
Total amount of support: Varies.

NO. MOST RECENT APPLICANTS: Varies.

NO. AWARDS: Varies.

APPLICATION INFO:
The application form and guidelines are available on the League web site.
Duration: One-time award.
Deadline: January 15 and March 15. Awards announced February 15 and April 15, respectively.

ADDRESS INQUIRIES TO:
Sherwin Little, Executive Director
(See address above.)

AMERICAN INSTITUTE OF INDIAN STUDIES [599]
1130 East 59th Street
Chicago, IL 60637
(773) 702-8638
E-mail: aiis@uchicago.edu
Web Site: www.indiastudies.org

FOUNDED: 1961

AREAS OF INTEREST:
Indian studies.

NAME(S) OF PROGRAMS:
● **Advanced Language Program in India**

TYPE:
Fellowships. Awards for studies in India in an Indian language.

YEAR PROGRAM STARTED: 1969

PURPOSE:
To provide advanced language training in India.

LEGAL BASIS:
Cooperative, nonprofit organization of 90 American colleges and universities.

ELIGIBILITY:
Open to graduate and junior or senior-level undergraduate students in U.S. colleges and universities who have had a minimum of two years or 240 class hours of classroom instruction in Bengali, Hindi or Tamil and intend to pursue teaching degrees. Applicants for other Indian languages may be considered, but they should contact the AIIS for further information and advice. Applicants must be U.S. citizens.

FINANCIAL DATA:
Grants will be awarded on a competitive basis and will include round-trip airfare to India and a maintenance allowance sufficient to cover living expenses. No funding will be provided for dependents.

APPLICATION INFO:
Application forms are available online. All applications must include a $25 processing fee.
Duration: Nine months.
Deadline: December 31.

EXECUTIVE STAFF:
Elise Auerbach, Administrator

ADDRESS INQUIRIES TO:
Elise Auerbach, Administrator
(See address above.)

AMERICAN RESEARCH INSTITUTE IN TURKEY, INC.
c/o The University of Pennsylvania Museum
3260 South Street
Philadelphia, PA 19104-6324
(215) 898-3474
Fax: (215) 898-0657
E-mail: leinwand@sas.upenn.edu
Web Site: ccat.sas.upenn.edu/ARIT/index.html

TYPE:
Fellowships. Bogazici University Summer Language Program: For summer study in Turkey. Also offer travel, stipend and tuition grants. This intensive program offers the

equivalent of one full academic year of study in advanced Turkish language at the college level.

See entry 806 for full listing.

THE JAPAN FOUNDATION, NEW YORK
1700 Broadway
15th Floor
New York, NY 10019
(212) 489-0299
Fax: (212) 489-0409
E-mail: info@jfny.org
Web Site: www.jfny.org

TYPE:
Conferences/seminars; Fellowships; Professorships; Project/program grants; Research grants; Travel grants. The Japanese Studies Fellowship Program has three components: Doctoral Fellowship, Long-term Research Fellowship, and Short-term Research Fellowship.

See entry 775 for full listing.

KOBE COLLEGE CORPORATION-JAPAN EDUCATION EXCHANGE
540 West Frontage Road, Suite 3335
Northfield, IL 60093
(847) 386-7661
Fax: (847) 386-7662
E-mail: programs@kccjee.org
Web Site: www.kccjee.org

TYPE:
Awards/prizes. The KCC-JEE High School Essay Contest includes a one-month trip to Japan. It incorporates intensive language study, college credit and a home stay with a Japanese family.

See entry 837 for full listing.

LUSO-AMERICAN EDUCATION FOUNDATION [600]
7080 Donlon Way
Suite 200
Dublin, CA 94568
(925) 828-3883
Fax: (925) 828-4554
E-mail: education@luso-american.org
Web Site: www.luso-american.org/laef

FOUNDED: 1963

AREAS OF INTEREST:
Perpetuation of the Portuguese language and culture in the U.S.

NAME(S) OF PROGRAMS:
● **Luso-American Education Foundation Scholarships**

TYPE:
Scholarships.

LEGAL BASIS:
Tax-exempt corporation.

ELIGIBILITY:
For the General Youth Scholarship, the applicant must currently be a high school graduating senior enrolled in a junior or four-year college or university, or in a trade or business school, and an official U.S. resident. He or she must also meet one of the following requirements:
(1) being of Portuguese descent, with a minimum grade point average of 3.5;
(2) currently taking Portuguese classes at

high school level, with a minimum grade point average of 3.0 or;
(3) having attended the Luso-American Education Foundation Cultural Youth Summer Camp for a minimum of two years, with a minimum grade point average of 3.0.

FINANCIAL DATA:
Amount of support per award: $1,000 per year.

NO. AWARDS: 19 for the year 2021.

APPLICATION INFO:
The following materials must be submitted:
(1) a completed scholarship application;
(2) an official transcript of all completed high school work (proof of grade point average); these must be issued and certified by a school official;
(3) two letters of recommendation from a personal acquaintance, teacher, or counselor who can speak of applicant's character and/or financial need and;
(4) a recent wallet-size photo of applicant. Photo can be e-mailed to educatopn@luso-american.org, but must include applicant's full name.
Duration: One year. Renewable for one to three additional years, depending on type of institution.
Deadline: Key dates are posted on the Foundation web site.

PUBLICATIONS:
Program announcement.

ADDRESS INQUIRIES TO:
Bernice Pelicas
Administrative Director
(See address or e-mail above.)

LUSO-AMERICAN EDUCATION FOUNDATION   [601]
7080 Donlon Way
Suite 200
Dublin, CA 94568
(925) 828-3883
Fax: (925) 828-4554
E-mail: education@luso-american.org
Web Site: www.luso-american.org/laef

FOUNDED: 1963

AREAS OF INTEREST:
Perpetuation of the Portuguese language and culture in the U.S., Portuguese education and the teaching of Portuguese in California schools and universities.

CONSULTING OR VOLUNTEER SERVICES:
Provides advisory and reference services, assists teachers and school districts in setting up Portuguese language and literature courses, choosing texts, etc., makes referrals to other sources of information, permits on-site use of collection and holds annual Conference on Portuguese-American Education for educators, administrators and community persons. Services are free and available to people across the U.S.

NAME(S) OF PROGRAMS:
● **Educational Grant Program**

TYPE:
Grants-in-aid; Research grants. The Foundation provides a variety of grant programs: research grants, Portuguese language-program grants, study-abroad (in Portugal) grants, and educator (of Portuguese language and/or culture) grants.

YEAR PROGRAM STARTED: 1970

PURPOSE:
To lead initiatives for the advances of the Portuguese culture and language; to support qualified students in accessing higher education; and to foster life-long learning programs.

LEGAL BASIS:
Tax-exempt corporation.

ELIGIBILITY:
Varies with the program.

FINANCIAL DATA:
Amount of support per award: Grants vary in amount, depending on the applicant's need and Foundation funds allocated.
Total amount of support: Varies.

NO. AWARDS: Varies.

APPLICATION INFO:
Form can be downloaded from the Foundation web site.
Deadline: Key days are posted on the Foundation web site.

PUBLICATIONS:
The Luso-American, annual; *Portuguese Presence in California*; *Literatura de Expressao Portuguesa Nos Estados Unidos*; bibliographies; annual report.

ADDRESS INQUIRIES TO:
Bernice Pelicas
Administrative Director
(See address or e-mail above.)

MODERN LANGUAGE ASSOCIATION OF AMERICA   [602]
85 Broad Street, Suite 500
New York, NY 10004-2434
(646) 576-5000
(646) 576-5141
Fax: (646) 458-0030
E-mail: awards@mla.org
Web Site: www.mla.org

FOUNDED: 1883

AREAS OF INTEREST:
Literary studies, languages and education.

NAME(S) OF PROGRAMS:
● **Morton N. Cohen Award for a Distinguished Edition of Letters**
● **Kenneth W. Mildenberger Prize**
● **Modern Language Association Prize for a Scholarly Edition**
● **Modern Language Association Prize for Independent Scholars**
● **Mina P. Shaughnessy Prize**

TYPE:
Awards/prizes.

PURPOSE:
To recognize outstanding scholarly work.

LEGAL BASIS:
Membership association.

ELIGIBILITY:
Authors are not required to be members of the Association.

The Morton N. Cohen Award is presented biennially in odd-numbered years for important collections of letters published in either of the two preceding years. A multivolume edition is eligible if at least one volume was published during that period. Editors can apply regardless of the fields they and the authors of the letters represent. The winning collection will be one that provides a clear, accurate and readable text, necessary

background information, and succinct and eloquent introductory material and annotations. The collection should be in itself a work of literature.

The Kenneth W. Mildenberger Prize is presented biennially in odd-numbered years for an outstanding publication in the field of teaching foreign languages and literatures.

The Modern Language Association Prize for a Scholarly Edition will be given biennially in odd-numbered years to a book published in either of the two preceding years without regard to the field or language either of the editor or of the text presented in the edition. To qualify for the award, an edition should be based on an examination of all available relevant textual sources; the source texts and the edited text's deviations from them should be fully described; the edition should employ editorial principles appropriate to the materials edited, and those principles should be clearly articulated in the volume; the text should be accompanied by appropriate textual and other historical contextual information; the edition should exhibit the highest standards of accuracy in the presentation of its text and apparatus; and the text and apparatus should be presented as accessibly and elegantly as possible.

The Modern Language Association Prize for Independent Scholars is awarded biennially in even-numbered years for a distinguished scholarly book published in the field of English or another modern language or literature. Authors enrolled in a program leading to an academic degree and authors holding a tenured, tenure-accruing or tenure-track position in a postsecondary institution at the time of publication of the book are not eligible. Tenure is understood to include any comparable provision for job security in a postsecondary educational institution.

The Mina P. Shaughnessy Prize is presented biennially in even-numbered years for an outstanding scholarly book in the fields of language, culture, literacy and literature that has a strong application to the teaching of English.

FINANCIAL DATA:
Amount of support per award: Varies.
Total amount of support: Varies.

APPLICATION INFO:
Application form is required for submissions to the Prize for Independent Scholars. To enter book into competition for other prizes, no special form or procedure is needed. Shipments of books should be preceded or accompanied by letters identifying the works.
Duration: One-time award.
Deadline: May 1.

ADDRESS INQUIRIES TO:
Annie M. Reiser, Coordinator of Book Prizes
(See address above.)

MODERN LANGUAGE ASSOCIATION OF AMERICA   [603]
85 Broad Street, Suite 500
New York, NY 10004-2434
(646) 576-5000
(646) 576-5141
Fax: (646) 458-0030
E-mail: awards@mla.org
Web Site: www.mla.org

FOUNDED: 1883

AREAS OF INTEREST:
  Literary studies, languages and education.

NAME(S) OF PROGRAMS:
  - **Matei Calinescu Prize**
  - **Katherine Singer Kovacs Prize**
  - **Fenia and Yaakov Leviant Memorial Prize in Yiddish Studies**
  - **James Russell Lowell Prize**
  - **Howard R. Marraro Prize**
  - **MLA Prize for a First Book**
  - **MLA Prize for an Edited Collection**
  - **MLA Prize for Collaborative, Bibliographical or Archival Scholarship**
  - **MLA Prize in United States Latina and Latino and Chicana and Chicano Literary and Cultural Studies**
  - **Lois Roth Award for a Translation of a Literary Work**
  - **Aldo and Jeanne Scaglione Prize for a Translation of a Literary Work**
  - **Aldo and Jeanne Scaglione Prize for a Translation of a Scholarly Study of Literature**
  - **Aldo and Jeanne Scaglione Prize for Comparative Literary Studies**
  - **Aldo and Jeanne Scaglione Prize for French and Francophone Studies**
  - **Aldo and Jeanne Scaglione Prize for Italian Studies**
  - **Aldo and Jeanne Scaglione Prize for Studies in Slavic Languages and Literatures**
  - **Aldo and Jeanne Scaglione Prize for Studies in Germanic Languages and Literatures**
  - **Aldo and Jeanne Scaglione Publication Award for a Manuscript in Italian Literary Studies**
  - **William Sanders Scarborough Prize**

TYPE:
  Awards/prizes. To recognize outstanding scholarly works in the fields of English, French, Italian, Germanic languages and Slavic languages, Yiddish literature and culture, Black American literature and culture, Latino/Latina and Chicana/Chicano literature and culture. Germanic languages include Danish, Dutch, German, Icelandic, Norwegian, Swedish and Yiddish.

  The Fenia and Yaakov Leviant Memorial Prize in Yiddish Studies, the Howard R. Marraro Prize, the Aldo and Jeanne Scaglione Prize for a Translation of a Literary Work and the Aldo and Jeanne Scaglione Prize for Studies in Germanic Languages and Literatures are offered biennially in even-numbered years. The MLA Prize in United States Latina and Latino and Chicana and Chicano Literary and Cultural Studies, the Lois Roth Award for a Translation of a Literary Work, the Aldo and Jeanne Scaglione Prize for a Translation of a Scholarly Study of Literature, the Aldo and Jeanne Scaglione Prize for Italian Studies, and the Aldo and Jeanne Scaglione Prize for Studies in Slavic Languages and Literatures are offered biennially in odd-numbered years. All others are awarded annually.

PURPOSE:
  To recognize outstanding scholarly work.

LEGAL BASIS:
  Membership association.

ELIGIBILITY:
  For all awards, works of literary history, literary criticism, philology or literary theory are eligible. Except for translation prizes, books that are primarily translations are ineligible. For French, Germanic, Italian,

Lowell, First Book and Marraro Prizes, books must be written by a current member of the Association.

FINANCIAL DATA:
  Amount of support per award: Varies.

APPLICATION INFO:
  To enter books into competition for prizes, no special form or procedure is needed. Four to six copies of each work are required, depending upon the prize. Shipments of books should be preceded or accompanied by letters identifying the works and where necessary, confirming the author's membership in the MLA.

  Duration: One-time awards.

  Deadline: James Russell Lowell Prize and Prize for a First Book: March 1. Matei Calinescu Prize, Lois Roth Award and Scaglione Prize for a Translation of a Literary Work: April 1. Scaglione Publication Award for a Manuscript in Italian Literary Studies: June 1. All other awards: May 1.

ADDRESS INQUIRIES TO:
  Annie M. Reiser, Coordinator of Book Prizes (See address above.)

NATIONAL SCIENCE FOUNDATION   [604]
Division of Behavioral and Cognitive Sciences
2415 Eisenhower Avenue, W13
Alexandria, VA 22314
(703) 292-2434
E-mail: tkendall@nsf.gov
Web Site: www.nsf.gov

FOUNDED: 1950

NAME(S) OF PROGRAMS:
  - **Linguistics Program**
  - **Linguistics Program-Doctoral Dissertation Research Improvement Grants (Ling-DDRI)**
  - **NSF Dynamic Language Infrastructure-NEH Documenting Endangered Languages (DLI-DEL)**
  - **Dynamic Language Infrastructure-Doctoral Dissertation Research Improvement Grants (DLI-DDRI)**

TYPE:
  Research grants. Conferences/workshops. Awards provide support for research into the syntactic, morphological, semantic, phonological and phonetic properties of individual languages and of language in general. Research into the acquisition of language, the psychological processes in the production and perception of language, the social influences on language and dialect variation, and the formal and mathematical properties of language models is also supported.

YEAR PROGRAM STARTED: 1975

PURPOSE:
  To support scientific research and education to strengthen research potential in language sciences.

LEGAL BASIS:
  National Science Foundation Act of 1950.

ELIGIBILITY:
  Applicants may be U.S. colleges and universities on behalf of their staff members, nonprofit, nonacademic research institutions, such as independent museums, observatories, research laboratories and similar

organizations, private profit organizations and, under special circumstances, unaffiliated U.S. scientists.

FINANCIAL DATA:
  Support may cover research assistantships, staff benefits if a direct cost, permanent equipment, travel, publication costs, computer costs and certain other direct and indirect costs.

  Amount of support per award: Averages $350,000 over three-year grant period; DLI-DDRI: Not more than $15,000 in direct costs; Ling-DDRI: Not more than $12,000 in direct costs.

  Total amount of support: Approximately $6,250,000 for fiscal year 2019; $3,100,000 for DLI-DEL.

CO-OP FUNDING PROGRAMS: DLI-DEL in partnership with the National Endowment for the Humanities.

NO. MOST RECENT APPLICANTS: Approximately 250 for the year 2019; 80 for DLI-DEL.

APPLICATION INFO:
  Proposal should include information about the institution, principal investigator and business administrator, title and description of proposed research, desired effective date of grant, duration of support, facilities, personnel, biographical sketches, current support and pending applications and budget.

  Duration: Most grants are for two to three years.

  Deadline: Linguistics Program, including DDRIs: Target dates are July 15 for Fall review and January 15 for Spring review. Proposals received too late for one round of review will be reviewed in the following round with a corresponding delay in the availability of funding. DLI-DDRI dissertation proposals may be submitted at any time. DLI-DEL: February 15 and September 15.

PUBLICATIONS:
  NSF Proposal & Award Policies & Procedures Guide (PAPPG).

STAFF:
  Tyler Kendall, Program Director

ADDRESS INQUIRIES TO:
  Tyler Kendall, Program Director (See address above.)

PEN AMERICA   [605]
588 Broadway, Suite 303
New York, NY 10012
(212) 334-1660 ext. 4813
Fax: (212) 334-2181
E-mail: awards@pen.org
Web Site: pen.org

FOUNDED: 1922

AREAS OF INTEREST:
  Translated prose from any language into English.

NAME(S) OF PROGRAMS:
  - **PEN Translation Prize**

TYPE:
  Awards/prizes. Translation prize awarded for a distinguished translation into English from any language published in the U.S. during the award year.

YEAR PROGRAM STARTED: 1962

PURPOSE:
  To promote the art of translation; to pay tribute to the profession.

LEGAL BASIS:
Nonprofit organization affiliated with
International PEN.

ELIGIBILITY:
Although all eligible books must have been
published in the U.S. in 2021, translators
may be of any nationality; U.S. residency or
citizenship is not required. There are no
restrictions on the subject matter of translated
works, although eligible titles should be of a
literary character; technical, scientific, or
bibliographical translations will not be
considered. Translators and authors may not
submit their own work. Submissions will
only be accepted from publishers and literary
agents.

FINANCIAL DATA:
Amount of support per award: $3,000.
Total amount of support: $3,000 annually.

NO. MOST RECENT APPLICANTS: Approximately
200.

NO. AWARDS: 1 each year.

REPRESENTATIVE AWARDS:
Emma Ramadan, translator of *A Country for
Dying: A Novel*, by Abdellah Taia.

APPLICATION INFO:
Online application form can be found on the
Center web site beginning June 1. One copy
of a book-length literary translation published
during the calendar year under consideration
may be submitted by publishers or literary
agents. Early submissions are strongly
recommended.
Deadline: August 1.

ADDRESS INQUIRIES TO:
See e-mail address above.

THE PHI BETA KAPPA SOCIETY
1606 New Hampshire Avenue, N.W.
Washington, DC 20009
(202) 745-3287
Fax: (202) 986-1601
E-mail: awards@pbk.org
Web Site: www.pbk.org

TYPE:
Fellowships. Fellowship for at least six
months of study in France. One award given
annually.

See entry 847 for full listing.

SOUTH ATLANTIC MODERN LANGUAGE ASSOCIATION [606]
Georgia State University
Department of English
25 Park Place, N.E., Suite 2425
Atlanta, GA 30303
(404) 413-5816
Fax: (404) 413-5830
E-mail: samla@gsu.edu
Web Site: samla.memberclicks.net

FOUNDED: 1928

AREAS OF INTEREST:
All humanities.

NAME(S) OF PROGRAMS:
• **Graduate Student Creative Writing Award**
• **Graduate Student Essay Prize**
• **Harper Fund Award**
• **SAMLA Studies Award**
• **SAR Prize**
• **Undergraduate Essay Award**

TYPE:
Assistantships; Awards/prizes;
Conferences/seminars; Internships;
Professorships; Travel grants. SAMLA
Studies Award is for the best scholarly book
written by a SAMLA member. Presses and
individual members may nominate their
recent publications in the year prior to the
year of the convention.

YEAR PROGRAM STARTED: 1934

PURPOSE:
To encourage and honor distinguished
scholarship in the modern languages and
literatures.

LEGAL BASIS:
Nonprofit organization.

ELIGIBILITY:
Open to SAMLA members.

FINANCIAL DATA:
Amount of support per award: Graduate
Student Creative Writing Award and
Graduate Student Essay Prize: $250 per
award; Harper Fund Award: Based on annual
donations and not to exceed $500; SAMLA
Studies Award: $1,000; SAR Prize: $500;
Undergraduate Essay Award: $125.
Total amount of support: Varies.

NO. MOST RECENT APPLICANTS: Varies.

NO. AWARDS: Varies.

APPLICATION INFO:
SAMLA Studies Award: Applicants must be
SAMLA members who have a scholar
nominate their recent publications.
Duration: One-time award. Nonrenewable.
Deadline: Varies.

PUBLICATIONS:
South Atlantic Review, quarterly journal;
SAMLA News, newsletter.

IRS I.D.: 62-0800246

OFFICERS:
Rudyard Alcocer, President
Christina McDonald, First Vice President
Adam Parkes, Second Vice President

EXECUTIVE COMMITTEE:
Leticia Perez Alonso
Martine Boumtje
Bryan Giemza
Amy Hodges Hamilton
E. Nicole Meyer
Horacio Sierra

ADDRESS INQUIRIES TO:
Dan Abitz, Associate Director
(See address above.)

U.S. DEPARTMENT OF EDUCATION [607]
International and Foreign Language Education
Advanced Training and Research Division
400 Maryland Avenue, S.W.
Washington, DC 20202
(202) 453-7854
Fax: (202) 453-5780
E-mail: ifle@ed.gov
Web Site: www.ed.gov/ope/iegps

AREAS OF INTEREST:
Foreign language and area studies.

NAME(S) OF PROGRAMS:
• **Foreign Language and Area Studies Fellowships**

TYPE:
Fellowships. The Foreign Language and Area
Studies Fellowships program provides

allocations of academic year and summer
fellowships to institutions of higher education
or consortia of institutions of higher
education to assist meritorious undergraduate
students and graduate students undergoing
training in modern foreign languages and
related international or area studies.

YEAR PROGRAM STARTED: 1959

LEGAL BASIS:
Section 602, Title VI of the Higher
Education Act of 1965, as amended.

ELIGIBILITY:
FLAS grants are awarded to institutions for a
four-year project period. Institutions conduct
competitions to select eligible undergraduate
and graduate students to receive fellowships.
Funds may be used overseas with prior
approval from IFLE.

GEOG. RESTRICTIONS: United States.

FINANCIAL DATA:
Each fellowship includes an institutional
payment and a subsistence allowance.
Amount of support per award: The estimated
institutional payment for 2020-21 academic
year fellowship is $18,000 for a graduate
student and $10,000 for an undergraduate
student. The estimated institutional payment
for summer 2020 fellowship is $5,000 for
graduate and undergraduate students.
The estimated subsistence allowance for
academic year 2020-21 fellowship is $15,000
for a graduate student and $5,000 for an
undergraduate student. The subsistence
allowance for summer 2020 fellowship is
$2,500 for graduate and undergraduate
students.

APPLICATION INFO:
An electronic application form is available at
the web site.
Duration: Institutions: Four years.
Individuals: Academic year or summer.

ADDRESS INQUIRIES TO:
Carolyn Collins, Program Officer
(See address above.)

*PLEASE NOTE:
The next competition will take place in 2022.

U.S. DEPARTMENT OF EDUCATION [608]
International and Foreign Language Education
400 Maryland Avenue, S.W.
Room 258-24
Washington, DC 20202
(202) 453-6891
Fax: (202) 453-5780
E-mail: ddra@ed.gov
Web Site: www.ed.
gov/programs/iegpsddrap/index.html

AREAS OF INTEREST:
Foreign languages.

NAME(S) OF PROGRAMS:
• **Fulbright-Hays Doctoral Dissertation Research Abroad**

TYPE:
Fellowships. Fellowships to support doctoral
dissertation research abroad in modern
foreign languages and related area studies.
For the purpose of these programs, area
studies is defined as a program of
comprehensive study of the aspects of a
society or societies, including the study of
their geography, history, culture, economy,
politics, international relations and languages.
The program is designed to develop research
knowledge and capability in world areas not

widely included in American curricula. Awards will not be available for projects focusing on Western Europe.

YEAR PROGRAM STARTED: 1964

PURPOSE:
To enable graduate students who plan to teach in the U.S. to undertake doctoral dissertation research in the field of modern foreign languages and area studies; to assist with the development of language and area studies specialists.

LEGAL BASIS:
The Mutual Educational and Cultural Exchange Act of 1961, Public Law 87-256, as amended (commonly known as the Fulbright-Hays Act), Section 102(b)(6).

ELIGIBILITY:
A student is eligible to receive a fellowship if he or she:
(1) is a citizen or national of the U.S. or is a permanent resident of the U.S.;
(2) is a graduate student in good standing at an institution of higher education who, when the fellowship begins, is admitted to candidacy in a doctoral program in modern foreign languages and area studies at that institution;
(3) is planning a teaching career in the U.S. upon graduation and;
(4) possesses adequate skills in the language(s) necessary to carry out the dissertation project.

FINANCIAL DATA:
Travel expenses, including excess baggage to and from the residence of the fellow to the host country of research. Maintenance allowance based on the cost of living in country(ies) of research for the fellow and his or her dependent(s). Project allowance for research-related expenses such as books, affiliation fees, local travel and other incidental expenses. Health and accident insurance premiums. $100 administrative fee to applicant institution.

Amount of support per award: $33,461 average for the year 2020.

Total amount of support: $4,265,723 for the year 2020.

NO. MOST RECENT APPLICANTS: 300.

NO. AWARDS: 117 for the year 2020.

APPLICATION INFO:
Official application materials are available from college and university graduate schools concerned with the fellowship program. Prospective applicants must apply electronically through their institutions. The completed materials are then forwarded electronically by the institution to the U.S. Education Department's G5 e-Application system.

Duration: Fellowships provide support for a minimum period of six months and a maximum period of 12 months.

Deadline: Refer to web site or contact the Department of Education.

ADDRESS INQUIRIES TO:
Dr. Pamela Maimer
(See e-mail address above.)

U.S. DEPARTMENT OF EDUCATION [609]
Office of Postsecondary Education
International and Foreign Language Education (IFLE)
400 Maryland Avenue, S.W.
Mail Stop 257-09
Washington, DC 20202
(202) 453-5690
E-mail: IFLE@ed.gov
Web Site: www2.ed.gov/programs/iegpsnrc

AREAS OF INTEREST:
Area studies, international studies, and modern foreign languages.

NAME(S) OF PROGRAMS:
● **National Resource Centers (NRC) Program**

TYPE:
Project/program grants; Training grants. The NRC Program provides grants to institutions of higher education and consortia of institutions to establish, strengthen and operate comprehensive and undergraduate centers that will be national resources for:
(1) teaching of any modern foreign language;
(2) instruction in fields needed to provide full understanding of areas, regions or countries in which the modern foreign language is commonly used;
(3) research and training in international studies and the international and foreign language aspects of professional and other fields of study and;
(4) instruction and research on issues in world affairs that concern one or more countries.

This program operates on a four-year grant cycle.

PURPOSE:
To establish, strengthen and operate language and area or international studies centers that will be national resources for teaching any modern foreign language.

LEGAL BASIS:
Authorized under Section 602, Title VI of the Higher Education Act, as amended.

ELIGIBILITY:
Any institution of higher education or a combination of institutions of higher education may apply.

FINANCIAL DATA:
Amount of support per award: $188,000 to $270,000 (estimated) per year.

Total amount of support: $22,743,107 (estimated) for the year 2020.

NO. MOST RECENT APPLICANTS: 141.

NO. AWARDS: 100 institutional grants for fiscal year 2018.

APPLICATION INFO:
Guidelines are available on the NRC Program web site in late fall.
Duration: Four years.

ADDRESS INQUIRIES TO:
Cheryl E. Gibbs, Senior Director
International Foreign Language Education Office
(See address above.)

*PLEASE NOTE:
The NRC Program competes every four years. The next competition will be in fiscal year 2022. This is not a cost-share or matching grant program.

U.S. DEPARTMENT OF EDUCATION [610]
International and Foreign Language Education (IFLE)
Language Resource Centers Program
400 Maryland Avenue, S.W.
Mail Stop 258-40
Washington, DC 20202
(202) 453-7854
E-mail: carolyn.collins@ed.gov
Web Site: www2.ed.gov/programs/iegpslrc/index.html

AREAS OF INTEREST:
Foreign language education.

NAME(S) OF PROGRAMS:
● **Language Resource Centers Program**

TYPE:
General operating grants. Language Resource Centers Program provides grants for establishing, strengthening and operating centers that serve as resources for improving the nation's capacity for teaching and learning foreign languages through teacher training, research, materials development and dissemination projects.

PURPOSE:
To provide grants to institutions of higher education to establish, strengthen and operate resource centers that serve to improve the nation's capacity to teach and learn foreign languages.

ELIGIBILITY:
Applicant organizations must be institutions of higher education.

FINANCIAL DATA:
Amount of support per award: Average award: $171,673.

Total amount of support: $2,746,768 appropriated for fiscal year 2020.

NO. AWARDS: 16 for the year 2020.

APPLICATION INFO:
Details are available on the Program web site. Applications are submitted through grants.gov.
Duration: Four-year cycle.

ADDRESS INQUIRIES TO:
Carolyn Collins, Program Officer
Language Resource Centers Program
(See address above.)

*PLEASE NOTE:
The next competition will be in fiscal year 2022.

U.S. DEPARTMENT OF EDUCATION
International and Foreign Language Education
400 Maryland Avenue, S.W.
Mail Stop 258-40
Washington, DC 20202
(202) 453-6950
E-mail: gpa@ed.gov
Web Site: www2.ed.gov/programs/iegpsgpa/index.html

TYPE:
Exchange programs; Project/program grants; Seed money grants; Training grants; Travel grants. Also, study grants and grants for foreign language and area study programs of educational development for projects to be undertaken abroad. Grants are awarded to higher education institutions, nonprofit educational organizations, state department of education and consortium of such institutions, departments, organizations and

institutions which, in turn, enable professors, college and elementary and secondary school teachers and advanced students to attend seminars abroad and to travel and study in foreign countries in order to strengthen the institution's programs in foreign languages, area studies and world affairs.

See entry 854 for full listing.

U.S. DEPARTMENT OF EDUCATION

International and Foreign Language Education
400 Maryland Avenue, S.W.
Washington, DC 20202
(202) 453-6391
E-mail: tanyelle.richardson@ed.gov
Web Site: www.ed.gov/ope/iegps

TYPE:
Project/program grants; Seed money grants. Grants to plan, develop, and carry out a program to strengthen and improve undergraduate instruction in international studies and foreign languages. Projects primarily focus on curriculum and faculty development. Institutions of higher education and public and private nonprofit agencies and organizations may apply for funds to develop projects which have the potential for making an especially significant contribution to the improvement of undergraduate instruction in international and foreign language studies in the U.S.

See entry 1464 for full listing.

YIVO INSTITUTE FOR JEWISH RESEARCH

15 West 16th Street, 3rd Floor
New York, NY 10011-6301
(917) 606-8290
Fax: (212) 292-1892
E-mail: bkaplan@yivo.cjh.org
Web Site: www.yivo.org

TYPE:
Fellowships. Fellowship in East European Arts, Music, and Theater is designed to assist an undergraduate, graduate or postgraduate researcher in the fields of Eastern European Jewish arts, music and theater.

Fellowship in East European Jewish Literature is designed to assist an undergraduate, graduate or postgraduate researcher in Eastern European Jewish literature.

The stipend is intended to defray expenses connected with research in YIVO's music, art and theater collections and library.

See entry 595 for full listing.

Literature

THE AMERICAN-SCANDINAVIAN FOUNDATION   [611]

58 Park Avenue
New York, NY 10016
(212) 847-9724
Fax: (212) 686-1157
E-mail: grants@amscan.org
Web Site: www.amscan.org/fellowships-grants/translation-competition

FOUNDED: 1910

AREAS OF INTEREST:
Translations of poetry, fiction, drama or literary prose by a Scandinavian author born after 1900.

NAME(S) OF PROGRAMS:
- **American-Scandinavian Foundation Translation Competition**

TYPE:
Awards/prizes. Prize for translation of fiction (50 double-spaced manuscript pages) or poetry (25 double-spaced manuscript pages).

YEAR PROGRAM STARTED: 1980

PURPOSE:
To encourage English translation of contemporary Scandinavian literature.

LEGAL BASIS:
Nonprofit educational institution qualifying under statutes 501(c)(3), 509(a)(1) and 170(c)(2) of the IRS code.

ELIGIBILITY:
Entry must be work by one author, though not necessarily from a single work. It should be conceived as part of a book manuscript. A table of contents for the proposed book should also be included.

FINANCIAL DATA:
Amount of support per award: First prize: $2,500; Second and Third Prize: $2,000 each.
Total amount of support: $6,500.

NO. MOST RECENT APPLICANTS: 15.

NO. AWARDS: 3.

APPLICATION INFO:
Request rules for Translation Prize Competition. Applicants should submit one copy of work in original language and one copy of translation, including title page and table of contents. Name, address and telephone number of translator and title and author of the manuscript with the original language specified should be on a separate page. Translator must include written permission from author or author's agent for translation to be entered in competition and published in *Scandinavian Review.* Manuscripts accompanied by self-addressed, stamped envelope will be returned.
Duration: One-time award.
Deadline: June 15. Awards announced by November 1.

PUBLICATIONS:
Competition rules.

OFFICER:
Edward P. Gallagher, President

ADDRESS INQUIRIES TO:
Translation Prize Committee
(See e-mail address above.)

THE ASCAP FOUNDATION   [612]

250 West 57th Street
New York, NY 10107
(212) 621-6000
Web Site: ascapfoundation.org

FOUNDED: 1914

AREAS OF INTEREST:
Writing on the subject of music.

NAME(S) OF PROGRAMS:
- **The ASCAP Foundation Deems Taylor/Virgil Thomson Awards**

TYPE:
Awards/prizes. The ASCAP Foundation Deems Taylor/Virgil Thomson Awards

program recognizes books, articles and liner notes on the subject of music selected for their excellence.

YEAR PROGRAM STARTED: 1967

PURPOSE:
To encourage, recognize and reward excellence in a field that is vital to the health and growth of America's musical heritage.

LEGAL BASIS:
Membership association.

ELIGIBILITY:
Eligible authors must be, at the time of entry, U.S. citizens, U.S. permanent residents or enrolled students with a valid and current U.S. student visa. Entrant must be at least 18 years of age or the age of majority in the state or country of residence, whichever is older.

Written works (i.e., concert articles, pop articles, and recording liner notes) must be written in English and published in the U.S. during the previous calendar year. The subject matter may be biographical or critical, reportorial or historical, about music and/or its creators. Instructional textbooks, how-to guides, compilations of articles or essays, or works of fiction will not be accepted. Reprints or translations of works that were previously published outside of the U.S. that were first published in the U.S. in the previous calendar year are eligible.

If an article submitted as part of the submission is co-written, all co-writers shall be considered entrants and must consent to participation in the award and satisfy all eligibility criteria and requirements.

GEOG. RESTRICTIONS: United States.

FINANCIAL DATA:
Amount of support per award: Several categories of cash prizes, from $200 to $500.
Total amount of support: $2,000.

NO. MOST RECENT APPLICANTS: 150.

NO. AWARDS: 11 for the year 2019.

APPLICATION INFO:
Entrants must complete and electronically submit an application, which is available on the ASCAP Foundation web site. Additionally, entrant must submit electronically copy(ies) of articles or recording liner notes pertaining to pop or concert music. Only one article or one recording liner notes may be submitted in each category per entrant.

For recording liner notes, entrants must submit digital copies of the work to the Foundation. Recording liner notes should be limited to 4,500 words.

For articles, entrants must submit their work by uploading the article as part of his or her Online Application. Entrant's full name and contact information should be submitted electronically.

Duration: Annual award.

Deadline: June 4.

ADDRESS INQUIRIES TO:
Malaika Alvaro
The ASCAP Foundation Deems Taylor/Virgil Thomson Awards
E-mail: malvaro@ascap.com

ASIAN AMERICAN WRITERS' WORKSHOP [613]

112 West 27th Street
Suite 600
New York, NY 10001
E-mail: desk@aaww.org
Web Site: aaww.org

FOUNDED: 1991

AREAS OF INTEREST:
Creative writing.

NAME(S) OF PROGRAMS:
- **The Margins Fellowship**
- **Open City Fellowship**

TYPE:
Fellowships; Grants-in-aid. The Margins Fellowship supports writers of fiction, creative nonfiction, and poetry through a year-long program that includes a grant, mentorship with an established writer, residency time at the Millay Colony for the Arts, publication opportunities, and career guidance.

The Open City Fellowship is awarded to journalists and nonfiction writers who write from and about New York City's Asian and Muslim immigrant neighborhoods, including Sunset Park, Bay Ridge, Richmond Hill, and Jackson Heights. Fellows receive a grant and publication on *Open City*.

PURPOSE:
To nurture a new generation of Asian diasporic writers.

ELIGIBILITY:
Fellowships are offered to emerging writers of color based in New York City.

GEOG. RESTRICTIONS: New York, New York.

FINANCIAL DATA:
Amount of support per award: The Margins Fellowship: $5,000; Open City Fellowship: $2,500.

NO. AWARDS: The Margins Fellowship: 4; Open City Fellowship: 2.

APPLICATION INFO:
Details are available online.

Duration: The Margins Fellowship: One year. Open City Fellowship: Nine months.

STAFF:
Jafreen Uddin, Executive Director
Jyothi Natarajan, Editor-in-Chief
Lily Philpott, Programs Manager
Yasmin Adele Majeed, Editorial Coordinator

BOARD OF DIRECTORS:
Manan Ahmed
Jin Auh
Mariko Gordon
Jennifer Hayashida
Hua Hsu
Anne Ishii
Kirby Kim
Jennifer 8. Lee
Tan Lin
Monica Youn

ADDRESS INQUIRIES TO:
Jafreen Uddin, Executive Director
(See address above.)

THE ASSOCIATION OF WRITERS & WRITING PROGRAMS [614]

5700 Rivertech Court, Suite 225
Riverdale Park, MD 20737-1250
(240) 696-7700
(240) 696-7683
E-mail: supriya@awpwriter.org
Web Site: www.awpwriter.org

FOUNDED: 1967

AREAS OF INTEREST:
Creative writing; four genres: short fiction, poetry, creative nonfiction and the novel.

CONSULTING OR VOLUNTEER SERVICES:
The office provides information on curricula for courses or programs in creative writing and members of the Board of Directors occasionally visit campuses in order to consult with departments wishing to establish or improve creative writing programs. The office also sponsors the INTRO Journals Project, an annual competition of fiction, nonfiction and poetry by students of creative writing; runs job placement service for members interested in obtaining teaching and writing-oriented positions.

NAME(S) OF PROGRAMS:
- **AWP Award Series in the Novel**
- **Donald Hall Prize for Poetry**
- **Grace Paley Prize for Short Fiction**
- **Sue William Silverman Prize for Creative Nonfiction**

TYPE:
Awards/prizes. Annual open competitions for book-length manuscripts: a collection of short stories, a collection of poems, or a work of creative nonfiction of more than 60,000 words. The award in each case is the publication of the winning manuscript by a university press and a cash honorarium from AWP in addition to royalties from the publisher.

YEAR PROGRAM STARTED: 1974

PURPOSE:
To support American writers and creative writing programs in U.S. colleges and universities; to encourage the publication and distribution of good fiction, poetry and other creative writing; to improve the quality of literary education primarily at the college level, as well as at the public school level; to disseminate information useful to writers and students of writing.

LEGAL BASIS:
Nonprofit, tax-exempt corporation.

ELIGIBILITY:
Original works written in English are eligible.

Only book-length manuscripts are eligible (poetry: 48 pages minimum; short story collection and creative nonfiction: 150 to 300 manuscript pages; novel: at least 60,000 words).

The AWP Award Series is open to all authors writing original works in English. No mixed-genre manuscripts can be accepted. Criticism and scholarly monographs are not acceptable for creative nonfiction, which the Award Series defines as factual and literary writing that has the narrative, dramatic, meditative and lyrical elements of novels, plays, poetry, and memoirs.

To avoid conflict of interest and to avoid the appearance of a conflict of interest, former students of a judge (former students who studied with a judge in an academic degree-conferring program or its equivalent) are ineligible to enter the competition in the genre for which their former teacher is serving as judge.

FINANCIAL DATA:
Negotiations regarding book royalties are left to the author and publisher, but AWP has established minimum standards.

Amount of support per award: AWP Prize for the Novel: $2,500 each; Donald Hall Prize in Poetry and Grace Paley Prize in Short Fiction: $5,500 each.

Total amount of support: $16,000.

NO. MOST RECENT APPLICANTS: Nonfiction: 171; Novel: 298; Poetry: 935; Short Fiction: 267.

NO. AWARDS: 1 winner per genre; 2 finalists per genre.

APPLICATION INFO:
For the Award Series, submissions are only accepted via Submittable (online submissions manager).

Manuscripts must be uploaded between January 1 and February 28. If the author's name appears anywhere except the cover page, the manuscript will be disqualified. Do not attach acknowledgement of previous publications or a biographical note. No manuscripts will be returned. There is a $30 entry/reading fee for nonmembers, $20 for AWP members. Please read guidelines on Association's web site before uploading one's manuscript through Submittable.

Deadline: Manuscripts are accepted only with postmark between January 1 and February 28.

PUBLICATIONS:
Guidelines; *The Writer's Chronicle*, six times per year.

IRS I.D.: 05-0314999

EXECUTIVE DIRECTOR:
Cynthia Sherman

ADDRESS INQUIRIES TO:
Supriya Bhatnagar
Director of Publications
(See address above.)

*PLEASE NOTE:
Reading period from February 1 to September 30 each year.

BREAD LOAF WRITERS' CONFERENCE [615]

Middlebury College
204 College Street
Middlebury, VT 05753
(802) 443-5286
Fax: (802) 443-2087
E-mail: blwc@middlebury.edu
Web Site: www.middlebury.edu/bread-loaf-conferences/bl_writers

FOUNDED: 1926

AREAS OF INTEREST:
Poetry, fiction and nonfiction.

NAME(S) OF PROGRAMS:
- **Fellowship and Scholarship Program for Writers**

TYPE:
Fellowships; Scholarships. Fellowships and scholarships pay all or part of conference fees.

YEAR PROGRAM STARTED: 1926

PURPOSE:
To encourage writers at the beginning of their careers.

LEGAL BASIS:
Nonprofit.

ELIGIBILITY:
Fellowship candidates must have had one or two original books published. Privately printed books are not considered.

Candidates for tuition scholarships must have had their work published in recognized literary periodicals, but will not have published in book form.

People under 18 are not eligible.

FINANCIAL DATA:
Fellowships pay all conference fees, tuition, room and board. Tuition scholarships pay all conference fees, tuition but not room and board. Working scholarships pay part of tuition and room and board; recipients earn the remainder.
Amount of support per award: Varies.
Total amount of support: Varies.

NO. MOST RECENT APPLICANTS: 2,000.

NO. AWARDS: 60.

APPLICATION INFO:
Information is available online.
Duration: Usually one-time award.
Deadline: February 15. Announcement in May.

DIRECTORS:
Jennifer Grotz, Director
Lauren Francis-Sharma, Assistant Director

ADDRESS INQUIRIES TO:
Jason Lamb, Coordinator
(See address above.)

THE WITTER BYNNER FOUNDATION FOR POETRY, INC.   [616]
P.O. Box 10169
Santa Fe, NM 87504-0169
(505) 699-5178
E-mail: witterb123@gmail.com
Web Site: bynnerfoundation.org

FOUNDED: 1972

AREAS OF INTEREST:
Poetry, with special interest in developing the poetry audience, the process of poetry translation, uses of poetry (including but not limited to dramatic, educational, therapeutic, etc.) and the support of individual poets through existing institutional programs.

TYPE:
Project/program grants.

YEAR PROGRAM STARTED: 1972

PURPOSE:
To develop the poetic art through grant support to nonprofit organizations and individuals represented by such organizations.

LEGAL BASIS:
Exempt, private foundation.

ELIGIBILITY:
Only applications from nonprofit tax-exempt organizations will be accepted. No grants to individuals. Publication projects, endowment funds, capital improvements, continued support and operating expenses are not generally funded.

GEOG. RESTRICTIONS: United States.

FINANCIAL DATA:
Amount of support per award: $1,000 to $10,000.
Total amount of support: $77,000 for the year 2019-20.

NO. MOST RECENT APPLICANTS: 115 letters of intent for the year 2019-20.

NO. AWARDS: 15 grant programs for the year 2019-20.

REPRESENTATIVE AWARDS:
$5,000 to New Mexico School for the Arts; $3,000 to Partners in Education; $5,000 to Reel Fathers; $6,000 to White Pine Press.

APPLICATION INFO:
Upon request, the Foundation's guidelines, an annual report, and a list of the most recent grants will be provided. Applicants must submit a letter of intent prior to application.
Duration: One-year grants only. May be renewed at the discretion of the Board of Directors.
Deadline: February 15 annually. Announcement in May. Letters of intent accepted from August 1 to December 31 annually.

PUBLICATIONS:
Annual report; application guidelines.

IRS I.D.: 23-7169999

ADDRESS INQUIRIES TO:
See e-mail address above.

*SPECIAL STIPULATIONS:
The Foundation is interested particularly in using its limited funds as a means to help attract additional monies from other sources to advance the art of poetry. Applications to support the development of seed-money proposals in each of the above areas, therefore, are especially encouraged. While the Foundation has traditionally been supportive of the four areas listed above, it may consider the support of other creative and innovative projects in poetry.

CARNEGIE FUND FOR AUTHORS   [617]
P.O. Box 409
Lenox Hill Station
New York, NY 10021
E-mail: carnegiefundforauthors@gmail.com
Web Site: www.carnegiefundforauthors.org

FOUNDED: 1942

AREAS OF INTEREST:
Literary interests.

TYPE:
Grants-in-aid.

YEAR PROGRAM STARTED: 1942

PURPOSE:
To award grants to authors whose need has come about because of illness or other emergency.

ELIGIBILITY:
Applicant must be a published American writer who has suffered an emergency to oneself or a family member. Applicant must have had at least one book of reasonable length published by a mainstream publisher. Applicant cannot use any publication they paid to have published.

Grants are made to individuals who must be U.S. citizens or residents. Applicants must live in the U.S.

Grants are for authors in acute pressing need, not for those with chronic problems.

FINANCIAL DATA:
Amount of support per award: No fixed sum; based on need.

NO. AWARDS: 20 for the year 2018.

APPLICATION INFO:
Applicants must request an application form and submit to the address above with all supporting documentation.
Duration: Lump-sum grant.
Deadline: Grants are voted on and distributed on a rolling basis.

IRS I.D.: 13-6084244

*PLEASE NOTE:
Grants are not given for travel, study or to complete projects.

CHILDREN'S LITERATURE ASSOCIATION   [618]
3525 Piedmont Road
Building 5, Suite 300
Atlanta, GA 30305
(630) 571-4520
Fax: (708) 876-5598
E-mail: info@childlitassn.org
Web Site: www.childlitassn.org

FOUNDED: 1973

AREAS OF INTEREST:
All aspects of children's literature scholarship, research and criticism.

NAME(S) OF PROGRAMS:
• **ChLA Diversity Research Grant**

TYPE:
Project/program grants; Research grants. ChLA Diversity Research Grant is a grant to support research related to children's and young adult cultural artifacts (including media, culture and texts) about populations that have been traditionally underrepresented or marginalized culturally and/or historically. Applications for this grant are to be considered annually and will be awarded as warranted.

YEAR PROGRAM STARTED: 2013

PURPOSE:
To promote scholarship and criticism in children's literature.

LEGAL BASIS:
International; tax-exempt 501(c)(3), nonprofit scholarly organization.

ELIGIBILITY:
Applications will be evaluated based upon the quality of the proposal and the potential of the project to enhance or advance Children's Literature studies. Funds may be used for - but are not restricted to - research-related expenses such as travel to special collections, subvention funds, or purchasing materials and supplies. The awards may not be used for obtaining advanced degrees, for researching or writing a thesis or dissertation, for textbook writing or for pedagogical projects. Winners must be members of the Children's Literature Association before they receive any funds. Winners must acknowledge ChLA in any publication or other presentation resulting from the grant.

Members of the ChLA Diversity Committee are not eligible to apply. Recipients of a Diversity Research Grant are not eligible to reapply until the third year from the date of the first award. (In the event the ChLA Board institutes another time interval - whether longer or shorter - the vote of the Board shall supersede the three-year interval rule.)

In a given year, if there are no proposals for the Diversity Research Grant that the Diversity and/or Grants Committee deems of sufficient quality to support ChLA's aims, no grants will be given; conversely, if there are multiple Diversity Research Grant proposals of high quality, it is possible that multiple grants will be made, in which case the award may be less than the proposed budget.

FINANCIAL DATA:
Amount of support per award: $500 to $1,500, depending upon the winning proposal's projected budgetary considerations.

APPLICATION INFO:
Forms and instructions are available on the Association's web site.
Deadline: Only applications that are complete and received as of midnight on February 1 will be considered. Winners will be notified in April, and the awards will be announced at the ChLA annual conference.

IRS I.D.: 38-2005828

ADDRESS INQUIRIES TO:
ChLA Grants Committee
(See address above.)

*SPECIAL STIPULATIONS:
Grant recipients are required to submit a progress report of the project to the chair of the Diversity Committee by April/May of the year following the award and a summary report of the completed project to the chair of the Diversity Committee by April/May of the second year, prior to the presentation of the ideas at the conference.

Each grant will be awarded with the expectation that the undertaking will lead to publication and make a significant contribution to the field of children's literature scholarship or criticism. Within two years of receiving the grant, the recipient will be asked to submit a paper proposal based upon the project for presentation at a ChLA annual conference.

CHILDREN'S LITERATURE ASSOCIATION   [619]
3525 Piedmont Road
Building 5, Suite 300
Atlanta, GA 30305
(630) 571-4520
Fax: (708) 876-5598
E-mail: info@childlitassn.org
Web Site: www.childlitassn.org

FOUNDED: 1973

AREAS OF INTEREST:
All aspects of children's literature scholarship, research and criticism.

NAME(S) OF PROGRAMS:
● **ChLA Beiter Graduate Student Research Grants**
● **ChLA Faculty Research Grants**

TYPE:
Conferences/seminars; Grants-in-aid; Project/program grants; Research grants. ChLA Beiter Graduate Student Research Grants are awarded for proposals of original scholarship with the expectation that the undertaking will lead to publication or a conference presentation and contribute to the field of children's literature criticism.

ChLA Faculty Research Grants are awarded for proposals dealing with criticism or original scholarship with the expectation that the undertaking will lead to publication and make a significant contribution to the field of children's literature in the area of scholarship or criticism. Proposals that deal with critical or original work in the areas of fantasy or science fiction for children or adolescents will be awarded the Margaret P. Esmonde Memorial Scholarship.

YEAR PROGRAM STARTED: 1978

PURPOSE:
To promote scholarship and criticism in children's literature.

LEGAL BASIS:
International; tax-exempt 501(c)(3), nonprofit scholarly organization.

ELIGIBILITY:
ChLA Beiter Research Grants for Graduate Students: Grant funds are not intended as income to assist in the completion of a graduate degree, but as support for research that may be related to the dissertation or Master's thesis. The grant may be used to purchase supplies and materials (e.g., books, videos, equipment), as research support (photocopying, etc.), or to underwrite travel to special collections or libraries. Winners must either be members of the Children's Literature Association or join the Association before they receive any funds. Students of ChLA Executive Board members or Scholarship Committee members are not eligible to apply.

ChLA Faculty Research Grants: Applications will be evaluated based upon the quality of the proposal and the potential of the project to enhance or advance children's literature studies. Funds may be used for (but are not restricted to) research-related expenses such as travel to special collections or purchasing materials and supplies. The awards may not be used for obtaining advanced degrees, for researching or writing a thesis or dissertation, for textbook writing, or for pedagogical projects. Winners must either be members of the Children's Literature Association or join the Association before they receive any funds. Members of the Executive Board of ChLA and of the Scholarship Committee are not eligible to apply.

FINANCIAL DATA:
ChLA Faculty Research Grants may be used for such expenses as transportation, living expenses or materials and supplies, but not for obtaining advanced degrees.
Amount of support per award: $500 to $1,500.
Total amount of support: Up to $10,000 annually for both grants.

NO. AWARDS: Varies.

APPLICATION INFO:
Forms and instructions are available on the Association's web site.
Duration: Varies. Usually a one-time award to run the length of the project or course of study.
Deadline: February 1. Announcement at the annual conference.

PUBLICATIONS:
Application guidelines.

IRS I.D.: 38-2005828

ADDRESS INQUIRIES TO:
ChLA Grants Committee
(See address above.)

*SPECIAL STIPULATIONS:
Winners should acknowledge ChLA in any publication resulting from the award.

GREAT LAKES COLLEGES ASSOCIATION NEW WRITERS AWARDS   [620]
535 West William Street
Suite 301
Ann Arbor, MI 48103
(734) 661-2350
Fax: (734) 661-2349
E-mail: wegner@glca.org
Web Site: www.glca.org

FOUNDED: 1962

AREAS OF INTEREST:
Education.

NAME(S) OF PROGRAMS:
● **New Writers Awards**

TYPE:
Awards/prizes. Winners invited to tour up to 13 Great Lakes Colleges. Honorarium and expenses included. Awards are made for yearly, first published best book of fiction, best book of poetry and best book of creative nonfiction. Judges of the awards are faculty members of literature and creative writing at member colleges.

YEAR PROGRAM STARTED: 1970

PURPOSE:
To promote new writers, literature and colleges.

LEGAL BASIS:
Association of independent, liberal arts colleges in Michigan, Indiana, Ohio and Pennsylvania.

ELIGIBILITY:
The book must be the first published volume in fiction, poetry, or creative nonfiction by the author. Only publishers may submit, on behalf of the author, one book in each category, four copies.

Entries submitted must be written in English and published in the U.S. or Canada.

GEOG. RESTRICTIONS: United States and Canada.

FINANCIAL DATA:
The award also covers the costs of a writer's travel when visiting GLCA member colleges.
Amount of support per award: At least $500 per college visited.

NO. MOST RECENT APPLICANTS: 150.

NO. AWARDS: 1 each for creative nonfiction, fiction and poetry.

APPLICATION INFO:
Visit the GLCA web site to download submission packet.
Deadline: June 25.

ADDRESS INQUIRIES TO:
New Writers Awards
(See address above.)

ITALIAN AMERICAN STUDIES ASSOCIATION
The Calandra Institute
25 West 43rd Street, 17th Floor
New York, NY 10036
(212) 642-2094
E-mail: webmaster@italianamericanstudies.net
Web Site: www.italianamericanstudies.net

TYPE:
Fellowships.

See entry 551 for full listing.

JEWISH BOOK COUNCIL   [621]
520 Eighth Avenue, 4th Floor
New York, NY 10018-4393
(212) 201-2920
Fax: (212) 532-4952
E-mail: info@jewishbooks.org
Web Site: www.jewishbookcouncil.org

FOUNDED: 1943

AREAS OF INTEREST:
Jewish literature.

NAME(S) OF PROGRAMS:
- **National Jewish Book Award-American Jewish Studies**
- **National Jewish Book Award-Anthologies and Collections**
- **National Jewish Book Award-Autobiography and Memoir**
- **National Jewish Book Award-Biography**
- **National Jewish Book Award-Book Club**
- **National Jewish Book Award-Children's Literature**
- **National Jewish Book Award-Contemporary Jewish Life and Practice**
- **National Jewish Book Award-Debut Fiction**
- **National Jewish Book Award-Education and Jewish Identity**
- **National Jewish Book Award-Fiction**
- **National Jewish Book Award-Food Writing and Cookbooks**
- **National Jewish Book Award-History**
- **National Jewish Book Award-Holocaust**
- **National Jewish Book Award-Modern Jewish Thought and Experience**
- **National Jewish Book Award-Poetry**
- **National Jewish Book Award-Scholarship**
- **National Jewish Book Award-Sephardic Culture**
- **National Jewish Book Award-Visual Arts**
- **National Jewish Book Award-Women's Studies**
- **National Jewish Book Award-Writing Based on Archival Material**
- **National Jewish Book Award-Young Adult Literature**

TYPE:
Awards/prizes. National Jewish Book Awards:
(1) Award to the author of a nonfiction book about the Jewish experience in North America;
(2) Award to the author of a book of essays, biographies, short stories, or other collected works by more than one author;
(3) Award to the author of an autobiography or personal memoir. The subject need not be a Jewish person or family, but must have significant relevance to the Jewish experience.
(4) Award to the author of a biography or family history. The subject need not be a Jewish person or family, but must have significant relevance to the Jewish experience;
(5) Award recognizing the power of books to inspire Jewish community and thought-provoking discussions.
(6) Award to the author of a book on a Jewish theme that is intended for children;

(7) Award to the author of a nonfiction book about current tools and resources of Jewish living within the greater Ashkenazic and Sephardic communities. These include, but are not limited to, cookbooks, holiday how-to books and life-cycle books;
(8) Award to the author of a debut novel or short-story collection with Jewish content;
(9) Award to the author of a nonfiction work that focuses on theory, history and/or practice of Jewish education. Textbooks are not eligible;
(10) Award to the author of a novel or short-story collection with Jewish content;
(11) Award to honor books that illuminate Jewish life, identity, and culture through a culinary lens.
(12) Award to the author of a nonfiction work about the Jewish historical experience. Books focusing primarily on the Holocaust do not belong in this category;
(13) Award to the author of a nonfiction book concerning the Holocaust including autobiographies, memoirs and academic studies;
(14) Award to the author of a nonfiction work addressing Sephardic and/or Ashkenazic Jewish thought and experience;
(15) Award to the author of a book of verse consisting primarily of poems of Jewish concern;
(16) Award to the author of a nonfiction selection that makes an original contribution to Jewish learning. This includes, but is not limited to, works on Bible, Rabbinics and Jewish Law;
(17) Award to the author of a book that explores the traditions and practices unique to Sephardic Jews;
(18) Award to the author of a work of one or more visual artists (painters, weavers, sculptors, photographers, etc.) which includes illustrations and images of Jewish content as a dominant component;
(19) Award to the author of a nonfiction book about women's role in the Jewish experience;
(20) Award to the author of a book of modern historical writing published in English based on archival material including footnotes and bibliography and;
(21) Award to the author of a book on a Jewish theme that is intended for young adults.

YEAR PROGRAM STARTED: 1949

PURPOSE:
To promote greater awareness of works of Jewish literature and scholarship.

LEGAL BASIS:
Not-for-profit organization.

ELIGIBILITY:
Books published during the current calendar year will be eligible, except anthologies of previously published material or collections of writings by various authors or reprints and revised editions, unless otherwise specified. No manuscripts are accepted.

Books must be published in the English language unless otherwise specified. This includes books translated into English from any other language.

FINANCIAL DATA:
Amount of support per award: Varies.
Total amount of support: Varies.

NO. MOST RECENT APPLICANTS: 400.

NO. AWARDS: 18 to 20 each year. Some awards are biennial.

APPLICATION INFO:
Guidelines and submission forms are available online in June.
Duration: One year.
Deadline: Submissions accepted early summer to late September.

PUBLICATIONS:
Application guidelines.

EXECUTIVE DIRECTOR:
Naomi Firestone-Teeter

ADDRESS INQUIRIES TO:
Naomi Firestone-Teeter, Executive Director
or
Evie Saphire-Bernstein, Program Director
(See address above.)

ROBERT F. KENNEDY HUMAN RIGHTS   [622]
1300 19th Street, N.W.
Suite 750
Washington, DC 20036
(202) 463-7575
Fax: (202) 463-6606
E-mail: info@rfkhumanrights.org
Web Site: rfkhumanrights.org

FOUNDED: 1968

NAME(S) OF PROGRAMS:
- **RFK Book Award**
- **RFK Journalism Awards**

TYPE:
Awards/prizes. The RFK Book Award recognizes authors whose works of moral insight and imagination uphold a vision of political inclusion, compassion and justice.

The RFK Journalism Awards celebrate excellence in journalism in 13 categories, from investigative journalism to satirical cartoons and documentary film.

YEAR PROGRAM STARTED: 1980

PURPOSE:
To carry forward the mission of Robert F. Kennedy.

LEGAL BASIS:
Tax-exempt public charity.

ELIGIBILITY:
Fiction and nonfiction books published in the U.S. in the previous calendar year are eligible.

FINANCIAL DATA:
Amount of support per award: Book Award: $2,500 Grand Prize; Journalism Awards: $1,000 to individual or news organization and $500 to college and high school winners.
Total amount of support: Varies.

NO. MOST RECENT APPLICANTS: Over 325.

NO. AWARDS: Varies.

APPLICATION INFO:
Entries may be made by either individual authors or publishers. There is a handling fee of $75 per entry. Books must be submitted in quadruplicate with an entry form clipped inside the front cover of each book.
Duration: One-time award.
Deadline: February.

PUBLICATIONS:
Rules for entry.

ADDRESS INQUIRIES TO:
Monica Duran, Development Associate
(See address above.)

KNIGHTS OF COLUMBUS VATICAN FILM LIBRARY AT ST. LOUIS UNIVERSITY [623]

Pius XII Memorial Library
St. Louis University
3650 Lindell Boulevard
St. Louis, MO 63108-3302
(314) 977-3090
Fax: (314) 977-3108
E-mail: vfl@slu.edu
Web Site: lib.slu.edu/special-collections/research/fellowship

AREAS OF INTEREST:
History, philosophy, theology, literature, art, science, paleogeography, codicology, illumination, text editing, and library history.

NAME(S) OF PROGRAMS:
- **Vatican Film Library Mellon Fellowship**

TYPE:
Fellowships; Travel grants. Stipendiary fellowship which includes cost of air travel within the continental U.S.

YEAR PROGRAM STARTED: 1976

PURPOSE:
To conduct research into Medieval and Renaissance manuscripts containing microfilm in the Vatican Film Library.

ELIGIBILITY:
Applicants must be at the postdoctoral level or be a graduate student formally admitted to Ph.D. candidacy and working on their dissertation. U.S. citizens and foreign nationals are eligible.

FINANCIAL DATA:
Fellowship provides the cost of air travel within the continental U.S.
Amount of support per award: $2,250 per month living allowance.
Total amount of support: Varies. Maximum allowance of $4,500 plus air travel.

NO. AWARDS: Varies.

APPLICATION INFO:
Applicants must write a brief project description and notify of the manuscripts to be consulted (for availability), including dates of proposed study, a curriculum vitae, as well as a select bibliography on titles related to project. Proposals should not exceed more than two to three pages. Doctoral applicants must include a letter of recommendation from their advisor.
Duration: Two to eight weeks. Fellows can reapply the following year.
Deadline: March 1 for June to August. June 1 for September to December. October 1 for January to May.

STAFF:
Gregory A. Pass, Ph.D., Assistant Dean for Special Collections and Director, Vatican Film Library

ADDRESS INQUIRIES TO:
See e-mail address above.

STEPHEN LEACOCK ASSOCIATES [624]

P.O. Box 854
Orillia ON L3V 6K8 Canada
E-mail: bettewalkerca@gmail.com
info@leacock.ca
Web Site: www.leacock.ca

FOUNDED: 1946

AREAS OF INTEREST:
Writing of humour by Canadians.

NAME(S) OF PROGRAMS:
- **Stephen Leacock Memorial Medal for Humour**

TYPE:
Awards/prizes. Stephen Leacock Memorial Medal for Humour is presented for a book of humour published in the current calendar year and written by a Canadian. A cash prize accompanies this award.

YEAR PROGRAM STARTED: 1947

PURPOSE:
To promote the writing of Canadian humour.

LEGAL BASIS:
Nonprofit charitable organization.

ELIGIBILITY:
The major emphasis of each entry must be on humor, but literary merit and insightful comment are also important. Books of cartoons and graphic novels are eligible only if they contain a substantial amount of textual material. All entries must carry an ISBN, and have been published in the current year. The language of the entry must be English. In the case of a translation from another language, the translation must have been published in the current year.

The author or authors must be Canadian citizens or landed immigrants and living at the time of publication.

FINANCIAL DATA:
Amount of support per award: Awardee receives a sterling silver medal plus a $15,000 (CAN) cash prize; two runners-up receive $3,000 (CAN) each.
Total amount of support: $21,000 (CAN).

NO. MOST RECENT APPLICANTS: 68.

NO. AWARDS: 1.

APPLICATION INFO:
There is an entry fee of $200 per entry to be sent by check in Canadian funds. Send eight copies of each title plus author biography to Stephen Leacock Associates. Work must be published in previous calendar year. Books are nonreturnable. Entries should be sent to: Mrs. Bette Walker, 149 Peter Street North, Orillia, ON L3V 4Z4 Canada.
Deadline: December 31.

PUBLICATIONS:
Newspacket.

BOARD OF DIRECTORS:
Michael Hill, President
Daphne Mainprize, Vice President and Chairman, Award Committee
John Hughes, Treasurer
Anne Kallin, Secretary

ADDRESS INQUIRIES TO:
Bette Walker
Chairman, Award Committee
E-mail: awardschair@leacock.ca
(See address above.)

*SPECIAL STIPULATIONS:
Authors must agree to be present for the Gala dinner.

WILLIAM MORRIS SOCIETY IN THE U.S.

P.O. Box 53263
Washington, DC 20009
E-mail: wmsusmembership@gmail.com
mroberts@tcnj.edu
Web Site: www.morrissociety.org

TYPE:
Fellowships; Research grants; Scholarships; Travel grants; Visiting scholars; Research contracts. Supports scholarly, creative, and translation projects about William Morris and his designs, writings and other work.

See entry 432 for full listing.

NATIONAL FEDERATION OF STATE POETRY SOCIETIES, INC. [625]

49 Kitchen Avenue
Harveys Lake, PA 18618
E-mail: paperlesspoets@gmail.com
Web Site: www.nfsps.com

FOUNDED: 1989

AREAS OF INTEREST:
Poetry.

NAME(S) OF PROGRAMS:
- **NFSPS College Undergraduate Poetry (CUP) Competition**

TYPE:
Awards/prizes; Travel grants. The College Undergraduate Poetry Competition consists of two awards: The Edna Meudt Memorial Award and the Florence Kahn Memorial Award.

YEAR PROGRAM STARTED: 1989

PURPOSE:
To encourage the study and writing of poetry.

ELIGIBILITY:
All undergraduate levels of study at an accredited U.S. university or college are eligible (freshman through senior).

GEOG. RESTRICTIONS: United States.

FINANCIAL DATA:
Amount of support per award: Each awardee receives $500 plus 75 copies of published manuscript and an additional $300 stipend for travel to the NFSPS Convention to give a reading.

NO. MOST RECENT APPLICANTS: Up to 25.

NO. AWARDS: 2.

APPLICATION INFO:
Applicant must submit a manuscript of 10 original poems. Consult web site for complete application information. Submissions may be made online via submittable.com.
Deadline: Applications are accepted December 1 to January 31. One anonymous, highly qualified judge will evaluate, judge and select scholarship winners on or before March 12.

ADDRESS INQUIRIES TO:
Steven Concert, Chairperson
College Undergraduate Poetry Competition
(See address above.)

THE NATIONAL POETRY SERIES [626]

57 Mountain Avenue
Princeton, NJ 08540
(609) 430-0999
Fax: (609) 430-9933
E-mail: npspoetry@gmail.com
Web Site: nationalpoetryseries.org

FOUNDED: 1978

AREAS OF INTEREST:
Poetry.

NAME(S) OF PROGRAMS:
- **National Poetry Series Open Competition**

TYPE:
Awards/prizes.

YEAR PROGRAM STARTED: 1978

PURPOSE:
To recognize and promote excellence in contemporary poetry.

LEGAL BASIS:
Nonprofit, private.

ELIGIBILITY:
The National Poetry Series seeks book-length manuscripts of poetry written by American residents or American citizens living abroad. All manuscripts must be previously unpublished, although some or all of the individual poems may have appeared in periodicals. Translations, chapbooks, small groups of poems and books previously self-published are not eligible. Manuscript length is not limited; however, a length of 48 to 64 pages is suggested.

GEOG. RESTRICTIONS: United States.

FINANCIAL DATA:
Arrangements are between author and publisher.
Amount of support per award: $10,000 and book publication.
Total amount of support: $50,000.

NO. MOST RECENT APPLICANTS: 1,850.

NO. AWARDS: 5.

APPLICATION INFO:
Manuscripts are submitted online via the web site. Each manuscript must be accompanied by an entrance fee of $35.

Manuscripts must include two cover pages: (1) title of manuscript, author's name, address and telephone number (this should be the only page with author's identification) and;
(2) title of manuscript only.

Manuscripts must be paginated and contain a Table of Contents. Do not include acknowledgments, explanatory statements, resumes, autobiographical statements, photographs, illustrations or artwork. These will not be considered.

A list of previous publications or appearances in periodicals should not be included.
Duration: One-time award.
Deadline: March 15.

PUBLICATIONS:
Guidelines.

STAFF:
Daniel Halpern, Director
Beth Dial, Coordinator

ADDRESS INQUIRIES TO:
Coordinator, National Poetry Series
(See address above.)

PEN AMERICA   [627]
588 Broadway, Suite 303
New York, NY 10012
(212) 334-1660 ext. 4813
Fax: (212) 334-2181
E-mail: awards@pen.org
Web Site: pen.org

NAME(S) OF PROGRAMS:
- **PEN/Hemingway Award for a Debut Novel**

TYPE:
Awards/prizes. Awarded annually for the first published book-length work of fiction by an American writer.

YEAR PROGRAM STARTED: 1976

PURPOSE:
To recognize literary excellence and to honor debut fiction.

LEGAL BASIS:
Nonprofit organization affiliated with International PEN.

ELIGIBILITY:
First published novel by an American citizen or resident, published in the U.S. in 2021. Self-published books are not eligible.

GEOG. RESTRICTIONS: United States.

FINANCIAL DATA:
Amount of support per award: $10,000.
Total amount of support: $10,000.

NO. MOST RECENT APPLICANTS: 150.

NO. AWARDS: 1 winner and 2 honorable mentions.

APPLICATION INFO:
Application process begins on June 1. Submissions are only accepted from publishers or literary agents. Authors may not submit their own book. Full guidelines are available on the web site.
Duration: One-time award.
Deadline: August 1.

ADDRESS INQUIRIES TO:
See e-mail address above.

*SPECIAL STIPULATIONS:
Self-published books, electronic submissions or e-books are not eligible for consideration.

PEN AMERICA   [628]
588 Broadway, Suite 303
New York, NY 10012-5258
(212) 334-1660
Fax: (212) 334-2181
E-mail: prisonwriting@pen.org
Web Site: pen.org

FOUNDED: 1922

AREAS OF INTEREST:
Writing of literature and poetry.

NAME(S) OF PROGRAMS:
- **PEN Prison Writing Program**

TYPE:
Awards/prizes.

YEAR PROGRAM STARTED: 1971

PURPOSE:
To help incarcerated writers develop their writing talents and to promote writing as a means of rehabilitation.

LEGAL BASIS:
Tax-exempt, nonprofit organization.

ELIGIBILITY:
U.S. federal, state or county prisoners in the year before the deadline may apply. Only unpublished manuscripts will be considered, except those that have appeared in a prison publication.

GEOG. RESTRICTIONS: United States.

FINANCIAL DATA:
In addition to prize money, all winners are awarded the opportunity to correspond with a writing mentor.

Amount of support per award: First prize: $250, Second prize: $150, Third prize: $100, honorable mention: $25. Prizes are given for each of five categories: Poetry, Fiction, Essay, Memoir and Drama.

NO. MOST RECENT APPLICANTS: 1,500.

NO. AWARDS: Approximately 35 annually.

APPLICATION INFO:
Manuscripts must be typewritten (double-spaced) or clearly printed on standard letter-size paper. Also accept alternative submissions. Authors must not submit more than one entry in each category except in poetry. Name, inmate number and address must appear on each submission.
Duration: One-time award.
Deadline: September 1. Winners announced in Spring.

PUBLICATIONS:
PEN Handbook for Writers in Prison (lists resources available to inmates and journals interested in prison writing).

STAFF:
Robert Pollock, Prison and Justice Writing Program Manager

ADDRESS INQUIRIES TO:
PEN Writing Award for Prisoners
(See address above.)

PEN AMERICA   [629]
588 Broadway, Suite 303
New York, NY 10012
(212) 334-1660
Fax: (212) 334-2181
E-mail: writersfund@pen.org
Web Site: pen.org/writers-emergency-fund

FOUNDED: 1922

AREAS OF INTEREST:
Literature, free expression and international literary fellowship.

NAME(S) OF PROGRAMS:
- **PEN America Writers' Emergency Fund**

TYPE:
Grants-in-aid. Emergency fund for professional (published or produced) writers in acute, emergency financial crisis.

YEAR PROGRAM STARTED: 1958

PURPOSE:
To assist professional literary writers in times of short-term financial emergency and also to assist writers and editors with AIDS or HIV; to advance literature, defend free expression and foster international literary fellowship.

LEGAL BASIS:
Nonprofit organization affiliated with International PEN.

ELIGIBILITY:
The fund aims to assist professional (published or produced) writers facing unexpected financial and medical emergencies, and those who are HIV-positive. The fund does not exist for research purposes, for completing projects or to support publications or organizations. Must be a permanent U.S. resident or citizen. Self-published writers are not eligible.

GEOG. RESTRICTIONS: United States.

FINANCIAL DATA:
Amount of support per award: $500 to $1,000.

NO. AWARDS: Varies.

APPLICATION INFO:
Applicants should submit a completed application form, published writing samples, documentation of financial emergency and professional resume. Applications are accepted year-round and are reviewed every three months by the Writers' Fund Committee.

Application can be found at the above web site address.

Deadline: Mid-March, mid-June, mid-September and mid-December.

PUBLICATIONS:
Application; guidelines.

ADDRESS INQUIRIES TO:
See e-mail address above.

*SPECIAL STIPULATIONS:
Repeat grants to any one individual will not be given within a three-year period since last grant.

PEN AMERICA   [630]
588 Broadway, Suite 303
New York, NY 10012
(212) 334-1660 ext. 4813
Fax: (212) 334-2181
E-mail: awards@pen.org
Web Site: pen.org

FOUNDED: 1922

AREAS OF INTEREST:
Fiction, literary nonfiction, biography/memoir and poetry.

NAME(S) OF PROGRAMS:
● **PEN Open Book Award**

TYPE:
Awards/prizes. Invites submissions of book-length writings by authors of color, published during the calendar year.

PURPOSE:
To encourage racial and ethnic diversity within the literary and publishing communities.

ELIGIBILITY:
Open to authors of color who have not received wide media coverage. U.S. residency or citizenship is not required. Works of fiction, literary nonfiction, biography/memoir, poetry, and other works of literary character are strongly preferred. Authors may not submit their own work. Submissions will only be accepted from publishers or literary agents.

FINANCIAL DATA:
Amount of support per award: $10,000.

NO. MOST RECENT APPLICANTS: Approximately 250.

NO. AWARDS: 1.

APPLICATION INFO:
Online application form can be found on the Center web site beginning June 1. Publishers and agents may submit one copy of a book-length writing by an author of color published during the calendar year under consideration, with an official letter of recommendation. Self-published books are not eligible. Early submissions are strongly recommended.

Deadline: August 1 of each year.

ADDRESS INQUIRIES TO:
See e-mail address above.

PEN AMERICA   [631]
588 Broadway, Suite 303
New York, NY 10012
(212) 334-1660 ext. 4813
Fax: (212) 334-2181
E-mail: awards@pen.org
Web Site: pen.org

FOUNDED: 1922

AREAS OF INTEREST:
Children's/young adult fiction.

NAME(S) OF PROGRAMS:
● **PEN/Phyllis Naylor Grant for Children's and Young Adult Novelists**

TYPE:
Awards/prizes. The Fellowship is offered annually to an author of children's or young adult fiction for a novel-in-progress.

PURPOSE:
To recognize the fact that many writers' work is of high literary caliber but has not yet attracted a broad readership.

ELIGIBILITY:
A candidate is a writer of children's or young adult fiction demonstrating financial need. Candidate must have published at least one novel for children or young adults which have been warmly received by literary critics, but have not generated sufficient income to support the author. The writer's books must be published by a U.S. publisher.

FINANCIAL DATA:
Amount of support per award: $5,000.

NO. MOST RECENT APPLICANTS: 20.

NO. AWARDS: 1.

APPLICATION INFO:
Nomination process begins on April 1. Writers may nominate themselves or a fellow writer. This Fellowship will be judged blindly - the administrators will be aware of the nominee's names, but the judges will not. The application process is entirely online. Hard copy materials will no longer be accepted. The online application will require the following materials:
(1) a letter describing in some detail how they meet the criteria for the Fellowship, including a list of their published novel(s) for children or young adults;
(2) copies of at least three reviews of their novel(s) from professional publications;
(3) a letter of recommendation from an editor or fellow writer;
(4) one copy of the outline of the current novel in progress;
(5) one copy of 50 to 75 pages of the text. Picture books are not eligible. The writers' name should not appear anywhere on the manuscript, in order to ensure anonymity for the judging process and;
(6) on a separate piece of paper, a brief description of the candidate's recent earnings and a statement about why monetary support will make a particular difference in the applicant's writing life at this time. If the candidate is married or living with a domestic partner, please include a brief description of total family income and expense.

Deadline: June 1.

ADDRESS INQUIRIES TO:
See e-mail address above.

PEN AMERICA   [632]
588 Broadway, Suite 303
New York, NY 10012
(212) 334-1660 ext. 4813
Fax: (212) 334-2181
E-mail: awards@pen.org
Web Site: pen.org

FOUNDED: 1922

AREAS OF INTEREST:
Poetry in translation.

NAME(S) OF PROGRAMS:
● **PEN Award for Poetry in Translation**

TYPE:
Awards/prizes. The award recognizes book-length translations of poetry from any language into English published during the current calendar year and is judged by a single translator of poetry appointed by the PEN Translation Committee. The award was made possible originally by a bequest from the late translator and PEN member Rae Dalven, and has received current support from The Kaplen Foundation. It is conferred every spring in New York.

YEAR PROGRAM STARTED: 1963

PURPOSE:
To recognize book-length translations of poetry from any language into English published during the current calendar year.

ELIGIBILITY:
Eligible titles must be original book-length poetry translations by a single original author published between January 1 and December 31 of the award year by a U.S. trade publisher. Eligible books must be previously published in a language other than English. Translators may be of any nationality. U.S. residency or citizenship is not required. Books may have no more than two translators.

If a book is submitted for this award, submission for any additional PEN America Literary Awards, with the exception of the PEN Open Book Prize, is not permitted. PEN/Faulkner Award is not considered a PEN America Literary Award.

Prose, self-published books, reprints or retranslations, books with more than two translators, and translations-in-progress are not accepted.

FINANCIAL DATA:
Amount of support per award: $3,000.

NO. MOST RECENT APPLICANTS: 50.

NO. AWARDS: 1.

APPLICATION INFO:
Application process opens on June 1. PEN America will only accept submissions from publishers or literary agents. Authors may not submit their own book for this award. One copy of book-length translations of poetry published during the calendar year under consideration may be submitted. Early submissions are strongly recommended.

Deadline: August 1.

ADDRESS INQUIRIES TO:
See e-mail address above.

PEN AMERICA   [633]
588 Broadway, Suite 303
New York, NY 10012
(212) 334-1660 ext. 4813
Fax: (212) 334-2181
E-mail: awards@pen.org
Web Site: pen.org

FOUNDED: 1922

AREAS OF INTEREST:
Poetry.

NAME(S) OF PROGRAMS:
• **PEN/Voelcker Award for Poetry Collection**

TYPE:
Awards/prizes. The PEN/Voelcker Award for Poetry Collection, established by a bequest from Hunce Voelcker, is given annually to a poet whose distinguished and growing body of work to date represents a notable and accomplished presence in American literature, for whom the promise seen in earlier work has been fulfilled, and who has matured with each successive volume of poetry.

PURPOSE:
To recognize an exceptional poetry collection.

ELIGIBILITY:
A candidate's work must be a collection of poetry published by a U.S. trade publisher during the previous calendar year (January 1 to December 31). The book must be a series of individual poems published by a single living author. Anthologies with multiple authors are ineligible. Individual poems may have been previously published elsewhere; however, if the submitted book includes work previously published in a collection by the author, the submitted book should include significant new work.

The author must be a permanent U.S. resident or citizen.

Submissions for this award may not be submitted for any additional PEN America Literary Award, with the exception of the PEN Open Book Award. Please note that the PEN/Faulkner Award is not considered a PEN America Literary Award.

Self-published books are not eligible.

FINANCIAL DATA:
Amount of support per award: $5,000.

NO. AWARDS: 1.

APPLICATION INFO:
All letters of nomination (one to two pages is expected) should describe the scope and literary caliber of the candidate's work, and summarize the candidate's publications. Most importantly, nominations should articulate the degree of accomplishment the nominated poet has attained, and the esteem in which the candidate's work is held within the American literary community. Letters of nomination must be submitted through PEN's online nomination portal.

ADDRESS INQUIRIES TO:
See e-mail address above.

PEN AMERICA   [634]
588 Broadway, Suite 303
New York, NY 10012
(212) 334-1660 ext. 4813
Fax: (212) 334-2181
E-mail: awards@pen.org
Web Site: pen.org

FOUNDED: 1922

AREAS OF INTEREST:
Debut short story collections.

NAME(S) OF PROGRAMS:
• **PEN/Robert W. Bingham Prize for Debut Short Story Collection**

TYPE:
Awards/prizes. The PEN/Robert W. Bingham Prize is awarded annually and honors an exceptionally talented fiction writer whose debut work of short stories published in the prior year represents distinguished literary achievement and suggests great promise.

YEAR PROGRAM STARTED: 1990

PURPOSE:
To promote the professional careers of exceptionally talented fiction writers.

LEGAL BASIS:
Nonprofit organization affiliated with International PEN.

ELIGIBILITY:
Candidate's first (and only first) collection of short fiction must have been published by a U.S. trade publisher between January 1 and December 31 of the prior year. Candidates must be U.S. residents. American citizenship is not required. There are no restrictions on the candidate's age or on the style of his or her work. Self-published books are not eligible. Authors may not submit their own work. Submissions will only be accepted from publishers and literary agents.

FINANCIAL DATA:
Amount of support per award: $25,000.

NO. MOST RECENT APPLICANTS: 75.

NO. AWARDS: 1.

APPLICATION INFO:
Application process begins June 1. Submissions will only be accepted from publishers and literary agents. Submitter is expected to mail one copy of book to mailing address provided.
Deadline: August 1 of each year.

ADDRESS INQUIRIES TO:
See e-mail address above.

PEN AMERICA   [635]
588 Broadway, Suite 303
New York, NY 10012
(212) 334-1660 ext. 4813
Fax: (212) 334-2181
E-mail: awards@pen.org
Web Site: pen.org

FOUNDED: 1922

AREAS OF INTEREST:
Promoting the professional development of talented fiction writers.

NAME(S) OF PROGRAMS:
• **PEN/Robert J. Dau Short Story Prize for Emerging Writers**

TYPE:
Awards/prizes. The PEN/Robert J. Dau Short Story Prize for Emerging Writers recognizes emerging fiction writers for their debut short story published in a literary magazine, journal or cultural web site and aims to support the launch of their careers as fiction writers.

PURPOSE:
To recognize emerging fiction writers for their debut short story published in a literary magazine or journal.

LEGAL BASIS:
Nonprofit organization affiliated with International PEN.

ELIGIBILITY:
Submissions must be from editors of eligible publications. Authors may not submit their own work. Stories must have been published (or forthcoming) in the applicable calendar year. Participating publications may be online magazines, print magazines distributed in the U.S., or cultural web sites.

Editors from eligible publications may only submit a short story by a debut writer. The story must be the writer's first English publication of any genre that has undergone an editorial review process and been accepted and published in a literary journal, book, media outlet, or other publication that the author is not academically or professionally associated with. Editors from eligible publications may submit up to four eligible stories (up to 12,000 word) from eligible authors in a given award year.

The editor and author must agree to the award's declaration of eligibility and consent, which outlines serials rights for *Catapult's* forthcoming anthology.

FINANCIAL DATA:
Total amount of support: $2,000 and publication in an anthology.

NO. MOST RECENT APPLICANTS: 150.

NO. AWARDS: 12.

APPLICATION INFO:
Submissions are accepted from June 1 to November 15. Submissions will not be considered unless officially submitted via the online form and received at the PEN America New York office with the corresponding declaration of eligibility and consent.
Deadline: November 15.

ADDRESS INQUIRIES TO:
See e-mail address above.

PEN AMERICA   [636]
588 Broadway, Suite 303
New York, NY 10012
(212) 334-1660 ext. 4813
Fax: (212) 334-2181
E-mail: awards@pen.org
Web Site: pen.org

FOUNDED: 1922

AREAS OF INTEREST:
Promoting the professional development of talented writers.

NAME(S) OF PROGRAMS:
• **PEN/Diamonstein-Spielvogel Award for the Art of the Essay**

TYPE:
Awards/prizes. The PEN/Diamonstein-Spielvogel Award for the Art of the Essay honors a writer whose collection of individual essays, published in the current calendar year, is an expansion of their exceptional body of work focusing on the essay as an art form. This is considered a mid- to late career achievement award.

YEAR PROGRAM STARTED: 1991

PURPOSE:
To recognize a writer whose collection of individual essays expands their exceptional body of work focusing on the essay as an art form.

LEGAL BASIS:
Nonprofit organization affiliated with International Pen.

ELIGIBILITY:
Author must be a permanent U.S. resident or U.S. citizen. Eligible titles must have been published by a U.S. trade publisher during

the applicable calendar year. There are no restrictions on the subject matter. Essays may deal with a range of subjects or may explore one specific theme.

The book must be a series of individual essays published by a single author. Anthologies with multiple authors are ineligible.

Individual essays may have been previously published in magazines, journals, or anthologies.

Books submitted for this award may not be submitted to any additional PEN America Literary Award, with the exception of the PEN Open Book Award.

Self published books and single book-length works of nonfiction are not eligible.

FINANCIAL DATA:
Amount of support per award: $15,000.

NO. MOST RECENT APPLICANTS: 100.

NO. AWARDS: 1.

APPLICATION INFO:
Submissions are only accepted from publishers or literary agents. Authors may not submit their own book. Book submissions will not be considered unless officially submitted via the online form and received at the PEN America New York office with the corresponding Declaration of Eligibility.
Duration: One-time award.
Deadline: August 15.

ADDRESS INQUIRIES TO:
See e-mail address above.

PEN AMERICA   [637]
588 Broadway, Suite 303
New York, NY 10012
(212) 334-1660 ext. 4813
Fax: (212) 334-2181
E-mail: awards@pen.org
Web Site: pen.org

FOUNDED: 1922

AREAS OF INTEREST:
Promoting the professional development of talented writers.

NAME(S) OF PROGRAMS:
● **PEN/E.O. Wilson Prize for Literary Science Writing**

TYPE:
Awards/prizes. The PEN/E.O. Wilson Literary Science Award was founded by scientist and author Dr. Edward O. Wilson, activist and actor Harrison Ford, and the E.O. Wilson Biodiversity Foundation. The award celebrates writing that exemplifies literary excellence on the subject of the physical or biological sciences and communicates complex scientific concepts to a lay audience.

YEAR PROGRAM STARTED: 2011

PURPOSE:
To recognize the art of literary science writing.

LEGAL BASIS:
Nonprofit organization affiliated with International PEN.

ELIGIBILITY:
Eligible titles must have been published between January 1 and December 1 of the current award cycle. Authors of the work must be permanent U.S. residents or U.S. citizens.

Books submitted for this award may not be submitted for any additional PEN America Literary Award, with the exception of the PEN Open Book Award.

Anthologies and self-published books are not eligible.

FINANCIAL DATA:
Amount of support per award: $10,000.

NO. MOST RECENT APPLICANTS: 80.

NO. AWARDS: 1.

APPLICATION INFO:
Submissions will only be accepted from publishers and literary agents. Authors may not submit their own book for this award. Book submissions will not be considered unless officially submitted via the online form and received at the PEN America New York office with the corresponding Declaration of Eligibility.
Duration: One-time award.
Deadline: August 1.

ADDRESS INQUIRIES TO:
See e-mail address above.

PEN AMERICA   [638]
588 Broadway, Suite 303
New York, NY 10012
(212) 334-1660 ext. 4813
Fax: (212) 334-2181
E-mail: awards@pen.org
Web Site: pen.org

FOUNDED: 1922

AREAS OF INTEREST:
Promoting the professional development of talented writers.

NAME(S) OF PROGRAMS:
● **PEN/Jacqueline Bograd Weld Award for Biography**

TYPE:
Awards/prizes. The PEN/Jacqueline Bograd Weld Award for Biography is awarded for excellence in the art of biography. This prize goes to the author of a distinguished work published in the U.S. during the previous calendar year. The winning title is considered by the judges to be a work of exceptional literary, narrative, and artistic merit, based on scrupulous research.

PURPOSE:
To recognize a work of exceptional literary, narrative, and artistic merit, based on scrupulous research.

LEGAL BASIS:
Nonprofit organization affiliated with International PEN.

ELIGIBILITY:
A candidate's book of nonfiction must have been published by a trade publisher in the U.S. between January 1 and December 31 of the award year. Candidates need not be U.S. residents.

Books must be works by an author about another person.

Books submitted for this award may not be submitted for any additional PEN America Literary Award, with the exception of the PEN Open Book Award.

Memoirs, autobiographies, and self-published books are not eligible.

FINANCIAL DATA:
Amount of support per award: $5,000.

NO. MOST RECENT APPLICANTS: 120.

NO. AWARDS: 1.

APPLICATION INFO:
Submissions will only be accepted from publishers or literary agents. Authors may not submit their own book for this award. Book submissions will not be considered unless officially submitted via the online form and received at the PEN America New York office with the corresponding Declaration of Eligibility.
Duration: One-time award.
Deadline: August 1.

ADDRESS INQUIRIES TO:
See e-mail address above.

PEN AMERICA   [639]
588 Broadway, Suite 303
New York, NY 10012
(212) 334-1660 ext. 4813
Fax: (212) 334-2181
E-mail: awards@pen.org
Web Site: pen.org

FOUNDED: 1922

AREAS OF INTEREST:
Promoting the professional development of talented nonfiction writers.

NAME(S) OF PROGRAMS:
● **PEN/Jean Stein Grant for Literary Oral History**

TYPE:
Grants-in-aid; Project/program grants. The PEN/Jean Stein Grant for Literary Oral History recognizes a literary work of nonfiction that uses oral history to illuminate an event, individual, place, or movement. The grant is meant to help the author maintain or complete their ongoing project.

This grant is made possible by a substantial contribution from American author and editor Jean Stein, whose groundbreaking work helped popularize literary oral history.

PURPOSE:
To recognize the work of talented nonfiction writers.

LEGAL BASIS:
Nonprofit organization affiliated with International PEN.

ELIGIBILITY:
The submitted project must be the work of a single individual, written in English, and must be an unpublished work-in-progress. The project must be a work of literary nonfiction. Oral history must be a significant component of the project and its research.

Scholarly or academic writing is not eligible.

FINANCIAL DATA:
Amount of support per award: $15,000.

NO. MOST RECENT APPLICANTS: 60.

NO. AWARDS: 2.

APPLICATION INFO:
Application process is entirely online. Hard copy applications will not be accepted. The online submission form requires the following, submitted as one PDF file: (1) a one- to two-page, single-spaced description of the work, its importance, and why the author chose to undertake this project. One can additionally use this space to discuss relevant permissions, contracts, rights, or other aspects of the project; (2) a one- to two-page, single-spaced statement explaining why and how oral

history was used in the project;
(3) a 300- to 500-word statement explaining how a grant would aid in the completion of the project;
(4) a curriculum vitae for the author of the project, which should include information on any previous publications;
(5) an outline that includes the work completed thus far and the work remaining. The outline should include the names of all participants;
(6) transcripts of the project interviews (six to 10 pages) and;
(7) a writing sample from the project (20 to 40 pages, double-spaced).
Duration: One-time award.
Deadline: June 1.

ADDRESS INQUIRIES TO:
See e-mail address above.

PEN AMERICA   [640]
588 Broadway, Suite 303
New York, NY 10012
(212) 334-1660 ext. 4813
Fax: (212) 334-2181
E-mail: awards@pen.org
Web Site: pen.org

FOUNDED: 1922

AREAS OF INTEREST:
Promoting the professional development of talented writers.

NAME(S) OF PROGRAMS:
● **PEN/Heim Translation Fund Grant**

TYPE:
Grants-in-aid. The PEN/Heim Translation Fund was established by an endowed gift from Michael Henry Heim and Pricilla Heim, in response to the dismayingly low number of literary translations currently appearing in English.

YEAR PROGRAM STARTED: 2003

PURPOSE:
To promote the publication and reception of translated international literature in English.

LEGAL BASIS:
Nonprofit organization affiliated with International PEN.

ELIGIBILITY:
Grants support the translation of book-length works of fiction, creative nonfiction, poetry, or drama that have not previously appeared in English in print or have appeared only in an outdated or otherwise flawed translation. Works should be translations-in-progress, as the grant aims to provide support for completion. Preference will be given to translators at the beginning of their career, and to works by underrepresented writers working in underrepresented languages.

There are no restrictions on the nationality or citizenship of the translator, but the works must be translated into English.

The Fund seeks to encourage translators to undertake projects they might not otherwise have had the means to attempt.

Works with multiple translators, literary criticism, and scholarly or technical texts do not quality.

Translators may only submit one project per year.

FINANCIAL DATA:
Amount of support per award: $2,000 to $4,000.

NO. MOST RECENT APPLICANTS: 250.

NO. AWARDS: 10 to 12.

APPLICATION INFO:
Application must be submitted with the following:
(1) a one- to two-page, single-spaced statement outlining the work and describing its importance;
(2) a biography and bibliography of the author, including information on translations of his or her work into other languages and;
(3) curriculum vitae of the translator, no longer than three pages.

If the book is not in the public domain and the project is not yet under contract, include a photocopy of the copyright notice from the book published in its original language and a letter from the copyright holder stating that English-language rights to the book are available. A letter or copy of an e-mail from the copyright holder is sufficient. If the translation is currently under contract with a publisher, submit a copy of the contract.

Translator must also include a eight- to 10-page, single-spaced sample of the translation and the same passage in the original language. If the work has been previously translated, the same passage in the earlier version.
Deadline: June 1.

ADDRESS INQUIRIES TO:
See e-mail address above.

*PLEASE NOTE:
Translators who have previously been awarded grants by the Fund are ineligible to reapply for three years after the year in which they receive a grant. Projects that have been previously submitted and have not received a grant are unlikely to be reconsidered in a subsequent year.

PEN/FAULKNER FOUNDATION   [641]
6218 Georgia Avenue, N.W.
Unit 1062
Washington, DC 20011
(202) 898-9063
E-mail: ngwydion@penfaulkner.org
Web Site: www.penfaulkner.org

FOUNDED: 1980

AREAS OF INTEREST:
Fiction.

NAME(S) OF PROGRAMS:
● **PEN/Faulkner Award for Fiction**

TYPE:
Awards/prizes. Cash awards for a published winning author and four finalists.

YEAR PROGRAM STARTED: 1981

PURPOSE:
To honor literary excellence.

LEGAL BASIS:
Nonprofit 501(c)(3) organization.

ELIGIBILITY:
Candidates must be living American permanent residents. Books must be published within the calendar year of the award. No self-published books.

GEOG. RESTRICTIONS: United States.

FINANCIAL DATA:
Amount of support per award: $15,000 for the winner. $5,000 to each of four finalists.
Total amount of support: $35,000.

NO. MOST RECENT APPLICANTS: 450.

NO. AWARDS: 5.

APPLICATION INFO:
Candidates should submit four copies of their book. Complete information is available on the Foundation web site.
Deadline: Submissions must be postmarked by October 31. Announcement by mid-March.

IRS I.D.: 52-1431622

OFFICER:
Tracy B. McGillvary, President

EXECUTIVE DIRECTOR:
Gwydion Suilebhan

ADDRESS INQUIRIES TO:
Shahenda Helmy
Director of Literary Programs
Awards Department
(See address above.)

*PLEASE NOTE:
This is not a grant program, but a prize for published work.

PERPETUAL TRUSTEE COMPANY LTD.   [642]
Level 6, 123 Pitt Street
Sydney N.S.W. 2000 Australia
(61) 1800 501 227
Fax: (61) 02 8256 1471
E-mail: philanthropy@perpetual.com.au
Web Site: www.perpetual.com.au/milesfranklin

FOUNDED: 1954

AREAS OF INTEREST:
The advancement, improvement and betterment of Australian literature.

NAME(S) OF PROGRAMS:
● **Miles Franklin Literary Award**

TYPE:
Awards/prizes. Annual cash award for a published book on Australian life.

YEAR PROGRAM STARTED: 1957

PURPOSE:
To improve the educational style of authors; to help and give incentive to authors and to provide them with additional monetary support to enable them to improve their literary efforts.

LEGAL BASIS:
Trustees of estate of the late Miles Franklin.

ELIGIBILITY:
All works must be in English. No special requirements as regards nationality, age, etc. The book must be published in the year of entry of the award and be of the highest literary merit and must present Australian life in any of its phases. More than one entry may be submitted by each author. Novels or plays written by two or more authors in collaboration are eligible.

Biographies, collections of short stories, children's books and poetry are not eligible. Judges will not consider any text that has only had Internet publication.

FINANCIAL DATA:
Amount of support per award: $60,000 (AUD) for the year 2021.

NO. AWARDS: 1 per year.

APPLICATION INFO:
Application information is available on the web site when the award cycle opens. Publishers are required to submit the novels on the authors' behalf.

PUBLICATIONS:
Application guidelines.

ADDRESS INQUIRIES TO:
Scholarship and Awards
Miles Franklin Literary Award
(See e-mail address above.)

THE PHI BETA KAPPA
SOCIETY   [643]
1606 New Hampshire Avenue, N.W.
Washington, DC 20009
(202) 745-3287
Fax: (202) 986-1601
E-mail: awards@pbk.org
Web Site: www.pbk.org

FOUNDED: 1776

NAME(S) OF PROGRAMS:
● **The Phi Beta Kappa Book Awards**

TYPE:
Awards/prizes. The Phi Beta Kappa Book
Awards consist of three book awards given
annually to outstanding scholarly books that
have been published in the U.S. in the fields
of the humanities, the social sciences, the
natural sciences and mathematics.

The Ralph Waldo Emerson Book Award is
offered annually for scholarly studies that
contribute significantly to interpretations of
the intellectual and cultural condition of
humanity. This award may recognize work in
the fields of history, philosophy and religion;
these fields are conceived in sufficiently
broad terms to permit the inclusion of
appropriate work in related fields such as
anthropology and the social sciences.
Biographies of public figures may be eligible
if their critical emphasis is primarily on the
intellectual and cultural condition of
humanity.

The Christian Gauss Award is offered for
books in the field of literary scholarship or
criticism. The prize honors the late Christian
Gauss, the distinguished Princeton University
scholar, teacher, and dean, who also served
as president of the Phi Beta Kappa Society.
To be eligible, a literary biography must have
a predominantly critical emphasis.

Phi Beta Kappa Book Award in Science is
offered for outstanding contributions by
scientists to the literature of science. The
Award's intent is to encourage literate and
scholarly interpretations of the physical and
biological sciences and mathematics;
monographs and compendiums are not
eligible. To be eligible, biographies of
scientists must have a substantial critical
emphasis on their scientific research.

PURPOSE:
To recognize outstanding printed work in
several fields including the social sciences,
humanities, natural science and math.

LEGAL BASIS:
National scholarly honorary society.

ELIGIBILITY:
Awards are given for works published in the
U.S. during the previous calendar year.
Entries must be original publications.
Translations and works previously published
as a whole are not eligible. Books that
contain chapters or sections previously
published as articles in periodicals will be
considered only if they have very clear,
unifying themes and are not random
collections. Books that consist entirely of
previously published articles are unlikely to
qualify.

Entries ordinarily will be the work of a
single writer. Exceptions may be made for
books written by small teams of scholars
working in close collaboration. Books that
are collections of chapters by several
different authors are not eligible. Entries
should not be highly technical in character,
nor should they treat subjects of narrowly
limited interest. Monographs and reports on
research as such are not eligible. In all cases,
the subject and style of the entries should be
accessible to the general, literate reader.

Authors must be citizens or residents of the
U.S. Entries must have been published
originally in the U.S. A book may not be
entered for more than one of the awards. All
entries must be submitted by the publisher.
Publishers may submit no more than one
entry for each award.

GEOG. RESTRICTIONS: United States.

FINANCIAL DATA:
Amount of support per award: $10,000 to the
winning author.

Total amount of support: $30,000 annually.

NO. MOST RECENT APPLICANTS: Varies.

NO. AWARDS: 1 award in each category each
year.

APPLICATION INFO:
Inquiries and entries should be addressed to
the appropriate award committee at the
address above. Entries must be submitted by
the publisher.
Duration: No renewal.
Deadline: January 31.

PUBLICATIONS:
Application guidelines.

ADDRESS INQUIRIES TO:
Aurora Sherman, Executive Assistant to the
Secretary and Awards Coordinator
(See address above.)

PITT POETRY SERIES   [644]
University of Pittsburgh Press
7500 Thomas Boulevard
Pittsburgh, PA 15260
(412) 383-2456
Fax: (412) 383-2466
E-mail: info@upress.pitt.edu
Web Site: upittpress.org

FOUNDED: 1967

AREAS OF INTEREST:
Contemporary American poetry.

NAME(S) OF PROGRAMS:
● **Agnes Lynch Starrett Poetry Prize**

TYPE:
Awards/prizes. Cash prize, plus publication in
the Pitt Poetry Series.

YEAR PROGRAM STARTED: 1980

LEGAL BASIS:
University.

ELIGIBILITY:
Starrett Prize awarded annually for a
manuscript in English by a writer who has
not previously published a full-length book
of poetry.

FINANCIAL DATA:
Amount of support per award: $5,000, plus
book publication.

Total amount of support: $5,000.

NO. MOST RECENT APPLICANTS: 600 for the
year 2019.

NO. AWARDS: 1 each year.

REPRESENTATIVE AWARDS:
Eleanor Boudreau, *Earnest, Earnest*?

APPLICATION INFO:
Send one copy of manuscript on good quality
white paper, with no fewer than 48 and no
more than 100 typescript pages. Clean,
legible photocopies are acceptable. Name,
address, telephone number, and e-mail
address should be on the title page. Also
include curriculum vitae. A $25 reading fee
per manuscript is required.

Application can also be submitted through
www.submittable.com.

Deadline: Between March 1 and April 30
only. Announcement in the fall.

PUBLICATIONS:
Competition rules.

OFFICERS:
Ed Ochester, Editor, Pitt Poetry Series

ADDRESS INQUIRIES TO:
See e-mail address above.

*SPECIAL STIPULATIONS:
Competition for the Starrett Prize is severe.
Casual submissions are not encouraged.
Publisher cannot provide critiques of
manuscripts.

Manuscripts will not be returned.

THE PLAYWRIGHTS'
CENTER   [645]
2301 Franklin Avenue East
Minneapolis, MN 55406
(612) 332-7481 ext. 1115
Fax: (612) 332-6037
E-mail: info@pwcenter.org
juliab@pwcenter.org
Web Site: pwcenter.org

FOUNDED: 1971

AREAS OF INTEREST:
Playwriting.

CONSULTING OR VOLUNTEER SERVICES:
Advice on career development, jobs and
production for playwrights.

NAME(S) OF PROGRAMS:
● **Affiliated Writer Program**
● **Core Apprentice Program**
● **Core Writer Program**
● **Jerome Fellowships**
● **Many Voices Fellowships**
● **Many Voices Mentorships**
● **McKnight Fellowships in Playwriting**
● **McKnight National Residency and
Commission**
● **McKnight Theater Artist Fellowships**
● **New Plays on Campus**

TYPE:
Awards/prizes; Conferences/seminars;
Development grants; Fellowships;
Internships; Project/program grants. Core
Apprentice Program provides student
playwrights with such benefits as a year of
mentorship with a professional playwright
and a full workshop of a new play at the
Playwrights' Center.

Core Writer Program confers additional
membership benefits to committed
professional playwrights.

Jerome Fellowships provide grants to
emerging playwrights, who receive access to
Center's developmental services.

Many Voices Fellowships are awarded to playwrights of color.

Many Voices Mentorships are awarded to Minnesota-based beginning writers of color.

McKnight Fellowships in Playwriting provide grants to midcareer Minnesota-based playwrights.

McKnight National Residency and Commission aids in the creation and development of new works from nationally recognized playwrights not residing in Minnesota.

McKnight Theater Artist Fellowships are awarded to Minnesota theater artists (other than playwrights).

YEAR PROGRAM STARTED: 1971

PURPOSE:
To assist playwrights.

LEGAL BASIS:
Tax-exempt and nonprofit.

ELIGIBILITY:
Core Writer Program is open to professional playwrights in the U.S.

Jerome Fellowships are open to emerging playwrights in the U.S. (citizens or permanent residents).

Many Voices Fellowships are available to national and local writers of color.

Many Voices Mentorships are available to Minnesota-based beginning playwrights.

McKnight Fellowships in Playwriting are open to Minnesota residents only.

McKnight Theater Artist Fellowships are open to Minnesota writers only.

McKnight National Residency and Commission is for playwrights residing outside of Minnesota.

Additional criteria vary for each program.

GEOG. RESTRICTIONS: Many Voices Mentorships, McKnight Fellowships in Playwriting and McKnight Theater Artist Fellowships: Minnesota.

FINANCIAL DATA:
Amount of support per award: Varies.
Total amount of support: Over $250,000.

NO. MOST RECENT APPLICANTS: 200 for fellowships. 500 for all programs.

NO. AWARDS: For the year 2018-19: Core Apprentices: 3; Core Writers: 29; Jerome Fellowships: 3; Many Voices Fellowships: 2; Many Voices Mentorship: 1; McKnight Fellowships in Playwriting: 2; McKnight National Residency and Commission: 1; McKnight Theater Artist Fellowships: 3.

APPLICATION INFO:
Application information is available on the web site.
Duration: Core Writer: Three years; All other fellowships: One year.
Deadline: Varies.

PUBLICATIONS:
Annual report; newsletter.

IRS I.D.: 41-6170139

STAFF:
Jeremy Cohen, Producing Artistic Director
Hayley Finn, Associate Artistic Director
Julia Brown, Artistic Programs Administrator

ADDRESS INQUIRIES TO:
Julia Brown, Artistic Programs Administrator
(See address above.)

*SPECIAL STIPULATIONS:
Playwright must be in residence in Minnesota for one year for Jerome Fellowship. Recipients of McKnight Advancement Fellowships, McKnight Theater Artist Fellowships, and Many Voices Fellowships must maintain residence in Minnesota during program year.

SOCIETY OF CHILDREN'S BOOK WRITERS AND ILLUSTRATORS   [646]
6363 Wilshire Boulevard
Suite 425
Los Angeles, CA 90048
(323) 782-1010
Fax: (323) 782-1892
E-mail: scbwi@scbwi.org
Web Site: www.scbwi.org

FOUNDED: 1968

AREAS OF INTEREST:
Writers, editors and illustrators of children's books.

NAME(S) OF PROGRAMS:
* **Don Freeman Memorial Grant-in-Aid**
* **Work-In-Progress Grants**

TYPE:
Grants-in-aid; Project/program grants. The Freeman Memorial Grant-In-Aid has been established to enable picture-book artists to further their understanding, training and work in any aspect of the picture-book genre.

Work-In-Progress Grants have been established to assist children's book writers to complete a specific project. Grants are given in seven categories: Picture Book Text, Chapter Books/Early Readers, Middle Grade, Young Adult Fiction, Nonfiction, Multicultural Fiction or Nonfiction, and Translation.

YEAR PROGRAM STARTED: 1974

PURPOSE:
To encourage continuing excellence in the creation of children's literature and to provide assistance and support to those working in the children's book field.

LEGAL BASIS:
Corporation.

ELIGIBILITY:
Both grants are available to full and associate members of the Society of Children's Book Writers. The SCBW Grant Committee reserves the right to withhold the grants for any given year.

FINANCIAL DATA:
Amount of support per award: Freeman Memorial Grant-In-Aid: $1,000.
Total amount of support: Freeman Memorial Grant-In-Aid: $2,000.

NO. MOST RECENT APPLICANTS: 285.

NO. AWARDS: Freeman Memorial Grant-In-Aid: 2; Work-In-Progress Grant: 1 in each category.

APPLICATION INFO:
All applications must be digital and sent as a single PDF. Full details are available on the Society's web site.
Duration: One-time grant.
Deadline: April 15. Work-In-Progress Grant recipients announced in September.

PUBLICATIONS:
Grants brochure.

EXECUTIVE DIRECTOR:
Lin Oliver

ADDRESS INQUIRIES TO:
For the Freeman Memorial Grant-In-Aid:
E-mail: sarahbaker@scbwi.org

For the Work-In-Progress Grants:
SCBW Grant Committee
(See address above.)

SYRACUSE UNIVERSITY   [647]
English Graduate Office
420 Hall of Languages
Syracuse, NY 13244-1170
(315) 443-2174
Fax: (315) 443-3660
E-mail: tazollo@syr.edu
Web Site: english.syr.edu

FOUNDED: 1861

AREAS OF INTEREST:
American and British literature and culture, creative writing, critical theory, gender studies, cultural studies and film and screen studies.

NAME(S) OF PROGRAMS:
* **Graduate Program in Creative Writing**

TYPE:
Assistantships; Awards/prizes; Fellowships; Scholarships; Travel grants. Fellowships and teaching assistantships in creative writing.

YEAR PROGRAM STARTED: 1963

PURPOSE:
To assist talented writers to pursue graduate degrees at Syracuse University.

ELIGIBILITY:
Applicants must be an outstanding Arts and Sciences seniors with minimum 3.6 grade point average and must be nominated to the Arts and Sciences selection committee by department chairpersons or program directors, or individuals designated by them.

FINANCIAL DATA:
Fellowships and assistantships include remission of tuition costs for graduate study.
Amount of support per award: Annual stipend of $17,500. University Fellowships: $25,290.
Total amount of support: Varies.

APPLICATION INFO:
Applications must be submitted online through CollegeNET's ApplyWeb. Additional information required varies by program.
Duration: Three years.
Deadline: December 15.

ADDRESS INQUIRIES TO:
Terri Zollo
Graduate English Office Coordinator
(See e-mail address above.)

TOWSON UNIVERSITY   [648]
College of Liberal Arts
8000 York Road
Towson, MD 21252
(410) 704-2128
Fax: (410) 704-6392
E-mail: cla@towson.edu
Web Site: www.towson.edu/cla

FOUNDED: 1866

NAME(S) OF PROGRAMS:
* **Towson University Prize for Literature**

TYPE:
Awards/prizes. Awarded to Maryland writer of a single book or book-length manuscript of fiction, poetry, drama or imaginative nonfiction.

YEAR PROGRAM STARTED: 1980

PURPOSE:
To honor a published work of fiction, poetry or imaginative nonfiction by a Maryland resident.

LEGAL BASIS:
Special endowment.

ELIGIBILITY:
Applicant must be a Maryland resident for at least three years at the time of the award. Prize is awarded on the basis of literary and aesthetic excellence. Book must have been published in the three years prior to the award.

The winning author must be willing to be present at the awards ceremony and to grant to Towson State University the right to quote from the winning work in any publicity related to the prize.

GEOG. RESTRICTIONS: Maryland.

FINANCIAL DATA:
Amount of support per award: Generally $1,000.
Total amount of support: $1,000.

NO. MOST RECENT APPLICANTS: 15.

NO. AWARDS: 1 annually.

APPLICATION INFO:
Any individual, institution, group or publisher may nominate one or more works for the prize. Submit three copies of the work by certified mail, bound if published or typewritten if manuscript. If manuscript, proof of acceptance by a publisher and proposed date of publication must be provided. A completed nomination form must accompany entry.
Duration: One-time award.
Deadline: June 15 each year. Announcement in early Spring.

ADDRESS INQUIRIES TO:
Dean, College of Liberal Arts, LA 2213
Towson University
(See address above.)

THE UNIVERSITY OF IOWA [649]
Iowa Writers' Workshop
102 Dey House
507 North Clinton Street
Iowa City, IA 52242-1000
(319) 335-0416
Fax: (319) 335-0420
E-mail: deb-west@uiowa.edu
Web Site: writersworkshop.uiowa.edu

AREAS OF INTEREST:
Short story collection.

NAME(S) OF PROGRAMS:
● **The Iowa Short Fiction Award**
● **The John Simmons Short Fiction Award**

TYPE:
Awards/prizes. Publication of short story collection/manuscript.

YEAR PROGRAM STARTED: 1969

PURPOSE:
To encourage writing of short stories.

ELIGIBILITY:
Any writer who has not previously published a volume of prose fiction is eligible. Revised manuscripts which have been previously entered may be resubmitted. Writers who have published a volume of poetry are eligible.

The manuscript must be a collection of short stories of at least 150 word-processed, double-spaced pages. Stories previously published in periodicals are eligible.

CO-OP FUNDING PROGRAMS: The awards are provided with cooperation of the Iowa Writers' Workshop and the University of Iowa Press.

NO. MOST RECENT APPLICANTS: 400.

NO. AWARDS: 1 of each annually.

APPLICATION INFO:
No application forms are necessary. Manuscripts should be mailed to: Iowa Short Fiction Award, Iowa Writers' Workshop, at the address listed above. Do not send the only copy of the manuscript. Xeroxed copies are encouraged. Stamped, self-addressed packaging may be included for return of the manuscript, but is not required.
Deadline: Entries should be postmarked between August 1 and September 30. Announcement of the winners will be made early in the following year.

STAFF:
Lan Samantha Chang, Director

ADDRESS INQUIRIES TO:
Sasha Khmelnik, Program Associate
(See address above.)

UNIVERSITY OF MINNESOTA [650]
Room 113, Elmer L. Andersen Library
222 21st Avenue South
Minneapolis, MN 55455
(612) 624-4576
E-mail: asc-clrc@umn.edu
Web Site: www.lib.umn.edu/clrc

AREAS OF INTEREST:
Children's book artist development.

NAME(S) OF PROGRAMS:
● **The Ezra Jack Keats/Kerlan Memorial Fellowship**

TYPE:
Research grants; Travel grants; Visiting scholars. Award to travel to Kerlan Collection, University of Minnesota, plus per diem.

YEAR PROGRAM STARTED: 1985

PURPOSE:
To fund the artist development of a talented writer and/or illustrator of children's books.

ELIGIBILITY:
Grants are awarded to individuals based on need. Special consideration will be given to those who would find it difficult to finance a visit to the Kerlan Collection. Candidates do not have to be U.S. citizens or residents.

FINANCIAL DATA:
Recipient will receive transportation cost and a per diem allotment.
Amount of support per award: Up to $3,000.
Total amount of support: Up to $3,000.

NO. AWARDS: 1.

APPLICATION INFO:
Electronic application acceptable by deadline.

Duration: Grants are awarded annually and are nonrenewable.
Deadline: January 30 (postmark).

ADDRESS INQUIRIES TO:
Ezra Jack Keats/Kerlan Collection Memorial Fellowship Committee
(See address above.)

THE UNIVERSITY OF SOUTHERN MISSISSIPPI [651]
118 College Drive
Box 5148
Hattiesburg, MS 39406
(601) 266-4349
Fax: (601) 266-6269
E-mail: ellen.ruffin@usm.edu
Web Site: www.degrummond.org/fellowships

FOUNDED: 1966

AREAS OF INTEREST:
American and British children's literature.

NAME(S) OF PROGRAMS:
● **Ezra Jack Keats/Janina Domanska Children's Literature Research Fellowship**

TYPE:
Fellowships; Research grants.

PURPOSE:
To encourage imaginative and productive research in children's literature.

ELIGIBILITY:
Applicants of any discipline who engage in projects which require substantial use of the de Grummond Collection may apply. Awards will be based upon the applicant's scholarly qualifications, the merits of the proposal submitted, and the appropriateness of the proposal to the resources of the de Grummond Collection. Preference will be given to projects which have a good likelihood of being published.

FINANCIAL DATA:
Fellowship monies can be used for travel, lodging, and meals.
Amount of support per award: Up to $1,600.
Total amount of support: Varies.

NO. MOST RECENT APPLICANTS: Average 5 to 7.

NO. AWARDS: 1 for the year 2019.

APPLICATION INFO:
Application information is available on the web site.
Duration: One year. Grants not renewable.
Deadline: October 15.

ADDRESS INQUIRIES TO:
Ellen H. Ruffin, Curator
de Grummond Children's Literature Collection
(See address above.)

UNIVERSITY OF VIRGINIA PRESS [652]
210 Sprigg Lane
Charlottesville, VA 22903
(434) 924-3361
Fax: (434) 982-2655
E-mail: arh2h@virginia.edu
Web Site: www.upress.virginia.edu

FOUNDED: 1963

AREAS OF INTEREST:
18th century studies.

NAME(S) OF PROGRAMS:
● **Walker Cowen Memorial Prize**

TYPE:
Awards/prizes.

YEAR PROGRAM STARTED: 1989

LEGAL BASIS:
University.

ELIGIBILITY:
Submissions should be a work in 18th century studies in history, literature, philosophy or the arts. The work may cover Europe, the Americas, or the Atlantic world. Translation candidates must submit any unpublished, book-length manuscript in English.

FINANCIAL DATA:
Amount of support per award: $5,000 and an advance publishing contract.

NO. MOST RECENT APPLICANTS: Approximately 10.

NO. AWARDS: 1 annually.

APPLICATION INFO:
Applicant must include three copies of their curriculum vitae and a description (one to two typescript pages) of the manuscript's content, scope, and intended readership. For new manuscripts, two identical copies of the manuscript must be submitted simultaneously. For translation candidates, one copy of the work in the original language must be submitted together with copies of any published reviews. If possible, submit an introduction or other sample material from the book translated into English.
Deadline: November 1 (postmark). Award announcement in the following March.

ADDRESS INQUIRIES TO:
Angie Hogan, Acquiring Editor
(See address above.)

THE WORD WORKS, INC.   [653]
P.O. Box 42164
Washington, DC 20015
E-mail: editor@wordworksbooks.org
Web Site: www.wordworksbooks.org

FOUNDED: 1974

AREAS OF INTEREST:
Poetry and literature.

NAME(S) OF PROGRAMS:
• **The Washington Prize**

TYPE:
Awards/prizes.

YEAR PROGRAM STARTED: 1981

PURPOSE:
To encourage and promote contemporary American poetry.

LEGAL BASIS:
Nonprofit corporation.

ELIGIBILITY:
The Washington Prize is awarded for a volume of original poetry in English by a living American or Canadian writer.

GEOG. RESTRICTIONS: Canada and United States.

FINANCIAL DATA:
Amount of support per award: $1,500 plus book publication.

NO. AWARDS: 1 each year.

APPLICATION INFO:
Application must be submitted online. There is an entry fee of $25 (U.S.) drawn on a U.S. bank only, payable to The Word Works.

Deadline: January 15 to March 15. Decision by August.

IRS I.D.: 52-1042022

BOARD OF DIRECTORS:
Karren L. Alenier, Chairperson of the Board
Nancy White, President
Dr. James Beall
Jacqueline Johnson
JoAnne McFarland

ADDRESS INQUIRIES TO:
Andrea Carter-Brown
Washington Prize Series Editor
P.O. Box 42164
Washington, DC 20015

*PLEASE NOTE:
The Washington Prize is for support of poets. It is not an academic scholarship for higher education.

THE WORD WORKS, INC.   [654]
P.O. Box 42164
Washington, DC 20015
E-mail: editor@wordworksbooks.org
Web Site: www.wordworksbooks.org

FOUNDED: 1974

AREAS OF INTEREST:
Poetry.

NAME(S) OF PROGRAMS:
• **Tenth Gate Prize**

TYPE:
Awards/prizes. Award is given to a living poet with at least two full-length collections of poetry published by literary presses.

PURPOSE:
To encourage and promote contemporary American poetry.

ELIGIBILITY:
Submitted work must be a volume of original poetry written in English. Applicant must have had at least two full-length collections of poetry published by literary presses.

FINANCIAL DATA:
Amount of support per award: $1,000 plus standard publishing contract.

APPLICATION INFO:
Application must be made online. There is an entry fee of $25 (U.S.). Detailed information can be found on the web site.
Deadline: June 1 to July 15. Decision by October 1.

ADDRESS INQUIRIES TO:
Nancy White, Series Director
Tenth Gate Prize
Adirondack Community College
640 Bay Road
Queensbury, NY 12804

*PLEASE NOTE:
Include a self-addressed, stamped envelope with all regular mail inquiries.

Museums and libraries

ALABAMA LIBRARY ASSOCIATION SCHOLARSHIP FUND, INC.   [655]
Alabama Library Association
6030 Monticello Drive
Montgomery, AL 36117
(334) 414-0113
E-mail: allaadmin@allanet.org
Web Site: www.allanet.org

FOUNDED: 1904

AREAS OF INTEREST:
Library science.

NAME(S) OF PROGRAMS:
• **Scholarships in Library Science**

TYPE:
Scholarships. Scholarships for graduate study in library science/library media.

YEAR PROGRAM STARTED: 1945

PURPOSE:
To provide professional training for librarians and prospective librarians.

LEGAL BASIS:
Nonprofit corporation.

ELIGIBILITY:
Residents of Alabama who have been accepted by an accredited institution offering a graduate course in library science are eligible to apply. Recipients will be selected based on academic achievement, potential service to the library profession and financial need.

GEOG. RESTRICTIONS: Alabama.

FINANCIAL DATA:
Amount of support per award: ALLA Centennial Memorial Scholarship: Minimum $500, with additional funds up to $1,000 based on contributions to the scholarship fund each year; ALLA Memorial Scholarship: Up to $1,000 per award.
Total amount of support: Up to $2,500.

NO. AWARDS: 2.

APPLICATION INFO:
Applicant must submit:
(1) an application form;
(2) a certified final transcript from the institution that awarded applicant's undergraduate degree;
(3) a certified transcript of any graduate work undertaken;
(4) a certified transcript of test scores on the GRE or MAT;
(5) proof of acceptance at an ALA-accredited library school and;
(6) recommendation forms from three references.
Duration: One academic year.
Deadline: June 1.

PUBLICATIONS:
Brochure; application guidelines.

AMERICAN ASSOCIATION OF LAW LIBRARIES   [656]
105 West Adams Street
Suite 3300
Chicago, IL 60603
(312) 939-4764
Fax: (312) 431-1097
E-mail: membership@aall.org
Web Site: www.aallnet.org

FOUNDED: 1906

AREAS OF INTEREST:
Librarianship, law librarianship and law.

NAME(S) OF PROGRAMS:
• **Library Degree for Law School Graduates**
• **Library Degree for Non-Law School Graduates**

- **Library School Graduates Attending Law School**
- **Library School Graduates Seeking a Non-Law Degree**

TYPE:
Scholarships. For study of law or librarianship, with support intended for prospective law librarians.

YEAR PROGRAM STARTED: 1966

PURPOSE:
To assist qualified persons who are interested in becoming professional law librarians.

LEGAL BASIS:
Not-for-profit corporation.

ELIGIBILITY:
Preference is given to AALL members, but scholarships are not restricted to members. Evidence of financial need must be submitted.

GEOG. RESTRICTIONS: United States.

FINANCIAL DATA:
Amount of support per award: $1,000 to $3,000. Amounts vary according to available funds and may be limited at the discretion of the Scholarships Committee.
Total amount of support: Varies.

NO. MOST RECENT APPLICANTS: 30.

NO. AWARDS: Varies.

APPLICATION INFO:
Application information is available on the web site.
Duration: Varies by scholarship.
Deadline: April 1.

ADDRESS INQUIRIES TO:
Kylie Weller
Membership Services Manager
(See address above.)

AMERICAN ASSOCIATION OF LAW LIBRARIES   **[657]**
105 West Adams Street
Suite 3300
Chicago, IL 60603
(312) 939-4764
Fax: (312) 431-1097
E-mail: membership@aall.org
Web Site: www.aallnet.org

FOUNDED: 1906

AREAS OF INTEREST:
Librarianship, law librarianship and minorities.

NAME(S) OF PROGRAMS:
- **George A. Strait Minority Stipend Scholarship Endowment**

TYPE:
Scholarships. Stipend for graduate study leading to a degree at an accredited school of library or information science or an accredited law school. Preference will be given to individuals with previous service to, or interest in, law librarianship.

YEAR PROGRAM STARTED: 1966

PURPOSE:
To assist qualified persons who are interested in becoming professional law librarians.

LEGAL BASIS:
Not-for-profit corporation.

ELIGIBILITY:
Application is limited to minority group members defined by current guidelines of the

U.S. government. Applicant must be a degree candidate in an ALA-accredited library school or ABA-accredited law school and intend to have a career in law librarianship.

GEOG. RESTRICTIONS: United States.

FINANCIAL DATA:
Amount of support per award: Up to $2,500.
Total amount of support: Varies.

NO. MOST RECENT APPLICANTS: 11.

NO. AWARDS: Varies.

APPLICATION INFO:
Application packet must include:
(1) an official transcript or unofficial copy of transcript from the school where applicant completed most recent degree;
(2) a letter from the Admissions Officer of the library school, stating the program for which the applicant has been accepted and the date the courses begin, or, if applicant has already begun pursuing the degree, a transcript showing they are a degree candidate in good standing, or, if the applicant is attending law school, a transcript showing they are a degree candidate in good standing;
(3) two letters of recommendation from persons who have knowledge of the applicant's abilities and who can evaluate and comment upon law library employment experience;
(4) a personal statement discussing the applicant's interest in law librarianship, reason for applying for this scholarship, career goals as a law librarian, and statement of financial need and;
(5) a resume.
Duration: One year.
Deadline: April 1.

ADDRESS INQUIRIES TO:
Kylie Weller
Membership Services Manager
(See address above.)

AMERICAN ASSOCIATION OF SCHOOL LIBRARIANS   **[658]**
225 North Michigan Avenue
Suite 1300
Chicago, IL 60601
(312) 280-4385
(800) 545-2433 ext. 4382
Fax: (312) 280-4385
E-mail: aasl@ala.org
Web Site: www.ala.org/aasl

FOUNDED: 1951

AREAS OF INTEREST:
Libraries and librarianship.

NAME(S) OF PROGRAMS:
- **AASL Collaborative School Library Award**
- **AASL Frances Henne Award**
- **AASL Innovative Reading Grant**
- **AASL National School Library of the Year Award**
- **ABC-CLIO Leadership Grant**

TYPE:
Awards/prizes; Development grants; Project/program grants.

PURPOSE:
To honor distinguished service and foster professional growth in the school library profession.

ELIGIBILITY:
Requirements vary by award or grant.

FINANCIAL DATA:
Amount of support per award: $1,250 to $10,000.
Total amount of support: Varies.

NO. MOST RECENT APPLICANTS: 50.

NO. AWARDS: Varies.

APPLICATION INFO:
Application form and information are available from the Association.
Deadline: AASL National School Library of the Year Award: January 1; AASL Collaborative School Library Award, AASL Frances Henne Award, AASL Innovative Reading Grant and ABC-CLIO Leadership Grant: February 1.

EXECUTIVE DIRECTOR:
Sylvia Norton

ADDRESS INQUIRIES TO:
Allison Cline, Deputy Executive Director
(See e-mail address above.)

AMERICAN LIBRARY ASSOCIATION (ALA)   **[659]**
225 North Michigan Avenue
Suite 1300
Chicago, IL 60601
(312) 280-3247
(800) 545-2433 ext. 3247
E-mail: awards@ala.org
Web Site: www.ala.org

FOUNDED: 1876

AREAS OF INTEREST:
Librarianship.

NAME(S) OF PROGRAMS:
- **ALA Awards**

TYPE:
Awards/prizes; Conferences/seminars; Development grants; Fellowships; Research grants; Scholarships; Seed money grants; Travel grants. Cash and noncash awards for achievement/distinguished service, authors/illustrators/publishers, exhibits, funding, intellectual freedom, literacy, professional development, public relations, publications/articles and special services, as well as scholarships, fellowships and research grants sponsored by ALA and its units.

PURPOSE:
To honor distinguished service and foster professional growth.

FINANCIAL DATA:
Amount of support per award: Awards: $250 to $10,000; Research Grants and Fellowships: $500 to $10,000.
Total amount of support: Varies.

NO. AWARDS: Varies.

REPRESENTATIVE AWARDS:
Academic or Research Librarian of the Year Award for outstanding contribution to academic and research librarianship and library development, $3,000 (donated by Baker & Taylor); EBSCO Information Services Library Staff Development Award to library organization for a program to further its goals and objectives, $3,500 (donated by EBSCO Publishers); Frances Henne Research Grant to provide seed money to an individual, institution or group for a project to encourage research on library service to young adults, $500 minimum (donated by Voice of Youth Advocates); David H. Clift Scholarship to worthy U.S. or Canadian citizen to begin an M.L.S. degree in an

ALA-accredited program, $3,000 (donated by scholarship endowment interest, individual contributions).

APPLICATION INFO:
Application information is available on the web site.
Duration: Varies.
Deadline: Varies.

ADDRESS INQUIRIES TO:
Cheryl Malden, Program Officer
(See address above.)

ASSOCIATION FOR LIBRARY AND INFORMATION SCIENCE EDUCATION (ALISE)   [660]
4 Lan Drive, Suite 310
Westford, MA 01886
(978) 674-6190
Fax: (978) 250-1117
E-mail: office@alise.org
Web Site: www.alise.org

FOUNDED: 1915

AREAS OF INTEREST:
Library and information science education.

NAME(S) OF PROGRAMS:
● **ALISE Research Awards**

TYPE:
Awards/prizes; Research grants. Award for an outstanding research proposal in the field of librarianship and information science.

YEAR PROGRAM STARTED: 1976

PURPOSE:
To provide support for research which will help to promote excellence in education for librarianship and information science.

LEGAL BASIS:
Nonprofit 501(c)(3) corporation.

ELIGIBILITY:
Determined on the basis of the project's appropriateness to the goals of the ALISE, evidence of an established methodology and a viable research design, likelihood of completion in 12 to 18 months and on the qualifications of the researcher, who should be an ALISE member. Evidence that other funds are not available for the project should be presented.

The award cannot be used to support a doctoral dissertation. At least one applicant in a group submitting a proposal must be a personal member of the Association as of the deadline date. Staff training, general operating or overhead expenses, and other indirect costs are not funded.

Recipients of the award must present a progress report at the ALISE Annual Conference, submit written quarterly reports to the Executive Director of ALISE, who will pay the grant in periodic installments as the research progresses, submit the results of the funded study to the Association's *Journal of Education for Library and Information Science* (JELIS) for possible publication prior to submission to other publications, that is, the Journal will have first option on publication, acknowledge the support of ALISE in any publicity or presentation based on the funded study and inform the Executive Director if they receive research funding in addition to that provided by ALISE.

FINANCIAL DATA:
Staff training, general operating or overhead expenses, and other indirect costs are not funded.

Amount of support per award: Up to $5,000.
Total amount of support: $5,000 annually.

NO. AWARDS: 1 or more.

REPRESENTATIVE AWARDS:
Lynn Bowker, University of Ottawa, for "Against the Clock: Developing and Testing a Framework for Speed Training in LIS Education."

APPLICATION INFO:
Proposals should be succinct and precise. No more than 20 double-spaced, typed pages. If necessary, supporting information may be included in an appendix. Proposals must include the following information to be considered in the competition:
(1) abstract of the project in no greater than 200 words;
(2) problem statement and literature review including justification and need for the research;
(3) project objectives;
(4) project description;
(5) research design, methodology and analysis techniques;
(6) detailed budget (including institutional or departmental contributions, if any);
(7) expected benefits and impact from the research and;
(8) vita(e) of project investigator(s).
Duration: One year.
Deadline: March 15.

PUBLICATIONS:
Application guidelines.

IRS I.D.: 51-0193882

STAFF:
Cambria Happ, MPA, CAE, Executive Director

BOARD OF DIRECTORS AND OFFICERS:
Sandy Hirsh, President
Lisa O'Connor, President-Elect
Heather Moulaison Sandy, Secretary/Treasurer
Lilia Pavlovsky, Director, Community Building
Denice Adkins, Director, Membership
Mega Subramaniam, Director, Programming

ADDRESS INQUIRIES TO:
ALISE Awards
(See address above.)

*SPECIAL STIPULATIONS:
The Research Grant award cannot be used to support a doctoral dissertation.

ASSOCIATION FOR LIBRARY AND INFORMATION SCIENCE EDUCATION (ALISE)   [661]
4 Lan Drive, Suite 310
Westford, MA 01886
(978) 674-6190
Fax: (978) 250-1117
E-mail: office@alise.org
Web Site: www.alise.org

FOUNDED: 1915

AREAS OF INTEREST:
Library and information science education.

NAME(S) OF PROGRAMS:
● **ALISE/ProQuest Methodology Paper Competition**
● **The Eugene Garfield/ALISE Doctoral Dissertation Competition**
● **Bohdan S. Wynar Research Paper Competition**

TYPE:
Awards/prizes. Awards for an outstanding unpublished research paper, methodology paper and for each of two outstanding doctoral dissertations, respectively.

YEAR PROGRAM STARTED: 1977

PURPOSE:
To encourage research in the field of library and information science education and related areas.

LEGAL BASIS:
Nonprofit 501(c)(3) corporation.

ELIGIBILITY:
ALISE/ProQuest Methodology Paper Competition is open to all types of methodology. Papers must be limited to description and discussion of a research method or a technique associated with a particular research method. Papers must explain the particular method/technique, including methodological implications for library and information science. Examples to illustrate its value can come from LIS-related published studies, proposed studies, and works in progress. Papers that stress findings are not eligible.

The Eugene Garfield/ALISE Doctoral Dissertation Competition is open to doctoral students who have recently graduated in any field of study, or who will have completed their dissertations by the deadline. Dissertations must deal with substantive issues related to library and information science, but applicants may be from within or outside LIS programs.

Bohdan S. Wynar Research Paper Competition is open to research papers concerning any aspect of library and information science. This competition is not limited to research regarding LIS education. Any research methodology is acceptable.

FINANCIAL DATA:
Amount of support per award:
ALISE/ProQuest Methodology Paper and The Eugene Garfield/ALISE Doctoral Dissertation Competitions: $500 each.

NO. AWARDS: ALISE/ProQuest Methodology Paper Competition: 1; The Eugene Garfield/ALISE Doctoral Dissertation and Bohdan S. Wynar Research Paper Competitions: Up to 2 each.

APPLICATION INFO:
Application information is available on the web site.
Deadline: March 15.

IRS I.D.: 51-0193882

STAFF:
Cambria Happ, MPA, CAE, Executive Director

BOARD OF DIRECTORS AND OFFICERS:
Sandy Hirsh, President
Lisa O'Connor, President-Elect
Heather Moulaison Sandy, Secretary/Treasurer
Lilia Pavlovsky, Director, Community Building
Denice Adkins, Director, Membership Services
Mega Subramaniam, Director, Programming

ADDRESS INQUIRIES TO:
ALISE Awards
(See address above.)

BETA PHI MU [662]

P.O. Box 42139
Philadelphia, PA 19101
(267) 361-5018
E-mail: headquarters@betaphimu.org
Web Site: www.betaphimu.org

FOUNDED: 1948

AREAS OF INTEREST:
Library and information studies.

NAME(S) OF PROGRAMS:
- **Eugene Garfield Doctoral Dissertation Fellowship**
- **Harold Lancour Foreign Research Fellowship**
- **Sarah Rebecca Reed Scholarship**
- **Frank B. Sessa Scholarship for Continuing Professional Education of Beta Phi Mu Members**
- **Blanche E. Woolls Scholarship for School Library Media Service**

TYPE:
Fellowships; Scholarships. Eugene Garfield Doctoral Dissertation Fellowship is funded through the generosity of Eugene Garfield, and provides fellowships for up to six students per year. They are awarded to foster high-quality research in the field and to expedite the movement of new Doctorates into teaching positions.

The Harold Lancour Fellowship is given for foreign study.

The Sarah Rebecca Reed Scholarship is given to a beginning student at the Master's level accepted in an American Library Association-accredited program.

The Frank B. Sessa Scholarship is given for Continuing Education for a Beta Phi Mu member.

The Blanche Woolls Scholarship is given to a beginning student at the Master's level accepted in an American Library Association-Accredited Program majoring in School Media Services.

PURPOSE:
To assist qualified persons who are interested in completing a course of advanced study in library and information studies.

LEGAL BASIS:
Nonprofit organization.

FINANCIAL DATA:
Amount of support per award: Garfield Doctoral Dissertation Fellowship: $3,000; Lancour Fellowship: $1,750; Reed and Woolls Scholarships: $2,250 each; Sessa Scholarship: $150.
Total amount of support: Varies.

NO. AWARDS: Garfield Doctoral Dissertation Fellowship: 6; Lancour Fellowship, Reed Scholarship and Woolls Scholarship: 1 per award; Sessa Scholarship: 10.

APPLICATION INFO:
Forms are available on the Society's web site.
Duration: One-time award. Nonrenewable.
Deadline: March 15.

PUBLICATIONS:
The Pipeline, online newsletter.

STAFF:
Alison M. Lewis, Ph.D., Executive Director

ADDRESS INQUIRIES TO:
Alison M. Lewis, Ph.D., Executive Director
(See address above.)

GLADYS BROOKS FOUNDATION

1055 Franklin Avenue
Suite 208
Garden City, NY 11530-2903
(516) 746-6103
Fax: (516) 877-1758
E-mail: kathy@gladysbrooksfoundation.org
Web Site: www.gladysbrooksfoundation.org

TYPE:
Capital grants; Challenge/matching grants; Demonstration grants; Development grants; Endowments; Matching gifts; Project/program grants; Scholarships. Grants to private, not-for-profit publicly supported libraries, educational institutions, hospitals and clinics in the eastern U.S.
See entry 1075 for full listing.

CALIFORNIA LIBRARY ASSOCIATION [663]

1055 East Colorado Boulevard
Suite 500
Pasadena, CA 91106
(626) 204-4071
E-mail: info@cla-net.org
Web Site: www.cla-net.org

FOUNDED: 1896

AREAS OF INTEREST:
Librarianship.

NAME(S) OF PROGRAMS:
- **Begun Scholarship**
- **CLA Scholarship for Minority Students in Memory of Edna Yelland**

TYPE:
Scholarships. Support for minority library school students. Support for graduate students in reference/information service librarianship.

YEAR PROGRAM STARTED: 1973

PURPOSE:
To help support the educational goals of minority students in the library service field.

LEGAL BASIS:
Nonprofit.

ELIGIBILITY:
Applicant must be accepted by a graduate library school in California, accredited by the American Library Association, be of ethnic origin and show financial need. California residents and U.S. citizens or permanent U.S. residents may apply.

GEOG. RESTRICTIONS: California.

FINANCIAL DATA:
Amount of support per award: Generally $2,500 per Edna Yelland Scholarship; $3,000 for Begun Scholarship.
Total amount of support: $10,500.

NO. MOST RECENT APPLICANTS: 25.

NO. AWARDS: 4.

APPLICATION INFO:
Application information can be found on the Association's web site.
Duration: One-time award.
Deadline: Mid-March.

CAMBRIDGE UNIVERSITY LIBRARY [664]

West Road
Cambridge CB3 9DR England
(44) 01223 333000
Fax: (44) 01223 333160
E-mail: universitylibrarian@lib.cam.ac.uk
Web Site: www.lib.cam.ac.uk/munby

FOUNDED: 1400

AREAS OF INTEREST:
Bibliographic research.

NAME(S) OF PROGRAMS:
- **The Munby Fellowship in Bibliography**

TYPE:
Fellowships. Graduate fellowships for bibliographical research based on the collections of Cambridge libraries.

YEAR PROGRAM STARTED: 1977

LEGAL BASIS:
University.

ELIGIBILITY:
Open to university graduates in any discipline, with preference given to scholars of postdoctoral or equivalent level, of any nationality or age. Research must be bibliographical.

FINANCIAL DATA:
Amount of support per award: GBP 35,845, plus GBP 1,500 expense allowance for the year 2021-22.

NO. MOST RECENT APPLICANTS: 50.

NO. AWARDS: 2 for the year 2020-21.

APPLICATION INFO:
Applications are accepted through the Cambridge University Job Opportunities link. Applicant must log on to create an online application form. Statement outlining research proposal (maximum two pages), cover letter, and curriculum vitae must be uploaded with the application form.
Duration: 10 months, October 1 to July 31.
Deadline: Advertised in autumn for post to begin October the following year. Election normally made by early January.

PUBLICATIONS:
Application guidelines.

ADDRESS INQUIRIES TO:
Library Syndicate
(See address above.)

CONNECTICUT LIBRARY ASSOCIATION [665]

55 North Main Street
Unit 49
Belchertown, MA 01007
(860) 346-2444
Fax: (860) 344-9199
E-mail: mscheier@ctlibraryassociation.org
Web Site: www.ctlibraryassociation.org

AREAS OF INTEREST:
Library conferences, workshops and professional level opportunities.

NAME(S) OF PROGRAMS:
- **Proficiency Enhancement Grants (PEG)**

TYPE:
Grants-in-aid. Grants for personnel at all levels of library work.

YEAR PROGRAM STARTED: 1976

PURPOSE:
To support the educational goals of library science students in Connecticut.

LEGAL BASIS:
Nonprofit organization.

ELIGIBILITY:
Grants are made to CLA members only.

GEOG. RESTRICTIONS: Connecticut.

FINANCIAL DATA:
Amount of support per award: Maximum $400.

Total amount of support: Up to $2,500 annually.

NO. AWARDS: Up to 4 or 5 grants per year.

APPLICATION INFO:
Application form is available online. Apply to the Chairperson, Program for Educational Grants, at the address above.

Duration: One year. Not renewable.

Deadline: January 2, July 1, September 1 and November 1.

ADDRESS INQUIRIES TO:
Peter F. Ciparelli, PEG Chairman
E-mail: petercip73@gmail.com

*PLEASE NOTE:
Only for continuing education, workshops and seminars. Any other applications will be considered at the discretion of the committee.

COOPERSTOWN GRADUATE PROGRAM   [666]
SUNY College at Oneonta
Cooperstown Graduate Program in Museum Studies
5838 State Route 80
Cooperstown, NY 13326-2502
(607) 547-2586
Fax: (607) 547-8926
E-mail: melanie.bruce@oneonta.edu
gretchen.sorin@oneonta.edu
Web Site: www.oneonta.edu/academics/cgp

FOUNDED: 1964

AREAS OF INTEREST:
History museum studies and science museum studies.

TYPE:
Assistantships; Fellowships; Scholarships. Awards for museum studies for Cooperstown Graduate Program students only.

YEAR PROGRAM STARTED: 1964

PURPOSE:
To provide professionally trained individuals for the museum field.

ELIGIBILITY:
Applicants must have a strong academic record, an interest in public service, excellent writing skills and a demonstrated commitment to the field through museum work in either staff or volunteer capacity.

FINANCIAL DATA:
Amount of support per award: $4,000 to $12,000 per year.

Total amount of support: $175,000.

CO-OP FUNDING PROGRAMS: Co-sponsored with SUNY College at Oneonta.

NO. MOST RECENT APPLICANTS: Approximately 60.

NO. AWARDS: Approximately 50 awards for students.

APPLICATION INFO:
Applications and further information may be obtained from the web site. Applications are to be submitted online.

Duration: Tenable in Cooperstown, NY, for 24 months.

Deadline: May 1 for fellowship application.

PUBLICATIONS:
Viewbook.

ADDRESS INQUIRIES TO:
Melanie Bruce
Outreach and Engagement Coordinator
P.O. Box 4
Cooperstown, NY 13326-0004

THE FOUNDATION FOR ADVANCEMENT IN CONSERVATION (FAIC)   [667]
727 15th Street, N.W.
Suite 500
Washington, DC 20005
(202) 452-9545
Fax: (202) 452-9328
E-mail: cap@culturalheritage.org
Web Site: www.culturalheritage.org/cap

FOUNDED: 1973

AREAS OF INTEREST:
Conservation assessment of museum collections.

CONSULTING OR VOLUNTEER SERVICES:
Professional consulting services.

NAME(S) OF PROGRAMS:
● **Collections Assessment for Preservation (CAP)**

TYPE:
Technical assistance. Provides funds for an independent, professional conservation assessment of a museum's collections and building environment. The assessor's resulting report will identify conservation priorities to assist the museum in developing a long-term plan for collections care and management.

YEAR PROGRAM STARTED: 2017

PURPOSE:
To make collections care and conservation a fundamental priority of museums and historical societies.

LEGAL BASIS:
Private and nonprofit.

ELIGIBILITY:
Institutions including museums, zoos, aquariums, botanical gardens and arboreta are eligible for assistance. CAP will also support the on-site participation of an architectural assessor. Zoos and aquariums that do not have an assessment of the animals' physical conditions and habitats can use the program for a general assessment of those collections.

GEOG. RESTRICTIONS: United States.

FINANCIAL DATA:
Institutions will normally pay travel costs and a portion of assessors fees.

Amount of support per award: $3,600 to $8,000.

Total amount of support: Varies.

CO-OP FUNDING PROGRAMS: Program funded through Institute of Museum and Library Services.

NO. MOST RECENT APPLICANTS: 110.

NO. AWARDS: 75.

APPLICATION INFO:
Notification of the release of CAP application online will be publicized on the FAIC web site.

Duration: One year.

Deadline: Submission deadlines are posted online.

PUBLICATIONS:
CAP brochure.

STAFF:
Tiffani Emig, Program Director and Administrative Manager

ADDRESS INQUIRIES TO:
Collections Assessment for Preservation (See address above.)

GEORGIA LIBRARY ASSOCIATION   [668]
P.O. Box 30324
Savannah, GA 31410
(912) 376-9155
E-mail: scholarship@georgialibraryassociation.org
Web Site: gla.georgialibraries.org/resources/scholarships

FOUNDED: 1897

AREAS OF INTEREST:
Library professional development.

NAME(S) OF PROGRAMS:
● **Beard Scholarship**
● **Hubbard Scholarship**

TYPE:
Scholarships. Awards for graduate study of library science.

PURPOSE:
To recruit excellent librarians for Georgia.

LEGAL BASIS:
Professional association.

ELIGIBILITY:
Applicants must be accepted for admission to a Master's program at an ALA-accredited library school and must indicate intention to complete the Master's program within three years. Recipient must work in a library in Georgia for at least one year after graduation from ALA-accredited library school. Beard Scholarship is for candidates who demonstrate leadership potential.

GEOG. RESTRICTIONS: Georgia.

FINANCIAL DATA:
Amount of support per award: Beard Scholarship: $1,500; Hubbard Scholarship: $3,000.

Total amount of support: $4,500 annually.

NO. AWARDS: 1 each annually.

APPLICATION INFO:
Applicant must submit to the Chair the following:
(1) one official application form (applicant may be considered for both scholarships via one form and other accompanying documentation; do not submit duplicate materials);
(2) proof of admission to an American Library Association-accredited Master's program/library school, i.e., a letter from the dean of the school/program certifying acceptance (photocopy is acceptable);
(3) three letters of reference sent directly from the reference to the Committee Chair and;
(4) official transcripts of all academic work sent directly to the Chair from each college or university attended.

Duration: Remainder of MLIS Program.

Deadline: May 14.

ADDRESS INQUIRIES TO:
GLA Scholarship Fund
Georgia Library Association
(See address above.)

*SPECIAL STIPULATIONS:
The scholarship winners must agree to work in Georgia for one year following receipt of the Master's degree or agree to pay back a prorated amount of the award plus interest. Repayment must be made within two years.

HARTFORD PUBLIC LIBRARY   [669]
500 Main Street
Hartford, CT 06103-3075
(860) 695-6300
Fax: (860) 722-6900
E-mail: mjarry@hplct.org
Web Site: www.hplct.org

FOUNDED: 1774

AREAS OF INTEREST:
Children's librarianship.

NAME(S) OF PROGRAMS:
● The Caroline M. Hewins Scholarship

TYPE:
Scholarships. Awarded to candidates for M.L.S. who will work with children.

YEAR PROGRAM STARTED: 1926

PURPOSE:
To assist in graduate Library Science study, leading to a career in library service with children.

ELIGIBILITY:
Students who plan to specialize in library work with children, who have received or are about to receive a four-year undergraduate degree and who have been admitted to or are attending an ALA-accredited library school are eligible. Preference is given to applicants who plan to pursue a career in public library service.

FINANCIAL DATA:
Amount of support per award: Up to $4,000.
Total amount of support: Up to $4,000 annually.

NO. MOST RECENT APPLICANTS: 52.

NO. AWARDS: 1 annually.

APPLICATION INFO:
The application form can be downloaded from the Library's web site.
Deadline: Completed applications must be submitted by between July 1 and September 1.

ADDRESS INQUIRIES TO:
Marie Jarry, Director of Public Services
(See address above.)

INDIANA LIBRARY FEDERATION   [670]
941 East 86th Street
Suite 260
Indianapolis, IN 46240
(317) 257-2040
Fax: (317) 257-1389
E-mail: askus@ilfonline.org
Web Site: www.ilfonline.org

FOUNDED: 1891

AREAS OF INTEREST:
Librarian education and training.

NAME(S) OF PROGRAMS:
● The Esther Schlundt Memorial Fund
● The Sue Marsh Weller Fund

TYPE:
Scholarships. Awards for graduate study of library science at ALA-accredited schools.

PURPOSE:
To aid students in financial need who have strong undergraduate records and who show unusual ability in the library field either public or academic.

LEGAL BASIS:
Professional association.

ELIGIBILITY:
Applicants must be legal residents of Indiana who intend to work in an Indiana library for at least one year after completing library education and must be enrolled in an ALA-accredited graduate program of library science.

GEOG. RESTRICTIONS: Indiana.

FINANCIAL DATA:
Amount of support per award: Up to $1,000.
Total amount of support: Varies.

NO. MOST RECENT APPLICANTS: 7 for the year 2020.

NO. AWARDS: 7 for the year 2020.

APPLICATION INFO:
Application must be made in writing. Further information may be requested from the Federation.
Deadline: April 30.

ADDRESS INQUIRIES TO:
Lucinda Nord, Executive Director
(See address above.)

INSTITUTE OF MUSEUM AND LIBRARY SERVICES   [671]
955 L'Enfant Plaza North, S.W.
Suite 4000
Washington, DC 20024
(202) 653-4657
TTY: (202) 606-8636
E-mail: imlsinfo@imls.gov
Web Site: www.imls.gov

FOUNDED: 1996

AREAS OF INTEREST:
Museums in all disciplines including art, history, science, as well as aquariums and zoological parks, botanical gardens, arboretums, planetariums, nature centers, natural history and children's museums.

NAME(S) OF PROGRAMS:
● Inspire! Grants for Small Museums
● Museum Assessment Program
● Museum Grants for African American History and Culture
● Museums Empowered: Professional Development Opportunities for Museum Staff
● Museums for America
● National Leadership Grants for Museums
● National Medal for Museum and Library Service
● Native American/Native Hawaiian Museum Services Program

TYPE:
Awards/prizes; Challenge/matching grants; Conferences/seminars; Demonstration grants; Development grants; Fellowships; Formula grants; Internships; Project/program grants; Research grants; Scholarships; Seed money grants; Technical assistance; Training grants; Research contracts. Museum Assessment Program (MAP) grants help strengthen museum operations, plan for the future and meet national standards through self-study and a site visit from a peer reviewer.

Museum Grants for African American History and Culture strengthen African American museums by improving care of collections, developing professional management or providing internships and fellowship opportunities.

Museums for America grants support activities that strengthen museums as active resources for lifelong learning, vital components of livable communities and good stewards of the nation's collections.

National Leadership Grants for Museums support projects that address challenges or needs of the museum field, have broad impact and demonstrate innovation and collaboration.

National Medal for Museum and Library Service is the nation's highest honor for libraries and museums and is awarded by IMLS to outstanding institutions that make exceptional contributions to their communities.

Native American/Native Hawaiian Museum Services Program grants enhance museum services to sustain heritage, culture and knowledge.

YEAR PROGRAM STARTED: 1977

PURPOSE:
To foster leadership, innovation and lifetime learning by supporting museums and libraries.

LEGAL BASIS:
Federal independent agency within the Executive Branch.

ELIGIBILITY:
All types of museums, large and small, are eligible for funding. An eligible museum must be a public or private nonprofit institution that exists on a permanent basis for educational or aesthetic purposes.

Funds cannot be used for construction, renovation of facilities, endowment or acquisition of objects. Contact IMLS for program-specific eligibility.

GEOG. RESTRICTIONS: United States, American Samoa, Guam, the Marshall Islands, Micronesia, Northern Mariana Islands, Palau, Puerto Rico and the Virgin Islands.

FINANCIAL DATA:
Amount of support per award: Varies.
Total amount of support: Varies.

CO-OP FUNDING PROGRAMS: The Museum Assessment Program is funded by the Institute of Museum and Library Services and administered by the American Alliance for Museums.

NO. MOST RECENT APPLICANTS: Varies.

NO. AWARDS: Varies.

APPLICATION INFO:
Grant program guidelines and application instructions are available at IMLS web site.
Deadline: Varies.

PUBLICATIONS:
Annual report.

ADDRESS INQUIRIES TO:
E-mail: imls-museumgrants@imls.gov

228

MUSEUMS AND LIBRARIES

INSTITUTE OF MUSEUM AND LIBRARY SERVICES [672]
955 L'Enfant Plaza North, S.W.
Suite 4000
Washington, DC 20024
(202) 653-4657
E-mail: imlsinfo@imls.gov
Web Site: www.imls.gov

FOUNDED: 1996

AREAS OF INTEREST:
Libraries, including public libraries, school libraries, state libraries, college and university libraries, digital libraries, research libraries and archives that are not an integral part of an institution of higher education and that make publicly available library services and materials, and private or special libraries deemed eligible to participate by the state in which the library is located. Organizations, including graduate schools of library and information science, library consortia and library associations. There are special funding categories for state library administrative agencies, tribal libraries and organizations providing library services to Native Hawaiians.

NAME(S) OF PROGRAMS:
- **Laura Bush 21st Century Librarian Program**
- **Grants to State Library Administrative Agencies**
- **National Leadership Grants for Libraries**
- **National Medal for Museum and Library Service**
- **Native American Library Services: Basic Grants and Enhancement Grants**
- **Native Hawaiian Library Services Grant**

TYPE:
Project/program grants. Laura Bush 21st Century Librarian Program: Grants support professional development, graduate education and continuing education to help libraries and archives develop human capital capacity.

Grants to State Library Administrative Agencies: This is the largest grant program run by IMLS. It provides funds to State Library Administrative Agencies (SLAAs) using a population-based formula.

National Leadership Grants for Libraries: This program supports projects that address challenges faced by the library and archive fields and that have the potential to advance practice in those fields.

Native American Library Services: Basic Grants and Enhancement Grants: Provide funds for core library operations, technical assistance, and innovative project grants for libraries serving Native Americans and Alaska Native villages.

A Native Hawaiian Library Services Grant is awarded annually to organizations providing library services to Native Hawaiians.

PURPOSE:
To foster leadership, innovation and lifetime learning by supporting museums and libraries.

LEGAL BASIS:
Federal independent agency within the Executive Branch.

ELIGIBILITY:
Restricted funding categories exist for state library administrative agencies and for library services to Native Americans and Native Hawaiians.

Funds cannot be used for construction, renovation of facilities, endowment or acquisition of objects. Contact IMLS for program-specific eligibility.

GEOG. RESTRICTIONS: United States and territories.

FINANCIAL DATA:
Amount of support per award: Varies.
Total amount of support: Varies.

NO. MOST RECENT APPLICANTS: Varies.

NO. AWARDS: Varies.

APPLICATION INFO:
Application information is available online.
Duration: Varies per award.
Deadline: Varies.

ADDRESS INQUIRIES TO:
E-mail: ilms-librarygrants@imls.gov

MEDICAL LIBRARY ASSOCIATION [673]
225 West Wacker Drive
Suite 650
Chicago, IL 60606
(312) 419-9094
E-mail: awards@mail.mlahq.org
Web Site: www.mlanet.org

FOUNDED: 1898

AREAS OF INTEREST:
Health sciences librarianship.

NAME(S) OF PROGRAMS:
- **MLA Doctoral Fellowship**
- **MLA Scholarship**

TYPE:
Fellowships; Scholarships. Awarded for study and doctoral work in health sciences librarianship.

YEAR PROGRAM STARTED: 1986

PURPOSE:
To support and encourage individuals who are qualified to make a contribution to librarianship.

LEGAL BASIS:
Nonprofit.

ELIGIBILITY:
Citizens or permanent residents of the U.S. or Canada are eligible to apply.

For the MLA Doctoral Fellowship, applicants must be members of MLA and graduates of an ALA-accredited library school or have equivalent graduate credentials in related information science disciplines (i.e., computer science, biomedical informatics). They must also have been accepted to candidacy in a Ph.D. program in health sciences librarianship with an emphasis on biomedical and health-related information science. A past recipient of the MLA Doctoral Fellowship is ineligible.

Applicants for the MLA Scholarship must be entering an ALA-accredited graduate library school Master's program or, at the time of the granting of the scholarship (February), have completed no more than one-half of the academic requirements of the graduate program. An applicant who is a past recipient of the MLA Scholarship or the MLA Scholarship for Underrepresented Students is ineligible.

GEOG. RESTRICTIONS: United States and Canada.

FINANCIAL DATA:
Amount of support per award: MLA Doctoral Fellowship: $2,000; MLA Scholarship: Up to $5,000.

NO. AWARDS: MLA Doctoral Fellowship: 1 every two years; MLA Scholarships: 1 each per year.

APPLICATION INFO:
MLA Doctoral Fellowship, applicant must submit the following:
(1) application form and pertinent documentation;
(2) signed statement of terms and conditions;
(3) two letters of reference, submitted by the reference directly to MLA, Professional Development Department;
(4) transcripts of graduate work or proof of enrollment in the graduate program and a list of courses completed and;
(5) name, title, address, telephone and e-mail of doctoral advisor.

For the MLA Scholarship, applicant must submit an application form, essay, and all related documents plus a single copy of transcripts, two letters of reference and a copy of applicant's library school catalog or web page, which states the number of credits needed for one's degree.

Application and all supporting documents must be received by the deadline to be valid.
Duration: One year.
Deadline: December 1.

STAFF:
Maria Lopez, Grants, Scholarships and Awards Coordinator

ADDRESS INQUIRIES TO:
Coordinator
Grants, Scholarships and Awards
(See address above.)

MEDICAL LIBRARY ASSOCIATION [674]
225 West Wacker Drive
Suite 650
Chicago, IL 60606
(312) 419-9094
E-mail: awards@mail.mlahq.org
Web Site: www.mlanet.org

FOUNDED: 1898

AREAS OF INTEREST:
Health sciences librarianship.

NAME(S) OF PROGRAMS:
- **Estelle Brodman Award for the Academic Medical Librarian of the Year**
- **Lois Ann Colaianni Award for Excellence and Achievement in Hospital Librarianship**
- **Louise Darling Medal for Distinguished Achievement in Collection Development in the Health Sciences**
- **Janet Doe Lectureship**
- **Ida and George Eliot Prize**
- **Erich Meyerhoff Prize**
- **Marcia C. Noyes Award**
- **Rittenhouse Award**
- **Frank Bradway Rogers Information Advancement Award**

TYPE:
Awards/prizes; Visiting scholars. Awards to honor service to libraries and librarianship.

The Estelle Brodman Award for the Academic Medical Librarian of the Year recognizes an academic medical librarian at the midcareer level who demonstrates significant achievement or the potential for leadership and continuing excellence.

The Lois Ann Colaianni Award for Excellence and Achievement in Hospital Librarianship is given to an MLA-member who has made significant contributions to the profession in the area of hospital librarianship.

The Louise Darling Medal for Distinguished Achievement in Collection Development in the Health Sciences is given annually for outstanding collection development in the health sciences.

The Janet Doe Lectureship chooses an individual to present the lecture at the MLA's annual meeting. Recipients are chosen for their unique perspective on the history or philosophy of medical librarianship.

The Ida and George Eliot Prize is presented annually for a work published in the preceding calendar year that has been judged most effective in furthering medical librarianship.

The Erich Meyerhoff Prize is awarded annually for the best unpublished essay on the history of medicine and allied health sciences written by a health sciences librarian.

The Marcia C. Noyes Award is the highest professional distinction of the MLA. It recognizes a career that has resulted in lasting and outstanding contributions to medical librarianship.

The Rittenhouse Award recognizes an outstanding unpublished paper written by a library student or intern on health sciences librarianship or medical informatics.

Fellows and Honorary Members are selected for outstanding lifetime contributions to the advancement of the purposes of the MLA and are ordinarily chosen from members at or near the close of an active professional career. Honorary members are nonmembers who have made outstanding contributions to the advancement of the purposes of the Association.

The Frank Bradway Rogers Information Advancement Award is presented annually to recognize the application of technology to the delivery of health sciences information to the science of information, or to the facilitation of the delivery of health sciences information.

PURPOSE:
To honor those who have rendered distinguished service to libraries and medical librarianship.

LEGAL BASIS:
Nonprofit organization.

ELIGIBILITY:
Applicants must be health science librarians. Essays submitted must be on the history of medicine or the allied sciences and must be unpublished.

Membership in MLA is required.

FINANCIAL DATA:
Amount of support per award: Brodman Award, Colaianni Award for Excellence and Achievement in Hospital Librarianship, Rittenhouse Award and Rogers Award: $500 each; Darling Medal: $1,000; Janet Doe Lectureship: $500 and up to $1,700 for travel, lodging and registration; Eliot Prize: $200; Meyerhoff Prize: $500.

CO-OP FUNDING PROGRAMS: The Rittenhouse Award established and sponsored by the Rittenhouse Book Distributors, Philadelphia, PA.

NO. AWARDS: 1 per award each year.

APPLICATION INFO:
Nominations forms and guidelines are available on the web site.
Deadline: November 1.

PUBLICATIONS:
Honors and awards program announcement.

STAFF:
Maria Lopez, Grants, Scholarships and Awards Coordinator

ADDRESS INQUIRIES TO:
Coordinator
Grants, Scholarships and Awards
(See address above.)

MEDICAL LIBRARY ASSOCIATION

225 West Wacker Drive
Suite 650
Chicago, IL 60606
(312) 419-9094
E-mail: awards@mail.mlahq.org
Web Site: www.mlanet.org

TYPE:
Fellowships; Travel grants; Work-study programs. Work-study program for medical librarians from countries other than the U.S. or Canada for a time period of at least two weeks.

See entry 875 for full listing.

MEDICAL LIBRARY ASSOCIATION

225 West Wacker Drive
Suite 650
Chicago, IL 60606
(312) 419-9094
E-mail: awards@mail.mlahq.org
Web Site: www.mlanet.org

TYPE:
Awards/prizes; Scholarships. Awarded for study in health sciences librarianship.

See entry 906 for full listing.

THE METROPOLITAN MUSEUM OF ART   [675]

1000 Fifth Avenue
New York, NY 10028-0198
(212) 650-2763
E-mail: academic.programs@metmuseum.org
Web Site: www.metmuseum.org

AREAS OF INTEREST:
Art conservation and research.

NAME(S) OF PROGRAMS:
● **Conservation and Scientific Research Fellowships**

TYPE:
Fellowships. Fellowship awards for recent Master's graduates, Ph.D. candidates, postdoctoral scholars, and senior scientists in the fields of conservation and scientific research.

ELIGIBILITY:
Applicants should have reached an advanced level of experience or training.

FINANCIAL DATA:
Amount of support per award: $52,000 stipend for senior fellows for one year, $42,000 for predoctoral fellows, and up to an additional $6,000 for travel and miscellaneous expenses.

APPLICATION INFO:
Applications must be completed through the Museum's online portal. No hard copies will be accepted.
Duration: Normally, a fellow will be in residence at The Metropolitan Museum of Art for a maximum of one year. Shorter terms are available for senior fellows.
Deadline: Application and required letters of recommendation must be received by the first Friday in December. Announcements of awards will be made by late March.

STAFF:
Marcie Karp, Senior Managing Educator, Academic and Professional Programs, Education Department

ADDRESS INQUIRIES TO:
See e-mail address above.

*SPECIAL STIPULATIONS:
All fellowship recipients will be expected to spend the fellowship in residence in the department with which they are affiliated.

MINNESOTA DEPARTMENT OF EDUCATION   [676]

1500 Highway 36 West
Roseville, MN 55113-4266
(651) 582-8791
Fax: (651) 582-8752
E-mail: mde.lst@state.mn.us
Web Site: education.mn.gov/MDE/dse/Lib/sls/

FOUNDED: 1899

AREAS OF INTEREST:
Supporting innovation in library services, cooperation among all types of libraries, public library accessibility, library technology and resource sharing.

CONSULTING OR VOLUNTEER SERVICES:
Assistance provided on a range of library issues.

NAME(S) OF PROGRAMS:
● **Library Construction Grants**
● **Library Services and Technology Act Competitive Grants**
● **Multi-Type Library Cooperation Aid**
● **Regional Library Telecommunications Aid**
● **Regional Public Libraries Systems Support**

TYPE:
Capital grants; Development grants; Formula grants; General operating grants; Project/program grants; Seed money grants; Technical assistance; Training grants. Matching capital grants for library accessibility and improvement. Competitive grants that address activities and priorities in the Minnesota Five-Year Plan.

YEAR PROGRAM STARTED: 1957

PURPOSE:
To extend and improve library and information services for the people of Minnesota through public libraries and cooperation among all types of libraries.

LEGAL BASIS:
Government agency.

ELIGIBILITY:
Specific requirements vary by program and include local public libraries; Minnesota

county and regional public library systems; and multicounty, multitype library systems meeting minimum support requirements. Academic libraries and school library media centers are also eligible to apply. Contact the Department for details.

GEOG. RESTRICTIONS: Minnesota.

FINANCIAL DATA:
Amount of support per award: Varies by grant program.
Total amount of support: Varies by year.
Matching fund requirements: Varies by program.

NO. MOST RECENT APPLICANTS: Varies by grant program.

NO. AWARDS: Varies by grant program.

APPLICATION INFO:
Applications are available online.
Duration: Varies by grant program.
Deadline: Varies by grant program.

ADDRESS INQUIRIES TO:
State Library Services
(See address above.)

NATIONAL HOME LIBRARY FOUNDATION [677]
3804 Williams Lane, Lower Level
Chevy Chase, MD 20815
(301) 986-4854
Fax: (301) 986-4855
E-mail: grants@homelibraryfoundation.org
Web Site: homelibraryfoundation.org

FOUNDED: 1932

AREAS OF INTEREST:
Literacy.

TYPE:
Project/program grants. Grants in support of libraries, books and publications.

PURPOSE:
To assist in the distribution of books and other literacy-related resources to libraries and community groups with limited access to sources of specific areas of information; to assist in support, promotion and development of programs with the goal of combating illiteracy and/or encouraging an interest in reading and the literacy arts among all ages; to encourage development of programs relating primarily to literary or cultural topics that utilize various means of communications.

ELIGIBILITY:
Applicants must be tax-exempt groups with appropriate interests and activities.

GEOG. RESTRICTIONS: United States, with preference to Maryland, Virginia and Washington, DC, areas.

FINANCIAL DATA:
Amount of support per award: $500 to $5,000. Average grant approximately $2,000.
Total amount of support: $30,300 for the year 2019.

REPRESENTATIVE AWARDS:
$4,000 to Loudon Literacy Council, Leesburg, VA, for the purchase of books and communications materials; $1,600 to All Ages Read Together, Herndon, VA, for the purchase of books and communications materials; $4,500 to Camp Fire Patuxent Area Council, Bowie, MD, for the purchase of books and communications materials.

APPLICATION INFO:
Application takes the form of a proposal stating the nature of the project and its sponsors, along with a budget and financial statement.
Duration: Typically one year.
Deadline: Applications may be submitted at any time and are reviewed in the spring and fall.

IRS I.D.: 52-6051013

ADDRESS INQUIRIES TO:
Aisha Karimah, Executive Director
(See address above.)

NEW HAMPSHIRE LIBRARY ASSOCIATION [678]
c/o NH State Library
20 Park Street
Concord, NH 03301-6314
(603) 624-6550
E-mail: cpearman@manchesternh.gov
Web Site: nhlibrarians.org

FOUNDED: 1889

AREAS OF INTEREST:
Library and information science education.

NAME(S) OF PROGRAMS:
• Rosalie Norris Scholarship
• F. Mabel Winchell Loan Fund

TYPE:
Scholarships. The Norris Scholarship is awarded to New Hampshire residents or individuals working in a New Hampshire library for graduate library study. The Winchell Loan Fund provides for interest-free loans to New Hampshire residents or individuals working in a New Hampshire library to attend graduate library schools.

YEAR PROGRAM STARTED: 1949

PURPOSE:
To promote good library service from all types of libraries to all people of the state.

LEGAL BASIS:
Nonprofit.

ELIGIBILITY:
An applicant must be a member of the New Hampshire Library Association and have been accepted into the appropriate program. Applicant must live in New Hampshire or be employed by a New Hampshire library and must be enrolled in an ALA- accredited program.

GEOG. RESTRICTIONS: New Hampshire.

FINANCIAL DATA:
Amount of support per award: Scholarship grant provides a maximum of $1,000. Loan provides $2,000 (interest-free) to be repaid in four years.
Total amount of support: Varies.

NO. AWARDS: 2 Norris Scholarships for the year 2020.

APPLICATION INFO:
Applications are approved by the New Hampshire Library Association Scholarship Committee. Mail applications to: Carlos Pearman, Scholarship Chairperson, New Hampshire Library Association, c/o Manchester City Library, 405 Pine Street, Manchester, NH 03104.
Duration: One year.
Deadline: April 1 and September 1.

ADDRESS INQUIRIES TO:
Carlos Pearman, Scholarship Chairperson
(See address above.)

NEW JERSEY LIBRARY ASSOCIATION [679]
163 U.S. Highway 130 North
Building 1, Suite 1C
Bordentown, NJ 08505
(609) 482-1282
Fax: (609) 379-6278
E-mail: njla_office@njla.org
jmachie@njla.org
Web Site: www.njla.org

FOUNDED: 1890

AREAS OF INTEREST:
Education, training of members and recruitment into the profession.

NAME(S) OF PROGRAMS:
• Scholarships

TYPE:
Scholarships. Offered to residents of New Jersey for study leading to a degree in library science at a graduate library school with an ALA-accredited degree program.

YEAR PROGRAM STARTED: 1926

PURPOSE:
To give financial support for tuition to worthy candidates, of New Jersey residency, desiring to work toward a graduate degree in library service as a profession.

LEGAL BASIS:
Nonprofit status.

ELIGIBILITY:
Applicants for scholarships must:
(1) be residents of New Jersey at the time of application or have worked in any New Jersey library for at least 12 months on a full-time or part-time basis;
(2) show substantial financial need and;
(3) present worthy scholarship, as shown by official transcript, a written essay describing what the applicant can contribute to librarianship, and two recommendations by people in the field of librarianship if possible.

FINANCIAL DATA:
Scholarships are awarded in the spring for the following school year for full- or part-time study. Funds must be used for tuition only and are sent directly to the college. Any unused monies are refunded to the treasurer of the New Jersey Library Association.
Amount of support per award: Varies depending on funding.

APPLICATION INFO:
Applications and guidelines are available on the Association web site.
Duration: One year.
Deadline: March. Announcement in winter.

ADDRESS INQUIRIES TO:
See e-mail address above.

NEW MEXICO LIBRARY ASSOCIATION [680]

P.O. Box 26074
Albuquerque, NM 87125
(505) 400-7309
Fax: (505) 544-5740
E-mail: education@nmla.org
Web Site: www.nmla.wildapricot.
org/scholarships-grants

FOUNDED: 1923

AREAS OF INTEREST:
Promoting libraries and librarianship in New Mexico.

NAME(S) OF PROGRAMS:
● **College Scholarship Fund**
● **Continuing Education Grants**
● **Marion Dorroh Memorial Scholarship**

TYPE:
Scholarships. The scholarships support study in an accredited library school program. The continuing grants support attending workshops, conferences and educational activities of practicing New Mexico librarians.

YEAR PROGRAM STARTED: 1953

PURPOSE:
To support and promote libraries and the development of library personnel.

LEGAL BASIS:
Nonprofit corporation.

ELIGIBILITY:
College Scholarship Fund: Application is intended for New Mexico library workers who are pursuing an undergraduate program culminating in a degree in Library Technology or school library certification. It can also be used for graduate study toward a teacher-librarian endorsement.

Marion Dorroh Memorial Scholarship: Applicant must be accepted or currently enrolled in an ALA-accredited college or university as a full- or part-time student for an advanced degree in Library and Information Science.

The Continuing Education Grants support is based upon financial need. The Grants are intended for New Mexico library workers to promote professional development. They may be used to attend workshops, conferences and related activities.

GEOG. RESTRICTIONS: New Mexico.

FINANCIAL DATA:
Amount of support per award: Continuing Education Grants: Up to $200.
Total amount of support: Varies.

NO. AWARDS: 1 per award.

APPLICATION INFO:
Application forms are available on the Association web site.
Duration: One year.
Deadline: College Scholarship and Marion Dorroh Memorial Scholarship: May 31. Continuing Education Grants: Applications are accepted on a rolling basis.

IRS I.D.: 23-7024820

ADDRESS INQUIRIES TO:
Chairperson
NMLA Education Committee
(See address above.)

NORTH CAROLINA LIBRARY ASSOCIATION [681]

c/o NCLA Scholarships Committee
265 East Chester Drive
Suite 133, No. 364
High Point, NC 27262
E-mail: admin@nclaonline.org
Web Site: nclaonline.org/about/awards

FOUNDED: 1904

AREAS OF INTEREST:
The promotion of libraries and library service in North Carolina.

NAME(S) OF PROGRAMS:
● **The Appalachian Scholarship**
● **The North Carolina Library Association Memorial Scholarship**
● **The Query-Long Scholarship**

TYPE:
Scholarships. Scholarships and loans to promote the education of qualified librarians.

PURPOSE:
To promote libraries, library and information services, librarianship, intellectual freedom and literacy.

LEGAL BASIS:
Professional association.

ELIGIBILITY:
Applicants must have been a legal resident of North Carolina for two years, have a genuine interest in professional library work, demonstrate need of financial assistance, hold an undergraduate degree and be accepted by a library school. (Persons whose library school applications are pending may apply for the scholarships.)

GEOG. RESTRICTIONS: North Carolina.

FINANCIAL DATA:
Amount of support per award: $1,000 per award.
Total amount of support: $3,000.

NO. MOST RECENT APPLICANTS: Approximately 20.

NO. AWARDS: 1 per award.

APPLICATION INFO:
Application forms and instructions can be found on the Association web site.
Deadline: May 31. Notification in the summer. Awarded biennially in Conference years.

ADDRESS INQUIRIES TO:
Amy Funderburk
Scholarships Committee Chair
North Carolina Library Association
(See address above.)

ROCK ISLAND ARSENAL MUSEUM

Rock Island Arsenal Historical Society
R. Maguire Scholarship Committee
One Rock Island Arsenal
Rock Island, IL 61299-5000
(309) 782-5021
Fax: (309) 782-3598
E-mail: contact@arsenalhistoricalsociety.org
rhist37@gmail.com
Web Site: www.arsenalhistoricalsociety.org

TYPE:
Scholarships.

See entry 580 for full listing.

STATE LIBRARY AND ARCHIVES OF FLORIDA [682]

R.A. Gray Building
500 South Bronough Street
Tallahassee, FL 32399-0250
(850) 245-6620
Fax: (850) 245-6643
E-mail: marian.deeney@dos.myflorida.com
Web Site: dos.myflorida.com/library-archives/services-for-libraries/grants/lsta

FOUNDED: 1925

AREAS OF INTEREST:
Public libraries, public elementary school or secondary school libraries, academic libraries, research libraries, private libraries, or library consortium.

CONSULTING OR VOLUNTEER SERVICES:
Provide advice to public and institution libraries and libraries for the blind and handicapped.

NAME(S) OF PROGRAMS:
● **Library Services and Technology Act**

TYPE:
Project/program grants. Project grants congruent with the state long-range plan.

YEAR PROGRAM STARTED: 1997

PURPOSE:
To stimulate excellence and promote access to learning and information resources in all types of libraries for individuals of all ages; to promote library services that provide all users access to information through state, regional, national, and international electronic networks; to provide linkages among and between libraries; to promote targeted library services to people of diverse geographic, cultural, and socioeconomic backgrounds, to individuals with disabilities and to people with limited functional literacy or information skills.

LEGAL BASIS:
Based on U.S. Library Services and Technology Act (P.L. 104-208, as amended) and Florida Statutes 257.12, 257.191 and 257.192.

ELIGIBILITY:
Applicants must be Florida libraries that provide free library service or institution libraries that are operated or substantially supported by the state.

GEOG. RESTRICTIONS: Florida.

FINANCIAL DATA:
Amount of support per award: Varies.
Total amount of support: $8,971,754 for fiscal year 2020-21.
Matching fund requirements: At least one-third of the grant request or award must be met with matching funds.

NO. MOST RECENT APPLICANTS: 40.

APPLICATION INFO:
Application must be submitted online. Applicants should supply project proposal.
Duration: One year. Must reapply for each year.
Deadline: Varies.

PUBLICATIONS:
Grant guidelines.

IRS I.D.: 59-3466865

ADDRESS INQUIRIES TO:
David Beach, Library Program Specialist
Tel: (850) 245-6630
E-mail: david.beach@dos.myflorida.com

TEXAS LIBRARY ASSOCIATION [683]
3355 Bee Cave Road, Suite 401
Austin, TX 78746-6763
(512) 328-1518
(800) 580-2852
E-mail: tla@txla.org
Web Site: www.txla.org

FOUNDED: 1902

AREAS OF INTEREST:
Library and information science.

NAME(S) OF PROGRAMS:
- Walter H. Escue Memorial Scholarship
- Vivian Greenfield Education Award
- Ray C. Janeway Scholarship
- TLA Summer School Scholarship
- Van Dusen-Tobin-Kaiser Scholarship

TYPE:
Scholarships. Awards for graduate study leading to a Master's degree in library science.

YEAR PROGRAM STARTED: 1998

PURPOSE:
To help support the educational goals of students who want to get an advanced degree in library science.

LEGAL BASIS:
Professional association.

ELIGIBILITY:
Applicants must be members of TLA.

Walter Escue Scholars must be Texas residents concentrating studies in technical services, systems administration or library automation, attained at least a "B" average during the last two years of a Baccalaureate degree program and have been accepted as a graduate student to a Texas ALA-accredited library education program.

Vivian Greenfield Award applicants must reside in Texas and write a goals statement outlining a desired educational endeavor revolving around youth services.

Janeway Scholarship applicants must be Texas residents, attained at least a "B" average during the last two years of a Baccalaureate program and have been accepted as a graduate student at a Texas ALA-accredited library education program.

TLA Summer School Scholar must be a Texas resident, attained at least a "B" average during the last two years of a Baccalaureate degree program, and must be registered for MLS degree courses during a summer session at a Texas ALA-accredited library education program. (The scholarship applies only to the summer session.)

Van Dusen-Tobin-Kaiser Scholars must be Texas residents and must be pursuing graduate studies leading to a career as an elementary school or children's librarian, attained at least a "B" average during the last two years of a Baccalaureate degree program, and accepted as a graduate student at a Texas ALA-accredited library education program.

GEOG. RESTRICTIONS: Texas.

FINANCIAL DATA:
Amount of support per award: Escue Scholarship: $1,000; Greenfield Award: $1,500; Janeway Scholarship: $2,000, awarded annually; TLA Summer School Scholarship: $500; Van Dusen-Tobin-Kaiser Scholarship: $1,000, awarded biennially in even-numbered years.
Total amount of support: Varies.

NO. AWARDS: Varies.

APPLICATION INFO:
Application must be submitted online.
Duration: One year.
Deadline: Completed applications must be submitted no later than January 31.

IRS I.D.: 74-6014110

ADDRESS INQUIRIES TO:
Michele Santos, Marketing Specialist
E-mail: micheles@txla.org or
Shirley Robinson, Executive Director
(See address above.)

*SPECIAL STIPULATIONS:
Scholarships and grants are to be awarded to Texas residents only and only to applicants attending an institution of higher learning in Texas with an accredited School of Library Science.

UNITED STATES HOLOCAUST MEMORIAL MUSEUM - JACK, JOSEPH AND MORTON MANDEL CENTER FOR ADVANCED HOLOCAUST STUDIES
100 Raoul Wallenberg Place, S.W.
Washington, DC 20024-2126
E-mail: vscholars@ushmm.org
Web Site: www.ushmm.org/research/opportunities-for-academics

TYPE:
Exchange programs; Fellowships. The Jack, Joseph and Morton Mandel Center for Advanced Holocaust Studies awards several types of fellowships to support significant research and writing about the Holocaust and related topics. A fellowship at the Mandel Center not only provides time to research and access to world-renowned archives, but also an extensive network of people and institutions. Visiting scholars at the Mandel Center have access to more than 120 million pages of Holocaust-related archival documents; library resources in more than 60 languages; hundreds of thousands of oral history, film, photo, art, artifacts and memoir collections; the Database of Holocaust Survivor and Victim Names; more than 200 million images from the ITS Digital Archive; plus more. Applications from all disciplines are welcome.

See entry 590 for full listing.

UNIVERSITY OF ARIZONA SCHOOL OF INFORMATION [684]
University of Arizona
1103 East Second Street, Room 409
Tucson, AZ 85721
(520) 621-3565
Fax: (520) 621-3279
E-mail: si_info@email.arizona.edu
Web Site: ischool.arizona.edu

FOUNDED: 1963

AREAS OF INTEREST:
Information science.

TYPE:
Assistantships; Internships; Scholarships. Graduate assistantships; Research assistantships; Undergraduate internships and scholarships. Awarded to qualified students to attend the School of Information.

YEAR PROGRAM STARTED: 1963

PURPOSE:
To prepare students to tackle the challenges of an information-based society; to enable students to seize opportunities to succeed in emerging industries.

LEGAL BASIS:
Nonprofit, tax-exempt.

ELIGIBILITY:
Any student receiving financial aid must be accepted into the SI degree program. Awards are made to students who meet the criteria set by the School. (This includes students participating in the program online.) The School requires that the student be enrolled for the required number of hours for the semester of award. Assistance is awarded on a semester basis.

A new financial aid form must be completed each semester that a student wishes to be considered for aid. To be considered for financial assistance, an applicant must meet the deadlines posted. Criteria for financial aid are: stellar academic performance, financial status, and other qualifications as defined by specific scholarships.

FINANCIAL DATA:
Amount of support per award: Varies by program.
Total amount of support: Varies.

APPLICATION INFO:
Applicant must complete the Financial Assistance Application section of Library Science Application for Admission.
Duration: One or two semesters.
Deadline: Varies.

ADDRESS INQUIRIES TO:
See e-mail address above.

THE UNIVERSITY OF DELAWARE-HAGLEY GRADUATE PROGRAM
Department of History, John Munroe Hall
University of Delaware
Newark, DE 19716
(302) 831-8226
Fax: (302) 831-1538
E-mail: dianec@udel.edu
Web Site: www.udel.edu/hagley
www.history.udel.edu

TYPE:
Assistantships; Fellowships. The University of Delaware, in association with the Hagley Museum, sponsors a premier graduate resident program for the study of technology, business, consumption, and work in industrial and post-industrial societies leading to a Master of Arts or Ph.D. in History. Students have access to faculty with international reputations in American, European and non-Western history, and benefit from strong interdisciplinary ties to museum studies and material culture programs, as well as the Hagley Museum and Library.

See entry 591 for full listing.

UNIVERSITY OF TORONTO [685]
Faculty of Information
140 St. George Street
Toronto ON M5S 3G6 Canada
(416) 978-3234
Fax: (416) 978-5762
E-mail: awards.ischool@utoronto.ca
Web Site: www.ischool.utoronto.ca

FOUNDED: 1928

AREAS OF INTEREST:
Education.

NAME(S) OF PROGRAMS:
- **Patricia Fleming Visiting Fellowship in Bibliography and Book History**

TYPE:
Fellowships. Fellowship is awarded biennially in even-numbered years.

YEAR PROGRAM STARTED: 2005

PURPOSE:
To encourage outstanding scholars to conduct research in the field of bibliographical studies or book history.

LEGAL BASIS:
University.

GEOG. RESTRICTIONS: Canada.

FINANCIAL DATA:
Amount of support per award: $2,000 (CAN).

NO. MOST RECENT APPLICANTS: 7.

NO. AWARDS: 1.

APPLICATION INFO:
Applicants should submit a resume, two letters of recommendation, a one- to two-page research proposal describing the project, and the proposed timing of the fellowship.
Duration: One month.
Deadline: March 31.

ADDRESS INQUIRIES TO:
Student Services
(See address above.)

UTAH DIVISION OF ARTS & MUSEUMS

617 East South Temple
Salt Lake City, UT 84102
(801) 236-7550
Fax: (801) 236-7556
E-mail: lalder@utah.gov
Web Site: artsandmuseums.utah.gov

TYPE:
General operating grants; Project/program grants.

See entry 464 for full listing.

Music

ACCADEMIA MUSICALE CHIGIANA   [686]

Via di Città, 89
53100 Siena Italy
(39) 0577 22091
Fax: (39) 0577 288124
E-mail: accademia.chigiana@chigiana.it
Web Site: www.chigiana.it

FOUNDED: 1932

AREAS OF INTEREST:
Music.

NAME(S) OF PROGRAMS:
- **Scholarships for Summer Music Courses**

TYPE:
Awards/prizes; Scholarships. Merit scholarships to those who are registered as active students at the Academy, which offers various summer music master courses in orchestral conducting, composition, voice and various instruments.

In addition, there are other scholarships financed by public institutions or private donors and are awarded at the discretion of the Accademia Chigiana Direction.

YEAR PROGRAM STARTED: 1932

PURPOSE:
To allow young musicians from all over the world to perfect themselves in the principal instruments, studying with many world famous musicians.

ELIGIBILITY:
Applicants can be students of any nationality. Active students must hold an Italian music diploma or an equivalent foreign certificate (exception made for the courses of guitar and singing) and must pass an entrance examination. Age limits are as follows: Conducting, 30 years for the session dedicated to the classical orchestral repertoire; 40 years for the session dedicated to the modern symphonic repertoire; Voice, 32 years (sopranos and tenors), 34 years (mezzo sopranos, baritones and basses); Instruments, 30 years; Chamber Music, average of 30 years. The Italian government also finances scholarships for attendance of summer master classes at the Accademia Chigiana.

Scholarships offered by the Accademia Musicale Chigiana are awarded on the basis of the results of the entrance examination and student merit.

No scholarship will be granted to students already benefiting from financial help from other institutions or to those who do not take the entrance examination on the established date.

FINANCIAL DATA:
Amount of support per award: Scholarships consist of reimbursement of tuition fees (after detraction of the added value tax) plus a daily grant of EUR 35 gross.

Total amount of support: EUR 60,000 (with funds of the Academy) plus EUR 30,000 (by public institutions or private donors).

APPLICATION INFO:
Detailed information and application forms are available from the address above. For details of requirements and application formalities about scholarships awarded by the Italian government, candidates should write directly to the Italian Culture Institute or to the Italian Embassy in their own country.
Deadline: May 15 for the Orchestral Conducting Course; May 31 for Composition Course; June 10 for all other courses.

PUBLICATIONS:
Courses booklet (information and application form).

OFFICERS:
Carlo Rossi, President
Angelica Lippi Piccolomini, Vice President
Angelo Armiento, Administrative Director
Nicola Sani, Artistic Director

ADDRESS INQUIRIES TO:
Fondazione Accademia Musicale Chigiana
(See address above.)

AMERICAN ACADEMY OF ARTS AND LETTERS   [687]

633 West 155th Street
New York, NY 10032-7599
(212) 368-5900
Fax: (212) 491-4615
E-mail: academy@artsandletters.org
Web Site: www.artsandletters.org

FOUNDED: 1898

NAME(S) OF PROGRAMS:
- **The Richard Rodgers Awards**

TYPE:
Awards/prizes. Completed musical scripts are accepted by the Academy for this annual competition. The award subsidizes staged readings, studio productions or productions in New York City by a not-for-profit theater group of a musical play by composers and writers who are not already established in this field.

YEAR PROGRAM STARTED: 1978

PURPOSE:
To further the art of the musical theater in the U.S.

LEGAL BASIS:
Nonprofit Internal Revenue Code 501(c)(3).

ELIGIBILITY:
Open only to U.S. citizens or permanent residents of any age. While students may enter the competition, it is primarily intended for work at a professional level.

GEOG. RESTRICTIONS: United States.

FINANCIAL DATA:
Award money is given to the not-for-profit theater for production expenses.
Amount of support per award: Varies.

NO. MOST RECENT APPLICANTS: 133.

NO. AWARDS: 1 to 4.

APPLICATION INFO:
Application form can be downloaded from the Academy web site. The name(s) of the author(s) must be blocked out on each of the items submitted, with the exception of the application form. Write only the title of the work on the script, plot summary and CD. Entries must include the following items:
(1) script with lyrics, preferably with no binders or metal clips. Do not send score, videos or visuals;
(2) half-page synopsis of the action and a list of characters;
(3) CD which must contain at least 45 minutes of music, including a minimum of eight songs, recorded in chronological order. Orchestrations are not necessary; piano and vocals are sufficient. Songs must be in sequence on the CD and each song clearly keyed into the script. Please include a separate track sheet of recorded songs with page numbers indicating where they appear in the script, and specify the total number of minutes recorded. Audio tapes will not be accepted and;
(4) application form signed by all collaborators in a sealed envelope with the title of the work on the outside. Applicants submitting work which has already been produced must give full information concerning these productions, including programs. A work is not eligible if one of the collaborators is deceased.

If the submitted work (or a portion thereof) is an adaptation of material which is not in the public domain, candidates must submit licenses, permissions, or authorizations necessary to permit the work to be produced in conformity with applicable copyright laws. The music must be original.

Materials will be returned if a self-addressed, stamped mailer is enclosed. Addresses must be valid for at least six months. The Academy will take all due care of materials, but it cannot be held responsible for their safe return.

Deadline: November 1. Notification by March.

PUBLICATIONS:
Application guidelines.

STAFF:
Cody Upton, Executive Director
Ashley Fedor, Coordinator, Richard Rodgers Awards

ADDRESS INQUIRIES TO:
The Richard Rodgers Awards
(See address above.)

*SPECIAL STIPULATIONS:
Musical submitted may not be entered again, even if revised.

AMERICAN ACCORDION MUSICOLOGICAL SOCIETY   [688]
322 Haddon Avenue
Westmont, NJ 08108
(856) 854-6628
E-mail: acmeaccordion@gmail.com
Web Site: aamsaccordionfestival.com

FOUNDED: 1968

AREAS OF INTEREST:
Research and symposiums on accordion history in the U.S.

CONSULTING OR VOLUNTEER SERVICES:
Library services, books and music on the accordion, and records, CDs and DVDs for rental.

NAME(S) OF PROGRAMS:
● **Annual Symposium and Festival**

TYPE:
Awards/prizes; Work-study programs. The Annual Symposium and Festival is held on a weekend in March.

YEAR PROGRAM STARTED: 1970

PURPOSE:
To help and stimulate young composers to write for the accordion.

LEGAL BASIS:
Nonprofit professional association.

ELIGIBILITY:
Composer must be acquainted with the various types of accordions.

FINANCIAL DATA:
Amount of support per award: $300.

NO. AWARDS: 1.

APPLICATION INFO:
Applicants should write for entry forms or send an e-mail to the address above.

Deadline: Contact the Society.

ADDRESS INQUIRIES TO:
Joanna Darrow, Director
(See address above.)

THE AMERICAN BANDMASTERS ASSOCIATION   [689]
2602 Pine Valley Drive
Champaign, IL 61822
(217) 721-5156
E-mail: caneva@bsu.edu
Web Site: www.americanbandmasters.org

FOUNDED: 1929

AREAS OF INTEREST:
Concert band and band music.

NAME(S) OF PROGRAMS:
● **Sousa/ABA/Ostwald Award**

TYPE:
Awards/prizes. Prize sponsored by the American Bandmasters Association and Sousa Foundation, involving cash award and performance of the winning band or wind ensemble composition. One award is presented in odd years for grades 1-4; one award is presented in even years for grades 5-6.

YEAR PROGRAM STARTED: 1955

PURPOSE:
To enrich the spectrum of concert band activity.

ELIGIBILITY:
Details are available on the Association web site.

FINANCIAL DATA:
Amount of support per award: $5,000.
Total amount of support: $5,000.

NO. MOST RECENT APPLICANTS: 99.

NO. AWARDS: 1.

APPLICATION INFO:
Send scores (PDFs only) and recordings (mp3 of live performances only) and direct all inquiries to the Chairman of the Contest Committee at the e-mail address above. Additional requirements are provided on the Association web site.

Deadline: August 1. Announcement on October 1.

PUBLICATIONS:
Journal of Band Research.

IRS I.D.: 36-6112860

OFFICERS:
Jay Gephart, President
Kerry Taylor, President-Elect
Michael Colburn, Vice President
Thomas V. Fraschillo, Secretary-Treasurer
Lowell Graham, Chairperson, Nominating Committee

BOARD OF DIRECTORS:
Linda Moorhouse, Chairman
Dr. Daniel Bolin
Bobby R. Francis
Mark Heidel
J. Steven Moore
Michael Nakasone
Stephen Peterson
Robert W. Smith

ADDRESS INQUIRIES TO:
Tom Caneva, Chairperson
Sousa/ABA/Ostwald Committee
(See e-mail address above.)

*SPECIAL STIPULATIONS:
All inquiries and correspondence must be in the form of an e-mail.

AMERICAN MATTHAY ASSOCIATION FOR PIANO   [690]
Albion College
611 East Porter Street
Albion, MI 49224
E-mail: dabbott@albion.edu
Web Site: www.matthay.org

FOUNDED: 1925

AREAS OF INTEREST:
Piano performance and teaching.

NAME(S) OF PROGRAMS:
● **Clara Wells Fellowships**

TYPE:
Conferences/seminars; Scholarships; Work-study programs. Two annual awards, one for high school and one for collegiate, for travel to and accommodation at the Matthay Annual Piano Festival. The award includes attendance at the festival, mentoring by members, a recital performance, performance in a master class, a collection of books and CDs.

YEAR PROGRAM STARTED: 1970

PURPOSE:
To foster the teaching principles of Tobias Matthay.

LEGAL BASIS:
Nonprofit organization.

ELIGIBILITY:
Candidates must be between 15 to 30 years of age, as of the application deadline.

FINANCIAL DATA:
Amount of support per award: $1,000.
Total amount of support: $2,000.

NO. MOST RECENT APPLICANTS: 6 to 10 per year.

NO. AWARDS: 2.

APPLICATION INFO:
Application must contain:
(1) a cover letter which includes applicant's name, age, school grade, address, telephone and e-mail contacts; length of piano study and names of teachers; experience (performances, awards, scholarships, etc.); a brief statement explaining why applicant wants to be a Clara Wells Scholar; and the name and contact information for applicant's current teacher;
(2) a performance video (unedited) submitted through the YouTube link;
(3) written answers to the Reading Requirement;
(4) evidence of age (PDF file of birth certificate or passport);
(5) application fee of $20 (nonrefundable) for students of active members of the American Matthay Association or $60 (nonrefundable) for students of non-members of the American Matthay Association. Make checks payable to the American Matthay Association and;
(6) a teacher's letter of recommendation. Additional supporting letters may be sent as well, but all must be sent under separate cover by e-mail.

Deadline: March. Notification no later than April 1.

PUBLICATIONS:
The Matthay News.

ADDRESS INQUIRIES TO:
Dr. David Abbott
Competition Chairperson
Attn.: Clara Wells
(See e-mail address above.)

AMERICAN MUSICOLOGICAL SOCIETY [691]

20 Cooper Square, 2nd Floor
New York, NY 10003
(212) 992-6340
(877) 679-7648
Fax: (877) 679-7648
E-mail: ams@amsmusicology.org
Web Site: www.amsmusicology.org

FOUNDED: 1934

AREAS OF INTEREST:
Scholastic work in musicology.

NAME(S) OF PROGRAMS:
- **AMS Teaching Award**
- **The Philip Brett Award**
- **The H. Robert Cohen/RIPM Award**
- **Early Music Award**
- **The Alfred Einstein Award**
- **Noah Greenberg Award**
- **Thomas Hampson Award**
- **The Roland Jackson Award**
- **The Otto Kinkeldey Award**
- **Lewis Lockwood Award**
- **Music in American Culture Award**
- **Claude V. Palisca Award**
- **Paul A. Pisk Prize**
- **H. Colin Slim Award**
- **Ruth A. Solie Award**
- **Robert M. Stevenson Award**
- **Judy Tsou Critical Race Studies Award**

TYPE:
Awards/prizes. AMS Teaching Award honors an exceptional pedagogical resource for musicology published during the previous two years. By "resource" is meant a published article, book (including textbook), digital, or online material that best exemplifies the highest qualities of originality, theory, application, and communication for the teaching of musicology or music history.

The Philip Brett Award honors exceptional musicological work in the field of gay, lesbian, bisexual, transgender/transsexual studies completed during the previous two calendar years in any country and in any language. By "work" is meant a published article, book, edition, annotated translation, a paper read at a conference, teaching materials (course descriptions and syllabi), and other scholarly work accepted by the award committee that best exemplifies the highest qualities of originality, interpretation, theory and communication in this field of study.

The H. Robert Cohen/RIPM Award honors a publication related to the goals of RIPM (Retrospective Index to Music Periodicals). Works include, but are not limited to, books, articles, or widely-disseminated databases focusing on one or more journals, music critics and criticism, reception history, critical and cultural histories, and issues of access and preservation.

Early Music Award honors a substantial, single-author work of scholarship on music before 1550. By "work" is meant a variety of formats: articles, books, and scholarly editions with significant editorial commentaries published during the preceding three calendar years in any language and in any country.

The Alfred Einstein Award honors a musicological article of exceptional merit, published during the previous year in any language and in any country, by a scholar in the early stages of his or her career.

The Noah Greenberg Award is intended as a grant-in-aid to stimulate active cooperation between scholars and performers by recognizing and fostering outstanding contributions to historical performing practices. Both scholars and performers may apply, since the Award may subsidize the publication costs of articles, monographs, or editions, as well as public performance, recordings, or other projects.

The Thomas Hampson Award is dedicated to fostering editions and scholarship on classic song in all its contexts as well as new and innovative technologies for promoting and understanding classic song via interactive media and the Internet.

The Roland Jackson Award recognizes an article in the English language of exceptional merit in the field of music analysis. Awards are made in three separate subject categories, in successive years, on music from circa 1800 to the present, music circa 1600 to 1800, and music before 1600.

The Otto Kinkeldey Award will honor each year a musicological book of exceptional merit published during the previous year in any language and in any country by a scholar who is past the early stages of his or her career.

The Lewis Lockwood Award honors each year a musicological book of exceptional merit published during the previous year in any language and in any country by a scholar in the early stages of his or her career who is a member of the AMS or a citizen or permanent resident of Canada or the U.S.

The Music in American Culture Award honors each year a book of exceptional merit that both illuminates some important aspect of the music of the U.S. and places that music in a rich cultural context. Books published in the previous year in any language and in any country are eligible. The author must be a citizen or permanent resident of the U.S. or Canada.

The Claude V. Palisca Award honors each year a scholarly edition or translation in the field of musicology published during the previous year in any language and in any country by a scholar who is a member of the AMS or a citizen or permanent resident of Canada or the U.S., deemed by a committee of scholars to best exemplify the highest qualities of originality, interpretation, logic and clarity of thought, and communication.

The Paul A. Pisk Prize is awarded annually to a graduate music student for a scholarly paper to be presented at the Annual Meeting of the Society.

The H. Colin Slim Award honors each year a musicological article of exceptional merit, published during the previous year in any language and in any country by a scholar who is past the early stages of his or her career and who is a member of the AMS or a citizen or permanent resident of Canada or the U.S.

The Ruth A. Solie Award honors each year a collection of musicological essays of exceptional merit published during the preceding calendar year in any language and in any country and edited by a scholar or scholars who are members of the AMS or citizens or permanent residents of Canada or the U.S.

The Robert M. Stevenson Award recognizes outstanding scholarship in Iberian music. The prize will be awarded annually to a book, monograph, edition, or journal article by a member of the AMS. The publication must be written in English and must have been published during the preceding three calendar years.

Judy Tsou Critical Race Studies Award honors outstanding musicological work in the field of critical race and/or critical ethnic studies. By "work" is meant a published article, book, edition, or other scholarly entity that best exemplifies the highest qualities of originality, interpretation, theory, and communication in this area. Work must have been published during the preceding three calendar years.

Winners of all awards receive a monetary prize, conferred at the Annual Business Meeting and Awards Presentation of the Society by the chair of the committee.

YEAR PROGRAM STARTED: 1967

LEGAL BASIS:
Private.

GEOG. RESTRICTIONS: United States and Canada.

FINANCIAL DATA:
Amount of support per award: Varies.
Total amount of support: Varies.

APPLICATION INFO:
Application information is available on the web site.
Deadline: Noah Greenburg Award and Thomas Hampson Award: August 15. Paul A. Pisk Prize: October 1. Claude V. Palisca Award: January 31. All others; May 1.

IRS I.D.: 23-1577392

ADDRESS INQUIRIES TO:
See e-mail address above.

AMERICAN MUSICOLOGICAL SOCIETY [692]

20 Cooper Square, 2nd Floor
New York, NY 10003
(212) 992-6340
(877) 679-7648
Fax: (877) 679-7648
E-mail: ams@amsmusicology.org
Web Site: www.amsmusicology.org

FOUNDED: 1934

AREAS OF INTEREST:
Research in the various fields of music as a branch of learning and scholarship.

NAME(S) OF PROGRAMS:
- **Howard Mayer Brown Fellowship**
- **Holmes/D'Accone Dissertation Fellowship in Opera Studies**
- **Alvin H. Johnson AMS 50 Dissertation Fellowships**

TYPE:
Fellowships. The Howard Mayer Brown Fellowship is intended to increase the presence of minority scholars and teachers in musicology. The fellowship supports one year of graduate work for a member of a historically underrepresented group.

The Holmes/D'Accone Fellowship for dissertation research recognizes academic achievement and future promise in the study of opera. An approved dissertation proposal in the subfield of opera studies is required.

The Alvin H. Johnson AMS 50 Dissertation Fellowships are not intended for support of the early stages of research; it is expected that a Fellow's dissertation be completed within the fellowship year. Any submission for a doctoral degree in which the emphasis is on musical scholarship will be considered.

YEAR PROGRAM STARTED: 1989

PURPOSE:
To support the advancement of research in various fields of music.

LEGAL BASIS:
Nonprofit organization.

ELIGIBILITY:
For the AMS Fellowship, applicants must be registered for a Doctorate at a North American university and have completed all formal degree requirements except the dissertation.

The Howard Mayer Brown Fellowship will be awarded to a student who has completed at least one year of graduate work, and who intends to complete a Ph.D. in the field. Applications are encouraged from African-Americans, Native Americans, Latinos, Asian-Americans and, in Canada, visible minorities. There are no restrictions as to age or sex.

FINANCIAL DATA:
Amount of support per award: Varies.
Total amount of support: Varies.

APPLICATION INFO:
Applications must be submitted electronically.
Duration: One year.
Deadline: December 15.

IRS I.D.: 23-1577392

ADDRESS INQUIRIES TO:
See e-mail address above.

ARD INTERNATIONAL MUSIC COMPETITION   [693]
Internationaler Musikwettbewerb der ARD
Bayerischer Rundfunk
Rundfunkplatz 1
D-80335 Munich Germany
(49) 89 5900 42471
Fax: (49) 89 5900 3573
E-mail: ard.musikwettbewerb@br.de
Web Site: www.br.de/ard-musikwettbewerb

FOUNDED: 1952

AREAS OF INTEREST:
International music competition.

TYPE:
Awards/prizes. Cash prizes; Competition for music.

Intended for a selection of young musicians who are interested in following an international career. The standards are, therefore, high and the prizes are awarded only for outstanding performances. Program categories differ each year. For 2021: voice, horn, violin and piano duo.

YEAR PROGRAM STARTED: 1952

PURPOSE:
To create gifted musicians and international soloists.

ELIGIBILITY:
The competition is open to musicians of all nations. Horn and flute: Applicant must have been born between 1992 and 2004. Voice: Applicant must have been born between 1989

and 2001. Piano duo: Total age maximum 60, single members not younger than 17 and not older than 35.

FINANCIAL DATA:
Amount of support per award: Soloists: First prize, EUR 10,000; Second prize, EUR 7,500; Third prize, EUR 5,000. Wind Quintet: First prize, EUR 25,000; Second prize, EUR 20,000; Third prize, EUR 15,000. Piano Duo: First prize, EUR 12,000; Second prize, EUR 9,000; Third prize, EUR 6,000. String Quartet: First prize, EUR 24,000; Second prize, EUR 18,000; Third prize, EUR 12,000. Piano Trio: First Prize, EUR 18,000; Second prize, EUR 13,500; Third prize, EUR 9,000.

Total amount of support: EUR 124,500 for the year 2021.

CO-OP FUNDING PROGRAMS: Theodor - Rogler - Foundation, Alice - Rosner - Foundation, Siemens Arts Program and others.

NO. MOST RECENT APPLICANTS: Approximately 400 each year.

NO. AWARDS: 12.

APPLICATION INFO:
A valid statement of type and duration of study should accompany the entry form. Students must have permission from their current teacher to participate. A list of the applicant's complete repertoire is required. Upon arrival in Munich, each competitor should present a birth certificate or a valid passport at the Competition Office.

Preselections with videos are obligatory for all categories.

Due to Covid-19, the first round will be held digitally.
Deadline: March 31.

PUBLICATIONS:
Annual prospectus with application guidelines and programs.

OFFICERS:
Oswald Beaujean, Artistic Director
Meret Forster, Artistic Director
Elisabeth Kozik, Managing Director
Anja Krainz, Project Management

ADDRESS INQUIRIES TO:
Competition Office
(See address above.)

THE ASCAP FOUNDATION
250 West 57th Street
New York, NY 10107
(212) 621-6000
Web Site: ascapfoundation.org

TYPE:
Awards/prizes. The ASCAP Foundation Deems Taylor/Virgil Thomson Awards program recognizes books, articles and liner notes on the subject of music selected for their excellence.

See entry 612 for full listing.

THE ASCAP FOUNDATION   [694]
250 West 57th Street
New York, NY 10107
(212) 621-6000
E-mail: concertmusic@ascap.com
Web Site: www.ascapfoundation.org

FOUNDED: 1975

AREAS OF INTEREST:
Music, music composition and music education.

NAME(S) OF PROGRAMS:
● **The ASCAP Foundation Morton Gould Young Composer Awards**

TYPE:
Awards/prizes.

YEAR PROGRAM STARTED: 1978

PURPOSE:
To encourage talented young American composers.

LEGAL BASIS:
Publicly supported foundation, 501(c)(3) organization.

ELIGIBILITY:
Entrants must be, at the time of entry, at least 13 years of age and a U.S. citizen, permanent resident or enrolled student with a valid and current U.S. student visa. Entrants must also be under the age of 30 as of the application deadline.

No co-written submissions will be considered for this award.

GEOG. RESTRICTIONS: United States.

FINANCIAL DATA:
Amount of support per award: $500 to $3,500, at discretion of judges.
Total amount of support: $25,000.

NO. MOST RECENT APPLICANTS: Approximately 700.

NO. AWARDS: 15 or more.

APPLICATION INFO:
Entrants must complete and submit an Online Application, which is available on the ASCAP web site. Application shall include: (1) a score of one published or unpublished original concert work (no arrangements) and; (b) an mp3 (if available) of an electronic realization or recording of the musical work.

If entrant is under the age of majority in their state, district, or territory of resident at the time of entry, such entrant's parent or legal guardian must complete and submit the Online Application on such entrant's behalf and download, complete, and return a copy of the signed Parental Consent form to the e-mail or physical address listed above.
Deadline: February 1.

PUBLICATIONS:
Annual report; contributions policy; application guidelines.

BOARD OF DIRECTORS:
Paul Williams, President
Irwin Z. Robinson, Vice President
Dean Kay, Treasurer
Ginny Mancini, Secretary
Marilyn Bergman
Charles Bernstein
Bruce Broughton
Tita Cahn
Desmond Child
Dan Foliart
Arthur Hamilton
James M. Kendrick
Robert Kimball
Tania Leon
Michelle Lewis
James McBride
Roger McNulty
Marcus Miller
Betsy Perez
Michael Price
Geoffrey Sargeant

Stephen Schwartz
Alex Shapiro
Valerie Simpson
Doug Wood

ADMINISTRATION:
Colleen McDonough, Executive Director

ADDRESS INQUIRIES TO:
Cia Toscanini
Vice President, Concert Music
(See address above.)

BRANDON UNIVERSITY   [695]
School of Music
270 18th Street
Brandon MB R7A 6A9 Canada
(204) 727-7388
Fax: (204) 728-6839
E-mail: music@brandonu.ca
Web Site: www.brandonu.ca/music

AREAS OF INTEREST:
Music education, performance and literature
(piano, collaborative piano, strings,
composition, clarinet, trumpet, conducting
and jazz).

TYPE:
Assistantships; Scholarships.

YEAR PROGRAM STARTED: 1980

PURPOSE:
To afford graduate students the opportunity
to gain professional experience while
studying and to provide monetary assistance.

ELIGIBILITY:
Open to candidates with a Bachelor's degree
in music or music education with a minimum
grade point average of 3.0 during the final
year.

FINANCIAL DATA:
Amount of support per award: Up to $5,000
per year.
Total amount of support: $20,000 per year.

NO. MOST RECENT APPLICANTS: 15.

NO. AWARDS: 9.

APPLICATION INFO:
Applications available both online and from
the Graduate Music Office.
Duration: Two years.
Deadline: May 1.

ADDRESS INQUIRIES TO:
Greg Gatien, Chairperson
Graduate Music Department
(See address above.)

CHAMBER MUSIC
AMERICA   [696]
12 West 32nd Street, 7th Floor
New York, NY 10001
(212) 242-2022 ext. 102
E-mail: sdadian@chamber-music.org
Web Site: www.chamber-music.org

FOUNDED: 1977

AREAS OF INTEREST:
The promotion of public interest in and
appreciation of chamber music and the
promotion of cooperation among and
advancement of professional American
chamber music ensembles and presenters.

NAME(S) OF PROGRAMS:
● **Chamber Music America Classical
   Commissioning Program**

TYPE:
Project/program grants. Classical
Commissioning provides support to U.S.
member ensembles and presenters for
commissions of new chamber works by
American composers. Grants are made for
commissioning fees, copying costs and
ensemble rehearsal honoraria.

YEAR PROGRAM STARTED: 1983

PURPOSE:
To stimulate the composition of new works
for chamber ensembles.

LEGAL BASIS:
Nonprofit arts service organization.

ELIGIBILITY:
Ensembles and presenters must be
organizational members of Chamber Music
America. Compositions must be written for
small ensembles (two to 10 musicians)
performing one to a part, and may represent
a diverse musical spectrum, including
contemporary art music, world music, and
works that include electronics.

GEOG. RESTRICTIONS: United States and its
territories.

FINANCIAL DATA:
Amount of support per award: Up to $20,000
for composer fee, copying allotment of
$1,000 and subsidy of $1,000 per musician.
Total amount of support: Varies.

NO. MOST RECENT APPLICANTS: 190.

NO. AWARDS: 16.

APPLICATION INFO:
Guidelines may be obtained in January from
the web site listed above.
Duration: Applicants may reapply after one
cycle.
Deadline: 9 P.M., April 23.

PUBLICATIONS:
Guidelines and applications.

ADDRESS INQUIRIES TO:
Susan Dadian, Program Director
CMA Classical/Contemporary
(See address above.)

CHOPIN FOUNDATION OF THE
U.S.   [697]
1440 79th Street Causeway, Suite 117
Miami, FL 33141
(305) 868-0624
Fax: (305) 865-5150
E-mail: info@chopin.org
Web Site: www.chopin.org

FOUNDED: 1977

AREAS OF INTEREST:
Chopin and the promotion of classical music
in the community by the support of young
American pianists.

NAME(S) OF PROGRAMS:
● **Scholarship Program for Young
   Pianists**

TYPE:
Scholarships. Scholarship program supporting
young American pianists, 14 to 17 years of
age.

YEAR PROGRAM STARTED: 1997

PURPOSE:
To support talented young American
musicians in their struggle for career
recognition; to make classical music available
to the community.

ELIGIBILITY:
Open to qualified American pianists (citizens
or legal residents) not younger than 14 and
not older than 17 years of age on the
application deadline, whose field of study is
music and whose major is piano. If applicant
is older than 17 years of age, he or she may
only be accepted if currently in this
scholarship program.

GEOG. RESTRICTIONS: United States.

FINANCIAL DATA:
Amount of support per award: $1,000.
Total amount of support: $18,000 for the
year 2018-19.

NO. AWARDS: 18 for the year 2018-19.

APPLICATION INFO:
Scholarship applications must be submitted
online. The following documents are required
and must be uploaded with the application:
(1) statement of career goals;
(2) two recommendations from piano
teachers or professional piano performers;
(3) an unedited video recording of Chopin's
works as required for Years One to Four.
Video must be recorded in one session, but
must be saved and uploaded as separate files.
Uploaded file must be labeled with the name
of the piece and the edition used;
(4) proof of current school enrollment or
statement of being homeschooled;
(5) copy of birth certificate or proof of U.S.
naturalization/legal residency and;
(6) non-refundable $25 application fee.

Incomplete applications will not be
considered.
Duration: One year. Renewable up to four
years as long as the recipient continues to
study piano, maintains satisfactory progress,
and each year submits an audiocassette, CD
or DVD recording of unedited performances
of Chopin's works for evaluation as per
renewal information.
Deadline: May 15.

IRS I.D.: 59-1778404

ADDRESS INQUIRIES TO:
Barbara Muze, Executive Director
(See address above.)

*SPECIAL STIPULATIONS:
Registration fee of $25 must be included
with application.

CIVIC ORCHESTRA OF
CHICAGO   [698]
220 South Michigan Avenue
Chicago, IL 60604
(312) 294-3400
Fax: (312) 294-3329
E-mail: civic@cso.org
Web Site: cso.org/civic

FOUNDED: 1919

AREAS OF INTEREST:
Training young musicians for professional
work in the orchestral field at the highest
level with an emphasis on artistic excellence,
community engagement and advocacy.

NAME(S) OF PROGRAMS:
● **Civic Orchestra Lesson Scholarship
   Stipends**

TYPE:
Fellowships; Scholarships. Stipends to help
defray cost of private study with Chicago
Symphony members and additional music

training-related costs. Scholarship funds may be used for full-time two-year graduate-level study at a local academic institution.

YEAR PROGRAM STARTED: 1919

PURPOSE:
To promote the development of aesthetic sensitivity and playing technique through personal instruction with skilled pedagogues.

LEGAL BASIS:
The Civic Orchestra is a training orchestra under the auspices of the Chicago Symphony Orchestra, which is incorporated as a nonprofit, tax-exempt organization.

ELIGIBILITY:
Scholarships are available to all Civic Orchestra members.

FINANCIAL DATA:
Amount of support per award: $8,500 average for 30-week season.
Total amount of support: Varies.

NO. MOST RECENT APPLICANTS: 565.

NO. AWARDS: 90 each season.

APPLICATION INFO:
Application forms can be filled out when auditioning for the Civic Orchestra. Membership application forms are available from the Civic Orchestra office. Auditions are held in February and March.
Duration: 30 weeks, September to June. Renewal possible for up to two years.
Deadline: Mid-January.

OFFICERS:
Helen Zell, Chairperson
Jeff Alexander, President, Chicago Symphony Orchestra

ADDRESS INQUIRIES TO:
Jonathan McCormick
Director of Education
(See address above.)

COLUMBIA UNIVERSITY

709 Pulitzer Hall
2950 Broadway
New York, NY 10027
(212) 854-3841
E-mail: pulitzer@pulitzer.org
Web Site: www.pulitzer.org

TYPE:
Awards/prizes; Fellowships. Awards in journalism, books and music.

Pulitzer Prizes in Journalism are awarded based on material appearing in a text-based U.S. newspaper or news site that publishes at least once a week during the year. Awards given for:
(1) meritorious public service by a newspaper through the use of its journalistic resources which may include editorials, cartoons, photographs, graphics and online material;
(2) local, state or national reporting of breaking news;
(3) investigative reporting by an individual or team, presented as a single article or series;
(4) explanatory journalism that illuminates a significant or complex subject, demonstrating mastery of the subject, lucid writing and clear presentation;
(5) reporting on significant issues of local concern;
(6) reporting on national affairs;
(7) reporting on international affairs, including United Nations correspondence;
(8) feature writing giving prime consideration to high literary quality and originality;

(9) commentary;
(10) criticism;
(11) editorial writing;
(12) cartoon or portfolio of cartoons;
(13) breaking news photography in black and white or color, which may consist of a photograph or photographs, a sequence or an album;
(14) feature photography in black and white or color with the same stipulations as above and;
(15) audio journalism that serves the public interest.

Prizes in Letters are restricted to works first published in the U.S. during the year in book form and available for purchase by the general public. Awards given for:
(1) fiction by an American author, preferably dealing with American life;
(2) a play by an American author, preferably original in its source and dealing with American life, produced in the U.S. January 1 to December 31;
(3) appropriately documented book on the history of the U.S.;
(4) appropriately documented biography or autobiography by an American author;
(5) volume of original verse by an American author and;
(6) appropriately documented book of nonfiction by an American author that is not eligible for consideration in any other category.

A prize in music is given for distinguished musical composition by an American that has had its first performance in the U.S. during the year.

Four fellowships enable outstanding graduates to travel, report and study abroad. One fellowship is given to an outstanding graduate who wishes to specialize in drama, music, literary, film or television criticism.

See entry 1729 for full listing.

CONTEMPORARY MUSIC FESTIVAL   [699]

School of Music
Indiana State University
Terre Haute, IN 47809
(812) 237-2743
Fax: (812) 237-3009
E-mail: kurt.fowler@indstate.edu
Web Site: www.indstate.edu/cas/cmf

FOUNDED: 1966

AREAS OF INTEREST:
Contemporary orchestra music.

NAME(S) OF PROGRAMS:
● **Competition for Orchestral Compositions**

TYPE:
Awards/prizes; Conferences/seminars. Performance of new music by the Indianapolis Chamber Orchestra. Winning composers will take part in seminars that are part of the festival and will receive an honorarium to cover expenses.

YEAR PROGRAM STARTED: 1966

PURPOSE:
Performance of new orchestral music.

ELIGIBILITY:
Contestants must be citizens or legal residents of the U.S. Winners of the competition within the last five years are not eligible.

FINANCIAL DATA:
Amount of support per award: First place: $1,000.

NO. MOST RECENT APPLICANTS: 50.

NO. AWARDS: 1.

APPLICATION INFO:
Guidelines are available on the web site.
Deadline: July 1.

ADDRESS INQUIRIES TO:
Indianapolis Chamber Orchestra
4603 Clarendon Road, Suite 36
Indianapolis, IN 46208
Tel: (317) 940-9607

AARON COPLAND FUND FOR MUSIC, INC.   [700]

254 West 31st Street, 15th Floor
New York, NY 10001
(212) 461-6956
Fax: (212) 810-4567
E-mail: onlinegrants@coplandfund.org
Web Site: www.coplandfund.org

FOUNDED: 1992

AREAS OF INTEREST:
Music.

NAME(S) OF PROGRAMS:
● **Performance Program**
● **Recording Program**
● **Supplemental Program**

TYPE:
General operating grants; Project/program grants. Performance Program: Provides support to performing organizations whose artistic excellence encourages and improves public knowledge and appreciation of serious contemporary American music. Organizations whose principal function is to support a specific performing ensemble should apply to this program.

Recording Program: Documents and provides wider exposure for the music of contemporary American composers, develops audiences for contemporary American music through record distribution and other retail markets, and supports the release and dissemination of recordings of previously unreleased contemporary American music and the reissuance of recordings that are no longer available.

Supplemental Program: Provides support to nonprofit organizations that have a history of substantial commitment to contemporary American music but whose needs are not addressed by the Fund's programs of support for performing organizations and recording projects, such as presenters and music service organizations.

YEAR PROGRAM STARTED: 1992

PURPOSE:
To encourage and improve public knowledge and appreciation of contemporary American music.

LEGAL BASIS:
Foundation.

ELIGIBILITY:
For the Performance Program, applicants must be nonprofit professional performing ensembles with a history of substantial commitment to contemporary American music and with plans to continue that commitment. Ensembles must have been in existence for at least two years at the time of application. Festivals are only eligible to apply for their professional core ensembles.

Individuals, student ensembles, presenters without a core ensemble are not eligible. Grants will not be made for the purpose of commissions to composers.

For the Recording Program, applicants must be nonprofit performance ensembles, presenting institutions or nonprofit or commercial recording companies. Any applicant who, as of the deadline date, has one or more Recording Program grants that have been paid but that have not been released within two years after receiving funds will not be eligible to apply for a Recording Program grant. Grants will not be made for the purpose of commissions to composers.

Supplemental Program: Applications may be submitted by nonprofit organizations that have a history of substantial commitment to contemporary American music but whose needs are not addressed by the Fund's programs of support for performing organizations and recording projects. Organizations must have been in existence for at least two years at the time of application.

FINANCIAL DATA:
Amount of support per award: $1,000 to $20,000 for Performance Program and Supplemental Program; Up to $20,000 for the Recording Program.
Total amount of support: Varies.

NO. MOST RECENT APPLICANTS: Approximately 550.

NO. AWARDS: Varies.

APPLICATION INFO:
Fund guidelines and application procedures are available to prospective applicants on the Fund's web site.
Duration: Varies depending on needs and nature of the request.

ADDRESS INQUIRIES TO:
Grants Manager
E-mail: grantsmanager@coplandfund.org
(See address above.)

CURTIS INSTITUTE OF MUSIC [701]

1726 Locust Street
Philadelphia, PA 19103
(215) 717-3167
E-mail: admissions@curtis.edu
Web Site: www.curtis.edu

FOUNDED: 1924

AREAS OF INTEREST:
Music performance.

NAME(S) OF PROGRAMS:
● **Bachelor of Music**
● **Diploma**
● **Master of Music**
● **Post-Baccalaureate Diploma**
● **Professional Studies Certificate**

TYPE:
Scholarships. The Curtis Institute of Music educates and trains exceptionally gifted young musicians to engage a local and global community through the highest level of artistry. To ensure that admissions are based solely on artistic promise, Curtis makes an investment in each admitted student so that no tuition is charged for their studies.

Master of Music and Professional Studies Certificate are only offered in opera.

YEAR PROGRAM STARTED: 1924

PURPOSE:
To train exceptionally gifted young musicians for careers as performing artists on the highest professional level.

LEGAL BASIS:
The school is operated under a Charter granted by the Commonwealth of Pennsylvania and is also included in the list of "Colleges and Universities in Pennsylvania approved by the State Council of Education for the Granting of Degrees."
The U.S. Government has duly approved the Curtis Institute of Music as an institution of learning for the attendance of nonimmigrant students, under the Immigration and Nationality Act.

ELIGIBILITY:
All are eligible for the competitive audition, regardless of race, origin or geographic distribution.

For Bachelor of Music Degree Program and Diploma Program, eligibility requirements consist of a competitive audition, high school diploma or GED, SAT Scores, English achievement scores and TOEFL for foreign students.

For Master of Music Degree Programs, eligibility requirements consist of a competitive audition and previous Bachelor's degree.

Full requirements are detailed online.

FINANCIAL DATA:
Curtis makes an investment in each student so that no tuition is charged for their studies. Generous financial aid likewise ensures that no student accepted to Curtis will be unable to attend because of financial need. Student fees apply.
Amount of support per award: Scholarship valued at $47,143 for undergraduate students and $58,535 for graduate students for the academic year 2020-21.
Total amount of support: Varies based on individual needs.

NO. MOST RECENT APPLICANTS: 640.

NO. AWARDS: 155 scholarships awarded each year.

APPLICATION INFO:
The application, required supporting documents, and $150 application fee must be submitted online.

Invited applicants must participate in an audition process and select studies require pre-screening.
Duration: Scholarships are renewed each year of a student's enrollment.
Deadline: Mid-December.

PUBLICATIONS:
The Curtis Institute of Music Catalogue (includes application form).

IRS I.D.: 23-1585611

ADDRESS INQUIRIES TO:
Belmary Lorcas, Admissions and Recruitment Manager
(See telephone number and e-mail address above.)

EASTMAN SCHOOL OF MUSIC OF THE UNIVERSITY OF ROCHESTER [702]

26 Gibbs Street
Rochester, NY 14604
(585) 274-1560
Fax: (585) 274-1088
E-mail: gdean@esm.rochester.edu
Web Site: www.esm.rochester.edu

AREAS OF INTEREST:
Music.

NAME(S) OF PROGRAMS:
● **Eastman School of Music Graduate Awards**

TYPE:
Assistantships; Awards/prizes; Fellowships; Internships; Scholarships; Visiting scholars.

PURPOSE:
To support the School's academic programs.

ELIGIBILITY:
Open to nationals of all countries. Candidates should have the qualifications necessary for admission to the Eastman School of Music. Non-U.S. citizens are usually offered service scholarships in ensemble work at graduate level.

FINANCIAL DATA:
Amount of support per award: Up to $21,000 in stipend and $43,680 in tuition scholarship per year.
Total amount of support: Approximately $9,000,000 annually.

NO. AWARDS: 350.

APPLICATION INFO:
Applicants must complete an application form. In addition, awards require an interview in Rochester or at one of the regional auditions.
Duration: One academic year. Renewable.
Deadline: December 1.

ADDRESS INQUIRIES TO:
Admissions Office
Eastman School of Music
(See address above.)

AVERY FISHER ARTIST PROGRAM [703]

c/o Veronique Firkusny
155 West 68th Street, Suite 1130
New York, NY 10023
(917) 363-4380
E-mail: averyfisherartistprogram@firkusny.org
Web Site: www.averyfisherartistprogram.org

FOUNDED: 1974

AREAS OF INTEREST:
Music, specifically classical instrumentalists.

NAME(S) OF PROGRAMS:
● **The Avery Fisher Career Grants**
● **The Avery Fisher Prize**

TYPE:
Awards/prizes; Grants-in-aid. Awards for excellence and help in launching major careers. The Program is administered by the Lincoln Center for the Performing Arts, Inc.

YEAR PROGRAM STARTED: 1974

PURPOSE:
To recognize outstanding classical instrumentalists and chamber ensembles.

LEGAL BASIS:
Not-for-profit, tax-exempt.

ELIGIBILITY:
Instrumentalists who are U.S. citizens or permanent residents may be nominated. Small U.S.-based chamber ensembles are also eligible for consideration.

FINANCIAL DATA:
Amount of support per award: Avery Fisher Career Grants: $25,000 each; Avery Fisher Prize: $100,000.
Total amount of support: Varies.

NO. AWARDS: Up to 5 Career Grants per year. Avery Fisher Prize is considered every year, but awarded at the discretion of the Executive Committee.

APPLICATION INFO:
Individual artists may not apply directly. Nominations are made by the Recommendation Board, which comprises nationally known instrumentalists, conductors, chamber ensembles, music educators and presenters. Final selections are made by the Executive Committee.
Deadline: Varies.

EXECUTIVE COMMITTEE:
Emanuel Ax
Deborah Borda
Marylou Falcone
David Finckel
Henry Fogel
Anthony Fogg
Pamela Frank
Jeremy Geffen
Ara Guzelimian
Wu Han
Yo-Yo Ma
Anthony McGill
Chad Smith
Matias Tarnopolsky
Henry Timms

ADDRESS INQUIRIES TO:
Veronique Firkusny, Executive Director
(See address above.)

FONDATION DES ETATS-UNIS [704]
15, boulevard Jourdan
75014 Paris France
(33) 1 53 80 68 80
Fax: (33) 1 53 80 68 99
E-mail: culture@fondationdesetatsunis.org
Web Site: fondationdesetatsunis.org/hhw-scholarship

FOUNDED: 1929

AREAS OF INTEREST:
Grants for musicians, artists, and psychiatry residents.

CONSULTING OR VOLUNTEER SERVICES:
Office of Cultural Affairs.

NAME(S) OF PROGRAMS:
• **Harriet Hale Woolley Scholarship**

TYPE:
Awards/prizes; Development grants; Scholarships. Bequeathed to the Fondation des Etats-Unis, Cite Internationale Universitaire de Paris in the early 1930s, the Harriet Hale Woolley Scholarship is awarded annually to a select number of exceptional American artists and musicians who plan to pursue their studies in Paris.

A scholarship is also available to French, Swiss and American medical postgraduates specializing in psychiatry with an internship in a Parisian hospital.

The scholarship is not intended for research in art history or musicology, nor for dance or theater.

YEAR PROGRAM STARTED: 1933

PURPOSE:
To promote artistic and cultural exchange between the U.S. and France.

LEGAL BASIS:
Fondation Reconnue d'Utilite Publique (FRUP).

ELIGIBILITY:
Requirements include:
(1) American citizenship;
(2) between 21 and 30 years of age;
(3) graduation with high academic standing from an American college, university, or professional school of recognized standing;
(4) evidence of accomplishment in the candidate's field of expertise;
(5) proposal of a unique and detailed artistic project related to one's field of study that requires a one-year residency in Paris and;
(6) good moral character, personality and adaptability, plus good physical health and emotional stability.

Scholarship recipient must reside at the Fondation des Etats-Unis for the academic year.

FINANCIAL DATA:
The Scholarship is designed to assist with living expenses while in Paris.
Amount of support per award: Stipend of EUR 10,000 (may vary subject to fund earnings), payable in four installments during the academic year (October 1 to June 30).

NO. MOST RECENT APPLICANTS: 15 to 20.

NO. AWARDS: Artists and musicians: Up to 4; Postgraduates in Psychiatry: 1.

APPLICATION INFO:
Application should be made by e-mail. Instructions are available online.
Duration: One academic year.
Deadline: All application dossiers and their supporting materials must be received no later than January 31, for the current academic year.

STAFF:
Dr. Anne Cremieux, Director
Dr. Sophie Vasset, Director
Noëmi Haire-Sievers, Culture and International Relations Manager

ADDRESS INQUIRIES TO:
Harriet Hale Woolley Scholarship
(See address above.)

*SPECIAL STIPULATIONS:
As this project should include enrollment in a recognized institution, it is strongly suggested that the candidate establish a significant contact with a teacher or institution prior to arriving in France and to show evidence of this contact in his or her application dossier.

FROMM MUSIC FOUNDATION AT HARVARD [705]
Department of Music
3 Oxford Street
Harvard University
Cambridge, MA 02138
(617) 495-2791
Fax: (617) 496-8081
E-mail: musicdpt@fas.harvard.edu
Web Site: frommfoundation.fas.harvard.edu

FOUNDED: 1972

AREAS OF INTEREST:
Commissioning and performance of contemporary music.

TYPE:
Commission and grant-in-aid.

YEAR PROGRAM STARTED: 1952

PURPOSE:
To bring contemporary music closer to the public by providing support to composers and performers.

LEGAL BASIS:
Private foundation.

ELIGIBILITY:
Composers must be citizens or residents of the U.S. For these purposes, "residents" shall be deemed to include only lawful permanent residents, temporary residents, asylees, refugees and nonimmigrants who have lawfully been admitted to the U.S. for a term of one year or more.

FINANCIAL DATA:
Amount of support per award: $12,000.

NO. MOST RECENT APPLICANTS: 250.

NO. AWARDS: 12 annually.

APPLICATION INFO:
Applicants must contact the Foundation for an application.
Deadline: June 1 for consideration in following fall. Commissions will be awarded in December.

PUBLICATIONS:
Application guidelines.

STAFF:
Enrique Marquez, Administrator

DIRECTORS:
Ingrid Monson, Chairperson
George Lewis
Chen Yi

ADDRESS INQUIRIES TO:
Enrique Marquez, Administrator
(See address above.)

*SPECIAL STIPULATIONS:
For those who have previously received a Fromm Commission, there is a 15-year waiting period before you can apply again. The Fromm Commission cannot be applied to projects that have been awarded other commissions.

THE GRAMMY MUSEUM [706]
888 South Figueroa Street
Los Angeles, CA 90017
(310) 581-1260
E-mail: grants@grammymuseum.org
Web Site: www.grammymuseum.org/national-reach/grant-program

FOUNDED: 1989

AREAS OF INTEREST:
Music research, archiving and preserving and the medical and occupational well-being of music professionals.

TYPE:
Challenge/matching grants; Project/program grants; Research grants. The GRAMMY Museum Grant Program funds the following areas:
(1) Scientific Research Projects - Grants to organizations and individuals to support efforts that advance the research and/or broad reaching implementations of original scientific research projects related to the impact of music on the human condition, such as the links between music study and

early childhood development, the effects of music therapy and the medical and occupational well-being of music professionals.

(2) Archiving and Preservation Projects - Grants to organizations and individuals to support efforts that advance the archiving and preservation of the music and recorded sound heritage of the Americas. The Archiving and Preservation area has two funding categories: (a) Preservation Implementation and (b) Planning, Assessment and/or Consultation.

YEAR PROGRAM STARTED: 1989

PURPOSE:
To cultivate the understanding, appreciation and advancement of the contribution of recorded music to American culture.

ELIGIBILITY:
Priority is given to music projects of national significance that achieve a broad reach and whose final results are accessible to the general public.

The GRAMMY Museum, Inc., will not fund:
(1) chapters, trustees, officers or staff;
(2) organizations that discriminate on the basis of race, sex, religion, national origin, disability or age;
(3) recording projects, demo tapes or live performances designed to promote the career of an individual or group;
(4) faculty and staff salaries unrelated to the project;
(5) performance events;
(6) purchase or repairs of music instruments or equipment;
(7) competitions and related expenses;
(8) work toward academic degrees;
(9) regular ongoing business activities of corporate clients;
(10) organizations or individuals for more than three consecutive years;
(11) organizations not based in the U.S. or;
(12) documentaries, endowments and web sites.

FINANCIAL DATA:
Amount of support per award: Up to $20,000.
Total amount of support: Varies.

NO. AWARDS: 13 for the year 2020.

APPLICATION INFO:
Letters of inquiry are only accepted online. Guidelines are available on the Foundation web site. Applicants must use current grant application only and should also include:
(1) evidence of organization's nonprofit status and copy of IRS tax determination letter;
(2) general description, history and accomplishments of the organization;
(3) current resume for individual applicants and organization's key personnel;
(4) two letters of support for the project and;
(5) an itemized budget.

Late or incomplete applications will not be reviewed.
Duration: Six to 24 months.
Deadline: November 1. Announcement in May.

ADDRESS INQUIRIES TO:
Derek Spencer, Program Manager
(See address above.)

*SPECIAL STIPULATIONS:
Projects must be completed and a final report submitted within 12 to 24 months of project start date. A full set of the completed project is due to The GRAMMY Museum within 90 days of the project completion date. Grantees

must formally credit The GRAMMY Museum in all published materials and announcements.

GUITAR FOUNDATION OF AMERICA   [707]
P.O. Box 2900
Palos Verdes Peninsula, CA 90274
(877) 570-1651
E-mail: info@guitarfoundation.org
Web Site: www.guitarfoundation.org

FOUNDED: 1973

AREAS OF INTEREST:
Classical guitar.

NAME(S) OF PROGRAMS:
● **International Concert Artists Competition**
● **International Youth Competition**
● **Regional Events**

TYPE:
Awards/prizes; Conferences/seminars. International Youth Competition awarded in two divisions: Division I for ages 15 to 18 years old and Division II for ages 14 years old and under.

PURPOSE:
To support the serious study of the guitar in its historic and performance aspects; to promote the guitar as an ensemble instrument; to encourage composition and arrangements of ensemble music involving the guitar; to preserve and make available literature on the guitar.

LEGAL BASIS:
501(c)(3).

ELIGIBILITY:
Open to competitors worldwide.

FINANCIAL DATA:
Amount of support per award: Varies.
Total amount of support: Varies.

NO. AWARDS: 3 grand prize winners annually.

IRS I.D.: 51-0147668

ADDRESS INQUIRIES TO:
E-mail: ekhamas@guitarfoundation.org

THE KOSCIUSZKO FOUNDATION, INC.   [708]
15 East 65th Street
New York, NY 10065
(212) 734-2130 ext. 414
E-mail: chopin@thekf.org
Web Site: www.kfchopin.org

FOUNDED: 1925

AREAS OF INTEREST:
Polish culture in the U.S., friendship and understanding between the U.S. and Poland through educational and cultural programs.

NAME(S) OF PROGRAMS:
● **Chopin Piano Competition**

TYPE:
Awards/prizes; Scholarships.

YEAR PROGRAM STARTED: 1949

PURPOSE:
To encourage gifted young pianists to further their studies and perform the works of Chopin, Szymanowski and other Polish composers.

LEGAL BASIS:
501(c)(3) not-for-profit organization.

ELIGIBILITY:
The competition is open to pianists of all nationalities representing a professional level of performance, born between January 1, 1989 and December 31, 2001. It is expected that applicants will have demonstrated exceptional talent and artistic achievement. Contestants may apply to compete in the preliminaries in New York. Each contestant should have a program of at least 60 minutes and is expected to perform complete works from memory.

GEOG. RESTRICTIONS: United States.

FINANCIAL DATA:
Amount of support per award: $10,000 first prize; $5,000 second prize; $3,000 third prize.
Total amount of support: $20,000.

APPLICATION INFO:
Official application materials are available upon request to the Foundation. Send business-size, self-addressed, stamped envelope. These materials are also available on the web site.
Deadline: January 1.

PUBLICATIONS:
KF newsletter; annual report.

IRS I.D.: 13-1628179

STAFF:
Marek Skulimowski, President and Executive Director

ADDRESS INQUIRIES TO:
Chopin Piano Competition
(See address above.)

THE LEEDS INTERNATIONAL PIANO COMPETITION   [709]
The Piano Competition Office
The University of Leeds
169B Woodhouse Lane
Leeds LS2 9JT England
(44) 0113 244 6586
Fax: (44) 0113 234 6106
E-mail: info@leedspiano.com
Web Site: www.leedspiano.com

FOUNDED: 1961

AREAS OF INTEREST:
Piano.

TYPE:
Awards/prizes. Prizes in piano awarded every third year.

YEAR PROGRAM STARTED: 1963

PURPOSE:
To provide a competition for professional pianists.

LEGAL BASIS:
Charity.

ELIGIBILITY:
The Competition is open to professional pianists of all nationalities born between September 19, 1991 and April 4, 2001.

FINANCIAL DATA:
Amount of support per award: GBP 2,000 to GBP 25,000.
Total amount of support: Prize money in excess of GBP 70,000.

APPLICATION INFO:
Application may be made online. Competitors must complete the form in English and upload both an audio recording of a performance from the audition repertoire and a set of documents as specified online.

All applications must include references which support the applicant's readiness for a professional career as a pianist.

Deadline: October 31.

ADDRESS INQUIRIES TO:
Linda Wellings, Operations Director
(See e-mail address above.)

THE LESCHETIZKY ASSOCIATION, INC.   [710]

880 West 181st Street
Apartment 3H
New York, NY 10033
(212) 781-5377
E-mail: tleschetizky@gmail.com
alison.thomas@verizon.net
alison.thomas109@gmail.com
Web Site: www.leschetizky.org
www.concertocompetitionTL.org

FOUNDED: 1942

AREAS OF INTEREST:
Piano playing and instruction.

CONSULTING OR VOLUNTEER SERVICES:
Performance opportunities and workshops.

NAME(S) OF PROGRAMS:
● **Concerto Competition "Theodor Leschetizky" for Gifted Young Pianists**

TYPE:
Awards/prizes. First prize winner plays full concerto with orchestra in New York City.

PURPOSE:
To perpetuate Theodor Leschetizky's principles of pianism and teaching by offering programs and performing opportunities for pianists, piano teachers and students.

LEGAL BASIS:
Tax-exempt organization under the IRS code 501(c)(3).

ELIGIBILITY:
Open to pianists aged 17 and younger, internationally.

FINANCIAL DATA:
Amount of support per award: $300 to $1,000.
Total amount of support: $10,000.

NO. MOST RECENT APPLICANTS: Varies.

NO. AWARDS: First and second prize; other awards at the discretion of judges.

APPLICATION INFO:
Information is available online. Entry materials may be mailed to Alison Thomas at the address below.
Deadline: February 11, 2022.

PUBLICATIONS:
Annual bulletin.

OFFICERS:
Zelma Bodzin, President
Dr. Alison Thomas, Competition Chairman

ADDRESS INQUIRIES TO:
Dr. Alison Thomas, Competition Chairman
(See address above.)

LONG-THIBAUD-CRESPIN COMPETITION   [711]

32, avenue Matignon
75008 Paris France
(33) 1 42 66 66 80
Fax: (33) 1 42 66 06 43
E-mail: contact@long-thibaud-crespin.org
Web Site: www.long-thibaud-crespin.org

FOUNDED: 1943

AREAS OF INTEREST:
Music.

TYPE:
Awards/prizes. International competition for piano, violin and voice. The competition varies yearly: The Long Piano Competition (2022); The Crespin Singing Competition (2023); The Thibaud Violin Competition (2024).

ELIGIBILITY:
Candidate maximum age of 30 years on January 1 of the year of the contest.

FINANCIAL DATA:
Amount of support per award: First Grand Prize: EUR 25,000. There are other prizes also in each competition.

NO. MOST RECENT APPLICANTS: 57.

NO. AWARDS: Varies with the competition.

APPLICATION INFO:
Information about the various competitions can be found on the web site.
Duration: One week.
Deadline: Varies.

PUBLICATIONS:
Brochures.

OFFICERS:
Bernard Volker, President

ADDRESS INQUIRIES TO:
Delegate General
Long-Thibaud-Crespin Competition
(See address above.)

E. NAKAMICHI FOUNDATION   [712]

10736 Jefferson Boulevard
P.M.B. 523
Culver City, CA 90230
(714) 771-9677
E-mail: enakamichi.foundation@gmail.com
Web Site: www.enfoundation.com

FOUNDED: 1985

AREAS OF INTEREST:
Music.

TYPE:
Project/program grants. Performance of music by classical and romantic period composers.

YEAR PROGRAM STARTED: 1986

PURPOSE:
To support appreciation of music by classical and romantic period composers.

LEGAL BASIS:
Private foundation.

ELIGIBILITY:
Eligible organizations must be 501(c)(3) tax-exempt. Individuals and religious organizations are ineligible.

GEOG. RESTRICTIONS: Japan and United States.

FINANCIAL DATA:
Amount of support per award: $3,000 to $10,000.
Total amount of support: Generally $100,000 to $200,000 per year.

NO. MOST RECENT APPLICANTS: 60.

NO. AWARDS: 25.

APPLICATION INFO:
Contact the Foundation for application procedures.

Duration: Single/multiple performances.
Deadline: March 15 and October 15.

IRS I.D.: 95-3870341

ADDRESS INQUIRIES TO:
Gayle Yamazaki, President
(See address above.)

*PLEASE NOTE:
The Foundation is only accepting grant applications from those organizations that were successfully awarded a grant in the years 2000 through 2007.

NATIONAL ASSOCIATION OF COMPOSERS, USA (NACUSA)   [713]

445 S.W. Spindrift
Depoe Bay, OR 97341-9530
(541) 418-1182
E-mail: gregsteinke@mail.music-usa.org
Web Site: nacusa.us

FOUNDED: 1932

AREAS OF INTEREST:
The performance, publication, broadcasting and archiving of new American concert hall music.

NAME(S) OF PROGRAMS:
● **Young Composers' Competition**

TYPE:
Awards/prizes; Conferences/seminars. Cash awards and guaranteed performances.

YEAR PROGRAM STARTED: 1978

PURPOSE:
To recognize and encourage young talent.

LEGAL BASIS:
501(c)(3) nonprofit organization.

ELIGIBILITY:
Open to all NACUSA members who are American citizens or residents, who have reached their 18th birthday, but have not yet reached their 32nd birthday by the submission deadline. Compositions submitted should not exceed 10 to 12 minutes. Compositions should not be published nor have won other competitions. Two works may be submitted.

Instrumentation varies from year to year; check NACUSA web site for current instrumentation and other details.

GEOG. RESTRICTIONS: United States.

FINANCIAL DATA:
Amount of support per award: First prize: $500 and a guaranteed performance at a NACUSA concert; Second prize: $400; Third prize: $300 and possible performances at a NACUSA concert.

CO-OP FUNDING PROGRAMS: Contest is supported, in part, by grants from ASCAP and BMI.

NO. MOST RECENT APPLICANTS: 30.

NO. AWARDS: 3 annually.

APPLICATION INFO:
Complete information and electronic application submission is available on the Association web site.
Deadline: December 15.

PUBLICATIONS:
Composer/USA, newsletter.

IRS I.D.: 51-0166704

ADDRESS INQUIRIES TO:
Dr. Greg A. Steinke, Secretary
(See address above.)

NATIONAL FEDERATION OF MUSIC CLUBS [714]

1646 West Smith Valley Road
Greenwood, IN 46142
(317) 882-4003
Fax: (317) 882-4019
E-mail: info@nfmc-music.org
Web Site: www.nfmc-music.org

FOUNDED: 1898

AREAS OF INTEREST:
Vocal and instrumental music, dance and composition.

NAME(S) OF PROGRAMS:
● **NFMC Competitions and Awards**

TYPE:
Awards/prizes. Competitions. Awards for students and adults who show proficiency in the fields of voice, instrumental performance, dance, composition, etc. The Federation provides a wide range of awards.

PURPOSE:
To support performance and promotion of American music.

LEGAL BASIS:
Nonprofit.

ELIGIBILITY:
Competitions cover a wide range of age groups from age 10 through adult. In general, applicants must be native-born or naturalized American citizens and must be members or become members of the National Federation of Music Clubs either by individual or group affiliation before applications are accepted.

GEOG. RESTRICTIONS: United States.

FINANCIAL DATA:
Amount of support per award: $25 to $20,000.
Total amount of support: Over $750,000 at the local, state and national level.

APPLICATION INFO:
Award requirements and application forms are available on the NFMC web site or contact the Chair of the specific award. All award applications must be submitted online by uploading them to the NFMC web site.
Duration: One-time award.

PUBLICATIONS:
Competitions and awards chart; *Junior Keynotes Magazine*; *Music Club Magazine*.

OFFICERS:
Frances Nelson, President
Suzanne Carpenter, Treasurer
Linda Lind, Recording Secretary

STAFF:
Jennifer Griffin, Executive Director

ADDRESS INQUIRIES TO:
Jennifer Griffin, Executive Director
(See address above.)

NATIONAL FEDERATION OF MUSIC CLUBS [715]

1646 West Smith Valley Road
Greenwood, IN 46142
(317) 882-4003
Fax: (317) 882-4019
E-mail: info@nfmc-music.org
Web Site: www.nfmc-music.org

FOUNDED: 1898

AREAS OF INTEREST:
Vocal and instrumental music and composition.

NAME(S) OF PROGRAMS:
● **Award Program for Summer Music Festivals and Music Centers**

TYPE:
Awards/prizes. Prizes for the performance and promotion of American music at summer music festivals.

PURPOSE:
To support performance and promotion of American music.

LEGAL BASIS:
Nonprofit.

ELIGIBILITY:
Program open to summer music festivals, centers and camps in the U.S. and its territories. In general, applicants must be native-born or naturalized American citizens and must be members or become members of the National Federation of Music Clubs either by individual or group affiliation before applications are accepted.

GEOG. RESTRICTIONS: United States.

FINANCIAL DATA:
Amount of support per award: Average $200 to $3,000.

NO. AWARDS: Approximately 35.

OFFICERS:
Frances Nelson, President
Suzanne Carpenter, Treasurer
Linda Lind, Recording Secretary

STAFF:
Jennifer Griffin, Executive Director

ADDRESS INQUIRIES TO:
Jennifer Griffin, Executive Director
(See address above.)

NATIONAL FEDERATION OF MUSIC CLUBS [716]

1646 West Smith Valley Road
Greenwood, IN 46142
(317) 882-4003
Fax: (317) 882-4019
E-mail: info@nfmc-music.org
Web Site: www.nfmc-music.org

FOUNDED: 1898

AREAS OF INTEREST:
Dedicated to finding and fostering young musical talent.

NAME(S) OF PROGRAMS:
● **Dorothy Dann Bullock Music Therapy Award**

TYPE:
Grants-in-aid. Financial assistance.

PURPOSE:
To support performance and promotion of American music.

LEGAL BASIS:
Nonprofit.

ELIGIBILITY:
Offered to Music Therapy Majors (college sophomores, juniors or seniors) in accredited schools offering Music Therapy degrees approved by American Music Therapy Association. Applicants must be native-born or naturalized American citizens and must be members or become members of NFMC either by individual or group affiliation before applications are accepted.

GEOG. RESTRICTIONS: United States.

FINANCIAL DATA:
Amount of support per award: $1,500.
Total amount of support: $1,500 annually.

NO. AWARDS: 1 annually.

APPLICATION INFO:
Application information is available on the web site.
Deadline: March 1.

OFFICERS:
Frances Nelson, President
Suzanne Carpenter, Treasurer
Linda Lind, Recording Secretary

STAFF:
Jennifer Griffin, Executive Director

ADDRESS INQUIRIES TO:
Bullock Music Therapy Award
(See address above.)

NATIONAL OPERA ASSOCIATION, INC. [717]

100 Baits Drive
Ann Arbor, MI 48109
(734) 615-3784
E-mail: ksevert@noa.org
Web Site: www.noa.org

FOUNDED: 1955

AREAS OF INTEREST:
Opera production, opera composition, promotion of operatic talent and opera education.

CONSULTING OR VOLUNTEER SERVICES:
Distinguished members available for consultation and workshops.

NAME(S) OF PROGRAMS:
● **Carolyn Bailey and Dominick Argento Vocal Competition**
● **Biennial Dissertation Competition**
● **Chamber Opera Competition**
● **Collegiate Opera Scenes Competition**
● **Opera Production Competition**
● **Scholarly Paper Competition**

TYPE:
Awards/prizes. Cash prizes awarded to Artist Division winners and Scholarship Division winners. Also scholarships to AIMS, awarded in both divisions. Productions of winning operas in Chamber Opera Competition will be scheduled for annual convention.

YEAR PROGRAM STARTED: 1977

PURPOSE:
To assist young opera singers in furthering their training for an operatic career and to honor the best of the new chamber operas and the outstanding opera productions by universities and colleges.

LEGAL BASIS:
Nonprofit organization.

ELIGIBILITY:
All applicants must submit an entrance fee depending on category and membership status.

FINANCIAL DATA:
Amount of support per award: Minimum $500 for singing competitors.
Total amount of support: Approximately $10,000.

NO. MOST RECENT APPLICANTS: 180 for vocal competition, 80 for opera production competition and 45 for chamber opera competition.

NO. AWARDS: Approximately 10.

APPLICATION INFO:
Application information is available on the web site.
Duration: Varies.
Deadline: Varies by contest.

PUBLICATIONS:
Opera Journal; NOA Newsletter.

ADDRESS INQUIRIES TO:
Kirk Severtson, Executive Director
(See address above.)

NATIONAL ORCHESTRAL INSTITUTE   [718]
3800 Clarice Smith Performing Arts Center
University of Maryland School of Music
College Park, MD 20742
(301) 405-2317
Fax: (301) 405-5977
E-mail: noi@umd.edu
Web Site: theclarice.umd.edu/noi

FOUNDED: 1988

AREAS OF INTEREST:
Orchestral music.

TYPE:
Residencies; Scholarships; Training grants; Visiting scholars. Advanced orchestral training program offering talented musicians on the threshold of their professional careers a four-week opportunity to study and perform under internationally renowned conductors and principal musicians from leading American orchestras.

YEAR PROGRAM STARTED: 1988

PURPOSE:
To prepare musicians for professional orchestral careers.

LEGAL BASIS:
University.

ELIGIBILITY:
Applicants must be between the ages of 18 and 28 with appropriate orchestral music skill.

FINANCIAL DATA:
Support includes tuition at the Institute.
Amount of support per award: Over $4,000.
Total amount of support: Varies.

NO. AWARDS: Approximately 750.

APPLICATION INFO:
Applicants should submit an application, resume and one letter of recommendation. They should also audition at one of the audition centers in cities across the U.S. between January and March.
Duration: June 1 to June 30.
Deadline: Varies by audition location.

PUBLICATIONS:
Program announcement.

ADDRESS INQUIRIES TO:
Richard Scerbo, Director
(See address above.)

THE WALTER W. NAUMBURG FOUNDATION, INC.   [719]
120 Claremont Avenue
New York, NY 10027
(917) 493-4040
E-mail: naumburgfoundation@gmail.com
Web Site: www.naumburg.org

FOUNDED: 1925

AREAS OF INTEREST:
Sponsorship of international competitions for various musical instruments and voice.

TYPE:
Awards/prizes.

ELIGIBILITY:
This competition is open to musicians of all nationalities. Requirements differ by category.

FINANCIAL DATA:
Amount of support per award: $25,000 first prize, $15,000 second prize and $10,000 third prize.

APPLICATION INFO:
Application forms may be obtained online.
Duration: One-time award.

ADDRESS INQUIRIES TO:
Debra Kinzler, Associate Director
(See address above.)

*PLEASE NOTE:
The solo competition disciplines rotate from year to year.

NEW MUSIC USA   [720]
40 Wall Street, 6th Floor
New York, NY 10005
(212) 645-6949
Fax: (646) 490-0998
E-mail: info@newmusicusa.org
Web Site: www.newmusicusa.org

FOUNDED: 2011

AREAS OF INTEREST:
Living composers and contemporary music of all kinds.

NAME(S) OF PROGRAMS:
• **Amplifying Voices**
• **New Music Capacity Building Program**
• **New Music Creator Development Fund**
• **Organizational Development Fund**
• **Reel Change: The Fund for Diversity in Film Scoring**

TYPE:
Awards/prizes; General operating grants; Project/program grants; Residencies. Amplifying Voices is a five-year residency and commissioning program that places composers of color with mid-sized orchestras to encourage collaboration and collective action toward equitable representing of artists of color in the contemporary classical canon.

New Music Capacity Building Program is a two-year program offering financial support and professional development opportunities for small- to medium-sized New York City based music groups and venues.

New Music Creator Development Fund offers project-specific funding to individual music creators.

Organizational Development Fund offers grants to nonprofit organizations, performance groups, dance organizations, festivals, presenters, and venues to support their new music programming.

Reel Change provides funding and mentorship for midcareer composers working on film projects currently in production.

PURPOSE:
To increase opportunities for composers by fostering the creation, performances, dissemination, and appreciation for their music; to fund the creation of new work; to support direct contact between composers and audiences; to create education programs that deepen the understanding of composers and their work; to establish innovative private- and public-sector partnerships that create new opportunities.

LEGAL BASIS:
Nonprofit corporation.

GEOG. RESTRICTIONS: United States.

FINANCIAL DATA:
Amount of support per award: New Music Capacity Building Program: $10,000; New Music Creator Development Fund: Average $5,000; Organizational Development Fund: Maximum $20,000, average $10,000; Reel Change: Average $14,000.
Total amount of support: Approximately $1,000,000 annually.

NO. MOST RECENT APPLICANTS: New Music Creator Development Fund: 1,100; Organizational Development Fund: Over 400.

NO. AWARDS: New Music Capacity Building Program: 10; New Music Creator Development Fund: 53; Organizational Development Fund: 50; Reel Change: 5.

APPLICATION INFO:
Guidelines are available online.
Duration: Varies.
Deadline: Varies.

IRS I.D.: 13-0432981

BOARD OF DIRECTORS:
Reena Esmail, Chairperson
Joseph Walker, Chairperson
Amy Iwano, Vice Chairperson
Steven Tresnan, Treasurer
Matias Tarnopolsky, Secretary

ADDRESS INQUIRIES TO:
Scott Winship, Director of Grantmaking Programs or
Monisha Chowdhary, Grantmaking Manager
(See address above.)

ORCHESTRE SYMPHONIQUE DE MONTREAL (OSM)   [721]
1600, rue Saint-Urbain
Montreal QC H2X 0S1 Canada
(514) 840-7400 ext. 7415
Fax: (514) 842-0728
E-mail: concours@osm.ca
Web Site: www.osm.ca/en/competition

FOUNDED: 1937

AREAS OF INTEREST:
Music.

NAME(S) OF PROGRAMS:
• **OSM Competition**

TYPE:
Awards/prizes; Scholarships. Grand prize includes money prize, a performance with the Orchestre symphonique de Montreal, concert opportunities with various organizations throughout Canada, scholarships at leading North American summer academies and a professional recording by ICI Musique.

YEAR PROGRAM STARTED: 1940

PURPOSE:
To encourage young Canadian musicians.

LEGAL BASIS:
Symphony orchestra.

ELIGIBILITY:
Open to Canadian citizens or landed immigrants in the following categories: Piano and Strings, up to 25 years of age; Woodwinds and Brass, 16 to 25 years of age

(except tuba, 16 to 30 years of age); Percussion, 16 to 30 years of age; Voice, 22 to 30 years of age.

Each year is for a different category.

FINANCIAL DATA:
Amount of support per award: One grand prize: $15,000 (CAN); two first prizes: $10,000 (CAN). Three second prizes: $5,000 (CAN). Three third prizes: $2,500 (CAN). Three prizes for the best interpretation of a Canadian work: $2,500 (CAN).
Total amount of support: More than $100,000 (CAN) in prizes, scholarships and concert opportunities.

NO. MOST RECENT APPLICANTS: 85 to 95.

NO. AWARDS: Approximately 15 annually.

APPLICATION INFO:
Include application form, registration fee, proof of age and of Canadian citizenship and curriculum vitae. Applicants must contact OSM Competition to acquire full details of application process.
Deadline: May 10.

ADDRESS INQUIRIES TO:
OSM Competition
(See address above.)

*PLEASE NOTE:
Musical program approved by the jury members of the competition.

PERCUSSIVE ARTS SOCIETY [722]
110 West Washington Street
Suite A
Indianapolis, IN 46204
(317) 974-4488
Fax: (317) 974-4499
E-mail: percarts@pas.org
Web Site: www.pas.org

FOUNDED: 1961

AREAS OF INTEREST:
Percussive arts, including music education, performance and literature related to percussion instruments.

CONSULTING OR VOLUNTEER SERVICES:
The Society has consulting committees on acoustics, education curricula, literature, etc.

NAME(S) OF PROGRAMS:
● **Jim Chapin Memorial Teacher Scholarship**
● **John E. Grimes Timpani Scholarship**
● **Freddie Gruber Scholarship**
● **Internship Program**
● **Larrie Londin Memorial Scholarship**
● **PASIC International Scholarship**
● **PASIC Scholarships**
● **PAS/Armand Zildjian Percussion Scholarship**
● **PAS/Remo, Inc. Fred Hoey Memorial Scholarship**
● **Percussion Composition Contest**
● **Zildjian Family Opportunity Fund**

TYPE:
Awards/prizes; Internships; Project/program grants; Scholarships.

YEAR PROGRAM STARTED: 1961

PURPOSE:
To promote percussion education, research, performance and appreciation.

LEGAL BASIS:
Not-for-profit corporation.

ELIGIBILITY:
Applicants must be members of the Society.

Internships are open to enrolled music business major students in an accredited university program.

FINANCIAL DATA:
Amount of support per award: Varies.
Total amount of support: Approximately $60,000 in grants and scholarships annually.

APPLICATION INFO:
Application may be submitted online. Consult Society web site.
Duration: Education scholarships and grants: One year.
Deadline: Varies.

PUBLICATIONS:
Percussive Notes, magazine; *Rhythm! Scene,* digital magazine.

IRS I.D.: 73-1385751

STAFF:
Joshua Simonds, Executive Director

ADDRESS INQUIRIES TO:
Amber Fox, Programs Manager
(See address above.)

THE PITTSBURGH NEW MUSIC ENSEMBLE, INC. [723]
Wellington Square, Suite 102
1225 South Main Street
Greensburg, PA 15601
(512) 785-6255
E-mail: kevin@pnme.org
Web Site: www.pnme.org

FOUNDED: 1975

AREAS OF INTEREST:
New music.

NAME(S) OF PROGRAMS:
● **Harvey Gaul Music Composition Contest**

TYPE:
Awards/prizes.

YEAR PROGRAM STARTED: 1975

PURPOSE:
To promote new music and support composers.

LEGAL BASIS:
Nonprofit corporation.

ELIGIBILITY:
Contestants must be U.S. citizens.

FINANCIAL DATA:
Amount of support per award: $6,000 commission.

NO. AWARDS: 1.

APPLICATION INFO:
An entry form is required. An entry fee of $20 must accompany each composition. Contestants should send a score and CD of a representative instrumental work, along with a current biography and contact information. No MIDI realizations.

PUBLICATIONS:
Application guidelines.

IRS I.D.: 25-1364030

OFFICERS:
Samantha Bennett, Executive Director
Catherine Noe'Rourke, Executive Director
Kevin Noe, Artistic Director

ADDRESS INQUIRIES TO:
Kevin Noe, Artistic Director
(See address above.)

*PLEASE NOTE:
Contest is on an as needed basis, not every year.
The Ensemble does not award scholarships.

PRESSER FOUNDATION [724]
1501 Cherry Street
Philadelphia, PA 19102
(267) 519-5350
E-mail: trodgers@presserfoundation.org
Web Site: www.presserfoundation.org

FOUNDED: 1939

AREAS OF INTEREST:
Music education and music philanthropy.

NAME(S) OF PROGRAMS:
● **Advancement of Music**
● **Assistance to Worthy Music Teachers**
● **Capital Support**
● **The Presser Foundation Graduate Music Award**
● **The Presser Foundation Undergraduate Scholar Award**
● **Special Projects**

TYPE:
Awards/prizes; General operating grants; Project/program grants.

YEAR PROGRAM STARTED: 1939

PURPOSE:
To provide financial awards to promising undergraduate and graduate students at qualified higher education institutions; to provide grants for the construction and renovation of suitable buildings for musical instruction and performance; to administer emergency aid to worthy music teachers in distress; to provide support to innovative projects and collaborations between music organizations; to provide operating support to worthy music organizations in the Greater Philadelphia area.

LEGAL BASIS:
Private foundation.

GEOG. RESTRICTIONS: United States.

FINANCIAL DATA:
Total amount of support: Advancement of Music: $2,500 to $60,000; Capital Support: $25,000 to $500,000; The Presser Foundation Graduate Music Award: $10,000; The Presser Foundation Undergraduate Scholar Award: Approximately $4,000; Special Projects: $5,000 to $100,000.

APPLICATION INFO:
Applicant must apply through the online grant management system.
Duration: Varies.
Deadline: Advancement of Music: November 15. Capital Support: February 1. The Presser Foundation Undergraduate Scholar Award: September 1. Special Projects: October 15.

ADDRESS INQUIRIES TO:
Teresa Araco Rodgers, Executive Director
(See e-mail address above.)

THE QUEEN ELISABETH INTERNATIONAL MUSIC COMPETITION OF BELGIUM [725]
20, rue aux Laines
B-1000 Brussels Belgium
(32) 2 213 40 50
E-mail: info@queenelisabethcompetition.be
Web Site: queenelisabethcompetition.be
concoursreineelisabeth.de/en

FOUNDED: 1951

AREAS OF INTEREST:
Voice, violin, piano and cello.

TYPE:
Awards/prizes.

PURPOSE:
To support young artists and thus help to establish their reputations with both professionals and the public through an international competition for music interpretation.

LEGAL BASIS:
Nonprofit organization.

ELIGIBILITY:
Programs alternate each year. The competition is dedicated to the piano in 2021, the cello in 2022, and voice in 2023.

The competition is open to musicians of all nationalities. The minimum age for applicants is 18. Maximum age is 30 for pianists, violinists, and cellists, and 32 for singers. Instrumental competitors play both assigned works and pieces of their own selection. The competition is divided into selection rounds and final round.

FINANCIAL DATA:
Amount of support per award: Varies.

NO. MOST RECENT APPLICANTS: 331 pianists for the year 2021.

NO. AWARDS: 24 for the year 2021.

APPLICATION INFO:
Applications for registration should be downloaded online and accompanied by the following:
(1) a copy of birth certificate;
(2) proof of nationality;
(3) one photograph in the form of a TIFF file (minimum 300 dpi) for the programme;
(4) curriculum vitae;
(5) documentation providing proof of his or her skill (for example, higher diplomas, repertoire list with works performed in public, prizes and diplomas received from other competitions, press reviews, etc.) and;
(6) a video recording (image and sound) with appropriate music programme.
Deadline: Early December of the year preceding the competition.

PUBLICATIONS:
Competition announcement and rules; brochures.

OFFICERS:
Baron Jan Huyghebaert, Chairman
Nicolas Dernoncourt, Secretary General

ADDRESS INQUIRIES TO:
The Secretariat of the Competition
(See address above.)

SAN FRANCISCO CONSERVATORY OF MUSIC   [726]
50 Oak Street
San Francisco, CA 94102
(415) 503-6214
Fax: (415) 503-6299
E-mail: dhoward@sfcm.edu
Web Site: www.sfcm.edu

FOUNDED: 1917

AREAS OF INTEREST:
Music.

NAME(S) OF PROGRAMS:
• **Performance Scholarships in Music for Students in Bachelor and Master of Music Programs**

TYPE:
Assistantships; Scholarships; Work-study programs. Awards for the study of music at the Conservatory.

YEAR PROGRAM STARTED: 1917

PURPOSE:
To enable talented, needy students to attend the Conservatory.

LEGAL BASIS:
Conservatory of Music.

ELIGIBILITY:
U.S. and foreign citizens may apply. Candidates must have had considerable experience in musical performance and must attend the Conservatory on a full-time basis.

FINANCIAL DATA:
Scholarships are to be applied toward tuition at the Conservatory.
Amount of support per award: $1,000 and up.
Total amount of support: $11,016,000 for the academic year 2018-19.

NO. MOST RECENT APPLICANTS: 950.

NO. AWARDS: 456 for the academic year 2018-19.

APPLICATION INFO:
Applicants must submit the San Francisco Conservatory of Music Application and either the Free Application for Federal Student Aid or International Student Certification of Finances. CSS/Financial Aid Profile is required for all international students and domestic students under the age of 26.
Duration: Tenable for one year and may be renewed.
Deadline: February 15.

OFFICER:
Doris Howard, Director of Financial Aid

ADDRESS INQUIRIES TO:
Financial Aid
E-mail: finaid@sfcm.edu
(See address above.)

SAN FRANCISCO OPERA CENTER   [727]
War Memorial Opera House
301 Van Ness Avenue
San Francisco, CA 94102-4509
(415) 565-3244
Fax: (415) 551-6305
E-mail: sfoperacenter@sfopera.com
Web Site: sfopera.com/about-us/opera-center/

FOUNDED: 1954

AREAS OF INTEREST:
Young professional singers, pianists/accompanists and stage directors interested in a sequence of opera performance and career development opportunities.

CONSULTING OR VOLUNTEER SERVICES:
Board of Directors of Merola Opera Program and a full staff of conductors, coaches, stage directors and instructors in singing, acting, movement, stage combat, auditioning, career development and other activities.

NAME(S) OF PROGRAMS:
• **Adler Fellowships**
• **Merola Opera Program**

TYPE:
Fellowships; Internships; Technical assistance. Auditions by application are held in the fall of each year for the following summer's Merola Opera Program in various cities throughout the U.S. Participants will also be considered for Adler Fellowships (singers/pianists).

YEAR PROGRAM STARTED: 1977

PURPOSE:
To provide professional opera training and performance opportunities for talented young opera professionals.

LEGAL BASIS:
Nonprofit.

ELIGIBILITY:
Open to all singers, pianists/accompanists and stage directors. All voice types are eligible, between the ages of 20 and 34.

To participate in the Adler Fellowships, applicants must complete one month of the Merola Summer Program.

FINANCIAL DATA:
Merola Opera Program participants receive shared housing accommodations, weekly allowance and round-trip airfare from place of residence to San Francisco. Adler Fellowships are for a salaried 12-month contract.
Total amount of support: Varies.

APPLICATION INFO:
Auditions are held nationally. Details are available on the web site.
Duration: Adler Fellowships: 12-month contract. Merola Opera Program: June through August.
Deadline: Refer to the National Auditions page on the Center's web site.

PUBLICATIONS:
Application guidelines.

OFFICERS:
Sheri Greenawald, Director

ADDRESS INQUIRIES TO:
Chris Bragg, Administrative Director
(See e-mail address above.)

SIGMA ALPHA IOTA PHILANTHROPIES, INC.   [728]
One Tunnel Road
Asheville, NC 28805-1229
(828) 251-0606
Fax: (828) 251-0644
E-mail: nh@sai-national.org
Web Site: www.sai-national.org

FOUNDED: 1903

AREAS OF INTEREST:
Music, new compositions.

CONSULTING OR VOLUNTEER SERVICES:
Local volunteers in music.

NAME(S) OF PROGRAMS:
• **Inter-American Music Awards**

TYPE:
Awards/prizes. Music composition contest.

YEAR PROGRAM STARTED: 1948

PURPOSE:
To give to the fraternity, and to the public, compositions of high musical merit; to bring distinction to winning composers; to offer royalties and other benefits coincident with publication of winning music.

LEGAL BASIS:
Nonprofit corporation.

ELIGIBILITY:
Requirements change each triennium; however, applicants must be residents of North, Central or South America.

GEOG. RESTRICTIONS: North, Central and South America.

FINANCIAL DATA:
Amount of support per award: $2,500 prize, plus winning composition published by a major music publisher.

NO. MOST RECENT APPLICANTS: 45.

NO. AWARDS: 1.

APPLICATION INFO:
Application information is available on the web site.
Duration: One-time award.
Deadline: September 1.

PUBLICATIONS:
Brochure.

STAFF:
Ruth Sieber Johnson, SAI Executive Director

ADDRESS INQUIRIES TO:
Ruth Sieber Johnson
SAI Executive Director
(See address above.)

SYMPHONY OF THE MOUNTAINS [729]
Kingsport Renaissance Center, Suite 311
1200 East Center Street
Kingsport, TN 37660
(423) 392-8423
E-mail: info@symphonyofthemountains.org
Web Site: www.symphonyofthemountains.org

FOUNDED: 1946

AREAS OF INTEREST:
Symphonic concerts and educational and social activities.

NAME(S) OF PROGRAMS:
● **Elizabeth Harper Vaughn Concerto Competition**

TYPE:
Awards/prizes. Cash prize and appearance with the Symphony of the Mountains Orchestra.

YEAR PROGRAM STARTED: 1969

PURPOSE:
To recognize excellence in music performance, with the potential for career advancement.

LEGAL BASIS:
Not-for-profit corporation.

ELIGIBILITY:
Open to musicians 25 years of age and under, with recommendation of private instructor.

FINANCIAL DATA:
Amount of support per award: $750.
Total amount of support: $750.

NO. MOST RECENT APPLICANTS: 10.

NO. AWARDS: 1 in odd-numbered years.

APPLICATION INFO:
Requires recommendation of private instructor and CD or DVD of performance (full concerto or other appropriate musical arrangement with orchestral accompaniment).
Duration: One-time award.
Deadline: September 1.

PUBLICATIONS:
Posters, postcards, programs for subscription concerts.

IRS I.D.: 62-0534228

STAFF:
Cornelia Laemmli Orth, Music Director/Chief Operating Officer

ADDRESS INQUIRIES TO:
Cornelia Laemmli Orth
Music Director/Chief Operating Officer
(See address above.)

THE RICHARD TUCKER MUSIC FOUNDATION, INC. [730]
1790 Broadway
Suite 715
New York, NY 10019-1412
(212) 757-2218
Fax: (212) 757-2347
E-mail: info@richardtucker.org
Web Site: www.richardtucker.org

FOUNDED: 1975

AREAS OF INTEREST:
Financial aid to American opera singers and opera companies with development programs for American singers.

NAME(S) OF PROGRAMS:
● **Richard Tucker Award**
● **Richard Tucker Career Grants**
● **Sara Tucker Study Grants**

TYPE:
Awards/prizes.

YEAR PROGRAM STARTED: 1978

PURPOSE:
To help further the careers of young American singers.

LEGAL BASIS:
Tax-exempt, not-for-profit organization.

ELIGIBILITY:
Nominees must already be performing in opera. Open to males and females in all vocal categories. Singers cannot apply; they must be recommended by a professional in the field. Applicants must also be U.S.-born.

GEOG. RESTRICTIONS: United States.

FINANCIAL DATA:
Amount of support per award: Richard Tucker Award: $50,000. Richard Tucker Career Grants: Unrestricted grant of $10,000. Sara Tucker Study Grants: Unrestricted grant of $5,000.
Total amount of support: Approximately $105,000.

NO. MOST RECENT APPLICANTS: 100 to 120.

NO. AWARDS: Richard Tucker Award: 1. Richard Tucker Career Grants and Sara Tucker Study Grants: 3 to 5 each.

APPLICATION INFO:
Information on the nominating process for the awards is available on the web site or by telephoning the Foundation. Application is via a confidential anonymous nomination process.
Duration: Varies, but most of the awards are one-time awards.
Deadline: Recommendations are due December 31.

IRS I.D.: 23-7431029

BOARD OF DIRECTORS:
Jeffrey Manocherian, Chairman
Barry Tucker, President

Sherrill Milnes, Vice President
John A. Petts, Vice President
Samuel Ramey, Vice President
Robert S. Tucker, Vice President

ADDRESS INQUIRIES TO:
Peter H. Carwell, Executive Director
(See address above.)

THE VIOLIN SOCIETY OF AMERICA [731]
14070 Proton Road
Suite 100
Dallas, TX 75244
(972) 233-9107 ext. 224
Fax: (972) 490-4219
E-mail: info@vsaweb.org
Web Site: www.vsaweb.org

FOUNDED: 1973

AREAS OF INTEREST:
Making and restoring stringed instruments and their bows, the history of stringed instruments and performers, technique, performance practice, repertory and the acoustics of bowed stringed instruments. The Society also sponsors conventions that include lectures, demonstrations, symposia and concerts, biennial international competitions for new stringed instruments and their bows, a Music Fair and a periodical covering all aspects of bowed string instruments.

NAME(S) OF PROGRAMS:
● **Kaplan-Goodkind Memorial Scholarship Fund**
● **Kun Scholarship Fund**
● **Aram and Rose Nigogosian Fund**

TYPE:
Scholarships. Tuition grants to students of violin-making and bow-making enrolled in a full-time violin-making school.

YEAR PROGRAM STARTED: 1982

PURPOSE:
To bring together people from various fields to exchange ideas and skills and to help people learn about the making of bows and stringed instruments.

LEGAL BASIS:
Tax-exempt educational organization.

ELIGIBILITY:
Students must be U.S. citizens, have satisfactorily completed at least one full year of study in the program, have shown serious effort, talent and future promise, and have financial need.

GEOG. RESTRICTIONS: United States.

FINANCIAL DATA:
Amount of support per award: $1,000 average.
Total amount of support: Varies.

NO. MOST RECENT APPLICANTS: 15.

NO. AWARDS: 8 to 12 annually.

APPLICATION INFO:
Apply through the program director of an approved program.
Duration: One-time tuition grant.
Deadline: Grants made on a continuing basis.

PUBLICATIONS:
The Journal, newsletter.

IRS I.D.: 23-7354645

OFFICERS:
Marilyn Wallin, President
Zachary Moen, President-Elect/Secretary
Nicholas Lampo, First Vice President

Julian Cossman Cooke, Second Vice
President
Richard Dodson, Treasurer

ADDRESS INQUIRIES TO:
Lewis Martinez, General Manager
(See address above.)

YOUNG CONCERT ARTISTS, INC. [732]

1776 Broadway
Suite 1500
New York, NY 10019
(212) 307-6655
Fax: (212) 581-8894
E-mail: yca@yca.org
Web Site: www.yca.org

FOUNDED: 1961

AREAS OF INTEREST:
Young composers, young solo classical
musicians (instruments and voice) and string
quartets.

NAME(S) OF PROGRAMS:
● **Young Concert Artists International
   Auditions**

TYPE:
Awards/prizes. Artist management. YCA
sponsors the Young Concert Artists Series in
New York City at Carnegie's Zankel Hall,
Lincoln Center's Alice Tully Hall, Kaufman
Music Center's Merkin Hall, and in
Washington, DC at the Kennedy Center;
books concert engagements in the U.S. and
abroad; offers career guidance and
development; and provides all promotion and
publicity materials, at no cost to the artists.
YCA membership generally continues until
the artists are signed by commercial
management. The organization's work is
made possible by contributions from
corporations, foundations, individuals and
government agencies.

YEAR PROGRAM STARTED: 1961

PURPOSE:
To discover and launch the careers of
exceptional young musicians.

LEGAL BASIS:
Nonprofit, tax-exempt.

ELIGIBILITY:
Instrumentalists and singers must perform
required repertoire and have letters of
recommendation.

NO. MOST RECENT APPLICANTS: 275.

NO. AWARDS: Varies. Winners are selected only
against a standard of excellence; any number
can win who are selected by the jury.

APPLICATION INFO:
Auditions dates, application form and
requirements are available online.
Duration: Each winner signs a multiyear
renewable contract with Young Concert
Artists, which may be extended by mutual
consent.
Deadline: Contact the organization.

PUBLICATIONS:
Brochure.

IRS I.D.: 13-1951681

OFFICER:
Daniel Kellogg, President

ADDRESS INQUIRIES TO:
Daniel Kellogg, President

Auditions:
Mr. Erol Gurol
(See address above.)

THE LOREN L. ZACHARY SOCIETY FOR THE PERFORMING ARTS [733]

2250 Gloaming Way
Beverly Hills, CA 90210-1717
(310) 276-2731
Fax: (310) 275-8245
E-mail: infoz@zacharysociety.org
Web Site: www.zacharysociety.org

FOUNDED: 1972

AREAS OF INTEREST:
Performing arts and operatic vocal.

NAME(S) OF PROGRAMS:
● **Annual Loren L. Zachary National
   Vocal Competition for Young Opera
   Singers**

TYPE:
Awards/prizes.

YEAR PROGRAM STARTED: 1973

PURPOSE:
To assist in the development of the careers of
young opera singers through financial support
and performance opportunities.

LEGAL BASIS:
Educational, tax-exempt, nonprofit
corporation.

ELIGIBILITY:
Open to singers between the ages of 21 and
35, who have completed proper operatic
training and are prepared to pursue
professional stage careers. Awards are
available only through participation in the
annual vocal competition in New York and
Los Angeles. All singers with completed
applications are guaranteed an audition.

GEOG. RESTRICTIONS: United States and
Canada.

FINANCIAL DATA:
Amount of support per award: Top six
awards for the year 2019: $18,000, $12,000,
$8,000, $5,000, $3,500, and $2,500.
Remaining four grants $2,000 each.
Total amount of support: $56,650 for the
year 2019.

NO. MOST RECENT APPLICANTS: 150.

NO. AWARDS: 10 for the year 2019.

APPLICATION INFO:
Application and rules are available at the
web site, or submit a letter requesting
audition information and applications in
October. Singers must be present in Los
Angeles or New York for all phases of the
Competition. Recordings are not acceptable.
No fax or e-mail requests.

For more information, contact the
Competition Director at the telephone
number above.
Duration: February to May.
Deadline: January (for New York Auditions)
and February (for Los Angeles Auditions);
exact date varies each year.

PUBLICATIONS:
Application; guidelines.

IRS I.D.: 95-2800160

OFFICERS:
Nedra Zachary, President and Founder
Peter Hubner, Vice President

Allan J. Stephan, Vice President
Michele Patazkis, Secretary
Joseph Givens, Treasurer

ADVISORY BOARD:
John DeMain
Stephen De Maio
Michael Fabiano
Dr. George Fritthum
Peter Guth
Michael Hampe
Ioan Holender
Marilyn Horne
David Hulme
Marjan Kiepura
Mrs. George London
Peter Mark
Thea Musgrave
Arlene Shrut
Barbara Ann Testa

ADDRESS INQUIRIES TO:
Nedra Zachary, Director of Competition
(See address above.)

Religion and theology

AMERICAN ACADEMY OF RELIGION [734]

825 Houston Mill Road, N.E.
Suite 300
Atlanta, GA 30329
(404) 727-3049
Fax: (404) 727-7959
E-mail: info@aarweb.org
Web Site: www.aarweb.org

FOUNDED: 1909

AREAS OF INTEREST:
Religion and theology.

NAME(S) OF PROGRAMS:
● **Collaborative Research Grants**
● **Individual Research Grants**
● **International Dissertation Research
   Grant**

TYPE:
Research grants. Collaborative Research
Grants and Individual Research Grants
provide support for important aspects of
research such as travel to archives and
libraries, research assistance, field work and
released time. However, funds are not
provided for dissertation research.

International Dissertation Research Grants
support AAR student members whose
dissertation research requires them to travel
outside of the country in which their school
or university is located. Grants are intended
to help candidates complete their doctoral
degrees by offsetting costs of travel, lodging,
and other dissertation research-related
expenses.

YEAR PROGRAM STARTED: 1989

PURPOSE:
To promote research and scholarship in the
field of religion; to foster excellence in
teaching in the field of religion; to support
and encourage members' professional
development; to develop programming and
participation in AAR regional groups; to
advance publication and scholarly
communication in the field of religion; to
contribute to the public understanding of
religion; to welcome the various voices in the
field of religion and to support and encourage

diversity within the AAR; to help to advance and secure the future of the academic study of religion.

LEGAL BASIS:
501(c)(3).

ELIGIBILITY:
Applicants must be current AAR members who have been in good standing for the previous three years and have not received an AAR Research Award in the previous five years.

FINANCIAL DATA:
Amount of support per award: Collaborative and Individual Research Grants: $500 to $5,000; International Dissertation Research Grant: $5,000.

APPLICATION INFO:
Individual or Collaborative grant applicants should submit through the Academy's electronic system:
(1) cover page that includes the following: (a) name, (b) institutional affiliation, (c) title of the project and, (d) grant type - Individual or Collaborative;
(2) abstract of 50 words or fewer describing the project;
(3) project budget;
(4) two-page focused description of the research project that details its aims and significance and explains how the award would be used. Collaborative project descriptions should include brief descriptions of the scholarly role of each collaborator and a plan to have the research published and;
(5) curriculum vitae of no more than two pages.

International Dissertation Research Grant applicants must submit the following materials through the online form:
(1) letter of application (no longer than three pages) that describes their research project and how support for on-site research is critical for the completion of their dissertation;
(2) current curriculum vitae;
(3) proposed budget and project timeline and;
(4) letter of support from their dissertation supervisor.
Duration: Individual or Collaborative Grant: Research projects may be undertaken any time within that academic year and up to the end of the following calendar year. International Dissertation Research Grant: Funds must be expended by the end of the calendar year awarded.
Deadline: Collaborative Grant and Individual Research Grant: August 1; International Dissertation Grant: December 1.

IRS I.D.: 25-6063005

STAFF:
Elizabeth Hardcastle, Service Coordinator

ADDRESS INQUIRIES TO:
Elizabeth Hardcastle, Service Coordinator
(See address above.)

AMERICAN ACADEMY OF RELIGION [735]
825 Houston Mill Road, N.E.
Suite 300
Atlanta, GA 30329
(404) 727-3049
Fax: (404) 727-7959
E-mail: info@aarweb.org
Web Site: www.aarweb.org

FOUNDED: 1909

AREAS OF INTEREST:
To support projects within the regions that promise to benefit the scholarly and professional life of AAR members and the work of the regions.

NAME(S) OF PROGRAMS:
● **Regional Development Grants**

TYPE:
Development grants. Workshops, special programs, training events and other innovative regional projects may be funded through this source.

PURPOSE:
To promote research and scholarship in the field of religion; to foster excellence in teaching in the field of religion; to support and encourage members' professional development; to develop programming and participation in AAR regional groups; to advance publication and scholarly communication in the field of religion; to contribute to the public understanding of religion; to welcome into our conversation the various voices in the field of religion and to support and encourage diversity within the AAR; to help to advance and secure the future of the academic study of religion.

LEGAL BASIS:
501(c)(3).

ELIGIBILITY:
Applicant must be a current member of AAR and maintain their membership throughout the grant period.

GEOG. RESTRICTIONS: United States.

FINANCIAL DATA:
Amount of support per award: Maximum $4,000.

NO. MOST RECENT APPLICANTS: 15.

NO. AWARDS: 4.

APPLICATION INFO:
Grant applications must be submitted electronically through the Online Submissions System. Proposals should include the following:
(1) complete contact information for all parties involved in developing the grant proposal;
(2) a narrative description of the project detailing how the project promises to benefit the scholarly and professional life of AAR members and the work of the region;
(3) a statement on how this project or activities may be adapted to other regional groups or a brief explanation of why this project is region-specific;
(4) a clear timeline for the completion of the grant. Please note that projects are to be completed within one year of award announcement, unless other arrangements have been made with the AAR Executive Office and;
(5) a detailed budget, including office expenses, travel expenses, honoraria, stipend, and other expenses. Institutional overhead costs may not be included in this budget.

Duration: One year.

Deadline: June 1.

IRS I.D.: 20-5478525

ADDRESS INQUIRIES TO:
Regional Coordinator

AMERICAN CATHOLIC HISTORICAL ASSOCIATION [736]
Mount St. Mary's University
16300 Old Emmitsburg Road
Emmitsburg, MD 21727
(301) 447-5799
E-mail: acha@achahistory.org
Web Site: achahistory.org

FOUNDED: 1919

AREAS OF INTEREST:
The history of Catholicism from antiquity to the present.

NAME(S) OF PROGRAMS:
● **The Peter Guilday Prize**

TYPE:
Awards/prizes; Challenge/matching grants; Conferences/seminars; Travel grants. A prize awarded annually to the author whose article, dealing with the history of the Catholic Church, is the first of his or her professional career and is judged to be the best of those in that category accepted for publication in any given year by the editors of the *Catholic Historical Review.*

YEAR PROGRAM STARTED: 1972

PURPOSE:
To stimulate interest in the history of Catholicism among young scholars.

LEGAL BASIS:
Learned society.

ELIGIBILITY:
The article must deal with some aspect of the history of the Catholic Church broadly considered. Anyone who has already published an historical book or an article in a learned journal will not be eligible for competition. Articles based on doctoral dissertations will be welcome, provided they are self-contained studies. The author must be a citizen or permanent resident of the U.S. or Canada.

GEOG. RESTRICTIONS: United States and Canada.

FINANCIAL DATA:
Amount of support per award: $250.
Total amount of support: $250 per annum.

NO. MOST RECENT APPLICANTS: 3.

NO. AWARDS: 1 per annum.

APPLICATION INFO:
Inquiries and manuscripts should be sent to the editors of the *Catholic Historical Review.* Manuscripts must not exceed 30 typewritten pages (footnotes included).
Deadline: September 1.

ADDRESS INQUIRIES TO:
Nelson Minnich
Editor, *Catholic Historical Review*
(See address above.)

AMERICAN CATHOLIC HISTORICAL ASSOCIATION [737]
Mount St. Mary's University
16300 Old Emmitsburg Road
Emmitsburg, MD 21727
(301) 447-5799
E-mail: acha@achahistory.org
Web Site: achahistory.org

FOUNDED: 1919

AREAS OF INTEREST:
The history of Catholicism from antiquity to the present.

NAME(S) OF PROGRAMS:
• **The John Gilmary Shea Prize**

TYPE:
Awards/prizes. This Prize is given annually to the author of a book, published during a preceding 12-month period, which is judged by a committee of experts to have made the most original and distinguished contribution to knowledge of the history of the Catholic Church.

YEAR PROGRAM STARTED: 1945

PURPOSE:
To stimulate interest in the history of Catholicism among young scholars.

LEGAL BASIS:
Learned society.

ELIGIBILITY:
Any author who is a citizen or permanent resident of the U.S. or Canada is eligible to apply. The work submitted must have been published within the previous calendar year.

GEOG. RESTRICTIONS: United States and Canada.

FINANCIAL DATA:
Amount of support per award: $1,500.
Total amount of support: $1,500 per annum.

NO. AWARDS: 1 per annum.

APPLICATION INFO:
No formal application is required. Publishers or authors may enter by sending three copies of the work to be considered. Write or e-mail to the above address for further details.
Deadline: May 15.

ADDRESS INQUIRIES TO:
Katie Stirling-Harris
Shea Prize Committee Chairperson
E-mail: akharris@ucdavis.edu

AMERICAN CATHOLIC HISTORICAL ASSOCIATION [738]
Mount St. Mary's University
16300 Old Emmitsburg Road
Emmitsburg, MD 21727
(301) 447-5799
E-mail: acha@achahistory.org
Web Site: achahistory.org

FOUNDED: 1919

AREAS OF INTEREST:
The history of Catholicism from antiquity to the present.

NAME(S) OF PROGRAMS:
• **John Tracy Ellis Dissertation Award**
• **Presidential Graduate Travel Grant**
• **Summer Research and Writing Grant**

TYPE:
Awards/prizes; Challenge/matching grants; Conferences/seminars; Research grants; Travel grants. John Tracy Ellis Dissertation Award memorializes the scholarship and teaching of Monsignor Ellis (1905-1992) and is awarded to a doctoral student in the field of Catholic Studies with a promising, but not-yet-completed dissertation.

Presidential Graduate Travel Grant was created in 2010 by the Association from donations from former presidents. This cash grant is awarded to a graduate student presenting at the Annual Meeting to assist with travel expenses.

Summer Research and Writing Grant is awarded to an ACHA member who is a graduate student or contingent faculty member to support writing or travel expenses.

PURPOSE:
To stimulate interest in the history of Catholicism among young scholars.

LEGAL BASIS:
Learned society.

ELIGIBILITY:
John Tracy Ellis Dissertation Award: Applicants must be citizens or authorized residents of the U.S. or Canada, and must be enrolled in a doctoral program at a recognized institution of higher education.

Presidential Graduate Travel Grant: Given on a competitive basis to two graduate students who are current members of the Association and who have papers accepted at either the Annual or Spring meetings.

Summer Research and Writing Grant: Awarded to an ACHA graduate student member who has completed all requirements for the Doctorate except the dissertation and is attending an accredited institution of higher learning.

FINANCIAL DATA:
Amount of support per award: John Tracy Ellis Dissertation Award: A purse of $1,500; Presidential Graduate Travel Grant: $1,000 per award; Summer Research and Writing Grant: $1,500 per award.

NO. AWARDS: John Tracy Ellis Dissertation Award: 1; Presidential Graduate Travel Grant: 2 for the Annual Meeting and 2 for the Spring Meeting; Summer Research and Writing Grant: 4.

APPLICATION INFO:
John Tracy Ellis Dissertation Award: Applicant must submit the online application form, along with the required materials.

Presidential Graduate Travel Grant and Summer Research and Writing Grant: Applicants should complete the online form and have a letter of recommendation e-mailed.
Deadline: John Tracy Ellis Dissertation Award: May 15; Presidential Graduate Travel Grant: Fall 2021; Summer Research and Writing Grant: March 30.

ADDRESS INQUIRIES TO:
Charles Strauss
Executive Secretary-Treasurer
(See e-mail address above.)

THE CHATLOS FOUNDATION, INC. [739]
P.O. Box 915048
Longwood, FL 32791-5048
(407) 862-5077
E-mail: info@chatlos.org
Web Site: www.chatlos.org

FOUNDED: 1953

AREAS OF INTEREST:
Bible colleges, seminaries, religion, liberal arts colleges, medical and social concerns.

TYPE:
General operating grants; Project/program grants; Scholarships; Technical assistance; Training grants. Scholarships are not provided directly to individuals but rather to colleges and seminaries which in turn provide monies to the students of their choice.

YEAR PROGRAM STARTED: 1953

LEGAL BASIS:
Private foundation.

ELIGIBILITY:
The Foundation only funds nonprofit organizations which are tax-exempt for U.S. federal income tax purposes around the globe. Less emphasis on grant requests for bricks and mortar, endowments, conference and administrative expenses and multiyear grants. No grants for medical research, individual church congregations, primary/secondary schools, organizations in existence for less than two years, arts organizations or individuals. Contributions cannot be made to organizations which discriminate on the basis of race, color, sex, creed, age or national origin.

FINANCIAL DATA:
Amount of support per award: Bible colleges: $5,000 to $20,000; Religious causes and medical concerns: $5,000 to $15,000; Liberal arts colleges: $2,500 to $7,500; Social concerns: $2,000 to $5,000.

Initially, the Foundation tends to fund requests for amounts around $10,000.
Total amount of support: Approximately $2,000,000 for the year 2020.

NO. MOST RECENT APPLICANTS: 695 for the year 2020.

NO. AWARDS: 76 grants for the year 2020.

APPLICATION INFO:
Application may be submitted by mail or online. Details are available on the Foundation web site.
Duration: Varies, although multiyear grants are rarely considered.
Deadline: Applications are accepted throughout the year.

PUBLICATIONS:
Application guideline brochure.

IRS I.D.: 13-6161425

BOARD OF DIRECTORS:
Kathryn A. Randle, Chairman of the Board
William J. Chatlos, President
Michele C. Roach, Senior Vice President and Secretary
William J. Chatlos, III, Vice President
Cindee Random, Treasurer and Trustee
Janet A. Chatlos, Trustee
Cherlyn Dannhaeuser, Trustee
Kimberly Grimm, Trustee
Charles O. Morgan, Jr., Trustee

ADDRESS INQUIRIES TO:
Grants Administrator
(See address above.)

EPISCOPAL CHURCH FOUNDATION [740]
475 Riverside Drive, Suite 750
New York, NY 10115
(212) 870-2852
(800) 697-2858
Fax: (212) 297-0142
E-mail: fellows@episcopalfoundation.org
Web Site: www.episcopalfoundation.org

FOUNDED: 1949

AREAS OF INTEREST:
Innovative programs in leadership development, education and philanthropy for the clergy and laity of the Episcopal Church.

CONSULTING OR VOLUNTEER SERVICES:
Capital campaigns, planned giving and endowment management services.

NAME(S) OF PROGRAMS:
● **ECF Fellowship Partners Program**

TYPE:
Fellowships. Religious studies. Fellowship Partners Program consists of two tracks: Academic Fellowships and Ministry Fellowships.

YEAR PROGRAM STARTED: 1964

PURPOSE:
To support doctoral study for Episcopalians planning teaching careers in theological education in the Episcopal Church in the U.S.

ELIGIBILITY:
Applications from both lay and ordained Episcopalians are welcome.

Academic Fellowship applicants on the academic track must be engaged in or embarking on a course of study at the graduate level, except for first professional degrees (e.g., M.Div., J.D., M.D.). Acceptable courses of study include doctoral- and Master's-level programs, as well as clinical study or training at the postundergraduate level.

Ministry Fellowship applicants will be asked to demonstrate how their ministry has the potential to transform community at the grassroots level, and special consideration will be given to programs in locations with limited resources or among underserved communities.

GEOG. RESTRICTIONS: United States.

FINANCIAL DATA:
Amount of support per award: Up to $15,000 per year.
Total amount of support: Varies.

NO. AWARDS: 2 for the year 2020.

APPLICATION INFO:
Application information is available on the web site.
Duration: One year. Fellowship is renewable for two more years.
Deadline: Early March. Notification by late May.

PUBLICATIONS:
ECF Vital Practices.

ADDRESS INQUIRIES TO:
Kjerstin Besser
Associate Program Director
(See address above.)

GENERAL BOARD OF HIGHER EDUCATION AND MINISTRY, THE UNITED METHODIST CHURCH   [741]

1001 19th Avenue South
Nashville, TN 37212
(615) 340-7338
Fax: (615) 340-7529
E-mail: mbigord@gbhem.org
Web Site: www.gbhem.org

AREAS OF INTEREST:
Religion.

NAME(S) OF PROGRAMS:
● **Georgia Harkness Scholarships**

TYPE:
Awards/prizes; Scholarships. Awards to encourage women over age 35 to prepare for ordained ministry as an Elder in the United Methodist Church as a second career. The scholarship is to be used for study toward the basic seminary degree in an accredited school of theology.

YEAR PROGRAM STARTED: 1975

PURPOSE:
To support and encourage women for ordained ministry as an Elder in the United Methodist Church.

LEGAL BASIS:
Nonprofit organization.

ELIGIBILITY:
Applicant must be a member of the United Methodist Church for a minimum of three years and be a certified candidate for Elder in the year they are applying. Women over age 35 who have received a Bachelor of Arts or equivalent degree, have been accepted in an accredited school of theology, and have affirmed a specific interest in preparation for ordination as an Elder in the United Methodist Church are eligible. A 3.0 grade point average is required.

FINANCIAL DATA:
Amount of support per award: $5,000.

NO. AWARDS: Varies.

APPLICATION INFO:
Applicants can access the application at the Board web site.
Duration: One year.
Deadline: Early March.

ADDRESS INQUIRIES TO:
Marcie Bigord, Assistant Director
Office of Loans and Scholarships
(See address above.)

*PLEASE NOTE:
Full-time enrollment required.

GENERAL COMMISSION ON ARCHIVES AND HISTORY OF THE UNITED METHODIST CHURCH   [742]

36 Madison Avenue
Madison, NJ 07940
(973) 408-3189
Fax: (973) 408-3909
E-mail: adreff@gcah.org
Web Site: www.gcah.org

FOUNDED: 1968

AREAS OF INTEREST:
History of the United Methodist Church and antecedent bodies.

NAME(S) OF PROGRAMS:
● **John Harrison Ness Memorial Award**

TYPE:
Awards/prizes. Awards to the students of accredited seminaries whose professor submits the best papers on various aspects of United Methodist denominational history. In general, comprehensive subjects on the history of some phase of the denomination will be preferred, but papers on local church or annual conference subjects will be accepted if approved by the professor advising the project.

YEAR PROGRAM STARTED: 1979

PURPOSE:
To stimulate interest in history of the United Methodist Church.

LEGAL BASIS:
Private church-related organization.

ELIGIBILITY:
The paper must have been appraised by the professor of church history under whom the student has been studying and who will submit the paper. The paper must be properly annotated and be a minimum length of 3,000 words. It is desired that the project be undertaken only after the student has had a course in United Methodist history or at least during the enrollment in such.

FINANCIAL DATA:
Amount of support per award: First prize: $500; Second prize: $300.
Total amount of support: $800 annually.

NO. AWARDS: 2.

APPLICATION INFO:
Details are available online.
Duration: Annual. A recipient may resubmit if he or she is still in seminary.
Deadline: February 1. Announcement approximately three months later.

OFFICERS:
Ashley Boggan Dreff, General Secretary

ADDRESS INQUIRIES TO:
Ashley Boggan Dreff, General Secretary
(See address above.)

THE STEWART HUSTON CHARITABLE TRUST   [743]

50 South 1st Avenue
Coatesville, PA 19320
(610) 384-2666
Fax: (610) 384-3396
E-mail: admin@stewarthuston.org
Web Site: www.stewarthuston.org

FOUNDED: 1989

AREAS OF INTEREST:
Historic preservation, health and human services, civic and Protestant Christian organizations.

CONSULTING OR VOLUNTEER SERVICES:
General nonprofit organizational issues. Finance and fund-raising.

TYPE:
Capital grants; Challenge/matching grants; General operating grants; Matching gifts; Project/program grants.

YEAR PROGRAM STARTED: 1989

PURPOSE:
To provide funds, technical assistance and collaboration on behalf of nonprofit organizations engaged exclusively in religious, charitable or educational work; to extend opportunities to deserving needy persons.

LEGAL BASIS:
Private foundation.

ELIGIBILITY:
Applicants must be tax-exempt and address a particular community need. Grants are not awarded for scholarship support to individuals, endowment purposes, purchase of tickets or advertising for benefit purposes, coverage of continuing operating deficits, and document publication costs. Support is not provided to intermediate or pass-through organizations (other than United Way), groups such as fraternal organizations,

political campaigns, veterans, labor or local civic groups, volunteer fire companies, and groups engaged in influencing legislation.

According to Stewart Huston's Indenture of Trust, 60% of distributions go to Trinitarian/Evangelical organizations as defined by the Chester County Orphans Court: "The grant applicant must be organized and operated exclusively to further religious and charitable activities carried on by Protestant churches, other than Unitarian churches, and affiliated or related organizations; grant proceeds must be used exclusively for one or both of the following two activities: dissemination of the Christian Gospel by preaching and conducting religious services, offering a Christian education, etc.; and promotion of Christian principles through charity."

The remaining 40% is to be distributed for secular purposes within a 100-mile radius from Coatesville, PA.

GEOG. RESTRICTIONS: Chester County, Pennsylvania and Savannah, Georgia areas.

FINANCIAL DATA:
Amount of support per award: Maximum grant: $20,000; Average $5,000 to $10,000.
Total amount of support: $650,000 in grants for the year ended December 31, 2018.

NO. MOST RECENT APPLICANTS: 130.

NO. AWARDS: 44.

REPRESENTATIVE AWARDS:
$10,000 to The Living Vine; $5,000 to Chester County Food Bank; $20,000 to Christ Church Episcopal; $15,000 to Bridge of Hope; $10,000 to Habitat for Humanity.

APPLICATION INFO:
Online application will require a summary of the organization, a description of the project, and the following attachments in PDF format:
(1) IRS tax-exempt letter;
(2) statement that there has been no change in purpose, character or method of operation since the Agency's IRS tax ruling was issued;
(3) statement of Christian ministry faith-based initiatives;
(4) current by-laws;
(5) current board of directors list (with professional affiliation);
(6) most recent independent financial audit;
(7) list of public/private funding sources during the past fiscal year;
(8) current semi-annual or annual report;
(9) examples of published media reviews;
(10) strategic plan;
(11) organizational flow chart and;
(12) overall operating budget for the current fiscal year.
Duration: No multiyear commitments.
Deadline: April 1 for civic and health organizations; April 1 and October 1 for Trinitarian Evangelical and secular groups.

PUBLICATIONS:
Program announcement; guidelines; annual report.

IRS I.D.: 23-2612599

TRUSTEES:
Charles L. Huston, III
Harriet Cann Connolly
Elinor Lashley

ADDRESS INQUIRIES TO:
Scott G. Huston, Executive Director
(See address above.)

IMMANUEL BIBLE FOUNDATION   [744]
1301 South Fell Avenue
Normal, IL 61761
(309) 452-6710
Fax: (309) 862-4121
E-mail: immanuelbiblefoundation@yahoo.com
Web Site: www.ibfoundation.org

FOUNDED: 1944

AREAS OF INTEREST:
Local charities and youth-serving organizations.

TYPE:
General operating grants. Special needs grants.

YEAR PROGRAM STARTED: 1949

PURPOSE:
To promote the gospel and serve as a resource for the Christian community.

LEGAL BASIS:
Tax-exempt private foundation.

ELIGIBILITY:
Tax-exempt organizations, entirely local to the Foundation's immediate area, may apply. Out-of-state applications are not accepted. No grants to individuals.

GEOG. RESTRICTIONS: McLean County, Illinois.

FINANCIAL DATA:
Amount of support per award: $500.
Total amount of support: Up to $7,500.

APPLICATION INFO:
Grant applications are available for download on the Foundation web site.
Duration: Varies by need.
Deadline: Applications accepted January 1 to May 1. Announcement by September 1.

IRS I.D.: 37-0688539

ADDRESS INQUIRIES TO:
Annette Klinzing, Executive Director
(See address above.)

KOCH FOUNDATION, INC.   [745]
4421 N.W. 39th Avenue
Building 1, Suite 1
Gainesville, FL 32606
(352) 373-7491
Fax: (352) 337-1548
E-mail: staff@thekochfoundation.org
Web Site: www.thekochfoundation.org

FOUNDED: 1979

AREAS OF INTEREST:
Roman Catholic evangelization.

TYPE:
Fellowships; Grants-in-aid; Project/program grants; Training grants. Grants are made for direct evangelization programs, preparation of evangelists, resource-poor Catholic schools that are the principal means of evangelization in the community.

YEAR PROGRAM STARTED: 1979

PURPOSE:
To provide financial support for evangelization efforts to Catholic organizations throughout the world that propagate the Roman Catholic faith.

LEGAL BASIS:
Not-for-profit corporation.

ELIGIBILITY:
U.S. Catholic organizations must be 501(c)(3) and appear in the Official Catholic Directory. Non-U.S. Catholic organizations must have a fiscal agent in the U.S. who is willing to disburse grant funds for them, should a grant be awarded.

FINANCIAL DATA:
Amount of support per award: Varies depending on needs and nature of the request; typical grant $15,000.
Total amount of support: $4,717,100 in total support for fiscal year 2018-19.

NO. MOST RECENT APPLICANTS: 455 for fiscal year 2016-17.

NO. AWARDS: 342 approved grants for fiscal year 2018-19.

APPLICATION INFO:
Application forms are available January 1 to May 1. Briefly describe the project when writing for a grant application. All requests must be in English to assure appropriate attention. Faxed requests are not accepted. Completed applications must be returned within 90 days. Applications must include a budget, a statement of the desired impact on evangelization and, if international, the country and diocese where the program will take place and the U.S. fiscal agent who will be responsible for distributing the funds. Applications for a continuing project must be accompanied by a six-month progress report or yearly evaluation.
Duration: Varies.
Deadline: May 1. Announcement in mid-March.

PUBLICATIONS:
Application guidelines.

IRS I.D.: 59-1885997

BOARD OF DIRECTORS:
William A. Bomberger, President
Inge L. Vraney, Vice President
Carolyn L. Bomberger, Treasurer
Rachel A. Bomberger, Secretary
Lawrence E. Vraney, Jr., Assistant Treasurer
Michelle H. Bomberger, Assistant Secretary
Matthew A. Bomberger
Charlotte L. Spacinsky
Jeffrey Vraney
Lori Vraney
Maura J. Vraney

ADDRESS INQUIRIES TO:
Executive Director
(See address above.)

LUTHERAN FOUNDATION OF ST. LOUIS   [746]
8860 Ladue Road
Suite 200
St. Louis, MO 63124
(314) 231-2244
Fax: (314) 727-7688
E-mail: info@lutheranfoundation.org
Web Site: www.lutheranfoundation.org

FOUNDED: 1984

AREAS OF INTEREST:
Christian voluntarism, congregation social service outreach, Lutheran education, services to ex-offenders and their families, foreign-born populations, and older adults maintaining independence.

TYPE:
Project/program grants.

YEAR PROGRAM STARTED: 1984

PURPOSE:
To help assure a creative Jewish future throughout the world by encouraging Jewish scholarship, Jewish education and Jewish cultural creativity.

LEGAL BASIS:
IRS Section 501(c)(3) charity; not a private foundation.

ELIGIBILITY:
Individual requirements vary according to the scholarship or fellowship.

FINANCIAL DATA:
Amount of support per award: Up to $10,000 per year.

APPLICATION INFO:
Guidelines and application forms for scholarships and fellowships are available on written request to the Foundation at the address above.
Duration: One academic year.
Deadline: October 31 for doctoral scholarships and fellowships.

OFFICERS:
Marlene Bethlehem, President
Jeni S. Friedman, Executive Vice President

ADDRESS INQUIRIES TO:
Jeni S. Friedman
Executive Vice President
(See address above.)

PONTIFICAL INSTITUTE OF MEDIAEVAL STUDIES

59 Queen's Park Crescent East
Toronto ON M5S 2C4 Canada
(416) 926-7142
Fax: (416) 926-7292
E-mail: allan.smith@utoronto.ca
Web Site: www.pims.ca

TYPE:
Fellowships.

See entry 579 for full listing.

PRESBYTERIAN CHURCH (U.S.A.) [750]

100 Witherspoon Street
Louisville, KY 40202-1396
(502) 569-5224
(800) 728-7228 ext. 5224
Fax: (502) 569-8766
E-mail: finaid@pcusa.org
Web Site: www.pcusa.org/financialaid

NAME(S) OF PROGRAMS:
• **Presbyterian Study Grants**

TYPE:
Grants-in-aid; Scholarships.

PURPOSE:
To assist graduate students who are communicant members of the Presbyterian Church (U.S.A.) in their preparation for professional church occupations.

ELIGIBILITY:
Applicants must demonstrate financial need, be enrolled on a full-time basis, be in good academic standing, be studying in a Presbyterian Church (U.S.A.) seminary, and must be studying in one of the two categories listed below:
(1) students preparing for ordination must be full-time M.Div. and must be enrolled as an inquirer with or received as a candidate by a Presbyterian Church (U.S.A.) presbytery for a church occupation or;

(2) students preparing for occupations as a Christian educator must be full-time M.A.C.E. students.

GEOG. RESTRICTIONS: United States.

FINANCIAL DATA:
Grants are meant to be supplemental to other assistance a student has sought and is receiving from presbytery, seminary, home church, etc. Grants are not available for summer study, intern year or studying abroad.
Amount of support per award: Up to $7,000 for the academic year, depending upon demonstrated need and availability of funds.
Total amount of support: Varies.

APPLICATION INFO:
Detailed information and forms are available on the web site.
Duration: One academic year. Renewals possible (annually).
Deadline: May 15 for Part 1.

*SPECIAL STIPULATIONS:
No grants are available for doctoral study.

RASKOB FOUNDATION FOR CATHOLIC ACTIVITIES [751]

P.O. Box 4019
Wilmington, DE 19807
(302) 655-4440
Fax: (302) 655-3223
E-mail: info@rfca.org
Web Site: www.rfca.org

FOUNDED: 1945

AREAS OF INTEREST:
Catholic activities.

TYPE:
Project/program grants.

YEAR PROGRAM STARTED: 1945

PURPOSE:
To engage in such exclusively religious, charitable, literary and educational activities as will aid the Roman Catholic Church and institutions and organizations identified with it.

LEGAL BASIS:
Nonprofit foundation.

ELIGIBILITY:
Applicants must be Catholic organizations with nonprofit status.

FINANCIAL DATA:
Since inception, the Foundation has awarded over $200,000,000, both domestically and internationally, for a wide variety of causes.
Amount of support per award: $5,000 to $60,000.
Total amount of support: $6,706,778 for the year 2019.

NO. MOST RECENT APPLICANTS: 739 for the year 2019.

NO. AWARDS: 223 for the year 2019.

APPLICATION INFO:
Process and requirements for Domestic and International Programs are available on the Foundation's web site. The International Program is comprised of two phases. The abstract phase is open to organizations/projects meeting the outlined requirements. After abstracts are reviewed, the Foundation will notify each organization whether or not they are invited to the application phase.

Duration: Varies.
Deadline: Domestic applications: Applications are accepted from January 1 through the last business day in January for Board decision at the Foundation's May meeting and from June 1 through the last business day in June for Board decision at the Foundation's November meeting. International applications: Abstracts may be submitted from May 7 through the last business day of May. Decisions regarding abstracts will be sent in mid-September.

PUBLICATIONS:
Application guidelines.

IRS I.D.: 51-0070060

STAFF:
Theresa G. Robinson, Executive Director

ADDRESS INQUIRIES TO:
Janine Harlam, Grants Administrator
(See address above.)

SUBCOMMITTEE ON CATHOLIC HOME MISSIONS [752]

United States Conference of Catholic Bishops
3211 4th Street, N.E.
Washington, DC 20017-1194
(202) 541-5400
Fax: (202) 541-3473
E-mail: homemissions@usccb.org
Web Site: www.usccb.org

FOUNDED: 1924

AREAS OF INTEREST:
Catholic missions and diocesan programs in America, including evangelization, catechesis, parish life, Hispanic ministry, youth outreach, prison ministry, and personnel training.

TYPE:
General operating grants; Project/program grants; Seed money grants; Training grants. Annual grants to fund home mission and diocesan activities, such as evangelization through proclamation of the Word, pastoral services, personnel training and the formation of faith communities in the U.S. and its territories. Home mission activities may be centered at the national, regional, diocesan or local level and may address the country as a whole, a particular group of people or a particular place.

YEAR PROGRAM STARTED: 1924

ELIGIBILITY:
Eligible applicants may come from diocesan bishops of home mission dioceses for activities that serve to establish or strengthen the church in their dioceses. No funds are available for endowments or loans.

GEOG. RESTRICTIONS: United States and its Caribbean and Pacific territories.

FINANCIAL DATA:
Amount of support per award: Varies depending on needs and nature of the request.
Total amount of support: $9,950,000 for the year 2020.

NO. AWARDS: 77.

APPLICATION INFO:
Application materials are available January of each year. Contact office for other requirements.
Duration: Grants are renewable.
Deadline: April 1. Announcement in October. Disbursements are made semiannually, January to December.

PUBLICATIONS:
Annual report; guidelines; *Neighbors*, quarterly newsletter.

OFFICERS:
Bishop Shawn McKnight, Chairman
Kevin Day, Director

ADDRESS INQUIRIES TO:
Kevin Day, Director
(See telephone and e-mail address above.)

*PLEASE NOTE:
Currently considering grants from dioceses only.

UNITED JEWISH APPEAL-FEDERATION OF JEWISH PHILANTHROPIES OF NEW YORK   [753]

130 East 59th Street
New York, NY 10022
(212) 980-1000
(212) 836-1321
Fax: (212) 836-1353
E-mail: feinsteinl@ujafedny.org
Web Site: www.ujafedny.org

FOUNDED: 1917

AREAS OF INTEREST:
Human services, Jewish identity and education, rescue and resettlement of Jewish communities in distress.

CONSULTING OR VOLUNTEER SERVICES:
Offers numerous opportunities to volunteer. Please call Resource Line: (212) 836-1447.

TYPE:
Awards/prizes; Block grants; Capital grants; Challenge/matching grants; Conferences/seminars; Demonstration grants; Development grants; Fellowships; General operating grants; Internships; Matching gifts; Project/program grants; Research grants; Scholarships; Technical assistance; Travel grants; Research contracts.

YEAR PROGRAM STARTED: 1917

PURPOSE:
To care for people in need; to inspire a passion for Jewish life and learning; to strengthen Jewish communities in New York, in Israel, and around the world.

LEGAL BASIS:
501(c)(3).

ELIGIBILITY:
No grants to individuals. Applicants must be 501(c)(3) organizations.

GEOG. RESTRICTIONS: New York including the five boroughs, Nassau, Suffolk and Westchester counties.

FINANCIAL DATA:
Amount of support per award: Varies depending upon needs and nature of the request.
Total amount of support: $138,193,071 for fiscal year 2020.

APPLICATION INFO:
Application form required. Organizations must include documentation of IRS nonprofit status with their application.
Duration: One year. Renewal possible.
Deadline: January for most programs.

PUBLICATIONS:
Annual Report to the Community.

IRS I.D.: 51-0172429

ADDRESS INQUIRIES TO:
E-mail: grants@ujafedny.org

UNITED METHODIST COMMUNICATIONS

810 12th Avenue South
Nashville, TN 37203-4704
(615) 742-5400
E-mail: rjames@umcom.org
Web Site: www.umcom.org

TYPE:
Fellowships. Assists one United Methodist student in postgraduate study at an accredited U.S. college or university who intends to pursue a career in religious journalism.

See entry 1760 for full listing.

THE WABASH CENTER FOR TEACHING AND LEARNING IN THEOLOGY AND RELIGION   [754]

301 West Wabash Avenue
Crawfordsville, IN 47933
(765) 361-6047
Fax: (765) 361-6051
E-mail: wabashcenter@wabash.edu
Web Site: www.wabashcenter.wabash.edu

FOUNDED: 1995

AREAS OF INTEREST:
Teaching religion and theology, higher education pedagogy in theology and religion.

NAME(S) OF PROGRAMS:
● **Educational Environments**
● **Faculty Practices and Vocation**

TYPE:
Conferences/seminars; Fellowships; Project/program grants; Research grants.

YEAR PROGRAM STARTED: 1995

PURPOSE:
To strengthen and enhance the teaching of religion and theology in North American theological schools and religion departments in colleges and universities.

ELIGIBILITY:
Full-time faculty members in religion departments of colleges and universities in North America and in theological schools accredited by the Association of Theological Schools are eligible to apply for these grants.

GEOG. RESTRICTIONS: United States and Canada.

FINANCIAL DATA:
Amount of support per award: Up to $30,000.

NO. MOST RECENT APPLICANTS: Approximately 200.

NO. AWARDS: 60.

APPLICATION INFO:
Grant proposals should consist of an application form, project proposal (including budget) and letter of support. Specific format for grant proposals is explained in detail on the Center's web site.
Deadline: February 15.

PUBLICATIONS:
Teaching Theology and Religion, published quarterly by Wiley-Blackwell Publishers.

ADDRESS INQUIRIES TO:
Paul O. Myhre, Senior Associate Director
(See address above.)

INTERNATIONAL AFFAIRS AND AREA STUDIES

International affairs and area studies

AMERICAN INSTITUTE OF PAKISTAN STUDIES [755]

University of Wisconsin-Madison
B488 Medical Sciences Center
1300 University Avenue
Madison, WI 53706
(608) 265-1471
Fax: (608) 265-3302
E-mail: aips@pakistanstudies-aips.org
Web Site: www.pakistanstudies-aips.org

FOUNDED: 1973

AREAS OF INTEREST:
All fields of humanities and social sciences if engaged in research on Pakistan and relations between Pakistan and other countries.

NAME(S) OF PROGRAMS:
- **AIPS Post Doctoral Fellowship**
- **AIPS Pre-Doctoral Fellowship**
- **Community College Faculty Exchange**
- **Lecture Series**
- **Workshop Series**

TYPE:
Awards/prizes; Conferences/seminars; Fellowships; Travel grants; Visiting scholars. Awarded in several categories including predoctoral research, postdoctoral study, library service and professional development.

YEAR PROGRAM STARTED: 1973

PURPOSE:
To promote research on Pakistan.

ELIGIBILITY:
Applicants must be scholars and advanced graduate students who are American citizens and are engaged in research on Pakistan in ancient, medieval and modern times, in all fields of the humanities and social sciences. Research topics comparing aspects of Pakistan with other Muslim countries are especially encouraged.

Graduate student applicants must have fulfilled all residence, language and preliminary examination requirements for the Doctorate and have an approved dissertation topic.

FINANCIAL DATA:
The award will provide a maintenance allowance for the scholar and dependents, plus travel and other benefits.
Amount of support per award: Varies.
Total amount of support: Approximately $100,000.

NO. MOST RECENT APPLICANTS: 15.

NO. AWARDS: Varies.

APPLICATION INFO:
Predoctoral applications should include a proposal (five pages), curriculum vitae, a transcript, a letter from the dissertation advisor and contact information for two references. Postdoctoral applications should include a proposal (five pages), curriculum vitae, and contact information for two referees.
Duration: Two to nine months.
Deadline: Varies.

STAFF:
Laura Hammond, U.S. Director

ADDRESS INQUIRIES TO:
Laura Hammond, U.S. Director
(See address above.)

THE KATHRYN AMES FOUNDATION [756]

c/o Pierson & Pierson
305 West Chesapeake Avenue, Suite 308
Towson, MD 21204
(410) 821-3006
Fax: (410) 821-3007
E-mail: info@kathrynames.org
Web Site: www.kathrynames.org

FOUNDED: 1993

AREAS OF INTEREST:
Israel, education, health care, poverty relief and pluralism.

TYPE:
General operating grants; Project/program grants.

YEAR PROGRAM STARTED: 1993

PURPOSE:
To benefit organizations located in Israel which are working for charitable and benevolent purposes.

LEGAL BASIS:
Private foundation.

ELIGIBILITY:
Eligible organizations must be nonprofit and located in Israel.

GEOG. RESTRICTIONS: Israel.

FINANCIAL DATA:
Amount of support per award: $7,500 to $40,000; Average: $11,389.
Total amount of support: $439,381 for the year 2020.

NO. MOST RECENT APPLICANTS: Letters of Inquiry: 230; Full Applications: 43 for the year 2020.

NO. AWARDS: 37 for the year 2020.

APPLICATION INFO:
Application form is available online.
Duration: Typically one year.

PUBLICATIONS:
Application guidelines.

ADDRESS INQUIRIES TO:
Stacy Friedman, Grants Administrator
(See address above.)

ARCHAEOLOGICAL INSTITUTE OF AMERICA [757]

44 Beacon Street
Boston, MA 02108
(857) 305-9360
Fax: (857) 233-4270
E-mail: fellowships@archaeological.org
Web Site: www.archaeological.org

FOUNDED: 1879

AREAS OF INTEREST:
Archaeological research and publication.

NAME(S) OF PROGRAMS:
- **The Archaeology of Portugal Fellowship**

TYPE:
Fellowships. The Fellowship supports projects pertaining to the archaeology of Portugal. These include, but are not limited to, research projects, colloquia, symposia, publication, research-related travel, or travel to academic meetings for the purpose of presenting papers on the archaeology of Portugal.

PURPOSE:
To promote archaeological studies pertaining to Portugal.

ELIGIBILITY:
Portuguese, American and other international scholars are invited to apply. Applicants must have been AIA members in good standing for at least two consecutive years (one year for graduate students).

FINANCIAL DATA:
Amount of support per award: Award may vary based on the merit of the proposal. Typically $4,000.
Total amount of support: Typically $2,000 to $8,000.

NO. MOST RECENT APPLICANTS: 8.

NO. AWARDS: 1 for the year 2020.

APPLICATION INFO:
Application information is available on the web site.
Duration: One year; work to be conducted between July 1 of the award year and the following June 30.
Deadline: November 1. Announcement by February 1.

ADDRESS INQUIRIES TO:
Laurel Nilsen Sparks
Lecture and Fellowship Coordinator
(See address above.)

ASHBURN INSTITUTE INC. [758]

198 Okatie Village Drive
Suite 103, PMB 301
Bluffton, SC 29909
(703) 728-6482
Fax: (843) 705-7643
E-mail: info@ashburninstitute.org
Web Site: www.ashburninstitute.org

FOUNDED: 1940

AREAS OF INTEREST:
International relations, political science, Middle Eastern studies, and international security.

NAME(S) OF PROGRAMS:
- **Frank Educational Fund**

TYPE:
Research grants; Scholarships. The Institute carries out its own scholarship program for graduate students through an annual endowment received in perpetuity. Half of the funds must be awarded to U.S. citizens. The best papers which meet the goals of the conference, as outlined in the "Call for Papers," will reimburse the graduate authors by covering their conference travel and lodging expenses. Locations for the conference may be anywhere in the world. The top papers are selected for publication with due credit to the authors.

Funding is provided by the gracious endowment left by Mayme and Herb Frank for the purpose of promoting international integration and harmonization.

YEAR PROGRAM STARTED: 1991

PURPOSE:
To support the study of federalism and international integration at the graduate and postgraduate level.

ELIGIBILITY:
Open to graduate students of good academic standing working on a thesis or dissertation relating to international integration and federalism or doing coursework that places major weight on international integration and

federalism. International (foreign institutions) graduate students are eligible, as well as U.S. students.

FINANCIAL DATA:
Amount of support per award: $1,000 to $2,000.

Total amount of support: $20,000 annually.

APPLICATION INFO:
Application information can be found on the Institute's web site. Please submit abstract paper for consideration at the International Conference.

Deadline: Determined by future conference dates.

ADDRESS INQUIRIES TO:
Frank Fund Manager
(See address above.)

AUSTRO-AMERICAN ASSOCIATION OF BOSTON [759]
34 Cutting Cross Way
Wayland, MA 01778
(978) 579-2191
E-mail: scholarship@austria-boston.org
Web Site: www.austria-boston.org

FOUNDED: 1944

AREAS OF INTEREST:
All aspects of Austrian society, especially culture; music; and Austrian-American relations.

TYPE:
Research grants; Scholarships. Scholarship award provides support for a project relating to Austrian music, history, literature, science, art, architecture, contemporary life or other aspects of the Austrian contribution to culture.

YEAR PROGRAM STARTED: 1976

PURPOSE:
To further interest in Austrian culture.

LEGAL BASIS:
Organized and established as of July 6, 1970 by the Secretary of the Commonwealth.

ELIGIBILITY:
The project must be related to Austria.

Undergraduate or graduate students at New England colleges or universities are eligible. They must be willing to present the results of their project at an event of the Austro-American Association.

GEOG. RESTRICTIONS: New England.

FINANCIAL DATA:
The scholarship award does not support tuition or other expenses related to a course of study.

Amount of support per award: $3,000.

Total amount of support: $3,000.

NO. MOST RECENT APPLICANTS: 6.

NO. AWARDS: 1 per year (when funds are available).

APPLICATION INFO:
Applications should include a curriculum vitae, a detailed description of the proposed project and two letters of recommendation from faculty members well acquainted with the applicant's background and potential. Applicants will be invited to present the results of their project at a meeting of the Association. A personal interview will be required.

Duration: One year.

Deadline: March 23.

OFFICERS:
Traude Schieber-Acker, President
Marta Stasa, Vice President
Hana Sittler, Treasurer
Judy Zohn, Secretary

ADDRESS INQUIRIES TO:
Traude Schieber-Acker, President and Chairperson, Scholarship Panel
Austro-American Association of Boston, Inc.
(See address and e-mail above.)

*PLEASE NOTE:
E-mail correspondence and electronic submission are requested.

CENTER FOR INTERNATIONAL SECURITY AND COOPERATION (CISAC)   [760]
Freeman Spogli Institute for International Studies
Stanford University
Encina Hall, C222, 616 Serra Street
Stanford, CA 94305-6165
(650) 736-4566
Fax: (650) 723-0089
E-mail: cisacfellowship@stanford.edu
Web Site: cisac.fsi.stanford.edu

FOUNDED: 1970

AREAS OF INTEREST:
CISAC fellows may focus on any of the following topics: nuclear weapons policy and nonproliferation; nuclear energy; digital security; biosecurity and global health; insurgency; terrorism; civil conflict; national security strategies; and global governance.

NAME(S) OF PROGRAMS:
● **Cybersecurity and International Security Fellowship**
● **Human-Centered Artificial Intelligence (HAI)**
● **The MacArthur Foundation Nuclear Security Fellowship**
● **Natural Sciences or Engineering International Security Fellowship**
● **Social Sciences or Humanities International Security Fellowship**
● **Stanford International Observatory Research Fellowship**
● **The Stanton Nuclear Security Fellowship**

TYPE:
Fellowships.

PURPOSE:
To produce policy-relevant research on international security topics; to teach and train the next generation of security specialists; to influence policymaking in international security; to develop a more informed public discussion.

LEGAL BASIS:
University.

ELIGIBILITY:
Must be in Ph.D. program, have a Ph.D. or equivalent, or extraordinary professional experience.

FINANCIAL DATA:
Amount of support per award: Varies.

Total amount of support: Varies.

NO. MOST RECENT APPLICANTS: Over 220.

NO. AWARDS: 10 to 20.

APPLICATION INFO:
Application information is available on the CISAC web site.

Duration: Nine to 11 months.

Deadline: January.

ADDRESS INQUIRIES TO:
CISAC Fellowship Program
(See address above.)

CENTER FOR U.S.-MEXICAN STUDIES, UNIVERSITY OF CALIFORNIA, SAN DIEGO   [761]
School of Global Policy and Strategy
9500 Gilman Drive, No. 0519
La Jolla, CA 92093-0519
(858) 822-1696
Fax: (858) 534-6447
E-mail: usmex@ucsd.edu
Web Site: usmex.ucsd.edu

FOUNDED: 1979

AREAS OF INTEREST:
The study of U.S. and Mexico relations and the study of Mexico within the social sciences and history.

NAME(S) OF PROGRAMS:
● **USMEX Visiting Fellows Program**

TYPE:
Fellowships.

YEAR PROGRAM STARTED: 1980

PURPOSE:
To support the write-up of a Ph.D. dissertation or the write-up of a postdoctoral research project.

ELIGIBILITY:
Applications are accepted from Ph.D. candidates who are ABD and have completed a substantial portion of their dissertations and professors on sabbatical. Applicant must be concurrently enrolled/employed at their home university.

Priority will be given to proposals that are policy-relevant, show a feasible plan of action, and/or will contribute towards a better understanding of Mexico and/or U.S.-Mexico relations. Applications from Mexican scholars are particularly welcome.

GEOG. RESTRICTIONS: United States and Mexico.

FINANCIAL DATA:
Amount of support per award: Stipends average $1,000 per month for visiting professors and $2,500 per month for predoctoral students.

Total amount of support: $150,000.

NO. AWARDS: 8 for the year 2020-21.

APPLICATION INFO:
Call for Letters of Intent will be posted on the USMEX web site by September. Applicants must describe the work to be completed during residence.

Duration: Four to nine months. Former Visiting Fellows are eligible to apply again after five years.

Deadline: November.

ADDRESS INQUIRIES TO:
Greg Mallinger, Fellows Coordinator
(See address above.)

THE CHRISTENSEN FUND
660 Fourth Street, No. 235
San Francisco, CA 94107
(415) 644-1600
Fax: (415) 644-1601
E-mail: info@christensenfund.org
Web Site: www.christensenfund.org

TYPE:
General operating grants; Project/program grants.

See entry 57 for full listing.

COUNCIL FOR EUROPEAN STUDIES AT COLUMBIA UNIVERSITY [762]

475 Riverside Drive
Office 308i
New York, NY 10115
(646) 745-8550
E-mail: awards@ces-europe.org
Web Site: councilforeuropeanstudies.org

FOUNDED: 1970

AREAS OF INTEREST:
The study of Europe.

NAME(S) OF PROGRAMS:
● **Book Award**
● **CES Small Event Grants**
● **Conference Travel Grants**
● **First Article Prize in Humanities and Social Sciences**
● **Mellon-CES Dissertation Completion Fellowship in European Studies**
● **SAE-CES Pre-Dissertation Research Fellowships**

TYPE:
Awards/prizes; Conferences/seminars; Fellowships; Internships; Scholarships; Travel grants. The CES Book Award honors talented emerging scholars with an award for the best first book on any subject in European studies. The award is given every two years.

CES Conference Travel Grants support transcontinental travel for junior faculty and graduate students already scheduled to present at the Council's International Conference of Europeanists.

CES Small Event Grants support workshops, lectures, symposia and other small events that share research on Europe with a wider community.

First Article Prize awards one prize to a scholar working in the humanities and one to a scholar working in the social sciences. These prizes will honor the writers of the best first articles on European studies published within a two-year period.

Mellon-CES Dissertation Completion Fellowships are intended to facilitate the timely completion of the doctoral degree by late-stage graduate students focused on topics in European studies.

SAE-CES Pre-Dissertation Research Fellowships are intended to fund student's first major research project in Europe.

YEAR PROGRAM STARTED: 1971

ELIGIBILITY:
Book Award: Must be scholar's first book on any subject in European studies. Books may be nominated by the author, a CES member, or by a publisher.

Pre-Dissertation Research Fellowships are limited to graduate students currently enrolled in a doctoral program at a university that is a member of the Council for European Studies Academic Consortium. Member universities and additional eligibility requirements can be found online.

First Article Prize nominees meet the following criteria:
(1) be the first article published by the nominee in the field of European studies in a peer-reviewed journal;
(2) be published between October 1, 2019 and September 30, 2021;
(3) be the work of one author only or be an article on which the nominee is the first author and;
(4) be authored by a member of the Council for European Studies or a faculty/student of an institution that is a member. Nominations may be submitted by the publisher, editor, author, or admiring colleagues.

To be eligible for the Mellon-CES Dissertation Completion Fellowship, the applicant must be ABD, be enrolled at a higher education institution in the U.S., and can have no more than one full year of dissertation work remaining at the start of the fellowship year as certified by his or her dissertation advisor. The applicant must also have exhausted the dissertation completion funding normally provided by his or her academic department or university, and he or she must be working on a topic within or substantially overlapping European studies. To be eligible to receive the fellowship, applicants must also be enrolled in an institution that is a member of the CES Academic Consortium. However, students whose universities are not currently members of the CES consortium may apply, but they are encouraged to apply early in the application season so that every effort may be made to enroll the institution in the CES member consortium and, thus, establish the student's eligibility by the application deadline.

FINANCIAL DATA:
Book Award recipient receives a certificate, $1,000 and all-expenses-paid trip to International Conference and award ceremony. Fellowship recipients receive a stipend, travel support for attending and presenting at the CES International Conference of Europeanists, and the opportunity to publish in *Perspectives on Europe.*
Amount of support per award: Book Award: $1,000; CES Small Event Grants: $300 to $1,000; Conference Travel Grant: equivalent of $725, $500 cash grant and waiver of registration fee; First Article Prize: $250; Mellon-CES Dissertation Completion Fellowship: $27,500 stipend to be paid in six bimonthly installments; Pre-Dissertation Research Fellowship: $5,000 stipend.
Total amount of support: Varies.

APPLICATION INFO:
Applications and guidelines are available online.
Deadline: Book Award: Mid-October; CES Small Event Grants: December 1 for spring and July 15 for fall; Conference Travel Grant: January 9; First Article Prize: October 1; Mellon-CES Dissertation Completion Fellowship and Pre-Dissertation Research Fellowship: January.

COUNCIL ON FOREIGN RELATIONS [763]

58 East 68th Street
New York, NY 10065
(212) 434-9400
Fax: (212) 434-9870
E-mail: fellowships@cfr.org
Web Site: www.cfr.org/fellowships

FOUNDED: 1921

AREAS OF INTEREST:
International relations, international affairs, Japan, U.S.-Japan relations, U.S.-Japan politics, Japanese studies, Japanese-American relations, foreign policy, policymaking, and public service.

NAME(S) OF PROGRAMS:
● **International Affairs Fellowship in Japan (IAF-J)**

TYPE:
Fellowships. The International Affairs Fellowship (IAF) in Japan, sponsored by Hitachi, Ltd., seeks to strengthen mutual understanding and cooperation between the rising generations of leaders in the U.S. and Japan. The program provides a select group of midcareer professionals the opportunity to carry out research while affiliated with appropriate institutions in Japan and to establish long-term professional and personal ties through their activities. Fellows are drawn from academia, business, government, media, NGOs, and think tanks. In cooperation with CFR, the program's sponsor assists fellows in finding suitable host organizations in Japan. CFR cannot guarantee placement at any specific agency or organization.

YEAR PROGRAM STARTED: 1997

PURPOSE:
To strengthen mutual understanding and cooperation between the rising generations of leaders in the U.S. and Japan.

ELIGIBILITY:
The IAF in Japan Program is only open to early to midcareer professionals with a demonstrated commitment to a career in foreign policy. The program is intended primarily for those without substantial prior experience in Japan, although the selection committee has made exceptions when it considered that the fellowship would allow an individual to add a significant new dimension to his or her career. Knowledge of the Japanese language is not a requirement. Candidates must be U.S. citizens to be considered for the fellowship.

FINANCIAL DATA:
Fellows are considered independent contractors rather than employees of CFR, and are not eligible for employment benefits, including health insurance.
Amount of support per award: Monthly stipend of $7,700, along with a $5,000 travel grant.

CO-OP FUNDING PROGRAMS: Hitachi, Ltd.

NO. AWARDS: Approximately 3 to 5 per year.

APPLICATION INFO:
Interested candidates who meet the program's eligibility requirements can apply online via the CFR web site between July 1 and October 31 on an annual basis. Candidates who are selected as IAF-J finalists will be notified between December and January, with finalist interviews scheduled between January and February. Official selections and announcement of IAF-J awards will be made between February and March.
Duration: Three to 12 months.
Deadline: October 31, 2022.

ADDRESS INQUIRIES TO:
See telephone or e-mail address above.

COUNCIL ON FOREIGN RELATIONS
58 East 68th Street
New York, NY 10065
(212) 434-9740
Fax: (212) 434-9870
E-mail: fellowships@cfr.org
Web Site: www.cfr.org/fellowships

TYPE:
Fellowships. The Edward R. Murrow Press Fellowship seeks to promote the quality of responsible and discerning journalism that exemplified the work of Edward R. Murrow. One resident fellowship is awarded each year to a distinguished foreign correspondent or editor. The fellow spends 10 months full-time in residence at CFR's headquarters in New York. The program enables the fellow to engage in sustained analysis and writing, expand his or her intellectual and professional horizons, and participate in CFR's active program of meetings and events. The fellow is part of the David Rockefeller Studies Program, the CFR's think tank, alongside the program's full-time, adjunct, and visiting fellows, whose expertise extends across the broad range of significant foreign policy issues facing the U.S. and the international community.

See entry 1732 for full listing.

COUNCIL ON FOREIGN RELATIONS   [764]
58 East 68th Street
New York, NY 10065
(212) 434-9740
Fax: (212) 434-9800
E-mail: fellowships@cfr.org
Web Site: www.cfr.org/fellowships

FOUNDED: 1921

AREAS OF INTEREST:
International affairs, international relations, policymaking, U.S. foreign policy, foreign affairs, public service, government, and academia.

NAME(S) OF PROGRAMS:
• **International Affairs Fellowship (IAF)**

TYPE:
Fellowships. The International Affairs Fellowship (IAF) Program is the hallmark fellowship program of the Council on Foreign Relations. It aims to bridge the gap between the study and making of U.S. foreign policy by creating the next generation of scholar-practitioners. The program offers its fellows the unique chance to experience a new environment and gain a different perspective at a pivotal moment in their careers. Academics are thus placed in public service and policy-oriented settings and government officials in scholarly settings.

YEAR PROGRAM STARTED: 1967

PURPOSE:
To assist midcareer scholars and professionals in advancing their analytic capabilities and broadening their foreign policy experience.

ELIGIBILITY:
The IAF Program is only open to early and midcareer professionals with a demonstrated commitment to a career in foreign policy. The program welcomes applicants from a broad range of professional, academic, and personal backgrounds. Selected fellows possess a strong record of work experience as well as a firm grounding in the field of

foreign policy. A Ph.D. is not required for university-based applicants, though successful candidates from academia typically hold an advanced degree.

The program does not fund pre- or postdoctoral research, work toward a degree, or the completion of projects on which substantial progress has been made before the fellowship period.

For candidates from academia and the private sector looking to go into government, preference is given to candidates with no significant work experience in the U.S. government or at an international organization.

Candidates must be U.S. citizens to be considered for the fellowship.

FINANCIAL DATA:
Fellows are considered independent contractors rather than employees of CFR, and are not eligible for employment benefits, including health insurance.

Amount of support per award: Stipend of $105,000.

NO. AWARDS: 8 to 10 annually.

APPLICATION INFO:
Interested candidates who meet the program's eligibility requirements can apply online via the Council web site between June 1 and October 31 on an annual basis.

Duration: 12 months, preferably beginning in September.

Deadline: October 31. Notification between December and January. Announcement between February and March.

ADDRESS INQUIRIES TO:
See telephone or e-mail address above.

COUNCIL ON FOREIGN RELATIONS   [765]
58 East 68th Street
New York, NY 10065
(212) 434-9740
Fax: (212) 434-9870
E-mail: fellowships@cfr.org
Web Site: www.cfr.org/fellowships

FOUNDED: 1921

AREAS OF INTEREST:
Nuclear security, nuclear weapons, nuclear proliferation, nuclear terrorism, nuclear energy, nuclear force posture, nuclear arms, international relations, international affairs, foreign affairs, government, and public policy.

NAME(S) OF PROGRAMS:
• **Stanton Nuclear Security Fellowship Program (SNSF)**

TYPE:
Fellowships. The Stanton Nuclear Security Fellowship, sponsored by the Stanton Foundation, offers younger scholars studying nuclear security issues the opportunity to spend a period of 12 months at the CFR's offices in New York or Washington, DC, conducting policy-relevant research. While in residence full-time at CFR, selected fellows will be expected to lead a project of their own design, conduct original research, and write at least one policy-relevant document. The fellows will also be mentored by the fellows of CFR's David Rockefeller Studies Program.

YEAR PROGRAM STARTED: 2009

PURPOSE:
To stimulate the development of the next generation of thought leaders in nuclear security. The fellows could work on a wide range of issues, including nuclear terrorism, nuclear proliferation, nuclear weapons, nuclear force posture, and nuclear energy.

ELIGIBILITY:
Qualified candidates must be postdoctoral fellows or junior faculty in a tenure-track position at a recognized university and possess a strong record of professional achievement. Junior faculty at law schools or with a law degree as their terminal degree are also eligible. The program is only open to U.S. citizens.

FINANCIAL DATA:
Payment will be made in 12 equal monthly installments. Fellows are considered independent contractors rather than employees of CFR, and are not eligible for employment benefits, including health insurance.

Amount of support per award: A stipend of $110,000 for junior faculty and $80,000 for postdoctoral fellows.

CO-OP FUNDING PROGRAMS: The SNSF Program is made possible by a generous grant from the Stanton Foundation.

NO. AWARDS: 1 to 2 annually.

APPLICATION INFO:
Interested candidates who meet the program's eligibility requirements can apply online on or after October 1.

Duration: 12 months, preferably beginning in September.

Deadline: December 15.

ADDRESS INQUIRIES TO:
See telephone or e-mail address above.

CULTURAL VISTAS   [766]
1250 H Street, N.W.
Suite 300
Washington, DC 20005
(212) 497-3510
E-mail: alfa@culturalvistas.org
Web Site: www.culturalvistas.org/alfa
www.alfafellowship.org

FOUNDED: 2004

AREAS OF INTEREST:
Culture, business, law, politics, public policy, government, journalism, mass communications, finance and economics.

NAME(S) OF PROGRAMS:
• **Alfa Fellowship Program**

TYPE:
Exchange programs; Fellowships; Internships. The Alfa Fellowship Program is a distinguished international initiative that each year offers up to 18 accomplished Americans, Britons, and Germans the opportunity to complete a high-level professional development program in Russia. Over the course of the program, fellows complete work placements at leading institutions, attend professional seminars, and receive intensive language training. The fellowship provides a monthly stipend, accommodation, insurance, all program-related travel costs, language training in Russia, and private pre-departure tutoring.

YEAR PROGRAM STARTED: 2004

PURPOSE:
To foster a new generation of future American, British and German leaders with in-depth practical experience in the modern business and public policy environment of the Russian Federation.

ELIGIBILITY:
Open to U.S., U.K. and German citizens with a Bachelor's degree, work experience and professional interest or background in business, economics, journalism, law, public policy, arts/cultural management, human development, or other fields. Russian language proficiency preferred, but not required.

Applicants must:
(1) have U.S., U.K. or German citizenship;
(2) have a Bachelor's degree and;
(3) have relevant work experience in their field of expertise.

GEOG. RESTRICTIONS: United States, United Kingdom, Germany and Russia.

FINANCIAL DATA:
Monthly stipend, free accommodations in Russia, all in-country program-related travel, round-trip flight to Moscow, and limited international health, accident and liability insurance during the program in Russia.

NO. MOST RECENT APPLICANTS: Approximately 120.

NO. AWARDS: 18.

APPLICATION INFO:
Candidates must submit application online with all supporting materials by the deadline.
Duration: 11 months, June to April.
Deadline: December 1.

ADDRESS INQUIRIES TO:
Melissa Graves, Program Director
Alfa Fellowship Program
(See address above.)

J.W. DAFOE FOUNDATION [767]
Department of Political Studies
University of Manitoba
c/o 529 Fletcher Argue Building
Winnipeg MB R3T 5V5 Canada
(204) 474-8546
Fax: (204) 474-7645
E-mail: andrea.rounce@umanitoba.ca
Web Site: www.dafoefoundation.ca

AREAS OF INTEREST:
International relations, economics, history and political science.

NAME(S) OF PROGRAMS:
● **Dafoe Book Prize**
● **John W. Dafoe Graduate Fellowship**

TYPE:
Awards/prizes; Conferences/seminars; Fellowships; Project/program grants; Research grants. Dafoe Book Prize is awarded to the best book on Canada, Canadians, and/or Canada's place in the world published in the previous calendar year.

Graduate Fellowships for study in international relations, economics, history or political studies.

PURPOSE:
To encourage graduate study in international relations; to further international understanding.

LEGAL BASIS:
University association.

ELIGIBILITY:
Dafoe Book Prize: Distinguished writing by Canadians, or authors resident in Canada, that contributes to the understanding of Canada, Canadians, and/or Canada's place in the world are eligible. Co- or multiple-authored books are eligible, but not edited books consisting of chapters from many different authors.

Dafoe Graduate Fellowship will be offered to a graduate student who:
(1) is enrolled full-time in the Faculty of Graduate Studies entering the first or second year of a Master's program in any of the following departments: the Department of Economics, History, Political Studies, the Arthur V. Mauro Centre for Peace and Justice, or the Faculty of Law at the University of Manitoba;
(2) has achieved a minimum grade point average of 3.5 (or equivalent) in the previous 60 credit hours of study and;
(3) is pursuing a thesis stream program related to the field of international relations and/or international comparative studies.

GEOG. RESTRICTIONS: Canada.

FINANCIAL DATA:
Amount of support per award: $10,000 (CAN).
Total amount of support: $20,000 (CAN) annually.

NO. AWARDS: 1 per award.

APPLICATION INFO:
Dafoe Book Prize: Publishers and individuals are encouraged to submit their entries (in four copies), with the appropriate submission fee. Late entries for books published in later November and December will be accepted into the new year.

Dafoe Graduate Fellowship: Applicants are required to submit a cover letter, detailed research proposal, three letters of reference, and official transcripts to the Awards Office at the Faculty of Graduate Studies at the University of Manitoba.
Duration: Fellowships are for one year and are nonrenewable.
Deadline: Dafoe Book Prize: December 13. Dafoe Graduate Fellowship: May 1.

TRUSTEES:
Dr. Christopher Adams, Chairperson

*SPECIAL STIPULATIONS:
A submission fee of $50 per entry is required for the J.W. Dafoe Book Prize.

THE EAST-WEST CENTER [768]
1601 East West Road
Honolulu, HI 96848-1601
(808) 944-7735
Fax: (808) 944-7730 (Award Services Office)
E-mail: scholarships@eastwestcenter.org
Web Site: www.eastwestcenter.
org/studentprograms

FOUNDED: 1960

AREAS OF INTEREST:
Economics; environmental change, vulnerability and governance; population and health; politics, governance and security, at a local, national and/or regional level in the Asia Pacific region.

NAME(S) OF PROGRAMS:
● **East-West Center Graduate Degree Fellowship**

TYPE:
Fellowships.

YEAR PROGRAM STARTED: 1960

PURPOSE:
To strengthen relations and understanding among the peoples and nations of Asia, the Pacific and the U.S.; to serve as a vigorous hub for cooperative research, education and dialogue on critical issues of common concern to the Asia Pacific region and the U.S.

LEGAL BASIS:
Public, nonprofit educational corporation established in Hawaii in 1960 by the U.S. Congress.

ELIGIBILITY:
Candidates must have obtained a four-year Bachelor's degree or its equivalent, must be a citizen or permanent resident of the U.S. or a country in Asia or the Pacific, and must come to the Center on the exchange visitor (J-1) visa.

Priority in the student selection process is given to applicants with a commitment to the Asia Pacific region seeking degrees in fields of study related to research themes at the East-West Center.

GEOG. RESTRICTIONS: Hawaii.

FINANCIAL DATA:
Award may include housing, stipend, tuition, health insurance, when relevant, and book allowance as approved. Costs may be shared by collaborating institutions.
Amount of support per award: Varies.
Total amount of support: Varies.
Matching fund requirements: Cost-sharing on any Center award is actively sought.

CO-OP FUNDING PROGRAMS: Funding for the Center comes from the U.S. government, with additional support provided by private agencies, individuals, foundations, corporations, and the governments of the region.

NO. MOST RECENT APPLICANTS: 172.

NO. AWARDS: Varies based on funding.

APPLICATION INFO:
Applications are available online.
Duration: Initially 12 months with possible renewal up to two years for Master's Degree or doctoral studies, contingent upon funding, performance and academic progress.
Deadline: December 1 for forwarding to the Award Services Office.

ADDRESS INQUIRIES TO:
Award Services Office
(See address above.)

*SPECIAL STIPULATIONS:
Study must be at the University of Hawaii at Manoa.

THE EAST-WEST CENTER [769]
1601 East-West Road
Honolulu, HI 96848-1601
(808) 944-7646
Fax: (808) 944-7070 (Attn: APLP)
E-mail: aplp@eastwestcenter.org
Web Site: www.eastwestcenter.org/aplp

FOUNDED: 1960

AREAS OF INTEREST:
Issues related to the Asia Pacific region.

NAME(S) OF PROGRAMS:
● **Asia Pacific Leadership Program**

TYPE:
Fellowships. Links advanced and interdisciplinary analysis of emergent regional issues with experiential leadership learning.

YEAR PROGRAM STARTED: 2001

PURPOSE:
To create a network of action focused on building a peaceful, prosperous and just Asia Pacific community.

LEGAL BASIS:
Public, nonprofit educational corporation.

ELIGIBILITY:
Candidates must have at least a three-year Bachelor's degree or its equivalent from an accredited U.S. college or university or from a recognized institution of higher learning abroad, at least five years of work experience, a demonstrated commitment to promoting peace and prosperity in the Asia Pacific region, and a deep interest in experiential leadership development training.

Priority in the student selection process is given to candidates with professional work experience:
(1) international experience and aptitude, including overseas residence, language skills, intercultural and diversity exposure;
(2) leadership track record in professional, public and/or personal realms;
(3) volunteer and community service experience;
(4) Asia Pacific engagement and evidence of interest in the region, as well as commitment to its future prosperity; this might include classes taken at university, time spent in the region, languages spoken, membership and fellowships, specific projects, field studies and areas of research interest and;
(5) experience working collaboratively in small teams or in large groups.

GEOG. RESTRICTIONS: Hawaii.

FINANCIAL DATA:
Award includes program fees, living expenses, field study costs, and other academic expenses.
Amount of support per award: Varies.
Total amount of support: Varies.

NO. AWARDS: Approximately 25.

APPLICATION INFO:
Application form is available online.
Duration: Late June to November.
Deadline: Priority Deadline: December 1. Final Deadline: March 1.

PUBLICATIONS:
Annual report.

ADDRESS INQUIRIES TO:
Asia Pacific Leadership Program
(See address above.)

THE EISENHOWER INSTITUTE AT GETTYSBURG COLLEGE   [770]
818 Connecticut Avenue, N.W.
Suite 400
Washington, DC 20006
(202) 628-4444
Fax: (202) 628-4445
E-mail: ei@gettysburg.edu
Web Site: www.eisenhowerinstitute.org

FOUNDED: 1983

AREAS OF INTEREST:
World affairs.

NAME(S) OF PROGRAMS:
● **Eisenhower Institute Scholarship Programs**

TYPE:
Conferences/seminars; Endowments; Fellowships; Internships; Scholarships.

PURPOSE:
To promote sound and forward-looking policies that lay the intellectual and civic groundwork for the next generation of opinion-leaders, policy-shapers and public servants.

ELIGIBILITY:
Open to American high school, undergraduate, and graduate students.

FINANCIAL DATA:
Amount of support per award: Scholarships and fellowships: $4,000 to $10,000.

APPLICATION INFO:
Application procedures are available online.

IRS I.D.: 52-1306218

ADDRESS INQUIRIES TO:
Administrative Assistant
(See address above.)

GRADUATE INSTITUTE OF INTERNATIONAL AND DEVELOPMENT STUDIES   [771]
Chemin Eugene-Rigot 2A
P.O. Box 1672
CH - 1211 Geneva 1 Switzerland
(41) 22 908 57 00
Fax: (41) 22 908 57 10
E-mail: info@graduateinstitute.ch
Web Site: graduateinstitute.ch

FOUNDED: 1927

AREAS OF INTEREST:
Development, anthropology and sociology of development, and international relations.

NAME(S) OF PROGRAMS:
● **Financial Aid for Study at The Graduate Institute of International and Development Studies**

TYPE:
Assistantships; Awards/prizes; Exchange programs; Fellowships; Residencies; Scholarships; Visiting scholars. Financial aid in advanced study in international relations including intensive research and study towards the Master's degree and the Ph.D. Tenable at the Institute.

PURPOSE:
To support the scientific study of contemporary international relations and development studies and the pursuit of advanced studies based on personal work and research.

LEGAL BASIS:
Foundation.

ELIGIBILITY:
Each year, financial assistance is awarded by the Institute in the form of scholarships covering the minimum needs of students. They are allocated on the basis of applicants' academic performance and financial needs.

Scholarships also awarded for young lecturers from the global south.

FINANCIAL DATA:
Scholars are exempted from Institute fees, but not from the obligatory fees of the University of Geneva which confers the Doctorate.

Amount of support per award: Full scholarship: CHF 18,000 per academic year.

NO. AWARDS: 250 scholarships annually.

APPLICATION INFO:
Online application form is available from mid-September.
Duration: One academic year. Renewable.
Deadline: January 15.

PUBLICATIONS:
Annual report.

ADDRESS INQUIRIES TO:
E-mail: executive@graduateinstitute.ch

INSTITUTE OF CURRENT WORLD AFFAIRS   [772]
1818 N Street, N.W.
Suite 460
Washington, DC 20036
(202) 364-4068
E-mail: icwa@icwa.org
Web Site: www.icwa.org

FOUNDED: 1925

AREAS OF INTEREST:
International cultures and affairs.

TYPE:
Fellowships. Fellowships are not scholarships, and are not awarded to support work toward academic degrees or for collaborative research projects, or to write books.

YEAR PROGRAM STARTED: 1925

PURPOSE:
To provide talented and promising individuals with an opportunity to develop a deep understanding of an issue, country or region outside the U.S. and to share that understanding with a wider public.

ELIGIBILITY:
Fellowships are for self-designed independent study only. Applicants must have a good command of written and spoken English and be under 36 years of age who demonstrate initiative, integrity, outstanding character, good communications skills, seriousness of purpose and enthusiasm for their chosen fields.

FINANCIAL DATA:
The Institute provides sufficient, though not unlimited, financial support for its fellows and their immediate families, allowing them to live in good health and reasonable comfort in order to fulfill the purposes of the fellowship.
Amount of support per award: Varies.
Total amount of support: Varies.

NO. MOST RECENT APPLICANTS: 100.

NO. AWARDS: Varies.

APPLICATION INFO:
Applicants should write an initial letter of interest to the Executive Director explaining the personal background and professional experience that would qualify them for the fellowship they have in mind. They should describe the activities they would like to carry out during two years overseas and enclose a resume or curriculum vitae. Select candidates will be invited to submit a more detailed application.

Initial letter should be by e-mail, although regular mail will be accepted. Further information may be obtained from the Institute's web site.

Duration: Two years.
Deadline: Varies.

ADDRESS INQUIRIES TO:
Gregory Feifer, Executive Director
E-mail: apply@icwa.org

INSTITUTE OF INTERNATIONAL EDUCATION   [773]

1400 K Street, N.W.
Suite 700
Washington, DC 20005
(202) 686-8665
Fax: (202) 686-4029
E-mail: sir@iie.org
Web Site: www.cies.org/sir

FOUNDED: 1947

AREAS OF INTEREST:
Humanities or social sciences, or any field that will benefit from an international perspective.

NAME(S) OF PROGRAMS:
● **Fulbright Scholar-in-Residence Program**

TYPE:
Awards/prizes; Exchange programs; Visiting scholars. Grants support a visiting lecturer from outside the U.S. to teach regular courses or develop new ones, team teach or participate in special seminars or serve as a resource to faculty and students and, through outreach, to the community at large.

PURPOSE:
To initiate or develop international programs at colleges and universities by using a foreign scholar-in-residence to internationalize the curriculum, set up global studies or area-specific programs or otherwise expand contacts of students and faculty with other cultures and to strengthen or enrich existing international or area studies programs.

LEGAL BASIS:
Public Law 87-256, as amended, The Mutual Educational and Cultural Exchange Act of 1961.

ELIGIBILITY:
U.S. colleges and universities, including community colleges, are invited to submit proposals to obtain a foreign scholar-in-residence. Preference is given to proposals in the humanities or social sciences, although other fields focusing on international issues will be considered.

GEOG. RESTRICTIONS: United States.

FINANCIAL DATA:
Monthly stipend as well as round-trip international travel, excess baggage allowance, accident and sickness insurance, and allowances for books, professional development and dependents.
Amount of support per award:
Approximately $2,850 to $3,700 per month, depending on the cost of living in the city where the scholar will reside.
Total amount of support: Over $1,000,000 for the year 2020.
Matching fund requirements: Some cost sharing by the host institution is encouraged, either supplementary funding or in-kind support, such as housing.

CO-OP FUNDING PROGRAMS: U.S. Department of State.

NO. AWARDS: 30 to 35.

APPLICATION INFO:
Guidelines are available in February. Application must be submitted online.
Duration: One semester to one academic year.
Deadline: October.

PUBLICATIONS:
Directory of Visiting Scholars; descriptive brochure; annual report.

ADDRESS INQUIRIES TO:
Kailey Atwater, Program Manager
(See address above.)

THE INTERNATIONAL FOUNDATION   [774]

55 Lane Road
Suite 300
Fairfield, NJ 07004
E-mail: info@intlfoundation.org
Web Site: intlfoundation.org

FOUNDED: 1948

AREAS OF INTEREST:
Agriculture, health, education, social development, the environment and community development.

TYPE:
Development grants; Project/program grants; Seed money grants; Technical assistance; Training grants.

YEAR PROGRAM STARTED: 1948

PURPOSE:
To help people of the developing world in their endeavors to solve some of their problems, to attain a better standard of living, and to obtain a reasonable degree of self-sufficiency.

LEGAL BASIS:
Private foundation.

ELIGIBILITY:
The Foundation funds only projects of U.S.-based, IRS-certified philanthropies.

GEOG. RESTRICTIONS: United States.

FINANCIAL DATA:
Amount of support per award: Up to $25,000.

NO. AWARDS: Approximately 100.

APPLICATION INFO:
Applications are to be submitted on the Foundation's web site. Proposals must include a statement from IRS of not-for-profit status, a brief overview of the proposal, amount of funds requested from The Foundation, a brief background of organization applying, a statement of the problem addressed by project, objectives of the project, plan of operation/method of achieving objectives, beneficiaries of the project, methods of project evaluation and report, project budget, sources of other funding applied for or received and date.

All appropriate communications will be answered.
Duration: One year. Must reapply.
Deadline: Grant applications are accepted on a rolling basis.

PUBLICATIONS:
Brochure, includes application guidelines.

IRS I.D.: 13-1962255

BOARD OF DIRECTORS AND OFFICERS:
Letitia K. Butler, Chairperson
Douglas P. Walker, Vice Chairperson
John D'A. Tyree, Treasurer
Matthew H. Hurlock, Secretary
Hilda Arellano
Gary Dicovitsky

ADDRESS INQUIRIES TO:
Hilda Arellano
Grants Committee Chairperson
(See address above.)

THE JAPAN FOUNDATION, NEW YORK   [775]

1700 Broadway
15th Floor
New York, NY 10019
(212) 489-0299
Fax: (212) 489-0409
E-mail: info@jfny.org
Web Site: www.jfny.org

FOUNDED: 1972

AREAS OF INTEREST:
Arts and cultural exchange, Japanese studies, intellectual exchange and grassroots exchange and education.

NAME(S) OF PROGRAMS:
● **Abe Fellowship for Journalists Program**
● **Abe Fellowship Program**
● **CGP Grant Program - Discretionary Grants**
● **CGP Grant Program - Education Grants**
● **CGP Grant Program - Grassroots Program**
● **CGP Grant Program - Intellectual Exchange**
● **Exhibitions Abroad Support Program**
● **Institutional Project Support Grant Program for Japanese Studies**
● **Institutional Project Support Small Grant Program for Japanese Studies**
● **Japanese Studies Fellowship Program**
● **JFNY Grant for Japanese Studies**
● **JFNY Grant Program - Arts and Culture**
● **Performing Arts Japan Program**
● **Support Program for Translation and Publication on Japan**
● **U.S.-Southeast Asia-Japan Collaboration and Exchange Initiative**

TYPE:
Conferences/seminars; Fellowships; Professorships; Project/program grants; Research grants; Travel grants. The Japanese Studies Fellowship Program has three components: Doctoral Fellowship, Long-term Research Fellowship, and Short-term Research Fellowship.

PURPOSE:
To promote international cultural exchange and mutual understanding between Japan and other countries by providing assistance for Arts and Cultural Exchange, Japanese Studies, Intellectual Exchange, and Grassroots Exchange and Education programs in the U.S.

LEGAL BASIS:
Independent administrative institution.

ELIGIBILITY:
Varies according to program.

FINANCIAL DATA:
For Fellowships, the Foundation will provide a round-trip, economy-class airfare to and from Japan. The stipend is determined in accordance with the grantee's professional status.

Amount of support per award: Varies according to program.

Matching fund requirements: Varies according to program.

APPLICATION INFO:
Program announcements and application forms are available on the web site. Arts and Culture grant applications from Alaska, Arizona, California, Colorado, Hawaii, Idaho, Montana, Nevada, New Mexico, Oregon, Utah, Washington and Wyoming should be sent to the Japan Foundation, Los Angeles Office, 5700 Wilshire Boulevard, Suite 100, Los Angeles, CA 90036; Tel: (323) 761-7510; Fax: (323) 761-7517; E-mail: jflainfo@jflalc.org. Arts and Culture Grant applications from all other states should be sent directly to the Japan Foundation New York Office. Grant applications for all other programs should be sent to the New York office to the section in charge of the grant program.

Duration: Varies according to program.

Deadline: Varies according to program.

PUBLICATIONS:
Annual report.

IRS I.D.: 13-2974222

STAFF:
Takeshi Yoshida, Director General
Kenji Matsumoto, Deputy Director General
Koji Nozaki, Program Director, Arts and Cultural Exchange
Moto Ono, Program Director, Intellectual Exchange
Kanako Mabuchi, Program Director, Japanese Studies and Japanese-Language Course

ADDRESS INQUIRIES TO:
See e-mail address above.

JAPAN-U.S. FRIENDSHIP COMMISSION   [776]
1201 15th Street, N.W.
Suite 330
Washington, DC 20005
(202) 653-9800
Fax: (202) 653-9802
E-mail: jusfc@jusfc.gov
Web Site: www.jusfc.gov

FOUNDED: 1976

AREAS OF INTEREST:
Cultural and educational activities between Japan and the U.S., including language and area studies, economic relations, media and public education.

TYPE:
Project/program grants. Programs of institutional support. Grants for projects of research, training and exchange with Japan.

YEAR PROGRAM STARTED: 1977

PURPOSE:
To enhance reciprocal people-to-people understanding and friendship between the U.S. and Japan.

LEGAL BASIS:
Independent agency of the U.S. government.

ELIGIBILITY:
Grants are offered to cultural and educational institutions in the U.S. and Japan.

GEOG. RESTRICTIONS: United States and Japan.

FINANCIAL DATA:
U.S. government trust fund of $40,000,000.
Amount of support per award: Varies.

Total amount of support: Varies.

CO-OP FUNDING PROGRAMS: NEA.

NO. MOST RECENT APPLICANTS: Varies by program.

NO. AWARDS: Approximately 30 annually.

APPLICATION INFO:
Application forms are available on the web site.
Duration: One year.
Deadline: July 1. Notification in October.

PUBLICATIONS:
Biennial report; program information/guidelines; application form.

OFFICERS:
Dr. Sheila Smith, Chairman
Dr. Edward Lincoln
Dr. Patricia Maclachlan
Dr. Deanna Marcum
Dr. Samuel C. Morse
Dr. Leonard J. Schoppa, Jr.
David Sneider
Dr. William M. Tsutsui

ADDRESS INQUIRIES TO:
Paige Cottingham-Streater, Executive Director
(See address above.)

*SPECIAL STIPULATIONS:
Institution grants only.

THE JAPANESE AMERICAN CITIZENS LEAGUE (JACL)   [777]
Washington, DC Office
1629 K Street, N.W., Suite 400
Washington, DC 20006
(202) 223-1240
Fax: (202) 296-8082
E-mail: dinoue@jacl.org
Web Site: www.jacl.org

FOUNDED: 1929

AREAS OF INTEREST:
Cultural exchange.

NAME(S) OF PROGRAMS:
• **JACL Kakehashi Program**

TYPE:
Travel grants. The Kakehashi Program is a new international program, part of JACL's leadership development. It is for college students and consists of five webinars and a nine-day trip to Japan.

PURPOSE:
To strengthen cultural ties between Japan and the U.S.

ELIGIBILITY:
This Program is for college students in good standing between the ages of 18 and 25. Students are selected for their community service, leadership experience and academic accomplishments. Eligible students must be either of Japanese ancestry or Asian ancestry, and must be a U.S. citizen. Students who have previously participated in a program sponsored by the government of Japan are ineligible.

NO. AWARDS: 185 students are to be selected for the Program.

APPLICATION INFO:
Contact JACL.

ADDRESS INQUIRIES TO:
David Inoue, Executive Director
E-mail: japanprogram@jacl.org
(See address above.)

A.J. MUSTE MEMORIAL INSTITUTE
168 Canal Street, 6th Floor
New York, NY 10013
(212) 533-4335
E-mail: info@ajmuste.org
Web Site: www.ajmuste.org

TYPE:
Grants-in-aid. The Institute's regular grant fund annually funds international, national and local projects in the U.S. and around the world. It gives priority to those with small budgets and little chance of funding from more traditional sources. It also offers fiscal sponsorship. The Institute does not provide academic scholarships.

See entry 1349 for full listing.

THE NATIONAL COUNCIL FOR EURASIAN AND EAST EUROPEAN RESEARCH   [778]
1828 L Street, N.W.
Suite 1200
Washington, DC 20036
(202) 572-9095
Fax: (866) 937-9872
E-mail: info@nceeer.org
Web Site: www.nceeer.org

FOUNDED: 1978

AREAS OF INTEREST:
The program is limited to research designed to contribute to knowledge of current developments and analysis of their significance in Eastern Europe and the successor states of the former Soviet Union.

TYPE:
Research grants; Research contracts. Institutional grants and research contracts and policy research scholarships and related activities, such as meetings and conferences, research-specific training, contact among scholars and specialists in government and private enterprise, development of databanks and other reference aids and dissemination of research data, methodology and findings, both in scholarly forms and through public media.

YEAR PROGRAM STARTED: 1978

PURPOSE:
To encourage and sustain high-quality research on Eastern Europe, the former Soviet Union and its successor states, in the social sciences (including geography, demography and environmental studies) and history.

LEGAL BASIS:
Incorporated, nonprofit, autonomous academic body.

ELIGIBILITY:
Limited to scholars at the postdoctoral level for academic participants and to an equivalent degree of maturity and professional employment for those from other fields. Applicant must be a U.S. citizen. Applications must be submitted to the Council by U.S. nonprofit institutions in the form of grant or contract proposals.

Dissertation completion grants may be available.

GEOG. RESTRICTIONS: United States.

FINANCIAL DATA:
Amount of support per award: Varies; normally not more than $40,000 for any individual project.

Matching fund requirements: Cost sharing at a minimum of 20% from non-federal funds is mandatory.

APPLICATION INFO:
Application guidelines, compliance with which is required, should be obtained from the Council, at the address above. Required documentation includes:
(1) identification form;
(2) one-page summary;
(3) detailed description of project;
(4) curriculum vitae and bibliographies for principal personnel;
(5) description of proposed written or other products and dissemination methods;
(6) budget and;
(7) letters of recommendation.
Duration: Varies.
Deadline: December 31.

PUBLICATIONS:
Guidelines.

BOARD OF DIRECTORS:
Bruce Grant, Chairperson
Elizabeth Wood, Vice Chairperson
Maria Carlson
Ted Gerber
Mary Kruger
Martha Lampland
Susan Linz
Mieke Meurs
Joanna Regulska
James Richter
Edward Schatz

ADDRESS INQUIRIES TO:
President
(See address above.)

NUCLEAR AGE PEACE FOUNDATION [779]
1622 Anacapa Street
Santa Barbara, CA 93101
(805) 965-3443
Fax: (805) 568-0466
E-mail: cwarner@napf.org
Web Site: www.wagingpeace.org

FOUNDED: 1982

AREAS OF INTEREST:
Achieving a nuclear weapon-free world, international law, international relations, liberty, justice, human dignity, human rights, nonviolence, responsible use of technology, peace education, and youth empowerment.

NAME(S) OF PROGRAMS:
● **Barbara Mandigo Kelly Peace Poetry Awards**

TYPE:
Awards/prizes; Internships. An annual series of awards to encourage poets to explore and illuminate positive visions of peace and the human spirit.

PURPOSE:
To play an important role in making the 21st century a time of peace and justice, and a time in which the rights of all individuals to peace, security and a healthy environment will be realized.

FINANCIAL DATA:
Amount of support per award: Adults: $1,000; Youth (13-18): $200; Youth (12 and under): $200.
Total amount of support: $1,400.

APPLICATION INFO:
Application information and guidelines are available at www.peacecontests.org.

Deadline: April 30.

ORGANIZATION OF AMERICAN STATES [780]
1889 F Street, N.W.
Seventh Floor
Washington, DC 20006
(202) 370-9771
Fax: (202) 458-3967
E-mail: scholarships@oas.org
Web Site: www.oas.org/scholarships

FOUNDED: 1890

AREAS OF INTEREST:
To promote the economic, social, scientific and cultural development of the Member States in order to achieve a stronger bond and better understanding among the peoples of the Americas through the advanced training of its citizens in the priority areas requested by the countries.

NAME(S) OF PROGRAMS:
● **Academic Studies**
● **Professional Development**

TYPE:
Fellowships; Scholarships; Technical assistance. Awarded for graduate academic studies and/or research, and last two years of undergraduate studies for students in the English-speaking Caribbean, for training in areas contributing to the economic, social, technical and cultural development of OAS member countries.

YEAR PROGRAM STARTED: 1958

PURPOSE:
Program of Scholarships and Training: to assist the member states with their domestic efforts in pursuit of integral development goals by supporting human resource development in the priority areas established by the member countries.

ELIGIBILITY:
Candidates must be citizens or permanent residents of an OAS member country, with a university degree in the case of academic studies, or who have demonstrated ability to pursue advanced training in the field chosen for professional development courses. Scholarships are for graduate or undergraduate studies, research, or professional training in any field, with the exception of the medical sciences and related areas and introductory language studies. Candidates must know the language of the study country. Studies must be undertaken at an institution in a member country of the OAS, with the exception of the country of which the candidate is a citizen or permanent resident.

Graduate scholarships are offered for study towards a Master's or Doctorate degree. They may also be used for research, if required by a specific academic program. Scholarships are awarded for an initial period of one academic year and may be extended subsequently for up to one additional year. Under the Self-Placed in an OAS Non-Consortium University, candidates apply directly for admission to the universities or educational institutions of their choice, and present their application for an OAS scholarship. Only one candidate per country will be awarded with this type of scholarship. In the Self-Placed in an OAS Consortium University, candidates apply directly to up to three programs in different universities, part of the OAS Consortium University, located in

three different countries. Applying to this type of scholarship increases the applicant's chances of being offered an OAS scholarship. Undergraduate scholarships are available only to citizens of the English-speaking Caribbean member countries for the last two years of study for an undergraduate degree.

No fellowships will be awarded retroactively, and no benefits will be provided to the family of the fellowship holder.

FINANCIAL DATA:
Fellowship may include, depending upon the circumstances of each fellow, a round-trip ticket, tuition fees, study materials, health insurance, and partial subsistence allowance (which varies from country to country).
Amount of support per award: Academic Studies: Minimum U.S. $10,000 for one year, maximum not to exceed U.S. $20,000 for up to two years; Professional Development: Varies.
Matching fund requirements: Students are responsible for covering a portion of their subsistence costs.

APPLICATION INFO:
Application materials are available at the web site. Except for applicants in the U.S., applications must be presented to the National Liaison Offices (ONEs) of the applicant's country of origin or permanent residence. The ONE is the official channel identified by each government for submission of applications for OAS scholarships. U.S. citizens can send applications directly to the Organization's mailing address.
Duration: Fellowships are tenable for not less than one year nor more than two years.
Deadline: For presentation of applications to the National Liaison Office (ONE): Differs from country to country and should therefore be confirmed with the National Liaison Office (ONE) in the applicant's country of origin or permanent residence.

ADDRESS INQUIRIES TO:
Department of Human Development, Education and Employment
(See address above.)

*SPECIAL STIPULATIONS:
For countries other than the U.S., the fellowship form must be presented to the General Secretariat of the OAS in Washington, DC, through the official channels established by each government.

HERBERT SCOVILLE, JR. PEACE FELLOWSHIP [781]
820 First Street, N.E.
Suite LL-180
Washington, DC 20002
(202) 446-1565
E-mail: info@scoville.org
Web Site: scoville.org

FOUNDED: 1987

AREAS OF INTEREST:
Climate and security, emerging technology threats, nuclear nonproliferation and weapons of mass destruction, and peace building and conflict resolution.

TYPE:
Fellowships.

YEAR PROGRAM STARTED: 1987

PURPOSE:
To provide an opportunity for college graduates to gain practical knowledge and

experience by contributing to the efforts of nonprofit, public-interest organizations working on peace and security issues.

LEGAL BASIS:
Nonprofit program.

ELIGIBILITY:
Prospective Fellows are expected to demonstrate excellent academic accomplishments and a strong interest in issues of peace and security. Graduate study, a college major, course work, or substantial independent reading that reflects the substantive focus of the Fellowship is also a plus. Prior experience with public-interest activism or advocacy is highly desirable. It is preferred, but not required, that such activities be focused on peace and security issues.

Candidates are required to have completed a Baccalaureate degree by the time the Fellowship commences. Preference is given to U.S. citizens, although a Fellowship to a foreign national residing in the U.S. is awarded periodically based on availability of funding. The Scoville Fellowship is not intended for students or scholars interested in pursuing independent research in Washington, DC.

Preference will be given to individuals who have not had substantial prior public-interest or government experience in the Washington, DC area.

FINANCIAL DATA:
Amount of support per award: $3,450 per month, plus travel expenses to the Washington, DC area to begin fellowship, health insurance, and up to $1,000 in professional development.
Total amount of support: Varies.

NO. MOST RECENT APPLICANTS: 300 to 350.

NO. AWARDS: 6 to 8 per year.

APPLICATION INFO:
Information is available on the web site. Reference letters and transcripts must be submitted by e-mail to apply@scoville.org.
Duration: Six to nine months.
Deadline: Spring Fellowship: October 1; Fall Fellowship: January 7.

PUBLICATIONS:
Application guidelines; organization description.

ADDRESS INQUIRIES TO:
Paul Revsine, Executive Director
(See address above.)

SOCIAL SCIENCE RESEARCH COUNCIL   [782]
One Pierrepont Plaza
15th Floor
Brooklyn, NY 11201
(212) 377-2700 ext. 3672
E-mail: japan@ssrc.org
Web Site: www.ssrc.org/fellowships/jsps-fellowship

FOUNDED: 1923

AREAS OF INTEREST:
Social sciences and humanities.

NAME(S) OF PROGRAMS:
● **SSRC/JSPS Long-Term Fellowship**
● **SSRC/JSPS Short-Term Fellowship**

TYPE:
Fellowships; Research grants. The Japan Society for the Promotion of Science (JSPS)

Postdoctoral Fellowship for Foreign Researchers provides promising and highly qualified recent Ph.Ds. and ABDs with funding to conduct research in Japan. JSPS guidelines target the applicant who wishes to conduct cooperative research under the leadership of a host researcher, thereby advancing the Fellow's own research and at the same time stimulating Japanese academic circles through close collaboration with young Japanese researchers.

YEAR PROGRAM STARTED: 1967

PURPOSE:
To stimulate Japanese academic circles through close collaboration with young foreign researchers.

LEGAL BASIS:
Not-for-profit organization.

ELIGIBILITY:
Applicants must be U.S. citizens or permanent residents at the time of application and not be of Japanese descent. Citizens of other countries are eligible for short-term fellowships if they have completed a Master's or Ph.D. course at an institution of higher education in the U.S. and, upon completing the course, have for at least three continuous years conducted high-level research at a university in the U.S. Japanese nationals are not eligible for a fellowship regardless of current residency status. Applicants currently in Japan are not eligible for short-term fellowships.

Applicants for long-term fellowships must submit a copy of a Ph.D. diploma from a university outside Japan dated no more than six years prior to April 1, 2020.

Applicants for short-term fellowships must submit a copy of a Ph.D. diploma from a university outside Japan dated no more than six years prior to April 1, 2020 or a letter from their institution stating that the applicant is a Ph.D. candidate within two years of receiving a Ph.D.

Scholars who have previously received funding from JSPS for the Short-Term Fellowship are eligible to apply for the JSPS Long-Term Fellowship.

FINANCIAL DATA:
Grants are to be used for maintenance, travel and research expenses.
Amount of support per award: Varies based on length of research term and doctoral status.
Total amount of support: Varies.

NO. MOST RECENT APPLICANTS: Long-Term and Short-Term Fellowships: 21.

NO. AWARDS: Long-Term Fellowships: 4; Short-Term Fellowships: 5.

APPLICATION INFO:
Application information is available on the web site.
Duration: Long-Term Fellowships: 12 to 24 months; Short-Term Fellowships: One to 12 months.
Deadline: December 1.

PUBLICATIONS:
Annual report; *Items,* newsletter; *Fellowships and Grants for Training and Research,* brochure.

STAFF:
Nicole Levit, Japan Associate Director
Bree Brinson, Program Assistant

ADDRESS INQUIRIES TO:
Bree Brinson, Program Assistant
Japan Program
Social Science Research Council
(See address above.)

SOCIAL SCIENCE RESEARCH COUNCIL   [783]
300 Cadman Plaza West
15th Floor
Brooklyn, NY 11201
(212) 377-2700 ext. 3644
Fax: (212) 377-2727
E-mail: idrf@ssrc.org
Web Site: www.ssrc.org/programs/idrf

FOUNDED: 1923

AREAS OF INTEREST:
Fellowships in the humanities and humanistic social sciences.

NAME(S) OF PROGRAMS:
● **International Dissertation Research Fellowship Program (IDRF)**

TYPE:
Fellowships. Support to graduate students in the humanities and humanistic social sciences who are enrolled in doctoral programs in the U.S. and conducting dissertation research outside of the U.S.

YEAR PROGRAM STARTED: 1997

PURPOSE:
To support the advancement of social science and humanistic research.

LEGAL BASIS:
Not-for-profit corporation.

ELIGIBILITY:
Applicants must be enrolled in a full-time doctoral program at a U.S. university. U.S. citizenship is not required. Research must be conducted outside of the U.S. and on a non-U.S. topic.

FINANCIAL DATA:
Amount of support per award: Average $23,000.

NO. MOST RECENT APPLICANTS: More than 1,000.

NO. AWARDS: 70.

APPLICATION INFO:
Application information is available on the web site usually the first week in August.
Duration: Nine to 12 months.
Deadline: Typically the first week in November.

ADDRESS INQUIRIES TO:
See e-mail address above.

SOCIAL SCIENCE RESEARCH COUNCIL   [784]
One Pierrepont Plaza
15th Floor
Brooklyn, NY 11201
(212) 377-2700 ext. 3672
E-mail: abe@ssrc.org
Web Site: www.ssrc.org/fellowships/abe-fellowship

FOUNDED: 1923

AREAS OF INTEREST:
International multidisciplinary research on topics of pressing global concern.

NAME(S) OF PROGRAMS:
● **Abe Fellowship Program**

TYPE:
Fellowships; Research grants. The program encourages international multidisciplinary research on topics of pressing global concern and fosters the development of a new generation of researchers interested in policy-relevant topics of long-range importance and willing to become key members of a bilateral and global research network built around such topics.

The Abe Fellowship Program administers an annual fellowship competition that provides scholars and nonacademic research professionals in the social sciences and related disciplines with support for research projects addressing one or more of three themes: (1) Threats to Personal, Societal and International Security; (2) Growth and Sustainable Development; (3) Social, Scientific and Cultural Trends and Transformations and; (4) Governance, Empowerment and Participation.

YEAR PROGRAM STARTED: 1991

PURPOSE:
To encourage international multidisciplinary research on topics of pressing global concern.

ELIGIBILITY:
Competition is open to citizens of the U.S. and Japan as well as to nationals of other countries who can demonstrate strong and serious long-term affiliations with research communities in Japan or the U.S. Applicants must hold the Ph.D. or the terminal degree in their field, or have attained an equivalent level of professional experience. Applications from researchers in professions other than academia are encouraged. Previous language training is not a prerequisite for this Fellowship. However, if the research project requires language ability, the applicant should provide evidence of adequate proficiency to complete the project. Projects proposing to address key policy issues or seeking to develop a concrete policy proposal must reflect nonpartisan positions.

GEOG. RESTRICTIONS: Japan and United States.

FINANCIAL DATA:
Awards may be used for maintenance, travel and research expenses.

Amount of support per award: Varies.

Total amount of support: Varies.

NO. MOST RECENT APPLICANTS: 71 for the year 2019.

NO. AWARDS: 10.

APPLICATION INFO:
Applications are available by early summer and must be submitted online at applications.ssrc.org.

Duration: Three to 12 months of full-time support over a 24-month period. Fellowship tenure must begin between April 1 and December 31 of a given year.

Deadline: Typically late fall.

STAFF:
Nicole Levit, Associate Director
Bree Brinson, Program Assistant

ADDRESS INQUIRIES TO:
Abe Fellowship Program
Social Science Research Council
(See address above.)

SOCIETY FOR FRENCH HISTORICAL STUDIES

Colorado College, Department of History
Palmer Hall, No. 215D
14 East Cache La Poudre Street
Colorado Springs, CO 80903
E-mail: bragan@coloradocollege.edu
Web Site: www.
societyforfrenchhistoricalstudies.net

TYPE:
Awards/prizes. The Chinard Prize is for a recent book on historical relations between France and the Americas.

Davis Graduate Student Award is given for the best paper presented by a graduate student at the Society's annual meeting.

Farrar Award is for dissertation research.

The Institut Francais d'America Fund Research Fellowships are for research in France for a period of at least one month.

The Koren Prize is for a recent journal article written on French history.

The Pinkney Prize is for a recent book written on French history.

Research Travel Award is for recent recipients of Doctorates (awarded jointly with Western Society for French History).

See entry 584 for full listing.

SWEDISH WOMEN'S EDUCATIONAL ASSOCIATION INC. [785]

P.O. Box 4128
Fort Lauderdale, FL 33338-4128
E-mail: litstip@swea.org
Web Site: swea.org

AREAS OF INTEREST:
Sweden's culture, history and language.

NAME(S) OF PROGRAMS:
● **SWEA Scholarship in Literature, Language and Area Studies**

TYPE:
Scholarships. Funds may be used to study in Sweden. Previous trips to Sweden, or lack thereof, are of no consideration. Willingness to travel to Sweden for dissertation work is a plus, but not a requirement.

PURPOSE:
To promote and preserve the Swedish language, cultures and traditions.

ELIGIBILITY:
The applicant must:
(1) be a well-merited doctoral candidate, studying at a non-Swedish university and reside permanently outside of Sweden;
(2) have filed a dissertation topic and;
(3) have a good knowledge of the Swedish language (written and spoken).

FINANCIAL DATA:
Amount of support per award: $10,000.
Total amount of support: $10,000.

NO. AWARDS: 1.

APPLICATION INFO:
The applicant must submit an application, curriculum vitae, a detailed description of the dissertation project, a statement explaining how the scholarship money will be used, a presentation of himself or herself in Swedish, and three letters of recommendation. Applications are available online.

Duration: One year. Recipients may reapply.

Deadline: January 15.

ADDRESS INQUIRIES TO:
SWEA International Committee for Literary Scholarship
(See e-mail address above.)

*SPECIAL STIPULATIONS:
There is no discrimination on the basis of gender, race, color, age, religion or nationality.

TINKER FOUNDATION INC. [786]

55 East 59th Street
Suite 21C
New York, NY 10022
(212) 421-6858
Fax: (212) 223-3326
E-mail: tinker@tinker.org
Web Site: www.tinker.org

FOUNDED: 1959

AREAS OF INTEREST:
Institutional grants for projects addressing democratic governance, sustainable resource management, and education, with a geographic focus on the Spanish- and Portuguese-speaking countries of Latin America.

NAME(S) OF PROGRAMS:
● **Institutional Grants**
● **Tinker Field Research Grants**
● **Tinker Visiting Professor**

TYPE:
Travel grants; Visiting scholars. Travel grants (issued to universities) are to be used to support brief periods of individual research in Latin America by graduate students.

YEAR PROGRAM STARTED: 1979

PURPOSE:
To enable emerging scholars to work in the Spanish- and Portuguese-speaking countries of Latin America, enabling them to acquire a comprehensive knowledge of language, cultures and terrain, and to gather research data and develop contacts with scholars and institutions in their respective fields.

LEGAL BASIS:
Private foundation.

ELIGIBILITY:
Open to all recognized Centers or Institutes of Latin American Studies with graduate doctoral programs at accredited U.S. universities. Field Research Grants, awarded to individuals by the appropriate university institutes/centers, are to reflect the Foundation's broad areas of interest.

The Foundation's selection criteria include the quality of the overall graduate program in Latin American studies, the immediate benefits to the Latin American studies program that will result from the availability of Field Research Grants at the university and the level of general university support for Latin American studies as demonstrated by past commitments and future projects.

Institutional Grants: Open to any 501(c)(3) (or equivalent foreign) organization doing work in and on the Spanish- and Portuguese-speaking countries of Latin America.

GEOG. RESTRICTIONS: Latin America, excluding Puerto Rico.

FINANCIAL DATA:
Amount of support per award: Field Research Grants: $10,000 and $15,000; Institutional Grants: Up to $150,000.

Total amount of support: $3,500,000 annually.

Matching fund requirements: Field Research Grant Awards require the university to match the award on a 1:1 ratio.

NO. MOST RECENT APPLICANTS: Field Research Grants: 11; Institutional Grants: Approximately 500.

NO. AWARDS: Field Research Grants: Up to 6 new annually; Institutional Grants: Varies.

APPLICATION INFO:
Application instructions and forms can be accessed via the web site.
Duration: Maximum of three years.
Deadline: Field Research Grants: October 1. Institutional Grants: January or February and July or August.

STAFF:
Margaret J. Cushing, Associate Director
Susan Vega, Director of Administration and Finance
Avi Richman, Education Program Officer
Angelina Pienczykowski, Grants Manager

DIRECTORS AND OFFICERS:
Alan Stoga, Chairman
Caroline B. Kronley, President
Kathleen Waldron, Treasurer
Luis Rubio, Secretary
Tatiana R. Martins
Shannon K. O'Neil
Arturo C. Porzecanski
Susan L. Segal
Bradford K. Smith

ADDRESS INQUIRIES TO:
Angelina Pienczykowski, Grants Manager
(See address above.)

U.S. DEPARTMENT OF EDUCATION
International and Foreign Language Education
Advanced Training and Research Division
400 Maryland Avenue, S.W.
Washington, DC 20202
(202) 453-7854
Fax: (202) 453-5780
E-mail: ifle@ed.gov
Web Site: www.ed.gov/ope/iegps

TYPE:
Fellowships. The Foreign Language and Area Studies Fellowships program provides allocations of academic year and summer fellowships to institutions of higher education or consortia of institutions of higher education to assist meritorious undergraduate students and graduate students undergoing training in modern foreign languages and related international or area studies.

See entry 607 for full listing.

U.S. DEPARTMENT OF EDUCATION
International and Foreign Language Education
400 Maryland Avenue, S.W.
Room 258-24
Washington, DC 20202
(202) 453-6891
Fax: (202) 453-5780
E-mail: ddra@ed.gov
Web Site: www.ed.
gov/programs/iegpsddrap/index.html

TYPE:
Fellowships. Fellowships to support doctoral dissertation research abroad in modern foreign languages and related area studies.

For the purpose of these programs, area studies is defined as a program of comprehensive study of the aspects of a society or societies, including the study of their geography, history, culture, economy, politics, international relations and languages. The program is designed to develop research knowledge and capability in world areas not widely included in American curricula. Awards will not be available for projects focusing on Western Europe.

See entry 608 for full listing.

U.S. DEPARTMENT OF EDUCATION
Office of Postsecondary Education
International and Foreign Language Education (IFLE)
400 Maryland Avenue, S.W.
Mail Stop 257-09
Washington, DC 20202
(202) 453-5690
E-mail: IFLE@ed.gov
Web Site: www2.ed.gov/programs/iegpsnrc

TYPE:
Project/program grants; Training grants. The NRC Program provides grants to institutions of higher education and consortia of institutions to establish, strengthen and operate comprehensive and undergraduate centers that will be national resources for:
(1) teaching of any modern foreign language;
(2) instruction in fields needed to provide full understanding of areas, regions or countries in which the modern foreign language is commonly used;
(3) research and training in international studies and the international and foreign language aspects of professional and other fields of study and;
(4) instruction and research on issues in world affairs that concern one or more countries.

This program operates on a four-year grant cycle.

See entry 609 for full listing.

U.S. DEPARTMENT OF EDUCATION   [787]
International and Foreign Language Education
400 Maryland Avenue, S.W.
Mail Stop 257-09
Washington, DC 20202
(202) 453-5690
E-mail: cheryl.gibbs@ed.gov
Web Site: www2.ed.gov/programs/iegpsaorc

AREAS OF INTEREST:
Area studies, international studies and postgraduate research.

NAME(S) OF PROGRAMS:
● **American Overseas Research Centers (AORC) Program**

TYPE:
Project/program grants; Research grants; Training grants. The AORC Program provides grants to consortia of U.S. institutions of higher education to establish or operate an AORC that promotes postgraduate research, exchanges and area studies.

LEGAL BASIS:
Authorized under Section 609 of the Higher Education Act of 1965, as amended.

ELIGIBILITY:
Any American overseas research center can qualify that meets the following conditions:

(1) be a consortium of U.S. institutions of higher education that receives more than 50% of its funding from public or private U.S. sources;
(2) have a permanent presence in the country in which the center is located and;
(3) be an organization described in Section 501(c)(3) of the Internal Revenue Code of 1993, which is exempt from taxation under Section 501(a) of the Code.

FINANCIAL DATA:
AORC grants may be used to pay all or a portion of the cost of establishing or operating a center or program including:
(1) the cost of operation and maintenance of overseas facilities;
(2) the cost of organizing and managing conferences;
(3) the cost of teaching and research materials;
(4) the cost of acquisition, maintenance and preservation of library collections;
(5) the cost of bringing visiting scholars and faculty to the center to teach or to conduct research;
(6) the cost of faculty and staff stipends and salaries;
(7) the cost of faculty, staff and student travel and;
(8) the cost of publication and dissemination of materials for the scholarly and general public.

Amount of support per award: Average annual grant: $65,000.

Total amount of support: $1,000,000 in non-competing continuation awards for fiscal year 2021.

NO. AWARDS: 15.

APPLICATION INFO:
Applications must be submitted through grants.gov.
Duration: Up to 48 months.

ADDRESS INQUIRIES TO:
Cheryl E. Gibbs, Senior Director
International Foreign Language Education Office
(See address above.)

*PLEASE NOTE:
The AORC Program competes every four years. The next competition for new grants will be held in 2024.

U.S. INSTITUTE OF PEACE   [788]
Jennings Randolph Fellowship
Programs for International Peace
2301 Constitution Avenue, N.W.
Washington, DC 20037-2900
(202) 429-7812
Fax: (202) 429-6063
E-mail: jrprogram@usip.org
Web Site: www.usip.org

FOUNDED: 1984

AREAS OF INTEREST:
Topics and disciplines related to international peace, conflict and conflict management.

NAME(S) OF PROGRAMS:
● **Jennings Randolph Senior Fellowship Programs for International Peace**
● **USIP Peace Scholar Dissertation Fellowship**

TYPE:
Fellowships; Residencies. Residential program for senior fellows, but not for Peace Scholars. The U.S. Institute of Peace is an independent, nonpartisan institution created

by Congress to strengthen the nation's capacity to promote the peaceful resolution of international conflict.

Under the Jennings Randolph Senior Fellowship Programs for International Peace, Senior Fellowships and Peace Scholar Dissertation Fellowships are awarded on a competitive basis.

Senior Fellowships are awarded annually to scholars and practitioners from a variety of professions, including college and university faculty, journalists, diplomats, writers, educators, military officers, international negotiators and lawyers, and staff of civil society organizations. Fellows are supported for varying periods of time to conduct research on themes defined by USIP centers in their Calls for Applications, which will be published on USIP's web site, consult with staff and contribute to the ongoing work of the Institute.

Peace Scholar program supports doctoral dissertations that explore the sources and nature of international conflict, and strategies to prevent or end conflict and to sustain peace. Peace Scholars work at their university or appropriate field research sites. Successful applicants must demonstrate that their work is relevant for policy and/or practice in the field of conflict analysis, prevention and management, and postconflict peacebuilding.

YEAR PROGRAM STARTED: 1986

PURPOSE:
To enable outstanding scholars, practitioners and doctoral students to focus their efforts on critical problems of international peace and conflict.

Fellows undertake research and education projects that will increase knowledge and spread awareness among the public and policymakers and the public about topics concerning the sources and nature of international conflict and the full range of ways to end or prevent conflict and to sustain peace.

LEGAL BASIS:
Independent, nonpartisan and educational institution created by the U.S. Congress.

ELIGIBILITY:
Senior Fellowships: The competition is open to citizens of all nations. Fellowship topics will vary.

Peace Scholar Dissertation Fellowships: Citizens of all countries are eligible, but must be enrolled in an accredited college or university registered in the U.S. Applicants must have completed all requirements for the degree except the dissertation by the commencement of the award (September 1). Priority will be given to projects that contribute knowledge relevant to the formulation of policy or to understanding of best practices on international peace and conflict issues.

FINANCIAL DATA:
Senior Fellows receive a stipend that will vary according to the particular call for applications.
Amount of support per award: Senior Fellows receive stipend of $11,500 per month; Peace Scholar Dissertation Fellows receive a $20,000 flat stipend, which may be used to support writing or field research.
Total amount of support: Varies each year.

NO. MOST RECENT APPLICANTS: 50 for Jennings Randolph Senior Fellowships; 115 for Peace Scholar Awards.

NO. AWARDS: Jennings Randolph Senior Fellowships: Up to 3; Peace Scholar Awards: 6 to 12 per year.

APPLICATION INFO:
For application forms for either the Senior Fellowships or the Peace Scholar Dissertation Fellowships, please visit the Institute's web site or contact the Jennings Randolph Fellowship Programs at the address above. Please note that the applications for both competitions are online only.
Duration: Senior Fellowships: Varies; Peace Scholar Dissertation Fellowships: Ten months.
Deadline: Jennings Randolph Senior Fellowships: Varies. There may be up to four competitions per year. Peace Scholar Fellows: November.

PUBLICATIONS:
Program Description with guidelines; application form; brochure.

STAFF:
Kathleen Kuehnast, Director
Jeremy Moore, Senior Program Officer
Tina Hegadorn, Senior Program Specialist

ADDRESS INQUIRIES TO:
Jennings Randolph Fellowship Programs for International Peace
(See address above.)

*PLEASE NOTE:
Research on conflict within the U.S. may not be supported under the terms of the Institute's mandate.

*SPECIAL STIPULATIONS:
No telephone calls please.

U.S. INSTITUTE OF PEACE   [789]
2301 Constitution Avenue, N.W.
Washington, DC 20037
(202) 457-1700
E-mail: jrprogram@usip.org
Web Site: www.usip.org/grants-fellowships

FOUNDED: 1984

AREAS OF INTEREST:
International peace and conflict management and related fields. Topic areas of interest include, but are not restricted to, international conflict resolution, diplomacy, negotiation theory, functionalism and "track two" diplomacy, methods of third-party dispute settlement, international law, international organizations and collective security, deterrence and balance of power, arms control, psychological theories about international conflict, the role of nonviolence and nonviolent sanctions, moral and ethical thought about conflict and conflict resolution and theories about relationships among political institutions, human rights and conflict.

NAME(S) OF PROGRAMS:
• **U.S. Institute of Peace Grants & Fellows Program**

TYPE:
Conferences/seminars; Project/program grants; Research grants; Research contracts. Support for research, education and training and the dissemination of information on international peace and conflict resolution.

YEAR PROGRAM STARTED: 1986

PURPOSE:
To carry out basic and applied research on the causes of war and other international conflicts; to develop curricula and texts for high school through postgraduate study and to conduct teacher-training institutes, workshops and seminars; to conduct training, symposia and continuing education programs for practitioners, policymakers, policy implementers and the public; to undertake public information efforts; to increase the store of information on international peace and conflict resolution.

LEGAL BASIS:
Independent, nonpartisan federal institution created and funded by the U.S. Congress.

ELIGIBILITY:
Grant applicants must be nonprofit organizations, official public institutions and, both U.S. and foreign nationals, including the following: institutions of postsecondary, community and secondary education, public and private education, training or research institutions and libraries and public departments and agencies (including state and territorial departments of education and commerce).

Individuals requesting support for degree work are not eligible.

For additional questions regarding eligibility, please contact the appropriate program center at USIP listed online.

FINANCIAL DATA:
Amount of support per award: The amount of any grant is based on the proposed budget and on negotiations with successful applicants.

NO. MOST RECENT APPLICANTS: 200.

NO. AWARDS: 16.

APPLICATION INFO:
Application information is available on the web site.
Duration: One to two years.
Deadline: Varies by program. Specific dates are posted online.

PUBLICATIONS:
Program announcement.

STAFF:
Kathleen Kuehnast, Director
Jeremy Moore, Senior Program Officer
Tina Hegadorn, Senior Program Specialist

ADDRESS INQUIRIES TO:
The Grant Program
United States Institute of Peace
(See address above.)

*SPECIAL STIPULATIONS:
The Institute does not support funding for degree work.

U.S. INSTITUTE OF PEACE   [790]
2301 Constitution Avenue, N.W.
Washington, DC 20037
(202) 457-1700
Fax: (202) 429-6063
E-mail: publiceducation@usip.org
Web Site: www.usip.org/public-education/students/AFSAEssayContest

FOUNDED: 1984

AREAS OF INTEREST:
International affairs, peace, conflict resolution, history, writing and research.

NAME(S) OF PROGRAMS:
• **AFSA National High School Essay Contest**

TYPE:
Awards/prizes; Scholarships. The American Foreign Service Association's National High School Essay Contest engages high school students in learning and writing about issues of peace and conflict. It encourages an appreciation for diplomacy's role in building partnerships that can advance peacebuilding and protect national security.

YEAR PROGRAM STARTED: 1987

PURPOSE:
To have students research and write about issues dealing with international conflict resolution and peacemaking.

LEGAL BASIS:
Independent, nonpartisan institution created by the U.S. Congress.

ELIGIBILITY:
Students whose parents are not in the Foreign Service are eligible to participate if they are in grades nine to 12 in any of the 50 states, the District of Columbia, the U.S. territories, or if they are U.S. citizens attending high school overseas. Students may be attending a public, private or parochial school. Entries from home students are also accepted.

Previous first-place winners and immediate relatives of directors or staff of the American Foreign Service Association and Semester at Sea are not eligible to participate.

FINANCIAL DATA:
First-place winner receives an all-expense-paid, two-day trip to Washington, DC to meet members of the Senior State Department Leadership and tour the U.S. Institute of Peace, as well as a full-tuition-paid voyage with Semester at Sea upon his or her enrollment at an accredited university.

Runner-up receives a full scholarship to participate in the International Diplomacy Program of the National Student Leadership Conference, held annually in Washington, DC.

Amount of support per award: First-place winner: $2,500. Runner-up: $1,250.

CO-OP FUNDING PROGRAMS: The National High School Essay Contest is conducted in conjunction with the U.S. Institute of Peace, Semester at Sea, and the National Student Leadership Conference.

NO. MOST RECENT APPLICANTS: 450.

APPLICATION INFO:
Up-to-date information and details can be found on the American Foreign Service Association's web site (www.afsa.org/essay-contest).

Duration: One-time award. This is an annual contest.

Deadline: March 15.

ADDRESS INQUIRIES TO:
Theo Horn
Awards Manager
American Foreign Service Association
2101 E Street, N.W.
Washington, DC 20037
E-mail: horn@afsa.org

UNITED STATES-JAPAN FOUNDATION   [791]
145 East 32nd Street
12th Floor
New York, NY 10016
(212) 481-8753
(212) 481-8757
Fax: (212) 481-8762
E-mail: programs@us-jf.org
Web Site: www.us-jf.org

FOUNDED: 1980

AREAS OF INTEREST:
Precollege education and policy studies, communication and public opinion.

NAME(S) OF PROGRAMS:
● **Grants**
● **Elgin Heinz Outstanding Teacher Award**
● **U.S.-Japan Leadership Program**

TYPE:
Awards/prizes; General operating grants; Project/program grants; Research grants; Travel grants. In the area of Precollege Education, the Foundation supports the improvement and enhancement of instruction of Japan in the U.S. and on the U.S. in Japan in secondary and elementary schools through programs which foster the creative use of the Internet in education, teacher training, professional development, intensive study tours, and curriculum design. The Foundation also supports the improvement of Japanese language instruction.

In the area of Policy Studies, the Foundation supports joint policy research and has established several nongovernmental channels for ongoing discussions between small groups of prominent experts. Policy projects have been active in such fields as trade and international finance, the environment, multilateral crisis management, and Northeast Asian security.

The Foundation will consider communication/public opinion projects that not only raise awareness about Japan in the U.S. and of the U.S. in Japan, but also deal with concrete issues that affect the bilateral relationship. Using creative approaches, these programs should reach broad audiences to stimulate balanced, in-depth and quality media coverage of issues that are central to U.S.-Japan relations.

Projects that link civil society organizations in the two countries are also supported.

YEAR PROGRAM STARTED: 1980

PURPOSE:
To promote stronger ties between Americans and Japanese through education, communication, policy studies and similar activities that foster greater mutual knowledge and understanding regarding each other and issues of common concern.

LEGAL BASIS:
Not-for-profit private foundation.

ELIGIBILITY:
Certain types of programs fall outside the Foundation's current interests. These include undergraduate education, cultural performances or exhibitions, sports exchanges, publication subsidies, scientific research and research conferences. As a rule, grants cannot be made to individuals applying on their own behalf for independent study, research, travel or participation in meetings; grants also cannot be made to for-profit organizations.

Because the Foundation is interested primarily in supporting program activities, it does not award grants as contributions to capital campaigns, endowment funds or deficit operations. In addition, it does not award grants for the construction or maintenance of buildings or other physical premises or for the purchase of equipment.

The Foundation does not administer programs which it supports. Foundation grants may not be used to influence legislation or election to public office.

GEOG. RESTRICTIONS: United States or Japan.

FINANCIAL DATA:
Amount of support per award: Varies.
Total amount of support: Approximately $2,000,000 annually.

NO. MOST RECENT APPLICANTS: 150 to 200.

NO. AWARDS: Approximately 45.

REPRESENTATIVE AWARDS:
Education: $30,000 to Concordia Language Villages, Moorhead, MN, to support a program to strengthen the teaching of the Japanese language in the U.S.; Community/Public Opinion: JPY 300,000 to Sapporo Cultural Arts Foundation, Hokkaido, Japan, to support workshops and lessons during the Sapporo Junior Jazz School.

APPLICATION INFO:
Applicants should submit a preproposal letter of inquiry, including a brief description of the proposed project and its objectives, any necessary background information on the project and applicant, and a brief budget estimate. If there is interest, the applicant will be invited to prepare a full proposal.

Duration: 12 months. Annual renewal possible.

ADDRESS INQUIRIES TO:
Director of Foundation Grants
(See address above.)

WORLD LEARNING INC.   [792]
1015 15th Street, N.W.
7th Floor
Washington, DC 20005
(202) 408-5420
(202) 464-6490
E-mail: fulbrightspecialist@worldlearning.org
Web Site: fulbrightspecialist.worldlearning.org

FOUNDED: 1947

AREAS OF INTEREST:
Scholarly exchange.

NAME(S) OF PROGRAMS:
● **Fulbright Specialist Program**

TYPE:
Exchange programs; Project/program grants. The Fulbright Specialist Program is designed to provide short-term project opportunities for U.S. faculty and professionals. Grant recipients have a chance to participate in a variety of new and exciting activities: collaborate with counterparts in other countries on curriculum and faculty development, assist in institutional planning, deliver a series of lectures or provide other expertise, etc.

YEAR PROGRAM STARTED: 2001

PURPOSE:
To promote mutual understanding and scholarship.

LEGAL BASIS:
Private, nonprofit organization that receives funding from the U.S. State Department.

ELIGIBILITY:
The Fulbright Specialist Program is open to qualified U.S. scholars and professionals in various fields. Applicants will be considered without regard to race, color, religion, sex, age, national origin and/or physical impairment.

Applicants must meet all of the following minimum eligibility requirements:
(1) U.S. citizen at the time of application; permanent resident status is not sufficient;
(2) for academics, a Ph.D. or equivalent professional/terminal degree at the time of application plus a minimum of five years of postdoctoral teaching or professional experience in the field in which person is applying;
(3) for professionals and artists outside academe, recognized professional standing and substantial professional accomplishments plus a minimum of five years of professional experience in the field in which person is applying;
(4) disclosure of prior conviction, current indictment or arrest for commission of a felony or misdemeanor (excluding minor traffic violations); prior conviction or current indictment may result in disqualification and;
(5) U.S. residency required at the time of selection for a grant.

In matching candidates with grant opportunities, preference will be given to candidates with the most relevant professional experience.

FINANCIAL DATA:
Grants awarded will include travel and per diem plus a $200 per day honorarium. Per diem costs, which are in-country costs for lodging, meals and in-country transportation, will be covered by the host institution.
Amount of support per award: Varies.

NO. MOST RECENT APPLICANTS: 600.

NO. AWARDS: Approximately 350 to 450 per year.

APPLICATION INFO:
Qualified U.S. scholars and professionals apply throughout the calendar year for candidacy on the Fulbright Specialists Roster. Peer review is conducted six times each year. CIES builds lists of qualified Specialist candidates for each eligible discipline and facilitates matching Specialist candidates with project requests. There is a two-tier application process for U.S. scholars.

Non-U.S. postsecondary degree-granting academic institutions and other eligible institutions with education-focused programming submit Specialist project requests through the appropriate Fulbright agency in their country. Once approved by the Fulbright Commission or U.S. Embassy, the Specialist project request is forwarded to the U.S. Department of State for final approval.
Duration: Two to six weeks.

ADDRESS INQUIRIES TO:
See e-mail address above.

International studies and research abroad

AFS INTERCULTURAL PROGRAMS/USA [793]
120 Wall Street, 4th Floor
New York, NY 10005
(800) 237-4636
(646) 751-2011
Fax: (212) 299-9090
E-mail: studyabroad@afsusa.org
Web Site: www.afsusa.org

FOUNDED: 1947

AREAS OF INTEREST:
International exchange of high school students who live with host families and attend local schools. Participants go to and from 60 countries.

CONSULTING OR VOLUNTEER SERVICES:
More than 100,000 volunteers around the world.

NAME(S) OF PROGRAMS:
● **AFS Faces of America Diversity Scholarship Program**
● **AFS Global Prep**
● **AFS Semester Program**
● **AFS Summer Program**
● **AFS Year Program**
● **AFSNext**
● **Congress-Bundestag Youth Exchange (CBX)**
● **Kennedy-Lugar Youth Exchange and Study Abroad (YES Abroad)**
● **National Securities Languages Initiative for Youth (NSLI-Y)**

TYPE:
Exchange programs; Scholarships. U.S. students abroad. Scholarships are for AFS-run programs only.

YEAR PROGRAM STARTED: 1947

PURPOSE:
To provide cross-cultural learning experiences for young people in another environment.

LEGAL BASIS:
Incorporated under the Not-for-Profit Corporation Laws of the state of New York. Exempt from New York state, New York City and federal taxes.

ELIGIBILITY:
Age, health, academic background, motivation and personality are considered.

FINANCIAL DATA:
Amount of support per award: Varies depending on merit and need.
Total amount of support: Approximately $3,000,000.

NO. AWARDS: Nearly 50% of all participants receive financial aid. AFS deals with 4,400 students each year.

APPLICATION INFO:
Candidate must submit health record, school record, applicant essay, screening group recommendation, interview forms and parental essay.
Duration: Two to six weeks to one year. Nonrenewable.
Deadline: Dependent on program.

PUBLICATIONS:
Annual report; application forms; AFS program catalog; *Partnerships*, newsletter.

IRS I.D.: 39-1711417

ADDRESS INQUIRIES TO:
See e-mail address above.

ALBRIGHT INSTITUTE OF ARCHAEOLOGICAL RESEARCH (AIAR) [794]
Department of Classics, UNC-Chapel Hill
212 Murphey Hall, CB 3145
Chapel Hill, NC 27599-3145
(919) 962-7191
Fax: (919) 962-4036
E-mail: gatesfos@email.unc.edu
Web Site: www.aiar.org

FOUNDED: 1900

AREAS OF INTEREST:
Fellowships are open to those in Near Eastern studies from prehistory through the early Islamic period, including the fields of anthropology, archaeology, art history, Bible, epigraphy, historical geography, history, language, literature, philology and religion, and related disciplines.

NAME(S) OF PROGRAMS:
● **Fellowships at the Albright Institute of Archaeological Research in Jerusalem**

TYPE:
Fellowships; Professorships; Scholarships; Travel grants; Visiting scholars. Fellowships are for study at the Albright Institute in Jerusalem, Israel.

The ACLS Recent Doctoral Recipients Fellowship is available to awardees and alternates of the Mellon/ACLS Dissertation Completion Fellowships the prior year.

The Marcia and Oded Borowski Research Fellowship provides a one-month fellowship to doctoral and postdoctoral candidates of all nationalities.

The Council of American Overseas Research Centers (CAORC) Multi-Country Research Fellowships are open to U.S. doctoral candidates and scholars who have already earned their Ph.D. in fields in the humanities, social sciences, or allied natural sciences and wish to conduct research of regional or transregional significance. Fellowships require scholars to conduct research in more than one country, at least one of which hosts a participating American overseas research center. (Apply at www.caorc.org/programs/index.html.)

Educational and Cultural Affairs Fellowships (ECA): (1) Junior Research Fellowships consist of two fellowships of up to four months each; these fellowships are open to doctoral students and recent Ph.D. recipients who are U.S. citizens and; (2) Associate

Fellowships consist of 13 administrative fee awards for senior and junior fellows (one or two semesters).

Ernest S. Frerichs Annual Professorship is for four months and is open to doctoral and postdoctoral scholars of all nationalities. Recipient is expected to assist the Albright's Director in planning and implementing the Ernest S. Frerichs Program for Albright Fellows, which requires a working knowledge of living and traveling in Israel.

The Seymour Gitin Distinguished Professorship is open to internationally recognized senior scholars of all nationalities who have made significant contributions to their field of study.

Carol and Eric Meyers Doctoral Dissertation Fellowship provides one month of study for doctoral students whose research involves the study of archaeology and society in the biblical or early postbiblical periods. Topics dealing with society at the household level are encouraged.

The Lydie T. Shufro Summer Research Fellowship is for one month during the summer and open to scholars at all levels and nationalities.

YEAR PROGRAM STARTED: 1940

PURPOSE:
To help scholars undertake high-quality research and field projects in the Near East; to encourage interdisciplinary study and communication among scholars.

LEGAL BASIS:
Nonprofit, archaeological research corporation.

ELIGIBILITY:
Fellowships are open to those in Near Eastern studies from prehistoric through the early Islamic period, including the fields of archaeology, anthropology, art history, Bible, epigraphy, gender studies, historical geography, history, language, literature, philology and religion and related disciplines. The research period should be continuous, without frequent trips outside the country. Residence at the Albright is required. The option to accommodate dependents is subject to space available at the Albright.

FINANCIAL DATA:
Amount of support per award: Varies.
Total amount of support: Up to $200,000 in fellowships and awards.

CO-OP FUNDING PROGRAMS: With various organizations and foundations, such as the NEH.

NO. AWARDS: Up to 20 in fellowships and awards from the Institute; 50 Associate Fellows receive funding from other sources.

APPLICATION INFO:
All eligible persons are encouraged to apply for as many awards as they wish, but each awardee can hold only one AIAR award at a time. Persons who have received an award in one year can reapply for the same or other awards the following year, but new applicants will be given priority.
Duration: One to four months.
Deadline: January 15 and October 15.

PUBLICATIONS:
Applications.

STAFF:
Dr. Matthew J. Adams, Director

ADDRESS INQUIRIES TO:
Dr. Jennifer Gates-Foster, Chair
Albright Fellowship Committee
(See e-mail address above.)

THE AMERICAN ACADEMY IN BERLIN   [795]
Am Sandwerder 17-19
D-14109 Berlin Germany
(49) 30 804 83 106
Fax: (49) 30 804 83 111
E-mail: cs@americanacademy.de
Web Site: www.americanacademy.de

FOUNDED: 1994

AREAS OF INTEREST:
History, political science, literature, economics, German studies, art history, musicology, anthropology, law, writing, journalism, religious studies and sociology.

NAME(S) OF PROGRAMS:
● **Berlin Prize Fellowship**

TYPE:
Fellowships. Academic semester fellowship in Berlin with residence at the Hans Arnhold Center.

YEAR PROGRAM STARTED: 1998

PURPOSE:
To further scholarly professional development; to foster greater understanding between the people of the U.S. and the people of Germany.

LEGAL BASIS:
Private, independent, nonprofit center.

ELIGIBILITY:
Must be either a U.S. citizen or permanent resident, and have completed their Doctorate or equivalent professional degree. Open to scholars, artists, and professionals who wish to engage in independent study in Berlin for an academic semester or, in rare cases, for an entire academic year. Candidates need not work on German topics, but their project descriptions should explain how a residency in Berlin will contribute to further professional development. Writers must have published at least one book at time of application.

FINANCIAL DATA:
Amount of support per award: Stipend of $5,000 per month, round-trip airfare, and an apartment and partial board at the Hans Arnhold Center.

NO. MOST RECENT APPLICANTS: 300 to 400.

NO. AWARDS: Approximately 20.

APPLICATION INFO:
General Application is available online from late May to the end of September.
Duration: One academic semester.
Deadline: September.

STAFF:
Carol Scherer, Manager of Fellows Selection

ADDRESS INQUIRIES TO:
Carol Scherer
Manager of Fellows Selection
(See address above.)

AMERICAN ACADEMY IN ROME
7 East 60th Street
New York, NY 10022-1001
(212) 751-7200
Fax: (212) 751-7220
E-mail: info@aarome.org
Web Site: www.aarome.org

TYPE:
Awards/prizes; Fellowships; Residencies. Fellowships for independent work in architecture, landscape architecture, design, musical composition, visual arts, historic preservation/conservation, literature, ancient studies, medieval studies, renaissance and early modern studies, and modern Italian studies. Supported projects must be conducted at American Academy in Rome facilities.

See entry 303 for full listing.

AMERICAN ACADEMY IN ROME
7 East 60th Street
New York, NY 10022
(212) 751-7200
Fax: (212) 751-7220
E-mail: info@aarome.org
Web Site: www.aarome.org

TYPE:
Awards/prizes; Fellowships; Residencies. Provides a residential year at the American Academy in Rome for an American landscape architect for advanced study, travel and association with other fellows in the arts and humanities.

See entry 1956 for full listing.

THE AMERICAN CENTER OF RESEARCH   [796]
209 Commerce Street
Alexandria, VA 22314
(703) 789-9231
E-mail: usa.office@acorjordan.org
Web Site: www.acorjordan.org

FOUNDED: 1968

AREAS OF INTEREST:
The study of humanistic disciplines, such as art and architecture, literature, philology, prehistory and topography, relating in particular to the Middle East from prehistoric times to the modern era. Projects involving Islamic studies are especially encouraged.

The American Center of Oriental Research in Amman, Jordan serves as a center of operations for scholars of all nationalities wishing to conduct research in Jordan.

NAME(S) OF PROGRAMS:
● **ACOR-CAORC Fellowship**
● **ACOR-CAORC Postdoctoral Fellowships**
● **Pierre and Patricia Bikai Fellowship**
● **Bert and Sally de Vries Fellowship**
● **Lawrence T. Geraty Travel Scholarship**
● **Jennifer C. Groot Fellowships in the Archaeology of Jordan**
● **Harrell Family Fellowship**
● **MacDonald/Sampson Fellowship**
● **National Endowment for the Humanities (NEH) Fellowship**
● **Kenneth W. Russell Fellowship**
● **James A. Sauer Fellowship**

TYPE:
Fellowships; Research grants; Visiting scholars. ACOR-CAORC Fellowships are for M.A. and doctoral students. Fields of study include all areas of the humanities and the natural and social sciences. Topics should contribute to scholarship in Near Eastern studies; U.S. citizenship required.

ACOR-CAORC Postdoctoral Fellowships are for postdoctoral scholars and scholars with a terminal degree in their field, pursuing research or publication projects in the natural and social sciences, humanities, and associated disciplines relating to the Near East; U.S. citizenship required.

Pierre and Patricia Bikai Fellowship is for a residency at ACOR in Amman and is open to enrolled graduate students of any nationality, except Jordanian citizens, participating in an archaeological project or conducting archaeological work in Jordan.

Bert and Sally de Vries Fellowship supports a student for participation on an archaeological project or research in Jordan. Senior project staff members whose expenses are being borne largely by the project are ineligible. Open to enrolled undergraduate or graduate students of any nationality except Jordanian citizens.

The Lawrence T. Geraty Travel Scholarship is for an undergraduate or graduate student from an accredited institution to conduct ASOR- or CAP-affiliated excavation and/or research in Jordan.

The Jennifer C. Groot Fellowships support beginners in archaeological fieldwork who have been accepted as team members on archaeological projects with ASOR/CAP affiliation in Jordan. Open to undergraduate or graduate students of U.S. or Canadian citizenship.

Harrell Family Fellowship supports a graduate student for participation on an archaeological project or research in Jordan. Senior project staff members whose expenses are being borne largely by the project are ineligible. Open to enrolled graduate students of any nationality except Jordanian citizens.

MacDonald/Sampson Fellowship is for a residency at ACOR for research in the fields of Ancient Near Eastern languages and history, archaeology, Bible studies, or comparative religion, or a travel grant to assist with participation in an archaeological field project in Jordan. Open to enrolled undergraduate or graduate students of Canadian citizenship or landed immigrant status.

The National Endowment for the Humanities (NEH) Fellowship is for scholars who have a Ph.D. or have completed their professional training. Fields of research include modern and classical languages, linguistics, literature, history, jurisprudence, philosophy, archaeology, comparative religion, ethics, and the history, criticism and theory of the arts. Social and political scientists are encouraged to apply. Applicants must be U.S. citizens or foreign nationals living in the U.S. three years immediately preceding the application deadline.

James A. Sauer Fellowship is open to enrolled graduate students of U.S. or Canadian citizenship participating on an archaeological project or research in Jordan.

YEAR PROGRAM STARTED: 1968

PURPOSE:
To help scholars undertake high-quality research and field projects in the Middle East; to encourage interdisciplinary study and communication among scholars.

LEGAL BASIS:
Nonprofit, archaeological research corporation.

ELIGIBILITY:
Most fellowships are restricted to U.S. or Canadian citizens.

CAORC, NEH, MacDonald/Sampson and Bikai Fellows will reside at the ACOR facility in Amman while conducting their research. Recipients are expected to participate actively in the formal and informal activities of the Center.

FINANCIAL DATA:
Amount of support per award:
ACOR-CAORC Fellowships: $23,800 maximum; ACOR-CAORC Postdoctoral Fellowships: $32,400 maximum; Pierre and Patricia Bikai Fellowship: $600 monthly stipend plus room and board at ACOR; Bert and Sally de Vries Fellowship and Groot Fellowships: $1,500; Lawrence T. Geraty Scholarship and James A. Sauer Fellowship: $1,250; Harrell Family Fellowship: $2,000; MacDonald/Sampson Fellowship: $400 stipend, plus room and board at ACOR, or travel grant of $2,000 to help with any project-related expenses; National Endowment for the Humanities (NEH) Fellowship: $50,000 maximum; Kenneth W. Russell Fellowship: $1,800.

Total amount of support: Varies.

CO-OP FUNDING PROGRAMS: With various organizations and foundations, such as the NEH.

NO. MOST RECENT APPLICANTS: 88 for all fellowships.

NO. AWARDS: ACOR-CAORC Fellowships and ACOR-CAORC Postdoctoral Fellowships: 2 or more each; Bikai Fellowship: 1 to 2; Bert and Sally de Vries, Harrell Family, MacDonald/Sampson, NEH and Sauer Fellowships: 1 each; Groot Fellowships: Up to 4.

APPLICATION INFO:
Prospective applicants are encouraged to consult with the ACOR Administrative Director about application procedures, the competitiveness of their applications, or any other questions they might have about the awards program.

Online application portal can be found at orcfellowships.fluidreview.com.

All eligible persons are encouraged to apply for as many awards as they wish, but each awardee can hold only one ACOR award at a time. Persons who have received an award in one year can reapply for the same or other awards the following year, but new applicants will be given priority.

Duration: ACOR-CAORC Fellowships/Postdoctoral Fellowships: Two to six months; Bikai Fellowship: One to two months; National Endowment for the Humanities (NEH) Fellowship: Four to 10 months; Sauer Fellowship: One month.

Deadline: February 1.

PUBLICATIONS:
Program announcements.

IRS I.D.: 23-7084091

ADDRESS INQUIRIES TO:
ACOR Fellowship Committee
(See address above.)

AMERICAN FRIENDS OF THE ALEXANDER VON HUMBOLDT FOUNDATION   [797]
1401 K Street
Suite 1005
Washington, DC 20005
(202) 783-1907
E-mail: info@americanfriendsofavh.org
Web Site: www.americanfriendsofavh.org

FOUNDED: 1953

AREAS OF INTEREST:
Intercultural exchange.

NAME(S) OF PROGRAMS:
● **German Chancellor Fellowship**

TYPE:
Exchange programs; Fellowships; Project/program grants. Fellowship for one-year stay in Germany for professional development, study or research. Applicants design individual projects specific to Germany and decide at which institutions to pursue them.

YEAR PROGRAM STARTED: 1990

PURPOSE:
To strengthen ties between Germany and the U.S. through fellowship recipient's profession or studies.

ELIGIBILITY:
Intended for career-oriented individuals from any profession or field of study who show outstanding potential for U.S. leadership. Selected fellows represent the private, public, not-for-profit, cultural and academic sectors. Applicant must be from (and current national of) the U.S., Russia, China or Brazil.

FINANCIAL DATA:
Stipend covers housing and living expenses. In addition, the Fellowship also covers travel expenses to and from Germany and the costs of a German language course, introductory seminar, study tour, and final meeting in Bonn.

Amount of support per award: Monthly stipend of EUR 2,150 to EUR 2,750, based on qualifications.

Total amount of support: Varies.

NO. MOST RECENT APPLICANTS: 37 (from U.S.).

NO. AWARDS: 10 annually (from U.S.).

APPLICATION INFO:
Applications must be submitted to the Foundation's Bonn, Germany office.

Duration: One year.

Deadline: September 15. Fellowship period begins the following year on September 1.

STAFF:
Brian Craft, Alumni Relations and Annual Fund Program Coordinator
Alexis Brouwer-Ancher, Communications and Events Program Coordinator

ADDRESS INQUIRIES TO:
Program Coordinator
(See address above.)

*SPECIAL STIPULATIONS:
Prior to submitting an application, applicants are expected to have established contact with a mentor in Germany who agrees to provide professional and/or scholarly assistance throughout the program year.

AMERICAN FRIENDS OF THE ALEXANDER VON HUMBOLDT FOUNDATION [798]

1401 K Street
Suite 1005
Washington, DC 20005
(202) 783-1907
E-mail: info@americanfriendsofavh.org
Web Site: www.americanfriendsofavh.org

FOUNDED: 1953

AREAS OF INTEREST:
Postgraduate research in Germany.

NAME(S) OF PROGRAMS:
- **Humboldt Research Fellowship for Experienced Researchers**

TYPE:
Fellowships; Project/program grants; Research grants. This program allows a researcher to carry out a long-term research project (six to 18 months) at a research institution in Germany which the applicant has selected in cooperation with an academic host.

PURPOSE:
To support highly qualified scholars and scientists of all nationalities and disciplines so that they may carry out a long-term research project.

ELIGIBILITY:
Open to scientists and scholars from outside Germany, with above-average qualifications, who:
(1) have completed their Doctorate less than 12 years ago;
(2) already have his or her own research profile and;
(3) are working at least at the level of Assistant Professor or Junior Research Group Leader or have a record of several years of independent academic work.

Fellowships are awarded on the basis of academic achievement, the quality and feasibility of the proposed research and the candidate's publications.

FINANCIAL DATA:
In addition to a monthly stipend, special allowances are available for accompanying family members, travel expenses, and German language instruction.
Amount of support per award: EUR 3,150 monthly stipend.
Total amount of support: Varies.

NO. MOST RECENT APPLICANTS: Approximately 1,800.

NO. AWARDS: Approximately 600.

APPLICATION INFO:
Application documents can be downloaded from www.humboldt-foundation.de.
Duration: Six to 18 months. Fellowships may be divided into a maximum of three visits of at least three months each.
Deadline: Applications may be submitted at any time to the Humboldt Foundation in Bonn, Germany. The review process takes four to seven months, and the selection committee meets three times a year to review applications.

STAFF:
Brian Craft, Alumni Relations and Annual Fund Program Coordinator
Alexis Brouwer-Ancher, Communications and Events Program Coordinator

ADDRESS INQUIRIES TO:
Program Coordination
(See address above.) or

Alexander von Humboldt Stiftung
Jean-Paul-Strasse 12
D-53173 Bonn
Germany
Tel: 49 (0228) 833-0
Fax: 49 (0228) 833-199
E-mail: info@avh.de

*SPECIAL STIPULATIONS:
Applicant must have received Ph.D. within 12 years.

AMERICAN INSTITUTE FOR SRI LANKAN STUDIES (AISLS) [799]

155 Pine Street
Belmont, MA 02478
E-mail: us.director.aisls@gmail.com
Web Site: www.aisls.org

FOUNDED: 1996

AREAS OF INTEREST:
The promotion of scholarly excellence in Sri Lankan studies.

NAME(S) OF PROGRAMS:
- **AISLS Fellowship Program**

TYPE:
Fellowships. Program supports research in Sri Lanka by U.S. citizens who already hold a Ph.D. or the equivalent at the time they begin their fellowship tenure.

PURPOSE:
To foster excellence in American research and teaching on Sri Lanka; to promote the exchange of scholars and scholarly information between the U.S. and Sri Lanka.

ELIGIBILITY:
Applicants must hold U.S. citizenship and a Ph.D. or equivalent academic degree, or show that they will hold such a degree before taking up the fellowship. Scholars at all ranks are eligible. Applicants must plan to spend at least two months in Sri Lanka and complete the fellowship within the time frame listed under eligibility guidelines. Projects in all fields in the social sciences and humanities are eligible.

FINANCIAL DATA:
Fellowship includes reimbursement up to $2,000 for round-trip airfare between the U.S. and Colombo via U.S. carriers, and a limited budget for research expenses, to be negotiated.
Amount of support per award: Per diem of $3,700 per month.

APPLICATION INFO:
The completed application should contain the following items:
(1) AISLS Fellowship Application Cover Sheet;
(2) curriculum vitae, not to exceed three pages;
(3) description of the proposed study, not to exceed three single-spaced pages. This is the most important part of the application. It should cover the questions to be addressed by the project, the approach to be taken, work done to date, work to be accomplished during the fellowship period, the applicant's competence to carry out the project, how the project addresses the criteria of the competition, and a statement of other support received or being sought for the project and;
(4) one-page bibliography, including a selected list of publications by other scholars or primary sources that have been or will be used in the project.

Completed application must be sent directly to John Rogers at the e-mail address listed above.
Duration: Two to six months.
Deadline: December 1.

ADDRESS INQUIRIES TO:
John Rogers, U.S. Director
(See e-mail address above.)

*PLEASE NOTE:
AISLS requires all communication through e-mail.

AMERICAN INSTITUTE FOR SRI LANKAN STUDIES (AISLS) [800]

155 Pine Street
Belmont, MA 02478
E-mail: us.director.aisls@gmail.com
Web Site: www.aisls.org

FOUNDED: 1996

AREAS OF INTEREST:
The promotion of scholarly excellence in Sri Lankan studies.

NAME(S) OF PROGRAMS:
- **AISLS Dissertation Planning Grant**

TYPE:
Research grants. Grant to assist graduate students intending to do dissertation research in Sri Lanka.

YEAR PROGRAM STARTED: 2006

PURPOSE:
To enable graduate students to make a pre-dissertation visit to Sri Lanka to investigate the feasibility of their topic, to sharpen their research design, or to make other practical arrangements for future research.

ELIGIBILITY:
Applicants must be enrolled in a Ph.D. program (or equivalent) in a U.S. university, or be a U.S. citizen enrolled in a Ph.D. program in any other country. Applicants should have completed most of their graduate coursework by the time they take up their grant. The grant is especially intended for students who are in the process of completing their dissertation proposals and preparing applications for funds to support their dissertation research, but other purposes may be proposed. Applicants should plan to spend at least six weeks in Sri Lanka.

FINANCIAL DATA:
Grant includes reimbursement up to $2,000 for round-trip airfare between U.S. and Colombo, reimbursement for any visa fees paid to the Sri Lankan government, and a per diem for six to eight weeks.
Amount of support per award: Per diem of $560 per week.

APPLICATION INFO:
The completed application should contain the following items:
(1) AISLS Dissertation Planning Grant Application Cover Sheet;
(2) curriculum vitae, not to exceed two pages, which should include the name and e-mail address of the applicant's dissertation supervisor;
(3) copy of the applicant's graduate transcript. An unofficial copy is acceptable;
(4) project narrative, not to exceed two single-spaced pages. This is the most important part of the application and should contain a summary of the proposed dissertation project, or, if the purpose of the

planning grant is to define a dissertation project, a summary of the more general questions the applicant hopes to address in his or her dissertation, a description of what the applicant intends to do during the grant period, and the applicant's competence to carry out his or her proposed project, including language training;
(5) one-page project bibliography, including a selected list of publications by other scholars or primary sources that have been or will be used in the project and;
(6) a confidential letter of recommendation from the applicant's dissertation supervisor. This letter should cover the applicant's academic record and be specific about the applicant's progress to date within the graduate program concerned.

Letter of recommendation and completed application must be sent directly to John Rogers at the e-mail address listed above.

Duration: Six to eight weeks.

Deadline: December 1. Early submission is encouraged.

ADDRESS INQUIRIES TO:
John Rogers, U.S. Director
(See e-mail address above.)

*PLEASE NOTE:
AISLS requires all communication through e-mail.

AMERICAN INSTITUTE OF BANGLADESH STUDIES   [801]
Berkley Center for Religion, Peace and World Affairs
3307 M Street, N.W.
Suite 200
Washington, DC 20007
(202) 687-6444
E-mail: sudiptaroy.aibs@gmail.com
Web Site: www.aibs.net

FOUNDED: 1989

AREAS OF INTEREST:
Bangladesh culture and society.

NAME(S) OF PROGRAMS:
● **Junior Fellowship**
● **Pre-Dissertation Fellowships**
● **Seminar and Conference Support**
● **Senior Fellowship**

TYPE:
Awards/prizes; Conferences/seminars; Fellowships; Research grants; Travel grants. Junior Fellowship is for those who are in the ABD phase of their Ph.D. program. Applicants must be prepared to commence field research at the start of the fellowship period.

Pre-Dissertation Fellowships are short-term grants offered to graduate students pursuing studies of Bangladesh or another country outside the U.S. The grant provides a stay of between two and four months in Bangladesh that may be used for language study, resource assessment, or network building to aid the completion of a competitive dissertation proposal.

The Senior Fellowship is for those who have a Ph.D. They may already have research experience in Bangladesh or may be interested in developing a research area on Bangladesh.

YEAR PROGRAM STARTED: 1989

PURPOSE:
To improve the scholarly understanding of Bangladesh culture and society in the U.S. and to promote educational exchange between the U.S. and Bangladesh.

ELIGIBILITY:
Applicants must be U.S. citizens enrolled, employed or affiliated with a U.S. or non-U.S. academic institution. Independent scholars are also welcome to apply.

Pre-Dissertation Fellowship: At the time of application, students must have completed at least one year of graduate study in a recognized Ph.D.-granting institution.

FINANCIAL DATA:
Amount of support per award: Junior Fellowship: $1,150 monthly allowance; Senior Fellowship: $1,400 per month, plus research and dependents' allowances in non-convertible Bangladesh Taka. Round-trip air transportation will be provided via the most direct route and using the Bangladesh carrier whenever possible.
Total amount of support: Varies.

NO. AWARDS: 4 fellowships for the year 2019-20.

APPLICATION INFO:
Application link is available online.
Duration: Junior and Senior Fellowship: Two to 12 months; Pre-Dissertation Fellowship: Two to four months.
Deadline: Varies depending upon program.

ADDRESS INQUIRIES TO:
See e-mail address above.

AMERICAN INSTITUTE OF INDIAN STUDIES
1130 East 59th Street
Chicago, IL 60637
(773) 702-8638
E-mail: aiis@uchicago.edu
Web Site: www.indiastudies.org

TYPE:
Fellowships. Awards for studies in India in an Indian language.

See entry 599 for full listing.

AMERICAN INSTITUTE OF INDIAN STUDIES   [802]
1130 East 59th Street
Chicago, IL 60637
(773) 702-8638
E-mail: aiis@uchicago.edu
Web Site: www.indiastudies.org

FOUNDED: 1961

AREAS OF INTEREST:
Indian studies.

NAME(S) OF PROGRAMS:
● **AIIS Fellowships**

TYPE:
Fellowships; Research grants. Senior (postdoctoral) Research Fellowships are awarded to academic specialists in Indian studies who possess the Ph.D. or equivalent. While in India, each Senior Research Fellow will be formally affiliated with an Indian university.

Fellowships for Senior Scholarly Development are awarded to established scholars who have not previously specialized in Indian studies and to established professionals who have not previously

worked or studied in India. Proposals in this category should have a substantial research or project component and the anticipated results should be clearly defined. While in India, each Fellow will be formally affiliated with an Indian university.

Junior (dissertation) Fellowships are awarded to graduate students from all academic disciplines whose dissertation research requires study in India. Junior Fellows will have formal affiliation with Indian universities and Indian research supervisors.

Senior Performing Arts Fellowships are awarded to accomplished practitioners of the performing arts of India who demonstrate that studying in India will enhance their skills, develop their capabilities to teach or perform in the U.S., enhance American involvement with India's artistic traditions and strengthen their links with peers in India.

YEAR PROGRAM STARTED: 1962

PURPOSE:
To support the advancement of knowledge and understanding of India, its people and culture, primarily through research conducted in India by American scholars.

LEGAL BASIS:
Cooperative, nonprofit organization of 90 American colleges and universities.

ELIGIBILITY:
U.S. citizens are eligible for AIIS grants, as are foreign nationals enrolled or teaching full-time at American colleges or universities. U.S. and Indian government employees are ineligible for AIIS grants. Eligible applicants who are unaffiliated or who are from nonmember institutions are encouraged to apply.

FINANCIAL DATA:
Fellowships include a maintenance allowance and international travel. Fellowships for four months or less have significant travel restrictions. Fellowships for six months or more may include limited dependent coverage if funds are available. Award funds are generally made available in foreign currency only.

NO. AWARDS: Determined by the amount of support received by AIIS.

APPLICATION INFO:
Application forms are available online. All applications must include a $25 processing fee.
Duration: Up to nine months for Senior Research Fellowships, Fellowships for Senior Scholarly Development and Senior Performing Arts Fellowships; Up to 11 months for Junior Fellowships.
Deadline: November 15. Awards are announced the following March. Awards begin as early as that September.

EXECUTIVE STAFF:
Elise Auerbach, Administrator

ADDRESS INQUIRIES TO:
Elise Auerbach, Administrator
(See address above.)

THE AMERICAN JEWISH JOINT DISTRIBUTION COMMITTEE [803]

P.O. Box 4124
New York, NY 10163
(212) 687-6200
E-mail: jdcentwine@jdc.org
miriam.bader@jdc.org
Web Site: www.jdcentwine.org/lead/rigfellow

AREAS OF INTEREST:
International Jewish communal service.

NAME(S) OF PROGRAMS:
● **The Ralph I. Goldman Fellowship**

TYPE:
Fellowships. Premier leadership opportunity awarded to one person annually for young thinkers and doers - writers, artists, policy shapers, business innovators and community builders.

YEAR PROGRAM STARTED: 1987

PURPOSE:
To provide young Jewish leaders with an insider's perspective on JDC's global programs, while also giving them the opportunity to participate in the life of international Jewish communities.

ELIGIBILITY:
Candidates should have the following credentials:
(1) Bachelor's degree or equivalent and proven academic excellence;
(2) professional achievement in the candidate's chosen career;
(3) demonstrated exceptional leadership and communication skills;
(4) strong interest in international Jewish affairs and public service;
(5) knowledge of foreign language(s) is a plus, but not a requirement and;
(6) formal and/or informal Jewish education.

FINANCIAL DATA:
Amount of support per award:
Approximately $50,000 stipend plus international travel expenses.

NO. AWARDS: 1 annually.

APPLICATION INFO:
Candidates should send an e-mail to the address above. Application includes a short personal essay, two letters of recommendation, and a 90-second video.
Duration: One year, beginning in January.

AMERICAN RESEARCH CENTER IN EGYPT, INC. [804]

909 North Washington Street
Suite 320
Alexandria, VA 22314
(703) 721-3479
E-mail: info@arce.org
fellows@arce.org
Web Site: www.arce.org

FOUNDED: 1948

AREAS OF INTEREST:
Research on Egypt and in Egypt on all phases of Egyptian civilization and culture from earliest times to the present.

NAME(S) OF PROGRAMS:
● **Fellowships for Research in Egypt**

TYPE:
Fellowships; Research grants; Travel grants. Fellowships awarded to doctoral students in the all-but-dissertation (ABD) stage as well as to postdoctoral scholars. Topics for research fellowship encompass the humanities, social sciences and art and archaeology and cover periods from ancient times to the present. A limited number of predissertation travel grants are awarded in the same categories as fellowships.

YEAR PROGRAM STARTED: 1974

PURPOSE:
To obtain a fresh and more profound knowledge of Egypt and the Near East through scholarly research; to train American specialists in Near Eastern Studies in academic disciplines which require familiarity with Egypt; to disseminate knowledge of Egypt and thus understanding of the whole Near East and promote American-Egyptian cultural relations.

LEGAL BASIS:
Nonprofit organization.

ELIGIBILITY:
Criteria for selections rest on the Committee's judgment of the applicant's intellectual capacity and maturity, fitness for field work in Egypt, the significance and relevance of the proposed topic and its potential contribution to scholarly research in Egypt. No special consideration is given to applicants from member institutions and candidates need not be members of the ARCE. Awards are open to all qualified candidates without regard to sex, race and religion. All applicants, pre- and postdoctoral, must be U.S. citizens due to funding guidelines. Under certain circumstances, funding is available through the NEH for non-U.S. postdoctoral scholars living in the U.S. for more than three consecutive years to receive funding. Therefore, it is advisable to contact fellows@arce.org for further clarification.

GEOG. RESTRICTIONS: Egypt.

FINANCIAL DATA:
Monthly per diem plus round-trip airfare between the U.S. and Cairo. Fellows may receive stipends only for the period of time during which they are present in Egypt. A small dependent allowance for accompanying family members is available.
Amount of support per award:
ARCE/CAORC: $2,200 to $3,520 monthly per diem; ARCE/NEH: $5,000 per month.
Total amount of support: Varies.

CO-OP FUNDING PROGRAMS: NEH and CAORC/ECA.

NO. AWARDS: ARCE/CAORC: 4 to 6; ARCE/NEH: 1.

APPLICATION INFO:
Electronic submission is preferred. Original letters of recommendation and transcripts, if applicable, may also be scanned and sent electronically.

All applicants must submit three letters of recommendation. Predoctoral applicants must submit a fourth recommendation attesting to their capacity in ancient or modern languages as related to their proposed research.
Duration: ARCE/CAORC: Three to 12 months. ARCE/NEH: Four months.
Deadline: Mid-January.

PUBLICATIONS:
Annual report; application guidelines; journal; bulletin; e-newsletter.

IRS I.D.: 04-2319500

GOVERNING BOARD:
Betsy Bryan, President
David Anderson, Vice President
Paul Stanwick, Treasurer

ADDRESS INQUIRIES TO:
Academic Programs Manager
E-mail: fellows@arce.org

AMERICAN RESEARCH INSTITUTE IN TURKEY, INC. [805]

c/o The University of Pennsylvania Museum
3260 South Street
Philadelphia, PA 19104-6324
(215) 898-3474
Fax: (215) 898-0657
E-mail: leinwand@sas.upenn.edu
Web Site: ccat.sas.upenn.edu/ARIT/index.html

FOUNDED: 1964

AREAS OF INTEREST:
Research and study in Turkey, including all fields of the humanities and social sciences.

NAME(S) OF PROGRAMS:
● **ARIT Fellowship Program**

TYPE:
Fellowships. ARIT offers a number of fellowships for research in Turkey in humanities and social sciences. Grants for tenures of up to one academic year will be considered; some preference is given to projects of shorter duration. ARIT operates hostel, research and study facilities for researchers in Turkey at its branch centers in Istanbul and Ankara.

YEAR PROGRAM STARTED: 1964

PURPOSE:
To support research in humanities and social sciences in Turkey.

LEGAL BASIS:
Funded in part by grants from U.S. Department of State, Bureau of Educational and Cultural Affairs.

ELIGIBILITY:
Scholars and advanced graduate students engaged in research on ancient, medieval or modern times in Turkey, in any field of the humanities and social sciences, are eligible. Student applicants must have fulfilled all preliminary requirements for the Doctorate except the dissertation by June of the program year, and before beginning any ARIT-sponsored research. Non-U.S. applicants who currently reside in the U.S. or Canada are expected to maintain an affiliation with an educational institution in the U.S. or Canada. For questions of eligibility and procedures, please check with the ARIT office in Philadelphia.

FINANCIAL DATA:
Awards cover international travel to and from Turkey and provide a stipend based on Turkish living standards and the fellow's academic status.
Amount of support per award: Generally $2,500 to $15,500.
Total amount of support: Varies.

CO-OP FUNDING PROGRAMS: The Fellowship program is supported in part by a grant from the U.S. Department of State, Bureau of Educational and Cultural Affairs.

NO. AWARDS: 4 for the year 2019-20.

APPLICATION INFO:
Turkish law requires foreign scholars to obtain formal permission for any research to be carried out at institutions in Turkey. ARIT fellowship applicants are responsible for

obtaining the appropriate research permissions and visas. In general, researchers should seek permission to carry out research directly from the director(s) of the institution(s) where they intend to work; this includes researchers who wish to work in libraries housed in Turkish museums. For archival and library research with tenures of less than three months, some foreign scholars may enter Turkey on a tourist visa and apply for the research permit and visa from within Turkey, or scholars may choose to procure a research visa from the Turkish embassy in advance of their arrival. Scholars wishing to carry out research in Turkey for terms longer than three months should apply for the research permit and in addition secure a research visa prior to entering Turkey. Non-U.S. researchers should consult the Turkish Consulate for specific procedures.

Researchers who wish to work with collections housed in the Turkish archaeological museums, however, should make their applications through the Ministry of Culture and Tourism, General Directorate for Cultural Heritage and Museums. In addition, if the material they wish to work with is part of an excavation, researchers must submit a letter with their application signed by the excavation director giving permission to carry out the research. The research permit application regulations and format for researchers are posted on the ARIT web site. ARIT reserves the right to withhold payment of fellowship stipends if appropriate research permission is not obtained.

Please include three letters of reference with one's application. Graduate student applicants must provide a copy of their graduate transcript.

Duration: Up to one academic year.

Deadline: November 1.

OFFICERS:
C. Brian Rose, President
Beatrice Manz, Vice President
Brian Peasnall, Treasurer
Nikolay Antov, Secretary

ADDRESS INQUIRIES TO:
Nancy W. Leinwand
(See telephone and e-mail above.)

AMERICAN RESEARCH INSTITUTE IN TURKEY, INC. [806]

c/o The University of Pennsylvania Museum
3260 South Street
Philadelphia, PA 19104-6324
(215) 898-3474
Fax: (215) 898-0657
E-mail: leinwand@sas.upenn.edu
Web Site: ccat.sas.upenn.edu/ARIT/index.html

FOUNDED: 1964

AREAS OF INTEREST:
Turkey.

NAME(S) OF PROGRAMS:
● **Bogazici University Summer Language Program for Intensive Advanced Turkish Language Study**

TYPE:
Fellowships. Bogazici University Summer Language Program: For summer study in Turkey. Also offer travel, stipend and tuition grants. This intensive program offers the

equivalent of one full academic year of study in advanced Turkish language at the college level.

YEAR PROGRAM STARTED: 1981

PURPOSE:
To support the study of advanced Turkish language.

LEGAL BASIS:
Consortium of universities. Funding from the U.S. Department of Education.

ELIGIBILITY:
Full-time students and scholars affiliated at academic institutions are eligible to apply. To be a fellowship applicant, one must:
(1) be a citizen, national or permanent resident of the U.S.;
(2) be enrolled in an undergraduate- or graduate-level academic program, or be faculty;
(3) have a minimum B average in one's studies, if still a student and;
(4) perform at the high-intermediate level on a proficiency-based admissions examination.

FINANCIAL DATA:
Fellowships cover round-trip airfare to Istanbul, application and tuition fees, and a maintenance stipend.

CO-OP FUNDING PROGRAMS: Funded by U.S. Department of Education, Office of Post-Secondary Education.

NO. MOST RECENT APPLICANTS: Approximately 40.

NO. AWARDS: Approximately 18 for the year 2021.

APPLICATION INFO:
Application information is available on the web site.
Duration: Approximately eight weeks (late June through early August).
Deadline: Early February.

OFFICERS:
C. Brian Rose, President
Beatrice Manz, Vice President
Brian Peasnall, Treasurer
Nikolay Antov, Secretary

ADDRESS INQUIRIES TO:
Dr. Sylvia Onder
Eastern Mediterranean Languages
Department of Arabic and Islamic Studies
Georgetown University
210 North Poulton Hall
1437 37th Street, N.W.
Washington, DC 20007
E-mail: aritfellowship@georgetown.edu or

Nancy Leinwand
American Research Institute in Turkey
(See address and e-mail above.)

AMERICAN RESEARCH INSTITUTE IN TURKEY, INC. [807]

c/o The University of Pennsylvania Museum
3260 South Street
Philadelphia, PA 19104-6324
(215) 898-3474
Fax: (215) 898-0657
E-mail: leinwand@sas.upenn.edu
Web Site: ccat.sas.upenn.edu/ARIT/index.html

FOUNDED: 1964

AREAS OF INTEREST:
Turkey covering all periods of history in the general range of the humanities and including humanistically oriented aspects of the social

sciences, prehistory, history, art, archaeology, literature and linguistics, as well as interdisciplinary aspects of cultural history.

NAME(S) OF PROGRAMS:
● **NEH Fellowships for Research in Turkey**

TYPE:
Fellowships. These advanced fellowships are made possible by support from the National Endowment for the Humanities. The fields of study cover all periods of history in the general range of the humanities and include humanistically oriented aspects of the social sciences, prehistory, history, art, archaeology, literature and linguistics, as well as interdisciplinary aspects of cultural history.

ARIT maintains two research institutes in Turkey. ARIT in Istanbul has a research library concentrated on Byzantine and Ottoman Turkey. The ARIT Ankara center focuses on art, archaeology, and ancient history in its library, and serves Turkish and American archaeologists through its programs. Both institutes have residential facilities for fellows and provide general assistance as well as introductions to colleagues, institutions and authorities in Turkey.

YEAR PROGRAM STARTED: 1991

PURPOSE:
To support long-term postdoctoral research in Turkey in the humanities.

LEGAL BASIS:
Consortium of universities. Funding from the National Endowment for the Humanities.

ELIGIBILITY:
Scholars who have completed their formal academic training by the application deadline and plan to carry out research in Turkey may apply. Applicants may be U.S. citizens or three-year residents of the U.S. Please consult ARIT headquarters on questions of eligibility. Advanced scholars may also apply for ARIT Fellowships in the Humanities and Social Sciences.

FINANCIAL DATA:
Amount of support per award: Stipend of $4,200 per month, awarded on the basis of individual proposals.

NO. MOST RECENT APPLICANTS: 12.

NO. AWARDS: 1 to 3 advanced fellowships for the 2020-21 academic year.

APPLICATION INFO:
In order to be considered, applicants must provide complete application information. Application materials and three letters of recommendation must be submitted by e-mail to aritoffice@gmail.com. Letters of reference can be sent by mail or e-mail. Letters should support the proposed research and applicant's capacity to carry out the project.
Duration: Four to 12 continuous months.
Deadline: November 1 for the following academic year. Applicants will be notified by the end of January of that following year.

PUBLICATIONS:
Program announcement.

OFFICERS:
C. Brian Rose, President
Beatrice Manz, Vice President
Brian Peasnall, Treasurer
Nikolay Antov, Secretary

ADDRESS INQUIRIES TO:
Nancy W. Leinwand
(See telephone number above.)

THE AMERICAN-SCANDINAVIAN FOUNDATION   [808]

58 Park Avenue
New York, NY 10016
(212) 779-3587
(615) 881-1532
Fax: (212) 686-1157
E-mail: grants@amscan.org
Web Site: www.amscan.org

FOUNDED: 1910

AREAS OF INTEREST:
   Advanced study in Scandinavia.

NAME(S) OF PROGRAMS:
   • **ASF Awards for Study in Scandinavia**

TYPE:
   Fellowships; Research grants. Short-term
   project grants and long-term fellowships for
   advanced study in a field which may be
   pursued with particular merit in one of the
   Scandinavian countries (Denmark, Finland,
   Iceland, Norway or Sweden).

   Fellowships are intended to support an
   academic year-long stay. Priority is given to
   candidates at the graduate level for
   dissertation-related study or research.

   Grants are considered especially suitable for
   postgraduate scholars, professionals and
   candidates in the arts to carry out research or
   study visits of one to three months' duration.

YEAR PROGRAM STARTED: 1911

PURPOSE:
   To advance cultural and intellectual
   understanding between the U.S. and
   Scandinavia, primarily through exchange
   programs, cultural programs and publications.

LEGAL BASIS:
   Nonprofit educational institution qualifying
   under statutes 501(c)(3), 509(a)(1) and
   170(c)(2) of the IRS code.

ELIGIBILITY:
   Applicants must have a well-defined research
   or study project that makes a stay in
   Scandinavia essential. Applicants must be
   U.S. citizens or permanent residents who will
   have completed their undergraduate education
   by the start of their project in Scandinavia.
   Team projects are eligible, but each member
   must apply as an individual, submitting a
   separate, fully documented application. First
   priority will be given to applicants who have
   not previously received an ASF award. Only
   in exceptional cases will a third award be
   considered. The ASF considers it desirable
   that all candidates have at least some ability
   in the language of the host country, even if it
   is not essential for the execution of the
   research plan. For projects that require a
   command of one or more Scandinavian (or
   other) languages, candidates should defer
   application until they have the necessary
   proficiency. Evidence of a confirmed
   invitation or affiliation is an important factor
   in award consideration.

   ASF does not fund the following:
   (1) travel for attendance at professional
   meetings, conferences, seminars or
   conventions;
   (2) performances or exhibitions;
   (3) publication costs;
   (4) equipment purchases, including personal
   computers, software and cell phones;
   (5) research assistants;
   (6) institutional overhead costs;
   (7) tuition fees from U.S. home institution;
   (8) foregone salary;

(9) supplementation of substantial sabbatical
support;
(10) support for dependents;
(11) personal obligations, including
repayment of loans and mortgages;
(12) acquisition of language skills;
(13) study in programs especially designed
for English-speaking students, or at
English-language institutions;
(14) beginning studies in any subject or;
(15) retroactive program support.

   Projects must be undertaken in Denmark,
   Finland, Iceland, Norway or Sweden.

FINANCIAL DATA:
   The awards support project-related costs,
   including maintenance, transatlantic
   round-trip travel, in-country travel, tuition
   and fees (where applicable) and materials
   expenditures (e.g., books, photocopying, art
   supplies).

   Amount of support per award: Grants
   normally up to $5,000, especially suited for
   short visits of one to three months and
   fellowships of up to $23,000, intended for a
   full academic year of study or research.

   Total amount of support: Over $400,000 for
   the 2018-19 competition.

NO. MOST RECENT APPLICANTS: 84.

NO. AWARDS: Varies each year according to
   total funds available. Awards were made to
   26 Americans in the 2018-19 competition.

APPLICATION INFO:
   Only applications on current official ASF
   forms will be considered. Such applications
   are available online. Incomplete applications
   cannot be processed. Unsuccessful
   applications will be discarded.

   Applicants for Awards for Study in
   Scandinavia are urged to arrange their
   academic or professional affiliations as far in
   advance as possible. Applicants must secure
   these placements or affiliations on their own;
   the ASF cannot assist in establishing
   contacts. The ASF requires confirmation of
   invitation or affiliation from the institution or
   individuals detailed in the proposal. Since
   July and August are traditionally holiday
   months in Scandinavia, many people may not
   be available for consultation. Applicants are
   cautioned to plan their projects accordingly.
   Applicants are expected to devote full-time to
   their proposed study or research, and must
   justify the length of time needed to complete
   their project. Awards are based on the
   application submitted; subsequent changes in
   the proposal are discouraged and may not be
   considered.

   Duration: Grants: One to three months.
   Fellowships: One academic year.

   Deadline: November 1 for receipt of fully
   documented applications. Awards announced
   by the following April 15.

PUBLICATIONS:
   Annual report; fellowship and grant
   application guidelines; *Scandinavian Review*;
   Scan, newsletter; *Study in Scandinavia*,
   guide.

ADMINISTRATION:
   Edward P. Gallagher, President
   Lynn Carter, Secretary to the Board

ADDRESS INQUIRIES TO:
   Fellowships and Grants
   (See address above.)

*SPECIAL STIPULATIONS:
   ASF awards may require supplementation
   from other sources, but they should not

duplicate the benefits of additional awards
(and vice versa). Candidates must notify the
ASF if they have received other award offers.
The ASF will not provide funds if, in its
judgment, a proposal can be carried out
without its assistance.

AMERICAN SCHOOL OF CLASSICAL STUDIES AT ATHENS   [809]

6-8 Charlton Street
Princeton, NJ 08540-5232
(609) 683-0800
Fax: (609) 924-0578
E-mail: application@ascsa.org
Web Site: www.ascsa.edu.gr

FOUNDED: 1881

AREAS OF INTEREST:
   Classical studies.

NAME(S) OF PROGRAMS:
   • **National Endowment for the
     Humanities Fellowships**

TYPE:
   Fellowships. Fellowships for postdoctoral
   scholars and professionals in the humanities.

LEGAL BASIS:
   Graduate research and teaching center.

ELIGIBILITY:
   Postdoctoral scholars and professionals in
   relevant fields including architecture and art
   history who are U.S. citizens or foreign
   nationals who have lived in the U.S. for the
   three years immediately preceding the
   application deadline may apply. Applicants
   must already hold their Ph.D. or have
   completed all requirements, except for the
   actual conferral of the degree, by the
   application deadline.

FINANCIAL DATA:
   School fees are waived and the award
   provides lunches at Loring Hall five days per
   week. The NEH fellow will pay for travel
   costs, housing, residence permit, and other
   living expenses from the stipend.

   Amount of support per award: Stipend of
   $4,200 per month.

   Total amount of support: $75,600 annually.

NO. MOST RECENT APPLICANTS: 31.

NO. AWARDS: 2 to 4.

APPLICATION INFO:
   Correspondence about fellowships and
   admission to membership in the school
   should be directed to the address above.
   Applicants must submit an online application
   form, a short abstract of the project, a
   statement of the project (up to five pages),
   curriculum vitae, and the names of three
   recommenders who will write letters of
   reference.

   Applicants should indicate their preference
   for the length and dates of tenure of the
   award to coincide with the American
   School's academic year: September to June
   for a nine-month fellowship, January to June
   for a five-month fellowship, or September to
   December for a four-month fellowship.

   Duration: Four, five or nine months.

   Deadline: October 31.

STAFF:
   Jenifer Neils, Director

ADDRESS INQUIRIES TO:
   See e-mail address above.

AMERICAN SCHOOL OF CLASSICAL STUDIES AT ATHENS [810]

6-8 Charlton Street
Princeton, NJ 08540-5232
(609) 683-0800
Fax: (609) 924-0578
E-mail: application@ascsa.org
Web Site: www.ascsa.edu.gr

FOUNDED: 1881

AREAS OF INTEREST:
Late Antique through Modern Greek Studies, including but not limited to the Byzantine, Frankish, Post-Byzantine, and Ottoman periods.

NAME(S) OF PROGRAMS:
- **M. Alison Frantz Fellowship in Post-Classical Studies at the Gennadius Library**

TYPE:
Fellowships. The M. Alison Frantz Fellowship is part of the Student Associate Program, which is open to advanced graduate students in the same fields as the Regular Academic Program (classical studies and ancient Mediterranean studies and related fields such as history of art, anthropology, prehistory, studies in postclassical Greece, etc.), who plan to pursue independent research projects and who do not wish to commit to the full Regular Academic Program.

YEAR PROGRAM STARTED: 1963

PURPOSE:
To provide financial assistance to advanced graduate students who plan to pursue independent research projects but do not wish to commit to the American School's full Regular Academic Program.

LEGAL BASIS:
Graduate educational institution (non-degree granting).

ELIGIBILITY:
Ph.D. candidates and recent Ph.Ds. (up to five years) from a U.S. or Canadian institution may apply. Candidates should demonstrate their need to work in the Gennadius Library.

FINANCIAL DATA:
Amount of support per award: Stipend of $11,500, plus room, board and waiver of School fees.

NO. AWARDS: 1.

APPLICATION INFO:
Application must be made online on the ASCSA web site. Applicants must submit the Fellowship Application Form, a curriculum vitae, a description of the proposed project (up to 750 words), and three letters of reference online. Students must submit transcripts.
Duration: One academic year (September to June).
Deadline: January 15.

STAFF:
Jenifer Neils, Director

ADDRESS INQUIRIES TO:
Chair, Committee on Libraries and Archives
(See address above.)

*SPECIAL STIPULATIONS:
Fellows are expected to be in residence at the School for the full academic year. A final report is due at the end of the award period,

and the ASCSA expects that copies of all publications that result from research conducted as a Fellow of the ASCSA be contributed to the Gennadius Library.

AMERICAN SCHOOL OF CLASSICAL STUDIES AT ATHENS [811]

6-8 Charlton Street
Princeton, NJ 08540-5232
(609) 683-0800
Fax: (609) 924-0578
E-mail: application@ascsa.org
Web Site: www.ascsa.edu.gr

FOUNDED: 1881

AREAS OF INTEREST:
Classical studies, history of art, history of architecture, pottery, Mycenaean archaeology, Athenian architecture and archaeology.

NAME(S) OF PROGRAMS:
- **Advanced Fellowships**

TYPE:
Fellowships. Several Fellowships awarded by the School for the full academic year: the Samuel H. Kress Fellowship in art and architecture of antiquity, the Gorham Phillips Stevens Fellowship in the history of architecture; the Ione Mylonas Shear Fellowship in Mycenaean archaeology or Athenian architecture and/or archaeology; the Homer A. and Dorothy B. Thompson Fellowship in the study of pottery. Additionally, three Fellowships are unrestricted as to field: the Edward Capps, the Doreen Canaday Spitzer, and the Eugene Vanderpool Fellowships.

PURPOSE:
To support work on a specific project by students who wish to study at the School for a year.

ELIGIBILITY:
Students who have completed the Regular Program or one year as a Student Associate Member at the ASCSA and plan to return to the School to pursue independent research, usually for the Ph.D. dissertation, may apply. Given only if candidates meet a standard acceptable to the Director and the Committee.

School programs are generally open to qualified students and scholars at colleges or universities in the U.S. or Canada; restrictions may apply for specific fellowships and programs. The American School of Classical Studies at Athens does not discriminate on the basis of race, age, sex, sexual orientation, color, religion, ethnic origin, or disability when considering admission to any form of membership.

GEOG. RESTRICTIONS: United States and Canada.

FINANCIAL DATA:
Stipend, plus room, board and waiver of fees.
Amount of support per award: Kress Fellowship: Stipend of $15,000; All others: Stipend of $11,500.

NO. MOST RECENT APPLICANTS: 9.

NO. AWARDS: 7.

APPLICATION INFO:
Submit application form, curriculum vitae, transcripts, letters of recommendation and a detailed statement of the project to be pursued in Greece. Application must be made online on the ASCSA web site.

Duration: One year.
Deadline: February 15.

STAFF:
Jenifer Neils, Director

ADDRESS INQUIRIES TO:
See e-mail address above.

*SPECIAL STIPULATIONS:
Membership application to the ASCSA must be made online on the web site at the same time one applies to any outside funding organization for work at the School.

AMERICAN SCHOOL OF CLASSICAL STUDIES AT ATHENS [812]

6-8 Charlton Street
Princeton, NJ 08540-5232
(609) 683-0800
Fax: (609) 924-0578
E-mail: application@ascsa.org
Web Site: www.ascsa.edu.gr

FOUNDED: 1881

AREAS OF INTEREST:
Ancient Greek law.

NAME(S) OF PROGRAMS:
- **The Harry Bikakis Fellowship**

TYPE:
Fellowships. Research fellowship awarded periodically, but not more frequently than once a year.

PURPOSE:
To promote research.

ELIGIBILITY:
North American or Greek graduate students researching ancient Greek law, or Greek graduate students working on a School excavation.

School programs are generally open to qualified students and scholars at colleges or universities in the U.S. or Canada; restrictions may apply for specific fellowships and programs. The American School of Classical Studies at Athens does not discriminate on the basis of race, age, sex, sexual orientation, color, religion, ethnic origin, or disability when considering admission to any form of membership.

FINANCIAL DATA:
Amount of support per award: Stipend of $1,875. School fees are waived.

NO. MOST RECENT APPLICANTS: 1.

NO. AWARDS: 1.

APPLICATION INFO:
Submit Associate Member application, including an outline of the proposed project, and two letters of reference online on the ASCSA web site.
Deadline: January 15.

STAFF:
Jenifer Neils, Director

ADDRESS INQUIRIES TO:
See e-mail address above.

*SPECIAL STIPULATIONS:
Membership application to the ASCSA must be made online on the web site at the same time one applies to any outside funding organization for work at the School.

AMERICAN SCHOOL OF CLASSICAL STUDIES AT ATHENS   [813]

6-8 Charlton Street
Princeton, NJ 08540-5232
(609) 683-0800
Fax: (609) 924-0578
E-mail: application@ascsa.org
Web Site: www.ascsa.edu.gr

FOUNDED: 1881

AREAS OF INTEREST:
Gennadeion collections.

NAME(S) OF PROGRAMS:
- **Cotsen Traveling Fellowship for Research in Greece**

TYPE:
Fellowships. Short-term grant.

PURPOSE:
To assist students and scholars in the pursuit of research topics requiring the use of Gennadeion collections.

ELIGIBILITY:
Senior scholars and graduate students for projects and research at the Gennadius Library. Requires residency in Athens of at least one month during the academic year from September 1 to June 1. The recipient is expected to take part in the activities of the Library and of the School in addition to pursuing research.

School programs are generally open to qualified students and scholars at colleges or universities in the U.S. or Canada; restrictions may apply for specific fellowships and programs. The American School of Classical Studies at Athens does not discriminate on the basis of race, age, sex, sexual orientation, color, religion, ethnic origin, or disability when considering admission to any form of membership.

FINANCIAL DATA:
Fellowship does not include costs for School trips, housing or board.
Amount of support per award: Stipend of $2,000. School fees are waived for a maximum of two months.

NO. MOST RECENT APPLICANTS: 10.

NO. AWARDS: 1.

APPLICATION INFO:
Application must be made online and should include the following:
(1) curriculum vitae;
(2) letter (up to 750 words) describing the project, proposed dates, budget, and explanation of the relation of the Gennadius Library's collection to the research project and;
(3) two letters of recommendation.
Duration: Minimum one month.
Deadline: January 15.

STAFF:
Dr. Maria Georgopoulou, Director, Gennadius Library

ADDRESS INQUIRIES TO:
Director, Gennadius Library
(See address above.)

*SPECIAL STIPULATIONS:
Membership application to the ASCSA must be made online on the web site at the same time one applies to any outside funding organization for work at the School.

AMERICAN SCHOOL OF CLASSICAL STUDIES AT ATHENS   [814]

6-8 Charlton Street
Princeton, NJ 08540-5232
(609) 683-0800
Fax: (609) 924-0578
E-mail: ascsa@ascsa.org (for information)
application@ascsa.org (to apply)
Web Site: www.ascsa.edu.gr

FOUNDED: 1881

AREAS OF INTEREST:
Skeletal, faunal, geoarchaeological, environmental studies and archaeological science.

NAME(S) OF PROGRAMS:
- **Wiener Laboratory Post-Doctoral Fellowship**
- **Wiener Laboratory Pre-Doctoral Fellowship**
- **Wiener Laboratory Programmatic Post-Doctoral Fellowship**
- **Wiener Laboratory Research Associateships**

TYPE:
Fellowships; Research grants. The Malcolm H. Wiener Laboratory for Archaeological Science at ASCSA provides funding for scholars pursuing interdisciplinary research on archaeological questions pertaining to the ancient Greek world and adjacent areas. Three different types of funding are offered: Post-Doctoral (three-year term), Pre-Doctoral (two-year term), and Programmatic Post-Doctoral (three-year term). The School also offers shorter-duration, more focused Research Associate positions.

PURPOSE:
To promote laboratory research pertinent to the American School of Classical Studies at Athens.

ELIGIBILITY:
Applicants are welcome from any college or university worldwide. The American School of Classical Studies at Athens does not discriminate on the basis of race, age, sex, sexual orientation, color, religion, ethnic origin, or disability when considering admission to any form of membership or application for employment.

Post-Doctoral Fellowship: Eligibility limited to individuals who have received their Ph.D. within the last seven years.

Pre-Doctoral Fellowship: Eligibility limited to individuals actively enrolled in a graduate program who have passed all qualifying exams and have an approved Ph.D. proposal.

Programmatic Post-Doctoral Research Fellowship: Eligibility limited to individuals who received their Ph.Ds. and are applying to work on material related to an ASCSA archaeological project.

Research Associateships: Eligibility limited to individuals actively enrolled in a graduate program and individuals with a higher-level degree in a relevant discipline.

FINANCIAL DATA:
Amount of support per award: Post-Doctoral and Programmatic Post-Doctoral Fellowship: Stipend of $35,000 per year; Pre-Doctoral Fellowship: Stipend up to $20,000 per year; Research Associateships: Stipend variable up to $7,000.

NO. AWARDS: Varies.

APPLICATION INFO:
Applicants should consult the web site for updated information about the application process. Application must be made online on the ASCSA web site.
Duration: Post-Doctoral and Programmatic Post-Doctoral Fellowship: Three-year term. Pre-Doctoral Fellowship: Two-year term. Research Associateships: Up to nine months.
Deadline: January 15. Announcement by March 15.

ADDRESS INQUIRIES TO:
Dr. Panagiotis Karkanas
Director, Wiener Laboratory
E-mail: TKarkanas@ascsa.edu.gr

*SPECIAL STIPULATIONS:
Membership application to the ASCSA must be made online on the web site at the same time one applies to any outside funding organization for work at the School.

AMERICAN SCHOOL OF CLASSICAL STUDIES AT ATHENS   [815]

6-8 Charlton Street
Princeton, NJ 08540-5232
(609) 683-0800
Fax: (609) 924-0578
E-mail: application@ascsa.org
Web Site: www.ascsa.edu.gr

FOUNDED: 1881

AREAS OF INTEREST:
Research at the ASCSA excavations at Ancient Corinth in Greece.

NAME(S) OF PROGRAMS:
- **Henry S. Robinson Corinth Research Fellowship**

TYPE:
Fellowships. Fellowship for research on a doctoral dissertation or primary publication, specifically on Corinth. Program is offered every other year. Robinson Fellowship for 2022-23 to be announced in the fall of 2021.

PURPOSE:
To revive field work at Corinth.

ELIGIBILITY:
Open to established scholars or Ph.D. candidates, for research on a doctoral dissertation or primary publication specifically on Corinth, requiring the use of the resources, archaeological site and collections at the ASCSA excavations at Ancient Corinth in Greece. Open to all nationalities.

FINANCIAL DATA:
The Fellowship does not allow travel costs (to and from country of origin or within Greece). Funding is for research activities at Corinth, to be used to cover living expenses, including room, board, fees and other costs associated with the study, such as photography and drawings. Availability of rooms and work space is limited during the excavation season from April to June.
Amount of support per award: Stipend up to $4,000 for one or more individuals. School fees are waived.

NO. MOST RECENT APPLICANTS: 8.

NO. AWARDS: 1 or more.

APPLICATION INFO:
Submit Associate Membership application online, including curriculum vitae and proposal statement, which should have the

following items:
(1) project outline;
(2) explanation of goals;
(3) statement of the significance of the project;
(4) work completed to date;
(5) schedule for completion;
(6) dates for project;
(7) budget and;
(8) two letters of support, including one from dissertation advisor if applicant is a Ph.D. candidate.

Duration: Up to three months within the 12-month period July 1 to June 30. Nonrenewable.

Deadline: January 15. Announcement mid-March.

*SPECIAL STIPULATIONS:
The Robinson Fellowship may not be held concurrently with another School fellowship. Preference is given to candidates who have not previously held the Robinson Fellowship or received substantial ASCSA funding for the same project.

AMERICAN SCHOOL OF CLASSICAL STUDIES AT ATHENS [816]

6-8 Charlton Street
Princeton, NJ 08540-5232
(609) 683-0800
Fax: (609) 924-0578
E-mail: application@ascsa.org
Web Site: www.ascsa.edu.gr

FOUNDED: 1881

AREAS OF INTEREST:
Archaeology.

NAME(S) OF PROGRAMS:
● **Jacob Hirsch Fellowship**

TYPE:
Fellowships.

PURPOSE:
To provide an opportunity for students who are Ph.D. candidates writing their dissertations in archaeology or recent Ph.Ds. completing a project, such as a revision of a dissertation for publication, who require a lengthy residence in Greece.

LEGAL BASIS:
Graduate educational institution (non-degree granting).

ELIGIBILITY:
Students who hold U.S. or Israeli citizenship, and who are Ph.D. candidates writing their dissertations in archaeology or recent Ph.Ds. completing a project may apply.

FINANCIAL DATA:
Stipend plus room, board, and waiver of School fees.
Amount of support per award: Stipend of $11,500.

NO. AWARDS: 1.

APPLICATION INFO:
Applicant must submit "Associate Membership with Fellowship" application online. The application should include a curriculum vitae, a detailed description of the project to be pursued in Greece (250-word abstract and a statement up to three pages, single-spaced), and three letters of recommendation. Student applicants are required to submit legible PDF scans of academic transcripts as part of the online application.

Duration: One academic year (September to June).
Deadline: January 15.

STAFF:
Jenifer Neils, Director

ADDRESS INQUIRIES TO:
Chair, Committee on Admissions and Fellowships
(See address above.)

*SPECIAL STIPULATIONS:
A final report is due at the end of the award period, and the ASCSA expects that copies of all publications that result from research conducted as a Fellow of the ASCSA be contributed to the relevant library of the School.

AMERICAN SCHOOL OF CLASSICAL STUDIES AT ATHENS [817]

6-8 Charlton Street
Princeton, NJ 08540-5232
(609) 683-0800
Fax: (609) 924-0578
E-mail: application@ascsa.org
Web Site: www.ascsa.edu.gr

FOUNDED: 1881

AREAS OF INTEREST:
Archaeology, classical studies, history, classical literature, art history, and Bronze Age archaeology.

NAME(S) OF PROGRAMS:
● **Regular Member Program Fellowships**

TYPE:
Fellowships. The Heinrich Schliemann and the John Williams White Fellowships in Archaeology are awarded based on the student's performance on the archaeology examination.

The Thomas Day Seymour Fellowship in History and Literature is awarded based on the student's combined performance on the history and literature examination.

Nine fellowships are unrestricted to field. These are the Virginia Grace, the Michael Jameson, the Philip Lockhart, the Lucy Shoe Meritt, the Fowler Merle-Smith, the Martin Ostwald, and the James Rignall Wheeler Fellowships. The Bert Hodge Hill Fellowship is unrestricted, but with a preference for a student in art history. The Emily Townsend Vermeule Fellowship is unrestricted, but with a preference for Bronze Age archaeology.

PURPOSE:
To provide members with full funding and lodging to pursue research.

LEGAL BASIS:
Graduate educational institution (non-degree granting).

ELIGIBILITY:
Open to students at colleges or universities in the U.S. or Canada who have completed a B.A., but not a Ph.D., who are preparing for an advanced degree in classical or ancient Mediterranean studies, or a related field. Although preference is given to those who have completed at least one year of graduate study, well-qualified students who have received a B.A. will be considered for admission and fellowships.

Student must first be accepted into the Regular Member Program.

GEOG. RESTRICTIONS: United States and Canada.

FINANCIAL DATA:
Stipend plus room, board, and waiver of School fees.
Amount of support per award: Stipend of $11,500.

NO. AWARDS: Up to 12.

APPLICATION INFO:
Students will automatically be considered for these fellowships upon the submission of their application and completion of the ASCSA Entrance Exams.
Duration: One academic year (September to June 1).
Deadline: January 15.

AMERICAN SCHOOLS OF ORIENTAL RESEARCH (ASOR) [818]

209 Commerce Street
Alexandria, VA 22314
(703) 789-9229
E-mail: info@asor.org
Web Site: www.asor.org

FOUNDED: 1900

AREAS OF INTEREST:
The study of humanistic disciplines, such as anthropology, archaeology, Biblical studies, epigraphy, history, history of art and architecture, literature, philology, prehistory and topography, relating in particular to the Middle East from prehistoric times to the modern era.

NAME(S) OF PROGRAMS:
● **William G. Dever Fellowship for Biblical Scholars**
● **Foundation for Biblical Archaeology Scholarships**
● **Harris Grants**
● **Heritage Fellowships**
● **P.E. MacAllister Fellowships**
● **Member Supported Fellowships**
● **Mesopotamian Fellowship**
● **Eric and Carol Meyers Fellowships**
● **Shirlee Meyers/G. Ernest Wright Fellowships**
● **Platt Fellowships**
● **Harva L. Sheeler Excavation Fellowships**
● **Strange/Midkiff Families Fellowships**
● **Student Travel Grants**
● **Study of Collections Fellowships**

TYPE:
Conferences/seminars; Fellowships; Scholarships; Travel grants.

YEAR PROGRAM STARTED: 1940

PURPOSE:
To encourage scholars to undertake study and research about the ancient Near East.

LEGAL BASIS:
Nonprofit, archaeological research corporation.

ELIGIBILITY:
The Fellowship is open to qualified students and scholars from any country. Applicants must be or become individual professional members of ASOR, or must be affiliated with an institution that is a member of ASOR.

FINANCIAL DATA:
Amount of support per award: Dever Fellowship: $7,000; Foundation for Biblical Archaeology Scholarships: $700; Harris Grants: $5,000; Heritage, MacAllister, Member-Supported, Meyers, Meyers/Wright,

Platt, Sheeler, Strange/Midkiff and Study of Collections Fellowships: $2,000 each; Mesopotamian Fellowship: $9,000; Student Travel Grants: $250.

Total amount of support: Approximately $63,000.

NO. MOST RECENT APPLICANTS: Varies.

NO. AWARDS: Varies.

APPLICATION INFO:
All eligible persons are encouraged to apply for as many fellowships and professorships as they wish, but a person can hold only one award at a time. Persons who have received an award in one year can reapply for the same or other awards the following year, but new applicants will have priority.

Deadline: Dever, Heritage, MacAllister, Member Supported, Meyers, Meyers/Wright, Platt, Sheeler and Strange/Midkiff Fellowships: February. Foundation for Biblical Archaeology Scholarships and Student Travel Grants: Mid-August. Harris Grants: January. Mesopotamian Fellowships: November 1.

STAFF:
Andrew G. Vaughn, Ph.D., Executive Director

ADDRESS INQUIRIES TO:
Office Coordinator
(See address above.)

*SPECIAL STIPULATIONS:
Applicants must be or become members of ASOR or attend an ASOR-affiliated institution.

THE AMERICAN SWEDISH INSTITUTE   [819]
2600 Park Avenue South
Minneapolis, MN 55407
(612) 871-4907
Fax: (612) 871-8682
E-mail: info@asimn.org
Web Site: asimn.org

FOUNDED: 1929

AREAS OF INTEREST:
Swedish culture.

NAME(S) OF PROGRAMS:
● **Lilly Lorénzen Scholarship**

TYPE:
Scholarships; Travel grants.

YEAR PROGRAM STARTED: 1980

PURPOSE:
To foster and preserve Swedish culture in America.

ELIGIBILITY:
Must be a Minnesota resident with demonstrated achievement in their field of study who plans to study in Sweden, has a working knowledge of the Swedish language and will contribute to American-Swedish exchange.

FINANCIAL DATA:
Amount of support per award: $1,000.
Total amount of support: $1,000.

NO. MOST RECENT APPLICANTS: 10.

NO. AWARDS: 1.

APPLICATION INFO:
Updated information and application are available on the ASI web site.
Duration: One-time award.
Deadline: May 1.

ADDRESS INQUIRIES TO:
Britta Walstron, ASI Programs Manager
E-mail: brittaw@asimn.org

BELGIAN AMERICAN EDUCATIONAL FOUNDATION, INC.   [820]
195 Church Street
New Haven, CT 06510
(203) 785-4055
E-mail: emile.boulpaep@yale.edu
Web Site: www.baef.us
www.baef.be

FOUNDED: 1920

AREAS OF INTEREST:
Educational exchange between the U.S. and Belgium.

NAME(S) OF PROGRAMS:
● **B.A.E.F. Fellowships for Study in Belgium**

TYPE:
Fellowships. Predoctoral and postdoctoral fellowships for advanced study in most fields of knowledge with supported work to be undertaken at a Belgian university or an institution of higher learning. Fellowships for Belgian students are also available.

YEAR PROGRAM STARTED: 1920

PURPOSE:
To allow American candidates to pursue independent study and research in Belgium on projects for which Belgium provides special advantages.

LEGAL BASIS:
Public foundation.

ELIGIBILITY:
The applicant must be a citizen or permanent resident of the U.S. and either have a Bachelor's degree, Master's degree or equivalent degree, or be working towards a Ph.D. or equivalent degree while holding the B.A.E.F. Fellowship. Preference is given to applicants under the age of 30. Knowledge of Dutch, French or German is optional.

FINANCIAL DATA:
Fellowships carry a fixed stipend for living expenses, travel and tuition, if any. Health insurance coverage is also provided.
Amount of support per award: $29,000 for Master's or Ph.D. student; $33,000 for Postdoctoral Fellows for 12 months.

NO. MOST RECENT APPLICANTS: 50 U.S. applicants per academic year.

NO. AWARDS: Up to 11 awards to American students per academic year.

APPLICATION INFO:
Applicant shall furnish a completed application form with all its appropriate attachments. Application blanks are available on www.baef.us. Completed applications must be submitted electronically with attachments in PDF format to the e-mail address above.
Duration: 12 months preferred; no less than six months.
Deadline: October 31, for the following academic year. Fellowship starting as early as July 1 of that following year.

DIRECTORS:
Dr. Emile L. Boulpaep, President and Chairman
Marcel Crochet, Vice President
Olivier Trouveroy, Treasurer

L. Gilles Sion, Secretary
Maryan Ainsworth
Alexia Bertrand
Diego du Monceau
Susan Friberg
Margaret Hoover
Daniel Janssen
Filip Moerman
William S. Moody
Frans van Daele
Dirk Wauters
Jacques Willems

ADDRESS INQUIRIES TO:
Dr. Emile L. Boulpaep, President
(See address above.)

BRUCEBO FINE ART SCHOLARSHIP FOUNDATION
Concordia University
1455 De Maisonneuve Boulevard West
Montreal QC H3G 1M8 Canada
(514) 848-2424 ext. 4600
E-mail: fineartsresearch@concordia.ca
Web Site: www.bruceboscholarships.ca
www.concordia.ca/finearts

TYPE:
Development grants; Research grants; Residencies; Scholarships; Travel grants. Grant principally in the fields of fine arts, visual art and design. Grant is either for stay at the Brucebo Studio on the Island of Hanseatic Gotland, Sweden, in the Baltic Sea, for three months during the summer annually, or for undertaking a European Fine Art Travel-Study journey.

See entry 497 for full listing.

CANADIAN BUREAU FOR INTERNATIONAL EDUCATION (CBIE)   [821]
220 Laurier Avenue West, Suite 1550
Ottawa ON K1P 5Z9 Canada
(613) 237-4820
Fax: (613) 237-1073
E-mail: scholarships-bourses@cbie.ca
Web Site: www.educanada.ca/scholarships-bourses

FOUNDED: 1981

AREAS OF INTEREST:
All disciplines at the Master's or doctoral levels.

NAME(S) OF PROGRAMS:
● **Foreign Government Awards Program**

TYPE:
Scholarships. The Government of the Republic of Korea, through the National Institute for International Education Development (NIIED), offers scholarships for study or research at the Master's or Ph.D. level in Korean studies, humanities, social sciences, natural sciences, engineering, and other fields of study.

PURPOSE:
To provide opportunities for Canadians to pursue studies or research at institutions of higher education abroad.

ELIGIBILITY:
Applicants must:
(1) be Canadian citizens. Neither the applicant nor their parents can hold Korean citizenship;
(2) be under 40 years of age as of the beginning of the scholarship period;
(3) hold or be expecting to hold an undergraduate or Master's degree by August

31 preceding the start of the scholarship;
(4) not have completed an undergraduate,
Master's, or doctoral degree program in
South Korea;
(5) have a minimum A- average from the
previously attended institution;
(6) select the university and subject of study
from the list of eligible universities and
programs designated by NIIED and;
(7) be in good health, both mentally and
physically, to complete the program of study
successfully.

Priority may be given to candidates who have
certified scores on their proficiency in Korean
or who apply for studies in natural sciences
and engineering.

FINANCIAL DATA:
Funding includes airfare, tuition and monthly
living allowances. These scholarships are
subject to the availability of funding.

NO. AWARDS: 5 for the academic year 2021-22.

APPLICATION INFO:
Further information and application forms are
available on the web site above.
Duration: Up to two years at the Master's
level, plus up to 12 months for language
training (if necessary); Up to three years at
the doctoral level, plus up to 12 months for
language training (if necessary).
Deadline: March.

ADDRESS INQUIRIES TO:
Program Coordinator
International Scholarships Program
(See address above.)

*SPECIAL STIPULATIONS:
Candidates may not hold other awards
concurrently.

CANADIAN BUREAU FOR INTERNATIONAL EDUCATION (CBIE) [822]

220 Laurier Avenue West, Suite 1550
Ottawa ON K1P 5Z9 Canada
(613) 237-4820
Fax: (613) 237-1073
E-mail: scholarships-bourses@cbie.ca
Web Site: www.educanada.ca/scholarships-bourses

FOUNDED: 1981

AREAS OF INTEREST:
All disciplines at the Master's, doctoral or
postdoctoral levels.

NAME(S) OF PROGRAMS:
● **Canada-China Scholars' Exchange Program**

TYPE:
Exchange programs; Scholarships. Global
Affairs Canada and the Chinese Ministry of
Education offer short-term scholarships to
Canadians wishing to study abroad in China.
Scholarships are awarded for studies,
research, language studies or a combination
of studies and language studies at
participating Chinese institutions.

PURPOSE:
To provide opportunities for Canadians to
pursue studies or research at institutions of
higher education abroad.

ELIGIBILITY:
Applicants must:
(1) be Canadian citizens residing in Canada;
(2) be a full-time professor or research staff
at a recognized postsecondary education or
research institution in Canada, a student

enrolled in either a college, undergraduate or
graduate program at a recognized
postsecondary education institution in
Canada, or a midcareer professional from a
Canadian government, media or cultural
organization, or national education
association, who has a graduate (Master's or
doctoral) degree and has managerial, policy
development or decision making
responsibilities for at least three years with
the organization;
(3) have achieved the required level of
written and spoken Chinese by the host
institution in China (if applicable);
(4) undertake studies in an approved subject
area in a Chinese institution;
(5) not be seeking a degree in China and;
(6) be under 45 years of age for "General
Scholar" category or under 50 years of age
for "Senior Scholar" category.

FINANCIAL DATA:
Funding includes tuition, accommodation,
and comprehensive medical insurance.
Amount of support per award: Varies by
level of study.

APPLICATION INFO:
Applicant must complete the following
two-step process:
(1) Applicants must first complete and submit
the online application form of the
Department of Foreign Affairs, Trade and
Development (DFATD) available on the
CBIE web site and provide the supporting
documents as requested and;
(2) Applicants must complete and submit the
CSC online application from the China
Scholarship Council web site, as well as an
application package submitted by mail.
Duration: Four to 12 months for students;
Eight weeks to 12 months for midcareer
professionals and faculty members.
Deadline: January 20.

ADDRESS INQUIRIES TO:
Program Coordinator
International Scholarships Program
(See address above.)

CANADIAN INSTITUTE FOR ADVANCED LEGAL STUDIES

P.O. Box 43538, Leaside Post Office
1601 Bayview Avenue
Toronto ON M4G 4G8 Canada
(416) 429-3292
Fax: (416) 429-9805
E-mail: info@canadian-institute.com
Web Site: www.canadian-institute.com

TYPE:
Scholarships.

See entry 1770 for full listing.

CANADIAN INSTITUTE IN GREECE/L'INSTITUT CANADIEN EN GRECE

Wilfred Laurier University
Department of Archaeology and Heritage
Studies
75 University Avenue West
Waterloo ON N2L 3C5 Canada
(519) 884-0710 ext. 4260
E-mail: sgallimore@wlu.ca
Web Site: www.cig-icg.gr

TYPE:
Fellowships; Internships; Travel grants.
Intended to support the graduate work of a
person who needs to study in Greece.

See entry 315 for full listing.

WINSTON CHURCHILL FOUNDATION OF THE UNITED STATES [823]

600 Madison Avenue, Suite 1601
New York, NY 10022-1737
(212) 752-3200
Fax: (212) 246-8330
E-mail: info@churchillscholarship.org
Web Site: www.churchillscholarship.org

FOUNDED: 1959

AREAS OF INTEREST:
Science, math and engineering.

NAME(S) OF PROGRAMS:
● **Churchill Scholarship**

TYPE:
Scholarships. Scholarship for one year of
graduate work at University of Cambridge.
Churchill Scholarship may also include a
Special Research Grant.

YEAR PROGRAM STARTED: 1963

PURPOSE:
To encourage Anglo-American cooperation
and American scientific and technological
talent.

LEGAL BASIS:
Public charity.

ELIGIBILITY:
Candidate must be a citizen of the U.S.,
either native born or naturalized, and must be
a senior who is enrolled in one of the
institutions participating in the Scholarship
Program, or a student who has graduated
from one of those institutions within the past
12 months. Upon taking up the Scholarship,
a scholar must hold a Bachelor's degree or
an equivalent, and may not have attained a
Doctorate.

FINANCIAL DATA:
Amount of support per award: Churchill
Scholarship: Tuition, plus GBP 14,777 living
allowance, $1,500 travel allowance and
reimbursement of visa application fees. Total
individual package is approximately $60,000;
Churchill Scholars may also receive a Special
Research Grant of up to $2,000.
Total amount of support: Approximately
$900,000 for the year 2020.

NO. MOST RECENT APPLICANTS: 125.

NO. AWARDS: 17 scholarships for the year 2021.

APPLICATION INFO:
Application forms are available from
Foundation representatives at participating
institutions. Information also available on
Foundation's web site.
Duration: One year.
Deadline: November 1.

OFFICERS:
John L. Loeb, Jr., Chairman
Patrick A. Gerschel, President
Michael Morse, Executive Director
David D. Burrows, Treasurer
James A. Fitzpatrick, Jr., Secretary

ADDRESS INQUIRIES TO:
Michael Morse, Executive Director
(See address above.)

COUNCIL OF AMERICAN OVERSEAS RESEARCH CENTERS (CAORC)   [824]

P.O. Box 37012
MRC 178
Washington, DC 20013-7012
(202) 633-1599
E-mail: fellowships@caorc.org
Web Site: www.caorc.org

FOUNDED: 1981

AREAS OF INTEREST:
Promoting the work of American overseas research centers.

NAME(S) OF PROGRAMS:
- **Multi-Country Research Fellowship Program**

TYPE:
Fellowships; Research grants. Requires scholars to conduct research in two or more countries outside the U.S., at least one of which hosts a participating American overseas research center.

YEAR PROGRAM STARTED: 1993

PURPOSE:
To advance higher learning and scholarly research by providing a forum for communication and cooperation among American overseas advanced research centers; to provide general and continuing publicity about the importance and contributions of the centers; to exchange operational and administrative information among the centers; to exchange scholarly and research information among the centers; to encourage joint research projects.

LEGAL BASIS:
501(c)(3) organization.

ELIGIBILITY:
Program is open to U.S. doctoral candidates and scholars who have already earned their Ph.D. in fields in the humanities, social sciences, or allied natural sciences and wish to conduct research of regional or trans-regional significance. Must be U.S. citizen or permanent resident.

U.S. State Department travel restrictions apply. U.S. citizens may not travel to Afghanistan, Iraq, Yemen or Pakistan (senior scholars allowed only).

FINANCIAL DATA:
Amount of support per award: Up to $11,000.

NO. AWARDS: 9.

APPLICATION INFO:
A complete application consists of:
(1) application form;
(2) project description (1,500 words or less) describing the nature of the proposal and competence to carry out the required research;
(3) project bibliography/literature review (one page maximum);
(4) two signed letters of recommendation;
(5) curriculum vitae (three pages maximum) and;
(6) graduate transcripts (Ph.D. candidates only).

Applicants are urged to review the Application Instructions before submitting the application.
Duration: Ph.D./Postdoctoral: Minimum of 90 days.
Deadline: Late January.

ADDRESS INQUIRIES TO:
Program Manager
(See address above.)

*SPECIAL STIPULATIONS:
Fellows must complete their research within a specific time.

COUNCIL ON FOREIGN RELATIONS

58 East 68th Street
New York, NY 10065
(212) 434-9740
Fax: (212) 434-9870
E-mail: fellowships@cfr.org
Web Site: www.cfr.org/fellowships

TYPE:
Fellowships. The International Affairs Fellowship (IAF) in Japan, sponsored by Hitachi, Ltd., seeks to strengthen mutual understanding and cooperation between the rising generations of leaders in the U.S. and Japan. The program provides a select group of midcareer professionals the opportunity to carry out research while affiliated with appropriate institutions in Japan and to establish long-term professional and personal ties through their activities. Fellows are drawn from academia, business, government, media, NGOs, and think tanks. In cooperation with CFR, the program's sponsor assists fellows in finding suitable host organizations in Japan. CFR cannot guarantee placement at any specific agency or organization.

See entry 763 for full listing.

CULTURAL VISTAS   [825]

1250 H Street, N.W.
Suite 300
Washington, DC 20005
(212) 497-3500
E-mail: dvillanueva@culturalvistas.org
Web Site: culturalvistas.org

FOUNDED: 1968

AREAS OF INTEREST:
All career areas, including the humanities and arts, business, technical, and engineering.

NAME(S) OF PROGRAMS:
- **Congress-Bundestag Youth Exchange for Young Professionals**

TYPE:
Exchange programs; Fellowships; Internships; Scholarships; Work-study programs. Language learning. Scholarship program with a strong focus on cultural exchange. One-year scholarship for work/study program to Germany including German language training, academic semester in Germany and internship component.

YEAR PROGRAM STARTED: 1983

PURPOSE:
To give participants understanding for everyday life, education and professional training in Germany.

ELIGIBILITY:
Requirements include:
(1) U.S. citizenship;
(2) 18 and one-half to 24 years of age at start of program;
(3) at least high school diploma or equivalent and;
(4) clear career goals, a solid academic background, and relevant work experience or internships in field strongly preferred.

German language proficiency preferred, but not required.

FINANCIAL DATA:
Funding provided for international airfare, language training and study costs, living expenses during study phases, all seminars, and sickness and accident insurance while abroad.

CO-OP FUNDING PROGRAMS: Funded in U.S. by the Bureau of Educational and Cultural Affairs of the Department of State and through the Administration of the Bundestag in Germany.

NO. MOST RECENT APPLICANTS: 420.

NO. AWARDS: 75.

APPLICATION INFO:
Electronic submission only.
Duration: 11 months (July to June).
Deadline: November 1 for the following program year.

ADDRESS INQUIRIES TO:
Congress-Bundestag Youth Exchange for Young Professionals
(See address above.)

*SPECIAL STIPULATIONS:
Must be U.S. citizens, 18 and one-half to 24 years of age at the start of the program. Previous recipients of Congress-Bundestag scholarships are not eligible for this program.

CYPRUS AMERICAN ARCHAEOLOGICAL RESEARCH INSTITUTE   [826]

209 Commerce Street
Alexandria, VA 22314
(703) 789-9235
E-mail: usa.office@caari.org.cy
Web Site: www.caari.org

FOUNDED: 1900

AREAS OF INTEREST:
The study of humanistic disciplines, such as anthropology, archaeology, Biblical studies, epigraphy, history, history of art and architecture, literature, philology, prehistory and topography, relating in particular to the Middle East from prehistoric times to the modern era.

Cyprus American Archaeological Research Institute is the only residential archaeological institute on the island of Cyprus and serves as a center for the dissemination of information about the archaeology of Cyprus.

NAME(S) OF PROGRAMS:
- **The Anita Cecil O'Donovan Fellowship**
- **The Danielle Parks Memorial Fellowship**
- **The Helena Wylde Swiny and Stuart Swiny Fellowship**

TYPE:
Fellowships; Research grants; Residencies; Travel grants. There are a large variety of fellowships available through the Near Eastern Fellowship Program for the American Schools of Oriental Research and affiliated overseas research centers. Besides The Cyprus American Archaeological Research Institute in Nicosia, Cyprus (CAARI), there are also The American Center of Oriental Research in Amman, Jordan (ACOR) and the W.F. Albright Institute of Archaeological Research in Jerusalem, Israel (AIAR). Contact the American Schools of Oriental Research for full details.

The Anita Cecil O'Donovan Fellowship is an award to a graduate student of any nationality, enrolled in a graduate program in any nation, to pursue research on a project relevant to the archaeology and/or culture of Cyprus.

The Danielle Parks Memorial Fellowship is for a graduate student of any nationality who needs to work in Cyprus to further his or her research on a subject of relevance to Cypriot archaeology and culture.

The Helena Wylde Swiny and Stuart Swiny Fellowship is a grant to a graduate student of any nationality in a U.S. or Canadian university or college to pursue a research project relevant to an ongoing field project in Cyprus or that requires work on Cyprus itself.

YEAR PROGRAM STARTED: 1940

PURPOSE:
To help scholars undertake high-quality research and field projects in the Middle East; to encourage interdisciplinary study and communication among scholars.

LEGAL BASIS:
Nonprofit, archaeological research corporation.

ELIGIBILITY:
All ASOR awards are open to qualified students and scholars from any country. Applicants must be affiliated with an institution that is a member of the ASOR corporation or must be an individual professional member. Prime consideration is given to applicants whose projects are affiliated with ASOR.

ASOR does not conduct the competition nor take part in the selection process for the Fulbright Fellowships, but encourages qualified scholars to apply for these awards.

FINANCIAL DATA:
The Anita Cecil O'Donovan Fellowship and The Helena Wylde Swiny and Stuart Swiny Fellowship will be used to fund research time in residence at CAARI and to help defray costs of travel.

The Danielle Parks Memorial Fellowship covers travel to and living expenses in Cyprus.
Amount of support per award: $2,000 each.
Total amount of support: $6,000.

NO. MOST RECENT APPLICANTS: 13 for the year 2020.

NO. AWARDS: 1 each.

APPLICATION INFO:
Application form is available on the Institute web site. All eligible persons are encouraged to apply for as many fellowships and professorships as they wish, but a person can hold only one award at a time. Persons who have received an award in one year can reapply for the same or other awards the following year, but new applicants will have priority.
Duration: One-time awards.
Deadline: December.

ADDRESS INQUIRIES TO:
See e-mail address above.

*SPECIAL STIPULATIONS:
For the O'Donovan, Parks and Swiny Fellowships, residence at CAARI is mandatory.

For the Danielle Parks Memorial Fellowship, the fellow is expected during his or her stay to give a presentation at CAARI on a subject related to his or her research. The fellow will periodically keep the Director of CAARI apprised of his or her research activities and will acknowledge CAARI and the Danielle Parks Memorial Fellowship in any publication that emerges from the research carried during the Fellowship.

CYPRUS AMERICAN ARCHAEOLOGICAL RESEARCH INSTITUTE [827]
209 Commerce Street
Alexandria, VA 22314
(703) 789-9235
E-mail: usa.office@caari.org.cy
Web Site: www.caari.org

FOUNDED: 1900

AREAS OF INTEREST:
The study of humanistic disciplines, such as anthropology, archaeology, Biblical studies, epigraphy, history, history of art and architecture, literature, philology, prehistory and topography, relating in particular to the Middle East from prehistoric times to the modern era.

Cyprus American Archaeological Research Institute is the only residential archaeological institute on the island of Cyprus and serves as a center for the dissemination of information about the archaeology of Cyprus.

NAME(S) OF PROGRAMS:
● **CAARI/CAORC Research Fellowships**
● **Edgar J. Peltenburg Postdoctoral Research Fellowship in Cypriot Prehistory**

TYPE:
Fellowships; Research grants; Travel grants. CAARI/CAORC Research Fellowships are designed for scholars who already have their Ph.Ds., whose research engages the archaeology, history, culture, or geography of Cyprus, and who would derive significant benefits from a month's research time on the island.

The Edgar J. Peltenburg Postdoctoral Research Fellowship honors the late Professor Edgar Peltenburg and provides a stipend to conduct research on Cypriot prehistory (from the first visitors to the transition to the Iron Age).

PURPOSE:
To help scholars undertake high-quality research and field projects in the Middle East; to encourage interdisciplinary study and communication among scholars.

LEGAL BASIS:
Nonprofit, archaeological research corporation.

ELIGIBILITY:
CAARI/CAORC Research Fellowship: Scholars who already have their Ph.D., whose research engages the archaeology, history, culture, or geography of Cyprus, may apply. Applicants must be U.S. citizens. Particular consideration is given to applicants whose projects enable them to include Cyprus in their teaching.

Edgar J. Peltenburg Postdoctoral Research Fellowship: Applicants of all nationalities are encouraged to apply provided they have been awarded a Ph.D. by the start of the fellowship. Although the fellowship is open to scholars of all ages, priority will be given to early career candidates who have received their Ph.D. within five years of the start of the fellowship.

FINANCIAL DATA:
Amount of support per award:
CAARI/CAORC Research Fellowship: $5,500 (up to $1,500 for transportation and up to $4,000 for research expenses on the island); Peltenburg Fellowship: $14,000 stipend and up to $1,500 travel expenses for those traveling to Cyprus from abroad.

NO. AWARDS: CAARI/CAORC Research Fellowship: 2.

APPLICATION INFO:
Application form is available on the Institute web site. All eligible persons are encouraged to apply for as many fellowships as they wish, but a person can hold only one award at a time. Persons who have received an award in one year can reapply for the same or other awards the following year, but new applicants will have priority.
Duration: CAARI/CAORC Research Fellowship: Minimum one month. Peltenburg Fellowship: Nine months. Renewable in exceptional cases for an additional nine months.
Deadline: January.

ADDRESS INQUIRIES TO:
See e-mail address above.

*SPECIAL STIPULATIONS:
A minimum of 30 days residence at CAARI is required for the CAARI/CAORC Research Fellowship.

Peltenburg Fellow will normally be expected to reside at CAARI for the duration of the fellowship. In addition, he or she is expected to play an active role in the CAARI community and contribute to the academic environment with research-related and/or outreach events.

THE LADY DAVIS FELLOWSHIP TRUST [828]
The Sprinzak Building, Room 103
The Edmond Safra Campus, Hebrew University
Jerusalem 91904 Israel
(972) 2-651-2306 (voice mail)
(972) 2-658-4723
Fax: (972) 2-566-3848
E-mail: ld.fellows@mail.huji.ac.il
Web Site: ldft.huji.ac.il

FOUNDED: 1973

NAME(S) OF PROGRAMS:
● **Postdoctoral Researchers Fellowship**
● **Visiting Professorships Fellowship**

TYPE:
Fellowships.

YEAR PROGRAM STARTED: 1973

LEGAL BASIS:
University association.

ELIGIBILITY:
Postdoctoral Researchers: If applying for academic year 2021-22, must have received Doctorate no earlier than October 1, 2016.

Visiting Professorships: Must be a full or associate professor and have an academic sponsor.

FINANCIAL DATA:
The Trust pays round-trip airfare from the fellow's country of origin to Israel and half the medical insurance if purchased and paid for in Israel.

Amount of support per award: Postdoctoral Researchers: $1,834 (per month) plus $303 rental allowance (per month); Visiting Professorships: $3,032 (per month).

APPLICATION INFO:
Prospective candidates must establish contact with the relevant department at the Hebrew University, and ensure that there is a faculty member willing to sponsor the application.

Duration: Postdoctoral Researchers: Nine to 12 months. May request an extension of one year only. Visiting Professorships: Two or three months.

Deadline: Postdoctoral Researchers: December 31. Visiting Professorships: November 30.

*SPECIAL STIPULATIONS:
Fellowships may not be deferred from one year to the next.

Fellows who have won another concurrent fellowship must disclose this to the Trust, whereupon the amount of the award will be reviewed.

A Fellow is expected to take up the Fellowship within the period of the academic year for which he has applied (in other words, between October 1 and September 30 in the following year). Attempts are made to be as elastic as possible should a Fellow expect to arrive before or after October 1.

EMBASSY OF FRANCE IN THE U.S., SCAC   [829]
4101 Reservoir Road, N.W.
Washington, DC 20007
(202) 944-6000
Fax: (202) 944-6268
Web Site: frenchhighereducation.org

FOUNDED: 1980

AREAS OF INTEREST:
Higher education, study abroad, research, France, and French language.

NAME(S) OF PROGRAMS:
 ● **Chateaubriand Humanities & Social Sciences (HSS) Fellowship Program**
 ● **France on Campus Award**
 ● **Teaching Assistant Program in France**
 ● **Transatlantic Mobility Program**

TYPE:
Assistantships; Exchange programs; Fellowships; Grants-in-aid; Project/program grants; Research grants; Training grants; Travel grants. Chateaubriand Fellowship Program: Offered by the embassy of France in the U.S., each year this program allows doctoral students enrolled in American universities to conduct research in France for up to nine months.

Teaching Assistant Program in France: The French Ministry of Education and the Cultural Services Department of the French Embassy in Washington, DC offer over 1,500 teaching assistantships each year for American citizens and permanent residents of the U.S. to teach English in French schools. Assistants may work in primary schools or secondary schools.

YEAR PROGRAM STARTED: 1980

PURPOSE:
To promote the exchange of ideas between France and the U.S.

LEGAL BASIS:
Embassy.

ELIGIBILITY:
Details are available online.

FINANCIAL DATA:
Amount of support per award: Chateaubriand Fellowship Program: EUR 1,500 monthly, a round-trip ticket to France and health insurance; France on Campus Award: $500 to $2,000 per project; Teaching Assistant Program in France: EUR 785 per month (net); Transatlantic Mobility Program: Up to $15,000 per U.S. higher education institution.

NO. AWARDS: Chateaubriand Fellowship Program: 15 to 20; France on Campus Award: 3 to 10; Teaching Assistant Program in France: Over 1,500; Transatlantic Mobility Program: 4 for the year 2020.

APPLICATION INFO:
Details are available online.

Duration: Chateaubriand Fellowship Program: Four or eight months; Teaching Assistant Program in France: Seven months.

Deadline: Details are available online.

ADDRESS INQUIRIES TO:
Chateaubriand Fellowship Program
E-mail: admin@chateaubriand-fellowship.org
France on Campus Award
E-mail: franceoncampus@frenchculture.org
Teaching Assistant Program in France:
E-mail: erin.glaser@frenchculture.org
Transatlantic Mobility Program
E-mail: anna.malan@frenchculture.org

THE GARDEN CLUB OF AMERICA
14 East 60th Street, Third Floor
New York, NY 10022
(212) 753-8287
Fax: (212) 753-0134
E-mail: scholarshipapplications@gcamerica.org
Web Site: www.gcamerica.org/scholarships

TYPE:
Exchange programs; Fellowships. A graduate academic year in the U.S. for a British student and a work-study program for an American at universities and botanical gardens in the U.K. in fields related to horticulture, botany and landscape design.

See entry 1966 for full listing.

THE GARDEN CLUB OF AMERICA
14 East 60th Street, Third Floor
New York, NY 10022
(212) 753-8287
Fax: (212) 753-0134
E-mail: scholarshipapplications@gcamerica.org
Web Site: www.gcamerica.org/scholarships

TYPE:
Research grants. Financial assistance to college seniors and graduate students to study habitat-related issues that will benefit threatened or endangered bird species and lend useful information for land management decisions.

See entry 1967 for full listing.

GERMAN ACADEMIC EXCHANGE SERVICE   [830]
871 United Nations Plaza, 14th Floor
New York, NY 10017
(212) 758-3223
Fax: (212) 755-5780
E-mail: daadny@daad.org
Web Site: www.daad.org

FOUNDED: 1925

AREAS OF INTEREST:
International exchanges in education, research in higher education, and academic teaching staff; scholarships to German and foreign students.

CONSULTING OR VOLUNTEER SERVICES:
DAAD serves on a consultancy service in the field of international academic mobility.

NAME(S) OF PROGRAMS:
 ● **DAAD Emigre Memorial German Internship Program (EMGIP-Bundestag)**
 ● **DAAD German Studies Research Grant**
 ● **DAAD Research Grant**
 ● **DAAD Research Internships in Science and Engineering (RISE)**
 ● **DAAD Research Stays for University Academics and Scientists**
 ● **DAAD RISE Professional**
 ● **DAAD Study Scholarship**
 ● **DAAD University Summer Course Grant**
 ● **DAAD Visiting Professorship**

TYPE:
Awards/prizes; Conferences/seminars; Exchange programs; Fellowships; Internships; Professorships; Project/program grants; Research grants; Scholarships; Visiting scholars. The German Academic Exchange Service is the New York office of the Deutscher Akademischer Austausch Dienst (DAAD), a German organization with its head office in Bonn. DAAD offers a wide range of opportunities to students, scholars and higher education institutions of the U.S. and Canada, from undergraduate students to faculty, for study and research in Germany.

PURPOSE:
To provide information on study and research opportunities in higher education at home and abroad; to promote international higher education and research through scholarships; to recruit and place German academic teaching staff from all disciplines at foreign institutions of higher education; to maintain a network of former scholarship holders abroad.

LEGAL BASIS:
Registered association under private law.

ELIGIBILITY:
DAAD grants are available to faculty and students in the U.S. and Canada to participate in a wide variety of academic activities. Funding is restricted to travel to Germany, including German higher education institutions, research institutions and archives in Germany.

GEOG. RESTRICTIONS: United States and Canada.

FINANCIAL DATA:
Amount of support per award: Varies.
Total amount of support: Varies.

APPLICATION INFO:
Application information is available on the web site.
Duration: Varies.
Deadline: Varies.

PUBLICATIONS:
Grants for Study and Research in Germany.

ADDRESS INQUIRIES TO:
See contact form on DAAD web site.

GERMAN HISTORICAL INSTITUTE

1607 New Hampshire Avenue, N.W.
Washington, DC 20009-2562
(202) 387-3355
E-mail: fellowships@ghi-dc.org
Web Site: www.ghi-dc.org

TYPE:
Fellowships. The Institute awards short-term fellowships to German and American doctoral students as well as postdoctoral scholars/Habilitanden in the fields of German and European history, the history of German-American relations, and the role of Germany and the U.S. in international relations.

See entry 542 for full listing.

GRADUATE WOMEN INTERNATIONAL (GWI)

Chemin du Grand-Montfleury, 48
CH-1290 Versoix Geneva Switzerland
(41) 22 731 23 80
Fax: (41) 22 738 04 40
E-mail: gwi@graduatewomen.org
Web Site: www.graduatewomen.org

TYPE:
Awards/prizes; Fellowships; Internships; Research grants; Training grants. Graduate Women International fellowships and grants are awarded triennially to encourage and enable women graduates to undertake original research or obtain further training in the humanities, social sciences and natural sciences.

See entry 978 for full listing.

THE HAGUE ACADEMY OF INTERNATIONAL LAW

Peace Palace
Carnegieplein 2
2517 KJ The Hague The Netherlands
(31) 70 3024242
E-mail: registration@hagueacademy.nl
Web Site: www.hagueacademy.nl

TYPE:
Project/program grants. Study programs. Residential scholarships for doctoral candidates from developing countries whose thesis, in private international law or public international law, is in the process of completion, who reside in their home country and who do not have access to scientific sources.

See entry 1775 for full listing.

THE HAGUE ACADEMY OF INTERNATIONAL LAW

Peace Palace
Carnegieplein 2
2517 KJ The Hague The Netherlands
(31) 70 3024242
E-mail: registration@hagueacademy.nl
Web Site: www.hagueacademy.nl

TYPE:
Project/program grants; Scholarships. Study programs. A limited number of scholarships are given to cover tuition and living expenses while studying at the three-week summer session of the Hague Academy of International Law. Because of the limited number, granting of scholarships is based solely on academic merit.

See entry 1776 for full listing.

THE HAGUE ACADEMY OF INTERNATIONAL LAW

Peace Palace
Carnegieplein 2
2517 KJ The Hague The Netherlands
(31) 70 3024242
E-mail: centre@hagueacademy.nl
Web Site: www.hagueacademy.nl

TYPE:
Project/program grants.

See entry 1773 for full listing.

THE HAGUE ACADEMY OF INTERNATIONAL LAW

Peace Palace
Carnegieplein 2
2517 KJ The Hague The Netherlands
(31) 70 3024242
E-mail: info@hagueacademy.nl
Web Site: www.hagueacademy.nl

TYPE:
Project/program grants. External Programme is held each year, in turn in Africa, Asia and Latin America, upon the invitation of host governments or international organizations. It is designed for approximately 20 participants from the countries in the region (who are resident in their own country), whose traveling expenses and accommodations are financed by the government of the host state or organization. In addition, 20 participants come from the host state itself.

See entry 1774 for full listing.

HEINRICH HERTZ-STIFTUNG [831]

Ministerium fuer Kultur und Wissenschaft des Landes Nordrhein-Westfalen
Heinrich Hertz-Stiftung
Voelklinger Strasse 49
D-40221 Duesseldorf Germany
(49) 211 896-4266
Fax: (49) 211 896-4407
E-mail: martina.schoeler@heinrich-hertz-stiftung.nrw.de
Web Site: www.heinrich-hertz-stiftung.de

FOUNDED: 1961

AREAS OF INTEREST:
International exchange of scientists.

TYPE:
Exchange programs; Scholarships. Scholarships to promote the sciences through the exchange of university teachers and young scientists (without special restrictions).

YEAR PROGRAM STARTED: 1962

PURPOSE:
To promote sciences.

LEGAL BASIS:
Public foundation.

ELIGIBILITY:
University teachers and young scientists are eligible. Non-German citizens should have a working knowledge of German and German citizens a working knowledge of the language of the host country.

GEOG. RESTRICTIONS: Land Nordrhine-Westphalia.

FINANCIAL DATA:
Amount of support per award: Award values are dependent upon individual needs.
Total amount of support: Varies.

NO. MOST RECENT APPLICANTS: 10.

NO. AWARDS: 10 for the year 2020.

APPLICATION INFO:
Applications should be submitted only by third persons. A curriculum vitae, examination record, two references and a full description of the planned project with a timetable are to be included. Further information may be obtained on request.
Duration: Dependent upon individual needs. Two years maximum.

PUBLICATIONS:
Hinweise auf die Antragstellung; *Die Heinrich Hertz-Stiftung*, booklet; Heinrich Hertz-Stiftung, folder.

STAFF:
Susanne Schneider-Salomon, Chief Executive Officer
Martina Schoeler, Head of Office

ADDRESS INQUIRIES TO:
Ministerium fuer Kultur und Wissenschaft des Landes Nordrhein-Westfalen
Heinrich Hertz-Stiftung
(See address above.)

INSTITUTE FOR THE INTERNATIONAL EDUCATION OF STUDENTS (IES)

33 West Monroe Street
Suite 2300
Chicago, IL 60603-5405
(312) 944-1750
(800) 995-2300
Fax: (312) 944-1448
E-mail: info@IESabroad.org
Web Site: www.IESabroad.org

TYPE:
Awards/prizes; Scholarships. Boren and Gilman Scholarship Support Grants: This program offers recipients of these prestigious scholarships the opportunity to apply for additional financial support.

Disability Grants: This program's purpose is to enhance study abroad opportunities for students with disabilities. It offers grants to students whose disabilities may add significant costs to their study abroad experience.

Diversity Scholarships: This program offers one way to encourage and support students from a range of institutions and underrepresented populations. Underrepresented students include students from underrepresented racial and ethnic groups, first-generation-to-college students, students from low-income families and students with a history of overcoming adversity.

Donor Funded Scholarships: These scholarship opportunities have been created through the generosity of various donors who support the important mission of IES Abroad.

Need Based Aid: This program is available to students with demonstrated financial need. Priority is given to Pell Grant recipients.

Partner University Scholarships: These scholarships are funded by IES Abroad partner universities in countries where IES has programs.

Public University Grants: This program offers an automatic $2,000 credit toward a semester or academic year program.

See entry 1514 for full listing.

INSTITUTE OF INTERNATIONAL EDUCATION   [832]

One World Trade Center, 36th Floor
New York, NY 10007
(800) 272-6994
E-mail: fbstudent@iie.org
Web Site: www.us.fulbrightonline.org

FOUNDED: 1919

AREAS OF INTEREST:
International educational and cultural exchange for graduating seniors, graduate-level students and early career professionals.

NAME(S) OF PROGRAMS:
● **Fulbright U.S. Student Program**

TYPE:
Exchange programs; Scholarships. Grants for graduate study, research or English Teaching Assistantships abroad.

YEAR PROGRAM STARTED: 1946

PURPOSE:
To give U.S. students the opportunity to live, study, teach or do research in a foreign country for one academic year and to increase mutual understanding between the people of the U.S. and other countries through the exchange of persons, knowledge and skills.

LEGAL BASIS:
Nonprofit, as described under Internal Revenue Code 501(c)(3).

ELIGIBILITY:
The program is open to all disciplines and fields of study, except medical degree study. Candidates must possess U.S. citizenship, a Bachelor's degree by the beginning date of the grant, language proficiency sufficient to carry out the project overseas and good health. Preference in selecting candidates is for those who have had the majority of high school and undergraduate college education at educational institutions in the U.S and little experience living, studying or working in the country of application. Candidates may not hold a doctoral degree at the time of application.

FINANCIAL DATA:
Fulbright Grants provide round-trip transportation, orientation program, books, maintenance for one academic year and health benefits package. Some country programs may provide tuition and language study courses. The maintenance allowance is based on living costs in the host country and is sufficient to meet normal expenses of a single person at the graduate-study level. Dependents allowances vary by country.
Amount of support per award: Varies by country.

CO-OP FUNDING PROGRAMS: Funds from other scholarships, fellowships or grants in dollars or foreign currency received concurrently with a Fulbright Grant will be deducted if they duplicate the Fulbright benefits. No deduction is made if other grants are for assistance in meeting family expenses of grantees or other expenses not covered by the grant.

NO. MOST RECENT APPLICANTS: 11,700.

NO. AWARDS: Approximately 2,500.

APPLICATION INFO:
Enrolled students should contact the Fulbright Program Adviser on their campus. Candidates who are not enrolled in an educational institution should contact IIE, U.S. Student Programs Division, at the address above.
Duration: One academic year.
Deadline: Enrolled students should submit their applications to their campus Fulbright Program Advisers by the dates set by them. At-large candidates must submit their applications to the IIE office in October.

ADDRESS INQUIRIES TO:
Daniel Kramer, Director of Fulbright U.S. Student Program
(See address above.)

INTERNATIONAL DEVELOPMENT RESEARCH CENTRE (IDRC)

150 Kent Street
Ottawa ON K1P 0B2 Canada
(613) 696-2098
E-mail: awards@idrc.ca
Web Site: www.idrc.ca
www.crdi.ca

TYPE:
Internships. Program provides training in research management and grant administration under the guidance of Centre program staff. Approximately 50% of the time spent on own research project.

See entry 1184 for full listing.

INTERNATIONAL DEVELOPMENT RESEARCH CENTRE (IDRC)

150 Kent Street
Ottawa ON K1P 0B2 Canada
(613) 696-2098
E-mail: awards@idrc.ca
Web Site: www.idrc.ca
www.crdi.ca

TYPE:
Fellowships. Fellowship is awarded for research on the relationship between forest resources and the social, economic, cultural and environmental welfare of people in developing countries.

See entry 1185 for full listing.

INTERNATIONAL RESEARCH & EXCHANGES BOARD (IREX)   [833]

1275 K Street, N.W.
Suite 600
Washington, DC 20005
(202) 628-8188
Fax: (202) 628-8189
E-mail: communications@irex.org
Web Site: www.irex.org

FOUNDED: 1968

AREAS OF INTEREST:
Academic research exchanges and professional training programs in Europe, Eurasia, the Middle East and North Africa, and Asia.

TYPE:
Conferences/seminars; Exchange programs; Fellowships; Project/program grants; Research grants; Training grants; Travel grants; Visiting scholars.

YEAR PROGRAM STARTED: 1968

PURPOSE:
To promote advanced field research and professional training programs between the U.S. and the countries of Europe, Eurasia, Asia and the Middle East and North Africa.

LEGAL BASIS:
Nonprofit organization.

ELIGIBILITY:
Varies by program.

GEOG. RESTRICTIONS: United States, Europe, Eurasia, the Middle East, Asia and North Africa.

FINANCIAL DATA:
Amount of support per award: Varies per program.

APPLICATION INFO:
Application information is available upon request.

PUBLICATIONS:
Policy papers, application materials.

ADDRESS INQUIRIES TO:
Program Coordinator
(See address above.)

ISTITUTO ITALIANO PER GLI STUDI STORICI

Via Benedetto Croce, 12
80134 Naples Italy
(39) 081 5517159
(39) 081 5512390
Fax: (39) 081 5514813
E-mail: info@iiss.it
Web Site: www.iiss.it

TYPE:
Awards/prizes; Conferences/seminars; Research grants; Scholarships. Awards for historical, literature and philosophical studies at the Istituto Italiano per gli Studi Storici in Naples.

Federico II Scholarship: Funded by the Universita di Napoli Federico II for graduates from Italian universities with medieval studies final dissertation.

See entry 550 for full listing.

JAPAN INFORMATION CENTER   [834]

Consulate General of Japan
299 Park Avenue, 18th Floor
New York, NY 10171
(212) 418-4463
E-mail: scholarship@ny.mofa.go.jp
Web Site: www.ny.us.emb-japan.go.jp

FOUNDED: 1955

AREAS OF INTEREST:
Japanese language and cultural studies.

NAME(S) OF PROGRAMS:
● **Japanese Government (Monbukagakusho) Scholarships for Japanese Studies**

TYPE:
Scholarships. Undergraduate scholarships awarded to foreign students who wish to pursue Japanese language and cultural studies in Japan. The program offers students an

intensive course of Japanese language and introduction to Japanese studies in various aspects.

YEAR PROGRAM STARTED: 1955

PURPOSE:
To provide funding for non-Japanese students who want to pursue a course of Japanese and cultural studies in Japan.

LEGAL BASIS:
Japanese government agency.

ELIGIBILITY:
Applicants must:
(1) be nationals of the country to which the scholarships are offered;
(2) be at least 18 years and less than 29 years of age as of April 1 of the year of application;
(3) be regular students who follow an undergraduate course at a university in their own country or a third country and who are mainly first- to third-year Bachelor's students or above in that course;
(4) be specializing in a field concerning Japanese language or Japanese culture at their university;
(5) have good knowledge of the Japanese language and;
(6) be in good health.

Applicants must have a background in Japanese studies to qualify. A written Japanese examination will be given to selected applicants before being considered by the government offices in Japan.

FINANCIAL DATA:
Amount of support per award: Varies.
Total amount of support: Varies.

NO. AWARDS: Varies.

APPLICATION INFO:
Applicants should contact the appropriate Japanese consulate. Consulates General are located in Anchorage, Atlanta, Boston, Chicago, Denver, Detroit, Hagatna (Guam), Honolulu, Houston, Los Angeles, Miami, Nashville, New York City, Portland, Saipan, San Francisco, Seattle, and Washington, DC.
Duration: One academic year.
Deadline: Varies.

PUBLICATIONS:
Application guidelines.

ADDRESS INQUIRIES TO:
Local Japanese Consulate General

*PLEASE NOTE:
Placement of grantees to universities will be decided by Monbukagakusho after consultation with the universities concerned.

JAPAN INFORMATION CENTER [835]
Consulate General of Japan
299 Park Avenue, 18th Floor
New York, NY 10171
(212) 418-4463
Fax: (212) 371-1294
E-mail: scholarship@ny.mofa.go.jp
Web Site: www.ny.us.emb-japan.go.jp

FOUNDED: 1955

AREAS OF INTEREST:
Humanities and social sciences: literature, history, aesthetics, law, politics, economics, commerce, pedagogy, psychology, sociology, music, fine arts, natural sciences, pure science, engineering, agriculture, fisheries, pharmacology, medicine, dentistry and home economics.

NAME(S) OF PROGRAMS:
● **Japanese Government (Monbukagakusho) Scholarships for Research Students**

TYPE:
Scholarships. Graduate scholarships awarded to foreign students who wish to study at Japanese universities as nondegree research students.

PURPOSE:
To help students wishing to pursue Japan-related studies.

LEGAL BASIS:
Japanese government agency.

ELIGIBILITY:
Applicants must:
(1) be nationals of the country to which the scholarships are offered;
(2) be under 36 years of age as of April 1 of the year of the award;
(3) be university or college Bachelor or Master's degree graduates;
(4) be willing to study the Japanese language and to receive instruction in that language and;
(5) be in good health.

The study area must be in the same field as the applicant has studied (or is now studying) or a related one.

FINANCIAL DATA:
Amount of support per award: Varies.
Total amount of support: Varies.

NO. AWARDS: Varies.

APPLICATION INFO:
Applicants should contact the appropriate Japanese consulate. Consulates General are located in Anchorage, Atlanta, Boston, Chicago, Denver, Detroit, Hagatna (Guam), Honolulu, Houston, Los Angeles, Miami, Nashville, New York City, Portland, Saipan, San Francisco, Seattle, and Washington, DC.
Duration: 18 months to two years, including a six-month language course.
Deadline: Varies.

PUBLICATIONS:
Application guidelines.

ADDRESS INQUIRIES TO:
Local Japanese Consulate General

*PLEASE NOTE:
Field of study must be one of those available at the Japanese universities and practical training given by factories or companies is excluded.

HERBERT D. KATZ CENTER FOR ADVANCED JUDAIC STUDIES [836]
420 Walnut Street
Philadelphia, PA 19106
(215) 746-1290
E-mail: carrielo@upenn.edu
Web Site: katz.sas.upenn.edu

AREAS OF INTEREST:
Advanced research in Judaic and related studies.

NAME(S) OF PROGRAMS:
● **Judaic and Related Studies Postdoctoral Fellowships**

TYPE:
Fellowships.

PURPOSE:
To support education in Judaic and related studies.

ELIGIBILITY:
Postdoctoral scholars in the humanities, social sciences and the arts at all levels may apply. All scholars whose work fits within the proposed research topics are eligible to apply. National and international scholars who meet the application terms may apply. International scholars are appointed under a J-1 visa only. No exceptions can be made. Applicants should consult the international programs office at their current university to confirm eligibility before applying for this fellowship.

Fellowships may be granted for one semester or the full academic year. Scholars are required to spend the term of the fellowship in residence in Philadelphia at the Katz Center.

FINANCIAL DATA:
Amount of support per award: Up to $60,000.

NO. AWARDS: 20.

APPLICATION INFO:
Application information is available on the web site.
Duration: Up to one year. Fellowships are not renewable.
Deadline: Mid-September.

ADDRESS INQUIRIES TO:
Carrie Love
Fellowship Program Administrator
(See address above.)

KOBE COLLEGE CORPORATION-JAPAN EDUCATION EXCHANGE [837]
540 West Frontage Road, Suite 3335
Northfield, IL 60093
(847) 386-7661
Fax: (847) 386-7662
E-mail: programs@kccjee.org
Web Site: www.kccjee.org

AREAS OF INTEREST:
Japanese culture and language.

NAME(S) OF PROGRAMS:
● **The KCC-JEE High School Essay Contest**

TYPE:
Awards/prizes. The KCC-JEE High School Essay Contest includes a one-month trip to Japan. It incorporates intensive language study, college credit and a home stay with a Japanese family.

YEAR PROGRAM STARTED: 1995

PURPOSE:
To provide American high school students the opportunity to experience Japanese culture firsthand, enhancing their Japanese language skills and deepening their appreciation of Japanese culture and values by living in Japan for one month.

ELIGIBILITY:
Applicant must meet the following requirements:
(1) be an American citizen or permanent resident alien, 16 years of age by June 1 of the year contest is held;
(2) must have had at least one year of accredited Japanese language study;
(3) attend a public or private high school in

the U.S. and;

(4) be available to study during the four weeks established for this program.

GEOG. RESTRICTIONS: United States.

FINANCIAL DATA:
Prize includes round-trip airfare, tuition, and room and board in a Japanese home.
Amount of support per award:
Approximately $4,000.

APPLICATION INFO:
Application and complete information can be found online.
Duration: One summer month (typically July). Nonrenewable.
Deadline: February.

THE KOSCIUSZKO FOUNDATION, INC.   [838]
15 East 65th Street
New York, NY 10065
(212) 734-2130 ext. 412
E-mail: addy@thekf.org
Web Site: www.thekf.org/kf/programs/study

FOUNDED: 1925

AREAS OF INTEREST:
Strengthening of cultural and educational bonds between the U.S. and Poland through an exchange program to Poland for the purpose of Polish language, culture and history studies.

NAME(S) OF PROGRAMS:
● **Summer Study Abroad Programs**

TYPE:
Exchange programs; Scholarships. Summer programs. The Summer Study Abroad Programs offer a variety of courses from July through August at the Jagiellonian University in Krakow and at the John Paul II Catholic University of Lublin, Poland. Polish language, culture, history, art and many other subjects are available. The Foundation sponsors this program mainly for paying students; however, the Tomaszkiewicz-Florio and Frances E. Wyszynski Scholarships are available for the program at the Jagiellonian University in Krakow.

YEAR PROGRAM STARTED: 1970

PURPOSE:
To enable American students to pursue a short-term course of Polish language, culture, history and art studies abroad.

LEGAL BASIS:
501(c)(3) not-for-profit organization.

ELIGIBILITY:
The Summer Study Abroad Programs are open to U.S. undergraduate and graduate students as well as graduating high school students who will be 18 years of age by the first day of the program.

Students of Polish descent can apply for funding to attend the Foundation's three-week program at the Jagiellonian University via the Foundation's Tomaszkiewicz-Florio Scholarship.

GEOG. RESTRICTIONS: United States.

FINANCIAL DATA:
Program fee includes tuition, course materials, cultural events and sightseeing trips, a language placement test, language classes, afternoon classes, shared dormitory room, two meals a day and assistance from Polish university students. The scholarships which are available cover program fees for three-week programs at the Jagiellonian University in Krakow.
Amount of support per award: Varies.
Total amount of support: $31,860 awarded towards Summer Studies in Krakow for the year 2019.

NO. AWARDS: 18 for the year 2019.

APPLICATION INFO:
Required forms are available on the Summer Study Abroad Programs web page. There is a nonrefundable fee of $35.
Duration: Two- to eight-week programs are available.
Deadline: Mid-April for scholarship applicants. Mid-May for students who wish to pay their own way.

PUBLICATIONS:
KF Newsletter; annual report.

IRS I.D.: 13-1628179

STAFF:
Marek Skulimowski, President and Executive Director

ADDRESS INQUIRIES TO:
Addy Tymczyszyn, Coordinator
Summer Study Abroad Programs
(See e-mail address above.)

*PLEASE NOTE:
Students submit scholarship applications to the Foundation's chapters. Pay-to-go applicants must submit application materials to Kosciuszko Foundation's headquarters in New York City.

*SPECIAL STIPULATIONS:
Students who receive scholarships are required to submit a report upon completion of the program. The report is forwarded to the donors of the scholarship.

THE KOSCIUSZKO FOUNDATION, INC.   [839]
15 East 65th Street
New York, NY 10065
(212) 734-2130 ext. 413
E-mail: exchangetopoland@thekf.org
Web Site: www.thekf.
org/kf/scholarships/exchange-poland/year-abroad

FOUNDED: 1925

AREAS OF INTEREST:
Strengthening of cultural and educational bonds between the U.S. and Poland through an exchange program to Poland for the purpose of Polish language, culture and history studies.

NAME(S) OF PROGRAMS:
● **The Kosciuszko Foundation Year Abroad Program**

TYPE:
Exchange programs; Scholarships. The Year Abroad Program at the Center for Polish Language and Culture in the World, Jagiellonian University (Krakow) offers American students the opportunity to study Polish language, history, literature and culture for one academic year or one semester. This program allows students to spend their undergraduate junior or senior year in Poland. Undergraduate credit may be transferred. Students at the Master's level may also apply.

PURPOSE:
To enable American students to pursue an undergraduate course of Polish language,

literature, history and culture at the Center for Polish Language and Culture, Jagiellonian University, Krakow.

LEGAL BASIS:
501(c)(3) not-for-profit organization.

ELIGIBILITY:
U.S. citizens enrolled at a U.S. college or university who will be entering their junior or senior year can apply. Graduate students, with the exception of those at the dissertation level, can also apply. Minimum grade point average of 3.0 is required.

GEOG. RESTRICTIONS: United States.

FINANCIAL DATA:
Scholarship offers a tuition waiver, housing and a monthly stipend of 1,600 Polish zloty per month from the Polish government towards living expenses. Recipients also receive $900 per semester from the Foundation for living expenses. Transportation to and from Poland and other personal expenses are not included.
Amount of support per award: $900 per semester plus additional funding from the Polish National Agency for Academic Exchange in the amount of 1,600 Polish zloty per month of study.
Total amount of support: Varies.

NO. MOST RECENT APPLICANTS: 18.

NO. AWARDS: 7.

APPLICATION INFO:
Details are available on the Foundation web site.
Duration: One semester (October to February or February to June) or one academic year (October to June).
Deadline: February 20. Notification in May. Funding is for the following academic year.

PUBLICATIONS:
Guidelines; *KF Newsletter;* annual report.

IRS I.D.: 13-1628179

STAFF:
Marek Skulimowski, President and Executive Director
Gosia Szymanska, Exchange Program Officer

ADDRESS INQUIRIES TO:
Gosia Szymanska, Exchange Program Officer
(See e-mail address above.)

THE KOSCIUSZKO FOUNDATION, INC.   [840]
15 East 65th Street
New York, NY 10065
(212) 734-2130 ext. 413
E-mail: exchangetopoland@thekf.org
Web Site: www.thekf.
org/kf/scholarships/exchange-poland/research

FOUNDED: 1925

AREAS OF INTEREST:
Strengthening of cultural and educational bonds between the U.S. and Poland through an exchange program for graduate-level students and scholars who wish to conduct research programs in Poland.

NAME(S) OF PROGRAMS:
● **The Kosciuszko Foundation Graduate Studies and Research in Poland**

TYPE:
Exchange programs; Research grants; Scholarships. This program enables American students and scholars to pursue a course of graduate or postgraduate study and research

in Poland. It is also open to university faculty who wish to spend a sabbatical conducting research in Poland.

Research may be conducted during the Polish academic year, October through June only.

PURPOSE:
To assist Americans in continuing their graduate and postgraduate studies and research at institutions of higher learning in Poland.

LEGAL BASIS:
501(c)(3) not-for-profit organization.

ELIGIBILITY:
U.S. citizens with strong Polish language skills who wish to conduct research in Poland may apply. Funding is granted for research at institutions of higher learning in Poland which fall under the jurisdiction of the Polish National Agency for Academic Exchange.

GEOG. RESTRICTIONS: United States.

FINANCIAL DATA:
Scholarship does not cover tuition costs. Participants receive a stipend from the Polish government towards housing and living expenses. No provisions are made for dependents. Transportation to and from Poland is at the expense of the participant. Personal expenses are not included.
Amount of support per award: $300 per month of approved study/research, plus 1,600 zloty per month from the Polish National Agency for Academic Exchange.
Total amount of support: Varies.

NO. MOST RECENT APPLICANTS: Approximately 10.

NO. AWARDS: 5.

APPLICATION INFO:
Details are available on the Foundation web site.
Duration: Maximum of nine months. Research may be conducted from October to June.
Deadline: February 20. Notification in May for funding in the following academic year.

PUBLICATIONS:
KF Newsletter; annual report.

IRS I.D.: 13-1628179

STAFF:
Marek Skulimowski, President and Executive Director

ADDRESS INQUIRIES TO:
Gosia Szymanska, Exchange Program Officer (See e-mail address above.)

THE KOSCIUSZKO FOUNDATION, INC. [841]
15 East 65th Street
New York, NY 10065
(212) 734-2130 ext. 407
E-mail: dorwat@thekf.org
Web Site: www.thekf.
org/kf/programs/teaching_english_in_poland

FOUNDED: 1925

AREAS OF INTEREST:
Educational and cultural exchange program in Poland.

NAME(S) OF PROGRAMS:
● **Teaching English in Poland**

TYPE:
Summer educational and cultural exchange program for American teachers and teaching assistants in Poland.

YEAR PROGRAM STARTED: 1991

PURPOSE:
To provide Polish students with English language experiences within an American cultural context; to familiarize Polish students with various aspects of American life and culture; to introduce American teachers and teaching assistants to Polish culture, history, traditions and people of Poland so that their knowledge and impressions will be shared.

LEGAL BASIS:
501(c)(3) not-for-profit organization.

ELIGIBILITY:
Experienced teachers/administrators certified in the U.S., educators with private/parochial school or other verifiable teaching experience, college/university faculty, and those engaged in student services (school nurse, social worker, guidance counselor, school psychologist, etc.) are eligible for participation. Group flight arrangements will be made by the Foundation. Participants are encouraged to travel to Poland with the group.

GEOG. RESTRICTIONS: United States.

FINANCIAL DATA:
Registration fee of $300 for teachers and $250 for teaching assistants and peer tutors. Medical insurance, required by The Kosciuszko Foundation, is covered. This is a volunteer opportunity. Applicant pays for airfare. Room and board during the teaching program as well as sightseeing in Poland after the program's end are covered by Polish hosts.
Amount of support per award: Varies.
Matching fund requirements: In-kind donations such as art and sport equipment towards the program are accepted.

CO-OP FUNDING PROGRAMS: Delta Kappa Gamma support in the amount of $14,000.

NO. MOST RECENT APPLICANTS: 120.

NO. AWARDS: 31.

APPLICATION INFO:
Applications must be completed on the Foundation's web site.
Duration: Two and one-half to four weeks.
Deadline: January 31.

PUBLICATIONS:
KF Newsletter; Annual Report.

IRS I.D.: 13-1628179

STAFF:
Mary Kay Pieski, Ph.D.

ADDRESS INQUIRIES TO:
Teaching English in Poland Program (See address above.)

THE ROBERTO LONGHI FOUNDATION FOR THE STUDY OF THE HISTORY OF ART
Via Benedetto Fortini, 30
50125 Florence Italy
(39) 055 6580794
Fax: (39) 055 6580794
E-mail: longhi@fondazionelonghi.it
Web Site: www.fondazionelonghi.it

TYPE:
Fellowships.
See entry 508 for full listing.

MARSHALL AID COMMEMORATION COMMISSION [842]
ACU
Woburn House
20-24 Tavistock Square
London WC1H 9HF England
(44) 207 380 6704
(44) 207 380 6703
E-mail: apps@marshallscholarship.org
Web Site: www.marshallscholarship.org

FOUNDED: 1953

NAME(S) OF PROGRAMS:
● **Marshall Scholarships**

TYPE:
Scholarships. Tenable at any university in the U.K. in any subject leading to the award of a British university degree, which recipients are required to take.

Marshall Scholarships finance young Americans of high ability to study for a degree in the U.K. in a system of higher education recognized for its excellence. These grants have been established to express British gratitude for the European Recovery Program (the Marshall Plan) instituted by General of the Army George C. Marshall.

YEAR PROGRAM STARTED: 1954

PURPOSE:
To enable intellectually distinguished young Americans to study in the U.K.; to contribute to the advancement of knowledge in science, technology, the humanities and social sciences and the creative arts at Britain's centers of academic excellence.

LEGAL BASIS:
Programme established by British Parliamentary Act.

ELIGIBILITY:
Scholarships are offered to U.S. citizens for study in the U.K. Graduates of a degree-granting college or university who have graduated from their undergraduate college or university no more than three years before the year the award will be taken up are eligible (e.g., for awards tenable from October 2022, candidates must have graduated after April 2019). Candidates must be American citizens at the time of application and must have obtained a grade point average of not less than 3.7 (or A-).

FINANCIAL DATA:
Scholarships include a personal allowance, tuition fees, grants for books, travel, thesis and fares to and from Britain.
Amount of support per award: Currently GBP 1,110 per month (GBP 1,362 for those registered within the London Metropolitan Police district).
Total amount of support: GBP 2,550,000 for the year ended March 31, 2019.

NO. MOST RECENT APPLICANTS: Approximately 1,000.

NO. AWARDS: Up to 50 awards annually.

APPLICATION INFO:
Application should be made to a British Consulate-General (in Atlanta, Boston, Chicago, Houston, Los Angeles, New York and San Francisco) or to the British Embassy in Washington, DC.

Duration: One to two years. May be extended for a third year.

Deadline: Early October of the year preceding the award.

OFFICERS:
Caroline Harrison, Executive Secretary
Mary C. Denyer, Assistant Secretary

COMMISSION MEMBERS:
John Raine, Chairperson
Alan Bookbinder
Prof. Judith Buchanan
Adrian Greer
Suzanne McCarthy
Dr. Alice Prochaska
Prof. Adam Smith
Dr. Leslie Vinjamuri
Xenia Wickett
Lord Wood of Anfield

THE MATSUMAE INTERNATIONAL FOUNDATION   [843]
4-14-46, Kamiogi, Suginami-ku
Tokyo 167-0043 Japan
(81) 3-3301-7600
Fax: (81) 3-3301-7601
E-mail: contact@mif-japan.org
Web Site: www.mif-japan.org

FOUNDED: 1979

AREAS OF INTEREST:
Natural sciences, engineering and medicine are given first priority.

NAME(S) OF PROGRAMS:
● **Fellowship Program**

TYPE:
Fellowships; Research grants.

YEAR PROGRAM STARTED: 1980

PURPOSE:
To provide opportunity to foreign scientists to conduct research at Japanese institutions.

LEGAL BASIS:
Private foundation.

ELIGIBILITY:
Citizenship is unrestricted. Those of non-Japanese nationality who meet all of the following eligibility requirements are invited to submit the required application documents:
(1) Applicants must hold a Ph.D. degree, or be recognized by the Foundation as possessing equivalent academic qualifications;
(2) Applicants must be 49 years of age or under at the time of application;
(3) Applicants must have sufficient conversational ability in English or Japanese to prevent insurmountable difficulties during their research activities in Japan;
(4) Applicants should not have been in Japan in the past and/or in the present and;
(5) Applicants should have firm positions and professions in their home countries and should return to their countries upon completion of their fellowship stay by the Foundation.

FINANCIAL DATA:
Awards include stipend for research and stay, lump sum on arrival, round-trip travel and insurance.
Amount of support per award: Monthly allowance of JPY 220,000; lump sum on arrival of 120,000 JPY.

NO. MOST RECENT APPLICANTS: 852 researchers from 119 countries for the year 2019.

NO. AWARDS: Up to 10.

APPLICATION INFO:
Applicant must obtain acceptance from a host institution prior to submitting the application. Applicant must submit the required documents in accordance with the latest announcement, which can be downloaded from MIF's web site.

All of the documents must be typed in English, converted to Adobe PDF, and submitted by e-mail to the address listed above. Required documents include:
(1) original application form, which can be downloaded from the MIF web site;
(2) a detailed description of the research project, including content, purpose and methodology of the research, as well as the road map of the research project;
(3) the most significant publication by the applicant. If not available in English, then attach an abstract or summary in English;
(4) curriculum vitae;
(5) a recommendation letter from applicant's home institution written on their letterhead;
(6) soft copies of academic certificates and diplomas for Bachelor, Master's and Ph.D. degrees. If the documents are not available in English, please attach English translations and;
(7) the invitation letter from the host professor or scholar in charge at the host institution in Japan and written on their letterhead. Name of host, name of host institution, e-mail address of host, and postal code, mailing address and telephone number of the host institution must be mentioned in Japanese.

Applications will not be accepted before or after the application period.
Duration: Three to six months; extension/reduction of the granted period is not allowed.
Deadline: Applications must be received by the Foundation by June 30 for the following year's fellowship.

PUBLICATIONS:
Program announcement.

ADDRESS INQUIRIES TO:
Fellowship Program
(See address above.)

*PLEASE NOTE:
To promote deeper understanding of Japan, the Foundation organizes a Study Tour during the invitation period in Japan.

Each year, the Foundation issues a "Research Report" containing summaries of research activities or results which are kindly submitted by the Fellows.

In order to keep in touch with Fellows after their return home, the Foundation issues a "Newsletter" and "Fellowship Directory" annually.

MICHIGAN STATE UNIVERSITY   [844]
Office for Education Abroad
427 North Shaw Lane, Room 109
East Lansing, MI 48824
(517) 353-8920
Fax: (517) 432-2082
E-mail: abroad@msu.edu
Web Site: educationabroad.msu.edu

NAME(S) OF PROGRAMS:
● **MSU Education Abroad Scholarships**

TYPE:
Scholarships. Academic study abroad scholarships for college-level credit. The program includes over 275 overseas study programs in more than 60 countries in a wide variety of academic fields.

PURPOSE:
To assist Michigan State University students who will benefit from study abroad.

LEGAL BASIS:
University.

ELIGIBILITY:
Applicants must be MSU students. Participation in study abroad program is:
(1) based on financial need. Applicant must have FAFSA application on file with MSU office of financial aid and have a minimum 2.0 grade point average and;
(2) based on academic performance. Applicant must have a minimum 3.5 grade point average and submit an essay explaining how study abroad would enhance the student's education.

FINANCIAL DATA:
Amount of support per award: $250 to $1,750 available per student.
Total amount of support: Approximately $400,000 annually.

NO. MOST RECENT APPLICANTS: Approximately 1,200.

NO. AWARDS: Approximately 400 per year.

APPLICATION INFO:
Application information is available on the web site.
Duration: Varies.
Deadline: October 1 and March 1.

STAFF:
Lynn Aguado, Study Abroad Program Coordinator

ADDRESS INQUIRIES TO:
Kelsey Pink, Budget and Financial Manager
E-mail: pinkkels@msu.edu

NATIONAL SECURITY EDUCATION PROGRAM   [845]
Institute of International Education
1400 K Street, N.W., Suite 700
Washington, DC 20005-2403
(800) 618-6737
E-mail: boren@iie.org
Web Site: www.borenawards.org

FOUNDED: 1991

AREAS OF INTEREST:
Languages and cultures of world regions that are critical to U.S. interests and underrepresented in study abroad, including Africa, Asia, Central and Eastern Europe, Eurasia, Latin America, and the Middle East.

NAME(S) OF PROGRAMS:
● **Boren Scholarships**

TYPE:
Scholarships. Boren Scholarships provide funding for U.S. undergraduate students to study less commonly taught languages in world regions that are critical to U.S. interests and underrepresented in study abroad.

PURPOSE:
To provide American undergraduates with the resources and encouragement they need to acquire language skills and cultural experiences in areas of the world critical to national security, broadly defined. In

exchange for funding, recipients commit to working in the federal government for a minimum of one year after graduation.

ELIGIBILITY:
Must be a U.S. citizen at the time of application. Open to high school graduates, or those who have earned a GED, and are matriculated as a freshman, sophomore, junior, or senior in a U.S. postsecondary institution, including universities, colleges, and community colleges. Applicant must plan to study abroad in Africa, Asia, Central and Eastern Europe, Eurasia, or the Middle East. The countries of Western Europe, Canada, Australia, and New Zealand are excluded. The study abroad program must meet home institution standards and end prior to graduation.

FINANCIAL DATA:
Amount of support per award: Summer: Up to $8,000; Semester: Up to $12,500; Full academic year: Up to $25,000.

NO. MOST RECENT APPLICANTS: 784.

NO. AWARDS: 217.

APPLICATION INFO:
Complete details and application information can be found on the Boren Awards web site.
Duration: Summer (eight to 11 weeks), fall or spring semester (12 to 24 weeks), and full academic year (25 to 52 weeks).
Deadline: February 3.

ADDRESS INQUIRIES TO:
See e-mail address or telephone number above.

*SPECIAL STIPULATIONS:
In exchange for funding, recipients agree to the National Security Education Program (NSEP) Service Requirement. The NSEP Service Requirement stipulates that an award recipient work for a minimum of one year in the federal government in a position with national security responsibilities. The Departments of Defense, Homeland Security, State, or any element of the Intelligence Community are priority agencies.

NATIONAL SECURITY EDUCATION PROGRAM [846]
Institute of International Education
1400 K Street, N.W., Suite 700
Washington, DC 20005-2403
(800) 618-6737
E-mail: boren@iie.org
Web Site: www.borenawards.org

FOUNDED: 1991

AREAS OF INTEREST:
Boren Fellowships support study and research in areas of the world that are critical to U.S. interests, including Africa, Asia, Central and Eastern Europe, Eurasia, Latin America, and the Middle East.

NAME(S) OF PROGRAMS:
● **Boren Fellowships**

TYPE:
Fellowships. Fellowships for U.S. graduate students to provide support for overseas study or a combination of overseas and domestic study.

PURPOSE:
To encourage U.S. graduate students to add an important international and language component to their graduate education through specialization in area study, language study, or increased language proficiency; to

support study and research in areas of the world that are critical to U.S. interests, including Africa, Asia, Central and Eastern Europe, Eurasia, Latin America, and the Middle East.

ELIGIBILITY:
Must be a U.S. citizen at the time of application. Applicants must be matriculated in or applying to a graduate degree program at an accredited U.S. college or university located within the U.S. Boren Fellows must remain matriculated in their graduate programs for the duration of the fellowship. Applicant must plan an overseas program that meets home institution standards in Africa, Asia, Central and Eastern Europe, Eurasia, Latin America, and the Middle East. The countries of Western Europe, Canada, Australia, and New Zealand are excluded.

FINANCIAL DATA:
Amount of support per award: Up to $12,000 for summer domestic study; Up to $25,000 for overseas study; Up to $30,000 for a combination of domestic and overseas study.

NO. MOST RECENT APPLICANTS: 268.

NO. AWARDS: 119.

APPLICATION INFO:
Complete details and application information can be found on the Boren Awards web site.
Duration: Minimum 12 weeks for overseas study. Preference will be given to programs of 25 to 52 weeks.
Deadline: January 27.

ADDRESS INQUIRIES TO:
See e-mail address or telephone number above.

*SPECIAL STIPULATIONS:
In exchange for funding, recipients agree to the National Security Education Program (NSEP) Service Requirement. The NSEP Service Requirement stipulates that an award recipient work for a minimum of one year in the federal government in a position with national security responsibilities. The Departments of Defense, Homeland Security, State, or any element of the Intelligence Community are priority agencies.

THE PHI BETA KAPPA SOCIETY [847]
1606 New Hampshire Avenue, N.W.
Washington, DC 20009
(202) 745-3287
Fax: (202) 986-1601
E-mail: awards@pbk.org
Web Site: www.pbk.org

AREAS OF INTEREST:
French language, literature and culture.

NAME(S) OF PROGRAMS:
● **The Walter J. Jensen Fellowship for French Language, Literature and Culture**

TYPE:
Fellowships. Fellowship for at least six months of study in France. One award given annually.

YEAR PROGRAM STARTED: 2001

PURPOSE:
To help educators and researchers improve education in standard French language, literature and culture, and in the study of standard French in the U.S.

ELIGIBILITY:
Candidates must be U.S. citizens under 40 years of age who can demonstrate their career does or will involve active use of the French language. They must have earned a Baccalaureate degree from an accredited four-year institution, and have a 3.0 minimum grade point average in French language and literature as a major. They must demonstrate superior competence in French, according to the standards established by the American Association of Teachers of French. Preference may be given to members of Phi Beta Kappa and educators at the secondary school level or above.

GEOG. RESTRICTIONS: United States.

FINANCIAL DATA:
Includes single round-trip, economy-class ticket for travel to France.
Amount of support per award: $16,400 for the year 2018.

NO. MOST RECENT APPLICANTS: Varies.

NO. AWARDS: Minimum 1 annually.

APPLICATION INFO:
The application booklet contains:
(1) the Application for the Walter J. Jensen Fellowship;
(2) two Transcript Request forms and;
(3) the Letter of Recommendation Form.

Applicant must submit three complete sets of documents. The Letter of Recommendation and Transcript Request forms may be duplicated. Please indicate the Fellowship name on all correspondence.

Applicant should send the application, official transcripts, and confidential letters of recommendation (in sealed envelopes) to the Walter J. Jensen Fellowship Committee in care of the Phi Beta Kappa Society.
Duration: At least six months.
Deadline: January 15.

ADDRESS INQUIRIES TO:
Aurora Sherman, Executive Assistant to the Secretary and Awards Coordinator
(See address above.)

THE ROTARY FOUNDATION OF ROTARY INTERNATIONAL [848]
One Rotary Center
1560 Sherman Avenue
Evanston, IL 60201-3698
(847) 866-3000
E-mail: rotarypeacecenters@rotary.org
Web Site: www.rotary.org/en/peace-fellowships

FOUNDED: 2002

AREAS OF INTEREST:
Higher education.

NAME(S) OF PROGRAMS:
● **Rotary Peace Fellowships**

TYPE:
Fellowships. The Rotary Peace Centers offer individuals committed to peace and cooperation the opportunity to pursue a one- to two-year Master's-level degree or a three-month professional certificate in international studies, peace studies and conflict resolution at one of the six Rotary Peace Centers. The university partners are: Duke University and the University of North Carolina at Chapel Hill (North Carolina, U.S.A.); International Christian University (Tokyo, Japan); University of Bradford (West Yorkshire, England); University of Queensland (Brisbane, Queensland,

Australia); Uppsala University (Uppsala, Sweden); and Chulalongkorn University (Bangkok, Thailand).

YEAR PROGRAM STARTED: 2002

PURPOSE:
To further peace and international understanding.

LEGAL BASIS:
Incorporated not-for-profit foundation.

ELIGIBILITY:
For the Master's Degree Program, applicants must have:
(1) a minimum of three years of related full-time work or volunteer experience and a Bachelor's degree;
(2) proficiency in English; proficiency in a second language is strongly recommended;
(3) a strong commitment to international understanding and peace as demonstrated through professional and academic achievements and personal or community service and;
(4) excellent leadership skills.

For the Professional Development Certificate Program, applicants must have:
(1) a minimum of five years of relevant full-time work or volunteer experience and a strong academic background;
(2) proficiency in English; proficiency in a second language is strongly recommended;
(3) a strong commitment to international understanding and peace demonstrated through professional and academic achievements and personal and community service activities and;
(4) excellent leadership skills.

Rotary Peace Fellowship may not be used for doctoral study. The following people are not eligible for the Master's Degree Program:
(1) active Rotarians;
(2) employees of a Rotary club, Rotary International, or other Rotary entity;
(3) spouses, lineal descendants (children or grandchildren by blood or legal adoption), spouses of lineal descendants or ancestors (parents or grandparents by blood) of any living person in the categories above and;
(4) former Rotarians and their relatives as described above.

FINANCIAL DATA:
Fellowship will include funding for tuition and required fees, room and board, transportation, contingency expenses and other funding, including paid internship experience.
Amount of support per award: Master's Program: Average $75,000; Professional Development Certificate: Average $11,000.
Total amount of support: Varies.

NO. MOST RECENT APPLICANTS: 700.

NO. AWARDS: Approximately 130 each year.

APPLICATION INFO:
Applicants are required to submit their application and all supplementary materials to a Rotary district. Rotary clubs can help to connect applicants with a Rotary district. It is strongly recommended that applicants connect to a club near their legal or permanent place of residence, full-time study, or employment to assist with the application process. Applications must be submitted to the applicant's chosen Rotary district by May 31, and it is recommended that the applicants contact a club and/or district when they begin the application process.

Application checklist and essay requirements are available on the Rotary web site.

Duration: Master's Program: 15 to 24 months. Professional Development Certificate: One year.
Deadline: May 31.

PUBLICATIONS:
Application; brochure.

ADDRESS INQUIRIES TO:
Local Rotary Club or Rotary Peace Centers Staff
(See e-mail address above.)

ST. ANDREW'S SOCIETY OF THE STATE OF NEW YORK [849]
150 East 55th Street, 3rd Floor
New York, NY 10022
(212) 223-4248
Fax: (212) 233-0748
E-mail: office@standrewsny.org
Web Site: standrewsny.org

FOUNDED: 1756

AREAS OF INTEREST:
Charitable support of needy persons of Scottish descent and scholarship program.

NAME(S) OF PROGRAMS:
● **Scholarship Program for Graduate Study in Scotland**

TYPE:
Scholarships. Scholarships for American students of Scottish descent for one year of graduate study in any Scottish university.

YEAR PROGRAM STARTED: 1956

PURPOSE:
To promote cultural interchange and goodwill between Scotland and the U.S.

LEGAL BASIS:
Tax-exempt charitable organization.

ELIGIBILITY:
An applicant must be in senior year of undergraduate study, exhibit financial need, possess an outstanding scholastic and activity record, provide evidence of Scottish descent, and reside within a 250-mile radius of New York state.

GEOG. RESTRICTIONS: New Jersey, New York, Pennsylvania and the New England states.

FINANCIAL DATA:
Award is to be used initially against tuition, then board, room, transportation and other expenses.
Amount of support per award: $35,000.
Total amount of support: Varies each year.

NO. MOST RECENT APPLICANTS: 100.

NO. AWARDS: 3 per year (for U.S. applicants).

APPLICATION INFO:
The applicant must contact the Fellowships Office at their current academic institution. Each college or university is invited to send only one candidate forward to the St. Andrew's Society Selection Committee. Referral must be by the president of the institution the applicant is attending.
Duration: One year. Nonrenewable.
Deadline: December 15. Announcement in early March.

PUBLICATIONS:
Quarterly newsletter.

IRS I.D.: 13-5602329

OFFICERS:
David M. Murphy, President
Richard Porter, First Vice President

John H. Blankley, Second Vice President
John A.D. Needham, Treasurer
Thomas Burt, Secretary

ADDRESS INQUIRIES TO:
Samuel S. Abernethy, Scholarship Chairman
(See address above.)

*SPECIAL STIPULATIONS:
Candidates must be from northeastern U.S. and of Scottish descent, and must be U.S. citizens.

SCUOLA NORMALE SUPERIORE   [850]
Piazza dei Cavalieri, 7
56126 Pisa Italy
(39) 050 509237
(39) 050 509111
Fax: (39) 050 563513
E-mail: mario.landucci@sns.it
phd@sns.it
Web Site: www.sns.it

FOUNDED: 1813

AREAS OF INTEREST:
Classical philology, linguistics and history, modern philology and linguistics, history, art history, philosophy, mathematics and physics and their applications in chemistry and biology.

NAME(S) OF PROGRAMS:
● **Graduate School Scholarships for Study in Italy**

TYPE:
Scholarships. Scholarships for study at the Scuola Normale Superiore, Pisa, Italy, for postgraduate study in the disciplinary areas of the humanities and of mathematics, physics and natural sciences listed above.

PURPOSE:
To promote research and study in Italy.

LEGAL BASIS:
State-owned university.

ELIGIBILITY:
Citizens of all countries who have an M.A. degree and know Italian may apply. Students over 30 at the time of application cannot be admitted to the graduate courses. Applicants may not be receiving other forms of assistance.

FINANCIAL DATA:
Amount of support per award:
Perfezionamento (Ph.D.): Study grant of EUR 17,000 per year.

NO. AWARDS: 76 for the year 2020-21.

APPLICATION INFO:
Information is available online. The new announcement appears around May to June each year.
Duration: Up to three years; fellowship may be extended for an additional year for justified academic and/or scientific reasons if possible within the budget.
Deadline: Varies by faculty.

ADDRESS INQUIRIES TO:
Student Secretariat
Dott. Mario Landucci
(See address above.)

SHASTRI INDO-CANADIAN INSTITUTE (SICI) [851]
1418 Education Tower
2500 University Drive, N.W.
Calgary AB T2N 1N4 Canada
(403) 220-3220
E-mail: maldeen@ucalgary.ca
Web Site: www.shastriinstitute.org

AREAS OF INTEREST:
Knowledge creation and mobilization, faculty and student mobility, building institutional partnerships and understanding between India and Canada.

TYPE:
Fellowships; Internships; Travel grants. Collaborative research grants; Publication grants.

YEAR PROGRAM STARTED: 1968

PURPOSE:
To promote understanding between Canada and India, mainly through facilitating academic activities.

ELIGIBILITY:
Applicants must be Canadian citizens or permanent residents.

FINANCIAL DATA:
Amount of support per award: Varies.
Total amount of support: Varies.

CO-OP FUNDING PROGRAMS: Department of Education, Ministry of Human Resources, Government of India.

NO. MOST RECENT APPLICANTS: 30 to 70 per grant.

NO. AWARDS: Varies.

APPLICATION INFO:
Application information is available on the web site.
Duration: Three months to two years.
Deadline: Varies.

ADDRESS INQUIRIES TO:
See e-mail address above.

SOMMERHOCHSCHULE - UNIVERSITY OF VIENNA [852]
Campus of the University of Vienna
Alser Strasse 4/Hof 1/Tuer 1.16
1090 Vienna Austria
43-(0)1-4277-24131
E-mail: sommerhochschule@univie.ac.at
Web Site: shs.univie.ac.at

FOUNDED: 1949

AREAS OF INTEREST:
European Studies (with focus on legal, economic, political and cultural aspects) taught in English; German Language Courses (A1, A2, B1, B2).

NAME(S) OF PROGRAMS:
- **univie: summer school for International and European Studies**

TYPE:
Scholarships. The European Studies courses focus on the political, economic and legal, but also historical and cultural, aspects of Europe and the EU. The German language courses are offered at four different levels of proficiency (beginners to advanced).

YEAR PROGRAM STARTED: 1949

PURPOSE:
To contribute to an increased understanding of the EU and its possible future shape and to create an environment which encourages intercultural and social exchange and favors mutual understanding among participants.

LEGAL BASIS:
A subcompany of the University of Vienna.

ELIGIBILITY:
Applicants have to be at least 18 years old and must have completed at least two years of studies at college or university level in their countries of residence or have an educational background equivalent to one year at a European university before the beginning of the program.

FINANCIAL DATA:
A limited number of partial scholarships are available for the European Studies section of the program. The scholarships are awarded on the basis of academic excellence and financial need.
Amount of support per award: EUR 400 to 2,800.

NO. MOST RECENT APPLICANTS: 90 to 110.

NO. AWARDS: Varies based on the scholarship budget available.

APPLICATION INFO:
Applicants must submit the following documents:
(1) application form;
(2) transcript of grades;
(3) letter of recommendation;
(4) official proof of proficiency in English;
(5) statement of purpose and;
(6) two passport-size photos taken within the past year.

All documents have to be submitted either in original or as a certified copy and have to be translated into English or German.

Application material must be sent to the office of the Sommerhochschule (e-mailed applications cannot be accepted).
Duration: Four weeks, middle of July to middle of August.
Deadline: Regular Applications: April 30. Scholarship Applications: February 28.

PUBLICATIONS:
Annual brochures and leaflets for the univie: summer school of the Sommerhochschule.

STAFF:
Dr. Franz-Stefan Meissel, Director
Verena Bauer, Program Coordinator
Nina Gruber, Program Coordinator

ADDRESS INQUIRIES TO:
Nina Gruber, Program Coordinator
(See address above.)

SOMMERHOCHSCHULE - UNIVERSITY OF VIENNA [853]
Campus of the University of Vienna
Alser Strasse 4/Hof 1/Tuer 1.16
1090 Vienna Austria
43-(0)1-4277-24131
E-mail: sommerhochschule@univie.ac.at
Web Site: shs.univie.ac.at/winter-school

FOUNDED: 1949

AREAS OF INTEREST:
History and society of the late Habsburg Monarchy, as well as fine arts, architecture and design of the same period, and developments in psychology, literature and music.

NAME(S) OF PROGRAMS:
- **univie: winter school for Cultural Historical Studies**

TYPE:
Scholarships. The winter school courses provide a well-structured introduction into the culture of the fin-de-siecle. The program offers six courses about the history and society of the late Habsburg Monarchy, as well as fine arts, architecture and design of the same period. The courses are held by distinguished scholars with international teaching experience. The interdisciplinary lectures will lead to a thorough understanding of the input of the fin-de-siecle on the modernization of Europe.

YEAR PROGRAM STARTED: 2015

PURPOSE:
To increase the understanding of the input of the fin-de-siecle on the modernization of Europe; to promote intercultural and social exchange among participants.

LEGAL BASIS:
A subcompany of the University of Vienna.

ELIGIBILITY:
Applicants must be at least 18 years old and must have completed one year of studies at college or university level before the beginning of the program.

FINANCIAL DATA:
Participants have the opportunity to receive a tuition waiver (scholarship) for the winter school from the International Office of the University of Vienna.

NO. MOST RECENT APPLICANTS: 60.

NO. AWARDS: 4 per year.

APPLICATION INFO:
Applicants must submit the following documents:
(1) application form;
(2) statement of purpose;
(3) transcript of grades;
(4) official proof of proficiency in English;
(5) two passport-size photos and;
(6) passport scan.

All documents have to be submitted either in original or as a certified copy and have to be translated into English or German. Application materials must be sent to the office of the Sommerhochschule. E-mailed applications cannot be accepted.
Duration: Two weeks in February.
Deadline: November 30.

PUBLICATIONS:
Annual folders for the univie: winter school of the Sommerhochschule.

STAFF:
Dr. Franz-Stefan Meissel, Director
Verena Bauer, Program Coordinator
Nina Gruber, Program Coordinator

ADDRESS INQUIRIES TO:
Nina Gruber, Program Coordinator
(See e-mail address above.)

U.S. DEPARTMENT OF EDUCATION [854]
International and Foreign Language Education
400 Maryland Avenue, S.W.
Mail Stop 258-40
Washington, DC 20202
(202) 453-6950
E-mail: gpa@ed.gov
Web Site: www2.ed.gov/programs/iegpsgpa/index.html

FOUNDED: 1967

AREAS OF INTEREST:
Foreign languages and area studies.

NAME(S) OF PROGRAMS:
- **Fulbright-Hays Group Projects Abroad Program**

TYPE:
Exchange programs; Project/program grants; Seed money grants; Training grants; Travel grants. Also, study grants and grants for foreign language and area study programs of educational development for projects to be undertaken abroad. Grants are awarded to higher education institutions, nonprofit educational organizations, state department of education and consortium of such institutions, departments, organizations and institutions which, in turn, enable professors, college and elementary and secondary school teachers and advanced students to attend seminars abroad and to travel and study in foreign countries in order to strengthen the institution's programs in foreign languages, area studies and world affairs.

YEAR PROGRAM STARTED: 1967

PURPOSE:
To contribute to the development and improvement of the study of foreign languages and area studies in the U.S. by providing opportunities for faculty, teachers, upperclassmen and/or graduate students to travel to foreign countries in group projects for research, training and curriculum development.

LEGAL BASIS:
The Mutual Educational and Cultural Exchange Act of 1961, Public Law 87-256 (Fulbright Hays Act), Section 102(b)(6).

ELIGIBILITY:
Under the program, grants are awarded to institutions of higher education, state departments of education, private nonprofit educational organizations and consortiums of such institutions, departments and organizations to conduct overseas group projects in research, training and curriculum development, by groups of individuals engaged in a common endeavor.

A participant must be a citizen, national or permanent resident of the U.S. and either a faculty member in modern foreign languages or area studies, an experienced educator responsible for planning, conducting or supervising programs in modern foreign languages or area studies at the elementary, secondary or postsecondary levels, a graduate student or upperclassman who plans a teaching career in modern foreign languages or area studies.

The grant does not provide funds for project-related expenses within the U.S. Funds may be used only for a maintenance stipend based on 50% of the amount established in the U.S. Department of State publication, *Maximum Travel Per Diem Allowances for Foreign Areas*, round-trip international travel, a local travel allowance for necessary project-related transportation within the country of study, exclusive of the purchase of transportation equipment, the purchase of project-related artifacts, books and other teaching materials in the country of study, rent for instructional facilities in the country of study, and clerical and professional services performed by resident instructional personnel in the country of study.

FINANCIAL DATA:
Amount of support per award: Varies.
Total amount of support: $2,670,500 appropriated for fiscal year 2020.

APPLICATION INFO:
Application information is available on the web site.
Duration: Four weeks to one year. No renewals.
Deadline: March.

ADDRESS INQUIRIES TO:
Cory Neal, Program Officer
(See e-mail address above.)

*PLEASE NOTE:
Annual competition contingent upon receiving a Congressional Appropriation.

UNIVERSITY OF BRISTOL   [855]
Senate House
Tyndall Avenue
Bristol BS8 1TH England
(44) 0117 928 9000
(44) 0117 331 7972
Fax: (44) 0117 331 7873
E-mail: student-funding@bristol.ac.uk
Web Site: www.bristol.ac.uk

FOUNDED: 1909

AREAS OF INTEREST:
Faculties of arts, engineering, biomedical sciences, health sciences, science, social sciences and law.

NAME(S) OF PROGRAMS:
- **Postgraduate Research Scholarships**

TYPE:
Scholarships. Postgraduate research scholarships for study toward the Ph.D. degree in one of the Schools of the University of Bristol.

YEAR PROGRAM STARTED: 1989

PURPOSE:
To attract excellent research students.

LEGAL BASIS:
University.

ELIGIBILITY:
Scholarships are available for the U.K., Europe and overseas students.

APPLICATION INFO:
Information is available from the Student Funding Office at the University of Bristol or online.
Duration: Up to four years, subject to satisfactory academic progress and according to the particular discipline and training programme.
Deadline: Varies.

PUBLICATIONS:
Annual report; research prospectus.

ADDRESS INQUIRIES TO:
Student Funding Office
(See address above.)

UNIVERSITY OF ILLINOIS AT URBANA-CHAMPAIGN
College of Fine and Applied Arts
608 East Lorado Taft Drive, Suite 100
Champaign, IL 61820
(217) 333-1661
(217) 333-1660
E-mail: faa@illinois.edu
Web Site: www.faa.illinois.edu/alumni-friends/kate-neal-kinley-memorial-fellowship

TYPE:
Fellowships. Awarded for advanced study in the fine arts in the U.S. or abroad, in an

approved educational institution, with an approved private teacher or in independent study.

Three major Fellowships will be awarded:
(1) one in any field of music;
(2) one in architectural design and history, art and design, theatre, dance, or instrumental or vocal music and;
(3) one in art, architecture, dance, landscape architecture, theatre, or urban and regional planning.

See entry 522 for full listing.

THE UNIVERSITY OF MANCHESTER   [856]
Manchester Doctoral College
Oxford Road
Manchester M13 9PL England
(44) 0161 275 8792
E-mail: mdc@manchester.ac.uk
Web Site: www.manchester.ac.uk/study/postgraduate-research/funding

FOUNDED: 1824

AREAS OF INTEREST:
Arts, economic, social and legal studies, education, science, engineering, medicine and biological sciences.

NAME(S) OF PROGRAMS:
- **British Marshall Scholarships**
- **Fulbright - University of Manchester Award**
- **North American Foundation Awards**
- **President's Doctoral Scholar Award**

TYPE:
Assistantships; Awards/prizes; Block grants; Conferences/seminars; Endowments; Exchange programs; Fellowships; Research grants; Scholarships; Training grants; Travel grants; Visiting scholars. Research studentships for postgraduate-taught and research programmes in the fields above.

North American Foundation Awards are for postgraduate study at the University of Manchester (NAFUM).

The University of Manchester is also a recognized institution for the purpose of U.S. federal loans and Canadian student loans.

FINANCIAL DATA:
Studentships include payment of fees at U.K. level and/or maintenance allowance.
Amount of support per award: Varies.

ADDRESS INQUIRIES TO:
Student Services Centre
E-mail: ssc@manchester.ac.uk

UNIVERSITY OF OSLO INTERNATIONAL SUMMER SCHOOL   [857]
Oslo International Summer School
c/o St. Olaf College
1520 St. Olaf Avenue
Northfield, MN 55057-1098
(507) 786-3269
(800) 639-0058
E-mail: iss@stolaf.edu
Web Site: www.uio.no/summerschool

FOUNDED: 1947

AREAS OF INTEREST:
The International Summer School offers undergraduate and graduate courses in the following areas:
General course offerings - Norwegian language, Norwegian art history, Norwegian architecture and design, Norwegian literature,

history, political science, culture and society, international relations and gender equality in Nordic countries;
Graduate courses - peace research, international development, gender equality, international community health, energy and sustainable development, human rights, and a changing Arctic.

TYPE:
Scholarships.

YEAR PROGRAM STARTED: 1947

PURPOSE:
To offer academic instruction to a gathering of many nationalities in the hope of a modest but concrete increase in understanding and goodwill among nations.

LEGAL BASIS:
Part of the University of Oslo.

ELIGIBILITY:
Scholarships awarded only to students accepted into the Oslo International Summer School program. Scholarship applicants must meet the entrance requirements of the International Summer School and must present evidence of attending or having attended a recognized university and have a good academic record. One year or more of college or university is required. In addition, seriousness of academic purpose and personal qualities likely to make the applicant a good representative of his or her country.

FINANCIAL DATA:
Amount of support per award: Varies.

Total amount of support: Varies.

NO. MOST RECENT APPLICANTS: Approximately 30.

NO. AWARDS: Varies.

APPLICATION INFO:
A financial aid application form and the application for admission to the International Summer School and the supporting letters of recommendation are used by the Financial Aid Committee to choose financial aid recipients.

Duration: Six weeks during the summer, from late June to early August. No renewal possibilities.

Deadline: February 1. Results are announced the first week in April.

PUBLICATIONS:
ISS catalog.

ADMINISTRATION:
Nita Kapoor, Director, International Summer School Norwegian Office
Michelle Fredrickson, Program Administrator, North American Admissions Office

ADDRESS INQUIRIES TO:
Non-North American students should request information from:
International Summer School
Postbox 1082
NO-0317 Oslo, Norway
Tel: (011) 47 2285-6385

All other applicants can use the North American address above.

THE UNIVERSITY OF SYDNEY [858]
Scholarships Office
Level 4, Jane Foss Russell Building G02
The University of Sydney N.S.W. 2006
Australia
61 (02) 8627 1444
E-mail: scholarships.officer@sydney.edu.au
Web Site: www.sydney.edu.au/scholarships

FOUNDED: 1850

NAME(S) OF PROGRAMS:
● **Research Training Program (RTP)**

TYPE:
Scholarships. Awarded for research leading to a higher degree. Tenable at the University of Sydney.

LEGAL BASIS:
University.

ELIGIBILITY:
The scholarships are awarded on academic merit and research ability to qualified candidates. Open to qualified foreign graduates from any country eligible to commence a higher degree by research. Australian and New Zealand citizens or permanent residents are not eligible.

FINANCIAL DATA:
Amount of support per award: $35,629 AUD for the year 2021.

NO. AWARDS: Varies.

APPLICATION INFO:
Application information is available on the web site.
Duration: Two years for a Master's research degree and three years for a Ph.D. Extension of up to six months possible for Ph.D. candidate subject to satisfactory progress.

VILLA I TATTI: THE HARVARD UNIVERSITY CENTER FOR ITALIAN RENAISSANCE STUDIES [859]
Via di Vincigliata, 26
50135 Florence Italy
E-mail: fellowships@itatti.harvard.edu
Web Site: itatti.harvard.edu/i-tatti-fellowship

FOUNDED: 1961

AREAS OF INTEREST:
All aspects of the Italian Renaissance: fine arts, literature, music, science, philosophy, religion and political, intellectual, economic and social history.

CONSULTING OR VOLUNTEER SERVICES:
Library, photographic collection and archive.

NAME(S) OF PROGRAMS:
● **I Tatti Fellowship**

TYPE:
Fellowships. I Tatti Fellowship supports postdoctoral research in any aspect of the Italian Renaissance, broadly understood to include the period from the 14th to the 17th century and geographically to include transnational dialogues between Italy and other cultures (e.g., Latin American, Mediterranean, African, Asian, etc.).

YEAR PROGRAM STARTED: 1961

PURPOSE:
To promote advanced interdisciplinary study in Renaissance fields.

LEGAL BASIS:
Part of Harvard University.

ELIGIBILITY:
Fellows are selected by an international and interdisciplinary committee that welcomes applications from scholars from all nations. At the time of application, scholars must hold a Ph.D., dottorato di ricerca, or an equivalent degree. Applicants must be conversant in either English or Italian and able to understand both languages. Applicants should be in the early stages of their career, having received a Ph.D. between January 1, 2011 and September 1, 2021, and have a solid background in Italian Renaissance studies. Candidates may not be working on a second Ph.D. at the time of application.

The project must represent advanced research in the Italian Renaissance. Subjects covered include art and architecture, history, literature, material culture, music and performance, philosophy, religion, and science. Scholars can also apply to work on the transmission and circulation of ideas, objects, and people during the Renaissance, into and beyond the Italian peninsula, or on the historiography of the Italian Renaissance, including the rebirth of interest in the Renaissance in later periods.

Preference is given to a postdoctoral research project, but projects could also represent a significant reworking of a dissertation. Special consideration may be given to candidates without regular access to research materials and facilities available in Italy.

FINANCIAL DATA:
Amount of support per award: $60,000, plus relocation supplement and housing or housing supplement.

NO. AWARDS: 15.

APPLICATION INFO:
Applications can be written in English or Italian and must be submitted electronically. Scholars can apply for only one type of I Tatti fellowship per academic year. Applicants must have two scholars who know their work well submit recommendations online by October 22. These recommendations can be written in English or Italian.
Duration: One year from July 1 to June 30.
Deadline: October 15.

IRS I.D.: 04-2103580

ADDRESS INQUIRIES TO:
Alina Payne, Director
(See address above.)

*SPECIAL STIPULATIONS:
In light of the residential nature of this fellowship, Fellows must live in the Florence area and be present at the Villa and at lunch at least three days a week beginning the first week of September. They are expected to engage fully in the scholarly life of the institution, and attendance at lectures, Fellows' seminars and other events sponsored by I Tatti is assumed of every Fellow.

VILLA I TATTI: THE HARVARD UNIVERSITY CENTER FOR ITALIAN RENAISSANCE STUDIES [860]
Via di Vincigliata, 26
50135 Florence Italy
E-mail: fellowships@itatti.harvard.edu
Web Site: itatti.harvard.edu/wallace-fellowship

FOUNDED: 1961

AREAS OF INTEREST:
All aspects of the Italian Renaissance: fine arts, literature, music, science, philosophy, religion and political, intellectual, economic and social history.

CONSULTING OR VOLUNTEER SERVICES:
Library, photographic collection and archive.

NAME(S) OF PROGRAMS:
- **Wallace Fellowship**

TYPE:
Fellowships. Wallace Fellowships are designed for scholars who explore the historiography and impact of the Italian Renaissance in the Modern Era (19th to 21st centuries).

PURPOSE:
To promote advanced interdisciplinary study in Renaissance fields.

LEGAL BASIS:
Part of Harvard University.

ELIGIBILITY:
At the time of application, scholars must have a Ph.D. in hand. They may not be working on a second Ph.D. at the time of application. Applicants must be conversant in English and have familiarity with Italian. Priority will be given to early and midcareer scholars.

Projects can address the historiography or impact of the Renaissance on any field, including art and architecture, landscape architecture, history, literature, material culture, music, philosophy, religion, and science.

FINANCIAL DATA:
Amount of support per award: $4,200 stipend per month, up to $1,500 relocation supplement, plus housing or housing supplement.

CO-OP FUNDING PROGRAMS: Lila Wallace-Reader's Digest Fund.

NO. AWARDS: Up to 4.

APPLICATION INFO:
Applications can be written in English or Italian and must be submitted electronically. Scholar can apply to only one type of fellowship at I Tatti per academic year.

Applicants must have two scholars who know their work well submit recommendations online by November 20. These recommendations can be written in English or Italian.

Duration: One semester (four to six months).
Deadline: November 16.

IRS I.D.: 04-2103580

ADDRESS INQUIRIES TO:
Alina Payne, Director
(See address above.)

VILLA I TATTI: THE HARVARD UNIVERSITY CENTER FOR ITALIAN RENAISSANCE STUDIES   [861]
Via di Vincigliata, 26
50135 Florence Italy
E-mail: fellowships@itatti.harvard.edu
Web Site: itatti.harvard.edu/berenson-fellowship

FOUNDED: 1961

AREAS OF INTEREST:
All aspects of the Italian Renaissance: fine arts, literature, music, science, philosophy, religion and political, intellectual, economic and social history.

CONSULTING OR VOLUNTEER SERVICES:
Library, photographic collection and archive.

NAME(S) OF PROGRAMS:
- **Berenson Fellowship**

TYPE:
Fellowships. The Berenson Fellowship is designed for scholars who explore "Italy in the World." Projects should address the transnational dialogues between Italy and other cultures (e.g., Latin American, Mediterranean, African, Asian, etc.) during the Renaissance, broadly understood historically to include the period from the 14th to the 17th century.

PURPOSE:
To promote advanced interdisciplinary study in Renaissance fields.

LEGAL BASIS:
Part of Harvard University.

ELIGIBILITY:
Scholars working in all fields supported by I Tatti are encouraged to apply. At the time of application, scholars must have a Ph.D. in hand. They may not be working on a second Ph.D. at the time of application. Applicants must be conversant in English and have familiarity with Italian. Priority will be given to early and midcareer scholars. I Tatti welcomes applications from scholars from all nations and gives special consideration to candidates without regular access to research materials and facilities in Italy.

FINANCIAL DATA:
Amount of support per award: $4,200 stipend per month, up to $1,500 relocation supplement, plus housing or housing supplement.

CO-OP FUNDING PROGRAMS: Lila Wallace-Reader's Digest Fund.

NO. AWARDS: Up to 4.

APPLICATION INFO:
Applications can be written in English or Italian and must be submitted electronically. Scholars can apply to only one type of fellowship at I Tatti per academic year.

Applicants must have two scholars who know their work submit recommendations online by November 20. These recommendations can be written in English or Italian.

Duration: One semester (four to six months).
Deadline: November 16.

IRS I.D.: 04-2103580

ADDRESS INQUIRIES TO:
Alina Payne, Director
(See address above.)

VILLA I TATTI: THE HARVARD UNIVERSITY CENTER FOR ITALIAN RENAISSANCE STUDIES   [862]
Via di Vincigliata, 26
50135 Florence Italy
E-mail: fellowships@itatti.harvard.edu
Web Site: itatti.harvard.edu/fellowship-digital-humanities

FOUNDED: 1961

AREAS OF INTEREST:
All aspects of the Italian Renaissance: fine arts, literature, music, science, philosophy, religion and political, intellectual, economic and social history.

CONSULTING OR VOLUNTEER SERVICES:
Library, photographic collection and archive.

NAME(S) OF PROGRAMS:
- **Fellowship in the Digital Humanities**

TYPE:
Fellowships. Fellowship in the Digital Humanities supports the work of scholars in the humanities or social sciences, librarians, archivists, and data science professionals whose research interests or practice cut across traditional disciplinary boundaries and actively employ technology in their work. Projects can address any aspect of the Italian Renaissance, broadly understood to include the period from the 14th to the 17th century, and geographically to include translational dialogues between Italy and other cultures (e.g., Latin American, Mediterranean, African, Asian, etc.). Projects should apply digital technologies such as mapping, textual analysis, visualization, or the semantic web to topics in fields such as art and architecture, history, literature, material culture, music, philosophy, religion, and the history of science.

PURPOSE:
To promote advanced interdisciplinary study in Renaissance fields.

LEGAL BASIS:
Part of Harvard University.

ELIGIBILITY:
Applicants must be conversant in English and have familiarity with Italian. At the time of application, a Ph.D. is required for scholars in the humanities and social sciences. A Master's degree is required for librarians, archivists, and data science professionals. A background in programming, library sciences, computer graphics, computational linguistics, or other fields relevant to digital humanities research is high desirable.

Candidates must possess the technical skills to carry out their project at the time of application, and it must be possible for applicants to carry out most of their research in Florence.

Priority will be given to early and midcareer scholars. I Tatti welcomes applications from scholars from all nations and gives special consideration to candidates without regular access to research materials and facilities in Italy.

FINANCIAL DATA:
Amount of support per award: $4,200 stipend per month, up to $1,500 relocation supplement, plus housing or housing supplement.

NO. AWARDS: Up to 2.

APPLICATION INFO:
Applications must be written in English and must be submitted electronically. Scholars can apply for only one type of fellowship at I Tatti per academic year.

Applicants must have two scholars who know their work submit recommendations online by November 20. These recommendations can be written in English or Italian.

Duration: One semester (four to six months).

Deadline: November 16.

IRS I.D.: 04-2103580

ADDRESS INQUIRIES TO:
Alina Payne, Director
(See address above.)

VILLA I TATTI: THE HARVARD UNIVERSITY CENTER FOR ITALIAN RENAISSANCE STUDIES [863]

Via di Vincigliata, 26
50135 Florence Italy
E-mail: fellowships@itatti.harvard.edu
Web Site: itatti.harvard.edu/david-and-julie-tobey-fellowship

FOUNDED: 1961

AREAS OF INTEREST:
Research on drawings, prints and illustrated manuscripts from the Italian Renaissance.

CONSULTING OR VOLUNTEER SERVICES:
Library, photographic collection and archive.

NAME(S) OF PROGRAMS:
● **David and Julie Tobey Fellowship**

TYPE:
Fellowships. The David and Julie Tobey Fellowship supports research on drawings, prints, and illustrated manuscripts from the Italian Renaissance, and especially the role that these works played in the creative process, the history of taste and collecting, and questions of connoisseurship.

PURPOSE:
To promote advanced interdisciplinary study in Renaissance fields.

LEGAL BASIS:
Part of Harvard University.

ELIGIBILITY:
Proposals on a variety of subjects with a substantive component of research on drawings, prints, and illustrated manuscripts done on paper or parchment types are welcome.

At the time of application, scholars must have a Ph.D. in hand. They may not be working on a second Ph.D. at the time of application. Applicants must be conversant in English and have familiarity with Italian.

Priority will be given to early and midcareer scholars. It must be possible for applicants to carry out most of their research in Florence. I Tatti welcomes applications from scholars from all nations and gives special consideration to candidates without regular access to research materials and facilities in Italy.

FINANCIAL DATA:
Amount of support per award: $4,200 stipend per month, up to $1,500 relocation supplement, plus housing or housing supplement.

NO. AWARDS: 1.

APPLICATION INFO:
Applications can be written in English or Italian and must be submitted electronically. Scholars can apply to only one type of fellowship at I Tatti per academic year.

Applicants must have two scholars who know their work submit recommendations online by November 20. These recommendations can be written in English or Italian.

Duration: One semester (four to six months).

Deadline: November 16.

IRS I.D.: 04-2103580

ADDRESS INQUIRIES TO:
Alina Payne, Director
(See address above.)

VILLA I TATTI: THE HARVARD UNIVERSITY CENTER FOR ITALIAN RENAISSANCE STUDIES [864]

Via di Vincigliata, 26
50135 Florence Italy
E-mail: fellowships@itatti.harvard.edu
Web Site: itatti.harvard.edu/craig-hugh-smyth-fellowship

FOUNDED: 1961

AREAS OF INTEREST:
All aspects of the Italian Renaissance: fine arts, literature, music, science, philosophy, religion and political, intellectual, economic and social history.

CONSULTING OR VOLUNTEER SERVICES:
Library, photographic collection and archive.

NAME(S) OF PROGRAMS:
● **Craig Hugh Smyth Fellowship**

TYPE:
Fellowships. The Craig Hugh Smyth Fellowship is designed for curators and conservators pursuing advanced research in any aspect of the Italian Renaissance.

PURPOSE:
To promote advanced interdisciplinary study in Renaissance fields.

LEGAL BASIS:
Part of Harvard University.

ELIGIBILITY:
Applicants should be scholars who work for an educational or cultural institution as a curator or conservator. They may apply to carry out research on behalf of their home institution or propose projects relating to their personal research interests.

Applicant must be conversant in English and have familiarity with Italian. Priority will be given to early and midcareer scholars. It must be possible for applicants to carry out most of their research in Florence. I Tatti welcomes applications from scholars of all nations and gives special consideration to candidates without regular access to research materials and facilities in Italy.

FINANCIAL DATA:
Amount of support per award: $4,200 stipend per month, up to $1,500 relocation supplement, plus housing or housing supplement.

NO. AWARDS: 2.

APPLICATION INFO:
Applications can be written in English or Italian and must be submitted electronically. Scholars can apply to only one type of fellowship at I Tatti per academic year.

Applicants must have two scholars who know their work well submit recommendations online by November 20. These recommendations can be written in English or Italian.

Duration: One semester (four to six months).

Deadline: November 16.

IRS I.D.: 04-2103580

ADDRESS INQUIRIES TO:
Alina Payne, Director
(See address above.)

VILLA I TATTI: THE HARVARD UNIVERSITY CENTER FOR ITALIAN RENAISSANCE STUDIES [865]

Via di Vincigliata, 26
50135 Florence Italy
E-mail: fellowships@itatti.harvard.edu
Web Site: itatti.harvard.edu/i-tattimuseo-nacional-del-prado-joint-fellowship

FOUNDED: 1961

AREAS OF INTEREST:
Art history, with preference given to advanced research projects that address the relationship between Spain and Italy, including transnational connections and dialogues with Latin America, during the Renaissance.

CONSULTING OR VOLUNTEER SERVICES:
Library, photographic collection and archive.

NAME(S) OF PROGRAMS:
● **I Tatti/Museo Nacional del Prado Joint Fellowship**

TYPE:
Fellowships. Joint fellowship designed to support early and midcareer scholars in the field of art history.

PURPOSE:
To promote advanced interdisciplinary study in Renaissance fields.

LEGAL BASIS:
Part of Harvard University.

ELIGIBILITY:
Applicants must have their Ph.D. certificate by the time they apply. They must be conversant in English and Spanish and have at least a reading knowledge of Italian, with a solid background in Italian and/or Spanish and Latin American studies.

Priority will be given to applicants with no previous association with either I Tatti or the Museo del Prado.

FINANCIAL DATA:
Amount of support per award: Stipend for autumn semester in Madrid is EUR 3,000 per month; stipend for the spring semester in Florence is $4,000 per month, plus a one-time supplement (maximum $1,500) towards relocation expenses. An additional $1,000 per month will be offered to offset rental costs, if applicable.

CO-OP FUNDING PROGRAMS: Centro de Estudios de Europa Hispanica.

NO. AWARDS: 1.

APPLICATION INFO:
Applications must be written in English and must be submitted electronically. Scholars can apply to only one type of fellowship at I Tatti per academic year.

Duration: Fall semester (September to December) in Madrid and spring semester (January to June) in Florence.

Deadline: November 15.

IRS I.D.: 04-2103580

ADDRESS INQUIRIES TO:
Alina Payne, Director
(See address above.)

VILLA I TATTI: THE HARVARD UNIVERSITY CENTER FOR ITALIAN RENAISSANCE STUDIES [866]

Via di Vincigliata, 26
50135 Florence Italy
E-mail: fellowships@itatti.harvard.edu
Web Site: itatti.harvard.edu/warburgi-tatti-joint-fellowship

FOUNDED: 1961

AREAS OF INTEREST:
History, with preference given to advanced research projects that address the history of science and knowledge related to early modern Italy, including transnational connections between Italy and other cultures.

CONSULTING OR VOLUNTEER SERVICES:
Library, photographic collection and archive.

NAME(S) OF PROGRAMS:
● **Warburg/I Tatti Joint Fellowship**

TYPE:
Fellowships. Villa I Tatti - The Harvard University Center for Italian Renaissance Studies in Florence, Italy, and the Warburg Institute School of Advanced Study at the University of London offer a joint, residential fellowship. Fellows will spend the fall term (September to December) in London and the spring term (January to June) in Florence. The fellowship is designed for early and midcareer scholars in the field of history, with preference given to advanced research projects that address the history of science and knowledge related to early modern Italy, including transnational connections between Italy and other cultures. Scholars can also apply to work on the transmission and circulation of ideas, objects, and people during the Renaissance, into and beyond the Italian peninsula, or on the historiography of the Italian Renaissance, including the rebirth of interest in the Renaissance in later periods.

PURPOSE:
To promote advanced interdisciplinary study in Renaissance fields.

LEGAL BASIS:
Part of Harvard University.

ELIGIBILITY:
Applicants must have their Ph.D. in hand by the time they apply. Applicants must be conversant in English and have at least a reading knowledge of Italian, with a solid background in Italian Renaissance Studies. Each successful candidate must be approved by both the Warburg Institute and Villa I Tatti.

Priority will be given to applicants with no previous association with either I Tatti or the Warburg Institute.

Applications will not be accepted from candidates proposing to revise their doctoral dissertation for publication.

FINANCIAL DATA:
Amount of support per award: Spring Term at Villa I Tatti: Stipend of $4,000 per month, plus up to $1,500 for relocation expenses. An additional $1,000 per month will be offered to offset rental costs, if applicable; Autumn Term at Warburg Institute: Stipend of GBP 1,500 per month.

NO. AWARDS: 1.

APPLICATION INFO:
Applications must be written in English and must be submitted electronically. Scholars can apply to only one type of fellowship at I Tatti per academic year.

Applicants must have two scholars who know their work well submit recommendations online by the deadline. These recommendations must be written in English.

Duration: 10 months.

Deadline: November 15.

IRS I.D.: 04-2103580

ADDRESS INQUIRIES TO:
Director
(See address above.)

THOMAS J. WATSON FELLOWSHIP PROGRAM

233 Broadway
Suite 2709
New York, NY 10279
(212) 245-8859
E-mail: tjw@watson.foundation
Web Site: watson.foundation

TYPE:
Fellowships. The Foundation provides Fellows an opportunity for a focused and disciplined "Wanderjahr" of their own devising or design-time in which to explore with thoroughness a particular interest, test their aspirations and abilities, view their lives and American society in greater perspective and concomitantly, to develop a more informed sense of international concern. The Fellowship experience is intended to provide Fellows an opportunity to immerse themselves in cultures other than their own for an entire year. The candidate's proposed project should involve investigation into an area of demonstrated concern and personal interest.

See entry 1468 for full listing.

WEIZMANN INSTITUTE OF SCIENCE [867]

Feinberg Graduate School
David Lopatie Hall of Graduate Studies
P.O. Box 26
234 Herzl Street
Rehovot 7610001 Israel
(972) 8-934-2924
Fax: (972) 8-934-4114
E-mail: FGS@weizmann.ac.il
Web Site: www.weizmann.ac.il/feinberg

FOUNDED: 1934

AREAS OF INTEREST:
Life sciences, chemistry, physics, mathematics, computer science and science teaching.

NAME(S) OF PROGRAMS:
● **Postdoctoral Fellowships Program at the Weizmann Institute of Science**

TYPE:
Fellowships. The Feinberg Graduate School of the Weizmann Institute of Science offers a limited number of postdoctoral fellowships in all areas of research in which the Weizmann Institute is engaged. The fellowships are offered in various fields of biology, chemistry, physics, biochemistry-biophysics, mathematics, computer science and science teaching.

YEAR PROGRAM STARTED: 1976

PURPOSE:
To train postgraduate research students to senior positions in academia, scientific research, medical research, industry, education, and government systems.

LEGAL BASIS:
Research institute.

ELIGIBILITY:
Postdoctoral fellowship applicants must have received a Ph.D. or equivalent degree within seven years of the start of the fellowship program. Candidates may be citizens of any country.

FINANCIAL DATA:
The annual stipend is adjusted periodically in accordance with living costs. Also offered is a small relocation allowance and a one-way, economy-class airfare (round-trip airfare in case the fellowship is extended to two years).
Amount of support per award:
Approximately $31,000 per year.

APPLICATION INFO:
Application forms and additional information may be obtained from the Feinberg Graduate School, Weizmann Institute of Science and from the web site.

Duration: 12 months. Possible renewal for a second and third year.

Deadline: Applications may be submitted year-round.

STAFF:
Prof. Gilad Perez, Dean
Prof. Michael Fainzilber, Chairperson, Postdoctoral Fellowship Program

ADDRESS INQUIRIES TO:
Feinberg Graduate School
(See address above.)

YOUTH FOR UNDERSTANDING USA [868]

6856 Eastern Avenue, N.W.
Suite 310
Washington, DC 20012
(202) 774-5200 ext. 5203
(800) 833-6243
Fax: (202) 588-7571
E-mail: info@yfu.org
mckendree@yfu.org
Web Site: www.yfuusa.org

FOUNDED: 1957

AREAS OF INTEREST:
The exchange of U.S. and international high school students in more than 60 countries.

CONSULTING OR VOLUNTEER SERVICES:
Intercultural education and training and research.

NAME(S) OF PROGRAMS:
● **Americans Overseas Summer, Semester and Year Programs**
● **Congress-Bundestag Youth Exchange Program**
● **Corporate Scholarship Program**
● **International Semester and Year Programs**
● **Japan-U.S. Senate Youth Exchange Program**

TYPE:
Exchange programs; Grants-in-aid; Scholarships; Travel grants. Students on summer semester and year programs live with volunteer host families overseas. Students on semester and academic year programs also attend school. International students live and study at U.S. high schools or community colleges. Competitive, full and partial scholarships for Corporate, Japan-U.S. Senate Programs and Japan-America Friendship Scholars Program.

YEAR PROGRAM STARTED: 2001

PURPOSE:
To advance intercultural understanding, mutual respect and social responsibility through educational exchanges for youth, families and communities.

LEGAL BASIS:
Tax-exempt, 501(c)(3) international educational organization.

ELIGIBILITY:
Applicants must be U.S. or international high school students between the ages of 15 and 18. Full scholarships for special programs are awarded through merit competition. Partial scholarships (10 to 25%) are awarded on the basis of need.

FINANCIAL DATA:
Amount of support per award: From $500 to full support.

CO-OP FUNDING PROGRAMS: Funding sources for scholarships include a multitude of governments, corporations, foundations and individuals.

NO. AWARDS: Approximately 250.

APPLICATION INFO:
Applicants for programs involving full scholarships must complete special application materials. For corporate programs, applicants must meet special eligibility requirements. Applicants for partial scholarships must complete financial aid forms.
Duration: Scholarships awarded for the program period.
Deadline: Scholarships: December 1. Programs: March 1. Announcement between February and April.

IRS I.D.: 02-0557010

OFFICERS AND TRUSTEES:
Andrew Towne, Chairman
Mamiko Reeves, Vice-Chairman
Ambassador Laurence Wohlers, Vice-Chairman
Bastian Von Beschwitz, Treasurer
Susan Harcourt, Secretary
Eric Biga
Jyarland Daniels
William Dant
Gloria Garcia
Kristan McMahon
Seena Mortazavi
Martin Nichols
Daryl Weinert

ADDRESS INQUIRIES TO:
Jennifer McKendree, National Director of Marketing and Study Abroad
(See address and toll-free telephone number above.)

Programs for foreign scholars

AMERICA-ISRAEL CULTURAL FOUNDATION [869]
25 West 39th Street, 8th Floor
New York, NY 10018
(212) 557-1600
Fax: (212) 557-1611
E-mail: admin@aicf.org
Web Site: www.aicf.org

FOUNDED: 1939

AREAS OF INTEREST:
Music, dance, theater, visual arts, film and television.

TYPE:
Awards/prizes; Endowments; Fellowships; Project/program grants; Scholarships. For study in the arts of music, painting and sculpture, dance and drama, film and television, to be pursued either in Israel or in other countries.

YEAR PROGRAM STARTED: 1952

PURPOSE:
To further Israeli talent in the fields of music, visual arts, dance and drama, film and television.

ELIGIBILITY:
Only Israeli nationals that live and study in Israel are eligible to apply for domestic scholarships. Israeli nationals studying abroad are able to apply for scholarships to any international location of study.

FINANCIAL DATA:
Amount of support per award: $600 to $10,000.
Total amount of support: $1,300,000 per year.

NO. MOST RECENT APPLICANTS: Approximately 2,500.

NO. AWARDS: Approximately 600.

APPLICATION INFO:
Application materials are available upon request to America-Israel Cultural Foundation, 20 Dr. George Wise Street, Broshim Center, Tel Aviv 6997712, Israel.
Duration: Grants are awarded for one to two years of study. Teachers of the arts may also apply for up to six-month fellowships.
Deadline: Varies.

IRS I.D.: 13-1664048

ADDRESS INQUIRIES TO:
Scholarships: Iris Reff Ronen
Executive Director
20 Dr. George Wise Street
Broshim Center
Tel Aviv 6997712, Israel

AMERICAN ASSOCIATION OF FAMILY AND CONSUMER SCIENCES (AAFCS) [870]
107 South West Street
Suite 816
Alexandria, VA 22314
(703) 706-4600
(800) 424-8080
Fax: (703) 636-7648
E-mail: awards@aafcs.org
Web Site: www.aafcs.org/resources/recognition

FOUNDED: 1909

AREAS OF INTEREST:
Family and consumer sciences.

NAME(S) OF PROGRAMS:
• **National Fellowship**

TYPE:
Fellowships. AAFCS awards fellowships to individuals who have exhibited the potential to make contributions to the family and consumer sciences profession.

PURPOSE:
To support graduate study in the field of family and consumer sciences.

LEGAL BASIS:
501(c)(3) nonprofit charity.

FINANCIAL DATA:
Amount of support per award: $5,000 fellowship, plus up to $1,000 of support.
Total amount of support: Varies.

NO. MOST RECENT APPLICANTS: 15.

NO. AWARDS: 1 to 5.

APPLICATION INFO:
Application information is available on the web site.
Duration: One academic year.
Deadline: Varies.

PUBLICATIONS:
Brochure.

ADDRESS INQUIRIES TO:
See e-mail address above.

AMERICAN ASSOCIATION OF UNIVERSITY WOMEN [871]
1310 L Street, N.W.
Suite 1000
Washington, DC 20005
E-mail: fellowships@aauw.org
Web Site: www.aauw.org

FOUNDED: 1888

AREAS OF INTEREST:
Advancement of educational and professional opportunities for women in the U.S. and around the globe.

NAME(S) OF PROGRAMS:
• **AAUW International Fellowships**

TYPE:
Fellowships. Awarded to women pursuing full-time graduate or postdoctoral study in the U.S. who are not U.S. citizens or permanent residents.

YEAR PROGRAM STARTED: 1917

PURPOSE:
To provide advanced study and training for women, who are not U.S. citizens or permanent residents, of outstanding academic ability who return to their home countries to become leaders.

ELIGIBILITY:
International Fellowships are awarded for full-time study or research in the U.S. to women who are not U.S. citizens or permanent residents. Both graduate and postgraduate studies at accredited U.S. institutions are supported. Applicants must have earned the equivalent of a U.S. Bachelor's degree and must have applied to their proposed institutions of study by the time of the application. Up to five International Master's/First Professional Degree Fellowships are renewable for a second year.

Recipients are selected for academic achievement and demonstrated commitment to women and girls. Recipients return to their home countries to become leaders in business, government, academia, community activism, the arts and sciences.

FINANCIAL DATA:
Amount of support per award: $18,000 to $30,000.

APPLICATION INFO:
Applicant must create an account through the "apply now" link to the vendor site located on the funding opportunity page.
Deadline: November 15.

ADDRESS INQUIRIES TO:
E-mail: aauw@applyists.com

THE AMERICAN SOCIETY OF MECHANICAL ENGINEERS AUXILIARY, INC.

2 Park Avenue, MS-RB
New York, NY 10016-5990
(212) 591-7650
E-mail: bigleyr@asme.org
Web Site: go.asme.org/scholarships

TYPE:
Scholarships. Lucy and Charles W.E. Clarke Scholarship is for high school seniors participating on a FIRST team.

Baldwin, Cartwright, Chenoweth, Farny, Kezios, Scharp and Zamrik Scholarships are for undergraduate students in mechanical engineering.

Parsons and Rothermel Scholarships are for graduate students with a degree in mechanical engineering, to be used to pursue a Master's or Ph.D. degree in mechanical engineering.

Student Loan Fund is for juniors, seniors or graduate students enrolled as degree candidates in good standing.

See entry 2387 for full listing.

BELGIAN AMERICAN EDUCATIONAL FOUNDATION, INC.

195 Church Street
New Haven, CT 06510
(203) 785-4055
E-mail: emile.boulpaep@yale.edu
Web Site: www.baef.us
www.baef.be

TYPE:
Fellowships. Predoctoral and postdoctoral fellowships for advanced study in most fields of knowledge with supported work to be undertaken at a Belgian university or an institution of higher learning. Fellowships for Belgian students are also available.

See entry 820 for full listing.

INTERNATIONAL ROAD FEDERATION   [872]

500 Montgomery Street, Suite 525
Alexandria, VA 22314
(703) 535-1001
Fax: (703) 535-1007
E-mail: psankey@irf.global
info@irf.global
Web Site: www.irf.global

FOUNDED: 1948

AREAS OF INTEREST:
Highway engineering, management and policy.

NAME(S) OF PROGRAMS:
● **IRF Fellowship Program**

TYPE:
Fellowships; Scholarships. Annual awards for graduate study in highway and traffic engineering for graduate engineers and policymakers.

YEAR PROGRAM STARTED: 1949

PURPOSE:
To train personnel in the field of highways and highway transport.

LEGAL BASIS:
Private foundation.

ELIGIBILITY:
Open to non-U.S. graduate students. Qualified civil engineers must return to home country following completion of program.

FINANCIAL DATA:
Amount of support per award: $2,500 to $15,000 to defray partially one year of graduate study.

Total amount of support: Approximately $90,000 annually.

Matching fund requirements: Home country donors must make up differential.

NO. AWARDS: Varies.

APPLICATION INFO:
Applications must be submitted directly to the IRF web site during the open enrollment period.

Duration: One year.

Deadline: October 15.

PUBLICATIONS:
Annual Report; *Directory of Students.*

IRS I.D.: 52-0793883

STAFF:
C. Patrick Sankey, President and Chief Executive Officer

ADDRESS INQUIRIES TO:
C. Patrick Sankey, President
(See address above.)

THE KENNEDY MEMORIAL TRUST   [873]

3 Birdcage Walk
Westminster
London SW1H 9JJ England
(44) 020 7222 1151
Fax: (44) 020 7222 7189
E-mail: emily@kennedytrust.org.uk
Web Site: www.kennedytrust.org.uk

FOUNDED: 1966

NAME(S) OF PROGRAMS:
● **Kennedy Scholarships**

TYPE:
Scholarships. Awarded for postgraduate work for one year at Harvard University or the Massachusetts Institute of Technology (MIT). Field of study is unrestricted.

YEAR PROGRAM STARTED: 1966

PURPOSE:
To award graduate scholarships as part of the British memorial to President Kennedy.

LEGAL BASIS:
Private.

ELIGIBILITY:
Those applying for the Kennedy Scholarships must be all of the following:
(1) British citizens at the time of application;
(2) ordinarily resident in the U.K.;
(3) wholly or mainly educated in the U.K. and;
(4) graduates of a British university.

Awards will not be made to postdoctoral candidates wishing to pursue further research in their own field. Applications cannot be accepted from those already in the U.S. Marriage is not a bar to the award of a Kennedy Scholarship, but there is no extra funding for a spouse.

FINANCIAL DATA:
Full tuition and health insurance fees, plus a stipend for living costs and a grant for vacation travel within the U.S.

Amount of support per award: Means-tested stipend of up to $27,250.

NO. MOST RECENT APPLICANTS: 160.

NO. AWARDS: 10 for the year 2020-21.

APPLICATION INFO:
Applications for awards are available on The Trust web site starting in mid- to late August. In the same application season, candidates should make a separate and independent application to the programme(s) of their choice at Harvard and/or MIT.

Applications must be submitted online. In addition to completing an online form, applicants will be asked to submit an essay (not to exceed 1,000 words) giving an account of their academic pursuits and intellectual interests, their general activities, their reasons for their choice of course and institution, and their current plans for the future.

Duration: One year.

Deadline: Late October.

OFFICERS AND TRUSTEES:
Prof. Sir Mark Walport, FRS, Chairman
Dr. Emily Charnock, Director
Matt Clifford
Dr. Peter Englander
Stephanie Flanders
Tilly Franklin
Prof. Maya Jasanoff
Prof. Fiona Macpherson
Mary Ann Sieghart
Moira Wallace
Prof. Andrew Whittle

ADDRESS INQUIRIES TO:
Dr. Emily Charnock, Director
(See address above.)

LASPAU, INC.   [874]

25 Mount Auburn Street
Suite 200
Cambridge, MA 02138-6095
(617) 495-5255
Fax: (617) 495-8990
E-mail: laspau-webmaster@calists.harvard.edu
Web Site: www.laspau.harvard.edu

FOUNDED: 1965

AREAS OF INTEREST:
Designing and administering academic and professional exchange programs in Latin America, the Caribbean, Canada and the U.S.

CONSULTING OR VOLUNTEER SERVICES:
Specialized educational consulting services are offered by Laspau.

TYPE:
Exchange programs; Fellowships; Project/program grants; Scholarships; Technical assistance; Training grants; Travel grants. Laspau administers school programs, institutional development programs through executive training, and graduate admission tests. Laspau is involved in these exchange areas: professional/business, students/educators and training.

YEAR PROGRAM STARTED: 1966

PURPOSE:
To strengthen human capital in Latin America and the Caribbean through educational and professional development opportunities.

LEGAL BASIS:
Nonprofit organization.

ELIGIBILITY:
In most cases, individuals wishing to apply for a scholarship must be nominated through the program sponsor by a participating Latin American, Caribbean or other institution. (Similarly, all scholarship and loan recipients agree to return promptly to their home institutions.)

Laspau gives special priority to regional, socio-economic and ethnic diversity in order to broaden opportunities for underserved populations. Independent applications are accepted only for certain programs; details are available at the Programs section on the web site.

GEOG. RESTRICTIONS: Latin America and the Caribbean.

FINANCIAL DATA:
Laspau provides grantees and their sponsors with comprehensive financial services, disbursement of scholarship grants and regular reports to sponsoring agencies.
Amount of support per award: Varies.
Total amount of support: Approximately $13,000,000.

APPLICATION INFO:
Application procedures vary by program. Check the Programs section on the web site for details.

PUBLICATIONS:
eNewsletter, annual report; newsletter; brochures; grantee guides.

MEDICAL LIBRARY ASSOCIATION [875]
225 West Wacker Drive
Suite 650
Chicago, IL 60606
(312) 419-9094
E-mail: awards@mail.mlahq.org
Web Site: www.mlanet.org

FOUNDED: 1898

AREAS OF INTEREST:
Health sciences librarianship.

NAME(S) OF PROGRAMS:
● **Cunningham Memorial International Fellowship**

TYPE:
Fellowships; Travel grants; Work-study programs. Work-study program for medical librarians from countries other than the U.S. or Canada for a time period of at least two weeks.

YEAR PROGRAM STARTED: 1972

PURPOSE:
To assist in the education and training of medical librarians from countries outside the continental U.S. and Canada in areas where improved medical library service is essential to the health and welfare of the people through the education of physicians and scientists.

LEGAL BASIS:
Nonprofit.

ELIGIBILITY:
Candidate must be working in a medical library or be preparing to work in one in their country and must have an undergraduate and a Master's-level library degree. (The latter requirement may be waived.) Candidate must have a statement from a responsible official of the institution where they are working or plans to work that they will be guaranteed a position in a medical library when they return to their country; they must also pass the TOEFL exam to demonstrate competence in English and he or she must present three letters of recommendation and a health certificate. Past recipients of the Fellowship are ineligible.

FINANCIAL DATA:
The Fellowship pays a stipend toward living, travel and tuition expenses in the U.S. and Canada. These funds are for the fellow only. No support is provided for spouses or dependents. Payment for travel to and from the U.S. or Canada is the responsibility of the fellow.
Amount of support per award: Up to $4,000.
Matching fund requirements: Candidate may need additional resources during the period of this fellowship.

NO. AWARDS: 1 per year.

APPLICATION INFO:
Applicant must submit the following:
(1) three letters of reference, in English, from responsible persons who are familiar with the applicant's qualifications;
(2) a signed statement, in English, from a responsible official of the institution where he or she is working or plans to work, guaranteeing a position in a health sciences library upon his or her return;
(3) a certificate of good physical health, written in English, from a licensed physician;
(4) a video with a typed transcript and;
(5) an essay.
Duration: At least two to three weeks.
Deadline: December 1. Announcement in March.

STAFF:
Maria Lopez, Grants, Scholarships and Awards Coordinator

ADDRESS INQUIRIES TO:
Coordinator
Grants, Scholarships and Awards
(See address above.)

ORGANIZATION OF AMERICAN STATES
1889 F Street, N.W.
Seventh Floor
Washington, DC 20006
(202) 370-9771
Fax: (202) 458-3967
E-mail: scholarships@oas.org
Web Site: www.oas.org/scholarships

TYPE:
Fellowships; Scholarships; Technical assistance. Awarded for graduate academic studies and/or research, and last two years of undergraduate studies for students in the English-speaking Caribbean, for training in areas contributing to the economic, social, technical and cultural development of OAS member countries.

See entry 780 for full listing.

ORGANIZATION OF AMERICAN STATES [876]
Department of Human Development, Education and Employment
1889 F Street, N.W., Seventh Floor
Washington, DC 20006
(202) 370-9760
Fax: (202) 458-3167
E-mail: rowefund@oas.org
Web Site: www.oas.org/en/rowefund

FOUNDED: 1948

AREAS OF INTEREST:
Any field of study.

NAME(S) OF PROGRAMS:
● **The Leo S. Rowe Pan American Fund**

TYPE:
Assistantships; Awards/prizes; Scholarships; Visiting scholars. Loan program. The Leo S. Rowe Pan American Fund awards interest-free student loans to citizens from Latin America and the Caribbean countries, to help them finance their higher studies or research in accredited universities across the U.S. The Rowe Fund Program is available to foreign students and foreign scholars in U.S. universities.

YEAR PROGRAM STARTED: 1948

PURPOSE:
To provide a loan program to qualified citizens from Latin America and the Caribbean countries to help them finance their higher education or research at accredited institutions in the U.S. by awarding interest-free loans.

ELIGIBILITY:
Rowe Fund loans are granted to individuals currently studying or wishing to pursue graduate, postgraduate or the last two years of undergraduate studies. Additionally, professionals or university faculty who are currently pursuing, or wish to pursue, advanced training, research or technical certificates at accredited institutions in the U.S. are also eligible. This includes semester-abroad programs and professional development courses, with the exception of English-as-a-Second-Language courses. Most fields of study are accepted.

Applicants must be citizens of the following countries: Antigua and Barbuda, Argentina, Barbados, Belize, Bolivia, Brazil, Chile, Colombia, Costa Rica, Dominica (Commonwealth of), Dominican Republic, Ecuador, El Salvador, Grenada, Guatemala, Guyana, Haiti, Honduras, Jamaica, Mexico, Nicaragua, Panama, Paraguay, Peru, Saint Kitts and Nevis, Saint Lucia, Saint Vincent and the Grenadines, Suriname, The Bahamas (Commonwealth of), Trinidad and Tobago, Uruguay or Venezuela (Bolivarian Republic of).

Candidates must:
(1) be nationals of a Latin American or Caribbean member state of the OAS (U.S. and Canadian citizens are not eligible);
(2) have an international student visa (F or J) allowing them to study full-time in the U.S.;
(3) be accepted as a full-time student in an accredited institution of higher learning in the U.S.;
(4) have adequate academic records (grade point average greater than or equal to 3.0);
(5) be able to demonstrate other sources of financing (such as savings, employment, fellowship, funds supplied by the university or relatives, etc.) to cover the greater portion of their academic expenses;
(6) ensure that loans are underwritten by a guarantor (citizen or permanent resident of the U.S.) and;
(7) promise that upon completion of his or her studies, he or she will repay the loan in full and return to his or her country; (if OPT is granted, the return date can be extended up to a year upon completion of studies).

FINANCIAL DATA:

Loans can be used to cover a portion of the tuition and other university fees, essential books and supplies, room and board and/or emergencies not covered by their principal source of funding. No application or processing fees. Funding is sent directly to the student after approval.

Amount of support per award: Up to U.S. $7,500 per academic semester. Loan recipients may apply for additional loans for subsequent academic semesters, providing the total amount of loans granted does not exceed U.S. $15,000 over the course of the studies for which the loan is granted.

Total amount of support: $15,000 (U.S.) per Rowe Fund recipient.

Matching fund requirements: The prospective applicant must demonstrate other sources of financing (such as savings, employment, a fellowship, funds supplied by the university or relatives, etc.), to cover the greater part of their academic expenses and must present a guarantor.

NO. AWARDS: Averaging 100.

APPLICATION INFO:

Instructions are available on the Rowe Fund web site.

Duration: Two years maximum.

Deadline: A person may apply for a Rowe Fund loan at any time during the course of their studies in the U.S.

STAFF:

Lina M. Sevillano, Program Coordinator

ADDRESS INQUIRIES TO:

Leo S. Rowe Pan American Fund
(See address above.)

*SPECIAL STIPULATIONS:

Repayment is deferred while the loan recipient is in school. Loan repayment is scheduled in 50 equal monthly payments starting three months after completion of studies.

These loans are made with the understanding that, upon completing those studies, loan recipients commit to repay the loan in full and return to their home countries within a year to apply their knowledge and training as well as continue fostering friendship and communication among the peoples of the Americas.

P.E.O. SISTERHOOD   [877]

P.E.O. Executive Office
3700 Grand Avenue
Des Moines, IA 50312
(515) 255-3153
Fax: (515) 255-3820
E-mail: ips@peodsm.org
Web Site: www.peointernational.org

FOUNDED: 1869

NAME(S) OF PROGRAMS:

● **P.E.O. International Peace Scholarship**

TYPE:

Scholarships. Awards for selected women from countries other than the U.S. and Canada to pursue graduate study in the U.S. or Canada. Support is available for advanced study in any field except for research. No new applications at the dissertation level.

YEAR PROGRAM STARTED: 1949

PURPOSE:

To promote world peace and understanding through scholarship aid to selected women from other countries to further their education in the U.S. and Canada.

LEGAL BASIS:

Nonprofit organization.

ELIGIBILITY:

Prerequisites for applicants:
(1) Applicant must be qualified for admission to full-time graduate study, working toward a graduate degree in the accredited college or university she will attend in the U.S. or Canada;
(2) A copy of the applicant's confirmation of admission must be submitted with the application. This notice must specify the graduate degree program. No consideration will be given to applicants lacking evidence of admission and;
(3) Prerequisites 1 and 2 do not apply to the applicant who enrolls at Cottey College (Nevada, MO), which is owned and operated by the P.E.O. Sisterhood. The applicant shall present evidence of admission to Cottey.

In order to qualify for her first scholarship, an applicant must have a full year of coursework remaining and be enrolled and on campus for the entire school year. Doctoral students who have completed coursework and are working on dissertations only are not eligible as first-time applicants. Doctoral students in medicine or dentistry will be considered only in the final two years of coursework, internship or residency.

Upon completion of the degree program or Optional Practical Training, the applicant must promise to return to her home country or to a location outside the U.S. or Canada within 60 days, depending on visa status.

A student holding citizenship or permanent residency in the U.S. or Canada is ineligible. Scholarships are not given for online courses, research, internships or for practical training if not combined with coursework. Scholarships are not awarded for travel or repayment of past debt.

FINANCIAL DATA:

Scholarships to students studying in Canadian universities will be paid in Canadian dollars.

Amount of support per award: $12,500 maximum per year, based upon need.

NO. MOST RECENT APPLICANTS: Approximately 450.

NO. AWARDS: Approximately 180.

APPLICATION INFO:

In order to be considered for an IPS Scholarship, a student must submit an eligibility form electronically through the P.E.O. International web site. Paper forms sent to the P.E.O. International office will not be accepted. The online eligibility form can be submitted from September 15 to December 15.

Duration: Initial support is for a period not to exceed one year (two semesters fall-spring), with one renewal possible. Not to exceed a total of two years.

Deadline: To establish eligibility: December 15. Final date to submit completed application materials from applicants already enrolled in the graduate program and school for which their scholarship is intended: March 1. Final date to submit completed application materials from applicants not yet enrolled in the graduate program or school

for which the scholarship is intended: April 1. Last date to submit completed application materials for applicants who will be attending Cottey College: April 1. Notification of scholarships: May. Final date for student acceptance of scholarships: June 1.

No eligibility information will be accepted before September 15 or after December 15.

PUBLICATIONS:

Information sheet.

ADDRESS INQUIRIES TO:

Project Supervisor
(See address above.)

*SPECIAL STIPULATIONS:

Applicant must have round-trip or return travel expense guaranteed at the time of application.

THE UNIVERSITY OF
SYDNEY   [878]

Scholarships Office
Level 4, Jane Foss Russell Building G02
The University of Sydney N.S.W. 2006
Australia
61 (02) 8627 1444
E-mail: scholarships.officer@sydney.edu.au
Web Site: www.sydney.edu.au/scholarships

FOUNDED: 1850

NAME(S) OF PROGRAMS:

● **Walter Mersh Strong Scholarship**

TYPE:

Scholarships. Awarded for studies at postgraduate level. Tenable at the University of Sydney. The scholarship is available for a Master by coursework program in agriculture, education and social work, or public health.

YEAR PROGRAM STARTED: 1946

PURPOSE:

To provide opportunities for graduate students from Papua New Guinea to attend the University of Sydney to undertake a Master by coursework program in agriculture, education and social work, or public health.

LEGAL BASIS:

University.

ELIGIBILITY:

Only citizens from Papua New Guinea may apply. Applicants must have completed the equivalent of an Australian Bachelor degree qualification with outstanding results based on the Australian grading system.

Students who have already commenced postgraduate studies or students transferring with credit exemptions and/or advanced standing are not eligible.

GEOG. RESTRICTIONS: Papua New Guinea.

FINANCIAL DATA:

Amount of support per award: Tuition fees and living allowance of $35,629 AUD per annum for the year 2021.

NO. AWARDS: 1.

APPLICATION INFO:

Application information is available on the web site.

Deadline: As advertised, when funds are available.

Technical assistance and cooperative research

NATIONAL INSTITUTES OF HEALTH [879]

Division of International Relations
Fogarty International Center
Building 31, Room B2C11
31 Center Drive, MSC 2220
Bethesda, MD 20892-2220
(301) 496-4784
Fax: (301) 480-3414
E-mail: tina.chung@nih.gov
Web Site: www.fic.nih.
gov/programs/pages/japan-fellowships.aspx

AREAS OF INTEREST:
Biomedical and behavioral sciences.

NAME(S) OF PROGRAMS:
- **Japan Society for the Promotion of Science Postdoctoral Research Fellowships (Extramural)**

TYPE:
Fellowships. A limited number of postdoctoral research fellowships are provided by the Japan Science and Technology Agency (JSTA) to U.S. scientists to conduct research in Japan. Types of activity supported include collaboration in basic or clinical research and familiarization with or utilization of special techniques and equipment not otherwise available to the applicant.

YEAR PROGRAM STARTED: 1987

PURPOSE:
To provide a research experience in the biomedical, clinical and behavioral sciences in Japanese laboratories.

LEGAL BASIS:
Government agency.

ELIGIBILITY:
Applicants for the program must be U.S. citizens or permanent U.S. residents, hold a Doctorate in one of the clinical, behavioral or biomedical sciences and make prior arrangements with the appropriate Japanese host researcher as to the research plan.

The program does not provide support for activities that have as their principal purpose brief observational visits, attendance at scientific meetings or independent study.

NO. AWARDS: Up to 10 short-term, 2 long-term.

APPLICATION INFO:
Application information is available on the web site.
Duration: Short-term: One to 12 months; Long-term: 12 to 24 months.
Deadline: Short-term: March 31 and October 1. Long-term: March 31.

ADDRESS INQUIRIES TO:
Tina Chung, M.P.H., Program Officer
(See address above.)

NORTH ATLANTIC TREATY ORGANIZATION [880]

Emerging Security Challenges Division (ESCD)
NATO HQ, Boulevard Leopold III
B-1110 Brussels Belgium
Fax: (32) 2 707 4232
E-mail: sps.info@hq.nato.int
Web Site: www.nato.int/science

FOUNDED: 1958

AREAS OF INTEREST:
Scientific cooperation between NATO Allies and partner countries.

NAME(S) OF PROGRAMS:
- **Science for Peace and Security (SPS) Programme**

TYPE:
Multiyear projects; workshops and training.

Offers grants to scientists in NATO and Partner countries to collaborate on priority research topics, which include NATO priorities and additional Partner country priorities.

In addition to activities funded by the NATO international budget, the Science for Peace and Security Programme also engages in activities funded directly by one or more nations. These consist of pilot studies, short-term projects and topical workshops which are aligned with NATO's Strategic Objectives and are in areas of priority to NATO or Partner countries. Any NATO or Partner country can initiate a new proposal. The initiating nation seeks the participation of other NATO and Partner nations and this participation is always voluntary. Support Grant Programme is open to experts from both NATO countries and those Partner countries eligible for support.

YEAR PROGRAM STARTED: 1960

PURPOSE:
To stimulate collaboration between laboratories in different countries and thus enhance the effectiveness of research.

GEOG. RESTRICTIONS: NATO countries: Albania, Belgium, Bulgaria, Canada, Croatia, Czech Republic, Denmark, Estonia, France, Germany, Greece, Hungary, Iceland, Italy, Latvia, Lithuania, Luxembourg, Montenegro, Netherlands, Norway, Poland, Portugal, Republic of North Macedonia, Romania, Slovakia, Slovenia, Spain, Turkey, United Kingdom and United States.

FINANCIAL DATA:
Covering project-related costs, organizational costs, travel and living expenses.
Amount of support per award: Typical three-year projects are EUR 150,000 to EUR 350,000.

APPLICATION INFO:
Applications should be presented on the official application forms that can be downloaded from the Science for Peace and Security web site. Applications should be submitted via e-mail to sps.applications@hq.nato.int.
Duration: Depends on the mechanism. Up to three years for the multiyear projects.
Deadline: February 1, June 1 and October 1. Applications may be submitted at any time. Applications received later than this deadline date will be considered during the next evaluation cycle.

PUBLICATIONS:
NATO Science Series.

ADDRESS INQUIRIES TO:
See e-mail address above.

U.S.-ISRAEL BINATIONAL SCIENCE FOUNDATION (BSF) [881]

P.O. Box 45086 (Hamarpeh Street, No. 8)
Har Hotzvim
Jerusalem 91450 Israel
(972) 2-582-8239
Fax: (972) 2-582-8306
E-mail: bsf@bsf.org.il
Web Site: www.bsf.org.il

FOUNDED: 1972

AREAS OF INTEREST:
Science.

TYPE:
Research grants. Promotes cooperation between the countries in research concerned with science and technology for peaceful purposes through grants to cooperative research projects. Grants are for bilateral, cooperative research between U.S. and Israeli scientists for research conducted in either country.

YEAR PROGRAM STARTED: 1974

PURPOSE:
To strengthen U.S.-Israel science cooperation.

LEGAL BASIS:
Established by government-to-government agreement.

ELIGIBILITY:
Any scientist on the staff of a U.S. or Israel nonprofit research institution may apply by submitting a cooperative research proposal.

Eligible research areas are health sciences, life sciences, physics, chemistry, mathematical sciences, atmospheric and earth sciences, oceanography and limnology, materials research, environmental research, energy research, biomedical engineering, economics, sociology, social and developmental psychology, and computer sciences.

Submission of grant applications is on a split-program basis; namely, eligibility is limited, in alternate years, to either health and life sciences or to exact, natural and social sciences.

FINANCIAL DATA:
Awards are made to cover the direct cost of executing the approved research, i.e., salaries for research assistants, supplies, travel, etc. Salaries of principal investigators are not included.
Amount of support per award: Regular Grant: Up to $230,000 for four years; Start-up Grant: Up to $75,000 over two years.
Total amount of support: Approximately $17,000,000.

APPLICATION INFO:
Proposals are unsolicited and should be submitted jointly by the collaborating scientists via the prospective grantee institution where the research will be performed. Proposals should be submitted via the BSF web site.
Duration: Up to four years.
Deadline: The completed application form must reach the BSF by November 15 for a grant to be awarded in the following year. Awards are made annually and are announced in July.

OFFICERS:
Prof. Anton Post, Executive Director
Dr. Rachel Haring, Assistant Executive Director

ADDRESS INQUIRIES TO:
Prof. Anton Post, Executive Director
(See address above.)

SPECIAL POPULATIONS

Special Populations

THE ABLE TRUST [882]
3320 Thomasville Road
Suite 200
Tallahassee, FL 32308
(850) 224-4493
Fax: (850) 224-4496
E-mail: info@abletrust.org
Web Site: www.abletrust.org

FOUNDED: 1991

AREAS OF INTEREST:
Disabilities and handicapped persons.

NAME(S) OF PROGRAMS:
- **Board Directed Initiative Grants**
- **General Support for Employment Placement Programs**
- **Strategic Employment Placement Initiatives**

TYPE:
Project/program grants. Board Directed Initiative Grants: This program is defined through an announcement by the Board of Directors for proposals that address a specific issue. The release of an Initiative Request is at the discretion of the Board and may occur at any time during a fiscal year. Funding parameters in this category will be described in the published Initiative Request and will correspond to the described objective of the Board Directed Initiative.

General Support for Employment Placement Programs: This program is for general support of employment programs for a grant year. Requests should result in employment placement for participating individuals with disabilities and could encompass equipment and/or staffing needs of an applicant organization to expand an existing program in a new way or create a new program. Awards for this category will occur twice a year at the Fall and Summer Board Meetings.

Strategic Employment Placement Initiatives: This is the primary grant program of The Foundation, and such proposals address the employment placement of Floridians with disabilities. Consideration for these large grants will occur at the Third Quarter Board Meeting of The Foundation.

YEAR PROGRAM STARTED: 1990

PURPOSE:
To be a key leader in providing Floridians with disabilities opportunities for successful employment.

LEGAL BASIS:
501(c)(3) public-private partnership foundation.

ELIGIBILITY:
Proposals will be accepted from Florida-based nonprofit organizations with 501(c)(3) status serving disabled Florida citizens. Each organization may have only one active grant in any one-year time period.

GEOG. RESTRICTIONS: Florida.

FINANCIAL DATA:
Amount of support per award: Average award is $50,000 for organizations. General Support for Employment Placement Programs: Up to $65,000. Strategic Employment Placement Initiatives: Up to $250,000.
Total amount of support: $2,544,484 for fiscal year 2019-20.

NO. MOST RECENT APPLICANTS: 90.

NO. AWARDS: 78.

APPLICATION INFO:
Application guidelines are available on the Able Trust web site.
Duration: Board Directed Initiative Grants and General Support for Employment Placement Programs: One year. Strategic Employment Placement Initiatives: Three years.
Deadline: General Support for Employment Placement Programs: April 5 and July 5. Strategic Employment Placement Initiatives: December 6.

IRS I.D.: 59-3052307

STAFF:
Allison Chase, President
Guenevere Crum, Senior Vice President, Grants and Donor Relations

ADDRESS INQUIRIES TO:
Allison Chase, President
(See address above.)

THE ACTUARIAL FOUNDATION
475 North Martingale Road
Suite 600
Schaumburg, IL 60173-2226
(847) 706-3535
Fax: (847) 706-3599
E-mail: Scholarships@ActFnd.org
Web Site: www.actuarialfoundation.org

TYPE:
Scholarships. This scholarship promotes diversity in the profession through an annual scholarship program for Black/African American, Hispanic, Native North American and Pacific Islander students. The scholarship award recognizes and encourages academic achievements by awarding scholarships to full-time undergraduate students pursuing a degree that may lead to a career in the actuarial profession.

See entry 1880 for full listing.

ALZHEIMER'S DRUG DISCOVERY FOUNDATION
57 West 57th Street
Suite 904
New York, NY 10019
(212) 901-8000
Fax: (212) 901-8010
E-mail: info@alzdiscovery.org
grants@alzdiscovery.org
Web Site: www.alzdiscovery.org

TYPE:
Awards/prizes; Conferences/seminars; Research grants.

See entry 1995 for full listing.

AMERICAN ASSOCIATION OF LAW LIBRARIES
105 West Adams Street
Suite 3300
Chicago, IL 60603
(312) 939-4764
Fax: (312) 431-1097
E-mail: membership@aall.org
Web Site: www.aallnet.org

TYPE:
Scholarships. Stipend for graduate study leading to a degree at an accredited school of library or information science or an accredited law school. Preference will be given to individuals with previous service to, or interest in, law librarianship.

See entry 657 for full listing.

AMERICAN BAR FOUNDATION [883]
750 North Lake Shore Drive
Fourth Floor
Chicago, IL 60611
(312) 988-6500
Fax: (312) 988-6579
E-mail: fellowships@abfn.org
Web Site: www.americanbarfoundation.org

FOUNDED: 1952

AREAS OF INTEREST:
Law and social science.

NAME(S) OF PROGRAMS:
- **Summer Undergraduate Research Fellowships**

TYPE:
Internships. Fellows spend the summer gaining hands-on research experience, touring legal institutions and law schools, and meeting with legal practitioners and scholars.

YEAR PROGRAM STARTED: 1988

PURPOSE:
To promote access to legal education and the academy for historically underrepresented individuals by immersing highly talented diverse students in a rigorous empirical and interdisciplinary research environment, while introducing multiple career paths to the legal profession and the academy.

LEGAL BASIS:
Private foundation.

ELIGIBILITY:
Must be a U.S. citizen or permanent resident. The program is open, but not limited to, persons who are African-American, Hispanic/Latino, Native American, or Puerto Rican. Applicants must be sophomores or juniors in college with a grade point average of at least 3.0 on a scale of 4.0 and must be moving toward an academic major in one of the social science or humanities disciplines.

GEOG. RESTRICTIONS: United States.

FINANCIAL DATA:
Amount of support per award: $3,600.

NO. MOST RECENT APPLICANTS: 160.

NO. AWARDS: 4 each year.

APPLICATION INFO:
Application form is available online.
Duration: Eight weeks during the summer.
Deadline: January.

PUBLICATIONS:
Annual report, application guidelines and forms.

ADDRESS INQUIRIES TO:
Marcilena Shaeffer, Program Coordinator
(See address above.)

AMERICAN COUNCIL FOR POLISH CULTURE (ACPC)
911 Saddleback Court
McLean, VA 22102
(301) 717-0662
Web Site: www.polishcultureacpc.org

TYPE:
Scholarships.

See entry 1473 for full listing.

AMERICAN COUNCIL OF THE BLIND

1703 North Beauregard Street
Suite 420
Alexandria, VA 22311
(612) 332-3242
(800) 866-3242
Fax: (703) 465-5085
E-mail: info@acb.org
Web Site: www.acb.org

TYPE:
Assistantships; Awards/prizes; Internships; Scholarships. Scholarships for outstanding blind students enrolled in academic, vocational, technical or professional training programs beyond the high school level.

See entry 1474 for full listing.

THE AMERICAN GEOSCIENCES INSTITUTE (AGI)

4220 King Street
Alexandria, VA 22302-1502
(703) 379-2480
Fax: (703) 379-7563
E-mail: keane@americangeosciences.org
Web Site: www.americangeosciences.
org/workforce/harriet-evelyn-wallace-scholarship

TYPE:
Scholarships. Open to all women pursuing a Master's or Doctorate degree in geosciences at an accredited institution of higher education in a recognized geoscience program.

See entry 1866 for full listing.

THE AMERICAN HELLENIC EDUCATIONAL PROGRESSIVE ASSOCIATION   [884]

1909 Q Street, N.W.
Suite 500
Washington, DC 20009
(202) 232-6300
Fax: (202) 232-2140
E-mail: ahepa@ahepa.org
Web Site: www.ahepa.org

FOUNDED: 1922

AREAS OF INTEREST:
Culture, history, and issues relating to Greece and Cyprus.

TYPE:
Scholarships.

PURPOSE:
To promote, encourage, induce and advance education at the college, university and graduate school level.

ELIGIBILITY:
Applicants must be of Hellenic heritage, although their ancestry does not have to be 100% Greek. The applicant must be a member in good standing of AHEPA or affiliated organizations, demonstrate financial need and have no criminal record.

FINANCIAL DATA:
Amount of support per award: Up to $2,000.
Total amount of support: $100,000 for the year 2020.

NO. AWARDS: Varies.

APPLICATION INFO:
Scholarship application is posted online.
Duration: One year. Renewal possible.
Deadline: March 31.

ADDRESS INQUIRIES TO:
Basil Mossaidis, Executive Director
(See address above.)

AMERICAN INSTITUTE OF CHEMICAL ENGINEERS (AICHE)

120 Wall Street, Floor 23
New York, NY 10005-4020
(800) 242-4363
Fax: (646) 495-1503
E-mail: awards@aiche.org
Web Site: www.aiche.org

TYPE:
Scholarships.

See entry 2377 for full listing.

AMERICAN PLANNING ASSOCIATION   [885]

205 North Michigan Avenue
Suite 1200
Chicago, IL 60601
(312) 786-6345
E-mail: foundation@planning.org
Web Site: www.planning.
org/foundation/scholarships

FOUNDED: 1909

AREAS OF INTEREST:
Urban and regional planning and the promotion of the art and science of planning.

NAME(S) OF PROGRAMS:
● **APA Foundation Scholarship**

TYPE:
Scholarships.

YEAR PROGRAM STARTED: 1970

PURPOSE:
To celebrate planning by providing partial funding for all women and minority (African American, Hispanic American or Native American) students.

LEGAL BASIS:
Private, nonprofit educational association.

ELIGIBILITY:
Applicants must be citizens of the U.S. and enrolled or accepted for enrollment in a planning program accredited by the Planning Accreditation Board (PAB). Applicants must document the need for financial assistance.

GEOG. RESTRICTIONS: United States.

FINANCIAL DATA:
Scholarship provides partial funding for tuition and one-year student membership in the American Planning Association.
Amount of support per award: $4,000 to $5,000 paid directly to the student's school.
Total amount of support: Varies.

NO. MOST RECENT APPLICANTS: 86.

NO. AWARDS: 4 annually.

APPLICATION INFO:
Contact the Association.
Duration: One academic year.
Deadline: June.

PUBLICATIONS:
Program announcement.

ADDRESS INQUIRIES TO:
See e-mail address above.

AMERICAN POLITICAL SCIENCE ASSOCIATION

1527 New Hampshire Avenue, N.W.
Washington, DC 20036
(202) 483-2512
Fax: (202) 483-2657
E-mail: kmealy@apsanet.org
Web Site: www.apsanet.org/mfp

TYPE:
Fellowships; Grants-in-aid; Scholarships. Awards to aid prospective African American, Asian Pacific, Latino/Latina and Native American political science students beginning the doctoral study of political science.

See entry 1783 for full listing.

AMERICAN PSYCHOLOGICAL ASSOCIATION

Minority Fellowship Program/APA
750 First Street, N.E.
Washington, DC 20002-4242
(202) 336-6127
Fax: (202) 336-6012
E-mail: mfp@apa.org
Web Site: www.apa.org/pi/mfp

TYPE:
Fellowships. Fellowship is geared to those pursuing careers as practitioners specializing in the delivery of behavioral health services to ethnic minority populations. Students specializing in clinical, school and counseling psychology are encouraged to apply.

See entry 2315 for full listing.

AMERICAN PSYCHOLOGICAL ASSOCIATION

Minority Fellowship Program/APA
750 First Street, N.E.
Washington, DC 20002-4242
(202) 336-6127
Fax: (202) 336-6012
E-mail: mfp@apa.org
Web Site: www.apa.org/pi/mfp

TYPE:
Fellowships.

See entry 2313 for full listing.

AMERICAN SOCIETY FOR MICROBIOLOGY

Education Department
1752 N Street, N.W.
Washington, DC 20036
(202) 942-9282
Fax: (202) 942-9329
E-mail: fellowships@asmusa.org
Web Site: www.asm.org

TYPE:
Fellowships. Research Capstone Fellowship provides funding for professional development and career networking to underrepresented minority students.

Undergraduate Research Fellowships provide undergraduate, community college and post-Baccalaureate students the opportunity to perform summer research with an ASM faculty member, in addition to receiving professional development training at the Microbe Academy for Professional Development (MAPD).

See entry 1934 for full listing.

AMERICAN SOCIOLOGICAL ASSOCIATION [886]

1430 K Street, N.W.
Suite 600
Washington, DC 20005
(202) 383-9005
TDD: (202) 638-0981
E-mail: diversity@asanet.org
Web Site: www.asanet.org

FOUNDED: 1905

AREAS OF INTEREST:
All areas of sociology.

NAME(S) OF PROGRAMS:
● **Minority Fellowship Program**

TYPE:
Fellowships. Predoctoral training fellowships for minority-group members studying sociology.

YEAR PROGRAM STARTED: 1974

PURPOSE:
To provide predoctoral students with financial support, academic and research training, and mentoring, in coordination with university graduate programs, in order to increase the talent pool of minority sociologists in the U.S.

LEGAL BASIS:
Nonprofit professional association.

ELIGIBILITY:
Applicants must be citizens, noncitizen nationals of the U.S. or have been lawfully admitted to the U.S. for permanent residence, DACA eligible, and have in their possession an Alien Registration Card, and they must be enrolled in (and have completed one full academic year) in a program that grants the Ph.D. in sociology.

In addition, applicants must be members of an underrepresented racial and ethnic group, including African Americans, Latinos (e.g., Mexican, Cuban, Puerto Rican), American Indians or Alaskan Natives and Asians (e.g., Chinese, Japanese, Korean, Southeast Asian) or Pacific Islanders (e.g., Hawaiian, Guamanian, Samoan, Filipino).

GEOG. RESTRICTIONS: United States.

FINANCIAL DATA:
Award includes stipend and some tuition assistance.
Amount of support per award: $18,000.
Total amount of support: Varies.

NO. MOST RECENT APPLICANTS: 100.

NO. AWARDS: Up to 5 annually.

APPLICATION INFO:
Applicants must submit completed application forms, transcripts, letters of recommendation and two essays. Selection is based upon evidence of scholarship, writing ability, research potential, financial need and racial and ethnic minority identification.
Duration: Fellowships are tenable for one calendar year.
Deadline: January 31. Announcement by April 30.

ADDRESS INQUIRIES TO:
Minority Program
(See address above.)

THE ARCHITECTS FOUNDATION

1735 New York Avenue, N.W.
Washington, DC 20006-5292
(202) 626-7514
E-mail: scholarships@architectsfoundation.org
Web Site: www.aia.org
architectsfoundation.org

TYPE:
Scholarships. Scholarships provide the opportunity for financially disadvantaged and/or minority groups to pursue a professional degree in architecture.

See entry 368 for full listing.

ARMENIAN GENERAL BENEVOLENT UNION

55 East 59th Street, 7th Floor
New York, NY 10022-1112
(212) 319-6383
E-mail: scholarship@agbu.org
Web Site: www.agbu-scholarship.org

TYPE:
Fellowships; Scholarships.

See entry 1481 for full listing.

ARMENIAN RELIEF SOCIETY OF EASTERN U.S.A., INC. [887]

80 Bigelow Avenue
Suite 200
Watertown, MA 02472
(617) 926-3801
Fax: (617) 924-7238
E-mail: arseastus@gmail.com
Web Site: www.arseastusa.org

FOUNDED: 1910

NAME(S) OF PROGRAMS:
● **A.R.S. Lazarian Graduate Scholarship**
● **A.R.S. Undergraduate Scholarship**

TYPE:
Awards/prizes; Scholarships. Scholarships to assist students of Armenian ancestry in their higher education studies.

PURPOSE:
To aid Armenian students residing in the U.S.

LEGAL BASIS:
Nonprofit organization.

ELIGIBILITY:
Undergraduate students must meet the following requirements:
(1) must be of Armenian descent;
(2) must be an undergraduate student who has completed at least one college semester at an accredited four-year college or university in the U.S. or must be enrolled in a two-year college and transferring to a four-year college or university as a full-time student in the fall.

Applicants for the Lazarian Scholarship must be of Armenian descent, have graduated from an accredited four-year college or university in the U.S., and be in need of financial assistance. Applicants must be pursuing their studies at the graduate level (Master's or Doctorate degree) in the field of law, history, political science, international relations, journalism, government, economics, business administration, medicine public service, or a similar field.

Scholarships are awarded on the basis of financial need, academic merit and involvement in the Armenian community.

FINANCIAL DATA:
Amount of support per award: Varies, according to donations.

NO. MOST RECENT APPLICANTS: Undergraduate: 25; Graduate: 20.

APPLICATION INFO:
Application form must be downloaded from the web site and mailed to the address listed above.

Undergraduate Scholarship applicant must submit the following with the completed application:
(1) first two pages of their parent's most recent income tax returns;
(2) first two pages of their most recent income tax returns;
(3) sealed official transcript;
(4) two letters of recommendation and;
(5) tuition costs (submit one copy of the school's cost for the academic year).

Lazarian Graduate Scholarship applicant must submit the following with a completed application:
(1) official transcript of undergraduate, as well as graduate, college grades. No faxes or copies will be accepted;
(2) tuition costs (submit one copy of the school's costs for the current academic year);
(3) applicant's most recent income tax return (form 1040). If an income tax return has not been filed, a copy of FAFSA, SAR, or the parents' income tax return must be submitted;
(4) three letters of recommendation and;
(5) proof of enrollment in a graduate program or proof of acceptance into a graduate program.
Duration: One year. No automatic renewal. An individual who receives an award may apply for a scholarship during the following year. Applicants may receive a total of two awards.
Deadline: April 1.

STAFF:
Vart Chiloyan, Executive Secretary

ADDRESS INQUIRIES TO:
Scholarship Committee
(See address above.)

ASTRAEA LESBIAN FOUNDATION FOR JUSTICE [888]

116 East 16th Street, 7th Floor
New York, NY 10003
(212) 529-8021
Fax: (212) 982-3321
E-mail: info@astraeafoundation.org
Web Site: www.astraeafoundation.org

FOUNDED: 1977

AREAS OF INTEREST:
Racial, economic and gender justice for lesbian, gay, bisexual, transgender, and intersex (LGBTI) peoples in the global south and east.

NAME(S) OF PROGRAMS:
● **International Fund**

TYPE:
General operating grants; Grants-in-aid; Project/program grants.

PURPOSE:
To provide critically needed financial support to lesbian-led, LGBTI and progressive organizations striving to eliminate oppression based on race, age, sex, religion, sexual

orientation, gender identity, economic exploitation, physical and mental ability, anti-semitism, and other such factors.

ELIGIBILITY:
Must be charitable nongovernmental organizations and meet the criteria used in determining 501(c)(3) status in the U.S. Those eligible to apply are:
(1) groups led by and/or for LGBTI communities;
(2) groups doing work towards social change on issues affecting LGBTI people;
(3) nongovernmental, not-for-profit groups with organizational budgets of $500,000 (U.S.) or less and;
(4) groups active for at least one year at the time of proposal.

Organizations applying must not have a budget of over $500,000 (U.S.).

GEOG. RESTRICTIONS: Africa, Asia and the Pacific, Eastern Europe/Commonwealth of Independent States, Latin America and the Caribbean, and the Middle East.

FINANCIAL DATA:
Amount of support per award: $7,000 to $20,000; Average grant: $10,000.
Total amount of support: Varies.

APPLICATION INFO:
Organizations must submit letter of interest. Full applications are by invitation only.
Duration: One year. Must reapply.

ADDRESS INQUIRIES TO:
Mariam Gagoshashvili, Associate Director International Fund
(See address above.)

ASTRAEA LESBIAN FOUNDATION FOR JUSTICE   [889]
116 East 16th Street, 7th Floor
New York, NY 10003
(212) 529-8021
Fax: (212) 982-3321
E-mail: info@astraeafoundation.org
Web Site: www.astraeafoundation.org

FOUNDED: 1977

AREAS OF INTEREST:
Social change organizations and projects (including film, video, media and cultural projects) that directly address the depth and complexity of critical issues in LGBTQ communities.

NAME(S) OF PROGRAMS:
● **U.S. General Fund**

TYPE:
General operating grants; Grants-in-aid; Project/program grants. Grants are provided to LGBTQ people of color-led organizations fighting for racial and economic justice.

PURPOSE:
To provide critically needed financial support to lesbian-led, LGBTQ and progressive organizations striving to eliminate oppression based on race, age, sex, religion, sexual orientation, gender identity, economic exploitation, physical and mental ability, anti-semitism, and other such factors.

ELIGIBILITY:
501(c)(3) organizations. No grants to individuals.

GEOG. RESTRICTIONS: United States and its territories.

FINANCIAL DATA:
Amount of support per award: $7,000 to $30,000; Average grant: $10,000
Total amount of support: Varies.

APPLICATION INFO:
Unsolicited proposals are not accepted.
Duration: One year. Must reapply.

ASTRAEA LESBIAN FOUNDATION FOR JUSTICE   [890]
116 East 16th Street, 7th Floor
New York, NY 10003
(212) 529-8021
Fax: (212) 982-3321
E-mail: info@astraeafoundation.org
Web Site: www.astraeafoundation.org

FOUNDED: 1977

AREAS OF INTEREST:
Impactful art by LGBTQI people and organizations.

NAME(S) OF PROGRAMS:
● **Global Arts Fund**

TYPE:
Awards/prizes.

YEAR PROGRAM STARTED: 2013

PURPOSE:
To recognize the work of LGBTQI artists and organizations by providing support to those who show artistic merit and whose art and perspective reflect a commitment to Astraea's mission and efforts to promote LGBTQI visibility and social justice in marginalized LGBTQI communities in the face of exploitations wrought by globalization, imperialism, and neocolonialism.

ELIGIBILITY:
LGBTQI people and organizations with limited access to resources are eligible. The Fund will consider submissions, requested through a nomination process, in many artistic expressions: video, film, poetry, fictional prose, photography, painting, performance, dance, theater, music and other interdisciplinary expressions.

GEOG. RESTRICTIONS: United States, the Global East and the Global South.

FINANCIAL DATA:
Amount of support per award: $5,000 to $30,000.

NO. AWARDS: 4 to 10.

APPLICATION INFO:
The Fund only considers submissions through a nomination process, nominators having been grantees.
Deadline: Varies.

ADDRESS INQUIRIES TO:
E-mail: loi@astraeafoundation.org

ALEXANDER GRAHAM BELL ASSOCIATION FOR THE DEAF AND HARD OF HEARING   [891]
3417 Volta Place, N.W.
Washington, DC 20007
(202) 337-5220
E-mail: scholarships@agbell.org
Web Site: www.agbell.org

FOUNDED: 1890

AREAS OF INTEREST:
All areas of study.

NAME(S) OF PROGRAMS:
● **Alexander Graham Bell College Scholarship Awards**

TYPE:
Scholarships.

YEAR PROGRAM STARTED: 1967

PURPOSE:
To assist students with pre-lingual, bilateral hearing loss, who use listening and spoken language, to attend mainstream colleges.

ELIGIBILITY:
Based on age of diagnosis, degree of hearing loss and grade point average.

FINANCIAL DATA:
Amount of support per award: $1,500 to $2,500.
Total amount of support: Varies.

NO. MOST RECENT APPLICANTS: Approximately 200.

NO. AWARDS: Approximately 10.

APPLICATION INFO:
Applicants should download the application (preferred) or request via e-mail. Photocopies are not accepted.
Duration: One year. Nonrenewable.
Deadline: Varies. Details posted online in December.

IRS I.D.: 53-0196644

ADDRESS INQUIRIES TO:
College Scholarships
(See address and e-mail above.)

BEN & JERRY'S FOUNDATION   [892]
30 Community Drive
South Burlington, VT 05403-6828
(802) 846-1500
E-mail: info@benandjerrysfoundation.org
Web Site: www.benandjerrysfoundation.org

FOUNDED: 1985

AREAS OF INTEREST:
Economic, environmental, social justice and grassroots organizing.

TYPE:
General operating grants; Project/program grants. Grants to nonprofit organizations which facilitate progressive social change by addressing the underlying conditions of societal and/or environmental problems using organizing as a strategy to create change.

YEAR PROGRAM STARTED: 1986

PURPOSE:
To support and encourage organizations that facilitate progressive social change by addressing the underlying conditions of societal and environmental problems.

LEGAL BASIS:
Private foundation.

ELIGIBILITY:
The Foundation generally funds organizations with budgets less than $500,000. Applicant must be a nonprofit 501(c)(3) organization or have a sponsoring agent that has this status. No grants to support basic services. Applicants need to demonstrate that their projects will lead to societal, institutional or environmental change, help ameliorate an unjust or destructive situation by empowering constituents and address the root causes of social and/or environmental problems.

No funding for discretionary or emergency requests, colleges or universities, individuals or scholarships, research projects, religious projects, state agencies, international or foreign programs or direct-service programs.

GEOG. RESTRICTIONS: United States and its territories.

FINANCIAL DATA:
Amount of support per award: Community Action Team Grants: Up to $2,000; Economic Justice Grants: Up to $20,000; National Grants: Up to $30,000.
Total amount of support: $3,398,783 for the year 2020.

NO. AWARDS: 381 for the year 2020.

REPRESENTATIVE AWARDS:
$18,000 to 350 New Hampshire, Dover, NH, for the Youth Climate Organizing Team; $20,000 to Beyond Toxics, Eugene, OR, for general support for intersectionality in environmental justice; $20,000 to I Have A Future, Dorchester, MA, for general support.

APPLICATION INFO:
Guidelines and application process are detailed online.
Duration: One year. Must reapply.
Deadline: National Grassroots Organizing Program: February 1, June 1 and October 1. Vermont Community Action Team Program: Applications are reviewed monthly. Vermont Economic Justice Program: July 1.

PUBLICATIONS:
Annual report; application guidelines; grant recipients list.

IRS I.D.: 03-0300865

STAFF:
Lisa Pendolino, Director of Finance and Operations
Rebecca Golden, Director of Programs
Dana Jeffery, Administrative and Grants Management Coordinator

*PLEASE NOTE:
The Foundation does not accept mailed letters of interest. Please apply online.

JACOB AND HILDA BLAUSTEIN FOUNDATION   [893]
One South Street
Suite 2900
Baltimore, MD 21202
(410) 347-7201
Web Site: www.blaufund.org

FOUNDED: 1957

AREAS OF INTEREST:
Jewish life and Israel, education, human rights, health and mental health, and the arts.

TYPE:
General operating grants; Matching gifts; Project/program grants.

ELIGIBILITY:
Grants are made to organizations that have tax-exempt status under Section 501(c)(3) of the Internal Revenue Code. No grants are made to individuals.

GEOG. RESTRICTIONS: United States (primarily Baltimore, Maryland) and Israel.

FINANCIAL DATA:
Amount of support per award: Varies.
Total amount of support: $8,554,000 for the year 2020.

APPLICATION INFO:
Application information is available on the Foundation's web site.
Duration: Typically one to two years.

ADDRESS INQUIRIES TO:
Betsy F. Ringel
Executive Director
(See address above.)

CALIFORNIA LIBRARY ASSOCIATION
1055 East Colorado Boulevard
Suite 500
Pasadena, CA 91106
(626) 204-4071
E-mail: info@cla-net.org
Web Site: www.cla-net.org

TYPE:
Scholarships. Support for minority library school students. Support for graduate students in reference/information service librarianship.
See entry 663 for full listing.

CARING FOR MILITARY FAMILIES: THE ELIZABETH DOLE FOUNDATION   [894]
600 New Hampshire Avenue, N.W.
10th Floor
Washington, DC 20037
(202) 249-7171
E-mail: molly@elizabethdolefoundation.org
Web Site: www.elizabethdolefoundation.org

FOUNDED: 2012

AREAS OF INTEREST:
Military and veteran caregivers.

NAME(S) OF PROGRAMS:
● **Hidden Heroes Fund**

TYPE:
Project/program grants; Research grants. The Elizabeth Dole Foundation provides grants to qualified nonprofits as part of the Hidden Heroes Fund. This fund is dedicated to supporting innovative programs that make a direct impact on the lives of America's military and veteran caregivers.

YEAR PROGRAM STARTED: 2016

PURPOSE:
To spur targeted support for military caregivers, providing funding to leading nonprofit organizations with an exemplary track record.

ELIGIBILITY:
Organizations must be 501(c)(3) registered, and projects must directly impact the lives of military and veteran caregivers, the spouses, parents, and other loved-ones caring for our nation's wounded warriors at home. Projects must fall under one or more of the Foundation's five pillars of impact: families and communities, education and training, employment and workplace support, financial and/or legal support, and health and well-being.

Use of the Foundation's RAND study data or other relevant research in designing and implementing the project is highly encouraged.

FINANCIAL DATA:
The Foundation has awarded $1,000,000 in grants since inception.
Amount of support per award: Varies depending on the project.

NO. MOST RECENT APPLICANTS: Over 150.

NO. AWARDS: 10.

APPLICATION INFO:
Information may be obtained by contacting the Foundation at the e-mail address above.
Duration: Funding until completion of the specific project. Project duration is negotiated during the application process. Grant not renewable; however, organizations are allowed to apply more than once.
Deadline: Applications are accepted on a year-round basis.

ADDRESS INQUIRIES TO:
Molly Ramsey
Manager, Policy and Programs
(See address above.)

*SPECIAL STIPULATIONS:
The program or project must support military caregivers directly. Programs supporting veterans, with incidental or tangential support for their caregivers, will not be considered.

THE CENTER FOR LGBTQ STUDIES   [895]
The Graduate Center/CUNY
365 Fifth Avenue, Room 7115
New York, NY 10016
(212) 817-1955
E-mail: clagsfellowships@gmail.com
Web Site: clags.org

FOUNDED: 1991

AREAS OF INTEREST:
Scholarly research on the lesbian, gay, bisexual, transgender, and queer experience.

NAME(S) OF PROGRAMS:
● **The Duberman-Zal Fellowship**

TYPE:
Awards/prizes; Fellowships. An endowed fellowship named for CLAGS founder and first executive director, Martin Duberman, and partner, Eli Zal.

PURPOSE:
To promote the study of historical, cultural, and political issues of vital concern to lesbian, gay, bisexual, and transgendered individuals.

ELIGIBILITY:
Graduate students, independent scholars, or adjunct from any country doing scholarly research on the lesbian/gay/bisexual/transgender/queer (LGBTQ) experience may apply. University affiliation is not necessary.

FINANCIAL DATA:
Amount of support per award: $2,500.

NO. AWARDS: 1.

APPLICATION INFO:
Applications must include the following:
(1) a cover letter with contact information (address, telephone number, and e-mail), project title, names of recommenders, and the fellowship being applied for;
(2) a research proposal of seven to 10 pages (double-spaced) including references;
(3) a brief statement of how the funds will be used;
(4) a curriculum vitae and;
(5) two letters of recommendation.

All submissions must be sent electronically to the e-mail listed above.

Letters of recommendation should be electronically directly from recommenders to the e-mail listed above.

Deadline: Mid-November. Final decisions are made in Spring.

PUBLICATIONS:
Annual report.

ADDRESS INQUIRIES TO:
Jasmina Sinanovic, Director of Finance and Development
(See address above.)

*SPECIAL STIPULATIONS:
Fellowship recipient may be asked to participate in CLAG's programming the following academic year to present their research project.

CINTAS FOUNDATION
8724 Sunset Drive
P.M.B. 528
Miami, FL 33173
E-mail: info@cintasfoundation.org
Web Site: www.cintasfoundation.org

TYPE:
Awards/prizes; Fellowships. Awarded to persons of Cuban citizenship or lineage residing outside Cuba for achievement of a creative nature in architecture, painting, sculpture, printmaking, music composition and literature.

See entry 395 for full listing.

THE CONSORTIUM FOR GRADUATE STUDY IN MANAGEMENT
229 Chesterfield Business Parkway
Chesterfield, MO 63005
(636) 681-5553
Fax: (636) 681-5499
E-mail: recruiting@cgsm.org
Web Site: www.cgsm.org

TYPE:
Fellowships. Competitive Advantage is a career and graduate school readiness program for underrepresented minority college students.

Graduate fellowships for minority students interested in management careers in business.

See entry 1701 for full listing.

COUNCIL ON SOCIAL WORK EDUCATION [896]
333 John Carlyle Street
Suite 400
Alexandria, VA 22314
(703) 683-8080
Fax: (703) 683-8099
E-mail: dnguyen@cswe.org
Web Site: www.cswe.org

FOUNDED: 1952

AREAS OF INTEREST:
Improvement of social services and mental health.

NAME(S) OF PROGRAMS:
● **The Mental Health and Substance Abuse Fellowship Program**

TYPE:
Fellowships. Awards for doctoral-level studies in social work, specializing in mental health and substance abuse-related education, research, policy and practice.

YEAR PROGRAM STARTED: 1974

PURPOSE:
To reduce health disparities and improve health care outcomes of racially and ethnically diverse populations by increasing the number of culturally competent behavioral health professionals available to underserved populations in the public and private nonprofit sectors.

LEGAL BASIS:
Nonprofit organization.

ELIGIBILITY:
Applicants must be American citizens, noncitizen nationals, or have permanent residence status. International students, Deferred Action for Childhood Arrivals students, and work visa holders are not eligible to apply. The fellowship targets, but is not limited to, minority ethnic and racial groups.

Applicant must have a Master's degree in social work from a CSWE-accredited program and be starting full-time study leading to a doctoral degree in social work, or be currently enrolled as a full-time student in a doctoral social work program.

Applicant's career goals should center on leadership in practice, research, teaching, or policy promulgation with underrepresented and underserved persons facing mental health and/or substance abuse challenges.

FINANCIAL DATA:
Fellowship awards include a monthly stipend for one year to help meet living and doctoral study expenses.
Amount of support per award: Varies.
Total amount of support: Varies.

CO-OP FUNDING PROGRAMS: Funded by the Center for Mental Health Services, Center for Substance Abuse Prevention, and the Center for Substance Abuse Treatment in the Substance Abuse and Mental Health Services Administration (SAMHSA).

NO. AWARDS: Up to 25.

APPLICATION INFO:
Complete information is available at the Council web site.
Duration: Three years maximum. Renewable each year subject to availability of funds and progress in program.
Deadline: February 28.

ADDRESS INQUIRIES TO:
E-mail: mfp@cswe.org
(See telephone number above.)

DARTMOUTH COLLEGE [897]
Office of Graduate Studies
Eastman/Marshall
37 Dewey Field Road, Suite 6062, Room 437
Hanover, NH 03755-3526
(603) 646-2106
Fax: (603) 646-8762
E-mail: amy.l.gallagher@dartmouth.edu
Web Site: graduate.dartmouth.edu

FOUNDED: 1769

AREAS OF INTEREST:
Fellowships for underrepresented minority scholars (including African-American and Native American scholars) and other graduate scholars with a demonstrated commitment and ability to advance educational diversity.

NAME(S) OF PROGRAMS:
● **Eastman/Marshall Dissertation Fellowships**

TYPE:
Exchange programs; Fellowships.

YEAR PROGRAM STARTED: 1991

PURPOSE:
To increase the number of underrepresented minority faculty in American higher education by supporting African-American, Native American and other scholars with a demonstrated commitment to the advancement of educational diversity.

LEGAL BASIS:
University.

ELIGIBILITY:
Applicants will be chosen on the basis of academic achievement and promise, membership in a racial or ethnic group that is currently underrepresented among faculty in the applicant's academic field, demonstrated commitment to increasing opportunities for underrepresented minorities and increasing cross-racial understanding, and potential for serving as an advocate and mentor for minority undergraduate and graduate students.

GEOG. RESTRICTIONS: United States and Canada.

FINANCIAL DATA:
Fellowship provides stipend, office space, library privileges and research assistance.
Amount of support per award: $36,000 stipend and $2,500 research assistance.
Total amount of support: $77,000 annually.

NO. AWARDS: 2.

APPLICATION INFO:
Application form required. Contact the Office of Graduate Studies. Supporting documentation includes abstract of dissertation prospectus, statement of academic career plan, curriculum vitae, transcripts and three letters of reference.
Duration: Two years.
Deadline: February 18. Announcement April 1.

PUBLICATIONS:
Program announcement.

ADDRESS INQUIRIES TO:
Amy Gallagher, Assistant Graduate Registrar and
Office Manager
(See address above.)

*SPECIAL STIPULATIONS:
Fellows are expected to complete the dissertation during the tenure of the Fellowship and may have the opportunity to participate in teaching, either as a primary instructor or as part of a team.

DAUGHTERS OF PENELOPE FOUNDATION, INC. [898]
1909 Q Street, N.W., Suite 500
Washington, DC 20009
(202) 234-9741
Fax: (202) 483-6983
E-mail: president@dopfoundationinc.com
dophq@ahepa.org
Web Site: www.dopfoundationinc.com
www.daughtersofpenelope.org

FOUNDED: 1983

AREAS OF INTEREST:
Philanthropic, educational and cultural activities pertaining to Greek culture.

NAME(S) OF PROGRAMS:
● **Daughters of Penelope National Scholarship Awards**

TYPE:
Scholarships. Academic and Financial Need.

YEAR PROGRAM STARTED: 1984

PURPOSE:
To promote the social, ethical and intellectual interests of members; to perpetuate the study of American ideals and to encourage Hellenic study; to cultivate citizenship and patriotism.

ELIGIBILITY:
Applicant must be a woman and have a current member of their immediate family or legal guardian (court-appointed) in the Daughters of Penelope or the Order of Ahepa, in good standing for a minimum of two years, or be a member in good standing for two years in the Daughters of Penelope or the Maids of Athena.

FINANCIAL DATA:
Amount of support per award: $500 to $2,500 depending on scholarship.
Total amount of support: Varies.

NO. MOST RECENT APPLICANTS: Varies.

NO. AWARDS: 8 for the year 2018.

APPLICATION INFO:
Application is available on the Foundation web site.
Duration: One year.
Deadline: May 1.

ADDRESS INQUIRIES TO:
E-mail:
dopfoundationscholarship@gmail.com

EDUCATIONAL TESTING SERVICE
660 Rosedale Road
Princeton, NJ 08541
E-mail: internfellowships@ets.org
Web Site: www.ets.org/research/internship-fellowship

TYPE:
Internships. Interns in this 10-week program participate in research under the guidance of ETS mentors in one of the areas of interest listed above at ETS office located in Princeton, N.J. Interns also participate in seminars and workshops on a variety of topics.

See entry 1384 for full listing.

LOIS AND RICHARD ENGLAND FAMILY FOUNDATION
P.O. Box 34-1077
Bethesda, MD 20827
(301) 657-7737
Fax: (301) 657-7738
E-mail: englandfamilyfdn@gmail.com
Web Site: fdnweb.org/england

TYPE:
Capital grants; Challenge/matching grants; Development grants; General operating grants; Matching gifts; Project/program grants; Seed money grants; Technical assistance; Training grants.

See entry 1013 for full listing.

FEDERAL HIGHWAY ADMINISTRATION
Center of Transportation Workforce Development
1200 New Jersey Avenue, S.E.
Washington, DC 20590
(703) 235-0538
E-mail: transportationedu@dot.gov
Web Site: www.fhwa.dot.gov/ugp

TYPE:
Fellowships; Internships; Research grants. Dwight David Eisenhower Transportation Fellowship Program's objectives are to attract the nation's brightest minds to the field of transportation, to enhance the careers of transportation professionals by encouraging them to seek advanced degrees, and to retain top talent in the transportation industry of the U.S. This Program encompasses all areas of transportation. The Program has seven award categories:
(1) Eisenhower Graduate (GRAD) Fellowships enable students to pursue Master's degrees or Doctorates in transportation-related fields at the university of their choice;
(2) Eisenhower Grants for Research (GRF) Fellowships acquaint undergraduate and graduate students with transportation research, development and technology-transfer activities at the U.S. Department of Transportation facilities;
(3) Eisenhower Historically Black Colleges and Universities (HBCU) Fellowships provide HBCU students with additional opportunities to enter careers in transportation. The Fellowships also serve as a feeder for other Eisenhower fellowships;
(4) Eisenhower Hispanic Serving Institutions (HSI) Fellowships provide HSI students with additional opportunities to enter careers in transportation. The Fellowships also serve as a feeder for other Eisenhower fellowships;
(5) Eisenhower Tribal College and Universities Fellowships (TCU) provides students with additional opportunities to enter careers in transportation. The Fellowships also serve as a feeder for other Eisenhower fellowships;
(6) Eisenhower Intern Fellowships (EIF) provides students with opportunities to perform a wide range of transportation-related activities at public and private-sector transportation organizations and;
(7) Eisenhower Community College Fellowships provide students at community colleges with opportunities to enter careers in transportation. The Fellowships also serve as a feeder for other Eisenhower fellowships.

See entry 2353 for full listing.

FEEA SCHOLARSHIP PROGRAM
1641 Prince Street
Alexandria, VA 22314
(202) 554-0007
Fax: (202) 559-1298
E-mail: fedshelpingfeds@feea.org
Web Site: feea.org

TYPE:
Scholarships. Merit-based scholarship competition program open exclusively to federal employees, their spouses and their children.

See entry 1500 for full listing.

FOUNDATION FOR SCIENCE AND DISABILITY [899]
503 N.W. 89th Street
Gainesville, FL 32607
(352) 374-5774
E-mail: rmankin1@ufl.edu
Web Site: stemd.org

FOUNDED: 1978

AREAS OF INTEREST:
Science, mathematics, medicine, engineering and computer science.

TYPE:
Grants-in-aid; Research grants.

YEAR PROGRAM STARTED: 1978

PURPOSE:
To assist disabled students who are interested in obtaining a graduate degree in one of the above fields.

LEGAL BASIS:
Affiliate of American Association for Advancement of Science.

ELIGIBILITY:
Open to college seniors and graduate students who have some physical or sensory disability and who have been accepted to graduate or professional school. Selection is based on purpose of fund usage, scholarly success, and research ability.

FINANCIAL DATA:
Funds may be used for an assistive device or instrument, or as financial support to work with a professor on an individual research project, or for some other special need.
Amount of support per award: $1,000.

NO. MOST RECENT APPLICANTS: 7.

NO. AWARDS: At least 1.

APPLICATION INFO:
Application forms may be obtained by writing or e-mailing Dr. Richard Mankin, as listed above, or can be downloaded from the Foundation web site.

Applicants should submit a copy of college transcript, two letters of recommendation, 250-word summary of educational goals including what the funds will be used for, if awarded, and a copy of a U.S. birth or naturalization certificate.
Deadline: December 1.

ADDRESS INQUIRIES TO:
Dr. Richard Mankin, Chairperson
Science Student Grant Committee
(See address above.)

THE FOUNDATION OF THE AMERICAN COLLEGE OF HEALTHCARE EXECUTIVES
300 South Riverside Plaza
Suite 1900
Chicago, IL 60606-6698
(312) 424-9400
Fax: (312) 424-9405
E-mail: contact@ache.org
Web Site: www.ache.org/scholarships

TYPE:
Scholarships. Offered annually, the Albert W. Dent and the Foster G. McGaw Graduate Student Scholarships are designated for students enrolled in their final year of classroom work in a health care management graduate program.

Albert W. Dent Graduate Student Scholarship is only available to minority students.

See entry 1291 for full listing.

4A'S [900]
1065 Avenue of the Americas, 16th Floor
New York, NY 10018
(212) 682-2500
Fax: (212) 682-8391
E-mail: maip@aaaa.org
Web Site: foundation.aaaa.org

FOUNDED: 1917

AREAS OF INTEREST:
Advertising, media, marketing, data/analytics
and design.

NAME(S) OF PROGRAMS:
● **Multicultural Advertising Intern
Program (MAIP)**

TYPE:
Fellowships; Scholarships.

YEAR PROGRAM STARTED: 1973

PURPOSE:
To assist multicultural students in attaining
skills and knowledge necessary for careers in
advertising and to assist advertising agencies
in recruiting multicultural persons for the
professional level.

LEGAL BASIS:
Nonprofit organization.

ELIGIBILITY:
Open to any Black, Native Hawaiian or
Pacific Islander, American Indian or Alaska
Native, Asian, Hispanic, multiracial or
multiethnic student. Students must be
currently enrolled in an undergraduate or
graduate program at any accredited,
degree-granting college or university, or a
student attending a participating 4A's
portfolio school and have completed at least
their junior year by the time of the
internship. Applicants must have a grade
point average minimum of 3.0 on a scale of
4.0 and must be citizens or permanent
residents of the U.S. Applicants must be able
to show their passion to launch an
advertising career through their essays.

Students have the opportunity to work in one
of the basic career areas of advertising
including account management, media buying
and planning, art direction, community
management, copywriting, design,
production, project management, public
relations and strategy.

GEOG. RESTRICTIONS: United States.

FINANCIAL DATA:

Amount of support per award: $12 per hour.
Total amount of support: Varies.

NO. MOST RECENT APPLICANTS: 342.

NO. AWARDS: 100 to 200.

APPLICATION INFO:
Candidates must submit an application,
resume, letters of recommendation, school
transcripts and supporting materials (such as
artwork). $25 application fee required.
Semi-finalists are interviewed before final
selections are made.
Duration: 22 weeks (12-week online Spring
Training and a 10-week internship).
Deadline: Mid- to end of October.

ADDRESS INQUIRIES TO:
Reema Elghossain, Vice President
Talent, Engagement and Inclusion
(See e-mail address above.)

GSBA SCHOLARSHIP FUND [901]
400 East Pine Street, Suite 322
Seattle, WA 98122
(206) 363-9188
Fax: (206) 568-3123
E-mail: scholarship@thegsba.org
Web Site: www.thegsba.org

FOUNDED: 1991

AREAS OF INTEREST:
Leadership and service in the LGBTQ
community.

TYPE:
Awards/prizes; Scholarships. Scholarships are
intended for college, creative study,
vocational training and postsecondary
education.

YEAR PROGRAM STARTED: 1991

PURPOSE:
To expand economic opportunities for the
Lesbian, Gay, Bisexual and Transgender
community and those who support equality
for all.

LEGAL BASIS:
501(c)(3) nonprofit.

ELIGIBILITY:
Applicants must demonstrate proven
leadership skills, strong academic
achievement and a commitment to making a
positive difference in the world. Applicant
must be a current Washington state resident
pursuing a postsecondary degree in the U.S.

GEOG. RESTRICTIONS: Washington state.

FINANCIAL DATA:
The Fund has awarded over $4,000,000 since
its founding.
Amount of support per award: Up to
$13,000.
Total amount of support: $500,000 for the
year 2019.

NO. MOST RECENT APPLICANTS: 800 for the
year 2019.

NO. AWARDS: 50 for the year 2019.

APPLICATION INFO:
Applicants must submit the online application
form, letters of recommendation and
transcripts.
Duration: One year. Renewable up to four
years.
Deadline: January 10.

PUBLICATIONS:
Guide/Directory, business listing and
resources; *Perspective,* monthly newsletter.

IRS I.D.: 94-3138514

STAFF:
Louise Chernin, President and Chief
Executive Officer
Ilona Lohrey, Vice President of Membership
and Programs
Rachel Chernin, Vice President of Operations
and Finance
Matt Landers, Director of Public Policy and
Government Affairs
Mark Rosen, Deputy Director
Amy Burdick, Senior Business Relationship
Manager
Jeff Boyer, Senior Development Officer
Christine Arrington, Development Manager
and Capitol Hill Specialist
Levi Coffin, Grant Manager and Business
Training Specialist
Toraya Miller, Membership and Program
Manager

Joey Chapman, Membership Development
Manager
Carlos Chavez, Program Events Manager
Taylor Briggs, Scholarship Program Manager
Cade Schmidt, Marketing Specialist

BOARD OF DIRECTORS:
Stephanie Dallas, Chairman
Jay Petterson, Vice Chairman
Carolyn Hojaboom, Treasurer
Brandon Chun, Secretary
Carrie Carson, Scholarship Chairperson
David Blandford
Leda Chahim
Danny Cords
Linda DiLello-Morton
Roz Edison
Rigo Garcia Ortega
Gladys Gillis
Eve Gourley
Jenny Harding
Andrew Held
James Hing
Katie Mooney
Mike Novasio
Alex Oh
Dustin O'Quinn
Lisa Sterritt
Masoud Torabi
Barb Wilson
Beto Yarce

MYRTLE E. AND WILLIAM G. HESS CHARITABLE TRUST [902]
c/o JPMorgan
28660 Northwestern Highway
Southfield, MI 48034
(248) 738-6169
Fax: (800) 919-3085
E-mail: kimberly.l.thomas@jpmorgan.com
Web Site: www.jpmorgan.com/onlinegrants

FOUNDED: 1985

AREAS OF INTEREST:
Catholic charitable organizations located in
Oakland County, MI; Catholic charitable,
educational and scientific objectives.

TYPE:
Capital grants; Development grants;
Endowments; General operating grants;
Project/program grants.

YEAR PROGRAM STARTED: 1985

PURPOSE:
To provide funds in perpetuity for charitable
purposes.

LEGAL BASIS:
Private foundation.

ELIGIBILITY:
Limited to Catholic organizations with
charitable, educational and scientific
objectives. Particular preference being given
to such objectives within the confines of
Waterford and White Lake Townships.

GEOG. RESTRICTIONS: Waterford and White
Lake townships in Oakland County,
Michigan.

FINANCIAL DATA:
Amount of support per award: $2,500 to
$25,000.
Total amount of support: Varies.

NO. MOST RECENT APPLICANTS: 28.

NO. AWARDS: 26.

APPLICATION INFO:
Only online applications are accepted.
Duration: One year. Renewals possible.
Deadline: April 30.

ADDRESS INQUIRIES TO:
Kimberly Thomas, Trust Officer
(See address above.)

IMMUNE DEFICIENCY FOUNDATION [903]

110 West Road
Suite 300
Towson, MD 21204
(800) 296-4433
Fax: (410) 321-9165
E-mail: dantilla@primaryimmune.org
Web Site: www.primaryimmune.org

FOUNDED: 1980

AREAS OF INTEREST:
Immunodeficiency diseases.

NAME(S) OF PROGRAMS:
● **The Varun Bhaskaran (WAS) Scholarship Program of IDF**

TYPE:
Scholarships.

YEAR PROGRAM STARTED: 2013

ELIGIBILITY:
Scholarship for undergraduate or graduate students living with Wiskott-Aldrich Syndrome.

GEOG. RESTRICTIONS: United States.

FINANCIAL DATA:
Amount of support per award: Varies.
Total amount of support: Varies.

APPLICATION INFO:
Contact the Foundation for application procedures.
Duration: Renewable yearly based on financial need and academic participation.
Deadline: Usually February 1 to April 1.

ADDRESS INQUIRIES TO:
Dan Antilla, Program Manager
(See address above.)

INSTITUTE OF INDUSTRIAL AND SYSTEMS ENGINEERS (IISE)

3577 Parkway Lane
Building 5, Suite 200
Norcross, GA 30092
(770) 349-1102
Fax: (770) 441-3295
E-mail: bcameron@iise.org
Web Site: www.iise.org

TYPE:
Fellowships; Scholarships. The Institute supports the advancement of engineering education and research through scholarships and fellowships to recognize and support these types of endeavors.

See entry 2392 for full listing.

THE JAPANESE AMERICAN CITIZENS LEAGUE (JACL)

Washington, DC Office
1629 K Street, N.W., Suite 400
Washington, DC 20006
(202) 223-1240
Fax: (202) 296-8082
E-mail: dinoue@jacl.org
Web Site: www.jacl.org

TYPE:
Travel grants. The Kakehashi Program is a new international program, part of JACL's leadership development. It is for college students and consists of five webinars and a nine-day trip to Japan.

See entry 777 for full listing.

JEWISH COMMUNITY FOUNDATION OF LOS ANGELES

6505 Wilshire Boulevard
Suite 1200
Los Angeles, CA 90048
(323) 761-8700
Fax: (323) 761-8720
E-mail: info@jewishfoundationla.org
Web Site: www.jewishfoundationla.org

TYPE:
Awards/prizes; Capital grants; Project/program grants; Seed money grants.
Capital Grants: Construction and renovation projects for facilities that predominantly serve members of the Los Angeles Jewish community.

Cutting Edge Grants: New programs with the potential for transformative impact that address critical needs in the Los Angeles Jewish community.

General Community Grants: Programs by organizations outside of the Jewish community which address high-priority concerns in the Los Angeles community.

Israel Grants: Programs that have an impact on economic development and pluralistic Jewish identity in Israel.

Next Stage Grants: Capacity building support for select former Cutting Edge Grant recipients to get to the next stage of their success.
Reimagine Grants provide support for organizations and synagogues to reimagine Jewish Los Angeles in response to Covid-19.

See entry 1186 for full listing.

JEWISH FEDERATION OF METROPOLITAN CHICAGO ACADEMIC SCHOLARSHIP PROGRAM

JVS Career and Employment/JCFS Chicago
216 West Jackson Boulevard, Suite 700
Chicago, IL 60606-6921
(312) 673-3444
Fax: (312) 553-5544
E-mail: jvsscholarship@jcfs.org
Web Site: www.jcfs.org/jvsscholarships

TYPE:
Awards/prizes; Scholarships. Awards to individuals for the academic year.

See entry 1520 for full listing.

THE LUCIUS N. LITTAUER FOUNDATION, INC. [904]

220 Fifth Avenue, 19th Floor
New York, NY 10001-7708
(646) 237-5158
E-mail: adivack@littauerfoundation.org
Web Site: littauerfoundation.org

FOUNDED: 1929

AREAS OF INTEREST:
Access to opportunity for low-income and marginalized populations in New York and Israel, support for Jewish communal life in New York, and Judaica libraries and archives.

TYPE:
General operating grants; Project/program grants; Seed money grants; Training grants; Loan forgiveness programs.

YEAR PROGRAM STARTED: 1929

PURPOSE:
To support education, health care and social welfare in the Jewish world and beyond.

LEGAL BASIS:
Independent foundation.

ELIGIBILITY:
Funds are awarded to nonprofit 501(c)(3) institutions. No grants to individuals.

GEOG. RESTRICTIONS: New York, New York and Israel.

FINANCIAL DATA:
Amount of support per award: Varies.
Total amount of support: $3,980,350 for the year 2020.

NO. MOST RECENT APPLICANTS: 206 for the year 2020.

NO. AWARDS: 112 for the year 2020.

APPLICATION INFO:
All grant requests must be made online through the Foundation web site. Application includes a full description of project, budget request, timetable for completion, institution which will administer grant and contact person.
Duration: Varies. Renewal possible.
Deadline: Applications are accepted on a rolling basis.

PUBLICATIONS:
Guidelines.

IRS I.D.: 13-1688027

TRUSTEES AND OFFICERS:
Robert D. Frost, President
Geula R. Solomon, Treasurer
Noah B. Perlman, Secretary
Charles Berlin
Mark A. Bilski
Teri Horowitz
Sarah Levy
Peter J. Solomon
Dr. David Stern

ADDRESS INQUIRIES TO:
Alan Divack, Program Director
(See address above.)

LUSO-AMERICAN EDUCATION FOUNDATION

7080 Donlon Way
Suite 200
Dublin, CA 94568
(925) 828-3883
Fax: (925) 828-4554
E-mail: education@luso-american.org
Web Site: www.luso-american.org/laef

TYPE:
Scholarships.

See entry 600 for full listing.

MARINE BIOLOGICAL LABORATORY

7 MBL Street
Woods Hole, MA 02543
(508) 289-7173
Fax: (508) 289-7934
E-mail: researchprograms@mbl.edu
Web Site: www.mbl.edu

TYPE:
Research grants.

See entry 1941 for full listing.

MAURICE J. MASSERINI TRUST [905]
c/o Wells Fargo Private Bank
4365 Executive Drive, 18th Floor
San Diego, CA 92121
(858) 622-6958
Fax: (858) 622-6848
E-mail: grantadministration@wellsfargo.com
Web Site: www.wellsfargo.com/private-foundations/masserini-trust

AREAS OF INTEREST:
Underprivileged children, the elderly, religious, human services, health, environment/animals, education, and arts and culture.

TYPE:
Project/program grants.

ELIGIBILITY:
Eligible organizations must be IRS 501(c)(3) tax-exempt and be located in San Diego County, CA. Start-up organizations or salaries are generally not supported.

GEOG. RESTRICTIONS: San Diego County, California.

FINANCIAL DATA:
Amount of support per award: Generally $5,000 to $15,000.
Total amount of support: Varies.

NO. AWARDS: 20 per year.

APPLICATION INFO:
Applications are submitted through an online application process.
Duration: One year. Renewable by reapplication.
Deadline: June 30.

ADDRESS INQUIRIES TO:
Wells Fargo Philanthropic Services
(See e-mail address above.)

MEDICAL LIBRARY ASSOCIATION [906]
225 West Wacker Drive
Suite 650
Chicago, IL 60606
(312) 419-9094
E-mail: awards@mail.mlahq.org
Web Site: www.mlanet.org

FOUNDED: 1898

AREAS OF INTEREST:
Health sciences librarianship.

NAME(S) OF PROGRAMS:
● MLA Scholarship for Underrepresented Students

TYPE:
Awards/prizes; Scholarships. Awarded for study in health sciences librarianship.

YEAR PROGRAM STARTED: 1964

PURPOSE:
To contribute to the support of underrepresented individuals who are qualified to make a contribution to health sciences librarianship.

LEGAL BASIS:
Nonprofit.

ELIGIBILITY:
Applicant must be:
(1) a member of an underrepresented group;
(2) entering a Master's program at an ALA-accredited graduate library school or must have completed no more than half of their graduate program academic requirements at the time the award is made and;
(3) a citizen of or have permanent residence status in the U.S. or Canada.

A past recipient of the MLA Scholarship or the MLA Scholarship for Underrepresented Students is ineligible. Membership in MLA is not required.

FINANCIAL DATA:
Amount of support per award: Up to $5,000.

NO. AWARDS: 1 per year.

APPLICATION INFO:
Applicant must submit the following:
(1) a completed online application;
(2) two letters of reference from persons not related to the applicant who are knowledgeable about the applicant's character, education and abilities;
(3) official transcript from each college or university attended, sent directly from the respective institution that grants either Baccalaureate degree or library study degree and;
(4) copy of catalog or web page of applicant's library school, which states the number of credits needed for applicant's degree.
Duration: One year.
Deadline: December 1.

STAFF:
Maria Lopez, Grants, Scholarships and Awards Coordinator

ADDRESS INQUIRIES TO:
Coordinator
Grants, Scholarships and Awards
(See address above.)

MICHIGAN STATE UNIVERSITY, THE GRADUATE SCHOOL [907]
Chittenden Hall
466 West Circle Drive
East Lansing, MI 48824
(517) 353-3220
E-mail: gradschool@grd.msu.edu
Web Site: grad.msu.edu

FOUNDED: 1855

AREAS OF INTEREST:
Higher education.

NAME(S) OF PROGRAMS:
● Academic Achievement Graduate Assistantships
● Education Opportunity Fellowship
● University Distinguished Fellowships
● University Enrichment Fellowships

TYPE:
Assistantships; Fellowships.

YEAR PROGRAM STARTED: 1970

PURPOSE:
To increase participation by all U.S. students in graduate programs leading to advanced degrees in fields that do not yet reflect the inclusive diversity of the U.S. population; to enhance their retention and degree completion.

LEGAL BASIS:
University.

ELIGIBILITY:
Candidates are considered for the Academic Achievement Graduate Assistantship if nominated by the academic unit of the graduate program. Candidates for the Education Opportunity Fellowship may apply directly upon admission into a graduate program.

Candidate must be admitted to or enrolled in a graduate/professional degree-granting program at Michigan State University. Some programs require a student to demonstrate financial need. To be considered for financial support under the Graduate Education Opportunity Programs, all recipients must be able to prove U.S. citizenship or permanent residency. Funding based on financial need.

University Distinguished Fellowship and University Enrichment Fellowship are merit-based recruitment fellowships. Students must be nominated by a department/college.

GEOG. RESTRICTIONS: United States.

FINANCIAL DATA:
Amount of support per award: Academic Achievement Graduate Assistantship (AAGA): Level I, half-time, $13,032 to $23,361, plus nine credits (Fall/Spring), including health care; Education Opportunity Fellowship (EOF): $1,500 per semester; University Distinguished Fellowships (UDF) and University Enrichment Fellowships (UEF): $29,000, plus six to 10 credits (Fall/Spring) or three to five credits (Summer), including health care.
Total amount of support: Approximately $270,000.

APPLICATION INFO:
Contact the Graduate School.
Duration: Five to 11 semesters.
Deadline: April 15.

ADDRESS INQUIRIES TO:
Aida Montalvo, Secretary
(See address above.)

*SPECIAL STIPULATIONS:
Students must be enrolled in a graduate/professional program at Michigan State University.

MITSUBISHI ELECTRIC AMERICA FOUNDATION
1300 Wilson Boulevard
Suite 825
Arlington, VA 22209
(703) 276-8240
E-mail: mea.foundation@meus.mea.com
Web Site: www.meaf.org

TYPE:
Demonstration grants; Internships; Matching gifts; Project/program grants; Seed money grants; Technical assistance; Training grants. Grants are offered to make a better world for all by helping young people with disabilities to maximize their potential and participation in society.

See entry 1435 for full listing.

THE NATIONAL ACADEMIES OF SCIENCES, ENGINEERING, AND MEDICINE [908]
Fellowships Office
Ford Foundation Fellowship Programs
500 Fifth Street, N.W.
Washington, DC 20001
(202) 334-2872
E-mail: FordApplications@nas.edu
Web Site: www.nationalacademies.org/ford

FOUNDED: 1979

AREAS OF INTEREST:
Behavioral and social sciences, humanities, engineering, mathematics, physical sciences, biological sciences, education and interdisciplinary programs comprised of two or more eligible disciplines supported by the fellowship program.

NAME(S) OF PROGRAMS:
● **Ford Foundation Fellowship Programs**

TYPE:
Fellowships. Awards for study in research-based doctoral programs leading to the Ph.D. or Sc.D. degrees, as well as postdoctoral studies.

YEAR PROGRAM STARTED: 1986

PURPOSE:
To increase the diversity of the nation's college and university faculties by increasing their ethnic and racial diversity, to maximize the educational benefits of diversity, and to increase the number of professors who can and will use diversity as a resource for enriching the education of all students.

LEGAL BASIS:
Private foundation.

ELIGIBILITY:
Applicants to these Ford Foundation Fellowships must be U.S. citizens, U.S. permanent residents, or U.S. nationals, individuals granted deferred action status under Deferred Action for Childhood Arrivals Program, Indigenous individuals exercising rights associated with the Jay Treaty of 1794, individuals granted Temporary Protected Status, asylees, or refugees by the application deadline.

Predoctoral Fellowships are intended for students who plan to work toward the Ph.D. or Sc.D. degree in selected academic disciplines that lead to careers in teaching and research at the college or university level, and who have at least three years remaining in their program. They may be college seniors, or individuals who have completed undergraduate study, or who have completed some graduate study, or who have already enrolled in a Ph.D. or Sc.D. program.

Dissertation Fellowships are intended for Ph.D. or Sc.D. degree candidates who, by the application deadline, have completed all departmental and institutional requirements for the Ph.D. or Sc.D., except for the writing and defense of the dissertation. Fellowship support is intended for the final year of dissertation writing.

Predoctoral and Dissertation Fellowships: Persons holding a doctoral degree earned at any time and in any field are not eligible to apply. Applicants must be Ph.D. or Sc.D. degree candidates studying one of the fields in the behavioral and social sciences, humanities, social sciences, life sciences, chemistry, earth sciences, physics and astronomy, engineering, mathematics, computer science, education, or interdisciplinary programs composed of two or more eligible disciplines supported by the fellowship program. They must aspire to a teaching and research career. Awards are not made for practice-oriented programs in business administration and management, health sciences, public health, home economics, library science, speech pathology and audiology, personnel and guidance, social work, fine arts and performing arts and education.

Postdoctoral Fellowships are intended for fellows to engage in a year of postdoctoral research and scholarship in an environment free from the interference of their normal professional duties. Applicants are required to have earned a Ph.D. or Sc.D. degree from a U.S. educational institution within a specified time period. Only those individuals already engaged in a teaching and research career or those planning such a career are eligible to apply in this program. Previous Ford Foundation postdoctoral fellows may not reapply. Awards will be made in research-based areas of the behavioral and social sciences, humanities, life sciences, chemistry, earth sciences, physics and astronomy, engineering, mathematics, computer science, education, or for interdisciplinary programs composed of two or more eligible disciplines supported by the fellowship program.

FINANCIAL DATA:
Amount of support per award: Dissertation Fellowships: $28,000 for one year and invitation to attend one Conference of Ford Fellows; Predoctoral Fellowships: Annual $27,000 stipend, invitation to attend at least one Conference of Ford Fellows; Postdoctoral Fellowships: $50,000 stipend and invitation to attend one Conference of Ford Fellows.

CO-OP FUNDING PROGRAMS: Program funded by the Ford Foundation.

NO. MOST RECENT APPLICANTS: Approximately 3,000 reviewed applicants.

NO. AWARDS: 70 Predoctoral Fellowships, 36 Dissertation Fellowships, and 24 Postdoctoral Fellowships.

APPLICATION INFO:
Applications are to be submitted online.
Duration: Predoctoral Fellowships: Three years; Dissertation and Postdoctoral Fellowships: Nine or 12 months.
Deadline: Predoctoral Fellowships: December 16, 5 P.M.; Dissertation and Postdoctoral Fellowships: December 9, 5 P.M.

PUBLICATIONS:
Program announcement.

ADDRESS INQUIRIES TO:
See e-mail address above.

NATIONAL ACTION COUNCIL FOR MINORITIES IN ENGINEERING, INC. (NACME)
1432 Duke Street
Alexandria, VA 22314
(914) 539-4010
Fax: (914) 539-4032
E-mail: scholarships@nacme.org
Web Site: www.nacme.org

TYPE:
Block grants; Scholarships. The NACME Bridge Scholarship program is designed to support students who have received and accepted freshman admission to an undergraduate engineering or computer science program at a NACME Partner Institution and have been invited to attend a residential academic program the summer prior to freshman matriculation. The scholarship covers the published cost of participation of the Bridge program.

See entry 2394 for full listing.

NATIONAL ACTION COUNCIL FOR MINORITIES IN ENGINEERING, INC. (NACME)
1432 Duke Street
Alexandria, VA 22314
(914) 539-4010
Fax: (914) 539-4032
E-mail: scholarships@nacme.org
Web Site: www.nacme.org

TYPE:
Fellowships; Scholarships. Chevron/Diversity Association Scholarship Program awards current matriculating students in engineering, specifically mechanical, chemical, electrical, civil and petroleum as well as computer science (and qualifying information technology programs), who have the potential to excel as scholars, leaders and potential contributors to Chevron Corporation. Assessment will be based on academic merit and leadership potential.

Sidney and Katherine Friend Scholarship is a joint endowment established between NACME and New York University, Tandon School of Engineering.

William Randolph Hearst Endowment Scholarship is supported by the William Randolph Hearst Foundation.

Phillip D. Reed Undergraduate Endowment Fellowship is made possible through an endowment from the Phillip D. Reed Foundation.

See entry 2395 for full listing.

NATIONAL ASSOCIATION OF HISPANIC JOURNALISTS   [909]
1050 Connecticut Avenue, N.W.
5th Floor
Washington, DC 20036
(202) 853-7760
(202) 909-6880
E-mail: nahj@nahj.org
lafrank@nahj.org
Web Site: nahj.org

FOUNDED: 1984

AREAS OF INTEREST:
English or Spanish language print, photo, broadcast or online journalism.

NAME(S) OF PROGRAMS:
● **Jonathan Camuy Scholarship**
● **Getty Images Inclusion Scholarship**
● **Luis Gomez Scholarship**
● **NAHJ Ana Real Scholarship**
● **NAHJ Cecilia Alvear Scholarship**
● **NAHJ Facebook Journalism Project Scholarship**
● **NAHJ General Scholarships (Ruben Salazar Fund)**
● **NAHJ Maria Elena Salinas Scholarship**
● **NAHJ/NBC News Summer Fellows Program**

TYPE:
Awards/prizes; Conferences/seminars; Fellowships; General operating grants; Internships; Matching gifts; Project/program grants; Research grants; Scholarships; Seed money grants; Training grants; Travel grants.

YEAR PROGRAM STARTED: 1986

PURPOSE:
To encourage the study and practice of journalism and mass communications by Hispanics.

ELIGIBILITY:
Open to high school seniors, college undergraduates and first-year graduate students pursuing careers in English or Spanish-language print, broadcast, digital or photojournalism. Grade point average of 3.0 or higher is required.

GEOG. RESTRICTIONS: United States and Puerto Rico.

FINANCIAL DATA:
Amount of support per award: Jonathan Camuy Scholarship: $1,500; NAHJ Ana Real Scholarship: $5,000; NAHJ Cecilia Alvear Scholarship and NAHJ Maria Elena Salinas Scholarship: $2,500; Getty Images Inclusion Scholarship and NAHJ Facebook Journalism Scholarship: $10,000; Luis Gomez Scholarship and NAHJ General Scholarships: $2,000.

NO. MOST RECENT APPLICANTS: Approximately 230.

NO. AWARDS: 50 scholarships.

APPLICATION INFO:
Scholarship applications are available online in January of each year.
Duration: One year.
Deadline: March.

IRS I.D.: 95-3927141

ADDRESS INQUIRIES TO:
Scholarships Department
(See address above.)

NATIONAL FEDERATION OF THE BLIND   [910]
NFB Scholarship Program
200 East Wells Street at Jernigan Place
Baltimore, MD 21230
(410) 659-9314 ext. 2415
E-mail: scholarships@nfb.org
Web Site: www.nfb.org/scholarships

FOUNDED: 1940

AREAS OF INTEREST:
Improving the quality of life for blind persons by creating opportunity and combating discrimination.

CONSULTING OR VOLUNTEER SERVICES:
Major programs in scholarships, promoting employment for the blind, civil rights litigation, helping parents of blind children, public education, etc.

NAME(S) OF PROGRAMS:
• **National Federation of the Blind Scholarship Program**

TYPE:
Scholarships. Awarded on the basis of academic excellence, service to the community and leadership. Provides a one-time grant plus a continuing program of mentors and seminars for blind college students.

PURPOSE:
To create opportunities for blind persons residing in and attending college or university in the U.S. or Puerto Rico.

LEGAL BASIS:
Nonprofit, tax-deductible, nationwide membership organization of the blind.

ELIGIBILITY:
Applicants residing in the U.S. or Puerto Rico must be legally blind and pursuing or planning to pursue a full-time postsecondary course of study in the upcoming fall semester

in the U.S or Puerto Rico. One scholarship, however, may be given to a person working full-time while attending school part-time. In addition, some scholarships have been further restricted by the donor. Recipients of Federation scholarships need not be members of the National Federation of the Blind. International students are not eligible unless they reside in the U.S. or Puerto Rico.

GEOG. RESTRICTIONS: United States and Puerto Rico.

FINANCIAL DATA:
Scholarship includes financial assistance to attend the NFB Annual Convention and other gifts.
Amount of support per award: $3,000 to $12,000; other gifts vary in value.
Total amount of support: Over $120,000 annually.

NO. MOST RECENT APPLICANTS: 470.

NO. AWARDS: 29 (1 $10,000 scholarship, 2 $8,000 scholarships, 4 $5,000 scholarships and 22 $3,000 scholarships).

APPLICATION INFO:
Application information is available on the web site. Those interested in applying should read the rules of eligibility, the timeline, the Submission Checklist and the Scholarship FAQ, then fill in the online Scholarship Application Form. Supply the required documents and complete one telephone interview with the NFB representative.
Duration: One year. Renewals possible upon reapplication.
Deadline: Scholarship applications are accepted from November 1 of the previous year to March 31 of the year in which the scholarship is to be awarded. All documentation and the interview request must be received by the deadline. Notification by June 1.

ADDRESS INQUIRIES TO:
Scholarship Committee
(See address above.)

*SPECIAL STIPULATIONS:
Applicants must be legally blind in both eyes. Winners are assisted to attend the NFB Annual Convention in July. Attendance is required and a part of the prize awarded to each winner.

THE NATIONAL GEM CONSORTIUM   [911]
1430 Duke Street
Alexandria, VA 22314
(703) 562-3646
Fax: (202) 207-3518
E-mail: info@gemfellowship.org
Web Site: www.gemfellowship.org

FOUNDED: 1976

AREAS OF INTEREST:
Engineering at the Master's and Doctorate levels and science at the Doctorate level.

CONSULTING OR VOLUNTEER SERVICES:
Mentor/protege training, graduate study preparedness training, success training, programs and publications designed to promote graduate education in engineering and science.

NAME(S) OF PROGRAMS:
• **Future Faculty and Professionals (FFP) Travel Grant**
• **The GEM M.S. Engineering Fellowship**

• **The GEM Ph.D. Engineering Fellowship**
• **The GEM Ph.D. Science Fellowship**
• **GRAD Lab**

TYPE:
Fellowships; Internships; Travel grants. Future Faculty and Professionals (FFP) Symposium is a career development program for future faculty members and industry professionals. The goal is to provide graduate students with improved research and career competitiveness, tools and metrics for greater control in career planning, and to gain access to a powerful network of peers and mentors. Travel grants provide current GEM Fellow or non-Fellow graduate students the opportunity to take advantage of the program focused specifically on their needs, and support successful matriculation to completion of their graduate STEM degree.

G.E.M Fellowships provide all-expenses for graduate study (tuition and stipend) and paid summer work experience in a scientific or engineering environment.

YEAR PROGRAM STARTED: 1976

PURPOSE:
To increase the number of minorities with graduate degrees in engineering and science.

LEGAL BASIS:
Incorporated in the State of Virginia; 501(c)(3) tax-exempt.

ELIGIBILITY:
Must be a U.S. citizen or permanent resident and an American Indian/Native, African American/Black, or Hispanic American/Latino.

FINANCIAL DATA:
Amount of support per award: FFP Travel Grant: $1,750 per student; M.S. Fellowship: Tuition and fees, plus a $16,000 stipend over entire M.S. program. Master's-level students also are assigned to a paid internship. Ph.D. Fellowships: $16,000 stipend applied in one academic year. Additional stipend support from GEM University.
Total amount of support: Varies.

NO. AWARDS: 174 full fellowships and 153 associate/university fellowships for the year 2019.

APPLICATION INFO:
Three recommendations, GRE scores, and unofficial transcript of all college work.
Duration: Average four semesters or six quarters for Master's; five years renewable for Doctorate.
Deadline: November 13. Announcement May 31.

PUBLICATIONS:
Annual report; application brochure.

BOARD OF DIRECTORS:
Michael A. Greene, Chairperson
Felicia Benton-Johnson, Ed.D., Vice Chairperson
Johney B. Green, Jr., Ph.D., Vice Chairperson
Anthony Jackson, Treasurer
Darryll Pines, Ph.D., Secretary
Greg Anderson
Sharnnia Artis, Ph.D.
Romayne Botti
Terrence Buck
Avery H. Demond, Ph.D.
Sheri Depp
Percy Gilbert, Ph.D.
Jorge Leis, Ph.D.
John Lesko, Ph.D

Bruce Lindvall, Ph.D.
Christine Ortiz, Ph.D.
Sara Perkovic, Ph.D.
Gregory Singleton
La'Tonia Stiner-Jones, Ph.D.
Mark Vaughn, Ph.D.

ADDRESS INQUIRIES TO:
Fellowship Administration Team
(See address above.)

NATIONAL INSTITUTE OF GENERAL MEDICAL SCIENCES

National Institutes of Health
45 Center Drive, MSC 6200
Bethesda, MD 20892-6200
(301) 496-7301
Fax: (301) 402-0224
E-mail: info@nigms.nih.gov
Web Site: www.nigms.nih.gov

TYPE:
Fellowships; Research grants; Training grants; Research contracts. Capacity building. The National Institute of General Medical Sciences (NIGMS) supports basic research that increases understanding of biological processes and lays the foundation for advances in disease diagnosis, treatment and prevention. NIGMS-funded scientists investigate how living systems work at a range of levels, from molecules and cells to tissues, whole organisms and populations. The Institute also supports research in certain clinical areas, primarily those that affect multiple organ systems. To assure the vitality and continued productivity of research enterprise, NIGMS provides leadership in training the next generation of scientists, in enhancing the diversity of scientific workforce, and in developing research capacities throughout the country.

See entry 2052 for full listing.

NATIONAL INSTITUTE OF GENERAL MEDICAL SCIENCES

Center for Research Capacity Building
45 Center Drive, MSC 6200
Bethesda, MD 20892-6200
(301) 594-3900
Fax: (301) 480-2753
E-mail: irina.krasnova@nih.gov
Web Site: www.nigms.nih.gov

TYPE:
Development grants; Research grants. Grants to assist eligible institutions to strengthen the institutions' biomedical research capabilities and provide opportunities to students to engage in biomedical or behavioral research and other activities in preparation for Ph.D. training in these areas.

See entry 2053 for full listing.

NATIONAL INSTITUTE ON MINORITY HEALTH AND HEALTH DISPARITIES [912]

6707 Democracy Boulevard, Suite 800
MSC 5465
Bethesda, MD 20892-5465
(301) 402-1366
Fax: (301) 480-4049
Web Site: www.nimhd.nih.gov

AREAS OF INTEREST:
Minority opportunities in biomedical and behavioral science.

NAME(S) OF PROGRAMS:
- **Minority Health and Health Disparities Research Training Program (MHRT)**

TYPE:
Research grants; Training grants. The NIMHD Minority Health Research Training Program (MHRT) funds U.S. institutions to offer short-term research training opportunities in international and domestic settings to undergraduate and graduate students, postdoctoral and medical students from health disparity backgrounds. Institutions with MHRT funding provide training and international and domestic exposure to students to conduct research at foreign and domestic sites in the biomedical, clinical, social, or behavioral sciences. Although the training time of the 10- to 12-week (or longer) training period varies by institution, it often takes place during the summer or for one semester during the academic year.

YEAR PROGRAM STARTED: 1993

PURPOSE:
To provide research training opportunities for minority undergraduate students, minority medical students and postdoctorates in biomedical and behavioral research; to support faculty members to serve as mentors to students abroad and at home.

ELIGIBILITY:
Minority participants must be from underrepresented minority groups including African Americans, Asian Americans, Native Americans, Hispanic Americans, Alaskan Natives, Native Hawaiians and Pacific Islanders.

Applicants must be undergraduate or graduate students pursuing a doctoral degree in the biomedical or behavioral sciences, a medical degree, or a postdoctorate pursuing a degree in the biomedical or behavioral sciences.

GEOG. RESTRICTIONS: United States and its territories.

FINANCIAL DATA:
Amount of support per award: Up to $250,000 in direct costs annually.

Total amount of support: Approximately $5,000,000 in grants annually.

NO. AWARDS: Up to 12.

APPLICATION INFO:
NIMHD does not work directly with students interested in the MHRT Program. Students who are interested in MHRT must apply through the MHRT Program at a specific college or university (see roster of programs on the NIMHD web site).

Duration: Up to five years.

Deadline: Varies.

PUBLICATIONS:
Program announcement; guidelines.

ADDRESS INQUIRIES TO:
Richard Berzon, Ph.D.
Health Scientist Administrator
(See address above.)

THE NATIONAL ITALIAN AMERICAN FOUNDATION

1860 19th Street, N.W.
Washington, DC 20009-5501
(202) 939-3114
Fax: (202) 387-0800
E-mail: scholarships@niaf.org
Web Site: www.niaf.org/scholarships

TYPE:
Scholarships. The National Italian American Foundation (NIAF) will award scholarships and grants to outstanding students for use during the following academic year. The awards will be made on the basis of academic merit to Italian American students studying a wide range of subjects.

See entry 1536 for full listing.

NATIONAL MEDICAL FELLOWSHIPS, INC.

P.O. Box 3875
New York, NY 10163
(212) 483-8880
Fax: (212) 483-8897
E-mail: scholarships@nmfonline.org
Web Site: www.nmfonline.org

TYPE:
Awards/prizes; Project/program grants; Scholarships. Service learning. NMF supports underrepresented minority medical students and health professions students enrolled in U.S. accredited programs as they matriculate. Awards are available to students M1 to M4/5. In addition to financial support, NMF provides opportunities for aspiring doctors to take their learning into the community.

See entry 2062 for full listing.

NATIONAL TAXIDERMISTS ASSOCIATION [913]

1615 Montana Street
Missoula, MT 59801
(406) 721-1214
E-mail: nationaltaxidermistassoc@gmail.com
Web Site: www.nationaltaxidermists.com

AREAS OF INTEREST:
Taxidermy and education.

NAME(S) OF PROGRAMS:
- **Charlie Fleming Scholarship**

TYPE:
Scholarships.

PURPOSE:
To promote higher education and taxidermy education.

ELIGIBILITY:
Students must be a member, spouse or dependent of the NTA for three consecutive years.

FINANCIAL DATA:
Amount of support per award: $1,500.

NO. AWARDS: 2 per year.

APPLICATION INFO:
Contact the Organization for application procedures.

Applicant must submit an essay incorporating the MTA mission statement, their personal desires and ambitions and the educator the applicant wishes to study under.

Duration: One year.

Deadline: August 1.

NEW JERSEY OFFICE OF THE SECRETARY OF HIGHER EDUCATION (OSHE)

One John Fitch Plaza
P.O. Box 542
Trenton, NJ 08625-0542
(609) 341-3808
Fax: (609) 292-7225
E-mail: hasani.carter@oshe.nj.gov
Web Site: www.state.nj.
us/highereducation/EOF/EOF_Description.shtml

TYPE:
Grants-in-aid. Student support. The Educational Opportunity Fund (EOF) is administered through the Office of the Secretary of Higher Education (OSHE). Created by law in 1968, EOF is one of the state's most comprehensive student support programs that provides access to higher education for those who come from low income and educationally disadvantaged backgrounds. EOF is not an entitlement grant program.

See entry 1547 for full listing.

NEWMEXICOWOMEN.ORG [914]

1807 2nd Street, Suite 76
Santa Fe, NM 87505
(505) 750-1732
E-mail: sarah@newmexicowomen.org
Web Site: newmexicowomen.org

FOUNDED: 2012

AREAS OF INTEREST:
Gender justice and healing.

TYPE:
General operating grants.

PURPOSE:
To advance opportunities for women and girls statewide so they can lead self-sufficient, healthy and empowered lives.

ELIGIBILITY:
Tax-exempt, nonprofit organizations may apply.

GEOG. RESTRICTIONS: New Mexico.

FINANCIAL DATA:
Amount of support per award: $1,000 to $20,000.
Total amount of support: $173,000 for the year 2020.

NO. AWARDS: 36 for the year 2020.

APPLICATION INFO:
Instructions are available online.
Duration: One year.
Deadline: July 26.

ADDRESS INQUIRIES TO:
Sarah Ghiorse, Executive Director
(See address above.)

ORDER SONS OF ITALY IN AMERICA, GRAND LODGE OF FLORIDA

2021 Pine Needle Trail
Kissimmee, FL 34746
(321) 286-6787
E-mail: gertd830@gmail.com
Web Site: osiaflorida.org

TYPE:
Awards/prizes; Grants-in-aid; Scholarships. Scholarships are provided to high school students entering college.

Financial aid is given in support of charitable programs, such as Alzheimer's disease, Cooley's anemia, autism, and cancer.

See entry 1559 for full listing.

PEN AMERICA

588 Broadway, Suite 303
New York, NY 10012
(212) 334-1660 ext. 4813
Fax: (212) 334-2181
E-mail: awards@pen.org
Web Site: pen.org

TYPE:
Awards/prizes. Invites submissions of book-length writings by authors of color, published during the calendar year.

See entry 630 for full listing.

PRIDE FOUNDATION [915]

2014 East Madison Street
Suite 300
Seattle, WA 98122
(206) 323-3318
Fax: (206) 323-1017
E-mail: grants@pridefoundation.org
Web Site: www.pridefoundation.org

FOUNDED: 1985

AREAS OF INTEREST:
Arts and recreation; education outreach and advocacy; HIV/AIDS; lesbian health; youth and family; and other health and community services.

TYPE:
Endowments; General operating grants; Project/program grants; Scholarships; Seed money grants. Short-term grants.

YEAR PROGRAM STARTED: 1987

PURPOSE:
To inspire giving; to expand opportunities and advance full equality for LGBTQ people across the Northwest.

ELIGIBILITY:
Organizations applying for grant funds must have 501(c)(3) nonprofit tax status, or be affiliated with an organization that has 501(c)(3) status that will assume responsibility for administering all funds received and expended.

Organizations and/or projects must encompass LGBTQ issues and/or populations.

GEOG. RESTRICTIONS: Alaska, Idaho, Montana, Oregon and Washington.

FINANCIAL DATA:
Amount of support per award: $2,500 to $10,000.
Total amount of support: $550,000.

NO. MOST RECENT APPLICANTS: Approximately 130 annually.

NO. AWARDS: Approximately 30 annually.

APPLICATION INFO:
Detailed instructions are available on the Foundation web site.
Duration: One year.
Deadline: Varies.

PUBLICATIONS:
e-Newsletter, bimonthly.

IRS I.D.: 91-1325007

ADDRESS INQUIRIES TO:
Jeremiah Allen, Director of Programs
(See address above.)

PROSPANICA [916]

2711 LBJ Freeway
Suite 800
Dallas, TX 75234
(877) 467-4622
E-mail: info@prospanica.org
Web Site: www.prospanica.org

AREAS OF INTEREST:
Business administration.

NAME(S) OF PROGRAMS:
● **Prospanica Scholarship Program**

TYPE:
Awards/prizes; Conferences/seminars; Scholarships.

YEAR PROGRAM STARTED: 1989

PURPOSE:
To empower Hispanic business professionals to achieve their full educational, economic and social potential.

LEGAL BASIS:
501(c)(3) organization.

ELIGIBILITY:
Applicant must:
(1) be a U.S. citizen or legal permanent resident;
(2) be of Hispanic/Latino heritage;
(3) have a minimum grade point average of 3.0 on a 4.0 scale (or equivalent) or have a minimum 2.75 grade point average on a 4.0 scale (or equivalent) in combination with two years of full-time work experience;
(4) have a Prospanica membership (member ID required);
(5) for the Graduate Awards, be enrolled in a Master's degree program in the business school at a college or university in the U.S. or Puerto Rico accredited by AACSB and;
(6) for the Undergraduate Awards, be a sophomore or higher pursuing a Bachelor's degree within the business school at a college or university in the U.S. or Puerto Rico accredited by AACSB.

GEOG. RESTRICTIONS: United States and Puerto Rico.

FINANCIAL DATA:
Amount of support per award: $2,000 to $5,000.

APPLICATION INFO:
Applications are submitted on the Prospanica web site. Round 1 requires no outside documentation. For Round 2, the following information will be needed for the application process:
(1) personal statement (maximum 300 words or 3,000 characters);
(2) Prospanica essay;
(3) college academic information, including complete transcripts of grades from all colleges attended;
(4) list of work, Prospanica participation, and community service experience and;
(5) financial information from the family's most recently submitted tax return.

Applicants should review their application before submission. All application pages with required fields must be completed in the format described in order to submit the application. It is recommended the applicant print a hard copy for their records. Once the application is submitted, no further revisions can be made.

To complete the application process, the following documents must be uploaded or mailed to Prospanica before the deadline: (1) complete undergraduate and graduate school transcripts of grades from all colleges attended. Online transcripts must display student name, school name, grades and credit hours for each course and term in which each course was taken and; (2) two recommendation forms from professors, advisors or employers.

It is the applicant's responsibility to gather and submit all required information. An e-mail confirmation will be generated when the application is successfully submitted. Late submissions and incomplete applications will not be considered. Applicant should contact Prospanica to check on the completeness of their application.

Duration: One academic year.

Deadline: Round 1: April 20. Round 2: June 11, by invitation only.

RIGHTEOUS PERSONS FOUNDATION [917]

400 South Beverly Drive, Suite 420
Beverly Hills, CA 90212
(310) 314-8393
E-mail: grants@righteouspersons.org
Web Site: www.righteouspersons.org

FOUNDED: 1994

AREAS OF INTEREST:
Primarily Jewish organizations.

TYPE:
General operating grants; Matching gifts; Project/program grants; Seed money grants; Technical assistance.

PURPOSE:
To strengthen Jewish life in America.

LEGAL BASIS:
Nonprofit.

ELIGIBILITY:
Applicants must be tax-exempt organizations. Priority is given to national organizations and projects which create meaningful experiences for Jewish youth, promote Jewish learning, provide leadership training grounded in Jewish tradition, employ the arts and media to explore the relevance of modern Jewish identity, promote tolerance and understanding between Jews and non-Jews, and encourage Jews to participate in the work of social justice.

The Foundation does not make grants to individuals. Also, the Foundation does not support university faculty chairs, individual synagogues or day schools, research, the publication of books or magazines, or organizations or projects based outside of the U.S. In addition, the Foundation generally does not support endowments, capital campaigns, building funds, or social service projects.

GEOG. RESTRICTIONS: United States.

FINANCIAL DATA:
Amount of support per award: Varies.
Total amount of support: Varies.

APPLICATION INFO:
Applicants should submit a two- to three-page letter of inquiry including:
(1) a description of the proposed project including the issues the project will address and the target population(s);
(2) a brief description of the organization's mission, activities and history;
(3) the total amount of the organization's operating budget;
(4) the total amount requested from the Foundation;
(5) the name, mailing address and telephone number of a contact person;
(6) a detailed project budget;
(7) a list of the organization's board of directors;
(8) documentation of the organization's 501(c)(3) status;
(9) the total amount requested from the Foundation and;
(10) a list of the organization/project's primary sources of support over the last two years including names of foundations and amounts provided each year.

If there is a fiscal sponsor for the project, include a current copy of the sponsor's tax-exempt letter from the IRS as well as a letter of support from the sponsor acknowledging their responsibilities. Do not send full proposals or video or audio tapes unless otherwise requested. Faxed applications will not be considered.

Duration: Varies.

PUBLICATIONS:
Program announcement; guidelines.

STAFF:
Rachel Levin, Executive Director
Shayna Rose Triebwasser, Senior Program Officer

BOARD OF DIRECTORS:
Steven Spielberg, Chairman
Gerald Breslauer, President
Tammy Anderson

ADDRESS INQUIRIES TO:
Shayna Rose Triebwasser, Program Officer
(See address above.)

JACKIE ROBINSON FOUNDATION (JRF) [918]

75 Varick Street, 2nd Floor
New York, NY 10013-1917
(212) 290-8600
Fax: (212) 290-8081
E-mail: general@jackierobinson.org
Web Site: www.jackierobinson.org

FOUNDED: 1973

AREAS OF INTEREST:
Providing college education and a comprehensive set of support services for academically gifted, highly motivated students of color with financial need.

NAME(S) OF PROGRAMS:
● **Extra Innings Fellowship Program (EIF)**
● **Mentoring and Leadership Program**
● **Rachel Robinson International Fellowship Program (RRIF)**

TYPE:
Conferences/seminars; Fellowships; Scholarships. The Foundation Scholarship Program (Mentoring and Leadership Program) is designed to address the financial needs of college students and provide comprehensive mentoring services through its 42 Strategies for Success Curriculum.

The Fellowship programs are follow-up programs to the JRF Scholars program (Mentoring and Leadership Program).

The Extra Innings Fellowship Program helps highly motivated JRF Scholars to fund the cost of advanced professional or graduate training.

The Rachel Robinson International Fellowship Program promotes and supports international service and study opportunities for JRF Scholars.

PURPOSE:
To award four-year college scholarships to academically gifted students of color with financial need, enabling them to attend the college of their choice.

ELIGIBILITY:
Applicants must complete the JRF Scholars Program (Mentoring and Leadership Program) to be eligible for the Fellowship Programs. Foundation Scholar applicants must meet all of the following criteria:
(1) have U.S. citizenship;
(2) be a minority student;
(3) be a high school senior enrolling in college in the coming fall;
(4) have a SAT score (combined math and critical reading sections) of 1,000 or above, an ACT of 21 or above;
(5) have leadership potential and;
(6) be in financial need.

FINANCIAL DATA:
JRF Scholars program includes financial sponsorship to attend JRF's annual, four-day "Mentoring and Leadership Conference " in New York City as well as other regional events throughout the year.

Amount of support per award: Scholarships: Up to $7,000 per year; maximum $28,000 over four years.

NO. MOST RECENT APPLICANTS: Scholarships: Approximately 5,000 per year.

NO. AWARDS: Scholarships: 60 per year.

APPLICATION INFO:
Application information is available at the Foundation web site. Scholarship application is available for online review on October 15, and goes live on November 1.

Duration: Four years.

Deadline: The application is due February 1. Applicants are notified of status April 30; final selection of Scholars is announced on June 15.

ADDRESS INQUIRIES TO:
Mentoring and Leadership Program
Jackie Robinson Foundation
(See address above.)

RRF FOUNDATION FOR AGING [919]

8765 West Higgins Road
Suite 430
Chicago, IL 60631-4170
(773) 714-8080
Fax: (773) 714-8089
E-mail: info@rrf.org
Web Site: www.rrf.org

FOUNDED: 1950

AREAS OF INTEREST:
Aging.

NAME(S) OF PROGRAMS:
● **Organizational Capacity Building**
● **Responsive Grants**

TYPE:
Project/program grants; Research grants; Technical assistance; Training grants. Grants program support projects that have a

significant focus on older adults, ages 65 and older, in the following areas:

Advocacy - Achieve enduring social change around issues that affect older Americans; Direct Service - Improve availability and quality of community-based and residential long-term services and supports; Professional Education and Training - Increase the competency of professionals and paraprofessionals who serve older adults and; Research - Seek causes and solutions to significant problems for older adults.

Organizational Capacity Building - Designed to strengthen the effectiveness of Illinois nonprofit groups serving older people Priority is given to proposals addressing caregiving, economic security in later life, housing, and social and intergenerational connectedness.

YEAR PROGRAM STARTED: 1979

PURPOSE:
To improve the quality of life for the nation's older population.

LEGAL BASIS:
Private foundation.

ELIGIBILITY:
To be eligible for support, organizations, congregations and institutions must qualify under the regulations of the IRS.

GEOG. RESTRICTIONS: Direct-service grants limited to Florida, Illinois, Iowa, Kentucky, Michigan, Missouri and Wisconsin; OCB Grants are limited to the Chicago, Illinois area.

FINANCIAL DATA:
Assets of $136,091,407 for the year 2018.
Amount of support per award: $46,400 average for the year 2019.
Total amount of support: $6,403,453 for the year 2019.

NO. MOST RECENT APPLICANTS: 245 for the year 2019.

NO. AWARDS: 138 for the year 2019.

APPLICATION INFO:
The Foundation has an online application process. Visit the Foundation web site to find information about submitting a proposal.
Deadline: Responsive Grants: February 1, May 1 and August 1, with award announcement three to four months after submission date.

TRUSTEES AND OFFICERS:
Ruth Ann Watkins, Chairman of the Board
Irene Frye, President
Downey R. Varey, Treasurer
Michael J. Starshak, Secretary
John Bouman
Kathleen Kolodgy
Thomas D. Kuczmarski
Adrienne D. Mims, M.D.
Anthony J. Perry, M.D.
Thomas R. Prohaska, Ph.D.

ADDRESS INQUIRIES TO:
See e-mail address above.

SANTA FE COMMUNITY FOUNDATION   [920]
501 Halona Street
Santa Fe, NM 87505
(505) 988-9715
Fax: (505) 988-1829
E-mail: foundation@santafecf.org
Web Site: www.santafecf.org

FOUNDED: 1981

AREAS OF INTEREST:
Animal welfare, cultural vibrancy, educational success and career pathways, economic opportunity, health, lesbian, gay, bisexual and transgender community, Native Americans, sustainable agriculture and stewardship of resources, and well-being.

NAME(S) OF PROGRAMS:
● **Community Leadership Fund**
● **Dollars 4 Schools**
● **Envision Fund**
● **Local Impact Investing Initiative**
● **MoGro**
● **Native American Advised Fund**
● **NM Health Equity Partnership**
● **Santa Fe Baby Fund**

TYPE:
General operating grants; Project/program grants.

YEAR PROGRAM STARTED: 1981

PURPOSE:
To promote charitable community outreaches.

LEGAL BASIS:
Community foundation.

ELIGIBILITY:
The Foundation awards grants to nonprofit organizations only. The Foundation does not award grants for religious or political purposes, capital outlay, endowment or to individuals.

GEOG. RESTRICTIONS: Santa Fe and northern New Mexico.

FINANCIAL DATA:
Amount of support per award: $5,000 to $15,000.
Total amount of support: $10,000,000 (including donor-advised funds) for the year 2019.

CO-OP FUNDING PROGRAMS: Hispanics in Philanthropy, Opportunity Santa Fe, Law Enforcement Assisted Diversion, Early Childhood Funders Network, All Together New Mexico Fund, COVID-19 Response Fund, and Empty Pantry Fund.

NO. MOST RECENT APPLICANTS: Approximately 200 for the year 2019.

NO. AWARDS: 75 for the year 2019.

APPLICATION INFO:
Applicants must submit proof of IRS 501(c)(3) status.
Duration: Varies.
Deadline: Spring and Fall.

PUBLICATIONS:
Giving Together, catalogue.

IRS I.D.: 85-0303044

OFFICER:
Christa Coggins, Acting President and Chief Executive Officer

ADDRESS INQUIRIES TO:
Diane Hamamoto, Grants Officer
(See address above.)

SONS OF ITALY FOUNDATION   [921]
219 E Street, N.E.
Washington, DC 20002
(202) 547-2900
Fax: (202) 546-8168
E-mail: scholarships@osia.org
Web Site: www.osia.org/sons-of-italy-foundation

FOUNDED: 1959

AREAS OF INTEREST:
Cultural preservation and advancement for Italian Americans; education.

NAME(S) OF PROGRAMS:
● **National Leadership Grant Competition**

TYPE:
Awards/prizes; Scholarships. The Foundation provides Italian language scholarships, study-abroad scholarships and merit-based higher education scholarships.

YEAR PROGRAM STARTED: 1959

PURPOSE:
To help educate Italian Americans and improve their lives.

LEGAL BASIS:
Public, tax-exempt organization as defined by Section 501(c)(3) and Section 509(a)(1) of the Internal Revenue Code.

ELIGIBILITY:
Applicants must be U.S. citizens of Italian descent (at least one Italian or Italian-American grandparent) enrolled in a four-year undergraduate program or a graduate program at an accredited academic institution for the fall term.

FINANCIAL DATA:
Amount of support per award: Scholarships: $4,000 to $25,000.
Total amount of support: Varies.

NO. MOST RECENT APPLICANTS: 1,000.

NO. AWARDS: 10 to 12.

APPLICATION INFO:
General requirements are posted online.
Duration: One year.
Deadline: February 28.

PUBLICATIONS:
Annual report; *Grant Priorities, Guidelines and Procedures,* booklet.

ADDRESS INQUIRIES TO:
Michelle Ment, Chairperson
Scholarship, Education and
Culture Committee
(See address above.)

U.S. DEPARTMENT OF EDUCATION
Office of English Language Acquisition
LBJ Education Building, MS-6510
400 Maryland Avenue, S.W.
Washington, DC 20202-6510
(202) 401-1433 (NPD Program)
(202) 453-6054 (NAM Program)
Web Site: www.ed.gov/offices/oela

TYPE:
Formula grants. National Professional Development Program provides grants for eligible entities to implement professional development activities intended to improve instruction for English Learners (ELs) and assists education personnel working with ELs to meet high professional standards. Professional development activities may include both pre-service and in-service activities.

Native American and Alaska Native Children in School Program awards grants to eligible entities to develop and enhance capacity to provide effective instruction and support to Native American students who are identified as English Learners (ELs). The goal of this program is to support the teaching, learning and studying of Native American languages while also increasing the English language proficiency of students served to achieve the same challenging state academic content and achievement standards for all students.

See entry 1424 for full listing.

UCLA INSTITUTE OF AMERICAN CULTURES (IAC) [922]

2329 Murphy Hall, Box 957244
Los Angeles, CA 90095-7244
(310) 825-6815
Fax: (310) 825-3994
E-mail: iaccoordinator@conet.ucla.edu
Web Site: www.iac.ucla.edu

FOUNDED: 1969

AREAS OF INTEREST:
Advancing knowledge, strengthening and integrating interdisciplinary research and enriching instruction on African Americans, American Indians, Asian Americans and Chicanos.

NAME(S) OF PROGRAMS:
- **Institute of American Cultures Visiting Research Scholar Fellowship Program in Ethnic Studies**

TYPE:
Fellowships. Deals with arts and humanities, education and teacher training, fine arts, applied arts, law, social sciences, and sciences. The IAC, in cooperation with UCLA's four Ethnic Studies Research Centers (American Indian Studies Center, Asian American Studies Center, Bunche Center for African American Studies, and Chicano Studies Research Center), offers awards to visiting scholars to support research on African Americans, American Indians, Asian Americans and Chicanas/os.

PURPOSE:
To enable Ph.D. scholars wishing to work in association with the American Indian Studies Center, the Bunche Center for African American Studies, the Asian American Studies Center, and the Chicano Studies Research Center, in order to conduct research and publish books or manuscripts.

ELIGIBILITY:
Open to U.S. citizens or permanent residents of the U.S. who hold a Ph.D. from an accredited college or university (or, in the case of the arts, a terminal degree) in the appropriate field at the time of appointment. UCLA faculty, staff and currently enrolled students are not eligible to apply.

FINANCIAL DATA:
Amount of support per award: Up to $35,000 stipend and up to $4,000 in research support. Amount contingent upon rank, experience and date of completion of terminal degree.

NO. AWARDS: Up to 4.

APPLICATION INFO:
Applicants are encouraged to contact the Studies Research Center of interest prior to applying. Application process begins in November.
Duration: Up to three quarters (nine months).
Deadline: Dates are posted on the IAC web site.

ADDRESS INQUIRIES TO:
IAC Coordinator
(See address above.)

UNITED METHODIST COMMUNICATIONS [923]

810 12th Avenue South
Nashville, TN 37203-4744
(615) 742-5400
E-mail: rjames@umcom.org
Web Site: www.umcom.org

FOUNDED: 1948

AREAS OF INTEREST:
Religious communications.

NAME(S) OF PROGRAMS:
- **The Leonard M. Perryman Communications Scholarship for Ethnic Minority Students**

TYPE:
Fellowships; Scholarships. Award for junior or senior undergraduate study in religion journalism or mass communications. The term *communications* is meant to cover various media as audio-visual, electronic and print journalism.

PURPOSE:
To enable the recipient to continue his or her studies in communication; to promote a level of excellence in communication on the undergraduate level by an ethnic minority student.

ELIGIBILITY:
Applicants must be United Methodist ethnic minority undergraduate students, junior or senior, who have an intention to pursue a career in religion journalism or mass communications and are enrolled in an accredited U.S. college or university.

FINANCIAL DATA:
Amount of support per award: $2,500.
Total amount of support: $2,500 per academic year.

NO. AWARDS: 1.

APPLICATION INFO:
Applicant must submit:
(1) an application form (completed and submitted electronically or printed and mailed);
(2) official transcripts from the current institution of higher education and any others attended. Transcripts should be mailed by the school directly to the address listed in the application packet;
(3) three letters of recommendation, one from the local church pastor or a denominational official, one from the chairperson of the department in which the applicant is majoring as an undergraduate student, and one from an employer or supervisor in a position to evaluate the applicant's communications skills;
(4) an essay (no more than 500 words) about the applicant's commitment to the Christian faith and interest in communications, and how the applicant sees the two intersecting in their life presently and in the future;
(5) three examples of journalistic work (audiovisual, electronic, print). If requested in writing, these materials will be returned after the committee has completed its selection and;
(6) a recent photograph, preferably head and shoulders, suitable for publicity use if awarded the scholarship.
Duration: One academic year.
Deadline: March 15 (postmarked).

PUBLICATIONS:
Application guidelines.

ADDRESS INQUIRIES TO:
Relationship Team
(See address above.)

*SPECIAL STIPULATIONS:
Candidates must be in their junior or senior year to qualify.

UNIVERSITY OF CALIFORNIA [924]

President's Postdoctoral Fellowship Program
402 Sproul Hall
Berkeley, CA 94720-1508
(510) 643-8235
E-mail: ppfpinfo@berkeley.edu
Web Site: ppfp.ucop.edu/info

FOUNDED: 1869

AREAS OF INTEREST:
Education and research.

NAME(S) OF PROGRAMS:
- **University of California President's Postdoctoral Fellowship Program**

TYPE:
Fellowships. Awarded for research conducted under faculty sponsorship on any one of the University of California's 10 campuses.

YEAR PROGRAM STARTED: 1984

PURPOSE:
To encourage outstanding women and minority Ph.D. recipients to pursue academic careers at the University of California; to offer research fellowships to all qualified candidates who are committed to university careers in research, teaching and service that will enhance the diversity of the academic community at the University of California.

LEGAL BASIS:
University.

ELIGIBILITY:
Applicants must be U.S. citizens or permanent residents and must hold or receive a Ph.D. from an accredited university. Applicants should expect to have earned their Ph.D. degree by June 30 of the year for which they are applying.

The program will prefer candidates who have research interests focusing on underserved populations and understanding issues of racial or gender inequalities.

The program also prefers candidates with a record of leadership or significant experience teaching and mentoring students from groups that have been historically underrepresented in higher education.

FINANCIAL DATA:
The award includes salary, health, vision and dental benefits, and up to $5,000 for research-related and program travel expenses.
Amount of support per award:
Approximately $54,540 per fellow, depending upon the field and level of experience, plus benefits for self and dependents.

NO. AWARDS: 42 new for the year 2020-21.

APPLICATION INFO:
Application consists of curriculum vitae, research proposal, dissertation abstract, personal statement, writing sample, mentor support letter and thesis advisor letter.
Duration: Initially one academic year beginning July 1. Renewal for a second year will be granted upon demonstration of academic productivity and participation in program events.
Deadline: November 1. Announcement of awardees in the spring.

STAFF:
Mark A. Lawson, Ph.D., Director
Kimberly M. Adkinson, Assistant Director

ADDRESS INQUIRIES TO:
Kimberly M. Adkinson, Assistant Director
President's Postdoctoral Fellowship Program
(See address above.)

UNIVERSITY OF CALIFORNIA, LOS ANGELES [925]

Asian American Studies Center
3230 Campbell Hall
Los Angeles, CA 90095-1546
(310) 825-2974
Fax: (310) 206-9844
E-mail: melanyd@ucla.edu
Web Site: www.aasc.ucla.edu/scholarships

FOUNDED: 1969

AREAS OF INTEREST:
Asian American studies, policy, social science, public health, law, education, and humanities research on Asian Americans and Pacific Islanders.

NAME(S) OF PROGRAMS:
● **Ethnic Studies Fellowships**

TYPE:
Awards/prizes; Conferences/seminars; Fellowships; Research grants; Scholarships; Visiting scholars; Work-study programs. Support for visiting scholars and researchers.

YEAR PROGRAM STARTED: 1969

PURPOSE:
To provide funding for studies in the field of Asian American arts, humanities, social sciences and applied research.

LEGAL BASIS:
University.

ELIGIBILITY:
Applicants must have the Ph.D. in place at the time Fellowship is awarded. UCLA faculty members are not eligible for support.

FINANCIAL DATA:
Visiting Scholars may use the funds to supplement sabbatical support, though the total available will not exceed the maximum stipend levels, and when combined with sabbatical funds may not exceed the candidate's current institutional salary.

Visiting Scholars will be paid through their home institutions and will be expected to continue their health benefits through that source. Awardees may receive up to $4,000 in research support (through reimbursements of research expenses).

Amount of support per award: Maximum stipend of $35,000, contingent upon rank, experience and date of completion of terminal degree.
Total amount of support: Varies.

NO. MOST RECENT APPLICANTS: 10.

NO. AWARDS: 1.

APPLICATION INFO:
Contact the University.
Duration: Nine months.
Deadline: Approximately January 10, 2021.

STAFF:
Melany De La Cruz-Viesca, Associate Director/IAC Coordinator

ADDRESS INQUIRIES TO:
Melany De La Cruz-Viesca
Associate Director/IAC Coordinator
Asian American Studies Center
(See address above.)

UNIVERSITY OF SOUTHERN CALIFORNIA

USC Graduate School
3601 Trousdale Parkway, STU 301
Los Angeles, CA 90089-0894
(213) 740-9033
Fax: (213) 740-9048
E-mail: gradfllw@usc.edu
Web Site: graduateschool.usc.edu

TYPE:
Fellowships. Merit fellowships. Fellowships will be combined with matching funds from individual schools to provide four or more years of funding toward the Ph.D.

See entry 1608 for full listing.

VIRGINIA POLYTECHNIC INSTITUTE AND STATE UNIVERSITY [926]

MAOP Office
Media Annex, Room 103A
130 Otey Street
Blacksburg, VA 24061
(540) 231-5023
E-mail: maop@vt.edu
Web Site: www.maop.vt.edu

AREAS OF INTEREST:
Graduate programs particularly in science, math and technology.

NAME(S) OF PROGRAMS:
● **Multicultural Academic Opportunity Graduate Student Scholars Program**

TYPE:
Assistantships; Fellowships; Internships; Scholarships. The program assists with graduate school financing in exchange for assistance to MAOP administration. Graduate students assist with programming implementation such as mentoring to undergraduate students.

YEAR PROGRAM STARTED: 1973

PURPOSE:
To improve professional and educational opportunities for minority students in architecture, planning, public and international affairs, and landscape architecture.

ELIGIBILITY:
Candidate must maintain a 3.0 cumulative grade point average, attend and participate in monthly Graduate Scholar workshops, and remain engaged with the MAOP program.

FINANCIAL DATA:
Amount of support per award: $6,000 to $16,000 per academic year.

NO. AWARDS: 12.

APPLICATION INFO:
Complete application includes a 500-word essay, two letters of recommendation and departmental commitment of funding.
Duration: One year. Renewable.
Deadline: April 1.

ADDRESS INQUIRIES TO:
Monica Hunter, Director
MAOP Office
(See address above.)

WIDENER MEMORIAL FOUNDATION IN AID OF HANDICAPPED CHILDREN [927]

4060 Butler Pike
Suite 225
Plymouth Meeting, PA 19462
(610) 825-8900
Fax: (610) 825-8904
E-mail: jhagerty@erdixon.com

FOUNDED: 1912

AREAS OF INTEREST:
Orthopedically handicapped children.

TYPE:
Capital grants.

PURPOSE:
To benefit orthopedically handicapped children.

LEGAL BASIS:
Special interest foundation.

ELIGIBILITY:
Applicants must be 501(c)(3) organizations that are not classified as private foundations. Organizations must benefit orthopedically handicapped children in some way.

GEOG. RESTRICTIONS: Greater Delaware Valley area (including the city of Philadelphia, Pennsylvania), and Bucks, Burlington, Camden, Chester, Delaware, Gloucester, Montgomery and Philadelphia counties.

FINANCIAL DATA:
Amount of support per award: Varies.
Total amount of support: Approximately $900,000 to $1,000,000 annually.

NO. MOST RECENT APPLICANTS: 26.

NO. AWARDS: 17.

APPLICATION INFO:
Applicant should include a letter describing the purpose for which grant would be used, persons who would benefit from the activity for which the grant is requested, specifically orthopedically handicapped children, and statements showing that the organization is exempt under 501(c)(3) of the Internal Revenue Code and also not classified as a private foundation.
Duration: Typically one year. Must reapply.
Deadline: May 15 and October 15. Board meets in May or June and November to approve grant requests.

IRS I.D.: 23-6267223

OFFICERS:
Edith D. Miller, President
Heike Sullivan, Esq., Vice President and Trustee
Edith R. Dixon, Treasurer and Trustee
George W. Dixon, Secretary
Mark S. DePillis, Esq., Trustee
Linda Grobman, Ed.D., Trustee
John Keleher, Trustee
Robert Mack, Ed.D., Trustee

ADDRESS INQUIRIES TO:
Edith D. Miller, President
P.O. Box 178
Lafayette Hill, PA 19444-0178

WITH FOUNDATION [928]

2225 East Bayshore Road, Suite 200
Palo Alto, CA 94303
(650) 320-1715
Fax: (650) 320-1716
E-mail: info@withfoundation.org
Web Site: withfoundation.org

FOUNDED: 2002

AREAS OF INTEREST:
Health care access and health care research benefiting adults with developmental disabilities.

TYPE:
Challenge/matching grants; Conferences/seminars; General operating grants; Project/program grants; Research grants; Technical assistance.

YEAR PROGRAM STARTED: 2002

PURPOSE:
To provide financial support to organizations that promote the establishment of comprehensive health care for adults with developmental disabilities.

ELIGIBILITY:
Organizations must be nonprofit 501(c)(3). Only grant proposals consistent with the Foundation's mission statement will be eligible for funding. No grants are made to individuals.

GEOG. RESTRICTIONS: United States.

FINANCIAL DATA:
Amount of support per award: $30,000 to $50,000.

Total amount of support: Approximately $750,000 annually.

Matching fund requirements: By invitation only.

NO. MOST RECENT APPLICANTS: 171 for fiscal year 2020.

NO. AWARDS: 31 for fiscal year 2020.

APPLICATION INFO:
Letter of interest must be completed online during open grant cycles.
Duration: Typically one year.

ADDRESS INQUIRIES TO:
E-mail: grants@withfoundation.org

African-American

CONGRESSIONAL BLACK CAUCUS FOUNDATION, INC. [929]
1720 Massachusetts Avenue, N.W.
Washington, DC 20036
(202) 263-2800
Fax: (202) 263-0846
E-mail: scholarships@cbcfinc.org
Web Site: www.cbcfinc.org

FOUNDED: 1976

AREAS OF INTEREST:
Promoting educational and leadership opportunities for African Americans.

NAME(S) OF PROGRAMS:
● **CBC Spouses Education Scholarship**

TYPE:
Scholarships. The CBC Spouses Education Scholarship is a national program that awards scholarships to academically talented and highly motivated students who intend to pursue full-time undergraduate, graduate or doctoral degrees.

PURPOSE:
To provide support to students, particularly African-Americans, who exhibit leadership skills, are involved in their community, and are pursuing higher education.

LEGAL BASIS:
Nonpartisan, nonprofit foundation.

ELIGIBILITY:
Undergraduate or graduate students residing or attending school in district of CBC member may apply.

FINANCIAL DATA:
Amount of support per award: Varies.
Total amount of support: Varies.

NO. AWARDS: Varies.

APPLICATION INFO:
The Foundation utilizes an online application process.
Duration: One year. Must reapply.
Deadline: End of May.

PUBLICATIONS:
Policy review; annual report.

IRS I.D.: 52-1160561

ADDRESS INQUIRIES TO:
Leadership Institute for Public Service
(See address or e-mail above.)

CONGRESSIONAL BLACK CAUCUS FOUNDATION, INC. [930]
1720 Massachusetts Avenue, N.W.
Washington, DC 20036
(202) 263-2800
Fax: (202) 263-0846
E-mail: scholarships@cbcfinc.org
Web Site: www.cbcfinc.org

FOUNDED: 1976

NAME(S) OF PROGRAMS:
● **CBC Spouses Performing Arts Scholarship**
● **CBC Spouses Visual Arts Scholarship**

TYPE:
Scholarships. CBC Spouses Performing Arts Scholarship, developed in honor of the late Curtis Mayfield, is intended to ensure that students pursuing a career in the performing arts receive the financial assistance to achieve their goals.

CBC Spouses Visual Arts Scholarship was established for students who are pursuing a career in the visual arts.

PURPOSE:
To encourage education in the performing and visual arts among minority students.

ELIGIBILITY:
Applicant must:
(1) be a U.S. citizen or permanent U.S. resident;
(2) be preparing to pursue an undergraduate degree full-time, or be a current full-time student in good academic standing at a U.S. accredited college or university;
(3) have a minimum 2.5 grade point average and;
(4) exhibit leadership ability and participate in community service activities.

The scholarships do not have a residency requirement.

GEOG. RESTRICTIONS: United States.

FINANCIAL DATA:
Amount of support per award: $3,000.
Total amount of support: Up to $60,000.

NO. AWARDS: Up to 10 scholarships annually.

APPLICATION INFO:
The Foundation utilizes an online application process.

Duration: One year. Must reapply.
Deadline: Late April to early May.

ADDRESS INQUIRIES TO:
Leadership Institute for Public Service
(See address or e-mail above.)

CONGRESSIONAL BLACK CAUCUS FOUNDATION, INC. [931]
1720 Massachusetts Avenue, N.W.
Washington, DC 20036
(202) 263-2800
Fax: (202) 263-0846
E-mail: info@cbcfinc.org
internships@cbcfinc.org
Web Site: www.cbcfinc.org

AREAS OF INTEREST:
Promoting educational and leadership opportunities for African Americans.

NAME(S) OF PROGRAMS:
● **The CBCF Congressional Fellows Program**
● **The CBCF Congressional Internship Program**

TYPE:
Fellowships; Internships. The CBCF Congressional Fellows Program helps participants gain invaluable experience as they assist in the development of legislation and public policy initiatives while working as congressional staff for a year. This program targets early career policy professionals who have completed a professional and/or graduate degree and have demonstrated commitment to improving the lives and services for individuals living in underserved communities. Fellows work on Capitol Hill in the office of a Congressional Black Caucus member.

The CBCF Congressional Internship Program provides undergraduate students with an in-depth orientation to Capitol Hill and the legislative process through actual work experience in the offices of Congressional Black Caucus Members. In this way interns prepare to become decision makers in the policymaking process.

PURPOSE:
To increase the number of African Americans on congressional committees and subcommittees by providing students the opportunity to participate in all aspects of the legislative process.

LEGAL BASIS:
Nonpartisan, nonprofit foundation.

ELIGIBILITY:
Fellows Program applicants must have completed graduate coursework. Internship Program applicants must be college undergraduates.

FINANCIAL DATA:
Fellows are responsible for their own travel arrangements, expenses and housing accommodations. CBCF provides health and dental insurance coverage during term of fellowship. Interns receive a stipend and housing at a local university.

Amount of support per award: Fellows Program: $40,000 annual stipend; Internship Program: $3,000 stipend.

Total amount of support: Varies.

NO. AWARDS: 6 to 9 fellowships per year.

APPLICATION INFO:
Submit a completed application with detailed resume, certificate of academic standing

and/or faculty certification, a writing sample of up to 10 pages, three letters of recommendation, one of which must be from the dean, department chairperson, faculty or advisor and an official transcript from each school attended.

Duration: Fellowships: 20 months; Internships: Nine weeks during the Summer, 16 weeks during the Spring and Fall.

Deadline: Spring: November; Summer: March; Fall: July.

IRS I.D.: 52-1160561

ADDRESS INQUIRIES TO:
Leadership Institute for Public Service (See address above.)

FREDERICK DOUGLASS INSTITUTE FOR AFRICAN AND AFRICAN-AMERICAN STUDIES

311 Morey Hall
University of Rochester
P.O. Box 270440
Rochester, NY 14627-0440
(585) 276-5744
Fax: (585) 256-2594
E-mail: FDI@rochester.edu
Web Site: www.sas.rochester.edu/aas

TYPE:
Awards/prizes; Conferences/seminars; Fellowships.

See entry 1383 for full listing.

FLORIDA DEPARTMENT OF EDUCATION   [932]

Office of Student Financial Assistance
325 West Gaines Street, Suite 1314
Tallahassee, FL 32399-0400
(888) 827-2004
Fax: (850) 487-1809
E-mail: osfa@fldoe.org
Web Site: www.floridastudentfinancialaidsg.org

NAME(S) OF PROGRAMS:
● **Rosewood Family Scholarship Program**

TYPE:
Scholarships. Financial assistance for descendants of the Rosewood family affected by the incidents of January 1923, to attend a state university, public community college or public postsecondary vocational-technical school.

PURPOSE:
To encourage and assist minority students to continue on to higher education.

LEGAL BASIS:
Governmental agency.

ELIGIBILITY:
To receive funding, the applying student must meet the following initial eligibility requirements:
(1) not owe a repayment or be in default under any state or federal grant, loan or scholarship program unless satisfactory arrangements to repay have been made;
(2) not have previously received a Baccalaureate degree;
(3) enroll full-time at an eligible participating postsecondary institution in a program of study leading to an undergraduate degree, a certificate or a diploma and;
(4) must provide copies of documents of ancestry by April 1; mail copies to Florida Department of Education, Office of Student Financial Assistance, State Scholarship and Grant Programs.

FINANCIAL DATA:
Amount of support per award: Varies; may not exceed $6,100.

NO. MOST RECENT APPLICANTS: 258 for the year 2019-20.

NO. AWARDS: 29 for the year 2019-20.

APPLICATION INFO:
Detailed program information can be found on the web site.
Duration: Renewable for 100% of student's programs.
Deadline: April 1 for submitting a fully completed, error-free Florida Financial Aid Application. Florida residents must complete and submit the Free Application for Federal Student Aid (FAFSA) online in time to be processed error-free by the U.S. Department of Education on or before May 15. Florida nonresidents must complete and submit the FAFSA in time to receive the Student Aid Report (SAR) from the processor and postmark a copy of the SAR to OSFA by May 15.

ADDRESS INQUIRIES TO:
State Scholarship and Grant Programs (See address above.)

THE JACK AND JILL OF AMERICA FOUNDATION   [933]

1930 17th Street, N.W.
Washington, DC 20009-6207
(202) 232-5290
Fax: (202) 232-1747
E-mail: administration@jackandjillfoundation.org
Web Site: www.jackandjillfoundation.org

FOUNDED: 1968

AREAS OF INTEREST:
African American families, education, and health and wellness.

CONSULTING OR VOLUNTEER SERVICES:
Volunteer services.

NAME(S) OF PROGRAMS:
● **Heart and Mind**
● **Hidden Talent Grants**
● **Our Village**
● **Reading Corner Literacy Grant**
● **Teen Community Service Award**

TYPE:
Project/program grants; Scholarships. Volunteer opportunities.

YEAR PROGRAM STARTED: 1968

PURPOSE:
To influence the ongoing positive development of children.

LEGAL BASIS:
Public charity.

ELIGIBILITY:
Grants are made to 501(c)(3), 501(c)(4) and IRS charitable organizations.

GEOG. RESTRICTIONS: United States.

FINANCIAL DATA:
Amount of support per award: $3,000 to $10,000.
Total amount of support: Varies.

NO. MOST RECENT APPLICANTS: 500.

NO. AWARDS: Varies.

APPLICATION INFO:
Applicant should carefully read the Information for Grant Applicants on the Foundation web site before submitting an

application on the designated form. Furthermore, answers on the application coversheet must be given in the space provided; no additional sheets can be attached. Type the application (using at least 10-point type). Applications may not be faxed. All signatures should be signed in blue ink. A complete application consists of an application coversheet along with the following materials:
(1) proposal;
(2) copy of IRS 501(c)(3) letter or documentation of 501(c)(4) status, whichever is applicable;
(3) most recent audited income statement or 990 tax return, if 501(c)(3) organization, or most recent year-end statement of income and expenses, if 501(c)(4) organization and;
(4) brief resume or bio of the organization's Project Director and other relevant supporting material.
Duration: One year.
Deadline: April 21.

PUBLICATIONS:
Newsletter; annual report; application guidelines.

IRS I.D.: 51-0224656

STAFF:
Pier A.H. Blake, Executive Director

ADDRESS INQUIRIES TO:
Pier A.H. Blake, Executive Director (See address above.)

THE NAACP LEGAL DEFENSE AND EDUCATIONAL FUND, INC.   [934]

40 Rector Street
5th Floor
New York, NY 10006
(212) 965-2244
Fax: (212) 226-7592
E-mail: scholarships@naacpldf.org
eanderson@naacpldf.org
Web Site: www.naacpldf.org/scholarships

FOUNDED: 1964

AREAS OF INTEREST:
Financial assistance for African-American undergraduates and for law students with a demonstrable interest in civil rights.

NAME(S) OF PROGRAMS:
● **LDF Herbert Lehman Education Fund Scholarship Program**
● **LDF Earl Warren Legal Training Program**

TYPE:
Awards/prizes; Grants-in-aid; Internships; Scholarships. LDF Herbert Lehman Education Fund Scholarship Program: Scholarships for African-American high school seniors, high school graduates and college freshmen to attend four-year accredited colleges and universities.

LDF Earl Warren Legal Training Program: Scholarships for law students to attend three-year accredited law schools.

YEAR PROGRAM STARTED: 1964

PURPOSE:
To encourage students to continue the work of the Legal Defense Fund; to encourage young people to be involved in public service; to increase the presence of African-American students in colleges, universities and law schools in the U.S.

LEGAL BASIS:
501(c)(3) corporation.

ELIGIBILITY:
Applicants must be U.S. citizens. Candidates must have outstanding potential evidenced by their recommendations, high school academic records, test scores and essays. They must understand their educational goals and academic abilities. Candidates should have a clear commitment to working in the public service as exemplified by their community and school involvements. Candidates should have exceptional leadership potential with an ability to work well in diverse settings.

Law students already enrolled in law school are not eligible to apply for the LDF Earl Warren Legal Training Program.

Applicants are encouraged to visit the Fund's web site.

GEOG. RESTRICTIONS: United States.

FINANCIAL DATA:
Amount of support per award: LDF Herbert Lehman Education Fund Scholarship Program: $2,000 per year; LDF Earl Warren Legal Training Program: $10,000 per year.

NO. MOST RECENT APPLICANTS: Over 2,000.

NO. AWARDS: Herbert Lehman Scholarship: 25; Earl Warren Program: 5 annually.

APPLICATION INFO:
Applications will be available for online submission by November 30 of each year. Applicants who do not meet the basic criteria for eligibility or do not satisfy program requirements for the completion of applications will not be considered.
Duration: Herbert Lehman Scholarship: Up to four years depending upon availability of funds. Renewable during undergraduate career, if student remains in good standing with their college or university. Earl Warren Program: Three years provided scholar remains in good academic standing and meets scholarship criteria.
Deadline: April 1 for the Lehman Scholarship and May 1 for the Warren Legal Training Program. Notification normally takes place at the end of July, prior to the fall semester of the student's first academic year.

STAFF:
Eve Anderson, Program Assistant

ADDRESS INQUIRIES TO:
Eve Anderson, Program Assistant
(See address above.)

NATIONAL ASSOCIATION FOR EQUAL OPPORTUNITY IN HIGHER EDUCATION (NAFEO) [935]
110 Maryland Avenue, N.E.
Suite 509
Washington, DC 20002
(202) 552-3300
Fax: (202) 552-3330
Web Site: www.nafeonation.org

FOUNDED: 1969

AREAS OF INTEREST:
Equal opportunity in higher education.

NAME(S) OF PROGRAMS:
● **NAFEO Internship Program**

TYPE:
Internships. NAFEO Internship Program offers full-time paid internships in the summer, spring and fall.

YEAR PROGRAM STARTED: 1997

PURPOSE:
To provide lifelong learning experiences that enhance personal and professional development.

ELIGIBILITY:
Preference will be given to students enrolled in undergraduate or graduate programs at historically or predominantly black colleges and universities. A grade point average of 3.0 or above on a 4.0 scale is required. (Some internships require U.S. citizenship.)

FINANCIAL DATA:
Stipends are paid according to a student's classification at the time of application. Round-trip travel: Students selected for summer internships only who reside outside of the Washington, DC, metropolitan area will receive a travel allowance. A housing stipend will be provided. Local travel: Interns receive an allowance to subsidize daily travel to and from their work assignments.
Amount of support per award: Undergraduate students, $11 per hour; graduate students, $13 to $15 per hour.

NO. AWARDS: Approximately 20.

APPLICATION INFO:
Applicant must submit:
(1) complete application;
(2) current resume;
(3) unofficial transcript - by request only;
(4) official transcript - by request only and;
(5) two completed faculty recommendation forms - by request only.

In conjunction with NAFEO member institutions, NAFEO staff reviews applications to ensure that applicants are eligible and that the applications are complete. NAFEO staff then refers applications to employing agencies based on the academic disciplines they are seeking. Employing agencies review the applications, conduct interviews if necessary, and make all final selections.

Selected students will be notified by NAFEO staff and provided with an official internship offer.
Duration: Summer: 10 weeks; Fall and spring: 15 weeks.
Deadline: Varies.

ADDRESS INQUIRIES TO:
Internship Coordinator
(See address above.)

THE NATIONAL ASSOCIATION OF BLACK SOCIAL WORKERS, INC. [936]
2305 Martin Luther King Jr. Avenue, S.E.
Washington, DC 20020
(202) 678-4570
Fax: (202) 678-4572
E-mail: officemanager@nabsw.org
Web Site: www.nabsw.org

FOUNDED: 1968

AREAS OF INTEREST:
Social work and community advocacy.

NAME(S) OF PROGRAMS:
● **Office of Student Affairs Community Leadership Tuition Scholarship**
● **Cenie Jomo Williams Tuition Scholarship**

TYPE:
Scholarships.

YEAR PROGRAM STARTED: 1968

PURPOSE:
To promote the welfare, survival and liberation of communities of African ancestry.

LEGAL BASIS:
Nonprofit membership association.

ELIGIBILITY:
Student must:
(1) be an active paid member of NABSW;
(2) have a 3.0 grade point average on a 4.0 scale;
(3) express research interest in African Americans or those of African ancestry and;
(4) be enrolled for full-time study at an accredited U.S. social work program for the semester that the award will be granted.

GEOG. RESTRICTIONS: United States.

FINANCIAL DATA:
Amount of support per award: Office of Student Affairs Scholarship: $1,000; Williams Scholarship: $1,500.
Total amount of support: $2,500 for the academic year 2021-22.

NO. AWARDS: 1 per award.

APPLICATION INFO:
Scholarship applications can be obtained from the National Office.
Duration: One-time award.
Deadline: June 28.

PUBLICATIONS:
Quarterly newsletters.

IRS I.D.: 13-2779773

ADDRESS INQUIRIES TO:
Terrence A. Bradford, National Office Manager
(See address above.)

NATIONAL BLACK MBA ASSOCIATION [937]
400 West Peachtree Street, N.W.
Suite 203
Atlanta, GA 30308
(404) 260-5444
E-mail: scholarship@nbmbaa.org
Web Site: nbmbaa.org

FOUNDED: 1970

AREAS OF INTEREST:
The economic and intellectual wealth of the black community.

NAME(S) OF PROGRAMS:
● **NBMBAA Undergraduate Scholarship Program**

TYPE:
Scholarships.

PURPOSE:
To help create economic and intellectual wealth for the Black community; to identify and increase the pool of Black talent for business, public, private and nonprofit sectors.

ELIGIBILITY:
Applicant must:
(1) be a student in their first, second, third or fourth year enrolled full-time at an accredited college or university at the time of award (September);
(2) be a financially active member of the National Black MBA Association;
(3) be a U.S. or Canadian citizen;
(4) submit an essay on provided topic;
(5) submit a current resume;

(6) have a grade point average of 3.0 or above;
(7) demonstrate academic excellence;
(8) demonstrate exceptional leadership potential;
(9) be actively involved in their local communities through service to others and;
(10) be recommended by faculty advisor.

GEOG. RESTRICTIONS: United States and Canada.

FINANCIAL DATA:
Amount of support per award: Up to $5,000 for the 2021-22 academic year.
Total amount of support: Over $500,000.

NO. MOST RECENT APPLICANTS: 350.

NO. AWARDS: Minimum of 10.

APPLICATION INFO:
Applicant is strongly advised to contact the Association at the e-mail address above for up-to-date details.

The following application materials must be submitted:
(1) application (must be completed online);
(2) a 500-word essay completed on the selected topic (submitted online only);
(3) a current resume no more than two pages long;
(4) a copy uploaded of applicant's most recent official transcript(s) and;
(5) a professional headshot (photograph) in jpeg format (image should be at least 1024 x 768).

Deadline: March 31.

ADDRESS INQUIRIES TO:
See e-mail address above.

*SPECIAL STIPULATIONS:
Scholarship recipients are required to agree to participate in limited public relations activities.

NATIONAL BLACK NURSES ASSOCIATION, INC.
8630 Fenton Street
Suite 910
Silver Spring, MD 20910
(301) 589-3200
Fax: (301) 589-3223
E-mail: info@nbna.org
Web Site: www.nbna.org

TYPE:
Scholarships.

See entry 2240 for full listing.

NATIONAL SOCIETY OF BLACK ENGINEERS
205 Daingerfield Road
Alexandria, VA 22314
(703) 549-2207
Fax: (703) 683-5312
E-mail: scholarships@nsbe.org
rgoodine@nsbe.org
Web Site: www.nsbe.org

TYPE:
Awards/prizes; Scholarships. The Society offers a variety of NSBE and corporate-sponsored scholarship and award opportunities to its precollege, collegiate undergraduate and graduate student members as well as technical professional members.

See entry 1541 for full listing.

NEED   [938]
The Law and Finance Building
429 Fourth Avenue, 20th Floor
Pittsburgh, PA 15219
(412) 566-2760
Fax: (412) 471-6643
E-mail: needpgh@gmail.com
Web Site: www.needld.org

FOUNDED: 1963

AREAS OF INTEREST:
Higher education, college access services.

CONSULTING OR VOLUNTEER SERVICES:
Counseling for postsecondary education; assistance to students and parents needing help with the completion of financial aid forms; mentoring services.

NAME(S) OF PROGRAMS:
● **Access to College and Career Education (ACE) Program**
● **African American Male Mentoring Initiative (AAMMI)**
● **Future NEED Scholars**
● **The NEED HBCU (Historically Black Colleges and Universities) Educational Tour**
● **Science, Technology, Engineering, Art and Math (STEAM) Female Mentoring Program**
● **Unmet NEED Grants and Scholarships**

TYPE:
Internships; Matching gifts; Scholarships. Supplemental grants for postsecondary education at colleges and business, trade and technical schools.

YEAR PROGRAM STARTED: 1963

PURPOSE:
To provide career and college access services which empower youth from the Pittsburgh region to aspire to, learn about, prepare for, and complete higher education.

LEGAL BASIS:
Incorporated nonprofit, tax-exempt.

ELIGIBILITY:
Applicant must meet the following requirements:
(1) be a high school student planning to enroll, or a student already enrolled, full-time in a college or university;
(2) be a resident of a county in the Pittsburgh area for one year prior to entering a school or college;
(3) have a minimum cumulative grade point average of 2.0;
(4) be a U.S. citizen;
(5) demonstrate unmet financial need of at least $1,000 after the financial aid award package has been determined and;
(6) have an Expected Family Contribution (EFC) less than $5,000.

GEOG. RESTRICTIONS: Allegheny, Armstrong, Beaver, Butler, Fayette, Greene, Lawrence, Washington and Westmoreland counties, Pennsylvania.

FINANCIAL DATA:
Amount of support per award: $1,000 to $3,500.
Total amount of support: Varies.

APPLICATION INFO:
Applicant must submit:
(1) NEED application;
(2) high school, college or school transcript (whichever is most recent) and;
(3) photo.

Duration: Academic year. May reapply in subsequent years.

Deadline: May 31.

PUBLICATIONS:
Annual report.

OFFICERS:
TiAnda Blount, Chairperson of the Board

ADDRESS INQUIRIES TO:
Student Services Department
(See address above.)

THE SCHOMBURG CENTER FOR RESEARCH IN BLACK CULTURE, NEW YORK PUBLIC LIBRARY
515 Malcolm X Boulevard
New York, NY 10037-1801
(212) 491-2228
E-mail: sir@nypl.org
Web Site: www.nypl.org/about/locations/schomburg/fellowships

TYPE:
Fellowships. Awarded to scholars and professionals whose research in African diasporic studies can benefit from extended access to the Center's collections. Seminars, colloquia, forums, symposia and conferences complement the residency program.

See entry 353 for full listing.

UNITED NEGRO COLLEGE FUND (UNCF)   [939]
1805 Seventh Street, N.W.
Washington, DC 20001
(800) 331-2244
(202) 810-0258
E-mail: scholarships@uncf.org
Web Site: www.uncf.org

FOUNDED: 1944

TYPE:
Fellowships; Internships; Scholarships; Technical assistance. The Fund, since its founding, has raised money for 37 private, historically Black colleges and universities.

Faculty fellowship programs make it possible for hundreds of instructors to earn doctoral degrees.

Mentoring and internship opportunities are provided for hundreds of UNCF students.

Scholarships are offered to a pool of more than 60,000 talented students attending UNCF colleges and universities. The Fund oversees more than 450 scholarship programs in the following general categories:
(1) geographically based scholarships;
(2) scholarships based on academic major;
(3) scholarships based on merit and need and;
(4) financial aid for graduate study.

PURPOSE:
To provide low-cost quality education in an environment that enables students to excel.

FINANCIAL DATA:
Amount of support per award: Scholarships: $500 to $10,000.
Total amount of support: Varies.

APPLICATION INFO:
Contact the Fund for detailed information.

OFFICERS:
Michael L. Lomax, Ph.D, President and Chief Executive Officer

ADDRESS INQUIRIES TO:
James Lander, Senior Director of Program Management
(See address above.)

Native American

AMERICAN INDIAN COLLEGE FUND [940]

8333 Greenwood Boulevard
Denver, CO 80221
(303) 426-8900
Fax: (303) 426-1200
E-mail: scholarships@collegefund.org
Web Site: collegefund.org

FOUNDED: 1989

AREAS OF INTEREST:
Scholarship funding for Native American and Alaska Native students.

NAME(S) OF PROGRAMS:
● **Full Circle Scholarship Program**
● **TCU Scholarship Program**

TYPE:
Scholarships.

YEAR PROGRAM STARTED: 1989

PURPOSE:
To educate the mind and spirit of Native American communities by providing undergraduate and graduate Native student scholarships and programmatic support for the nation's 35 accredited tribal colleges and universities to provide access to an affordable, quality higher education while preserving Native cultures and languages; to make scholarships available to undergraduate and graduate Native students at any accredited public or private (nonprofit) college.

ELIGIBILITY:
Minimum requirements for all American Indian College Fund Full Circle Scholarships include:
(1) U.S. citizenship;
(2) enrollment full-time in an accredited tribal, public or private (nonprofit) college or university;
(3) ability to trace Indian ancestry; registered as a member of a federal- or state-recognized tribe, or a descendant of at least one grandparent or parent who is an enrolled tribal member; Alaska Natives may use Native Corporation membership;
(4) minimum grade point average of 2.0 mandatory (many Full Circle Scholarships funded by Fund's partners are more competitive) and;
(5) submission of a completed online application.

GEOG. RESTRICTIONS: United States.

FINANCIAL DATA:
Amount of support per award: Scholarships: Average $1,200 per year.

APPLICATION INFO:
Guidelines and application form are available on the web site.
Deadline: Full Circle Scholarship: Applications accepted January 1 to May 31 each year. TCU Scholarship: Varies by college.

STAFF:
Tiffany Gusbeth, Director of Student Success Services

ADDRESS INQUIRIES TO:
See e-mail address above.

AMERICAN INDIAN GRADUATE CENTER [941]

3701 San Mateo Boulevard, N.E.
Suite 200
Albuquerque, NM 87110
(505) 881-4584
Fax: (505) 884-0427
E-mail: fellowships@aigcs.org
Web Site: www.aigcs.org

FOUNDED: 1969

AREAS OF INTEREST:
Graduate and undergraduate-level education in any field.

NAME(S) OF PROGRAMS:
● **Fellowships for American Indians or Alaskan Natives**

TYPE:
Fellowships; Grants-in-aid; Scholarships. Grants on an academic year basis. Summer funding available to continuing students only; these are students who are currently in the fellowship program.

YEAR PROGRAM STARTED: 1969

PURPOSE:
To help open doors to graduate education and help tribes obtain the educated professionals they need to become more self-sufficient and exercise their rights to self-determination.

LEGAL BASIS:
IRS status 501(c)(3), tax-exempt, incorporated in New Mexico.

ELIGIBILITY:
An applicant must be an enrolled member of a U.S. federally recognized American Indian tribe or Alaska Native group, or possess one-fourth degree Indian blood from a federally recognized tribe. Applicant must be pursuing a Master's, Doctorate or professional degree as a full-time graduate student at an accredited graduate school in the U.S. and must be in financial need. They must submit an essay as described in the application packet. Applicants must apply for federal financial and campus-based aid at the financial aid office of the university they plan to attend.

GEOG. RESTRICTIONS: United States.

FINANCIAL DATA:
Awards are based on each applicant's unmet financial need as verified by the applicant's college financial aid office. Fellowships are supplementary grants and are only a percentage of a student's total unmet financial need.
Amount of support per award: Varies.
Total amount of support: Varies.
Matching fund requirements: Universities are encouraged to provide assistance.

CO-OP FUNDING PROGRAMS: The organization works with other scholarship agencies to assure that there will be no overfunding of students.

NO. AWARDS: Varies.

APPLICATION INFO:
Application must be submitted online.
Duration: One academic year at a time. Students may reapply each year.
Deadline: Varies depending on scholarship.

PUBLICATIONS:
Annual report; newsletter; brochure.

IRS I.D.: 85-0222386

STAFF:
Marveline Vallo Gabbard, Scholarship Operations Manager

Josh Lucio, Scholarship Operations Manager
Lakota Coriz, Scholarship Operations Assistant

ADDRESS INQUIRIES TO:
See e-mail address above.

AMERICAN INDIAN SCIENCE AND ENGINEERING SOCIETY (AISES) [942]

6899 Winchester Circle
Suite 102A
Boulder, CO 80301
(720) 552-6123
Fax: (720) 526-6940
E-mail: info@aises.org
Web Site: www.aises.org

FOUNDED: 1977

AREAS OF INTEREST:
American Indian education in the science and engineering fields.

TYPE:
Academic and travel scholarships. AISES scholarships are intended to partially defray tuition and other educational expenses, thereby increasing access to higher education and improving college retention rates for AISES members.

AISES scholarships are made possible by corporations, government agencies, foundations, and individuals who wish to support the advancement of American Indians/Alaskan Natives. Scholarships are distributed in two disbursements and awarded for one academic year, unless otherwise specified. Recipients cannot receive more than one scholarship in any of the programs.

Scholarships are also awarded to members of AISES who are American Indian/Alaskan Native college students who meet the eligibility requirements for each scholarship.

YEAR PROGRAM STARTED: 1983

PURPOSE:
To significantly increase the number of American Indian/Alaskan Native scientists and engineers, and develop knowledgeable leaders within native communities; to foster the building of community by bridging science and technology with traditional native values.

LEGAL BASIS:
Private, nonprofit corporation.

ELIGIBILITY:
Each scholarship has its own eligibility requirements regarding grade point average, majors and academic status. Minimum requirements include:
(1) Applicant must be an AISES member at the time of application and;
(2) Applicant must be an enrolled member or a descendant of an enrolled member of a federal or state recognized American Indian Tribe or Alaska Native Village, or Native Hawaiian or descendant from a Native Hawaiian, or Pacific Islander or descendant from a Pacific Islander, or Indigenous person of Canada. Enrollment documents and/or a copy of birth certificate(s) showing descendancy from an enrolled citizen, Indigenous group of Canada, Native Hawaiian, or Pacific Islander are acceptable. Applicant may also, instead, provide a copy of their Certificate of Degree of Indian Blood or Certificate of Degree of Alaska Native Blood (CDIB) card.

GEOG. RESTRICTIONS: United States and Canada.

FINANCIAL DATA:
Amount of support per award: Varies.
Total amount of support: Varies.

NO. AWARDS: 301 scholarships for the year 2019.

APPLICATION INFO:
Student must complete a General Applicant Profile through the Online Scholarship Application Information System (OASIS) provided by Indigenous Education, Inc., which is located at cobellscholar.academicworks.com.
Duration: One academic year.
Deadline: May 31.

PUBLICATIONS:
AISES Scholarship Program brochure.

IRS I.D.: 73-1023474

ADDRESS INQUIRIES TO:
Dr. Johnny Poolaw, Associate Director of Student Success Services
(See address above.)

AMERICAN PHILOSOPHICAL SOCIETY [943]
104 South Fifth Street
Philadelphia, PA 19106-3387
(215) 440-3429
E-mail: lmusumeci@amphilsoc.org
Web Site: www.amphilsoc.org/grants/phillips-fund-native-american-research

FOUNDED: 1743

AREAS OF INTEREST:
Scholarly research.

NAME(S) OF PROGRAMS:
● **Phillips Fund for Native American Research**

TYPE:
Grants-in-aid; Research grants. Postgraduate grants for research in Native American linguistics, ethnohistory and the history of studies of Native Americans in the continental U.S. and Canada. The Committee prefers supporting the work of younger scholars/graduate students for research on Master's or doctoral dissertations. Grants are for travel costs, tapes, films and consultants' fees.

YEAR PROGRAM STARTED: 1940

LEGAL BASIS:
Nonprofit learned society.

ELIGIBILITY:
Open to graduate students and postdoctoral candidates.

The grants described above are for research in Native American linguistics and ethnohistory, as well as in the history of studies of Native Americans. There are no ethnic restrictions on applicants. Work must be on groups located in the continental U.S. and Canada.

The Committee sometimes approves more than two awards to the same person within a five-year period. Grants are not made for projects in archaeology, ethnography, psycholinguistics, or for the preparation of pedagogical materials, general maintenance or purchase of permanent equipment (tape recorders, books, etc.).

FINANCIAL DATA:
The grants are intended for such extra costs as travel, tapes, films, consultants' fees, etc., but not for the purchase of permanent equipment (tape recorders, computers, etc.)

Amount of support per award: Awards average $3,000; grants do not exceed $3,500.
Total amount of support: $49,900 for the year 2020.

NO. MOST RECENT APPLICANTS: 32.

NO. AWARDS: 17 for the year 2020.

APPLICATION INFO:
Application must be submitted electronically through the Society's online portal. Up to two additional pages may be submitted for the project statement.

Two letters of support are required.

The application and both letters of reference must be received by the deadline.
Duration: One year.
Deadline: March 1. Notification by May.

ADDRESS INQUIRIES TO:
Linda Musumeci
Director of Grants and Fellowships
(See address above.)

ASSOCIATION ON AMERICAN INDIAN AFFAIRS [944]
6030 Daybreak Circle
Suite A150-217
Clarksville, MD 21029
(240) 314-7155
E-mail: general@indian-affairs.org
Web Site: www.indian-affairs.org/scholarships.html

FOUNDED: 1922

AREAS OF INTEREST:
Sovereignty, culture preservation, youth education and capacity building of Indian country.

NAME(S) OF PROGRAMS:
● **Association on American Indian Affairs Scholarship Program**

TYPE:
Scholarships. Undergraduate and graduate scholarships for citizens of federally recognized Tribes and unrecognized Tribes.

PURPOSE:
To promote the welfare of American Indians and Alaska Natives by supporting efforts to sustain and perpetuate their cultures and languages; to protect their sovereignty, constitutional, legal and human rights and natural resources; to improve their health, education and economic and community development.

LEGAL BASIS:
Charitable nonprofit foundation.

ELIGIBILITY:
The applicant must meet the following basic requirements:
(1) be enrolled in one's tribe;
(2) be attending an accredited school full-time both fall and spring semesters;
(3) be seeking a Master's degree in any curriculum, Ph.D., law degree or medical degree and;
(4) have a minimum 2.5 grade point average.

Scholars should be able to show how they are connected to their Native Nations and/or Indian Country and plan to utilize their degree to support their Nation or Indian Country.

GEOG. RESTRICTIONS: Continental United States and Alaska.

FINANCIAL DATA:
Amount of support per award: Varies.

NO. AWARDS: 30.

APPLICATION INFO:
Application period opens February 1. Information is available online.
Duration: Life of the student's academic career, as long as the student maintains a 2.5 grade point average and full-time status.
Deadline: May 31.

BNSF RAILWAY FOUNDATION [945]
2500 Lou Menk Drive
Building AOB-2
Fort Worth, TX 76131-2830
(817) 867-6458
E-mail: bnsffoundation@bnsf.com
Web Site: www.bnsffoundation.org

NAME(S) OF PROGRAMS:
● **Native American Scholarship Program**

TYPE:
Scholarships. Awarded annually to outstanding Native American high school seniors from funds provided by the Foundation, for up to four years or until undergraduate degree requirements are completed, whichever occurs first. Scholarship winners may attend any accredited college (two-year leading to a four-year degree) or university in the U.S.

LEGAL BASIS:
Corporate foundation.

ELIGIBILITY:
High school seniors having one-fourth or more Indian blood are eligible. Applicants need not be related to Burlington Northern Santa Fe personnel to qualify. Two scholarships are provided exclusively for members of the Navajo Tribe and the other three are available to any Native American high school students residing in Arizona, California, Colorado, Kansas, Minnesota, Montana, New Mexico, North Dakota, Oklahoma, Oregon, South Dakota, or Washington.

Winners are selected on the basis of strong academic performance in high school, with award preference being given to the study of any of the sciences such as medicine, engineering, natural and physical sciences, as well as business, education and health administration.

GEOG. RESTRICTIONS: Arizona, California, Colorado, Kansas, Minnesota, Montana, New Mexico, North Dakota, Oklahoma, Oregon, South Dakota and Washington.

FINANCIAL DATA:
Amount of support per award: $1,000 to $2,500 annually for up to four years or until undergraduate degree requirements are completed, whichever occurs first (but not to exceed five years). Financial need determines the amount awarded.

NO. AWARDS: 5.

APPLICATION INFO:
The scholarship is administered by the American Indian Science and Engineering Society (AISES) and all winners are selected by the organization. Applications may be obtained by writing American Indian Science and Engineering Society, P.O. Box 9828, Albuquerque, NM 87119-9828. All correspondence and questions should be directed to AISES.

Duration: Up to four years or until undergraduate degree requirements are completed, whichever occurs first, but not to exceed five years.

ADDRESS INQUIRIES TO:
American Indian Science and Engineering Society
(See address above.)

BUREAU OF INDIAN AFFAIRS [946]
Office of Indian Services
Division of Workforce Development
1849 C Street, N.W., Room 4520
Washington, DC 20240
(202) 513-7625
E-mail: Terrence.Parks@bia.gov
Web Site: www.indianaffairs.gov

FOUNDED: 1824

AREAS OF INTEREST:
Vocational training, job placement, education, childcare and related services.

NAME(S) OF PROGRAMS:
- **Indian Employment Assistance**
- **Public Law 102-477**

TYPE:
Project/program grants; Training grants. Vocational training and job placement, advisory services and counseling, education, childcare and youth development programs.

YEAR PROGRAM STARTED: 1956

PURPOSE:
To provide individual grants for adult vocational training and job placement services for Indians.

LEGAL BASIS:
Public Law 67-85, The Snyder Act of November 2, 1921; Public Law 84-959, Indian Adult Vocational Training Act of August 3, 1956; Public Law 102-477.

ELIGIBILITY:
Applicant must be a member of a federally recognized tribe, band or group of Indians, whose residence is on or near an Indian reservation under the jurisdiction of BIA.

GEOG. RESTRICTIONS: United States.

FINANCIAL DATA:
Total amount of support: Over $100,000,000 annually.

CO-OP FUNDING PROGRAMS: Indian Education, Training and Employment.

NO. MOST RECENT APPLICANTS: 6,500.

NO. AWARDS: 455 for the year 2017.

APPLICATION INFO:
Applicants should make application to the nearest Agency or Tribal Employment Assistance. Contact tribal office nearest to place of residence.
Duration: One year. Renewal possible if continuing training.

STAFF:
Terrence Parks, Division Chief

ADDRESS INQUIRIES TO:
Terrence Parks, Division Chief
(See address above.)

BUREAU OF INDIAN AFFAIRS [947]
Office of Indian Energy and Economic Development
Division of Energy and Mineral Development
13922 Denver West Parkway, Suite 200
Lakewood, CO 80401
(720) 999-1414
Fax: (303) 969-5278
E-mail: IEEDgrants@bia.gov
Web Site: www.bia.gov/as-ia/ieed

AREAS OF INTEREST:
Energy development; renewable energy; development capacity; oil, gas and coal development.

NAME(S) OF PROGRAMS:
- **Tribal Energy Development Capacity (TEDC) Grant**

TYPE:
Project/program grants.

PURPOSE:
To help tribes in assessing, developing or obtaining the managerial, organizational and technical capacity needed to develop energy resources on Indian land and to properly account for resulting energy production and revenues, as provided for in Title V, Section 503, of the Energy Policy Act.

LEGAL BASIS:
Public Law 67-85, The Snyder Act of November 2, 1921; The Energy Policy Act of 2005 (25 U.S.C. 3501 et seq.)

ELIGIBILITY:
Federally recognized Indian tribes and tribal energy resource development organizations.

GEOG. RESTRICTIONS: United States.

FINANCIAL DATA:
Amount of support per award: $10,000 to $1,000,000.

NO. AWARDS: Up to 15.

APPLICATION INFO:
Applicants should refer to the solicitation notice on www.grants.gov.
Duration: 12 months; renewal possible.

STAFF:
Stephen Manydeeds, Division Chief
Winter Jojola-Talburt, Deputy Division Chief
Payton Batliner, Program Coordinator

ADDRESS INQUIRIES TO:
Payton Batliner, Program Coordinator
(See address above.)

BUREAU OF INDIAN AFFAIRS [948]
Office of Indian Energy and Economic Development
Division of Energy and Mineral Development
13922 Denver West Parkway, Suite 200
Lakewood, CO 80401
(720) 999-1414
Fax: (303) 969-5278
E-mail: IEEDgrants@bia.gov
Web Site: www.bia.gov/as-ia/ieed

AREAS OF INTEREST:
Energy development; mineral development; feasibility study; renewable energy; oil, gas and coal development.

NAME(S) OF PROGRAMS:
- **Energy and Mineral Development Program (EMDP) Grant**

TYPE:
Project/program grants.

PURPOSE:
To promote energy and mineral development projects that explore for energy and mineral resources, inventory or assess known resources, or perform feasibility or market studies that tend to promote the use and development of known energy and mineral resources.

LEGAL BASIS:
Public Law 67-85, The Snyder Act of November 2, 1921; The Energy Policy Act of 2005 (25 U.S.C. 3501 et seq.)

ELIGIBILITY:
Federally recognized Indian tribes and tribal energy resource development organizations.

GEOG. RESTRICTIONS: Indian land within the United States.

FINANCIAL DATA:
Amount of support per award: Up to $600,000 appropriated annually.
Total amount of support: Over $5,000,000; total funds are contingent on annual appropriations.

NO. AWARDS: Approximately 15.

APPLICATION INFO:
Applicants should refer to the solicitation notice on www.grants.gov.
Duration: 12 months; renewal possible.
Deadline: May.

STAFF:
Stephen Manydeeds, Division Chief
Winter Jojola-Talburt, Deputy Division Chief
Payton Batliner, Program Coordinator

ADDRESS INQUIRIES TO:
Payton Batliner, Program Coordinator
(See address above.)

BUREAU OF INDIAN AFFAIRS [949]
Office of Indian Energy and Economics Development (IEED)
U.S. Department of the Interior, Room 4138 MIB
1849 C Street, N.W.
Washington, DC 20240
(202) 595-4766
E-mail: jamesr.west@bia.gov
Web Site: www.bia.gov/service/grants/nabdi

AREAS OF INTEREST:
Economic development, feasibility study.

NAME(S) OF PROGRAMS:
- **Native American Business Development Institute (NABDI)**

TYPE:
Project/program grants.

PURPOSE:
To study the viability of an economic development project or business or the practicality of a technology an eligible recipient may choose to pursue.

LEGAL BASIS:
Public Law 67-85, The Snyder Act of November 2, 1921.

ELIGIBILITY:
Federally recognized Indian tribes.

GEOG. RESTRICTIONS: United States.

FINANCIAL DATA:
Amount of support per award: Approximately $35,000 to $50,000.
Total amount of support: Varies. Total funds are contingent on annual appropriations.

NO. MOST RECENT APPLICANTS: 50 to 80.

NO. AWARDS: 12 to 22.

APPLICATION INFO:
Applicants should refer to the solicitation notice on www.grants.gov.
Duration: 12 months. Renewal possible.
Deadline: Varies.

STAFF:
James R. West, IEED Grant Manager

ADDRESS INQUIRIES TO:
James R. West, IEED Grant Manager
(See e-mail address above.)

BUREAU OF INDIAN EDUCATION   [950]
12220 Sunrise Valley Drive
Reston, VA 20191
(703) 390-6697
E-mail: katherine.campbell@bie.edu
Web Site: www.bie.edu

FOUNDED: 1824

AREAS OF INTEREST:
Elementary and secondary education tribal colleges.

NAME(S) OF PROGRAMS:
- **Higher Education Grant Program for American Indians and Alaska Natives**

TYPE:
Fellowships; Scholarships.

YEAR PROGRAM STARTED: 1949

PURPOSE:
To provide financial aid to eligible Indian students enabling them to attend accredited institutions of higher education.

LEGAL BASIS:
Snyder Act.

ELIGIBILITY:
Applicant must be a member of a tribe eligible for services from the Bureau, enrolled or accepted for enrollment in an accredited college and have financial need as determined by the institution's financial aid office.

FINANCIAL DATA:
The grants are intended to supplement the financial aid package prepared by the educational institution's financial aid officer. The grant meets the unmet need portion of the package.
Amount of support per award: Varies.
Total amount of support: Varies.
Matching fund requirements: Meets the unmet need portion of the institution's financial aid package.

CO-OP FUNDING PROGRAMS: Other donor's funding programs are a part of the financial aid package.

NO. MOST RECENT APPLICANTS: 20,000.

NO. AWARDS: 15,000.

APPLICATION INFO:
Candidates should request an application from a home agency or tribal Higher Education Grant Program (HEGP). Contact the BIA/Tribal census office to obtain a Certificate of Degree of Indian Blood (CDIB) and tribal enrollment and submit with the application. Write to the admissions office of the chosen school for an application. Request a financial aid packet from the school's Financial Aid Officer, who will prepare a financial aid package based on the applicant's need. Then submit all these forms to the appropriate offices well in advance of the deadline.
Duration: One academic year. Must renew annually.
Deadline: Varies.

ADDRESS INQUIRIES TO:
Home agency or tribally administered Higher Education Grant Program

CATCHING THE DREAM   [951]
8200 Mountain Road, N.E.
Suite 103
Albuquerque, NM 87110
(505) 262-2351
Fax: (505) 262-0534
E-mail: NScholarsh@aol.com
Web Site: www.catchingthedream.org

FOUNDED: 1986

AREAS OF INTEREST:
Scholarships for Native college students and improvement of Indian schools and postsecondary education for Native American students in the fields of math, engineering, science, business, education and computers.

CONSULTING OR VOLUNTEER SERVICES:
The Fund assists Native American students who need help in locating other sources of funding and provides fund-raising, management training, conferences, and seminars.

NAME(S) OF PROGRAMS:
- **Math and Science Teaching (MAST)**
- **MESBEC (Math, Engineering, Science, Business, Education and Computers) Program**
- **Native American Leadership in Education (NALE) Program**
- **Reading Award Program (RAP)**
- **Tribal Business Management (TBM) Program**

TYPE:
Conferences/seminars; Development grants; Grants-in-aid; Scholarships; Technical assistance. CTD also works to improve Indian schools through a program of grants and technical assistance. This work has led to the development of 40 Exemplary Programs in Indian education since 1988. The annual Exemplary Institute is a meeting of these Exemplary Programs, where they teach other people how to develop similar programs.

MAST program makes grants of $5,000 to Indian high schools to improve their math and science teaching.

MESBEC Program consists of competitive scholarships for high-potential Native Americans studying in math, engineering, science, business, education and computers.

NALE Program consists of competitive scholarships for high-potential paraprofessional Native Americans who plan to complete their degrees and obtain credentials as teachers, counselors or administrators.

RAP makes grants to Indian schools to improve the reading ability of their students.

Tribal Business Management (TBM) Program consists of competitive scholarships for Native students in all fields of business.

YEAR PROGRAM STARTED: 1986

PURPOSE:
To help tribes prepare young people to work in the fields which are critical for economic, social, business and political development in Indian Country.

LEGAL BASIS:
Nonprofit organization.

ELIGIBILITY:
Applicants must be at least one-quarter blood member of a federally recognized, state recognized or terminated Indian tribe. They must have high potential for the field of study and work for which they are preparing. They must attend an accredited U.S. college or university. They must have clear goals in mind and have done some work toward accomplishing these goals. The goals must be related to the betterment of Indian people or the betterment of an Indian tribe or community. Progress toward accomplishing a goal may be demonstrated by study, by work, by volunteer work or by other means.

Students with no clear goals are discouraged from applying. Normally, successful applicants will plan to earn a four-year degree or a graduate degree. In a few cases, associate degrees are approved. Applicants must apply for all other sources of funding for which they are eligible, including private scholarship sources, corporate traineeships, federal funds, loans, jobs, grants and so forth.

Students can contact CTD up to three years in advance.

GEOG. RESTRICTIONS: United States.

FINANCIAL DATA:
Amount of support per award: $500 to $5,000.
Total amount of support: Approximately $202,000 for the year 2017-18.

NO. AWARDS: Varies by program.

APPLICATION INFO:
Contact Catching the Dream.
Duration: Until completion of degree.
Deadline: March 15 for summer school. September 15 for winter quarter and spring semester. April 30 for fall semester.

PUBLICATIONS:
The National Indian Grant Directory; Reading for College; Racism in Indian Country; The Secret of No Face; Basic Fund Raising; How to Write Winning Proposals; Literacy in Indian Country.

IRS I.D.: 85-0360858

BOARD OF DIRECTORS:
James Lujan, President
Dr. Lester Sandoval, Vice President
John Tohtsoni, Jr., Treasurer
Jodie Palmer, Secretary
Dr. Dean Chavers
Ms. Lynn Okon Scholnick

CHEROKEE NATION   [952]
P.O. Box 948
Tahlequah, OK 74465
(918) 453-5000
(918) 453-5465
Fax: (918) 458-6286
E-mail: collegeresources@cherokee.org
Web Site: www.cherokee.org

FOUNDED: 1904

AREAS OF INTEREST:
Planning and development (individual and tribal), health, education and welfare.

CONSULTING OR VOLUNTEER SERVICES:
Tribal government administration consultants and volunteers in all interest areas available to eligible tribal members.

NAME(S) OF PROGRAMS:
● **College Resource Center**

TYPE:
Project/program grants; Scholarships; Technical assistance. Financial and other support through all programs to eligible tribal members.

YEAR PROGRAM STARTED: 1964

PURPOSE:
To serve its tribes and members in the areas indicated.

LEGAL BASIS:
Federally recognized Indian tribe.

ELIGIBILITY:
Tribal membership is required.

GEOG. RESTRICTIONS: Primarily northeast Oklahoma.

FINANCIAL DATA:
Amount of support per award: Varies.
Total amount of support: Varies.

APPLICATION INFO:
Guidelines and application form are available on the web site.
Duration: Varies.
Deadline: Varies.

ADDRESS INQUIRIES TO:
College Resource Center
(See e-mail address above.)

FIRST NATIONS DEVELOPMENT INSTITUTE [953]
2432 Main Street, Second Floor
Longmont, CO 80501
(303) 774-7836
Fax: (303) 774-7841
E-mail: grantmaking@firstnations.org
Web Site: www.firstnations.org

FOUNDED: 1980

AREAS OF INTEREST:
Nourishing Native foods and health, investing in Native youth, achieving Native financial empowerment, strengthening tribal and community institutions, stewarding native lands, and advancing household and community asset building strategies.

CONSULTING OR VOLUNTEER SERVICES:
Yes.

TYPE:
Program development grants. First Nations works to improve economic conditions for Native Americans through technical assistance and training, advocacy and policy, and direct financial grants in the six key areas of interest.

YEAR PROGRAM STARTED: 1993

PURPOSE:
To strengthen American Indian economies to support healthy Native communities.

LEGAL BASIS:
Nonprofit organization.

ELIGIBILITY:
Eligible organizations include:
(1) fiscally sponsored Native community organizations;
(2) Native controlled nonprofit organizations;

(3) Native 7871 organizations and;
(4) Federal and state recognized tribal government and tribal government programs.

Grants are not made to individuals for for-profit businesses, programs serving exclusively urban Native communities, programs serving Natives but not controlled by a majority of Natives, for-profit Native consulting firms, for-profit Native businesses except those associated with a nonprofit Native enterprise, or religious organizations (except for traditional Native American spiritual programs).

GEOG. RESTRICTIONS: United States and its territories.

FINANCIAL DATA:
Amount of support per award: Varies.
Total amount of support: Varies.

NO. MOST RECENT APPLICANTS: 358.

NO. AWARDS: 136 program grants and 291 COVID-19 Emergency Response Fund grants for the year 2020.

APPLICATION INFO:
Application must be made online. Complete information is available on the web site.
Duration: Typically one year.
Deadline: Varies.

PUBLICATIONS:
List of publications; annual report.

IRS I.D.: 54-1254491

ADDRESS INQUIRIES TO:
Jacque Demko, Grants Officer
(See address above.)

NATIONAL SOCIETY DAUGHTERS OF THE AMERICAN REVOLUTION
1776 D Street, N.W.
Washington, DC 20006-5303
(202) 879-3263
E-mail: scholarships@nsdar.org
Web Site: www.dar.org

TYPE:
Scholarships. Intended to help Native American college/university and technical school students at the undergraduate or graduate level.

See entry 1538 for full listing.

NATIONAL SOCIETY DAUGHTERS OF THE AMERICAN REVOLUTION
1776 D Street, N.W.
Washington, DC 20006-5303
(202) 879-3263
E-mail: scholarships@nsdar.org
Web Site: www.dar.org

TYPE:
Scholarships. Intended to help Native American students enrolled full-time at a two- or four-year college or university.

See entry 1539 for full listing.

THE NEWBERRY LIBRARY [954]
Newberry Institute for Research and Education
60 West Walton Street
Chicago, IL 60610
(312) 255-3666
E-mail: research@newberry.org
Web Site: www.newberry.org/fellowships

AREAS OF INTEREST:
Native American women, humanities and social sciences.

NAME(S) OF PROGRAMS:
● **Frances C. Allen Fellowship**

TYPE:
Fellowships; Visiting scholars. The Frances C. Allen Fellowship supports women of American Indian heritage. Recipients are expected to work closely with members of the D'Arcy McNickle Center for American Indian and Indigenous Studies during their residency.

PURPOSE:
To encourage study by Native American women of the humanities and social sciences.

LEGAL BASIS:
Private research library.

ELIGIBILITY:
Preference is given to non-tenured women working in any graduate or pre-professional field. This fellowship is open to all fields of study.

FINANCIAL DATA:
Amount of support per award: $3,000 per month stipend.

NO. MOST RECENT APPLICANTS: 5.

NO. AWARDS: 1 to 2.

APPLICATION INFO:
Applications must be submitted through the online webform.
Duration: One to two months.
Deadline: December 15.

STAFF:
Keelin Burke, Director of Fellowships and Academic Programs

ADDRESS INQUIRIES TO:
See e-mail address above.

*SPECIAL STIPULATIONS:
Allen Fellows are expected to spend a significant part of their tenure in residence at the D'Arcy McNickle Center for American Indian and Indigenous Studies.

RUNNING STRONG FOR AMERICAN INDIAN YOUTH [955]
8301 Richmond Highway
Alexandria, VA 22309
(703) 317-9881
Fax: (703) 659-6231
E-mail: info@indianyouth.org
Web Site: www.indianyouth.org

FOUNDED: 1986

AREAS OF INTEREST:
Native Americans.

TYPE:
Capital grants; Challenge/matching grants; General operating grants; Project/program grants; Seed money grants.

YEAR PROGRAM STARTED: 1986

PURPOSE:
To help American Indian people meet their immediate survival needs - food, water and shelter - while implementing and supporting programs designed to create opportunities for self-sufficiency and self-esteem, particularly for tribal youth.

ELIGIBILITY:
No grants are made to individuals or fund-raising events. Grants made only to programs that support Native Americans.

GEOG. RESTRICTIONS: United States.

FINANCIAL DATA:
Amount of support per award: Up to $5,000 for new applicants.
Total amount of support: Varies.

NO. AWARDS: Varies.

APPLICATION INFO:
E-mail or call for grant guidelines.
Duration: Up to five years. Must reapply each year.

PUBLICATIONS:
Annual report; application guidelines.

IRS I.D.: 54-1594578

ADDRESS INQUIRIES TO:
Lauren Haas Finkelstein
Executive Director
(See address above.)

U.S. DEPARTMENT OF EDUCATION   [956]
Office of Indian Education
400 Maryland Avenue, S.W.
LBJ Building, 3W101
Washington, DC 20202-6335
(202) 260-3774
Fax: (202) 205-0606
E-mail: indian.education@ed.gov
Web Site: www2.ed.gov/programs/indianformula/index.html

NAME(S) OF PROGRAMS:
● **Indian Education-Formula Grants to Local Education Agencies (LEAs)**

TYPE:
Formula grants. Grants to provide financial assistance to LEAs and tribal schools to address the unique cultural, language and educationally related academic needs of American Indian and Alaska Native students, including preschool children.

LEGAL BASIS:
Public Law 92-318, Title IV, Part A, as amended (25 U.S.C. 2601-2606, 2651).

ELIGIBILITY:
Local educational agencies which have at least 10 Indian children or in which Indians constitute at least 25% of the total enrollment may apply. However, these enrollment requirements do not apply to an LEA in Alaska, California or Oklahoma that serves Indian children or an LEA on, or in proximity to, an Indian reservation. An Indian tribe or an organization controlled or sanctioned by an Indian tribal government and that operates a school for children of that tribe is eligible if that school provides its students an educational program that meets the standards established by the Bureau of Indian Affairs (BIA) or is operated by that tribe or organization under a contract with the BIA.

FINANCIAL DATA:
Amount of support per award: Varies.
Total amount of support: Varies.

NO. AWARDS: Varies.

APPLICATION INFO:
Application instructions and forms are available upon request.
Duration: One year, July 1 to June 30.
Deadline: Varies.

ADDRESS INQUIRIES TO:
Indian Education Programs
(See address above.)

U.S. DEPARTMENT OF HEALTH AND HUMAN SERVICES   [957]
Mary E. Switzer Memorial Building
Room 4126
330 C Street, S.W.
Washington, DC 20416
(877) 922-9262 (Help Desk)
Fax: (202) 690-8145
E-mail: anacomments@acf.hhs.gov
Web Site: www.acf.hhs.gov/ana

FOUNDED: 1974

AREAS OF INTEREST:
General community programming, training and technical assistance and research, demonstration and evaluation.

NAME(S) OF PROGRAMS:
● **Environmental Regulatory Enhancement**
● **Native Languages**
● **Social and Economic Development Strategies (SEDS) for Native Americans**

TYPE:
Demonstration grants; Development grants; Project/program grants; Research grants; Seed money grants; Technical assistance; Training grants. Financial Assistance grants may be used for such purposes as, but not limited to, Governance Projects, development of codes and ordinances and status clarification activities; Economic Development Projects, to promote business starts for Native-owned businesses and improve Native American housing management; and Social Development Projects, to assume local control of planning and delivering social services in Native American communities, developing local models related to comprehensive planning and delivery of social services and developing or coordinating activities with state-funded projects in decreasing the incidence of child abuse, neglect and fetal alcohol syndrome.

YEAR PROGRAM STARTED: 1973

PURPOSE:
To support projects that improve social and economic conditions of Native Americans within their communities and increase the effectiveness of Indian Tribes and Native American organizations in meeting their economic and social goals.

LEGAL BASIS:
Native American Programs Act of 1974, as amended, Public Law 93-644; Older Americans Act Amendments of 1987, Title V, Public Law 100-175; Indian Reorganization Act Amendments, Section 215, Public Law 100-581; Older Americans Act Amendments of 1992, Title VIII, Public Law 102-375; 42 U.S.C. 2991 et. seq.

ELIGIBILITY:
Governing bodies of Indian tribes, Alaskan Native villages and regional associations established by the Alaska Native Claims Settlement Act, Indian and Alaska Native Organizations in urban or rural nonreservation areas, public and nonprofit agencies serving Native Hawaiians and other Native American Pacific Islanders which include the Native peoples from Guam, American Samoa, Palau or the Commonwealth of the Northern Mariana Islands. The populations served may be located on those islands or in the U.S.

GEOG. RESTRICTIONS: United States.

FINANCIAL DATA:
Amount of support per award: Approximately $250,000 average.
Total amount of support: Approximately $38,500,000 annually.
Matching fund requirements: A matching share of 20% is required unless waived in accordance with criteria which is published in 45 CFR, Part 1336.50. This program has maintenance of effort requirements.

NO. AWARDS: 58 for the year 2019.

APPLICATION INFO:
In order to apply for a grant, an organization must complete the grants.gov registration process.
Duration: One year with possibility of multiyear funding.
Deadline: Varies.

STAFF:
Jeannie Hovland, Commissioner

ADDRESS INQUIRIES TO:
Administration for Native Americans
(See address above.)

THE MORRIS K. UDALL AND STEWART L. UDALL FOUNDATION   [958]
130 South Scott Avenue
Tucson, AZ 85701
(520) 901-8564
Fax: (520) 901-8570
E-mail: curley@udall.gov
Web Site: www.udall.gov

FOUNDED: 1992

AREAS OF INTEREST:
Educating young Americans in our nation's heritage, environmental studies, Native American affairs and public policy conflict resolution.

NAME(S) OF PROGRAMS:
● **Congressional Internships**

TYPE:
Internships. Congressional Internships: Native American college, graduate and law students work in congressional offices and federal agencies to gain a firsthand understanding of the federal government. The Foundation arranges meetings with elected officials, staff at Native American advocacy and public interest organizations, and Native American professionals in Washington, DC. They also take field trips and meet with congressional members, agency heads and cabinet secretaries.

YEAR PROGRAM STARTED: 1996

PURPOSE:
To educate a new generation of Americans to preserve and protect their national heritage through studies in the environment, Native American health and tribal policy and effective public policy conflict resolution.

LEGAL BASIS:
The Foundation is an executive branch agency. The President of the U.S. appoints its board of trustees with the advice and consent of the U.S. Senate.

ELIGIBILITY:
Interns will be selected by an independent committee. Applicants must demonstrate a commitment to learning about the federal government. They must be self-motivated and interested in taking advantage of the rich and diverse resources available to them in

Washington, DC. Additionally, candidates for the internship program must:
(1) be an enrolled member of a recognized tribe or state-recognized tribe;
(2) be a college junior, senior, graduate student, law student or graduating from a tribal college;
(3) have a minimum 3.0 grade point average or a "B" average and;
(4) have an interest in tribal government and policy.

FINANCIAL DATA:
Interns are provided with airfare to and from Washington, DC, lodging convenient to Capitol Hill, and a daily allowance sufficient for meals, transportation and incidentals.
Amount of support per award: $1,200 educational stipend to be paid at the conclusion of the internship.

NO. MOST RECENT APPLICANTS: 50.

NO. AWARDS: 12.

APPLICATION INFO:
Application information is available on the web site.
Duration: 10 weeks.
Deadline: January 31 (postmark).

STAFF:
Jason Curley, Program Manager

ADDRESS INQUIRIES TO:
Jason Curley, Program Manager
(See address above.)

UNITED SOUTH AND EASTERN TRIBES, INC. [959]
711 Stewarts Ferry Pike
Suite 100
Nashville, TN 37214
(615) 872-7900
Fax: (615) 872-7417
E-mail: lestolt@usetinc.org
Web Site: www.usetinc.org

FOUNDED: 1969

AREAS OF INTEREST:
Indian tribes.

TYPE:
Scholarships.

PURPOSE:
To enhance the development of Indian Tribes; to improve the capabilities of Tribal governments; to assist the member Tribes and their governments in dealing effectively with public policy issues and in serving the broad needs of Indian people.

ELIGIBILITY:
Supplemental monies are awarded to USET area Indian students who are enrolled members of one of the 33 USET member Tribal Nations.

Must be an Indian student that meets the following criteria:
(1) satisfactory scholastic standing and;
(2) current enrollment or acceptance in a postsecondary educational institution.

FINANCIAL DATA:
Amount of support per award: Selected undergraduate applicants receive an equal amount in any award period in increments of no less than $750. In addition, selected graduate applicants receive an equal amount in any award period in increments of no less than $1,000.
Total amount of support: Varies.

NO. MOST RECENT APPLICANTS: 36.

NO. AWARDS: 22.

APPLICATION INFO:
Contact the Organization for application procedures. Information is also available online.
Duration: Annual supplemental scholarship. Must reapply for additional term.
Deadline: January 15.

ADDRESS INQUIRIES TO:
USET Scholarship Fund
Attn: Loren Estolt
(See address above.)

UNIVERSITY OF CALIFORNIA, LOS ANGELES [960]
American Indian Studies Center
UCLA - 3220 Campbell Hall, Box 951548
Los Angeles, CA 90095-1548
(310) 825-7315
Fax: (310) 206-7060
E-mail: aisc@ucla.edu
Web Site: www.aisc.ucla.edu

FOUNDED: 1970

AREAS OF INTEREST:
American Indian studies and related topics in policy, education, economics, culture and community.

NAME(S) OF PROGRAMS:
● **Institute of American Cultures Grant**

TYPE:
Fellowships; Research grants; Visiting scholars.

YEAR PROGRAM STARTED: 1969

PURPOSE:
To conduct research in Native American Studies.

LEGAL BASIS:
University research organization; nonprofit organization.

ELIGIBILITY:
Applicants must be citizens or permanent residents of the U.S. and hold a Ph.D. from an accredited college or university (or, in the case of the arts, an appropriate terminal degree) in a relevant field at the time of appointment. UCLA faculty, staff and currently enrolled students are not eligible to apply.

FINANCIAL DATA:
Visiting Researchers may use funds to supplement sabbatical support for a total that does not exceed the candidate's current institutional salary. Visiting Researchers will be paid through their home institutions and will be expected to continue their health benefits through that source as well. Awardees may receive up to $4,000 in research support (through reimbursement of research expenses).
Amount of support per award: Maximum stipend $35,000.
Total amount of support: Varies.

APPLICATION INFO:
Application information is available on the web site.
Duration: Nine to 12 months. Nonrenewable.
Deadline: Varies.

PUBLICATIONS:
American Indian Culture and Research Journal; brochures; books.

IRS I.D.: 95-6006143

STAFF:
Shannon Speed, Director
Pam Grieman, Assistant Director

ADDRESS INQUIRIES TO:
AISC Coordinator
(See address above.)

WASHINGTON STUDENT ACHIEVEMENT COUNCIL [961]
American Indian Endowed Scholarship
917 Lakeridge Way
Olympia, WA 98502
(360) 753-7843
Fax: (360) 704-6243
E-mail: aies@wsac.wa.gov
Web Site: wsac.wa.gov/american-indian-endowed-scholarship

AREAS OF INTEREST:
Student financial aid.

NAME(S) OF PROGRAMS:
● **American Indian Endowed Scholarship Program**

TYPE:
Scholarships.

YEAR PROGRAM STARTED: 1993

PURPOSE:
To create an educational opportunity for students with close social and cultural ties to the American Indian community to pursue undergraduate and graduate studies who might not be able otherwise to attend and graduate from higher education institutions in Washington state.

LEGAL BASIS:
Government agency.

ELIGIBILITY:
Applicants must be students of an in-state institution with close social and cultural ties to the American Indian community in the state. Must be a resident of the state of Washington and in financial need. Applicant must have applied for financial aid via FAFSA. Applicant must intend to return service to the state Native American community. Academic merit is also a consideration.

FINANCIAL DATA:
Amount of support per award: $500 to $2,000.
Total amount of support: Varies.

APPLICATION INFO:
Application includes statement of commitment to return service to Washington American Indian communities, statement of close social and cultural ties, three letters of recommendation, completed application and release of information form and transcripts.
Duration: One year. Must reapply for renewal for a maximum of four additional years.
Deadline: February 1. Announcement will be made by late Spring.

ADDRESS INQUIRIES TO:
Ann Voyles, Program Associate
American Indian Endowed Scholarship
P.O. Box 43430
Olympia, WA 98504-3430
E-mail: aies@wsac.wa.gov

Spanish-speaking

CONGRESSIONAL HISPANIC CAUCUS INSTITUTE [962]

1128 16th Street, N.W.
Washington, DC 20036
(202) 543-1771
Fax: (202) 546-2143
E-mail: programs@chci.org
Web Site: www.chci.org

FOUNDED: 1978

AREAS OF INTEREST:
Leadership training in the legislative process for promising Latino undergraduates.

NAME(S) OF PROGRAMS:
● **CHCI Congressional Internship**

TYPE:
Internships. Internships provide college students with a paid work placement in a congressional office or federal agency for a period of 12 weeks (Spring and Fall Programs) or 10 weeks (Summer Program), as well as extensive professional development and leadership trainings.

PURPOSE:
To expose young Latinos to the legislative process and to strengthen their professional leadership skills, ultimately promoting the presence of Latinos on Capitol Hill and in federal agencies.

ELIGIBILITY:
Students must currently be enrolled full-time and working towards their undergraduate degree.

Student must display:
(1) high academic achievement (preference of 3.0 grade point average or higher);
(2) evidence of leadership skills and potential for leadership growth;
(3) demonstrated commitment to public service-oriented activities and;
(4) superior analytical skills, outstanding oral and written communication skills.

Applicants must be U.S. citizens, lawful permanent residents, asylees, or individuals who are lawfully authorized to work full-time without restriction for any U.S. employer and who, at the time of application, possess lawful evidence of employment authorization.

GEOG. RESTRICTIONS: United States.

FINANCIAL DATA:
Internship includes stipend, domestic round-trip transportation to Washington, DC, housing (all expenses covered) and academic credit if eligible.

Amount of support per award: Spring and Fall Programs: $3,750 stipend; Summer Program: $3,125.

NO. AWARDS: 70 per year.

APPLICATION INFO:
A complete application consists of a one-page PDF resume, curriculum vitae, most recent unofficial transcript, and two letters of recommendation.

Duration: Spring and Fall Programs: 12 weeks; Summer Program: 10 weeks. Internships are not renewable.

Deadline: Spring Program: October 21. Fall Program: February 21. Summer Program: December 1.

CONGRESSIONAL HISPANIC CAUCUS INSTITUTE [963]

1128 16th Street, N.W.
Washington, DC 20036
(202) 543-1771
(202) 548-8796
Fax: (202) 546-8799
E-mail: programs@chci.org
Web Site: chci.org

FOUNDED: 1978

AREAS OF INTEREST:
Higher education, secondary education, health, housing, law, and public policy.

NAME(S) OF PROGRAMS:
● **CHCI Graduate Fellowship Program**
● **CHCI Public Policy Fellowship**

TYPE:
Fellowships. Graduate Fellowship Program offers exceptional Latinos who have earned a graduate degree or higher related to a chosen policy issue area within three years of program start date unparalleled exposure to hands-on experience in public policy.

Public Policy Fellowship offers talented Latinos who have earned a Bachelor's degree within two years of the program start date the opportunity to gain hands-on experience at the national level in public policy.

PURPOSE:
To help increase opportunities for Hispanics to participate in and contribute to the American policymaking process.

ELIGIBILITY:
Applicants must:
(1) demonstrate high academic achievement (preference of 3.0 grade point average or higher);
(2) show evidence of leadership skills and potential for leadership growth;
(3) demonstrate commitment to public service-oriented activities and;
(4) possess superior analytical skills, outstanding oral and written communication skills.

Graduate Fellowship Program applicants must have completed a Master's degree or postgraduate degree prior to the program start date.

Public Policy Fellowship applicants must have earned a Bachelor's degree within two years of the program start date.

Applicants must be U.S. citizens, lawful permanent residents, asylees, or individuals who are lawfully authorized to work full-time without restriction for any U.S. employer and who, at the time of application, possess lawful evidence of employment authorization.

GEOG. RESTRICTIONS: United States.

FINANCIAL DATA:
Amount of support per award: CHCI Graduate Fellowship Program: Stipend of $29,700; CHCI Public Policy Fellowship: Stipend of $26,100.

APPLICATION INFO:
A complete application consists of a one-page PDF resume, curriculum vitae, most recent unofficial transcript, and a letter of recommendation.

Duration: Nine months: Late August to late May.

Deadline: January 30.

FLORIDA DEPARTMENT OF EDUCATION [964]

Office of Student Financial Assistance
325 West Gaines Street, Suite 1314
Tallahassee, FL 32399-0400
(888) 827-2004
Fax: (850) 487-1809
E-mail: osfa@fldoe.org
Web Site: www.floridastudentfinancialaidsg.org

NAME(S) OF PROGRAMS:
● **Jose Marti Scholarship Challenge Grant Fund**

TYPE:
Challenge/matching grants; Grants-in-aid. Jose Marti Scholarship Challenge Grant Fund is a need-based merit scholarship that provides financial assistance to eligible students of Hispanic origin who will attend Florida public or eligible private institutions.

YEAR PROGRAM STARTED: 1986

PURPOSE:
To provide financial assistance to Hispanic-American high school seniors and graduate students in Florida.

LEGAL BASIS:
Florida Department of Education.

ELIGIBILITY:
Applicants for undergraduate study must apply during their senior year of high school. Graduate students may apply; however, priority for the scholarship is given to graduating high school seniors.

For the applying student, initial eligibility requirements to receive funding are as follows:
(1) be a Florida resident and a U.S. citizen or eligible noncitizen; a student's residency and citizenship status are determined by the postsecondary institution; consult the financial aid office or admissions office of the institution the student plans to attend for questions;
(2) not owe a repayment or be in default under any state or federal grant, loan or scholarship program unless satisfactory arrangements to repay have been made;
(3) be of Spanish culture, born in or having a natural parent who was born in either Mexico, or a Hispanic country of the Caribbean, Central or South America, regardless of race;
(4) have earned, by the end of the seventh semester, a minimum unweighted cumulative grade point average of 3.0 on a 4.0 scale in high school for an undergraduate scholarship, or a 3.0 institutional cumulative grade point average for undergraduate college work if applying for a graduate-level scholarship;
(5) enroll as a degree-seeking student at an eligible postsecondary institution and enroll each academic term for a minimum of 12 credit hours for undergraduate study or nine credit hours for graduate study and;
(6) demonstrate a minimum $2,000 in financial need by timely completing and submitting the FAFSA.

GEOG. RESTRICTIONS: Florida.

FINANCIAL DATA:
Amount of support per award: Typically $2,000.

Total amount of support: $124,000 for the year 2019-20.

NO. MOST RECENT APPLICANTS: 28,482 for the year 2019-20.

NO. AWARDS: 65 for the year 2019-20.

APPLICATION INFO:
Detailed program information can be found on the web site.

Duration: One academic year.

Deadline: For undergraduate study, submit a fully completed error-free Florida Financial Aid Application during the student's last year in high school by April 1. For graduate study, submit a fully completed error-free Florida Financial Aid Application by April 1 prior to the year of graduate study.

ADDRESS INQUIRIES TO:
State Scholarship and Grant Programs
(See address above.)

THE HISPANIC NATIONAL BAR FOUNDATION

1900 K Street, N.W.
Suite 100
Washington, DC 20006
(786) 340-9991
E-mail: info@hnbf.org
Web Site: www.hnbf.org

TYPE:
Conferences/seminars; Training grants. Nine-day program held by the Foundation in Washington, DC which provides Latino high school students with the opportunity to learn more about the legal profession. The Summer Law Institute offers students the chance to come to the nation's capital and learn more about the college application process, meet influential Latino leaders, and tour national monuments and various government agencies.

See entry 1778 for full listing.

HISPANIC SCHOLARSHIP FUND [965]

1411 West 190th Street
Suite 700
Gardena, CA 90248
(877) 473-4636
(310) 975-3700
Fax: (310) 349-3328
E-mail: info@hsf.net
scholar1@hsf.net
Web Site: www.hsf.net

FOUNDED: 1975

AREAS OF INTEREST:
College scholarships for Hispanic American students.

NAME(S) OF PROGRAMS:
● **General College Scholarship Program**

TYPE:
Scholarships. Awarded to Hispanic community college, undergraduate and graduate students.

YEAR PROGRAM STARTED: 1975

PURPOSE:
To strengthen America by generating support for the educational advancement of Hispanics by increasing the rate of Hispanics earning a college degree.

LEGAL BASIS:
Nonprofit 501(c)(3) organization.

ELIGIBILITY:
Applicant must:
(1) be of Hispanic heritage;
(2) be a U.S. citizen or legal permanent resident;
(3) have a minimum 3.0 cumulative grade

point average (on a 4.0 scale) and;
(4) apply for federal financial aid using FAFSA.

FINANCIAL DATA:
Amount of support per award: $500 to $5,000.

Total amount of support: Approximately $500,000,000.

NO. MOST RECENT APPLICANTS: 50,000.

NO. AWARDS: 1,000.

APPLICATION INFO:
Electronic application only; forms available at the web site.

Duration: Students may reapply until they obtain a degree, providing they satisfy full-time enrollment.

Deadline: February 15.

PUBLICATIONS:
Annual report; newsletter.

IRS I.D.: 52-1051044

BOARD OF DIRECTORS:
Gene Camarena, Chairperson
Elizabeth Oliver-Farrow, Vice Chairperson
Anthony Salcido, Treasurer
Fidel A. Vargas, President and Chief Executive Officer
Daniel J. Acosta
Michael J. Bender
Walter Dolhare
Nely Galan
Phillip Hyun
James McNamara
Angel Luis Morales
Ida Nieto
Bea Perez
Adam Rodriguez
Gina Rodriguez
Maria Elena Salinas
Peggy Turner
Cesar Vargas

UCLA CHICANO STUDIES RESEARCH CENTER [966]

193 Haines Hall
Box 951544
Los Angeles, CA 90095
(310) 825-2363
Fax: (310) 206-1784
E-mail: csrcinfo@chicano.ucla.edu
Web Site: www.chicano.ucla.edu
www.iac.ucla.edu

FOUNDED: 1969

AREAS OF INTEREST:
Chicano Studies and relevant fields.

NAME(S) OF PROGRAMS:
● **Institute of American Cultures Visiting Research Scholar Program in Ethnic Studies**

TYPE:
Fellowships; Visiting scholars.

YEAR PROGRAM STARTED: 1976

PURPOSE:
To foster learning and scholarship pertaining to the Chicano-Latino community.

LEGAL BASIS:
University program.

ELIGIBILITY:
Applicant must be a U.S. citizen or permanent resident. At the time of appointment, applicant must hold a Ph.D. from an accredited college or university, or in the case of the arts, an appropriate terminal degree.

UCLA faculty, staff and currently enrolled students are not eligible to apply.

FINANCIAL DATA:
Amount of support per award: Up to $35,000 to home institution and up to $4,000 research grant.

Total amount of support: Up to $39,000.

NO. AWARDS: 1.

APPLICATION INFO:
Application information available upon request.

Duration: Up to nine months.

Deadline: January. Notification in March.

OFFICERS:
Chon A. Noriega, Director

ADDRESS INQUIRIES TO:
Grants and Fellowships Coordinator
(See address above.)

Women

THE ISABEL ALLENDE FOUNDATION [967]

116 Caledonia Street
Sausalito, CA 94965
(415) 289-0992
E-mail: lori@isabelallende.com
Web Site: www.isabelallendefoundation.org

FOUNDED: 1996

AREAS OF INTEREST:
Reproductive rights, economic independence and freedom from violence for women and girls.

NAME(S) OF PROGRAMS:
● **Esperanza Grants**

TYPE:
Project/program grants. Promotes and preserves the fundamental rights of women and children to be empowered and protected.

PURPOSE:
To invest in the power of women and girls to secure reproductive rights, economic independence and freedom from violence.

ELIGIBILITY:
Nonprofit 501(c)(3) grassroots organizations and equivalent international organizations that benefit the San Francisco Bay area and/or Chile are eligible to apply. No grants to individuals.

The Foundation does not fund capital campaigns, individual trips or tours, conferences or events, and projects that benefit political, religious, and/or military organizations.

GEOG. RESTRICTIONS: San Francisco Bay area, California and Chile.

FINANCIAL DATA:
Amount of support per award: Typically $1,000 to $10,000.

Total amount of support: Varies.

APPLICATION INFO:
New organization proposals are not being accepted at this time. Current grantees may apply for renewal and will receive instructions from the Foundation on how to apply.

Duration: One year. Must submit report for renewal.

Deadline: Varies.

ADDRESS INQUIRIES TO:
Lori Barra, Executive Director
(See address above.)

AMERICAN ASSOCIATION OF UNIVERSITY WOMEN [968]
1310 L Street, N.W.
Suite 1000
Washington, DC 20005
E-mail: fellowships@aauw.org
Web Site: www.aauw.org

FOUNDED: 1888

AREAS OF INTEREST:
Advancement of educational and professional opportunities for women in the U.S.

NAME(S) OF PROGRAMS:
● **AAUW Selected Professions Fellowships**

TYPE:
Fellowships. Awarded to women who are U.S. citizens or permanent residents who are pursuing full-time study in a Master's or professional degree program in which women are underrepresented, including STEM, law, business and medicine.

YEAR PROGRAM STARTED: 1970

PURPOSE:
To encourage women's participation in fields where they have been traditionally underrepresented.

ELIGIBILITY:
The Association awards Selected Professions Fellowships to women who are citizens or permanent residents of the U.S. who have achieved high standards of academic excellence and show promise of distinction in their respective fields. Applicants must be full-time students at an accredited U.S. institution during the fellowship year, and should be pursuing a course of study in the U.S. over the full academic year. Priority is given to women who do not already hold a Master's or first professional degree.

Selected Professions Fellowships are awarded for the following Master's programs:
(1) Architecture;
(2) Computer/information sciences;
(3) Engineering and;
(4) Mathematics/statistics.

Fellowships in the following degree programs are restricted to women of color, who have been underrepresented in these fields:
(1) Master's in business administration - applicants may apply for second year of study only;
(2) Law - applicants may apply for third year of study only and;
(3) Doctorate in medicine - applicants may apply for third or fourth year of study only.

GEOG. RESTRICTIONS: United States.

FINANCIAL DATA:
Amount of support per award: $5,000 to $18,000.

APPLICATION INFO:
Applicant must create an account through the "apply now" link to the vendor site located on the funding opportunity page.
Deadline: December 1.

AMERICAN ASSOCIATION OF UNIVERSITY WOMEN [969]
1310 L Street, N.W.
Suite 1000
Washington, DC 20005
E-mail: fellowships@aauw.org
Web Site: www.aauw.org

FOUNDED: 1888

AREAS OF INTEREST:
Advancement of educational and professional opportunities for women in the U.S. and around the globe.

NAME(S) OF PROGRAMS:
● **Research Publication Grants in Engineering, Medicine and Science**

TYPE:
Research grants.

PURPOSE:
To help women overcome gender stereotypes and bias by funding research projects that will culminate in scholarly publications.

ELIGIBILITY:
Research publication grants are open to scholars who identify as women who are conducting basic research in engineering, medicine or the physical or biological sciences and have a Doctorate degree in one of those fields. The grantee must publish their research in a scholarly publication and be listed as the primary author.

Grants are not open to previous recipients of any AAUW national fellowship or grant (not including branch or local awards or Community Action Grants).

FINANCIAL DATA:
Amount of support per award: $10,000 to $35,000.

APPLICATION INFO:
Applicant must create an account through the "apply now" link to the vendor site located on the funding opportunity page.
Deadline: December 1.

ADDRESS INQUIRIES TO:
E-mail: aauw@applyists.com

AMERICAN ASSOCIATION OF UNIVERSITY WOMEN [970]
1310 L Street, N.W.
Suite 1000
Washington, DC 20005
E-mail: fellowships@aauw.org
Web Site: www.aauw.org

FOUNDED: 1888

AREAS OF INTEREST:
Advancement of educational and professional opportunities for women in the U.S. and around the globe.

NAME(S) OF PROGRAMS:
● **American Fellowships**

TYPE:
Fellowships; Visiting scholars. Awarded to women who are U.S. citizens or permanent residents pursuing full-time study to complete dissertations, conducting postdoctoral research full-time, or preparing research for publication for eight consecutive weeks.

YEAR PROGRAM STARTED: 1888

PURPOSE:
To support women scholars who are completing dissertations, planning research leave from accredited institutions or preparing research for publication.

ELIGIBILITY:
Applicants must be citizens or permanent residents of the U.S. There are no restrictions as to place of study or age. Fellowship is open to women who will have completed all requirements for the Doctorate, except the writing of the dissertation, by November 15 preceding the fellowship year, July 1 to June 30, or who hold the Ph.D. at the time of application. Applicants are evaluated by academic professionals on the scholarly excellence of their proposals, quality and originality of project design, and experience teaching or mentoring female students. In addition, applicants will be asked to outline their commitment to helping women and girls through community service, service in their profession and/or service in their field of research.

GEOG. RESTRICTIONS: United States.

FINANCIAL DATA:
Amount of support per award: $6,000 to $30,000.

APPLICATION INFO:
Applicant must create an account through the "apply now" link to the vendor site located on the funding opportunity page.
Deadline: November 1.

AMERICAN ASSOCIATION OF UNIVERSITY WOMEN
1310 L Street, N.W.
Suite 1000
Washington, DC 20005
E-mail: fellowships@aauw.org
Web Site: www.aauw.org

TYPE:
Fellowships. Awarded to women pursuing full-time graduate or postdoctoral study in the U.S. who are not U.S. citizens or permanent residents.

See entry 871 for full listing.

AMERICAN ASSOCIATION OF UNIVERSITY WOMEN [971]
1310 L Street, N.W.
Suite 1000
Washington, DC 20005
E-mail: fellowships@aauw.org
Web Site: www.aauw.org

FOUNDED: 1888

AREAS OF INTEREST:
Nontraditional fields.

NAME(S) OF PROGRAMS:
● **AAUW Career Development Grants**

TYPE:
Grants-in-aid. Awarded to women who are U.S. citizens or permanent residents pursuing a certificate or degree to advance their careers, change careers or re-enter the workforce and whose Bachelor's degree was received a number of years before the award period.

YEAR PROGRAM STARTED: 1972

PURPOSE:
To assist women who are continuing their self-development through higher education.

ELIGIBILITY:
Career Development Grants provide funding to women who hold a Bachelor's degree and are preparing to advance or change careers or re-enter the workforce. Primary consideration

is given to women of color and women pursuing their first advanced degree or credentials in nontraditional fields.

Applicants must be U.S. citizens or permanent residents whose last degree was received a number of years before the award period. Funds are available for tuition, fees, books, supplies, local transportation and dependent care.

Grants provide support for course work beyond a Bachelor's degree, including a Master's degree, second Bachelor's degree, certification program or specialized training in technical or professional fields. Course work must be taken at an accredited two- or four-year college or university in the U.S. or at a technical school that is fully licensed or accredited by the U.S. Department of Education. Funds are not available for Doctorate-level work.

Current requirements are posted on the AAUW web site.

GEOG. RESTRICTIONS: United States.

FINANCIAL DATA:
Amount of support per award: $2,000 to $12,000.

APPLICATION INFO:
Applicant must create an account through the "apply now" link to the vendor site located on the funding opportunity page.
Deadline: November 15.

AMERICAN NUCLEAR SOCIETY (ANS)

555 North Kensington Avenue
LaGrange Park, IL 60526
(708) 352-6611
Fax: (708) 352-0499
E-mail: scholarships@ans.org
Web Site: www.ans.org

TYPE:
Scholarships. Delayed Education for Women Scholarship is designed for women in a nuclear-related field whose formal studies have been delayed or interrupted for at least one year.

Landis Scholarships are administered by the ANS NEED Committee, and are awarded to undergraduate and graduate students who have greater-than-average financial need.

See entry 2378 for full listing.

BERKSHIRE CONFERENCE OF WOMEN HISTORIANS

Penn State Brandywine
Vairo Library, 124
25 Yearsley Mill Road
Media, PA 19063
(610) 892-1464
E-mail: secretary@berksconference.org
Web Site: www.berksconference.org

TYPE:
Awards/prizes. The Berkshire Conference of Women Historians awards two annual book and article prizes in the following categories: A first book that deals substantially with the history of women, gender, and/or sexuality; A first book in any field of history that does not focus on the history of women, gender, and/or sexuality; An article in the fields of the history of women, gender, and/or sexuality and;

An article in any field of history other than the history of women, gender, and/or sexuality.

See entry 529 for full listing.

BOSTON WOMEN'S FUND   [972]

678 Massachusetts Avenue
Suite 700
Cambridge, MA 02139
(617) 725-0035
Fax: (617) 725-0277
E-mail: info@bostonwomensfund.org
Web Site: bostonwomensfund.org

FOUNDED: 1984

AREAS OF INTEREST:
Women organized for racial, economic and social justice.

TYPE:
Grants-in-aid; Project/program grants; Seed money grants.

PURPOSE:
To pool funds from individuals; to channel money to support women's and girls' organizations for economic and social justice.

LEGAL BASIS:
Public foundation.

ELIGIBILITY:
Applicants or their fiscal agents must be 501(c)(3) organizations. Also funded are direct-service projects which have an organizing component. Groups just getting started are encouraged to apply, particularly those women who are most vulnerable and have the least access to other resources including women of color, low-income women, disabled women, lesbians, girls, older women, transgender people, immigrant and refugee women. Applicants with organizational budgets of less than $350,000 per year are preferred. No grants to individuals.

GEOG. RESTRICTIONS: Preference given to the Boston metropolitan area, and to selected outlying areas such as Brockton, Lawrence, Lowell and Worcester, Massachusetts.

FINANCIAL DATA:
Amount of support per award: Up to $15,000.

NO. MOST RECENT APPLICANTS: Varies.

NO. AWARDS: Varies.

APPLICATION INFO:
Send an e-mail to request the application.
Duration: Typically one year.

PUBLICATIONS:
Application guidelines; donor contribution information in annual report.

ADDRESS INQUIRIES TO:
E-mail: programs@bostonwomensfund.org

BROOKHAVEN WOMEN IN SCIENCE   [973]

P.O. Box 183
Upton, NY 11973
(631) 344-7153
E-mail: bwischasmanaward@bnl.gov
Web Site: www.bnl.gov/bwis/scholarships.php

FOUNDED: 1979

AREAS OF INTEREST:
Advancement of women in the natural sciences, engineering or mathematics fields.

NAME(S) OF PROGRAMS:
● **Renate W. Chasman Scholarship for Women**

TYPE:
Awards/prizes; Scholarships. These scholarships are offered to encourage women to pursue careers in the sciences technology, engineering or mathematics.

YEAR PROGRAM STARTED: 1986

PURPOSE:
To encourage women to resume their formal education in a technical field.

LEGAL BASIS:
Tax-exempt, incorporated under the Educational Laws of New York state.

ELIGIBILITY:
Applicants must be:
(1) women;
(2) graduate students at an accredited educational institution;
(3) performing research at Brookhaven National Laboratory in the STEM disciplines (science, technology, engineering or mathematics) and;
(4) receiving their degree not prior to May of the competition year.

FINANCIAL DATA:
Amount of support per award: $2,500.

NO. AWARDS: 1 per year.

APPLICATION INFO:
Application form is available online.
Duration: One-time award.
Deadline: February 28. Announcement in spring.

ADDRESS INQUIRIES TO:
Chasman Scholarship Fund
Brookhaven Women in Science
(See address or e-mail above.)

CANADIAN FEDERATION OF UNIVERSITY WOMEN   [974]

331 Cooper Street, Suite 502
Ottawa ON K2P 0G5 Canada
(613) 234-8252
(888) 220-9606
Fax: (613) 234-8221
E-mail: cfuwfls@rogers.com
Web Site: www.cfuw.org
www.cfuwcharitabletrust.ca

FOUNDED: 1919

AREAS OF INTEREST:
Graduate education for women.

NAME(S) OF PROGRAMS:
● **Ruth Binnie Fellowship**
● **Canadian Home Economics Association (CHEA) Fellowship**
● **CFUW Aboriginal Women's Award (AWA)**
● **CFUW Bourse Georgette Lemoyne**
● **CFUW Dr. Alice E. Wilson Awards**
● **CFUW Dr. Margaret McWilliams Pre-Doctoral Fellowship**
● **CFUW Elizabeth and Rachel Massey Award**
● **CFUW Linda Souter Humanities Award**
● **CFUW Memorial Fellowship**
● **CFUW 1989 Ecole Polytechnique Commemorative Awards**
● **CFUW 100th Anniversary Legacy Fellowship**

TYPE:
Awards/prizes; Fellowships. The Ruth Binnie Fellowship is for Master's studies with a

focus on one or more aspects of the field of home economics. The candidate may be studying abroad.

Canadian Home Economics Association Fellowship candidate must be studying one or more aspects in the field of home economics at the Master's or doctoral level in Canada.

CFUW Aboriginal Women's Award candidate must be a Canadian Aboriginal woman studying in Canada, who holds an undergraduate university degree or equivalent and has applied to be a full-time student in any year of an eligible program at a recognized or accredited Canadian post-secondary degree-granting institution. Eligible programs include: programs leading to a first degree in law, i.e., Bachelor of Laws (LLB) or Juris Doctor (JD); programs leading to first degrees in medicine, i.e., Medical Doctor (M.D.) or Doctor of Optometry (O.D.); programs leading to qualifying for a license to practice as a Nurse Practitioner in the province or territory of the graduate's choice; and programs leading to a Master's degree in fields dealing with important Canadian aboriginal issues at the time the AWA is given as defined by most recent Canadian report by the United Nations Special Rapporteur on the rights of indigenous peoples.

CFUW Bourse Georgette Lemoyne Fellowship is for graduate study at a Canadian university. The candidate must be studying in French.

CFUW Dr. Alice E. Wilson Award is for graduate studies in any field, with special consideration given to mature students returning to study after at least three years.

CFUW Dr. Margaret McWilliams Pre-Doctoral Fellowship candidate must have completed at least one full calendar year as a full-time student in doctoral-level studies and be a full-time student in Canada or abroad at the time of application.

CFUW Elizabeth and Rachel Massey Award is for postgraduate studies in the visual arts such as painting, sculpture or in music in Canada or abroad.

CFUW Linda Souter Humanities Award is for Master's or doctoral students. Generally, study in the humanities is theoretical and does not involve empirical methodology. Humanities could include English language and literature, history, languages study, classics, philosophy, film studies, communication studies and culture studies.

CFUW Memorial Fellowship candidate must be enrolled in a Master's degree program in science, mathematics, or engineering in Canada or abroad.

CFUW 1989 Ecole Polytechnique Commemorative Award is for graduate studies in any field. The candidate must justify the relevance of her work to women.

CFUW 100th Anniversary Legacy Fellowship is awarded to a woman who has completed one calendar year of a doctoral program at the time of application. The Ph.D. thesis research/project must focus on advancing gender equality. It is not restricted to a specific field of studies. The Fellowship is tenable in Canada or abroad.

YEAR PROGRAM STARTED: 1921

PURPOSE:
To support the education of women at the postgraduate level in Canada and abroad.

LEGAL BASIS:
Foundation of a nonprofit organization.

ELIGIBILITY:
Candidates must hold at least a Bachelor's degree or equivalent from a recognized university, have been accepted into the proposed program and place of study, and be a Canadian citizen or permanent resident.

FINANCIAL DATA:
Amount of support per award: $5,000 to $25,000 (CAN).

Total amount of support: Approximately $100,000.

NO. MOST RECENT APPLICANTS: 200 for the year 2020.

NO. AWARDS: 11 different categories, with 15 awards.

APPLICATION INFO:
Application form and guidelines are posted in August on the Federation's web site.

Duration: One year. Grants not renewable, except the CFUW Aboriginal Women's Award.

Deadline: January 14. Announcement April 15.

PUBLICATIONS:
CFUW Charitable Trust Annual Report;
CFUW Club Action News, e-newsletter;
CFUW Fellowships and Awards, e-newsletter;
CFUW External Annual Report.

ADDRESS INQUIRIES TO:
Betty Dunlop
Fellowships Program Manager
(See e-mail address above.)

*PLEASE NOTE:
Applicants are encouraged to confirm deadline on the Federation web site.

THE COORDINATING COUNCIL FOR WOMEN IN HISTORY, INC.   [975]
3118 Chaucer Drive
Charlotte, NC 28210
(773) 960-2092
E-mail: execdir@theccwh.org
Web Site: www.theccwh.org

FOUNDED: 1969

AREAS OF INTEREST:
Women's history, gender and sexuality, and activism for women.

NAME(S) OF PROGRAMS:
● **Catherine Prelinger Award**

TYPE:
Awards/prizes. The Catherine Prelinger Award is given to a scholar, with a Ph.D. or ABD, whose career has not followed a traditional academic path through secondary and higher education and whose work has contributed to women in the historical profession.

YEAR PROGRAM STARTED: 1998

PURPOSE:
To explore the diverse experiences and histories of all women; to honor scholars that have not followed a traditional academic path of uninterrupted and completed secondary, undergraduate, and graduate degrees leading into a tenured faculty position and whose work has contributed to women in the historical profession; to promote research and interpretation in areas of women's history; to recognize or to enhance the ability of the

recipient to contribute significantly to women in history, whether in the profession in the present or in the study of women in the past.

ELIGIBILITY:
The applicant:
(1) must be a member in good standing of the Coordinating Council for Women in History;
(2) must hold either ABD status or the Ph.D. at the time of application;
(3) shall be actively engaged in scholarship that is historical in nature, although the degree may be in related fields;
(4) shall have already contributed or shown potential for contributing significantly to women in history, whether in the profession in the present or in the study of women in the past and;
(5) has not followed a traditional academic path of uninterrupted and completed secondary, undergraduate and graduate degrees leading to a tenure-track faculty position.

FINANCIAL DATA:
Funds issued in U.S. dollars only.
Amount of support per award: $20,000.

NO. MOST RECENT APPLICANTS: 30 to 50.

NO. AWARDS: 1.

APPLICATION INFO:
Contact the organization.
Deadline: May 15.

ADDRESS INQUIRIES TO:
Elizabeth Everton, Ph.D., Executive Director
(See e-mail address above.)

*SPECIAL STIPULATIONS:
All recipients will be required to submit a final paper to CCWH on how the award was expended and summarizing the scholarly work completed.

THE COORDINATING COUNCIL FOR WOMEN IN HISTORY, INC.
3118 Chaucer Drive
Charlotte, NC 28210
(773) 960-2092
E-mail: execdir@theccwh.org
Web Site: www.theccwh.org

TYPE:
Awards/prizes; Fellowships.

See entry 534 for full listing.

DAUGHTERS OF PENELOPE FOUNDATION, INC.   [976]
1909 Q Street, N.W., Suite 500
Washington, DC 20009
(202) 234-9741
Fax: (202) 483-6983
E-mail: dophq@ahepa.org
Web Site: www.dopfoundationinc.com

FOUNDED: 1983

AREAS OF INTEREST:
Education, health and philanthropy.

NAME(S) OF PROGRAMS:
● **Paula J. Alexander Memorial Scholarship (Undergraduate)**
● **Helen J. Beldecos, Past Grand President, Scholarship (Undergraduate)**
● **The Big Five Graduate Scholarship**
● **Daughters of Penelope Past Grand Presidents Memorial Scholarship (Undergraduate)**

- **Daughters of Penelope Past Grand Presidents Undergraduate Scholarship**
- **Daughters of Penelope - St. Basil's Academy**
- **Eos #1 Mother Lodge Chapter Scholarship (Undergraduate)**
- **Joanne V. Hologgitas, Ph.D., Past Grand President, Scholarship (Undergraduate)**
- **Hopewell Agave Chapter #224 Scholarship (Undergraduate)**
- **Mary Kandaras Memorial Scholarship (Undergraduate)**
- **Kottis Family Scholarship (Undergraduate)**
- **Clara R. Payne Memorial Scholarship**
- **Dorothy Lillian Quincey Memorial Graduate Scholarship**
- **Alexandra Apostolides Sonenfeld Memorial Undergraduate Scholarship**
- **Sonja B. Stefanadis Graduate Student Scholarship**
- **Barbara Edith Quincey Thorndyke Memorial Undergraduate Scholarship**
- **Mary M. Verges, Past Grand President, Scholarship (Undergraduate)**
- **The Sotiri Zervoulias & Lea Soupata Scholarship (St. Basil's Academy)**

TYPE:
Scholarships.

YEAR PROGRAM STARTED: 1983

PURPOSE:
To support education for women of Greek descent.

LEGAL BASIS:
The Foundation is a recognized 501(c)(3) organization; tax-exempt.

ELIGIBILITY:
Scholarships are based on financial need or academic merit (or both). Contact the organization for full details.

GEOG. RESTRICTIONS: Canada, Greece and United States.

FINANCIAL DATA:
Amount of support per award: $500 to $2,500.

Total amount of support: Varies.

NO. AWARDS: 15 for the year 2018.

APPLICATION INFO:
Information and guidelines are available online.

Deadline: May 1.

PUBLICATIONS:
President's Bulletin, monthly publication.

IRS I.D.: 52-1346043

ADDRESS INQUIRIES TO:
Elena Saviolakis
Executive Director
(See address above.)

*SPECIAL STIPULATIONS:
Scholarship may not be deferred to be used at a later date. These awards are not renewable and must be used strictly for tuition and/or books. Application must be typewritten. All requirements must be met and all questions answered or applicant will be disqualified.

DAUGHTERS OF THE CINCINNATI
271 Madison Avenue
Suite 1408
New York, NY 10016
(212) 991-9945
E-mail: scholarships@daughters1894.org
Web Site: www.daughters1894.org

TYPE:
Scholarships. Undergraduate scholarships.

See entry 1496 for full listing.

DREXEL UNIVERSITY COLLEGE OF MEDICINE   [977]
The Legacy Center
Archives and Special Collections
2900 West Queen Lane
Philadelphia, PA 19129
(215) 991-8340
Fax: (215) 991-8172
E-mail: com_archives@drexel.edu
Web Site: archives.drexelmed.edu

FOUNDED: 1977

AREAS OF INTEREST:
Medicine as it relates to women in professional practice.

NAME(S) OF PROGRAMS:
- **M. Louise Gloeckner, M.D., Summer Research Fellowship**

TYPE:
Fellowships. For four to six weeks of research at The Legacy Center. Collections house the business and academic records of the Woman's Medical College of Pennsylvania, the Medical College of Pennsylvania, and Drexel University College of Medicine, the personal papers of women physicians, records of national and international women's medical organizations, schools, associations, hospitals and a historic photograph collection.

YEAR PROGRAM STARTED: 1985

PURPOSE:
To encourage the use of the institution's archival collections in the study of women in medicine, and history generally.

LEGAL BASIS:
University.

ELIGIBILITY:
Applicants must be either undergraduate or graduate students, medical students, faculty members or independent researchers. Preference is given to researchers with well-defined projects to be completed in one summer.

FINANCIAL DATA:
Total amount of support: $4,000.

NO. AWARDS: 1 annually.

APPLICATION INFO:
Guidelines and application form are available on the web site.
Duration: Four to six weeks depending on project.
Deadline: April 1.

PUBLICATIONS:
Program announcement.

STAFF:
Margaret Graham, Director

ADDRESS INQUIRIES TO:
Margaret Graham, Director
(See address above.)

THE EDUCATIONAL FOUNDATION FOR WOMEN IN ACCOUNTING
7946 Clyo Road, Suite A
Centerville, OH 45459
(937) 424-3391
E-mail: info@efwa.org
Web Site: www.efwa.org

TYPE:
Scholarships. Laurels Fund provides a one-year academic scholarship for women pursuing a Ph.D. in accounting.

Women in Need Scholarship is available to women in their third, fourth or fifth year of academic pursuit who need the financial support to complete their degrees. It is renewable annually upon satisfactory completion of course requirements.

Women in Transition Scholarship is intended for women returning to school as freshmen to earn a Bachelor's degree in accounting. It is renewable annually upon satisfactory completion of course requirements.

See entry 1704 for full listing.

GENERAL BOARD OF HIGHER EDUCATION AND MINISTRY, THE UNITED METHODIST CHURCH
1001 19th Avenue South
Nashville, TN 37212
(615) 340-7338
Fax: (615) 340-7529
E-mail: mbigord@gbhem.org
Web Site: www.gbhem.org

TYPE:
Awards/prizes; Scholarships. Awards to encourage women over age 35 to prepare for ordained ministry as an Elder in the United Methodist Church as a second career. The scholarship is to be used for study toward the basic seminary degree in an accredited school of theology.

See entry 741 for full listing.

GRADUATE WOMEN IN SCIENCE
P.O. Box 7
Mullica Hill, NJ 08062
E-mail: fellowships@gwis.org
Web Site: www.gwis.org

TYPE:
Fellowships.

See entry 1630 for full listing.

GRADUATE WOMEN INTERNATIONAL (GWI)   [978]
Chemin du Grand-Montfleury, 48
CH-1290 Versoix Geneva Switzerland
(41) 22 731 23 80
Fax: (41) 22 738 04 40
E-mail: gwi@graduatewomen.org
Web Site: www.graduatewomen.org

FOUNDED: 1919

AREAS OF INTEREST:
Secondary, tertiary, continuing and nontraditional education for girls and women, human rights, status of women.

CONSULTING OR VOLUNTEER SERVICES:
At the international level, Graduate Women International has working relationships with a

number of nongovernmental organizations, consultative status with ECOSOC, ILO and UNESCO, as well as periodic cooperation with other United Nations bodies. At the national level, affiliates in 58 countries work to accomplish Graduate Women International's goals and to address issues of global concern, both through project work and interaction with their governments and other interested groups.

NAME(S) OF PROGRAMS:
- **BFWG Marjorie Shaw Fellowship**
- **FfWG Crosby Hall Fellowship**
- **NZFGW Daphne Purves Grant**
- **Caroline Spurgeon Centenary Fellowship**

TYPE:
Awards/prizes; Fellowships; Internships; Research grants; Training grants. Graduate Women International fellowships and grants are awarded triennially to encourage and enable women graduates to undertake original research or obtain further training in the humanities, social sciences and natural sciences.

YEAR PROGRAM STARTED: 1919

PURPOSE:
To promote understanding and friendship among the university women of the world, irrespective of their race, nationality, religion or political opinions; to encourage international cooperation; to further the development of education; to represent university women in international organizations; to encourage the full application of members' skills to the problems which arise at all levels of public life, whether local, national, regional or worldwide; to encourage their participation in the solving of these problems.

LEGAL BASIS:
International nongovernmental organization, based in Geneva, Switzerland.

ELIGIBILITY:
Open to women graduates:
(1) who are members of Graduate Women International enrolled in a Ph.D. programme of which they have completed the first year and;
(2) who are nonmembers and independent members of less than the nominated period of membership; these may apply subject to payment of an administrative fee.

Applications are welcomed from the humanities, social sciences and natural sciences. Membership in a national association is also an eligibility factor.

FINANCIAL DATA:
Candidates must provide evidence of adequate budgetary provision to meet the costs of their studies over and above the amount requested for the GWI award.

Amount of support per award: Fellowships: CHF 2,000 to 12,000; Grants: CHF 3,000 to 6,000.

NO. AWARDS: 5 to 15 fellowships and grants are offered in each competition.

APPLICATION INFO:
All applications must be submitted electronically. Application forms are available on the web site. Members of one of GWI's national affiliates must submit applications when completed with required supporting documentation to their NFA. Independent members and nonmembers must submit their

completed applications directly to the GWI Office in Geneva with any administrative fee that is required.

Duration: Fellowships are intended to cover eight to 12 months of work. Grants are awarded for a minimum of two months of work. The awards are not renewable.

Deadline: June 30.

ADDRESS INQUIRIES TO:
See e-mail address above.

*SPECIAL STIPULATIONS:
Women graduates only.

KENTUCKY FOUNDATION FOR WOMEN   [979]
505 West Ormsby Avenue
Louisville, KY 40203
(502) 562-0045
E-mail: team@kfw.org
Web Site: www.kfw.org

FOUNDED: 1985

AREAS OF INTEREST:
Arts, social change and feminism.

NAME(S) OF PROGRAMS:
- **Art Meets Activism**
- **Artist Enrichment**
- **Hopscotch House Artist Retreat and Residency Center**

TYPE:
Awards/prizes; Project/program grants; Residencies.

YEAR PROGRAM STARTED: 1985

PURPOSE:
To promote positive social change through support of feminist expression in the arts.

ELIGIBILITY:
Individuals engaging in arts-based activities may apply. Applicants must be residents of Kentucky.

GEOG. RESTRICTIONS: Kentucky.

FINANCIAL DATA:
Amount of support per award: $1,000 to $7,500.
Total amount of support: $250,000 annually.

NO. MOST RECENT APPLICANTS: Varies.

NO. AWARDS: Varies.

APPLICATION INFO:
Guidelines and application form are available on the Foundation web site.

Duration: One year.

Deadline: Art Meets Activism: First Friday of March; Artist Enrichment: First Friday of September.

STAFF:
Sharon LaRue, Executive Director
Avery Guess, Grant Program Manager

ADDRESS INQUIRIES TO:
Sharon LaRue, Executive Director
(See address above.)

THE LALOR FOUNDATION, INC.
c/o GMA Foundations
2 Liberty Square, Suite 500
Boston, MA 02109
(617) 426-7080
(617) 391-3088
E-mail: gsullivan@gmafoundations.com
Web Site: lalorfound.org

TYPE:
Project/program grants.

See entry 2250 for full listing.

THE LEEWAY FOUNDATION   [980]
1315 Walnut Street
Suite 832
Philadelphia, PA 19107
(215) 545-4078
Fax: (215) 545-4021
E-mail: info@leeway.org
Web Site: www.leeway.org

FOUNDED: 1993

AREAS OF INTEREST:
Women and trans artists creating art for social change.

NAME(S) OF PROGRAMS:
- **Art and Change Grant**
- **Leeway Transformation Award**

TYPE:
Awards/prizes; Project/program grants. Art and Change Grants provide project-based grants to fund art for social change projects.

Leeway Transformation Award is an unrestricted award (not project-based) for women and trans people demonstrating a commitment of five years or more to art for social change work.

YEAR PROGRAM STARTED: 1998

PURPOSE:
To support women and trans artists who create art for social change.

ELIGIBILITY:
Women and trans artists living in the Delaware Valley region may apply. The Transformation Award is open to women and trans people working in any art form who create art and social change and have done so for the past five years or more, demonstrating a commitment to art for social change work.

GEOG. RESTRICTIONS: Camden County, New Jersey; Bucks, Chester, Delaware, Montgomery and Philadelphia counties, Pennsylvania.

FINANCIAL DATA:
Amount of support per award: Art and Change Grant: Up to $2,500; Leeway Transformation Award: $15,000.
Total amount of support: Varies.

NO. MOST RECENT APPLICANTS: Varies.

NO. AWARDS: Varies.

APPLICATION INFO:
Contact the Foundation for application or download a copy of the current application and guideline procedures from the web site.

Duration: Varies based on project need.

Deadline: Art and Change Grant: March 1 and August 1; Leeway Transformation Award: May 15.

STAFF:
Denise Brown, Executive Director

ADDRESS INQUIRIES TO:
Melissa Hamilton, Program Director
(See address above.)

MICHIGAN WOMEN FORWARD [981]

1155 Brewery Park Boulevard
Suite 350
Detroit, MI 48207
(313) 962-1920
Fax: (313) 962-1926
E-mail: info@miwf.org
Web Site: www.miwf.org

FOUNDED: 1986

AREAS OF INTEREST:
Needs of women and girls.

NAME(S) OF PROGRAMS:
● **Young Women for Change**

TYPE:
General operating grants; Project/program grants; Seed money grants. Specific focus changes yearly and is determined by each of seven chapters.

YEAR PROGRAM STARTED: 1986

PURPOSE:
To develop young women through the process of philanthropy and grantmaking into successful, fiscally responsible and socially responsive women.

LEGAL BASIS:
Nonprofit 501(c)(3) organization.

ELIGIBILITY:
Eligible organizations must be IRS 501(c)(3) tax-exempt.

GEOG. RESTRICTIONS: Michigan.

FINANCIAL DATA:
Amount of support per award: $500 to $5,000.
Total amount of support: Varies.

APPLICATION INFO:
Guidelines and application form are available on the web site.
Duration: One year.

PUBLICATIONS:
Trillium, newsletter.

IRS I.D.: 38-2689979

ADDRESS INQUIRIES TO:
See e-mail address above.

MONEY FOR WOMEN/BARBARA DEMING MEMORIAL FUND, INC. [982]

P.O. Box 717
Bearsville, NY 12409
E-mail: demingfund@gmail.com
Web Site: demingfund.org

FOUNDED: 1975

AREAS OF INTEREST:
Visual art, fiction, nonfiction and poetry.

NAME(S) OF PROGRAMS:
● **Individual Artist Support Grants**

TYPE:
Awards/prizes. Small grants awarded annually to individual feminists in the arts.

YEAR PROGRAM STARTED: 1975

PURPOSE:
To support feminists in the arts.

LEGAL BASIS:
Private foundation.

ELIGIBILITY:
Open to individual feminist women in the arts, in visual art, fiction (prose), nonfiction (prose) and poetry whose work addresses women's concerns and/or speaks for peace and justice from a feminist perspective. Applicants must be citizens with primary residence in the U.S. or Canada. No educational or study scholarships.

GEOG. RESTRICTIONS: United States and Canada.

FINANCIAL DATA:
Amount of support per award: $500 to $1,500.
Total amount of support: Varies.

NO. MOST RECENT APPLICANTS: 550.

NO. AWARDS: 17 for the year 2020.

REPRESENTATIVE AWARDS:
Makenzie Brown (fiction), Buena Vista, CO, *The Y*; Ursula Gullow (art), Asheville, NC, *By Her Own Hand: A Self-Portrait Series*; Jean Ho (fiction), Los Angeles, CA, *Fiona and Jane*.

APPLICATION INFO:
Visit the Fund web site to complete electronic application. Completed applications require an application/processing fee of $25.
Deadline: January 1 to January 31, 2022 for fiction, visual art and mixed genre. January 1 to January 31, 2023 for nonfiction and poetry. Announcement by May.

PUBLICATIONS:
Newsletter.

IRS I.D.: 51-0176956

BOARD OF DIRECTORS:
Elvia R. Arriola
Maureen Brady
Gabrielle Calvocoressi
Daisy Hernandez
Martha Ellen Hughes
Alice Templeton
Crystal Williams

ADDRESS INQUIRIES TO:
See e-mail address above.

MS. FOUNDATION FOR WOMEN [983]

12 MetroTech Center
26th Floor
Brooklyn, NY 11201
(212) 742-2300
Fax: (212) 742-1653
E-mail: info@ms.foundation.org
Web Site: forwomen.org

FOUNDED: 1972

AREAS OF INTEREST:
Economic justice, women's health, and safety.

NAME(S) OF PROGRAMS:
● **Economic Justice**
● **Women's Health**
● **Women's Safety**

TYPE:
Project/program grants; Technical assistance. General support. Capacity building.

YEAR PROGRAM STARTED: 1976

PURPOSE:
To support the efforts of women and girls to govern their own lives and influence the world around them; to champion an equitable society by effecting change in public consciousness, law, philanthropy and social policy through its leadership, expertise and financial support.

LEGAL BASIS:
Public foundation.

ELIGIBILITY:
Funding is by invitation only. Within its funding priorities, the Foundation gives priority to:
(1) efforts that engage women and girls in crafting activist solutions to the particular challenges they face in their communities based on gender, race, ethnicity, class, age, disability, sexual orientation and culture and;
(2) national-, regional- or state-level public policy advocacy informed by local organizing work and undertaken by organizations with strong linkages to a grassroots constituency.

Special consideration is given to the organizations that:
(1) are pro-women's empowerment, proactively antiracist and working to dismantle heterosexism, class oppression and discrimination based on disability;
(2) address the particular challenges faced by low-income women and girls;
(3) clearly articulate and respond to issues of gender as related to class and race/ethnicity;
(4) are multi-issue and involved in a form of cross-constituency organizing and coalition work;
(5) encourage intergenerational work that empowers younger as well as older women;
(6) include in leadership positions those who are affected most directly by the issues addressed and;
(7) have limited access to other funding sources.

The Foundation does not fund direct-service projects, stand-alone cultural or media projects, publications, individuals, scholarships, religious institutions, conferences, university-based research or government agencies.

GEOG. RESTRICTIONS: United States.

FINANCIAL DATA:
Amount of support per award: Varies.
Total amount of support: Varies.

NO. AWARDS: Over 100.

APPLICATION INFO:
Applications are accepted by invitation only through targeted Requests for Proposals. From time to time, however, the Foundation will launch open calls for proposals, which will be posted on the Foundation web site.
Duration: Generally one-time grants. Some renewal funding.
Deadline: Varies per program.

PUBLICATIONS:
Annual report; application guidelines; most recent grants list.

BOARD OF DIRECTORS:
Alicia Lara, Chairperson
Jenna Skinner Scalan, Vice Chairperson
Jenna Bussman-Wise, Treasurer
Danielle Moodie, Secretary
Angela Glover Blackwell
Alex Busansky
Wade Davis
Susan Dickler
Lauren Embrey
Jocelyn Frye
Cathy Hartnett
Suzanne Lerner
Yin Ling Leung
Rinku Sen
Candi Castleberry Singleton
Gail Wasserman
Tom Watson
Catherine Yelverton

NATIONAL FEDERATION OF REPUBLICAN WOMEN   [984]

124 North Alfred Street
Alexandria, VA 22314
(703) 548-9688
E-mail: scholarships@nfrw.org
Web Site: www.nfrw.org

FOUNDED: 1938

AREAS OF INTEREST:
The political process.

NAME(S) OF PROGRAMS:
- **Dorothy Kabis Internship**
- **National Pathfinder's Scholarship**
- **Betty Rendel Scholarship**

TYPE:
Internships; Scholarships. Dorothy Kabis Internship includes a six- to eight-week internship in Washington, DC, housing, travel and stipend.

National Pathfinder's Scholarships are given to the best nominated candidates.

Betty Rendel Scholarships are given to undergraduate women who are majoring in political science, government or economics.

PURPOSE:
To involve more women in the political process and provide educational opportunities.

ELIGIBILITY:
National Pathfinder's Scholarship is open to young women seeking undergraduate or postgraduate degrees, college sophomores, juniors, seniors and students enrolled in a Master's program. Recent high school graduates and first-year college women are not eligible.

Betty Rendel Scholarship applicants must be undergraduate women who are majoring in political science, government or economics. Open only to women who have successfully completed two years of college work.

GEOG. RESTRICTIONS: United States.

FINANCIAL DATA:
Dorothy Kabis Internship includes a small stipend, housing and airfare.
Amount of support per award: National Pathfinder's Scholarship: $2,500; Betty Rendel Scholarship: $1,000.

NO. AWARDS: 3 per scholarship and 2 internships.

APPLICATION INFO:
All grant information, including a printable version of the application, can be found online.
Duration: One-time award.
Deadline: June 1 for the National Pathfinder's Scholarship and Betty Rendel Scholarship. December 1 for Dorothy Kabis Internship.

ADDRESS INQUIRIES TO:
Scholarship Coordinator
(See address above.)

*SPECIAL STIPULATIONS:
Applicants must be U.S. citizens and may only apply to one program in a given year. Winners may not reapply.

THE NEWBERRY LIBRARY

Newberry Institute for Research and Education
60 West Walton Street
Chicago, IL 60610
(312) 255-3666
E-mail: research@newberry.org
Web Site: www.newberry.org/fellowships

TYPE:
Fellowships; Visiting scholars. The Frances C. Allen Fellowship supports women of American Indian heritage. Recipients are expected to work closely with members of the D'Arcy McNickle Center for American Indian and Indigenous Studies during their residency.

See entry 954 for full listing.

OPEN MEADOWS FOUNDATION   [985]

P.O. Box 150584
Brooklyn, NY 11215
E-mail: openmeadowsfdn@gmail.com
Web Site: sites.google.com/site/openmeadowsfoundation

FOUNDED: 1986

AREAS OF INTEREST:
Projects led by and benefiting women and girls, reflecting community diversity, building community power, and promoting racial, social, economic and environmental justice.

TYPE:
Development grants; Project/program grants; Training grants. International program for women and girls.

PURPOSE:
To promote gender, racial and economic justice.

ELIGIBILITY:
Applicant organization must be nonprofit 501(c)(3) or have a fiscal sponsor that is tax-exempt 501(c)(3). Small and start-up organizations are given priority. Proposals for projects that have limited financial access or have encountered obstacles in their search for funding are eligible to apply. Applicant's organizational budget should not exceed $75,000. Projects must be led by and benefit women and girls. No grants are made to individuals.

FINANCIAL DATA:
Amount of support per award: Up to $2,000.
Total amount of support: Varies.

NO. MOST RECENT APPLICANTS: 500.

NO. AWARDS: Approximately 40 per year.

APPLICATION INFO:
Proposals must be submitted via e-mail. Guidelines are available on the Foundation web site.
Duration: One year. Must reapply.
Deadline: February 15 and August 15 each year, 12 midnight.

ADDRESS INQUIRIES TO:
See e-mail address above.

P.E.O. SISTERHOOD

P.E.O. Executive Office
3700 Grand Avenue
Des Moines, IA 50312
(515) 255-3153
Fax: (515) 255-3820
E-mail: ips@peodsm.org
Web Site: www.peointernational.org

TYPE:
Scholarships. Awards for selected women from countries other than the U.S. and Canada to pursue graduate study in the U.S. or Canada. Support is available for advanced study in any field except for research. No new applications at the dissertation level.

See entry 877 for full listing.

THE PHI BETA KAPPA SOCIETY   [986]

1606 New Hampshire Avenue, N.W.
Washington, DC 20009
(202) 745-3287
Fax: (202) 986-1601
E-mail: awards@pbk.org
Web Site: www.pbk.org

FOUNDED: 1776

AREAS OF INTEREST:
French language, literature and culture; Greek language, literature and history.

NAME(S) OF PROGRAMS:
- **Mary Isabel Sibley Fellowship**

TYPE:
Fellowships. Grant to women scholars made in alternate years for advanced research dealing with Greek language, literature, history or archaeology (odd-numbered years) or with French language or literature (even-numbered years).

YEAR PROGRAM STARTED: 1934

PURPOSE:
To assist women scholars conducting original research.

LEGAL BASIS:
National scholarly honorary society.

ELIGIBILITY:
Unmarried women between 25 and 35 years of age (inclusive) are eligible to apply. They must hold the Doctorate or have fulfilled all requirements for the Doctorate except the dissertation. Applicants must have demonstrated ability to carry on original research and must plan to devote full-time work to research during the fellowship year. Eligibility is not restricted to members of the Society or to U.S. citizens.

FINANCIAL DATA:
The Fellowship carries a $20,000 stipend with one-half of the amount payable after July following announcement of the Fellowship and the balance after another six months have elapsed.
Amount of support per award: $20,000.
Total amount of support: $20,000.

NO. MOST RECENT APPLICANTS: Varies.

NO. AWARDS: 1 each year.

APPLICATION INFO:
Official application materials are available upon request to the Awards Coordinator or on the web site. Fellowships are awarded alternately in the fields of Greek language, literature, history or archaeology (odd-numbered years) and French language or literature (even-numbered years). Send brief description of intended research project when requesting an application.
Duration: The Fellowship is tenable for one year.
Deadline: January 15.

ADDRESS INQUIRIES TO:
Mary Isabel Sibley Fellowship Committee
(See address above.)

ROCHESTER AREA COMMUNITY FOUNDATION [987]

500 East Avenue
Rochester, NY 14607-1912
(585) 271-4100
Fax: (585) 271-4292
E-mail: racf@racf.org
Web Site: www.racf.org

FOUNDED: 1972

AREAS OF INTEREST:
Women in poverty, organizational capacity building, aging, arts, the environment, civic engagement, youth and families, historical preservation, health, racial equity, concentrated poverty, academic and achievement gap.

TYPE:
Project/program grants; Scholarships.

PURPOSE:
To support community responsibility and leadership, healthy options for young people and their families, early childhood development and quality of life.

LEGAL BASIS:
Tax-exempt public charity.

GEOG. RESTRICTIONS: Genesee, Livingston, Monroe, Ontario, Orleans, Seneca, Wayne and Yates counties, New York.

FINANCIAL DATA:
Amount of support per award: Varies.
Total amount of support: Approximately $28,000,000 for the year 2019.

IRS I.D.: 23-7250641

ADDRESS INQUIRIES TO:
Jennifer Leonard, President and Chief Executive Officer
(See address above.)

SKILLBUILDERS FUND [988]

4707 College Boulevard, Suite 201
Leawood, KS 66211
(913) 608-7545
E-mail: info@skillbuildersfund.org
Web Site: www.skillbuildersfund.org

FOUNDED: 1983

AREAS OF INTEREST:
Programs benefiting low-income women and girls.

TYPE:
Project/program grants; Scholarships. Programs that help women and girls with economic self-sufficiency. Scholarships are only given to organizations, not to individuals.

YEAR PROGRAM STARTED: 1984

PURPOSE:
To enhance the capabilities of women and girls of all ages in the Kansas City metropolitan area and to realize their full potential.

LEGAL BASIS:
Private foundation.

ELIGIBILITY:
Organizations must be IRS 501(c)(3) not-for-profit. Funding primarily is directed to 501(c)(3) organizations that specifically benefit women and girls. Individuals, businesses and other for-profit organizations do not qualify.

GEOG. RESTRICTIONS: Kansas City metropolitan area, including Cass, Clay, Jackson, Johnson, Leavenworth, Platte, Ray and Wyandotte counties.

FINANCIAL DATA:
Amount of support per award: $10,000 to $25,000.
Total amount of support: Varies.

NO. AWARDS: 3 to 9 annually.

APPLICATION INFO:
Application information is available on the web site. Applicants must include a copy of their IRS tax determination letter with the application.
Duration: One year.
Deadline: Varies from year to year.

PUBLICATIONS:
Information brochure with application procedures.

IRS I.D.: 48-0984713

ADDRESS INQUIRIES TO:
Jennifer Sullivan, Grants Administrator and Executive Assistant
(See address above.)

SOCIETY OF DAUGHTERS OF THE U.S. ARMY

11804 Grey Birch Place
Reston, VA 20191-4223
E-mail: DUSAscholarships@gmail.com
Web Site: armydaughters.org

TYPE:
Scholarships.

See entry 1572 for full listing.

SOCIETY OF WOMEN ENGINEERS [989]

130 East Randolph Street
Suite 3500
Chicago, IL 60601
(312) 596-5223
(877) 793-4636
Fax: (312) 312-9550
E-mail: scholarships@swe.org
Web Site: swe.org/scholarships

FOUNDED: 1950

AREAS OF INTEREST:
Engineering.

NAME(S) OF PROGRAMS:
• **Society of Women Engineers Scholarship Program**

TYPE:
Awards/prizes; Conferences/seminars; Scholarships. Support for undergraduate and graduate engineering studies including women who have been out of the engineering job market and out of school for a minimum of two years and who will return to school for an engineering program.

PURPOSE:
To encourage women to achieve their utmost in careers as professional engineers and as the leaders of tomorrow and to attain high levels of education.

LEGAL BASIS:
Nonprofit educational organization under IRS 501(c)(3) classification.

ELIGIBILITY:
Scholarships are open only to students identifying as female studying an accredited engineering program in a school, college, or university. Candidate is evaluated on the basis of scholastic standing in high school and/or activity.

Some scholarships require applicant to be a U.S. citizen.

Additional criteria can be found on the Society web site.

FINANCIAL DATA:
Scholarship payments are made directly to academic institutions on the recipient's behalf.
Amount of support per award: $1,000 to $17,000.
Total amount of support: Over $810,000 for the year 2019.

NO. AWARDS: 260 new and renewed for the year 2019.

APPLICATION INFO:
Completed application form and letters of reference are required.
Duration: One year. Possible renewal.
Deadline: May 1 for freshmen. February 15 for sophomore, junior, senior and graduate. Announcement in late spring and summer, respectively, for use during the following academic year.

PUBLICATIONS:
Applications; *SWE* magazine.

IRS I.D.: 13-1947735

ADDRESS INQUIRIES TO:
See e-mail address above.

TEXAS WOMEN'S FOUNDATION [990]

Campbell Centre II
8150 North Central Expressway, Suite 110
Dallas, TX 75206
(214) 965-9977
Fax: (214) 526-3633
E-mail: ldelagarza@txwf.org
Web Site: www.txwf.org

FOUNDED: 1985

AREAS OF INTEREST:
Leadership and education, economic security, health and safety, and women's issues.

TYPE:
General operating grants; Project/program grants.

YEAR PROGRAM STARTED: 1985

PURPOSE:
To invest in women and girls; to empower women's philanthropy to build a better world.

LEGAL BASIS:
Community organization.

ELIGIBILITY:
Applicants must be 501(c)(3) organizations with 50% of the recipients residing in Collin, Dallas, Denton, Tarrant and surrounding counties, TX. The applying program must serve at least 75% women and/or girls, inclusive of sexual orientation, gender identity and gender expression.

GEOG. RESTRICTIONS: Collin, Dallas, Denton, Tarrant and surrounding counties, Texas.

FINANCIAL DATA:
Amount of support per award: Up to $30,000.
Total amount of support: Approximately $6,300,000 per year.

APPLICATION INFO:
The guidelines and application form are available online.

Duration: One year.

Deadline: Varies according to program area.

IRS I.D.: 75-2048261

STAFF:
Roslyn Dawson Thompson, President and Chief Executive Officer
Dawn Hooper, Vice President of Operations and Chief Financial Officer
Ashley Harris, Vice President of Development
Lisa De La Garza, Vice President of Programs
Mary Valadez, Associate Vice President of Grants

ADDRESS INQUIRIES TO:
Shonda Barnett, Senior Manager
E-mail: sbarnett@txwf.org

WASHINGTON UNIVERSITY IN ST. LOUIS
Office of the Provost
One Brookings Drive, Campus Box 1072
St. Louis, MO 63130
(314) 935-3000
E-mail: olinfellowship@wustl.edu
Web Site: graduateschool.wustl.edu/olin-fellowship

TYPE:
Fellowships. The Olin Fellowship is open to candidates for any of the following graduate and professional schools at Washington University: architecture, art, arts and sciences, business, engineering, law, medicine, and social work.

See entry 1613 for full listing.

WELLESLEY COLLEGE [991]
Career Education
Green Hall 439, 106 Central Street
Wellesley, MA 02481-8203
(781) 283-2347
Fax: (781) 283-3674
E-mail: fellowships@wellesley.edu
Web Site: www.wellesley.edu/careereducation/fellowships-and-scholarships

AREAS OF INTEREST:
Graduate education.

NAME(S) OF PROGRAMS:
- **Anne Louise Barrett Fellowship**
- **Margaret Freeman Bowers Fellowship**
- **The Eugene L. Cox Fellowship**
- **Professor Elizabeth F. Fisher Fellowship**
- **Ruth Ingersoll Goldmark Fellowship**
- **Horton-Hallowell Fellowship**
- **Peggy Howard Fellowship in Economics**
- **Edna V. Moffett Fellowship**
- **Alice Freeman Palmer Fellowship**
- **Kathryn Conway Preyer Fellowship**
- **Vida Dutton Scudder Fellowship**
- **Harriet A. Shaw Fellowship**
- **Mary Elvira Stevens Traveling Fellowship**
- **Maria Opasnov Tyler '52 Scholarship**
- **Sarah Perry Wood Medical Fellowship**
- **Fanny Bullock Workman Fellowship**

TYPE:
Fellowships; Research grants. The Anne Louise Barrett Fellowship is given preferably in music and primarily for study or research in musical theory, composition, or in the history of music, abroad or in the U.S.

The Margaret Freeman Bowers Fellowship is given for graduate/professional study in fields leading to a career of service to others. Fields include social work, law, public health, policy and administration, and development studies. Business, medicine, and science also qualify, as long as they are dedicated to addressing social challenges in the U.S. and around the world.

The Eugene L. Cox Fellowship is for graduate study in medieval or renaissance history and culture abroad or in the U.S.

The Professor Elizabeth F. Fisher Fellowship is given for research or further study in geology or geography, including urban, environmental or ecological studies.

The Ruth Ingersoll Goldmark Fellowship is awarded for graduate study in English literature, English composition or in the classics.

The Horton-Hallowell Fellowship is awarded for graduate study in any field, preferably in the last two years of candidacy for the Ph.D. degree, or its equivalent, or for private research of equivalent standard.

The Peggy Howard Fellowship in Economics is given to provide financial aid for Wellesley students or alumnae continuing their study of economics. Administered by the economics faculty who may name one or two recipients depending on the income available.

The Edna V. Moffett Fellowship is given to a young alumna, preferably for a first year of graduate study in history.

The Alice Freeman Palmer Fellowship is awarded for study or research abroad or in the U.S.

The Kathryn Conway Preyer Fellowship is for advanced study in history.

The Vida Dutton Scudder Fellowship is given for study in the field of social science, political science or literature.

The Harriet A. Shaw Fellowship is given for study or research in music and the allied arts, in the U.S. or abroad.

Mary Elvira Stevens Traveling Fellowship is awarded for travel or study outside the U.S.

The Maria Opasnov Tyler '52 Scholarship is for graduate study in Russian studies.

The Sarah Perry Wood Medical Fellowship is awarded for the study of medicine at an accredited medical school approved by the American Medical Association.

The Fanny Bullock Workman Fellowship is given for graduate study in any field.

ELIGIBILITY:
Open to seniors graduating from Wellesley College and Wellesley graduates. Additional requirements are available on the College web site.

FINANCIAL DATA:
Amount of support per award: Varies.
Total amount of support: Varies.

APPLICATION INFO:
Details are posted online.

Deadline: Peggy Howard Fellowship: Early April. Mary Elvira Stevens Fellowship: Mid-February. All other awards: Early January.

PUBLICATIONS:
Program announcement.

*PLEASE NOTE:
Eligibility requirements change frequently. Wellesley College prefers applicants use the web site as the main source of information.

*SPECIAL STIPULATIONS:
These fellowships are for study at institutions other than Wellesley College. Applicants must be graduating seniors or alumnae of Wellesley College for all fellowships.

WELLESLEY COLLEGE [992]
Career Education
Green Hall 439, 106 Central Street
Wellesley, MA 02481-8203
(781) 283-2347
Fax: (781) 283-3674
E-mail: fellowships@wellesley.edu
Web Site: www.wellesley.edu/careereducation/fellowships-and-scholarships

AREAS OF INTEREST:
Graduate study for women.

NAME(S) OF PROGRAMS:
- **Mary McEwen Schimke Scholarship**
- **M.A. Cartland Shackford Medical Fellowship**

TYPE:
Fellowships; Scholarships. Awards are made to female applicants who plan for full-time graduate study for the coming year.

The Mary McEwen Schimke Scholarship is a supplemental award given to afford relief from household and child care expenses while pursuing graduate study.

The M.A. Cartland Shackford Medical Fellowship is given for study of medicine with a view to general practice, not psychiatry.

ELIGIBILITY:
Open to women graduates of any American institution. Additional requirements are posted on the College web site.

FINANCIAL DATA:
Amount of support per award: Varies.
Total amount of support: Varies.

APPLICATION INFO:
Application information is available on the web site.

Duration: One year.

Deadline: Mid-January.

PUBLICATIONS:
Announcement.

*PLEASE NOTE:
Eligibility requirements change from year to year. Wellesley College prefers applicants use the web site as their main source of information.

WOMEN IN DEFENSE [993]
WID HORIZONS
2101 Wilson Boulevard, Suite 700
Arlington, VA 22201
(703) 247-2563
Fax: (703) 522-1885
E-mail: awebster@ndia.org
Web Site: www.womenindefense.net

AREAS OF INTEREST:
Increasing women's participation in national security fields.

NAME(S) OF PROGRAMS:
- **Horizons Foundation Scholarship Program**

TYPE:
Scholarships. The Horizons Foundation Scholarship Program is supported by accredited colleges and universities. Awards are made on an annual basis. The Foundation selects all scholarship recipients based on criteria it sets. Scholarships are awarded to applicants who require financial assistance, demonstrate strong academic credentials and a commitment to a career in national security.

YEAR PROGRAM STARTED: 1988

PURPOSE:
To encourage women to pursue careers related to the national security interests of the U.S.; to provide development opportunities to women who are already working in national security fields.

ELIGIBILITY:
Scholarship Program applicants should be pursuing studies in engineering, computer science, security studies, military history, government relations, cyber security, physics, mathematics, business, law, international relations, political science, operations research or economics. Other disciplines will be considered if the applicant can successfully demonstrate relevance to a career in the areas of national security or defense.

Scholarship Program applicants also must meet the following criteria (no exceptions will be considered):
(1) be a female currently enrolled at an accredited university or college, either full-time or part-time;
(2) undergraduate and graduate students are eligible; undergraduates must have attained at least junior-level status (60 credits);
(3) demonstrate interest in pursuing a career related to national security/national defense;
(4) demonstrate financial need;
(5) have a minimum grade point average of 3.25 and;
(6) be a citizen of the U.S.

Recipients of past awards may apply for future financial assistance.

FINANCIAL DATA:
Amount of support per award: Varies.
Total amount of support: Varies.

NO. MOST RECENT APPLICANTS: 90.

NO. AWARDS: 11 for the academic year 2020-21.

APPLICATION INFO:
Applications must be completed in full and include only the following requested items:
(1) one essay in three segments (no more than 500 words);
(2) official academic transcripts;
(3) two recommendation letters and;
(4) proof of U.S. citizenship.

Do not include copies of awards, certificates or photographs. Only students meeting eligibility requirements will be considered.
Deadline: March 12.

ADDRESS INQUIRIES TO:
Ann Webster, Associate Director
E-mail: awebster@ndia.org

*PLEASE NOTE:
Interested applicants should monitor WID's web site for detailed instructions and application deadlines.

WOMEN IN FILM   [994]
4221 Wilshire Boulevard
Suite 130
Los Angeles, CA 90010
(323) 935-2211
Fax: (323) 935-2212
E-mail: mverdugo@wif.org
Web Site: womeninfilm.org

FOUNDED: 1973

AREAS OF INTEREST:
Filmmaking.

NAME(S) OF PROGRAMS:
- **Women in Film Finishing Fund**

TYPE:
Project/program grants. Awards for completion of films on subjects that meet the stated guidelines of WIF on an annual basis.

YEAR PROGRAM STARTED: 1985

PURPOSE:
To increase employment and promote equal opportunities for women; to encourage individual creative projects by women; to enhance media images of women; to further the professional development of women; to influence prevailing attitudes and practices regarding and on behalf of women.

LEGAL BASIS:
Nonprofit organization.

ELIGIBILITY:
Filmmaker must have completed 90% of principal photography and have a rough cut at the time of application. Membership in Women In Film is not required. Writer and Director must identify as female or the Writer or Director must identify as female and the Protagonist must be female.

Applications are encouraged from around the world.

Student projects and web series are not eligible for funding.

FINANCIAL DATA:
Amount of support per award: Up to $25,000 in cash and/or in-kind services.
Total amount of support: Varies.

NO. AWARDS: 10 for the year 2020.

APPLICATION INFO:
Detailed guidelines and application form may be obtained from the Foundation's web site.
Duration: Varies.
Deadline: July 7.

ADDRESS INQUIRIES TO:
Melissa Verdugo, Manager of Programs
(See e-mail address above.)

*SPECIAL STIPULATIONS:
Projects must be in post-production by the deadline. Filmmakers must submit a rough cut of their films to be considered.

WOMEN'S CONGRESSIONAL POLICY INSTITUTE (WCPI) [995]
409 12th Street, S.W.
Suite 702
Washington, DC 20024
(202) 554-2323
Fax: (202) 554-2346
E-mail: cindy@wcpinst.org
Web Site: www.wcpinst.org

FOUNDED: 1995

AREAS OF INTEREST:
Public policy.

NAME(S) OF PROGRAMS:
- **Congressional Fellowships on Women and Public Policy**

TYPE:
Fellowships.

YEAR PROGRAM STARTED: 1980

PURPOSE:
To develop a cadre of talented leaders experienced in public policymaking at the national level; to encourage more effective participation by women in policy formation at all levels of government; to examine how policies affect women and men differently and encourage the formulation of policy options that recognize the needs of all people; to promote activities that encourage the translation of research into policy; to raise awareness that domestic and international issues affecting women are interdependent; to increase understanding that those issues often defined as "women's issues" are, in fact, issues of equal importance to men and women.

LEGAL BASIS:
501(c)(3) nonprofit organization.

ELIGIBILITY:
Only students who are currently enrolled in a Master's, doctoral, or professional degree program at an accredited institution, or who have completed such a program within two years of applying, are eligible. Applicant must be legally eligible to work in the U.S.

It is strongly recommended that applicants complete at least nine hours of graduate coursework before applying.

Applicant must have a demonstrated interest in research or political activity relevant to issues of interest to women and their families.

FINANCIAL DATA:
Amount of support per award:
Approximately $3,400 per month, plus $1,000 health care allowance for the year 2021.

NO. MOST RECENT APPLICANTS: Approximately 100.

NO. AWARDS: Approximately 3.

APPLICATION INFO:
Applications are available in early spring. Applicants must submit all academic transcripts, three letters of recommendation, completed application form and essay. Applications may be submitted online.
Duration: January through August. No renewals.
Deadline: Approximately June 1. Applicant should confirm exact date on the WCPI web site. Regional interviews of semi-finalists are held in June and awards made by July 31.

IRS I.D.: 52-1914894

STAFF:
Cindy Hall, President
Cheryl Williams, Vice President

ADDRESS INQUIRIES TO:
Cindy Hall, President
(See address above.)

WOMEN'S FOUNDATION OF MINNESOTA [996]

105 Fifth Avenue South
Suite 300
Minneapolis, MN 55401-6050
(612) 337-5010
Fax: (612) 337-0404
E-mail: contactus@wfmn.org
Web Site: www.wfmn.org

FOUNDED: 1983

AREAS OF INTEREST:
Women and girls in Minnesota.

NAME(S) OF PROGRAMS:
- **Community Response Fund**
- **girlsBEST Fund**
- **Ripley Memorial Foundation**
- **WFMN Fund for Safety**
- **Young Women's Initiative**

TYPE:
General operating grants; Project/program grants; Technical assistance. Responsive grants. The Women's Foundation of Minnesota has grant opportunities for organizations working in the three impact areas of economic opportunity, safety, and leadership.

YEAR PROGRAM STARTED: 1986

PURPOSE:
To invest in innovation to drive gender and racial equity in Minnesota; to make grants, invest in research, advocate policy, and forge cross-sector partnerships to ensure community-based, community-led solutions across Minnesota.

LEGAL BASIS:
Public foundation.

ELIGIBILITY:
Must primarily benefit women and girls and be not-for-profit or informal not-for-profit. Foundation does not fund direct service programs.

The Foundation applies an Intersectional Equity Framework inclusive of gender, race, place, and additional identities (ethnicity, sovereignty, socioeconomic class, age, disability, LGBTQ+, immigration status) to its research, grantmaking, public policy agenda, and internal work.

GEOG. RESTRICTIONS: Minnesota.

FINANCIAL DATA:
Amount of support per award: $5,000 to $25,000.
Total amount of support: Over $3,000,000 total funding in all programs.

NO. MOST RECENT APPLICANTS: 500.

APPLICATION INFO:
Detailed instructions and guidelines are available on the web site.
Duration: One to three years.
Deadline: Varies.

PUBLICATIONS:
Annual report; equality report; brochure; grant guidelines; research/issue reports.

IRS I.D.: 41-1635761

BOARD OF TRUSTEES:
Susan Segal, Chairperson
Nevada Littlewolf, Vice Chairperson
Gail Polley-Nordhaus, Treasurer
Chanda Smith-Baker, Secretary
Jennifer Alstad
Julia Classen
Joanne Green
Katharine L. Kelly

Rebecca Klevan
George Martin
Elena Brito Sifferlin
Roderic Southall
Valerie Spencer
Pheng Thao
Sandy Vargas

ADDRESS INQUIRIES TO:
Jasmine Sanchez
Senior Program Officer and
Grants Manager
(See address above.)

*SPECIAL STIPULATIONS:
Funds only in Minnesota.

WOMEN'S SPORTS FOUNDATION [997]

247 West 30th Street, 5th Floor
New York, NY 10001
(516) 542-4700
(800) 227-3988
Fax: (212) 967-2757
E-mail: info@womenssportsfoundation.org
Web Site: www.womenssportsfoundation.org

FOUNDED: 1974

AREAS OF INTEREST:
The Foundation - the leading authority on the participation of women and girls in sports - advocates for equality, educates the public, conducts research and offers grants to promote sports and physical activity for girls and women.

NAME(S) OF PROGRAMS:
- **Travel & Training Fund**

TYPE:
Training grants; Travel grants.

YEAR PROGRAM STARTED: 1984

PURPOSE:
To advance the lives of girls and women through sports and physical activity; to provide direct financial assistance to aspiring female athletes with successful competitive records who have potential to achieve even higher performance levels and rankings.

LEGAL BASIS:
501(c)(3) nonprofit organization.

ELIGIBILITY:
Individual applicants and all members of a team must be female U.S. citizens or legal residents and be eligible to compete for a U.S. national team. Applicants must have amateur status.

GEOG. RESTRICTIONS: United States.

FINANCIAL DATA:
Amount of support per award: $2,500 to $10,000.
Total amount of support: Minimum $75,000 annually.

NO. AWARDS: Varies.

APPLICATION INFO:
Contact the Foundation for guidelines.
Duration: One year.

PUBLICATIONS:
Annual report; research reports; educational guides; educational curriculum.

IRS I.D.: 23-7380557

OFFICERS:
Dr. Deborah Antonine, Chief Executive Officer
Phaidra Knight, President

ADDRESS INQUIRIES TO:
Anne Peltier, Coordinator
Community Impact
(See address above.)

*SPECIAL STIPULATIONS:
Applicants must demonstrate accomplishments and potential to be considered. No travel grants outside the U.S. An individual or team may be awarded only one grant per calendar year and a maximum of three grants in a lifetime.

ZONTA FOUNDATION FOR WOMEN

1200 Harger Road, Suite 330
Oak Brook, IL 60523
(630) 928-1400
E-mail: programs@zonta.org
Web Site: www.zonta.org

TYPE:
Fellowships. Awarded annually to women pursing a Ph.D./doctoral degree conducting research applied to aerospace engineering or space sciences.

See entry 1846 for full listing.

ZONTA FOUNDATION FOR WOMEN

1200 Harger Road, Suite 330
Oak Brook, IL 60523
(630) 928-1400
E-mail: programs@zonta.org
Web Site: www.zonta.org

TYPE:
Awards/prizes; Scholarships. For women of any nationality pursuing degrees in business who demonstrate outstanding potential in the field of business.

See entry 1722 for full listing.

ZONTA FOUNDATION FOR WOMEN [998]

1200 Harger Road, Suite 330
Oak Brook, IL 60523
(630) 928-1400
E-mail: programs@zonta.org
Web Site: www.zonta.org

FOUNDED: 1919

AREAS OF INTEREST:
Encouraging women's involvement in public affairs.

NAME(S) OF PROGRAMS:
- **Young Women in Public Affairs Awards**

TYPE:
Awards/prizes.

YEAR PROGRAM STARTED: 1990

PURPOSE:
To encourage young women's involvement and interest in public affairs.

LEGAL BASIS:
Incorporated in the state of Illinois as a nonprofit organization.

ELIGIBILITY:
Women of ages 16 to 19 on April 1 of each year, living in a Zonta district/region, or a citizen of a Zonta country, who demonstrate evidence of the following, are eligible to apply:
(1) active commitment to volunteerism;
(2) experience in local government, student government or workplace leadership (paid or unpaid);

(3) volunteer leadership achievements;
(4) knowledge of Zonta International and its programs and;
(5) advocating for Zonta International's mission of advancing the status of women worldwide.

Applicants from geographic areas within a Zonta district/region where no clubs are located will be considered and also eligible to apply for the district/region award.

FINANCIAL DATA:
Amount of support per award: District award recipients receive $1,500 (U.S.) from the Zonta Foundation for Women YWPA Fund. Districts may choose to add to this award amount. Also, 10 international award recipients are selected from district recipients and receive an additional $4,000 (U.S.)

Total amount of support: Varies.

NO. MOST RECENT APPLICANTS: 32.

NO. AWARDS: 32.

APPLICATION INFO:
The YWPA Awards program operates at the club, district and international levels of Zonta International and is managed by Zonta members. To apply, contact the Zonta Club within the applicant's district/region for deadlines and an address to mail application. (Such contact information is available on the web site.) Alternatively, one can e-mail one's name and contact information to the Young Women in Public Affairs Committee Chairman at ywpachairman@zonta.org.

Deadline: Must contact Zonta Club directly for deadline.

ADDRESS INQUIRIES TO:
Programs Senior Coordinator
(See e-mail address above.)

URBAN AND REGIONAL AFFAIRS

Children and youth

THE JOHN W. ALDEN TRUST [999]

c/o Emma M. Greene, Senior V.P.
Philanthropic Client Dir., U.S. Trust
Bank of America Private Wealth Management
225 Franklin Street, MA1-225-04-02
Boston, MA 02110
(617) 951-1108
E-mail: susan.t.monahan@gmail.com
Web Site: www.cybergrants.com/alden

AREAS OF INTEREST:
Education and therapy for children who are blind, retarded, disabled, mentally or physically ill; medical and scientific research for the prevention and/or cure of the conditions.

TYPE:
Capital grants; Challenge/matching grants; Conferences/seminars; Demonstration grants; Development grants; Matching gifts; Project/program grants; Research grants; Seed money grants; Technical assistance; Training grants.

LEGAL BASIS:
Private foundation.

ELIGIBILITY:
Organizations must be IRS 501(c)(3) tax-exempt and serve residents of eastern Massachusetts.

FINANCIAL DATA:
Amount of support per award: Generally up to $20,000.
Total amount of support: $555,500 for fiscal year 2020.
Matching fund requirements: Determined on a case-by-case basis.

NO. AWARDS: 44 grants for the year 2020.

REPRESENTATIVE AWARDS:
$10,000 to Silver Lining Mentoring; $10,000 to Triangle; $20,000 to House of Possibilities.

APPLICATION INFO:
All applications must be submitted online.
Duration: Varies.
Deadline: Approximately January 5, April 5, July 5 and October 5.

PUBLICATIONS:
Guidelines.

TRUSTEES:
Emma Green
Susan T. Monahan, Grants Coordinator

ADDRESS INQUIRIES TO:
Susan T. Monahan
Grants Coordinator and Trustee
(See e-mail address above.)

THE ISABEL ALLENDE FOUNDATION

116 Caledonia Street
Sausalito, CA 94965
(415) 289-0992
E-mail: lori@isabelallende.com
Web Site: www.isabelallendefoundation.org

TYPE:
Project/program grants. Promotes and preserves the fundamental rights of women and children to be empowered and protected.

See entry 967 for full listing.

AMERICAN ACADEMY OF CHILD AND ADOLESCENT PSYCHIATRY

3615 Wisconsin Avenue, N.W.
Washington, DC 20016-3007
(202) 966-7300 ext. 117
Fax: (202) 966-5894
E-mail: aarcher@aacap.org
Web Site: www.aacap.org

TYPE:
Conferences/seminars; Fellowships; Research grants; Travel grants. Educational Outreach Program provides travel support for residents and CAP fellows to travel to the Annual Meeting and network with child and adolescent psychiatrists.

Joshi International Scholar Awards recognize midcareer international physicians who primarily work with children and adolescents providing mental health services outside the U.S.

Junior Investigator Award is offered for one child and adolescent psychiatry junior faculty to pursue innovative research. The research may be basic or clinical in nature but must be relevant to the understanding, treatment and prevention of child and adolescent mental health disorders. The award also includes the cost of attending AACAP's Annual Meeting for five days.

Life Members Mentorship Grant for Medical Students provides travel support for medical student recipients to receive a formal overview of child and adolescent psychiatry, establish mentor relationships with child and adolescent psychiatrists, and experience AACAP's Annual Meeting.

Pilot Awards are offered to members with a career interest in child and adolescent mental health research.

Ülgür International Scholar Award recognizes a child and adolescent psychiatrist or a physician in the international community who has made significant contributions to the enhancement of mental health services for children and adolescents.

See entry 2308 for full listing.

AMERICAN ACADEMY OF CHILD AND ADOLESCENT PSYCHIATRY

3615 Wisconsin Avenue, N.W.
Washington, DC 20016-3007
(202) 966-7300 ext. 117
Fax: (202) 966-5894
E-mail: aarcher@aacap.org
Web Site: www.aacap.org

TYPE:
Project/program grants; Research grants; Travel grants. The Marilyn B. Benoit, M.D., Child Maltreatment Mentorship Award facilitates the completion of a project in which the applicant collaborates with a mentor specializing in the areas of child welfare, foster care, and/or children maltreatment prevention/intervention.

The Psychodynamic Faculty Training and Mentorship Initiative provides a reimbursable travel stipend to cover travel support for attending the required program events during AACAP's Annual Meeting.

See entry 2309 for full listing.

AMERICAN ACADEMY OF CHILD AND ADOLESCENT PSYCHIATRY

3615 Wisconsin Avenue, N.W.
Washington, DC 20016-3007
(202) 966-7300 ext. 117
Fax: (202) 966-5894
E-mail: aarcher@aacap.org
Web Site: www.aacap.org

TYPE:
Awards/prizes; Conferences/seminars; Fellowships; Research grants; Travel grants. Jeanne Spurlock Minority Medical Student Research Fellowship in Substance Abuse and Addiction provides support for research training in substance abuse and addiction under a mentor with experience in the type of research that is being proposed, and whose work includes children and adolescents participants.

Summer Medical Student Fellowship provides clinical or research training under a child and adolescent psychiatrist mentor.

See entry 2307 for full listing.

ANDRUS FAMILY FUND

200 Madison Avenue, 25th Floor
New York, NY 10016
(212) 687-6975
E-mail: jkaizer@affund.org
info@affund.org
Web Site: affund.org

TYPE:
Project/program grants.

See entry 1056 for full listing.

BAINUM FAMILY FOUNDATION [1000]

7735 Old Georgetown Road, Suite 1000
Bethesda, MD 20814
(240) 450-0000
Fax: (240) 450-4115
E-mail: swhite@bainumfdn.org
Web Site: www.bainumfdn.org

FOUNDED: 1968

AREAS OF INTEREST:
Early learning (birth to three years of age), wrap-around support, and knowledge building.

TYPE:
Practice, policy, and research programs.

YEAR PROGRAM STARTED: 1968

PURPOSE:
To support educational programs assisting underserved children/youth.

LEGAL BASIS:
Private foundation.

ELIGIBILITY:
Eligible organizations must be IRS 501(c)(3) tax-exempt.

GEOG. RESTRICTIONS: Baltimore, Maryland and Washington, DC metropolitan areas.

FINANCIAL DATA:
Amount of support per award: Approximately $50,000.
Total amount of support: $20,000,000.

NO. AWARDS: Approximately 400.

APPLICATION INFO:
Applications are accepted by invitation only.
Duration: Varies.
Deadline: Varies.

ADDRESS INQUIRIES TO:
Shantelice White, Director of
Grants Management
(See address above.)

THE BOY SCOUTS OF AMERICA, NATIONAL EAGLE SCOUT ASSOCIATION [1001]

1325 West Walnut Hill Lane
P.O. Box 152079
Irving, TX 75015-2079
(972) 580-2000
E-mail: nesa@scouting.org
Web Site: www.nesa.org

AREAS OF INTEREST:
Scouting and youth.

NAME(S) OF PROGRAMS:
• **Hall/McElwain Merit Scholarships**
• **Robert and Rebeca Palmer Scholarship**

TYPE:
Scholarships.

PURPOSE:
To serve Eagle Scouts and through them, the
entire movement of Scouting.

ELIGIBILITY:
Must be graduating high school senior or an
undergraduate college student no later than
completion of their junior year. Applicant
must have demonstrated leadership ability in
scouting and a strong record of participation
in activities outside of scouting.

Applicant must be a member of the National
Eagle Scout Association and must supply
Scout history and participation. Award is not
based on financial need or grades.

FINANCIAL DATA:
Scholarships are for tuition, room, board and
books.
Amount of support per award: $2,500 to
$5,000.
Total amount of support: Varies.

NO. AWARDS: Varies, depending on funds
available.

APPLICATION INFO:
Application process begins December 1.
Information is available on the Association
web site. Application must be submitted
online.
Duration: One-time award.
Deadline: February 12.

ADDRESS INQUIRIES TO:
See e-mail address above.

*PLEASE NOTE:
This scholarship is not available to students
attending any of the U.S. military academies.

*SPECIAL STIPULATIONS:
Applicant must fill out new application each
year.

THE BOY SCOUTS OF AMERICA, NATIONAL EAGLE SCOUT ASSOCIATION [1002]

1325 West Walnut Hill Lane
P.O. Box 152079
Irving, TX 75015-2079
(972) 580-2000
E-mail: nesa@scouting.org
Web Site: www.nesa.org

AREAS OF INTEREST:
Scouting and youth.

NAME(S) OF PROGRAMS:
• **Mabel and Lawrence S. Cooke
Scholarship**
• **National Eagle Scout Scholarship Fund**

TYPE:
Scholarships.

PURPOSE:
To serve Eagle Scouts and through them, the
entire movement of Scouting.

ELIGIBILITY:
For the Mabel and Lawrence S. Cooke
Scholarship, applicant must register and
maintain status as a full-time student at a
college/university. The scholarship is not
available to students attending any of the
U.S. military academies, because the U.S.
government pays expenses that are covered
by NESA scholarships at these academies.

National Eagle Scout Scholarship Fund
applicants must register and maintain status
as a full-time student at a college/university.
Applicant must be a member of the National
Eagle Scout Association.

FINANCIAL DATA:
Funds are for tuition, room, board, and
books.
Amount of support per award: Mabel and
Lawrence S. Cooke Scholarship: One
scholarship of up to $48,000 (up to $12,000
per year for four years) and four $25,000
scholarships ($6,250 per year for four years)
are given annually; National Eagle Scout
Scholarship Fund: $5,000.
Total amount of support: Varies.

NO. AWARDS: Varies.

APPLICATION INFO:
Application information is available on the
web site. Application must be submitted
online.
Duration: Up to four years.
Deadline: Applications open December 1;
submit no later than February 12.

ADDRESS INQUIRIES TO:
See e-mail address above.

THE LOUIS CALDER FOUNDATION [1003]

999 18th Street
Suite 2350S
Denver, CO 80202
(720) 943-9865
E-mail: proposals@calderfdn.org
Web Site: www.louiscalderfoundation.org

FOUNDED: 1951

AREAS OF INTEREST:
Education reform.

TYPE:
Capital grants; Project/program grants.
Curriculum development.

YEAR PROGRAM STARTED: 1951

PURPOSE:
To promote scholastic development of
children and youth by improving elementary
and secondary education through its support
of charter and parochial schools.

LEGAL BASIS:
Private foundation.

ELIGIBILITY:
The Foundation typically gives funding
consideration to education programs in the
areas of development of new charter and
independent parochial K-8 schools, expansion

of existing, high-performing charter
management organizations, and teacher and
leadership development.

GEOG. RESTRICTIONS: Continental United States.

FINANCIAL DATA:
Amount of support per award: Average
$100,000.
Total amount of support: Approximately
$6,500,000 annually.

NO. AWARDS: Over 50.

APPLICATION INFO:
The Foundation does not accept unsolicited
proposals. Organizations unfamiliar to the
Foundation, or those that are not current
grantees, are encouraged to submit a letter of
inquiry via the web site. If the organization's
programming falls within the parameters of
the current grantmaking strategy and is
selected for further review, a full proposal
will be requested.
Duration: Varies.

PUBLICATIONS:
Annual report.

IRS I.D.: 13-6015562

TRUSTEES:
M. Alexander Calder
Peter D. Calder
Frank E. Shanley

ADDRESS INQUIRIES TO:
Holly Nuechterlein, Program Director
(See e-mail address above.)

CAMPBELL FOUNDATION, INC. [1004]

705 York Road
Towson, MD 21204
(410) 828-1961
Fax: (410) 821-8814
E-mail: lcasciero@stoycpa.com

AREAS OF INTEREST:
Social services, education, arts and cultural
programs.

TYPE:
Capital grants; General operating grants;
Project/program grants.

PURPOSE:
To provide support for cultural, educational
and social services and institutions.

LEGAL BASIS:
Nonprofit foundation.

ELIGIBILITY:
Organization must have 501(c)(3) status.

GEOG. RESTRICTIONS: Maryland, primarily
Baltimore.

FINANCIAL DATA:
Amount of support per award: $2,500 to
$5,000 general operating grant; $15,000 to
$20,000 capital grant.
Total amount of support: Average $190,000
per year.

NO. AWARDS: Average 80 per year.

APPLICATION INFO:
Organizations must submit a written
proposal, up to two pages in length,
including program specifications. Proof of
501(c)(3) status required.
Duration: One year. Renewal by
reapplication.
Deadline: November 15.

ADDRESS INQUIRIES TO:
Virginia T. Campbell, President
(See address above.)

THE CARSON SCHOLARS FUND, INC.
305 West Chesapeake Avenue
Suite 310
Towson, MD 21204
(410) 828-1005
Fax: (410) 828-1007
E-mail: lrichards@carsonscholars.org
Web Site: carsonscholars.org

TYPE:
Scholarships. The Carson Scholars Fund awards college scholarships to students in grades 4-11 who excel academically and are dedicated to serving their communities.

See entry 1490 for full listing.

THOMAS AND AGNES CARVEL FOUNDATION   [1005]
35 East Grassy Sprain Road
Yonkers, NY 10710
(914) 793-7300
Fax: (914) 793-7381
E-mail: tacarvelfoundation@gmail.com

AREAS OF INTEREST:
Children, youth, health and religion.

TYPE:
General operating grants; Grants-in-aid; Matching gifts; Project/program grants; Research grants.

ELIGIBILITY:
Applicants must be 501(c)(3) tax-exempt organizations. Grants may be given to religious organizations that meet geographic requirements. No grants to individuals.

GEOG. RESTRICTIONS: Connecticut, New Jersey and New York.

FINANCIAL DATA:
Amount of support per award: Varies, depending on needs and nature of the request.

APPLICATION INFO:
No application form required. Applicants must provide IRS tax-exempt documentation.
Duration: One year. Renewable.

ADDRESS INQUIRIES TO:
Peter A. Smith, President
(See address above.)

THE CENTER AT SIERRA HEALTH FOUNDATION
1321 Garden Highway
Suite 210
Sacramento, CA 95833
(916) 993-7701
E-mail: impact@shfcenter.org
Web Site: www.shfcenter.org

TYPE:
Matching gifts; Project/program grants.

See entry 1334 for full listing.

CHILDREN'S BUREAU   [1006]
Administration on Children, Youth and Families
330 C Street, S.W.
Washington, DC 20201
(202) 205-8172
E-mail: jan.shafer@acf.hhs.gov
Web Site: www.acf.hhs.gov/cb

FOUNDED: 1974

AREAS OF INTEREST:
Prevention, identification, assessment and treatment of child abuse and neglect, sexual abuse, incidence of abuse and neglect.

NAME(S) OF PROGRAMS:
● **Child Abuse Prevention and Treatment Act (CAPTA) Discretionary Grants**

TYPE:
Demonstration grants; Project/program grants; Research grants; Technical assistance; Training grants.

YEAR PROGRAM STARTED: 1974

PURPOSE:
To assist state, local and voluntary agencies and organizations to strengthen their capacities to prevent child abuse and neglect, identify and assess abused and neglected children and provide necessary ameliorative services to them and their families.

LEGAL BASIS:
Public Law 102-295, 45 CFR Subtitle B, part 1340.

ELIGIBILITY:
Grants for demonstration programs or projects and research projects may be made to states, public agencies, community-based organizations, or public or private organizations.

FINANCIAL DATA:
Amount of support per award: Average $400,000.
Total amount of support: $25,310,000 budgeted for fiscal year 2019.

APPLICATION INFO:
Standard grant application forms provided by the agency must be used. Complete instructions and necessary forms are issued with each announcement or solicitation, which is published on grants.gov.
Duration: Normally 36 to 60 months.
Deadline: Varies.

ADDRESS INQUIRIES TO:
Jan Shafer, Director
Division of Program Innovation
(See address above.)

*SPECIAL STIPULATIONS:
Financial and program progress reports are required semiannually; a final report and an expenditure report are required no later than 90 days after the completion of the project. Audits conducted. Records must be maintained for three years.

ADOLPH COORS FOUNDATION   [1007]
215 St. Paul Street, Suite 300
Denver, CO 80206
(303) 388-1636
Fax: (303) 388-1684
E-mail: info@acoorsfdn.org
Web Site: coorsfoundation.org

FOUNDED: 1976

AREAS OF INTEREST:
Primarily youth, job training, and self-sufficiency.

TYPE:
Capital grants; General operating grants; Project/program grants.

PURPOSE:
To build a stronger, healthier society.

ELIGIBILITY:
Organizations must be classified as 501(c)(3) and operate within the U.S. The Foundation does not consider grants to organizations that in policy or practice discriminate on the basis of race, creed or gender. No grants to religious organizations or individuals.

GEOG. RESTRICTIONS: Colorado.

FINANCIAL DATA:
Amount of support per award: Varies.
Total amount of support: $7,700,000 for the year 2020.

NO. AWARDS: 146 for the year 2020.

APPLICATION INFO:
Applications may only be submitted online.
Duration: One year.
Deadline: March 1, July 1 and November 1.

ADDRESS INQUIRIES TO:
Carrie Tynan, Executive Director
(See address above.)

THE CRAIL-JOHNSON FOUNDATION   [1008]
461 West 6th Street
Suite 300
San Pedro, CA 90731
(310) 519-7413
Fax: (310) 519-7221
Web Site: www.crail-johnson.org

FOUNDED: 1987

AREAS OF INTEREST:
Underserved children, youth and families in the areas of health, education and human services.

TYPE:
General operating grants; Project/program grants.

YEAR PROGRAM STARTED: 1987

PURPOSE:
To promote the well-being of children in need through effective application of human and financial resources.

LEGAL BASIS:
Private foundation.

ELIGIBILITY:
Applicants must be tax-exempt 501(c)(3) organizations. No grants to individuals.

GEOG. RESTRICTIONS: Los Angeles, California.

FINANCIAL DATA:
Amount of support per award: $50 to $30,000.

APPLICATION INFO:
Consult applications procedure page of web site.
Duration: Typically one year.
Deadline: Varies.

PUBLICATIONS:
Guidelines.

OFFICERS:
Craig C. Johnson, Chairman
Alan C. Johnson, President
Byung Kim, Chief Financial Officer

MICHAEL AND SUSAN DELL FOUNDATION   [1009]
4417 Westlake Drive
Austin, TX 78746
Fax: (512) 600-5501
E-mail: info@dell.org
Web Site: www.dell.org

AREAS OF INTEREST:
Education, family economic stability, and childhood health.

TYPE:
Project/program grants. Grants to support and initiate programs that directly serve the needs of children living in urban poverty.

PURPOSE:
To improve outcomes for children, living in urban poverty around the world, in a measurable way.

ELIGIBILITY:
Eligible organizations must be 501(c)(3) or have a fiscal sponsor which is 501(c)(3).

GEOG. RESTRICTIONS: United States, India and South Africa.

FINANCIAL DATA:
Foundation will not fund more than 25% of a project's budget or more than 10% of an organization's total annual operating expenses.
Amount of support per award: Varies.
Total amount of support: Varies.

APPLICATION INFO:
All grant requests should be submitted via online form.
Duration: Varies.

THE CLEVELAND H. DODGE FOUNDATION, INC. [1010]
420 Lexington Avenue, Suite 2331
New York, NY 10170
(212) 972-2800
E-mail: emommsen@chdodgefoundation.org
Web Site: www.chdodgefoundation.org

FOUNDED: 1917

AREAS OF INTEREST:
Educational and supportive services for youth in under-resourced communities.

TYPE:
Project/program grants.

YEAR PROGRAM STARTED: 1917

PURPOSE:
To support projects and programs with community organizations and institutions that provide educational and supportive services for youth in under-resourced communities.

LEGAL BASIS:
Private foundation.

ELIGIBILITY:
Grants are made to nonprofit, 501(c)(3) organizations in the Foundation's areas of interest. No grants are made to individuals.

GEOG. RESTRICTIONS: New York City, New York.

FINANCIAL DATA:
Amount of support per award: $5,000 to $50,000; average grant: $25,000.
Total amount of support: $2,500,000 for the year 2019.

NO. MOST RECENT APPLICANTS: Approximately 100.

NO. AWARDS: 45.

APPLICATION INFO:
Applicants must provide:
(1) a letter describing the organization and grant request, including budget;
(2) annual report and;
(3) proof of 501(c)(3) status.
Duration: Typically one year. Multiyear commitments are few in number.
Deadline: April 15 and September 15.

IRS I.D.: 13-6015087

ADDRESS INQUIRIES TO:
Emily Mommsen, Executive Director
(See address above.)

EAST TENNESSEE FOUNDATION [1011]
520 West Summit Hill Drive
Suite 1101
Knoxville, TN 37902
(865) 524-1223
(877) 524-1223
Fax: (865) 637-6039
E-mail: etf@etf.org
Web Site: www.easttennesseefoundation.org

FOUNDED: 1986

AREAS OF INTEREST:
Arts and culture, youth-at-risk, community development, affordable housing construction, and scholarships.

CONSULTING OR VOLUNTEER SERVICES:
A variety of technical assistance to applicants and grantees.

TYPE:
Project/program grants; Scholarships; Seed money grants; Technical assistance. The Foundation is comprised of 474 philanthropic funds and nine supporting organizations.

PURPOSE:
To make the region a better place today and for future generations.

LEGAL BASIS:
Community foundation; 501(c)(3) organization.

ELIGIBILITY:
Grants are awarded to 501(c)(3) public charities, units of government, or educational institutions. The Foundation does not make grants or loans to individuals.

GEOG. RESTRICTIONS: Counties in East Tennessee.

FINANCIAL DATA:
Amount of support per award: Funding support generally $500 to $10,000 per year for competitive grants and scholarships; $15,000 to $140,000 in Affordable Housing Trust Fund (AHTF) grants.
Total amount of support: Varies.

APPLICATION INFO:
Applications are accepted online.
Duration: Varies.
Deadline: Varies.

PUBLICATIONS:
Connect, quarterly newsletter; annual reports; documents; brochures.

IRS I.D.: 62-0807696

STAFF:
Michael McClamroch, President and Chief Executive Officer
Carolyn Schwenn, Executive Vice President and Secretary
Tamara Boyer, Vice President for Advancement
Jan Elston, Vice President for Competitive Grant Program
Deanene Catani, Director of Communications

ADDRESS INQUIRIES TO:
Michael McClamroch
President and Chief Executive Officer
(See address above.)

*PLEASE NOTE:
Organizations located outside of the Foundation's service area are not eligible for funding.

THE EISNER FOUNDATION [1012]
9401 Wilshire Boulevard
Suite 735
Beverly Hills, CA 90212
(310) 228-6808
E-mail: info@eisnerfoundation.org
Web Site: eisnerfoundation.org

FOUNDED: 1996

AREAS OF INTEREST:
Intergenerational programs.

TYPE:
Capital grants; General operating grants; Project/program grants. The Eisner Foundation supports organizations offering intergenerational solutions to society's greatest challenges through its grant-making programs.
Capacity-Building Grants support training or planning.
Capital Project Grants support buying, constructing or renovating facilities.
General Operating Grants offer unrestricted support.
Opportunity Grants aim to help smaller organizations grow and gain credibility, and encourage organizations to be innovative and entrepreneurial in developing new intergenerational solutions.
Project Support Grants offer funding for specific projects or initiatives.

PURPOSE:
To identify, advocate for, and invest in high-quality and innovative programs that unite multiple generations for the betterment of our communities.

LEGAL BASIS:
501(c)(3) organization.

ELIGIBILITY:
Tax-exempt 501(c)(3) organizations based in Los Angeles County or doing work that benefits populations in Los Angeles County are eligible to apply. Grants are available for general operating expenses, project support, capacity-building, and capital projects.

Opportunity Grants are offered to smaller organizations or larger organizations launching new intergenerational initiatives.

GEOG. RESTRICTIONS: Los Angeles County, California.

FINANCIAL DATA:
Amount of support per award: Typically $100,000 to $300,000; Opportunity Grants: Up to $25,000.

Total amount of support: Approximately $7,500,000 per year.

REPRESENTATIVE AWARDS:
$125,000 to CASA of Los Angeles to recruit volunteer court advocates for children in the child welfare system; $50,000 to Heart of Los Angeles to increase access to services for seniors and create volunteer opportunities that will facilitate intergenerational connections with HOLA youth; $150,000 (over two years) to Turnaround Arts to bring high-quality arts education resources to Los Angeles County's lowest performing elementary and middle schools.

APPLICATION INFO:
Before submitting a Letter of Inquiry, organization must answer brief questions online to determine eligibility.

Duration: One year or multiyear. Opportunity Grants are available for one-year terms and are renewable for small organizations. Large organizations with successful initiatives may apply for additional grant funds after one year, but cannot renew an Opportunity Grant.

Deadline: Letters of Intent are accepted year-round. Full grant proposals are presented to the Board for quarterly review with the exception of Opportunity Grant proposals, which are presented in June and December.

IRS I.D.: 95-4607191

STAFF:
Trent Stamp, Chief Executive Officer
Cathy Choi, Senior Director of Programs
Chelsea Mason, Director of External Relations
Christine Dragan, Foundation Administrator

ADDRESS INQUIRIES TO:
Trent Stamp, Chief Executive Officer
(See address above.)

LOIS AND RICHARD ENGLAND FAMILY FOUNDATION   [1013]
P.O. Box 34-1077
Bethesda, MD 20827
(301) 657-7737
Fax: (301) 657-7738
E-mail: englandfamilyfdn@gmail.com
Web Site: fdnweb.org/england

FOUNDED: 1990

AREAS OF INTEREST:
Arts and culture, education and youth development, justice reform, reproductive health, Jewish community life, and voting rights.

TYPE:
Capital grants; Challenge/matching grants; Development grants; General operating grants; Matching gifts; Project/program grants; Seed money grants; Technical assistance; Training grants.

YEAR PROGRAM STARTED: 1994

PURPOSE:
To improve the lives of those in need in the Washington, DC metropolitan area; to strengthen Jewish life and institutions locally, nationally and in Israel.

LEGAL BASIS:
Private family foundation.

ELIGIBILITY:
Organizations must be classified by the IRS as public charities and tax-exempt under Section 501(c)(3) of the IRS Code of 1986. Unsolicited proposals are not considered. No grants to individuals.

GEOG. RESTRICTIONS: Washington, DC and Israel.

FINANCIAL DATA:
Amount of support per award: Typically, $20,000 to $50,000.
Total amount of support: Approximately $2,000,000 for the year 2018.

NO. MOST RECENT APPLICANTS: 80.

NO. AWARDS: Approximately 50.

REPRESENTATIVE AWARDS:
Jewish Giving: $15,000 to American Jewish Committee. Washington, DC Giving: $25,000 to Heads Up. Discretionary Grants: $30,000 to Lymphoma Research Foundation.

APPLICATION INFO:
The Foundation does not accept unsolicited proposals. Any organization interested in applying should first submit the online Letter of Inquiry.
Duration: Annual grants.
Deadline: Educational and Youth Development grants: Spring; Jewish Community Life grants: Fall.

BOARD OF DIRECTORS:
Rick England, President
Nonie Akman, Vice President
Jonathan Akman, Treasurer
Leah Gelb, Secretary

ADDRESS INQUIRIES TO:
Alexis Connolly, Grants Management
(See address above.)

FOSTER CARE TO SUCCESS
23811 Chagrin Boulevard
Suite 210
Cleveland, OH 44122
(571) 203-0270
E-mail: scholarships@fc2success.org
Web Site: www.fc2success.org

TYPE:
Scholarships.

See entry 1387 for full listing.

H.B. FULLER COMPANY FOUNDATION   [1014]
1200 Willow Lake Boulevard
St. Paul, MN 55110
(651) 236-5900
E-mail: hbfullerfoundation@hbfuller.com
Web Site: www.hbfuller.com/community

FOUNDED: 1974

AREAS OF INTEREST:
STEM education for youth (science, technology, engineering and math), youth leadership development, and racial equity.

NAME(S) OF PROGRAMS:
● **Leadership Development for Youth**
● **Racial Equity**
● **STEM Education**

TYPE:
Project/program grants. Leadership Development for Youth supports organizations and programs that help young people become successful, productive adults.

Racial Equity supports programs focused on addressing racial inequities in the areas of employment, education and community safety.

STEM Education supports youth education initiatives in the areas of science, technology, engineering and math (STEM).

PURPOSE:
To support charitable activities of the company.

ELIGIBILITY:
Must be an eligible, tax-exempt 501(c)(3) organization. Projects must be aligned with the Company's focus areas and must aim to benefit people where employees live and work.

GEOG. RESTRICTIONS: Greater Atlanta, Georgia; Aurora, Illinois; South Bend, Indiana; Paducah, Kentucky; Peabody, Massachusetts; Grand Rapids and Michigan Center, Michigan; Twin Cities metropolitan area, Minnesota; Rexdale, Ontario; Simpsonville, South Carolina; and Vancouver, Washington.

FINANCIAL DATA:
Amount of support per award: Varies. Individual grants typically are from $5,000 to $10,000.
Total amount of support: Varies.

APPLICATION INFO:
Online application process.
Duration: Typically one year.
Deadline: Leadership Development for Youth and STEM Education: Proposals accepted March 1 to 31 and August 1 to 31. Racial Equity: Proposals accepted May 1 to May 31.

ADDRESS INQUIRIES TO:
H.B. Fuller Community Affairs
(See e-mail address above.)

THE GERBER FOUNDATION   [1015]
4747 West 48th Street
Suite 153
Fremont, MI 49412
(231) 924-3175
Fax: (231) 924-7906
E-mail: tgf@gerberfoundation.org
Web Site: www.gerberfoundation.org

FOUNDED: 1952

AREAS OF INTEREST:
Enhancing the quality of life of infants and young children in nutrition, care and development.

TYPE:
Matching gifts; Research grants. Grants to ensure the continuity of scientific and educational research in infant nutrition and child health. Matching gifts to 501(c)(3) educational, health and human services institutions within the U.S.

YEAR PROGRAM STARTED: 1952

PURPOSE:
To enhance the quality of life of infants and young children.

LEGAL BASIS:
Private foundation.

ELIGIBILITY:
Must be 501(c)(3).

GEOG. RESTRICTIONS: United States.

FINANCIAL DATA:
Amount of support per award: Matching Gifts: $75 to $2,250; Research Grants: $20,000 to $350,000.
Total amount of support: $3,794,288 for the year 2019.
Matching fund requirements: Must be a Gerber Products Company retiree and have retired before July 1, 2002.

NO. MOST RECENT APPLICANTS: 57 Matching Gifts and 244 Research Grants for the year 2019.

NO. AWARDS: 201 Matching Gifts and 14 Research Grants for the year 2019.

APPLICATION INFO:
Research grant applicants should submit a two- to three-page letter of inquiry initially. Applications for all programs are submitted through the gerberfoundation.smartsimple.com web site.
Duration: One-time award with annual review.
Deadline: Letters of inquiry due May 15 and November 15.

PUBLICATIONS:
Guidelines; application.

IRS I.D.: 38-6068090

OFFICERS:
Barbara J. Ivens, President
Fernando Flores-New, Vice President
Stan VanderRoest, Treasurer
Tracy Baker, Secretary

ADDRESS INQUIRIES TO:
Catherine Obits, Program Manager
(See address above.)

THE WILLIAM T. GRANT FOUNDATION   [1016]
One Grand Central Place, 43rd Floor
60 East 42nd Street
New York, NY 10165
(212) 752-0071
Fax: (212) 752-1398
E-mail: info@wtgrantfdn.org
Web Site: wtgrantfoundation.org

FOUNDED: 1936

AREAS OF INTEREST:
Supporting research to improve the lives of
young people in the U.S.

NAME(S) OF PROGRAMS:
- **William T. Grant Scholars Program**
- **Institutional Challenge Grant**
- **Research Grants Program**
- **Youth Service Improvement Grants Program**

TYPE:
Project/program grants; Research grants.
William T. Grant Scholars Program supports
promising early career researchers from
diverse disciplines. The award is intended to
facilitate the professional development of
early career scholars who have demonstrated
success in conducting high-quality research
and are seeking to further develop their skills
and research program.

The Institutional Challenge Grant encourages
university-based research institutes, schools
and centers to build sustained
research-practice partnerships with public
agencies or nonprofit organizations to reduce
inequality in youth outcomes.

The Youth Service Improvement Grants
Program supports activities conducted by
community-based organizations in the five
boroughs of New York City to improve the
quality of services for young people ages 8
to 25.

YEAR PROGRAM STARTED: 1936

PURPOSE:
To help create a society that values young
people and enables them to reach their full
potential. In pursuit of this goal, the
Foundation invests in research and in people
and projects that use evidence-based
approaches.

LEGAL BASIS:
Private foundation.

ELIGIBILITY:
Organization must have 501(c)(3) status. No
grants to individuals.

GEOG. RESTRICTIONS: United States.

FINANCIAL DATA:
Amount of support per award: William T.
Grant Scholars Program: Up to $350,000;
Institutional Challenge Grant: $650,000;

Research Grants: $100,000 to $600,000;
Youth Service Improvement Grants Program:
$25,000.
Total amount of support: Varies.

NO. AWARDS: William T. Grant Scholars
Program: 4 to 6 annually; Institutional
Challenge Grant: 1 annually; Youth Service
Improvement Grants Program: Varies.

APPLICATION INFO:
Application, requirements and procedures are
available online.
Duration: William T. Grant Scholars
Program: Five years; Institutional Challenge
Grant: Three years; Investigator Initiated
Grants: Two to three years.
Deadline: Varies.

PUBLICATIONS:
Annual report; guidelines; *William T. Grant
Scholars,* brochure.

TRUSTEES:
Russell P. Pennoyer, Chairperson
Andres A. Alonso
Margaret R. Burchinal
Prudence L. Carter
Greg Duncan
Scott Evans
Adam Gamoran
Kenji Hakuta
Mary Patillo
Judson Reis
Estelle B. Richman
Mark Soler
Noah Walley

STAFF:
Adam Gamoran, President
Vivian Tseng, Senior Vice President,
Programs
Rosanna Aybar, Vice President, Finance and
Administration
Lauren Supplee, Senior Program Officer
Tricia Denton, Director, Grantmaking
Operations
Sharon Brewster, Grants Coordinator,
Discretionary Grants
Nancy Rivera-Torres, Grants Coordinator,
Major Grants
Irene Williams, Grants Coordinator, William
T. Grant Scholars

HASBRO CHILDREN'S FUND   [1017]
One Hasbro Place
Providence, RI 02903
(401) 727-5084
Fax: (401) 721-7275
Web Site: globalphilanthropy.hasbro.com

FOUNDED: 2006

AREAS OF INTEREST:
The welfare and development of children.

NAME(S) OF PROGRAMS:
- **Community Grants**

TYPE:
Product donations; Project/program grants.
Grants made by the Hasbro Children's Fund
focus on three core principles:
(1) Programs which provide hope to children
who need it most;
(2) Play for children who otherwise would
not be able to experience that joy and;
(3) Empowerment of youth through service.

YEAR PROGRAM STARTED: 1985

PURPOSE:
To assist children in triumphing over critical
life obstacles as well as bringing the joy of
play into their lives.

ELIGIBILITY:
U.S.-based 501(c)(3) organizations who
deliver programs to children in Los Angeles,
CA; Boulder, CO; Miami, FL; Renton, WA;
and Rhode Island.

FINANCIAL DATA:
Amount of support per award: Varies.
Total amount of support: Varies.

APPLICATION INFO:
All interested organizations are asked to
apply through the Fund's online application
system.

CHARLES HAYDEN FOUNDATION   [1018]
140 Broadway, 51st Floor
New York, NY 10005
(212) 785-3677
Fax: (212) 785-3689
E-mail: fdn@chf.org
Web Site: www.charleshaydenfoundation.org

FOUNDED: 1937

AREAS OF INTEREST:
Education and youth agencies.

TYPE:
Project/program grants. Grant priorities focus
on institutions and programs primarily
serving youth at risk of not reaching their
full potential, especially youth in low-income
communities. Support is provided for youth
development programs, charter schools,
independent and parochial schools, and
informal educational enrichment programs.

YEAR PROGRAM STARTED: 1937

PURPOSE:
To promote the mental, moral and physical
development of children and youth three to
18 years of age in the New York and Boston
metropolitan areas.

LEGAL BASIS:
Private foundation.

ELIGIBILITY:
Grants are restricted to institutions and
organizations in the New York and Boston
metropolitan areas, as defined by the
Foundation. The Foundation focuses on those
grants primarily serving children and youth,
five to 21 years of age, that are most at-risk
of not reaching their full potential, especially
youth in low-income communities. Grants are
available for capital and program support.
Program grants must have clear goals to be
met within the specified time frame. Program
support goes mainly for new and expanded
programs. No grants are awarded to
individuals.

GEOG. RESTRICTIONS: New York and Boston,
Massachusetts metropolitan areas.

FINANCIAL DATA:
Amount of support per award: Varies.
Total amount of support: $10,054,947 for the
year 2021.

APPLICATION INFO:
Applicants should submit a request online
through the Foundation web site.

Interviews, if required or requested, are not
arranged until the written grant application
has been submitted and the preliminary
review is completed.
Duration: Most grants are for one year.
Grant renewals are sometimes considered.

IRS I.D.: 13-5562237

OFFICERS:
Dean H. Steeger, Chairman of the Board

Kenneth D. Merin, President and Chief
Executive Officer
Kristen J. McCormack, Treasurer
Robert Andrews, Secretary
Carol Argento, Assistant Secretary
Sonni Holland, Assistant Secretary

BOARD OF TRUSTEES:
Robert Andrews
Jose Claxton
Robert Howitt
Kristen J. McCormack
Kenneth D. Merin
Lorenzo Smith
Dean H. Steeger
Peg Tyre
William Wachenfeld

ADDRESS INQUIRIES TO:
Kenneth D. Merin
President and Chief Executive Officer
(See address above.)

*SPECIAL STIPULATIONS:
Institutions receiving capital support must
wait two years before seeking additional
assistance.

THE JACK AND JILL OF AMERICA FOUNDATION

1930 17th Street, N.W.
Washington, DC 20009-6207
(202) 232-5290
Fax: (202) 232-1747
E-mail: administration@jackandjillfoundation.
org
Web Site: www.jackandjillfoundation.org

TYPE:
Project/program grants; Scholarships.
Volunteer opportunities.

See entry 933 for full listing.

KANSAS HEALTH FOUNDATION

309 East Douglas
Wichita, KS 67202
(316) 262-7676
(800) 373-7681
Fax: (316) 262-2044
E-mail: info@khf.org
Web Site: kansashealth.org

TYPE:
Project/program grants.

See entry 1304 for full listing.

THE KLINGENSTEIN THIRD GENERATION FOUNDATION

80 8th Avenue
Suite 1400
New York, NY 10011
(332) 219-0601
E-mail: info@klingenstein.org
Web Site: www.ktgf.org

TYPE:
Fellowships; Research grants. The
Foundation funds research and other
programs related to childhood and adolescent
ADHD and depression. All funding is
directed towards three research fellowship
programs (funding postdoctoral research in
ADHD, depression and access to care) and
the medical student training program. The
Foundation does not accept general
applications for project or research funding.

See entry 2329 for full listing.

THE AGNES M. LINDSAY TRUST [1019]

10 North Road, Suite 2
Chelmsford, MA 01824
(978) 445-7818
E-mail: admin@lindsaytrust.org
Web Site: www.lindsaytrust.org

FOUNDED: 1939

AREAS OF INTEREST:
Broad charitable giving and special
community needs, including handicapped,
elderly, children's homes, youth
organizations, homeless shelters and food
banks.

NAME(S) OF PROGRAMS:
- **Camp Scholarships**
- **Dental Health**
- **Education**
- **Food Banks**
- **Health and Welfare**
- **Homeless Shelters**

TYPE:
Capital grants. Awards grants for capital
campaigns, capital items and renovation
needs. Also, supports a number of health and
welfare organizations, health projects, dental
projects, special needs including blind, deaf
and learning-disabled, elderly, homeless
shelters, food banks, Covid-19, children's
hospitals, children's homes, youth
organizations, youth and family services and
summer camperships (summer enrichment
programs).

YEAR PROGRAM STARTED: 1939

PURPOSE:
To support the education of poor and
deserving students from rural communities;
to relieve suffering through child welfare.

ELIGIBILITY:
Eligible organizations must be IRS 501(c)(3)
tax-exempt and be located in the New
England states of Maine, Massachusetts, New
Hampshire and Vermont. The Trust does not
fund in Connecticut or Rhode Island.

The Trust does not make grants to
individuals.

The Trust rarely, if ever, approves grants for
general operating funds, nor does it fund
grant requests from public entities,
municipalities, sectarian organizations, or
individuals.

GEOG. RESTRICTIONS: Maine, Massachusetts,
New Hampshire and Vermont.

FINANCIAL DATA:
$29,000,000 in assets for the year ended
2020.

Amount of support per award: $1,000 to
$5,000.

Total amount of support: $962,236 in total
grants for the year 2020.

NO. AWARDS: 234 for the year 2020.

APPLICATION INFO:
Guidelines are available online. Application,
including financial statements or Form 990,
must be downloaded and e-mailed to the
address listed above.

Duration: One year.

Deadline: Trustees meet monthly. It generally
takes two months from time of submission of
application to receipt of letter of decision.

IRS I.D.: 02-6004971

TRUSTEES:
Michael S. DeLucia

Ernest E. Dion
Alan G. Lampert

ADDRESS INQUIRIES TO:
Amy Lampert, Administrative Director
(See address above.)

*PLEASE NOTE:
It is highly recommended that applicants
review the information available online prior
to submission of a grant proposal.

*SPECIAL STIPULATIONS:
If your organization is awarded a grant, the
Trust requests that your organization wait one
year before applying for future funding.

LOS ANGELES RAMS FOUNDATION [1020]

29899 Agoura Road
Agoura Hills, CA 91301
(818) 540-2016
Web Site: www.therams.com/community

FOUNDED: 1997

AREAS OF INTEREST:
Youth health, fitness and character education.

TYPE:
General operating grants; Project/program
grants.

YEAR PROGRAM STARTED: 1997

PURPOSE:
To support programs designed to engage
youth in activities that promote health, fitness
and character development.

ELIGIBILITY:
Grants are made to organizations that have
tax-exempt status under Section 501(c)(3) of
the Internal Revenue Code. No unsolicited
grants are accepted.

FINANCIAL DATA:
Since 1997, the Foundation has donated more
than $10,000,000 in cash, grants,
merchandise and tickets to area charities.

Amount of support per award: Varies based
on program or project scope.

Total amount of support: Up to $250,000
annually.

NO. AWARDS: 30 to 50.

APPLICATION INFO:
Proposals are accepted by invitation only;
however, letters and collateral material from
potential grant recipients are welcome.

ADDRESS INQUIRIES TO:
Director of Community Outreach
(See address above.)

THE DR. JOHN T. MACDONALD FOUNDATION, INC. [1021]

1550 Madruga Avenue, Suite 215
Coral Gables, FL 33146
(305) 667-6017
Fax: (305) 667-9135
E-mail: info@jtmacdonaldfdn.org
Web Site: www.jtmacdonaldfdn.org

FOUNDED: 1992

AREAS OF INTEREST:
Health education, prevention and early
detection of disease, children, economically
disadvantaged, and medical rehabilitation.

TYPE:
Project/program grants.

YEAR PROGRAM STARTED: 1992

PURPOSE:
To provide funding for programs and projects designed to improve, preserve or restore the health and health care of people in Miami-Dade County, FL.

LEGAL BASIS:
Private.

ELIGIBILITY:
Must be designated as a 501(c)(3) organization and registered to solicit funds under Florida law. The Foundation funds projects for medical and health-related programs. The Foundation does not fund national projects, multiyear funding requests, for-profit organizations, political candidates or campaigns, religious projects, support for individuals, or other grantmaking foundations.

GEOG. RESTRICTIONS: Miami-Dade County, Florida.

FINANCIAL DATA:
Amount of support per award: $5,000 to $50,000.

Total amount of support: $1,500,000 for the year 2020.

NO. AWARDS: 19, plus 4 scholarships and awards; 1 major multimillion-dollar award.

APPLICATION INFO:
Letter of Inquiry must be filed electronically. Application information and instructions are available on the Foundation web site.

Deadline: Letters of inquiry are accepted February 1 to April 15.

PUBLICATIONS:
Program announcement; guidelines; application packet (online).

IRS I.D.: 59-0818918

ADDRESS INQUIRIES TO:
John Edward Smith
Managing Director
(See address above.)

MAURICE J. MASSERINI TRUST

c/o Wells Fargo Private Bank
4365 Executive Drive, 18th Floor
San Diego, CA 92121
(858) 622-6958
Fax: (858) 622-6848
E-mail: grantadministration@wellsfargo.com
Web Site: www.wellsfargo.com/private-foundations/masserini-trust

TYPE:
Project/program grants.

See entry 905 for full listing.

R.J. MCELROY TRUST   [1022]

425 Cedar Street, Suite 312
Waterloo, IA 50701-1351
(319) 287-9102
Fax: (319) 287-9105
E-mail: megan@mcelroytrust.org
Web Site: www.mcelroytrust.org

FOUNDED: 1965

AREAS OF INTEREST:
Education, children and youth.

TYPE:
Capital grants; Challenge/matching grants; General operating grants; Internships; Project/program grants; Scholarships; Seed money grants; Technical assistance.

PURPOSE:
To invest in nonprofit and public organizations that inspire and transform youth.

LEGAL BASIS:
Private.

ELIGIBILITY:
The Trust only supports programs, projects or endeavors that help young people. Applicant must be nonprofit or tax-exempt.

The Trust does not make grants to religious organizations for religious programming or to schools or school districts for one-to-one technology/computers for students.

GEOG. RESTRICTIONS: Allamakee, Black Hawk, Bremer, Buchanan, Butler, Chickasaw, Clayton, Delaware, Fayette, Grundy, Tama and Winneshiek counties, Iowa.

FINANCIAL DATA:
Amount of support per award: Varies per project.

Total amount of support: Approximately $1,900,000 for the year 2019.

Matching fund requirements: The Trust seldom funds 100% of a project.

NO. AWARDS: Approximately 60 per year.

APPLICATION INFO:
Applications are available online.

Duration: One year. Renewal possible.

Deadline: Applications accepted on a rolling basis.

IRS I.D.: 42-6173496

TRUSTEES:
Dr. Raleigh D. Buckmaster
Kathy Flynn
Sally Hollis
Robert Smith, Jr.
James B. Waterbury
Mike Young
Rick Young

STAFF:
Megan McKenzie, Executive Director
Shanlee McNally, Program Officer

ADDRESS INQUIRIES TO:
Megan McKenzie, Executive Director
(See address above.)

*PLEASE NOTE:
Contact the Executive Director before applying.

THE MCJ AMELIOR FOUNDATION   [1023]

310 South Street
Morristown, NJ 07960
(973) 540-1946

AREAS OF INTEREST:
Youths at risk, children, community empowerment and mentoring.

TYPE:
Challenge/matching grants; General operating grants; Project/program grants; Seed money grants.

LEGAL BASIS:
Private foundation.

ELIGIBILITY:
Applicants must be 501(c)(3) organizations.

GEOG. RESTRICTIONS: Newark, New Jersey.

FINANCIAL DATA:
Amount of support per award: Varies.

Total amount of support: Varies.

APPLICATION INFO:
The Foundation does not accept unsolicited proposals.

Duration: Varies.

STAFF:
Suzanne Spero, Executive Director
Christine C. Gilfillan, President

ADDRESS INQUIRIES TO:
Suzanne Spero, Executive Director
(See address above.)

MEBANE CHARITABLE FOUNDATION, INC.   [1024]

232 South Main Street
Mocksville, NC 27028
(336) 936-0041
Fax: (336) 936-0038
E-mail: lcolbourne@mebanefoundation.com
Web Site: www.mebanefoundation.com

FOUNDED: 1992

AREAS OF INTEREST:
Children's education.

NAME(S) OF PROGRAMS:
- **The Early Childhood Development Program**
- **Literacy Interventions PreK-3rd Grades**
- **The Teacher Training and Professional Development Program**

TYPE:
Project/program grants.

PURPOSE:
To teach children first to read then to further their education at all levels of learning, thereby attempting to break the cycle of poverty.

ELIGIBILITY:
Organizations qualified for exemption under Section 501(c)(3) of the IRS Code and not private foundations as defined by Section 509(a).

GEOG. RESTRICTIONS: Mainly North Carolina, Southeast.

FINANCIAL DATA:
Amount of support per award: $250 to $298,499.

Total amount of support: $2,027,150 for the year 2019.

NO. MOST RECENT APPLICANTS: Over 100 for the year 2019.

NO. AWARDS: 54.

APPLICATION INFO:
Organization must first complete a telephone interview with the President to determine if their proposal is within the objectives and interest of the Foundation.

Duration: Varies.

Deadline: Application must be postmarked by July 1 for fall meeting of the board of directors, or by January 1 for spring meeting.

ADDRESS INQUIRIES TO:
Larry Colbourne, President
(See address above.)

MLB-MLBPA YOUTH DEVELOPMENT FOUNDATION   [1025]

1271 Avenue of the Americas
New York, NY 10020
(212) 931-7886
E-mail: ydf@mlb.com
Web Site: mlbplayers.com/ydf

FOUNDED: 1999

AREAS OF INTEREST:
Youth baseball and softball.

TYPE:
Capital grants; Challenge/matching grants; Project/program grants. Grants are offered to promote and enhance the growth of youth baseball and softball in the U.S., Canada and throughout the world.

YEAR PROGRAM STARTED: 2000

PURPOSE:
To expand the access of youth participation in baseball and softball.

ELIGIBILITY:
The Foundation encourages submission of proposals from organizations and individuals that have bold, innovative and creative ideas to increase opportunities for youth (elementary through high school), youth who are minorities, girls and/or located in underserved communities, to play baseball and/or softball.

FINANCIAL DATA:
Amount of support per award: Varies.

NO. MOST RECENT APPLICANTS: Varies.

NO. AWARDS: Varies.

APPLICATION INFO:
Letter of Inquiry must be written and submitted in English. No more than three pages and the project budget will be reviewed. Letter of Inquiry must include in the following order:
(1) contact information (name, title, e-mail, telephone, and organization address);
(2) brief sentence on how the organization heard of this grant opportunity;
(3) short summary of the organization;
(4) short description of the proposed project and need;
(5) amount of grant being requested;
(6) statement of need;
(7) methodology of how this project and grant request will solve the described need;
(8) a list of leadership staff and board of directors;
(9) photos and professional renderings for capital projects, if applicable and;
(10) completed project budget template (download from YDF web site).

ADDRESS INQUIRIES TO:
See e-mail address above.

NATIONAL FOOTBALL LEAGUE FOUNDATION

345 Park Avenue
New York, NY 10154
(212) 450-2000
E-mail: alexia.gallagher@nfl.com
Web Site: www.nflfoundation.org

TYPE:
Awards/prizes; Challenge/matching grants; General operating grants; Project/program grants; Research grants; Seed money grants; Training grants.

See entry 1211 for full listing.

NATIONAL FOSTER PARENT ASSOCIATION   [1026]

14508 Owen Tech Boulevard, No. 129
Austin, TX 78728
(512) 686-1948
(800) 557-5238
Fax: (888) 925-5634
E-mail: info@nfpaonline.org
Web Site: www.nfpaonline.org

FOUNDED: 1972

AREAS OF INTEREST:
Foster parents and children in foster care.

NAME(S) OF PROGRAMS:
● **NFPA Youth Scholarship**
● **Walk Me Home Program**

TYPE:
Conferences/seminars; Scholarships. Scholarships for youth living in foster families whose foster parents are members of NFPA.

Walk Me Home Program is a walk program to raise awareness of foster care and the need for more foster families, as well as to raise funds for recruitment and other activities.

YEAR PROGRAM STARTED: 1972

PURPOSE:
To support foster youth and children of foster parents that wish to further their education beyond high school, including college or university studies, vocational and job training, and correspondence courses, including the GED.

LEGAL BASIS:
Nonprofit, volunteer organization established in 1972, with tax-exempt status under Section 501(c)(3) of the Internal Revenue Code.

ELIGIBILITY:
Must be a foster youth or an adoptive or birth child of foster parent members who is a college- or university-bound senior or is 17 years of age (either in school or out) in pursuit of vocational/job training/correspondence GED/other educational advancement.

GEOG. RESTRICTIONS: United States and territories.

FINANCIAL DATA:
Amount of support per award: $500.
Total amount of support: $2,500.

NO. MOST RECENT APPLICANTS: 23.

NO. AWARDS: 5 scholarships; 3 to foster children, 1 to an adoptive child, and 1 to a biological child of foster parents.

APPLICATION INFO:
Application is available from the Association at the address above. A minimum of two letters of recommendation and a typewritten statement of 300 to 500 words on "Why I want to further my education and why I should be considered for a National Foster Parent Association Scholarship" is also required.
Duration: Possible renewal.
Deadline: Applications must be postmarked on or before March 15.

IRS I.D.: 06-0894870

ADDRESS INQUIRIES TO:
Irene Clements, Executive Director
(See address above.)

NATIONAL JEWISH COMMITTEE ON SCOUTING

1325 West Walnut Hill Lane
Irving, TX 75038
(972) 580-2425
Fax: (972) 580-2535
E-mail: anthony.berger@scouting.org
Web Site: www.jewishscouting.org

TYPE:
Scholarships.

See entry 1537 for full listing.

ORLANDO MAGIC YOUTH FOUNDATION   [1027]

8701 Maitland Summit Boulevard
Orlando, FL 32810
(407) 916-2400
Fax: (407) 916-2985
E-mail: omyf@orlandomagic.com
Web Site: www.omyf.org

FOUNDED: 1988

AREAS OF INTEREST:
Children and families at risk in central Florida in the areas of child and youth education, health and wellness with a specific focus on childhood obesity prevention, and homelessness.

TYPE:
Development grants; General operating grants; Project/program grants.

PURPOSE:
To nourish the minds and bodies of children who need it most in central Florida.

ELIGIBILITY:
Organizations must be classified as 501(c)(3) or 170(c)(3) by the IRS and have a constituency open to all segments of the community with a focus on low income. The Fund does not typically provide funding for private schools, legal aid societies, political, lobbying or advocacy groups, or capital requests for building and/or major improvements, except those for equipment/supplies that are critical to the delivery of a program or service.

GEOG. RESTRICTIONS: Orange, Osceola and Seminole counties, Florida.

FINANCIAL DATA:
Amount of support per award: $10,000 to $100,000.
Total amount of support: $1,000,000 annually.

NO. MOST RECENT APPLICANTS: 75.

NO. AWARDS: 15.

APPLICATION INFO:
Applicants are invited to submit Letter of Inquiry.
Duration: One year. May reapply.
Deadline: Letter of Inquiry: Late April.

LUCILE PACKARD FOUNDATION FOR CHILDREN'S HEALTH   [1028]

400 Hamilton Avenue, Suite 340
Palo Alto, CA 94301
(650) 736-0675
(650) 497-8365
Fax: (650) 498-2619
E-mail: grants@lpfch.org
Web Site: www.lpfch-cshcn.org

FOUNDED: 1997

AREAS OF INTEREST:
Children's health.

TYPE:
Project/program grants.

YEAR PROGRAM STARTED: 2000

PURPOSE:
To promote the health and well-being of children through statewide and local

partnerships; to improve the system of health care for children, especially those with chronic or complex health problems.

ELIGIBILITY:
Organizations must be 501(c)(3) nonprofit.

GEOG. RESTRICTIONS: California.

FINANCIAL DATA:
Amount of support per award: Varies.

NO. MOST RECENT APPLICANTS: 20.

NO. AWARDS: Varies.

APPLICATION INFO:
The Foundation generally invites specific applications for proposals. However, unsolicited proposals for projects that contribute to achieving the program's goals are welcome. Proposals initiated by applicants should be presented to the Foundation as a letter of inquiry. It is strongly recommended that applicants carefully review the program goals, priorities and restrictions before submitting a letter of inquiry.
Duration: Typically six months to two years.

ADDRESS INQUIRIES TO:
Jenny Ly, Grants Manager
(See address above.)

THE PINKERTON FOUNDATION   [1029]
610 Fifth Avenue
Suite 316
New York, NY 10020
(212) 332-3385
E-mail: grantsmanager@pinkertonfdn.org
Web Site: www.thepinkertonfoundation.org

FOUNDED: 1966

AREAS OF INTEREST:
After-school and summer learning, career readiness, education, youth and family justice.

TYPE:
General operating grants; Internships; Project/program grants. Support for programs that develop individual competencies, instill values and increase opportunities to participate in society.

Support for community-based programs with preference given to projects for children, youth and families that intervene before a pattern of failure has been established.

YEAR PROGRAM STARTED: 1968

PURPOSE:
To improve the lives of young people in poor neighborhoods throughout New York City.

LEGAL BASIS:
Not-for-profit corporation organized in the state of Delaware in 1966.

ELIGIBILITY:
Grant applicants must be nonprofit public charitable organizations which are tax-exempt under Section 501(c)(3) of the Internal Revenue Code. The Foundation does not make grants to individuals or give loans or emergency assistance, nor does it support medical research or the direct provision of health care or religious education. It generally does not make grants to support conferences, publications, media or to building renovations or other capital projects, unless they are integrally related to the Foundation's program objectives or are an outgrowth of one of its grantee's programs.

GEOG. RESTRICTIONS: New York, New York.

FINANCIAL DATA:
Amount of support per award: $25,000 to $480,000; average $75,000.
Total amount of support: Approximately $30,518,200.

NO. AWARDS: Approximately 250 annually.

APPLICATION INFO:
Applications must be submitted through the Foundation's Grant Portal.
Duration: Usually up to three years.
Deadline: Letters of inquiry are accepted at any time. Decisions are made immediately following board meetings in May and December.

OFFICERS:
Daniel L. Mosley, Chairman
Richard M. Smith, President
James Piereson, Treasurer
Marnie S. Pillsbury, Secretary

STAFF:
Laurie Dien, Vice President, Programs
Julie Peterson, Senior Program Officer
Jennifer Negron, Program Officer

ADDRESS INQUIRIES TO:
Yvonne Schonborg, Grants Manager
(See e-mail address above.)

PRITCHETT TRUST   [1030]
BMO Harris Bank
790 North Water Street, Floor 11
Milwaukee, WI 53202
(414) 287-7250
Fax: (414) 287-8580
E-mail: trust.custody@bmo.com

AREAS OF INTEREST:
Children, families and youth.

TYPE:
Project/program grants; Seed money grants.

YEAR PROGRAM STARTED: 1995

PURPOSE:
To improve the quality of life in Crawford County and southeast Kansas by supporting initiatives that serve these populations.

LEGAL BASIS:
Private trust.

ELIGIBILITY:
Applicants for grants must be located or operating in southeastern Kansas and a strong, if not exclusive, preference is given to applicants located or operating in Crawford County. The applicant must qualify as a charitable organization described in Section 501(c)(3) of the Internal Revenue Code or as a political subdivision of the State of Kansas including municipalities, school districts and Pittsburg State University.

GEOG. RESTRICTIONS: Southeast Kansas, with an emphasis on Crawford County.

FINANCIAL DATA:
Amount of support per award: Varies.
Total amount of support: $400,000 to $500,000.

NO. MOST RECENT APPLICANTS: 72.

NO. AWARDS: 43.

APPLICATION INFO:
Requests should be submitted in the form of a one-page synopsis, together with a package containing the full proposal.
Duration: One year. Renewal possible.
Deadline: June 1.

ADDRESS INQUIRIES TO:
BMO Trust and Custody Services
(See address above.)

RONALD MCDONALD HOUSE CHARITIES   [1031]
110 North Carpenter Street
Chicago, IL 60607
(630) 623-7048
E-mail: info@rmhc.org
Web Site: www.rmhc.org

FOUNDED: 1984

AREAS OF INTEREST:
Primarily, the health and well-being of children.

NAME(S) OF PROGRAMS:
* **Africa and South Asia: Child and Maternal Health**
* **U.S. Grants: Children's Oral Health Care**

TYPE:
Challenge/matching grants; Grants-in-aid; Project/program grants; Training grants.

YEAR PROGRAM STARTED: 1984

PURPOSE:
To directly improve the health and well-being of children.

LEGAL BASIS:
Nonprofit, 501(c)(3) tax-exempt organization.

ELIGIBILITY:
Not-for-profit tax-exempt organizations, based in the U.S. but operating either domestically or internationally. Projects must be sustainable and measurable. Proposed projects must directly benefit children. No grants to individuals, political campaigns, secular religious activities, for salaries, travel or ongoing expenses, or capital expenses. Projects must include a "Train-the-Trainer" component in the methodology.

Grant requests from organizations more regional in nature will be referred to the closest local chapter.

FINANCIAL DATA:
Amount of support per award: $100,000 and up.
Total amount of support: Approximately $4,000,000.

NO. MOST RECENT APPLICANTS: 150.

NO. AWARDS: 11.

REPRESENTATIVE AWARDS:
$169,043 over two years to Curamericas, Liberia; $179,800 to Lwala Community Alliance, Kenya; $627,637 to Resurge, Nepal and India; $50,000 to Wyman Center, U.S.

APPLICATION INFO:
Application information is available on the web site.
Duration: One-year to multiyear funding.

PUBLICATIONS:
Application form; annual report; application guidelines.

BOARD OF TRUSTEES:
Steven Ramirez, Chairman of the Board
Sheila Musolino, President and Chief Executive Officer

*SPECIAL STIPULATIONS:
Applications only accepted online.

HENRY AND RUTH BLAUSTEIN ROSENBERG FOUNDATION

One South Street, Suite 2900
Baltimore, MD 21202
(410) 347-7201
Fax: (410) 347-7210
E-mail: info@blaufund.org
Web Site: www.blaufund.org

TYPE:
Capital grants; General operating grants; Project/program grants. Programs of benefit to the underserved community in the Baltimore, MD area.

See entry 1233 for full listing.

THE SAIGH FOUNDATION [1032]

231 South Bemiston Avenue
Suite 735
St. Louis, MO 63105
(314) 862-3055
Fax: (314) 862-9288
E-mail: saigh@thesaighfoundation.org
Web Site: thesaighfoundation.org

FOUNDED: 2000

AREAS OF INTEREST:
Children and youth in the field of education and health care in the St. Louis metropolitan area.

TYPE:
Development grants; Endowments; General operating grants; Internships; Project/program grants; Research grants; Scholarships; Technical assistance; Training grants.

PURPOSE:
To enhance the quality of life in St. Louis metropolitan region through support for charitable projects and initiatives which primarily benefit children and youth through education and health care.

LEGAL BASIS:
501(c)(3).

ELIGIBILITY:
St. Louis area nonprofit organizations benefiting children and youth in the areas of education and health care may apply.

GEOG. RESTRICTIONS: St. Louis, Missouri metropolitan area.

FINANCIAL DATA:
Amount of support per award: Varies.
Total amount of support: Varies.

NO. MOST RECENT APPLICANTS: Approximately 225.

APPLICATION INFO:
Applications are to be submitted through the Foundation's online portal.
Deadline: January 15, April 15, July 15 and October 15.

STAFF:
Elke Buckland, Executive Director
Julie Hantman, Assistant Director

ADDRESS INQUIRIES TO:
Elke Buckland, Executive Director
(See address above.)

THE SCHUMANN FUND FOR NEW JERSEY [1033]

21 Van Vleck Street
Montclair, NJ 07042
(973) 509-9883
E-mail: astrickland@schumannfund.org
Web Site: fdnweb.org/schumann

FOUNDED: 1988

AREAS OF INTEREST:
Children and youth, education, racial and economic equity, and public policy (statewide) as well as social services in Essex County, NJ.

TYPE:
Demonstration grants; General operating grants; Project/program grants. Priorities include early childhood development, supporting efforts to heighten the chances of academic and social success for young children, especially the urban poor. Other focus areas include public policy and local activities directed at solving community problems, with particular concern for families with young children and education.

YEAR PROGRAM STARTED: 1988

LEGAL BASIS:
Tax-exempt, private foundation.

ELIGIBILITY:
Organizations seeking grants must be designated 501(c)(3) by the IRS. No applications for capital campaigns, annual giving, endowment, direct support of individuals and local programs in counties other than Essex. Projects in the arts, health care and housing development normally fall outside the Schumann Fund priority areas.

GEOG. RESTRICTIONS: New Jersey, with special emphasis on Essex County.

FINANCIAL DATA:
Amount of support per award: $15,000 to $50,000.
Total amount of support: Approximately $500,000.

APPLICATION INFO:
There is no standard application form to be used in presenting a request to the Schumann Fund. The Fund, however, encourages the use of the New York/New Jersey Common Application Form. A written proposal should be submitted which includes a detailed description of the purpose for which assistance is desired and the plan for accomplishment. The proposal should be accompanied by a copy of the organization's latest financial statement, an expense budget which identifies all sources of income, the project's time frame and future funding plans, a list of the organization's Board of Directors, IRS documents confirming the organization's status as a 501(c)(3) tax-exempt organization and not a private foundation, and the most recent audit.
Duration: Usually one year. Multiyear grants possible.
Deadline: January 15, April 15, July 15 and October 15.

PUBLICATIONS:
Annual report.

IRS I.D.: 52-1556076

TRUSTEES:
Anthony Cicatello
Barbara Bell Coleman
Leonard S. Coleman, Jr.
Christopher J. Daggett
Martha Day
Roger Pratt

EXECUTIVE DIRECTOR:
Annette Strickland

ADDRESS INQUIRIES TO:
Annette Strickland, Executive Director
(See address above.)

*PLEASE NOTE:
Grants are restricted to projects in New Jersey.

THE SEYBERT FOUNDATION [1034]

P.O. Box 52758
Philadelphia, PA 19115
(215) 821-8144
E-mail: admin@seybertfoundation.org
Web Site: www.seybertfoundation.org

FOUNDED: 1914

AREAS OF INTEREST:
Disadvantaged children and youth who are residents of the city of Philadelphia.

TYPE:
General operating grants. Operating support for nonprofit organizations serving disadvantaged children and youth who are residents of the city of Philadelphia. The Institution is limited under the terms of the will setting up the fund to disadvantaged boys and girls of the city of Philadelphia only.

LEGAL BASIS:
501(c)(3) charitable foundation.

ELIGIBILITY:
Grants are limited to nonprofit organizations serving disadvantaged young people through the high school ages who are residents of the city of Philadelphia. Grants are made to qualifying tax-exempt organizations under Sections 501(c)(3) and 509(a) of the Internal Revenue Code. Priority is given to organizations with operating budgets of less than $1,500,000.

GEOG. RESTRICTIONS: Philadelphia, Pennsylvania.

FINANCIAL DATA:
Amount of support per award: $10,000 per year.

NO. AWARDS: 28 for the year 2020.

REPRESENTATIVE AWARDS:
Big Picture Alliance; Mighty Writers; Philadelphia Youth Basketball.

APPLICATION INFO:
Guidelines are available on the Foundation web site.
Duration: Two years.
Deadline: May 17. No more than one request will be considered per calendar year except under special circumstances.

PUBLICATIONS:
Application guidelines.

IRS I.D.: 23-6260105

OFFICERS AND BOARD OF DIRECTORS:
Marissa Meyers, President
Matthew A. Grande, Vice President
Rich Sedmak, Treasurer
Cat Lavigne, Secretary
Noor Bowman
Jill Fink
Landon Jones, Esq.
Lamia Makkar
Miguel Morel
Cicely Peterson-Mangum, Esq.

ADDRESS INQUIRIES TO:
Theresa Jackson, Manager
(See address above.)

*PLEASE NOTE:
Grants must benefit poor boys and girls of the city of Philadelphia.

SIERRA HEALTH FOUNDATION
1321 Garden Highway
Sacramento, CA 95833
(916) 922-4755
Fax: (916) 922-4024
E-mail: info@sierrahealth.org
Web Site: www.sierrahealth.org

TYPE:
Project/program grants. Sponsorship. Specific to funding opportunities - solicited.

See entry 1359 for full listing.

SILICON VALLEY COMMUNITY FOUNDATION
2440 West El Camino Real
Suite 300
Mountain View, CA 94040-1498
(650) 450-5400
Fax: (650) 450-5401
E-mail: info@siliconvalleycf.org
Web Site: www.siliconvalleycf.org

TYPE:
General operating grants; Project/program grants; Scholarships; Seed money grants. Nonprofit organizations that provide services or programs related to the specific five grantmaking strategies in San Mateo and Santa Clara counties may be eligible to apply for funding from the Foundation's endowment. Scholarships for college-bound students are also open to application.

See entry 1247 for full listing.

STUART FOUNDATION   [1035]
500 Washington Street
Eighth Floor
San Francisco, CA 94111
(415) 393-1551
Fax: (415) 568-9815
E-mail: operations@stuartfoundation.org
Web Site: www.stuartfoundation.org

FOUNDED: 1985

NAME(S) OF PROGRAMS:
• **Education**

TYPE:
Development grants; General operating grants; Project/program grants; Research grants; Technical assistance; Training grants. Systematic change and collaborative service delivery.

YEAR PROGRAM STARTED: 1985

PURPOSE:
To provide a coordinated set of programs, activities, research, and policy analysis that improve opportunities for children and youth in California and Washington to become self-reliant, responsible and contributing members of their communities.

LEGAL BASIS:
Private foundation.

ELIGIBILITY:
No grants to individuals.

GEOG. RESTRICTIONS: California and Washington.

FINANCIAL DATA:
Amount of support per award: Average grant of $100,000.
Total amount of support: Approximately $16,000,000 annually.

APPLICATION INFO:
The Foundation does not accept unsolicited requests for funding.

Duration: Grants are approved for one year at a time, although projects can be funded for several years.

IRS I.D.: 20-0882784

BOARD MEMBERS:
Dwight L. Stuart, Jr., Chairman

ADDRESS INQUIRIES TO:
Jade Nelson, Grants and Operations Manager
(See address above.)

*PLEASE NOTE:
The Foundation does not accept unsolicited requests for funding.

SUBARU OF AMERICA FOUNDATION, INC.
One Subaru Drive
Camden, NJ 08103
(856) 488-5099
Fax: (856) 254-1367
E-mail: foundation@subaru.com
Web Site: www.subaru.com/about-subaru/subaru-foundation

TYPE:
General operating grants; Project/program grants. Employee matching gift program.

See entry 1419 for full listing.

THE FRANK M. TAIT FOUNDATION   [1036]
40 North Main Street
Suite 1530
Dayton, OH 45423
(937) 222-2401
E-mail: taitfoundation@gmail.com

FOUNDED: 1955

AREAS OF INTEREST:
Early childhood intervention and education.

TYPE:
Project/program grants.

YEAR PROGRAM STARTED: 1956

PURPOSE:
To provide programs that develop youth (particularly early childhood development programs); to provide cultural enrichment experiences for underserved youth.

LEGAL BASIS:
Ohio corporation, not for profit.

ELIGIBILITY:
The Foundation seeks to fund high-quality, innovative and evidence-based early childhood intervention and education programs that:
(1) serve under-resourced families and children ages 0-8 in Montgomery County, OH and;
(2) demonstrate the potential to make measurable improvements in early childhood intervention and education outcomes.

Organizations must be exempt under 501(c)(3). No private foundations.

The Foundation does not fund:
(1) medical research or equipment;
(2) operating budgets or annual fund drives;
(3) emergency requests for crash programs;
(4) endowment funds;
(5) religious programs or activities or;
(6) lobbying or propaganda activities.

GEOG. RESTRICTIONS: Montgomery County, Ohio.

FINANCIAL DATA:
Amount of support per award: Typically $5,000 to $50,000.
Total amount of support: $348,000 for the year 2019.

NO. AWARDS: 15.

APPLICATION INFO:
Must contact the Executive Director at the telephone number or e-mail address above to discuss the prospective grant proposal and to obtain approval for its subsequent submission.
Duration: Usually one year. Reapply for renewal.
Deadline: Requests are reviewed quarterly. Contact the Executive Director at the telephone number above to confirm deadlines.

PUBLICATIONS:
Guidelines.

IRS I.D.: 31-6037499

ADDRESS INQUIRIES TO:
Executive Director
(See address above.)

TURRELL FUND   [1037]
21 Van Vleck Street
Montclair, NJ 07042-2358
(973) 783-9358
E-mail: turrell@turrellfund.org
Web Site: www.turrellfund.org

FOUNDED: 1935

AREAS OF INTEREST:
Agencies rendering direct services to at-risk children in the state of Vermont, and, primarily, in the New Jersey counties of Essex, Hudson, Passaic and Union; policy initiatives for the very young child. While there are exceptions, the Fund's emphasis is on programs serving children, from birth to five years of age, and advocacy programs which support children in the same age range.

TYPE:
General operating grants; Project/program grants.

YEAR PROGRAM STARTED: 1935

PURPOSE:
To financially and strategically support organizations which directly provide or foster the creation and delivery of high-quality, developmental and educational services to at-risk children, especially the youngest and their families in Vermont and designated areas of New Jersey.

LEGAL BASIS:
Tax-exempt private foundation.

ELIGIBILITY:
Tax-exempt 501(c)(3) organizations in New Jersey and Vermont only may apply. In New Jersey, emphasis is on northern urban areas centered in Essex, Hudson, Passaic and Union counties only. No grants are awarded for lobbying, endowments or research. No grants to individuals and most hospital work and health delivery services. Only organizations providing direct services and advocacy for children and youth are eligible.

GEOG. RESTRICTIONS: Essex, Hudson, Passaic and Union counties, New Jersey and Vermont.

FINANCIAL DATA:
Amount of support per award: $500 to $451,000 for the year 2019.

Total amount of support: $3,809,800 for the year 2019.

NO. MOST RECENT APPLICANTS: Approximately 400 per year.

NO. AWARDS: Approximately 250 per year.

APPLICATION INFO:
Applications are accepted online only. The following documents are to be submitted as attachments to the online application:
(1) copy of the IRS determination letter;
(2) Form 990 for the most recent year available;
(3) operating budget for the coming year;
(4) list of the names of the Board of Directors and their affiliations;
(5) audited financial statement for the most recent year available;
(6) expense and income budget for the particular project or program and;
(7) independent auditor's communication of internal control identified in the audit (Management Letter).
Duration: One year.
Deadline: August 1 and February 1. Announcement in early June and early December.

PUBLICATIONS:
Annual report.

IRS I.D.: 22-1551936

OFFICERS:
S. Lawrence Prendergast, Chairman of the Board
Richard A. Ribeiro, Treasurer
Curtland E. Fields, Secretary
Kim Keiser, Assistant Secretary

TRUSTEES:
Robert E. Angelica
Elizabeth W. Christie
Curtland E. Fields
Rev. William S. Gannon
William H. Hammond
Junlei Li
Matthew E. Melmed
Dr. Julia A. Miller
Rev. Dr. John P. Mitchell
John Morning
S. Lawrence Prendergast
Mark Sustic

ADDRESS INQUIRIES TO:
Curtland E. Fields
President and Chief Executive Officer
(See address above.)

U.S. DEPARTMENT OF HEALTH AND HUMAN SERVICES   [1038]
Administration for Children and Families
300 C Street, S.W., 4th Floor
Washington, DC 20024
(866) 763-6481
(202) 205-8573
Fax: (202) 205-9721
E-mail: headstart@eclkc.info
Web Site: www.acf.HHS.gov/ohs

NAME(S) OF PROGRAMS:
● **Head Start**

TYPE:
Project/program grants. Grants for comprehensive programs focused primarily upon children from low-income families who have not reached the age of compulsory school attendance. Supported projects should involve:
(1) comprehensive health (including medical and dental examinations), nutritional, social, psychological, educational and mental health

services;
(2) appropriate activities to encourage and provide opportunities for participation of parents and effective use of provided services and;
(3) other pertinent training, technical assistance, evaluation and follow-through activities.

YEAR PROGRAM STARTED: 1965

PURPOSE:
To promote school readiness for children in low-income families by offering educational, nutritional, health, social and other services.

LEGAL BASIS:
Omnibus Budget and Reconciliation Act of 1981 (Public Law 97-35).

ELIGIBILITY:
Public or private nonprofit organizations, including community-based and faith-based organizations, or for-profit agencies within a community that wish to compete for funds, are eligible to apply.

FINANCIAL DATA:
Federal funds may not exceed 80% except in certain limited situations where grantees may be relieved of all or part of the nonfederal share.
Amount of support per award: Varies.
Total amount of support: $10,028,460,690 (federal appropriation) for fiscal year 2019.
Matching fund requirements: Grantees are required to provide 20% of the total cost of the project.

APPLICATION INFO:
Applications from organizations which are not current grantees are accepted only in response to announcements in the *Federal Register.* Applicants for a Head Start grant should contact the Health and Human Services regional office in their area. Parents wishing to enroll their children should consult the local Head Start Program in their Community.

U.S. DEPARTMENT OF HEALTH AND HUMAN SERVICES   [1039]
Administration for Children and Families
Family and Youth Services Bureau
330 C Street, S.W.
Washington, DC 20201
(202) 205-8102
Fax: (202) 260-9333
Web Site: www.acf.hhs.gov/fysb

FOUNDED: 1974

AREAS OF INTEREST:
Crisis and referral services for runaway and homeless youth.

NAME(S) OF PROGRAMS:
● **Runaway and Homeless Youth (RHY) Programs**

TYPE:
Development grants; General operating grants; Project/program grants; Technical assistance. Title III of the Juvenile Justice and Delinquency Prevention Act of 1974, et seq., to authorize the Runaway and Homeless Youth Program.

Basic Center, Street Outreach, and Transitional Living are components of this Program.

Through Basic Center, the Bureau provides financial assistance to establish or strengthen community-based programs that address the immediate needs of runaway and homeless

youth and their families. These programs are designed to provide youth with emergency shelter, food, clothing, counseling and referrals for health care.

Through Street Outreach, the Bureau awards grants to private, nonprofit agencies to conduct outreach designed to build relationships between grantee staff and street youth. These efforts are intended to help young people leave the streets.

Through Transitional Living, the Bureau targets LGBTQ projects that provide longer-term residential services to homeless youth, 16 to 21 years of age, for up to 18 months. Services are intended to help homeless youth make a successful transition to self-sufficient living. Transitional Living also supports youth maternity group home.

YEAR PROGRAM STARTED: 1974

PURPOSE:
To establish or strengthen locally controlled community programs that address the immediate needs of runaway and homeless youth and their families. Services must be provided outside of the law enforcement, juvenile justice system, child welfare or mental health. The program is designed to alleviate problems of RHY youth, reunite youth with their families, and encourage the resolution of intrafamily problems through counseling and other services, strengthen family relationships and encourage stable living conditions for youth and help youth decide upon constructive courses of action.

ELIGIBILITY:
Grants are available to states, localities, nonprofit private agencies, coordinated networks and Indian Tribes.

GEOG. RESTRICTIONS: United States and its territories.

FINANCIAL DATA:
Amount of support per award: Basic Center: $50,000 to $200,000; Street Outreach: $90,000 to $150,000; Transitional Living: $100,000 to $250,000.
Total amount of support: Over $28,000,000 for the year 2019.

NO. MOST RECENT APPLICANTS: Varies.

NO. AWARDS: Basic Center: 89; Street Outreach: 55; Transitional Living: 18.

APPLICATION INFO:
Guidelines available on the web site.
Duration: Three years for Basic Center and Street Outreach. Five years for Transitional Living.
Deadline: July.

ADDRESS INQUIRIES TO:
National Clearinghouse on Families and Youth
8120 Woodmont Avenue, Suite 850
Bethesda, MD 20814

U.S. DEPARTMENT OF HEALTH AND HUMAN SERVICES   [1040]
Administration for Children and Families
Children's Bureau
330 C Street, S.W.
Washington, DC 20201
(202) 205-8618
Fax: (202) 205-9721
Web Site: www.acf.hhs.gov/cb

AREAS OF INTEREST:
Adoption, child abuse and neglect, child welfare services, foster care, guardianship and tribes.

NAME(S) OF PROGRAMS:
- **Child Welfare Waiver Demonstration Projects**
- **Discretionary Grant Programs**
- **State & Tribal Grant Programs**

TYPE:
Formula grants; Project/program grants. The Child Welfare Waiver Demonstration authority provides states with an opportunity to use federal funds more flexibly in order to test innovative approaches to child welfare service delivery and financing. The states can design and demonstrate a wide range of approaches to reforming child welfare and improving outcomes in the areas of safety, permanency, and well-being.

Discretionary Grants are awarded for research and program development through a competitive peer-review process, to State, Tribal and local agencies, faith-based and community-based organizations, and other nonprofit and for-profit groups.

State & Tribal Grant Programs provide matching funds to States and Tribes to help them operate every aspect of their child welfare systems - from prevention of child abuse and neglect to adoption and the information systems necessary to support these programs.

PURPOSE:
To fund projects, programs and research that serve children, families or the community to states, territories and tribes.

ELIGIBILITY:
Discretionary Grants: States, local governments, tribes, public agencies or private agencies or organizations with expertise in providing technical assistance related to family preservation, family support, time-limited family reunification and adoption promotion and support.

State & Tribal Grant Programs: States, territories and certain Indian Tribes are eligible.

FINANCIAL DATA:
Amount of support per award: Varies.

Total amount of support: Varies.

APPLICATION INFO:
ACF requires electronic submission of applications. Information on applying electronically is available at Grants.gov. Applicants who do not have an Internet connection or sufficient capacity to upload large files to the Internet may contact ACF for an exception that will allow these applicants to submit an application in paper format.

Duration: Discretionary Grants are generally for a 12-, 24- or 36-month period; some may be renewed for up to five years.

Deadline: Contact the headquarters or regional office, as appropriate, for application deadlines.

ADDRESS INQUIRIES TO:
Catherine Heath, Program Specialist
(See address above.)

U.S. DEPARTMENT OF JUSTICE
Office of Juvenile Justice and
Delinquency Prevention
810 Seventh Street, N.W., 7th Floor
Washington, DC 20531
(202) 307-5911
Fax: (202) 353-9093
E-mail: lynnell.clarke@usdoj.gov
Web Site: www.ojjdp.gov

TYPE:
Block grants; Challenge/matching grants; Demonstration grants; Formula grants; Internships; Project/program grants; Research grants; Technical assistance; Training grants. Grants to increase the capacity of state and local governments to conduct effective juvenile justice and delinquency prevention programs as developed in the state comprehensive action plan.

See entry 1280 for full listing.

USDA FOOD AND NUTRITION SERVICE   [1041]
Child Nutrition Service
1320 Braddock Place, 4th Floor
Alexandria, VA 22314
(703) 305-2054
Web Site: www.fns.usda.gov

FOUNDED: 1969

AREAS OF INTEREST:
Child nutrition.

NAME(S) OF PROGRAMS:
- **The Child and Adult Care Food Program**
- **The Fresh Fruit and Vegetable Program**
- **The National School Lunch Program**
- **The School Breakfast Program**
- **The Special Milk Program**
- **The Summer Food Service Program**

TYPE:
Formula grants; Grants-in-aid; Project/program grants. Reimbursement for the support of food service in schools, child and adult care institutions to improve nutrition.

The Child and Adult Care Food Program helps child care facilities and institutions serve nutritious meals and snacks to preschool and school-age children. To participate, facilities and institutions must be licensed or approved to provide child care services. They must also meet certain other eligibility requirements. The program operates in nonresidential day care centers, settlement houses, outside-school-hours care centers, family day care homes, institutions providing day care for handicapped children and others. Participating facilities and institutions get cash assistance, USDA-donated foods and technical guidance. In child care centers, the amount of cash assistance varies according to the family size and income of children served. In day care homes, the amount of cash assistance is based on a food service payment rate. Similar benefits are also now available to adult day care centers which serve functionally impaired adults or persons 60 years of age or older.

The Fresh Fruit and Vegetable Program introduces school children to a variety of produce that they otherwise might not have the opportunity to sample. The goal is to improve children's overall diet and create healthier eating habits to impact their present and future health.

The National School Lunch Program makes well-planned nutritious meals available to school children. Any public or nonprofit private schools of high school grade or under and licensed public or nonprofit private residential child care institutions are eligible to participate in the National School Lunch and School Breakfast Programs. Schools that participate are required to provide free and reduced-price meals to children unable to pay the full price. Eligibility is based on application information submitted by a parent or guardian. The household income limit for free lunches is set at or below 130% of the federal poverty level and for reduced price lunches household income must be above 130% or at or below 185% of the federal poverty level. Children from households not eligible for free or reduced-price meals must pay the school's full price charge for lunch. Cash and donated commodities are provided to participating schools and institutions according to the number of meals served.

The School Breakfast Program makes nutritious breakfasts available to school children under the same eligibility guidelines and general requirements as the National School Lunch Program.

The Special Milk Program makes it possible for all children attending a participating school or institution to purchase milk at a reduced price or receive it free, if they are eligible. Reimbursement is provided for each half-pint of milk served under the program. Schools and institutions that participate in other federal child nutrition programs authorized under the National School Lunch Act or the Child Nutrition Act of 1966 may not participate in the Special Milk Program, except for split-session kindergarten programs conducted in schools in which the children do not have access to the other meal program.

The Summer Food Service Program helps communities serve meals to needy children when school is not in session. The program is sponsored by public or private nonprofit school food authorities or local, municipal, county or state governments. Public or private nonprofit residential camps, other private nonprofit organizations, colleges and universities which participate in the National Youth Sports Program also may be sponsors. The program operates in areas in which at least 50% of the children meet the income criteria for free and reduced-price school meals. USDA reimburses sponsors for operating costs of food services up to a specified maximum rate for each meal served. In addition, sponsors receive some reimbursement for planning, operating and supervising expenses.

YEAR PROGRAM STARTED: 1946

PURPOSE:
To help safeguard the health and well-being of the nation's children and to encourage the domestic consumption of nutritious agricultural commodities and other foods.

LEGAL BASIS:
The National School Lunch Act as amended and the Child Nutrition Act of 1966, as amended.

ELIGIBILITY:
Family size and number of children based on income poverty levels.

GEOG. RESTRICTIONS: United States and its territories.

FINANCIAL DATA:
Amount of support per award: Varies.
Total amount of support: Varies.
Matching fund requirements: Varies.

APPLICATION INFO:
Official application materials are available upon request to state educational agencies or other state-designated agency. In states where education agencies do not administer the programs for nonprofit private schools, contact the appropriate Food and Nutrition Service Regional Office of the Department of Agriculture for more information.
Deadline: Applications are accepted throughout the year.

VETERANS OF FOREIGN WARS AUXILIARY
National Headquarters
406 West 34th Street, 10th Floor
Kansas City, MO 64111
(816) 561-8655
E-mail: info@vfwauxiliary.org
Web Site: vfwauxiliary.org

TYPE:
Awards/prizes.

See entry 467 for full listing.

JOSEPH B. WHITEHEAD FOUNDATION [1042]
191 Peachtree Street, Suite 3540
Atlanta, GA 30303
(404) 522-6755
Fax: (404) 522-7026
E-mail: fdns@woodruff.org
Web Site: jbwhitehead.org

FOUNDED: 1937

AREAS OF INTEREST:
Human services, public education, children and youth services, and early childhood education.

TYPE:
Capital grants; Project/program grants.

LEGAL BASIS:
Private foundation.

ELIGIBILITY:
Organization must:
(1) be a 501(c)(3) charity;
(2) be located or operating in metropolitan Atlanta, as defined by the United Way of Greater Atlanta to include Butts, Cherokee, Clayton, Cobb, Coweta, DeKalb, Douglas, Fayette, Fulton, Gwinnett, Henry, Paulding, and Rockdale counties and;
(3) align with the Foundation's program interests in early childhood education, K-12 education, children and youth, human services, or health.

GEOG. RESTRICTIONS: Metropolitan Atlanta, Georgia.

FINANCIAL DATA:
Amount of support per award: $40,000 to $15,000,000 for the year 2019.
Total amount of support: $62,868,379 for the year 2019.

NO. MOST RECENT APPLICANTS: 57 for the year 2019.

NO. AWARDS: 42 for the year 2019.

APPLICATION INFO:
Applicants are encouraged to review the eligibility requirements, grantmaking guidelines and program interests and submit

an informal inquiry to the Foundation's e-mail address to determine grant eligibility before submitting a formal request. Formal proposals should be submitted through the online grant portal and should include the following information:
(1) a description of the organization, its purposes, programs, staffing and governing board;
(2) organization's latest financial statements, including the most recent report;
(3) a description of the proposed project and full justification for its funding;
(4) an itemized project budget, including other sources of support in hand anticipated and;
(5) evidence from the IRS of the organization's tax-exempt status and the applying organization itself is not a private foundation.
Duration: One year.
Deadline: February 1 and August 15.

TRUSTEES:
E. Jenner Wood, III, Chairman
Lawrence L. Gellerstedt, III, Vice Chairman

OFFICERS:
P. Russell Hardin, President
Erik S. Johnson, Vice President and Secretary
Eli Niepoky, Treasurer

ADDRESS INQUIRIES TO:
P. Russell Hardin, President
(See address above.)

WIDENER MEMORIAL FOUNDATION IN AID OF HANDICAPPED CHILDREN
4060 Butler Pike
Suite 225
Plymouth Meeting, PA 19462
(610) 825-8900
Fax: (610) 825-8904
E-mail: jhagerty@erdixon.com

TYPE:
Capital grants.

See entry 927 for full listing.

Community development and services

ABEL FOUNDATION [1043]
1815 Y Street
Lincoln, NE 68508
(402) 434-1212
Fax: (402) 434-1799
Web Site: www.abelfoundation.org

AREAS OF INTEREST:
Health and human services, higher education and community development programs.

TYPE:
Capital grants; Matching gifts; Project/program grants.

PURPOSE:
To improve the quality of life, particularly in communities where the company has facilities.

ELIGIBILITY:
Grants are made to organizations that have tax-exempt status under Section 501(c)(3) of the Internal Revenue Code. No grants are made to individuals.

GEOG. RESTRICTIONS: Nebraska, particularly Lincoln.

FINANCIAL DATA:
Amount of support per award: Varies.
Total amount of support: $555,133 for the year 2020.

APPLICATION INFO:
Applicants are requested to use the Lincoln/Lancaster County Grant Maker Common Application Form.
Duration: One year. Renewal possible.
Deadline: March 31, July 15 and October 31. Foundation meets in May, September and December, respectively, to review funding requests.

ADDRESS INQUIRIES TO:
J. Ross McCown, Vice President
(See address above.)

AKRON COMMUNITY FOUNDATION [1044]
345 West Cedar Street
Akron, OH 44307-2407
(330) 376-8522
Fax: (330) 376-0202
E-mail: jgarofalo@akroncf.org
Web Site: www.akroncf.org

FOUNDED: 1955

AREAS OF INTEREST:
Arts and culture, civic affairs, health and human services, and education.

TYPE:
Capital grants; General operating grants; Project/program grants; Scholarships; Seed money grants.

YEAR PROGRAM STARTED: 1955

PURPOSE:
To embrace and enhance the work of charitable people who make a permanent commitment to the good of the community.

LEGAL BASIS:
Community foundation.

ELIGIBILITY:
Organizations must be tax-exempt.

GEOG. RESTRICTIONS: Summit County, Ohio.

FINANCIAL DATA:
Assets of $264,594,000 for the year ended December 31, 2019.
Amount of support per award: Average $15,000 to $17,000.
Total amount of support: $11,241,228 for the year 2019.

CO-OP FUNDING PROGRAMS: County of Summit.

NO. AWARDS: 1,977 for the year 2019.

APPLICATION INFO:
Applicants must contact the Foundation before submitting an application.
Duration: One year.
Deadline: Arts and Culture: April 1; Civic Affairs: July 1; Health and Human Services: October 1; Education: December 15.

PUBLICATIONS:
Guidelines.

IRS I.D.: 34-1087615

ADDRESS INQUIRIES TO:
John F. Garofalo
Vice President of Community Investment
(See address above.)

ALBION COMMUNITY FOUNDATION [1045]

P.O. Box 156
Albion, MI 49224-0156
(517) 629-3349
Fax: (517) 629-8027
E-mail: foundation@albionfoundation.org
Web Site: www.albionfoundation.org

FOUNDED: 1969

AREAS OF INTEREST:
Promoting philanthropy addressing community needs through grantmaking, and providing leadership on key community issues.

TYPE:
Capital grants; Challenge/matching grants; Development grants; Project/program grants.

PURPOSE:
To provide a favorable ratio between the amount of money requested and the number of people served, show innovation and creativity in addressing a community need that demonstrates careful planning that provides for successful completion of the project.

LEGAL BASIS:
501(c)(3).

ELIGIBILITY:
Any nonprofit charity, as defined by Sections 501(c)(3) and 509(a) of the Internal Revenue Code, located within the greater Albion area or directly serving residents of the greater Albion area is eligible to apply for funding. Faith institutions, public entities, and schools directly serving the great Albion area community are also eligible for specific projects subject to restrictions.

GEOG. RESTRICTIONS: Greater Albion, Michigan area.

FINANCIAL DATA:
Amount of support per award: $150 to $10,000, depending on the fund.
Total amount of support: Approximately $80,000 to $100,000 each year.

APPLICATION INFO:
Details for applying are available online. The Foundation uses an online application system. Applicants should e-mail or call to have an account set up or to discuss the proposed project.
Deadline: January 10, March 10, May 10 and September 10.

ALBUQUERQUE COMMUNITY FOUNDATION [1046]

624 Tijeras, N.W.
Albuquerque, NM 87102
(505) 883-6240
Fax: (505) 883-3629
E-mail: khia@abqcf.org
Web Site: abqcf.org

FOUNDED: 1981

AREAS OF INTEREST:
Arts and culture, education, environmental and historic preservation, economic and workforce development, health and human services.

TYPE:
Challenge/matching grants; General operating grants; Project/program grants; Scholarships; Seed money grants; Technical assistance.

YEAR PROGRAM STARTED: 1983

PURPOSE:
To improve the quality of life in the greater Albuquerque area by providing support for projects and organizations that serve the community.

LEGAL BASIS:
Community foundation.

ELIGIBILITY:
Grants are made to nonprofit organizations. Foundation grants are generally not made to individuals, for political or religious purposes, to retire indebtedness, for the payment of interest or taxes, annual campaigns, endowments, emergency funding, to influence legislation or elections, to private foundations and other grantmaking organizations, or to organizations that discriminate on the basis of race, creed or sex.

GEOG. RESTRICTIONS: Bernalillo, Sandoval, Torrance and Valencia counties, New Mexico.

FINANCIAL DATA:
Amount of support per award: Varies.
Total amount of support: Varies.

APPLICATION INFO:
Current guidelines and criteria are available on the web site.
Duration: One year.

PUBLICATIONS:
Report to the Community.

IRS I.D.: 85-0295444

STAFF:
Randy Royster, President and Chief Executive Officer
Nick Williams, Chief Financial Officer
Marisa Magallenez, Vice President of Strategy

BOARD OF TRUSTEES:
Steve Maestas, Chairperson
Beverly R. Bendicksen, Chairperson-elect and Treasurer
Marcus Mims, C.P.A., Secretary
Patricia Apodaca
Arellana Cordero
Paul DiPaola
Anna Doss
Debbie Harmes
Rebecca Harrington
William P. Lang
Kenneth C. Leach
Linda H. Parker
Anne Sapon
Charlotte Schoenmann
Walter E. Stern
Jose Viramontes

ADDRESS INQUIRIES TO:
Joanna Colangelo, Vice President of Community Impact
(See address above.)

ALGER REGIONAL COMMUNITY FOUNDATION [1047]

P.O. Box 39
Munising, MI 49862
(906) 387-3900
E-mail: algercf@yahoo.com
Web Site: www.algercf.com

FOUNDED: 1992

AREAS OF INTEREST:
Cultural arts, community service, education, the environment and conservation, health and human services, and youth.

TYPE:
Endowments; Project/program grants; Scholarships.

YEAR PROGRAM STARTED: 1995

PURPOSE:
To provide support to organizations that enhance the quality of life in Alger County.

ELIGIBILITY:
Grants are made to organizations that have tax-exempt status under Section 501(c)(3) of the Internal Revenue Code. Nonsectarian religious programs may apply. Organizations must serve or be located in Alger County, MI. No grants are made to individuals.

GEOG. RESTRICTIONS: Alger County, Michigan.

FINANCIAL DATA:
Amount of support per award: Varies.

APPLICATION INFO:
Foundation staff members are available to talk with potential applicants who are interested in learning about opportunities and needs in the community.
Deadline: Varies.

ALLEGAN COUNTY COMMUNITY FOUNDATION [1048]

112 Locust Street
Allegan, MI 49010
(269) 673-8344
E-mail: lwittkop@alleganfoundation.org
Web Site: www.alleganfoundation.org

FOUNDED: 1965

AREAS OF INTEREST:
Education, health and human services, culture, community development, environmental issues and art.

TYPE:
General operating grants; Project/program grants; Scholarships; Technical assistance. Grants fall into the following categories: youth and general.

PURPOSE:
To positively impact the Allegan County community through the establishment of permanently endowed funds.

LEGAL BASIS:
Community foundation.

ELIGIBILITY:
Applications accepted from charitable organizations serving Allegan County, MI residents. No funding for individuals except for scholarships.

GEOG. RESTRICTIONS: Allegan County, Michigan.

FINANCIAL DATA:
Amount of support per award: $500 to $20,000.

APPLICATION INFO:
Applications must include a copy of the IRS 501(c)(3) tax determination letter.
Duration: One year.
Deadline: TAG: First Friday in September; Legacy: December.

IRS I.D.: 38-6189947

ADDRESS INQUIRIES TO:
Lee Wittkop, Executive Director
(See address above.)

*SPECIAL STIPULATIONS:
Potential applicants must meet with the Executive Director before receiving the grant application(s).

ALTMAN FOUNDATION [1049]

8 West 40th Street
19th Floor
New York, NY 10018-2263
(212) 682-0970
Fax: (212) 682-1648
E-mail: info@altman.org
Web Site: www.altmanfoundation.org

FOUNDED: 1913

AREAS OF INTEREST:
Strengthening communities, health,
education, independent and non-public
schools, arts and culture.

TYPE:
Project/program grants.

YEAR PROGRAM STARTED: 1913

PURPOSE:
To support programs and organizations
within the five boroughs of New York City
working in the Foundation's program areas.

LEGAL BASIS:
Private foundation.

ELIGIBILITY:
Must have a current IRS 501(c)(3)
tax-exemption letter. No grants to individuals.
No grants for bricks and mortar or capital
equipment.

GEOG. RESTRICTIONS: Five boroughs of New
York City.

FINANCIAL DATA:
Amount of support per award: Varies.
Total amount of support: Varies.

NO. MOST RECENT APPLICANTS: Approximately
300.

APPLICATION INFO:
Applicants should review material on the
Foundation's web site regarding funding
approach, guidelines, limitations and
procedures.
Duration: One year. Renewal possible.

PUBLICATIONS:
Annual report.

IRS I.D.: 13-1623879

STAFF:
Deborah T. Velazquez, President
Megan McAllister, Senior Program Officer
Rachael N. Pine, J.D., Senior Program
Officer

ADDRESS INQUIRIES TO:
Deborah T. Velasquez, President
(See address above.)

AMARILLO AREA FOUNDATION [1050]

801 South Fillmore
Suite 700
Amarillo, TX 79101
(806) 376-4521
Fax: (806) 373-3656
E-mail: kathie@aaf-hf.org
Web Site: www.amarilloareafoundation.org

FOUNDED: 1957

AREAS OF INTEREST:
Community, arts and culture, education,
health and human services, teen pregnancy
prevention, youth-oriented programs and
elderly services.

TYPE:
Project/program grants; Scholarships.
Discretionary grants.

PURPOSE:
To exercise leadership on charitable issues,
advance the cause of philanthropy throughout
the region and promote efficient and effective
delivery of services from nonprofit
organizations.

LEGAL BASIS:
501(c)(3).

ELIGIBILITY:
No grants to individuals. Scholarships go to
educational institutions.

GEOG. RESTRICTIONS: 26 northernmost counties
in the Texas panhandle.

FINANCIAL DATA:
Amount of support per award: $2,500 to
$300,000.
Total amount of support: Varies.

APPLICATION INFO:
Contact Grants Coordinator for counseling
prior to submitting application. Application is
available online for download as a Word
document.
Duration: Typically one year.

ADDRESS INQUIRIES TO:
Kathie Grant, Grant Administrator
(See address above.)

AMERICAN PLANNING ASSOCIATION

205 North Michigan Avenue
Suite 1200
Chicago, IL 60601
(312) 786-6345
E-mail: foundation@planning.org
Web Site: www.planning.
org/foundation/scholarships

TYPE:
Scholarships.

See entry 885 for full listing.

AMERICAN PLANNING ASSOCIATION [1051]

205 North Michigan Avenue
Suite 1200
Chicago, IL 60601
(312) 786-6705
E-mail: foundation@planning.org
Web Site: www.planning.
org/foundation/scholarships

FOUNDED: 1909

AREAS OF INTEREST:
Urban and regional planning and promotion
of the art and science of planning.

NAME(S) OF PROGRAMS:
● **Charles Abrams Scholarship Program**

TYPE:
Scholarships. For a student enrolled in a
graduate planning program, leading to a
Master's degree, who attends one of the
following schools:
(1) Columbia University, Division of Urban
Planning;
(2) Harvard University, Urban Planning
Program, Harvard Graduate School of
Design;
(3) Massachusetts Institute of Technology,
Department of Urban Studies and Planning;
(4) New School University, Urban Policy
Analysis and Management Program, Robert
J. Milano Graduate School of Management
and Urban Policy or;
(5) University of Pennsylvania, Department
of City and Regional Planning.

PURPOSE:
To aid students who will pursue careers as
practicing planners.

LEGAL BASIS:
Private, nonprofit educational association.

ELIGIBILITY:
An applicant must be a U.S. citizen and have
been accepted into the graduate planning
program of one of the five eligible schools.
Incoming students are eligible. An applicant
must be in need of financial assistance, as
determined by a review of the applicant's
financial needs. A nomination by the
department chair is required.

FINANCIAL DATA:
Student also receives one-year membership in
the American Planning Association.
Amount of support per award: $2,000 paid
directly to the student's school to defray
tuition costs.
Total amount of support: $2,000 each year.

NO. MOST RECENT APPLICANTS: 5.

NO. AWARDS: 1 each year.

APPLICATION INFO:
An eligible applicant should apply through
one of the five designated schools on forms
supplied to the participating university by
APA. Applicant needs to be nominated by
Department Chair.
Duration: One academic year.
Deadline: June.

ADDRESS INQUIRIES TO:
See e-mail address above.

AMPCO-PITTSBURGH CHARITABLE FOUNDATION [1052]

726 Bell Avenue, Suite 301
Carnegie, PA 15106
(412) 456-4418
Fax: (412) 456-4436
E-mail: rhoover@ampcopgh.com

AREAS OF INTEREST:
Universities and community funds.

TYPE:
Cash contributions.

PURPOSE:
To provide support for community funds and
higher education.

ELIGIBILITY:
Organizations classified as 501(c)(3) by the
IRS can apply. No grants to individuals.

GEOG. RESTRICTIONS: United States.

FINANCIAL DATA:
Amount of support per award: $250 to
$1,000.
Total amount of support: $400,000 per year.

APPLICATION INFO:
Request should be in letter format.
Deadline: October 31.

ADDRESS INQUIRIES TO:
Rose Hoover
Chairman of Board and Trustee
(See address above.)

THE ANDERSEN CORPORATE FOUNDATION [1053]
White Pine Building
342 Fifth Avenue North, Suite 200
Bayport, MN 55003
(651) 275-4450
Fax: (651) 439-9480
E-mail: andersencorpfdn@srinc.biz
Web Site: www.andersencorporation.
com/sustainability/community

FOUNDED: 1941

AREAS OF INTEREST:
Education and youth development, health and safety, human services, and affordable housing.

TYPE:
Capital grants; General operating grants; Project/program grants.

YEAR PROGRAM STARTED: 1941

PURPOSE:
To better people's lives and strengthen communities, focusing primarily where Andersen employees live and work.

LEGAL BASIS:
Private foundation.

ELIGIBILITY:
Qualified tax-exempt organizations. Primary focus on Washington County, MN and portions of western Wisconsin.

GEOG. RESTRICTIONS: Washington County, Minnesota; Dunn, Polk and St. Croix counties, Wisconsin. Limited support to organizations serving Ramsey County, Minnesota.

FINANCIAL DATA:
$50,000,000 in assets as of December 31, 2019.

Amount of support per award: $1,500 to $100,000.

Total amount of support: $2,100,000 for the year 2018-19.

NO. AWARDS: 138 for the year 2018-19.

APPLICATION INFO:
Applications are accepted by invitation only. New organizations must complete the Inquiry Form available on the web site and submit to the e-mail address listed above.

Duration: One year. Renewal by reapplication.

Deadline: November 15, February 15 and June 15.

PUBLICATIONS:
Application guidelines.

IRS I.D.: 41-6020912

OFFICERS AND BOARD OF DIRECTORS:
Karen Richard, President
Eliza Chlebeck, Vice President
Chris Galvin, Treasurer
Phil Donaldson
Jeanne Junker
Jay Lund

ADDRESS INQUIRIES TO:
Chloette Haley, Program Officer
(See address above.)

*PLEASE NOTE:
Foundation prefers that the proposal be sent to the address above.

FRED C. AND KATHERINE B. ANDERSEN FOUNDATION [1054]
P.O. Box 80
Bayport, MN 55003
(651) 264-7355
Fax: (651) 264-7245
E-mail: marygillstrom@sbcglobal.net

FOUNDED: 1959

AREAS OF INTEREST:
Education, youth, elderly and health programs.

TYPE:
Capital grants; Challenge/matching grants; General operating grants; Project/program grants. The Foundation supports four-year accredited colleges and universities that do not accept state or federal funding.

YEAR PROGRAM STARTED: 1959

PURPOSE:
To support organizations of higher learning that are four-year institutions that do not accept state or federal funding.

LEGAL BASIS:
Private foundation.

ELIGIBILITY:
Grants are made to organizations that have tax-exempt status under Section 501(c)(3) of the Internal Revenue Code. No grants are made to individuals. No grants for endowment.

GEOG. RESTRICTIONS: Washington County, Minnesota; Pierce, Polk and St. Croix counties, Wisconsin.

FINANCIAL DATA:
Total market value of $800,000 for the year 2019.

Amount of support per award: Varies by need.

Total amount of support: $35,967,000 for the year 2019.

APPLICATION INFO:
Organizations should submit a letter of intent to the Foundation.

Duration: One year. Must reapply for future grants.

Deadline: March 15, June 15 and September 15.

IRS I.D.: 41-6020920

ADDRESS INQUIRIES TO:
Mary Gillstrom, Vice President/Secretary
(See address above.)

HUGH J. ANDERSEN FOUNDATION [1055]
342 Fifth Avenue North, Suite 200
Bayport, MN 55003-4502
(651) 275-4489
Fax: (651) 439-9480
E-mail: hjafdn@srinc.biz
Web Site: www.srinc.biz/foundations/hugh-j-andersen-foundation

FOUNDED: 1962

AREAS OF INTEREST:
Humanities, arts/culture, elementary and secondary education, health care, human services, women and homelessness.

TYPE:
Capital grants; General operating grants; Project/program grants. Supports focused efforts that foster inclusivity, promotes equality, and lends to increased human independence, self-sufficiency and dignity.

PURPOSE:
To improve the quality of life in the St. Croix Valley.

LEGAL BASIS:
Private organization.

ELIGIBILITY:
Eligible organizations must be IRS 501(c)(3) tax-exempt.

GEOG. RESTRICTIONS: Primarily Washington County, Minnesota and Pierce, Polk, and St. Croix counties in Wisconsin, with secondary focus in St. Paul, Minnesota.

FINANCIAL DATA:
Amount of support per award: $500 to $75,000.

Total amount of support: $4,404,000 for fiscal year ended February 28, 2019.

NO. AWARDS: 244.

APPLICATION INFO:
The Foundation requires a full proposal when applying for a grant. A full proposal consists of:
(1) Request Cover Form;
(2) Proposal Checklist and;
(3) all documentation as indicated on the Checklist.

Although the Foundation prefers the use of the Hugh J. Andersen Foundation Request Cover Form and Checklist for a complete proposal, the Minnesota Common Grant Application Form will be accepted provided the Foundation's Request Cover Form and Proposal Checklist are also included.

Duration: One year. Renewal by reapplication.

Deadline: March 15, June 15, August 15 and November 15.

PUBLICATIONS:
Annual report; application guidelines.

IRS I.D.: 41-6020914

ADDRESS INQUIRIES TO:
Brad Kruse, Philanthropy Director
(See address above.)

ANDRUS FAMILY FUND [1056]
200 Madison Avenue, 25th Floor
New York, NY 10016
(212) 687-6975
E-mail: jkaizer@affund.org
info@affund.org
Web Site: affund.org

FOUNDED: 2000

AREAS OF INTEREST:
Juvenile justice and foster care.

NAME(S) OF PROGRAMS:
● **Foster Care Program**
● **Juvenile Justice Program**

TYPE:
Project/program grants.

YEAR PROGRAM STARTED: 2000

PURPOSE:
To contribute to the body of knowledge and experience about what is necessary to create and sustain effective social change.

LEGAL BASIS:
501(c)(3).

ELIGIBILITY:
Groups must be tax-exempt under Section 501(c)(3) of the IRS. Organizations can also submit Letters of Inquiry through a sponsoring organization if the sponsor has a 501(c)(3) status.

The Andrus Family Fund does not fund individuals, capital campaigns or building construction, purchasing of equipment, or conference scholarships.

GEOG. RESTRICTIONS: United States.

FINANCIAL DATA:
Amount of support per award: $50,000 to $200,000.
Total amount of support: $3,500,000 to $4,000,000.

APPLICATION INFO:
Applicants are encouraged to review the guidelines on the Foundation web site thoroughly before submitting a grant application.
Deadline: Grants are awarded by the trustees, who meet in September.

ADDRESS INQUIRIES TO:
Manuela Arciniegas, Director
(See address above.)

ANN ARBOR AREA COMMUNITY FOUNDATION   [1057]

301 North Main Street
Suite 300
Ann Arbor, MI 48104-1133
(734) 663-0401
(734) 436-7587
Fax: (734) 663-3514
E-mail: info@aaacf.org
kvideto@aaacf.org
Web Site: www.aaacf.org

FOUNDED: 1963

AREAS OF INTEREST:
Environment, arts, health and human services, youth and seniors.

NAME(S) OF PROGRAMS:
● **The African American Endowment Fund**
● **The Anna Botsford Bach Fund**
● **Community Grantmaking**
● **Coordinated Funding**
● **Cultural Economic Development**
● **Youth Council**
● **The Ypsilanti Area Community Fund**

TYPE:
Demonstration grants; Development grants; General operating grants; Project/program grants; Scholarships; Seed money grants; Technical assistance.

YEAR PROGRAM STARTED: 1963

PURPOSE:
To improve the quality of life in the Foundation's region.

ELIGIBILITY:
AAACF welcomes grant applications from 501(c)(3) nonprofit organizations whose programs and services benefit the people of Washtenaw County, MI.

GEOG. RESTRICTIONS: Washtenaw County, Michigan.

FINANCIAL DATA:
Amount of support per award: Varies.
Total amount of support: Varies.

APPLICATION INFO:
A guideline on how to apply and application form are available on the Foundation web site.
Duration: One year.
Deadline: Varies.

OFFICER:
Neel Hajra, President and Chief Executive Officer

ADDRESS INQUIRIES TO:
Jillian Rosen, Vice President for Community Investment
E-mail: jrosen@aaacf.org

THE ANNENBERG FOUNDATION

2000 Avenue of the Stars
Suite 1000 S
Los Angeles, CA 90067
(310) 209-4560
Fax: (310) 209-1631
E-mail: info@annenberg.org
requests@annenberg.org
Web Site: www.annenberg.org

TYPE:
General operating grants; Grants-in-aid; Project/program grants; Technical assistance.

See entry 15 for full listing.

ARIZONA COMMUNITY FOUNDATION   [1058]

2201 East Camelback Road
Suite 405-B
Phoenix, AZ 85016
(602) 381-1400
(800) 222-8221
Fax: (602) 381-1575
E-mail: info@azfoundation.org
Web Site: www.azfoundation.org

FOUNDED: 1978

AREAS OF INTEREST:
Children's mental health and prevention programs, economic development, arts and culture, youth agencies and health agencies.

NAME(S) OF PROGRAMS:
● **Communities for All Ages**

TYPE:
Project/program grants.

YEAR PROGRAM STARTED: 1978

PURPOSE:
To benefit the quality of life in the Phoenix, AZ community and the surrounding area.

LEGAL BASIS:
Community foundation.

ELIGIBILITY:
Tax-exempt, nonprofit organizations. No grants are made to individuals.

GEOG. RESTRICTIONS: Arizona.

FINANCIAL DATA:
Amount of support per award: $10,000 average.

APPLICATION INFO:
Application information is available on the web site.
Duration: Typically, one year.

PUBLICATIONS:
Annual report.

OFFICERS:
Stephen O. Evans, Chairman
Robbin M. Coulon, Esq., Vice Chairman
Rufus Glasper, Treasurer
Leezie Kim, Esq., Secretary

ADDRESS INQUIRIES TO:
Lora Golke
Senior Director, Philanthropic Services
(See address above.)

ARKANSAS COMMUNITY FOUNDATION   [1059]

5 Allied Drive
Suite 51110
Little Rock, AR 72202
(501) 372-1116
Fax: (501) 372-1166
E-mail: arcf@arcf.org
Web Site: www.arcf.org

FOUNDED: 1976

AREAS OF INTEREST:
Grants are made in all fields.

TYPE:
Project/program grants; Scholarships.

PURPOSE:
To promote smart giving to improve communities.

LEGAL BASIS:
Community foundation.

ELIGIBILITY:
Applicants must be nonprofit organizations with projects to benefit Arkansans. Few unrestricted grants are made. Only Arkansas organizations need apply.

Most funds are restricted or designated for specific organizations. Very few unrestricted grants are made.

GEOG. RESTRICTIONS: Arkansas.

FINANCIAL DATA:
Total amount of support: $53,092,015 for the year 2020.

APPLICATION INFO:
Application information is available on the web site.
Duration: One year.

PUBLICATIONS:
Annual report; newsletter.

IRS I.D.: 52-1055743

BOARD OF DIRECTORS:
Don Greenland, Chairperson
Heather Larkin, President and Chief Executive Officer
Ramsay Ball
Kandice Bell
Alison Bradford-White
Tracy Cude
Holly Dunsworth
Eric Hutchinson
Heather Loftis
Creshelle Nash, M.D.
Steve Nipper
Paige Partridge-Hix
Andy Peeler
Vance Smiley
Philip Tappan
Robert Thompson
Scott Van Horn
Sharon Wilson
Robert Zunick

ADDRESS INQUIRIES TO:
Grants Coordinator
(See address above.)

THE AUSTIN COMMUNITY FOUNDATION   [1060]

4315 Guadalupe Street
Suite 300
Austin, TX 78751
(512) 472-4483
Fax: (512) 472-4486
E-mail: info@austincf.org
Web Site: www.austincf.org

FOUNDED: 1977

AREAS OF INTEREST:
Arts and culture, community engagement, education, recreation and animal-related services, environment and public space, human services/basic needs, and health and wellness.

NAME(S) OF PROGRAMS:
● **Community Grant Program**

TYPE:
Project/program grants; Scholarships.

YEAR PROGRAM STARTED: 1977

PURPOSE:
To promote philanthropy in central Texas; to improve the quality of life now and in the future.

ELIGIBILITY:
Organizations must be 501(c)(3) or 170(b)(1)(a)(vi) and located in the central Texas area, including Bastrop, Burnet, Caldwell, Hays, Travis and Williamson counties. Funds are not given to individuals.

GEOG. RESTRICTIONS: Central Texas.

FINANCIAL DATA:
Amount of support per award: Varies; average competitive grant is $25,000.
Total amount of support: $42,200,000 in grants and $319,000 in scholarships for the year 2020.

NO. MOST RECENT APPLICANTS: 240.

NO. AWARDS: 95.

APPLICATION INFO:
Applications is available on the Foundation web site.
Duration: One year. Must reapply.
Deadline: Proposals are reviewed on an ongoing basis; four- to five-month process.

IRS I.D.: 74-1934031

ADDRESS INQUIRIES TO:
Meagan A. Longley
Vice President Community Impact
(See address above.)

AUTRY FOUNDATION   [1061]
4383 Colfax Avenue
Studio City, CA 91604
(818) 752-7770
Fax: (818) 752-7779
E-mail: mhansen@autry.com

AREAS OF INTEREST:
Culture, education, children's and seniors' groups, hunger and health.

TYPE:
Project/program grants.

PURPOSE:
To offer assistance to communities in southern California.

LEGAL BASIS:
Private foundation.

ELIGIBILITY:
Eligible organizations must be IRS 501(c)(3) tax-exempt.

GEOG. RESTRICTIONS: Southern California.

FINANCIAL DATA:
Amount of support per award: Varies.
Total amount of support: Varies.

ADDRESS INQUIRIES TO:
Maxine Hansen, Director
(See address above.)

*PLEASE NOTE:
The Foundation is only funding existing programs at this time.

BADGER METER FOUNDATION, INC.   [1062]
4545 West Brown Deer Road
Milwaukee, WI 53223-2479
(414) 371-5742

AREAS OF INTEREST:
Social services, education, conservation and community funds.

TYPE:
Capital grants.

PURPOSE:
To support education and community service organizations, health associations, the handicapped, the arts and conservation.

ELIGIBILITY:
Organizations classified as 501(c)(3) by the IRS can apply. No grants to individuals and religious organizations.

GEOG. RESTRICTIONS: Southeastern Milwaukee area, Wisconsin.

FINANCIAL DATA:
Amount of support per award: Varies.
Total amount of support: Varies.

NO. AWARDS: 40 for the year 2019.

APPLICATION INFO:
Request must be submitted on organization's letterhead paper.
Duration: One year. Grants are renewable.

ADDRESS INQUIRIES TO:
John Biever, Treasurer and Secretary
(See address above.)

BALTIMORE COMMUNITY FOUNDATION
11 East Mount Royal Avenue
2nd Floor
Baltimore, MD 21202
(410) 332-4171
Fax: (410) 837-4701
E-mail: info@bcf.org
Web Site: www.bcf.org

TYPE:
Scholarships. Neighborhood grants. Education grants.

See entry 29 for full listing.

BARAGA COUNTY COMMUNITY FOUNDATION   [1063]
100 Hemlock Street
Baraga, MI 49908
(906) 353-7898
E-mail: baragacf@up.net
Web Site: www.baragacountyfoundation.org

FOUNDED: 1994

AREAS OF INTEREST:
Arts and culture, community development, education, senior well-being, and youth development.

TYPE:
Capital grants; Challenge/matching grants; Endowments; Project/program grants; Scholarships; Seed money grants; Technical assistance. Community convening.

YEAR PROGRAM STARTED: 1994

PURPOSE:
To enhance the quality of life for the citizens of the community.

LEGAL BASIS:
501(c)(3).

ELIGIBILITY:
Grants are made to organizations that have tax-exempt status under Section 501(c)(3) of the Internal Revenue Code.

GEOG. RESTRICTIONS: Baraga County, Michigan.

FINANCIAL DATA:
Amount of support per award: Varies depending upon the needs and nature of the request; $1,500 common.
Total amount of support: $27,000 for the year 2019.

NO. AWARDS: Varies.

APPLICATION INFO:
Application information is available online.
Duration: One year. Renewal possible.
Deadline: Varies.

IRS I.D.: 38-3198122

ADDRESS INQUIRIES TO:
Gordette Cote Leutz, Executive Director
(See address above.)

BARNES GROUP FOUNDATION   [1064]
123 Main Street
Bristol, CT 06010
(860) 583-7070
E-mail: info@bginc.com
Web Site: www.barnesgroupinc.com

FOUNDED: 1945

AREAS OF INTEREST:
Cultural arts, education, and health and welfare.

TYPE:
General operating grants; Scholarships. Employee scholarship program.

PURPOSE:
To support higher education, cultural arts, and health and welfare.

ELIGIBILITY:
Organizations classified as 501(c)(3) by the IRS can apply. Individuals and religious organizations are ineligible.

GEOG. RESTRICTIONS: United States, with emphasis on Connecticut and New England.

FINANCIAL DATA:
Amount of support per award: Varies.
Total amount of support: Varies.

APPLICATION INFO:
Applicants must write to the Foundation for an application form.
Duration: One year. Grants are renewable.

ADDRESS INQUIRIES TO:
Tom Barnes, Secretary
(See address above.)

BARR FOUNDATION   [1065]
2 Atlantic Avenue, Lewis Wharf
Fourth Floor
Boston, MA 02110
(617) 854-3500
Fax: (617) 854-3501
E-mail: info@barrfoundation.org
Web Site: www.barrfoundation.org

FOUNDED: 1987

AREAS OF INTEREST:
Education, the environment, arts and cultural activities with a focus on Boston, MA.

TYPE:
Capital grants; Challenge/matching grants; Conferences/seminars; Development grants; Endowments; Fellowships; General operating grants; Matching gifts; Project/program grants; Technical assistance. The work of the Foundation focuses on three critical areas with a focus on Boston, MA:
(1) closing education opportunity gaps;
(2) mitigating climate change and;
(3) enhancing cultural vitality.

PURPOSE:
To enhance the quality of life for all of Boston's citizens.

ELIGIBILITY:
Barr does not make grants to individuals or for scholarships. It is also rare to fund capital projects, event sponsorships, program-related investments, or organizations not classified as public charities and tax-exempt under Section 501(c)(3) of the Internal Revenue Code.

GEOG. RESTRICTIONS: Regional Boston, Massachusetts and New England areas.

FINANCIAL DATA:
Amount of support per award: Varies.
Total amount of support: $85,115,402 in grants and matching gifts for the year 2020.

NO. MOST RECENT APPLICANTS: Approximately 330 grant applicants.

NO. AWARDS: 495 grants and matching gifts.

APPLICATION INFO:
Generally, by invitation only. From time to time, Barr issues open requests for proposals, to provide broad access to funding opportunities, and to ensure the Foundation remains open to new ideas and new partnerships. Organizations are encouraged to subscribe to the Foundation's newsletter to stay informed about future RFP opportunities.
Duration: Varies.
Deadline: Grants are approved quarterly at the Trustee Meeting and also monthly by the President and Vice President for Strategy and Programs.

PUBLICATIONS:
Newsletter.

IRS I.D.: 04-6579815

ADDRESS INQUIRIES TO:
Kerri Ann Hurley
Director of Grants Management
(See address above.)

BAYER FUND   [1066]
800 North Lindbergh Boulevard
Creve Coeur, MO 63141
E-mail: grantquestions@bayer.com
Web Site: www.fund.bayer.us

FOUNDED: 1964

AREAS OF INTEREST:
Community development, STEM education, health and wellness, and food and nutrition.

TYPE:
Project/program grants.

PURPOSE:
To strengthen communities where Bayer customers and employees live and work; to address families in underresourced areas, with an emphasis on children.

ELIGIBILITY:
Applicants must be nonprofit 501(c)(3) or units of government 170(c)(1). Proposed projects must fit within one of the focus areas. Must be an experienced, established and reputable organization (not a start-up organization), financially sound with a diverse funding base, and be audited annually.

Grants are not given to religious organizations.

GEOG. RESTRICTIONS: Primarily Berkeley, California; St. Louis, Missouri; northern New Jersey; and Pittsburgh, Pennsylvania.

FINANCIAL DATA:
Amount of support per award: Varies.
Total amount of support: $17,000,000 for the year 2020.

APPLICATION INFO:
Application information is available online.
Duration: One to two years.
Deadline: Varies.

NORWIN S. AND ELIZABETH N. BEAN FOUNDATION   [1067]
40 Stark Street
Manchester, NH 03101
(603) 493-7257
E-mail: kcook@beanfoundation.org
Web Site: www.beanfoundation.org

FOUNDED: 1967

AREAS OF INTEREST:
Arts and humanities, education, environment, health and human services, and public benefit.

TYPE:
Capital grants; Challenge/matching grants; Project/program grants. Grants to tax-exempt charitable organizations operating in Amherst or Manchester, NH, for broad charitable purposes. Generally, at least two-thirds of available funds are awarded as grants for programs undertaken by nonprofit organizations and public agencies.

General operating support grants are rarely made to ongoing programs, and awards are not made to eliminate previously incurred deficits. Short-term operating support may be provided to new organizations or for new program initiatives of established organizations. Generally, grants are provided for expenditure over a period of one year.

YEAR PROGRAM STARTED: 1967

PURPOSE:
To promote the general welfare.

LEGAL BASIS:
Private foundation.

ELIGIBILITY:
Applications are accepted from nonprofit 501(c)(3) organizations, municipal and public agencies serving the communities of Amherst or Manchester, NH. Priority consideration is given to organizations operating primarily in those two communities. However, the Foundation will consider applications from statewide or regional organizations which provide a substantial and documented level of service to Manchester and Amherst. The Foundation does not make grants to individuals or provide scholarship aid.

GEOG. RESTRICTIONS: Amherst or Manchester, New Hampshire.

FINANCIAL DATA:
Amount of support per award: $1,000 to $50,000.
Total amount of support: $413,100 for fiscal year 2019.

NO. MOST RECENT APPLICANTS: 45.

NO. AWARDS: 29 for the year 2019.

REPRESENTATIVE AWARDS:
$5,000 to Currier Museum of Art to support the Earn and Learn Teen Volunteer Program; $10,000 to MY TURN to support paid work-based learning opportunities for youth in its Manchester HiSET Program; $5,000 to The Chill Foundation for operating funds for Manchester youth participating in Chill Snow and Skate programs; $25,000 to Webster House to employ a nonprofit management consultant to develop a strategic plan for the next five years, including a transition plan for the Executive Director.

APPLICATION INFO:
Applications must be submitted electronically. Applications should include a completed cover letter sheet and proposal with appropriate enclosures explaining the purpose of the project, describing how the project will be accomplished, and indicating the amount of grant support sought.
Duration: Grants are usually awarded for a one-year period only. The Foundation does not consider multiyear grants except in very rare circumstances.
Deadline: April 1, September 1 and December 1 for decisions made in February, June and November, respectively.

PUBLICATIONS:
Guidelines.

STAFF:
Kathleen D. Cook, Grant Manager

BOARD OF TRUSTEES:
Michael Delaney, Chairperson
John F. Dinkel, Jr.
Thomas J. Donovan
Robert Heaton
Katy Easterly Martey
Kris McCracken

ADDRESS INQUIRIES TO:
Kathleen D. Cook, Grant Manager
(See address above.)

BERKS COUNTY COMMUNITY FOUNDATION   [1068]
237 Court Street
Reading, PA 19601
(610) 685-2223
E-mail: info@bccf.org
Web Site: www.bccf.org

FOUNDED: 1994

AREAS OF INTEREST:
Community, health, energy, smart growth and public policy.

TYPE:
Project/program grants; Scholarships.

PURPOSE:
To promote philanthropy and improve the quality of life in Berks County; to encourage and nurture performing artists at critical points in their careers.

LEGAL BASIS:
501(c)(3).

ELIGIBILITY:
Tax-exempt or nonprofit organizations, individuals, associations and public or private agencies are eligible to apply. Grant must be used for charitable purposes only.

GEOG. RESTRICTIONS: Berks County, Pennsylvania.

FINANCIAL DATA:
$86,733,408 in assets for the year ended July 1, 2020.

Amount of support per award: Varies, depending on fund.

Total amount of support: Varies.

APPLICATION INFO:
Applications are submitted through the Foundation's Grant Application System.

Duration: Varies.

PUBLICATIONS:
Annual report.

ADDRESS INQUIRIES TO:
See e-mail address above.

WILLIAM BLAIR AND COMPANY FOUNDATION [1069]

150 North Riverside Plaza
Chicago, IL 60606
(312) 364-8037
E-mail: lcoy@williamblair.com
Web Site: www.williamblair.com

AREAS OF INTEREST:
Cultural programs, education, health and human services, social services, youth and entrepreneurship.

TYPE:
Matching gifts; Project/program grants.

ELIGIBILITY:
Organizations must be classified as 501(c)(3) by the IRS. No grants to individuals. Limited to employees of William Blair. Not open to the public.

FINANCIAL DATA:
Amount of support per award: Varies.

Total amount of support: Varies.

Matching fund requirements: Employee donations are matched 1:1 up to $1,500 per calendar year. The Foundation also had a nonprofit board match and a volunteer grants match of up to $250 per calendar year for eight hours of service.

NO. MOST RECENT APPLICANTS: Varies.

NO. AWARDS: Over 500.

APPLICATION INFO:
Contact the Foundation.

Duration: One year.

ADDRESS INQUIRIES TO:
Laura Coy, Head of Philanthropy Strategy and ESG Integration
(See address above.)

*PLEASE NOTE:
All Foundation grants are employee inspired.

BLOWITZ-RIDGEWAY FOUNDATION [1070]

1701 East Woodfield Road
Suite 201
Schaumburg, IL 60173-5127
(847) 330-1020
E-mail: serena@blowitzridgeway.org
Web Site: blowitzridgeway.org

FOUNDED: 1984

AREAS OF INTEREST:
Health care and housing.

TYPE:
General operating grants; Project/program grants.

YEAR PROGRAM STARTED: 1984

PURPOSE:
To improve the health of the uninsured, underinsured and low-income metropolitan Chicago residents and the community through increased access to community-based preventive and primary health services, such as medical, dental, vision, mental health, and case management; to support housing programs and services that provide access to prevention, intervention, follow-up, supportive services, and employment training for individuals and families who are homeless or at-risk of being homeless.

LEGAL BASIS:
Private independent foundation.

ELIGIBILITY:
Organizations classified as 501(c)(3) by the IRS can apply. Preference will be given to organizations in Illinois and to programs or services which benefit youth, seniors or individuals lacking sufficient resources to care for themselves. No grants to individuals, religious or political organizations, government agencies, organizations that subsist mainly on third-party funding nor for the production or writing of audio-visual materials.

GEOG. RESTRICTIONS: City of Chicago and the six collar counties of Cook, DuPage, Kane, Lake, McHenry, and Will, Illinois.

FINANCIAL DATA:
Assets of $39,100,000 for the year ended September 30, 2020.

Amount of support per award: Generally, $10,000 to $15,000; some larger grants.

Total amount of support: Approximately $1,044,500 for fiscal year 2020.

NO. MOST RECENT APPLICANTS: 168 for the year 2020.

NO. AWARDS: 84 for the year 2020.

APPLICATION INFO:
The Blowitz-Ridgeway Foundation no longer accepts paper applications or applications submitted by mail. Applications are only accepted through the online grant program. If declined, applicants must reapply the following year.

Duration: One year. Grants are renewable.

PUBLICATIONS:
Annual report; application guidelines.

IRS I.D.: 36-2488355

ADDRESS INQUIRIES TO:
Serena Moy, Executive Director
(See address above.)

BLUE MOUNTAIN COMMUNITY FOUNDATION [1071]

P.O. Box 603
Walla Walla, WA 99362-0015
(509) 529-4371
Fax: (509) 529-5284
E-mail: bmcf@bluemountainfoundation.org
Web Site: www.bluemountainfoundation.org

FOUNDED: 1984

AREAS OF INTEREST:
Social and community services, education, health, and the arts and humanities.

TYPE:
Endowments; Project/program grants; Scholarships. The Foundation administers and awards scholarships to local area students to enable them to attend college, graduate school or trade school.

PURPOSE:
To seek, steward and share charitable gifts in the Blue Mountain area.

ELIGIBILITY:
The Foundation awards grants to nonprofit, tax-exempt organizations in the Foundation's service area which includes the counties of Columbia, Garfield and Walla Walla in the state of Washington and the communities in Umatilla County, OR. It strives to make awards to agencies and programs that meet community needs and bring the most benefit to people in the Blue Mountain area.

GEOG. RESTRICTIONS: Columbia, Garfield and Walla Walla counties in Washington, and Umatilla County in Oregon.

FINANCIAL DATA:
Amount of support per award: Varies.

Total amount of support: Approximately $2,000,000 annually.

APPLICATION INFO:
Grant guidelines and application forms can be obtained through the Foundation's web site. Application must be submitted electronically.

Duration: Typically one year.

Deadline: Grants: July 1; Scholarships: March 2.

THE BNY MELLON FOUNDATION OF SOUTHWESTERN PENNSYLVANIA [1072]

P.O. Box 185
Pittsburgh, PA 15230-0185
(412) 234-0023
Fax: (412) 236-1662
Web Site: www.bnymellon.com

FOUNDED: 1974

AREAS OF INTEREST:
Humanitarian and social impact through pro bono volunteerism and donations.

TYPE:
Project/program grants; Technical assistance.

YEAR PROGRAM STARTED: 1974

PURPOSE:
To identify and support initiatives that improve the social and economic conditions of residents where the company does business and where employees live and work. Through powering potential, the company's strategic philanthropic investments.

LEGAL BASIS:
Corporate foundation, part of BNY Mellon's Charitable Giving Program.

ELIGIBILITY:
Organizations requesting support must have 501(c)(3) tax-exempt charitable status and must be public charities as defined under Section 509(a)(1) of the Internal Revenue Code.

No support is available for loans or direct grants to individuals, religious programs of churches or other sectarian organizations and political parties, campaigns or candidates. As a general rule, support is not available for fraternal organizations, such as police or fire associations, scholarships, fellowships and travel grants, conference or seminar attendance, specialized health campaigns, endowment campaigns, individual United Way agencies which already benefit from the Corporation's gift to the United Way appeal, national organizations, projects or programs or those which operate outside the U.S. and multiyear commitments.

GEOG. RESTRICTIONS: Southwestern Pennsylvania.

FINANCIAL DATA:
Amount of support per award: Varies.
Total amount of support: Approximately $4,000,000 for the year 2018.

NO. MOST RECENT APPLICANTS: Approximately 500.

NO. AWARDS: Approximately 125.

APPLICATION INFO:
Contact the Foundation.
Duration: One year.
Deadline: Requests are considered upon receipt.

PUBLICATIONS:
Annual report which contains contributions policy and application guidelines.

STAFF:
Daisey Holmes, President

ADDRESS INQUIRIES TO:
Daisey Holmes, President
(See address above.)

THE BOSTON FOUNDATION   [1073]
75 Arlington Street, Third Floor
Boston, MA 02116-3936
(617) 338-1700
Fax: (617) 338-1604
E-mail: grantsinfo@tbf.org
Web Site: www.tbf.org

FOUNDED: 1915

AREAS OF INTEREST:
Health, welfare, educational, cultural, planning and housing needs of the Boston metropolitan area community.

TYPE:
General operating grants; Project/program grants; Technical assistance. Capacity building. Grants for new or experimental programs of both new and established institutions.

LEGAL BASIS:
Community foundation established in 1915 in Massachusetts by agreement and declaration of trust. Incorporated in 1917.

ELIGIBILITY:
Grants are made to organizations or for programs in the Boston standard metropolitan statistical area only. Organizations must be 501(c)(3) public charity or have federal tax-exempt status or a fiscal nonprofit agent. No grants are made to individuals. Grants are not made for scholarship, travel, medical or scientific research, religious purposes, publications or films or for national/international organizations.

GEOG. RESTRICTIONS: Greater Boston, Massachusetts.

FINANCIAL DATA:
Amount of support per award: Averages approximately $10,000 to $150,000.

Total amount of support: Approximately $16,000,000 annually.
Matching fund requirements: Varies.

NO. MOST RECENT APPLICANTS: Approximately 550.

NO. AWARDS: Approximately 220.

APPLICATION INFO:
Information may be obtained from the Foundation web site.
Duration: Up to five years.

PUBLICATIONS:
Annual report; application guidelines; quarterly newsletters.

OFFICERS:
Linda Mason, Chairperson
T.J. Rose, Vice Chairperson
M. Lee Pelton, President and Chief Executive Officer
Alfred F. Van Ranst, Jr., Treasurer and Chief Financial Officer
Stephen Chan, Secretary
George C. Wilson, Assistant Treasurer
John Ho, Assistant Secretary

BOARD MEMBERS:
Zamawa Arenas
Andrew Arnott
Vanessa Calderon-Rosado, Ph.D.
Elyse Cherry
Brian Conway
Pam Y. Eddinger, Ph.D.
Michael R. Eisenson
Betty Francisco
Paul C. Gannon
Paul W. Lee
Linda Mason
Dr. Myechia Minter-Jordan
J. Keith Motley, Ph.D.
Peter Nessen
Ron O'Hanley
Tracy Palandjian
Dwight Poler
T.J. Rose
Scott E. Squillace, Esq.
C.A. Webb

ADDRESS INQUIRIES TO:
Grants Manager or Program Officer
(See address above.)

OTTO BREMER TRUST   [1074]
30 East 7th Street
Suite 2900
St. Paul, MN 55101
(651) 227-8036
(888) 291-1123
Fax: (651) 312-3665
E-mail: twilliams@ottobremer.org
Web Site: ottobremer.org

AREAS OF INTEREST:
Community economic, civic, and social betterment.

TYPE:
Capital grants; Challenge/matching grants; General operating grants; Project/program grants.

PURPOSE:
To assist people in achieving full economic, civic and social participation in and for the betterment of their communities.

ELIGIBILITY:
Grants are restricted to private nonprofit or public tax-exempt organizations for purposes defined under Section 501(c)(3) of the Internal Revenue Code. Grants are only made to organizations whose beneficiaries are

residents of Minnesota, Montana, North Dakota or Wisconsin. Grants are not made to individuals.

GEOG. RESTRICTIONS: Minnesota, Montana, North Dakota and western Wisconsin.

FINANCIAL DATA:
Amount of support per award: $1,000 to $500,000; average $35,000.
Total amount of support: Approximately $71,000,000 for the year 2020.

NO. AWARDS: Approximately 900 for the year 2020.

APPLICATION INFO:
Applicants must complete the eligibility questions through the link on the Trust web site. Those encouraged to continue the application process will be directed to the landing page.
Duration: One year. Must reapply.
Deadline: Varies.

GLADYS BROOKS FOUNDATION   [1075]
1055 Franklin Avenue
Suite 208
Garden City, NY 11530-2903
(516) 746-6103
Fax: (516) 877-1758
E-mail: kathy@gladysbrooksfoundation.org
Web Site: www.gladysbrooksfoundation.org

FOUNDED: 1981

AREAS OF INTEREST:
Libraries, education, hospitals and clinics.

TYPE:
Capital grants; Challenge/matching grants; Demonstration grants; Development grants; Endowments; Matching gifts; Project/program grants; Scholarships. Grants to private, not-for-profit publicly supported libraries, educational institutions, hospitals and clinics in the eastern U.S.

YEAR PROGRAM STARTED: 1981

PURPOSE:
To provide for the intellectual, moral and physical welfare of the people of this country by establishing and supporting nonprofit libraries, educational institutions, hospitals and clinics.

ELIGIBILITY:
Applicants must be publicly supported, not-for-profit tax-exempt organizations. Generally speaking, grant applications will only be considered where outside funding, including governmental, is not available. The project will be largely funded by the grant unless the grant request covers a discrete component of a larger project. The funds will be used for capital projects including equipment or endowments. Applications for direct salary support will not be accepted.

Grant applications will be considered for major expenditures generally between $50,000 and $150,000 and greater or lesser amounts in certain circumstances.

GEOG. RESTRICTIONS: Connecticut, Florida, Illinois, Indiana, Louisiana, Maine, Maryland, Massachusetts, New Jersey, New York, Pennsylvania, Rhode Island and Tennessee.

FINANCIAL DATA:
Amount of support per award: $50,000 to $150,000.

APPLICATION INFO:
The initial step in seeking a grant is completion of the Request Form and

submitting it electronically to the Foundation. In doing so, the applicant will automatically be provided with all the information required for the Grant Proposal Letter. This step will also initiate the two-week period by the end of which the Grant Proposal Letter must be submitted.

Duration: One year.

Deadline: May 31.

PUBLICATIONS:
Annual report.

GOVERNING BOARD:
James J. Daly, Chairman
Michael P. Connors
Thomas Q. Morris, M.D.

*PLEASE NOTE:
All grant awards are made on the condition that the entirety of the funds advanced shall be utilized in direct furtherance of the project and that no portion thereof shall be appropriated by the grantee as an administrative or processing fee, for overseeing the project or for its general overhead.

BRUNSWICK FOUNDATION, INC.   [1076]

26125 North Riverwoods Boulevard
Suite 500
Mettawa, IL 60045
(847) 735-4306
Fax: (847) 735-4765
E-mail: brunswick.foundation@brunswick.com
Web Site: www.brunswick.com

FOUNDED: 1957

AREAS OF INTEREST:
Organizations that support the company's products.

NAME(S) OF PROGRAMS:
• **Brunswick Employee Sons and Daughters Scholarship**
• **Dollars for Doers Volunteer Program**

TYPE:
General operating grants. Scholarships to employee's children.

PURPOSE:
To support causes and/or projects that are related to fitness activities.

LEGAL BASIS:
Private foundation.

ELIGIBILITY:
Organizations in areas of company operation classified as 501(c)(3) by the IRS will be considered. Scholarship applicants must be children of current employees at the company.

FINANCIAL DATA:
Amount of support per award: Dollars for Doers: $75 to $1,000.
Total amount of support: Approximately $250,000.

NO. MOST RECENT APPLICANTS: 250.

NO. AWARDS: Varies.

APPLICATION INFO:
Applications are sent out by invitation only.
Duration: One year.
Deadline: End of February.

IRS I.D.: 36-6033576

DIRECTORS:
Christopher Dekker, President
Brenna Preisser, Vice President

William L. Metzger, Treasurer
Julianne Foran, Secretary

THE BUHL FOUNDATION   [1077]

650 Smithfield Street
Suite 2300
Pittsburgh, PA 15222
(412) 566-2711
Fax: (412) 566-2714
E-mail: buhl@buhlfoundation.org
Web Site: www.buhlfoundation.org
www.onenorthsidepgh.org

FOUNDED: 1927

AREAS OF INTEREST:
Education, youth development, human services and economic and community development, particularly with regard to the Northside of Pittsburgh.

CONSULTING OR VOLUNTEER SERVICES:
Wide variety of community initiatives to improve quality of life in the greater Pittsburgh area in general, and the Northside of Pittsburgh in particular.

TYPE:
Demonstration grants; Development grants; Grants-in-aid; Project/program grants; Seed money grants; Training grants. Capacity building. Grants-in-aid, primarily to institutions in the Pittsburgh metropolitan area, Allegheny County and western Pennsylvania for developmental and innovative projects in education, children and youth, and community services. More recently, a place-based granting focus on the Northside of Pittsburgh.

YEAR PROGRAM STARTED: 1928

PURPOSE:
To support efforts that contribute to the vibrancy and well-being of the Northside and the Pittsburgh region, create learning environments so that young people will thrive and be prepared for adulthood, encourage innovation and entrepreneurial solutions to improve quality of life, and make a definitive difference in addressing persistent community challenges or unmet needs of at-risk neighborhoods.

LEGAL BASIS:
Independent private foundation established by will probated on June 20, 1927.

ELIGIBILITY:
Tax-exempt, nonprofit institutions with appropriate interests in southwestern Pennsylvania are eligible to apply. Emphasis is on grants to institutions in the Pittsburgh metropolitan area, with a particular focus on the Northside of Pittsburgh. Programs and projects which combine different professional interests and relate agencies in cooperative endeavors are often recognized as worthy of a grant. Grants are not made to individuals.

GEOG. RESTRICTIONS: Southwestern Pennsylvania, including Pittsburgh and Allegheny counties, with a focus on the Northside of Pittsburgh.

FINANCIAL DATA:
Total amount of support: $2,706,653 for the year ended June 30, 2018.

NO. MOST RECENT APPLICANTS: 110.

NO. AWARDS: 69.

REPRESENTATIVE AWARDS:
$175,000 to New Sun Rising to support the administration of the 2018 One Northside Neighbor-to-Neighbor Mini-Grant program;

$180,000 to Auberle to provide a workforce solution for Northside residents by launching the Northside Employment Institute; $105,875 to United Way of Southwestern Pennsylvania to support a stipend-based program to encourage community participation in One Northside education efforts; $75,000 to Foundation of HOPE to implement a diversion program on the Northside for low- to medium-risk, nonviolent offenders intended to decrease the participant's likelihood of re-offending.

APPLICATION INFO:
Grant applications are submitted online. Details are available on the Foundation web site under "How to Apply."
Duration: Usually one year. Some grants cover two or three years.

PUBLICATIONS:
Annual report; application procedures.

IRS I.D.: 25-0378910

OFFICERS:
Diana A. Bucco, President

TRUSTEES:
Peter F. Mathieson, Chairperson
Saleem H. Ghubril, Vice Chairperson
Kim Tillotson Fleming, Secretary and Treasurer
Quintin B. Bullock
Carolyn Duronio
Anne Lewis
Lara E. Washington

ADDRESS INQUIRIES TO:
Diana A. Bucco, President
(See address above.)

PATRICK AND AIMEE BUTLER FAMILY FOUNDATION   [1078]

2356 University Avenue West
Suite 420
St. Paul, MN 55114
(651) 222-2565
E-mail: roberth@butlerfamilyfoundation.org
Web Site: butlerfamilyfoundation.org

FOUNDED: 1951

AREAS OF INTEREST:
Arts and culture, environment, and human services.

TYPE:
General operating grants; Project/program grants.

YEAR PROGRAM STARTED: 1951

PURPOSE:
To foster safety, opportunity, and growth for individuals and families by supporting effective, nonprofit organizations in the arts, environment and human services.

LEGAL BASIS:
Private foundation.

ELIGIBILITY:
Eligible organizations must be IRS 501(c)(3) tax-exempt. The Foundation does not fund criminal justice, economic development or education, employment or vocational programs, films or videos, health, hospitals or medical research, loans or grants to individuals, secondary or elementary education, theater or dance, or projects outside the U.S.

GEOG. RESTRICTIONS: Twin Cities Metropolitan area, Minnesota.

FINANCIAL DATA:
Amount of support per award: Average $30,000.

Total amount of support: $8,468,090 for the year 2020.

NO. MOST RECENT APPLICANTS: 174 for the year 2020.

NO. AWARDS: 172 for the year 2020.

APPLICATION INFO:
Must apply online through web site link.
Duration: Two years.
Deadline: April 1.

PUBLICATIONS:
Guidelines.

TRUSTEES:
Sara Rottunda, Chairperson
Temple Peterson, Vice Chairperson
John K. Butler, Treasurer
Bridget A. O'Brien, Secretary
Catherine C. Butler
Maddie Butler
Patrick Butler, Jr.
Paul S. Butler
Kathleen LeFevour
Suzanne A. LeFevour
Bridget E. McElroy

STAFF:
Robert Hybben, Foundation Co-Director
JoAnne Peters, Foundation Co-Director

ADDRESS INQUIRIES TO:
Robert Hybben
Foundation Co-Director
(See address above.)

CALIFORNIA COMMUNITY FOUNDATION [1079]
221 South Figueroa Street, Suite 400
Los Angeles, CA 90012
(213) 413-4130
Fax: (213) 383-2046
E-mail: info@calfund.org
Web Site: www.calfund.org

FOUNDED: 1915

AREAS OF INTEREST:
Education, health, housing and homelessness, and immigration.

NAME(S) OF PROGRAMS:
● **Education**
● **Health**
● **Housing**
● **Immigration**

TYPE:
Fellowships; General operating grants; Project/program grants; Scholarships. Policy analysis and advocacy.

YEAR PROGRAM STARTED: 1915

PURPOSE:
To lead positive systemic change that strengthens Los Angeles communities.

LEGAL BASIS:
Community foundation, designated a public charity by the IRS.

ELIGIBILITY:
The Foundation will consider applications that are consistent with current program priorities and goals. Eligible organizations are:
(1) nonprofit agencies with evidence of tax-exempt status under Section 501(c)(3) of the Internal Revenue Code and not classified as a private foundation;
(2) located within and primarily serving residents of Los Angeles County, with the exception of regional, statewide or national public policy efforts that may benefit a

substantial portion of the local population and;
(3) operated and organized so that they do not discriminate in the hiring of staff or the provision of services on the basis of race, religion, gender, sexual orientation, age, national origin or disability.

GEOG. RESTRICTIONS: Los Angeles County, California.

FINANCIAL DATA:
Amount of support per award: Nonprofit Organization Grants: Generally $50,000 to $100,000; Scholarships: Generally $250 to $15,000; Fellowship for Visual Artists Awards: $15,000 to $20,000.
Total amount of support: $247,000,000 for the year 2017-18.

CO-OP FUNDING PROGRAMS: Building a Lifetime of Options and Opportunities for Men - BLOOM; Early Childhood Alliance; Home L.A. Fund; L.A. Justice Fund.

NO. AWARDS: 8,747.

APPLICATION INFO:
Information about how to apply can be found on the web site.
Duration: Varies.
Deadline: Varies.

PUBLICATIONS:
Annual report; application form; application guidelines; philanthropic white papers; fund brochures.

IRS I.D.: 95-3510055

STAFF:
Antonia Hernandez, President and Chief Executive Officer
Steven J. Cobb, Chief Financial Officer
Jarrett Tomas Barrios, Senior Vice President of Community and Programmatic Initiatives
Teresa Mosqueda, Vice President, Development and Donor Relations
Efrain Escobeda, Vice President, Education and Immigration
Summer Moore, Vice President, Operations
Carol Bradford, Senior Counsel and Charitable Advisor

BOARD OF DIRECTORS:
James E. Berliner, Chairperson
Peter Adamson
Gwen Baba
Louise Henry Bryson
Alejandra Campoverdi
William C. Choi
Elyssa Elbaz
Antonia Hernandez
Eva Ho
Ji Hee Hu
Melvin D. Lindsey
Robert Lovelace
Hon. Gloria Molina
David Wheeler Newman
Crystal Nix-Hines
Thomas A. Saenz
Miguel A. Santana
Therese Tucker
Karim Webb
Daniel G. Weiss

CALLAWAY FOUNDATION, INC. [1080]
209 Broome Street
LaGrange, GA 30240
(706) 884-7348
Fax: (706) 884-0201
E-mail: tpenn@callawayfoundation.org
Web Site: www.callawayfoundation.org

FOUNDED: 1943

AREAS OF INTEREST:
Charitable, religious and educational interests.

TYPE:
Capital grants; Challenge/matching grants; Matching gifts. Matching grants focus on construction.

YEAR PROGRAM STARTED: 1943

PURPOSE:
To improve the quality of life in the city of LaGrange and Troup County, Georgia.

LEGAL BASIS:
Private foundation.

ELIGIBILITY:
Eligible organizations must be IRS 501(c)(3). Each application is considered on its merits.

GEOG. RESTRICTIONS: City of LaGrange and Troup County, Georgia.

FINANCIAL DATA:
Amount of support per award: Varies.
Total amount of support: Varies.

NO. MOST RECENT APPLICANTS: 100.

NO. AWARDS: Varies.

REPRESENTATIVE AWARDS:
$3,000,000 to LaGrange College; $450,000 to Downtown LaGrange Development Authority; $155,000 to Lafayette Society for Performing Arts.

APPLICATION INFO:
Applicants may submit a written proposal and must include a copy of the IRS tax determination letter. Application can be found on Foundation's web site.
Duration: Varies.
Deadline: March 15, June 15, September 15 and December 15.

PUBLICATIONS:
Annual report.

IRS I.D.: 58-0566147

ADDRESS INQUIRIES TO:
Paul S. (Tripp) Penn, III, President
(See address above.)

CAPITAL REGION COMMUNITY FOUNDATION [1081]
330 Marshall Street
Suite 300
Lansing, MI 48912
(517) 272-2870
Fax: (517) 272-2871
E-mail: chales@ourcommunity.org
Web Site: www.ourcommunity.org

FOUNDED: 1987

AREAS OF INTEREST:
Arts, education, environment, health care, human services, humanities and youth.

TYPE:
Capital grants; Project/program grants; Scholarships. Impact grants. Capacity building grants.

YEAR PROGRAM STARTED: 1989

PURPOSE:
To build a permanent endowment; to meet charitable needs in the tri-county area.

LEGAL BASIS:
Community foundation.

ELIGIBILITY:
Eligible organizations must be IRS 501(c)(3) tax-exempt and be located in the tri-county area.

GEOG. RESTRICTIONS: Clinton, Eaton and Ingham counties, Michigan.

FINANCIAL DATA:
Amount of support per award: Varies.
Total amount of support: Varies.

NO. MOST RECENT APPLICANTS: 110.

NO. AWARDS: 50.

APPLICATION INFO:
Application information is available on the web site.
Duration: One year.
Deadline: Early February.

PUBLICATIONS:
Annual report; grant guidelines.

IRS I.D.: 38-2776652

ADDRESS INQUIRIES TO:
Cindy Hales
Director of Community Investment
(See address above.)

*PLEASE NOTE:
No grants are made to individuals. Do not apply for college scholarships.

THE CARPENTER FOUNDATION   [1082]

824 East Main Street
Suite 102
Medford, OR 97504
(541) 772-5851
(541) 772-5732
Fax: (541) 773-3970
E-mail: pwilliams@carpenter-foundation.org
Web Site: www.carpenter-foundation.org

FOUNDED: 1958

AREAS OF INTEREST:
Arts, education, human services and public interest issues.

TYPE:
Capital grants; Challenge/matching grants; Demonstration grants; Development grants; General operating grants; Matching gifts; Project/program grants; Scholarships; Technical assistance; Training grants.

YEAR PROGRAM STARTED: 1958

PURPOSE:
To add opportunity, choice, inclusiveness, enrichment and a climate for change for those living in the Rogue Valley.

LEGAL BASIS:
Private family foundation.

ELIGIBILITY:
Grant applications will be accepted from tax-exempt agencies only. No grants are made to individuals. Only one grant per year to any agency is usually considered. The Foundation makes grants within Jackson and Josephine counties, with the exception of a few statewide public interest issues directly affecting persons living in these counties. The Foundation rarely makes multiyear grants, grants for historical applications, hospital construction or equipment, group or individual trips, or activities for religious purposes.

GEOG. RESTRICTIONS: Jackson and Josephine counties, Oregon.

FINANCIAL DATA:
Total assets of $19,400,710 for fiscal year ended June 30, 2019.
Amount of support per award: Varies.

Total amount of support: $747,232 in grants for fiscal year ended June 30, 2019.

CO-OP FUNDING PROGRAMS: The Foundation works in partnership with other agencies, organizations and public entities.

NO. MOST RECENT APPLICANTS: Approximately 150.

NO. AWARDS: 90.

APPLICATION INFO:
Cover letter (no more than one page) from the applicant organization summarizing the scope of the project, the amount of the request, and the name, address, telephone number and e-mail address of the person to contact regarding the request is required.

Proposal information (no more than four pages) including:
(1) description of proposal or project, and the community needs or strengths that it addresses;
(2) review of the applicant agency, its purpose and services to the community, its staffing and use of volunteers;
(3) the project budget, showing specifically how the grant funds will be used, as well as other possible funding sources for this project;
(4) description of how the project will be funded in the future (if applicable);
(5) the planning process, staffing and timeline for the project;
(6) result expected and proposed evaluation method and;
(7) any recent independent board fund-raising efforts.

Required attachments (do not staple or clip):
(1) detailed budget for the agency's current year and the year for which the project is proposed (if different);
(2) income statement and balance sheet from the most recently completed fiscal year (or audit, if available); no 990s please;
(3) list of board of directors, occupations and addresses;
(4) approval of the application by the agency's board of directors and;
(5) copy of the IRS exemption letter under Section 501(c)(3).
Duration: One year.
Deadline: Applications are reviewed on a quarterly basis.

BOARD OF TRUSTEES:
Emily C. Mostue, President
Karen C. Allan, Vice President/Secretary
Dan Thorndike, Treasurer
Brian Gross
Sue Naumes
Paul Nicholson
Teresa Sayre

ADDRESS INQUIRIES TO:
Polly Williams, Program Officer
Tel: (541) 772-5732
(See e-mail address above.)

CATERPILLAR FOUNDATION   [1083]

100 N.E. Adams Street
Peoria, IL 61629-1480
(309) 675-1000
Web Site: www.caterpillar.
com/en/company/caterpillar-foundation.html
www.togetherstronger.com

FOUNDED: 1952

AREAS OF INTEREST:
Poverty alleviation via programs with measurable outcomes in the areas of basic human needs, education and environment.

TYPE:
General operating grants; Project/program grants.

PURPOSE:
To support local and community activities where the company has a major manufacturing presence, as well as national and international organizations; to alleviate poverty and place people on the path to prosperity.

ELIGIBILITY:
Organizations in areas of company manufacturing operations and classified as 501(c)(3) by the IRS can apply. No grants to individuals and religious organizations.

FINANCIAL DATA:
Amount of support per award: Varies.

APPLICATION INFO:
Applicant must complete eligibility questionnaire. Grant application process is by invitation only.
Duration: One year. Grants are renewable.

CATHOLIC CAMPAIGN FOR HUMAN DEVELOPMENT   [1084]

3211 4th Street, N.E.
Washington, DC 20017
(202) 541-3210
Fax: (202) 541-3329
E-mail: cchdgrants@usccb.org
Web Site: www.usccb.org/cchd

FOUNDED: 1970

AREAS OF INTEREST:
Humanitarianism.

NAME(S) OF PROGRAMS:
● **Community Development Grant**
● **Economic Development Grant**

TYPE:
Project/program grants.

YEAR PROGRAM STARTED: 1970

PURPOSE:
To address the root causes of poverty by nurturing solidarity between the poor and non-poor and facilitating the participation of people living in poverty.

LEGAL BASIS:
Roman Catholic Church-sponsored funding agency.

ELIGIBILITY:
To qualify for CCHD funds, applicant organizations must not promote, in any way, activities that work against Catholic values. CCHD's grants to local anti-poverty efforts are screened, awarded and monitored in close partnership with local Catholic dioceses. CCHD grants to groups in a local community require the explicit approval of the Bishop of that diocese.

GEOG. RESTRICTIONS: United States and territories.

FINANCIAL DATA:
Amount of support per award: $25,000 to $75,000.

Total amount of support: Varies.

NO. AWARDS: Approximately 180 for the year 2018.

APPLICATION INFO:
Contact CCHD for guidelines.

Duration: Community Development Grant:
Six years; Economic Development Grant:
Three years.

Deadline: Proposals accepted September 1 to
November 1.

ADDRESS INQUIRIES TO:
Grants Administrator
(See address above.)

CENTRAL INDIANA COMMUNITY FOUNDATION [1085]

615 North Alabama Street
Suite 300
Indianapolis, IN 46204
(317) 634-2423 ext. 138
Fax: (317) 684-0943
E-mail: info@cicf.org
Web Site: www.cicf.org

FOUNDED: 1997

AREAS OF INTEREST:
Arts, culture, civic affairs, education,
environment, parks, and health and human
services.

TYPE:
General operating grants; Project/program
grants; Scholarships.

PURPOSE:
To strengthen Marion and Hamilton counties
by attracting charitable endowments; to
maximize benefits to donors; to make
effective grants; to provide leadership to
address community needs by developing
productive citizens, building strong
neighborhoods, embracing inclusiveness, and
promoting community amenities.

LEGAL BASIS:
Community foundation.

ELIGIBILITY:
Grants are made to nonprofit charitable
organizations exempt from federal taxation
under Section 501(c)(3) of the Internal
Revenue Code. Priority is given to programs
and projects which expect to have a positive
effect on Marion and Hamilton counties.

GEOG. RESTRICTIONS: Mostly Marion and
Hamilton counties, Indiana.

FINANCIAL DATA:
Amount of support per award: $250 to
$100,000.

Total amount of support: Varies.

APPLICATION INFO:
Application information is available on the
web site.

Duration: Typically one year.

Deadline: Varies.

PUBLICATIONS:
Annual report; newsletter.

IRS I.D.: 35-1793630

ADDRESS INQUIRIES TO:
Hector Morales Hernandez
Grants Coordinator
E-mail: hectormh@cicf.org

CENTRAL NEW YORK COMMUNITY FOUNDATION [1086]

431 East Fayette Street
Suite 100
Syracuse, NY 13202-3314
(315) 422-9538
Fax: (315) 471-6031
E-mail: info@cnycf.org
Web Site: cnycf.org

FOUNDED: 1927

AREAS OF INTEREST:
Literacy, poverty, lead poisoning, capacity
building, leadership development, and
strengthening nonprofit capacity.

TYPE:
Capital grants; Project/program grants.
Capital, programmatic, and organizational
development grants that support new ideas
and scale up projects with proven impact.

PURPOSE:
To support programs that strengthen
nonprofits and prepare leaders for the future;
to build, sustain, and share community
knowledge; to promote collaboration to
address community issues.

LEGAL BASIS:
Community foundation.

ELIGIBILITY:
Applicants must be tax-exempt, 501(c)(3)
not-for-profit organizations in Madison and
Onondaga counties which will fund
innovative programs that address unmet
community needs.

The Foundation encourages proposals that:
(1) suggest practical solutions to community
problems;
(2) promote cooperation among
not-for-profits without duplicating existing
services;
(3) generate community support, both
professional and volunteer;
(4) strengthen the organization's effectiveness
or stability;
(5) demonstrate the organization's ability to
secure realistic funding and;
(6) address prevention as well as remediation.

The Foundation does not make grants for
annual operating budgets, endowments,
sectarian purposes, loans or assistance to
individuals, medical or academic research
except when directed by donor, or activities
that occurred before the Community
Foundation's decision date.

GEOG. RESTRICTIONS: Madison and Onondaga
counties, New York.

FINANCIAL DATA:
Amount of support per award: Varies.
Total amount of support: Over $15,000,000
for the year ended March 31, 2020.

NO. AWARDS: 3,340 grants to 1,288 nonprofits
for the year ended March 31, 2020.

APPLICATION INFO:
Standard application forms are available.
Foundation staff is available to answer
questions or discuss with any prospective
applicant the appropriateness of a request.
Duration: Varies.
Deadline: March and October.

PUBLICATIONS:
Annual report.

OFFICERS:
Peter A. Dunn, President and Chief Executive
Officer

Kim Sadowski, Senior Vice President and
Chief Financial Officer
Katrina M. Crocker, Vice President,
Communications
Frank M. Ridzi, Vice President, Community
Investment

ADDRESS INQUIRIES TO:
Peter Dunn, Chief Executive Officer
(See address above.)

THE CH FOUNDATION

6102 82nd Street
Suite 8A
Lubbock, TX 79424
(806) 792-0448
Fax: (806) 792-7824
E-mail: hhocker@chfoundation.com
Web Site: www.chfoundationlubbock.com

TYPE:
Capital grants; Project/program grants.

See entry 1907 for full listing.

HARRY CHAPIN FOUNDATION [1087]

16 Gerard Street
Huntington, NY 11743
(631) 423-7558
Fax: (631) 423-7596
E-mail: harrychapinfound@aol.com
Web Site: harrychapinfoundation.org

FOUNDED: 1981

AREAS OF INTEREST:
Community education, arts-in-education,
agriculture and environment.

TYPE:
Challenge/matching grants; Project/program
grants.

YEAR PROGRAM STARTED: 1981

PURPOSE:
To address the problems of the disadvantaged
and promote educational programs that lead
to a greater understanding of human
suffering.

ELIGIBILITY:
Only programs operating in the U.S. will be
funded. Applicants must be 501(c)(3)
nonprofit. Organizations with annual budgets
less than $500,000 are favored. Complete
description of focus areas is available on the
Foundation web site.

No grants to individuals.

GEOG. RESTRICTIONS: United States.

FINANCIAL DATA:
Amount of support per award: Up to
$10,000.

NO. AWARDS: 35 for the year 2020.

APPLICATION INFO:
Application should be made in a brief e-mail
or written proposal to Ms. Leslie Ramme,
Executive Director, at the HCF Office. HCF
also accepts the New York/New Jersey Area
Common Grant Application Form.
Duration: One year. Must reapply.
Deadline: Applications are accepted on an
ongoing basis.

EXECUTIVE DIRECTOR:
Leslie Ramme

ADDRESS INQUIRIES TO:
Leslie Ramme, Executive Director
(See address or e-mail above.)

CHARLESTON AREA CHARITABLE FOUNDATION [1088]

c/o Gilbert, Metzger & Madigan
P.O. Box 677
Charleston, IL 61920
(217) 345-2128
Fax: (217) 345-2315

AREAS OF INTEREST:
Community and education.

TYPE:
Grants-in-aid; Project/program grants.

PURPOSE:
To enhance and support the quality of life in Charleston, IL area.

ELIGIBILITY:
Grants are made to organizations that have tax-exempt status under Section 501(c)(3) of the Internal Revenue Code. No grants are made to individuals.

GEOG. RESTRICTIONS: Charleston, Illinois and surrounding area.

FINANCIAL DATA:
Amount of support per award: Grants vary in amount, depending upon the needs and nature of the request.
Total amount of support: Varies.

APPLICATION INFO:
Applicants must submit a brief letter outlining the purpose of the grant.
Duration: One-time grants.
Deadline: Quarterly; two weeks prior to Board meetings to be held in February, May, August and November.

ADDRESS INQUIRIES TO:
Michael Metzger, President
(See address above.)

THE CHAUTAUQUA REGION COMMUNITY FOUNDATION [1089]

418 Spring Street
Jamestown, NY 14701
(716) 661-3390
E-mail: info@crcfonline.org
Web Site: www.crcfonline.org

FOUNDED: 1978

AREAS OF INTEREST:
Community development and services.

TYPE:
Awards/prizes; Capital grants; Challenge/matching grants; Endowments; General operating grants; Matching gifts; Project/program grants; Scholarships; Seed money grants; Technical assistance; Training grants. Community Service Grants support programming, capital and technology needs.

General Grants support emerging and one-time costs.

Strategic Project Grants support larger initiatives with wide-reaching and longer term community impact.

YEAR PROGRAM STARTED: 1978

PURPOSE:
To enrich the quality of life in the Chautauqua region.

LEGAL BASIS:
501(c)(3).

ELIGIBILITY:
Grants are available to 501(c)(3) nonprofit organizations. Scholarships are provided to students for higher education.

GEOG. RESTRICTIONS: Chautauqua region, New York.

FINANCIAL DATA:
Amount of support per award: Varies.
Total amount of support: $3,700,000 for the year 2020.
Matching fund requirements: Varies depending on the request.

APPLICATION INFO:
Details are available on the Foundation web site.
Duration: One calendar year.
Deadline: Varies by process.

PUBLICATIONS:
Annual report; newsletters; scholarship booklet.

IRS I.D.: 16-1116837

STAFF:
Tory L. Irgang, Executive Director
Elizabeth Jones, Community Impact Officer
Michelle Frederickson, Scholarship Officer
Michelle Tambascio, Program Associate

ADDRESS INQUIRIES TO:
Tory L. Irgang, Executive Director
(See address above.)

CHESTER COUNTY COMMUNITY FOUNDATION [1090]

28 West Market Street
West Chester, PA 19382
(610) 696-8211
Fax: (610) 696-8213
E-mail: grants@chescocf.org
Web Site: www.chescocf.org

FOUNDED: 1994

AREAS OF INTEREST:
Quality of life in the Chester County, Pennsylvania area.

TYPE:
Capital grants; General operating grants; Grants-in-aid; Project/program grants; Scholarships.

YEAR PROGRAM STARTED: 1994

PURPOSE:
To improve the quality of life in communities within Chester County, PA.

LEGAL BASIS:
501(c)(3) public charity.

GEOG. RESTRICTIONS: Primarily Chester County, Pennsylvania.

FINANCIAL DATA:
Approximately $64,000,000 in assets.
Amount of support per award: $1,000 to $15,000.
Total amount of support: $2,900,000 in grants and scholarships for fiscal year 2020.

NO. AWARDS: 700 grants and 225 scholarships for fiscal year 2020.

APPLICATION INFO:
Information may be obtained from the Foundation web site.
Duration: One year. Renewal by reapplication.
Deadline: Proposals are accepted year-round.

ADDRESS INQUIRIES TO:
Stephenie Stevens
Grants and Outreach Officer
(See address above.)

THE CHICAGO COMMUNITY TRUST [1091]

225 North Michigan Avenue
Suite 2200
Chicago, IL 60601
(312) 616-8000
Fax: (312) 616-7955
E-mail: grants@cct.org
Web Site: www.cct.org

FOUNDED: 1915

AREAS OF INTEREST:
The well-being of the residents of Cook County, IL in the fields of health, basic human needs, community development, education, cultural arts, sustainability and the environment.

TYPE:
General operating grants; Project/program grants; Technical assistance. Grants to tax-exempt institutions and organizations for charitable purposes. Special initiatives are developed periodically.

YEAR PROGRAM STARTED: 1915

PURPOSE:
To provide for the broad charitable needs of the community in a manner which will assure response to the most pressing problems of the day.

LEGAL BASIS:
Community foundation.

ELIGIBILITY:
Applicants must be tax-exempt, 501(c)(3) organizations. Funded projects must benefit the residents of Cook County, IL. Some grants are made for the region.

GEOG. RESTRICTIONS: Cook County, Illinois.

FINANCIAL DATA:
Amount of support per award: Varies.
Total amount of support: Approximately $369,700,000 in combined grant commitments for the year 2019.

NO. MOST RECENT APPLICANTS: 700 to 800.

APPLICATION INFO:
Applicants must register through the online grant system. Paper letters of inquiry will not be accepted.
Duration: One year.

PUBLICATIONS:
Guidelines; annual report.

STAFF:
Helene D. Gayle, President and Chief Executive Officer

ADDRESS INQUIRIES TO:
See e-mail address above.

ROBERT STERLING CLARK FOUNDATION [1092]

135 East 64th Street
New York, NY 10065
(212) 288-8900
Fax: (212) 288-1033
E-mail: rscf@rsclark.org
Web Site: www.rsclark.org

FOUNDED: 1952

AREAS OF INTEREST:
Leadership and leadership development.

TYPE:
Project/program grants.

PURPOSE:
To support, encourage and invest in people and the nonprofit organizations that develop them in communities across New York City.

LEGAL BASIS:
501(c)(3).

ELIGIBILITY:
Applicants must be nonprofit organizations.

FINANCIAL DATA:
Amount of support per award: Varies.

NO. AWARDS: Varies.

PUBLICATIONS:
Annual report; guidelines.

BOARD OF DIRECTORS:
James Allen Smith, Chairman
Julie Muraco, Treasurer
Paul Dolan, Secretary
Daisy Auger-Dominguez
Diahann Billings-Burford
Gregg Bishop
Vincent McGee
Adriana Rocha

OFFICER:
Philip Li, President

ADDRESS INQUIRIES TO:
Philip Li, President
(See address above.)

THE CLEVELAND FOUNDATION [1093]

1422 Euclid Avenue
Suite 1300
Cleveland, OH 44115-2001
(216) 861-3810
Fax: (216) 861-1729
E-mail: grantsmgmt@clevefdn.org
Web Site: www.clevelandfoundation.org

FOUNDED: 1914

AREAS OF INTEREST:
Economic development, public education reform, neighborhood and housing, human services and youth development strengthening the quality of life in early childhood, strengthening the arts and cultural community and greater university circle.

TYPE:
Project/program grants; Scholarships.

YEAR PROGRAM STARTED: 1914

PURPOSE:
To enhance the quality of life for all citizens of greater Cleveland, now and for generations to come, by building endowment, addressing needs through grantmaking and providing leadership on key community issues.

LEGAL BASIS:
Community foundation.

ELIGIBILITY:
Grantmaking is restricted to programs and services in the Greater Cleveland community, Cuyahoga, Geauga and Lake counties. Requests are considered from tax-exempt agencies in the following areas: civic affairs, economic development, education, health, social services, arts and culture, and environment. Careful consideration is given to such criteria as benefit the entire community and applicant's ability to successfully carry out the proposed activity. Applicant must be a nonprofit organization.

Giving is limited to the Greater Cleveland area unless specified by the donor. No grants to individuals or religious institutions for

religious purposes. No support for community services such as fire and police protection, fund-raising campaigns, memberships and travel. No support for publications or audiovisual materials unless they are an integral part of a key program. Capital support for buildings, major equipment, land or renovation is only provided when there is strong evidence that the project has high priority for the community.

GEOG. RESTRICTIONS: Greater Cleveland, Cuyahoga, Geauga and Lake counties, Ohio.

FINANCIAL DATA:
Amount of support per award: $200 to $4,000,000; average $50,000.
Total amount of support: $114,000,000 in grants authorized for the year 2019.
Matching fund requirements: Depending upon proposal, grants may be authorized contingent upon receipt of matching funds from agency's own or other sources.

CO-OP FUNDING PROGRAMS: Neighborhood Connections Program.

NO. AWARDS: 5,059 grants authorized for the year 2019.

APPLICATION INFO:
The Foundation requires organizations to submit inquiries and applications electronically. Guidelines can be found on the web site.
Duration: Usually one year.

PUBLICATIONS:
Annual report; *Giving Voice,* quarterly; Grantee e-newsletter.

IRS I.D.: 34-0714588

COASTAL COMMUNITY FOUNDATION OF SOUTH CAROLINA [1094]

1691 Turnbull Avenue
North Charleston, SC 29405
(843) 723-3635
Fax: (843) 577-3671
E-mail: info@coastalcommunityfoundation.org
Web Site: www.coastalcommunityfoundation.org

FOUNDED: 1974

AREAS OF INTEREST:
Community development, health, education, human needs, environment and arts.

NAME(S) OF PROGRAMS:
● **Regional Grants**
● **Specialized Grants**

TYPE:
Challenge/matching grants; Endowments; Project/program grants; Scholarships; Technical assistance; Training grants.

YEAR PROGRAM STARTED: 1974

PURPOSE:
To help create vibrant communities by uniting people and investing resources.

ELIGIBILITY:
Generally, applicants must be charitable 501(c)(3) organizations in Beaufort, Berkeley, Charleston, Colleton, Dorchester, Georgetown, Hampton and Jasper counties, South Carolina.

GEOG. RESTRICTIONS: Coastal South Carolina.

FINANCIAL DATA:
Amount of support per award: Generally $20,000 maximum.

Total amount of support: Varies.

NO. MOST RECENT APPLICANTS: Approximately 550 for the year 2018.

NO. AWARDS: Approximately 330 for the year 2018.

APPLICATION INFO:
Application and instructions are available online.
Duration: Grantees typically have 12 months from receipt to expend their awards.
Deadline: Mid-January and early June.

IRS I.D.: 23-7390313

THE COLUMBUS FOUNDATION [1095]

1234 East Broad Street
Columbus, OH 43205
(614) 251-4000
Fax: (614) 251-4009
E-mail: contactus@columbusfoundation.org
Web Site: www.columbusfoundation.org

FOUNDED: 1943

AREAS OF INTEREST:
Advancing philanthropy, arts and humanities, urban affairs, conservation, education, health and social services.

NAME(S) OF PROGRAMS:
● **Fund for Capital Improvements**
● **Fund for Financial Innovation**
● **Fund for Innovative Operations**
● **Fund for Targeted Needs**

TYPE:
Capital grants; Development grants; Fellowships; General operating grants; Project/program grants; Scholarships. The Foundation awards competitive grants from the unrestricted and field-of-interest funds created by donors.

The Fund for Capital Improvements supports projects designed to improve the delivery, quality, and efficiency of nonprofit programs and services that serve vulnerable populations.

The Fund for Financial Innovation will support nonprofit leaders and their organizations to adapt to the new economic reality.

The Fund for Innovative Operations addresses significant needs of local organizations through grants supporting continuous improvement, capacity-building, and arts and cultural efforts.

The Fund for Targeted Needs addresses basic needs, disadvantaged children, developmental disabilities (traditional grants program), as well as more narrow and specific grant programs.

YEAR PROGRAM STARTED: 1943

PURPOSE:
To assist donors and others in strengthening and improving the community for the benefit of all its residents.

LEGAL BASIS:
Community foundation, exempt under Section 501(c)(3) of the Internal Revenue Code.

ELIGIBILITY:
Organizations in the central Ohio region having recognition under Section 501(c)(3) of the Internal Revenue Code. No grants are made to individuals.

GEOG. RESTRICTIONS: Primarily Franklin County and surrounding area.

FINANCIAL DATA:
Amount of support per award: $250 to $1,250,000.
Total amount of support: Varies.

NO. MOST RECENT APPLICANTS: 403.

NO. AWARDS: 292.

REPRESENTATIVE AWARDS:
Capacity Building and Leadership Grants: $6,000 to Jeanne B. McCoy Community Center for the Arts Corporation to support the fund-raising planning component of the business plan; Innovative Operations-Continuous Improvement: $273,500 to Ohio Association of Second Harvest Foodbanks to support overall operations; Basic Needs: $95,000 to Community Shelter Board to support general operating expenses to address homelessness.

APPLICATION INFO:
Those seeking grants may submit a Letter of Intent or a Full Proposal to the Foundation by accessing its online grant application system through its web site.
Duration: Typically one year.
Deadline: Varies.

PUBLICATIONS:
Annual yearbook; application guidelines.

IRS I.D.: 31-6044264

STAFF:
Douglas F. Kridler, President and Chief Executive Officer
Scott G. Heitkamp, Vice President and Chief Financial Officer
Dan A. Sharpe, Vice President, Community Research and Grants Management

ADDRESS INQUIRIES TO:
Melissa McCool
Grants Management Coordinator
(See address above.)

COLUMBUS JEWISH FOUNDATION   [1096]

Robins Center for Philanthropy
1175 College Avenue
Columbus, OH 43209
(614) 338-2365
Fax: (614) 338-2361
E-mail: susan@jewishcolumbus.org
Web Site: www.jewishcolumbus.org

FOUNDED: 1955

AREAS OF INTEREST:
Jewish education, Jewish leadership development and the preservation of the integrity of the Jewish family.

TYPE:
Challenge/matching grants; Demonstration grants; Seed money grants.

YEAR PROGRAM STARTED: 1955

PURPOSE:
To develop sustainable financial resources to fulfill the Foundation's mission to ensure continuity of Jewish life and to meet changing needs locally, in Israel, and in our worldwide community.

LEGAL BASIS:
Public charity.

ELIGIBILITY:
Applicants must be 501(c)(3) organizations. Money will be designated for pilot projects or as seed money only. Particular emphasis on central Ohio Jewish organizations.

No grants to individuals. No operating support.

FINANCIAL DATA:
Amount of support per award: Varies depending on needs and nature of the request.
Total amount of support: $473,300 for fiscal year ended June 30, 2019.

CO-OP FUNDING PROGRAMS: The Foundation prefers to set up networks for funding with other organizations.

NO. MOST RECENT APPLICANTS: 22.

NO. AWARDS: 14 anticipated for the year 2019.

REPRESENTATIVE AWARDS:
Columbus Torah Academy Experiential Learning Initiative; Columbus Jewish Day School Math and English Arts Coaching; Columbus Jewish Cemetery Association for cemetery repairs and geo-tagging.

APPLICATION INFO:
Formal request forms are available from the Foundation.
Duration: Generally one year.
Deadline: September 15 and February 15.

PUBLICATIONS:
Annual report; guidelines.

IRS I.D.: 31-1384772

OFFICERS:
Jim Bowman, President
Harlan W. Robins, Vice President
William Byers, Treasurer
Michael Schlonsky, Secretary

ADDRESS INQUIRIES TO:
Susan Tanur, Director of Grants
(See address and e-mail above.)

COMMON COUNSEL FOUNDATION   [1097]

1624 Franklin Street
Suite 1022
Oakland, CA 94612
(510) 834-2995
Fax: (510) 834-2998
E-mail: info@commoncounsel.org
Web Site: www.commoncounsel.org

FOUNDED: 1988

AREAS OF INTEREST:
Economic, environmental and social justice.

TYPE:
General operating grants; Training grants; Travel grants.

PURPOSE:
To offer strategic philanthropic advisory services to donors and family foundations while serving the community at large.

ELIGIBILITY:
501(c)(3) nonprofit organizations. Religious organizations must be working in interfaith coalitions. Grants are not made to individuals. Also, must involve low- and moderate-income members in grassroots community organizing to bring about long-term policy change. Organizational budget must be $400,000 or less except for the small Grassroots Exchange Fund (travel grants), which considers requests from organizations with budgets up to $1,000,000 (higher priority is given to those with budgets less than $750,000).

FINANCIAL DATA:
Amount of support per award: Travel and training grants: $500 to $1,000 with an average of approximately $800; General operating grants: $5,000 to $15,000.

CO-OP FUNDING PROGRAMS: Abelard Foundation West; Acorn Foundation; Victor and Lorraine Honig Fund; Grassroots Exchange Fund; Native Voices Rising; Social and Economic Justice Fund; Still We Rise Fund.

NO. MOST RECENT APPLICANTS: 280.

APPLICATION INFO:
Applicant should submit a letter of inquiry. Full proposals for most of the Funds are by invitation only.
Deadline: January 15 and June 15 (or February through November for Grassroots Exchange Fund).

COMMUNITY FOUNDATION FOR A GREATER RICHMOND   [1098]

3409 Moore Street
Richmond, VA 23230
(804) 330-7400
Fax: (804) 330-5992
E-mail: sblackwell@cfrichmond.org
info@cfrichmond.org
Web Site: www.cfrichmond.org

FOUNDED: 1968

AREAS OF INTEREST:
Children, families, communities, health care, education and arts.

NAME(S) OF PROGRAMS:
● **The Jenkins Foundation: Improving the Health of Greater Richmond**
● **R.E.B. Awards for Teaching Excellence**
● **Sheltering Arms Fund**

TYPE:
Project/program grants; Scholarships. Competitive grants.

YEAR PROGRAM STARTED: 1968

PURPOSE:
To improve life for generations of children; to improve public education; to support innovative health care projects.

LEGAL BASIS:
Charitable trust.

ELIGIBILITY:
Proposals are accepted from charitable 501(c)(3) organizations serving residents of Greater Richmond and/or the Tri-Cities.

GEOG. RESTRICTIONS: Richmond and central Virginia.

FINANCIAL DATA:
Amount of support per award: Jenkins Fund: Up to $75,000; R.E.B. Awards: $4,000 to $12,000; Sheltering Arms: $5,000 to $20,000.
Total amount of support: Varies.

APPLICATION INFO:
Guidelines and application forms are available on the web site.
Duration: Typically one year.
Deadline: Varies per program.

PUBLICATIONS:
Annual report.

OFFICERS:
Pamela J. Royal, M.D., Chairperson
Austin Brockenbrough, IV, Vice Chairperson
Sherrie Armstrong, President and Chief Executive Officer

Philip M. Goodpasture, Treasurer
Kristen Hager, Secretary

ADDRESS INQUIRIES TO:
Jenkins Foundation and Sheltering Arms:
Eric Clay, Senior Program Officer
Health Initiatives

R.E.B. Awards:
Stacey Keeley, Director of
Philanthropic Services
(See address above.)

COMMUNITY FOUNDATION FOR GREATER ATLANTA, INC. [1099]

191 Peachtree Street, N.E.
Suite 1000
Atlanta, GA 30303
(404) 688-5525
Fax: (404) 688-3060
E-mail: rrodriguez@cfgreateratlanta.org
Web Site: www.cfgreateratlanta.org

FOUNDED: 1951

AREAS OF INTEREST:
Operational grants to nonprofits serving a
23-county region in Georgia.

NAME(S) OF PROGRAMS:
- **A Place to Perform**
- **An Extra Wish**
- **Atlanta AIDS Fund**
- **Civic Engagement Fund**
- **Metropolitan Atlanta Arts Fund**
- **Neighborhood Fund**
- **Newton Fund**
- **Nonprofit Toolbox**
- **Strategic Restructuring Fund**

TYPE:
General operating grants; Project/program
grants; Scholarships; Technical assistance;
Training grants. Project/program grants
support organizations implementing creative
and impactful programs and policies that
increase the equity of opportunity.

YEAR PROGRAM STARTED: 1951

PURPOSE:
To provide quality services to donors and
innovative leadership on community issues.

LEGAL BASIS:
501(c)(3) community foundation.

ELIGIBILITY:
Applicant organizations must have 501(c)(3)
status. Project must be within the
metropolitan Atlanta area. Request for
funding may not exceed 10% of
organization's operational budget. For general
operation grants, organization must have an
operating budget of $100,000.

Grant funds cannot be used for regranting,
fund-raising or capital campaigns. No grants
to individuals.

GEOG. RESTRICTIONS: 23 counties in the
metropolitan Atlanta area.

FINANCIAL DATA:
Amount of support per award: Maximum
$75,000.

NO. MOST RECENT APPLICANTS: 290 for
discretionary monies.

APPLICATION INFO:
Grant application guidelines are available
online.

Duration: No grants are awarded on a
continuing basis. Generally, grants are one or
two years.

Deadline: Arts Fund and Common Good:
May; Grants: February and October.

PUBLICATIONS:
Annual report; policy and application
guidelines.

IRS I.D.: 58-1344646

STAFF:
Alicia Philipp, President
Diana Champ Davis, Chief Financial Officer
and Vice President, Capacity
Lita Ugarte Pardi, Vice President,
Community
Elyse Hammett, Vice President, Marketing
and Communications

BOARD MEMBERS:
Susan Grant, Chairperson
Frank Bell
Rabbi Peter S. Berg
Millard Choate
Bert Clark
Richard W. Courts, IV
Patrice Greer
Doug Hooker
Julia A. Houston
Wonya Lucas
Jeffrey S. Muir
Barbara Bing Pliner
Bryan Rand
John C. Reid
Dave Stockert
Ramon Tome
Dr. Gregory J. Vaughn
Benjamin T. White, Legal Counsel
Jerry Wilkinson
Studie Young

ADDRESS INQUIRIES TO:
Ryan Rodriguez, Grants Manager
(See address above.)

COMMUNITY FOUNDATION FOR GREATER BUFFALO [1100]

726 Exchange Street
Suite 525
Buffalo, NY 14210
(716) 852-2857
Fax: (716) 852-2861
E-mail: mail@cfgb.org
Web Site: cfgb.org

FOUNDED: 1919

TYPE:
Grants-in-aid; Scholarships. Grants to
organizations in the eight counties of western
New York state.

YEAR PROGRAM STARTED: 1919

PURPOSE:
To connect people, ideas and resources to
improve lives in western New York state. The
four community goals of the Foundation are:
(1) Improve educational achievement for
students living in low-income households;
(2) Increase racial/ethnic equity;
(3) Protect and restore significant
environmental resources and promote
equitable access and;
(4) Strengthen the region as a center for
architecture, arts and culture.

LEGAL BASIS:
Community trust; 501(c)(3) tax
determination; public charity under Section
170(b)(1)(a)(vi).

ELIGIBILITY:
Programs and agencies must benefit residents
of the eight counties of western New York
state.

GEOG. RESTRICTIONS: Eight counties of western
New York state.

FINANCIAL DATA:
Amount of support per award: $5,522 to
$45,000 for the year 2018.

Total amount of support: $529,622.

NO. MOST RECENT APPLICANTS: 114 for the
year 2018.

NO. AWARDS: 23.

APPLICATION INFO:
Application information is available on the
web site.

Deadline: Letters of Intent accepted from
January 1 to February 1. Selected Letters of
Intent invited to submit a full proposal by
May 3. Applicants notified by mid-July.

STAFF:
Clotilde Perez-Bode Dedecker,
President/Chief Executive Officer
Brendan Harrington, Chief Financial
Officer/Chief Administrative Officer
Cindy Odom, Chief Community Impact
Officer
Betsy Constantine, Executive Vice President,
Giving Strategies
Jean McKeown, Vice President, Community
Impact
Myra Lawrence, Vice President, Finance
Colleen Becht, Controller
Kate Masiello, Senior Director, Client
Relations
Mary Bradach, Senior Director, Gift Planning
Felicia Beard, Senior Director, Racial Equity
Initiatives
Leah Angel Daniel, Director, Communities of
Giving Legacy Initiative
Bridget Niland, Director, Youth Sports
Initiatives
Ba Zin Lin, Senior Program Officer
Darren Penoyer, Senior Program Officer
Sira Faye, Program Officer
Allie Urbanski, Program Officer
Alexandra Warner, Program Officer
Aubrey Hammond, Scholarship Officer
Linda Gallagher, Accounting Manager
Alicia Dziak, Communications Content
Manager
Mark Vanderwerken, Operations Manager
Mary Sheehan, Senior Accountant
Nora Kennon, Giving Strategies Associate
Laura Schwamborn, Giving Strategies
Associate

BOARD OF DIRECTORS:
Tamara O. Alsace, Ph.D.
Jennifer Chalmers Balbach
Melissa Baumgart
James Biltekoff
Gary Crosby
Bonnie R. Durand, Ph.D.
Ross J. Eckert
Steve Finch
Lawrence C. Franco
Dottie Gallagher
Allen (Pete) Grum
Alice Jacobs, J.D.
Cheryl A. Jankowski
William Joyce
Alex Montante
Gary L. Mucci
Hal D. Payne
Hon. Rose H. Sconiers
John F. Somers
Francisco M. Vasquez, Ph.D.
John N. Walsh, III

ADDRESS INQUIRIES TO:
Darren Penoyer, Senior Program Officer
(See address above.)

THE COMMUNITY FOUNDATION FOR GREATER NEW HAVEN [1101]

70 Audubon Street
New Haven, CT 06510-9755
(203) 777-2386
Fax: (203) 787-6584
E-mail: contactus@cfgnh.org
Web Site: www.cfgnh.org

FOUNDED: 1928

AREAS OF INTEREST:
Health, education, community development, regional and economic development, arts and culture, youth, environment, and food and shelter.

TYPE:
Capital grants; General operating grants; Matching gifts; Project/program grants; Scholarships. Capacity building grants. Support for youth and welfare agencies, social services, hospitals and health agencies, educational institutions, community funds and the humanities, including music and art, to organizations serving the residents of greater New Haven.

PURPOSE:
To create positive and sustainable change in greater New Haven, CT.

LEGAL BASIS:
Community foundation established in Connecticut by Resolution and Declaration of Trust.

ELIGIBILITY:
The Foundation welcomes grant requests from greater New Haven area organizations that are defined as tax-exempt under Section 501(c)(3) or any applicable statute of the Internal Revenue Code. While grants are occasionally made to governmental agencies, local nonprofits receive priority.

GEOG. RESTRICTIONS: Greater New Haven, Connecticut: Ansonia, Bethany, Branford, Cheshire, Derby, East Haven, Guilford, Hamden, Madison, Milford, New Haven, North Branford, North Haven, Orange, Oxford, Seymour, Shelton, Wallingford, West Haven, Woodbridge.

FINANCIAL DATA:
Amount of support per award: Varies.
Total amount of support: Over $20,000,000 each year.

NO. MOST RECENT APPLICANTS: Varies.

NO. AWARDS: Varies.

REPRESENTATIVE AWARDS:
$50,000 to Bridges Healthcare, Inc., to provide general operating support for a comprehensive range of prevention, mental health and addiction recovery programs for adults, children and families; $120,000 to New Haven Reads to provide general operating support for the promotion of literacy through tutoring, family engagement, college preparation and a free book bank; $30,000 to JUNTA for Progressive Action to support leadership transition activities including a national Executive Search, a staff retreat and board development.

APPLICATION INFO:
Application information is available on the Foundation's web site.
Duration: One year with multiyears considered annually.
Deadline: Varies from year to year.

PUBLICATIONS:
Annual report; grant guidelines; newsletters.

IRS I.D.: 06-6032106

STAFF:
William W. Ginsberg, President and Chief Executive Officer
Christina M. Ciociola, Senior Vice President for Grantmaking and Strategy
A.F. Drew Alden, Senior Vice President for Investments, Chief Financial Officer and Chief Compliance Officer

ADDRESS INQUIRIES TO:
Denise Canning, Director of Grant Operations
(See address above.)

COMMUNITY FOUNDATION FOR MONTEREY COUNTY [1102]

2354 Garden Road
Monterey, CA 93940
(831) 375-9712
Fax: (831) 375-4731
E-mail: info@cfmco.org
Web Site: www.cfmco.org/grants

FOUNDED: 1945

AREAS OF INTEREST:
Animal welfare, arts and culture, community development, education, environment, health, human services, historic preservation and youth development.

NAME(S) OF PROGRAMS:
- **Community Impact Grants Program**
- **Neighborhood Grants Program**
- **Opportunity Grants**
- **Organizational Development Grants**

TYPE:
Capital grants; General operating grants; Project/program grants; Scholarships; Technical assistance.

PURPOSE:
To inspire philanthropy and be a catalyst for strengthening communities throughout Monterey County.

LEGAL BASIS:
Community foundation.

ELIGIBILITY:
Community-based, nonprofit organizations whose programs benefit the residents of Monterey County, CA.

The Foundation does not make Community Impact Grants to support individuals, for normal operating costs usually covered by operating income, for endowment funds, to support sectarian religious programs, for annual campaigns, dinners, or special events, to pay off past debts or existing obligations, for scholarships, fellowships or travel grants, or for technical or specialized research.

GEOG. RESTRICTIONS: Monterey County, California.

FINANCIAL DATA:
Amount of support per award: Varies depending on type of grant.
Total amount of support: Varies.

APPLICATION INFO:
Detailed guidelines and application form can be obtained at the Foundation web site.
Duration: One year. Reapplication annually.
Deadline: Varies.

IRS I.D.: 94-1615897

ADDRESS INQUIRIES TO:
Director of Grantmaking or Grants and Programs Coordinator
E-mail: grants@cfmco.org

THE COMMUNITY FOUNDATION FOR NORTHEAST FLORIDA [1103]

245 Riverside Avenue
Suite 310
Jacksonville, FL 32202
(904) 356-4483
Fax: (904) 356-7910
E-mail: kshaw@jaxcf.org
Web Site: www.jaxcf.org

AREAS OF INTEREST:
Early childhood, seniors, and the arts.

TYPE:
Project/program grants.

PURPOSE:
To stimulate philanthropy to build a better community.

ELIGIBILITY:
Eligible organizations must be IRS 501(c)(3) tax-exempt.

GEOG. RESTRICTIONS: Baker, Clay, Duval, Nassau and St. Johns counties in northern Florida.

FINANCIAL DATA:
Amount of support per award: Varies.
Total amount of support: Varies.

APPLICATION INFO:
Application information is available on the web site.
Duration: Up to 24 months.
Deadline: Varies.

PUBLICATIONS:
Newsletter; annual report.

STAFF:
John Zell, Vice President, Development
Kathleen Shaw, Vice President, Programs

ADDRESS INQUIRIES TO:
Kathleen Shaw
Vice President, Programs
(See address above.)

COMMUNITY FOUNDATION FOR NORTHEAST GEORGIA [1104]

6500 Sugarloaf Parkway, Suite 220
Duluth, GA 30097
(770) 813-3380
Fax: (770) 813-3375
E-mail: rredner@cfneg.org
Web Site: www.cfneg.org

FOUNDED: 1985

AREAS OF INTEREST:
The quality of life in northeast Georgia.

TYPE:
Grants-in-aid.

PURPOSE:
To improve the quality of life throughout northeast Georgia.

ELIGIBILITY:
Grants can be made to tax-exempt private agencies that the IRS classifies as 501(c)(3) organizations, public charities and government agencies. The Foundation will consider organizations that serve people in the areas of education, health and human services, community service and the arts.

GEOG. RESTRICTIONS: Northeast Georgia.

FINANCIAL DATA:
Approximately $80,000,000 has been granted since inception.
Amount of support per award: Varies.
Total amount of support: Varies.

NO. AWARDS: Varies.

APPLICATION INFO:
The grant request must be completed according to the standard Grant Proposal Guidelines issued by the Foundation. Application can be downloaded from the web site.
Duration: Typically one year.
Deadline: March.

ADDRESS INQUIRIES TO:
Margaret Bugbee, Chief Financial Officer
(See address above.)

COMMUNITY FOUNDATION FOR NORTHEAST MICHIGAN [1105]
100 North Ripley
Suite F
Alpena, MI 49707
(989) 354-6881
Fax: (989) 356-3319
E-mail: pheraghty@cfnem.org
Web Site: www.cfnem.org

FOUNDED: 1974

AREAS OF INTEREST:
Education, health, youth services, arts, community needs and issues important to women.

TYPE:
Conferences/seminars; Development grants; Endowments; Project/program grants; Scholarships; Seed money grants; Training grants. Tobacco-related programs/projects. Women's Giving Circle for issues important to women. Youth-related programs/projects.

YEAR PROGRAM STARTED: 1974

PURPOSE:
To provide resources for community projects.

LEGAL BASIS:
Community foundation.

ELIGIBILITY:
Eligible organizations must be IRS 501(c)(3) tax-exempt, government schools or churches, providing the project is nonsectarian. No grants to individuals.

GEOG. RESTRICTIONS: Alcona, Alpena, Montmorency and Presque Isle counties, Michigan.

FINANCIAL DATA:
Amount of support per award: Community Impact Grant: Up to $5,000; Women's Giving Circle and Youth-related programs/projects: Up to $2,500.
Total amount of support: Over $250,000 in grants for fiscal year 2018-19.

CO-OP FUNDING PROGRAMS: Collaboration between organizations is encouraged.

NO. MOST RECENT APPLICANTS: Approximately 225.

NO. AWARDS: Varies.

REPRESENTATIVE AWARDS:
High School Orchard Project; Eighth Grade University Visits; Elementary School and High School Robotics; Safety and Mobility for Seniors; Fiftieth Anniversary Capital Campaign.

APPLICATION INFO:
Applications may be obtained online.
Duration: One year, with the possibility of a six-month extension.
Deadline: Varies.

PUBLICATIONS:
Annual report; biannual newsletter; brochures; application guidelines.

IRS I.D.: 23-7384822

EXECUTIVE DIRECTOR:
Patrick Heraghty

ADDRESS INQUIRIES TO:
For Grants:
Kara LeMonds, Program Officer

For Women's Giving Circle:
Julie Wiesen, Program Director
(See address above.)

COMMUNITY FOUNDATION FOR PALM BEACH AND MARTIN COUNTIES [1106]
700 South Dixie Highway
Suite 200
West Palm Beach, FL 33401-5854
(561) 659-6800
Fax: (561) 832-6542
E-mail: info@cfpbmc.org
Web Site: www.yourcommunityfoundation.org

FOUNDED: 1972

AREAS OF INTEREST:
Community revitalization, positive youth development, education attainment, arts and culture, hunger and capacity building, and environment.

TYPE:
Challenge/matching grants; Conferences/seminars; Development grants; Project/program grants; Scholarships; Technical assistance; Training grants.

PURPOSE:
To develop a shared vision of building a sense of community.

ELIGIBILITY:
501(c)(3) organizations are eligible to apply for grants.

GEOG. RESTRICTIONS: Martin and Palm Beach counties, Florida.

FINANCIAL DATA:
Amount of support per award: Varies.
Total amount of support: $9,200,000 for the year ended June 30, 2018.
Matching fund requirements: Varies.

NO. MOST RECENT APPLICANTS: Approximately 600 grant applicants and 450 scholarship applicants for the year ended June 30, 2017.

NO. AWARDS: 618 grants and scholarships for the year ended June 30, 2017.

APPLICATION INFO:
Applicants must complete a proposal summary and budget form. Check online for application and submission information.
Duration: Scholarships: Up to four years. Grants: Varies.
Deadline: Scholarships: February 1. Grants: Varies.

PUBLICATIONS:
Annual report; newsletter.

IRS I.D.: 23-7181875

OFFICERS:
Bradley Hurlburt, President and Chief Executive Officer
Steve Erjavec, Chief Financial Officer

ADDRESS INQUIRIES TO:
Daryl Houston
Senior Community Impact Officer
(See address above.)

THE COMMUNITY FOUNDATION FOR THE GREATER CAPITAL REGION [1107]
2 Tower Place
Albany, NY 12203
(518) 446-9638
Fax: (518) 446-9708
E-mail: info@cfgcr.org
Web Site: www.cfgcr.org

FOUNDED: 1968

AREAS OF INTEREST:
Health, science, education, youth and environment.

NAME(S) OF PROGRAMS:
• **Capacity-Building Grant Initiative**
• **Regular Competitive Grants**

TYPE:
Capital grants; Challenge/matching grants; General operating grants; Matching gifts; Project/program grants; Research grants; Scholarships; Technical assistance. Small, flexible grants to support some of the costs associated with organizational capacity-building.

The Foundation creates networks of opportunity - opportunities to bring together interested donors and community service providers to address a particular problem or need in the local community served. It serves the Capital Region of New York state by funding creative, visionary and sensitive projects - often seed money for innovative programs - that address the evolving needs of the community. The Foundation also serves as a vehicle for individuals, families, corporations, private foundations and nonprofit organizations to use in carrying out their long-term philanthropic plans.

Homelessness: Grants are designed to eliminate homelessness in the Capital Region.

Disabilities: The purpose of these grants is to serve the needs of the mentally and/or physically disabled, including the hearing- and sight-impaired.

Health: Program and capital grants are available for health care organizations working to improve the health of residents of the four-county region around Albany, NY.

Science: This program makes grants to support and promote discovery and development in medicine, science and technology in the Capital District.

PURPOSE:
To support capacity-building efforts of organizations including projects that are designed to generate new thinking about ways to improve an organization's ability to serve the community, more effectively carry out its mission, and plan for the future.

LEGAL BASIS:
Classified by the Internal Revenue Code as a public charity.

ELIGIBILITY:
Grants are made to applicants that qualify under Section 501(c)(3) of the Internal Revenue Code as a nonprofit organization, or operate under the fiscal sponsorship of an organization that does, and serve residents and be located within the ten-county Greater Capital Region. No grants are made to individuals. Nonsectarian religious programs may apply.

The Foundation's competitive grants support organizations that do not discriminate in their employment practices, volunteer opportunities, or delivery of programs or services on the basis of race, color, religion, gender, national origin, ancestry, age, medical condition, disability, veteran status, marital status, sexual orientation, or any other characteristic protected by law.

GEOG. RESTRICTIONS: Albany, Columbia, Fulton, Greene, Montgomery, Rensselaer, Saratoga, Schenectady, Schoharie, or Washington counties, New York.

FINANCIAL DATA:
Assets of over $83,000,000.
Amount of support per award: $1,000 to $30,000.
Total amount of support: $6,400,000 in grants and scholarships for the year 2019.

NO. AWARDS: Over 1,374 grants and scholarships for the year 2019.

APPLICATION INFO:
An application form is required and may be obtained online. Prospective applicants may discuss their plans with the Foundation's program staff prior to submitting an application.
Duration: Varies.
Deadline: Varies.

PUBLICATIONS:
Grantmaking Guidelines.

ADDRESS INQUIRIES TO:
See e-mail address above.

COMMUNITY FOUNDATION OF ABILENE   [1108]
850 North First
Abilene, TX 79601
(325) 676-3883
Fax: (325) 676-4206
E-mail: mparrish@cfabilene.org
Web Site: www.cfabilene.org

FOUNDED: 1986

AREAS OF INTEREST:
Human services, arts and culture, education, health, community development and civic affairs.

TYPE:
Capital grants; Challenge/matching grants; Project/program grants; Technical assistance.

PURPOSE:
To increase the quality of life in Abilene, TX; to increase the awareness of philanthropy in the area.

ELIGIBILITY:
Eligible organizations must be IRS 501(c)(3) tax-exempt and be located in the immediate Abilene, TX area.

GEOG. RESTRICTIONS: Abilene, Texas.

FINANCIAL DATA:
Amount of support per award: $1,000 to $25,000.

Total amount of support: Approximately $5,400,000.

NO. MOST RECENT APPLICANTS: 75.

NO. AWARDS: 50.

APPLICATION INFO:
Applicants must submit required documentation online.
Duration: One year.
Deadline: Spring and fall.

ADDRESS INQUIRIES TO:
Michelle Parrish, Grants Director
(See address above.)

COMMUNITY FOUNDATION OF COLLIER COUNTY   [1109]
1110 Pine Ridge Road, Suite 200
Naples, FL 34108
(239) 649-5000
Fax: (239) 649-5337
E-mail: ekeesler@cfcollier.org
Web Site: www.cfcollier.org

FOUNDED: 1985

AREAS OF INTEREST:
Health, human services, basic needs, education, civic affairs, environment, arts and humanities, women and girls, economic development and animal welfare.

TYPE:
Development grants; Matching gifts; Project/program grants; Scholarships. Capacity-building grants. Community Grant Programs in the area of professional development.

YEAR PROGRAM STARTED: 1985

PURPOSE:
To improve the quality of life in Collier County by connecting donors to community needs; to provide leadership on critical community issues.

LEGAL BASIS:
Public foundation.

ELIGIBILITY:
Eligible organizations must be IRS 501(c)(3) tax-exempt.

GEOG. RESTRICTIONS: Primarily Collier County, Florida.

FINANCIAL DATA:
Amount of support per award: Varies.
Total amount of support: Varies.

APPLICATION INFO:
Guidelines are available on the Foundation web site. Applications must be submitted through the online grant portal.
Duration: Varies.
Deadline: Varies.

PUBLICATIONS:
Guidelines; annual report; newsletter; *Vital Signs*, report; *Donor Advised Fund Handbook*; issue papers.

STAFF:
Eileen Connolly-Keesler, President and Chief Executive Officer
Lisette Holmes, Chief Financial Officer
Laura Simmelink, Senior Director of Programs

ADDRESS INQUIRIES TO:
Eileen Connolly-Keesler
President and Chief Executive Officer
(See address above.)

COMMUNITY FOUNDATION OF EASTERN CONNECTICUT [1110]
68 Federal Street
New London, CT 06320
(860) 442-3572
Fax: (860) 442-0584
E-mail: jennob@cfect.org
Web Site: www.cfect.org

FOUNDED: 1982

AREAS OF INTEREST:
Arts and culture, civic affairs, community needs and development, education, empowering youth, promoting basic needs and rights, preserving the environment, and advancing animal welfare.

NAME(S) OF PROGRAMS:
● **Animal Welfare Grants**
● **Community Foundation Scholarships**
● **Environmental Grants**
● **Northeast Area Women and Girls Fund**
● **Norwich Area Women and Girls Fund**
● **Norwich Youth Grants**
● **Southeast Area Women and Girls Fund**
● **Southeastern General Grants**
● **Windham Area Women and Girls Fund**

TYPE:
General operating grants; Project/program grants; Scholarships.

YEAR PROGRAM STARTED: 1982

PURPOSE:
To connect the generosity of private donors with the changing needs of the residents of eastern Connecticut by promoting local philanthropy and funding local projects.

ELIGIBILITY:
Federally recognized 501(c)(3) organizations and most charitable, educational and civic institutions that serve the towns listed below.

GEOG. RESTRICTIONS: Towns of Ashford, Bozrah, Brooklyn, Canterbury, Chaplin, Colchester, Columbia, Coventry, Eastford, East Lyme, Franklin, Griswold, Groton, Hampton, Killingly, Lebanon, Ledyard, Lisbon, Lyme, Mansfield, Montville, New London, North Stonington, Norwich, Old Lyme, Plainfield, Pomfret, Preston, Putnam, Salem, Scotland, Sprague, Stafford, Sterling, Stonington, Thompson, Union, Voluntown, Waterford, Willington, Windham, and Woodstock, Connecticut.

FINANCIAL DATA:
Amount of support per award: Grants: $1,000 to $50,000; Scholarships: $500 to $12,000.

Total amount of support: Varies.

NO. MOST RECENT APPLICANTS: Grants: 200; Scholarships: Over 500.

NO. AWARDS: Approximately 150 grants and 300 scholarships.

APPLICATION INFO:
Information is available on the Foundation web site or contact the Foundation for specific details on the various grant programs.
Duration: Typically one to four years.
Deadline: Varies by program.

ADDRESS INQUIRIES TO:
Jennifer O'Brien, Program Director
(See address above.)

THE COMMUNITY FOUNDATION OF FREDERICK COUNTY, MD, INC. [1111]

312 East Church Street
Frederick, MD 21701
(301) 695-7660
Fax: (301) 695-7775
E-mail: info@frederickcountygives.org
Web Site: www.frederickcountygives.org

FOUNDED: 1986

AREAS OF INTEREST:
Community development.

TYPE:
Project/program grants; Scholarships.

YEAR PROGRAM STARTED: 1986

PURPOSE:
To make charitable dreams come true by working with donors to establish funds that award grants and scholarships.

ELIGIBILITY:
Requirements can be found on the Foundation web site.

GEOG. RESTRICTIONS: Frederick County, Maryland.

FINANCIAL DATA:
Amount of support per award: Varies depending on need.
Total amount of support: Grants: Over $5,000,000 for fiscal year ended June 30, 2019; Scholarships: Over $1,000,000 annually.

NO. AWARDS: Over 280 grants to nonprofits for the year ended June 30, 2019; 430 scholarships to 314 individuals for the academic year 2019-20.

APPLICATION INFO:
Information may be found on the Foundation web site.
Duration: Grants: Varies. Scholarships: One academic year.
Deadline: Varies.

PUBLICATIONS:
Annual report; newsletters; grant applications.

IRS I.D.: 52-1488711

ADDRESS INQUIRIES TO:
See e-mail address above.

THE COMMUNITY FOUNDATION OF GREATER CHATTANOOGA, INC. [1112]

1400 Williams Street
Chattanooga, TN 37408
(423) 265-0586 ext. 11
Fax: (423) 265-0587
E-mail: rsuttles@cfgc.org
Web Site: cfgc.org

FOUNDED: 1963

AREAS OF INTEREST:
Nonprofit organizations.

TYPE:
Scholarships.

YEAR PROGRAM STARTED: 1963

PURPOSE:
To encourage giving and inspire action to improve lives in the Chattanooga area.

LEGAL BASIS:
501(c)(3).

ELIGIBILITY:
Each scholarship fund has specific eligibility criteria. Most funds require the applicant:

(1) be a graduating high school senior from a Hamilton County, TN high school;
(2) demonstrate financial need;
(3) applied to or have been accepted to attend a regionally accredited two- or four-year, technical, nonproprietary or community college or university and;
(4) have at least a cumulative grade point average of 2.5 or higher.

GEOG. RESTRICTIONS: Hamilton County, Tennessee.

FINANCIAL DATA:
Amount of support per award: Varies.

APPLICATION INFO:
Students must complete an eligibility quiz before being provided access to the scholarship application.
Duration: Varies.
Deadline: Varies.

IRS I.D.: 62-6045999

STAFF:
Meaghan Jones, President
Marisa Ogles, Vice President, Donor Services and Engagement
Rebecca Suttles, Director of Scholarships

BOARD OF DIRECTORS:
Julie Stowe, Chairperson
John Clark, Vice Chairperson
Dallas Joseph, Vice Chairperson
Elizabeth Williams, Vice Chairperson
Barry Large, Treasurer
Ansley Moses, Corporate Secretary
Ben Brown
Rondell Crier
Stacy Johnson
Cheryl Key
Travis Lytle
Gladys Pineda
Chantelle Roberson
Ray Ryan
Greg Willett

ADDRESS INQUIRIES TO:
Rebecca Suttles
Director of Scholarships
(See address above.)

THE COMMUNITY FOUNDATION OF GREATER CHATTANOOGA, INC. [1113]

1400 Williams Street
Chattanooga, TN 37408
(423) 265-0586 ext. 15
Fax: (423) 265-0587
E-mail: rposey@cfgc.org
Web Site: cfgc.org

FOUNDED: 1963

AREAS OF INTEREST:
Improving the quality of life in the Chattanooga, TN area.

TYPE:
Project/program grants.

PURPOSE:
To inspire giving and encourage action to improve lives in the Chattanooga area.

LEGAL BASIS:
501(c)(3).

ELIGIBILITY:
Organizations have to be 501(c)(3) public charities located in Hamilton County, TN and/or primarily serving Hamilton County.

GEOG. RESTRICTIONS: Hamilton County, Tennessee.

FINANCIAL DATA:
Amount of support per award: Varies.
Total amount of support: Approximately $900,000.

APPLICATION INFO:
Application information is available on the Foundation web site.
Duration: Generally one year.
Deadline: Contact Foundation for exact date.

ADDRESS INQUIRIES TO:
Robin Posey
Director of Community Impact
(See address above.)

COMMUNITY FOUNDATION OF GREATER GREENSBORO [1114]

330 South Greene Street
Suite 100
Greensboro, NC 27401
(336) 379-9100
Fax: (336) 378-0725
E-mail: info@cfgg.org
Web Site: cfgg.org

FOUNDED: 1983

AREAS OF INTEREST:
Capacity-building for nonprofits serving the Greater Greensboro, NC area.

NAME(S) OF PROGRAMS:
- **College and University Scholarships**
- **Community Grants Program**
- **Pre-College Scholarships**

TYPE:
Challenge/matching grants; Conferences/seminars; Demonstration grants; Development grants; Endowments; General operating grants; Project/program grants; Scholarships. Recognition Awards.

ELIGIBILITY:
Grant applicant must be a 501(c)(3) nonprofit organization located in or serving the greater Greensboro area. No grants to individuals.

GEOG. RESTRICTIONS: Greater Greensboro, North Carolina area.

FINANCIAL DATA:
Amount of support per award: Average grant: $3,000 to $5,000. Scholarships: Varies.
Total amount of support: Varies.

APPLICATION INFO:
Applications and guidelines are available online.
Duration: Varies.
Deadline: Varies.

IRS I.D.: 56-1380249

ADDRESS INQUIRIES TO:
H. Walker Sanders, President
(See address above.)

COMMUNITY FOUNDATION OF GREATER ROCHESTER [1115]

P.O. Box 80431
Rochester, MI 48308-0431
(248) 608-2804
Fax: (248) 608-2826
E-mail: director@cfound.org
Web Site: www.cfound.org

FOUNDED: 1983

AREAS OF INTEREST:
Arts, conservation of natural resources, community needs and development, culture, education, environment, health, historic preservation and human services.

TYPE:
Endowments; Project/program grants; Scholarships; Travel grants. Community grants.

PURPOSE:
To enhance the quality of life for the citizens of Greater Rochester area by serving as a community endowment builder, grantmaker and leader.

ELIGIBILITY:
Grants are made to organizations that have tax-exempt status under Section 501(c)(3) of the Internal Revenue Code. Nonsectarian religious programs may apply.

GEOG. RESTRICTIONS: Primarily Greater Rochester, Michigan and surrounding area.

FINANCIAL DATA:
Amount of support per award: Varies.
Total amount of support: Varies.

APPLICATION INFO:
Contact the Foundation for application procedures.
Duration: Varies.
Deadline: Varies.

ADDRESS INQUIRIES TO:
Johanna Allen, Executive Director
(See address above.)

THE COMMUNITY FOUNDATION OF HERKIMER & ONEIDA COUNTIES, INC.   [1116]
2608 Genesee Street
Utica, NY 13502
(315) 735-8212
Fax: (315) 735-9363
E-mail: info@foundationhoc.org
Web Site: foundationhoc.org

FOUNDED: 1952

AREAS OF INTEREST:
Economic development, education, health and wellness, arts and culture.

TYPE:
Capital grants; Challenge/matching grants; Project/program grants; Scholarships; Seed money grants; Technical assistance; Training grants.

PURPOSE:
To improve the quality of life of the residents of Herkimer and Oneida counties in New York.

LEGAL BASIS:
Community foundation.

ELIGIBILITY:
Applications are entertained from organizations that are tax-exempt under Section 501(c)(3) of the Internal Revenue Code. Grants may be made for program or capital expenses. Operating funds will receive consideration on a short-term or emergency basis, with the understanding that applicants must submit a clear, realistic plan to secure alternative funding at the end of a specific time.

The Community Foundation does not make grants for religious purposes, nor does it provide financial assistance or scholarships directly to individuals, support for nonemergency expenses already incurred or ongoing operating support.

GEOG. RESTRICTIONS: Herkimer and Oneida counties, New York.

FINANCIAL DATA:
Amount of support per award: Average $34,000.
Total amount of support: $8,087,000.

NO. MOST RECENT APPLICANTS: 475.

NO. AWARDS: 891 grants and scholarships.

APPLICATION INFO:
Details are available on the Foundation web site.
Duration: One year; multiyear grants available occasionally on case-by-case basis.
Deadline: Grant requests are accepted on an ongoing basis.

PUBLICATIONS:
Annual report; newsletters.

IRS I.D.: 15-6016932

ADDRESS INQUIRIES TO:
Jan Squadrito
Senior Community Investment Manager
(See address above.)

COMMUNITY FOUNDATION OF JACKSON HOLE   [1117]
245 East Simpson Avenue
Jackson, WY 83001
(307) 739-1026
Fax: (307) 734-2841
E-mail: info@cfjacksonhole.org
Web Site: www.cfjacksonhole.org

FOUNDED: 1989

AREAS OF INTEREST:
Art, civic involvement, education, environment, health and human services, and recreation.

TYPE:
Development grants; General operating grants; Grants-in-aid; Project/program grants; Research grants.

PURPOSE:
To improve lives through philanthropic leadership.

LEGAL BASIS:
501(c)(3).

ELIGIBILITY:
Must be a 501(c)(3) corporation.

GEOG. RESTRICTIONS: Teton County, Wyoming.

FINANCIAL DATA:
Amount of support per award: Varies.
Total amount of support: Approximately $23,000,000 for the year 2018.

APPLICATION INFO:
Application information is available on the web site.
Deadline: Varies.

IRS I.D.: 83-0308856

ADDRESS INQUIRIES TO:
Laurie Andrews, President
(See address above.)

THE COMMUNITY FOUNDATION OF LORAIN COUNTY   [1118]
9080 Leavitt Road
Elyria, OH 44035
(440) 984-7390
Fax: (440) 984-7399
E-mail: foundation@peoplewhocare.org
Web Site: www.peoplewhocare.org

FOUNDED: 1980

AREAS OF INTEREST:
Arts and culture, civic affairs, education, health, and social services.

TYPE:
General operating grants; Project/program grants. Grants are given to improve the quality of life in Lorain County.

YEAR PROGRAM STARTED: 1980

PURPOSE:
To connect people who care with causes that matter.

ELIGIBILITY:
Organization or sponsor must be 501(c)(3). Funding must serve the people of Lorain County.

GEOG. RESTRICTIONS: Lorain County, Ohio.

FINANCIAL DATA:
Amount of support per award: Varies.
Total amount of support: Varies.

APPLICATION INFO:
Application is available on the web site.
Deadline: Dates are posted online.

ADDRESS INQUIRIES TO:
Linda Styer, Senior Program Officer
E-mail: grants@peoplewhocare.org

COMMUNITY FOUNDATION OF NORTH CENTRAL WISCONSIN   [1119]
500 First Street
Suite 2600
Wausau, WI 54403
(715) 845-9555
E-mail: info@cfoncw.org
Web Site: www.cfoncw.org

FOUNDED: 1987

AREAS OF INTEREST:
Arts, education, health and human services, and resource preservation.

TYPE:
Capital grants; Development grants; Project/program grants; Scholarships; Seed money grants; Technical assistance.

YEAR PROGRAM STARTED: 1987

PURPOSE:
To enhance the quality of north central Wisconsin.

ELIGIBILITY:
Consideration is given primarily to those organizations that are tax-exempt under Section 501(c)(3) of the Internal Revenue Code.

GEOG. RESTRICTIONS: Greater Wausau area, Marathon County, Wisconsin.

FINANCIAL DATA:
Amount of support per award: $1,000 to $50,000.
Total amount of support: Varies.

CO-OP FUNDING PROGRAMS: Community Arts Grants are funded through the Wisconsin Arts Board; B.A. and Esther Greenheck Foundation and Community Foundation.

NO. MOST RECENT APPLICANTS: Average 100 per year.

NO. AWARDS: Average 50 to 60 per year.

REPRESENTATIVE AWARDS:
Medical College of Wisconsin; Boys & Girls Club; United Way.

APPLICATION INFO:
Application information is available on the web site.

Duration: One year.

Deadline: Applications are due the first business day of March, June, September and December.

STAFF:
Jean Tehan, President/Chief Executive Officer
Sue Nelson, Program Officer
Pam Eckmann, Director of Finance

ADDRESS INQUIRIES TO:
Sue Nelson, Program Officer
(See address above.)

COMMUNITY FOUNDATION OF SAINT JOSEPH COUNTY   [1120]

P.O. Box 837
South Bend, IN 46624
(574) 232-0041
Fax: (574) 233-1906
E-mail: info@cfsjc.org
Web Site: www.cfsjc.org

AREAS OF INTEREST:
Arts and culture; community development and urban affairs; health and human services; parks, recreation, and environment; youth and education.

NAME(S) OF PROGRAMS:
- **African American Community Fund**
- **ArtsEverywhere Fund**
- **Leighton Award for Nonprofit Excellence**
- **Senior Living Initiative**
- **Special Project Challenge Grant**

TYPE:
Capital grants; Challenge/matching grants; Project/program grants; Scholarships. Donor-advised grants.

PURPOSE:
To promote organizations whose programs benefit the residents of St. Joseph County; to assist existing agencies to better respond to the needs of the community.

ELIGIBILITY:
Grants are made to organizations that have tax-exempt status under Section 501(c)(3) of the Internal Revenue Code. No grants are made to individuals. Nonsectarian religious programs may apply. Funded projects should benefit a significant constituency within the community and the organization must exhibit the ability to raise the required matching funds, if applicable.

GEOG. RESTRICTIONS: Saint Joseph County, Indiana.

FINANCIAL DATA:
Amount of support per award: Varies per award.
Matching fund requirements: Some programs require matching funds.

APPLICATION INFO:
Application information is available on the web site.
Duration: Varies.
Deadline: Special Project Challenge Grant: March 1 and October 1; Senior Living Initiative and ArtsEverywhere Fund: May 1 and November 1; Leighton Award for Nonprofit Excellence: August 1 of odd-numbered years.

STAFF:
Rose Meissner, President

ADDRESS INQUIRIES TO:
Emily Slatt, Program Officer
(See address above.)

THE COMMUNITY FOUNDATION OF SHELBY COUNTY   [1121]

Courtview Center, Suite 202
100 South Main Avenue
Sidney, OH 45365-2771
(937) 497-7800
Fax: (937) 497-7799
E-mail: info@commfoun.com
Web Site: www.commfoun.com

FOUNDED: 1952

AREAS OF INTEREST:
Arts and culture, family and community, education, environment, and health.

TYPE:
Capital grants; Project/program grants; Scholarships; Seed money grants.

PURPOSE:
To improve the quality of life and to cultivate, administer and distribute legacy gifts for the benefit of its local community.

ELIGIBILITY:
Organizations must have 501(c)(3) status.

GEOG. RESTRICTIONS: Shelby County, Ohio.

FINANCIAL DATA:
Amount of support per award: Discretionary grants: $500 to $5,000.
Total amount of support: $88,000 in discretionary grants for the year 2020; $2,700,000 in total grantmaking for fiscal year 2018.

NO. MOST RECENT APPLICANTS: Varies.

NO. AWARDS: Varies.

APPLICATION INFO:
Applicants must call the Executive Director of the Foundation to discuss the grant request idea and whether the project appears to fit within the Foundation's guidelines. Preliminary Grant Proposals and Full Proposals will not be accepted if they have not been requested by the Executive Director.

Applications for most of the scholarships are available online.
Deadline: Grants: Approximately February 1 and August 1. Scholarships: Varies.

ADDRESS INQUIRIES TO:
Marian Spicer, Executive Director
(See address above.)

THE COMMUNITY FOUNDATION OF SOUTH ALABAMA   [1122]

212 St. Joseph Street
Mobile, AL 36602
(251) 438-5591
Fax: (251) 438-5592
E-mail: jberson@communityfoundationsa.org
Web Site: communityfoundationsa.org

FOUNDED: 1976

AREAS OF INTEREST:
Arts and culture, economic opportunity, civic engagement, and health and wellness.

TYPE:
Project/program grants; Scholarships. Capacity-building grants. Special initiative grants.

PURPOSE:
To assemble and direct philanthropic assets to make Southwestern Alabama a better place.

LEGAL BASIS:
Alabama not-for-profit corporation/community foundation.

ELIGIBILITY:
Eligible organizations must be IRS 501(c)(3) tax-exempt and located in southwest Alabama.

GEOG. RESTRICTIONS: Southwestern Alabama (Baldwin, Choctaw, Clarke, Conecah, Escambia, Mobile, Monroe and Washington counties).

FINANCIAL DATA:
Amount of support per award: Varies.
Total amount of support: Varies.

APPLICATION INFO:
Guidelines and application form are available online.
Duration: Typically one year. Renewal by reapplication. Some multiyear grants may be awarded.
Deadline: Varies.

PUBLICATIONS:
Annual report; newsletter; application guidelines; *Charitable Gift Annuity*; *Real Estate Gifts*.

IRS I.D.: 63-0695166

STAFF:
Rebecca Byrne, President and Chief Executive Officer
Jena Berson, Director of Communications and Programs
Carolyn Marston, Director of Operations

ADDRESS INQUIRIES TO:
Jena Berson, Director of Communications and Programs
(See address and telephone number above.)

COMMUNITY FOUNDATION OF THE EASTERN SHORE   [1123]

1324 Belmont Avenue, Suite 401
Salisbury, MD 21804
(410) 742-9911
Fax: (410) 742-6638
E-mail: hmahler@cfes.org
Web Site: www.cfes.org

FOUNDED: 1984

AREAS OF INTEREST:
Arts, civic affairs, community needs, conservation, culture, education, health and historic preservation.

NAME(S) OF PROGRAMS:
- **Community Needs Grants**
- **Education Grants Program**
- **Richard A. Henson Award of Excellence**
- **Mini Grants**
- **Frank H. Morris Humanitarian Award**
- **Nonprofit Support Program**
- **Women's Fund Grants**
- **Workforce Development Grants**

TYPE:
Awards/prizes; Challenge/matching grants; Demonstration grants; Project/program grants; Scholarships; Seed money grants; Technical assistance; Training grants.

YEAR PROGRAM STARTED: 1984

PURPOSE:
To improve the quality of life in the area by acting as a funding source for present and future generations.

ELIGIBILITY:
Grants are made to organizations that have tax-exempt status under Section 501(c)(3) of

the Internal Revenue Code and not classified as a private foundation that is located or serves the residents of the counties. No grants are made to individuals. Nonsectarian religious programs may apply. Agencies must be operated and organized so that they do not discriminate in the hiring of staff on the basis of race, religion, gender, sexual orientation, age, national origin or disability.

GEOG. RESTRICTIONS: Somerset, Wicomico and Worcester counties, Maryland.

FINANCIAL DATA:
Amount of support per award: Community Needs, Education Grants and Women's Fund Grants: Maximum $5,000; Henson and Morris Awards: Approximately $1,000; Mini Grants: Maximum $1,500.
Total amount of support: Over $5,000,000 in grants and scholarships annually.

APPLICATION INFO:
Varies by program. All request for funding must be submitted through the Foundation's e-grant portal.
Duration: One year.
Deadline: Community Needs: February 1 and August 1; Education Grants Program: August; Henson and Morris Awards: September 1; Mini Grants: 15th of each month; Women's Fund: March 30; Workforce Development: October 1.

STAFF:
Heather Mahler, Program Director

ADDRESS INQUIRIES TO:
Heather Mahler, Program Director
(See address above.)

COMMUNITY FOUNDATION OF THE FOX RIVER VALLEY [1124]
111 West Downer Place
Suite 312
Aurora, IL 60506
(630) 896-7800
Fax: (630) 896-7811
E-mail: info@cffrv.org
Web Site: www.cffrv.org

AREAS OF INTEREST:
Education, health care, social services, the arts, and other charitable fields.

TYPE:
Capital grants; Scholarships.

PURPOSE:
To support worthwhile projects in the served communities.

ELIGIBILITY:
Grants are made to organizations that have tax-exempt status under Section 501(c)(3) of the Internal Revenue Code. No grants are made to individuals.

GEOG. RESTRICTIONS: Aurora, southern Kane County, and Kendall County, Illinois.

FINANCIAL DATA:
Amount of support per award: Varies.
Total amount of support: Varies.

NO. MOST RECENT APPLICANTS: Scholarships: Approximately 700 for the year 2019.

NO. AWARDS: Scholarships: Approximately 380 for the year 2019.

APPLICATION INFO:
Applications may be obtained from the Foundation web site.
Duration: Varies.

Deadline: Letter of Intent: March 31 and September 30. Grant proposals: May 1 and November 1. Scholarships: January.

ADDRESS INQUIRIES TO:
Julie Christman, President and Chief Executive Officer
(See address above.)

COMMUNITY FOUNDATION OF THE NORTH STATE [1125]
1335 Arboretum Drive, Suite B
Redding, CA 96003
(530) 244-1219
E-mail: megan@cfnorthstate.org
Web Site: www.cfnorthstate.org

FOUNDED: 2000

AREAS OF INTEREST:
Arts and culture, community development, education, health and human services.

NAME(S) OF PROGRAMS:
● **The McConnell Fund**
● **Redding Rancheria Community Fund**

TYPE:
Project/program grants.

PURPOSE:
To enhance the quality of life of Shasta, Siskiyou and Tehama counties through philanthropy, education and information.

ELIGIBILITY:
To be eligible for funding, the applicant must be a nonprofit 501(c)(3) organization or public agency and provide specific and direct benefits to residents of Shasta, Siskiyou or Tehama counties, primarily, or to Modoc or Trinity counties.

GEOG. RESTRICTIONS: Primarily Shasta, Siskiyou and Tehama counties, California. Limited funding to Modoc and Trinity counties, California.

FINANCIAL DATA:
Net investment assets of $33,300,000 in 2020.
Amount of support per award: Varies.
Total amount of support: $4,300,000 in grants and $272,300 in scholarships awarded in 2019.

NO. AWARDS: Grants: Varies; Scholarships: More than 200 annually.

APPLICATION INFO:
Consult the Foundation web site.
Duration: Varies.
Deadline: Varies.

ADDRESS INQUIRIES TO:
Grants:
Megan Conn, Program Officer
(See e-mail address above.)

Scholarships:
Miriam Leal, Program Associate
(See telephone number above.)

*PLEASE NOTE:
Formerly known as the Shasta Regional Community Foundation.

COMMUNITY FOUNDATION OF THE OZARKS [1126]
425 East Trafficway
Springfield, MO 65806
(417) 864-6199
Fax: (417) 864-8344
E-mail: bdierks@cfozarks.org
Web Site: cfozarks.org

AREAS OF INTEREST:
Health and social services; arts, culture and environment; education and community development.

TYPE:
Challenge/matching grants; Demonstration grants; Development grants; Endowments; Project/program grants; Scholarships. Initiative grants. Technical/Capacity-building grants.

PURPOSE:
To build a community endowment; to provide leadership; to prompt collaboration on community issues; to improve the quality of life for citizens in Greene County, MO and the surrounding region.

LEGAL BASIS:
Community foundation.

ELIGIBILITY:
Eligible organizations must be IRS 501(c)(3) tax-exempt and located in Greene County, MO or counties represented by the Foundation's affiliate organizations which are located throughout the central and southern half of Missouri.

GEOG. RESTRICTIONS: Central and southern Missouri.

FINANCIAL DATA:
Amount of support per award: Grants: $1,500 to $25,000; Initiative Awards: $100,000 to $1,000,000.
Total amount of support: Discretionary Grants and Scholarships Programs: $2,000,000.

APPLICATION INFO:
Complete application information is available online.
Duration: Typically one year.
Deadline: Varies.

ADDRESS INQUIRIES TO:
Bridget Dierks, Vice President of Programs
(See address above.)

COMMUNITY FOUNDATION OF THE TEXAS HILL COUNTRY [1127]
420 Water Street
Suite 108
Kerrville, TX 78028
(830) 896-8811
E-mail: austin@communityfoundation.net
Web Site: www.communityfoundation.net

FOUNDED: 1982

AREAS OF INTEREST:
Art and heritage, religion, basic human needs and youth development.

TYPE:
Challenge/matching grants; Development grants; Grants-in-aid; Matching gifts; Project/program grants; Scholarships; Technical assistance.

PURPOSE:
To improve the quality of life in the Texas Hill Country of Texas.

LEGAL BASIS:
Corporation.

ELIGIBILITY:
Organization must be located in or provide services to Bandera, Blanco, Edwards, Gillespie, Kendall, Kerr, Kimble, Mason, Real or Uvalde County, TX. Organization must be IRS 501(c)(3) tax-exempt. Grants are not awarded to individuals.

FINANCIAL DATA:
More than $23,000,000 in assets for the year ended December 31, 2018.

Amount of support per award: Varies.

Total amount of support: Varies.

NO. AWARDS: Varies.

APPLICATION INFO:
Application information is available on the Foundation web site.

IRS I.D.: 74-2225369

STAFF:
Austin Dickson, Executive Director
Amy Rector, Business Manager
Ingrid Cunyus, Grants and Scholarships Manager
Jayne Zirkel, Marketing and Events Manager

ADDRESS INQUIRIES TO:
Austin Dickson, Executive Director
(See address above.)

COMMUNITY FOUNDATION OF WEST TEXAS   [1128]

6102 82nd Street, Suite 8B
Lubbock, TX 79424
(806) 762-8061
E-mail: tami@
communityfoundationofwesttexas.org
Web Site: www.cfwtx.org

FOUNDED: 1981

AREAS OF INTEREST:
Charitable organizations and community development.

NAME(S) OF PROGRAMS:
● **Mini Grant for Teachers Program**

TYPE:
Project/program grants; Scholarships; Technical assistance. Responsiveness to changing or emerging community needs approach for solving community problems in South Plains area.

YEAR PROGRAM STARTED: 1981

PURPOSE:
To improve the quality of life in the South Plains area of Texas.

ELIGIBILITY:
Organizations must be 501(c)(3) not-for-profit.

GEOG. RESTRICTIONS: Lubbock and the surrounding 14 counties of Texas.

FINANCIAL DATA:
Amount of support per award: Grant awards: Up to $5,000; Mini Grant for Teachers Program: Up to $1,000.

Total amount of support: Varies.

CO-OP FUNDING PROGRAMS: Affiliate Endowment Challenges, Community Endowment Challenge, Mini Grant for Teachers.

APPLICATION INFO:
Application information is available on the web site.

Duration: One year. Must reapply.

Deadline: Mini Grant for Teachers: June 15. All others: Varies.

ADDRESS INQUIRIES TO:
See e-mail address above.

COMMUNITY FOUNDATION OF WESTERN MASSACHUSETTS (CFWM)   [1129]

333 Bridge Street
Springfield, MA 01103
(413) 732-2858
Fax: (413) 733-8565
E-mail: wmass@communityfoundation.org
Web Site: communityfoundation.org

FOUNDED: 1991

AREAS OF INTEREST:
Human services, economic development, education, arts and culture, health, housing and environment.

TYPE:
Capital grants; Project/program grants; Scholarships. Capacity building. Equipment.

YEAR PROGRAM STARTED: 1991

PURPOSE:
To enrich the quality of life of the people of our region.

ELIGIBILITY:
Grants are restricted to worthy public charities serving residents of Franklin, Hampden and Hampshire counties in Massachusetts.

GEOG. RESTRICTIONS: Franklin, Hampden and Hampshire counties, Massachusetts.

FINANCIAL DATA:
Amount of support per award: Varies.

Total amount of support: Approximately $2,000,000 awarded annually through competitive grant opportunities.

CO-OP FUNDING PROGRAMS: Informal linkages as well as funds established by family foundations within the community foundation.

NO. MOST RECENT APPLICANTS: 129 for the year 2018.

NO. AWARDS: 106 for the year 2018.

APPLICATION INFO:
Contact the Foundation for application procedures.

Duration: One year. Nonrenewable.

Deadline: Varies.

PUBLICATIONS:
Annual report; newsletter; brochures for donors and applicants.

STAFF:
Katie Allan Zobel, President and Chief Executive Officer
James Ayres, Vice President for Programs and Strategy

ADDRESS INQUIRIES TO:
James Ayres
Vice President for Programs and Strategy
(See address above.)

COMMUNITY FOUNDATIONS OF THE HUDSON VALLEY [1130]

80 Washington Street, Suite 201
Poughkeepsie, NY 12601
(845) 452-3077
Fax: (845) 452-3083
E-mail: grant@communityfoundationshv.org
Web Site: www.communityfoundationshv.org

FOUNDED: 1969

AREAS OF INTEREST:
Health, education and social services.

NAME(S) OF PROGRAMS:
● **Community Response Grants**
● **Farm Fresh Food Initiatives**
● **Fund for Excellence in Education Grants**

TYPE:
Project/program grants; Scholarships; Training grants. Equipment to improve office operations.

PURPOSE:
To improve the quality of life in Dutchess, Putnam and Ulster counties, New York.

ELIGIBILITY:
Eligible organizations must be IRS 501(c)(3) tax-exempt or have a fiscal sponsor.

GEOG. RESTRICTIONS: Primarily Dutchess, Putnam and Ulster counties, New York.

FINANCIAL DATA:
Amount of support per award: Varies.

Total amount of support: Approximately $27,000,000 for the year 2019.

APPLICATION INFO:
Application information is available on the web site. Applications are submitted through the online application system.

PUBLICATIONS:
Annual report; newsletters.

IRS I.D.: 23-7026859

ADDRESS INQUIRIES TO:
See e-mail address above.

*SPECIAL STIPULATIONS:
Review web site, if possible, for grant information. Applicants may contact the organization for details of its grants.

COMMUNITYGIVING   [1131]

101 7th Avenue South, No. 100
St. Cloud, MN 56301
(320) 253-4380
(877) 253-4380
Fax: (320) 240-9215
E-mail: kgrochow@communitygiving.org
Web Site: www.communitygiving.org

FOUNDED: 1985

AREAS OF INTEREST:
Philanthropy to support arts and culture, education, environment, youth and families, and human services.

TYPE:
Challenge/matching grants; Conferences/seminars; General operating grants; Project/program grants; Scholarships; Seed money grants; Technical assistance.

PURPOSE:
To attract and administer funds to improve the quality of life for citizens of central Minnesota.

LEGAL BASIS:
Community foundation.

ELIGIBILITY:
Eligible organizations must be IRS 501(c)(3) tax-exempt and located within Benton, Sherburne and Stearns counties, Minnesota. Funding to religious organizations of a nonsectarian nature, which benefits the entire community. No grants to individuals.

GEOG. RESTRICTIONS: Benton, Sherburne and Stearns counties, Minnesota.

FINANCIAL DATA:
$149,000,000 in assets as of June 30, 2019.

Amount of support per award: Average: $5,096.

Total amount of support: $13,746,040 in grants paid as of June 30, 2019.

NO. AWARDS: 2,697.

APPLICATION INFO:
Online application and required documents
are available online. Applicant must include a
copy of the IRS 501(c)(3) tax determination
letter.
Duration: One year.
Deadline: Varies.

PUBLICATIONS:
Annual report; application guidelines.

IRS I.D.: 36-3412544

ADDRESS INQUIRIES TO:
Kathy Grochow
Director of Community Programs
(See address above.)

CONNECTICUT COMMUNITY FOUNDATION   [1132]
43 Field Street
Waterbury, CT 06702
(203) 753-1315
Fax: (203) 756-3054
E-mail: info@conncf.org
Web Site: www.conncf.org

FOUNDED: 1923

AREAS OF INTEREST:
Arts and culture, cradle to career (youth
development/education), economic vitality,
environment, grassroots engagement, healthy
communities, older adults, technology and
women's issues.

CONSULTING OR VOLUNTEER SERVICES:
Nonprofit advisor services available.

NAME(S) OF PROGRAMS:
● **Capacity Building Grants**
● **Nonprofit Assistance Initiative**
● **Program Grants**
● **Scholarships**
● **Training Programs**

TYPE:
Capital grants; Challenge/matching grants;
Project/program grants; Scholarships; Seed
money grants; Technical assistance.
Sponsorships. Organizational development.

YEAR PROGRAM STARTED: 1923

PURPOSE:
To serve the people of the Greater Waterbury
and Litchfield Hills to improve the quality of
life.

LEGAL BASIS:
Community foundation.

ELIGIBILITY:
Applicant must:
(1) be a not-for-profit organization
recognized under Section 501(c)(3) of the
Internal Revenue Code, or a municipal entity
seeking a grant for public purposes;
(2) have a board, representative of the
community, of which a majority is neither
employees nor relatives of employees;
(3) be located within and/or providing
services to residents of the Foundation's
21-town service area: Beacon Falls,
Bethlehem, Bridgewater, Cheshire, Goshen,
Litchfield, Middlebury, Morris, Naugatuck,
New Milford, Oxford, Prospect, Roxbury,
Southbury, Thomaston, Warren, Washington,
Waterbury, Watertown, Wolcott or Woodbury
and;
(4) have a Nonprofit Registration to Solicit
Funds (or exemption, if appropriate) from the
Connecticut Department of Consumer
Protection. Registration must be renewed
annually.

Grant requests for political or religious
purposes or for capital expenditures on
buildings not owned by a nonprofit are not
accepted. Religious organizations or
municipalities are not eligible to apply for
grants for buildings or expenses related to
buildings. However, they may apply for
equipment that is specifically part of an
eligible programmatic request.

GEOG. RESTRICTIONS: Greater Waterbury and
Litchfield Hills, Connecticut.

FINANCIAL DATA:
Amount of support per award: Varies.
Total amount of support: Approximately
$4,000,000 in grants and scholarships.

NO. AWARDS: Over 900 grants and scholarships.

APPLICATION INFO:
Guidelines and application form may be
obtained online.
Duration: One year. Multiyear funding
should be applied for at the outset and is
subject to review.
Deadline: Varies.

PUBLICATIONS:
Annual report.

IRS I.D.: 06-6038074

ADDRESS INQUIRIES TO:
Josh Carey, Director of Grants Management
(See address above.)

COOK FAMILY FOUNDATION   [1133]
120 West Exchange Street
Suite 202
Owosso, MI 48867
(989) 725-1621
Fax: (989) 936-5910
E-mail: tom@cookfamilyfoundation.org
Web Site: www.cookfamilyfoundation.org

FOUNDED: 1978

AREAS OF INTEREST:
Community organizations, education and
youth, environment, and University of
Michigan.

TYPE:
Capital grants; Challenge/matching grants;
Demonstration grants; Development grants;
Matching gifts; Project/program grants;
Scholarships; Seed money grants; Technical
assistance. Educational support.

YEAR PROGRAM STARTED: 1978

PURPOSE:
To strengthen and invest in the future of
community institutions in Shiawassee
County; to support the University of
Michigan.

LEGAL BASIS:
Family (private) foundation.

ELIGIBILITY:
Eligible organizations must be IRS 501(c)(3)
tax-exempt. The Foundation does not give
grants for religious purposes and upholds
federal law which prohibits the expenditure
of funds for political campaigns or direct
lobbying activities. With the exception of
scholarships, the Foundation does not give
grants to individuals.

GEOG. RESTRICTIONS: Shiawassee County,
Michigan.

FINANCIAL DATA:
Amount of support per award: Typically
$5,000 to $50,000.

Total amount of support: $1,483,644 in
grants for the year 2020.
Matching fund requirements: Varies based on
grant; average 20% cash/in-kind.

APPLICATION INFO:
Applicants should submit a short letter of
inquiry.
Deadline: First consideration will be given to
grant applications submitted by April 1.
Applications should be made no later than
November 1.

STAFF:
Yvette Collard, Associate Director

ADDRESS INQUIRIES TO:
Thomas Cook, Executive Director
P.O. Box 278
Owosso, MI 48867

*PLEASE NOTE:
The Foundation establishes a total annual
grant budget in January for that year and
addresses applications on a first-come,
first-served basis within that budget.

COOPERATIVE DEVELOPMENT FOUNDATION   [1134]
1775 I Street, N.W.
Eighth Floor
Washington, DC 20006
(202) 442-2302
E-mail: kboyette@ncba.coop
Web Site: www.cdf.coop
www.heroes.coop

FOUNDED: 1944

AREAS OF INTEREST:
Community, economic and social
development through cooperative enterprise.

TYPE:
Grants-in-aid. The Foundation makes grants
and loans for cooperative development
through its various funds.

PURPOSE:
To promote self-help and mutual aid in
community, economic and social
development through cooperative enterprise.

LEGAL BASIS:
501(c)(3) organization.

ELIGIBILITY:
The Foundation does not award grants for
purely personal needs. It works only in the
cooperative sector.

GEOG. RESTRICTIONS: Primarily the United
States.

FINANCIAL DATA:
Amount of support per award: Varies.
Total amount of support: Varies.

NO. MOST RECENT APPLICANTS: Approximately
70.

NO. AWARDS: 45.

APPLICATION INFO:
Contact the Foundation after reviewing the
various fund descriptions to determine if the
proposed project fits within the Foundation's
funding priorities. The Foundation supports
cooperative development only.

PUBLICATIONS:
Annual report.

STAFF:
Leslie Mead, Executive Director
Kirstie Boyette, Fund-raising and Fund
Manager

ADDRESS INQUIRIES TO:
See e-mail address above.

*SPECIAL STIPULATIONS:
The Foundation supports cooperative development only.

ADOLPH COORS FOUNDATION
215 St. Paul Street, Suite 300
Denver, CO 80206
(303) 388-1636
Fax: (303) 388-1684
E-mail: info@acoorsfdn.org
Web Site: coorsfoundation.org

TYPE:
Capital grants; General operating grants; Project/program grants.

See entry 1007 for full listing.

CORPORATION FOR NATIONAL AND COMMUNITY SERVICE (AMERICORPS) [1135]
250 E Street, S.W.
Washington, DC 20525
(202) 606-5000
(800) 942-2677
E-mail: VISTA@americorps.gov
Web Site: www.nationalservice.gov/programs/americorps/americorps-programs/americorps-vista

FOUNDED: 1965

AREAS OF INTEREST:
Anti-poverty activities, particularly food security, housing and economic justice.

NAME(S) OF PROGRAMS:
• AmeriCorps VISTA

TYPE:
Project/program grants. Provides full-time, full-year members at the request of community groups to work on clearly defined tasks that lead to mobilization of the community's resources. The members live among the people they serve at subsistence levels of support.

YEAR PROGRAM STARTED: 1965

PURPOSE:
To supplement efforts to eliminate poverty and poverty-related problems.

LEGAL BASIS:
Domestic Volunteer Service Act of 1973, as amended (P.L. 93-113).

ELIGIBILITY:
Sponsors applying for AmeriCorps VISTA must be nonprofit organizations, tribal, state or local governments.

GEOG. RESTRICTIONS: United States and its territories.

FINANCIAL DATA:
Organizations receive AmeriCorps VISTA member slots. Those VISTA members receive a basic monthly substance allowance. An end-of-service stipend or the Segal AmeriCorps Educational Award is paid upon completion of service.
Amount of support per award: Approximately $22,000 per VISTA slot.
Total amount of support: Varies.

NO. MOST RECENT APPLICANTS: Organizations: Approximately 1,000; Individuals: Approximately 5,500.

NO. AWARDS: Organizations: Approximately 850.

APPLICATION INFO:
Application information is available online.

Duration: One to five years.
Deadline: Applications accepted on an ongoing basis.

ADDRESS INQUIRIES TO:
E-mail: VISTA@cns.gov

THE DALLAS FOUNDATION [1136]
3000 Pegasus Park Drive
Suite 930
Dallas, TX 75247
(214) 741-9898
Fax: (214) 741-9848
E-mail: info@dallasfoundation.org
Web Site: www.dallasfoundation.org

FOUNDED: 1929

AREAS OF INTEREST:
Arts, education, health and human services, social services, and public/civic benefit.

TYPE:
Capital grants; Project/program grants; Scholarships.

YEAR PROGRAM STARTED: 1929

PURPOSE:
To improve the quality of life for residents of the city and county of Dallas.

LEGAL BASIS:
Community foundation.

ELIGIBILITY:
Applicant organizations must be tax-exempt nonprofit focused on needs within Dallas County. Grants from the field of interest funds require a match between the purpose of the grant and the purpose of the available funds. Grants from the unrestricted funds may be given to any type of need within Dallas County.

Funds are not available from discretionary funds for individuals, endowments, research, debt retirement, annual campaigns or underwriting of fund-raising events.

GEOG. RESTRICTIONS: City and county of Dallas, Texas.

FINANCIAL DATA:
Amount of support per award: Varies.
Total amount of support: Varies.

NO. MOST RECENT APPLICANTS: 400.

NO. AWARDS: 50.

APPLICATION INFO:
Letters of Inquiry are available through the Foundation's online grant application portal. Access to the portal is found on the Foundation's web site. Grant applications are provided directly to nonprofits after approval of their letter of inquiry.
Duration: Varies.
Deadline: Field of Interest Funds cycle generally opens in February and decisions are made in May. Community Impact Fund cycle generally opens in August and decisions are made in November.

PUBLICATIONS:
Annual report; application guidelines.

ADDRESS INQUIRIES TO:
Brittani Trusty, Director of Community Impact
(See address above.)

DANIELS FUND
101 Monroe Street
Denver, CO 80206-4467
(303) 393-7220
E-mail: info@danielsfund.org
grantsinfo@danielsfund.org
Web Site: www.danielsfund.org

TYPE:
Capital grants; General operating grants; Project/program grants; Scholarships. Daniels Fund Ethics Initiative delivers principle-based ethics education and reinforces the value of ethical business and personal conduct. The Ethics Initiative consists of a Collegiate Program, High School Program, Middle School Program, Community College Program, Elementary School Program, Law Enforcement Program, Business Program, and an online Case Bank. Each of the Ethics Initiative's components utilizes a specific approach to reach its target audience. Funding is provided through the Daniels Fund Grants Program.

Daniels Fund Grants Program supports highly effective nonprofit organizations in Colorado, New Mexico, Utah and Wyoming.

Daniels Fund Scholarship Program consists of the Daniels Scholarship Program and the Boundless Opportunity Scholarship Program. The Daniels Scholarship Program provides a comprehensive, four-year annually-renewable college scholarship for highly motivated students to earn a Bachelor's degree that helps them build a successful career and rewarding life. Daniels Scholars are honest, respectful, self-reliant, and compassionate. They are proud Americans who value our free enterprise system and are prepared to give the world their very best shot. The scholarship applies toward the expense of attaining a Bachelor's degree at any nonprofit, accredited college or university in the U.S. The Boundless Opportunity Scholarship Program provides college scholarships for non-traditional students of all ages, awarded by select colleges and universities using funds provided by the Daniels Fund.

See entry 83 for full listing.

IRENE E. AND GEORGE A. DAVIS FOUNDATION [1137]
One Monarch Place
Suite 1300
Springfield, MA 01144-1300
(413) 734-8336
Fax: (413) 734-7845
E-mail: info@davisfdn.org
Web Site: www.davisfdn.org

FOUNDED: 1970

AREAS OF INTEREST:
Community, social services and early education.

TYPE:
Capital grants; General operating grants; Project/program grants.

PURPOSE:
To make strategically significant investments in organizations and projects that promise demonstrable long-range benefits improving the quality of life of citizens residing in Hampden County, MA.

LEGAL BASIS:
Private foundation.

ELIGIBILITY:
Grants are made to organizations that have tax-exempt status under Section 501(c)(3) of the Internal Revenue Code. Catholic organizations may apply. No grants are made to individuals.

GEOG. RESTRICTIONS: Hampden County, Massachusetts.

FINANCIAL DATA:
Amount of support per award: Varies.
Total amount of support: Varies.

NO. MOST RECENT APPLICANTS: 200.

NO. AWARDS: 125.

APPLICATION INFO:
Guidelines and application form are available on the Foundation web site. An initial Letter of Inquiry is required to determine the interest and appropriateness of a full proposal.
Duration: Typically one year.
Deadline: Proposals are accepted throughout the year.

ADDRESS INQUIRIES TO:
See telephone number above.

DEARBORN COMMUNITY FOUNDATION, INC.   [1138]
322 Walnut Street
Lawrenceburg, IN 47025
(812) 539-4115
E-mail: fmccarter@dearborncf.org
Web Site: www.dearborncf.org

FOUNDED: 1997

AREAS OF INTEREST:
Art, culture and humanities, community and public benefit, education, environment and animal protection, human services, public safety, and youth programs.

TYPE:
Capital grants; Challenge/matching grants; Development grants; General operating grants; Project/program grants; Scholarships; Seed money grants; Technical assistance; Training grants.

YEAR PROGRAM STARTED: 1997

PURPOSE:
To connect people who care with causes that improve the quality of life in the community by advancing cultural, educational and social opportunities, while preserving the community's heritage and helping donors create a permanent legacy in Dearborn County, IN.

ELIGIBILITY:
Grants are made to organizations that are tax-exempt under Section 501(c)(3) of the Internal Revenue Code and recognized by the state of Indiana as current and active not-for-profit organizations. No grants are made to individuals outside of scholarships and/or educational grants. Nonsectarian religious programs may apply.

GEOG. RESTRICTIONS: Dearborn County, Indiana.

FINANCIAL DATA:
Amount of support per award: Varies.

APPLICATION INFO:
Applications are submitted online.
Duration: One year.
Deadline: Varies.

STAFF:
Fred McCarter, Executive Director

ADDRESS INQUIRIES TO:
Fred McCarter, Executive Director
(See address above.)

DELAWARE COUNTY FOUNDATION   [1139]
737 Enterprise Drive
Suite A
Lewis Center, OH 43035
(614) 764-2332
Fax: (614) 764-2333
E-mail: foundation@delawarecf.org
Web Site: www.delawarecf.org

FOUNDED: 1995

AREAS OF INTEREST:
Arts, civic affairs, community needs, culture, education, environment, health and human services.

NAME(S) OF PROGRAMS:
● **Designated Funds**
● **Donor Advised Funds**
● **Field of Interest Funds**
● **Organizational Endowment Funds**
● **Scholarship Funds**
● **Special Project Funds**
● **Unrestricted Funds**

TYPE:
Project/program grants; Scholarships.

PURPOSE:
To enhance the quality of life for Delaware County residents.

ELIGIBILITY:
Grants are made to organizations that have tax-exempt status under Section 501(c)(3) of the Internal Revenue Code that serve Delaware County. No grants are made to individuals, religious programs, political groups or for deficit reduction.

GEOG. RESTRICTIONS: Delaware County, Ohio.

FINANCIAL DATA:
Amount of support per award: $400 to $200,000.
Total amount of support: $1,158,559 in grants and scholarships for the year 2020.

NO. AWARDS: 201 grants and 174 scholarships for the year 2020.

APPLICATION INFO:
Information may be obtained from the Foundation web site.
Duration: Typically one year.
Deadline: Grants: July 10. Scholarships: February 15 and June 1.

STAFF:
Chris Baker, President and Chief Executive Officer

ADDRESS INQUIRIES TO:
See e-mail address above.

CHIEF JUSTICE ROGER L. DELL AND AGNES C. DELL CHARITABLE TRUST   [1140]
800 Nicollet Mall
Suite 800
Minneapolis, MN 55402
(855) 452-4015
E-mail: charitableservicesgroupmpls@usbank.com

AREAS OF INTEREST:
Arts and culture, education and youth in the Fergus Falls, MN region.

TYPE:
Capital grants; General operating grants; Project/program grants.

PURPOSE:
To improve the quality of life in Fergus Falls, MN and the surrounding area.

ELIGIBILITY:
Eligible organizations must be IRS 501(c)(3) tax-exempt.

GEOG. RESTRICTIONS: Fergus Falls, Minnesota and the surrounding area.

FINANCIAL DATA:
Amount of support per award: Varies.
Total amount of support: Varies.

APPLICATION INFO:
Application should be submitted in writing outlining the nature of the request.
Deadline: Varies.

ADDRESS INQUIRIES TO:
Matt McGovern
Pemberton Sorlie Rufer Kershner PLLP
110 North Mill Street
P.O. Box 866
Fergus Falls, MN 56538-0866

*SPECIAL STIPULATIONS:
Unsolicited proposals not accepted.

DEPAUW UNIVERSITY INTERNATIONAL BONNER SCHOLARSHIP   [1141]
204 East Seminary Street
Greencastle, IN 46135
(765) 658-4187
(800) 447-2495
Fax: (765) 658-4137
E-mail: financialaid@depauw.edu

AREAS OF INTEREST:
Leadership and community service.

NAME(S) OF PROGRAMS:
● **Bonner Scholarship**

TYPE:
Scholarships.

PURPOSE:
To encourage youth to become actively involved in the community around them.

ELIGIBILITY:
Selection is based on academic achievement, commitment to community service, and leadership.

Women, ethnic minorities, and high-need students are encouraged to apply.

GEOG. RESTRICTIONS: United States.

FINANCIAL DATA:
Amount of support per award: $3,000.

CO-OP FUNDING PROGRAMS: Corella and Bertram F. Bonner Foundation.

NO. MOST RECENT APPLICANTS: 125.

NO. AWARDS: 20.

APPLICATION INFO:
Details are available on the DePauw University web site.
Duration: Four years.
Deadline: March 1 for early consideration; however, applications will be received until all selections are made.

ADDRESS INQUIRIES TO:
DePauw University Office of Admission
Bonner Scholarship Program
Greencastle, IN 46135-1778

*SPECIAL STIPULATIONS:
Bonner scholars are expected to maintain good academic standing at DePauw (2.5 grade point average or better), participate in educational and enrichment activities, successfully complete the Bonner Program First-Year Student Seminar, as well as participate in community-service programs for an average of eight hours per week during the school year, and complete two summer internships consisting of 280 hours each.

DICKINSON AREA COMMUNITY FOUNDATION [1142]
333 South Stephenson Avenue
Suite 204
Iron Mountain, MI 49801
(906) 774-3131
Fax: (906) 774-7640
E-mail: tjuul@dickinsonareacf.org
information@dickinsonareacf.org
Web Site: www.dickinsonareacommunityfoundation.org

FOUNDED: 1995

AREAS OF INTEREST:
Arts, community needs and development, culture, education, environment, health and human services.

TYPE:
Grants-in-aid; Scholarships.

PURPOSE:
To encourage philanthropic investment in Dickinson County and surrounding Wisconsin communities.

LEGAL BASIS:
501(c)(3) tax-exempt organization.

ELIGIBILITY:
Grants are made to organizations that have tax-exempt status under Section 501(c)(3) of the Internal Revenue Code. No grants are made to individuals. Nonsectarian religious programs may apply.

GEOG. RESTRICTIONS: Dickinson County, Michigan and surrounding Wisconsin and Michigan communities.

FINANCIAL DATA:
Amount of support per award: Varies by fund or scholarship.
Total amount of support: Varies.

APPLICATION INFO:
When grants are available, application information is available on the web site.

Scholarship applicants can apply at their local schools.
Duration: One year.
Deadline: Scholarships: March 15. Grants: October 15.

PUBLICATIONS:
Brochures.

ADDRESS INQUIRIES TO:
Tamara Juul, Executive Director
(See address above.)

THE DIXON FOUNDATION [1143]
One Chase Corporate Center
Suite 400
Birmingham, AL 35244-7001
(205) 313-6501
E-mail: joy.levio@dixon-group.com

FOUNDED: 1986

AREAS OF INTEREST:
Local community.

TYPE:
General operating grants.

PURPOSE:
To support social services in northern Alabama and northern Georgia.

ELIGIBILITY:
Eligible organizations must be IRS 501(c)(3) tax-exempt. No funding to individuals.

GEOG. RESTRICTIONS: Central Alabama and northern Georgia.

FINANCIAL DATA:
Amount of support per award: Varies.

APPLICATION INFO:
Applicants should send in a brief summary, budget, and copy of IRS 501(c)(3) tax determination letter.
Duration: One year. Grants renewable by reapplication.
Deadline: September 30.

ADDRESS INQUIRIES TO:
Joy Levio, Vice President and Treasurer
(See address above.)

THE JEAN AND LOUIS DREYFUS FOUNDATION, INC. [1144]
64 West 48th Street
Suite 1408
New York, NY 10036
(212) 599-1931
Fax: (646) 992-8091
E-mail: jk@jldreyfus.org
Web Site: www.jldreyfus.org

FOUNDED: 1979

AREAS OF INTEREST:
Aging and disadvantaged, arts-in-education, education and literacy, and social services.

TYPE:
Challenge/matching grants; General operating grants; Project/program grants. Funding to direct-service organizations and those projects which will produce systemic change.

PURPOSE:
To enhance the quality of life of New Yorkers, particularly the aging and disadvantaged.

ELIGIBILITY:
Nonprofit 501(c)(3) direct-service organizations focusing on enhancing the quality of life of New Yorkers.

GEOG. RESTRICTIONS: New York City (five boroughs), New York.

FINANCIAL DATA:
Total amount of support: $745,300 in grants for the year 2020.

NO. AWARDS: 48.

APPLICATION INFO:
Initially, a two-page letter of inquiry describing the grantee organization and outlining the project in question. Letters should be sent by e-mail to the attention of Jessica Keuskamp, Executive Director.

Letters of inquiry from organizations not previously funded are not being accepted at this time.
Duration: One year. Must reapply.
Deadline: Letter of Inquiry: January 15 and July 15.

ADDRESS INQUIRIES TO:
Jessica Keuskamp, Executive Director
(See address above.)

*PLEASE NOTE:
Do not send unsolicited printed materials.

DULUTH SUPERIOR AREA COMMUNITY FOUNDATION [1145]
324 West Superior Street
Suite 700
Duluth, MN 55802
(218) 726-0232
Fax: (218) 726-0257
E-mail: grantsinfo@dsacommunityfoundation.com
Web Site: www.dsacommunityfoundation.org

FOUNDED: 1982

AREAS OF INTEREST:
Arts, community and economic development, education, environment and human services.

TYPE:
Challenge/matching grants; Development grants; Project/program grants; Scholarships; Seed money grants.

YEAR PROGRAM STARTED: 1983

PURPOSE:
To improve the quality of life in Duluth, Superior and surrounding counties.

LEGAL BASIS:
Community foundation.

ELIGIBILITY:
Eligible organizations must be IRS 501(c)(3) tax-exempt.

GEOG. RESTRICTIONS: Aitkin, Carlton, Cook, Itasca, Koochiching, Lake and St. Louis counties, Minnesota; Ashland, Bayfield and Douglas counties, Wisconsin.

FINANCIAL DATA:
Amount of support per award: Varies.
Total amount of support: Varies.

APPLICATION INFO:
Information regarding the inquiry process is available online.
Duration: Grants: Usually one year. Nonrenewable. Scholarships: One year. Most are renewable.
Deadline: Varies according to program.

PUBLICATIONS:
Elements, newsletter; annual report.

ADDRESS INQUIRIES TO:
See e-mail address above.

THE JOHN G. DUNCAN TRUST [1146]
c/o Wells Fargo Wealth Management
100 North Main Street, 6th Floor
MAC D4001-065
Winston-Salem, NC 27101
(888) 235-4351
Fax: (877) 746-5889
E-mail: grantadministration@wellsfargo.com
Web Site: www.wellsfargo.com/private-foundations/duncan-charitable-trust

FOUNDED: 1955

AREAS OF INTEREST:
Animals, environment, culture and humanities, human services, health, education, religion, arts and public/society benefit.

TYPE:
Project/program grants.

YEAR PROGRAM STARTED: 1956

PURPOSE:
To support charitable, benevolent, educational and religious purposes within the state of Colorado.

LEGAL BASIS:
Private foundation.

ELIGIBILITY:
501(c)(3) tax-exempt organizations in Colorado may apply. Grants are not made for individuals, general operating expenses, endowments, organizations outside of Colorado, or other grantmaking organizations.

Organizations receiving a grant are not eligible to apply for a grant in the following calendar year.

GEOG. RESTRICTIONS: Colorado.

FINANCIAL DATA:
Amount of support per award: Average grant $10,000 to $20,000.

Total amount of support: Approximately $300,000 per year.

APPLICATION INFO:
Applications must be submitted online during the application periods for specific program areas in order to be reviewed at the grant meetings held after each application deadline date.

Duration: No grants are made on a continuing basis.

Deadline: Arts, Culture, Humanities and Education: March 31. Environment, Animals and Human Services: June 30. Health, Public/Society Benefit and Religion: September 30.

ADDRESS INQUIRIES TO:
See e-mail address above.

*SPECIAL STIPULATIONS:
Periodic progress reports and final reports may be required for funded projects.

THE EAST BAY COMMUNITY FOUNDATION [1147]
De Domenico Building
200 Frank H. Ogawa Plaza
Oakland, CA 94612
(510) 836-3223
Fax: (510) 836-7418
E-mail: grantmaking@eastbaycf.org
Web Site: www.ebcf.org

FOUNDED: 1928

AREAS OF INTEREST:
Early childhood success, arts and environment, economic empowerment, and policy advocacy and civic engagement.

TYPE:
Project/program grants. Building leadership capacity grants.

YEAR PROGRAM STARTED: 1928

PURPOSE:
To transform the lives of people in the East Bay with pressing needs.

LEGAL BASIS:
Public foundation.

ELIGIBILITY:
Eligible organizations must be IRS 501(c)(3) tax-exempt.

GEOG. RESTRICTIONS: Alameda and Contra Costa counties, California.

FINANCIAL DATA:
Amount of support per award: Varies.

Total amount of support: Over $69,000,000 in grants and over $46,000 in scholarships for the year 2019.

APPLICATION INFO:
Guidelines and application are available online.

Duration: Varies.

PUBLICATIONS:
Guidelines.

EAST TEXAS COMMUNITIES FOUNDATION [1148]
315 North Broadway Avenue
Suite 210
Tyler, TX 75702-5712
(903) 533-0208
Fax: (903) 533-0258
E-mail: ddurman@etcf.org
Web Site: etcf.org

FOUNDED: 1989

AREAS OF INTEREST:
Community development.

TYPE:
Grants-in-aid; Scholarships. The Foundation administers scholarship funds for donors, nonprofit organizations, civic clubs, service groups and businesses.

PURPOSE:
To promote charitable giving which enhances the quality of life for the people of east Texas.

ELIGIBILITY:
Grants are made to 501(c)(3) organizations. Scholarship applicants must be citizens or permanent residents of the U.S.

GEOG. RESTRICTIONS: East Texas.

FINANCIAL DATA:
Amount of support per award: Varies.

Total amount of support: Varies.

APPLICATION INFO:
Application information is available on the web site. Scholarship applications must be submitted electronically.

Duration: Varies.

Deadline: Varies.

ADDRESS INQUIRIES TO:
Dana Durman, Program Officer
(See address above.)

EAU CLAIRE COMMUNITY FOUNDATION [1149]
306 South Barstow Street, Suite 104
Eau Claire, WI 54701
(715) 552-3801
Fax: (715) 552-3802
E-mail: info@eccfwi.org
Web Site: www.eccfwi.org

FOUNDED: 1997

AREAS OF INTEREST:
Serving the charitable needs of the Eau Claire, WI area.

TYPE:
Project/program grants.

YEAR PROGRAM STARTED: 1997

PURPOSE:
To strengthen our community by offering donors opportunities to establish charitable legacies, by making grants, and by serving as a catalyst to address community needs.

LEGAL BASIS:
Nonprofit community foundation.

ELIGIBILITY:
Eligible organizations must have 501(c)(3) status. Grants are available to religious organizations when recipients of services are not required to profess membership or belief in the religious organization.

GEOG. RESTRICTIONS: Eau Claire County, Wisconsin.

FINANCIAL DATA:
Amount of support per award: Varies.

Total amount of support: $2,500,000 (unaudited) for the year 2019.

CO-OP FUNDING PROGRAMS: Women's Giving Circle.

NO. MOST RECENT APPLICANTS: 60 for the year 2019.

NO. AWARDS: 43 full or partial grant awards for the year 2019.

APPLICATION INFO:
Application must be submitted online.
Duration: One year.
Deadline: January 15 and July 1.

PUBLICATIONS:
Annual report; newsletters.

IRS I.D.: 39-1891064

STAFF:
Sue Bornick, Executive Director

ADDRESS INQUIRIES TO:
Sue Bornick, Executive Director
(See address above.)

ECOLAB FOUNDATION [1150]
One Ecolab Place
St. Paul, MN 55102
(651) 250-2923
E-mail: ecolabfoundation@ecolab.com
Web Site: www.ecolab.com/corporate-responsibility/social/community-involvement

FOUNDED: 1986

AREAS OF INTEREST:
Arts and culture, youth and education, environment and conservation, and civic and community development.

CONSULTING OR VOLUNTEER SERVICES:
501(c)(3) organizations.

TYPE:
General operating grants; Project/program grants. Employee matching gifts.

YEAR PROGRAM STARTED: 1986

PURPOSE:
To enrich the quality of life in communities where Ecolab operates.

LEGAL BASIS:
Corporate foundation.

ELIGIBILITY:
Eligible organizations must be IRS 501(c)(3) tax-exempt.

Employee matching gifts to accredited schools only.

GEOG. RESTRICTIONS: City of Industry, California; Jacksonville, FL; McDonough, Georgia; Clearing, Elk Grove Village, Joliet and Naperville, Illinois; Huntington, Indiana; Garyville, Louisiana; St. Paul, Minnesota; Greensboro, North Carolina; Ellwood City,

Pennsylvania; Fort Worth, Garland and Sugar Land, Texas; Martinsburg, West Virginia; and Beloit, Wisconsin.

FINANCIAL DATA:
Amount of support per award: $5,000 to $60,000.

Total amount of support: $23,000,000 total giving for the year 2020.

Matching fund requirements: Must be a full-time Ecolab employee.

NO. MOST RECENT APPLICANTS: 300.

NO. AWARDS: 200.

APPLICATION INFO:
Application form is available online.
Duration: One year.
Deadline: Varies per geographic region.

ADDRESS INQUIRIES TO:
Lisa Maloney-Vinz, Program Director
Global Community Relations
(See address above.)

*PLEASE NOTE:
Requests for matching gifts must be made through the Ecolab Giving Site (employees only).

EL PASO COMMUNITY FOUNDATION [1151]
333 North Oregon Street
2nd Floor
El Paso, TX 79901
(915) 533-4020
Fax: (915) 532-0716
E-mail: info@epcf.org
Web Site: www.epcf.org

FOUNDED: 1977

AREAS OF INTEREST:
Arts and humanities, education, economic development, health and disabilities, environment and animals, and human services.

TYPE:
General operating grants; Scholarships. A charitable fund established at the Foundation by individuals, corporations or organizations.

PURPOSE:
To improve the quality of life in the El Paso region, TX.

LEGAL BASIS:
Permanent endowment.

ELIGIBILITY:
Grant request will be considered only from 501(c)(3) agencies located within or offering services to the community which includes far west Texas, southern New Mexico and northern Chihuahua, Mexico. Grants are not made to individuals or religious organizations.

GEOG. RESTRICTIONS: Far west Texas, southern New Mexico and northern Chihuahua, Mexico.

FINANCIAL DATA:
Amount of support per award: Most awards $1,000 to $10,000.

Total amount of support: $15,032,708 in grants and projects for the year 2020.

APPLICATION INFO:
The Foundation utilizes an online application process.
Duration: One year.
Deadline: Grants: February 1 and August 1.

ADDRESS INQUIRIES TO:
Bonita Johnson, Grants Manager
(See address above.)

FRED L. EMERSON FOUNDATION, INC. [1152]
5654 South Street Road
Auburn, NY 13021
(315) 253-9621
E-mail: info@emersonfoundation.com
Web Site: www.emersonfoundation.com

FOUNDED: 1932

AREAS OF INTEREST:
Education (primarily private higher education), hospital and health programs, community agencies, cultural institutions, youth and community service programs, and social welfare agencies.

TYPE:
Capital grants; Challenge/matching grants; Endowments; Project/program grants; Research grants.

PURPOSE:
To improve the quality of life in Auburn, Cayuga County and upstate New York.

ELIGIBILITY:
Organizations must be tax-exempt. No grants are made to individuals or for-profit organizations. No sponsorship of fund-raising events or political activities. Proposals seeking support solely for recurring operating expenses of an organization are strongly discouraged.

GEOG. RESTRICTIONS: Focus on upstate New York with a concentration in the community of Auburn, Cayuga County and the surrounding region.

FINANCIAL DATA:
Amount of support per award: Varies.
Total amount of support: $3,514,094 for the year 2020.

NO. AWARDS: 126 for the year 2020.

APPLICATION INFO:
All proposals submitted for consideration must be completed through the Foundation's Online Application portal or using the printable Grant Proposal Submission Form.
Duration: Varies.
Deadline: Colleges and universities: March 1 and September 1. All other proposals are accepted on an ongoing basis.

PUBLICATIONS:
Guidelines.

ADDRESS INQUIRIES TO:
Daniel J. Fessenden
Executive Director
(See address above.)

ENTERPRISE COMMUNITY PARTNERS
334 Boylston Street, Suite 400
Boston, MA 02116
(781) 235-2006
E-mail: rosefellowship@enterprisecommunity.org
Web Site: www.enterprisecommunity.org/rose

TYPE:
Fellowships. The Rose Fellowship partners community-engaged architects and artists with local community development organizations. Architectural fellows are designers with an accredited degree in

architecture and a passion for applying their skills in a community development context. Artists are defined as socially-engaged creative practitioners, teaching artists, and culture bearers working in all disciplines.

See entry 371 for full listing.

ESSEX COUNTY COMMUNITY FOUNDATION [1153]
175 Andover Street
Suite 101
Danvers, MA 01923
(978) 777-8876 ext. 133
Fax: (978) 777-9454
E-mail: c.lavoieschuster@eccf.org
Web Site: www.eccf.org

FOUNDED: 1999

AREAS OF INTEREST:
Arts and culture, education, environment, health, social and community services and youth services.

CONSULTING OR VOLUNTEER SERVICES:
Nonprofit organizations in Essex County, MA.

NAME(S) OF PROGRAMS:
● **Emergency Fund**
● **Essex County Land and Environment Initiative**
● **First Jobs Fund**
● **Fund for Excellence in Essex County**
● **Greater Lawrence Community Fund**
● **Greater Lawrence Summer Fund**
● **Greater Newburyport Fund for the Blind**
● **Institute for Trustees**
● **Merrimack Valley Municipal Business Development and Recovery Fund**
● **North Shore Community Health Network**
● **Dee & King Webster Memorial Fund for Greater Lawrence**
● **The Women's Fund of Essex County**

TYPE:
Capital grants; Conferences/seminars; Endowments; General operating grants; Project/program grants; Scholarships; Technical assistance. Capacity-building grants. Various grantmaking funds. Mostly project/program grants. Agencies can establish endowment funds.

The Foundation has 235 grant funds and 30 scholarship programs.

YEAR PROGRAM STARTED: 1999

PURPOSE:
To promote philanthropy in Essex County by managing charitable funds for donors; to provide grants and services to nonprofit organizations; to engage in community leadership activities.

LEGAL BASIS:
Public 501(c)(3) charity.

ELIGIBILITY:
Organizations offering programs and services in Essex County (MA) communities, recognized as tax-exempt under Section 501(c)(3) of the Internal Revenue Code and, in some cases, to agencies of local or state government. Organizations with a qualified fiscal sponsor are also considered.

GEOG. RESTRICTIONS: Primarily Essex County, Massachusetts.

FINANCIAL DATA:
Approximately $97,000,000 in assets under management.

Amount of support per award: $2,000 to $20,000 for competitive grants; donor-advised funds may award larger grants.

Total amount of support: Over $21,000,000 for fiscal year 2020.

NO. AWARDS: 1,701 grants for fiscal year 2020.

REPRESENTATIVE AWARDS:
$15,000 (over three years) to Raw Art Works to support after-school and out-of-school arts programs for underserved girls and women; $7,500 to Essex County Greenbelt Association to determine meaningful collectible data sets for strategic decision making.

APPLICATION INFO:
Competitive grant applications are accepted online. Scholarship applicants should inquire at their local school.
Duration: Up to three years, depending on fund.
Deadline: Varies.

PUBLICATIONS:
Annual report; newsletter; brochure.

IRS I.D.: 04-3407816

STAFF:
Beth Francis, President and Chief Executive Officer

ADDRESS INQUIRIES TO:
Carol Lavoie Schuster, Vice President for Grants, Nonprofit and Services
(See address above.)

SAMUEL S. FELS FUND   [1154]
1528 Walnut Street
Suite 1002
Philadelphia, PA 19102
(215) 731-9455
E-mail: info@samfels.org
Web Site: www.samfels.org

FOUNDED: 1935

AREAS OF INTEREST:
Refugees and immigrants, arts and community, and social, racial and economic justice.

NAME(S) OF PROGRAMS:
● **Arts and Culture**
● **Focused Populations**
● **Social, Racial and Economic Justice**

TYPE:
General operating grants; Project/program grants. In the area of Arts and Culture, the Fund invests in arts and cultural organizations whose primary mission is to preserve, strengthen and/or share social or cultural identities and traditions and those that amplify marginalized voices and perspectives in pursuit of social change.

In the area of Focused Populations, the Fund supports developing services and policies that improve integration, opportunity and advancement for refugees and immigrants or improve safety, stability and opportunity for youth in and exiting the child welfare system.

In the area of Social, Racial and Economic Justice, the Fund supports new ideas and proven approaches, including legal and other direct services for marginalized communities (excluding those that fall under one of the previous focus areas), that address social inequities, protect civil liberties and human rights, and advance diversity and inclusion within and among nonprofits.

YEAR PROGRAM STARTED: 1936

PURPOSE:
To improve conditions and opportunities for marginalized communities within the city of Philadelphia; to support services, advocacy and activities that move us towards a more socially, racially and economically just society with opportunities for all.

LEGAL BASIS:
Private foundation.

ELIGIBILITY:
Applicants must be agencies located in the city of Philadelphia. Excluded from the Fund's program of grants are contributions to national organizations, capital campaigns, scholarships, fellowships and grants-in-aid for travel, research and publication, or grants to individual day care or afterschool programs. No grants are made to individuals.

GEOG. RESTRICTIONS: Philadelphia, Pennsylvania.

FINANCIAL DATA:
Amount of support per award: $20,000 to $35,000.
Total amount of support: $2,905,000 for the year 2020.

NO. AWARDS: 142 for the year 2020.

APPLICATION INFO:
Guidelines are available on the web site.
Duration: Primarily one year.

PUBLICATIONS:
Annual report; guidelines for applicants.

TRUSTEES:
John L. Jackson, Jr., Chairperson
Fariha Khan, Vice-Chairperson
Tamer Makary, Treasurer
Dannyelle Austin
Ida K. Chen
Will Gonzalez
Pari Hashemi Magura
Michael O'Bryan

STAFF:
Sarah Martinez-Helfman, President
Tim Murray, Proposal and Budget Officer
Michelle Currica, Grants and Operations Manager

ADDRESS INQUIRIES TO:
Michelle Currica, Grants and Operations Manager
(See e-mail address above.)

THE FLINN FOUNDATION
1802 North Central Avenue
Phoenix, AZ 85004
(602) 744-6800
E-mail: info@flinn.org
Web Site: flinn.org

TYPE:
Demonstration grants; Fellowships; Project/program grants; Scholarships; Seed money grants. The arts and culture grants program assists Arizona's large arts and culture organizations in generating capital through creative programming and fiscal planning.

The Foundation's biosciences grant projects aim to strengthen Arizona's biosciences infrastructure and thereby improve the state's capacity to compete nationally and internationally in the biosciences economy.

The Arizona Center for Civic Leadership seeks to strengthen civic leadership in Arizona.

The Flinn Scholars Program annually awards top Arizona high school graduates full scholarship support.

See entry 111 for full listing.

THE FOUNDATION FOR ENHANCING COMMUNITIES   [1155]
200 North Third Street, 8th Floor
Harrisburg, PA 17101
(717) 236-5040
Fax: (717) 231-4463
E-mail: info@tfec.org
Web Site: www.tfec.org

FOUNDED: 1920

AREAS OF INTEREST:
Education, human services, arts and culture, children and youth, environment and community development.

CONSULTING OR VOLUNTEER SERVICES:
Offers consulting services.

TYPE:
Challenge/matching grants; Conferences/seminars; Endowments; Internships; Matching gifts; Project/program grants; Scholarships; Seed money grants; Technical assistance. Management services.

YEAR PROGRAM STARTED: 1920

PURPOSE:
To inspire giving by partnering with donors to achieve their charitable goals; to strengthen our local communities by investing in them now and for future generations.

LEGAL BASIS:
Community foundation.

ELIGIBILITY:
Eligible organizations must have 501(c)(3) status. No grants are made to individuals or religious organizations for religious purposes.

GEOG. RESTRICTIONS: Dillsburg area, Cumberland, Dauphin, Franklin, Lebanon and Perry counties, Pennsylvania.

FINANCIAL DATA:
Assets of $123,110,000 for the year ended December 31, 2020.
Amount of support per award: $3,453 average.
Total amount of support: Approximately $1,035,776 annually.

NO. MOST RECENT APPLICANTS: 452.

NO. AWARDS: 300.

APPLICATION INFO:
Applicants should:
(1) review the grantmaking guidelines for each regional foundation;
(2) contact the Program Officer to determine eligibility to apply and discuss the proposal and;
(3) submit a grant application according to the guidelines provided on the Foundation's web site.
Duration: One year. Nonrenewable.

PUBLICATIONS:
Annual report.

IRS I.D.: 01-0564355

STAFF:
Janice Black, President and Chief Executive Officer
Kirk Demyan, Vice President and Chief Financial Officer

Jennifer Doyle, Vice President of
Philanthropy and Community Investment
Michael Blymier, Marketing and
Communications Officer
Dawn Brotherton, Philanthropic Officer
Debbie Garrison, Philanthropic Officer
Andrea Iquina-Perez, Program Officer for
Community Investment
Jim Martin, Senior Financial Services
Associate
Yamit Friedman, Community Investment
Associate
Kara Gunderman, Donor Services Associate
Raeann Buskey, Marketing and
Communications Associate
Ashlee Morley, Scholarship Associate
Faith Elmes, Scholarship Coordinator
Leslie Fick, Early Education Specialist
Jeane Predmore, Early Education Specialist

ADDRESS INQUIRIES TO:
Program Officer for Community Investment
(See address above.)

*SPECIAL STIPULATIONS:
All discretionary grants must be awarded in
the five-county region of Cumberland,
Dauphin, Franklin, Lebanon and Perry
counties or the Dillsburg area.

FOUNDATION FOR THE
CAROLINAS [1156]
220 North Tryon Street
Charlotte, NC 28202
(704) 973-4500
(800) 973-7244
Fax: (704) 973-7244
E-mail: bcollier@fftc.org
Web Site: www.fftc.org

FOUNDED: 1958

AREAS OF INTEREST:
Education, human services, health and
medical research, arts, environment and
historical preservation, youth, senior
programs and social capital.

TYPE:
Demonstration grants; General operating
grants; Project/program grants; Scholarships;
Seed money grants.

YEAR PROGRAM STARTED: 1958

PURPOSE:
To advance philanthropy by serving donors,
increasing charitable giving and improving
communities in its area of service.

LEGAL BASIS:
Community foundation.

ELIGIBILITY:
Grants will be made only to organizations
recognized by the IRS as 501(c)(3) in the
greater Charlotte area.

The Foundation generally does not fund
capital campaigns and buildings, computers,
vehicles and similar equipment, publication
of books and production of videos,
conferences and travel, grants to individuals
or endowment funds.

GEOG. RESTRICTIONS: Greater Charlotte,
13-county region in North and South
Carolina.

FINANCIAL DATA:
Amount of support per award: $2,500 to
$100,000.

Total amount of support: Varies.

APPLICATION INFO:
Grant requests are submitted online. The
application must include information about

the needs to be addressed, how results will
be evaluated, and budget including other
funding sources.

Duration: One year.

Deadline: Varies.

BOARD OF DIRECTORS:
Jewell D. Hoover, Chairperson
Kendall Alley
Cathy Bessant
Chantay Bouler
Marian Steele Clark
Jesse Cureton
Al de Molina
Jada Grandy-Mock
Barnes Hauptfuhrer
Kelly Katterhagen
Kelly King
Susan Kluttz
Arrington Mixon
Janice Patrick
Chris Poplin
Ruth Shaw
Fred Whitfield

ADDRESS INQUIRIES TO:
Brian Collier, Executive Vice President
(See address above.)

FOUNDATION FOR THE MID
SOUTH [1157]
134 East Amite Street
Jackson, MS 39201
(601) 355-8167
Fax: (601) 355-6499
E-mail: iallen@fndmidsouth.org
Web Site: www.fndmidsouth.org

FOUNDED: 1989

AREAS OF INTEREST:
Improving the quality of life for residents in
the states of Arkansas, Louisiana and
Mississippi, with a primary focus on
education, community development, health
and wellness, and wealth building.

NAME(S) OF PROGRAMS:
● **Community Development**
● **Education**
● **Health & Wellness**
● **Wealth Building**

TYPE:
Conferences/seminars; General operating
grants; Internships; Project/program grants;
Training grants.

PURPOSE:
To nurture families and children; to improve
schools; to build the economy for all people
in the region.

ELIGIBILITY:
Applicants must be tax-exempt organizations
under Section 501(c)(3) of the Internal
Revenue Code.

GEOG. RESTRICTIONS: Arkansas, Louisiana and
Mississippi.

FINANCIAL DATA:
Amount of support per award: Varies.

Total amount of support: Varies.

APPLICATION INFO:
Details are available on the Foundation web
site.

Duration: One to three years.

Deadline: 12 weeks prior to award periods in
February, May and November.

FOUNDATION FOR THE
TRI-STATE COMMUNITY,
INC. [1158]
855 Central Avenue
Suite 300
Ashland, KY 41101
(606) 324-3888
Fax: (606) 324-5961
E-mail: grants@tristatefoundation.org
Web Site: www.tristatefoundation.org

FOUNDED: 1972

AREAS OF INTEREST:
Arts and cultural programs, education,
science and charity.

NAME(S) OF PROGRAMS:
● **21st Century Endowment Fund**

TYPE:
Challenge/matching grants; Project/program
grants; Seed money grants; Technical
assistance.

YEAR PROGRAM STARTED: 1980

PURPOSE:
To engage donors to build community wealth
for a stronger region.

LEGAL BASIS:
Community foundation.

ELIGIBILITY:
Priority will be given to organizations which
are 501(c)(3) and other organizations that
meet the Foundation's special charitable grant
guidelines. The Foundation does not fund
sectarian activities or individuals.

GEOG. RESTRICTIONS: Boyd and Greenup
counties, Kentucky; Lawrence County, Ohio;
Cabell and Wayne counties, West Virginia.

FINANCIAL DATA:
Amount of support per award: $500 to
$5,000.

Total amount of support: Approximately
$15,000 per quarter.

NO. AWARDS: 16 for the year 2018.

APPLICATION INFO:
Contact Foundation for grant application and
to discuss proposed project.

Duration: One-time award. Applicants may
reapply after a one-year period.

Deadline: January 10, April 10, July 10 and
October 10.

PUBLICATIONS:
Annual report; *How We've Grown*; grant
guidelines.

IRS I.D.: 61-0729266

STAFF:
Mary Witten Wiseman, Chief Executive
Officer
Kathryn Lamp, President

ADDRESS INQUIRIES TO:
Kathryn Lamp, President
(See address above.)

THE FRIST FOUNDATION [1159]
3100 West End Avenue, Suite 1200
Nashville, TN 37203-1348
(615) 292-3868
Fax: (615) 292-5843
E-mail: askfrist@fristfoundation.org
Web Site: www.fristfoundation.org

FOUNDED: 1982

AREAS OF INTEREST:
Health, human services, education,
technology, civic affairs and the arts.

CONSULTING OR VOLUNTEER SERVICES:
Management consulting.

NAME(S) OF PROGRAMS:
- **The Frist Foundation Awards of Achievement**
- **The Frist Foundation Technology Grants Program**

TYPE:
Capital grants; General operating grants; Technical assistance. The Foundation makes direct grants to tax-exempt organizations in the greater Nashville area in the fields of health, human services, education, civic affairs and the arts, with a special emphasis on vulnerable populations.

In addition to conducting a grantmaking program responsive to external requests, the Frist Foundation actively seeks out and initiates programs addressing particular needs. Among these programs are the Center for Nonprofit Management, a community-wide effort to provide specialized management training and consulting to nonprofit community organizations.

Operating grants are given to organizations that offer management assistance, training, volunteers, goods or services to large numbers of Nashville agencies.

YEAR PROGRAM STARTED: 1983

PURPOSE:
To invest its resources in selected not-for-profit organizations in the greater Nashville area in ways that strengthen their ability to provide services; to enhance unique community assets in Nashville; to develop new sources of revenue through social enterprise.

LEGAL BASIS:
509(a) private foundation.

ELIGIBILITY:
Grantees must be tax-exempt under Section 501(c)(3) of the Internal Revenue Code and not private foundations as described in Section 509(a). The Foundation ordinarily does not make grants or provide support to:
(1) international, regional or local organizations outside the Nashville area;
(2) projects, programs or organizations that serve a limited audience or a relatively small number of people;
(3) hospitals, biomedical or clinical research, or disease-specific organizations seeking support for national projects and programs;
(4) organizations during their first three years of operation;
(5) endowments;
(6) social events, fund-raising activities or telethons;
(7) individuals or their projects;
(8) political activities;
(9) religious organizations for religious purposes;
(10) private foundations;
(11) advertising sponsorships or;
(12) schools below the college level, except for projects intended to serve the broader community.

Special emphasis is placed on organizations that provide services to vulnerable populations.

GEOG. RESTRICTIONS: Nashville, Tennessee area.

FINANCIAL DATA:
Amount of support per award: $500 to $100,000. Average $3,500.
Total amount of support: $18,110,484 for the year 2020.

NO. MOST RECENT APPLICANTS: Approximately 200 for the year 2019.

NO. AWARDS: 148 for the year 2019.

APPLICATION INFO:
If an organization wishes to apply for support, it should make contact by telephone, by letter of inquiry, or by completing an application through the web site. If applying by mail, the letter should describe in no more than two pages:
(1) the organization and its record of accomplishment;
(2) the objectives of the program to be funded and whom it would benefit;
(3) the amount sought from the Foundation in relation to the total need;
(4) exactly how Foundation funds would be used and;
(5) the proposed method to evaluate the program's success.

The initial inquiry should also include an annual report, if available, and a copy of the IRS letter confirming that the organization is tax-exempt under Section 501(c)(3) of the Internal Revenue Code and not a private foundation as described in Section 509(a).
Duration: Up to three years. Renewals are not automatic. Applications from organizations supported in the past will be considered new requests.

IRS I.D.: 62-1134070

STAFF:
Peter F. Bird, Jr., President and Chief Executive Officer
Colette R. Easter, Treasurer
Corinne C. Bergeron, Program Officer

DIRECTORS:
William R. Frist, Chairman
Peter F. Bird, Jr.
Chuck Elcan
Lauren Elcan
Patricia Frist Elcan
Jennifer Frist
Julie D. Frist
Thomas F. Frist, III

ADDRESS INQUIRIES TO:
Peter F. Bird, Jr.
President and Chief Executive Officer
P.O. Box 90906
Nashville, TN 37209

THE GIFFORD FOUNDATION [1160]
100 Clinton Square
126 North Salina Street, 3rd Floor
Syracuse, NY 13202
(315) 474-2489
Fax: (315) 475-4983
E-mail: sheena@giffordfoundation.org
Web Site: www.giffordfoundation.org

FOUNDED: 1954

AREAS OF INTEREST:
Youth development, education and job readiness, and capacity building.

TYPE:
Challenge/matching grants; Conferences/seminars; Demonstration grants; Development grants; Project/program grants; Research grants; Training grants. Capacity building grants; Professional development grants; Succession planning; Technology grants.

YEAR PROGRAM STARTED: 1954

PURPOSE:
To provide funds for general charitable purposes.

LEGAL BASIS:
Private.

ELIGIBILITY:
Only tax-exempt organizations may apply. Organizations must show evidence of problems to be solved and how proposed solution will benefit constituency and the community. No grants to individuals.

FINANCIAL DATA:
Amount of support per award: Varies.
Total amount of support: Varies.

APPLICATION INFO:
The Foundation only invites community grant proposals after reviewing a letter of inquiry.
Duration: One year.

PUBLICATIONS:
Application guidelines; statement of policies; mission statement.

STAFF:
Sheena Solomon, Executive Director
Lindsay McClung, Associate Director
Sheria Walker, Program Administrator
Maximilian Eyle, Communications Specialist and Grants Management

ADDRESS INQUIRIES TO:
Lindsay McClung, Associate Director
(See address above.)

LISA AND DOUGLAS GOLDMAN FUND [1161]
One Montgomery Street, Suite 3440
San Francisco, CA 94104
(415) 771-1717
E-mail: grantsmanager@ldgfund.org
Web Site: www.ldgfund.org

FOUNDED: 1992

AREAS OF INTEREST:
Democracy and civil liberties, education and literacy, environment, health and recreation, Jewish community, and reproductive health and rights.

TYPE:
Capital grants; Project/program grants.

YEAR PROGRAM STARTED: 1992

PURPOSE:
To improve the quality of life, primarily in San Francisco.

LEGAL BASIS:
Private foundation.

ELIGIBILITY:
Eligible organizations must be IRS 501(c)(3) tax-exempt.

GEOG. RESTRICTIONS: Primarily San Francisco area, California.

FINANCIAL DATA:
Amount of support per award: $20,000 to $100,000.
Total amount of support: Generally $11,000,000.

NO. MOST RECENT APPLICANTS: 241.

NO. AWARDS: 312.

APPLICATION INFO:
Online application process. Applicants must include a copy of the IRS tax determination letter. Letter of inquiry must be submitted before proposal.
Duration: Varies.

PUBLICATIONS:
Annual report; application guidelines.

ADDRESS INQUIRIES TO:
See e-mail address above.

GOLDSEKER FOUNDATION [1162]

1040 Park Avenue
Suite 310
Baltimore, MD 21201
(410) 837-5100
E-mail: kate@goldsekerfoundation.org
Web Site: www.goldsekerfoundation.org

FOUNDED: 1973

AREAS OF INTEREST:
Community development and the nonprofit sector.

TYPE:
Challenge/matching grants; General operating grants; Matching gifts; Project/program grants; Technical assistance. Project grants and ongoing operating support.

The Foundation maintains a two-track grantmaking program that designates two priority areas, but retains the ability to initiate and respond to new ideas and opportunities within established program areas, namely community affairs, education, and human services. In each of the priority grant areas - community development and the nonprofit sector - the Foundation is a directly engaged and active partner. Grants include a mix of Foundation initiatives and projects submitted independently by potential grantees.

YEAR PROGRAM STARTED: 1976

PURPOSE:
To support programs which directly benefit the people of the Baltimore metropolitan area.

LEGAL BASIS:
Private, nonprofit.

ELIGIBILITY:
Qualified nonprofit, charitable and educational organizations as defined under federal and state laws as permissible grantees of private foundations. Support is limited to institutions in the Baltimore metropolitan area with special emphasis on disadvantaged persons, giving priority to programs intended to assist children and families and to strengthen neighborhoods.

No support for endowment, capital, deficits, annual giving, publications, religious purposes, arts and culture, specific diseases or disabilities or projects typically supported with public funds.

GEOG. RESTRICTIONS: Metropolitan Baltimore, Maryland.

FINANCIAL DATA:
No distribution in any calendar year to any single institution is to exceed five percent of the Foundation's net income for that year.
Amount of support per award: Varies.
Total amount of support: Approximately $4,200,000 for the year 2020.
Matching fund requirements: Varies with specific request.

NO. AWARDS: 143 for the year 2020.

REPRESENTATIVE AWARDS:
$100,000 to CASA de Maryland; $100,000 to Urban Teachers; $36,000 to Baltimore Community Lending; $10,000 to Digital Equity Initiative for Baltimore.

APPLICATION INFO:
Applicants must submit a brief letter describing their program. It should include:
(1) evidence of 501(c)(3) and 509(a) tax-exempt status;
(2) background information about the applicant;
(3) objectives of the proposed project;
(4) methods for accomplishing objectives and;
(5) projected program budget and amount sought from the Foundation.

The Foundation welcomes telephone inquiries about funding throughout the year.
Duration: Typically one year. Occasional multiyear grants.
Deadline: Requests will be considered at one of four quarterly meetings of the Board of Directors.

PUBLICATIONS:
Annual report; program guidelines.

IRS I.D.: 52-0983502

OFFICERS:
Sheldon Goldseker, Chairman
Deby Goldseker, Vice Chairman
Matthew D. Gallagher, President and Chief Executive Officer
Sharna Goldseker, Treasurer
Ana Goldseker, Secretary

STAFF:
Kate Essex, Program Officer

BOARD OF DIRECTORS:
Ana Goldseker
Deby Goldseker
Sharna Goldseker
Sheldon Goldseker
Shelley Goldseker
Susan B. Katzenberg
Howard M. Weiss

ADDRESS INQUIRIES TO:
Program Officer
(See address above.)

*SPECIAL STIPULATIONS:
Grantmaking is limited to the metropolitan area of Baltimore, MD.

THE GRACO FOUNDATION [1163]

P.O. Box 1441
Minneapolis, MN 55440-1441
E-mail: gracofoundation@graco.com
Web Site: www.graco.com/foundation

FOUNDED: 1956

AREAS OF INTEREST:
Education, especially STEM; workforce development; youth development.

CONSULTING OR VOLUNTEER SERVICES:
Through established community programs.

NAME(S) OF PROGRAMS:
● **Financial Grants of Support**

TYPE:
Capital grants; Scholarships. Technology grants.

YEAR PROGRAM STARTED: 1956

PURPOSE:
To help organizations grow their ability to serve community needs through grants focused on capital projects, specific programs and technology needs.

LEGAL BASIS:
Established under the Minnesota Nonprofit Corporation Act as a nonprofit corporation

under the provisions of Chapter 317, Minnesota Statutes 1953 and Acts amendatory thereof.

ELIGIBILITY:
Priority is placed on organizations that have a proven track record of enabling people to become self-sufficient and more productive, with emphasis on educational programs, especially STEM (science, technology, engineering and math) programs; human service programs promoting workforce development; and youth development programs. The Foundation especially likes to reach out to communities close to its U.S. facilities.

FINANCIAL DATA:
Amount of support per award: Varies.
Total amount of support: $1,274,679 in grants for the year 2020.

APPLICATION INFO:
New grant applications by invitation only.

PUBLICATIONS:
Annual report/guidelines available on web site.

IRS I.D.: 41-6023537

BOARD OF DIRECTORS:
Janel French, Treasurer
Charlotte Boyd, Secretary

ADDRESS INQUIRIES TO:
Charlotte Boyd, Foundation Manager
(See address above.)

*PLEASE NOTE:
Unsolicited requests are not accepted.

GRAND HAVEN AREA COMMUNITY FOUNDATION [1164]

One South Harbor Drive
Grand Haven, MI 49417
(616) 842-6378
Fax: (616) 842-9518
E-mail: info@ghacf.org
Web Site: www.ghacf.org

FOUNDED: 1971

AREAS OF INTEREST:
Arts and culture, diversity and inclusion, economic and community betterment, education, environment, and health and human services.

TYPE:
Project/program grants; Scholarships; Seed money grants. Pool of funds contributed by donors for the benefit of the Northwest Ottawa County area.

YEAR PROGRAM STARTED: 1971

PURPOSE:
To enrich and enhance the quality of life in the Northwest Ottawa County area; to link donors' interests with the needs of the community.

LEGAL BASIS:
Community foundation.

ELIGIBILITY:
Grant applicants must be charitable organizations recognized under Section 501(c)(3) of the Internal Revenue Code. Grants are also awarded to units of government, educational institutions and churches that are providing services which benefit the Tri-Cities community.

GEOG. RESTRICTIONS: Northwest Ottawa
County, Michigan.

FINANCIAL DATA:
Amount of support per award: Varies
depending on needs and nature of the
request.
Total amount of support: $7,997,765 in
competitive and donor-advised grants for the
year 2019.

NO. AWARDS: 1,358 for the year 2019.

REPRESENTATIVE AWARDS:
$100,000 to No More Sidelines for the
Building Belongings Campaign to renovate
the athletic facilities at the Folkert
Community Hub; $75,000 (over three years)
to Grand Rapids Community Foundation to
support organizations and programs designed
to combat youth homelessness; $24,832 to
Pathways of Arbor Circle for Ottawa
Substance Abuse Prevention NW Quadrant
Rebuilding.

APPLICATION INFO:
Applicant must submit Letter of Inquiry form
online. Upon staff review and determination
of project alignment with Foundation's
priorities, applicant will be prompted to
submit a full application.
Duration: Varies.
Deadline: Letter of Inquiry: November 18,
February 17, May 26 and August 18.

PUBLICATIONS:
Annual report; application.

STAFF:
Hadley Streng, President
Patty McDonald, Vice President of Finance
and Administration
Holly Cole, Vice President of Grants and
Program

BOARD OF TRUSTEES:
Chad Bush, Chairperson
Barb VanHeest, Vice Chairperson
Mark Pereira, Treasurer
Anil Mandala, Secretary
Cindy Anderson
Mary Carole Cotter
Nelson Jacobson
Keith Konarska
David Swain
Pat VerDuin
Shirley Woodruff

ADDRESS INQUIRIES TO:
Holly Cole, Vice President of
Grants and Program
(See address above.)

THE GREATER CEDAR RAPIDS COMMUNITY FOUNDATION [1165]
324 Third Street, S.E.
Cedar Rapids, IA 52401
(319) 366-2862
Fax: (319) 366-2912
E-mail: grants@gcrcf.org
Web Site: www.gcrcf.org

FOUNDED: 1948

AREAS OF INTEREST:
Arts and culture, community development,
education, environment, health and human
services.

NAME(S) OF PROGRAMS:
- **Endowment Challenge Fund**
- **Linn County Fund**
- **Nonprofit Network**
- **Organization Support Fund**

- **President's Fund**
- **Program Support Fund**

TYPE:
Challenge/matching grants; General operating
grants; Project/program grants; Scholarships;
Seed money grants; Technical assistance.

YEAR PROGRAM STARTED: 1989

PURPOSE:
To enrich the quality of life in Linn County,
IA.

LEGAL BASIS:
Community foundation.

ELIGIBILITY:
Eligible organizations must be IRS 501(c)(3)
tax-exempt, public agencies/units of
government or have a fiscal sponsor.

GEOG. RESTRICTIONS: Cedar Rapids and
surrounding Linn County, Iowa.

FINANCIAL DATA:
Amount of support per award: $250 to
$30,000 depending on fund.
Total amount of support: $11,000,000 for the
year 2019.

CO-OP FUNDING PROGRAMS: A variety of donor
advisors operate competitive funds.

NO. MOST RECENT APPLICANTS: Varies.

NO. AWARDS: 1,761 for the year 2019.

APPLICATION INFO:
Applications must be made online.
Duration: One to three years for most funds.
Renewal by reapplication.
Deadline: Approximately February 15, July 1
and October 1.

PUBLICATIONS:
Annual report; "Community" newsletter;
guidelines.

ADDRESS INQUIRIES TO:
See e-mail address above.

*SPECIAL STIPULATIONS:
The Foundation makes competitive grant
awards only within Linn County, IA and its
immediate vicinity.

GREATER CINCINNATI FOUNDATION [1166]
720 East Pete Rose Way
Suite 120
Cincinnati, OH 45202
(513) 241-2880
Fax: (513) 768-6133
E-mail: werisetogether@gcfdn.org
Web Site: www.gcfdn.org

FOUNDED: 1963

AREAS OF INTEREST:
Racial equity and justice, affordable housing
production, preservation and protection,
women's economic mobility, arts, education,
environment, community organizing and
advocacy, and safety net services.

NAME(S) OF PROGRAMS:
- **All-In Cincinnati Racial Equity Coalition**
- **Community-Wide Affordable Housing Strategy**
- **COVID-19 Response**
- **Racial Equity Matters**
- **Women's Fund of Greater Cincinnati Foundation**

TYPE:
Capital grants; Development grants;
Project/program grants. Funds for capacity

building, programmatic support, and
transformative projects addressing systemic
issues.

PURPOSE:
To lead the charge toward a more vibrant
Greater Cincinnati for everyone, now and for
generations to come.

LEGAL BASIS:
Tax-exempt under Section 501(c)(3) of IRS
code.

ELIGIBILITY:
Recipient must be a local agency in the
Greater Cincinnati area and must be
tax-exempt under Section 501(c)(3) of the
IRS code.

GEOG. RESTRICTIONS: Greater Cincinnati, Ohio,
northern Kentucky and southeast Indiana.

FINANCIAL DATA:
Amount of support per award: $1,000 to
$100,000.
Total amount of support: Over $80,000,000
for the year 2019.

CO-OP FUNDING PROGRAMS: Over 800 for the
year 2019.

NO. MOST RECENT APPLICANTS: Over 600 for
the year 2019.

REPRESENTATIVE AWARDS:
Dan Beard Council, Boy Scouts of America;
Children's Protective Service, Cincinnati
Association for the Blind.

APPLICATION INFO:
Application information is available on the
web site.

Unsolicited proposals are not accepted under
the Community Grants program.
Duration: One to three years.
Deadline: Varies.

IRS I.D.: 31-0669700

STAFF:
Ellen Katz, President and Chief Executive
Officer
Will Woodward, Chief Financial Officer
Philip Lanham, Vice President for Giving
Strategy
Ronald C. Christian, Esq., Legal Counsel

GOVERNING BOARD:
Delores Hargrove-Young, Chairperson
George H. Vincent, Esq., Vice Chairperson
Calvin Buford
Robin F. Chatman, M.D.
Thomas Croft
John Domaschko
Steven Jemison
Mike Keating
Uma R. Kotagal, M.D.
Timothy J. Maloney
Ernest F. McAdams, Jr., Esq.
David Osborn, C.F.A.
Maribeth Rahe
Dianne M. Rosenberg
Ryan Rybolt
Ann Schwister
Ellen van der Horst
Sally Westheimer

ADDRESS INQUIRIES TO:
Inquiries must be submitted through
www.gcfdn.org/submitinquiry

GREATER GREEN BAY COMMUNITY FOUNDATION   [1167]

320 North Broadway
Suite 260
Green Bay, WI 54303
(920) 432-0800
Fax: (920) 432-5577
E-mail: amberpaluch@ggbcf.org
Web Site: www.ggbcf.org

FOUNDED: 1991

AREAS OF INTEREST:
Community initiatives.

TYPE:
General operating grants; Project/program grants; Scholarships. Capacity-building grants; Donor-advised funds.

YEAR PROGRAM STARTED: 1991

PURPOSE:
Tto provide smart and effective giving tools for donors, impactful grants for nonprofit organizations and collaborative leadership around critical community initiatives.

LEGAL BASIS:
Nonprofit corporation.

ELIGIBILITY:
Eligible organizations must have 501(c)(3) not-for-profit status. Schools and governmental entities may also apply. No grants are made to individuals.

GEOG. RESTRICTIONS: Brown, Door, Kewaunee and Oconto counties, Wisconsin.

FINANCIAL DATA:
Amount of support per award: Varies.
Total amount of support: Approximately $9,000,000 annually.

NO. AWARDS: 2,000 annually.

APPLICATION INFO:
All applicants should share their ideas with the Foundation prior to the submission of a formal application.
Duration: Varies by grant program.
Deadline: Varies by grant program.

IRS I.D.: 39-1699966

ADDRESS INQUIRIES TO:
Vice President of Community Engagement (See address above.)

THE GREATER KANAWHA VALLEY FOUNDATION   [1168]

178 Summer Street
Charleston, WV 25301
(304) 346-3620
Fax: (304) 346-3640
E-mail: shyre@tgkvf.org
Web Site: www.tgkvf.org

FOUNDED: 1962

AREAS OF INTEREST:
Education, health, community economic development, basic needs, and arts and culture.

TYPE:
Project/program grants; Scholarships.

YEAR PROGRAM STARTED: 1962

PURPOSE:
To serve the greater Kanawha Valley and surrounding areas.

LEGAL BASIS:
501(c)(3).

ELIGIBILITY:
Grant applicant must be a 501(c)(3) nonprofit organization as determined by the IRS or a government entity located in or directly benefiting residents of the Greater Kanawha Valley.

GEOG. RESTRICTIONS: Boone, Clay, Fayette, Kanawha, Lincoln and Putnam, West Virginia.

FINANCIAL DATA:
Amount of support per award: Varies.
Total amount of support: $7,304,646 in donor-advised and donor-designated grants and $3,287,372 in discretionary grants for the year ended December 31, 2019; $740,612 in scholarships for the academic year 2019-20.
Matching fund requirements: Must have a match, in-kind or cash, not a specific percent.

NO. MOST RECENT APPLICANTS: Varies.

NO. AWARDS: 440 donor-advised and donor-designated grants for the year 2019; 368 scholarships for the academic year 2019-20.

APPLICATION INFO:
Applications are accepted by invitation only and must be submitted online.
Duration: Varies.
Deadline: Grants: Varies. Scholarships: January 15.

PUBLICATIONS:
Annual report.

IRS I.D.: 55-6024430

STAFF:
Stephanie Hyre, Senior Program Officer, Education and Arts
Derek Vance, Program Officer, Basic Needs and Special Initiatives
Todd Dorcas, Program Officer, Community Economic Development
Megan Simpson, Program Officer, Health
Susan Hoover, Scholarship Program Officer
Candace Krell, Grants Manager

ADDRESS INQUIRIES TO:
Candace Krell, Grants Manager
E-mail: ckrell@tgkvf.org

For Basic Needs and Special Initiative Grants:
Derek Vance, Program Officer
E-mail: dvance@tgkvf.org

For Community Economic Development Grants:
Todd Dorcas, Program Officer
E-mail: tdorcas@tgkvf.org

For Education and Arts Grants:
Stephanie Hyre, Senior Program Officer
E-mail: shyre@tgkvf.org

For Health Program Grants:
Megan Simpson, Program Officer
E-mail: msimpson@tgkvf.org

For scholarships:
Susan Hoover, Scholarship Program Officer
E-mail: shoover@tgkvf.org

GREATER KANSAS CITY COMMUNITY FOUNDATION   [1169]

1055 Broadway Boulevard, Suite 130
Kansas City, MO 64105
(816) 842-0944
(866) 719-7886
(816) 627-3417
Fax: (816) 842-8079
E-mail: info@growyourgiving.org
Web Site: www.growyourgiving.org

FOUNDED: 1978

CONSULTING OR VOLUNTEER SERVICES:
Grantmaking services.

TYPE:
Project/program grants; Scholarships. Grants in the areas of public education and life sciences and scholarships are given to make a positive support of the nonprofit sector and to promote philanthropy for the benefit of the community.

PURPOSE:
To improve the quality of life in greater Kansas City by increasing charitable giving, connecting donors to community needs they care about, and providing leadership on critical community issues.

LEGAL BASIS:
Public foundation.

ELIGIBILITY:
The Community Foundation does not ordinarily fund endowment campaigns, debt reduction, annual appeals and membership contributions, operating expenses and fund-raising projects of religious organizations, capital fund drives, including brick and mortar, land acquisition, equipment purchases, renovation or purchase of buildings, construction or the improvement of public spaces or financial assistance for individuals.

GEOG. RESTRICTIONS: Greater Kansas City, Missouri.

FINANCIAL DATA:
Amount of support per award: Varies.
Total amount of support: $464,000,000 for the year 2019.

NO. MOST RECENT APPLICANTS: 1,734 grant applicants for the year 2019.

NO. AWARDS: 841 grants for the year 2019.

APPLICATION INFO:
Unsolicited applications will not be accepted.
Duration: Typically one year.
Deadline: Varies.

IRS I.D.: 43-1152398

OFFICERS:
Deborah L. Wilkerson, President and Chief Executive Officer
Brenda Chumley, Senior Vice President of Foundation Relations and Operations
Katie Gray, Senior Vice President of Finance and Foundation Services

*PLEASE NOTE:
Unsolicited requests will not be accepted.

GREATER MILWAUKEE FOUNDATION   [1170]

101 West Pleasant Street
Suite 210
Milwaukee, WI 53212
(414) 272-5805
Fax: (414) 272-6235
E-mail: info@greatermilwaukeefoundation.org
Web Site: www.greatermilwaukeefoundation.org

FOUNDED: 1915

AREAS OF INTEREST:
Unrestricted grantmaking in the areas of strengthening neighborhoods, strengthening education, increasing economic opportunities, and promoting equity and inclusion.

TYPE:
Awards/prizes; Capital grants;
Challenge/matching grants; Demonstration
grants; Development grants; Matching gifts;
Professorships; Project/program grants;
Research grants; Scholarships; Seed money
grants; Technical assistance; Training grants.
The Foundation's unrestricted grantmaking
does not support general operations.

The Foundation operates as a community
trust, a public nonprofit organization
established to administer charitable funds for
the benefit of the people of the community. It
is composed of more than 1,200 funds, each
created by donors to serve the charitable
causes of their choice. Donors can make
grants locally, nationally or around the world.

The component funds are of several types,
depending upon the wishes of the donor
expressed at the time the originating gift or
bequest was made:
(1) Unrestricted funds are those in which the
Foundation's Board is given full discretion in
determining how income can best be
disbursed each year for charitable purposes;
(2) Field of interest funds are administered
with a particular charitable purpose in mind,
such as support of the arts, child welfare or
education;
(3) Designated funds have been established
to favor specific charitable agencies and
institutions; the income earned by this type
of fund is paid annually to a particular
agency or agencies named by the donor;
grants are usually intended to provide general
sustaining support for current agency
operations and;
(4) Donor-advised funds are those established
by gifts from individuals, foundations or
corporations in which the original
contributors make suggestions to the
Foundation Board about grant distributions.

YEAR PROGRAM STARTED: 1915

PURPOSE:
To inspire philanthropy, serve donors, and
strengthen communities now and for future
generations.

LEGAL BASIS:
Public nonprofit organization exempt from
federal taxation under Section 501(c)(3) of
the Internal Revenue Code.

ELIGIBILITY:
The Greater Milwaukee Foundation Board
welcomes grant applications from agencies
serving the people of the greater Milwaukee
community. Details regarding grantmaking
criteria are available online.

The Foundation is committed to promoting
equity and inclusion with a focus on racial
equity in its community. This commitment
applies to its grantmaking. Nonprofit board
diversity is the first of many things it
considers. Eligible nonprofits must have
board membership that is at least 10% people
of color (African Americans, Asian
Americans, Hispanic/Latino Americans and
all other persons not categorized as white by
the U.S. Census).

GEOG. RESTRICTIONS: Greater Milwaukee,
Wisconsin, including Milwaukee, Ozaukee,
Washington and Waukesha counties.

FINANCIAL DATA:
The funds vary in size from $25,000 to
$33,800,000.

Amount of support per award: $9,300
average for the year 2020.

Total amount of support: $65,610,846 for the
year 2020.

CO-OP FUNDING PROGRAMS: Nonprofit
Management Fund; Milwaukee Teen
Pregnancy Prevention Initiative Collaborative
Fund; Milwaukee Succeeds Funders
Collaborative.

NO. AWARDS: 6,922 grants for the year 2020.

APPLICATION INFO:
Applicant organization should update or add
its information to the Foundation's online
Grants Portal. Details for grant seekers are
available online.
Duration: Generally, one year.
Deadline: Funding decisions are made
quarterly.

PUBLICATIONS:
Newsletter; magazine; annual report.

IRS I.D.: 39-6036407

STAFF:
Kenneth Robertson, Executive Vice President,
Chief Operating Officer and Chief Financial
Officer
Kathryn Dunn, Senior Vice President and
Chief Strategy Officer
Janel Hines, Vice President, Community
Impact
Kristen Mekemson, Vice President,
Development and Philanthropic Services
Wendy Ponting, Vice President, Finance and
Controller
Michael D. Hoffman, Vice President, Human
Resources and Organizational Learning
Laura Porfilio Glawe, Vice President,
Marketing and Communications
Danae Davis, Executive Director, Milwaukee
Succeeds

BOARD OF DIRECTORS:
Jacqueline Herd-Barber, Chairperson
Paul J. Jones, Vice Chairperson
Wendy Reed Bosworth
Pedro Colon
David J. Drury
Susan Ela
Thomas W. Florsheim, Jr.
Cecelia Gore
Dale Kent
David J. Kundert
Gregory S. Marcus
Darryl D. Morin
Cory L. Nettles
Greg Oberland
Marie L. O'Brien
Mary Ellen Stanek
Derek L. Tyus
Gregory M. Wesley

OFFICER:
Ellen M. Gilligan, President and Chief
Executive Officer

ADDRESS INQUIRIES TO:
Laura Porfilio Glawe
Vice President, Marketing and
Communications
(See address above.)

THE GREATER NEW ORLEANS FOUNDATION   [1171]

919 St. Charles Avenue
New Orleans, LA 70130
(504) 598-4663
Fax: (504) 598-4676
E-mail: richard@gnof.org
Web Site: www.gnof.org

AREAS OF INTEREST:
Housing, environment, health, workforce
development, arts and culture, and children
and youth.

TYPE:
Project/program grants; Scholarships. The
Foundation provides start-up funds for
promising new organizations or programs. It
also funds demonstration grants to new or
established organizations with innovative
program models and offers transition grants
to nonprofit organizations moving into a new
state of organizational development.

PURPOSE:
To create a resilient, sustainable, vibrant
community for all in the greater New Orleans
region.

ELIGIBILITY:
The Foundation makes grants to nonprofit,
tax-exempt organizations that serve the
greater New Orleans area.

GEOG. RESTRICTIONS: Southeastern Louisiana
and greater New Orleans region.

FINANCIAL DATA:
Amount of support per award: Varies.
Total amount of support: Varies.

APPLICATION INFO:
Guidelines are available online.
Duration: Typically one year. Renewal by
reapplication.
Deadline: Varies.

PUBLICATIONS:
Guidelines.

*SPECIAL STIPULATIONS:
Upon completion of the funded project, or
within one year, grant recipients must
provide an end-of-grant report based on their
proposed program evaluation.

GREATER TOLEDO COMMUNITY FOUNDATION   [1172]

300 Madison Avenue, Suite 1300
Toledo, OH 43604
(419) 241-5049
E-mail: toledocf@toledocf.org
Web Site: www.toledocf.org

FOUNDED: 1973

AREAS OF INTEREST:
Education, social services, physical and
mental health, neighborhood and urban
affairs, natural resources and the arts.

TYPE:
Challenge/matching grants; Project/program
grants; Seed money grants. The Foundation
has a particular interest in providing seed
money for new programs designed to meet
emerging community needs or to expand
existing successful programs. Emphasis is
placed on programs that will:
(a) create safe, positive living environments;
(b) enable families to develop the
skills/resources needed to support and nurture
each member and;
(c) foster the development of responsible
young people who are capable of achieving
their fullest potential.

PURPOSE:
To enrich the quality of life for individuals
and families in the greater Toledo, OH
service area.

ELIGIBILITY:
Grants are awarded only to nonprofit,
charitable organizations that are IRS

501(c)(3) tax-exempt. The Foundation usually will not make grants from its unrestricted funds to support general operating budgets (or budget deficits) of established organizations, annual campaigns, capital campaigns, purchase of equipment such as computer hardware/software or motor vehicles, production of films, videos, television programs, etc., or for sectarian activities of religious organizations.

GEOG. RESTRICTIONS: Northwest Ohio and southeast Michigan, with particular emphasis on the greater Toledo, Ohio area.

FINANCIAL DATA:
Amount of support per award: Varies.

APPLICATION INFO:
Online grant application must be completed. No hard copies accepted.
Duration: Generally one year.
Deadline: January 15 and September 15.

PUBLICATIONS:
Guidelines.

ADDRESS INQUIRIES TO:
Patrick Johnston
Vice President, Community Investments
(See address above.)

THE GRUNDY FOUNDATION [1173]

680 Radcliffe Street
Bristol, PA 19007
(215) 788-5460
Fax: (215) 788-0915
E-mail: ejw@grundyfoundation.com
Web Site: www.grundyfoundation.com

FOUNDED: 1961

AREAS OF INTEREST:
Arts and culture, education and human services.

TYPE:
Capital grants; General operating grants; Project/program grants. Capital grants for 501(c)(3) organizations throughout Bucks County, PA, primarily Lower Bucks County. Operating/programmatic support only for preselected organizations primarily in Bristol, PA and other parts of Lower Bucks County.

YEAR PROGRAM STARTED: 1961

PURPOSE:
To promote the well-being of the Commonwealth of Pennsylvania, with a particular emphasis in Bucks County.

LEGAL BASIS:
501(c)(3) private foundation.

ELIGIBILITY:
Applicants must be nonprofit organizations that have public charity status. No grants to individuals or for fellowships or loans.

GEOG. RESTRICTIONS: Primarily Lower Bucks County, Pennsylvania.

FINANCIAL DATA:
Amount of support per award: Excluding two impact grants each year, average grant $2,600.
Total amount of support: Varies.
Matching fund requirements: Stipulated with specific programs.

NO. AWARDS: 7 for the year 2019.

APPLICATION INFO:
Applicants should use the Philanthropy Network of Greater Philadelphia Common Grant Form found at www.philanthropynetwork.org.

Duration: No grants are awarded on a continuing basis.

PUBLICATIONS:
Application guidelines.

ADDRESS INQUIRIES TO:
Eugene J. Williams, Executive Director
(See address above.)

GULF COAST COMMUNITY FOUNDATION [1174]

601 Tamiami Trail South
Venice, FL 34285
(941) 486-4600
Fax: (941) 486-4699
E-mail: info@gulfcoastcf.org
Web Site: www.gulfcoastcf.org

FOUNDED: 1995

AREAS OF INTEREST:
Arts and culture, civic and economic development, the environment, education, and health and human services.

TYPE:
Project/program grants.

YEAR PROGRAM STARTED: 1995

PURPOSE:
To improve the quality of life in communities the Foundation serves.

LEGAL BASIS:
Community foundation.

ELIGIBILITY:
Nonprofit organizations, 501(c)(3) tax-exempt, are eligible to apply.

GEOG. RESTRICTIONS: Charlotte, DeSoto, Lee, Manasota and Sarasota counties, Florida.

FINANCIAL DATA:
Amount of support per award: Varies.
Total amount of support: Varies.
Matching fund requirements: Varies.

REPRESENTATIVE AWARDS:
Charlotte County Homeless Coalition to provide first-year operating support for Safe House Shelter; Legal Aid of Manasota to provide free legal representation for southern Sarasota County homeowners facing foreclosure on their homes; United Way of Sarasota County to fund site coordinators who will facilitate the new Volunteer Income Tax Assistance Program.

APPLICATION INFO:
Application information is available on the web site.
Duration: Varies.
Deadline: Varies.

PUBLICATIONS:
Annual report; application guidelines.

ADDRESS INQUIRIES TO:
See e-mail address above.

HALL FAMILY FOUNDATION

P.O. Box 419580
Mail Drop 323
Kansas City, MO 64141-6580
(816) 274-8516
Fax: (816) 274-8547
E-mail: hff@hallmark.com
Web Site: www.hallfamilyfoundation.org

TYPE:
Capital grants; Project/program grants; Training grants.

See entry 132 for full listing.

HAMILTON COMMUNITY FOUNDATION [1175]

120 King Street West, Suite 700
Hamilton ON L8P 4V2 Canada
(905) 523-5600
Fax: (905) 523-0741
E-mail: grants@hamiltoncommunityfoundation.ca
Web Site: www.hamiltoncommunityfoundation.ca

FOUNDED: 1954

AREAS OF INTEREST:
Arts and culture, education, environment, health and human service, and recreation.

TYPE:
Project/program grants.

YEAR PROGRAM STARTED: 1954

PURPOSE:
To foster the growth of community philanthropy; to build and prudently manage community endowments; to provide exceptional services to donors; to address needs through strategic grantmaking and organizational support; to provide leadership on key community issues.

LEGAL BASIS:
Community foundation.

ELIGIBILITY:
Grants only to registered Canadian charities and others qualified as described in Section 110 of the Income Tax Act. On occasion, not-for-profit organizations without charitable status may be sponsored by a registered charity.

GEOG. RESTRICTIONS: Community of Hamilton, Ontario, Canada.

FINANCIAL DATA:
Amount of support per award: Varies.
Total amount of support: $11,500,000 in grants and community leadership for the year 2019-20.

NO. AWARDS: 893 grants to 318 organizations for the year 2019-20.

APPLICATION INFO:
Application information is available on the web site.
Duration: Varies by fund.

STAFF:
Terry Cooke, President and Chief Executive Officer

ADDRESS INQUIRIES TO:
Rudi Wallace, Vice President
Grants and Community Initiatives
(See address above.)

THE HAMPTON ROADS COMMUNITY FOUNDATION [1176]

101 West Main Street
Suite 4500
Norfolk, VA 23510
(757) 622-7951
Fax: (757) 622-1751
E-mail: grants@hamptonroadscf.org
Web Site: www.hamptonroadscf.org

FOUNDED: 1950

AREAS OF INTEREST:
Community development, education and social welfare.

TYPE:
Capital grants; Development grants; Project/program grants; Research grants; Scholarships. Planning grants. Grants for Vibrant Places (facilities and capital campaigns), environmental stewardship, educational success, cultural vitality, health and wellness, economic stability, and special interest.

YEAR PROGRAM STARTED: 1950

PURPOSE:
To provide opportunity for all through leadership, philanthropy and civic engagement.

LEGAL BASIS:
Nonprofit corporation.

ELIGIBILITY:
501(c)(3) nonprofit organizations that provide benefits to the residents.

GEOG. RESTRICTIONS: Southeastern Virginia.

FINANCIAL DATA:
Amount of support per award: $500 to $650,000.

Total amount of support: Approximately $19,000,000 for the year 2020.

NO. MOST RECENT APPLICANTS: Approximately 125.

NO. AWARDS: Approximately 80.

APPLICATION INFO:
Application information is available on the web site.

Duration: Grants: One year to multiyear; Scholarships: One to four years.

Deadline: Varies depending upon program.

PUBLICATIONS:
Annual report; application guidelines; quarterly newsletter.

IRS I.D.: 54-2035996

STAFF:
Deborah M. DiCroce, President and Chief Executive Officer
Robin Foreman, Vice President for Administration
Leigh Evans Davis, Vice President for Donor Engagement
Linda Rice, Vice President for Grantmaking
Vivian Oden, Vice President for Special Projects
Gina Kelly, Grants Manager

ADDRESS INQUIRIES TO:
See e-mail address above.

HAWAII COMMUNITY FOUNDATION   [1177]
827 Fort Street Mall
Honolulu, HI 96813
(808) 537-6333
(888) 731-3863 (Hawaii)
Fax: (808) 521-6286
E-mail: give@hawaiicommunityfoundation.org
Web Site: www.hawaiicommunityfoundation.org

FOUNDED: 1916

AREAS OF INTEREST:
Culture and art, natural resources conservation, education, health and medical research, human services, disability, mentoring and media, scholarships, neighbor island assistance, persons in need and the FLEX Program.

TYPE:
Development grants; Project/program grants; Scholarships; Seed money grants; Technical assistance; Training grants; Travel grants.

PURPOSE:
To build community among the people of Hawaii.

LEGAL BASIS:
Community foundation.

ELIGIBILITY:
Grantseeker must be a tax-exempt organization, either a unit of government or one classified by the IRS as a 501(c)(3) charity which is not a private foundation. The organization must serve Hawaii's people and environment and have leadership which represents the community served. It must make a request that is time-limited or has other source of future funding.

The Foundation supports innovative and creative programs that fit within specific areas. It also provides scholarships for college studies.

GEOG. RESTRICTIONS: Hawaii.

FINANCIAL DATA:
Amount of support per award: Varies.
Total amount of support: Varies.

APPLICATION INFO:
Grant and scholarship applications must be submitted online.
Duration: Varies.
Deadline: Varies by program.

PUBLICATIONS:
Annual report.

THE HEALTH FOUNDATION OF GREATER INDIANAPOLIS, INC.
429 East Vermont Street, Suite 400
Indianapolis, IN 46202-3698
(317) 630-1805
Fax: (317) 630-1806
E-mail: rmcconnell@thfgi.org
Web Site: www.thfgi.org

TYPE:
Project/program grants.

See entry 1337 for full listing.

THE HEALTHCARE FOUNDATION FOR ORANGE COUNTY
1505 East 17th Street
Suite 113
Santa Ana, CA 92705
(714) 245-1650
Fax: (714) 245-1653
E-mail: info@hfoc.org
Web Site: www.hfoc.org

TYPE:
Demonstration grants; Development grants; General operating grants; Project/program grants; Technical assistance; Training grants.

See entry 1299 for full listing.

HILLSDALE COUNTY COMMUNITY FOUNDATION   [1178]
2 South Howell
Hillsdale, MI 49242-1634
(517) 439-5101
Fax: (517) 439-5109
E-mail: s.bisher@abouthccf.org
Web Site: www.abouthccf.org

FOUNDED: 1991

AREAS OF INTEREST:
Arts, education, community needs, scholarships and philanthropy.

TYPE:
Project/program grants; Scholarships.

YEAR PROGRAM STARTED: 1991

PURPOSE:
To improve the quality of life in Hillsdale County.

LEGAL BASIS:
Community foundation.

ELIGIBILITY:
For grants, organizations must be in and benefit Hillsdale County and be IRS 501(c)(3) tax-exempt. For scholarships, students must be graduates of Hillsdale County High School, residents of Hillsdale County and citizens of the U.S.

GEOG. RESTRICTIONS: Hillsdale County, Michigan.

FINANCIAL DATA:
Amount of support per award: $300 to $25,000.
Total amount of support: Varies.

NO. MOST RECENT APPLICANTS: 15 to 20.

NO. AWARDS: 10.

APPLICATION INFO:
Applications are available at the address above and must include all required documentation, completed application according to requirements, and a copy of the IRS 501(c)(3) tax determination letter.
Duration: One year.
Deadline: Foundation Grants: May 1 and November 1.

ADDRESS INQUIRIES TO:
Sharon Bisher, President and Chief Executive Officer
(See address above.)

THE HOME DEPOT FOUNDATION   [1179]
2455 Paces Ferry Road, C-17
Atlanta, GA 30339
Fax: (770) 384-3908
E-mail: hd_foundation@homedepot.com
Web Site: corporate.homedepot.com/community

FOUNDED: 1978

AREAS OF INTEREST:
Affordable housing, sustainable community development and community affairs.

CONSULTING OR VOLUNTEER SERVICES:
Team Depot volunteer program.

NAME(S) OF PROGRAMS:
● **Community Impact Grants Program**
● **Disaster Relief Program**
● **National Partner Grants Program**
● **Team Depot**
● **Veteran Housing Grants Program**

TYPE:
Challenge/matching grants; Development grants; Product donations; Project/program grants. Environmental research grants.

YEAR PROGRAM STARTED: 2002

PURPOSE:
To improve the homes and lives of U.S. military veterans and their families; to respond to communities in disaster.

LEGAL BASIS:
Corporate giving program.

ELIGIBILITY:
Most grants are made in communities where The Home Depot operates stores. No grants to individuals, religious, fraternal, political, labor, athletic, social or veterans groups, fund-raising benefits, dinners, exhibits, conferences and sports events, charities sponsored solely by a single civic organization, courtesy or journal advertising campaigns, multiyear commitments, or organizations that are not 501(c)(3) or Revenue Canada-designated charities.

GEOG. RESTRICTIONS: United States, Canada and Mexico.

FINANCIAL DATA:
Amount of support per award: Community Impact Grants: Up to $5,000; Veteran Housing Grants Program: $100,000 to $500,000.

Matching fund requirements: Employees making contributions to recognized nonprofits may apply for matching gifts up to $500 through The Home Depot Matching Gift Program.

APPLICATION INFO:
Contact the Foundation for application guidelines.
Duration: Varies.
Deadline: Varies according to program.

PUBLICATIONS:
Brochure; *Social Responsibility Report.*

ADDRESS INQUIRIES TO:
See e-mail address above.

HOUSING EDUCATION AND RESEARCH ASSOCIATION (HERA) [1180]
581 Stargazer Way
Florence, MT 59833
(406) 580-4836
E-mail: heraballen@gmail.com
Web Site: www.housingeducators.org

AREAS OF INTEREST:
Housing education.

NAME(S) OF PROGRAMS:
● **Tessie Agan Award Competition**

TYPE:
Awards/prizes.

ELIGIBILITY:
Open to graduate and undergraduate students.

FINANCIAL DATA:
Amount of support per award: Graduate Award: $750 presented at the HERA Annual Meeting; Undergraduate Award: $250.

APPLICATION INFO:
Information and specific guidelines pertaining to all grants can be found online.
Duration: One-time award.

ADDRESS INQUIRIES TO:
Barbara Allen, Executive Director
(See address above.)

*SPECIAL STIPULATIONS:
Award is contingent upon attending the meeting and presenting the paper. Conference registration fees are waived.

HUDSON-WEBBER FOUNDATION [1181]
333 West Fort Street
Suite 1310
Detroit, MI 48226-3134
(313) 963-7777
Fax: (313) 963-2818
Web Site: hudson-webber.org

FOUNDED: 1943

AREAS OF INTEREST:
The primary concern of the Foundation is the vitality of the metropolitan Detroit community. The Foundation's Trustees have defined four specific program missions in which they will concentrate their efforts and resources: Community and Economic Development, Safe and Just Communities, Built Environment, and Arts and Culture.

TYPE:
Project/program grants.

YEAR PROGRAM STARTED: 1943

PURPOSE:
To improve the quality of life of the metropolitan Detroit community.

LEGAL BASIS:
Private foundation.

ELIGIBILITY:
The Foundation assigns highest priority of support to programs in the city of Detroit. Programs outside of Detroit generally are not supported.

The Foundation does not make grants for endowments, fund-raising social events, conferences or exhibits. With the exception of the Foundation's program for Hudsonians, the Foundation does not make grants to individuals.

GEOG. RESTRICTIONS: Southeastern Michigan, specifically the city of Detroit.

FINANCIAL DATA:
Amount of support per award: $5,000 to $1,000,000.

Total amount of support: $7,321,475 for the year 2018.

NO. AWARDS: 63.

APPLICATION INFO:
Information may be obtained from the Foundation's web site.
Duration: One year.

BOARD OF TRUSTEES:
Jennifer Hudson Parke, Chairperson
Melanca D. Clark, President and Chief Executive Officer
David E. Meador, Treasurer
Amanda Van Dusen, Secretary
Toby Barlow
Matthew P. Cullen
Stephen R. D'Arcy
Stephen Henderson
Gilbert Hudson
Joseph L. Hudson, IV
Barbara McQuade
Joseph R. Parke
Robert G. Riney
Matthew Simoncini
Reginald M. Turner
Jean Hudson Witmer

ADDRESS INQUIRIES TO:
Stephanie Armes, Grants Manager
(See address above.)

HUMBOLDT AREA FOUNDATION [1182]
363 Indianola Road
Bayside, CA 95524
(707) 442-2993
Fax: (707) 442-3811
E-mail: craigw@hafoundation.org
Web Site: www.hafoundation.org

FOUNDED: 1972

AREAS OF INTEREST:
Children, youth and families; community, economy and the environment; health and well-being; arts and humanities; native cultures; racial equity.

NAME(S) OF PROGRAMS:
● **Community Response Grant**
● **Holiday Funding Program**
● **Victor Thomas Jacoby Award**
● **Robert Lochtie Memorial Fund**
● **Native Cultures Fund**
● **School Enrichment Grant Program**
● **Senior Citizens Grant**
● **Summer Youth Program**
● **Youth Leadership Fund**

TYPE:
Capital grants; Challenge/matching grants; General operating grants; Project/program grants; Seed money grants.

YEAR PROGRAM STARTED: 1972

PURPOSE:
To support a thriving, just, healthy and equitable region through thriving youth and families, economic development, healthy ecosystems and racial equity.

ELIGIBILITY:
Eligible organizations must be IRS 501(c)(3) tax-exempt, a public benefit organization (public schools, government agencies, federally recognized tribes), or community group with a qualified fiscal sponsor.

GEOG. RESTRICTIONS: Curry, Del Norte, Humboldt and Trinity counties, California.

FINANCIAL DATA:
Amount of support per award: Varies.
Total amount of support: Varies.

NO. AWARDS: Varies.

APPLICATION INFO:
Information, guidelines and applications are available online.
Duration: Varies.
Deadline: Varies.

PUBLICATIONS:
Guidelines.

IRS I.D.: 23-7310660

ADDRESS INQUIRIES TO:
Craig Woods, Director of Grants and Scholarships
(See address above.)

INTERNATIONAL DEVELOPMENT RESEARCH CENTRE (IDRC) [1183]
150 Kent Street
Ottawa ON K1P 0B2 Canada
(613) 696-2098
E-mail: awards@idrc.ca
Web Site: www.idrc.ca
www.crdi.ca

FOUNDED: 1970

AREAS OF INTEREST:
Agriculture and environment, inclusive economies, technology and innovation.

NAME(S) OF PROGRAMS:
- **IDRC Doctoral Research Awards (IDRA)**

TYPE:
Awards/prizes. These awards are offered once a year and are intended for field research in one or more developing countries. Candidates must conduct their research in areas corresponding to IDRC's research priorities.

PURPOSE:
To support the field research of Canadian graduate students and developing country nationals enrolled in a Canadian university for doctoral research on a topic of relevance to sustainable and equitable development.

ELIGIBILITY:
Applicants must meet the following conditions for eligibility:
(1) hold Canadian citizenship (or permanent residency status), or hold citizenship of a developing country;
(2) be enrolled at a Canadian university at the doctoral level;
(3) research proposal is for a doctoral thesis and has been approved by the thesis supervisor;
(4) proposed field research must take place in one or more developing countries and be conducted for a doctoral dissertation;
(5) provide evidence of affiliation with an institution or organization in the developing-country region(s) in which the research will take place and;
(6) have completed course work and passed comprehensive examinations before taking up the award.

FINANCIAL DATA:
Total amount of support: Up to $20,000 (CAN).

NO. AWARDS: Approximately 20 per year.

APPLICATION INFO:
Applications are to be submitted online from the IDRC funding page. E-mail applications are not accepted.
Duration: 10 weeks to 12 months.
Deadline: June.

ADDRESS INQUIRIES TO:
IDRC Centre Awards
(See e-mail address above.)

INTERNATIONAL DEVELOPMENT RESEARCH CENTRE (IDRC)   [1184]
150 Kent Street
Ottawa ON K1P 0B2 Canada
(613) 696-2098
E-mail: awards@idrc.ca
Web Site: www.idrc.ca
www.crdi.ca

FOUNDED: 1970

AREAS OF INTEREST:
Research for international development.

NAME(S) OF PROGRAMS:
- **IDRC Research Awards**

TYPE:
Internships. Program provides training in research management and grant administration under the guidance of Centre program staff. Approximately 50% of the time spent on own research project.

PURPOSE:
To provide exposure to research for international development through a program of training in research management and grant administration.

ELIGIBILITY:
Canadian citizens, permanent residents of Canada, and citizens of developing countries are eligible. Applicant must be registered in a Master's or Ph.D. program or have completed a Master's or Ph.D. degree in a recognized university.

Additional requirements are available on the IDRC funding page.

FINANCIAL DATA:
Amount of support per award: $42,033 to $48,659.

NO. AWARDS: 6 for the year 2021.

APPLICATION INFO:
Applications must be submitted online from the IDRC funding page.
Duration: One year.
Deadline: Posted on the IDRC web site in June.

ADDRESS INQUIRIES TO:
IDRC Centre Awards
(See e-mail address above.)

INTERNATIONAL DEVELOPMENT RESEARCH CENTRE (IDRC)   [1185]
150 Kent Street
Ottawa ON K1P 0B2 Canada
(613) 696-2098
E-mail: awards@idrc.ca
Web Site: www.idrc.ca
www.crdi.ca

FOUNDED: 1970

AREAS OF INTEREST:
Research for international development.

NAME(S) OF PROGRAMS:
- **IDRC John G. Bene Research Fellowship in Developing Countries**

TYPE:
Fellowships. Fellowship is awarded for research on the relationship between forest resources and the social, economic, cultural and environmental welfare of people in developing countries.

PURPOSE:
To support field research in all developing countries.

ELIGIBILITY:
Applicant must meet the following criteria:
(1) hold Canadian citizenship or permanent residency status;
(2) be registered at a Canadian university at the Master's or doctoral level;
(3) have an academic background that combines forestry or agroforestry with social sciences. Applicants from interdisciplinary programs (e.g., environmental studies) may also be eligible;
(4) have approval of the research proposal by applicant's supervisor;
(5) proposed field research must take place in a developing country;
(6) applicant must be affiliated with an institution or organization in the region in which the research will take place and provide proof and;
(7) applicant must have completed course work and passed comprehensive examinations before taking up the award.

FINANCIAL DATA:
Amount of support per award: Up to $15,000 (CAN).

NO. AWARDS: 1.

APPLICATION INFO:
Application forms are available on the funding page of the IDRC web site.
Duration: 10 weeks to 12 months.
Deadline: June or July. Exact date is posted online in April.

ADDRESS INQUIRIES TO:
IDRC Centre Awards
(See e-mail address above.)

JEWISH COMMUNITY FOUNDATION OF LOS ANGELES   [1186]
6505 Wilshire Boulevard
Suite 1200
Los Angeles, CA 90048
(323) 761-8700
Fax: (323) 761-8720
E-mail: info@jewishfoundationla.org
Web Site: www.jewishfoundationla.org

FOUNDED: 1954

AREAS OF INTEREST:
Jewish life, community and health services, education, social services, arts and culture, and civic life.

CONSULTING OR VOLUNTEER SERVICES:
Center for Designed Philanthropy - consultation with family foundations and individual funders regarding the effectiveness of their grantmaking.

NAME(S) OF PROGRAMS:
- **Capital Grants**
- **Cutting Edge Grants**
- **General Community Grants**
- **Israel Grants**
- **Next Stage Grants**
- **Reimagine Grants**

TYPE:
Awards/prizes; Capital grants; Project/program grants; Seed money grants. Capital Grants: Construction and renovation projects for facilities that predominantly serve members of the Los Angeles Jewish community.

Cutting Edge Grants: New programs with the potential for transformative impact that address critical needs in the Los Angeles Jewish community.

General Community Grants: Programs by organizations outside of the Jewish community which address high-priority concerns in the Los Angeles community.

Israel Grants: Programs that have an impact on economic development and pluralistic Jewish identity in Israel.

Next Stage Grants: Capacity building support for select former Cutting Edge Grant recipients to get to the next stage of their success.
Reimagine Grants provide support for organizations and synagogues to reimagine Jewish Los Angeles in response to Covid-19.

YEAR PROGRAM STARTED: 1976

PURPOSE:
To provide endowment resources to enable the community to initiate model programs, assist agencies to address the diverse and demanding challenges to face emergencies and the needs of the Jewish community and the Los Angeles community at large.

LEGAL BASIS:
Jewish community foundation.

ELIGIBILITY:
Grants are made to nonprofit 501(c)(3) organizations.

GEOG. RESTRICTIONS: Primarily Los Angeles and Israel.

FINANCIAL DATA:
The Foundation currently manages assets of approximately 1.1 billion.

Amount of support per award: Capital Grants: Up to $200,000 over a two-year period; Cutting Edge Grants: Up to $300,000; General Community Grants: $10,000 to $25,000; Israel Grants: $100,000 to $250,000; Next Stage Grants: Up to $250,000 over a three-year period; Reimagine Grants: $50,000 to $200,000 to organizations and $25,000 to $50,000 to synagogues.

Total amount of support: The Foundation and its donors distribute approximately $81,000,000 in grants.

REPRESENTATIVE AWARDS:
$70,000 to Chrysalis for Direct Hire Program; $250,000 to the Jewish Federation of Greater Los Angeles for the Campaign for Civil Discourse; $250,000 to Project Miracle for the Miracle Masters Program.

APPLICATION INFO:
Application information is available on the web site. General Community Grants and Israel Grants are by invitation only.

Duration: Most grants one to three years. No renewals. Cutting Edge Grants: Three to five years. Reimagine Grants: One to two years.

Deadline: Varies.

PUBLICATIONS:
Annual report.

IRS I.D.: 95-6111928

OFFICERS:
Evan Schlessinger, Chairperson
Marvin I. Schotland, President and Chief Executive Officer
Abby Feinman, Vice President
Marcia Weiner Mankoff, Vice President
Harold Masor, Vice President
Scott Richland, Vice President
Mark Schwartz, Vice President
Eugene Stein, Vice President
Adlai Wertman, Vice President
Anthony Chanin, Treasurer
Selwyn Gerber, Secretary

EXECUTIVE STAFF:
Marvin I. Schotland, President and Chief Executive Officer
Daniel M. Rothblatt, Executive Vice President, Philanthropic Services
David Carroll, Senior Vice President, Finance and Administration/Chief Financial Officer
Ellen Rosen, Vice President and General Counsel
Lewis Groner, Vice President, Marketing and Communications
Naomi Strongin, Acting Director, Center for Designed Philanthropy
Natella Royzman, Director, Charitable Gift Planning

## THE KANTZLER FOUNDATION			[1187]
Pere Marquette Depot
1000 Adams Street, Suite 200
Bay City, MI 48708
(989) 893-4438
Fax: (989) 893-4448
E-mail: kathy@kantzler.org
Web Site: www.kantzler.org

FOUNDED: 1974

AREAS OF INTEREST:
Education, science, arts, culture, human services, conservation, beautification and recreation projects in the Bay County area.

TYPE:
Capital grants; Development grants; Project/program grants.

YEAR PROGRAM STARTED: 1974

PURPOSE:
To provide financial support for charitable projects and programs that directly benefit the residents of Bay County, MI.

LEGAL BASIS:
Michigan nonprofit corporation.

ELIGIBILITY:
Organizations must be IRS 501(c)(3) tax-exempt. Priority is given to projects that will have a multiplier effect upon the community. The grants must be used to finance the cost of special projects and capital improvements and not to defray current operating expenses. The Foundation will not provide the entire support for a project and will expect that others will share the costs.

GEOG. RESTRICTIONS: Bay County area, Michigan.

FINANCIAL DATA:
Assets of approximately $6,000,000.
Amount of support per award: $1,000 to $250,000.
Total amount of support: Varies.

APPLICATION INFO:
Organizations wishing to submit a grant request must first call the Foundation to register their intent to submit the request. At that time they will be provided helpful information and assistance. If the request meets preliminary qualification criteria, the applicant will be assigned a login and password to the online application form. Applications must be completed and filed online, but supporting documents, endorsement letters, financial documents and public filings may be submitted in hard copy form.

Duration: Usually one year.
Deadline: Mid-March, early June, early September and late November.

PUBLICATIONS:
Brochure.

ADDRESS INQUIRIES TO:
Administrator for the Board of Trustees (See address above.)

## EDWARD BANGS KELLEY & ELZA KELLEY FOUNDATION, INC.			[1188]
261 Whites Path, Unit 2
South Yarmouth, MA 02664
(508) 775-3117
Fax: (508) 760-3640
E-mail: contact@kelleyfoundation.org
Web Site: www.kelleyfoundation.org

FOUNDED: 1954

AREAS OF INTEREST:
Health, psychology, sociology, education, culture, and environment.

TYPE:
Capital grants; Challenge/matching grants; Development grants; Matching gifts; Project/program grants.

YEAR PROGRAM STARTED: 1954

PURPOSE:
To promote the health and welfare of the residents of Barnstable County.

LEGAL BASIS:
Private foundation.

ELIGIBILITY:
Applicants must be U.S. citizens, residents of Barnstable County, or organizations who serve Barnstable County. Grants must benefit health and welfare of Barnstable County (MA) residents.

GEOG. RESTRICTIONS: Barnstable County, Massachusetts.

FINANCIAL DATA:
Amount of support per award: Varies.
Total amount of support: Approximately $250,000.

CO-OP FUNDING PROGRAMS: Cape Cod Grantmakers Collaborative, other foundations.

APPLICATION INFO:
Grant applicants should contact Robert Talerman, President of the Foundation, for information and application forms. Additional information is available on the web site.

Duration: One year.
Deadline: Applications are accepted on a rolling basis.

IRS I.D.: 04-6039660

ADDRESS INQUIRIES TO:
Dara Gannon, Administrative Manager (See e-mail address above.)

## THE KETTERING FUND			[1189]
40 North Main Street
Suite 1480
Dayton, OH 45423
(937) 228-1021
E-mail: info@ketteringfamilyphilanthropies.org
Web Site: www.cfketteringfamilies.com

FOUNDED: 1958

AREAS OF INTEREST:
The environment, medical research, teaching, the arts, human services, and higher education.

TYPE:
Capital grants; Challenge/matching grants; Development grants; Endowments; Matching gifts; Project/program grants; Research grants.

YEAR PROGRAM STARTED: 1958

PURPOSE:
To support scientific, medical, social and educational studies and research conducted by nonprofit, charitable organizations that are located in Ohio.

LEGAL BASIS:
Private foundation.

ELIGIBILITY:
Applicants must be tax-exempt 501(c)(3) nonprofit organizations. The Fund does not support individuals, partisan political causes or candidates, public elementary or secondary schools, scholarships or travel.

GEOG. RESTRICTIONS: Ohio.

FINANCIAL DATA:
Amount of support per award: Varies.
Total amount of support: $3,698,227 in grants paid for the year 2020.

NO. AWARDS: 10 to 15.

REPRESENTATIVE AWARDS:
$40,000 to Ohio Arts Council; $20,000 to Ohio Foundation of Independent Colleges.

APPLICATION INFO:
The Kettering Fund requires a Request Summary, to be submitted online, as a preliminary step before an application is requested. Check online for availability of funding.
Duration: Varies with project.
Deadline: Letter of inquiry: Generally late January and July.

PUBLICATIONS:
Application guidelines.

ADDRESS INQUIRIES TO:
Kathy Reed, Administrative Director
(See address above.)

KEWEENAW COMMUNITY FOUNDATION   [1190]
236 Quincy Street
Hancock, MI 49930
(906) 482-9673
Fax: (906) 482-9679
E-mail: mail@keweenawfoundation.org
Web Site: www.keweenawgives.org

FOUNDED: 1994

AREAS OF INTEREST:
Environment, health, arts, recreation, and youth.

TYPE:
Awards/prizes; Challenge/matching grants; Development grants; Endowments; Project/program grants; Scholarships.

YEAR PROGRAM STARTED: 1994

PURPOSE:
To inspire giving that invests in our community's quality of life.

ELIGIBILITY:
Grants are made to organizations that have tax-exempt status under Section 501(c)(3) of the Internal Revenue Code. No grants are made to individuals. Religious programs may apply. Grants can also be given to governmental units or eligible educational institutions.

GEOG. RESTRICTIONS: Houghton and Keweenaw counties, Michigan.

FINANCIAL DATA:
Amount of support per award: Grants vary in amount, depending upon the needs and nature of the request.
Total amount of support: Varies.

APPLICATION INFO:
Information is available on the web site.
Duration: One year. Renewal possible.

IRS I.D.: 38-3223079

STAFF:
Charles Ouellette, Executive Director
Lisa Broemer, Finance and Fund Development
Andrew Ranville, Communications Coordinator

ADDRESS INQUIRIES TO:
Lisa Broemer, Finance and Fund Development
(See address above.)

KITSAP COMMUNITY FOUNDATION   [1191]
9657 Levin Road, N.W.
Suite 220
Silverdale, WA 98383
(360) 698-3622
E-mail: info@kitsapfoundation.org
Web Site: www.kitsapfoundation.org

FOUNDED: 1993

AREAS OF INTEREST:
Arts and culture, children and youth development, education, environment and animal welfare, and health and human services.

NAME(S) OF PROGRAMS:
● **Annual Competitive Grant Program**

TYPE:
General operating grants; Project/program grants; Scholarships.

YEAR PROGRAM STARTED: 1999

PURPOSE:
To improve the quality of life in the community.

LEGAL BASIS:
501(c)(3).

ELIGIBILITY:
Grant support mostly for nonprofit organizations serving Kitsap County, WA and surrounding areas.

GEOG. RESTRICTIONS: Kitsap County, Washington and its surrounding areas.

FINANCIAL DATA:
$13,400,000 in assets as of September 30, 2020.
Amount of support per award: $500 to $5,000.
Total amount of support: $80,000 in grants for the year 2019.

NO. MOST RECENT APPLICANTS: 62.

NO. AWARDS: 17 for the year 2019.

APPLICATION INFO:
Applications are to be submitted online at commongrantapplication.com.
Duration: One year.
Deadline: September 28.

PUBLICATIONS:
Newsletter; annual report.

IRS I.D.: 94-3205217

STAFF:
Shaine Schramling, Funds and Grants Officer

ADDRESS INQUIRIES TO:
Shaine Schramling
Funds and Grants Officer
(See address above.)

THE KROGER COMPANY FOUNDATION   [1192]
1014 Vine Street
Cincinnati, OH 45202-1100
(513) 762-4000
Fax: (513) 762-1100
E-mail: krogerfoundation@kroger.com
Web Site: www.thekrogerco.com/community

FOUNDED: 1987

AREAS OF INTEREST:
Hunger relief.

TYPE:
General operating grants.

YEAR PROGRAM STARTED: 1987

PURPOSE:
To feed the hungry and assist local grassroots organizations.

LEGAL BASIS:
Corporate giving program.

ELIGIBILITY:
Only proposals from 501(c)(3) organizations located in communities where the Kroger Company has operations are considered.

FINANCIAL DATA:
Amount of support per award: Typically $10,000.

APPLICATION INFO:
Grant request must be submitted at www.communitygifts.com. All requests must include a 501(c)(3) tax determination letter from the IRS.

PUBLICATIONS:
Program announcement; application guidelines.

ADDRESS INQUIRIES TO:
Foundation Administrator
(See address above.)

*SPECIAL STIPULATIONS:
Funding limited to organizations serving communities where Kroger operates.

LAWRENCE COUNTY COMMUNITY FOUNDATION   [1193]
1324 K Street, Suite 150
Bedford, IN 47421
(812) 279-2215
Fax: (812) 279-1984
E-mail: lccf@cfpartner.org
Web Site: www.cfpartner.org

AREAS OF INTEREST:
Community improvement.

TYPE:
Endowments; Project/program grants; Scholarships. Collaborative projects. Classroom grants.

PURPOSE:
To be proactive in creating and growing an enduring source of charitable assets that will help to identify and respond to the emerging and changing needs of the community.

ELIGIBILITY:
Organizations and agencies who may or may not be tax-exempt according to Section 501(c)(3) of the Internal Revenue Code or for-profit entities interested in funding a charitable, not-for profit program are eligible. Population served by the program must be within Lawrence County, IN.

GEOG. RESTRICTIONS: Lawrence County, Indiana.

FINANCIAL DATA:
Amount of support per award: Varies.
Total amount of support: Varies.

APPLICATION INFO:
Application form can be requested from the Foundation or downloaded from the web site. Applicants must submit the following documents with the application form:
(1) concise summary of the proposed project, two or three paragraphs in length, stating the community need to be addressed by the project and why the organization is qualified to address the need, the target population and estimated number to be served, the organization's experience with similar projects, and a description of how the project will fit into and further the organization's overall mission;

(2) description of the activities or steps that will be taken to carry out the project, including project timeline;
(3) summary of funding details, including how the funds will be used, as well as other funding sources. Attach a detailed budget sheet showing projected income and expenses for the project;
(4) an explanation of how the success of this project will be evaluated. If the organization plans to continue the project, explain how will it be sustained after grant funding is expended and;
(5) list of names and amounts from sources contributing 10% or more of the organization's budget in the past two years. Also list affiliations with religious groups.

Application must be signed by the organization President and another nonpaid board officer. Staple or clip each grant application copy.
Duration: Funding for a multiyear project will usually be considered on an annual basis and not extend beyond three years.

ADDRESS INQUIRIES TO:
Hope Flores, Chief Executive Officer
(See address above.)

THE JOHN J. LEIDY FOUNDATION   [1194]
305 West Chesapeake Avenue
Suite 308
Towson, MD 21204
(410) 821-3006
Fax: (410) 821-3007
E-mail: info@leidyfoundation.org
Web Site: www.leidyfoundation.org

FOUNDED: 1957

AREAS OF INTEREST:
Education, health care, arts/culture, food services, human services, children and youth.

TYPE:
General operating grants; Project/program grants.

PURPOSE:
To improve the quality of life in the Baltimore area.

LEGAL BASIS:
Private foundation.

ELIGIBILITY:
Organizations must be IRS 501(c)(3) tax-exempt and be located in Maryland. The Foundation does not fund individuals.

GEOG. RESTRICTIONS: Baltimore metropolitan area.

FINANCIAL DATA:
Amount of support per award: $1,000 to $25,000.
Total amount of support: $777,443 for the year 2020.

NO. MOST RECENT APPLICANTS: 125.

NO. AWARDS: 90 for the year 2020.

APPLICATION INFO:
Applications must include the proposed budget and a copy of the IRS tax-exempt letter. Application submission via e-mail is preferred.
Duration: Typically one year.

PUBLICATIONS:
Application guidelines.

OFFICER:
Robert L. Pierson, President

ADDRESS INQUIRIES TO:
Stacy Friedman, Grants Administrator
(See address above.)

LOCAL INITIATIVES SUPPORT CORPORATION   [1195]
28 Liberty Street
34th Floor
New York, NY 10005
(212) 455-9800
Fax: (212) 682-5929
E-mail: info@lisc.org
Web Site: www.lisc.org

FOUNDED: 1980

AREAS OF INTEREST:
Urban and rural community revitalization.

TYPE:
Project/program grants; Technical assistance. Equity. Organizational support.

YEAR PROGRAM STARTED: 1980

PURPOSE:
To support community development; to equip struggling communities with the capital, strategy and know-how to become places where people can thrive; to build sustainable communities, which are good places to work, do business and raise children.

ELIGIBILITY:
Nonprofit 501(c)(3) IRS status.

GEOG. RESTRICTIONS: United States.

FINANCIAL DATA:
Amount of support per award: Varies.
Total amount of support: Varies.
Matching fund requirements: A strict matching requirement, dollar-for-dollar of new money from local private sources.

APPLICATION INFO:
Contact LISC local offices or the Corporation.
Duration: Varies.

IRS I.D.: 13-3030229

LONG ISLAND COMMUNITY FOUNDATION   [1196]
900 Walt Whitman Road
Suite 205
Melville, NY 11747
(631) 991-8800 ext. 233
Fax: (631) 991-8801
E-mail: jdemaio@licf.org
Web Site: www.licf.org

FOUNDED: 1978

AREAS OF INTEREST:
Arts, education, community development, environment, health, mental health, hunger, technical assistance, and youth development.

TYPE:
Project/program grants.

YEAR PROGRAM STARTED: 1978

PURPOSE:
To provide leadership in identifying current and future community needs, and building a permanent endowment to address these needs.

LEGAL BASIS:
501(c)(3) or fiscal agent.

ELIGIBILITY:
Programs and projects benefiting Long Island, NY. Nonprofit organizations

headquartered outside of Nassau and Suffolk Counties may apply if the project benefits Nassau and Suffolk counties.

GEOG. RESTRICTIONS: Nassau and Suffolk counties, New York.

FINANCIAL DATA:
Amount of support per award: Generally $15,000 to $25,000.
Total amount of support: $5,500,000 for the year 2020.

APPLICATION INFO:
The Foundation has three grant cycles throughout the year. Detailed instructions are provided on the Foundation's web site. Applicants should review the instructions carefully before submitting an application.
Duration: One year.

STAFF:
Marie Smith, Director of Donor and Media Relations
Sol Marie Alfonso-Jones, Senior Program Officer
Jeannie DeMaio, Grants Administrator

EXECUTIVE DIRECTOR:
David Okorn

ADDRESS INQUIRIES TO:
Jeannie DeMaio, Grants Administrator
(See address above.)

M & M AREA COMMUNITY FOUNDATION   [1197]
1110 10th Avenue, Suite L-1
Menominee, MI 49858
(906) 864-3599
E-mail: info@mmacf.org
Web Site: www.mmacf.org

FOUNDED: 1994

AREAS OF INTEREST:
Arts, charity, civic affairs, community development, culture, education, health, historic preservation and human services.

TYPE:
Project/program grants; Scholarships.

YEAR PROGRAM STARTED: 1997

PURPOSE:
To inspire people to provide lasting legacies which enrich our communities.

ELIGIBILITY:
Grants are made to organizations that have tax-exempt status under Section 501(c)(3) of the Internal Revenue Code. No grants are made to individuals.

GEOG. RESTRICTIONS: Menominee County, Michigan and Marinette County, Wisconsin.

FINANCIAL DATA:
Amount of support per award: Varies.
Total amount of support: $500,000 in grants and scholarships annually.

NO. AWARDS: 75 scholarships in fiscal year 2020.

APPLICATION INFO:
Applications must be submitted online.
Duration: Varies.
Deadline: Varies.

ADDRESS INQUIRIES TO:
Paula Gruszynski
Executive Director
(See e-mail address above.)

MADISON COMMUNITY FOUNDATION [1198]
111 North Fairchild Street
Suite 260
Madison, WI 53703
(608) 232-1763
Fax: (608) 232-1772
E-mail: tlinfield@madisongives.org
grants@madisongives.org
Web Site: www.madisongives.org

FOUNDED: 1942

AREAS OF INTEREST:
Arts and culture, community development, environment, capacity building, and learning.

TYPE:
Capital grants; Project/program grants. Endowment challenge grants. Program grants support new programs or expansion of existing programs. Capital grants support the construction, acquisition and renovation of facilities and the purchase of equipment. Investments in technology are given to significantly enhance the organization's ability to operate or to improve services. Endowment grants are 1:2 or 1:3 challenge grants to grow agency endowment funds.

PURPOSE:
To enhance the quality of life for residents in Dane County.

LEGAL BASIS:
Community foundation.

ELIGIBILITY:
Organizations must be nonprofit IRS 501(c)(3) tax-exempt, serve the people of Dane County, employ a staff, elect a governing board, and conduct business without discrimination on the basis of race, religion, gender, sexual preference, age, marital status, disability or national origin.

Generally grants are not made for operating expenses, individuals, debt retirement, lobbying, annual campaigns, scholarships, religious organizations for religious purposes, conferences, fund-raising, celebrations or substance abuse treatment.

GEOG. RESTRICTIONS: Dane County, Wisconsin.

FINANCIAL DATA:
Approximately 25% of grant applications are funded at some level. The Foundation is rarely the sole funder of projects; other sources will be sought to accomplish project goals.
Amount of support per award: Program average: $35,000; Capital average: $55,000.
Total amount of support: Approximately $2,000,000 in unrestricted and field-of-interest grants.

NO. MOST RECENT APPLICANTS: 130.

NO. AWARDS: 70.

REPRESENTATIVE AWARDS:
Neighborhood Center STEM Project; Madison Public Library Capital Campaign; Madison Parks Foundation; Boys and Girls Club; Madison Opera.

APPLICATION INFO:
Guidelines and applications are available from the Foundation. Full proposals must be submitted in both paper and electronic form. Proposals by fax are not accepted. An online letter of inquiry (LOI) is required.
Duration: One to two years.
Deadline: Letter of Inquiry: August 1. Those asked to submit a full proposal: October 1.

PUBLICATIONS:
Grantmaking Guidelines.

ADDRESS INQUIRIES TO:
Tom Linfield
Vice President, Community Impact
(See address above.)

MARIETTA COMMUNITY FOUNDATION [1199]
100 Putnam Street
Marietta, OH 45750
(740) 373-3286
E-mail: heather@mcfohio.org
Web Site: www.mcfohio.org

FOUNDED: 1974

AREAS OF INTEREST:
Civic affairs, the elderly, community needs and education.

TYPE:
Challenge/matching grants; Conferences/seminars; Development grants; Endowments; Grants-in-aid; Matching gifts; Scholarships; Seed money grants; Technical assistance; Training grants.

YEAR PROGRAM STARTED: 1974

PURPOSE:
To support philanthropy and the efforts of citizens to improve natural, human and civic resources.

LEGAL BASIS:
Community foundation.

ELIGIBILITY:
Must be a 501(c)(3) organization in or serving Washington County, OH.

GEOG. RESTRICTIONS: Greater Washington County, Ohio, and surrounding area.

FINANCIAL DATA:
Amount of support per award: $200 to $20,000.

NO. MOST RECENT APPLICANTS: 60.

NO. AWARDS: 35.

APPLICATION INFO:
Organizations may either send a one-page letter of inquiry or submit a formal application form.
Duration: Varies.
Deadline: Proposals are accepted at any time during the year. To be considered in a particular quarter, the in-hand deadlines are February 15 and September 15. Applicants should allow 45 to 75 days for processing and response.

PUBLICATIONS:
Annual report; grant guidelines; memorial brochure.

FREDA MAYTAG-GRACE CRAWFORD TRUST
c/o JPMorgan Private Foundation Services
P.O. Box 227237, TX1-2963
Dallas, TX 75222-7237
(214) 965-2901
Fax: (800) 888-7695
E-mail: jpmorgan.pcs.grants@jpmchase.com
Web Site: www.jpmorgan.com/onlinegrants

TYPE:
Project/program grants.

See entry 1307 for full listing.

LUTHER T. MCCAULEY CHARITABLE TRUST [1200]
c/o JPMorgan
370 17th Street, Suite 3200
Denver, CO 80202
(303) 607-7810
Fax: (303) 607-7761
E-mail: julie.golden@jpmorgan.com
Web Site: www.jpmorgan.com/onlinegrants

AREAS OF INTEREST:
Economically deprived, the socially disadvantaged, mentally and physically handicapped citizens, with preference made toward the youth of the community for their educational, social, recreational and medical needs.

TYPE:
Project/program grants.

ELIGIBILITY:
Qualifying charities, agencies and institutions which direct their attention to the economically deprived, the socially disadvantaged and the mentally and physically handicapped citizens of El Paso County, CO. No grants to individuals.

Organization must provide copy of current IRS determination letter showing tax-exempt status under Section 501(c)(3) and public charity status under Section 509(a).

GEOG. RESTRICTIONS: El Paso County, Colorado.

FINANCIAL DATA:
Total amount of support: Average: $7,500.

APPLICATION INFO:
Applications must be submitted online. No physical applications will be accepted.
Duration: One year. No renewals.
Deadline: November 1. Decision by end of first quarter of the following year.

ADDRESS INQUIRIES TO:
Julie Golden, Trust Advisor
(See address above.)

RICHARD KING MELLON FOUNDATION [1201]
BNY/Mellon Center
500 Grant Street, Suite 4106
Pittsburgh, PA 15219-2502
(412) 392-2800
Fax: (412) 392-2837
E-mail: lreed@rkmf.org
Web Site: www.rkmf.org

FOUNDED: 1947

AREAS OF INTEREST:
Conservation; regional economic development; education; human services and nonprofit capacity building.

TYPE:
Capital grants; Challenge/matching grants; Grants-in-aid; Project/program grants. Grant program for improving the quality of life in southwestern Pennsylvania.

PURPOSE:
To promote conservation, economic development, education, human services and programs in the public interest.

ELIGIBILITY:
Must be 501(c)(3) nonprofit organizations. Priority is given to projects and programs that have clearly defined outcomes and an evaluation component. Funding is almost exclusively committed to southwestern Pennsylvania. Preference is given for support of established organizations with specific

objectives, and for partnering with other donors rather than solely underwriting the entire cost of projects.

GEOG. RESTRICTIONS: Southwestern Pennsylvania.

FINANCIAL DATA:
Amount of support per award: Varies.
Total amount of support: $127,591,006 in grants paid for the year 2018.

NO. AWARDS: 180 for the year 2018.

APPLICATION INFO:
Applications must be submitted online.
Duration: Varies.
Deadline: Applications accepted on a rolling basis.

ADDRESS INQUIRIES TO:
Lisa Reed, Information and Grants Manager
(See address above.)

EUGENE AND AGNES E. MEYER FOUNDATION [1202]
1250 Connecticut Avenue, N.W.
Suite 800
Washington, DC 20036
(202) 483-8294
E-mail: jward@meyerfdn.org
Web Site: www.meyerfoundation.org

FOUNDED: 1944

AREAS OF INTEREST:
Housing, employment, education, asset building, and capacity-building.

TYPE:
General operating grants; Project/program grants. Capacity-building grants. Grants for a wide variety of projects in the above areas of interest in the Washington, DC metropolitan area.

YEAR PROGRAM STARTED: 1944

PURPOSE:
To pursue and invest in solutions that build on equitable greater Washington, DC community in which economically vulnerable people thrive.

LEGAL BASIS:
Private foundation.

ELIGIBILITY:
The Foundation distributes its funds to and through tax-exempt nonprofit organizations. It does not make grants for projects that are primarily sectarian in character. Grants are seldom made for projects outside the geographical boundaries of Greater Washington and are never made to individuals. The Foundation does not support endowment drives, scientific or medical research, scholarship programs, seasonal programs, special or annual events or conferences.

GEOG. RESTRICTIONS: Montgomery and Prince George's counties, Maryland; Arlington, Fairfax and Prince William counties and the cities of Alexandria, Falls Church, Manassas and Manassas Park, Virginia; Washington, DC.

FINANCIAL DATA:
Amount of support per award: Most grants $10,000 to $50,000.
Total amount of support: $8,100,000 in grants authorized for the year 2018.

CO-OP FUNDING PROGRAMS: Occasional joint funding.

NO. MOST RECENT APPLICANTS: Approximately 425.

NO. AWARDS: Approximately 220 grants annually.

APPLICATION INFO:
Applications must be submitted online via link on the Foundation's web site.
Duration: Generally one-year support from date of award.

PUBLICATIONS:
E-newsletter.

IRS I.D.: 53-0241716

STAFF:
Nicky Goren, President and Chief Executive Officer
Karen FitzGerald, Vice President, Community Partnerships and Learning
Janice Thomas, Vice President, Finance and Operations
Jane Ward, Grants Director
Nadine Duplessy Kearns, Program Director, DC
Julian A. Haynes, Program Director, Maryland
Sonia Quinonez, Program Director, Northern Virginia
Melody Fitzgerald, Executive Office and Governance Manager
Andrew Brown, Grants Manager
Jenny Burke, Operations Manager
Edward Erskine, Finance and Operations Associate
Kari Den Otter, Partnerships Associate
Alexis Martinez, Partnerships Coordinator

OFFICERS AND BOARD OF DIRECTORS:
Charlene M. Dukes, Chairperson
Bo Menkiti, Vice Chairperson
Nicky Goren, President and Chief Executive Officer
Tram Nguyen, Treasurer
Tori O'Neil-McElrath, Secretary
Winell Belfonte
William Dunbar
David Harrington
Lidia Soto-Harmon
Karen Wawrzaszek
Ryan Young

ADDRESS INQUIRIES TO:
Nicky Goren, President and Chief Executive Officer
(See address above.)

MICHIGAN GATEWAY COMMUNITY FOUNDATION [1203]
111 Days Avenue
Buchanan, MI 49107-1609
(269) 695-3521
E-mail: info@mgcf.org
Web Site: mgcf.org

FOUNDED: 1978

AREAS OF INTEREST:
Health, culture, education and community development.

TYPE:
Challenge/matching grants; Development grants; Project/program grants; Scholarships; Seed money grants.

YEAR PROGRAM STARTED: 1978

PURPOSE:
To address the changing needs of the community in Cass and South Berrien counties; to foster a community of philanthropy, for good, forever.

LEGAL BASIS:
501(c)(3) nonprofit foundation.

ELIGIBILITY:
Eligible organizations must be IRS 501(c)(3) tax-exempt.

GEOG. RESTRICTIONS: Cass and South Berrien counties, Michigan.

FINANCIAL DATA:
Amount of support per award: Varies.
Total amount of support: Varies.

APPLICATION INFO:
Applicants may use the Common Grant Application Form of the Council of Michigan Foundations. Applications must include a copy of the IRS tax determination letter. Applications for grants and scholarships are available on the web site.

Applicants for grants are strongly encouraged to contact the Foundation for an appointment before completing an application.
Duration: One year. Most grants not renewable.
Deadline: Grants from unrestricted grant sources: February 1 and August 1.

PUBLICATIONS:
Annual report; scholarship programs.

IRS I.D.: 38-2180730

ADDRESS INQUIRIES TO:
Michael Rowland
President and Chief Executive Officer
(See address above.)

THE MINNEAPOLIS FOUNDATION [1204]
800 IDS Center
80 South Eighth Street
Minneapolis, MN 55402
(612) 672-3878
Fax: (612) 672-3846
E-mail: e-mail@mplsfoundation.org
Web Site: www.minneapolisfoundation.org

FOUNDED: 1915

AREAS OF INTEREST:
Economic mobility, arts and culture, climate and environment, education, civic leadership, criminal justice, and health and wellness.

CONSULTING OR VOLUNTEER SERVICES:
Philanthropic services for other foundations.

NAME(S) OF PROGRAMS:
- **Catalyst Initiative**
- **Fourth Generation**
- **Racial and Economic Justice**
- **Reimagine Education**

TYPE:
General operating grants; Project/program grants.

PURPOSE:
To invest the Foundation's unrestricted resources towards specific results in order to achieve social, economic and racial equity for Minneapolis residents.

LEGAL BASIS:
Community foundation incorporated in Minnesota.

ELIGIBILITY:
Organizations must advance social, economic, and/or racial equity to be eligible for funding. The Foundation grants to 501(c)(3) organizations, some 501(c)(4) nonprofits, governmental or tribal organizations, and groups organized for nonprofit purposes (informal, emerging or collaborative groups).

The Foundation does not fund individuals, organizations/activities outside of Minnesota, conference registration fees, memberships, direct religious activities, political organizations or candidates' fund-raising efforts, conferences, events or sponsorships, financial deficits, replacement of public sector funds, emergency/safety net services, regranting/loans, production of housing units, or purchase or repair of vehicles.

GEOG. RESTRICTIONS: Primarily Minneapolis, Minnesota.

FINANCIAL DATA:
Amount of support per award: Varies.

NO. AWARDS: Varies.

REPRESENTATIVE AWARDS:
$35,000 to African Development Center of Minnesota to produce affordable housing opportunities and support a more competitive workforce; $40,000 to State Voices to increase voter participation in communities of color; $50,000 to EMPOWER to recruit, prepare, train and mobilize a cohort of underserved and underrepresented low-income and communities of color across Minneapolis to advocate for high-quality educational options for all children.

APPLICATION INFO:
Application information and updates on the Foundation grantmaking cycle are available on the web site.
Duration: Varies.
Deadline: Varies.

IRS I.D.: 41-6029402

OFFICERS:
R.T. Rybak, President and Chief Executive Officer

ADDRESS INQUIRIES TO:
Community Grantmaking
(See address above.)

MIZUHO USA FOUNDATION, INC.   [1205]
Mizuho Americas
1271 Avenue of the Americas, 4th Floor
New York, NY 10020-1104
(212) 282-4192
E-mail: mizuho.usa.foundation@mizuhogroup.com
Web Site: www.mizuhoamericas.com/foundation

FOUNDED: 2003

AREAS OF INTEREST:
Community development, with a focus on affordable housing, economic development and workforce development.

NAME(S) OF PROGRAMS:
- **Fostering Economic Self-Sufficiency**
- **Mizuho Community Involvement Grants Program**
- **Mizuho Matching Gifts Program**
- **Promoting Economic Development**
- **Strengthening Affordable Housing**

TYPE:
Demonstration grants; Matching gifts; Project/program grants; Seed money grants. The Foundation awards grants to not-for-profit charitable organizations for community development programs that help sustain and revitalize economically distressed urban communities, and assist individuals who live in these neighborhoods.

Mizuho Community Involvement Grants Program makes small grants available to the not-for-profit charitable organizations with which Mizuho Corporate Bank volunteer activities take place.

Mizuho Matching Gifts Program is for qualifying contributions made by eligible Mizuho Financial Group U.S. employees to qualifying not-for-profit charitable organizations in the areas of education, arts and culture, health and community affairs.

YEAR PROGRAM STARTED: 2003

PURPOSE:
To provide grants to not-for-profit charitable organizations to support community development programs that contribute to the strength and vitality of urban neighborhoods; to serve as a catalyst for innovative programs in the U.S. that strengthen urban communities.

LEGAL BASIS:
Corporate foundation.

ELIGIBILITY:
Organizations applying to the Foundation must:
(1) be recognized as tax-exempt under Section 501(c)(3) of the Internal Revenue Code and classified as a public charity under Section 509(a)(1) or (2) of the Internal Revenue Code and not a supporting organization under Section 509(a)(3);
(2) present a proposal that satisfies the Foundation's guidelines;
(3) not discriminate against a person or group on the basis of age, race, national origin, ethnicity, gender, disability, sexual orientation, political affiliation or religious belief and;
(4) be in full compliance with U.S. anti-terrorism laws and regulations, including the USA Patriot Act and Executive Order 13224, pertaining to U.S.-based, not-for-profit charitable organizations conducting activities outside of the U.S.

The Foundation does not fund:
(1) general operating support;
(2) individuals;
(3) religious, sectarian, fraternal, veteran, athletic or labor groups;
(4) organizations or programs outside the U.S.;
(5) political organizations, political candidates or political activity;
(6) organizations whose primary purpose is to influence legislation;
(7) fund-raising activities such as charitable dinners or sporting events;
(8) advertising and;
(9) endowment or capital campaigns.

GEOG. RESTRICTIONS: New York City, New York.

FINANCIAL DATA:
Foundation's endowment is approximately $15,000,000 as of December 31, 2020.
Amount of support per award: $10,000 to $100,000; average $50,000.
Total amount of support: $640,000, including approximately $440,000 in program grants, for the year 2020.
Matching fund requirements: Mizuho Matching Gifts Program: 1:1 match for qualifying contributions. Requests for matching gifts must come from eligible employees of the Mizuho Financial Group in the U.S.

CO-OP FUNDING PROGRAMS: Neighborhood Opportunities Fund (New York City, NY) and New York City Workforce Development Fund.

NO. AWARDS: 21 grants for the year 2020.

REPRESENTATIVE AWARDS:
$25,000 to Association for Neighborhood and Housing Development to support community organizations by providing trainings that advance their skills, knowledge, and abilities to tackle complex community development issues; $50,000 to The Door to expand a program to help more young people who are at greatest risk of not succeeding in college gain admission and make a successful transition to college; $30,000 to Local Initiatives Support Coalition to support the expansion of a program that helps affordable housing developers in New York City integrate green, health measures and energy efficiency retrofits in their buildings to reduce building costs and improve the health of residents.

APPLICATION INFO:
Qualifying organizations must submit a short concept paper of up to three pages for preliminary review. The concept paper should include:
(1) a brief description of the organization including its legal name, history, mission/goals, activities and web address;
(2) copy of the IRS determination letter indicating 501(c)(3) tax-exempt status and 509(1) public charity classification and;
(3) a description of the program for which funding is sought, including statement of need, goals and objectives of the program, expected outcomes and evaluation methods, projected time frame, population(s)/geographies served, grant amount requested, and a preliminary program budget, with projected expenses and revenues, including funding commitments received to date for the program as well as pending requests (may be provided in attachment form).

The Foundation staff will review all initial submissions and invite organizations on a selective basis to submit more detailed proposals. Each applicant will be notified of the Foundation's interest within eight weeks of the annual deadline. Selected proposals are presented to the Foundation's Board of Directors, which makes funding decisions each fall.
Duration: Usually one year; some multiyear grants may be awarded.
Deadline: July 1 or first business day in July, to be considered for funding in the same year.

PUBLICATIONS:
Brochure; application guidelines.

IRS I.D.: 13-3550008

OFFICERS:
Martin Mand, Chairman
Hiroyuki Kasama, President
Paul Dankers, Treasurer
Atsushi Shibukawa, Secretary
Lesley H. Palmer, Executive Director
Albert Scarola, Assistant Treasurer
Leah Markham, Program Officer

BOARD OF DIRECTORS:
Jill Considine
Hiroyuki Kasama
Martin Mand
Shuji Matsuura
Atsushi Shibukawa

ADDRESS INQUIRIES TO:
Lesley H. Palmer, Executive Director
(See address above.)

MONTANA COMMUNITY FOUNDATION [1206]
33 South Last Chance Gulch
Suite 2A
Helena, MT 59601
(406) 443-8313
Fax: (406) 442-0482
E-mail: info@mtcf.org
Web Site: www.mtcf.org

FOUNDED: 1988

AREAS OF INTEREST:
General charitable purposes.

NAME(S) OF PROGRAMS:
● Women's Foundation of Montana

TYPE:
Grants-in-aid; Scholarships. The Foundation provides $2,000,000 annually in grants and scholarships, with almost all of that money designated. It also has a large number of donor-advised and scholarship funds.

The mission of the Women's Foundation of Montana is to promote economic self-sufficiency and a brighter future for women and girls.

PURPOSE:
To cultivate a culture of giving so Montana communities can flourish.

LEGAL BASIS:
501(c)(3) organization.

ELIGIBILITY:
Applicants must be 501(c)(3) tax-exempt organizations or an exempt government unit.

GEOG. RESTRICTIONS: Montana.

FINANCIAL DATA:
Assets of approximately $124,000,000 as of June 30, 2020.
Amount of support per award: Women's Foundation of Montana: Up to $10,000; Scholarships: Generally $500 to $5,000; Snowbird Fund: $500.
Total amount of support: $2,400,000 in grants and scholarships distributed in fiscal year 2020.

APPLICATION INFO:
Application information is posted online. Only one application per organization will be accepted.
Duration: Varies.
Deadline: Scholarships: March 18.

ADDRESS INQUIRIES TO:
Jessica Stewart-Kuntz, Vice President
(See address above.)

THE MORTON-KELLY CHARITABLE TRUST [1207]
c/o Jensen Baird Gardner & Henry
10 Free Street
Portland, ME 04112
(207) 775-7271
Fax: (207) 775-7935
E-mail: mquinlan@jbgh.com
Web Site: www.morton-kelly.org

FOUNDED: 1988

AREAS OF INTEREST:
Educational programs, cultural projects, historic preservation projects and environmental initiatives.

TYPE:
Capital grants; Challenge/matching grants; Development grants; Project/program grants; Seed money grants. One-time cash award.

YEAR PROGRAM STARTED: 1988

PURPOSE:
To support organizations in the arts, education, environment and history.

LEGAL BASIS:
Private foundation.

ELIGIBILITY:
Organizations must be IRS 501(c)(3) tax-exempt and be located in Maine.

GEOG. RESTRICTIONS: Maine.

FINANCIAL DATA:
Amount of support per award: Varies.
Total amount of support: $957,000 for the year 2020.

NO. MOST RECENT APPLICANTS: 79 for the year 2020.

NO. AWARDS: 71 for the year 2020.

REPRESENTATIVE AWARDS:
$5,000 to 317 Main Community Music Center; $5,000 to Kennebec Estuary Land Trust; $4,000 to Friends of L.C. Bates Museum; $15,000 to Maine Humanities Council; $5,000 to Penobscot Theatre Council.

APPLICATION INFO:
Application can be found on the Trust web site.
Duration: One year.
Deadline: October 1.

IRS I.D.: 01-0442078

ADDRESS INQUIRIES TO:
Erik Jorgensen, Administrative Trustee
Tel: (207) 939-7120
E-mail: eric.c.jorgensen@gmail.com

*PLEASE NOTE:
Applications not accepted before July 1 each year.

CHARLES STEWART MOTT FOUNDATION [1208]
Mott Foundation Building
503 South Saginaw Street, Suite 1200
Flint, MI 48502-1851
(810) 238-5651
Fax: (810) 766-1753
E-mail: info@mott.org
Web Site: www.mott.org

FOUNDED: 1926

AREAS OF INTEREST:
Civil society, environment, education and Flint, MI area, besides exploratory interests.

TYPE:
Challenge/matching grants; Demonstration grants; General operating grants; Project/program grants; Seed money grants; Technical assistance; Training grants. Grants for improvement of the quality of living in the community through pilot ventures in a number of human service areas. Emphasis is on improving opportunity for the individual, partnership with the community, effectiveness of community systems and leadership.

PURPOSE:
To support efforts that promote a just, equitable and sustainable society.

LEGAL BASIS:
Private foundation.

ELIGIBILITY:
Applicants must be organizations and institutions with appropriate interests. No grants to individuals. Tax-exempt status is required.

FINANCIAL DATA:
Amount of support per award: $15,000 to $250,000.
Total amount of support: $133,000,000 for the year 2019.

NO. AWARDS: 364 for the year 2019.

APPLICATION INFO:
Letter of Inquiry form must be completed on the Foundation web site.
Duration: One year; occasionally multiyear.

PUBLICATIONS:
Annual report.

TRUSTEES:
Ridgway H. White, Chairman and Chief Executive Officer
Frederick S. Kirkpatrick, Vice Chairman
A. Marshall Acuff, Jr.
Lizabeth Ardisana
Tiffany W. Lovett
Webb F. Martin
Olivia P. Maynard
John Morning
Maryanne Mott
Charlie Nelms
Douglas X. Patiño
Jeremy Piper
William H. Piper
George E. Ross
Marise M.M. Stewart
Helen Taylor

ADDRESS INQUIRIES TO:
Office of Proposal Entry
(See address above.)

MUSKINGUM COUNTY COMMUNITY FOUNDATION [1209]
534 Putnam Avenue
Zanesville, OH 43701
(740) 453-5192
Fax: (740) 453-5734
E-mail: giving@mccf.org (grants)
scholarshipcentral@mccf.org (scholarships)
Web Site: www.mccf.org

FOUNDED: 1985

AREAS OF INTEREST:
Improving the quality of life in Muskingum County, OH.

CONSULTING OR VOLUNTEER SERVICES:
Assistance to college-bound students, grantseekers and grantmakers in the Muskingum County, OH area.

NAME(S) OF PROGRAMS:
● Scholarship Central

TYPE:
Awards/prizes; Challenge/matching grants; Conferences/seminars; Development grants; Endowments; Project/program grants; Scholarships; Seed money grants; Technical assistance; Visiting scholars. Scholarships for Muskingum County, OH residents and others designated in fund agreements.

YEAR PROGRAM STARTED: 1985

PURPOSE:
To improve the quality of life and to serve the charitable needs of the community by attracting and administering charitable funds.

LEGAL BASIS:
Ohio nonprofit corporation classified by the IRS as a 501(c)(3) entity.

ELIGIBILITY:
Organization with primary or sole impact on Muskingum County, OH.

GEOG. RESTRICTIONS: Muskingum and contiguous counties, Ohio.

FINANCIAL DATA:
Amount of support per award: Varies.
Total amount of support: Approximately $1,000,000 annually.

NO. AWARDS: Grants and scholarships: Over 100 yearly.

APPLICATION INFO:
Varies per grant or scholarship.
Duration: Grants and scholarships: Varies.
Deadline: Varies.

ADDRESS INQUIRIES TO:
Brian Wagner, Chief Executive Officer
(See address above.)

NATIONAL BLACK MBA ASSOCIATION   [1210]
400 West Peachtree Street, N.W.
Suite 203
Atlanta, GA 30308
(404) 260-5444
E-mail: scholarship@nbmbaa.org
Web Site: nbmbaa.org

FOUNDED: 1970

AREAS OF INTEREST:
The economic and intellectual wealth of the black community.

NAME(S) OF PROGRAMS:
● **NBMBAA Graduate Scholarship Program**

TYPE:
Scholarships.

PURPOSE:
To help create economic and intellectual wealth for the black community; to identify and increase the pool of Black talent for business, public, private and nonprofit sectors.

ELIGIBILITY:
Applicant must:
(1) be a financially active member of the National Black MBA Association;
(2) be a U.S. or Canadian citizen;
(3) be a student entering their first year, or continuing in a full or part-time Master's program at an accredited college or university at the time of award;
(4) have a 3.0 or above grade point average;
(5) demonstrate academic excellence;
(6) demonstrate exceptional leadership potential;
(7) be actively involved in their local communities through service to others and;
(8) be recommended by a faculty member or individual familiar with applicant's academic achievements or supervisor in a business workplace.

GEOG. RESTRICTIONS: United States and Canada.

FINANCIAL DATA:
The Association has awarded over $5,000,000 in scholarships to deserving youth and minority students (undergraduate, graduate and doctoral).
Amount of support per award: Up to $5,000 for the 2021-22 academic year.

Total amount of support: Over $500,000.

NO. MOST RECENT APPLICANTS: 550.

NO. AWARDS: Minimum of 10.

APPLICATION INFO:
Application materials include:
(1) application (must be completed online);
(2) essay (500 words on the selected topic, submitted online only);
(3) current resume no more than two pages long;
(4) copy of most recent official transcript(s) uploaded and;
(5) headshot in jpeg format (image should be at least 1024 x 768).
Deadline: March 31.

ADDRESS INQUIRIES TO:
See e-mail address above.

NATIONAL BLACK MBA ASSOCIATION
400 West Peachtree Street, N.W.
Suite 203
Atlanta, GA 30308
(404) 260-5444
E-mail: scholarship@nbmbaa.org
Web Site: nbmbaa.org

TYPE:
Scholarships.

See entry 937 for full listing.

NATIONAL FOOTBALL LEAGUE FOUNDATION   [1211]
345 Park Avenue
New York, NY 10154
(212) 450-2000
E-mail: alexia.gallagher@nfl.com
Web Site: www.nflfoundation.org

FOUNDED: 1973

AREAS OF INTEREST:
Health and safety, youth football, and community.

NAME(S) OF PROGRAMS:
● **Field Grants**
● **Player Foundation Grants**
● **Pro Bowl Grants**
● **Youth Football Grants**

TYPE:
Awards/prizes; Challenge/matching grants; General operating grants; Project/program grants; Research grants; Seed money grants; Training grants.

YEAR PROGRAM STARTED: 1973

PURPOSE:
To support youth-oriented programs that promote education, physical fitness and the value of a healthy lifestyle.

LEGAL BASIS:
Private foundation.

ELIGIBILITY:
Grants will be awarded to organizations that focus on youth-centered educational and recreational programming on a national scale.

GEOG. RESTRICTIONS: United States.

FINANCIAL DATA:
Amount of support per award: Varies.
Total amount of support: Varies.

NO. MOST RECENT APPLICANTS: Approximately 1,200.

NO. AWARDS: Varies.

APPLICATION INFO:
Application information is available on the web site.
Deadline: Varies.

IRS I.D.: 23-7315236

ADDRESS INQUIRIES TO:
Alexia Gallagher, Executive Director
(See address above.)

NATIONAL TRUST FOR HISTORIC PRESERVATION
2600 Virginia Avenue, N.W.
Suite 1100
Washington, DC 20037
(202) 588-6277
E-mail: grants@savingplaces.org
Web Site: forum.savingplaces.org/build/funding

TYPE:
Challenge/matching grants; Project/program grants; Seed money grants; Technical assistance; Training grants. Education program curricula. Project grants to support consultants with professional expertise in areas such as architecture, law, planning, economics, archeology and graphic design. Conferences that address subjects of particular importance to historic preservation also are funded. In addition, grants are made for curriculum development in preservation education directed at select audiences.

See entry 564 for full listing.

NBCC FOUNDATION, INC.
3 Terrace Way
Greensboro, NC 27403
(336) 232-0376
Fax: (336) 232-0010
E-mail: foundation@nbcc.org
Web Site: www.nbccf.org

TYPE:
Fellowships; Scholarships. Academic scholarships for individuals pursuing a graduate-level degree in professional counseling.

See entry 1543 for full listing.

NEW MEXICO FOUNDATION   [1212]
8 Calle Medico
Santa Fe, NM 87505
(505) 820-6860
E-mail: edavila@newmexicofoundation.org
info@newmexicofoundation.org
Web Site: www.newmexicofoundation.org

FOUNDED: 1983

AREAS OF INTEREST:
New Mexico's communities and their people.

NAME(S) OF PROGRAMS:
● **Education and Leadership**
● **Emergency Grants**

TYPE:
Endowments; Grants-in-aid; Scholarships. New Mexico Community Foundation provides grants that help nonprofit organizations, community groups and charities statewide expand their efforts, increase their impact and advance their unique mission and vision to achieve success today and tomorrow. Although the Foundation does not have a regular open or revolving grant cycle, programmatic grant opportunities are available from time to time. It has the following program areas of focus:

Education and Leadership: Included in this program area are College Scholarships, which have originated through donor-advised funds and which assist high school graduates to pursue their academic goals; Fiscal Sponsorship Program, which enables new organizations to raise money for programs and provides guidance and oversight as needed to expand capacity and develop best practices; and Native American Preparatory Scholars Fund, an initiative and endowment fund of the Foundation that supports increasing the number of New Mexico Native American students who shall aspire to, be prepared for, and graduate from colleges and universities.

Emergency Grants provide help for individuals and families facing crisis situations.

LEGAL BASIS:
501(c)(3) organization.

GEOG. RESTRICTIONS: New Mexico.

FINANCIAL DATA:
Amount of support per award: Varies.

ADDRESS INQUIRIES TO:
Erika Davila, Program Manager
(See address above.)

THE NORCLIFFE FOUNDATION
600 University Street
Suite 2003
Seattle, WA 98101
(206) 682-4820
E-mail: info@norcliffefoundation.org
Web Site: www.norcliffefoundation.org

TYPE:
Capital grants; General operating grants; Project/program grants.

See entry 217 for full listing.

NORTHEAST AGRICULTURAL EDUCATION FOUNDATION
220 South Warren Street
9th Floor
Syracuse, NY 13202
(315) 671-0588
Fax: (315) 671-0589
E-mail: info@northeastagriculture.org
Web Site: www.northeastagriculture.org

TYPE:
Project/program grants.

See entry 1921 for full listing.

NORTHERN TRUST CORPORATION [1213]
50 South LaSalle Street, L7
Chicago, IL 60603
(312) 630-6000
Fax: (312) 630-1809
E-mail: corporate_philanthropy@ntrs.com
Web Site: www.northerntrust.com

FOUNDED: 1889

AREAS OF INTEREST:
Education, social welfare, and culture and the arts.

NAME(S) OF PROGRAMS:
- **The Northern Trust Company Charitable Trust**
- **The Northern Trust Matching Gift Program**
- **Volunteer Grants Program**

TYPE:
Capital grants; Endowments; General operating grants; Matching gifts; Project/program grants; Technical assistance; Training grants. Grants within the Bank's areas of interest, including matching gifts to hospitals, educational institutions, cultural institutions and social welfare organizations.

YEAR PROGRAM STARTED: 1966

PURPOSE:
To reach out to people in the Chicago area who are in need or face obstacles that impede their full participation in society.

LEGAL BASIS:
Northern Trust Company is a multi-bank holding company.

ELIGIBILITY:
Applicant must be a not-for-profit organization, tax-exempt under IRS requirements and located in the U.S., Chicago metropolitan area.

Normally, contributions will not be made to support individuals, fraternal groups, individual churches or sectarian organizations, political activity, research, tickets or advertising for fund-raising benefits and agencies receiving more than 5% of their funding from the United Way.

GEOG. RESTRICTIONS: Chicago, Illinois.

FINANCIAL DATA:
Amount of support per award: Typical grant is $10,000 to $15,000.

Total amount of support: $4,499,271 in grants for the year 2017.

Matching fund requirements: Will match 100% of any gifts at least $25 to a maximum of $2,000 per person per year.

APPLICATION INFO:
New applicants must submit an online letter of inquiry eight weeks before application deadline. If proposal is approved, then applicant must submit:
(1) a completed application form;
(2) a copy of organization's IRS 501(c)(3) notification letter;
(3) a copy of organization's operating budget and specific project budget, if applicable;
(4) financial information for previous two years;
(5) a list of Chicago-area corporate and foundation contributors and amounts given in the last and the current year;
(6) a list of board members, with affiliations and;
(7) a list of organization's management staff and their qualifications.

Prior successful applicants are not required to submit the letter of inquiry.

Duration: Grants are annual. Multiyear pledges for capital or endowments. Requests for renewals are considered annually.

Deadline: Varies.

PUBLICATIONS:
Annual report.

IRS I.D.: 36-6147253

STAFF:
Deborah Liverett, Senior Vice President
Alexis Sutton, Vice President
Chastity Davis, Officer
Edrea Jones, Coordinator
Dawn McGovern, Coordinator

ADDRESS INQUIRIES TO:
See e-mail address above.

THE NORTHWEST MINNESOTA FOUNDATION [1214]
201 Third Street, N.W.
Bemidji, MN 56601
(218) 759-2057
Fax: (218) 759-2328
E-mail: info@nwmf.org
Web Site: www.nwmf.org

FOUNDED: 1986

AREAS OF INTEREST:
Community planning, civic engagement, business development, housing, child care, health equity, and philanthropy.

TYPE:
Challenge/matching grants; Demonstration grants; Project/program grants; Research grants; Scholarships; Seed money grants; Technical assistance.

YEAR PROGRAM STARTED: 1986

PURPOSE:
To invest resources, facilitate collaboration, and promote philanthropy to make the region a better place to live and work.

ELIGIBILITY:
Applicants must be a public agency or private nonprofit organization with a 501(c)(3) federal tax-exempt status. If an organization does not meet these criteria, it may work with an affiliated tax-exempt organization that may be the applicant and fiscal agent for the project. The affiliate must be a parent organization, provide similar services and/or define in writing its participation in project implementation. No grants are made to individuals.

GEOG. RESTRICTIONS: Beltrami, Clearwater, Hubbard, Kittson, Lake of the Woods, Mahnomen, Marshall, Norman, Pennington, Polk, Red Lake and Roseau counties, Minnesota.

FINANCIAL DATA:
Amount of support per award: Varies depending on the grant type.
Total amount of support: Varies.
Matching fund requirements: 50% typically required.

NO. MOST RECENT APPLICANTS: 40.

NO. AWARDS: 30.

APPLICATION INFO:
A preproposal must be submitted on the NMF preproposal application form. Applicants are encouraged to contact NMF staff to discuss projects prior to submission. Once a project has been determined to be eligible, a full application is invited and NMF staff will explain the process for submitting additional information.
Duration: Up to two years; multiyear depending upon grant.
Deadline: Preproposals may be submitted at any time.

ADDRESS INQUIRIES TO:
Michael Neusser, Vice President for Operations
(See address above.)

THE NORTHWESTERN MUTUAL FOUNDATION [1215]
720 East Wisconsin Avenue
Milwaukee, WI 53202
(414) 665-2200
Fax: (414) 662-7519
E-mail: foundationonline@northwesternmutual.com
Web Site: foundation.northwesternmutual.com

FOUNDED: 1992

AREAS OF INTEREST:
Education, childhood cancer, building neighborhood capacity and volunteerism.

CONSULTING OR VOLUNTEER SERVICES:
MutualFriends is the name of the corporate employee volunteer program.

TYPE:
Project, program and capacity-building support, matching gifts, scholarships, disaster relief, United Way and UPAF support.

PURPOSE:
To improve the lives of children and families in need.

ELIGIBILITY:
Organization must have tax-exempt classification under Section 501(c)(3) of the Internal Revenue Code. No grants to organizations that advocate, support or practice activities inconsistent with Northwestern Mutual's nondiscrimination policies.

GEOG. RESTRICTIONS: Milwaukee, Wisconsin. United States for National Childhood Cancer Program.

FINANCIAL DATA:
Amount of support per award: Varies.

APPLICATION INFO:
Guidelines and deadlines are communicated annually on the Foundation web site. Foundation accepts online applications only through its web site.
Duration: One year. Must reapply.

OFFICER:
Eric Christophersen, President

ADDRESS INQUIRIES TO:
See e-mail address above.

OKLAHOMA CITY COMMUNITY FOUNDATION, INC.   [1216]
P.O. Box 1146
Oklahoma City, OK 73101-1146
(405) 235-5603
Fax: (405) 235-5612
E-mail: info@occf.org
Web Site: occf.org

FOUNDED: 1969

AREAS OF INTEREST:
Beautification, education, the arts, social services and civic organizations.

TYPE:
Project/program grants; Scholarships. Support for philanthropic agencies designated by donors. Discretionary grants by the Foundation's trustees are relatively modest.

PURPOSE:
To serve the charitable purposes of its donors and the charitable needs of the Oklahoma City area through the development and administration of endowment and other charitable funds with the goal of preserving capital and enhancing value.

LEGAL BASIS:
Public foundation.

ELIGIBILITY:
Applicants can be any IRS 501(c)(3) organization.

GEOG. RESTRICTIONS: Oklahoma City, Oklahoma and surrounding area.

FINANCIAL DATA:
Assets of $1,175,030,000 for the year ended June 30, 2019.
Amount of support per award: Varies.
Total amount of support: $37,521,000 in grant distributions for fiscal year ended June 30, 2019.

APPLICATION INFO:
Application information is available on the web site.
Duration: Varies.

IRS I.D.: 23-7024262

ADDRESS INQUIRIES TO:
Nancy Anthony, President
(See address above.)

OMAHA COMMUNITY FOUNDATION
3555 Farnam Street
Suite 222
Omaha, NE 68131
(402) 342-3458
Fax: (402) 342-3582
E-mail: info@omahafoundation.org
Web Site: www.omahafoundation.org

TYPE:
Capital grants; General operating grants; Project/program grants; Technical assistance. Donors can contribute through the Omaha Community Foundation to any nonprofit agency. The OCF also has 10 discretionary grant programs.

See entry 223 for full listing.

OPEN SOCIETY INSTITUTE - BALTIMORE   [1217]
201 North Charles Street
Suite 1300
Baltimore, MD 21201
(410) 234-1091
Fax: (410) 234-2816
E-mail: osi.baltimore@opensocietyfoundations. org
Web Site: www.osibaltimore.org

AREAS OF INTEREST:
Drug addiction.

NAME(S) OF PROGRAMS:
• **Addiction and Health Equity Program**

TYPE:
Project/program grants. The Drug Addiction Treatment Program seeks to ensure universal access to treatment services for all in need regardless of income or insurance status.

YEAR PROGRAM STARTED: 1998

PURPOSE:
To focus on critical national urban issues as they are expressed locally.

LEGAL BASIS:
Foundation.

ELIGIBILITY:
Grants are made to organizations that have tax-exempt status under Section 501(c)(3) of the Internal Revenue Code. No grants are made to individuals. Nonsectarian religious programs may apply.

GEOG. RESTRICTIONS: Baltimore City, Maryland.

FINANCIAL DATA:
Amount of support per award: Varies.
Total amount of support: Varies.

APPLICATION INFO:
Applicants should submit a letter of inquiry of two to three pages which includes:
(1) a description of the program to be funded;
(2) the qualifications of the organization to carry out the program;
(3) the ways in which the program reflects the priorities of The Drug Addiction Treatment Program;
(4) the amount requested and;
(5) a copy of the IRS letter stating the organization's tax-exempt status.
Duration: Varies.
Deadline: Grant applications are accepted on an ongoing basis.

ADDRESS INQUIRIES TO:
Scott Nolen, Program Director
Drug Addiction Treatment
(See address above.)

THE ORDEAN FOUNDATION   [1218]
501 Ordean Building
424 West Superior Street
Duluth, MN 55802
(218) 726-4785
E-mail: dness@ordean.org
Web Site: www.ordean.org

FOUNDED: 1933

AREAS OF INTEREST:
Social services, education and health, services to low-income, mentally and physically handicapped, elderly, mentally ill, chemically dependent, prevention of delinquency, and scholarships for certain health-related majors at Duluth colleges.

TYPE:
Challenge/matching grants; Demonstration grants; General operating grants; Project/program grants; Scholarships.

YEAR PROGRAM STARTED: 1933

LEGAL BASIS:
Private foundation.

ELIGIBILITY:
Applicants must be nonprofit, tax-exempt IRS 501(c)(3) organizations located or providing services in Greater City of Duluth, MN.

GEOG. RESTRICTIONS: Greater City of Duluth, Minnesota.

FINANCIAL DATA:
Amount of support per award: $5,000 to $170,000.
Total amount of support: $1,400,000 for the year 2020.

NO. AWARDS: Approximately 45.

REPRESENTATIVE AWARDS:
$125,000 to Lake Superior Community Health Center; $100,000 to Mentor North to match caring adults with at-risk youths.

APPLICATION INFO:
Guidelines are available from the Foundation office at the address above.
Duration: Varies.
Deadline: January 15, February 15, May 15, August 15, October 15 and November 15 for the February, March, June, September, November and December meetings, respectively.

STAFF:
Don Ness, Executive Director
Joe Everett, Program Director

ADDRESS INQUIRIES TO:
Joe Everett, Program Director
(See address above.)

THE OREGON COMMUNITY FOUNDATION [1219]

1221 S.W. Yamhill Street, Suite 100
Portland, OR 97205-2108
(503) 227-6846
E-mail: info@oregoncf.org
Web Site: www.oregoncf.org

FOUNDED: 1973

AREAS OF INTEREST:
Health and well-being, education, arts and culture, economic vitality, and community livability, environment and engagement.

NAME(S) OF PROGRAMS:
• **Community Grants Program**

TYPE:
Capital grants; Challenge/matching grants; Matching gifts; Project/program grants; Scholarships.

YEAR PROGRAM STARTED: 1974

PURPOSE:
To strengthen the social fabric of our communities by awarding grants that build civic leadership and engagement and address evolving, community-identified needs.

LEGAL BASIS:
Community foundation.

ELIGIBILITY:
Applicants for programs must be nonprofit, tax-exempt organizations in Oregon.

Applicants must have received a community grant only once during the previous 12 months and must have completed evaluation reports for all prior grants. The Foundation gives preference to projects that demonstrate strong local support and promise tangible benefits or means of solving community problems or concerns.

GEOG. RESTRICTIONS: Oregon.

FINANCIAL DATA:
Amount of support per award: $5,000 to $50,000. Average grant $20,000.
Total amount of support: $110,000,000 in grants, including $10,000,000 in scholarships and $7,000,000 for the Community Grants Program.

NO. MOST RECENT APPLICANTS: 600 to 700 proposals per year.

NO. AWARDS: Community Grants: Approximately 350 annually.

APPLICATION INFO:
Application information is available on the web site. Application must be submitted via the online system.
Duration: Small grants: One year; Large grants: One to three years.
Deadline: Community Grants Program: January 15 and July 15.

IRS I.D.: 23-7315673

ADDRESS INQUIRIES TO:
Program Officer
(See address above.)

*SPECIAL STIPULATIONS:
Generally funds only in Oregon.

OUTER BANKS COMMUNITY FOUNDATION [1220]

13 Skyline Road
Southern Shores, NC 27949
(252) 261-8839
Fax: (252) 261-0371
E-mail: info@obcf.org
Web Site: www.obcf.org

FOUNDED: 1982

AREAS OF INTEREST:
Outer Banks, from Corolla to Ocracoke Island.

TYPE:
Project/program grants; Scholarships. 55 different scholarship funds available to local students. Grants available for local nonprofit programs and projects.

YEAR PROGRAM STARTED: 1982

PURPOSE:
To help meet local needs in the Outer Banks of North Carolina, from Corolla to Ocracoke Island.

LEGAL BASIS:
501(c)(3).

GEOG. RESTRICTIONS: Corolla area of Currituck County, Dare County and Ocracoke Island in Hyde County, North Carolina.

FINANCIAL DATA:
Amount of support per award: Varies.
Total amount of support: Varies.

APPLICATION INFO:
Application information is available on the web site.
Deadline: Varies.

IRS I.D.: 58-1516313

ADDRESS INQUIRIES TO:
Lorelei Costa, Executive Director
(See address above.)

PERMIAN BASIN AREA FOUNDATION [1221]

3312 Andrews Highway
Midland, TX 79703
(432) 617-3213
Fax: (432) 617-0151
E-mail: mharris@pbaf.org
Web Site: www.pbaf.org

FOUNDED: 1989

AREAS OF INTEREST:
Community development.

TYPE:
Grants-in-aid; Scholarships.

PURPOSE:
To enrich the quality of life for the communities of the Permian Basin area of Texas.

LEGAL BASIS:
501(c)(3) organization.

GEOG. RESTRICTIONS: Communities of the Permian Basin region of Texas.

FINANCIAL DATA:
The Foundation has awarded nearly $100,000,000 in grants and scholarships since inception.
Amount of support per award: Grants: Average $15,000; Scholarships: $1,000 to $2,500.

APPLICATION INFO:
Organizations wishing to apply for a grant must fully complete and submit one copy of the Pre-Application Summary (SF-1). Organizations that have received funding during a previous grant cycle must also complete and submit the Grant Award Follow-up Form (SF-FW). Do not include a cover letter with the application.

A full application will be complete when one copy of the appropriate Standard Forms and additional documents indicated on the Standard Form Checklist are completed and submitted to the Foundation by the full application due date. (The list of required forms differs depending on the purpose of the grant request.) Upon receiving a full application, the Foundation will conduct a full application review which may include an applicant interview, a site visit, and/or a request for additional information.

All scholarship applications must contain the following:
(1) transcript with fall semester grades;
(2) college transcript if student is enrolled in concurrent college courses and;
(3) at least one letter of recommendation, but not more than three.

Some applications require an essay. Check the individual scholarship criteria to determine if an essay is required and the designated topic.
Duration: Grants: Typically one year. Can reapply every two years.
Deadline: Grant proposals: April 1 for Spring and October 1 for Fall.

ADDRESS INQUIRIES TO:
Grants Administrator
(See address above.)

PETOSKEY-HARBOR SPRINGS AREA COMMUNITY FOUNDATION [1222]

616 Petoskey Street, Suite 203
Petoskey, MI 49770
(231) 348-5820
Fax: (231) 348-5883
E-mail: info@phsacf.org
Web Site: www.phsacf.org

FOUNDED: 1992

AREAS OF INTEREST:
Arts, education, environment, health, human service and community development.

TYPE:
Grants-in-aid; Scholarships. Grants are given for scholarships or for charitable needs.

YEAR PROGRAM STARTED: 1992

PURPOSE:
To build an endowment to serve community needs.

LEGAL BASIS:
Community foundation.

ELIGIBILITY:
Grants must be for charitable purposes, but not for individuals.

GEOG. RESTRICTIONS: Emmet County, Michigan.

FINANCIAL DATA:
Over $50,000,000 in assets.
Amount of support per award: $500 to $15,000.
Total amount of support: Varies.

APPLICATION INFO:
Applicants are required to call the Foundation before applying.
Duration: One year.
Deadline: March 1 and October 1.

PUBLICATIONS:
Annual report; application guidelines.

ADDRESS INQUIRIES TO:
Director of Community Philanthropy
(See address above.)

THE PHILADELPHIA FOUNDATION   [1223]

1835 Market Street
Suite 2410
Philadelphia, PA 19103-2968
(215) 563-6417
Fax: (215) 563-6882
E-mail: info@philafound.org
Web Site: www.philafound.org

FOUNDED: 1918

AREAS OF INTEREST:
Arts, culture, humanities, education, environment, health, human services and public/community development.

NAME(S) OF PROGRAMS:
- **Advocacy Program**
- **Advocacy Unrestricted**
- **Direct Service**
- **Impact Grant**
- **Leadership Grant**

TYPE:
General operating grants; Project/program grants; Scholarships. The Philadelphia Foundation's grantmaking strategies are sensitive to the needs of diverse population groups in the community and reflect a commitment to stabilizing the infrastructure of nonprofit organizations.

YEAR PROGRAM STARTED: 1918

PURPOSE:
To serve as a vehicle and resource for philanthropy in the greater Philadelphia area, PA; to develop, manage and allocate community resources in partnership with donors and grantees to build on community assets, to respond to the needs of the entire community, and to promote empowerment, leadership, and civic participation among underserved groups; to practice and encourage diversity, equity, and inclusiveness as fundamental values of community life.

LEGAL BASIS:
Community foundation established in Pennsylvania by bank resolution.

ELIGIBILITY:
Organization must be IRS 501(c)(3), located in five-county area of southeastern Pennsylvania.

GEOG. RESTRICTIONS: Greater Philadelphia area, Pennsylvania.

FINANCIAL DATA:
Amount of support per award: $3,000 to $50,000 (but not more than 10% of an organization's budget).
Total amount of support: $25,000,000 annually.

CO-OP FUNDING PROGRAMS: The Nonprofit Repositioning Fund.

NO. AWARDS: 1,000 annually.

APPLICATION INFO:
Applicants must take the Eligibility Wizard quiz as the initial step.
Duration: Usually one year.
Deadline: Varies.

PUBLICATIONS:
Newsletters; annual report.

OFFICERS:
Pedro A. Ramos, Esq., President and Chief Executive Officer
Orlando C. Esposito, Chief Financial Officer

ADDRESS INQUIRIES TO:
Grantmaking Services Department
E-mail: grantmakingservices@philafound.org
(See address above.)

THE PITTSBURGH FOUNDATION   [1224]

5 PPG Place
Suite 250
Pittsburgh, PA 15222
(412) 391-5122
Fax: (412) 391-7259
E-mail: contactus@pghfdn.org
Web Site: www.pittsburghfoundation.org

FOUNDED: 1945

AREAS OF INTEREST:
Education, family life, economic development, health care and the arts.

TYPE:
Capital grants; General operating grants; Project/program grants; Research grants; Scholarships. The Foundation promotes and champions the betterment of the greater Pittsburgh community and the quality of life for all its citizens by helping a wide variety of donors fulfill significant community needs and providing a vehicle to make giving easy, personally satisfying and effective. The Foundation awards grants through restricted and unrestricted funds. Purposes for which unrestricted grants are awarded include: organizational capacity building; systemic change; improved service delivery; planning and program development; capital and equipment (in limited and special circumstances) through one targeted fund; operating (in very limited and defined circumstances); research (in special circumstances).

Scholarships and medical research grants are awarded from specific funds established for this purpose.

PURPOSE:
To achieve educational excellence and equity; to support families; to foster economic development; to eliminate disparities in health outcomes; to advance the arts.

LEGAL BASIS:
Community foundation established in Pennsylvania by bank resolution and declaration of trust.

ELIGIBILITY:
Grant applicants must be tax-exempt, public charitable organizations and institutions located in Pittsburgh and southwestern Pennsylvania. Generally, grants are nonrecurring and are not granted for operating budgets and not made to individuals.

GEOG. RESTRICTIONS: Pittsburgh and southwestern Pennsylvania.

FINANCIAL DATA:
Amount of support per award: Varies.
Total amount of support: Approximately $15,000,000 in unrestricted funds; $20,000,000 in donor-directed funds.

NO. MOST RECENT APPLICANTS: Approximately 2,380.

NO. AWARDS: 2,255.

APPLICATION INFO:
Application form is available online and must be submitted electronically.
Duration: Up to three years.

PUBLICATIONS:
Annual report; newsletter; donor information; application guidelines; scholarship brochure.

IRS I.D.: 25-0965466

STAFF:
Lisa Schroeder, President and Chief Executive Officer
Jonathan Brelsford, Senior Vice President of Finance and Investments

BOARD OF DIRECTORS:
Edith L. Shapira, M.D., Chairperson
John C. Harmon, Esq., Vice Chairperson
John R. McGinley, Jr., Vice Chairperson
Kim Tillotson Fleming, Treasurer
Walter H. Smith, Jr., Ph.D., Secretary
Edward J. Donnelly, III, M.D.
Patrick Dowd, Ph.D.
Laura Ellsworth
Lee B. Foster, II
William Generett, Jr.
Rev. Glenn Grayson
Laura Shapira Karet
Brian R. Lenart
Anne Lewis
Terry Miller, M.S.W.
Kamal Nigam
William Strickland

ADDRESS INQUIRIES TO:
Lisa Schroeder
President and Chief Executive Officer
(See address above.)

PRINCETON AREA COMMUNITY FOUNDATION   [1225]

15 Princess Road
Lawrenceville, NJ 08648
(609) 219-1800
Fax: (609) 219-1850
E-mail: info@pacf.org
Web Site: pacf.org

FOUNDED: 1991

AREAS OF INTEREST:
Arts and culture, housing, social services, civil rights and public policy, religion, health, education, and children, youth and families.

TYPE:
General operating grants; Project/program grants; Scholarships.

PURPOSE:
To connect people who care with causes that matter across central New Jersey.

LEGAL BASIS:
A public benefit (nonprofit) organization.

ELIGIBILITY:
Eligible organizations must have 501(c)(3) status.

FINANCIAL DATA:
Since its founding, the Foundation has granted nearly $126,000,000 to its community area of service.
Amount of support per award: Varies.
Total amount of support: Over $20,000,000 in grants and $330,000 in scholarships for the year 2018.

NO. AWARDS: 2,080 grants for the year 2017.

APPLICATION INFO:
Application information is available on the web site.
Duration: One year. Renewable.

STAFF:
Jeffrey M. Vega, President and Chief Executive Officer
Laura J. Longman, MBA, Chief Financial Officer
Marcia Schakelford, Chief Philanthropy Officer

ADDRESS INQUIRIES TO:
Grants and Programs
Princeton Area Community Foundation
(See address above.)

PROLITERACY WORLDWIDE [1226]

101 Wyoming Street
Syracuse, NY 13204
(315) 422-9121
Fax: (315) 422-6369
E-mail: nbf@proliteracy.org
Web Site: www.proliteracy.org

FOUNDED: 1955

AREAS OF INTEREST:
Literacy, adult basic education, English as a second language, and family literacy.

NAME(S) OF PROGRAMS:
• **National Book Fund (NBF)**

TYPE:
Project/program grants; Technical assistance.

YEAR PROGRAM STARTED: 1995

PURPOSE:
To provide grants for books and other materials local programs can use to expand their current volunteer literacy programs; to develop, promote and expand literacy programs in the U.S.

LEGAL BASIS:
Nonprofit organization.

ELIGIBILITY:
Adult literacy and adult basic education programs only.

GEOG. RESTRICTIONS: United States.

FINANCIAL DATA:
Amount of support per award: Typically $500 to $2,000.
Total amount of support: Varies.
Matching fund requirements: Up to 20% match required for non-ProLiterary members.

NO. MOST RECENT APPLICANTS: More than 100 annually.

NO. AWARDS: 92 for the year 2019-20.

APPLICATION INFO:
Application information is available online. Applications may be submitted beginning February 1.
Duration: One year. NBF grantee eligible again in three years or two full funding cycles.

Deadline: March 15.

PUBLICATIONS:
Guidelines.

IRS I.D.: 16-1214734

ADDRESS INQUIRIES TO:
Alicia Suskin
National Book Fund Program Director
(See e-mail address above.)

RANCHO SANTA FE FOUNDATION [1227]

162 South Rancho Santa Fe Road
Suite B-30
Encinitas, CA 92024
(858) 756-6557
Fax: (858) 756-6561
E-mail: christy@rsffoundation.org
Web Site: www.rsffoundation.org

FOUNDED: 1981

AREAS OF INTEREST:
Military, workforce development for at-risk youth, human trafficking prevention, and capacity building support for regional nonprofits.

NAME(S) OF PROGRAMS:
• **The Patriots Connection**
• **Rancho Santa Fe Women's Fund**

TYPE:
Challenge/matching grants; Development grants; Endowments; General operating grants; Project/program grants; Scholarships.

YEAR PROGRAM STARTED: 1981

PURPOSE:
To connect donors with regional and global needs through visionary community leadership, personalized service and effective grantmaking.

LEGAL BASIS:
Community foundation.

ELIGIBILITY:
Organizations must have tax-exempt status under Section 501(c)(3) of the Internal Revenue Code. Additional requirements are listed on the Foundation web site.

FINANCIAL DATA:
Amount of support per award: $5,000 to $100,000.
Total amount of support: Varies.

NO. MOST RECENT APPLICANTS: 60 to 75.

NO. AWARDS: Varies.

APPLICATION INFO:
The Foundation accepts applications by invitation only. The Foundation does not accept unsolicited grant requests, except for the Rancho Santa Fe Women's Fund. Women's Fund application process opens August 1.
Duration: Typically one year.
Deadline: Patriots Connection: Mid-April. Awarded in June; Women's Fund: August 1. Awarded in May.

PUBLICATIONS:
Annual report.

IRS I.D.: 95-3709639

STAFF:
Christina P. Wilson, President and Chief Executive Officer
Karen Sprigle, Chief Operations Officer
Debbie Anderson, Programs Director
Megan Fletcher, Communications Manager

Jeff Peterson, Senior Accountant
Korri Ball, Administrative Coordinator, Women's Fund

ADDRESS INQUIRIES TO:
Christina P. Wilson, President and Chief Executive Officer
(See address above.)

RBC FOUNDATION - U.S.A. [1228]

RBC Plaza
60 South Sixth Street
Minneapolis, MN 55402-4422
(612) 371-2936
Fax: (612) 371-7933
E-mail: fndapplications@rbc.com
Web Site: www.rbcwealthmanagement.com

AREAS OF INTEREST:
Arts and culture, youth, health and human services.

NAME(S) OF PROGRAMS:
• **RBC Emerging Artists Project**
• **RBC Youth Mental Well-being Project**

TYPE:
Project/program grants. In the area of arts and culture, the Emerging Artists Program supports initiatives that help artists in their early years of development and that bridge the gap between their academic experiences to professional careers in the arts.

In the area of health and human services, grants are exclusively directed to the RBC Youth Mental Well-being Project focusing on programs that are helping youth and families access the right care at the right time. To foster economic independence and promote self-sufficiency, the Foundation also focuses on organizations providing emergency food, shelter and basic needs, and adult literacy and employment training programs.

In the area of youth, grants are focused on programs that prepare students for future success.

PURPOSE:
To improve the quality of life in communities where the company has facilities.

LEGAL BASIS:
Corporate foundation.

ELIGIBILITY:
Organizations must have their 501(c)(3) registered nonprofit status for a minimum of three years, a minimum annual operating budget of $100,000 and an established relationship with an RBC Wealth Management employee, preferably board involvement.

The Foundation does not support capital and endowment campaigns, multiyear commitments, or start-up organizations.

FINANCIAL DATA:
Total amount of support: $2,800,000 for the year 2020.

APPLICATION INFO:
Guidelines and application forms are available on the web site.
Duration: One year.
Deadline: Varies.

ADDRESS INQUIRIES TO:
Julie Allen
E-mail: julie.allen@rbc.com

THE REINBERGER FOUNDATION   [1229]

30000 Chagrin Boulevard, Suite 300
Cleveland, OH 44124
(216) 292-2790
E-mail: info@reinbergerfoundation.org
Web Site: www.reinbergerfoundation.org

FOUNDED: 1968

AREAS OF INTEREST:
Arts, education and human service.

NAME(S) OF PROGRAMS:
- **Arts, Culture and Humanities**
- **Education**
- **Human Service**

TYPE:
Capital grants; Challenge/matching grants;
General operating grants; Matching gifts;
Project/program grants.

PURPOSE:
To help individuals move toward
self-sufficiency; to provide opportunity for
enrichment in the community.

LEGAL BASIS:
Private foundation.

ELIGIBILITY:
Eligible organizations must be IRS 501(c)(3)
tax-exempt. Priority will be given to those
organizations who received Reinberger
Foundation support in the past five years.

GEOG. RESTRICTIONS: Northeast Ohio or greater
Columbus area.

FINANCIAL DATA:
Since its beginning, the Foundation has
provided more than $120,000,000 in funding
support to the community.
Amount of support per award: $2,500 to
$150,000 for the year 2020.
Total amount of support: $2,949,682 for the
year 2020.

NO. AWARDS: 120 for the year 2020.

APPLICATION INFO:
Online application is available on the web
site.
Duration: Up to five years.
Deadline: March 15 for Education, July 15
for Human Service and November 15 for Art.

ADDRESS INQUIRIES TO:
Karen L. Hooser, President
(See address above.)

LUTHER I. REPLOGLE FOUNDATION   [1230]

1720 N Street, N.W.
Washington, DC 20036-2907
(202) 213-1657
Fax: (202) 580-6579
E-mail: gwenn@lirf.org
Web Site: reploglefoundation.org

FOUNDED: 1966

AREAS OF INTEREST:
At-risk youth, children and families, with
particular attention to improving educational
opportunities for inner-city children.

TYPE:
General operating grants; Project/program
grants. The Foundation supports programs
that:
(1) address the needs of youth and children
living in, or at risk of, long-term poverty,
especially children of inner-city residents. Of
particular interest are programs for teen
pregnancy prevention, counseling,

broad-spectrum social services, and other
programs that help young people improve
their own lives and;
(2) improve educational opportunities for
inner-city children, including enrichment
programs in the arts and sciences, alternative
schools, after-school tutoring and mentoring,
and scholarship programs.

PURPOSE:
To address the needs of youth and children
living in, or at risk of, long-term poverty; to
improve educational opportunities for
inner-city children; to support programs for
affordable and supportive housing that reach
groups of people frequently left out of
traditional shelter programs.

ELIGIBILITY:
Organizations must be not-for-profit
501(c)(3) with revenues less than $3,000,000.

GEOG. RESTRICTIONS: Washington, DC;
Chicago, Illinois; Minneapolis/St. Paul,
Minnesota.

FINANCIAL DATA:
Amount of support per award: Usually
$5,000 to $10,000.
Total amount of support: $417,000 for the
year 2020.

NO. MOST RECENT APPLICANTS: Over 50.

NO. AWARDS: 1 new, 31 programmatic renewals
and 12 discretionary renewals.

APPLICATION INFO:
Application is available on the Foundation
web site.
Duration: Renewable if grantee sends report.
Deadline: August 15 for new requests.
September 15 for renewals.

IRS I.D.: 36-6141697

ADDRESS INQUIRIES TO:
Gwenn H.S. Gebhard, Executive Director
(See address above.)

ROCHESTER AREA FOUNDATION   [1231]

12 Elton Hills Drive, N.W.
Rochester, MN 55901
(507) 282-0203
Fax: (507) 616-7608
E-mail: raf-info@rochesterarea.org
giving@rochesterarea.org
Web Site: www.rochesterarea.org

FOUNDED: 1944

AREAS OF INTEREST:
General grants to benefit residents of the
Greater Rochester area.

TYPE:
Capital grants; Challenge/matching grants;
Project/program grants; Scholarships; Seed
money grants.

YEAR PROGRAM STARTED: 1944

PURPOSE:
To use its resources to improve the quality of
life, promote greater equality of opportunities
and to support development of effective
methods to assist those in need in the Greater
Rochester area.

LEGAL BASIS:
Community foundation.

ELIGIBILITY:
Applicants must be 501(c)(3) organizations
or units of government agencies or

government-created public agencies located
in or serving the Greater Rochester area.
Grants are not given to individuals.

GEOG. RESTRICTIONS: Greater Rochester,
Minnesota.

FINANCIAL DATA:
Amount of support per award: Varies.
Total amount of support: $2,612,649 for the
year 2019.

NO. AWARDS: 976 for the year 2019.

APPLICATION INFO:
Pre-approved and approved application forms
are required. Applicant organizations must
include an IRS letter of tax determination.
Duration: One-time grants.
Deadline: January and August.

PUBLICATIONS:
Annual report with consolidated financials.

ROSE COMMUNITY FOUNDATION   [1232]

4500 Cherry Creek Drive South
Suite 900
Denver, CO 80246
(303) 398-7400
Fax: (303) 398-7430
E-mail: grantsmanager@rcfdenver.org
kcostello@rcfdenver.org
Web Site: www.rcfdenver.org

FOUNDED: 1995

AREAS OF INTEREST:
Equity, justice and inclusion; policy
advocacy; Jewish life; nonprofit strength and
support.

TYPE:
Capital grants; Challenge/matching grants;
General operating grants; Project/program
grants; Seed money grants; Technical
assistance. Capacity-building grants.

YEAR PROGRAM STARTED: 1995

PURPOSE:
To enhance the quality of life of the greater
Denver community through leadership,
resources, traditions and values.

ELIGIBILITY:
Applicants must be charitable, nonprofit
organizations classified as 501(c)(3) by the
IRS or be a tax-supported institution, such as
a school or government agency. New or
emerging organizations are permitted to
apply through a sponsoring tax-exempt
organization. Applicants (including university
departments) may have only one proposal
pending at any given time.

The Foundation will not support grants to
individuals or endowments, including
academic chairs, grants to one organization
to be passed to another, annual appeals or
membership drives, fund-raising events, or
political candidates.

GEOG. RESTRICTIONS: Denver metropolitan area,
specifically Adams, Arapahoe, Boulder,
Broomfield, Denver, Douglas and Jefferson
counties, Colorado.

FINANCIAL DATA:
Amount of support per award: Varies
depending on needs and nature of the
request.
Total amount of support: Approximately
$17,000,000 for the year 2019.
Matching fund requirements: Varies by nature
of award.

NO. AWARDS: Approximately 600.

APPLICATION INFO:
It is recommended to speak with a Program Officer prior to submitting an application to discuss the program, project or organization.
Duration: Varies.

IRS I.D.: 84-0920862

ADDRESS INQUIRIES TO:
Kelly Costello, Grants Manager
(See address above.)

HENRY AND RUTH BLAUSTEIN ROSENBERG FOUNDATION [1233]

One South Street, Suite 2900
Baltimore, MD 21202
(410) 347-7201
Fax: (410) 347-7210
E-mail: info@blaufund.org
Web Site: www.blaufund.org

FOUNDED: 1959

AREAS OF INTEREST:
Arts and culture, youth development, and adult self-sufficiency.

TYPE:
Capital grants; General operating grants; Project/program grants. Programs of benefit to the underserved community in the Baltimore, MD area.

PURPOSE:
To promote arts and culture, youth development, and adult self-sufficiency within the underserved community.

ELIGIBILITY:
Grantees must be 501(c)(3) nonprofit organizations. No grants to individuals.

GEOG. RESTRICTIONS: Baltimore, Maryland.

FINANCIAL DATA:
Amount of support per award: $3,000 to $75,000.
Total amount of support: Approximately $3,460,000 for the year 2019.

APPLICATION INFO:
Send two- to three-page letter of intent or application. IRS tax status determination letter is required. Faxed and e-mailed letters of intent are not accepted.
Duration: One to two years. Prior grantee organizations may be renewable.

ADDRESS INQUIRIES TO:
Betsy F. Ringel, Executive Director
(See address above.)

ROSS FOUNDATION [1234]

202 South Fifth Street
Arkadelphia, AR 71923
(870) 246-9881
Fax: (870) 246-9674
E-mail: info@rossfoundation.us
Web Site: www.rossfoundation.us

FOUNDED: 1966

AREAS OF INTEREST:
Education, culture, conservation and community activities.

TYPE:
Conferences/seminars; Matching gifts; Project/program grants; Research grants.

YEAR PROGRAM STARTED: 1966

LEGAL BASIS:
Private foundation.

ELIGIBILITY:
Applicants must be IRS 501(c)(3) organizations located in Clark County or Arkadelphia, AR. No grants to individuals.

GEOG. RESTRICTIONS: Clark County or Arkadelphia, Arkansas.

FINANCIAL DATA:
Amount of support per award: Generally $500 to $25,000.
Total amount of support: $679,000 for the year 2018.
Matching fund requirements: Varies.

CO-OP FUNDING PROGRAMS: Arkadelphia Promise Foundation.

NO. MOST RECENT APPLICANTS: Approximately 30.

NO. AWARDS: Approximately 20.

APPLICATION INFO:
Application form is available online.
Duration: Typically one year.
Deadline: Proposals are reviewed March, July and October.

ADDRESS INQUIRIES TO:
Mary Elizabeth Eldridge
Director of Programs or
Amanda Fenocchi, Assistant Grants Officer
(See address above.)

THE RUSSELL FAMILY FOUNDATION [1235]

3025 Harborview Drive
Gig Harbor, WA 98335
(253) 858-5050
Fax: (253) 851-0460
E-mail: info@trff.org
Web Site: www.trff.org

FOUNDED: 1999

AREAS OF INTEREST:
Elimination of poverty, healthy educational and extracurricular activities for youth, and social justice.

NAME(S) OF PROGRAMS:
● **Jane's Fellowship Program**

TYPE:
Fellowships. Fellowship program for individuals who plan to work in the Foundation's areas of interest.

YEAR PROGRAM STARTED: 2004

PURPOSE:
To support grassroots leaders in Pierce County and Tacoma, WA.

ELIGIBILITY:
Must be a grassroots leader who has demonstrated exceptional creativity, courage and commitment in serving diverse needs in Tacoma and countywide.

GEOG. RESTRICTIONS: Pierce County and Tacoma, Washington.

FINANCIAL DATA:
Amount of support per award: Varies.
Total amount of support: Varies.

NO. AWARDS: Up to 13.

APPLICATION INFO:
Application information is available on the web site.
Duration: 15 months.
Deadline: Varies.

ADDRESS INQUIRIES TO:
E-mail: jfp.app@trff.org

SAGINAW COMMUNITY FOUNDATION [1236]

One Tuscola Street, Suite 100
Saginaw, MI 48607
(989) 755-0545
Fax: (989) 755-6524
E-mail: brian@saginawfoundation.org
Web Site: www.saginawfoundation.org

FOUNDED: 1984

AREAS OF INTEREST:
Arts, community development, culture, education, health, youth and human services.

CONSULTING OR VOLUNTEER SERVICES:
Seminars, group presentations and one-on-one consultation.

TYPE:
Grants-in-aid; Project/program grants; Scholarships.

YEAR PROGRAM STARTED: 1984

PURPOSE:
To fulfill donor wishes and enable community initiatives to come to life, now and forever; to provide strategic leadership in the community; to practice impactful grantmaking in the areas of youth development, early education, and community improvement; to provide stewardship of the Foundation's resources, human and financial.

ELIGIBILITY:
Grants are made to organizations that have tax-exempt status under Section 501(c)(3) of the Internal Revenue Code, local units of government and religious institutions to support projects or programs benefiting the citizens and communities of Saginaw County. Except for scholarships, no grants are made to individuals. Nonsectarian religious programs may apply.

GEOG. RESTRICTIONS: Saginaw County, Michigan.

FINANCIAL DATA:
Amount of support per award: Grants vary in amount, depending upon the needs and nature of the request.
Total amount of support: $3,770,651 for the year 2018.
Matching fund requirements: Varies by program.

NO. MOST RECENT APPLICANTS: 6,800.

NO. AWARDS: 627.

APPLICATION INFO:
Application information is available on the web site.

ADDRESS INQUIRIES TO:
Program Officer
(See address above.)

ST. CROIX VALLEY FOUNDATION [1237]

516 Second Street, Suite 214
Hudson, WI 54016
(715) 386-9490
Fax: (715) 386-1250
E-mail: info@scvfoundation.org
Web Site: www.scvfoundation.org

FOUNDED: 1995

AREAS OF INTEREST:
Arts, civic affairs, community needs and development, environment, health and human services, and education.

NAME(S) OF PROGRAMS:
- **Health and Wellness Grant**
- **Music Education Grant**
- **Valley Arts Initiative Grant**

TYPE:
Project/program grants; Scholarships. Environmental and humane grants.

YEAR PROGRAM STARTED: 1995

PURPOSE:
To advance the quality of life in the St. Croix Valley of Wisconsin and Minnesota.

LEGAL BASIS:
501(c)(3).

ELIGIBILITY:
Grants are made to organizations that have tax-exempt status under Section 501(c)(3) of the Internal Revenue Code or serving the St. Croix Valley of Wisconsin and Minnesota. Nonsectarian religious programs may apply.

GEOG. RESTRICTIONS: Burnett, Pierce, Polk and St. Croix counties in St. Croix Valley, Wisconsin; Chisago and Washington counties in Minnesota.

FINANCIAL DATA:
Amount of support per award: Maximum $5,000.

Total amount of support: Approximately $100,000 per year.

NO. MOST RECENT APPLICANTS: Approximately 80.

NO. AWARDS: Approximately 40.

APPLICATION INFO:
For full guidelines, refer to the Foundation web site.

Duration: Varies depending on the field of interest.

Deadline: Music Education Grant: October. Health and Wellness Grant: March. Valley Arts Initiative Grant: December. Exact dates will be posted online.

IRS I.D.: 41-1817315

ADDRESS INQUIRIES TO:
Angela Pilgrim
Grants and Programs Officer
E-mail: apilgrim@scvfoundation.org

SAINT-GOBAIN CORPORATION FOUNDATION [1238]
20 Moores Road
Malvern, PA 19355
(610) 893-5484
Fax: (855) 639-6629
E-mail: SGNorthAmericaInfo@saint-gobain.com
Web Site: www.saint-gobain-northamerica.com

FOUNDED: 2001

AREAS OF INTEREST:
Education, energy conservation, environmental concerns, STEM (science, technology, engineering and math), local communities, housing and community development.

NAME(S) OF PROGRAMS:
- **Direct Grants Program**

TYPE:
Project/program grants.

PURPOSE:
To play a vital role in the economic, social and educational development of the community.

LEGAL BASIS:
Corporation foundation.

ELIGIBILITY:
Eligible organizations must be IRS 501(c)(3) tax-exempt and be located in areas where Saint-Gobain Corporation has manufacturing locations.

GEOG. RESTRICTIONS: Massachusetts and Pennsylvania.

FINANCIAL DATA:
Amount of support per award: Varies.
Total amount of support: Varies.

APPLICATION INFO:
Applicants must complete the online Direct Grants Application Form. All completed applications must include the following in order to be considered:
(1) full details of the proposed program;
(2) a brief overview of the organization and a description of its history, mission, goals and key achievements;
(3) IRS letter confirming tax-exempt status as 501(c)(3);
(4) proof of accreditation and IRS Tax Identification Number for education institutions;
(5) current listing of organization's officers and board of directors, including their affiliations;
(6) current board-approved organizational budget and the budget for the proposed project;
(7) major sources of funding and;
(8) a copy of the most recent audited financial statement.

Duration: Typically one year.
Deadline: Applications must be submitted by end of February for April Board Meeting and by end of July for September Board Meeting.

ADDRESS INQUIRIES TO:
Patty Tarantino, Communications Coordinator
E-mail: patricia.a.tarantino@saint-gobain.com

SAN ANGELO AREA FOUNDATION [1239]
221 South Irving Street
San Angelo, TX 76903
(325) 947-7071
Fax: (325) 947-7322
E-mail: infosaaf@saafound.org
Web Site: www.saafound.org

FOUNDED: 2002

AREAS OF INTEREST:
Community development.

TYPE:
Grants-in-aid; Scholarships. To build a legacy of philanthropy by attracting and prudently managing endowed gifts in order to match donor interests with community needs of the area.

PURPOSE:
To improve the quality of life in the San Angelo, TX area.

LEGAL BASIS:
Community foundation.

ELIGIBILITY:
Must be a 501(c)(3) nonprofit organization. Grant funds must be used within and for the benefit of residents and communities of the 17 counties of the San Angelo area.

GEOG. RESTRICTIONS: San Angelo area, Texas.

FINANCIAL DATA:
Amount of support per award: Varies.

Total amount of support: Varies.

APPLICATION INFO:
Application and proposal forms are available online.

Duration: Grants: Typically one year. Scholarships: One to eight semesters.

Deadline: Grants: February 1 for spring cycle and September 1 for fall cycle. Scholarships: March 1.

ADDRESS INQUIRIES TO:
Matt Lewis, President and Chief Executive Officer
(See address above.)

SAN ANTONIO AREA FOUNDATION [1240]
303 Pearl Parkway
Suite 114
San Antonio, TX 78215
(210) 225-2243
Fax: (210) 225-1980
E-mail: info@saafdn.org
Web Site: www.saafdn.org

FOUNDED: 1964

AREAS OF INTEREST:
Cultural vibrancy, livable and resilient communities, successful aging, and youth success.

NAME(S) OF PROGRAMS:
- **Annual Responsive Grants**
- **San Antonio Area African-American Community Fund**
- **Special and Urgent Needs**
- **Women and Girls Development Fund**

TYPE:
Capital grants; General operating grants; Project/program grants; Research grants; Scholarships; Technical assistance.

YEAR PROGRAM STARTED: 1964

PURPOSE:
To help donors achieve their charitable goals for the greater benefit of the community.

LEGAL BASIS:
Community foundation.

ELIGIBILITY:
Eligible organizations must be IRS 501(c)(3) tax-exempt and located in Bexar County or surrounding counties. Endowments and debt reduction will not be funded. The Foundation does not provide grants to individuals.

GEOG. RESTRICTIONS: Bexar County and surrounding counties, Texas.

FINANCIAL DATA:
Amount of support per award: Varies.
Total amount of support: $41,696,698 in grants and scholarships for the year 2018.

APPLICATION INFO:
Application and guidelines are available on the web site.

Duration: One year. Must reapply for additional funding.
Deadline: Varies.

PUBLICATIONS:
Newsletter; annual report.

IRS I.D.: 74-6065414

ADDRESS INQUIRIES TO:
Community, Engagement and Impact Team
(See e-mail address above.)

*SPECIAL STIPULATIONS:
The Foundation does not fund statewide; only in Bexar County and surrounding counties.

THE SAN DIEGO FOUNDATION [1241]

2508 Historic Decatur Road
Suite 200
San Diego, CA 92106-6138
(619) 235-2300
Fax: (619) 239-1710
E-mail: info@sdfoundation.org
Web Site: www.sdfoundation.org

FOUNDED: 1975

AREAS OF INTEREST:
Civil society, economic/employment development, education, health and human services, environment, arts and culture, capacity building, science and technology.

TYPE:
Awards/prizes; Capital grants; Challenge/matching grants; Demonstration grants; Development grants; Fellowships; General operating grants; Project/program grants; Research grants; Scholarships; Seed money grants; Technical assistance; Training grants.

YEAR PROGRAM STARTED: 1975

PURPOSE:
To improve the quality of life for all San Diegans through effective responsible philanthropy.

LEGAL BASIS:
Community foundation.

ELIGIBILITY:
Applicant organizations must be IRS 501(c)(3).

GEOG. RESTRICTIONS: San Diego County, California.

FINANCIAL DATA:
Amount of support per award: Varies.
Total amount of support: Over $40,000,000 annually.
Matching fund requirements: On a case-by-case basis.

NO. AWARDS: 3,000.

APPLICATION INFO:
Impact proposals must meet the guidelines posted and be submitted through the Foundation's web site. Unsolicited proposals are not accepted for Donor-Advised Funds.
Duration: Generally, one year.
Deadline: Varies.

PUBLICATIONS:
Annual report; newsletters.

IRS I.D.: 95-2942582

ADDRESS INQUIRIES TO:
E-mail: communityimpact@sdfoundation.org

*SPECIAL STIPULATIONS:
Most grants made only in San Diego region.

SAN FRANCISCO FOUNDATION [1242]

One Embarcadero Center
Suite 1400
San Francisco, CA 94111
(415) 733-8500
Fax: (415) 477-2783
E-mail: info@sff.org
Web Site: sff.org

FOUNDED: 1948

AREAS OF INTEREST:
Societal and civic issues, health and environment, and arts and humanities.

NAME(S) OF PROGRAMS:
● **Community Leadership Awards**

TYPE:
Awards/prizes.

YEAR PROGRAM STARTED: 1963

PURPOSE:
To recognize individuals and organizations whose leadership has made a significant impact in the Bay Area.

LEGAL BASIS:
Community foundation.

ELIGIBILITY:
Applicants must be based in and serve residents in one or more of the five Bay Area counties. Individuals may work in any industry and must be nominated by a third party. Organizations must have an IRS 501(c)(3) tax-exempt status or be a fiscally sponsored project of another nonprofit entity.

GEOG. RESTRICTIONS: Alameda, Contra Costa, Marin, San Francisco and San Mateo counties, California.

FINANCIAL DATA:
Amount of support per award: Individual leaders: $10,000; Organizations: $20,000.
Total amount of support: Varies.

NO. MOST RECENT APPLICANTS: 275.

NO. AWARDS: Varies.

APPLICATION INFO:
Each year, members of the public are asked to nominate outstanding individuals and nonprofit organizations in the Bay Area for one of four awards. Eligible nominees are then asked to submit an application.
Deadline: Varies.

ADDRESS INQUIRIES TO:
Community Leadership Award Program
E-mail: vgoode@sff.org

SANTA BARBARA FOUNDATION [1243]

1111 Chapala Street, Suite 200
Santa Barbara, CA 93101
(805) 963-1873
Fax: (805) 966-2345
E-mail: info@sbfoundation.org
Web Site: www.sbfoundation.org

FOUNDED: 1928

AREAS OF INTEREST:
Arts and culture expression, living and dying with dignity, lifelong learning, safety, education, civic engagement, sustainable protection of environment/historic places, and the local food system.

NAME(S) OF PROGRAMS:
● **Children, Early Care and Education Grants**
● **Community Disaster Relief Fund**
● **Get Together Grant Program**
● **Small Impact Building Grants**

TYPE:
Capital grants; Challenge/matching grants; Development grants; General operating grants; Project/program grants.

YEAR PROGRAM STARTED: 1928

PURPOSE:
To enrich the lives of the people of Santa Barbara County, CA.

LEGAL BASIS:
Community foundation incorporated in California.

ELIGIBILITY:
501(c)(3) organizations only. Funds must be used to benefit the people of Santa Barbara County, CA.

GEOG. RESTRICTIONS: Santa Barbara County, California.

FINANCIAL DATA:
Amount of support per award: Children, Early Care and Education Grants: $5,000 to $20,000; Community Grants: Up to $50,000; Small Capacity Building Grants: Up to $5,000.
Total amount of support: Approximately $3,700,000 in discretionary grants for the year ended December 31, 2018.
Matching fund requirements: Varies.

APPLICATION INFO:
Application information is available on the web site.
Duration: One year. No guarantee for continuation.
Deadline: Community Grants: First Monday of each month, February to November.

PUBLICATIONS:
Annual report; application guidelines; quarterly newsletter.

IRS I.D.: 95-1866094

STAFF:
Jackie Carrera, President and Chief Executive Officer
Pedro Paz, Director of Grantmaking

ADDRESS INQUIRIES TO:
Grants Associate
(See address above.)

CHARLES AND LYNN SCHUSTERMAN FAMILY PHILANTHROPIES [1244]

110 West Seventh Street, Suite 2000
Tulsa, OK 74119
(202) 289-7000
Fax: (918) 392-9724
E-mail: information@schusterman.org
Web Site: www.schusterman.org

FOUNDED: 1987

AREAS OF INTEREST:
Criminal justice, education, gender and reproductive equity, Jewish community, and voting rights.

TYPE:
Capital grants; General operating grants; Project/program grants.

PURPOSE:
To fund projects of interest to the Foundation including, but not limited to, those working with education, community life and Jewish affairs.

LEGAL BASIS:
Family foundation.

ELIGIBILITY:
Tax-exempt U.S. and international organizations that enhance Jewish life and nonsectarian Oklahoma-based organizations focused on child advocacy, education and youth leadership through service are eligible.

FINANCIAL DATA:
Amount of support per award: Varies.
Total amount of support: Varies.

NO. AWARDS: 117.

APPLICATION INFO:
Grants are by invitation only.

Duration: One year; seldom more than three years. Must reapply for renewal based on performance.

Deadline: Applications are received on a rolling basis.

ADDRESS INQUIRIES TO:
See e-mail address above.

SCRANTON AREA COMMUNITY FOUNDATION   [1245]
615 Jefferson Avenue, Suite 102
Scranton, PA 18510
(570) 347-6203
E-mail: info@safdn.org
Web Site: www.safdn.org

FOUNDED: 1954

AREAS OF INTEREST:
Arts and culture, education, environment, human services, and civic and cultural organizations in northeastern Pennsylvania.

TYPE:
Challenge/matching grants; Demonstration grants; Grants-in-aid; Project/program grants; Scholarships; Seed money grants; Training grants.

PURPOSE:
To enhance the quality of life for all people in northeastern Pennsylvania.

ELIGIBILITY:
Grants to 501(c)(3) nonprofits serving Lackawanna County, PA.

GEOG. RESTRICTIONS: The city of Scranton, Lackawanna County and northeastern Pennsylvania.

FINANCIAL DATA:
Amount of support per award: Varies.
Total amount of support: Varies.

APPLICATION INFO:
Applicant must submit a letter of intent through the Foundation web site.
Duration: Varies.

ADDRESS INQUIRIES TO:
Cathy Fitzpatrick, Grant and Scholarship Manager
E-mail: cathyf@safdn.org

THE SELF FAMILY FOUNDATION   [1246]
120 Main Street
Greenwood, SC 29646
(864) 941-4011
(864) 953-2441
E-mail: mamienic@selffoundation.org
Web Site: www.selffoundation.org

FOUNDED: 1942

AREAS OF INTEREST:
Community wellness, education, with emphasis on early childhood development and youth, and health with emphasis on prevention.

TYPE:
Challenge/matching grants; Project/program grants. Project grants in areas of the Foundation's interest.

YEAR PROGRAM STARTED: 1942

PURPOSE:
To help people to help themselves in South Carolina.

LEGAL BASIS:
Tax-exempt, private foundation.

ELIGIBILITY:
Applicants must be tax-exempt organizations in South Carolina only. No grants are awarded directly to individuals.

GEOG. RESTRICTIONS: South Carolina, with preference to Greenwood.

FINANCIAL DATA:
Amount of support per award: $1,000 to $500,000. Typical grant: $25,000.
Total amount of support: $1,157,000 for the year 2020.
Matching fund requirements: Stipulated with specific programs.

NO. AWARDS: 40 for the year 2020.

REPRESENTATIVE AWARDS:
$300,000 to Humane Society of Greenwood County for the spay and neuter clinic; $25,000 to Healthy Learners for the Healthy Learners Greenwood program; $10,000 to Greenwood Performing Arts for the Inter-generational Outreach Program.

APPLICATION INFO:
Application form is available on the Foundation web site.
Duration: No grants on a continuing basis.
Deadline: March 1, June 1, September 1 and November 1. Announcements in April, July, October and December.

IRS I.D.: 57-0400594

OFFICERS:
J.C. Self, III, Chairman
Sally E. Self, M.D., Vice Chairman
Mamie Nicholson, President
W.M. Self, Jr., Treasurer
Cade Jackson, Secretary

TRUSTEES:
Virginia Self Goldsmith
Cade Jackson
Matt Logan, M.D.
Laurie Self Pulver, M.D.
Furman C. Self
J.C. Self, III
Sally E. Self, M.D.
W.M. Self, Jr.
Jerry Stevens
Mary Andrews Self Whittington

ADDRESS INQUIRIES TO:
Mamie Nicholson, President
(See address above.)

SILICON VALLEY COMMUNITY FOUNDATION   [1247]
2440 West El Camino Real
Suite 300
Mountain View, CA 94040-1498
(650) 450-5400
Fax: (650) 450-5401
E-mail: info@siliconvalleycf.org
Web Site: www.siliconvalleycf.org

FOUNDED: 2007

AREAS OF INTEREST:
This community foundation utilizes five grantmaking strategies: economic security; education (closing the middle school achievement gap in mathematics); immigrant integration; regional planning (land use and transportation planning); and a community opportunity fund currently focused on safety-net services of food and shelter.

TYPE:
General operating grants; Project/program grants; Scholarships; Seed money grants. Nonprofit organizations that provide services

or programs related to the specific five grantmaking strategies in San Mateo and Santa Clara counties may be eligible to apply for funding from the Foundation's endowment. Scholarships for college-bound students are also open to application.

YEAR PROGRAM STARTED: 2008

PURPOSE:
To advance philanthropic solutions to challenging problems, engaging donors to make our region and world a better place for all.

LEGAL BASIS:
Community foundation.

ELIGIBILITY:
To be eligible for a grant, an organization should have current evidence of tax-exempt status under Section 501(c)(3) from the IRS, be a public entity or have a fiscal sponsor with tax-exempt status.

In general, the Foundation does not make grants from its endowment for or to:
(1) activities not directly benefiting the residents of San Mateo and Santa Clara counties;
(2) organizations that are discriminatory;
(3) individuals (contact the Foundation for exceptions to this rule);
(4) costs already incurred;
(5) fraternal organizations, unless sponsoring a specific program open to the entire community;
(6) religious purposes; however, organizations with religious affiliations will be considered for grants if their programs seek to address the needs of the wider community without regard to religious beliefs;
(7) fund-raising events such as walk-a-thons, tournaments and fashion shows and general fund-raising solicitations;
(8) organizations and programs designed to elect candidates to public office or;
(9) out-of-area travel.

GEOG. RESTRICTIONS: San Mateo and Santa Clara counties, California.

FINANCIAL DATA:
Amount of support per award: $10,000 to $250,000, with average grant size less than $100,000. Grant size varies according to the type of project, needs of the organization, and the Foundation's annual giving budget and program concentration.
Total amount of support: Dependent on the Foundation's annual giving budget.

NO. MOST RECENT APPLICANTS: 360.

APPLICATION INFO:
The first step for any potential applicant is to learn the specific components of the grantmaking strategies. If the potential applicant's organization does work or plans to do work related to one of the grantmaking strategies and a Request for Proposal (RFP) regarding that strategy is open for application, then a representative should attend a grant information session. This will give the potential applicant an opportunity to learn more about the grantmaking strategy, the RFP process and talk with a program officer.

The second step would be to submit a proposal with all the required information outlined in the RFP application checklist. The Foundation encourages submission of proposals via e-mail and accepts proposals postmarked and submitted electronically by the respective deadline date.

Duration: Grants are usually for one year, and should not be considered a source of ongoing support.

Deadline: Contact the Foundation for the appropriate grantmaking strategy application.

PUBLICATIONS:
Annual report; RFP guidelines; research papers; *One Magazine.*

IRS I.D.: 20-5205488

BOARD OF DIRECTORS:
Wade W. Loo, Chairperson
Nicole Taylor, President and Chief Executive Officer
Alan Zafran, Secretary/Treasurer
Rebecca Guerra
Greta S. Hansen
Marie Oh Huber
Larry Kramer
Julie Miraglia Kwon
Judy Minor
Kate Mitchell
Shannon Nash
Daniel Perez
Mauricio Simbeck
Luz Urrutia
Isaac Vaughn

*SPECIAL STIPULATIONS:
Funding limited to San Mateo and Santa Clara counties only.

SOUTHWEST FLORIDA COMMUNITY FOUNDATION [1248]

2031 Jackson Street
Suite 100
Fort Myers, FL 33901
(239) 274-5900
Fax: (239) 274-5930
E-mail: info@floridacommunity.com
bkelly@floridacommunity.com
Web Site: collaboratory.org

FOUNDED: 1976

AREAS OF INTEREST:
Community design, arts communities and culture, economy and jobs, education, health safety, animals, environment, equity empowerment, climate change, resources for change, philanthropy and community trust.

TYPE:
Demonstration grants; Project/program grants; Scholarships.

PURPOSE:
To connect donors and their philanthropic aspirations with evolving community needs.

LEGAL BASIS:
501(c)(3).

ELIGIBILITY:
Grants are made to organizations that have tax-exempt status under Section 501(c)(3) of the Internal Revenue Code. No grants are made to individuals. Nonsectarian religious programs may apply. Must serve the needs of the communities listed below.

GEOG. RESTRICTIONS: Charlotte, Collier, Glades, Hendry and Lee counties, Florida.

FINANCIAL DATA:
Amount of support per award: $5,000 to $25,000; Initiative Grant Awards: Up to $50,000.

Total amount of support: $5,200,000 in grants and $901,729 in scholarships for fiscal year 2018.

NO. MOST RECENT APPLICANTS: Varies.

NO. AWARDS: Grants: 20; Scholarships: 135.

APPLICATION INFO:
Contact the Foundation for application procedures.
Duration: One year.
Deadline: Varies per program.

PUBLICATIONS:
Annual report; quarterly newsletter.

IRS I.D.: 59-6580974

ADMINISTRATORS:
Sarah Owen, President and Chief Executive Officer

ADDRESS INQUIRIES TO:
Barbara Kelly, Impact Coordinator
(See address above.)

STARK COMMUNITY FOUNDATION [1249]

400 Market Avenue North
Suite 200
Canton, OH 44702-2107
(330) 454-3426
Fax: (330) 454-5855
E-mail: info@starkcf.org
Web Site: www.starkcf.org

FOUNDED: 1963

AREAS OF INTEREST:
Advancement of the health, social welfare, education, culture or civic improvement of the community.

TYPE:
Capital grants; Challenge/matching grants; Demonstration grants; Development grants; General operating grants; Matching gifts; Project/program grants; Research grants; Scholarships; Seed money grants; Technical assistance; Training grants; Loan forgiveness programs.

YEAR PROGRAM STARTED: 1965

PURPOSE:
To improve the quality of life for residents of Stark County, OH.

LEGAL BASIS:
Community foundation.

ELIGIBILITY:
Organizations with 501(c)(3) status serving Stark County, OH, are eligible. The Foundation will not support operating expenses of well-established organizations, deficit programs, or capital expenditures, endowment funds, religious organizations or religious purposes, annual appeal or membership contributions, conferences or recognition events.

GEOG. RESTRICTIONS: Stark County, Ohio.

FINANCIAL DATA:
Approximately $305,000,000 in total assets as of January 31, 2020.

Amount of support per award: $1,000 to $225,000.

Total amount of support: Approximately $15,300,000 for the year 2020.

Matching fund requirements: No general requirements.

NO. AWARDS: 650 grants and 315 scholarships for the year 2020.

APPLICATION INFO:
Application information is available on the web site.
Duration: One year.
Deadline: Varies.

PUBLICATIONS:
Annual report; guidelines and policies; *Community and Commitment,* newsletter.

STAFF:
Mark Samolczyk, President

ADDRESS INQUIRIES TO:
Mark Samolczyk, President
(See address above.)

THE STEELE-REESE FOUNDATION [1250]

32 Washington Square West
New York, NY 10011
(917) 331-2741
Fax: (212) 286-8513
E-mail: charles@steele-reese.org
Web Site: www.steele-reese.org

FOUNDED: 1955

AREAS OF INTEREST:
Education, health, social welfare, the humanities and the environment.

TYPE:
General operating grants; Project/program grants. Funding is only provided for rural projects of interest to the Foundation. The projects must serve people in the geographic area served by the Foundation.

In Appalachian Kentucky, grants are awarded for elementary and secondary school education purposes only.

YEAR PROGRAM STARTED: 1955

LEGAL BASIS:
Private foundation.

ELIGIBILITY:
Funding is provided to nonprofit organizations servicing communities in Appalachian Kentucky and the western states of Idaho and Montana.

All organizations seeking funds must demonstrate additional local community support for their programming.

GEOG. RESTRICTIONS: Appalachian Kentucky, Idaho and Montana.

FINANCIAL DATA:
Amount of support per award: Typically $5,000 to $50,000. Larger grants are typically for multiyear support.

Matching fund requirements: Some grants require that an organization raise a specific matching amount.

NO. MOST RECENT APPLICANTS: 200 to 250.

NO. AWARDS: Approximately 60.

APPLICATION INFO:
The Foundation welcomes proposals that are accurately aimed. The Foundation's policies and guidelines in detail are available for review online. All applicants must submit proposal materials electronically through the Foundation's web site.

Duration: Grants payable over one to three years. Absolutely no renewals.

Deadline: Appalachian Kentucky: March 1 for consideration during the current fiscal year. Idaho and Montana: Approximately January 9.

PUBLICATIONS:
Annual report.

ADDRESS INQUIRIES TO:
For general inquiries about Foundation policies:

William T. Buice, Trustee
The Steele-Reese Foundation
(See address above.) or

Charles U. Buice, Trustee
The Steele-Reese Foundation
123 Fort Greene Place, No. 4
Brooklyn, NY 11217
(See e-mail address above.)

For Kentucky:
Judy Owens, Appalachian Director
2613 Clubside Court
Lexington, KY 40513
Tel & Fax: (859) 313-5225
E-mail: jkowensjd@aol.com

For Idaho or Montana:
Linda Tracy, Western Program Director
P.O. Box 8311
Missoula, MT 59807-8311
Tel: (406) 207-7984
Fax: (207) 470-3872
E-mail: linda@steele-reese.org

THE ABBOT AND DOROTHY H. STEVENS FOUNDATION [1251]
P.O. Box 111
North Andover, MA 01845
(978) 688-7211
E-mail: grantprocess@stevensfoundation.com

AREAS OF INTEREST:
Education, community welfare, arts and youth programs.

TYPE:
Capital grants; General operating grants; Project/program grants.

PURPOSE:
To improve the quality of life in greater Lawrence and Merrimack Valley.

ELIGIBILITY:
Eligible organizations must be IRS 501(c)(3) tax-exempt.

GEOG. RESTRICTIONS: Greater Lawrence and Merrimack Valley, Massachusetts.

FINANCIAL DATA:
Amount of support per award: $8,000 average.
Total amount of support: Varies.

APPLICATION INFO:
Applicants must include a copy of their IRS 501(c)(3) tax determination letter.
Duration: One year.
Deadline: Trustees meet monthly with the exception of July and August.

PUBLICATIONS:
Guidelines.

ADDRESS INQUIRIES TO:
Joshua Miner, Executive Director
(See address above.)

THE NATHANIEL AND ELIZABETH P. STEVENS FOUNDATION [1252]
P.O. Box 111
North Andover, MA 01845
(978) 688-7211
E-mail: grantprocess@stevensfoundation.com

AREAS OF INTEREST:
Education, community welfare, arts and youth programs.

TYPE:
Capital grants; General operating grants; Project/program grants.

PURPOSE:
To improve the quality of life in the greater Lawrence and Merrimack Valley.

ELIGIBILITY:
Eligible organizations must be IRS 501(c)(3) tax-exempt.

GEOG. RESTRICTIONS: Greater Lawrence and Merrimack Valley, Massachusetts.

FINANCIAL DATA:
Amount of support per award: $8,000 average.
Total amount of support: Varies.

APPLICATION INFO:
Applications must include a copy of the IRS 501(c)(3) tax determination letter.
Duration: One year.
Deadline: Trustees meet monthly with the exception of July and August.

PUBLICATIONS:
Guidelines.

ADDRESS INQUIRIES TO:
Joshua Miner, Executive Director
(See address above.)

H. CHASE STONE TRUST
c/o JPMorgan
370 17th Street, Suite 3200
Denver, CO 80202
(303) 607-7810
Fax: (303) 607-7761
E-mail: julie.golden@jpmorgan.com
Web Site: www.jpmorgan.com/onlinegrants

TYPE:
Project/program grants.

See entry 457 for full listing.

SUDBURY FOUNDATION [1253]
326 Concord Road
Sudbury, MA 01776
(978) 443-0849
Fax: (978) 579-9536
E-mail: contact@sudburyfoundation.org
Web Site: www.sudburyfoundation.org

FOUNDED: 1952

AREAS OF INTEREST:
Scholarships, environment, food initiatives and charitable grants for communities in the Sudbury area; children, youth and families.

NAME(S) OF PROGRAMS:
● **The Atkinson Scholarship Program**
● **Children, Youth and Families Program**
● **Farm and Local Food Program**
● **The Sudbury Program**

TYPE:
Project/program grants; Scholarships. Capacity-building grants.

YEAR PROGRAM STARTED: 1952

PURPOSE:
To improve the quality of life in Sudbury and the surrounding communities.

ELIGIBILITY:
Eligible organizations must be IRS 501(c)(3) tax-exempt. The Foundation funds projects in Sudbury and the 10 communities surrounding Sudbury that address the issues of Youth Development and Opportunity, Community Building, and Preservation of Community Character and Assets.

The Atkinson Scholarship Program provides college financial aid to students connected to Sudbury, MA.

Farm and Local Food program focuses on food and local farm initiatives in Massachusetts.

GEOG. RESTRICTIONS: Sudbury, Massachusetts and surrounding areas.

FINANCIAL DATA:
Scholarships are administered to the schools earmarked for specific students.
Amount of support per award: Scholarships: Up to $5,000 annually; Grants: $5,000 to $150,000.
Total amount of support: Varies.

NO. AWARDS: Scholarships: 59 for the year 2019; Grants to nonprofits: Approximately 35 per year.

APPLICATION INFO:
Details are available on the Foundation web site.
Duration: Typically one year.
Deadline: Varies.

ADDRESS INQUIRIES TO:
Marilyn Martino, Executive Director
(See address above.)

*SPECIAL STIPULATIONS:
Scholarship program open to local high school seniors only for undergraduate education.

THE SUMMERLEE FOUNDATION [1254]
5556 Caruth Haven Lane
Dallas, TX 75225
(214) 363-9000
Fax: (214) 363-1941
E-mail: info@summerlee.org
Web Site: www.summerlee.org

FOUNDED: 1988

AREAS OF INTEREST:
Animal protection and Texas history.

NAME(S) OF PROGRAMS:
● **Animal Protection Program**
● **Texas History**

TYPE:
Project/program grants; Research grants; Technical assistance.

YEAR PROGRAM STARTED: 1988

PURPOSE:
To promote animal protection and the prevention of cruelty to animals; to research and document all facets of Texas history.

LEGAL BASIS:
Charitable foundation.

ELIGIBILITY:
No grants are made for religious purposes or to individuals. Must be 501(c)(3).

FINANCIAL DATA:
Amount of support per award: $5,000 to $10,000.

NO. MOST RECENT APPLICANTS: Approximately 200.

NO. AWARDS: 84.

APPLICATION INFO:
Guidelines are available on the Foundation web site.
Duration: Generally one year; occasionally multiyear.
Deadline: Varies.

IRS I.D.: 75-2252355

OFFICERS:
John W. Crain, Chairman

Mary Volcansek, Ph.D., Vice Chairman
Gary N. Smith, President
Jim Bruseth, Ph.D., Treasurer
Hon. David D. Jackson, Assistant Secretary

BOARD OF DIRECTORS:
Melanie K. Anderson
Jim Bruseth, Ph.D.
Joan Casey
John W. Crain
Hon. Nikki DeShazo
Ron Tyler, Ph.D.
Mary Volcansek, Ph.D.

ADDRESS INQUIRIES TO:
Melanie K. Anderson
Program Director-Animal Protection or
Gary N. Smith
Program Director-Texas History
(See address above.)

THE SUMMIT FOUNDATION [1255]

103 South Harris Street
Breckenridge, CO 80424
(970) 453-5970
E-mail: info@summitfoundation.org
Web Site: www.summitfoundation.org

FOUNDED: 1984

AREAS OF INTEREST:
Art and culture, health and human service, education, environment and sports.

TYPE:
Capital grants; Challenge/matching grants; Endowments; General operating grants; Project/program grants; Scholarships; Technical assistance. The Foundation supports scholarship programs at Summit High School and neighboring community high schools. Scholarships are available to graduating seniors each year.

YEAR PROGRAM STARTED: 1984

PURPOSE:
To improve the quality of life for residents and guests of Summit County and neighboring communities.

LEGAL BASIS:
Community foundation.

ELIGIBILITY:
Grants are made to organizations that have tax-exempt status under Section 501(c)(3) of the Internal Revenue Code. No grants are made to individuals.

GEOG. RESTRICTIONS: Summit County and neighboring communities of Alma, Fairplay, Kremmling and Leadville, Colorado.

FINANCIAL DATA:
Amount of support per award: Varies.
Total amount of support: Approximately $4,000,000 for the year 2019.

NO. AWARDS: Over 100.

APPLICATION INFO:
Applications are accepted through the online grant portal.
Deadline: Typically April and October.

IRS I.D.: 74-2341399

ADDRESS INQUIRIES TO:
Tara Dew, Program Manager
E-mail: tara@summitfoundation.org

SYNTHOMER/OMNOVA SOLUTIONS FOUNDATION [1256]

25435 Harvard Road
Beachwood, OH 44122-6201
(216) 682-7067
Fax: (216) 453-0113
E-mail: theresa.carter@omnova.com
Web Site: www.omnova.com

FOUNDED: 1999

AREAS OF INTEREST:
Support of educational, cultural and 501(c)(3) organizations in areas where Synthomer/OMNOVA Solutions has large concentrations of employment.

TYPE:
Capital grants; Development grants; Endowments; General operating grants; Matching gifts; Product donations; Project/program grants; Scholarships.

YEAR PROGRAM STARTED: 1999

PURPOSE:
To support education and other charitable organizations in the communities where Synthomer/OMNOVA Solutions has facilities.

LEGAL BASIS:
Nonprofit corporation, private foundation.

ELIGIBILITY:
501(c)(3) tax-exempt organizations are eligible.

GEOG. RESTRICTIONS: Georgia, Massachusetts, North Carolina, Ohio, Pennsylvania and South Carolina.

FINANCIAL DATA:
Amount of support per award: $100 to $50,000. Average $5,000.
Total amount of support: $1,195,689 for the year 2019.

NO. AWARDS: Approximately 271 for the year 2019.

REPRESENTATIVE AWARDS:
American Red Cross; Akron Community Service Center and Urban League; Akron Symphony Orchestra; United Way; Great Akron and Greater Cleveland Food Banks.

APPLICATION INFO:
Application is available on the Foundation web site.
Duration: One year. Renewable.
Deadline: October 30.

PUBLICATIONS:
Application guidelines; annual report.

IRS I.D.: 34-1909350

TRUSTEES:
Paul DeSantis, Chairman
Christopher Weber, Treasurer
Erin Hagen
Jackie Laurich
Marshall Moore

STAFF:
Kim Huff, Community Relations Representative

ADDRESS INQUIRIES TO:
Theresa Carter, President
(See address above.)

THOMAS THOMPSON TRUST [1257]

c/o Rackemann, Sawyer & Brewster
160 Federal Street, 15th Floor
Boston, MA 02110-1700
(617) 951-1108
Fax: (617) 542-7437
E-mail: smonahan@rackemann.com
Web Site: www.thomasthompsontrust.org

AREAS OF INTEREST:
Education, health/mental health, social services and cultural.

TYPE:
Capital grants; Challenge/matching grants; Conferences/seminars; Demonstration grants; Development grants; Endowments; Professorships; Project/program grants; Seed money grants; Technical assistance; Training grants; Research contracts. Support for special programs, capital support, new construction, renovation and equipment.

PURPOSE:
To promote health, education, or general social and civic betterment.

LEGAL BASIS:
Private foundation.

ELIGIBILITY:
Eligible organizations must be in operation for three consecutive years prior to submitting an application.

GEOG. RESTRICTIONS: Dutchess County, New York, particularly in Rhinebeck; and Windham County, Vermont, particularly in Brattleboro.

FINANCIAL DATA:
Amount of support per award: $5,000 to $25,000.
Total amount of support: $775,950 for fiscal year ended May 31, 2020.
Matching fund requirements: Determined on case-by-case basis.

NO. MOST RECENT APPLICANTS: 59.

NO. AWARDS: 41 for fiscal year ended May 31, 2020.

REPRESENTATIVE AWARDS:
Brattleboro Boys and Girls Club; Windham Housing Trust; Groundworks Collaborative; Culture Connect.

APPLICATION INFO:
Applications must be submitted online.
Duration: Varies.
Deadline: Generally January 5, April 1, July 1 and October 1.

PUBLICATIONS:
Application guidelines.

TRUSTEES:
Susan T. Monahan
Maura E. Murphy, Esq.
Michael F. O'Connell, Esq.

ADDRESS INQUIRIES TO:
Susan T. Monahan
Grants Coordinator and Trustee
(See address or e-mail above.)

TIDES FOUNDATION [1258]

P.O. Box 399389
San Francisco, CA 94139-9389
(415) 561-6400
Fax: (415) 561-6401
E-mail: info@tides.org
Web Site: www.tides.org

FOUNDED: 1976

AREAS OF INTEREST:
Civic participation, economic development, economic and racial justice, environment, environmental justice, LGBTIQ communities, HIV/AIDS, native communities, progressive media, arts and culture, violence prevention, women's empowerment and reproductive health, and youth organizing and development.

NAME(S) OF PROGRAMS:
- **Antonio Pizzigati Prize for Software in the Public Interest**

TYPE:
General operating grants; Project/program grants.

YEAR PROGRAM STARTED: 1976

PURPOSE:
To partner with donors to increase and organize resources for social change.

LEGAL BASIS:
Public foundation.

FINANCIAL DATA:
Amount of support per award: Varies.
Total amount of support: $291,149,400 in grants (U.S. and international) in 2018.

NO. AWARDS: Approximately 2,350 grants for the year 2018.

APPLICATION INFO:
The Fund does not accept unsolicited grant requests.

IRS I.D.: 51-0198509

THE TRULL FOUNDATION [1259]

404 Fourth Street
Palacios, TX 77465
(361) 972-5241
E-mail: info@trullfoundation.org
Web Site: www.trullfoundation.org

FOUNDED: 1967

AREAS OF INTEREST:
Children, substance abuse problems, Texas coastal environment, and The Palacios County area.

CONSULTING OR VOLUNTEER SERVICES:
Assists local projects and organizations in Texas, with a priority to rural Texas.

TYPE:
Challenge/matching grants; Development grants; General operating grants; Project/program grants; Scholarships.

YEAR PROGRAM STARTED: 1948

PURPOSE:
To support charitable and educational programs.

LEGAL BASIS:
Private (family) foundation.

ELIGIBILITY:
Applicants must have federal tax-exemption letter from IRS.

GEOG. RESTRICTIONS: Primarily in rural Texas.

FINANCIAL DATA:
Amount of support per award: $2,000 to $5,000 average.
Total amount of support: Approximately $1,000,000 to $2,000,000.

NO. AWARDS: 116 for the year 2020.

APPLICATION INFO:
Guidelines are available on the Foundation web site.

Duration: Usually no more than one year per project.
Deadline: Announcement within three months after receipt of proposal.

PUBLICATIONS:
Biennial report; application guidelines; proposal fact sheet.

IRS I.D.: 23-7423943

ADDRESS INQUIRIES TO:
Nellie Lee, Executive Director
(See address above.)

U.S. BANCORP FOUNDATION [1260]

BC-MN-H21B
800 Nicollet Mall
Minneapolis, MN 55402
(612) 303-4000
E-mail: usbankgrants@usbank.com
Web Site: www.usbank.com/community/index.aspx

FOUNDED: 1979

AREAS OF INTEREST:
Workforce education and economic prosperity, neighborhood stability and revitalization, and artistic and cultural enrichment and learning through play.

NAME(S) OF PROGRAMS:
- **Community Possible**

TYPE:
Capital grants; Development grants; General operating grants; Matching gifts; Project/program grants.

PURPOSE:
To improve the quality of life in communities where U.S. Bancorp employees live and work.

LEGAL BASIS:
Corporate foundation.

ELIGIBILITY:
Organizations must be IRS 501(c)(3) tax-exempt and must be located in communities where United States Bank operates.

The Foundation charitable contributions program will not provide funding for:
(1) organizations not tax-exempt under Internal Revenue Code Section 501(c)(3);
(2) fraternal organizations, merchant associations, chamber memberships or programs, or 501(c)(4) or (6) organizations;
(3) fund-raising events or sponsorships, "pass through" organizations or private foundations;
(4) organizations outside U.S. Bancorp communities;
(5) programs operated by religious organizations for religious purposes;
(6) political organizations or organizations designed primarily to lobby;
(7) individuals;
(8) travel and related expenses;
(9) endowment campaigns;
(10) deficit reduction;
(11) organizations receiving primary funding from the United Way or;

(12) organizations whose practices are not in keeping with the Company's equal opportunity policy.

GEOG. RESTRICTIONS: Communities where United States Bank has operations.

FINANCIAL DATA:
Amount of support per award: Varies.
Total amount of support: Varies.

APPLICATION INFO:
Organizations that are new to the Foundation must submit a Letter of Interest online. Applications are accepted by invitation only.
Duration: One year.

PUBLICATIONS:
Guidelines; Corporate Citizenship Report.

IRS I.D.: 41-1359579

ADDRESS INQUIRIES TO:
See e-mail address above.

U.S. DEPARTMENT OF HEALTH AND HUMAN SERVICES [1261]

Office of Innovation
330 C Street, S.W.
Washington, DC 20201
(202) 401-4634
Web Site: www.acl.gov

AREAS OF INTEREST:
Developmental disabilities.

NAME(S) OF PROGRAMS:
- **Projects of National Significance for Persons with Developmental Disabilities**

TYPE:
Demonstration grants; Technical assistance; Training grants. Model demonstration grants. Support for persons with developmental disabilities.

YEAR PROGRAM STARTED: 1975

PURPOSE:
To support policy development and awards funding that enhance the independence, productivity, inclusion and integration of people with developmental disabilities and their families.

LEGAL BASIS:
Government agency.

ELIGIBILITY:
Applicants must be nonprofit organizations, state agencies, or consortia.

GEOG. RESTRICTIONS: United States and its territories.

FINANCIAL DATA:
Amount of support per award: Varies.
Total amount of support: $8,000,000 budgeted for the year 2018.
Matching fund requirements: 25% local match.

NO. AWARDS: Varies.

APPLICATION INFO:
Application information is available on the web site.
Duration: 12 to 60 months.
Deadline: Varies.

OFFICERS:
Julie Hocker, Commissioner, Administration on Disabilities

ADDRESS INQUIRIES TO:
Allison Cruz, Director
(See address above.)

U.S. DEPARTMENT OF HOUSING AND URBAN DEVELOPMENT [1262]
Entitlement Communities Division
451 7th Street, S.W., Room 7282
Washington, DC 20410
(202) 708-3587 (Office of Block Grant Assistance)
(202) 708-1577 (Entitlement Division)
(202) 708-1322 (State/Small Cities Division)
Fax: (202) 401-2044
E-mail: gloria.l.coates@hud.gov
Web Site: www.hudexchange.info

FOUNDED: 1974

AREAS OF INTEREST:
Community development.

NAME(S) OF PROGRAMS:
● **Community Development Block Grant Program: Entitlement Program**

TYPE:
Block grants; Project/program grants. Acquisition, construction of certain public works, facilities and improvements, clearance, housing rehabilitation, relocation and demolition, public services (limited), activities relating to conservation and renewable energy resources, neighborhood revitalization and economic development projects, including assistance to micro enterprises.

YEAR PROGRAM STARTED: 1975

PURPOSE:
To develop viable urban communities, including decent housing and a suitable living environment and expand economic opportunities, principally for persons of low and moderate income.

LEGAL BASIS:
Units of general local government under Title I of the Housing and Community Development Act of 1974 (PL 93-383).

ELIGIBILITY:
The following units of general local government and states are all entitled to receive block grants from the CDBG Entitlement Program and State and Small Cities Program. Grant amounts are determined by a statutory formula:
(1) principal cities of Metropolitan Statistical Areas (MSAs);
(2) other metropolitan cities with a population of at least 50,000 and;
(3) qualified urban counties, as defined in the Act, with populations of at least 200,000 (excluding the population of entitled cities).

Under the HUD Administered Small Cities Program, HUD directly awards grants to non-entitled units of general local government within the state of Hawaii by formula. The total value of grants awarded through this Program is determined by statutory formula.

FINANCIAL DATA:
Amount of support per award: Varies from city to city.
Total amount of support: Approximately $3 billion for fiscal year 2019.

APPLICATION INFO:
For the CDBG Entitlement Program, a grantee must develop and submit to HUD its consolidated plan, which is a jurisdiction's comprehensive planning document and application for funding under the Community Planning and Development formula grant programs: CDBG, HOME, Emergency Shelter Grants (ESG) and Housing

Opportunities for Persons with AIDS (HOPWA). In its consolidated plan, the jurisdiction must identify its goals for these community planning and development programs, as well as for housing programs. These goals will serve as the criteria against which HUD will evaluate a jurisdiction's plan and its performance under the plan. In addition, the consolidated plan must include required certifications, including that not less than 70% of the CDBG funds expended over a one-, two- or three-year period specified by the grantee, will be used for activities that benefit low- and moderate-income persons. A consolidated plan submission will be approved by HUD unless the plan (or a portion of it) is inconsistent with the purposes of the National Affordable Housing Act or it is substantially incomplete.

Under the HUD Administered Small Cities Program, to receive a grant, the counties of Hawaii, Maui and Kauai in Hawaii must prepare and submit a consolidated plan to HUD.

ADDRESS INQUIRIES TO:
Office of Block Grant Assistance
(See address above.)

*SPECIAL STIPULATIONS:
Block grants made to states and local governments, not individuals.

THE UNITY FOUNDATION OF LAPORTE COUNTY [1263]
422 Franklin Street
Suite C
Michigan City, IN 46360
(219) 879-0327
Fax: (219) 210-3881
E-mail: unity@uflc.net
Web Site: www.uflc.net

FOUNDED: 1992

AREAS OF INTEREST:
Community development in LaPorte County, IN.

CONSULTING OR VOLUNTEER SERVICES:
Technical assistance to nonprofits and donors.

NAME(S) OF PROGRAMS:
● **Community Fund**

TYPE:
Challenge/matching grants; Grants-in-aid; Project/program grants; Scholarships; Technical assistance. Community Fund makes grants to education, the arts, health and human services, and the environment to the whole community. Grants are based on what the community needs at a given time.

YEAR PROGRAM STARTED: 1992

PURPOSE:
To improve the quality of life in LaPorte County, IN.

LEGAL BASIS:
Indiana corporation 501(c)(3).

ELIGIBILITY:
Nonprofits serving people of LaPorte County, IN.

GEOG. RESTRICTIONS: LaPorte County, Indiana.

FINANCIAL DATA:
Amount of support per award: Community grants: Up to $3,000.
Total amount of support: More than $700,000 in community grants and more than $130,000 in scholarships each year.

NO. MOST RECENT APPLICANTS: Grants: 89.

NO. AWARDS: 81.

APPLICATION INFO:
Applications should follow the format outlined in the online directions. The following information is required:
(1) narrative describing the program or specific need to be addressed, its significance to the community and its particular benefit to those living in the LaPorte County area, and the names and qualifications of those persons who will carry it out;
(2) complete budget for the project, including funding plan, amount of the request, and names of other funding sources the organization has applied to for assistance and;
(3) description of applicant organization(s) including the name, address, telephone and fax number of the contact person, a list of the officers and board members, a copy of the IRS letter designating the organization as 501(c)(3) federal tax-exempt, latest annual financial report, and any descriptive brochures or promotional literature.
Deadline: Grants: April 1; Scholarships: January 1.

PUBLICATIONS:
Report to Community.

STAFF:
Maggi Spartz, President

ADDRESS INQUIRIES TO:
Maggi Spartz, President
(See address above.)

VAN LOBEN SELS/REMBEROCK FOUNDATION [1264]
131 Steuart Street
Suite 301
San Francisco, CA 94105
(415) 512-0500
Fax: (415) 371-0227
E-mail: nwiltsek@vlsrr.org
Web Site: www.vlsrr.org

FOUNDED: 1964

AREAS OF INTEREST:
Legal services.

TYPE:
General operating grants; Project/program grants; Seed money grants.

YEAR PROGRAM STARTED: 1964

PURPOSE:
To support projects that will test potentially useful innovations in the areas of public interest law.

LEGAL BASIS:
Private independent foundation.

ELIGIBILITY:
Grants are restricted to northern California. Grants are not ordinarily made for projects requiring medical, scientific or other technical knowledge for evaluation, operating budgets of well-established organizations, capital expenditures, to national organizations unless for a specific local project, to individuals or for scholarships.

GEOG. RESTRICTIONS: Northern California.

FINANCIAL DATA:
Amount of support per award: Most grants $7,500 to $30,000.
Total amount of support: $1,812,500 for the year 2019.

NO. AWARDS: 85 for the year 2019.

REPRESENTATIVE AWARDS:
$40,000 to Bay Area Legal Aid to support their work providing access to the civil justice system through accessible quality legal assistance; $20,000 to Eviction Defense Collaborative to support their work providing tenants with legal representation and rental assistance; $10,000 to LGBT Asylum Project for affirmative and defensive immigration legal services for LGBT clients fleeing persecution and seeking asylum in the U.S.

APPLICATION INFO:
Application information is available on the web site.

Duration: Most grants are awarded on a single-year basis, but may be renewed if warranted.

Deadline: Proposals are considered every two to three months. Deadlines are four times a year, dates of which are posted on the Foundation web site. Announcement several days after Board meetings.

BOARD OF DIRECTORS:
Toni Rembe, President
Brian Wong, Treasurer
Julie Divola, Secretary
Irma Herrera
Thomas C. Layton

EXECUTIVE DIRECTOR:
Nancy Wiltsek

ADDRESS INQUIRIES TO:
Nancy Wiltsek, Executive Director
(See address above.)

VENTURA COUNTY COMMUNITY FOUNDATION   [1265]

4001 Mission Oaks Boulevard
Suite A
Camarillo, CA 93012
(805) 330-6672
Fax: (805) 484-2700
E-mail: pwiggins@vccf.org
Web Site: www.vccf.org

FOUNDED: 1987

AREAS OF INTEREST:
Community needs and development, culture, education, health, human services, women's issues and Latino issues.

TYPE:
Project/program grants; Scholarships.

YEAR PROGRAM STARTED: 1987

PURPOSE:
To promote and enable philanthropy to improve our community, for good, forever.

ELIGIBILITY:
Must qualify under the Internal Revenue Code Section 501(c)(3) as a nonprofit organization, or operate under the fiscal sponsorship of an organization that does, and serve residents of Ventura County, CA.

GEOG. RESTRICTIONS: Ventura County, California.

FINANCIAL DATA:
Amount of support per award: Varies.
Total amount of support: Varies.

NO. AWARDS: 802.

APPLICATION INFO:
Applications accepted only in response to an open request for proposals.

Duration: Varies per program.

ADDRESS INQUIRIES TO:
Appropriate program officer, as outlined in the Request for Proposals.

VICTORIA FOUNDATION, INC.   [1266]

31 Mulberry Street, Fifth Floor
Newark, NJ 07102
(973) 792-9200
Fax: (973) 792-1300
E-mail: info@victoriafoundation.org
Web Site: www.victoriafoundation.org

FOUNDED: 1924

AREAS OF INTEREST:
Education, neighborhood revitalization, youth and families in Newark, NJ, as well as statewide environmental issues.

TYPE:
Capital grants; Challenge/matching grants; General operating grants; Project/program grants. The focus in Education includes after-school programs, educational enrichment, teacher training and curriculum development.

Neighborhood Revitalization includes community development, employment training, housing programs and community organizing.

The focus in Youth and Families includes youth development programs and efforts to strengthen families.

The concentration in Environment includes open space preservation in New Jersey, particularly in the Highlands and Pinelands.

YEAR PROGRAM STARTED: 1924

PURPOSE:
To promote education, urban environment, neighborhood development and urban revitalization, and youth and families in the city of Newark; to preserve and conserve resources including land and water in the state of New Jersey and within the city of Newark.

LEGAL BASIS:
Independent foundation.

ELIGIBILITY:
Organizations must be nonprofit per Internal Revenue Code 501(c)(3) and must address the Foundation's interests. No grants are made to individuals or for programs dealing with specific diseases, afflictions or geriatric needs. Proposals from arts organizations will be considered only if they directly bear on education.

General programs are focused within Newark, NJ. Environmental programs encompass the areas of New Jersey Highlands, Pine Barrens, Kittatinny Ridge and Valley Regions of New Jersey.

GEOG. RESTRICTIONS: Newark, New Jersey.

FINANCIAL DATA:
Amount of support per award: Varies.
Total amount of support: Varies.

NO. MOST RECENT APPLICANTS: Approximately 300.

NO. AWARDS: Varies.

REPRESENTATIVE AWARDS:
$75,000 to New Jersey Symphony Orchestra to support the Newark Early Strings Program, which provides Suzuki violin instruction to over 500 elementary school children;

$130,000 to Ironbound Community Corporation towards general operating support.

APPLICATION INFO:
Application information is available on the web site. Applicants must apply through the online portal. No mail-in applications will be accepted.

Duration: One year. Renewal based upon careful trustee and staff review of subsequent proposal submissions.

Deadline: Current grantees: Mid-January and mid-July; New applicants: Early January and mid- to late June; School applications: February 1; Summer camp: First week of September. Announcements in late June and December; Environment land acquisitions accepted on a rolling basis.

PUBLICATIONS:
Annual report.

IRS I.D.: 22-1554541

OFFICERS:
Frank Alvarez, President
Margaret H. Parker, Vice President
Gary M. Wingens, Treasurer
Irene Cooper-Basch, Executive Officer and Secretary

TRUSTEES:
Frank Alvarez
Henry Amoroso
Ana Baptista
Michael Catania
Sally Chubb
Robert Holmes
Robert L. Johnson, M.D.
Franklin E. Parker, IV
John F. Parker
Margaret H. Parker
Denise Rodgers
Sara Chubb Sauvayre
Bei Saville
Grizel Ubarry
Gary M. Wingens
A. Zachery Yamba

ADDRESS INQUIRIES TO:
Irene Cooper-Basch, Executive Officer
(See address above.)

THE WACO FOUNDATION   [1267]

1227 North Valley Mills Drive
Suite 235
Waco, TX 76710
(254) 754-3404
(254) 752-9457 (MAC Program)
Fax: (254) 753-2887
E-mail: mac@wacofoundation.org
Web Site: www.wacofoundation.org

FOUNDED: 1958

AREAS OF INTEREST:
Residents of McLennan County, TX.

NAME(S) OF PROGRAMS:
● **MAC College Money Program**

TYPE:
Scholarships. Intended to promote postsecondary educational opportunities in the community, and thereby promote greater employment opportunities for those of working age.

YEAR PROGRAM STARTED: 1995

PURPOSE:
To make a positive difference in the lives and future of the people who live in Waco and McLennan County through grantmaking, promotion of community philanthropy, and support of the not-for-profit sector.

ELIGIBILITY:
Must have graduated from McLennan County high schools and have family income of less than $50,000.

GEOG. RESTRICTIONS: McLennan County, Texas.

FINANCIAL DATA:
Amount of support per award: Varies.
Total amount of support: $500,000 in contributions annually.

APPLICATION INFO:
High school seniors must submit completed application form and FAFSA.
Duration: Two years. Renewable for two years.
Deadline: May 1 of student's senior year of high school.

ADDRESS INQUIRIES TO:
Maria Arevalo, MAC and Scholarships Coordinator
(See address above.)

DENNIS & PHYLLIS WASHINGTON FOUNDATION [1268]
P.O. Box 16630
Missoula, MT 59808
(406) 523-1300
E-mail: info@dpwfoundation.org
Web Site: www.dpwfoundation.org

FOUNDED: 1987

AREAS OF INTEREST:
Direct service, youth-focused programs in arts and culture, community service, health and human services, and education.

TYPE:
Project/program grants; Scholarships.

YEAR PROGRAM STARTED: 1987

PURPOSE:
To invest in people to improve the quality of their lives.

LEGAL BASIS:
Private foundation.

ELIGIBILITY:
Eligible organizations must be IRS 501(c)(3) tax-exempt. Low administrative costs required. Indirect or overhead costs not directly related to implementation of a grant are not allowed.

GEOG. RESTRICTIONS: Montana and communities where Washington has services.

FINANCIAL DATA:
Amount of support per award: Varies.
Total amount of support: Varies.

APPLICATION INFO:
Grant applicants must complete the online application process which includes reading grant guidelines and completion of a short eligibility review. If qualified, the organization will be invited to submit a full application online.

Scholarship applicants can review application guidelines on the Foundation's web site.
Duration: One to three years.
Deadline: Applications are accepted on a rolling basis.

ADDRESS INQUIRIES TO:
See e-mail address above.

WASHINGTON FORREST FOUNDATION [1269]
2407 Columbia Pike, Suite 200
Arlington, VA 22204
(703) 920-3688
Fax: (703) 920-0130
E-mail: allison@washingtonforrest.org
Web Site: washingtonforrest.org

FOUNDED: 1968

AREAS OF INTEREST:
Human services, education and community development organizations or programs serving South Arlington, VA.

TYPE:
Capital grants; General operating grants; Project/program grants; Seed money grants. Pilot project grants.

PURPOSE:
To improve and enhance the quality of life in South Arlington, VA.

LEGAL BASIS:
Public foundation.

ELIGIBILITY:
Eligible organizations must be IRS 501(c)(3) tax-exempt and be located in northern Virginia.

Capital grants to existing grantees only.

Pilot project grants and seed money grants are usually awarded to existing organizations for unique programs.

GEOG. RESTRICTIONS: South Arlington, Virginia.

FINANCIAL DATA:
Amount of support per award: $5,000 to $30,000.
Total amount of support: Approximately $850,000.

NO. MOST RECENT APPLICANTS: 59.

NO. AWARDS: 59.

APPLICATION INFO:
Applicants should first call the Foundation to discuss the proposal. Applications must include a copy of the IRS tax determination letter.
Duration: One year. Renewal by reapplication.
Deadline: One month prior to board meetings held in September, December and March. Dates will be posted online.

ADDRESS INQUIRIES TO:
Allison A. Erdle, Executive Director
(See address above.)

*SPECIAL STIPULATIONS:
Organization must be located in or have a program operating in South Arlington, VA.

WEGE FOUNDATION [1270]
99 Monroe Avenue, N.W.
Suite 902
Grand Rapids, MI 49503
(616) 957-0480
Fax: (616) 957-0616
E-mail: kfurtado@wegefoundation.org
Web Site: www.wegefoundation.org

FOUNDED: 1968

AREAS OF INTEREST:
Education, environment, arts and culture, and community health and well-being.

TYPE:
Capital grants; Endowments; General operating grants; Project/program grants.

YEAR PROGRAM STARTED: 1968

PURPOSE:
To assist programs and projects in the areas of education, environment, health care, arts and culture, and human services.

ELIGIBILITY:
Grants are made to tax-exempt, nonprofit organizations which meet the Foundation's current program priorities and are located in the west Michigan area.

GEOG. RESTRICTIONS: Grand Rapids, Kent County and west Michigan.

FINANCIAL DATA:
Amount of support per award: $500 to $40,000.
Total amount of support: Approximately $20,000,000 annually.

NO. MOST RECENT APPLICANTS: 299 for the year 2020.

NO. AWARDS: 261 for the year 2020.

APPLICATION INFO:
Applications must be submitted through the Foundation's web site.
Duration: One year. Renewal possible. Some multiyear grants are approved.
Deadline: Proposals are accepted twice per year for Spring and Fall grant review.

BOARD OF DIRECTORS AND TRUSTEES:
Jonathan Wege, Chairman
Mark Van Putten, President and Chief Executive Officer
Christopher Carter
Mary Goodwillie Nelson
Juan Olivarez
Johanna Osman
Caitlin Wege
Christopher Wege
Diana Wege
Laura Wege

THE HARRY AND JEANETTE WEINBERG FOUNDATION, INC. [1271]
7 Park Center Court
Owings Mills, MD 21117
(410) 654-8500
Fax: (410) 654-3943
E-mail: claumann@hjweinberg.org
Web Site: www.hjweinbergfoundation.org

FOUNDED: 1959

AREAS OF INTEREST:
Housing, health, jobs, education, and community services.

TYPE:
Capital grants; Challenge/matching grants; General operating grants; Matching gifts; Project/program grants.

ELIGIBILITY:
Grants are made to nonprofit 501(c)(3) organizations that provide direct services to low-income and vulnerable individuals and families, primarily in the U.S. and Israel. Grants are focused on meeting basic needs and enhancing an individual's ability to meet those needs with emphasis on older adults, the Jewish community and the hometown communities of Maryland, northeastern Pennsylvania and Hawaii.

Religious organizations are eligible to apply.

The Foundation does not give grants to individuals.

FINANCIAL DATA:
Amount of support per award: Varies.
Total amount of support: Varies.

NO. AWARDS: 724.

APPLICATION INFO:
Applicants must first determine eligibility by completing the online questionnaire.
Duration: Varies.
Deadline: Grant requests are accepted throughout the year.

ADDRESS INQUIRIES TO:
E-mail: grantsintake@hjweinberg.org

THOMAS H. WHITE FOUNDATION   [1272]
1422 Euclid Avenue, Suite 966
Cleveland, OH 44115-1952
(216) 696-7273
(216) 621-2901
Fax: (216) 621-8198
E-mail: sclancy@fmscleveland.com
Web Site: thomaswhitefoundation.org

FOUNDED: 1913

AREAS OF INTEREST:
Early childhood education, middle school to high school education, high school to higher education, and human services.

TYPE:
Project/program grants. The Foundation will focus its grantmaking in two major areas: Education and Human Services. Specifically, the Foundation is interested in supporting programs that address four critical areas:
(1) Workforce readiness: programs that emphasize science and technology education, adequate employment preparation, support systems and the relationship to earning potential;
(2) School retention: programs that emphasize the critical transition issues that occur during early teenage years and affect family relationships and school attendance;
(3) Early childhood enrichment: programs which enhance the learning environment; provide support, training and ancillary services to parents; and/or enhance the recruitment and training of day care providers and;
(4) Programs that support education in science, technology, engineering and math.

Organizations and programs that contribute generally to the quality of life in Greater Cleveland may also be considered at the Foundation's discretion.

YEAR PROGRAM STARTED: 1913

PURPOSE:
To improve educational resources and support charitable purposes in the city of Cleveland, OH.

LEGAL BASIS:
Private foundation.

ELIGIBILITY:
Grants awarded to tax-exempt, nonprofit charitable and educational institutions located within Cuyahoga County, OH, if such organizations, and their services and facilities, primarily serve residents of the city of Cleveland.

Applicants are discouraged from submitting requests for endowment, general operating support, research, symposia or seminars. No grants are awarded to individuals. The Foundation does not respond to general solicitations or annual fund-raising campaigns.

GEOG. RESTRICTIONS: Cuyahoga County, Ohio; primarily the city of Cleveland.

FINANCIAL DATA:
Amount of support per award: $5,000 to $25,000.
Total amount of support: Approximately $500,000 for the year 2020.
Matching fund requirements: Stipulated with individual programs.

APPLICATION INFO:
Application forms and guidelines are available on the Foundation web site.
Deadline: December 1, April 1 and August 1, for meetings held in March, June and October, respectively.

ADDRESS INQUIRIES TO:
Sherri Clancy, Consultant
(See address above.)

*SPECIAL STIPULATIONS:
Local giving only.

WICHITA COMMUNITY FOUNDATION   [1273]
301 North Main Street
Suite 100
Wichita, KS 67202
(316) 264-4880
Fax: (316) 264-7592
E-mail: wcf@wichitacf.org
Web Site: www.wichitacf.org

FOUNDED: 1986

AREAS OF INTEREST:
Arts, conservation, education, environmental health, humanities and social services.

TYPE:
Project/program grants; Scholarships; Seed money grants.

PURPOSE:
To provide a permanent resource for building community philanthropy.

LEGAL BASIS:
Community foundation.

ELIGIBILITY:
Grants are made to organizations that have tax-exempt status under Section 501(c)(3) of the Internal Revenue Code. No grants are made to individuals.

GEOG. RESTRICTIONS: Sedgwick County, Kansas.

FINANCIAL DATA:
Amount of support per award: $10,000 to $100,000.
Total amount of support: Approximately $5,500,000 for the year 2019.

APPLICATION INFO:
Grant application information is available on the web site. High school students may apply for scholarships online.
Duration: Typically one year.
Deadline: Grant applications are accepted throughout the year; deadlines vary. Scholarship applications: March 15.

ADDRESS INQUIRIES TO:
James Woods
Director of Nonprofit Services
(See address above.)

WOODS CHARITABLE FUND, INC.   [1274]
1248 O Street, Suite 1130
Lincoln, NE 68508
(402) 436-5971
E-mail: twoods@woodscharitable.org
Web Site: www.woodscharitable.org

FOUNDED: 1941

AREAS OF INTEREST:
Arts and culture, civic and community, education, and human services.

TYPE:
Challenge/matching grants; Demonstration grants; General operating grants; Project/program grants; Seed money grants; Technical assistance. Grants to support organizations and projects located in and directly serving the residents of Lincoln, NE.

YEAR PROGRAM STARTED: 1941

PURPOSE:
To strengthen the community by improving opportunities and life outcomes for all people in Lincoln, NE.

LEGAL BASIS:
Private foundation.

ELIGIBILITY:
Grants are made only to tax-exempt organizations described in Section 501(c)(3) of the IRS Code and which have a written ruling from the IRS that they also qualify under 509(a)(1), (2) or (3) of the Code (publicly supported organizations and their affiliates).

Geographically, grants are limited to organizations in Lincoln. Occasionally, the Fund reviews proposals from outside the city if the proposed activities have statewide impact and a significant Lincoln component. While the Fund makes grants in very diverse fields, fund-raising benefits or program advertising, individual needs, endowments, scholarships or fellowships are not eligible for grant review.

GEOG. RESTRICTIONS: Lincoln, Nebraska.

FINANCIAL DATA:
Amount of support per award: $5,000 to $300,000; average payment $32,270 for the year 2020.
Total amount of support: $1,645,750 in grants paid for the year 2020.

NO. MOST RECENT APPLICANTS: Approximately 180.

NO. AWARDS: 44.

REPRESENTATIVE AWARDS:
$20,000 to ACLU Nebraska Foundation, Inc., for a court-watching project in Lancaster County and related educational outreach; $15,000 to Leadership Lincoln, Inc., in support of the organization's Advocate's cohort, which develops strong leaders advocating for underrepresented voices; $20,000 to National Audubon Society, Inc., to support educational outreach that conserves and restores the tallgrass prairie ecosystem.

APPLICATION INFO:
Guidelines are available on the Fund web site. Before submitting a full proposal, applicants should contact the Fund with a two-page summary request and budget or a telephone call. If the request appears suitable, a full proposal will be requested.
Deadline: April 15 to 30 for November Board Meeting. October 15 to 31 for May Board Meeting. Proposals that arrive well before the deadline have a better chance for careful review.

IRS I.D.: 47-6032847

STAFF:
Tom Woods, President and Secretary

Kathy Steinauer Smith, Senior Community
Investment Director
Nicole Juranek, Community Investment
Director
Joan Stolle, Operations Manager

DIRECTORS:
Nelle Woods Jamison, Chairperson
Ed Wimes, Vice Chairperson
Hank Woods, Treasurer
Michael J. Tavlin, Assistant Treasurer
Pablo Cervantes
Jay Conrad
Michelle Suarez
Suk Wortman

ADDRESS INQUIRIES TO:
Tom Woods, President
(See address above.)

WOODS FUND CHICAGO   [1275]

200 West Madison Street
3rd Floor
Chicago, IL 60606
(312) 600-0948
E-mail: dclark@woodsfund.org
Web Site: www.woodsfund.org

FOUNDED: 1941

AREAS OF INTEREST:
Racial equity, economic justice, public policy
advocacy, and integration of community
organizing.

TYPE:
General operating grants; Project/program
grants.

PURPOSE:
To advance racial equity and economic
justice.

LEGAL BASIS:
Nonprofit.

ELIGIBILITY:
The Woods Fund will support organizations
that:
(1) have an explicit racial equity and
economic justice focus. The organization's
commitment to racial equity and economic
justice should be present in their mission,
vision, and/or values;
(2) prioritize and engage people most
impacted by structural racism and economic
injustice to lead the process of defining
problems and developing solutions;
(3) have the majority of people of color in
their leadership, including senior staff and
board membership and;
(4) lead with community organizing and/or
public policy advocacy as the strategies for
change.

GEOG. RESTRICTIONS: Metropolitan Chicago,
Illinois.

FINANCIAL DATA:
Amount of support per award: Funding
amounts depend on the size, capacity and
demonstrated efficacy of the organization.
Typically grants are $15,000 to $55,000. New
applicants generally receive $15,000 to
$25,000 annually for the initial year(s) of
funding.
Total amount of support: Typically
$2,300,000 in grants annually.

APPLICATION INFO:
Instructions are available at the Fund web
site.
Duration: One to two years.

*PLEASE NOTE:
Contact program officer prior to applying for
grant.

WYOMING ARTS COUNCIL

2301 Central Avenue
Barrett Building, 2nd Floor
Cheyenne, WY 82002
(307) 214-7819
E-mail: karen.merklin@wyo.gov
Web Site: wyoarts.state.wy.us

TYPE:
Awards/prizes; Conferences/seminars;
Development grants; Fellowships; General
operating grants; Project/program grants;
Technical assistance. Individual fellowships
are provided in visual, literary and
performing arts to Wyoming residents.

Folk & Traditional Arts Mentoring Project
Grants are designed to support the
transmission of Wyoming's finest folk and
traditional skills through the natural process
of in-person, hands-on instruction from a
master artist to a worthy apprentice.

Pattie Layser Fellowship is a national call
open to writers and journalists and seeks to
intersect science, education, current events,
and conservation to effectively communicate
the Greater Yellowstone's natural history and
singular importance to society through
creative and exceptional writing and subject
communication.

Native Art Fellowship is an unrestricted
award of merit, based on the artist's
portfolio, honoring the work of Native artists
based within Wyoming. Artists working
across any artistic discipline or medium
(visual, literary, performing, folk and
traditional, etc.) may apply. This fellowship
is designed to raise the profiles of the highly
talented Native artists in Wyoming and
celebrate their artistry. Recipients will be
given support to find a venue to showcase
their work.

See entry 479 for full listing.

Crime prevention

INTERNATIONAL CENTRE FOR COMPARATIVE CRIMINOLOGY   [1276]

University of Montreal
C.P. 6128, Succursale Centre-Ville
Montreal QC H3C 3J7 Canada
(514) 343-7065
Fax: (514) 343-2269
E-mail: cicc@umontreal.ca
Web Site: www.cicc-iccc.org

FOUNDED: 1969

AREAS OF INTEREST:
Sociology of crime and deviance,
comparative studies on criminal justice,
police, courts, prisons, victims, national and
international research, terrorism and
counterterrorism.

CONSULTING OR VOLUNTEER SERVICES:
In all the fields of criminal justice.

NAME(S) OF PROGRAMS:
● **Research Fieldwork**

TYPE:
Conferences/seminars; Exchange programs;
Fellowships. The Centre brings visiting
professors and specialists to confer on
projects and cooperate on research

investigation and invites graduate and
postgraduate students to do fieldwork at the
Centre.

YEAR PROGRAM STARTED: 1969

PURPOSE:
To provide funding to encourage continued
study in the field of crime and criminal
justice.

LEGAL BASIS:
University.

ELIGIBILITY:
Applicant must:
(1) hold a Ph.D. degree before starting the
postdoctoral research and for no more than
three years prior to the proposed starting date
of the fellowship;
(2) be supervised by a regular researcher
from the CICC. The researcher must formally
agree to supervise the candidate in the
postdoctoral research and will guarantee the
feasibility of the project;
(3) have completed university studies in a
field relevant or related to criminology:
anthropology, forensics, law, history,
psychiatry, psycho-education, psychology,
political science, sociology, applied social
sciences statistics, and social work are the
principal related fields and;
(4) master French or English. Applicant must
be able to write scientific papers, either in
French or English.

Priority will be given to candidates who are
co-supervised.

FINANCIAL DATA:
Amount of support per award: Postdoctoral
Fellowships: $33,485 (CAN) for the year
2019.

NO. MOST RECENT APPLICANTS: 6.

NO. AWARDS: Postdoctoral Fellowships: 1 or 2
per year.

APPLICATION INFO:
Detailed instructions are available on the
Centre's web site.
Duration: One year, January to December.
Deadline: July 15.

PUBLICATIONS:
Annual report; Revue *Criminologie.*

OFFICERS:
M. Remi Boivin, Director

ADDRESS INQUIRIES TO:
See e-mail address above.

NATIONAL INSTITUTE OF JUSTICE, U.S. DEPARTMENT OF JUSTICE   [1277]

810 Seventh Street, N.W.
Washington, DC 20531
(202) 307-2942
Web Site: www.nij.gov

FOUNDED: 1968

AREAS OF INTEREST:
Criminal justice research and evaluation,
program development, dissemination of
research-based criminal justice, and
fellowships.

NAME(S) OF PROGRAMS:
● **Research Grants**

TYPE:
Research grants. Grants and contracts related
to topics in criminal justice and social
science, physical science, and forensic
science, including those for evaluative

research; research and development grants and contracts in science and technology for criminal justice applications.

The focus of NIJ research is on generating information that is useful to state and local public officials in developing policies related to crime reduction.

YEAR PROGRAM STARTED: 1968

PURPOSE:
To increase knowledge of the causes, prevention, and control of crime, the effectiveness and efficiency of the criminal justice system, and the responsiveness of the nation's law enforcement and justice administration systems; to disseminate this knowledge to the federal, state, and local policymakers.

LEGAL BASIS:
Omnibus Crime Control and Safe Streets Act of 1968; Homeland Security Act of 2002.

ELIGIBILITY:
NIJ awards grants to or enters into cooperative agreements with educational institutions, nonprofit organizations, public agencies, individuals, and profit-making organizations that are willing to waive their fees. Special eligibility criteria are indicated in NIJ's solicitations for proposals.

GEOG. RESTRICTIONS: United States.

FINANCIAL DATA:
All NIJ awards must be used to supplement existing funds, not to replace those already appropriated for the same purpose.
Amount of support per award: $10,000 to $500,000.
Total amount of support: Approximately $250,000,000 annually.
Matching fund requirements: Units of state and local governments are encouraged to contribute matching funds and other applicants are encouraged to seek matching contributions from government agencies or private organizations.

NO. AWARDS: Approximately 400.

APPLICATION INFO:
Guidelines, applications, and information about specific solicitations for proposals are available on the web site.
Duration: Normally two years maximum. Renewal possible.
Deadline: Varies.

ADDRESS INQUIRIES TO:
National Criminal Justice Reference Service
P.O. Box 6000
Rockville, MD 20849-6000
Tel: (800) 851-3420

U.S. DEPARTMENT OF JUSTICE [1278]
Bureau of Justice Statistics
810 7th Street, N.W.
Washington, DC 20531
(202) 307-0765
E-mail: askbjs@usdoj.gov
Web Site: www.bjs.gov

FOUNDED: 1969

AREAS OF INTEREST:
Statistics on crime, victims of crime, criminal offenders and operations of justice systems at all levels of government throughout the U.S.

NAME(S) OF PROGRAMS:
● **State Justice Statistics for Statistical Analysis Centers**

TYPE:
Development grants; Research grants. Cooperative agreements for the development of statistical methods and techniques and the aggregation and analysis of statistical information on crime and criminal justice in the states.

YEAR PROGRAM STARTED: 1972

PURPOSE:
To develop and enhance the capabilities of the states in gathering, analyzing and using statistical information pertaining to crime and the criminal justice system and to obtain selected types of data for multistate aggregation.

LEGAL BASIS:
Government agency formed under the Justice System Improvement Act of 1979.

ELIGIBILITY:
Applicants must be state agencies whose activities include statistical analysis at the state level.

FINANCIAL DATA:
Amount of support per award: $75,000 to $210,000.
Total amount of support: Varies.

NO. MOST RECENT APPLICANTS: Approximately 39 for the year 2018.

APPLICATION INFO:
Applicants must register in the OJP Grants Management System prior to submitting an application.
Duration: 12 to 36 months.
Deadline: March 29.

ADDRESS INQUIRIES TO:
Devon Adams, Chief, Criminal Justice Data Improvement Program
(See address above.)

U.S. DEPARTMENT OF JUSTICE [1279]
Office of Juvenile Justice and Delinquency Prevention
810 Seventh Street, N.W., 7th Floor
Washington, DC 20531
(202) 307-5911
Fax: (202) 353-9093
E-mail: lynnell.clarke@usdoj.gov
Web Site: www.ojjdp.gov

FOUNDED: 1975

AREAS OF INTEREST:
Delinquency prevention research, juvenile gangs, serious violent juvenile offenders and juvenile justice statistics.

NAME(S) OF PROGRAMS:
● **Juvenile Justice and Delinquency Prevention Program**

TYPE:
Conferences/seminars; Development grants; Fellowships; Internships; Project/program grants; Research grants; Residencies; Visiting scholars; Research contracts. Grants to conduct research, evaluation and development on juvenile justice and delinquency prevention activities, including the development of new or improved approaches, techniques, systems and program models to conduct behavioral research on the causes of juvenile crime, means of, intervention and prevention, and to evaluate juvenile programs and procedures.

YEAR PROGRAM STARTED: 1975

PURPOSE:
To encourage, coordinate and conduct research and evaluation of juvenile justice and delinquency prevention activities; to provide a clearinghouse and information center for collecting, publishing and distributing information on juvenile delinquency; to conduct a national training program; to establish standards for the administration on juvenile justice. Current emphasis is work in the area of serious and violent juvenile crime, drug involvement by youth and missing children.

LEGAL BASIS:
Juvenile Justice Reform Act of 2018, Public Law 115-385, as amended.

ELIGIBILITY:
Public or private agencies, organizations, including institutions of higher learning, or individuals.

GEOG. RESTRICTIONS: United States and its territories.

FINANCIAL DATA:
Amount of support per award: Varies.
Total amount of support: Varies.

NO. MOST RECENT APPLICANTS: 100.

NO. AWARDS: 80.

REPRESENTATIVE AWARDS:
Law Enforcement Agencies Policies Regarding Missing Children; School Crime and Discipline Research and Discipline; Causes and Correlates of Delinquency.

APPLICATION INFO:
Contact the U.S. Department of Justice.
Duration: Generally one to three years.
Deadline: Varies.

PUBLICATIONS:
Annual report; annual program plan; various project reports.

ADDRESS INQUIRIES TO:
Juvenile Justice Clearinghouse
National Criminal Justice Reference Service
P.O. Box 6000
Rockville, MD 20849-6000
Tel: (800) 851-3420
Fax: (301) 240-5830

U.S. DEPARTMENT OF JUSTICE [1280]
Office of Juvenile Justice and Delinquency Prevention
810 Seventh Street, N.W., 7th Floor
Washington, DC 20531
(202) 307-5911
Fax: (202) 353-9093
E-mail: lynnell.clarke@usdoj.gov
Web Site: www.ojjdp.gov

AREAS OF INTEREST:
Juvenile justice, delinquency prevention and child protection.

NAME(S) OF PROGRAMS:
● **Juvenile Justice and Delinquency Prevention Allocation to States**

TYPE:
Block grants; Challenge/matching grants; Demonstration grants; Formula grants; Internships; Project/program grants; Research grants; Technical assistance; Training grants. Grants to increase the capacity of state and local governments to conduct effective juvenile justice and delinquency prevention programs as developed in the state comprehensive action plan.

YEAR PROGRAM STARTED: 1974

LEGAL BASIS:
Juvenile Justice Reform Act of 2018, Public Law 115-385, as amended.

ELIGIBILITY:
To receive an award, states must, each year, satisfy 28 state plan requirements. If a state does not meet these requirements, it is not eligible to receive its Formula Grants program allocation for that year.

GEOG. RESTRICTIONS: United States and its territories.

FINANCIAL DATA:
Amount of support per award: Varies.
Total amount of support: Varies.
Matching fund requirements: Formula is based upon population of people under age 18. No match is required except for construction programs, where the match is 50%. Seven and one half percent administrative funds are matched 100%.

NO. MOST RECENT APPLICANTS: 60.

NO. AWARDS: 60.

APPLICATION INFO:
Contact the U.S. Department of Justice.
Duration: One to three years from the fiscal year of awards.
Deadline: Varies.

ADDRESS INQUIRIES TO:
Juvenile Justice Clearinghouse
National Criminal Justice
Reference Service
P.O. Box 6000
Rockville, MD 20849-6000
Tel: (800) 851-3420
Fax: (301) 240-5830

Public health

AGENCY FOR HEALTHCARE RESEARCH AND QUALITY (AHRQ) [1281]
Office of Management Services
Division of Grants Management
5600 Fishers Lane, 7th Floor
Rockville, MD 20857
(301) 427-1104 (specify funding area)
(301) 427-1450
E-mail: gmi@ahrq.hhs.gov
Web Site: www.ahrq.gov

FOUNDED: 1968

AREAS OF INTEREST:
AHRQ is the primary source of federal support for research on problems related to the quality and delivery of health services.

NAME(S) OF PROGRAMS:
● AHRQ Research Grants

TYPE:
Conferences/seminars; Development grants; Fellowships; Project/program grants; Research grants; Training grants. Dissertation support highlighting primary care, market forces, cost containment, managed care, the cost of treating AIDS, the improvement of treatment for persons with HIV, rural health care, infant mortality, medical liability, malpractice reform, health care of the aged and disabled and policy studies.

YEAR PROGRAM STARTED: 1969

PURPOSE:
To support research to improve the quality, effectiveness, accessibility and cost effectiveness of health care.

LEGAL BASIS:
AHCPR Research Grants: Section 304, 5, 7, 8, of the Public Health Service Act.

ELIGIBILITY:
Any academic institution, agency of a state or local government, nonprofit organization or individual is eligible to submit grant proposals under this program. For-profit entities are not eligible.

FINANCIAL DATA:
Amount of support per award: Varies according to the project type and nature of the individual research proposal.
Total amount of support: Varies.

APPLICATION INFO:
Contact the Agency.
Duration: One to five years.
Deadline: Varies.

STAFF:
Priti Mehrotra, Director, Division of Scientific Review

ADDRESS INQUIRIES TO:
Office of Management Services
Division of Grants Management
(See address above.)

THE AMERICAN FOUNDATION FOR SUICIDE PREVENTION
199 Water Street
11th Floor
New York, NY 10038
(212) 363-3500 ext. 2015
Fax: (212) 363-6237
E-mail: grantsmanager@afsp.org
Web Site: afsp.org/research-grant-information

TYPE:
Research grants.

See entry 1364 for full listing.

THE AMERICAN FOUNDATION FOR SUICIDE PREVENTION
199 Water Street
11th Floor
New York, NY 10038
(212) 363-3500 ext. 2015
Fax: (212) 363-6237
E-mail: grantsmanager@afsp.org
Web Site: afsp.org/research-grant-information

TYPE:
Fellowships; Research grants; Training grants.

See entry 1365 for full listing.

THE AMERICAN FOUNDATION FOR SUICIDE PREVENTION
199 Water Street
11th Floor
New York, NY 10038
(212) 363-3500 ext. 2015
Fax: (212) 363-6237
E-mail: grantsmanager@afsp.org
Web Site: afsp.org/research-grant-information

TYPE:
Research grants.

See entry 1366 for full listing.

THE AMERICAN FOUNDATION FOR SUICIDE PREVENTION
199 Water Street
11th Floor
New York, NY 10038
(212) 363-3500 ext. 2015
Fax: (212) 363-6237
E-mail: grantsmanager@afsp.org
Web Site: afsp.org/research-grant-information

TYPE:
Research grants. Standard Research Innovation Grants are awarded to individual investigators. An additional annual stipend is available for mentors on Young Investigator Innovation Grants in which the investigator is at the level of Assistant Professor or lower.

See entry 1367 for full listing.

AMERICAN MEDICAL WOMEN'S ASSOCIATION, INC.
1100 East Woodfield Road
Suite 350
Schaumburg, IL 60173
(847) 517-2801
Fax: (847) 517-7229
E-mail: associatedirector@amwa-doc.org
Web Site: www.amwa-doc.org

TYPE:
Awards/prizes; Conferences/seminars; General operating grants; Project/program grants; Training grants; Travel grants. Support for clinics serving the poor in medically underserved areas, scholarships and loans to qualifying women medical students, and continuing medical education for physicians in areas related to women's health.

See entry 2002 for full listing.

AMERICAN PSYCHOLOGICAL ASSOCIATION
Government Relations Office
Public Interest Directorate
750 First Street, N.E.
Washington, DC 20002-4242
(202) 336-6166
Fax: (202) 336-6063
E-mail: abishop@apa.org
Web Site: www.apa.org/about/awardes/congress-fellow

TYPE:
Fellowships. Program provides trained scientists and practitioners an opportunity for enhanced understanding of and involvement in the federal policymaking process by serving as congressional staff in Washington, DC.

See entry 2314 for full listing.

ARCHSTONE FOUNDATION [1282]
301 East Ocean Boulevard
Suite 1850
Long Beach, CA 90802
(562) 590-8655
Fax: (562) 495-0317
E-mail: archstone@archstone.org
Web Site: www.archstone.org

FOUNDED: 1985

AREAS OF INTEREST:
Aging in community, depression in late life, and family caregiving.

TYPE:
Challenge/matching grants;
Conferences/seminars; Demonstration grants;
Development grants; Project/program grants;
Technical assistance; Training grants.

YEAR PROGRAM STARTED: 1985

PURPOSE:
To contribute toward the preparation of
society in meeting the needs of an aging
population.

ELIGIBILITY:
501(c)(3) organizations. Individuals may not
apply. No funding available for capital
expenditures, fund-raisers or research.

GEOG. RESTRICTIONS: Southern California.

FINANCIAL DATA:
Limited indirect costs to 10%.
Amount of support per award: Varies.
Total amount of support: $1,778,903 in
grants payable for the year ended June 30,
2018.

NO. AWARDS: 51 during fiscal years 2018 and
2019.

APPLICATION INFO:
Application forms and reporting guidelines
are available on the Foundation's web site.
Duration: One year. May be renewed for up
to three years.

IRS I.D.: 33-0133359

BOARD OF DIRECTORS:
Diana M. Bonta, Chairperson
Cynthia D. Banks
Hon. Lynn Daucher
Christopher A. Langston, Ph.D.
Amye L. Leong, MBA
Theresa J. Marino
Hon. Renee B. Simon, M.S., M.L.S.
Rocky Suares, C.F.P.
Peter C. Szutu, M.P.H.
Heather M. Young, Ph.D., R.N.

ADDRESS INQUIRIES TO:
Tanisha Davis, Grants Manager
(See address above.)

BRIGHAM AND WOMEN'S HOSPITAL   [1283]
75 Francis Street
Boston, MA 02115
(617) 732-5500
Fax: (617) 582-6112
E-mail: bwhdeland@partners.org
Web Site: www.brighamandwomens.org

AREAS OF INTEREST:
Health care.

NAME(S) OF PROGRAMS:
● **Deland Fellowship Program in Health
Care and Society**

TYPE:
Fellowships.

YEAR PROGRAM STARTED: 1988

PURPOSE:
To train outstanding future leaders in health
care.

ELIGIBILITY:
It is anticipated that candidates will come
from a variety of careers and educational
backgrounds including business, law,
economics, public policy, medicine and
nursing. Candidates are required to have an
advanced degree from a U.S. accredited
institution.

NO. AWARDS: 2 annually.

APPLICATION INFO:
Brigham and Women's Hospital is using the
National Council on Administrative
Fellowship's centralized application system.
Candidates can apply at
nafcas.liaisoncas.com. If there is a reason
that the potential candidate cannot apply
through NAFCAS, please contact the
program director for consideration of a direct
application.
Duration: One year.
Deadline: First Monday in October.
Notification in November.

ADDRESS INQUIRIES TO:
Director, Deland Fellowship Program
(See e-mail address above.)

BRIGHT FOCUS FOUNDATION   [1284]
22512 Gateway Center Drive
Clarksburg, MD 20871
(301) 948-3244
(800) 437-2423
Fax: (301) 948-4403
E-mail: researchgrants@brightfocus.org
Web Site: www.brightfocus.org

FOUNDED: 1997

AREAS OF INTEREST:
Macular degeneration.

NAME(S) OF PROGRAMS:
● **Macular Degeneration Research
Program**

TYPE:
Research grants.

YEAR PROGRAM STARTED: 1998

PURPOSE:
To fund research on and educate the public
about macular degeneration.

LEGAL BASIS:
501(c)(3) nonprofit charitable organization.

ELIGIBILITY:
Grants are awarded on the basis of the
proposal's scientific merit and its relevance to
understanding the diseases studied. No funds
for large equipment, institutional overhead
cost, construction or building expenses.

The Foundation is particularly interested in
receiving letters from new investigators and
from established investigators seeking to
explore new directions in macular
degeneration research.

FINANCIAL DATA:
Amount of support per award: Innovative
Research Grant: Up to $600,000; New
Investigator Grant: Up to $450,000;
Postdoctoral Fellowship: Up to $200,000.
Total amount of support: Varies.

NO. MOST RECENT APPLICANTS: 170 letters of
intent for fiscal year 2021.

NO. AWARDS: 53 invited to submit proposals for
fiscal year 2020.

APPLICATION INFO:
Must send initial letter of intent. Subsequent
proposal by invitation.
Duration: Innovative Research Grant and
New Investigator Grant: Up to three years;
Postdoctoral Fellowship: Up to two years.
Deadline: Letter of Intent: July 29.

PUBLICATIONS:
Annual report; newsletters; clinical brochures.

ADDRESS INQUIRIES TO:
See e-mail address above.

THE CALIFORNIA ENDOWMENT   [1285]
1000 North Alameda Street
Los Angeles, CA 90012
(800) 449-4149
E-mail: gms@calendow.org
Web Site: www.calendow.org

FOUNDED: 1996

AREAS OF INTEREST:
Health care access, disparities in health,
public health, multicultural health, health and
well-being, cultural competency and work
force diversity.

NAME(S) OF PROGRAMS:
● **Building Healthy Communities
Initiative**

TYPE:
Challenge/matching grants; General operating
grants; Matching gifts; Project/program
grants.

YEAR PROGRAM STARTED: 1998

PURPOSE:
To improve access to affordable, quality
health care for underserved individuals and
communities; to promote fundamental
improvements in the health status of the
people of California; to improve the health of
Californians through community-based
programs, collaborations and partnerships
that strengthen leadership, stimulate policy
development and contribute to systems
change.

ELIGIBILITY:
Grants are awarded to tax-exempt
organizations only. No grants to individuals.

GEOG. RESTRICTIONS: California.

FINANCIAL DATA:
Amount of support per award: Varies.

APPLICATION INFO:
Applications by invitation only.

IRS I.D.: 95-4523232

CALIFORNIA HEALTHCARE FOUNDATION   [1286]
1438 Webster Street
Suite 400
Oakland, CA 94612
(510) 238-1040
Fax: (510) 238-1388
E-mail: grants@chcf.org
Web Site: www.chcf.org

FOUNDED: 1996

AREAS OF INTEREST:
Affordable health care.

NAME(S) OF PROGRAMS:
● **Health Innovation Fund**
● **Improving Access**
● **People-Centered Care**

TYPE:
Project/program grants.

PURPOSE:
To advance meaningful, measurable
improvements in the way the health care
delivery system provides care to the people
of California, particularly those with low
incomes and those whose needs are not well
served by the status quo.

GEOG. RESTRICTIONS: California.

FINANCIAL DATA:
Amount of support per award: Varies.
Total amount of support: Varies.

NO. AWARDS: 425.

APPLICATION INFO:
Most grants are solicited. Letters of inquiry are preferred for unsolicited projects with description, timeline and estimated budget.
Duration: Varies.

ADDRESS INQUIRIES TO:
Lisa Kang
Director, Grants Administration
(See address above.)

THE CALIFORNIA WELLNESS FOUNDATION   [1287]
City National Plaza, Suite 1100
515 South Flower Street
Los Angeles, CA 90071
(818) 702-1900
Fax: (818) 702-1999
E-mail: grants@calwellness.org
info@calwellness.org
Web Site: www.calwellness.org

FOUNDED: 1991

AREAS OF INTEREST:
Access and quality health care, healthy and safe neighborhoods, and education and employment.

NAME(S) OF PROGRAMS:
● **Advancing Wellness Grants Program**

TYPE:
Conferences/seminars; Demonstration grants; General operating grants; Project/program grants; Seed money grants.

YEAR PROGRAM STARTED: 1992

PURPOSE:
To improve the health of the people of California by making grants for health promotion, wellness education and disease prevention.

LEGAL BASIS:
Private foundation.

ELIGIBILITY:
Applicants must be nonprofit organizations that are exempt under Section 501(c)(3) of the IRS and are defined as "not a private foundation" under Section 509(a)(1). The Foundation also funds government agencies.

The Foundation does not fund Section 509(a)(3) Type III non-functionally integrated supporting organizations and does not provide international funding or fund organizations located outside of the U.S. Grants are not made for annual fund drives, building campaigns, major equipment, biomedical research or to activities that exclusively benefit members of sectarian or religious organizations.

GEOG. RESTRICTIONS: California.

FINANCIAL DATA:
Amount of support per award: Varies depending on needs and nature of the request.
Total amount of support: Approximately $35,000,000 annually.

NO. AWARDS: 332 for the year 2020.

APPLICATION INFO:
Applicant must submit a Letter of Interest through Cal Wellness' Grants Portal. If asked to submit a full proposal, guidance will be provided about how to submit the proposal.

Duration: Varies.

PUBLICATIONS:
Annual report; brochure; quarterly newsletter.

IRS I.D.: 95-4292101

STAFF:
Rochelle Witharana, Chief Financial Officer
Arun Baheti, Vice President of Operations
Fatima Angeles, Vice President of Programs
Alex M. Johnson, Program Director
Jeffrey S. Kim, Program Director
Karren Lane, Program Director
Earl Lui, Program Director

BOARD OF DIRECTORS:
Dr. Pamela J. Simms-Mackey, Chairperson
Judy Belk, President and Chief Executive Officer
Terence Mulligan, Treasurer
Angelica Salas, Secretary
Xochitl Castaneda
Irma Cota
Virginia Hedrick
Katherine Katcher
Joseph M. Lumarda
Debra Nakatomi
Arnold X.C. Perkins
Ernest J. Wilson, III
Geri Yang-Johnson

EXECUTIVE STAFF:
Judy Belk, President and Chief Executive Officer
Richard Tate, Executive Vice President

ADDRESS INQUIRIES TO:
Grants Management
E-mail: grants@calwellness.org
(See telephone number above.)

CENTER FOR SCIENCE IN THE PUBLIC INTEREST
1220 L Street, N.W.
Suite 300
Washington, DC 20005
(202) 332-9110
Fax: (202) 265-4954
E-mail: hr@cspinet.org
Web Site: www.cspinet.org

TYPE:
Internships. These unpaid internships allow interns to work on specific projects under the direction of a Project Director or the Executive Director.

See entry 2413 for full listing.

CHICAGO BOARD OF TRADE FOUNDATION   [1288]
141 West Jackson Boulevard
Suite 1404
Chicago, IL 60604
(312) 789-8225
Fax: (312) 604-6118
E-mail: cbotfoundation@gmail.com
Web Site: www.cbotfoundation.org

AREAS OF INTEREST:
Youth, education, seniors, wildlife, social and human services.

TYPE:
General operating grants; Project/program grants.

PURPOSE:
To assist children in need, seniors, people with disabilities, social and human services within the Chicago community.

ELIGIBILITY:
Organizations classified as 501(c)(3) by the IRS can apply. Individuals and religious organizations are ineligible. Must be nondiscriminatory in its practices and may not give funds to ancillary organizations.

GEOG. RESTRICTIONS: Greater Chicago, Illinois metropolitan area.

FINANCIAL DATA:
Amount of support per award: Up to $25,000.

NO. MOST RECENT APPLICANTS: 125 for the year 2020.

NO. AWARDS: 30 for the year 2020.

APPLICATION INFO:
Applicant must submit a copy of proposal, 501(c)(3), (4) or (10) documentation, and a recent financial statement.
Duration: One year. Grants are renewable.
Deadline: September 31.

ADDRESS INQUIRIES TO:
Dawn Andersen
(See address above.)

THE CULLEN TRUST FOR HEALTH CARE   [1289]
2727 Allen Parkway, Suite 1000
Houston, TX 77019
(713) 651-8837
E-mail: gina@cullenfdn.org
Web Site: www.cullentrust.org

FOUNDED: 1978

AREAS OF INTEREST:
Health care.

TYPE:
Capital grants; Development grants; Endowments; General operating grants; Project/program grants. Clinical-based research grants.

YEAR PROGRAM STARTED: 1978

PURPOSE:
To provide financial assistance and to benefit institutions providing health care.

LEGAL BASIS:
Charitable trust.

ELIGIBILITY:
Applicants must be tax-exempt 501(c)(3).

GEOG. RESTRICTIONS: Primarily Houston, Texas area.

FINANCIAL DATA:
Amount of support per award: Average $50,000.
Total amount of support: Varies.

APPLICATION INFO:
Applications are only accepted through the Trust web site.
Duration: One to three years.
Deadline: February 15 and September 1.

ADDRESS INQUIRIES TO:
Gina McEvily, Grant Administrator
(See address above.)

THE FOUNDATION FOR SPIRITUALITY AND MEDICINE   [1290]
c/o Daniel Ford, M.D.
5 Bafford Court
Glen Arm, MD 21057
(410) 614-0986
E-mail: dford@jhmi.edu
Web Site: www.foundationspiritmed.com

FOUNDED: 1981

AREAS OF INTEREST:
Health, health education and spirituality.

TYPE:
Challenge/matching grants;
Conferences/seminars; Demonstration grants;
Development grants; General operating
grants; Project/program grants; Research
grants; Seed money grants; Training grants.

YEAR PROGRAM STARTED: 1995

PURPOSE:
To promote the integration of spirituality into
health care.

ELIGIBILITY:
Grants are given to any nonprofit
organization whose mission is the training of
professionals in the healing arts, the delivery
of health care, or the provision of spiritual
services. Preference may be given to
applicants who demonstrate matching funds
by their organization or from other sources.

GEOG. RESTRICTIONS: Primarily Maryland.

FINANCIAL DATA:
Amount of support per award: Maximum
$25,000 per year.

Total amount of support: Approximately
$100,000 per year.

Matching fund requirements: The Foundation
prefers matching funds.

NO. AWARDS: Varies.

APPLICATION INFO:
Applications must be no more than 10 pages
in length (double-spaced) and should include
the following:
(1) description and history of the project;
(2) description of organization and personnel;
(3) rationale for proposed project;
(4) goals and objectives of the project;
(5) short-term and long-term benefits
expected from the project;
(6) plans for a continuation of the project;
(7) timetable and;
(8) budget.

Grantees must meet Foundation requirements
for regular financial and project reporting,
and submit an annual and final written report.
An oral presentation to the board of directors
of the Foundation may be requested as part
of the application process and/or as part of
the report.

Applicants are requested to submit
applications electronically to
smdcdaneker@comcast.net. In addition,
applicants are required to mail at least two
paper copies of the application to the
Foundation's address.

Duration: Up to two years.

Deadline: January 15 and July 15.
Announcements April 1 and October 1.

PUBLICATIONS:
Brochure.

IRS I.D.: 52-1238713

ADDRESS INQUIRIES TO:
David C. Daneker, Chairman
(See address above.)

THE FOUNDATION OF THE AMERICAN COLLEGE OF HEALTHCARE EXECUTIVES [1291]

300 South Riverside Plaza
Suite 1900
Chicago, IL 60606-6698
(312) 424-9400
Fax: (312) 424-9405
E-mail: contact@ache.org
Web Site: www.ache.org/scholarships

FOUNDED: 1933

AREAS OF INTEREST:
Health care management.

NAME(S) OF PROGRAMS:
● **Albert W. Dent Graduate Student
Scholarship**
● **Foster G. McGaw Graduate Student
Scholarship**

TYPE:
Scholarships. Offered annually, the Albert W.
Dent and the Foster G. McGaw Graduate
Student Scholarships are designated for
students enrolled in their final year of
classroom work in a health care management
graduate program.

Albert W. Dent Graduate Student Scholarship
is only available to minority students.

YEAR PROGRAM STARTED: 1969

PURPOSE:
To provide financial aid, increase the
enrollment in health care management
graduate programs and to encourage students
to obtain positions in the middle and upper
levels of health care management.

ELIGIBILITY:
An applicant must:
(1) be a full-time student entering the final
year of classroom work in a health care
management graduate program;
(2) be able to demonstrate financial need;
(3) be a U.S. or Canadian citizen;
(4) have not been a previous recipient of the
scholarship and;
(5) be a minority if applying for the Albert
W. Dent Graduate Student Scholarship.

GEOG. RESTRICTIONS: United States and
Canada.

FINANCIAL DATA:
Amount of support per award: $5,000.

Total amount of support: Varies.

CO-OP FUNDING PROGRAMS: The initial gift for
the McGaw Student Scholarship was from
the Foster G. McGaw Charitable Fund.
Additional gifts were made by Mr. McGaw
from his personal funds before his death in
1986.

NO. MOST RECENT APPLICANTS: 200 to 250.

NO. AWARDS: Up to 15 scholarships awarded
per year.

APPLICATION INFO:
Application is submitted online via the
Foundation web site.

Duration: One year.

Deadline: March 31.

ADDRESS INQUIRIES TO:
Scholarship Committee
Division of Member Services
(See address above.)

THE DAVID GEFFEN FOUNDATION [1292]

12011 San Vicente Boulevard
Suite 606
Los Angeles, CA 90049
(310) 581-5955
E-mail: ddishman@geffenco.com

FOUNDED: 1986

AREAS OF INTEREST:
AIDS/HIV, civil liberties, health and health
care, the arts and issues of concern to the
Jewish community.

TYPE:
General operating grants; Project/program
grants.

PURPOSE:
To support the arts, health care, issues of
concern to the Jewish community, HIV/AIDS
and civil liberties.

LEGAL BASIS:
Private foundation.

ELIGIBILITY:
Applicants must be 501(c)(3) organizations.
No grants for documentaries, audio-visual
programming or publications. No grants to
individuals.

GEOG. RESTRICTIONS: Primarily New York City
and Los Angeles, California.

FINANCIAL DATA:
Amount of support per award: Varies
depending on needs and nature of the
request.

Total amount of support: $41,175,591 for the
year 2019.

APPLICATION INFO:
No application form. Proposals should
include summary and description of the
project or program, background information
of the organization, description of key staff,
list of Board of Directors, IRS letter
confirming tax-exempt status and financial
information including annual operating and
project budgets. Applicants should not send
videotapes or additional materials unless
otherwise requested.

Duration: One-time grant and multiyear
support. Renewal possible.

Deadline: Applications accepted throughout
the year. Each request may take up to three
months to evaluate.

PUBLICATIONS:
Application guidelines.

IRS I.D.: 95-4085811

STAFF:
J. Dallas Dishman, Ph.D., Executive Director

ADDRESS INQUIRIES TO:
J. Dallas Dishman, Ph.D., Executive Director
(See address above.)

HCR MANORCARE FOUNDATION [1293]

333 North Summit Street
Toledo, OH 43604
(419) 252-5989
Fax: (419) 252-5521
E-mail: gives@hcr-manorcare.com
Web Site: www.hcr-manorcare.com

FOUNDED: 1997

AREAS OF INTEREST:
Community service and outreach,
hospice-related programs, research and public
education for diseases and disorders that

affect the elderly, those requiring post-acute services and those requiring hospice or end-of-life care.

TYPE:
Challenge/matching grants; Project/program grants.

YEAR PROGRAM STARTED: 1997

PURPOSE:
To support organizations involved in research and public education about diseases and disorders affecting the elderly, and organizations which provide community service and outreach to such individuals; to provide support to programs addressing end-of-life care; to provide support for hospice.

LEGAL BASIS:
Corporate foundation.

ELIGIBILITY:
Preference is given to organizations in states where HCR ManorCare Corporation has strategic operations. Organizations must be IRS 501(c)(3) tax-exempt and have one other source of support.

HCR ManorCare will not fund advertising or fund-raising events, individuals, for-profit organizations, building or capital campaigns, endowments, organizations with primary service areas in non-HCR ManorCare states, multiyear commitments, research projects with overhead fees in excess of 10% or organizations that have applied for funding within the last 12 months.

GEOG. RESTRICTIONS: United States.

FINANCIAL DATA:
Amount of support per award: Varies.
Total amount of support: Varies.

NO. MOST RECENT APPLICANTS: 300.

NO. AWARDS: 150.

APPLICATION INFO:
The Foundation does not accept unsolicited applications. Grants are only given through HCR ManorCare Corporation locations.
Duration: One year.

IRS I.D.: 52-2031975

ADDRESS INQUIRIES TO:
Bill White, Executive Director
(See address above.)

HEALTH EFFECTS INSTITUTE (HEI) [1294]

75 Federal Street
Suite 1400
Boston, MA 02110-1817
(617) 488-2338
Fax: (617) 488-2335
E-mail: jrutledge@healtheffects.org
Web Site: www.healtheffects.org

FOUNDED: 1980

AREAS OF INTEREST:
Health effects of air pollution.

NAME(S) OF PROGRAMS:
● **Health Effects of Air Pollution**
● **Walter A. Rosenblith New Investigator Award**

TYPE:
Research contracts.

YEAR PROGRAM STARTED: 1980

PURPOSE:
To provide high-quality, impartial, and relevant science on the health effects of air pollution.

LEGAL BASIS:
Public/Private partnership.

ELIGIBILITY:
Requirements vary according to program.

FINANCIAL DATA:
Amount of support per award: Health Effects of Air Pollution: $500,000 to $800,000; Rosenblith New Investigator Award: Up to $500,000 over three years.
Total amount of support: Varies.

APPLICATION INFO:
Application information is available online.
Duration: Up to three years.
Deadline: Varies.

ADDRESS INQUIRIES TO:
For Health Effects:
Lissa McBurney
Tel: (617) 488-2345

For Walter A. Rosenblith New Investigator Award:
Dr. Dan Crouse
E-mail: dcrouse@healtheffects.org
(See address above.)

THE HEALTH FOUNDATION OF GREATER INDIANAPOLIS, INC. [1295]

429 East Vermont Street, Suite 400
Indianapolis, IN 46202-3698
(317) 630-1805
Fax: (317) 630-1806
E-mail: rmcconnell@thfgi.org
Web Site: www.thfgi.org

FOUNDED: 1985

AREAS OF INTEREST:
Childhood obesity, school-based health and HIV/AIDS.

NAME(S) OF PROGRAMS:
● **Indiana AIDS Fund**

TYPE:
Grants-in-aid.

YEAR PROGRAM STARTED: 2019

PURPOSE:
To serve the community's most vulnerable citizens by funding health-related projects and organizations not easily supported by other means.

ELIGIBILITY:
Any Indiana-based nonprofit 501(c)(3) group, organization or agency that provides HIV/AIDS-related programs or services to local constituencies may apply for funding.

GEOG. RESTRICTIONS: Indiana.

FINANCIAL DATA:
Amount of support per award: Varies.
Total amount of support: Varies.

NO. MOST RECENT APPLICANTS: 58.

NO. AWARDS: 57.

APPLICATION INFO:
The Foundation does not accept unsolicited proposals.
Duration: 12 months.
Deadline: Varies.

ADDRESS INQUIRIES TO:
Jason Grisell, MBA
President and Chief Executive Officer
(See address above.)

HEALTH FOUNDATION OF SOUTH FLORIDA [1296]

One Biscayne Tower
2 South Biscayne Boulevard, Suite 1710
Miami, FL 33131
(305) 374-7200
Fax: (305) 374-7003
E-mail: fkuchkarian@hfsf.org
Web Site: www.hfsf.org

FOUNDED: 1993

AREAS OF INTEREST:
Access to care, health coverage, healthy safety-net, social determinants of health, social needs, health and housing, anchor institutions, systems change, policy and advocacy, and racial equity and inclusion.

NAME(S) OF PROGRAMS:
● **Cash Grants**
● **Mission Related Investments Contracts**
● **Officers and Trustees Discretionary Grants**

TYPE:
Challenge/matching grants; General operating grants; Project/program grants. Foundation-administered program/awards; Program related investments.

PURPOSE:
To invest in and be a catalyst for collaborations, policy, and systems change that improves the health of South Florida communities, with a focus on vulnerable, low- to moderate income populations.

ELIGIBILITY:
Eligible organizations must be IRS 501(c)(3) tax-exempt and be located in south Florida.

GEOG. RESTRICTIONS: Broward and Miami-Dade counties, Florida.

FINANCIAL DATA:
Amount of support per award: Typically $30,000 to $500,000.
Total amount of support: $4,250,000.

NO. AWARDS: 52.

APPLICATION INFO:
Concept proposals must be submitted electronically through the Foundation's web site. Applicants are encouraged to reach out to the Foundation program staff before applying.
Duration: Multiyear.
Deadline: Proposals are accepted year-round.

ADDRESS INQUIRIES TO:
Fernanda Kuchkarian
Director, Programs
(See address above.)

THE HEALTH TRUST [1297]

3180 Newberry Drive
Suite 200
San Jose, CA 95118
(408) 513-8700
Fax: (408) 448-4055
E-mail: grants@healthtrust.org
Web Site: www.healthtrust.org

FOUNDED: 1996

AREAS OF INTEREST:
Public health.

NAME(S) OF PROGRAMS:
● **Community Grants**

TYPE:
Project/program grants.

YEAR PROGRAM STARTED: 1996

PURPOSE:
To support events and projects that build health equity in Silicon Valley.

LEGAL BASIS:
Nonprofit, public charity, qualifying as IRS 501(c)(3) organization.

ELIGIBILITY:
The organization must be tax-exempt and nonprofit. Health services must be provided within Santa Clara County and the following three zip codes of San Benito County: 95045, 95023 and 95024.

GEOG. RESTRICTIONS: Santa Clara and northern San Benito counties, California.

FINANCIAL DATA:
Amount of support per award: $250 to $2,500.
Total amount of support: Varies.

NO. MOST RECENT APPLICANTS: Approximately 38.

APPLICATION INFO:
Guidelines are available on the Trust web site. Event Grant application must be submitted online.
Duration: One year.
Deadline: Applications are accepted on a rolling basis.

STAFF:
Maria Garcia, Program Officer

ADDRESS INQUIRIES TO:
Program Associate
(See address above.)

THE HEALTH TRUST [1298]
3180 Newberry Drive
Suite 200
San Jose, CA 95118
(408) 513-8700
Fax: (408) 448-4055
E-mail: grants@healthtrust.org
Web Site: www.healthtrust.org

FOUNDED: 1996

AREAS OF INTEREST:
Public health.

NAME(S) OF PROGRAMS:
● **Health Partnership Grants**

TYPE:
Project/program grants.

PURPOSE:
To make grants to programs and projects that advance specific priorities under three focus areas: Improving Health Through Food, Making Chronic Conditions More Preventable and Manageable, and Prioritizing Health Through Housing.

LEGAL BASIS:
Nonprofit, public charity.

ELIGIBILITY:
Organization must be tax-exempt and nonprofit. Health services must be provided within Santa Clara County and the following three zip codes of San Benito County: 95045, 95023 and 95024.

GEOG. RESTRICTIONS: Santa Clara and northern San Benito counties, California.

FINANCIAL DATA:
Amount of support per award: Varies.
Total amount of support: Varies.

APPLICATION INFO:
Applications must be submitted online.
Duration: Varies.

Deadline: Varies.

ADDRESS INQUIRIES TO:
Program Associate
(See address above.)

THE HEALTHCARE FOUNDATION FOR ORANGE COUNTY [1299]
1505 East 17th Street
Suite 113
Santa Ana, CA 92705
(714) 245-1650
Fax: (714) 245-1653
E-mail: info@hfoc.org
Web Site: www.hfoc.org

FOUNDED: 1996

AREAS OF INTEREST:
Health care and community health.

CONSULTING OR VOLUNTEER SERVICES:
Some training and technical assistance.

NAME(S) OF PROGRAMS:
● **Partnership for a Healthy Orange County**

TYPE:
Demonstration grants; Development grants; General operating grants; Project/program grants; Technical assistance; Training grants.

YEAR PROGRAM STARTED: 1999

PURPOSE:
To promote health and support health care for the benefit of the people of Orange County, CA; to improve the health of the neediest and most underserved residents of the county.

LEGAL BASIS:
Private 501(c)(3) foundation.

ELIGIBILITY:
Grants are made to nonprofit organizations that are exempt from taxation under Section 501(c)(3) of the Internal Revenue Code and that are defined as "not a private foundation" under Section 509(a). Government agencies may also be funded.

Grants are not generally awarded for annual fund drives, building campaigns, major equipment or biomedical research. Activities that exclusively benefit the members of a religious or fraternal organization are not funded.

GEOG. RESTRICTIONS: Primarily Anaheim, Orange, Santa Ana and Tustin, California.

FINANCIAL DATA:
Amount of support per award: Varies.
Total amount of support: $660,000 for the year 2019.

CO-OP FUNDING PROGRAMS: Health Funders Partnership.

NO. MOST RECENT APPLICANTS: 29 for the year 2018.

NO. AWARDS: 15 for the year 2018.

APPLICATION INFO:
Requests for proposals may be obtained from the Foundation.
Duration: One year; multiyear funding at the Board's discretion.
Deadline: September 6.

IRS I.D.: 33-0644620

ADDRESS INQUIRIES TO:
Foundation Coordinator
(See address above.)

HUGOTON FOUNDATION [1300]
900 Park Avenue, Suite 17E
New York, NY 10075
(212) 734-5447
Fax: (212) 734-5447

AREAS OF INTEREST:
Patient care and health.

TYPE:
Project/program grants.

PURPOSE:
To improve patient care.

LEGAL BASIS:
Nonprofit organization.

ELIGIBILITY:
Eligible organizations must be IRS 501(c)(3) tax-exempt and be located in Miami, FL or the borough of Manhattan, NY.

GEOG. RESTRICTIONS: Miami, Florida and borough of Manhattan, New York.

FINANCIAL DATA:
Amount of support per award: $1,000 to $250,000.

APPLICATION INFO:
Written request must include organization description, tax-exempt certificate, detailed cost and specific need.
Duration: One year. Nonrenewable.

ADDRESS INQUIRIES TO:
Joan K. Stout, President
(See address above.)

THE JENKINS FOUNDATION [1301]
3409 Moore Street
Richmond, VA 23230
(804) 330-7400
Fax: (804) 330-5992
E-mail: info@cfrichmond.org
Web Site: www.jenkinsfoundation-va.org

FOUNDED: 1995

AREAS OF INTEREST:
Access to primary care, access to mental health care, and the prevention and treatment of substance use disorders in the greater Richmond, VA area.

TYPE:
General operating grants; Project/program grants.

YEAR PROGRAM STARTED: 1996

PURPOSE:
To expand access to community-based health care programs and improved health care in the greater Richmond area.

LEGAL BASIS:
Supporting organization of The Community Foundation Serving Richmond and Central Virginia.

ELIGIBILITY:
Eligible organizations must be IRS 501(c)(3) tax-exempt and serve the greater Richmond, VA area.

GEOG. RESTRICTIONS: Richmond and the counties of Chesterfield, Goochland, Hanover, Henrico and Powhatan, Virginia.

FINANCIAL DATA:
Amount of support per award: Up to $75,000.
Total amount of support: $2,129,153 for the year 2019.

NO. AWARDS: 40.

APPLICATION INFO:
Application forms are available online.
Duration: Annually. May reapply.

PUBLICATIONS:
Guidelines; annual report (online).

ADDRESS INQUIRIES TO:
Arnette Cousins
Tel: (804) 409-5594
E-mail: acousins@cfrichmond.org

THE JEWISH HEALTHCARE FOUNDATION OF PITTSBURGH [1302]

EQT Tower, Suite 2500
625 Liberty Avenue
Pittsburgh, PA 15222
(412) 594-2550
Fax: (412) 232-6240
E-mail: info@jhf.org
Web Site: www.jhf.org

FOUNDED: 1990

AREAS OF INTEREST:
Aging and long-term care, Jewish
community, professional education and
workforce, public health, and quality and
safety.

CONSULTING OR VOLUNTEER SERVICES:
Research, planning, convening and technical
assistance.

TYPE:
Challenge/matching grants; Demonstration
grants; Fellowships; Project/program grants;
Research grants; Seed money grants;
Technical assistance; Training grants.

YEAR PROGRAM STARTED: 1991

PURPOSE:
To improve health outcomes for elderly, poor
and disabled residents in and beyond the
Pittsburgh region; to improve health care
quality, cost and efficiency.

LEGAL BASIS:
Public charity.

ELIGIBILITY:
Applicants must be 501(c)(3) organizations.
No grants to programs without a health care
component, general operations, endowments,
capital campaigns, retirement of debt,
scholarships, fellowships, travel or individual
research grants.

GEOG. RESTRICTIONS: Pittsburgh region,
Pennsylvania.

FINANCIAL DATA:
Amount of support per award: Average
$50,000.
Total amount of support: Over $2,500,000
for the year 2019.

REPRESENTATIVE AWARDS:
United Way of Allegheny County; WESA;
Jewish Federation of Greater Pittsburgh.

APPLICATION INFO:
Send letter of intent (not to exceed six
pages), including program objectives,
timetable, long-term plans, board of directors
list, budget, documentation of 501(c)(3)
status and most recent financial statements.

The Foundation also accepts the common
grant application designed by Grantmakers of
Western Pennsylvania.
Duration: Varies.
Deadline: Applications accepted on a
continual basis.

PUBLICATIONS:
Annual report; *Roots*, reports; *Branches*,
periodical.

IRS I.D.: 25-1624347

STAFF:
Karen Wolk Feinstein, Ph.D., President and
Chief Executive Officer
Nancy D. Zionts, MBA, Chief Operating
Officer and Chief Program Officer

ADDRESS INQUIRIES TO:
Nancy D. Zionts, Chief Operating Officer
and Chief Program Officer
(See address above.)

THE JOHNS HOPKINS CENTER FOR ALTERNATIVES TO ANIMAL TESTING [1303]

Johns Hopkins University
615 North Wolfe Street, Room W7032
Baltimore, MD 21205
(410) 614-4990
Fax: (410) 614-2871
E-mail: caat@jhu.edu
Web Site: altweb.jhsph.edu

FOUNDED: 1981

AREAS OF INTEREST:
Health and safety.

TYPE:
Development grants; Research grants.

YEAR PROGRAM STARTED: 1982

PURPOSE:
To develop innovative non-whole animal
methods to evaluate fully commercial and/or
therapeutic products to ensure the health and
safety of the public. CAAT accomplishes this
goal by funding research which will lead to
the refinement, replacement or reduction of
animals in toxicity testing and by
disseminating scientifically correct
information about these methods and their
applications.

LEGAL BASIS:
University research program.

ELIGIBILITY:
Grants are made to institutions which have
an established mechanism for handling
private funding. Grant proposals should
provide the fundamental knowledge base to
develop alternative methods to whole animals
for the safety evaluation of commercial
products. CAAT encourages the development
of in vitro approaches to toxicity evaluation
including, but not limited to, methods using
human cells/cell lines and studies in the areas
of skin hypersensitivity/toxicity,
phototoxicity, target organ toxicity (e.g.,
neurotoxicity) and structure-activity
relationships.

FINANCIAL DATA:
Amount of support per award: $40,000
maximum per year, including 15% overhead
or actual costs, whichever is less.

APPLICATION INFO:
Applicants must submit and receive approval
of preproposal by deadline date using CAAT
preproposal form.
Duration: Up to two years.
Deadline: April 19 for preproposal abstracts.

PUBLICATIONS:
CAAT Newsletter; technical reports;
Alternatives in Toxicology, book series.

IRS I.D.: 52-0595110

ADDRESS INQUIRIES TO:
Michele Downes, Grants Coordinator
(See address above.)

KANSAS HEALTH FOUNDATION [1304]

309 East Douglas
Wichita, KS 67202
(316) 262-7676
(800) 373-7681
Fax: (316) 262-2044
E-mail: info@khf.org
Web Site: kansashealth.org

FOUNDED: 1985

AREAS OF INTEREST:
Health equity and civic health.

NAME(S) OF PROGRAMS:
● **Impact Capacity Grant**

TYPE:
Project/program grants.

YEAR PROGRAM STARTED: 2017

PURPOSE:
To improve the health of all Kansans.

ELIGIBILITY:
Applicants must be tax-exempt under Section
501(c)(3), a government entity, or a church
(with certain exclusions), located within the
state, and not a previous recipient of a grant
within the calendar year.

GEOG. RESTRICTIONS: Kansas.

FINANCIAL DATA:
Amount of support per award: Up to $25,000
per organization.
Total amount of support: Up to $2,000,000
annually in two cycles per year.

NO. AWARDS: Varies.

APPLICATION INFO:
Proposals are to be submitted using the
online portal.
Duration: One year.
Deadline: Varies.

PUBLICATIONS:
Grant announcement press release.

IRS I.D.: 48-0873431

ADDRESS INQUIRIES TO:
Chan Brown, Program Officer
(See address above.)

LA84 FOUNDATION [1305]

2141 West Adams Boulevard
Los Angeles, CA 90018
(323) 730-4600
Fax: (323) 730-9637
E-mail: info@la84.org
Web Site: la84.org

FOUNDED: 1984

AREAS OF INTEREST:
Youth sports.

TYPE:
Capital grants; Project/program grants. Field
of play activities.

PURPOSE:
To promote and enhance youth sports
opportunities in southern California.

LEGAL BASIS:
Private nonprofit foundation.

ELIGIBILITY:
Grants are made only to organizations with
nonrestrictive membership operating open to

all, regardless of race, creed, sex, sexual orientation, religious affiliation, or nationality. No grants to individuals. Grants are discouraged for endowments, travel outside of southern California, general operating expenses, land purchases, or debt recovery and liability. Grants are need-based.

GEOG. RESTRICTIONS: Imperial, Los Angeles, Orange, Riverside, San Bernardino, San Diego, Santa Barbara and Ventura counties, California.

FINANCIAL DATA:
Amount of support per award: Small grants: Generally $10,000 or less. Other grants: Average $25,000 to $50,000.
Total amount of support: Approximately $4,000,000 per year.

NO. AWARDS: Approximately 80 per year.

REPRESENTATIVE AWARDS:
$36,400 to Aceing Autism Inc. for personnel, equipment and facility fees for a tennis program serving autistic youth; $25,000 to Catholic Charities of Los Angeles, Inc. for program personnel and referees for a middle school soccer program; $80,000 to Play Rugby, Inc. for personnel, administrative expenses and equipment for a rugby program.

APPLICATION INFO:
Guidelines are posted on the Foundation web site.
Duration: One year.
Deadline: Applications are accepted year-round.

PUBLICATIONS:
Biannual report.

IRS I.D.: 95-3792725

OFFICERS:
Renata Simril, President and Chief Executive Officer
Marcia Suzuki, Chief Financial Officer
Anne-Marie Jones, Chief Strategy Officer
Oscar Delgado, Vice President, Partnerships and Development

STAFF:
Nolan Ortiz, Director, Grants and Programs

ADDRESS INQUIRIES TO:
Nolan Ortiz
Director, Grants and Programs
E-mail: grants@la84.org

LIVINGSTON MEMORIAL FOUNDATION [1306]
c/o Musick, Peeler and Garrett
2801 Townsgate Road, Suite 200
Westlake Village, CA 91361-5842
(805) 418-3115
Fax: (805) 418-3101
E-mail: l.mcavoy@mpglaw.com
Web Site: www.livingstonmemorialfoundation.org

FOUNDED: 1974

AREAS OF INTEREST:
Medical and health care in Ventura County, CA.

NAME(S) OF PROGRAMS:
• **Operational Program Grants**
• **Special Project Grants**

TYPE:
Capital grants; General operating grants; Project/program grants; Travel grants. Capital grants are for medical and health care services.

Operational grants support well-established programs that continue to provide positive results.

Special project grants support those agencies and institutions that can demonstrate the need for assistance in funding a special project or with the cost of medical equipment that promises significant positive results.

YEAR PROGRAM STARTED: 1976

PURPOSE:
To promote medical and health-related services of benefit to the underserved and uninsured people of Ventura County, CA.

LEGAL BASIS:
Private Foundation under the Internal Revenue Code.

ELIGIBILITY:
Grant applications are assessed according to criteria that include giving preferential treatment to programs or projects that offer measurable medical benefits, are patient-specific or involve hands-on care.

Grants are not usually made to individuals, for projects or programs normally financed from government sources, conferences, seminars, workshops, exhibits, travel, or publishing activities.

GEOG. RESTRICTIONS: Ventura County, California.

FINANCIAL DATA:
Amount of support per award: $1,500 to $200,000.
Total amount of support: $435,500 for the year 2020-21.

NO. MOST RECENT APPLICANTS: 22 for the year 2020-21.

NO. AWARDS: 18.

APPLICATION INFO:
Organizations should first submit a brief introductory letter, not to exceed three pages. The letter should include a concise statement of the need for the funds, the amount requested, pertinent factual information, and state the desired type of grant. Current verification of tax-exempt status should also be included. After review, eligible organizations may be invited to submit a formal grant application.
Duration: One year.
Deadline: Formal applications are received in late November. Awards are announced in April of each year.

IRS I.D.: 23-7364623

DIRECTORS AND OFFICERS:
Laura K. McAvoy, Esq., President and Chairman
Richard M. Loft, M.D., Vice President and Vice Chairman
Thomas P. Pecht, Vice President, Vice Chairman and Assistant Secretary
Kathleen F. Deutschman, Secretary and Assistant Chief Financial Officer
John R. Walters, M.D., Chief Financial Officer

ADDRESS INQUIRIES TO:
Laura K. McAvoy, Esq.
President and Chairman
(See address above.)

THE DR. JOHN T. MACDONALD FOUNDATION, INC.
1550 Madruga Avenue, Suite 215
Coral Gables, FL 33146
(305) 667-6017
Fax: (305) 667-9135
E-mail: info@jtmacdonaldfdn.org
Web Site: www.jtmacdonaldfdn.org

TYPE:
Project/program grants.

See entry 1021 for full listing.

FREDA MAYTAG-GRACE CRAWFORD TRUST [1307]
c/o JPMorgan Private Foundation Services
P.O. Box 227237, TX1-2963
Dallas, TX 75222-7237
(214) 965-2901
Fax: (800) 888-7695
E-mail: jpmorgan.pcs.grants@jpmchase.com
Web Site: www.jpmorgan.com/onlinegrants

AREAS OF INTEREST:
Tuberculosis and other respiratory diseases; preservation of a clean and healthy environment.

TYPE:
Project/program grants.

PURPOSE:
To provide medical and nursing care for individuals in the Colorado Springs community who are afflicted with tuberculosis or other respiratory diseases.

ELIGIBILITY:
Grants to 501(c)(3) nonprofit organizations. No grants to individuals.

GEOG. RESTRICTIONS: Colorado Springs, Colorado.

FINANCIAL DATA:
Amount of support per award: Varies.

APPLICATION INFO:
Application and guidelines are available online.
Duration: Varies.
Deadline: March 20, June 20, September 20 and December 20.

ADDRESS INQUIRIES TO:
Stephany Lewis, Trust Officer
E-mail: stephany.n.lewis@jpmorgan.com

MT. SINAI HEALTH CARE FOUNDATION [1308]
11000 Euclid Avenue
Cleveland, OH 44106-1714
(216) 421-5500
E-mail: mitchell.balk@case.edu
Web Site: www.mtsinaifoundation.org

FOUNDED: 1996

AREAS OF INTEREST:
Urban health, Jewish community, health policy, academic medicine and bioscience.

TYPE:
Challenge/matching grants; Demonstration grants; Development grants; Project/program grants; Seed money grants.

YEAR PROGRAM STARTED: 1997

PURPOSE:
To improve the health of the citizens in the greater Cleveland, OH area.

LEGAL BASIS:
Public charity.

ELIGIBILITY:
Eligible organizations must be IRS 501(c)(3) tax-exempt.

GEOG. RESTRICTIONS: Greater Cleveland, Ohio.

FINANCIAL DATA:
Amount of support per award: Varies.
Total amount of support: $7,300,000 for the year 2019.

APPLICATION INFO:
Application information may be obtained by contacting the Foundation or visiting the web site listed above.
Duration: Varies.
Deadline: January 1, April 1, July 1 and October 1.

PUBLICATIONS:
Guidelines; annual report; *Legacy*, newsletter.

IRS I.D.: 34-1777878

ADDRESS INQUIRIES TO:
Mitchell Balk, President
(See address above.)

NATIONAL HEALTH SERVICE CORPS (NHSC)   [1309]
U.S. Department of Health and Human Services
Health Resources and Services Administration
5600 Fishers Lane
Rockville, MD 20857
(800) 221-9393
Web Site: bhw.hrsa.gov
nhsc.hrsa.gov

AREAS OF INTEREST:
Competitive scholarships for students enrolled in schools of osteopathic and allopathic medicine, family nurse practitioner, nurse midwifery and physician assistant training programs and dental school.

NAME(S) OF PROGRAMS:
● **National Health Service Corps Scholarship Program**

TYPE:
Scholarships. The scholarship award includes the payment of a monthly stipend, an amount for other reasonable educational expenses, tuition and required fees. Recipients owe one year of professional clinical service in a health professional shortage area (HPSA) for each year of support, with a two-year service minimum.

YEAR PROGRAM STARTED: 1973

PURPOSE:
To provide the National Health Service Corps with an adequate supply of trained health professionals to serve in health professional shortage areas.

ELIGIBILITY:
All applicants must be citizens or nationals of the U.S. at the time they apply, enrolled or accepted for enrollment in an accredited health professions education program.

GEOG. RESTRICTIONS: United States and its territories.

FINANCIAL DATA:
Scholarship recipients receive a monthly stipend, one annual payment for other reasonable educational expenses, and payment to the school, on their behalf, of tuition and required fees. The stipend is taxable only for certain scholarships.
Amount of support per award: Based on costs for every student in the program.
Total amount of support: Varies.

NO. MOST RECENT APPLICANTS: 2,068 for the year 2017.

NO. AWARDS: 181 for the year 2017.

APPLICATION INFO:
Complete information is available on the web site.
Duration: The scholarship award is only for one school year, with a two-year full-time or four-year half-time minimum service obligation.
Deadline: Varies.

PUBLICATIONS:
Applicant information bulletin.

ADDRESS INQUIRIES TO:
See telephone or e-mail address above.

*SPECIAL STIPULATIONS:
Recipients must serve where needed in a designated Health Professional Shortage Area (HPSA).

NATIONAL INSTITUTE ON AGING   [1310]
Division of Extramural Activities
7201 Wisconsin Avenue
Bethesda, MD 20892-9205
(301) 496-9322
E-mail: kenneth.santora@nih.gov
Web Site: www.nia.nih.gov

FOUNDED: 1975

AREAS OF INTEREST:
Biology of aging research, geriatrics and gerontology research, neuroscience research on aging, behavioral and social research on aging. Particular focus in Alzheimer's disease and related dementias.

NAME(S) OF PROGRAMS:
● **Aging Research**

TYPE:
Conferences/seminars; Fellowships; Grants-in-aid; Project/program grants; Research grants; Technical assistance; Training grants; Research contracts. Career development grants; Loan repayment programs.

PURPOSE:
To support biomedical, clinical, social, neuroscience, neuropsychology and behavioral research and research training directed toward greater understanding of the aging process and the needs and problems of older people. The primary goal is to improve the health and well-being of older people through the development of new knowledge.

LEGAL BASIS:
Government agency.

ELIGIBILITY:
Grants and contracts are available to universities, colleges, medical, dental and nursing schools, schools of public health, laboratories, hospitals, state and local health departments and other public or private profit or nonprofit institutions.
NRSA awards are provided for individual postdoctoral and institutional pre-and postdoctoral research training in health and health-related areas which are periodically specified by the National Institutes of Health. Individuals with a professional or scientific degree are eligible. Applicants must be citizens of the U.S. or be admitted for permanent residency.

GEOG. RESTRICTIONS: United States.

FINANCIAL DATA:
Amount of support per award: Average: $491,619 for research project grants.
Total amount of support: Varies.

NO. MOST RECENT APPLICANTS: 4,983 for fiscal year 2019.

NO. AWARDS: 1,001.

APPLICATION INFO:
Contact the Institute.
Duration: One year to multiyear.
Deadline: Varies.

OFFICERS:
Kenneth Santora, Ph.D., Director

ADDRESS INQUIRIES TO:
Division of Extramural Activities
(See address above.)

NATIONAL INSTITUTE ON ALCOHOL ABUSE AND ALCOHOLISM   [1311]
Office of Extramural Activities
6700B Rockledge Drive, Room 1458
Bethesda, MD 20817
(301) 443-9737
Fax: (301) 443-6077
E-mail: bautista@mail.nih.gov
Web Site: www.niaaa.nih.gov

FOUNDED: 1971

NAME(S) OF PROGRAMS:
● **Career Enhancement Award for Stem Cell Research (K18)**
● **Independent Scientist Awards (K02)**
● **Mentored Patient-Oriented Research Career Development Award (K23)**
● **Mentored Quantitative Research Career Development Award (K25)**
● **Midcareer Investigator Award in Patient-Oriented Research (K24)**
● **NIH Pathway to Independence Award (K99/R00)**
● **Scientist Development Awards for Mentored Clinical (K08)**
● **Scientist Development Awards for Mentored Research (K01)**

TYPE:
Research grants. Support for full-time research on a long-term (five years) basis for research scientists.

Career Enhancement Award for Stem Cell Research (K18) is to encourage investigators to obtain the training they need to appropriately use stem cells in their research.

Independent Scientist Awards (K02) support advanced research experience.

NIH Pathway to Independence (PI) Award (K99/R00) will provide up to five years of support consisting of two phases. The PI award is limited to postdoctoral trainees.

Scientist Development Awards for Mentored Research (K01) and Scientist Development Awards for Mentored Clinical (K08) support individuals with one to four years of postdoctoral training or experience, but no extensive research experience.

PURPOSE:
To provide salary support to talented investigators so that they can engage in full-time research on a long-term basis and develop their full research potential.

LEGAL BASIS:
PHS Act, Section 301 as amended (42 U.S.C. 241).

ELIGIBILITY:
Applicants can either be public or nonprofit private organizations and institutions located in the U.S. or its territories and possessions or U.S. citizens or permanent residents. Citizenship is mandatory for renewal beyond the initial five-year award.

FINANCIAL DATA:
Amount of support per award: Varies.
Total amount of support: Varies.

APPLICATION INFO:
Application kits are available at most institutional offices of sponsored research and may be obtained from the Grants Information Office.
Duration: Generally five years. Renewal possible.
Deadline: Standard due dates vary with specific grant. Consult web site.

PUBLICATIONS:
NIAAA additional information to the NIH Career Development Program Announcements (K Awards).

ADDRESS INQUIRIES TO:
Dr. Raye Litten, Director
Division of Treatment
and Recovery Research
Tel: (301) 443-0636 or

Dr. Michael Hilton, Deputy Director
Division of Epidemiology
and Prevention Research
Tel: (301) 402-9402 or

Dr. Kathy Jung
Division of Metabolism
and Health Effects
Tel: (301) 443-8744 or

Dr. Antonio Noronha
Division of Neuroscience and Behavior
Tel: (301) 443-4223
(See address above.)

NATIONAL INSTITUTE ON ALCOHOL ABUSE AND ALCOHOLISM [1312]
National Institutes of Health
6700 Rockledge Drive, Room 1324
Bethesda, MD 20892
(301) 443-4225
Fax: (301) 594-0673
E-mail: mryan1@mail.nih.gov
Web Site: www.niaaa.nih.gov/research/niaaa-sbir

FOUNDED: 1971

AREAS OF INTEREST:
Pharmaceuticals, diagnostic instruments, and the prevention and treatment of alcoholism and alcohol abuse.

NAME(S) OF PROGRAMS:
● **Small Business Innovation Research Program**

TYPE:
Research grants; Research contracts. Separate grant applications are awarded for Phase I and Phase II of the program. Phase I is designed to establish the feasibility of the technological innovation and determine the quality of performance. The objective of Phase II is to further demonstrate the efficacy of the product for commercial exploitation. Only funded applicants from Phase I are eligible to apply for Phase II.

YEAR PROGRAM STARTED: 1983

PURPOSE:
To stimulate technological innovation in the alcohol field, increase private-sector commercialization of innovations derived from federal research and development and foster and encourage participation by minority and disadvantaged firms in technological innovation.

LEGAL BASIS:
The Small Business Innovation Development Act, P.L. 97-219.

ELIGIBILITY:
Each organization must qualify as a small business in accordance with the stipulations set forth in the Omnibus Solicitation of the PHS Small Business Innovation Research Program. In general, the organization must be independently owned and operated, must be located in the U.S. and at least 51% of the ownership must be by U.S. citizens or lawfully admitted permanent resident aliens. The primary employment of the principal investigator must be with the firm at the time of award and during the conduct of the proposed project. The performance site must be in the U.S.

GEOG. RESTRICTIONS: United States.

FINANCIAL DATA:
Amount of support per award: May not exceed $150,000 for both direct and indirect costs for Phase I. May not exceed $1,000,000 for two years in total costs for Phase II. If costs exceed these amounts, contact the program officer named in the solicitation or the SBIR coordinator.

APPLICATION INFO:
The electronic submission process is multi-step. Details on applying can be found at sbir.nih.gov.
Duration: Varies for Phase I. Two years for Phase II.
Deadline: Contracts: Early November; Grants: April 5, September 5 and January 5.

PUBLICATIONS:
Omnibus solicitation for SBIR grant applications.

ADDRESS INQUIRIES TO:
Megan Ryan, SBIR Coordinator
(See address above.)

NATIONAL INSTITUTES OF HEALTH
Division of International Relations
Fogarty International Center
Building 31, Room B2C11
31 Center Drive, MSC 2220
Bethesda, MD 20892-2220
(301) 496-4784
Fax: (301) 480-3414
E-mail: tina.chung@nih.gov
Web Site: www.fic.nih.gov/programs/pages/japan-fellowships.aspx

TYPE:
Fellowships. A limited number of postdoctoral research fellowships are provided by the Japan Science and Technology Agency (JSTA) to U.S. scientists to conduct research in Japan. Types of activity supported include collaboration in basic or clinical research and familiarization with or utilization of special techniques and equipment not otherwise available to the applicant.

See entry 879 for full listing.

LUCILE PACKARD FOUNDATION FOR CHILDREN'S HEALTH
400 Hamilton Avenue, Suite 340
Palo Alto, CA 94301
(650) 736-0675
(650) 497-8365
Fax: (650) 498-2619
E-mail: grants@lpfch.org
Web Site: www.lpfch-cshcn.org

TYPE:
Project/program grants.

See entry 1028 for full listing.

THE PATRON SAINTS FOUNDATION [1313]
260 South Los Robles Avenue, No. 201
Pasadena, CA 91101
(626) 564-0444
Fax: (626) 564-0444
E-mail: patronsaintsfdn@sbcglobal.net
Web Site: patronsaintsfoundation.org

FOUNDED: 1986

AREAS OF INTEREST:
Health care.

TYPE:
Project/program grants. Limited operating support will be awarded at the discretion of the Board of Directors.

YEAR PROGRAM STARTED: 1986

PURPOSE:
To improve the health of individuals residing in the West San Gabriel Valley through health care programs that are consistent with the moral and religious teachings of the Roman Catholic Church.

LEGAL BASIS:
Private foundation.

ELIGIBILITY:
Organizations must be IRS 501(c)(3) tax-exempt.

GEOG. RESTRICTIONS: West San Gabriel Valley, California.

FINANCIAL DATA:
Amount of support per award: $5,000 to $15,000.
Total amount of support: $427,500 for fiscal year ended June 30, 2019.

NO. MOST RECENT APPLICANTS: 35.

NO. AWARDS: 28 for fiscal year ended June 30, 2019.

APPLICATION INFO:
Two copies of the application (not to exceed three pages, no less than 11-point type, one stapled and one paper-clipped) must be mailed to the Foundation, along with other required documents including financial statements, copy of the organization's 501(c)(3) determination letter and IRS Form 990.
Duration: One year. Renewal by reapplication.
Deadline: First Friday in March and first Friday in October.

PUBLICATIONS:
Grant guidelines; grant application form; brochure.

IRS I.D.: 95-3484257

EXECUTIVE DIRECTOR:
Kathleen T. Shannon

ADDRESS INQUIRIES TO:
Kathleen T. Shannon, Executive Director
(See address above.)

THE DOROTHY RIDER POOL HEALTH CARE TRUST   [1314]

645 West Hamilton Street
Suite 202
Allentown, PA 18101
(610) 770-9346
E-mail: info@pooltrust.org
Web Site: www.pooltrust.org

FOUNDED: 1975

AREAS OF INTEREST:
Community health, health services research, leadership development and medical education, recruitment and retention of outstanding health care providers, access to care, health studies, and clinical innovation.

TYPE:
Challenge/matching grants; Development grants; Project/program grants. Grants addressing at least one of the key components of the Trust's Philanthropic Agenda: improved health status of the citizens of the region, recruitment and retention of outstanding health care providers, clinical innovation, access to care, medical education, community health and health service research.

PURPOSE:
To serve as a resource that enables Lehigh Valley Hospital to be a superior regional hospital and improve the health of the citizens of the region it serves.

ELIGIBILITY:
The Trust considers proposals from nonprofit organizations and institutions within the Trust's interest areas.

GEOG. RESTRICTIONS: Allentown, Pennsylvania and surrounding area.

FINANCIAL DATA:
Amount of support per award: Varies.
Total amount of support: $840,447 for the year 2018.

APPLICATION INFO:
Funding requests should be initiated with a letter of intent from the applicant. The letter should be two to four pages summarizing the need, objective, strategy, evaluation, budget and duration.

Electronic application process is available on the web site.
Duration: Varies.

PUBLICATIONS:
Annual report.

IRS I.D.: 23-6627932

TRUSTEES:
Denise M. Gargan
John P. Jones, III
Peter M. Leibold, Esq.
Mary D. Naylor, Ph.D., FAAN
James O. Woolliscroft, M.D.

STAFF:
Edward F. Meehan, M.P.H., Executive Director
Ronald C. Dendas, M.S., Program Officer
Bridget I. Rassler, Manager, Finance and Administration
Regina M. Gabriel, Program Secretary

ADDRESS INQUIRIES TO:
Edward F. Meehan, M.P.H., Executive Director
(See address above.)

QUANTUM FOUNDATION   [1315]

2701 North Australian Avenue, Suite 200
West Palm Beach, FL 33407
(561) 832-7497
Fax: (561) 832-5794
E-mail: randy@quantumfnd.org
Web Site: www.quantumfnd.org

FOUNDED: 1995

AREAS OF INTEREST:
Health access, health education, health workforce, and basic needs to support health.

TYPE:
Capital grants; Challenge/matching grants; Demonstration grants; Matching gifts; Project/program grants; Seed money grants.

YEAR PROGRAM STARTED: 1997

PURPOSE:
To inspire and fund bold initiatives that improve the health of our communities through quality health.

LEGAL BASIS:
Private foundation.

ELIGIBILITY:
Eligible organizations must be IRS 501(c)(3) tax-exempt and defined as a public charity under Section 509(a)(1), (2) or (3), an accredited school or university, or a unit of government or public agency, typically tax-exempt under Section 107(c)(1) or Section 511(a)(2)(B), providing services in Palm Beach County.

GEOG. RESTRICTIONS: Palm Beach County, Florida.

FINANCIAL DATA:
Amount of support per award: Varies.
Total amount of support: Approximately $6,000,000 annually.

APPLICATION INFO:
Submit a Letter of Inquiry at the Foundation's web site.
Duration: One to three years.
Deadline: Varies.

STAFF:
Randy Scheid, Vice President of Programs
Shannon Hawkins, Senior Program Officer

ADDRESS INQUIRIES TO:
Randy Scheid, Vice President of Programs
(See e-mail address above.)

RESEARCH MANITOBA   [1316]

A201 Chown Building
753 McDermot Avenue
Winnipeg MB R3E 0T6 Canada
(204) 775-1096
E-mail: info@researchmb.ca
Web Site: researchmanitoba.ca

FOUNDED: 2014

AREAS OF INTEREST:
Research and innovation in health, natural and social sciences, engineering and the humanities in the province of Manitoba.

NAME(S) OF PROGRAMS:
- **CFI Matching Funds**
- **Innovative Proof-of-Concept Grants**
- **New Investigator Operating Grants**
- **NSERC Alliance-RM ACT Grant**
- **Strategic Partnership Program**
- **Trainee Awards**

TYPE:
Awards/prizes; Development grants; General operating grants.

YEAR PROGRAM STARTED: 2014

PURPOSE:
To promote, support and coordinate the funding of research in health, natural and social sciences, engineering and humanities in Manitoba.

LEGAL BASIS:
Established by an Act of the Provincial Legislature and provincially funded.

ELIGIBILITY:
Grants are awarded to academic researchers, postsecondary institutions and/or companies in the Province of Manitoba.

GEOG. RESTRICTIONS: Manitoba, Canada.

FINANCIAL DATA:
Amount of support per award: Varies.
Total amount of support: $12,000,000 budgeted annually.
Matching fund requirements: Innovative Proof-of-Concept Grant and NSERC Alliance-RM ACT Grant require matching funds from industry partners. Strategic Partnership Program matches industry and/or philanthropic dollars to support research programs/projects.

CO-OP FUNDING PROGRAMS: Canadian Foundation for Innovation; Natural Sciences and Engineering Council of Canada (NSERC).

NO. MOST RECENT APPLICANTS: 253.

NO. AWARDS: 91 for the year 2020-21.

APPLICATION INFO:
Applications must be made on the appropriate Research Manitoba forms online.
Duration: Varies.
Deadline: Specific deadlines for each program are posted on the Research Manitoba web site.

PUBLICATIONS:
Annual report; awards guide; GMS user guide.

STAFF:
Karen Dunlop, Chief Executive Officer
Nicole Barry, Director of Finance and Administration
Kristen Hooper, Communications Officer
Necole Sommersell, Manager, Evaluation and Impact
Jennifer Cleary, Manager, Programs
Freyja Arnason, Manager, RITHiM
Judi Bahl, Manager, Strategic Partnerships

BOARD MEMBERS:
Andrea Legary, Chairperson
Dr. Digvir Jayas, Vice-Chairperson
Dr. Rashid Ahmed
Dr. Athar Ata
Dr. Hani El-Gabalawy
Luis Escobar
Earl Gardiner
Cheryl Mayer
James Sandison

ADDRESS INQUIRIES TO:
See e-mail address above.

JOSEPHINE G. RUSSELL TRUST   [1317]

9 Bartlet Street, Suite 343
Andover, MA 01810
E-mail: russelltrust@yahoo.com
Web Site: jrusselltrust.org

FOUNDED: 1933

AREAS OF INTEREST:
Education, health care, poverty and social services.

TYPE:
General operating grants; Project/program grants; Scholarships.

PURPOSE:
To provide care, healing and nursing of the sick and injured; to provide relief and aid to the poor; to provide training and education of the young; to assist in any other manner of social service in the City of Lawrence.

LEGAL BASIS:
Private charitable trust.

ELIGIBILITY:
Eligible organizations must be IRS 501(c)(3) tax-exempt and serve the Lawrence area. No grants to individuals. No grants are made for endowments, equipment, capital campaigns, construction or renovations of buildings and facilities. No matching gifts.

Organizations intending to submit applications for funds must be able to demonstrate that, if funds are awarded by the Trust, the program will confer a direct benefit to Lawrence residents who are sick, injured or poor; or for education or in any other manner of social services upon the people of the city of Lawrence, MA.

GEOG. RESTRICTIONS: Lawrence, Massachusetts.

FINANCIAL DATA:
Total amount of support: $440,000 for the year 2019.

NO. MOST RECENT APPLICANTS: 55.

NO. AWARDS: 46.

APPLICATION INFO:
Updated guidelines may be requested from the e-mail address above. Applicants may submit a written proposal and must include a copy of the IRS tax determination letter, budget and list of trustees in the organization.

Once application is completed, individual copies must be sent to all designated trustees.
Duration: One year. Renewal possible.
Deadline: January 31.

PUBLICATIONS:
Guidelines.

STAFF:
Marsha E. Rich, Managing Trustee

ADDRESS INQUIRIES TO:
See e-mail address above.

*PLEASE NOTE:
Guidelines require submissions of grant proposals to all trustees.

*SPECIAL STIPULATIONS:
Funded organizations are required to submit expenditure letter by December 31 of funding year.

EUNICE KENNEDY SHRIVER NATIONAL INSTITUTE OF CHILD HEALTH AND HUMAN DEVELOPMENT [1318]
Division of Extramural Research (DER)
6710B Rockledge Drive
Room 2314, MSC 7002
Bethesda, MD 20817
(800) 370-2943
(301) 945-7573
Fax: (866) 760-5947
E-mail: NICHDInformationResourceCenter@ mail.nih.gov
Web Site: www.nichd.nih.
gov/about/org/der/branches

FOUNDED: 1963

AREAS OF INTEREST:
All health sciences pertaining to mothers and children.

NAME(S) OF PROGRAMS:
- **Child Development and Behavior Branch (CDBB)**
- **Contraception Research Branch (CRB)**
- **Developmental Biology and Structural Variation Branch (DBSVB)**
- **Fertility and Infertility (FI) Branch**
- **Gynecologic Health and Disease Branch (GHDB)**
- **Intellectual and Developmental Disabilities Branch (IDDB)**
- **Maternal and Pediatric Infectious Disease Branch (MPIDB)**
- **Obstetric and Pediatric Pharmacology and Therapeutics Branch (OPPTB)**
- **Pediatric Growth and Nutrition Branch (PGNB)**
- **Pediatric Trauma and Critical Illness Branch (PTCIB)**
- **Population Dynamics Branch (PDB)**
- **Pregnancy and Perinatology Branch (PPB)**

TYPE:
Conferences/seminars; Development grants; Fellowships; General operating grants; Project/program grants; Training grants; Research contracts. Project grants and research contracts to expand the health and well-being of individuals from the moment of conception and extending through the later teenage years.

PURPOSE:
To discover new knowledge through research.

LEGAL BASIS:
Public Health Service Act, Sections 301(c), 444 and 472.

ELIGIBILITY:
Universities, colleges, medical, dental and nursing schools, schools of public health, laboratories, hospitals, state and local health departments, other public or private nonprofit institutions and commercial organizations are eligible. Individuals may apply for grants for academic and research training. They must have a professional or scientific degree and be citizens or permanent residents of the U.S.

FINANCIAL DATA:
Amount of support per award: Varies.

APPLICATION INFO:
Contact the Institute.
Duration: One year to multiyear funding.

ADDRESS INQUIRIES TO:
See e-mail address above.

SICKKIDS FOUNDATION [1319]
525 University Avenue, Suite 835
Toronto ON M5G 2L3 Canada
(416) 813-8104
(800) 661-1083 ext. 2354
E-mail: national.grants@sickkidsfoundation.com
Web Site: www.sickkidsfoundation.com/about-us/grants

FOUNDED: 1973

AREAS OF INTEREST:
Health and well-being of children.

NAME(S) OF PROGRAMS:
- **Community Conference Grants Program**
- **New Investigator Research Grants**

TYPE:
Awards/prizes; Conferences/seminars; Project/program grants; Research grants. Community Conference Grants program brings together families with researchers and clinicians for medical presentations and family-oriented discussions. It helps ensure knowledge exchange with families so that they are able to access the most up-to-date information about their children's health.

New Investigator Research Grants program focus is to ensure that there continues to be well-trained researchers across the country working to address the most pressing childhood diseases and conditions.

YEAR PROGRAM STARTED: 1974

PURPOSE:
To promote quality programs in child health, research and public health education in the field.

LEGAL BASIS:
Public foundation with charitable registration.

ELIGIBILITY:
Community Conference Grants: Eligible events must have a focus on information sharing between health professionals, community organizations and families. Academic conferences are not eligible for funding. Eligible events must:
(1) address issues that are relevant to child health in Canada;
(2) support the parent-child-professional partnership by having a focus on information sharing between families, health professionals, and community organizations;
(3) include knowledgeable and credible presenters;
(4) take place in Canada and;
(5) be sponsored by a registered Canadian charitable organization.

Preference will be given to events which are organized by smaller, community-based organizations, have interactive/knowledge exchange sessions with families, involve parents as panel/speakers, and have the potential to make an impact on practice or policy.

New Investigator Grants: Principal investigator must be eligible to apply for independent research grants and be formally affiliated with an eligible institution, where that institution is willing to financially administer the grant. The Principal Investigator will usually hold a doctoral degree (Ph.D.) or equivalent degree and have had formal research training. If there are two applicants, both must be eligible as a New Investigator. Eligible applicants are required to include a mentorship plan and to work with a clearly-identified mentor(s).

GEOG. RESTRICTIONS: Canada.

FINANCIAL DATA:
Amount of support per award: Community Conference Grants: Maximum $5,000; New Investigator Grants: Up to $100,000 per year.

Total amount of support: Varies.

NO. AWARDS: Community Conference Grants: Up to 12; New Investigator Research Grants: Up to 6.

APPLICATION INFO:
Application guidelines are available online. All applications are submitted through the Online Application Portal.

Duration: New Investigator Grants: Maximum of three years with annual review of progress. No renewals.

Deadline: Community Conference Grants: January 31, May 31 and September 30. New Investigator Research Grant: Mid-April.

SISTERS OF ST. JOSEPH HEALTHCARE FOUNDATION   [1320]

440 South Batavia
Orange, CA 92868-3998
(714) 633-8121 ext. 7109
E-mail: rfox@csjorange.org
Web Site: www.csjorange.org

FOUNDED: 1992

AREAS OF INTEREST:
Housing security, food security, family violence prevention and support, and related capacity-building efforts.

TYPE:
General operating grants; Project/program grants. The Foundation sponsors or supports long-term efforts which are closely identified with the Sisters of St. Joseph of Orange and their mission of bringing unity and healing where divisiveness and oppression exist.

PURPOSE:
To fund programs which directly serve the needs of the underserved, especially families and children at risk; to support programs and organizations that work to prevent violence and homelessness.

LEGAL BASIS:
Public foundation.

ELIGIBILITY:
Applicants must be nonprofit organizations operating in Humbolt County, southern California and San Francisco Bay area which have programs that directly serve the needs of the underserved, especially families and children at risk, as well as programs of education and advocacy which are directed at improving health and access to health care. Religious organizations also receive support. Capital projects will not be considered.

The Foundation desires to fund programs and organizations that:
(1) provide direct health-related services;
(2) support and transform the individual, social, economic, institutional, and cultural aspects of communities;
(3) provide change within larger societal systems to benefit low-income and at-risk populations and;
(4) develop the leadership and capacity for self-determination of those served by the Foundation's funding.

GEOG. RESTRICTIONS: Southern California, Humbolt County and San Francisco Bay area.

FINANCIAL DATA:
Amount of support per award: $15,000 to $50,000. Average award of $30,000.
Total amount of support: $1,917,000 for the year 2019.

NO. MOST RECENT APPLICANTS: 200 for the year 2019.

NO. AWARDS: 80 for the year 2019.

APPLICATION INFO:
Contact the Foundation.
Duration: One year.
Deadline: Contact Foundation for exact dates.

STAFF:
Sister Regina Fox, S.S.N.D., Executive Director
Mary Vagnone, Grants Manager

ADDRESS INQUIRIES TO:
Sister Regina Fox, S.S.N.D.
Executive Director
(See address above.)

GERTRUDE E. SKELLY CHARITABLE FOUNDATION

4600 North Ocean Boulevard
Suite 206
Boynton Beach, FL 33435
(561) 276-1008
Fax: (561) 272-2793
E-mail: ejoh@hhk.com

TYPE:
Challenge/matching grants; Conferences/seminars; Project/program grants; Research grants; Scholarships; Training grants. Emergency grants for continued education.

See entry 1461 for full listing.

THE CHRISTOPHER D. SMITHERS FOUNDATION, INC.   [1321]

P.O. Box 67
Mill Neck, NY 11765
(516) 676-0067
E-mail: info@smithersfoundation.org
Web Site: smithersfoundation.org

FOUNDED: 1952

AREAS OF INTEREST:
Education and prevention of alcohol use disorder and opioid use disorder.

TYPE:
Conferences/seminars; Project/program grants; Research grants; Technical assistance; Training grants.

YEAR PROGRAM STARTED: 1952

PURPOSE:
To prevent alcoholism and opioid abuse through education.

FINANCIAL DATA:
Amount of support per award: Varies.

APPLICATION INFO:
Grant proposal must include:
(1) a letter of introduction, addressed to Nikki Smithers, President;
(2) a brief description of the program and grant amount requested (budget);
(3) a copy of 501(c)(3) nonprofit status and;
(4) a copy of most recent annual report.

PUBLICATIONS:
Annual report.

OFFICERS:
Adele C. Smithers, Chairman
Nikki Smithers, President
Samuel B. Bacharach, Ph.D., Vice President
Stacia Murphy, Treasurer
Brinkley Smithers, Secretary

DIRECTORS:
Nicholas A. Pace, M.D.
M. Elizabeth Brothers, Honorary Director

ARTEMAS W. STEARNS TRUST   [1322]

9 Bartlet Street, Suite 343
Andover, MA 01810
E-mail: stearnstrust@yahoo.com
Web Site: stearnstrust.org

FOUNDED: 1896

AREAS OF INTEREST:
The aged and poor, health care in the Lawrence area, social services and education.

TYPE:
General operating grants; Project/program grants; Scholarships. Elder and infirm support.

YEAR PROGRAM STARTED: 1896

PURPOSE:
To pay income to such nonprofit and charitable homes, nursing homes, convalescent homes, retirement homes, sanitaria, homes for the aged, hospitals, agencies and such other similar institutions, organizations and agencies as may provide for or care, in whole or in part, for the indigent aged people of both sexes; to provide relief of the deserving poor of the City of Lawrence, without distinction of nationality or religious belief.

LEGAL BASIS:
Private charitable trust.

ELIGIBILITY:
Eligible organizations must be IRS 501(c)(3) tax-exempt. No grants to individuals. No grants are made for endowments, equipment, capital campaigns, construction or renovations of buildings and facilities.

Organizations intending to submit applications for funds must be able to demonstrate that, if funds are awarded by the Trust, the program will confer a direct benefit upon the indigent aged people or to the deserving poor of the city of Lawrence, MA exclusively.

GEOG. RESTRICTIONS: Lawrence, Massachusetts.

FINANCIAL DATA:
Amount of support per award: Varies.
Total amount of support: $187,000 for the year 2020.

NO. MOST RECENT APPLICANTS: 45.

NO. AWARDS: 40.

APPLICATION INFO:
Updated guidelines may be requested from the e-mail address above. Applicants may submit a written proposal and must include a copy of the IRS tax determination letter, budget and list of trustees in the organization.

Once application is completed, individual copies must be sent to all designated trustees.
Duration: One year. Renewal possible.
Deadline: January 31.

PUBLICATIONS:
Application guidelines.

STAFF:
Marsha E. Rich, Managing Trustee

ADDRESS INQUIRIES TO:
See e-mail address above.

*PLEASE NOTE:
Guidelines require submissions of grant proposals to all trustees.

*SPECIAL STIPULATIONS:
Funded organizations are required to submit expenditure letter by December 31 of funding year.

U.S. DEPARTMENT OF HEALTH AND HUMAN SERVICES [1323]

Health Resources and Services Administration
Bureau of Primary Health Care
Parklawn Building, 5600 Fishers Lane
Room 1874
Rockville, MD 20857
(301) 594-4300
(301) 594-4110
Web Site: bphc.hrsa.gov

FOUNDED: 1976

AREAS OF INTEREST:
Assisting communities located in medically underserved areas to develop needed primary health care services.

CONSULTING OR VOLUNTEER SERVICES:
Information and technical assistance is available from U.S. Public Health Service Regional Office staff.

NAME(S) OF PROGRAMS:
• The Health Center Program

TYPE:
Project/program grants. Grants may be made for planning and development of a community health center and for operations.

YEAR PROGRAM STARTED: 1975

PURPOSE:
To provide primary health care in ambulatory care settings located in severely medically underserved areas and to develop a network of services involving as many other health programs and facilities operating in the area as possible; to arrange for other federal programs not operating in the area to establish services within the federally funded primary care center whenever possible.

LEGAL BASIS:
Government agency.

ELIGIBILITY:
Grants may be made to public or private not-for-profit entities. Area to be served must be medically underserved. Priority will be given to areas of highest need.

GEOG. RESTRICTIONS: United States.

FINANCIAL DATA:
Amount of support per award: Approximately $650,000.

Matching fund requirements: The applicant must assume part of the project costs determined on a case-by-case basis.

CO-OP FUNDING PROGRAMS: Funding along with other federal programs, such as Migrant Health Centers, National Health Service Corps, MCH, or Mental Health Alcohol and Drug Abuse is encouraged, as well as cooperation with state and local programs.

APPLICATION INFO:
Information available from HRSA Grant Application Center, 901 Russell Avenue, Suite 450, Gaithersburg, MD 20879, or call (877) 477-2123.

Duration: Project periods may be up to three years, with annual budget periods.

PUBLICATIONS:
Application guidelines.

STAFF:
Jim Macrae, Associate Administrator to Bureau of Primary Health Care Director

U.S. DEPARTMENT OF HEALTH AND HUMAN SERVICES [1324]

Centers for Medicare and Medicaid Services
7500 Security Boulevard
Baltimore, MD 21244-1850
(410) 786-3000
(877) 267-2323
Fax: (410) 786-1008
E-mail: medicaid.gov@cms.hhs.gov
Web Site: www.medicaid.gov

FOUNDED: 1967

NAME(S) OF PROGRAMS:
• Medicaid

TYPE:
Formula grants. Financial assistance to states for in- and outpatient hospital services, other laboratory services, home health care, family planning, physicians' services and early diagnosis and treatment for persons who are medically needy.

LEGAL BASIS:
Title XIX, Social Security Act as amended; Public Law 89-97; Public Law 90-248; Public Law 91-56; 42 U.S.C. 1396, et seq. Public Law 92-223; Public Law 92-603.

ELIGIBILITY:
State and local welfare agencies operating under an approved Medicaid plan are eligible for support.

GEOG. RESTRICTIONS: United States.

FINANCIAL DATA:
Amount of support per award: Varies.
Total amount of support: Varies.

APPLICATION INFO:
Application forms are available from the address above or from regional or local offices of the Medical Services Administration to whom applications should be submitted.

Duration: Quarterly.

Deadline: States must submit quarterly estimates of funds no later than May 15, August 15, November 15 and February 15 in order to receive quarterly grant awards.

UNITED HOSPITAL FUND OF NEW YORK [1325]

1411 Broadway, 12th Floor
New York, NY 10018
(212) 494-0761
Fax: (212) 494-0801
E-mail: hholmes@uhfnyc.org
Web Site: uhfnyc.org

FOUNDED: 1879

AREAS OF INTEREST:
Expanding health insurance coverage, improving quality of care, and redesigning health care services.

NAME(S) OF PROGRAMS:
• Health Care Improvement Grant Program

TYPE:
Project/program grants; Seed money grants.

YEAR PROGRAM STARTED: 1938

PURPOSE:
To provide support to innovative projects by nonprofit hospitals and health care and other organizations to improve the quality of health care for all New Yorkers.

LEGAL BASIS:
Public charity.

ELIGIBILITY:
Nonprofit 501(c)(3) tax-exempt organizations in or to the benefit of New York City are eligible for support. No grants to individuals, capital or endowment campaigns or general operating grants.

GEOG. RESTRICTIONS: Primarily New York, New York, including the five boroughs.

FINANCIAL DATA:
Amount of support per award: Typically $50,000 to $125,000.

Total amount of support: Approximately $1,000,000 annually.

Matching fund requirements: Varies.

NO. MOST RECENT APPLICANTS: 60.

REPRESENTATIVE AWARDS:
$75,833 to BronxCare Health System; $79,948 to Mount Sinai Hospital; $72,691 to St. John's Episcopal Hospital.

APPLICATION INFO:
The Foundation is not accepting Letters of Intent or unsolicited proposals at this time.

Duration: One to two years. Nonrenewable.

PUBLICATIONS:
Annual report; application guidelines.

OFFICERS:
John C. Simons, Chairman
Anthony Shih, M.D., M.P.H., President
Sally J. Rogers, Senior Vice President
Chad Shearer, Senior Vice President
Jo Ivey Boufford, M.D., Vice Chairman
Quincy McLain, C.P.A., Vice President and Treasurer
Vaughn R. Muria, Vice President
Amanda A. Williams, Corporate Secretary

BOARD OF DIRECTORS:
Jo Ivey Boufford, M.D.
Dale C. Christensen, Jr.
J. Barclay Collins, II
Margaret Crotty
Samuel J. Daniel, M.D.
Christophe Durand
Robert S. Galvin, M.D.
Jennifer L. Howse, Ph.D.
Eugene Keilin
Cary A. Kravet
Josh N. Kuriloff
Meera Mani, M.D., Ph.D.
Howard P. Milstein
Susana R. Morales, M.D.
Robert C. Osborne, Jr.
Seun Salami
Anthony Shih, M.D., M.P.H.
Anthony Shorris
John C. Simons
Eileen M. Sullivan-Marx, Ph.D.
Mary Beth C. Tully
Barbara A. Yastine

ADDRESS INQUIRIES TO:
Hollis Holmes, Grants Manager
(See address above.)

US COMMUNITY PARTNERSHIPS [1326]

GSK
5 Moore Drive
Research Triangle Park, NC 27709
E-mail: us.communitypartnerships@gsk.com
Web Site: us.gsk.com

AREAS OF INTEREST:
Nutrition and physical activity for children and youth, STEM education, and disaster preparedness and response.

TYPE:
Project/program grants.

PURPOSE:
To foster increased understanding of scientific, clinical and health care issues; to contribute to improving patient care.

LEGAL BASIS:
Corporate foundation.

ELIGIBILITY:
Applicants must be nonprofit organizations with proposals consistent with guidelines and interest areas. No grants for capital projects, operating expenses, conferences, symposia, publications, fund-raising events, lobbying to influence legislation, religious organizations, sporting events, universities, free-standing research centers, scholar aid, expeditions or individuals.

GEOG. RESTRICTIONS: United States.

FINANCIAL DATA:
Amount of support per award: Varies depending on needs and nature of the request.

APPLICATION INFO:
Applicants must first register on the U.S. Community Partnerships Charitable Grant Request System. Once registration is approved (approximately 10 days), organization may be required to submit additional information including:
(1) copy of 501(c)(3) or 501(c)(1), if a public school, IRS letter of determination;
(2) member list for the Board of Directors;
(3) program literature;
(4) program evaluation (if an ongoing program for three or more years);
(5) most recent audited financials and;
(6) additional information as required per Impact Awards or Impact Grants programs.
Duration: Typically one year.
Deadline: Applications accepted throughout the year.

THE WHITEHORSE FOUNDATION [1327]
Westlake Tower
1601 Fifth Avenue, Suite 1900
Seattle, WA 98101
(206) 515-2131
(206) 622-2294
Fax: (206) 622-7673
E-mail: c.erickson@seattlefoundation.org
Web Site: www.seattlefoundation.org

FOUNDED: 1990

AREAS OF INTEREST:
Preventative human services to improve the lives of children, youth and families in Snohomish County, WA.

TYPE:
Project/program grants.

YEAR PROGRAM STARTED: 1990

PURPOSE:
To fund comprehensive preventive social service programs in Snohomish County, WA.

LEGAL BASIS:
Community foundation.

ELIGIBILITY:
Applicant organizations must be IRS 501(c)(3) tax-exempt. No grants to individuals.

GEOG. RESTRICTIONS: Snohomish County, Washington.

FINANCIAL DATA:
Amount of support per award: $25,000 to $100,000.
Total amount of support: $1,500,000.

NO. MOST RECENT APPLICANTS: 50.

NO. AWARDS: 25.

APPLICATION INFO:
Applications guidelines are available on the web site. Letter of Inquiry must be submitted to grantmaking@seattlefoundation.org.
Duration: Multiyear grants.
Deadline: Prior to board meetings held in June and December.

STAFF:
Ceil Erickson, Program Director

ADDRESS INQUIRIES TO:
Ceil Erickson, Program Director
(See address above.)

MR. AND MRS. P.A. WOODWARD'S FOUNDATION [1328]
1055 West Hastings Street, Suite 300
Vancouver BC V6E 2E9 Canada
(604) 682-8116
E-mail: pawoodwardfoundation@gmail.com
Web Site: www.woodwardfoundation.ca

FOUNDED: 1951

AREAS OF INTEREST:
Health care.

TYPE:
The Foundation supports those projects which affect the people of the Province of British Columbia where there is clear indication of the health benefit anticipated. The Foundation is charged with aiding in the purchase of the latest medical equipment of proven performance that provides direct benefit to the patient. A preference was expressed to fund items with direct patient benefit, as contrasted to research done in the laboratory with uncertain or delayed benefits and programs that create awareness.

PURPOSE:
To assist in projects which could contribute to better health care.

LEGAL BASIS:
Charitable foundation.

ELIGIBILITY:
Organizations applying for funding must be domiciled within the Province of British Columbia. All individuals and organizations applying must be in possession of a Charitable Gift Registration Number as issued by the Department of National Revenue of Canada.

The Foundation will consider applications in the following general areas:
(1) health care equipment of proven effectiveness and;
(2) special projects which will benefit the health of British Columbians.

The Foundation will not support routine operational budgets, fundamental research not directly related to patient care, conferences or annual meetings, endowments, capital building costs, or renovations.

GEOG. RESTRICTIONS: British Columbia, Canada.

FINANCIAL DATA:
Amount of support per award: Grants vary in amount, depending upon the needs and nature of the request.

NO. AWARDS: Varies.

APPLICATION INFO:
Applications will be received by invitation only. Organizations must e-mail a Letter of Intent indicating what they would like to apply for. Organizations may then be invited to submit a full application.
Deadline: Beginning of February for March Board meeting; beginning of May for June Board meeting; Middle of September for October Board meeting. Actual dates are posted on the Foundation web site.

OFFICERS:
Christopher C. Woodward, President
Jill Leversage, Treasurer
Paul Langley, Secretary
Jim Allworth

MEMBERS AND DIRECTORS:
Jim Allworth
Paul Langley
Jill Leversage
Gregory J.D. McKinstry
Hon. Madam Justice Mary V. Newbury
David N. Ostrow
Elizabeth Watson
Christopher C. Woodward

ADDRESS INQUIRIES TO:
Executive Director
(See address above.)

Social welfare

THE ABELARD FOUNDATION-EAST [1329]
P.O. Box 148
Lincoln, MA 01773
E-mail: eastabel@aol.com
Web Site: fdnweb.org/abelardeast

AREAS OF INTEREST:
Progressive social change, community organizing, civil and human rights.

TYPE:
General operating grants; Project/program grants.

PURPOSE:
To support local progressive social change activities that expand and protect civil liberties and civil and human rights, and promote and strengthen community involvement in, and control over, the decisions that affect their lives.

ELIGIBILITY:
Applicants must represent or be associated with a nonprofit, 501(c)(3) tax-exempt organization. Priority is given to projects that are in their first years of development and have budgets less than $350,000.

GEOG. RESTRICTIONS: Eastern United States, east of the Mississippi River.

FINANCIAL DATA:
Amount of support per award: Average $10,000.
Total amount of support: Approximately $150,000 annually.

NO. AWARDS: Approximately 15 new and renewals.

APPLICATION INFO:
Applicants should submit one copy of a proposal (no more than seven to 10 pages) which includes:
(1) background of the organization;

(2) description of the work for which funds are being sought;

(3) explanation of need;

(4) impact the project will have;

(5) brief bios of key staff and board officers;

(6) data about board and staff;

(7) current organizational budget and;

(8) current private supporters list with names and grant amounts.

Proposals prepared in a "common application" format will also be accepted.

Applying organizations must include IRS 501(c)(3) determination letter.

Duration: One year. Up to two renewals possible.

Deadline: Applications mailed by March 15 will be reviewed for the spring meeting. Applications mailed by September 15 will be reviewed for the fall meeting.

ADDRESS INQUIRIES TO:
Susan Collins, Trustee
The Abelard Foundation-East
(See address above.)

EMMA J. ADAMS MEMORIAL FUND, INC. [1330]

328 Eldert Lane
Brooklyn, NY 11208
(347) 789-6717
Fax: (347) 789-6717

FOUNDED: 1933

AREAS OF INTEREST:
Geriatric institutions, welfare, elderly, and needy, mostly through organizations.

TYPE:
Grants-in-aid. Financial support and organized aid to geriatric, needy and/or elderly institutional agencies and occasionally to referred respectable, aged indigent persons in financial difficulty through no fault of their own, in the greater New York City area.

YEAR PROGRAM STARTED: 1936

PURPOSE:
To aid elderly, needy and indigent people and geriatric institutions.

LEGAL BASIS:
Nonprofit corporation.

ELIGIBILITY:
Most grants are awarded to operating geriatric institutions.

No scholarships, program grants, administrative expenses, and no brick-and-mortar grants.

GEOG. RESTRICTIONS: Greater New York area.

FINANCIAL DATA:
Amount of support per award: Varies.
Total amount of support: Average $40,000 per year.

NO. MOST RECENT APPLICANTS: Over 150.

NO. AWARDS: 15 to 20.

APPLICATION INFO:
Application forms available upon request. The letter must indicate the referral source. No telephone requests honored.

Duration: Varies.

Deadline: September 1.

IRS I.D.: 13-6116503

DIRECTORS:
Jill Harvey
Betsy Rowe

Sally Saran
Elizabeth H.J. Scott
Carolyn Swayze

ADDRESS INQUIRIES TO:
Sally Saran, President
(See address above.)

JUDD S. ALEXANDER FOUNDATION [1331]

500 First Street, Suite 10
Wausau, WI 54403
(715) 845-4556
Fax: (715) 843-9018
E-mail: office@alexanderprop.org
Web Site: juddsalexanderfoundation.org

FOUNDED: 1978

AREAS OF INTEREST:
Education, recreation, human services, children's services and economic development.

TYPE:
Capital grants; Challenge/matching grants; Project/program grants; Seed money grants. Support is provided for capital building and emergency funds.

YEAR PROGRAM STARTED: 1978

PURPOSE:
To support quality of life and economic development in Marathon County, WI.

LEGAL BASIS:
Private foundation.

ELIGIBILITY:
Organizations classified as 501(c)(3) by the IRS can apply. The Foundation does not make grants to individuals or private businesses.

GEOG. RESTRICTIONS: Marathon County, Wisconsin.

FINANCIAL DATA:
Amount of support per award: Varies.
Total amount of support: Varies.

APPLICATION INFO:
Five copies, unbound, of the proposal should be submitted. Proposal material should not be placed in protective covers or other presentation formats. Videos and other supplementary materials are not encouraged and will not be returned to applicants. A fully reviewable proposal will include:
(1) a cover page with the exact name and location of the proposed grant recipient, along with the name, title, address and telephone number of an individual at the organization;
(2) a project overview, which includes a description of the organization's main activities and whether it is a public, private or not-for-profit entity, a description of the project or activity for which funding is requested, and specific outcomes and goals and;
(3) a project budget which includes revenue and expense pages and a budget narrative.

The following items must also be attached:
(1) the organization's current annual operating budget, including revenues and expenses;
(2) a list of the organization's governing body and its officers, showing business, professional and/or community affiliations, along with officers' financial contributions to the organization;
(3) letters of support and letters from other agencies indicating their intent to collaborate

(as appropriate);
(4) other documents to supplement the above information, provided it is not duplicative of other material or information contained in the narratives or budget presentation;
(5) the most recent audited financial statements and;
(6) the most recent IRS determination letter.

The Foundation does not accept proposals by fax or e-mail.

Duration: Typically one year. Must reapply.

ADDRESS INQUIRIES TO:
Gary W. Freels, President
(See address above.)

THE ALLSTATE FOUNDATION [1332]

3075 Sanders Road
Northbrook, IL 60062
E-mail: foundation@allstate.com
Web Site: www.allstatefoundation.org

FOUNDED: 1952

AREAS OF INTEREST:
Domestic violence, youth empowerment, nonprofit leadership and volunteerism.

TYPE:
Matching gifts; Project/program grants. Program support in the Foundation's areas of focus; matching gifts for higher education only.

YEAR PROGRAM STARTED: 1952

PURPOSE:
To assist deserving organizations serving the fields of domestic violence and youth empowerment.

LEGAL BASIS:
Corporate foundation.

ELIGIBILITY:
If invited to apply, an organization must be exempt under Section 501(c)(3) of the IRS code, or be a municipal, state or federal government entity.

GEOG. RESTRICTIONS: United States.

FINANCIAL DATA:
Amount of support per award: National programs: $100,000; Local/regional grants: $5,000 to $20,000.
Total amount of support: Approximately $25,000,000 in grants for the year 2018.
Matching fund requirements: For colleges and universities.

APPLICATION INFO:
Unsolicited grant applications will not be accepted.

Duration: One year. Renewal based on program outcome and results.

PUBLICATIONS:
Guidelines.

IRS I.D.: 36-6116535

ADDRESS INQUIRIES TO:
See e-mail address above.

AMERICORPS [1333]

250 E Street, S.W.
Washington, DC 20024
(202) 606-5000
(800) 942-2677
Fax: (202) 606-3475
TTY: (800) 833-3722
E-mail: info@cns.gov
Web Site: americorps.gov/serve/americorps-seniors

FOUNDED: 1971

AREAS OF INTEREST:
Volunteer service.

NAME(S) OF PROGRAMS:
- **Foster Grandparent Program**
- **Retired and Senior Volunteer Program (RSVP)**
- **Senior Companion Program**

TYPE:
Demonstration grants; General operating grants; Grants-in-aid; Project/program grants; Technical assistance. Grants to provide meaningful opportunities for low-income persons age 55 years and over, specifically providing person-to-person service to children with special needs as Foster Grandparents and providing services to adults with special needs as Senior Companions. The Retired and Senior Volunteer Program helps people 55 and older put their skills and life experience to work in their communities.

PURPOSE:
To provide volunteer service opportunities for older Americans.

LEGAL BASIS:
Federal agency.

ELIGIBILITY:
State and local public agencies, private nonprofit organizations, and tribal entities may apply.

GEOG. RESTRICTIONS: United States and territories.

FINANCIAL DATA:
Amount of support per award: Foster Grandparent Program: $328,000 average. Retired Senior Volunteer Program: $77,000 average. Senior Companion Program: $204,000 average.

Matching fund requirements: 10% for Foster Grandparent Program and Senior Companion Program. For Retired Senior Volunteer Program, 10-20-30%.

CO-OP FUNDING PROGRAMS: Local public and private nonprofit agencies receive grants to sponsor and operate FGP, RSVP and SCP.

APPLICATION INFO:
Contact the Corporation.
Duration: Three years with opportunity to amend annually.
Deadline: Varies.

PUBLICATIONS:
Grant application; guidelines.

IRS I.D.: 53-0260397

THE CALIFORNIA ENDOWMENT
1000 North Alameda Street
Los Angeles, CA 90012
(800) 449-4149
E-mail: gms@calendow.org
Web Site: www.calendow.org

TYPE:
Challenge/matching grants; General operating grants; Matching gifts; Project/program grants.

See entry 1285 for full listing.

CAMPBELL FOUNDATION, INC.
705 York Road
Towson, MD 21204
(410) 828-1961
Fax: (410) 821-8814
E-mail: lcasciero@stoycpa.com

TYPE:
Capital grants; General operating grants; Project/program grants.

See entry 1004 for full listing.

THE CENTER AT SIERRA HEALTH FOUNDATION   [1334]
1321 Garden Highway
Suite 210
Sacramento, CA 95833
(916) 993-7701
E-mail: impact@shfcenter.org
Web Site: www.shfcenter.org

AREAS OF INTEREST:
Improving health outcomes and reducing health disparities.

NAME(S) OF PROGRAMS:
- **Asthma Mitigation Project**
- **Building Healthy Communities**
- **California Funders for Boys and Men of Color**
- **Census 2020 Outreach**
- **Elevate Youth California**
- **Leadership Development for Racial Equity**
- **Medi-Cal Health Navigator Project**
- **Medication Assisted Treatment Access Points Project**
- **My Brother's Keeper Sacramento Collaborative**
- **Oak Park Project**
- **Positive Youth Justice Initiative**
- **San Joaquin Valley Health Fund**
- **San Joaquin Valley Impact Investment Fund**
- **Steering Committee on Reducation of African American Child Deaths**
- **Youth and Community PopUps**

TYPE:
Matching gifts; Project/program grants.

PURPOSE:
To eradicate health inequities across the state; to bring people, ideas and infrastructure together to create positive change.

LEGAL BASIS:
501(c)(3) nonprofit.

ELIGIBILITY:
Applicant must be a public entity or designated 501(c)(3) organization by the IRS with 509(a)(1) or 509(a)(2) status. No grants to individuals, endowments or activities which exclusively benefit members of private or religious organizations.

GEOG. RESTRICTIONS: California, with a focus on underserved San Joaquin Valley.

FINANCIAL DATA:
Amount of support per award: Varies.

OFFICERS:
Chet P. Hewitt, President and Chief Executive Officer
Gil Alvarado, Senior Vice President of Finance and Administration
Kaying Hang, Vice President of Programs and Partnerships

BOARD OF DIRECTORS:
Debra McKenzie, Chairman
Jose Hermocillo, Vice Chairman
David W. Gordon
Chet P. Hewitt
Nancy P. Lee
Robert Petersen, C.P.A.
Dr. Claire Pomeroy
Carol Whiteside

ADDRESS INQUIRIES TO:
See e-mail address above.

THE COMMONWEALTH FUND   [1335]
One East 75th Street
New York, NY 10021
(212) 606-3800
Fax: (212) 606-3500
E-mail: grants@cmwf.org
Web Site: www.commonwealthfund.org

FOUNDED: 1918

AREAS OF INTEREST:
Supporting independent research on health care issues, and making grants to improve health care practice and policy.

NAME(S) OF PROGRAMS:
- **Advancing Medicare**
- **Controlling Health Care Costs**
- **Federal and State Health Policy**
- **Health Care Coverage and Access**
- **Health Care Delivery System Reform**
- **International Health Policy and Practice Innovations**
- **Tracking Health System Performance**

TYPE:
Fellowships; Project/program grants; Research grants; Scholarships; Research contracts.

YEAR PROGRAM STARTED: 1918

PURPOSE:
To promote a high-performing health care system that achieves better access, improved quality, and greater efficiency, particularly for society's most vulnerable, including low-income people, the uninsured, minority Americans, young children and elderly adults.

The Fund carries out this mandate by supporting independent research on health care issues and making grants to improve health care practice and policy. An international program in health policy is designed to stimulate innovative policies and practices in the U.S. and other industrialized countries.

LEGAL BASIS:
Private foundation.

ELIGIBILITY:
The Fund makes grants only to tax-exempt organizations and public agencies. No grants to individuals.

FINANCIAL DATA:
Amount of support per award: Varies.

Total amount of support: $19,600,000 in grants for fiscal year 2017-18.

NO. MOST RECENT APPLICANTS: 850.

NO. AWARDS: 170.

REPRESENTATIVE AWARDS:
$20,000 to Grantmakers in Aging, Inc., for engaging philanthropy in complex care; $345,900 to Issues Research, Inc., for case studies and tools to support the spread of promising practices in health care delivery and cost control; $121,771 to Bipartisan Policy Center, Inc., for development of policy options for addressing barriers to care improvement for patients with complex care needs.

APPLICATION INFO:
The Fund requests letters of inquiry to initiate the grant application process. Applicants are encouraged to submit letters of inquiry using the online form. While the

Fund will continue to accept letters of inquiry via regular mail and fax, such submissions will take longer to process than those received online. Letters of inquiry are acknowledged when received. Applicants are typically advised of the results of an initial staff review within two months. Program staff will contact applicants if more detailed information is required.

Duration: Typically one year, although some multiyear funding available.

Deadline: Applications may be submitted at any time.

IRS I.D.: 13-1635260

STAFF:
David Blumenthal, M.D., President
Kathleen Regan, Executive Vice President and Chief Operating Officer
Donald Moulds, Executive Vice President for Programs
Eric C. Schneider, M.D., Senior Vice President for Policy and Research
Barry A. Scholl, Senior Vice President for Communications and Publishing
Andrea Landes, Vice President of Grants Management

BOARD OF DIRECTORS:
Benjamin K. Chu, M.D., Chairman
Maureen Bisognano
David Blumenthal, M.D.
Mitchell J. Blutt, M.D.
Sheila P. Burke, R.N.
Michael V. Drake, M.D.
Margaret A. Hamburg, M.D.
Kathryn D. Haslanger
Vivian S. Lee, M.D.
Lois Quam
Mark D. Smith, M.D.
Simon Stevens
Laura Walker, MBA
William Y. Yun

ADDRESS INQUIRIES TO:
Andrea Landes
Vice President of Grants Management
(See address above.)

COMMUNITY FOUNDATION OF THE VERDUGOS [1336]
111 East Broadway, Suite 200
Glendale, CA 91205
(818) 241-8040
Fax: (818) 241-8045
E-mail: info@cfverdugos.org
Web Site: www.cfverdugos.org

FOUNDED: 1956

AREAS OF INTEREST:
Arts and culture, children, education, health, homeless services, human services, senior services and environment.

TYPE:
Capital grants; Development grants; Project/program grants; Scholarships.

YEAR PROGRAM STARTED: 1956

PURPOSE:
To meet current and changing needs in the community; to provide grants that create impact on the community.

LEGAL BASIS:
Community foundation.

ELIGIBILITY:
Eligible organizations must be schools or IRS 501(c)(3) tax-exempt.

GEOG. RESTRICTIONS: Burbank, Glendale, La Canada/Flintridge, La Crescenta, Montrose and Verdugo City, California.

FINANCIAL DATA:
Amount of support per award: Grants: $5,000 minimum; average grant $8,000 to $12,000; Scholarships: Varies.
Total amount of support: Approximately $400,000 to $500,000 annually.

CO-OP FUNDING PROGRAMS: Through restricted, donor-advised funds within the Foundation.

APPLICATION INFO:
Guidelines and application form are available on the Foundation web site.
Duration: One year. Agency can reapply one year after the grant ends.
Deadline: June 1.

PUBLICATIONS:
Annual report; quarterly newsletters.

IRS I.D.: 95-6068137

ADDRESS INQUIRIES TO:
Chief Executive Officer
(See address above.)

CARL M. FREEMAN FOUNDATION
31255 Americana Parkway
Selbyville, DE 19975
(302) 483-7639
Fax: (302) 483-7639
E-mail: grantsmanager@freemanfoundation.org
Web Site: www.carlfreemanfoundation.org

TYPE:
Capital grants; General operating grants.

See entry 407 for full listing.

THE HEALTH FOUNDATION OF GREATER INDIANAPOLIS, INC. [1337]
429 East Vermont Street, Suite 400
Indianapolis, IN 46202-3698
(317) 630-1805
Fax: (317) 630-1806
E-mail: rmcconnell@thfgi.org
Web Site: www.thfgi.org

FOUNDED: 1985

AREAS OF INTEREST:
Childhood obesity, school-based health and HIV/AIDS.

TYPE:
Project/program grants.

PURPOSE:
To serve the community's most vulnerable citizens by funding health-related projects and organizations not easily supported by other means.

ELIGIBILITY:
Applicant must be a 501(c)(3) group, organization or agency that provides health-related programs or services within Indiana. Must also function without discrimination or segregation based on race, gender, age, religion, national origin, sexual orientation, disability, military or marital status in hiring, termination, assignment and promotion of staff, selection of board members or provisions of services. No grants are made to individuals. Nonsectarian religious programs may apply.

GEOG. RESTRICTIONS: Indiana.

FINANCIAL DATA:
Amount of support per award: Varies.
Total amount of support: Varies.

NO. MOST RECENT APPLICANTS: 38.

NO. AWARDS: 36.

APPLICATION INFO:
The Foundation does not accept unsolicited proposals. The Board of Directors identify relevant health issues and direct the staff to connect organizations to one another.
Duration: One year.
Deadline: Varies.

IRS I.D.: 35-6203550

ADDRESS INQUIRIES TO:
Jason Grisell, MBA
President and Chief Executive Officer
(See address above.)

VICTOR AND LORRAINE HONIG FUND [1338]
1624 Franklin Street
Suite 1022
Oakland, CA 94612
(510) 834-2995
Fax: (510) 834-2998
E-mail: info@commoncounsel.org
Web Site: www.commoncounsel.org

AREAS OF INTEREST:
Social change, community development, environment, public policy and empowerment.

TYPE:
General operating grants; Project/program grants.

PURPOSE:
To support community organizations that are working to advance equality, opportunity, justice and civil rights for low-income communities and communities of color in the San Francisco Bay area and beyond; to support organizations that connect local social justice efforts with national and international movements for peace and justice.

LEGAL BASIS:
Family foundation.

ELIGIBILITY:
Grants made only to IRS 501(c)(3) tax-exempt organizations. No grants are made to social service programs offering ongoing or direct delivery of services, medical, educational or cultural institutions, emergency funding, scholarship funds or other aids to individuals, organizations which have sophisticated fund-raising capabilities, capital expenditure, construction or renovation programs or programs undertaken at government initiative. Priority is given to grassroots community organizations in low-income areas.

GEOG. RESTRICTIONS: California.

FINANCIAL DATA:
Amount of support per award: $1,000 to $25,000.
Total amount of support: Varies.

NO. MOST RECENT APPLICANTS: 50 to 100.

NO. AWARDS: Varies.

APPLICATION INFO:
Letters of Inquiry and Proposals are by invitation only.
Duration: Most grants are for one year.

ADDRESS INQUIRIES TO:
Grants Administrator
(See address above.)

A.V. HUNTER TRUST, INC. [1339]

650 South Cherry Street
Suite 535
Glendale, CO 80246
(303) 399-5450
Fax: (303) 399-5499
E-mail: news@avhuntertrust.org
Web Site: avhuntertrust.org

FOUNDED: 1924

AREAS OF INTEREST:
Disabled, seniors, youth, indigent, and
individuals with medical needs.

NAME(S) OF PROGRAMS:
● **Direct Operating Grants**
● **Funds for One**

TYPE:
General operating grants. Grants to
qualifying nonprofit organizations offering
direct services to assist those in need.

Funds for One assists qualified individuals
with the purchase of eyeglasses, hearing aids,
durable medical equipment, and limited
dental procedures through applications from a
Case Manager.

YEAR PROGRAM STARTED: 1924

PURPOSE:
To give aid, comfort, support or assistance to
children or aged persons or indigent adults.

LEGAL BASIS:
Private foundation.

ELIGIBILITY:
Applicants must be organizations classified as
501(c)(3) by the IRS. The Trust will consider
only one request from an organization during
any 12-month period. Institutions or
organizations supported by tax-derived
monies, including those which have lost
governmental funding, will not be
considered. The Trustees will not consider
grants or loans to individuals, developmental
or start-up funds, research, publications, films
or other media projects, capital campaigns or
acquisitions, including construction and
renovations, education or scholarship aid,
grants to cover deficits or retirement of debt,
purchase of memberships or blocks of
tickets, endowments, recruiting and training
of staff or gathering and disseminating
information.

GEOG. RESTRICTIONS: Colorado.

FINANCIAL DATA:
Amount of support per award: $2,500 to
$30,000. Average: $15,000.
Total amount of support: $2,543,930 for the
year 2020.

NO. AWARDS: 161 grants to organizations and
206 grants to individuals for the year 2020.

REPRESENTATIVE AWARDS:
$10,000 to Boys & Girls Clubs of Fremont
County; $10,000 to Greeley Transitional
Housing; $10,000 to Senior Resource
Services.

APPLICATION INFO:
Organizations are encouraged to call the
Trust's office to discuss eligibility and the
grant application process. Unsolicited
applications will not be accepted.

STAFF:
Janet Willson, Executive Director
Charlotte A. Gillespie, Senior Program
Officer
Kary L. Cramer, Program Officer, Funds for
One
Ryan O. Campbell, Program Officer, Grants

BOARD OF TRUSTEES:
Allan B. Adams, President
Mary K. Anstine, Vice President
Jeremy O. May, Treasurer
Bruce K. Alexander
W. Robert Alexander

ADDRESS INQUIRIES TO:
Janet Willson, Executive Director
(See address above.)

THE STEWART HUSTON CHARITABLE TRUST

50 South 1st Avenue
Coatesville, PA 19320
(610) 384-2666
Fax: (610) 384-3396
E-mail: admin@stewarthuston.org
Web Site: www.stewarthuston.org

TYPE:
Capital grants; Challenge/matching grants;
General operating grants; Matching gifts;
Project/program grants.

See entry 743 for full listing.

THE HYAMS FOUNDATION, INC. [1340]

50 Federal Street, 9th Floor
Boston, MA 02110
(617) 426-5600
Fax: (866) 497-2260
E-mail: info@hyamsfoundation.org
Web Site: www.hyamsfoundation.org

FOUNDED: 1921

AREAS OF INTEREST:
Community issues, racial justice, equitable
housing, fair wages and benefits, and
school-to-prison.

TYPE:
General operating grants; Project/program
grants; Technical assistance. General
operating.

PURPOSE:
To reduce racial and ethnic disparaties in
Boston and Chelsea, MA.

LEGAL BASIS:
Nonprofit foundation.

ELIGIBILITY:
Applicants must be Massachusetts charitable
corporations, tax-exempt under Section
501(c)(3) and designated as not a private
foundation under Section 509(a). No grants
will be made to one organization for the
programs of another organization which has
not itself received both such determinations.
The Foundation ordinarily will consider only
one application from an organization in any
given 12-month period. However, a single
application may include a request for more
than one program or purpose.

Grants are not given to individuals,
educational institutions for standard
educational or capital programs, any
municipal, state or federal agency, hospital
capital campaigns, endowments and religious
organizations for sectarian religious purposes.

Grants are rarely made for curriculum
development, conferences, film production,
scholarships or to national or international
organizations.

GEOG. RESTRICTIONS: Boston and Chelsea,
Massachusetts.

FINANCIAL DATA:
Total amount of support: $4,374,466 in
grants for the year 2018.

NO. AWARDS: 106 for the year 2018.

APPLICATION INFO:
Application form required. Organizations
which are unsure about whether they meet
the Foundation's funding priorities and
criteria are encouraged to submit a one-page
letter of interest to the Foundation. This letter
should describe the reason for seeking
support and the geographic area(s) and
population(s) to be served.

Application form is available online.
Duration: Typically one year. Multiyear
grants also given.
Deadline: March 1, September 1 and
December 1.

TRUSTEES:
Penn S. Loh, Chairperson
Willma H. Davis, Treasurer
Omar Simmons, Assistant Treasurer
Iris Gomez, Clerk
Julie Goodridge
Lucas H. Guerra
Rahsaan D. Hall
Karen L. Mapp
Martella Wilson-Taylor

STAFF:
Lisa Owens, Executive Director
David Moy, Deputy Director
Mark Paley, Director of Administration and
Finance
R. Shani Pankam, Grants Manager
Nahir Torres, Senior Program Officer, Teen
Development
Sergio Marin Luna, Program Officer
Maria Mulkeen, Program Officer, Affordable
Housing

ADDRESS INQUIRIES TO:
R. Shani Pankam, Grants Manager
(See address above.)

ITTLESON FOUNDATION, INC. [1341]

15 East 67th Street
New York, NY 10065
(212) 794-2008
Fax: (212) 794-0351
Web Site: www.ittlesonfoundation.org

FOUNDED: 1932

AREAS OF INTEREST:
Mental health, environment and AIDS.

TYPE:
Demonstration grants; Project/program
grants; Seed money grants. Seed money for
the start-up of innovative programs in the
fields of mental health, AIDS, and the
environment.

In the area of AIDS, the Foundation supports
cutting-edge prevention efforts. It is also
particularly interested in new model, pilot,
and demonstration efforts which address the
needs of underserved at-risk populations,
respond to the challenges facing
community-based AIDS service
organizations, provide meaningful
school-based sex education, make treatment
information accessible, available, and easily
understandable to those in need of it, and
address the psycho-social needs of those
infected and affected by AIDS, especially
adolescents.

In the area of environment, the Foundation
supports innovative pilot, model and
demonstration projects that will help move

individuals, communities and organizations from environmental awareness to environmental activism. The Foundation seeks to support the present generation of environmental activists, educate and engage the next generation, strengthen the infrastructure of the environmental movement with a particular focus on efforts at the grassroots and statewide levels, and activate new constituencies.

In the area of mental health, the Foundation continues to support efforts to address the needs of underserved populations. It also seeks pilot, model and demonstration projects which fight the stigma associated with mental illness, utilize new knowledge and current technological advances to improve programs and services for people with mental illness, bring the full benefits of this new knowledge and technology to those who presently do not have access to them, and advance preventative mental health efforts, especially those targeted to youth and adolescents.

PURPOSE:
To launch and disseminate innovative projects in the areas of mental health, AIDS and the environment.

ELIGIBILITY:
Grants are available to nonprofit organizations within the U.S. Preference is given to pilot projects, test and demonstration projects and applied research which ideally should inform public policy, if successful. The Foundation also supports dissemination projects.

The Foundation does not usually support capital building projects, endowments, grants to individuals, scholarships or internships (except as part of a program), or continuing support to existing programs. Moreover, the Foundation does not support programs of direct service to individuals with only a local focus or constituency. The Foundation does not make international grants.

GEOG. RESTRICTIONS: United States.

FINANCIAL DATA:
Amount of support per award: Average $45,000 to $90,000.
Total amount of support: $375,000 for the year 2019.

APPLICATION INFO:
There are no application forms. Applicants should write a brief letter to the Executive Director describing the basic organization and the work for which funds are being sought, along with a budget and evidence of tax-exempt status. If the activity falls within the current scope of the Foundation's interests, the applicant will be asked to supply additional information as required. Applicant should consult web site for current year's focus.
Duration: Generally one year. Multiyear when appropriate. No renewals.
Deadline: Letters of Intent must be received by September 1.

OFFICERS AND DIRECTORS:
H. Anthony Ittleson, Chairman and President
Andrew Auchincloss, Vice Chairman and Director
Pamela Syrmis, Vice President and Director
H. Davison, Treasurer
Anthony C. Wood, Secretary and Executive Director
H. Philip Ittleson, Director
Stephanie Ittleson, Director

Christina Ittleson Smith, Director
Victor Talbot, M.D., Director

ADDRESS INQUIRIES TO:
Anthony C. Wood, Executive Director
(See address above.)

JACKSONVILLE JAGUARS FOUNDATION
One TIAA Bank Field Drive
Jacksonville, FL 32202
(904) 633-5437
Fax: (904) 633-5683
Web Site: www.jaguars.com/community

TYPE:
General operating grants; Project/program grants. Limited capital grants that target economically and socially "at-risk" youths in northeast Florida.

See entry 148 for full listing.

THE CARL W. AND CARRIE MAE JOSLYN CHARITABLE TRUST [1342]
c/o JPMorgan Private Foundation Services
2200 Ross Avenue, Floor 5
Dallas, TX 75201
Fax: (800) 883-7695
E-mail: grant.reports@jpmorgan.com
Web Site: www.jpmorgan.com/onlinegrants

FOUNDED: 1975

AREAS OF INTEREST:
Children, elderly and handicapped persons of El Paso County, CO.

TYPE:
Project/program grants. Small project grants and general operating support.

YEAR PROGRAM STARTED: 1975

LEGAL BASIS:
Tax-exempt charitable trust.

ELIGIBILITY:
Organizations serving children, the elderly and persons suffering from blindness and cancer in El Paso County, CO, are eligible to apply.

GEOG. RESTRICTIONS: El Paso County, Colorado.

FINANCIAL DATA:
Amount of support per award: Varies.
Total amount of support: Varies.

NO. MOST RECENT APPLICANTS: 50.

NO. AWARDS: 10.

APPLICATION INFO:
Application must be made online; paper applications will not be accepted.
Duration: One year. Nonrenewable.
Deadline: November 1.

ADDRESS INQUIRIES TO:
Stephany Lewis, Executive Director
JPMorgan
(See address above.)

LIBERTY HILL FOUNDATION [1343]
941 East 2nd Street, No. 106
Los Angeles, CA 90012
(323) 556-7200
Fax: (323) 556-7240
E-mail: info@libertyhill.org
Web Site: www.libertyhill.org

FOUNDED: 1976

AREAS OF INTEREST:
Economic justice, environmental justice, LGBTQ justice, racial justice, youth justice, and youth development.

NAME(S) OF PROGRAMS:
- **California Funders for Boys and Men of Color (CFBMOC)**
- **emPOWER**
- **Fund for Change (FFC)**
- **Wally Marks Leadership Institute for Change**
- **Ready to Rise**
- **Stay Housed LA**

TYPE:
General operating grants; Project/program grants; Seed money grants; Technical assistance. emPOWER is a coordinated Los Angeles County-wide outreach program with a mission to overcome barriers to sustainable energy usage commonly experienced in low-income and working class communities of color. emPOWER matches household needs with local and statewide resources to help residents maximize potential savings and use of available incentive programs.

Fund for Change supports high-impact social change through cultivating effective community leaders, seeding emerging organizations, and developing a base of grassroots activists within the areas of economic and racial justice, environmental justice and LGBTQ justice.

The Wally Marks Leadership Institute for Change invests in community leaders at the front lines of change with intensive on-the-job training for community organizers.

YEAR PROGRAM STARTED: 1976

PURPOSE:
To advance social change through a strategic combination of grants, leadership training and campaigns.

LEGAL BASIS:
Public foundation.

ELIGIBILITY:
Fund for Change: The Foundation considers applications from nonprofit 501(c)(3) organizations, or those organizations having a fiscal sponsorship agreement with a nonprofit organization which complies with Liberty Hill's policy on fiscal sponsorship, in Los Angeles County, CA, that actively work toward a more just distribution of resources and power, develop grassroots activism and leadership, are building their organizational infrastructure and promote a society free from discrimination.

The Foundation does not fund capital campaigns for land or buildings, individual efforts, films or video projects, profit-making ventures, direct union organizing, electioneering for candidates in public office, one-time events or conferences that are not linked to social change organizing strategies, or projects that only serve communities outside Los Angeles County.

GEOG. RESTRICTIONS: Primarily Los Angeles County, California.

FINANCIAL DATA:
Amount of support per award: Average grant of $27,000 in fiscal year 2020.
Total amount of support: $5,400,000 in program grants for fiscal year 2020.

CO-OP FUNDING PROGRAMS: Donor-advised program.

NO. MOST RECENT APPLICANTS: 194 for the year 2020.

NO. AWARDS: 103 for the year 2020.

APPLICATION INFO:
Varies by program area. Unsolicited proposals will not be accepted.
Duration: One to two years.
Deadline: Letter of Inquiry: Varies.

PUBLICATIONS:
Guidelines; newsletter.

IRS I.D.: 51-0181191

STAFF:
Shane Goldsmith, President and Chief Executive Officer
Joanna Kabat, Director of Grantmaking and Capacity Building

ADDRESS INQUIRIES TO:
Joanna Kabat, Director of Grantmaking and Capacity Building
E-mail: programs@libertyhill.org

*PLEASE NOTE:
Unsolicited proposals will not be accepted.

THE AGNES M. LINDSAY TRUST
10 North Road, Suite 2
Chelmsford, MA 01824
(978) 445-7818
E-mail: admin@lindsaytrust.org
Web Site: www.lindsaytrust.org

TYPE:
Capital grants. Awards grants for capital campaigns, capital items and renovation needs. Also, supports a number of health and welfare organizations, health projects, dental projects, special needs including blind, deaf and learning-disabled, elderly, homeless shelters, food banks, Covid-19, children's hospitals, children's homes, youth organizations, youth and family services and summer camperships (summer enrichment programs).

See entry 1019 for full listing.

LUTHERAN FOUNDATION OF ST. LOUIS
8860 Ladue Road
Suite 200
St. Louis, MO 63124
(314) 231-2244
Fax: (314) 727-7688
E-mail: info@lutheranfoundation.org
Web Site: www.lutheranfoundation.org

TYPE:
Project/program grants.

See entry 746 for full listing.

M & M AREA COMMUNITY FOUNDATION
1110 10th Avenue, Suite L-1
Menominee, MI 49858
(906) 864-3599
E-mail: info@mmacf.org
Web Site: www.mmacf.org

TYPE:
Project/program grants; Scholarships.

See entry 1197 for full listing.

MAINE INITIATIVES [1344]
56 North Street, Suite 100
Portland, ME 04101
(207) 607-4070
E-mail: info@maineinitiatives.org
Web Site: www.maineinitiatives.org

FOUNDED: 1993

AREAS OF INTEREST:
Supporting social change in Maine.

NAME(S) OF PROGRAMS:
● **Grants for Change**

TYPE:
General operating grants; Seed money grants; Technical assistance. Grants provide funding to Maine groups advancing social, economic, and environmental justice at the grassroots level.

YEAR PROGRAM STARTED: 1994

PURPOSE:
To cultivate social, economic and environmental justice through grants and other support to grassroots organizations in Maine communities.

ELIGIBILITY:
Organization must be tax-exempt. Religious organizations are eligible but not for religious purposes.

GEOG. RESTRICTIONS: Maine.

FINANCIAL DATA:
Amount of support per award: Up to $25,000 over three years.
Total amount of support: Varies.

NO. AWARDS: 20 for the year 2020.

APPLICATION INFO:
Copies of IRS 501(c)(3) designation letters are requested. Contact the organization for application.
Duration: Up to three years.
Deadline: July 15.

PUBLICATIONS:
Newsletter; annual report.

IRS I.D.: 01-0484310

STAFF:
Phil Walsh, Executive Director

ADDRESS INQUIRIES TO:
See e-mail address above.

MAZON: A JEWISH RESPONSE TO HUNGER [1345]
10850 Wilshire Boulevard
Suite 400
Los Angeles, CA 90024
(310) 442-0020
Fax: (310) 442-0030
E-mail: mazonmail@mazon.org
amiller@mazon.org
Web Site: www.mazon.org

FOUNDED: 1986

AREAS OF INTEREST:
Anti-hunger advocacy pertaining to local, state and federal nutrition safety-net services.

NAME(S) OF PROGRAMS:
● **Quick Reaction Fund (QRF)**

TYPE:
Demonstration grants; General operating grants; Internships; Project/program grants. Capacity building grants. Quick Reaction Fund, launched in September of 2017, recognizes the need for anti-hunger movement leaders to respond quickly to

pressing issues that will disproportionally impact the lives of food insecure people. QRF addresses this need by providing one-time grants to leaders to help leverage immediate, innovative and time-sensitive advocacy opportunities in response to unforeseen legislation, political development, public attacks, or public messaging opportunities.

YEAR PROGRAM STARTED: 1986

PURPOSE:
To prevent and alleviate hunger among people of all faiths and backgrounds.

GEOG. RESTRICTIONS: United States and Israel.

FINANCIAL DATA:
Amount of support per award: QRF: $500 to $15,000; All others: Varies.
Total amount of support: Varies.

NO. MOST RECENT APPLICANTS: 171.

NO. AWARDS: 153.

APPLICATION INFO:
All MAZON applications are by invitation only.
Duration: One year.

PUBLICATIONS:
Program announcement; guidelines.

ADDRESS INQUIRIES TO:
Alexis Miller, Program Officer
E-mail: amiller@mazon.org

THE MCKNIGHT FOUNDATION [1346]
710 South Second Street
Suite 400
Minneapolis, MN 55401
(612) 333-4220
Fax: (612) 332-3833
E-mail: info@mcknight.org
Web Site: www.mcknight.org

FOUNDED: 1953

AREAS OF INTEREST:
Regional economic and community development, Minnesota's arts and artists, education equity, Midwest climate and energy, Mississippi River water quality, neuroscience research, and international crop research.

NAME(S) OF PROGRAMS:
● **Arts**
● **Education**
● **International**
● **Midwest Climate and Energy**
● **Neuroscience**

TYPE:
General operating grants; Project/program grants.

YEAR PROGRAM STARTED: 1953

PURPOSE:
To advance climate solutions in the Midwest; to support the arts, international crop research, and neuroscience.

LEGAL BASIS:
Family foundation.

ELIGIBILITY:
Applicants must be classified as tax-exempt, nonprofit organizations by the IRS.

GEOG. RESTRICTIONS: Minnesota, with emphasis on the Minneapolis-St. Paul area, Mississippi River Corridor, and select international areas of work.

FINANCIAL DATA:
Total amount of support: Approximately $200,000 for the year 2018.

NO. AWARDS: 315 for the year 2019.

APPLICATION INFO:
Applications are available online.
Deadline: Varies. Specific dates are posted on the Foundation web site.

PUBLICATIONS:
Annual report, including grants list; grantmaking guidelines for all programs.

OFFICERS:
Pamela Wheelock, President
Nichol Higdon, Vice President of Finance and Compliance

BOARD:
Dana Anderson
Anne Binger
Erika Binger
Meghan Binger Brown
Phyllis Goff
Debby Landesman
Perry Moriearty
Luther Ragin, Jr.
Roger Sit
Noa Staryk
Ted Staryk
Kathy Tunheim

ADDRESS INQUIRIES TO:
Stephanie Duffy, Director of Grants and Information Management
(See address above.)

MARIETTA MCNEILL MORGAN AND SAMUEL TATE MORGAN, JR. TRUST   [1347]
Bank of America Private Bank
1800 K Street, N.W., Mail Code DC1-842-05-01
Washington, DC 20006
(202) 442-7460
E-mail: dc.grantmaking@ustrust.com
Web Site: www.bankofamerica.com/grantmaking

FOUNDED: 1962

AREAS OF INTEREST:
Arts, culture and humanities, education, and human services.

TYPE:
Capital grants.

PURPOSE:
To support and promote quality educational and human services programming in the Commonwealth of Virginia.

LEGAL BASIS:
Private foundation.

ELIGIBILITY:
Nonprofit organizations in the Commonwealth of Virginia who are classified by IRS as tax-exempt and are not private foundations. Grants for capital only. No grants to individuals, for endowment funds or operating funds.

GEOG. RESTRICTIONS: Virginia.

FINANCIAL DATA:
Amount of support per award: $5,000 to $75,000 dispersed in a single payment; average $40,000.
Total amount of support: Varies.

CO-OP FUNDING PROGRAMS: Other funding sources encouraged.

NO. MOST RECENT APPLICANTS: 58.

NO. AWARDS: 29.

APPLICATION INFO:
Applications are submitted online.
Duration: One year.
Deadline: March 1. Notification by June 30.

ADDRESS INQUIRIES TO:
Lee Parker, Senior Vice President
(See address above.)

MRG FOUNDATION   [1348]
P.O. Box 12489
Portland, OR 97212
(503) 289-1517
Fax: (503) 232-1731
E-mail: grants@mrgf.org
Web Site: www.mrgfoundation.org

FOUNDED: 1976

AREAS OF INTEREST:
Community-based groups working for progressive social, racial, economic and environmental justice change.

NAME(S) OF PROGRAMS:
- **Capacity Building Grants**
- **Critical Response Grants**
- **General Fund Grants**
- **Travel Grants**

TYPE:
General operating grants; Internships; Seed money grants; Travel grants. Funds special project grants and general support.

Critical Response Grants provide community-based groups with the additional capacity needed to organize a progressive response to an unexpected crisis or opportunity for organizing.

Travel Grants help MRG grantees make national and regional connections and develop the leadership and skills needed for effective organizational development and organizing.

YEAR PROGRAM STARTED: 1976

PURPOSE:
To empower those impacted by injustice; to promote social change.

LEGAL BASIS:
Nonprofit, tax-exempt 501(c)(3) public foundation.

ELIGIBILITY:
Organizations must do tax-exempt activities in the state of Oregon and fit criteria of social change work listed in fields of interest. No grants to individuals. The Foundation does not fund food co-ops, health centers, schools or social services.

Grant applicants for the Critical Response Grant and the Travel Grant must have an organizational budget under $500,000 to be eligible.

GEOG. RESTRICTIONS: Oregon.

FINANCIAL DATA:
Amount of support per award: Critical Response Grants: Up to $2,000; General Fund: $2,000 to $20,000; Travel Grants: Up to $1,000.
Total amount of support: $470,000.

NO. MOST RECENT APPLICANTS: 100.

NO. AWARDS: 34.

REPRESENTATIVE AWARDS:
Center for Intercultural Organizing;
Community Alliance of Tenants;
Salem/Keizer Coalition for Equality.

APPLICATION INFO:
Application forms and information are available upon request.
Duration: Six to 12 months.
Deadline: Critical Response Grants and Travel Grants have no application deadline, but are subject to exhaustion of annual funding monies. General Fund: September and March.

PUBLICATIONS:
Applying for a Grant from MRG.

OFFICERS:
Lizzie Martinez, Chairperson

*PLEASE NOTE:
Formerly known as the McKenzie River Gathering Foundation.

A.J. MUSTE MEMORIAL INSTITUTE   [1349]
168 Canal Street, 6th Floor
New York, NY 10013
(212) 533-4335
E-mail: info@ajmuste.org
Web Site: www.ajmuste.org

FOUNDED: 1974

AREAS OF INTEREST:
Peace and disarmament, social and economic justice, racial and gender equality, human rights, and the labor movement.

TYPE:
Grants-in-aid. The Institute's regular grant fund annually funds international, national and local projects in the U.S. and around the world. It gives priority to those with small budgets and little chance of funding from more traditional sources. It also offers fiscal sponsorship. The Institute does not provide academic scholarships.

YEAR PROGRAM STARTED: 1974

PURPOSE:
To promote peace and disarmament, social and economic justice, racial and sexual equality, and the labor movement.

ELIGIBILITY:
The Institute funds projects which seek to advance nonviolent grassroots education and action for social and economic justice. The Institute does not make grants for general support of ongoing operations. It does not generally accept proposals from organizations with annual budgets over $500,000 or for projects with budgets over $50,000. It will also not accept a new request from a previously funded group for two years after a grant. Grants are not made to individuals and generally not to religious organizations or development projects.

FINANCIAL DATA:
Amount of support per award: Average grant: $5,000.
Total amount of support: Varies.

NO. AWARDS: Varies.

APPLICATION INFO:
Complete information is available on the Institute web site.
Duration: Varies.
Deadline: Varies according to program.

ADDRESS INQUIRIES TO:
Heidi Boghosian, Executive Director
(See address above.)

NATIONAL COUNCIL ON FAMILY RELATIONS [1350]

661 LaSalle Street
Suite 200
St. Paul, MN 55114
(763) 781-9331
Fax: (763) 781-9348
E-mail: info@ncfr.org
Web Site: www.ncfr.org

FOUNDED: 1938

AREAS OF INTEREST:
Family science, family research, family practice, family education, sociology, psychology, social work, human development, child development, and certified family life education.

NAME(S) OF PROGRAMS:
- **Felix Berardo Mentoring Award**
- **Czaplewski Fellowship Award**
- **Ruth Jewson Award**
- **NCFR Student Award**
- **Cindy Winter Scholarship Award**

TYPE:
Awards/prizes. Awards given for contributions to the area of family science. All of the awards require NCFR membership.

YEAR PROGRAM STARTED: 1938

PURPOSE:
To share in the development and dissemination of knowledge about families and family relationships; to establish professional standards; to work to promote family well-being.

LEGAL BASIS:
501(c)(3) education and research association.

ELIGIBILITY:
Criteria are posted on the Council web site.

FINANCIAL DATA:
Amount of support per award: $250 to $500.
Total amount of support: Varies.

NO. MOST RECENT APPLICANTS: 150.

NO. AWARDS: 45 to 50.

APPLICATION INFO:
Application information is available on the web site.
Duration: One year.
Deadline: Berardo Award, Jewson Award, NCFR Student Award and Winter Award: May 1.

PUBLICATIONS:
Journal of Marriage and Family; Family Relations; Journal of Family Theory and Review.

OFFICERS:
Leigh A. Leslie, President

ADDRESS INQUIRIES TO:
E-mail: membership@ncfr.org

*PLEASE NOTE:
Czaplewski Fellowship Award will be awarded only when there is a request for support, but not more often than once very other year.

JESSIE SMITH NOYES FOUNDATION

122 East 42nd Street
Suite 2501
New York, NY 10168
(212) 684-6577
Fax: (212) 689-6549
E-mail: noyes@noyes.org
Web Site: noyes.org

TYPE:
General operating grants; Project/program grants.

See entry 1979 for full listing.

OPEN SOCIETY INSTITUTE - BALTIMORE [1351]

201 North Charles Street
Suite 1300
Baltimore, MD 21201
(410) 234-1091
Fax: (410) 234-2816
E-mail: osi.baltimore@opensocietyfoundations.org
Web Site: www.osibaltimore.org

AREAS OF INTEREST:
Criminal justice reform.

NAME(S) OF PROGRAMS:
- **Criminal and Juvenile Justice Program**

TYPE:
Project/program grants. The Criminal and Juvenile Justice Program seeks to reduce the use of incarceration and its social and economic costs without compromising public safety, and promote justice systems that are fair, are used as a last resort, and offer second chances. The Program supports advocacy, public education, research, grassroots organizing, litigation and demonstration projects that focus on reforming racial and social inequities at critical stages of the criminal and juvenile justice systems - from arrest to re-entry into the community.

YEAR PROGRAM STARTED: 1998

PURPOSE:
To reduce Maryland's overuse of incarceration and its social and economic costs without compromising public safety.

LEGAL BASIS:
Foundation.

ELIGIBILITY:
Grants are made to organizations that have tax-exempt status under Section 501(c)(3) of the Internal Revenue Code. No grants are made to individuals.

GEOG. RESTRICTIONS: Baltimore City, Maryland.

FINANCIAL DATA:
Amount of support per award: Varies.
Total amount of support: Varies.

APPLICATION INFO:
Applicants should submit a letter of inquiry of two to three pages which includes:
(1) a description of the program to be funded;
(2) the qualifications of the organization to carry out the program;
(3) the ways in which the program reflects the priorities of the Criminal and Juvenile Justice Program;
(4) the amount of the budget and the funds requested and;
(5) a copy of the IRS letter stating the organization's tax-exempt status.
Duration: Varies.
Deadline: Grant applications are accepted on an ongoing basis.

ADDRESS INQUIRIES TO:
Tara Huffman, Program Director
Criminal and Juvenile Justice Program
(See address above.)

PASADENA COMMUNITY FOUNDATION [1352]

301 East Colorado Boulevard
Suite 810
Pasadena, CA 91101
(626) 796-2097
Fax: (626) 583-4738
E-mail: jdevoll@pasadenacf.org
Web Site: pasadenacf.org

FOUNDED: 1954

AREAS OF INTEREST:
Charitable organizations (Pasadena area only), children, youth and family, community development, environment education, arts and the humanities, health and people with special needs.

TYPE:
Capital grants; Project/program grants. Grants for non-recurring capital needs, such as equipment, building repairs and vehicles.

YEAR PROGRAM STARTED: 1954

PURPOSE:
To support charitable organizations in the Pasadena area.

LEGAL BASIS:
Nonprofit public benefit corporation.

ELIGIBILITY:
Applicants must be 501(c)(3) organizations. No personal grants to individuals, churches or schools. No grants out of the Pasadena area.

GEOG. RESTRICTIONS: Greater Pasadena area, California.

FINANCIAL DATA:
Amount of support per award: Capital grants: Up to $25,000; Project/program grants: Up to $30,000.
Total amount of support: $5,334,738 in grants awarded for the year 2018.

REPRESENTATIVE AWARDS:
$15,632 to Kidspace Children's Museum; $12,361 to Peace Over Violence; $30,000 to Pasadena Educational Foundation.

APPLICATION INFO:
Guidelines are available on the Foundation web site.
Duration: One year.
Deadline: Project/program grants: Early February or late March. Capital grants: Early August.

PUBLICATIONS:
Application guidelines; formal application form; newsletter.

IRS I.D.: 20-0253310

ADDRESS INQUIRIES TO:
Mike deHilster, Program Officer
E-mail: mdehilster@pasadenacf.org

JAY AND ROSE PHILLIPS FAMILY FOUNDATION OF MINNESOTA [1353]

615 First Avenue, N.E.
Suite 400
Minneapolis, MN 55413
(612) 623-1654
Fax: (612) 623-1653
E-mail: info@phillipsfamilymn.org
Web Site: phillipsfamilymn.org

FOUNDED: 1944

AREAS OF INTEREST:
Education, small business development and entrepreneurship.

TYPE:
Project/program grants. Grants to improve organizational effectiveness.

YEAR PROGRAM STARTED: 1944

PURPOSE:
To provide support for organizations and projects that address unmet human and social needs.

LEGAL BASIS:
Private foundation.

ELIGIBILITY:
Grants are made to organizations that have tax-exempt status under Section 501(c)(3) of the Internal Revenue Code. No grants are made to individuals.

The Foundation's preference is to support projects that represent new thinking about community needs and innovative efforts.

GEOG. RESTRICTIONS: North Minneapolis, Minnesota.

FINANCIAL DATA:
Amount of support per award: Typically, $15,000 to $50,000.
Total amount of support: Varies.

NO. AWARDS: Varies.

APPLICATION INFO:
Application by invitation only.
Duration: Typically one year.

PUBLICATIONS:
Annual report; application guidelines.

IRS I.D.: 27-4196509

ADDRESS INQUIRIES TO:
Tracy Lamparty
Grants and Operations Manager
(See address above.)

*SPECIAL STIPULATIONS:
Unsolicited requests are not accepted.

PLOUGH FOUNDATION   [1354]
62 North Main, Suite 201
Memphis, TN 38103
(901) 521-2779
Fax: (901) 529-4063
E-mail: mail@plough.org
Web Site: www.plough.org

FOUNDED: 1960

AREAS OF INTEREST:
Families in crisis, public education and youth, crime, health and economic development.

TYPE:
Capital grants; Challenge/matching grants; Seed money grants.

YEAR PROGRAM STARTED: 1960

PURPOSE:
To make payments or distributions to charitable organizations or for charitable purposes which will benefit the greatest number of people in the City of Memphis and/or Shelby County, TN.

LEGAL BASIS:
Private, independent foundation.

ELIGIBILITY:
No grants for assistance to address a crisis management situation caused by poor initial planning, individuals and projects outside the Memphis/Shelby County (TN) area. No grants for funding for private schools K-12, public charter schools, funding for annual fund-raising, or to individuals.

GEOG. RESTRICTIONS: Shelby County, Tennessee.

FINANCIAL DATA:
Amount of support per award: Varies.
Total amount of support: Varies.

REPRESENTATIVE AWARDS:
University of Memphis; Memphis Child Advocacy Center; Memphis College of Art; Memphis Shelby Crime Commission.

APPLICATION INFO:
Applications are accepted by invitation only.
Duration: One to three years.
Deadline: Dates are posted on the Foundation web site.

PUBLICATIONS:
Brochure.

IRS I.D.: 23-7175983

BOARD OF TRUSTEES:
Diane Rudner, Chairperson
Patricia R. Burnham
Eugene J. Callahan
D.D. Eisenberg
Johnny B. Moore, Jr.
Peter Pettit
Steven Wishnia

ADDRESS INQUIRIES TO:
Bob Wallace, Chief Operating Officer and Chief Financial Officer
(See address above.)

PRITCHETT TRUST
BMO Harris Bank
790 North Water Street, Floor 11
Milwaukee, WI 53202
(414) 287-7250
Fax: (414) 287-8580
E-mail: trust.custody@bmo.com

TYPE:
Project/program grants; Seed money grants.

See entry 1030 for full listing.

KATE B. REYNOLDS
CHARITABLE TRUST   [1355]
128 Reynolda Village
Winston-Salem, NC 27106-5123
(336) 397-5500
Fax: (336) 723-7765
E-mail: laura@kbr.org
Web Site: kbr.org

FOUNDED: 1947

AREAS OF INTEREST:
Improving the health and quality of life for communities in Forsyth County and across North Carolina.

NAME(S) OF PROGRAMS:
● **Health Improvement in North Carolina**
● **Local Impact in Forsyth County**

TYPE:
Capital grants; Challenge/matching grants; Conferences/seminars; Demonstration grants; Fellowships; Project/program grants; Seed money grants; Technical assistance; Training grants; Research contracts. Capacity building. The Trust supports promising programs, systems change work, and innovative ideas that help residents and communities thrive, increase equitable access to health care, and achieve equitable health outcomes.

Local Impact and Health Improvement program areas are structured around strategic goals. The Trust invests at the program, community, town, county, and state level to

foster long-term change. The most intensive efforts are focused on two long-term, place-based initiatives - Healthy Places NC and Great Expectations - and three key bodies of work - Equitable Access to Care, Equitable Health Outcomes, and Inclusive Economy.

YEAR PROGRAM STARTED: 1947

PURPOSE:
To improve the quality of life and quality of health for the financially needy of North Carolina; to accelerate positive movement on critical community issues and to effect enduring systemic change.

LEGAL BASIS:
Private foundation.

ELIGIBILITY:
Organizations eligible for grants are those that have qualified for exemption under Section 501(c)(3) and are not private foundations or a Type III supporting organization. Grants are not made to individuals or for medical research. Advance consultations are required prior to accepting an application.

GEOG. RESTRICTIONS: North Carolina.

FINANCIAL DATA:
Amount of support per award: Average $20,000 to $200,000.
Total amount of support: Approximately $25,000,000 per year.

APPLICATION INFO:
Applicants are urged to visit the funding opportunity page on the Trust web site. The Trust requires prospective applicants to contact the program coordinator for a phone consultation to determine if the proposed idea is a fit in advance of submitting an application.
Duration: Generally one to three years.
Deadline: Usually February, April, August and October.

PUBLICATIONS:
Newsletter.

IRS I.D.: 56-6036515

STAFF:
Laura Gerald, President
Stephanie Cooper-Lewter, Executive Vice President, Programs and Administration
Joel T. Beeson, Director of Administration
Nora Ferrell, Director of Communications
Adam Linker, Director of Programs
Debra Hall, Grants Manager
Alan G. Welch, Information Systems Manager

ADDRESS INQUIRIES TO:
Laura Gerald, President
(See address above.)

SAILORS' SNUG HARBOR OF
BOSTON   [1356]
c/o GMA Foundations
Two Liberty Square, Suite 500
Boston, MA 02109
(617) 391-3097
Fax: (617) 426-7087
E-mail: phall@gmafoundations.com
Web Site: www.sailorssnugharbor.org

FOUNDED: 1852

AREAS OF INTEREST:
Elderly and fishing families.

TYPE:
General operating grants; Project/program grants.

PURPOSE:
To address the social service needs of fishermen, their families, and low-income elders residing in coastal communities of Massachusetts.

LEGAL BASIS:
Private foundation.

ELIGIBILITY:
Grants are made to organizations that have tax-exempt status under Section 501(c)(3) of the Internal Revenue Code. No grants are made to individuals. Nonsectarian religious programs may apply.

GEOG. RESTRICTIONS: Massachusetts.

FINANCIAL DATA:
Amount of support per award: Typical one-year grant: $10,000; Multiyear grants: Up to $50,000 per year.
Total amount of support: $407,400 for the year 2019.

NO. AWARDS: 17 for the year 2019.

APPLICATION INFO:
Applications must be submitted online.
Duration: One or three years. One-year grant is renewable by reapplication.
Deadline: August 15.

ADDRESS INQUIRIES TO:
Phil Hall, Foundation Administrator
(See address above.)

GEORGE J. AND EFFIE L. SEAY MEMORIAL TRUST [1357]
Mail Code TAOBFB
P.O. Box 1517
Pennington, NJ 08534
(202) 442-7460
E-mail: dc.grantmaking@ustrust.com
Web Site: www.bankofamerica.com/philanthropic/foundation.go

FOUNDED: 1959

AREAS OF INTEREST:
Arts, culture, humanities, education, and human services.

TYPE:
Project/program grants. Grants for specific needs.

PURPOSE:
To enhance the quality of life in the Commonwealth of Virginia.

LEGAL BASIS:
Private foundation.

ELIGIBILITY:
Nonprofit organizations only in the Commonwealth of Virginia. No grants to individuals or to endowment funds.

GEOG. RESTRICTIONS: Virginia.

FINANCIAL DATA:
Amount of support per award: $10,000 to $50,000.
Total amount of support: Varies.
Matching fund requirements: Stipulated for specific grants.

CO-OP FUNDING PROGRAMS: Other funding sources are encouraged.

APPLICATION INFO:
Guidelines are available online. Application must be submitted through the "Apply Now" link.

Duration: One year.
Deadline: April 1. Decision by June 30.

PUBLICATIONS:
Application guidelines.

ADDRESS INQUIRIES TO:
See e-mail address above.

*SPECIAL STIPULATIONS:
Grants made only to organizations in Virginia.

SHARE OUR STRENGTH [1358]
1030 15th Street, N.W.
Suite 1100 W
Washington, DC 20005
(800) 969-4767
E-mail: info@strength.org
Web Site: www.nokidhungry.org

FOUNDED: 1984

AREAS OF INTEREST:
Domestic childhood hunger, hunger prevention and alleviation limited to summer meals, after-school meals, school breakfast and nutrition education.

NAME(S) OF PROGRAMS:
● **No Kid Hungry**

TYPE:
Project/program grants. Grants are focused on increasing participation in the federal nutrition programs, including summer meals, after-school meals, and school breakfast, as well as nutritional education and early childhood nutrition.

YEAR PROGRAM STARTED: 1984

PURPOSE:
To end childhood hunger in the United States.

LEGAL BASIS:
Nonprofit organization.

ELIGIBILITY:
Applicants must be 501(c)(3) organizations, schools/school districts, churches/faith-based organizations or other organizations/agencies eligible to receive grants.

GEOG. RESTRICTIONS: United States.

FINANCIAL DATA:
Amount of support per award: Varies.
Total amount of support: $33,000,000 in grants payable for fiscal year 2020.

NO. AWARDS: 1,483 grants approved in fiscal year 2020.

APPLICATION INFO:
Applications will be accepted by invitation only.
Duration: One year. Renewal possible.
Deadline: Varies.

PUBLICATIONS:
Annual report.

SIERRA HEALTH FOUNDATION [1359]
1321 Garden Highway
Sacramento, CA 95833
(916) 922-4755
Fax: (916) 922-4024
E-mail: info@sierrahealth.org
Web Site: www.sierrahealth.org

FOUNDED: 1984

AREAS OF INTEREST:
Improving health outcomes and reducing health disparities.

NAME(S) OF PROGRAMS:
● **Conference and Education Center**
● **Health Leadership Program**
● **Healthy Sacramento Coalition**
● **Nonprofit Event Sponsorships**
● **Responsive Grants Program**

TYPE:
Project/program grants. Sponsorship. Specific to funding opportunities - solicited.

YEAR PROGRAM STARTED: 1984

PURPOSE:
To invest in and serve as a catalyst for ideas, partnerships and programs that improve health and quality of life in northern California through convening, educating and strategic grantmaking.

LEGAL BASIS:
Private foundation.

ELIGIBILITY:
Applicant must be a public entity or designated 501(c)(3) organization by the IRS with 509(a)(1) or 509(a)(2) status. No grants to individuals, endowments or activities which exclusively benefit members of private or religious organizations.

GEOG. RESTRICTIONS: Northern California counties.

FINANCIAL DATA:
Amount of support per award: Varies by program.
Total amount of support: Varies.

IRS I.D.: 68-0050036

OFFICERS:
Chet P. Hewitt, President and Chief Executive Officer
Gil Alvarado, Senior Vice President of Finance and Administration and Chief Financial Officer
Kaying Hang, Senior Vice President of Programs and Partnerships

BOARD OF DIRECTORS:
David W. Gordon
Jose Hermocillo
Chet P. Hewitt
Nancy P. Lee
Debra McKenzie
Robert Petersen, C.P.A.
Dr. Claire Pomeroy
Shamus Roller

ADDRESS INQUIRIES TO:
See e-mail address above.

SOCIAL JUSTICE FUND NORTHWEST [1360]
1904 Third Avenue, Suite 806
Seattle, WA 98101
(206) 624-4081 ext. 127
Fax: (206) 382-2640
E-mail: info@socialjusticefund.org
Web Site: socialjusticefund.org

FOUNDED: 1978

AREAS OF INTEREST:
Funding community-based groups to promote social justice activities and organizations attempting to establish a society that is politically and economically democratic, equitable and environmentally sound.

CONSULTING OR VOLUNTEER SERVICES:
Facilitates regional networking and general foundation information.

TYPE:
General operating grants; Project/program grants; Seed money grants; Training grants. Rapid response grants.

YEAR PROGRAM STARTED: 1978

PURPOSE:
To be a resource for organizations working for social justice in the states of Idaho, Montana, Oregon, Washington and/or Wyoming attempting to establish a society that is politically and economically democratic, equitable and environmentally just.

LEGAL BASIS:
Nonprofit, 501(c)(3), public foundation.

ELIGIBILITY:
An organization or project must:
(1) be an organized group of people (those not incorporated or fiscally sponsored must speak with program staff first);
(2) use a community organizing approach;
(3) be led by people who are most directly affected by the problems that the organization or project is addressing;
(4) carry out most of its work in Idaho, Montana, Oregon, Washington and/or Wyoming and;
(5) satisfy evaluation requirements for any previous Social Justice Fund grants.

GEOG. RESTRICTIONS: Idaho, Montana, Oregon, Washington and Wyoming.

FINANCIAL DATA:
Amount of support per award: Average grant: $15,000.
Total amount of support: $1,545,588 in giving project grants for the year 2019.

NO. AWARDS: 55 giving project grants for the year 2019.

APPLICATION INFO:
Application information is available on the web site.
Duration: Two years.
Deadline: Varies.

PUBLICATIONS:
Guidelines; monthly e-mail newsletter; annual report.

IRS I.D.: 91-1036971

BOARD OF DIRECTORS:
Yen Baynes
Emily Bookstein
Rebecca Chan
Monica Foucher
Maria Hernandez
Gita Mehrotra
Aaron Oravillo
Carolanne Sanders
Ranfis Giannettino Villatoro

ADDRESS INQUIRIES TO:
E-mail: grants@socialjusticefund.org
Tel: (206) 624-4081 ext. 103

THE STODDARD CHARITABLE TRUST   [1361]
370 Main Street. 12th Floor
Worcester, MA 01608
(508) 459-8032
E-mail: wfletcher@fletchertilton.com

FOUNDED: 1939

AREAS OF INTEREST:
Culture, private education and social services.

TYPE:
Capital grants. Grants to support activities in the Trustees' areas of interest.

YEAR PROGRAM STARTED: 1939

PURPOSE:
To provide funding to worthy causes in the Worcester, MA area and to help that community during times of need.

LEGAL BASIS:
Private, charitable foundation.

ELIGIBILITY:
Nonprofit organizations.

GEOG. RESTRICTIONS: Worcester, Massachusetts.

FINANCIAL DATA:
Amount of support per award: Varies.
Total amount of support: Approximately $4,500,000 for the year 2019.

APPLICATION INFO:
Any organization who has never before received a grant from the Trust, who is considering applying for a grant, should first contact Warner Fletcher before going to the time and effort of putting a request together.
Duration: One year.
Deadline: No later than the 15th of the month preceding one of the four annual distribution meetings held in March, June, September and December.

OFFICERS AND TRUSTEES:
Warner S. Fletcher, Chairman
Judith S. King, Treasurer
Valerie S. Loring, Secretary
Allen W. Fletcher
Justin L. Fletcher
Megan Fletcher
Robert S. Loring
Jennifer Paradee

ADDRESS INQUIRIES TO:
Warner S. Fletcher, Chairman
(See address above.)

THE SUMMIT FOUNDATION
103 South Harris Street
Breckenridge, CO 80424
(970) 453-5970
E-mail: info@summitfoundation.org
Web Site: www.summitfoundation.org

TYPE:
Capital grants; Challenge/matching grants; Endowments; General operating grants; Project/program grants; Scholarships; Technical assistance. The Foundation supports scholarship programs at Summit High School and neighboring community high schools. Scholarships are available to graduating seniors each year.

See entry 1255 for full listing.

SUNNEN FOUNDATION   [1362]
7910 Manchester Avenue
St. Louis, MO 63143
(314) 781-2100

FOUNDED: 1953

AREAS OF INTEREST:
Grants for specific goal-oriented activities to protect reproductive and First Amendment rights and for youth and family services.

TYPE:
Capital grants; Challenge/matching grants; Development grants; Matching gifts; Project/program grants.

YEAR PROGRAM STARTED: 1953

LEGAL BASIS:
Private foundation.

ELIGIBILITY:
Limited to those organizations having tax-exempt status. No scholarship, research or travel grants are made to or for specific individuals.

GEOG. RESTRICTIONS: St. Louis, Missouri.

FINANCIAL DATA:
Assets of $14,959,248 (unaudited) as of December 31, 2018.
Amount of support per award: $5,000 to $168,000 for the year 2018.
Total amount of support: $594,800 for the year 2018.

NO. MOST RECENT APPLICANTS: Approximately 30.

NO. AWARDS: 15 for the year 2018.

REPRESENTATIVE AWARDS:
$155,000 to Planned Parenthood of St. Louis.

APPLICATION INFO:
The Sunnen Foundation has no formal application form. Proposal should include:
(1) summary page that describes the project and amount of funds requested;
(2) organizational background that includes mission, history, types of programs offered and constituencies served;
(3) project description that justifies the need, outlines specific goals, objectives and activities planned to meet the goals and objectives, a project timeline and specific methods of evaluation;
(4) project budget that notes anticipated expenses, including details of how the Sunnen Foundation funds will be used and anticipated income, including information about other grantmakers approached for funding;
(5) organizational budget that notes the current year budget and proposed budget for project year(s) showing income and expenses, the organization's most recent audited financial statement and public and private sources of funds and;
(6) supporting documents that should include a list of current board members, annual report and evidence of 501(c)(3) status.

Five copies of the proposal should be submitted.
Duration: Varies.
Deadline: August 1.

PUBLICATIONS:
Guidelines.

IRS I.D.: 43-6029156

OFFICERS:
Kurt J. Kallaus, President and Director
Matthew S. Kreider, Vice President and Director
Susan S. Brasel, Treasurer and Director
Ruth Cardinale, Secretary and Director
Kathryn Dando, Director

ADDRESS INQUIRIES TO:
Kurt J. Kallaus, President
(See address above.)

TIDES FOUNDATION
P.O. Box 399389
San Francisco, CA 94139-9389
(415) 561-6400
Fax: (415) 561-6401
E-mail: info@tides.org
Web Site: www.tides.org

TYPE:
General operating grants; Project/program grants.

See entry 1258 for full listing.

UNITED JEWISH APPEAL-FEDERATION OF JEWISH PHILANTHROPIES OF NEW YORK

130 East 59th Street
New York, NY 10022
(212) 980-1000
(212) 836-1321
Fax: (212) 836-1353
E-mail: feinsteinl@ujafedny.org
Web Site: www.ujafedny.org

TYPE:
Awards/prizes; Block grants; Capital grants; Challenge/matching grants; Conferences/seminars; Demonstration grants; Development grants; Fellowships; General operating grants; Internships; Matching gifts; Project/program grants; Research grants; Scholarships; Technical assistance; Travel grants; Research contracts.

See entry 753 for full listing.

UNITED METHODIST HEALTH MINISTRY FUND [1363]

100 East First Avenue
Hutchinson, KS 67501
(620) 662-8586
Fax: (620) 662-8597
E-mail: healthfund@healthfund.org
Web Site: healthfund.org

FOUNDED: 1986

AREAS OF INTEREST:
Health care.

NAME(S) OF PROGRAMS:
- **Access to Health Care-System Change and Advocacy**
- **Early Childhood Development**
- **Healthy Congregations Program**

TYPE:
Challenge/matching grants; Conferences/seminars; Demonstration grants; General operating grants; Project/program grants; Seed money grants; Technical assistance; Training grants.

YEAR PROGRAM STARTED: 1986

PURPOSE:
To advance health, healing and wholeness for persons within and beyond the bounds of the former Kansas West Conference of the United Methodist Church.

LEGAL BASIS:
Church foundation.

ELIGIBILITY:
Projects and partners are chosen based on their potential to impact the health of Kansans.

GEOG. RESTRICTIONS: Kansas.

FINANCIAL DATA:
Amount of support per award: Approximately $20,000 average grant.
Total amount of support: $1,500,000 to $2,000,000.

NO. MOST RECENT APPLICANTS: Approximately 130.

NO. AWARDS: Approximately 100.

REPRESENTATIVE AWARDS:
$250,000 to Enroll America to support expanded outreach efforts-Affordable Care Act enrollment; $150,400 to Prairie View, Inc., Newton, KS, for a Tri-County Mental Health Project to improve and increase mental health services.

APPLICATION INFO:
Grant proposals are accepted by invitation only.
Duration: Varies.
Deadline: January, March, July and October. Contact Fund for exact dates.

PUBLICATIONS:
Annual report; special publications.

IRS I.D.: 48-1019578

STAFF:
David Jordan, President
Katie Schoenhoff, Director of Programs
Dashinika Poindexter, Program Coordinator

ADDRESS INQUIRIES TO:
Katie Schoenhoff, Director of Programs
(See address above.)

*SPECIAL STIPULATIONS:
Preference for United Methodist Churches and agencies in Kansas.

WICHITA COMMUNITY FOUNDATION

301 North Main Street
Suite 100
Wichita, KS 67202
(316) 264-4880
Fax: (316) 264-7592
E-mail: wcf@wichitacf.org
Web Site: www.wichitacf.org

TYPE:
Project/program grants; Scholarships; Seed money grants.

See entry 1273 for full listing.

EDUCATION

Educational projects and research (general)

THE AMERICAN FOUNDATION FOR SUICIDE PREVENTION   [1364]
199 Water Street
11th Floor
New York, NY 10038
(212) 363-3500 ext. 2015
Fax: (212) 363-6237
E-mail: grantsmanager@afsp.org
Web Site: afsp.org/research-grant-information

FOUNDED: 1987

AREAS OF INTEREST:
Suicide prevention.

NAME(S) OF PROGRAMS:
● **Pilot Innovation Grant**

TYPE:
Research grants.

PURPOSE:
To provide seed funding for new projects that have the potential to lead to larger investigations.

ELIGIBILITY:
Grants are awarded to investigators at any level affiliated with not-for-profit institutions or organizations. Grant applications are not accepted from for-profit organizations, or from federal or state government agencies. Applications from the Veterans Administration are eligible.

FINANCIAL DATA:
Amount of support per award: Up to $30,000.

NO. MOST RECENT APPLICANTS: 30.

NO. AWARDS: Varies.

APPLICATION INFO:
Applications must be submitted online at the Foundation web site.
Duration: One or two years.
Deadline: Mid-November.

ADDRESS INQUIRIES TO:
Carl Niedzielski, Director, Grants and Researcher Development
(See address above.)

THE AMERICAN FOUNDATION FOR SUICIDE PREVENTION   [1365]
199 Water Street
11th Floor
New York, NY 10038
(212) 363-3500 ext. 2015
Fax: (212) 363-6237
E-mail: grantsmanager@afsp.org
Web Site: afsp.org/research-grant-information

FOUNDED: 1987

AREAS OF INTEREST:
Suicide prevention.

NAME(S) OF PROGRAMS:
● **Postdoctoral Research Fellowship Innovation Grants**

TYPE:
Fellowships; Research grants; Training grants.

YEAR PROGRAM STARTED: 1987

PURPOSE:
To enable young investigators to quality for independent careers in suicide research.

ELIGIBILITY:
Postdoctoral Research Fellowships are awarded for full-time training projects by investigators who have received an M.D. or Ph.D. degree within the preceding six years and have not had more than three years of fellowship support.

FINANCIAL DATA:
Amount of support per award: Up to $132,900 (stipend $54,450 per year and $12,000 per year institutional allowance).

NO. MOST RECENT APPLICANTS: 15.

NO. AWARDS: Varies.

APPLICATION INFO:
Applications must be submitted online at the Foundation web site.
Duration: Two years.
Deadline: Mid-November.

ADDRESS INQUIRIES TO:
Carl Niedzielski, Director, Grants and Researcher Development
(See address above.)

THE AMERICAN FOUNDATION FOR SUICIDE PREVENTION   [1366]
199 Water Street
11th Floor
New York, NY 10038
(212) 363-3500 ext. 2015
Fax: (212) 363-6237
E-mail: grantsmanager@afsp.org
Web Site: afsp.org/research-grant-information

FOUNDED: 1987

AREAS OF INTEREST:
Suicide prevention.

NAME(S) OF PROGRAMS:
● **Distinguished Investigator Innovation Grants**

TYPE:
Research grants.

YEAR PROGRAM STARTED: 1987

PURPOSE:
To advance knowledge of suicide and the ability to prevent it; to fund new directions and initiatives in suicidology.

ELIGIBILITY:
Applicant must be an associate professor or higher with a proven history of research and publication in the area of suicide.

FINANCIAL DATA:
Amount of support per award: Up to $125,000 ($62,500 per year).

NO. MOST RECENT APPLICANTS: 10.

NO. AWARDS: Varies.

APPLICATION INFO:
Applications must be submitted online at the Foundation web site.
Duration: Up to two years.
Deadline: Mid-November.

ADDRESS INQUIRIES TO:
Carl Niedzielski, Director, Grants and Researcher Development
(See address above.)

THE AMERICAN FOUNDATION FOR SUICIDE PREVENTION   [1367]
199 Water Street
11th Floor
New York, NY 10038
(212) 363-3500 ext. 2015
Fax: (212) 363-6237
E-mail: grantsmanager@afsp.org
Web Site: afsp.org/research-grant-information

FOUNDED: 1987

AREAS OF INTEREST:
Suicide prevention.

NAME(S) OF PROGRAMS:
● **Standard Research Innovation Grants**
● **Young Investigator Innovation Grants**

TYPE:
Research grants. Standard Research Innovation Grants are awarded to individual investigators. An additional annual stipend is available for mentors on Young Investigator Innovation Grants in which the investigator is at the level of Assistant Professor or lower.

YEAR PROGRAM STARTED: 1987

PURPOSE:
To advance the knowledge of suicide and the ability to prevent it; to promote the study of clinical, biological and psychosocial aspects of suicide.

ELIGIBILITY:
Standard Research Innovation Grants are awarded to individual investigators at any level. Young Investigator Innovation Grants are awarded to investigators at or below the level of assistant professor.

FINANCIAL DATA:
Amount of support per award: Up to $100,000 for a Standard Research Innovation Grant; Up to $90,000 for a Young Investigator Innovation Grant, with $10,000 allocated to the mentor.

NO. MOST RECENT APPLICANTS: Standard Research Innovation Grants: 80; Young Investigator Innovation Grants: 30.

NO. AWARDS: Varies.

APPLICATION INFO:
Applications must be submitted online at the Foundation web site.
Duration: Two years.
Deadline: Mid-November.

ADDRESS INQUIRIES TO:
Carl Niedzielski, Director, Grants and Researcher Development
(See address above.)

AMERICAN HONDA FOUNDATION   [1368]
1919 Torrance Boulevard
Torrance, CA 90501
(310) 781-4090
E-mail: ahf@ahm.honda.com
Web Site: www.honda.com/community

FOUNDED: 1984

AREAS OF INTEREST:
Youth education in the areas of science, technology, engineering, mathematics, environment, job training and literacy.

TYPE:
Challenge/matching grants; General operating grants; Project/program grants.

YEAR PROGRAM STARTED: 1984

PURPOSE:
To fund programs which strive to educate communities in the process of problem solving and planning; to educate minority youth in the areas of science and math.

LEGAL BASIS:
501(c)(3) corporate foundation.

ELIGIBILITY:
Applicants must be 501(c)(3) organizations, national in scope, impact and outreach and focused on youth and scientific education. To be considered for possible funding, programs related to youth and scientific education should be dedicated to improving the human condition of all mankind, soundly managed and administered by enthusiastic and dedicated individuals who approach their jobs in a youthful way, look to the future or foresightful programs, innovative and creative programs that propose untried methods which ultimately may result in providing solutions to the complex cultural, educational, scientific and social concerns currently facing American society, broad in scope, intent, impact and outreach, possess a high potential for success with a relatively low incidence of duplication of effort, operate from a position of financial soundness, in urgent need of funding from a priority basis (not necessarily financial need), i.e., the relative importance of the program or project to the public and represent a minimal risk in terms of venture capital investment.

Grants are not given to individuals or for scholarships, politics, fund-raising activities, religious activities, arts and culture, medical or educational research, sponsorships for nonprofit, or disaster relief.

No in-kind contributions from the Foundation. No donations of Honda products.

GEOG. RESTRICTIONS: United States.

FINANCIAL DATA:
Amount of support per award: $20,000 to $75,000 per year; $45,000 average.
Total amount of support: $1,220,590 for fiscal year 2019.

APPLICATION INFO:
Proposals must be submitted online. No paper or faxed applications will be accepted.
Duration: One year.
Deadline: February 1 and August 1 for organizations that have never received funding from the Foundation. May 1 for organizations that have received at least one year of funding support in the last 10 years.

ADDRESS INQUIRIES TO:
See e-mail address above.

*SPECIAL STIPULATIONS:
One proposal per year, per grant seeker.

AMERICAN INSTITUTE OF CERTIFIED PUBLIC ACCOUNTANTS (AICPA)   [1369]
220 Leigh Farm Road
Durham, NC 27707
(919) 402-4473
E-mail: scholarships@aicpa.org
Web Site: thiswaytocpa.com/scholarships

AREAS OF INTEREST:
Accounting.

NAME(S) OF PROGRAMS:
● **AICPA Scholarship for Minority Accounting Students**

TYPE:
Scholarships.

YEAR PROGRAM STARTED: 1969

PURPOSE:
To provide financial assistance to minority students who show significant potential to become C.P.As.

ELIGIBILITY:
An applicant must meet the following requirements:
(1) be an underrepresented minority in the accounting profession (e.g., Black or African American, Hispanic or Latino, Native American or Asian American);
(2) enrolled as a full-time undergraduate (12 semester-hours or equivalent) or a full-time graduate-level student (nine semester-hours or equivalent) for the 2021-22 academic year; an exception may be granted if the student plans to participate in an internship;
(3) pursuing an undergraduate- or graduate-level degree in an "accounting-related" major ("accounting-related" shall be as determined by Sponsor in Sponsor's sole discretion);
(4) planning to pursue the C.P.A. licensure but not presently be a C.P.A.;
(5) completed at least 30 semester-hours (or equivalent) of college coursework, including at least six semester-hours (or equivalent) in accounting, by end of spring 2020;
(6) applied to or been accepted into a public or private, 501(c) four-year college or university located in the U.S. or its territories; the business program must be accredited by the AACSB and/or ACBSP;
(7) maintained an overall and major grade point average of at least 3.0 (on a 4.0 scale);
(8) be an AICPA student affiliate member (or have submitted a new member application); those interested can apply on the web site at no cost;
(9) be a U.S. citizen or permanent resident (green card holder) and;
(10) have some financial need (i.e., not receiving a full or partial scholarship(s) and/or grant(s) that cover and/or exceed one's educational expenses).

AICPA staff and their family members are not eligible to receive this scholarship.

GEOG. RESTRICTIONS: United States and its territories.

FINANCIAL DATA:
Amount of support per award: $3,000 to $5,000.
Total amount of support: Approximately $450,000 for the academic year 2018-19.

NO. AWARDS: Up to 90 per academic year.

APPLICATION INFO:
Information is available online.
Duration: One year. Renewable.
Deadline: March 1.

ADDRESS INQUIRIES TO:
AICPA Scholarship for Minority Accounting Students Program
(See e-mail address above.)

*SPECIAL STIPULATIONS:
Students selected to receive an AICPA scholarship must participate in the AICPA Legacy Scholars program, which includes performing at least eight hours of community service per semester to advocate for the C.P.A. profession. Through their community service efforts, AICPA Legacy Scholars enhance their leadership and communication skills by building relationships with both aspiring and seasoned C.P.As.

THE AMERICAN SOCIETY FOR NONDESTRUCTIVE TESTING, INC.   [1370]
1711 Arlingate Lane
Columbus, OH 43228
(614) 274-6003
(800) 222-2768 ext. 233 (U.S. and Canada)
Fax: (614) 274-6899
E-mail: james@asnt.org
Web Site: www.asnt.org

FOUNDED: 1997

AREAS OF INTEREST:
Promotion of nondestructive testing.

NAME(S) OF PROGRAMS:
● **ASNT Faculty Grant Award**

TYPE:
Development grants. The Society sponsors an annual award that will provide grants to foster the development of nondestructive testing and evaluation courses (NDT & NDE) as an integral part of its engineering curricula.

PURPOSE:
To provide incentive to faculty members of engineering or science programs at U.S. universities or colleges to revise their existing NDT courses or to develop new courses to teach NDT by providing financial resources in the form of a grant.

LEGAL BASIS:
501(c)(3) corporation.

ELIGIBILITY:
Faculty members from engineering or science programs at U.S. universities and colleges are encouraged to apply.

FINANCIAL DATA:
Amount of support per award: $10,000.
Total amount of support: Varies.

NO. AWARDS: Up to 2.

APPLICATION INFO:
Guidelines and application are available online.
Duration: One year.
Deadline: December 1. Funding will begin the following July.

ADDRESS INQUIRIES TO:
Jessica Ames, ASNT Program Specialist
(See address above.)

THE KATHRYN AMES FOUNDATION
c/o Pierson & Pierson
305 West Chesapeake Avenue, Suite 308
Towson, MD 21204
(410) 821-3006
Fax: (410) 821-3007
E-mail: info@kathrynames.org
Web Site: www.kathrynames.org

TYPE:
General operating grants; Project/program grants.

See entry 756 for full listing.

ARCHAEOLOGICAL INSTITUTE OF AMERICA
44 Beacon Street
Boston, MA 02108
(857) 305-9360
Fax: (857) 233-4270
E-mail: fellowships@archaeological.org
Web Site: www.archaeological.org

TYPE:
Fellowships. The Fellowship supports projects pertaining to the archaeology of Portugal. These include, but are not limited to, research projects, colloquia, symposia, publication, research-related travel, or travel to academic meetings for the purpose of presenting papers on the archaeology of Portugal.

See entry 757 for full listing.

ARIZONA STATE UNIVERSITY   [1371]
P.O. Box 870901
Tempe, AZ 85287-0901
(480) 965-9139
E-mail: lsp@asu.edu
Web Site: eoss.asu.edu/lsp

AREAS OF INTEREST:
Leadership.

NAME(S) OF PROGRAMS:
● **ASU Leadership Scholarship Program**

TYPE:
Scholarships.

YEAR PROGRAM STARTED: 1977

PURPOSE:
To recognize outstanding high school graduating seniors who have achieved excellence in leadership.

ELIGIBILITY:
Applicant must be nominated by their high school counselor. Only one applicant per high school will be considered. Additionally, applicant must:
(1) have an unweighted grade point average of 3.25;
(2) have a history of community service or volunteering and involvement with clubs and organizations and;
(3) have a completed ASU application for undergraduate admission on file.

FINANCIAL DATA:
Amount of support per award: In-state: $10,000 per year; Out-of-state: $13,000 per year.

NO. AWARDS: 25 per year.

APPLICATION INFO:
Guidelines are available on the University web site.
Duration: Eight consecutive semesters.
Deadline: Early January.

ADDRESS INQUIRIES TO:
Lara Klinkner, Assistant Director
(See e-mail address above.)

ASSOCIATION OF INTERNATIONAL CERTIFIED PROFESSIONAL ACCOUNTANTS (THE ASSOCIATION)
220 Leigh Farm Road
Durham, NC 27707
(919) 402-4682
E-mail: scholarships@aicpa.org
academics@aicpa.org
Web Site: www.aicpa.org

TYPE:
Fellowships. Awarded annually to full-time minority accounting scholars who demonstrate significant potential to become accounting educators.

See entry 1485 for full listing.

BAT CONSERVATION INTERNATIONAL   [1372]
500 North Capital of Texas Highway
Building One
Austin, TX 78746
(512) 327-9721
E-mail: scholarships@batcon.org
Web Site: www.batcon.org/grants

FOUNDED: 1982

AREAS OF INTEREST:
Mammals, ecology, conservation and biology; specifically bats.

NAME(S) OF PROGRAMS:
● **BCI Student Research Scholarships**

TYPE:
Research grants; Scholarships. Support graduate students in research.

YEAR PROGRAM STARTED: 1990

PURPOSE:
To conserve bats and their habitat worldwide; to support research that specifically provides for bat conservation progress.

ELIGIBILITY:
Must be currently enrolled in a degree-granting program.

FINANCIAL DATA:
Amount of support per award: $3,000.
Total amount of support: Varies.
Matching fund requirements: Varies.

NO. MOST RECENT APPLICANTS: 70 to 90.

NO. AWARDS: 10 to 15.

APPLICATION INFO:
Open Request for Proposals is posted online. Request for student proposals will be open from October 1 to October 31.
Duration: One year.
Deadline: Varies.

IRS I.D.: 74-2553144

ADDRESS INQUIRIES TO:
Amanda Adams
Conservation Research Program Manager
(See address above.)

BATON ROUGE AREA FOUNDATION
100 North Street
Suite 900
Baton Rouge, LA 70802
(225) 387-6126
E-mail: lsmyth@braf.org
Web Site: www.braf.org

TYPE:
Capital grants; Challenge/matching grants; Conferences/seminars; Demonstration grants; Development grants; Matching gifts; Project/program grants; Scholarships; Seed money grants; Technical assistance; Training grants; Visiting scholars.

See entry 393 for full listing.

BETHESDA LUTHERAN COMMUNITIES   [1373]
600 Hoffmann Drive
Watertown, WI 53094
(920) 261-3050
Fax: (920) 261-8441
E-mail: jenna.wegner@bethesdalc.org
Web Site: bethesdalc.org

AREAS OF INTEREST:
Developmental disabilities.

NAME(S) OF PROGRAMS:
● **Intellectual and Developmental Disabilities Scholastic Achievement Scholarships**

TYPE:
Scholarships.

PURPOSE:
To encourage Lutheran youth to develop God-pleasing attitudes and actions toward people with individual differences, and to consider careers in the field of intellectual and developmental disabilities services.

ELIGIBILITY:
Must be an active, communicant member of a Lutheran congregation, be classified as a freshman, sophomore or junior at an accredited four-year college or university, have a minimum 3.0 grade point average on a 4.0 scale, and have a career objective in the field of intellectual and developmental disabilities services.

GEOG. RESTRICTIONS: United States.

FINANCIAL DATA:
Amount of support per award: $3,000.
Total amount of support: Varies.

NO. MOST RECENT APPLICANTS: 30.

NO. AWARDS: Up to 10.

APPLICATION INFO:
Application requirements include:
(1) a completed application form;
(2) documentation of 100 hours of service to people with intellectual and/or developmental disabilities, volunteer or paid. Service must be completed within the past two years;
(3) a 250- to 300-word essay on how the intended academic course of study will support their career in the field of intellectual and/or developmental disabilities;
(4) four letters of recommendation (pastor, professor/teacher and two unrelated others);
(5) an official college/university transcript(s) and;
(6) a photograph showing applicant in service of someone with developmental disabilities (not required, but helpful).

Applicant may include any other material that will assist the committee to better know them.
Deadline: May 15. Announcement end of July.

ADDRESS INQUIRIES TO:
Jenna Wegner
Executive Administrative Assistant
(See address above.)

BIBLIOGRAPHICAL SOCIETY OF AMERICA   [1374]
67 West Street
Suite 401, Unit C-17
Brooklyn, NY 11222
(212) 452-2710
E-mail: bsa@bibsocamer.org
Web Site: www.bibsocamer.org/awards/fellowships

FOUNDED: 1904

AREAS OF INTEREST:
Study of books and manuscripts and other textual artifacts in traditional and emerging formats.

NAME(S) OF PROGRAMS:
● **BSA Fellowship Program**

TYPE:
Fellowships. Stipend in support of travel, living and research expenses.

YEAR PROGRAM STARTED: 1983

PURPOSE:
To support bibliographical inquiry as well as research in the history of the book trades and in publishing history.

ELIGIBILITY:
Open to Doctorates, postdoctorates and postgraduates, as well as professionals in the book trades and library fields without doctoral degrees. Applicants of any nationality can apply, with some restrictions (details online). Eligible topics may concentrate on books and documents in any field, but should focus on the book or manuscript (the physical object) as historical evidence. Such topics may include establishing a text or studying the history of book production, publication, distribution, collecting, or reading.

FINANCIAL DATA:
Amount of support per award: Varies.
Total amount of support: Varies.

NO. MOST RECENT APPLICANTS: 60.

NO. AWARDS: 20.

APPLICATION INFO:
Instructions on how to apply are available on the Society's web site.
Deadline: October 1.

ADDRESS INQUIRIES TO:
Hope Mayo, Chair of the
Fellowship Committee
E-mail: bsafellowships@bibsocamer.org

BROWARD EDUCATION FOUNDATION   [1375]
600 S.E. Third Avenue, First Floor
Fort Lauderdale, FL 33301
(754) 321-2030
Fax: (754) 321-2706
E-mail: befinfo@browardschools.com
Web Site: browardeducationfoundation.org

FOUNDED: 1983

AREAS OF INTEREST:
Education.

NAME(S) OF PROGRAMS:
• **Broward Education Foundation School Supply Center**
• **Innovative Teacher Grants**
• **Student Scholarships**

TYPE:
Grants-in-aid; Scholarships.

YEAR PROGRAM STARTED: 1983

PURPOSE:
To provide resources for Broward County Public Schools students and teachers that increase achievement success in education.

LEGAL BASIS:
501(c)(3) education foundation.

GEOG. RESTRICTIONS: Broward County, Florida.

FINANCIAL DATA:
Amount of support per award: Varies.
Total amount of support: Approximately $3,864,555 for fiscal year 2021.

NO. MOST RECENT APPLICANTS: 1,300.

NO. AWARDS: Innovative Teacher Grants: 235; School Supply Center: 4,108; Student Scholarships: 360.

APPLICATION INFO:
Contact the Foundation for program-specific information.
Duration: Varies.
Deadline: Varies.

PUBLICATIONS:
Financial report.

ADDRESS INQUIRIES TO:
Coco Burns, Program Director
(See address above.)

THE BROWN FOUNDATION, INC.   [1376]
P.O. Box 130646
Houston, TX 77219-0646
(713) 523-6867
E-mail: bfi@brownfoundation.org
Web Site: www.brownfoundation.org

FOUNDED: 1951

AREAS OF INTEREST:
Education, arts and humanities, civic/public affairs, medicine and science, and human services.

TYPE:
Capital grants; General operating grants; Project/program grants; Seed money grants.

YEAR PROGRAM STARTED: 1951

PURPOSE:
To distribute funds for public charitable purposes, principally for the support, encouragement and assistance to education, the arts and community service.

LEGAL BASIS:
Private foundation.

ELIGIBILITY:
Funding given to 501(c)(3) nonprofit institutions only. No grants to individuals.

GEOG. RESTRICTIONS: Primarily Texas.

FINANCIAL DATA:
Amount of support per award: Varies.
Total amount of support: Approximately $70,000,000.

APPLICATION INFO:
Instructions are available on the Foundation web site.
Duration: Typically one year.

PUBLICATIONS:
Application guidelines.

OFFICERS AND TRUSTEES:
William N. Mathis, Chairman
Isabel Lummis, President
Holbrook F. Dorn, Treasurer
Louisa Sarofim, Secretary

ADDRESS INQUIRIES TO:
Ann Ziker, Executive Director
(See address above.)

FRITZ B. BURNS FOUNDATION   [1377]
21800 Oxnard Street
Suite 490
Woodland Hills, CA 91367
(818) 313-8818
Fax: (818) 313-8821

FOUNDED: 1955

AREAS OF INTEREST:
Education.

TYPE:
Capital grants; Scholarships. Grants are educational in nature. The emphasis is on

buildings, equipment, endowments (not for operational expenses), scholarships, faculty fellowships, hospitals and hospital equipment and medical research.

YEAR PROGRAM STARTED: 1955

LEGAL BASIS:
Private foundation.

ELIGIBILITY:
Eligible organizations must have IRS 501(c)(3) not-for-profit status. Grants are not made to individuals or to religious organizations.

GEOG. RESTRICTIONS: California and Nevada.

FINANCIAL DATA:
Amount of support per award: $500 to $100,000.
Total amount of support: Varies.

APPLICATION INFO:
Applicant organizations must provide IRS 501(c)(3) documentation. Financial statements and a list of the organization's board of directors must be included with the application.
Duration: One year.
Deadline: September 30.

OFFICER:
Rex Rawlinson, President

ADDRESS INQUIRIES TO:
Rex Rawlinson, President
(See address above.)

THE CEMALA FOUNDATION   [1378]
330 South Greene Street, Suite 101
Greensboro, NC 27401
(336) 274-3541
Fax: (336) 272-8153
E-mail: cemala@cemala.org
Web Site: www.cemala.org

FOUNDED: 1986

AREAS OF INTEREST:
Early childhood development, workforce development, and transformational spaces and opportunities.

TYPE:
Capital grants; Challenge/matching grants; Development grants; Grants-in-aid; Project/program grants; Seed money grants; Technical assistance.

PURPOSE:
To better the quality of life for the citizens of Greensboro, NC.

LEGAL BASIS:
Private foundation.

ELIGIBILITY:
Eligible organizations must be IRS 501(c)(3) tax-exempt.

GEOG. RESTRICTIONS: Primarily Greensboro, North Carolina.

FINANCIAL DATA:
Amount of support per award: Varies.
Total amount of support: Varies.

APPLICATION INFO:
The Cemala Foundation is no longer accepting unsolicited grant proposals. It is making strategic investments in projects compatible with the Foundation's vision. Consult its web site for additional information.
Duration: Typically one year. Renewal possible.

Deadline: March 1 and September 1.

STAFF:
Susan Schwartz, Executive Director
Melissa Burroughs, Assistant Treasurer

ADDRESS INQUIRIES TO:
Susan Schwartz, Executive Director
(See address above.)

THE COCA-COLA FOUNDATION, INC. [1379]

P.O. Box 1734
Atlanta, GA 30301
(404) 676-2121
E-mail: cocacolacommunityrequest@coca-cola.com
Web Site: www.coca-colacompany.com/shared-future/communities/the-coca-cola-foundation

FOUNDED: 1984

AREAS OF INTEREST:
Empowering women, protecting the environment, and enhancing communities.

TYPE:
Project/program grants.

PURPOSE:
To help develop and maintain vibrant, sustainable and local communities; to support initiatives and programs that respond in a meaningful way to community needs and priorities.

LEGAL BASIS:
Corporate foundation.

ELIGIBILITY:
Grants are made only to nonprofit 501(c)(3) or equivalent organizations. No grants to individuals, religious organizations or endeavors, or political, legislative, lobbying or fraternal organizations.

FINANCIAL DATA:
Amount of support per award: Varies.
Total amount of support: Varies.

APPLICATION INFO:
Applications must be submitted through the online application system.
Duration: Typically one year.
Deadline: Requests accepted and reviewed on a year-round basis.

PUBLICATIONS:
Annual report.

THE COMMUNITY FOUNDATION FOR THE GREATER CAPITAL REGION [1380]

2 Tower Place
Albany, NY 12203
(518) 446-9638
Fax: (518) 446-9708
E-mail: info@cfgcr.org
Web Site: www.cfgcr.org

AREAS OF INTEREST:
Education.

TYPE:
Scholarships.

YEAR PROGRAM STARTED: 1968

PURPOSE:
To assist outstanding students who plan to pursue postsecondary education in college and vocational programs.

LEGAL BASIS:
Community foundation.

ELIGIBILITY:
Eligible students must be high school seniors enrolling in a full-time undergraduate course of study at an accredited college, university, or vocational-technical school.

GEOG. RESTRICTIONS: Varies according to scholarship opportunity.

FINANCIAL DATA:
Amount of support per award: Varies.
Total amount of support: Varies.

NO. AWARDS: Varies.

APPLICATION INFO:
Applications are posted online as they become available.
Duration: One year.
Deadline: Generally March to May.

ADDRESS INQUIRIES TO:
See e-mail address above.

COMMUNITY FOUNDATION OF THE LOWCOUNTRY, INC. [1381]

4 Northridge Drive, Suite A
Hilton Head Island, SC 29926
(843) 681-9100
Fax: (843) 681-9101
E-mail: ksmith@cf-lowcountry.org
Web Site: www.cf-lowcountry.org

FOUNDED: 1994

TYPE:
Community impact grants. Community investment grants. Opportunity grants. Organization development grants.

PURPOSE:
To maintain and enhance the educational, social, culture, health, civic and environmental resources of the community.

LEGAL BASIS:
501(c)(3) and SC Secretary of State annual registration.

ELIGIBILITY:
501(c)(3) organizations.

GEOG. RESTRICTIONS: Hilton Head area, South Carolina.

FINANCIAL DATA:
Amount of support per award: Community Impact Grants and Community Investment Grants: $10,000 or more; Organizational Development Grants: Up to $5,000.
Total amount of support: Approximately $5,000,000 for fiscal year 2018.

APPLICATION INFO:
Applicants must attend a grants information session and register on the Giving Marketplace. In order to determine project eligibility, applicants are then required to meet with the Vice President for Grantmaking. Those eligible are invited to apply.
Duration: One year.
Deadline: January 15, May 15 and September 15.

ADDRESS INQUIRIES TO:
Kevin Smith, Grants
(See e-mail address above.)

COUNCIL ON TECHNOLOGY AND ENGINEERING TEACHER EDUCATION (CTETE) [1382]

Rhode Island College
Department of Educational Studies
600 Mount Pleasant Avenue
Providence, RI 02809-1991
(401) 456-8793
E-mail: cmclaughlin@ric.edu
Web Site: ctete.org

FOUNDED: 1950

AREAS OF INTEREST:
Technology and engineering teacher education.

CONSULTING OR VOLUNTEER SERVICES:
NCATE state guideline preparation found on web site.

NAME(S) OF PROGRAMS:
● **Outstanding Research Award**

TYPE:
Research grants.

YEAR PROGRAM STARTED: 1996

PURPOSE:
To discover philosophical rationales, theoretical models, principles and/or practices that potentially increase the effectiveness and efficiency of pre-service or in-service engineering and technology teacher education.

LEGAL BASIS:
Special-interest foundation.

ELIGIBILITY:
Applicants must be members of the Council on Technology and Engineering Teacher Education.

FINANCIAL DATA:
Amount of support per award: $500.
Total amount of support: $500.

NO. AWARDS: 1.

APPLICATION INFO:
Candidates may nominate themselves or be nominated by someone else. The application process consists of an initial screening by the CTETE Research and Scholarship Committee based on a brief abstract, followed by a peer review of papers submitted by selected finalists.
Duration: One year.
Deadline: December 31.

ADDRESS INQUIRIES TO:
Charles McLaughlin, Past President
(See address above.)

THE DANA FOUNDATION

505 Fifth Avenue, Sixth Floor
New York, NY 10017
(212) 223-4040
Fax: (212) 317-8721
E-mail: danainfo@dana.org
grantsinfo@dana.org
Web Site: www.dana.org

TYPE:
Awards/prizes; Research grants.

See entry 2025 for full listing.

FREDERICK DOUGLASS INSTITUTE FOR AFRICAN AND AFRICAN-AMERICAN STUDIES   [1383]

311 Morey Hall
University of Rochester
P.O. Box 270440
Rochester, NY 14627-0440
(585) 276-5744
Fax: (585) 256-2594
E-mail: FDI@rochester.edu
Web Site: www.sas.rochester.edu/aas

FOUNDED: 1986

AREAS OF INTEREST:
African and African-American studies and graduate education through advanced research at the University of Rochester.

NAME(S) OF PROGRAMS:
● **FDI Postdoctoral Fellowship**

TYPE:
Awards/prizes; Conferences/seminars; Fellowships.

PURPOSE:
To promote the development of African and African-American studies and graduate education through advanced research at the University of Rochester; specifically, to support the completion of a project.

ELIGIBILITY:
Open to scholars who hold a Ph.D. degree in a field related to African and African-American studies.

FINANCIAL DATA:
Amount of support per award: Annual stipend of $48,750 and a $3,000 fund for research-related activities.

NO. MOST RECENT APPLICANTS: Approximately 30 to 40.

NO. AWARDS: 2 annually.

APPLICATION INFO:
Application materials should be submitted at www.rochester.edu/faculty-recruiting/apply/10922. As part of the application, the following must be included: (1) a cover letter that describes applicant's research and how it relates to the yearly theme, a specific goal for the fellowship year, teaching experience, and a brief description of a proposed course applicant would offer at the 100- or 200-level undergraduate elective in African and African American Studies; (2) a writing sample related to the theme of anti-Blackness; (3) curriculum vitae and; (4) three letters of recommendation that comment upon the value and feasibility of the work proposed. Letters can be submitted online or sent to the e-mail address listed above.
Duration: One year with possibility of one year renewal.
Deadline: December 15. Announcement early March.

ADDRESS INQUIRIES TO:
Ghislaine Radegonde-Eison
Program Manager
(See e-mail address above.)

EDUCATIONAL TESTING SERVICE   [1384]

660 Rosedale Road
Princeton, NJ 08541
E-mail: internfellowships@ets.org
Web Site: www.ets.org/research/internship-fellowship

FOUNDED: 1947

AREAS OF INTEREST:
Psychometrics, validity, natural language processing and computational linguistics, cognitive psychology, learning sciences, linguistics, second language learning, teaching English as a second language, speech recognition and processing, teaching and classroom research, and statistics.

NAME(S) OF PROGRAMS:
● **Summer Internship Program for Graduate Students**

TYPE:
Internships. Interns in this 10-week program participate in research under the guidance of ETS mentors in one of the areas of interest listed above at ETS office located in Princeton, N.J. Interns also participate in seminars and workshops on a variety of topics.

YEAR PROGRAM STARTED: 1963

PURPOSE:
To provide research opportunities to individuals enrolled in a doctoral program in the fields described above.

LEGAL BASIS:
Not-for-profit organization.

ELIGIBILITY:
Graduate students who are currently enrolled in a full-time doctoral program in one of the areas listed above and who have completed a minimum of two years of coursework toward their Ph.D. or Ed.D. prior to the program start date are eligible to apply.

GEOG. RESTRICTIONS: Princeton, New Jersey.

FINANCIAL DATA:
Amount of support per award: $7,500 salary and transportation allowance for relocating to and from the Princeton area; housing will be provided for interns commuting more than 50 miles.

NO. MOST RECENT APPLICANTS: Average of 200.

NO. AWARDS: Approximately 10 to 15.

APPLICATION INFO:
The application process opens in November. Applicants must complete the electronic application form.
Duration: 10 weeks, June to August.
Deadline: February 1. Applicants will be notified by April 1.

PUBLICATIONS:
Program announcement.

STAFF:
Georgiana Weingart, Program Coordinator

ADDRESS INQUIRIES TO:
See e-mail address above.

FEDERATION OF AMERICAN CONSUMERS AND TRAVELERS   [1385]

318 Hillsboro Avenue
P.O. Box 104
Edwardsville, IL 62025
(618) 656-0454
(800) 872-3228
Fax: (618) 656-5369
E-mail: vrolens@usafact.org
Web Site: www.usafact.org

FOUNDED: 1984

AREAS OF INTEREST:
Education.

NAME(S) OF PROGRAMS:
● **Classroom and Community Grants**
● **Scholarship Program**

TYPE:
Project/program grants; Scholarships. Scholarship Program provides scholarships to members and their immediate families, with the hope of increasing accessibility to advanced education.

PURPOSE:
To help provide supplies or to otherwise support a classroom project for which funds may not be readily available somewhere else; to improve the teacher's ability to teach and the students' opportunity to learn.

ELIGIBILITY:
Classroom Grants: Any dues-paying member of FACT may nominate any teacher to apply for a grant. Only one nomination per year per member.

Scholarship Program: All applicants must be FACT members, their children or grandchildren.

GEOG. RESTRICTIONS: United States.

FINANCIAL DATA:
Amount of support per award: Classroom and Community Grants: $100 to $2,500; Scholarship Program: Varies.
Total amount of support: Varies.

APPLICATION INFO:
Contact the Federation for guidelines.
Duration: Annual awards.
Deadline: Classroom and Community Grants: January, April, July and October; Scholarship Program: Awarded quarterly.

ADDRESS INQUIRIES TO:
Vicki Rolens, Managing Director
(See address above.)

FLORIDA EDUCATION FUND   [1386]

201 East Kennedy Boulevard
Suite 1525
Tampa, FL 33602
(813) 272-2772 ext. 203
Fax: (813) 272-2784
E-mail: cjackson@fefonline.org
mdf@fefonline.org
Web Site: www.fefonline.org

FOUNDED: 1984

AREAS OF INTEREST:
Arts and sciences, mathematics, business, engineering, health sciences, nursing, higher education, visual and performing arts.

NAME(S) OF PROGRAMS:
● **McKnight Doctoral Fellowship**

TYPE:
Fellowships.

YEAR PROGRAM STARTED: 1984

PURPOSE:
To address the underrepresentation of African American and Hispanic faculty at colleges and universities in the state of Florida by increasing the pool of citizens qualified with Ph.D. degrees to teach at the college and university levels, thus expanding employment opportunities in the industry.

LEGAL BASIS:
Corporation.

ELIGIBILITY:
Applicants must be African American or Hispanic, U.S. citizens, and hold a minimum of a Bachelor's degree from a regionally accredited college or university. The Fellowship will be awarded only to persons who intend to seek the Ph.D. degree in one of the disciplines as described on the Fund's web site.

GEOG. RESTRICTIONS: United States.

FINANCIAL DATA:
Fellowships include a $12,000 stipend, plus up to $5,000 for tuition and fees. Any tuition and fees over $5,000 are waived.
Amount of support per award: Up to $17,000 per year.

NO. MOST RECENT APPLICANTS: 500.

NO. AWARDS: Up to 50 per academic year.

APPLICATION INFO:
Online application is available at the web site.
Duration: Three years, with fourth and fifth years supported by the institution if necessary.
Deadline: January 15.

PUBLICATIONS:
Annual report.

ADDRESS INQUIRIES TO:
Charles Jackson, Program Manager
(See address above.)

FOSTER CARE TO SUCCESS [1387]
23811 Chagrin Boulevard
Suite 210
Cleveland, OH 44122
(571) 203-0270
E-mail: scholarships@fc2success.org
Web Site: www.fc2success.org

FOUNDED: 1981

AREAS OF INTEREST:
Foster children.

NAME(S) OF PROGRAMS:
● **FCS Scholarship Fund**

TYPE:
Scholarships.

YEAR PROGRAM STARTED: 1986

PURPOSE:
To recognize outstanding scholarship and community service by a college student who has no family supporting their goals and efforts.

LEGAL BASIS:
501(c)(3), nonprofit organization.

ELIGIBILITY:
Applicants must:
(1) have been in public or private foster care for the 12 consecutive months leading up to and including their 18th birthday, or have been adopted or placed into legal guardianship from foster care after their 16th birthday, or they must have been orphaned for at least one year at the time of their 18th birthday;
(2) have been accepted into or expect to be accepted into an accredited, Pell-eligible college or other postsecondary school;
(3) be under the age of 25 on March 31 of the year in which they apply if they have not previously received scholarship funding from FC2S and;
(4) have been in foster care or orphaned while living in the U.S.

U.S. citizenship is not required.

GEOG. RESTRICTIONS: United States.

FINANCIAL DATA:
Funds may be used for tuition and books.
Amount of support per award: $2,500 to $5,000.
Total amount of support: Varies.

NO. MOST RECENT APPLICANTS: 2,200.

NO. AWARDS: 75 new; 300 repeat recipients.

APPLICATION INFO:
Information may be obtained from the address above or online from January 1 to March 31.
Duration: One academic year. Renewable up to five years if student remains eligible.
Deadline: March 31 for online application and postmark no later than April 15 for submission of additional materials required of applicant.

IRS I.D.: 52-1238437

EXECUTIVE DIRECTOR:
Eileen McCaffrey

ADDRESS INQUIRIES TO:
Dana Brown, Director of Scholarships and Grants
(See address above.)

FOUNDATION FOR TECHNOLOGY AND ENGINEERING EDUCATION [1388]
1914 Association Drive
Suite 201
Reston, VA 20191-1539
(703) 860-2100
Fax: (703) 860-0353
E-mail: kdelapaz@iteea.org
Web Site: www.iteea.org

FOUNDED: 1939

AREAS OF INTEREST:
STEM education.

NAME(S) OF PROGRAMS:
● **Maley/FTEE Scholarship Technology and Engineering Teacher Professional Development**

TYPE:
Scholarships.

PURPOSE:
To support teachers in their preparation to increase the positive outcomes of technology and engineering education.

ELIGIBILITY:
Applicant must be a technology and engineering teacher at any grade level who is beginning or continuing graduate study. Criteria includes evidence of teaching success, plans for action research, recommendations, plans for professional development, and the applicant's needs. Applicant must be a member of the International Technology and Engineering Educators Association.

FINANCIAL DATA:
Amount of support per award: $500.

NO. AWARDS: 1.

APPLICATION INFO:
Applicant must send an application package, which is to include the following required items:
(1) letter of application explaining plans for graduate study, plans for action research, the

applicant's need and the school's name, address, telephone, grade level, and home address;
(2) resume (not to exceed four pages) describing current position, professional activities and achievements;
(3) official college transcript(s);
(4) documentation of acceptance into graduate school and;
(5) three letters of recommendation from among the following: undergraduate faculty, graduate faculty and school administration.
Duration: One year.
Deadline: December 1.

ADDRESS INQUIRIES TO:
Maley/FTEE Scholarship
Foundation for Technology and Engineering Education
(See address above.)

*SPECIAL STIPULATIONS:
Applicant must be a member of the ITEEA.

THE GAMBLE FOUNDATION [1389]
1660 Bush Street, Suite 300
San Francisco, CA 94109
(415) 561-6540
E-mail: jwang@pfs-llc.net
Web Site: www.gamblefoundation.org

FOUNDED: 1968

AREAS OF INTEREST:
Environment and agriculture.

TYPE:
Project/program grants.

YEAR PROGRAM STARTED: 1968

PURPOSE:
To promote the holistic management of preserved lands through grants to organizations focused mainly in the San Francisco Bay, CA area.

LEGAL BASIS:
Private foundation.

ELIGIBILITY:
Grants are made to organizations that have tax-exempt status under Section 501(c)(3) of the Internal Revenue Code. No grants are made to individuals.

GEOG. RESTRICTIONS: San Francisco, Marin and Napa counties, California.

FINANCIAL DATA:
Amount of support per award: $1,500 to $40,000.
Total amount of support: Varies.

APPLICATION INFO:
Proposals are accepted by invitation only.
Duration: One to four years.

ADDRESS INQUIRIES TO:
Jane Wang, Grants Assistant
(See address above.)

HAMILTON FAMILY CHARITABLE TRUST [1390]
200 Eagle Road
Suite 308
Wayne, PA 19087
(610) 293-2225
Fax: (610) 293-0967
E-mail: nwingo@218enterprises.com
Web Site: www.hfctrust.org

FOUNDED: 1992

AREAS OF INTEREST:
Job skills training; education, youth and literacy-based education programs for underserved children and youth.

NAME(S) OF PROGRAMS:
- **After-School Programs**
- **In-School Programs**
- **Summer Programs**

TYPE:
Challenge/matching grants; Project/program grants.

YEAR PROGRAM STARTED: 1996

PURPOSE:
To promote quality programs of education for economically underserved youth; to support job skills training with a proven record of successful workforce placement.

LEGAL BASIS:
Private foundation.

ELIGIBILITY:
Grants are made to organizations that have tax-exempt status under Section 501(c)(3) of the Internal Revenue Code. No grants are made to individuals.

GEOG. RESTRICTIONS: Philadelphia, Pennsylvania and surrounding counties.

FINANCIAL DATA:
Amount of support per award: First-time grantees: $5,000 to $10,000; Others: $5,000 to $100,000.
Total amount of support: $7,736,750.

NO. MOST RECENT APPLICANTS: 108.

NO. AWARDS: 76.

APPLICATION INFO:
Application form and guidelines are available on the Trust web site.
Duration: One calendar year.
Deadline: December 1, February 1, May 1 and August 1.

STAFF:
Nancy Wingo, Executive Director

ADDRESS INQUIRIES TO:
Nancy Wingo, Executive Director
(See address above.)

HANNAFORD CHARITABLE FOUNDATION [1391]
145 Pleasant Hill Road
Scarborough, ME 04074
E-mail: hannafordcharitablefoundation@ hannaford.com
Web Site: www.hannaford.com

AREAS OF INTEREST:
Education, health through healthy communities and food security.

TYPE:
Capital grants; Project/program grants. Employee scholarships.

YEAR PROGRAM STARTED: 1994

PURPOSE:
To provide financial support to nonprofit organizations dedicated to improving the communities where Hannaford operates.

LEGAL BASIS:
Private foundation.

ELIGIBILITY:
Preference for funding is given to organizations or programs that involve Hannaford associates, are located in

Hannaford's marketing area, and have the potential to provide ongoing services to Foundation customers.

The Foundation does not offer support to individuals, tax-supported institutions or scholarship (employee) programs outside of their marketing area.

GEOG. RESTRICTIONS: Maine, Massachusetts, New Hampshire, New York and Vermont.

FINANCIAL DATA:
Amount of support per award: Varies.
Total amount of support: Varies.

NO. AWARDS: Varies.

APPLICATION INFO:
Instructions and requirements are available on the Foundation web site.
Duration: Typically one year.
Deadline: Grants submissions are reviewed quarterly.

HARBUS FOUNDATION [1392]
Harvard Business School
Soldiers Field
Boston, MA 02163
(617) 495-6528
Fax: (617) 495-8619
E-mail: foundation@harbus.org
Web Site: www.harbus.org/foundation

FOUNDED: 1997

AREAS OF INTEREST:
Education, journalism and literacy.

TYPE:
Project/program grants. The Foundation, which was formed by the student-run Harbus News Corporation at Harvard Business School, seeks to give back to the community by supporting programs of educational development in the communities where students live and learn.

PURPOSE:
To support small, community-based organizations, individuals, or local schools with limited resources to establish and sustain new and innovative programs in the areas of literacy, journalism, and/or education.

ELIGIBILITY:
Proposals will be accepted from individuals and tax-exempt organizations as defined by Section 501(c)(3) of the Internal Revenue Code for purposes to be carried out within the greater Boston area.

The Foundation does not fund scholarships and fellowships, religious organizations for religious purposes, city or state governments, capital campaigns, for-profit organizations or purely personal needs.

GEOG. RESTRICTIONS: Greater Boston, Massachusetts area with priority given to the communities of Allston and Brighton.

FINANCIAL DATA:
Amount of support per award: $20,000.
Total amount of support: $60,000 for the year 2018.

NO. AWARDS: 3 for the year 2018.

APPLICATION INFO:
Application for funding is by invitation only. However, if one's organization aligns with the Foundation mission, send e-mail with a brief description of this organization and desired use of the Foundation resources.

Duration: One year. Renewal possible by reapplication for a maximum of three years.
Deadline: December 1.

PUBLICATIONS:
Brochure.

THE PHIL HARDIN FOUNDATION [1393]
2750 North Park Drive
Meridian, MS 39305
(601) 483-4282
Fax: (601) 483-5665
E-mail: info@philhardin.org
Web Site: www.philhardin.org

FOUNDED: 1964

AREAS OF INTEREST:
Education with special (but not exclusive) emphasis on preK-12th grade.

TYPE:
Development grants; Endowments; General operating grants; Project/program grants. Foundation's current primary focus is improving student achievement for preK-12th grade.

YEAR PROGRAM STARTED: 1964

PURPOSE:
To improve educational and life outcomes for Mississippi children, with a special emphasis on Meridian and Lauderdale County; to expand access to high-quality educational opportunities.

LEGAL BASIS:
Tax-exempt, private foundation.

ELIGIBILITY:
Tax-exempt organizations in and out of Mississippi for projects to improve the education of Mississippians. No individual grants.

GEOG. RESTRICTIONS: Mississippi.

FINANCIAL DATA:
Amount of support per award: $10,000 to $500,000.
Total amount of support: $3,000,000 per year for all programs.
Matching fund requirements: Stipulated with specific program.

NO. MOST RECENT APPLICANTS: 68.

NO. AWARDS: 25 to 30.

APPLICATION INFO:
Proposals are to be based on current research and best practices. If not available, then prior approval to submit proposal must be obtained. Applications must be submitted online and include the following:
(1) IRS tax-exempt determination letter;
(2) list of board members, affiliations and contact information;
(3) most recent audited financial statement, including 990;
(4) copy of operating budget and;
(5) list of past and present funders.

The Foundation does not accept videotapes, faxed or e-mailed proposals.
Duration: One-time, one-year or multiyear grants. Some renewals possible.

OFFICERS:
Robert Ward, President and Chairperson
R.B. Deen, Jr., Senior Vice President
Marty Davidson, Vice President for Investments and Treasurer
Ronnie L. Walton, Secretary and General Counsel

DIRECTORS:
Kacey Bailey
Clair Huff
Jim McGinnis
Derron Radcliff
Michael Van Veckhoven

HEALTH RESOURCES AND SERVICES ADMINISTRATION [1394]
5600 Fishers Lane, Room 15-N78
Rockville, MD 20857
(301) 443-2909
Fax: (301) 451-5629
E-mail: SDSProgram@hrsa.gov
Web Site: bhw.hrsa.gov

AREAS OF INTEREST:
Health professions and nursing education.

NAME(S) OF PROGRAMS:
● **Scholarships for Disadvantaged Students**

TYPE:
Scholarships. Funds made available to eligible schools for the purpose of providing scholarships to full-time financially needy students from disadvantaged backgrounds. Students must apply at the financial aid office of school where enrolled or admitted for enrollment.

YEAR PROGRAM STARTED: 1991

PURPOSE:
To improve and expand health care services for underserved people.

LEGAL BASIS:
Government agency.

ELIGIBILITY:
Student must be a citizen or permanent resident of the U.S. enrolled in a health profession or nursing program and be from a disadvantaged background.

GEOG. RESTRICTIONS: United States.

FINANCIAL DATA:
Amount of support per award: Up to $40,000 per student.
Total amount of support: Varies.

NO. AWARDS: Approximately 79.

APPLICATION INFO:
Contact student financial aid office at the school attended for application procedure.
Duration: Four years. Must reapply for additional funding after four years.
Deadline: March.

WILLIAM G. AND MYRTLE E. HESS CHARITABLE TRUST [1395]
c/o JPMorgan
28660 Northwestern Highway
Southfield, MI 48034
(248) 738-6169
Fax: (800) 919-3085
E-mail: kimberly.l.thomas@jpmorgan.com
Web Site: www.jpmorgan.com/onlinegrants

FOUNDED: 1969

AREAS OF INTEREST:
Science, education and charity.

TYPE:
General operating grants; Grants-in-aid; Project/program grants.

YEAR PROGRAM STARTED: 1969

PURPOSE:
To benefit organizations in Michigan.

ELIGIBILITY:
Eligible organizations must be nonprofit, 501(c)(3) tax-exempt. Grants are not given to individuals or for religious or political purposes.

GEOG. RESTRICTIONS: Michigan.

FINANCIAL DATA:
Amount of support per award: $1,000 to $10,000.
Total amount of support: Varies.

APPLICATION INFO:
Applications are to be submitted online.
Duration: Typically one year.
Deadline: August 15. Decisions on grant requests made annually in September.

ADDRESS INQUIRIES TO:
Kimberly Thomas, Trust Officer
(See address above.)

*PLEASE NOTE:
Applications received late will be held until the following year.

HUTCHINSON COMMUNITY FOUNDATION
One North Main Street
Suite 501
Hutchinson, KS 67501
(620) 663-5293
E-mail: info@hutchcf.org
Web Site: hutchcf.org

TYPE:
Project/program grants; Seed money grants.

See entry 414 for full listing.

INTERNATIONAL ASSOCIATION OF ICE CREAM DISTRIBUTORS AND VENDORS (IAICDV) [1396]
3601 East Joppa Road
Baltimore, MD 21234
(410) 931-8100
Fax: (410) 931-8111
E-mail: info@iaicdv.org
Web Site: www.iaicdv.org/scholarship

FOUNDED: 1969

AREAS OF INTEREST:
The ice cream vending and distributing industries.

NAME(S) OF PROGRAMS:
● **IAICDV Annual Scholarship**

TYPE:
Scholarships.

YEAR PROGRAM STARTED: 1990

PURPOSE:
To award deserving applicants who are determined to further their profession, and our industry, through advanced education.

ELIGIBILITY:
The following criteria apply:
(1) Applicant must be an owner of a member company, employee of a member company or a dependent (natural or adopted) of a member company; the member company must be in good standing with the IAICDV;
(2) Applicant must be or have been working in the ice cream industry during the award year and;
(3) Applicant must use the scholarship for their postsecondary education, including university, college or trade school.

FINANCIAL DATA:
Total amount of support: Up to $3,000.

NO. MOST RECENT APPLICANTS: 5 to 7.

NO. AWARDS: 1 to 3.

APPLICATION INFO:
Contact the Association for detailed guidelines.
Duration: One-time award.
Deadline: June 30.

ADDRESS INQUIRIES TO:
IAICDV Scholarship Program
(See address above.)

INTERNATIONAL LITERACY ASSOCIATION (ILA) [1397]
P.O. Box 8139
Newark, DE 19714-8139
(800) 336-7323 (U.S. and Canada)
(302) 731-1600 (all other countries)
E-mail: ilaawards@reading.org
Web Site: www.literacyworldwide.org

FOUNDED: 1956

AREAS OF INTEREST:
Reading and literacy through professional development, advocacy, partnership, research, and global literacy development.

NAME(S) OF PROGRAMS:
● **Jeanne S. Chall Research Fellowship**
● **Corwin Literacy Leader Award**
● **Leaders Inspiring Readers Award**
● **Timothy and Cynthia Shanahan Outstanding Dissertation Award**
● **Steven A. Stahl Research Grant**

TYPE:
Awards/prizes; Fellowships; Grants-in-aid; Research grants. Jeanne S. Chall Research Fellowship encourages and supports reading research by promising scholars. Its special emphasis is to support research efforts in the areas of beginning reading, readability, reading difficulty, stages of reading development, the relation of vocabulary to reading, and diagnosing and teaching adults with limited reading ability.

Corwin Literacy Leader Award honors district or school administrators who offers literacy professional development, instructional resource support, and/or specific literacy programs. Must be an ILA member or nominated by an ILA member.

Leaders Inspiring Readers Award honors educators and researchers in the focus area of struggling readers. Must be an ILA member or nominated by their peers.

Timothy and Cynthia Shanahan Outstanding Dissertation Award honors ILA members who have completed dissertations in any aspect of the field of reading or literacy.

Steven A. Stahl Research Grant encourages and supports promising graduate students in their research. The grant will be awarded annually to a recipient with at least three years of teaching experience who is conducting classroom research (including action research) focused on improving reading instruction and children's reading achievement.

PURPOSE:
To promote reading by continuously advancing the quality of literacy instruction and research worldwide.

FINANCIAL DATA:
Amount of support per award: Jeanne S. Chall Grant: $2,000; Steven A. Stahl Grant: $1,000.
Total amount of support: Varies.

NO. AWARDS: 1 each annually. Research grants vary.

APPLICATION INFO:
Application guidelines are available online.
Deadline: March 15.

PUBLICATIONS:
Application guidelines.

ADDRESS INQUIRIES TO:
Dawn Roberts, Human Resources Associate
E-mail: mroberts@reading.org
(See address above.)

INTERNATIONAL LITERACY ASSOCIATION (ILA)   [1398]
P.O. Box 8139
Newark, DE 19714-8139
(800) 336-7323 (U.S. and Canada)
(302) 731-1600 (all other countries)
E-mail: ilaawards@reading.org
Web Site: www.literacyworldwide.org

FOUNDED: 1956

AREAS OF INTEREST:
Reading and literacy through professional development, advocacy, partnership, research, and global literacy development.

NAME(S) OF PROGRAMS:
● **Jerry Johns Outstanding Teacher Educator in Reading Award**

TYPE:
Awards/prizes; Research grants; Travel grants. The Jerry Johns Outstanding Teacher Educator in Reading Award honors an outstanding college or university teacher of reading methods or reading-related courses. Nominees must be Association members, affiliated with a college or a university, and engaged in teacher preparation in reading at the undergraduate and/or graduate levels.

PURPOSE:
To promote literacy worldwide.

FINANCIAL DATA:
Amount of support per award: $1,000.

APPLICATION INFO:
Forms and guidelines can be obtained at the Association web site.
Deadline: March 15.

ADDRESS INQUIRIES TO:
Dawn Roberts, Human Resources Associate
E-mail: mroberts@reading.org
(See address above.)

JELLISON BENEVOLENT SOCIETY   [1399]
P.O. Box 145
Junction City, KS 66441-0145
(785) 762-5566
E-mail: s_williams1948@yahoo.com

FOUNDED: 1947

AREAS OF INTEREST:
Higher education.

TYPE:
Scholarships.

PURPOSE:
To aid area students in pursuit of higher education.

LEGAL BASIS:
Private foundation.

ELIGIBILITY:
Must be a high school senior or older, preferably a resident of Geary County, KS.

GEOG. RESTRICTIONS: Typically Geary County, Kansas.

FINANCIAL DATA:
Amount of support per award: $500 to $1,500 per semester.
Total amount of support: Varies.

NO. MOST RECENT APPLICANTS: 75.

NO. AWARDS: 71.

APPLICATION INFO:
Contact the Society for guidelines.
Duration: One year. Renewable by supplying copy of grades above 2.0.
Deadline: June 20 and November 20.

IRS I.D.: 48-6106092

STAFF:
Dale Ann Clore, President
Susan E. Williams, Secretary

ADDRESS INQUIRIES TO:
Susan E. Williams, Secretary
(See address above.)

WILLIAM R. KENAN, JR. CHARITABLE TRUST   [1400]
360 Kenan Center Drive, Floor 5
Chapel Hill, NC 27599
(919) 391-7222
Fax: (919) 962-3331
E-mail: dzinn@kenancharitabletrust.org
Web Site: www.kenancharitabletrust.org

FOUNDED: 1965

AREAS OF INTEREST:
Education, arts and arts education, and basic human needs.

TYPE:
Project/program grants.

PURPOSE:
To support educational programs of interest to the Trust.

LEGAL BASIS:
Private foundation.

ELIGIBILITY:
The Foundation does not accept unsolicited proposals.

GEOG. RESTRICTIONS: United States, primarily within Florida, Kentucky, New York and North Carolina.

FINANCIAL DATA:
Amount of support per award: Varies.
Total amount of support: Varies.

APPLICATION INFO:
Trustee's statement of guidelines, areas of interest and required procedures are available on request.
Duration: Varies.

ADDRESS INQUIRIES TO:
Douglas Zinn, Executive Director
(See address above.)

*PLEASE NOTE:
The Trust does not accept unsolicited proposals.

CHARLES G. KOCH CHARITABLE FOUNDATION   [1401]
1320 North Courthouse Road
Suite 500
Arlington, VA 22201
(703) 875-1770
Fax: (703) 875-1766
E-mail: grants@charleskochfoundation.org
Web Site: www.charleskochfoundation.org

FOUNDED: 1980

AREAS OF INTEREST:
Criminal justice, economic opportunity, education, foreign policy, free speech and peace, health care, immigration, principled entrepreneurship, science of liberty, and technology and innovation.

TYPE:
Fellowships; Project/program grants; Research grants; Seed money grants; Travel grants. Dissertation grants.

YEAR PROGRAM STARTED: 1980

PURPOSE:
To advance an understanding of how economic freedom improves the well-being of people around the world.

LEGAL BASIS:
Private foundation.

ELIGIBILITY:
The Foundation primarily makes grants to Section 501(c)(3) public charities. The Foundation does not support for-profit corporations or individuals. Grant proposals for capital construction, debt reduction, or general fund-raising drives or events are discouraged. The Foundation does not make grants intended to support lobbying activities or candidates for political office, and rarely funds endowments.

Proposals will be considered for dissertations across a variety of disciplines that examine foundational, system-level and applied research questions.

The Foundation invites recent Ph.D.s and doctoral candidates with an expected graduation date of spring 2022 to apply for postdoctoral fellowships.

GEOG. RESTRICTIONS: United States.

FINANCIAL DATA:
Amount of support per award: Dissertation grants: Up to $5,000; All others: Varies depending on program.

APPLICATION INFO:
Organizations seeking grants must submit a proposal online. If the proposal meets the initial requirements, it is reviewed to assess whether it fits within the Foundation's priorities. Prospective grantees may be contacted for further information.
Duration: Varies depending on needs and nature of the request.
Deadline: Proposals are evaluated on a rolling basis.

STAFF:
Brian Hooks, President
Vonda Holliman, Secretary and Treasurer
Ryan Stowers, Executive Director
Matthew Brown, Policy Research Director
Teri Akpovi, Senior Programs Recruiter
Hussein Hussein, Program Officer
Elizabeth Brannen, Human Resource Coordinator

ADDRESS INQUIRIES TO:
Teri Akpovi, Senior Programs Recruiter
(See address above.)

THE JEAN AND E. FLOYD KVAMME FOUNDATION [1402]

P.O. Box 2494
Saratoga, CA 95070
(408) 395-2829
Fax: (408) 354-0804

AREAS OF INTEREST:
Arts, charitable and cultural, education, health, medical research and Christian religious organizations.

TYPE:
Capital grants; Development grants; General operating grants; Project/program grants. Medical grants are given primarily in the areas of Alzheimers, leukemia, arthritis, and spondylitis; however, grants for research in other areas are considered.

PURPOSE:
To support organizations and institutes that promote arts, cultural, education, health, medical, scientific and social advancement of the international communities.

LEGAL BASIS:
Corporate contributions.

ELIGIBILITY:
Grants are made to organizations that have tax-exempt status under Section 501(c)(3) of the Internal Revenue Code and international Christian organizations. No grants are made to individuals.

GEOG. RESTRICTIONS: Artistic and educational grants: Northern California.

FINANCIAL DATA:
Amount of support per award: Varies.
Total amount of support: Varies.

APPLICATION INFO:
Applicants must submit a brief (one-page) letter of intent with a brief description of the project, dollar amount and verification of 501(c)(3) status.
Duration: One year.

TRUSTEE:
Jean Kvamme

ADDRESS INQUIRIES TO:
Jean Kvamme, Trustee
(See address above.)

LEARNING FOR LIFE [1403]

1325 West Walnut Hill Lane
Irving, TX 75038
(972) 580-2433
Fax: (214) 256-4078
E-mail: exploring@lflmail.org
Web Site: www.learningforlife.org
www.exploring.org

AREAS OF INTEREST:
Career opportunities, life skills, service learning, character education and leadership experience.

NAME(S) OF PROGRAMS:
• **Exploring Program**

TYPE:
Awards/prizes; Scholarships. Exploring provides exciting activities and one-on-one mentorship for youth looking to discover their future.

PURPOSE:
To provide young men and women, ages 10 to 20, with an opportunity to learn about a wide variety of career fields and network with professionals already working in those fields; to offer hands-on experience, valuable networking contacts and interaction with other youth who share the same interests and aspirations.

ELIGIBILITY:
Open to young men and women 10 to 20 years old. Must be a participant in the Learning for Life Exploring Program to receive scholarship.

FINANCIAL DATA:
Amount of support per award: Varies per award.
Total amount of support: Varies.

APPLICATION INFO:
Guidelines are available on the web site.
Duration: One year. Must reapply.
Deadline: Varies per program.

ADDRESS INQUIRIES TO:
Tim Anderson, Senior Director of Exploring, Team Lead
(See address above.)

MARSHALL COMMUNITY FOUNDATION [1404]

614 Homer Road
Marshall, MI 49068
(269) 781-2273
Fax: (269) 781-9747
E-mail: info@marshallcf.org
Web Site: www.marshallcf.org

FOUNDED: 1970

AREAS OF INTEREST:
Arts and education, culture, environment, health and well-being, human services, youth and seniors, and community/economic development.

TYPE:
Project/program grants; Scholarships.

YEAR PROGRAM STARTED: 1985

PURPOSE:
To support projects that promote the educational, recreational, environmental and cultural development of the Marshall area and Calhoun County.

LEGAL BASIS:
Community foundation.

ELIGIBILITY:
Grants are made to organizations that have tax-exempt status under Section 501(c)(3) and 509(a)(1) or (2) of the Internal Revenue Code. Nonsectarian religious programs meeting a general community need may apply. No grants are made to individuals.

GEOG. RESTRICTIONS: Calhoun County, Michigan.

FINANCIAL DATA:
Amount of support per award: Varies.
Total amount of support: Varies.

APPLICATION INFO:
Application information is available online.
Duration: One year.
Deadline: January 1, April 1, July 1 and October 1.

ADDRESS INQUIRIES TO:
Shannon Tiernan, Executive Director
(See address above.)

THE NAACP LEGAL DEFENSE AND EDUCATIONAL FUND, INC.

40 Rector Street
5th Floor
New York, NY 10006
(212) 965-2244
Fax: (212) 226-7592
E-mail: scholarships@naacpldf.org
eanderson@naacpldf.org
Web Site: www.naacpldf.org/scholarships

TYPE:
Awards/prizes; Grants-in-aid; Internships; Scholarships. LDF Herbert Lehman Education Fund Scholarship Program: Scholarships for African-American high school seniors, high school graduates and college freshmen to attend four-year accredited colleges and universities.

LDF Earl Warren Legal Training Program: Scholarships for law students to attend three-year accredited law schools.

See entry 934 for full listing.

THE NATIONAL ACADEMY OF EDUCATION [1405]

500 Fifth Street, N.W.
Washington, DC 20001
(202) 334-2341
Fax: (202) 334-2350
E-mail: info@naeducation.org
Web Site: www.naeducation.org

FOUNDED: 1965

AREAS OF INTEREST:
All aspects of educational research.

NAME(S) OF PROGRAMS:
• **National Academy of Education/Spencer Dissertation Fellowship**
• **National Academy of Education/Spencer Postdoctoral Fellowship**

TYPE:
Fellowships. The Dissertation Fellowship seeks to encourage a new generation of scholars from a wide range of disciplines and professional fields to undertake research relevant to the improvement of education. These fellowships support individuals whose dissertations show potential for bringing fresh and constructive perspectives to the history, theory or practice of formal or informal education anywhere in the world. The program develops the careers of its recipients through professional development activities involving the National Academy of Education.

The Postdoctoral Fellowship is nonresidential and funds proposals that make significant scholarly contributions to the field of education. The program develops the careers of its recipients through professional development activities involving National Academy of Education members.

PURPOSE:
To support early career scholars working in critical areas of education research.

LEGAL BASIS:
Private operating foundation.

ELIGIBILITY:
Dissertation Fellowship: Open to students at U.S. institutions. Non-U.S. citizens enrolled at a graduate school in the U.S. are eligible to apply. The basic selection criteria are the importance of the research question to education, the quality of the research

approach and feasibility of the work plan, and the applicant's future potential as a researcher and interest in educational research.

Postdoctoral Fellowship: Primary criterion for selection is promise as an educational research scholar, with special emphasis on potential to make a significant contribution to our understanding of education. Applicant must have received Ph.D., Ed.D. or equivalent degree in the past five years.

FINANCIAL DATA:
Dissertation Fellowship: The Fellowship funding is to support the writing of the dissertation only. The Fellowship funding must not be spent on data collection.

Postdoctoral Fellowship: Terms of the award do not permit institutional overhead. If the scholar transfers institutions, the grant transfers with him or her. The money may be spent toward any salary, supplies, etc., that aid the grantee in pursuing research described in the Fellowship application.
Amount of support per award: Dissertation Fellowship: $27,500 for one year. Postdoctoral Fellowship: $70,000 over one year, 18 months or two years.

NO. MOST RECENT APPLICANTS: Dissertation Fellowship: Approximately 400 annually. Postdoctoral Fellowship: Approximately 200 annually.

NO. AWARDS: Dissertation Fellowship: 35. Postdoctoral Fellowship: 25.

APPLICATION INFO:
Application material is available in June.
Duration: Dissertation Fellowship: One or two years. Postdoctoral Fellowship: Up to two years.
Deadline: Dissertation Fellowship: October 7. Postdoctoral Fellowship: November 17.

ADDRESS INQUIRIES TO:
See e-mail address above.

NATIONAL CENTER FOR LEARNING DISABILITIES [1406]
1220 L Street, N.W.
Suite 100, Box 168
Washington, DC 20005
(301) 966-2234
E-mail: afscholarship@ncld.org
info@ncld.org
Web Site: www.ncld.org/what-we-do/scholarships

FOUNDED: 2001

AREAS OF INTEREST:
Education and learning disabilities.

NAME(S) OF PROGRAMS:
● **Anne Ford Scholarship**
● **Allegra Ford Thomas Scholarship**

TYPE:
Scholarships. Anne Ford Scholarship is a four-year scholarship granted to a graduating high school senior with a documented learning disability and/or ADHD who will be enrolled in a full-time Bachelor's degree program.

Allegra Ford Thomas Scholarship is a one-time scholarship awarded to a graduating high school senior with a documented learning disability and/or ADHD who will be enrolled in a two-year community college, a vocational or technical training program, or a specialized program for students with LD.

YEAR PROGRAM STARTED: 2001

PURPOSE:
To support a high school senior of high merit with a documented learning disability and/or ADHD, who is pursuing an undergraduate degree.

LEGAL BASIS:
Nonprofit organization.

ELIGIBILITY:
Anne Ford Scholarship applicant must:
(1) be a graduating high school senior who will be attending a four-year Bachelor's degree and;
(2) provide most current documentation of an identified learning disability and/or ADHD.

Allegra Ford Thomas Scholarship applicant must:
(1) be a graduating high school senior who will be attending a two-year community college, a vocational/technical training program, or specialized program for students with LD;
(2) demonstrate financial need;
(3) provide most current documentation of an identified learning disability and/or ADHD and;
(4) be a U.S. citizen.

GEOG. RESTRICTIONS: United States.

FINANCIAL DATA:
Amount of support per award: Anne Ford Scholarship: $10,000 ($2,500 per year over four years). Allegra Ford Thomas Scholarship: $5,000 ($2,500 per year over two years).

NO. MOST RECENT APPLICANTS: Approximately 2,200.

NO. AWARDS: 1 of each award per year.

APPLICATION INFO:
Application information is available on the web site.
Duration: Anne Ford Scholarship: Four years. Allegra Ford Thomas Scholarship: Two years.
Deadline: Varies. Check web site for specific dates.

ADDRESS INQUIRIES TO:
NCLD Team
E-mail: afscholarship@ncld.org

*SPECIAL STIPULATIONS:
The scholars will be required to submit annual reports detailing their progress in school and describing their insights about their personal growth.

NATIONAL COUNCIL FOR THE SOCIAL STUDIES
8555 16th Street, Suite 500
Silver Spring, MD 20910
(301) 588-1800 ext. 110
(800) 296-7840
Fax: (301) 588-2049
E-mail: awards@ncss.org
Web Site: www.socialstudies.org

TYPE:
Awards/prizes; Grants-in-aid. The Septima Clark Book Awards were first presented in 2019 and are intended to recognize the most distinguished books and encourage the writing, publishing and dissemination of outstanding social studies books for young readers that treat topics related to women's issues sensitively and accurately.

Exemplary Research in Social Studies Award acknowledges and encourages scholarly inquiry into significant issues and possibilities for social studies education. Research must be published and have a social education focus.

Jean Dresden Grambs Distinguished Career in Social Studies Award recognizes professionals who have made extensive contributions to knowledge concerning significant areas of social studies education through meritorious research.

Larry Metcalf Exemplary Dissertation Award recognizes outstanding research completed in pursuit of the doctoral degree and encourages scholarly inquiry into significant issues and possibilities for social studies education. Research must be published and have a social education focus.

The annual NCSS Outstanding Teacher of the Year Awards recognize exceptional classroom social studies teachers for grades K-6, 5-8 and 7-12 who teach social studies regularly and systematically in elementary school settings, and at least half-time in middle or junior high and high school settings.

Carter G. Woodson Book Award encourages the writing, publishing and dissemination of outstanding social studies books for young readers that treat topics related to ethnic minorities and relations sensitively and accurately.

See entry 1665 for full listing.

NATIONAL COUNCIL FOR THE SOCIAL STUDIES
8555 16th Street, Suite 500
Silver Spring, MD 20910
(301) 588-1800 ext. 110
(800) 296-7840
Fax: (301) 588-2049
E-mail: awards@ncss.org
Web Site: www.socialstudies.org

TYPE:
Awards/prizes. Annual award for projects representing excellence and innovation in social studies education and having the potential of serving as a model for other teachers.

See entry 1666 for full listing.

NATIONAL COUNCIL FOR THE SOCIAL STUDIES
8555 16th Street, Suite 500
Silver Spring, MD 20910
(301) 588-1800 ext. 110
(800) 296-7840
Fax: (301) 588-2049
E-mail: awards@ncss.org
Web Site: www.socialstudies.org

TYPE:
Awards/prizes. Award to promote school geography education programs that encourage the integration of geography into the social studies curriculum/classroom and enhance the geographic literacy of students at the classroom, district or statewide level.

See entry 1667 for full listing.

NATIONAL COUNCIL FOR THE SOCIAL STUDIES

8555 16th Street, Suite 500
Silver Spring, MD 20910
(301) 588-1800 ext. 110
(800) 296-7840
Fax: (301) 588-2049
E-mail: awards@ncss.org
Web Site: www.socialstudies.org

TYPE:
Awards/prizes. Award for Global
Understanding recognizes a social studies
educator (or a team of educators) who has
made notable contributions in helping social
studies students increase their understanding
of the world.

See entry 1668 for full listing.

NATIONAL COUNCIL OF TEACHERS OF ENGLISH RESEARCH FOUNDATION [1407]

340 North Neil Street
Suite 104
Champaign, IL 61820
(217) 328-3870
(877) 369-6283
E-mail: researchfoundation@ncte.org
Web Site: www.ncte.org/research-foundation

FOUNDED: 1911

AREAS OF INTEREST:
Teaching and learning of language, literacy
and culture.

TYPE:
Project/program grants; Research grants.
Support for projects related to the teaching
and learning of language, literacy and
culture.

YEAR PROGRAM STARTED: 1960

PURPOSE:
To encourage research, experimentation and
investigation in the teaching of English.

LEGAL BASIS:
Separate entity within nonprofit, tax-exempt
organization.

ELIGIBILITY:
Applicants must be members of NCTE.
Funds are not available for commercial
teaching materials, dissertation support,
tuition expenses, indirect overhead or benefit
costs, previously incurred expenses related to
the project, researcher salaries, or
refreshments.

GEOG. RESTRICTIONS: United States.

NO. MOST RECENT APPLICANTS: 15.

NO. AWARDS: 2.

REPRESENTATIVE AWARDS:
Hui Jiang, Special Education Itinerant
Teacher, Marie Pense Center, NJ for
"Bringing Funds of Knowledge to School:
Culturally Responsive Approaches that
Connect Home Culture with School Practice
for Preschool-Aged Children in Chinese
Immigrant Families;" Toby Emert, Associate
Professor and Chair, Department of
Education, Agnes Scott College for "ESL
Learners and High-Tech Storytelling:
Promoting Academic Confidence;" Jennifer
Escobar, English Instructor, Moreno Valley
College for "Examining the Effects of a
Critical Reading Selection Framework and
Process in the Community College
Classroom."

APPLICATION INFO:
Applicant must submit an application cover
sheet, grant proposal and one-page resume.
Duration: Generally one year. Applicants
may reapply to Trustees for extension.
Deadline: Research Grant: March 15 in
odd-numbered years. Notification by June 1.
Teacher Research Grant: October 1 in
odd-numbered years. Notification by
December 3.

PUBLICATIONS:
Application guidelines.

IRS I.D.: 37-0715886

ADDRESS INQUIRIES TO:
See e-mail address above.

*PLEASE NOTE:
Research grants are awarded in alternating
years. Next grant cycle is 2021.

NATIONAL FOSTER PARENT ASSOCIATION

14508 Owen Tech Boulevard, No. 129
Austin, TX 78728
(512) 686-1948
(800) 557-5238
Fax: (888) 925-5634
E-mail: info@nfpaonline.org
Web Site: www.nfpaonline.org

TYPE:
Conferences/seminars; Scholarships.
Scholarships for youth living in foster
families whose foster parents are members of
NFPA.

Walk Me Home Program is a walk program
to raise awareness of foster care and the need
for more foster families, as well as to raise
funds for recruitment and other activities.

See entry 1026 for full listing.

NATIONAL INSTITUTE ON DRUG ABUSE [1408]

6001 Executive Boulevard, Room 4246
MSC 9550
Bethesda, MD 20892-9550
(301) 443-1124
E-mail: tracy.waldeck@nih.gov
Web Site: www.drugabuse.gov/funding/research-training

AREAS OF INTEREST:
Drug abuse and addiction.

TYPE:
Awards/prizes. The Institute supports a
variety of training and career development
grant awards for all career stages.

PURPOSE:
To support research training and/or career
development at predoctoral, postdoctoral
(including postresident or research-track
resident), and junior faculty levels.

ELIGIBILITY:
Specific eligibility criteria vary based on the
award.

FINANCIAL DATA:
Amount of support per award: Varies.

ADDRESS INQUIRIES TO:
Tracy Waldeck, Ph.D., Director
(See address above.)

NATIONAL MOLE DAY FOUNDATION

3896 Leaman Court
Freeland, MI 48623
(989) 964-8020
E-mail: moleday@hotmail.com
Web Site: www.moleday.org

TYPE:
Grants-in-aid. The George Hague Memorial
Travel Award is given to financially support a
young chemistry instructor (with two to five
years of chemistry experience) in attending a
biennial ChemEd conference.

The National Mole of the Year Award
(MOTY) is given to a member of the
National Mole Day Foundation who has
contributed the most to furthering the cause
of Mole Day and chemistry education.

See entry 1859 for full listing.

NATIONAL OCEANIC AND ATMOSPHERIC ADMINISTRATION [1409]

200 Harry S. Truman Parkway
Suite 460
Annapolis, MD 21401
(410) 267-5660
Fax: (410) 267-5666
E-mail: andrew.w.larkin@noaa.gov
Web Site: chesapeakebay.noaa.gov

FOUNDED: 1985

AREAS OF INTEREST:
Fisheries habitat, ecosystem services, and
ecosystem-based fisheries research in
Chesapeake Bay.

NAME(S) OF PROGRAMS:
● **Chesapeake Bay Fisheries Research
Program**

TYPE:
Project/program grants; Research grants.
Research cooperative agreements.

YEAR PROGRAM STARTED: 1985

PURPOSE:
To support stock assessment, multispecies
and ecosystem-based fisheries research in
Chesapeake Bay.

LEGAL BASIS:
Government agency.

ELIGIBILITY:
Individuals who are U.S. citizens or residents
and organizations, including religious,
classified as 501(c)(3) by the IRS can apply.

GEOG. RESTRICTIONS: United States, with a
focus on Chesapeake Bay/mid-Atlantic.

FINANCIAL DATA:
Amount of support per award: Up to
$250,000.
Total amount of support: Up to $500,000.

NO. MOST RECENT APPLICANTS: 10.

NO. AWARDS: 2 to 4.

APPLICATION INFO:
Application information is available on the
web site. RFPs released between October and
February.
Duration: Multiyear.
Deadline: Varies each year.

PUBLICATIONS:
Application guidelines; annual report.

ADDRESS INQUIRIES TO:
Andrew Larkin, Grants Manager
National Marine Fisheries Service
(See address above.)

NATIONAL SCIENCE FOUNDATION

Directorate for Education and Human Resources
Division of Research on Learning in Formal and Informal Settings
2415 Eisenhower Avenue
Alexandria, VA 22314
(703) 292-8620
Fax: (703) 292-9044; (703) 292-9046
E-mail: acarroll@nsf.gov
Web Site: www.nsf.gov

TYPE:
Conferences/seminars; Demonstration grants; Development grants; Project/program grants; Research grants; Training grants. Advanced Informal STEM Learning (AISL) program invests in projects that develop and implement informal learning experiences designed to increase interest, engagement and understanding of science, technology, engineering and mathematics (STEM) by individuals of all ages and backgrounds, as well as projects that advance knowledge and practice of informal science education.

With an emphasis on two-year colleges, the Advanced Technological Education (ATE) program focuses on the education of technicians for the high-technology fields that drive the nation's economy.

Discovery Research PreK-12 (DR K12) funds research, development and evaluation activities through knowledge generation and application to improve PreK-12 learning and teaching.

Innovative Technology Experiences for Students and Teachers (ITEST) is designed to increase the opportunities for students and teachers to learn about, experience, and use information technologies within the context of science, technology, engineering and mathematics (STEM), including Information Technology (IT) courses. It is in direct response to the concern about shortages of information technology workers in the U.S.

Research and Evaluation on Education in Science and Engineering (REESE) supports basic and applied research and evaluation that enhances science, technology, engineering and mathematics (STEM) learning and teaching.

See entry 1436 for full listing.

NATIVE AMERICAN COMMUNITY BOARD (NACB)   [1410]
P.O. Box 572
Lake Andes, SD 57356-0572
(605) 487-7097
(605) 487-7072
Fax: (605) 487-7964
E-mail: charon@charles-mix.com
Web Site: www.nativeshop.org

AREAS OF INTEREST:
Native American women.

NAME(S) OF PROGRAMS:
● **NACB Internship Program**

TYPE:
Internships. Internships at the Native American Women's Health Education Resource Center and the Women's Lodge.

PURPOSE:
To support young women interested in learning about indigenous issues and willing to serve indigenous communities.

LEGAL BASIS:
Nonprofit tax-exempt 501(c)(3) organization.

ELIGIBILITY:
Internships are open to college and graduate students or recent graduates looking for some work experience. Applicants need to be interested in Native American rights and health issues and have a desire to actively promote civil rights, women's rights and a healthy environment. Priority will be given to those wishing to stay six months or longer.

FINANCIAL DATA:
Internship includes free room at the shelter and partial board from the Resource Center's food pantry.
Amount of support per award: $500 per month.
Total amount of support: Varies.

APPLICATION INFO:
A resume with references is required, and the Board needs to know the time frame in which the intern expects to serve. Applicant should mail personal resume to the Internship Coordinator; Native American Women's Health Education Resource Center; at the mailing address above, send it to the fax number above or e-mail it to the address above.
Duration: Three months to one year.
Deadline: Internship positions are available all year-round.

ADDRESS INQUIRIES TO:
Charon Asetoyer, Executive Director
(See e-mail address above.) or

The Native American Women's
Health Education Resource Center
(See telephone numbers above.)

*PLEASE NOTE:
Each intern will be assigned to the Resource Center and to the Domestic Violence Shelter, which is located nearby. After arrival and an orientation period, assignments will be given out based on the individual's experience, strengths, interests and, if necessary, academic requirements.

THE NEA FOUNDATION   [1411]
1201 16th Street, N.W., Suite 416
Washington, DC 20036
(202) 822-7840
Fax: (202) 822-7779
E-mail: neafoundation@nea.org
Web Site: www.neafoundation.org

AREAS OF INTEREST:
Public education.

NAME(S) OF PROGRAMS:
● **Awards for Teaching Excellence**

TYPE:
Awards/prizes. Recognizes and awards the excellence demonstrated by educators nationwide.

PURPOSE:
To advance student achievement, through the unique strength of the Foundation's partnership with educators, by investing in public education that will prepare each of America's children to learn and thrive in a rapidly changing world.

ELIGIBILITY:
Each NEA affiliate may nominate one educator. All current members of an NEA local affiliate or bargaining unit are eligible, including teachers, education support professionals, and higher education faculty and staff.

GEOG. RESTRICTIONS: United States.

FINANCIAL DATA:
Amount of support per award: State level: $650 gift to teacher's school and travel to Annual Salute to Excellence in Education Gala. Five finalists from the state level: $10,000 courtesy of the Horace Mann Educators Corporation. National awardee: $25,000 total from NEA Member Benefits Company.

APPLICATION INFO:
Applicants must complete proposals through the Foundation's online grant system.
Deadline: May 1.

THE NEA FOUNDATION   [1412]
1201 16th Street, N.W., Suite 416
Washington, DC 20036-3207
(202) 822-7840
Fax: (202) 822-7779
E-mail: neafoundation@nea.org
Web Site: www.neafoundation.org

FOUNDED: 1969

AREAS OF INTEREST:
Education.

NAME(S) OF PROGRAMS:
● **NEA Foundation Learning and Leadership Grants**
● **NEA Foundation Student Success Grants**

YEAR PROGRAM STARTED: 1999

PURPOSE:
To improve the academic achievement of students in U.S. public schools and public higher education institutions in any subject area(s); to support public school teachers, public education support professionals, and/or faculty and staff in public institutions of higher education.

ELIGIBILITY:
Applicants must be practicing U.S. public school teachers in grades PreK-12, public school education support professionals, or faculty or staff at public higher education institutions.

Applicants must be members of the National Education Association. The NEA Foundation encourages grant applications from education support professionals.

Learning and Leadership Grant: All professional development must improve practice, curriculum, and student achievement. Decisions regarding the content of the professional growth activities must be based upon an assessment of student work undertaken with colleagues, and must be integrated into the institutional planning process. Funds may not be used to pursue degrees, pay direct costs, grant administration fees, or salaries, or support travel costs or conference fees for more than one person.

Student Success Grant: The proposed work should engage students in critical thinking and problem solving that deepens their knowledge of standards-based subject matter. The work should also improve students' habits of inquiry, self-directed learning, and critical reflection. Proposals for work resulting in low-income and minority student success with honors, advanced placement, or other challenging curricula are particularly encouraged. Funds may be used for resource materials, supplies, equipment, transportation, software, or scholars-in-residence. Although some funds may be used to support the professional development necessary to implement the project, the majority of grant funds must be spent on materials or educational experiences for students.

GEOG. RESTRICTIONS: United States.

FINANCIAL DATA:
Amount of support per award: Learning and Leadership Grants: $2,000 (individuals) and $5,000 (groups engaged in collegial study); Student Success Grants: $2,000 and $5,000.

NO. AWARDS: Approximately 120 annually.

APPLICATION INFO:
All proposals must be submitted through the Foundation's online grant system.
Duration: Annual. Nonrenewable.
Deadline: February 28 and December 1.

ADDRESS INQUIRIES TO:
Jesse Graytock, Program Manager
(See address above.)

NELLIE MAE EDUCATION FOUNDATION [1413]
1250 Hancock Street, Suite 701N
Quincy, MA 02169
(781) 348-4200
E-mail: info@nmefoundation.org
Web Site: www.nmefoundation.org

FOUNDED: 1998

AREAS OF INTEREST:
Systems change and racial equity in public education.

TYPE:
Matching gifts; Research grants.

YEAR PROGRAM STARTED: 1998

PURPOSE:
To promote accessibility, quality and effectiveness of education, especially for underserved populations in the six New England states.

LEGAL BASIS:
Public charity.

ELIGIBILITY:
Organizations must be 501(c)(3) or public schools. No grants are made to individuals.

GEOG. RESTRICTIONS: Connecticut, Maine, Massachusetts, New Hampshire, Rhode Island and Vermont.

FINANCIAL DATA:
Amount of support per award: Varies.
Total amount of support: Varies.

APPLICATION INFO:
Open grant opportunities are posted online.
Duration: Varies.
Deadline: Varies.

ADDRESS INQUIRIES TO:
Ellen Wang, Senior Program Officer
E-mail: ewang@nmefoundation.org

NICSA [1414]
225 Franklin Avenue
26th Floor
Boston, MA 02110
(508) 485-1500
Fax: (508) 485-1560
E-mail: info@nicsa.org
Web Site: www.nicsa.org

FOUNDED: 1962

AREAS OF INTEREST:
Education.

NAME(S) OF PROGRAMS:
● **The NICSA/William T. Blackwell Scholarship Fund**

TYPE:
Scholarships.

PURPOSE:
To provide leadership and innovation in educational programming and information exchange within the operations sector of the mutual fund industry worldwide; to recognize outstanding students of the NICSA Family with financial support for postsecondary education.

ELIGIBILITY:
Applicants must be dependent children of full-time employees of NICSA member companies and be enrolled in or planning to pursue a full-time course of study leading to a Bachelor's degree from an accredited four-year college or university.

Must maintain a 3.0 grade point average for renewal.

FINANCIAL DATA:
Amount of support per award: Up to $5,000 per year.
Total amount of support: Maximum of $20,000 per student over four years.

NO. MOST RECENT APPLICANTS: 50.

NO. AWARDS: 5 new and 10 renewals.

APPLICATION INFO:
Application information is available online.
Duration: Up to four years.
Deadline: May 1.

ADDRESS INQUIRIES TO:
See e-mail address above.

NORTH CAROLINA GLAXOSMITHKLINE FOUNDATION [1415]
5 Moore Drive
P.O. Box 13398
Research Triangle Park, NC 27709
(919) 483-2140
Fax: (919) 315-3015
E-mail: info@ncgskfoundation.org
Web Site: www.ncgskfoundation.org

FOUNDED: 1986

AREAS OF INTEREST:
Science, health and education at all educational and professional levels.

NAME(S) OF PROGRAMS:
● **Child Health Recognition Awards**
● **Ribbon of Hope**
● **Traditional Grants**
● **Women in Science Scholars Program**

TYPE:
Project/program grants; Seed money grants. Support for activities which help meet the educational and health needs of today's society and future generations.

Child Health Recognition Awards program honors local health departments, public health staff, and individuals for innovative, collaborative programs that improve the lives of North Carolina's children.

Ribbon of Hope provides one-time grants to nonprofits for projects furthering health, science and education in their communities.

The Traditional Grants program provides for larger grants that may be multiyear in nature, to support programs advancing health, science and education throughout the state of North Carolina.

Women in Science Scholars Program offers an educational opportunity to young women by coupling college scholarships with a mentoring program.

YEAR PROGRAM STARTED: 1986

PURPOSE:
To provide programs that emphasize the understanding and applications of science, health and education at all academic and professional levels.

LEGAL BASIS:
Foundation.

ELIGIBILITY:
Ribbon of Hope: North Carolina community-based nonprofit, charitable organizations and institutions exempt under Section 501(c)(3) of the Internal Revenue Code are eligible to apply. Individuals may not apply. Nonprofits with proposals pertaining to science, health and education as well as collaborative partnerships between several community-based organizations are encouraged to apply.

Traditional Grants: Grant applicants must be nonprofit, charitable organizations and institutions exempt under Section 501(c)(3) of the Internal Revenue Code. No grants are made to individuals, for construction or restoration projects, or for international programs. The primary focus of the Foundation is to provide seed funds for new and worthwhile educational programs. This policy does not preclude the consideration and possible funding of ongoing projects.

GEOG. RESTRICTIONS: North Carolina.

FINANCIAL DATA:
Amount of support per award: Varies.
Total amount of support: Varies.

REPRESENTATIVE AWARDS:
Ribbon of Hope: Airlie Gardens Foundation, New Hanover County, to support the "Educator in the Gardens" program; Cradle of Forestry in America Interpretive Association, Transylvania County, to support programming that provides learning experiences on forest ecology, accessing public lands safely, and improving overall health through guided hikes, field trips, and natural science education classes; Anson County Partnership for Children, Anson County, to launch the Motheread program, providing parents with lessons to gain literacy skills and ways to also effectively teach their children literacy skills.

Traditional Grants: $1,577,718 (over five years) to The University of North Carolina-Asheville to support the Chemistry and Biology Fellows and Scholars undergraduate research; $1,100,000 (over four years) to The Hill Center to build statewide effectiveness, diversity, and scale their initiatives to provide educational support to struggling students; $125,000 to Bladen County Community College to develop a writing center for students.

APPLICATION INFO:
Applications are submitted through the Foundation web site.
Duration: Ribbon of Hope: One-time grant; Traditional Grants: Up to five years.
Deadline: Child Health Recognition Awards: May 31. Ribbon of Hope: April 1 and October 1. Traditional Grants: January 1, April 1, July 1 and October 1.

PUBLICATIONS:
Annual report; application; brochure.

IRS I.D.: 58-1698610

STAFF:
Marilyn E. Foote-Hudson, Executive Director

BOARD OF DIRECTORS:
Robert A. Ingram, Chairman
Margaret B. Dardess, President
Thomas R. Haber, Treasurer
Paul A. Holcombe, Jr., Secretary

ADDRESS INQUIRIES TO:
See e-mail address above.

OAK GROVE SCHOOL FOUNDATION   [1416]
P.O. Box 150
South China, ME 04358
(207) 445-3333
E-mail: austinlaw@fairpoint.net
Web Site: www.ogsfoundation.org

FOUNDED: 1989

AREAS OF INTEREST:
Education, secondary school curriculum
augmenting, limited secondary school
scholarships, and some not-for-profits.

NAME(S) OF PROGRAMS:
● **Grants Program**
● **Tuition Assistance**

TYPE:
Demonstration grants; General operating
grants; Grants-in-aid; Project/program grants;
Scholarships. Scholarships are for Quaker
high schools.

YEAR PROGRAM STARTED: 1991

PURPOSE:
To foster secondary education innovation in
proximate geographic area; to provide tuition
assistance.

LEGAL BASIS:
Private foundation.

ELIGIBILITY:
Secondary schools and 501(c)(3)
organizations in Central Maine. For tuition
assistance, candidates may be either currently
enrolled or accepted for enrollment in a
Quaker secondary school and must be a
resident of Maine.

GEOG. RESTRICTIONS: Central Maine.

FINANCIAL DATA:
Amount of support per award: Grants: $3,000
to $5,000; Scholarships: Varies.

Total amount of support: Approximately
$130,000 annually.

NO. MOST RECENT APPLICANTS: Approximately
150.

NO. AWARDS: Approximately 75 yearly.

APPLICATION INFO:
Application forms are available from the
Foundation web site.

Duration: Grants: One year. Renewal
possible upon review for up to two more
years.

Deadline: Large grants: April 1. Small
grants: Early October.

IRS I.D.: 01-0211537

ADDRESS INQUIRIES TO:
Joann Austin, Counselor and Attorney at Law
Austin Law
(See address above.)

THE MABEL LOUISE RILEY FOUNDATION   [1417]
2 Liberty Square
Suite 500
Boston, MA 02109
(617) 399-1850
Fax: (617) 399-1851
E-mail: info@rileyfoundation.com
Web Site: www.rileyfoundation.com

FOUNDED: 1972

AREAS OF INTEREST:
Emphasis on priority needs in social services,
human services and education, especially for
youth, community development including
cultural, housing and urban environmental
programs.

TYPE:
Capital grants; Challenge/matching grants;
Development grants; Project/program grants;
Seed money grants; Training grants.

LEGAL BASIS:
Private foundation.

ELIGIBILITY:
Requests are considered only from
corporations organized under the laws of
Massachusetts for purposes to be carried out
within Massachusetts and those who have a
501(c)(3) IRS determination.

GEOG. RESTRICTIONS: Greater Boston area, with
a primary focus on the city of Boston,
Massachusetts.

FINANCIAL DATA:
Amount of support per award: $50,000 to
$100,000.

Total amount of support: $3,163,333 for the
year 2019.

NO. AWARDS: 40.

APPLICATION INFO:
Applicants are required to submit a brief
summary (LOI) of their proposal, not more
than two pages, without a cover letter before
submitting a formal grant request. This
summary should briefly describe the purposes
and objectives of the proposal, a brief history
of the applicant and the amount requested
from the Foundation. In addition to the
two-page summary, a copy of the IRS
501(c)(3) Determination Letter and a
program budget relative to the request should
be included.

The Foundation will notify the applicant if
the submission of a formal grant request is
invited. Formal grant proposal must be made
using the Common Proposal Form of
Philanthropy Massachusetts.

Duration: One year. Renewals possible.
Two-year waiting period is requested before
applying again for those who have been
awarded a grant.

Deadline: Meetings are held in March, June,
September and December with deadlines for
receipt of full grant proposals set 60 days
prior to each meeting.

PUBLICATIONS:
Guidelines.

IRS I.D.: 04-6278857

TRUSTEES:
Grace Fey
Robert W. Holmes, Jr.
Joannie Jaxtimer

ADDRESS INQUIRIES TO:
Nancy A. Saunders, Administrator
(See address above.)

ROSS FOUNDATION
202 South Fifth Street
Arkadelphia, AR 71923
(870) 246-9881
Fax: (870) 246-9674
E-mail: info@rossfoundation.us
Web Site: www.rossfoundation.us

TYPE:
Conferences/seminars; Matching gifts;
Project/program grants; Research grants.

See entry 1234 for full listing.

GEORGE J. AND EFFIE L. SEAY MEMORIAL TRUST
Mail Code TAOBFB
P.O. Box 1517
Pennington, NJ 08534
(202) 442-7460
E-mail: dc.grantmaking@ustrust.com
Web Site: www.bankofamerica.
com/philanthropic/foundation.go

TYPE:
Project/program grants. Grants for specific
needs.

See entry 1357 for full listing.

SMITHSONIAN ENVIRONMENTAL RESEARCH CENTER (SERC)
647 Contees Wharf Road
Edgewater, MD 21037
(443) 482-2217
Fax: (443) 482-2380
E-mail: gustafsond@si.edu
Web Site: serc.si.edu

TYPE:
Fellowships; Internships. The Internship
Program enables undergraduates, recent
graduates and graduate students to work on
specific projects under the direction of the
Center's professional staff and is tailored to
provide the maximum educational benefit to
each participant. Graduate students and
undergraduates may conduct independent
projects with the approval of the staff
member with whom they plan to study.

Subject matter of the projects includes
terrestrial and estuarine environmental
research within the disciplines of
mathematics, chemistry, microbiology,
botany, zoology, and environmental
education.

Fellowships are offered annually at the
postdoctoral, predoctoral and graduate levels.

Internships are offered three times per year at
the undergraduate levels, recent graduate, or
beginning Master's student.

See entry 1983 for full listing.

SPENCER FOUNDATION   [1418]
625 North Michigan Avenue
Suite 1600
Chicago, IL 60611
(312) 337-7000
Fax: (312) 337-0282
E-mail: abrinkman@spencer.org
Web Site: www.spencer.org

FOUNDED: 1962

AREAS OF INTEREST:
Research on education as approached from scholars in the social sciences and humanities.

NAME(S) OF PROGRAMS:
- **Conference Grants**
- **Large Research Grants**
- **Research-Practice Partnershp Grants**
- **Small Research Grants**
- **Lyle Spencer Research Awards**

TYPE:
Research grants. Conference grants. Grants for research to expand knowledge and understanding of the problems and processes of education.

YEAR PROGRAM STARTED: 1970

PURPOSE:
To support research that gives promise of yielding new knowledge leading to the improvement of education, broadly defined.

LEGAL BASIS:
Independent foundation.

ELIGIBILITY:
The Foundation is interested in a wide variety of disciplinary and interdisciplinary approaches to the study of education. The principal investigator ordinarily must have an earned Doctorate in an academic discipline or in the field of education and must have an affiliation with a nonprofit organization such as a college or university, a research facility, or a cultural institution.

FINANCIAL DATA:
Amount of support per award: Varies.

Total amount of support: Approximately $24,000,000 annually.

NO. MOST RECENT APPLICANTS: Approximately 2,000.

NO. AWARDS: 150.

APPLICATION INFO:
Application procedures differ by program. Researchers seeking support should view the Foundation's web site for general program information.

Duration: Varies.

Deadline: Varies.

PUBLICATIONS:
Annual report.

OFFICERS:
Na'ilah Suad Nasir, President

BOARD OF DIRECTORS:
Pamela Grossman, Chairperson
Richard Murnane, Vice Chairperson
Carl Cohen
Na'ilah Suad Nasir
Erick Odmark
Eduardo Padron
Rob Reich
Cecilia Rios-Aguilar
Mark Vander Ploeg
Mike Williams

ADDRESS INQUIRIES TO:
Annie Brinkman, Director of Grants Administration
(See address above.)

SUBARU OF AMERICA FOUNDATION, INC. [1419]
One Subaru Drive
Camden, NJ 08103
(856) 488-5099
Fax: (856) 254-1367
E-mail: foundation@subaru.com
Web Site: www.subaru.com/about-subaru/subaru-foundation

FOUNDED: 1984

AREAS OF INTEREST:
Career exploration for at-risk middle and high school students and job training for unemployed and underemployed young adults, ages 16 to 26.

TYPE:
General operating grants; Project/program grants. Employee matching gift program.

YEAR PROGRAM STARTED: 1984

PURPOSE:
To help un- and low-employed young people become self-sufficient through job training, mentoring and work experience leading to obtaining and retaining employment.

LEGAL BASIS:
Corporate foundation.

ELIGIBILITY:
Only organizations that are tax exempt under section 501(c)(3) of the Internal Revenue Code may apply. The Foundation will consider partnerships with established organizations with proven records of success in training and gainful employment strategies that achieve the following:
(1) work with underserved communities and youth ages 16 to 26;
(2) help develop the soft and hard skills necessary to connect to employment pathways;
(3) provide STEAM-based training leading to employment opportunities;
(4) provide a support network for mentoring, coaching and counseling as it relates to building employment skills and eliminating barriers to success;
(5) assist in obtaining industry-appropriate certifications that may aid in getting employment;
(6) create and nurture partnerships for internships and job placement and;
(7) track employment of participants for at least one year past graduation.

GEOG. RESTRICTIONS: Only proposals serving the geographic locations listed will be considered:
Corporate Headquarters: southern New Jersey (mainly Camden and Burlington counties);
Eastern Region: Washington, District of Columbia; Orlando, Florida; Atlanta, Georgia; Frederick, Howard, Montgomery and Prince Georges counties in Maryland; Florence, New Jersey; Philadelphia, Pennsylvania and Fairfax, Loudon and Prince William counties in Virginia;
Central Region: Chicago, Illinois; Minneapolis, Minnesota; Columbus, Ohio; and Dallas, Texas;
Western Region: Phoenix, Arizona; Los Angeles, San Diego and San Francisco, California; Denver, Colorado; Portland, Oregon; and Seattle, Washington.

FINANCIAL DATA:
Amount of support per award: Varies.

Matching fund requirements: Contributions for the matching gift program must be made by Subaru of America employees at a $25 minimum or $2,000 maximum per employee per fiscal year.

APPLICATION INFO:
Application form is available online as a Word document. Grant application and all required supporting documentation must be submitted at the same time as one package and should be mailed to the address above to arrive by the deadline (not postmarked by the deadline). Grant applications with missing information or documentation will not be considered.
Deadline: March 30 and October 12.

IRS I.D.: 22-2531774

ADDRESS INQUIRIES TO:
Foundation Manager
(See address above.)

TAILHOOK EDUCATIONAL FOUNDATION [1420]
9696 Business Park Avenue
San Diego, CA 92131-1643
(858) 689-9223
Fax: (858) 578-8839
E-mail: rlw@tailhook.net
Web Site: tailhook.net/tef-home

FOUNDED: 1992

AREAS OF INTEREST:
Education.

NAME(S) OF PROGRAMS:
- **Tailhook Educational Foundation Scholarship Award**

TYPE:
Scholarships. The Foundation awards merit-based scholarships.

YEAR PROGRAM STARTED: 1992

PURPOSE:
To support dependents of the Naval Aviation community with their educational needs.

LEGAL BASIS:
501(c)(3).

ELIGIBILITY:
To be eligible for consideration, an individual must be a high school graduate and the natural, step, or adopted son, daughter, or grandchild of a current or former (U.S. Navy, U.S. Marine Corps or U.S. Coast Guard) Naval Aviator, Naval Flight Officer, or Naval Aircrewman. Also eligible are individuals or children/grandchildren of individuals who are serving or have served on board a U.S. Navy Aircraft Carrier in ship's company or the Air Wing. Eligible applicants must be accepted for undergraduate enrollment at an accredited college.

GEOG. RESTRICTIONS: United States.

FINANCIAL DATA:
Amount of support per award: $2,500 to $15,000.

Total amount of support: $311,000.

NO. MOST RECENT APPLICANTS: Approximately 700 for the year 2018.

NO. AWARDS: 107 for the year 2018.

APPLICATION INFO:
Application is available on the web site beginning December 15.
Duration: One year. Must reapply.
Deadline: March 1.

IRS I.D.: 33-0487778

TRIANGLE COMMUNITY FOUNDATION   [1421]

800 Park Offices Drive, Suite 201
Research Triangle Park, NC 27709
(919) 474-8370
Fax: (919) 941-9208
E-mail: rutina@trianglecf.org
Web Site: www.trianglecf.org

AREAS OF INTEREST:
Arts and culture, education, environment, health care, human services, foreign affairs, society, and religion.

TYPE:
Grants-in-aid; Scholarships. General grantmaking.

YEAR PROGRAM STARTED: 1984

PURPOSE:
To expand philanthropy.

ELIGIBILITY:
Organizations, including religious, classified as 501(c)(3) by the IRS can apply. No grants to individuals.

GEOG. RESTRICTIONS: Chatham, Durham, Orange and Wake counties, North Carolina.

FINANCIAL DATA:
Amount of support per award: Minimum $250.

Total amount of support: Varies.

NO. AWARDS: 4,488 grants for fiscal year 2019-20.

APPLICATION INFO:
Application must be submitted through the Online Grant Application Portal.
Duration: Grants are not renewable.

PUBLICATIONS:
Annual report.

ADDRESS INQUIRIES TO:
Rutina Bailey, Grants Manager or Sarah Battersby, Senior Scholarships and Education Officer
(See address above.)

U.S. DEPARTMENT OF EDUCATION   [1422]

550 12th Street, S.W.
Washington, DC 20024
(202) 245-7274
Fax: (202) 245-6752
E-mail: ies@ed.gov
ellie.pelaez@ed.gov
Web Site: ies.ed.gov

FOUNDED: 1972

AREAS OF INTEREST:
Basic and applied research, evaluations and analyses in education practice and policy.

NAME(S) OF PROGRAMS:
• **Education Research**

TYPE:
Project/program grants; Research grants. Grants competitions.

The Institute supports research on a diverse set of student outcomes including: school readiness for prekindergarten; academic outcomes in kindergarten through Grade 12 that include learning, achievement, and higher order thinking in the core academic content areas of reading, writing, mathematics, and science measured by specific assessments (e.g.,

researcher-developed assessments, standardized tests, grades, end of course exams, exit exams) as well as course completion, grade retention, high school graduation and dropout rates; social skills, dispositions, and behaviors that support academic outcomes for students from prekindergarten through high school; access to, retention in, and completion of postsecondary education; and reading, writing, and mathematics skills for adult learners (i.e., students at least 16 years old and outside of the K-12 system). The Institute supports research from prekindergarten through Grade 12 for the typically developing student. For postsecondary and adult learners the Institute supports research on typically developing students and students with disabilities. The Institute supports research on students with disabilities from birth through high school through a different grant program run by the Institute's National Center for Special Education Research.

LEGAL BASIS:
Public Law 92-318, as amended.

ELIGIBILITY:
Applicants must be colleges, universities, state departments of education, local education agencies, other public or private profit and nonprofit agencies, organizations, groups and individuals. Support is restricted to basic and applied research, planning studies, evaluations, investigations, experiments and developmental activities directly related to research in the field of education.

Most funds provide continuing support for long-term research and development programs. The remaining funds are used for new projects, announced as Grants Competitions in specific areas of interest.

FINANCIAL DATA:
Amount of support per award: Varies.
Total amount of support: Varies.

APPLICATION INFO:
Application information is available on the web site.
Duration: Varies.
Deadline: Specific date changes each year, but application deadlines generally fall between June and September.

ADDRESS INQUIRIES TO:
Ellie Pelaez
Management and Program Analyst
(See above address.)

U.S. DEPARTMENT OF EDUCATION   [1423]

Office of Career, Technical and Adult Education
550 12th Street, S.W., 11th Floor
Washington, DC 20202-7100
(202) 245-7700
Fax: (202) 245-7838
E-mail: octae@ed.gov
Web Site: www2.ed.gov/about/offices/list/ovae

FOUNDED: 1965

AREAS OF INTEREST:
Adult basic education, basic literacy skills, English as a second language and adult secondary education.

CONSULTING OR VOLUNTEER SERVICES:
Technical assistance is provided to state educational agencies.

TYPE:
Grants-in-aid. The program provides grants to states to fund local programs of adult education and literacy services, including workplace literacy services, family literacy services, English language learning and integrated English literacy/civics education programs. Basic grants to all states including the District of Columbia as well as the Virgin Islands, American Samoa, Guam, Northern Mariana Islands and Palau.

YEAR PROGRAM STARTED: 1965

PURPOSE:
To provide educational opportunities for educationally disadvantaged adults.

LEGAL BASIS:
The Adult Education and Family Literacy Act (AEFLA), enacted as Title II of the Workforce Investment Act (WIA) of 1998, is the principal source of federal support for adult basic and literacy education programs for adults who lack basic skills, a high school diploma, or proficiency in English.

ELIGIBILITY:
Individuals and local providers cannot receive grant money directly from the Office of Vocational and Adult Education (OVAE).

Adult education and literacy programs are funded through federal grants to the states. The amount each state receives is based on a formula established by Congress. States, in turn, distribute funds to local eligible entities to provide adult education and literacy services.

The Division provides assistance to states to improve program quality and capacity.

GEOG. RESTRICTIONS: United States and its territories.

FINANCIAL DATA:
AEFLA funds are distributed by formula to states using census data on the number of adults (ages 16 and older) in each state who lack a high school diploma and who are not enrolled in school. States must match 25% of the federal contribution with state or local funds, but many states contribute considerably more.

Amount of support per award: Varies.

Total amount of support: Approximately $1.9 billion annually.

Matching fund requirements: 25% of grant award.

NO. MOST RECENT APPLICANTS: 57.

NO. AWARDS: 57.

APPLICATION INFO:
Applicants interested in participating in the State-Administered Program should contact the appropriate state educational agency for information.

Duration: One year and continuing based on appropriations.

ADDRESS INQUIRIES TO:
Office of Career, Technical and Adult Education
Adult Education and Literacy Division
400 Maryland Avenue, S.W.
Washington, DC 20202-7100

U.S. DEPARTMENT OF EDUCATION [1424]

Office of English Language Acquisition
LBJ Education Building, MS-6510
400 Maryland Avenue, S.W.
Washington, DC 20202-6510
(202) 401-1433 (NPD Program)
(202) 453-6054 (NAM Program)
Web Site: www.ed.gov/offices/oela

AREAS OF INTEREST:
English language acquisition, language enhancement and academic achievement for Limited English Proficient (LEP) children.

NAME(S) OF PROGRAMS:
- **National Professional Development Program**
- **Native American and Alaska Native Children in School Program**

TYPE:
Formula grants. National Professional Development Program provides grants for eligible entities to implement professional development activities intended to improve instruction for English Learners (ELs) and assists education personnel working with ELs to meet high professional standards. Professional development activities may include both pre-service and in-service activities.

Native American and Alaska Native Children in School Program awards grants to eligible entities to develop and enhance capacity to provide effective instruction and support to Native American students who are identified as English Learners (ELs). The goal of this program is to support the teaching, learning and studying of Native American languages while also increasing the English language proficiency of students served to achieve the same challenging state academic content and achievement standards for all students.

YEAR PROGRAM STARTED: 1968

LEGAL BASIS:
Elementary and Secondary Education Act of 1965, as amended by No Child Left Behind Act of 2001.

ELIGIBILITY:
National Professional Development Program: Institutions of higher education in consortia with local education agencies or state education agencies may apply.

Native American and Alaska Native Children in School Program: Entities that operate the following kinds of elementary, secondary and postsecondary schools primarily for Native American children (including Alaska Native children) are eligible applicants under this program:
(1) Indian tribes;
(2) tribally sanctioned educational authorities;
(3) Native Hawaiian or Native American Pacific Islander native language educational organizations;
(4) elementary schools or secondary schools that are operated or funded by the Bureau of Indian Education (BIE), or a consortium of such schools;
(5) elementary schools or secondary schools operated under a contract with or grant from the BIE in consortium with another such school or a tribal or community organization and;
(6) elementary schools or secondary schools operated by the BIE and an institution of higher education (IHE), in consortium with elementary schools or secondary schools operated under a contract with or a grant from the BIE or a tribal or community organization.

GEOG. RESTRICTIONS: United States and its Commonwealths and territories.

FINANCIAL DATA:
Total amount of support: National Professional Development Program: $45,691,345 appropriated for fiscal year 2018; Native American and Alaska Native Children in School Program: $5,000,000.

STAFF:
Supreet Anand, Deputy Director

ADDRESS INQUIRIES TO:
National Professional Development Program:
Francisco Javier Lopez
Tel: (202) 401-1433

Native American and Alaska Native Children in School Program:
Celeste McLaughlin
Tel: (202) 453-6054

U.S. DEPARTMENT OF STATE, FULBRIGHT TEACHER EXCHANGES [1425]

1275 K Street, N.W.
Suite 600
Washington, DC 20005
(202) 628-8188
Fax: (202) 628-8189
E-mail: jbferguson@irex.org
Web Site: www.fulbrightteacherexchanges.org

FOUNDED: 1946

AREAS OF INTEREST:
K-12 education; all teaching disciplines including, but not limited to, mathematics, science, English, English as a Second Language (ESL), foreign language and history.

NAME(S) OF PROGRAMS:
- **Fulbright Teacher Exchanges**

TYPE:
Exchange programs; Travel grants. Fulbright Teacher Exchanges encompass the following programs:
Fulbright Distinguished Awards in Teaching Research Program, Fulbright Distinguished Awards in Teaching Short-Term Program and Fulbright Teachers for Global Classrooms Program are for U.S. educators;
Fulbright Leaders for Global Schools Program is for U.S. administrators and;
Fulbright Teaching Excellence & Achievement Program and Fulbright Distinguished Awards in Teaching for International Teachers Program are for international educators.

YEAR PROGRAM STARTED: 1946

PURPOSE:
To increase mutual understanding between the people of the U.S. and the people of other countries through the funding of K-12 educator exchanges.

LEGAL BASIS:
Mutual Educational and Cultural Exchange Act (Fulbright Hays Act) of 1961.

ELIGIBILITY:
Applicants must meet the following general requirements:
(1) be a U.S. citizen or hold citizenship and be a resident in one of the participating countries;
(2) be fluent in English;
(3) hold a Master's degree or higher (for U.S. educators; international applicant requirements vary);
(4) be employed full-time at an accredited school in the U.S., its territories, or in one of the participating countries;
(5) spend at least 50% of their time teaching or working directly with students and;
(6) have taught for at least five years.

FINANCIAL DATA:
In most cases, the U.S. educator secures a leave of absence with or without pay from his or her home institution (as does the foreign teacher). Exchange grants include a summer orientation program and round-trip transportation for grantee only.
Amount of support per award: Varies.
Total amount of support: Varies.

NO. MOST RECENT APPLICANTS: 1,000 across all programs.

NO. AWARDS: 400 annually.

APPLICATION INFO:
All applications must be submitted through the online application system.
Duration: U.S. Educators: Two weeks to six months; International Educators: Six weeks to four months.
Deadline: Varies. E-mail contact.fulbrightteachers@irex.org for information.

ADDRESS INQUIRIES TO:
See e-mail address above.

*PLEASE NOTE:
All programs are tentative and are subject to the availability of funds.

UNIVERSITY OF MANITOBA [1426]

Faculty of Graduate Studies
500 University Centre
Winnipeg MB R3T 2N2 Canada
(204) 474-6703
Fax: (204) 474-7553
E-mail: sara.sealey@umanitoba.ca
Web Site: umanitoba.ca/graduate_studies

AREAS OF INTEREST:
Teaching and cutting-edge research.

NAME(S) OF PROGRAMS:
- **University of Manitoba Graduate Fellowships**

TYPE:
Fellowships. Any discipline taught at graduate level at the university.

PURPOSE:
To reward academic excellence.

ELIGIBILITY:
At the time of application, students do not need to have been accepted by the department or faculty, but at the time of taking up the award must be regular full-time graduate students who have been admitted to and registered in advanced degree programmes, e.g., Master's or Ph.D., but not pre-Master's in any field of study or faculty of the University of Manitoba. Students beyond the second year in the Master's programme or beyond the fourth year in the Ph.D. programme are not eligible to apply for or hold a University of Manitoba Fellowship.

FINANCIAL DATA:
Amount of support per award: $18,000 for Ph.D.; $14,000 for Master's.

APPLICATION INFO:
Applicant must request information from the department to which he or she is applying at the University of Manitoba.

Duration: One year.

ADDRESS INQUIRIES TO:
Sara Sealey, Awards Officer
(See address above.)

DENNIS & PHYLLIS WASHINGTON FOUNDATION

P.O. Box 16630
Missoula, MT 59808
(406) 523-1300
E-mail: info@dpwfoundation.org
Web Site: www.dpwfoundation.org

TYPE:
Project/program grants; Scholarships.

See entry 1268 for full listing.

FRED B. AND RUTH B. ZIGLER FOUNDATION [1427]

P.O. Box 986
Jennings, LA 70546-0986
(337) 824-2413
Fax: (337) 824-2414
E-mail: ziglerfoundation@gmail.com

FOUNDED: 1956

AREAS OF INTEREST:
Education.

TYPE:
Project/program grants; Scholarships.

PURPOSE:
To benefit Jefferson-Davis Parish area.

LEGAL BASIS:
Private foundation.

ELIGIBILITY:
Grants are made to organizations that have tax-exempt status under Section 501(c)(3) of the Internal Revenue Code. No grants are made to individuals.

GEOG. RESTRICTIONS: Jefferson-Davis Parish area, Louisiana.

FINANCIAL DATA:
Amount of support per award: Varies.
Total amount of support: $100,000 to $400,000.

NO. AWARDS: Approximately 30 each year.

APPLICATION INFO:
Applicants must submit a brief letter outlining the purpose of the grant.

Duration: Up to four years.

Deadline: 30 days prior to the Board meeting. The Board meets every other month starting in January.

ADDRESS INQUIRIES TO:
Julie G. Berry, President
(See address above.)

Elementary and secondary education

ALTMAN FOUNDATION

8 West 40th Street
19th Floor
New York, NY 10018-2263
(212) 682-0970
Fax: (212) 682-1648
E-mail: info@altman.org
Web Site: www.altmanfoundation.org

TYPE:
Project/program grants.

See entry 1049 for full listing.

THE BELK FOUNDATION [1428]

6832 Morrison Boulevard
Suite 100
Charlotte, NC 28211
(704) 544-5444
E-mail: britt@belkfoundation.org
Web Site: www.belkfoundation.org

FOUNDED: 1928

AREAS OF INTEREST:
Education.

TYPE:
General operating grants; Project/program grants; Research grants; Training grants. Core achievement in grades K-3; Teacher and Leader development.

PURPOSE:
To invest in schools and organizations that work aggressively to ensure all students graduate from high school and continue on an intentional path toward college, career and life.

ELIGIBILITY:
Charitable organizations, with 501(c)(3) status, located in Charlotte, NC and select state-level initiatives in North Carolina.

No grants made to individuals, private elementary or secondary schools, international programs and/or organizations, and organizations for the primary purpose of fund-raising.

GEOG. RESTRICTIONS: North Carolina.

FINANCIAL DATA:
Amount of support per award: $5,000 to $500,000.
Total amount of support: Approximately $2,000,000.

NO. AWARDS: Approximately 20.

APPLICATION INFO:
Applications are accepted by invitation only. Applicant must complete online Eligibility Quiz. If prompted, applicant will submit Letter of Inquiry.

Duration: One to five years.

Deadline: April 1 and October 1.

STAFF:
Johanna Anderson, Executive Director
C.T. Anderson, Program Associate
Britt Benavidez, Program Associate

*PLEASE NOTE:
The Foundation dedicates its resources to two areas:
(1) Teaching and Leading and;
(2) K-3 Achievement.

*SPECIAL STIPULATIONS:
Currently the Foundation is only accepting Letters of Inquiry from organizations serving the community of Charlotte, NC and select state-level initiatives in North Carolina.

THE LOUIS CALDER FOUNDATION

999 18th Street
Suite 2350S
Denver, CO 80202
(720) 943-9865
E-mail: proposals@calderfdn.org
Web Site: www.louiscalderfoundation.org

TYPE:
Capital grants; Project/program grants. Curriculum development.

See entry 1003 for full listing.

SAMUEL N. AND MARY CASTLE FOUNDATION [1429]

733 Bishop Street, Suite 1275
Honolulu, HI 96813
(808) 522-1101
Fax: (808) 522-1103
E-mail: snandmarycastle@hawaii.rr.com
Web Site: fdnweb.org/castle/

FOUNDED: 1894

AREAS OF INTEREST:
Early education and care, cultural arts, human services for children, teacher training, and some maternal/child health support.

CONSULTING OR VOLUNTEER SERVICES:
Castle colleagues training for directors of early childhood centers.

TYPE:
Scholarships; Technical assistance; Training grants.

YEAR PROGRAM STARTED: 1894

PURPOSE:
To support training for early childhood education professionals; to support early education, preschools, scholarships, and select higher education programs in teacher training; to support early education.

LEGAL BASIS:
Private family foundation.

GEOG. RESTRICTIONS: Hawaii.

FINANCIAL DATA:
Amount of support per award: Typically $10,000 to $100,000.
Total amount of support: $2,500,000 for the year 2019.
Matching fund requirements: Varies.

NO. MOST RECENT APPLICANTS: 125.

NO. AWARDS: Approximately 50.

REPRESENTATIVE AWARDS:
$50,000 to Catholic Charities for families with children; $100,000 (over two years) to Chaminade University for student scholarships; $125,000 to University of Hawaii for scholarships.

APPLICATION INFO:
The applicant organization should review the Foundation's priorities and policies to determine whether it is eligible to be considered for funding and whether the type of activity proposed is in one of the Foundation's funding areas. Applicants are required to contact the Foundation's

Executive Director by letter, e-mail, telephone or personal visit before making fund application.

Proposals may be hand delivered or mailed and should include the following:
(1) proposal (one copy);
(2) one copy of each of the additional materials as defined on the Foundation's web site (e.g., IRS determination letter, audited financial statements);
(3) one- to two-page executive summary (two copies);
(4) budget (two copies) and;
(5) Board of Directors list (two copies).

Organizations which have submitted their charters, bylaws and 501(c)(3) may submit complete applications by e-mail attachment.

Applicant organizations should not bind their proposals or submit videos or other items which have not been requested by the Foundation.
Duration: One year. Renewal possible up to three years.
Deadline: January 15, May 15, and September 4.

OFFICERS:
Dr. Robert Peters, President
Dr. Kittredge A. Baldwin, Vice President
Alfred L. Castle, Treasurer and Executive Director
Cynthia Quisenberry, Secretary

ADDRESS INQUIRIES TO:
Alfred L. Castle, Executive Director
(See address above.)

*SPECIAL STIPULATIONS:
All applicants must be prescreened before applying.

HUGH AND HAZEL DARLING FOUNDATION
520 South Grand Avenue, Suite 395
Los Angeles, CA 90071
(213) 683-5200
Fax: (213) 627-7795
E-mail: rstack@darlingfoundation.org

TYPE:
Block grants; Capital grants; Challenge/matching grants; Matching gifts; Scholarships; Training grants.

See entry 1448 for full listing.

FIRSTENERGY FOUNDATION   [1430]
76 South Main Street
Akron, OH 44308
(330) 384-5022
Fax: (330) 245-5566
E-mail: fe_comm_involve@firstenergycorp.com
Web Site: www.firstenergycorp.com/community

AREAS OF INTEREST:
Science, technology, engineering and mathematics education.

NAME(S) OF PROGRAMS:
● **STEM Grants Program**

TYPE:
Project/program grants. Project/program grants in the classroom setting.

YEAR PROGRAM STARTED: 1985

PURPOSE:
To support classroom projects and teacher professional development initiatives focusing on STEM (science, technology, engineering and mathematics).

ELIGIBILITY:
Educators (grades preK-12) and youth group leaders in the service areas of FirstEnergy and communities where FirstEnergy has facilities are encouraged to apply. Any creative project dealing with science, technology, engineering and mathematics is eligible. Projects that involve students directly, incorporate matching funds, community resources, interdisciplinary or team-teaching and involve various age groups are highly favored. Teacher training projects are highly favored. Completed projects or those previously funded are not eligible.

GEOG. RESTRICTIONS: Maryland, New Jersey, Ohio, Pennsylvania and West Virginia.

FINANCIAL DATA:
Grants may be used to compensate experts who come to work with the students, but not to pay teachers or staff.
Amount of support per award: Up to $1,000.
Total amount of support: $97,000 for the year 2019.

NO. AWARDS: 116 for the year 2019.

APPLICATION INFO:
Application can be downloaded and completed electronically.
Duration: One school year.
Deadline: Usually third week in September.

PUBLICATIONS:
Bright Ideas for Educators.

ADDRESS INQUIRIES TO:
Community Involvement Department
(See address above.)

*SPECIAL STIPULATIONS:
Grants are only available to schools or groups in the FirstEnergy service area or in communities where it has facilities.

CHARLES HAYDEN FOUNDATION
140 Broadway, 51st Floor
New York, NY 10005
(212) 785-3677
Fax: (212) 785-3689
E-mail: fdn@chf.org
Web Site: www.charleshaydenfoundation.org

TYPE:
Project/program grants. Grant priorities focus on institutions and programs primarily serving youth at risk of not reaching their full potential, especially youth in low-income communities. Support is provided for youth development programs, charter schools, independent and parochial schools, and informal educational enrichment programs.

See entry 1018 for full listing.

INVESTED   [1431]
606 Oakesdale Avenue, S.W.
Suite C-202
Renton, WA 98057
(206) 352-1199 ext. 1
E-mail: jwalters@invested.org
Web Site: www.invested.org

FOUNDED: 1963

AREAS OF INTEREST:
Secondary schools and immediate support for disadvantaged students.

NAME(S) OF PROGRAMS:
● **InvestED School Partnership/Funding Program**

TYPE:
Grants-in-aid; Matching gifts. Support for partner schools only.

YEAR PROGRAM STARTED: 1963

PURPOSE:
To support middle and senior high school aid program providing for grants to both accredited public and private schools (grades 6-12) within the state of Washington to enable these schools to assist individual students who have needs their families cannot afford.

LEGAL BASIS:
Public charity.

ELIGIBILITY:
Grants are restricted to a program aiding students in Washington state.

School must submit year-end report May 1 to June 30 to be eligible for grant the following year.

GEOG. RESTRICTIONS: Washington state.

FINANCIAL DATA:
Amount of support per award: $350 to over $3,000 in initial funding; up to $500 matching grant per school, per school year.
Total amount of support: $510,000 initial funding and $175,000 in matching grants.

NO. MOST RECENT APPLICANTS: 660 schools.

NO. AWARDS: 660 schools.

APPLICATION INFO:
Contact the Organization for guidelines.
Duration: One year. Renewable.
Deadline: June 30.

IRS I.D.: 23-7189670

STAFF:
Joyce Walters, Executive Director
Christopher Coleman, Investments and Partnerships Officer
Zander Lyskin, Investments and Partnerships Officer
Andre Wesson, Director, Investments and Partnerships
Judy Simpson, Communications Manager

DIRECTORS:
Sandi Bennett-Scott, Ed.D., President
Patrick Leonard, First Vice President
Trish Millines Dziko, Second Vice President
Sourabh Mathur, Treasurer
Andy Knapp, Secretary
Angie Brotherton
Steven D. Brown
Trevor Carlson
Mia Coffman
Brian Kistler
Dr. Mark Lewis, D.P.M.
Marcie Maxwell
Mick Miller
Joe Osborne
Dr. Damien Pattenaude
Dr. Susana Reyes
Jeff Richards
Dave Wilson

ADDRESS INQUIRIES TO:
Executive Director
(See address above.)

MARTHA HOLDEN JENNINGS FOUNDATION   [1432]
The Halle Building
1228 Euclid Avenue, Suite 240
Cleveland, OH 44115-1811
(216) 589-5700
Web Site: www.mhjf.org

FOUNDED: 1959

AREAS OF INTEREST:
Ohio elementary and secondary education.

NAME(S) OF PROGRAMS:
- **Grants-to-Educators Program**
- **Open Grants**

TYPE:
Project/program grants. Project/program grants are for education only. Support to aide the improvement of elementary and secondary public school education in Ohio.

YEAR PROGRAM STARTED: 1959

PURPOSE:
To foster the development of individual capabilities of young people to the maximum extent through improving the quality of teaching in secular primary and secondary schools; to provide a means for greater accomplishment on the part of Ohio's teachers by encouraging creativity in teaching and bringing greater recognition to the teaching profession.

LEGAL BASIS:
Nonprofit foundation.

ELIGIBILITY:
For Grants-to-Educators, applicants must be teachers or public school administrators and are intended for classroom, schoolwide or districtwide projects. For other grants, applicants must be tax-exempt with 501(c)(3) status from the IRS.

Open Grants are available to any public school district, nonreligious private school working with public schools, or tax-exempt organization that assists elementary and secondary schools in Ohio. No grants for capital improvements or graduate study, and generally no grants for equipment or travel.

GEOG. RESTRICTIONS: Ohio.

FINANCIAL DATA:
Amount of support per award:
Grants-to-Educators: Up to $3,000; Open Grants: Varies depending on needs and nature of the request. Average: $15,000.

Total amount of support: $3,318,433 for the year 2019.

NO. MOST RECENT APPLICANTS: 279.

NO. AWARDS: 235 for the year 2019.

REPRESENTATIVE AWARDS:
$10,000 to Invent Now, Inc., North Canton, OH, for Camp Invention Program; $10,000 to Idea Stream, Cleveland, OH, for News Depth Program; $8,000 to Mount Vernon City Schools for STEM Robotics Program; $9,500 to Northwest Local Schools for LETRS Training.

APPLICATION INFO:
There are two funding categories within the Grants-to-Educators and Open Grants programs: Excellent Teaching and Deep Learning. Applicants need to understand the rationale behind these grant categories before completing a proposal. Applicants must indicate the category or categories for which they are seeking funds within each program.

All grant requests must be submitted online at the Foundation web site.
Duration: One year. Proposal may be resubmitted for a second or third year.
Deadline: Proposals must be submitted by the 15th of the month preceding the month in which they are to be considered.

Grants-to-Educators: The Distribution Committee meets ten months a year (not in July or December).

Open Grants: The Board of Directors does not meet in February, July, October or December. Decisions on grant applications are generally communicated within two months of submission.

PUBLICATIONS:
Guidelines; *Pro-Excellentia.*

STAFF:
Dr. Daniel J. Keenan, Executive Director

KLINGENSTEIN CENTER FOR INDEPENDENT SCHOOL LEADERSHIP   [1433]
Teachers College, Columbia University
525 West 120th Street, Box 125
New York, NY 10027-6696
(212) 678-3156
Fax: (212) 678-3156
E-mail: klingenstein@tc.columbia.edu
Web Site: klingensteincenter.org

FOUNDED: 1977

AREAS OF INTEREST:
Leadership development for independent and international education.

NAME(S) OF PROGRAMS:
- **Klingenstein Heads of Schools Program**
- **Klingenstein Summer Institute for Early Career Teachers**
- **Master's Degree in Private School Leadership**

TYPE:
Scholarships. The Klingenstein Heads of Schools Program gathers heads of independent and international schools from throughout the nation and the world for two weeks of intensive study among professional peers.

The Klingenstein Summer Institute gathers teachers in the beginning years of their careers for an exploration of teaching styles, educational philosophies and issues, and personal development.

The Master's Degree in Private School Leadership, with a focus in independent and international school leadership, gathers independent school teachers and administrators for a rigorous degree program. The Two Summers Master's Program is the two-summer version of the full-year degree program. Either program can be paired with an MBA from either Columbia Business School or INSEAD in France or Singapore to earn an M.A./MBA dual degree. The majority of students get generous tuition scholarships.

YEAR PROGRAM STARTED: 1978

PURPOSE:
To draw attention to outstanding leadership.

LEGAL BASIS:
Private foundation.

ELIGIBILITY:
Teachers and administrators working in an independent or international school with a nondiscriminatory admissions policy are eligible to apply. All programs are open to international applicants.

FINANCIAL DATA:
All programs offer tuition funding. The Heads of Schools Program and the Summer Institute for Early Career Teachers are

fully-funded fellowships. Students in Master's programs are eligible for financial aid and scholarships.
Amount of support per award: Varies.
Total amount of support: Varies.

APPLICATION INFO:
Applicant must submit application, transcripts, autobiographical information and recommendations from sponsoring school. Master's program applicants must submit GMAT or GRE scores.
Duration: Varies.
Deadline: Klingenstein Heads of Schools Program: May 1; Summer Institute and Full-Year Master's Degree: January 15; Two Summers Master's Program: November 1 of even-numbered years.

PUBLICATIONS:
Klingbrief.

ADDRESS INQUIRIES TO:
Assistant Director
(See address above.)

MCCARTHEY DRESSMAN EDUCATION FOUNDATION   [1434]
610 East South Temple Street
Suite 110
Salt Lake City, UT 84102
(801) 578-1260
Fax: (801) 578-1261
E-mail: info@mccartheydressman.org
Web Site: mccartheydressman.org

AREAS OF INTEREST:
Student learning and educational quality.

NAME(S) OF PROGRAMS:
- **Academic Enrichment Grants**
- **Student Teaching Scholarship**
- **Teacher Development Grants**

TYPE:
Development grants; Project/program grants; Scholarships. Academic Enrichment Grants aim to maximize innovation and results in classrooms and education departments.

Student Teaching Scholarships offer financial and mentoring support to educators who will be student teaching in their final year of a qualified teacher education program. Foundation mentors offer one-on-one guidance and attention to nurture the next generation of teachers. Scholarship recipients acquire and strengthen exemplary teaching practices that promote learning by their own students.

Teacher Development Grants aim to increase the effectiveness of individual educators and small teams of teachers. These grants provide opportunities for teachers to integrate fresh strategies that encourage critical inquiry and to observe their effects on students. Teachers have the opportunity to reflect and write about their projects, as well as to share their results with other teachers.

PURPOSE:
To serve as a catalyst in maximizing the skills and creativity of educators at the K-12 levels; to cultivate pioneering approaches to teaching that result in dynamic student learning.

ELIGIBILITY:
Applications for Academic Enrichment Grants are considered from educators who are employed by schools or nonprofit organizations, have the background and

experience to complete the project successfully, have direct and regular contact with students in grades preK-12, work with students from low-income households, and are willing to work in collaboration with the Foundation. A project may have one to many participants involved in its planning and implementation. However, the Foundation does require that each application by submitted in the name of one individual even if there are two or more participants involved in a single project.

Student Teaching Scholarship applicants must be full-time students in good standing and in the final year of the teacher education program at New Mexico State University, the University of California Santa Cruz, the University of Texas at Austin or the Stephen F. Austin State University. They must specialize in elementary or secondary education and have the background and experience to complete the project successfully. Applicant must be willing to work with a trustee of the Foundation during the student teaching experience.

Applications for Teacher Development Grants are considered from educators who are licensed K-12 teachers employed in public or private schools, have the background and experience to complete the project successfully, and are willing to work in collaboration with the Foundation. A project may have one to many participants involved in its planning and implementation. However, the Foundation does require that each application be submitted in the name of one individual even if there are two or more participants involved in a single project.

FINANCIAL DATA:
Amount of support per award: Academic Enrichment Grants and Teacher Development Grants: Up to $10,000 per year; Student Teaching Scholarship: $6,000.

NO. MOST RECENT APPLICANTS: Maximum 350 (175 Academic Enrichment, 50 Student Teaching and 125 Teacher Development).

NO. AWARDS: Academic Enrichment Grants: 5; Student Teaching Scholarship: 4; Teacher Development Grants: 4 for the year 2019-20.

APPLICATION INFO:
Applications are submitted online. Letters of recommendation are required.

Duration: Academic Enrichment Grants and Teacher Development Grants: Up to three years, provided eligibility requirements continue to be met. Student Teaching Scholarship: One year.

Deadline: April 15. Awards announced July 15.

TRUSTEES:
Judy A. Abbott
Michael Borish
Mark Dressman
Carmen Gonzales
Sarah McCarthey
Carolyn Schubach
Patrick Scott
Kip Tellez
Phil Wilder
Jo Worthy

MEBANE CHARITABLE FOUNDATION, INC.
232 South Main Street
Mocksville, NC 27028
(336) 936-0041
Fax: (336) 936-0038
E-mail: lcolbourne@mebanefoundation.com
Web Site: www.mebanefoundation.com

TYPE:
Project/program grants.

See entry 1024 for full listing.

MITSUBISHI ELECTRIC AMERICA FOUNDATION [1435]
1300 Wilson Boulevard
Suite 825
Arlington, VA 22209
(703) 276-8240
E-mail: mea.foundation@meus.mea.com
Web Site: www.meaf.org

FOUNDED: 1991

AREAS OF INTEREST:
People with disabilities, including education, employment, independence and community inclusion.

TYPE:
Demonstration grants; Internships; Matching gifts; Project/program grants; Seed money grants; Technical assistance; Training grants. Grants are offered to make a better world for all by helping young people with disabilities to maximize their potential and participation in society.

YEAR PROGRAM STARTED: 1991

PURPOSE:
To help young people with disabilities maximize their potential and participation in society.

LEGAL BASIS:
Foundation.

ELIGIBILITY:
Applicants must meet criteria as stated in Foundation guidelines. Priority given to applicants in communities where MEUS facilities are located.

GEOG. RESTRICTIONS: United States.

FINANCIAL DATA:
Amount of support per award: Typically $10,000 to $75,000 per year.
Total amount of support: $1,000,000 for the year 2021.
Matching fund requirements: Mitsubishi Electric employee must submit a request to match for qualified organizations.

NO. MOST RECENT APPLICANTS: 100.

NO. AWARDS: 6 to 12 annually.

APPLICATION INFO:
Submit a two-page concept paper (click on the "How to Apply" tab on the Foundation web site) including a budget summary and description of the need and objectives for the funds requested. Instructions for full proposals will be sent after initial screening. Concept papers are reviewed throughout the year.

Applicants are requested not to telephone the Foundation during the application process.
Duration: One to three years. Renewal possible on a case-by-case basis.
Deadline: October 15 to be considered for following year funding.

BOARD OF DIRECTORS:
Mike Corbo
Mike DeLano
Chris Gerdes
Brian Heery
Mark Kuntz
Nasahiro Oya
Perry Pappous
Scott Summerville
Dr. Richard C. Waters

ADDRESS INQUIRIES TO:
Kevin R. Webb, Senior Director
(See address above.)

NATIONAL ENDOWMENT FOR THE HUMANITIES
The Constitution Center
400 7th Street, S.W.
Washington, DC 20506
(202) 606-8424
Fax: (202) 606-8240
E-mail: communications@neh.gov
Web Site: www.neh.gov

TYPE:
Conferences/seminars. Grants support summer seminars and national institutes in the humanities for college and school teachers. These faculty development activities are conducted at colleges and universities across the country. Lists of pending seminars and institutes are available from the program.

See entry 338 for full listing.

NATIONAL SCIENCE FOUNDATION [1436]
Directorate for Education and Human Resources
Division of Research on Learning in Formal and Informal Settings
2415 Eisenhower Avenue
Alexandria, VA 22314
(703) 292-8620
Fax: (703) 292-9044; (703) 292-9046
E-mail: acarroll@nsf.gov
Web Site: www.nsf.gov

FOUNDED: 1950

AREAS OF INTEREST:
Science, mathematics, technology education content; pedagogy; applied research; development of resources and tools for instruction, assessment, evaluation and informal science.

NAME(S) OF PROGRAMS:
- **Advanced Informal STEM Learning (AISL)**
- **Advanced Technological Education (ATE)**
- **Discovery Research PreK-12 (DR K12)**
- **Innovative Technology Experiences for Students and Teachers (ITEST)**

TYPE:
Conferences/seminars; Demonstration grants; Development grants; Project/program grants; Research grants; Training grants. Advanced Informal STEM Learning (AISL) program invests in projects that develop and implement informal learning experiences designed to increase interest, engagement and understanding of science, technology, engineering and mathematics (STEM) by individuals of all ages and backgrounds, as well as projects that advance knowledge and practice of informal science education.

With an emphasis on two-year colleges, the Advanced Technological Education (ATE) program focuses on the education of technicians for the high-technology fields that drive the nation's economy.

Discovery Research PreK-12 (DR K12) funds research, development and evaluation activities through knowledge generation and application to improve PreK-12 learning and teaching.

Innovative Technology Experiences for Students and Teachers (ITEST) is designed to increase the opportunities for students and teachers to learn about, experience, and use information technologies within the context of science, technology, engineering and mathematics (STEM), including Information Technology (IT) courses. It is in direct response to the concern about shortages of information technology workers in the U.S.

Research and Evaluation on Education in Science and Engineering (REESE) supports basic and applied research and evaluation that enhances science, technology, engineering and mathematics (STEM) learning and teaching.

PURPOSE:
To promote quality programs of education in mathematics, science and technology for all the nation's youth, and informal learning opportunities in these fields for youth and adults.

LEGAL BASIS:
The National Science Foundation Act of 1950, Public Law 81-507, as amended.

GEOG. RESTRICTIONS: United States.

FINANCIAL DATA:
Amount of support per award: Grants vary in amount, depending upon the needs and nature of the request and availability of funds.
Total amount of support: $180,000,000.

APPLICATION INFO:
Application information is available on the Foundation's web site.
Duration: One to five years.
Deadline: Varies.

THE RADIANT PEACE FOUNDATION INTERNATIONAL, INC. [1437]
P.O. Box 40822
St. Petersburg, FL 33743-0822
(727) 343-8212
E-mail: radiantpeaceintl@gmail.com
Web Site: www.radiantpeace.org

FOUNDED: 1990

NAME(S) OF PROGRAMS:
● **Radiant Peace Education Awards**

TYPE:
Awards/prizes. Recognizes and awards children, teachers and schools for Radiant Peace essays, art, projects, and videos.

YEAR PROGRAM STARTED: 1990

PURPOSE:
To inspire, promote and encourage Radiant Peace worldwide.

LEGAL BASIS:
A 501(c)(3) nonprofit educational organization.

ELIGIBILITY:
All students grades one-12 including home schools and youth groups.

FINANCIAL DATA:
Amount of support per award: $25 to $500.
Total amount of support: Varies by year.

NO. AWARDS: 109.

APPLICATION INFO:
Invitations and guidelines posted online.
Deadline: December and April.

ADDRESS INQUIRIES TO:
Office Manager
(See address above.)

SONY CORPORATION OF AMERICA [1438]
25 Madison Avenue, 27th Floor
New York, NY 10010-8601
(212) 833-6826
E-mail: karen.kelso@sony.com
Web Site: www.sony.com

FOUNDED: 1972

AREAS OF INTEREST:
Arts, culture and technology, with primary focus in education; environmental issues; civic affairs; disaster relief.

TYPE:
General operating grants; Matching gifts; Product donations; Project/program grants.

YEAR PROGRAM STARTED: 1972

PURPOSE:
To meet the needs of the communities where Sony has a presence; to support national organizations which extend into Sony presence areas.

ELIGIBILITY:
No grants to individuals, political or religious organizations, labor unions, endowments, capital campaigns, lobbying groups, testimonial dinners, for-profit publications seeking advertisements and foreign or non-U.S. organizations.

GEOG. RESTRICTIONS: United States.

FINANCIAL DATA:
Amount of support per award: Varies.
Total amount of support: Varies.
Matching fund requirements: Sony matches contributions made by full-time employees to educational institutions, hospitals and health care organizations, cultural organizations, and environmental organizations.

APPLICATION INFO:
Send brief letter describing organization, amount requested, objectives of organization, recent audited financial statement and proof of tax-exempt status. Telephone calls are not accepted; only written requests.
Duration: One year. Must reapply for continued support.
Deadline: Requests accepted throughout the year. Notification within three months.

PUBLICATIONS:
Contribution guidelines.

OFFICERS:
Karen E. Kelso, Senior Director, Corporate Social Responsibility

ADDRESS INQUIRIES TO:
Karen E. Kelso, Senior Director
Corporate Social Responsibility
(See e-mail address above.)

STATE LIBRARY AND ARCHIVES OF FLORIDA
R.A. Gray Building
500 South Bronough Street
Tallahassee, FL 32399-0250
(850) 245-6620
Fax: (850) 245-6643
E-mail: marian.deeney@dos.myflorida.com
Web Site: dos.myflorida.com/library-archives/services-for-libraries/grants/lsta

TYPE:
Project/program grants. Project grants congruent with the state long-range plan.
See entry 682 for full listing.

W. CLEMENT & JESSIE V. STONE FOUNDATION [1439]
70 East Lake Street, Suite 1020
Chicago, IL 60601
(312) 366-2263
E-mail: info@wcstonefnd.org
Web Site: www.wcstonefnd.org

FOUNDED: 1958

AREAS OF INTEREST:
Education, early childhood and youth development.

TYPE:
General operating grants; Project/program grants; Technical assistance.

YEAR PROGRAM STARTED: 1958

PURPOSE:
To make the world a better place by supporting programs in education, early childhood and youth development.

ELIGIBILITY:
Grants are made to organizations that have tax-exempt status under Section 501(c)(3) of the Internal Revenue Code. Nonsectarian religious programs may apply. No grants are made to individuals.

GEOG. RESTRICTIONS: San Francisco Bay area, California; Chicago, Illinois; Boston, Massachusetts; New York City, New York; and Philadelphia, Pennsylvania.

FINANCIAL DATA:
Amount of support per award: $10,000 to $100,000, depending upon the program.
Total amount of support: Approximately $5,500,000 for the year 2019.

NO. MOST RECENT APPLICANTS: 50.

NO. AWARDS: 100.

REPRESENTATIVE AWARDS:
$100,000 to Strategies for Children, Boston, MA, for Early Education for All Campaign; $75,000 to National Equity Project, Oakland, CA, for general operating support; $50,000 to Bank Street College of Education, New York, NY, for TESOL Residency Program; $60,000 to Youth United for Change, Philadelphia, PA, for general operating support.

APPLICATION INFO:
The Foundation does not accept unsolicited proposals. Organizations may call if they feel there is a strong match between their work and the Foundation's grantmaking priorities.
Duration: One year. Renewal possible.
Deadline: Late April to early May and late October.

IRS I.D.: 36-2498125

OFFICERS AND DIRECTORS:
Amy Stone, Chairman
Sandra Stone, President
Steven M. Stone, Treasurer
Michael A. Stone, Secretary

Sara Slaughter, Executive Director
Barbara Stone
David Stone
Debbie Stone
Jeffrey Stone
Jennifer Stone
Sara Stone
Chad Tingley

ADDRESS INQUIRIES TO:
Sara Slaughter, Executive Director
(See address above.)

TOSHIBA AMERICA FOUNDATION [1440]

1251 Avenue of the Americas, 41st Floor
New York, NY 10020
(212) 596-0620
E-mail: tai-foundation@toshiba.com
Web Site: www.toshiba.com/taf

FOUNDED: 1990

AREAS OF INTEREST:
Mathematics and science education for
grades K-12.

TYPE:
Project/program grants.

YEAR PROGRAM STARTED: 1990

PURPOSE:
To improve science and math education at
the pre-college level (grades K-12 only).

LEGAL BASIS:
Corporate foundation.

ELIGIBILITY:
Grants are made to private or public schools.
Preference is given to programs or projects
that take place in science or math
classrooms. The Foundation does not fund
grants for general operating costs,
endowments, scholarships, conferences,
summer programs, purchase of equipment
(product or donations), sponsorships, or
individuals.

GEOG. RESTRICTIONS: United States.

FINANCIAL DATA:
Amount of support per award: $1,000 to
$20,000.
Total amount of support: Approximately
$500,000.

NO. AWARDS: 150 annually.

APPLICATION INFO:
Applications are available on the
Foundation's web site.
Duration: One year.
Deadline: Grades K-5: October 1. Grades
6-12: March 1, June 1, September 1 and
December 1 for requests up to $5,000; May
1 and November 1 for requests more than
$5,000.

IRS I.D.: 13-3596612

ADDRESS INQUIRIES TO:
Program Officer
(See address above.)

U.S. DEPARTMENT OF EDUCATION

Office of Indian Education
400 Maryland Avenue, S.W.
LBJ Building, 3W101
Washington, DC 20202-6335
(202) 260-3774
Fax: (202) 205-0606
E-mail: indian.education@ed.gov
Web Site: www2.ed.
gov/programs/indianformula/index.html

TYPE:
Formula grants. Grants to provide financial
assistance to LEAs and tribal schools to
address the unique cultural, language and
educationally related academic needs of
American Indian and Alaska Native students,
including preschool children.

See entry 956 for full listing.

U.S. DEPARTMENT OF EDUCATION

Office of Post Secondary Education
Federal TRIO Programs
400 Maryland Avenue, S.W.
Washington, DC 20202
(202) 453-6273
(202) 453-6914
Fax: (202) 502-7857
E-mail: OPE_TRIO@ed.gov
Web Site: www.ed.gov/ope/trio

TYPE:
Project/program grants. There are three types
of grants under the Upward Bound program:
Regular Upward Bound Grants, Veterans
Upward Bound Grants, and Upward Bound
Math and Science Grants.

The Regular Upward Bound projects are
designed to generate in participants the skills
and motivation necessary for success in
education beyond secondary school. The
Veterans Upward Bound projects are
designed to assist veterans in preparing for a
program of postsecondary education. The
Upward Bound Math and Science projects
are designed to prepare high school students
for postsecondary education programs that
lead to careers in the fields of math and
science.

See entry 1463 for full listing.

YOUTH FOR UNDERSTANDING USA

6856 Eastern Avenue, N.W.
Suite 310
Washington, DC 20012
(202) 774-5200 ext. 5203
(800) 833-6243
Fax: (202) 588-7571
E-mail: info@yfu.org
mckendree@yfu.org
Web Site: www.yfuusa.org

TYPE:
Exchange programs; Grants-in-aid;
Scholarships; Travel grants. Students on
summer semester and year programs live
with volunteer host families overseas.
Students on semester and academic year
programs also attend school. International
students live and study at U.S. high schools
or community colleges. Competitive, full and
partial scholarships for Corporate, Japan-U.S.
Senate Programs and Japan-America
Friendship Scholars Program.

See entry 868 for full listing.

Higher education projects and research

ABEL FOUNDATION

1815 Y Street
Lincoln, NE 68508
(402) 434-1212
Fax: (402) 434-1799
Web Site: www.abelfoundation.org

TYPE:
Capital grants; Matching gifts;
Project/program grants.

See entry 1043 for full listing.

AMERICAN FLORAL ENDOWMENT

1001 North Fairfax Street
Suite 201
Alexandria, VA 22314
(703) 838-5211
Fax: (703) 838-5212
E-mail: afe@endowment.org
Web Site: endowment.org

TYPE:
Internships; Project/program grants; Research
grants; Scholarships. The Endowment funds
research and educational development in
floriculture and environmental horticulture
designed to produce solutions to industry
needs and promote the growth and
improvement of the floral industry for the
benefit of the grower, wholesale, retail, allied
segments and the general public.

The Endowment supports educational
programs focused on attracting young people
to the industry, and educational endeavors to
identify and solve industry needs and/or
challenges. The programs are divided into
two major areas:
(1) paid floriculture internships/scholarships
for full-time college students and;
(2) general educational grants to national
programs.

See entry 1904 for full listing.

AMERICAN FOUNDATION FOR PHARMACEUTICAL EDUCATION (AFPE) [1441]

11325 Random Hills Road
Suite 360A-105
Fairfax, VA 22030
(703) 875-3095
Fax: (703) 875-3098
E-mail: fuentes@afpepharm.org
Web Site: afpepharm.org

FOUNDED: 1942

AREAS OF INTEREST:
Education.

NAME(S) OF PROGRAMS:
• **AFPE Predoctoral Fellowships in the
Pharmaceutical Sciences**

TYPE:
Fellowships.

YEAR PROGRAM STARTED: 1942

PURPOSE:
To encourage an outstanding pharmacy
school graduate to pursue an advanced
degree in the pharmaceutical sciences; to
identify and support students who have the
potential to become leaders in the
pharmaceutical profession.

ELIGIBILITY:
Eligible applicants must meet the following criteria:
(1) be a U.S. citizen or permanent resident;
(2) be a full-time student enrolled in a graduate Ph.D. program in pharmaceutical science administered by or officially affiliated with a U.S. college of pharmacy accredited by ACPE;
(3) have at least three semesters of study completed in the current Ph.D. program;
(4) have no more that three and a half years remaining to obtain the Ph.D. degree and;
(5) may be a joint Pharm.D./Ph.D. student who has completed the equivalent of three full semesters of graduate credit toward the Ph.D. and will be awarded the Ph.D. degree within three additional years.

GEOG. RESTRICTIONS: United States.

FINANCIAL DATA:
The Fellowship stipend may be used for a purpose decided by the awardee and college that will enable the student to make progress in their pursuit of the Ph.D., such as student stipend, laboratory supplies, books, materials, travel, etc. None of the funds shall be used for indirect costs by the institution.
Amount of support per award: $10,000 stipend.
Total amount of support: Varies.

NO. MOST RECENT APPLICANTS: 150.

NO. AWARDS: 42.

APPLICATION INFO:
Application and guidelines are available online.
Duration: One year, September to August. Renewable.

AMERICAN FOUNDATION FOR PHARMACEUTICAL EDUCATION (AFPE)
11325 Random Hills Road
Suite 360A-105
Fairfax, VA 22030
(703) 875-3095
Fax: (703) 875-3098
E-mail: fuentes@afpepharm.org
Web Site: afpepharm.org

TYPE:
Fellowships.
See entry 2289 for full listing.

AMERICAN FRIENDS OF THE ALEXANDER VON HUMBOLDT FOUNDATION   [1442]
1401 K Street
Suite 1005
Washington, DC 20005
(202) 783-1907
E-mail: info@americanfriendsofavh.org
Web Site: www.americanfriendsofavh.org

FOUNDED: 1953

AREAS OF INTEREST:
Postgraduate research in Germany.

NAME(S) OF PROGRAMS:
● **Humboldt Research Fellowship for Postdoctoral Researchers**

TYPE:
Fellowships; Project/program grants; Research grants; Scholarships. This program supports highly qualified scholars and scientists of all nationalities and disciplines

so that they may carry out long-term research projects that the applicant has selected in cooperation with an academic host the applicant has selected at a research institution in Germany.

PURPOSE:
To support highly qualified scholars and scientists of all nationalities and disciplines so that they may carry out long-term research projects in Germany.

ELIGIBILITY:
Open to scientists and scholars who completed a doctoral degree within four years prior to the application submission date.

Fellowships are awarded on the basis of academic achievement, the quality and feasibility of the proposed research and the candidate's publications.

FINANCIAL DATA:
In addition to a monthly stipend, special allowances are available for accompanying family members, travel expenses and German language instruction.
Amount of support per award: EUR 2,650 monthly.
Total amount of support: Varies.

NO. MOST RECENT APPLICANTS: Approximately 1,800.

NO. AWARDS: Approximately 600 total fellowships for postdoctoral researchers and experienced researchers each year.

APPLICATION INFO:
Application information is available on the web site.
Duration: Six to 24 months in Germany.
Deadline: Continuous. The review process takes several months, and the selection committee meets three times a year to review applications.

STAFF:
Brian Craft, Alumni Relations and Annual Fund Program Coordinator
Alexis Brouwer-Ancher, Communications and Events Program Coordinator

ADDRESS INQUIRIES TO:
Program Coordination
(See address above.) or

Alexander von Humboldt Stiftung
Jean-Paul-Strasse 12
D-53173 Bonn
Germany
Tel: 49 (0228) 833-0
Fax: 49 (0228) 833-199
E-mail: info@avh.de

*SPECIAL STIPULATIONS:
Applicant must have received Ph.D. within four years.

AMERICAN LIBRARY ASSOCIATION (ALA)   [1443]
225 North Michigan Avenue
Suite 1300
Chicago, IL 60601
(312) 280-4279
(800) 545-2433 ext. 4279
Fax: (312) 280-4279
E-mail: scholarships@ala.org
Web Site: www.ala.
org/educationcareers/scholarships

FOUNDED: 1969

AREAS OF INTEREST:
Library science.

NAME(S) OF PROGRAMS:
● **ALA Spectrum Scholarship**
● **ALA/Century Scholarship**
● **ALSC/Bound-to-Stay-Bound Books Scholarship**
● **ALSC/Frederic G. Melcher Scholarship**
● **David H. Clift Scholarship**
● **Tom and Roberta Drewes Scholarship**
● **Mary V. Gaver Scholarship**
● **Miriam L. Hornback Scholarship**
● **Christopher J. Hoy/ERT Scholarship**
● **Tony B. Leisner Scholarship**
● **LITA/Christian Larew Memorial Scholarship**
● **Peter Lyman Memorial/SAGE Scholarships**
● **W. David Rozkuszka Scholarship**

TYPE:
Scholarships. All scholarships are for librarians entering a Master's degree program.

ALA/Century Scholarship is for an individual with a disability entering a Master's degree or Ph.D. program.

ALSC and Gaver Scholarships are for a youth services librarian.

Clift, Hoy/ERT and Rozkuszka are general scholarships.

Drewes, Hornback and Leisner Scholarships are for paid library support staff currently working in a library.

SAGE Scholarship is for a new media services librarian.

PURPOSE:
To support library staff education.

ELIGIBILITY:
Applicants must be U.S. or Canadian citizens, or permanent residents thereof.

Applicants must demonstrate academic excellence, leadership qualities and evidence of commitment to a career in librarianship.

Applicants may not have completed more than 12 semester hours or the equivalent towards a Master's degree in library science prior to June 1.

GEOG. RESTRICTIONS: United States and Canada.

FINANCIAL DATA:
Amount of support per award: Varies.
Total amount of support: Over $300,000 annually.

APPLICATION INFO:
Applications and reference forms are submitted online. Applicants are required to submit their undergraduate transcripts.
Deadline: March 1.

STAFF:
Kimberly Redd, Program Manager

ADDRESS INQUIRIES TO:
Kimberly Redd, Program Manager
(See address above.)

THE AMERICAN-SCANDINAVIAN FOUNDATION   [1444]
58 Park Avenue
New York, NY 10016
(212) 779-3587
(615) 881-1532
Fax: (212) 686-1157
E-mail: grants@amscan.org
Web Site: www.amscan.org

FOUNDED: 1910

AREAS OF INTEREST:
Cross-cultural exchange at an academic level.

NAME(S) OF PROGRAMS:
● **Visiting Lectureships**

TYPE:
Exchange programs. The Foundation invites U.S. colleges and universities to apply for funding to host a visiting lecturer from Norway or Sweden. Lectureships should be in the area of contemporary studies with an emphasis in one of the following areas: (1) public policy; (2) conflict resolution; (3) environmental studies; (4) multiculturalism and; (5) health care.

PURPOSE:
To promote international understanding through educational and cultural exchange between the U.S. and Scandinavia.

ELIGIBILITY:
The competition is open to all American colleges and universities. The award is appropriate for any department or interdisciplinary program with an interest in incorporating a Scandinavian focus into its course offerings. The lecturer must be a Norwegian or Swedish citizen and a scholar or expert in a field appropriate to the host department or program.

FINANCIAL DATA:
Amount of support per award: $20,000 teaching/research stipend plus a $5,000 travel stipend for lecture appearances outside home institution.

NO. MOST RECENT APPLICANTS: 1.

NO. AWARDS: 1.

APPLICATION INFO:
Application and instructions are available on the Foundation web site.
Duration: One semester.
Deadline: February 15. Announcement April 15.

*SPECIAL STIPULATIONS:
The selected lecturer is expected to teach one course (undergraduate or graduate-level) and perform modest public activities (lectures, etc.) for which he or she will receive $20,000.

ARCHAEOLOGICAL INSTITUTE OF AMERICA [1445]
44 Beacon Street
Boston, MA 02108
(857) 305-9360
Fax: (857) 233-4270
E-mail: fellowships@archaeology.org
Web Site: www.archaeological.org

FOUNDED: 1879

AREAS OF INTEREST:
Archaeological research and publication.

NAME(S) OF PROGRAMS:
● **Helen M. Woodruff Fellowship of the AIA and the American Academy in Rome**

TYPE:
Fellowships. A predoctoral or postdoctoral fellowship for study of archaeology and classical studies established by the Institute at the American Academy in Rome. Award supports a Rome Prize.

PURPOSE:
To promote the study of archaeology and classical studies.

ELIGIBILITY:
Applicant must be a citizen or permanent resident of the U.S.

GEOG. RESTRICTIONS: United States.

FINANCIAL DATA:
Amount of support per award: $10,000.
Total amount of support: $10,000.

NO. AWARDS: 1 in odd-numbered years.

APPLICATION INFO:
Applications must be sent to the American Academy in Rome; 7 East 60th Street; New York, NY 10022.
Duration: One year.
Deadline: November 1 of even-numbered years.

ADDRESS INQUIRIES TO:
Fellowship Coordinator
Tel: (212) 571-7200

ARCHITECTURAL LEAGUE OF NEW YORK
594 Broadway, Suite 607
New York, NY 10012
(212) 753-1722
Fax: (212) 486-9173
E-mail: info@archleague.org
Web Site: archleague.org

TYPE:
Travel grants. The Deborah J. Norden Fund, established in 1995 in memory of architect and arts administrator Deborah Norden, awards travel/study grants to students and recent graduates in the field of architecture, architectural history, and urban studies.

See entry 369 for full listing.

ARCTIC INSTITUTE OF NORTH AMERICA [1446]
The University of Calgary
2500 University Drive, N.W., ES 1040
Calgary AB T2N 1N4 Canada
(403) 220-7515
Fax: (403) 282-4609
E-mail: arctic@ucalgary.ca
Web Site: www.arctic.ucalgary.ca

FOUNDED: 1945

AREAS OF INTEREST:
Arctic natural and social sciences.

NAME(S) OF PROGRAMS:
● **AINA Grants-in-Aid**

TYPE:
Grants-in-aid; Scholarships.

YEAR PROGRAM STARTED: 1945

PURPOSE:
To provide funding to young investigators, especially graduate students, to augment their research.

ELIGIBILITY:
Proposed projects can include field, library or office-intensive investigations. Although there is no limitation on the area of investigation, the Institute encourages applications focused on the natural sciences and social sciences, including anthropology and economics, in the North.

FINANCIAL DATA:
Funding can be used for travel, supplies, equipment and services, but not for salary or wages.
Amount of support per award: $1,000.

Total amount of support: Varies each year, depending on number of applications received.

NO. MOST RECENT APPLICANTS: 80.

NO. AWARDS: Varies.

APPLICATION INFO:
Applications may be submitted online.
Duration: One year.
Deadline: Varies. Check web site for current information.

PUBLICATIONS:
Arctic Journal.

ADDRESS INQUIRIES TO:
Arctic Institute of North America
(See e-mail address above.)

BARNES GROUP FOUNDATION
123 Main Street
Bristol, CT 06010
(860) 583-7070
E-mail: info@bginc.com
Web Site: www.barnesgroupinc.com

TYPE:
General operating grants; Scholarships. Employee scholarship program.

See entry 1064 for full listing.

ROY J. CARVER CHARITABLE TRUST [1447]
202 Iowa Avenue
Muscatine, IA 52761-3733
(563) 263-4010
Fax: (563) 263-1547
E-mail: info@carvertrust.org
Web Site: www.carvertrust.org

FOUNDED: 1982

AREAS OF INTEREST:
Biomedical and scientific research; elementary, secondary and higher education; youth recreation.

TYPE:
Capital grants; Challenge/matching grants; Professorships; Project/program grants; Research grants; Scholarships.

YEAR PROGRAM STARTED: 1982

PURPOSE:
To support medical and scientific research, scholarships, general education and programs addressing the needs of youth.

LEGAL BASIS:
Trust.

ELIGIBILITY:
Eligible organizations must be IRS 501(c)(3) tax-exempt.

GEOG. RESTRICTIONS: Iowa and portions of western Illinois.

FINANCIAL DATA:
Amount of support per award: Varies.
Total amount of support: Varies.

NO. AWARDS: Approximately 61.

APPLICATION INFO:
Detailed information is available online.
Duration: Varies.
Deadline: February 15, May 15, August 15 and November 15.

ADDRESS INQUIRIES TO:
Troy K. Ross, Ph.D., Executive Director
(See address above.)

CENTER FOR CALIFORNIA STUDIES, CAPITAL FELLOWS PROGRAMS

California State University, Sacramento
6000 J Street, MS 6081
Sacramento, CA 95819-6081
(916) 278-6906
Fax: (916) 278-5199
E-mail: calstudies@csus.edu
Web Site: www.csus.edu/center/center-california-studies

TYPE:
Fellowships. Sponsored by the Center for California Studies at California State University, Sacramento. Full-time fellowships for 64 fellows across four programs, 10 to 11 months, and graduate units earned from California State University, Sacramento.

See entry 1785 for full listing.

CORNELL UNIVERSITY

Society for the Humanities
A.D. White House
121 Presidents Drive
Ithaca, NY 14853-1101
(607) 255-9274
(607) 255-4086
Fax: (607) 255-1422
E-mail: humctr@cornell.edu
Web Site: societyhumanities.as.cornell.edu/fellowships

TYPE:
Fellowships. Postdoctoral teaching-research fellowships in the humanities, each awarded for a two-year period. While in residence at Cornell, postdoctoral fellows hold department affiliation and have limited teaching duties and the opportunity for scholarly work.

See entry 323 for full listing.

HUGH AND HAZEL DARLING FOUNDATION   [1448]

520 South Grand Avenue, Suite 395
Los Angeles, CA 90071
(213) 683-5200
Fax: (213) 627-7795
E-mail: rstack@darlingfoundation.org

FOUNDED: 1987

AREAS OF INTEREST:
Education.

TYPE:
Block grants; Capital grants; Challenge/matching grants; Matching gifts; Scholarships; Training grants.

YEAR PROGRAM STARTED: 1987

PURPOSE:
To support education in California, with principle emphasis on legal education.

LEGAL BASIS:
Private foundation.

ELIGIBILITY:
Grants are made only to tax-exempt 501(c)(3) organizations. No grants are made to individuals.

GEOG. RESTRICTIONS: California.

FINANCIAL DATA:
Amount of support per award: Varies.
Total amount of support: $1,950,000 for the year 2020.

NO. MOST RECENT APPLICANTS: 100.

NO. AWARDS: 25 for the year 2020.

APPLICATION INFO:
Send letter and literature.
Deadline: Applications accepted throughout the year.

IRS I.D.: 95-6874901

OFFICERS:
Richard L. Stack, Trustee

ADDRESS INQUIRIES TO:
Richard L. Stack, Trustee
(See address above.)

DELOITTE FOUNDATION   [1449]

695 East Main Street
Stamford, CT 06901
(203) 761-3413
Fax: (877) 366-1742
E-mail: plevine@deloitte.com
Web Site: www.deloitte.com/us/df

FOUNDED: 1928

AREAS OF INTEREST:
Higher education, specializing in accounting and business.

TYPE:
Conferences/seminars; Fellowships; Matching gifts; Professorships; Research grants.

YEAR PROGRAM STARTED: 1956

PURPOSE:
To support education through a variety of initiatives that help develop the talent of the future and their influencers and promote excellence in teaching, research and curriculum innovation.

LEGAL BASIS:
Foundation.

ELIGIBILITY:
Doctoral Fellowship Program applicants must be doctoral candidates pursuing a Ph.D. in accounting at U.S. colleges and universities.

GEOG. RESTRICTIONS: United States.

FINANCIAL DATA:
Amount of support per award: Doctoral Fellowship Program: $25,000.
Total amount of support: Fellowship: $250,000 each year.

NO. MOST RECENT APPLICANTS: Approximately 50.

NO. AWARDS: Doctoral Fellowship Program: Up to 10.

APPLICATION INFO:
Application required only for Doctoral Fellowship Program and can be obtained through head of university accounting program. Send letter for other grant requests.
Duration: Doctoral Fellowship Program: Up to two years.
Deadline: Doctoral Fellowships: October 15. Announcement in late January or early February. No deadline for Research Grants.

PUBLICATIONS:
Information brochure.

BOARD OF DIRECTORS:
Janet Foutty, Chairman
Erin Scanlon, President
Sam Silvers, Secretary and Treasurer

ADDRESS INQUIRIES TO:
Peg Levine, Senior Specialist
(See address above.)

HALBERT CENTRE FOR CANADIAN STUDIES   [1450]

Hebrew University of Jerusalem
Mount Scopus
Jerusalem 9190501 Israel
(972) 2-588-1344
Fax: (972) 2-582-6267
E-mail: mscanada@mail.huji.ac.il
Web Site: canadianstudies.huji.ac.il

FOUNDED: 1944

AREAS OF INTEREST:
Canadian studies.

NAME(S) OF PROGRAMS:
● **Halbert Centre for Canadian Studies Visiting Professors Program**

TYPE:
Professorships; Visiting scholars.

YEAR PROGRAM STARTED: 1945

PURPOSE:
To build bridges and strengthen ties between Canadian and Israeli scholars.

LEGAL BASIS:
Nonprofit.

ELIGIBILITY:
Applicants should hold university teaching positions in the social sciences, humanities or law. Applicants will be expected to combine broad teaching and research experience in their field with an ability to emphasize Canadian content. An expression of interest in participating in cooperative work to emphasize the development of joint Israel-Canada research will be of advantage to the applicant.

GEOG. RESTRICTIONS: Canada.

FINANCIAL DATA:
Remuneration includes up to $3,000 (CAN) for cost of airfare to Israel and housing.
Total amount of support: Varies.

NO. AWARDS: 4 for the academic year 2020-21.

APPLICATION INFO:
Application must be submitted by the chair of the hosting department at the Hebrew University. The hosting department is requested to submit a plan reflecting the nature and scope of the visit, as well as the applicant's curriculum vitae and a short bio.

Curriculum vitae should not exceed two pages in length, and should only include the candidate's experience in the last five years.
Duration: One to four weeks.
Deadline: February 20. Decision by end of March.

PUBLICATIONS:
Program announcement.

ADDRESS INQUIRIES TO:
See e-mail address above.

THE HALLETT CHARITABLE TRUSTS   [1451]

P.O. Box 14729
Minneapolis, MN 55414
(612) 346-7777
E-mail: info@halletttrusts.org
Web Site: www.halletttrusts.org

AREAS OF INTEREST:
Higher education, social services, children's services, health, economic and cultural services.

TYPE:
Project/program grants.

PURPOSE:
To directly impact the population of the community in a manner that will measurably enrich its educational, health, economic and cultural opportunities.

ELIGIBILITY:
Grants are made to organizations that have tax-exempt status under Section 501(c)(3) of the Internal Revenue Code. No grants are made to individuals.

GEOG. RESTRICTIONS: Cuyuna Lakes area, Minnesota.

FINANCIAL DATA:
Amount of support per award: Varies.
Total amount of support: Average $1,000,000 annually.

NO. AWARDS: 23 for the year 2020.

APPLICATION INFO:
Application information is available on the web site.
Duration: Typically one year. Trustees may make multiyear commitments for grants.
Deadline: October 31.

ADDRESS INQUIRIES TO:
Sally Godfrey, Executive Director
(See address above.)

HALLIBURTON FOUNDATION, INC. [1452]
Plaza 1, 3320 T
3000 North Sam Houston Parkway East
Houston, TX 77032
(281) 871-4000
Web Site: www.halliburton.com

FOUNDED: 1965

AREAS OF INTEREST:
Higher education and elementary/secondary education, health, and social services (health related).

TYPE:
Matching gifts; Project/program grants.

LEGAL BASIS:
Corporate giving program.

ELIGIBILITY:
Direct grant process is by invitation. Applicants are accredited junior colleges, colleges and universities or accredited elementary/secondary schools.

No grants are awarded for building programs, financial assistance to students or support of student activities and organizations.

GEOG. RESTRICTIONS: United States.

FINANCIAL DATA:
Amount of support per award: Varies.
Total amount of support: Varies.
Matching fund requirements: Contributions of directors, officers and employees of the Halliburton companies to accredited junior colleges, colleges/universities and elementary/secondary schools are matched 2.25:1 under certain conditions.

NO. AWARDS: Over 500.

APPLICATION INFO:
To be considered for a corporate grant, the organization must:
(1) provide evidence of 501(c)(3) tax-exempt status as granted by the IRS, or of a political subdivision (schools, municipal foundations, etc.);
(2) demonstrate that supporting the request will be of benefit to the company, employees,

the community and customers;
(3) indicate how many people will be impacted by the project;
(4) a summary of how the program or project will be accomplished and the expected results;
(5) a timeline for the project;
(6) budget information and other sources of funding for the project;
(7) a list of board of directors noting their business affiliations and;
(8) the most recent audited financial statement or form 990.
Duration: One year.

PUBLICATIONS:
Guidelines.

ADDRESS INQUIRIES TO:
Administrator
(See address above.)

THE HOROWITZ FOUNDATION FOR SOCIAL POLICY
P.O. Box 7
Rocky Hill, NJ 08553-0007
(732) 445-2280
E-mail: info@horowitz-foundation.org
Web Site: www.horowitz-foundation.org

TYPE:
Research grants. Grants to doctoral candidates at the dissertation level with emphasis on social policy-related studies.

See entry 1661 for full listing.

THE GEORGE A. AND ELIZA GARDNER HOWARD FOUNDATION [1453]
University Hall, Room 406
Brown University
One Prospect Street
Providence, RI 02912
(401) 863-2429
Fax: (401) 863-1339
E-mail: howard_foundation@brown.edu
Web Site: www.brown.edu/howard-foundation

FOUNDED: 1952

TYPE:
Fellowships. The Foundation awards a limited number of fellowships each year for independent projects in fields selected on a rotational basis.

YEAR PROGRAM STARTED: 1952

PURPOSE:
To aid the professional development of promising individuals at the crucial early-mid stages of their careers.

LEGAL BASIS:
Private foundation.

ELIGIBILITY:
Nominees should normally have the rank of assistant or associate professor or their nonacademic equivalents. Support is intended to augment paid sabbatical leaves, making it financially possible for grantees to have time off in which to pursue their projects, free of any other professional responsibilities. Accepted nominees should therefore be eligible for sabbaticals or other leave with guaranteed additional support.

The project undertaken by a Howard Fellow should also be comprehensible to persons outside the immediate field of specialization. Candidates, regardless of their country of

citizenship, must be professionally based in the U.S. either by affiliation with an institution or by residence.

GEOG. RESTRICTIONS: United States.

FINANCIAL DATA:
Amount of support per award: $35,000 for the year 2021-22.
Total amount of support: Approximately $315,000.

NO. MOST RECENT APPLICANTS: 200.

NO. AWARDS: Approximately 9 per year.

APPLICATION INFO:
Application process opens on July 1. Instructions are available on the web site.
Duration: One academic year, July 1 to June 30.
Deadline: November 1.

IRS I.D.: 05-0275563

ADMINISTRATION:
Joseph Meisel, Administrative Director
Edward Goll, Administrative Coordinator

ADDRESS INQUIRIES TO:
Edward Goll
Administrative Coordinator
George A. and Eliza
Gardner Howard Foundation
P.O. Box 1857
Brown University
Providence, RI 02912

INSTITUTE OF INTERNATIONAL EDUCATION/COUNCIL FOR INTERNATIONAL EXCHANGE OF SCHOLARS [1454]
1400 K Street, N.W.
Suite 700
Washington, DC 20005-2403
(202) 686-4000
Fax: (202) 686-4029
E-mail: iea@iie.org
Web Site: www.cies.org/iea

FOUNDED: 1947

AREAS OF INTEREST:
Scholarly exchange.

NAME(S) OF PROGRAMS:
● **Fulbright International Education Administrators Program**

TYPE:
Conferences/seminars; Exchange programs; Project/program grants; Research grants; Travel grants. Through its short-term seminars, the Fulbright International Education Administrators Program can help U.S. higher education administrators establish lasting connections within the social, cultural and education systems of other countries. Selected administrators have the opportunity to gain in-depth knowledge about the host country's higher education system as well as to establish networks of U.S. and international colleagues. Grantees return home with enhanced ability to serve international students and encourage prospective study-abroad students.

YEAR PROGRAM STARTED: 1947

PURPOSE:
To promote mutual understanding between people of the U.S. and people of other nations.

LEGAL BASIS:
Public Law 87-256, as amended, The Mutual Educational and Cultural Exchange Act of 1961.

ELIGIBILITY:
Applicants must be U.S. citizens.

U.S.-France IEA Program is open to experienced international education administrators and senior administrators responsible for enhancing the international dimensions of their institutions.

U.S.-Germany IEA Program is open to experienced administrators in international exchanges, foreign admissions, study-abroad, international education, career services, alumni affairs and development/fund-raising.

U.S.-Korea IEA Program is open to experienced international education administrators and senior administrators responsible for enhancing the international dimensions of their institutions. Preference is given to applicants who have an existing population of Korean students on campus.

Applicants to any of these IEA programs are not required to hold a Ph.D.

GEOG. RESTRICTIONS: United States.

FINANCIAL DATA:
Grants generally include round-trip airfare, travel within the host country, lodging, and a lump sum supplement for incidentals.
Amount of support per award: Varies.

NO. MOST RECENT APPLICANTS: Approximately 70 for the year 2022-23.

NO. AWARDS: U.S.-France IEA: Up to 12; U.S.-Germany IEA: Up to 15; U.S.-Korea IEA: Up to 8; U.S.-Russia IEA: 5.

APPLICATION INFO:
Guidelines are available on the CIES web site. Applications must be submitted online.
Duration: U.S.-France and U.S. Germany IEA: Two weeks in October; U.S.-Korea IEA: Two weeks in June; U.S.-Russia IEA: Two weeks in April.
Deadline: U.S.-France IEA, U.S.-Germany IEA and U.S.-Russia IEA: February 1; U.S.-Korea IEA: November 1.

PUBLICATIONS:
Descriptive brochure; annual awards catalog; annual report.

ADDRESS INQUIRIES TO:
Fulbright International Education Administrators Program
(See address and e-mail above.)

THE FLETCHER JONES FOUNDATION   [1455]
1055 East Colorado Boulevard
5th Floor
Pasadena, CA 91106
(626) 204-4012
Fax: (626) 535-9508
E-mail: mary@fletcherjonesfdn.org
Web Site: www.fletcherjonesfdn.org

FOUNDED: 1969

AREAS OF INTEREST:
Primarily, support to private independent colleges and universities in California.

TYPE:
Capital grants; Endowments; Fellowships; Grants-in-aid; Internships; Professorships; Project/program grants; Scholarships. Equipment grants. Academic programs.

YEAR PROGRAM STARTED: 1969

PURPOSE:
To assist private higher education in California.

LEGAL BASIS:
Private foundation.

ELIGIBILITY:
Grants are made to nonprofit, 501(c)(3) organizations. 90% of grants are for private colleges and universities in California. Grants are not made to carry on propaganda, to influence legislation or elections, to promote voter registration, to political candidates, to political campaigns, or to organizations engaged in such activities. Grants are not made to individuals.

The Foundation generally does not favor requests for projects which should be financed by government agencies, nor does it normally make grants to operating funds, elementary or secondary schools, deficit financing, or contingencies.

GEOG. RESTRICTIONS: California.

FINANCIAL DATA:
Amount of support per award: Varies.

NO. AWARDS: Varies.

REPRESENTATIVE AWARDS:
$1,000,000 to Pomona College; $300,000 to Biola University.

APPLICATION INFO:
The Foundation primarily supports private, nonprofit, degree-granting colleges and universities in California. An institution which believes it meets these criteria may contact the Executive Director for discussion. A link to the online application must be provided by the Executive Director after preliminary consultation.
Deadline: Applications are accepted throughout the year and reviewed quarterly.

IRS I.D.: 23-7030155

STAFF:
Mary Spellman, Executive Director and Treasurer

OFFICERS AND TRUSTEES:
Peter K. Barker, President
John D. Pettker, Vice President and Secretary
Samuel P. Bell, Vice President
Patrick C. Haden, Vice President
Parker S. Kennedy, Vice President
Daniel E. Lungren, Vice President
Donald E. Nickelson, Vice President
Hon. Rockwell Schnabel, Vice President
Stewart R. Smith, Vice President

ADDRESS INQUIRIES TO:
Mary Spellman
Executive Director and Treasurer
(See address above.)

LUMINA FOUNDATION   [1456]
30 South Meridian Street, Suite 700
Indianapolis, IN 46204-3503
(317) 951-5300
(800) 834-5756
Fax: (317) 951-5063
E-mail: gm@luminafoundation.org
Web Site: www.luminafoundation.org

FOUNDED: 2000

AREAS OF INTEREST:
Promoting educational improvements and access. Focus beginning in 2013: Mobilizing to reach Goal 2025 and designing and building a 21st-century higher education system.

TYPE:
Research contracts. Project/policy grants. The Foundation has worked with and made grants

to many colleges, universities, peer foundations, associations and other organizations that work to improve student outcomes across the nation.

PURPOSE:
To help people achieve their potential by expanding access to and success in education beyond high school. Specific goal: To increase the proportion of Americans with high-quality college degrees, certificates and credentials to 60% by 2025.

ELIGIBILITY:
Organizations that are classified as tax-exempt under Section 501(c)(3) of the Internal Revenue Code and as public charities under Section 509(a)(1), (2) or (3) or to public organizations that are designated under Section 170(c) of the Code, not individuals. Grants will not be made to supporting organizations controlled by disqualified persons to Lumina or Type III supporting organizations that are not functionally integrated Type III supporting organizations (as defined in the Internal Revenue Code).

GEOG. RESTRICTIONS: United States and its territories.

FINANCIAL DATA:
Amount of support per award: Average grant amount: $250,000.
Total amount of support: More than $55,000,000 for the year 2020.

NO. AWARDS: 143.

APPLICATION INFO:
Organizations new to Lumina, as well as existing grantees and consultants, are encouraged to complete a partner survey of demographic and related information. Responses are reviewed and made available so that Foundation staff may carefully review. Complete information can be found on the web site. Full proposals are by invitation.
Duration: One to three years. Grant is not renewable.

ADDRESS INQUIRIES TO:
Grants Management
P.O. Box 1806
Indianapolis, IN 46206-1806

NATIONAL ASSOCIATION OF SCHOLARS   [1457]
420 Madison Avenue
7th Floor
New York, NY 10017
(917) 551-6770
E-mail: contact@nas.org
Web Site: www.nas.org

NAME(S) OF PROGRAMS:
● **The Peter Shaw Memorial Award**

TYPE:
Awards/prizes. The Peter Shaw Memorial Award recognizes exemplary writing on issues pertaining to higher education and American intellectual culture.

PURPOSE:
To enrich the substance and strengthen the integrity of scholarship and teaching.

ELIGIBILITY:
Candidates must be chosen by the Association.

FINANCIAL DATA:
Award includes a plaque and travel expenses to attend the Association's National Conference and present a speech.

Amount of support per award: $1,000.

*PLEASE NOTE:
Awards are not given on an annual basis, but only when the Association holds a National Conference.

NATIONAL WILDLIFE FEDERATION

11100 Wildlife Center Drive
Reston, VA 20190-5362
(703) 438-6265
Fax: (703) 438-6468
E-mail: fellows@nwf.org
ecoleaders@nwf.org
Web Site: www.nwf.org
www.nwfecoleaders.org

TYPE:
Fellowships.

See entry 1977 for full listing.

THE SAMUEL ROBERTS NOBLE FOUNDATION [1458]

2510 Sam Noble Parkway
Ardmore, OK 73401
(580) 224-6213
Fax: (580) 224-6212
E-mail: granting@noblefoundation.org
Web Site: www.noblefoundation.org

FOUNDED: 1945

AREAS OF INTEREST:
Health, education and strong communities.

TYPE:
Capital grants; Challenge/matching grants; General operating grants; Project/program grants.

YEAR PROGRAM STARTED: 1946

PURPOSE:
To advance agricultural science and practice by conducting field and laboratory research, and by providing consultations to farmers, ranchers, and land managers in the Southern Great Plains; to foster sustainable agricultural practices; to support worthy charities through a program of grants with the aim of building stronger communities.

LEGAL BASIS:
Private foundation.

ELIGIBILITY:
Organizations must be classified as 501(c)(3) by the IRS and are primarily located in Oklahoma. No loans or grants are made to individuals.

GEOG. RESTRICTIONS: Oklahoma.

FINANCIAL DATA:
Amount of support per award: Varies.
Total amount of support: Varies.

NO. AWARDS: 31 grants approved for the year 2019.

APPLICATION INFO:
Letters of Inquiry must be submitted through the online grants management system.
Deadline: Letters of inquiry will be accepted online January 1 through June 1.

IRS I.D.: 73-0606209

STAFF:
Stacy Newman, Director of Philanthropy
Sarah Johnson, Program Coordinator

ADDRESS INQUIRIES TO:
Sarah Johnson, Program Coordinator
(See address above.)

NORTH CAROLINA ASSOCIATION OF EDUCATORS [1459]

NCAE Center for Instructional Advocacy
700 South Salisbury Street
Raleigh, NC 27601
(919) 832-3000
(800) 662-7924
Fax: (919) 829-1626
E-mail: awards@ncae.org
Web Site: www.ncae.org

FOUNDED: 1970

AREAS OF INTEREST:
Teaching.

NAME(S) OF PROGRAMS:
● **Mary Morrow/Edna Richards Scholarship Fund**

TYPE:
Scholarships. To be used for college expenses in senior year.

YEAR PROGRAM STARTED: 1994

PURPOSE:
To aid worthy students who plan to teach in North Carolina after graduation.

LEGAL BASIS:
Nonprofit organization.

ELIGIBILITY:
The applicant must be in their junior year in a North Carolina college or university, planning to teach and willing to teach in the public schools of North Carolina for at least two years following graduation. Selection is based on character, personality, scholastic achievement, evidence of promise as a teacher and financial need.

GEOG. RESTRICTIONS: North Carolina.

FINANCIAL DATA:
Amount of support per award: $1,000 per year.
Total amount of support: Varies.

NO. MOST RECENT APPLICANTS: Varies.

NO. AWARDS: Varies.

APPLICATION INFO:
Application forms are mailed in Fall to the heads of the department of education in colleges in North Carolina, both state-supported and private. The department head is requested to give the application forms to two juniors of his or her selection.
Duration: One year.
Deadline: January 30 (postmark).

ADDRESS INQUIRIES TO:
NCAE Center for Instructional Advocacy
(See address above.)

RADCLIFFE INSTITUTE FOR ADVANCED STUDY, HARVARD UNIVERSITY [1460]

Radcliffe Institute Fellowship Program
Byerly Hall
8 Garden Street
Cambridge, MA 02138
E-mail: fellowships@radcliffe.harvard.edu
Web Site: www.radcliffe.harvard.edu

FOUNDED: 1960

NAME(S) OF PROGRAMS:
● **Radcliffe Institute Fellowship Program**

TYPE:
Fellowships. The Radcliffe Institute for Advanced Study is a scholarly community where individuals pursue advanced work across a wide range of academic disciplines, professions or creative arts. Within this broad purpose, and in recognition of Radcliffe's historic contributions to the education of women and to the study of issues related to women, the Radcliffe Institute sustains a continuing commitment to the study of women, gender and society, although applicants' projects need not focus on gender.

Radcliffe Institute Fellowships are designed to support scholars, scientists, artists and writers of exceptional promise and demonstrated accomplishment who wish to pursue independent work in academic and professional fields, and in the creative arts.

YEAR PROGRAM STARTED: 1999

PURPOSE:
To offer support to The Radcliffe Institute for Advanced Study Fellowship programs for a scholarly community where individuals pursue advanced work across a wide range of academic disciplines, professions and creative arts.

LEGAL BASIS:
Department of Harvard University, nonprofit.

ELIGIBILITY:
For all programs, residence in the Boston area and participation in the Institute community are required during the fellowship appointment.

FINANCIAL DATA:
Some support for relocation expenses provided when relevant. If so directed, Radcliffe will pay stipend to home institution if the institution is U.S.-based.
Amount of support per award: Stipends up to $78,000 for one year, plus $5,000 to cover project expenses.

NO. MOST RECENT APPLICANTS: Over 1,350 for the year 2019.

NO. AWARDS: Up to 50 fellowships.

APPLICATION INFO:
Applications are available online in late Spring.
Duration: September 1 to May 31.
Deadline: Humanities and Social Sciences and Creative Arts: Mid-September. Science, Engineering and Mathematics: Early October.

STAFF:
Alison Ney, Administrator of Fellowships

ADDRESS INQUIRIES TO:
See e-mail address above.

*SPECIAL STIPULATIONS:
Fellows are expected to present their work-in-progress and to attend other fellows' events.

THE NELL J. REDFIELD FOUNDATION

P.O. Box 61
Reno, NV 89504
(775) 323-1373
Fax: (775) 323-4476
E-mail: gsmith@redfieldfoundation.org

TYPE:
Capital grants; Challenge/matching grants; Development grants; Matching gifts; Project/program grants. Grants for higher education. Medical and social welfare for disadvantaged children and seniors.

See entry 244 for full listing.

GERTRUDE E. SKELLY CHARITABLE FOUNDATION [1461]

4600 North Ocean Boulevard
Suite 206
Boynton Beach, FL 33435
(561) 276-1008
Fax: (561) 272-2793
E-mail: ejoh@hhk.com

FOUNDED: 1991

AREAS OF INTEREST:
Nursing education and medical care for indigents.

TYPE:
Challenge/matching grants; Conferences/seminars; Project/program grants; Research grants; Scholarships; Training grants. Emergency grants for continued education.

YEAR PROGRAM STARTED: 1991

PURPOSE:
To provide scholarships for individuals to obtain educational opportunities and/or medical care.

LEGAL BASIS:
Private foundation.

ELIGIBILITY:
Eligible applicants are colleges and universities, and other IRS 501(c)(3) tax-exempt organizations. No grants are given to agencies which do not provide direct services or scholarships.

GEOG. RESTRICTIONS: United States.

FINANCIAL DATA:
Amount of support per award: Maximum $50,000.
Total amount of support: $750,000 for the year 2020.
Matching fund requirements: Tailored to specific projects.

NO. MOST RECENT APPLICANTS: 100.

NO. AWARDS: 100.

APPLICATION INFO:
Write to the address above for application guidelines.
Duration: One year.
Deadline: June 30. Award announcement the following January or second quarter of the following year.

TRUSTEES:
Erik Edward Joh

ADDRESS INQUIRIES TO:
Erik Edward Joh, Trustee
(See address above.)

TARAKNATH DAS FOUNDATION [1462]

South Asia Institute
Columbia University
606 West 122nd Street, Room 213
New York, NY 10027
E-mail: lg17@columbia.edu
Web Site: www.sai.columbia.edu/taraknath-das-foundation

FOUNDED: 1930

AREAS OF INTEREST:
Indian national graduate students studying any field in a U.S. university.

TYPE:
Grants-in-aid.

YEAR PROGRAM STARTED: 1935

PURPOSE:
To promote friendly relations and cultural cooperation between the U.S. and India.

LEGAL BASIS:
Special interest foundation.

ELIGIBILITY:
Applicants are not limited by discipline or subject area. Applicants must be Indian nationals (holding Indian passports) and must have completed at least one year of graduate study in the U.S.

FINANCIAL DATA:
Amount of support per award: $5,000 to $7,000.
Total amount of support: Approximately $25,000.

NO. MOST RECENT APPLICANTS: Varies.

NO. AWARDS: 4 or 5 annually.

APPLICATION INFO:
Applicants must submit all application materials together. Only complete applications will be judged for the awards. Complete applications include:
(1) completed application form;
(2) transcript from most recent academic institution;
(3) three sealed letters of recommendation, including one from the applicant's academic advisor;
(4) academic plans of applicant and;
(5) photocopy of applicant's passport.
Duration: One year.
Deadline: October 31.

ADDRESS INQUIRIES TO:
Leonard Gordon, Director
(See address above.)

U.S. DEPARTMENT OF EDUCATION [1463]

Office of Post Secondary Education
Federal TRIO Programs
400 Maryland Avenue, S.W.
Washington, DC 20202
(202) 453-6273
(202) 453-6914
Fax: (202) 502-7857
E-mail: OPE_TRIO@ed.gov
Web Site: www.ed.gov/ope/trio

AREAS OF INTEREST:
Education for low-income youth.

NAME(S) OF PROGRAMS:
• **Upward Bound**

TYPE:
Project/program grants. There are three types of grants under the Upward Bound program: Regular Upward Bound Grants, Veterans Upward Bound Grants, and Upward Bound Math and Science Grants.

The Regular Upward Bound projects are designed to generate in participants the skills and motivation necessary for success in education beyond secondary school. The Veterans Upward Bound projects are designed to assist veterans in preparing for a program of postsecondary education. The Upward Bound Math and Science projects are designed to prepare high school students for postsecondary education programs that lead to careers in the fields of math and science.

YEAR PROGRAM STARTED: 1966

PURPOSE:
To generate participation skills and the motivation necessary for success in education beyond school.

LEGAL BASIS:
Title IV of the Higher Education Act of 1965, as amended.

ELIGIBILITY:
Institutions of higher education, public and private agencies and organizations including community-based organizations with experience serving disadvantaged youth, combinations of such institutions, agencies and organizations, and, as appropriate to the purposes of the program, secondary schools may apply. Students must have completed the eighth grade, be between the ages of 13 and 19, and have a need for academic support in order to pursue a program of postsecondary education. All students must be either from low-income families or be potential first-generation college students. The program requires that two-thirds of the participants in a project must be both low-income and potential first-generation students. The remaining one-third must be either low-income, first-generation college students, or students who have a high risk for academic failure.

GEOG. RESTRICTIONS: United States.

FINANCIAL DATA:
Amount of support per award: Average $355,442 for fiscal year 2019.
Total amount of support: $343,356,535 allocated for fiscal year 2019.

NO. MOST RECENT APPLICANTS: 70,744.

NO. AWARDS: 966.

APPLICATION INFO:
Applications are submitted through grants.gov.
Duration: Five-year grant award cycles.

ADDRESS INQUIRIES TO:
Kenneth Waters, Program Specialist
(See address above.)

U.S. DEPARTMENT OF EDUCATION [1464]

International and Foreign Language Education
400 Maryland Avenue, S.W.
Washington, DC 20202
(202) 453-6391
E-mail: tanyelle.richardson@ed.gov
Web Site: www.ed.gov/ope/iegps

NAME(S) OF PROGRAMS:
• **Undergraduate International Studies and Foreign Language Program**

TYPE:
Project/program grants; Seed money grants. Grants to plan, develop, and carry out a program to strengthen and improve undergraduate instruction in international studies and foreign languages. Projects primarily focus on curriculum and faculty development. Institutions of higher education and public and private nonprofit agencies and organizations may apply for funds to develop projects which have the potential for making an especially significant contribution to the improvement of undergraduate instruction in international and foreign language studies in the U.S.

YEAR PROGRAM STARTED: 1972

PURPOSE:
To assist institutions to internationalize the curriculum. Applicants may propose to

initiate a global studies program or a program focusing on a single world area and its languages; to develop a program which focuses on issues or topics, such as environmental studies or international business; to combine the teaching of international studies with professional or preprofessional training; to integrate undergraduate studies with Master's degree programs; to combine international studies with teacher training programs.

LEGAL BASIS:
Title VI, section 604A, Higher Education Act, as amended in 1986.

ELIGIBILITY:
Proposals are invited from institutions of higher education, including universities and two- to four-year colleges, and consortia of such institutions. The proposed program should include plans to initiate new or revised courses in international studies or area studies, and to improve or expand instruction in foreign languages. The program should be comparative or interdisciplinary in nature and strengthen linkages among disciplines and professional fields.

GEOG. RESTRICTIONS: United States.

FINANCIAL DATA:
Amount of support per award: Single Institutions: Average $89,000 per year; Organizations, Associations and Institutional Consortia: Average $140,000 per year.
Total amount of support: $2,800,000 for fiscal year 2020.
Matching fund requirements: Dollar-for-dollar primarily within in-kind contributions.

NO. MOST RECENT APPLICANTS: 92.

NO. AWARDS: Approximately 30 new awards for fiscal year 2020.

APPLICATION INFO:
Applications are required to be submitted electronically using the grants.gov system.
Duration: Single Institutions: Up to two years; Organizations, Associations and Institutional Consortia: Up to three years.
Deadline: Summer.

STAFF:
Tanyelle Richardson, Senior Program Officer

ADDRESS INQUIRIES TO:
Tanyelle Richardson
Senior Program Officer
(See e-mail address above.)

*PLEASE NOTE:
Competition held every two years contingent upon receiving a Congressional Appropriation.

U.S. DEPARTMENT OF EDUCATION
400 Maryland Avenue, S.W.
Washington, DC 20024
(202) 453-7521
E-mail: timothy.duvall@ed.gov
Web Site: www2.ed.
gov/programs/iegpscibe/index.html

TYPE:
Project/program grants. The program provides grants to eligible institutions of higher education or combinations of these institutions for planning, establishing and operating Centers for International Business Education.

See entry 1719 for full listing.

U.S. DEPARTMENT OF EDUCATION
International and Foreign Language Education (IFLE)
Language Resource Centers Program
400 Maryland Avenue, S.W.
Mail Stop 258-40
Washington, DC 20202
(202) 453-7854
E-mail: carolyn.collins@ed.gov
Web Site: www2.ed.
gov/programs/iegpslrc/index.html

TYPE:
General operating grants. Language Resource Centers Program provides grants for establishing, strengthening and operating centers that serve as resources for improving the nation's capacity for teaching and learning foreign languages through teacher training, research, materials development and dissemination projects.

See entry 610 for full listing.

UCLA INSTITUTE OF AMERICAN CULTURES (IAC)
2329 Murphy Hall, Box 957244
Los Angeles, CA 90095-7244
(310) 825-6815
Fax: (310) 825-3994
E-mail: iaccoordinator@conet.ucla.edu
Web Site: www.iac.ucla.edu

TYPE:
Fellowships. Deals with arts and humanities, education and teacher training, fine arts, applied arts, law, social sciences, and sciences. The IAC, in cooperation with UCLA's four Ethnic Studies Research Centers (American Indian Studies Center, Asian American Studies Center, Bunche Center for African American Studies, and Chicano Studies Research Center), offers awards to visiting scholars to support research on African Americans, American Indians, Asian Americans and Chicanas/os.

See entry 922 for full listing.

THE UNIVERSITY OF CALGARY [1465]
Faculty of Graduate Studies
Earth Sciences Building, Room 1010
2500 University Drive, N.W.
Calgary AB T2N 1N4 Canada
(403) 220-4938
Fax: (403) 289-7635
E-mail: gsaward@ucalgary.ca
Web Site: grad.ucalgary.ca/awards

AREAS OF INTEREST:
Management.

NAME(S) OF PROGRAMS:
● **Robert A. Willson Doctoral Management Scholarship**

TYPE:
Awards/prizes; Scholarships.

PURPOSE:
To produce a noteworthy leader in management teaching and research who has a broad appreciation of management's role in society, both nationally and internationally.

ELIGIBILITY:
Open to students registered full-time in a doctoral program in the Haskayne School of Business. While academic excellence is essential, candidates should also present evidence of leadership in their academic or

professional background. Students with international experience and orientation will be particularly considered.

FINANCIAL DATA:
Amount of support per award: $10,000.
Total amount of support: $10,000.

CO-OP FUNDING PROGRAMS: The donor of this scholarship program is the Haskayne School of Business.

NO. AWARDS: 1 per annum.

APPLICATION INFO:
Students should consult the Haskayne School of Business. A recommendation will be forwarded to the Graduate Scholarship Office. The recommendation is subject to final approval of the Graduate Scholarship Committee.
Duration: One year.
Deadline: May 15.

PUBLICATIONS:
Academic calendar.

ADDRESS INQUIRIES TO:
Graduate Scholarship Office
(See address above.)

UNIVERSITY OF CALIFORNIA
President's Postdoctoral Fellowship Program
402 Sproul Hall
Berkeley, CA 94720-1508
(510) 643-8235
E-mail: ppfpinfo@berkeley.edu
Web Site: ppfp.ucop.edu/info

TYPE:
Fellowships. Awarded for research conducted under faculty sponsorship on any one of the University of California's 10 campuses.

See entry 924 for full listing.

THE UNIVERSITY OF TEXAS AT AUSTIN [1466]
LBJ School of Public Affairs
P.O. Box Y
Austin, TX 78713-8925
(512) 471-4292
Fax: (512) 471-8455
E-mail: lbjadmit@austin.utexas.edu
Web Site: lbj.utexas.edu

AREAS OF INTEREST:
Public policy.

NAME(S) OF PROGRAMS:
● **Lyndon B. Johnson School of Public Affairs**

TYPE:
Assistantships; Fellowships. Merit fellowships are available to assist graduate students with financial support for education at the Master's and doctoral level.

ELIGIBILITY:
Applicants must be graduate students enrolled in Lyndon B. Johnson School of Public Affairs.

FINANCIAL DATA:
Amount of support per award: $4,000 to $60,000.

NO. AWARDS: Varies.

APPLICATION INFO:
Contact the University for application procedures.
Duration: One to two years. Grants not renewable.

Deadline: Varies.

ADDRESS INQUIRIES TO:
Office of Student Affairs and
Admissions
(See address above.)

THE WABASH CENTER FOR TEACHING AND LEARNING IN THEOLOGY AND RELIGION

301 West Wabash Avenue
Crawfordsville, IN 47933
(765) 361-6047
Fax: (765) 361-6051
E-mail: wabashcenter@wabash.edu
Web Site: www.wabashcenter.wabash.edu

TYPE:
Conferences/seminars; Fellowships;
Project/program grants; Research grants.

See entry 754 for full listing.

JEANNETTE K. WATSON FELLOWSHIP   [1467]

233 Broadway
Suite 2709
New York, NY 10279
(212) 245-8859
E-mail: jkw@watson.foundation
Web Site: watson.foundation

TYPE:
Fellowships. The program offers 15 students
each year, from 12 New York City colleges,
the opportunity for paid internships for three
consecutive summers. The internships offer
closely supervised, challenging work from
which the student can learn. The expectation
is that three summers in different sectors
(nonprofit organizations, public service and
for-profit firms) in New York City and
overseas will make fellows more compelling
candidates for national fellowships, graduate
admissions and good jobs.

YEAR PROGRAM STARTED: 2000

PURPOSE:
To develop talent, leadership and motivation
for service.

ELIGIBILITY:
Applicant must:
(1) be enrolled at one of the invited colleges
(Baruch College, Brooklyn College, City
College, College of Staten Island, Hunter
College, John Jay College, Lehman College,
Long Island University-Brooklyn Campus,
Marymount Manhattan College, Pace
University-Manhattan Campus, Queens
College, and St. John's University);
(2) be a second-semester freshman or a
sophomore;
(3) not be older than 25 on March 1 of
application year;
(4) be enrolled in a liberal arts program;
(5) be a U.S. citizen or a "green card" holder
and;
(6) be willing to participate in three
successive summer internships and their
collateral summer and term-time seminars.

FINANCIAL DATA:
Amount of support per award: $6,000 for the
first summer; $7,500 for the second summer,
and $8,500 for the third summer, plus $2,000
discovery fund.
Total amount of support: $360,000 annually.

APPLICATION INFO:
Application information is available on the
web site.

Duration: Three consecutive summer
internships of 10 weeks plus year-round
activities.
Deadline: February.

STAFF:
Chris Kasabach, Foundation Executive
Director

THOMAS J. WATSON FELLOWSHIP PROGRAM   [1468]

233 Broadway
Suite 2709
New York, NY 10279
(212) 245-8859
E-mail: tjw@watson.foundation
Web Site: watson.foundation

FOUNDED: 1968

AREAS OF INTEREST:
Independent study outside of the U.S. for
graduating college seniors.

TYPE:
Fellowships. The Foundation provides
Fellows an opportunity for a focused and
disciplined "Wanderjahr" of their own
devising or design-time in which to explore
with thoroughness a particular interest, test
their aspirations and abilities, view their lives
and American society in greater perspective
and concomitantly, to develop a more
informed sense of international concern. The
Fellowship experience is intended to provide
Fellows an opportunity to immerse
themselves in cultures other than their own
for an entire year. The candidate's proposed
project should involve investigation into an
area of demonstrated concern and personal
interest.

YEAR PROGRAM STARTED: 1968

PURPOSE:
To give exceptional college graduates the
freedom to engage in a year of independent
study, purposeful exploration and travel
outside of the U.S. in order to enhance their
capacity for resourcefulness, imagination,
openness and leadership, and to foster their
humane and effective participation in the
world community.

LEGAL BASIS:
Private foundation.

ELIGIBILITY:
The Foundation welcomes applicants from a
diverse range of backgrounds and academic
disciplines. Only graduating seniors at one of
40 partner colleges are eligible for
nomination by their institution.

GEOG. RESTRICTIONS: United States.

FINANCIAL DATA:
Amount of support per award: $36,000.
Total amount of support: Varies.

NO. MOST RECENT APPLICANTS: 220.

NO. AWARDS: Varies.

APPLICATION INFO:
Students must first be nominated by their
college or university, and then compete on a
national level. Application form required.
Duration: One year.
Deadline: Nominations and nominees'
completed applications should arrive by first
Tuesday in November. Announcement made
in mid-March.

PUBLICATIONS:
Guidelines.

IRS I.D.: 13-6038151

STAFF:
Sneha Subramanian, Program Manager

*SPECIAL STIPULATIONS:
All Fellows are required to maintain contact
with the fellowship office during their year
abroad. In addition to quarterly progress
reports, they must submit a final evaluation
of the Fellowship year together with a
financial accounting of the expenditure of
Fellowship funds. The Fellowship is taxable
and must be reported by recipients as
income. Taxes are not withheld by the
Foundation.

TODD WEHR FOUNDATION   [1469]

9212 Wilson Boulevard
Wauwatosa, WI 53226
(414) 258-6481

FOUNDED: 1954

AREAS OF INTEREST:
Education and inner-city Milwaukee capital
projects for the benefit of children.

TYPE:
Capital grants.

ELIGIBILITY:
Organizations must have 501(c)(3)
tax-exempt status. No grants to individuals.

GEOG. RESTRICTIONS: Wisconsin, with emphasis
on Milwaukee.

FINANCIAL DATA:
Amount of support per award: $5,000 to
$500,000.

NO. AWARDS: 1 to 10.

APPLICATION INFO:
Send brief letter of inquiry along with full
proposal.
Duration: One to 10 years.
Deadline: Applications accepted throughout
the year.

ADDRESS INQUIRIES TO:
Allan E. Iding, Chairman of the Board
(See address above.)

Scholar aid programs (all disciplines)

ALABAMA COMMISSION ON HIGHER EDUCATION   [1470]

100 North Union Street
Montgomery, AL 36104-3702
(334) 242-2273
Fax: (334) 242-2269
E-mail: cheryl.newton@ache.edu
Web Site: ache.edu

FOUNDED: 1977

AREAS OF INTEREST:
Continuing higher education.

NAME(S) OF PROGRAMS:
● **Senior Adult Scholarship Program**

TYPE:
Grants-in-aid; Scholarships. A free tuition
program for senior citizens who meet the
admission requirements.

ELIGIBILITY:
Alabama residents who are 60 years of age or older and who attend public two-year postsecondary educational institutions in Alabama are eligible to apply.

GEOG. RESTRICTIONS: Alabama.

APPLICATION INFO:
Applications can be obtained by contacting the financial aid office at any public two-year postsecondary educational institution in Alabama.

ADDRESS INQUIRIES TO:
Alabama Community College Systems
Tel: (334) 293-4500

ALABAMA COMMISSION ON HIGHER EDUCATION   [1471]

100 North Union Street
Montgomery, AL 36104-3702
(334) 242-2273
Fax: (334) 242-2269
E-mail: cheryl.newton@ache.edu
Web Site: ache.edu

FOUNDED: 1977

AREAS OF INTEREST:
Higher education.

NAME(S) OF PROGRAMS:
- **Alabama National Guard Educational Assistance Program**

TYPE:
Awards/prizes. An award to be used for tuition and educational fees for Alabama National Guard members to attend a public or private postsecondary educational institution in Alabama.

YEAR PROGRAM STARTED: 1984

ELIGIBILITY:
Students who are active members in good standing with a federally recognized unit of the Alabama National Guard are eligible to apply. Participants may receive federal veterans benefits, but must show a cost-less-aid amount of at least $100. Awards are based on need.

GEOG. RESTRICTIONS: Alabama.

FINANCIAL DATA:
Amount of support per award: Awards are limited to a maximum of $5,406 per term per year.
Total amount of support: $5,009,571 for the year 2019-20.

NO. AWARDS: 983 for the year 2019-20.

APPLICATION INFO:
Application forms are available from Alabama National Guard Units. Funds are limited, so students who are Guard members are encouraged to apply early. Forms must be signed by a representative of the Alabama Military Department and the financial aid officer at the college or university the student plans to attend. All applicants must have the Free Application for Federal Student Aid (FAFSA) on file.

ADDRESS INQUIRIES TO:
Cheryl B. Newton
Manager of Grants and Scholarships
(See address above.)

ALABAMA COMMISSION ON HIGHER EDUCATION   [1472]

100 North Union Street
Montgomery, AL 36104-3702
(334) 242-2273
Fax: (334) 242-2269
E-mail: cheryl.newton@ache.edu
Web Site: ache.edu

FOUNDED: 1977

AREAS OF INTEREST:
Higher education.

NAME(S) OF PROGRAMS:
- **Alabama Student Assistance Program**
- **Alabama Student Grant Program**

TYPE:
Awards/prizes; Grants-in-aid; Scholarships. The Alabama Student Assistance Program is a need-based, state grant. Awards are limited to undergraduate work.

The Alabama Student Grant Program is an award of grant assistance at an eligible independent Alabama college or university. Award is not based on need. Maximum amount available only when sufficient funds are available.

ELIGIBILITY:
Applicants for the Alabama Student Assistance Program must be undergraduate students who are Alabama residents attending eligible Alabama institutions. 55 Alabama institutions participate in the program.

Applicants for the Alabama Student Grant Program must be undergraduate students either half-time or full-time who are Alabama residents attending Amridge University, Birmingham-Southern College, Faulkner University, Huntington College, Judson College, Miles College, Oakwood University, Samford University, South University-Montgomery, Spring Hill College, Stillman College, U.S. Sports Academy or the University of Mobile.

GEOG. RESTRICTIONS: Alabama.

FINANCIAL DATA:
Amount of support per award: Student Assistance Program: $300 to $5,000; Student Grant Program: Up to $1,200.
Total amount of support: ASAP: $5,178,689; ASGP: $6,145,655 for the year 2019-20.

NO. AWARDS: ASAP: 6,746; ASGP: 5,467 for the year 2019-20.

APPLICATION INFO:
Application forms are available on the ACHE web site and at the institution that the applicant is planning on attending.

ADDRESS INQUIRIES TO:
Cheryl B. Newton
Manager of Grants and Scholarships
(See address above.)

AMERICAN ASSOCIATION OF UNIVERSITY WOMEN

1310 L Street, N.W.
Suite 1000
Washington, DC 20005
E-mail: fellowships@aauw.org
Web Site: www.aauw.org

TYPE:
Fellowships. Awarded to women who are U.S. citizens or permanent residents who are pursuing full-time study in a Master's or professional degree program in which women are underrepresented, including STEM, law, business and medicine.

See entry 968 for full listing.

AMERICAN COUNCIL FOR POLISH CULTURE (ACPC) [1473]

911 Saddleback Court
McLean, VA 22102
(301) 717-0662
Web Site: www.polishcultureacpc.org

NAME(S) OF PROGRAMS:
- **ACPC Scholarship, Summer Studies in Poland**
- **Polish Studies Scholarship**
- **Pulaski Scholarships for Advanced Studies**
- **Wladyslaw Zachariasiewicz Memorial Journalism Scholarship**

TYPE:
Scholarships.

ELIGIBILITY:
ACPC Scholarship, Summer Studies in Poland: American of Polish descent entering junior or senior year at accredited college or university. Must have an ACPC affiliation.

Polish Studies Scholarship: Intended for students pursuing some Polish studies (major may be in other fields) at universities in the U.S. who have completed at least two years of college or university work. Scholarships awarded for the fall term.

Pulaski Scholarships for Advanced Studies: Applicant must be of Polish heritage and have completed at least two years in advanced studies at a U.S. university.

Wladyslaw Zachariasiewicz Memorial Journalism Scholarship: Applicant must be a U.S. citizen, or one currently applying for U.S. citizenship, admitted for a fully accredited university in the U.S. or Poland. Special consideration will be given to students of Polish-American heritage and those of non-Polish heritage who have a clear and thorough understanding of Polish culture and values. Awards are based solely on professional and academic merit with an appreciation for issues that affect Polish-Americans.

FINANCIAL DATA:
Amount of support per award: ACPC Scholarship, Summer Studies in Poland: $2,000 toward transportation and tuition; Polish Studies Scholarship: $3,000; Pulaski Scholarships for Advanced Studies: $5,000; Zachariasiewicz Scholarship: $5,000 toward tuition and school-related expenses other than room and board.

APPLICATION INFO:
Instructions and application form, if required, are available online.
Deadline: ACPC Scholarship, Summer Studies in Poland: April 15. Polish Studies Scholarship: April 5. Pulaski Scholarships for Advanced Studies: March 16. Zachariasiewicz Scholarship: June 30.

ADMINISTRATION:
Raymond Glembocki, President

ADDRESS INQUIRIES TO:
ACPC Scholarship, Summer Studies in Poland:
Robert Synakowski
E-mail: syracusepolishhome@yahoo.com

Polish Studies Scholarship:
Deborah M. Majka
E-mail: dziecko2@comcast.net

Pulaski Scholarships for Advanced Studies:
Dr. Steven Medvec
E-mail: samedvec@comcast.net

Wladyslaw Zachariasiewicz Memorial
Scholarship Committee:
Mark G. Dillon, Chairperson
E-mail: mglendillon@aol.com

AMERICAN COUNCIL OF THE BLIND   [1474]
1703 North Beauregard Street
Suite 420
Alexandria, VA 22311
(612) 332-3242
(800) 866-3242
Fax: (703) 465-5085
E-mail: info@acb.org
Web Site: www.acb.org

FOUNDED: 1961

AREAS OF INTEREST:
Independence, security, equality of
opportunity and quality of life for all blind
and visually impaired.

NAME(S) OF PROGRAMS:
● **American Council of the Blind
Scholarships**

TYPE:
Assistantships; Awards/prizes; Internships;
Scholarships. Scholarships for outstanding
blind students enrolled in academic,
vocational, technical or professional training
programs beyond the high school level.

YEAR PROGRAM STARTED: 1982

PURPOSE:
To assist blind postsecondary students with
educational expenses.

LEGAL BASIS:
Nonprofit membership organization.

ELIGIBILITY:
Applicants must be legally blind persons
admitted or under consideration for
admission to postsecondary training programs
for the next school year, who are U.S.
citizens or resident aliens and who have
submitted a completed application and the
required supporting materials.

GEOG. RESTRICTIONS: United States.

FINANCIAL DATA:
Amount of support per award: $2,000 to
$7,500.
Total amount of support: $92,300 for the
year 2020.

NO. AWARDS: 21 for the year 2020.

APPLICATION INFO:
Application must be submitted through the
Council's web site.
Duration: One academic year. Nonrenewable,
but recipient may reapply.
Deadline: Mid-February.

PUBLICATIONS:
Annual report; *Braille Forum*; *Student
Advocate*.

IRS I.D.: 58-0914436

OFFICERS:
Dan Spoone, President
Mark Richert, First Vice President
Ray Campbell, Second Vice President

ADDRESS INQUIRIES TO:
Nancy Feela, Administrative Assistant
(See telephone numbers above.)

AMERICAN FRIENDS OF THE ALEXANDER VON HUMBOLDT FOUNDATION   [1475]
1401 K Street
Suite 1005
Washington, DC 20005
(202) 783-1907
E-mail: info@americanfriendsofavh.org
Web Site: www.americanfriendsofavh.org

FOUNDED: 1953

AREAS OF INTEREST:
Scholarly research and academic cooperation
through provision of awards and fellowships.
All countries and all disciplines.

NAME(S) OF PROGRAMS:
● **Humboldt Research Award Programme**

TYPE:
Awards/prizes; Fellowships; Project/program
grants; Research grants; Scholarships.
Research awards for outstanding
achievements in the fields of humanities and
social sciences, natural sciences, medicine
and engineering sciences providing for visits
to German research institutes.

YEAR PROGRAM STARTED: 1972

PURPOSE:
To strengthen scientific cooperation between
foreign and German researchers.

LEGAL BASIS:
Government agency run according to private
law.

ELIGIBILITY:
Open to internationally renowned scientists
and scholars having full professor or
equivalent standing.

FINANCIAL DATA:
Amount of support per award: Up to EUR
60,000, plus travel expenses for awardee and
accompanying family members.
Total amount of support: Varies.

NO. MOST RECENT APPLICANTS: Approximately
285.

NO. AWARDS: 100.

APPLICATION INFO:
Awards are made by nomination and by
eminent German scholars only. No
self-nomination is allowed.
Duration: Visits to German institutes from
six to 12 months. No renewal of the award is
possible, but recipient may be invited to
Germany again.
Deadline: Nominations may be submitted at
any time.

STAFF:
Brian Craft, Alumni Relations and Annual
Fund Program Coordinator
Alexis Brouwer-Ancher, Communications
and Events Program Coordinator

ADDRESS INQUIRIES TO:
See e-mail address above.

AMERICAN INDIAN COLLEGE FUND
8333 Greenwood Boulevard
Denver, CO 80221
(303) 426-8900
Fax: (303) 426-1200
E-mail: scholarships@collegefund.org
Web Site: collegefund.org

TYPE:
Scholarships.

See entry 940 for full listing.

AMERICAN INDIAN GRADUATE CENTER
3701 San Mateo Boulevard, N.E.
Suite 200
Albuquerque, NM 87110
(505) 881-4584
Fax: (505) 884-0427
E-mail: fellowships@aigcs.org
Web Site: www.aigcs.org

TYPE:
Fellowships; Grants-in-aid; Scholarships.
Grants on an academic year basis. Summer
funding available to continuing students only;
these are students who are currently in the
fellowship program.

See entry 941 for full listing.

AMERICAN INDIAN SCIENCE AND ENGINEERING SOCIETY (AISES)
6899 Winchester Circle
Suite 102A
Boulder, CO 80301
(720) 552-6123
Fax: (720) 526-6940
E-mail: info@aises.org
Web Site: www.aises.org

TYPE:
Academic and travel scholarships. AISES
scholarships are intended to partially defray
tuition and other educational expenses,
thereby increasing access to higher education
and improving college retention rates for
AISES members.

AISES scholarships are made possible by
corporations, government agencies,
foundations, and individuals who wish to
support the advancement of American
Indians/Alaskan Natives. Scholarships are
distributed in two disbursements and awarded
for one academic year, unless otherwise
specified. Recipients cannot receive more
than one scholarship in any of the programs.

Scholarships are also awarded to members of
AISES who are American Indian/Alaskan
Native college students who meet the
eligibility requirements for each scholarship.

See entry 942 for full listing.

AMERICAN INSTITUTE OF CERTIFIED PUBLIC ACCOUNTANTS (AICPA)
220 Leigh Farm Road
Durham, NC 27707
(919) 402-4473
E-mail: scholarships@aicpa.org
Web Site: thiswaytocpa.com/scholarships

TYPE:
Scholarships.

See entry 1369 for full listing.

AMERICAN LEGION AUXILIARY - DEPARTMENT OF WISCONSIN [1476]

P.O. Box 140
Portage, WI 53901-0140
(608) 745-0124
Fax: (608) 745-1947
E-mail: deptsec@amlegionauxwi.org
Web Site: www.amlegionauxwi.org

FOUNDED: 1921

AREAS OF INTEREST:
Scholar aid programs for children of Veterans.

NAME(S) OF PROGRAMS:
● **American Legion Auxiliary Badger Girls State Scholarships**
● **American Legion Auxiliary National Scholarships**
● **Child Welfare Scholarship**
● **Health Careers Scholarships**
● **Eileen Knox Memorial Scholarship**
● **H.S. and Angeline Lewis Scholarships**
● **Merit and Memorial Scholarships**
● **State President's Scholarships**
● **Della Van Deuren Scholarships**
● **Van Deuren Memorial Scholarship**

TYPE:
Scholarships.

PURPOSE:
To enable students to secure Baccalaureate degrees.

ELIGIBILITY:
Applicant must be a child, grandchild, great-grandchild, step-child, step grandchild, step great-grandchild, wife or widow of an honorably discharged American veteran. An applicant who is a member of the Wisconsin American Legion Family does not need to reside in Wisconsin. Applicant must:
(1) be in need of financial help to continue their education;
(2) have at least a 3.5 grade point average on a 4.0 grade base and;
(3) be a resident of Wisconsin, except as noted above.

Applicant may apply for more than one scholarship, but can only receive one scholarship from the American Legion Auxiliary-Department of Wisconsin, awarded on a one-time only basis, nonrenewable. School selected to attend must be an accredited school, but need not be located in Wisconsin. Judges reserve the right to determine the type of scholarship awarded and their decision is final.

GEOG. RESTRICTIONS: Wisconsin.

FINANCIAL DATA:
Amount of support per award: Varies depending on available funds.
Total amount of support: $21,000 for the year 2021.

NO. MOST RECENT APPLICANTS: Approximately 150.

NO. AWARDS: 21 for the year 2021.

APPLICATION INFO:
Applicants must use only the application form designated for the year that they are applying for. For the Lewis, State President's, Merit and Memorial, Child Welfare, Health Careers and Registered Nurse Scholarships, one application form may be used regardless of how many programs an applicant may be eligible for.
Duration: One year.
Deadline: March 15.

ADDRESS INQUIRIES TO:
Bonnie Dorniak
Executive Secretary/Treasurer
(See address above.)

AMERICAN MEDICAL ASSOCIATION FOUNDATION [1477]

330 North Wabash Avenue
Suite 39300
Chicago, IL 60611-5885
(312) 464-4200
Fax: (312) 464-4142
E-mail: amafoundation@ama-assn.org
Web Site: www.amafoundation.org

FOUNDED: 1950

AREAS OF INTEREST:
Public health and medical education.

NAME(S) OF PROGRAMS:
● **Excellence in Medicine Awards**
● **Joan F. Giambalvo Memorial Fund**
● **Leadership Development Institute**
● **LGBTQ+ Fellowship**
● **Physicians of Tomorrow Scholarship**

TYPE:
Awards/prizes; Project/program grants; Scholarships. Excellence in Medicine Awards are given to recognize physicians and medical students who are improving the health of their communities and the lives of those who are most in need.

The Joan F. Giambalvo Memorial Fund is presented in conjunction with the AMA's Women Physicians Section to provide a research grant to help researchers advance the progress of women in the medical profession and identify and address the needs of women physicians and medical students.

Leadership Development Institute offers a unique opportunity for participants to gain individualized skills needed to foster careers and the future of medicine. Participants will receive professional development opportunities as well as mentoring throughout the course of the program year.

LGBTQ+ Fellowship program, in partnership with medical and osteopathic-granting educational institutions, is a four-year medical fellowship program to address the social determinants of health specifically affecting LGBTQ+ individuals and create a pipeline of diverse health care providers who are knowledgeable and culturally competent in LGBTQ+ health.

The Physicians of Tomorrow Scholarships are awarded to rising fourth-year medical students based on financial need and academic excellence.

PURPOSE:
To bring together physicians and communities to improve our nation's health.

LEGAL BASIS:
Public foundation.

ELIGIBILITY:
Scholarships are based on academic excellence and financial need. Student must be nominated through the medical school dean's office designate and currently enrolled in an accredited U.S. allopathic or osteopathic medical school. Student must be a permanent resident or citizen of the U.S., or have DACA status.

GEOG. RESTRICTIONS: United States.

FINANCIAL DATA:
Amount of support per award: Joan F. Giambalvo Scholarship: Up to $10,000; LGBTQ+ Fellowship: Up to $750,000; Physicians of Tomorrow Scholarship: $10,000.

APPLICATION INFO:
Information is available on the Foundation web site.
Duration: Scholarships: One year.
Deadline: Varies.

PUBLICATIONS:
Brochure; program announcement; e-newsletter; quarterly newsletter.

ADDRESS INQUIRIES TO:
Emily Demko, Program Manager
(See address above.)

AMERICAN OSTEOPATHIC FOUNDATION

142 East Ontario Street, Suite 1450
Chicago, IL 60611-2864
(312) 202-8235
Fax: (312) 202-8216
E-mail: info@aof.org
Web Site: www.aof.org

TYPE:
Awards/prizes; Scholarships. Research, community service and international outreach grants.

See entry 2276 for full listing.

THE AMERICAN SOCIETY FOR NONDESTRUCTIVE TESTING, INC. [1478]

1711 Arlingate Lane
Columbus, OH 43228
(614) 274-6003
(800) 222-2768
Fax: (614) 274-6899
E-mail: james@asnt.org
Web Site: www.asnt.org

FOUNDED: 1941

AREAS OF INTEREST:
Nondestructive testing and engineering.

NAME(S) OF PROGRAMS:
● **Engineering Undergraduate Award**
● **Robert B. Oliver Scholarship**

TYPE:
Scholarships.

YEAR PROGRAM STARTED: 1998

PURPOSE:
To provide incentive to students in the field of nondestructive testing.

LEGAL BASIS:
501(c)(3) corporation.

ELIGIBILITY:
Engineering Undergraduate Award: Students enrolled in colleges and universities in the U.S. with recognized engineering department programs are eligible for the scholarship.

Oliver Scholarship: Students must be enrolled in an Associate degree or certificate program which includes studies in NDT.

FINANCIAL DATA:
Amount of support per award: Engineering Undergraduate Award: $3,000; Oliver Scholarship: $2,500.
Total amount of support: Engineering Undergraduate Award: $9,000; Oliver Scholarship: $7,500.

NO. AWARDS: Up to 3 per year per award.

APPLICATION INFO:
Information and application are available online.
Duration: One year.
Deadline: Engineering Undergraduate Award: December 15. Oliver Scholarship: February 15.

ADDRESS INQUIRIES TO:
Jessica Ames
ASNT Program Specialist
(See address above.)

AMERICAN SOCIETY OF HEMATOLOGY
2021 L Street, N.W.
Suite 900
Washington, DC 20036
(202) 776-0544
E-mail: awards@hematology.org
Web Site: www.hematology.org

TYPE:
Awards/prizes; Fellowships; Research grants; Scholarships.

See entry 2006 for full listing.

AMVETS   [1479]
4647 Forbes Boulevard
Lanham, MD 20706-4380
(301) 683-4027
Fax: (301) 683-3027
E-mail: klathroum@amvets.org
Web Site: www.amvets.org

FOUNDED: 1944

NAME(S) OF PROGRAMS:
● **AMVETS National Scholarship Program: Entering College Freshman Scholarship**
● **AMVETS National Scholarship Program: JROTC Scholarship**

TYPE:
Scholarships. National scholarship program for high school seniors who are children or grandchildren of veterans.

PURPOSE:
To make the goal of postsecondary education more attainable for the children and grandchildren of veterans by assisting deserving students who might not otherwise have the financial means to achieve their educational goals.

ELIGIBILITY:
Applicant must:
(1) be a graduating high school senior entering at the college freshman level in the upcoming fall or be an active JROTC cadet and currently a high school senior;
(2) have a minimum grade point average of 3.0 (or documented evidence of extenuating circumstances that caused a lower grade point average);
(3) be the child or grandchild of a U.S. veteran, active duty, National Guard, or Reservist;
(4) be a U.S. citizen;
(5) demonstrate academic promise and financial need and;
(6) agree to authorize AMVETS to publicize their scholarship award, if they are selected.

GEOG. RESTRICTIONS: United States.

FINANCIAL DATA:
Amount of support per award: Entering College Freshman Scholarship: $4,000 ($1,000 per year of a four-year program); JROTC Scholarship: $1,000.

NO. AWARDS: Entering College Freshman Scholarship: 6; JROTC Scholarship: 1.

APPLICATION INFO:
Applications must be completed online.
Duration: One to four years. Nonrenewable.
Deadline: April 30.

ADDRESS INQUIRIES TO:
Karla Lathroum
(See e-mail address above.)

ARCHAEOLOGICAL INSTITUTE OF AMERICA   [1480]
44 Beacon Street
Boston, MA 02108
(857) 305-9360
Fax: (857) 233-4270
E-mail: fellowships@archaeological.org
Web Site: www.archaeological.org

FOUNDED: 1879

AREAS OF INTEREST:
Archaeological research and publication.

NAME(S) OF PROGRAMS:
● **The AIA Publication Subvention Program**
● **Samuel H. Kress Grants for Research and Publication in Classical Art and Architecture**

TYPE:
Grants-in-aid. The AIA Publication Subvention Program offers subventions from the AIA's Bothmer Publication Fund in support of new book-length publications in the field of Greek, Roman, and Etruscan archaeology and art history.

Samuel H. Kress Grants for Research and Publication in Classical Art and Architecture funds publication preparation or research leading to publication undertaken by professional members of the AIA.

PURPOSE:
To support the scholarly publication of archaeological works.

ELIGIBILITY:
Applicants must have been AIA members in good standing for at least two consecutive years (one year for graduate students) before the application deadline.

FINANCIAL DATA:
Amount of support per award: AIA Publication Subvention Program: Average $5,000. Samuel H. Kress Grants: $3,000.
Total amount of support: Varies.

NO. MOST RECENT APPLICANTS: AIA Publication Subvention Program: 3; Samuel H. Kress Grants: 3.

NO. AWARDS: AIA Publication Subvention Program: 4; Samuel H. Kress Grants: 2.

APPLICATION INFO:
Applications must be completed online. Full details are available on the Institute web site.
Duration: Typically one year.
Deadline: March 1 and November 1.

ADDRESS INQUIRIES TO:
Laurel Nilsen Sparks
Lecture and Fellowship Coordinator
(See address above.)

ARMENIAN GENERAL BENEVOLENT UNION   [1481]
55 East 59th Street, 7th Floor
New York, NY 10022-1112
(212) 319-6383
E-mail: scholarship@agbu.org
Web Site: www.agbu-scholarship.org

AREAS OF INTEREST:
Education.

NAME(S) OF PROGRAMS:
● **Heritage Scholar Grant**
● **International Scholarship**
● **Performing Arts Scholarship**
● **Religious Studies Scholarship**
● **U.S. Graduate Scholarship**

TYPE:
Fellowships; Scholarships.

PURPOSE:
To provide financial assistance to students of Armenian descent.

ELIGIBILITY:
Students must be of Armenian descent enrolled in college or university.

FINANCIAL DATA:
Amount of support per award: Heritage Scholar Grant: Up to $2,000; International Scholarship: Up to $3,000; Performing Arts Scholarship: $1,000 to $5,000; Religious Studies Scholarship: Up to $5,000; U.S. Graduate Scholarship: $5,000 average.
Total amount of support: Approximately $1,000,000 annually.

NO. MOST RECENT APPLICANTS: Over 1,000.

NO. AWARDS: Over 500.

APPLICATION INFO:
Applicants must check their eligibility before gaining access to the application.
Deadline: Heritage Scholar Grant: April 15; International Scholarship: June 1; Performing Arts and Religious Studies Scholarships: May 31; U.S. Graduate Scholarship: April 30.

ADDRESS INQUIRIES TO:
Scholarship Program
(See address above.)

ASIAN AMERICAN JOURNALISTS ASSOCIATION   [1482]
1301 K Street, N.W.
Third Floor, Suite 443
Washington, DC 20005
(202) 729-8383
Fax: (202) 729-8383
E-mail: support@aaja.org
Web Site: www.aaja.org

FOUNDED: 1981

AREAS OF INTEREST:
Journalism.

NAME(S) OF PROGRAMS:
● **Stanford Chen Internship Grant**
● **Lloyd LaCuesta Internship Grant**
● **Sam Chu Lin Internship Grant**
● **William Woo Print & Online News Internship Grant**

TYPE:
Fellowships; Grants-in-aid; Scholarships.

YEAR PROGRAM STARTED: 1981

PURPOSE:
To encourage Asian-American students to pursue journalism careers.

ELIGIBILITY:
Must be a full-time college student pursuing journalism as a major.

Detailed information regarding each program is posted on the Association web site.

GEOG. RESTRICTIONS: United States.

FINANCIAL DATA:
Amount of support per award: Stanford Chen Internship Grant and William Woo Internship Grant: $2,000; Lloyd LaCuesta Internship Grant: $1,000; Sam Chu Lin Internship Grant: $500.
Total amount of support: Varies.

NO. MOST RECENT APPLICANTS: 20.

NO. AWARDS: 2.

APPLICATION INFO:
Application information is available on the web site.
Duration: One-time award. No renewals.
Deadline: April 21.

IRS I.D.: 95-3755203

STAFF:
April Siruno, Membership and Operations Associate

ADDRESS INQUIRIES TO:
April Siruno
Membership and Operations Associate
(See address above.)

ASIAN AMERICAN JOURNALISTS ASSOCIATION   [1483]
1301 K Street, N.W.
Third Floor, Suite 443
Washington, DC 20005
(202) 729-8383
Fax: (202) 729-8383
E-mail: support@aaja.org
Web Site: www.aaja.org

FOUNDED: 1981

AREAS OF INTEREST:
Journalism.

NAME(S) OF PROGRAMS:
- **Vincent Chin Memorial Scholarship**
- **CIC/Anna Chennault Scholarship**
- **Mary Quon Moy Ing Memorial Scholarship**
- **Sports Task Force/Al Young Sports Journalism Scholarship**
- **Jimmie & Suey Fong Yee Scholarship**

TYPE:
Fellowships; Internships; Scholarships. Vincent Chin Memorial Scholarship rewards an accomplished, community-minded student journalist for an insightful, articulate essay related to Vincent Chin and his legacy.

CIC/Anna Chennault Scholarship provides financial assistance to a student's college education. This scholarship encourages students to pursue journalism as a career.

Mary Quon Moy Ing Memorial Scholarship provides financial assistance to currently enrolled college students or graduating high school seniors pursuing journalism as a career.

The Sports Task Force/Al Young Sports Journalism Scholarship honors Al Young, a long-time member and ardent supporter of AAJA, who is an Asian American pioneer in sports media and is dedicated top empowering the voices of Asian American journalists.

Jimmie & Suey Fong Yee Scholarship offers a current college student and a young professional pursuing sports journalism and

media as a career the opportunity to pitch and produce a print, digital, audio or visual story about Asian Americans in sports, plus free registration for the annual AAJA National Convention.

PURPOSE:
To encourage Asian-American students to pursue journalism careers.

ELIGIBILITY:
Vincent Chin Memorial Scholarship applicant must be a current member and committed to AAJA's mission. Applicant must demonstrate journalistic excellence, a strong interest in pursuing journalism as a career, and a commitment to community involvement. Applicant must be a current undergraduate student enrolled full-time with at least 12 credit units each semester for the current year or the spring semester of the next year. Applicant must be currently taking or planning to take journalism courses and/or pursuing journalism as a career.

CIC/Anna Chennault Scholarship applicant must be committed to AAJA's mission and be a graduating high school senior that has been accepted to a U.S. college or a currently enrolled college student at the time of applying. AAJA membership is not required for the application but if selected, the student must sign up for student membership. Candidates will be judged on the basis of academic achievement, demonstrated journalistic ability, commitment to the field of journalism and/or sensitivity to Asian American and Pacific Islander issues.

Mary Quon Moy Ing Memorial Scholarship applicant must be committed to AAJA's mission. Applicant must demonstrate journalistic excellence, a strong interest in pursuing journalism as a career, and a commitment to community involvement. Applicant must be a graduating high school senior, undergraduate, or graduate student enrolled full-time with at least 12 credit units each semester for the fall or spring semester. Applicant must be currently taking or planning to take journalism courses and/or pursuing journalism as a career. AAJA student membership is encouraged for all applicants and required for the selected scholarship recipient. Candidates will be selected on the basis of academic achievement, demonstrated journalistic ability, financial need, commitment to the field of journalism and/or sensitivity to Asian American and Pacific Islander issues.

Sports Task Force/Al Young Sports Journalism Scholarship applicant must be an undergraduate student enrolled full-time with at least 12 credit units each semester at a junior college or university located in the U.S. Applicant must be currently taking or planning to take journalism courses and/or pursuing sports journalism as a career. Applicant must have a minimum 3.0 grade point average. Funds must be used to directly support or advance applicant's education. Applicants will be selected on the basis of academic achievement, demonstrated journalistic ability, financial need, a strong commitment to the pursuit of a sports journalism career and dedication to AAJA's mission of advancing Asian American and other underrepresented communities in media.

Jimmie & Suey Fong Yee Scholarship applicants must pitch a story they can realistically produce with their resources and time. Unique stories that humanize Asian

Americans in sports are highly preferred. Pitches can include stories that are local, regional or national. Currently enrolled students must be undergraduate or graduate students enrolled full-time with at least 12 credit units each semester at a junior college or university located in the U.S. Applicants must be currently taking or planning to take journalism courses and/or pursuing sports journalism as a career. A minimum 3.0 grade point average is required. Young professional applicants must have graduated from a community college or university, including graduate school, located in the U.S. within the past five years. Applicants must be currently and actively pursuing sports journalism as a career. Applicants will be selected on the basis of their unique and compelling story pitch, demonstrated journalistic ability, financial need, a strong commitment to the pursuit of a sports journalism career and dedication to AAJA's mission of advancing Asian Americans and other underrepresented communities in media.

GEOG. RESTRICTIONS: United States.

FINANCIAL DATA:
CIC/Anna Chennault Scholarship recipient will receive travel, lodging and registration to attend AAJA's annual convention. There is also an opportunity to be paired with a professional mentor.
Amount of support per award: Chin Scholarship: $1,500; CIC/Anna Chennault Scholarship: $5,000; Ing Scholarship: Up to $2,000; Sports Task Force/Al Young Sports Journalism Scholarship: $2,000; Yee Scholarship: $750.

APPLICATION INFO:
Requirements vary for each scholarship. Complete details are listed on the AAJA web site. Scholarship applications must be submitted online.
Deadline: January 31.

ADDRESS INQUIRIES TO:
April Siruno
Membership and Operations Associate
(See address above.)

*SPECIAL STIPULATIONS:
Yee Scholarship awardee must follow through with their story pitches, as well as commit to a minimum of five hours of volunteer work for the AAJA Sports Task Force.

ASIAN AMERICAN JOURNALISTS ASSOCIATION   [1484]
1301 K Street, N.W.
Third Floor, Suite 443
Washington, DC 20005
(202) 729-8383
Fax: (202) 729-8383
E-mail: support@aaja.org
Web Site: www.aaja.org

FOUNDED: 1981

AREAS OF INTEREST:
Journalism.

NAME(S) OF PROGRAMS:
- **Dinah Eng Leadership Fellowship**
- **Michael Kim Broadcast Fellowship**

TYPE:
Fellowships; Internships; Scholarships. The Dinah Eng Leadership Fellowship widens opportunities for midcareer AAJA members

pursuing the strategies and skills needed to enter news management and advance within its ranks. Fellowships are to be applied to event/seminar registration fees and, if applicable, can assist with travel, meals and hotel expenses.

Michael Kim Broadcast Fellowship supports a young sports broadcast journalist who has less than three years of professional experience. The scholarship is made possible by the Sports Task Force and an annual donation by Michael Kim.

PURPOSE:
To encourage Asian-Americans to pursue journalism careers.

ELIGIBILITY:
To quality for the Eng Fellowship, each applicant must:
(1) be a current, dues-paying AAJA member;
(2) demonstrate leadership potential, or currently hold a management position and;
(3) be recommended by their superior.

Kim Fellowship applicants must work in the broadcast sports industry in some form, either as on-camera talent or behind-the-scenes producer. Applicants must be within three years of college graduation and/or in their first television market. Applicants will be selected on the basis of demonstrated journalistic ability, financial need, a strong commitment to the pursuit of a sports journalism career and dedication to AAJA's mission of advancing Asian Americans and other underrepresented communities in media.

GEOG. RESTRICTIONS: United States.

FINANCIAL DATA:
Amount of support per award: Eng Fellowship: $1,000; Kim Fellowship: $2,000.

APPLICATION INFO:
Applications must be submitted online.
Deadline: Eng Fellowship: December 2. Kim Fellowship: January 31.

ADDRESS INQUIRIES TO:
April Siruno
Membership and Operations Associate
(See address above.)

*SPECIAL STIPULATIONS:
Kim Fellowship applicant must commit to a minimum of five hours of volunteer work for the AAJA Sports Task Force.

ASSOCIATION OF INTERNATIONAL CERTIFIED PROFESSIONAL ACCOUNTANTS (THE ASSOCIATION)   [1485]
220 Leigh Farm Road
Durham, NC 27707
(919) 402-4682
E-mail: scholarships@aicpa.org
academics@aicpa.org
Web Site: www.aicpa.org

AREAS OF INTEREST:
Accounting/doctoral program.

NAME(S) OF PROGRAMS:
● **AICPA Fellowship for Minority Doctoral Students**

TYPE:
Fellowships. Awarded annually to full-time minority accounting scholars who demonstrate significant potential to become accounting educators.

PURPOSE:
To ensure that C.P.As. of diverse backgrounds are visible in college and university classrooms; to increase the number of minority C.P.As. who serve as role models and mentors to young people in the academic environment.

ELIGIBILITY:
To be considered, applicants must meet the following requirements:
(1) have applied to a doctoral program and awaiting word on acceptance, or have been accepted into a doctoral program or already matriculated in a doctoral program and pursuing appropriate coursework;
(2) have earned a Master's degree and/or completed a minimum of three years of full-time experience in the practice of accounting;
(3) be a minority student of Black or African American, Hispanic or Latino, Native American, Native Hawaiian or Pacific Islander ethnicity;
(4) attend school on a full-time basis and plan to remain enrolled full-time until attaining one's doctoral degree;
(5) agree not to work full-time in a paid position or accept responsibility for teaching more than one course per semester as a teaching assistant, or dedicate more than one quarter of the time as a research assistant;
(6) be a C.P.A. or plan to pursue the C.P.A. credential and;
(7) be a U.S. citizen or permanent resident (green card holder).

GEOG. RESTRICTIONS: United States and its territories.

FINANCIAL DATA:
Amount of support per award: $12,000.
Total amount of support: $300,000 for the academic year 2020-21.

NO. AWARDS: 25 for the academic year 2020-21.

APPLICATION INFO:
Instructions are available online, or send an e-mail to the Association.
Duration: One year. Renewable up to five years.
Deadline: May 30.

ADDRESS INQUIRIES TO:
AICPA Minority Doctoral Fellowship Program
E-mail: academics@aicpa.org
(See address above.)

ASSOCIATION ON AMERICAN INDIAN AFFAIRS
6030 Daybreak Circle
Suite A150-217
Clarksville, MD 21029
(240) 314-7155
E-mail: general@indian-affairs.org
Web Site: www.indian-affairs.org/scholarships.html

TYPE:
Scholarships. Undergraduate and graduate scholarships for citizens of federally recognized Tribes and unrecognized Tribes.

See entry 944 for full listing.

ALEXANDER GRAHAM BELL ASSOCIATION FOR THE DEAF AND HARD OF HEARING
3417 Volta Place, N.W.
Washington, DC 20007
(202) 337-5220
E-mail: scholarships@agbell.org
Web Site: www.agbell.org

TYPE:
Scholarships.

See entry 891 for full listing.

BINC FOUNDATION
3135 South State Street
Suite 203
Ann Arbor, MI 48108
(866) 733-9064
Fax: (734) 477-2806
E-mail: info@bincfoundation.org
Web Site: www.bincfoundation.org

TYPE:
Challenge/matching grants; Grants-in-aid; Scholarships. Scholarships are awarded to bookstore and comic shop employees to pursue a variety of professional development opportunities.

See entry 38 for full listing.

BNSF RAILWAY FOUNDATION
2500 Lou Menk Drive
Building AOB-2
Fort Worth, TX 76131-2830
(817) 867-6458
E-mail: bnsffoundation@bnsf.com
Web Site: www.bnsffoundation.org

TYPE:
Scholarships. Awarded annually to outstanding Native American high school seniors from funds provided by the Foundation, for up to four years or until undergraduate degree requirements are completed, whichever occurs first. Scholarship winners may attend any accredited college (two-year leading to a four-year degree) or university in the U.S.

See entry 945 for full listing.

THE LYNDE AND HARRY BRADLEY FOUNDATION, INC.   [1486]
1400 North Water Street
Suite 300
Milwaukee, WI 53202
(414) 291-9915
Fax: (414) 291-9991
Web Site: www.bradleyfdn.org

FOUNDED: 1942

AREAS OF INTEREST:
Humanities, social sciences and law.

NAME(S) OF PROGRAMS:
● **Bradley Fellowship Program**

TYPE:
Fellowships. To strengthen America's "intellectual infrastructure" at a higher-education level, providing useful assistance to young scholars during a critical phase in their education.

YEAR PROGRAM STARTED: 1986

PURPOSE:
To encourage projects that focus on cultivating a renewed, healthier, and more

vigorous sense of citizenship among the American people, and among peoples of other nations, as well.

ELIGIBILITY:
Selected candidates must be intelligent doctoral and postdoctoral fellows within the discretion of participating professors or nominators. The principal consideration is excellence and merit. Candidates must also be U.S. citizens or residents.

GEOG. RESTRICTIONS: United States.

FINANCIAL DATA:
Amount of support per award: Up to $25,000 per academic year.

APPLICATION INFO:
Recipients must be nominated by participating professors or nominators.
Duration: One year.

ADDRESS INQUIRIES TO:
Senior Program Director
(See address above.)

BROADCAST EDUCATION ASSOCIATION
One M Street, S.E.
Washington, DC 20003
(202) 602-0587
Fax: (202) 609-9940
E-mail: help@beaweb.org
Web Site: www.beaweb.org

TYPE:
Scholarships. BEA is the professional development association for professors, industry professionals and students involved in teaching and research related to radio, television and other electronic media. BEA administers scholarships annually, to honor broadcasters and the entire electronic media profession.

John Bayliss and Abe Voron Awards: Study toward a career in radio.

BEA Founders, Richard Eaton, Edward O. Fritts, Peter B. Orlik and Vincent T. Wasilewski Awards: Study in any electronic media area. (Wasilewski Award is for graduate students only.)

Library of American Broadcasting Foundation Award is for graduate students focusing on broadcast history.

For the BEA Founders Award, preference is given to students enrolled in a BEA Two-Year/Small College Member Institution or graduates of these programs now enrolled in a BEA Four-Year Institution.

All other scholarships are awarded to juniors, seniors and graduate students at BEA Member institutions.

See entry 1724 for full listing.

BROADCAST EDUCATION ASSOCIATION
One M Street, S.E.
Washington, DC 20003
(202) 602-0586
Fax: (202) 609-9940
E-mail: help@beaweb.org
Web Site: www.beaweb.org

TYPE:
Scholarships. PILOT Media Technology and Innovation Scholarships are awarded to college sophomores, juniors, seniors entering graduate school and graduate students for pursuit of studies related to media technology and innovation.

See entry 1725 for full listing.

BUREAU OF INDIAN EDUCATION
12220 Sunrise Valley Drive
Reston, VA 20191
(703) 390-6697
E-mail: katherine.campbell@bie.edu
Web Site: www.bie.edu

TYPE:
Fellowships; Scholarships.

See entry 950 for full listing.

CALIFORNIA STUDENT AID COMMISSION   [1487]
P.O. Box 419027
Rancho Cordova, CA 95741-9027
(888) 224-7268
Fax: (916) 464-8004
E-mail: studentsupport@csac.ca.gov
Web Site: www.csac.ca.gov

FOUNDED: 1955

NAME(S) OF PROGRAMS:
• Cal Grants A, B and C

TYPE:
Assistantships; Grants-in-aid. Grant A will help pay for tuition and fees at public and private colleges, and some private career colleges. Grant B provides low-income students with a living allowance and assistance with tuition and fees. Most five-year students receive an allowance for books and living expenses. Grant C helps pay for tuition and training costs at occupational or career technical schools.

YEAR PROGRAM STARTED: 1956

PURPOSE:
To assist with tuition and books for students attending college in California.

LEGAL BASIS:
California Education Code.

ELIGIBILITY:
Student must be a U.S. citizen or eligible noncitizen and a California resident for at least one year.

GEOG. RESTRICTIONS: California.

FINANCIAL DATA:
Amount of support per award: Grants A and B: Varies by type of college; Grant C: Up to $2,462 for tuition and fees and $1,094 for books, tools and equipment.

NO. MOST RECENT APPLICANTS: 350,000.

NO. AWARDS: 75,000.

APPLICATION INFO:
Students should submit the Free Application for Federal Student Aid (FAFSA) or the California Dream Act Application and a verified Cal Grant grade point average. The FAFSA is available online.
Duration: Up to four years.
Deadline: March 2. California Community College students: March 2 and September 2.

PUBLICATIONS:
Fund Your Future; *Financial Aid for Students*, booklet.

CALIFORNIA STUDENT AID COMMISSION   [1488]
P.O. Box 419027
Rancho Cordova, CA 95741-9027
(888) 224-7268
Fax: (916) 464-8004
E-mail: specialized@csac.ca.gov
Web Site: www.csac.ca.gov

FOUNDED: 1955

AREAS OF INTEREST:
Dependents of law enforcement personnel.

NAME(S) OF PROGRAMS:
• Law Enforcement Personnel Dependents' Grant Program (LEPD)

TYPE:
Grants-in-aid. The program provides need-based educational grants to dependents and spouses of California peace officers (Highway Patrol, marshals, sheriffs, police officers), Department of Corrections and California Youth Authority employees and permanent/full-time firefighters, employed by public entities who have been killed in the performance of duty or totally disabled as a result of an accident or injury caused by external violence or physical force incurred in the performance of duty.

Grant awards are for attendance at WASC-accredited colleges in California.

YEAR PROGRAM STARTED: 1969

LEGAL BASIS:
California Labor Code, Section 4709. State agency.

ELIGIBILITY:
Dependents and spouses of California peace officers, Department of Corrections and California Youth Authority employees and permanent/full-time firefighters employed by public entities killed or totally disabled in the performance of duty.

GEOG. RESTRICTIONS: California.

FINANCIAL DATA:
Amount of support per award: $100 to $12,192.
Total amount of support: Varies.

APPLICATION INFO:
Eligible students must file the following documents with the Specialized Programs Branch:
(1) a Law Enforcement Personnel Dependent's Grant application;
(2) a copy of the Student Aid Report (SAR), which is generated after filing a FAFSA;
(3) birth certificate (not required for spouse);
(4) the death certificate of the parent or spouse and the coroner's report (if appropriate), police report, and any other documentation that shows evidence that the death or total disability was caused by external violence or physical force incurred in the line of duty (for peace and law enforcement officers), by the direct action of an inmate (for officers and employees of the Department of Corrections and Rehabilitation), or in the performance of duty (for firefighters);
(5) findings of the Workers' Compensation Appeals Board or other evidence that the fatality or 100% disabling accident or injury was compensable under Division 4.0 and 4.5 (commencing with Section 6100) of the Labor Code and;
(6) proof of enrollment at a California postsecondary institution as described above for the applicable academic year.
Duration: Up to four years.

PUBLICATIONS:
Financial Aid for Students, booklet.

STAFF:
Marlene L. Garcia, Executive Director

ADDRESS INQUIRIES TO:
See e-mail address above.

CANADIAN FRIENDS OF THE HEBREW UNIVERSITY   [1489]
4950 Yonge Street
Suite 1202
Toronto ON M2N 6K1 Canada
(416) 485-8000
(888) 432-7398
E-mail: inquiry@cfhu.org
Web Site: www.cfhu.org

FOUNDED: 1944

AREAS OF INTEREST:
Law, dentistry, social sciences, economics, humanities, the sciences, medicine and computer science.

TYPE:
Awards/prizes; Scholarships. The Canadian Friends of the Hebrew University sponsors Canadian college or university students who participate in programs at the Hebrew University of Jerusalem.

YEAR PROGRAM STARTED: 1944

PURPOSE:
To give the financial support necessary for Canadian students to study at Hebrew University in Jerusalem, Israel; to raise funds in support of the Hebrew University research programs.

LEGAL BASIS:
Nonprofit.

ELIGIBILITY:
Applicants must be Canadian citizens or landed immigrants. Awards are given based on need. Some scholarships are designated for Israeli students.

GEOG. RESTRICTIONS: Canada.

FINANCIAL DATA:
Amount of support per award: $1,000 to $3,000.
Total amount of support: Varies.

NO. AWARDS: Varies.

APPLICATION INFO:
Contact Chris Carabott at ccarabott@cfhu.org.
Duration: At least one year.
Deadline: May 1.

STAFF:
Rami Kleinmann, Chief Executive Officer and President

ADDRESS INQUIRIES TO:
Kris Hreczynski, Officer Manager
(See address above.)

THE CARSON SCHOLARS FUND, INC.   [1490]
305 West Chesapeake Avenue
Suite 310
Towson, MD 21204
(410) 828-1005
Fax: (410) 828-1007
E-mail: lrichards@carsonscholars.org
Web Site: carsonscholars.org

FOUNDED: 1994

AREAS OF INTEREST:
Education.

NAME(S) OF PROGRAMS:
● **Carson Scholarship Program**

TYPE:
Scholarships. The Carson Scholars Fund awards college scholarships to students in grades 4-11 who excel academically and are dedicated to serving their communities.

YEAR PROGRAM STARTED: 1994

PURPOSE:
To operate on the principle that if children could be taught early to excel, they would stay motivated and have a higher chance of educational success later in life.

ELIGIBILITY:
Students must be nominated by the principal at his or her school. Only one student from each school is able to apply. Carson Scholars must have a grade point average of 3.75 and display humanitarian qualities through community service. Scholarships are awarded solely on the basis of academic achievements and humanitarian qualities, without regard to financial need or ethnicity. Carson Scholars must be U.S. citizens or residents.

GEOG. RESTRICTIONS: United States.

FINANCIAL DATA:
Scholarship winners receive the honor of being named "Carson Scholars" and are awarded an Olympic-sized medal and a trophy for their school. Winners receive a recognition package and an invitation to attend an awards banquet.
Amount of support per award: $1,000.

NO. AWARDS: 477 for the year 2020.

APPLICATION INFO:
Students must be nominated by the principal of his or her school to compete. Only one student from each school is able to apply. Complete information is on the web site.
Duration: One-time award.
Deadline: Nominations open in October and close the beginning of January. Notification is made in March.

ADDRESS INQUIRIES TO:
Lacey Richards, Scholarship Director
(See e-mail address above.)

CATCHING THE DREAM
8200 Mountain Road, N.E.
Suite 103
Albuquerque, NM 87110
(505) 262-2351
Fax: (505) 262-0534
E-mail: NScholarsh@aol.com
Web Site: www.catchingthedream.org

TYPE:
Conferences/seminars; Development grants; Grants-in-aid; Scholarships; Technical assistance. CTD also works to improve Indian schools through a program of grants and technical assistance. This work has led to the development of 40 Exemplary Programs in Indian education since 1988. The annual Exemplary Institute is a meeting of these Exemplary Programs, where they teach other people how to develop similar programs.

MAST program makes grants of $5,000 to Indian high schools to improve their math and science teaching.

MESBEC Program consists of competitive scholarships for high-potential Native Americans studying in math, engineering, science, business, education and computers.

NALE Program consists of competitive scholarships for high-potential paraprofessional Native Americans who plan to complete their degrees and obtain credentials as teachers, counselors or administrators.

RAP makes grants to Indian schools to improve the reading ability of their students.

Tribal Business Management (TBM) Program consists of competitive scholarships for Native students in all fields of business.

See entry 951 for full listing.

CHATHAM UNIVERSITY   [1491]
Woodland Road
Berry Hall
Pittsburgh, PA 15232
(800) 837-1290
Fax: (412) 365-1825
E-mail: admission@chatham.edu
undergraduate@chatham.edu
Web Site: www.chatham.edu

FOUNDED: 1869

AREAS OF INTEREST:
Providing scholarship opportunities to students who have shown academic promise during their high school career and who are enrolled at Chatham University.

NAME(S) OF PROGRAMS:
● **The Chatham University Merit Scholarship Programs**

TYPE:
Awards/prizes; Endowments; Formula grants; General operating grants; Grants-in-aid; Internships; Scholarships. In addition to the Merit and Presidential Scholarships, other opportunities include the Heffer Family Scholarship, the Instrumental Music Scholarship, the Karen Lake Scholarship, the Legacy Award, the Minna Kaufmann Ruud Music Scholarship, the Pittsburgh Promise Housing Scholarship, and the Rachel Carson Scholarship.

YEAR PROGRAM STARTED: 1978

PURPOSE:
To attract outstanding students to Chatham University and to provide recognition of their academic performance.

ELIGIBILITY:
Chatham University Merit Scholars are chosen based on their performance in high school, grades, and SAT or ACT scores.

Grants are based strictly on need; many of the scholars are from families for whom the choice of a college such as Chatham would not be possible without this support.

FINANCIAL DATA:
Amount of support per award: Presidential Scholarship pays full tuition. Other Scholarships are from $3,000 per year to $18,000 per year.
Total amount of support: Varies.

NO. MOST RECENT APPLICANTS: Approximately 1,000 annually.

APPLICATION INFO:
Student must complete an admissions application, be granted acceptance to the University, and, in some cases, interview or audition.

Duration: Four years of the undergraduate career, provided the high academic criteria expected of such scholars is maintained. Renewable annually based on grade point average of 3.0 or higher for Presidential Scholarship and 2.0 or higher for the other scholarships, and full-time enrollment.

Deadline: February.

STAFF:
Amy Becher, Vice President for Enrollment Management
Dr. Jennifer Burns, Assistant Vice President of Financial Aid

ADDRESS INQUIRIES TO:
Office of Enrollment Management
(See address above.)

CHINESE AMERICAN MEDICAL SOCIETY

11 East Broadway, Suite 4-C
New York, NY 10038
(212) 334-4760
Fax: (646) 304-6373
E-mail: jlove@camsociety.org
Web Site: www.camsociety.org

TYPE:
Fellowships; Scholarships.

See entry 2024 for full listing.

THE CLARK FOUNDATION   [1492]

5229 State Highway 28
Cooperstown, NY 13326
(607) 547-9927
Fax: (607) 547-8598
E-mail: office@clarkscholarship.org
Web Site: clarkscholarship.org

FOUNDED: 1931

NAME(S) OF PROGRAMS:
● **Clark Foundation Scholarship Program**

TYPE:
Scholarships. Undergraduate college scholarships.

YEAR PROGRAM STARTED: 1961

PURPOSE:
To assist Cooperstown area students in their pursuit of higher education.

LEGAL BASIS:
Nonprofit foundation.

ELIGIBILITY:
Individual undergraduate college scholarships are awarded to graduates of Central School, Cooperstown, NY and 12 surrounding rural central school districts.

GEOG. RESTRICTIONS: Cooperstown and the 12 surrounding New York rural central school districts of Cherry Valley-Springfield, Edmeston, Gilbertsville, Laurens, Milford, Morris, Mount Markham, Mount Upton, Richfield Springs, Schenevus, Worcester and Owen D. Young.

FINANCIAL DATA:
Amount of support per award: Approximately $3,800.
Total amount of support: $3,800,000.

NO. MOST RECENT APPLICANTS: 331.

NO. AWARDS: 193.

APPLICATION INFO:
Students are recommended by their respective schools.

Duration: One year. Possible renewal each year for duration of undergraduate education.
Deadline: First week in February.

OFFICERS:
Jane Forbes Clark, President
Kevin S. Moore, Treasurer
Douglas Bauer, Executive Director and Secretary

ADDRESS INQUIRIES TO:
Gary Kuch, Director
Clark Foundation Scholarship Office
P.O. Box 427
Cooperstown, NY 13326

COCA-COLA SCHOLARS FOUNDATION   [1493]

P.O. Box 442
Atlanta, GA 30301-0442
(800) 306-2653
Fax: (404) 733-5439
E-mail: scholars@coca-cola.com
Web Site: www.coca-colascholars.org

FOUNDED: 1986

AREAS OF INTEREST:
Enhancing educational opportunities in the U.S.

NAME(S) OF PROGRAMS:
● **Coca-Cola Scholars Program**

TYPE:
Scholarships. Awards based on leadership, academics and community service.

YEAR PROGRAM STARTED: 1989

PURPOSE:
To enhance educational opportunities in the U.S. through scholarship awards and enrichment programs for young people who demonstrate, through academic excellence and leadership in their communities, their capacity for and commitment to making a difference in the world.

ELIGIBILITY:
Current high school (or home-schooled) seniors attending school in the U.S. (or select DoD schools). Applicant must not graduate prior to deadline.

GEOG. RESTRICTIONS: United States.

FINANCIAL DATA:
Program has awarded over $69,000,000 in scholarships since inception.
Amount of support per award: $20,000.
Total amount of support: Over $3,000,000 annually.

NO. MOST RECENT APPLICANTS: 50,000 to 100,000 annually.

NO. AWARDS: 150 annually.

APPLICATION INFO:
Application must be submitted online.
Duration: Four to 10 years.
Deadline: October 31.

ADDRESS INQUIRIES TO:
See e-mail address above.

CONCORDIA UNIVERSITY [1494]

1550 de Maisonneuve Boulevard West
Graduate Awards Office, Room GM 930.01
Montreal QC H3G 1M8 Canada
(514) 848-2424 ext. 3385
Fax: (514) 848-2812
E-mail: graduate-awards@concordia.ca
Web Site: www.concordia.ca/sgs.html

FOUNDED: 1974

AREAS OF INTEREST:
All disciplines.

NAME(S) OF PROGRAMS:
● **Concordia University Graduate Fellowships**

TYPE:
Assistantships; Awards/prizes; Conferences/seminars; Endowments; Fellowships; Scholarships. Postgraduate full-time fellowships.

PURPOSE:
To recruit highly qualified graduate students to doctoral programs.

ELIGIBILITY:
Candidates must be planning to pursue full-time doctoral studies at Concordia University. Academic merit is the prime consideration in the granting of the award.

All new admissions will be considered for awards.

GEOG. RESTRICTIONS: Canada.

FINANCIAL DATA:
Amount of support per award: $14,000 (CAN) per year.

NO. MOST RECENT APPLICANTS: Over 1,000.

NO. AWARDS: 100 or more.

APPLICATION INFO:
Guidelines are available on the University's web site.
Duration: One to four years.

COOK FAMILY FOUNDATION

120 West Exchange Street
Suite 202
Owosso, MI 48867
(989) 725-1621
Fax: (989) 936-5910
E-mail: tom@cookfamilyfoundation.org
Web Site: www.cookfamilyfoundation.org

TYPE:
Capital grants; Challenge/matching grants; Demonstration grants; Development grants; Matching gifts; Project/program grants; Scholarships; Seed money grants; Technical assistance. Educational support.

See entry 1133 for full listing.

JACK KENT COOKE FOUNDATION   [1495]

44325 Woodridge Parkway
Lansdowne, VA 20176-5297
(703) 723-8000
(800) 941-3300
Fax: (703) 723-8030
E-mail: scholarships@jkcf.org
Web Site: www.jkcf.org

FOUNDED: 2000

AREAS OF INTEREST:
Education.

NAME(S) OF PROGRAMS:
● **College Scholarship Program**
● **Undergraduate Transfer Scholarship**
● **Young Scholars Program**

TYPE:
Fellowships; Scholarships. College Scholarship Program is available to high-performing high school seniors with financial need who seek to attend and graduate from the nation's best four-year colleges and universities.

Undergraduate Transfer Scholarship honors excellence by supporting outstanding community college students with financial need to transfer to and complete their Bachelor's degrees at the nation's top four-year colleges and universities.

Young Scholars Program seeks high-achieving seventh-grade students with financial need, and cultivates their talents and abilities throughout high school by providing the personalized advising and financial support needed to secure challenging academic opportunities.

PURPOSE:
To help students of exceptional promise reach their full potential through education.

GEOG. RESTRICTIONS: United States.

FINANCIAL DATA:
Amount of support per award: College Scholarship Program and Undergraduate Transfer Scholarship: Up to $40,000 per year. Young Scholars Program: Varies.

NO. MOST RECENT APPLICANTS: College Scholarship Program: 5,520; Undergraduate Transfer Scholarship: 1,494; Young Scholars Program: 2,302 for the year 2019.

NO. AWARDS: College Scholarship Program: Approximately 60; Undergraduate Transfer Scholarship: Approximately 60; Young Scholars: Approximately 50.

APPLICATION INFO:
An application form needs to be completed. Application information is available on the web site.

Duration: College Scholarship Program: Up to four years. Undergraduate Transfer Scholarship: Two to three years.

Deadline: College Scholarship Program and Undergraduate Transfer Scholarship: Opens August, closes late November. Young Scholars Program: Opens January, closes April.

ADDRESS INQUIRIES TO:
See e-mail address above.

DARTMOUTH COLLEGE

Office of Graduate Studies
Eastman/Marshall
37 Dewey Field Road, Suite 6062, Room 437
Hanover, NH 03755-3526
(603) 646-2106
Fax: (603) 646-8762
E-mail: amy.l.gallagher@dartmouth.edu
Web Site: graduate.dartmouth.edu

TYPE:
Exchange programs; Fellowships.

See entry 897 for full listing.

DAUGHTERS OF PENELOPE FOUNDATION, INC.

1909 Q Street, N.W., Suite 500
Washington, DC 20009
(202) 234-9741
Fax: (202) 483-6983
E-mail: dophq@ahepa.org
Web Site: www.dopfoundationinc.com

TYPE:
Scholarships.

See entry 976 for full listing.

DAUGHTERS OF THE CINCINNATI   [1496]

271 Madison Avenue
Suite 1408
New York, NY 10016
(212) 991-9945
E-mail: scholarships@daughters1894.org
Web Site: www.daughters1894.org

FOUNDED: 1894

NAME(S) OF PROGRAMS:
● **Daughters of the Cincinnati Scholarship Program**

TYPE:
Scholarships. Undergraduate scholarships.

YEAR PROGRAM STARTED: 1906

PURPOSE:
To assist high school seniors entering college with financial aid (annually for the four years).

LEGAL BASIS:
Nonprofit, tax-exempt organization.

ELIGIBILITY:
Applicant must be a senior in high school who is the daughter of a career officer commissioned in the regular Army, Navy, Air Force, Coast Guard or Marine Corps (active, retired or deceased). The daughters of officers in the Reserves, National Guard and State Militia are not eligible to apply for this scholarship.

FINANCIAL DATA:
Aid for tuition and room and board.
Amount of support per award: Average $4,000 to $5,000 annually.
Total amount of support: Varies.

NO. MOST RECENT APPLICANTS: Approximately 100.

NO. AWARDS: Approximately 3 to 4 annually.

APPLICATION INFO:
The application is accessible from the web site after supplying the parent's branch of service and rank.

Duration: Four years, or as long as the student attends college up to that length of time. Reviewed annually.

Deadline: Postmarked by March 15. Announcement in mid-May.

PUBLICATIONS:
Information sheet.

ADDRESS INQUIRIES TO:
Scholarship Administrator
(See address above.)

DAVIDSON INSTITUTE   [1497]

9665 Gateway Drive, Suite B
Reno, NV 89521
(775) 852-3483
E-mail: tmoessner@davidsongifted.org
davidsonfellows@davidsongifted.org
Web Site: www.davidsongifted.org/Fellows-Scholarship

FOUNDED: 1999

AREAS OF INTEREST:
Encouraging the development of academically gifted students.

NAME(S) OF PROGRAMS:
● **Davidson Fellows**

TYPE:
Awards/prizes; Scholarships.

YEAR PROGRAM STARTED: 2001

PURPOSE:
To award students working at the college graduate level on projects that have the potential to benefit society.

ELIGIBILITY:
Students must be 18 or younger as of application deadline, must be U.S. citizens or permanent residents residing in the U.S. and must have completed a significant piece of work.

FINANCIAL DATA:
Amount of support per award: Scholarships of $10,000, $25,000 or $50,000 to be used at an accredited college or university.
Total amount of support: $480,000 for the year 2020.

NO. MOST RECENT APPLICANTS: 600.

NO. AWARDS: 20.

APPLICATION INFO:
Application categories are Science, Technology, Engineering, Mathematics, Literature, Music, Philosophy and Outside the Box. The application is completely online. Students must submit a project, two essays and a video; they must also have two nominators.

Duration: The scholarship is available for 10 years and is not renewable.

Deadline: The second Wednesday in February.

ADDRESS INQUIRIES TO:
Tacie Moessner, Director
Davidson Fellows Scholarship Program
(See e-mail address above.)

MICHAEL AND SUSAN DELL FOUNDATION   [1498]

4417 Westlake Drive
Austin, TX 78746
(877) 600-5587
(800) 294-2039 (apply)
Fax: (512) 600-5501
E-mail: info@dell.org
Web Site: www.dell.org
www.dellscholars.org

NAME(S) OF PROGRAMS:
● **Dell Scholars Program**

TYPE:
Scholarships. Need-based scholarship that recognizes academic potential in lower-income and underserved students. Applicants must demonstrate a drive to succeed while overcoming personal obstacles.

YEAR PROGRAM STARTED: 2004

PURPOSE:
To assist students who have worked hard to prepare themselves for higher education yet may have lower grade point averages and test scores because of adverse personal situations or surroundings.

ELIGIBILITY:
Applicants must:
(1) be high school seniors who have participated in a Michael and Susan Dell Foundation-approved college readiness program;
(2) be a U.S. citizen or legal permanent resident;
(3) have financial need confirmed through eligibility for a Federal Pell Grant;
(4) have a minimum 2.4 grade point average on a 4.0 scale and;
(5) be planning to enroll full-time in a

Bachelor's degree program at an accredited higher education institution in the fall directly after high school graduation.

Scholarship may be used at any accredited two- or four-year institution in the U.S. where credits can be earned towards a Baccalaureate degree, including community and junior colleges. Technical colleges and vocational programs are not eligible.

GEOG. RESTRICTIONS: United States.

FINANCIAL DATA:
Award may be applied to any cost of acquiring an education. Also provide other means of support, such as mentoring.
Amount of support per award: $20,000 over a maximum of six years.
Total amount of support: Varies.

NO. AWARDS: 500 annually.

APPLICATION INFO:
Application, which becomes available in October, must be completed online. No paper applications will be accepted.
Duration: Up to six years.
Deadline: December 1.

ADDRESS INQUIRIES TO:
E-mail: apply@dellscholars.org

THE EBELL OF LOS ANGELES [1499]
743 South Lucerne Boulevard
Los Angeles, CA 90005-3707
(323) 931-1277 ext. 184
Fax: (323) 937-0272
E-mail: Scholarship@ebelloflosangeles.com
Web Site: www.ebellla.org

FOUNDED: 1894

AREAS OF INTEREST:
Higher education.

NAME(S) OF PROGRAMS:
● **Ebell/Flint Scholarship**

TYPE:
Scholarships.

YEAR PROGRAM STARTED: 1919

PURPOSE:
To support scholarships for qualified college students.

LEGAL BASIS:
Private foundation.

ELIGIBILITY:
To be eligible for an Ebell scholarship, applicant must:
(1) be a U.S. citizen;
(2) be a permanent resident of Los Angeles County;
(3) be at least a full-time freshman attending an accredited Los Angeles County college or university;
(4) achieve at least a 3.25 cumulative grade point average;
(5) demonstrate community commitment and;
(6) be available for an in-person interview with the Ebell Scholarship Committee on the Ebell campus.

GEOG. RESTRICTIONS: Los Angeles County, California.

FINANCIAL DATA:
Amount of support per award: Four-year colleges: $5,000 per year (12 months) paid semiannually in September and February; Two-year colleges: $3,000 per year.
Total amount of support: Over $200,000 annually.

NO. AWARDS: 53.

APPLICATION INFO:
Guidelines and application form are available on the web site.
Duration: Three years or when the student attains Bachelor's degree, whichever comes first.
Deadline: April 2.

IRS I.D.: 23-7049580

ADDRESS INQUIRIES TO:
See e-mail address above.

THE EISENHOWER FOUNDATION
200 S.E. 4th Street
Abilene, KS 67410
(785) 263-6771
Fax: (785) 263-6715
E-mail: info@eisenhowerfoundation.net
Web Site: www.EisenhowerFoundation.net

TYPE:
Travel grants. Travel grants are awarded to individual researchers on a competitive basis to cover a portion of expenses while in Abilene, KS, using the presidential library.

See entry 1789 for full listing.

FEEA SCHOLARSHIP PROGRAM [1500]
1641 Prince Street
Alexandria, VA 22314
(202) 554-0007
Fax: (202) 559-1298
E-mail: fedshelpingfeds@feea.org
Web Site: feea.org

AREAS OF INTEREST:
Education.

TYPE:
Scholarships. Merit-based scholarship competition program open exclusively to federal employees, their spouses and their children.

PURPOSE:
To financially aid hard-working federal employees, their spouses and their children in their college education.

ELIGIBILITY:
Children, step-children and legal dependents of full- or part-time permanent federal civilian or postal workers employed with the federal government for more than three years, as well as their spouses may apply. Dependents may first apply as high school seniors. Dependents must be full-time students enrolled in or planning to enroll in an accredited postsecondary school in a course of study that leads to a two-year, four-year or graduate degree. 3.0 grade point average on a 4.0 scale is required.

GEOG. RESTRICTIONS: United States.

FINANCIAL DATA:
Amount of support per award: $1,000 to $5,000.

NO. MOST RECENT APPLICANTS: 2,700.

NO. AWARDS: 217.

APPLICATION INFO:
Scholarship catalog and application instructions are available on the FEEA web site. Required material includes:
(1) complete high school or college transcripts;
(2) one written recommendation or letter of

reference;
(3) a short essay (topic changes annually);
(4) a list of community service, extracurricular activities and awards and;
(5) a copy of the employee sponsor's most recent SF-50.

Specific instructions and any additional requirements are listed on each year's application.
Duration: One year. May reapply each year if still eligible.
Deadline: End of March. Exact date will be posted online.

THE JAMES MARSTON FITCH CHARITABLE FOUNDATION
c/o Municipal Art Society
488 Madison Avenue, Suite 1900
New York, NY 10022
(212) 252-6809
Fax: (212) 471-9987
E-mail: cpena@fitchfoundation.org
Web Site: fitchfoundation.org

TYPE:
Research grants. Richard L. Blinder Award was created to promote studies that explore the architecture of cultural buildings which integrate historic preservation and new construction - past, present and future; presented biennially.

Mid-Career Fellowship: This grant is the primary mission and the signature grant of this Foundation. The grants are intended to support projects of innovative original research or creative design that advance the practice of historic preservation in the U.S.

See entry 372 for full listing.

FLORIDA DEPARTMENT OF EDUCATION
Office of Student Financial Assistance
325 West Gaines Street, Suite 1314
Tallahassee, FL 32399-0400
(888) 827-2004
Fax: (850) 487-1809
E-mail: osfa@fldoe.org
Web Site: www.floridastudentfinancialaidsg.org

TYPE:
Scholarships. Financial assistance for descendants of the Rosewood family affected by the incidents of January 1923, to attend a state university, public community college or public postsecondary vocational-technical school.

See entry 932 for full listing.

FLORIDA DEPARTMENT OF EDUCATION [1501]
Office of Student Financial Assistance
325 West Gaines Street, Suite 1314
Tallahassee, FL 32399-0400
(888) 827-2004
Fax: (850) 487-1809
E-mail: osfa@fldoe.org
Web Site: www.floridastudentfinancialaidsg.org

AREAS OF INTEREST:
Financial aid for Florida undergraduate students.

NAME(S) OF PROGRAMS:
● **Access to Better Learning and Education Grant Program (ABLE)**
● **Mary McLeod Bethune Scholarship Program (MMB)**

- **Effective Access to Student Education (EASE)**
- **First Generation Matching Grant Program (FGMG)**
- **Florida Farmworker Student Scholarship Program**
- **Florida Student Assistance Grant Program (FSAG)**
- **Florida Work Experience Program (FWEP)**
- **Scholarships for Children and Spouses of Deceased or Disabled Veterans (CSDDV)**

TYPE:
Challenge/matching grants; Grants-in-aid; Scholarships. The Access to Better Learning and Education (ABLE) Grant Program provides tuition assistance to Florida undergraduate students enrolled in degree programs at eligible private Florida colleges or universities. ABLE is a decentralized program, and each participating institution determines application procedures, deadlines and student eligibility.

The Mary McLeod Bethune Scholarships (MMB) are awarded to undergraduate students who meet scholastic requirements attending Bethune-Cookman University, Edward Waters College, Florida A&M University, or Florida Memorial University.

The Effective Access to Student Education (EASE) grants are provided to full-time Florida undergraduates attending an eligible private, nonprofit Florida college or university.

The First Generation Matching Grant Program (FGMG) provides need-based grants to degree-seeking, resident, undergraduate students who demonstrate financial need, are enrolled in participating postsecondary institutions, and whose parents have not earned Baccalaureate or higher degrees.

The Florida Farmworker Student Scholarship Program requires one parent to be a farmer.

The Florida Student Assistance Grant Program (FSAG) is a need-based grant program available to degree-seeking and certificate-seeking, resident, undergraduate students who demonstrate substantial financial need and are enrolled in participating postsecondary institutions.

The Florida Work Experience Program (FWEP) provides eligible Florida students the opportunity to secure work experiences that will complement and reinforce the students' educational and career goals.

Scholarships for Children and Spouses of Deceased or Disabled Veterans (CSDDV) provides scholarships for dependent children and unremarried spouses of Florida veterans who died as a result of service-connected injuries, diseases, or disabilities sustained while on active duty or have been certified by the Florida Department of Veterans' Affairs as having service-connected 100% total and permanent disabilities.

PURPOSE:
To provide financial assistance to Florida students continuing their education.

LEGAL BASIS:
State agency.

GEOG. RESTRICTIONS: Florida.

FINANCIAL DATA:
Amount of support per award: Varies per program.
Total amount of support: Varies.

NO. AWARDS: Access to Better Learning and Education Grant Program: 2,290 disbursed; Mary McLeod Bethune Scholarship Program: 147 disbursed; Effective Access to Student Education: 46,026 disbursed; First Generations Matching Grant Program: 10,912 disbursed; Florida Student Assistance Grant Program: 174,887 disbursed; Florida Work Experience Program: 728 disbursed; Scholarships for Children and Spouses of Deceased or Disabled Veterans: 1,966 disbursed.

APPLICATION INFO:
Applicant must submit a completed, error-free Florida Financial Aid Application (FFAA) or Free Application for Federal Student Aid (FAFSA) as designated online.
Duration: Varies.
Deadline: CSDDV: April 1. All others: Determined by institution.

ADDRESS INQUIRIES TO:
See telephone and e-mail address above.

FLORIDA DEPARTMENT OF EDUCATION

Office of Student Financial Assistance
325 West Gaines Street, Suite 1314
Tallahassee, FL 32399-0400
(888) 827-2004
Fax: (850) 487-1809
E-mail: osfa@fldoe.org
Web Site: www.floridastudentfinancialaidsg.org

TYPE:
Challenge/matching grants; Grants-in-aid. Jose Marti Scholarship Challenge Grant Fund is a need-based merit scholarship that provides financial assistance to eligible students of Hispanic origin who will attend Florida public or eligible private institutions.

See entry 964 for full listing.

FLORIDA DEPARTMENT OF EDUCATION [1502]

Office of Student Financial Assistance
325 West Gaines Street, Suite 1314
Tallahassee, FL 32399-0400
(888) 827-2004
Fax: (850) 487-1809
E-mail: osfa@fldoe.org
Web Site: www.floridastudentfinancialaidsg.org

NAME(S) OF PROGRAMS:
- **Florida Bright Futures Scholarship Program**

TYPE:
Scholarships. The Florida Bright Futures Scholarship Program is the umbrella program for three state-funded scholarships based on academic achievement in high school: Florida Academic Scholars (FAS) Award, Florida Medallion Scholars (FMS) Award, Florida Gold Seal Vocational Scholars (GSV) Award, and Florida Gold Seal Cape Award.

YEAR PROGRAM STARTED: 1997

PURPOSE:
To reward Florida's high school graduates who merit recognition of high academic achievement.

LEGAL BASIS:
State agency.

ELIGIBILITY:
Initial eligibility requirements to receive funding are as follows:
(1) be a Florida resident and a U.S. citizen or

eligible noncitizen; student's residency and citizenship status are determined by the postsecondary institution; consult the financial aid office or admissions office of the institution one plans to attend; (2) meet specific coursework, volunteer service hours, and minimum grade point average and test score requirements and; (3) not be found guilty of, or pled nolo contendere to, a felony charge, unless the student has been granted clemency by the Governor and Cabinet sitting as the Executive Office of Clemency.

GEOG. RESTRICTIONS: Florida.

FINANCIAL DATA:
Amount of support per award: Varies.
Total amount of support: Varies.

NO. MOST RECENT APPLICANTS: 138,160 for the year 2019-20.

NO. AWARDS: 113,957 disbursed for the year 2019-20.

APPLICATION INFO:
Detailed program information can be found on the web site.
Duration: One year; renewable up to five years from high school graduation or a first Baccalaureate degree, whichever comes first.
Deadline: Florida Financial Aid Application must be submitted no later than December 1 after high school graduation.

ADDRESS INQUIRIES TO:
State Scholarship and Grant Programs (See address above.)

FOUNDATION FOR TECHNOLOGY AND ENGINEERING EDUCATION [1503]

1914 Association Drive
Suite 201
Reston, VA 20191-1539
(703) 860-2100
Fax: (703) 860-0353
E-mail: kdelapaz@iteea.org
Web Site: www.iteea.org

FOUNDED: 1939

AREAS OF INTEREST:
STEM education.

NAME(S) OF PROGRAMS:
- **FTEE Undergraduate Scholarship**

TYPE:
Scholarships. The scholarship is for an undergraduate student majoring in technology and engineering education teacher preparation.

PURPOSE:
To support teacher preparation in technology and engineering education.

ELIGIBILITY:
Applicant must be a member of the International Technology and Engineering Educators Association and be a current, full-time undergraduate majoring in technology and engineering education teacher preparation. Applicant must not be a senior by application deadline.

FINANCIAL DATA:
Amount of support per award: $500.
Total amount of support: $500.

NO. AWARDS: 1.

APPLICATION INFO:
Applicants must submit the application package, which is to include the following required items:
(1) letter of transmittal that includes a statement about personal interest in teaching technology and engineering and applicant's address with day and evening telephone numbers;
(2) resume or vitae which indicate career goals, current professional and college activities and achievements (maximum three pages);
(3) photocopy of college transcript (required 2.5 grade point average on 4.0 scale) and;
(4) three faculty letters of recommendation from among his or her professors and/or advisor.

Application may be submitted electronically to the e-mail address listed above.

Duration: One year.

Deadline: December 1.

ADDRESS INQUIRIES TO:
FTEE Undergraduate Scholarship
Foundation for Technology and
Engineering Education
(See address above.)

*SPECIAL STIPULATIONS:
Applicant must be a member of the ITEEA.

FOUNDATION FOR TECHNOLOGY AND ENGINEERING EDUCATION   [1504]
1914 Association Drive
Suite 201
Reston, VA 20191-1539
(703) 860-2100
Fax: (703) 860-0353
E-mail: kdelapaz@iteea.org
Web Site: www.iteea.org

FOUNDED: 1939

AREAS OF INTEREST:
STEM education.

NAME(S) OF PROGRAMS:
- **Litherland/FTEE Scholarship Undergraduate Major in Technology and Engineering Education**

TYPE:
Scholarships.

PURPOSE:
To assist an undergraduate student majoring in technology education and engineering teacher preparation.

ELIGIBILITY:
Applicant must be member of the International Technology and Engineering Educators Association and a current, full-time undergraduate majoring in technology education and engineering teacher preparation. The student must not be a senior by application deadline. The award is based upon interest in teaching, academic ability, need and faculty recommendations.

FINANCIAL DATA:
Amount of support per award: $500.

NO. AWARDS: 1.

APPLICATION INFO:
Applicants must submit an application package, which is to include the following required items:
(1) a letter of transmittal that includes a statement about his or her personal interest in

teaching technology and engineering and applicant's address with day and evening telephone numbers;
(2) resume or vitae identifying career goals, current professional activities and achievements;
(3) photocopy of college transcript and;
(4) three faculty letters of recommendation from among his or her professors and/or advisor.

Duration: One year.

Deadline: December 1.

ADDRESS INQUIRIES TO:
Litherland/FTEE Scholarship
Foundation for Technology and
Engineering Education
(See address above.)

*SPECIAL STIPULATIONS:
Applicant must be a member of the ITEEA.

FREEDOM ALLIANCE   [1505]
22570 Markey Court, Suite 240
Dulles, VA 20166
(703) 444-7940
(800) 475-6620 ext. 301
Fax: (703) 444-9893
E-mail: wanda.cruz@freedomalliance.org
Web Site: www.fascholarship.com

FOUNDED: 1990

AREAS OF INTEREST:
Scholarship aid to the children of American military personnel who have been killed or injured in military service.

NAME(S) OF PROGRAMS:
- **Freedom Alliance Scholarship Fund**

TYPE:
Scholarships. Freedom Alliance Scholarship Fund provides college scholarships to the sons and daughters of America's military heroes - those who sacrifice life or limb in defense of America's freedom.

YEAR PROGRAM STARTED: 1990

PURPOSE:
To honor the bravery and dedication exhibited by Americans in the U.S. armed forces who have sacrificed life and limb by providing educational scholarships to their children.

LEGAL BASIS:
501(c)(3) educational and charitable foundation.

ELIGIBILITY:
Students must be a dependent child of a service member who was killed or was permanently disabled (100% rating) in the line of duty, or who is currently certified as POW or MIA. The applicant must also be a senior in high school, a high school graduate, or enrolled in an institution of higher learning, including colleges, universities or vocational schools.

FINANCIAL DATA:
Amount of support per award: Varies.
Total amount of support: $2,300,000.

NO. MOST RECENT APPLICANTS: 750 for the year 2020.

NO. AWARDS: 558 for the year 2020.

APPLICATION INFO:
Eligible students seeking a Freedom Alliance scholarship must first complete an application form. Applications will not be considered by the scholarship committee unless all required materials listed below accompany the

application package:
(1) certificate of death/disability or proof of POW/MIA status as defined in the instructions;
(2) proof of dependency as defined in the instructions;
(3) 500-word essay as explained in the instructions;
(4) official transcripts from high school and all post-high school educational institutions;
(5) photo of applicant and;
(6) photo of parent.

DD Form 214 is also required in the case of a student whose parent is permanently disabled, in addition to the VA rating letter demonstrating permanent disability in the application packet.

Duration: Scholarships are awarded annually and are renewable for a total of four scholarships.

Deadline: Applications are accepted on a rolling basis.

STAFF:
Thomas Kilgannon, President
Calvin Coolidge, Executive Director

BOARD OF DIRECTORS AND OFFICERS:
Gerald Lindholm, Chairman
Rita Scott, Secretary/Treasurer
Lt Gen Jerry Boykin, USA (Ret.)
Ed Daily
Bob Garthwait

FOUNDERS:
Lt Col Oliver L. North, USMC (Ret.), Honorary Chairman
Lt Gen Edward J. Bronars, USMC

ADDRESS INQUIRIES TO:
Wanda Cruz, Program Assistant
(See address above.)

*PLEASE NOTE:
No graduate scholarships are provided.

GOLDEN KEY INTERNATIONAL HONOUR SOCIETY, INC.   [1506]
4470 Chamblee Dunwoody Road
Suite 304
Atlanta, GA 30338
(678) 689-2200
(800) 377-2401
E-mail: awards@goldenkey.org
Web Site: goldenkey.org

AREAS OF INTEREST:
Nonprofit academic honors organization that recognizes the top 15% of juniors and seniors in all undergraduate fields.

NAME(S) OF PROGRAMS:
- **The Golden Key Graduate Scholarship Award**
- **Golden Key Humanitarian/Service Response Award**
- **Golden Key Outstanding Member Award**
- **Golden Key Professional Development Grant**
- **Joan Nelson Study Abroad Scholarship**
- **Undergraduate Achievement Scholarship**

TYPE:
Awards/prizes; Scholarships; Travel grants. The Golden Key Graduate Scholar Award: Golden Key's premier scholarship program. Supports members' post-Baccalaureate study at accredited universities anywhere in the world.

Golden Key Humanitarian/Service Response Award showcases members during a pandemic and supports member commitment to a service.

Golden Key Professional Development Grant allows current Golden Key chapter advisors the ability to attend professional development conferences or pursue research within their academic disciplines.

Joan Nelson Study Abroad Scholarships assist members who are going to participate in a study abroad program.

Undergraduate Achievement Scholarship recognizes members for their excellence throughout their undergraduate careers.

PURPOSE:
To enable members to realize their potential.

ELIGIBILITY:
Open to Golden Key members.

FINANCIAL DATA:
Amount of support per award: $500 to $10,000.
Total amount of support: Varies.

APPLICATION INFO:
Golden Key's scholarships and awards require a formal application. Each scholarship has a unique submission deadline and application process. Details about each of the scholarship programs can be found under the Scholarships Listing on the web site. All scholarship submissions must be written in English.
Deadline: Varies.

ADDRESS INQUIRIES TO:
Chris Yarbrough
Director, Programs and Operations
(See address above.)

*SPECIAL STIPULATIONS:
Only Golden Key members may apply for these scholarships and awards.

THE GREATER KANAWHA VALLEY FOUNDATION

178 Summer Street
Charleston, WV 25301
(304) 346-3620
Fax: (304) 346-3640
E-mail: shyre@tgkvf.org
Web Site: www.tgkvf.org

TYPE:
Project/program grants; Scholarships.

See entry 1168 for full listing.

THE HIGHER EDUCATION STUDENT ASSISTANCE AUTHORITY [1507]

P.O. Box 540
Trenton, NJ 08625-0540
(609) 588-3300
E-mail: client_services@hesaa.org
Web Site: www.hesaa.org

FOUNDED: 1959

AREAS OF INTEREST:
State financial assistance for college students.

NAME(S) OF PROGRAMS:
● **Law Enforcement Officer Memorial Scholarship**
● **New Jersey Governor's Industry Vocations Scholarship for Women and Minorities (NJ-GIVS)**
● **New Jersey Student Tuition Assistance Reward Scholarship (NJ STARS)**

● **New Jersey Student Tuition Assistance Reward Scholarship II (NJ STARS II)**
● **New Jersey World Trade Center Scholarship**
● **NJBEST Scholarship**
● **Survivor Tuition Benefits Program**

TYPE:
Scholarships. Law Enforcement Officer Memorial Scholarship provides financial aid for eligible children of law enforcement officers killed in the line of duty.

New Jersey Governor's Industry Vocations Scholarship for Women and Minorities pays for an eligible certificate or degree-granting program in a construction-related field at one of New Jersey's eligible institutions.

New Jersey Student Tuition Assistance Reward Scholarship provides access to higher education for the state's highest achieving students.

New Jersey Student Tuition Assistance Reward Scholarship II enables successful NJ STARS scholars to transfer to a New Jersey four-year college or university and earn a Bachelor's degree.

New Jersey World Trade Center Scholarship benefits dependent children and surviving spouses of New Jersey residents who were killed in or who died of the terrorist attacks against the U.S. on September 11, 2001.

NJBEST Scholarship is a one-time scholarship to beneficiaries in the NJBEST 529 college savings plan, who are enrolled at least half-time in his or her first year, first semester of postsecondary education at a New Jersey institution.

Survivor Tuition Benefits Program benefits dependent children and surviving spouses of New Jersey firefighters, emergency service workers or law enforcement officers who were killed in the line of duty.

PURPOSE:
To provide financial assistance to college students demonstrating academic proficiency, and/or need.

ELIGIBILITY:
Student must be a U.S. citizen or eligible noncitizen and registered with the Selective Service. For some programs, New Jersey residency and a current-year FAFSA are required. Application deadlines, years of eligibility and payment limits apply to all programs. Contact HESAA for details.

GEOG. RESTRICTIONS: New Jersey.

FINANCIAL DATA:
Amount of support per award: New Jersey Governor's Industry Vocations Scholarship for Women and Minorities: Up to $2,000 per year or up to the cost of tuition, less any federal, state or institutional aid. NJBEST Scholarship: Varies depending upon the number of years open and level of contributions. Survivor Tuition Benefits Program: Covers the cost of tuition at any New Jersey public college or university. Students enrolled at an independent New Jersey college or university may receive up to the highest tuition charges at a New Jersey public institution.

APPLICATION INFO:
Application information as well as applications are available on the HESAA web site. Some programs require a FAFSA to be filed before applying.
Deadline: All programs have deadline dates for fall and spring terms. Contact HESAA for application deadline dates.

STAFF:
Jean M. Hathaway, Director, Grants and Scholarships

THE HIGHER EDUCATION STUDENT ASSISTANCE AUTHORITY [1508]

P.O. Box 540
Trenton, NJ 08625-0540
(609) 588-3300
E-mail: client_services@hesaa.org
Web Site: www.hesaa.org

FOUNDED: 1959

AREAS OF INTEREST:
State financial assistance for college students.

NAME(S) OF PROGRAMS:
● **Tuition Aid Grant (TAG)**

TYPE:
Grants-in-aid. The Higher Education Student Assistance Authority (HESAA) is a New Jersey authority that provides students and families with the financial and informational resources for students to pursue their education beyond high school. With roots dating back to 1959, HESAA's singular focus has always been to benefit the students it serves. HESAA provides state supplemental loans, grants and scholarships. HESAA also administers the state's college savings plan.

YEAR PROGRAM STARTED: 1969

PURPOSE:
To provide financial assistance to needy students attending approved New Jersey institutions. This is calculated by estimating what a family can contribute from income and assets plus a contribution from the student's earnings and savings. The amount and type of aid will depend upon program eligibility, available funds and the degree of need.

LEGAL BASIS:
New Jersey Higher Education Tuition Aid Act.

ELIGIBILITY:
Applicants must be New Jersey residents for at least 12 consecutive months prior to receiving an award, and will be enrolled in an approved New Jersey institution. Student must be a U.S. citizen or eligible noncitizen and be registered with the Selective Service, if applicable. Grants are renewable annually based upon satisfactory academic progress and continued financial need. Students who have received a Baccalaureate degree are not eligible.

GEOG. RESTRICTIONS: New Jersey.

FINANCIAL DATA:
Amount of support per award: Award amounts are based on the student's New Jersey Eligibility Index, tuition charged and appropriated funds.

NO. AWARDS: Based upon appropriations.

APPLICATION INFO:
Applicants must file the Free Application for Federal Student Aid (FAFSA), including the additional New Jersey questions.
Duration: Renewable for four years of undergraduate study providing eligibility continues and an application is filed.
Deadline: February 15 for fall and spring terms. September 15 for spring term only. Renewals April 15 for fall and spring terms.

PUBLICATIONS:
State and Federal Financial Aid Programs for New Jersey Students, brochure.

HISPANIC SCHOLARSHIP FUND

1411 West 190th Street
Suite 700
Gardena, CA 90248
(877) 473-4636
(310) 975-3700
Fax: (310) 349-3328
E-mail: info@hsf.net
scholar1@hsf.net
Web Site: www.hsf.net

TYPE:
Scholarships. Awarded to Hispanic community college, undergraduate and graduate students.

See entry 965 for full listing.

THE HONOR SOCIETY OF PHI KAPPA PHI [1509]

7576 Goodwood Boulevard
Baton Rouge, LA 70806
(225) 388-4917 ext. 235
(800) 804-9880 ext. 235
Fax: (225) 388-4900
E-mail: kpartin@phikappaphi.org
Web Site: www.phikappaphi.org

FOUNDED: 1897

AREAS OF INTEREST:
Scholastic excellence in all academic fields.

NAME(S) OF PROGRAMS:
● **The Phi Kappa Phi Fellowship**

TYPE:
Fellowships. Support for the first year of graduate or professional school.

YEAR PROGRAM STARTED: 1932

PURPOSE:
To stimulate members of Phi Kappa Phi to go to graduate or professional school.

LEGAL BASIS:
Honor Society incorporated in Michigan, May 20, 1972. Authorized to operate in Louisiana, September 1978. Tax-exempt under IRS 501(c)(3). Companion organization, the Phi Kappa Phi Foundation, incorporated in California, December 17, 1969, as a Public Benefit Foundation, tax-exempt under IRS 501(c)(3).

ELIGIBILITY:
Applicant must be a member of Phi Kappa Phi, maintain high scholastic standing and be recommended by a chapter of Phi Kappa Phi.

FINANCIAL DATA:
Amount of support per award: $8,500 to $35,000.
Total amount of support: $615,000 for the year 2018.

CO-OP FUNDING PROGRAMS: Awards made through Phi Kappa Phi Foundation, a companion organization to the Society.

NO. AWARDS: 58 (50 valued at $8,500, 6 valued at $20,000 and 2 valued at $35,000) for the year 2018.

APPLICATION INFO:
Completed application packet must be returned to the local chapter on or before the deadline.
Duration: One academic year. Nonrenewable.

IRS I.D.: 95-1856406

STAFF:
Kelli Partin, Awards Manager

ADDRESS INQUIRIES TO:
Kelli Partin, Awards Manager
(See address above.)

HORTICULTURAL RESEARCH INSTITUTE, INC. [1510]

2130 Stella Court
Columbus, OH 43215
(614) 487-1117
Fax: (614) 487-1216
E-mail: jenniferg@americanhort.org
Web Site: www.hriresearch.org

AREAS OF INTEREST:
Nursery, landscape research and horticulture.

NAME(S) OF PROGRAMS:
● **Carville M. Akehurst Memorial Scholarship**
● **Timothy Bigelow and Palmer W. Bigelow, Jr. Scholarship**
● **Bryan A. Champion Memorial Scholarship**
● **Muggets Scholarship**
● **Spring Meadow Nursery Scholarship**
● **Usrey Family Scholarship**
● **Susie and Bruce Usrey Education Scholarship**

TYPE:
Scholarships.

YEAR PROGRAM STARTED: 1988

PURPOSE:
To aid students seeking a career in the horticulture industry.

LEGAL BASIS:
Nonprofit organization.

ELIGIBILITY:
Varies.

GEOG. RESTRICTIONS: Varies.

FINANCIAL DATA:
Amount of support per award: $500 to $5,000.
Total amount of support: Varies.

NO. AWARDS: 9 for the academic year 2019-20.

APPLICATION INFO:
Applications are available online.
Deadline: September 8.

IRS I.D.: 52-1052547

ADDRESS INQUIRIES TO:
See e-mail address above.

ILLINOIS RESTAURANT ASSOCIATION EDUCATIONAL FOUNDATION [1511]

33 West Monroe, Suite 250
Chicago, IL 60603
(312) 787-4000
E-mail: khodges@illinoisrestaurants.org
Web Site: www.illinoisrestaurants.org

FOUNDED: 1973

AREAS OF INTEREST:
Foodservice/restaurant/hospitality.

NAME(S) OF PROGRAMS:
● **IRA Educational Foundation Scholarship Program**
● **IRAEFF Restaurant Employee Relief Fund**

TYPE:
Product donations; Scholarships. Grants for impacted food service employees.

YEAR PROGRAM STARTED: 1973

PURPOSE:
To build the Illinois hospitality workforce through the ProStart® curriculum, career exploration, workforce development and scholarships for high school students; to provide emergency assistance and direct financial support to restaurant industry workers.

LEGAL BASIS:
Not-for-profit organization.

ELIGIBILITY:
Applicants for the Restaurant Employee Relief Fund must be permanent residents of the state of Illinois who are diagnosed with coronavirus (COVID-19), a caregiver for an immediate family member who has been diagnosed with COVID-19, quarantined with a doctor's note, or out of work for three weeks or more without unemployment benefits. Requirements are subject to change.

Applicants for the scholarship program must be permanent residents of the state of Illinois who are applying to or enrolled in an accredited culinary school, college or university and who are enrolled full-time or substantial part-time, taking a minimum of nine credit hours each term, majoring in a culinary restaurant management or foodservice-related program.

GEOG. RESTRICTIONS: Illinois.

FINANCIAL DATA:
Grants provide assistance to cover necessary living expenses such as rent, food and utilities. Scholarships provide assistance toward tuition and materials.
Amount of support per award: Restaurant Employee Relief Fund: $500; Scholarship: Varies.

NO. AWARDS: 69 scholarships for the year 2020.

APPLICATION INFO:
Application forms for scholarships and the relief fund are available on the web site.
Duration: Scholarship: One academic year. Renewal is not automatic.
Deadline: Scholarship: May 2.

IRS I.D.: 36-3271510

ADDRESS INQUIRIES TO:
ProStart® Manager
Tel: 312-380-4117
Fax: 312-787-4792
(See address above.)

INDIANA COMMISSION FOR HIGHER EDUCATION, DIVISION OF STUDENT FINANCIAL AID [1512]

101 West Ohio Street
Suite 300
Indianapolis, IN 46204-4206
(317) 464-4400
(888) 528-4719
Fax: (317) 232-3260
E-mail: awards@che.in.gov
Web Site: www.in.gov/che/state-financial-aid

FOUNDED: 1965

AREAS OF INTEREST:
Student financial aid.

NAME(S) OF PROGRAMS:
● **William A. Crawford Minority Teacher Scholarship**
● **Mitch Daniels Early Graduation Scholarship**

- **EARN Indiana (State Work Study)**
- **National Guard Supplemental Grant**
- **Next Generation Hoosier Educators Scholarship**
- **The Frank O'Bannon Grant**
- **Earline S. Rogers Student Teaching Stipend for Minorities**
- **Student Teaching Stipend for High-Needs Fields**
- **21st Century Scholars Program**

TYPE:
Grants-in-aid; Project/program grants; Scholarships; Work-study programs. Monetary grants awarded annually toward the cost of tuition.

The Crawford Minority Teacher Scholarship was created to address the critical shortage of Black and Hispanic teachers in Indiana.

The Next Generation Hoosier Educators Scholarship provides high-achieving high school and college students interested in pursuing a career in education the opportunity to earn a renewable scholarship. In exchange, students agree to teach for five years at an eligible Indiana school or repay the corresponding, prorated amount of the scholarship.

The Rogers Student Teaching Stipend for Minorities is for minority students (defined as Black and Hispanic) who plan to teach.

Student Teaching Stipend for High-Needs Fields is for students who plan to teach in "high-need" fields, which means a teaching specialty that affects the economic vitality of Indiana and in which there is a shortage of candidates.

21st Century Scholars Program was created as Indiana's way of raising the educational aspirations of low- and moderate-income families.

YEAR PROGRAM STARTED: 1971

PURPOSE:
To provide financial assistance to students attending colleges within the state of Indiana.

LEGAL BASIS:
Indiana Scholarship Act, I.C. 20-12-21. I.C. 20-12-21.1.

ELIGIBILITY:
An applicant must be an Indiana resident, a U.S. citizen or eligible noncitizen and must attend an eligible institution located within the state of Indiana as a full-time undergraduate student (12 to 15 hours per term).

Next Generation Hoosier Educators Scholarship applicant must be a current high school senior or college student. Applicant must rank in the top 20% of SAT or ACT scores. Student must enroll at an eligible Indiana institution.

21st Century Scholars Program applicant must complete the Scholar Success Program in high school and during college. Applicant must enroll as a full-time student and maintain Indiana residency.

GEOG. RESTRICTIONS: Indiana.

FINANCIAL DATA:
Amount of support per award: Varies.
Total amount of support: Varies.
Matching fund requirements: Only in EARN Indiana.

NO. AWARDS: Varies.

APPLICATION INFO:
Free Application for Federal Student Aid (FAFSA) must be received by April 15 for The Frank O'Bannon Grant and the 21st Century Scholars Program.
Duration: Four years. Reapplication required annually.
Deadline: Mitch Daniels Early Graduation and Minority Teacher Scholarships: August 31. EARN Indiana and The Frank O'Bannon Grant: April 15. Next Generation Hoosier Education Scholarship: January 31. Student Teaching Stipend: September 30 for fall term and January 31 for spring term. 21st Century Scholars Program: June 30.

PUBLICATIONS:
Application guidelines.

ADDRESS INQUIRIES TO:
Indiana Commission for Higher Education (See address above.)

INSTITUTE FOR CITIZENS & SCHOLARS   [1513]
104 Carnegie Center
Suite 301
Princeton, NJ 08540
(609) 452-7007 ext. 142
E-mail: newcombe@woodrow.org
Web Site: www.woodrow.org

FOUNDED: 1945

AREAS OF INTEREST:
Higher education.

NAME(S) OF PROGRAMS:
- **Charlotte W. Newcombe Doctoral Dissertation Fellowships**

TYPE:
Awards/prizes; Fellowships; Scholarships. Awards to support and encourage original and significant study of ethical and/or religious values in the humanities and social sciences.

YEAR PROGRAM STARTED: 1981

PURPOSE:
To encourage study of ethical or religious values.

LEGAL BASIS:
Publicly supported charity.

ELIGIBILITY:
Doctoral candidates enrolled in a U.S. university, located in the U.S., working on topics of religious or ethical values in the Humanities or Social Sciences may apply.

FINANCIAL DATA:
Amount of support per award: $27,000 for 12 months of dissertation writing.

CO-OP FUNDING PROGRAMS: Program made available by funds from the Charlotte W. Newcombe Foundation.

NO. MOST RECENT APPLICANTS: 500.

NO. AWARDS: Minimum of 22.

APPLICATION INFO:
Applications are accepted beginning September 1 and must be submitted electronically.
Duration: Tenure of the award is for the academic year following the announcement of the winners.
Deadline: November 15.

ADDRESS INQUIRIES TO:
See e-mail address above.

*PLEASE NOTE:
Until 2020, known as The Woodrow Wilson National Fellowship Foundation.

*SPECIAL STIPULATIONS:
Fellowship is for humanities and social sciences. Applicants in highly quantitative fields should not apply.

INSTITUTE FOR THE INTERNATIONAL EDUCATION OF STUDENTS (IES)   [1514]
33 West Monroe Street
Suite 2300
Chicago, IL 60603-5405
(312) 944-1750
(800) 995-2300
Fax: (312) 944-1448
E-mail: info@IESabroad.org
Web Site: www.IESabroad.org

FOUNDED: 1950

AREAS OF INTEREST:
International education.

NAME(S) OF PROGRAMS:
- **Boren and Gilman Scholarship Support Grants**
- **Disability Grants**
- **Diversity Scholarships**
- **Donor Funded Scholarships**
- **Need Based Aid**
- **Partner University Scholarships**
- **Public University Grants**

TYPE:
Awards/prizes; Scholarships. Boren and Gilman Scholarship Support Grants: This program offers recipients of these prestigious scholarships the opportunity to apply for additional financial support.

Disability Grants: This program's purpose is to enhance study abroad opportunities for students with disabilities. It offers grants to students whose disabilities may add significant costs to their study abroad experience.

Diversity Scholarships: This program offers one way to encourage and support students from a range of institutions and underrepresented populations. Underrepresented students include students from underrepresented racial and ethnic groups, first-generation-to-college students, students from low-income families and students with a history of overcoming adversity.

Donor Funded Scholarships: These scholarship opportunities have been created through the generosity of various donors who support the important mission of IES Abroad.

Need Based Aid: This program is available to students with demonstrated financial need. Priority is given to Pell Grant recipients.

Partner University Scholarships: These scholarships are funded by IES Abroad partner universities in countries where IES has programs.

Public University Grants: This program offers an automatic $2,000 credit toward a semester or academic year program.

YEAR PROGRAM STARTED: 1950

PURPOSE:
To provide study opportunities abroad for qualified undergraduate students from U.S. colleges and universities.

LEGAL BASIS:
Not-for-profit educational organization organized under the laws of Illinois.

ELIGIBILITY:
All aid categories require applicants to be accepted to and attend an IES Abroad standard program. (Customized programs are not eligible for IES Abroad aid.)

Some aid categories require that applicants attend a college or university that is part of the IES Abroad Consortium and that transfers at least 75% of institutional aid for study abroad expenses.

FINANCIAL DATA:
Amount of support per award: Boren and Gilman Scholarship Support Grants: $500 for summer program; $1,000 for fall or spring program. Disability Grants: Up to $2,500. Diversity Scholarships: Up to $5,000 depending on category. Donor Funded Scholarships: Award amounts vary by category. Need Based Aid: Up to $5,000 (fall or spring programs); up to $1,000 (summer programs). Public University Grants: $2,000.

APPLICATION INFO:
Applications may be submitted online.
Duration: Academic year, one semester, or summer (need-based only). Nonrenewable.
Deadline: May 1 for fall semester and academic year; November 1 for spring semester; April 1 for summer.

PUBLICATIONS:
Annual report; IES Abroad Alumni Exchange Newsletter; IES Abroad catalogs; IES MAP©.

IRS I.D.: 36-2251912

GOVERNING BOARD:
Ezio Vergani, Chairperson
Robert Browne
Mary Cahillane
Dr. Cecilia A. Conrad
James Crawford
Debora de Hoyos
Marie Fioramonti
Dr. Pamela Brooks Gann
Phyllis Haberman
Dr. J. Kline Harrison
Dr. Gregory D. Hess
Rhonda Jordan
Brian Kelly
Mary O'Brien Pearlman
Dr. Marla Salmon
Alan Schwartz
Dr. John D. Simon
Sheila A. Stamps
Peter E. Sundman
Dr. Lara Tiedens
Monica Vachher

ADDRESS INQUIRIES TO:
Lauren Kreibich
Director of Enrollment Management
(See address above.)

INTERNATIONAL ASSOCIATION OF FIRE CHIEFS FOUNDATION, INC. [1515]

4795 Meadow Wood Lane
Suite 100
Chantilly, VA 20151
(703) 273-0911
Fax: (703) 273-9363
E-mail: foundation@iafc.org
Web Site: www.iafcf.org

FOUNDED: 1974

AREAS OF INTEREST:
Fire prevention and research.

NAME(S) OF PROGRAMS:
● **International Association of Fire Chiefs Foundation Scholarship Program**

TYPE:
Scholarships. Scholarships for advanced study in fire science, fire department administration and operation, public administration or any fire-related program.

YEAR PROGRAM STARTED: 1974

PURPOSE:
To aid in better fire service administration and to support training in this area.

ELIGIBILITY:
Under the regulations, any member of the fire service who is an active member of U.S. or Canadian Fire Service in a state, county, provincial, municipal, community, industrial or federal fire department, and who has demonstrated proficiency as a member, is eligible to apply for a scholarship to a recognized institution of higher education of his or her choice. Applicants must have the approval of their department chiefs. Dependents are not eligible.

GEOG. RESTRICTIONS: United States.

FINANCIAL DATA:
Amount of support per award: Generally $250 to $2,000, providing a maximum of this dollar amount toward tuition costs.
Total amount of support: Approximately $45,000 per year.

NO. MOST RECENT APPLICANTS: 75.

NO. AWARDS: 42 for the year 2020.

APPLICATION INFO:
Application information is available on the web site.
Duration: One year.
Deadline: June 25.

PUBLICATIONS:
Application guidelines.

ADDRESS INQUIRIES TO:
John W. Morris, Program Manager
International Fellowship Program
Tel: (703) 217-8116
E-mail: jmorris@iafc.org

INTERNATIONAL DEVELOPMENT RESEARCH CENTRE (IDRC)

150 Kent Street
Ottawa ON K1P 0B2 Canada
(613) 696-2098
E-mail: awards@idrc.ca
Web Site: www.idrc.ca
www.crdi.ca

TYPE:
Awards/prizes. These awards are offered once a year and are intended for field research in one or more developing countries. Candidates must conduct their research in areas corresponding to IDRC's research priorities.

See entry 1183 for full listing.

IODE [1516]

40 Orchard View Boulevard, Suite 219
Toronto ON M4R 1B9 Canada
(416) 487-4416
Fax: (416) 487-4417
E-mail: iodecanada@bellnet.ca
Web Site: www.iode.ca

FOUNDED: 1900

AREAS OF INTEREST:
Education, social service and citizenship.

NAME(S) OF PROGRAMS:
● **War Memorial Scholarships**

TYPE:
Scholarships. Postgraduate scholarships tenable in any university in Canada and the Commonwealth.

YEAR PROGRAM STARTED: 1920

PURPOSE:
To provide scholarships for educational purposes as a memorial to Canadian men and women who gave their lives in defense of freedom during World Wars I and II.

LEGAL BASIS:
Charitable organization.

ELIGIBILITY:
Candidates must be Canadian citizens. At the time of application, candidates must hold a first degree from a Canadian university and be enrolled in at least the second year of a doctoral program.

GEOG. RESTRICTIONS: Canada and the Commonwealth.

FINANCIAL DATA:
Amount of support per award: $15,000 (CAN) for study in Canada and for study overseas within the Commonwealth for the 2021-22 academic year.

NO. AWARDS: 3 for the 2021-22 academic year.

APPLICATION INFO:
A candidate must apply to the War Memorial Convener in the province in which the first degree was obtained. The names of Conveners change from year to year, but appear in the scholarship folder. Application must be submitted online.
Duration: One year.
Deadline: Applications must reach the Convener of the province from which the first degree was obtained by November 1.

OFFICERS:
Hazel MacLeod, National War Memorial Officer

TRUSTEES:
Carol McCall, National President

ADDRESS INQUIRIES TO:
E-mail: iodewarmemorial@gmail.com

THE JAPAN FOUNDATION, LOS ANGELES [1517]

5700 Wilshire Boulevard
Suite 100
Los Angeles, CA 90036
(323) 761-7510
Fax: (323) 761-7517
E-mail: culture@jflalc.org
Web Site: www.jflalc.org

FOUNDED: 1983

AREAS OF INTEREST:
Japanese arts, culture and language education.

NAME(S) OF PROGRAMS:
● **Arts & Culture Grants**
● **J-LEAP**
● **Japanese Language Grants**

TYPE:
Conferences/seminars; Exchange programs; Fellowships; Grants-in-aid; Product donations; Project/program grants; Research grants; Training grants; Visiting scholars.

PURPOSE:
To support grants that promote Japanese arts, culture, language and education.

ELIGIBILITY:
Candidates must be citizens or permanent residents of the U.S.

GEOG. RESTRICTIONS: United States.

FINANCIAL DATA:
Amount of support per award: Varies.
Total amount of support: Varies.

APPLICATION INFO:
Guidelines are available online.
Duration: Arts & Culture Grants and Japanese Language Grants: One year; J-LEAP: Two years.
Deadline: Varies.

THE JAPANESE AMERICAN CITIZENS LEAGUE (JACL) [1518]

JACL National Office
1629 K Street, Suite 400
Washington, DC 20006
(202) 223-1240
E-mail: sfjacl@yahoo.com
policy@jacl.org
Web Site: www.jacl.org

FOUNDED: 1929

AREAS OF INTEREST:
Education, cultural preservation, and civil rights.

NAME(S) OF PROGRAMS:
● **JACL National Scholarship and Awards Program**

TYPE:
Scholarships. JACL offers more than 30 scholarships and student aid awards (financial aid).

Scholarship categories: Entering Freshman (High School Senior), Undergraduate, Graduate, Law, Creative and Performing Arts, and Financial Aid.

YEAR PROGRAM STARTED: 1946

PURPOSE:
To recognize education as a key to greater opportunities for its members.

ELIGIBILITY:
Applicant must be an active National JACL member at either an individual or student/youth level. Applicants must be planning to attend full-time an institution of higher learning within the U.S. at the undergraduate or graduate school level. Applicants may apply under only one scholarship category. Entering freshman applicants must be high school seniors. Creative and performing arts applicants cannot be professional artists.

JACL membership is open to everyone of any ethnic background.

FINANCIAL DATA:
Amount of support per award: $1,000 to $5,000.
Total amount of support: Over $70,000 in scholarships.

APPLICATION INFO:
Information brochure and applications are posted on the JACL web site annually in November.

Freshman applications must be postmarked and mailed to the local JACL chapter to which the applicant belongs. All other applications must be postmarked and mailed to the address on the application form.

Duration: One year. Limited to a total of two awards.
Deadline: Freshman Application: March 1; All others: First week of April.

ADDRESS INQUIRIES TO:
Patty Wada, Regional Director
E-mail: pwada@jacl.org

JEWISH FAMILY AND CHILDREN'S SERVICES   [1519]

2150 Post Street
San Francisco, CA 94115
(415) 449-1226
TDD: (415) 567-1044
E-mail: michellel@jfcs.org
Web Site: www.jfcs.org

FOUNDED: 1850

AREAS OF INTEREST:
Education, vocational training, and business and professional endeavors in the Greater Bay area.

NAME(S) OF PROGRAMS:
● **Educational Loans and Grants Program**

TYPE:
Grants-in-aid. Loans and grants for eligible Jewish individuals and families with financial need for college tuition, vocational training and camperships. In addition, JFCS offers loans for qualified Jewish businesses and professional endeavors in the Greater Bay area.

PURPOSE:
To provide educational loans and grants to Jewish graduate and undergraduate students.

LEGAL BASIS:
Nonprofit.

ELIGIBILITY:
Applicants must be students of Jewish descent who have demonstrated academic achievement (generally demonstrated by a 3.0 grade point average on a 4.0 scale), financial need, broad-based extracurricular activities and in-depth community involvement and acceptance to an accredited college, university or vocational school.

GEOG. RESTRICTIONS: Marin, San Francisco, San Mateo, Santa Clara, or Sonoma counties, California.

FINANCIAL DATA:
Amount of support per award: Need-based grants of $500 to $3,000 and loans of $1,000 to $6,000 for undergraduate students; Need-based grants of $500 to $1,500 and loans of $1,000 to $10,000 for graduate students.

NO. MOST RECENT APPLICANTS: 53.

NO. AWARDS: Varies per year.

APPLICATION INFO:
Application information is available on the web site beginning the first week of May. Contact the organization's Director of Financial Aid Center for more information.
Duration: One academic year.
Deadline: First week of July. However, applications will be accepted until funding is exhausted.

PUBLICATIONS:
Program announcement.

ADDRESS INQUIRIES TO:
Michelle Lamphere
Director, JFCS Financial Aid Center
(See address above.)

JEWISH FEDERATION OF METROPOLITAN CHICAGO ACADEMIC SCHOLARSHIP PROGRAM   [1520]

JVS Career and Employment/JCFS Chicago
216 West Jackson Boulevard, Suite 700
Chicago, IL 60606-6921
(312) 673-3444
Fax: (312) 553-5544
E-mail: jvsscholarship@jcfs.org
Web Site: www.jcfs.org/jvsscholarships

FOUNDED: 1959

AREAS OF INTEREST:
Higher education for Jewish students in full-time academic programs in the helping professions, legally domiciled in the metropolitan Chicago (IL) area.

TYPE:
Awards/prizes; Scholarships. Awards to individuals for the academic year.

YEAR PROGRAM STARTED: 1959

PURPOSE:
To provide financial support to Jewish men and women for their full-time academic programs.

LEGAL BASIS:
Tax-exempt private foundation.

ELIGIBILITY:
Scholarships are awarded on the basis of financial need. Applicants must be full-time students of Jewish background, legally domiciled in the metropolitan Chicago area. Applicants must have demonstrated career promise. Assistance is available for the fields listed below, including but not limited to:
(1) the helping professions such as medicine, dentistry, social work, education, psychology, the rabbinate and noncorporate areas of law;
(2) mathematics, engineering and other sciences and;
(3) communications within the College of Media at the University of Illinois at Urbana-Champaign.

Additional requirements:
(1) undergraduates entering or who have entered the junior year in career-specific programs which require no postgraduate education for professional-level employment in one of the professional areas mentioned above or;
(2) students entering or who have entered a graduate or professional school in a helping profession described above or;
(3) students in a vocational training program with a specific educational goal in the helping professions.

Newcomers who are refugees or asylees are encouraged to apply. Citizenship is not a prerequisite.

FINANCIAL DATA:
Amount of support per award: Up to $8,000.

Total amount of support: Approximately $500,000 per year.

CO-OP FUNDING PROGRAMS: Program is administered by JVS Career and Employment/JCFS Chicago.

NO. MOST RECENT APPLICANTS: Approximately 130 for the year 2018.

NO. AWARDS: Approximately 90.

APPLICATION INFO:

Application submission must include application form, budget worksheet, personal and financial data, IRS Form 1040, proof of (Cook County) legal domicility, two reference letters, autobiography and official academic transcript. Applicants must be available for a personal interview at JVS Career and Employment/JCFS Chicago offices located throughout the Chicago metropolitan area prior to April 20.

Applications are available in the fall and can be downloaded from the JVS Career and Employment/JCFS Chicago web site. (Click on "Scholarship Services.").

Duration: One academic year. Recipients may reapply for renewal.

Deadline: February 1 for submission of applications.

OFFICERS:

Sally Yarberry, Scholarship Coordinator

ADDRESS INQUIRIES TO:

Scholarship Coordinator
(See address and telephone number above.)

*SPECIAL STIPULATIONS:

All applicants must be available for a personal interview at the JVS Career and Employment/JCFS Chicago offices located throughout the Chicago metropolitan area.

KANSAS BOARD OF REGENTS   [1521]

1000 S.W. Jackson, Suite 520
Topeka, KS 66612-1368
(785) 430-4240
Fax: (785) 430-4233
E-mail: dlindeman@ksbor.org
Web Site: www.kansasregents.org

FOUNDED: 1925

AREAS OF INTEREST:

Higher education.

NAME(S) OF PROGRAMS:

- **Kansas Comprehensive Grant**

TYPE:

Grants-in-aid. Grant-in-aid is available to students with demonstrated financial need attending the four-year public and independent colleges and universities in Kansas.

YEAR PROGRAM STARTED: 1999

PURPOSE:

To provide access and choice for needy students attending either public or independent four-year colleges and universities in the state.

ELIGIBILITY:

Students must be U.S. citizens or residents and Kansas resident undergraduates, attending either a four-year public or independent college/university, and have demonstrated financial need as determined by the Free Application for Federal Student Aid (FAFSA) need analysis.

GEOG. RESTRICTIONS: Kansas.

FINANCIAL DATA:

Amount of support per award: Eligible students attending four-year public colleges and universities may be awarded up to $1,500 annually. Eligible students attending four-year independent colleges and universities may be awarded up to $3,500 annually.

Total amount of support: $16,658,338 for the 2019-20 academic year.

NO. MOST RECENT APPLICANTS: 24,314.

NO. AWARDS: 9,545.

APPLICATION INFO:

No application other than the FAFSA.

Duration: Annual award. Students need to file their FAFSA annually.

Deadline: Priority deadline is April 1 annually.

ADDRESS INQUIRIES TO:

Diane Lindeman
Director of Student Financial Assistance
(See address above.)

KENTUCKY HIGHER EDUCATION ASSISTANCE AUTHORITY (KHEAA)   [1522]

P.O. Box 798
Frankfort, KY 40602-0798
(800) 928-8926
Fax: (502) 696-7373
E-mail: studentaid@kheaa.com
Web Site: www.kheaa.com

FOUNDED: 1966

AREAS OF INTEREST:

Postsecondary student financial assistance.

NAME(S) OF PROGRAMS:

- **College Access Program (CAP)**
- **Kentucky Educational Excellence Scholarship (KEES)**
- **Kentucky Tuition Grant (KTG)**

TYPE:

Grants-in-aid; Scholarships. Need-based or incentive-based student aid; College Access Program helps Kentucky's financially needy undergraduate students attend eligible public and private Kentucky colleges, universities, proprietary schools and technical colleges.

Kentucky Educational Excellence Scholarship awards scholarships to Kentucky high school students based on grade point average and ACT/SAT scores to encourage them to attend a college or university in Kentucky. Low-income students may earn additional awards based on Advanced Placement (AP) or International Baccalaureate (IB) exam scores.

Kentucky Tuition Grant provides a tuition equalization grant to help Kentucky residents attend eligible Kentucky private colleges.

PURPOSE:

To provide financial aid to students.

ELIGIBILITY:

Applicant must be a U.S. citizen or resident.

College Access Program: Student must reside in Kentucky, demonstrate financial need, attend a participating college or university in Kentucky, have no past due financial obligations to KHEAA or any Title IV program, and be enrolled at least half-time in a program of study at least two years in length.

Kentucky Educational Excellence Scholarship: Student must earn at least a 2.5 grade point average in any year of high school in Kentucky while meeting Kentucky Educational Excellence Scholarship curriculum requirements. Student must reside in Kentucky and attend and graduate from a certified Kentucky high school. Student must

have an ACT composite score of 15 or higher for ACT bonus. Convicted felons will be disqualified.

Kentucky Tuition Grant: Student must reside in Kentucky, demonstrate financial need, attend a participating college or university in Kentucky, have no past due financial obligations to KHEAA or any Title IV program, and be enrolled full-time in an Associate or Bachelor's degree program.

FINANCIAL DATA:

Amount of support per award: College Access Program: Up to $2,000 per academic year at two-year schools, up to $2,200 per academic year at four-year schools; Kentucky Educational Excellence Scholarship: Varies by student; Kentucky Tuition Grant: Up to $3,000 per academic year.

Total amount of support: College Access Program: $91,600,000; Kentucky Educational Excellence Scholarship: $118,800,000; Kentucky Tuition Grant: $35,700,000 for the academic year 2019-20.

NO. MOST RECENT APPLICANTS: CAP: 234,500; KEES: 70,500; KTG: 54,500 for the academic year 2019-20.

NO. AWARDS: CAP: 59,200; KEES: 70,500; KTG: 14,100.

APPLICATION INFO:

College Access Program and Kentucky Tuition Grant : Applicant must complete the Free Application for Federal Student Aid (FAFSA) (available at www.fafsa.ed.gov).

Duration: College Access Program and Kentucky Tuition Grant: Awarded on an annual basis. Nonrenewable. Kentucky Educational Excellence Scholarship: Funds awarded based on high school academic performance. Renewal requirements must be met annually once the student is in college.

Deadline: College Access Program and Kentucky Tuition Grant: End of FAFSA processing year, which is the end of the academic year.

ADDRESS INQUIRIES TO:

KHEAA Student Aid
(See e-mail address above.)

KENTUCKY HIGHER EDUCATION ASSISTANCE AUTHORITY (KHEAA)   [1523]

P.O. Box 798
Frankfort, KY 40602-0798
(800) 928-8926
Fax: (502) 696-7373
E-mail: studentaid@kheaa.com
Web Site: www.kheaa.com

FOUNDED: 1966

AREAS OF INTEREST:

Postsecondary student financial assistance.

NAME(S) OF PROGRAMS:

- **Kentucky National Guard Tuition Award Program**

TYPE:

Need-based student aid; Military service grant. Kentucky National Guard Tuition Award Program provides tuition assistance for active members of the Kentucky National Guard to attend a Kentucky college or university.

PURPOSE:

To provide financial aid to students.

ELIGIBILITY:
Applicants must be U.S. citizens or residents. Student must be an active member of the Kentucky National Guard, maintain all minimum eligibility standards, be eligible for all positive personnel actions, and have completed basic training or its equivalent.

Limited to participating postsecondary institutions in Kentucky.

FINANCIAL DATA:
Amount of support per award: Up to in-state tuition for full- or part-time study at a Kentucky public university.

Total amount of support: $7,230,000 for the academic year 2019-20.

NO. MOST RECENT APPLICANTS: 1,800.

NO. AWARDS: 1,800.

APPLICATION INFO:
Application available online (https://ky.ngb.army.mil/tuitionstudent) or contact the Boone National Guard at (502) 607-1039.

ADDRESS INQUIRIES TO:
Student Aid
Kentucky Higher Education
Assistance Authority
(See address or telephone number above.)

KNIGHTS OF COLUMBUS [1524]
One Columbus Plaza
New Haven, CT 06510
(203) 752-4332
Fax: (203) 752-4103
E-mail: scholarships@kofc.org
Web Site: www.kofc.org/scholarships

AREAS OF INTEREST:
Educational support.

NAME(S) OF PROGRAMS:
- **Bishop Charles P. Greco Graduate Fellowships**
- **John W. McDevitt (Fourth Degree) Scholarships**
- **Pro Deo and Pro Patria Scholarships**

TYPE:
Fellowships; Project/program grants; Scholarships. Scholarships and fellowships are awarded to members of The Knights of Columbus in good standing, a son or daughter of such a member or deceased member, or to a member of the Columbian Squires.

The Bishop Greco Graduate Fellowships are for full-time graduate study leading to a Master's degree in a program for classroom teachers of persons with intellectual disabilities.

The John W. McDevitt (Fourth Degree) Scholarships are awarded to students entering the freshman class of undergraduate study at a Catholic college or university in the U.S.

For the Pro Deo and Pro Patria Scholarships, students must be entering the freshman class in a college program leading to a Bachelor's degree. Scholarships are available at The Catholic University of America in Washington, DC and to students entering other Catholic colleges in the U.S.

PURPOSE:
To provide support for community activities, education; to provide financial assistance to children of members in good standing.

ELIGIBILITY:
For Bishop Greco Graduate Fellowships, applicants must be enrolled in a graduate study program leading to a Master's degree in a program designed for the preparation of classroom teachers of persons with intellectual disabilities. Membership requirements as listed for the scholarship above also apply for this award.

For McDevitt (Fourth Degree) Scholarships, applicants must be members in good standing of the Knights of Columbus or the wife, widow, son or daughter of such a member or deceased member.

For Pro Deo and Pro Patria Scholarships, applicants must be students entering in the freshman class in a Catholic college program leading to a Bachelor's degree. An applicant must be a member in good standing of the Knights of Columbus or the son or daughter of such a member, a deceased member or a member in good standing of the Columbian Squires.

GEOG. RESTRICTIONS: United States.

FINANCIAL DATA:
Amount of support per award: Bishop Greco Graduate Fellowships: $2,000 maximum per year; McDevitt (Fourth Degree) Scholarships: $1,500; Pro Deo and Pro Patria Scholarships: $1,500 per year.

Total amount of support: $711,519 in scholarships for the academic year 2017-18.

NO. AWARDS: 450 for the academic year 2017-18.

APPLICATION INFO:
Application order form required. Candidates are required to submit supporting documents to substantiate eligibility.

To be considered on a financial basis, applicant must include SAR report (within the FAFSA).

Duration: Pro Deo and Pro Patria Scholarships: Up to four years. Greco Graduate Fellowship: Up to two years.

Deadline: March 1 for U.S. students. May 1 for Canadian students.

ADDRESS INQUIRIES TO:
Department of Scholarships
(See address above.)

*SPECIAL STIPULATIONS:
Candidates for Educational Trust Fund scholarships will be required to submit supporting documents to substantiate the claim.

THE KOSCIUSZKO FOUNDATION, INC. [1525]
15 East 65th Street
New York, NY 10065
(212) 734-2130 ext. 412
E-mail: addy@thekf.org
Web Site: www.thekf.org/kf/scholarships/tuition/

FOUNDED: 1925

AREAS OF INTEREST:
Scholarships and grant support for Americans of Polish descent and to Americans whose majors focus on Polish language, history and culture; funding for graduate-level studies in the U.S.

NAME(S) OF PROGRAMS:
- **The Kosciuszko Foundation Tuition Scholarship**

TYPE:
Scholarships. Offers funding to American citizens of Polish descent and to Polish citizens who have permanent residency status in the U.S. Scholarships are for Master's and Ph.D. students for full-time studies only. Undergraduate seniors may apply for a scholarship towards their first year of Master's-level studies. Americans (non-Polish descent) are eligible for graduate-level studies when majoring in Polish language, history or culture.

All majors are supported. However, the Kosciuszko Foundation has special funding allocated in the following areas: law and engineering studies at DePaul University and nonpublic colleges and universities in Illinois, Indiana, Iowa, Kansas, Michigan, Minnesota, Missouri, Nebraska, North Dakota, Ohio, South Dakota, Wisconsin and Bayonne, NJ residents; residents of Connecticut, particularly Fairfield and New Haven counties; Amsterdam, NY, Chicopee, MA and New Hampshire and; for violin and piano.

Contact Foundation for additional funding opportunities.

YEAR PROGRAM STARTED: 1950

PURPOSE:
To promote higher education of Americans of Polish descent and Polish studies.

LEGAL BASIS:
501(c)(3) not-for-profit organization which is engaged in educational and cultural relations between the U.S. and Poland.

ELIGIBILITY:
Applicants must:
(1) be U.S. citizens of Polish descent or;
(2) be Polish citizens who have legal permanent residency status in the U.S. or;
(3) be Americans of non-Polish descent who are pursuing Polish majors and;
(4) have a minimum grade point average of 3.0.

Scholarships are awarded on the basis of academic excellence and evidence of identification with the Polish-American community. Financial need is taken into consideration. Scholarships are for full-time graduate study in the U.S. and certain programs in Poland.

Within the parameters of the scholarship program are special opportunities for studies in journalism, nursing, teaching, business, piano performance, law, arts, social sciences and education.

GEOG. RESTRICTIONS: United States and Poland.

FINANCIAL DATA:
Funding for tuition and educational expenses such as books and fees associated with attendance at colleges and universities.

Amount of support per award: $1,000 to $7,000.

Total amount of support: $267,435 for the academic year 2019.

NO. AWARDS: 91.

APPLICATION INFO:
Detailed instructions are available on the Foundation web site. Completed applications must be accompanied by a nonrefundable $35 application fee.

Duration: One academic year. Possible renewal for a second year upon reapplication.

Deadline: Mid-January. Notification in May. Funding for the following academic year.

PUBLICATIONS:
Guidelines; *KF Newsletter*; grants brochure; annual report.

IRS I.D.: 13-1628179

STAFF:
Marek Skulimowski, President and Executive
Director

ADDRESS INQUIRIES TO:
Addy Tymczyszyn, Coordinator
(See e-mail address above.)

*SPECIAL STIPULATIONS:
Scholarship checks are issued upon proof of
full-time status.

THE KOSCIUSZKO FOUNDATION, INC.   [1526]
15 East 65th Street
New York, NY 10065
(212) 734-2130 ext. 412
E-mail: addy@thekf.org
Web Site: www.thekf.
org/kf/programs/study/wsips

AREAS OF INTEREST:
Strengthening of cultural and educational
bonds between the U.S. and Poland through
an exchange program to Poland for the
purpose of Polish language and culture
studies.

NAME(S) OF PROGRAMS:
● **Wisconsin Study in Poland (WSIP)**

TYPE:
Scholarships. The Wisconsin Study in Poland
program offers a four- or six-week Polish
language and culture scholarship at the
Jagiellonian University in Krakow during the
summer session.

PURPOSE:
To enable Wisconsin residents of Polish
descent the opportunity to pursue a
short-term course of Polish language and
culture studies abroad.

LEGAL BASIS:
501(c)(3) not-for-profit organization.

ELIGIBILITY:
Applicant must meet all requirements for the
Summer Study Abroad Program. Applicant
must be a Wisconsin resident of Polish
descent. Consideration may also be given to
nonresident Wisconsin students of Polish
descent if they are attending Wisconsin
college or university. Candidate must have a
cumulative grade point average of 3.0 or
higher.

Previous knowledge of the Polish language is
not required.

FINANCIAL DATA:
Scholarship covers the cost of program fees,
including tuition, course materials and
textbooks, a shared room, two meals per day,
and complementary programs such as
sightseeing. Scholarship recipients will be
responsible for their own transportation,
health care coverage and all other costs.
Total amount of support: $4,840 for the year
2019.

NO. AWARDS: 2 scholarships per year.

APPLICATION INFO:
Details are available on the Foundation web
site. A $35 nonrefundable scholarship
application fee is required.
Duration: Four- or six-week program, to
begin in July.
Deadline: Mid-April. E-mail notification in
May.

PUBLICATIONS:
KF Newsletter; annual report.

IRS I.D.: 13-1628179

STAFF:
Marek Skulimowski, President and Executive
Director

ADDRESS INQUIRIES TO:
Addy Tymczyszyn, Coordinator
Wisconsin Study in Poland
(See e-mail address above.)

*PLEASE NOTE:
Students who receive scholarship funding
will be required to submit a $95
nonrefundable registration fee, as well as
additional application materials.

LORAN SCHOLARS FOUNDATION   [1527]
460 Richmond Street West, Suite 502
Toronto ON M5V 1Y1 Canada
(416) 646-2120
Fax: (416) 646-0846
E-mail: info@loranscholar.ca
Web Site: www.loranscholar.ca
www.boursierloran.ca

FOUNDED: 1988

AREAS OF INTEREST:
Higher education.

NAME(S) OF PROGRAMS:
● **Loran Awards**

TYPE:
Scholarships. Grants for graduating high
school students about to enter a university in
Canada. These awards include an annual
stipend and matching tuition waiver, access
to $10,000 in funding for summer
internships, one-on-one mentorship, and
annual retreats and scholar gatherings.

PURPOSE:
To identify and support talented students who
demonstrate character, promise of leadership
and a strong commitment to service in the
community; to fund these citizens to study on
Canadian campuses, to the benefit of their
future and ours.

ELIGIBILITY:
Applicant must:
(1) be in the graduating year of uninterrupted
full-time studies in high school or CEGEP.
Exceptions may be considered for those who
have undertaken a gap year for academic
pursuits or community service-based
activities;
(2) present a minimum cumulative average of
85%;
(3) hold Canadian citizenship or permanent
resident status and;
(4) be at least 16 years of age by September
1 of the following year.

GEOG. RESTRICTIONS: Canada.

FINANCIAL DATA:
Amount of support per award: Valued at
$100,000 for four years.
Total amount of support: $3,700,000 (CAN).

NO. AWARDS: 130 to 140 annually.

APPLICATION INFO:
Applications are available early September
and can be completed online. Students should
speak to their guidance counselor about their
school's nomination process.
Duration: Up to four years.
Deadline: Mid-October.

ADDRESS INQUIRIES TO:
See e-mail address above.

*PLEASE NOTE:
Loran Award Finalist and Provincial Awards
are tenable at any public university in
Canada. Loran Awards are tenable at
participating Canadian consortium
universities only.

LOUISIANA DIVISION OF THE ARTS, DEPARTMENT OF CULTURE, RECREATION AND TOURISM
1051 North Third Street, Room 405
Baton Rouge, LA 70802
(225) 342-8200
Fax: (225) 342-8173
E-mail: arts@crt.la.gov
Web Site: www.crt.state.la.us/cultural-
development/arts

TYPE:
General operating grants.

See entry 423 for full listing.

MARINE CORPS SCHOLARSHIP FOUNDATION, INC.   [1528]
909 North Washington Street
Suite 400
Alexandria, VA 22314
(703) 549-0060
Fax: (703) 549-9474
E-mail: scholarship@mcsf.org
Web Site: www.mcsf.org

FOUNDED: 1962

AREAS OF INTEREST:
Scholarships to eligible children of Marines
and children of qualifying Navy Corpsmen,
chaplains, and religious program specialists.

TYPE:
Scholarships. Scholarships are for accredited
undergraduate (post-high school) college or
career technical education (CTE).

YEAR PROGRAM STARTED: 1962

PURPOSE:
To provide need-based scholarships to the
children of Marines and qualifying Navy
Corpsmen who attend college or career
training; to honor Marines by educating their
children.

LEGAL BASIS:
Nonprofit, tax-exempt corporation.

ELIGIBILITY:
Applicant must be the child of an active duty
or reserve U.S. Marine, or a veteran U.S.
Marine who has received an honorable
discharge or who was killed while serving in
the U.S. Marine Corps. Children of U.S.
Navy Corpsmen, chaplains, or religious
specialists attached to a Marine unit may also
qualify. Applicant must be planning to attend,
or already attending, an accredited college or
vocational/technical institution, have a grade
point average of at least 2.0, and pursuing
their first degree or technical certificate.
Graduate study is not eligible. An income
requirement must be met. Special funding is
available for children of those who were
wounded or killed in combat.

FINANCIAL DATA:
The Scholarship Foundation has provided
over 40,000 scholarships valued at over
$135,000,000 since 1962.
Amount of support per award: $1,500 to
$10,000 per year.
Total amount of support: $8,200,000 for the
2019-20 academic year.

NO. MOST RECENT APPLICANTS: Over 2,900 for the 2019-20 academic year.

NO. AWARDS: Over 2,300 for the 2019-20 academic year.

APPLICATION INFO:
Application available online beginning January 1.
Duration: One year. Renewable for up to three years. Recipients must reapply.
Deadline: March 1.

PUBLICATIONS:
Annual report; guidelines; yearbook; trifold; newsletter.

IRS I.D.: 22-1905062

STAFF:
Steven D. Peterson, Chief Operating Officer
Jeanna Adams, Director, Scholarship Programs

ADDRESS INQUIRIES TO:
Director of Scholarship Programs
(See address above.)

*SPECIAL STIPULATIONS:
Cannot violate civil or campus law.

THURGOOD MARSHALL COLLEGE FUND (TMCF)   [1529]
901 F Street, N.W.
Suite 700
Washington, DC 20004
(202) 507-4861
Fax: (202) 652-2934
E-mail: scholarships@tmcf.org
Web Site: tmcf.org

FOUNDED: 1987

AREAS OF INTEREST:
Business, teaching, communications and public relations.

NAME(S) OF PROGRAMS:
• TMCF Scholarships

TYPE:
Scholarships. Scholarship for full-time students pursuing a degree at one of the 47 TMCF "member schools."

ELIGIBILITY:
Students must:
(1) have a minimum cumulative grade point average of 3.0 on a 4.0 scale;
(2) apply for financial aid using the Free Application for Federal Student Aid;
(3) attend one of the 47 TMCF member-schools (unless otherwise stated on the application);
(4) be a U.S. citizen or legal permanent resident with a valid permanent resident card or passport stamped;
(5) demonstrate leadership qualities and service experience and;
(6) be recommended by a faculty or staff member of one's current school.

Awards are merit-based.

GEOG. RESTRICTIONS: United States.

FINANCIAL DATA:
TMCF scholarships are restricted for payment of tuition, on-campus room and board, and books and fees.
Amount of support per award: Average $3,100 per semester.
Total amount of support: Varies.

NO. AWARDS: Nearly 500 scholarships per year.

APPLICATION INFO:
Apply online only.

Duration: Usually one academic year.
Deadline: Varies.

MARYLAND HIGHER EDUCATION COMMISSION   [1530]
Office of Student Financial Assistance (OSFA)
6 North Liberty Street
Baltimore, MD 21201
(410) 767-3301
(410) 767-3300
(800) 974-0203 (toll-free)
Fax: (410) 332-0250; (410) 332-0252
TTY: (800) 735-2258
E-mail: osfamail.mhec@maryland.gov
Web Site: mhec.maryland.gov

FOUNDED: 1961

NAME(S) OF PROGRAMS:
• Maryland State Scholarships

TYPE:
Grants-in-aid; Scholarships; Loan forgiveness programs. Career and occupational programs. The Howard P. Rawlings Program of Educational Excellence Awards is the state's largest need-based program. It has two components: the Educational Assistance Grant and the Guaranteed Access Grant. The Educational Assistance Grant is targeted to low- to moderate-income families and is based on financial need (40% of calculated financial need for four-year institutions, 60% for community colleges). The Guaranteed Access Grant is for very low-income high school students and requires a 2.5 high school grade point average (100% of student need up to a maximum of $19,100).

The Part-Time Grant supports part-time, degree-seeking, undergraduate students.

The Graduate and Professional School Scholarship provides support to full-time and part-time graduate and professional students in nursing, pharmacy, dentistry, law, medicine, veterinary science, and social work.

Senatorial Scholarships: Each member of the state senate may award scholarships each year.

Delegate Scholarships: Each member of the House of Delegates may award scholarships to students attending approved Maryland postsecondary institutions.

Maryland also offers a number of career/occupational and unique population financial assistance programs.

LEGAL BASIS:
Government agency.

ELIGIBILITY:
Candidate must be a resident of the state and generally enrolled or intending to enroll in a college or university in Maryland.

GEOG. RESTRICTIONS: Maryland.

FINANCIAL DATA:
Amount of support per award: Educational Assistance Grant: $400 to $3,000;
Guaranteed Access Grant: Up to $19,100;
Part-Time Grant: $200 to $2,000; Graduate and Professional School Scholarship: $1,000 to $5,000; Senatorial Scholarships: $400 to $11,800 annually per member of the state senate; Delegate Scholarships: Minimum $200.

Total amount of support: $1,110,000 for all aid programs (including loan repayment programs) for the 2017-18 award year.

Educational Assistance Grant: $54,500,000;
Guaranteed Access Grant: $21,520,592;
Part-Time Grant: $5,087,780; Graduate and Professional School Scholarship: $1,168,030;
Senatorial Scholarships: $6,913,562; Delegate Scholarships: $6,148,599.

NO. MOST RECENT APPLICANTS: One-time FAFSA applications: 121,243.

NO. AWARDS: 51,687, including all state grant and loan repayment programs.

APPLICATION INFO:
Use the Free Application for Federal Student Aid (FAFSA) or special program application.
Duration: Up to four years. Renewable.
Deadline: March 1 for state-administered, need-based aid program; other deadlines vary throughout the year.

PUBLICATIONS:
A Quick Guide to Cash for College and How to Get it; *Student Guide to Higher Education and Financial Aid In Maryland*; *6 Steps to Choosing the Right School.*

ADDRESS INQUIRIES TO:
See e-mail address above.

MASSACHUSETTS MEDICAL SOCIETY (MMS)   [1531]
860 Winter Street
Waltham Woods Corporate Center
Waltham, MA 02451-1411
(781) 893-4610
(800) 322-2303
Fax: (781) 893-8009
E-mail: info@massmed.org
Web Site: www.massmed.org

FOUNDED: 1781

NAME(S) OF PROGRAMS:
• Massachusetts Medical Society International Health Studies Grant Program
• Massachusetts Medical Society (MMS) Annual Scholars Program
• MMS Medical Information Technology Awards
• MMS Student Section Community Service Grants

TYPE:
Awards/prizes; Grants-in-aid; Research grants; Scholarships. Massachusetts Medical Society International Health Studies Grant Program: Grants to defray the costs of study abroad.

Massachusetts Medical Society (MMS) Annual Scholars Program: Awarded to four students from each of the four Massachusetts medical schools.

MMS Medical Information Technology Awards: Given annually to one medical student and one resident physician.

MMS Student Section Community Service Grants: Funding for each of two service projects per medical school chapter of the Section, per calendar year.

PURPOSE:
To advance medical knowledge; to develop and maintain the highest professional and ethical standards of medical practice and health care; to promote medical institutions formed on liberal principles for the health, benefit, and welfare of the citizens of the Commonwealth.

ELIGIBILITY:
Massachusetts Medical Society International Health Studies Grant Program: MMS medical

student or resident; preference given to applicants planning a career serving underprivileged populations. Massachusetts Medical Society (MMS) Annual Scholars Program: MMS member; fourth-year medical students expected to graduate each year and enrolled in a Massachusetts medical school. MMS Medical Information Technology Awards: MMS member; medical students or residents enrolled in one of the four Massachusetts Medical Schools or a Massachusetts hospital or training program. MMS Student Section Community Service Grants: Current medical student members of the MMS whose projects meet objectives in community and social service, public health activism and education or volunteer mentorship activities.

FINANCIAL DATA:
Amount of support per award: Massachusetts Medical Society International Health Studies Grant Program: Up to $2,000. Massachusetts Medical Society (MMS) Annual Scholars Program: $10,000. MMS Medical Information Technology Awards: $5,000 annually. MMS Student Section Community Service Grants: Up to $250.

NO. AWARDS: Massachusetts Medical Society International Health Studies Grant Program: 5 to 7. Massachusetts Medical Society (MMS) Annual Scholars Program: 16. MMS Medical Information Technology Awards: 1 medical student and 1 resident physician. MMS Student Section Community Service Grants: 2 service projects per medical school chapter of the Section, per calendar year.

APPLICATION INFO:
Application information is available on the web site.
Deadline: Massachusetts Medical Society International Health Studies Grant Program: Mid-November. Massachusetts Medical Society (MMS) Annual Scholars Program: Mid-January. MMS Medical Information Technology Awards: Mid-November. MMS Student Section Community Service Grants: Accepted on a rolling deadline basis.

PUBLICATIONS:
Application guidelines.

ADDRESS INQUIRIES TO:
MMS International Health Studies Grant Program:
Jennifer Day, MMS and Alliance Charitable Foundation Director
Tel: (781) 434-7044
E-mail: jday@mms.org.

MMS Annual Scholars Program:
Applicant's Office of Student Affairs or Lisa Smith, Membership Services Specialist
MMS Membership Communications and Marketing
Tel: (781) 434-7759
E-mail: lsmith@mms.org

MMS Medical Information Technology Awards
Leon Q. Barzin, MMS Technical Program Portfolio Director
Tel: (800) 322-2303 ext. 7048
E-mail: lbarzin@mms.org

MMS Student Section Community Service Grants:
Colleen Hennessey
Manager, Member Relations
Tel: (781) 434-7315
E-mail: chennessey@mms.org

MASSACHUSETTS OFFICE OF STUDENT FINANCIAL ASSISTANCE [1532]
75 Pleasant Street
Malden, MA 02148
(617) 391-6070
Fax: (617) 391-6085
E-mail: cmccurdy@dhe.mass.edu
Web Site: www.mass.edu/osfa

FOUNDED: 1980

AREAS OF INTEREST:
Financial assistance to Massachusetts students.

NAME(S) OF PROGRAMS:
● **Massachusetts Cash Grant**
● **Massachusetts Gilbert Matching Student Grant Program**
● **MASSGrants**

TYPE:
Grants-in-aid. Massachusetts Cash Grant is intended to assist needy students in meeting institutionally held charges such as mandatory fees and non-state-supported tuition. Designed as an offset of the Tuition Waiver Program, these grants provide financial support to those individuals who would otherwise be denied the opportunity for higher education.

Massachusetts Gilbert Matching Student Grant Program is based on financial need and awarded to Massachusetts residents enrolled in nonprofit private colleges.

MASSGrants are state grants in all undergraduate fields, based solely on financial need, renewable for up to four years of undergraduate study. State grants must be used at accredited institutions in Massachusetts and reciprocal states.

PURPOSE:
To assist those who are unable to meet the costs of postsecondary education.

ELIGIBILITY:
For Massachusetts Cash Grant, applicant must be a permanent legal resident of Massachusetts for one year prior to the academic year for which the grant is awarded, be a U.S. citizen or eligible noncitizen, and be in compliance with applicable laws. For Massachusetts Gilbert Matching Student Grant Program, applicants must be permanent Massachusetts residents for at least one year, attending full-time in Massachusetts. MASSGrant applicants may attend school in Massachusetts, Pennsylvania, Vermont or Washington, DC.

GEOG. RESTRICTIONS: Primarily Massachusetts.

FINANCIAL DATA:
Amount of support per award: Massachusetts Cash Grant and MASSGrant: Varies; Massachusetts Gilbert Matching Student Grant Program: $200 to $2,500 per academic year.
Total amount of support: Varies.

APPLICATION INFO:
Applicants must file the Free Application for Federal Student Aid (FAFSA) after October 1.
Deadline: Massachusetts Cash Grant and Massachusetts Gilbert Matching Student Grant Program is determined by college. MASSGrant: FAFSA must be completed by May 1 each year.

Students must meet the FAFSA priority date for Massachusetts Cash Grant, Massachusetts Gilbert Matching Student Grant Program and other state financial aid programs that are awarded directly by the college.

PUBLICATIONS:
Guidelines.

ADDRESS INQUIRIES TO:
Clantha McCurdy
Senior Deputy Commissioner
(See address above.)

MICHIGAN STATE UNIVERSITY, THE GRADUATE SCHOOL
Chittenden Hall
466 West Circle Drive
East Lansing, MI 48824
(517) 353-3220
E-mail: gradschool@grd.msu.edu
Web Site: grad.msu.edu

TYPE:
Assistantships; Fellowships.

See entry 907 for full listing.

MISSOURI DEPARTMENT OF HIGHER EDUCATION AND WORKFORCE DEVELOPMENT [1533]
P.O. Box 1469
Jefferson City, MO 65102-1469
(573) 751-2361
(800) 473-6757 (option 4)
Fax: (573) 751-6635
E-mail: info@dhewd.mo.gov
Web Site: dhewd.mo.gov

FOUNDED: 1986

NAME(S) OF PROGRAMS:
● **Missouri Higher Education Academic Scholarship Program ("Bright Flight")**

TYPE:
Scholarships. Provides undergraduate student financial aid to qualified Missouri students who wish to attend qualified Missouri institutions of higher education, both public and private.

PURPOSE:
To enable qualified full-time students to attend a participating postsecondary institution (public and private).

LEGAL BASIS:
RSMO Supp. 173.250. Government agency.

ELIGIBILITY:
Applicant must be a resident of Missouri and a U.S. citizen or permanent resident and enrolled in an eligible Missouri institution, be a high school senior who plans to enroll as a first-time, full-time student and have a composite score on the American College Testing Program (ACT) or the Scholastic Aptitude Test (SAT) in the top five percent of all Missouri students taking the tests.

Student must take the ACT or SAT assessment and receive the required test score on or before the June test date of their senior year. GED and home-schooled students may also qualify. The Missouri Department of Higher Education will obtain the ACT or SAT assessment records, whichever the student has taken, and will notify students, high schools and postsecondary institutions of scholarship awards. Scholarships may not be used for theology for divinity studies.

GEOG. RESTRICTIONS: Missouri.

FINANCIAL DATA:
Amount of support per award: Statutory maximum award for an academic year is $3,000 for the top three percent and $1,000 for the fourth/fifth percentile.

Total amount of support: $21,254,230 for the 2019-20 academic year.

NO. AWARDS: 7,470 for the 2019-20 academic year.

APPLICATION INFO:
Eligible students will receive approval letters for qualifying scores.

Duration: One academic year. Renewable annually until students have obtained a Baccalaureate degree or completed a total of 10 semesters.

Deadline: Student applicant has to achieve the qualified score by the June test date.

ADDRESS INQUIRIES TO:
Information Center
(See address above.)

MISSOURI DEPARTMENT OF HIGHER EDUCATION AND WORKFORCE DEVELOPMENT [1534]
P.O. Box 1469
Jefferson City, MO 65102-1469
(573) 751-2361
(800) 473-6757 (option 4)
Fax: (573) 751-6635
E-mail: info@dhewd.mo.gov
Web Site: dhewd.mo.gov

FOUNDED: 1986

NAME(S) OF PROGRAMS:
● **Access Missouri Financial Assistance Program**

TYPE:
Grants-in-aid. Undergraduate student financial aid to qualified Missouri students who wish to attend qualified Missouri institutions of higher education, both public and private.

YEAR PROGRAM STARTED: 2007

PURPOSE:
To enable full-time students to attend a participating postsecondary institution (public and private).

LEGAL BASIS:
Section 173.1101-173.1107, RSMo. Government agency.

ELIGIBILITY:
Initially, applicants must meet the following requirements:
(1) have a FAFSA on file by April 1;
(2) have any FAFSA corrections made by July 31 (if one is eligible, school choices may be added until September 30 by contacting the MDHE);
(3) be a U.S. citizen or permanent resident and a Missouri resident;
(4) be an undergraduate student enrolled full-time at a participating Missouri school (students with documented disabilities who are enrolled in at least six credit hours may be considered to be enrolled full-time);
(5) have an Expected Family Contribution (EFC) of $12,000 or less;
(6) not be pursuing a degree or certificate in theology or divinity and;
(7) not have received the first Bachelor's degree, completed the required hours for a Bachelor's degree, or completed 150 semester credit hours.

Renewal students must continue to meet the eligibility requirements for initial students and additionally:
(1) continue to meet the eligibility requirements for initial students;
(2) maintain a minimum cumulative grade point average of 2.5 and otherwise maintain satisfactory academic progress as defined by the applicant's school (if this is the first academic year in which one has received an Access Missouri payment, this requirement does not apply) and;
(3) not have received an Access Missouri award for a maximum of five semesters at a two-year school or 10 semesters at any combination of two-year or four-year schools, whichever occurs first.
If Charles Gallagher or Missouri College Guarantee awardee in past semesters, those semesters are counted in the 10-semester limit, along with any semester in which the applicant has received an Access Missouri award.

GEOG. RESTRICTIONS: Missouri.

FINANCIAL DATA:
Amount of support per award: Award amounts are based on the type of school one is attending when award is received. If applicant transfers to a different school, his or her award amount may change based on the type of school to which he or she transfers. Public two-year: $300 to $940. Public four-year and State Technical College of Missouri: $1,500 to $2,050. Private: $1,500 to $2,050. (Note: Maximum award amounts may be less than these figures; it depends on the amount of funding that is available for the program.)

Total amount of support: $67,909,710 for the 2019-20 academic year.

NO. AWARDS: 44,208 for the 2019-20 academic year.

APPLICATION INFO:
Contact the Department or consult the web site.

Duration: One academic year. Renewable.

Deadline: FAFSA on file by April 1. Priority deadline: February 1. Final deadline: April 1.

ADDRESS INQUIRIES TO:
Information Center
(See address above.)

NATIONAL FEDERATION OF THE BLIND
NFB Scholarship Program
200 East Wells Street at Jernigan Place
Baltimore, MD 21230
(410) 659-9314 ext. 2415
E-mail: scholarships@nfb.org
Web Site: www.nfb.org/scholarships

TYPE:
Scholarships. Awarded on the basis of academic excellence, service to the community and leadership. Provides a one-time grant plus a continuing program of mentors and seminars for blind college students.

See entry 910 for full listing.

NATIONAL INSTITUTE FOR LABOR RELATIONS RESEARCH [1535]
5211 Port Royal Road
Suite 510
Springfield, VA 22151
(703) 321-9606
(703) 770-2247
Fax: (703) 321-0676
E-mail: clj@nrtw.org
Web Site: www.nilrr.org

FOUNDED: 1975

AREAS OF INTEREST:
Organization of public opposition to compulsory unionism in the education community.

NAME(S) OF PROGRAMS:
● **Applegate-Jackson-Parks Future Teacher Scholarship**

TYPE:
Scholarships. Scholarship awarded annually to the education student who exemplifies dedication to principle and high professional standards.

YEAR PROGRAM STARTED: 1989

PURPOSE:
To promote awareness of compulsory unionism.

LEGAL BASIS:
Nonprofit 501(c)(3) organization.

ELIGIBILITY:
Applicants are limited to undergraduates and graduate students majoring in education in institutions of higher learning throughout the U.S. Foreign students may apply, as long as they are attending an institution of higher learning in the U.S. Applicants who will be considered must demonstrate potential for successful completion of educational requirements in a college or university Department of Education program and the potential of successful application for a teaching license and demonstrate, by means of a written essay, an understanding of the individual freedom issue as it applies to the problem of compulsory unionism in the education community.

GEOG. RESTRICTIONS: United States.

FINANCIAL DATA:
Amount of support per award: $1,000 per scholarship.

Total amount of support: $1,000.

NO. MOST RECENT APPLICANTS: Approximately 212.

NO. AWARDS: 1.

APPLICATION INFO:
Applications may be submitted electronically. A total application will consist of a completed application form and a typewritten essay of approximately 500 words clearly demonstrating an interest in and a knowledge of the Right to Work principle as it applies to educators. All applicants will be requested to submit an official copy of his or her most recent transcript of grades.

Duration: One year. Nonrenewable.

Deadline: Applications must be postmarked on or by January 31.

ADDRESS INQUIRIES TO:
Cathy Jones, Scholarship Administrator
(See address above.)

*SPECIAL STIPULATIONS:
Applicant must be an education major attending college or have been admitted to an institution of higher learning in the U.S.

THE NATIONAL ITALIAN AMERICAN FOUNDATION [1536]
1860 19th Street, N.W.
Washington, DC 20009-5501
(202) 939-3114
Fax: (202) 387-0800
E-mail: scholarships@niaf.org
Web Site: www.niaf.org/scholarships

NAME(S) OF PROGRAMS:
● **NIAF Scholarship Program**

TYPE:
Scholarships. The National Italian American Foundation (NIAF) will award scholarships and grants to outstanding students for use during the following academic year. The awards will be made on the basis of academic merit to Italian American students studying a wide range of subjects.

PURPOSE:
To assist Italian American students or those interested in Italian studies.

ELIGIBILITY:
To be eligible for a NIAF scholarship, a student must meet the following criteria:
(1) be a member of NIAF or have a parent, grandparent or guardian with an active NIAF membership;
(2) be enrolled in a U.S. accredited institution of higher education for the fall semester;
(3) have a grade point average of at least 3.5 out of 4.0 (or the equivalent). Some scholarships require a lower grade point average requirement for eligibility. Students that are part of a pass-fail system are also eligible to apply;
(4) be a U.S. citizen or permanent resident alien and;
(5) must have at least one ancestor who has immigrated from Italy.

NIAF offers a variety of scholarships with specific eligibility requirements. Applicants should visit the scholarship page to review all criteria.

GEOG. RESTRICTIONS: United States.

FINANCIAL DATA:
Each scholarship award can only cover tuition and university-provided room and board. Scholarship monies not used during the academic year are not transferable to the following academic year and must be returned to the Foundation.
Amount of support per award: $2,500 to $12,000.
Total amount of support: Varies.

NO. MOST RECENT APPLICANTS: Over 4,000.

NO. AWARDS: 60 to 70.

APPLICATION INFO:
In order to be complete, an application must include the following:
(1) completed online application form;
(2) recent transcripts (either official or unofficial);
(3) recent resume outlining academic achievement, awards received, extracurricular involvement and work experience and;
(4) one letter of recommendation uploaded through the letter of recommendation provider.

Students applying for need-based scholarships will be required to upload their FAFSA Student Aid Report (SAR).
Duration: One academic year.
Deadline: March 1.

PUBLICATIONS:
Scholarship brochure.

ADDRESS INQUIRIES TO:
See e-mail address above.

NATIONAL JEWISH COMMITTEE ON SCOUTING [1537]
1325 West Walnut Hill Lane
Irving, TX 75038
(972) 580-2425
Fax: (972) 580-2535
E-mail: anthony.berger@scouting.org
Web Site: www.jewishscouting.org

NAME(S) OF PROGRAMS:
● **Rick Arkans Eagle Scout Scholarship**
● **Chester M. Vernon Memorial Eagle Scout Scholarship**
● **Frank L. Weil Memorial Eagle Scout Scholarship**

TYPE:
Scholarships.

PURPOSE:
To promote Boy Scouting among Jewish youth; to help Jewish institutions and local council Jewish committees to provide Scouting opportunities for Jewish youth; to promote Jewish values in Scouting.

ELIGIBILITY:
Applicants must:
(1) be a registered, active member of a Boy Scout troop, Varsity Scout team, or Venturing crew;
(2) have received the Eagle Scout Award;
(3) be an active member of a synagogue and must have received the Ner Tamid or Etz Chaim religious emblem;
(4) have demonstrated practical citizenship in his synagogue, school, Scouting unit, and community and;
(5) be enrolled in an accredited high school and in his final year at the time of selection, except Scouts whose Eagle Scout boards of review are held the same year of their high school graduation may apply in that calendar year. They may receive a scholarship one time only.

Applicants for Rick Arkans and Chester M. Vernon Memorial Eagle Scout Scholarships must also demonstrate financial need.

GEOG. RESTRICTIONS: United States.

FINANCIAL DATA:
Amount of support per award: Rick Arkans Eagle Scout Scholarship: $1,000; Chester M. Vernon Memorial Eagle Scout Scholarship: $1,000 per year; Frank L. Weil Memorial Eagle Scout Scholarship: $1,000 first place award and two $500 second place awards.

NO. AWARDS: 6.

APPLICATION INFO:
Applicants for the Arkans and Vernon Scholarships must submit a copy of the Free Application for Federal Student Assistance (FAFSA).

All sections of the scholarship application should be completed with as much information as possible. However, except for the required letter of recommendation (and FAFSA), no additional pages may be attached.
Duration: One year. Chester M. Vernon Memorial Eagle Scout Scholarship: Up to four years.

Deadline: Application submitted no later than January 31. Announcements by June 1.

ADDRESS INQUIRIES TO:
Anthony Berger, Staff Advisor
(See address above.)

NATIONAL SOCIETY DAUGHTERS OF THE AMERICAN REVOLUTION [1538]
1776 D Street, N.W.
Washington, DC 20006-5303
(202) 879-3263
E-mail: scholarships@nsdar.org
Web Site: www.dar.org

FOUNDED: 1890

AREAS OF INTEREST:
Furthering the education of Native Americans.

NAME(S) OF PROGRAMS:
● **American Indian Scholarship**

TYPE:
Scholarships. Intended to help Native American college/university and technical school students at the undergraduate or graduate level.

PURPOSE:
To provide scholarship assistance to Native American students of any age or tribe, in any state, striving to get an education.

ELIGIBILITY:
Applicants must:
(1) be Native Americans (proof required by letter or proof papers) in financial need;
(2) be U.S. citizens/residents and;
(3) have a grade point average of 3.25 or higher.

Graduate students are eligible; however, undergraduate students are given preference.

GEOG. RESTRICTIONS: United States.

FINANCIAL DATA:
Amount of support per award: $4,000.
Total amount of support: Varies.

NO. AWARDS: Up to 5.

APPLICATION INFO:
Applicants must use the DAR Scholarship Committee's online submission process found on the DAR public web site. Once applicants have set up their scholarship profile, they will be able to complete the application. If necessary, applicants will be able to provide access to individuals wishing to submit confidential letters of recommendations or school transcripts.
Duration: One-time award.
Deadline: January 31.

ADDRESS INQUIRIES TO:
National Vice Chairman
E-mail: americanindianschol@nsdar.org

NATIONAL SOCIETY DAUGHTERS OF THE AMERICAN REVOLUTION [1539]
1776 D Street, N.W.
Washington, DC 20006-5303
(202) 879-3263
E-mail: scholarships@nsdar.org
Web Site: www.dar.org

FOUNDED: 1890

AREAS OF INTEREST:
Furthering the education of Native Americans.

NAME(S) OF PROGRAMS:
- **Frances Crawford Marvin American Indian Scholarship**

TYPE:
Scholarships. Intended to help Native American students enrolled full-time at a two- or four-year college or university.

PURPOSE:
To provide scholarship assistance to Native American students.

ELIGIBILITY:
Applicants must:
(1) be enrolled full-time at a two- or four-year college or university;
(2) be Native Americans (proof required by letter or proof papers);
(3) be U.S. citizens/residents;
(4) demonstrate financial need and academic achievement and;
(5) have a grade point average of 3.25 or higher.

A recipient may reapply and be considered along with members of the applicant pool.

GEOG. RESTRICTIONS: United States.

FINANCIAL DATA:
Amount of support per award: Varies.

NO. AWARDS: 1.

APPLICATION INFO:
Applicants must use the DAR Scholarship Committee's online submission process found on the DAR public web site. Once applicants have set up their scholarship profile, they will be able to complete the application. If necessary, applicants will be able to provide access to individuals wishing to submit confidential letters of recommendations or school transcripts.

Duration: One year. Renewable.

Deadline: January 31.

ADDRESS INQUIRIES TO:
National Vice Chairman
E-mail: fcmarvinamericanindianscholarship@nsdar.org

NATIONAL SOCIETY OF ACCOUNTANTS SCHOLARSHIP FOUNDATION [1540]
1330 Braddock Place
Suite 540
Alexandria, VA 22314
(703) 549-6400
(800) 966-6679
Fax: (703) 549-2984
E-mail: members@nsacct.org
Web Site: www.nsacct.org

FOUNDED: 1969

AREAS OF INTEREST:
Accounting.

NAME(S) OF PROGRAMS:
- **NSA Scholarships**
- **The Stanley H. Stearman Award**

TYPE:
Endowments; Scholarships.

PURPOSE:
To provide financial encouragement to students who select accounting as a career.

LEGAL BASIS:
501(c)(3) charitable organization.

ELIGIBILITY:
Must be an undergraduate accounting major who is a U.S. or Canadian citizen that attends a U.S.-accredited school and maintains a "B" or better overall grade point average.

For the Stearman Award, applicant must be the spouse, son, daughter, grandchild, niece, nephew, daughter-in-law or son-in-law of an active or retired NSA living or deceased member. The member must have held membership for at least one year prior to the annual distribution of applications in October.

GEOG. RESTRICTIONS: United States.

FINANCIAL DATA:
Amount of support per award: Endowments: $1,000 to $2,000; Scholarships: $500 to $2,200.

Total amount of support: $95,650 for the year 2019.

NO. AWARDS: 45 for the year 2019.

APPLICATION INFO:
Guidelines are available on the Foundation web site.

Duration: One year. Nonrenewable, except for the Stearman Award which cannot exceed three years.

Deadline: March 31 (postmark).

NATIONAL SOCIETY OF BLACK ENGINEERS [1541]
205 Daingerfield Road
Alexandria, VA 22314
(703) 549-2207
Fax: (703) 683-5312
E-mail: scholarships@nsbe.org
rgoodine@nsbe.org
Web Site: www.nsbe.org

FOUNDED: 1975

AREAS OF INTEREST:
All areas of engineering.

TYPE:
Awards/prizes; Scholarships. The Society offers a variety of NSBE and corporate-sponsored scholarship and award opportunities to its precollege, collegiate undergraduate and graduate student members as well as technical professional members.

PURPOSE:
To increase the number of culturally responsible Black engineers who excel academically, succeed professionally and positively impact the community.

ELIGIBILITY:
For scholarships, applicant must be an active, paid NSBE member.

FINANCIAL DATA:
Amount of support per award: $500 to $16,000.

Total amount of support: Approximately $658,800 given annually in scholarships.

NO. MOST RECENT APPLICANTS: 1,925.

NO. AWARDS: Approximately 250 scholarships annually.

APPLICATION INFO:
Application information is available on the web site. Application must be submitted online.

Duration: One year. Nonrenewable.

Deadline: Spring cycle: Applications open in April with a deadline of June 30. Fall cycle: Applications open September 1 with a deadline of January 8.

*SPECIAL STIPULATIONS:
Each scholarship recipient cannot be awarded more than two scholarships in a given program year. Members that apply for more than one scholarship that has an internship requirement must rank acceptance of scholarship for awarding, if selected as a recipient. (A member cannot accept both internships for a given time period; thus he or she must decide prior to selection which scholarship/internship they would want to accept in priority order.)

NATSO FOUNDATION [1542]
Bill and Carolyn Moon Scholarships
1330 Braddock Place, Suite 501
Alexandria, VA 22314
(703) 549-2100
Fax: (703) 684-4525
E-mail: billmoonscholarship@natsofoundation.org
Web Site: www.natso.com/natsofoundation/billmoonscholarship

FOUNDED: 1989

AREAS OF INTEREST:
Research, scholarships and public outreach.

NAME(S) OF PROGRAMS:
- **Bill and Carolyn Moon Scholarships**

TYPE:
Scholarships. These scholarships provide much needed and deserved assistance to industry students planning for their postsecondary education.

PURPOSE:
To aid travel plaza employees and their dependents with educational expenses.

ELIGIBILITY:
Must be a truck stop/travel plaza employee or the legal dependent of a truck stop/travel plaza employee.

FINANCIAL DATA:
Amount of support per award: $5,000.

Total amount of support: Varies.

NO. AWARDS: 5.

APPLICATION INFO:
Applications are submitted online.

Duration: One semester.

Deadline: Mid-May.

ADDRESS INQUIRIES TO:
See e-mail address above.

NBCC FOUNDATION, INC. [1543]
3 Terrace Way
Greensboro, NC 27403
(336) 232-0376
Fax: (336) 232-0010
E-mail: foundation@nbcc.org
Web Site: www.nbccf.org

FOUNDED: 2005

AREAS OF INTEREST:
Philanthropy, mental health care, professional counseling, credentialing, scholarships and grant funding.

NAME(S) OF PROGRAMS:
- **ACS Training Award**
- **BCC Training Award**
- **CCE Professional Development Award**
- **Doctoral Minority Fellowship**
- **GCDF Scholarship**
- **Master's Youth Addictions Minority Fellowship**
- **Master's Youth Minority Fellowship**

- **NBCC Foundation Military Scholarship**
- **NBCC Foundation Rural Scholarship**

TYPE:
Fellowships; Scholarships. Academic scholarships for individuals pursuing a graduate-level degree in professional counseling.

YEAR PROGRAM STARTED: 2009

PURPOSE:
To increase the availability of counselors in underserved areas, with the current priority areas of minority, rural and military communities. Military Scholarship: To increase the number of counselors available to serve active duty service members and veterans. Minority Fellowship: To increase counseling resources available to underserved minority populations. Rural Scholarship: To increase access to needed counseling services in remote areas.

ELIGIBILITY:
For the ACS Training Award, the applicant must:
(1) currently hold the NCC certification maintained with no ethical holds or missed payments for a minimum of one year;
(2) have extensive clinical experience in providing mental health or substance abuse counseling services and;
(3) commit to applying for the ACS credential within one year of the award.

For the BCC Training Award, the applicant must:
(1) not be currently or previously certified as a BCC;
(2) commit to applying for the BCC and;
(3) demonstrate exceptional coaching potential through one or more of the following: having access to the population in need of coaching or working in a setting conducive to coaching; having a background in leadership; and holding or pursuing a degree from a relevant program.

For the CCE Professional Development Award, applicant must:
(1) currently hold a CCE credential maintained in good standing for a minimum of one year and;
(2) promote their CCE credential or contribute to the related field through one or more of the following: providing credential-related training for others; bringing programs that promote the credential to their campus or organization; delivering a presentation at a relevant conference; conducting relevant research; writing for a relevant publication; holding leadership positions in relevant groups or associations; and mentoring another who is pursuing the credential.

For the Doctoral Minority Fellowship, the applicant must:
(1) be a U.S. citizen or have permanent resident status;
(2) not receive any other federal funds (except for federal loans) or work for a federal agency;
(3) must currently hold the National Certified Counselor (NCC) certification and be in good standing or document all of the following: a full state license as a professional counselor; a passing score on the National Counselor Examination for Licensure and Certification (NCE) or the National Clinical Mental Health Counseling Examination (NCMHCE); and a commitment to obtain the NCC certification within three months if awarded a fellowship;

(4) be enrolled full-time and be in good standing in a CACREP-accredited, doctoral-level counseling program;
(5) have demonstrated knowledge and experience with racially and ethnically diverse populations and;
(6) commit to provide mental health and substance abuse services to underserved minority populations in the private nonprofit and public sectors through direct practice or the training of direct practitioners.
African Americans, Alaska Natives, American Indians, Asian Americans, Hispanics/Latinos, Native Hawaiians and Pacific Islanders are especially encouraged to apply.

For the GCDF Scholarship, the applicant must:
(1) (if a U.S. applicant) hold an active GCDF credential in good standing and be enrolled in a Master's-level program accredited by the Council for Accreditation of Counseling & Related Educational Programs (CACREP);
(2) (if an international applicant) either hold an active GCDF credential in good standing and be enrolled in an advanced education program in counseling or be a student currently enrolled in both a GCDF training program and a post-Bachelor's counseling program, as appropriate to their country and;
(3) commit to providing career counseling services for two years.

For the Master's Youth Addictions Minority Fellowship, the applicant must:
(1) be a U.S. citizen or have permanent resident status;
(2) not receive any other federal funds (except for federal student loans) or work for a federal agency;
(3) be entering their last year of study in the upcoming fall academic year;
(4) be enrolled full-time in either an accredited addictions counseling Master's program or a CACREP-accredited Master's program with a concentration in addictions counseling;
(5) demonstrate knowledge of and experience with racially and ethnically diverse populations;
(6) commit to applying for the National Certified Counselor (NCC) certification prior to graduation and to completing the application process and;
(7) commit to providing addictions counseling services to underserved minority transition-age youth (16 to 25) populations for two years.
African Americans, Alaska Natives, American Indians, Asian Americans, Hispanics/Latinos, Native Hawaiians and Pacific Islanders are especially encouraged to apply.

For the Master's Youth Minority Fellowship, the applicant must:
(1) be a U.S. citizen or have permanent resident status;
(2) not receive any other federal funds (except for federal student loans) or work for a federal agency;
(3) be enrolled full-time in a CACREP-accredited counseling Master's program;
(4) must demonstrate knowledge of and experience with racially and ethnically diverse populations;
(5) must commit to applying for the National Certified Counselor (NCC) certification prior to graduation and to completing the application process and;
(6) must commit to providing mental health

services to underserved minority transition-age youth (16 to 25) populations for two years.
African Americans, Alaska Natives, American Indians, Asian Americans, Hispanics/Latinos, Native Hawaiians and Pacific Islanders are especially encouraged to apply.

For the Military Scholarship, the applicant must:
(1) be enrolled full-time in a CACREP-accredited counseling Master's program;
(2) be former or current active duty U.S. military service members or spouses of a military service member whose service was within the past five years; veterans must have served in the military within the past five years and have received an honorable discharge;
(3) commit to applying for the National Certified Counselor (NCC) certification prior to graduation and to completing the application process and;
(4) commit to providing mental health services to service members and/or veterans for at least two years.

For the Rural Scholarship, the applicant must:
(1) be enrolled full-time in a CACREP-accredited counseling Master's program;
(2) reside in a rural area as defined by the Health Resources and Services Administration (HRSA);
(3) commit to applying for the National Certified Counselor (NCC) certification prior to graduation and to completing the application process and;
(4) commit to providing mental health services in a rural area for at least two years.

FINANCIAL DATA:
Awards go directly to recipients for any expenses associated with educational pursuit.
Amount of support per award: ACS Training Award: $500. BCC Training Award: Up to $3,000. CCE Professional Development Award: $500. Doctoral Minority Fellowship: Up to $20,000. GCDF Scholarship: $5,000. Master's Youth Addictions Minority Fellowship: Up to $11,000. Master's Youth Minority Fellowship: Up to $8,000. Military and Rural Scholarships: $5,000 (subject to change upon annual review).

APPLICATION INFO:
Application information is available on the web site.
Duration: One-time scholarship award. Not renewable.
Deadline: Varies from year to year.

ADDRESS INQUIRIES TO:
Program Coordinator
(See address above.)

NEBRASKA'S COORDINATING COMMISSION FOR POSTSECONDARY EDUCATION   [1544]
140 North 8th Street, Suite 300
Lincoln, NE 68508
(402) 471-2847
E-mail: ritchie.morrow@nebraska.gov
Web Site: www.ccpe.nebraska.gov

FOUNDED: 1991

AREAS OF INTEREST:
Higher education in Nebraska.

NAME(S) OF PROGRAMS:
- **Nebraska Opportunity Grant**

TYPE:
Scholarships. Nebraska Opportunity Grant is a need-based aid program to assist Nebraska students working on an undergraduate degree.

YEAR PROGRAM STARTED: 2003

PURPOSE:
To assist with costs of attending a Nebraska college or university.

ELIGIBILITY:
Applicant must be a Nebraska resident who has not earned a Bachelor's, Master's or professional degree. He or she must complete Free Application for Federal Student Aid (FAFSA) and have an Expected Family Contribution (EFC) equal to or less than the yearly maximum.

GEOG. RESTRICTIONS: Nebraska.

FINANCIAL DATA:
Amount of support per award: Varies.
Total amount of support: $17,978,264 for the year 2018-19.

NO. AWARDS: 12,753 for the year 2018-19.

APPLICATION INFO:
Must complete the FAFSA. Institutions may have additional application requirements.
Duration: Up to one academic year. Renewable.
Deadline: Applications are accepted on a rolling basis.

ADDRESS INQUIRIES TO:
J. Ritchie Morrow, M.S.Ed.
Financial Aid Officer
Nebraska's Coordinating Commission for Postsecondary Education
P.O. Box 95005
Lincoln, NE 68509-5005
(See telephone number above.)

NEED
The Law and Finance Building
429 Fourth Avenue, 20th Floor
Pittsburgh, PA 15219
(412) 566-2760
Fax: (412) 471-6643
E-mail: needpgh@gmail.com
Web Site: www.needld.org

TYPE:
Internships; Matching gifts; Scholarships. Supplemental grants for postsecondary education at colleges and business, trade and technical schools.

See entry 938 for full listing.

NEW JERSEY DEPARTMENT OF MILITARY AND VETERANS AFFAIRS [1545]
DVS-VBB
P.O. Box 340
Trenton, NJ 08625-0340
(609) 530-6854
Fax: (609) 530-6970
E-mail: patty.richter@dmava.nj.gov
Web Site: www.nj.gov/military

FOUNDED: 1959

AREAS OF INTEREST:
State financial assistance for postsecondary students.

NAME(S) OF PROGRAMS:
- **Veterans Tuition Credit Program (VTCP)**

TYPE:
Grants-in-aid. Tuition assistance grant for attendance at any eligible undergraduate, graduate or vocational institution in the U.S.

YEAR PROGRAM STARTED: 1977

PURPOSE:
To provide tuition assistance to U.S. veterans of the Armed Forces of the U.S. who served on active duty between December 31, 1960 and May 7, 1975 who were, or are, eligible for federal veterans' educational assistance (G.I. Bill).

LEGAL BASIS:
Entitlement.

ELIGIBILITY:
Applicant must be a veteran of the armed forces of the U.S. who is or was eligible for veterans educational assistance pursuant to federal law and served on active duty in the armed forces of the U.S. between December 31, 1960 and May 7, 1975. Applicant must have been a legal New Jersey resident at the time of induction into the armed forces, or at the time of discharge from active duty or for at least one year prior to the time of application, excluding the time spent in active duty. If a veteran was not a New Jersey resident at time of induction or separation, veteran must provide documentation reflecting residency – copy of NJ Income Tax Return, letter from postmaster, home mortgage or apartment lease. Applicant must be currently enrolled in an approved state approving agency course of study at any eligible academic, professional or vocational institution in the U.S.

GEOG. RESTRICTIONS: New Jersey.

FINANCIAL DATA:
Amount of support per award: Eligible veterans may receive a maximum award of $400 a year for full-time attendance or $200 a year for half-time attendance as provided by regulations and available appropriations.

NO. MOST RECENT APPLICANTS: 17.

NO. AWARDS: Based upon appropriations.

APPLICATION INFO:
Applications are available at campus Veterans Affairs offices or by calling the New Jersey Department of Military and Veterans Information Number, Tel: (888) 865-8387, available from any location in New Jersey, Monday through Friday, 8:30 A.M. to 4:30 P.M.
Duration: Eligible veterans may receive up to four academic years of payment.
Deadline: October 1 for fall and spring terms. March 1 for spring term only.

OFFICERS:
Tom DeShields, Director, Fiscal Operations

ADDRESS INQUIRIES TO:
Patricia Richter, Bureau Chief, VBB
(See address above.)

NEW JERSEY DEPARTMENT OF MILITARY AND VETERANS AFFAIRS [1546]
DVS-VBB
P.O. Box 340
Trenton, NJ 08625-0340
(609) 530-6854
Fax: (609) 530-6970
E-mail: patty.richter@dmava.nj.gov
Web Site: www.nj.gov/military

FOUNDED: 1959

AREAS OF INTEREST:
State financial assistance for college students, 16 to 21 years of age.

NAME(S) OF PROGRAMS:
- **Prisoner of War/Missing in Action (POW/MIA) Program**

TYPE:
Grants-in-aid; Scholarships.

YEAR PROGRAM STARTED: 1978

LEGAL BASIS:
Entitlement.

ELIGIBILITY:
Applicants must be dependent children (any child born before, during or after the period of time its parent was a POW/MIA) of military service personnel who were officially declared "Prisoner of War" or "Person Missing in Action" after January 1, 1960. The POW or MIA must have been a resident of New Jersey at the time he or she entered the Armed Forces of the U.S. or whose official residence is New Jersey.

GEOG. RESTRICTIONS: New Jersey.

FINANCIAL DATA:
Amount of support per award: Full tuition costs will be paid on behalf of the eligible dependent to any New Jersey public or independent college or university upon certification of full-time enrollment.

APPLICATION INFO:
Applications are available by contacting the New Jersey Department of Military and Veterans Affairs, Veterans Service Office, located in Mercer County.
Deadline: October 1 for fall and spring term benefits. March 1 for spring term benefits only.

OFFICERS:
Tom DeShields, Director, Fiscal Operations

ADDRESS INQUIRIES TO:
Patricia Richter, Bureau Chief, VBB
(See address above.)

NEW JERSEY OFFICE OF THE SECRETARY OF HIGHER EDUCATION (OSHE) [1547]
One John Fitch Plaza
P.O. Box 542
Trenton, NJ 08625-0542
(609) 341-3808
Fax: (609) 292-7225
E-mail: hasani.carter@oshe.nj.gov
Web Site: www.state.nj.us/highereducation/EOF/EOF_Description.shtml

FOUNDED: 1968

AREAS OF INTEREST:
State financial and student support assistance for low-income college students.

NAME(S) OF PROGRAMS:
- **The New Jersey Educational Opportunity Fund (EOF) Program**

TYPE:
Grants-in-aid. Student support. The Educational Opportunity Fund (EOF) is administered through the Office of the Secretary of Higher Education (OSHE). Created by law in 1968, EOF is one of the state's most comprehensive student support programs that provides access to higher education for those who come from low

income and educationally disadvantaged backgrounds. EOF is not an entitlement grant program.

YEAR PROGRAM STARTED: 1968

PURPOSE:
To ensure meaningful access to higher education for those who come from backgrounds of economic and educational disadvantage.

LEGAL BASIS:
New Jersey Educational Opportunity Act of 1968.

ELIGIBILITY:
Applicants must meet both the EOF statewide and institutional requirements. Applicants must be New Jersey residents for at least 12 consecutive months prior to receiving an award. Applicants must be full-time, matriculated students in an approved New Jersey college or university in an approved program of study. Household income cannot exceed established guidelines. The amount of the grant varies based on financial need, cost of attendance and available funding.

GEOG. RESTRICTIONS: New Jersey.

FINANCIAL DATA:
Amount of support per award: Dependent upon annual appropriations, financial need, cost of attendance, and enrollment status.

Public four-year institution: $800 a semester for a resident student; $675 a semester for a commuter student. County/community college: $625 a semester. Independent college/university: $1,350 a semester.

Total amount of support: $32,679,000.

NO. AWARDS: 13,200 undergraduates, unduplicated.

APPLICATION INFO:
Space is limited and admission into EOF is conducted at the campus level. Applicants should contact the participating institution for more information regarding their respective EOF admission process. Participating institutions are listed at www.nj.gov/highereducation/EOF/EOF_programs.shtml.

Duration: Financial assistance is renewable for four years of undergraduate study providing student is making satisfactory academic progress, demonstrates unmet need, and an application is filed by the deadline.

Deadline: September 15 for fall term and February 15 for spring term.

PUBLICATIONS:
State and Federal Financial Aid Programs for New Jersey Students, brochure.

ADDRESS INQUIRIES TO:
Dr. Hasani Carter
EOF Executive Director
Office of the Secretary
of Higher Education
(See address above.)

NEW YORK STATE EDUCATION DEPARTMENT   [1548]
Office of Postsecondary
Access, Support and Success
89 Washington Avenue, EBA 960
Albany, NY 12234
(518) 474-3719
Fax: (518) 474-7468
E-mail: scholar@nysed.gov
Web Site: www.nysed.gov/postsecondary-services

NAME(S) OF PROGRAMS:
● **Regents Physician Loan Forgiveness Award Program**
● **Scholarships for Academic Excellence**

TYPE:
Scholarships. Regents Physician Loan Forgiveness Award Program: Designed to increase the number of physicians practicing in areas of New York state designated by the Regents as having a shortage of physicians. Emphasis is placed on primary care.

Scholarships for Academic Excellence: For use only at colleges and universities within New York state. Students are nominated by their high schools for this award.

PURPOSE:
To encourage specially talented youth to continue their education.

GEOG. RESTRICTIONS: New York state.

FINANCIAL DATA:
Amount of support per award: Regents Physician Loan Forgiveness Award Program: Up to $10,000 per year for two years, then reapply for up to two more years at same amount; Scholarships for Academic Excellence: $500 to $1,500.

Total amount of support: Varies.

NO. AWARDS: Regents Physician Loan Forgiveness Award Program: Minimum of 80; Scholarships for Academic Excellence; 2,000 $1,500 scholarships, 6,000 $500 scholarships.

APPLICATION INFO:
Regents Physician Loan Forgiveness Award Program: Consult the Department web site. Scholarships for Academic Excellence: Available through the student's high school.

Duration: Regents Physician Loan Forgiveness Award Program: Two years, after which the physician must reapply; physician then may be able to get two more years of funding. Scholarships for Academic Excellence: Four years.

Deadline: Regents Physician Loan Forgiveness Award Program: Posted online. Scholarships for Academic Excellence: February 15.

ADDRESS INQUIRIES TO:
See telephone or e-mail address above.

NEW YORK STATE HIGHER EDUCATION SERVICES CORPORATION   [1549]
99 Washington Avenue
Albany, NY 12255
(888) 697-4372
(518) 473-1574
Fax: (518) 474-3749
Web Site: www.hesc.ny.gov

FOUNDED: 1975

AREAS OF INTEREST:
Postsecondary student financial aid.

NAME(S) OF PROGRAMS:
● **Military Enhanced Recognition Incentive and Tribute (MERIT)**
● **NYS Memorial Scholarships**

TYPE:
Grants-in-aid; Scholarships. Military Enhanced Recognition Incentive and Tribute (MERIT) provides financial aid to children, spouses and financial dependents of members of the armed forces of the U.S. or of a state-organized militia who, at any time on or

after August 2, 1990, while a New York state resident, died or became severely and permanently disabled while performing their military duties, whether in combat or not.

NYS Memorial Scholarships (NYS Memorial Scholarships for Families of Deceased Firefighters, Volunteer Firefighters, Police Officers, Peace Officers, and Emergency Medical Service Workers) provides financial aid to children, spouses and financial dependents of deceased members of these branches of public service who have died as the result of injuries sustained in the line of duty in service to the state of New York. It is for study in New York state.

The Corporation administers more than 25 grant, scholarship, award and other programs providing college financial aid for New York state residents.

YEAR PROGRAM STARTED: 2004

PURPOSE:
To provide special financial assistance for postsecondary study for children in certain categories.

LEGAL BASIS:
Article 13 of the Education Law. New York state agency.

ELIGIBILITY:
Students must:
(1) study at an approved postsecondary institution in New York state;
(2) have graduated from high school in the U.S., earned a GED, or passed a federally approved "Ability to Benefit" test as defined by the Commissioner of the State Education Department;
(3) be enrolled as a full-time student taking 12 or more credits per semester;
(4) be matriculated in an approved program of study and be in good academic standing and;
(5) not be in default on a student loan guaranteed by HESC or any repayment of state awards.

GEOG. RESTRICTIONS: New York state.

FINANCIAL DATA:
Amount of support per award: Varies.

Total amount of support: Varies.

APPLICATION INFO:
Applicants must complete and submit either the MERIT Scholarships Web Supplement or the NYS Memorial Scholarship Web Supplement. Be sure to print the Web Supplement confirmation, sign the supplement, and submit it along with the required documentation according to the instructions. FAFSA must be completed after eligibility is established and applicant has been assigned an account number.

Duration: Four years of full-time undergraduate study or five years of undergraduate study if the student is enrolled in an approved five-year program.

Deadline: June 30.

ADDRESS INQUIRIES TO:
E-mail: scholarships@hesc.ny.gov

NEW YORK STATE HIGHER EDUCATION SERVICES CORPORATION [1550]

99 Washington Avenue
Albany, NY 12255
(888) 697-4372
(518) 473-1574
Fax: (518) 474-3749
E-mail: edward.gilbert@hesc.ny.gov
Web Site: www.hesc.ny.gov

FOUNDED: 1975

AREAS OF INTEREST:
Postsecondary student financial aid.

NAME(S) OF PROGRAMS:
- **NYS Aid for Part-Time Study (APTS)**

TYPE:
Grants-in-aid. College-based program providing grant assistance for eligible part-time students enrolled in approved undergraduate studies.

YEAR PROGRAM STARTED: 1984

PURPOSE:
To help pay tuition for eligible students enrolled in approved certificate or degree programs.

LEGAL BASIS:
State agency.

ELIGIBILITY:
To be considered for an award, a student must enroll part-time in a degree or an approved certificate program at a degree-granting institution, meet specific income limits, be a New York state resident, be either a U.S. citizen or eligible noncitizen, have a tuition charge of at least $100 per year, and not have used up Tuition Assistance Program (TAP) eligibility.

For this program, part-time study means being enrolled for at least three, but less than 12, semester-hours per semester, or four, but less than eight, credit hours per trimester. A participating college selects recipients from among eligible students.

GEOG. RESTRICTIONS: New York state.

FINANCIAL DATA:
Award amount is based on the student's need and the amount of money available at the institution.
Amount of support per award: Up to $2,000 per year.

APPLICATION INFO:
Awards are made through each college offering the program. Students should contact the college financial aid office to find out how to apply at their school.
Duration: Renewable up to four years.
Deadline: Varies.

ADDRESS INQUIRIES TO:
E-mail: scholarships@hesc.ny.gov

NEW YORK STATE HIGHER EDUCATION SERVICES CORPORATION [1551]

99 Washington Avenue
Albany, NY 12255
(888) 697-4372
(518) 473-1574
Fax: (518) 474-3749
E-mail: edward.gilbert@hesc.ny.gov
Web Site: www.hesc.ny.gov

FOUNDED: 1975

AREAS OF INTEREST:
Postsecondary student financial aid.

NAME(S) OF PROGRAMS:
- **New York State Tuition Assistance Program (TAP)**

TYPE:
Grants-in-aid. New York's largest grant program, the Tuition Assistance Program helps eligible New York residents attending in-state postsecondary institutions pay for tuition. TAP grants are based on the applicant's and his or her family's New York state net taxable income.

YEAR PROGRAM STARTED: 1976

PURPOSE:
To partially defray tuition charges to students.

LEGAL BASIS:
Article 13 of the Education Law.

ELIGIBILITY:
Legal New York state residents who are U.S. citizens or eligible noncitizens, who are full-time students at an approved postsecondary institution in New York state, and who meet income eligibility limitations are eligible to apply.

Student must attend an institution charging at least $200 annual tuition.

GEOG. RESTRICTIONS: New York state.

FINANCIAL DATA:
Amount of support per award: Up to $5,665; grant varies according to New York net taxable income of the applicant and family.
Total amount of support: Varies.

NO. AWARDS: Unlimited.

APPLICATION INFO:
Student must complete the annual FAFSA online application; from there he or she can proceed via online link to the HESC TAP application, which must also be completed. The TAP application is also available by accessing the HESC web site (above).
Duration: Up to four or five years of undergraduate study if the student is enrolled in an approved five-year program.
Deadline: June 30 of the current school year.

ADDRESS INQUIRIES TO:
Student Information
(See address above.)

THE CHARLOTTE W. NEWCOMBE FOUNDATION [1552]

35 Park Place
Princeton, NJ 08542-6918
(609) 924-7022
Fax: (609) 252-1773
E-mail: info@newcombefoundation.org
Web Site: www.newcombefoundation.org

FOUNDED: 1979

AREAS OF INTEREST:
College scholarship funds to colleges and universities.

NAME(S) OF PROGRAMS:
- **Newcombe Fellowships**
- **Newcombe Scholarships for Mature Students**
- **Newcombe Scholarships for Students with Disabilities**
- **Special Scholarship Endowment Grants**

TYPE:
Challenge/matching grants; Endowments; Fellowships; Internships; Scholarships. Endowment challenges build up current Newcombe Scholarship Endowments at colleges in a Newcombe program.

Newcombe Fellowships are designed to encourage original and significant study of ethical and religious values in all areas of human endeavor. The selection process and all administration for this continuing fellowship program are handled by the Institute for Citizens & Scholars. All doctoral requirements except the dissertation must be completed by November of the year preceding the Fellowship award. Student must be attending a graduate school in the U.S.

Newcombe Scholarships for Mature Students are for students age 25 and older who have completed half the credits required for their Bachelor's degrees. These scholarships are available at selected colleges which offer support services for mature students. Preference in this program is given to four-year colleges with excellent support services for mature students. It is Foundation policy not to provide grants in this program to professional schools, including theological seminaries and those training health care professionals; 28 colleges are in this program.

Newcombe Scholarships for Students with Disabilities are intended to recognize the extraordinary expenses these students incur because of their disabilities and to supplement other sources of aid. The Newcombe Foundation offers special disability expense scholarships, internship scholarships and partial tuition scholarships through the counseling offices of colleges which provide excellent support services for disabled students. Preference in this program is given to four-year colleges which render exceptional service to large numbers of disabled students. 12 colleges are in the Newcombe Program.

Special Scholarship Endowment Grants are awarded to selected institutions to benefit students from a specified economically disadvantaged population that the institution serves.

The Foundation makes no awards to individual students. All grants are made to colleges, universities and other institutions of higher education.

YEAR PROGRAM STARTED: 1981

PURPOSE:
To provide selected colleges and universities with scholarship funds for specifically targeted groups of students.

LEGAL BASIS:
Private.

ELIGIBILITY:
No grants to individuals. Scholarship aid only. No funds for program development staffing or support. The Foundation provides grants to colleges, universities and foundations to create scholarships for designated undergraduate and graduate students. No aid is available for postdoctoral fellowships.

GEOG. RESTRICTIONS: Scholarships for Disabled Students and Mature Students are generally limited to the mid-Atlantic states.

FINANCIAL DATA:
Amount of support per award: Varies.

Total amount of support: $2,300,000 for the year 2018-19.

Matching fund requirements: Varies.

NO. AWARDS: Varies.

APPLICATION INFO:
For Newcombe Fellowships, contact Institute for Citizens & Scholars, 104 Carnegie Center, Suite 301, Princeton, NJ 08540 for application materials. Tel: (609) 452-7007. Web site: www.woodrow.org/newcombe.

For Newcombe Scholarships for Mature Students and Students with Disabilities, colleges within geographic area should contact the Foundation for applications. Individuals should contact their college of choice for availability of these scholarships.

Duration: Varies.

Deadline: Inquiries are accepted on an ongoing basis. Proposals by invitation.

PUBLICATIONS:
Annual report.

IRS I.D.: 23-2120614

STAFF:
Dr. Gianna Durso-Finley, Executive Director
Lindsey G. Bohra, Associate Executive Director

BOARD OF TRUSTEES:
Dale Robinson Anglin
John R. Bowlin
Elizabeth T. Frank
Louise U. Johnson
J. Barton Luedeke

ADDRESS INQUIRIES TO:
Dr. Gianna Durso-Finley, Executive Director
(See address above.)

*PLEASE NOTE:
No grants to individuals.

*SPECIAL STIPULATIONS:
Grants are made to colleges and universities exclusively for student scholarships. Two programs (Mature Students and Students with Disabilities) are generally limited to mid-Atlantic states.

NORTH CAROLINA STATE EDUCATION ASSISTANCE AUTHORITY/COLLEGE FOUNDATION OF NORTH CAROLINA   [1553]

P.O. Box 14103
Research Triangle Park, NC 27709
(919) 549-8614
(866) 866-2362
E-mail: programinformation@cfnc.org
Web Site: www.cfnc.org

AREAS OF INTEREST:
Financial aid for North Carolina students.

TYPE:
Grants-in-aid; Scholarships.

PURPOSE:
To provide access to higher education and information for the citizens of North Carolina.

ELIGIBILITY:
Varies with program. All applicants must be North Carolina residents and intend to use funds for tuition purposes only.

GEOG. RESTRICTIONS: North Carolina.

FINANCIAL DATA:
Amount of support per award: Varies.
Total amount of support: Varies.

APPLICATION INFO:
Students and families are urged to consult the CFNC web site for information regarding state grants, scholarships and student loans. Applications may be obtained online or by telephone request.

Duration: Varies.

Deadline: Varies.

ADDRESS INQUIRIES TO:
Administrative questions:
NCSEAA Grants Training and Outreach
(See address above.)

NORTHERN CHAUTAUQUA COMMUNITY FOUNDATION   [1554]

212 Lake Shore Drive West
Dunkirk, NY 14048
(716) 366-4892
Fax: (716) 366-3905
E-mail: nccf@nccfoundation.org
Web Site: www.nccfoundation.org

FOUNDED: 1986

AREAS OF INTEREST:
Youth development and economic development.

TYPE:
Challenge/matching grants; Project/program grants; Scholarships. Youth Development and Economic Development grants.

YEAR PROGRAM STARTED: 1986

PURPOSE:
To enhance the northern Chautauqua community.

LEGAL BASIS:
Community foundation.

ELIGIBILITY:
Applicants must be registered 501(c)(3) organizations that serve the northern Chautauqua County community.

GEOG. RESTRICTIONS: Northern Chautauqua County, New York.

FINANCIAL DATA:
Amount of support per award: $25 to $10,000.

Total amount of support: $1,404,933 in grants and scholarships for the year 2019.

APPLICATION INFO:
Call the Foundation for information or visit its web site.

Deadline: Community Grants: March 1 and September 1.

PUBLICATIONS:
Annual report; Spring and Fall newsletters.

IRS I.D.: 16-1271663

STAFF:
Diane E. Hannum, Executive Director
Eileen Ardillo, Program Coordinator
Leslie Wille, Community Engagement Coordinator
Victoria Howell, Scholarship and Administrative Coordinator

ADDRESS INQUIRIES TO:
Eileen Ardillo, Program Coordinator or
Victoria Howell
Scholarship and Administrative Coordinator
(See address above.)

THE NRA   [1555]

11250 Waples Mill Road
Fairfax, VA 22030
(703) 267-1087
(866) 672-6986
Fax: (703) 267-1083
E-mail: jebrayscholarship@nrahq.org
Web Site: awards.nra.org

NAME(S) OF PROGRAMS:
• **Jeanne E. Bray Memorial Scholarship**

TYPE:
Scholarships. For children of peace officers.

YEAR PROGRAM STARTED: 1988

PURPOSE:
To assist children of peace officers, who are current NRA members, in furthering their education.

ELIGIBILITY:
Must be an adult or junior member of the NRA and the son or daughter of a currently serving, full-time/deceased, full-time/retired, full-time, or disabled and retired commissioned peace officer who is also a current NRA member or was at the time of death. Eligible students can be senior high school students through senior college students. Applicants must have a satisfactory academic record and be enrolled full-time. Must be U.S. citizens or residents.

GEOG. RESTRICTIONS: United States.

FINANCIAL DATA:
Amount of support per award: $3,000 per semester (up to $6,000 per year).

NO. AWARDS: Varies.

APPLICATION INFO:
Applicant will need to contact Chandra Bolland to receive the personal reference forms.

Duration: Up to four semesters.

Deadline: November 15.

ADDRESS INQUIRIES TO:
Jeanne E. Bray Memorial
Scholarship Committee
(See address and e-mail above.)

OHIO DEPARTMENT OF HIGHER EDUCATION   [1556]

Office of Financial Aid
25 South Front Street
Columbus, OH 43215
(614) 752-9528
Fax: (614) 466-5866
E-mail: hotline@highered.ohio.gov
rchurch@highered.ohio.gov
Web Site: www.ohiohighered.org/ohio-war-orphans

NAME(S) OF PROGRAMS:
• **Ohio War Orphan and Severely Disabled Veterans' Children Scholarships**

TYPE:
Scholarships. Full-time undergraduate scholarships.

YEAR PROGRAM STARTED: 1954

PURPOSE:
To provide tuition assistance to the children of deceased or severely disabled Ohio veterans who served in the armed forces during a period of declared war or conflict.

LEGAL BASIS:
State agency.

ELIGIBILITY:
Applicant must be 16 to 24 years of age and a child of disabled or deceased Ohio war veteran or child of Vietnam conflict MIA or POW. Veteran parent must have at least a 60% combined disability rating. Applicant must also be enrolled as a full-time student in an eligible institution of higher education.

GEOG. RESTRICTIONS: Ohio.

FINANCIAL DATA:
Students attending Ohio nonprofit and profitmaking institutions of higher education will receive amounts no greater than the average amount paid for students attending public institutions; tuition coverage at public institutions varies each year.
Amount of support per award: Varies.
Total amount of support: $11,777,388 for the year 2019-20.

NO. AWARDS: 1,500 for the year 2019-20.

APPLICATION INFO:
Student must submit a completed application form.
Duration: Scholarships are automatically renewable for up to five years of undergraduate education.
Deadline: May 15. Announcements in early August.

STAFF:
Ramah Church, Program Manager

ADDRESS INQUIRIES TO:
Ramah Church, Program Manager
(See address above.)

*SPECIAL STIPULATIONS:
This program is not for graduate students.

OHIO DEPARTMENT OF HIGHER EDUCATION   [1557]
Office of Financial Aid
25 South Front Street
Columbus, OH 43215
(614) 466-6000
Fax: (614) 752-5903
E-mail: ocog_admin@highered.ohio.gov
Web Site: www.ohiohighered.org/ocog

FOUNDED: 1963

NAME(S) OF PROGRAMS:
● **Ohio College Opportunity Grant Program (OCOG)**

TYPE:
General operating grants. Grants for Ohio students who demonstrate the highest levels of financial need.

YEAR PROGRAM STARTED: 2006

PURPOSE:
To assist in achieving the goals of access and choice for low-income and middle-income students.

LEGAL BASIS:
State agency.

ELIGIBILITY:
Applicant must be an Ohio resident, demonstrate financial need, and be seeking an Associate's degree, a Bachelor's degree, or nursing diploma at an eligible institution.

GEOG. RESTRICTIONS: Ohio and Pennsylvania.

FINANCIAL DATA:
Amount of support per award: Varies.
Total amount of support: $94,341,562 for the year 2019.

NO. AWARDS: 60,756 for the year 2019.

APPLICATION INFO:
Student must submit a Free Application for Federal Student Aid (FAFSA).
Duration: One academic year. Renewable for a maximum of 10 semesters of full-time study.
Deadline: October 1.

ADDRESS INQUIRIES TO:
Tamika Braswell, Director
(See address above.)

*SPECIAL STIPULATIONS:
This program is not for graduate students.

OHIO NATIONAL GUARD SCHOLARSHIP PROGRAM [1558]
The Adjutant General's Department
2825 West Dublin Granville Road
Columbus, OH 43235-2789
(614) 336-7143
(888) 400-6484
Fax: (614) 336-7195
E-mail: ng.oh.oharng.mbx.ong-scholarship@mail.mil
lonny.r.kirby.nfg@mail.mil
Web Site: www.ong.ohio.gov/information/education/scholarship_index.html

FOUNDED: 1977

AREAS OF INTEREST:
Associate or undergraduate general education.

TYPE:
Scholarships. Grants for undergraduate students attending three credit hours or more.

YEAR PROGRAM STARTED: 1978

PURPOSE:
To encourage enlistment in Ohio National Guard.

LEGAL BASIS:
Ohio Revised Code. Nonprofit.

ELIGIBILITY:
Applicants must possess a high school diploma or a GED certificate and enlist, re-enlist or extend their current enlistment in the Ohio National Guard for a minimum of three years and up to six years.

GEOG. RESTRICTIONS: Ohio.

FINANCIAL DATA:
Instructional and general fees paid 100% for student attending public institution. For private institutions, the amount paid is equivalent to the average cost of public schools.
Amount of support per award: Varies.
Total amount of support: $21,000,000 annually.

NO. MOST RECENT APPLICANTS: 3,500.

APPLICATION INFO:
An applicant must apply each term so that the application is received in the Scholarship Program Office no later than the established deadlines, which are no later than the close of business (4:30 P.M.).
Duration: A three- to five-year enlistment will qualify applicants for 48 semester hours towards an Associate or Bachelor's degree. A six-year enlistment will qualify applicants for 96 semester hours towards an Associate or Bachelor's degree.
Deadline: July 1 for fall; November 1 for winter/quarter, semester, trimester/spring semester; February 1 for spring quarter; April 1 for summer.

PUBLICATIONS:
Regulation AGOR 621-1(Army); *35-1*(Air).

STAFF:
Lonny Kirby, Program Coordinator

ADDRESS INQUIRIES TO:
Lonny Kirby, Program Coordinator
(See address above.)

*SPECIAL STIPULATIONS:
Applicant must enlist in Ohio National Guard for not less than three years. Must enroll minimum three credit hours in degree-granting program.

ORDER SONS OF ITALY IN AMERICA, GRAND LODGE OF FLORIDA   [1559]
2021 Pine Needle Trail
Kissimmee, FL 34746
(321) 286-6787
E-mail: gertd830@gmail.com
Web Site: osiaflorida.org

FOUNDED: 1953

AREAS OF INTEREST:
Culture, charity and education.

TYPE:
Awards/prizes; Grants-in-aid; Scholarships. Scholarships are provided to high school students entering college.

Financial aid is given in support of charitable programs, such as Alzheimer's disease, Cooley's anemia, autism, and cancer.

YEAR PROGRAM STARTED: 1988

PURPOSE:
To share and help those in need; to support high school students entering college; to support charitable programs.

ELIGIBILITY:
Scholarship program: Applying student must be a U.S. citizen or resident who resides in the state of Florida, be of Italian heritage, and achieve high scholastic grades.

Applying organizations must have 501(c)(3) not-for-profit status. No grants are made to religious organizations.

GEOG. RESTRICTIONS: Florida.

FINANCIAL DATA:
Amount of support per award: Scholarship program: $2,000 per student.
Total amount of support: $10,000.

NO. AWARDS: Scholarship program: Varies with funding; 5 scholarships in 2018.

APPLICATION INFO:
Scholarship application form can be obtained on the web site or at applying student's local high school. Completed application materials must be submitted to the State Scholarship Chairperson.
Duration: One-time awards. Grants are not renewable.
Deadline: March 31.

ADDRESS INQUIRIES TO:
Gertrude Dorries, State Scholarship Chairperson
(See e-mail address above.)

PARAPSYCHOLOGY FOUNDATION, INC.
P.O. Box 1562
New York, NY 10021-0043
(212) 628-1550
Fax: (212) 628-1559
E-mail: office@parapsychology.org
Web Site: parapsychology.org

TYPE:
Scholarships. Assists students attending an accredited college or university in pursuing the academic study of the science of parapsychology.

See entry 2334 for full listing.

PENNSYLVANIA HIGHER EDUCATION ASSISTANCE AGENCY [1560]
1200 North Seventh Street
Harrisburg, PA 17102-1398
(717) 720-2800
(800) 692-7392 (Pennsylvania only)
Fax: (717) 720-3786
E-mail: granthelp@pheaa.org
Web Site: www.pheaa.org

FOUNDED: 1964

NAME(S) OF PROGRAMS:
● **Pennsylvania State Grant Program**

TYPE:
Grants-in-aid. The Pennsylvania State Grant Program allows eligible Pennsylvania residents to obtain financial assistance for undergraduate study at any PHEAA-approved institution of higher education. The Free Application for Federal Student Aid (FAFSA) serves as the program's application.

YEAR PROGRAM STARTED: 1964

PURPOSE:
To assist needy students in obtaining higher education.

LEGAL BASIS:
Government agency.

ELIGIBILITY:
The student applying for Pennsylvania State Grants must:
(1) meet criteria for financial need;
(2) be enrolled on at least a half-time basis in a PHEAA-approved undergraduate program of study and not already have a four-year (or more) undergraduate degree;
(3) be a high school graduate or the recipient of a GED;
(4) demonstrate academic progress (for continued aid) and;
(5) be a Pennsylvania resident (domiciliary).

Summer school students may also qualify for State Grant funds.

GEOG. RESTRICTIONS: Pennsylvania.

FINANCIAL DATA:
Amount of support per award: Varies annually.

NO. AWARDS: Approximately 130,000.

APPLICATION INFO:
Submit the Free Application for Federal Student Aid (FAFSA) and Pennsylvania State Grant Form. Most renewal students do not have to complete the State Grant Form.
Duration: One academic year. Renewal contingent upon continued eligibility and financial need.
Deadline: Varies.

EXECUTIVE OFFICERS:
James H. Steeley, President and Chief Executive Officer
Elizabeth McCloud, Vice President of State Grants and Special Programs

ADDRESS INQUIRIES TO:
Elizabeth McCloud, Vice President of State Grants and Special Programs
(See address above.)

THE PHI BETA KAPPA SOCIETY [1561]
1606 New Hampshire Avenue, N.W.
Washington, DC 20009
(202) 745-3287
Fax: (202) 986-1601
E-mail: awards@pbk.org
Web Site: www.pbk.org

AREAS OF INTEREST:
Philosophy.

NAME(S) OF PROGRAMS:
● **The Romanell-Phi Beta Kappa Professorship in Philosophy**

TYPE:
Fellowships. Professorship awarded to scholars in the field of philosophy, without restriction to any one school of philosophical thought.

YEAR PROGRAM STARTED: 1983

PURPOSE:
To recognize not only distinguished achievement, but also the recipient's contribution or potential contribution to public understanding of philosophy.

ELIGIBILITY:
Scholar need not be a member of Phi Beta Kappa, but must be on the faculty of an institution sheltering a chapter of Phi Beta Kappa and must be nominated by that chapter.

GEOG. RESTRICTIONS: United States.

FINANCIAL DATA:
In addition to the stipend, the award includes a lecture series and publishing deal with Oxford University Press.
Amount of support per award: $7,500 stipend for the awardee and $1,000 for his or her chapter.

NO. AWARDS: 1 annually.

APPLICATION INFO:
Recipient must be nominated by the chapter of Phi Beta Kappa at the institution in which they are on faculty.
Duration: One year. Nonrenewable.
Deadline: June 30.

ADDRESS INQUIRIES TO:
Aurora Sherman, Executive Assistant to the Secretary and Awards Coordinator
(See address above.)

*SPECIAL STIPULATIONS:
Recipient will be expected to give a series of three special lectures during the year of the Professorship. Such lectures are to be given at the sheltering institution and to be open to the general public as well as to the academic community.

PI GAMMA MU, INTERNATIONAL HONOR SOCIETY IN SOCIAL SCIENCE [1562]
1001 Millington, Suite B
Winfield, KS 67156
(620) 221-3128
E-mail: executivedirector@pigammamu.org
Web Site: www.pigammamu.org

FOUNDED: 1924

AREAS OF INTEREST:
Economics, history, political science, sociology, anthropology, international relations, social work, psychology, social philosophy, history of education and criminal justice, law and human/cultural geography.

NAME(S) OF PROGRAMS:
● **Pi Gamma Mu Scholarships**

TYPE:
Scholarships. Awarded for graduate study.

YEAR PROGRAM STARTED: 1951

PURPOSE:
To promote scholarship in the Society's areas of interest.

LEGAL BASIS:
Nonprofit.

ELIGIBILITY:
Applicant must be a member of Pi Gamma Mu.

FINANCIAL DATA:
Amount of support per award: $1,000 or $2,000.
Total amount of support: Up to $13,000 annually.

NO. MOST RECENT APPLICANTS: Approximately 47.

NO. AWARDS: Up to 10.

APPLICATION INFO:
Resume, personal statement, transcript and three letters of recommendation required.
Duration: One year.
Deadline: February 15. Announcement: Spring. Distribution: Fall.

PUBLICATIONS:
Application guidelines.

OFFICERS:
Dr. C. Laurence Heck, President
Dr. Susan Kinsella, First Vice President
Dr. Clara Small, Second Vice President
Dr. Mari Plikuhn, Secretary and Treasurer
Dr. Charles Hartwig, Chancellor
Katherine Im, Chancellor
Allison G.S. Knox, Chancellor
Dr. Brad Tennant, Chancellor

ADDRESS INQUIRIES TO:
Executive Director

MINNIE STEVENS PIPER FOUNDATION [1563]
1250 N.E. Loop 410, Suite 810
San Antonio, TX 78209-1539
(210) 525-8494
Fax: (210) 341-6627
E-mail: mspf@mspf.org
Web Site: www.mspf.org

FOUNDED: 1950

NAME(S) OF PROGRAMS:
● **Piper Professor Program**
● **Piper Scholar Program**
● **Student Loan Program**

TYPE:
Awards/prizes; Scholarships. Piper Professor Program: Annual awards to professors for superior teaching at the college level.

Piper Scholars: Four-year scholarships awarded to academically promising and superior high school seniors in amounts that assist them in attending the college or university of their choice within the state of Texas.

Student Loan Program: Loans to worthy and needy students at the junior, senior, undergraduate or graduate college level.

PURPOSE:
To support charitable, scientific, or educational undertakings by providing for, or contributing toward, the education of financially limited but worthy students; to assist young men and women residents of Texas, attending or wishing to attend colleges and universities in the state of Texas, to complete their education and obtain degrees; to contribute to community chests; to support any other nonprofit organization or activity dedicated to promoting the general welfare within the state of Texas.

LEGAL BASIS:
Private foundation with Letter Ruling under Section 4945 of the Tax Reform Act of 1969.

ELIGIBILITY:
Piper Professor Program: Candidates must be U.S. citizens and nominated through college/university President's office.

Piper Scholar Program: Participation is by invitation only to high schools in certain geographic areas. Student must be nominated by their high school counselor.

Student Loan Program: Must be full-time status. Restricted to Texas residents attending a college or university within the state of Texas.

GEOG. RESTRICTIONS: Texas.

FINANCIAL DATA:
Amount of support per award: Piper Professor Program: $5,000.

NO. AWARDS: Piper Professor Program: 10; Piper Scholar Program: 25.

APPLICATION INFO:
Student Loan application can be downloaded from the Foundation web site.
Duration: Piper Scholar Program: Four years.

ADDRESS INQUIRIES TO:
Joyce M. Ellis, Executive Director
(See address above.)

*SPECIAL STIPULATIONS:
Piper Professor and Piper Scholars Programs are by invitation only.

THE PLANNING AND VISUAL EDUCATION PARTNERSHIP   [1564]
4651 Sheridan Street, Suite 470
Hollywood, FL 33021
(954) 241-4800
(954) 241-4834
Fax: (954) 893-8375
E-mail: info@paveglobal.org
Web Site: paveglobal.org

FOUNDED: 1992

AREAS OF INTEREST:
Retail design planning, industrial design and visual merchandising.

TYPE:
Awards/prizes; Capital grants; Conferences/seminars; Product donations; Project/program grants; Scholarships. Student educational support. Mentorships.

PURPOSE:
To encourage students to study in the field of retail design, interior design, and planning and visual merchandising.

FINANCIAL DATA:
Amount of support per award: PAVE Global Shop Design Project: $15,000; Student Aid Program: $25,000; Student Design Competition: $8,000 for first place, $5,500 for second place, $3,000 for third place and $1,000 for honorable mention.
Total amount of support: $115,000 for the year 2018-19.

NO. AWARDS: 13.

ADDRESS INQUIRIES TO:
Dash Nagel, Managing Director
(See address above.)

PRESBYTERIAN CHURCH (U.S.A.)   [1565]
100 Witherspoon Street
Louisville, KY 40202-1396
(888) 728-7228 ext. 5224
Fax: (502) 569-8766
E-mail: finaid@pcusa.org
Web Site: www.pcusa.org/financialaid

AREAS OF INTEREST:
Majors in health services/sciences, religious studies, sacred music, social services and social sciences.

NAME(S) OF PROGRAMS:
● **Student Opportunity Scholarship**

TYPE:
Scholarships. Need-based.

YEAR PROGRAM STARTED: 1956

PURPOSE:
To assist undergraduate sophomores, juniors and seniors already in college, with preference to racial ethnic students.

ELIGIBILITY:
Scholarship preference to African Americans, Asian Americans, Middle Eastern Americans and Hispanic Americans. Applicants must:
(1) demonstrate financial need;
(2) be a member of the Presbyterian Church (U.S.A.);
(3) be a sophomore, junior or senior already in college;
(4) have a 2.5 grade point average or greater and;
(5) be seeking a Bachelor's degree.

GEOG. RESTRICTIONS: United States.

FINANCIAL DATA:
Amount of support per award: Up to $4,000 per academic year.
Total amount of support: Approximately $160,000 annually.

NO. MOST RECENT APPLICANTS: 120.

NO. AWARDS: 80.

APPLICATION INFO:
Applications can be downloaded from the web site, beginning April 1.
Duration: Renewable up to three years depending on need and maintenance of a 2.5 grade point average.
Deadline: May 15 for "getting started" part; June 15 for financial information.

PUBLICATIONS:
Financial Aid Programs.

ADDRESS INQUIRIES TO:
Financial Aid for Service
(See address above.)

PRESBYTERIAN CHURCH (U.S.A.)   [1566]
100 Witherspoon Street
Louisville, KY 40202-1396
(888) 728-7228 ext. 5224
Fax: (502) 569-8766
E-mail: finaid@pcusa.org
Web Site: www.pcusa.org/financialaid

NAME(S) OF PROGRAMS:
● **Samuel Robinson Award**

TYPE:
Awards/prizes. Essay contest, awarded to junior or senior undergraduate students enrolled full-time in one of the colleges/universities related to the Presbyterian Church (U.S.A.).

YEAR PROGRAM STARTED: 1940

PURPOSE:
To instill an interest in the work of the Presbyterian Church throughout the U.S.

LEGAL BASIS:
Nonprofit.

ELIGIBILITY:
Must be a member of the Presbyterian Church (U.S.A.) and a junior or senior attending a Presbyterian-related college or university.

GEOG. RESTRICTIONS: United States.

FINANCIAL DATA:
Amount of support per award: $1,500 to $7,500.
Total amount of support: Varies.

NO. MOST RECENT APPLICANTS: 2.

NO. AWARDS: Up to 10.

APPLICATION INFO:
Applications by request. Contact the Presbyterian Church (U.S.A.) or refer to web site.
Duration: One-time award.
Deadline: Proposals are reviewed on a rolling basis. Applications will be reviewed quarterly.

ADDRESS INQUIRIES TO:
Financial Aid for Service
(See address above.)

*SPECIAL STIPULATIONS:
Open to Presbyterian students attending a Presbyterian-related school.

THE PRESS CLUB OF ST. LOUIS CHARITABLE FUND - ST. LOUIS PRESS CLUB   [1567]
c/o The Press Club of St. Louis
P.O. Box 410522
Creve Couer, MO 63141
(314) 449-8029
Fax: (314) 317-0031
E-mail: info@stlpressclub.org
Web Site: stlpressclub.org

FOUNDED: 1956

AREAS OF INTEREST:
Journalism.

NAME(S) OF PROGRAMS:
● **Joe Bonwich Media Scholarship**

- **Donald R. Burris Journalism Scholarship**
- **Joan Foster Dames Women's Journalism Scholarship**
- **Fourth Estate Scholarships**
- **Karl Heinz and Doris Finzel Photojournalism Scholarship**
- **High School Journalism Scholarship**
- **Journalism Foundation Scholarships**
- **David S. Lipman Scholarship**
- **Sarah Bryan Miller Scholarship**
- **Press Club and St. Louis Post-Dispatch Ronald Wade Journalism Scholarship**
- **Press Club Internship Scholarships**
- **Press Club Journalism Scholarship**
- **Press Club Media Summer Internship Scholarships**
- **Press Club Neiman Marcus Media Scholarship**

TYPE:
Capital grants; Fellowships; Internships; Project/program grants; Scholarships.

YEAR PROGRAM STARTED: 1970

PURPOSE:
To award scholarships to those entering sophomore, junior and senior years of college or graduate school preparing for journalism/communications careers at recognized schools, majoring in journalism, broadcasting, English or related fields; to award fellowships for journalists to do investigative stories for publication.

LEGAL BASIS:
Incorporated as nonprofit organization in state of Missouri.

ELIGIBILITY:
Applicants for scholarships must be currently enrolled as full-time students who are intending to pursue a career in journalism, media communications or a related field; graduate students must carry at least six hours. Press Club Fellowship Program: Journalists with an investigative project concerning the St. Louis region.

GEOG. RESTRICTIONS: St. Louis, Missouri and counties of Franklin, Jefferson, Lincoln, St. Charles, St. Louis and Warren, and Illinois counties of Bond, Clinton, Jersey, Madison, Monroe and St. Clair.

FINANCIAL DATA:
Amount of support per award: Fellowship/Grants Program: Up to $10,000. Scholarships: $1,000 to $4,000.

CO-OP FUNDING PROGRAMS: Grants from member organizations.

NO. AWARDS: Grants: 1; Scholarships: Approximately 15.

APPLICATION INFO:
Consult the Press Club web site.
Deadline: Scholarships: April 15.

PUBLICATIONS:
Courier, newsletter.

IRS I.D.: 43-1489003

STAFF:
Glenda Partlow, Executive Director
Laura Schnarr, Development and Social Media Coordinator

ADDRESS INQUIRIES TO:
Glenda Partlow
Executive Director, Press Club
(See address above.)

RONALD REAGAN PRESIDENTIAL FOUNDATION AND INSTITUTE [1568]
40 Presidential Drive
Simi Valley, CA 93065
(571) 213-7970
E-mail: ekorsvall@reaganfoundation.org
Web Site: www.reaganfoundation.org/scholarships

FOUNDED: 1987

NAME(S) OF PROGRAMS:
- **GE-Reagan Foundation Scholarship Program**

TYPE:
Scholarships. The GE-Reagan Foundation Scholarship Program rewards college-bound students who demonstrate exemplary leadership, drive, integrity and citizenship with financial assistance to pursue higher education.

PURPOSE:
To honor the legacy and character of America's 40th president.

ELIGIBILITY:
Open to current high school seniors.

GEOG. RESTRICTIONS: United States.

FINANCIAL DATA:
Amount of support per award: $10,000 for each scholarship.

NO. AWARDS: Varies.

APPLICATION INFO:
Application information is available on the web site.
Duration: One academic year. Renewable for up to three additional years.
Deadline: Application is available in the fall and is due the first week of January. The scholarship will then be awarded for the next full academic year. Contact the Foundation for exact details.

ADDRESS INQUIRIES TO:
E-mail: ge-reagan@scholarshipamerica.org
Tel: (844) 402-0354

SID RICHARDSON MEMORIAL FUND [1569]
309 Main Street
Fort Worth, TX 76102
(817) 336-0494
Fax: (817) 339-7245
E-mail: mkuykendall@sidrichardson.org
Web Site: www.sidrichardsonmemorialfund.org

FOUNDED: 1965

AREAS OF INTEREST:
Academic and vocational scholarships.

TYPE:
Scholarships. Scholarships are for both academic and vocational studies.

YEAR PROGRAM STARTED: 1965

LEGAL BASIS:
Tax-exempt.

ELIGIBILITY:
Limited funds are available to assist in defraying the cost of college education or of vocational training. These scholarships are awarded on a competitive basis according to academic achievement and/or financial need.

Those eligible to apply for a Sid Richardson Memorial Fund scholarship are direct descendants (children or grandchildren) of persons who qualified for Early Retirement,

Normal Retirement, Disability Retirement, or Death Benefits from The Bass Retirement Plan (formerly The Retirement Plan For Employees of Bass Enterprises Production Co.), Retirement Plan for Employees of Barbnet/San Jose Cattle Co., Retirement Plan for Employees of City Center Development Co., City Club Retirement Plan, Retirement Plan for Employees of Richardson Aviation, G.P., Retirement Plan for Employees of Sid W. Richardson Foundation, or Retirement Plan for Employees of Sundance Square. Those eligible also include direct descendants (children or grandchildren) of persons presently employed with a minimum of three years' full-time service (as of March 31) with any of the following employers: Barbnet Investment Co., BBT Capital Management, LLC, BEPCO, L.P., City Club of Fort Worth, Richardson Aviation, San Jose Cattle Co., SHSM Partners, L.P., Sid Richardson Carbon Co. (SRCE, L.P.), Sid W. Richardson Foundation, and Sundance Square Management, L.P.

FINANCIAL DATA:
Amount of support per award: $1,000 to $25,000 per student per academic year.
Total amount of support: $545,000 for the year 2019.

NO. MOST RECENT APPLICANTS: Varies.

NO. AWARDS: 77 for the year 2019.

APPLICATION INFO:
Application request may be submitted via the Fund's web site. Follow "How to Apply" tab. You may also direct a written request for an application to Mary Kuykendall, Sid Richardson Memorial Fund, at the address, e-mail or fax number listed above. Include the student name, address, e-mail and telephone number, as well as the qualifying employee's name, last four digits of Social Security Number, qualifying company name and dates of employment, as well as relationship to the student.
Duration: Considered for renewal annually if a 2.0 grade point average is maintained for each semester.
Deadline: Completed applications must be postmarked no later than March 31 annually for the following academic year. Announcement of awards by May 31.

IRS I.D.: 75-1220266

OFFICERS:
Pete Geren, Executive Director
Shanda Ranelle, Treasurer
Mary Kuykendall, Secretary

BOARD OF DIRECTORS:
Thomas White, Chairman
Johnny Campbell, Vice President
William Jones, Vice President
Heidi McDonald, Vice President
Mitchell Roper, Vice President

ADDRESS INQUIRIES TO:
Mary Kuykendall, Scholarship Coordinator
(See address above.)

JACKIE ROBINSON FOUNDATION (JRF)
75 Varick Street, 2nd Floor
New York, NY 10013-1917
(212) 290-8600
Fax: (212) 290-8081
E-mail: general@jackierobinson.org
Web Site: www.jackierobinson.org

TYPE:
Conferences/seminars; Fellowships; Scholarships. The Foundation Scholarship Program (Mentoring and Leadership Program) is designed to address the financial needs of college students and provide comprehensive mentoring services through its 42 Strategies for Success Curriculum.

The Fellowship programs are follow-up programs to the JRF Scholars program (Mentoring and Leadership Program).

The Extra Innings Fellowship Program helps highly motivated JRF Scholars to fund the cost of advanced professional or graduate training.

The Rachel Robinson International Fellowship Program promotes and supports international service and study opportunities for JRF Scholars.

See entry 918 for full listing.

THE ROTARY CLUB OF BRYN MAWR [1570]
P.O. Box 84
Bryn Mawr, PA 19010
(484) 254-6377
E-mail: info@brynmawrrotary.org
Web Site: www.brynmawrrotary.org

FOUNDED: 1969

AREAS OF INTEREST:
To serve others and satisfy Rotary principles.

NAME(S) OF PROGRAMS:
● **Harry H. Cabell Scholarship Program**

TYPE:
Awards/prizes; Scholarships.

YEAR PROGRAM STARTED: 1985

PURPOSE:
To recognize and reward college students who meet trust requirements.

LEGAL BASIS:
Not-for-profit society.

ELIGIBILITY:
Financial need, high academic standards and leadership qualities, service to others and achievement qualities are important factors in the decision process. Applicants must be in an area college or university.

GEOG. RESTRICTIONS: Metropolitan Philadelphia and surrounding counties.

FINANCIAL DATA:
Amount of support per award: $2,500 for the year 2017.
Total amount of support: Varies.

NO. AWARDS: 2 for the year 2017.

APPLICATION INFO:
Application form must include recommendation from faculty, statement of good standing from dean, transcript of grades and 300-word essay.
Duration: One year. No renewals.
Deadline: Early March. Announcement approximately April 30.

ADDRESS INQUIRIES TO:
Richard Cuff, Scholarship Committee
Harry H. Cabell Scholarship Awards
(See address above.)

SHASTRI INDO-CANADIAN INSTITUTE (SICI)
1418 Education Tower
2500 University Drive, N.W.
Calgary AB T2N 1N4 Canada
(403) 220-3220
E-mail: maldeen@ucalgary.ca
Web Site: www.shastriinstitute.org

TYPE:
Fellowships; Internships; Travel grants. Collaborative research grants; Publication grants.

See entry 851 for full listing.

HORACE SMITH FUND [1571]
16 Union Avenue
Suite 2K
Westfield, MA 01085
(413) 739-4222
Fax: (413) 739-1108
E-mail: info@horacesmithfund.org
Web Site: www.horacesmithfund.org

FOUNDED: 1899

AREAS OF INTEREST:
Education, scholarships and fellowships.

TYPE:
Fellowships; Scholarships.

YEAR PROGRAM STARTED: 1899

PURPOSE:
To help students obtain scholarships and fellowships.

ELIGIBILITY:
For scholarships, students must have graduated from a high school in Hampden County. For fellowships, students must be legal residents of Hampden County.

GEOG. RESTRICTIONS: Hampden County, Massachusetts.

FINANCIAL DATA:
Amount of support per award: Scholarships: $3,000 per year for four years; Fellowships: $5,000 per year for up to three years.
Total amount of support: Varies.

NO. MOST RECENT APPLICANTS: Approximately 300 for the year 2019.

NO. AWARDS: Fellowships: 3; Scholarships: 20.

APPLICATION INFO:
Applications are available in September.
Duration: One year. Scholarships renewable up to four years; Fellowships up to three years.
Deadline: March 15.

PUBLICATIONS:
Annual report; contributions policy; application guidelines.

ADDRESS INQUIRIES TO:
Josephine Sarnelli, Executive Director
(See address above.)

*SPECIAL STIPULATIONS:
Hampden County, MA residents only.

SOCIETY OF DAUGHTERS OF THE U.S. ARMY [1572]
11804 Grey Birch Place
Reston, VA 20191-4223
E-mail: DUSAscholarships@gmail.com
Web Site: armydaughters.org

FOUNDED: 1928

NAME(S) OF PROGRAMS:
● **Society of Daughters of the United States Army Scholarships**

TYPE:
Scholarships.

PURPOSE:
To help daughters or granddaughters (including adopted or step) of career warrant and commissioned Army officers (Warrant Officers through General) who are on active duty, retired after at least 20 years of active service, were medically retired, or died while on active duty or after eligible retirement.

LEGAL BASIS:
Nonprofit corporation.

ELIGIBILITY:
For the Roberts, Wagner, Prickett, Simpson and DUSA Scholarships, applicants must be a daughter or granddaughter (including step or adopted) of a career warrant (WO 1-5) or commissioned (Second & First LT, CPT, MAJ, LTC, COL and BG, MG, LT or full General) officer of the U.S. Army who either:
(1) is currently on active duty;
(2) retired after at least 20 years of active service;
(3) was medically retired before 20 years of active service;
(4) died while on active duty or;
(5) died after retiring with 20 or more years of active service.

U.S. Army must have been the officer's primary occupation. These scholarships are for undergraduate study only and cover academic expenses only. Minimum grade point average is 3.0.

FINANCIAL DATA:
Amount of support per award: $1,500 per year.

NO. MOST RECENT APPLICANTS: 50.

NO. AWARDS: 11.

APPLICATION INFO:
Mail one request with the officer's name, rank, component (active, reserve, retired), inclusive dates of active duty, and the relationship to the applicant, along with a stamped, self-addressed envelope, to the Scholarship Chairman. Do not send any documentation. Requests for applications must be postmarked between November 1 and March 1 for awards in the next academic year. Office is closed between March 2 and October 31. Application is not available when office is closed. Application will not be sent without qualifying information.

Do not send by registered/certified or commercial mail; delivery will be delayed. All application submissions become the property of DUSA.
Duration: One year. The scholarships may be renewed annually for four years, provided a student maintains eligibility.
Deadline: March 1.

STAFF:
Mary P. Maroney, Chairman, Memorial and Scholarship Funds

ADDRESS INQUIRIES TO:
Mary P. Maroney, Scholarship Chairman
Daughters of the United States Army
(See address above.)

SOCIETY OF PHYSICS STUDENTS [1573]

One Physics Ellipse
College Park, MD 20740-3843
(301) 209-3007
E-mail: sps@aip.org
Web Site: www.spsnational.org

FOUNDED: 1968

AREAS OF INTEREST:
Physics.

NAME(S) OF PROGRAMS:
● **Society of Physics Students Leadership Scholarship**

TYPE:
Scholarships.

YEAR PROGRAM STARTED: 1985

PURPOSE:
To encourage the study of physics and the pursuit of high scholarship.

LEGAL BASIS:
Not-for-profit, 501(c)(3).

ELIGIBILITY:
Applicants must be a junior according to their institution's definition and plan to be enrolled as an undergraduate for at least one more semester. Only Society of Physics Students members are eligible. Scholarship is awarded on the basis of academic performance and leadership in the Society of Physics Students.

GEOG. RESTRICTIONS: United States.

FINANCIAL DATA:
Amount of support per award: $2,000 to $5,000.

NO. MOST RECENT APPLICANTS: 23.

NO. AWARDS: 17.

APPLICATION INFO:
Completed application form, official transcript of grades, and two letters of recommendation required. Applications are accepted through the online application system only.
Duration: One year. No renewals.
Deadline: March 15.

STAFF:
Mikayla Cleaver, Senior Programs Coordinator

ADDRESS INQUIRIES TO:
Mikayla Cleaver, Senior Programs Coordinator
(See address above.)

*SPECIAL STIPULATIONS:
Applicant must be an active member of the Society of Physics Students.

THE PAUL & DAISY SOROS FELLOWSHIPS FOR NEW AMERICANS [1574]

11 West 42nd Street, 3rd Floor
New York, NY 10036
(212) 405-8234
E-mail: pdsoros@pdsoros.org
Web Site: www.pdsoros.org

FOUNDED: 1997

AREAS OF INTEREST:
Graduate education support for New Americans.

TYPE:
Fellowships.

PURPOSE:
To provide graduate school support to promising New Americans who will go on and make distinctive contributions to American society, culture, or their field.

ELIGIBILITY:
A New American is defined as an individual who:
(1) has been naturalized as a U.S. citizen;
(2) is a resident alien (i.e., holds a Green Card);
(3) was adopted from abroad;
(4) has refugee or asylee status or;
(5) if none of these statuses, then graduated from both high school and college in the U.S. (including DACA recipients).

Whether born abroad or in the U.S., both birth parents must have been born abroad as non-U.S. citizens.

If applicant was raised by only one parent (single parent household), then they are eligible if:
(1) the parent who raised them was born abroad as a non-U.S. citizen and;
(2) the second birth parent was not part of their life growing up and they do not have contact with them.

GEOG. RESTRICTIONS: United States.

FINANCIAL DATA:
Amount of support per award: Fellow receives maintenance grant of $25,000 and a tuition grant of one-half tuition cost of U.S. graduate program attended, up to a maximum of $20,000 per annum.

NO. MOST RECENT APPLICANTS: Over 2,400 annually.

NO. AWARDS: 30 per year.

APPLICATION INFO:
Applications must be submitted via the online application system.
Duration: Up to two years.
Deadline: October 28.

ADDRESS INQUIRIES TO:
Yulian Ramos, Deputy Director
(See e-mail address above.)

*SPECIAL STIPULATIONS:
Must be 30 years old or younger by deadline in order to be eligible.

SOUTH CAROLINA HIGHER EDUCATION TUITION GRANTS COMMISSION [1575]

111 Executive Center Drive
Suite 242
Columbia, SC 29210
(803) 896-1120
E-mail: info@sctuitiongrants.org
Web Site: www.sctuitiongrants.org

FOUNDED: 1970

AREAS OF INTEREST:
Undergraduate student financial aid to eligible South Carolina residents attending in-state, independent colleges on a full-time basis.

CONSULTING OR VOLUNTEER SERVICES:
Assistance to South Carolina high schools and colleges with questions and problems pertaining to student financial aid.

NAME(S) OF PROGRAMS:
● **South Carolina Tuition Grants Program**

TYPE:
Grants-in-aid.

YEAR PROGRAM STARTED: 1970

PURPOSE:
To increase the level of college attendance in South Carolina and to better utilize the existing educational resources of the state; to give students a choice of attending the college that best meets their academic needs.

LEGAL BASIS:
Established by state statute.

ELIGIBILITY:
Applicant must be a South Carolina resident, demonstrate good moral character, be accepted by or enrolled full-time in an eligible South Carolina private college and have financial need. Incoming freshmen must rank in the upper three-quarters of their class or score 900 or higher on the re-centered SAT, score 19 or higher on the ACT, or graduate with a minimum 2.7 grade point average on the SC Uniform Grading Scale. Renewal applicants must complete at least 24 semester-hours per year.

GEOG. RESTRICTIONS: South Carolina.

FINANCIAL DATA:
Awards cannot exceed tuition and fees at the institution, the need of the student and the average per-pupil expenditure by the state at a public college.
Amount of support per award: $100 to $3,600 per year. Average grant $3,100 for the year 2019-20.
Total amount of support: Approximately $44,100,000 total state appropriations for the 2019-20.

NO. MOST RECENT APPLICANTS: 34,531 for the year 2019-20.

NO. AWARDS: 12,850 for the year 2019-20.

APPLICATION INFO:
Application available online.
Duration: One year. Renewable if need continues for up to eight semesters. Must reapply each year.
Deadline: June 30.

PUBLICATIONS:
Annual report; general brochure.

GRANTS COMMITTEE:
Dr. Darrell Parker, Chairperson
Dr. Rosalyn Clark Artis, Vice Chairperson
Scott Cochran, Secretary
Dr. Robert Gustafson
Dr. Ronnie Hopkins
Dr. Rusty Monhollon
Steve Pettit
Dr. Leroy Staggers
Dr. Dwaun Warmack

ADDRESS INQUIRIES TO:
Zachary Christian, Deputy Director
(See address above.)

STATE COUNCIL OF HIGHER EDUCATION FOR VIRGINIA [1576]

James Monroe Building, 10th Floor
101 North 14th Street
Richmond, VA 23219
(804) 225-2600
Fax: (804) 225-2604
E-mail: communications@schev.edu
Web Site: www.schev.edu

FOUNDED: 1956

AREAS OF INTEREST:
Statewide coordination of higher education.

NAME(S) OF PROGRAMS:
- **Virginia Tuition Assistance Grant Program (VTAG)**

TYPE:
Grants-in-aid.

YEAR PROGRAM STARTED: 1972

PURPOSE:
To assist Virginia residents who attend accredited private, nonprofit colleges and universities in Virginia.

LEGAL BASIS:
State agency. Program mandated by state law.

ELIGIBILITY:
Recipients must be domiciliary residents of Virginia who are enrolled full-time at an approved private college or university within the state. Not available at Virginia public institutions, for-profit institutions or non-Virginia institutions. Awards are not based on financial need.

Graduate students must be enrolled in a health-related professional program.

Students may not be enrolled in a program of religious training or theological education.

GEOG. RESTRICTIONS: Virginia.

FINANCIAL DATA:
Funding is specified biennially by the Appropriations Act.
Amount of support per award: Up to $4,000 for Undergraduate and $2,000 for Graduate for the academic year 2021-22, depending on amount of appropriation and number of recipients (less for students enrolled in online programs).
Total amount of support: $71,098,303 for the academic year 2020-21.

NO. AWARDS: Approximately 22,000 for the academic year 2020-21.

APPLICATION INFO:
Application is available from participating private colleges or universities in Virginia.
Duration: Nine months (academic year). Renewals are reviewed by the institutions.
Deadline: July 31. December 1 for late applications.

ADDRESS INQUIRIES TO:
Applicants should contact the financial aid officer at the participating private Virginia college or university they plan to attend.

STATE OF IDAHO BOARD OF EDUCATION   [1577]
650 West State Street, No. 307
Boise, ID 83720-0037
(208) 332-1595
Fax: (208) 334-2632
E-mail: scholarshiphelp@osbe.idaho.gov
Web Site: www.boardofed.idaho.
gov/scholarship/idaho-opportunity-scholarship

FOUNDED: 1891

AREAS OF INTEREST:
Idaho education.

NAME(S) OF PROGRAMS:
- **Idaho Opportunity Scholarship**

TYPE:
Scholarships. Scholarships are available for high school and college students.

YEAR PROGRAM STARTED: 2009

PURPOSE:
To provide scholarships for Idaho citizens who have graduated from an Idaho high school or earned their GED in Idaho.

LEGAL BASIS:
Idaho Code Title 33, Chapter 43 (33-4303).

ELIGIBILITY:
The following scholarship application requirements apply:
(1) Idaho residency;
(2) graduation from an Idaho high school;
(3) grade point average of 3.0;
(4) demonstration of need by completion of Free Application for Federal Student Aid (FAFSA) and;
(5) U.S. citizenship or residency.

GEOG. RESTRICTIONS: Idaho.

FINANCIAL DATA:
Scholarship award cannot exceed cost of attendance.
Amount of support per award: $3,500.
Total amount of support: $20,777,300 for the year 2019.

NO. MOST RECENT APPLICANTS: 5,261.

NO. AWARDS: 6,438 new and renewals for the year 2019.

APPLICATION INFO:
An application form needs to be completed. Apply online at the web site address above from December 1 to March 1 of the following year.
Duration: Four years. Scholarship is renewable.
Deadline: March 1.

STAFF:
Joy Miller, Scholarships Program Manager

ADDRESS INQUIRIES TO:
Scholarships Program Manager
(See address above.)

STATE OF IDAHO BOARD OF EDUCATION   [1578]
P.O. Box 983
Boise, ID 83701
(208) 342-0777
(208) 334-2270
E-mail: scholarshiphelp@osbe.idaho.gov
Web Site: www.idahogovernorscup.org
www.boardofed.idaho.gov/scholarship/idaho-governors-cup-scholarship

FOUNDED: 1891

AREAS OF INTEREST:
Idaho education.

NAME(S) OF PROGRAMS:
- **Idaho Governor's Cup Scholarship**

TYPE:
Scholarships. Scholarships are available for high school seniors and home school students throughout Idaho.

YEAR PROGRAM STARTED: 1974

PURPOSE:
To provide scholarships for Idaho citizens who have graduated from an Idaho high school or earned their GED in Idaho.

LEGAL BASIS:
Idaho Code Title 33, Chapter 43 (33-4303).

ELIGIBILITY:
To qualify for the scholarship, a student must meet all of the following criteria:
(1) be a resident of Idaho;
(2) be a graduating senior of an Idaho high school or home school;
(3) enroll as a full-time student in an academic or technical program at an Idaho college or university, taking the ACT or SAT if enrolling in an academic program;

(4) have a cumulative grade point average of 2.8 or above and;
(5) attend the first semester of college following graduation.

High consideration for selection will be based on a demonstrated commitment to public service. Documentation of volunteer work, leadership, and public service is required.

GEOG. RESTRICTIONS: Idaho.

FINANCIAL DATA:
Amount of support per award: $3,000.

NO. AWARDS: Approximately 25.

APPLICATION INFO:
Application requires:
(1) completion of the online application;
(2) two letters of recommendation from individuals who are unrelated to the applicant, yet know of their interests, achievements and commitment to public service;
(3) an essay of no more than 500 words sharing a little information about the applicant. Make sure to include academic interests and what the applicant hopes to accomplish individually and for others in the future and;
(4) completed online forms detailing a commitment to public service including, but not limited to, school, community and church volunteer service projects, and participation in other service organizations and volunteer work.
Duration: One year. Renewable up to four years for academic programs and up to three years for career technical programs.
Deadline: February 15 for academic programs; March 15 for career technical programs.

STAFF:
Carlie Foster, Executive Director
Mikayla Mitzel, Scholarship Manager

BOARD OF DIRECTORS AND OFFICERS:
Doug Sayer, President
Mike Reynoldson, Vice President
Cordell Chigbrow, Treasurer
Jeremy Pisca, Secretary
Mike Brassey
Ken Dey
Scott Madison
Jason Kreizenbeck
Jayson Ronk
Pat Sullivan
Anna Torma
Tim Vedder

ADDRESS INQUIRIES TO:
High school counselor or scholarship program manager
(See e-mail address above.)

STATE OF MICHIGAN DEPARTMENT OF TREASURY   [1579]
P.O. Box 30462
Lansing, MI 48909-7962
(888) 447-2687
Fax: (517) 241-5835
E-mail: mistudentaid@michigan.gov
Web Site: www.michigan.gov/mistudentaid

AREAS OF INTEREST:
Promoting and aiding student higher education in the state of Michigan.

NAME(S) OF PROGRAMS:
- **Children of Veterans Tuition Grant (CVTG)**
- **Dual Enrollment**
- **Fostering Futures Scholarship**
- **Michigan Competitive Scholarship (MCS)**
- **Michigan Gear Up**

TYPE:
Grants-in-aid; Scholarships.

ELIGIBILITY:
All state of Michigan programs require: (1) high school diploma, certificate of completion, or GED; (2) Michigan residency of at least one year prior to enrollment; (3) U.S. citizenship, permanent residency or approved refugee status; (4) at least half-time enrollment at an approved Michigan college or university; (5) student not being in default on a federal student loan and; (6) the student meeting Satisfactory Academic Progress (SAP) standards as set by the institution.

Children of Veterans Tuition Grant: Student must be the natural or adopted child of a Michigan veteran who is totally and permanently disabled, deceased or missing in action. Student must be at least 16 and less than 21 years old and must maintain a cumulative grade point average of 2.25 for renewal.

Dual Enrollment: Students attending a private high school are determined eligible by the Michigan Department of Education (MDE).

Fostering Futures Scholarship: Student must have been in foster care after the 13th birthday. There is no upper age limit and student can receive funding at any age. Student must be attending a Michigan public or private four-year college/university or a community college. Funding can be used along with the Education Training Voucher.

Michigan Competitive Scholarship: Student must have an SAT score of 1200 and a qualifying ACT score of at least 23 (composite) or 90 (scaled score) and cannot be attending an institution whose primary purpose is to prepare students for ordination or appointment as a member of the clergy of a church, denomination or religious sect. Student must maintain a minimum cumulative 2.0 grade point average.

Michigan Gear Up: Only nominated participants will be eligible for a scholarship.

FINANCIAL DATA:
Fostering Futures provides eligible foster youth with scholarship funds for tuition, fees, room/board, books and supplies/equipment required for enrollment. Michigan Competitive Scholarship program is both merit- and need-based. Limited to tuition and mandatory fees.
Amount of support per award: Children of Veterans Tuition Grant: Up to $2,800 per academic year (award limited to tuition and mandatory fees); Fostering Futures Scholarship: Up to $3,000; Michigan Competitive Scholarship: Up to $1,000 per academic year; Michigan Gear Up: Maximum $1,000.

APPLICATION INFO:
Fostering Futures Scholarship: Application must be submitted with copies of student financial aid award letter, most recent transcripts, and documentation supporting any off-campus expenses requested.

Duration: Children of Veterans Tuition Grant and Michigan Gear Up: Up to four academic years. Michigan Competitive Scholarship: Limited to 10 semesters or 15 terms.
Deadline: Varies.

ADDRESS INQUIRIES TO:
State of Michigan
Student Scholarships and Grants
(See address and e-mail above.)

STATE OF MICHIGAN DEPARTMENT OF TREASURY [1580]

P.O. Box 30462
Lansing, MI 48909-7962
(888) 447-2687
Fax: (517) 241-5835
E-mail: mistudentaid@michigan.gov
Web Site: www.michigan.gov/mistudentaid

NAME(S) OF PROGRAMS:
- **Michigan Tuition Grant (MTG)**
- **Police Officer's and Fire Fighter's Survivor Tuition Grant (STG)**
- **Tuition Incentive Program (TIP)**

TYPE:
Grants-in-aid.

ELIGIBILITY:
Michigan Tuition Grant: Program is need-based. Student must be enrolled at an approved independent, degree-granting Michigan institution. However, student cannot be enrolled in a course of study leading to a degree in theology, divinity or religious education.

Police Officer's and Fire Fighter's Survivor Tuition Grant: For children and surviving spouses of Michigan police officers and firefighters killed in the line of duty. Must provide satisfactory proof. Child must be less than 21 at the time of the police officer's or firefighter's death and must apply before age 21. Award recipient must enroll at least half-time in a program leading to a certificate or degree at an approved Michigan community college or public university. Applicant must, excluding death benefits, be below 400% of the federal poverty level (must demonstrate financial need).

Tuition Incentive Program: Student must have received Medicaid coverage, as determined by The Michigan Department of Human Services (DHS), for 24 months within any 36 consecutive months between the ages of 9 and high school graduation. Awardee must begin using program within four years from high school graduation. Eligibility ends after six years from the date of high school graduation.

FINANCIAL DATA:
Police Officer's and Fire Fighter's Survivor Tuition Grant: Award limited to tuition only. Tuition Incentive Program: Award limited to tuition and mandatory fees; eligible mandatory fees cannot exceed $250 per semester or term.
Amount of support per award: Michigan Tuition Grant: Up to $2,400 per academic year. Award limited to tuition and mandatory fees.

APPLICATION INFO:
Details are available online.
Duration: Michigan Tuition Grant: Limited to 10 semesters or 15 terms. Police Officer's and Fire Fighter's Survivor Tuition Grant: Limited to 9 semesters or 14 terms (124

semester- or 180 term-credits). Tuition Incentive Program: Pays up to 24 semester- or 36 term-credits per academic year; cannot exceed 80 semester- or 120 term-credits.
Deadline: Michigan Tuition Grant: March 1. Tuition Incentive Program: August 31.

ADDRESS INQUIRIES TO:
State of Michigan
Student Scholarships and Grants
(See address and e-mail above.)

SUDBURY FOUNDATION

326 Concord Road
Sudbury, MA 01776
(978) 443-0849
Fax: (978) 579-9536
E-mail: contact@sudburyfoundation.org
Web Site: www.sudburyfoundation.org

TYPE:
Project/program grants; Scholarships. Capacity-building grants.

See entry 1253 for full listing.

SYRACUSE UNIVERSITY [1581]

Graduate School
304 Lyman Hall
Syracuse, NY 13244-1200
(315) 443-1701
E-mail: gradawd@syr.edu
Web Site: www.syr.edu

AREAS OF INTEREST:
Student work/study programs.

NAME(S) OF PROGRAMS:
- **Syracuse University Graduate Assistantships**

TYPE:
Assistantships. Syracuse University Graduate Assistantships are of a teaching or research nature.

FINANCIAL DATA:
Amount of support per award: Determined by department.

APPLICATION INFO:
Applicants must apply through departments.
Duration: One year. Renewable, depending upon student's performance and departmental need.
Deadline: Varies by program and is dependent upon admission deadline.

ADDRESS INQUIRIES TO:
Academic department of interest.

SYRACUSE UNIVERSITY [1582]

Graduate School
304 Lyman Hall
Syracuse, NY 13244-1200
(315) 443-1701
E-mail: gradawd@syr.edu
Web Site: www.syr.edu

AREAS OF INTEREST:
Graduate university education.

NAME(S) OF PROGRAMS:
- **African American Graduate Fellowship**
- **STEM Doctoral Fellowships**
- **Syracuse University Fellowship**

TYPE:
Fellowships.

PURPOSE:
To provide a full support package during a student's term of study.

ELIGIBILITY:
African American Graduate Fellowships: Awarded annually to new and continuing students across disciplines whose work supports that of the African American Studies Program.

STEM Doctoral Fellowships: Science, technology, engineering and math disciplines. Open to members of an underrepresented group who are U.S. citizens or permanent residents.

Syracuse University Fellowships: Open to nationals of any country.

FINANCIAL DATA:
Fellowships include up to 30 credits of tuition.

Amount of support per award: $15,425 for Master's stipend plus full tuition; $25,290 for Ph.D. stipend for full tuition.

NO. AWARDS: African American Graduate Fellowship: 6 new per year; STEM Doctoral Fellowships: Up to 5 new per year; Syracuse University Fellowship: Number of awards determined by each academic college, varies yearly.

APPLICATION INFO:
Applicants must apply through admission application.

Duration: Varies by fellowship type, one to five years.

Deadline: January 1, unless earlier date determined by specific department.

ADDRESS INQUIRIES TO:
See e-mail address above.

TENNESSEE STUDENT ASSISTANCE CORPORATION   [1583]

312 Rosa Parks Avenue, 9th Floor
Nashville, TN 37243
(615) 741-1346
(800) 342-1663
Fax: (615) 741-6101
E-mail: tsac.aidinfo@tn.gov
Web Site: www.tn.gov/collegepays

FOUNDED: 1974

NAME(S) OF PROGRAMS:
- **Dependent Children Scholarship Program**
- **Graduate Nursing Loan-Forgiveness Program**
- **Ned McWherter Scholars Program**
- **Minority Teaching Fellows Program**
- **Tennessee Education Lottery Scholarship Program**
- **Tennessee Math & Science Teachers Loan Forgiveness Program**
- **Tennessee Promise**
- **Tennessee Reconnect**
- **Tennessee Student Assistance Award**
- **Tennessee Teaching Scholars Program**

TYPE:
Grants-in-aid; Scholarships; Loan forgiveness programs. Need-based grants for undergraduate Tennessee residents enrolled in an eligible Tennessee institution.

Dependent Children Scholarship Program provides aid for Tennessee residents who are dependent children of a Tennessee law enforcement officer, fireman or an emergency medical service technician who has been killed or totally and permanently disabled while performing duties within the scope of such employment.

Graduate Nursing Loan-Forgiveness Program is designed to encourage Tennessee residents who are nurses to become teachers and administrators in Tennessee nursing education programs. Participants in this program incur an obligation to enter a faculty or administrative position in a nursing education program, in Tennessee, immediately upon completion of the education program.

The Ned McWherter Scholars Program is intended to encourage academically superior Tennessee high school graduates to attend college in Tennessee.

Minority Teaching Fellows Program is intended to encourage talented minority Tennesseans to enter the teaching field in Tennessee.

Tennessee Education Lottery Scholarship Program is for those who have been a Tennessee resident for one year by September 1 of the year of application date.

Tennessee Math & Science Teachers Loan Forgiveness Program provides financial assistance to Tennessee public school teachers seeking an advanced degree in a math or a science, or a certification to teach a math or a science. Loan forgiveness requires employment in a Tennessee public school system two years for each year of the loan funding received.

Tennesee Promise is both a scholarship and mentoring program focused on increasing the number of students that attend college in the state. It provides students a last-dollar scholarship, meaning the scholarship will cover tuition and fees not covered by the Pell grant, the HOPE scholarship, or state student assistance funds. Students may use the scholarship at any of the state's 13 community colleges, 27 colleges of applied technology, or other eligible institutions offering an Associate's degree program.

Tennessee Reconnect is Governor Bill Haslam's initiative to help more of the state's adults enter higher education to gain new skills, advance in the workplace, and fulfill lifelong dreams of completing a degree or credential.

Tennessee Student Assistance Award provides nonrepayable financial assistance to financially needy undergraduate students who are residents of Tennessee.

Tennessee Teaching Scholars Program is intended to encourage exemplary students to enter the teaching field in Tennessee.

YEAR PROGRAM STARTED: 1976

PURPOSE:
To provide grants based on financial need for Tennessee residents.

LEGAL BASIS:
State agency.

ELIGIBILITY:
Applicants for the Ned McWherter Scholars Program must be high school seniors with a 3.5 grade point average, a GED score of 570 and 29 ACT or 1280 SAT, and planning to attend an eligible Tennessee institution.

Applicants for the Minority Teaching Fellows Program are preferably high school seniors with a 2.75 grade point average and 18 ACT or be at the top 25% of their graduating class. Undergraduate applicants must have a 2.5 college grade point average.

Applicants for the Tennessee Education Lottery Scholarship Program must:
(1) be entering freshmen who are Tennessee residents for one year prior to application;
(2) enroll in a Tennessee public college/university or enroll in a Tennessee private college/university that is accredited by the Southern Association of Colleges and Schools and;
(3) be enrolled full-time (part-time prorated), leading to a certificate in the Tennessee Technology Centers or degree in approved colleges and universities. Satisfactory academic progress required.

Applicants for the Tennessee Teaching Scholars Program must be college juniors or seniors or post-Baccalaureate students admitted to teacher education programs in Tennessee colleges or universities and U.S. citizens.

GEOG. RESTRICTIONS: Tennessee.

FINANCIAL DATA:
Amount of support per award: Varies.
Matching fund requirements: For Ned McWherter Scholars Program, the institution must match $3,000.

NO. MOST RECENT APPLICANTS: Ned McWherter Scholars: 900; Minority Teaching Fellows: 150; Tennessee Teaching Scholars: 400.

NO. AWARDS: Ned McWherter Scholars: 50; Minority Teaching Fellows: 29; Tennessee Education Lottery Scholarship Program: 40,000; Tennessee Teaching Scholars: 160.

APPLICATION INFO:
Detailed information is available online.
Duration: Renewable each academic year.
Deadline: Ned McWherter Scholars: February 15; Minority Teaching Fellows: April 15; Tennessee Education Lottery Scholarship Program: September 1 for fall term, February 1 for spring and summer terms; Tennessee Teaching Scholars: April 15.

ADDRESS INQUIRIES TO:
See telephone numbers above.

*SPECIAL STIPULATIONS:
Loan Forgiveness Programs, Tennessee Teaching Scholars and Minority Teaching Fellows: Recipients agree to teach one year for each year of funding in a public Tennessee grades K-12 school or appropriate learning institution or repayment will be required.

TWO TEN FOOTWEAR FOUNDATION   [1584]

Scholarship Department
1466 Main Street
Waltham, MA 02451
(781) 736-1500
Fax: (781) 736-1554
E-mail: socialservices@twoten.org
Web Site: twoten.org

FOUNDED: 1939

AREAS OF INTEREST:
All disciplines of study.

NAME(S) OF PROGRAMS:
- **Two Ten Footwear Foundation Scholarship Program**

TYPE:
Scholarships. Offered to footwear employees and their dependents.

YEAR PROGRAM STARTED: 1969

PURPOSE:
To provide financial assistance to people in the footwear, leather and allied industries.

LEGAL BASIS:
Private foundation.

ELIGIBILITY:
Scholarship applicant must work in or be the dependent of an employee in the footwear, leather or allied industries:
(1) either the student must be employed in the above industries, or have a parent (natural, step or adopted) who must be employed in these industries for a minimum of two years prior to January 1 (student must be considered a dependent);
(2) student must display financial need for college costs as calculated by the federal method of need analysis and the Two Ten Selection Committee;
(3) student must be a U.S. citizen or eligible noncitizen and;
(4) student must enroll at an accredited college, university, nursing or vocational/technical school, earning a two- or four-year undergraduate degree.

FINANCIAL DATA:
Amount of support per award: Generally, up to $4,000; Members of National Shoe Travelers and retailers of the National Shoe and Shoe Retailers Association: Up to $5,000.
Total amount of support: Approximately $999,500 for the year 2019.

NO. AWARDS: 300 for the year 2019.

APPLICATION INFO:
Contact the Foundation.
Duration: Up to four years.
Deadline: April 1.

ADDRESS INQUIRIES TO:
See e-mail address above.

*SPECIAL STIPULATIONS:
Eligible companies must do at least 50% of their business in footwear, or applicant or parent must work in a specific footwear division.

TWO TEN FOOTWEAR FOUNDATION   [1585]
1466 Main Street
Waltham, MA 02451
(781) 736-1500
Fax: (781) 736-1554
E-mail: socialservices@twoten.org
Web Site: twoten.org

AREAS OF INTEREST:
Footwear design.

NAME(S) OF PROGRAMS:
● **Two Ten Footwear Foundation Design Scholarship Program**

TYPE:
Scholarships. Intended for students who are interested in pursuing a career in footwear design.

YEAR PROGRAM STARTED: 2003

PURPOSE:
To provide financial aid to those studying footwear design.

ELIGIBILITY:
Applicant must:
(1) demonstrate an interest and commitment to a career in footwear design;
(2) be a U.S. citizen or eligible noncitizen;
(3) display financial need as calculated by the

federal method of need analysis and the Design Scholarship Selection Committee (applicant can estimate Expected Family Contribution at www.finaid.com) and;
(4) attend or plan to attend an approved postsecondary institution.

GEOG. RESTRICTIONS: United States.

FINANCIAL DATA:
Amount of support per award: Up to $4,000.
Total amount of support: Varies.

NO. AWARDS: Varies.

APPLICATION INFO:
Applicants for consideration must submit a portfolio. Interested candidates must contact the director of scholarship for further information.
Duration: Up to four years.
Deadline: April 1.

ADDRESS INQUIRIES TO:
See e-mail address above.

U.S. DEPARTMENT OF EDUCATION   [1586]
Federal Student Aid Programs
830 First Street, N.E.
Washington, DC 20202
(800) 433-3243
TTY: (800)-730-8913
E-mail: studentaid@ed.gov
Web Site: studentaid.gov

AREAS OF INTEREST:
Student financial aid.

NAME(S) OF PROGRAMS:
● **Pell Grant**

TYPE:
Grants-in-aid. Student aid grants for higher education. Available almost exclusively to undergraduates. Grant does not have to be repaid.

YEAR PROGRAM STARTED: 1973

PURPOSE:
To help undergraduates pay for education after high school.

LEGAL BASIS:
Title IV, Higher Education Act of 1965, as amended.

ELIGIBILITY:
In general, the aid recipient must:
(1) show financial need;
(2) enroll as a regular student in an eligible degree or certificate program;
(3) be a U.S. citizen or eligible noncitizen and;
(4) meet the school's satisfactory academic progress standards in his or her course of study.

The student also must register with the Selective Service, if required.

FINANCIAL DATA:
Amount of support per award: Depends on student's financial need, the cost of attendance (COA) at the student's school, status as full-time or part-time student and how long the student will be enrolled in the academic year in question. The financial aid office at student's college or career school will determine how much financial aid he or she is eligible to receive.

APPLICATION INFO:
Applicants should contact the financial aid office at each school they are considering attending to determine which forms must be

submitted. Students can request a copy of the *Student Guide* at the toll-free telephone number.
Duration: One year. Renewable. Student can receive Federal Pell Grant for no more than 12 semesters or the equivalent (roughly six years).

PUBLICATIONS:
Funding Education Beyond High School: The Guide to Federal Student Aid.

ADDRESS INQUIRIES TO:
Federal Student Aid Programs
P.O. Box 84
Washington, DC 20044

*PLEASE NOTE:
Applicant may receive only one Pell Grant in an award year, and may not receive Pell Grant funds from more than one school at a time.

U.S. DEPARTMENT OF EDUCATION   [1587]
Federal Student Aid Programs
830 First Street, N.E.
Washington, DC 20202
(800) 433-3243
TTY: (800) 730-8913
E-mail: studentaid@ed.gov
Web Site: studentaid.gov

AREAS OF INTEREST:
Student financial aid.

NAME(S) OF PROGRAMS:
● **Federal Work-Study**

TYPE:
Work-study programs. Federal Work-Study program provides part-time jobs for undergraduate and graduate students with financial need. This allows them to earn money to help pay education expenses. Jobs can be on- or off-campus and are available to full-time or part-time students. Students are paid at least federal minimum wage. The money earned does not have to be repaid. The program is administered by schools participating in the Federal Work-Study Program. Interested students should check with their school's financial aid office to determine if their school does participate.

PURPOSE:
To enable students to earn a part of educational expenses.

LEGAL BASIS:
Government agency.

ELIGIBILITY:
In general, the aid recipient must:
(1) show financial need;
(2) be a U.S. citizen or eligible noncitizen with a valid Social Security number (SSN);
(3) be working toward a degree or certificate in an eligible program;
(4) demonstrate one is qualified to obtain a postsecondary education;
(5) register (if not already done so) with the Selective Service, if one is a male between the ages of 18 and 25 and;
(6) maintain satisfactory academic progress once in school.

FINANCIAL DATA:
Federal Work-Study wages will be at least the current federal minimum wage, but may be higher, depending on the type of work and the skills required. The total Federal Work-Study award depends on when a student applies, one's level of need, and the funding level of one's school.
Amount of support per award: Varies.

Total amount of support: Varies.

APPLICATION INFO:
The interested student should consult with his or her school's financial aid office.

Duration: One year. Renewable.

PUBLICATIONS:
Funding Your Education: The Guide to Federal Student Aid.

ADDRESS INQUIRIES TO:
Federal Student Aid Programs
P.O. Box 84
Washington, DC 20044

U.S. DEPARTMENT OF EDUCATION   [1588]
Federal Student Aid Programs
830 First Street, N.E.
Washington, DC 20202
(800) 433-3243
TTY: (800) 730-8913 (for hearing-impaired)
E-mail: studentaid@ed.gov
Web Site: studentaid.gov

AREAS OF INTEREST:
Student financial aid.

NAME(S) OF PROGRAMS:
● **Federal Supplemental Educational Opportunity Grant (FSEOG)**

TYPE:
Grants-in-aid. Federal Supplemental Educational Opportunity Grant (FSEOG) is a grant for undergraduate students with exceptional financial need. This grant does not need to be repaid. The program is administered directly by the financial aid office at each participating school and is therefore called "campus-based" aid. Not all schools participate.

PURPOSE:
To help undergraduates with exceptional financial need.

ELIGIBILITY:
FSEOG is awarded to undergraduate students who have exceptional financial need and who have not earned a Bachelor's or graduate degree. Federal Pell Grant recipients receive priority.

FINANCIAL DATA:
Amount of support per award: $100 to $4,000 a year, depending on student's financial need, when student applied, the amount of other aid student has received, and the availability of funds at student's school.

APPLICATION INFO:
Student should check with his or her school's financial aid office to ascertain if the school offers the FSEOG.

Deadline: Each school sets its own deadlines for campus-based funds.

*PLEASE NOTE:
Each participating school receives a certain amount of FSEOG funds each year from the U.S. Department of Education's office of Federal Student Aid. Once the full amount of the school's FSEOG funds has been awarded to students, no more FSEOG awards can be made for that year.

U.S. DEPARTMENT OF EDUCATION   [1589]
Federal Student Aid Programs
830 First Street, N.E.
Washington, DC 20202
(800) 433-3243
TTY: (800) 730-8913 (for hearing-impaired)
E-mail: studentaid@ed.gov
Web Site: studentaid.gov

AREAS OF INTEREST:
Student financial aid.

NAME(S) OF PROGRAMS:
● **Teacher Education Assistance for College and Higher Education (TEACH) Grant**

TYPE:
Grants-in-aid. Grant does not have to be repaid unless recipient fails to carry out the service obligation.

PURPOSE:
To help undergraduate, post-Baccalaureate and graduate students with financial need.

ELIGIBILITY:
The TEACH Grant is intended for undergraduate, post-Baccalaureate and graduate students who plan to become elementary or secondary teachers. Recipient must sign Agreement to Serve saying he or she will teach full-time in a high-need field for four complete years (within eight years of completing the academic program) at an elementary school, secondary school or educational service agency serving children from low-income families. Grant recipient must attend a participating college and meet certain academic achievement requirements. Failure to complete the teaching service commitment will result in the grant being converted to a Direct Unsubsidized Loan that must be repaid.

FINANCIAL DATA:
Amount of support per award: Up to $4,000 per year.

APPLICATION INFO:
Those interested in applying must contact the financial aid office at the school where they will be enrolled to find out whether the school participates in the TEACH Grant Program and to learn about the programs of study at the school that are TEACH-grant eligible.

THE MORRIS K. UDALL AND STEWART L. UDALL FOUNDATION   [1590]
130 South Scott Avenue
Tucson, AZ 85701
(520) 901-8564
Fax: (520) 901-8570
E-mail: curley@udall.gov
Web Site: www.udall.gov

FOUNDED: 1992

AREAS OF INTEREST:
Environment, including policy, engineering, science, education, urban planning and renewal, business, justice and economics; Native American health care and tribal public policy, including policy, engineering, science, education and business.

NAME(S) OF PROGRAMS:
● **Udall Scholarship**

TYPE:
Scholarships. The Udall Foundation seeks future leaders across a wide spectrum of

environmental fields, including policy, engineering, science, education, urban planning and renewal, business, justice and economics.

The Udall Foundation also seeks future Native American and Alaska Native leaders in Native American health care and tribal public policy. Tribal policy includes fields related to tribal sovereignty, tribal governance, tribal law, Native American education, Native American justice, natural resource management, cultural preservation and revitalization, Native American economic development and other areas affecting Native American communities. Native American health care includes health care administration, social work, medicine and research into health conditions affecting Native American communities.

YEAR PROGRAM STARTED: 1996

PURPOSE:
To educate a new generation of Americans to preserve and protect their national heritage through studies in the environment, Native American health and tribal policy, and effective public policy conflict resolution.

LEGAL BASIS:
The Foundation is an executive branch agency. The President of the U.S. appoints its board of trustees with the advice and consent of the U.S. Senate.

ELIGIBILITY:
Citizens, nationals or permanent residents of the U.S. are eligible to apply. The scholarship awards are made on the basis of merit to two groups of students:
(1) those who are college sophomores or juniors in the current academic year, have outstanding potential and who study the environment and related fields and;
(2) Native American and Alaska Native students who are college sophomores or juniors in the current academic year, have outstanding potential and are in fields related to health care or tribal public policy.

FINANCIAL DATA:
Amount of support per award: Up to $7,000.
Total amount of support: Varies.

NO. AWARDS: Approximately 55 for the year 2021.

APPLICATION INFO:
Application information is available on the web site.

Duration: One year.

Deadline: Approximately early March each year.

STAFF:
Jason Curley, Program Manager

ADDRESS INQUIRIES TO:
Jason Curley, Program Manager
(See address above.)

*SPECIAL STIPULATIONS:
Students must have support from a faculty or staff member at their college.

UNICO NATIONAL, INC.   [1591]
271 U.S. Highway 46 West
Suite F-103
Fairfield, NJ 07004
(973) 808-0035
Fax: (973) 808-0043
E-mail: uniconational@unico.org
Web Site: www.unico.org

FOUNDED: 1922

NAME(S) OF PROGRAMS:

- **Maria and Paolo Alessio Southern Italy Scholarship**
- **Sargeant John Basilone Memorial Graduate Scholarship**
- **Cottone Postgraduate Scholarship (Medical Only)**
- **William C. Davini Scholarship**
- **DiMattio Celli Undergraduate Study Abroad Program**
- **Major Don S. Gentile Scholarship**
- **Ella Grasso Literary Scholarship**
- **Inserra Scholarships**
- **Guglielmo Marconi Engineering Scholarship**
- **Theodore Mazza Scholarship**
- **Alphonse A. Miele Scholarship**
- **Robert J. Tarte Scholarship for Italian Studies**
- **Bernard and Carolyn Torraco Nursing Scholarships**
- **Louise Torraco Memorial Scholarship for Science**
- **Ralph J. Torraco Fine Arts Scholarship**
- **Ralph J. Torraco Scholarship**
- **Ralph J. Torraco Scholarship for Special Education**
- **Ralph J. Torraco Scholarship for Therapy Sciences**

TYPE:
Scholarships. Postgraduate scholarships and undergraduate scholarships.

PURPOSE:
To give financial aid to students of outstanding merit so they may complete their education.

ELIGIBILITY:
Candidates must reside in the home state of an active UNICO Chapter, unless otherwise indicated. Candidates must meet the eligibility requirements stated on each of the respective applications. Online degree programs are not eligible for UNICO scholarships.

Scholarship candidates must, in general, be of Italian heritage, i.e., must have one parent or grandparent of Italian heritage. The Tarte and Torraco Scholarships are open to all ethnicities. The extent to which a candidate has contributed to the life and welfare of school and/or community will be taken into account in the assessment of merit. UNICO member's children are eligible. Each chapter of UNICO National may submit applications for each of the UNICO Foundation scholarships.

A candidate for the undergraduate scholarships must be a citizen of the U.S. and have Italian heritage. An applicant must be a graduating senior at a public or private secondary school.

Applicants to the Alessio Scholarship must be currently attending, full-time students at an accredited campus based college or university program in the U.S. pursuing a degree. Applicant must be of Southern Italian descent, specifically including the regions of Abruzzo, Basilicata, Calabria, Campania, Latium, Molise, Puglia, Sardinia, and Sicilia.

The Basilone Scholarship requires that the applicant be a senior in college or a graduate beginning postgraduate studies.

The Cottone Scholarship requires that a candidate be a college senior or graduate who is beginning postgraduate studies in the field of medicine or is currently enrolled in an accredited medical school in the U.S.

A candidate for either postgraduate program (Basilone or Cottone Scholarship) must be a U.S. citizen of Italian heritage.

A candidate for the Inserra Scholarship must be a full-time student enrolled in an accredited college or university in the U.S. pursuing a degree. Candidate must be a citizen of Italian heritage.

A candidate for the Guglielmo Marconi Engineering Scholarship must be a sophomore, junior or senior student enrolled full-time, in an accredited college/university program in the U.S. majoring in engineering. Applicant must be a U.S. citizen of Italian heritage.

Robert J. Tarte Scholarship is given to a student enrolled full-time in an accredited college or university program in the U.S. pursuing Italian studies.

A candidate for the Bernard and Carolyn Torraco Memorial Nursing Scholarship must currently be enrolled in an accredited nursing degree program in the U.S., completing core nursing courses, at one of the following: An Associate Degree School of Nursing; A Collegiate School of Nursing; A Diploma School of Nursing. Proof of enrollment must be provided. The candidate must have a minimum grade point average of 3.0 or B to qualify. Preference will be given to applicants demonstrating financial need.

A candidate for the Louise Torraco Memorial Scholarship for Science must be enrolled full-time in an accredited college/university program in the U.S. pursuing study in the physical sciences or life sciences. Nominee must hold U.S. citizenship.

Ralph J. Torraco Fine Arts Scholarship is given to students enrolled full-time in an accredited college/university program in the U.S. pursuing a degree in the fine arts. Nominee must hold U.S. citizenship.

Ralph J. Torraco Scholarship requires students to be enrolled full-time in an accredited college/university program in the U.S. pursuing a degree. Nominees must hold U.S. citizenship.

Ralph J. Torraco Scholarship for Special Education requires students to be currently attending, full-time, an accredited campus based college/university program in the U.S. pursuing a degree in the field of special education. A candidate must hold U.S. citizenship.

Ralph J. Torraco Scholarship for Therapy Sciences requires students to be currently attending, full-time, an accredited campus based college/university program in the U.S. pursuing a degree in the field of therapy sciences. A candidate must hold U.S. citizenship.

FINANCIAL DATA:
Amount of support per award: Alessio, Inserra, Torraco Nursing, Louise Toracco Memorial and all Ralph J. Torraco Scholarships: $2,500; Basilone, Davini, Gentile, Mazza and Miele Scholarships: $1,500 per year; Cottone Postgraduate Scholarship: $5,000; DiMattio Celli Program and Guglielmo Marconi Engineering Scholarship: $1,250; Grasso and Tarte Scholarships: $1,000.

Total amount of support: Varies.

NO. AWARDS: Alessio, Cottone, Davini, Gentile, Marconi, Mazza, Miele and Tarte Scholarships: 1; Basilone, DiMattio, Grasso, Inserra, Louise Torraco and all Ralph J. Torraco Scholarships: 2; Bernard and Carolyn Torraco Scholarship: Up to 10.

APPLICATION INFO:
Applications are to be submitted online. Students will find complete information and submission instructions under the Scholarship tab on the UNICO National web site. Paper applications cannot be accepted.

Duration: Basilone Scholarship: Maximum of two years; Cottone Postgraduate Scholarship: One-time only; Undergraduate scholarships: Maximum of four years.

Deadline: DiMattio Celli Undergraduate Study Abroad Program: March 1. All others: April 15.

ADDRESS INQUIRIES TO:
UNICO National Scholarship Director
(See address above.)

UNITED NEGRO COLLEGE FUND (UNCF)
1805 Seventh Street, N.W.
Washington, DC 20001
(800) 331-2244
(202) 810-0258
E-mail: scholarships@uncf.org
Web Site: www.uncf.org

TYPE:
Fellowships; Internships; Scholarships; Technical assistance. The Fund, since its founding, has raised money for 37 private, historically Black colleges and universities.

Faculty fellowship programs make it possible for hundreds of instructors to earn doctoral degrees.

Mentoring and internship opportunities are provided for hundreds of UNCF students.

Scholarships are offered to a pool of more than 60,000 talented students attending UNCF colleges and universities. The Fund oversees more than 450 scholarship programs in the following general categories:
(1) geographically based scholarships;
(2) scholarships based on academic major;
(3) scholarships based on merit and need; and;
(4) financial aid for graduate study.

See entry 939 for full listing.

THE UNIVERSITY OF BRITISH COLUMBIA   [1592]
Faculty of Graduate and Postdoctoral Studies
170-6371 Crescent Road
Vancouver BC V6T 1Z2 Canada
(604) 822-2848
Fax: (604) 822-5802
E-mail: graduate.awards@ubc.ca
Web Site: www.grad.ubc.ca/scholarships-awards-funding

AREAS OF INTEREST:
All areas of advanced study.

NAME(S) OF PROGRAMS:
- **Affiliated Fellowships**

TYPE:
Fellowships. For postgraduate studies leading to a Master's or Doctorate degree at the University of British Columbia.

PURPOSE:
To allow outstanding students to devote full-time to research and study leading to a Master's or Doctorate degree.

LEGAL BASIS:
University.

ELIGIBILITY:
Citizens of any country may apply. Applicants must have outstanding academic records.

FINANCIAL DATA:
Amount of support per award: Master's: $175 to $16,000 (CAN); Doctoral: $175 to $30,000 (CAN) per annum. Most approximately $16,000 (CAN).
Total amount of support: Approximately $600,000 (CAN) per annum.

NO. MOST RECENT APPLICANTS: Approximately 800.

NO. AWARDS: Approximately 50 per year.

APPLICATION INFO:
Fellowships are awarded on the basis of applications submitted to graduate programs.
Duration: One or two years.
Deadline: Early December for Master's Program and mid-September for Doctoral Program.

ADDRESS INQUIRIES TO:
See e-mail address above.

THE UNIVERSITY OF BRITISH COLUMBIA   [1593]
Faculty of Graduate and Postdoctoral Studies
170-6371 Crescent Road
Vancouver BC V6T 1Z2 Canada
(604) 822-2848
Fax: (604) 822-5802
E-mail: graduate.awards@ubc.ca
Web Site: www.grad.ubc.ca/scholarships-awards-funding

AREAS OF INTEREST:
Research-based Master's and doctoral studies.

NAME(S) OF PROGRAMS:
● **Graduate Support Initiative**

TYPE:
Scholarships.

YEAR PROGRAM STARTED: 2008

PURPOSE:
To provide funding for graduate students through entrance scholarships, multiyear funding packages, tuition awards, and scholarship top-ups.

LEGAL BASIS:
University.

ELIGIBILITY:
Students in all fields of graduate study at the University of British Columbia-Vancouver may apply. Funding is available to both domestic and international students.

FINANCIAL DATA:
Amount of support per award: Set by graduate programs.
Total amount of support: Approximately $6,500,000 annually.

APPLICATION INFO:
Student should submit research proposal and academic record to the graduate department of interest.
Duration: Up to four years.
Deadline: Inquiry to graduate program of interest accepted throughout the year. Most funding decisions are made January to March.

ADDRESS INQUIRIES TO:
See e-mail address above.

THE UNIVERSITY OF BRITISH COLUMBIA   [1594]
Faculty of Graduate and Postdoctoral Studies
170-6371 Crescent Road
Vancouver BC V6T 1Z2 Canada
(604) 822-2848
Fax: (604) 822-5802
E-mail: graduate.awards@ubc.ca
Web Site: www.grad.ubc.ca/scholarships-awards-funding

AREAS OF INTEREST:
Doctoral study in all disciplines.

NAME(S) OF PROGRAMS:
● **Four Year Doctoral Fellowships**

TYPE:
Fellowships.

YEAR PROGRAM STARTED: 2009

PURPOSE:
To attract and retain outstanding doctoral students by offering stable, base-level funding for four years of their Ph.D. studies and research.

ELIGIBILITY:
Open to doctoral students in any discipline. Citizens of any country may apply.

FINANCIAL DATA:
Amount of support per award: Ensures student receives financial support of at least $18,200 (CAN) per year plus tuition.
Total amount of support: Approximately $14,000,000.

NO. AWARDS: 200 new fellowships offered by graduate programs each year.

APPLICATION INFO:
Applicant must first contact graduate program of interest. Fellowships are awarded on basis of nomination made by graduate program.
Duration: Up to four years.
Deadline: Most funding decisions made in January to March.

ADDRESS INQUIRIES TO:
See e-mail address above.

THE UNIVERSITY OF CALGARY   [1595]
Faculty of Graduate Studies
Earth Sciences Building, Room 1010
2500 University Drive, N.W.
Calgary AB T2N 1N4 Canada
(403) 220-4938
Fax: (403) 289-7635
E-mail: gsaward@ucalgary.ca
Web Site: grad.ucalgary.ca/awards

FOUNDED: 1966

AREAS OF INTEREST:
Petroleum industry.

NAME(S) OF PROGRAMS:
● **The Archibald Waynne Dingman Memorial Graduate Scholarship**

TYPE:
Awards/prizes; Scholarships. Graduate scholarship for study in all areas relevant to the petroleum industry. Tenable at The University of Calgary. Award endowed through a bequest of the late Corinne Patteson.

ELIGIBILITY:
Open to students registered full-time in a thesis-based graduate program in the Faculty of Graduate Studies at The University of Calgary.

FINANCIAL DATA:
Amount of support per award: $3,500 (CAN).
Total amount of support: $3,500 (CAN).

NO. AWARDS: 1.

APPLICATION INFO:
Students should consult the Graduate Award Competition Guidelines and complete the Graduate Award Application through the Student Centre.
Duration: One year.
Deadline: Varies. Students should contact their Graduate Program Administrator.

ADDRESS INQUIRIES TO:
Graduate Scholarship Office
(See address above.)

THE UNIVERSITY OF CALGARY   [1596]
Faculty of Graduate Studies
Earth Sciences Building, Room 1010
2500 University Drive, N.W.
Calgary AB T2N 1N4 Canada
(403) 220-4938
Fax: (403) 289-7635
E-mail: gsaward@ucalgary.ca
Web Site: grad.ucalgary.ca/awards

FOUNDED: 1966

AREAS OF INTEREST:
Medical sciences.

NAME(S) OF PROGRAMS:
● **William H. Davies Medical Research Scholarships**

TYPE:
Awards/prizes; Scholarships. Awards for study in the medical sciences. Tenable at The University of Calgary. Award endowed through a bequest of the late William H. Davies.

ELIGIBILITY:
Open to students registered full-time in a thesis-based graduate program in the Cumming School of Medicine and/or students registered full-time in a thesis-based program who are supervised by a faculty member with a primary appointment in the Cumming School of Medicine.

FINANCIAL DATA:
Amount of support per award: $3,000 to $11,000 (CAN), depending upon the candidate's qualifications, experience and graduate program.

NO. AWARDS: Varies.

APPLICATION INFO:
Students should apply to the Associate Dean, Graduate Science Education. Recommendations will be forwarded to the Graduate Scholarship Office. The recommendations are subject to final approval of the Graduate Scholarship Committee.
Duration: One year.
Deadline: June 15.

ADDRESS INQUIRIES TO:
Graduate Scholarship Office
(See address above.)

THE UNIVERSITY OF CALGARY [1597]

Faculty of Graduate Studies
Earth Sciences Building, Room 1010
2500 University Drive, N.W.
Calgary AB T2N 1N4 Canada
(403) 220-4938
Fax: (403) 289-7635
E-mail: gsaward@ucalgary.ca
Web Site: grad.ucalgary.ca/awards

FOUNDED: 1966

AREAS OF INTEREST:
All fields of study, except art.

NAME(S) OF PROGRAMS:
- **Izaak Walton Killam Doctoral Scholarships**

TYPE:
Awards/prizes; Scholarships.

YEAR PROGRAM STARTED: 1967

PURPOSE:
To encourage advanced study, to increase the scientific and scholastic attainment of Canadians and to promote sympathetic understanding between Canadians and the peoples of other countries. Those receiving scholarships would likely contribute to the advancement of learning or win distinction in their profession.

ELIGIBILITY:
Scholarships are normally awarded to students who will be in their first, second, or third year of doctoral studies during the tenure of the award. Fourth year students may be considered under exceptional circumstances. The recipients must be registered full-time in a doctoral program at the University of Calgary. Applicants must have completed at least one year of graduate study before taking up an award.

GEOG. RESTRICTIONS: Canada.

FINANCIAL DATA:
$3,000 of this award (a Killam Research Scholarship) is reserved to cover costs associated with special equipment, conferences and/or travel in direct connection with the Ph.D. research.

Amount of support per award: $36,000 (CAN).

Total amount of support: Varies.

NO. AWARDS: Varies.

APPLICATION INFO:
Students should consult the Graduate Award Competition Guidelines and Application. In order to receive the Killam Research Scholarship portion of the award, the student must submit a letter outlining the proposed use of funds. This statement must be signed by the supervisor approving the use. No receipts are required.

Duration: Two years.

Deadline: Varies by program. Students should contact their Graduate Program Administrator.

ADDRESS INQUIRIES TO:
Graduate Scholarship Office
(See address above.)

THE UNIVERSITY OF CALGARY [1598]

Faculty of Graduate Studies
Earth Sciences Building, Room 1010
2500 University Drive, N.W.
Calgary AB T2N 1N4 Canada
(403) 220-4938
Fax: (403) 289-7635
E-mail: gsaward@ucalgary.ca
Web Site: grad.ucalgary.ca/awards

FOUNDED: 1966

AREAS OF INTEREST:
Cellular, molecular, microbial and biochemical biology.

NAME(S) OF PROGRAMS:
- **Bettina Bahlsen Memorial Graduate Scholarship**

TYPE:
Awards/prizes; Scholarships. Award for study in the fields of cellular, molecular, microbial or biochemical biology. Tenable at The University of Calgary, Department of Biological Sciences.

PURPOSE:
To assist graduate students from outside Canada who require financial assistance for their first year of study.

ELIGIBILITY:
Open to full-time graduate students entering or enrolled in a doctoral program in the Department of Biological Sciences. Selection will be based on academic excellence. Preference will be accorded to an international student and, if possible, to a student entering the first year of graduate studies.

FINANCIAL DATA:
Amount of support per award: $22,500 (CAN).

Total amount of support: $22,500 (CAN).

NO. AWARDS: 1.

APPLICATION INFO:
Students should consult the Department of Biological Sciences. A recommendation will be forwarded to the Graduate Scholarship Office. The recommendation is subject to final approval of the Graduate Scholarship Committee.

Duration: One year.

Deadline: February 1.

ADDRESS INQUIRIES TO:
Graduate Scholarship Office
(See address above.)

THE UNIVERSITY OF CALGARY [1599]

Faculty of Graduate Studies
Earth Sciences Building, Room 1010
2500 University Drive, N.W.
Calgary AB T2N 1N4 Canada
(403) 220-4938
Fax: (403) 289-7635
E-mail: gsaward@ucalgary.ca
Web Site: grad.ucalgary.ca/awards

FOUNDED: 1966

AREAS OF INTEREST:
Business, management and related areas.

NAME(S) OF PROGRAMS:
- **John Labatt Limited Scholarship**
- **ScotiaMcLeod Scholarship**

TYPE:
Awards/prizes; Scholarships. Awards for study in the fields of business, management and related areas. Tenable at the University of Calgary. Awards are endowed through gifts from John Labatt Limited and ScotiaMcLeod Inc. Matching grants provided from the Province of Alberta's Advanced Education Endowment Fund.

ELIGIBILITY:
Open to students registered full-time in the MBA program at the Haskayne School of Business. Awardees must be engaged in full-time study during the tenure of the award.

FINANCIAL DATA:
Amount of support per award: Labatt Scholarship: $3,600 (CAN); ScotiaMcLeod Scholarship: $4,000 (CAN).

Total amount of support: $7,600 (CAN).

NO. AWARDS: 1 per award.

APPLICATION INFO:
Student should consult with the Haskayne School of Business. A recommendation will be forwarded to the Graduate Scholarship Office. The recommendation is subject to final approval of the Graduate Scholarship Committee.

Duration: One year.

Deadline: May 15.

ADDRESS INQUIRIES TO:
Graduate Scholarship Office
(See address above.)

THE UNIVERSITY OF CALGARY [1600]

Faculty of Graduate Studies
Earth Sciences Building, Room 1010
2500 University Drive, N.W.
Calgary AB T2N 1N4 Canada
(403) 220-4938
Fax: (403) 289-7635
E-mail: gsaward@ucalgary.ca
Web Site: grad.ucalgary.ca/awards

FOUNDED: 1966

NAME(S) OF PROGRAMS:
- **The University of Calgary Silver Anniversary Graduate Fellowships**

TYPE:
Awards/prizes; Fellowships. Graduate fellowships in all fields of study tenable in The Faculty of Graduate Studies at The University of Calgary. Award endowed by an anonymous donor and matched by the Province of Alberta.

ELIGIBILITY:
Open to students who are registered full-time in a doctoral program at The University of Calgary. Candidates must be residents of Canada. Awards are granted on the basis of academic standing and demonstrated potential for advanced study and research.

FINANCIAL DATA:
Amount of support per award: $16,000 to $20,000.

Total amount of support: Varies.

NO. AWARDS: Varies depending on funds.

APPLICATION INFO:
Students should consult the Graduate Award Competition guidelines and application, which are posted on the web site.

Duration: Two years.

Deadline: Varies by program. Students should contact their Graduate Program Administrator.

ADDRESS INQUIRIES TO:
Graduate Scholarship Office
(See address above.)

THE UNIVERSITY OF
CALGARY [1601]
Faculty of Graduate Studies
Earth Sciences Building, Room 1010
2500 University Drive, N.W.
Calgary AB T2N 1N4 Canada
(403) 220-4938
Fax: (403) 289-7635
E-mail: gsaward@ucalgary.ca
Web Site: grad.ucalgary.ca/awards

FOUNDED: 1966

AREAS OF INTEREST:
Creative writing in English, English
literature, and related literary fields.

NAME(S) OF PROGRAMS:
• **The A.T.J. Cairns Memorial
Scholarship**

TYPE:
Awards/prizes; Scholarships. Graduate
scholarship tenable at The University of
Calgary. Award endowed through the estate
of the late A.T.J. Cairns, with a matching
grant provided by the Province of Alberta's
Advanced Education Endowment Fund.

ELIGIBILITY:
Open to students registered full-time in a
graduate program in the Department of
English.

FINANCIAL DATA:
Amount of support per award: $1,000 to
$5,000.
Total amount of support: Varies.

NO. AWARDS: Determined annually.

APPLICATION INFO:
Students interested in the award should
consult the Department of English. A
recommendation will be forwarded to the
Graduate Scholarship Office. The
recommendation is subject to final approval
of the Graduate Scholarship Committee.
Duration: One year.
Deadline: April 30.

ADDRESS INQUIRIES TO:
Graduate Scholarship Office
(See address above.)

THE UNIVERSITY OF
CALGARY [1602]
Faculty of Graduate Studies
Earth Sciences Building, Room 1010
2500 University Drive, N.W.
Calgary AB T2N 1N4 Canada
(403) 220-4938
Fax: (403) 289-7635
E-mail: gsaward@ucalgary.ca
Web Site: grad.ucalgary.ca/awards

FOUNDED: 1966

NAME(S) OF PROGRAMS:
• **Graduate Faculty Council Scholarship**

TYPE:
Awards/prizes; Scholarships. Graduate
scholarship in all fields of study tenable at
The University of Calgary. Award endowed
by The University of Calgary Graduate
Faculty Council.

ELIGIBILITY:
Open to students registered full-time in a
doctoral program.

FINANCIAL DATA:
Amount of support per award: $10,000.
Total amount of support: Varies depending
on funds available.

NO. AWARDS: Varies.

APPLICATION INFO:
Students should consult the Graduate Award
Competition guidelines and application,
which are available online.
Duration: One year.
Deadline: Varies by program. Students
should contact their Graduate Awards
Administrator.

ADDRESS INQUIRIES TO:
Graduate Scholarship Office
(See address above.)

THE UNIVERSITY OF
CALGARY [1603]
Faculty of Graduate Studies
Earth Sciences Building, Room 1010
2500 University Drive, N.W.
Calgary AB T2N 1N4 Canada
(403) 220-4938
Fax: (403) 289-7635
E-mail: gsaward@ucalgary.ca
Web Site: grad.ucalgary.ca/awards

FOUNDED: 1966

AREAS OF INTEREST:
Humanities.

NAME(S) OF PROGRAMS:
• **Peter C. Craigie Memorial Scholarship**

TYPE:
Awards/prizes; Scholarships. Graduate
scholarship tenable at The University of
Calgary. Award endowed by friends, family
and colleagues of Peter Craigie, who was
Vice President (Academic) at the University;
matching grant provided from the Province
of Alberta's Advanced Education Endowment
Fund.

ELIGIBILITY:
Open to students registered full-time who
have completed one term of study in a
Master's program in one of the following
departments: Classics and Religion; English;
French, Italian and Spanish; Linguistics,
Languages and Cultures; and Philosophy. The
recipient must have an outstanding scholastic
record and have been or be involved in
activities contributing to the general welfare
of the university community.

FINANCIAL DATA:
Amount of support per award: $6,000.
Total amount of support: $6,000.

NO. AWARDS: 1.

APPLICATION INFO:
Applicants must complete a statement of
eligibility (approximately 400 words)
describing their activities contributing to the
general welfare of the University of Calgary
community. Students should consult the
Graduate Awards Competition Guidelines and
complete the Graduate Award Scholarship
Application through the Student Centre.
Duration: One year.
Deadline: Varies by program. Candidates
should contact their Graduate Program
Administrator.

ADDRESS INQUIRIES TO:
Graduate Scholarship Office
(See address above.)

THE UNIVERSITY OF
CALGARY [1604]
Faculty of Graduate Studies
Earth Sciences Building, Room 1010
2500 University Drive, N.W.
Calgary AB T2N 1N4 Canada
(403) 220-4938
Fax: (403) 289-7635
E-mail: gsaward@ucalgary.ca
Web Site: grad.ucalgary.ca/awards

FOUNDED: 1966

AREAS OF INTEREST:
Economics, geoscience, engineering and
management.

NAME(S) OF PROGRAMS:
• **Canadian Natural Resources Limited
Graduate Scholarship**

TYPE:
Awards/prizes; Scholarships. Graduate
scholarship tenable at the University of
Calgary. This Scholarship recognizes the
importance training and education play in
helping students take advantage of the career
and economic prospects available in the oil
and gas industry.

PURPOSE:
To recognize the importance training and
education play in helping students take
advantage of the career and economic
prospects available in the oil and gas
industry.

ELIGIBILITY:
Open to students who are registered full-time
in a thesis-based program in the Faculty of
Graduate Studies at the University of
Calgary.

FINANCIAL DATA:
Amount of support per award: $10,400.
Total amount of support: $10,400.

CO-OP FUNDING PROGRAMS: Endowed by
Canadian Natural Resources Ltd (formerly
Sceptre Resources Limited); matching grant
provided from the Province of Alberta's
Advanced Education Endowment Fund.

NO. AWARDS: 1.

APPLICATION INFO:
Students should consult the Graduate Award
Competition Guidelines on the web site and
complete the Graduate Award Scholarship
Application through the Student Centre.
Duration: One year.
Deadline: Varies by program. Candidates
should contact their Graduate Program
Administrator.

ADDRESS INQUIRIES TO:
Graduate Scholarship Office
(See address above.)

THE UNIVERSITY OF
CALGARY [1605]
Faculty of Graduate Studies
Earth Sciences Building, Room 1010
2500 University Drive, N.W.
Calgary AB T2N 1N4 Canada
(403) 220-4938
Fax: (403) 289-7635
E-mail: gsaward@ucalgary.ca
Web Site: grad.ucalgary.ca/awards

AREAS OF INTEREST:
Natural resources, energy and environmental
law.

NAME(S) OF PROGRAMS:
- **Faculty of Law Graduate Scholarship**

TYPE:
Awards/prizes; Scholarships.

ELIGIBILITY:
Open to students registered full-time in a graduate program in the Faculty of Law. If, in the opinion of the University of Calgary Graduate Scholarship Committee, no suitable applications are received, no awards will be made.

FINANCIAL DATA:
Amount of support per award: $12,500.
Total amount of support: $12,500.

CO-OP FUNDING PROGRAMS: Endowed through contributions made to the Focus on Natural Resources Law Campaign; matching grant provided from the Province of Alberta.

NO. AWARDS: 1.

APPLICATION INFO:
Students should consult the Faculty of Law. A recommendation will be forwarded to the Graduate Scholarship Office. The recommendation is subject to final approval of the Graduate Scholarship Committee.
Duration: One year. Nonrenewable.
Deadline: December 15.

PUBLICATIONS:
Academic calendar.

ADDRESS INQUIRIES TO:
Graduate Scholarship Office
(See address above.)

UNIVERSITY OF KANSAS CHILD LANGUAGE DOCTORAL PROGRAM [1606]
1000 Sunnyside Avenue
Room 3031, Dole Center
Lawrence, KS 66045-7555
(785) 864-0661
Fax: (785) 864-4571
E-mail: childlang@ku.edu
Web Site: clp.ku.edu

AREAS OF INTEREST:
Early childhood education and language research.

NAME(S) OF PROGRAMS:
- **Child Language Doctoral Program**

TYPE:
Conferences/seminars; Research grants; Scholarships.

PURPOSE:
To train individuals on language impairment across the life span.

ELIGIBILITY:
Applicants must have U.S. citizenship or permanent residency status, admission to the Child Language Doctoral Program or Intercampus Program in Speech-Language-Hearing or a related program, submission of a significant research plan of high quality, demonstrated high academic achievements and potential, and research interests congruent with those of one or more of the training program faculty members.

FINANCIAL DATA:
Amount of support per award: $21,180 per year predoctoral award.
Total amount of support: Varies.

APPLICATION INFO:
Applicants must submit:
(1) a curriculum vitae;

(2) a list of all courses taken in relevant areas such as language impairment of children, linguistics, psychology, special education, and speech and hearing sciences;
(3) a research plan describing the applicant's plans for research on language impairments of children;
(4) two official transcripts;
(5) names and telephone numbers of three references who can evaluate the applicant's research potential;
(6) scores from the Graduate Record Examinations and;
(7) letter of intent stating willingness to participate in continuous research practicum.
Duration: One year.
Deadline: Beginning of February.

STAFF:
Dr. Mabel L. Rice, Director
Suzanne Scales, Program Assistant

ADDRESS INQUIRIES TO:
Dr. Mabel L. Rice, Director
(See address above.)

UNIVERSITY OF SOUTHERN CALIFORNIA [1607]
3720 South Flower Street, Third Floor
CUB 303
Los Angeles, CA 90089-0701
(213) 740-8336
Fax: (213) 740-6070
E-mail: jeri.muniz@usc.edu
Web Site: research.usc.edu

AREAS OF INTEREST:
Art history.

TYPE:
Fellowships; Grants-in-aid.

PURPOSE:
To support graduate education in art history at USC.

ELIGIBILITY:
Admission to Ph.D. program in art history.

GEOG. RESTRICTIONS: California.

FINANCIAL DATA:
Amount of support per award: Varies.

APPLICATION INFO:
Applicants must submit the Graduate School Application and the Supplemental Application form along with Graduate Record Exam (GRE) scores and letters of recommendation.
Duration: One year. Renewal possible based on academic progress.
Deadline: December 1.

ADDRESS INQUIRIES TO:
Contracts and Grants
(See address above.)

UNIVERSITY OF SOUTHERN CALIFORNIA [1608]
USC Graduate School
3601 Trousdale Parkway, STU 301
Los Angeles, CA 90089-0894
(213) 740-9033
Fax: (213) 740-9048
E-mail: gradfllw@usc.edu
Web Site: graduateschool.usc.edu

NAME(S) OF PROGRAMS:
- **Annenberg Graduate Fellowship Program**
- **Global Ph.D. Fellowship**
- **Provost's Ph.D. Fellowship Program**
- **Rose Hills Ph.D. Fellowship**

TYPE:
Fellowships. Merit fellowships. Fellowships will be combined with matching funds from individual schools to provide four or more years of funding toward the Ph.D.

YEAR PROGRAM STARTED: 1982

PURPOSE:
To allow outstanding students to devote full-time to research and study at USC leading to a career in university teaching and research.

LEGAL BASIS:
University.

ELIGIBILITY:
Excellent incoming Ph.D. applicants who show outstanding promise for academic careers in research and training.

FINANCIAL DATA:
Amount of support per award: Varies by department and school.

APPLICATION INFO:
Nomination by department only.
Duration: Two years, awarded annually with at least two years subsequent departmental/school support, based upon continued superior performance.
Deadline: Varies.

PUBLICATIONS:
Program announcements.

ADDRESS INQUIRIES TO:
Kate Tegmeyer, Assistant Director
(See address above.)

VERMONT STUDENT ASSISTANCE CORPORATION [1609]
10 East Allen Street
Winooski, VT 05404-2601
(800) 642-3177 (continental U.S.)
(802) 655-9602 (Burlington area)
Fax: (802) 654-3765
TDD: (800) 281-3341
E-mail: walshr@vsac.org
Web Site: www.vsac.org

FOUNDED: 1965

AREAS OF INTEREST:
Students in need.

NAME(S) OF PROGRAMS:
- **Vermont Incentive Grants and Scholarships**
- **Vermont Outreach Programs**

TYPE:
Conferences/seminars; Grants-in-aid; Scholarships. Grants and loans for students enrolled in approved postsecondary institutions.

YEAR PROGRAM STARTED: 1965

PURPOSE:
To ensure that all Vermonters have the necessary financial and informational resources to pursue their educational goals beyond high school.

LEGAL BASIS:
Nonprofit, public corporation.

ELIGIBILITY:
For Incentive Grant, applicant must be a Vermont resident, enrolled full-time at an approved postsecondary institution, and must meet need test.

For Part-Time Grant, applicant must be a Vermont resident, taking fewer than 12 credit hours, have not received a Bachelor's degree, and must meet need test.

For Non-Degree Grant, applicant must be a Vermont resident, not matriculated, and must meet need test.

GEOG. RESTRICTIONS: Vermont.

FINANCIAL DATA:
    Amount of support per award: Incentive Grant: $1,000 to $12,500 for the academic year 2020-21; Non-Degree Grant: Varies; Part-Time Grant: $500 to $9,300 for the academic year 2020-21.
    Total amount of support: $20,168,796 for fiscal year 2019.

NO. MOST RECENT APPLICANTS: 20,283 for fiscal year 2019.

NO. AWARDS: 11,766 need-based grants for the year 2019.

APPLICATION INFO:
    FAFSA and Vermont Grant application required for Incentive and Part-Time Grant.
    Duration: One academic year. Renewal possible under annual reapplication for up to 10 semesters.
    Deadline: Applications accepted on a rolling basis for all grants.

ADDRESS INQUIRIES TO:
    VSAC Research Department
    (See address above.)

VERTICAL FLIGHT FOUNDATION
2700 Prosperity Avenue, Suite 275
Fairfax, VA 22031
(703) 684-6777
Fax: (703) 739-9279
E-mail: bchen@vtol.org
Web Site: www.vtol.org/vff

TYPE:
    Awards/prizes; Scholarships. Annual scholarships to undergraduate senior, Master's or Ph.D. students interested in pursuing careers in some technical aspect of helicopter or vertical flight engineering.

See entry 2374 for full listing.

VIRGINIA POLYTECHNIC INSTITUTE AND STATE UNIVERSITY
MAOP Office
Media Annex, Room 103A
130 Otey Street
Blacksburg, VA 24061
(540) 231-5023
E-mail: maop@vt.edu
Web Site: www.maop.vt.edu

TYPE:
    Assistantships; Fellowships; Internships; Scholarships. The program assists with graduate school financing in exchange for assistance to MAOP administration. Graduate students assist with programming implementation such as mentoring to undergraduate students.

See entry 926 for full listing.

WASHINGTON STUDENT ACHIEVEMENT COUNCIL [1610]
917 Lakeridge Way, S.W.
Olympia, WA 98502
(360) 753-7848
Fax: (855) 480-8718
E-mail: sws@wsac.wa.gov
Web Site: readysetgrad.wa.gov

FOUNDED: 1969

NAME(S) OF PROGRAMS:
● **Washington State Need Grant Program**
● **Washington State Work-Study Program**

TYPE:
    Work-study programs. Subsidized employment opportunities.

YEAR PROGRAM STARTED: 1974

PURPOSE:
    To provide financial assistance to needy students attending eligible postsecondary institutions in the state of Washington by stimulating and promoting their employment and to provide such needy students, wherever possible, with employment related to their academic pursuits.

LEGAL BASIS:
    State agency.

ELIGIBILITY:
    Applicants must demonstrate financial need, be enrolled or accepted for enrollment as at least half-time undergraduate, graduate or professional students and be capable, in the opinion of the institution, of maintaining good standing in a course of study while employed under the program.

GEOG. RESTRICTIONS: Washington state.

FINANCIAL DATA:
    Amount of support per award: Varies.
    Total amount of support: Approximately $7,800,000 for the 2018-19 academic year.

APPLICATION INFO:
    There is no separate application for this program. Students are awarded automatically by their school on the basis of their financial need as evidenced from their Free Application for Federal Student Aid (FAFSA) results or Washington Application for State Financial Aid (WASFA).
    Duration: Renewable.

STAFF:
    Jeffrey Powell, Program Administrator
    Debbie Jackson, Program Manager

ADDRESS INQUIRIES TO:
    Financial Aid Office at the college or Washington Student Achievement Council
    (See address above.)

WASHINGTON STUDENT ACHIEVEMENT COUNCIL [1611]
917 Lakeridge Way, S.W.
Olympia, WA 98504-3430
(888) 535-0747 (option 5)
E-mail: health@wsac.wa.gov
Web Site: www.wsac.wa.gov/health

AREAS OF INTEREST:
    Primary and integrated health care.

NAME(S) OF PROGRAMS:
● **Washington Health Corps**

TYPE:
    Loan repayment program.

YEAR PROGRAM STARTED: 1991

PURPOSE:
    To encourage health professionals to work in rural or underserved urban areas of the state of Washington by providing loan repayment.

LEGAL BASIS:
    Government agency.

ELIGIBILITY:
    Many types of health care providers are eligible, in a variety of clinical settings. Health care sites must apply and be approved as part of the competitive yearly application process.

GEOG. RESTRICTIONS: Washington state.

FINANCIAL DATA:
    Amount of support per award: $70,000 with a two-year service commitment and $75,000 with a three-year service commitment.
    Total amount of support: $6,500,000 annually.

NO. MOST RECENT APPLICANTS: 362.

NO. AWARDS: 98.

APPLICATION INFO:
    Instructions are available on the Washington Health Corps web site.

STAFF:
    Melisa Ziegler, Associate Director for Workforce Programs
    Jaclyn Cook, Program Manager
    Kristen Jenkins, Program Coordinator

ADDRESS INQUIRIES TO:
    Jaclyn Cook, Program Manager
    (See address above.)

*SPECIAL STIPULATIONS:
    Must commit to employment at a preapproved site in Washington state.

WASHINGTON UNIVERSITY IN ST. LOUIS [1612]
Office of the Provost
One Brookings Drive, Campus Box 1072
St. Louis, MO 63130-4899
(314) 935-3000
E-mail: cgfp@wustl.edu
Web Site: graduateschool.wustl.edu/cgfp

FOUNDED: 1853

AREAS OF INTEREST:
    Anthropology, architecture, art history, archaeology, biology, biomedical sciences, business administration, chemistry, Chinese/Japanese and comparative literature, creative writing, earth and planetary sciences, economics, education, engineering, English, fine arts, German, history, material science and engineering, mathematics, movement science, music, philosophy, physics, political science, psychology, romance languages, statistics, social work, and visual arts.

NAME(S) OF PROGRAMS:
● **The Chancellor's Graduate Fellowship Program at Washington University in St. Louis**

TYPE:
    Fellowships; Research grants; Scholarships; Travel grants.

YEAR PROGRAM STARTED: 1991

PURPOSE:
    To facilitate training for students interested in becoming college or university professors, and who can contribute to diversity on the Washington University campus.

LEGAL BASIS:
    University.

ELIGIBILITY:
Open to students who are admissible into any of Washington University's Ph.D. programs in Arts and Sciences, Business, Engineering or Social Work. Also eligible are students admissible to other Washington University programs providing final disciplinary training for prospective college professors (e.g., M.F.A. in Creative Writing, M.F.A. in Art). Students must be able to contribute to the diversity on the Washington University campus.

Applicants must be in the process of receiving, or will receive, an undergraduate degree from a four-year institution in the U.S. International students may apply, as long as they meet all admissions criteria.

FINANCIAL DATA:
Amount of support per award: Doctoral candidates are provided stipends and allowances of $38,220 per twelve-month year for program length, plus full tuition scholarships, with a total value in excess of $450,000. This combines a fellowship stipend of $36,720 and a $1,500 educational allowance.

NO. MOST RECENT APPLICANTS: 400.

NO. AWARDS: Varies.

APPLICATION INFO:
Application information is available on the web site.
Duration: Program length for doctoral candidates, contingent upon satisfactory academic progress. Two years for graduate students in MFA (in Writing, Visual Art and Dance) and M.Arch. (Master of Architecture) programs. Three years for J.D. in Law.
Deadline: January 25.

PUBLICATIONS:
Program announcement.

ADDRESS INQUIRIES TO:
See e-mail address above.

*SPECIAL STIPULATIONS:
Fellows will meet as a community on a regular basis to discuss trends and activities within their various disciplines. Scholars will lead discussions on a multitude of topics and the fellows will participate in an annual conference.

WASHINGTON UNIVERSITY IN ST. LOUIS [1613]
Office of the Provost
One Brookings Drive, Campus Box 1072
St. Louis, MO 63130
(314) 935-3000
E-mail: olinfellowship@wustl.edu
Web Site: graduateschool.wustl.edu/olin-fellowship

FOUNDED: 1974

AREAS OF INTEREST:
Anthropology, architecture, art history, archaeology, biology, biomedical sciences, business administration, chemistry, Chinese, classics, comparative literature, creative writing, dance, earth and planetary sciences, economics, education, engineering, English, French, German, Hispanic studies, history, Japanese, law, materials science, mathematics, medicine, movement science, music, nursing science, occupational therapy, philosophy, physics, political science, psychology, public health, rehabilitation and participation science, social work, sociology, statistics, urban design and visual arts.

NAME(S) OF PROGRAMS:
● **Spencer T. and Ann W. Olin Fellowship for Women in Graduate Study**

TYPE:
Fellowships. The Olin Fellowship is open to candidates for any of the following graduate and professional schools at Washington University: architecture, art, arts and sciences, business, engineering, law, medicine, and social work.

YEAR PROGRAM STARTED: 1974

PURPOSE:
To encourage women of exceptional promise to prepare for careers in higher education and the professions; to continue and extend the historically important contributions of Monticello College to the education of women; to extend the influence of Washington University by assisting in the advanced education of outstanding young women who are likely to make significant contributions to higher education and the professions.

LEGAL BASIS:
Joint program of a private foundation (The Monticello College Foundation) and of Washington University in St. Louis.

ELIGIBILITY:
Any female graduate of a Baccalaureate institution in the U.S. who plans to prepare for a career in higher education or the professions by full-time advanced study at Washington University is eligible to apply. Applicants are considered without regard to age, handicap, religious creed, race, sexual orientation or national origin and only with regard to the excellence of their qualifications. Applicants must meet the admission requirements of the graduate or professional school of Washington University. Preference will be given to those who wish to study for the highest earned degree in their chosen field.

FINANCIAL DATA:
The Olin Fellowships are tenable only at Washington University. They carry awards which compare favorably in each discipline with the most attractive financial aid (full tuition remission), stipend support, travel support, and health coverage (90% health subsidy) offer packages available in that discipline at Washington University.
Amount of support per award: $36,720 stipend over 12 months.

NO. MOST RECENT APPLICANTS: 1,142.

NO. AWARDS: Varies.

APPLICATION INFO:
Application and instructions are available online.
Duration: Up through, but not to exceed, program length, contingent upon satisfactory academic progress.
Deadline: Applications, with all supporting documents, must be submitted online no later than January 25 preceding the academic year for which application has been made.

ADDRESS INQUIRIES TO:
See e-mail address above.

WELLESLEY COLLEGE
Career Education
Green Hall 439, 106 Central Street
Wellesley, MA 02481-8203
(781) 283-2347
Fax: (781) 283-3674
E-mail: fellowships@wellesley.edu
Web Site: www.wellesley.edu/careereducation/fellowships-and-scholarships

TYPE:
Fellowships; Research grants. The Anne Louise Barrett Fellowship is given preferably in music and primarily for study or research in musical theory, composition, or in the history of music, abroad or in the U.S.

The Margaret Freeman Bowers Fellowship is given for graduate/professional study in fields leading to a career of service to others. Fields include social work, law, public health, policy and administration, and development studies. Business, medicine, and science also qualify, as long as they are dedicated to addressing social challenges in the U.S. and around the world.

The Eugene L. Cox Fellowship is for graduate study in medieval or renaissance history and culture abroad or in the U.S.

The Professor Elizabeth F. Fisher Fellowship is given for research or further study in geology or geography, including urban, environmental or ecological studies.

The Ruth Ingersoll Goldmark Fellowship is awarded for graduate study in English literature, English composition or in the classics.

The Horton-Hallowell Fellowship is awarded for graduate study in any field, preferably in the last two years of candidacy for the Ph.D. degree, or its equivalent, or for private research of equivalent standard.

The Peggy Howard Fellowship in Economics is given to provide financial aid for Wellesley students or alumnae continuing their study of economics. Administered by the economics faculty who may name one or two recipients depending on the income available.

The Edna V. Moffett Fellowship is given to a young alumna, preferably for a first year of graduate study in history.

The Alice Freeman Palmer Fellowship is awarded for study or research abroad or in the U.S.

The Kathryn Conway Preyer Fellowship is for advanced study in history.

The Vida Dutton Scudder Fellowship is given for study in the field of social science, political science or literature.

The Harriet A. Shaw Fellowship is given for study or research in music and the allied arts, in the U.S. or abroad.

Mary Elvira Stevens Traveling Fellowship is awarded for travel or study outside the U.S.

The Maria Opasnov Tyler '52 Scholarship is for graduate study in Russian studies.

The Sarah Perry Wood Medical Fellowship is awarded for the study of medicine at an accredited medical school approved by the American Medical Association.

The Fanny Bullock Workman Fellowship is given for graduate study in any field.

See entry 991 for full listing.

WELLESLEY COLLEGE

Career Education
Green Hall 439, 106 Central Street
Wellesley, MA 02481-8203
(781) 283-2347
Fax: (781) 283-3674
E-mail: fellowships@wellesley.edu
Web Site: www.wellesley.
edu/careereducation/fellowships-and-
scholarships

TYPE:

Fellowships; Scholarships. Awards are made
to female applicants who plan for full-time
graduate study for the coming year.

The Mary McEwen Schimke Scholarship is a
supplemental award given to afford relief
from household and child care expenses
while pursuing graduate study.

The M.A. Cartland Shackford Medical
Fellowship is given for study of medicine
with a view to general practice, not
psychiatry.

See entry 992 for full listing.

WEST VIRGINIA HIGHER EDUCATION POLICY COMMISSION   [1614]

1018 Kanawha Boulevard East, Suite 700
Charleston, WV 25301
(304) 558-4016
Fax: (855) 292-1415
E-mail: brian.weingart@wvhepc.edu
Web Site: www.wvhepc.edu

FOUNDED: 1969

AREAS OF INTEREST:
Education.

NAME(S) OF PROGRAMS:
- **West Virginia Higher Education Grant Program**

TYPE:
Grants-in-aid. Monetary grants awarded to
undergraduate students attending approved
institutions of higher education.

YEAR PROGRAM STARTED: 1968

PURPOSE:
To guarantee that the most able and needy
students are given the opportunity to continue
their program of self-improvement at the
postsecondary level by assisting in the
removal of financial barriers through
monetary awards.

LEGAL BASIS:
West Virginia Higher Education Grant
Program is a government program
administered under the authority of West
Virginia Code 18-C-5-1.

ELIGIBILITY:
An applicant must be a citizen of the U.S.,
have been a resident of West Virginia for at
least one year immediately preceding the date
of application for a grant or renewal of a
grant, require financial assistance to pursue a
college education, possess academic promise
or be making satisfactory progress and enroll
as a full-time undergraduate in an approved
educational institution.

Grants are restricted to approved educational
institutions located in West Virginia and
Pennsylvania.

GEOG. RESTRICTIONS: West Virginia and
Pennsylvania.

FINANCIAL DATA:
Amount of support per award: Average
award of $2,379.

Total amount of support: $37,312,270 total
funding for student awards for academic year
2019-20 in state-appropriated funds, special
fee revenues allocated by the governing
Board.

NO. AWARDS: Approximately 15,682 for
academic year 2019-20.

APPLICATION INFO:
Applicants must submit the Free Application
for Federal Student Aid (FAFSA).

Duration: Total of eight semesters or 12
quarters. The eight semesters do not have to
be consecutive. Receipt of a grant in a given
year does not guarantee its continuance in a
subsequent year even though eligibility may
be maintained. Students must reapply each
year.

Deadline: April 15 for priority consideration.

IRS I.D.: 55-0517092

STAFF:
Matt Turner, Executive Vice Chancellor for
Administration
Brian Weingart, Senior Director of Financial
Aid

ADDRESS INQUIRIES TO:
Brian Weingart
Senior Director of Financial Aid
(See address above.)

WOMEN IN DEFENSE

WID HORIZONS
2101 Wilson Boulevard, Suite 700
Arlington, VA 22201
(703) 247-2563
Fax: (703) 522-1885
E-mail: awebster@ndia.org
Web Site: www.womenindefense.net

TYPE:
Scholarships. The Horizons Foundation
Scholarship Program is supported by
accredited colleges and universities. Awards
are made on an annual basis. The Foundation
selects all scholarship recipients based on
criteria it sets. Scholarships are awarded to
applicants who require financial assistance,
demonstrate strong academic credentials and
a commitment to a career in national
security.

See entry 993 for full listing.

SCIENCES (multiple disciplines)

Sciences (multiple disciplines)

THE ACADEMY OF NATURAL SCIENCES OF PHILADELPHIA [1615]

1900 Benjamin Franklin Parkway
Philadelphia, PA 19103-1101
(215) 299-1065
Fax: (215) 299-1079
E-mail: kepics@ansp.org
Web Site: ansp.org/research/fellowships-endowments/gallagher

FOUNDED: 1812

AREAS OF INTEREST:
Research, exhibition and education in natural sciences.

NAME(S) OF PROGRAMS:
- **John J. and Anna H. Gallagher Fellowship**

TYPE:
Fellowships; Project/program grants; Research grants; Residencies; Training grants; Visiting scholars. The Gallagher Fellowship provides support for original postdoctoral or sabbatical research on the systematics of microscopic invertebrates, with priority for the study of rotifers.

YEAR PROGRAM STARTED: 1990

LEGAL BASIS:
Private, nonprofit natural science museum.

ELIGIBILITY:
Candidates must have a Ph.D. in zoology or in ecology, evolution and biodiversity from a major university. Applicants must provide a research proposal involving microscopic freshwater invertebrate animals, including development of expertise in one or more taxonomic groups and the names of three references who are acknowledged scholars in the field. Preference will be given to candidates specializing in Rotifera.

Work must take place primarily at the Academy of Natural Sciences of Philadelphia and/or in the field and should emphasize utilization of the Academy's collections of literature and specimens. Projects should be scaled for completion during the one-year duration of the fellowship.

FINANCIAL DATA:
Fellowship includes salary, benefits, travel expenses, field and laboratory supplies.
Total amount of support: Varies.

NO. MOST RECENT APPLICANTS: 9.

NO. AWARDS: 1.

APPLICATION INFO:
Research proposal should include:
(1) curriculum vitae;
(2) statement of research interests;
(3) a three- to five-page description of the project (including salary request, research project costs and a timeline) and;
(4) names and contact information of three references.
Duration: Up to 12 months.
Deadline: Proposals are accepted on a rolling basis.

ADDRESS INQUIRIES TO:
Kristen Kepics, Department Administrator
(See e-mail address above.)

ALABAMA ACADEMY OF SCIENCE, INC. [1616]

2108 Fox Valley Circle
Birmingham, AL 35216
(205) 936-0823
E-mail: krannich@uab.edu
Web Site: www.alabamaacademyofscience.org

FOUNDED: 1924

AREAS OF INTEREST:
Chemistry, biology, archaeology, earth science, forestry, geography, conservation, physics, industry, economics, mathematics, computer science, anthropology, engineering, psychology, behavioral and social sciences, physical sciences, health sciences and ecology.

CONSULTING OR VOLUNTEER SERVICES:
Visiting Scientist Speaker Program for elementary schools, high schools and colleges.

NAME(S) OF PROGRAMS:
- **Gorgas Scholarship**
- **Mason Science Teaching Fellowships**
- **Student Research Grants**
- **Student Travel Awards**

TYPE:
Assistantships; Awards/prizes; Conferences/seminars; Fellowships; Project/program grants; Research grants; Scholarships; Travel grants; Visiting scholars. Grants to college and university students for small research projects and for travel to scientific meetings to present papers.

Fellowships are for teaching science for Alabama teachers.

The Gorgas Scholarships are awarded to high school senior students who were Alabama Science Scholar Search entrants for any Alabama college or university.

YEAR PROGRAM STARTED: 1924

PURPOSE:
To stimulate student science study and research; to promote the development of interested scientific matter in the state; to render public service in scientific matters.

LEGAL BASIS:
Tax-exempt membership organization.

ELIGIBILITY:
Open to individuals committed to the purpose of the Academy.

GEOG. RESTRICTIONS: Alabama.

FINANCIAL DATA:
Amount of support per award: MST Fellowship: $1,000 for teacher and $50 to $100 per award for student research; Student Research Grants: $250; Student Travel Awards: $50; $10,000 in scholarships to high school seniors.
Total amount of support: Up to $13,000 annually.

CO-OP FUNDING PROGRAMS: Gorgas Scholarship Program is supported by an endowment. All other programs are funded by membership dues, meeting registrations, exhibits, contributions and university memberships.

NO. MOST RECENT APPLICANTS: 100.

NO. AWARDS: Gorgas Scholarship: 12; MST Fellowship: 1 teacher award and 40 for student research competition; Student Research Grants: 4; Student Travel Awards: 30.

APPLICATION INFO:
Contact the Academy.

Duration: One year.
Deadline: Approximately February 1. Award announcement at annual meeting in March.

PUBLICATIONS:
Journal of the Alabama Academy of Sciences.

IRS I.D.: 63-6050246

ADDRESS INQUIRIES TO:
Larry K. Krannich, Ph.D.
Executive Director
(See address above.)

ALTERNATIVES RESEARCH AND DEVELOPMENT FOUNDATION [1617]

801 Old York Road, Suite 316
Jenkintown, PA 19046
(215) 887-8076
E-mail: grants@ardf-online.org
Web Site: www.ardf-online.org

FOUNDED: 1993

AREAS OF INTEREST:
Development, validation and adoption of non-animal methods in biomedical research, product testing and education.

NAME(S) OF PROGRAMS:
- **Annual Open Grant Program**
- **William and Eleanor Cave Award**

TYPE:
Awards/prizes; Research grants.

YEAR PROGRAM STARTED: 1993

PURPOSE:
To fund and promote the development, validation and adoption of non-animal methods in biomedical research, product testing and education.

ELIGIBILITY:
Nonsectarian religious programs may apply. Preference is given to universities and research institutions in the U.S. No grants are made to individuals.

FINANCIAL DATA:
Amount of support per award: Up to $40,000.
Total amount of support: Varies.

NO. MOST RECENT APPLICANTS: 29.

NO. AWARDS: 7.

APPLICATION INFO:
All application information must be submitted using ARDF's online application portal in ProposalCentral. The applicant will need to provide the project title, project period, names and contact information for primary investigator(s), and institution information. This information will be entered into the proposal submission site, along with:
(1) an abstract (up to 300 words) describing

the proposed research and explaining how the project would contribute to reducing or replacing current uses of laboratory animals in biomedical research, product safety testing, or educational demonstrations and;

(2) the project proposal, which includes a research plan (no more than 10 pages), budget and justification, applicant biosketch or curriculum vitae, and relevant publications (optional), uploaded as separate PDF documents.

Duration: One year.

Deadline: April 30.

ADDRESS INQUIRIES TO:
Sue Leary, President
(See address above.)

AMERICAN INSTITUTE OF CHEMICAL ENGINEERS (AICHE)   [1618]
120 Wall Street, Floor 23
New York, NY 10005-4020
(203) 702-7660
(646) 495-1348
Fax: (203) 775-5177
E-mail: awards@aiche.org
Web Site: www.aiche.org

AREAS OF INTEREST:
Chemical engineering.

NAME(S) OF PROGRAMS:
● **Food, Pharmaceutical and Bioengineering Division Award in Chemical Engineering**

TYPE:
Awards/prizes.

YEAR PROGRAM STARTED: 1970

PURPOSE:
To recognize an individual's outstanding chemical engineering contribution in the food, pharmaceutical and/or bioengineering industry.

LEGAL BASIS:
Professional association.

ELIGIBILITY:
Contribution may have been made in industry, government, or academic areas, or with other organizations.

FINANCIAL DATA:
Amount of support per award: $2,000 and a plaque.
Total amount of support: $2,000.

NO. AWARDS: 1 annually.

APPLICATION INFO:
Nomination form is available on the AIChE web site.
Deadline: April 30.

ADDRESS INQUIRIES TO:
Dr. Wilfred Chen, Gore Professor of Chemical Engineering
224 Colburn Laboratory
Department of Chemical and Biomedical Engineering
University of Delaware
Newark, DE 19716
E-mail: wilfred@udel.edu

THE AMERICAN MUSEUM OF NATURAL HISTORY   [1619]
Richard Gilder Graduate School
Central Park West at 79th Street
New York, NY 10024-5192
(212) 769-5017
Fax: (212) 769-5257
E-mail: fellowships-rggs@amnh.org
assistantdirector-rggs@amnh.org
Web Site: www.amnh.org/our-research/richard-gilder-graduate-school

FOUNDED: 1869

AREAS OF INTEREST:
Anthropology, paleontology and zoology.

NAME(S) OF PROGRAMS:
● **Collection Study Grants**
● **Lerner-Gray Grants for Marine Research**
● **Theodore Roosevelt Memorial Grants**

TYPE:
Grants-in-aid; Research grants. Collection Study Grants enable predoctoral and recent postdoctoral investigators to study any of the scientific collections at the American Museum in the departments of anthropology, earth and planetary sciences, entomology, herpetology, ichthyology, invertebrates, mammalogy, ornithology, and vertebrate paleontology.

The Lerner-Gray Grants for Marine Research provide support to highly qualified persons starting careers in marine zoology.

The Theodore Roosevelt Memorial Grants support research on North American fauna in wildlife conservation or related fields of North American fauna.

YEAR PROGRAM STARTED: 1976

PURPOSE:
To provide modest short-term awards to advanced graduate students and postdoctoral researchers who are commencing their careers in the fields of zoology, paleontology and anthropology.

ELIGIBILITY:
Applicants should be advanced graduate students and postdoctoral researchers who are beginning their careers in the interest areas listed above. Research projects need not be carried out at the American Museum.

FINANCIAL DATA:
Amount of support per award: $500 to $3,500.
Total amount of support: Varies.

NO. AWARDS: Collection Study Grants: 23; Lerner-Gray Grants: 28; Theodore Roosevelt Grants: 34 for the year 2019.

APPLICATION INFO:
Application information is available on the web site.
Duration: Collection Study Grants: Projects of four days or longer are encouraged; Lerner-Gray and Theodore Roosevelt Grants: One year.
Deadline: Collection Study Grants: May 1; Lerner-Gray Grants: March 14; Theodore Roosevelt Memorial Grants: February 15.

ADDRESS INQUIRIES TO:
Maria Rios, Assistant Director
Fellowships and Student Affairs
(See address above.)

THE AMERICAN MUSEUM OF NATURAL HISTORY   [1620]
Richard Gilder Graduate School
Central Park West at 79th Street
New York, NY 10024-5192
(212) 769-5017
Fax: (212) 769-5257
E-mail: fellowships-rggs@amnh.org
assistantdirector-rggs@amnh.org
Web Site: www.amnh.org/our-research/richard-gilder-graduate-school

FOUNDED: 1869

AREAS OF INTEREST:
Vertebrate and invertebrate zoology, paleozoology, anthropology, earth and planetary sciences.

NAME(S) OF PROGRAMS:
● **Postdoctoral Research Fellowship Program**

TYPE:
Fellowships.

YEAR PROGRAM STARTED: 1960

PURPOSE:
To advance the training of recent postdoctoral investigators and established scientists.

LEGAL BASIS:
Nonprofit.

ELIGIBILITY:
Provides training to postdoctoral investigators and established scientists to carry out a specific project, which must fit into the Museum's areas of interest. Postdoctoral Fellows are expected to be in residence at the Museum.

FINANCIAL DATA:
Salary, health insurance and research expenses, as per budget, are provided.
Amount of support per award: Varies.
Total amount of support: Varies.

NO. MOST RECENT APPLICANTS: 50.

NO. AWARDS: 5.

APPLICATION INFO:
Applications require a project description with bibliography, budget, curriculum vitae including a list of publications, and letters of recommendation.
Duration: Up to two years.
Deadline: November 15.

PUBLICATIONS:
Grants and Fellowships of the American Museum of Natural History, booklet.

ADDRESS INQUIRIES TO:
Maria Rios, Assistant Director
Fellowships and Student Affairs
(See address above.)

AMERICAN TINNITUS ASSOCIATION (ATA)   [1621]
8300 Boone Boulevard
Suite 500
Vienna, VA 22182
(800) 634-8978
E-mail: tinnitus@ata.org
Web Site: www.ata.org

FOUNDED: 1971

AREAS OF INTEREST:
Tinnitus.

NAME(S) OF PROGRAMS:
● **ATA Student Research Grant Program**
● **ATA Tinnitus Research Grant Program**

TYPE:
Research grants; Seed money grants.
Financially supports scientific studies about
tinnitus.

YEAR PROGRAM STARTED: 1980

PURPOSE:
To identify the mechanisms of tinnitus or to
improve tinnitus treatments.

LEGAL BASIS:
501(c)(3) nonprofit association.

ELIGIBILITY:
Tinnitus Research Grant: Postdoctorate.
Student Grant: Doctorate or medical student.
ATA will consider the subject of research,
quality of its design, potential for significant
advances in basic knowledge or clinical
application, available facilities and personnel
at the institution and qualifications of
investigators. Facility must be nonprofit.

GEOG. RESTRICTIONS: United States.

FINANCIAL DATA:
Amount of support per award: Tinnitus
Research Grant: Up to $150,000 ($50,000 per
year); Student Grant: $10,000.

APPLICATION INFO:
In addition to the application form, applicants
must submit a concisely written research
proposal containing detailed descriptions of
the following elements:
(1) introduction, statement of the problem
and specific aims of the research;
(2) background and significance of the issue;
(3) relevant preliminary or pilot studies;
(4) the facility that will house the study
and/or administer the funds;
(5) discussion of relevant literature and,
where appropriate, standardized tinnitus
measures;
(6) outline of intended study procedures
including study design, sampling and
measurement data to be used, and description
of analysis and evaluation plan and;
(7) outcomes expected from the study and
the study's use.
Duration: Tinnitus Research Grant: Up to
three years. Student Grant: One year.
Deadline: November 1.

STAFF:
Torryn Brazell, Chief Executive Officer

ADDRESS INQUIRIES TO:
Torryn Brazell, Chief Executive Officer
(See address above.)

ARGONNE NATIONAL
LABORATORY   [1622]
Human Resources Service
9700 South Cass Avenue
Argonne, IL 60439-4845
(630) 252-4114
Fax: (630) 252-3193
E-mail: lisareed@anl.gov
undergrad@anl.gov
Web Site: www.dep.anl.gov

FOUNDED: 1968

AREAS OF INTEREST:
Basic physical and life sciences,
mathematics, computer science, engineering,
applied research relating to coal,
conservation, environmental impact and
technology, fission and fusion energy.

NAME(S) OF PROGRAMS:
● **Science Undergraduate Laboratory**
Internships

TYPE:
Internships.

PURPOSE:
To encourage the further study of science.

LEGAL BASIS:
Research center of the U.S. Department of
Energy.

ELIGIBILITY:
Applicants must be U.S. citizens or legal
permanent residents who are full-time
students at accredited U.S. colleges or
universities. Applicants must have completed
at least one year as a matriculated
undergraduate student at the time of
applying, with an undergraduate cumulative
minimum grade point average of 3.0 on a 4.0
scale. Applicants must be 18 years of age or
older at the time the internship begins.

GEOG. RESTRICTIONS: United States.

FINANCIAL DATA:
Amount of support per award: $600 per
week stipend.
Total amount of support: Varies.

NO. MOST RECENT APPLICANTS: 100.

APPLICATION INFO:
Applications must be submitted at the
Department of Energy web site.
Duration: 10 weeks during the summer; 15
weeks during fall or spring.
Deadline: Summer: January 10. Fall:
Approximately May 30. Spring: October 30.

ADDRESS INQUIRIES TO:
Lisa Reed, Program Coordinator
(See address above.)

ARGONNE NATIONAL
LABORATORY   [1623]
Human Resources Service
9700 South Cass Avenue
Argonne, IL 60439-4845
(630) 252-4114
Fax: (630) 252-3193
E-mail: lisareed@anl.gov
graduate@anl.gov
Web Site: www.dep.anl.gov

FOUNDED: 1946

AREAS OF INTEREST:
Basic physical and life sciences,
mathematics, computer science and
engineering, applied research relating to coal,
conservation, environmental science and
energy technologies and fission and fusion
energy.

NAME(S) OF PROGRAMS:
● **Graduate Research Program**

TYPE:
Fellowships. Graduate Research Program
provides Master's and Ph.D. level candidates
an opportunity to conduct work within an
Argonne research group or on a specific
project for the purpose of supporting the
student's thesis work. The university sets the
academic standards and awards the degree. In
practice, the participation of the faculty
member varies from full partnership in the
research to general supervision of the
student's thesis work. The Argonne staff
member keeps the faculty member at the
university informed on the student's progress.

YEAR PROGRAM STARTED: 1968

PURPOSE:
To encourage the advanced study of science.

LEGAL BASIS:
Research center of the U.S. Department of
Energy.

ELIGIBILITY:
Appointments are available to qualified U.S.
and non-U.S. university graduate students
who wish to carry out their thesis research at
Argonne National Laboratory under the
co-sponsorship of an Argonne staff member
and a faculty member at the student's home
institution.
Applicant must be currently enrolled
full-time at an accredited institution and be
18 years of age or older at the time the
appointment begins.

GEOG. RESTRICTIONS: United States.

FINANCIAL DATA:
Appointees receive an hourly wage, which is
determined by the hiring division and the
Educational Programs Office. Travel
reimbursement is determined by the hiring
division in accordance with laboratory policy.
All travel arrangements must be made by the
hiring division in order to receive any
reimbursement.
Total amount of support: Varies.

NO. AWARDS: Approximately 15.

APPLICATION INFO:
Applications must be submitted
electronically.
Duration: Three months to one year.
Possibility of renewal.

ADDRESS INQUIRIES TO:
Lisa Reed, Program Coordinator
(See address above.)

BROOKHAVEN WOMEN IN
SCIENCE
P.O. Box 183
Upton, NY 11973
(631) 344-7153
E-mail: bwischasmanaward@bnl.gov
Web Site: www.bnl.gov/bwis/scholarships.php

TYPE:
Awards/prizes; Scholarships. These
scholarships are offered to encourage women
to pursue careers in the sciences technology,
engineering or mathematics.

See entry 973 for full listing.

CARNEGIE INSTITUTION FOR
SCIENCE   [1624]
1530 P Street, N.W.
Washington, DC 20005
(202) 939-1120
E-mail: tmcdowell@carnegiescience.edu
Web Site: www.carnegiescience.edu

FOUNDED: 1902

AREAS OF INTEREST:
Astronomy, physics, chemistry, earth
sciences, materials science, plant biology,
developmental biology and global ecology.

NAME(S) OF PROGRAMS:
● **Predoctoral and Postdoctoral**
Fellowships at the Carnegie Institution

TYPE:
Fellowships; Internships; Technical
assistance; Visiting scholars; Research
contracts. Predoctoral and Postdoctoral
fellowships for research training in the fields
of astronomy, geophysics, physics and related
sciences, plant biology, genetics and

developmental biology in residence at one of the Carnegie Institution's six operating centers.

PURPOSE:
To encourage in the broadest and most liberal manner investigation, research and discovery and the application of knowledge to the improvement of mankind.

LEGAL BASIS:
Exempt under Section 501(c)(3) of the Internal Revenue Code.

ELIGIBILITY:
Qualified scientists who have obtained the doctoral degree or are in the process are eligible. Candidates are evaluated on the basis of academic record, recommendations of professors and associates and the complementing nature of their research to work in progress at the Carnegie department. Women and minorities are encouraged to apply.

FINANCIAL DATA:
Amount of support per award: Varies by department.

APPLICATION INFO:
Fellowship applications are submitted online to the Directors of the Departments of Carnegie Institution.
Duration: Fellowships are usually awarded for one to two years with the possibility of renewal for another year.
Deadline: Varies.

PUBLICATIONS:
Newsletter.

OFFICERS:
Eric D. Isaacs, President
Timothy Doyle, Chief Operating Officer

DIRECTORS:
Dr. Yixian Zheng, Director, Department of Embryology
Dr. Richard Carlson, Director, Earth and Planets Laboratory
Dr. John Mulchaey, Director, Observatories of the Carnegie Institution
Dr. Anna Michalak, Acting Director, Department of Global Ecology
Dr. Zhi-yong Wang, Acting Director, Department of Plant Biology
Dr. Michael Walter, Deputy Director, Earth and Planets Laboratory

ADDRESS INQUIRIES TO:
Call first to determine to whom inquiry should be directed.

Dr. Yixian Zheng
Director, Department of Embryology
3520 San Martin Drive
Baltimore, MD 21218 or

Dr. Richard Carlson
Director, Earth and Planets Laboratory
5241 Broad Branch Road, N.W.
Washington, DC 20015 or

Dr. Michael Walter
Deputy Director, Earth and Planets Laboratory
5251 Broad Branch Road, N.W.
Washington, DC 20015 or

Dr. John Mulchaey
Director, Observatories of the Carnegie Institution
813 Santa Barbara Street
Pasadena, CA 91101 or

Dr. Anna Michalak
Acting Director, Department of Global Ecology

260 Panama Street
Stanford, CA 94305
Tel: (650) 646-3830 or

Dr. Zhi-yong Wang
Acting Director, Department of Plant Biology
260 Panama Street
Stanford, CA 94305

*SPECIAL STIPULATIONS:
Fellowships are tenable only at one of the Institution's facilities. No extracurricular grants.

EARTHWATCH INSTITUTE   [1625]
1380 Soldiers Field Road
Suite 2700
Boston, MA 02135
(800) 776-0188
E-mail: research@earthwatch.org
Web Site: earthwatch.org/research/apply-for-research-funding

FOUNDED: 1971

AREAS OF INTEREST:
Earthwatch supports rigorous research that responds to global challenges - from climate change to human-wildlife coexistence to environmental sustainability - while engaging with local communities.

NAME(S) OF PROGRAMS:
● **Earthwatch Funding for Field Research**

TYPE:
Research grants. Financial support for field research projects. Earthwatch's overarching goal is to support projects that produce rigorous, relevant, and impactful science, address global change, and actively involve citizen-scientist participants. Through Earthwatch's citizen science model, research teams are provided with funding and volunteers needed to support data collection in marine, terrestrial, freshwater, and urban ecosystems. Volunteers take action to help scientists accomplish their research goals and contribute to tangible outcomes that advance conservation.

YEAR PROGRAM STARTED: 1971

PURPOSE:
To engage people worldwide in scientific field research and education to promote understanding and action necessary for a sustainable environment.

LEGAL BASIS:
Incorporated as a nonprofit, tax-exempt organization, 501(c)(3) of the IRS Code.

ELIGIBILITY:
All Principal Investigators must have a Ph.D. and an affiliation with a university, government agency or science-focused NGP. Earthwatch strongly encourages graduate student participation on projects and is particularly interested in helping support early-career scientists and scientists local to the research nation.

Proposals are evaluated on the basis of scientific merit, appropriateness of citizen-scientist activities, expected project outcomes and impacts, safety, and logistics.

GEOG. RESTRICTIONS: Due to safety concerns, Earthwatch is not able to support any research projects in certain regions of the world. More information is provided during the application process.

FINANCIAL DATA:
Amount of support per award: Field grants vary based on project needs. Typical field grants are $20,000 to $80,000 per year per project.
Total amount of support: $1,598,000 for the year 2019.

NO. MOST RECENT APPLICANTS: 80 for the year 2021.

NO. AWARDS: 5 new for the year 2021.

APPLICATION INFO:
Pre-proposals for new projects are solicited by an annual Request for Proposals in late April.
Duration: Three years, subject to passing an annual performance review. Funding is renewable, upon submitting a research renewal proposal.

PUBLICATIONS:
Earthwatch, magazine; *Project Briefings*; proposal guidelines; grants list.

STAFF:
Dr. Stan Rullman, Director of Research

ADDRESS INQUIRIES TO:
Research Department
(See address above.)

EARTHWATCH INSTITUTE   [1626]
1380 Soldiers Field Road
2nd Floor
Boston, MA 02135
(800) 776-0188
E-mail: fellowshipawards@earthwatch.org
Web Site: www.earthwatch.org/education

FOUNDED: 1971

AREAS OF INTEREST:
Promoting a sustainable environment.

NAME(S) OF PROGRAMS:
● **Earthwatch Educator Program**
● **Earthwatch Teach Earth USA Program**

TYPE:
Fellowships. Teachers in grades K-12 apply for seven- to 14-day Earthwatch expedition fellowships that take place during the summer. Earthwatch selects teachers from all subject areas across the U.S. to assist scientists on expeditions by collecting data on climate change and sustainable resource management. Funding for these fellowships comes from a variety of donors, e.g., individuals, corporations, family foundations, community organizations and nonprofits. On their return from the field, these teachers must develop a lesson or action plan that ties their experience back to their classroom or community.

YEAR PROGRAM STARTED: 1971

PURPOSE:
To inspire young people to become environmental ambassadors by engaging educators and empowering them to be role models regarding environmental issues and science research; to accomplish this, the Teach Earth USA Fellowship program focuses on engaging teachers from all subject areas and grade levels to assist scientists with research on climate change and sustainable resource management.

LEGAL BASIS:
Incorporated as a nonprofit, tax-exempt organization, 501(c)(3) of the IRS Code.

ELIGIBILITY:
All U.S. teachers that currently teach grades K-12. These teachers must be passionate

about teaching, looking to learn more about environmental issues, are interested in how scientific research is conducted, excited to collaborate with a team of teachers, and committed to engaging students and the community outside the classroom. Earthwatch searches for evidence of passionate teaching that stretches beyond the basics of the classroom and engages professionals who may not identify as science experts but are willing to learn and do more.

GEOG. RESTRICTIONS: United States.

FINANCIAL DATA:
Fellowship covers the full cost of the assigned expedition including meals and accommodations and on-site transportation. The fellowship also includes a travel award to offset out-of-pocket travel expenses to and from the expedition. Partially-funded fellowships are also offered.
Amount of support per award: $6,500.
Total amount of support: $377,006.

NO. MOST RECENT APPLICANTS: Approximately 450.

NO. AWARDS: 30.

APPLICATION INFO:
Applicants may contact Earthwatch at the e-mail address listed above.
Duration: Seven- to 14-day expedition.
Deadline: Applications are typically sent out during the fall. Deadline is mid-January to mid-February.

PUBLICATIONS:
Earthwatch, magazine; Project Briefings; proposal guidelines; grants list.

THE ELECTROCHEMICAL SOCIETY   [1627]
65 South Main Street, Building D
Pennington, NJ 08534-2839
(609) 737-1902 ext. 124
Fax: (609) 737-2743
E-mail: awards@electrochem.org
Web Site: www.electrochem.org/awards

FOUNDED: 1902

AREAS OF INTEREST:
Advancement of the theory and practice of electrochemical and solid-state science and technology, and allied subjects.

NAME(S) OF PROGRAMS:
• **Edward Goodrich Acheson Award**
• **Allen J. Bard Award**
• **Vittorio de Nora Award**
• **Henry B. Linford Award for Distinguished Teaching**
• **Gordon E. Moore Medal for Outstanding Achievement in Solid State Science and Technology**
• **Olin Palladium Award**
• **Charles W. Tobias Young Investigator Award**
• **Carl Wagner Memorial Award**

TYPE:
Awards/prizes. Edward Goodrich Acheson Award is for distinguished contributions to discoveries, research, inventions, or theory or practice of electrochemical and/or solid state science and technology, as well as distinguished service to The Electrochemical Society.

Allen J. Bard Award recognizes distinguished paradigm shifting contributions in the fields of electrochemical science and for

exceptionally creative experimental or theoretical studies that have opened new directions in electroanalytical chemistry or electrocatalysis.

Vittorio de Nora Award is for contributions to the field of electrochemical engineering and technology.

Henry B. Linford Award for Distinguished Teaching recognizes excellence in teaching in subject areas of interest to the Society.

Gordon E. Moore Medal for Outstanding Achievement in Solid State Science and Technology is for distinguished contributions to the field of solid state science and technology.

Olin Palladium Award is for distinguished contributions to the field of electrochemical or corrosion science.

Charles W. Tobias Young Investigator Award recognizes outstanding scientific and/or engineering work in fundamental or applied electrochemistry or solid state science and technology by a young scientist or engineer.

Carl Wagner Memorial Award recognizes a midcareer achievement and excellence in research areas of interest of the Society and significant contributions in the teaching or guidance of students or colleagues in education, industry or government.

PURPOSE:
To advance the theory and practice of electrochemical and solid-state science and technology, and allied subjects.

ELIGIBILITY:
Varies by award.

FINANCIAL DATA:
All awards include complimentary meeting registration and a dinner held in recipient's honor during the designated meeting and Life Membership in The Electrochemical Society.
Amount of support per award: Edward Goodrich Acheson Award: Gold medal, a plaque containing a bronze replica of the medal, and a $10,000 prize; Allen J. Bard Award: Wall plaque containing a glass carbon medal and a prize of $7,500; Vittorio de Nora Award: Gold medal, wall plaque containing a bronze replica of the medal and a prize of $7,500; Henry B. Linford Award for Distinguished Teaching: Silver medal, wall plaque containing a bronze replica of the medal, and a prize of $2,500; Olin Palladium Award: Palladium medal, wall plaque containing a bronze replica of the medal, and a prize of $7,500; Gordon E. Moore Medal for Outstanding Achievement in Solid State Science and Technology: Silver medal, wall plaque containing a bronze replica of the medal and a prize of $7,500; Charles W. Tobias Young Investigator Award: Framed certificate, prize of $5,000 and up to $1,000 in travel assistance to attend the designated meeting; Carl Wagner Memorial Award: Silver medal, framed certificate and up to $1,000 in travel assistance to attend the designated meeting.

NO. MOST RECENT APPLICANTS: 15 to 20.

NO. AWARDS: 4 annually; only 1 winner per award given in any of the award cycles.

APPLICATION INFO:
Application information is available on the web site.
Deadline: April or October, depending on award cycle.

ADDRESS INQUIRIES TO:
E-mail: awards@electrochem.org

THE ELECTROCHEMICAL SOCIETY   [1628]
65 South Main Street, Building D
Pennington, NJ 08534-2839
(609) 737-1902 ext. 111
Fax: (609) 737-2743
E-mail: awards@electrochem.org
jessica.wisniewski@electrochem.org
Web Site: www.electrochem.org

FOUNDED: 1902

AREAS OF INTEREST:
Advancement of the theory and practice of electrochemistry, electrometallurgy, solid-state science, electrothermics and allied subjects.

NAME(S) OF PROGRAMS:
• **ECS Summer Fellowships**

TYPE:
Awards/prizes; Conferences/seminars; Development grants; Fellowships; Grants-in-aid; Project/program grants; Research grants; Training grants; Travel grants. Summer Fellowships assist students in pursuit of work in a field of interest to the The Electrochemical Society.

YEAR PROGRAM STARTED: 1928

PURPOSE:
To stimulate and encourage participation and education in the fields of electrochemical science and technology as well as other interests to the Society.

LEGAL BASIS:
Scientific, educational, nonprofit, tax-exempt organization.

ELIGIBILITY:
For Fellowships, the applicant must be a graduate student (between B.S. and Ph.D.) in a college or university who will continue studies following the summer months the award is given.

No limitations on sex, race, nationality or religion.

FINANCIAL DATA:
Amount of support per award: Varies upon approval from the Board of Directors; usually $5,000 each.
Total amount of support: Varies.

NO. MOST RECENT APPLICANTS: 49.

NO. AWARDS: Up to 4 Summer Fellowships annually.

APPLICATION INFO:
Submit a brief statement of educational objectives, work accomplished on thesis, work planned, transcript of undergraduate and graduate work, two letters of recommendation and a letter of agreement not to hold other appointments or fellowships simultaneously.
Duration: June to September.
Deadline: Fellowships: January 15. Notification for Fellowships will be made on or before March 15.

PUBLICATIONS:
Interface Magazine.

STAFF:
Jessica Wisniewski, Human Resources and Operations Manager

ADDRESS INQUIRIES TO:
The Electrochemical Society
Awards/ECS
(See address above.)

FATS AND PROTEINS RESEARCH FOUNDATION, INC. [1629]
500 Montgomery Street
Suite 310
Alexandria, VA 22314
(703) 683-2633
E-mail: dmeeker@nara.org
Web Site: www.fprf.org

FOUNDED: 1962

AREAS OF INTEREST:
Use of rendered product in animal nutrition and other applications; feed safety, biosecurity, and efficiency of processes.

TYPE:
Research grants; Research contracts.

YEAR PROGRAM STARTED: 1962

PURPOSE:
To promote scientific and technological research into new and expanded uses for fats and proteins from animal by-products and processing technology; to encourage cooperative studies.

LEGAL BASIS:
Nonprofit foundation, 501(c)(6).

ELIGIBILITY:
Colleges, universities and research institutes with appropriate interests and capabilities are eligible to apply.

FINANCIAL DATA:
Amount of support per award: Average $35,000.
Total amount of support: $300,000 to $400,000 annually.

CO-OP FUNDING PROGRAMS: Encouraged.

NO. MOST RECENT APPLICANTS: 14 for the year 2019.

NO. AWARDS: 10 for the year 2020.

APPLICATION INFO:
Request proposal format from the above address or visit the web site. Prospective applicants should submit a brief outline of the proposed project (including background information, objectives, scope and mode of approach) along with a statement of the required budget and a brief biographical sketch of personnel to be involved in the research.
Duration: Varies.
Deadline: March 15 and September 15 for review of applications.

PUBLICATIONS:
Annual report; contributions policy; application guidelines.

IRS I.D.: 39-2497869

ADDRESS INQUIRIES TO:
Dr. David L. Meeker, Research Director
(See e-mail address above.)

FLORIDA EDUCATION FUND
201 East Kennedy Boulevard
Suite 1525
Tampa, FL 33602
(813) 272-2772 ext. 203
Fax: (813) 272-2784
E-mail: cjackson@fefonline.org
mdf@fefonline.org
Web Site: www.fefonline.org

TYPE:
Fellowships.

See entry 1386 for full listing.

FOUNDATION FOR SCIENCE AND DISABILITY
503 N.W. 89th Street
Gainesville, FL 32607
(352) 374-5774
E-mail: rmankin1@ufl.edu
Web Site: stemd.org

TYPE:
Grants-in-aid; Research grants.

See entry 899 for full listing.

GRADUATE WOMEN IN SCIENCE [1630]
P.O. Box 7
Mullica Hill, NJ 08062
E-mail: fellowships@gwis.org
Web Site: www.gwis.org

FOUNDED: 1922

AREAS OF INTEREST:
Science and research.

CONSULTING OR VOLUNTEER SERVICES:
A great deal of volunteering is provided by 22 chapters of the organization (e.g., science fair judges, girl scout support in science, etc.).

NAME(S) OF PROGRAMS:
● GWIS Fellowships Program

TYPE:
Fellowships.

YEAR PROGRAM STARTED: 1941

PURPOSE:
To increase knowledge in the natural sciences; to encourage research careers in the sciences by women.

ELIGIBILITY:
Applicants must be women scientists who have already completed a Bachelor's degree and are conducting research in the natural sciences. Applicants are encouraged to become SDE/GWIS members at the time of application.

FINANCIAL DATA:
Amount of support per award: Up to $10,000.
Total amount of support: Approximately $50,000 for the year 2020-21.

NO. MOST RECENT APPLICANTS: 210 for the year 2020-21.

NO. AWARDS: 7 for the year 2020-21.

APPLICATION INFO:
Information about the application process is available online.
Duration: One year. No renewals.
Deadline: January 11.

PUBLICATIONS:
GWIS Bulletin; *GWIS e-news*, monthly electronic newsletter.

IRS I.D.: 24-0825560

ADDRESS INQUIRIES TO:
Vicky Cattani, Fellowships Coordinator
(See address above.)

HARVARD TRAVELLERS CLUB, PERMANENT FUND [1631]
170 Hubbard Street
Lenox, MA 01240
E-mail: jackdeary@harvardtravellersclub.org
Web Site: www.travellersfund.org

FOUNDED: 1937

AREAS OF INTEREST:
Various scientific fields.

TYPE:
Project/program grants; Research grants. Small grants for research projects.

YEAR PROGRAM STARTED: 1937

PURPOSE:
To foster research and/or exploration which involves travel.

LEGAL BASIS:
501(c)(3) nonprofit organization.

ELIGIBILITY:
Applicants must have ability to make a competent contribution in the field of research. The Fund does not pay travel expenses unless it is intimately involved with the research and/or exploration. Preference is given to applicants working on advanced degrees.

FINANCIAL DATA:
Amount of support per award: Up to $5,000.
Total amount of support: Maximum $10,000 annually.

NO. MOST RECENT APPLICANTS: 15.

NO. AWARDS: 2.

APPLICATION INFO:
Applicants should submit a curriculum vitae and proposal of travel/studies.
Duration: Usually one-time grant.
Deadline: Late February. Decision in April.

IRS I.D.: 04-6115589

AWARDS COMMITTEE:
Nils Bonde-Henricksen
Peter Creighton
Jack Deary

ADDRESS INQUIRIES TO:
Jack Deary, Trustee
(See address above.)

*SPECIAL STIPULATIONS:
No scholarships for study at educational institutions.

THE HERB SOCIETY OF AMERICA, INC.
9019 Kirtland Chardon Road
Kirtland, OH 44094
(440) 256-0514
Fax: (440) 256-0541
E-mail: director@herbsociety.org
Web Site: www.herbsociety.org

TYPE:
Research grants.

See entry 1917 for full listing.

HISTORY OF SCIENCE SOCIETY
440 Geddes Hall
University of Notre Dame
Notre Dame, IN 46556
(574) 631-1194
E-mail: info@hssonline.org
Web Site: www.hssonline.org

TYPE:
Awards/prizes. The Davis Prize honors books in the history of science directed to a wide public and was established through a long-term pledge from Miles and Audrey Davis.

The Joseph H. Hazen Education Prize recognizes excellence in teaching in the history of science.

The Levinson Prize is awarded in even-numbered years to an outstanding book in the life sciences and natural history.

The Philip J. Pauly Prize is awarded to the best first book on the history of science in the Americas.

The Pfizer Prize honors the best English-language work related to the history of science published in the preceding three years.

The Ronald Rainger Prize is awarded for early career work in the history of earth and environmental sciences.

The Nathan Reingold Prize is given for an original essay in the history of science and its cultural influences.

The Margaret W. Rossiter History of Women in Science Prize honors an outstanding book, or in even-numbered years an article, published in the preceding four years.

See entry 548 for full listing.

HISTORY OF SCIENCE SOCIETY

440 Geddes Hall
University of Notre Dame
Notre Dame, IN 46556
(574) 631-1194
E-mail: info@hssonline.org
Web Site: www.hssonline.org

TYPE:
Awards/prizes. Prize for the best scholarly article published in *Isis* during the past three years.

See entry 547 for full listing.

ILLINOIS STATE ACADEMY OF SCIENCE [1632]

c/o Research and Collections Center
1011 East Ash Street
Springfield, IL 62703
(217) 782-6436
E-mail: robyn.myers@illinoisstatemuseum.org
Web Site: ilacadofsci.com

FOUNDED: 1907

AREAS OF INTEREST:
Promotion of science in the state of Illinois.

NAME(S) OF PROGRAMS:
● **Scientific Research Grants/Proposal Writing Contest**

TYPE:
Awards/prizes; Grants-in-aid; Project/program grants; Research grants; Seed money grants. Cash grants and certificates to Illinois high school, junior college or college students for writing a scientific proposal and conducting the proposed research.

YEAR PROGRAM STARTED: 1981

PURPOSE:
To promote science in the state of Illinois.

LEGAL BASIS:
Nonprofit organization.

ELIGIBILITY:
All public or private high school, junior college or college students in the state of Illinois who are sponsored by a signing instructor are eligible. ISAS membership is required. Proposals do not have to be

original. They can be a spin-off of a lab experiment from class or something the student is interested in as a hobby.

GEOG. RESTRICTIONS: Illinois.

FINANCIAL DATA:
Amount of support per award: High School students: Up to $200; Undergraduate students: Up to $500; Graduate students: Up to $1,000.
Total amount of support: Varies each year.

NO. AWARDS: Varies.

APPLICATION INFO:
Students must submit application electronically through the Academy's web site.
Duration: One-time award.
Deadline: Application deadline is posted on the Academy's web site.

PUBLICATIONS:
Transactions of the Illinois State Academy of Science.

IRS I.D.: 37-6043007

ADDRESS INQUIRIES TO:
Dr. Kurt Schulz, Student Grants Coordinator
E-mail: kschulz@siue.edu or
Robyn L. Myers, Executive Secretary
(See address above.)

INSTITUTE OF FOOD TECHNOLOGISTS FOUNDATION

525 West Van Buren Street
Suite 1000
Chicago, IL 60607
(312) 782-8424
Fax: (312) 416-7919
E-mail: feedingtomorrow@ift.org
Web Site: www.ift.org

TYPE:
Scholarships. Freshman Scholarships and Undergraduate Scholarships encourage undergraduate enrollment in food science and technology. Graduate Scholarships support advanced study in the field of food science and technology.

See entry 2356 for full listing.

INTERNATIONAL FOUNDATION FOR ETHICAL RESEARCH, INC. (IFER) [1633]

444 North Wells Street
Suite 406
Chicago, IL 60654
(312) 427-6065
Fax: (312) 427-6524
E-mail: ifer@ifer.org
Web Site: www.ifer.org

FOUNDED: 1985

AREAS OF INTEREST:
Scientifically valid alternatives to the use of animals in research, product testing, and education.

NAME(S) OF PROGRAMS:
● **Graduate Fellowship Program for Alternatives to the Use of Animals in Science**

TYPE:
Fellowships; Research grants. Graduate Fellowships in Humane Science support research in, but not limited to, tissue, cell and organ cultures, clinical studies using animals or humans, epidemiological studies, enhanced use of extensive tissue repositories

and patient databases, public education, and computer modeling to replace the use of animals used in science.

YEAR PROGRAM STARTED: 1985

PURPOSE:
To provide financial incentives to graduate students in science that encourage them at the earliest stages of their career to integrate innovation and discovery with ethics and respect for animals.

LEGAL BASIS:
Nonprofit.

ELIGIBILITY:
Application is open to students enrolled in Master's and Ph.D. programs in the sciences and human or veterinary medicine. Projects in other fields that show promise to increase public awareness or promote changes in the legal system or public policy regarding the use of animals in research, testing and education are also eligible.

Fellowships are awarded to those candidates whose program of study shows the greatest potential to replace the use of animals in science.

FINANCIAL DATA:
Amount of support per award: Up to $12,500 stipend, plus up to $2,500 for supplies per year.

APPLICATION INFO:
Information and preproposal guidelines are available from the Foundation.
Duration: The fellowships are renewable for up to three years.
Deadline: Preproposal: Usually spring. Exact date will be posted online.

PUBLICATIONS:
Newsletter.

IRS I.D.: 22-2628153

THE LALOR FOUNDATION, INC. [1634]

c/o GMA Foundations
2 Liberty Square, Suite 500
Boston, MA 02109
(617) 426-7080
(617) 391-3088
E-mail: fellowshipmanager@gmafoundations.com
Web Site: lalorfound.org

FOUNDED: 1935

AREAS OF INTEREST:
Basic postdoctoral research in mammalian reproductive physiology and biochemistry bearing on sterilization and/or prevention or termination of pregnancy.

NAME(S) OF PROGRAMS:
● **The Lalor Foundation Postdoctoral Fellowship Program**

TYPE:
Fellowships. Fellowships to institutions for basic postdoctoral research in mammalian reproductive biology as related to the regulation of fertility.

YEAR PROGRAM STARTED: 1937

PURPOSE:
To promote intensive research in mammalian reproductive biology.

LEGAL BASIS:
Tax-exempt philanthropic foundation.

ELIGIBILITY:
Domestic institutions must be exempt from federal income taxes under Section 501(c)(3) of the Internal Revenue Code. Domestic and foreign institutions must qualify under Section 509(a)(1), (2) or (3). Individuals who are nominated by the applicant institution may be citizens of any country and should have training and experience at least equal to the Ph.D. or M.D. level. Potential fellows may not have held the doctoral degree more than two years.

The applicant institution may make its nomination of a fellow from among its own personnel or elsewhere, but, qualifications being equal, candidates from other than the proposing institution itself may carry modest preference. The application must name the institution's nominee for fellowship and include his or her performance record.

FINANCIAL DATA:
Grants for coverage of fellowship stipend and institutional expenses.
Amount of support per award: $50,000 per year.
Total amount of support: Approximately $500,000.

NO. AWARDS: 10 for fiscal year 2018.

APPLICATION INFO:
Application and appendices are to be submitted online.
Duration: One year. Renewable under some circumstances.
Deadline: January 15. Notification by April 15.

IRS I.D.: 51-6000153

ADDRESS INQUIRIES TO:
Fellowship Manager
(See e-mail address above.)

LOS ALAMOS NATIONAL LABORATORY   [1635]
P.O. Box 1663
MS-P290
Los Alamos, NM 87545
(505) 665-6406
E-mail: hrstaffing-postdocs@lanl.gov
Web Site: www.lanl.gov/science/postdocs

FOUNDED: 1943

AREAS OF INTEREST:
Biosciences, chemistry, computing, Earth and space science, engineering, materials science, mathematics and physics.

NAME(S) OF PROGRAMS:
● **Richard P. Feynman Postdoctoral Fellowship in Theory and Computing**
● **J. Robert Oppenheimer Postdoctoral Fellowship**
● **Frederick Reines Postdoctoral Fellowship in Experimental Sciences**

TYPE:
Fellowships. The Distinguished Postdoctoral Fellowships provide the opportunity for the recipients to collaborate with LANL scientists and engineers on staff-initiated research. Candidates for these awards must display extraordinary ability in scientific research and show clear and definite promise of becoming outstanding leaders in the research they pursue.

YEAR PROGRAM STARTED: 1960

ELIGIBILITY:
Candidates must have a doctoral degree within the last five years or will have

completed all Ph.D. requirements by commencement of their appointment. The Feynman and Reines Fellowships require the ability to obtain a DOE "Q" clearance, which normally requires U.S. citizenship.

Every candidate must be sponsored by a technical staff member before being reviewed by the Postdoctoral Committee.

FINANCIAL DATA:
A generous and comprehensive salary and benefits package is provided, including incoming relocation.
Amount of support per award: Feynman, Oppenheimer and Reines Postdoctoral Fellowships provide a starting salary of $111,000.

NO. AWARDS: Up to 2 in each fellowship category.

APPLICATION INFO:
Details are available online.
Duration: Appointments are for three years.
Deadline: January.

ADDRESS INQUIRIES TO:
See e-mail address above.

MICHIGAN SOCIETY OF FELLOWS
University of Michigan
0540 Rackham Building
915 East Washington Street
Ann Arbor, MI 48109-1070
(734) 763-1259
E-mail: society.of.fellows@umich.edu
Web Site: www.societyoffellows.umich.edu

TYPE:
Fellowships. Fellows are appointed as Assistant Professors in appropriate departments and as Postdoctoral Scholars in the Michigan Society of Fellows. They are expected to be in residence in Ann Arbor during the academic years of the fellowship, to teach for the equivalent of one academic year, to participate in the informal intellectual life of the Society, and to devote time to their independent research or artistic projects.

See entry 334 for full listing.

MICRON TECHNOLOGY FOUNDATION, INC.
P.O. Box 6
Boise, ID 83707-0006
(208) 363-3675
Fax: (208) 368-4435
E-mail: mtf@micron.com
Web Site: www.micron.com/foundation

TYPE:
Matching gifts; Professorships; Project/program grants; Research grants.

See entry 1886 for full listing.

MICROSCOPY SOCIETY OF AMERICA   [1636]
11130 Sunrise Valley Drive
Suite 350
Reston, VA 20191
(703) 234-4115
E-mail: associationmanagement@microscopy.org
Web Site: www.microscopy.org/awards

FOUNDED: 1942

AREAS OF INTEREST:
Microscopy.

NAME(S) OF PROGRAMS:
● **Undergraduate Research Scholarship Program**

TYPE:
Scholarships.

PURPOSE:
To foster educational and research potential in full-time undergraduate students intent on pursuing microscopy as a career or major research tool.

LEGAL BASIS:
Nonprofit society.

ELIGIBILITY:
The applicant must be a full-time undergraduate student and must have achieved junior or senior standing by the time the work is initiated. Research must be completed prior to graduation. Scholarship funds must be expended within one year of award date.

Applicants may receive only one scholarship and may perform research at an institution other than the one in which the applicant is enrolled. Successful applicants must agree to furnish MSA with an abstract for publication in the Society Journal, *Microscopy & Microanalysis,* describing the results and status of their project within two months after the conclusion of the award period, to acknowledge the award in all resulting publications, and to provide reprints of any other resulting publications to the Society.

FINANCIAL DATA:
Amount of support per award: Up to $3,000.
Total amount of support: Varies.

NO. MOST RECENT APPLICANTS: 20.

NO. AWARDS: Average 5.

APPLICATION INFO:
Required application form should include:
(1) a research proposal not to exceed three pages in length, including a brief introduction, a short methods section and description and itemized goals of the study;
(2) a budget indicating how the awarded funds will be expended;
(3) two letters of reference from scientists or university faculty familiar with the applicant's capabilities;
(4) a letter from the laboratory supervisor where the proposed research will be performed, confirming that the applicant and research project are acceptable;
(5) a curriculum vitae detailing previous education and/or training in microscopy and a brief statement of career goals and;
(6) a letter of recommendation from an MSA member.

An original and four copies of a completed application form and attachments are required, unless all materials are being submitted electronically to the e-mail address above.

Duration: One year. No renewals.
Deadline: December 1. Award announcement January 15.

PUBLICATIONS:
Program announcement.

ADDRESS INQUIRIES TO:
Ashley Carey, Managing Director
(See address above.)

MICROSCOPY SOCIETY OF AMERICA [1637]
11130 Sunrise Valley Drive
Suite 350
Reston, VA 20191
(703) 234-4115
E-mail: associationmanagement@microscopy.org
Web Site: www.microscopy.org/awards

FOUNDED: 1942

AREAS OF INTEREST:
All phases of microscopy.

NAME(S) OF PROGRAMS:
● **Microscopy & Microanalysis (M & M) Student Award**

TYPE:
Travel grants. Awards are given to outstanding students selected on the basis of the quality and originality of their research abstracts submitted for the Annual MSA Scientific Program. The award consists of free registration for the meeting, a copy of *Proceedings*, and an invitation to the Sunday social event.

PURPOSE:
To promote student interest in microscopy and exchange of information.

LEGAL BASIS:
Nonprofit.

ELIGIBILITY:
Applicants must be bona fide students at a recognized college or university at the time of the meeting. Awards are based on the quality of the paper submitted for presentation at the meeting and the applicant must be the submitted paper's first author. Successful applicants must present their papers personally at the meeting in order to receive the award. They are expected to attend and participate in the entire meeting. Candidates should be juniors or seniors at the time the work is initiated. Former winners are ineligible.

FINANCIAL DATA:
Awardees will be reimbursed up to $1,000 for travel (round-trip, lowest-fare, continental U.S.) and complimentary full-meeting registration to the Microscopy & Microanalysis meeting, and invitation to the Presidential Reception.

Amount of support per award: Varies.

Total amount of support: $30,000.

NO. AWARDS: Varies.

APPLICATION INFO:
Applications consist of a completed Advanced Reservation Form, payment for student registration, a supporting letter from a member of MSA, preferably a research advisor, attesting to the applicant's status, and a scientific paper for presentation accompanied by a completed Data Form.

Deadline: February 15.

PUBLICATIONS:
The MSA Proceedings.

ADDRESS INQUIRIES TO:
See e-mail address above.

NATIONAL CENTER FOR ATMOSPHERIC RESEARCH [1638]
1850 Table Mesa Drive
Boulder, CO 80305
(303) 497-1607
Fax: (303) 497-1646
E-mail: sbriggs@ucar.edu
Web Site: www.asp.ucar.edu

FOUNDED: 1960

AREAS OF INTEREST:
Research in atmospheric sciences, including such topics as atmospheric dynamics (on all scales) and models, climate science, cloud physics, atmospheric chemistry and radiation, turbulence, upper-atmosphere physics, solar and solar-terrestrial physics (including ionospheric studies and aeronomy), oceanography and atmospheric technology. Also included are studies of the interaction of the atmosphere with the oceans, the cryosphere, the Earth's surface and human society and application of biology, ecology, geology, economics and political science skills to atmospheric issues.

NAME(S) OF PROGRAMS:
● **Postdoctoral Fellowships at NCAR**

TYPE:
Fellowships. The fellowships cover a year's appointment, with a likely extension to two years, at NCAR to take advantage of its educational programs and/or research facilities in the broad field of atmospheric sciences.

YEAR PROGRAM STARTED: 1964

PURPOSE:
To provide an opportunity for talented scientists who have recently received their Ph.Ds. to continue to pursue their research interests and to develop expertise in new areas; to enrich the research talent in the atmospheric sciences by offering an opportunity for highly qualified Ph.D. physicists, chemists, applied mathematicians, engineers and specialists from other disciplines such as biology, geology, science education, economics and geography, as well as atmospheric science, to apply their training to research in the atmospheric sciences.

LEGAL BASIS:
Research institution operated by the nonprofit University Corporation for Atmospheric Research (UCAR) under sponsorship of the National Science Foundation (NSF).

ELIGIBILITY:
Interested scientists who have received their Ph.D., Sc.D. or equivalent are eligible. NCAR encourages applications from women and minorities. There are no restrictions for foreign applicants.

Primary criteria in selection of postdoctoral appointees are the applicant's scientific capability and potential, originality and independence, and the ability to take advantage of the research opportunities at NCAR.

Appointments are tenable only in residence in Boulder, CO.

FINANCIAL DATA:
All appointees are eligible for life and health insurance in addition to excellent retirement benefits. Travel expenses to NCAR will be reimbursed for the fellow and his or her family. A small allowance for moving and storage is provided.

Amount of support per award: Basic stipend of $68,220 for the first year and $69,910 for the second year, plus a minimum of $3,500 for annual scientific travel support.

NO. MOST RECENT APPLICANTS: 100.

NO. AWARDS: Approximately 10 per year.

APPLICATION INFO:
Contact the Center.

Duration: Two years.

Deadline: January, to be considered for fellowship awards to begin the following summer or fall. Selections announced in March.

PUBLICATIONS:
Program announcement.

ADDRESS INQUIRIES TO:
Scott Briggs, Coordinator
Advanced Study Program
(See address above.)

*SPECIAL STIPULATIONS:
Appointments are tenable only in residence at the National Center for Atmospheric Research.

NATIONAL INVENTORS HALL OF FAME [1639]
3701 Highland Park, N.W.
North Canton, OH 44720-4535
(800) 968-4332 (option 5)
E-mail: collegiate@invent.org
Web Site: www.invent.org/collegiate-inventors

AREAS OF INTEREST:
Creative invention: science, engineering, mathematics, technology and related fields.

NAME(S) OF PROGRAMS:
● **Collegiate Inventors Competition**

TYPE:
Awards/prizes. National competition in the U.S. that recognizes and rewards innovations, discoveries, and research by college and university students and their faculty advisors.

YEAR PROGRAM STARTED: 1990

PURPOSE:
To promote exploration in invention, science, engineering, technology, and other creative endeavors and provide a window on the future technologies from which society will benefit in the future.

ELIGIBILITY:
Open to students who are enrolled part-time or full-time in any U.S. college or university at least part of the 12-month period prior to the date the entry is submitted. In the case of a team (maximum of four students), at least one member must meet the eligibility criteria.

Entry must be the original idea and work product of the student/advisor team, and must not have been:
(1) made available to the public as a commercial product or process or;
(2) patented or published more than one year prior to the date of competition submission.

Entries must be written in English.

GEOG. RESTRICTIONS: United States.

FINANCIAL DATA:
Finalists will win an all-expense-paid trip in the fall to present their work to a panel of expert judges, including National Inventors Hall of Fame inductees.

Amount of support per award: Up to $15,000.

Total amount of support: Up to $100,000.

NO. MOST RECENT APPLICANTS: 300.

NO. AWARDS: 5.

APPLICATION INFO:
All entries must be submitted on the official application form, which is available online.

Deadline: Mid-June.

ADDRESS INQUIRIES TO:
Collegiate Inventors Competition
(See e-mail address above.)

NATIONAL OCEANIC AND ATMOSPHERIC ADMINISTRATION   [1640]

NOAA/Sea Grant, R/SG
1315 East-West Highway, Room 11735
Silver Spring, MD 20910
(301) 734-1066
Fax: (301) 713-0799
E-mail: sgweb@noaa.gov
Web Site: www.seagrant.noaa.gov

FOUNDED: 1966

AREAS OF INTEREST:
Marine resource development.

NAME(S) OF PROGRAMS:
● **National Sea Grant College Program**

TYPE:
Research grants. Grants for research, education and outreach in oceanography, fisheries science and environmental studies; marine commerce and engineering and marine biotechnology; economic, legal and sociological considerations related to the management and development of natural resources in the marine environment; and development, conservation and economic utilization of resources in the marine environment.

The grant provides training and advisory service activities in order to increase the understanding, development and wise use of ocean, coastal and Great Lakes resources. The Secretary of Commerce, through NOAA, awards grants on a competitive basis for these purposes.

The program is carried out through a network of 34 Sea Grant programs, located in coastal and Great Lakes states, involving hundreds of universities nationwide.

YEAR PROGRAM STARTED: 1966

PURPOSE:
To promote wise utilization of marine and coastal resources.

LEGAL BASIS:
The National Sea Grant College and Program Act of 1966, Public Law 89-688, as amended. (33 U.S.C. 1121, et seq.)

ELIGIBILITY:
Universities and colleges, junior colleges, technical schools, institutes, laboratories and other public or private agencies with appropriate interests are eligible to apply.

FINANCIAL DATA:
Amount of support per award: Varies.

Total amount of support: Approximately $76,500,000 in grant funds for the year 2018.

APPLICATION INFO:
Detailed information is available on the web site.

Duration: Generally one to three years.

Deadline: Varies.

ADDRESS INQUIRIES TO:
Jonathan Pennock, Director
(See address above.)

NATIONAL RESEARCH COUNCIL OF CANADA   [1641]

1200 Montreal Road, Building M-58
Room E-109
Ottawa ON K1A 0R6 Canada
(613) 993-9101
E-mail: info@nrc-cnrc.gc.ca
racoordinator.hrb@nrc-cnrc.gc.ca
Web Site: www.nrc-cnrc.gc.ca

FOUNDED: 1916

AREAS OF INTEREST:
Science and engineering.

NAME(S) OF PROGRAMS:
● **National Research Council Research Associate Program**

TYPE:
Associateships. Research Associate Program provides promising scientists and engineers with the opportunity to work in a challenging research environment during the early stages of their career. Applicants will be selected competitively and must demonstrate the ability to perform original, high-quality research in their chosen field.

Research Associates will be offered appointments to the staff of the National Research Council on a term basis and will be offered salaries and benefits currently available to Research Officers.

YEAR PROGRAM STARTED: 1975

PURPOSE:
To undertake, assist or promote scientific and engineering research to further Canada's economic and social development and to give promising scientists and engineers an opportunity to work on challenging research problems.

LEGAL BASIS:
Federal government agency.

ELIGIBILITY:
Applicant must possess a Ph.D. in natural science or engineering or a Master's degree in an engineering field earned within the last five years, or expect to obtain the degree within six months. Applicant must have a demonstrated ability to perform original high-quality research in their chosen field.

Although preference will be given to Canadian citizens and permanent residents, Associateships are open to nationals of all countries. An Associateship does not ensure foreign nationals permanent residency in Canada.

FINANCIAL DATA:
Salaries commensurate with experience are taxable and subject to other deductions.

Amount of support per award: Current annual Ph.D. recruiting rate is $68,997.

Total amount of support: Varies.

APPLICATION INFO:
Applicants must apply online. All applicants must submit university transcripts, two letters of recommendation and resume. Application is valid for one year.

Duration: Two years. Renewal to a maximum of five years.

ADDRESS INQUIRIES TO:
Research Associates Program Coordinator
(See address above.)

NATIONAL SCIENCE FOUNDATION   [1642]

Directorate for Education and Human Resources
Division of Graduate Education
2415 Eisenhower Avenue
Alexandria, VA 22314
(703) 292-8630
(866) 673-4737
Fax: (703) 292-9048
E-mail: info@nsfgrfp.org
Web Site: www.nsf.gov/grfp (official program information)
www.nsfgrfp.org (application assistance)

FOUNDED: 1950

AREAS OF INTEREST:
Science, technology, engineering and math.

NAME(S) OF PROGRAMS:
● **NSF Graduate Research Fellowship Program**

TYPE:
Fellowships. Awarded for graduate study leading to research-based Master's and doctoral degrees in science and engineering. The GRFP provides three years of support for the graduate education of individuals who have demonstrated their potential for significant achievements in science and engineering. The ranks of NSF Fellows include individuals who have made transformative breakthrough discoveries in science and engineering, become leaders in their chosen careers and been honored as Nobel laureates.

YEAR PROGRAM STARTED: 1952

PURPOSE:
To help ensure the vitality and diversity of the scientific and engineering workforce in the U.S.

LEGAL BASIS:
Government agency.

ELIGIBILITY:
Applicant must meet all of the following eligibility criteria by the application deadline:
(1) be a U.S. citizen, national or permanent resident;
(2) intend to enroll or be enrolled full-time in a research-based graduate degree program in an eligible field of study in STEM or STEM education;
(3) have never previously accepted a GRFP award, or if previously offered a GRFP award, have declined by the deadline;
(4) have never earned a doctoral or terminal degree in any field;
(5) have never earned a Master's or professional degree in any field, unless returning to graduate study after an interruption of two or more consecutive years immediately preceding the deadline, and are not enrolled in a graduate degree program at the application deadline and;
(6) not be a current NSF employee.

GEOG. RESTRICTIONS: United States.

FINANCIAL DATA:
Amount of support per award: $138,000 per award; $46,000 annually (includes $34,000 stipend to the Fellow and $12,000 cost of education allowance to the institution).

NO. MOST RECENT APPLICANTS: 12,000 for the year 2018.

NO. AWARDS: Approximately 1,600.

APPLICATION INFO:
Application must be completed online.

The following material is required from all applicants:
(1) personal, relevant background and future goals statement;
(2) graduate research plan statement;
(3) three reference letters and;
(4) academic transcripts.

Duration: The fellowship period is five years, during which NSF provides three years of support. Normal tenure is 12 months for each fellowship year. Availability of the second and third years of a support is contingent upon certification by the fellowship institution that progress is being made and availability of appropriated funds.

Deadline: October.

ADDRESS INQUIRIES TO:
Graduate Research Fellowship Program
(See address above.)

*PLEASE NOTE:
Program eligibility requirements subject to change each year.

NATIONAL SCIENCE FOUNDATION [1643]

2415 Eisenhower Avenue
Alexandria, VA 22314
(703) 292-7283
Fax: (703) 292-9068
E-mail: fkronz@nsf.gov
Web Site: www.nsf.gov

FOUNDED: 1950

AREAS OF INTEREST:
Research that uses historical, philosophical, and social scientific methods to investigate the intellectual, material, or social facets of STEM (Science, Technology, Engineering and Mathematics) disciplines. It encompasses a broad spectrum of topics including interdisciplinary studies of ethics, equity, governance, and policy issues closely related to STEM disciplines.

NAME(S) OF PROGRAMS:
• **Science and Technology Studies**

TYPE:
Conferences/seminars; Research grants. Doctoral dissertation research improvement grants; Professional development grants; Research community development grants; Scholars awards; Standard grants and grants for collaborative research. The proposals that are considered for support use methods from a variety of disciplines including anthropology, communications, history, philosophy, political science, and sociology to investigate STEM theory and practice with regards to their history, socio-cultural formation, philosophical underpinnings, and impacts on quality of life, culture, and society.

YEAR PROGRAM STARTED: 1976

PURPOSE:
To provide educational opportunities for graduate students.

LEGAL BASIS:
Government agency.

ELIGIBILITY:
Open to U.S. institutions of higher education and U.S. nonprofit, non-academic organizations.

FINANCIAL DATA:
Amount of support per award: Generally, $12,000 to $500,000.

Total amount of support: Approximately $6,200,000 for fiscal year 2020.

CO-OP FUNDING PROGRAMS: National Institutes of Health; Department of Energy.

NO. AWARDS: Approximately 40.

APPLICATION INFO:
Proposers should consult the Science and Technology Studies (STS) Announcement 19-610 and appropriate NSF brochures such as Grant Proposal Guide, available from the address above.
Duration: One to five years.
Deadline: February 2 and August 3.

ADDRESS INQUIRIES TO:
Frederick Kronz, Program Director
(See address above.)

NATIONAL SCIENCE FOUNDATION [1644]

Directorate of Geosciences
Office of Polar Programs
2415 Eisenhower Avenue
Alexandria, VA 22314
(703) 292-8030
Fax: (703) 292-9081
E-mail: pmaiden@nsf.gov
Web Site: www.nsf.gov

FOUNDED: 1950

AREAS OF INTEREST:
Antarctic natural sciences.

NAME(S) OF PROGRAMS:
• **U.S. Antarctic Research Program**

TYPE:
Fellowships; Project/program grants; Research grants. Grants for research projects in all fields of science pertinent to the Antarctic, including both field work in the Antarctic and study in the U.S. of already gathered data and specimens. Support is provided for research projects in astronomy, astrophysics, the behavioral sciences, biology, cartography, geology, glaciology, meteorology, oceanography, solid earth geophysics, upper atmospheric physics and magnetospheric physics. Logistics and support in Antarctica are arranged by the Foundation.

YEAR PROGRAM STARTED: 1959

PURPOSE:
To fund, coordinate and arrange for support of research in all fields of science pertinent to Antarctica.

LEGAL BASIS:
Federal agency under the National Science Foundation Act of 1950, Public Law 81-507, as amended. Also White House memo 6646 dated February 5, 1982.

ELIGIBILITY:
U.S. universities and colleges are the primary participants in the program. Other eligible participants include nonacademic research institutions, profit or nonprofit, and unaffiliated scientists or scientists employed by other federal agencies.

GEOG. RESTRICTIONS: United States.

FINANCIAL DATA:
Amount of support per award: Varies with need.
Total amount of support: $55,000,000.
Matching fund requirements: Grantee institutions are generally required to share in project costs by a contribution to any cost element in the project, direct or indirect.

NO. AWARDS: Approximately 50.

APPLICATION INFO:
Applications are submitted in the form of a proposal with a detailed research plan and budget. Information concerning proposal preparation is available in the PAPPG, NSF 17-1, *Grant Proposal Guide, Antarctic Research Program Announcement.* Information regarding guidelines for the Office of Polar Programs can be found on the web site under the tab "Geosciences."
Deadline: Proposals are accepted on a rolling basis.

ADDRESS INQUIRIES TO:
Cognizant Program Officer
(See address above.)

NATIONAL SCIENCE FOUNDATION [1645]

Directorate of Geosciences
Office of Polar Programs
2415 Eisenhower Avenue
Alexandria, VA 22314
(703) 292-8030
Fax: (703) 292-9081
E-mail: pmaiden@nsf.gov
Web Site: www.nsf.gov

FOUNDED: 1950

AREAS OF INTEREST:
Arctic natural sciences, social sciences, Arctic system science, and Arctic observing network.

NAME(S) OF PROGRAMS:
• **Arctic Research Program**

TYPE:
Conferences/seminars; Research grants; Research contracts. Grants and contracts to support scientific research projects relating to the Arctic as well as the subsequent analysis of data. Research may be concerned with problems of marine research, including the polar pack ice; terrestrial biology, including analysis of the ecosystem; meteorology; solar-terrestrial physics; glaciology, including permafrost; geology and geophysics; social sciences; and data and information.

YEAR PROGRAM STARTED: 1971

PURPOSE:
To increase man's knowledge of the Arctic environment and its dynamic parameters; to increase cooperation in research with other agencies and nations having Arctic interests.

LEGAL BASIS:
The National Science Foundation Act of 1950, Public Law 81-507, as amended; Arctic Research and Policy Act of 1984.

ELIGIBILITY:
Proposals may be submitted by U.S. colleges and universities and by academically related nonprofit research organizations. Industry and other organizations are also eligible for support.

GEOG. RESTRICTIONS: United States.

FINANCIAL DATA:
Amount of support per award: Varies.
Total amount of support: $40,000,000 annually.
Matching fund requirements: Cost sharing is not required.

NO. AWARDS: 75 per year, pending availability of funds.

APPLICATION INFO:
Application information may be requested from the Foundation. Information regarding

guidelines for the Office of Polar Programs can be found on the web site under the tab "Geosciences."

Because of far-reaching scientific, logistic and international implications of Arctic research projects, it is essential that scientists specify all field needs when submitting proposals. Special procedures and a longer lead time apply to research proposed for Greenland. Proposers should also consult the Foundation's *Proposal and Award Procedures Guide* (PAPPG) (NSF 17-1).

Deadline: Proposals are accepted on a rolling basis.

ADDRESS INQUIRIES TO:
Cognizant Program Officer
(See address above.)

THE ROYAL SOCIETY OF CANADA [1646]

Walter House
282 Somerset Street West
Ottawa ON K2P 0J6 Canada
(613) 998-9920 ext. 106
Fax: (613) 991-6996
E-mail: nominations@rsc-src.ca
Web Site: www.rsc-src.ca

FOUNDED: 1883

AREAS OF INTEREST:
Arts and humanities, social sciences and science.

NAME(S) OF PROGRAMS:
● **Yvan Allaire Medal**
● **The Bancroft Award**
● **The Pierre Chauveau Medal**
● **The Sir John William Dawson Medal**
● **The Flavelle Medal**
● **Ursula Franklin Award in Gender Studies**
● **The Jason A. Hannah Medal**
● **The Innis-Gérin Medal**
● **The McLaughlin Medal**
● **Willet G. Miller Medal**
● **The Lorne Pierce Medal**
● **The Miroslaw Romanowski Medal**
● **The Rutherford Memorial Medals**
● **The John L. Synge Award**
● **The Henry Marshall Tory Medal**
● **The J.B. Tyrrell Historical Medal**

TYPE:
Awards/prizes. The Yvan Allaire Medal is awarded in recognition of outstanding research in governance of public and private organizations.

The Bancroft Award is given for publication, instruction and research in the earth sciences that have conspicuously contributed to public understanding and appreciation of the subject.

The Pierre Chauveau Medal is awarded for a distinguished contribution to knowledge in the humanities.

The Sir John William Dawson Medal is awarded for important contributions of knowledge in multiple domains.

The Flavelle Medal is awarded for an outstanding contribution to biological science during the preceding 10 years or for significant additions to a previous outstanding contribution to biological science.

The Ursula Franklin Award in Gender Studies is intended to recognize significant contributions by a Canadian scholar in the humanities and social sciences to furthering our understanding of issues concerning gender.

The Jason A. Hannah Medal is awarded for an important publication in the history of medicine.

The Innis-Gérin Medal is presented for a distinguished and sustained contribution to the literature of the social sciences.

The McLaughlin Medal is awarded for important research of sustained excellence in any branch of the medical sciences.

The Willet G. Miller Medal is given for outstanding research in any branch of earth sciences.

The Lorne Pierce Medal is awarded for an achievement of special significance and conspicuous merit in imaginative or critical literature written in either English or French (critical literature dealing with Canadian subjects has priority over critical literature of equal merit that does not deal with Canadian subjects).

The Miroslaw Romanowski Medal is awarded for significant contributions to the resolution of scientific aspects of environmental problems or for important improvements to the quality of an ecosystem in all aspects - terrestrial, atmospheric and aqueous - brought about by scientific means.

The Rutherford Memorial Medals are awarded for outstanding research in any branch of physics and chemistry.

The John L. Synge Award is given to acknowledge outstanding research in any of the branches of the mathematical sciences.

The Henry Marshall Tory Medal is given for outstanding research in any branch of astronomy, chemistry, mathematics, physics or an allied science.

The J.B. Tyrrell Historical Medal is awarded for outstanding work in the history of Canada.

YEAR PROGRAM STARTED: 1955

PURPOSE:
To annually recognize Canadian citizens for contributions to Canadian academic excellence in various branches.

LEGAL BASIS:
Nonprofit.

ELIGIBILITY:
Awarded to Canadian citizens or those who have had status for at least three years as Canadian Permanent Residents.

GEOG. RESTRICTIONS: Canada.

FINANCIAL DATA:
Amount of support per award: Varies with every medal.

APPLICATION INFO:
Open call for nominations takes place January 15 to March 31.
Duration: The Bancroft Award, The Chauveau Medal, The Sir John William Dawson Medal, The Flavelle Medal, Ursula Franklin Award in Gender Studies, The Jason A. Hannah Medal, The Innis-Gérin Medal, Willet G. Miller Medal, The Lorne Pierce Medal, The Henry Marshall Tory Medal and The J.B. Tyrrell Historical Medal: Every two years. Allaire, McLaughlin, Romanowski and Rutherford Memorial Medals: Every year. The John L. Synge Award: Varies.
Deadline: March 31.

ADDRESS INQUIRIES TO:
Christopher Dragan, Membership and Engagement Coordinator
(See address above.)

SIGMA XI: THE SCIENTIFIC RESEARCH HONOR SOCIETY [1647]

3200 East NC Highway 54
Suite 300
Research Triangle Park, NC 27709
(919) 549-4691 ext. 206
Fax: (919) 549-0090
E-mail: giar@sigmaxi.org
Web Site: www.sigmaxi.org

FOUNDED: 1886

AREAS OF INTEREST:
Life sciences, physical sciences, engineering, social, behavioral and life sciences.

NAME(S) OF PROGRAMS:
● **Grants in Aid of Research**

TYPE:
Grants-in-aid; Project/program grants; Research grants. Grants in Aid support research projects in any field of scientific investigation. Assistance is available for such research-related activities as travel to research location or supplies.

YEAR PROGRAM STARTED: 1922

PURPOSE:
To encourage scientific research.

LEGAL BASIS:
Nonprofit organization.

ELIGIBILITY:
Graduate and undergraduate students with proposals for specific research projects are eligible to apply. Student faculty advisor (first recommender) should be a full, active member of Sigma Xi to compete for Sigma Xi funds. NAS funds in the program are unrestricted and cover the physical, life and medical sciences (excluding the social sciences).

Grants do not cover overhead costs. No grants for publication/presentation costs, travel to meetings or stipends. Will fund travel to a research site.

FINANCIAL DATA:
Amount of support per award: Up to $1,000 for most areas of the sciences and engineering; Up to $5,000 for astronomy; Up to $2,500 for eye/vision research.
Total amount of support: Approximately $200,000.

CO-OP FUNDING PROGRAMS: National Academy of Sciences.

NO. MOST RECENT APPLICANTS: 1,600.

NO. AWARDS: 200.

APPLICATION INFO:
Contact the Society for details.
Duration: Applicants may apply for a second grant after submitting a report on the outcome of the project supported by a first grant.
Deadline: Applications and supporting letters must be received by March 15 or October 1. Awards are announced within 12 weeks.

PUBLICATIONS:
Annual report; application guidelines.

STAFF:
Dr. Janelle Simmons, Manager of Programs
Lindsay Holton, Programs Coordinator

ADDRESS INQUIRIES TO:
Dr. Janelle Simmons, Manager of Programs
E-mail: jsimmons@sigmaxi.org

SMITHSONIAN INSTITUTION [1648]
Office of Fellowships and Internships
470 L'Enfant Plaza, S.W., Suite 7102
MRC 902, P.O. Box 37012
Washington, DC 20013-7012
(202) 633-7070
E-mail: siofi@si.edu
Web Site: www.smithsonianofi.com

FOUNDED: 1846

AREAS OF INTEREST:
Animal behavior, ecology and environmental science, including an emphasis on the tropics; anthropology, including archaeology; astrophysics and astronomy; earth sciences and paleobiology; evolutionary and systematic biology; history of science and technology; history of art, especially American, contemporary, African and Asian art; 20th-century American crafts and decorative arts; social and cultural history of the U.S.; and folklore.

NAME(S) OF PROGRAMS:
- **Smithsonian Graduate Student Fellowships**
- **Smithsonian Postdoctoral Fellowships**
- **Smithsonian Predoctoral Fellowships**
- **Smithsonian Senior Fellowships**

TYPE:
Fellowships. Offered to qualified scholars for research to be conducted in residence at the Smithsonian in association with the staff, using collections and research facilities.

YEAR PROGRAM STARTED: 1964

PURPOSE:
To provide students and scholars in the sciences, arts and humanities with an opportunity for research utilizing the unique collections and facilities of the Smithsonian, while working with the institution's research staff.

LEGAL BASIS:
Act of Congress approved August 10, 1846; 20 U.S.C. 41 et seq.

ELIGIBILITY:
Smithsonian Fellowships are open to both U.S. citizens and foreign nationals. Fluency in English is required.

For the graduate fellowships, students must be formally enrolled and engaged in a graduate program of study at a degree-granting institution, have completed at least one semester and have not yet been advanced to candidacy if in a Ph.D. program.

For the predoctoral fellowships, students must be enrolled in a university as candidates for the Ph.D. or equivalent. At the time of appointment, the university must approve the undertaking of dissertation research at the Smithsonian and indicate that requirements for the Doctorate, other than the dissertation, have been met.

For the postdoctoral fellowships, applicants must have received the Ph.D., or equivalent, within seven years of the program deadline and must have completed the degree or certificate at the time the fellowship commences.

For the senior fellowships, applicants must have received the Ph.D., or equivalent, seven or more years before the program deadline.

Research must be conducted while in residence at the Smithsonian.

The Smithsonian Institution does not offer financial assistance for degree-granting programs at academic institutions. All forms of financial assistance are to support research in residence at the Smithsonian and its facilities.

FINANCIAL DATA:
Amount of support per award: Varies.

APPLICATION INFO:
Official application materials are available upon request. Specify the fellowship corresponding to your academic level.
Duration: Varies.
Deadline: November 1.

PUBLICATIONS:
Smithsonian Opportunities for Research and Study.

ADDRESS INQUIRIES TO:
Office of Fellowships and Internships
(See address above.)

SOCIETY FOR SCIENCE AND THE PUBLIC [1649]
1719 N Street, N.W.
Washington, DC 20036
(202) 785-2255
E-mail: sts@societyforscience.org
Web Site: www.societyforscience.org

FOUNDED: 1921

AREAS OF INTEREST:
Sciences, mathematics, engineering and medicine.

NAME(S) OF PROGRAMS:
- **Regeneron Science Talent Search**

TYPE:
Awards/prizes. Competition for high school seniors excelling in science, math and engineering.

YEAR PROGRAM STARTED: 1942

PURPOSE:
To discover at the high school senior year level, those who have the potential to become the scientists, mathematicians and engineers of the future; to make the public aware of the impact that a quality science, mathematics or engineering education has on our future and the future of our nation.

LEGAL BASIS:
Nonprofit educational institution.

ELIGIBILITY:
Student must be in the last year of secondary school in the U.S., Puerto Rico, Guam, Virgin Islands, American Samoa, Wake and Midway Islands, the Marianas, DOD Schools or American schools abroad or for citizens studying abroad.

FINANCIAL DATA:
Amount of support per award: National Semifinalists receive $2,000 and their schools receive $2,000. Top 10 awarded $40,000 to $250,000. Remainder of top 40 receive $25,000.
Total amount of support: Varies.

NO. AWARDS: 300 National Semifinalists; 40 Finalists.

APPLICATION INFO:
There are four components of the application: (1) Applicants enter responses to the basic information and essay questions directly into the text boxes on the web pages of the

application;
(2) Documents such as the research report, IRB summary, and IACUC approvals, where applicable, will be uploaded to the application as Word documents or PDF's;
(3) Each student must request at least one Project Recommendation, one High School Report, and one Educator Recommendation. Each applicant has the option of requesting a second recommendation of each type and;
(4) Applicants may mail their transcripts to the Society in hard copy form or ask their High School Report provider to upload a scanned copy to their High School Report. In either case, the timely receipt of the transcript is the responsibility of the student.
Deadline: November.

PUBLICATIONS:
Science News, magazine.

ADDRESS INQUIRIES TO:
Allie Stifel, Program Director
(See address above.)

THE SOCIETY FOR THE SCIENTIFIC STUDY OF SEXUALITY [1650]
881 Third Street, Suite B-5
Whitehall, PA 18052
(610) 443-3100
E-mail: thesociety@sexscience.org
Web Site: sexscience.org

FOUNDED: 1957

AREAS OF INTEREST:
Sex research, sex therapy and sex education.

NAME(S) OF PROGRAMS:
- **Grants-in-Aid Project**
- **Student Research Grants**

TYPE:
Grants-in-aid; Research grants. Grants-in-Aid Project supports scientific sexuality research in areas not likely to receive support from other sources.

Student Research Grant supports an SSSS student member who is doing human sexuality research.

YEAR PROGRAM STARTED: 1985

PURPOSE:
To assist with the development of quality research projects in the area of sex research.

LEGAL BASIS:
Tax-exempt, private, not-for-profit corporation.

ELIGIBILITY:
Grants-in-Aid Project is open to all professionals conducting research related to human sexuality.

Student Research Grants are open to students who are enrolled in a degree-granting program and student members of SSSS.

FINANCIAL DATA:
Amount of support per award: Grants-in-Aid: $1,000; Student Research Grants: $2,000.

NO. MOST RECENT APPLICANTS: 25.

NO. AWARDS: Varies.

APPLICATION INFO:
Applications and additional information can be found online.
Deadline: Grants-in-Aid Project: Proposals may be submitted at any time during the year. Student Research Grants: September 1.

PUBLICATIONS:
Application guidelines.

IRS I.D.: 13-2642753

SYSTEMS PLUS, INC.
One Research Court
Suite 360
Rockville, MD 20850
(301) 948-4232
E-mail: afsffp.pmo@sysplus.com
Web Site: afsffp.sysplus.com

TYPE:
Fellowships. Research fellowship.

See entry 2406 for full listing.

TOURETTE ASSOCIATION OF AMERICA, INC.
42-40 Bell Boulevard
Suite 205
Bayside, NY 11361-2820
(718) 224-2999
Fax: (718) 279-9596
E-mail: support@tourette.org
Web Site: www.tourette.org

TYPE:
Fellowships; General operating grants;
Research grants; Seed money grants;
Technical assistance. Research grants
available for Ph.D. and M.D. researchers in
the following categories:
(1) proposals in basic neuroscience
specifically relevant to Tourette Syndrome
and;
(2) clinical studies related to the etiology,
pathophysiology and treatment of Tourette
Syndrome.

Fellowships provide one-year postdoctoral
training.

See entry 2233 for full listing.

U.S. ARMY RESEARCH OFFICE   [1651]
800 Park Office Drive
Research Triangle Park, NC 27703
(919) 549-0641
Fax: (919) 549-4310
Web Site: www.arl.army.mil

FOUNDED: 1951

AREAS OF INTEREST:
Biosciences, chemistry, electronics,
engineering, environmental sciences,
materials sciences, mathematical and
computer sciences and physics.

TYPE:
Conferences/seminars; Research grants;
Research contracts. Grants and contracts for
scientific research in such areas of interest to
the U.S. Army as chemistry, engineering,
biology, mathematics, metallurgy and
materials, physics, electronics and
environmental sciences. Support is also
provided for symposia on particular aspects
of scientific investigation, the results of
which further Department of the Army
objectives.

YEAR PROGRAM STARTED: 1951

PURPOSE:
To increase knowledge of natural phenomena
and environment in an attempt to solve
problems in the physical, engineering,
environmental and life sciences.

LEGAL BASIS:
Government agency.

ELIGIBILITY:
Organizations with appropriate interests are
eligible to apply.

FINANCIAL DATA:
Amount of support per award: Grants and
contracts vary in amount, depending upon the
needs and nature of the request; $136,000
yearly average.
Total amount of support: $500,000,000 to
$550,000,000 including both grants and
contracts.

NO. MOST RECENT APPLICANTS: Approximately
550.

NO. AWARDS: Approximately 350.

APPLICATION INFO:
Research awards are selected from proposals
submitted in response to an open-ended
Broad Agency Announcement (BAA).
Contractors interested in submitting proposals
should go to the ARL web site and download
the ARO BAA.
Duration: One to three years. Continuations
possible if work has not been completed.
Deadline: Varies.

ADDRESS INQUIRIES TO:
RDECOM Acquisitions Center
(See address above.)

U.S. DEPARTMENT OF ENERGY
3610 Collins Ferry Road
P.O. Box 880
Morgantown, WV 26507-0880
(304) 285-4764
Fax: (304) 285-4403
Web Site: www.netl.doe.gov

TYPE:
Assistantships; Project/program grants;
Research grants. Topics change annually. In
general, the program areas could include high
performance materials, sensors and controls,
simulation-based engineering, and water
management research and development.

See entry 2408 for full listing.

U.S. DEPARTMENT OF THE NAVY   [1652]
Office of Naval Research, One Liberty Center
875 North Randolph Street, Suite 1425
Arlington, VA 22203-1995
(703) 696-5031
Fax: (703) 696-5940
E-mail: onrpublicaffairs@navy.mil
Web Site: www.onr.navy.mil

FOUNDED: 1946

AREAS OF INTEREST:
Advanced materials, ocean sciences,
mathematics, information sciences, physics,
electronics, chemistry, mechanics, cognitive
and neural sciences.

NAME(S) OF PROGRAMS:
● **University Research Initiative**
● **Young Investigator Program**

TYPE:
Research grants; Research contracts. ONR
sponsors long-range scientific research,
applied research and advanced technology
development which offer potential for
advancement and improvement of naval
operations. Programs include physics,
electronic and solid state sciences,
mathematics, operations research, statistics

and probability, information science, fluid
dynamics, physiology, biochemistry,
biophysics, microbiology, naval biology,
cognitive and neural sciences research,
personnel and training research, Arctic
research, coastal sciences, earth and
environmental physics, atmospheric sciences,
metallurgy and ceramics research, chemistry,
energy research, structural mechanics,
physical and chemical oceanography, marine
geology and geophysics, ocean biology,
ocean acoustics and ocean engineering.

YEAR PROGRAM STARTED: 1946

PURPOSE:
To support research in various scientific
fields including ocean science and physics.

LEGAL BASIS:
Public Law 588, as amended and Public Law
85-934, as amended.

ELIGIBILITY:
Nonprofit institutions of higher education and
organizations whose primary purpose is the
conduct of scientific research may apply for
contracts or grants. Nonprofit and
profit-making institutions, organizations or
industrial establishments, as well as qualified
individuals, are eligible for contract support.

FINANCIAL DATA:
Amount of support per award: Varies,
depending upon the needs and nature of the
request.
Total amount of support: Varies.

NO. MOST RECENT APPLICANTS: Approximately
4,000 inquiries.

NO. AWARDS: Approximately 2,500 annually.

APPLICATION INFO:
Before submitting a proposal, interested
individuals are encouraged to assess the
relevance of their research interests to Navy
research priorities by consulting the ONR
web page and talking to the relevant ONR
Program Manager. Applications are submitted
in the form of a proposal which should
include:
(1) general statement requesting consideration
of the proposal;
(2) brief review of the scientific background
of the proposed research;
(3) technical description of the project,
including statement of objectives and
scientific methods to be employed;
(4) description of available facilities;
(5) background of principal investigator(s)
and associates;
(6) bibliography of pertinent publications;
(7) proposed duration of project and annual
itemized budget;
(8) other research projects currently
undertaken by the principal investigator;
(9) other agencies to whom the proposal is
being submitted for possible financial support
and;
(10) cost breakdown by year.

WEIZMANN INSTITUTE OF SCIENCE
Feinberg Graduate School
David Lopatie Hall of Graduate Studies
P.O. Box 26
234 Herzl Street
Rehovot 7610001 Israel
(972) 8-934-2924
Fax: (972) 8-934-4114
E-mail: FGS@weizmann.ac.il
Web Site: www.weizmann.ac.il/feinberg

TYPE:
Fellowships. The Feinberg Graduate School of the Weizmann Institute of Science offers a limited number of postdoctoral fellowships in all areas of research in which the Weizmann Institute is engaged. The fellowships are offered in various fields of biology, chemistry, physics, biochemistry-biophysics, mathematics, computer science and science teaching.

See entry 867 for full listing.

THE HELEN HAY WHITNEY FOUNDATION [1653]

20 Squadron Boulevard
Suite 630
New City, NY 10956-5247
(845) 639-6799
Fax: (845) 639-6798
E-mail: office@hhwf.org
Web Site: hhwf.org

FOUNDED: 1947

AREAS OF INTEREST:
Biomedical sciences.

NAME(S) OF PROGRAMS:
● **Early Postdoctoral Research Fellowship Program in Biomedical Sciences**

TYPE:
Fellowships. Postdoctoral research fellowships.

YEAR PROGRAM STARTED: 1957

PURPOSE:
To provide beginning postdoctoral research training to young M.Ds. and Ph.Ds. to further their careers in research in biomedical sciences.

LEGAL BASIS:
Independent foundation.

ELIGIBILITY:
Candidates living in North America or foreign nationals that pursue their fellowship in the U.S., who hold the M.D., Ph.D. or equivalent degree, who are seeking beginning postdoctoral training in basic biomedical research and have no more than two years of postdoctoral experience by June 15 are eligible. U.S. citizenship is not a requirement, but fellowships to resident noncitizens are awarded only for training in the U.S. Citizens may train abroad.

Applications from established scientists or advanced fellows will not be considered. Applicants who have already had one year's postdoctoral laboratory training at the time of deadline will not be considered for a Whitney Fellowship.

FINANCIAL DATA:
Amount of support per award: Fellowships provide stipends as follows: $56,000 for the first year, $59,000 for the second year and $62,000 for the third year, plus a $1,500 research allowance to the department for each year of tenure, travel to fellowship location and annual meeting of all fellows. Additionally, there is a dependent child allowance of $1,500 per each dependent child.

NO. MOST RECENT APPLICANTS: 500.

APPLICATION INFO:
Online application is available at the Foundation web site.
Duration: Three years. Contingent upon satisfactory performance.
Deadline: Applications accepted April 15 to June 15. Fellowships begin the following April 1 through September 1.

PUBLICATIONS:
Annual report.

WOODS HOLE OCEANOGRAPHIC INSTITUTION [1654]

Academic Programs Office
Clark 223, MS No. 31
360 Woods Hole Road
Woods Hole, MA 02543-1541
(508) 289-3379
E-mail: education@whoi.edu
Web Site: www.whoi.edu/main/summer-student-fellowship

FOUNDED: 1930

AREAS OF INTEREST:
Research in biological oceanography, marine chemistry and geochemistry, marine geology and geophysics, applied ocean physics and engineering, physical oceanography and marine policy.

NAME(S) OF PROGRAMS:
● **Summer Student Fellowship Program in Oceanography**

TYPE:
Fellowships. Awards for independent research in oceanography/ocean engineering and marine policy projects pursued under the guidance of a member of the research staff of the Woods Hole Oceanographic Institution. Fellowship is for a 10- to 12-week summer study at Woods Hole Oceanographic Institution.

YEAR PROGRAM STARTED: 1954

PURPOSE:
To give a small group of qualified undergraduate science and engineering students experience that will enable them to determine whether they wish to devote lifetime careers to studying the oceans.

LEGAL BASIS:
Charter under the Commonwealth of Massachusetts.

ELIGIBILITY:
Summer Student Fellowships are awarded to undergraduate students who will have completed their junior year at colleges or universities by the start of the fellowship period. Students who will graduate before the fellowship begins are not eligible to apply. Preference is given to students studying in any of the fields of science or engineering including but not limited to the fields of biology, chemistry, engineering, geology, geophysics, mathematics, meteorology, physics, oceanography, and marine policy. Students must have at least a tentative interest in the ocean sciences, oceanographic engineering, mathematics, or marine policy.

Persons from underrepresented groups are encouraged to apply. WHOI actively recruits underrepresented minorities in ocean science as defined by the National Science Foundation (African-, Hispanic- and Native-Americans, and Pacific Islanders).

Fellows are selected based on the applicant's previous academic and scientific achievements and promise as future ocean scientists or ocean engineers. Important consideration is given to matching each fellow with an appropriate advisor on WHOI's Scientific or Senior Technical Staff.

FINANCIAL DATA:
Award includes weekly stipend, travel allowance of $700 and institutional housing.
Amount of support per award: Stipend of $650 per week.
Total amount of support: Varies.

NO. AWARDS: 25 to 30.

APPLICATION INFO:
Applications must be submitted online. A complete application should include an application form, transcripts of college and university records, at least three personal references, a concise statement of the applicant's research plans and interests, future education and career plans, and reasons for applying to the Institution.
Duration: 10 to 12 weeks.
Deadline: February 5. Notification by March 15.

STAFF:
Margaret K. Tivey, Vice President for Academic Programs and Dean

ADDRESS INQUIRIES TO:
See e-mail address above.

*SPECIAL STIPULATIONS:
Fellows are required to present a mid-summer progress report. At the end of the summer, each fellow is required to prepare a written report describing their research.

SOCIAL SCIENCES

Social sciences (general)

AGENCY FOR HEALTHCARE RESEARCH AND QUALITY (AHRQ)

Office of Management Services
Division of Grants Management
5600 Fishers Lane, 7th Floor
Rockville, MD 20857
(301) 427-1104 (specify funding area)
(301) 427-1450
E-mail: gmi@ahrq.hhs.gov
Web Site: www.ahrq.gov

TYPE:
Conferences/seminars; Development grants; Fellowships; Project/program grants; Research grants; Training grants. Dissertation support highlighting primary care, market forces, cost containment, managed care, the cost of treating AIDS, the improvement of treatment for persons with HIV, rural health care, infant mortality, medical liability, malpractice reform, health care of the aged and disabled and policy studies.

See entry 1281 for full listing.

AMERICAN BAR FOUNDATION

750 North Lake Shore Drive
Fourth Floor
Chicago, IL 60611
(312) 988-6500
Fax: (312) 988-6579
E-mail: fellowships@abfn.org
Web Site: www.americanbarfoundation.org

TYPE:
Internships. Fellows spend the summer gaining hands-on research experience, touring legal institutions and law schools, and meeting with legal practitioners and scholars.

See entry 883 for full listing.

AMERICAN BAR FOUNDATION

750 North Lake Shore Drive
Fourth Floor
Chicago, IL 60611-4403
(312) 988-6500
Fax: (312) 988-6579
E-mail: fellowships@abfn.org
Web Site: www.americanbarfoundation.org

TYPE:
Fellowships. The American Bar Foundation (ABF), in partnership with AccessLex Institute (ALI), is committed to developing the next generation of scholars interested in empirical and interdisciplinary research on legal and higher education. This is a residential fellowship at the ABF.

See entry 1768 for full listing.

BRETT FAMILY FOUNDATION   [1655]

1123 Spruce Street
Boulder, CO 80302
(303) 442-1200
E-mail: info@brettfoundation.org
Web Site: www.brettfoundation.org

FOUNDED: 2000

AREAS OF INTEREST:
Social justice, equal rights and access to opportunity for individuals and families.

NAME(S) OF PROGRAMS:
● **Nonprofit Media Grant Program**
● **Social Justice Grant Program**

TYPE:
General operating grants.

PURPOSE:
To promote caring communities by investing in organizations throughout Colorado working for social justice and nonprofit media.

GEOG. RESTRICTIONS: Colorado.

FINANCIAL DATA:
Amount of support per award: $2,500 to $10,000.
Total amount of support: Approximately $500,000 annually.

REPRESENTATIVE AWARDS:
$7,500 to Colorado Civic Engagement Roundtable; $3,500 to Family Learning Center; $10,000 to Colorado Public Radio.

APPLICATION INFO:
By invitation only.
Duration: One year. Must reapply.
Deadline: Varies.

ADDRESS INQUIRIES TO:
Senior Advisor
(See address above.)

CANADIAN FEDERATION FOR THE HUMANITIES AND SOCIAL SCIENCES   [1656]

141 Laurier Avenue West
Suite 200
Ottawa ON K1P 5J3 Canada
(613) 238-6112 ext. 319
Fax: (613) 238-6114
E-mail: aspp-paes@ideas-idees.ca
Web Site: www.ideas-idees.ca

FOUNDED: 1941

AREAS OF INTEREST:
Social sciences and humanities.

NAME(S) OF PROGRAMS:
● **Awards to Scholarly Publications Program**

TYPE:
Grants-in-aid. Grants to support the publication of scholarly books in the social sciences and humanities.

YEAR PROGRAM STARTED: 1941

PURPOSE:
To assist the publication of books of advanced scholarship in the humanities and social sciences that make an important contribution to knowledge.

LEGAL BASIS:
NGO, nonprofit.

ELIGIBILITY:
Scholarly works in English or French of at least 40,000 words in length authored by Canadian citizens or permanent residents of Canada. The following works are not eligible: unrevised theses, conference proceedings, scholarly journals or articles, textbooks, technical reports, concordances, memoires and autobiographies. Approved works must be published in Canada by ASPP-approved publishers.

GEOG. RESTRICTIONS: Canada.

FINANCIAL DATA:
Grants are paid following publication directly to the publisher.

Amount of support per award: Publication Grant: $8,000. Translation Grant: $12,000.

NO. MOST RECENT APPLICANTS: 226.

NO. AWARDS: 180 Publication Grants and 5 Translation Grants per year.

APPLICATION INFO:
Publishers usually apply on the behalf of authors, though authors may also apply directly. Visit the program web site to download the most up-to-date guidelines and application forms.

PUBLICATIONS:
Application guidelines; application forms.

ADDRESS INQUIRIES TO:
Program Officer, ASPP
(See address above.)

*SPECIAL STIPULATIONS:
Non-Canadians may be eligible for ASPP support if their work is on a Canadian subject and is based on Canadian sources.

CANADIAN INSTITUTE OF UKRAINIAN STUDIES

University of Alberta
4-30 Pembina Hall
Edmonton AB T6G 2H8 Canada
(780) 492-2972
E-mail: cius@ualberta.ca
Web Site: www.cius.ca

TYPE:
Fellowships; Research grants; Scholarships. The Helen Darcovich Memorial Doctoral Fellowship is awarded annually to a student writing a dissertation on a Ukrainian or Ukrainian-Canadian topic in education, history, humanities, social sciences, law or library sciences.

The Neporany Doctoral Fellowship, offered by the Canadian Foundation for Ukrainian Studies, is awarded to one ore more doctoral students specializing on Ukraine in political science, economics, and related fields.

Research Grants are awarded in support of projects that have scholarly value, well-defined work plans, and modest budgets.

See entry 531 for full listing.

COUNCIL FOR EUROPEAN STUDIES AT COLUMBIA UNIVERSITY

475 Riverside Drive
Office 308i
New York, NY 10115
(646) 745-8550
E-mail: awards@ces-europe.org
Web Site: councilforeuropeanstudies.org

TYPE:
Awards/prizes; Conferences/seminars; Fellowships; Internships; Scholarships; Travel grants. The CES Book Award honors talented emerging scholars with an award for the best first book on any subject in European studies. The award is given every two years.

CES Conference Travel Grants support transcontinental travel for junior faculty and graduate students already scheduled to present at the Council's International Conference of Europeanists.

CES Small Event Grants support workshops, lectures, symposia and other small events that share research on Europe with a wider community.

First Article Prize awards one prize to a scholar working in the humanities and one to a scholar working in the social sciences. These prizes will honor the writers of the best first articles on European studies published within a two-year period.

Mellon-CES Dissertation Completion Fellowships are intended to facilitate the timely completion of the doctoral degree by late-stage graduate students focused on topics in European studies.

SAE-CES Pre-Dissertation Research Fellowships are intended to fund student's first major research project in Europe.

See entry 762 for full listing.

CROSSROADS FUND   [1657]

3411 West Diversey Avenue, Suite 20
Chicago, IL 60647-1245
(773) 227-7676
Fax: (773) 227-7790
E-mail: info@crossroadsfund.org
Web Site: www.crossroadsfund.org

FOUNDED: 1981

AREAS OF INTEREST:
Racial, social and economic justice.

TYPE:
General operating grants; Project/program grants; Seed money grants; Technical assistance.

PURPOSE:
To support grassroots organizations working to alleviate underlying causes of social ills.

LEGAL BASIS:
Public foundation.

ELIGIBILITY:
Projects must be run by community organizations or nonprofits. No individuals. The Foundation only funds groups with annual expenses under $300,000.

GEOG. RESTRICTIONS: Chicago, Illinois metropolitan area and northwestern Indiana.

FINANCIAL DATA:
Amount of support per award: Up to $10,000.
Total amount of support: $1,200,000 for fiscal year 2020.

NO. AWARDS: 121 organizations funded for fiscal year 2020.

APPLICATION INFO:
Application information is available on the web site.
Duration: One year.

PUBLICATIONS:
Application guidelines; newsletter; brochure; annual report.

ADDRESS INQUIRIES TO:
Jane Kimondo, Executive Director
(See address above.)

THE HARRY FRANK GUGGENHEIM FOUNDATION   [1658]

120 West 45th Street
New York, NY 10036
(646) 428-0971
Fax: (646) 428-0981
E-mail: info@hfg.org
Web Site: www.hfg.org

FOUNDED: 1929

AREAS OF INTEREST:
Scholarly research on violence and aggression.

NAME(S) OF PROGRAMS:
● **The Harry Frank Guggenheim Foundation Emerging Scholars Award**

TYPE:
Fellowships. Awarded to individuals who will complete the writing of the dissertation within the award year. Support is for dissertations pertaining to the causes of violence or aggression.

YEAR PROGRAM STARTED: 1990

PURPOSE:
To further understanding of human social problems related to violence and aggression.

LEGAL BASIS:
Private foundation.

ELIGIBILITY:
Fellowships are for students in the final year of their doctoral programs. They are designed to support the write-up stage of the dissertation. They are available to citizens of any country in the world.

Recipients of the Dissertation Fellowship must submit a copy of the dissertation, approved and accepted by their institution, within six months after the end of the award year. Any papers, books, articles, or other publications based on the research should also be sent to the Foundation.

FINANCIAL DATA:
Amount of support per award: $25,000.
Total amount of support: Approximately $300,000.

NO. MOST RECENT APPLICANTS: Average 225.

NO. AWARDS: 10 or more.

APPLICATION INFO:
Guidelines and application forms are available on the web site.
Duration: One-time award. Nonrenewable.
Deadline: February 1.

PUBLICATIONS:
Guidelines and Report.

OFFICERS:
Daniel Wilhelm, President
Deirdre Hamill, Director, Finance and Administration
Joel Wallman, Director of Research
Nyeleti Honwana, Program Officer

ADDRESS INQUIRIES TO:
Emerging Scholars Award
(See address above.)

THE HARRY FRANK GUGGENHEIM FOUNDATION   [1659]

120 West 45th Street
New York, NY 10036
(646) 428-0971
Fax: (646) 428-0981
E-mail: info@hfg.org
Web Site: www.hfg.org

FOUNDED: 1929

AREAS OF INTEREST:
Research on violence and aggression.

NAME(S) OF PROGRAMS:
● **The Harry Frank Guggenheim Foundation Distinguished Scholar Award**

TYPE:
Research grants. Support for research on the causes or reduction of violence or aggression.

YEAR PROGRAM STARTED: 1972

PURPOSE:
To further understanding of human social problems related to violence and aggression.

LEGAL BASIS:
Private, operating foundation.

ELIGIBILITY:
The Foundation awards research grants to individuals (or a few principal investigators at most) for individual projects and does not award grants to institutions for institutional programs.

Applicants for a research grant may be citizens of any country. While almost all recipients of a Foundation research grant possess a Ph.D., M.D., or equivalent degree, there are no formal degree requirements for the grant. The grant, however, may not be used to support research undertaken as part of the requirements for a graduate degree. Applicants need not be affiliated with an institution of higher learning, although most are college or university professors.

FINANCIAL DATA:
Amount of support per award: Usually $15,000 to $45,000 per year.
Total amount of support: Grants and Fellowships: $400,000 to $500,000.

NO. MOST RECENT APPLICANTS: 250.

NO. AWARDS: 10 to 15.

APPLICATION INFO:
Guidelines and application form are available at the Foundation web site.
Duration: One to two years. Renewal is possible if requested in original application, but not guaranteed.
Deadline: August 1.

PUBLICATIONS:
Guidelines; Annual Report.

OFFICERS:
Daniel Wilhelm, President
Deirdre Hamill, Director, Finance and Administration
Joel Wallman, Director of Research
Nyeleti Honwana, Program Officer

ADDRESS INQUIRIES TO:
Distinguished Scholar Award
(See address above.)

THE JOHN RANDOLPH HAYNES AND DORA HAYNES FOUNDATION   [1660]

888 West Sixth Street, Suite 1150
Los Angeles, CA 90017-2737
(213) 623-9151
Fax: (213) 623-3951
E-mail: info@haynesfoundation.org
Web Site: www.haynesfoundation.org

FOUNDED: 1926

AREAS OF INTEREST:
Public policy for Los Angeles.

TYPE:
Fellowships; Research grants.

YEAR PROGRAM STARTED: 1926

PURPOSE:
To strengthen research in the social sciences into public policy issues of the Los Angeles region.

LEGAL BASIS:
Independent private foundation.

ELIGIBILITY:
501(c)(3) organizations only.

No grants are made to individuals.

GEOG. RESTRICTIONS: California, specifically Los Angeles, Orange, Riverside, San Bernardino, and Ventura counties.

FINANCIAL DATA:
Amount of support per award: $5,000 to $250,000.

Total amount of support: Up to $3,000,000.

NO. AWARDS: 13 grants and 14 fellowships for fiscal year 2020-21.

REPRESENTATIVE AWARDS:
$138,954 to University of Southern California; $68,593 to University of California, Los Angeles; $159,091 to University of California, Riverside.

APPLICATION INFO:
Application information is available on the web site.

Duration: One to two years.

Deadline: Varies.

PUBLICATIONS:
Annual report.

IRS I.D.: 95-1644020

BOARD OF TRUSTEES:
Dr. Jane G. Pisano, President
Robert Ecker
Gil Garcetti
Philip M. Hawley
Enrique Hernandez, Jr.
Robin Kramer
Dr. Daniel A. Mazmanian
Gilbert T. Ray
Roberto Suro

ADDRESS INQUIRIES TO:
See e-mail address above.

THE HOROWITZ FOUNDATION FOR SOCIAL POLICY [1661]
P.O. Box 7
Rocky Hill, NJ 08553-0007
(732) 445-2280
E-mail: info@horowitz-foundation.org
Web Site: www.horowitz-foundation.org

FOUNDED: 1997

AREAS OF INTEREST:
Social sciences, including anthropology, area studies, economics, political science, psychology, sociology, urban studies, as well as newer areas such as evaluation research.

TYPE:
Research grants. Grants to doctoral candidates at the dissertation level with emphasis on social policy-related studies.

YEAR PROGRAM STARTED: 1997

PURPOSE:
To support the advancement of research and understanding in the major fields of the social sciences.

ELIGIBILITY:
Awards are only open to aspiring Ph.Ds. at the dissertation level whose project has received approval from their appropriate department head/university. Applicants are not required to be U.S. citizens or U.S. residents.

Preference will be given to projects that deal with contemporary issues in the social sciences and issues of policy relevance.

Awards are not allocated so as to insure a representative base of disciplines, but are approved solely on merit.

FINANCIAL DATA:
Amount of support per award: $7,500 plus additional special grants; Additional $5,000 for best overall project.

CO-OP FUNDING PROGRAMS: Determined on a case-by-case basis.

NO. MOST RECENT APPLICANTS: 855 for the year 2019.

NO. AWARDS: Approximately 25 annually.

APPLICATION INFO:
Application guidelines and eligibility criteria can be found at the Foundation web site. Applications must be submitted through the online system. All materials must be submitted, in English, prior to the closing date.

Duration: One year. Nonrenewable.

Deadline: December 1.

IRS I.D.: 31-1612153

BOARD OF TRUSTEES:
Ayse Akincigil
David J. Armor
Hans Martin Boehmer
Jonathan D. Breul
Mary E. Curtis Horowitz
Richard Edwards
Pearl Eliadis
Michal Grinstein-Weiss
Melissa Jonson-Reid
Mary McKay
Nandini Ramanujam
Ray C. Rist
William Rodgers
Jos Vaessen

ADDRESS INQUIRIES TO:
Mary E. Curtis Horowitz
Chairman and Trustee
(See address above.)

INSTITUTE FOR ADVANCED STUDY [1662]
One Einstein Drive
Princeton, NJ 08540
(609) 734-8250
Fax: (609) 951-4457
E-mail: donne@ias.edu
Web Site: www.sss.ias.edu

FOUNDED: 1930

AREAS OF INTEREST:
Economics, political science, sociology, education, anthropology and history.

NAME(S) OF PROGRAMS:
• **School of Social Science Fellowships**

TYPE:
Fellowships. Postdoctoral research fellowships at the School of Social Science.

YEAR PROGRAM STARTED: 1970

PURPOSE:
To support fundamental research and scholarship in the social sciences and humanities.

LEGAL BASIS:
Private, nonprofit research center.

ELIGIBILITY:
Scholars of any nationality who have obtained their highest degree and whose work is relevant to any aspect of the social sciences are urged to apply.

FINANCIAL DATA:
Amount of support per award:
Approximately $35,000 to $75,000.

Total amount of support: Varies.

Matching fund requirements: Institute strongly encourages applicants to apply for outside funds as well.

NO. MOST RECENT APPLICANTS: 400.

NO. AWARDS: 26.

APPLICATION INFO:
Applications must be submitted online.

Duration: One academic year.

Deadline: November 1.

PUBLICATIONS:
Annual report.

STAFF:
Donne Petito, Administrative Officer

ADDRESS INQUIRIES TO:
School of Social Science
(See address above.)

*SPECIAL STIPULATIONS:
This is a residential (on-site) fellowship.

INSTITUTE FOR QUANTITATIVE SOCIAL SCIENCE, HARVARD UNIVERSITY [1663]
Henry A. Murray Research Archive
CGIS Knafel Building, Room 318
1737 Cambridge Street
Cambridge, MA 02138
(617) 496-6528
E-mail: support@dataverse.org
Web Site: www.murray.harvard.edu
www.iq.harvard.edu/dissertation-awards

FOUNDED: 1976

AREAS OF INTEREST:
Social sciences, psychology and human development, and education.

NAME(S) OF PROGRAMS:
• **Jeanne Humphrey Block Dissertation Award**

TYPE:
Awards/prizes. The Block Dissertation Award is offered by the Henry A. Murray Research Archive.

YEAR PROGRAM STARTED: 1990

PURPOSE:
To support research that best embodies Henry A. Murray's commitment to the in-depth study of individuals in context, over time and from a variety of perspectives.

LEGAL BASIS:
University or research association.

ELIGIBILITY:
Applicant must be a Harvard Ph.D. candidate (third year or above) in the social sciences.

FINANCIAL DATA:
Amount of support per award: $2,500.

Total amount of support: $2,500.

NO. AWARDS: 1.

APPLICATION INFO:
Detailed information and application guidelines are available upon request to the Institute or can be found on its web site.

Duration: One year.

Deadline: March 13.

PUBLICATIONS:
Program announcement.

IRS I.D.: 04-2103589

ADDRESS INQUIRIES TO:
E-mail: funding@iq.harvard.edu

*SPECIAL STIPULATIONS:
 Dissertation must utilize data archived in the
 Harvard Dataverse.

KAPPA OMICRON NU HONOR SOCIETY
P.O. Box 798
Okemos, MI 48805-0798
(727) 940-2658 ext. 2003
E-mail: info@kon.org
Web Site: www.kon.org

TYPE:
 Fellowships; Project/program grants;
 Research grants; Scholarships. Awarded to
 members for graduate or postgraduate study
 and research in human sciences or one of its
 specializations at colleges or universities with
 strong research programs and supporting
 disciplines for the chosen major or topic.

See entry 2416 for full listing.

MADDIE'S FUND   [1664]
6150 Stoneridge Mall Road
Suite 125
Pleasanton, CA 94588
(925) 310-5450
E-mail: grants@maddiesfund.org
Web Site: www.maddiesfund.org

AREAS OF INTEREST:
 Animal welfare.

TYPE:
 Project/program grants; Training grants.

PURPOSE:
 To revolutionize the status and well-being of
 companion animals.

ELIGIBILITY:
 To be considered for a grant, an organization
 must meet the following criteria:
 (1) be a U.S.-based 501(c)(3) or government
 animal welfare organization focused on dogs
 and/or cats;
 (2) publicly share annual animal statistics on
 their web site;
 (3) publicly share lifesaving percentage and
 the formula for how it was calculated on
 their web site;
 (4) be an active participant in Shelter
 Animals Count and;
 (5) be an active participant in the Million Cat
 Challenge.

GEOG. RESTRICTIONS: United States.

FINANCIAL DATA:
 Amount of support per award: Varies by
 program.
 Total amount of support: $9,698,519 for the
 year 2020.

NO. AWARDS: 381 for the year 2020.

APPLICATION INFO:
 Applications will be made available when
 each individual grant opportunity is
 announced. Potential applicants can sign up
 for the Maddie Network to receive an e-mail
 when new grant opportunities or application
 periods are open.
 Duration: Varies by program.
 Deadline: Varies by program.

ADDRESS INQUIRIES TO:
 Kelly Clardy, Senior Grants Specialist
 (See address above.)

THE NATIONAL ASSOCIATION OF BLACK SOCIAL WORKERS, INC.
2305 Martin Luther King Jr. Avenue, S.E.
Washington, DC 20020
(202) 678-4570
Fax: (202) 678-4572
E-mail: officemanager@nabsw.org
Web Site: www.nabsw.org

TYPE:
 Scholarships.

See entry 936 for full listing.

NATIONAL COUNCIL FOR THE SOCIAL STUDIES   [1665]
8555 16th Street, Suite 500
Silver Spring, MD 20910
(301) 588-1800 ext. 110
(800) 296-7840
Fax: (301) 588-2049
E-mail: awards@ncss.org
Web Site: www.socialstudies.org

FOUNDED: 1921

AREAS OF INTEREST:
 Social studies education.

NAME(S) OF PROGRAMS:
 ● **Septima Clark Book Awards**
 ● **Exemplary Research in Social Studies**
 ● **Jean Dresden Grambs Distinguished Career in Social Studies**
 ● **The Larry Metcalf Exemplary Dissertation Award**
 ● **Outstanding Social Studies Teacher of the Year Awards (Elementary, Middle and Secondary Levels)**
 ● **Carter G. Woodson Book Awards**

TYPE:
 Awards/prizes; Grants-in-aid. The Septima
 Clark Book Awards were first presented in
 2019 and are intended to recognize the most
 distinguished books and encourage the
 writing, publishing and dissemination of
 outstanding social studies books for young
 readers that treat topics related to women's
 issues sensitively and accurately.

 Exemplary Research in Social Studies Award
 acknowledges and encourages scholarly
 inquiry into significant issues and
 possibilities for social studies education.
 Research must be published and have a
 social education focus.

 Jean Dresden Grambs Distinguished Career
 in Social Studies Award recognizes
 professionals who have made extensive
 contributions to knowledge concerning
 significant areas of social studies education
 through meritorious research.

 Larry Metcalf Exemplary Dissertation Award
 recognizes outstanding research completed in
 pursuit of the doctoral degree and encourages
 scholarly inquiry into significant issues and
 possibilities for social studies education.
 Research must be published and have a
 social education focus.

 The annual NCSS Outstanding Teacher of the
 Year Awards recognize exceptional classroom
 social studies teachers for grades K-6, 5-8
 and 7-12 who teach social studies regularly
 and systematically in elementary school
 settings, and at least half-time in middle or
 junior high and high school settings.

 Carter G. Woodson Book Award encourages
 the writing, publishing and dissemination of
 outstanding social studies books for young

readers that treat topics related to ethnic
minorities and relations sensitively and
accurately.

PURPOSE:
 To provide leadership, service and support
 for all social studies educators.

ELIGIBILITY:
 NCSS membership is required, except for the
 Septima Clark and Carter G. Woodson Book
 Awards.

GEOG. RESTRICTIONS: United States.

FINANCIAL DATA:
 Amount of support per award: Grants-in-Aid:
 Up to $3,000; Outstanding Social Studies
 Teacher of the Year Awards: $2,500 and up
 to $500 in transportation/lodging
 reimbursement to attend the annual
 conference.
 Total amount of support: Varies.

NO. MOST RECENT APPLICANTS: Varies.

NO. AWARDS: Exemplary Research in Social
 Studies, Jean Dresden Grambs Award and
 Larry Metcalf Award: 1 per award annually;
 Outstanding Social Studies Teacher Award: 1
 annually per category; Septima Clark Award
 and Carter G. Woodson Award: 3 annually.

APPLICATION INFO:
 Applications must be submitted through the
 online system.
 Deadline: Dates are posted online.

ADDRESS INQUIRIES TO:
 See e-mail address above.

NATIONAL COUNCIL FOR THE SOCIAL STUDIES   [1666]
8555 16th Street, Suite 500
Silver Spring, MD 20910
(301) 588-1800 ext. 110
(800) 296-7840
Fax: (301) 588-2049
E-mail: awards@ncss.org
Web Site: www.socialstudies.org

FOUNDED: 1921

AREAS OF INTEREST:
 Social studies education.

NAME(S) OF PROGRAMS:
 ● **Christa McAuliffe Reach for the Stars Award**

TYPE:
 Awards/prizes. Annual award for projects
 representing excellence and innovation in
 social studies education and having the
 potential of serving as a model for other
 teachers.

YEAR PROGRAM STARTED: 1986

PURPOSE:
 To help a social studies educator make his or
 her dream of innovative social studies a
 reality; to assist classroom teachers in
 developing and implementing imaginative,
 innovative, and illustrative social studies
 teaching strategies; to assist classroom
 teachers in supporting student implementation
 of innovative social studies, citizenship
 projects, field experiences, and community
 connections.

ELIGIBILITY:
 NCSS membership is required. Applicant
 must be a full-time social studies teacher or
 social studies teacher educator currently
 engaged with K-12 students.

GEOG. RESTRICTIONS: United States.

FINANCIAL DATA:
Amount of support per award: $2,500, commemorative gift, presentation session at annual conference, and publicity.

NO. MOST RECENT APPLICANTS: 4.

NO. AWARDS: 1 annually.

APPLICATION INFO:
Applications must be submitted through the online system. No mail-in copies will be allowed.

Deadline: Dates are posted online.

ADDRESS INQUIRIES TO:
See e-mail address above.

NATIONAL COUNCIL FOR THE SOCIAL STUDIES   [1667]

8555 16th Street, Suite 500
Silver Spring, MD 20910
(301) 588-1800 ext. 110
(800) 296-7840
Fax: (301) 588-2049
E-mail: awards@ncss.org
Web Site: www.socialstudies.org

FOUNDED: 1921

AREAS OF INTEREST:
Social studies education.

NAME(S) OF PROGRAMS:
- **Grant for the Enhancement of Geographic Literacy in Honor of James F. Marren**

TYPE:
Awards/prizes. Award to promote school geography education programs that encourage the integration of geography into the social studies curriculum/classroom and enhance the geographic literacy of students at the classroom, district or statewide level.

PURPOSE:
To promote geography education in the schools; to enhance the geographic literacy of students at the classroom, district, or statewide level; to encourage integration of geography into the social studies curriculum/classroom.

ELIGIBILITY:
Programs, not individuals, individual lessons or units, which will enhance the geographic literacy of students at the classroom, district, or statewide levels. Recipients may be individuals or groups in school districts, public institutions, or universities.

GEOG. RESTRICTIONS: United States.

FINANCIAL DATA:
Amount of support per award: $2,500, commemorative gift, presentation session at annual conference, and publicity.

NO. MOST RECENT APPLICANTS: 6.

NO. AWARDS: 1.

APPLICATION INFO:
Instructions and application form are available on the NCSS web site.

Deadline: Dates are posted online.

ADDRESS INQUIRIES TO:
See e-mail address above.

NATIONAL COUNCIL FOR THE SOCIAL STUDIES   [1668]

8555 16th Street, Suite 500
Silver Spring, MD 20910
(301) 588-1800 ext. 110
(800) 296-7840
Fax: (301) 588-2049
E-mail: awards@ncss.org
Web Site: www.socialstudies.org

FOUNDED: 1921

AREAS OF INTEREST:
Social studies education.

NAME(S) OF PROGRAMS:
- **Award for Global Understanding in Honor of James M. Becker**

TYPE:
Awards/prizes. Award for Global Understanding recognizes a social studies educator (or a team of educators) who has made notable contributions in helping social studies students increase their understanding of the world.

PURPOSE:
To recognize a social studies educator (or a team of educators) who has made notable contributions in helping social studies students increase their understanding of the world.

ELIGIBILITY:
NCSS membership is required. Anyone may nominate. Nominees must be social studies educators who are affecting the global understanding of preK-12 students.

FINANCIAL DATA:
Amount of support per award: $2,000 cash award, up to $700 in transportation/lodging reimbursement, a complimentary NCSS conference registration, publicity for a session to present at the NCSS annual conference, and a commemorative gift.

NO. MOST RECENT APPLICANTS: 8.

NO. AWARDS: 1 annually.

APPLICATION INFO:
Instructions and application form are available on the NCSS web site.

Deadline: Dates are posted online.

ADDRESS INQUIRIES TO:
See e-mail address above.

NATIONAL COUNCIL ON FAMILY RELATIONS

661 LaSalle Street
Suite 200
St. Paul, MN 55114
(763) 781-9331
Fax: (763) 781-9348
E-mail: info@ncfr.org
Web Site: www.ncfr.org

TYPE:
Awards/prizes. Awards given for contributions to the area of family science. All of the awards require NCFR membership.

See entry 1350 for full listing.

NATIONAL INSTITUTE OF MENTAL HEALTH   [1669]

Division of Translational Research (DTR)
6001 Executive Boulevard
Room 7111, MSC 9632
Bethesda, MD 20892-9632
(301) 443-9232
E-mail: ftuma@nih.gov
Web Site: www.nimh.nih.gov/about/organization/dtr

AREAS OF INTEREST:
Psychopathology related to trauma, including research on neurobiological, behavioral, cognitive, and other risk and protective factors for psychopathology after traumatic events and the development of interventions for post-traumatic psychopathology.

NAME(S) OF PROGRAMS:
- **Traumatic Stress Research Program**

TYPE:
Fellowships; Project/program grants; Research grants; Technical assistance; Training grants.

YEAR PROGRAM STARTED: 1969

PURPOSE:
To plan, support and administer programs of research, research training and resource development aimed at understanding the pathophysiology of mental illness and hastening the translation of behavioral science and neuroscience advances into innovations in clinical care.

LEGAL BASIS:
Section 301 of the Public Health Service Act, as amended; Public Law 78-410, 42 U.S.C. 241.

ELIGIBILITY:
Applicants can be any public or nonprofit institution such as a university, college, hospital or a community agency, unit of state or local government, an authorized unit of the federal government or a for-profit institution and/or entity.

FINANCIAL DATA:
Amount of support per award: Funding amounts vary by grant type.

APPLICATION INFO:
Forms and instructions are available online.

Duration: Average three to five years.

Deadline: Varies.

ADDRESS INQUIRIES TO:
See e-mail address above.

NATIONAL SCIENCE FOUNDATION

2415 Eisenhower Avenue
Alexandria, VA 22314
(703) 292-7283
Fax: (703) 292-9068
E-mail: fkronz@nsf.gov
Web Site: www.nsf.gov

TYPE:
Conferences/seminars; Research grants. Doctoral dissertation research improvement grants; Professional development grants; Research community development grants; Scholars awards; Standard grants and grants for collaborative research. The proposals that are considered for support use methods from a variety of disciplines including anthropology, communications, history, philosophy, political science, and sociology to investigate STEM theory and practice with regards to their history, socio-cultural formation, philosophical underpinnings, and impacts on quality of life, culture, and society.

See entry 1643 for full listing.

NATIONAL SOCIETY DAUGHTERS OF THE AMERICAN REVOLUTION [1670]

1776 D Street, N.W.
Washington, DC 20006-5303
(202) 879-3263
E-mail: scholarships@nsdar.org
Web Site: www.dar.org

FOUNDED: 1895

AREAS OF INTEREST:
Political science, history, government and economics.

NAME(S) OF PROGRAMS:
- **Enid Hall Griswold Memorial Scholarship**

TYPE:
Scholarships. Undergraduate scholarships awarded to a deserving junior or senior accepted or enrolled in an accredited college or university in the U.S. who is majoring in either political science, history, government or economics.

YEAR PROGRAM STARTED: 1982

PURPOSE:
To provide ways and means to aid students to attain higher education.

LEGAL BASIS:
Incorporated historical society.

ELIGIBILITY:
Scholarships are awarded without regard to race, religion, sex or national origin. Candidates must be U.S. citizens and must attend an accredited college or university in the U.S. No affiliation or relationship to DAR is required for qualification. Awards are judged on the basis of academic excellence, commitment to field of study, as required, and financial need.

Candidate must major in political science, history, government or economics.

GEOG. RESTRICTIONS: United States.

FINANCIAL DATA:
Amount of support per award: $5,000.
Total amount of support: $10,000.

NO. AWARDS: 2.

APPLICATION INFO:
Applicants must use the DAR Scholarship Committee's online submission process found on the DAR public web site. Once applicants have set up their scholarship profile, they will be able to complete the application. If necessary, applicants will be able to provide access to individuals wishing to submit confidential letters of recommendations or school transcripts.
Duration: One academic year. Nonrenewable.
Deadline: January 31.

PUBLICATIONS:
American Spirit, magazine.

ADDRESS INQUIRIES TO:
National Vice Chairman
E-mail:
enidhallmemorialscholarship@nsdar.org

THE PHI BETA KAPPA SOCIETY [1671]

1606 New Hampshire Avenue, N.W.
Washington, DC 20009
(202) 265-3808
Fax: (202) 986-1601
E-mail: awards@pbk.org
Web Site: www.pbk.org

AREAS OF INTEREST:
Philosophy.

NAME(S) OF PROGRAMS:
- **The Dr. Martin R. Lebowitz and Eve Lewellis Lebowitz Prize for Philosophical Achievement and Contribution**

TYPE:
Awards/prizes. In conjunction with the American Philosophical Association, the award is presented to a pair of philosophers who hold contrasting views of an important philosophical question that is of current interest both to the field and to an educated public audience. The Lebowitz symposium program ordinarily consists of two annual lectures to be delivered sequentially at a divisional meeting selected by the honorees, or lacking their agreement, by the Phi Beta Kappa Society.

PURPOSE:
To promote the discipline of philosophy.

ELIGIBILITY:
The committee is encouraged to consider candidates who address important philosophical issues using diverse methodologies and perspectives and who, in so doing, are able to communicate important philosophical ideas to specialist and non-specialist audiences.

FINANCIAL DATA:
Amount of support per award:
Approximately $25,000 per person.

Total amount of support: Approximately $50,000 annually.

NO. AWARDS: 1 annually for 1 pair.

APPLICATION INFO:
American Philosophical Association members are eligible to nominate or self-nominate. A complete nomination will consist of the following, and can be uploaded into the form:
(1) two 300-word abstracts, one for each speaker, which details the proposed topic and the approach that will be taken in the symposium;
(2) a complete curriculum vitae for both proposed speakers and;
(3) two letters of recommendation. Ideally, the reference will have knowledge of both proposed speakers. Letters should address the stature of the candidates and the relevance of the selected topic.
Deadline: December 1.

ADDRESS INQUIRIES TO:
Eva Caldera, Associate Secretary
Tel: (202) 745-3244
E-mail: ecaldera@pbk.org

PI GAMMA MU, INTERNATIONAL HONOR SOCIETY IN SOCIAL SCIENCE

1001 Millington, Suite B
Winfield, KS 67156
(620) 221-3128
E-mail: executivedirector@pigammamu.org
Web Site: www.pigammamu.org

TYPE:
Scholarships. Awarded for graduate study.

See entry 1562 for full listing.

SMITH RICHARDSON FOUNDATION, INC. [1672]

60 Jesup Road
Westport, CT 06880
(203) 222-6222
Fax: (203) 222-6282
E-mail: jhollings@srf.org
Web Site: www.srf.org

FOUNDED: 1935

AREAS OF INTEREST:
Improvement of public policy in the fields of social welfare, economic and regulatory schemes and education issues; improvement of American foreign policy, particularly as it relates to national security.

NAME(S) OF PROGRAMS:
- **Domestic Public Policy Program**
- **International Security and Foreign Policy Program**

TYPE:
Conferences/seminars; Project/program grants; Research grants. The Domestic Policy Program primarily supports research on ways to improve public policy in the fields of social welfare, economic and regulatory schemes and education issues. The program has a particular interest in research that examines the effectiveness of institutions which serve children and families at-risk.

The Foreign Policy Program supports projects in national security and defense policy, in military history and strategy, in the political, military and economic affairs of Eastern Europe and the states of the former Soviet Union, economic and security developments in the Asia Pacific, and also in international economic issues of vital interest to American policymakers. The program aims to define the nature of the post-cold war security environment.

YEAR PROGRAM STARTED: 1935

PURPOSE:
To support and promote a vigorous and free society.

LEGAL BASIS:
Private foundation.

ELIGIBILITY:
Organizations sponsoring projects appropriate to the Foundation's interests are eligible. The Foundation originates many of the grant commitments which are made, and the vast majority of unsolicited requests for funding must be rejected. Because of fund limitations, no grants are available for deficit funding of previously established operations, projects relating to building construction (i.e., "brick and mortar"), programs related to the arts, historic restoration projects, or research in the physical sciences. No grants are made directly to individuals or to advocacy organizations. The Foundation does not provide support for the operating costs of direct-service programs or charities. The Foundation rarely provides general support for any organization or funding for conferences and documentaries.

The Foundation awards grants for policy research with national implications. Some small grants are available to support innovative service and educational programs in Connecticut and North Carolina which assist children and families at-risk. Nearly all such local grants are solicited by the staff and the Board of the Foundation. Service programs in states other than Connecticut and North Carolina are ineligible for funding.

GEOG. RESTRICTIONS: Connecticut and North Carolina.

FINANCIAL DATA:
Amount of support per award: Varies.

APPLICATION INFO:
The Foundation has a two-stage application process. Initial inquiries should be submitted by mail to the address above in the form of a concept paper. If the project is determined to be a good candidate for a grant, applicants will be asked to prepare a full-length proposal.
Duration: Varies.
Deadline: Grants are reviewed on an ongoing basis.

PUBLICATIONS:
Annual report.

IRS I.D.: 56-0611550

STAFF:
Allan Song, Senior Program Officer
Mark Steinmeyer, Senior Program Officer
Olga Ramous, Grants Coordinator
Kathy Lavery, Records Coordinator

OFFICERS AND TRUSTEES:
Peter L. Richardson, Chairman of the Board
W. Winburne King, III, Vice-Chairman of the Board, General Counsel and Chief Investment Officer
Marin J. Strmecki, Ph.D., Senior Vice President, Director of Programs
Ross F. Hemphill, Vice President and Chief Financial Officer
Arvid R. Nelson, Ph.D., Secretary
Karla W. Frank, Assistant Secretary
Michael Blair
John Richardson
Nico Richardson
Tyler B. Richardson
E. William Stetson, III

ADDRESS INQUIRIES TO:
Domestic Policy or Foreign Policy Program
(See address above.)

THE ROYAL TOWN PLANNING INSTITUTE [1673]

41 Botolph Lane
London EC3R 8DL England
(020) 7929-9494
Fax: (020) 7929-9490
E-mail: marketing@rtpi.org.uk
Web Site: www.rtpi.org.uk

FOUNDED: 1914

AREAS OF INTEREST:
Urban and regional planning, land use, transport and housing, industrial strategy on planning, rural planning, conservation and recreational planning.

NAME(S) OF PROGRAMS:
● **George Pepler International Award**

TYPE:
Travel grants. This biennial award is made to individuals in their first 10 years of post-qualification experience, who wish to visit Britain or, as residents of Britain, desire to visit another country for a short period to study the theory and practice of town and country planning or some particular aspect of planning.

YEAR PROGRAM STARTED: 1973

PURPOSE:
To provide an international travelling award for young people of any nationality who wish to visit another country in order to study town planning or a related subject.

LEGAL BASIS:
Charitable trust.

ELIGIBILITY:
Young people of any nationality under the age of 30 are eligible to apply. Professional qualifications are not necessary. Each applicant is required to complete a prescribed application form and submit to a panel of advisers a statement showing the nature of the study and suggested itinerary.

FINANCIAL DATA:
Amount of support per award: GBP 3,000 paid in two equal installments.

NO. MOST RECENT APPLICANTS: 15.

NO. AWARDS: 1 biennially.

APPLICATION INFO:
Contact the Institute through its e-mail address for an entry form and details. Application and information can be found online.
Duration: Three to four weeks.
Deadline: September 30.

ADDRESS INQUIRIES TO:
Rebecca Hildreth, Director of Communications
(See address above.)

RUSSELL SAGE FOUNDATION [1674]

112 East 64th Street
New York, NY 10065
(212) 750-6000
Fax: (212) 371-4761
E-mail: info@rsage.org
Web Site: www.russellsage.org

FOUNDED: 1907

AREAS OF INTEREST:
Behavioral economics; future of work; race, ethnicity, and immigration; and social inequality. Special initiatives on integrating biology and social science knowledge, computational social science, immigrant and immigrant integration, and non-standard employment.

TYPE:
Research grants; Visiting scholars.
Presidential grants.

YEAR PROGRAM STARTED: 1907

PURPOSE:
To improve social and living conditions in the U.S. by conducting and supporting social science research relevant to public policy issues.

LEGAL BASIS:
Private operating foundation.

ELIGIBILITY:
The Foundation supports focused, empirical research projects under the direction of a principal investigator. Under the terms of the contract, the research must be coordinated through a fiscal agency (university, college or 501(c)(3) organization under the Internal Revenue Code).

The Foundation's awards are restricted to support for basic social science research within its announced programs. These currently include research on the future of work, immigration and the social psychology of social contact.

The Foundation conducts a Visiting Scholar program under which persons working in the areas of current interest to the Foundation join the staff for one year to consult and continue their own research and writing.

GEOG. RESTRICTIONS: United States.

FINANCIAL DATA:
Amount of support per award: Presidential grants: Up to $50,000; Research grants: Up to $175,000.
Total amount of support: Approximately $4,800,000 for the year 2019.

NO. MOST RECENT APPLICANTS: Approximately 875.

NO. AWARDS: Approximately 90.

APPLICATION INFO:
Applications for awards should be preceded by a letter of inquiry to the Foundation. Guidelines and other details are available on the web site.
Duration: One to three years.
Deadline: Eight weeks prior to Board meetings to be held March, June and November.

PUBLICATIONS:
Biennial report; scholarly books.

IRS I.D.: 13-1635303

OFFICERS:
Sheldon Danziger, President
Claire Gabriel, Secretary

ADDRESS INQUIRIES TO:
E-mail: programs@rsage.org

SOCIAL SCIENCES AND HUMANITIES RESEARCH COUNCIL OF CANADA [1675]

350 Albert Street
Ottawa ON K1P 6G4 Canada
(613) 943-7777
Fax: (613) 943-1329
E-mail: fellowships@sshrc-crsh.gc.ca
Web Site: www.sshrc-crsh.gc.ca

FOUNDED: 1977

AREAS OF INTEREST:
The development and support of research, research training, and scholarly activities in the social sciences and humanities.

NAME(S) OF PROGRAMS:
● **Doctoral Awards**

TYPE:
Awards/prizes; Fellowships; Scholarships. Through its Doctoral Awards program, SSHRC offers two types of funding for doctoral students:
(1) SSHRC Doctoral Fellowships and;
(2) Joseph-Armand Bombardier (JAB) Canada Graduate Scholarships (CGS) program - Doctoral Scholarships.

YEAR PROGRAM STARTED: 1977

PURPOSE:
To develop research skills and assist in the training of highly qualified personnel by supporting students who demonstrate a high standard of scholarly achievement in undergraduate and graduate studies in the social sciences and humanities.

LEGAL BASIS:
Government agency.

ELIGIBILITY:
Applicants must be Canadian citizens or permanent residents of Canada. SSHRC Doctoral Fellowships are tenable at any recognized university in Canada, or abroad,

in which case the award holder has to have at least one previous degree from a Canadian university.

Joseph-Armand Bombardier Canada Graduate Scholarships-Doctoral Scholarships are tenable only at Canadian universities.

FINANCIAL DATA:
Amount of support per award: SSHRC Doctoral Fellowships: $20,000 (CAN) per year; Joseph-Armand Bombardier Canada Graduate Scholarships-Doctoral Scholarships: $35,000 (CAN) per year.

NO. AWARDS: SSHRC Doctoral Fellowships: 508; Joseph-Armand Bombardier Canada Graduate Scholarships-Doctoral Scholarships: 430 for the year 2019-20.

APPLICATION INFO:
On university campuses, information may be obtained from the Faculty of Graduate Studies, the Office of Research Administration, the Registrar, or the Student Awards Office. Inquiries may also be addressed directly to the Research Training Portfolio of the Council, at the address above. Detailed program and application information is available online.
Duration: SSHRC Doctoral Fellowships: One to four years; Joseph-Armand Bombardier Canada Graduate Scholarships-Doctoral Scholarships: Three years. Nonrenewable.
Deadline: For applicants registered at a Canadian university, in the fall on the date set by the university; for other applicants, usually in October.

ADDRESS INQUIRIES TO:
Research Training Portfolio
(See address above.)

SOCIAL SCIENCES AND HUMANITIES RESEARCH COUNCIL OF CANADA   [1676]
350 Albert Street
Ottawa ON K1P 6G4 Canada
(613) 943-7777
Fax: (613) 943-1329
E-mail: fellowships@sshrc-crsh.gc.ca
Web Site: www.sshrc-crsh.gc.ca

FOUNDED: 1977

AREAS OF INTEREST:
The development and support of research, research training, and scholarly activities in the social sciences and humanities.

NAME(S) OF PROGRAMS:
● **SSHRC Postdoctoral Fellowships**

TYPE:
Fellowships. For Canadian citizens or permanent residents of Canada, to support postdoctoral research in the humanities and social sciences.

YEAR PROGRAM STARTED: 1977

PURPOSE:
To support promising new scholars in the social sciences and humanities and to assist them in establishing a research base at an important time in their research careers.

LEGAL BASIS:
Government agency.

ELIGIBILITY:
Competition is open to persons who have been awarded an earned Doctorate within the two years preceding competition closing date (or up to five years if the applicant's career was interrupted or delayed for the purpose of

maternity, childrearing, illness or health-related family responsibilities). Applicants must demonstrate that all doctoral requirements will be completed before the proposed starting date of tenure. Awards are for postdoctoral study or research within a university or research institution.

Applicants must be Canadian citizens or permanent residents of Canada at the time of application.

FINANCIAL DATA:
Amount of support per award: $45,000 (CAN) per year for up to two years.

NO. MOST RECENT APPLICANTS: 751 for the year 2019-20.

NO. AWARDS: 160 for the year 2019-20.

APPLICATION INFO:
Before submitting an application, applicants must ensure that they meet the requirements specified under Eligibility on the Council web site. Applicants must complete and submit only one application form, together with the curriculum vitae and required attachments. Instructions for filling out the application form and curriculum vitae are available within the form used by applicants to create their online submission.
Duration: Period of tenure is 12 to 24 months. Nonrenewable.
Deadline: Usually in mid-September. Announcement in February.

ADDRESS INQUIRIES TO:
Research Training Portfolio
(See address or e-mail above.)

SOCIAL SCIENCES AND HUMANITIES RESEARCH COUNCIL OF CANADA   [1677]
350 Albert Street
Ottawa ON K1P 6G4 Canada
(613) 943-7777
Fax: (613) 943-1329
E-mail: fellowships@sshrc-crsh.gc.ca
Web Site: www.sshrc-crsh.gc.ca

FOUNDED: 1977

AREAS OF INTEREST:
The development and support of research, research training, and scholarly activities in the social sciences and humanities.

NAME(S) OF PROGRAMS:
● **Joseph-Armand Bombardier Canada Graduate Scholarships Program - Master's Scholarships**
● **Master's Awards**

TYPE:
Awards/prizes; Fellowships; Scholarships.

YEAR PROGRAM STARTED: 2003

PURPOSE:
To develop research skills and assist in the training of highly qualified personnel by supporting students who demonstrate a high standard of scholarly achievement in undergraduate and graduate studies in the social sciences and humanities.

LEGAL BASIS:
Government agency.

ELIGIBILITY:
Applicants must be Canadian citizens or permanent residents of Canada.
Joseph-Armand Bombardier Canada Graduate Scholarships-Master's Scholarships are tenable only at Canadian universities.

FINANCIAL DATA:
Amount of support per award: Joseph-Armand Bombardier Canada Graduate Scholarships - Master's Scholarships: $17,500 (CAN).

NO. AWARDS: 1,501 Joseph-Armand Bombardier Canada Graduate Scholarships - Master's Scholarships for the year 2020-21.

APPLICATION INFO:
Information may be obtained from the Faculty of Graduate Studies or sent directly to the Research Training Portfolio at the e-mail address listed above. Detailed program and application information is available online. Applications must be submitted online using the Research Portal.
Duration: One year. Nonrenewable.
Deadline: December 1.

ADDRESS INQUIRIES TO:
Research Training Portfolio
(See address above.)

SOCIAL SCIENCES AND HUMANITIES RESEARCH COUNCIL OF CANADA   [1678]
350 Albert Street
Ottawa ON K1P 6G4 Canada
(613) 943-7777
Fax: (613) 943-1329
E-mail: vanier@cihr-irsc.gc.ca
Web Site: www.vanier.gc.ca

FOUNDED: 2008

AREAS OF INTEREST:
The development and support of research, research training, and scholarly activities in the social sciences and humanities.

NAME(S) OF PROGRAMS:
● **Vanier Canada Graduate Scholarships (CGS)**

TYPE:
Awards/prizes; Fellowships; Scholarships. For doctoral students in the humanities and social sciences. Administered by the Canadian Institutes of Health Research, the Natural Sciences and Engineering Research Council and the Social Sciences Research Council.

YEAR PROGRAM STARTED: 2008

PURPOSE:
To attract and retain world-class doctoral students by supporting students who demonstrate both leadership skills and a high standard of scholarly achievement in graduate studies in social sciences and humanities, natural sciences and engineering, and health.

LEGAL BASIS:
Government agency.

ELIGIBILITY:
Applicants can be citizens or permanent residents of Canada, as well as international students. For full eligibility criteria, visit www.vanier.gc.ca/en/eligibility-admissibilite.html.

GEOG. RESTRICTIONS: Canada.

FINANCIAL DATA:
Amount of support per award: $50,000 (CAN) per year.

NO. MOST RECENT APPLICANTS: 179 for the year 2019-20.

NO. AWARDS: 56 for the year 2019-20.

APPLICATION INFO:
Candidates must be nominated by a Canadian institution with a quota at which they want to study. On university campuses, information

may be obtained from the Dean or Faculty of
Graduate Studies, the Office of Research
Administration, the Registrar, or the Student
Awards Office. Inquiries may also be
addressed directly to the Vanier Banting
Secretariat at the e-mail address above.

Duration: Three years. Nonrenewable.

Deadline: Nomination deadline is set by the
university. The Vanier Banting Secretariat's
deadline for nominations submitted by the
universities is usually early November.

ADDRESS INQUIRIES TO:
See e-mail address above.

SOCIAL SCIENCES AND HUMANITIES RESEARCH COUNCIL OF CANADA   [1679]
350 Albert Street
Ottawa ON K1P 6G4 Canada
(613) 943-7777
Fax: (613) 943-1329
E-mail: fellowships@sshrc-crsh.gc.ca
Web Site: www.sshrc-crsh.gc.ca

FOUNDED: 2010

AREAS OF INTEREST:
The development and support of research,
research training, and scholarly activities in
the social sciences and humanities.

NAME(S) OF PROGRAMS:
● **Banting Postdoctoral Fellowships**

TYPE:
Fellowships. For Canadian citizens,
permanent residents of Canada and foreign
citizens to support postdoctoral research in
the humanities and social sciences.

YEAR PROGRAM STARTED: 2010

PURPOSE:
To support promising new scholars in the
social sciences and humanities and to assist
them in establishing a research base at an
important time in their research careers.

LEGAL BASIS:
Government agency.

ELIGIBILITY:
Competition is open to persons who have
been awarded an earned Doctorate within the
three years preceding competition. Applicants
can be citizens or permanent residents of
Canada, as well as international students.

Without exception, the Banting Postdoctoral
Fellowships:
(1) are tenable only at the institution which
supported the original application for the
program;
(2) must be taken up no earlier than April 1
and no later than October 1 of the year
following the application deadline and;
(3) are for two years from the date of
up-take.

FINANCIAL DATA:
Amount of support per award: $70,000
(CAN) per year for two years.

NO. MOST RECENT APPLICANTS: 162 for the
year 2019-20.

NO. AWARDS: 25.

APPLICATION INFO:
On university campuses, information may be
obtained from the Dean or Faculty of
Graduate Studies, the Office of Research
Administration, the Registrar, or the Student
Awards Office.

For more information, visit
www.banting.fellowships-bourses.gc.ca.

Duration: Period of tenure is 24 months.
Nonrenewable.

Deadline: Usually mid-September.

ADDRESS INQUIRIES TO:
Research Training Portfolio
(See address above.)

THE SOCIETY FOR THE PSYCHOLOGICAL STUDY OF SOCIAL ISSUES (SPSSI)   [1680]
700 Seventh Street, S.E.
Washington, DC 20003
(202) 675-6956
E-mail: awards@spssi.org
Web Site: www.spssi.org

FOUNDED: 1936

AREAS OF INTEREST:
Social psychology research.

NAME(S) OF PROGRAMS:
● **Gordon Allport Intergroup Relations Prize**

TYPE:
Awards/prizes. The Gordon Allport
Intergroup Relations Prize honors the
memory of the late Dr. Gordon W. Allport, a
founder and past president of SPSSI.

LEGAL BASIS:
Independently incorporated society.

ELIGIBILITY:
Entries must be works published during the
calendar year preceding the year of
submission. Submissions are limited to
articles, chapters or other works published in
their primary form (e.g., appearing in print
for print journals or books or online for
online-only journals or other volumes) with a
formal publication date of the prior year. An
individual or group may only submit one
paper to SPSSI awards (including the
Allport, Klineberg and Dissertation Awards)
per award year (January 1 to December 31).
All entries must be submitted in English.

The award is given to "the best paper or
article of the year on intergroup relations."
Originality of the contribution, whether
theoretical or empirical, will be given special
weight. The research area of intergroup
relations includes such dimensions as age,
gender, and socioeconomic status, as well as
ethnicity.

FINANCIAL DATA:
Amount of support per award: $1,000.

CO-OP FUNDING PROGRAMS: The Award is
sponsored by The Gordon W. Allport
Memorial Fund of Harvard University and
SPSSI.

NO. AWARDS: 1 for the year 2019.

APPLICATION INFO:
Online submissions are the preferred method.
Limit the number and size of files uploaded
when applying online.

For hard-copy submissions, send five copies
to SPSSI.

Duration: Annual award.

Deadline: June 15. Notification by October
15.

ADDRESS INQUIRIES TO:
See e-mail address above.

THE SOCIETY FOR THE PSYCHOLOGICAL STUDY OF SOCIAL ISSUES (SPSSI)   [1681]
700 Seventh Street, S.E.
Washington, DC 20003
(202) 675-6956
E-mail: awards@spssi.org
Web Site: www.spssi.org

FOUNDED: 1936

AREAS OF INTEREST:
Social psychology research.

NAME(S) OF PROGRAMS:
● **Innovative Teaching Award**

TYPE:
Awards/prizes. SPSSI confers an annual
award for innovative teaching in areas related
to the psychological study of social issues.

PURPOSE:
To recognize effective courses, assignments
or classroom activities addressing social
issues.

LEGAL BASIS:
Independently incorporated society.

ELIGIBILITY:
Nominees should be SPSSI members who
have developed innovative pedagogical
products that aid in teaching the
psychological study of social issues.
Nominees may teach at graduate
degree-granting institutions, four-year
undergraduate colleges and universities,
two-year and community colleges, or as
contingent or adjunct faculty.

FINANCIAL DATA:
Recipients will be recognized in the Teaching
and Learning column in the SPSSI *Forward*
newsletter. Honorable Mention awardees will
receive one year of free SPSSI membership.

Amount of support per award: $1,000 and a
plaque.

NO. MOST RECENT APPLICANTS: 4.

NO. AWARDS: 1.

APPLICATION INFO:
Application instructions are available on the
web site.

Deadline: March 1.

ADDRESS INQUIRIES TO:
See e-mail address above.

THE SOCIETY FOR THE PSYCHOLOGICAL STUDY OF SOCIAL ISSUES (SPSSI)   [1682]
700 Seventh Street, S.E.
Washington, DC 20003
(202) 675-6956
E-mail: awards@spssi.org
Web Site: www.spssi.org

FOUNDED: 1936

AREAS OF INTEREST:
Social issues and psychology.

NAME(S) OF PROGRAMS:
● **Awards for Outstanding Teaching and Mentoring**

TYPE:
Awards/prizes. SPSSI confers one or two
annual awards for outstanding teaching and
mentoring in areas related to the
psychological study of social issues. The
award recognizes teaching excellence in a
variety of contexts.

PURPOSE:
To recognize outstanding teaching in areas related to the psychological study of social issues.

LEGAL BASIS:
Independently incorporated society.

ELIGIBILITY:
Nominees should be SPSSI members who have made substantial contributions to students in the psychological study of social issues. To be eligible, individuals must have been teaching and/or mentoring students for at least five years full-time since the doctoral degree. Nominees may teach at graduate degree-granting institutions, Bachelor's degree universities and colleges, or two-year and community colleges. Self-nominations are encouraged.

FINANCIAL DATA:
Amount of support per award: $1,000 plus a plaque.

NO. MOST RECENT APPLICANTS: 6.

NO. AWARDS: 1 or 2.

APPLICATION INFO:
Application information is available on the web site.
Deadline: February 15.

PUBLICATIONS:
Application guidelines.

ADDRESS INQUIRIES TO:
See e-mail address above.

THE SOCIETY FOR THE PSYCHOLOGICAL STUDY OF SOCIAL ISSUES (SPSSI)   [1683]
700 Seventh Street, S.E.
Washington, DC 20003
(202) 675-6956
E-mail: awards@spssi.org
Web Site: www.spssi.org

FOUNDED: 1936

AREAS OF INTEREST:
Social psychology research.

NAME(S) OF PROGRAMS:
● **SPSSI Action Teaching Grants**

TYPE:
Grants-in-aid.

PURPOSE:
To develop, enhance, or measure the impact of an innovative action teaching classroom activity, student assignment, field experience, or web-based resource.

LEGAL BASIS:
Independently incorporated society.

ELIGIBILITY:
Open to regular dues-paying members of SPSSI, including graduate students. Proposed projects will be judged on originality, feasibility, potential teaching effectiveness, and potential impact with respect to one or more social issues.

FINANCIAL DATA:
Amount of support per award: $100 to $1,500.

NO. AWARDS: Maximum 3 annually.

APPLICATION INFO:
Online submissions are the preferred method. Application should include:
(1) SPSSI Action Teaching Grant Application Form;
(2) curriculum vitae or resume;

(3) an abstract of 75 to 100 words summarizing the grant proposal and;
(4) a description of the project, including a statement of what students will learn from the action teaching resource or activity developed with grant funding, how the action teaching resource or activity will contribute to society or others beyond the class, how student learning will be assessed and its broader impact, why grant funding is needed to develop the action teaching resource or activity, and a budget describing each item and rationale.
Deadline: April 15. Decision by May 15.

ADDRESS INQUIRIES TO:
See e-mail address above.

THE SOCIETY FOR THE PSYCHOLOGICAL STUDY OF SOCIAL ISSUES (SPSSI)   [1684]
700 Seventh Street, S.E.
Washington, DC 20003
(202) 675-6956
E-mail: awards@spssi.org
Web Site: www.spssi.org

FOUNDED: 1936

AREAS OF INTEREST:
Social psychology research.

NAME(S) OF PROGRAMS:
● **SPSSI James Marshall Fellowship in Public Policy**

TYPE:
Fellowships. Fellowship provides support for a postdoctoral level fellow to work full-time for one year in the U.S. Congress in Washington, DC. The fellow should expect to use psychological research to inform the public policymaking process while working full-time in a congressional office.

PURPOSE:
To train early career scientists to contribute to the effective use of scientific knowledge about social issues in the formation of public policy at the federal level; to educate the scientific community about how research can contribute to the development of public policy; to establish a more effective liaison between social scientists and various policymaking mechanisms.

LEGAL BASIS:
Independently incorporated society.

ELIGIBILITY:
Fellowship is open to postdoctoral scientists from any discipline relevant to the psychological study of social issues. Candidates must hold a Ph.D. or Psy.D. before the start of the fellowship and be a member of SPSSI. Candidates must demonstrate interest or involvement in the application of social science to social issues and policies, have a sound scientific background, and demonstrate sensitivity toward policy issues. Candidates must be able to communicate effectively, both orally and in writing. Individual initiative and an ability to work cooperatively with others having diverse viewpoints are critical. Knowledge of policy processes at the national level, along with placement goals, is desirable, but not essential.

FINANCIAL DATA:
Fellowship includes health benefits and paid attendance at the annual SPSSI Conference in June of the fellowship year.

Amount of support per award: Stipend of $60,000.

CO-OP FUNDING PROGRAMS: Supported, in part, by an endowment provided by the James Marshall Fund.

NO. MOST RECENT APPLICANTS: 16.

NO. AWARDS: 1.

APPLICATION INFO:
Applications for the 2021-22 fellowship year are available beginning December 1, 2020. The following documents will be required:
(1) a personal statement (1,000-word limit) describing the applicant's interest and experience in policy activities or social issues, their interest in the fellowship program, how the fellowship fits into their career goals, and what the desired objectives are;
(2) curriculum vitae and;
(3) three letters of reference. Letters should address the applicant's abilities, experience and motivation as related to the fellowship program.
Duration: One year, September to August.
Deadline: February 1.

ADDRESS INQUIRIES TO:
Sarah Mancoll, Policy Director
(See address above.)

THE SOCIETY FOR THE PSYCHOLOGICAL STUDY OF SOCIAL ISSUES (SPSSI)   [1685]
700 Seventh Street, S.E.
Washington, DC 20003
(202) 675-6956
E-mail: awards@spssi.org
Web Site: www.spssi.org

FOUNDED: 1936

AREAS OF INTEREST:
Social psychology research.

NAME(S) OF PROGRAMS:
● **Small-Scale Events Advancing SPSSI (SEAS) Grants**

TYPE:
Conferences/seminars; Development grants. Grants for support of small-scale events hosted at a member's institution or other local venue related to the psychological study of social issues. These events may include, but are not limited to, departmental or institutional speakers or speaker series, research symposia, brown-bag events or series, or mini-conferences. Initiatives that enhance SPSSI membership and pre-conferences or small meetings attached to larger conferences where the theme and content of the meeting is related to the psychological study of social issues are also supported.

PURPOSE:
To promote awareness of the Society; to identify potential new members.

LEGAL BASIS:
Independently incorporated society.

ELIGIBILITY:
Current regular dues-paying members of SPSSI may apply. If not a current member of SPSSI, a membership application may be submitted along with the grant application. Graduate student members may apply, with faculty mentor or advisor serving as a co-applicant.

Proposals will be evaluated on the event's potential to attract new SPSSI members, promote SPSSI's basic interests and goals, and to facilitate research links, networks and capacity. Proposals for events drawing attendees from two or more institutions, departments or disciplines are highly encouraged.

FINANCIAL DATA:
Funds may be used to publicize the event, pay speakers' honoraria, reimburse speakers' travel expenses, print collateral materials, or other expenses related to the specific project. Funds may not be used for paying SPSSI membership dues, honoraria for organizers, or costs not directly related to the project or event.

Amount of support per award: Up to $1,000.

NO. AWARDS: 1 for the year 2019.

APPLICATION INFO:
Application should include:
(1) a cover letter;
(2) a brief proposal (up to 1000 words) outlining the purpose of the event and its anticipated outcomes and;
(3) a detailed budget (one page or less) outlining the use of funds, and including additional sources of funding that will be sought to support the event.

Online submissions are the preferred method.
Duration: One year.
Deadline: September 15.

ADDRESS INQUIRIES TO:
See e-mail address above.

THE SOCIETY FOR THE PSYCHOLOGICAL STUDY OF SOCIAL ISSUES (SPSSI)   [1686]
700 Seventh Street, S.E.
Washington, DC 20003
(202) 675-6956
E-mail: awards@spssi.org
Web Site: www.spssi.org

FOUNDED: 1936

AREAS OF INTEREST:
Social psychology research.

NAME(S) OF PROGRAMS:
● **Local- and State-Level Policy Work Grants**

TYPE:
Research grants.

YEAR PROGRAM STARTED: 2015

PURPOSE:
To influence policy at the local and state levels through applied research; to increase the availability of policy opportunities for SPSSI members who are interested in applied research; to encourage younger scholars to become more involved in SPSSI.

LEGAL BASIS:
Independently incorporated society.

ELIGIBILITY:
To be eligible, a group must meet the following criteria:
(1) at least one member of the group must be a current SPSSI member;
(2) the group must consist of a minimum of three social scientists who live in the same state or similar regionally-based jurisdiction outside of the U.S.;
(3) the group members must be working on the same issue, broadly defined and;
(4) the group must compellingly demonstrate that the members are interested in the policy applications of psychological science and other social science research.

Preference will be given to groups that demonstrate either existing policy expertise or the willingness to learn more about policy work at the local or state level.

FINANCIAL DATA:
Amount of support per award: Up to $2,000 per award.
Total amount of support: Up to $6,000.

NO. MOST RECENT APPLICANTS: 4.

NO. AWARDS: Up to 3.

APPLICATION INFO:
To apply for funding, the group should submit a short proposal (no more than 3,000 words) that:
(1) addresses the criteria delineated above;
(2) explains the outcomes or deliverables;
(3) provides a budget for the year;
(4) specifies agreement to submit a presentation of the work for the annual SPSSI Conference and;
(5) specifies agreement to deliver a summary of the work completed at the end of the grant period. Such a document may take the form of a five- to 10-page summary of the work completed, a policy paper, a research report, or another suitable report.

Duration: One year.
Deadline: June 1 for spring award cycle; September 1 for fall award cycle.

ADDRESS INQUIRIES TO:
Sarah Mancoll, Policy Director
E-mail: smancoll@spssi.org

THE SOCIETY FOR THE PSYCHOLOGICAL STUDY OF SOCIAL ISSUES (SPSSI)   [1687]
700 Seventh Street, S.E.
Washington, DC 20003
(202) 675-6956
E-mail: awards@spssi.org
Web Site: www.spssi.org

FOUNDED: 1936

AREAS OF INTEREST:
Social psychology research.

NAME(S) OF PROGRAMS:
● **Dalmas A. Taylor Memorial Summer Minority Policy Fellowship**

TYPE:
Fellowships. This fellowship is to honor the memory of Dalmas A. Taylor, who passed away during his term as President of SPSSI. It provides an opportunity for a graduate student of color to work on public policy issues in Washington, DC.

PURPOSE:
To provide an opportunity for a graduate student of color to work on public policy issues in Washington, DC.

LEGAL BASIS:
Independently incorporated society.

ELIGIBILITY:
Applicants must be currently enrolled and in good standing in an accredited graduate program in psychology or a related field. They must be members of an ethnic minority group (African American, Alaskan Native, American Indian, Asian American, Hispanic and Pacific Islander) or have demonstrated a commitment to a career with a focus on ethnic minority issues. Applicants should not have completed their graduate program by the time they begin the fellowship.

FINANCIAL DATA:
Fellowship includes travel expenses and up to $1,500 for living expenses to relocate to Washington, DC.
Amount of support per award: Stipend of $3,000.

CO-OP FUNDING PROGRAMS: This fellowship is administered in conjunction with APA and the APA Minority Fellowship Program.

NO. MOST RECENT APPLICANTS: 10.

NO. AWARDS: 1.

APPLICATION INFO:
Application should include:
(1) a cover page stating name, institution, address, telephone number, fax number (if applicable) and e-mail address;
(2) a statement (no more than 1,000 words) which details the reason for interest in this fellowship, previous and current research experiences, indication of interest in ethnic minority psychological issues and statement of how this fellowship would contribute to the applicant's career goals;
(3) two letters of recommendation, which can be uploaded with application materials or sent directly to the e-mail address listed above and;
(4) current curriculum vitae.

A link to the application will be available online beginning January 1. Online submission is the preferred method.
Duration: Typically eight to 12 weeks.
Deadline: March 1. Announcement will be made on or about April 15.

ADDRESS INQUIRIES TO:
See e-mail address above.

THE SOCIETY FOR THE PSYCHOLOGICAL STUDY OF SOCIAL ISSUES (SPSSI)   [1688]
700 Seventh Street, S.E.
Washington, DC 20003
(202) 675-6956
E-mail: awards@spssi.org
Web Site: www.spssi.org

FOUNDED: 1936

AREAS OF INTEREST:
Social psychology research.

NAME(S) OF PROGRAMS:
● **SPSSI Grants-in-Aid**

TYPE:
Grants-in-aid.

YEAR PROGRAM STARTED: 1956

PURPOSE:
To support scientific research in social problem areas related to the basic interests and goals of SPSSI and particularly those that are not likely to receive support from traditional sources.

LEGAL BASIS:
Independently incorporated society.

ELIGIBILITY:
The applicant must be a member of SPSSI. Applicants may submit only one application per deadline. If an applicant has applied to the Clara Mayo Grant in the same award year (July 1 to June 30), he or she is not eligible to apply for Grants-in-Aid. Individuals may submit a joint application.

The SPSSI Committee on Grants-in-Aid especially encourages proposals involving:
(1) unique and timely research opportunities;
(2) underrepresented institutions, graduate

students and junior scholars;
(3) volunteer research teams and;
(4) actual, not pilot, projects.

SPSSI's Grants-in-Aid program will include grants earmarked especially in support of research related to SPSSI's current policy priorities: interpersonal violence, marriage equality, and immigration reform. Proposals within these priorities will receive special consideration, though submissions are not limited to these areas of focus.

FINANCIAL DATA:
Funds are normally not provided for travel to conventions, travel or living expenses while conducting research, stipends of principal investigators, costs associated with manuscript preparation, or the indirect costs of institutions.
Amount of support per award: Usually, up to $2,000 for postdoctoral work and up to $1,000 for predoctoral work.
Total amount of support: Varies.
Matching fund requirements: Applicant is required to submit evidence of a request to match amount offered.

NO. AWARDS: 42 for the year 2019.

APPLICATION INFO:
Application information is available on the web site.
Duration: One year.
Deadline: Spring round May 15, with announcement by July 20. Fall round October 15, with announcement by December 15.

PUBLICATIONS:
Application guidelines.

ADDRESS INQUIRIES TO:
See e-mail address above.

THE SOCIETY FOR THE PSYCHOLOGICAL STUDY OF SOCIAL ISSUES (SPSSI)   [1689]
700 Seventh Street, S.E.
Washington, DC 20003
(202) 675-6956
E-mail: awards@spssi.org
Web Site: www.spssi.org

FOUNDED: 1936

AREAS OF INTEREST:
Intergroup relations, social issues and psychology.

NAME(S) OF PROGRAMS:
● **The Applied Social Issues Internship Program**

TYPE:
Internships.

PURPOSE:
To encourage research that is conducted in cooperation with a community or government organization, public interest group or other not-for-profit entity that will benefit directly from the project.

LEGAL BASIS:
Independently incorporated society.

ELIGIBILITY:
College seniors, graduate students and first-year postdoctorates in psychology, applied social science, and related disciplines are eligible. Applicant must be an SPSSI member.

FINANCIAL DATA:
Amount of support per award: $300 to $2,500 to cover research costs, community organizing and, in unusual cases, a stipend for the intern.
CO-OP FUNDING PROGRAMS: Cost sharing by sponsoring department or organization is desirable.

NO. MOST RECENT APPLICANTS: 10.

NO. AWARDS: 6.

APPLICATION INFO:
Application information may be obtained from the web site.
Duration: One year.
Deadline: March 15. Announcement by May 15.

ADDRESS INQUIRIES TO:
See e-mail address above.

THE SOCIETY FOR THE PSYCHOLOGICAL STUDY OF SOCIAL ISSUES (SPSSI)   [1690]
700 Seventh Street, S.E.
Washington, DC 20003
(202) 675-6956
E-mail: awards@spssi.org
Web Site: www.spssi.org

FOUNDED: 1936

AREAS OF INTEREST:
Intergroup relations, social issues and psychology.

NAME(S) OF PROGRAMS:
● **Clara Mayo Grants**

TYPE:
Research grants. Supports Master's theses and predissertation research on sexism, racism or prejudice, with preference given to students enrolled in a terminal Master's program.

PURPOSE:
To support Master's theses or predissertation research on aspects of sexism, racism or prejudice, with preference given to students enrolled in a terminal Master's program. Studies of the application of theory or the design of interventions or treatments to address these problems are welcome.

LEGAL BASIS:
Independently incorporated society.

ELIGIBILITY:
Individuals who are SPSSI members and who have matriculated in graduate programs in psychology, applied social science and related disciplines are eligible to apply. Self-nominations are encouraged. A student who is applying for the Grants-In-Aid program may not apply for the Clara Mayo award in the same award year. Applicants may submit only one Mayo application per calendar year.

Studies of the application of theory or the design of interventions or treatments to address these problems are welcome. Proposals that include a college or university agreement to match the amount requested will be favored, but proposals without matching funds will also be considered.

FINANCIAL DATA:
Amount of support per award: $1,000 maximum.
Total amount of support: Varies.

NO. MOST RECENT APPLICANTS: Approximately 28 per cycle.

NO. AWARDS: Up to 6 each cycle.

APPLICATION INFO:
Application information is available on the web site.
Duration: One to two years.
Deadline: Spring round May, with announcement by July. Fall round October, with announcement by December.

ADDRESS INQUIRIES TO:
See e-mail address above.

THE SOCIETY FOR THE PSYCHOLOGICAL STUDY OF SOCIAL ISSUES (SPSSI)   [1691]
700 Seventh Street, S.E.
Washington, DC 20003
(202) 675-6956
E-mail: awards@spssi.org
Web Site: www.spssi.org

FOUNDED: 1936

AREAS OF INTEREST:
Intergroup relations, social issues and psychology.

NAME(S) OF PROGRAMS:
● **The SAGES Program**

TYPE:
Research grants. Program to encourage retired members to apply their knowledge to helping solve social problems or to assist policymakers to solve social problems. Proposals are invited that use social science research findings to address social problems through direct action projects, consulting with not-for-profit groups, or through preparing reviews of existing social science literature that could be used by policymakers.

LEGAL BASIS:
Independently incorporated society.

ELIGIBILITY:
Applicants must be retired SPSSI members. Members nearing retirement may be considered. Proposals will be evaluated in terms of how well they build on existing social science research and theory, the feasibility of the project, and the importance of the project.

FINANCIAL DATA:
Funding can be submitted for direct costs related to the project. This can be spent over a two-year period. Money can be used for hiring staff (including clerical assistance), computing fees, travel, telephone, or other justifiable expenses. Funding cannot be used as a stipend for the applicant.
Amount of support per award: $2,000 to $3,000; rarely, up to $10,000.

NO. AWARDS: 2 for the year 2019.

APPLICATION INFO:
Online submissions are the preferred method. Please limit the number and size of files uploaded when applying online.

Proposals should include a brief review of the relevant literature underlying the project (no more than five pages), a timetable, a detailed budget, and the curriculum vitae of the applicant. The applicant's employment status must be clearly specified, along with a statement of SPSSI membership. Projects that involve collaboration with some organization should include a letter from the sponsoring organization.

Duration: Up to two years.
Deadline: April 15. Announcement by June 15.

ADDRESS INQUIRIES TO:
See e-mail address above.

THE SOCIETY FOR THE PSYCHOLOGICAL STUDY OF SOCIAL ISSUES (SPSSI) [1692]
700 Seventh Street, S.E.
Washington, DC 20003
(202) 675-6956
E-mail: awards@spssi.org
Web Site: www.spssi.org

FOUNDED: 1936

AREAS OF INTEREST:
Intergroup relations, social issues and psychology.

NAME(S) OF PROGRAMS:
● **The Louise Kidder Early Career Award**

TYPE:
Awards/prizes. This award is named in honor of Louise Kidder for her early career accomplishments and contributions to SPSSI.

PURPOSE:
To recognize social issues researchers who have made substantial contributions to the field early in their careers.

LEGAL BASIS:
Independently incorporated society.

ELIGIBILITY:
Nominees should be investigators who have made substantial contributions to social issues research within 10 years of receiving a graduate degree and who have demonstrated the potential to continue such contributions. Nominees need not be current Society members. Applicants must be scholars who are within 10 years of obtaining their doctoral degree.

FINANCIAL DATA:
Amount of support per award: $500 and plaque.

NO. MOST RECENT APPLICANTS: 17.

NO. AWARDS: 1.

APPLICATION INFO:
Online submissions are the preferred method.
Deadline: June 1. Decisions announced by August 1.

ADDRESS INQUIRIES TO:
See e-mail address above.

THE SOCIETY FOR THE PSYCHOLOGICAL STUDY OF SOCIAL ISSUES (SPSSI) [1693]
700 Seventh Street, S.E.
Washington, DC 20003
(202) 675-6956
E-mail: awards@spssi.org
Web Site: www.spssi.org

FOUNDED: 1936

AREAS OF INTEREST:
Intergroup relations, social issues and psychology.

NAME(S) OF PROGRAMS:
● **The Social Issues Dissertation Award**

TYPE:
Awards/prizes. The Social Issues Dissertation Award is given for the best psychological

dissertation concerned with social issues. It is judged upon scientific excellence and potential application to social problems.

PURPOSE:
To encourage excellence in socially relevant research.

LEGAL BASIS:
Independently incorporated society.

ELIGIBILITY:
Any doctoral dissertation in psychology (or in a social science with psychological subject matter) accepted between March 1 of the previous year and up to the deadline of the current year is eligible. Applicants must have successfully defended their dissertation prior to the current year's award deadline. An individual or group may only submit one paper to one SPSSI award (including the Allport, Klineberg and Dissertation Awards) per award year. Applicants may not submit to the Dissertation Prize more than one time.

FINANCIAL DATA:
Amount of support per award: First prize: $1,000; Second prize: $500.

NO. MOST RECENT APPLICANTS: 47.

NO. AWARDS: 2.

APPLICATION INFO:
Online applications are the preferred method. Limit the number and size of files uploaded when applying online. For hard-copy submissions, mail the complete application to SPSSI, at the address above; Attn: Social Issues Dissertation.

The application should include a 500-word summary of the dissertation. The summary should include title, rationale, methods, and results of dissertation, as well as its implications for social problems. Please also include a cover sheet that states the title of one's dissertation, applicant's name, postal and e-mail addresses, telephone number and university granting the degree.
Deadline: May 1. Announcement of finalist status by July 13.

PUBLICATIONS:
Application guidelines.

ADDRESS INQUIRIES TO:
See e-mail address above.

STIFTELSEN RIKSBANKENS JUBILEUMSFOND
Kungstradgardsgatan 18
111 47 Stockholm Sweden
(46) 08-50 62 64 00
E-mail: rj@rj.se
Web Site: www.rj.se

TYPE:
Conferences/seminars; Research grants.

See entry 355 for full listing.

U.S. ARMY RESEARCH INSTITUTE FOR BEHAVIORAL AND SOCIAL SCIENCES [1694]
Building 1464
6000 6th Street
Fort Belvoir, VA 22060-5586
(703) 545-2410
Fax: (703) 806-2151
E-mail: gregory.a.ruark.civ@mail.mil

FOUNDED: 1940

AREAS OF INTEREST:
Leadership, team and multi-team systems, interactive training and simulation, individual performance and information comprehension, and social structures affecting army performance.

TYPE:
Fellowships; Research grants; Visiting scholars.

PURPOSE:
To contribute to the cumulative knowledge base in behavioral science, with an eye to building new technologies capable of improving the effectiveness of Army personnel and their units.

LEGAL BASIS:
Government agency.

ELIGIBILITY:
Both single-investigator and collaborative research efforts will be considered, and multidisciplinary approaches to a central problem are encouraged. Collaborative efforts may involve researchers at a single institution or in cooperating institutions and joint university/industry partnerships are welcomed. Interest is welcomed from the widest range of institutions, including historically Black colleges and universities and minority institutions.

No consideration will be given to applied research or investigations whose primary focus is on physiological or chemical mechanisms or psychopathology. Another consideration determining support for the research is the judgment that findings have the potential for feeding into development of new behavioral technologies capable of improving the effectiveness of Army personnel and their units.

FINANCIAL DATA:
Amount of support per award: Grant amounts vary according to funds available and Army requirements. Generally $100,000 to $800,000. Average $200,000 per year.
Total amount of support: $5,600,000 for the year 2019.

NO. MOST RECENT APPLICANTS: 38.

NO. AWARDS: 5.

APPLICATION INFO:
Interested individuals should seek ARI's Broad Agency Announcement issued biennially on odd years with an open period of 15 months. Preliminary concept papers (three to five pages) as well as formal proposals may be submitted. Concept papers should describe the problem to be addressed, justify the effort's theoretical significance and uniqueness, briefly describe the approach to the problem and state potential benefits to the Army. An estimated budget and project duration should be included, along with brief vitae of the principal investigators.

Concept papers will be reviewed within ARI for their relevance to Army priorities, theoretical significance and technical merit. Offers of highly rated concept papers will be invited to submit formal proposals.
Duration: Maximum five years for base period. Average three years.
Deadline: Varies.

PUBLICATIONS:
Program announcement.

ADDRESS INQUIRIES TO:
Chief of Foundational Science Research Unit (See address above.)

U.S. DEPARTMENT OF JUSTICE

Office of Juvenile Justice and
Delinquency Prevention
810 Seventh Street, N.W., 7th Floor
Washington, DC 20531
(202) 307-5911
Fax: (202) 353-9093
E-mail: lynnell.clarke@usdoj.gov
Web Site: www.ojjdp.gov

TYPE:
Conferences/seminars; Development grants;
Fellowships; Internships; Project/program
grants; Research grants; Residencies; Visiting
scholars; Research contracts. Grants to
conduct research, evaluation and development
on juvenile justice and delinquency
prevention activities, including the
development of new or improved approaches,
techniques, systems and program models to
conduct behavioral research on the causes of
juvenile crime, means of, intervention and
prevention, and to evaluate juvenile programs
and procedures.

See entry 1279 for full listing.

UKRAINIAN RESEARCH INSTITUTE AT HARVARD UNIVERSITY

34 Kirkland Street
Cambridge, MA 02138
(617) 495-4053
Fax: (617) 495-8097
E-mail: huri@fas.harvard.edu
Web Site: www.huri.harvard.edu/fellowships

TYPE:
Fellowships. The Jacyk Distinguished
Fellowship is designed to bring senior
scholars to Harvard University for focused
research in Ukrainian history, literature,
philology, culture, and other related areas of
study in the humanities and social sciences
fields. This fellowship is awarded biennially.

See entry 358 for full listing.

UKRAINIAN RESEARCH INSTITUTE AT HARVARD UNIVERSITY

34 Kirkland Street
Cambridge, MA 02138
(617) 495-4053
Fax: (617) 495-8097
E-mail: huri@fas.harvard.edu
Web Site: www.huri.harvard.edu/fellowshiups

TYPE:
Fellowships.

See entry 359 for full listing.

WOODROW WILSON INTERNATIONAL CENTER FOR SCHOLARS

One Woodrow Wilson Plaza
1300 Pennsylvania Avenue, N.W.
Washington, DC 20004-3027
(202) 691-4170
Fax: (202) 691-4001
E-mail: fellowships@wilsoncenter.org
Web Site: www.wilsoncenter.org

TYPE:
Fellowships; Research grants; Residencies;
Scholarships; Visiting scholars. The Center
seeks to commemorate, through its residential
fellowship program of advanced research,
both the scholarly depth and the public

concerns of Woodrow Wilson. The Center
welcomes outstanding project proposals in
the social sciences and humanities on global
issues - topics that intersect with questions of
public policy or provide the historical
framework to illume policy issues of
contemporary importance. The Center
especially welcomes projects likely to foster
communication between the world of ideas
and the world of public affairs.

Projects should have relevance to the world
of public policy. Fellows should be prepared
to interact with policymakers in Washington
and with the Center's staff working on
similar areas.

Fellowships are tenable in residence only at
the Woodrow Wilson International Center for
Scholars. The Center will not provide support
for research to be carried out elsewhere.
Fellows devote their full time to research and
writing.

See entry 361 for full listing.

CARTER G. WOODSON INSTITUTE FOR AFRICAN-AMERICAN AND AFRICAN STUDIES

University of Virginia
McCormick Road, 108 Minor Hall
Charlottesville, VA 22903
(434) 924-3109
Fax: (434) 924-8820
E-mail: woodson@virginia.edu
Web Site: woodson.as.virginia.edu

TYPE:
Fellowships. The Woodson Institute offers
residential fellowships to predoctoral and
postdoctoral scholars. These fellowships are
designed to facilitate the completion of works
in progress by providing scholars with
unencumbered leave.

Afro-American and African Studies is
considered to cover Africa, Africans and
peoples of African descent in North, Central
and South America and the Caribbean, past
and present.

See entry 364 for full listing.

Business and economics

THE ACTUARIAL FOUNDATION

475 North Martingale Road
Suite 600
Schaumburg, IL 60173-2226
(847) 706-3535
Fax: (847) 706-3599
E-mail: Scholarships@ActFnd.org
Web Site: www.actuarialfoundation.org

TYPE:
Scholarships.

See entry 1881 for full listing.

THE ACTUARIAL FOUNDATION

475 North Martingale Road
Suite 600
Schaumburg, IL 60173-2226
(847) 706-3535
Fax: (847) 706-3599
E-mail: Scholarships@ActFnd.org
Web Site: www.actuarialfoundation.org

TYPE:
Scholarships. Originally named the John
Culver Wooddy Scholarship, the Curtis E.
Huntington Memorial Scholarship is awarded
annually to undergraduate seniors enrolled as
full-time students at an accredited U.S.
educational institution.

See entry 1882 for full listing.

AMERICAN INSTITUTE OF CERTIFIED PUBLIC ACCOUNTANTS (AICPA)   [1695]

220 Leigh Farm Road
Durham, NC 27707
(919) 402-4473
E-mail: scholarships@aicpa.org
Web Site: thiswaytocpa.com/scholarships

FOUNDED: 1887

AREAS OF INTEREST:
Accounting.

NAME(S) OF PROGRAMS:
● **AICPA Foundation Scholarship for Future CPAs**

TYPE:
Scholarships.

YEAR PROGRAM STARTED: 2019

PURPOSE:
To provide financial assistance to outstanding
students to encourage their pursuit of
accounting as a major and their ultimate
entry into the profession; to support
undergraduate or graduate students interested
in pursuing the CPA license after graduation.

ELIGIBILITY:
Applicant must be a U.S. citizen or
permanent resident and an AICPA Student
Affiliate member. Applicant must be enrolled
as a full-time undergraduate (12 semester
hours or equivalent) or full-time graduate
level student (nine semester hours or
equivalent) pursuing an undergraduate or
graduate-level degree in accounting or an
accounting-related major at a public or
private, not-for-profit four-year college or
university in the U.S. or its territories.
Student must have completed at least 30
semester hours (or equivalent) of college
coursework, including at least six semester
hours (or equivalent) in accounting. Student
must maintain an overall grade point average
of at least 3.0 on a 4.0 scale.

Applicant must be planning to pursue the
CPA licensure, but not presently be a CPA.

GEOG. RESTRICTIONS: United States and its
territories.

FINANCIAL DATA:
Amount of support per award: $5,000.

NO. AWARDS: 25.

APPLICATION INFO:
Application must be submitted online.

Duration: One academic year. Nonrenewable.

Deadline: March 1.

ADDRESS INQUIRIES TO:
AICPA Scholarship Manager
(See address above.)

AMERICAN INSTITUTE OF CERTIFIED PUBLIC ACCOUNTANTS (AICPA)   [1696]
220 Leigh Farm Road
Durham, NC 27707
(919) 402-4473
E-mail: scholarships@aicpa.org
Web Site: thiswaytocpa.com/scholarships

AREAS OF INTEREST:
Accounting and accounting-related fields.

NAME(S) OF PROGRAMS:
● **AWSCPA Scholarship Award**

TYPE:
Scholarships. AWSCPA Scholarship Award provides financial assistance to outstanding female students majoring in accounting or an accounting-related field.

YEAR PROGRAM STARTED: 2019

PURPOSE:
To support the success of women in the accounting profession.

ELIGIBILITY:
Applicant must:
(1) be a woman pursuing an undergraduate or graduate-level degree in an accounting or accounting-related major;
(2) be planning to pursue the C.P.A. licensure, but not presently be a C.P.A.;
(3) attend a public or private, not-for-profit 501(c) four-year college or university in the U.S. or its territories for the full academic year;
(4) be enrolled in a business and/or accounting program that is accredited by the AACSB and/or ACBSP for the full academic year;
(5) have completed at least 30 semester hours (or equivalent) of college coursework, including at least six semester hours (or equivalent) in accounting by spring of the award year;
(6) maintain an overall grade point average of a least 3.0 on a 4.0 scale;
(7) be an AICPA Student Affiliate member, or have submitted a new member application;
(8) be a U.S. citizen or permanent resident;
(9) exhibit some financial need and;
(10) plan to participate in the AICPA Legacy Scholars program for the full academic year.

FINANCIAL DATA:
Amount of support per award: $5,000.
Total amount of support: Up to $20,000 annually.

NO. AWARDS: Varies.

APPLICATION INFO:
Guidelines are available on the web site.
Duration: One academic year. Nonrenewable.
Deadline: March 1.

ADDRESS INQUIRIES TO:
See e-mail address above.

AMERICAN INSTITUTE OF CERTIFIED PUBLIC ACCOUNTANTS (AICPA)   [1697]
220 Leigh Farm Road
Durham, NC 27707
(919) 402-4473
E-mail: scholarships@aicpa.org
Web Site: thiswaytocpa.com/scholarships

AREAS OF INTEREST:
Accounting.

NAME(S) OF PROGRAMS:
● **AICPA/Robert Half Student Scholarships**

TYPE:
Scholarships. Awarded to accounting majors to encourage them to become a C.P.A.

PURPOSE:
To provide financial assistance to students who are currently majoring in accounting, finance or information systems; to encourage students to consider careers in accounting and business.

ELIGIBILITY:
An applicant must meet the following requirements:
(1) pursuing an undergraduate- or graduate-level degree in an "accounting-related" major ("accounting-related" shall be as determined by Sponsors in Sponsors' sole discretion);
(2) planning to pursue the C.P.A. licensure but not presently be a C.P.A.;
(3) applied to or been accepted into a public or private, 501(c) four-year college or university located in the U.S. or its territories; the business program must be accredited by the AACSB and/or ACBSP;
(4) completed at least 30 semester-hours (or equivalent) of college coursework, including at least six semester-hours (or equivalent) in accounting, by end of spring 2021;
(5) maintained an overall and major grade point average of at least 3.0 (on a 4.0 scale);
(6) enrolled as a full-time undergraduate (12 semester-hours or equivalent) or a full-time graduate-level student (nine semester-hours or equivalent) for the 2021-22 academic year; an exception may be made if one plans to participate in an internship program;
(7) be an AICPA student affiliate member (or have submitted a new member application); those interested can apply on the web site at no cost;
(8) be a U.S. citizen or permanent resident (green card holder) and;
(9) have some financial need (i.e., not receiving a full or partial scholarship(s) and/or grant(s) that cover and/or exceed one's educational expenses).

AICPA and RHI/Accountemps staff and their family members are not eligible to receive this scholarship.

GEOG. RESTRICTIONS: United States and its territories.

FINANCIAL DATA:
Amount of support per award: $10,000.
Total amount of support: Up to $40,000 annually.

NO. AWARDS: Varies.

APPLICATION INFO:
Guidelines are available on the web site.
Duration: One year. Nonrenewable.
Deadline: March 1.

ADDRESS INQUIRIES TO:
See e-mail address above.

*SPECIAL STIPULATIONS:
Students selected to receive an AICPA scholarship must participate in the AICPA Legacy Scholars program, which includes performing at least eight hours of community service per semester to advocate for the C.P.A. profession. Through their community service efforts, AICPA Legacy Scholars enhance their leadership and communication skills by building relationships with both aspiring and seasoned C.P.As.

AMERICAN INSTITUTE OF CERTIFIED PUBLIC ACCOUNTANTS (AICPA)   [1698]
220 Leigh Farm Road
Durham, NC 27707
(919) 402-4473
E-mail: scholarships@aicpa.org
Web Site: thiswaytocpa.com/scholarships

AREAS OF INTEREST:
Accounting and accounting-related fields.

NAME(S) OF PROGRAMS:
● **AICPA Foundation Two-Year Transfer Scholarship**

TYPE:
Scholarships. AICPA Foundation Two-Year Transfer Scholarship provides financial assistance to students who have earned an Associate's degree in business, accounting, finance or economics with a declared intent to major in accounting at a four-year college or university.

PURPOSE:
To provide financial assistance to students who are currently majoring in accounting, finance or information systems; to encourage students to consider careers in accounting and business.

ELIGIBILITY:
An eligible applicant must be/have:
(1) earned an Associate's degree in business, accounting, finance or economics with a declared intent to major in accounting or an "accounting-related field" at a four-year college or university ("accounting-related" shall be as determined by Sponsors in Sponsors' sole discretion);
(2) planning to pursue the C.P.A. licensure but not presently be a C.P.A.;
(3) proof of acceptance into a public or private, not-for-profit 501(c) four-year college or university located in the U.S. states or territories for the full upcoming academic year; the business program must be accredited by the AACSB and/or ACBSP; (exception may be granted, but not guaranteed, at the discretion of Sponsor; inquire at the e-mail address above if one is unsure of one's eligibility);
(4) maintained an overall and major grade point average of at least 3.0 (on a 4.0 scale);
(5) enrolled as a full-time undergraduate (12 semester hours or equivalent); an exception may be made if one plans to participate in an internship program;
(6) an AICPA student affiliate member (or have submitted a new member application); one can apply online at no cost at the web site above;
(7) a U.S. citizen or permanent resident (green card holder) and;
(8) some financial need (i.e., not receiving a full or partial scholarship(s) and/or grant(s) that cover and/or exceed one's educational expenses).

AICPA staff and their family members are not eligible to receive this scholarship.

FINANCIAL DATA:
Scholarship aid may be used only for the payment of expenses that directly relate to obtaining an accounting education (e.g., tuition, fees, room and board and/or books and materials only). Scholarship payments are sent directly to the student's financial aid office on behalf of the student.
Amount of support per award: $5,000.
Total amount of support: Up to $125,000 annually.

NO. AWARDS: Varies.

APPLICATION INFO:
Guidelines are available on the web site.
Duration: One academic year. Nonrenewable.
Deadline: March 1.

ADDRESS INQUIRIES TO:
See e-mail address above.

*SPECIAL STIPULATIONS:
Students selected to receive an AICPA scholarship must participate in the AICPA Legacy Scholars program, which includes performing at least eight hours of community service per semester to advocate for the C.P.A. profession. Through their community service efforts, AICPA Legacy Scholars enhance their leadership and communication skills by building relationships with both aspiring and seasoned C.P.As.

AMERICAN INSTITUTE OF CERTIFIED PUBLIC ACCOUNTANTS (AICPA)   [1699]
220 Leigh Farm Road
Durham, NC 27707
(919) 402-4473
E-mail: scholarships@aicpa.org
Web Site: thiswaytocpa.com/scholarships

AREAS OF INTEREST:
Accounting.

NAME(S) OF PROGRAMS:
• **John L. Carey Scholarship**

TYPE:
Scholarships.

YEAR PROGRAM STARTED: 2013

PURPOSE:
To provide financial assistance to liberal arts or other nonbusiness-related degree holders pursuing graduate studies in accounting and the C.P.A. designation; to encourage students with little or no previous accounting education to consider professional accounting careers.

ELIGIBILITY:
An applicant must meet the following requirements:
(1) have obtained a liberal arts or other nonbusiness undergraduate degree from a regionally accredited institution in the U.S. prior to enrolling in a graduate accounting program;
(2) have not earned more than 12 credits in accounting or business during his or her undergraduate program;
(3) planning to pursue the C.P.A. licensure but not presently be a C.P.A.;
(4) planning to pursue a graduate-level degree in an "accounting-related" major ("accounting-related" shall be as determined by Sponsor in Sponsor's sole discretion); this program will enable a student to sit for the C.P.A. exam;
(5) applied to or been accepted into a public or private, 501(c) four-year college or university located in the U.S. or its territories; the business program must be accredited by the AACSB and/or ACBSP;
(6) not actively participating in a graduate accounting program;
(7) enrolled as a full-time graduate-level student (nine semester-hours or equivalent) for the 2021-22 academic year; an exception may be granted if one plans to participate in an internship program;
(8) be an AICPA student affiliate member (or have submitted a new member application)

by the beginning of the 2021-22 academic year; those interested can apply on the web site at no cost;
(9) be a U.S. citizen or permanent resident (green card holder) and;
(10) have some financial need (i.e., not already be receiving a full or partial scholarship(s) that covers or exceeds one's educational expenses).
Note: AICPA staff and their family members are not eligible to receive this scholarship.

GEOG. RESTRICTIONS: United States and its territories.

FINANCIAL DATA:
Amount of support per award: $5,000.
Total amount of support: Up to $25,000 annually.

NO. AWARDS: Varies.

APPLICATION INFO:
Guidelines are available on the web site.
Duration: One year. Nonrenewable.
Deadline: March 1.

ADDRESS INQUIRIES TO:
See e-mail address above.

*SPECIAL STIPULATIONS:
Students selected to receive an AICPA scholarship must participate in the AICPA Legacy Scholars program, which includes performing at least eight hours of community service per semester to advocate for the C.P.A. profession. Through their community service efforts, AICPA Legacy Scholars enhance their leadership and communication skills by building relationships with both aspiring and seasoned C.P.As.

APPRAISAL INSTITUTE OF PROFESSIONAL RESOURCES   [1700]
200 West Madison Street
Suite 1500
Chicago, IL 60606
(312) 335-4226
Fax: (312) 335-4134
E-mail: aierf@appraisalinstitute.org
Web Site: www.aiedtrust.org

NAME(S) OF PROGRAMS:
• **Appraisal Institute Education and Relief Foundation Scholarship**

TYPE:
Scholarships. Graduate and undergraduate scholarships to help worthy and qualified students finance the cost of college work leading to a degree in the fields of real estate appraisal, land economics, real estate and allied fields.

PURPOSE:
To help finance the educational endeavors of individuals concentrating their studies in real estate appraisal, land economics, real estate or allied fields.

ELIGIBILITY:
Applicants must be citizens of the U.S., attending a full-time college, U.S. university or community college, and have the expressed intention of majoring in real estate evaluation and related subjects. Related subjects may include land economics, economics, economic geography, and others similarly related. Levels of education for the scholarship must be sophomore, junior, senior and graduate year of college.

Preference will be given to those applicants whose previous training and whose future course of study indicate that they intend to

follow a field of endeavor which comes within the scope of the objectives of the Appraisal Institute. Applicants must also demonstrate qualities of leadership and scholarly attainments.

GEOG. RESTRICTIONS: United States.

FINANCIAL DATA:
Amount of support per award: Graduate: $2,000; Undergraduate: $1,000.

NO. AWARDS: Approximately 20 per year.

APPLICATION INFO:
Scholarship applications are available on the web site.
Duration: One academic year.
Deadline: April 15 for the following academic year.

OFFICERS:
Jim Amorin, Chief Executive Officer

BOARD OF TRUSTEES:
Shelly Tanaka, Chairperson
Miles Hamrick, Sr., Vice Chairperson

ADDRESS INQUIRIES TO:
Scott Brody
Supervisor of Professional Resources
(See address above.)

THE CONSORTIUM FOR GRADUATE STUDY IN MANAGEMENT   [1701]
229 Chesterfield Business Parkway
Chesterfield, MO 63005
(636) 681-5553
Fax: (636) 681-5499
E-mail: recruiting@cgsm.org
Web Site: www.cgsm.org

FOUNDED: 1966

NAME(S) OF PROGRAMS:
• **Competitive Advantage**
• **Fellowships for Under-Represented Minorities in Management**

TYPE:
Fellowships. Competitive Advantage is a career and graduate school readiness program for underrepresented minority college students.

Graduate fellowships for minority students interested in management careers in business.

YEAR PROGRAM STARTED: 1967

PURPOSE:
To hasten the entry of minorities into management positions in business.

LEGAL BASIS:
Not-for-profit, IRS 501(c)(3) status.

ELIGIBILITY:
U.S. citizenship and permanent residence in the U.S. is required. Applicant must present evidence of their commitment to the Consortium's mission of promoting the inclusion of African Americans, Hispanic Americans and Native Americans in American Business. The undergraduate degree need not be in business or economics.

Fellowships are awarded only by Consortium institutions, including University of California-Berkeley, Carnegie-Mellon University, Dartmouth College, Emory University, Indiana University (Bloomington), New York University, Rice University, University of Michigan (Ann Arbor), University of North Carolina (Chapel Hill), University of Rochester, University of Southern California, University of Texas

(Austin), University of Virginia, University of Wisconsin (Madison) and Washington University (St. Louis).

There are no fellowships awarded for part-time study.

FINANCIAL DATA:
The fellowship includes full tuition and required fees.
Total amount of support: $46,681,738 for the year 2020-21.

NO. MOST RECENT APPLICANTS: 1,250.

NO. AWARDS: 425.

APPLICATION INFO:
Guidelines and application form are available on the web site.
Duration: Fellowships are awarded for a maximum of four semesters of full-time study.
Deadline: November 15 and January 5.

IRS I.D.: 43-0962198

STAFF:
Peter Aranda, Chief Executive Officer
Glenn Wilen, Vice President of Finance and Administration

DECA INC. [1702]
1908 Association Drive
Reston, VA 20191
(703) 860-5000
Fax: (703) 860-4013
E-mail: cindy@deca.org
Web Site: www.deca.org

FOUNDED: 1946

AREAS OF INTEREST:
Marketing education, management and entrepreneurship.

TYPE:
Scholarships.

YEAR PROGRAM STARTED: 1962

PURPOSE:
To prepare emerging leaders and entrepreneurs in marketing, finance, hospitality and management in high schools and colleges around the globe.

LEGAL BASIS:
Nonprofit association.

ELIGIBILITY:
Applicant must be a current member of DECA.

GEOG. RESTRICTIONS: United States.

FINANCIAL DATA:
Amount of support per award: Varies.
Total amount of support: Over $200,000 in scholarships provided at the International Career Development Conference (ICDC) each year.

NO. MOST RECENT APPLICANTS: 5,000.

NO. AWARDS: 100.

APPLICATION INFO:
Information is available at the web site.
Duration: One year. Renewals are considered. Must reapply.
Deadline: January.

ADDRESS INQUIRIES TO:
Cindy Allen
Director of Sponsorships
(See e-mail address above.)

ECONOMIC HISTORY ASSOCIATION [1703]
Department of Economics
University of Wisconsin-La Crosse
1725 State Street
La Crosse, WI 54601
(608) 785-6863
E-mail: mhaupert@uwlax.edu
Web Site: www.eh.net/eha

FOUNDED: 1940

AREAS OF INTEREST:
Economic history.

NAME(S) OF PROGRAMS:
● **Arthur H. Cole Grants-in-Aid**

TYPE:
Grants-in-aid. Grants for advanced research in any aspect of economic history.

YEAR PROGRAM STARTED: 1972

PURPOSE:
To support individual research in the field of economic history.

LEGAL BASIS:
Nonprofit.

ELIGIBILITY:
Applicants must have completed their Ph.D. and must be members of the Economic History Association. Preference is given to recent Ph.D. recipients.

FINANCIAL DATA:
Amount of support per award: Up to $5,000.
Total amount of support: $15,000 to $20,000.

NO. MOST RECENT APPLICANTS: 18.

NO. AWARDS: 6.

APPLICATION INFO:
Application information is available on the Association web site.
Duration: One year.
Deadline: Early March.

PUBLICATIONS:
The Journal of Economic History.

IRS I.D.: 13-6128711

THE EDUCATIONAL FOUNDATION FOR WOMEN IN ACCOUNTING [1704]
7946 Clyo Road, Suite A
Centerville, OH 45459
(937) 424-3391
E-mail: info@efwa.org
Web Site: www.efwa.org

FOUNDED: 1966

AREAS OF INTEREST:
Women in the accounting field.

NAME(S) OF PROGRAMS:
● **Laurels Fund**
● **Michelle L. McDonald Scholarship**
● **Moss Adams LLP Scholarship**
● **Rhonda J. O'Leary Scholarship**
● **Women in Need Scholarship**
● **Women in Transition Scholarship**

TYPE:
Scholarships. Laurels Fund provides a one-year academic scholarship for women pursuing a Ph.D. in accounting.

Women in Need Scholarship is available to women in their third, fourth or fifth year of academic pursuit who need the financial support to complete their degrees. It is renewable annually upon satisfactory completion of course requirements.

Women in Transition Scholarship is intended for women returning to school as freshmen to earn a Bachelor's degree in accounting. It is renewable annually upon satisfactory completion of course requirements.

YEAR PROGRAM STARTED: 1966

PURPOSE:
To provide scholarships and mentoring, supporting equitable access to education and the advancement of women who are pursuing careers in accounting.

LEGAL BASIS:
501(c)(3) organization.

ELIGIBILITY:
Women who are pursuing accounting degrees at the undergraduate, graduate and postgraduate levels. U.S. citizenship required.

GEOG. RESTRICTIONS: United States.

FINANCIAL DATA:
Amount of support per award: Varies.
Total amount of support: Varies.

NO. AWARDS: Vary annually.

APPLICATION INFO:
Applications are available on the web site.
Duration: Laurels Fund, Michelle L. McDonald, Moss Adams LLP and Rhonda J. O'Leary Scholarships: One year; Women in Need Scholarship: Two years; Women in Transition Scholarship: Four years.
Deadline: Laurels Fund: May 15. All others: April 30.

IRS I.D.: 36-6149364

ADDRESS INQUIRIES TO:
Foundation Administrator
(See address above.)

ERNST & YOUNG FOUNDATION [1705]
200 Plaza Drive
Secaucus, NJ 07094
(201) 872-5686
E-mail: ellen.glazerman@ey.com

FOUNDED: 1937

AREAS OF INTEREST:
Higher education, with specific interests in accounting, business, computer science, engineering and information systems.

TYPE:
Fellowships; Matching gifts; Scholarships.

YEAR PROGRAM STARTED: 1937

PURPOSE:
To support higher education.

LEGAL BASIS:
Public charity.

ELIGIBILITY:
No grants to individuals. No cold requests.

GEOG. RESTRICTIONS: United States and its territories.

FINANCIAL DATA:
Amount of support per award: Varies.
Total amount of support: Varies.
Matching fund requirements: Ernst & Young Foundation will only match contributions to not-for-profit accredited colleges, junior colleges, community colleges, universities, graduate schools or professional schools.

APPLICATION INFO:
The Foundation does not accept unsolicited requests for funding.
Duration: Varies.

Deadline: Varies.

ADDRESS INQUIRIES TO:
Ellen J. Glazerman, Executive Director
(See address and e-mail above.)

FEDERATION OF AMERICAN CONSUMERS AND TRAVELERS [1706]
318 Hillsboro Avenue
P.O. Box 104
Edwardsville, IL 62025
(618) 656-0454
(800) 872-3228
Fax: (618) 656-5369
E-mail: vrolens@usafact.org
Web Site: www.usafact.org

NAME(S) OF PROGRAMS:
• **Community and Business Project Grants**

TYPE:
Project/program grants; Seed money grants.

PURPOSE:
To support civic club, church, and community projects that are nominated by members.

ELIGIBILITY:
Projects are nominated by members.

GEOG. RESTRICTIONS: United States.

FINANCIAL DATA:
Amount of support per award: $100 to $2,500, based on funding availability and the needs of the specific proposal.
Total amount of support: Varies.

APPLICATION INFO:
Contact the Federation for guidelines.
Duration: One-time award.
Deadline: Quarterly.

ADDRESS INQUIRIES TO:
Vicki Rolens, Managing Director
(See address above.)

*SPECIAL STIPULATIONS:
Applicant must be a FACT member or have been nominated by a FACT member.

4A'S
1065 Avenue of the Americas, 16th Floor
New York, NY 10018
(212) 682-2500
Fax: (212) 682-8391
E-mail: maip@aaaa.org
Web Site: foundation.aaaa.org

TYPE:
Fellowships; Scholarships.

See entry 900 for full listing.

HAGLEY MUSEUM AND LIBRARY
Hagley Library
298 Buck Road
Wilmington, DE 19807
(302) 658-2400 ext. 243
E-mail: clockman@hagley.org
Web Site: www.hagley.org

TYPE:
Fellowships; Research grants; Travel grants; Visiting scholars. Grants to support short-term research in the imprint, manuscript, pictorial and artifact collections of the Hagley Museum and Library.

The Henry Belin du Pont Dissertation Fellowship in Business, Technology, and Society supports research and writing by candidates for doctoral degrees. Projects should demonstrate superior intellectual quality and make substantial use of Hagley's collections.

Henry Belin du Pont Research Grants support research in the collections of the museum and library.

Hagley Exploratory Research Grant supports a one-week visit by scholars who believe that their project will benefit from Hagley research collections, but need the opportunity to explore them on-site to determine if a Henry Belin du Pont research grant application is warranted.

See entry 543 for full listing.

THE S.S. HUEBNER FOUNDATION FOR INSURANCE EDUCATION [1707]
Department of Risk Management and Insurance
Georgia State University
P.O. Box 4036
Atlanta, GA 30302-4036
(404) 413-7466
E-mail: jthielman@gsu.edu
Web Site: www.huebnerfoundation.com

FOUNDED: 1940

AREAS OF INTEREST:
Insurance and risk management.

TYPE:
The Foundation's program goals are:
(1) to support the Ph.D. program at Georgia State University that is training the next generation of scholars who will conduct academic research on insurance economics specifically and the efficient allocation of risk in the economy more generally;
(2) to sponsor a periodic summer symposium or occasional lecture series facilitated by leading scholars designed to build collaborative research relationships among young researchers at Georgia State University and elsewhere who are interested in risk-related topics and;
(3) to provide assistance for professionals who seek to develop the research skills necessary to address contemporary insurance and risk problems in such areas as regulation, policy or industry practice.

YEAR PROGRAM STARTED: 1940

PURPOSE:
To advance university-level risk management and insurance scholarship and learning.

APPLICATION INFO:
Contact the Foundation for guidelines.

IRS I.D.: 23-6297325

ADDRESS INQUIRIES TO:
John P. Thielman, Executive Director
(See address above.)

INSTITUTE FOR SUPPLY MANAGEMENT [1708]
309 West Elliot Road, Suite 113
Tempe, AZ 85284-1556
(480) 752-6276
Fax: (480) 752-7890
E-mail: membersvcs@ismworld.org
Web Site: www.ismworld.org

AREAS OF INTEREST:
Supply management, supply chain management and procurement.

NAME(S) OF PROGRAMS:
• **R. Gene Richter Scholarship Program**

TYPE:
Scholarships.

YEAR PROGRAM STARTED: 2008

PURPOSE:
To identify the future leaders of supply management and fast-track those individuals into the profession through a program of tuition assistance, executive mentoring, junior mentoring and networking.

ELIGIBILITY:
Eligible students are:
(1) enrolled full-time in an accredited supply chain management curriculum;
(2) entering their senior year during the academic year of the scholarship award;
(3) graduating either in December or Spring of scholarship award year;
(4) a citizen of the U.S. or Canada, or possess a valid green card;
(5) available to attend the Institute for Supply Management Annual International Conference and;
(6) willing to sign a contract pledging that the monetary award will be used for educational expenses.

Scholarship recipients will be chosen based on attained high academic achievement, demonstrated strong leadership ability, demonstrated high ethical standards, and a strong commitment to pursuing a career in the field of supply chain management.

FINANCIAL DATA:
Amount of support per award: $10,000 ($5,000 for December graduates).
Total amount of support: Varies.

CO-OP FUNDING PROGRAMS: R. Gene Richter Scholarship Fund and the R. Gene and Nancy D. Richter Foundation.

NO. MOST RECENT APPLICANTS: 56.

NO. AWARDS: 4 for the year 2019-20.

APPLICATION INFO:
Application is available online.
Duration: One academic year.
Deadline: December 31.

ADDRESS INQUIRIES TO:
See e-mail address above.

THE CALVIN K. KAZANJIAN ECONOMICS FOUNDATION, INC. [1709]
P.O. Box 300
Dallas, PA 18612-0330
(602) 456-0214
E-mail: director@kazanjian.org
Web Site: www.kazanjian.org

FOUNDED: 1947

AREAS OF INTEREST:
Promoting the understanding of economics and addressing the issue of economic illiteracy.

TYPE:
Challenge/matching grants; Demonstration grants. Grants for economic education.

PURPOSE:
To aid in bringing greater happiness and prosperity to all through a better understanding of economics.

ELIGIBILITY:
The Foundation will only give serious consideration to those projects which directly advance its immediate purposes and meet its guidelines. It will only support nonprofit 501(c)(3) organizations and will not support overhead or indirect costs.

GEOG. RESTRICTIONS: United States.

FINANCIAL DATA:
Amount of support per award: $10,000 to $25,000.

Total amount of support: Approximately $400,000.

APPLICATION INFO:
Organizations wishing to be considered for funding need to complete the Letter of Interest online. Please review Grant Instructions for submission requirements.
Duration: Varies.
Deadline: March 10 and September 10.

IRS I.D.: 06-0665174

ADDRESS INQUIRIES TO:
Elena Zee, Managing Director
(See address above.)

*PLEASE NOTE:
The Foundation does not give scholarships.

KPMG FOUNDATION   [1710]
3 Chestnut Ridge Road
Montvale, NJ 07645-0435
(201) 307-7932
Fax: (201) 624-7763
E-mail: tperino@kpmg.com
Web Site: www.kpmgfoundation.org
www.phdproject.org

FOUNDED: 1968

AREAS OF INTEREST:
Academic research, education and professional development in the area of business.

TYPE:
Conferences/seminars; Matching gifts; Professorships; Project/program grants. Special grants, made on the recommendations of the Firm's college relations partners, are for specific projects that create new educational opportunities.

YEAR PROGRAM STARTED: 1968

PURPOSE:
To recognize outstanding achievement in accounting education and research; to recognize academic excellence and community achievement; to help minority students obtain careers in business and industry; to promote research that will benefit the profession now and in the future.

LEGAL BASIS:
501(c)(3) public charity.

ELIGIBILITY:
The Foundation restricts grants to educational purposes related to its firm's functional areas, including accounting, auditing and tax.

GEOG. RESTRICTIONS: United States.

FINANCIAL DATA:
Matching fund requirements: The Matching Gift Program only matches employee/partner gifts to colleges and universities from which the donors are alumni or where KPMG recruits. Minimum $50 for employees and maximum $7,500 per institution per fiscal year.

PUBLICATIONS:
Annual report.

IRS I.D.: 13-6262199

BOARD OF TRUSTEES:
Robert F. Arning, Chairperson
Blane Ruschak, President
Darren H. Burton
David DiCristofaro
Gabriel De La Rosa
Maureen Evers-Willox
Ben Garfunkel
Tandra C. Jackson
Christine M. Kachinsky
Heidi Murdy-Michael
James Powell
Bradley N. Sprong
Sandra B. Torchia

ADDRESS INQUIRIES TO:
Tara Perino, Senior Director
(See address above.)

THE GERALD LOEB AWARDS
UCLA Anderson School of Management
110 Westwood Plaza
Gold Hall, Suite B307
Los Angeles, CA 90095-1481
(310) 825-4478
Fax: (310) 825-4479
E-mail: loeb@anderson.ucla.edu
Web Site: www.anderson.ucla.edu/gerald-loeb-awards

TYPE:
Awards/prizes. Awards to recognize business and financial journalists for important contributions to the understanding of business, finance and the economy.

See entry 1742 for full listing.

MARKETING EDGE   [1711]
500 Seventh Avenue, 8th Floor
New York, NY 10018
(212) 790-1510
E-mail: admin@marketingedge.org
Web Site: www.marketingedge.org

FOUNDED: 1966

NAME(S) OF PROGRAMS:
- **Collegiate ECHO Marketing Challenge**
- **Collegiate Summit**
- **Robert Kestnbaum Research Program**
- **Marketing EDGE Scholarship Program**
- **Professor's Institute**
- **Shankar-Spiegel Award for the Best Dissertation Proposal in Direct/Interactive Marketing**
- **Student Career Forums**

TYPE:
Awards/prizes; Conferences/seminars; Internships; Research grants; Scholarships; Research contracts. Collegiate ECHO Marketing Challenge provides students worldwide with experiential learning, crafting an integrated marketing plan.

Collegiate Summit is an annual conference focused on digital and data-focused marketing for undergraduate students.

Robert Kestnbaum Research Program is intended to generate leading-edge academic research to impact the future of direct/interactive marketing.

Marketing EDGE Scholarship Program provides education funding support to undergraduate and graduate students nationwide.

Professor's Institute is an invitation-only conference held in conjunction with SMU's Brierly Institute for Customer Engagement, to bring marketing academics and practitioners together to engage in thought-provoking conversations that have the potential to influence marketing curricula and current marketing practice.

Shankar-Spiegel Award for the Best Dissertation Proposal in Direct/Interactive Marketing recognizes doctoral candidates with the best dissertation proposal in direct/interactive marketing. Doctoral students from accredited doctoral programs are eligible to receive this award.

Student Career Forums provides opportunity for college students to meet and network with marketing professionals.

YEAR PROGRAM STARTED: 1966

PURPOSE:
To educate, develop, grow and employ college students in the marketing field.

LEGAL BASIS:
Nonprofit, tax-exempt organization.

ELIGIBILITY:
Varies by program.

GEOG. RESTRICTIONS: United States.

FINANCIAL DATA:
Amount of support per award: $5,000 to $50,000.

CO-OP FUNDING PROGRAMS: Corporate Leadership Program.

APPLICATION INFO:
Form and guidelines are available online.

PUBLICATIONS:
Annual report; conference materials; *Journal of Interactive Marketing*®.

IRS I.D.: 13-6222757

STAFF:
Terri L. Bartlett, Chief Executive Officer and President
Marie Adolphe, Senior Vice President, Program Development

ADDRESS INQUIRIES TO:
Administration Assistant
(See address above.)

THE BURTON D. MORGAN FOUNDATION   [1712]
22 Aurora Street
Hudson, OH 44236
(330) 655-1660
Fax: (330) 655-1673
E-mail: grantsmanager@bdmorganfdn.org
Web Site: www.bdmorganfdn.org

FOUNDED: 1967

AREAS OF INTEREST:
Entrepreneurship and entrepreneurship education.

TYPE:
Challenge/matching grants; Conferences/seminars; Endowments; General operating grants; Project/program grants.

YEAR PROGRAM STARTED: 1967

PURPOSE:
To champion the entrepreneurial spirit.

LEGAL BASIS:
Private foundation.

ELIGIBILITY:
Grants are made to organizations classified as public charities and tax-exempt under Section

501(c)(3) of the IRS Code. For-profit companies and startups are not eligible to apply for funding directly from the Foundation. The Foundation does not make grants to individuals.

Projects with national impact are occasionally considered.

GEOG. RESTRICTIONS: Primarily Northeast Ohio.

FINANCIAL DATA:
Amount of support per award: Varies.
Total amount of support: Varies.
Matching fund requirements: Varies.

NO. MOST RECENT APPLICANTS: 299.

NO. AWARDS: 198.

APPLICATION INFO:
Details on how to apply for grants can be found on the Foundation web site.
Duration: One year.
Deadline: Requests greater than $20,000: May 1 for September consideration, September 1 for January or February consideration, and February 1 for June consideration. Requests under $20,000 are considered on a rolling basis.

PUBLICATIONS:
Pipeline, e-newsletter; annual report.

IRS I.D.: 34-6598971

OFFICER:
Deborah D. Hoover, President and Chief Executive Officer

ADDRESS INQUIRIES TO:
Grants Manager
(See address above.)

NASDAQ FOUNDATION   [1713]
805 King Farm Boulevard
Rockville, MD 20850
(800) 842-0356
Fax: (301) 978-8472
E-mail: foundation@nasdaq.com
Web Site: www.nasdaq.com/nasdaq-foundation

FOUNDED: 1994

AREAS OF INTEREST:
Financial literacy and entrepreneurship.

TYPE:
Development grants; Fellowships; Project/program grants; Research grants; Seed money grants. The Foundation works to support women and underrepresented minority communities by focusing on two goals:
(1) Reimagining investor engagement to equip underrepresented communities with the financial knowledge to share in the wealth that markets create and;
(2) Leveraging investment in the Nasdaq Entrepreneurial Center alongside new strategic partnerships with organizations that can help build a deeper, data-led understanding where the challenges are greatest, what existing efforts could be amplified, and how the Nasdaq Foundation can make new and distinctive contributions.

PURPOSE:
To advance diversity in investor engagement.

ELIGIBILITY:
The Foundation will accept proposals from organizations designated as tax-exempt according to Section 501(c)(3) of the Internal Revenue Code or a for-profit business or consultant acting on behalf of a qualified tax-exempt entity.

FINANCIAL DATA:
Amount of support per award: Varies.
Total amount of support: Varies.

APPLICATION INFO:
Applicant must submit:
(1) a one-page cover sheet;
(2) a proposal (not more than five pages, excluding attachments) which describes the project and the organization;
(3) a conflict of interest disclosure and;
(4) required supporting documents.

A single e-mail of the completed proposal (including attachments, letters and other supporting material) must be sent to the e-mail address listed above.
Duration: One year, unless otherwise specified.
Deadline: March 31, May 31, August 31 and November 30.

NATIONAL ENDOWMENT FOR FINANCIAL EDUCATION (NEFE)   [1714]
1331 17th Street, Suite 1200
Denver, CO 80202
(303) 741-6333
Fax: (303) 220-0838
E-mail: nefegrantrequest@nefe.org
Web Site: www.nefe.org

FOUNDED: 1997

AREAS OF INTEREST:
Financial education for the American public.

NAME(S) OF PROGRAMS:
● **NEFE Research Funding Program**

TYPE:
Fellowships; Research grants. NEFE Research Funding Program recruits qualified individuals from diverse backgrounds who share a common interest in working on projects within NEFE's broad scope of activities and in gaining nonprofit operations and management experience. The program also awards grants for research projects that will expand the body of knowledge in the field of financial literacy.

YEAR PROGRAM STARTED: 1998

PURPOSE:
To fund innovative research that can make a profound contribution to the field of financial literacy.

ELIGIBILITY:
To be considered for a fellowship opportunity, candidates must be:
(1) in good standing with their academic institution and;
(2) a currently registered graduate degree-seeking student.

Grants are awarded to organizations that have been designated tax-exempt status according to Internal Revenue Code Section 501(c)(3) or its equivalent for colleges and universities. Grants are not awarded to:
(1) individuals;
(2) organizations that have not been designated tax-exempt under Section 501(c)(3) or its equivalent;
(3) organizations that discriminate on the basis of age, color, disability, marital status, nationality, race, religion, sex, sexual orientation, or veteran status;
(4) organizations and/or project principals and team members who fail to meet NEFE's Strategy Statement and Procedures requirements concerning the U.S.A. Patriot

Act and related regulations;
(5) foreign organizations;
(6) international programs or projects or;
(7) organizations whose projects include re-grant of NEFE funding.

Project outcomes should be in the field of financial literacy and directly relevant to the public's well-being.

GEOG. RESTRICTIONS: United States.

FINANCIAL DATA:
Amount of support per award: Fellowships: $3,000 per semester; Grants: Generally $100,000 up.
Total amount of support: Varies.

NO. MOST RECENT APPLICANTS: 25.

NO. AWARDS: 3.

APPLICATION INFO:
Fellowship Program does not accept unsolicited applications. Applicants to the Grant Program must first submit a Letter of Inquiry. Those projects appearing to have strong potential will move to a proposal phase; applicants for those selected projects will be given further instruction at that time.
Duration: Varies.
Deadline: First Tuesday in December for spring funding and first Tuesday in June for fall funding.

PUBLICATIONS:
NEFE Digest.

IRS I.D.: 84-0632115

ADDRESS INQUIRIES TO:
Grants Manager
(See address above.)

THE NATIONAL RESTAURANT ASSOCIATION EDUCATIONAL FOUNDATION   [1715]
2055 L Street, N.W.
Washington, DC 20036
(202) 973-3672
E-mail: scholars@nraef.org
Web Site: www.chooserestaurants.org/programs-and-scholarships

FOUNDED: 1987

AREAS OF INTEREST:
Foodservice education and training.

NAME(S) OF PROGRAMS:
● **Professional Development Grants for Educators**

TYPE:
Training grants; Travel grants.

PURPOSE:
To support foodservice educators earning their Certified Secondary Educators Foodservice certification; to provide financial support to attend an NRA Summer Institute or participate in a "hands-on" industry work experience.

ELIGIBILITY:
Must be an educator of a restaurant and/or foodservice-related program in a secondary school and submit a signed letter of recommendation on school letterhead that also verifies employment by an immediate supervisor or program director. Applicants must be U.S. citizens/residents.

GEOG. RESTRICTIONS: United States.

FINANCIAL DATA:
Amount of support per award: $1,675.
Total amount of support: Varies.

NO. MOST RECENT APPLICANTS: 150.

NO. AWARDS: Varies.

APPLICATION INFO:
Application information is available online.
Duration: Varies.
Deadline: January 31.

THE NATIONAL RESTAURANT ASSOCIATION EDUCATIONAL FOUNDATION
2055 L Street, N.W.
Washington, DC 20036
(202) 973-3672
E-mail: scholars@nraef.org
Web Site: www.chooserestaurants.org/programs-and-scholarships

TYPE:
Scholarships. Provides scholarships for students who are pursuing an education and career in the foodservice industry.

See entry 2419 for full listing.

PHI CHI THETA EDUCATIONAL FOUNDATION   [1716]
1508 East Beltline Road, Suite 104
Carrollton, TX 75006
(972) 245-7202
E-mail: foundationinfo@phichitheta.org
Web Site: www.phichitheta.org/foundation

FOUNDED: 1999

AREAS OF INTEREST:
Business and economics.

NAME(S) OF PROGRAMS:
● **Educational and Scholastic Advancement Programs**

TYPE:
Scholarships. Grants.

YEAR PROGRAM STARTED: 2000

PURPOSE:
To provide scholarships and grants to members of the Phi Chi Theta Fraternity.

LEGAL BASIS:
Public charity, 501(c)(3) organization.

ELIGIBILITY:
Open to students who are members of Phi Chi Theta in approved courses in colleges and universities in the U.S. leading to Bachelor's, Master's or doctoral degrees in the fields of business administration and/or economics. Applicants must have completed at least one semester of college-level study. Selection is based on scholastic achievement, motivation, leadership potential and financial need.

GEOG. RESTRICTIONS: United States.

FINANCIAL DATA:
Amount of support per award: $500 to $1,000.
Total amount of support: Varies.

NO. MOST RECENT APPLICANTS: Over 20.

NO. AWARDS: Varies.

APPLICATION INFO:
Applicants must submit an official transcript and two letters of recommendation.
Duration: One year. Nonrenewable.
Deadline: May 1.

PUBLICATIONS:
Application guidelines.

IRS I.D.: 31-1672618

OFFICERS:
Melissa Bolin, President
Mary Ellen Lewis, Treasurer

PROSPANICA
2711 LBJ Freeway
Suite 800
Dallas, TX 75234
(877) 467-4622
E-mail: info@prospanica.org
Web Site: www.prospanica.org

TYPE:
Awards/prizes; Conferences/seminars; Scholarships.

See entry 916 for full listing.

CHARLES SCHWAB FOUNDATION   [1717]
211 Main Street, SF211 MN-16-205
San Francisco, CA 94105-1905
E-mail: charlesschwabfoundation@schwab.com
Web Site: www.aboutschwab.com/citizenship
www.schwabmoneywise.com

FOUNDED: 1993

AREAS OF INTEREST:
Financial literacy and cultural and social needs.

NAME(S) OF PROGRAMS:
● **Schwab Moneywise**

TYPE:
General operating grants; Matching gifts; Project/program grants. The Charles Schwab Foundation awards strategic financial support through direct grants to selected nonprofit organizations that respond to local cultural and social needs or support Schwab's commitment to financial literacy. These grants provide employees with a voice and role in supporting the community groups they care about most.

YEAR PROGRAM STARTED: 1993

PURPOSE:
To give back to communities by supporting employee-selected causes and fostering financial literacy through funding, involvement and expertise.

LEGAL BASIS:
Corporate foundation.

ELIGIBILITY:
The Foundation provides direct grants to select nonprofit organizations that support Schwab's commitment to financial literacy and respond to local cultural and social needs.

Applicants must meet at least one of the following selection criteria:
(1) be recommended by a Schwab employee who is an active volunteer in the organization;
(2) be performing community work that corresponds to the Foundation's initiatives or;
(3) promote financial capability.

Greater consideration will be given to those organizations that already have Schwab employee volunteer involvement. The more employees involved, the greater the opportunity to be considered for a direct grant.

To qualify for a direct grant, an organization must:
(1) be based in the U.S. or one of its territories;
(2) be recognized as a tax-exempt public

charity under Section 501(c)(3) of the U.S. Internal Revenue Code (per Section 170) and;
(3) (if an educational institution) be accredited by a regional accrediting association or by a recognized independent accrediting group.

GEOG. RESTRICTIONS: United States.

FINANCIAL DATA:
Total amount of support: $12,200,000 in direct support to nonprofit organizations; $5,980,000 in employee gifts and matching donations in 2020.

NO. AWARDS: Over 3,193 nonprofit organizations received financial support in 2020.

APPLICATION INFO:
The Foundation is currently accepting grant requests by invitation only.
Deadline: Proposals are reviewed on a quarterly basis.

PUBLICATIONS:
Program brochure with application guidelines.

IRS I.D.: 94-1737782

ADDRESS INQUIRIES TO:
Direct Grant Program
(See address above.)

SIMON FRASER UNIVERSITY   [1718]
Maggie Benston Student Services Centre 1100
8888 University Drive
Burnaby BC V5A 1S6 Canada
(778) 782-3042
Fax: (778) 782-3080
E-mail: gradstdy@sfu.ca
Web Site: www.sfu.ca/dean-gradstudies.html

NAME(S) OF PROGRAMS:
● **SFU Graduate Fellowships**

TYPE:
Fellowships.

PURPOSE:
To offer financial support to the University's students enrolled in a Master's or Ph.D. program.

ELIGIBILITY:
Open to current or entering Master's or Ph.D. program students with a grade point average of 3.5 or above.

FINANCIAL DATA:
Amount of support per award: $3,500 to $7,000 (CAN).

APPLICATION INFO:
Eligible students apply through their department of enrollment by completing an application through the Graduate Award Application and Adjudication System.
Duration: One term or more. Must reapply.
Deadline: Varies.

ADDRESS INQUIRIES TO:
Specific Department of Enrollment
Simon Fraser University
(Request specific department's address.)

SOCIETY OF ACTUARIES (SOA)
475 North Martingale Road
Suite 600
Schaumburg, IL 60173-2226
(847) 706-3509
Fax: (847) 273-8605
E-mail: ttatsumi@soa.org
Web Site: www.soa.org/doctoral-stipend

TYPE:
Awards/prizes; Scholarships. Society of Actuaries' James C. Hickman Scholar Doctoral Stipend Program is designed to provide stipends to doctoral students who will, through their studies, address research and education needs of the profession, including both the theoretical and practical aspects.

See entry 1887 for full listing.

U.S. DEPARTMENT OF EDUCATION [1719]
400 Maryland Avenue, S.W.
Washington, DC 20024
(202) 453-7521
E-mail: timothy.duvall@ed.gov
Web Site: www2.ed.gov/programs/iegpscibe/index.html

AREAS OF INTEREST:
International business education.

CONSULTING OR VOLUNTEER SERVICES:
Offers technical assistance.

NAME(S) OF PROGRAMS:
• **Centers for International Business Education Program**

TYPE:
Project/program grants. The program provides grants to eligible institutions of higher education or combinations of these institutions for planning, establishing and operating Centers for International Business Education.

YEAR PROGRAM STARTED: 1989

PURPOSE:
To provide funding to U.S. institutions of higher education for curriculum development, research, and training on issues of importance to U.S. trade and competitiveness.

LEGAL BASIS:
Government agency.

ELIGIBILITY:
An applicant must be a U.S. institution of higher education or a combination of such institutions that establishes a Center Advisory Council prior to the date that federal assistance is received. The Center Advisory Council shall conduct extensive planning prior to the establishment of the Center for International Business Education concerning the scope of the Center's activities and the design of its programs. Programs and activities to be conducted by Centers for International Business Education must meet the programmatic requirements listed above.

FINANCIAL DATA:
Grant funds may be used to pay the federal share of costs of faculty and staff travel in foreign areas, regions or countries, teaching and research materials, curriculum planning and development, bringing visiting scholars and faculty to the center to teach or to conduct research, training and improvement of the staff for the purpose of and subject to such conditions as the Secretary finds necessary for carrying out the objectives of this program and other costs consistent with planning, establishing or operating a center.
Amount of support per award: $305,000 average award for fiscal year 2018.
Total amount of support: $4,571,400 for fiscal year 2018.

NO. MOST RECENT APPLICANTS: 26.

NO. AWARDS: Approximately 15.

APPLICATION INFO:
The Department of Education provides an application package upon request to the Office of Postsecondary Education. Applications become available in May.
Duration: Four years.
Deadline: June. Competition held every four years.

PUBLICATIONS:
Application guidelines; abstracts of grantees.

ADDRESS INQUIRIES TO:
Tim Duvall, Ph.D.
(See address above.)

THE UNIVERSITY OF CALGARY
Faculty of Graduate Studies
Earth Sciences Building, Room 1010
2500 University Drive, N.W.
Calgary AB T2N 1N4 Canada
(403) 220-4938
Fax: (403) 289-7635
E-mail: gsaward@ucalgary.ca
Web Site: grad.ucalgary.ca/awards

TYPE:
Awards/prizes; Scholarships. Awards for study in the fields of business, management and related areas. Tenable at the University of Calgary. Awards are endowed through gifts from John Labatt Limited and ScotiaMcLeod Inc. Matching grants provided from the Province of Alberta's Advanced Education Endowment Fund.

See entry 1599 for full listing.

UNIVERSITY OF NEBRASKA AT OMAHA [1720]
Mammel Hall, Room 300
6708 Pine Street
Omaha, NE 68182-0048
(402) 554-2341
E-mail: mba@unomaha.edu
Web Site: www.unomaha.edu/college-of-business-administration

AREAS OF INTEREST:
UNO MBA Program and MS Economics.

NAME(S) OF PROGRAMS:
• **UNO Graduate Assistantships**

TYPE:
Assistantships. Graduate, MBA scholarships in all subjects.

ELIGIBILITY:
Graduate assistantships are available for qualified students who are enrolled in a graduate degree program in the College of Business Administration.

FINANCIAL DATA:
Amount of support per award: Waiver of tuition costs for a minimum of six semester-hours of graduate credit per semester up to a maximum of 12.

NO. MOST RECENT APPLICANTS: Varies.

NO. AWARDS: Varies.

APPLICATION INFO:
Applicants should complete the Graduate Assistantship application that is available on the web site. Application must be submitted to the e-mail address above, along with a resume and letters of recommendation.
Deadline: Varies.

THE DEAN WITTER FOUNDATION [1721]
c/o Kramer, Blum and Associates
P.O. Box 6106
San Rafael, CA 94903
(415) 981-2966
Fax: (415) 981-5218
E-mail: admin@deanwitterfoundation.org
Web Site: www.deanwitterfoundation.org

FOUNDED: 1952

AREAS OF INTEREST:
Research and higher education in finance, wildlife research and conservation projects, and K-12 education.

TYPE:
Challenge/matching grants; Fellowships; General operating grants; Internships; Matching gifts; Professorships; Project/program grants; Research grants; Scholarships; Seed money grants.

YEAR PROGRAM STARTED: 1952

PURPOSE:
To help fund research and higher education in areas of special interest to the Foundation, as well as K-12 education.

LEGAL BASIS:
Private foundation.

ELIGIBILITY:
Grants are made to tax-exempt 501(c)(3) institutions. No grants are made to individuals.

GEOG. RESTRICTIONS: Northern California.

FINANCIAL DATA:
Amount of support per award: Typically $10,000 to $25,000.
Total amount of support: Approximately $3,500,000.

NO. AWARDS: 12 for the year 2020-21.

APPLICATION INFO:
The Foundation does not accept unsolicited proposals.
Duration: One year. Renewal possible.

OFFICERS AND TRUSTEES:
Dean Witter, III, Chairman
Malcolm G. Witter, President
Allison Frey, Secretary
Brooke Witter, Trustee

ADDRESS INQUIRIES TO:
Kenneth J. Blum, Administrative Director
(See address above.)

*PLEASE NOTE:
The Foundation does not accept unsolicited proposals.

ZONTA FOUNDATION FOR WOMEN [1722]
1200 Harger Road, Suite 330
Oak Brook, IL 60523
(630) 928-1400
E-mail: programs@zonta.org
Web Site: www.zonta.org

FOUNDED: 1919

AREAS OF INTEREST:
Financial support for women of any nationality pursuing degrees in business leading to a business management career.

NAME(S) OF PROGRAMS:
• **Jane M. Klausman Women in Business Scholarships**

TYPE:
Awards/prizes; Scholarships. For women of any nationality pursuing degrees in business who demonstrate outstanding potential in the field of business.

YEAR PROGRAM STARTED: 1998

PURPOSE:
To provide financial support for women of any nationality pursuing degrees in business leading to a business management career.

LEGAL BASIS:
Incorporated in the state of Illinois as a nonprofit organization.

ELIGIBILITY:
Applicant must meet the following minimum requirements:
(1) be undertaking a business and/or business-related program at an accredited university, college or institute;
(2) be enrolled in at least the second year of an undergraduate program through the final year of a Master's program at the time the application is submitted (applicants must still be attending school to receive this award in November);
(3) have achieved an outstanding academic record during her academic studies, including business-related subjects;
(4) have demonstrated initiative, ambition and commitment to pursuing a career in business and;
(5) be living or studying in a Zonta region/district.

FINANCIAL DATA:
The scholarship award may be used for tuition, books or living expenses at any university, college or institution offering accredited business courses and degrees.

Amount of support per award: Up to $2,000 at the District Level and 6 international scholarships for $8,000.

Total amount of support: Varies.

NO. MOST RECENT APPLICANTS: Varies.

NO. AWARDS: Up to 32.

APPLICATION INFO:
Applications must be completed in English. English translations must accompany all non-English documents. The Jane M. Klausman Women in Business Scholarship program operates at the club, district and international levels of Zonta International. To apply, contact the Zonta Club within the applicant's district/region for deadlines and an address to mail application. (Such contact information is also available on the web site.) Alternatively, one can e-mail one's name and contact information to Zonta International Headquarters at the address above. Applicants must be nominated by a local Zonta Club first.

Deadline: Must contact Zonta Club for deadlines.

ADDRESS INQUIRIES TO:
Programs Senior Coordinator
(See e-mail address above.)

Communications

AMERICAN ASSOCIATION FOR THE ADVANCEMENT OF SCIENCE [1723]
1200 New York Avenue, N.W.
Washington, DC 20005
(202) 326-6431
E-mail: sja@aaas.org
Web Site: sjawards.aaas.org

FOUNDED: 1848

AREAS OF INTEREST:
Science and engineering.

NAME(S) OF PROGRAMS:
● **AAAS Kavli Science Journalism Awards**

TYPE:
Awards/prizes. Global awards for stories of life, physical and social sciences, engineering and mathematics, published in newspapers, general magazines, aired on radio or podcasts, on video, and online. Entries should be intended for general, nontechnical audiences. There is also an award recognizing excellence in science news reporting for children. Since 2015, the contest has been open to journalists worldwide in all categories.

YEAR PROGRAM STARTED: 1945

PURPOSE:
To encourage newspaper, magazine, audio, video and online science writing.

LEGAL BASIS:
Nonprofit scientific organization.

ELIGIBILITY:
Qualified individuals may apply with appropriate single stories or series published in newspapers or general circulation magazines, or aired on podcasts, radio or video, and online. Awards may not be presented to the same entrant in any two consecutive years, and individuals who have already won three of the annual awards are no longer eligible to apply.

FINANCIAL DATA:
Amount of support per award: Gold Award: $5,000; Silver Award: $3,500.
Total amount of support: $68,000.

CO-OP FUNDING PROGRAMS: Sponsored by The Kavli Foundation.

NO. MOST RECENT APPLICANTS: 1,250.

NO. AWARDS: 16 for the 2021 contest year. Two each for eight categories, including large newspaper, small newspaper, magazine, video in-depth reporting, video spot news/feature reporting, audio, online and children's science news.

APPLICATION INFO:
Online application information and FAQ can be found at the web site.
Deadline: August 1.

OFFICERS:
Dr. Sudip Parikh, Chief Executive Officer

ADDRESS INQUIRIES TO:
Earl Lane, Executive Director
AAAS Kavli Science Journalism Awards
(See address above.)

AMERICAN POLITICAL SCIENCE ASSOCIATION
1527 New Hampshire Avenue, N.W.
Washington, DC 20036
(202) 483-2512
Fax: (202) 483-2657
E-mail: cfp@apsanet.org
Web Site: www.apsanet.org/cfp

TYPE:
Fellowships. Awards to political science professors and journalists in early-career to midcareer status; the award provides an opportunity for support as a full-time aide to a member of the House or Senate or as a staff member for a Congressional committee.

See entry 1782 for full listing.

BROADCAST EDUCATION ASSOCIATION [1724]
One M Street, S.E.
Washington, DC 20003
(202) 602-0587
Fax: (202) 609-9940
E-mail: help@beaweb.org
Web Site: www.beaweb.org

FOUNDED: 1923

AREAS OF INTEREST:
Electronic media.

NAME(S) OF PROGRAMS:
● **John Bayliss Scholarship Award**
● **BEA Founders Award**
● **Richard Eaton Foundation Award**
● **Edward O. Fritts Award**
● **Library of American Broadcasting Foundation Award**
● **Peter B. Orlik Award**
● **Abe Voron Award**
● **Vincent T. Wasilewski Award**

TYPE:
Scholarships. BEA is the professional development association for professors, industry professionals and students involved in teaching and research related to radio, television and other electronic media. BEA administers scholarships annually, to honor broadcasters and the entire electronic media profession.

John Bayliss and Abe Voron Awards: Study toward a career in radio.

BEA Founders, Richard Eaton, Edward O. Fritts, Peter B. Orlik and Vincent T. Wasilewski Awards: Study in any electronic media area. (Wasilewski Award is for graduate students only.)

Library of American Broadcasting Foundation Award is for graduate students focusing on broadcast history.

For the BEA Founders Award, preference is given to students enrolled in a BEA Two-Year/Small College Member Institution or graduates of these programs now enrolled in a BEA Four-Year Institution.

All other scholarships are awarded to juniors, seniors and graduate students at BEA Member institutions.

YEAR PROGRAM STARTED: 1962

PURPOSE:
To secure mutual advantages that flow from a continuing relationship between broadcasters and institutions of higher learning which offer a high standard of training and guidance for those who plan to enter the electronic media.

LEGAL BASIS:
Private association.

ELIGIBILITY:
Scholarships will be awarded for full-time degree work for the full academic year. One-semester grants are not made. Scholarships must be used exclusively for tuition, student fees, university bookstore course purchases, dormitory and related items eligible to be charged to a student's official campus account. Current scholarship holders are not eligible to reapply in the year following their award. All scholarships must be applied to study at a campus where at least one department is a BEA institutional member. Applicant can visit the Association web site (click on "Scholarship") or call the telephone number above to verify that one's campus is a member.

The applicant should be able to show substantial evidence of superior academic performance and potential to be an outstanding electronic media professional. There should be compelling evidence that the applicant possesses high integrity and a well-articulated sense of personal and professional responsibility.

FINANCIAL DATA:
Amount of support per award: Bayliss and Orlik Awards: $3,500; BEA Founders Award: $1,500 each; Eaton Foundation and Wasilewski Awards: $4,000; Fritts Award: $1,000; Library of American Broadcasting Foundation and Voron Awards: $3,000 each.

Total amount of support: $31,000 for the year 2022-23.

NO. MOST RECENT APPLICANTS: 45 to 90.

NO. AWARDS: Bayliss, Eaton, Fritts, Library of American Broadcasting Foundation, Orlik and Wasilewski Awards: 1 each; BEA Founders Award: 2; Voron Award: 3.

APPLICATION INFO:
Application forms and directions are available under the "Scholarship" tap on the BEA web site.

Duration: One full-time academic year.

Deadline: Application forms and materials must be received by Dr. Orlik by the close of business on October 15.

PUBLICATIONS:
Journal of Broadcasting & Electronic Media; *Journal of Education Media*; *Journal of Radio Studies*.

ADDRESS INQUIRIES TO:
Dr. Peter B. Orlik, Scholarships
613 Kane Street
Mount Pleasant, MI 48858
E-mail: orlik1pb@cmich.edu
(See address above.)

*PLEASE NOTE:
Due to the large volume of scholarship-related business, telephone calls cannot be returned.

*SPECIAL STIPULATIONS:
All scholarships must be applied to study at a campus where at least one department is a BEA institutional member. Applications listing ineligible schools will be disqualified.

BROADCAST EDUCATION ASSOCIATION [1725]
One M Street, S.E.
Washington, DC 20003
(202) 602-0586
Fax: (202) 609-9940
E-mail: help@beaweb.org
Web Site: www.beaweb.org

FOUNDED: 1923

AREAS OF INTEREST:
Electronic media.

NAME(S) OF PROGRAMS:
● **PILOT Media Technology and Innovation Scholarships**

TYPE:
Scholarships. PILOT Media Technology and Innovation Scholarships are awarded to college sophomores, juniors, seniors entering graduate school and graduate students for pursuit of studies related to media technology and innovation.

PURPOSE:
To secure mutual advantages that flow from a continuing relationship between broadcasters and institutions of higher learning which offer a high standard of training and guidance for those who plan to enter the electronic media.

LEGAL BASIS:
Private association.

ELIGIBILITY:
Applicant must be a current college sophomore, junior, senior entering graduate school or continuing graduate student pursuing studies related to media technology and innovation. Eligible academic areas include broadcast television or radio engineering/technology, sports media production or other broadcast content creation, web/online media, mobile media, media-related information technology, audience measurement and media technology research.

FINANCIAL DATA:
Amount of support per award: $2,500.
Total amount of support: Up to $10,000 for the year 2021-22.

NO. AWARDS: Up to 4.

APPLICATION INFO:
Application form requires the following information:
(1) personal contact information;
(2) academic history;
(3) supportive statements from two references;
(4) a 250-word statement of career goals;
(5) listing of relevant accomplishments and experience and;
(6) college transcripts.
Duration: One full-time academic year.
Deadline: January 15.

PUBLICATIONS:
Journal of Broadcasting & Electronic Media; *Journal of Media Education*; *Journal of Radio & Audio Media*.

ADDRESS INQUIRIES TO:
Traci Bailey
Manager, Business Operations
(See address above.)

*PLEASE NOTE:
Due to the large volume of scholarship-related business, telephone calls cannot be returned.

COLUMBIA JOURNALISM SCHOOL [1726]
2950 Broadway
New York, NY 10027
(212) 854-6468
Fax: (212) 854-3148
E-mail: cm3443@columbia.edu
Web Site: journalism.columbia.edu/oakes

FOUNDED: 1960

AREAS OF INTEREST:
Environmental journalism.

NAME(S) OF PROGRAMS:
● **John B. Oakes Award**

TYPE:
Awards/prizes. Awarded for distinguished excellence in environmental journalism.

YEAR PROGRAM STARTED: 1993

ELIGIBILITY:
To be considered for this Award, submitted articles must have been written between January 1 and December 31 of previous year. The article must have been published in a U.S.-based publication. An online publication is acceptable.

GEOG. RESTRICTIONS: United States.

FINANCIAL DATA:
Amount of support per award: $5,000 and a certificate.

NO. AWARDS: 1 award yearly.

APPLICATION INFO:
Nomination instructions are available online. Entry fee of $50 required for each nomination (non-refundable).
Duration: Recipients of the Oakes Award can win it a second time.
Deadline: January 31.

ADDRESS INQUIRIES TO:
Caroline Wernecke
Assistant Director, Professional Prizes
(See address above.)

COLUMBIA JOURNALISM SCHOOL [1727]
2950 Broadway
New York, NY 10027-7004
(212) 854-6468
E-mail: cm3443@columbia.edu
Web Site: journalism.columbia.edu/berger

FOUNDED: 1960

NAME(S) OF PROGRAMS:
● **Mike Berger Award**

TYPE:
Awards/prizes. A newspaper competition, covering the previous calendar year, open to reporters nationwide.

YEAR PROGRAM STARTED: 1960

PURPOSE:
To honor distinguished newspaper reporting in the tradition of the late Meyer Berger of the New York Times.

LEGAL BASIS:
University.

ELIGIBILITY:
All newspaper reporters across the country are eligible whether they report for dailies, weeklies, monthlies, newspaper magazines, radio broadcast, digital reporting or online publications. Members of the ethnic press should submit copies of original stories with an English translation.

FINANCIAL DATA:
Winners receive a cash award along with a certificate and hotel and travel expenses to New York.
Amount of support per award: $1,500.

NO. AWARDS: 1 annually.

APPLICATION INFO:
Nominations are solicited from the editors of all daily newspapers across the country, as well as ethnic, weekly and online publications. Judges request that a nominating exhibit include two copies of a letter from the editor, a brief biographical resume of the reporter, and two copies of not more than five clippings.
Deadline: Early March. Notification in the spring. Presented at Columbia University in May.

ADDRESS INQUIRIES TO:
Caroline Wernecke
Assistant Director, Professional Prizes
(See address above.)

COLUMBIA JOURNALISM SCHOOL [1728]

2950 Broadway
New York, NY 10027
(212) 854-5047
Fax: (212) 854-3148
E-mail: lm3105@columbia.edu
Web Site: journalism.columbia.edu/cabot

AREAS OF INTEREST:
Journalism and inter-American relations.

NAME(S) OF PROGRAMS:
• **Maria Moors Cabot Prizes**

TYPE:
Awards/prizes. The prize program recognizes distinguished journalistic contributions to inter-American understanding. Prizes are awarded annually by the Trustees of Columbia University on recommendations made by the Dean of the Graduate School of Journalism and the Cabot Board.

YEAR PROGRAM STARTED: 1938

PURPOSE:
To recognize sustained and distinguished contributions of journalists to the advancement of understanding among the peoples of the Western Hemisphere.

LEGAL BASIS:
University.

ELIGIBILITY:
Although awards have been made to publishers or others in managerial positions, the board is particularly interested in working journalists throughout the Americas whose writings or broadcasts have contributed to mutual understanding and freedom of the press over a period of time.

GEOG. RESTRICTIONS: Western Hemisphere.

FINANCIAL DATA:
Amount of support per award: $5,000 and a Cabot medal, plus round-trip transportation to Columbia University for the award ceremonies.

NO. AWARDS: 5 for the year 2019.

APPLICATION INFO:
The Committee appreciates the submission of at least five, but no more than 10, newspaper or magazine articles, television or radio programs or Internet stories that are

representative of the nominee's work. Complete nomination instructions are available online.
Deadline: March 16.

ADDRESS INQUIRIES TO:
Lauren Meregildo-Santos
Program Coordinator
(See address above.)

COLUMBIA UNIVERSITY [1729]

709 Pulitzer Hall
2950 Broadway
New York, NY 10027
(212) 854-3841
E-mail: pulitzer@pulitzer.org
Web Site: www.pulitzer.org

FOUNDED: 1917

AREAS OF INTEREST:
Excellence in journalism, books, drama and music.

NAME(S) OF PROGRAMS:
• **Pulitzer Fellowships**
• **Pulitzer Prizes**

TYPE:
Awards/prizes; Fellowships. Awards in journalism, books and music.

Pulitzer Prizes in Journalism are awarded based on material appearing in a text-based U.S. newspaper or news site that publishes at least once a week during the year. Awards given for:
(1) meritorious public service by a newspaper through the use of its journalistic resources which may include editorials, cartoons, photographs, graphics and online material;
(2) local, state or national reporting of breaking news;
(3) investigative reporting by an individual or team, presented as a single article or series;
(4) explanatory journalism that illuminates a significant or complex subject, demonstrating mastery of the subject, lucid writing and clear presentation;
(5) reporting on significant issues of local concern;
(6) reporting on national affairs;
(7) reporting on international affairs, including United Nations correspondence;
(8) feature writing giving prime consideration to high literary quality and originality;
(9) commentary;
(10) criticism;
(11) editorial writing;
(12) cartoon or portfolio of cartoons;
(13) breaking news photography in black and white or color, which may consist of a photograph or photographs, a sequence or an album;
(14) feature photography in black and white or color with the same stipulations as above and;
(15) audio journalism that serves the public interest.

Prizes in Letters are restricted to works first published in the U.S. during the year in book form and available for purchase by the general public. Awards given for:
(1) fiction by an American author, preferably dealing with American life;
(2) a play by an American author, preferably original in its source and dealing with American life, produced in the U.S. January 1 to December 31;
(3) appropriately documented book on the history of the U.S.;
(4) appropriately documented biography or autobiography by an American author;

(5) volume of original verse by an American author and;
(6) appropriately documented book of nonfiction by an American author that is not eligible for consideration in any other category.

A prize in music is given for distinguished musical composition by an American that has had its first performance in the U.S. during the year.

Four fellowships enable outstanding graduates to travel, report and study abroad. One fellowship is given to an outstanding graduate who wishes to specialize in drama, music, literary, film or television criticism.

YEAR PROGRAM STARTED: 1917

PURPOSE:
To recognize excellence in journalism, letters, drama and music.

LEGAL BASIS:
University.

ELIGIBILITY:
Competition for prizes is limited to work done during the calendar year ending December 31.

FINANCIAL DATA:
Amount of support per award: $7,500 for fellowships; $15,000 for prizes.

NO. AWARDS: Fellowships: 5; Prizes in Letters, Drama and Music: 7; Prizes in Journalism: 15.

APPLICATION INFO:
Application form and $75 handling fee required with entries.
Duration: One-time awards. Previous winners are eligible for consideration each year for any award.
Deadline: Prizes in Books: June 15 and October 1; Prizes in Drama and Prize in Music: December 31; Prizes in Journalism: Fourth Friday of January.

PUBLICATIONS:
Award announcement; brochure.

BOARD:
Elizabeth Alexander
Nancy Barnes
Robert Blau
Lee C. Bollinger
Katherine Boo
Neil Brown
Dana Canedy
Nicole Carroll
Steve Coll
Gail Collins
John Daniszewski
Stephen Engelberg
Aminda Marques Gonzales
Steven Hahn
Carlos Lozada
Emily Ramshaw
David Remnick
Tommy Shelby

ADDRESS INQUIRIES TO:
The Pulitzer Prize Board
(See address above.)

COLUMBIA UNIVERSITY [1730]

Graduate School of Journalism
2950 Broadway, Mail Code 3850
New York, NY 10027
(212) 854-271
E-mail: ann.grimes@columbia.edu
Web Site: www.journalism.columbia.edu/kb

FOUNDED: 1975

AREAS OF INTEREST:
Economics and business journalism for midcareer journalists.

NAME(S) OF PROGRAMS:
● **Knight-Bagehot Fellowship in Economics and Business Journalism**

TYPE:
Awards/prizes; Fellowships. Awarded to midcareer professional journalists to study business and economics at Columbia University.

YEAR PROGRAM STARTED: 1975

PURPOSE:
To improve the quality of business and economics journalism.

LEGAL BASIS:
University-affiliated fellowship program.

ELIGIBILITY:
Applicants must have at least four years' experience in journalism.

FINANCIAL DATA:
The Fellowship includes free tuition plus a stipend to cover living expenses.
Amount of support per award: Up to $60,000.

NO. AWARDS: Up to 10.

APPLICATION INFO:
Application information is available online.
Duration: One academic year.
Deadline: February 15.

PUBLICATIONS:
Annual report.

ADDRESS INQUIRIES TO:
Ann Grimes, Director
Knight-Bagehot Fellowship
(See address above.)

COUNCIL FOR THE ADVANCEMENT OF SCIENCE WRITING, INC. [1731]
P.O. Box 17337
Seattle, WA 98127
(206) 880-0177
E-mail: info@casw.org
Web Site: www.casw.org

FOUNDED: 1959

AREAS OF INTEREST:
Writing about science, medicine, health, technology, energy, the environment, etc., for the general public via the mass media (distinct from technical writing or technical journalism).

NAME(S) OF PROGRAMS:
● **Evert Clark/Seth Payne Award for Young Science Journalists**
● **The Victor Cohn Prize for Excellence in Medical Science Reporting**
● **Rennie Taylor/Alton Blakeslee Fellowships for Graduate Study in Science Writing**

TYPE:
Awards/prizes; Fellowships. Evert Clark/Seth Payne Award recognizes outstanding reporting and writing in any field of science.

The Victor Cohn Prize salutes general excellence in medical science writing for the mass media. The prize, to be given annually, seeks to honor a writer for a body of work published or broadcast within the last five years which, for reasons of uncommon clarity, accuracy, breadth of coverage, enterprise, originality, insight and narrative

power, has made a profound and lasting contribution to public awareness and understanding of critical advances in medical science and their impact on human health and well-being.

Rennie Taylor/Alton Blakeslee Fellowships support graduate students in science journalism and experienced reporters who wish to study science writing at the graduate level.

PURPOSE:
To increase public understanding of science by upgrading the quality and quantity of science and medical writing and by improving relationships between scientists and the press.

LEGAL BASIS:
Nonprofit 501(c)(3).

ELIGIBILITY:
Evert Clark/Seth Payne Award is limited to non-technical, print and online journalism. Articles published in newspapers (including college newspapers), magazines, newsletters and web sites are eligible. Both freelancers and staff writers are eligible. Books, as well as articles in technical journals and trade association publications, are not eligible. Entries will be judged on the basis of accuracy, clarity, insightfulness, fairness, resourcefulness, and timeliness. Applicants must be age 30 or younger.

The Victor Cohn Prize: Editors, colleagues, scientists and others familiar with the candidate's body of work may proffer nominations. Individuals may nominate themselves.

Rennie Taylor/Alton Blakeslee Fellowships: Journalists with two years of experience who wish to specialize in science writing will receive priority selection. Such applicants should be employed by daily newspapers, wire services, news magazines, radio stations, or television stations or networks. Students must have undergraduate degrees in science or journalism and prove to the satisfaction of a selection committee that they have the motivation and ability to pursue a career in science writing. Fellows may attend school full- or part-time.

Fellowships are not available to those who are pursuing or plan to pursue careers in public relations or public information work.

GEOG. RESTRICTIONS: United States.

FINANCIAL DATA:
Amount of support per award: Evert Clark/Seth Payne Award: $1,000 and expenses to attend ScienceWriters Conference; The Victor Cohn Prize: $3,000 and a framed certificate; Rennie Taylor/Alton Blakeslee Fellowships: $5,000.

NO. MOST RECENT APPLICANTS: Evert Clark/Seth Payne Award: 71; Rennie Taylor/Alton Blakeslee Fellowships: 29 for the year 2020.

NO. AWARDS: Evert Clark/Seth Payne Award and The Victor Cohn Prize: 1; Rennie Taylor/Alton Blakeslee Fellowships: 5 full fellowships.

APPLICATION INFO:
Applicants must apply on the CASW web site.
Duration: One academic year. Nonrenewable.
Deadline: Evert Clark/Seth Payne Award and The Victor Cohn Prize: June 30. Rennie Taylor/Alton Blakeslee Fellowships: March.

PUBLICATIONS:
Guide to Careers in Science Writing.

IRS I.D.: 13-1953314

OFFICERS AND DIRECTORS:
Robin Lloyd, President
Christie Aschwanden, Vice President
Richard Harris, Treasurer
Betsy Mason, Secretary
Rosalind Reid, Executive Director
Deborah Blum
Alan Boyle
William Kearney
Maggie Koerth
Celeste LeCompte
Thomas Lin
Tariq Malik
Debbie Ponchner
Cristine Russell
Ashley Smart
Kenneth P. Trevett
Dan Vergano

ADDRESS INQUIRIES TO:
Rosalind Reid, Executive Director
(See address above.)

*SPECIAL STIPULATIONS:
U.S. citizens only.

COUNCIL ON FOREIGN RELATIONS [1732]
58 East 68th Street
New York, NY 10065
(212) 434-9740
Fax: (212) 434-9870
E-mail: fellowships@cfr.org
Web Site: www.cfr.org/fellowships

FOUNDED: 1921

AREAS OF INTEREST:
International relations, international news, foreign policy, journalism, international journalism, war reporting, foreign affairs, international affairs, and international media.

NAME(S) OF PROGRAMS:
● **Edward R. Murrow Press Fellowship**

TYPE:
Fellowships. The Edward R. Murrow Press Fellowship seeks to promote the quality of responsible and discerning journalism that exemplified the work of Edward R. Murrow. One resident fellowship is awarded each year to a distinguished foreign correspondent or editor. The fellow spends 10 months full-time in residence at CFR's headquarters in New York. The program enables the fellow to engage in sustained analysis and writing, expand his or her intellectual and professional horizons, and participate in CFR's active program of meetings and events. The fellow is part of the David Rockefeller Studies Program, the CFR's think tank, alongside the program's full-time, adjunct, and visiting fellows, whose expertise extends across the broad range of significant foreign policy issues facing the U.S. and the international community.

YEAR PROGRAM STARTED: 1949

PURPOSE:
To promote the quality of responsible and discerning journalism that exemplified the work of Edward R. Murrow.

ELIGIBILITY:
The program is only open to applicants who have distinguished credentials in the field of journalism and who have covered international news as a working journalist for

COMMUNICATIONS601

print, broadcast or online media widely available in the U.S. Candidates must be U.S. citizens to be considered for the fellowship.

FINANCIAL DATA:
The Fellow is considered an independent contractor rather than an employee of CFR, and is not eligible for employment benefits, including health insurance.

Amount of support per award: A stipend of $75,000, as well as a modest travel grant.

CO-OP FUNDING PROGRAMS: CBS Foundation and Ford Foundation.

NO. AWARDS: 1 per year.

APPLICATION INFO:
Interested candidates who meet the program's eligibility requirements can apply online between January 1 and March 1 on an annual basis.

Duration: Nine months, beginning in September.

Deadline: March 1. Official selections and announcement will be made in April.

ADDRESS INQUIRIES TO:
See telephone or e-mail address above.

THE DOW JONES NEWS FUND [1733]
4300 Route One North
Monmouth Junction, NJ 08852
(609) 452-2820
Fax: (609) 520-5477
E-mail: djnf@dowjones.com
Web Site: dowjonesnewsfund.org

FOUNDED: 1958

AREAS OF INTEREST:
Journalism.

NAME(S) OF PROGRAMS:
• **Multimedia Training Academies**
• **Summer High School Journalism Workshops**
• **Summer Journalism Intern Programs**

TYPE:
Internships. Multimedia Training Academies for professors at historically Black colleges and universities and Hispanic-serving institutions.

Free week-long skills training boot camp, followed by paid Summer Journalism Intern Programs for college juniors, seniors and graduate students.

PURPOSE:
To encourage students to consider careers in journalism.

LEGAL BASIS:
Nonprofit foundation.

ELIGIBILITY:
Internships: Applicants must be juniors, seniors or graduate students at any college who have a sincere interest in professional newsroom work. Working on a school publication is not a stated requirement, but highly recommended. Applicants must also be U.S. citizens or have a working Visa permitting them to work in the U.S.

GEOG. RESTRICTIONS: United States.

FINANCIAL DATA:
Interns will receive regular wages (minimum $450 per week) from the news organizations for which they work. After the summer of work, a $1,500 scholarship check is awarded to interns returning to school or can be used towards federal student loans.

Amount of support per award: Program grants: $3,000 to $25,000; Scholarships: $1,500.

Total amount of support: Approximately $390,000.

NO. MOST RECENT APPLICANTS: 700.

NO. AWARDS: Internships and Scholarships: Up to 85; Multimedia Training Academies: 25 college faculty; Workshops: 150 participants.

APPLICATION INFO:
Internships: Applicants must submit a resume and complete a skills test and 500-word essay.

Duration: Internships: 10 to 12 weeks. Workshops and training programs: Five to 10 days. All programs occur during the summer.

Deadline: November 1.

OFFICERS:
Richard J. Levine, President
Paul Schmidt, Treasurer
Diana Mitsu Klos, Secretary

STAFF:
Shirley Carswell, Executive Director
Denise Jester, Finance and Administration Manager
Heather Taylor, Digital Media and Programs Manager

DIRECTORS:
LaSharah S. Bunting
Thomas E. Engleman
Gail Griffin
Garry D. Howard
Neal Lipschutz
Kamilah Mitchell-Thomas
Laurence G. O'Donnell
Dr. Reginald Owens
Karen Miller Pensiero
Anna Sedgley
Dr. Russell G. Todd

ADDRESS INQUIRIES TO:
Internship Coordinator
Intern Programs
(See address above.)

FUND FOR INVESTIGATIVE JOURNALISM [1734]
1110 Vermont Avenue, N.W.
Suite 500
Washington, DC 20005
(202) 378-0953
E-mail: fundfij@gmail.com
Web Site: www.fij.org

FOUNDED: 1969

AREAS OF INTEREST:
Promoting the work of investigative journalism.

TYPE:
Project/program grants. The Fund gives grants to investigative reporters working outside the protection and backing of major news organizations.

PURPOSE:
To provide funding for reporters engaged in investigative journalism.

ELIGIBILITY:
Projects on domestic issues are eligible. To be considered, foreign-based story proposals must come from U.S.-based reporters or have a strong U.S. angle involving American citizens, government or business. All stories must be published in English and have a media outlet in the U.S.

FINANCIAL DATA:
Amount of support per award: Up to $10,000.

Total amount of support: Varies.

APPLICATION INFO:
Applications are to be submitted online. Applicant must write a proposal letter outlining the story, what he or she expects to prove, how this will be done, and the type of sources for the proof. For projects, include the anticipated completion date.

The letter must be supported by a resume, a detailed budget to justify the size of the grant, no more than two writing samples or one sample chapter in the case of a book applicant, and a letter of commitment from an editor or publisher or an executive of a broadcast news operation or online news outlet stating that the project will be published or broadcast if completed according to the proposal.

A letter of commitment is required for all applicants and is a nonnegotiable requirement. In the case of individuals seeking grants for books, a signed copy of a contract with a publisher is required and should be substituted for the commitment letter.

Deadline: Varies.

ADDRESS INQUIRIES TO:
Eric Ferrero, Executive Director
(See address above.)

WILLIAM RANDOLPH HEARST FOUNDATION [1735]
90 New Montgomery Street, Suite 1212
San Francisco, CA 94105
(415) 908-4565
(800) 841-7048 ext. 4565
Fax: (415) 243-0760
E-mail: jwatten@hearstfdn.org
Web Site: www.hearstawards.org

FOUNDED: 1948

AREAS OF INTEREST:
Writing, photojournalism, broadcast journalism and multimedia.

NAME(S) OF PROGRAMS:
• **Hearst Journalism Awards Program**

TYPE:
Awards/prizes; Scholarships. Awards to the top 10 winners of 14 monthly competitions: five writing, two photojournalism, one radio news coverage, two television news coverage and four multimedia. Entrants must be journalism majors attending one of the 105 accredited schools of journalism. The schools receive a matching grant.

YEAR PROGRAM STARTED: 1960

PURPOSE:
To provide support, encouragement and assistance to education in journalism at the undergraduate college level.

LEGAL BASIS:
Nonprofit foundation.

ELIGIBILITY:
Participation in the program is open only to journalism majors who are undergraduates at the colleges and universities that are members of the Association of Schools of Journalism and Mass Communication.

GEOG. RESTRICTIONS: United States.

FINANCIAL DATA:
Amount of support per award: $3,000 to $10,000, depending upon placement of winners.

Total amount of support: Over $700,000 for the year 2020-21.

NO. MOST RECENT APPLICANTS: 1,400.

NO. AWARDS: 150 scholarships and grants.

APPLICATION INFO:
Full application information may be obtained through individual departments of journalism at participating schools. A list of accredited schools is available at Hearst Foundation's San Francisco address.
Duration: Varies.
Deadline: Monthly during academic year.

STAFF:
Dino Dinovitz, Executive Director
Jan C. Watten, Program Director
Yasi Haerizadeh, Deputy Program Director

BOARD OF DIRECTORS:
William R. Hearst, III, President
James Asher
Annissa Balson
David Barrett
Frank A. Bennack, Jr.
John G. Conomikes
Lisa Hagerman
George R. Hearst, Jr.
Gilbert C. Maurer
Mark Miller
Virginia Randt
Mitchell Scherzer
Steven Swartz

ADDRESS INQUIRIES TO:
Jan C. Watten, Program Director
(See address above.)

THE SIDNEY HILLMAN FOUNDATION, INC.   [1736]
330 West 42nd Street
Suite 900
New York, NY 10036
(646) 448-6413
E-mail: alex@hillmanfoundation.org
Web Site: www.hillmanfoundation.org

FOUNDED: 1950

AREAS OF INTEREST:
Civil liberties, civil rights, labor movement, social welfare, housing, economic security and international understanding.

NAME(S) OF PROGRAMS:
● **Hillman Prizes for Journalism**
● **Sidney Awards**

TYPE:
Awards/prizes. Monetary awards for outstanding contributions in the fields of daily or periodical journalism, nonfiction, radio and television, blogs and commentary.

YEAR PROGRAM STARTED: 1950

PURPOSE:
To recognize outstanding contributions to the field of journalism dealing with themes relating to the ideals which Sidney Hillman held throughout his life, including the protection of individual civil liberties, improved race relations, a strengthened labor movement, the advancement of social welfare, housing and economic security, greater world understanding and related problems.

LEGAL BASIS:
Private foundation.

ELIGIBILITY:
Only work published in English in the previous calendar year and distributed in the U.S. and Canada is eligible for consideration.

Radio and television contributions must have been produced under professional auspices in the previous calendar year.

GEOG. RESTRICTIONS: United States and Canada.

FINANCIAL DATA:
Amount of support per award: Hillman Prize: $5,000; Sidney Award: $500.

NO. MOST RECENT APPLICANTS: 600.

NO. AWARDS: Hillman Prizes: 7; Sidney Awards: 12.

APPLICATION INFO:
Nominations may be submitted by the author, editor or publication. The entry must be accompanied by a brief cover letter.
Deadline: Hillman Prizes: January 30. Sidney Awards: Last day of each month.

STAFF:
Alexandra Lescaze, Executive Director
Lindsay Beyerstein, Lead Writer

ADDRESS INQUIRIES TO:
Alexandra Lescaze, Executive Director
(See address above.)

INTER AMERICAN PRESS ASSOCIATION (IAPA)   [1737]
3511 N.W. 91st Avenue
Miami, FL 33172
(305) 987-3363
Fax: (305) 860-4264
E-mail: info@sipiapa.org
Web Site: www.sipiapa.org

FOUNDED: 1942

AREAS OF INTEREST:
Press freedom.

NAME(S) OF PROGRAMS:
● **IAPA Scholarship Fund**

TYPE:
Exchange programs; Fellowships; Scholarships. Scholarships for American and Canadian working journalists, journalism graduates or journalism students to study in Latin America and for journalists who are citizens or residents of countries outside the U.S. or Canada to study in the U.S. or Canada.

YEAR PROGRAM STARTED: 1954

PURPOSE:
To support the exchange of journalists and journalism students between countries of the Western Hemisphere.

LEGAL BASIS:
Nonprofit association, tax-exempt under Internal Revenue Code 501(c)(3).

ELIGIBILITY:
Applicants must be native to countries in North and South America or the Caribbean, reporters, editors or managers at newspapers, broadcasters or digital news media platforms, between the ages of 21 and 35 year old at the date of application, with mastery of the language of the program of study. Applicants from the U.S. and Canada must provide certification from a recognized authority of proficiency in Spanish or Portuguese for those going to Brazil. Latin American applicants must pass a TOEFL language exam.

FINANCIAL DATA:
Amount of support per award: Up to $20,000 plus reimbursement for round-trip airfare (economy class).

NO. MOST RECENT APPLICANTS: 95.

NO. AWARDS: 4.

APPLICATION INFO:
Application is available on the web site or by writing to the Association.
Duration: One academic year.
Deadline: January 31.

STAFF:
Ricardo Trotti, Executive Director
Emilio Sanchez, Coordinator of Scholarship Fund

ADDRESS INQUIRIES TO:
Emilio Sanchez
Coordinator of Scholarship Fund
(See address above.)

INTERNATIONAL DOCUMENTARY ASSOCIATION
3600 Wilshire Boulevard
Suite 1810
Los Angeles, CA 90010
(213) 232-1660
Fax: (213) 232-1669
E-mail: grants@documentary.org
Web Site: www.documentary.org

TYPE:
Awards/prizes; Internships. IDA Documentary Awards celebrate the best nonfiction films and programs of the year. Prize awarded in seven categories: feature, short, episodic series, curated series, short film series, limited series, and the David L. Wolper Student Documentary Award.

IDA/David L. Wolper Student Documentary Achievement Award recognizes exceptional achievement in nonfiction film and video production at the university level and brings greater public and industry awareness to the work of students in the documentary field.

The Pare Lorentz Award is awarded for films that reflect the spirit and tradition of Pare Lorentz's work. The film should demonstrate one or more of Lorentz's central concerns (the appropriate use of the natural environment, justice for all, and the illumination of pressing social problems) presented as a compelling story by skillful filmmaking.

Pare Lorentz Documentary Fund supports full-length documentary films that reflect the spirit and nature of Pare Lorentz's work, exhibiting objective research, artful storytelling, strong visual style, high production values, artistic writing and outstanding music composition, as well as skillful direction, camerawork and editing.

Los Angeles County Arts Commission Internships are offered to undergraduate students who currently reside or are enrolled in a college or university located in Los Angeles County, CA. Those interested should consult the Association web site for up-to-date details.

See entry 417 for full listing.

INVESTIGATIVE REPORTERS AND EDITORS   [1738]
141 Neff Annex
Missouri School of Journalism
Columbia, MO 65211
(573) 882-6668
Fax: (573) 882-5431
E-mail: rescntr@ire.org
Web Site: www.ire.org

FOUNDED: 1975

AREAS OF INTEREST:
Journalism across all media.

NAME(S) OF PROGRAMS:
- **Investigative Reporters and Editors Contest**

TYPE:
Awards/prizes; Fellowships. Investigative Reporters and Editors Contest is an annual investigative reporting contest. The Tom Renner Award (one of the 17 categories of this Contest) is given to the best investigative reporting in print, broadcast or book form, covering crime and its impact on society.

IRE also offers fellowships to minority journalism students and professionals to attend IRE national or regional conferences. There are also fellowships available for small newspaper staffers and for journalism students.

PURPOSE:
To promote high-quality, in-depth journalism.

LEGAL BASIS:
University.

ELIGIBILITY:
Individual journalists and news organizations may submit entries for the Renner Award. No more than 10 stories can be entered. Entries that disregard the rules will be disqualified. Qualifications for IRE minority fellowships include financial need, references and answers to essay questions.

FINANCIAL DATA:
Amount of support per award: Renner Award: $500; Student Award: $250.
Total amount of support: Varies.

NO. MOST RECENT APPLICANTS: 550.

NO. AWARDS: 17.

APPLICATION INFO:
All entry materials are entered online through the IRE Award contest platform. There is no limit on the number of entries allowed from individual journalists.
Deadline: Mid-January. Deadline for fellowships depends on conference dates.

PUBLICATIONS:
Program announcement; entry form.

IRS I.D.: 51-0166741

ADDRESS INQUIRIES TO:
Lauren Grandestaff, Contest Coordinator
(See address above.)

JOURNAL OF THE AMERICAN MEDICAL ASSOCIATION [1739]
330 North Wabash Avenue
Suite 39300
Chicago, IL 60611
(312) 464-4186
Fax: (312) 464-5824
E-mail: robert.golub@jamanetwork.org
fishbein@jamanetwork.org
Web Site: jamanetwork.org

FOUNDED: 1847

AREAS OF INTEREST:
Public health, physician and health care personnel education and medical publications.

NAME(S) OF PROGRAMS:
- **Morris Fishbein Fellowship in Medical Editing**

TYPE:
Fellowships. Award granted to physicians exclusively as a one-year, full-time editorial fellowship with *The Journal of the American Medical Association*. The successful candidate will work with the editorial and production staff in all facets of editing and publishing a major weekly medical journal. At the completion of the program, it is expected that the candidate will be proficient in all aspects of manuscript selection, peer review, issue makeup, copy editing and styling, issue planning and managing, in addition to the many other elements of medical journal publication.

YEAR PROGRAM STARTED: 1978

PURPOSE:
To provide physicians with an opportunity to learn the editorial functions of a major medical journal.

LEGAL BASIS:
Not-for-profit organization serving members in the medical profession.

ELIGIBILITY:
Applicants must be physicians. Candidates also must have proven writing ability at the time of application because they will be required during the course of the year to prepare articles for publication. Although the fellow will work under the supervision of a physician-editor, ability to work independently is a must. Ability to use a resource library is a strong plus.

Fellow must live in Chicago during the 12-month full-time fellowship (July to June).

FINANCIAL DATA:
Amount of support per award: $73,000.
Total amount of support: $73,000 annually.

NO. MOST RECENT APPLICANTS: 12.

NO. AWARDS: 1 annually.

APPLICATION INFO:
Application forms may be obtained from the address or e-mail listed above.
Duration: One year.
Deadline: Early January.

ADDRESS INQUIRIES TO:
Robert M. Golub, M.D., Deputy Editor
(See e-mail and address above.)

KAPPA TAU ALPHA [1740]
76 Gannett Hall
School of Journalism
University of Missouri
Columbia, MO 65211-1200
(573) 882-7685
E-mail: umcjourkta@missouri.edu
Web Site: www.kappataualpha.org

FOUNDED: 1910

AREAS OF INTEREST:
Journalism research and mass communication.

NAME(S) OF PROGRAMS:
- **Frank Luther Mott KTA Research/Book Award**

TYPE:
Awards/prizes. Annual award for a published book concerned with journalism and mass communications research.

YEAR PROGRAM STARTED: 1944

PURPOSE:
To recognize the top book published in the field of journalism and mass communications research; to promote interest in Kappa Tau Alpha among students and faculty.

LEGAL BASIS:
National society honoring scholarship in journalism and mass communication.

ELIGIBILITY:
Qualified individuals may apply for the award with an appropriate book published during the year.

FINANCIAL DATA:
Amount of support per award: $1,000 and a plaque.

NO. MOST RECENT APPLICANTS: 15 to 20 annually.

NO. AWARDS: 1 annually.

APPLICATION INFO:
Interested applicants should submit six copies of the published work to be considered.
Deadline: December 9.

OFFICERS:
Edward Carter, President
Bill Cassidy, Vice President
Beverly Horvit, Executive Director

JUDGES:
Edward Carter
Bill Cassidy
Beverly Horvit

ADDRESS INQUIRIES TO:
Beverly Horvit, Executive Director
(See address above.)

LIVINGSTON AWARDS [1741]
Wallace House, University of Michigan
620 Oxford Road
Ann Arbor, MI 48104
(734) 998-7575
Fax: (734) 998-7979
E-mail: livawards@umich.edu
Web Site: wallacehouse.umich.edu/livingston-awards

FOUNDED: 1981

AREAS OF INTEREST:
Broadcast, print and online journalism.

NAME(S) OF PROGRAMS:
- **Livingston Awards for Young Journalists**

TYPE:
Awards/prizes; Challenge/matching grants; Endowments.

YEAR PROGRAM STARTED: 1981

PURPOSE:
To recognize the best young journalists; to support the work of young journalists; to create modern role models for the next generation of news consumers; to advance excellence in journalism.

LEGAL BASIS:
Foundation.

ELIGIBILITY:
The Livingston Awards recognize the best journalists under the age of 35 with prizes for local, national and international reporting. Open to all forms of journalism - text, video, audio, data visualization and multi-media - entries must consist of materials prepared in the ordinary course of the journalist's professional production. One entry per individual. Individuals may apply on their own, or be entered by their organization.

Multiple bylines are eligible, but all must meet age criteria. Materials prepared by journalists specifically for submission to the Livingston Awards will not qualify and may not be considered. Student media are not eligible.

All entries will be judged on the basis of either a single piece, or in the case of series, a maximum of three related pieces.

FINANCIAL DATA:
Amount of support per award: $10,000.
Total amount of support: $30,000.

NO. AWARDS: 3.

APPLICATION INFO:
Detailed information is available online.
Deadline: February 1. Announcement in June.

PUBLICATIONS:
Program brochure.

STAFF:
Melissa Riley, Program Manager

ADDRESS INQUIRIES TO:
See e-mail address above.

THE GERALD LOEB AWARDS   [1742]
UCLA Anderson School of Management
110 Westwood Plaza
Gold Hall, Suite B307
Los Angeles, CA 90095-1481
(310) 825-4478
Fax: (310) 825-4479
E-mail: loeb@anderson.ucla.edu
Web Site: www.anderson.ucla.edu/gerald-loeb-awards

FOUNDED: 1957

AREAS OF INTEREST:
Business, economic and financial news writing and journalism.

TYPE:
Awards/prizes. Awards to recognize business and financial journalists for important contributions to the understanding of business, finance and the economy.

YEAR PROGRAM STARTED: 1957

PURPOSE:
To recognize journalists who make significant contributions to the understanding of business and finance.

LEGAL BASIS:
University.

ELIGIBILITY:
Entries submitted must have been published or broadcast for the first time during the previous calendar year in the U.S.

FINANCIAL DATA:
Amount of support per award: $2,000; $500 Honorable Mention.

APPLICATION INFO:
Guidelines are available on the web site. Application must be submitted online.
Deadline: February 13.

PUBLICATIONS:
Entry brochure.

ADDRESS INQUIRIES TO:
Jonathan Daillak, Executive Director
(See address above.)

MASSACHUSETTS INSTITUTE OF TECHNOLOGY   [1743]
77 Massachusetts Avenue
E19-623
Cambridge, MA 02139
(617) 452-3513
E-mail: knight-info@mit.edu
Web Site: ksj.mit.edu

AREAS OF INTEREST:
Science journalism.

NAME(S) OF PROGRAMS:
● **Knight Science Journalism Fellowship**

TYPE:
Fellowships. Access to courses, laboratories and researchers for 10 months.

YEAR PROGRAM STARTED: 1983

PURPOSE:
To recognize excellence in explaining science, medicine, technology and the environment to the public; to provide a deeper familiarity with the processes of research and development to widen the fellows' acquaintance with leading engineers, scientists and medical researchers experienced in explaining complex issues.

LEGAL BASIS:
University.

ELIGIBILITY:
Applicants must be full-time journalists, whether they are on staff or freelance. They must have at least three years of full-time experience covering science, technology, medicine or environment. Candidates may be reporters, writers, editors, producers, illustrators, filmmakers or photojournalists. They may work for newspapers, magazines, television, radio, the Web or other media. Journalists from all countries are eligible to apply.

FINANCIAL DATA:
Fellowship includes stipend. During their residence, fellows receive MIT affiliate and extended health plan for individuals, spouses and families.
Amount of support per award: $70,000 plus $2,500 housing stipend.

CO-OP FUNDING PROGRAMS: Sponsored by the John S. and James L. Knight Foundation.

NO. AWARDS: 10 annually.

APPLICATION INFO:
Online submission only.
Duration: Nine months, August to May.
Deadline: January 15. Interviews will begin in March with public announcement in April.

ADDRESS INQUIRIES TO:
Bettina Urcuioli
Program Administrator
Tel: (617) 452-3513
E-mail: bma@mit.edu

NATIONAL ASSOCIATION OF FARM BROADCASTERS FOUNDATION   [1744]
1100 Platte Falls Road
Platte City, MO 64079
(816) 431-4032
Fax: (816) 431-4087
E-mail: susan@nafb.com
Web Site: www.nafbfoundation.com

AREAS OF INTEREST:
Agricultural journalism and communications.

NAME(S) OF PROGRAMS:
● **Glenn Kummerow Memorial Scholarship**
● **The George Logan Scholarship**
● **Orion Samuelson Scholarship**

TYPE:
Scholarships. Since 1977, the NAFB Foundation has provided financial support and educational opportunities in the form of college scholarships to assist students in pursuit of careers in agricultural communications. These scholarships are recognized at the National NAFB Convention.

YEAR PROGRAM STARTED: 1975

PURPOSE:
To provide financial support and educational opportunities for students in pursuit of careers in agricultural communications.

ELIGIBILITY:
Must be at least junior-year college students, enrolled in an agricultural journalism/agricultural communications curriculum, or plan to transfer to a university which offers a designated professional program of study in agricultural radio-television broadcasting. Selection is by application and is based on agricultural communications aptitude and leadership achievements, academic record and career plans.

FINANCIAL DATA:
Winners receive an expense-paid trip to attend the convention as part of the award.
Amount of support per award: $7,500 per scholarship.
Total amount of support: $30,110 for the year 2020.

NO. AWARDS: 4 for the year 2020.

APPLICATION INFO:
Applications are available in April on the Foundation web site.
Duration: One academic year.
Deadline: June 11.

ADDRESS INQUIRIES TO:
NAFB Member Services Manager
(See address above.)

NATIONAL ASSOCIATION OF HISPANIC JOURNALISTS
1050 Connecticut Avenue, N.W.
5th Floor
Washington, DC 20036
(202) 853-7760
(202) 909-6880
E-mail: nahj@nahj.org
lafrank@nahj.org
Web Site: nahj.org

TYPE:
Awards/prizes; Conferences/seminars; Fellowships; General operating grants; Internships; Matching gifts; Project/program grants; Research grants; Scholarships; Seed money grants; Training grants; Travel grants.
See entry 909 for full listing.

NATIONAL ASSOCIATION OF SCIENCE WRITERS, INC.   [1745]
P.O. Box 7905
Berkeley, CA 94707
(510) 859-7229
E-mail: director@nasw.org
Web Site: www.nasw.org

FOUNDED: 1934

AREAS OF INTEREST:
Dissemination of scientific and medical information to a general lay audience and professional development for science writers.

NAME(S) OF PROGRAMS:
• **Science in Society Awards**

TYPE:
Conferences/seminars; Fellowships; Project/program grants; Seed money grants; Training grants; Travel grants. Separate monetary prizes and awards for writers in five categories:
(1) books;
(2) commentary or opinion;
(3) science reporting (short, medium or long);
(4) science reporting for a local or regional market and;
(5) science reporting series.

YEAR PROGRAM STARTED: 1972

PURPOSE:
To recognize investigative or interpretive reporting about the sciences and their impact on society.

LEGAL BASIS:
Professional membership organization.

ELIGIBILITY:
Any writer (or team) is eligible to submit not more than one entry in each category. Material may be single article or broadcast or a series. Books with a copyright date of 2021 are eligible. Works must be written or spoken, in English, intended for the layperson and published or broadcast in North America between January 1, 2021 and December 31, 2021.

GEOG. RESTRICTIONS: North America.

FINANCIAL DATA:
Amount of support per award: $2,000 and Certificates of Recognition in each category.
Total amount of support: $14,000.

NO. MOST RECENT APPLICANTS: 360.

NO. AWARDS: 7 annually.

APPLICATION INFO:
Details are available online.
Deadline: February 1.

ADDRESS INQUIRIES TO:
Tinsley Davis, Executive Director
(See address above.)

NATIONAL ASSOCIATION OF SCIENCE WRITERS, INC. [1746]
P.O. Box 7905
Berkeley, CA 94707
(510) 859-7229
E-mail: director@nasw.org
Web Site: www.nasw.org

FOUNDED: 1934

AREAS OF INTEREST:
Dissemination of scientific and medical information to a general audience and professional development for science writers.

NAME(S) OF PROGRAMS:
• **NASW Idea Grants**

TYPE:
Project/program grants. Grants to support projects or programs designed to help science writers in their professional lives and/or benefit the field of science writing.

YEAR PROGRAM STARTED: 2010

PURPOSE:
To award the creativity and initiative of science writers; to create projects and programs that benefit the field and the writers in it.

LEGAL BASIS:
Professional membership organization.

ELIGIBILITY:
Individuals or groups are eligible to apply. Proposals can serve non-members, as well as members. Creative thinking is encouraged.

GEOG. RESTRICTIONS: North America.

FINANCIAL DATA:
Amount of support per award: $1,000 to $20,000.
Total amount of support: Varies.

NO. AWARDS: 3 to 5.

APPLICATION INFO:
Details are available online.
Deadline: Varies.

ADDRESS INQUIRIES TO:
Tinsley Davis, Executive Director
(See address above.)

NATIONAL ASSOCIATION OF SCIENCE WRITERS, INC. [1747]
P.O. Box 7905
Berkeley, CA 94707
(510) 859-7229
E-mail: director@nasw.org
Web Site: www.nasw.org

FOUNDED: 1934

AREAS OF INTEREST:
Dissemination of scientific and medical information to a general lay audience and professional development for science writers.

NAME(S) OF PROGRAMS:
• **Excellence in Institutional Writing Awards**

TYPE:
Awards/prizes. Monetary prizes and awards for writers in two categories:
(1) Short form and;
(2) Long form.

YEAR PROGRAM STARTED: 2018

PURPOSE:
To recognize high-caliber, publicly accessible science writing produced on behalf of an institution or other non-media organization.

LEGAL BASIS:
Professional membership organization.

ELIGIBILITY:
Material must be published or broadcast in January to December preceding the deadline.

FINANCIAL DATA:
Amount of support per award: $2,000 and Certificates of Recognition in each category.
Total amount of support: $4,000.

NO. MOST RECENT APPLICANTS: Over 200.

NO. AWARDS: 2 annually.

APPLICATION INFO:
Details are available online December 1.
Deadline: February 1.

ADDRESS INQUIRIES TO:
Tinsley Davis, Executive Director
(See address above.)

NATIONAL ENDOWMENT FOR THE HUMANITIES [1748]
The Constitution Center
400 7th Street, S.W.
Washington, DC 20506
(202) 606-8269
Fax: (202) 606-8557
E-mail: publicpgms@neh.gov
Web Site: www.neh.gov

FOUNDED: 1965

AREAS OF INTEREST:
Scholarship, research, education and public programs in the humanities. In the act that established the Endowment, the term humanities includes, but is not limited to, the study of history, philosophy, languages, linguistics, literature, archaeology, jurisprudence, the history, theory and criticism of the arts, ethics, comparative religion and those aspects of the social sciences that employ historical or philosophical approaches.

NAME(S) OF PROGRAMS:
• **Public Humanities Projects**

TYPE:
Project/program grants. Public Humanities Projects grants support projects that bring the ideas and insights of the humanities to life for general audiences. Projects must engage humanities scholarship to illuminate significant themes in disciplines such as history, literature, ethics and art, or to address challenging issues in contemporary life. NEH encourages projects that involve members of the public in collaboration with humanities scholars or that invite contributions from the community in the development and delivery of humanities programming. The grant program supports a variety of forms of audience engagement: Community Conversations: This format supports one- to three-year-long series of community-wide public discussions in which diverse residents creatively address community challenges, guided by the perspectives of the humanities; Exhibitions: This format supports permanent exhibitions that will be on view for at least three years, or traveling exhibitions that will be available to public audiences in at least two venues in the U.S. (including the originating location) and; Historic Places: This format supports the interpretation of historic sites, houses, neighborhoods and regions, which might include living history presentations, guided tours, exhibitions and public programs.

YEAR PROGRAM STARTED: 1969

PURPOSE:
To create an understanding and appreciation of the humanities among the general public.

LEGAL BASIS:
The National Foundation on the Arts and Humanities Act of 1965, Public Law 89-209, as amended.

ELIGIBILITY:
Any U.S. nonprofit organization with IRS tax-exempt status is eligible, as are state and local governmental agencies and federally recognized Indian tribal governments.

GEOG. RESTRICTIONS: United States.

FINANCIAL DATA:
Amount of support per award: Planning: Mostly up to $40,000, with a maximum of $75,000 for complex projects that will reach large national audiences. Implementation: Typically up to $400,000 ($460,000 for

projects requesting a Position in Public Humanities); up to $1,000,000 for Chairman's Special Awards.

Total amount of support: Varies.

NO. MOST RECENT APPLICANTS: Average 99.

NO. AWARDS: Average 16.

APPLICATION INFO:
All applications must be submitted via Grants.gov. Applications should follow the parameters set out in one of the three formats listed above. Details are provided on the NEH web site.
Duration: Varies.
Deadline: August. NEH strongly recommends that applicant complete or verify one's Grants.gov registration at least six weeks before the application deadline, as it takes time to process one's registration.

PUBLICATIONS:
Annual report; *Grant Programs*; *Humanities Magazine*.

IRS I.D.: 52-1098584

ADDRESS INQUIRIES TO:
Division of Public Programs
(See telephone or e-mail address above.)

NATIONAL INSTITUTE FOR LABOR RELATIONS RESEARCH [1749]

5211 Port Royal Road
Suite 510
Springfield, VA 22151
(703) 321-9606
(703) 770-2247
Fax: (703) 321-0676
E-mail: CLJ@nrtw.org
Web Site: www.nilrr.org

FOUNDED: 1985

AREAS OF INTEREST:
Research and analysis exposing the economic and social inequities of compulsory unionism.

NAME(S) OF PROGRAMS:
● The William B. Ruggles Journalist Scholarship

TYPE:
Scholarships. Unrestricted scholarship awarded annually to the student who exemplifies the dedication to principle and high journalistic standards of the late William B. Ruggles, the well-known and respected Texas journalist who contributed significantly to the Right to Work movement.

YEAR PROGRAM STARTED: 1974

PURPOSE:
To honor the late William B. Ruggles, former editorial page editor of *The Dallas Morning News*.

LEGAL BASIS:
Nonpartisan coalition of citizens.

ELIGIBILITY:
Applicants are limited to graduate or undergraduate students majoring in journalism or other related majors (communications, multimedia, film, etc.) in institutions of higher learning throughout the U.S. Foreign students are eligible, as long as they are attending an institution of higher learning in the U.S. Graduating high school seniors may apply, if accepted to a journalism or communications school. To be considered, applicants must demonstrate the potential for a successful completion of

educational requirements in an accredited journalism program and an understanding of voluntarism and of the problems of compulsory unionism.

GEOG. RESTRICTIONS: United States.

FINANCIAL DATA:
Amount of support per award: $2,000.
Total amount of support: $2,000 each year.

NO. MOST RECENT APPLICANTS: 50.

NO. AWARDS: 1 annually.

APPLICATION INFO:
A total application will consist of a completed formal application form, available from the address above, an official grade transcript from essay finalists and a typewritten essay of approximately 500 words clearly demonstrating an interest in and a knowledge of the Right to Work principle. Application may be submitted electronically or by mail. Online applications are encouraged.
Deadline: Postmark by January 31.

ADDRESS INQUIRIES TO:
Cathy Jones, Scholarship Administrator
(See address above.)

NATIONAL PRESS FOUNDATION [1750]

1211 Connecticut Avenue, N.W.
Suite 310
Washington, DC 20036
(202) 663-7280
E-mail: jenny@nationalpress.org
Web Site: nationalpress.org

AREAS OF INTEREST:
Journalism.

NAME(S) OF PROGRAMS:
● **Clifford K. and James T. Berryman Award for Editorial Cartoons**
● **Benjamin C. Bradlee Editor of the Year Award**
● **Chairman's Citation**
● **Everett McKinley Dirksen Award for Distinguished Reporting of Congress**
● **The Feddie Reporting Award**
● **Hinrich Foundation Award for Distinguished Reporting on Trade**
● **Innovative Storytelling Award**
● **W.M. Kiplinger Distinguished Contributions to Journalism Award**
● **Carolyn C. Mattingly Award for Mental Health Reporting**
● **Sol Taishoff Award for Excellence in Broadcast Journalism**
● **Technology in Journalism Award**

TYPE:
Awards/prizes; Fellowships. International programs. Each year, the National Press Foundation recognizes the best in American Journalism across 11 award categories.

Benjamin C. Bradlee Editor of the Year Award recognizes significant achievements that enhance the quality of journalism in the U.S.

Chairman's Citation, selected at the sole discretion of the NPF chairman, confers recognition on individuals whose accomplishments fall outside the traditional categories of excellence.

Everett McKinley Dirksen Award for Distinguished Reporting of Congress is intended to recognize U.S.-based journalists whose work shows thoughtful appraisal and

insight into the workings of the U.S. Congress and represents the highest standards of journalism.

The Feddie Reporting Award recognizes outstanding reporting about the impact of federal laws and regulations on local communities.

The Hinrich Foundation Award recognizes exemplary journalism that illuminates and advances the public's understanding of international business and trade.

The Innovative Storytelling Award recognizes digital journalism of the highest quality that re-invents the way stories are told to present a compelling audience experience.

W.M. Kiplinger Distinguished Contributions to Journalism Award honors persons who have, through their vision and leadership, strengthened American journalism and furthered the efforts to establish the highest qualify of American journalism.
Carolyn C. Mattingly Award for Mental Health Reporting recognized exemplary journalism that illuminates and advances the understanding of mental health issues and treatments for the illness.

Sol Taishoff Award for Excellence in Broadcast Journalism is awarded to a U.S.-based broadcaster for a body of quality work in video or audio journalism that represents the highest standards of journalism. This award may recognize an individual's accomplishment in field reporting, producing, writing or work at the anchor desk.

Technology in Journalism Award recognizes individuals or organizations that develop, adapt or creatively apply specific tools or technologies in the gathering and reporting of impactful journalism of the highest quality.

PURPOSE:
To help journalists better understand the issues about which they write and broadcast.

ELIGIBILITY:
Clifford K. and James T. Berryman Award for Editorial Cartoons is open to U.S.-based editorial cartoonists for work that exhibits power to influence public opinion, plus good drawing and striking effect.

Benjamin C. Bradlee Editor of the Year Award is open to any U.S.-based editor at any level of a news organization. It recognizes imagination, professional skill, ethics and an ability to motivate staff.

The Feddie Reporting Award is open to any U.S.-based journalist whose work represents the highest standards of journalism.

The Hinrich Award is open to any professional journalist whose work exemplifies the highest standards of journalism and is published by a reputable news organization. This includes print, broadcast and digital journalists.

Innovative Storytelling Award is open to any U.S. journalist or U.S. news organization. Judges will take into consideration the originality of the nominated presentation, and how re-imagined delivery vehicles enhanced the audience's understanding of the underlying journalism.

Technology in Journalism Award is open to anyone at a U.S. news organization. A vendor or technology partner may apply if submitted jointly with a news organization. Judges will take into consideration the originality of the nominated tool or technology, its criticality to shaping the story, and how it is used within larger journalistic efforts.

FINANCIAL DATA:
Amount of support per award: Berryman and Kiplinger Awards: $2,500; Bradlee, Dirksen, Feddie, Innnovative Storytelling, Taishoff and Technology in Journalism Awards: $5,000; Chairman's Citation: $1,000; Hinrich Award and Mattingly Award: $10,000.
Total amount of support: $55,000 in cash prizes.

NO. AWARDS: 1 per award category.

APPLICATION INFO:
Application information is available on the Foundation's web site.

STAFF:
Sonni Efron, President
Jason Zaragoza, Director of Operations

NEW YORK STATE SENATE
Legislative Office Building, Suite 1426
Albany, NY 12247
(518) 455-2611
Fax: (518) 426-6827
E-mail: students@nysenate.gov
Web Site: www.nysenate.gov/student-programs

TYPE:
Fellowships. These fellowships are intended for the graduate/postgraduate level. Stipends are for bipartisan opportunities to train in government while on-site in Albany, NY. Fellows spend almost a year immersed in the work of the Senate, learning techniques associated with policymaking and legislative process. Placement is usually in the office of an elected Senate member. The Senate Legislative Fellows Program, Biggane Fellowship, Roth Journalism Fellowship and Wiebe Public Service Fellowship constitute the Senate Graduate/Post-Graduate Fellowships.

See entry 1801 for full listing.

NIEMAN FOUNDATION FOR JOURNALISM AT HARVARD   [1751]
Walter Lippmann House
One Francis Avenue
Cambridge, MA 02138
(617) 495-2238
E-mail: nieman_applications@harvard.edu
Web Site: www.nieman.harvard.edu

FOUNDED: 1938

AREAS OF INTEREST:
Journalism.

NAME(S) OF PROGRAMS:
● **Nieman Fellowships in Journalism**

TYPE:
Fellowships. Provides journalists with the opportunity to spend a year of study at Harvard University. Awards are for U.S. and international journalists.

The Foundation also offers short-term Knight Visiting Nieman Fellowships to journalists and other professionals working on projects to advance journalism. Contact the Foundation for further details.

YEAR PROGRAM STARTED: 1938

PURPOSE:
To provide an opportunity for journalists to deepen their knowledge in a field of

specialty, broaden their knowledge in several areas, or prepare for a new journalistic assignment.

LEGAL BASIS:
A foundation of Harvard University.

ELIGIBILITY:
Print, broadcast and online reporters, editors, photographers, producers, editorial writers, columnists, filmmakers and cartoonists with at least five years of full-time, professional experience in the news media are invited to apply.

During the two years prior to applying, an applicant should not have participated in a fellowship or taken a leave of absence from work that lasted for four months or longer. There are no age limits or academic prerequisites, and a college degree is not required.

All prospective fellows must speak, read and write English fluently.

FINANCIAL DATA:
Nieman Fellows receive a stipend plus housing, child care and health insurance allowance, if applicable.
Amount of support per award: $75,000 stipend.

NO. AWARDS: Approximately 24 annually (around 12 to journalists from the U.S. and around 12 to journalists from other countries).

APPLICATION INFO:
Contact the Foundation.
Duration: Nine months.
Deadline: U.S. applications due January 31 for the academic year beginning in August. International applications are due December 1 for the academic year beginning the following August.

PUBLICATIONS:
Nieman Reports.

STAFF:
Nicole Arias, Fellowship Administrator

ADDRESS INQUIRIES TO:
Nicole Arias, Fellowship Administrator
(See address above.)

NIEMAN FOUNDATION FOR JOURNALISM AT HARVARD   [1752]
Walter Lippmann House
One Francis Avenue
Cambridge, MA 02138
(617) 496-6333
Fax: (617) 495-8976
E-mail: christine_kaye@harvard.edu
Web Site: www.nieman.harvard.edu

FOUNDED: 1938

AREAS OF INTEREST:
Journalism.

NAME(S) OF PROGRAMS:
● **Taylor Family Award for Fairness in Journalism**

TYPE:
Awards/prizes. Established through gifts for an endowment by members of the Taylor family, which published *The Boston Globe* from 1872 to 1999.

YEAR PROGRAM STARTED: 2001

PURPOSE:
To encourage fairness in news coverage by America's journalists and news organizations.

ELIGIBILITY:
Nominations are for a single article, editorial, commentary, photograph, or a series of stories, photographs, editorials, commentaries, or a body of work by an individual journalist. The work must have been published in a U.S. newspaper or magazine or on the newspaper or magazine's web site during the previous calendar year.

GEOG. RESTRICTIONS: United States.

FINANCIAL DATA:
Amount of support per award: $10,000, plus two $1,000 finalist awards.
Total amount of support: $12,000.

APPLICATION INFO:
All entries must be submitted online using the Foundation's online application form.
Deadline: Date will be posted on the Foundation web site.

ADDRESS INQUIRIES TO:
Christine Kaye, Event Manager
(See address above.)

NIEMAN FOUNDATION FOR JOURNALISM AT HARVARD   [1753]
Walter Lippmann House
One Francis Avenue
Cambridge, MA 02138
(617) 496-6333
Fax: (617) 495-8976
E-mail: christine_kaye@harvard.edu
Web Site: nieman.harvard.edu

FOUNDED: 1938

AREAS OF INTEREST:
Journalism and investigative reporting.

NAME(S) OF PROGRAMS:
● **Worth Bingham Prize for Investigative Journalism**

TYPE:
Awards/prizes. Honors investigative reporting of stories of national significance where the public interest is being ill-served. These stories may involve state, local or national government, lobbyists or the press itself wherever there exists an "atmosphere of easy tolerance" that journalist Worth Bingham himself once described in his reporting on the nation's capital. The investigative reporting may cover actual violations of the law, rule or code; lax or ineffective administration or enforcement; or activities which create conflicts of interest, entail excessive secrecy or otherwise raise questions of propriety.

YEAR PROGRAM STARTED: 1967

PURPOSE:
To honor exceptional investigative reporting of stories of national significance where the public interest is being ill-served.

ELIGIBILITY:
All submissions must have been published in a U.S. newspaper or magazine or on the newspaper or magazine's web site during the calendar year. Web-based news organizations that follow a strict code of journalistic ethics and publish original reporting on a regular basis may also submit entries. No broadcast-only entries are allowed.

Entries may include a single story, a related series of stories, or up to three unrelated stories. Columns and editorials are eligible. Individuals are encouraged to submit their own entries. In the case of a series, at least half the individual stories must have been published during the contest year.

Winners in any one year will be eligible for future awards without restriction.

GEOG. RESTRICTIONS: United States.

FINANCIAL DATA:
Amount of support per award: $20,000 annually.

NO. AWARDS: 1.

APPLICATION INFO:
Application must be made online. All entries must be accompanied by a $50 entry fee, payable online.

ADDRESS INQUIRIES TO:
Christine Kaye, Award Coordinator
(See address above.)

THE ALICIA PATTERSON FOUNDATION [1754]
1100 Vermont Avenue, N.W.
Suite 900
Washington, DC 20005
(202) 393-5995
Fax: (301) 951-8512
E-mail: info@aliciapatterson.org
Web Site: www.aliciapatterson.org

FOUNDED: 1961

AREAS OF INTEREST:
Journalism.

NAME(S) OF PROGRAMS:
● **Fellowship Program for Journalists**

TYPE:
Fellowships. Awarded to working print journalists for six months or one year of travel and inquiry. On leave from their normal writing, editing or photographing duties, Fellows examine their chosen subjects (areas or problems of significant interest, foreign or domestic) and write quarterly articles for the *APF Reporter*. These articles may be reprinted.

YEAR PROGRAM STARTED: 1965

PURPOSE:
To foster, promote, sustain and improve the best traditions of American journalism; to provide a few talented and promising American journalists with the opportunity to pursue independent projects.

LEGAL BASIS:
Section 501(c)(3) of the IRS Code and Not For Profits Corporation Law: New York State.

ELIGIBILITY:
The program is open to U.S. citizens who are full-time print journalists or to non-U.S. citizens who work full-time for U.S. print publication, either in America or abroad.

FINANCIAL DATA:
Amount of support per award: $20,000 stipend for six months or $40,000 stipend for the year.
Total amount of support: Varies.

NO. MOST RECENT APPLICANTS: Varies.

NO. AWARDS: 7 to 10 per year.

APPLICATION INFO:
Application forms are available in June. Information may be requested from the address above throughout the year.

Duration: Fellowships support a one-year or six-month leave of absence. The fellowship typically begins within the first three months of the calendar year.
Deadline: October 1 (postmark).

PUBLICATIONS:
APF Reporter, quarterly online magazine.

IRS I.D.: 13-6092124

ADDRESS INQUIRIES TO:
Margaret Engel, Executive Director
(See address above.)

THE PRESS CLUB OF ST. LOUIS CHARITABLE FUND - ST. LOUIS PRESS CLUB
c/o The Press Club of St. Louis
P.O. Box 410522
Creve Couer, MO 63141
(314) 449-8029
Fax: (314) 317-0031
E-mail: info@stlpressclub.org
Web Site: stlpressclub.org

TYPE:
Capital grants; Fellowships; Internships; Project/program grants; Scholarships.

See entry 1567 for full listing.

PULLIAM JOURNALISM FELLOWSHIP [1755]
Indiana Star
130 South Meridian Street
Indianapolis, IN 46225
(317) 213-9830
E-mail: russell.pulliam@indystar.com
Web Site: www.indystar.com/pjf

FOUNDED: 1974

AREAS OF INTEREST:
Journalism awards.

TYPE:
Fellowships. Newswriting internship program at *The Indianapolis Star* and *The Arizona Republic*, which are owned by Gannett Co.

YEAR PROGRAM STARTED: 1974

PURPOSE:
To offer on-the-job experience, plus seminars and writing criticism, to college students seriously pursuing a newspaper journalism career.

LEGAL BASIS:
Corporate-sponsored.

ELIGIBILITY:
Applicants are generally college journalism majors or liberal arts majors with part-time newspaper experience, outstanding character references, proven writing ability and a solid academic record.

GEOG. RESTRICTIONS: United States.

FINANCIAL DATA:
Amount of support per award: $6,500 ($650 per week for 10-week program).

NO. MOST RECENT APPLICANTS: 200.

NO. AWARDS: 25.

APPLICATION INFO:
Brochures are available from the address above. View the instructions and download the application at the web site.
Duration: 10 weeks, June to August. No renewals.
Deadline: November 1 (postmark).

PUBLICATIONS:
Brochure.

ADDRESS INQUIRIES TO:
Russ Pulliam, Director
(See address above.)

QUILL AND SCROLL FOUNDATION [1756]
School of Journalism and Mass Communication
The University of Iowa
100 Adler Journalism Building, Room W111
Iowa City, IA 52242-2004
(319) 335-3457
(319) 335-3321
E-mail: quill-scroll@uiowa.edu
Web Site: www.quillandscroll.org

FOUNDED: 1926

AREAS OF INTEREST:
Journalism, high school media, media law and ethics, and scholastic journalism education.

CONSULTING OR VOLUNTEER SERVICES:
Coordinate judging of K-12 writing, journalism and media contests.

TYPE:
Scholarships; Training grants.

YEAR PROGRAM STARTED: 1964

PURPOSE:
To improve the quality of secondary school journalism.

LEGAL BASIS:
Nonprofit special-interest foundation.

ELIGIBILITY:
Qualified scholars or educational departments with appropriate interests are eligible to apply.

GEOG. RESTRICTIONS: Primarily United States.

FINANCIAL DATA:
Amount of support per award: $500 to $1,500.
Total amount of support: $2,500 for the year 2020.

NO. MOST RECENT APPLICANTS: More than 100.

NO. AWARDS: 4 for the year 2020.

APPLICATION INFO:
Applications are available online.
Duration: One-time award.
Deadline: Students: May 10; Teachers: April 15.

PUBLICATIONS:
Application guidelines.

IRS I.D.: 42-0795095

TRUSTEES:
Richard P. Johns, Chairperson
Yuxing Zheng, Vice Chairperson
William Casey
Erica Hernandez
John Humenik
Patrick Johnson
Jack Kennedy
Anthony Whitten
Jessica Young

OFFICER:
Jeff Browne, Executive Director

ADDRESS INQUIRIES TO:
Jeff Browne, Executive Director
(See address above.)

RADIO TELEVISION DIGITAL NEWS ASSOCIATION FOUNDATION [1757]

The National Press Building
529 14th Street, N.W., Suite 1240
Washington, DC 20045
(202) 662-7254
E-mail: katem@rtdna.org
Web Site: www.rtdna.org

FOUNDED: 1946

AREAS OF INTEREST:
Electronic journalism.

NAME(S) OF PROGRAMS:
● **N.S. Biestock Fellowship**
● **Ed Bradley Scholarship**
● **Michele Clark Fellowship**
● **George Foreman Tribute to Lyndon B. Johnson**
● **Bob Horner Scholarship**
● **Jacque I. Minnotte Fellowship**
● **Vada and Barney Oldfield Fellowship for National Security Reporting**
● **Lou and Carole Prato Sports Reporting Scholarship**
● **The President's Scholarships**
● **Mike Reynolds Journalism Scholarship**
● **Carole Simpson Scholarship**
● **Lee Thornton Scholarship**
● **Pete Wilson Scholarship**

TYPE:
Fellowships; Scholarships. Scholarship awards for one year of undergraduate and/or graduate study in broadcast journalism.

YEAR PROGRAM STARTED: 1967

PURPOSE:
To aid in advanced learning of electronic journalism.

LEGAL BASIS:
Incorporated.

ELIGIBILITY:
For scholarships, applicants must be officially enrolled in college and have at least one full academic year remaining, must be a fully enrolled college sophomore or higher, may apply for only one scholarship, and may be enrolled in any major so long as their career intent is television or radio news. Fellowships are available to young professionals with fewer than 10 years in the field. U.S. citizens and international applicants are eligible.

International applicants must have a U.S. Taxpayer ID Number (TIN).

FINANCIAL DATA:
Amount of support per award: Scholarships: $1,000 to $10,000; Fellowships: $1,000 and $2,500.

NO. MOST RECENT APPLICANTS: 250.

NO. AWARDS: Undergraduate: 10; Fellowships: 4.

APPLICATION INFO:
Application must be submitted online.
Duration: Scholarships: One year.
Deadline: Varies.

PUBLICATIONS:
Annual report.

IRS I.D.: 38-1860090

ADDRESS INQUIRIES TO:
Kate McGarrity, Program and Award Manager
(See address above.)

REPORTERS COMMITTEE FOR FREEDOM OF THE PRESS [1758]

1156 15th Street, N.W.
Suite 1020
Washington, DC 20005
(202) 795-9306
Fax: (202) 795-9310
E-mail: kpoole@rcfp.org
Web Site: www.rcfp.org

FOUNDED: 1970

AREAS OF INTEREST:
First Amendment interests of the news media.

NAME(S) OF PROGRAMS:
● **The Reporters Committee Legal Fellowships**

TYPE:
Fellowships. Legal fellows monitor significant developments in First Amendment media law, assist with legal defense requests from reporters, prepare legal memoranda, amicus briefs and other special projects. The Fellowship focuses on media law.

YEAR PROGRAM STARTED: 1987

PURPOSE:
To protect the right to gather and distribute news; to keep government accountable by ensuring access to public records, meetings and courtrooms; to preserve the principles of free speech and unfettered press, as guaranteed by the First Amendment of the U.S. Constitution.

ELIGIBILITY:
Candidates must have received a law degree by August of the year the Fellowship begins. Strong legal research and writing skills are required, and a background in news reporting is very strongly preferred.

FINANCIAL DATA:
Fellowship includes fully paid health benefits.
Amount of support per award: Minimum of $65,000.

NO. AWARDS: 6 to 8 annually.

APPLICATION INFO:
Contact the Committee by e-mail.
Duration: One year, September to August.
Deadline: November 3.

ADDRESS INQUIRIES TO:
E-mail: fellowship@rcfp.org

KURT SCHORK MEMORIAL FUND [1759]

4441 MacArthur Boulevard, N.W.
Washington, DC 20007
(202) 333-2545
E-mail: enquiries@ksmfund.org
Web Site: www.ksmfund.org

FOUNDED: 2001

AREAS OF INTEREST:
International journalism.

NAME(S) OF PROGRAMS:
● **Kurt Schork Awards in International Journalism**

TYPE:
Awards/prizes. Awards for print reporters whose stories shed new light on controversial issues. Three prizes are awarded each year, one to a local reporter in a developing country or nation in transition, one to a freelance journalist covering international news, and one to recognize the unsung work of news fixers.

The awards are underwritten by the Kurt Schork Memorial Fund and Reuters, and administered by the Columbia University Graduate School of Journalism.

YEAR PROGRAM STARTED: 2002

PURPOSE:
To honor Kurt Schork, an American freelance journalist, killed in a military ambush while on assignment for Reuters on May 24, 2000 in Sierra Leone.

ELIGIBILITY:
Local Reporter: Print journalists employed by a local news outlet and residing in a developing country or nation in transition (non-OECD or EU countries), whose work has been published in a local publication, are eligible.

Freelance Journalist: All freelance print journalists and those contracted by news organizations are eligible.

Eligible Media: Entries are welcomed from all types of print-based media including newspapers and magazines and established online publications.

FINANCIAL DATA:
Amount of support per award: $5,000.

NO. AWARDS: 3.

APPLICATION INFO:
Complete information may be found on the Fund web site.
Deadline: May 31.

ADDRESS INQUIRIES TO:
See e-mail address above.

UNITED METHODIST COMMUNICATIONS

810 12th Avenue South
Nashville, TN 37203-4744
(615) 742-5400
E-mail: rjames@umcom.org
Web Site: www.umcom.org

TYPE:
Fellowships; Scholarships. Award for junior or senior undergraduate study in religion journalism or mass communications. The term *communications* is meant to cover various media as audio-visual, electronic and print journalism.

See entry 923 for full listing.

UNITED METHODIST COMMUNICATIONS [1760]

810 12th Avenue South
Nashville, TN 37203-4704
(615) 742-5400
E-mail: rjames@umcom.org
Web Site: www.umcom.org

FOUNDED: 1948

AREAS OF INTEREST:
Religion communications.

NAME(S) OF PROGRAMS:
● **The Stoody-West Fellowship**

TYPE:
Fellowships. Assists one United Methodist student in postgraduate study at an accredited U.S. college or university who intends to pursue a career in religious journalism.

YEAR PROGRAM STARTED: 1964

PURPOSE:
To enable the recipient to continue graduate studies in religion journalism; to promote a level of excellence in communication at the graduate level.

LEGAL BASIS:
Nonprofit.

ELIGIBILITY:
Applicant must be a United Methodist student who intends to pursue a career in religion journalism and is enrolled in graduate study at an accredited U.S. college or university (includes electronic and broadcast media as well as print). Employees of United Methodist Communications and members of the General Commission on Communication are not eligible for the Fellowship.

FINANCIAL DATA:
Amount of support per award: $6,000.
Total amount of support: $6,000.

NO. AWARDS: 1 annually.

APPLICATION INFO:
Application forms are available online.

Applicant must submit:
(1) completed application form;
(2) official transcripts of schools attended, including evidence of enrollment as a graduate student in the journalism or communications department of a duly accredited college or university in the U.S.;
(3) three letters of recommendation;
(4) an essay of not more than 500 words about their commitment to the Christian Faith, interest in religion communication, and how they see the two intersecting in their life, presently and in the future;
(5) three writing samples and;
(6) recent personal photograph.

If materials must be mailed, use the following address:
Stoody-West Fellowship Committee
United Methodist Communications
P.O. Box 320
Nashville, TN 37202-0320.

If submitting by FedEx or UPS, send to:
Stoody-West Fellowship Committee, United Methodist Communications, at the street address above.

Duration: One academic year.
Deadline: March 15 (postmark).

PUBLICATIONS:
Application guidelines.

ADDRESS INQUIRIES TO:
Relationship Team
(See address above.)

*PLEASE NOTE:
Religious journalism is interpreted to include news writing for secular press, church press and for church institutions. Appropriate news and journalism forms will be considered, including electronic and broadcast media, as well as print.

UNIVERSITY FILM AND VIDEO ASSOCIATION   [1761]
Bentley University
Department of English and Media Studies
AAC 087
Waltham, MA 02452
(781) 891-2862
E-mail: chayward@bentley.edu
Web Site: www.ufva.org

AREAS OF INTEREST:
Film, video and multimedia production.

NAME(S) OF PROGRAMS:
● **Carole Fielding Student Grants**

TYPE:
Project/program grants; Research grants. Annual support for student projects in film, video and multimedia productions or research activities in historical, critical, theoretical or experimental studies in film or video.

YEAR PROGRAM STARTED: 1993

PURPOSE:
To support and promote student film and video makers.

LEGAL BASIS:
UFVA membership funded.

ELIGIBILITY:
An applicant must be a graduate or undergraduate student at the time the application is made, be sponsored by a faculty member who is an active member of the University Film and Video Association and agree to present, or have presented by his or her representative, a report on the project or production at the next annual meeting of the Association.

The judges reserve the right not to make an award if quality or quantity of submissions so justify.

FINANCIAL DATA:
Amount of support per award: Varies.
Total amount of support: $2,500 per year.

NO. MOST RECENT APPLICANTS: 75.

NO. AWARDS: Varies.

APPLICATION INFO:
Applicants should submit materials online. The proposal must include a one-page description of the production or project which includes a statement of purpose, an indication of the resources available to complete the work and a summary of the proposed film, video production or study. If a narrative film is proposed, submit a copy of the script. A documentary proposal should include a short treatment. An experimental or animated film proposal should include a treatment (or script) and/or story boards. Also include a one-page budget, indicating what portion of the total project will be supported by this grant and a statement by a faculty member who is an active member of the University Film and Video Association assessing the feasibility of the project or production and indicating his or her willingness to serve as faculty supervisor or consultant.

Deadline: December 15. Announcements by March 31.

OFFICERS:
Christina Lane, President

ADDRESS INQUIRIES TO:
Prof. Casey Hayward, UFVA Grants Office
(See e-mail address above.)

THE UNIVERSITY OF CALGARY   [1762]
Faculty of Graduate Studies
Earth Sciences Building, Room 1010
2500 University Drive, N.W.
Calgary AB T2N 1N4 Canada
(403) 220-4938
Fax: (403) 289-7635
E-mail: gsaward@ucalgary.ca
Web Site: grad.ucalgary.ca/awards

FOUNDED: 1966

AREAS OF INTEREST:
Communication and media studies.

NAME(S) OF PROGRAMS:
● **Cogeco Inc. Graduate Scholarship**

TYPE:
Awards/prizes; Scholarships.

LEGAL BASIS:
University scholarship program.

ELIGIBILITY:
Open to students registered in a Master's program in Communication and Media Studies at the University of Calgary. Awards will be made on the basis of academic excellence.

FINANCIAL DATA:
Amount of support per award: $10,000.
Total amount of support: $10,000.

CO-OP FUNDING PROGRAMS: Scholarship is financed by Cogeco Inc.

NO. AWARDS: 1 each year.

APPLICATION INFO:
Candidates should consult the Communication and Media Studies Program. A recommendation will be forwarded to the Graduate Scholarship Office. The recommendation is subject to final approval of the Graduate Scholarship Committee.
Duration: One year.
Deadline: February 1.

ADDRESS INQUIRIES TO:
Graduate Scholarship Office
(See address above.)

UNIVERSITY OF MICHIGAN   [1763]
Knight-Wallace Fellowships
Wallace House
620 Oxford Road
Ann Arbor, MI 48104-2635
(734) 998-7666
Fax: (734) 998-7979
E-mail: kwfellows@umich.edu
Web Site: www.wallacehouse.umich.edu/knight-wallace

AREAS OF INTEREST:
Journalism, arts, sciences and professions.

NAME(S) OF PROGRAMS:
● **Knight-Wallace Fellowships for Journalists**

TYPE:
Fellowships. The Knight-Wallace Fellowships offer accomplished journalists a year of study and collaborative learning at the University of Michigan to deepen their skills and meet the challenges of a changing industry.

YEAR PROGRAM STARTED: 1973

PURPOSE:
To offer a full academic year to midcareer journalists at the University of Michigan.

LEGAL BASIS:
A part of the Provost's office at the University of Michigan.

ELIGIBILITY:
Status of eligibility extends to all full-time print, broadcast, online, photo and film journalists with five years' experience whose work appears regularly in U.S.-controlled news organizations. Freelancers are included. Work may be related or unrelated to professional objectives.

FINANCIAL DATA:
Fellowship includes tuition and fees to audit courses at the University of Michigan.
Amount of support per award: $75,000 stipend.

NO. AWARDS: Maximum 18 fellows per year.

APPLICATION INFO:
Application form, a leave of absence (if possible) for the period of the Fellowship, and a support letter from direct supervisor is required. Two statements, an intellectual autobiography, and a proposed program of study must be included. Do not submit more than five examples of applicant's work.
Duration: Eight-month academic year, September through April.
Deadline: Typically February 1 for U.S. applicants. International applicants deadline may vary.

PUBLICATIONS:
Wall House Journal.

ADDRESS INQUIRIES TO:
Lynette Clemetson, Director or Robert Yoon, Associate Director
(See e-mail address above.)

Labor

IMAGINE AMERICA FOUNDATION [1764]
14200 Park Meadow Drive
Suite 117 S
Chantilly, VA 20151
(571) 267-3015
E-mail: studentservices@imagine-america.org
Web Site: www.imagine-america.org

FOUNDED: 1982

AREAS OF INTEREST:
Private career education, trade schools, and vocational schools.

NAME(S) OF PROGRAMS:
● **Imagine America Adult Skills Education Program (ASEP)**
● **Imagine America High School Scholarship Program**
● **Imagine America Military Award Program (MAP)**

TYPE:
Awards/prizes; Scholarships; Research contracts. Sponsorships. For the Imagine America High School Scholarship Program, three scholarships are given to each high school listed on the Foundation web site above.

YEAR PROGRAM STARTED: 1982

PURPOSE:
To provide research, scholarship and training for America's career colleges.

LEGAL BASIS:
501(c)(3) nonprofit organization.

ELIGIBILITY:
Applicants for the Adult Skills Education Program must be 19 years of age or older.

Applicants for the Military Award Program must be honorably discharged, active duty, reservist or retired military.

Scholarship applicants must be graduating high school seniors.

GEOG. RESTRICTIONS: United States and Puerto Rico.

FINANCIAL DATA:
Amount of support per award: Adult Skills Education Program, High School Scholarship Program and Military Award Program: $1,000.
Total amount of support: $10,000,000.

NO. AWARDS: 10,000.

PUBLICATIONS:
Career College Central, magazine.

ADDRESS INQUIRIES TO:
Lee Doubleday
Director of Operations
(See address above.)

U.S. DEPARTMENT OF HEALTH AND HUMAN SERVICES/ADMINISTRATION FOR CHILDREN AND FAMILIES/OFFICE OF FAMILY ASSISTANCE [1765]
Mary E. Switzer Building
330 C Street, S.W.
Washington, DC 20201
(877) 696-6775
Fax: (202) 205-5887
E-mail: rachel.johnson@acf.hhs.gov
info.ofa@acf.hhs.gov
Web Site: www.acf.hhs.gov/ofa

FOUNDED: 1996

AREAS OF INTEREST:
Education, employment and support services, and financial assistance.

NAME(S) OF PROGRAMS:
● **State Family Assistance Grants**
● **Temporary Assistance for Needy Families (TANF)**

TYPE:
Block grants; Internships; Technical assistance. Block grants to states, the District of Columbia, territories, and federally recognized Indian tribes and Alaska Native Organizations for education, employment, training and supportive services to help eligible families move to work and self-sufficiency.

YEAR PROGRAM STARTED: 1996

PURPOSE:
To help needy families achieve self-sufficiency.

LEGAL BASIS:
Social Security Act, Title IV-A and Title IV-F, as amended (42 USC 602-603, 681-687 and 1302) and Public Law 100-485.

ELIGIBILITY:
Grants are awarded to states, the District of Columbia, territories, and federally recognized Indian tribes and Alaska Native Organizations based on a complete TANF plan. Statute precludes any grantees other than those stated above.

FINANCIAL DATA:
Amount of support per award: Calculated share of federal block grant.
Total amount of support: $16.5 billion.

NO. AWARDS: 54 states, the District of Columbia and U.S. territories.

PUBLICATIONS:
TANF Annual Report to Congress; policy announcements; program instructions; information memoranda.

ADDRESS INQUIRIES TO:
Rachel Johnson, Program Analyst
(See address above.)

U.S. DEPARTMENT OF LABOR [1766]
Office of Apprenticeship
Room N-5311
200 Constitution Avenue, N.W.
Washington, DC 20210
(202) 693-2796
E-mail: apprenticeship@dol.gov
Web Site: www.dol.gov/apprenticeship

FOUNDED: 1937

AREAS OF INTEREST:
Apprenticeship, skill and technical training.

CONSULTING OR VOLUNTEER SERVICES:
Provides technical assistance at no cost.

NAME(S) OF PROGRAMS:
● **National Apprenticeship System**

TYPE:
Technical assistance. Management and labor, along with government and the education system, work together at the national, state and local levels to formulate and promote effective apprenticeship programs. The program must be an organized, written plan embodying training and supervision of one or more apprentices in an apprenticeable occupation, as defined in 29 CFR 29.4 and subscribed to by a sponsor who has undertaken to carry out the apprenticeship program.

YEAR PROGRAM STARTED: 1937

PURPOSE:
To formulate, promote and publish labor standards necessary to safeguard the welfare of apprentices, encourage the inclusion of such standards in apprenticeship contracts, bring together employers and labor to create apprenticeship programs, cooperate with state agencies in formulating and promoting apprenticeship standards, and cooperate with the U.S. Department of Education on vocational education and related instruction in apprenticeship.

LEGAL BASIS:
National Apprenticeship Act of 1937 (P.L. 308-75); Title 29, CFR Part 30; Title 29, CFR Part 29.

ELIGIBILITY:
To be eligible as a sponsor, apprenticeship programs must meet the basic standards and established criteria set forth by the Secretary of Labor and may be registered upon request of the program sponsor. Registration of programs and apprentices in states having apprenticeship agencies recognized by the U.S. Department of Labor is performed by the state apprenticeship agencies. Programs in states not having recognized apprenticeship agencies will be registered by the Bureau of Apprenticeship and Training.

To be eligible as a beneficiary, applicants for apprenticeship must be at least 16 years of age. They must have the ability and aptitude to master the occupations and sufficient education to complete satisfactorily the required hours of related theoretical instruction.

GEOG. RESTRICTIONS: United States.

FINANCIAL DATA:
The Department of Labor does not finance apprenticeships. Program sponsors bear the expenses of the program.

NO. MOST RECENT APPLICANTS: 100,000.

APPLICATION INFO:
Notices for accepting applications are published locally by apprenticeship program sponsors. Information may be obtained from local One Stop Centers or may be requested by contacting regional, state or area offices of the Office of Apprenticeship, U.S. Department of Labor, or the ETA Grants Office.

PUBLICATIONS:
Apprenticeship Past and Present; *National Apprenticeship Program*.

ADDRESS INQUIRIES TO:
Grants Department
Division of Grants and Contracts
(See address above.)

W.E. UPJOHN INSTITUTE FOR EMPLOYMENT RESEARCH [1767]

300 South Westnedge Avenue
Kalamazoo, MI 49007-4686
(269) 343-5541
Fax: (269) 343-3308
E-mail: communications@upjohn.org
Web Site: www.upjohn.org

FOUNDED: 1945

AREAS OF INTEREST:
Policy-relevant research on employment and unemployment at the international, national, state and local levels. The Institute is also receptive to international studies for the purpose of drawing lessons for U.S. policy. Topics of interest include job creation, job stabilization, matching of jobs and people, alleviation of unemployment hazards, the political science of manpower programs and the quality of work life.

CONSULTING OR VOLUNTEER SERVICES:
Both consulting and volunteer services are available, though the latter are limited.

NAME(S) OF PROGRAMS:
• **Early Career Research Awards**

TYPE:
Conferences/seminars; Research grants; Visiting scholars; Research contracts. Early Career Research Awards are intended to provide resources to junior faculty (untenured and within six years of earning the Ph.D.) to carry out policy-related research on labor market issues. The Institute supports and encourages research on all issues related to labor markets and public workforce policy.

YEAR PROGRAM STARTED: 1976

PURPOSE:
To conduct research into the causes and effects of unemployment and measures for the alleviation of unemployment at the national, state and local levels.

LEGAL BASIS:
Public nonprofit organization.

ELIGIBILITY:
Award proposals will be evaluated according to the following criteria:
(1) contribution to important labor market policy issues and to the professional literature and;
(2) technical merit.

FINANCIAL DATA:
The Institute does not pay indirect costs but will entertain any legitimate research expense as part of the budget. Acceptable items include costs for professional, technical, and support personnel, data acquisition, materials and supplies, computer services, and travel. The Institute does not fund dissertation research although it does have a Dissertation Award program. Grant payments are made to the individual upon award.

Amount of support per award: Up to $5,000.

NO. MOST RECENT APPLICANTS: 84.

NO. AWARDS: 15.

APPLICATION INFO:
Applicants should submit a proposal of up to 1,200 words (approximately four double-spaced pages) describing the proposed research and its relevance to labor market policy. The proposal should include an abstract and a brief budget. Applications must also include a current curriculum vitae.

Submissions are to be made through www.upjohn.org/form/ecra.

Duration: Ordinarily one year, which includes research and writing of paper to be submitted to a scholarly journal.

Deadline: Applications: Late January. Announcement: March or April.

PUBLICATIONS:
Program announcement; proposal guidelines.

IRS I.D.: 38-1360419

TRUSTEES:
Donald R. Parfet, Chairman
Marilyn Schlack, Vice Chairman
B. Joseph White, Secretary-Treasurer
John M. Dunn
Sydney Parfet
Frank J. Sardone
Amanda Van Dusen
Dr. Eileen Wilson-Oyelaran

ADDRESS INQUIRIES TO:
Richard Wyrwa, Manager of Publications and Marketing
(See address above.)

*PLEASE NOTE:
Awards are essentially performance-based contracts. Applications and all work submitted under Early Career Research Awards become the property of the Institute. It is Institute policy to require submission of the research paper to its working paper series. Unaccepted proposals and rejected research papers will be returned upon request, without restrictions on further use by others. It is also Institute policy to encourage publication of the sponsored research in scholarly journals following submission of the research paper to the Institute. Submission of any material waives all rights to make any claim because of any use thereof by the W.E. Upjohn Unemployment Trustee Corporation, its agents and employees.

*SPECIAL STIPULATIONS:
Award recipients are expected to write a research paper based on the funded work for submission to the Institute's working paper series, submit the paper to a peer-reviewed journal, and prepare a synopsis of the research for possible publication in the Institute's newsletter, *Employment Research*.

Law

AMERICAN ASSOCIATION OF LAW LIBRARIES

105 West Adams Street
Suite 3300
Chicago, IL 60603
(312) 939-4764
Fax: (312) 431-1097
E-mail: membership@aall.org
Web Site: www.aallnet.org

TYPE:
Scholarships. For study of law or librarianship, with support intended for prospective law librarians.

See entry 656 for full listing.

AMERICAN BAR FOUNDATION [1768]

750 North Lake Shore Drive
Fourth Floor
Chicago, IL 60611-4403
(312) 988-6500
Fax: (312) 988-6579
E-mail: fellowships@abfn.org
Web Site: www.americanbarfoundation.org

FOUNDED: 1952

AREAS OF INTEREST:
Law, legal institutions, and legal processes and their impact on society.

NAME(S) OF PROGRAMS:
• **ABF/ALI Doctoral Fellowship Program in Legal & Higher Education**

TYPE:
Fellowships. The American Bar Foundation (ABF), in partnership with AccessLex Institute (ALI), is committed to developing the next generation of scholars interested in empirical and interdisciplinary research on legal and higher education. This is a residential fellowship at the ABF.

YEAR PROGRAM STARTED: 2017

PURPOSE:
To assist emerging scholars who are studying issues of access, affordability or value in legal or higher education; to assemble and coordinate a professional network of scholars who will produce innovative, objective, empirical and interdisciplinary research in the field.

LEGAL BASIS:
Private foundation.

ELIGIBILITY:
Applications are invited from outstanding students who are candidates for Ph.D. degrees, across a broad range of disciplines. Doctoral research must address significant issues in the field and show promise of a major contribution to social scientific understanding of legal or higher education. Students from underrepresented minority groups are especially encouraged to apply. There are no citizenship requirements for this fellowship. Non-U.S. nationals are welcome to apply; however, the ABF is unable to sponsor an H-1B visa.

FINANCIAL DATA:
Fellows will receive a stipend for up to 24 months. Fellows may also request up to $3,500 per year to reimburse for expenses associated with research, travel to meet with advisors, or travel to conferences at which

papers are presented. Doctoral Fellows may request reimbursement of reasonable relocation expenses up to $2,500.

Amount of support per award: Varies.

NO. AWARDS: Varies.

APPLICATION INFO:
Application form is available online.
Duration: One year.
Deadline: Current deadlines are posted on the Foundation web site.

ADDRESS INQUIRIES TO:
Marcilena Shaeffer, Program Coordinator
(See address above.)

*PLEASE NOTE:
Fellowships are held in residence at the ABF. Appointments to fellowships are full-time. Fellows are expected to participate fully in the academic life of the ABF so that they may develop close collegial ties with ABF faculty and other scholars in residence.

AMERICAN COLLEGE OF LEGAL MEDICINE
515 North Dearborn Street
Chicago, IL 60654
(312) 670-2550
E-mail: info@aclm.org
Web Site: theaclm.org

TYPE:
Awards/prizes. The Hirsh Award is awarded to a law, dentistry, podiatry, nursing, pharmacy, health science, health care administration, or public health student.

See entry 1997 for full listing.

THE CANADIAN BAR ASSOCIATION   [1769]
66 Slater Street
Suite 1200
Ottawa ON K1P 5H1 Canada
(613) 237-2925
(800) 267-8860
Fax: (613) 237-0185
E-mail: info@cba.org
Web Site: www.cba.org

FOUNDED: 1914

AREAS OF INTEREST:
Law and the administration of justice, promoting access to justice and promotion of equality in the professional justice system.

NAME(S) OF PROGRAMS:
● **Viscount Bennett Fellowship**

TYPE:
Awards/prizes; Fellowships. Award is offered annually to one student for postgraduate studies in law.

YEAR PROGRAM STARTED: 1946

PURPOSE:
To encourage a high standard of legal education, training and ethics.

ELIGIBILITY:
Canadian citizens who have graduated from an approved law school in Canada or who, at the time of application, are pursuing final-year studies as undergraduate students at such approved law school. All applicants must be CBA members in good standing. Candidates must have completed and filed an application for graduate studies with the institution of higher learning of their choice before submitting the fellowship application to the CBA.

GEOG. RESTRICTIONS: Canada.

FINANCIAL DATA:
Amount of support per award: $25,000 (CAN) paid in two equal installments.
Total amount of support: $25,000 (CAN).

NO. MOST RECENT APPLICANTS: 27.

NO. AWARDS: 1.

APPLICATION INFO:
Each applicant must submit a Viscount Bennett Application Form with relevant attachments. Applications must be accompanied by:
(1) a birth or citizenship certificate;
(2) a certified copy of all law school transcripts;
(3) a one-page synopsis highlighting pertinent information from university transcripts;
(4) a synopsis of extracurricular activities during postsecondary studies;
(5) a statement of the course of study to be pursued and;
(6) two letters of reference.

Completed application forms must be submitted to the address above:
Viscount Bennett Fellowship
c/o Senior Director of Communications and Marketing.
Duration: One year. Nonrenewable.
Deadline: November 15 (postmark).

ADDRESS INQUIRIES TO:
Senior Director of
Communications and Marketing
(See address above.)

*SPECIAL STIPULATIONS:
As a condition of the Fellowship, recipient(s) of the Viscount Bennett Fellowship must submit a written report at midterm and at the end of the year of graduate study, and must submit a copy of their final thesis at year end.

CANADIAN INSTITUTE FOR ADVANCED LEGAL STUDIES   [1770]
P.O. Box 43538, Leaside Post Office
1601 Bayview Avenue
Toronto ON M4G 4G8 Canada
(416) 429-3292
Fax: (416) 429-9805
E-mail: info@canadian-institute.com
Web Site: www.canadian-institute.com

FOUNDED: 1979

AREAS OF INTEREST:
Law.

NAME(S) OF PROGRAMS:
● **French Language Scholarship**
● **The Right Honourable Paul Martin Sr. Scholarship**

TYPE:
Scholarships.

YEAR PROGRAM STARTED: 1983

PURPOSE:
French Language Scholarship: To study for the equivalent of a Master's or doctoral degree from a Canadian university at a European university where instruction is given in French.

The Right Honourable Paul Martin Sr. Scholarship: To study for an LLM at the University of Cambridge.

ELIGIBILITY:
French Language Scholarship: The Institute annually awards a scholarship for graduate

studies in law toward a second-cycle or third-cycle diploma (the equivalent of a Master's or doctoral degree from a Canadian university) at a European university where instruction is given in French, to a person who has (in the four years before the candidate will commence the proposed studies) been awarded a Bachelor's degree in law from a Canadian university. An applicant must be accepted into a French-language European university for graduate studies in law in order to receive this Scholarship, although such acceptance need not be confirmed at the time of the application for the Scholarship or at the time that the Institute provides the candidate with notice that he or she has been selected to receive the Scholarship.

The Right Honourable Paul Martin Sr. Scholarship: The Institute annually awards two full scholarships for the LLM degree at the University of Cambridge (Cambridge, England) to candidates who have been awarded a law degree from a three- or four-year program at a faculty of law in a Canadian university in the four years before the candidate will commence his or her studies at the University of Cambridge (supported by The Right Honourable Paul Martin Sr. Scholarship). An applicant must be accepted into the University of Cambridge and a College of the University of Cambridge for the LLM in order to receive this Scholarship, although such acceptance need not be confirmed at the time of the application for the Scholarship nor at the time that the Institute provides the candidate with notice that he or she has been selected to receive the Scholarship.

FINANCIAL DATA:
French Language Scholarship: Scholarship includes full tuition and includes an allowance to cover a portion of living expenses and reasonable travel expenses to and from the European university, subject to any other awards received by the successful candidate.

The Right Honourable Paul Martin Sr. Scholarship: Scholarships include full tuition at the University of Cambridge, a monthly living allowance, the Immigration Health Surcharge and one return airfare, subject to any other awards received by the successful candidate.

Total amount of support: French Language Scholarship: Up to $20,000 (CAN); The Right Honourable Paul Martin Sr. Scholarship: Approximately GBP 42,000.

NO. MOST RECENT APPLICANTS: French Language Scholarship: 2. The Right Honourable Paul Martin Sr. Scholarship: 20.

NO. AWARDS: French Language Scholarship: 1. The Right Honourable Paul Martin Sr. Scholarship: 2.

APPLICATION INFO:
French Language Scholarship: Applications must include:
(1) curriculum vitae;
(2) a personal statement indicating why the applicant wishes to undertake graduate studies in law and why the applicant is suited to undertake such studies;
(3) a copy of transcripts for undergraduate and graduate studies, for studies in law or for a Bar Admission Course, as applicable, as well as an understanding that the proposed program of study is conducted principally in

the French language;
(4) a maximum of three letters of reference and;
(5) a statement of tuition fees and anticipated living and travel expenses.

The Right Honourable Paul Martin Sr. Scholarship: Applications must include:
(1) curriculum vitae;
(2) a personal statement indicating why the applicant wishes to undertake graduate studies in law at the University of Cambridge and why the applicant is suited to undertake such studies;
(3) a copy of transcripts for undergraduate and graduate studies, for studies in law and for a Bar Admissions Course, as applicable, and;
(4) a maximum of three letters of reference.

Applications may be submitted by mail or e-mail.

Duration: One year.

Deadline: December 31. Notification by April 15.

ADDRESS INQUIRIES TO:
See e-mail address above.

ENVIRONMENTAL LAW INSTITUTE   [1771]
1730 M Street, N.W.
Suite 700
Washington, DC 20036
(202) 939-3800
Fax: (202) 939-3868
E-mail: law@eli.org
Web Site: www.eli.org

FOUNDED: 1969

AREAS OF INTEREST:
Environmental law, management and policy, including economic and scientific aspects and protection of natural areas.

CONSULTING OR VOLUNTEER SERVICES:
Variety of services including tuition scholarships to continuing legal education programs, consulting services and technical assistance.

TYPE:
Scholarships. Scholarships to annual Environmental Law Course.

YEAR PROGRAM STARTED: 1970

PURPOSE:
To provide access to education on environmental law and policy; to improve the level of practice and raise the quality of debate on key legal/policy questions.

LEGAL BASIS:
Nonprofit corporation, 501(c)(3).

ELIGIBILITY:
Open to public interest lawyers, attorneys doing substantial pro bono work, and state and local government attorneys involved in environmental law.

FINANCIAL DATA:
Amount of support per award: Approximately $800 to $900 per scholarship applicant approved.
Total amount of support: Approximately $25,000 annually.

CO-OP FUNDING PROGRAMS: Environmental Law Conference with ALI-CLE.

NO. MOST RECENT APPLICANTS: Approximately 25.

NO. AWARDS: Approximately 25.

APPLICATION INFO:
Send letter of application stating need and expected benefit.

PUBLICATIONS:
Annual report; *Environmental Law Reporter*; *The Environmental Forum*; *National Wetlands Newsletter*.

IRS I.D.: 52-0901863

OFFICERS:
Scott Fulton, President

ADDRESS INQUIRIES TO:
See e-mail address above.

FOOD AND DRUG LAW INSTITUTE (FDLI)   [1772]
1155 15th Street, N.W., Suite 910
Washington, DC 20005-2706
(202) 371-1420
(800) 956-6293
E-mail: info@fdli.org
Web Site: www.fdli.
org/resources/career/austern-writing-competition

FOUNDED: 1949

AREAS OF INTEREST:
Food and drug law issues.

NAME(S) OF PROGRAMS:
● **H. Thomas Austern Writing Competition**

TYPE:
Awards/prizes. The subject matter of the competition is an in-depth analysis of a current issue relevant to the food and drug field, including a relevant case law, legislative history and other authorities, particularly where the U.S. Food and Drug Administration is involved.

YEAR PROGRAM STARTED: 1978

PURPOSE:
To encourage law students interested in the areas of law affecting FDA regulated industries, foods, drugs, medical devices, dietary supplements, cosmetics, veterinary, cannabis or tobacco and nicotine products, and biologics; to provide a marketplace for discussing food and drug law issues.

LEGAL BASIS:
Nonprofit educational association.

ELIGIBILITY:
The level of study is postgraduate. Entrants must currently be enrolled in a J.D. program at any of the U.S. ABA-accredited law schools.

GEOG. RESTRICTIONS: United States.

FINANCIAL DATA:
Amount of support per award: $750 first prize; $500 second prize; $250 third prize.
Total amount of support: $1,500.

NO. AWARDS: 3 annually.

APPLICATION INFO:
Applicants must submit all materials electronically. Instructions can be found on the web site.
Duration: One year.
Deadline: Mid-June.

PUBLICATIONS:
Food and Drug Law Journal.

ADDRESS INQUIRIES TO:
Paige Samson
E-mail: paige.samson@fdli.org

THE HAGUE ACADEMY OF INTERNATIONAL LAW   [1773]
Peace Palace
Carnegieplein 2
2517 KJ The Hague The Netherlands
(31) 70 3024242
E-mail: centre@hagueacademy.nl
Web Site: www.hagueacademy.nl

FOUNDED: 1914

AREAS OF INTEREST:
Public and private international law.

NAME(S) OF PROGRAMS:
● **Centre for Studies and Research in International Law and International Relations**

TYPE:
Project/program grants.

YEAR PROGRAM STARTED: 1957

PURPOSE:
To bring together young international lawyers of a high standard from all over the world, to undertake original research on a common general theme which is determined each year by the Academy.

ELIGIBILITY:
The program is open to academics or lawyers of a high standard. Applications are open only to those persons who hold advanced university degrees (a Doctorate or the Academy's diploma) or to those who provide evidence of their actual involvement, for at least three years, in international legal matters. Candidates must have real practical experience and an ability to undertake research.

FINANCIAL DATA:
Registration is free of charge and all participants receive a partial reimbursement of travel expenses.

NO. AWARDS: 24.

APPLICATION INFO:
Candidates should upload the following documents to the online registration form:
(1) a copy of their valid passport or identification;
(2) an identity photograph;
(3) a copy of their highest degree certificate or an official document from their university certifying that the applicant is preparing to obtain a degree;
(4) a curriculum vitae with, if applicable, a list of publications;
(5) a short letter stating the reasons for the application (one to two pages) and;
(6) a recommendation letter from a professor of international law.
Duration: Three weeks.
Deadline: September 1.

PUBLICATIONS:
Books of the Centre for Studies and Research - Hague Academy of International Law.

OFFICERS:
Prof. Yves Daudet, President
Jean-Marc Thouvenin, Secretary-General of the Academy

ADDRESS INQUIRIES TO:
Registration Office
(See address and e-mail above.)

*PLEASE NOTE:
The research work undertaken at the Centre may be included in a collective work published by the Academy.

*SPECIAL STIPULATIONS:
In principle, no person may participate more than once in the Centre's activities. Each participant must write an article on a subject arising out of the general theme of the year, which will be determined by the Director of Research. This report must be sent to the relevant Director of Research, within an established deadline.

THE HAGUE ACADEMY OF INTERNATIONAL LAW   [1774]
Peace Palace
Carnegieplein 2
2517 KJ The Hague The Netherlands
(31) 70 3024242
E-mail: info@hagueacademy.nl
Web Site: www.hagueacademy.nl

FOUNDED: 1914

AREAS OF INTEREST:
Public and private international law.

NAME(S) OF PROGRAMS:
• **External Programme**

TYPE:
Project/program grants. External Programme is held each year, in turn in Africa, Asia and Latin America, upon the invitation of host governments or international organizations. It is designed for approximately 20 participants from the countries in the region (who are resident in their own country), whose traveling expenses and accommodations are financed by the government of the host state or organization. In addition, 20 participants come from the host state itself.

YEAR PROGRAM STARTED: 1969

ELIGIBILITY:
This programme is aimed at persons having studied international law (young university teachers and young civil servants from the ministry of foreign affairs or other ministries), selected by the Secretary-General in the name of the Curatorium on exclusively scientific criteria. Candidates should come from countries in the region of the host country. A list of the eligible nationalities is published every year.

FINANCIAL DATA:
Regional participants are provided with accommodation and a reimbursement of their travel expenses, as well as a daily allowance by the host state.

NO. MOST RECENT APPLICANTS: 50.

NO. AWARDS: 20.

APPLICATION INFO:
Candidates should apply online with the following:
(1) a curriculum vitae with, if applicable, a list of publications;
(2) a copy of candidate's highest degree certificate or an official document from candidate's university certifying candidate is preparing to obtain a degree. If the original document is not in English or French, please add a translation;
(3) a short letter giving reasons for the application (one to two pages);
(4) a recommendation letter from a professor of international law sent separately;
(5) a copy of candidate's valid passport or ID and;
(6) an identity photograph.
Duration: Eight days.
Deadline: Typically, July 31.

OFFICERS:
Prof. Yves Daudet, President
Jean-Marc Thouvenin, Secretary-General of the Academy

ADDRESS INQUIRIES TO:
Secretariat
(See address above.)

*SPECIAL STIPULATIONS:
One is not allowed to participate more than once in the External Programme. Candidates should reside in their home country when applying.

THE HAGUE ACADEMY OF INTERNATIONAL LAW   [1775]
Peace Palace
Carnegieplein 2
2517 KJ The Hague The Netherlands
(31) 70 3024242
E-mail: registration@hagueacademy.nl
Web Site: www.hagueacademy.nl

FOUNDED: 1914

AREAS OF INTEREST:
Private and public international law.

NAME(S) OF PROGRAMS:
• **Doctoral Scholarships in International Law**

TYPE:
Project/program grants. Study programs. Residential scholarships for doctoral candidates from developing countries whose thesis, in private international law or public international law, is in the process of completion, who reside in their home country and who do not have access to scientific sources.

YEAR PROGRAM STARTED: 1923

PURPOSE:
To facilitate the completion of the theses through the use of the Academy, and especially the resources of the Library of the Peace Palace.

LEGAL BASIS:
Non-governmental organization.

ELIGIBILITY:
The candidates' doctoral thesis should be in the process of completion. Applicant should be a national of a non-member state of the OECD, who is a resident in their own country.

FINANCIAL DATA:
Help in the form of a daily allowance and contribution towards travelling expenses may be granted to participants, taking into account the distance of their country of normal residence.
Amount of support per award: EUR 2,250 plus half of the traveling expenses, up to a maximum of EUR 910.

NO. MOST RECENT APPLICANTS: 30.

NO. AWARDS: 4.

APPLICATION INFO:
Application online only. Applications should be accompanied by a recommendation from the professor under whose direction the thesis is being written which mentions the title of the thesis. It should also contain a curriculum vitae, a copy of the highest degree certificate (translated in French or English) and a short letter giving reasons for application.
Duration: Eight weeks, July to September.
Deadline: January 31.

PUBLICATIONS:
Programme de la Session; Collected Courses, series of published lectures.

ADDRESS INQUIRIES TO:
Registration Office
(See address above.)

*SPECIAL STIPULATIONS:
The Academy will verify that recipients of scholarships are effectively resident in The Hague without interruption and that they use the Peace Palace Library on a regular basis.

No person may receive more than one scholarship.

THE HAGUE ACADEMY OF INTERNATIONAL LAW   [1776]
Peace Palace
Carnegieplein 2
2517 KJ The Hague The Netherlands
(31) 70 3024242
E-mail: registration@hagueacademy.nl
Web Site: www.hagueacademy.nl

FOUNDED: 1914

AREAS OF INTEREST:
Private and public international law.

NAME(S) OF PROGRAMS:
• **Hague Academy of International Law Summer Courses**

TYPE:
Project/program grants; Scholarships. Study programs. A limited number of scholarships are given to cover tuition and living expenses while studying at the three-week summer session of the Hague Academy of International Law. Because of the limited number, granting of scholarships is based solely on academic merit.

YEAR PROGRAM STARTED: 1923

PURPOSE:
To support personal and effective participation of members in scientific work related to international law and international affairs.

ELIGIBILITY:
Candidates must have completed at least four consecutive years of university studies, which must have included lectures on International Law, or must hold a three-year law degree on the date of the opening of the courses. All candidates must master one of the two working languages of the Academy - English or French.

FINANCIAL DATA:
Amount of support per award: EUR 2,000 (including registration fees of EUR 1,150) covering accommodation expenses incurred during the three weeks of one of the teaching periods. Travelling expenses will be partially reimbursed either by the relevant donor or by the Academy.

NO. MOST RECENT APPLICANTS: 680.

NO. AWARDS: 100.

APPLICATION INFO:
Application for scholarship should be made through the online registration form. The application must contain an identity photograph, a curriculum vitae, a copy of the highest degree certificate (translated in English or French), a short letter giving reason for the application and a recommendation from a professor of international law, sent separately.
Duration: Three weeks in public international law; three weeks in private international law.

Deadline: Complete files of scholarship candidates should be in the possession of the Secretariat before January 31.

PUBLICATIONS:
Collected Courses, series of published lectures.

OFFICERS:
Prof. Yves Daudet, President
Jean-Marc Thouvenin, Secretary-General of the Academy

ADDRESS INQUIRIES TO:
Registration Office
(See address above.)

*SPECIAL STIPULATIONS:
No person may receive more than one scholarship for the Summer Courses. Recipients of scholarships are required to attend the Academy's courses throughout the session.

THE HISPANIC BAR ASSOCIATION OF D.C. FOUNDATION [1777]
1341 G Street, N.W.
Suite 500
Washington, DC 20005
(202) 466-8585
Fax: (202) 463-4803
E-mail: foundation@hbadc.org
Web Site: www.hbadc.org

FOUNDED: 1995

AREAS OF INTEREST:
Law and public interest.

NAME(S) OF PROGRAMS:
● **The HBA-DC Foundation Fellowship**

TYPE:
Fellowships.

PURPOSE:
To provide students with valuable work experience and exposure to an area of public interest law.

ELIGIBILITY:
First- and second-year law students attending accredited law schools in the District of Columbia metropolitan area are eligible to apply, once having obtained a job offer from a sponsoring organization.

GEOG. RESTRICTIONS: District of Columbia and the metropolitan area.

FINANCIAL DATA:
Amount of support per award: Minimum $5,000.
Total amount of support: Varies.

NO. AWARDS: 1 or more.

APPLICATION INFO:
Application information is available on the web site. Completed application must be submitted by e-mail to fellowships@hbadc.org.
Duration: Annual.
Deadline: Dates are posted on the Foundation web site.

ADDRESS INQUIRIES TO:
See e-mail address above.

THE HISPANIC NATIONAL BAR FOUNDATION [1778]
1900 K Street, N.W.
Suite 100
Washington, DC 20006
(786) 340-9991
E-mail: info@hnbf.org
Web Site: www.hnbf.org

FOUNDED: 1985

AREAS OF INTEREST:
Promoting the legal education of persons of Hispanic heritage throughout the U.S. and Puerto Rico.

NAME(S) OF PROGRAMS:
● **Future Latino Leaders Summer Law Institute**

TYPE:
Conferences/seminars; Training grants.
Nine-day program held by the Foundation in Washington, DC which provides Latino high school students with the opportunity to learn more about the legal profession. The Summer Law Institute offers students the chance to come to the nation's capital and learn more about the college application process, meet influential Latino leaders, and tour national monuments and various government agencies.

YEAR PROGRAM STARTED: 2005

PURPOSE:
To provide tools and resources necessary to ensure full and equal opportunity for Hispanics to become leaders in the global community, thereby ensuring a brighter future for all.

LEGAL BASIS:
Section 501(c)(3) organization dedicated to charitable and educational purposes.

ELIGIBILITY:
Applicants must meet the following criteria: (1) be a high school student entering the sophomore, junior or senior year, or be a recent graduate;
(2) have an interest in learning about law school and becoming a lawyer;
(3) be a U.S. citizen, legal permanent resident or be a legal U.S. visitor with a valid visa and passport and;
(4) have a demonstrated interest in helping one's community and building one's leadership skills.

FINANCIAL DATA:
There is no cost to participate in the Summer Law Institute. However, accepted students must pay a $50 application fee, unless a waiver of this fee is requested and granted. Students are also responsible for arranging transportation to Washington, DC. The cost of transportation should not deter one from applying. Upon acceptance to the program, the Foundation is committed to working with the attendee and his or her family in order to ensure that person's ability to attend.
Amount of support per award: Valued at over $3,000 per person.

NO. MOST RECENT APPLICANTS: 100.

NO. AWARDS: 32.

APPLICATION INFO:
Application process begins mid-February. Application can be completed online or sent by mail and must include:
(1) Applicant Information Form;
(2) signed Rules and Regulations Form;
(3) two essays;
(4) two letters of recommendation (from teachers, counselors or employers);
(5) resume (may include community service, leadership positions or civic activities);
(6) certified copy of academic record from high school and;
(7) $50 application fee or fee waiver approval.
Duration: Nine days.

ADDRESS INQUIRIES TO:
See e-mail address above.

JOHN M. LLOYD FOUNDATION [1779]
11777 San Vicente Boulevard
Suite 745
Los Angeles, CA 90049
(310) 622-1050
E-mail: truejustice@johnmlloyd.org
Web Site: johnmlloyd.org

FOUNDED: 1991

AREAS OF INTEREST:
Criminal justice reform primarily in Los Angeles County, CA.

TYPE:
General operating grants.

YEAR PROGRAM STARTED: 1992

PURPOSE:
To promote one just criminal justice system in Los Angeles County, CA, a system centered on strong communities and practical resources, not prisons; to help Los Angeles County become a leader in a movement toward true justice nationwide.

LEGAL BASIS:
Private, family foundation.

ELIGIBILITY:
The Foundation does not accept unsolicited requests for funding at this time.

GEOG. RESTRICTIONS: Primarily Los Angeles County, California.

FINANCIAL DATA:
Amount of support per award: Varies; most grants are about $30,000.

Total amount of support: $735,000 for the year 2020.

NO. AWARDS: 25 new grants for the year 2020.

REPRESENTATIVE AWARDS:
Dignity and Power Now; Youth Justice Coalition; Healing Dialogue and Action.

APPLICATION INFO:
Unsolicited formal proposals will not be considered.

Duration: One year and multiyear grants.

IRS I.D.: 36-3766003

BOARD OF DIRECTORS:
Mark-Anthony Clayton-Johnson
Eliot Estrin
Jesse Estrin
Robert L. Estrin
Griff Foxley
Zoe Lloyd Foxley
Trish Devine Karlin
Linda Dorn Klein
Heidi Mage Lloyd
Pricilla Ocen
Gabrielle Zhuang
Diana Zuniga

ADDRESS INQUIRIES TO:
Melanie Havelin, Executive Director
(See e-mail address above.)

*SPECIAL STIPULATIONS:
Unsolicited formal proposals will not be considered.

MCGILL UNIVERSITY [1780]
Chancellor Day Hall
3644 Peel Street
Montreal QC H3A 1W9 Canada
(514) 398-6616
E-mail: staffappointments.law@mcgill.ca
Web Site: www.mcgill.ca/law

AREAS OF INTEREST:
Law.

NAME(S) OF PROGRAMS:
● **Maxwell Boulton Q.C. Fellowship**

TYPE:
Fellowships.

YEAR PROGRAM STARTED: 1983

PURPOSE:
To provide younger scholars with an
opportunity to pursue a major research
project or to complete the research
requirement for a higher degree.

ELIGIBILITY:
Open to candidates who have completed
residency requirements for a doctoral degree
in law.

FINANCIAL DATA:
Amount of support per award: $40,000
(CAN) per year.

NO. MOST RECENT APPLICANTS: 25.

NO. AWARDS: 1.

APPLICATION INFO:
Information is available on the web site.
Duration: One year.
Deadline: February 1.

ADDRESS INQUIRIES TO:
See e-mail address above.

REPORTERS COMMITTEE FOR FREEDOM OF THE PRESS
1156 15th Street, N.W.
Suite 1020
Washington, DC 20005
(202) 795-9306
Fax: (202) 795-9310
E-mail: kpoole@rcfp.org
Web Site: www.rcfp.org

TYPE:
Fellowships. Legal fellows monitor
significant developments in First Amendment
media law, assist with legal defense requests
from reporters, prepare legal memoranda,
amicus briefs and other special projects. The
Fellowship focuses on media law.

See entry 1758 for full listing.

RHODE ISLAND STATE GOVERNMENT INTERNSHIP PROGRAM
State House, Room 8AA
Providence, RI 02903
(401) 222-6782
Fax: (401) 222-4447
E-mail: intern@rilegislature.gov
blanzi@rilegislature.gov
Web Site: www.rilegislature.gov/internship

TYPE:
Internships. The Internship Program is run
through the Joint Committee on Legislative
Services (JCLS). Students are connected with
internship experiences throughout state
government. This includes the Legislative,
Executive and Judicial branches, as well as
state departments of government, municipal
agencies and community and nonprofit
organizations. Students are placed in areas of
interest where they work with their
placement supervisor on a variety of projects
and tasks that enable them to meet
educational learning objectives.

Many colleges and universities grant credit
for the internship experience. The amount of
credit granted to each student differs based
on school and hours of service.

See entry 1805 for full listing.

THE UNIVERSITY OF CALGARY [1781]
Faculty of Graduate Studies
Earth Sciences Building, Room 1010
2500 University Drive, N.W.
Calgary AB T2N 1N4 Canada
(403) 220-4938
Fax: (403) 289-7635
E-mail: gsaward@ucalgary.ca
Web Site: grad.ucalgary.ca/awards

FOUNDED: 1966

AREAS OF INTEREST:
Law.

NAME(S) OF PROGRAMS:
● **The Honourable N.D. McDermid
Graduate Scholarships in Law**

TYPE:
Awards/prizes; Scholarships. Graduate
scholarships in law tenable at The University
of Calgary. Awards endowed by the
McDermid Law Fund in memory of the late
Honourable Neil Douglas McDermid, Q.C.,
who was a prominent member of the legal
profession of Alberta and the Calgary
community for many years.

PURPOSE:
To financially assist students who want to
study law at the university.

LEGAL BASIS:
University.

ELIGIBILITY:
Open to students registered full-time in a
graduate program in the Faculty of Law at
The University of Calgary. If, in the opinion
of the Graduate Scholarship Committee, no
suitable applications are received, no awards
will be made.

GEOG. RESTRICTIONS: Canada.

FINANCIAL DATA:
Amount of support per award: $14,000
(award may be divided further to $7,000).
Total amount of support: $28,000.

NO. AWARDS: 2 to 4.

APPLICATION INFO:
Students should consult the Faculty of Law.
Recommendations will be made to the
Graduate Scholarship Office. The
recommendations are subject to final
approval of the Graduate Scholarship
Committee.
Duration: One year. Nonrenewable.
Deadline: December 15.

ADDRESS INQUIRIES TO:
Graduate Scholarship Office
(See address above.)

THE UNIVERSITY OF CALGARY
Faculty of Graduate Studies
Earth Sciences Building, Room 1010
2500 University Drive, N.W.
Calgary AB T2N 1N4 Canada
(403) 220-4938
Fax: (403) 289-7635
E-mail: gsaward@ucalgary.ca
Web Site: grad.ucalgary.ca/awards

TYPE:
Awards/prizes; Scholarships.

See entry 1605 for full listing.

Political science

AMERICAN POLITICAL SCIENCE ASSOCIATION [1782]
1527 New Hampshire Avenue, N.W.
Washington, DC 20036
(202) 483-2512
Fax: (202) 483-2657
E-mail: cfp@apsanet.org
Web Site: www.apsanet.org/cfp

FOUNDED: 1903

AREAS OF INTEREST:
Political science.

NAME(S) OF PROGRAMS:
● **Congressional Fellowship Program**

TYPE:
Fellowships. Awards to political science
professors and journalists in early-career to
midcareer status; the award provides an
opportunity for support as a full-time aide to
a member of the House or Senate or as a
staff member for a Congressional committee.

YEAR PROGRAM STARTED: 1953

PURPOSE:
To equip outstanding young political
scientists and journalists with a better
understanding of the national legislative
process.

LEGAL BASIS:
Nonprofit association.

ELIGIBILITY:
Open to U.S. political scientists and
journalists. Political scientists must have
completed their Ph.D. within the last 15
years or will have defended a dissertation by
the start of the fellowship year. Applicant
journalists must have a Bachelor's degree and
between two and 10 years of full-time
professional experience in newspaper,
magazine, radio or television work. Special
fellowships are available for Ph.D.-level
scholars of any discipline or journalists with
demonstrated professional interest in
telecommunications.

FINANCIAL DATA:
Amount of support per award: $52,500
stipend plus travel.

NO. MOST RECENT APPLICANTS: Varies.

NO. AWARDS: Varies.

APPLICATION INFO:
Official application materials are available on
the web site.
Duration: 10 months, November to August.
Deadline: Early December

ADDRESS INQUIRIES TO:
See e-mail address above.

AMERICAN POLITICAL SCIENCE ASSOCIATION [1783]

1527 New Hampshire Avenue, N.W.
Washington, DC 20036
(202) 483-2512
Fax: (202) 483-2657
E-mail: kmealy@apsanet.org
Web Site: www.apsanet.org/mfp

FOUNDED: 1903

AREAS OF INTEREST:
Political science.

NAME(S) OF PROGRAMS:
● APSA Minority Fellows Program

TYPE:
Fellowships; Grants-in-aid; Scholarships.
Awards to aid prospective African American,
Asian Pacific, Latino/Latina and Native
American political science students beginning
the doctoral study of political science.

YEAR PROGRAM STARTED: 1969

PURPOSE:
To increase the number of minority scholars
in the discipline; to assist minority students
in completing their Doctorates by
concentrating not only on the recruitment of
minorities, but also on the retention of these
groups within the profession.

LEGAL BASIS:
Nonprofit association.

ELIGIBILITY:
Applicants must:
(1) be minority students applying to enter a
doctoral program in political science for the
first time;
(2) be members of one of the following
racial/ethnic minority groups: African
Americans, Asian Pacific Americans,
Latinos/Latinas, and Native Americans
(federal and state recognized tribes);
(3) demonstrate an interest in teaching and
potential for research in political science and;
(4) be a U.S. citizen, U.S. national,
permanent resident or an individual granted
Deferred Action for Childhood Arrivals
(DACA) program status at time of
application.

FINANCIAL DATA:
Amount of support per award: $4,000,
disbursed in two $2,000 payments, one at the
end of their first graduate year and one at the
end of their second, provided that they
remain in good academic standing.

NO. MOST RECENT APPLICANTS: 20.

NO. AWARDS: 16 for the year 2019-20.

APPLICATION INFO:
Forms can be downloaded from the web site.
Duration: One year.
Deadline: Varies.

ADDRESS INQUIRIES TO:
Kimberly Mealy
Senior Director, Diversity and Inclusion
(See address above.)

AMERICAN POLITICAL SCIENCE ASSOCIATION [1784]

1527 New Hampshire Avenue, N.W.
Washington, DC 20036
(202) 483-2512
Fax: (202) 483-2657
E-mail: centennial@apsnet.org
Web Site: www.apsanet.org/smallresearchgrant

AREAS OF INTEREST:
Political science.

NAME(S) OF PROGRAMS:
● **Small Research Grant Program**

TYPE:
Project/program grants; Research grants;
Seed money grants; Technical assistance;
Travel grants. The Association Small
Research Grant Program supports research in
all fields of political science.

PURPOSE:
To support the research of political scientists
who are not employed at Ph.D.-granting
departments in the field, or who are in
non-tenure track or contingent positions
ineligible for departmental funding.

ELIGIBILITY:
Applicants must be Association members at
the time of application and when the funds
are dispersed. The principal investigator and
any coauthor must be one of the following:
(1) a Ph.D. faculty member at a college or
university that does not award a Ph.D. in
political science, public administration, public
policy, international relations, government or
politics and whose primary appointment is in
one of these departments or;
(2) a Ph.D. faculty member at a college or
university that awards the Ph.D. in political
science who is on a non-tenure or contingent
track, and ineligible for departmental funding
or;
(3) a political scientist not affiliated with an
academic institution who is unemployed or
working in a research organization such as a
think tank.

This grant does not provide support for
dissertation research or writing. Graduate
students are not eligible to apply. Applicants
do not have to be U.S. citizens or residents.

FINANCIAL DATA:
Funds may be used for travel to archives,
travel to conduct interviews, administration
and coding of instruments, research
assistance, and purchase of data-sets. Travel
to professional meetings, secretarial costs
except for preparation of the final
manuscripts for publication, and salary
support for the principal investigator are
excluded from funding. Overhead or indirect
costs are not allowable expenses.
Amount of support per award: Up to $2,500.

APPLICATION INFO:
Complete proposal and application
procedures as well as sample proposals can
be found on the web site. Application must
be submitted through the link on the Small
Research Grant Program web page.
Duration: One year. Nonrenewable.
Deadline: Submission date will be posted
online.

*SPECIAL STIPULATIONS:
Funds must be expended between the time
they are received (usually in May) and the
end of the following fiscal year (June 30).

ASHBURN INSTITUTE INC.

198 Okatie Village Drive
Suite 103, PMB 301
Bluffton, SC 29909
(703) 728-6482
Fax: (843) 705-7643
E-mail: info@ashburninstitute.org
Web Site: www.ashburninstitute.org

TYPE:
Research grants; Scholarships. The Institute
carries out its own scholarship program for
graduate students through an annual

endowment received in perpetuity. Half of
the funds must be awarded to U.S. citizens.
The best papers which meet the goals of the
conference, as outlined in the "Call for
Papers," will reimburse the graduate authors
by covering their conference travel and
lodging expenses. Locations for the
conference may be anywhere in the world.
The top papers are selected for publication
with due credit to the authors.

Funding is provided by the gracious
endowment left by Mayme and Herb Frank
for the purpose of promoting international
integration and harmonization.

See entry 758 for full listing.

CENTER FOR CALIFORNIA STUDIES, CAPITAL FELLOWS PROGRAMS [1785]

California State University, Sacramento
6000 J Street, MS 6081
Sacramento, CA 95819-6081
(916) 278-6906
Fax: (916) 278-5199
E-mail: calstudies@csus.edu
Web Site: www.csus.edu/center/center-california-studies

FOUNDED: 1982

AREAS OF INTEREST:
California state government and public
service.

NAME(S) OF PROGRAMS:
● **Executive Fellowship Program**
● **Judicial Fellowship Program**
● **Senate Fellowship Program**
● **Jesse M. Unruh Assembly Fellowship Program**

TYPE:
Fellowships. Sponsored by the Center for
California Studies at California State
University, Sacramento. Full-time fellowships
for 64 fellows across four programs, 10 to 11
months, and graduate units earned from
California State University, Sacramento.

PURPOSE:
To provide insight into the legislative
process, including exposing people with
diverse life experience and backgrounds to
the legislative process; to provide research
and other professional staff assistance to the
Assembly or Senate; to provide an
experiential learning opportunity in California
state government within the Executive
branch, whereby Fellows gain valuable
insight and experience in the realm of public
policy and politics; to enable fellows to
conduct research, advocate on behalf of the
judiciary, develop and implement programs,
seek grants, and engage in education
outreach, strategic, planning, and policy
analysis.

LEGAL BASIS:
University/government program funded by
State Budget-General Budget Fund.

ELIGIBILITY:
Must be 20 years of age by September 1 of
fellowship year and have a minimum
four-year Bachelor's degree with graduation
by September 1 of fellowship year. Graduate,
postgraduate and midcareer applicants are
welcome.

FINANCIAL DATA:
In addition to the stipend, full medical, vision
and dental benefits are provided.

Amount of support per award: $2,794 monthly stipend (taxable income).

NO. MOST RECENT APPLICANTS: 1,300.

NO. AWARDS: 64.

APPLICATION INFO:
Applications will only be accepted online. Applicants must submit all transcripts, three letters of recommendation (minimum), and required writing prompts.
Duration: 10 to 11 months.
Deadline: February. Interviews in southern California and Sacramento in April/May. Fellowship announcement in May.

ADDRESS INQUIRIES TO:
Leonor Ehling, Executive Director
(See address above.)

*SPECIAL STIPULATIONS:
International fellows must have a valid work visa.

CITY OF NEW YORK [1786]
Department of Citywide Administrative Services
One Centre Street, Room 2425
New York, NY 10007
(212) 386-0058
E-mail: urbanfellows@dcas.nyc.gov
Web Site: www.nyc.gov/fellowships

FOUNDED: 1969

AREAS OF INTEREST:
City government and New York City government.

NAME(S) OF PROGRAMS:
● **New York City Urban Fellows Program**

TYPE:
Fellowships. Stipend for full-time work in New York City government agencies. Fellows work closely with city officials on long- and short-term projects and attend weekly seminars to get an academic perspective on the workings and problems of local government. Assignments range over fields such as urban planning, housing, health and social sciences, economic and financial administration, youth service, intergovernmental relations, criminal justice, cultural affairs and innumerable others. Positions are at relatively high levels as assistants to administrators and staff within the various city agencies.

YEAR PROGRAM STARTED: 1969

PURPOSE:
To attract qualified college graduates to participate in a management training program in New York City government.

LEGAL BASIS:
City Government agency.

ELIGIBILITY:
As of September of the program year, applicants must be recent college graduates (no more than two full years out of college). Fellows participate on a full-time basis. Applicants must be able to demonstrate their eligibility to work in the U.S. after graduation and for the entire fellowship period.

FINANCIAL DATA:
A choice of paid health insurance plans is provided.
Amount of support per award: $31,563 for the year 2021-22.

NO. MOST RECENT APPLICANTS: Approximately 300.

NO. AWARDS: 25 annually.

APPLICATION INFO:
Application information is available on the web site.
Duration: Nine months, September to May.
Deadline: Second Friday in January.

PUBLICATIONS:
Application guidelines.

ADDRESS INQUIRIES TO:
New York City Urban Fellows Program
(See address above.)

CONGRESSIONAL BLACK CAUCUS FOUNDATION, INC.
1720 Massachusetts Avenue, N.W.
Washington, DC 20036
(202) 263-2800
Fax: (202) 263-0846
E-mail: scholarships@cbcfinc.org
Web Site: www.cbcfinc.org

TYPE:
Scholarships. The CBC Spouses Education Scholarship is a national program that awards scholarships to academically talented and highly motivated students who intend to pursue full-time undergraduate, graduate or doctoral degrees.

See entry 929 for full listing.

CONGRESSIONAL BLACK CAUCUS FOUNDATION, INC.
1720 Massachusetts Avenue, N.W.
Washington, DC 20036
(202) 263-2800
Fax: (202) 263-0846
E-mail: info@cbcfinc.org
internships@cbcfinc.org
Web Site: www.cbcfinc.org

TYPE:
Fellowships; Internships. The CBCF Congressional Fellows Program helps participants gain invaluable experience as they assist in the development of legislation and public policy initiatives while working as congressional staff for a year. This program targets early career policy professionals who have completed a professional and/or graduate degree and have demonstrated commitment to improving the lives and services for individuals living in underserved communities. Fellows work on Capitol Hill in the office of a Congressional Black Caucus member.

The CBCF Congressional Internship Program provides undergraduate students with an in-depth orientation to Capitol Hill and the legislative process through actual work experience in the offices of Congressional Black Caucus Members. In this way interns prepare to become decision makers in the policymaking process.

See entry 931 for full listing.

CONGRESSIONAL HISPANIC CAUCUS INSTITUTE
1128 16th Street, N.W.
Washington, DC 20036
(202) 543-1771
Fax: (202) 546-2143
E-mail: programs@chci.org
Web Site: www.chci.org

TYPE:
Internships. Internships provide college students with a paid work placement in a congressional office or federal agency for a period of 12 weeks (Spring and Fall Programs) or 10 weeks (Summer Program), as well as extensive professional development and leadership trainings.

See entry 962 for full listing.

CONGRESSIONAL HISPANIC CAUCUS INSTITUTE
1128 16th Street, N.W.
Washington, DC 20036
(202) 543-1771
(202) 548-8796
Fax: (202) 546-8799
E-mail: programs@chci.org
Web Site: chci.org

TYPE:
Fellowships. Graduate Fellowship Program offers exceptional Latinos who have earned a graduate degree or higher related to a chosen policy issue area within three years of program start date unparalleled exposure to hands-on experience in public policy.

Public Policy Fellowship offers talented Latinos who have earned a Bachelor's degree within two years of the program start date the opportunity to gain hands-on experience at the national level in public policy.

See entry 963 for full listing.

THE DIRKSEN CONGRESSIONAL CENTER [1787]
2815 Broadway
Pekin, IL 61554
(309) 347-7113
E-mail: twhite@dirksencenter.org
Web Site: www.dirksencongressionalcenter.org

FOUNDED: 1963

AREAS OF INTEREST:
U.S. Congress and its leaders.

NAME(S) OF PROGRAMS:
● **Congressional Research Grants**

TYPE:
Research grants; Seed money grants; Travel grants. Financial awards to individuals conducting research about the U.S. Congress and its leaders.

YEAR PROGRAM STARTED: 1978

PURPOSE:
To foster study of Congress in order to enhance public understanding and appreciation of the legislative branch of the federal government.

LEGAL BASIS:
Independent, nonpartisan, not-for-profit research and educational organization.

ELIGIBILITY:
Open to anyone with a serious interest in studying Congress. The Center seeks applications specifically from political scientists, historians, biographers, scholars of public administration or American studies or journalists. Graduate students may also apply.

The program does not fund undergraduates or pre-Ph.D. study. Organizations are not eligible. No institutional overhead or indirect costs will be covered.

FINANCIAL DATA:
Total amount of support: $50,000 for the year 2020.

NO. MOST RECENT APPLICANTS: 45.

NO. AWARDS: Approximately 15 per year.

APPLICATION INFO:
Details on application are available on the web site.

Duration: Usually one year.

Deadline: Applications are accepted on a rolling basis. Announcements made no later than July of each year.

IRS I.D.: 36-6132816

ADDRESS INQUIRIES TO:
Tiffany White, Executive Director
(See address above.)

*SPECIAL STIPULATIONS:
This program does not fund tuition.

DONNER CANADIAN FOUNDATION   [1788]
8 Prince Arthur Avenue, 3rd Floor
Toronto ON M5R 1A9 Canada
(416) 920-6400
Fax: (416) 920-5577
E-mail: mclean@donner.ca
Web Site: www.donnerfoundation.org

FOUNDED: 1950

AREAS OF INTEREST:
Public policy research and education, environment and wildlife preservation, international development and human rights, and social services.

TYPE:
Project/program grants.

PURPOSE:
To determine how government handles public assets in delivering public services.

LEGAL BASIS:
Private foundation.

ELIGIBILITY:
The Foundation only makes grants to charitable organizations under the Income Tax Act of Canada. Grants are usually made for specific projects. The Foundation does not make grants for ongoing expenses, the acquisition of capital (equipment, buildings, land, etc.), endowments, fund-raising drives or to cover budget deficits. The Foundation does not accept unsolicited proposals.

GEOG. RESTRICTIONS: Canada.

FINANCIAL DATA:
Amount of support per award: Varies.

Total amount of support: Approximately $3,800,000 for the year 2019.

NO. AWARDS: More than 70 for the year 2019.

APPLICATION INFO:
The Foundation does not regularly respond to letters of inquiry or unsolicited requests for funding. Charitable organizations may send the Foundation's Executive Director a two- to three-page description of their goals and programs and if there is a potential match between this work and the interests of the Foundation, staff will contact the charity for more information.

Duration: One year.

EXECUTIVE DIRECTOR:
Helen McLean

ADDRESS INQUIRIES TO:
Helen McLean, Executive Director
(See address above.)

*PLEASE NOTE:
The Foundation only provides support to organizations recognized as charitable by the Canada Revenue Agency.

THE EISENHOWER FOUNDATION   [1789]
200 S.E. 4th Street
Abilene, KS 67410
(785) 263-6771
Fax: (785) 263-6715
E-mail: info@eisenhowerfoundation.net
Web Site: www.EisenhowerFoundation.net

AREAS OF INTEREST:
Scholarly research in the fields of history, government, economics, communications and international affairs.

NAME(S) OF PROGRAMS:
● **Travel Grants**

TYPE:
Travel grants. Travel grants are awarded to individual researchers on a competitive basis to cover a portion of expenses while in Abilene, KS, using the presidential library.

PURPOSE:
To assist scholars' research of primary sources in such fields as history, government, economics, communications and international affairs so they may provide informed leadership in American national life.

ELIGIBILITY:
Applicants must be graduate-level students.

FINANCIAL DATA:
Grants are not retroactive and travel must occur within one year of award.

Amount of support per award: Up to $1,000, dependent on application and review board recommendations.

Total amount of support: Varies.

NO. MOST RECENT APPLICANTS: 18.

NO. AWARDS: 17.

APPLICATION INFO:
Applications may be accessed online.

Deadline: Varies.

ADDRESS INQUIRIES TO:
Eisenhower Foundation
P.O. Box 295
Abilene, KS 67410
(See e-mail address above.)

*SPECIAL STIPULATIONS:
If grantee's research results in a thesis, dissertation, book or article, a copy of the final product must be submitted to the Eisenhower Library for its holdings.

GERALD R. FORD PRESIDENTIAL LIBRARY   [1790]
1000 Beal Avenue
Ann Arbor, MI 48109
(734) 205-0555
Fax: (734) 205-0571
E-mail: ford.library@nara.gov
Web Site: www.fordlibrarymuseum.gov

AREAS OF INTEREST:
Domestic issues, foreign policy and politics of the 1970s.

NAME(S) OF PROGRAMS:
● **Research Travel Grant Program**

TYPE:
Research grants; Travel grants. Research Travel Grants are awarded biannually to

scholars to help defray the expenses of travel to conduct archival research in the collections of the Ford Library. Library collections focus on federal policies, foreign relations, and politics in the 1970s.

PURPOSE:
To promote research in the holdings of the Ford Library.

ELIGIBILITY:
Overseas applicants are welcome to apply, but they are responsible for costs of travel from their home country to North America.

FINANCIAL DATA:
Amount of support per award: Maximum $2,200.

Total amount of support: Typically, $45,000 annually.

NO. MOST RECENT APPLICANTS: 40.

NO. AWARDS: Varies.

APPLICATION INFO:
Before applying, contact the Library for information about holdings related to your project. Applicants should submit the application form, a curriculum vitae, and a two- or three-page project proposal to the Library. The proposal should provide both a description of the project and the ways in which Ford Library resources can advance the research. Three professional references must submit supporting letters of recommendation.

Materials can be submitted electronically or sent by e-mail to: travelgrant@38foundation.org.

Duration: Research to be conducted within one year notice of award.

Deadline: March 15 and September 15 (postmark).

ADDRESS INQUIRIES TO:
Rachel Siglow, Grants Coordinator
303 Pearl Street, N.W.
Grand Rapids, MI 49504
Tel: (616) 254-0396
E-mail: travelgrant@38foundation.org

*SPECIAL STIPULATIONS:
The Gerald R. Ford Foundation expects acknowledgment of its support in resulting publication(s) and a donated copy of same to the Gerald R. Ford Presidential Library.

GERALD R. FORD PRESIDENTIAL LIBRARY   [1791]
1000 Beal Avenue
Ann Arbor, MI 48109
(734) 205-0558
Fax: (734) 205-0571
E-mail: ford.library@nara.gov
Web Site: www.fordlibrarymuseum.gov

FOUNDED: 1981

AREAS OF INTEREST:
The U.S. political process, broadly defined, since circa 1970. Of special interest is the role and analysis of public opinion in that process.

NAME(S) OF PROGRAMS:
● **Gerald R. Ford Scholar Award (Dissertation Award) in Honor of Robert M. Teeter**

TYPE:
Awards/prizes; Research grants. Annual award to a doctoral student doing dissertation research and writing on an aspect of the U.S. political process during the latter part of the

20th century. Robert Teeter spent over 30 years as a leader in public opinion analysis and campaign strategy, including the 1976 campaign of President Gerald R. Ford. The majority of written materials from Teeter's career are part of the Gerald R. Ford Presidential Library collections. The Robert M. Teeter Papers document public opinion analysis and political campaign strategy from 1972 to 2004. They also include NBC News and *Wall Street Journal* National Public Opinion Surveys from 1989 to 2004.

PURPOSE:
To promote research regarding the U.S. political process during the latter part of the 20th century.

ELIGIBILITY:
Applicants must have completed all requirements for the Ph.D. program (coursework and examinations) by the application deadline, except for the dissertation.

FINANCIAL DATA:
The Library will present the award when the recipient arrives at the Library to conduct research. The recipient determines use of the award money, including, but not limited to, travel, paper and audiovisual reproductions and administrative costs, and other research and writing expenses.
Amount of support per award: $5,000.

CO-OP FUNDING PROGRAMS: The Award has been made possible by the generous support of the Teeter family and friends, and the United Parcel Service.

NO. AWARDS: 1.

APPLICATION INFO:
Application can be downloaded from the web site listed above. Applicants must submit each of the following:
(1) an abstract describing the dissertation (no longer than 150 words);
(2) a five-page proposal;
(3) three letters of recommendation from individuals who can attest to the applicant's qualifications for the Award (one must be from their academic director that includes a statement approving the dissertation topic);
(4) unofficial transcripts from all graduate schools attended and;
(5) a curriculum vitae.
Deadline: March 31 postmark. Awards are made each spring. Applications may be submitted at any time, but those received after the deadline will automatically be entered for the following year's award.

STAFF:
Lauren White, Grant Coordinator

ADDRESS INQUIRIES TO:
Gerald R. Ford Scholar Award
in Honor of Robert M. Teeter
(See address above.)

THE FUND FOR AMERICAN STUDIES [1792]
1706 New Hampshire Avenue, N.W.
Washington, DC 20009
(202) 986-0384
Fax: (202) 986-0390
E-mail: dmccarthy@tfas.org
Web Site: www.tfas.org/programs/robert-novak-journalism-fellowship

FOUNDED: 1990

AREAS OF INTEREST:
Advancement of constitutional principles, a democratic society and a vibrant free enterprise system.

NAME(S) OF PROGRAMS:
• **Robert Novak Journalism Fellowship Program**

TYPE:
Fellowships. One-year writing project on a topic of applicant's choosing, focusing on journalism supportive of American culture and a free society.

YEAR PROGRAM STARTED: 1994

PURPOSE:
To award grants to working print and online journalists who share the Foundation's mission.

ELIGIBILITY:
Applicants must be U.S. citizens and working journalists with less than 10 years of professional experience in print and online journalism and who share the mission to advance constitutional principles, a democratic society and a vibrant free enterprise system.

FINANCIAL DATA:
Amount of support per award: Fellows: $30,000, plus up to $5,000 reimbursement for qualified project expenses; Full Fellows: $50,000 to $60,000, plus expense allowances between $10,000 and $15,000.
Total amount of support: Varies.

NO. AWARDS: Varies, depending upon funding available and the number of qualified applicants.

APPLICATION INFO:
Application materials must be submitted electronically.
Duration: One year.
Deadline: April 12.

IRS I.D.: 13-6223604

ADDRESS INQUIRIES TO:
Daniel McCarthy, Program Director
(See e-mail address above.)

HOOVER PRESIDENTIAL FOUNDATION [1793]
P.O. Box 696
West Branch, IA 52358
(319) 643-5327
Fax: (319) 643-2391
E-mail: info@hooverpf.org
Web Site: www.hooverpresidentialfoundation.org

FOUNDED: 1954

NAME(S) OF PROGRAMS:
• **Herbert Hoover Presidential Travel Grant Program**

TYPE:
Research grants; Travel grants. Money is only available for travel to the Hoover Presidential Library in West Branch, IA. The program seeks to encourage scholarly use of the holdings of the Herbert Hoover Presidential Library. It is specifically intended to promote the study of subjects of interest and concern to Herbert Hoover, Lou Henry Hoover, their associates and other public figures as reflected in the Library's 150 manuscript collections.

YEAR PROGRAM STARTED: 1978

PURPOSE:
To encourage historical research on Herbert Hoover and his connections.

LEGAL BASIS:
Tax-exempt, privately supported educational foundation.

ELIGIBILITY:
Current graduate students, postdoctoral scholars and independent researchers are eligible to apply. Applicant should contact archival staff to determine if Library holdings are pertinent to the applicant's research.

FINANCIAL DATA:
Amount of support per award: Up to $2,000. The Foundation will consider larger requests for extended graduate and postgraduate research at the Library.
Total amount of support: Varies.

NO. MOST RECENT APPLICANTS: 11.

NO. AWARDS: 9.

APPLICATION INFO:
Application materials are available on the web site or upon request from the Foundation. Applicants must consult with the archival staff concerning their topic prior to submitting a request for funding.
Duration: No grants made on a continuing basis. Reapplications for consecutive support periods are accepted. No more than two grants are allowed within a five-year period.
Deadline: March 1. Announcement April 30.

PUBLICATIONS:
Historical Materials in the Herbert Hoover Presidential Library.

ADDRESS INQUIRIES TO:
Delene W. McConnaha
Academic Programs Manager
(See address above.)

INSTITUTE FOR HUMANE STUDIES (IHS) [1794]
3434 Washington Boulevard, MS 1C5
Arlington, VA 22201
(703) 993-4880
Fax: (703) 993-4890
E-mail: hsf@theihs.org
Web Site: theihs.org/funding/humane-studies-fellowship

FOUNDED: 1961

AREAS OF INTEREST:
Individual liberty.

NAME(S) OF PROGRAMS:
• **Humane Studies Fellowships**

TYPE:
Fellowships; Research grants. Humane Studies Fellowships cover the fields of the social sciences and humanities.

PURPOSE:
To assist graduate students worldwide with a special interest in individual liberty.

ELIGIBILITY:
Graduate students in a Ph.D. program at a college or university may apply. Applicant must have a research interest that contributes to liberty-advancing scholarship.

FINANCIAL DATA:
Amount of support per award: Up to $15,000 per year.
Total amount of support: Varies.

APPLICATION INFO:
Application information is available on the web site.

Duration: One academic year. Renewable.

Deadline: April 1, August 1 and December 1.

ADDRESS INQUIRIES TO:
See e-mail address above.

THE INTERCOLLEGIATE STUDIES INSTITUTE [1795]

3901 Centerville Road
Wilmington, DE 19807
(302) 652-4600
Fax: (302) 652-6112
E-mail: jdavenport@isi.org
Web Site: isi.org/fellowships

FOUNDED: 1953

AREAS OF INTEREST:
Education.

NAME(S) OF PROGRAMS:
● **Richard M. Weaver Graduate Fellowship**

TYPE:
Awards/prizes; Fellowships; Scholarships. The Weaver Fellowship is granted to students who intend to use their advanced degree to teach.

PURPOSE:
To convey to successive generations of college students a better understanding of the values and institutions that sustain a free society.

LEGAL BASIS:
A nonprofit, nonpartisan, tax-exempt educational organization.

ELIGIBILITY:
Applicant must be a member of the Intercollegiate Studies Institute. Applicant must also engage in graduate studies for the purpose of teaching at the college level. Those attending preprofessional schools (such as law, business, medicine and divinity) are ineligible. Applicants must be U.S. citizens who will be enrolled in a full-time graduate program for the upcoming academic year. Applicants may apply for more than one fellowship in any given academic cycle.

FINANCIAL DATA:
Amount of support per award: Five at $15,000 each, five at $10,000 each, and five at $5,000 each.

Total amount of support: $150,000.

NO. AWARDS: 15.

APPLICATION INFO:
Application information is available on the web site.

Deadline: February 26.

ADDRESS INQUIRIES TO:
Academic Program Officer
Program and Fellowships
(See address above.)

THE JAPANESE AMERICAN CITIZENS LEAGUE (JACL) [1796]

Washington, DC Office
1629 K Street, N.W., Suite 400
Washington, DC 20006
(202) 223-1240
E-mail: dinoue@jacl.org
Web Site: www.jacl.org

FOUNDED: 1929

AREAS OF INTEREST:
Public service leadership development.

NAME(S) OF PROGRAMS:
● **Mike M. Masaoka Fellowship Fund Congressional Program**

TYPE:
Fellowships. Congressional fellowship established to help understand the importance of public service at the national level. The Masaoka fellow serves in the Washington, DC office of a member of Congress in either the U.S. House of Representatives or the U.S. Senate.

YEAR PROGRAM STARTED: 1988

PURPOSE:
To develop leaders for public service.

ELIGIBILITY:
Candidates must be U.S. citizens who are graduating college seniors or students in graduate or professional programs. Preference will be given to those who have demonstrated commitment to Asian American and Pacific Islander (AAPI) issues, particularly those affecting the Japanese American community. Membership in the JACL is required. Communication skills, especially in writing, are important.

GEOG. RESTRICTIONS: United States.

FINANCIAL DATA:
Fellowship includes round-trip airfare from fellow's home to Washington, DC.

Amount of support per award: $2,500 monthly stipend.

Total amount of support: Up to $30,000 per fellow.

NO. AWARDS: Up to 4 annually.

APPLICATION INFO:
Completed application materials may be sent via e-mail to dinoue@jacl.org.

Duration: Six to eight months.

Deadline: 11:59 P.M., July 31.

ADDRESS INQUIRIES TO:
David Inoue, Executive Director
E-mail: policy@jacl.org
(See address above.)

THE LYNDON BAINES JOHNSON FOUNDATION [1797]

2313 Red River Street
Austin, TX 78705-5702
(512) 721-0263
E-mail: grants@lbjfoundation.org
Web Site: www.lbjlibrary.org

FOUNDED: 1969

AREAS OF INTEREST:
Support for the LBJ Presidential Library and the LBJ School of Public Affairs at The University of Texas.

NAME(S) OF PROGRAMS:
● **Middleton Fellowship in Presidential Studies**
● **Moody Research Grants**

TYPE:
Fellowships; Research grants.

YEAR PROGRAM STARTED: 1972

PURPOSE:
To defray living, travel and related expenses incurred while conducting research at the LBJ Library during the period for which the grant is awarded.

LEGAL BASIS:
Nonprofit organization.

ELIGIBILITY:
In accepting a grant, an applicant must agree to the following conditions:
(1) that the product of the research which is made possible through these funds will not be used for any political purpose;
(2) that the funds are for the purpose of helping to defray expenses incurred while conducting research at the Johnson Library;
(3) that the grant must be used in the grant period in which it is awarded; and
(4) that the LBJ Foundation will be promptly provided with a copy of any publication, paper, article or book resulting from research made possible by this grant.

FINANCIAL DATA:
Amount of support per award: Middleton Fellowship: $5,000; Moody Research Grants: $600 to $3,000.

Total amount of support: Middleton Fellowship: $10,000 to $12,000; Moody Research Grants: Approximately $50,000 per grant period.

NO. MOST RECENT APPLICANTS: 3 Middleton Fellowships and 21 Moody Research Grants for Spring.

NO. AWARDS: Middleton Fellowship: 2; Moody Research Grants: 18.

APPLICATION INFO:
Application forms must be accompanied by a written proposal. Candidates should state clearly and precisely how the holdings of the LBJ Library will contribute to the completion of the project.

Middleton Fellowship applicants are also required to submit three letters of recommendation.

Duration: Eight months for spring grant period. Six months for fall grant period.

Deadline: September 15 for January to August grant period. March 15 for June to December grant period.

IRS I.D.: 74-1774063

STAFF:
Samantha Stone, Chief Operating Officer

ADDRESS INQUIRIES TO:
Samantha Stone, Chief Operating Officer
(See telephone or e-mail address above.)

NATIONAL ENDOWMENT FOR DEMOCRACY [1798]

1025 F Street, N.W.
Suite 800
Washington, DC 20004
(202) 378-9700
Fax: (202) 378-9407
E-mail: info@ned.org
Web Site: www.ned.org

FOUNDED: 1983

AREAS OF INTEREST:
Democracy throughout the world.

NAME(S) OF PROGRAMS:
● **National Endowment for Democracy Grants**

TYPE:
Project/program grants.

PURPOSE:
To strengthen democratic institutions throughout the world.

ELIGIBILITY:
Nongovernmental organizations, which include civic organizations, associations, independent media, and other similar

organizations, may apply. Individuals, governmental bodies, or state-supported institutions are also eligible.

FINANCIAL DATA:
Amount of support per award: Average $50,000 to $60,000.
Total amount of support: Varies.

NO. MOST RECENT APPLICANTS: Over 8,000.

NO. AWARDS: Approximately 1,600.

APPLICATION INFO:
Application information is available on the web site.
Duration: One year. Renewable.
Deadline: 10 to 12 weeks prior to board meetings held in January, March, June and September.

ADDRESS INQUIRIES TO:
E-mail: proposals@ned.org

NATIONAL FEDERATION OF REPUBLICAN WOMEN
124 North Alfred Street
Alexandria, VA 22314
(703) 548-9688
E-mail: scholarships@nfrw.org
Web Site: www.nfrw.org

TYPE:
Internships; Scholarships. Dorothy Kabis Internship includes a six- to eight-week internship in Washington, DC, housing, travel and stipend.

National Pathfinder's Scholarships are given to the best nominated candidates.

Betty Rendel Scholarships are given to undergraduate women who are majoring in political science, government or economics.

See entry 984 for full listing.

NEW YORK STATE ASSEMBLY INTERN COMMITTEE   [1799]
Legislative Office Building, Room 104A
Albany, NY 12248
(518) 455-4704
Fax: (518) 455-4705
E-mail: intern@nyassembly.gov
Web Site: www.nyassembly.gov/internship

FOUNDED: 1971

AREAS OF INTEREST:
Government.

NAME(S) OF PROGRAMS:
● **Assembly Session Internships**

TYPE:
Internships. Program provides firsthand knowledge of the legislative process and functions. The interns are assigned research and administrative responsibilities in an Assembly office. They receive a practical educational experience and attend weekly classes. The Assembly benefits from the new ideas and fresh perspectives of the interns. All intern placements are in Albany, NY.

YEAR PROGRAM STARTED: 1971

PURPOSE:
To encourage talented students from all fields to learn about and get involved in state government.

LEGAL BASIS:
Government legislature.

ELIGIBILITY:
Applicants must be matriculated in a U.S. college or university degree program as

juniors or seniors. Applications are welcome from students in any academic field. Colleges generally award a full semester of credit for participation. International students should have academic requirements in the U.S. to be eligible.

FINANCIAL DATA:
Session interns receive a stipend and semester of college credit.
Amount of support per award: $6,200 session term.

NO. MOST RECENT APPLICANTS: Over 200.

NO. AWARDS: 150.

APPLICATION INFO:
Applications are available from an Intern Program liaison officer on college campuses. Applications and all supporting documents must be submitted to the Intern Committee in a complete package.

The following documents must be included with the application:
(1) personal statement;
(2) official transcripts of all college courses completed and in progress;
(3) two letters of recommendation;
(4) a letter from an appropriate college official endorsing the student's participation and indicating the amount of credit to be granted by the college and;
(5) a concise writing sample.
Duration: January to mid-May.
Deadline: November 1.

STAFF:
Kathleen McCarty, Director, Assembly Intern Committee

ADDRESS INQUIRIES TO:
Kathleen McCarty, Director
Assembly Intern Committee
(See address above.)

NEW YORK STATE ASSEMBLY INTERN COMMITTEE   [1800]
Legislative Office Building, Room 104A
Albany, NY 12248
(518) 455-4704
Fax: (518) 455-4705
E-mail: intern@nyassembly.gov
Web Site: www.nyassembly.gov/internship

FOUNDED: 1971

AREAS OF INTEREST:
Government.

NAME(S) OF PROGRAMS:
● **Graduate Scholar Internship**

TYPE:
Internships. Assignments designed to provide up to 10 graduate students with full-time work placements as Assembly researchers and policy analysts with all the responsibilities and expectations of such positions. The work placements are with Assembly leaders. The interns will have the opportunity to develop a better understanding of the legislative process while contributing new ideas and fresh perspectives to the legislative decision making process.

YEAR PROGRAM STARTED: 1976

PURPOSE:
To bring the expertise and thinking of the state's best graduate students into the legislative process.

LEGAL BASIS:
Government.

ELIGIBILITY:
All students matriculated in or who have recently completed a graduate degree program may apply. Students with expertise in a variety of public policy issues are being sought. Issues include public finance, education, environmental conservation, etc. Students must work full-time in the Assembly. International students should have academic requirements in the U.S. to be eligible. Credit can often be arranged by the school.

GEOG. RESTRICTIONS: New York state.

FINANCIAL DATA:
Amount of support per award: $15,000 stipend per year.

NO. MOST RECENT APPLICANTS: 50.

NO. AWARDS: Up to 10 each year.

APPLICATION INFO:
Applications are available from graduate schools, directly from the Assembly Intern Committee, or on the web site. Applications must include two letters of recommendation, a letter from graduate program dean or director, official transcripts, a writing sample and a personal statement.
Duration: Six months (January to June). Nonrenewable.
Deadline: September 13 (postmark).

STAFF:
Kathleen McCarty, Director

ADDRESS INQUIRIES TO:
Kathleen McCarty, Director
(See address above.)

NEW YORK STATE SENATE   [1801]
Legislative Office Building, Suite 1426
Albany, NY 12247
(518) 455-2611
Fax: (518) 426-6827
E-mail: students@nysenate.gov
Web Site: www.nysenate.gov/student-programs

FOUNDED: 1965

AREAS OF INTEREST:
New York state government and education which includes improved public access to and understanding of government, resulting in enhanced citizenship, career staffing, government administration and leadership.

NAME(S) OF PROGRAMS:
● **James L. Biggane Fellowship in Finance**
● **New York State Senate Legislative Fellows Program**
● **Richard J. Roth Journalism Fellowship**
● **Richard A. Wiebe Public Service Fellowship**

TYPE:
Fellowships. These fellowships are intended for the graduate/postgraduate level. Stipends are for bipartisan opportunities to train in government while on-site in Albany, NY. Fellows spend almost a year immersed in the work of the Senate, learning techniques associated with policymaking and legislative process. Placement is usually in the office of an elected Senate member. The Senate Legislative Fellows Program, Biggane Fellowship, Roth Journalism Fellowship and Wiebe Public Service Fellowship constitute the Senate Graduate/Post-Graduate Fellowships.

YEAR PROGRAM STARTED: 1965

PURPOSE:
To provide an opportunity for career experience and learning for graduate assistants, career recruitment among superior fellows, and citizenship training in general.

LEGAL BASIS:
Legislative authority.

ELIGIBILITY:
Graduate/Postgraduate Fellowships: In most cases, Fellows must have completed graduate-level work at an accredited university during the immediately previous spring and fall semesters. Fellowships are open to all majors. Training in the history/politics/government of New York state is not required.

Biggane applicants need not be currently enrolled in graduate-level study, but must have obtained a previous graduate-level degree. Legislative Fellows will be talented and skilled graduate/postgraduate students from a variety of academic disciplines.

The Roth Fellow may be a student with experience and/or intentions in the fields of communications, journalism and/or public relations.

The Wiebe Fellow will be a student with legal training and a variety of other backgrounds.

Students are not required to presently reside in New York state or attend school in New York state.

FINANCIAL DATA:
The stipend is distributed in biweekly installments prorated from the first day to the last day of enrollment. Some benefit options are available (health, dental, vision, life insurance, and the retirement program). Fellows are not Senate employees; they do not earn vacation or personal leave.

All Senate Fellowships are on-site in Albany, NY. Fellowships are not financial aid for academic work, on-campus or classroom study. Housing in Albany is the responsibility of the Fellow.

Amount of support per award:
Grant-in-Study stipend of $40,000 for the fellowship year September 2021 to June 2022.

NO. MOST RECENT APPLICANTS: 35.

NO. AWARDS: Approximately 16 fellowships each year. Legislative Fellows Program: Up to 13; Biggane, Roth and Wiebe Fellowships: 1 each.

APPLICATION INFO:
Applications must include the following:
(1) course work-in-progress list signed by campus official (if not on transcript);
(2) calling of Office of Student Programs to indicate one's intent to apply;
(3) policy proposal;
(4) rebuttal of policy proposal;
(5) statement of purpose;
(6) writing sample essay;
(7) resume or curriculum vitae;
(8) all official transcripts (graduate and undergraduate) and;
(9) three letters of reference from persons familiar with the applicant's character, academic and/or professional abilities (at least two from faculty members).
Duration: Approximately one year, September through late June. No renewals.
Deadline: Last Friday in April.

PUBLICATIONS:
Program announcement.

ADDRESS INQUIRIES TO:
Director, Office of Student Programs
(See address above.)

NEW YORK STATE SENATE [1802]
Legislative Office Building, Suite 1426
Albany, NY 12247
(518) 455-2611
Fax: (518) 426-6827
E-mail: students@nysenate.gov
Web Site: www.nysenate.gov/student-programs

FOUNDED: 1978

AREAS OF INTEREST:
State government internships for undergraduates.

NAME(S) OF PROGRAMS:
● **Undergraduate Session Assistants Program**

TYPE:
Internships. Annual undergraduate internship running early January to late April.

YEAR PROGRAM STARTED: 1978

PURPOSE:
To provide on-site experience at the New York State Senate, Albany, NY.

ELIGIBILITY:
Applicant must be a full-time student in an accredited, undergraduate degree program on a campus in New York state. The program is intended and designed for college juniors and seniors; exceptional sophomores may occasionally be selected. Freshmen are ineligible.

The Senate welcomes majors in all accredited disciplines. Training in the history/politics/government of New York is neither a prerequisite of nor an advantage to selection. Skill and ability, initiative, eagerness to learn, discretion and mature flexibility are essential for success.

Each student should demonstrate a 3.0 grade point average or better and meet the campus/departmental standard for off-campus study; full-time enrollment in the immediately previous spring (not summer) and current fall semester/previous two trimesters. Each standard is to be certified by the Campus Liaison Officer (CLO), student's academic advisor, chairman, dean, or other duly authorized campus official.

Placements are ordinarily to the offices of individual senators. Students may observe, participate in, and/or acquire experience with state government procedures. Combined participation in the program and legislative placement is for a minimum of 35 hours per week. Longer hours are possible and should be expected.

Each applicant must be able to earn campus-awarded credit for participation in the program to be eligible. On-campus faculty is responsible for academic advisement, evaluation, grading and granting of credit for their student participant(s) enrolled in this Senate program.

GEOG. RESTRICTIONS: New York state.

FINANCIAL DATA:
Arrangement of housing in Albany is the responsibility of the individual enrollee.

Amount of support per award: A stipend of $6,600 to offset costs of moving to and living in Albany.

NO. MOST RECENT APPLICANTS: Approximately 40 to 45.

NO. AWARDS: Approximately 30.

APPLICATION INFO:
Enrollment is on-site at the New York State Senate in Albany, NY. Applications are available on campus, from the Student Programs Office, or at the web site.

If there is no CLO on campus, contact Nicholas J. Parrella, Director of Student Programs, at the address listed above.
Duration: Approximately four months.
Deadline: The last Friday in October. Expect an earlier on-campus deadline if one's school has a Campus Liaison Officer (CLO). Announcement of selections is approximately mid-November.

STAFF:
Nicholas J. Parrella, Director of Student Programs

ADDRESS INQUIRIES TO:
Nicholas J. Parrella
Director of Student Programs
(See address above.)

PIPER FUND [1803]
15 Research Drive
Suite B
Amherst, MA 01002
(413) 256-0349
E-mail: grantsmanager@proteusfund.org
Web Site: www.proteusfund.org

AREAS OF INTEREST:
Campaign finance reform in the American political system.

TYPE:
General operating grants; Project/program grants.

PURPOSE:
To help meet the needs of the growing movement for campaign finance reform in America.

GEOG. RESTRICTIONS: United States.

FINANCIAL DATA:
Amount of support per award: Typically $10,000 to $50,000.

Total amount of support: Approximately $38,000,000 since inception. Over $3,000,000 for the year 2018.

NO. AWARDS: 75 for the year 2019.

APPLICATION INFO:
Applications are accepted by invitation only.
Duration: One year.

ADDRESS INQUIRIES TO:
Kyrstin Thorson Rogers, Grants Manager
(See address above.)

*SPECIAL STIPULATIONS:
Grants are by invitation only.

PRESIDENT'S COMMISSION ON WHITE HOUSE FELLOWSHIPS [1804]
712 Jackson Place, N.W.
Washington, DC 20503
(202) 395-4522
Fax: (202) 395-6179
E-mail: whitehousefellows@who.eop.gov
Web Site: www.whitehouse.gov/get-involved/fellows

FOUNDED: 1964

AREAS OF INTEREST:
Leadership and public service for young professionals.

NAME(S) OF PROGRAMS:
● **White House Fellowships**

TYPE:
Fellowships. The White House Fellows program is America's most prestigious program for leadership and public service. White House Fellowships offer exceptional young men and women firsthand experience working at the highest levels of the federal government.

White House Fellows typically spend a year working as full-time, paid special assistants to senior White House staff, the Vice President, cabinet secretaries and other top-ranking government officials. Fellows also participate in an education program consisting of roundtable discussions with renowned leaders from the private and public sectors, and trips to study U.S. policy in action both domestically and internationally. Fellowships are awarded on a strictly nonpartisan basis.

PURPOSE:
To give those who participate in the program firsthand, high-level experience with the workings of the federal government and to increase their sense of participation in national affairs.

ELIGIBILITY:
The following criteria apply:
(1) applicants must be U.S. citizens;
(2) employees of the federal government are not eligible unless they are career military personnel;
(3) applicants must have completed their undergraduate education by the time they begin the application process and;
(4) there are no formal age restrictions; however, the fellowship program was created to give selected Americans the experience of government service early in their careers.

The Commission awards fellowships on a strict nonpartisan basis and encourages balance and diversity in all aspects of the program.

GEOG. RESTRICTIONS: United States.

FINANCIAL DATA:
Fellows are eligible to purchase health insurance through the Federal Employee Health Benefit Plans.

NO. MOST RECENT APPLICANTS: Up to 1,000.

NO. AWARDS: 11 to 19 fellowships per year.

APPLICATION INFO:
Application must be submitted online and is available beginning in the Fall.
Duration: Typically one year.
Deadline: Mid-January.

RHODE ISLAND STATE GOVERNMENT INTERNSHIP PROGRAM [1805]
State House, Room 8AA
Providence, RI 02903
(401) 222-6782
Fax: (401) 222-4447
E-mail: intern@rilegislature.gov
blanzi@rilegislature.gov
Web Site: www.rilegislature.gov/internship

FOUNDED: 1969

AREAS OF INTEREST:
All fields of study.

NAME(S) OF PROGRAMS:
● **Rhode Island State Government Internship Program**

TYPE:
Internships. The Internship Program is run through the Joint Committee on Legislative Services (JCLS). Students are connected with internship experiences throughout state government. This includes the Legislative, Executive and Judicial branches, as well as state departments of government, municipal agencies and community and nonprofit organizations. Students are placed in areas of interest where they work with their placement supervisor on a variety of projects and tasks that enable them to meet educational learning objectives.

Many colleges and universities grant credit for the internship experience. The amount of credit granted to each student differs based on school and hours of service.

YEAR PROGRAM STARTED: 1969

PURPOSE:
To provide a link between the public and state government; to open a channel for the potential recruitment of personnel for state government internship; to supplement college and university course offerings in state and local government; to enable students to develop a knowledge of the structure and procedure of state government.

LEGAL BASIS:
Chapter 47, General Laws, state of Rhode Island.

ELIGIBILITY:
The Program is open to students who are at least 18 years of age and currently enrolled in college, graduate school or law school. Students are required to be currently enrolled in an accredited institution and have a minimum 2.5 grade point average. The program accepts students who are Rhode Island residents attending an accredited in-state or out-of-state institution or a nonresident who is attending a Rhode Island accredited institution. All academic majors are accepted and student experience, academic background and educational goals are taken into consideration for placement.

FINANCIAL DATA:
Academic credit, up to a maximum of six credits, is available. For the Summer Internship, a student is required to work eight to 10 hours per week and receives a monthly stipend.

APPLICATION INFO:
Interns are selected by the academic committee and referred to Intern Staff.
Duration: Eight to 12 weeks in the spring and fall (one school semester) and eight weeks (July and August) for Summer Internship.
Deadline: August 28 for fall program, December 18 for spring program, and April 23 for summer program.

ADDRESS INQUIRIES TO:
Krystina Cesario
Office Administrative Assistant
E-mail: kcesario@rilegislature.gov

*SPECIAL STIPULATIONS:
Upon completion of the internship, placement supervisors complete an Intern Assessment and all interns are required to complete a Summary of Experience Essay.

FRANKLIN D. ROOSEVELT LIBRARY AND MUSEUM
4079 Albany Post Road
Hyde Park, NY 12538
(845) 486-7770
E-mail: grants.fdr@nara.gov
Web Site: fdrlibrary.org/research-grants

TYPE:
Grants-in-aid; Research grants. The Roosevelt Institute - the Library's nonprofit partner - supports a program of small grants-in-aid, in support of research on the "Roosevelt years" or clearly related subjects.

See entry 582 for full listing.

SARAH SCAIFE FOUNDATION, INC. [1806]
One Oxford Centre, Suite 3900
301 Grant Street
Pittsburgh, PA 15219-6402
(412) 392-2900
Web Site: www.scaife.com

FOUNDED: 1941

AREAS OF INTEREST:
Domestic and international public policy issues.

TYPE:
Challenge/matching grants; Fellowships; General operating grants; Project/program grants; Seed money grants.

YEAR PROGRAM STARTED: 1941

PURPOSE:
To direct money to programs that address major domestic and international issues.

LEGAL BASIS:
Private foundation.

ELIGIBILITY:
The Foundation does not make grants to individuals for any purpose, to nationally organized fund-raising groups, or to organizations that are not publicly supported nonprofit charitable organizations.

FINANCIAL DATA:
Amount of support per award: Average $25,000 to $250,000.

REPRESENTATIVE AWARDS:
$200,000 to American Civil Rights Union; $250,000 to Foundation for Individual Rights in Education, Inc.; $60,000 to New England Legal Foundation.

APPLICATION INFO:
Grant proposals to the Foundation must contain a cover letter signed by the organization's president or authorized representative and have the approval of the board of directors. The letter should include a concise description of the purpose of the requesting organization and of the specific project or program for which funds are requested (if applicable) along with the following:
(1) program or project budget (if applicable);
(2) timetable (if applicable);
(3) organization's annual budget;
(4) most recent audited financial statements;
(5) current Form 990;
(6) annual report;
(7) list of officers and directors with their affiliations;
(8) list of key supporters and;
(9) IRS determination letter evidencing 501(c)(3) tax-exempt status.
Duration: One year.

Deadline: Board meets quarterly in February, May, September and November. Notification within two to four weeks.

PUBLICATIONS:
Annual report.

OFFICERS:
Michael W. Gleba, Chairman, Chief Executive Officer and Treasurer
Linda M. Buckley, Secretary and Assistant Treasurer

ADDRESS INQUIRIES TO:
Michael W. Gleba
Chairman and Chief Executive Officer
(See address above.)

THE SOCIETY FOR THE PSYCHOLOGICAL STUDY OF SOCIAL ISSUES (SPSSI) [1807]

700 Seventh Street, S.E.
Washington, DC 20003
(202) 675-6956
E-mail: awards@spssi.org
Web Site: www.spssi.org

FOUNDED: 1936

AREAS OF INTEREST:
Public policy, social issues, psychology and international relations.

NAME(S) OF PROGRAMS:
● **Otto Klineberg Intercultural and International Relations Award**

TYPE:
Awards/prizes. The Klineberg Award is given for the best paper or article of the year on intercultural or international relations.

PURPOSE:
To award the best paper or article of the year on intercultural or international relations.

LEGAL BASIS:
Independently incorporated society.

ELIGIBILITY:
Entries can be either unpublished manuscripts, in press papers, book chapters, or journal articles published no more than 18 months prior to the submission deadline. Entries cannot be returned. The competition is open to nonmembers and members of SPSSI. Graduate students are especially urged to submit papers. Submissions from across the social sciences are encouraged, however the paper must clearly demonstrate its relevance for psychological theory and research in the domain of intercultural and international relations.

FINANCIAL DATA:
Amount of support per award: $1,000.

NO. MOST RECENT APPLICANTS: 24.

NO. AWARDS: 1.

APPLICATION INFO:
Online submissions are the preferred method. Please limit the number and size of files uploaded when applying online. For hard-copy submissions, send five (5) copies to the address listed above, "Attn: Klineberg Award."
Deadline: March 1.

PUBLICATIONS:
Program announcement; application guidelines.

ADDRESS INQUIRIES TO:
See e-mail address above.

HATTON W. SUMNERS FOUNDATION [1808]

325 North St. Paul Street
Suite 3920
Dallas, TX 75201
(214) 220-2128
Fax: (214) 953-0737
E-mail: info@hattonsumners.org
Web Site: www.sumnersfoundation.org

FOUNDED: 1949

AREAS OF INTEREST:
Self-government, political science and democracy.

TYPE:
Challenge/matching grants; Conferences/seminars; Endowments; Fellowships; Internships; Project/program grants; Scholarships. Scholarship programs at selected universities and grants to support other educational activities for both students and adults, which are designed to create an appreciation and understanding for the U.S. executive, legislative and judicial processes.

YEAR PROGRAM STARTED: 1949

PURPOSE:
To encourage the study, teaching and research into the science and art of self-government so that the American people may understand the fundamental principles of democracy and be guided thereby in shaping governmental policies.

LEGAL BASIS:
Private charitable foundation.

ELIGIBILITY:
Grants for purposes other than scholarships or fellowships are made only to organizations that are qualified charities under Section 501(c)(3) of the Internal Revenue Code.

GEOG. RESTRICTIONS: Arkansas, Kansas, Louisiana, Missouri, Nebraska, New Mexico, Oklahoma and Texas.

FINANCIAL DATA:
Amount of support per award: Varies.
Total amount of support: $2,357,750 in grants and $1,728,284 in scholarships for the year 2019.

NO. AWARDS: Varies.

REPRESENTATIVE AWARDS:
$20,000 to Bill of Rights Institute, Arlington, VA, for Constitutional Seminars and curriculum support for teachers in New Mexico; $150,000 to Institute for Policy Innovation, Irving, TX, for lecture series on public policy issues; $15,000 to The Arc of Collin, Dallas and Rockwall Counties, Dallas, TX, for funding of The Leadership Institute.

APPLICATION INFO:
The Foundation only accepts applications filed on its web site.
Duration: One year. Occasional multiyear funding.
Deadline: August 1. Decision in October.

PUBLICATIONS:
Annual report.

STAFF:
T. Charles Pierson, Executive Director

ADDRESS INQUIRIES TO:
T. Charles Pierson, Executive Director
(See address above.)

HARRY S. TRUMAN LIBRARY INSTITUTE [1809]

5151 Troost Avenue
Suite 300
Kansas City, MO 64110
(816) 400-1216
Fax: (816) 400-1213
E-mail: lisa.sullivan@trumanlibraryinstitute.org
Web Site: www.trumanlibraryinstitute.org

FOUNDED: 1957

AREAS OF INTEREST:
Harry S. Truman and the Truman Administration.

NAME(S) OF PROGRAMS:
● **Dissertation Year Fellowships**
● **Research Grant**
● **Scholar's Award**
● **Harry S. Truman Book Award**

TYPE:
Awards/prizes; Fellowships; Grants-in-aid; Research grants; Travel grants. The Dissertation Year Fellowships are given to encourage historical scholarship of the public career of Harry S. Truman or the Truman era. Support is given annually to one or two graduate students who have completed the dissertation research and are in the writing stage. Preference will be given to projects based on extensive research at the Truman Library. Successful applicants will be expected to deposit one copy of their completed dissertation, or any publication resulting therefrom, with the Truman Library.

Research Grants are intended to enable graduate students as well as postdoctoral scholars to come to the Library for one to three weeks to use its archival facilities.

The Scholar's Award is given every other year, even-numbered years only, to a scholar engaged in a study of either the public career of Harry S. Truman or some aspect of the history of the Truman administration or of the U.S. during that administration. The scholar's work must be based on extensive research at the Truman Library and must be designed to result in the publication of a book-length manuscript. One copy of such book (and/or any other publication resulting from work done under this award) shall be deposited by the author with the Harry S. Truman Library.

The Harry S. Truman Book Award is given in even years for the best book dealing with some aspect of history of the U.S. between April 12, 1945 and January 20, 1953 or with the public career of Harry S. Truman.

YEAR PROGRAM STARTED: 1959

PURPOSE:
To encourage study of the history of the Truman administration and the public career of Harry S. Truman; to promote the use of the Truman Library as a national center for historical scholarship.

ELIGIBILITY:
Undergraduate students, doctoral candidates and postdoctoral scholars with appropriate interests are eligible for support. Applicants must be competent researchers with viable topics for which pertinent materials are available at the Truman Library.

FINANCIAL DATA:
Amount of support per award: Dissertation Year Fellowships: $16,000 payable in two installments; Research Grants: Up to $2,500; Scholar's Award: $30,000; Truman Book Award: $2,500.
Total amount of support: $84,810.

NO. MOST RECENT APPLICANTS: 32.

NO. AWARDS: Dissertation Year Fellowships: Up to 2.

REPRESENTATIVE AWARDS:
Harry S. Truman Book Award: Derek Leebaert, "Grand Improvisation: America Confronts the British Superpower, 1945-1957."

APPLICATION INFO:
Applicants for the Scholar's Award should submit an application and proposal for preliminary screening. If selected, applicants must submit further information including a list of Truman files already utilized or planned to be utilized, a projected timeline for completion, and projected income for the academic year in which the award will be announced. Applicants for Research Grants may receive no more than two grants in this category in any one five-year period.

For the Harry S. Truman Book Award, five copies of each book entered must be submitted to the Book Award Administrator.

Duration: Research Grants: One to three weeks.

Deadline: Dissertation Year Fellowships: February 1. Announcement first week of April. Research Grants: April 1 and October 1. Results announced six weeks later. Scholar's Award: December 15 of odd-numbered years. Announcement no later than March 31. Harry S. Truman Book Award: Books must be received by January 20 in even-numbered years.

PUBLICATIONS:
Program announcement; *Whistle Stop*, newsletter.

OFFICERS:
Clyde F. Wendel, Chairman of the Board
Adam P. Sachs, Vice Chairperson
Jeannine Strandjord, Vice Chairperson
Hon. Eileen Weir, Vice Chairperson
John A. MacDonald, Treasurer
Lisa Hardwick, Secretary

BOARD OF DIRECTORS:
Clifton Truman Daniel, Honorary Chairperson
Merilyn K. Berenbom
Paul M. Black
Maureen McMeel Carroll
Robert P. Dunn
Josh Earnest
Susie S. Evans
Kari Frederickson
Greg Gunderson, Ph.D.
Harvey L. Kaplan
Charlotte L. Kemper
Kay Martin
Bridget McCandless, M.D.
Leigh Nottberg
James B. Nutter, Jr.
Patrick J. Ottensmeyer
Karen Pack
Jason C. Parker, Ph.D.
James D. Rine
Chris Rosson
Marny Sherman
Meyer J. Sosland
Timothy W. Triplett
David Von Drehle
Thomas R. Willard

ADDRESS INQUIRIES TO:
Grants Administrator
(See address above.)

THE HARRY S. TRUMAN SCHOLARSHIP FOUNDATION [1810]
712 Jackson Place, N.W.
Washington, DC 20006-4901
(202) 395-4831
Fax: (202) 395-6995
E-mail: office@truman.gov
Web Site: www.truman.gov

FOUNDED: 1975

AREAS OF INTEREST:
Local, state and national government service.

NAME(S) OF PROGRAMS:
● Harry S. Truman Scholarship Program

TYPE:
Awards/prizes. Awards for undergraduate students who demonstrate outstanding leadership potential, plan to pursue careers in government or elsewhere in public service and wish to attend graduate school to help prepare for their careers. At least one Truman Scholar is selected each year from each state, the District of Columbia, Puerto Rico and, considered as a single entity, Guam, the Virgin Islands, American Samoa and the Commonwealth of the Northern Mariana Islands. Scholars may attend graduate schools in the U.S. or in foreign countries.

YEAR PROGRAM STARTED: 1975

PURPOSE:
To develop increased opportunities for young Americans to prepare for and pursue careers in public service, whether it be at the local, county, state or national level, through an educational scholarship program. The Foundation defines public service as employment in government at any level, including uniformed services, public-interest organizations, non-governmental research and/or educational organizations and public-service oriented nonprofit organizations such as those whose primary purposes are to help needy or disadvantaged persons or to protect the environment.

LEGAL BASIS:
Authorized by Congress in 1975; the sole Federal memorial to President Harry S. Truman.

ELIGIBILITY:
To be considered for nomination as a Truman Scholar, a student must be:
(1) a full-time student as a junior at a four-year institution pursuing a Bachelor's degree;
(2) enrolled in a four-year accredited institution of higher education;
(3) committed to a career in government or in public service as defined above;
(4) in the upper quarter of his or her class and;
(5) a U.S. citizen or, in the case of nominees from American Samoa or the Commonwealth of the Northern Mariana Islands, a U.S. national.

FINANCIAL DATA:
The award may only be used for tuition, fees, books, room and board and other specifically approved expenses in graduate school.
Amount of support per award: Up to $30,000.

NO. MOST RECENT APPLICANTS: 845 for the year 2021.

NO. AWARDS: 62 for the year 2021.

APPLICATION INFO:
All candidates for scholarships are nominated by their institutions of higher education. The

Foundation neither solicits nor accepts direct candidate applications. Each participating institution must appoint a faculty representative to serve as liaison between the institution and the Foundation. The Foundation's nomination and supporting information forms are available from faculty representatives.
Duration: Up to four years.
Deadline: February 1.

THE MORRIS K. UDALL AND STEWART L. UDALL FOUNDATION
130 South Scott Avenue
Tucson, AZ 85701
(520) 901-8564
Fax: (520) 901-8570
E-mail: curley@udall.gov
Web Site: www.udall.gov

TYPE:
Internships. Congressional Internships: Native American college, graduate and law students work in congressional offices and federal agencies to gain a firsthand understanding of the federal government. The Foundation arranges meetings with elected officials, staff at Native American advocacy and public interest organizations, and Native American professionals in Washington, DC. They also take field trips and meet with congressional members, agency heads and cabinet secretaries.

See entry 958 for full listing.

WOMEN'S CONGRESSIONAL POLICY INSTITUTE (WCPI)
409 12th Street, S.W.
Suite 702
Washington, DC 20024
(202) 554-2323
Fax: (202) 554-2346
E-mail: cindy@wcpinst.org
Web Site: www.wcpinst.org

TYPE:
Fellowships.

See entry 995 for full listing.

Sociology and anthropology

AMERICAN SOCIOLOGICAL ASSOCIATION
1430 K Street, N.W.
Suite 600
Washington, DC 20005
(202) 383-9005
TDD: (202) 638-0981
E-mail: diversity@asanet.org
Web Site: www.asanet.org

TYPE:
Fellowships. Predoctoral training fellowships for minority-group members studying sociology.

See entry 886 for full listing.

L.S.B. LEAKEY FOUNDATION [1811]

1003B O'Reilly Avenue
San Francisco, CA 94129-1359
(415) 561-4646
Fax: (415) 561-4647
E-mail: grants@leakeyfoundation.org
Web Site: leakeyfoundation.org

FOUNDED: 1968

AREAS OF INTEREST:
Human evolution, including research into the environments, archaeology and human paleontology of the Miocene, Pliocene and Pleistocene, into the behavior, morphology, molecular anthropology and ecology of the great apes and other primate species when it contributes to the development or testing of models of human evolution and into the ecology and adaptations of living hunter-gatherer peoples.

NAME(S) OF PROGRAMS:
● **Leakey Foundation Grants**

TYPE:
Research grants. The General Research Grants priority is normally given to the exploratory phase of promising new projects that most closely meet the stated purpose of the Foundation.

YEAR PROGRAM STARTED: 1968

PURPOSE:
To conduct research related to human origins.

LEGAL BASIS:
Public foundation 501(c)(3).

ELIGIBILITY:
Grants are made to senior scientists and postdoctoral students with professional qualifications and demonstrated capability in the area of human evolution. Graduate students must be advanced to candidacy (ABD) in order to be considered.

FINANCIAL DATA:
Amount of support per award: General Research Grants are awarded up to $15,000 for Ph.D. candidate students (ABD), and up to $25,000 for senior scientists and postdoctoral students.

Total amount of support: Approximately $1,000,000 per year.

NO. AWARDS: Approximately 40 to 60 per year.

APPLICATION INFO:
Guidelines and application forms are available on the Foundation's web site. Applications are submitted and accepted online only.

All applications must be for research projects related to understanding human evolution.

Duration: One year.

Deadline: Session One (Fall): July 15, with notification in mid-December. Session Two (Spring): January 10, with notification in May.

PUBLICATIONS:
Application guidelines; newsletter.

IRS I.D.: 95-2536475

ADDRESS INQUIRIES TO:
See e-mail address above.

NATIONAL SCIENCE FOUNDATION [1812]

2415 Eisenhower Avenue
Alexandria, VA 22314
(703) 292-7783
Fax: (703) 292-9068
E-mail: jmantz@nsf.gov
Web Site: www.nsf.gov

FOUNDED: 1950

AREAS OF INTEREST:
Scientific research on the causes and consequences of human social and cultural variability.

NAME(S) OF PROGRAMS:
● **Cultural Anthropology Program**

TYPE:
Conferences/seminars; Grants-in-aid; Project/program grants; Research grants. The program supports a broad portfolio of research by both senior scholars and by graduate students.

YEAR PROGRAM STARTED: 1952

PURPOSE:
To support basic scientific research on the causes, consequences, and complexities of human social and cultural variability.

LEGAL BASIS:
National Science Foundation Act of 1950.

ELIGIBILITY:
The program does not fund research that takes as its primary goal improved clinical practice or applied policy.

Applicants may be colleges and universities on behalf of their staff members, nonprofit, U.S. nonacademic research institutions, such as independent museums, observatories, research laboratories, stock centers and similar organizations, private profit organizations, in exceptional circumstances, rarely, foreign institutions utilizing U.S. currency, and under special circumstances, unaffiliated U.S. scientists.

FINANCIAL DATA:
Support may cover salaries, research assistantships, staff benefits related directly to purpose, permanent equipment, travel, publication costs, computer costs and certain other direct and indirect costs.

Amount of support per award: $5,000 to $300,000; average $150,000.

Total amount of support: Approximately $4,000,000.

NO. AWARDS: 30 to 40.

APPLICATION INFO:
Application must be submitted online at FastLane or Grants.gov.

Duration: Up to 60 months, depending on the scientific merit and requirements of the project.

Deadline: August 15 and January 15.

STAFF:
Jeffrey Mantz, Program Director

ADDRESS INQUIRIES TO:
Jeffrey Mantz, Program Director
(See address above.)

NATIONAL SCIENCE FOUNDATION [1813]

Division of Behavioral and Cognitive Sciences
2415 Eisenhower Avenue
Alexandria, VA 22314
(703) 292-8759
E-mail: jyellen@nsf.gov
Web Site: www.nsf.gov

NAME(S) OF PROGRAMS:
● **Archaeology Program**
● **Archaeometry Program**

TYPE:
Conferences/seminars; Research grants. The programs provide support for anthropologically relevant archaeological research at both a "senior" and doctoral-dissertation level. It also funds anthropologically significant archaeometric research and high-risk exploratory research proposals.

FINANCIAL DATA:
Maximum of $20,000 in direct costs to meet expenses associated with doctoral dissertation research.

Amount of support per award: Varies.

Total amount of support: Approximately $7,200,000 for the year 2018.

APPLICATION INFO:
Instructions and application form are available on the web site above.

Duration: One to five years.

Deadline: Target dates: Archaeology: July 1 and December 20; Archaeometry: December 1. Dissertations may be submitted at any time.

STAFF:
Dr. John E. Yellen, Program Director

ADDRESS INQUIRIES TO:
Dr. John E. Yellen, Program Director
(See address above.)

*PLEASE NOTE:
All proposals must be submitted online.

SCHOOL FOR ADVANCED RESEARCH [1814]

P.O. Box 2188
Santa Fe, NM 87504-2188
(505) 954-7237
Fax: (505) 954-7214
E-mail: scholar@sarsf.org
seminar@sarsf.org
Web Site: sarweb.org

FOUNDED: 1907

AREAS OF INTEREST:
Anthropology and allied disciplines in the humanities and social sciences.

NAME(S) OF PROGRAMS:
● **Advanced Seminar Program**
● **Resident Scholar Fellowships**

TYPE:
Conferences/seminars; Fellowships; Residencies. Advanced Seminars promote in-depth communication among scholars who are at a critical stage of research on a common topic and whose interaction has the potential to move the discipline of anthropology forward with new insights into human evolution, behavior, culture or society, including critical contemporary issues. Each consists of up to 10 scholars who meet at SAR's Santa Fe campus for five days of intense discussion on a topic that provides new insights into human evolution, behavior, society or culture. Support is also available for two- and three-day short seminars, including a program funded by the National Science Foundation for research team seminars. Participants appraise ongoing research, assess recent innovations in theory and methods, and share data relevant to broad problems in anthropology and related disciplines.

Resident Scholar Fellowships are awarded each year to scholars in anthropology and related disciplines who have completed their research and who need time to prepare book-length manuscripts or doctoral dissertations on topics important to the understanding of humankind.

YEAR PROGRAM STARTED: 1973

PURPOSE:
To support advanced research in anthropology and related disciplines.

LEGAL BASIS:
Private, nonprofit.

ELIGIBILITY:
Proposals are sought for the Advanced Seminar Program.

Resident Scholar Program: Applications are evaluated on the basis of the overall excellence and significance of the proposed project, clarity of presentation and the applicant's academic accomplishments relative to subdiscipline and career stage. The program supports scholars whose work is broad, synthetic and interdisciplinary and promises to yield significant advances in understanding human culture, behavior, evolution or critical contemporary issues. Projects that are narrowly focused geographically and theoretically or that are primarily methodological seldom receive strong consideration. Each year the program supports a mix of scholars with scientific and humanistic orientations. Preference is given to applicants whose research and analysis are complete and who need time to prepare manuscripts. Applicants for postdoctoral fellowships must have their Ph.D. in hand at time of application. Immediate dissertation rewrites are not encouraged.

FINANCIAL DATA:
Advanced Seminars: SAR provides round-trip coach airfare within the U.S., lodging and all meals. Overseas airfare for up to two participants may also be offered.

Resident scholars are provided with an office, low-cost housing, a stipend, library assistance and other benefits during a nine-month tenure, from September through the following May. Books written by scholars may be considered for publication by SAR Press.

Amount of support per award: Resident Scholar Program: Maximum stipend up to $50,000.

Total amount of support: Varies.

CO-OP FUNDING PROGRAMS: Funding for the Resident Scholar Program is provided by the Weatherhead Foundation, the Katrin H. Lamon Endowment for Native American Art and Education, the Andrew H. Mellon Foundation and the Vera R. Campbell Foundation.

NO. MOST RECENT APPLICANTS: 200 for the year 2020.

NO. AWARDS: Advanced Seminars: 1 to 2 seminars annually (10 per seminar); Resident Scholar Fellowships: 5 to 6 annually.

APPLICATION INFO:
Submissions must be made via online application process. Guidelines and application form are available on the web site.
Duration: Advanced Seminars: Five days; Resident Scholar Fellowships: Nine months, September 1 through May 31.

Deadline: Resident Scholar Program: November 1. Announcement in April.

PUBLICATIONS:
Application guidelines.

OFFICERS:
Dr. Michael Brown, President and Chief Executive Officer
Paul Ryer, Director of Scholar Programs

ADDRESS INQUIRIES TO:
Maria Spray, Program Coordinator
(See address above.)

SCHOOL FOR ADVANCED RESEARCH [1815]
P.O. Box 2188
Santa Fe, NM 87504-2188
(505) 954-7237
Fax: (505) 954-7214
E-mail: staley@sarsf.org
Web Site: sarweb.org

FOUNDED: 1907

AREAS OF INTEREST:
Anthropology and related disciplines in the humanities and social sciences.

NAME(S) OF PROGRAMS:
● **J.I. Staley Prize**

TYPE:
Awards/prizes. Prize awarded annually to a living author of a ground-breaking book that exemplifies outstanding scholarship and writing in anthropology. The award recognizes innovative works that add new dimensions to the understanding of the human species.

YEAR PROGRAM STARTED: 1988

PURPOSE:
To acknowledge those innovative works that have gone beyond traditional frontiers and dominant schools of thought in anthropology and given new dimensions to our understanding of the human species; to honor books that cross subdisciplinary boundaries within anthropology and reach out in new and expanded interdisciplinary directions.

LEGAL BASIS:
Private, nonprofit.

ELIGIBILITY:
To be considered, a book must be currently in print and must have been in publication at least two years, but not more than eight years. Co-authored books may be nominated, but edited volumes and textbooks may not. The nomination must clearly be for a single book. The award is for one outstanding and influential publication, not for an author's lifetime achievement.

Nominated books are evaluated according to the following criteria:
(1) significant contribution to our understanding of humankind;
(2) innovative and rigorous thinking in terms of theory, research methods and/or application of findings;
(3) superior integration of subdisciplinary and/or interdisciplinary perspectives;
(4) exemplary writing and clarity of expression and;
(5) demonstrated or anticipated impact on the field of anthropology.

FINANCIAL DATA:
Amount of support per award: Cash award of $7,500.

Total amount of support: $7,500.

NO. MOST RECENT APPLICANTS: 10 for the year 2020.

NO. AWARDS: 1 annually.

APPLICATION INFO:
Detailed information is available on the web site.
Duration: One-time award.
Deadline: Nominations may be submitted at any time throughout the year. Nominations received by October 1 will be considered for next year's prize.

OFFICERS:
Dr. Michael Brown, President and Chief Executive Officer
Paul Ryer, Director of Scholar Programs

ADDRESS INQUIRIES TO:
Maria Spray, Program Coordinator
(See address above.)

THE AMAURY TALBOT FUND [1816]
Royal Anthropological Institute
50 Fitzroy Street
London W1T 5BT England
(44) 020 7387 0455
Fax: (44) 020 7388 8817
E-mail: admin@therai.org.uk
Web Site: www.therai.org.uk/awards/prizes/the-amaury-talbot-prize-for-african-anthropology/

FOUNDED: 1948

AREAS OF INTEREST:
Nigeria or West Africa.

NAME(S) OF PROGRAMS:
● **Amaury Talbot Prize for African Anthropology**

TYPE:
Awards/prizes. Prize for a significant book, article or work of anthropological research relating to West Africa.

YEAR PROGRAM STARTED: 1948

PURPOSE:
To recognize and support valuable works dealing with African anthropological research.

LEGAL BASIS:
Created under the terms of the will of Mrs. Miriam Winifred Florence Talbot.

ELIGIBILITY:
Works of anthropological research concerning Africa which were published during a calendar year, to be received no later than March 31 in succeeding year, are eligible for the prize. Although works relating to any region of Africa may be submitted, preference is given first to works focusing on Nigeria, then to those dealing with any other section of West Africa or to publications relating to West Africa in general.

FINANCIAL DATA:
The amount of the prize is determined by income from investments and is therefore not constant.
Amount of support per award: Approximately GBP 750 per annum.

NO. MOST RECENT APPLICANTS: 10.

NO. AWARDS: 1.

APPLICATION INFO:
No official application form is required, but copies of the prospectus are available upon request to the Coordinator at the address above. Entries must be accompanied by three copies of the book, article or work in question. Entries will not be returned.

Deadline: March 31 in the year following publication.

ADDRESS INQUIRIES TO:
Amaury Talbot Prize Coordinator
Royal Anthropological Institute
(See address above.)

WENNER-GREN FOUNDATION FOR ANTHROPOLOGICAL RESEARCH, INC.   [1817]

655 3rd Avenue, 23rd Floor
New York, NY 10017
(212) 683-5000
E-mail: inquiries@wennergren.org
Web Site: www.wennergren.org

FOUNDED: 1941

AREAS OF INTEREST:
All branches of anthropology, including cultural/social anthropology, ethnology, biological/physical anthropology, archaeology and anthropological linguistics, and closely related disciplines concerned with human origins, development and variation.

NAME(S) OF PROGRAMS:
● **Individual Research Grants**

TYPE:
Awards/prizes; Research grants. The Foundation offers Dissertation Fieldwork Grants, Post-Ph.D. Research Grants, and Hunt Postdoctoral Fellowships. Awards are available for basic research in all branches of anthropology. Grants are made to cover expenses or phases of a research project. The Foundation particularly invites projects employing comparative perspectives or integrating two or more subfields of anthropology.

The Hunt Postdoctoral Fellowship is awarded to scholars within 10 years of receipt of the Doctorate to aid the write-up of research results for publication.

Dissertation Fieldwork Grants are awarded to individuals to aid doctoral dissertation or thesis research.

Post-Ph.D. Research Grants are awarded to individual scholars holding the Doctorate or equivalent qualification in anthropology or a related discipline.

YEAR PROGRAM STARTED: 1941

PURPOSE:
To support anthropological research.

LEGAL BASIS:
Private operating foundation.

ELIGIBILITY:
Qualified scholars are eligible without regard to nationality or institutional affiliation for Dissertation Fieldwork, Post-Ph.D. Research Grants and Hunt Postdoctoral Fellowships.

Application for grants may be made by the scholar. Predoctoral grants application must be made jointly with a thesis advisor.

Dissertation Fieldwork Grants are for individuals enrolled in a doctoral program. These grants are contingent upon the applicant's successful completion of all requirements for the degree other than the dissertation/thesis.

Post-Ph.D. Research Grants are for individual scholars holding the Doctorate or equivalent qualification in anthropology or a related discipline.

Hunt Postdoctoral Fellowships are available to all scholars regardless of institutional affiliation and nationality. Applicants must have their Ph.D. in hand to apply and be within 10 years of receipt of their Doctorate.

FINANCIAL DATA:
Individual Research Grants, except for the Hunt Fellowship, are primarily for basic research. Grants cover research expenses directly related and essential to the project (i.e., travel, living expenses during fieldwork, equipment, supplies, research assistance and other relevant expenditures). Aid is not provided for salary and/or fringe benefits of applicant, tuition, nonproject personnel, travel to meetings, institutional overhead or institutional support. Expenses incurred prior to the effective date of an award will not be covered.

Amount of support per award: Dissertation Fieldwork Grants and Post Ph.D. Research Grants: Up to $20,000; May apply for a supplementary award, maximum $5,000. Hunt Fellowship: Up to $40,000.

Total amount of support: Approximately $5,000,000.

APPLICATION INFO:
Applicants are required to submit a formal application. Application forms must be submitted online through the Foundation's web site beginning three months prior to the application deadline.

Duration: Hunt Postdoctoral Fellowship: Up to one year (12 continuous months of full-time writing). Nonrenewable; Research Grants: Duration of the project.

Deadline: May 1 for funding during first half of the year. November 1 for projects scheduled to begin July or later. Announcement within six to eight months.

PUBLICATIONS:
Program announcement.

IRS I.D.: 13-1813827

OFFICERS:
Lauren Meserve, Chairman of the Board
Meredith Jenkins, Vice-Chairman and Treasurer
Dr. Danilyn Rutherford, President
Maugha Kenny, Vice-President for Finance and Secretary

TRUSTEES:
Cass Cliatt
Dr. Noah Feldman
Henry Gonzalez
Thomas Lenehan
Kiele Neas
Barbara Rockenbach
Barbara D. Savage
Dr. Leslie Vosshall
Justin Zaremby

WENNER-GREN FOUNDATION FOR ANTHROPOLOGICAL RESEARCH, INC.   [1818]

655 3rd Avenue, 23rd Floor
New York, NY 10017
(212) 683-5000
E-mail: dauston@wennergren.org
Web Site: www.wennergren.org

FOUNDED: 1941

AREAS OF INTEREST:
All branches of anthropology, including cultural/social anthropology, ethnology, biological/physical anthropology, archaeology, anthropological linguistics, and closely related disciplines concerned with human origins, development and variation.

NAME(S) OF PROGRAMS:
● **Conference and Workshop Grants**
● **Wenner-Gren Symposium Program**

TYPE:
Conferences/seminars. Workshops.

PURPOSE:
To support anthropological research.

LEGAL BASIS:
Private operating foundation.

ELIGIBILITY:
The Foundation provides conference support in two forms. Conference and workshop grants are made to the organizer(s). Priority is given to public conferences sponsored by international scholarly organizations (e.g., the IUAES and EASA) that serve as their annual or periodic meetings and to working conferences that address broad research issues in anthropology and provide for intensive interaction among participants. Funds are not normally provided for panels or sessions that are part of larger meetings.

The Foundation also sponsors and directly administers a limited number of conferences each year under the Wenner-Gren Symposium Program. These symposia are intended for topics of broad significance for anthropology. They are planned jointly by the organizer(s) and the Foundation president and follow a specific format developed by the Foundation.

Requests by individuals to support their own travel to meetings are not accepted.

FINANCIAL DATA:
The Foundation pays all costs related to the Wenner-Gren Symposium and actively manages it, including sending out invitations and making travel arrangements.

Amount of support per award: Conference and Workshop Grants: Up to $20,000.

Total amount of support: Varies.

NO. MOST RECENT APPLICANTS: 65.

NO. AWARDS: 30.

APPLICATION INFO:
Procedures are available on the Foundation web site.

Duration: Length of particular conference.

Deadline: Conference and Workshop Grants: June 1 and December 1.

PUBLICATIONS:
Annual report.

IRS I.D.: 13-1813827

OFFICERS:
Lauren Meserve, Chairman
Meredith Jenkins, Vice-Chairman and Treasurer
Dr. Danilyn Rutherford, President
Maugha Kenny, Vice-President and Secretary

ADDRESS INQUIRIES TO:
Donna Auston
Conference Program Associate
(See address above.)

PHYSICAL SCIENCES

Physical sciences (general)

AMERICAN CHEMICAL SOCIETY [1819]

1155 16th Street, N.W.
Washington, DC 20036
(202) 872-4481
Fax: (202) 872-6319
E-mail: prfinfo@acs.org
n_jensen@acs.org
Web Site: www.acs.org

FOUNDED: 1944

AREAS OF INTEREST:
Research in specified areas of fundamental research in chemistry, engineering and geology directly related to petroleum science.

NAME(S) OF PROGRAMS:
● **The Petroleum Research Fund**

TYPE:
Grants-in-aid; Research grants. The project must be pure science in one of the 10 specified areas which may afford a basis for subsequent research directly connected with the petroleum field.

Separate grant categories are available for professors in institutes that do not have doctoral programs.

YEAR PROGRAM STARTED: 1944

PURPOSE:
To support advanced scientific education and fundamental research in the petroleum field.

LEGAL BASIS:
Private trust established in 1944 with contributions of seven petroleum companies.

ELIGIBILITY:
Grants are made to nonprofit scientific or educational institutions, such as universities, on behalf of projects of their regularly appointed faculty.

FINANCIAL DATA:
Amount of support per award: Up to $110,000, depending upon the grant program.

Total amount of support: Approximately $17,500,000 for the year 2020.

Matching fund requirements: Varies.

NO. MOST RECENT APPLICANTS: Approximately 800 for the year 2020.

NO. AWARDS: 170 for the year 2020.

APPLICATION INFO:
Application information is available on the web site.

Duration: Up to three years. Most grants are awarded for two years.

Deadline: Approximately six months prior to each scheduled meeting. Specific deadlines are posted on the Society's web site.

PUBLICATIONS:
Annual report.

ADDRESS INQUIRIES TO:
Dr. Nancy Jensen, Assistant Director for Research Grants
(See address above.)

AMERICAN SOCIETY FOR MASS SPECTROMETRY [1820]

2019 Galisteo Street
Building I-1
Santa Fe, NM 87505
(505) 989-4517
Fax: (505) 989-1073
E-mail: info@asms.org
Web Site: www.asms.org

FOUNDED: 1969

AREAS OF INTEREST:
Mass spectrometry.

NAME(S) OF PROGRAMS:
● **ASMS Research Awards in Mass Spectrometry**

TYPE:
Project/program grants; Research grants.

YEAR PROGRAM STARTED: 1985

PURPOSE:
To promote academic research in mass spectrometry by young scientists.

LEGAL BASIS:
Nonprofit corporation.

ELIGIBILITY:
Grant applicants must be academic scientists within four years of joining the tenure track faculty or equivalent in a North American university for research in mass spectrometry.

Applicants must be members of ASMS.

GEOG. RESTRICTIONS: North America.

FINANCIAL DATA:
Grants are made to the university in the name of the selected individual.

Amount of support per award: $35,000.

Total amount of support: $105,000 for the year 2021.

NO. MOST RECENT APPLICANTS: 15.

NO. AWARDS: 3 for the year 2021.

APPLICATION INFO:
Applicants should submit applications electronically in a PDF format including a curriculum vitae, list of current research support, three-page proposal, one-page fiscal proposal and justification, and two letters of recommendation. Proposals are ranked primarily on scientific merit and secondarily on effectiveness of proposed use of funds.

Duration: Varies.

Deadline: November 30.

IRS I.D.: 23-7050068

ADDRESS INQUIRIES TO:
See e-mail address above.

AMERICAN SOCIETY OF NAVAL ENGINEERS (ASNE)

1423 Powhatan Street
Suite 1
Alexandria, VA 22314
(703) 836-6727
E-mail: scholarships@navalengineers.org
Web Site: www.navalengineers.org

TYPE:
Scholarships. Stipend for tuition, fees and expenses to follow a full-time or co-op program of study that applies to naval engineering, such as naval architecture, marine engineering, ocean engineering, mechanical engineering, structural engineering, electrical engineering, electronic engineering and the physical sciences, as well as other programs leading to careers

with civilian and military maritime organizations supporting and developing work and life at sea.

See entry 2388 for full listing.

ASPRS - THE IMAGING AND GEOSPATIAL INFORMATION SOCIETY [1821]

2151 Quail Run Drive
Suite B
Baton Rouge, LA 70808
(301) 493-0290
Fax: (225) 408-4422
E-mail: office@asprs.org
Web Site: www.asprs.org

FOUNDED: 1934

AREAS OF INTEREST:
Geospatial sciences, photogrammetry, remote sensing, geographic information systems (GIS), unmanned autonomous systems (UAS), Lidar and supporting technologies.

NAME(S) OF PROGRAMS:
● **Robert E. Altenhofen Memorial Scholarship**
● **Abraham Anson Memorial Scholarship**
● **John O. Behrens Institute for Land Information (ILI) Memorial Scholarship**
● **Robert N. Colwell Memorial Fellowship**
● **William A. Fischer Memorial Scholarship**
● **Ta Liang Memorial Award**
● **Francis H. Moffitt Memorial Scholarship**
● **The Kenneth J. Osborn Memorial Scholarship**
● **Paul R. Wolf Memorial Scholarship**

TYPE:
Assistantships; Awards/prizes; Fellowships; Internships; Scholarships; Travel grants. Robert E. Altenhofen Memorial Scholarship is for undergraduate or graduate study in photogrammetry.

Abraham Anson Memorial Scholarship is designed to encourage undergraduate students who have an exceptional interest in pursuing scientific research or education in geospatial science or technology related to photogrammetry, remote sensing, surveying and mapping to enter a professional field where they can use the knowledge of their discipline to excel in their profession.

John O. Behrens Institute for Land Information (ILI) Memorial Scholarship is an undergraduate award established by the Institute for Land Information to encourage those who have an exceptional interest in pursuing scientific research or education in geospatial science or technology or land information systems/records to enter a professional field where they can use the knowledge of this discipline.

Robert N. Colwell Memorial Fellowship is made to a graduate student (Master's or Ph.D. level) currently enrolled or intending to enroll in a college or university in the U.S. or Canada, who is pursuing a program of study aimed at starting a professional career where expertise is required in remote sensing or other related geospatial information technologies.

William A. Fischer Memorial Scholarship facilitates graduate-level studies and career goals adjudged to address new and innovative uses of remote sensing data/techniques that relate to the natural, cultural or agricultural resources of the Earth.

Ta Liang Memorial Award facilitates research-related travel by outstanding graduate students in remote sensing. Such travel includes field investigations, agency visits, participation in conferences, or any travel that enhances or facilitates a graduate research program.

Francis H. Moffitt Memorial Scholarship is for students currently enrolled or intending to enroll in a college or university in the U.S. or Canada, who are pursuing a program of study in surveying or photogrammetry leading to a career in the geospatial mapping profession.

The Kenneth J. Osborn Memorial Scholarship is made to an undergraduate student currently enrolled or intending to enroll in a college or university in the U.S., who is pursuing a program of study in preparation for entering the profession in the general area of surveying, mapping, photogrammetry or geospatial information and technology, and shows good collaboration skills.

The Paul R. Wolf Memorial Scholarship is designed for prospective teachers in the general area of surveying, mapping or photogrammetry.

PURPOSE:
To advance knowledge and improve understanding of mapping sciences; to promote the responsible applications of photogrammetry, remote sensing, geographic information systems (GIS) and supporting technologies.

LEGAL BASIS:
501(c)(3) organization.

ELIGIBILITY:
Requirements vary with the program. Applicant must be enrolled in an accredited college or university and be a student member of ASPRS.

FINANCIAL DATA:
Amount of support per award: Altenhofer, Anson, Behrens, Fischer, Liang and Osborn Scholarship: $2,000; Colwell Memorial Fellowship and Moffitt Memorial Scholarship: $7,000; Wolf Scholarship: $4,000.

NO. MOST RECENT APPLICANTS: 100.

NO. AWARDS: 1 for each award.

APPLICATION INFO:
Application information is available on the ASPRS web site. All complete applications, including reference letters and transcripts, must be submitted electronically.

Duration: One year.

Deadline: Contact the Society for dates.

PUBLICATIONS:
ASPRS Awards and Scholarships booklet (including application form).

STAFF:
Karen Schuckman, Managing Director

ADDRESS INQUIRIES TO:
Awards and Scholarships
(See address and e-mail above.)

COOPERATIVE INSTITUTE FOR RESEARCH IN ENVIRONMENTAL SCIENCES (CIRES)
CIRES Building, Room 201
University of Colorado
Boulder, CO 80309
(303) 497-3584
Fax: (303) 492-1149
E-mail: christine.wiedinmyer@colorado.edu
Web Site: cires.colorado.edu

TYPE:
Fellowships. The program provides opportunities for interactions between CIRES scientists and visiting fellows to pursue common research interests. CIRES research includes theoretical studies, laboratory experimentation, and field investigations which may affect the enhancement of air and water quality and prediction of weather climate fluctuations.

See entry 1963 for full listing.

JILA   [1822]
440 UCB
University of Colorado at Boulder
Boulder, CO 80309-0440
(303) 492-7789
Fax: (303) 492-5235
E-mail: kim.monteleone@jila.colorado.edu
Web Site: jila.colorado.edu

FOUNDED: 1962

AREAS OF INTEREST:
Atomic and molecular physics, chemical physics, laser physics, astrophysics, optical physics, precision measurements, geophysical measurement and other closely related areas.

NAME(S) OF PROGRAMS:
● **Postdoctoral Research Associateships**
● **Visiting Fellowships**

TYPE:
Assistantships; Fellowships. Postdoctoral Research Associateships provide advanced research experience in the years immediately after the Ph.D. degree. Visiting Fellowships support research and study for experienced scientists.

YEAR PROGRAM STARTED: 1963

PURPOSE:
To further scientific exchange.

LEGAL BASIS:
Jointly sponsored by the University of Colorado at Boulder and the National Institute of Standards and Technology.

ELIGIBILITY:
Postdoctoral Research Associateships are awarded on the basis of the applicants' scholarly qualifications, promise as research scientists, and research interests and experience in relation to those specific ongoing research programs for which financial support is available. There are no restrictions as to citizenship except as may be imposed by conditions of individual contracts. Ph.D. required.

Visiting Fellowships are available to scientists with extensive research experience beyond the doctoral degree, although younger persons with significant scientific achievements are also encouraged to apply. Awards are based on the fields of scientific interest and the scholarly achievements or promise of the applicants. There are no restrictions as to citizenship.

FINANCIAL DATA:
Amount of support per award: Varies.
Total amount of support: Varies.

APPLICATION INFO:
Application information is available on the web site.

Deadline: Varies.

ADDRESS INQUIRIES TO:
Kim Monteleone, Coordinator
Visiting Scientists Program
(See address above.)

LINK FOUNDATION   [1823]
c/o Binghamton University Foundation
P.O. Box 6005
Binghamton, NY 13902-6005
(607) 777-2210
Fax: (607) 777-2533
Web Site: www.linkfoundation.org

FOUNDED: 1953

AREAS OF INTEREST:
Energy, oceanographic, aerospace simulation research and fellowships.

NAME(S) OF PROGRAMS:
● **Energy Fellowship Program**
● **Oceanography Engineering Fellowship Program**
● **Simulation Fellowship Program**

TYPE:
Fellowships. Grants for research, development and training related to the mastery of air, sea and energy resources.

YEAR PROGRAM STARTED: 1953

PURPOSE:
To promote the general welfare through the advancement of scientific, technological and general educational projects.

ELIGIBILITY:
Nonprofit educational institutions and organizations with appropriate interests are eligible to apply. Grants are not awarded directly to individuals.

FINANCIAL DATA:
Amount of support per award: $6,000 to $32,500 for the year 2021-22.

APPLICATION INFO:
Information on applying for fellowships may be obtained from the administrators for the individual programs. Proof of an organization's tax-exempt status must accompany the application if not listed in the publication Cumulative List of Organizations described in Section 170(c) of the Internal Revenue Code.

The following documents must be submitted in the order indicated or they will not be accepted:
(1) cover sheet specific to the individual program;
(2) 500-word description of the project that places the research in the context of current activities in the field;
(3) two letters of recommendation, as specified for the individual program;
(4) two additional letters of reference (professional or educational);
(5) project objectives, timeline and projected budget (projected budget only for Energy Program) and;
(6) current resume.

Duration: Subject to annual review.

Deadline: January 15.

TRUSTEES:
Dr. Shelley D. Dionne, Chairman

Douglas R. Johnson, Treasurer
Dr. Thomas F. Kelly, Secretary
Dr. Andrew M. Clark
Lenny Genna

ADDRESS INQUIRIES TO:
Dr. Shelley D. Dionne, Chairman
(See address above.)

THE NATIONAL ACADEMIES OF SCIENCES, ENGINEERING, AND MEDICINE [1824]
500 Fifth Street, N.W.
Washington, DC 20001
(202) 334-2760
E-mail: rap@nas.edu
Web Site: www.nas.edu/rap

AREAS OF INTEREST:
All fields in science and engineering.

NAME(S) OF PROGRAMS:
● **NRC Research Associateship Programs**

TYPE:
Research scientists. Fellowships at the graduate, postdoctoral and senior levels for research-in-residence at U.S. federal laboratories and affiliated institutions.

YEAR PROGRAM STARTED: 1954

PURPOSE:
To provide research opportunities for qualified personnel.

LEGAL BASIS:
Not-for-profit agency.

ELIGIBILITY:
In most instances, applicants must be U.S. citizens. U.S. permanent residents and non-U.S. citizens are eligible to apply at select laboratories. Must have or expect to receive Ph.D., Sc.D. or other earned equivalent research Doctorate. Program also available for graduate-level applicants.

Awards are tenable only at participating U.S. federal laboratories and affiliated institutions.

GEOG. RESTRICTIONS: United States.

FINANCIAL DATA:
NRC Research Associateship awards include stipend, support for relocation, if eligible, and professional travel and health insurance.
Amount of support per award: Annual stipend for recent Ph.D. recipients: $45,000 to $80,000, with higher stipend for additional experience.
Total amount of support: Varies.

NO. MOST RECENT APPLICANTS: Approximately 500.

NO. AWARDS: Approximately 200 for the year 2020.

APPLICATION INFO:
Application information is available on the web site.
Duration: One to three years.
Deadline: February 1, May 1, August 1 and November 1.

STAFF:
Dr. Elizabeth Prescott, Director of Fellowships and Associateships

ADDRESS INQUIRIES TO:
NRC Research Associateship Programs
(See address above.)

NATIONAL INSTITUTE OF STANDARDS AND TECHNOLOGY, FIRE RESEARCH DIVISION [1825]
100 Bureau Drive, Stop 8660
Gaithersburg, MD 20899-8660
(301) 975-6689
Fax: (301) 975-4052
E-mail: nelson.bryner@nist.gov
Web Site: www.nist.gov/el/fire-research-division-73300

FOUNDED: 1974

AREAS OF INTEREST:
Exploratory fire research, furnishing flammability, fire performance and validation, smoke hazard calculation, fire growth and extinction, compartment fire models and fire safety performance.

NAME(S) OF PROGRAMS:
● **Fire Research Grants Program**

TYPE:
Research grants. The program includes the following: Fire Fighting Technology Group, Engineered Fire Safety Group, Flammability Reduction Group, Wildland Urban Interface Fire Group and National Fire Research Laboratory.

YEAR PROGRAM STARTED: 1981

PURPOSE:
To conduct research in the areas of fire analysis and prediction, fire metrology, fire fighting technology, integrated performance assessment, and materials and products.

LEGAL BASIS:
Public Law 93-498; Section 18.

ELIGIBILITY:
Institutions of higher education, hospitals, nonprofit organizations, commercial organizations, state, local, and Indian tribal governments, foreign governments, organizations under the jurisdiction of foreign governments, and international organizations are eligible. Joint programs with participation by more than one eligible entity are possible.

GEOG. RESTRICTIONS: United States.

FINANCIAL DATA:
Amount of support per award: Typically $50,000 to $100,000 per award.

NO. MOST RECENT APPLICANTS: 30.

NO. AWARDS: 3 to 5 annually.

APPLICATION INFO:
Prospective proposers are encouraged to contact the appropriate research group to determine the extent of interest prior to preparation of a detailed proposal. Electronic filing is accepted through www.grants.gov.
Duration: Up to three years.
Deadline: As listed in *Federal Register* notice.

NATIONAL SCIENCE FOUNDATION [1826]
Division of Atmospheric and Geospace Sciences
2415 Eisenhower Avenue
Alexandria, VA 22314
(703) 292-8520
E-mail: trozell@nsf.gov
Web Site: www.nsf.gov

FOUNDED: 1950

AREAS OF INTEREST:
The Atmospheric Sciences program supports research to add new understanding of the behavior of the Earth's atmosphere and its interactions with the Sun. Included are studies of the physics, chemistry and dynamics of the Earth's upper and lower atmosphere and its space environment, research on climate processes and variations and studies to understand the natural global cycles of gases and particles in the Earth's atmosphere.

TYPE:
Conferences/seminars; Research grants.

YEAR PROGRAM STARTED: 1962

PURPOSE:
To continue to build a base of fundamental knowledge of the atmospheres of the Earth and other planets and of the Sun.

LEGAL BASIS:
Government agency.

ELIGIBILITY:
Proposals may be submitted by academic institutions, nonacademic and nonprofit research organizations, profitmaking and private research organizations and individuals. Occasionally, NSF sponsors efforts by other government agencies, particularly for field programs.

GEOG. RESTRICTIONS: United States and its territories.

FINANCIAL DATA:
Amount of support per award: Varies.
Total amount of support: Varies.

APPLICATION INFO:
Application information is available on the web site.
Duration: Varies.
Deadline: Varies.

PUBLICATIONS:
NSF Guide to Programs.

ADDRESS INQUIRIES TO:
Tracy L. Rozell, Program Support Manager
(See address above.)

OAK RIDGE INSTITUTE FOR SCIENCE AND EDUCATION (ORISE)
100 ORAU Way
Oak Ridge, TN 37830
(865) 576-3424
E-mail: science.education@orau.org
Web Site: orise.orau.gov

TYPE:
Fellowships; Internships; Scholarships. ORISE administers a broad range of internships, scholarships, fellowships and research experiences. ORISE programs include research experiences at Department of Energy national laboratories as well as other federal agencies with research facilities located across the country as well as some positions outside the U.S.

See entry 2402 for full listing.

RESEARCH CORPORATION FOR SCIENCE ADVANCEMENT [1827]
4703 East Camp Lowell Drive
Suite 201
Tucson, AZ 85712-1281
(520) 571-1111
Fax: (520) 571-1119
E-mail: awards@rescorp.org
Web Site: www.rescorp.org

FOUNDED: 1912

AREAS OF INTEREST:
University research and education in physics, chemistry and astronomy.

NAME(S) OF PROGRAMS:
- **Cottrell Scholar Awards**
- **Scialog Awards**

TYPE:
Awards/prizes; Conferences/seminars; Research grants; Seed money grants. Cottrell Scholar Awards recognize early-career faculty in Ph.D.-granting universities and in primarily undergraduate institutions.

Scialog Awards provide seed funding for early-career academic scientists that work in highly innovative cross-disciplinary teams. Programs have included solar energy conversion research and cell biology and theoretical physics collaborations.

PURPOSE:
To promote excellence in both research and teaching in science departments in colleges and universities.

LEGAL BASIS:
Operating foundation.

ELIGIBILITY:
Cottrell Scholar Awards: Applicants must be tenure-track assistant professors in a Ph.D.-granting or primarily undergraduate institution in a department of astronomy, chemistry or physics. Additionally, they must be in their third academic year during the calendar year of application.

Scialog: Faculty in U.S. and Canadian colleges and universities may apply.

FINANCIAL DATA:
Cottrell Scholar and Scialog Awards: Grant awards can be used at discretion of awardee for most direct costs.
Amount of support per award: Cottrell Scholar Award: $100,000; Scialog: Varies, with typical award $100,000 per team of two to three members.
Total amount of support: Varies.

NO. MOST RECENT APPLICANTS: Varies.

NO. AWARDS: Cottrell Scholars Awards: Approximately 30; Scialog Awards: Varies with number of conferences.

APPLICATION INFO:
Application information is available on the web site.
Duration: Cottrell Scholars Awards: Three years; Scialog Awards: Varies.
Deadline: Varies.

PUBLICATIONS:
Annual report; newsletter; occasional publications and guidelines.

IRS I.D.: 13-1963407

STAFF:
Silvia Ronco, Ph.D., Senior Program Director, Cottrell Scholar Awards
Richard Wiener, Ph.D., Senior Program Director, Scialog Awards

BOARD OF DIRECTORS:
Lars Bildsten, Ph.D., Chairperson
Daniel Linzer, Ph.D., President
Joan B. Woodard, Ph.D., Secretary
G. Scott Clemons
Danielle Dana
James De Naut
Peter K. Dorhout, Ph.D.
Eugene Flood, Jr., Ph.D.
Nancy Haegel, Ph.D.
Brent L. Iverson, Ph.D.

Kristine Lipscomb
Catherine J. Murphy, Ph.D.

ALFRED P. SLOAN FOUNDATION [1828]
630 Fifth Avenue
Suite 2200
New York, NY 10111
(212) 649-1649
E-mail: researchfellows@sloan.org
Web Site: sloan.org/fellowships

FOUNDED: 1934

AREAS OF INTEREST:
Science, technology, mathematics, computer science, economics, ocean sciences, neuroscience, physics, and chemistry.

NAME(S) OF PROGRAMS:
- **Sloan Research Fellowships**

TYPE:
Awards/prizes; Fellowships. Research fellowships are awarded to young scholars in chemistry, computer science, economics, mathematics, neuroscience, and physics. The Fellow need not pursue a specified research project and is free to change the direction of his or her research at any time.

YEAR PROGRAM STARTED: 1955

PURPOSE:
To identify and support promising young scientists at an early stage.

LEGAL BASIS:
Private foundation.

ELIGIBILITY:
Candidates are required to hold a Ph.D. (or equivalent) in chemistry, physics, mathematics, computer science, economics, earth system science, neuroscience, or a related field, and must be members of the regular faculty of a U.S. or Canadian college or university.

Applicant must be employed at a U.S. or Canadian institution.

GEOG. RESTRICTIONS: United States and Canada.

FINANCIAL DATA:
Each fellowship is administered by the Fellow's institution and is designed to allow the greatest possible freedom and flexibility in its use. The award may be used for equipment, technical assistance, professional travel, or any other activity directly related to the Fellow's research.
Amount of support per award: $75,000 over a two-year period.
Total amount of support: $9,450,000 for fiscal year 2021.

NO. MOST RECENT APPLICANTS: Over 1,200.

NO. AWARDS: 118 fellowships: 23 for physics, 23 for chemistry, 20 for mathematics, 16 for neuroscience, 20 for computer science, 8 for economics, and 8 for earth system science.

APPLICATION INFO:
Candidates may not apply directly, but must be nominated by a department head or other senior researcher. The nominator should submit a letter describing the candidate's qualifications and must see that the Foundation receives three supporting letters directly from other researchers, preferably not all from the same institution. A curriculum vitae, a list of scientific publications plus one copy of two representative publications, and a one-page

statement by the candidate describing his or her significant scientific work and immediate research plans should accompany the nomination form and letter. Strong evidence in submitted publications and supporting letters of the nominee's independent creativity is one of the most important considerations in the review process.
Duration: Two years. One two-year extension is permitted on request.
Deadline: Selections are announced in February. Nominations must be received no later than September 15 for awards to begin the following September.

PUBLICATIONS:
Brochure; annual report.

ADMINISTRATIVE OFFICERS AND STAFF:
Adam F. Falk, President
Leisle Lin, Senior Vice President, Finance and Operations/Treasurer
Michelle Tepper, Controller

ADDRESS INQUIRIES TO:
Lauren von Eckartsberg
Grants Coordinator
(See e-mail address above.)

SOCIETY FOR THE STUDY OF AMPHIBIANS AND REPTILES [1829]
Department of Biology
Carroll University
Waukesha, WI 53186
(262) 951-3295
E-mail: rbrenes@carrollu.edu
Web Site: www.ssarherps.org

AREAS OF INTEREST:
Herpetology.

NAME(S) OF PROGRAMS:
- **Roger Conant Grants in Herpetology**

TYPE:
Awards/prizes; Research grants. Awards are given in six categories: Conservation of Amphibians and/or Reptiles, Field Research, Laboratory Research, Herpetological Education, Travel and International Research.

PURPOSE:
To advance research, conservation, and education concerning amphibians and reptiles; to provide financial support for deserving individuals or organizations involved in herpetological research, education, or conservation.

ELIGIBILITY:
Applicants applying for the International category must be students. Membership in SSAR is not required.

FINANCIAL DATA:
Amount of support per award: $500.
Total amount of support: $6,000 to $7,000 annually.

NO. MOST RECENT APPLICANTS: 52 for the year 2019.

NO. AWARDS: 12 to 14.

APPLICATION INFO:
Applicants may only apply for one category and must designate to which of the six their proposal is submitted. Each proposal must include the following:
(1) title page;
(2) background and objects of the proposed project;
(3) methods of carrying out the project;
(4) complete project budget;

(5) brief resume or curriculum vitae of the applicant or project coordinator and;
(6) letter of support.

Duration: One-time award.

Deadline: December 15.

ADDRESS INQUIRIES TO:
Dr. Roberto Brenes, Chairperson
(See address above.)

WILLIAM P. WHARTON TRUST [1830]

c/o Choate, Hall & Stewart
2 International Place
Boston, MA 02110
E-mail: williamwhartontrust@choate.com
Web Site: www.williampwhartontrust.org

AREAS OF INTEREST:
Conservation and nature.

TYPE:
Project/program grants.

YEAR PROGRAM STARTED: 1976

PURPOSE:
To support projects that directly promote the study, conservation and appreciation of nature.

ELIGIBILITY:
Organizations must be 501(c)(3) tax-exempt. No funding for individuals.

GEOG. RESTRICTIONS: United States and Canada.

FINANCIAL DATA:
Amount of support per award: Up to $15,000.

Total amount of support: Approximately $175,000 annually.

NO. MOST RECENT APPLICANTS: 72 for the year 2020.

NO. AWARDS: 11 for the year 2020.

APPLICATION INFO:
Complete application instructions are available on the Trust web site.

Duration: Varies.

Deadline: March 1 and September 15 for preliminary proposals. Early April and late October for final proposals. Specific dates are provided to applicants invited to final round.

ADDRESS INQUIRIES TO:
See e-mail address above.

Astronomy and aerospace science

AMERICAN ASTRONOMICAL SOCIETY [1831]

1667 K Street, N.W.
Suite 800
Washington, DC 20006
(202) 328-2010
Fax: (202) 234-2560
E-mail: marvel@aas.org
Web Site: www.aas.org/grants-and-prizes

FOUNDED: 1899

AREAS OF INTEREST:
The advancement of astronomy and closely related branches of science.

NAME(S) OF PROGRAMS:
● **Chrétien International Research Grant**

TYPE:
Research grants. Research grant(s) with preference given to individuals of high promise who are otherwise unfunded.

YEAR PROGRAM STARTED: 1982

PURPOSE:
To further international collaborative projects in observational astronomy, with emphasis on long-term international visits and the development of close working relationship with astronomers in other countries.

LEGAL BASIS:
Nonprofit, scientific corporation.

ELIGIBILITY:
Astronomers with a Ph.D. or equivalent are eligible. Graduate students are not eligible.

FINANCIAL DATA:
Amount of support per award: Up to $20,000.

Total amount of support: $20,000 each year.

NO. MOST RECENT APPLICANTS: 18.

NO. AWARDS: 1 or more individuals or groups.

APPLICATION INFO:
Application and all supporting materials should be submitted electronically to Sara Asfaw at grants@aas.org. Applications should include:
(1) a description of the research project (less than three pages in length), including an assessment of its importance to that particular subfield of astronomy and a statement enumerating all the aspects of international collaboration;
(2) a statement of the candidate's ability to do the proposed research, with special emphasis on international collaboration and foreign visits which have been arranged, including facilities available and observing time allocations, if any;
(3) the proposed budget, with brief justification for the amount requested;
(4) a description of other financial resources available;
(5) the candidate's curriculum vitae and bibliography of recent papers;
(6) two letters of reference from astronomers who know the candidate's work and;
(7) any special circumstances which might help in the decision process.

Duration: One year.

Deadline: April 1. Announcement the following September.

ADDRESS INQUIRIES TO:
Sara Asfaw, Grants Contact
E-mail: grants@aas.org

AMERICAN ASTRONOMICAL SOCIETY [1832]

1667 K Street, N.W.
Suite 800
Washington, DC 20006
(202) 328-2010
Fax: (202) 234-2560
E-mail: kevin.marvel@aas.org
Web Site: www.aas.org/grants-and-prizes

FOUNDED: 1899

AREAS OF INTEREST:
Astronomy and closely related branches of science.

NAME(S) OF PROGRAMS:
● **Newton Lacy Pierce Prize in Astronomy**

TYPE:
Awards/prizes. Given to recognize outstanding achievement during the five years preceding the award in observational astronomical research based on measurements of radiation from an astronomical object. A monetary prize and certificate are awarded annually.

YEAR PROGRAM STARTED: 1974

LEGAL BASIS:
Nonprofit, scientific corporation.

ELIGIBILITY:
Applicants must be residents of North America (including Hawaii or Puerto Rico) or a member of a North American institution stationed abroad. Applicants should also be under 36 years of age.

FINANCIAL DATA:
Amount of support per award: $1,500.

Total amount of support: $1,500.

NO. AWARDS: 1.

APPLICATION INFO:
Contact the Society regarding application materials and requirements.

Deadline: Nomination due by July 31.

PUBLICATIONS:
Program announcement.

ASTRONOMICAL SOCIETY OF THE PACIFIC [1833]

390 Ashton Avenue
San Francisco, CA 94112
(415) 337-1100
Fax: (415) 337-5205
E-mail: awards@astrosociety.org
lshore@astrosociety.org
Web Site: www.astrosociety.org

FOUNDED: 1889

AREAS OF INTEREST:
Astronomy and science education.

NAME(S) OF PROGRAMS:
● **Maria and Eric Muhlmann Award**

TYPE:
Awards/prizes. Maria and Eric Muhlmann Award recognizes important research results based upon development of groundbreaking instruments and techniques.

YEAR PROGRAM STARTED: 1995

PURPOSE:
To improve significant observational research, possibly through advances in astronomical instrumentation, software or support infrastructure.

ELIGIBILITY:
Award is available to individuals. Applicants do not have to be U.S. citizens or residents.

FINANCIAL DATA:
Award includes travel reimbursement and hotel accommodations to Annual Awards Gala.

Amount of support per award: $500 and plaque.

NO. MOST RECENT APPLICANTS: Varies.

NO. AWARDS: 1.

APPLICATION INFO:
Sponsors should submit a two-page nomination giving strong support to the choice.

Duration: One-time award.

Deadline: March 1.

ADDRESS INQUIRIES TO:
Dr. Linda Shore, Chief Executive Officer
(See address above.)

ASTRONOMICAL SOCIETY OF THE PACIFIC [1834]

390 Ashton Avenue
San Francisco, CA 94112
(415) 337-1100
Fax: (415) 337-5205
E-mail: awards@astrosociety.org
lshore@astrosociety.org
Web Site: www.astrosociety.org

AREAS OF INTEREST:
Astronomy.

NAME(S) OF PROGRAMS:
• **Klumpke-Roberts Award**

TYPE:
Awards/prizes.

PURPOSE:
To recognize outstanding contributions to the public understanding and appreciation of astronomy.

ELIGIBILITY:
There are no restrictions on nominations for this award. The contributions may be in the form of popular books and articles; lectures; radio, TV or movie productions; or service to public education in astronomy of any other nature.

FINANCIAL DATA:
Award includes travel reimbursement and hotel accommodation to Annual Awards Gala.
Amount of support per award: $500 and plaque.

NO. MOST RECENT APPLICANTS: Varies.

NO. AWARDS: 1.

APPLICATION INFO:
Nominations only. Self-nominations are not accepted.
Duration: One-time award.
Deadline: March 1.

ADDRESS INQUIRIES TO:
Dr. Linda Shore, Chief Executive Officer
(See e-mail address above.)

ASTRONOMICAL SOCIETY OF THE PACIFIC [1835]

390 Ashton Avenue
San Francisco, CA 94112
(415) 337-1100
Fax: (415) 337-5205
E-mail: awards@astrosociety.org
lshore@astrosociety.org
Web Site: www.astrosociety.org

AREAS OF INTEREST:
Astronomy.

NAME(S) OF PROGRAMS:
• **Thomas J. Brennan Award**

TYPE:
Awards/prizes.

PURPOSE:
To recognize exceptional achievement related to the teaching of astronomy at the high school level.

ELIGIBILITY:
Nominees must reside in North America.

GEOG. RESTRICTIONS: North America.

FINANCIAL DATA:
Award includes travel reimbursement and hotel accommodation to attend the Annual Awards Gala.
Amount of support per award: $500 and plaque.

NO. MOST RECENT APPLICANTS: Varies.

NO. AWARDS: 1.

APPLICATION INFO:
Nominations must be made on the Brennan Award form, available on the web site. Neither self-nominations nor nomination by a family member will be accepted.
Duration: One-time award.
Deadline: March 1.

ADDRESS INQUIRIES TO:
Dr. Linda Shore, Chief Executive Officer
(See e-mail address above.)

ASTRONOMICAL SOCIETY OF THE PACIFIC [1836]

390 Ashton Avenue
San Francisco, CA 94112
(415) 337-1100
Fax: (415) 337-5205
E-mail: awards@astrosociety.org
lshore@astrosociety.org
Web Site: www.astrosociety.org

AREAS OF INTEREST:
Astronomy and amateur astronomy.

NAME(S) OF PROGRAMS:
• **Las Cumbres Amateur Outreach Award**
• **The Gordon Myers Amateur Achievement Award**

TYPE:
Awards/prizes. Las Cumbres Amateur Outreach Award honors outstanding educational outreach by an amateur astronomer to K-12 children and the interested lay public.

The Gordon Myers Amateur Achievement Award recognizes significant observational or technological contributions to astronomy or amateur astronomy by an individual not employed in the field of astronomy in a professional capacity.

PURPOSE:
To award outstanding contribution or educational outreach in the field of astronomy or amateur astronomy.

ELIGIBILITY:
Las Cumbres Amateur Outreach Award: Nominee must not receive compensation (other than expenses) for their activitiy and not receive the majority of their income from a profession in astronomy.

The Gordon Myers Amateur Achievement Award: Nominees must not be employed as professional astronomers.

FINANCIAL DATA:
Awards include travel reimbursement and hotel accommodation to Annual Awards Gala.
Amount of support per award: $500 and plaque.

NO. MOST RECENT APPLICANTS: Varies.

NO. AWARDS: 1 per award.

APPLICATION INFO:
Nominations are made from the ASP Amateur Advisory Committee and by members of the astronomical community.

Self-nominations or nomination by a family member will not be accepted. Letters of support are required.
Duration: One-time award.
Deadline: March 1.

ADDRESS INQUIRIES TO:
Dr. Linda Shore, Chief Executive Officer
(See e-mail address above.)

ASTRONOMICAL SOCIETY OF THE PACIFIC [1837]

390 Ashton Avenue
San Francisco, CA 94112
(415) 337-1100
Fax: (415) 337-5205
E-mail: awards@astrosociety.org
lshore@astrosociety.org
Web Site: www.astrosociety.org

FOUNDED: 1889

AREAS OF INTEREST:
Astronomy and science education.

NAME(S) OF PROGRAMS:
• **Arthur B.C. Walker II Award**

TYPE:
Awards/prizes.

PURPOSE:
To improve significant observational research, possibly through advances in astronomical instrumentation, software or support infrastructure.

ELIGIBILITY:
Nominees can include a broad range of individuals of African descent from the U.S. or any country who are astronomers or space scientists whose research and educational efforts are of note in their field. Nominees must demonstrate a commitment to increasing the participation of underrepresented groups in STEM areas, especially astronomy and space science.

FINANCIAL DATA:
Amount of support per award: $500 and plaque.

NO. AWARDS: 1.

APPLICATION INFO:
Nominations are solicited from anyone familiar with or knowledgeable of the nominee's achievements. Self-nominations are not accepted. The nominator should submit a resume or curriculum vitae of the nominee, along with a letter of no more than two pages explaining in detail the specific contributions and achievements of the nominee that merit the Award. In addition to the nomination letter, two independent letters of support (no more than two pages each) must be submitted.
Deadline: March 1.

ADDRESS INQUIRIES TO:
See e-mail address above.

ASTRONOMICAL SOCIETY OF THE PACIFIC [1838]

390 Ashton Avenue
San Francisco, CA 94112
(415) 337-1100
Fax: (415) 337-5205
E-mail: awards@astrosociety.org
lshore@astrosociety.org
Web Site: www.astrosociety.org

FOUNDED: 1889

AREAS OF INTEREST:
Astronomy and science education.

NAME(S) OF PROGRAMS:
• **Richard H. Emmons Award**

TYPE:
Awards/prizes.

YEAR PROGRAM STARTED: 2006

PURPOSE:
To improve significant observational research, possibly through advances in astronomical instrumentation, software or support infrastructure.

ELIGIBILITY:
Nominees must be teachers of college-level introductory astronomy for non-science majors.

FINANCIAL DATA:
Amount of support per award: $500 and plaque.

NO. AWARDS: 1.

APPLICATION INFO:
Nominations are solicited from colleagues, students or others familiar with or knowledgeable of the nominee's achievements. Nominations may be made by anyone except the nominee or someone from the nominee's family. The nominator should submit a resume or curriculum vitae of the nominee, along with a letter of no more than two pages explaining in detail the specific contributions and achievements of the nominee that merit the Award. In addition to the nomination letter, two independent letters of support (no more than two pages each) must be submitted.
Deadline: March 1.

ADDRESS INQUIRIES TO:
See e-mail address above.

LUNAR AND PLANETARY INSTITUTE   [1839]
3600 Bay Area Boulevard
Houston, TX 77058
(281) 486-2159
Fax: (281) 486-2127
E-mail: internprogram@lpi.usra.edu
Web Site: www.lpi.usra.edu

FOUNDED: 1968

AREAS OF INTEREST:
Study of lunar exploration, planetary remote sensing and spectroscopy, image processing, planetary geology and surface processes, impact studies, geophysical data analysis and modeling, physics and chemistry of planetary atmospheres, meteorites and sample analysis, interplanetary dust and presolar grains, minerology/petrology and astrobiology.

NAME(S) OF PROGRAMS:
• **LPI Summer Intern Program in Planetary Science**

TYPE:
Conferences/seminars; Internships; Scholarships; Travel grants.

YEAR PROGRAM STARTED: 1969

PURPOSE:
To promote and assist in the analysis and interpretation of lunar and planetary data.

ELIGIBILITY:
College undergraduates with at least 50 semester hours of credit interested in pursuing a career in the sciences are eligible. Applicants will be considered for appointment without regard to race, creed, color, sex, national origin, age, handicap status or other non-merit factors.

Due to security issues, citizens of U.S. State Department designated countries are not eligible. See link under "ECP Notices" at oiir.hq.nasa.gov/nasaecp.

FINANCIAL DATA:
In addition to the stipend, financial support up to $1,000 (domestic travelers) or up to $1,500 (international travelers) is offered to interns who submit an accepted abstract as first author to the upcoming Lunar and Planetary Science Conference.
Amount of support per award: Selected interns will receive a $7,300 stipend to cover the costs associated with being in Houston for the duration of the program.
Total amount of support: Varies.

NO. AWARDS: 14 to 16.

APPLICATION INFO:
Applications are only accepted using the electronic application form found on the Institute web site.
Duration: 10-week program, June to August.
Deadline: January.

ADDRESS INQUIRIES TO:
See e-mail address above.

NATIONAL CENTER FOR ATMOSPHERIC RESEARCH   [1840]
High Altitude Observatory
P.O. Box 3000
Boulder, CO 80307-3000
(303) 497-1567
Fax: (303) 497-1589
E-mail: cquinn@ucar.edu
Web Site: www2.hao.ucar.edu

FOUNDED: 1940

AREAS OF INTEREST:
Solar physics, solar-terrestrial physics and related astrophysics. Specific research interests include coronal and interplanetary physics, solar activity and magnetic fields, the solar interior and terrestrial interactions.

NAME(S) OF PROGRAMS:
• **Newkirk Graduate Research Fellowship**

TYPE:
Fellowships.

PURPOSE:
To promote cooperative research between HAO and academic institutions by providing support for aspiring young scientists at formative stages in their careers.

ELIGIBILITY:
Applicants must be full-time graduate students enrolled in a university program leading to the Ph.D. Students must declare their intention of working on their thesis in cooperation with an HAO staff member and should expect to spend a significant fraction of their time in residence at HAO.

FINANCIAL DATA:
Fellowship includes airfare and travel expenses for the student's university advisor/mentor to visit HAO (one trip of up to two weeks' duration).
Amount of support per award: Stipend of $4,000 per month.
Total amount of support: Varies.

APPLICATION INFO:
Application includes cover letter, transcripts of undergraduate and graduate courses,

research statement (up to three pages), curriculum vitae, and two letters of recommendation.
Duration: Maximum nine months, which can be spread over three years.
Deadline: March 1.

PUBLICATIONS:
Brochure.

ADDRESS INQUIRIES TO:
Caitlyn Quinn Erdesz
HAO Visitor Committee
(See address above.)

*PLEASE NOTE:
Fellowship award is dependent upon funding.

NATIONAL RADIO ASTRONOMY OBSERVATORY   [1841]
520 Edgemont Road
Charlottesville, VA 22903-2475
(434) 296-0237
Fax: (434) 296-0278
E-mail: jutley@nrao.edu
Web Site: www.nrao.edu

FOUNDED: 1957

AREAS OF INTEREST:
Ground-based radio astronomy. Current areas of research include cosmology, theoretical and observational studies of radio sources, the interstellar and intergalactic medium, structure and dynamics of galactic and extragalactic sources, physics of HII regions, stars, solar system objects and astrometry.

NAME(S) OF PROGRAMS:
• **Jansky Fellowships at the NRAO**

TYPE:
Fellowships. Research appointments. Postdoctoral appointments with liberal support for research travel, data reduction and publication. Jansky Fellows may or may not be residents at NRAO sites.

YEAR PROGRAM STARTED: 1960

PURPOSE:
To provide postdoctoral opportunities for research in astronomy.

LEGAL BASIS:
Federally funded research organization.

ELIGIBILITY:
Fellows must have received their Ph.D. prior to beginning the appointment. Preference is given to recent Ph.D. recipients.

FINANCIAL DATA:
Vacation accrual, health insurance, a moving allowance and other benefits available.
Amount of support per award: Annual salary $68,500, plus $17,000 travel budget per year.

NO. MOST RECENT APPLICANTS: 52.

NO. AWARDS: 5 for the year 2020-21.

APPLICATION INFO:
Application should include a curriculum vitae and a statement of the type of research activity to be undertaken at the NRAO. The applicant should request letters of recommendation from three references. These letters should be sent directly to the NRAO.
Duration: Two years. Possibility of renewal for a third year if mutually agreeable.
Deadline: On or around November 1 of each year.

PUBLICATIONS:
Program announcement.

ADDRESS INQUIRIES TO:
Jessica Utley
Science Support and Research
(See address above.)

NATIONAL SCIENCE FOUNDATION   [1842]

Division of Astronomical Sciences
2415 Eisenhower Avenue
Alexandria, VA 22314
(703) 292-8820
Fax: (703) 292-9034
E-mail: jneff@nsf.gov
Web Site: www.nsf.gov

FOUNDED: 1950

AREAS OF INTEREST:
Astronomy and astrophysics of the Sun, the rest of the solar system, and/or extrasolar planets.

NAME(S) OF PROGRAMS:
● **Astronomy and Astrophysics Research Grants**

TYPE:
Awards/prizes; Challenge/matching grants; Conferences/seminars; Fellowships; Project/program grants; Research grants; Seed money grants; Travel grants; Research contracts. Broad base of support for fundamental research directed at explaining celestial objects and the cosmos in terms of physical principles.

Basic research support is provided under the following grant programs:

Planetary Astronomy - Objects studied in this program include the planets and their satellites, the asteroids and the comets. Ground-based observations are indispensable to the complete understanding of their structure, composition and origin.

Stellar Astronomy and Astrophysics - This program supports studies of the physical and chemical characteristics of the Sun and other stars, especially as they relate to the stars' past and future evolution. These studies make use of observations at many wavelengths, as well as laboratory measurements and theoretical modeling.

Galactic Astronomy - The topics studied in this program are the spatial and kinematics characteristics of the stars in our galaxy and the properties and distribution of the interstellar medium.

Extragalactic Astronomy and Cosmology - The objective of this program is the description of the nature, structure and evolution of external galaxies and quasars, as well as the implications of these data for the birth, expansion rate and future of the universe.

Advanced Technologies and Instrumentation - This program provides support for development of astronomical equipment at universities. In addition to supporting the acquisition of telescopes and auxiliary instrumentation, this program also supports the reduction of astronomical data by providing funds for minicomputers. Particular emphasis is being placed on the use of advanced technology detectors at radio, infrared and optical wavelengths.

PURPOSE:
To support research and education in astronomy and astrophysics.

LEGAL BASIS:
Government agency.

ELIGIBILITY:
NSF eligibility criteria apply.

GEOG. RESTRICTIONS: United States.

FINANCIAL DATA:
Amount of support per award: Varies.
Total amount of support: Estimated $48,500,000 for fiscal year 2019.

NO. AWARDS: Approximately 100 for fiscal year 2019.

APPLICATION INFO:
Application information is available on the Foundation web site.
Duration: Varies.
Deadline: November 15.

PUBLICATIONS:
Guide to Programs; *Grants for Scientific and Engineering Research*.

ADDRESS INQUIRIES TO:
James E. Neff, Deputy Director
(See address and e-mail above.)

SMITHSONIAN ASTROPHYSICAL OBSERVATORY   [1843]

60 Garden Street
Mail Stop 67
Cambridge, MA 02138
(617) 495-7103
Fax: (617) 496-7589
E-mail: predoc@cfa.harvard.edu
Web Site: www.cfa.harvard.edu/opportunities/fellowships/predoc

FOUNDED: 1890

AREAS OF INTEREST:
Astrophysical research, including the fields of astronomy, astrophysics and planetary sciences.

NAME(S) OF PROGRAMS:
● **Predoctoral Research Fellowships**

TYPE:
Exchange programs; Fellowships; Internships. Predoctoral fellowships for thesis research. Fellowships are designed to allow students from other institutions throughout the world to do all or part of their thesis research at the Observatory. A wide variety of research projects may be proposed. About 300 scientific staff conduct research in observation, theory and instrumentation, and in nearly all areas related to astronomy.

YEAR PROGRAM STARTED: 1985

ELIGIBILITY:
Applicants must be enrolled in a Ph.D. program in appropriate fields (i.e., astronomy or astrophysics) and have completed all course work and examinations.

Applicants must be ready to begin dissertation research at the time of the award. They must have the approval of their department head at their home institution to conduct their thesis research at the Observatory. Students from any country are eligible.

FINANCIAL DATA:
Some funds may be available for relocation, travel and other expenses.
Amount of support per award: $39,000 for the year 2022.

NO. MOST RECENT APPLICANTS: 20 for the year 2020.

NO. AWARDS: 14 for the year 2021.

APPLICATION INFO:
Application forms are available on the web site.
Duration: Six months. Renewable up to three years.
Deadline: Proposals are reviewed on an ongoing basis.

STAFF:
Charles R. Alcock, Director

ADDRESS INQUIRIES TO:
Christine A. Crowley
Fellowship Programs Coordinator
(See address above.)

SMITHSONIAN ASTROPHYSICAL OBSERVATORY   [1844]

60 Garden Street
Mail Stop 67
Cambridge, MA 02138
(617) 495-7103
Fax: (617) 496-7589
E-mail: postdoc@cfa.harvard.edu
Web Site: www.cfa.harvard.edu/opportunities/postdocs.html

FOUNDED: 1973

AREAS OF INTEREST:
Astrophysics, including the areas of theory, observation, instrumentation and/or laboratory research. Research programs at the Center are organized into seven divisions including atomic and molecular physics, high energy astrophysics, optical and infrared astronomy, radio and geoastronomy, solar, stellar and planetary sciences, theoretical astrophysics, and science education.

NAME(S) OF PROGRAMS:
● **Clay Postdoctoral Fellowship**

TYPE:
Fellowships. Postdoctoral fellowships for research in the Center's areas of interest.

YEAR PROGRAM STARTED: 1974

ELIGIBILITY:
Open to recent Ph.D. recipients with interests in any of the areas above.

FINANCIAL DATA:
Amount of support per award: Stipends of approximately $72,500; annual research budget of approximately $16,000 per appointee for the year 2022-23.

NO. AWARDS: 1.

APPLICATION INFO:
Application forms are available online.
Duration: Four years. Renewal possible for a fifth year.
Deadline: October 29.

PUBLICATIONS:
Observatory reports issue of the *Bulletin of the American Astronomical Society*.

STAFF:
Charles R. Alcock, Director

ADDRESS INQUIRIES TO:
Christine A. Crowley
Fellowship Programs Coordinator
(See address above.)

SPACE TELESCOPE SCIENCE INSTITUTE   [1845]

3700 San Martin Drive
Baltimore, MD 21218
(410) 338-2474
E-mail: nhfp@stsci.edu
Web Site: www.stsci.edu

FOUNDED: 1990

AREAS OF INTEREST:
Astronomy, astrophysics and related disciplines.

NAME(S) OF PROGRAMS:
● **NASA Hubble Fellowship Program**

TYPE:
Fellowships. Provides a limited number of recent postdoctoral scientists of unusual promise and ability with the opportunity to pursue research of their choice at a participating U.S. astronomical institution designated as host institution by the scientist.

YEAR PROGRAM STARTED: 1990

PURPOSE:
To expand and strengthen the research work of the astronomical community.

ELIGIBILITY:
Applicants must have earned a Doctorate degree, up to three years prior to application, in physics, astronomy or a related discipline. Applicants can be any nationality. Candidates are selected on the basis of their research proposal, publications and academic achievement. No more than one fellow per year is approved for any one academic location.

Fellowships must be held at U.S. institutions.

FINANCIAL DATA:
Amount of support per award: Annual stipend of approximately $70,500, plus $16,000 per year for research expenses, and up to $20,000 for health insurance.
Total amount of support: Varies.

CO-OP FUNDING PROGRAMS: NASA Exoplanet Science Institute and the Chandra X-ray Center.

NO. MOST RECENT APPLICANTS: Over 400 for the year 2021.

NO. AWARDS: Up to 24.

APPLICATION INFO:
Application information is available on the web site.
Duration: One year and two annual renewals contingent on satisfactory performance and availability of NASA funds.
Deadline: First week in November.

ADDRESS INQUIRIES TO:
NASA Hubble Fellowship Program Coordinator
(See address above.)

ZONTA FOUNDATION FOR WOMEN   [1846]

1200 Harger Road, Suite 330
Oak Brook, IL 60523
(630) 928-1400
E-mail: programs@zonta.org
Web Site: www.zonta.org

FOUNDED: 1919

AREAS OF INTEREST:
Aerospace engineering or space sciences.

NAME(S) OF PROGRAMS:
● **Amelia Earhart Fellowship**

TYPE:
Fellowships. Awarded annually to women pursing a Ph.D./doctoral degree conducting research applied to aerospace engineering or space sciences.

YEAR PROGRAM STARTED: 1938

PURPOSE:
To encourage and support the study and research of women scientists and engineers throughout the world and to improve the status of women.

LEGAL BASIS:
Incorporated in the state of Illinois as a nonprofit organization.

ELIGIBILITY:
Women of any nationality pursuing a Ph.D./doctoral degree who demonstrate a superior academic record in the field of aerospace-related sciences or aerospace-related engineering are eligible. Students must be registered in a full-time Ph.D./doctoral program and have completed at least one year of that program or have received a Master's degree in an aerospace applied field at the time the application is submitted. Applicants must not graduate from their Ph.D. or doctoral program before April 2022.

Postdoctoral research programs are not eligible for the fellowship. Members and employees of Zonta International or the Zonta Foundation for Women are also not eligible to apply for the fellowship. Previous Amelia Earhart Fellows are not eligible to apply to renew the fellowship for a second year.

FINANCIAL DATA:
Fellowship awards may be used for tuition, books, fees or living expenses.

Amount of support per award: $10,000 annually.

NO. MOST RECENT APPLICANTS: 183.

NO. AWARDS: Up to 35 annually.

APPLICATION INFO:
Applications may be submitted at zontainternational.awardspring.com and must include the following:
(1) biographical information;
(2) plan for intended study;
(3) list of schools attended, including official detailed transcripts of grades or equivalent records from all universities, colleges, or institutions attended, including undergraduate institutions and degrees received;
(4) scholarships, fellowships and honors received, if any;
(5) previous publications, if any;
(6) employment history;
(7) essay on academic program and professional goals and;
(8) three recommendations from university professors or supervisors who can assess applicant's ability to succeed in the program.

Duration: One academic year. Nonrenewable.

Deadline: November 15.

ADDRESS INQUIRIES TO:
Programs Senior Coordinator
(See address above.)

Chemistry

AMERICAN CHEMICAL SOCIETY   [1847]

Office of Research Grants
1155 16th Street, N.W.
Washington, DC 20036
(202) 872-4600
(202) 872-6207
(800) 227-5558
E-mail: a_fahr@acs.org
Web Site: www.acs.org

AREAS OF INTEREST:
Biology-chemistry interface.

NAME(S) OF PROGRAMS:
● **Irving S. Sigal Postdoctoral Fellowship**

TYPE:
Fellowships. The Sigal Fellowship is awarded every two years to a Ph.D. candidate who will pursue research at the chemistry and biology interface.

PURPOSE:
To advance research at the chemistry and biology interface.

ELIGIBILITY:
Nominee must be a scientist who has earned or will earn a doctoral degree in chemistry during the academic year of the competition or the preceding year in a graduate chemistry department within the U.S. Nominee must intend to pursue chemistry postdoctoral research at the biology-chemistry interface. There are no restrictions on the age or nationality of the fellow.

FINANCIAL DATA:
Amount of support per award: $75,000 per year.

NO. AWARDS: 1.

APPLICATION INFO:
Candidates are nominated by chairs of Ph.D.-granting Chemistry Departments in the U.S. During a competition, approximately one-fifth of the U.S. doctoral chemistry departments are invited to nominate one candidate for the Sigal Fellowship.

Individuals are not able to submit an application without being nominated.
Duration: Two years.

ADDRESS INQUIRIES TO:
E-mail: sigalinfo@acs.org or
Dr. Askar Fahr, Program Manager
(See e-mail address above.)

AMERICAN CHEMICAL SOCIETY   [1848]

1155 16th Street, N.W.
Washington, DC 20036
(800) 227-5558 ext. 6250
Fax: (202) 872-4361
E-mail: scholars@acs.org
Web Site: www.acs.org/content/acs/en/funding-and-awards.html

AREAS OF INTEREST:
Chemistry-related disciplines.

NAME(S) OF PROGRAMS:
● **ACS Scholars Program**

TYPE:
Scholarships.

PURPOSE:
To support the advancement of the chemical sciences through research, education, and community projects.

ELIGIBILITY:
To be considered for a scholarship, candidate
must:
(1) be a U.S. citizen or legal permanent
resident of the U.S.;
(2) be African-American/Black,
Hispanic/Latino, or American Indian;
(3) be a graduating high school senior or
college freshman, sophomore or junior.
Seniors can apply for their fifth year;
(4) intend to major or already major in
chemistry, biochemistry, chemical
engineering, chemical technology, or another
chemistry-related science and plan to pursue
a career in a chemistry-related science;
(5) be a full-time student at a high school or
accredited college, university or community
college and;
(6) demonstrate high academic achievement
in chemistry or science with a grade point
average 3.0 or higher.

FINANCIAL DATA:
Amount of support per award: $2,500 for
freshmen, $3,000 for sophomores, and $5,000
for juniors and seniors.

Total amount of support: Approximately
$900,000 annually.

NO. AWARDS: 350 annually.

APPLICATION INFO:
Application must include fall semester grades
or college transcripts. These must be sent
directly from the school either in a sealed
envelope or by transcript clearinghouse to the
address or e-mail listed above.

Two letters of recommendation are required.
One letter must be from a chemistry, science,
or math teacher or research advisor.

Applicant must also submit the Student Aid
Report (SAR) for the upcoming academic
year, after submission of the FAFSA form.
SAR must be sent to the e-mail address listed
above.

Duration: One year. Renewable.

Deadline: March 1.

ADDRESS INQUIRIES TO:
Mahalia Randle, Program Manager
(See address and e-mail above.)

AMERICAN CHEMICAL SOCIETY [1849]

1155 16th Street, N.W.
Washington, DC 20036-4801
(202) 872-4575
Fax: (202) 776-8008
E-mail: awards@acs.org
Web Site: www.acs.org/nationalawards

FOUNDED: 1876

AREAS OF INTEREST:
Chemical.

CONSULTING OR VOLUNTEER SERVICES:
Volunteer services.

NAME(S) OF PROGRAMS:
● **Nakanishi Prize**

TYPE:
Awards/prizes. Award presented in the U.S.
in odd years and Japan in even years.

YEAR PROGRAM STARTED: 1995

PURPOSE:
To recognize and stimulate significant work
that extends chemical and spectroscopic
methods to the study of important biological
phenomena.

LEGAL BASIS:
Nonprofit association.

ELIGIBILITY:
Individuals can apply. There are no limits on
age or nationality.

FINANCIAL DATA:
Amount of support per award: $5,000, plus
up to $2,500 travel allowance, medallion with
presentation box and certificate.

NO. AWARDS: 1.

APPLICATION INFO:
Application procedures are available online.

Duration: Nomination renewable.

Deadline: November 1.

ADDRESS INQUIRIES TO:
Awards Office
(See address above.)

*SPECIAL STIPULATIONS:
Special consideration will be given for work
that has contributed broadly on an
international scope.

AMERICAN CHEMICAL SOCIETY [1850]

1155 16th Street, N.W.
Washington, DC 20036-4801
(202) 872-4575
Fax: (202) 776-8008
E-mail: awards@acs.org
Web Site: www.acs.org/awards

FOUNDED: 1876

AREAS OF INTEREST:
Research in industrial and engineering
chemistry and chemical engineering
principles.

NAME(S) OF PROGRAMS:
● **E.V. Murphree Award in Industrial
and Engineering Chemistry**

TYPE:
Awards/prizes.

YEAR PROGRAM STARTED: 1955

PURPOSE:
To stimulate fundamental research in
industrial and engineering chemistry, the
development of chemical engineering
principles and their application to industrial
processes.

LEGAL BASIS:
Nonprofit association.

ELIGIBILITY:
Individuals can apply. Nominee must have
accomplished outstanding research of
theoretical or experimental nature in fields of
industrial chemistry or chemical engineering.
There are no limits on age or nationality.

FINANCIAL DATA:
Amount of support per award: $5,000,
certificate, and up to $1,000 travel expenses.

NO. AWARDS: 1.

APPLICATION INFO:
Application procedures are available online.

Duration: One year. Nominations renewable.

Deadline: November 1.

ADDRESS INQUIRIES TO:
Awards Office
(See address above.)

AMERICAN NUCLEAR SOCIETY (ANS) [1851]

555 North Kensington Avenue
LaGrange Park, IL 60526
(708) 352-6611
Fax: (708) 352-0499
E-mail: scholarships@ans.org
Web Site: www.ans.org

FOUNDED: 1954

AREAS OF INTEREST:
Radioanalytical chemistry or analytical
applications of nuclear science.

NAME(S) OF PROGRAMS:
● **James R. Vogt Radiochemistry
Scholarship**

TYPE:
Scholarships. Scholarship award to recognize
one outstanding undergraduate student or one
graduate student pursuing a career in
radioanalytical chemistry or analytical
applications of nuclear science.

YEAR PROGRAM STARTED: 1987

ELIGIBILITY:
U.S. and non-U.S. applicants must be ANS
student members. Applicants must have
completed a minimum of two years in an
accredited undergraduate program and be
enrolled in a four-year college or university
in the U.S. Undergraduates in their junior
and senior years are eligible to apply as are
graduate students in their first or second year
of graduate study.

Student must be engaged in proposing to
undertake graduate or undergraduate research
in radioanalytical chemistry or its
applications.

Applicants must be U.S. citizens or hold
permanent resident visa at the time of
application.

FINANCIAL DATA:
Scholarship funds may be used by the
student to defray any bona fide education
costs including tuition, fees, books, room and
board.

Amount of support per award: $3,000.

NO. AWARDS: 1 annually.

APPLICATION INFO:
Applications must be submitted online.
Applicant should include interest in
radioanalytical chemistry and its applications
in their Personal Statement of Future Plans.

Duration: One year. Nonrenewable.

Deadline: February 1.

ADDRESS INQUIRIES TO:
Scholarship Coordinator
(See address above.)

*PLEASE NOTE:
Scholarships are only offered to ANS student
members.

AMERICAN OIL CHEMISTS SOCIETY (AOCS) [1852]

2710 South Boulder Drive
Urbana, IL 61802-6996
(217) 693-4821
Fax: (217) 693-4865
E-mail: awards@aocs.org
Web Site: www.aocs.org/awards

FOUNDED: 1909

AREAS OF INTEREST:
Oils, fats, proteins, surfactants, lipid
chemistry, biochemistry, sterols and related
materials.

NAME(S) OF PROGRAMS:
- **Alton E. Bailey Award**
- **Stephen S. Chang Award**
- **Corporate Achievement Award**
- **Schroepfer Medal**
- **Supelco AOCS Research Award**
- **Young Scientist Research Award**

TYPE:
Awards/prizes.

YEAR PROGRAM STARTED: 1982

PURPOSE:
To annually recognize scientists, technologists or engineers who have made substantial accomplishments in lipid chemistry, either by one major breakthrough or by an accumulation of publications.

LEGAL BASIS:
Professional society.

ELIGIBILITY:
Nominations are accepted. Preference shall be given to individuals who are actively associated with research and who have made discoveries that have influenced their fields of endeavor.

FINANCIAL DATA:
Amount of support per award: Varies.
Total amount of support: Varies.

NO. MOST RECENT APPLICANTS: 20.

NO. AWARDS: Bailey Award, Chang Award, Supelco AOCS Research Award and Young Scientist Research Award: 1 of each annually. Corporate Achievement Award and Schroepfer Medal: 1 of each biennially in odd-numbered years.

APPLICATION INFO:
Nominations for the Chang Award must include a letter from the nominator describing the nominee's distinguished accomplishments in basic research and how they have been utilized by industry to help improve or develop products related to lipids. The nomination must include at least three letters of recommendation and biographical information, including the curriculum vitae.

Nominations for the Schroepfer Medal should include a 300- to 1,000-word summary describing the significance of the nominee's accomplishments in the steriod field, a current curriculum vitae including a full list of publications, and two supporting letters.

Duration: One-time awards.

Deadline: August 1.

PUBLICATIONS:
INFORM: International News on Fats, Oils, and Related Materials; *JAOCS: Journal of the American Oil Chemists' Society*; *Lipids*; *Journal of Surfactants and Detergents*.

ADDRESS INQUIRIES TO:
Victoria Santo, AOCS Program Manager
Membership Recognition
E-mail: victoria@aocs.org

CANADIAN SOCIETY FOR CHEMICAL TECHNOLOGY [1853]
222 Queen Street
Suite 1009
Ottawa ON K1P 5V9 Canada
(613) 232-6252
Fax: (613) 232-5862
E-mail: awards@cheminst.ca
Web Site: www.cheminst.ca/awards

AREAS OF INTEREST:
Chemistry, biochemistry, chemical engineering technology or chemical technology.

NAME(S) OF PROGRAMS:
- **Norman and Marion Bright Memorial Award**

TYPE:
Awards/prizes.

YEAR PROGRAM STARTED: 1980

PURPOSE:
To reward an individual who has made an outstanding contribution in Canada to the furtherance of chemical technology.

ELIGIBILITY:
The person honored must be either a chemical sciences technologist or a person from outside the field who had made a significant or noteworthy contribution to its advancement.

Membership in the Institute is not a prerequisite for this award.

GEOG. RESTRICTIONS: Canada.

FINANCIAL DATA:
Amount of support per award: $500.

NO. AWARDS: 1.

APPLICATION INFO:
A nomination package must be submitted electronically through ScholarOne. The package should include the following:
(1) a detailed outline of the contribution of the nominee to the advancement of chemical technology, and the reasons why the award is merited. Technical scientific achievement need not be the only consideration in the assessment of a nominee;
(2) curriculum vitae (maximum nine pages) and;
(3) supporting letters (one or more).
Deadline: December 1.

ADDRESS INQUIRIES TO:
Awards Manager
(See address above.)

CANADIAN SOCIETY FOR CHEMISTRY [1854]
222 Queen Street
Suite 1009
Ottawa ON K1P 5V9 Canada
(613) 232-6252
Fax: (613) 232-5862
E-mail: awards@cheminst.ca
Web Site: www.cheminst.ca/awards

AREAS OF INTEREST:
Biochemistry, organic and bioorganic chemistry.

NAME(S) OF PROGRAMS:
- **CCUCC Chemistry Doctoral Award**

TYPE:
Awards/prizes. CCUCC Chemistry Doctoral Award recognizes outstanding achievement and potential in research by a graduate student.

PURPOSE:
To recognize outstanding contributions by chemists for their research in a wide variety of fields.

ELIGIBILITY:
CCUCC Chemistry Doctoral Award is intended to recognize outstanding achievement and potential in research by a graduate student whose Ph.D. thesis in

chemistry was formally accepted by a Canadian university in the 12-month period preceding the nomination deadline. The formal convocation need not have occurred. In selecting candidates for the award, the Selection Committee shall be primarily concerned with demonstrated ability and achievements in research.

FINANCIAL DATA:
Amount of support per award: $2,000.

NO. AWARDS: 1.

APPLICATION INFO:
A nomination package must be submitted through ScholarOne. The package should include the following:
(1) letter of support by nominator;
(2) curriculum vitae (using NSERC guidelines);
(3) thesis synopsis;
(4) statement of merit and;
(5) one representative publication.
Deadline: September 15.

PUBLICATIONS:
Program announcement.

ADDRESS INQUIRIES TO:
Awards Manager
(See address above.)

*PLEASE NOTE:
No award will be given out if less than three nominations for the award are received or if the Committee considers that no suitable candidate has been nominated.

CANADIAN SOCIETY FOR CHEMISTRY [1855]
222 Queen Street
Suite 1009
Ottawa ON K1P 5V9 Canada
(613) 232-6252
Fax: (613) 232-5862
E-mail: awards@cheminst.ca
Web Site: www.cheminst.ca/awards

AREAS OF INTEREST:
Materials chemistry.

NAME(S) OF PROGRAMS:
- **Award for Research Excellence in Materials Chemistry**

TYPE:
Awards/prizes.

PURPOSE:
To recognize outstanding contributions to materials chemistry in Canada.

ELIGIBILITY:
Nominations may be made for candidates within 15 years of their first independent appointment. Nominee must be a Canadian citizen or landed immigrant who has made an outstanding contribution to materials chemistry while working in Canada.

Membership in the Chemical Institute of Canada is not a prerequisite for this award.

FINANCIAL DATA:
A framed scroll, an award lecture in a Materials Chemistry Division Symposium at the CSC conference and a lecture tour to two or more Canadian universities that are not in major centers, whose students normally do not travel to CSC meetings. Major travel costs for the award tour, to a maximum of $1,000, will be supported upon application to the Materials Chemistry Division Treasurer. Local costs (taxis, accommodation and meals) will be expected to be covered by the host institutions.

NO. AWARDS: 1.

APPLICATION INFO:
Nominations must include:
(1) a statement (250-word maximum) of why
the candidate should receive this award;
(2) a biographical sketch (maximum one
page), which provides background
information on the nominee and summarizes
past accomplishments;
(3) curriculum vitae (maximum nine pages)
and;
(4) three to five supporting letters, at least
two of which must be from outside the
nominee's organization.
Deadline: July 2.

ADDRESS INQUIRIES TO:
Awards Manager
(See address above.)

*SPECIAL STIPULATIONS:
The recipient will be required to present an
award lecture at the Canadian Chemistry
Conference and Exhibition.

CANADIAN SOCIETY FOR CHEMISTRY   [1856]
222 Queen Street
Suite 1009
Ottawa ON K1P 5V9 Canada
(613) 232-6252
Fax: (613) 232-5862
E-mail: awards@cheminst.ca
Web Site: www.cheminst.ca/awards

AREAS OF INTEREST:
Organic and biophysical chemistry.

NAME(S) OF PROGRAMS:
● **IntelliSyn Pharma Research Excellence Award**

TYPE:
Awards/prizes. The IntelliSyn Pharma
Research Excellence Award (formerly the
Boehringer Ingelheim Research Excellence
Award) is presented to a scientist residing in
Canada who has made a distinguished
contribution to medicinally relevant organic
or biophysical chemistry while working in
Canada.

PURPOSE:
To recognize distinguished contributions to
medicinally relevant organic or biophysical
chemistry.

ELIGIBILITY:
Candidates must have held their first
professional appointment as an independent
research for 12 years or less at the time of
initial nomination. Membership in the
Chemical Institute of Canada is not a
prerequisite for this award.

FINANCIAL DATA:
Amount of support per award: $2,000, which
can be used for travel to the CSC Conference
to present a lecture.

CO-OP FUNDING PROGRAMS: IntelliSyn RD

NO. AWARDS: 1.

APPLICATION INFO:
Nominations must include:
(1) a statement (250-word maximum) of why
the candidate should receive the award;
(2) a biographical sketch (maximum one
page), which provides background
information on the nominee and summarizes
past accomplishments;
(3) curriculum vitae (maximum nine pages)
and;
(4) three to five supporting letters, at least
two of which must be from outside the
nominee's organization.

Deadline: July 2.

ADDRESS INQUIRIES TO:
Awards Manager
(See address above.)

*SPECIAL STIPULATIONS:
The recipient will be required to present an
award lecture at the Canadian Chemistry
Conference and Exhibition.

CHEMICAL INSTITUTE OF CANADA   [1857]
222 Queen Street
Suite 1009
Ottawa ON K1P 5V9 Canada
(613) 232-6252
Fax: (613) 232-5862
E-mail: awards@cheminst.ca
Web Site: www.cheminst.ca/awards

AREAS OF INTEREST:
Environmental chemistry and environmental
chemical engineering.

NAME(S) OF PROGRAMS:
● **Environment Division Early Career Research Award**

TYPE:
Awards/prizes. The Environment Division
Early Career Research Award recognizes an
outstanding early career researcher who has
made distinguished contributions in the fields
of environmental chemistry or environmental
chemical engineering, while working in any
sector in Canada, e.g., academic, government,
industry, for-profit, non-for-profit, private or
public sector.

PURPOSE:
To recognize contributions in the fields of
environmental chemistry or environmental
chemical engineering.

ELIGIBILITY:
Early career researchers who received their
highest postgraduate or professional degree
(e.g., Ph.D.) in the preceding 12 years and
have demonstrated a strong track record of
independent productivity beyond research
conducted while working with a supervisor
are eligible for this award.

FINANCIAL DATA:
Awardee receives a framed scroll and up to
$1,000 for travel expenses to the Canadian
Chemistry Conference and Exhibition or
Canadian Chemical Engineering Conference
to present an award lecture.

NO. AWARDS: 1.

APPLICATION INFO:
Nominations must include:
(1) a statement (250-word maximum) of why
the candidate should receive the award;
(2) a biographical sketch (250-word
maximum), which provides background
information on the nominee and summarizes
past accomplishments;
(3) curriculum vitae (maximum nine pages);
(4) a summary of up to five key contributions
and advances in the field that best describe
the applicant's recent research progress and
impact (maximum one page) and;
(5) three to five supporting letters, two of
which must be from outside the nominee's
organization.
Deadline: July 2.

ADDRESS INQUIRIES TO:
Awards Manager
(See address above.)

GEORGETOWN UNIVERSITY   [1858]
Department of Chemistry
Box 571227
Washington, DC 20057-1227
(202) 687-6073
Fax: (202) 687-6209
E-mail: chemad@georgetown.edu
Web Site: chemistry.georgetown.edu

FOUNDED: 1789

AREAS OF INTEREST:
Graduate education in chemistry.

NAME(S) OF PROGRAMS:
● **Doctoral Program in Chemistry**

TYPE:
Assistantships; Awards/prizes;
Conferences/seminars; Exchange programs;
Fellowships; General operating grants;
Professorships; Research grants;
Scholarships; Visiting scholars.

YEAR PROGRAM STARTED: 1924

PURPOSE:
To enable graduate students to earn a Ph.D.
degree in chemistry, inorganic, organic,
analytical, physical or theoretical chemistry,
organometallic, synthetic, or nano-chemistry,
biochemistry, or structural crystallography.

LEGAL BASIS:
University.

ELIGIBILITY:
Fellowships are open to nationals of any
country. Bachelor's degree or the equivalent
is required.

FINANCIAL DATA:
Amount of support per award: $35,500
stipend, full-time tuition coverage and
comprehensive individual medical insurance.

NO. MOST RECENT APPLICANTS: 95.

NO. AWARDS: 10.

APPLICATION INFO:
Application information is available on the
web site.
Duration: Nine months to one year.
Renewable for as long as student continues
good progress toward the degree.
Deadline: January 15.

PUBLICATIONS:
Graduate Studies in Chemistry, booklet.

ADDRESS INQUIRIES TO:
Toshiko Ichiye, Chairperson
(See address above.)

NATIONAL MOLE DAY FOUNDATION   [1859]
3896 Leaman Court
Freeland, MI 48623
(989) 964-8020
E-mail: moleday@hotmail.com
Web Site: www.moleday.org

FOUNDED: 1991

AREAS OF INTEREST:
Chemistry education.

NAME(S) OF PROGRAMS:
● **The George Hague Memorial Travel Award**
● **National Mole of the Year Award (MOTY)**

TYPE:
Grants-in-aid. The George Hague Memorial
Travel Award is given to financially support a

young chemistry instructor (with two to five years of chemistry experience) in attending a biennial ChemEd conference.

The National Mole of the Year Award (MOTY) is given to a member of the National Mole Day Foundation who has contributed the most to furthering the cause of Mole Day and chemistry education.

PURPOSE:
To support Mole Day activities in classrooms, schools or communities.

ELIGIBILITY:
Must be a member of the National Mole Day Foundation and be involved with chemical education. Those receiving grants are not eligible again for the following three years.

FINANCIAL DATA:
Amount of support per award: The George Hague Memorial Travel Award: Up to $750; National Mole of the Year Award (MOTY): $250.

APPLICATION INFO:
Application information is available on the web site.
Deadline: March 1 of odd-numbered years.

ADDRESS INQUIRIES TO:
Rebecca Logan, Executive Director
(See address above.)

THE UNIVERSITY OF SYDNEY [1860]
Scholarships Office
Level 4, Jane Foss Russell Building G02
The University of Sydney N.S.W. 2006
Australia
61 (02) 8627 1444
E-mail: scholarships.officer@sydney.edu.au
Web Site: www.sydney.edu.au/scholarships

FOUNDED: 1850

AREAS OF INTEREST:
Chemistry in relation to agriculture and industry.

NAME(S) OF PROGRAMS:
● **Henry Bertie and Florence Mabel Gritton Postgraduate Research Scholarships**

TYPE:
Scholarships. Scholarships are awarded for research leading to a higher degree.

YEAR PROGRAM STARTED: 1957

PURPOSE:
To promote the knowledge and study of chemistry in relation to industry and agriculture, including chemistry connected with electrical engineering, metallurgical chemistry and chemistry in its application to mining and the winning and treatment of minerals and natural products of the soil.

LEGAL BASIS:
University.

ELIGIBILITY:
Open to graduates of universities which are members of the Association of Commonwealth Universities, graduates of any country who are citizens of a Commonwealth country, or Australian permanent residents. Candidates for scholarships must hold at least a first class honours degree.

Tenable at the University of Sydney.

FINANCIAL DATA:
Scholarship does not cover tuition fees payable by international students.

Amount of support per award: $35,629 AUD per annum for the year 2021.

APPLICATION INFO:
Application information is available on the web site.
Duration: Two years for a Master's research degree and three years for a Ph.D.
Deadline: September.

THE ROBERT A. WELCH FOUNDATION [1861]
5555 San Felipe
Suite 1900
Houston, TX 77056-2730
(713) 961-9884
Fax: (713) 961-5168
E-mail: info@welch1.org
Web Site: www.welch1.org

FOUNDED: 1954

AREAS OF INTEREST:
Basic research in chemistry.

NAME(S) OF PROGRAMS:
● **Departmental Grants**
● **Research Grants**
● **Welch Summer Scholar Program**

TYPE:
Research grants. Grants to support long-range fundamental research in the broad domain of chemistry.

The Welch Foundation supports chemical research at educational institutions within the state of Texas.

LEGAL BASIS:
Corporate.

ELIGIBILITY:
Full-time regular faculty members at Texas colleges or universities, who are tenured or on the tenured track, are eligible to apply for research grants.

GEOG. RESTRICTIONS: Texas.

FINANCIAL DATA:
Amount of support per award: Minimum $80,000 research grant per year.
Total amount of support: Varies.

NO. AWARDS: Varies.

APPLICATION INFO:
Application information is available on the web site.
Duration: Three years. Renewable.
Deadline: Departmental Grants: September 15; Research Grants: Last business day of January.

IRS I.D.: 76-0343128

ADDRESS INQUIRIES TO:
See e-mail address above.

Earth sciences

THE AMERICAN ASSOCIATION OF GEOGRAPHERS [1862]
1710 16th Street, N.W.
Washington, DC 20009
(202) 234-1450
Fax: (202) 234-2744
E-mail: grantsawards@aag.org
Web Site: www.aag.org

FOUNDED: 1904

NAME(S) OF PROGRAMS:
● **AAG Research Grant**

TYPE:
Research grants. Small grant to support research and fieldwork.

PURPOSE:
To support research and fieldwork proposals which offer the prospect of obtaining substantial subsequent support from private foundations or federal agencies and that address questions of major importance to the discipline.

ELIGIBILITY:
Must be an AAG member for at least two years at the time of application. Grants can be used only for direct expenses of research; salary and overhead costs are not allowed. The committee will not approve awards for Master's or doctoral dissertation research.

FINANCIAL DATA:
Amount of support per award: Up to $500.

APPLICATION INFO:
Digital submissions are required.
Deadline: December 31.

ADDRESS INQUIRIES TO:
See e-mail address above.

THE AMERICAN ASSOCIATION OF GEOGRAPHERS [1863]
1710 16th Street, N.W.
Washington, DC 20009
(202) 234-1450
Fax: (202) 234-2744
E-mail: grantsawards@aag.org
Web Site: www.aag.org

FOUNDED: 1904

NAME(S) OF PROGRAMS:
● **AAG Dissertation Research Grants**

TYPE:
Research grants.

PURPOSE:
To provide financial assistance to candidates preparing doctoral dissertations in geography.

ELIGIBILITY:
Applicant must:
(1) be an AAG member for at least one year at the time of application;
(2) not have a Doctorate at the time of the award and;
(3) have completed all Ph.D. requirements except the dissertation by the end of the semester or term following approval of the award. Dissertation supervisor must certify eligibility.

FINANCIAL DATA:
Amount of support per award: Up to $1,000.

APPLICATION INFO:
Digital submissions are required.
Deadline: December 31.

THE AMERICAN ASSOCIATION OF GEOGRAPHERS [1864]
1710 16th Street, N.W.
Washington, DC 20009
(202) 234-1450
Fax: (202) 234-2744
E-mail: grantsawards@aag.org
Web Site: www.aag.org

FOUNDED: 1904

Deadline: February 7.

ADDRESS INQUIRIES TO:
Workforce Development, Education,
Outreach and Scholarship Coordinator
The American Geosciences Institute (AGI)
(See address above.)

AMERICAN METEOROLOGICAL SOCIETY

45 Beacon Street
Boston, MA 02108-3693
(617) 227-2426 ext. 3907
Fax: (617) 742-8718
E-mail: dfernandez@ametsoc.org
Web Site: www.ametsoc.org

TYPE:
Fellowships; Scholarships. AMS Freshman
Undergraduate Scholarship Program awards
funding to high school seniors entering their
freshman year of undergraduate study in the
fall.

AMS Graduate Fellowship in the History of
Science is awarded to a student wishing to
complete a dissertation on the history of the
atmospheric and related oceanic or
hydrologic sciences.

AMS Graduate Fellowships are designed to
attract students entering their first year of
graduate study in the fall who wish to pursue
advanced degrees in the atmospheric and
related oceanic and hydrologic sciences.

AMS Minority Scholarship awards funding to
high school minority students entering
freshman year of undergraduate study in the
fall who have been traditionally
underrepresented in the sciences, especially
Hispanic, Native American and Black/African
American students.

AMS Senior Named Scholarships are
directed to students entering their final year
of undergraduate study in the fall.

The Father James B. Macelwane Annual
Awards in Meteorology is intended to
stimulate interest in meteorology among
college students through the submission of
original student papers concerned with some
phase of the atmospheric sciences. The
student must be enrolled as an undergraduate
at the time the paper was written.

See entry 2365 for full listing.

THE GEOLOGICAL SOCIETY OF AMERICA, INC.   [1867]

3300 Penrose Place
Boulder, CO 80301-9140
(303) 357-1025
(888) 443-4472
Fax: (303) 357-1070
E-mail: researchgrants@geosociety.org
Web Site: www.geosociety.org

FOUNDED: 1888

AREAS OF INTEREST:
Geoscience.

NAME(S) OF PROGRAMS:
● **GSA Research Grants**

TYPE:
Grants-in-aid; Project/program grants;
Research grants. Grants for projects
contributing to the science of geology.

YEAR PROGRAM STARTED: 1933

PURPOSE:
To provide partial support of Master's and
doctoral thesis research in earth science for
graduate students.

LEGAL BASIS:
Private membership association.

ELIGIBILITY:
Qualified investigators with appropriate
interests are eligible to apply. Graduate
students apply for support of Master's or
doctoral thesis work. The GSA strongly
encourages women, minorities and persons
with disabilities to participate in this grants
program.

Applicants must be members of GSA.

GEOG. RESTRICTIONS: North and Central
America.

FINANCIAL DATA:
Funds are intended as an aid to the research
project and not to sustain entire research
costs.
Amount of support per award: Generally
$500 to $2,500.

NO. MOST RECENT APPLICANTS: 750.

NO. AWARDS: 395.

APPLICATION INFO:
Official application materials are available
online.
Duration: One year.
Deadline: Applications must be submitted
electronically by February 1 for consideration
at the spring review meeting.

PUBLICATIONS:
Annual report; application guidelines.

OFFICERS:
Vicki McConnell, Executive Director

ADDRESS INQUIRIES TO:
Program Manager, Research Grants
(See address above.)

INTERNATIONAL WOMEN'S FISHING ASSOCIATION SCHOLARSHIP TRUST   [1868]

P.O. Box 530816
Miami Shores, FL 33153-0816
E-mail: scholarshiptrust@iwfa.org
Web Site: www.iwfa.org/scholarship

FOUNDED: 1965

AREAS OF INTEREST:
Marine science.

NAME(S) OF PROGRAMS:
● **IWFA Scholarship Trust**

TYPE:
Scholarships. For postgraduate educational
expense including tuition, supplies and
books.

YEAR PROGRAM STARTED: 1965

PURPOSE:
To aid needy students who are seeking
postgraduate degrees in marine science.

LEGAL BASIS:
501(c)(3) nonprofit organization.

ELIGIBILITY:
Applicant must be a graduate student in
marine science. Student must be matriculated
at a school in the U.S.

FINANCIAL DATA:
Amount of support per award: Typically
$1,000 to $3,000.

Total amount of support: $36,000 for the
year 2017.

NO. AWARDS: 23.

APPLICATION INFO:
Application must be entered electronically.
Duration: One year.
Deadline: March 1.

ADDRESS INQUIRIES TO:
Chairman, IWFA Scholarship Trust
(See address above.)

*SPECIAL STIPULATIONS:
For graduate students in the Marine Science
field only.

LUNAR AND PLANETARY INSTITUTE

3600 Bay Area Boulevard
Houston, TX 77058
(281) 486-2159
Fax: (281) 486-2127
E-mail: internprogram@lpi.usra.edu
Web Site: www.lpi.usra.edu

TYPE:
Conferences/seminars; Internships;
Scholarships; Travel grants.

See entry 1839 for full listing.

THE MINERALOGICAL SOCIETY OF AMERICA   [1869]

3635 Concorde Parkway, Suite 500
Chantilly, VA 20151-1110
(703) 652-9950
Fax: (703) 652-9951
E-mail: abenbow@minsocam.org
Web Site: www.minsocam.org

FOUNDED: 1919

AREAS OF INTEREST:
Crystallography, mineralogy and petrology.

NAME(S) OF PROGRAMS:
● **Research Grant in Crystallography,
Mineral Physics or Chemistry and
Mineralogy**
● **Student Research Grant in Mineralogy
and Petrology**

TYPE:
Research grants. Grants supported through
endowment funds.

YEAR PROGRAM STARTED: 1973

PURPOSE:
To encourage research in mineralogy,
crystallography, geochemistry, and petrology.

LEGAL BASIS:
501(c)(3) organization and Virginia
corporation.

ELIGIBILITY:
Crystallography grant is open to students, as
well as beginners, faculty and young
researchers. The mineralogy/petrology grant
is limited to students.

FINANCIAL DATA:
The grant is for research-related expenses
only. Travel to meetings, conferences, short
courses, nonresearch field trips, tuition,
nonresearch living (room and board)
expenses, etc., are not suitable uses of the
money. Neither should the money be used for
salary or wages for the researcher.
Amount of support per award: $5,000.
Total amount of support: $15,000.

NO. MOST RECENT APPLICANTS: 50 to 60
annually.

NO. AWARDS: 3.

APPLICATION INFO:

Proposal submissions are to be made online.

Duration: One year.

Deadline: March 1.

PUBLICATIONS:

American Mineralogist; Reviews in Mineralogy and Geochemistry; Elements.

IRS I.D.: 52-6044250

ADDRESS INQUIRIES TO:

Dr. Ann E. Benbow, Executive Director
(See address above.)

NATIONAL ASSOCIATION OF GEOSCIENCE TEACHERS [1870]

c/o Science Education Resource Center
200 Division Street, Suite 210
Northfield, MN 55057
(507) 222-4368
(507) 222-5339
Fax: (507) 222-5175
E-mail: nagtservice@nagt.org
acollette@carleton.edu
Web Site: www.nagt.org

FOUNDED: 1938

AREAS OF INTEREST:

Earth sciences.

NAME(S) OF PROGRAMS:

- **Scholarships for Field Study**
- **Dottie Stout Professional Development Grants**

TYPE:

Development grants; Scholarships.
Scholarships for Field Study: Cash award to undergraduate students to facilitate their study of field geoscience.

Dottie Stout Professional Development Grants will be awarded in support of the following activities:
(1) participation in earth science classes or workshops;
(2) attendance at professional scientific or science education meetings;
(3) participation in earth science field trips and;
(4) purchase of earth science materials for classroom use.

YEAR PROGRAM STARTED: 1970

PURPOSE:

To further geological education at the undergraduate level.

LEGAL BASIS:

Tax-exempt corporation.

ELIGIBILITY:

Scholarships for Field Study: Applicants must be full-time students with a geology major. The chief criterion for selection is advanced students with distinguished academic records within the major.

Dottie Stout Professional Development Grants: Community college faculty and K-12th grade teachers who teach one or more earth science courses and community college students actively pursuing a career in the earth sciences are encouraged to apply for these awards.

FINANCIAL DATA:

Amount of support per award: Scholarships for Field Study: $750; Dottie Stout Professional Development Grants: $750 each to a community college faculty member, a community college student and a K-12th grade educator.

Total amount of support: Varies.

NO. MOST RECENT APPLICANTS: Scholarships for Field Study: 32; Dottie Stout Professional Development Grants: 10.

NO. AWARDS: Scholarships for Field Study: 18; Dottie Stout Professional Development Grants: 3.

APPLICATION INFO:

Application information is available at the web site.

Deadline: Scholarships for Field Study: February 14; Dottie Stout Professional Development Grants: April 15.

PUBLICATIONS:

Journal of Geoscience Education; In The Trenches, magazine.

IRS I.D.: 74-6068050

OFFICERS:

Jennifer Wenner, President

NATIONAL CENTER FOR ATMOSPHERIC RESEARCH

1850 Table Mesa Drive
Boulder, CO 80305
(303) 497-1607
Fax: (303) 497-1646
E-mail: sbriggs@ucar.edu
Web Site: www.asp.ucar.edu

TYPE:

Fellowships. The fellowships cover a year's appointment, with a likely extension to two years, at NCAR to take advantage of its educational programs and/or research facilities in the broad field of atmospheric sciences.

See entry 1638 for full listing.

NATIONAL GEOGRAPHIC SOCIETY [1871]

Committee for Research and Exploration
1145 17th Street, N.W.
Washington, DC 20036
(202) 857-7000
E-mail: grantsinfo@ngs.org
Web Site: www.nationalgeographic.org/grants

FOUNDED: 1888

AREAS OF INTEREST:

Conservation, education, research, storytelling and technology.

NAME(S) OF PROGRAMS:

- **National Geographic Society Committee for Research and Exploration**

TYPE:

Grants-in-aid; Research grants; Seed money grants. Grants-in-aid for basic research in the sciences pertinent to geography (including, but not limited to, projects in geography). Support may also be provided for projects in these fields that depend on exploration. The Society is currently emphasizing multidisciplinary projects that address environmental issues.

YEAR PROGRAM STARTED: 1890

PURPOSE:

To further understanding of our planet and empower the global community to generate solutions for a healthier and more sustainable future.

LEGAL BASIS:

Nonprofit.

ELIGIBILITY:

Applicants are expected to have advanced degrees (Ph.D. or equivalent) and be associated with an educational organization or institution. Independent researchers or those pursuing a Ph.D.-level degree may apply, but competition is keen and awards to non-Ph.D. applicants are rare. As a general rule, all applicants are expected to have published a minimum of three articles in peer-reviewed scientific journals. Individuals between the ages of 18 and 25 are invited to apply to the Young Explorers Program. These applicants are not expected to have advanced degrees but should have a record of prior experience as it pertains to their proposed project. Citizens of any country are eligible.

Grants normally are made only for field research. Laboratory work is supported only to the extent that it may be a necessary follow-up to Society-funded field research.

Grants are awarded on the basis of the project's scientific merit. All proposed projects must have both a geographical dimension and relevance to other scientific fields and be of broad scientific interest. The Committee pays special attention to the significance of the research proposal in terms of its relationship to major scientific questions or problems. The Committee's priorities favor research that relates to environmental concerns and has relevance to global geographic issues.

FINANCIAL DATA:

Society funds may be used for transportation, supplies, and daily subsistence. Capital equipment (generally defined as any item costing more than U.S. $500) must be individually justified. Laboratory expenses are acceptable, provided the laboratory work is a logical extension of the field research.

Amount of support per award: Early Career Grants: $5,000 to $10,000; Exploration Grants: $10,000 to $30,000.

Total amount of support: $12,000,000 budgeted for research program annually.

Matching fund requirements: National Geographic Society funds are intended to function as complementary support. The committee strongly encourages applicants to seek additional, concurrent funding from other agencies.

NO. MOST RECENT APPLICANTS: 7,000.

NO. AWARDS: Approximately 600 per year.

APPLICATION INFO:

Project leader must submit a proposal using the online application in the Grants Portal. All application material must be in English.

To prepare the proposal, applicant will need:
(1) a primary project focus;
(2) curriculum vitae or resume, in English;
(3) a budget and;
(4) a list of the name, e-mail address, project role, affiliate organization, highest degree earned, and country of primary residence for all members of the project team. If applicant plans to work outside their home country, at least one local collaborator on the project team must be included. Early Career Grant applicants need to include the name and contact information of one advisor, mentor or supervisor.

Early Career Grant applicants must also submit a two-minute video that will be used to help evaluate the proposal. Applicant may speak in their primary language, but if that is not English, then it must include English subtitles or an English video transcript.

Duration: One year.

Deadline: At least six months in advance of anticipated project start date. Board meets quarterly in January, April, July and October.

PUBLICATIONS:
Program description; National Geographic Index 1888-1988.

*PLEASE NOTE:
Applicants are encouraged to confirm program online for recent changes.

NATIONAL OCEANIC AND ATMOSPHERIC ADMINISTRATION   [1872]
1315 East West Highway, 12th Floor
Silver Spring, MD 20910-5603
(301) 734-1206
Fax: (301) 713-0517
E-mail: cpograntss@noaa.gov
diane.brown@noaa.gov
Web Site: www.cpo.noaa.gov

FOUNDED: 1966

AREAS OF INTEREST:
Climate and atmospheric research.

NAME(S) OF PROGRAMS:
● **Climate Program**

TYPE:
Challenge/matching grants; Conferences/seminars; Formula grants. The Climate Program Office supports competitive research through three major program areas: Earth System Science and Modeling (ESSM), Climate and Societal Interactions (CS), and Communication, Education and Engagement (CEE). Several of these competitions are relevant to high-priority climate areas. The goal of these programs is to improve science understanding and/or capabilities that result in user-driven outcomes. The four initial risk areas are: Coastal Inundation, Marine Ecosystems, Water Resources and Extreme Heat.

PURPOSE:
To develop the knowledge required to establish a predictive capability for short- and long-term climate fluctuations and trends.

LEGAL BASIS:
Government agency.

ELIGIBILITY:
Applicants may be institutions of higher education, other nonprofits, commercial organizations, international organizations, state, local and Indian tribal governments. Federal agencies or institutions are ineligible.

FINANCIAL DATA:
Grants may be used for research and development, advisory services and operational systems as they relate to specific programs.
Amount of support per award: $50,000 to $300,000.
Total amount of support: Approximately $8,000,000 for the year 2021.

NO. AWARDS: Approximately 90 new awards for the year 2021.

APPLICATION INFO:
Applications are to be submitted through grants.gov.
Duration: One to three years.
Deadline: Varies.

ADDRESS INQUIRIES TO:
Diane Brown, Grants Manager
Climate Program Office
(See address above.)

NATIONAL OCEANIC AND ATMOSPHERIC ADMINISTRATION   [1873]
National Marine Fisheries Service
263 13th Avenue South
St. Petersburg, FL 33701
(727) 824-5324
Fax: (727) 824-5364
E-mail: dax.ruiz@noaa.gov
kelly.donnelly@noaa.gov
Web Site: www.fisheries.noaa.gov/funding-opportunities

AREAS OF INTEREST:
Southeast region.

NAME(S) OF PROGRAMS:
● **Bluefin Tuna Research Program Grants**
● **Cooperative Research Program Grants**
● **Marine Fisheries Initiative Grants**

TYPE:
Development grants; Research grants.

YEAR PROGRAM STARTED: 2003

PURPOSE:
To support research and development.

ELIGIBILITY:
Bluefin Tuna Research Program Grants are available to institutions of higher education, nonprofits, commercial organizations, individuals, and state, local, and Indian tribal governments. Federal agencies or institutions are not eligible.

Cooperative Research Program Grants: Applicants who are not commercial or recreational fishermen must have commercial or recreational fishermen participating in their project. There must be a written agreement with a fisherman describing the involvement in the project activity. Eligible applicants include institutions of higher education, other nonprofits, commercial organizations, state, local and Indian tribal governments and individuals. Federal agencies or institutions are not eligible.

Marine Fisheries Initiative Grants are available to institutions of higher education, other nonprofits, commercial organizations, state, local and Indian tribal governments. Federal agencies or institutions are not eligible.

Foreign governments, organizations under the jurisdiction of foreign governments, and international organizations are excluded for purposes of these solicitations since the objective of these programs is to optimize research and development benefits from U.S. marine fishery resources.

FINANCIAL DATA:
Amount of support per award: Bluefin Tuna: $25,000 to $600,000; CRP: $25,000 to $250,000; MARFIN: Up to $525,000.

Total amount of support: Bluefin Tuna: Approximately $600,000; CRP: Approximately $1,500,000 for the year 2020.

Matching fund requirements: Cost sharing is not required.

NO. MOST RECENT APPLICANTS: Bluefin Tuna: 7; CRP: 30, MARFIN: 30.

NO. AWARDS: Bluefin Tuna: 5; CRP: Approximately 8; MARFIN: 5.

APPLICATION INFO:
Applications are available on grants.gov. New applicants should contact the National Marine Fisheries Service Office.

Duration: Bluefin Tuna Research Program Grants and Cooperative Research Program Grants: One year; Marine Fisheries Initiative Grants: One to three years.

Deadline: Announced in NOAA solicitation and grant opportunities index.

PUBLICATIONS:
Annual report.

ADDRESS INQUIRIES TO:
Cooperative Research Program Grants:
Dax Ruiz, Federal Grants Program Officer

Marine Fisheries Initiative Grants:
Kelly Donnelly
Federal Grants Program Manager
(See address above.)

NATIONAL OCEANIC AND ATMOSPHERIC ADMINISTRATION   [1874]
Ocean Exploration and Research Program
SSMC3, R/OER, Room 10210
1315 East-West Highway
Silver Spring, MD 20910
(301) 734-1023
(301) 734-1017
Fax: (301) 713-1967
E-mail: frank.cantelas@noaa.gov
oceanexplorer@noaa.gov
Web Site: oceanexplorer.noaa.gov

AREAS OF INTEREST:
Marine research.

NAME(S) OF PROGRAMS:
● **Ocean Exploration and Research Program**

TYPE:
Project/program grants; Research grants.

ELIGIBILITY:
Eligible applicants are U.S. institutions of higher education, not-for-profit institutions, and federal, state, and local governments. Federal agencies may not charge salary or overhead.

GEOG. RESTRICTIONS: United States.

FINANCIAL DATA:
Amount of support per award: $10,000 to $750,000 projected for fiscal year 2020.

Total amount of support: Approximately $3,000,000 projected for fiscal year 2020.

NO. AWARDS: Approximately 10 for the year 2020.

APPLICATION INFO:
Each National Undersea Research Center has its own proposal forms and guidelines. Specific locations and instructions are available online.
Duration: Up to two years.
Deadline: Varies by Center.

ADDRESS INQUIRIES TO:
Frank Cantelas, Deputy Director
(See address above.)

NATIONAL SCIENCE FOUNDATION   [1875]
Division of Earth Sciences
2415 Eisenhower Avenue
Alexandria, VA 22314
(703) 292-8550
Fax: (703) 292-9025
Web Site: www.nsf.gov

FOUNDED: 1950

AREAS OF INTEREST:
Earth sciences.

TYPE:
Research grants. The Division of Earth Sciences supports proposals for research geared toward improving the understanding of the structure, composition, and evolution of the Earth and the processes that govern the formation and behavior of the Earth's materials.

YEAR PROGRAM STARTED: 1950

PURPOSE:
To create a better understanding of the Earth's changing environments and the natural distribution of its mineral, water and energy resources; to provide methods for predicting and mitigating the effects of geologic hazards such as earthquakes, volcanic eruptions, floods and landslides.

LEGAL BASIS:
Federal agency.

ELIGIBILITY:
Scientists and engineers, especially college and university faculty members, are eligible to apply.

GEOG. RESTRICTIONS: United States and its territories.

FINANCIAL DATA:
Amount of support per award: Varies.
Total amount of support: Varies.

NO. MOST RECENT APPLICANTS: 1,600.

NO. AWARDS: 500.

APPLICATION INFO:
Application information is available on the web site.
Duration: One to five years.

PUBLICATIONS:
Grant proposal guide (NSF 04-23).

NATIONAL SCIENCE FOUNDATION [1876]
Division of Ocean Sciences
2415 Eisenhower Avenue
Alexandria, VA 22314
(703) 292-8580
Fax: (703) 292-9449
E-mail: tquinn@nsf.gov
Web Site: www.nsf.gov

FOUNDED: 1950

AREAS OF INTEREST:
Biological, chemical and physical processes in the ocean.

NAME(S) OF PROGRAMS:
• Ocean Section

TYPE:
Research grants. Support for fundamental research in marine science, including physical oceanography and limnology, chemical oceanography, biological oceanography and marine geology, geophysics and ocean technology, with the objective of increasing knowledge and enhancing our understanding of the marine environment.

Most of the research supported is basic in character, although some applied research is also supported. This program also supports research workshops, symposia and conferences and purchases of scientific equipment related to projects supported.

YEAR PROGRAM STARTED: 1980

PURPOSE:
To improve understanding of the nature of the ocean and its influence on human activities and of human impacts on the marine environment.

LEGAL BASIS:
Government agency.

ELIGIBILITY:
Program is primarily for support of scientists in basic research in ocean sciences and instrumentation and the facilities to support it.

FINANCIAL DATA:
Amount of support per award: Varies.
Total amount of support: Varies.

APPLICATION INFO:
Application information is available at the web site.
Duration: Varies.
Deadline: Proposals may be submitted at any time. Approximately six months are required for review and processing. Target dates are February 15 and August 15.

STAFF:
Terrence M. Quinn, Division Director
Michael Sieracki, Program Director, Biological and Physical Oceanography

ADDRESS INQUIRIES TO:
Division of Ocean Sciences
(See address above.)

NATIONAL SOCIETY OF PROFESSIONAL SURVEYORS (NSPS)
5119 Pegasus Court
Suite Q
Frederick, MD 21704
(240) 439-4615 ext. 105
Fax: (240) 439-4952
E-mail: info@nsps.us.com
Web Site: www.nsps.us.com

TYPE:
Scholarships. Berntsen International Scholarship in Surveying Technology is for students enrolled in two-year degree programs in surveying technology. Scholarship awarded in even years only.

See entry 2397 for full listing.

NATIONAL SOCIETY OF PROFESSIONAL SURVEYORS (NSPS)
5119 Pegasus Court
Suite Q
Frederick, MD 21704
(240) 439-4615 ext. 105
Fax: (240) 439-4952
E-mail: info@nsps.us.com
Web Site: www.nsps.us.com

TYPE:
Scholarships. For students enrolled in four-year degree programs in surveying or in closely related degree programs such as geomatics or surveying engineering.

See entry 2398 for full listing.

NATIONAL SOCIETY OF PROFESSIONAL SURVEYORS (NSPS)
5119 Pegasus Court
Suite Q
Frederick, MD 21704
(240) 439-4615 ext. 105
Fax: (240) 439-4952
E-mail: info@nsps.us.com
Web Site: www.nsps.us.com

TYPE:
Scholarships.

See entry 2399 for full listing.

NATIONAL SOCIETY OF PROFESSIONAL SURVEYORS (NSPS) AMERICAN ASSOCIATION FOR GEODETIC SURVEYING (AAGS)
5119 Pegasus Court
Suite Q
Frederick, MD 21704
(240) 439-4615 ext. 105
Fax: (240) 439-4952
E-mail: info@nsps.us.com
Web Site: www.aagsmo.org
www.nsps.us.com

TYPE:
Fellowships. Annual fellowship award to support graduate study in a program with a significant focus on geodetic surveying or geodesy at a school of the recipient's choice.

See entry 2400 for full listing.

NATIONAL SOCIETY OF PROFESSIONAL SURVEYORS (NSPS) AMERICAN ASSOCIATION FOR GEODETIC SURVEYING (AAGS)
5119 Pegasus Court
Suite Q
Frederick, MD 21704
(240) 439-4615 ext. 105
Fax: (240) 439-4952
E-mail: info@nsps.us.com
Web Site: www.aagsmo.org
www.nsps.us.com

TYPE:
Scholarships. The award is intended for students enrolled in four-year degree programs in surveying or in closely related degree programs.

See entry 2401 for full listing.

V. KANN RASMUSSEN FOUNDATION [1877]
475 Riverside Drive, Suite 900
New York, NY 10115
(212) 812-4271
E-mail: grants@vkrf.org
Web Site: www.vkrf.org

FOUNDED: 1991

AREAS OF INTEREST:
Climate change and unsustainable consumption.

TYPE:
Project/program grants.

PURPOSE:
To support the transition to a more environmentally resilient, stable and sustainable planet.

LEGAL BASIS:
Private foundation.

ELIGIBILITY:
Eligible organizations must be IRS 501(c)(3) tax-exempt. Only projects that are global in scope will be considered.

GEOG. RESTRICTIONS: United States.

FINANCIAL DATA:
Amount of support per award: Varies.

APPLICATION INFO:
Application procedures can be found on the Foundation web site.
Duration: One to two years.
Deadline: Varies.

IRS I.D.: 22-3101266

STAFF:
Irene Krarup, Executive Director and Head of Programs

ADDRESS INQUIRIES TO:
Irene Krarup, Executive Director and Head of Programs
(See address above.)

THE PERCY SLADEN MEMORIAL FUND

c/o The Linnean Society of London
Burlington House, Piccadilly
London W1J 0BF England
(44) 020 7434 4479
Fax: (44) 020 7287 9364
E-mail: info@linnean.org
gina@linnean.org
Web Site: www.linnean.org

TYPE:
Awards/prizes; Project/program grants; Research grants; Travel grants. Field work grants in life and earth sciences (excludes any projects which are part of further education, e.g., a Doctorate or a Master's course).

See entry 1899 for full listing.

SOCIETY OF EXPLORATION GEOPHYSICISTS   [1878]

8801 South Yale Avenue
Suite 500
Tulsa, OK 74137
(918) 497-4630
Fax: (918) 497-5560
E-mail: scholarships@seg.org
Web Site: www.seg.org/foundation
www.seg.org/scholarships

FOUNDED: 1956

AREAS OF INTEREST:
Applied geophysics.

NAME(S) OF PROGRAMS:
● **SEG Scholarship Program**

TYPE:
Scholarships. Undergraduate and graduate scholarships for the study of geophysics.

YEAR PROGRAM STARTED: 1956

PURPOSE:
To assist young people in pursuing careers in the field of applied geophysics.

LEGAL BASIS:
Nonprofit society.

ELIGIBILITY:
Applicant must intend to pursue a college course directed toward a career in applied geophysics and must have an interest in and aptitude for physics, mathematics, and geology. Applicant must be:
(1) a high school student with above-average grades planning to enter college the next fall term;
(2) an undergraduate college student whose grades are above average or;
(3) a graduate college student whose studies are directed toward a career in applied geophysics in operations, teaching or research.

FINANCIAL DATA:
Amount of support per award: $500 to $10,000 per academic year, averaging $2,600 per academic year.
Total amount of support: $322,332 for the academic year 2020.

NO. MOST RECENT APPLICANTS: 494.

NO. AWARDS: 124 for the academic year 2020.

APPLICATION INFO:
Application must be submitted electronically. Transcripts and letters of recommendation may be submitted online or sent via regular mail. Results of aptitude tests are not required but should be included if taken.
Duration: One year. Renewable at the discretion of the SEG Scholarship Committee, subject to student's maintenance of satisfactory grades, funds available and continued study leading to a career in geophysics.
Deadline: March 1.

ADDRESS INQUIRIES TO:
Scholarship Administrator
(See address above.)

*SPECIAL STIPULATIONS:
Certain scholarships carry additional qualifications specified by the scholarships' donors.

THE UNIVERSITY OF CALGARY   [1879]

Faculty of Graduate Studies
Earth Sciences Building, Room 1010
2500 University Drive, N.W.
Calgary AB T2N 1N4 Canada
(403) 220-4938
Fax: (403) 289-7635
E-mail: gsaward@ucalgary.ca
Web Site: grad.ucalgary.ca/awards

NAME(S) OF PROGRAMS:
● **Harry and Laura Jacques Graduate Scholarship**

TYPE:
Scholarships.

ELIGIBILITY:
Open to students registered full-time in a thesis-based graduate program at the University of Calgary.

FINANCIAL DATA:
Amount of support per award: $5,200.
Total amount of support: $5,200.

NO. AWARDS: 1.

APPLICATION INFO:
Students should consult the Graduate Award Competition Guidelines and complete the Graduate Award Scholarship Application through the Student Centre.
Duration: One year.
Deadline: Varies by program. Students should contact their Graduate Program Administrator.

ADDRESS INQUIRIES TO:
Graduate Scholarship Office
(See address above.)

Mathematics

THE ACTUARIAL FOUNDATION   [1880]

475 North Martingale Road
Suite 600
Schaumburg, IL 60173-2226
(847) 706-3535
Fax: (847) 706-3599
E-mail: Scholarships@ActFnd.org
Web Site: www.actuarialfoundation.org

FOUNDED: 1994

AREAS OF INTEREST:
Actuarial science, a branch of mathematics based on calculus, probability and statistics, as well as business economics.

NAME(S) OF PROGRAMS:
● **Actuarial Diversity Scholarship**

TYPE:
Scholarships. This scholarship promotes diversity in the profession through an annual scholarship program for Black/African American, Hispanic, Native North American and Pacific Islander students. The scholarship award recognizes and encourages academic achievements by awarding scholarships to full-time undergraduate students pursuing a degree that may lead to a career in the actuarial profession.

YEAR PROGRAM STARTED: 2009

PURPOSE:
To promote diversity in the actuarial profession.

LEGAL BASIS:
Private- and corporate-funded.

ELIGIBILITY:
Each applicant must fulfill all of the following requirements:
(1) must have at least one birth parent who is a member of one of the following minority groups: Black/African American, Hispanic, Native North American, or Pacific Islander;
(2) enrolled as a full-time undergraduate student at a U.S.-accredited educational institution during the application academic year;
(3) minimum grade point average of 3.0 (on a 4.0 scale), emphasis on math or actuarial courses;
(4) entering college freshmen must have a minimum ACT math score of 28 or SAT math score of 620 and;
(5) intent on pursuing a career in the actuarial profession.

GEOG. RESTRICTIONS: United States.

FINANCIAL DATA:
Amount of support per award: $1,000 to $4,000.
Total amount of support: $157,000 for the year 2020.

NO. MOST RECENT APPLICANTS: 87.

NO. AWARDS: 62 for the year 2020.

APPLICATION INFO:
Applications are posted in early November. Application and guidelines are available online.
Duration: One academic year. Renewable based on academic performance.

Deadline: June 15.

IRS I.D.: 36-2136422

ADDRESS INQUIRIES TO:
Scholarship Coordinator
(See address above.)

*PLEASE NOTE:
Applicants must intend to pursue a career in the actuarial profession.

THE ACTUARIAL FOUNDATION   [1881]
475 North Martingale Road
Suite 600
Schaumburg, IL 60173-2226
(847) 706-3535
Fax: (847) 706-3599
E-mail: Scholarships@ActFnd.org
Web Site: www.actuarialfoundation.org

FOUNDED: 1994

AREAS OF INTEREST:
Actuarial science.

NAME(S) OF PROGRAMS:
● **Actuary of Tomorrow - Stuart A. Robertson Memorial Scholarship**

TYPE:
Scholarships.

YEAR PROGRAM STARTED: 2006

PURPOSE:
To recognize and encourage the academic achievements of undergraduate students pursuing a career in actuarial science.

ELIGIBILITY:
Applicant must:
(1) be a full-time undergraduate student entering as a sophomore, junior or senior in the fall term;
(2) have a minimum cumulative grade point average of 3.0 (on a 4.0 scale) and;
(3) have successfully completed two actuarial exams.

GEOG. RESTRICTIONS: United States.

FINANCIAL DATA:
Amount of support per award: Up to $9,000.
Total amount of support: $29,250 for the year 2020.

NO. MOST RECENT APPLICANTS: 10.

NO. AWARDS: 5 for the year 2020.

APPLICATION INFO:
Application is available online. Applicant should:
(1) attach a current unofficial copy of transcripts from attending college/university;
(2) provide a letter of recommendation supporting academic achievement, leadership and communication skills from professor or advisor;
(3) provide a letter of recommendation from an employer or previous employer and;
(4) submit a personal essay of approximately 500 words, focusing on why you want to be an actuary.
Duration: One academic year. Nonrenewable.
Deadline: June 1.

ADDRESS INQUIRIES TO:
Scholarship Coordinator
(See address and e-mail above.)

*SPECIAL STIPULATIONS:
Scholarships are awarded directly to the college/university of choice in the recipients' name.

THE ACTUARIAL FOUNDATION   [1882]
475 North Martingale Road
Suite 600
Schaumburg, IL 60173-2226
(847) 706-3535
Fax: (847) 706-3599
E-mail: Scholarships@ActFnd.org
Web Site: www.actuarialfoundation.org

FOUNDED: 1994

AREAS OF INTEREST:
Actuarial science, mathematics and statistics.

NAME(S) OF PROGRAMS:
● **Curtis E. Huntington Memorial Scholarship**

TYPE:
Scholarships. Originally named the John Culver Wooddy Scholarship, the Curtis E. Huntington Memorial Scholarship is awarded annually to undergraduate seniors enrolled as full-time students at an accredited U.S. educational institution.

YEAR PROGRAM STARTED: 2014

PURPOSE:
To recognize the remarkably positive impact Curtis E. Huntington had on the actuarial profession.

ELIGIBILITY:
Undergraduate seniors who are enrolled as full-time students at an accredited U.S. educational institution may apply. Student must have successfully completed at least one actuarial examination, have a minimum 3.0 grade point average on a 4.0 scale, and must be nominated by a professor at their school.

U.S. citizenship or permanent residency is required.

FINANCIAL DATA:
Amount of support per award: Up to $3,000.
Total amount of support: $22,500 for the year 2020.

NO. MOST RECENT APPLICANTS: 14.

NO. AWARDS: 10 for the year 2020.

APPLICATION INFO:
Student must be nominated by a professor at their school.
Duration: One academic year. Nonrenewable.
Deadline: March 31.

ADDRESS INQUIRIES TO:
Scholarship Coordinator
(See address and e-mail above.)

AMERICAN MATHEMATICAL SOCIETY   [1883]
201 Charles Street
Providence, RI 02904-2213
(800) 321-4267 ext. 4096
(401) 455-4096
Fax: (401) 455-4004
E-mail: fellows@ams.org
Web Site: www.ams.org

FOUNDED: 1888

AREAS OF INTEREST:
Research mathematics.

NAME(S) OF PROGRAMS:
● **American Mathematical Society Centennial Fellowship**

TYPE:
Fellowships. The AMS Centennial Research Fellowship Program makes awards annually to outstanding mathematicians to help further their careers in research.

YEAR PROGRAM STARTED: 1974

PURPOSE:
To help outstanding mathematicians further their careers in research.

LEGAL BASIS:
Nonprofit corporation.

ELIGIBILITY:
The primary selection criterion for the Centennial Fellowship is the excellence of the candidate's research. Preference will be given to candidates who have not had extensive fellowship support in the past. Recipients may not hold the Centennial Fellowship concurrently with another research fellowship such as a Sloan Fellowship, NSF Postdoctoral Fellowship, or Career Award. Under normal circumstances, the fellowship cannot be deferred. A recipient of the fellowship shall have held his or her doctoral degree for at least three years and not more than 12 years at the inception of the award. Applications will be accepted from those currently holding a tenured, tenure-track, postdoctoral, or comparable (at the discretion of the selection committee) position at an institution in North America.

GEOG. RESTRICTIONS: North America.

FINANCIAL DATA:
Amount of support per award: $50,000 for the academic year 2022-23.

CO-OP FUNDING PROGRAMS: The Society has a matching program so that funds for at least one fellowship are guaranteed.

NO. AWARDS: Usually 1 per academic year.

APPLICATION INFO:
Applications should include a cogent plan indicating how the fellowship will be used. The plan should include travel to at least one other institution and should demonstrate that the fellowship will be used for more than reduction of teaching at the candidate's home institution. The selection committee will consider the plan in addition to the quality of the candidate's research, and will try to award the fellowship to those for whom the award would make a real difference in the development of their research careers. Work in all areas of mathematics, including interdisciplinary work, is eligible.

Application forms can be accessed at the web site.
Duration: One year. Nonrenewable.
Deadline: December 1. Announcement in February.

PUBLICATIONS:
Application guidelines.

STAFF:
Kim Kuda, Senior Program Coordinator

ADDRESS INQUIRIES TO:
See e-mail address above.

*SPECIAL STIPULATIONS:
Acceptance of the Fellowship cannot be postponed.

CONFERENCE BOARD OF THE MATHEMATICAL SCIENCES   [1884]
1600 Grand Avenue
St. Paul, MN 55105
(651) 696-6559
E-mail: bressoud@macalester.edu
Web Site: www.cbmsweb.org

FOUNDED: 1960

AREAS OF INTEREST:
Mathematical sciences.

NAME(S) OF PROGRAMS:
● **NSF-CBMS Regional Conferences in the Mathematical Sciences**

TYPE:
Conferences/seminars. Grants given by NSF for five-day conferences in the mathematical sciences.

YEAR PROGRAM STARTED: 1969

PURPOSE:
To stimulate interest and activity in mathematical sciences research.

LEGAL BASIS:
A nonprofit professional society.

ELIGIBILITY:
Proposals may only be submitted by the following:
(1) Two- and four-year institutions of higher education accredited in, and having a campus located in the U.S., acting on behalf of their faculty members and;
(2) Nonprofit, non-academic organizations, independent museums, observatories, research labs, professional societies and similar organizations in the U.S. associated with educational or research activities.

FINANCIAL DATA:
Grants may include travel and lodging costs, director's and secretary's salaries, announcement costs and other miscellaneous expenses.
Amount of support per award: $35,000 per conference.

NO. AWARDS: Up to 10.

APPLICATION INFO:
Proposals must be submitted electronically via Fastlane to the Division of Mathematical Sciences (DMS) at NSF.
Duration: Five days during the summer or during a recess in the academic year.
Deadline: Last Friday in April. Announcement in October.

PUBLICATIONS:
Monographs of the conferences are available from the American Mathematical Society, the Society for Industrial and Applied Mathematics, the Institute of Mathematical Statistics and the American Statistical Association.

ADDRESS INQUIRIES TO:
Swatee Naik
Tel: (703) 292-4876
E-mail: snaik@nsf.gov

IBM THOMAS J. WATSON RESEARCH CENTER [1885]
Department of Mathematical Sciences
1101 Kitchawan Road
Yorktown Heights, NY 10598
E-mail: postdoc@us.ibm.com
Web Site: www.research.ibm.com/goldstine

AREAS OF INTEREST:
Research in pure and applied mathematics and in theoretical and exploratory computer science.

NAME(S) OF PROGRAMS:
● **IBM Herman Goldstine Memorial Postdoctoral Fellowship for Research in Mathematical and Computer Sciences**

TYPE:
Fellowships.

YEAR PROGRAM STARTED: 1972

PURPOSE:
To provide scientists of outstanding ability an opportunity to advance their scholarship as resident department members at the IBM Thomas J. Watson Research Center.

ELIGIBILITY:
Applicant must have a Ph.D. in science, engineering or mathematics received within the last five years, or must expect to receive one before the fellowship commences in the second half of the year (usually in September).

FINANCIAL DATA:
Allowance provided for moving expenses.
Amount of support per award:
Approximately $130,000 to $150,000 per year, depending on the length of experience.

NO. AWARDS: Up to 2 per year.

APPLICATION INFO:
Applicants are required to complete an online form and provide their full curriculum vitae, Ph.D. dissertation abstract, a two- to three-page research statement describing current research and the research they plan to pursue if offered the fellowship, and three or more letters of recommendation, including one from their thesis advisor.
Duration: One year. Renewable for a second year if of mutual interest.
Deadline: Applications accepted November to January (exact dates vary).

ADDRESS INQUIRIES TO:
See e-mail address above.

MICRON TECHNOLOGY FOUNDATION, INC. [1886]
P.O. Box 6
Boise, ID 83707-0006
(208) 363-3675
Fax: (208) 368-4435
E-mail: mtf@micron.com
Web Site: www.micron.com/foundation

FOUNDED: 1999

AREAS OF INTEREST:
Education with an emphasis on STEM (science, technology, engineering and mathematics).

TYPE:
Matching gifts; Professorships; Project/program grants; Research grants.

YEAR PROGRAM STARTED: 2000

PURPOSE:
To advance education and local communities; to partner with educators to spark a passion in youth for science, technology, engineering and mathematics; to engineer the future for students; to enrich the communities through strategic giving where team members live, work and volunteer.

LEGAL BASIS:
Private corporate foundation.

ELIGIBILITY:
Micron will consider projects or programs which:
(1) address an educational need, especially those which advance math and science;
(2) impact basic human needs for a large number of people;
(3) have long-term benefits and;
(4) are in a geographic area where Micron has operations.

Micron generally does not address individual sponsorships or donations, requests for assistance with travel or lodging expenses, religious organizations requesting funds for purposes other than nondenominational education or organizations located in areas where Micron has no operations.

GEOG. RESTRICTIONS: Boise, Idaho and Manassas, Virginia.

FINANCIAL DATA:
Amount of support per award: Varies.
Total amount of support: Varies.
Matching fund requirements: Micron may match employee donations at a 1:1 ratio, K-12 and higher education organizations up to $2,000 per employee per calendar year to qualified educational institutions.

NO. AWARDS: Varies.

REPRESENTATIVE AWARDS:
Boise State University; Leadership Prince William; Rochester Institute of Technology; Stanford University.

APPLICATION INFO:
Paper applications are no longer accepted. Applicants for K-12 grants and nonprofit community grants must apply online on the web site.
Higher education grants by invitation only.
Duration: Varies.

IRS I.D.: 82-0516178

ADDRESS INQUIRIES TO:
Micron Technology Foundation, M/S 407
Community and Academic Relations
8000 South Federal Way, P.O. Box 6
Boise, ID 83707-0006

SOCIETY OF ACTUARIES (SOA) [1887]
475 North Martingale Road
Suite 600
Schaumburg, IL 60173-2226
(847) 706-3509
Fax: (847) 273-8605
E-mail: ttatsumi@soa.org
Web Site: www.soa.org/doctoral-stipend

FOUNDED: 1949

AREAS OF INTEREST:
Actuarial science, a branch of mathematics based on calculus, probability and statistics, as well as business economics.

NAME(S) OF PROGRAMS:
● **Society of Actuaries' James C. Hickman Scholar Doctoral Stipend Program**

TYPE:
Awards/prizes; Scholarships. Society of Actuaries' James C. Hickman Scholar Doctoral Stipend Program is designed to provide stipends to doctoral students who will, through their studies, address research and education needs of the profession, including both the theoretical and practical aspects.

YEAR PROGRAM STARTED: 2009

PURPOSE:
To increase the number of academic actuaries who hold a Ph.D. and an actuarial designation, and who intend to pursue academic careers in the U.S. or Canada.

LEGAL BASIS:
Society-funded.

ELIGIBILITY:
Individuals who meet the following requirements may apply:
(1) enrolled full-time, have recently been admitted or are currently applying to a qualifying doctoral program in the U.S. or Canada; a qualifying doctoral program is one in actuarial science or a field related to actuarial science (e.g., business, demography, economics, financial economics, insurance, mathematics, risk management, statistics); applicants may apply at the same time they are applying for a doctoral program; if selected, these applicants will be awarded the stipend conditional upon enrollment in a qualifying doctoral program;
(2) hold a fellowship-level actuarial credential or are pursuing Associateship or Fellowship membership of an accrediting actuarial organization (i.e., AI, CAS, CIA, IFoA, SOA); applicants who are already Associate members (including those awarded the CERA designation) will be expected to pursue a Fellowship credential and;
(3) all applicants must have at least two actuarial exams passed.

While U.S. or Canadian citizenship is not expressly required, the applicant will attest to citizenship status on the application. An applicant's citizenship status may be used to evaluate the likelihood that the applicant will pursue an academic career in the U.S. or Canada.

FINANCIAL DATA:
The stipend is to be used at the discretion of the Ph.D. candidate for appropriate expenses related to the completion of the Ph.D. and the actuarial credential if not yet attained. Applicants should be aware that stipend funds are provided for qualified expenses (tuition, books, fees, etc.). Qualified expenses do not include room and board. Stipend funds not used for qualified expenses may be taxable. Please consult one's tax advisor if one has any questions.
Amount of support per award: Generally $20,000 per academic year.
Total amount of support: Varies.

NO. MOST RECENT APPLICANTS: 27.

NO. AWARDS: Varies.

APPLICATION INFO:
Applicants must submit an application and supporting documentation that includes the following:
(1) Applicants currently applying to doctoral programs must provide the names of the schools/programs to which they have applied, and the intended field of study in each school/program. (If a stipend is awarded, it will be conditional on enrollment in the specified program and for the field of study proposed in the application.);
(2) Applicants already enrolled in a doctoral program will indicate how many years they have been studying, and approximately how many more years they believe they need to complete their Doctorate. They will also provide a statement from their supervisor or program director attesting to progress in their doctoral program and;
(3) Applicant must submit a Statement of Interest. This may be the same statement submitted for the doctoral program, but additional language should be added for this application to clearly explain their goals regarding teaching, research and contributions to the actuarial profession.
Duration: One academic year. Renewable up to four times based on satisfactory progress.

Deadline: Completed application forms and supporting materials must be received at the Society no later than February 15. Recipients will be announced April 15. Recipients must notify the Society of acceptance of the stipend by May 15.

PUBLICATIONS:
Application guidelines.

ADDRESS INQUIRIES TO:
SOA James C. Hickman Scholar Doctoral Stipend Program
(See address above.)

Physics

AMERICAN INSTITUTE OF PHYSICS   [1888]
One Physics Ellipse
College Park, MD 20740-3843
(301) 209-3090
(301) 209-3092
E-mail: writing@aip.org
Web Site: www.aip.org/aip/awards/science-communication

FOUNDED: 1931

AREAS OF INTEREST:
The advancement and diffusion of the knowledge of physics and its application to human welfare.

NAME(S) OF PROGRAMS:
- **American Institute of Physics Science Communication Awards**

TYPE:
Awards/prizes. Four writing awards, one to a physicist, astronomer or member of an AIP society, one to a journalist for noteworthy writing about physics and astronomy in the print media, one to a journalist for noteworthy writing about physics and astronomy for broadcast media, and one for science writing aimed at children.

PURPOSE:
To stimulate distinguished reporting and writing that will improve public appreciation of the physical sciences, astronomy, math and related science fields.

ELIGIBILITY:
Entries must have been printed in any recognized international, national or local medium of communication such as newspapers, magazines or books. The media should normally be available to, and intended for, the general public. Purely scientific, technical and trade publications are excluded.

Entries must have been published or translated into English during the period one year immediately prior to the deadline date. No more than three entries may be submitted by any one individual. Persons other than the author may submit entries on behalf of an author in accordance with the rules.

FINANCIAL DATA:
Amount of support per award: $3,000.
Total amount of support: $12,000.

NO. AWARDS: 4.

APPLICATION INFO:
Application information is available on the web site.
Deadline: March 31.

OFFICERS AND STAFF:
Michael H. Moloney, Chief Executive Officer

Gigi Swartz, Chief Financial Officer
Alix Vance, Chief Executive Officer, Publishing
Nancy Rawles, Chief Human Resources Officer

ADDRESS INQUIRIES TO:
Marissa Nielsen, Programs Coordinator
(See address above.)

AMERICAN VACUUM SOCIETY (AVS)   [1889]
125 Maiden Lane, Suite 15B
New York, NY 10038-4714
(212) 248-0200
Fax: (212) 248-0245
E-mail: avsnyc@avs.org
Web Site: avs.org

FOUNDED: 1953

AREAS OF INTEREST:
Vacuum science and technology, thin film research, vacuum metallurgy, surface physics, electronic materials and processing, plasma science and technology and applied surface science.

NAME(S) OF PROGRAMS:
- **Graduate Research Awards**
- **Russell and Sigurd Varian Award**
- **Nellie Yeoh Whetten Award**

TYPE:
Awards/prizes; Fellowships. Cash awards and a one-year fellowship in recognition of scientific promise or excellence in graduate studies in vacuum science.

The Whetten Award is offered to encourage and recognize participation by women in science and engineering.

PURPOSE:
To recognize and encourage excellence in graduate studies in the sciences and technologies of interest to the Society.

LEGAL BASIS:
Nonprofit 501(c)(3) organization.

ELIGIBILITY:
All awards are open to students engaged in graduate studies in major fields of the organization's interest at accredited graduate schools in North America.

For the Whetten Award, the nominee must be a registered female graduate student in an accredited academic institution at the time when the applications are due. Criteria for selection of the awardee are research and academic excellence.

FINANCIAL DATA:
Amount of support per award: Graduate Research Awards: $1,000 per award; $1,500 each for the Whetten Award and for the Varian Award, plus reimbursed travel support (up to $750 maximum) to attend the International Symposium.
Total amount of support: Varies.

NO. MOST RECENT APPLICANTS: 11.

NO. AWARDS: Graduate Research Awards: Approximately 3 annually; Varian Award and Whetten Award: 1 each per year.

APPLICATION INFO:
Nomination guidelines are posted online.
Deadline: May 1.

ADDRESS INQUIRIES TO:
Angela Klink, Program Administrator
E-mail: angela@avs.org

NATIONAL SCIENCE FOUNDATION [1890]

Division of Physics
2415 Eisenhower Avenue
Alexandria, VA 22314
(703) 292-8890
Fax: (703) 292-9078
E-mail: info@nsf.gov
Web Site: www.nsf.gov

AREAS OF INTEREST:
Nuclear, theoretical, atomic and molecular, gravitational, and elementary particles, education and interdisciplinary research, physics of living systems, particle and nuclear astrophysics.

NAME(S) OF PROGRAMS:
• **Investigator-Initiated Research Projects**

TYPE:
Research grants.

PURPOSE:
To support physics research and the preparation of future scientists in U.S. colleges and universities across a broad range of physics disciplines.

ELIGIBILITY:
As specified in the NSF Grant Proposal Guidelines.

FINANCIAL DATA:
Amount of support per award: Varies.
Total amount of support: Approximately $90,000,000 in new awards annually, pending availability of funds.

NO. AWARDS: Approximately 300.

APPLICATION INFO:
Proposals must be submitted through FastLane or grants.gov.
Duration: Typically one to five years. Renewals by reapplication.
Deadline: Varies according to program.

ADDRESS INQUIRIES TO:
Cognizant Program Director
Division of Physics
(See address above.)

SOCIETY OF PHYSICS STUDENTS [1891]

American Institute of Physics
One Physics Ellipse
College Park, MD 20740
(301) 209-3007
E-mail: sps@aip.org
Web Site: www.spsnational.org/programs/awards/research.htm

AREAS OF INTEREST:
Physics.

NAME(S) OF PROGRAMS:
• **SPS Award for Outstanding Undergraduate Research**

TYPE:
Awards/prizes.

PURPOSE:
To promote interest in physics among students and the general public.

LEGAL BASIS:
Not-for-profit, 501(c)(3).

ELIGIBILITY:
Must participate in annual competition and must be SPS national member. Applicants must be undergraduate students at the time the application is due. Winners are chosen based on their research, letters of recommendation and SPS participation from among qualified applicants.

FINANCIAL DATA:
Amount of support per award: $500 honorarium for winner and $500 for the SPS chapter.
Total amount of support: Varies.

NO. MOST RECENT APPLICANTS: 9.

NO. AWARDS: 2.

APPLICATION INFO:
Consult the web site.
Duration: One year.
Deadline: March 15.

STAFF:
Mikayla Cleaver, Senior Programs Coordinator

ADDRESS INQUIRIES TO:
Mikayla Cleaver, Senior Programs Coordinator
(See address above.)

SOCIETY OF PHYSICS STUDENTS [1892]

One Physics Ellipse
College Park, MD 20740
(301) 209-3007
E-mail: sps@aip.org
Web Site: www.spsnational.org

FOUNDED: 1968

AREAS OF INTEREST:
Physics.

NAME(S) OF PROGRAMS:
• **Future Faces of Physics Awards**

TYPE:
Awards/prizes.

YEAR PROGRAM STARTED: 2011

PURPOSE:
To promote interest in physics across cultures.

LEGAL BASIS:
Not-for-profit, 501(c)(3).

ELIGIBILITY:
Applicant must be a Society of Physics Students member.

FINANCIAL DATA:
Amount of support per award: Up to $500.

NO. MOST RECENT APPLICANTS: 11.

NO. AWARDS: 8.

APPLICATION INFO:
Application information is available on the web site.
Duration: One year.
Deadline: November 15.

STAFF:
Mikayla Cleaver, Senior Programs Coordinator

ADDRESS INQUIRIES TO:
Mikayla Cleaver, Senior Programs Coordinator
(See address above.)

*SPECIAL STIPULATIONS:
Only one proposal may be submitted by an SPS chapter.

SOCIETY OF PHYSICS STUDENTS [1893]

One Physics Ellipse
College Park, MD 20740
(301) 209-3007
E-mail: sps@aip.org
Web Site: www.spsnational.org/awards

FOUNDED: 1968

AREAS OF INTEREST:
Physics.

NAME(S) OF PROGRAMS:
• **Marsh W. White Awards**

TYPE:
Awards/prizes.

YEAR PROGRAM STARTED: 1975

PURPOSE:
To support projects by SPS chapters that promote interest in physics among students and the general public.

LEGAL BASIS:
Not-for-profit, 501(c)(3).

ELIGIBILITY:
Applicants must be SPS chapters in good standing with the SPS national organization. The project leader must be a student that is a member of the SPS national organization.

FINANCIAL DATA:
Amount of support per award: Up to $500.

NO. MOST RECENT APPLICANTS: 16.

NO. AWARDS: 15.

APPLICATION INFO:
Consult the web site.
Duration: One year.
Deadline: November 15.

STAFF:
Mikayla Cleaver, Senior Programs Coordinator

ADDRESS INQUIRIES TO:
Mikayla Cleaver, Senior Programs Coordinator
(See address above.)

*SPECIAL STIPULATIONS:
Only one proposal may be submitted by an SPS chapter.

SOCIETY OF PHYSICS STUDENTS

One Physics Ellipse
College Park, MD 20740-3843
(301) 209-3007
E-mail: sps@aip.org
Web Site: www.spsnational.org

TYPE:
Scholarships.

See entry 1573 for full listing.

LIFE SCIENCES

Life sciences (general)

DJ & T FOUNDATION [1894]

P.O. Box 5109
West Hills, CA 91308
(323) 819-9295
Fax: (323) 446-7187
E-mail: info@djtfoundation.org
Web Site: www.djtfoundation.org

FOUNDED: 1995

AREAS OF INTEREST:
Animal population control.

TYPE:
Grants-in-aid. Fund grants to organizations
that operate low-cost spay/neuter clinics.

YEAR PROGRAM STARTED: 1995

PURPOSE:
To fund nonprofit, low-cost spay and neuter
clinics.

LEGAL BASIS:
Private foundation.

ELIGIBILITY:
Eligible organizations must be IRS 501(c)(3)
tax-exempt.

GEOG. RESTRICTIONS: United States.

FINANCIAL DATA:
Amount of support per award: Varies.
Total amount of support: Varies.

NO. MOST RECENT APPLICANTS: Approximately
80.

NO. AWARDS: 40 to 50.

APPLICATION INFO:
Applications are available at the web site and
must include a copy of the IRS tax
determination letter.
Duration: Varies.

ADDRESS INQUIRIES TO:
DJ & T Foundation
(See address above.)

THE HASTINGS CENTER [1895]

21 Malcolm Gordon Road
Garrison, NY 10524
(845) 424-4040
Fax: (845) 424-4545
E-mail: visitors@thehastingscenter.org
Web Site: www.thehastingscenter.org

FOUNDED: 1969

AREAS OF INTEREST:
Ethical issues in medicine, health care and
the life sciences. Recent research topics
include biotechnology, death and dying,
aging, neonatal care, allocation of resources,
occupational health, health
professional-patient relationships, chronic
illness, rehabilitation medicine, AIDS,
surrogate motherhood and artificial
reproduction, organ transplantation,
prospective payment systems,
deinstitutionalization, nursing homes, animal
experimentation, environmental protection,
civic education and the professions and the
public good.

NAME(S) OF PROGRAMS:
• **Visiting Scholars Program**

TYPE:
Residencies; Visiting scholars. Independent
study.

YEAR PROGRAM STARTED: 1969

PURPOSE:
To permit scholars and practitioners in the
humanities or the sciences to conduct
productive research on ethical issues in
medicine, the life sciences and the
professions.

LEGAL BASIS:
Nonprofit independent research association.

ELIGIBILITY:
Visiting Scholars Program is open to persons
with a degree in the humanities, sciences,
law or medicine and that are prepared to
pursue their own independent research
project in the Center's areas of interest.

NO. MOST RECENT APPLICANTS: Varies.

NO. AWARDS: Varies.

APPLICATION INFO:
Application information is available on the
web site.
Duration: Two to eight weeks.

PUBLICATIONS:
Annual report; application guidelines;
Hastings Center Report; *Hastings Center
Books in Print*; *IRB: Ethics and Human
Research*; *Bioethics Forum*.

ADDRESS INQUIRIES TO:
Visiting Scholars Program
(See address above.)

THOMAS F. AND KATE MILLER JEFFRESS MEMORIAL TRUST [1896]

Bank of America-Private Bank of America
DC1-842-0501
1800 K Street, N.W., Fifth Floor
Washington, DC 20006
(202) 442-7460
E-mail: dc.grantmaking@bofa.com
lee.parker@bofa.com
Web Site: hria.org/tmf/jeffress

FOUNDED: 1981

AREAS OF INTEREST:
Astronomy, biosciences, chemistry, computer
sciences, engineering, environmental
sciences, material science, mathematics and
physics.

NAME(S) OF PROGRAMS:
• **Jeffress Trust Awards Program in
Interdisciplinary Research**

TYPE:
Seed money grants. Administered by The
Medical Foundation, this awards program
supports high-impact, innovative one-year
projects that integrate computational and
quantitative scientific methodologies across a
broad range of scientific disciplines.

YEAR PROGRAM STARTED: 1982

PURPOSE:
To support basic research in chemical,
medical, or other scientific fields at
educational and research institutions in the
Commonwealth of Virginia.

LEGAL BASIS:
Trust.

ELIGIBILITY:
Grants are made to tax-exempt institutions
and organizations which are operated
exclusively for charitable, scientific purposes.
Grants are not made to private foundations.

GEOG. RESTRICTIONS: Virginia.

FINANCIAL DATA:
Amount of support per award: $100,000.

Total amount of support: Up to $1,000,000.

NO. MOST RECENT APPLICANTS: 24 for the year
2019.

NO. AWARDS: Up to 12 annually.

APPLICATION INFO:
Grant procedures and guidelines are available
at the web site above.
Duration: One year.
Deadline: Dates are posted on the Trust web
site.

PUBLICATIONS:
Guidelines.

ADDRESS INQUIRIES TO:
Jeanne Brown, Program Officer
E-mail: jbrown@hria.org
Tel: (617) 279-2240 ext. 709

*PLEASE NOTE:
The Trust grants funds only in Virginia.

THE NATIONAL ACADEMIES OF SCIENCES, ENGINEERING, AND MEDICINE

500 Fifth Street, N.W.
Washington, DC 20001
(202) 334-2760
E-mail: rap@nas.edu
Web Site: www.nas.edu/rap

TYPE:
Research scientists. Fellowships at the
graduate, postdoctoral and senior levels for
research-in-residence at U.S. federal
laboratories and affiliated institutions.

See entry 1824 for full listing.

NATIONAL DAIRY COUNCIL

10255 West Higgins Road
Suite 900
Rosemont, IL 60018-5616
(847) 803-2000
Fax: (847) 803-2077
E-mail: nutritionresearch@rosedmi.com
Web Site: researchsubmission.
nationaldairycouncil.org

TYPE:
Research contracts. The National Dairy
Council is the nutrition research, education
and communications arm of Dairy
Management Inc. On behalf of U.S. dairy
farmers, the National Dairy Council provides
science-based nutrition information to, and in
collaboration with, a variety of stakeholders
committed to fostering a healthier society,
including health professionals, educators,
school nutrition directors, academia, industry,
consumers and media. The National Dairy
Council comprises a staff of nutrition science
researchers, registered dietitians and
communications experts dedicated to
educating the public on the health benefits of
consuming milk and milk products
throughout a person's lifespan.

See entry 2418 for full listing.

NATIONAL EYE INSTITUTE

National Institutes of Health
6700B Rockledge Drive, MSC 6914
Bethesda, MD 20817
(301) 451-2020
E-mail: paek.lee@nih.gov
Web Site: www.nei.nih.gov

TYPE:
Conferences/seminars; Fellowships; Research
grants; Training grants. Research Project

Grants support individual investigators whose work is aimed at discovering means of improving the prevention, diagnosis and treatment of blinding and disabling eye and vision disorders.

Small Business Innovation Research Awards aim to stimulate technological innovations, to use small business to meet federal research-development needs that may ultimately lead to commercial products or services and to foster and encourage participation by minority and disadvantaged persons in technological innovations.

Areas of study include vision research, retinal diseases, corneal diseases, cataract, glaucoma, low vision and blindness rehabilitation, visual impairment and its rehabilitation, strabismus, amblyopia and visual processing.

See entry 2275 for full listing.

NATIONAL EYE INSTITUTE
National Institutes of Health
6700B Rockledge Drive, Suite 3400
Bethesda, MD 20817
(301) 451-2020
Fax: (301) 402-0528
E-mail: esl@nei.nih.gov
Web Site: www.nei.nih.gov

TYPE:
  Research grants.

See entry 2274 for full listing.

PFD RESEARCH
FOUNDATION   [1897]
1100 Wayne Avenue
Suite 670
Silver Spring, MD 20910
(301) 273-0570
Fax: (301) 273-0778
E-mail: info@augs.org
Web Site: www.pfdresearch.org

AREAS OF INTEREST:
  Incontinence and pelvic floor dysfunctions.

NAME(S) OF PROGRAMS:
  ● **PFD Research Foundation Grants Program**

TYPE:
  Research grants.

PURPOSE:
  To provide research training and experience for a candidate who exhibits significant evidence of talent and dedication to research.

ELIGIBILITY:
  Applicant must:
  (1) be an active, life, honorary or allied health member of the PFD Research Foundation;
  (2) be a current fellow in either an accredited or nonaccredited fellowship program;
  (3) have a senior research mentor or mentoring team. Mentors or co-investigators need not be members of the PFD Research Foundation and;
  (4) funding must remain at the same institution for the period of the research project.

FINANCIAL DATA:
  The award may be used for purchases of equipment and supplies, laboratory tests, technician/research assistant salaries, Institutional Review Board costs, and/or statistical report. Salary support for the applicant is not allowed.

Amount of support per award: Up to $25,000.
Total amount of support: Varies.

NO. MOST RECENT APPLICANTS: Average 20 per year.

NO. AWARDS: 3 for the year 2020.

APPLICATION INFO:
  Application requirements are available online.
  Duration: Two years.
  Deadline: March 15.

ADDRESS INQUIRIES TO:
  Tristan Wood, Manager, Membership and Community Programs
  (See e-mail address above.)

KENNETH A. SCOTT
CHARITABLE TRUST   [1898]
c/o KeyBank Nonprofit Services
100 Public Square, Suite 600
Cleveland, OH 44113
E-mail: director@kennethscottcharitabletrust.org
Web Site: www.kennethscottcharitabletrust.org

FOUNDED: 1995

AREAS OF INTEREST:
  Animal welfare.

TYPE:
  Project/program grants. Grants are available for projects of shelters and humane groups in Ohio and other Great Lakes states in the U.S.

YEAR PROGRAM STARTED: 1995

PURPOSE:
  To prevent cruelty to animals and promote the humane treatment of animals, particularly companion animals (dogs, cats) and other species commonly kept as household pets. Requests related to wildlife and animals in other settings may also be considered.

LEGAL BASIS:
  Private foundation.

ELIGIBILITY:
  Eligible organizations must be IRS 501(c)(3) tax-exempt. No grants to individuals.

GEOG. RESTRICTIONS: Ohio. Some grants in other Great Lakes states.

FINANCIAL DATA:
  Amount of support per award: $10,000 to $50,000.
  Total amount of support: $809,560 for the year 2020.

NO. AWARDS: 75 for the year 2020.

APPLICATION INFO:
  A one-page letter of inquiry, e-mail or telephone call to the Trust is required before submitting the application.
  Duration: One year.
  Deadline: January 15, May 15 and September 15 for proposals.

IRS I.D.: 34-7034544

ADDRESS INQUIRIES TO:
  Karen Kannenberg, Executive Director
  (See address above.)

THE PERCY SLADEN
MEMORIAL FUND   [1899]
c/o The Linnean Society of London
Burlington House, Piccadilly
London W1J 0BF England
(44) 020 7434 4479
Fax: (44) 020 7287 9364
E-mail: info@linnean.org
gina@linnean.org
Web Site: www.linnean.org

FOUNDED: 1904

AREAS OF INTEREST:
  Natural sciences, with a focus of support on field work in the life and earth sciences, both through expeditions and individual research projects overseas.

NAME(S) OF PROGRAMS:
  ● **Percy Sladen Memorial Fund Grants**

TYPE:
  Awards/prizes; Project/program grants; Research grants; Travel grants. Field work grants in life and earth sciences (excludes any projects which are part of further education, e.g., a Doctorate or a Master's course).

YEAR PROGRAM STARTED: 1904

PURPOSE:
  To support field work in life and earth sciences away from usual country of residence.

LEGAL BASIS:
  Registered charity.

ELIGIBILITY:
  There are no restrictions in award of grants based on nationality, age, sex or prior qualifications. No grants for field work undertaken as part of a higher degree or general support for undergraduate expeditions.

FINANCIAL DATA:
  Grants may be used toward a portion of total costs or for specific items of equipment.
  Amount of support per award: Up to GBP 1,500; generally less than GBP 1,000.
  Total amount of support: Approximately GBP 19,000 annually.

NO. MOST RECENT APPLICANTS: 44.

NO. AWARDS: 27.

APPLICATION INFO:
  Application form and referees reports are available from the Secretary to the Trustees at the address above.
  Duration: Grant must be taken up within one year of receipt.
  Deadline: January 30 and September 30.

ADDRESS INQUIRIES TO:
  Gina Douglas
  Secretary to the Trustees
  (See address above.)

*SPECIAL STIPULATIONS:
  No support for course work. No undergraduate expeditions. No grants for field work for completion of dissertations or higher degrees.

SOCIETY FOR THE STUDY OF
AMPHIBIANS AND REPTILES
Department of Biology
Carroll University
Waukesha, WI 53186
(262) 951-3295
E-mail: rbrenes@carrollu.edu
Web Site: www.ssarherps.org

TYPE:
  Awards/prizes; Research grants. Awards are given in six categories: Conservation of

Amphibians and/or Reptiles, Field Research, Laboratory Research, Herpetological Education, Travel and International Research.

See entry 1829 for full listing.

ROB AND BESSIE WELDER WILDLIFE FOUNDATION   [1900]

10429 Welder Wildlife
Sinton, TX 78387
(361) 364-2643
Fax: (361) 364-2650
E-mail: tblankenship@welderwildlife.org
Web Site: www.welderwildlife.org

FOUNDED: 1954

AREAS OF INTEREST:
Wildlife conservation, wildlife ecology, wildlife science and higher education (graduate level only).

TYPE:
Fellowships. Graduate research fellowships only in fields of wildlife ecology and management.

YEAR PROGRAM STARTED: 1956

PURPOSE:
To encourage and sponsor wildlife research and education.

LEGAL BASIS:
Private, nonprofit foundation.

ELIGIBILITY:
Graduate students at accredited universities seeking advanced degrees in the above-designated fields are eligible to apply. Undergraduates need not apply.

GEOG. RESTRICTIONS: Continental United States.

FINANCIAL DATA:
Fellowships are generally $1,800 (M.S.) to $2,000 (Ph.D.) per month, plus some funds for field supplies and travel. Living quarters are available for students doing research on the Foundation's refuge area near Sinton, TX, including utilities.
Amount of support per award: Normally $25,000 per calendar year.
Total amount of support: $140,000 available for the year 2020.

CO-OP FUNDING PROGRAMS: The Foundation participates in cooperative funding for approvable proposals not adequately financed through other sources, if and when surplus funds are available.

NO. MOST RECENT APPLICANTS: Over 20.

NO. AWARDS: 5 to 6.

APPLICATION INFO:
Initial contact with the Foundation may be submitted in an abbreviated outline of the research problem, a preliminary estimate of expenses, and letter signed by a qualified member of the faculty at the parent university. If the Foundation staff thereafter entertains the matter further, a more complete proposal will be requested along with material concerning the proposed fellowship recipient.
Duration: One year. May be renewed if progress is satisfactory.
Deadline: October 1.

PUBLICATIONS:
Biennial report of staff and student activities.

IRS I.D.: 74-1381321

OFFICERS:
Terry Blankenship, Ph.D., Director
Selma Glasscock, Ph.D., Assistant Director

TRUSTEES:
Hughes C. Thomas
H.C. Weil
John J. Welder, V

ADDRESS INQUIRIES TO:
Terry Blankenship, Ph.D., Director
(See address above.)

*SPECIAL STIPULATIONS:
Priority will be given to research proposals involving studies on the Foundation's refuge area and/or in south Texas.

THE WILEY FOUNDATION, INC.   [1901]

111 River Street
Hoboken, NJ 07030-5774
(201) 748-6000
E-mail: wileyfoundation@wiley.com
Web Site: www.wileyfoundation.org

FOUNDED: 2001

AREAS OF INTEREST:
Biomedical sciences.

NAME(S) OF PROGRAMS:
● **Wiley Prize in Biomedical Sciences**

TYPE:
Awards/prizes. The annual Wiley Prize in Biomedical Sciences has recognized breakthrough research in pure or applied life science research.

YEAR PROGRAM STARTED: 2002

PURPOSE:
To honor research that is distinguished by its excellence, originality and impact on the understanding of biological systems and processes.

ELIGIBILITY:
The Foundation invites the nomination of exceptional scientists or research teams whose work has achieved an impressive level of excellence in pure or applied life science research.

The Foundation encourages international nominations.

FINANCIAL DATA:
Amount of support per award: $50,000 prize and a luncheon in honor of the recipient.

NO. AWARDS: Varies.

APPLICATION INFO:
Each nomination should be submitted by someone other than the nominee. More than one nomination can be made from the same organization.
Duration: Annual award.
Deadline: September 30.

Agriculture, land resources, rural development

AGRICULTURAL HISTORY SOCIETY

Mount Royal University
Department of Humanities
4825 Mount Royal Gate, S.W.
Calgary AB T3E 6K6 Canada
(403) 440-8796
E-mail: aghistorysociety@gmail.com
Web Site: www.aghistorysociety.org

TYPE:
Awards/prizes. The Everett E. Edwards Award is presented to the graduate student who submits the best manuscript on any aspect of agricultural history and rural studies during the current calendar year.

The Gilbert C. Fite Dissertation Award will be presented to the author of the best dissertation on any aspect of agricultural history completed during the current calendar year.

The Wayne D. Rasmussen Award is given to the author of the best article on agricultural history published by a journal other than *Agricultural History* during the current calendar year.

The Theodore Saloutos Book Award is presented to the author of a book on any aspect of agricultural history in the U.S. within the current year, broadly interpreted.

The Henry A. Wallace Award is presented to the author of a book on any aspect of agricultural history outside of the U.S. within the current year, broadly interpreted.

See entry 524 for full listing.

THE AMERICAN CHESTNUT FOUNDATION   [1902]

50 North Merrimon Avenue
Suite 115
Asheville, NC 28804
(828) 281-0047
Fax: (828) 253-5373
E-mail: samantha.bowers@acf.org
Web Site: www.acf.org

FOUNDED: 1983

AREAS OF INTEREST:
Chestnut research.

TYPE:
Research grants.

YEAR PROGRAM STARTED: 1983

PURPOSE:
To restore the American chestnut to Eastern forests.

ELIGIBILITY:
Grants are reviewed on a case-by-case basis.

GEOG. RESTRICTIONS: United States.

FINANCIAL DATA:
Amount of support per award: Up to $10,000.
Total amount of support: $50,000 for the year 2019.

NO. MOST RECENT APPLICANTS: 15.

NO. AWARDS: 7 for the year 2019.

APPLICATION INFO:
Request for proposals are posted in May on the Foundation web site.
Duration: One year.
Deadline: August.

ADDRESS INQUIRIES TO:
Samantha Bowers, Grants Manager
(See address above.)

AMERICAN FARM BUREAU FOUNDATION FOR AGRICULTURE   [1903]
600 Maryland Avenue, S.W.
Suite 1000 West
Washington, DC 20024
(800) 443-8456
Fax: (202) 406-3600
E-mail: foundation@fb.org
Web Site: www.agfoundation.org

AREAS OF INTEREST:
  Agricultural, consumer education, classroom, consumer and farm safety programs.

NAME(S) OF PROGRAMS:
  • **White-Reinhardt Fund for Education**

TYPE:
  Conferences/seminars; Project/program grants; Research contracts. Teacher Scholarships to National Conference.

YEAR PROGRAM STARTED: 1967

PURPOSE:
  To provide travel expense funds to educators employed by a school system or to active agricultural literacy volunteers to attend the national conference; to provide funds for projects that will increase agricultural literacy in students grades K-12.

GEOG. RESTRICTIONS: United States.

FINANCIAL DATA:
  Amount of support per award: Grants: Up to $1,000; Scholarship: Up to $1,500 for reimbursement of expenses not covered by other funding source.
  Total amount of support: Varies.

APPLICATION INFO:
  Grant applications must be completed and submitted to the State Farm Bureau president, Agriculture in the Classroom coordinator or administrator for signature. All applications will be pre-screened for compliance with grant proposal guidelines. Any grant not meeting guidelines will be eliminated from the judging process prior to examination by judges.
  Duration: One year.
  Deadline: Grants: April 15 and October 15. Scholarship: October 15.

ADDRESS INQUIRIES TO:
  Sydney Andrews, Director of Project Management
  (See address above.)

AMERICAN FLORAL ENDOWMENT   [1904]
1001 North Fairfax Street
Suite 201
Alexandria, VA 22314
(703) 838-5211
Fax: (703) 838-5212
E-mail: afe@endowment.org
Web Site: endowment.org

FOUNDED: 1961

AREAS OF INTEREST:
  Floricultural/environmental horticulture research and development funding in the U.S.

TYPE:
  Internships; Project/program grants; Research grants; Scholarships. The Endowment funds research and educational development in floriculture and environmental horticulture designed to produce solutions to industry needs and promote the growth and improvement of the floral industry for the benefit of the grower, wholesale, retail, allied segments and the general public.

  The Endowment supports educational programs focused on attracting young people to the industry, and educational endeavors to identify and solve industry needs and/or challenges. The programs are divided into two major areas:
  (1) paid floriculture internships/scholarships for full-time college students and;
  (2) general educational grants to national programs.

YEAR PROGRAM STARTED: 1961

PURPOSE:
  To further the advancement of education and science in the field of floriculture through funding research and studies in the floriculture field, the results of which will be published; to finance scholarships and internships to students interested in floriculture.

LEGAL BASIS:
  Not-for-profit, nongovernmental organization.

GEOG. RESTRICTIONS: United States.

FINANCIAL DATA:
  Amount of support per award: Varies.
  Total amount of support: Varies.

APPLICATION INFO:
  Contact the Endowment.
  Duration: Typically one year; research grants can be multiyear.
  Deadline: Varies.

PUBLICATIONS:
  Update, quarterly newsletter; annual report.

AMERICAN SOCIETY FOR ENOLOGY AND VITICULTURE   [1905]
1724 Picasso Avenue, Suite E
Davis, CA 95618-0551
(530) 753-3142
Fax: (530) 753-3318
E-mail: info@asev.org
Web Site: www.asev.org

FOUNDED: 1951

AREAS OF INTEREST:
  A scientific society of enologists, viticulturists and others in the fields of wine and grape production, promoting technical advancement and integrated research in science and industry.

TYPE:
  Scholarships. Awards for undergraduate or graduate students enrolled in enology or viticulture or in a curriculum which emphasizes a science basic to the wine and grape industry and who intend to pursue a career in research for the wine or grape industry after graduation from college or university.

PURPOSE:
  To support education and research in enology, viticulture or related fields.

LEGAL BASIS:
  Professional, scientific association.

ELIGIBILITY:
  Undergraduate and graduate students who have been accepted at an accredited college or university in North America, are enrolled in an appropriate field of study and reside in North America may apply. Applicants must be at least junior level in academic status (60 quarter units or 45 semester units). Undergraduate students must have a minimum 3.0 overall grade point average on a scale of 4.0. Graduate students must have a minimum 3.2 overall grade point average on a scale of 4.0.

FINANCIAL DATA:
  Amount of support per award: Varies each academic year.
  Total amount of support: Varies each academic year.

APPLICATION INFO:
  Applications can be downloaded from the web site.
  Duration: One academic year. Renewable in open competition.
  Deadline: All completed forms, letters and transcripts must be received by March 1.

ADDRESS INQUIRIES TO:
  Scholarship Committee
  P.O. Box 1855
  Davis, CA 95617-1855

CENTER FOR PLANT CONSERVATION   [1906]
15600 San Pasqual Valley Road
Escondido, CA 92027-7000
(760) 796-5686
E-mail: info@saveplants.org
Web Site: www.saveplants.org

FOUNDED: 1984

AREAS OF INTEREST:
  Education.

NAME(S) OF PROGRAMS:
  • **Catherine H. Beattie Fellowship for Conservation Horticulture**

TYPE:
  Fellowships.

YEAR PROGRAM STARTED: 1984

PURPOSE:
  To promote conservation of rare and endangered flora in the U.S.

LEGAL BASIS:
  501(c)(3) nonprofit organization.

ELIGIBILITY:
  Open to graduate students in biology, horticulture, or a related field. Preference is given to students whose projects focus on the endangered flora of the Carolinas and southeastern U.S.

FINANCIAL DATA:
  Amount of support per award: Up to $4,500.

NO. MOST RECENT APPLICANTS: 10.

NO. AWARDS: 1.

APPLICATION INFO:
  Applicants must submit a project narrative detailing the proposed research. Items to submit include:
  (1) a one-page cover letter;
  (2) a two-page (maximum) project narrative;
  (3) a one-page project budget and timeline;
  (4) curriculum vitae and;
  (5) a letter of recommendation from their major advisor or equivalent.
  Duration: Varies.
  Deadline: January 31. Notification by mid-February.

PUBLICATIONS:
  Plant Conservation, newsletter.

THE CH FOUNDATION [1907]

6102 82nd Street
Suite 8A
Lubbock, TX 79424
(806) 792-0448
Fax: (806) 792-7824
E-mail: hhocker@chfoundation.com
Web Site: www.chfoundationlubbock.com

FOUNDED: 1976

AREAS OF INTEREST:
Agriculture, arts, community development, cultural education, health, ranching, research, social services and youth.

TYPE:
Capital grants; Project/program grants.

YEAR PROGRAM STARTED: 1991

PURPOSE:
To support programs that meet the needs of and improve the quality of life.

ELIGIBILITY:
Grants are limited to organizations whose services benefit the Lubbock area of Texas. Grants are made to organizations that have tax-exempt status under Section 501(c)(3) of the Internal Revenue Code. No grants are made to individuals or political organizations.

GEOG. RESTRICTIONS: Lubbock, Texas and surrounding counties.

APPLICATION INFO:
Contact the Foundation to determine the interest and appropriateness of a full proposal. Funding guidelines are available online.
Duration: One year. Renewal possible.
Deadline: May 1. Disbursements are made in December.

PUBLICATIONS:
Application guidelines.

IRS I.D.: 75-1534816

ADDRESS INQUIRIES TO:
Heather Hocker, Grants Administrator
(See address above.)

FARM AID [1908]

501 Cambridge Street
Third Floor
Cambridge, MA 02141
(617) 354-2922
Fax: (617) 354-6992
E-mail: grants@farmaid.org
Web Site: www.farmaid.org

FOUNDED: 1985

AREAS OF INTEREST:
Supporting organizations that help farm families stay on their land, build local markets, confront the threat of corporate control of agriculture, train new farmers and support farmer-to-farmer programs for more sustainable agricultural practices. Emergency and disaster assistance for farm families.

TYPE:
General operating grants; Project/program grants. Grants fall within three broad categories which make it possible for organizations to build long-term solutions to the problems farmers face.
(1) Growing the Good Food Movement: These grants fund organizations or projects that seek to strengthen what Farm Aid calls the Good Food Movement, the growing number of Americans reaching for and demanding family farm-identified, local, organic or humanely raised food. These grants build connections between farmers and consumers, creating new markets for family farmers.
(2) Helping Farmers Thrive: These grants fund organizations or projects that assist farmers in transitioning to more sustainable and profitable farming practices, finding alternative markets, or starting a new farming operation as well as providing support services to farm families in crisis. These organizations are the core of the Farmer Resource Network which responds to individual farmers as well as regional events such as natural disasters. (See www.farmaid.org/ideas.)
(3) Taking Action to Change the System: These grants fund organizations or projects that promote fair farm policies and organize grassroots campaigns to defend and bolster family farm-centered agriculture. These grants enable advocates to strengthen the voices of family farmers and promote their interests on a local, regional and national level.

YEAR PROGRAM STARTED: 1985

LEGAL BASIS:
Tax-exempt, charitable and educational organization.

ELIGIBILITY:
Applicants must be IRS 501(c)(3) nonprofit organizations and include a copy of their IRS 501(c)(3) tax-exempt verification letter. If organization does not have 501(c)(3) status, it must include the IRS 501(c)(3) letter and authorization from the organization acting as its fiscal agent.

The following types of projects are not eligible for Farm Aid funding:
(1) grants or loans to individuals;
(2) grants or loans to support commercial operation of a farming enterprise;
(3) production of book, film, television or radio projects;
(4) projects outside the U.S.;
(5) projects directed or substantially funded by government bodies (federal, state or local), including Resource Conservation & Development Councils (RC & Ds);
(6) legal defense funds;
(7) capital campaigns, equipment purchases, endowments or deficit financing;
(8) historic preservation of farmland or buildings;
(9) lobbying to influence elections or legislation and;
(10) conferences, publications or research projects unless they are directly connected to ongoing program activities.

GEOG. RESTRICTIONS: United States.

FINANCIAL DATA:
Amount of support per award: $3,000 to $30,000 for the year 2019.
Total amount of support: Varies.

NO. AWARDS: 95 for the year 2019.

APPLICATION INFO:
Up-to-date application information is available on the web site.
Deadline: August 1. Grants are awarded in December.

PUBLICATIONS:
Newsletter.

IRS I.D.: 36-3383233

ADDRESS INQUIRIES TO:
Grant Program
(See address above.)

THE GARDEN CLUB OF AMERICA [1909]

14 East 60th Street, Third Floor
New York, NY 10022
(212) 753-8287
Fax: (212) 753-0134
E-mail: scholarshipapplications@gcamerica.org
Web Site: www.gcamerica.org/scholarships

FOUNDED: 1913

AREAS OF INTEREST:
Public horticulture.

NAME(S) OF PROGRAMS:
● **The Garden Club of America Hope Goddard Iselin Fellowship in Public Horticulture**

TYPE:
Fellowships. Garden Club of America Hope Goddard Iselin Fellowship in Public Horticulture: Funds one or more students annually for practical research and training at a recognized public garden, botanic garden, arboretum or other institution directly engaged with connecting people, plants and gardening within the U.S.

YEAR PROGRAM STARTED: 2013

PURPOSE:
To further the study of public horticulture through experiential learning that takes place at a recognized public garden, botanic garden, arboretum or other closely aligned public horticulture institution within the U.S.

LEGAL BASIS:
Nonprofit national organization.

ELIGIBILITY:
Open to students enrolled in a graduate-level university program to study public horticulture. Student applicant must confirm ability to conduct research or otherwise utilize facility where study will be undertaken.

FINANCIAL DATA:
Amount of support per award: $5,000.

NO. AWARDS: 1 or more.

APPLICATION INFO:
Applications are available online and must be sent to the American Public Gardens Association (see address below).
Duration: One year.
Deadline: February 1 preceding the period of study.

PUBLICATIONS:
Program announcement.

ADDRESS INQUIRIES TO:
Ms. Joan Thomas
American Public Gardens Association
351 Longwood Road
Kennett Square, PA 19348
Tel: (610) 708-3010
E-mail: jthomas@publicgardens.org
Web Site: www.publicgardens.org

*PLEASE NOTE:
Only one GCA scholarship, fellowship or award may be applied for annually.

THE GARDEN CLUB OF AMERICA [1910]

14 East 60th Street, Third Floor
New York, NY 10022
(212) 753-8287
Fax: (212) 753-0134
E-mail: scholarshipapplications@gcamerica.org
Web Site: www.gcamerica.org/scholarships

FOUNDED: 1913

AREAS OF INTEREST:
Botany.

NAME(S) OF PROGRAMS:
- **The Garden Club of America Summer Scholarship in Field Botany**

TYPE:
Scholarships. Summer Scholarship in Field Botany offers students the opportunity to gain knowledge and experience beyond the regular course of study.

YEAR PROGRAM STARTED: 2000

PURPOSE:
To support student's field studies.

LEGAL BASIS:
Nonprofit national organization.

ELIGIBILITY:
Open to undergraduate and Master's degree students. Research must be conducted in the Western Hemisphere. Eligibility is open to U.S. citizens and permanent residents who are enrolled in a U.S.-based institution.

FINANCIAL DATA:
Amount of support per award: $3,000.

NO. AWARDS: 1 to 4.

APPLICATION INFO:
Application and instructions are available online.
Deadline: February 1.

ADDRESS INQUIRIES TO:
See e-mail address above.

THE GARDEN CLUB OF AMERICA [1911]

14 East 60th Street, Third Floor
New York, NY 10022
(212) 753-8287
Fax: (212) 753-0134
E-mail: scholarshipapplications@gcamerica.org
Web Site: www.gcamerica.org/scholarships

FOUNDED: 1913

AREAS OF INTEREST:
Medicinal botany.

NAME(S) OF PROGRAMS:
- **The Zeller Summer Scholarship in Medicinal Botany**

TYPE:
Scholarships. Zeller Scholarship encourages undergraduates to expand their knowledge of medicinal botany by pursuing summer study through coursework or internships.

YEAR PROGRAM STARTED: 2003

LEGAL BASIS:
Nonprofit national organization.

ELIGIBILITY:
Open to undergraduate students enrolled in an accredited U.S. college or university for study or work during the summer following the freshman, sophomore, junior or senior year. Applicant must be a U.S. citizen or permanent resident.

FINANCIAL DATA:
Amount of support per award: $3,000.

NO. AWARDS: 1.

APPLICATION INFO:
Application and instructions are available online.
Deadline: February 1.

ADDRESS INQUIRIES TO:
See e-mail address above.

THE GARDEN CLUB OF AMERICA [1912]

14 East 60th Street, Third Floor
New York, NY 10022
(212) 753-8287
Fax: (212) 753-0134
E-mail: scholarshipapplications@gcamerica.org
Web Site: www.gcamerica.org/scholarships

FOUNDED: 1913

AREAS OF INTEREST:
Botany.

NAME(S) OF PROGRAMS:
- **The Joan K. Hunt and Rachel M. Hunt Summer Scholarship in Field Botany**

TYPE:
Scholarships. Hunt Summer Scholarship offers an opportunity to gain knowledge and experience in the field beyond the regular course of study.

YEAR PROGRAM STARTED: 2003

PURPOSE:
To promote the importance of botany to horticulture by encouraging students to study field botany in the U.S.

LEGAL BASIS:
Nonprofit national organization.

ELIGIBILITY:
Open to undergraduate and graduate students up to the Master's degree level, with preference given to undergraduate students. Applicant must be a U.S. citizen or permanent resident enrolled in a U.S.-based institution.

FINANCIAL DATA:
Amount of support per award: $3,500.

NO. AWARDS: 1.

APPLICATION INFO:
Application and instructions are available online.
Deadline: February 1.

ADDRESS INQUIRIES TO:
See e-mail address above.

THE GARDEN CLUB OF AMERICA [1913]

14 East 60th Street, Third Floor
New York, NY 10022
(212) 753-8287
Fax: (212) 753-0134
E-mail: scholarshipapplications@gcamerica.org
Web Site: www.gcamerica.org/scholarships

FOUNDED: 1913

AREAS OF INTEREST:
Garden history and design.

NAME(S) OF PROGRAMS:
- **The Garden Club of America Internship in Garden History and Design**

TYPE:
Internships. Internship supports independent study in the field of landscape history and design.

YEAR PROGRAM STARTED: 1997

PURPOSE:
To encourage the study of garden history and design.

LEGAL BASIS:
Nonprofit national organization.

ELIGIBILITY:
Open to graduate students in museum studies, public history, or information studies with courses in collections management for archives and museums. Eligibility is open to U.S. citizens and permanent residents who are enrolled in a U.S.-based institution.

FINANCIAL DATA:
Amount of support per award: Up to $4,000.

NO. AWARDS: 1 or more.

APPLICATION INFO:
Application and instructions are available online. Applicants interested in applying for work at the Smithsonian's AAG must file an additional application with the Smithsonian.
Duration: 10 weeks.
Deadline: Winter and Spring: December 1. Summer: February 1. Fall: July 1.

ADDRESS INQUIRIES TO:
See e-mail address above.

THE GARDEN CLUB OF AMERICA [1914]

14 East 60th Street, Third Floor
New York, NY 10022
(212) 753-8287
Fax: (212) 753-0134
E-mail: scholarshipapplications@gcamerica.org
Web Site: www.gcamerica.org/scholarships

FOUNDED: 1913

AREAS OF INTEREST:
Horticulture.

NAME(S) OF PROGRAMS:
- **The Corliss Knapp Engle Scholarship in Horticulture**

TYPE:
Scholarships. Corliss Knapp Engle Scholarship encourages the development of research, documentation and teaching skills in the field of horticulture.

YEAR PROGRAM STARTED: 2010

PURPOSE:
To support study at an accredited college, university, or major botanic garden or arboretum.

LEGAL BASIS:
Nonprofit national organization.

ELIGIBILITY:
Project may include, but are not restricted to, plant propagation, photographic documentation of studies and research projects, the acquisition of skills for working with horticulture collections, and research in horticulture in the broadest sense.

FINANCIAL DATA:
Amount of support per award: $3,000.

NO. AWARDS: 1 or more.

APPLICATION INFO:
Application and instructions are available online.
Deadline: February 1.

ADDRESS INQUIRIES TO:
See e-mail address above.

THE GARDEN CLUB OF AMERICA [1915]

14 East 60th Street, Third Floor
New York, NY 10022
(212) 753-8287
Fax: (212) 753-0134
E-mail: scholarshipapplications@gcamerica.org
Web Site: www.gcamerica.org/scholarships

FOUNDED: 1913

AREAS OF INTEREST:
Horticulture, particularly native plants.

NAME(S) OF PROGRAMS:
- **The Garden Club of America Motine M. Freeman Scholarship in Native Plants**

TYPE:
Scholarships. Freeman Scholarship encourages the understanding, development and use of underutilized native plants.

YEAR PROGRAM STARTED: 2017

PURPOSE:
To encourage the development of research, documentation and teaching skills in the field of horticulture.

LEGAL BASIS:
Nonprofit national organization.

ELIGIBILITY:
Open to college undergraduate and graduate students, advanced degree candidates, or non-degree seeking applicants above the high school level. Applicant must be a U.S. citizen or permanent resident enrolled in a U.S.-based institution.

Projects may include, but are not restricted to, plant propagation and the acquisition of skills for working with native plant collections, including techniques for incorporating them in managed landscapes. Photographic and written documentation of studies and research projects may be considered.

FINANCIAL DATA:
Amount of support per award: $3,000 minimum.

NO. AWARDS: 1 or more.

APPLICATION INFO:
Application and instructions are available online.
Deadline: February 1.

ADDRESS INQUIRIES TO:
See e-mail address above.

THE FRED C. GLOECKNER FOUNDATION, INC. [1916]
550 Mamaroneck Avenue
Suite 510
Harrison, NY 10528-1609
(914) 698-2300
Fax: (914) 698-0848
E-mail: jsimone@fredgloeckner.com
Web Site: www.gloecknerfoundation.org

FOUNDED: 1960

AREAS OF INTEREST:
Floriculture and related fields such as plant pathology, plant breeding, agricultural engineering, agricultural economics, entomology and plant physiology related to floriculture.

TYPE:
Assistantships; Project/program grants; Research grants.

YEAR PROGRAM STARTED: 1961

PURPOSE:
To support floriculture research and education.

LEGAL BASIS:
Nonprofit educational corporation.

ELIGIBILITY:
Grants are awarded to nonprofit institutions, primarily colleges and universities, for research and education projects in the above fields. Research in basic plant physiology unrelated to floriculture is not considered. Grants may include assistantships for qualified graduate students seeking an M.S. or Ph.D. in the above fields. Grants are not made directly to students.

GEOG. RESTRICTIONS: United States.

FINANCIAL DATA:
Amount of support per award: $2,000 to $20,000.
Total amount of support: Varies.

NO. MOST RECENT APPLICANTS: 40 to 50.

NO. AWARDS: 14 for the year 2018.

REPRESENTATIVE AWARDS:
$13,000 to K. Nemali, Purdue University, for smartphone-based rapid, inexpensive, and accurate estimation of plant nitrogen status in floriculture production; $11,000 to B. Jackson, North Carolina University, for in situ, quantitative analysis of substrate rooting effects of poinsettia by x-ray microtomography; $10,000 to T. Colquhoun, University of Florida, for augmenting cut flowers with LEDs.

APPLICATION INFO:
Applications are available from the Foundation office, or can be downloaded from the web site.
Duration: One year. Renewals possible.
Deadline: April 1.

PUBLICATIONS:
Annual report; application guidelines.

OFFICERS:
Dr. Richard Craig, President
Dr. Paul Allen Hammer, Vice President
Martin D. Kortjohn, Treasurer
Joseph A. Simone, Secretary

DIRECTORS:
Dr. David G. Clark
Dr. Richard Craig
Margery Daughtery
Dr. Paul Allen Hammer
Shayne Johnson
J. Michael Klesa
Martin D. Kortjohn
Andrew Lee
Jay Sheely
Joseph A. Simone

ADDRESS INQUIRIES TO:
Joseph A. Simone, Secretary
(See e-mail address above.)

THE HERB SOCIETY OF AMERICA, INC. [1917]
9019 Kirtland Chardon Road
Kirtland, OH 44094
(440) 256-0514
Fax: (440) 256-0541
E-mail: director@herbsociety.org
Web Site: www.herbsociety.org

FOUNDED: 1933

AREAS OF INTEREST:
Furthering the knowledge and use of herbs and contributing the results of the experience and research of its members to the records of horticulture, science, literature, history, art or economics.

CONSULTING OR VOLUNTEER SERVICES:
Volunteer services including maintenance of public gardens and workshops.

NAME(S) OF PROGRAMS:
- **HSA Research Grant**

TYPE:
Research grants.

YEAR PROGRAM STARTED: 1971

PURPOSE:
To promote the knowledge, use and delight of herbs through educational programs, research, and sharing the experiences of its members with the community.

LEGAL BASIS:
Tax-exempt, nonprofit corporation under IRS 501(c)(3).

ELIGIBILITY:
Students, professionals and individuals engaged in research on the horticultural, scientific and/or social applications or use of herbs throughout history.

Funding does not cover indirect costs, purchase or maintenance of durable computer, laboratory or office equipment, expenses related to tuition, textbooks, or conference attendance, private garden development, or travel to/from research site.

Only U.S. residents may apply.

FINANCIAL DATA:
Amount of support per award: $5,000.
Total amount of support: $5,000.

NO. MOST RECENT APPLICANTS: 30.

NO. AWARDS: 1.

APPLICATION INFO:
Applications should include the following:
(1) application form;
(2) professional vitae, not to exceed two pages, listing qualifications for the project, academic degrees and honors;
(3) explanation, not to exceed 500 words, describing how the project will be completed, where the work will be done, and what facilities and equipment are available;
(4) detailed listing of all anticipated costs and;
(5) specific timeline for the project.

Successful applicants will be required to sign a Grant Acceptance Form prior to the award of a grant.
Duration: One year. No renewals.
Deadline: January 31. Announcement May 1.

PUBLICATIONS:
The Herbarist; newsletter; grant guidelines.

IRS I.D.: 34-1596261

*SPECIAL STIPULATIONS:
Under the terms of the grant, periodic progress reports are to be sent to the Research Grant Chairman. At the termination of the project, The Herb Society expects a complete copy of the finished product for the Herb Society Library and a summary of the work for publication in the Society's publication, *The Herbarist*. The Society reserves the right to reject or accept credit in any publication resulting from the grant.

HORTICULTURAL RESEARCH INSTITUTE, INC. [1918]
2130 Stella Court
Columbus, OH 43215
(614) 487-1117
Fax: (614) 487-1216
E-mail: jenniferg@americanhort.org
Web Site: www.hriresearch.org

FOUNDED: 1962

AREAS OF INTEREST:
Nursery and landscape research.

NAME(S) OF PROGRAMS:
- **HRI Competitive Research Grant Program**

TYPE:
Grants-in-aid; Research grants; Scholarships; Seed money grants; Research contracts.

YEAR PROGRAM STARTED: 1974

PURPOSE:
To direct, fund, promote and communicate research which increases the quality and value of plants, improves the productivity and profitability of the nursery and landscape industry and protects and enhances the environment.

LEGAL BASIS:
501(c)(3).

ELIGIBILITY:
Proposals are evaluated on the basis of their relevance to the nursery industry.

GEOG. RESTRICTIONS: North America.

FINANCIAL DATA:
Amount of support per award: $5,000 to $35,000 for the year 2021.
Total amount of support: Varies.
Matching fund requirements: Not required, but preferred.

NO. MOST RECENT APPLICANTS: 65.

NO. AWARDS: 12 for the year 2019.

APPLICATION INFO:
Completed proposals must be submitted using HRI's online application process. No hard copies or e-mailed applications will be accepted.
Deadline: May 31. Announcement in late January/early February.

PUBLICATIONS:
Application guidelines.

IRS I.D.: 52-1052547

ADDRESS INQUIRIES TO:
Jennifer Gray
Research Programs Administrator
(See address above.)

HORTICULTURAL RESEARCH INSTITUTE, INC.
2130 Stella Court
Columbus, OH 43215
(614) 487-1117
Fax: (614) 487-1216
E-mail: jenniferg@americanhort.org
Web Site: www.hriresearch.org

TYPE:
Scholarships.

See entry 1510 for full listing.

LAND O'LAKES FOUNDATION
4001 Lexington Avenue North
Arden Hills, MN 55126
(651) 375-2470
E-mail: landolakesfoundation@landolakes.com
Web Site: www.landolakesinc.com/responsibility

TYPE:
Scholarships. John Brandt Memorial Scholarship Program is a $5,000 scholarship available to graduate students pursuing dairy-related degrees. One or two scholarships are awarded annually to

deserving candidates who have demonstrated exceptional commitment and aptitude toward their field of study.

See entry 177 for full listing.

NATIONAL ASSOCIATION OF FARM BROADCASTERS FOUNDATION
1100 Platte Falls Road
Platte City, MO 64079
(816) 431-4032
Fax: (816) 431-4087
E-mail: susan@nafb.com
Web Site: www.nafbfoundation.com

TYPE:
Scholarships. Since 1977, the NAFB Foundation has provided financial support and educational opportunities in the form of college scholarships to assist students in pursuit of careers in agricultural communications. These scholarships are recognized at the National NAFB Convention.

See entry 1744 for full listing.

NATIONAL CATTLEMAN'S BEEF ASSOCIATION, A CONTRACTOR TO THE BEEF CHECKOFF
9110 East Nichols Avenue
Suite 300
Centennial, CO 80112-3450
(202) 879-9130
Fax: (303) 694-2851
E-mail: beefnutritionfp@beef.org
Web Site: www.beefresearch.org

TYPE:
Grants-in-aid; Research grants; Research contracts. Research contracts and grants-in-aid for experimental projects in the areas of:
(1) beef as part of a balanced diet;
(2) parity studies;
(3) health benefits of beef lipids and;
(4) contribution of beef nutrients to total diet.

Proposals solicited via specific RFPs (request for proposals).

See entry 2417 for full listing.

NATIONAL DAIRY SHRINE   [1919]
P.O. Box 68
Fort Atkinson, WI 53538
(920) 542-1003
E-mail: info@dairyshrine.org
Web Site: www.dairyshrine.org

FOUNDED: 1949

AREAS OF INTEREST:
Dairy production, research, milk products, milk marketing, genetics and education.

NAME(S) OF PROGRAMS:
- **National Dairy Shrine Student Recognition Program**
- **NDS/DMI Education and Communication Scholarship**
- **NDS/DMI Milk Marketing Scholarships**
- **NDS/Iager Scholarship**
- **NDS/Kildee Scholarships**
- **NDS/Lancaster Sophomore Scholarship**
- **NDS/Maurice E. Core Scholarship**
- **NDS/McCullough Scholarships**
- **NDS/Sowerby Junior Merit Scholarship**

TYPE:
Project/program grants; Scholarships. Awards made annually to students interested in careers in the dairy industry. Majors can include dairy science, animal science, agricultural economics, agricultural communications, agriculture education, agricultural marketing and sales, food and nutrition.

YEAR PROGRAM STARTED: 1951

PURPOSE:
To encourage students to pursue careers in the dairy industry.

LEGAL BASIS:
Nonprofit corporation.

ELIGIBILITY:
National Dairy Shrine Student Recognition Program: Graduating seniors planning a career related to dairy-production agriculture who have demonstrated leadership skills, academic ability and interest in dairy cattle.

NDS/DMI Education and Communication Scholarship: Available to undergraduate students (except previous winners) during his or her sophomore or junior year with an explicit interest in dairy products marketing. The applicants must have at least a cumulative 2.5 grade point average on a 4.0 scale.

NDS/DMI Milk Marketing Scholarships: Available to undergraduate students (except previous winners) during his or her sophomore or junior year with an explicit interest in dairy products marketing. The applicants must have at least a cumulative 2.5 grade point average on a 4.0 scale.

NDS/Iager Scholarship: Open to outstanding second-year college dairy students in a two-year agricultural college.

NDS/Kildee Scholarships: Applicants must have placed in Top 25 at National Intercollegiate or National 4-H Dairy Judging Contests. Platinum winners in the last three National Dairy Challenge Contests may apply for Kildee Graduate Study Scholarships.

NDS/Lancaster Sophomore Merit Scholarship: Applicants must be outstanding sophomore college students at a four-year agricultural college in a dairy related field.

NDS/Maurice E. Core Scholarship: Applicants must be outstanding freshman college students at a four-year agricultural college in a dairy related field.

NDS/McCullough Scholarships: The applicant must be a freshman in college with intent to major in Dairy/Animal Science with a Communications emphasis or Agricultural Journalism with a Dairy/Animal Science emphasis and be a U.S. citizen.

NDS/Sowerby Junior Merit Scholarship: Applicants must be outstanding junior college students at a four-year agricultural college in a dairy related field.

GEOG. RESTRICTIONS: United States.

FINANCIAL DATA:
Amount of support per award: National Dairy Shrine Student Recognition Program: $2,000, $1,500 and $1,000; NDS/DMI Education and Communication Scholarships, NDS/DMI Milk Marketing Scholarships, NDS/Lancaster Sophomore Scholarships and NDS/Sowerby Junior Scholarships: $1,500 and $1,000; NDS/Iager Scholarship, NDS/Maurice E. Core Scholarship and NDS/McCullough Scholarships: $1,000; NDS/Kildee Scholarships: $3,000.

Total amount of support: Over $45,000.

NO. MOST RECENT APPLICANTS: 110.

NO. AWARDS: National Dairy Shrine Student Recognition Program: 7 to 10; NDS/DMI Education and Communication Scholarships, NDS/DMI Milk Marketing Scholarships, NDS/Lancaster Sophomore Scholarships and NDS/Sowerby Junior Scholarships: 3 or 7 awards of $1,000 and 1 award of $1,500; NDS/Iager Scholarship: 2 or more; NDS/Kildee and NDS/McCullough Scholarships: 2; NDS/Maurice E. Core Scholarship: 2 to 5.

APPLICATION INFO:
All NDS scholarships and awards require the submission of a completed application form with additional requirements for some scholarships. Forms are available at the web site above. All requirements for the scholarship application and submission deadlines must be followed.

Duration: One year.

Deadline: Applications accepted March 1 to April 15 (postmarked). Announcements by July 1.

EXECUTIVE DIRECTOR:
Mike Opperman

ADDRESS INQUIRIES TO:
Mike Opperman, Executive Director
(See address above.)

*SPECIAL STIPULATIONS:
The second half of each scholarship will be awarded after successful completion of next year. Recipients will be asked to submit their most recent grade transcript and proof of enrollment in the first term of the following year.

NATIONAL FARMER'S ORGANIZATION   [1920]
528 Billy Sunday Road
Suite 100
Ames, IA 50010
(515) 292-2000
Fax: (866) 629-4853
E-mail: nfo@nfo.org
Web Site: nationalfarmers.com

AREAS OF INTEREST:
Agricultural careers.

NAME(S) OF PROGRAMS:
● **Farm Kids for College Scholarships**

TYPE:
Scholarships.

PURPOSE:
To assist students planning careers in agriculture and farming.

ELIGIBILITY:
Must be a high school senior that will major in an agricultural field at an accredited college or university. Winners in each state advance to the national competition.

GEOG. RESTRICTIONS: United States.

FINANCIAL DATA:
Some states offer monetary awards.
Amount of support per award: $1,000.
Total amount of support: $3,000.

NO. AWARDS: Approximately 15 national finalists; 3 awardees.

APPLICATION INFO:
Application information is available on the web site.

Duration: One year.

Deadline: Late February to early March.

ADDRESS INQUIRIES TO:
Helene Bergren
National Scholarship Coordinator
(See address above.)

NORTHEAST AGRICULTURAL EDUCATION FOUNDATION   [1921]
220 South Warren Street
9th Floor
Syracuse, NY 13202
(315) 671-0588
Fax: (315) 671-0589
E-mail: info@northeastagriculture.org
Web Site: www.northeastagriculture.org

FOUNDED: 1966

AREAS OF INTEREST:
Education, agriculture, farmers and rural community.

TYPE:
Project/program grants.

PURPOSE:
To support nonprofit organizations dedicated to serving the interests of farmers and rural communities in the Northeast.

LEGAL BASIS:
Private foundation.

ELIGIBILITY:
Grants are made to nonprofit organizations that have tax-exempt status under Section 501(c)(3) of the Internal Revenue Code. No grants are made to individuals.

GEOG. RESTRICTIONS: Primarily northeastern United States.

FINANCIAL DATA:
Amount of support per award: $1,000 to $20,000.
Total amount of support: Varies.

NO. AWARDS: 12 to 15 annually.

APPLICATION INFO:
Applicants to the Foundation should include the following materials in their submissions:
(1) Grant Summary Sheet, which can be downloaded with the Grant Guidelines (PDF);
(2) a letter, no longer than two pages, describing the organization, the proposed program or activity, the funding amount requested, and an evaluation methodology;
(3) most recent audited annual financial report;
(4) current operating budget summary, including fund-raising goals and a current donor list;
(5) detailed budget summary for the proposed project or program, indicating what portion would be funded by the grant request;
(6) current Board of Directors roster, including their affiliations;
(7) copy of the Section 501(c)(3) letter from the IRS;
(8) a statement of affiliation with the United Way or other federated fund-raising campaigns and;
(9) additional information about the organization and/or project.

Duration: Varies.

Deadline: May 1.

PUBLICATIONS:
Background and application guidelines; application requirements; grant request summary.

ADDRESS INQUIRIES TO:
Craig Buckhout, Administrator
(See e-mail address above.)

NORTHEASTERN LOGGERS' ASSOCIATION, INC.   [1922]
3311 State Route 28
Old Forge, NY 13420
(315) 369-3078
Fax: (315) 369-3736
E-mail: nela@northernlogger.com
Web Site: northernlogger.com

FOUNDED: 1952

AREAS OF INTEREST:
Forestry, wood science and technology.

NAME(S) OF PROGRAMS:
● **William J. Cox Memorial Fund Scholarship**

TYPE:
Scholarships. W.J. Cox Associates, through the William J. Fox Memorial Fund, has created a needs-based scholarship program for college students supported by business owners or employees in the forest products industry in Connecticut, Maine, Massachusetts, New Hampshire, New York, Pennsylvania and Vermont.

PURPOSE:
To provide support for students and employees of members.

LEGAL BASIS:
501(c)(6) giving program.

ELIGIBILITY:
Applicant must be a forest products industry worker or their dependent residing in the W.J. Cox Associates, Inc. area of operation (currently Connecticut, Maine, Massachusetts, New Hampshire, New York, Pennsylvania and Vermont). Applicant must be currently accepted or enrolled in any area of study in a U.S. institute of higher learning.

Applicant must demonstrate financial need by submitting a copy of their current Free Application for Federal Student Aid form.

FINANCIAL DATA:
Amount of support per award: $1,000.
Total amount of support: Varies.

NO. AWARDS: Varies.

APPLICATION INFO:
Applicant must complete the Student Personal Information and Industry Relationship Verification sections of the application form. Application is to be submitted to the NELA office with one document verifying school acceptance or enrollment and a copy of the student's current completed FAFSA. Additional circumstances the applicant may wish to be considered may be included on a separate sheet.

Deadline: March 31.

ADDRESS INQUIRIES TO:
See e-mail address above.

NORTHEASTERN LOGGERS' ASSOCIATION, INC.   [1923]
3311 State Route 28
Old Forge, NY 13420
(315) 369-3078
Fax: (315) 369-3736
E-mail: nela@northernlogger.com
Web Site: northernlogger.com

FOUNDED: 1952

AREAS OF INTEREST:
Forestry, wood science and technology.

NAME(S) OF PROGRAMS:
● **NELA Annual Scholarship Contest**

TYPE:
Scholarships. Essay scholarship contest.

YEAR PROGRAM STARTED: 1975

PURPOSE:
To provide support for students and employees of members.

LEGAL BASIS:
501(c)(6) giving program.

ELIGIBILITY:
Scholarships are available to the immediate families of individual members, or the immediate families of employees of Industrial and Associate Members of the Northeastern Loggers' Association. Applicants must be high school seniors, students in two-year Associate or technical school programs, or students in four-year Bachelor's programs.

GEOG. RESTRICTIONS: United States.

FINANCIAL DATA:
Amount of support per award: $500 to $1,000.
Total amount of support: Varies.

NO. AWARDS: Up to 8 annually.

APPLICATION INFO:
Applicants must prepare a 1,000-word essay, a captioned photo-essay, a seven-minute audio essay, or a seven-minute video essay presentation on the topic: "Why the Forest Products Industry is Important To Us All." Submit with completed application form and grade transcript.
Duration: One year.
Deadline: March 31. Notification in May.

ADDRESS INQUIRIES TO:
See e-mail address above.

RURAL HOUSING SERVICE   [1924]
1400 Independence Avenue, S.W.
Room 5014, Stop 0701
Washington, DC 20250-0701
(202) 692-0268
E-mail: elizabeth.green@usda.gov
Web Site: www.rd.usda.gov

FOUNDED: 1949

AREAS OF INTEREST:
Rural development.

NAME(S) OF PROGRAMS:
● **Rural Housing Grants (Section 504)**

TYPE:
Grants-in-aid; Project/program grants. Grants to assist elderly, very low-income owner-occupants in rural areas to repair or improve their dwellings to make such dwellings safe and sanitary and remove hazards.

RHS is the credit agency for rural development in USDA. RHS has offices at the state, district and county levels which serve every county or parish in the 50 states, plus the western Pacific areas, Guam, Puerto Rico and the Virgin Islands.

YEAR PROGRAM STARTED: 1961

PURPOSE:
To assist applicants who are unable to repay a loan amortized at one percent over 20 years.

LEGAL BASIS:
42 U.S.C. 1474.

ELIGIBILITY:
Open to counties and towns or places of 10,000 or less within SMA's and towns or places of up to 20,000 outside SMA's. Areas classified as rural prior to October 1, 1990, with a population in excess of 10,000 are eligible if the area population is 25,000 or less.

Applicants must own and occupy houses in rural areas that need repair to remove health or safety hazards. Grant recipients must be 62 years of age or older, very low-income households (under 50% of median income) owner-occupants, and unable to pay for that cost of repair with a loan.

FINANCIAL DATA:
Amount of support per award: Lifetime assistance cannot exceed $7,500.
Total amount of support: $30,000,000 for the year 2018.

NO. AWARDS: Approximately 4,500 annually.

APPLICATION INFO:
Applicants must apply at the local county Rural Development (RD) office. Awards are approved by Community Development Manager.

ADDRESS INQUIRIES TO:
Myron Wooden
E-mail: myron.wooden@usda.gov

TREE RESEARCH & EDUCATION ENDOWMENT FUND (TREE FUND)   [1925]
552 South Washington Street
Suite 109
Naperville, IL 60540
(630) 369-8300
Fax: (630) 369-8382
E-mail: treefund@treefund.org
Web Site: www.treefund.org

FOUNDED: 1975

AREAS OF INTEREST:
Research in areas of urban tree care, preservation and arboriculture education.

NAME(S) OF PROGRAMS:
● **Bonnie Appleton Memorial Scholarship**
● **Barborinas Family Fund Grant**
● **John Duling Grant**
● **Robert Felix Memorial Scholarship**
● **Hyland Johns Grant**
● **Jack Kimmel International Grant**
● **Ohio Chapter ISA Education Grant**
● **Safe Arborist Techniques Fund Grant**
● **Bob Skiera Memorial Fund Building Bridges Initiative Grant**
● **Tree and Soil Research Fund Grant**
● **Utility Arborist Research Fund Grant Program**
● **Fran Ward Women in Arboriculture Scholarship**
● **John Wright Memorial Scholarship**

TYPE:
Fellowships; Research grants; Scholarships; Seed money grants. Grants to further research relating to arboriculture. Scholarships are for arboriculture and horticulture students.

YEAR PROGRAM STARTED: 1976

PURPOSE:
To sustain the world's urban forests by providing funding for scientific research, education programs and scholarships related to arboriculture and urban forestry.

LEGAL BASIS:
Tax-exempt public-supported corporation, 501(c)(3) classification.

ELIGIBILITY:
Scholarships available for undergraduate study focusing on arboriculture or horticulture.

GEOG. RESTRICTIONS: Scholarships: United States.

FINANCIAL DATA:
Institutional overhead costs are capped at 10% of total grant value.
Amount of support per award: Appleton, Felix, Ward and Wright Scholarships: $5,000; Barborinas Family Fund Grant, Jack Kimmel International Grant and Tree and Soil Research Fund Grant: Up to $10,000; John Duling and Hyland Johns Grant: Up to $25,000; Ohio Chapter ISA Education Grant: Up to $5,000; Safe Arborist Techniques Fund Grant: Up to $15,000; Bob Skiera Memorial Fund Grant: Up to $30,000; Utility Arborist Research Fund Grant: Up to $50,000.
Matching fund requirements: 10% match or in-kind.

NO. MOST RECENT APPLICANTS: Varies.

NO. AWARDS: Varies.

APPLICATION INFO:
Completed application must be submitted via e-mail. Before applying for a grant, carefully read the Grant Guidelines. Applications that do not contain all the requested information may be denied.
Duration: Ohio Education Grants: One year. All other grants: Multiyear. Scholarships: Two years.
Deadline: Barborinas, John Duling, Jack Kimmel, Safe Arborist Techniques Fund and Bob Skiera Grants: October 1; Hyland Johns Grant, Ohio Education Grant, Scholarships and Utility Arborist Research Grant: March 15; Tree and Soil Research Fund Grant: October 31.

PUBLICATIONS:
Application guidelines.

IRS I.D.: 37-1018692

STAFF:
Russell King, President and Chief Executive Officer
Monika Otting, Business Relations Manager
Jonathan Cain, Community Engagement Manager
Barbara Duke, Grants and Operations Manager

ADDRESS INQUIRIES TO:
Barbara Duke, Grants and Operations Manager
E-mail: bduke@treefund.org

*SPECIAL STIPULATIONS:
No part of grant can be used for overhead expenses.

U.S. DEPARTMENT OF AGRICULTURE
1400 Independence Avenue, S.W.
Stop 0506
Washington, DC 20250-0510
(202) 690-1612
Fax: (202) 720-4619
E-mail: shanita.landon@usda.gov
Web Site: www.fsa.usda.gov

TYPE:
Grants-in-aid. Cost-share assistance with agricultural producers to rehabilitate agricultural lands damaged by natural disasters. Assistance may also be provided for carrying out emergency water conservation measures during periods of severe drought.

See entry 1988 for full listing.

U.S.-ISRAEL BINATIONAL AGRICULTURE RESEARCH AND DEVELOPMENT FUND (BARD) [1926]
P.O. Box 15159
Rishon LeZion 7505101 Israel
(972) 3-968-3834
(972) 3-968-3980
Fax: (972) 3-966-2506
E-mail: nitsan@bard-isus.com
Web Site: www.bard-isus.com

FOUNDED: 1977

AREAS OF INTEREST:
Agriculture.

NAME(S) OF PROGRAMS:
● **Graduate Student Fellowship Program**
● **Senior Research Fellowship Program**
● **Vaadia-BARD Postdoctoral Fellowship Program**

TYPE:
Fellowships; Research grants; Visiting scholars.

YEAR PROGRAM STARTED: 1977

PURPOSE:
To promote cooperative agriculture research between the U.S. and Israel; to provide BARD with input into new research areas; to enhance scientific competence in these areas.

LEGAL BASIS:
Nonprofit organization. Governmental Associations in U.S. and Israel.

ELIGIBILITY:
Citizens of the U.S. or Israel who are established research scientists, Ph.D. students and young scientists from American or Israeli nonprofit research institutions, universities, or federal or state agencies are eligible.

GEOG. RESTRICTIONS: United States and Israel.

FINANCIAL DATA:
Amount of support per award: Graduate Student Fellowship: $1,500 per month, plus $2,000 to cover travel costs. Postdoctoral Fellowship: $40,000, plus $9,000 for fellows with dependents. Research Grant: Approximately $310,000 over three years. Senior Research Fellowship: $3,000 per month, plus one-time allocation of $2,000 for travel.
Total amount of support: $7,30,000 for the year 2020.

NO. MOST RECENT APPLICANTS: 100.

NO. AWARDS: 38 for the year 2020.

APPLICATION INFO:
Guidelines and application forms are available online.
Duration: Graduate Student Fellowship: Two to six months. Postdoctoral Fellowship: One year; second year possible with agreement from mentor and shared on a matching basis between BARD and host lab. Research awards: Three years. Senior Research Fellowship: Two to 12 months.

Deadline: Research awards: Mid-September. Postdoctoral Fellowship, Senior Fellowship Program, and Graduate Student Fellowship Program: Mid-January.

PUBLICATIONS:
Application guidelines.

OFFICERS:
Yoram Kapulnik, Executive Director
Miriam Green, Controller

THE UNIVERSITY OF SYDNEY [1927]
Scholarships Office
Level 4, Jane Foss Russell Building G02
The University of Sydney N.S.W. 2006
Australia
61 (02) 8627 1444
E-mail: scholarships.officer@sydney.edu.au
Web Site: www.sydney.edu.au/scholarships

FOUNDED: 1850

AREAS OF INTEREST:
Veterinary science.

NAME(S) OF PROGRAMS:
● **F.H. Loxton Postgraduate Studentships**

TYPE:
Scholarships. Awarded for research leading to a higher degree. Tenable at the University of Sydney.

YEAR PROGRAM STARTED: 1960

PURPOSE:
To enable a male graduate of any university to engage in postgraduate research at the University of Sydney, within the Faculty of Veterinary Science.

LEGAL BASIS:
University.

ELIGIBILITY:
Open only to male graduates of any university enrolled in a higher degree by research in the Faculty of Veterinary Science.

FINANCIAL DATA:
Award does not cover tuition fees payable by international students. Relocation allowance within Australia and thesis allowance available.
Amount of support per award: $35,629 AUD per annum for the year 2021.

NO. AWARDS: Offered as vacancies occur. Awarded annually depending on the availability of funds in the area of Agriculture and Environment.

APPLICATION INFO:
Particulars are available from the Faculty of Veterinary Science, The University of Sydney.
Duration: Master's research degree: Two years; Ph.D. degree: Three years.
Deadline: Varies.

ADDRESS INQUIRIES TO:
The Faculty of Veterinary Science
The University of Sydney
N.S.W. 2006 Australia
E-mail: vetsci.education@sydney.edu.au

USDA - RURAL UTILITIES SERVICE [1928]
1400 Independence Avenue, S.W.
Stop 1548, Room 5143
Washington, DC 20250
(202) 720-0986
Web Site: www.rd.usda.gov

FOUNDED: 1935

AREAS OF INTEREST:
Rural areas and towns that have a population of up to 10,000.

NAME(S) OF PROGRAMS:
● **Water and Waste Disposal Systems for Rural Communities**

TYPE:
Capital grants; Development grants; Project/program grants. Loans. Provides funding for clean and reliable drinking water systems, sanitary sewage disposal, sanitary solid waste disposal, and storm water drainage to households and businesses in eligible rural areas.

YEAR PROGRAM STARTED: 1965

PURPOSE:
To provide funding for clean and reliable drinking water systems, sanitary sewage disposal, sanitary solid waste disposal and storm water drainage to households and businesses in eligible rural areas and towns.

LEGAL BASIS:
Government agency.

ELIGIBILITY:
Only rural areas and cities and towns with populations under 10,000 are eligible.

Applicants must:
(1) be a public entity, nonprofit corporation or Indian tribe;
(2) be unable to obtain needed funds from other sources at reasonable rates and terms;
(3) have legal capacity and;
(4) have adequate security for loans.

FINANCIAL DATA:
Amount of support per award: Varies.

CO-OP FUNDING PROGRAMS: Can cooperate with any other federal, state, local or private credit source.

APPLICATION INFO:
Applications must be filed electronically through RD Apply.
Deadline: Varies.

ADDRESS INQUIRIES TO:
Edna Primrose
Assistant Administrator
Water and Environmental Programs
(See address above.)

WOMAN'S NATIONAL FARM & GARDEN ASSOCIATION, INC. [1929]
367 Ferndale
Birmingham, MI 48009
E-mail: schwark@aol.com
Web Site: www.wnfga.org

FOUNDED: 1914

AREAS OF INTEREST:
Agriculture, horticulture, and related fields.

NAME(S) OF PROGRAMS:
● **Sarah Bradley Tyson Memorial Fellowship**

TYPE:
Fellowships; Internships; Scholarships. Awards for advanced study in the fields of agriculture, horticulture and allied subjects.

YEAR PROGRAM STARTED: 1928

PURPOSE:
To encourage better living around the world.

ELIGIBILITY:
Open to properly qualified young women (now including men) who have proven their

ability by several years of experience. Awards have been made in recognition of leadership in cooperative extension work and initiative in scientific research.

The Fellowship is to be used for advanced study (Master's or Doctorate) at an educational institution of recognized standing within the U.S. It is to be chosen by the candidate and with the approval of the Fellowship Committee.

FINANCIAL DATA:
Amount of support per award: $4,000 for the year 2021.

APPLICATION INFO:
There are no application forms. The e-mail letter of application should contain:
(1) an account of the applicant's educational training;
(2) a statement, in full, of the object in view and the plan of study;
(3) a certificate (transcript) from the registrar of the school, college or university awarding the degree or degrees received by the applicant;
(4) testimonials as to character, ability, personality and scholarship and;
(5) theses, papers or reports of investigations, published or unpublished, if available and; confidential letters sent to the Committee are retained.
Duration: One year.
Deadline: Applications and recommendations for the Fellowship must be received not later than March 15 of the year to be awarded.

IRS I.D.: 52-6073829

OFFICERS:
Mary Schwark, President
Audrey Ehrler, Corresponding Secretary
Fran Ralstrom, Recording Secretary

ADDRESS INQUIRIES TO:
Cindy Nuss, Chairman
Fellowship Committee
Woman's National Farm &
Garden Association, Inc.
3274 Susquehanna Road
Dresher, PA 19025
Tel: (215) 576-6524
E-mail: nussci56@gmail.com

*SPECIAL STIPULATIONS:
The acceptance of the Fellowship implies the obligation on the part of the student to devote herself or himself unreservedly to study or research as outlined in her or his application, and to submit any proposed change in her or his plan to the Chairman for approval.

Biology

THE ACADEMY OF NATURAL SCIENCES OF PHILADELPHIA   [1930]
1900 Benjamin Franklin Parkway
Philadelphia, PA 19103-1195
(215) 299-1065
Fax: (215) 299-1079
E-mail: kepics@ansp.org
Web Site: ansp.org/research/fellowships-endowments/jessup-mchenry

FOUNDED: 1812

AREAS OF INTEREST:
Research, exhibition and education in natural sciences.

NAME(S) OF PROGRAMS:
• **Jessup Fellowship**
• **McHenry Fellowship**

TYPE:
Fellowships. The Jessup Fellowship is for research support in any specialty in which the curatorial staff of the Academy have expertise. The McHenry Fellowship is for botanical research support.

PURPOSE:
To promote research in the natural sciences.

ELIGIBILITY:
Jessup funds are awarded competitively to students wishing to conduct studies at the postgraduate, doctoral and postdoctoral levels under the supervision or sponsorship of a member of the curatorial staff of the Academy. The Fellowships are not available for undergraduate study. These Fellowships are restricted to those who wish to conduct their study at the Academy and are intended to assist predoctoral and postdoctoral students within several years of receiving their Ph.Ds.

FINANCIAL DATA:
Costs for round-trip travel, lodging, scientific supplies, and equipment are negotiable and should be included in the application materials.

APPLICATION INFO:
Applicant is responsible to submit his or her application in time and to be sure that the three letters of recommendation also reach the Fund Chairman in time. One of these letters of recommendation must be from the Academy curator overseeing or sponsoring the student.
Duration: Two to 16 weeks.
Deadline: Applications for grants will be considered in March and October of each year. Applicants wishing to do their research between April 1 and October 31 should apply by March 1; those wishing to work between November 1 and March 31 should apply by October 1.

ADDRESS INQUIRIES TO:
Kristen Kepics, Department Administrator
(See e-mail address above.)

*SPECIAL STIPULATIONS:
Fellowship awardees are expected to give a seminar after their arrival and are encouraged to publish at least some of their work accomplished at the Academy.

AMERICAN ASSOCIATION OF ZOO KEEPERS   [1931]
8476 East Speedway
Suite 204
Tucson, AZ 85710-1728
(520) 298-9688
Fax: (520) 298-9688
E-mail: ed.hansen@aazk.org
Web Site: www.aazk.org

FOUNDED: 1968

AREAS OF INTEREST:
Animal care and the promotion of animal keeping as a profession.

NAME(S) OF PROGRAMS:
• **Bowling for Rhinos Conservation Resource Grant (BFR CRG)**
• **Conservation, Preservation and Restoration (CPR) Grant**
• **Latin American Professional AAZK Travel Grant**
• **Professional Development Grants**
• **Research Grant**
• **Trees for You and Me (TFYM) Reforestation Grant**

TYPE:
Challenge/matching grants; Conferences/seminars; Grants-in-aid; Research grants; Scholarships; Training grants; Travel grants. Grants in the area of zoology, with emphasis on contributions to improving animal management.

YEAR PROGRAM STARTED: 1980

PURPOSE:
To provide funds for original keeper-initiated research of behavioral and/or biomedical topics and general zoological park management principles.

LEGAL BASIS:
Nonprofit corporation.

ELIGIBILITY:
Candidates must be full-time, permanent keepers in the zoo and aquarium profession and must be AAZK professional members in good standing.

GEOG. RESTRICTIONS: United States and Canada.

FINANCIAL DATA:
Amount of support per award: BFR CRG Grant: $12,000; CPR Grant and Research Grant: Up to $1,000; Latin American Professional AAZK Travel Grant: $2,000; Professional Development Grants: Maximum $2,500; TFYM Reforestation Grant: Up to $20,000.
Total amount of support: Approximately $40,000.

NO. MOST RECENT APPLICANTS: 20.

NO. AWARDS: Professional Development Grants: 4; All others: Varies.

APPLICATION INFO:
Applications consist of an application form, brief research proposal and resume. Application materials and further information are available from the Committee chairperson or can be downloaded from the web site.
Duration: CPR Grant and Research Grant: One year. One-year extension is possible with status report and Committee approval.
Deadline: March 1. Successful applicants are notified within three months of the deadline.

PUBLICATIONS:
Application guidelines.

IRS I.D.: 23-7274856

BOARD OF DIRECTORS:
Bethany Bingham, President
Mary Ann Cisneros, Vice President
Paul Brandenburger
Hardy Kern
Nicole Pepo
Bill Steele
Ellen Vossekuil

ADDRESS INQUIRIES TO:
Ed Hansen, Chief Executive Officer/Chief Financial Officer
(See address above.)

*SPECIAL STIPULATIONS:
Noninvasive research results must be presented to the AAZK membership by either an oral presentation at an AAZK conference, a paper published in *Animal Keepers' Forum* or a research summary report published in *Animal Keepers' Forum.*

THE AMERICAN MUSEUM OF NATURAL HISTORY [1932]

Richard Gilder Graduate School
Central Park West at 79th Street
New York, NY 10024-5192
(212) 769-5017
Fax: (212) 769-5257
E-mail: assistantdirector-rggs@amnh.org
fellowships-rggs@amnh.org
Web Site: www.amnh.org/our-research/richard-gilder-graduate-school

FOUNDED: 1869

AREAS OF INTEREST:
Education of Ph.D. candidates in scientific disciplines.

NAME(S) OF PROGRAMS:
● **Graduate Student Fellowship Program**

TYPE:
Fellowships. An educational partnership with selected universities dedicated to the training of Ph.D. candidates. The university exercises educational jurisdiction over the program and awards the degree. The museum curator serves as a graduate advisor, co-major professor, or major professor. The student benefits by having the staff and facilities of both the university and the museum in order to carry on his or her training and research programs. Joint programs are with the following universities:
(1) Columbia University in astronomy, earth and planetary sciences, ecology, evolutionary and environmental biology;
(2) Cornell University in entomology;
(3) The Graduate Center of the City University of New York in earth and planetary sciences and evolutionary biology;
(4) New York University in molecular biology and;
(5) Stony Brook University in astronomy and astrophysics.

PURPOSE:
To encourage bright and promising students to enter the fields of science in which the museum participates.

ELIGIBILITY:
Applicants must have a Bachelor's degree and be able to fulfill university admission requirements, including TOEFL and Graduate Record Examinations. The program is not open to candidates for the Master's degree.

FINANCIAL DATA:
Fellowships cover stipend, tuition and health insurance.
Amount of support per award: Varies.
Total amount of support: Varies.

NO. MOST RECENT APPLICANTS: 40.

NO. AWARDS: 2.

APPLICATION INFO:
All applications are to be completed online only. All materials, including reference letters, must be submitted electronically, using the forms provided on the web site. Complete instructions are available on the web site.
Duration: One year. Renewable annually for up to four years.
Deadline: December 15.

PUBLICATIONS:
Program announcement; application.

ADDRESS INQUIRIES TO:
Maria Rios, Assistant Director
Fellowships and Student Affairs
(See address above.)

AMERICAN ORCHID SOCIETY [1933]

Fairchild Tropical Botanic Garden
10901 Old Cutler Road
Coral Gables, FL 33156
(305) 740-2010
E-mail: theaos@aos.org
Web Site: www.aos.org

FOUNDED: 1921

AREAS OF INTEREST:
Orchid research.

NAME(S) OF PROGRAMS:
● **American Orchid Society Grants for Orchid Research**

TYPE:
Awards/prizes; Block grants; Capital grants; Development grants; Grants-in-aid; Research grants. Grants and research contracts for experimental projects and applied and fundamental research pertaining to orchids and grants-in-aid to graduate students engaged in research on orchids. Support is given in such areas relevant to orchids as biological research (including taxonomy, anatomy, genetics, physiology development, tissue culture and pathology), conservation and education.

YEAR PROGRAM STARTED: 1966

PURPOSE:
To advance the scientific study of orchids in every aspect; to assist in the publication of scholarly and popular scientific literature on orchids.

LEGAL BASIS:
Corporation.

ELIGIBILITY:
Qualified personnel associated with accredited institutions or appropriate institutes or organizations may apply for grants. Support is not restricted to individuals or institutions within the U.S. The salaries of established scientists is not supported. Qualified graduate students with appropriate interests may apply for grants in support of their research.

In general, travel to collect orchids is not supported. Other types of travel may be supported on a case-by-case basis. Projects that involve commercial sales of plants are generally not supported.

FINANCIAL DATA:
Amount of support per award: Generally $1,000 to $10,000.
Total amount of support: $20,000 budgeted.

NO. MOST RECENT APPLICANTS: 21 for the year 2018.

NO. AWARDS: 4 for the year 2018.

APPLICATION INFO:
Detailed instructions are available on the Society's web site.
Duration: Although the duration of each grant depends upon the particular project, most grants are awarded for one year with the possibility of renewal.
Deadline: March 1.

PUBLICATIONS:
Application guidelines.

ADDRESS INQUIRIES TO:
Ron McHatton, Chief Education and Science Officer
(See address above.)

*SPECIAL STIPULATIONS:
Research application must involve orchids.

AMERICAN SOCIETY FOR MICROBIOLOGY [1934]

Education Department
1752 N Street, N.W.
Washington, DC 20036
(202) 942-9282
Fax: (202) 942-9329
E-mail: fellowships@asmusa.org
Web Site: www.asm.org

FOUNDED: 1899

AREAS OF INTEREST:
Biological research.

NAME(S) OF PROGRAMS:
● **Research Capstone Fellowship**
● **Undergraduate Research Fellowship**

TYPE:
Fellowships. Research Capstone Fellowship provides funding for professional development and career networking to underrepresented minority students.

Undergraduate Research Fellowships provide undergraduate, community college and post-Baccalaureate students the opportunity to perform summer research with an ASM faculty member, in addition to receiving professional development training at the Microbe Academy for Professional Development (MAPD).

PURPOSE:
To promote study and research in microbiology; to fulfill the later stages of undergraduate professional development for underrepresented minority students completing doctoral degrees in microbiology.

LEGAL BASIS:
Private, nonprofit science organization.

ELIGIBILITY:
Research Capstone Fellowship applicant must meet the following criteria:
(1) be an ASM member;
(2) be a U.S. citizen, permanent resident, or DACA eligible;
(3) be from an underrepresented minority group;
(4) have conducted research in the microbiological sciences;
(5) have submitted an abstract for presentation at ASM Microbe and;
(6) have a research mentor that is an ASM member (does not apply to the community college, undergraduate and post-Baccalaureate track).

To quality for consideration for the Undergraduate Research Fellowship, applicant must:
(1) be an ASM member;
(2) be a U.S. citizen, permanent resident, or DACA eligible;
(3) be erolled as a full-time matriculating undergraduate student during the 2019-20 academic year at an accredited U.S. institution;
(4) be involved in a research project;
(5) have an ASM member at applicant's home institution wiling to serve as a mentor and;
(6) not be receiving other financial support for research during the fellowship.

GEOG. RESTRICTIONS: United States.

FINANCIAL DATA:
Amount of support per award: Research Capstone Fellowship: Up to $2,000 to attend and present at the ASM Microbe Academy

for Professional Development and the ASM Microbe Meeting (contingent upon abstract acceptance). Doctoral candidates receive up to $2,000 in additional funding during years two and three of the fellowship to participate in professional development; Undergraduate Research Fellowship: Up to $4,000 stipend and $2,000 in travel funds to attend the MAPD.

Total amount of support: Varies.

PUBLICATIONS:
Application guidelines.

ADDRESS INQUIRIES TO:
See e-mail address above.

ATLANTIC SALMON
FEDERATION   [1935]
P.O. Box 5200
St. Andrews NB E5B 3S8 Canada
(506) 529-1062
Fax: (506) 529-1028
E-mail: emansfield@asf.ca
Web Site: www.asf.ca

FOUNDED: 1948

AREAS OF INTEREST:
Conservation of Atlantic salmon and its habitat through programs in education, research, enhancement, restoration and international cooperation.

NAME(S) OF PROGRAMS:
● **Olin Fellowships**

TYPE:
Awards/prizes; Block grants; Capital grants; Demonstration grants; Fellowships; General operating grants; Grants-in-aid; Internships; Project/program grants; Research grants; Scholarships; Training grants; Travel grants; Visiting scholars; Work-study programs. Fellowships are offered to individuals seeking to improve their knowledge or skills in advanced fields while looking for solutions to current problems in Atlantic salmon biology, management or conservation.

YEAR PROGRAM STARTED: 1971

PURPOSE:
To further salmon conservation.

LEGAL BASIS:
Tax-exempt, nonprofit organization.

ELIGIBILITY:
Applicants must be legal residents of the U.S. or Canada. The Fellowships are tenable at any accredited university or research laboratory or in an active management program and may be applied toward a wide range of endeavors including salmon management, graduate study and research. Applicants need not be enrolled in a degree program.

FINANCIAL DATA:
Amount of support per award: $1,000 to $3,000.
Total amount of support: Varies.

NO. AWARDS: Up to 3.

APPLICATION INFO:
Information and application forms may be obtained from the address above, from Atlantic Salmon Federation, P.O. Box 807, Calais, ME 04619 or from the web site.
Duration: One year. May be renewed.
Deadline: Applications must be received at the St. Andrews office by March 15. Applicants will be advised of awards by May 15.

PUBLICATIONS:
Atlantic Salmon Journal; annual report.

OFFICERS:
Bill Taylor, President
Alan Graham, Q.C., Chairman, ASF (Canada)
John Dillan, Chairman, ASF (U.S.)

ADDRESS INQUIRIES TO:
Ellen Mansfield, Office Manager
Research and Environment
(See address above.)

CALIFORNIA ACADEMY OF
SCIENCES   [1936]
55 Music Concourse Drive
San Francisco, CA 94118
(415) 379-8000
E-mail: ssi-bi@calacademy.org
Web Site: www.calacademy.org/scientists
www.calacademy.org/summer-systematics-institute

FOUNDED: 1853

AREAS OF INTEREST:
Biology, anthropology, aquatic biology, botany, entomology, geology, herpetology, ichthyology, invertebrate zoology, mammalogy, ornithology and paleontology.

NAME(S) OF PROGRAMS:
● **Summer Systematics Institute**

TYPE:
Internships. Matches students with Academy scientists to work on specific research projects. May include laboratory and molecular components.

YEAR PROGRAM STARTED: 1995

PURPOSE:
To allow students to gain hands-on experience in the labs and collections archive.

ELIGIBILITY:
Applicants must be undergraduates who are U.S. citizens or alien residents with an excellent academic record and demonstrated participation in a wide range of campus activities.

FINANCIAL DATA:
Travel costs to and from San Francisco will be provided. Housing will be provided in dormitories in San Francisco, with details to be disclosed upon selection of interns.
Amount of support per award: $5,400 stipend for the internship period.
Total amount of support: Varies.

NO. MOST RECENT APPLICANTS: 150.

NO. AWARDS: 7 to 10.

APPLICATION INFO:
Application information is available online.

Duration: Full-time (40 hours per week) for nine weeks (June to July).
Deadline: February.

PUBLICATIONS:
Program announcement.

IRS I.D.: 94-1156258

ADDRESS INQUIRIES TO:
Dr. Lauren Esposito, REU Site Director or
Dr. Rebecca Johnson, REU Site Director
(See address above.)

COLUMBIA UNIVERSITY   [1937]
Irving Medical Center, Vagelos College of Physicans and Surgeons
630 West 168th Street, Box 37b
New York, NY 10032
(212) 305-7970
E-mail: horwitzprize@columbia.edu
Web Site: www.cuimc.columbia.edu/research/louisa-gross-horwitz-prize

FOUNDED: 1754

AREAS OF INTEREST:
Biology and biochemistry.

NAME(S) OF PROGRAMS:
● **The Louisa Gross Horwitz Prize**

TYPE:
Awards/prizes. An annual prize designed to honor a major scientific contribution in basic research to the fields of biology or biochemistry.

YEAR PROGRAM STARTED: 1967

PURPOSE:
To honor a scientific investigator, or group of investigators, whose contributions to knowledge in either of these fields are deemed worthy of special recognition.

ELIGIBILITY:
The prize is open to scientists for outstanding basic research in the fields of biology or biochemistry.

NO. AWARDS: 3.

APPLICATION INFO:
Nomination must include the name, title, mailing address and e-mail address of the nominee and nominator, along with the following supporting documents:
(1) curriculum vitae;
(2) biographical sketch;
(3) 500-word research summary;
(4) 500-word research significance and;
(5) key publications list (up to 10).
Deadline: January 31.

ADDRESS INQUIRIES TO:
See e-mail address above.

HUMAN FRONTIER SCIENCE
PROGRAM
ORGANIZATION   [1938]
12 Quai St. Jean
67000 Strasbourg France
(33) 3-88-21-51-26 (Grants)
(33) 3-88-21-51-27 (Fellowships)
Fax: (33) 3-88-32-88-97
E-mail: grant@hfsp.org
fellow@hfsp.org
Web Site: www.hfsp.org

FOUNDED: 1989

AREAS OF INTEREST:
Interdisciplinary research into the complex mechanisms of biological functions.

APPLICATION INFO:
Applicants must submit:
(1) online application;
(2) letter of recommendation and;
(3) personal statement and research experience.

Undergraduate Research Fellowship applicants must also provide a research project overview.
Duration: Research Capstone Fellowship: Up to three years; Undergraduate Research Fellowship: 10 to 12 weeks.
Deadline: Research Capstone Fellowship: March 15; Undergraduate Research Fellowship: February 15.

NAME(S) OF PROGRAMS:
- **Cross-Disciplinary Fellowships**
- **Early Career Research Grants**
- **Long-Term Fellowships**
- **Program Grants**

TYPE:
Fellowships; Project/program grants; Research grants. Long-Term Fellowships are for young scientists within three years of obtaining their Ph.D. who wish to broaden their scientific experience in a foreign laboratory.

Cross-Disciplinary Fellowships are modeled on the Long-Term Fellowships but are specifically for scientists with Ph.Ds. in nonbiological disciplines who seek training in the life sciences.

Early Career Research Grants are collaborative research projects for interdisciplinary teams of young researchers who are within the first five years of their first independent positions and located in different countries.

Program Grants are collaborative research projects for interdisciplinary teams of researchers in different countries at any stage of their career.

YEAR PROGRAM STARTED: 1989

PURPOSE:
To foster international collaboration and postdoctoral training at the frontiers of the life sciences.

LEGAL BASIS:
Not-for-profit association.

ELIGIBILITY:
Scientists from all countries can apply, but with some restrictions. The principal applicant of grants must be from a member country. Fellowship candidates from nonmember countries can only apply to work in a member country.

FINANCIAL DATA:
Amount of support per award: Varies, depending upon the size of the grant team or the host country of the fellowship.

NO. MOST RECENT APPLICANTS:
Cross-Disciplinary Fellowships and Long-Term Fellowships: 544; Early Career Research Grants and Program Grants: 702 letters of intent, 85 full applications.

NO. AWARDS: Cross-Disciplinary Fellowships: 15; Early Career Research Grants: 8; Long-Term Fellowships: 50; Program Grants: 20.

APPLICATION INFO:
Application information is available on the web site.
Duration: Up to three years.

PUBLICATIONS:
Annual report.

ADDRESS INQUIRIES TO:
For fellowships: fellow@hfsp.org
For grants: grant@hfsp.org

INTERNATIONAL CRANE FOUNDATION, INC. [1939]
E-11376 Shady Lane Road
Baraboo, WI 53913
(608) 356-9462
Fax: (608) 356-9465
E-mail: info@savingcranes.org
Web Site: www.savingcranes.org

FOUNDED: 1973

AREAS OF INTEREST:
Aviculture, crane ecology and conservation education.

CONSULTING OR VOLUNTEER SERVICES:
Work with individuals who have specific questions regarding crane propagation, restoration of natural habitats, or conservation education on an informal basis and as the need arises.

TYPE:
Internships. Formal stipended internship programs in the fields of aviculture, crane ecology and conservation education.

YEAR PROGRAM STARTED: 1980

PURPOSE:
To act as the world center for the study and preservation of cranes and their natural habitats.

LEGAL BASIS:
Nonprofit corporation.

ELIGIBILITY:
College sophomores through recent college graduates in biology, zoology, botany or education who have a willingness to work at a variety of tasks and can work in a self-directed manner.

FINANCIAL DATA:
Amount of support per award: $567 stipend per month, plus housing.

NO. AWARDS: 4 for the year 2019.

APPLICATION INFO:
Letter of application indicating interest, relevant coursework and experience, plus three references. An interview will be required, although a telephone interview may suffice.
Duration: Six to eight months. Must submit additional application for renewal.

IRS I.D.: 39-1187711

ADDRESS INQUIRIES TO:
See e-mail address above.

LIFE SCIENCES RESEARCH FOUNDATION (LSRF) [1940]
P.O. Box 1482
Baltimore, MD 21030-7482
(410) 467-2597
E-mail: apply@lsrf.org
Web Site: www.lsrf.org

FOUNDED: 1984

AREAS OF INTEREST:
All areas of the life sciences, including biochemistry, cancer biology, cell biology, computational biology, developmental biology, immunology, microbiology, molecular biology, neurobiology, organismal population and evolutionary biology, physiology, plant biology, structural biology and virology.

NAME(S) OF PROGRAMS:
- **Three-Year Postdoctoral Fellowships**

TYPE:
Fellowships.

YEAR PROGRAM STARTED: 1984

PURPOSE:
To offer research support for aspiring scientists.

LEGAL BASIS:
Private organization.

ELIGIBILITY:
Individuals who have held a Ph.D. or M.D. degree for more than five years at the application deadline are not eligible for an LSRF fellowship.

FINANCIAL DATA:
Amount of support per award: $57,000 salary, plus $10,000 research allowance per year.

NO. MOST RECENT APPLICANTS: Over 900.

NO. AWARDS: 15 to 25.

APPLICATION INFO:
Applications are to be completed online and must contain all three components: Application Info, Research Proposal, and Letters of Reference and Support.
Duration: Three years.
Deadline: October 1.

ADDRESS INQUIRIES TO:
See e-mail address above.

MARINE BIOLOGICAL LABORATORY [1941]
7 MBL Street
Woods Hole, MA 02543
(508) 289-7173
Fax: (508) 289-7934
E-mail: researchprograms@mbl.edu
Web Site: www.mbl.edu

FOUNDED: 1888

AREAS OF INTEREST:
Cellular and molecular physiology, molecular biology, developmental biology, neurobiology, innate immunity, ecology, parasitology, microbiology, pharmacology, toxicology, cancer biology, regenerative biology, aging, molecular evolution, microbial biology, sensory physiology, aquaculture, metabolic diseases, environmental science, climate change, and plant physiology.

NAME(S) OF PROGRAMS:
- **Marine Biological Laboratory Research Awards**

TYPE:
Research grants.

PURPOSE:
To provide funding to scientists interested in conducting research projects in various scientific areas.

LEGAL BASIS:
Nonprofit organization.

ELIGIBILITY:
Applicants must be independent investigators. Working scientists must be willing to come to the Laboratory for a minimum six-week stay to conduct independent research in areas of interest to the Laboratory. Sabbaticals are encouraged.

FINANCIAL DATA:
Amount of support per award: Varies.
Total amount of support: Varies.
Matching fund requirements: Strongly encouraged from home institution.

CO-OP FUNDING PROGRAMS: APA, ASCB and HHMI.

NO. AWARDS: Varies.

APPLICATION INFO:
Application information is available on the web site.
Duration: Varies.
Deadline: Varies.

IRS I.D.: 04-2104690

ADDRESS INQUIRIES TO:
Diane Cook, Senior Grants and
Contracts Administrator
(See address above.)

MICROSCOPY SOCIETY OF AMERICA [1942]

11130 Sunrise Valley Drive
Suite 350
Reston, VA 20191
(703) 234-4115
E-mail: associationmanagement@microscopy.
org
Web Site: www.microscopy.org/awards

FOUNDED: 1942

AREAS OF INTEREST:
Microscopy.

NAME(S) OF PROGRAMS:
● **MSA Professional Technical Staff Awards**

TYPE:
Travel grants.

PURPOSE:
To stimulate attendance for those who
ordinarily might not participate; to encourage
supervisors to support their staff in
professional activities.

LEGAL BASIS:
Special interest society.

ELIGIBILITY:
Applicants must be regular, current members
of MSA at the time of submission. Awards
are based on the quality of the paper
submitted for presentation at the meeting.
Abstracts will be judged by the MSA
Technologist's Forum. The applicant must be
the first author of the submitted paper.

Successful applicants must present their
papers personally at the meeting in order to
receive the award. They are expected to
attend and participate in the entire meeting.
Former winners will not be eligible for
another award.

FINANCIAL DATA:
Amount of support per award: The award
consists of complimentary full registration for
the Microscopy and Microanalysis meeting
including proceedings and the social event
ticket. In addition, MSA will reimburse
awardees up to $1,000 for travel, lodging and
meeting expenses.
Total amount of support: Varies.

NO. AWARDS: Up to 4.

APPLICATION INFO:
Applications shall consist of a copy of the
abstract and data form to be sent to the
Technologist's Forum Committee and a
supporting letter from the applicant's
employer, manager or supervisor, attesting to
the applicant's status as a full-time,
professional staff member.
Duration: One-time award.
Deadline: February 8.

STAFF:
Ashley Carey, Managing Director

ADDRESS INQUIRIES TO:
See e-mail address above.

MUSEUM OF COMPARATIVE ZOOLOGY [1943]

Harvard University
26 Oxford Street
Cambridge, MA 02138
(617) 495-2460
E-mail: mczfunding@fas.harvard.edu
Web Site: www.mcz.harvard.edu/ernst-mayr-
travel-grants

FOUNDED: 1858

AREAS OF INTEREST:
Comparative zoology.

NAME(S) OF PROGRAMS:
● **Ernst Mayr Grants in Animal Systematics**

TYPE:
Awards/prizes; Research grants; Travel
grants.

YEAR PROGRAM STARTED: 1984

PURPOSE:
To enable animal systematists to make short
visits to museums for research needed to
complete taxonomic revisions and
monographs; to stimulate taxonomic work on
neglected taxa, including those with
numerous poorly described species, genera
and families known to have many
undescribed species in institutional
collections, taxa for which it is unknown
what proportion of the nominal species are
synonyms, and difficult genera without keys.

ELIGIBILITY:
Preference is given to studies that use the
Museum of Comparative Zoology collections,
although applications to work at other
museums also will be considered.

FINANCIAL DATA:
Grants may cover travel, lodging and meals
for up to a few months while conducting
research at the museums, services purchased
from the host institution, research supplies,
etc.
Amount of support per award: Up to $2,000.
Average grant is $1,000.
Total amount of support: Varies.

NO. AWARDS: Approximately 20.

APPLICATION INFO:
Proposals should consist of an application
form which includes a short project
description and explicit statement of the
goals of the research, itinerary, and budget, a
curriculum vitae, and three letters of support.
All applications should be written in English.
Proposals are submitted electronically.
Complete instructions are available on the
Museum web site.
Duration: Must be used within one year.
Deadline: April 1 and October 15.
Announcements typically within two months
following the application deadline.

STAFF:
Melissa Aja, Museum Projects Coordinator

ADDRESS INQUIRIES TO:
Melissa Aja
Museum Projects Coordinator
(See address and e-mail above.)

*SPECIAL STIPULATIONS:
Each grantee is required to submit a written
report summarizing the scientific
accomplishments achieved with the award
within one month of travel completion.

MYCOLOGICAL SOCIETY OF AMERICA [1944]

2424 American Lane
Madison, WI 53704
(608) 441-1060
Fax: (608) 443-2474
E-mail: msafungi@reesgroupinc.com
Web Site: msafungi.org

FOUNDED: 1932

AREAS OF INTEREST:
The study of fungi.

NAME(S) OF PROGRAMS:
● **Backus Award**
● **Salomon Bartnicki-Garcia Award**
● **Forest Fungal Ecology Awards**
● **International Travel Awards**
● **Martin-Baker Research Awards**
● **Mentor Student Travel Awards**
● **MSA Graduate Fellowship**
● **NAMA Memorial Fellowship**
● **John W. Rippon Research Award**
● **Clark T. Rogerson Research Award**
● **Alexander H. and Helen V. Smith Research Fund**
● **Undergraduate Research Award**

TYPE:
Awards/prizes; Conferences/seminars;
Fellowships; Travel grants. Supplementary
grant for an outstanding candidate awarded in
addition to any fellowship, scholarship or
assistantship support from other sources to
further undergraduate and graduate studies in
the field of mycology.

LEGAL BASIS:
Nonprofit organization.

ELIGIBILITY:
Applicants must be members of the
Mycological Society of America. In selecting
the recipient of the Fellowship, consideration
is given to scholastic merit, research ability
and promise shown as a future mycologist.

FINANCIAL DATA:
Amount of support per award: Backus and
Rogerson Research Awards: $1,000;
Bartnicki-Garcia, Rippon Research and
Undergraduate Research Awards: $500;
Forest Fungal Ecology Awards: $1,250 to
$2,500; International Travel Awards: $1,500
to $2,500; Martin Baker Research Award:
$3,000; Mentor Student Travel Awards:
Varies; MSA Graduate Fellowship and
NAMA Memorial Fellowship: $2,000.
Total amount of support: Approximately
$15,000 annually.

NO. MOST RECENT APPLICANTS: 78.

NO. AWARDS: 40.

APPLICATION INFO:
Application information is available on the
web site.
Duration: One year. Nonrenewable.
Deadline: February 15.

PUBLICATIONS:
Mycologia, research journal; *Inoculum,*
newsletter.

ADDRESS INQUIRIES TO:
MSA Distinctions Awards:
Distinguished Mycologist Award,
Alexopoulos Prize, Weston Award for
Excellence in Teaching, The Gordon and
Tina Wasson Award
Anne Pringle
E-mail: apringle2@wisc.edu

MSA Honorary Awards:
MSA Fellow, Honorary Member
Tom Volk
E-mail: volk.thom@uwlax.edu

Student Awards:
MSA Graduate Fellowships,
NAMA Memorial Fellowships, Backus
Award,
Undergraduate Research Award,
Best Oral and Poster Presentations by
Undergraduate and Graduate Students
Mia Maltz
E-mail: miarosequartz@gmail.com

NATIONAL ALOPECIA AREATA
FOUNDATION   [1945]

65 Mitchell Boulevard
Suite 200-B
San Rafael, CA 94903
(415) 472-3780
Fax: (415) 480-1800
E-mail: info@naaf.org
abby@naaf.org
Web Site: www.naaf.org

FOUNDED: 1981

AREAS OF INTEREST:
Baldness, hair loss and alopecia areata.

NAME(S) OF PROGRAMS:
● **Bridge Grants**
● **Mentored Investigator Awards**
● **Pilot and Feasibility Grants**
● **Research Grants**
● **Student Internship Awards**

TYPE:
Internships; Research grants. Bridge Grants
are intended to support researchers who have
submitted highly meritorious but unfunded
K-type (career development) and R-type
applications to the National Institutes of
Health with a focus on alopecia areata. This
grant is intended to provide a critical year of
additional support to near-miss applicants
whose projects were well-scored by the NIH,
but not funded so that they can collect data
that strengthens a future application.

Mentored Investigator Awards are intended to
support postdoctoral researchers training to
conduct alopecia areata research
independently. The goal is to put recipients
in a position to compete for larger grants in
the future and to establish successful
long-term careers with an enduring focus on
research relevant to alopecia areata.

Pilot and Feasibility Grants are intended to
support studies that explore preliminary ideas
and conduct proof-of-concept experiments.
The goal is to stimulate the development of
new research programs in the field of
alopecia areata capable of competing for
long-term funding from the NIH or similar
agencies in the future. Proposals must be
hypothesis-driven and reflect innovative
approaches to address critical questions in
alopecia areata research.

Research Grants are intended to support
studies focused on understanding the
mechanisms behind disease pathophysiology,
translational application of basic discoveries,
or provide insight into new therapies using
translational, clinical, or epidemiologic
approaches. Proposals must be
hypothesis-driven and provide sufficient
preliminary data to justify NAAF support.

Student Internship Awards are intended to
support students, residents and fellows
conducting short-term research projects
focused on alopecia areata under the
supervision of experienced investigators in
the field. The goal is to enable promising

young scientists and physicians to acquire
skills that will further their careers in
research relevant to alopecia areata.

YEAR PROGRAM STARTED: 1985

PURPOSE:
To support research to find an acceptable
treatment and studies that will lead to an
eventual cure for alopecia areata.

ELIGIBILITY:
Must be an Institute Review Board-approved
researcher who has submitted a proposal
about alopecia areata or hair biology. No
funding for established investigators.

FINANCIAL DATA:
Salaries only fellows, assistants, residents and
technicians.

Amount of support per award: Bridge Grants:
Maximum $100,000 per year for R-type and
maximum $75,000 for K-type; Mentored
Investigator Awards: Maximum $50,000 per
year; Pilot and Feasibility Grants: Maximum
$40,000; Research Grants: Maximum
$100,000 per year; Student Internship
Awards: Maximum $3,000.

Total amount of support: Over $5,700,000
since inception of program.

CO-OP FUNDING PROGRAMS: Joint grants with
other organizations.

NO. MOST RECENT APPLICANTS: Varies.

NO. AWARDS: Varies.

APPLICATION INFO:
Contact the Foundation for application
procedures.

Duration: Bridge Grants: Up to two years for
R-type and up to one year for K-type; Pilot
and Feasibility Grants and Student Internship
Awards: One year; Mentored Investigator
Awards: Up to three years; Research Grants:
Up to two years.

ADDRESS INQUIRIES TO:
Abby Ellison, Director of Research
(See address above.)

NATIONAL SCIENCE
FOUNDATION   [1946]

Division of Molecular and Cellular Biosciences
2415 Eisenhower Avenue
Alexandria, VA 22314
(703) 292-8440
Fax: (703) 292-9061
E-mail: tgood@nsf.gov
Web Site: www.nsf.gov

FOUNDED: 1950

AREAS OF INTEREST:
Molecular biophysics, cellular dynamics and
function, genetic mechanisms, and systems
and synthetic biology.

NAME(S) OF PROGRAMS:
● **Division of Molecular and Cellular**
  Biosciences Programs

TYPE:
Conferences/seminars; Project/program
grants; Research grants; Seed money grants.
The Division of Molecular and Cellular
Biosciences at the National Science
Foundation has the following clusters:

Molecular Biophysics, which encourages
proposals such as the following areas of
research:
(1) general principles of the relationship
between structure, dynamics and function of

biomolecules and;
(2) fundamental principles governing
biomolecular interactions and mechanisms.

Cellular Dynamics and Function, which
encourages proposals such as the following
areas of research:
(1) predictive understanding of the behavior
of living cells through integration of
modeling and experimentation;
(2) integrative cellular function across broad
spatiotemporal scales, from single molecules
to whole cells and;
(3) origin, evolution and function of cells,
organelles and microcompartments.

Genetic Mechanisms, which encourages
proposals such as the following areas of
research:
(1) gene expression, including epigenetics
and RNA-mediated regulation;
(2) chromosome dynamics, DNA replication,
repair, recombination and inheritance and;
(3) evolution of genes and genomes.

Systems and Synthetic Biology, which
encourages proposals such as the following
areas of research:
(1) systems-level, theory-driven analysis of
regulatory, signaling and metabolic networks;
(2) synthetic biology to address fundamental
biological questions including the origin of
life, minimal cell, emergent behavior in
complex systems, robustness in design and
organization and;
(3) tool development to facilitate systems and
synthetic biology studies.

YEAR PROGRAM STARTED: 1992

PURPOSE:
To increase our store of knowledge in these
fields and enhance our understanding of the
scientific aspects of major problems
confronting the nation.

LEGAL BASIS:
National Science Foundation Act of 1950,
Public Law 81-507, as amended.

ELIGIBILITY:
The principal recipients of scientific research
project support are academic institutions and
nonprofit research institutions. Grants may
also be awarded to other types of institutions
and to individuals. In these cases, preliminary
inquiry should be made to the cognizant
program officer before a proposal is
submitted. Support may be provided to
projects involving a single scientist or to
projects covering the activities of a number
of scientists. Awards are made for projects
confined to a single disciplinary area and for
projects which cross or merge disciplinary
interests. Clinically oriented research is not
supported.

FINANCIAL DATA:
Amount of support per award: Varies.
Total amount of support: Varies.

APPLICATION INFO:
Application information is available on the
web site.
Duration: Varies.
Deadline: Contact Foundation for specific
dates.

PUBLICATIONS:
Brochures.

DIRECTORS:
Dr. Theresa Good, Division Director

ADDRESS INQUIRIES TO:
Cognizant Program Officer

NATIONAL SCIENCE FOUNDATION   [1947]

Division of Environmental Biology
2415 Eisenhower Avenue
Alexandria, VA 22314
(703) 292-8480
Fax: (703) 292-9064
E-mail: shampton@nsf.gov
Web Site: www.nsf.gov/bio/deb/about.jsp

FOUNDED: 1950

AREAS OF INTEREST:
Population and community, ecology, ecosystem science, population and systematic biology, biodiversity inventories cluster and evolution processes.

NAME(S) OF PROGRAMS:
● Division of Environmental Biology

TYPE:
Conferences/seminars; Research grants; Training grants; Travel grants.

PURPOSE:
To increase our store of knowledge in these fields and enhance our understanding of the scientific aspects of major problems confronting the nation.

LEGAL BASIS:
National Science Foundation Act of 1950, Public Law 81-507, as amended.

ELIGIBILITY:
The principal recipients of scientific research project support are academic institutions and nonprofit research institutions. Grants may also be awarded to other types of institutions and to individuals. In these cases, preliminary inquiry should be made to the cognizant program officer before a proposal is submitted. Support may be provided to projects involving a single scientist or to projects covering the activities of a number of scientists. Awards are made for projects confined to a single disciplinary area and for projects which cross or merge disciplinary interests.

FINANCIAL DATA:
Amount of support per award: $108,000 average.

NO. MOST RECENT APPLICANTS: 2,500.

NO. AWARDS: 500.

APPLICATION INFO:
Application information is available on the web site.
Duration: 12 to 60 months, depending on the scientific merit and requirements of the project.

PUBLICATIONS:
Awards list; program description.

ADDRESS INQUIRIES TO:
Stephanie Hampton, Division Director
(See address above.)

SOCIETY FOR DEVELOPMENTAL BIOLOGY   [1948]

6120 Executive Boulevard
Suite 725
Rockville, MD 20852
(301) 634-7815
E-mail: sdb@sdbonline.org
Web Site: www.sdbonline.org

FOUNDED: 1939

AREAS OF INTEREST:
Developmental biology.

NAME(S) OF PROGRAMS:
● Edwin G. Conklin Medal
● Developmental Biology-SDB Lifetime Achievement Award
● John Doctor Best Education Award
● Viktor Hamburger Outstanding Educator Prize
● Elizabeth D. Hay New Investigator Award
● SDB Boot Camp for New Faculty
● SDB Education Activities Grant
● SDB Emerging Models Grant
● SDB Innovation Grant
● SDB International Scholarships
● SDB Meeting Grants
● SDB Trainee Science Communication Award
● SDB Travel Awards
● Teaching and Junior Faculty Travel Grants

TYPE:
Awards/prizes; Conferences/seminars; Scholarships.

PURPOSE:
To further the study of development in all organisms and at all levels; to represent and promote communication among students of development; to promote the field of developmental biology.

ELIGIBILITY:
Must be a student or investigator studying in the field of developmental biology.

FINANCIAL DATA:
Amount of support per award: John Doctor Best Education Award: $1,000; SDB International Scholarships: $2,000; Student/Postdoctoral Travel Awards: Varies; Teaching and Junior Faculty Travel Grants: $700.
Total amount of support: Varies.

NO. MOST RECENT APPLICANTS: 114 for Student/Postdoctoral Travel Awards.

NO. AWARDS: 86 Student/Postdoctoral Travel Awards.

APPLICATION INFO:
Nomination instructions and application guidelines may be obtained from the Society's web site.
Duration: One-time award. Reapplication possible for grants and scholarships.
Deadline: Varies.

ADDRESS INQUIRIES TO:
Ida Chow, Executive Director
(See address above.)

SOCIETY FOR THE STUDY OF AMPHIBIANS AND REPTILES

Department of Biology
Carroll University
Waukesha, WI 53186
(262) 951-3295
E-mail: rbrenes@carrollu.edu
Web Site: www.ssarherps.org

TYPE:
Awards/prizes; Research grants. Awards are given in six categories: Conservation of Amphibians and/or Reptiles, Field Research, Laboratory Research, Herpetological Education, Travel and International Research.

See entry 1829 for full listing.

THE UNIVERSITY OF CALGARY

Faculty of Graduate Studies
Earth Sciences Building, Room 1010
2500 University Drive, N.W.
Calgary AB T2N 1N4 Canada
(403) 220-4938
Fax: (403) 289-7635
E-mail: gsaward@ucalgary.ca
Web Site: grad.ucalgary.ca/awards

TYPE:
Awards/prizes; Scholarships. Award for study in the fields of cellular, molecular, microbial or biochemical biology. Tenable at The University of Calgary, Department of Biological Sciences.

See entry 1598 for full listing.

VIRGINIA SOCIETY OF ORNITHOLOGY   [1949]

P.O. Box 5994
Williamsburg, VA 23188
E-mail: danbieker@gmail.com
Web Site: www.virginiabirds.org

AREAS OF INTEREST:
Ornithology and bird conservation.

NAME(S) OF PROGRAMS:
● VSO Conservation Fund

TYPE:
Research grants.

YEAR PROGRAM STARTED: 2007

PURPOSE:
To benefit Virginia species and habitats.

ELIGIBILITY:
Awards are granted to worthy candidates conducting research in the field of bird conservation with potential benefits to Virginia species and habitats.

FINANCIAL DATA:
Amount of support per award: Generally $500 to $1,000.
Total amount of support: $2,500 annually.

NO. AWARDS: 5 for the year 2021.

ADDRESS INQUIRIES TO:
VSO Board of Directors
(See address above.)

THE WETLANDS INSTITUTE   [1950]

1075 Stone Harbor Boulevard
Stone Harbor, NJ 08247-1424
(609) 368-1211
Fax: (609) 368-3871
E-mail: research@wetlandsinstitute.org
Web Site: www.wetlandsinstitute.org

FOUNDED: 1969

AREAS OF INTEREST:
Environmental education and conservation research.

NAME(S) OF PROGRAMS:
● Coastal Conservation Research Program
● Environmental Education Internship

TYPE:
Internships. Coastal Conservation Research Program offers 10-week summer internships for field research on mid-Atlantic coastal organisms and environments at the Wetlands Institute.

Environmental Education Internships are for undergraduate students with an interest in environmental or outdoor education and/or classroom science education.

YEAR PROGRAM STARTED: 1969

PURPOSE:
To involve undergraduate students in a wide variety of research projects pertaining to the environment.

LEGAL BASIS:
Nonprofit organization that conducts research and education.

ELIGIBILITY:
Coastal Conservation Research Program applicants should be completing their sophomore, junior or senior year at a college or university and be interested in biological research as a career.

Environmental Education Internship applicants must have completed at least two years of college.

A science or education major is desired, but not required.

GEOG. RESTRICTIONS: United States.

FINANCIAL DATA:
Amount of support per award: Varies with project.
Total amount of support: Varies.

NO. MOST RECENT APPLICANTS: Over 100.

NO. AWARDS: 10.

APPLICATION INFO:
Contact the Institute for guidelines.
Duration: Late May to early August.
Deadline: March 1.

IRS I.D.: 23-7046783

ADDRESS INQUIRIES TO:
Coastal Conservation Research Program
E-mail: research@wetlandsinstitute.org

Environmental Education Internship
E-mail: education@wetlandsinstitute.org

WHITEHALL FOUNDATION, INC. [1951]
125 Worth Avenue
Suite 220
Palm Beach, FL 33480
(561) 655-4474
Fax: (561) 655-1296
E-mail: email@whitehall.org
Web Site: www.whitehall.org

FOUNDED: 1937

AREAS OF INTEREST:
Exclusive focus on assisting basic research in vertebrate (excluding clinical) and invertebrate neurobiology in the U.S.

TYPE:
Grants-in-aid; Research grants. Grants are available to established scientists of all ages working at accredited institutions in the U.S.

YEAR PROGRAM STARTED: 1937

PURPOSE:
To assist scholarly research in the life sciences; to assist those dynamic areas of basic biological research that are not heavily supported by federal agencies or other foundations with specialized missions.

LEGAL BASIS:
Not-for-profit corporation.

ELIGIBILITY:
Applications will be judged on the scientific merit and innovative aspects of the proposal, as well as on past performance and evidence of the applicant's continued productivity.

The Foundation does not award funds to investigators who have substantial existing or potential support (even if it is for an unrelated purpose), and applications may be held in abeyance until the results of other funding decisions are determined. In general, the Foundation currently defines "substantial" as approximately $200,000 per year (including both direct and indirect expense but excluding the principal investigator's salary). The principal investigator must hold no less than the position of assistant professor, or the equivalent, in order to make application.

GEOG. RESTRICTIONS: United States.

FINANCIAL DATA:
Amount of support per award: Research Grants: Up to $75,000 per year; Grants-in-aid: Up to $30,000.

APPLICATION INFO:
Application information is available on the Foundation web site.
Duration: Grants-in-aid: One year. Research Grants: Up to three years; a renewal grant with a maximum of two years is possible, but it will be awarded on a competitive basis.
Deadline: Dates are posted on the Foundation web site.

IRS I.D.: 13-5637595

ADDRESS INQUIRIES TO:
See e-mail address above.

*PLEASE NOTE:
The Foundation encourages the use of electronic mail. All correspondence and reports should be sent to the e-mail address above. The Letter of Intent must be submitted in hard copy on institutional letterhead.

THE WILEY FOUNDATION, INC.
111 River Street
Hoboken, NJ 07030-5774
(201) 748-6000
E-mail: wileyfoundation@wiley.com
Web Site: www.wileyfoundation.org

TYPE:
Awards/prizes. The annual Wiley Prize in Biomedical Sciences has recognized breakthrough research in pure or applied life science research.

See entry 1901 for full listing.

WILSON ORNITHOLOGICAL SOCIETY [1952]
Museum of Zoology
University of Michigan
1109 Geddes Avenue
Ann Arbor, MI 48109
(734) 764-0457
E-mail: wos@salve.edu
Web Site: wilsonsociety.org/awards

FOUNDED: 1888

AREAS OF INTEREST:
Ornithology.

NAME(S) OF PROGRAMS:
• **Louis Agassiz Fuertes Grant**
• **George A. Hall/Harold F. Mayfield Grant**
• **Research Grants**
• **Paul A. Stewart Grants**
• **Student Travel Awards**
• **Alexander Wilson Prize**

TYPE:
Grants-in-aid; Research grants. Fuertes, Hall/Mayfield and Stewart Grants provide for the promotion and encouragement of field research on birds. A research proposal is required.

Student Travel Awards provide funds for students to attend the annual meeting.

Alexander Wilson Prize is given to the best student paper presented at the annual meeting.

YEAR PROGRAM STARTED: 1947

PURPOSE:
To promote the scientific study of birds.

LEGAL BASIS:
Corporation.

ELIGIBILITY:
Each award requires a willingness of the awardee to report results of the research as an oral or poster paper at an annual meeting of the Wilson Ornithological Society.

Louis Agassiz Fuertes Grant: Available to all ornithologists, although graduate students and young professionals are preferred. Any avian research is eligible.

George A. Hall/Harold F. Mayfield Grant: Limited to independent researchers without access to funds and facilities available at colleges, universities or governmental agencies, and is restricted to nonprofessionals, including high school students. Any kind of avian research is eligible.

Research Grants are limited to research by Master's students for work in any area of ornithology.

Paul A. Stewart Grants: Preference will be given to proposals for studies of bird movements based on banding, analysis of recoveries and returns of banded birds, with an emphasis on economic ornithology.

Student Travel Awards: Students presenting an oral paper or poster at WOS Annual Meeting are invited to apply.

FINANCIAL DATA:
Amount of support per award: Fuertes Grant: $2,500; Hall/Mayfield Grant and Stewart Grant: $1,000; Research Grants: $1,500.

NO. MOST RECENT APPLICANTS: 113 for the year 2020.

NO. AWARDS: Fuertes Grant: Up to 2; Hall/Mayfield Grant: Up to 1; Research Grants and Stewart Grant: 4.

APPLICATION INFO:
Requirements and application instructions are available on the Society web site.
Duration: One-time grant. Nonrenewable.
Deadline: February 1.

PUBLICATIONS:
Wilson Journal of Ornithology; Wilson Bulletin; Guide to Graduate Programs in Ornithology; Manual of Ornithology.

ADDRESS INQUIRIES TO:
For Research Awards:
Letitia Reichart
E-mail: reichartlm@unk.edu

For Student Travel Grants:
Dennis Siegfried
E-mail: dsiegfried@sbuniv.edu

Environment

ACORN FOUNDATION [1953]

c/o Common Counsel Foundation
1624 Franklin Street, Suite 1022
Oakland, CA 94612
(510) 834-2995
Fax: (510) 834-2998
E-mail: info@commoncounsel.org
grantsadmin@commoncounsel.org
Web Site: www.commoncounsel.org

FOUNDED: 1978

AREAS OF INTEREST:
A sustainable ecological future and a healthy
global environment.

TYPE:
General operating grants.

YEAR PROGRAM STARTED: 1978

PURPOSE:
To advance community-based organizations
working for environmental conservation,
sustainability and environmental justice.

ELIGIBILITY:
The Foundation makes grants to grassroots
organizations. Organizational budget must be
$600,000 or less. The Foundation is
particularly interested in small and innovative
community-based projects that engage in
community organizing in order to:
(1) preserve and restore habitats supporting
biological diversity and wildlife;
(2) advocate for environmental justice,
particularly in low-income and indigenous
communities and;
(3) prevent or remedy toxic pollution.

GEOG. RESTRICTIONS: Western and southern
United States and Appalachia.

FINANCIAL DATA:
Amount of support per award: $5,000 to
$10,000.

NO. MOST RECENT APPLICANTS: More than 100.

NO. AWARDS: 10 to 14 per year.

APPLICATION INFO:
Organizations that meet the eligibility and
funding criteria are encouraged to submit a
letter of inquiry form.
Duration: 12 months.
Deadline: January 15 and June 15 for spring
and fall grantmaking meetings.

ADDRESS INQUIRIES TO:
Grants Administrator
(See address above.)

ALASKA CONSERVATION
FOUNDATION [1954]

1227 West Ninth Avenue
Suite 300
Anchorage, AK 99501
(907) 276-1917
Fax: (907) 274-4145
E-mail: grants@alaskaconservation.org
Web Site: www.alaskaconservation.org

AREAS OF INTEREST:
Conservation, ecosystem and lands
protection, marine conservation, linking
conservation with the economy and
organizational effectiveness.

NAME(S) OF PROGRAMS:
● **Rapid Response Grant**

TYPE:
Awards/prizes; General operating grants;
Internships; Project/program grants.

YEAR PROGRAM STARTED: 1977

PURPOSE:
To allow for a timely response to
fast-breaking, unforeseen environmental
threats of statewide or national significance.

ELIGIBILITY:
Applicants for Rapid Response Grants must
meet the following criteria:
(1) be a nonprofit organization engaged in
Alaska conservation advocacy;
(2) be based in Alaska, or have an
Alaska-based program;
(3) if a current ACF grantee, be in good
standing with required grants reports;
(4) grant must address an unforeseen
opportunity for action and;
(5) issue must be a statewide concern or have
statewide impact.

GEOG. RESTRICTIONS: Alaska.

FINANCIAL DATA:
Amount of support per award: $2,500 to
$10,000.

APPLICATION INFO:
Applicants should carefully review the Rapid
Response Grant Guidelines before starting
the application process. E-mail
adalton@alaskaconservation.org or call (907)
433-8213 prior to applying to ensure your
project is eligible.
Duration: Up to six months.

EXECUTIVE DIRECTOR:
Michael Barber

ADDRESS INQUIRIES TO:
See e-mail address above.

ALASKA CONSERVATION
FOUNDATION [1955]

1227 West Ninth Avenue
Suite 300
Anchorage, AK 99501
(907) 276-1917
Fax: (907) 274-4145
E-mail: grants@alaskaconservation.org
Web Site: www.alaskaconservation.org

FOUNDED: 1980

AREAS OF INTEREST:
Conservation, ecosystem and lands
protection, marine conservation, linking
conservation with the economy and
organizational effectiveness.

NAME(S) OF PROGRAMS:
● **Alaska Defense Fund**
● **Discovery Grants Program**

TYPE:
General operating grants; Internships;
Project/program grants.

YEAR PROGRAM STARTED: 1980

PURPOSE:
To build strategic leadership and support for
Alaskan efforts to take care of wild lands,
water and wildlife, which sustain diverse
cultures, healthy communities and prosperous
economies.

LEGAL BASIS:
501(c)(3) public foundation.

ELIGIBILITY:
Incorporate, tax-exempt organizations and
non-incorporated organizations may apply
according to program guidelines.

GEOG. RESTRICTIONS: Alaska.

FINANCIAL DATA:
Amount of support per award: Alaska
Defense Fund: Varies; Discovery Grants:
$500 to $2,000.
Total amount of support: $1,260,000 for the
year 2019.

NO. AWARDS: 81 for the year 2019.

APPLICATION INFO:
Alaska Defense Fund: Applications are
accepted by invitation only. Discovery Grant
applications must be submitted online.
Duration: Varies.
Deadline: Varies.

IRS I.D.: 92-0061466

EXECUTIVE DIRECTOR:
Michael Barber

ADDRESS INQUIRIES TO:
See e-mail address above.

*SPECIAL STIPULATIONS:
ACF funds only in Alaska.

AMERICAN ACADEMY IN
ROME [1956]

7 East 60th Street
New York, NY 10022
(212) 751-7200
Fax: (212) 751-7220
E-mail: info@aarome.org
Web Site: www.aarome.org

FOUNDED: 1894

AREAS OF INTEREST:
Landscape architecture.

NAME(S) OF PROGRAMS:
● **The Rome Prize Fellowship in
Landscape Architecture**

TYPE:
Awards/prizes; Fellowships; Residencies.
Provides a residential year at the American
Academy in Rome for an American
landscape architect for advanced study, travel
and association with other fellows in the arts
and humanities.

YEAR PROGRAM STARTED: 1920

PURPOSE:
To provide American landscape architects
with a special opportunity for advanced study
in Rome.

LEGAL BASIS:
Nonprofit, national organization.

ELIGIBILITY:
Applicants must hold an accredited degree in
landscape architecture, or equivalent
experience.

GEOG. RESTRICTIONS: United States.

FINANCIAL DATA:
Award consists of stipend, plus housing and
meals allowance.
Amount of support per award: $16,000 for
half-term fellowship; $28,000 for full-term
fellowship.

NO. MOST RECENT APPLICANTS: 25.

NO. AWARDS: 2 annually.

APPLICATION INFO:
Applications are submitted electronically.
Duration: Five and one-half months or 11
months.
Deadline: November 1. Announcement in
April.

PUBLICATIONS:
Program announcement.

STAFF:
Mark Robbins, President
Shawn Miller, Programs Director

ADDRESS INQUIRIES TO:
Programs Director
(See address above.)

AMERICAN ALPINE CLUB [1957]
710 10th Street
Suite 100
Golden, CO 80401
(303) 384-0110
E-mail: grants@americanalpineclub.org
Web Site: americanalpineclub.org/grants

FOUNDED: 1902

AREAS OF INTEREST:
Mountaineering, mountain environment and polar regions.

NAME(S) OF PROGRAMS:
- **Catalyst: Adventure Grants for Change**
- **Climbing Grief Grants**
- **Cornerstone Conservation Grant**
- **Cutting Edge Grant**
- **Jones Backcountry Adventure Grant**
- **Live Your Dream Grant**
- **Zack Martin Breaking Barriers Grant**
- **McNeill-Nott Award**
- **Mountaineering Fellowship Fund Grant**
- **Research Grants**
- **TINCUP Partner in Adventure**

TYPE:
Project/program grants; Research grants; Travel grants. Grants to support research in Arctic and alpine environments. Funds may also be used to assist in publication or other dissemination of the results of such research.

Cornerstone Conservation Grant aims to create healthy climbing landscape, promote respect for places to climb, and empowers local climbing communities.

Cutting Edge Grant supports advanced, seasoned climbers undertaking high-level climbing and mountaineering objectives.

Jones Backcountry Adventure Grant supports a multiday splitboarding expedition with a strong exploratory and adventure component. The project objective may focus on a single descent/summit or a tour/traverse of a region.

Live Your Dream Grant supports everyday adventurers looking to take their abilities to the next level, regardless of age, experience, or discipline.

Zack Martin Breaking Barriers Grant is a dual-purpose grant that focuses on projects with a humanitarian objective and an objective involving alpinism, iceclimbing, rock climbing or bouldering.

McNeill-Nott Award seeks to preserve the spirit of Sue Nott and her partner, Karen McNeill, by giving grants to amateur climbers exploring new routes or unclimbed peaks with small and lightweight teams.

Mountaineering Fellowship Fund grants encourage American climbers age 25 years and younger to go into remote areas and seek out climbs more difficult than they might ordinarily be able to do.

Research Grants support scientific endeavors in mountains and crags around the world. ACC funds projects that contribute vital knowledge to the climbing environment, enrich understanding of global climber

impacts, and support and improve the health and sustainability of mountain environments and habitats.

YEAR PROGRAM STARTED: 1945

PURPOSE:
To encourage and broaden scientific research in mountains and the polar regions.

LEGAL BASIS:
Membership organization.

ELIGIBILITY:
Individuals engaged in appropriate research are eligible to apply.

FINANCIAL DATA:
Amount of support per award: Cornerstone Conservation Grant: $1,000 to $8,000; Cutting Edge Grant: $5,000 to $15,000; Jones Grant: $1,500 plus a Jones splitboard, skins and backpack; Live Your Dream Grant: $200 to $1,000; McNeill-Nott Award: Up to $5,000; Mountaineering Fellowship Fund: $300 to $800; Research Grants: Varies.
Total amount of support: Over $130,000 annually.

APPLICATION INFO:
Application information is available on the web site.
Duration: One-time grant. New application required for ongoing projects.
Deadline: Copp-Dash Inspire Award: September 1. Cornerstone Conservation Grant: August 15. Cutting Edge Grant and Jones Grant: November 30. Live Your Dream Grant: March 31. Zack Martin Grant: April 15. McNeill-Nott Climbing Award: January 1. Mountaineering Fellowship Fund: April 1 and November 1. Research Grants: January 15.

PUBLICATIONS:
Application guidelines.

ADDRESS INQUIRIES TO:
Kenzie Schott, Grants Manager
(See e-mail address above.)

AMERICAN WATER RESOURCES ASSOCIATION [1958]
P.O. Box 2663
Woodbridge, VA 22195
(540) 687-8390
Fax: (540) 687-8395
E-mail: info@awra.org
Web Site: www.awra.org

FOUNDED: 1964

AREAS OF INTEREST:
Water resources.

NAME(S) OF PROGRAMS:
- **Richard A. Herbert Memorial Scholarship**

TYPE:
Scholarships.

YEAR PROGRAM STARTED: 1980

PURPOSE:
To advance multidisciplinary water resources management and research.

ELIGIBILITY:
Applicant must be a national AWRA member who is enrolled in a program related to water resources. May be a full-time undergraduate student working towards an undergraduate degree or a full-time graduate student.

The undergraduate scholarship will be awarded to the student most qualified by academic performance. The graduate scholarship will be awarded to the student most qualified by academic and/or research performance. Measures of academic performance include the cumulative grade point average, relevance of the student's curriculum to water resources, and leadership in extracurricular activities related to water resources.

FINANCIAL DATA:
Amount of support per award: $2,000.
Total amount of support: $8,000.

NO. MOST RECENT APPLICANTS: 40 undergraduate and 20 graduate applications.

NO. AWARDS: 3.

APPLICATION INFO:
Application must be submitted electronically as one document to the e-mail listed above. File cannot be greater that 10 MB in size to ensure delivery. A complete application includes:
(1) a title page;
(2) a two-page summary of academic interests and achievements, extracurricular interests, and career goals as they relate to the selection criteria;
(3) resume or curriculum vitae;
(4) three signed letters of reference from professors and/or advisors and;
(5) transcripts of all college courses (undergraduate and graduate).
Duration: One year.
Deadline: May.

ADDRESS INQUIRIES TO:
AWRA Scholarship Coordinator
(See e-mail address above.)

BEN & JERRY'S FOUNDATION
30 Community Drive
South Burlington, VT 05403-6828
(802) 846-1500
E-mail: info@benandjerrysfoundation.org
Web Site: www.benandjerrysfoundation.org

TYPE:
General operating grants; Project/program grants. Grants to nonprofit organizations which facilitate progressive social change by addressing the underlying conditions of societal and/or environmental problems using organizing as a strategy to create change.

See entry 892 for full listing.

BONNEVILLE ENVIRONMENTAL FOUNDATION [1959]
1500 S.W. 1st Avenue
Suite 885
Portland, OR 97201
(503) 248-1905
Fax: (503) 248-1908
E-mail: info@b-e-f.org
Web Site: www.b-e-f.org

FOUNDED: 1998

AREAS OF INTEREST:
Environmental conservation and the development of new sources of renewable energy.

NAME(S) OF PROGRAMS:
- **Model Watershed Program**
- **Renewable Energy Program**

TYPE:
Grants-in-aid. Model Watershed Program is intended to restore ecological integrity and native fish populations in watersheds across the western U.S.

Renewable Energy Program supports school solar projects and other renewable energy technologies that are taken up by utility and community-based renewable energy projects.

PURPOSE:
To support watershed restoration programs; to develop new sources of renewable energy.

ELIGIBILITY:
The Foundation does not fund residential projects.

FINANCIAL DATA:
Amount of support per award: Varies.
Total amount of support: Varies.

APPLICATION INFO:
Complete application information is available on the Foundation web site.
Duration: Varies.

STAFF:
Todd Reeve, Chief Executive Officer
Evan Ramsey, Senior Director for Renewable Energy Program
Robert Warren, Director, Model Watershed Program

BRUNSWICK PUBLIC FOUNDATION   [1960]
26125 North Riverwoods Boulevard
Suite 500
Mettawa, IL 60045
(847) 735-4306
Fax: (847) 735-4765
E-mail: brunswick.foundation@brunswick.com
Web Site: www.brunswick.com

FOUNDED: 1998

AREAS OF INTEREST:
Ocean conservancy, health and wellness.

TYPE:
Project/program grants.

PURPOSE:
To support community development primarily through contributions to preselected local United Way organizations; to support organizations that promote, preserve and restore our nation's waterways and ocean coastal areas and the aquatic and marine life that inhabits them.

ELIGIBILITY:
Grants are made to organizations that have tax-exempt status under Section 501(c)(3) of the Internal Revenue Code. Nonsectarian religious programs may apply. No grants are made to individuals.

FINANCIAL DATA:
Amount of support per award: $5,000 to $80,000.
Total amount of support: Approximately $215,000 for the year 2020.

NO. AWARDS: 5 for the year 2020.

APPLICATION INFO:
Contact the Foundation for guidelines.
Duration: One year.
Deadline: March 15, July 15 and October 15.

IRS I.D.: 36-4195390

BOARD OF DIRECTORS:
Jim Baugh
Kevin Grodzki

Jim Hubbard
Sarah Humphries

*SPECIAL STIPULATIONS:
By invitation only.

THE BULLITT FOUNDATION   [1961]
1501 East Madison, Suite 600
Seattle, WA 98122
(206) 343-0807
E-mail: grants@bullitt.org
Web Site: www.bullitt.org

FOUNDED: 1952

AREAS OF INTEREST:
Environment.

NAME(S) OF PROGRAMS:
● **Deep Green Buildings**
● **Energy, Climate and Materials**
● **Regional Ecosystem Health**
● **Resilient Cities, Healthy Communities**

TYPE:
Awards/prizes; Matching gifts; Project/program grants.

YEAR PROGRAM STARTED: 1952

PURPOSE:
To safeguard the natural environment by promoting responsible human activities and sustainable communities in the Pacific Northwest.

LEGAL BASIS:
Private foundation.

ELIGIBILITY:
Applicants must be organizations that have nonprofit tax status with clear, significant and achievable goals, as well as a cogent strategy to realize them. The trustees favor projects that avoid excessive reliance on any one source of funding. The Foundation cannot fund political elections or lobbying activities involving specific legislation. The Foundation does not fund university overhead costs or capital projects.

GEOG. RESTRICTIONS: Emerald Corridor: Vancouver, British Columbia to Portland, Oregon.

FINANCIAL DATA:
Amount of support per award: Grants: $5,000 to $100,000; $35,000 average.
Matching fund requirements: Employee and trustee donations will be matched.

NO. MOST RECENT APPLICANTS: 200.

NO. AWARDS: Approximately 125 annually.

REPRESENTATIVE AWARDS:
$50,000 to Justice Alliance Education Fund; $100,000 to Climate Solutions; $30,000 to Duwamish River Cleanup Coalition; $25,000 to Ecotrust.

APPLICATION INFO:
An organization must first submit a proposal inquiry via the web site. Complete application information is available online.
Duration: One year.
Deadline: Proposal inquiry: March 15 and September 15.

PUBLICATIONS:
Guidelines.

IRS I.D.: 91-6027795

TRUSTEES AND OFFICERS:
Denis Hayes, Chairperson
Jessie Woolley-Wilson, Vice Chairperson
Sally Anderson, Treasurer

Rob Pena, Secretary
Harriett Bullitt
Mark Edlen
Howard Frumkin
Erin Gomez
Lisa Graumlich
Martha Kongsgaard
Paul Schwer

ADDRESS INQUIRIES TO:
See e-mail address above.

LIZ CLAIBORNE ART ORTENBERG FOUNDATION   [1962]
1385 Broadway
23rd Floor
New York, NY 10018
(212) 333-2536
E-mail: lcaof@lcaof.org
Web Site: www.lcaof.org

FOUNDED: 1984

AREAS OF INTEREST:
Integration of conservation and development in the rural landscape.

TYPE:
Challenge/matching grants; Development grants; General operating grants; Project/program grants; Research grants; Seed money grants.

PURPOSE:
To conserve nature and relieve human distress; to redress the breakdown in the processes linking nature and humanity.

ELIGIBILITY:
The Foundation funds modest, carefully designed field projects, primarily in developing countries. No funding for general support or to underwrite institutional overhead. Local people should have a substantial proprietary interest in the project.

GEOG. RESTRICTIONS: Northern Rockies region of the United States.

FINANCIAL DATA:
Amount of support per award: $10,000 to $200,000.
Total amount of support: $6,233,638 for fiscal year 2019.

REPRESENTATIVE AWARDS:
$176,300 to African Conservation Centre for Amboseli Conservation Program in Kenya; $50,000 to National Wildlife Federation for Wildlife Conflict Resolution Program in Montana.

APPLICATION INFO:
Applications are accepted by invitation only.
Duration: One to three years.

PUBLICATIONS:
The View from Airlie; MONTANA: People and the Economy; brochure; *Next Year Country-View from Red Lodge; 9 Case Studies on the Interior West of U.S.*

TRUSTEES:
Victor Kovner
Alison Richard

ADVISORY BOARD:
Douglas Chadwick
William Conway
William deBuys
Ullas Karanth
Grant Parker
David Western

ADDRESS INQUIRIES TO:
Kent Wommack, Executive Director
Lori Cohen, Administrative Coordinator
(See address above.)

*PLEASE NOTE:
The Foundation is not accepting unsolicited
proposals at this time.

COLUMBIA JOURNALISM SCHOOL

2950 Broadway
New York, NY 10027
(212) 854-6468
Fax: (212) 854-3148
E-mail: cm3443@columbia.edu
Web Site: journalism.columbia.edu/oakes

TYPE:
Awards/prizes. Awarded for distinguished
excellence in environmental journalism.

See entry 1726 for full listing.

COOPERATIVE INSTITUTE FOR RESEARCH IN ENVIRONMENTAL SCIENCES (CIRES)   [1963]

CIRES Building, Room 201
University of Colorado
Boulder, CO 80309
(303) 497-3584
Fax: (303) 492-1149
E-mail: christine.wiedinmyer@colorado.edu
Web Site: cires.colorado.edu

FOUNDED: 1967

AREAS OF INTEREST:
Physics, chemistry and dynamics of the earth
system; global and regional environmental
change; climate system monitoring,
diagnostics, and modeling; development and
application of remote sensing and in-situ
measurement techniques for the earth and its
atmosphere, cryosphere, ecosystems, and
oceans.

NAME(S) OF PROGRAMS:
● **CIRES Visiting Fellowship Program in Environmental Sciences**

TYPE:
Fellowships. The program provides
opportunities for interactions between CIRES
scientists and visiting fellows to pursue
common research interests. CIRES research
includes theoretical studies, laboratory
experimentation, and field investigations
which may affect the enhancement of air and
water quality and prediction of weather
climate fluctuations.

YEAR PROGRAM STARTED: 1968

PURPOSE:
To provide support for scientists from around
the world to visit CIRES and collaborate in a
variety of research projects.

LEGAL BASIS:
Sponsored jointly by the University of
Colorado and National Oceanic and
Atmospheric Administration.

ELIGIBILITY:
Applicants must be Ph.D. scientists at all
levels; faculty planning sabbatical leave and
recent Ph.D. recipients are especially
encouraged to apply. Priority is given to
candidates with research experience at
institutions outside the Boulder scientific
community. The program is open to scientists

of all countries. The University of Colorado
is committed to diversity and equality in
education and employment.

FINANCIAL DATA:
Amount of support per award: Stipend is
flexible based on research experience.

NO. AWARDS: Up to 10.

APPLICATION INFO:
Applicant must send a resume, publications
list and a brief (two- to four-page)
description of the proposed research. In
addition, candidates should request three
letters of recommendation, to be sent directly
to CIRES, from persons familiar with their
qualifications. Postdoctoral-level applicants
must also submit undergraduate and graduate
transcripts.
Duration: Postdoctoral: Two years. Senior
Scientist: Three to 12 months.
Deadline: January 5. Selection the following
March.

ADDRESS INQUIRIES TO:
Christine Wiedinmyer
Associate Director for Science
(See address above.)

THE ENERGY FOUNDATION   [1964]

301 Battery Street, 5th Floor
San Francisco, CA 94111
(415) 561-6700
Fax: (415) 561-6709
E-mail: grants@ef.org
Web Site: www.ef.org

FOUNDED: 1991

AREAS OF INTEREST:
Energy efficiency and renewable energy.

NAME(S) OF PROGRAMS:
● **Buildings Program**
● **Climate Program**
● **Energy Foundation China**
● **Power Program**
● **Public Engagement Program**
● **Transportation Program**

TYPE:
Project/program grants. Promotes energy
efficiency and renewable energy.

Buildings Program supports policies to
increase the efficiency of U.S. homes and
businesses and to reduce carbon emissions
and utility bills.

Climate Program has a goal of putting the
U.S. on a path to meet or exceed its stated
target of reducing greenhouse gas emissions
by 17 percent below 2005 levels by 2020.

Energy Foundation China, with an emphasis
on both national policy and regional
implementation, assists agencies, experts and
entrepreneurs in solving that country's energy
challenges.

Power Program seeks to move the U.S.
toward cleaner, more affordable sources of
energy.

Public Engagement Program seeks to build
national and state support for clean energy
and strong climate policies.

Transportation Program works to reduce
energy use and carbon pollution through
policies that improve vehicle efficiency and
promote clean fuels.

YEAR PROGRAM STARTED: 1991

PURPOSE:
To assist in a national, and ultimately a
global, transition to a sustainable future by
promoting energy efficiency and renewable
energy.

LEGAL BASIS:
Public charity 501(c)(3).

ELIGIBILITY:
501(c)(3) organizations only. No grants to
individuals or for-profit organizations.
Projects must have broad regional or national
implications. No grants to religious
organizations, political parties or for
development of technology. No research and
development or demonstration grants.

GEOG. RESTRICTIONS: United States and China.

FINANCIAL DATA:
Amount of support per award: Varies.
Total amount of support: Approximately
$60,000,000 in grant payments for the year
2018.

NO. AWARDS: 427 for the year 2018.

APPLICATION INFO:
Program officers identify funding
opportunities in accordance with program
strategies. The Foundation does not accept
unsolicited proposals or letters of inquiry.
Duration: Typically one year. Renewal
possible.

PUBLICATIONS:
Annual report.

IRS I.D.: 94-3126848

BOARD OF DIRECTORS:
Rose McKinney-James, Chairperson
Melanie Audette
Robert Crane
Don Cravins, Jr.
Carlos Curbelo
Stephen Harper
Jason Mark
Kris Mayes
Gina McCarthy
Nicole Systrom
Sue Tierney

ADDRESS INQUIRIES TO:
Jason Mark, Chief Executive Officer
(See address above.)

ENVIRONMENTAL LAW INSTITUTE

1730 M Street, N.W.
Suite 700
Washington, DC 20036
(202) 939-3800
Fax: (202) 939-3868
E-mail: law@eli.org
Web Site: www.eli.org

TYPE:
Scholarships. Scholarships to annual
Environmental Law Course.

See entry 1771 for full listing.

FISHAMERICA FOUNDATION   [1965]

1001 North Fairfax Street, Suite 501
Alexandria, VA 22314
(703) 519-9691
Fax: (703) 519-1872
E-mail: fafgrants@asafishing.org
Web Site: www.fishamerica.org

FOUNDED: 1983

AREAS OF INTEREST:
Environment and conservation.

NAME(S) OF PROGRAMS:
- **Fisheries Conservation and Research Projects**

TYPE:
Challenge/matching grants; Project/program grants; Research grants; Seed money grants.

YEAR PROGRAM STARTED: 1983

PURPOSE:
To provide funding for on-the-ground projects aimed at enhancing fish populations, restoring fish habitat, improving water quality and advancing fisheries research to improve sportfishing success.

LEGAL BASIS:
Public foundation, 501(c)(3).

ELIGIBILITY:
Any nonprofit tax-exempt organization including conservation organizations, sporting clubs, civic groups, and local and state agencies can apply.

GEOG. RESTRICTIONS: United States and Canada.

FINANCIAL DATA:
Amount of support per award: Average $15,000 per grant.

Matching fund requirements: 1:1.

NO. MOST RECENT APPLICANTS: 162.

NO. AWARDS: 22.

REPRESENTATIVE AWARDS:
$20,000 to Mississippi Fish and Wildlife Foundation to improve water quality within the Bayou Pierre River and its tributaries; $50,000 to Toe River Valley Watch to implement the stream restoration project and greenway along Grassy Creek; $5,000 to New Hampshire B.A.S.S. Nation for the bass research project.

APPLICATION INFO:
Applicants should submit application, letter of support from the appropriate state resource agency biologist, and evidence of nonprofit status.

Duration: One year.

PUBLICATIONS:
Guidelines and application.

IRS I.D.: 36-3219015

BOARD OF DIRECTORS:
Chris Megan, Chairman
Zack Swanson, Vice Chairman
Jim Hubbard, Treasurer
Louis Chemi, Secretary
Bruce Akin
Dale Barnes
Ed Carter
Thomas Dammrich
Dan Ferris
Peter Foley
Patrick M. Gill
Kirk Immens
Carl Liederman
Dave J. Pfeiffer
Jesse Simpkins
Steve Smits

ADDRESS INQUIRIES TO:
Grants Manager
(See address above.)

THE GARDEN CLUB OF AMERICA   [1966]
14 East 60th Street, Third Floor
New York, NY 10022
(212) 753-8287
Fax: (212) 753-0134
E-mail: scholarshipapplications@gcamerica.org
Web Site: www.gcamerica.org/scholarships

FOUNDED: 1913

AREAS OF INTEREST:
Horticulture, botany, landscape architecture and environmental studies.

NAME(S) OF PROGRAMS:
- **The GCA and The Royal Horticultural Society Interchange Fellowships**

TYPE:
Exchange programs; Fellowships. A graduate academic year in the U.S. for a British student and a work-study program for an American at universities and botanical gardens in the U.K. in fields related to horticulture, botany and landscape design.

YEAR PROGRAM STARTED: 1948

PURPOSE:
To foster British-American relations through the interchange of scholars in horticulture, botany, landscape architecture and environmental studies.

LEGAL BASIS:
Nonprofit, national organization.

ELIGIBILITY:
GCA Fellowship is open to a British university graduate with a degree in horticulture, landscape architecture, botany, or environmental studies, or to a British student horticulturist with a recognized horticultural qualification.

RCA Fellowship is open to a single, unaccompanied American college graduate who has earned a B.A. or B.S. degree in horticulture, landscape architecture, or a related degree.

GEOG. RESTRICTIONS: United Kingdom and United States.

FINANCIAL DATA:
The Fellowship covers the cost of tuition, travel expenses, board, lodging and incidental college expenses. It also provides an allowance for personal needs.

Amount of support per award: Varies.

CO-OP FUNDING PROGRAMS: Sponsored jointly by The Garden Club of America and The Royal Horticultural Society.

NO. AWARDS: 2 annually.

APPLICATION INFO:
Guidelines and application forms are available online.

Duration: 10-month program.

Deadline: American scholars to the U.K.: January 15. British scholars to the U.S.: October 1.

PUBLICATIONS:
Program announcement.

ADDRESS INQUIRIES TO:
The Garden Club of America
Camila Bustos, Administrator
GCA/RHS Interchange Fellowships
(See address above.)

THE GARDEN CLUB OF AMERICA   [1967]
14 East 60th Street, Third Floor
New York, NY 10022
(212) 753-8287
Fax: (212) 753-0134
E-mail: scholarshipapplications@gcamerica.org
Web Site: www.gcamerica.org/scholarships

FOUNDED: 1913

AREAS OF INTEREST:
Native bird habitat.

NAME(S) OF PROGRAMS:
- **The Frances M. Peacock Scholarship for Native Bird Habitat**

TYPE:
Research grants. Financial assistance to college seniors and graduate students to study habitat-related issues that will benefit threatened or endangered bird species and lend useful information for land management decisions.

YEAR PROGRAM STARTED: 1994

PURPOSE:
To study areas in the U.S. that provide seasonal habitat for threatened or endangered native birds and to tend useful information for land-management decisions.

LEGAL BASIS:
Nonprofit, national organization.

ELIGIBILITY:
College seniors and graduate students only. (Second-semester juniors may apply for their senior year.)

GEOG. RESTRICTIONS: United States.

FINANCIAL DATA:
Amount of support per award: $4,500 annually. In special instances, because of two unusually fine candidates or two candidates working on one project, the award may be divided between two candidates.

NO. AWARDS: 1 to 2.

APPLICATION INFO:
Guidelines and application form are available online.

Duration: One year.

Deadline: March 31.

PUBLICATIONS:
Program announcement.

STAFF:
Camila Bustos, Administrator

ADDRESS INQUIRIES TO:
Frances M. Peacock Scholarship:
Prof. Irby Lovette
Cornell Lab of Ornithology
159 Sapsucker Woods Road
Ithaca, NY 14850-1999
E-mail: ijl2@cornell.edu
Web Site: www.birds.cornell.edu

*PLEASE NOTE:
Only one GCA scholarship, fellowship or award may be applied for annually.

THE GARDEN CLUB OF AMERICA   [1968]
14 East 60th Street, Third Floor
New York, NY 10022
(212) 753-8287
Fax: (212) 753-0134
E-mail: scholarshipapplications@gcamerica.org
Web Site: www.gcamerica.org/scholarships

FOUNDED: 1913

AREAS OF INTEREST:
Conservation, historic preservation and plant conservation, and tropical plant study.

NAME(S) OF PROGRAMS:
- **The Garden Club of America Award in Coastal Wetland Studies**

TYPE:
Fellowships. Funds one graduate student annually to support field-based wetlands research. A student may propose a wetlands program of his or her choice at a leading educational institution within the U.S. that specializes in wetlands studies. For the purposes of this scholarship, coastal wetlands are defined as those tidal or nontidal wetlands found within coastal states, including the Great Lakes.

YEAR PROGRAM STARTED: 1983

PURPOSE:
To promote wetlands conservation through the support of young scientists in their field work and research.

LEGAL BASIS:
Nonprofit, national organization.

ELIGIBILITY:
Graduate students pursuing advanced degrees in coastal wetlands science may apply. Applicant must be a U.S. citizen or permanent resident enrolled in a U.S.-based institution.

GEOG. RESTRICTIONS: United States.

FINANCIAL DATA:
Amount of support per award: $5,000.

NO. AWARDS: 1 annually.

APPLICATION INFO:
Guidelines and application form are available online.
Duration: One year.
Deadline: January 15 preceding the year of study.

PUBLICATIONS:
Program announcement.

ADDRESS INQUIRIES TO:
Camila Bustos, Administrator
The Garden Club of America
(See address above.)

*PLEASE NOTE:
Only one GCA scholarship, fellowship or award may be applied for annually.

THE GARDEN CLUB OF AMERICA [1969]
14 East 60th Street, Third Floor
New York, NY 10022
(212) 753-8287
Fax: (212) 753-0134
E-mail: scholarshipapplications@gcamerica.org
Web Site: www.gcamerica.org/scholarships

FOUNDED: 1913

AREAS OF INTEREST:
Conservation, historic preservation and plant conservation.

NAME(S) OF PROGRAMS:
- **GCA Awards for Summer Environmental Studies**

TYPE:
Scholarships.

YEAR PROGRAM STARTED: 1964

PURPOSE:
To encourage studies and careers in the environmental field.

LEGAL BASIS:
Nonprofit, national organization.

ELIGIBILITY:
Open to qualified undergraduates entering a summer program following their freshman, sophomore, or junior year.

FINANCIAL DATA:
Amount of support per award: $3,000.

NO. AWARDS: 1 or more.

APPLICATION INFO:
Application guidelines and form are available online.
Deadline: February 5.

PUBLICATIONS:
Program announcement.

ADDRESS INQUIRIES TO:
Camila Bustos, Administrator
(See address above.)

GREAT LAKES PROTECTION FUND [1970]
1560 Sherman Avenue
Suite 1370
Evanston, IL 60201
(847) 425-8150
Fax: (847) 424-9832
E-mail: info@glpf.org
Web Site: www.glpf.org

FOUNDED: 1989

AREAS OF INTEREST:
Health of the Great Lakes ecosystem.

TYPE:
Demonstration grants; Development grants; Seed money grants.

YEAR PROGRAM STARTED: 1990

PURPOSE:
To support projects that identify, demonstrate and promote regional action to enhance the health of the Great Lakes ecosystem.

LEGAL BASIS:
Nonprofit, multi-state endowment.

ELIGIBILITY:
The Great Lakes Protection Fund can support a wide variety of applicants. Nonprofit organizations (including environmental organizations, trade associations, and universities), for-profit businesses, government agencies, and individuals are eligible for Fund support. Successful applicants must maintain open access to certain project data, records and information.

All applicants must comply with the Fund's guidelines, show that the proposed work has clear public benefit to the Great Lakes basin, and that any related financial benefits will accrue to the public good. Government agencies must show that Fund support is not being used to replace or duplicate public funds.

FINANCIAL DATA:
Since inception, the Great Lakes Protection Fund has awarded more than $91,000,000 to support 296 projects with the goal of improving the health of the Great Lakes ecosystem.
Amount of support per award: Varies.
Total amount of support: Varies.

REPRESENTATIVE AWARDS:
$648,000 to Pennsylvania State University-Erie for Advancing Early Detection of Ballast-Mediated Invaders in the Great Lakes Program; $905,000 to Xylem,

Inc. for Great Lakes Impact Investment Platform Implementation Program; $1,230,000 to Environmental Consulting and Technology, Inc. for Great Lakes Resiliency and Finance Cluster Program.

APPLICATION INFO:
Potential applicants are encouraged to contact the Fund to discuss an idea, whether fully formed or not. If writing is preferred, the Fund will accept project concepts at any time. Applicant should review the funding guidelines for the characteristics of previously funded projects. Project concept should be no more than 1,500 words and should include the following information:
(1) environmental outcomes expected;
(2) proposed work;
(3) key personnel and;
(4) budget and funding plan.
Duration: Multiyear.

PUBLICATIONS:
Annual report; guidelines for funding; summary papers.

STAFF:
J. David Rankin, Executive Director
Drew Pfeifer, Vice President of Operations
Steve Cole, Vice President of Programs
Amy Elledge, Communications Manager
Shannon Donley, Project Implementation Manager
Janis Post, Business Manager

BOARD MEMBERS:
Kate Bartter
Timothy Bruno
Vita DeMarchi
Joanne So Young Dill
Tim Eder
Peter Gove
Richard Hylant
Jill Jedlicka
Kim Marotta
Andrew McElwaine
Don Ness
Laura Rubin
Kevin Shafer
Debra Shore

ADDRESS INQUIRIES TO:
E-mail: startaconversation@glpf.org (initial inquiry)
preproposal@glpf.org (preproposal submission)

THE JACOB AND TERESE HERSHEY FOUNDATION [1971]
3212 Smith Street
Suite 202
Houston, TX 77006-6622
(713) 529-7611
E-mail: dmueller@jthershey.org
Web Site: www.jthershey.org

FOUNDED: 1961

AREAS OF INTEREST:
Care facilities for domestic and wild animals, natural resources conservation, environmental preservation, parks and open space for public use, environmental education, land conservation, and reproductive rights, women's health, family planning and sex education.

TYPE:
Conferences/seminars; General operating grants; Matching gifts; Project/program grants; Seed money grants.

YEAR PROGRAM STARTED: 1961

PURPOSE:
To promote preservation and conservation of land, forests, streams, wetlands and habitat existing in a natural state and the defense of such resources; to establish, conserve and preserve parks and open space for public use; to help provide care facilities for animals and birds, both domestic and wild; to aid education efforts to promote environmental literacy and comprehension of the complexities of the web of life, particularly in museums and through citizen nonprofit organizations with similar purpose; to promote efforts toward population control.

LEGAL BASIS:
Private foundation.

ELIGIBILITY:
Grants are made to organizations that have tax-exempt status under Section 501(c)(3) of the Internal Revenue Code. Grants are not made to individuals, or for galas or fundraisers.

GEOG. RESTRICTIONS: Southwestern Colorado; Austin and Houston, Texas areas.

FINANCIAL DATA:
Amount of support per award: $2,000 to $50,000.
Total amount of support: $2,371,178 for the year 2019.

NO. MOST RECENT APPLICANTS: 72.

NO. AWARDS: 66.

APPLICATION INFO:
Guidelines are available on the Foundation web site.
Duration: One year. May reapply.
Deadline: Varies.

IRS I.D.: 74-6039126

ADDRESS INQUIRIES TO:
Deborah Mueller, Director of Operations and Grants Management
(See address above.)

THE HUDSON RIVER FOUNDATION [1972]
17 Battery Place, Suite 915
New York, NY 10004
(212) 483-7667
Fax: (212) 924-8325
E-mail: info@hudsonriver.org
Web Site: www.hudsonriver.org

FOUNDED: 1981

AREAS OF INTEREST:
Environmental, ecological and public policy aspects of the Hudson River estuary.

NAME(S) OF PROGRAMS:
• **Hudson River Fund**
• **Hudson River Improvement Fund**
• **New York City Environmental Fund**
• **New York-New Jersey Harbor & Estuary Program**

TYPE:
Capital grants; Fellowships; Research grants; Travel grants. The Hudson River Fund was created to meet the critical need for an independent institution to sponsor scientific research programs that would contribute to the development of sound public policy concerning the River's ecological system. The Hudson River Fund makes grants in five categories: Hudson River Research Grants, Travel Grants, Expedited Grants, Mark B. Baine Graduate Fellowship, and Tibor T. Polgar Fellowships.

The Hudson River Improvement Fund supports projects to enhance public use and enjoyment of the Hudson River's natural, scenic and cultural resources. The emphasis of the Improvement Fund is on physical projects requiring capital construction, development, or improvement.

The New York City Environmental Fund proposes to foster "restoration, care, public enjoyment of, and education about New York City's natural resources."

YEAR PROGRAM STARTED: 1983

PURPOSE:
To make science integral to decision-making with regard to the Hudson River and its watershed; to support competent stewardship of this extraordinary resource.

LEGAL BASIS:
Private foundation.

ELIGIBILITY:
Research must be focused on Hudson River.

FINANCIAL DATA:
Amount of support per award: Graduate Fellowships: Up to $16,000 for Master's students and up to $20,000 for doctoral students; Polgar Fellowships: $5,000.
Total amount of support: Varies.

NO. MOST RECENT APPLICANTS: 60 for research grants.

NO. AWARDS: 15.

APPLICATION INFO:
Guidelines are available online.
Duration: Hudson River Fund Research Fellowship: One to two years; Baine Graduate Fellowship: One year; Polgar Fellowship: One summer.
Deadline: Contact the Foundation.

PUBLICATIONS:
Annual Program Plan; *Hudson River Fund: Call for Proposals.*

EXECUTIVE DIRECTOR:
Clay Hiles

ILLINOIS CLEAN ENERGY COMMUNITY FOUNDATION [1973]
2 North LaSalle Street, Suite 1140
Chicago, IL 60602
(312) 372-5191
Fax: (312) 372-5190
E-mail: dobrien@illinoiscleanenergy.org
Web Site: www.illinoiscleanenergy.org

FOUNDED: 1999

AREAS OF INTEREST:
Improving the environmental quality of life in the state of Illinois and natural habitat preservation.

NAME(S) OF PROGRAMS:
• **Energy Program**
• **Natural Areas Program**

TYPE:
Grants-in-aid; Project/program grants. The Foundation provides financial support in two principal ways:
(1) Grantmaking: The Foundation provides grants on a competitive basis, in response to proposals submitted by organizations in accord with the Foundation's announced strategic priorities and the application process described below. The Foundation can provide several different types of financial support, including grants.

(2) Direct Initiatives: The Foundation identifies strategic opportunities to undertake large-scale, high-impact projects and special initiatives that further its program objectives in energy efficiency, renewable energy and natural areas conservation.

YEAR PROGRAM STARTED: 2001

PURPOSE:
To invest in clean energy development and land preservation efforts, working with communities and citizens to improve environmental quality in Illinois.

LEGAL BASIS:
Independent, nonprofit grantmaking institution.

ELIGIBILITY:
The Foundation provides funding to tax-exempt organizations, including governmental entities. The Foundation will not provide funding for remediation of environmentally impaired properties, technology research, promotion of proprietary products, reoccurring operating costs, political campaigns or lobbying, capital campaigns or support for an organization's endowment, or projects undertaken by individuals.

GEOG. RESTRICTIONS: Illinois.

FINANCIAL DATA:
Amount of support per award: Varies.
Matching fund requirements: Approximately $17,000,000 in grant obligations for the year 2019.

APPLICATION INFO:
Guidelines are available on the Foundation web site.
Duration: One to two years.

ADDRESS INQUIRIES TO:
Gabriela Martin
Program Director, Energy or
Frances Kane
Associate Program Officer, Natural Areas
(See address above.)

INTERNATIONAL CRANE FOUNDATION, INC.
E-11376 Shady Lane Road
Baraboo, WI 53913
(608) 356-9462
Fax: (608) 356-9465
E-mail: info@savingcranes.org
Web Site: www.savingcranes.org

TYPE:
Internships. Formal stipended internship programs in the fields of aviculture, crane ecology and conservation education.

See entry 1939 for full listing.

LANDSCAPE ARCHITECTURE FOUNDATION [1974]
1200 17th Street, N.W.
Suite 210
Washington, DC 20036
(202) 331-7070 ext. 14
E-mail: scholarships@lafoundation.org
Web Site: www.lafoundation.org/scholarship

FOUNDED: 1966

AREAS OF INTEREST:
The profession of landscape architecture.

NAME(S) OF PROGRAMS:
• **ASLA Council of Fellows Scholarship**
• **ASLA Florida Chapter Career Discovery Scholarships**

- ASLA-NY Designing in the Public Realm Scholarship
- EDSA Minority Scholarship
- Hawaii Chapter ASLA/David T. Woolsey Scholarship
- Steven G. King Play Environments Scholarship
- LAF Honor Scholarship for Inclusive Community Design
- LAF Honor Scholarship in Memory of Joe Lalli, FASLA
- Landscape Forms Scholarship in Memory of Peter Schaudt, FASLA
- Courtland Paul Scholarship
- Peridian International Inc./Rae L. Price, FASLA Scholarship
- Rain Bird Intelligent Use of Water Scholarship
- Douglas Dockery Thomas Fellowship in Garden History and Design

TYPE:
Fellowships; Scholarships. Awards for undergraduate and graduate students pursuing an education in landscape architecture.

PURPOSE:
To assist students enrolled in programs of landscape architecture.

LEGAL BASIS:
Nonprofit, tax-exempt foundation.

ELIGIBILITY:
Open to undergraduate and graduate students currently enrolled in a professional degree program in landscape architecture. Available to students in financial need who show promise and commitment to the profession.

GEOG. RESTRICTIONS: United States and Canada.

FINANCIAL DATA:
Amount of support per award: LAF Honor Scholarship for Inclusive Community Design: $10,000; LAF Honor Scholarship in Memory of Joe Lalli, FASLA: $20,000; All others: $2,000 to $5,000.
Total amount of support: Over $90,000 annually.

NO. MOST RECENT APPLICANTS: Varies.

NO. AWARDS: Varies.

APPLICATION INFO:
Application information is available on the web site.
Duration: One academic year.
Deadline: February 1.

PUBLICATIONS:
Guidelines.

ADDRESS INQUIRIES TO:
Program Manager
(See address and e-mail above.)

THE LEF FOUNDATION
P.O. Box 382066
Cambridge, MA 02238-2066
(617) 492-5333
E-mail: gen@lef-foundation.org
Web Site: lef-foundation.org

TYPE:
The Foundation gives grants for preproduction, production and post production of nonfiction film and video.

See entry 374 for full listing.

MARSHALL COMMUNITY FOUNDATION
614 Homer Road
Marshall, MI 49068
(269) 781-2273
Fax: (269) 781-9747
E-mail: info@marshallcf.org
Web Site: www.marshallcf.org

TYPE:
Project/program grants; Scholarships.

See entry 1404 for full listing.

NATIONAL FISH AND WILDLIFE FOUNDATION (NFWF)   [1975]
1133 15th Street, N.W.
Suite 1000
Washington, DC 20005
(202) 857-0166
Fax: (202) 857-0162
E-mail: info@nfwf.org
Web Site: www.nfwf.org

FOUNDED: 1984

AREAS OF INTEREST:
Sustaining, restoring and enhancing the nation's fish, wildlife, plants and habitats for current and future generations.

TYPE:
Challenge/matching grants; Project/program grants.

YEAR PROGRAM STARTED: 1986

PURPOSE:
To conserve natural resources through habitat protection, environmental education, natural resource management, species conservation and leadership training for conservation professionals.

LEGAL BASIS:
Private 501(c)(3) organization.

ELIGIBILITY:
Must be a 501(c)(3) organization. No grants to individuals.

GEOG. RESTRICTIONS: Primarily United States.

FINANCIAL DATA:
Amount of support per award: Varies.
Total amount of support: Approximately $750,000,000 in on-the-ground conservation impact.
Matching fund requirements: At least 1:1, preference for higher leverage.

NO. MOST RECENT APPLICANTS: Varies.

NO. AWARDS: Varies.

REPRESENTATIVE AWARDS:
$100,000 to Iowa Department of Natural Resources to restore 1,254 acres of bottomland hardwood forest in northeast Iowa on former agricultural lands. The project is working to reduce forest fragmentation, enhance water quality, and improve critical habitat for neo-tropical birds and other wildlife; $400,000 to Conservation Fund to reduce nutrient and sediment runoff entering Rockymarsh Run – a tributary to the Potomac River and ultimately the Chesapeake Bay.

APPLICATION INFO:
Application information may be obtained online.
Duration: Support usually lasts for one year. Renewals are on a case-by-case basis.

PUBLICATIONS:
Annual report; application guidelines.

IRS I.D.: 52-1384129

STAFF:
Jeff Trandahl, Executive Director/Chief Executive Officer
Lila Helms, Executive Vice President, External Affairs
Holly Bamford, Ph.D., Chief Conservation Officer
Tokunbo Falayi, Chief Financial Officer

BOARD OF DIRECTORS:
Edwin R. Rodriguez, Jr., Chairman
Sydney McNiff Johnson, Vice Chairperson
Reuben Mark, Vice Chairperson
Max C. Chapman, Jr.
J. Michael Cline
Bruce Culpepper
John Dane, III
John V. Faraci, Jr.
Blas Fonalledas
Dale Hall
Harold Hamm
Dr. Neil Jacobs
Ryan Lance
Don J. McGrath
R. King Milling
Kit Moncrief
Jennifer Mull Neuhaus
Trina Overlock
Chad Pike
Aurelia Skipwith
Federico Stubbe
John A. Tomke
Mark J. Vallely
K.C. Walsh

ADDRESS INQUIRIES TO:
Appropriate Partnership Office Director
(See address above.)

NATIONAL INSTITUTE OF ENVIRONMENTAL HEALTH SCIENCES   [1976]
Division of Extramural Research and Training
MD K3-05
111 T.W. Alexander Drive
Research Triangle Park, NC 27709
(984) 287-3285
E-mail: mastin@niehs.nih.gov
Web Site: www.niehs.nih.gov

FOUNDED: 1966

AREAS OF INTEREST:
Research on environmental agents and chemicals and their effects on human health.

NAME(S) OF PROGRAMS:
- Environmental Health Sciences Research and Training Grants

TYPE:
Conferences/seminars; Demonstration grants; Development grants; Fellowships; Project/program grants; Research grants; Training grants. NIEHS pursues its mission by supporting basic and applied research on the consequences of the exposure of humans to potentially toxic or harmful agents in the environment.

Research of interest encompasses studies that relate to the biological effects of environmental chemicals and physical factors including such agents as hazardous gases, suspended particles, aerosols, industrial by-products and intermediates, heavy metals, trace elements, food additives, adulterants and pesticides.

Research Training Programs support individuals at both the predoctoral and postdoctoral levels in the areas of environmental toxicology, environmental pathology, environmental mutagenesis and environmental epidemiology.

YEAR PROGRAM STARTED: 1966

PURPOSE:
To support research and research training in environmental health.

LEGAL BASIS:
Government agency authorized under Section 301(d), Public Health Services Act; 42 U.S.C. 241; 42 C.F.R. 52.

ELIGIBILITY:
Universities, research institutes and other public or private institutions may apply on behalf of qualified researchers. Small businesses may apply for SBIR grants.

GEOG. RESTRICTIONS: United States.

FINANCIAL DATA:
Funds are provided, as available, for all allowable expenses associated with approved research projects.
Amount of support per award: Varies.
Total amount of support: Varies.

NO. AWARDS: Approximately 1,200.

APPLICATION INFO:
Guidelines are available on the web site.
Duration: Total grant project periods may not exceed five years and are renewable on a competitive basis at the end of the project period. Average project period length is currently four years.
Deadline: Varies with the specific grant.

PUBLICATIONS:
Fact book; special announcements.

ADDRESS INQUIRIES TO:
J. Patrick Mastin, Ph.D.
Deputy Director
(See address above.)

NATIONAL WILDLIFE FEDERATION   [1977]
11100 Wildlife Center Drive
Reston, VA 20190-5362
(703) 438-6265
Fax: (703) 438-6468
E-mail: fellows@nwf.org
ecoleaders@nwf.org
Web Site: www.nwf.org
www.nwfecoleaders.org

FOUNDED: 1936

AREAS OF INTEREST:
Environment, conservation and sustainability.

NAME(S) OF PROGRAMS:
• **NWF EcoLeaders Fellowships**

TYPE:
Fellowships.

YEAR PROGRAM STARTED: 2014

PURPOSE:
To give well-qualified and highly motivated individuals substantive practical experience.

LEGAL BASIS:
Nonprofit organization able to carry on a defined amount of lobbying.

ELIGIBILITY:
Graduate students from any college or university within the U.S. may apply. Applications are invited from students in all disciplines and are not limited to environmental studies majors.

Current and former employees of National Wildlife Federation and former NWF Campus Ecology Fellows are ineligible to apply. Former NWF interns are eligible to apply following one year from their final work date.

Applicant must be enrolled in school through the duration of the four-month grant period.

GEOG. RESTRICTIONS: United States.

FINANCIAL DATA:
Amount of support per award: Up to $5,000.
Total amount of support: Varies.

NO. MOST RECENT APPLICANTS: Approximately 400.

NO. AWARDS: Varies.

APPLICATION INFO:
Information is available on the web site.
Duration: Four months.
Deadline: Varies.

PUBLICATIONS:
Program description.

OFFICERS:
Collin O'Mara, President and Chief Executive Officer

ADDRESS INQUIRIES TO:
E-mail: fellows@nwf.org

NEW YORK SEA GRANT   [1978]
125 Nassau Hall
SUNY at Stony Brook
Stony Brook, NY 11794-5001
(631) 632-6905
Fax: (631) 632-6917
E-mail: nyseagrant@stonybrook.edu
Web Site: seagrant.sunysb.edu

FOUNDED: 1971

AREAS OF INTEREST:
Coastal resource management, fisheries biology, contaminants and environmental quality, environmental processes and marine economics, seafood use and technology, recreation and tourism, human dimensions, marine aquaculture, youth education, biotech, and coastal processes.

TYPE:
Awards/prizes; Conferences/seminars; Development grants; Endowments; Fellowships; Internships; Project/program grants; Research grants; Scholarships; Technical assistance; Travel grants. Principally grants for laboratory and field studies, publications and communication and curriculum development.

YEAR PROGRAM STARTED: 1971

PURPOSE:
To foster the wise use and development of coastal resources through research, education and training.

LEGAL BASIS:
A cooperative research and education activity of the State University of New York and Cornell University, as well as NOAA's National Sea Grant College Program.

ELIGIBILITY:
Applicant must be a member of the faculty of an institution of higher learning or of a nonprofit organization. Projects must address issues relevant to New York state. In most cases, applicants are affiliated with New York institutions.

FINANCIAL DATA:
Amount of support per award: Varies.

Total amount of support: $1,000,000.
Matching fund requirements: 50% of funds requested must be provided by applicant from non-federal sources.

NO. MOST RECENT APPLICANTS: Around 100 for most biennial solicitations.

NO. AWARDS: Approximately 10 per year.

APPLICATION INFO:
Application information is available on the web site.
Duration: One or two years. Continuation possible.
Deadline: Biennial with occasional out-of-cycle.

ADDRESS INQUIRIES TO:
Lane Smith, Research Coordinator
E-mail: lane.smith@stonybrook.edu

JESSIE SMITH NOYES FOUNDATION   [1979]
122 East 42nd Street
Suite 2501
New York, NY 10168
(212) 684-6577
Fax: (212) 689-6549
E-mail: noyes@noyes.org
Web Site: noyes.org

FOUNDED: 1947

AREAS OF INTEREST:
Racial justice, environmental justice, and gender equity.

TYPE:
General operating grants; Project/program grants.

PURPOSE:
To support people-powered organizations participating in intersecting social-justice movements across the U.S.

LEGAL BASIS:
Family foundation.

ELIGIBILITY:
The Foundation makes grants to tax-exempt organizations with 501(c)(3) classification from the IRS for work within the U.S. It will not consider requests for endowments, capital construction, or deficit financing.

GEOG. RESTRICTIONS: United States, primarily Mississippi and New York.

FINANCIAL DATA:
Amount of support per award: Typically, $10,000 to $75,000.

NO. AWARDS: 78 for the year 2020.

REPRESENTATIVE AWARDS:
$37,000 to Black Love Resists in the Rust, Buffalo, NY; $35,00 to It Takes Roots, Takoma Park, MD; $25,00 to People's Advocacy Institute, Jackson, MS.

APPLICATION INFO:
The Foundation does not accept unsolicited proposals.
Duration: Varies.
Deadline: Most grants approved during spring, summer and fall Board meetings.

IRS I.D.: 13-5600408

STAFF:
Rini Banerjee, President
Gabby Dizon, Grants and Operations Manager

ADDRESS INQUIRIES TO:
Gabby Dizon
Grants and Operations Manager
(See address above.)

PATAGONIA INC. [1980]
259 West Santa Clara Street
Ventura, CA 93001
(805) 643-8616
E-mail: grants@patagonia.com
Web Site: www.patagonia.com/how-we-fund

AREAS OF INTEREST:
Preservation and protection of the natural environment.

NAME(S) OF PROGRAMS:
● **Environmental Grant Program**

TYPE:
General operating grants; Product donations; Project/program grants. Funds to help local groups working to protect local habitats and to force the government to abide by its own laws in regards to biodiversity and ecosystem protection.

YEAR PROGRAM STARTED: 1987

PURPOSE:
To assist groups who strive to preserve and restore the natural environment.

LEGAL BASIS:
Private corporation giving program.

ELIGIBILITY:
Applicants must be 501(c)(3) tax-exempt organizations. Support is given to small, grassroots, activist organizations with provocative direct-action agendas, working on multipronged campaigns to preserve and protect the environment. No grants for more general environmental education efforts. Contact Patagonia Inc. for complete details.

GEOG. RESTRICTIONS: Argentina, Australia, Austria, Belgium, Canada, Chile, Czechia, Denmark, France, Germany, Ireland, Italy, Japan, Korea, Luxembourg, The Netherlands, Norway, Spain, Sweden, Switzerland, United Kingdom and United States.

FINANCIAL DATA:
Company pledges one percent of sales to grassroots environmental groups.
Amount of support per award: $5,000 to $20,000.

NO. AWARDS: 954 grants to environmental groups in fiscal year 2017.

APPLICATION INFO:
Application information is available on the web site.
Duration: One year. Applicants must reapply for continued funding.
Deadline: Varies by program.

PUBLICATIONS:
Program guidelines.

ADDRESS INQUIRIES TO:
Lisa Myers
Senior Manager of Environmental Grants
(See address above.)

*PLEASE NOTE:
Telephone calls are discouraged.

RESOURCES FOR THE FUTURE [1981]
1616 P Street, N.W., Suite 600
Washington, DC 20036-1436
(202) 328-5000
Fax: (202) 939-3460
E-mail: info@rff.org
Web Site: www.rff.org

AREAS OF INTEREST:
Economics, policy sciences or issues relating to the environment and natural resources of energy.

NAME(S) OF PROGRAMS:
● **Summer Research Internship**

TYPE:
Awards/prizes; Internships. The Summer Research Internship is a paid internship for advanced graduates, graduates and early career professionals to prepare for careers that engage in academic and policy-relevant research.

PURPOSE:
To offer students and recent graduates the opportunity to experience working in a world renowned center for environmental and energy research.

ELIGIBILITY:
Candidates should display strong writing skills and a desire to understand complex environmental policy problems amenable to interdisciplinary methods. The ability to work without supervision in a careful and conscientious manner is essential. Highly motivated candidates in the social and natural sciences with training in economics and quantitative methods, or with keen interest in public policy, are encouraged to apply.

Priority consideration is given to graduate students.

FINANCIAL DATA:
Amount of support per award: $525 stipend per week. No housing assistance is provided.

APPLICATION INFO:
All applications must be submitted electronically. Completed application, supplemental questions and the following materials must be uploaded:
(1) a cover letter that explains applicant's interest in and how their qualifications match to a specific opening;
(2) resume summarizing applicant's qualifications for the position;
(3) copy of postsecondary academic transcripts (unofficial transcripts are acceptable at this stage);
(4) a writing sample of three to fives pages from a recent paper (excerpts are acceptable) and;
(5) the name, address, telephone number and e-mail information for two references.
Duration: 10 weeks during the summer.

THE RUSSELL FAMILY FOUNDATION [1982]
3025 Harborview Drive
Gig Harbor, WA 98335
(253) 858-5050
Fax: (253) 851-0460
E-mail: info@trff.org
Web Site: www.trff.org

FOUNDED: 1999

AREAS OF INTEREST:
Environmental sustainability.

NAME(S) OF PROGRAMS:
● **Environmental Education Fund**

TYPE:
General operating grants; Project/program grants. Grants focused on environmental education for grades five to 12 in Jefferson, King, Kitsap, Pierce and Thurston counties.

YEAR PROGRAM STARTED: 2001

PURPOSE:
To implement strategies that raise awareness and understanding of our environment and the importance of protecting it.

ELIGIBILITY:
Organizations must be 501(c)(3) or nonprofit entities such as public schools and school districts, and must be located in and/or provide services within the Puget Sound region. No grants to individuals.

GEOG. RESTRICTIONS: Western Washington state (Jefferson, King, Kitsap, Pierce and Thurston counties).

FINANCIAL DATA:
Amount of support per award: $10,000 to $40,000. Average grant: $25,000.

APPLICATION INFO:
Submit letter of inquiry through Foundation's online grantmaking system. Full proposals are accepted by invitation only.
Duration: One year. Renewal by reapplication.
Deadline: October.

ADDRESS INQUIRIES TO:
Linsey Sauer, Grants Manager
(See address above.)

SMITHSONIAN ENVIRONMENTAL RESEARCH CENTER (SERC) [1983]
647 Contees Wharf Road
Edgewater, MD 21037
(443) 482-2217
Fax: (443) 482-2380
E-mail: gustafsond@si.edu
Web Site: serc.si.edu

FOUNDED: 1965

AREAS OF INTEREST:
Environmental research and education.

NAME(S) OF PROGRAMS:
● **Professional Training**

TYPE:
Fellowships; Internships. The Internship Program enables undergraduates, recent graduates and graduate students to work on specific projects under the direction of the Center's professional staff and is tailored to provide the maximum educational benefit to each participant. Graduate students and undergraduates may conduct independent projects with the approval of the staff member with whom they plan to study.

Subject matter of the projects includes terrestrial and estuarine environmental research within the disciplines of mathematics, chemistry, microbiology, botany, zoology, and environmental education.

Fellowships are offered annually at the postdoctoral, predoctoral and graduate levels.

Internships are offered three times per year at the undergraduate levels, recent graduate, or beginning Master's student.

YEAR PROGRAM STARTED: 1972

PURPOSE:
To offer undergraduate and graduate-level students a unique opportunity to gain exposure to and experience in environmental research.

LEGAL BASIS:
Research unit of the Smithsonian Institution.

ELIGIBILITY:
Applicants must be qualified students from academic institutions in the U.S. or abroad. The SERC will accept applications from interested individuals who are in a position to commit themselves fully to the completion of

a project. Selection is based upon the student's academic credentials, extent of relevant training or experience, letters of recommendation and the congruence of the student's expressed goals with those of the Professional Training Program.

FINANCIAL DATA:
Dorm space is available for $105 per week and does not include board. Space is limited.
Amount of support per award: Interns receive $600 per week; $55,000 postdoctoral/senior stipend; $40,000 predoctoral stipend; $8,000 graduate student; research allowances are additional.

NO. MOST RECENT APPLICANTS: 49 fellowship applicants and 460 internship applicants for the year 2019.

NO. AWARDS: 1 to 3 fellowships and 35 to 50 internships for the year 2019.

APPLICATION INFO:
Application materials and additional information regarding fellowships can be obtained from the Smithsonian Institution Office of Fellowships and Grants, E-mail: siofg@ofg.si.edu.

Applicants must use the Smithsonian On-Line Academic Appointment (SOLAA) web site for application submittal: https://solaa.si.edu/solaa/solaahome.html.
Duration: Intern Appointments: Generally 10 to 16 weeks; Fellowships: One year, with renewal.
Deadline: November 1 for most fellowships; James Smithson Fellowship: January 15. Internships: November 15 for Winter/Spring Session; February 15 for Summer Session; June 1 for Fall Session.

PUBLICATIONS:
Application guidelines.

STAFF:
Anson H. Hines, Director
Patrick Megonigal, Associate Director of Research
Daniel E. Gustafson, Jr., Professional Training Coordinator

ADDRESS INQUIRIES TO:
Daniel E. Gustafson, Jr.
Professional Training Coordinator
(See address and e-mail above.)

SOIL AND WATER CONSERVATION SOCIETY [1984]
945 S.W. Ankeny Road
Ankeny, IA 50023-9723
(515) 289-2331
E-mail: awards@swcs.org
Web Site: www.swcs.org

AREAS OF INTEREST:
Soil, water and related natural resource management.

NAME(S) OF PROGRAMS:
● **Kenneth E. Grant Research Scholarship**

TYPE:
Research grants. Provides financial aid to members of the Society for graduate-level research on a specific conservation topic that will help the Society carry out its mission of fostering the science and the art of soil, water, and related natural resource management to achieve sustainability.

YEAR PROGRAM STARTED: 1978

PURPOSE:
To foster the science and the art of soil, water and related natural resource management to achieve sustainability; to promote and practice an ethic recognizing the interdependence of people and the environment.

ELIGIBILITY:
Open to members of the Society who have demonstrated integrity, ability and competence to complete the specified study topic. Applicants must be eligible for graduate work at an accredited institution and show reasonable need for financial assistance. Must be members of the Society for at least one year.

FINANCIAL DATA:
Amount of support per award: $500 for the year 2021.

NO. AWARDS: 1.

APPLICATION INFO:
Applicants must provide responses to questions in the online application. The following supplemental materials can be uploaded during the application process:
(1) a proposal (three pages maximum) that supports completing a specified research project related to this year's research and;
(2) budget for the project.
Included in the proposal should be material supporting the applicant's ability to meet the eligibility requirements outlined above.

Scholarship application can be completed and submitted electronically.
Duration: One year.
Deadline: April 23.

ADDRESS INQUIRIES TO:
See e-mail address above.

SOIL AND WATER CONSERVATION SOCIETY [1985]
945 S.W. Ankeny Road
Ankeny, IA 50023-9723
(515) 289-2331
E-mail: awards@swcs.org
Web Site: www.swcs.org

AREAS OF INTEREST:
Soil, water and related natural resource management.

NAME(S) OF PROGRAMS:
● **Melvin H. Cohee Student Leader Conservation Scholarship**

TYPE:
Scholarships. The Cohee Scholarship provides financial assistance to Society members who are in their junior or senior year of full-time undergraduate study or are pursuing graduate level studies with a natural resource conservation orientation at a properly accredited college or university.

PURPOSE:
To foster the science and the art of soil, water and natural resource management to achieve sustainability.

ELIGIBILITY:
Applicants must be a members of SWCS for at least one year prior to the application deadline and in their junior or senior year of full-time undergraduate study in fall of 2022 or pursuing graduate level studies in a natural resource field.

Members of the SWCS Awards Committee and their immediate families are not eligible.

FINANCIAL DATA:
Amount of support per award: Up to $500 for the year 2021.

NO. AWARDS: 1.

APPLICATION INFO:
Application form must be submitted electronically. All supporting materials are to be uploaded in the online application.
Duration: One year.
Deadline: April 23.

ADDRESS INQUIRIES TO:
See e-mail address above.

SOIL AND WATER CONSERVATION SOCIETY [1986]
945 S.W. Ankeny Road
Ankeny, IA 50023-9723
(515) 289-2331
E-mail: awards@swcs.org
Web Site: www.swcs.org

AREAS OF INTEREST:
Soil, water and related natural resource management.

NAME(S) OF PROGRAMS:
● **Donald A. Williams Soil Conservation Scholarship**

TYPE:
Scholarships. The Williams Scholarship provides financial assistance to Society members who are currently employed, but who wish to improve their technical or administrative competence in a conservation-related field through course work at an accredited college or through a program of special study.

PURPOSE:
To foster the science and the art of soil, water and natural resource management to achieve sustainability.

ELIGIBILITY:
Applicant must:
(1) be a member of SWCS for at least one year prior to the application deadline;
(2) have demonstrated integrity, ability, and competence in his or her work and possess skills gained through training or experience;
(3) have completed at least one year of full-time employment in a natural resource conservation endeavor and;
(4) be currently employed in a natural resource-related field.

Members of the SWCS Awards Committee and their immediate families are not eligible.

FINANCIAL DATA:
Amount of support per award: $1,000.

NO. AWARDS: 1.

APPLICATION INFO:
Application form is to be submitted electronically. All supporting materials must be uploaded in the online application.
Deadline: April 23.

ADDRESS INQUIRIES TO:
See e-mail address above.

THE ROBERT & PATRICIA SWITZER FOUNDATION [1987]
P.O. Box 293
Belfast, ME 04915-0293
(207) 338-5654
E-mail: erin@switzernetwork.org
Web Site: www.switzernetwork.org

FOUNDED: 1987

AREAS OF INTEREST:
Environment.

NAME(S) OF PROGRAMS:
- **Switzer Environmental Fellowship Program**

TYPE:
Fellowships; Project/program grants. Annual fellowship to recognize environmental leaders who have the ability and determination to make a significant impact on environmental quality.

YEAR PROGRAM STARTED: 1987

PURPOSE:
To support highly talented graduate students in California and New England whose studies are directed toward improving environmental quality and who demonstrate leadership in their field.

ELIGIBILITY:
Applicants must meet the following criteria: (1) be a U.S. citizen, permanent resident or Deferred Action for Childhood Arrivals (DACA) recipient; (2) be enrolled in an accredited institution in California or New England and; (3) have strong academic qualifications.

Master's degree candidates must have completed at least one semester of course work.

Ph.D. candidates must have completed at least three years of doctoral work or passed their qualifying exams.

GEOG. RESTRICTIONS: California and New England.

FINANCIAL DATA:
Amount of support per award: $15,000, paid in two equal installments, the first in June and the second in late January or early February.
Total amount of support: $300,000.

NO. MOST RECENT APPLICANTS: 300.

NO. AWARDS: 20 annually; 10 in California and 10 in New England.

APPLICATION INFO:
Application information is available on the web site.
Duration: One year.
Deadline: Early January.

ADDRESS INQUIRIES TO:
Erin Lloyd, Program Director
(See address above.)

U.S. DEPARTMENT OF AGRICULTURE [1988]

1400 Independence Avenue, S.W.
Stop 0506
Washington, DC 20250-0510
(202) 690-1612
Fax: (202) 720-4619
E-mail: shanita.landon@usda.gov
Web Site: www.fsa.usda.gov

FOUNDED: 1933

AREAS OF INTEREST:
The conservation of the nation's soil, forest and water resources.

CONSULTING OR VOLUNTEER SERVICES:
Technical assistance is provided by federal and state agencies cooperating with this program.

NAME(S) OF PROGRAMS:
- **Emergency Conservation Program (ECP)**

TYPE:
Grants-in-aid. Cost-share assistance with agricultural producers to rehabilitate agricultural lands damaged by natural disasters. Assistance may also be provided for carrying out emergency water conservation measures during periods of severe drought.

YEAR PROGRAM STARTED: 1957

PURPOSE:
To provide emergency funding and technical assistance for farmers and ranchers to rehabilitate farmland damaged by natural disasters and for carrying out emergency water conservation measures in periods of severe drought.

LEGAL BASIS:
Government agency, authorized by P.L. 95-334, August 1978.

ELIGIBILITY:
Applicants are limited to agricultural producers, such as owners, landlords, tenants or sharecroppers of farms or ranches used to produce grains, row crops, livestock, vegetables, hay, orchards, vineyards, seed crops or other agricultural commodities commercially.

All landowners, regardless of race, sex, religion, marital status, disability, color, age or national origin, may apply for cost-sharing.

GEOG. RESTRICTIONS: United States.

FINANCIAL DATA:
Amount of support per award: Maximum of $500,000 per person per disaster.
Matching fund requirements: Producers are required to contribute the difference between the cost-share amount and the total cost of each ECP practice.

ADDRESS INQUIRIES TO:
Contact the nearest FSA County Office where your land is located.

U.S. ENVIRONMENTAL PROTECTION AGENCY [1989]

Office of Superfund Remediation and Technology Innovation (5202P)
1200 Pennsylvania Avenue, N.W.
Washington, DC 20460
(703) 603-8714
E-mail: fine.ellyn@epa.gov
Web Site: www.epa.gov/superfund

FOUNDED: 1970

AREAS OF INTEREST:
Cleanup of hazardous waste releases into the environment.

NAME(S) OF PROGRAMS:
- **Superfund State and Indian Tribe Core Program Cooperative Agreements**
- **Superfund State, Political Subdivision, and Indian Tribe Site-Specific Cooperative Agreements**

TYPE:
Project/program grants. Superfund State and Indian Tribe Core Program Cooperative Agreements: This program seeks to effectively implement the statutory requirements of the Comprehensive Environmental Response, Compensation, and Liability Act (CERCLA), Section 121(f) for state involvement. It is intended to provide funds to conduct CERCLA activities which are not assignable to specific sites, but support a recipient's site-specific response program.

Superfund State, Political Subdivision, and Indian Tribe Site-Specific Cooperative Agreements: This program proposes to: (1) conduct site characterization activities at potential or confirmed hazardous waste sites; (2) undertake response planning and implementation actions at sites on the National Priorities List (NPL) to clean up the hazardous waste sites that are found to pose hazards to human health and; (3) effectively implement the statutory requirements of CERCLA 121(f) which mandates substantial and meaningful state involvement.

YEAR PROGRAM STARTED: 1981

PURPOSE:
To undertake removal actions at NPL and non-NPL sites to protect the public from the release of hazardous materials; to conduct preremedial activities to determine if sites require listing on the NPL; to perform remedial planning and remedial implementation actions in response to releases on the NPL; to clean up the hazardous waste sites that are found to pose the most imminent threat to human health; to support state involvement in the Superfund program.

LEGAL BASIS:
Comprehensive Environmental Response, Compensation and Liability Act of 1980 (Superfund) (P.L. 96-510), as amended by The Superfund Amendments and Reauthorization Act of 1986 (SARA) (P.L. 99-499), The Small Business Liability Relief and Brown Fields Revitalization Act (PL 107-118).

ELIGIBILITY:
States (and political subdivisions thereof), commonwealths, U.S. territories and possessions, and federally recognized Indian tribal governments, including intertribal consortia.

GEOG. RESTRICTIONS: United States and its territories.

FINANCIAL DATA:
Amount of support per award: Varies.

ADDRESS INQUIRIES TO:
Ellyn Fine, State Coordinator
(See address above.)

U.S. SOCIETY ON DAMS

9975 Wadsworth Parkway
Suite K-2, 145
Westminster, CO 80021
(303) 792-8753
Fax: (303) 792-8782
E-mail: info@ussdams.org
Web Site: www.ussdams.org

TYPE:
Awards/prizes; Scholarships.

See entry 2409 for full listing.

UNIVERSITY OF PITTSBURGH [1990]

Pymatuning Laboratory of Ecology
13142 Hartstown Road
Linesville, PA 16424
(814) 273-0416
Fax: (814) 683-2302
E-mail: pymlab@pitt.edu
Web Site: ple.pitt.edu

FOUNDED: 1949

AREAS OF INTEREST:
Ecology research.

NAME(S) OF PROGRAMS:
- **Leasure K. Darbaker Prize in Botany**
- **McKinley Research Fund**
- **Pape Research Fund**

TYPE:
Research grants. The Leasure K. Darbaker Prize in Botany is an annual award available for support of botanically related studies at the graduate or postdoctoral level.

The G. McKinley Research Fund and the Pape Research Fund of the Pittsburgh Foundation provide grants for support of graduate and postdoctoral research in ecology. Several are awarded each summer.

LEGAL BASIS:
Department of the University of Pittsburgh.

ELIGIBILITY:
Proposals are welcome at all academic graduate and postdoctoral levels for research in any area of ecology.

Awards are granted for work to be carried out at the facility in northwestern Pennsylvania.

FINANCIAL DATA:
Funds for travel, equipment, supplies, assistants and room and board at the laboratory may be included.
Amount of support per award: Up to $3,500 per award.
Total amount of support: Approximately $14,000 annually.

APPLICATION INFO:
Application information can be found at the web site.
Deadline: February 24.

PUBLICATIONS:
Application guidelines.

ADDRESS INQUIRIES TO:
Chris Davis, Assistant Director
(See address above.)

THE UNIVERSITY OF SYDNEY [1991]
Scholarships Office
Level 4, Jane Foss Russell Building G02
The University of Sydney N.S.W. 2006
Australia
61 (02) 8627 1444
E-mail: scholarships.officer@sydney.edu.au
Web Site: www.sydney.edu.au/scholarships

FOUNDED: 1850

AREAS OF INTEREST:
Water conservation.

NAME(S) OF PROGRAMS:
- **Richard Claude Mankin Scholarship**

TYPE:
Scholarships. Postdoctoral award for research and postgraduate for research leading to a higher degree. Tenable at the University of Sydney.

YEAR PROGRAM STARTED: 1973

PURPOSE:
To promote research related to water conservation at the University of Sydney.

LEGAL BASIS:
University.

ELIGIBILITY:
Candidates may be of postgraduate or postdoctoral standing at the University of Sydney.

FINANCIAL DATA:
The scholarship does not cover tuition fees payable by international students.
Amount of support per award: $35,629 AUD per annum for the year 2021.

NO. AWARDS: 1 offered as vacancy occurs and funds are available.

APPLICATION INFO:
Application information is available on the web site.
Duration: Two years for Master's candidate. Up to three years for Ph.D. candidate. In extraordinary circumstances, an additional six months may be granted to Ph.D. candidates.

VIRGINIA ENVIRONMENTAL ENDOWMENT [1992]
919 East Main Street, Suite 1070
Richmond, VA 23219
(804) 644-5000
Fax: (804) 644-0603
E-mail: info@vee.org
Web Site: www.vee.org

FOUNDED: 1977

AREAS OF INTEREST:
Environmental improvement.

NAME(S) OF PROGRAMS:
- **Community Conservation Program**
- **James River Water Quality Improvement Program**
- **Kanawha and Ohio River Valleys Program**
- **Virginia Program**

TYPE:
Challenge/matching grants; Demonstration grants; Project/program grants; Seed money grants. Provides grants to projects that demonstrate feasibility, innovation and appropriateness to the Endowment's purpose and priorities. Improvement of the quality of the environment in the Commonwealth of Virginia, especially on-the-ground water quality improvement and monitoring; land conservation; Chesapeake Bay conservation, outreach and education; and environmental literacy and climate resiliency. Programs addressing water quality and the effects of water pollution on public health and the environment in the Kanawha River and Ohio River valleys of Kentucky and West Virginia.

YEAR PROGRAM STARTED: 1977

PURPOSE:
To improve the quality of the environment by using its capital, expertise and resources to encourage all sectors to work together to prevent pollution, conserve natural resources and promote environmental literacy.

LEGAL BASIS:
Tax-exempt, grantmaking organization 501(c)(4).

ELIGIBILITY:
The Endowment makes grants to nonprofit, tax-exempt, charitable organizations and institutions, and governmental agencies. It encourages requests for specific projects that promise measurable results to improve the environment. Applicants should describe specifically how they propose to measure the success of a grant project. Grant funds are not provided for general support, overhead, indirect costs, capital projects, land purchases, building construction or renovation, endowments, lawsuits or to individuals.

GEOG. RESTRICTIONS: The state of Virginia and the Kanawha and Ohio River valleys of Kentucky and West Virginia.

FINANCIAL DATA:
Reviewed asset value: $38,636,833 as of March 31, 2018.
Amount of support per award: Varies.
Total amount of support: $542,970 for fiscal year ended March 31, 2018.
Matching fund requirements: At least a 1:1 match is normally required.

CO-OP FUNDING PROGRAMS: The Endowment welcomes opportunities for collaboration.

NO. MOST RECENT APPLICANTS: 70 for fiscal year 2018.

NO. AWARDS: 29 for fiscal year ended March 31, 2018.

APPLICATION INFO:
Two copies of the complete proposal, signed by the organization's chief executive officer or board chairman, must be received by the deadline date. The Endowment does not review or comment on preliminary proposals.

Each proposal must include the following information:
(1) a cover letter identifying the applicant, project title, grant request, matching funds, project schedule, and whether the proposal is being submitted to the Virginia Program, the James River Water Quality Improvement Program, or the Kanawha and Ohio River Valleys Program;
(2) a project description, limited to five pages, clearly stating the need for the project, goals and objectives and how they will be achieved, how project results will be measured, and relationship to other work being done in the field;
(3) a description of the organization, names and qualifications of key project staff, a list of the members of the governing board, the current operating budget, and a copy of the current tax-exempt ruling from the IRS, if applicable;
(4) a line-item budget for the proposed project showing total project costs, the amount and proposed allocation of grant funds requested from the Endowment, and all sources and amounts of matching funds, which must equal or exceed the requested grant;
(5) the project schedule, with specific beginning and ending dates for requested grant support and;
(6) a detailed plan for evaluating and disseminating project results, for continuing project activities, and for raising future financial support.

For delivery by U.S. Mail, address to Joseph Maroon, Executive Director, Virginia Environmental Endowment, P.O. Box 790, Richmond, VA 23218-0790.

The complete list of priorities, grant criteria and required documentation is available on the Endowment's web site listed above.

Duration: Stipulated with specific projects. One year preferred.

Deadline: Community Conservation Program: January 15; James River Water Quality Improvement Program: June 15; Kanawha and Ohio River Valleys Program: December 1; Virginia Program: June 15 and December 1.

PUBLICATIONS:
Annual report, including guidelines.

IRS I.D.: 54-1041973

STAFF:
Joseph Maroon, Executive Director

DIRECTORS:
Robin D. Baliles
Dixon M. Butler
Lawrence Kochard
Nina Randolph
Nancy N. Rogers
Robert B. Smith, Jr.
Blair Winbush

ADDRESS INQUIRIES TO:
Joseph Maroon, Executive Director
(See address above.)

*SPECIAL STIPULATIONS:
No preliminary proposal reviews are
provided; full proposals are required.

WEEDEN FOUNDATION [1993]
P.O. Box 606
Bedford Hills, NY 10507-0606
(914) 864-1375
Fax: (914) 864-1377
E-mail: info@weedenfoundation.org
Web Site: www.weedenfoundation.org

FOUNDED: 1963

AREAS OF INTEREST:
Biodiversity, environment, natural resources
conservation and consumption.

NAME(S) OF PROGRAMS:
● **Climate Crisis Activism**
● **Consumption**
● **Domestic Biodiversity**
● **International Biodiversity**

TYPE:
General operating grants; Project/program
grants.

YEAR PROGRAM STARTED: 1963

PURPOSE:
To embrace the protection of biodiversity.

LEGAL BASIS:
Nonprofit, family foundation.

ELIGIBILITY:
Applicants must be nonprofit, tax-exempt
organizations with 501(c)(3) status or
international equivalent.

GEOG. RESTRICTIONS: Chile, Northern California
and the High Divide.

FINANCIAL DATA:
Amount of support per award: Average:
$15,000 to $20,000.
Total amount of support: Varies.

NO. MOST RECENT APPLICANTS: 76 for the year
2020.

NO. AWARDS: 67 for the year 2020.

APPLICATION INFO:
Applications are submitted through the
Foundation web site.
Duration: One year. Renewal possible.
Deadline: Varies.

IRS I.D.: 94-6109313

STAFF:
Donald A. Weeden, Executive Director
Peggy Kennedy, Research Assistant

BOARD OF DIRECTORS:
Norm Weeden, Ph.D., President
John D. Weeden, Vice President
Bob Weeden, Treasurer
Leslie Weeden, Secretary
Barbara Daugherty

Nicholas Leibowitz
Malcolm Roux
Alan Weeden
William Weeden

ADDRESS INQUIRIES TO:
Donald A. Weeden, Executive Director
(See address above.)

THE DEAN WITTER FOUNDATION
c/o Kramer, Blum and Associates
P.O. Box 6106
San Rafael, CA 94903
(415) 981-2966
Fax: (415) 981-5218
E-mail: admin@deanwitterfoundation.org
Web Site: www.deanwitterfoundation.org

TYPE:
Challenge/matching grants; Fellowships;
General operating grants; Internships;
Matching gifts; Professorships;
Project/program grants; Research grants;
Scholarships; Seed money grants.

See entry 1721 for full listing.

Medicine (multiple disciplines)

A-T CHILDREN'S PROJECT [1994]
6810 State Road 7
Suite 125
Coconut Creek, FL 33073
(954) 481-6611
E-mail: grants@atcp.org
Web Site: www.atcp.org

FOUNDED: 1993

AREAS OF INTEREST:
Projects that, while drawing on basic
discoveries, apply innovative and novel
strategies for suggesting, developing and
evaluating specific disease-modifying and
symptomatic interventions for
ataxia-telangiectasia (A-T); clinical studies
for A-T.

NAME(S) OF PROGRAMS:
● **A-T Postdoctoral Fellowship Award**
● **A-T Research Grant Program**

TYPE:
Research grants.

YEAR PROGRAM STARTED: 1993

PURPOSE:
To accelerate first-rate, international scientific
research in an attempt to help find a cure or
life-improving therapies for children with
ataxia-telangiectasia.

ELIGIBILITY:
Open to all ages and nationalities. Proposal
for grant must have direct relevance to
ataxia-telangiectasia.

Applicants should be aware that meritorious
proposals may be rejected if:
(1) the proposed research is too far from
being relevant to a therapeutic intervention;
(2) the A-T Children's Project's scientific
advisors find the research redundant and in
no need of validation;
(3) the proposed research is likely to happen
anyway, without the A-T Children's Project's

support and;
(4) the research cannot realistically be
achieved with the proposed budget.

FINANCIAL DATA:
Amount of support per award: A-T
Postdoctoral Fellowship: $30,000 to $40,000
over two years; A-T Research Grant: Up to
$75,000 per year.
Total amount of support: Varies.

APPLICATION INFO:
Detailed information can be found on the
organization web site. A Letter of Intent
(LOI) is required prior to submission of a
full-length proposal. An LOI form can be
downloaded from the web site.
Duration: One to two years.
Deadline: Letter of Intent: August 1 for
September 1 deadline and February 1 for
March 1 deadline. Full proposal: March 1
and September 1.

ADDRESS INQUIRIES TO:
Jennifer Thornton, Executive Director
(See address above.)

THE JOHN W. ALDEN TRUST
c/o Emma M. Greene, Senior V.P.
Philanthropic Client Dir., U.S. Trust
Bank of America Private Wealth Management
225 Franklin Street, MA1-225-04-02
Boston, MA 02110
(617) 951-1108
E-mail: susan.t.monahan@gmail.com
Web Site: www.cybergrants.com/alden

TYPE:
Capital grants; Challenge/matching grants;
Conferences/seminars; Demonstration grants;
Development grants; Matching gifts;
Project/program grants; Research grants;
Seed money grants; Technical assistance;
Training grants.

See entry 999 for full listing.

ALZHEIMER'S DRUG DISCOVERY FOUNDATION [1995]
57 West 57th Street
Suite 904
New York, NY 10019
(212) 901-8000
Fax: (212) 901-8010
E-mail: info@alzdiscovery.org
grants@alzdiscovery.org
Web Site: www.alzdiscovery.org

FOUNDED: 2004

AREAS OF INTEREST:
Drug discovery and development for
Alzheimer's disease, related dementias and
cognitive decline.

NAME(S) OF PROGRAMS:
● **ADDF/NIH**
● **Biomarkers Development**
● **Drug Development**
● **Prevention Beyond the Pipeline**
● **Program to Accelerate Clinical Trials (PACT)**

TYPE:
Awards/prizes; Conferences/seminars;
Research grants.

PURPOSE:
To promote the research and development of
therapies to identify, treat and prevent
cognitive decline, Alzheimer's disease and
related dementias.

LEGAL BASIS:
Nonprofit Delaware corporation 501(c)(3) public charity.

ELIGIBILITY:
Applicant must be a university medical center or early-stage biotechnology company.

FINANCIAL DATA:
Amount of support per award: ADDF/NIH: Varies; Biomarkers Development and Drug Development: Up to $600,000; PACT and Prevention Beyond the Pipeline: Budget requests up to $3,000,000 are accepted for clinical trial submissions.
Total amount of support: Varies.

APPLICATION INFO:
Complete instructions are available on the Foundation web site.
Duration: Varies.
Deadline: Letters of Intent: February 5, May 28 and October 1. Invited full proposals: April 16, July 30 and December 3, respectively.

ADDRESS INQUIRIES TO:
Ashley Jones, Grants Manager
(See address above.)

AMERICAN ASSOCIATION FOR HAND SURGERY   [1996]
500 Cummings Center
Suite 4400
Beverly, MA 01915
(978) 927-8330
Fax: (978) 524-0498
E-mail: contact@handsurgery.org
Web Site: www.handsurgery.org

FOUNDED: 1970

AREAS OF INTEREST:
Hand surgery and hand therapy.

TYPE:
Research grants. International hand therapy outreach.

YEAR PROGRAM STARTED: 1970

PURPOSE:
To promote education and research; to foster creativity and innovation in basic and/or clinical research in all areas pertinent to hand surgery and hand therapy.

ELIGIBILITY:
Applications are open to AAHS members and candidates for membership. Residents and fellows sponsored by an AAHS member are also eligible to apply. One of the co-investigators must be an Active or Affiliate AAHS member. AAHS therapist and surgeon members are eligible to apply for the Vargas International Hand Therapy Teaching Award.

FINANCIAL DATA:
Amount of support per award: AAHS/PSF Combined Pilot Research Grant and AAHS Research Grant: $10,000; Vargas International Hand Therapy Teaching Award: Up to $5,000 in reimbursement for mission expenses.

CO-OP FUNDING PROGRAMS: Match grant with Plastic Surgery Foundation.

APPLICATION INFO:
Application information is available on the web site.
Duration: One year.
Deadline: Annual Research Grant: September 1.

ADDRESS INQUIRIES TO:
See e-mail address above.

AMERICAN COLLEGE OF LEGAL MEDICINE   [1997]
515 North Dearborn Street
Chicago, IL 60654
(312) 670-2550
E-mail: info@aclm.org
Web Site: theaclm.org

FOUNDED: 1960

AREAS OF INTEREST:
Legal medicine.

NAME(S) OF PROGRAMS:
● **American College of Legal Medicine's Student Writing Competition in Law, Medicine and Bioethics**

TYPE:
Awards/prizes. The Hirsh Award is awarded to a law, dentistry, podiatry, nursing, pharmacy, health science, health care administration, or public health student.

PURPOSE:
To promote interdisciplinary cooperation and an understanding of issues where law and medicine converge.

ELIGIBILITY:
Must be a student at an accredited school of law, medicine, dentistry, podiatry, nursing, pharmacy, health science, health care, administration, or public health that has written an outstanding original paper on Legal Medicine.

FINANCIAL DATA:
Amount of support per award: Hirsh Award: $1,000 first prize, $500 second prize and $250 third prize.
Total amount of support: $1,750.

NO. MOST RECENT APPLICANTS: 12 to 14.

NO. AWARDS: 3.

APPLICATION INFO:
Contact the College.
Deadline: January 15.

ADDRESS INQUIRIES TO:
Theodore Kanellakes, Executive Director
(See address above.)

AMERICAN FEDERATION FOR AGING RESEARCH (AFAR)   [1998]
55 West 39th Street
16th Floor
New York, NY 10018
(212) 703-9977
(888) 582-2327
Fax: (212) 997-0330
E-mail: grants@afar.org
Web Site: www.afar.org

FOUNDED: 1981

AREAS OF INTEREST:
Biomedical aging research.

NAME(S) OF PROGRAMS:
● **Glenn Foundation for Medical Research Postdoctoral Fellowships in Aging Research**

TYPE:
Fellowships; Research grants; Training grants. Glenn Foundation for Medical Research Postdoctoral Fellowships in Aging Research support basic and translational research that builds on early discoveries that

show translational potential for clinical relevant strategies. In partnership with the American Federation for Aging Research (AFAR), these fellowships aim to encourage and further the careers of postdoctoral fellows who are conducting research in the basic biology of aging, as well as translating advances in basic research from the laboratory to the clinic. The award is intended to provide significant research and training support to permit these postdoctoral fellows to become established in the field of aging.

PURPOSE:
To support basic biomedical research that promotes healthier aging and advances the understanding of the aging process and its associated diseases and disorders.

LEGAL BASIS:
Private foundation.

ELIGIBILITY:
Applicant must be a postdoctoral fellow (M.D. and/or Ph.D. or equivalent) at the start date of the award. Applicants whose total postdoctoral training period is great than five years must provide a justification for the additional training period.

The proposed research must be conducted at a qualified not-for-profit setting in the U.S.

Individuals who are employees in the NIH intramural program and individuals who are currently receiving financial support at a Paul F. Glenn Center for Biology of Aging Research are not eligible.

Fellows may not hold any concurrent not-for-profit or government funding for the same research project.

Applications from underrepresented groups in the biomedical sciences are encouraged.

GEOG. RESTRICTIONS: United States.

FINANCIAL DATA:
Amount of support per award: $60,000.

NO. AWARDS: Up to 10.

APPLICATION INFO:
Letter of Intent required. Guidelines are available on the AFAR web site.
Duration: One year.
Deadline: Letter of Inquiry: January. Invited Application: Mid-May.

PUBLICATIONS:
Program announcement.

STAFF:
Stephanie Lederman, Executive Director
Odette van der Willik, Director, Grant Programs
Hattie Herman, Program Officer
Catherine Cullar, Administrative Manager

ADDRESS INQUIRIES TO:
Hattie Herman, Program Officer
(See address above.)

AMERICAN FEDERATION FOR AGING RESEARCH (AFAR)   [1999]
55 West 39th Street
16th Floor
New York, NY 10018
(212) 703-9977
(888) 582-2327
Fax: (212) 997-0330
E-mail: grants@afar.org
Web Site: www.afar.org

FOUNDED: 1981

AREAS OF INTEREST:
Biomedical aging research.

NAME(S) OF PROGRAMS:
- **Paul Beeson Career Development Awards in Aging Research Program**
- **Glenn Foundation for Medical Research and AFAR Grants for Junior Faculty**
- **Glenn Foundation for Medical Research Breakthroughs in Gerontology (BIG) Awards**
- **Diana Jacobs Kalman/AFAR Scholarships for Research in the Biology of Aging**
- **Medical Student Training in Aging Research Program (MSTAR)**

TYPE:
Fellowships; Research grants; Scholarships; Training grants. The Paul Beeson Career Development Awards in Aging Research Program is intended to bolster the current and severe shortage of academic physicians who have the combination of medical, academic and scientific training relative to caring for older people.

The Glenn Foundation for Medical Research and AFAR Grants for Junior Faculty are given to provide one to two years of support for junior faculty to do research that will serve as the basis for longer-term research efforts.

The Glenn Foundation for Medical Research Breakthroughs in Gerontology Awards are to provide timely support to a small number of pilot research programs that may be of relatively high risk but which offer significant promise of yielding transforming discoveries in the fundamental biology of aging.

The Diana Jacobs Kalman/AFAR Scholarships for Research in the Biology of Aging aims to attract new generations of talented investigators to the field of aging research.

Medical Student Training in Aging Research Program (MSTAR) provides medical students, early in their training, with an enriching experience in aging-related research and geriatrics, under the mentorship of top experts in the field. Students participate in an eight- to 12-week structured research, clinical and didactic program in geriatrics.

PURPOSE:
To support basic biomedical research that promotes healthier aging and advances the understanding of the aging process and its associated diseases and disorders; to encourage the training of new scientists and physicians in geriatric research and in the practice of geriatric medicine.

LEGAL BASIS:
Private foundation.

ELIGIBILITY:
Paul Beeson Career Development Awards in Aging Research Program applicants are clinically trained individuals who are pursuing research careers in aging.

For the Glenn Foundation for Medical Research and AFAR Grants for Junior Faculty, applicants must be junior faculty (M.Ds. and Ph.Ds.).

For the Glenn Foundation for Medical Research Breakthroughs in Gerontology Awards, qualified applicants must be full-time faculty members at the rank of assistant professor or higher who can demonstrate a strong record of independence.

For the Diana Jacobs Kalman/AFAR Scholarships for Research in the Biology of Aging, student must be enrolled in an M.D., D.O., Ph.D., or combined-degree program.

The Medical Student Training in Aging Research Program (MSTAR) is intended for medical students and is built on the Medical Student Geriatric Scholars Program.

GEOG. RESTRICTIONS: United States.

FINANCIAL DATA:
Amount of support per award: Paul Beeson Career Development Awards in Aging Research: $200,000 per year; Glenn Foundation/AFAR Grants: Up to $100,000; Glenn Foundation for Medical Research BIG Awards: Up to $300,000; Diana Jacobs Kalman/AFAR Scholarships: $5,000.

NO. MOST RECENT APPLICANTS: Paul Beeson Career Development Awards in Aging Research: Varies; Glenn Foundation/AFAR Grants: 148; Glenn Foundation for Medical Research BIG Awards: 68.

NO. AWARDS: Paul Beeson Career Development Awards in Aging Research, Glenn Foundation/AFAR Grants and Diana Jacobs Kalman/AFAR Scholarships: Up to 10; Glenn Foundation for Medical Research BIG Awards: 2.

APPLICATION INFO:
Required application form is available on the web site.
Duration: Beeson Career Development Awards in Aging Research: Up to five years. Glenn Foundation/AFAR Grants: One to two years. Glenn Foundation for Medical Research BIG Awards: Three years. Diana Jacobs Kalman/AFAR Scholarships: Three to six months.
Deadline: Glenn Foundation/AFAR Grants and Glenn Foundation for Medical Research BIG Awards: Mid-December. Paul Beeson: Varies.

PUBLICATIONS:
Program announcement.

STAFF:
Stephanie Lederman, Executive Director
Odette van der Willik, Director, Grant Programs
Hattie Herman, Program Officer
Catherine Cullar, Administrative Manager

ADDRESS INQUIRIES TO:
Hattie Herman, Program Officer
(See address above.)

AMERICAN KIDNEY FUND [2000]
11921 Rockville Pike, Suite 300
Rockville, MD 20852
(800) 638-8299
(866) 300-2900 (Spanish/English HelpLine)
Fax: (301) 881-0898
E-mail: education@kidneyfund.org
Web Site: www.kidneyfund.org

FOUNDED: 1971

AREAS OF INTEREST:
Treatment, prevention and cure of kidney disease.

NAME(S) OF PROGRAMS:
- **Clinical Scientist in Nephrology (CSN)**

TYPE:
Fellowships.

YEAR PROGRAM STARTED: 1988

PURPOSE:
To improve the quality of care provided to kidney patients; to promote clinical research in nephrology.

ELIGIBILITY:
Applicant must be a current nephrologist at an institution that operates an accredited training program in nephrology or pediatric nephrology. Applicant must intend to pursue a professional career with emphasis on independent research and academia.

GEOG. RESTRICTIONS: United States and its territories.

FINANCIAL DATA:
Amount of support per award: Up to $80,000 per year.
Total amount of support: Up to $160,000.

NO. MOST RECENT APPLICANTS: 11.

NO. AWARDS: 1 to 2.

APPLICATION INFO:
Complete application information may be found on the web site.
Duration: One to two years.
Deadline: November 30.

ADDRESS INQUIRIES TO:
Michael Spigler, Vice President of Patient Services and Kidney Disease Education
(See address above.)

AMERICAN KIDNEY FUND [2001]
11921 Rockville Pike, Suite 300
Rockville, MD 20852
(800) 638-8299
(866) 300-2900 (Spanish/English HelpLine)
Fax: (301) 881-0898
E-mail: patientservice@kidneyfund.org
Web Site: www.kidneyfund.org

FOUNDED: 1971

AREAS OF INTEREST:
Treatment, prevention and cure of kidney disease.

NAME(S) OF PROGRAMS:
- **Patient Services Grants: Safety Net Grant Program**

TYPE:
Grants-in-aid. Medical Grants. Provides financial assistance to qualified dialysis patients who are referred by their physicians and social workers for treatment-specific expenses such as transportation, over-the-counter medicines, medication co-payments, kidney donor expenses, mobility aids and nutritional supplements.

YEAR PROGRAM STARTED: 1971

PURPOSE:
To provide aid in the treatment, prevention, and cure of kidney disease.

ELIGIBILITY:
Based on financial need. Kidney dialysis and transplant patients living in the U.S. are eligible. Additional requirements are available online.

GEOG. RESTRICTIONS: United States and its territories.

FINANCIAL DATA:
Amount of support per award: $100 per year.
Total amount of support: $496,621.40.

NO. MOST RECENT APPLICANTS: 4,988.

NO. AWARDS: 4,988.

APPLICATION INFO:
Applications must be submitted online via Grants Management System. Applications must be completed by the patient and a dialysis or transplant renal professional. Paper applications will no longer be accepted.

Duration: Renewable 12 months from the check date of the last grant.

IRS I.D.: 23-7124261

ADDRESS INQUIRIES TO:
Patient Services Department
Tel: (800) 795-3226
(See address above.)

AMERICAN MEDICAL ASSOCIATION FOUNDATION

330 North Wabash Avenue
Suite 39300
Chicago, IL 60611-5885
(312) 464-4200
Fax: (312) 464-4142
E-mail: amafoundation@ama-assn.org
Web Site: www.amafoundation.org

TYPE:
Awards/prizes; Project/program grants; Scholarships. Excellence in Medicine Awards are given to recognize physicians and medical students who are improving the health of their communities and the lives of those who are most in need.

The Joan F. Giambalvo Memorial Fund is presented in conjunction with the AMA's Women Physicians Section to provide a research grant to help researchers advance the progress of women in the medical profession and identify and address the needs of women physicians and medical students.

Leadership Development Institute offers a unique opportunity for participants to gain individualized skills needed to foster careers and the future of medicine. Participants will receive professional development opportunities as well as mentoring throughout the course of the program year.

LGBTQ+ Fellowship program, in partnership with medical and osteopathic-granting educational institutions, is a four-year medical fellowship program to address the social determinants of health specifically affecting LGBTQ+ individuals and create a pipeline of diverse health care providers who are knowledgeable and culturally competent in LGBTQ+ health.

The Physicians of Tomorrow Scholarships are awarded to rising fourth-year medical students based on financial need and academic excellence.

See entry 1477 for full listing.

AMERICAN MEDICAL WOMEN'S ASSOCIATION, INC. [2002]

1100 East Woodfield Road
Suite 350
Schaumburg, IL 60173
(847) 517-2801
Fax: (847) 517-7229
E-mail: associatedirector@amwa-doc.org
Web Site: www.amwa-doc.org

FOUNDED: 1915

AREAS OF INTEREST:
Women physicians, women medical students and women's health.

NAME(S) OF PROGRAMS:
● **American Women's Hospitals Service (AWHS)**

TYPE:
Awards/prizes; Conferences/seminars; General operating grants; Project/program grants; Training grants; Travel grants. Support for clinics serving the poor in medically underserved areas, scholarships and loans to qualifying women medical students, and continuing medical education for physicians in areas related to women's health.

YEAR PROGRAM STARTED: 1915

PURPOSE:
To advance women in medicine and improve women's health through advocacy, leadership, education, expertise and mentoring, and strategic alliances.

LEGAL BASIS:
AMWA: 501(c)(6) corporation. AWHS: 501(c)(3) foundation.

ELIGIBILITY:
Open to women who are enrolled in accredited medical schools in the U.S.

GEOG. RESTRICTIONS: United States.

FINANCIAL DATA:
Amount of support per award: Community Project Grants: Maximum $500; Overseas Clinic Support Grants: $2,000 to $3,500; Overseas Travel Grants: Up to $1,000.

NO. MOST RECENT APPLICANTS: Overseas Clinic Support Grants: 3; Overseas Travel and Community Project Grants: 11.

NO. AWARDS: Overseas Clinic Support Grants: 3; Overseas Travel and Community Project Grants: 7.

APPLICATION INFO:
Applications are available on the Association web site.
Duration: Overseas Clinic Support Grants: One year; Overseas Travel and Community Project Grants: One trip minimum four weeks or one project.
Deadline: Overseas Clinic Support Grants: July 30. Overseas Travel and Community Project Grants: January 5, May 5 and September 5.

OFFICER:
Janice Werbinski, M.D., President

ADDRESS INQUIRIES TO:
Danielle Carrier, Associate Director
(See address above.)

THE AMERICAN PORPHYRIA FOUNDATION [2003]

4915 St. Elmo Avenue
Suite 200
Bethesda, MD 20814
(301) 347-7166
(866) 273-3635
E-mail: info@porphyriafoundation.com
Web Site: www.porphyriafoundation.com

AREAS OF INTEREST:
Porphyria.

TYPE:
Research grants.

PURPOSE:
To improve the health and well-being of individuals and families affected by porphyria.

ELIGIBILITY:
Qualified investigators involved in porphyria research.

FINANCIAL DATA:
Amount of support per award: $5,000 to $10,000.
Total amount of support: Varies.

APPLICATION INFO:
Send a two-page summary of proposed research and research experience to the Foundation.
Duration: Typically one year.

PUBLICATIONS:
Newsletters.

ADDRESS INQUIRIES TO:
Desiree H. Lyon, Global Director
(See address above.)

AMERICAN ROENTGEN RAY SOCIETY [2004]

44211 Slatestone Court
Leesburg, VA 20176-5109
(703) 729-3353
Fax: (703) 729-4839
E-mail: scholarships@arrs.org
Web Site: www.arrs.org

FOUNDED: 1900

AREAS OF INTEREST:
Diagnostic radiology.

NAME(S) OF PROGRAMS:
● **ARRS Annual Scholarship Program**

TYPE:
Scholarships.

YEAR PROGRAM STARTED: 1992

PURPOSE:
To provide resources needed to acquire knowledge, skills and training in areas that are vital to radiology but have traditionally been outside the scope of diagnostic radiology.

ELIGIBILITY:
Candidates must have earned an M.D. or D.O. from an accredited institution and must have completed all residencies or fellowship training or equivalent.

Candidate must be a member of ARRS at the time the application is submitted and for the duration of the award.

FINANCIAL DATA:
Funds distributed to individual's institution.
Amount of support per award: $180,000.
Total amount of support: Varies.

NO. AWARDS: Up to 2.

APPLICATION INFO:
Submission of a curriculum vitae, summary of qualifications, goals and purposes of the study, estimated budget, and a statement from department regarding applicant's goals and commitment ensuring applicant's return to faculty upon completion.

Applications are to be submitted to scholarships@arrs.org with required documents attached.
Duration: One or two years.
Deadline: October.

ADDRESS INQUIRIES TO:
See e-mail address above.

AMERICAN SOCIETY OF HEMATOLOGY [2005]

2021 L Street, N.W.
Suite 900
Washington, DC 20036
(202) 776-0544
E-mail: awards@hematology.org
Web Site: www.hematology.org

AREAS OF INTEREST:
Hematology.

NAME(S) OF PROGRAMS:
- **Physician-Scientist Career Development Award**
- **Research Training Award for Fellows**

TYPE:
Awards/prizes. Physician-Scientist Career Development Award allows medical students to gain knowledge and perform research in between their first, second and third year of school.

Research Training Award for Fellows allows protected time for research.

PURPOSE:
To help medical students gain experience in hematology research; to encourage research in hematology, hematology/oncology, or other hematology-related training programs.

ELIGIBILITY:
Physician-Scientist Career Development Award applicant must:
(1) be a medical student member of ASH;
(2) be a first-, second- or third-year medical student actively enrolled in an M.D. or D.O. medical program in an LCME or AOA COCA (or its equivalent) accredited medical school in the U.S. or Canada. Applicant must be in good standing relative to their course work at the time of application and be between their first and second, second and third, or third and fourth year of medical school at the time the research is done;
(3) not be currently enrolled in a combined M.D.-Ph.D. program;
(4) be planning an investigative career in laboratory, translational, or clinical hematology research;
(5) have a mentor who is an active ASH member at the time of application and;
(6) not have any other concurrent funding for a similar experience.

Research Training Award for Fellows applicant must be a second-, third-, fourth- or fifth-year student at the time of the award, who is not yet eligible for the ASH Scholar Awards. Applicant must:
(1) possess an M.D. or D.O.;
(2) continue to maintain ASH membership and remain a member in good standing for the duration of the award term;
(3) plan to pursue an investigative career in hematology research;
(4) have a mentor who is an ASH member at the time the application is submitted and;
(5) not hold a position as an Assistant Professor.

FINANCIAL DATA:
Amount of support per award:
Physician-Scientist Award: $42,000; Research Training Award: $70,000.

NO. AWARDS: Physician-Scientist Award: Up to 5; Research Training Award: Up to 6.

APPLICATION INFO:
Guidelines are available on the Society's web site.
Duration: One year.

Deadline: Physician-Scientist Award: February 1; Research Training Award: January 15.

ADDRESS INQUIRIES TO:
Allie Samis, Awards Program Specialist
(See address above.)

AMERICAN SOCIETY OF HEMATOLOGY [2006]

2021 L Street, N.W.
Suite 900
Washington, DC 20036
(202) 776-0544
E-mail: awards@hematology.org
Web Site: www.hematology.org

FOUNDED: 1985

AREAS OF INTEREST:
Hematology, basic and clinical/translational research.

NAME(S) OF PROGRAMS:
- **Fellow Scholar Award**
- **Fellow to Faculty Scholar Award**
- **Junior Faculty Scholar Award**

TYPE:
Awards/prizes; Fellowships; Research grants; Scholarships.

PURPOSE:
To support hematologists who have chosen a career in research.

ELIGIBILITY:
Applicants must be a citizen of, or hold a visa in, the U.S. or Canada. Research must be conducted within the U.S. and Canada. Applicants are required to be members of ASH in good standing at the time of the Letter of Intent submission, and for the duration of the Scholar Award Program. Consideration will be given if membership application is pending at the time of the application deadline.

For the Fellow Scholar Award, Ph.D. or M.D./Ph.D. applicants must have fewer than five years of research experience after completion of their Ph.D. (including research performed during fellowship, but excluding clinical fellowship time). M.D. applicants should have more than three but fewer than five years of research experience (including research performed during fellowship, but excluding clinical fellowship time). M.D. applicants with fewer than three years research experience (inclusive of fellowship research time) should consider applying for the Senior RTAF award.

For the Fellow to Faculty Scholar Award, M.D./D.O., Ph.D. or M.D./D.O.-Ph.D. applicants must have more than five years (60 months) and eight or fewer years (96 months) of research experience after completion of their terminal degree (including research performed during fellowship, but excluding clinical fellowship time).

For the Junior Faculty Scholar Awards, M.D./D.O., Ph.D. or M.D./D.O.-Ph.D. applicants must have more than eight years (96 months) and 13 or fewer years (156 months) of research experience after completion of their terminal degree (including research performed during fellowship, but excluding clinical fellowship time).

Applicants with the title of Assistant Professor or equivalent must apply for the Junior Faculty Award, regardless of research experience.

GEOG. RESTRICTIONS: United States and Canada.

FINANCIAL DATA:
Amount of support per award: $150,000 for a Junior Faculty Scholar Award, $125,000 for a Fellow to Faculty Award or $100,000 for a Fellow Scholar Award. These awards can be spread over two or three years with an annual maximum not to exceed $75,000 for junior faculty, $62,500 for fellow to faculty and $50,000 for fellows.
Total amount of support: Approximately $3,800,000.

NO. MOST RECENT APPLICANTS: 221.

NO. AWARDS: 36.

APPLICATION INFO:
A letter of intent is required before submission of full proposal. Contact the Society for details.
Duration: Two to three years.
Deadline: Mandatory Letter of Intent: May 1.

ADDRESS INQUIRIES TO:
Vonnie Calemine
Awards Program Manager
(See address above.)

AMERICAN SOCIETY OF HEMATOLOGY [2007]

2021 L Street, N.W.
Suite 900
Washington, DC 20036
(202) 776-0544
E-mail: awards@hematology.org
Web Site: www.hematology.org

AREAS OF INTEREST:
Hematology.

NAME(S) OF PROGRAMS:
- **HONORS (Hematology Opportunities for the Next Generation of Research Scientists)**

TYPE:
Awards/prizes. Each scholarship provides the medical school with funds to cover the expenses for students to complete a program and travel support for students to attend the ASH annual meetings.

PURPOSE:
To provide medical students and residents with an introduction to the specialty of hematology by encouraging them to take time during their medical school curriculum to work on a project with a hematologist.

ELIGIBILITY:
Medical students and residents in the U.S., Mexico and Canada with an interest in hematology research may apply.

GEOG. RESTRICTIONS: United States, Mexico and Canada.

FINANCIAL DATA:
Amount of support per award: $5,000 cash award and $1,000 travel stipend for each of the two annual meetings.
Total amount of support: Varies.

APPLICATION INFO:
The institution is responsible for selecting student participants. Contact the Society for additional application information.
Duration: Summer project: Maximum three months; Flexible project: Three to 12 months.
Deadline: Mid-February.

ADDRESS INQUIRIES TO:
Allie Samis, Awards Program Specialist
(See address above.)

AMERICAN SOCIETY OF REGIONAL ANESTHESIA AND PAIN MEDICINE

3 Penn Center West
Suite 224
Pittsburgh, PA 15276
(412) 471-2718
Fax: (412) 471-7503
E-mail: asraassistant@asra.com
Web Site: www.asra.com

TYPE:
Research grants.

See entry 2291 for full listing.

AMERICAN SOCIETY OF REGIONAL ANESTHESIA AND PAIN MEDICINE   [2008]

3 Penn Center West
Suite 224
Pittsburgh, PA 15276
(412) 471-2718
Fax: (412) 471-7503
E-mail: asraassistant@asra.com
Web Site: www.asra.com

AREAS OF INTEREST:
Regional anesthesia and pain medicine.

NAME(S) OF PROGRAMS:
● **ASRA Early-Career Investigator Award**
● **ASRA Graduate Student Award**

TYPE:
Research grants.

PURPOSE:
To support research related to any aspect of regional anesthesia, acute and chronic pain medicine and their application to surgery, obstetrics and pain control; to encourage anesthesiologists and other researchers who are interested in the field.

ELIGIBILITY:
Applicant and co-investigators must be North Americans and members of ASRA.

For the Early-Career Investigator Award, the primary applicant must be an M.D. or D.O. within five years of graduating from a residency or fellowship program.

For the Graduate Student Award, the applicant must be a graduate or medical student.

FINANCIAL DATA:
Amount of support per award: Early-Career Investigator Award: Up to $30,000; Graduate Student Award: Up to $10,000.

NO. MOST RECENT APPLICANTS: 5.

NO. AWARDS: 1 per award.

APPLICATION INFO:
The application, which must be written by the applicant, should be accompanied by a complete narrative research protocol. The research proposal must be concerned with an original idea or concept. The research must be carried out primarily by the applicant.

Duration: Up to two years.

Deadline: Specific deadlines are posted on the ASRA web site.

ADDRESS INQUIRIES TO:
Angie Stengel, Executive Director
(See address above.)

AMERICAN VETERINARY MEDICAL ASSOCIATION   [2009]

AVMA Government Relations Division
1910 Sunderland Place, N.W.
Washington, DC 20036
(202) 289-3207
Fax: (202) 842-4360
E-mail: fellowship@avma.org
Web Site: www.avma.org/fellowship

AREAS OF INTEREST:
Veterinary medicine.

NAME(S) OF PROGRAMS:
● **AVMA Fellowship**

TYPE:
Fellowships.

YEAR PROGRAM STARTED: 1988

PURPOSE:
To support AVMA members to serve as a congressional fellow for one year in a personal or committee office of the U.S. Congress.

LEGAL BASIS:
Association.

ELIGIBILITY:
Applicants must be AVMA members and U.S. citizens who demonstrate special competence in an area of veterinary medicine, possess a broad professional background and exhibit an interest in applying scientific knowledge to solve societal/public policy problems.

Applicants must be articulate, literate, adaptable and capable of working on a wide range of policy issues.

Fellows must serve in Washington, DC.

FINANCIAL DATA:
Amount of support per award: Approximately $91,232.

NO. AWARDS: 2 for the year 2018-19.

APPLICATION INFO:
Applicants must submit:
(1) a letter of intent;
(2) a curriculum vitae;
(3) two letters of reference from professional colleagues;
(4) a letter of support from the applicant's local, state, specialty or allied veterinary medical organization and;
(5) a personal statement (not to exceed 750 words) describing the applicant's qualifications, commitment to veterinary medicine and why the fellowship is desired.

Duration: One year.

Deadline: Usually second Friday in February.

PUBLICATIONS:
Program announcement.

IRS I.D.: 36-6117739

ADDRESS INQUIRIES TO:
See e-mail address above.

ANIMAL ASSISTANCE FOUNDATION   [2010]

405 Urban Street
Suite 340
Lakewood, CO 80228
(303) 744-8396
E-mail: info@aaf-fd.org
Web Site: www.aaf-fd.org

FOUNDED: 1975

AREAS OF INTEREST:
Companion animal overpopulation, operational optimization, adoption and permanent homes, cruelty prevention and intervention, innovation and ingenuity and companion animals and unwanted horse issues.

TYPE:
Capital grants; General operating grants; Project/program grants. Operating and service grants. The Foundation offers charitable support through its grantmaking program to organizations located within the state of Colorado or an agency that has a direct impact on animals and their owners in Colorado. Direct impact on animals and their owners in Colorado applies to institutions conducting studies that result in new science, practice or knowledge significantly affecting animals living in Colorado.

YEAR PROGRAM STARTED: 1975

PURPOSE:
To provide leadership and support to make Colorado the Model State for animal welfare through philanthropy toward animals.

LEGAL BASIS:
Private foundation.

ELIGIBILITY:
Requirements vary by program and are outlined on the Foundation web site.

GEOG. RESTRICTIONS: Colorado.

FINANCIAL DATA:
Amount of support per award: Varies.
Total amount of support: More than $1,000,000 in grants for the year 2019.
Matching fund requirements: Varies.

NO. MOST RECENT APPLICANTS: 100.

NO. AWARDS: Approximately 60.

REPRESENTATIVE AWARDS:
$5,000 to Fort Collins Cat Rescue; $10,000 to Humane Society of Weld County.

APPLICATION INFO:
Application information is available on the Foundation web site.

Duration: One to two years. Renewable with reapplication.

Deadline: Letter of Intent: June 1 to August 1. Application (for approved LOIs): September 15.

IRS I.D.: 84-0715412

STAFF:
Katie Parker, Executive Director

ADDRESS INQUIRIES TO:
Rachel Gonzales, Program Director
E-mail: rgonzales@aaf-fd.org
(See address above.)

APLASTIC ANEMIA AND MDS INTERNATIONAL FOUNDATION   [2011]

4330 East West Highway
Suite 230
Bethesda, MD 20814
(301) 279-7202
(800) 747-2820
Fax: (240) 534-2231
E-mail: help@aamds.org
Web Site: aamds.org

FOUNDED: 1983

AREAS OF INTEREST:
Aplastic anemia, myelodysplastic syndrome (MDS) and paroxysmal nocturnal hemoglobinuria (PNH).

NAME(S) OF PROGRAMS:
● **AA&MDSIF Research Grant Program**

TYPE:
Research grants.

YEAR PROGRAM STARTED: 1989

PURPOSE:
To support research related to aplastic anemia, myelodysplastic syndrome (MDS) and paroxysmal nocturnal hemoglobinuria (PNH).

ELIGIBILITY:
Qualified investigators affiliated with appropriate institutions are eligible to apply.

FINANCIAL DATA:
Amount of support per award: $30,000 per year.
Total amount of support: $60,000.

NO. AWARDS: 2 for the year 2019.

APPLICATION INFO:
Letter of Intent is required prior to submitting a full application. Applicants will be invited to submit the full application based on their Letter of Intent.
Duration: Two years. Second-year funding pending approval by Medical Board.
Deadline: Letter of Intent: May 29. Full Application: September 30. Notification: December 1.

STAFF:
Alice Houk, Senior Director of Health Professional Programs

ADDRESS INQUIRIES TO:
Alice Houk, Senior Director of Health Professional Programs
(See address above.)

ARTHRITIS NATIONAL RESEARCH FOUNDATION (ANRF)   [2012]
19200 Von Karman Avenue
Suite 350
Irvine, CA 92612
(800) 588-2873
(562) 437-6808
E-mail: grants@curearthritis.org
Web Site: www.curearthritis.org

FOUNDED: 1952

AREAS OF INTEREST:
Research related to arthritis and related autoimmune diseases.

NAME(S) OF PROGRAMS:
● **ANRF Arthritis Research Grants**

TYPE:
Research grants; Travel grants. ANRF Arthritis Research Grants are intended to support basic and clinical research focusing on rheumatic and related autoimmune diseases, such as osteoarthritis and rheumatoid arthritis.

YEAR PROGRAM STARTED: 1952

PURPOSE:
To support basic and clinical research related to arthritis.

ELIGIBILITY:
Applicants must hold an M.D. and/or Ph.D. degree or equivalent. Applicants need not be U.S. citizens, but must conduct their research at U.S. nonprofit institutions.

FINANCIAL DATA:
No overhead expenses funded.
Amount of support per award: Up to $100,000.
Total amount of support: $1,600,000 for fiscal year 2020-21.

CO-OP FUNDING PROGRAMS: American Federation for Aging Research (AFAR) and National Psoriasis Foundation.

NO. AWARDS: 10 to 20 annually.

REPRESENTATIVE AWARDS:
$100,000 to study the role of autoantibodies in pulmonary manifestations of inflammatory arthritis.

APPLICATION INFO:
A standard cover sheet and budget page are required and provided on the Foundation's web site. Application must be submitted online. Hard copies are not accepted.
Duration: One year. May apply for second year of funding.
Deadline: January 15 or next business day.

IRS I.D.: 95-6043953

ADDRESS INQUIRIES TO:
See e-mail address above.

ASCP   [2013]
33 West Monroe, Suite 1600
Chicago, IL 60603
(312) 541-4110
E-mail: membership@ascp.org
Web Site: www.ascp.org/foundation

FOUNDED: 1922

AREAS OF INTEREST:
Laboratory medicine.

TYPE:
Development grants; Fellowships; Scholarships; Travel grants. American Society for Clinical Pathology (ASCP) and the ASCP Foundation offer a number of grants, scholarships and fellowships to their members, which include pathologists, pathology residents, medical students, laboratory professionals, and laboratory science students.

PURPOSE:
To support outstanding pathology residents and laboratory science students as they expand their knowledge, skills and professional networks.

LEGAL BASIS:
Professional society.

ELIGIBILITY:
Criteria vary per award. Details are available on the ASCP web site.

GEOG. RESTRICTIONS: United States.

FINANCIAL DATA:
Amount of support per award: Varies.
Total amount of support: Varies.

NO. AWARDS: Varies.

APPLICATION INFO:
Application form required. Contact ASCP.
Duration: Varies.
Deadline: Varies.

PUBLICATIONS:
Announcement.

ADDRESS INQUIRIES TO:
Angela Collier, Manager, Membership
(See address above.)

AUTISM SPEAKS INC.   [2014]
1060 State Road, 2nd Floor
Princeton, NJ 08540
(609) 228-7313
E-mail: jnew@autismspeaks.org
Web Site: www.autismspeaks.org

FOUNDED: 1994

AREAS OF INTEREST:
Autism.

TYPE:
Fellowships; Research grants. Autism Service Provider grants. Research grants that are in line with Autism Speaks research priorities.

YEAR PROGRAM STARTED: 2005

PURPOSE:
To promote solutions, across the spectrum and throughout the lifespan, for the needs of individuals with autism and their families through advocacy and support; to increase understanding and acceptance of people with autism spectrum disorder; to advance research into causes and better interventions for autism spectrum disorder and related conditions.

LEGAL BASIS:
National nonprofit, tax-exempt organization.

ELIGIBILITY:
Open to investigators at established research institutions.

GEOG. RESTRICTIONS: Non-Science Providers Grants: United States.

FINANCIAL DATA:
Amount of support per award: Varies.
Total amount of support: Varies.

NO. AWARDS: Varies.

APPLICATION INFO:
Applications are available online.
Duration: Varies.
Deadline: Varies.

IRS I.D.: 20-2329938

ADDRESS INQUIRIES TO:
Joan New, Grants Manager
(See address above.)

Non-Science Providers:
Serena Selkin, Grants Manager
E-mail: sselkin@autismspeaks.org

BATTEN DISEASE SUPPORT AND RESEARCH ASSOCIATION   [2015]
2780 Airport Drive
Suite 342
Columbus, OH 43219
(800) 448-4570
Fax: (866) 648-8718
E-mail: info@bdsra.org
Web Site: www.bdsra.org

FOUNDED: 1987

AREAS OF INTEREST:
Batten Disease research.

NAME(S) OF PROGRAMS:
● **Batten Disease Research Grant**

TYPE:
Fellowships; Research grants; Seed money grants.

YEAR PROGRAM STARTED: 1994

PURPOSE:
To further Batten Disease basic and translational research.

ELIGIBILITY:
Applications will be reviewed based upon the quality of the proposed science, the probability of achieving the specific aims proposed and the likelihood of securing federal funding for continued research.

APPLICATION INFO:
Guidelines are available on the Foundation web site.

Duration: One year.

IRS I.D.: 91-1397792

STAFF:
Amy Fenton Parker, Executive Director

ADDRESS INQUIRIES TO:
Amy Fenton Parker, Executive Director
(See address above.)

*SPECIAL STIPULATIONS:
Grants must not be used to cover indirect or overhead costs.

BRIGHAM AND WOMEN'S HOSPITAL
75 Francis Street
Boston, MA 02115
(617) 732-5500
Fax: (617) 582-6112
E-mail: bwhdeland@partners.org
Web Site: www.brighamandwomens.org

TYPE:
Fellowships.

See entry 1283 for full listing.

BURROUGHS WELLCOME FUND [2016]
21 T.W. Alexander Drive
Research Triangle Park, NC 27709
(919) 991-5100
Fax: (919) 991-0695
E-mail: info@bwfund.org
Web Site: www.bwfund.org

FOUNDED: 1955

AREAS OF INTEREST:
Biomedical research.

NAME(S) OF PROGRAMS:
• **Career Awards at the Scientific Interface**
• **Career Awards for Medical Scientists**
• **Investigators in the Pathogenesis of Infectious Disease**
• **Preterm Birth Initiative**

TYPE:
Awards/prizes; Conferences/seminars; Research grants. Career Awards at the Scientific Interface bridge advanced postdoctoral training and the first three years of faculty service. These awards are intended to foster the early career development of researchers with backgrounds in the physical/mathematical/computational sciences whose work addresses biological questions.

Career Awards for Medical Scientists provide funds to bridge advanced postdoctoral/fellowship training and the early years of faculty service. This award addresses the ongoing problem of increasing the number of physician scientists and will help facilitate the transition to a career in research.

Investigators in the Pathogenesis of Infectious Disease provides awards for opportunities for accomplished investigators at the assistant professor level to study pathogenesis, with a focus on the intersection of human and microbial biology. The program is intended to shed light on the overarching issues of how human hosts handle infectious challenge.

Preterm Birth Initiative brings together a diverse interdisciplinary group with expertise in genetics/genomics, immunology, microbiology and proteomics along with the more traditional areas of parturition research such as maternal fetal medicine, obstetrics and pediatrics to address the scientific issues related to preterm birth.

PURPOSE:
To advance the biomedical sciences by supporting research and other scientific and educational activities; to help scientists early in their careers develop as independent investigators; to advance fields in the basic biomedical sciences that are undervalued or in need of particular encouragement.

LEGAL BASIS:
Private foundation.

GEOG. RESTRICTIONS: United States and Canada.

FINANCIAL DATA:
Amount of support per award: Career Awards at the Scientific Interface and Investigators in Pathogenesis of Infectious Disease: $500,000; Career Awards for Medical Scientists: $700,000; Preterm Birth Initiative: Up to $500,000.
Total amount of support: Approximately $25,000,000 in grants awarded annually.

APPLICATION INFO:
Contact the Fund.
Duration: Preterm Birth Initiative: Four years. All others: Five years.
Deadline: Varies.

PUBLICATIONS:
FOCUS, newsletter; *Career Development Guides,* annual report.

IRS I.D.: 23-7225395

ADDRESS INQUIRIES TO:
Burroughs Wellcome Fund
P.O. Box 13901
Research Triangle Park, NC 27709-3901

CANADIAN BLOOD SERVICES [2017]
1800 Alta Vista Drive
Ottawa ON K1G 4J5 Canada
(613) 739-2496
Fax: (613) 739-2201
E-mail: centreforinnovation@blood.ca
Web Site: blood.ca

AREAS OF INTEREST:
Research in transfusion science.

NAME(S) OF PROGRAMS:
• **Canadian Blood Services Graduate Fellowship Program**
• **Canadian Blood Services Postdoctoral Fellowship Program**

TYPE:
Fellowships.

PURPOSE:
To attract and support young investigators to initiate or continue training in the field of transfusion science; to foster careers related to transfusion science in Canada.

ELIGIBILITY:
Graduate Fellowship: Applicants must be engaged in full-time training research in a graduate program at a Canadian university leading to a Ph.D. or combined health professional Ph.D. program. While priority will be given to applicants enrolled in a Ph.D. program, applications from applicants enrolled in an M.Sc. program will be considered. Applicants must not hold another stipend award at the same time as the Canadian Blood Services Graduate Fellowship.

Postdoctoral Fellowship: Applicants must hold a relevant prerequisite degree (Ph.D., M.D., D.D.S., or D.V.M.) from a recognized academic institution. Applicants must be within five years of completing their prerequisite degree. Applicants must secure the sponsorship of a primary academic supervisor who is either a Canadian Blood Services Scientist/Investigator, a Canadian Blood Services Adjunct Scientist, or a Medical Officer/Director. Applicants must not hold another salary or stipend award at the same time as the Postdoctoral Fellowship.

GEOG. RESTRICTIONS: Canada.

FINANCIAL DATA:
Postdoctoral fellowship offers one-time research allowance of $20,000.
Amount of support per award: Graduate Fellowship: $25,000 per annum (CIHR guidelines); Postdoctoral Fellowship: $21,000 to $50,000 per annum based on degree, licensure and experience.
Total amount of support: Graduate Fellowship: Approximately $300,000; Postdoctoral Fellowship: Approximately $200,000.

APPLICATION INFO:
Competition guidelines are posted on the web site.
Duration: Graduate Fellowship: Two to four years. Postdoctoral Fellowship: Three years.
Deadline: Graduate Fellowship Program: Spring and fall; Postdoctoral Fellowship: Summer.

ADDRESS INQUIRIES TO:
Centre for Innovation
Tel: (613) 739-2564
(See e-mail address above.)

*SPECIAL STIPULATIONS:
Awards must be held in Canada.

CANADIAN BLOOD SERVICES [2018]
1800 Alta Vista Drive
Ottawa ON K1G 4J5 Canada
(613) 739-2496
Fax: (613) 739-2201
E-mail: centreforinnovation@blood.ca
Web Site: blood.ca

AREAS OF INTEREST:
Research in transfusion science.

NAME(S) OF PROGRAMS:
• **Blood Efficiency Accelerator Program**

TYPE:
Research grants. The objective of the Blood Efficiency Accelerator Program is to improve the efficient and appropriate utilization of blood products, while maintaining the safety of the blood system.

PURPOSE:
To support innovative research projects that seek new knowledge or accelerate the application of existing knowledge in transfusion science.

ELIGIBILITY:
Primary applicant must be affiliated with a Canadian academic program as a faculty member or with Canadian Blood Services. All project teams require at least one Canadian Blood Services employee. All project team members must have a defined role in the project, and their expertise must be clearly required to adequately address project goals.

FINANCIAL DATA:
Amount of support per award: Up to $30,000.

NO. AWARDS: Varies.

APPLICATION INFO:
Applicants must complete the Canadian Blood Services Blood Efficiency Accelerator Program Application Form and prepare the supporting documents for the application package as per the instructions on the application form.

No applications, updates, or additional materials will be accepted after the deadline date.
Duration: One year.

ADDRESS INQUIRIES TO:
Centre for Innovation
Tel: (613) 739-2564
(See e-mail address above.)

CANADIAN BLOOD SERVICES [2019]
1800 Alta Vista Drive
Ottawa ON K1G 4J5 Canada
(613) 739-2496
Fax: (613) 739-2201
E-mail: centreforinnovation@blood.ca
Web Site: blood.ca

AREAS OF INTEREST:
Research in transfusion science.

NAME(S) OF PROGRAMS:
● **Intramural Research Grant Program**

TYPE:
Research grants. Canadian Blood Services Intramural Research Grant Program supports collaborative research projects that will generate knowledge and lead to new discoveries that will improve the safety and efficacy of blood products and the blood system in general.

PURPOSE:
To advance knowledge in blood product utilization, supply, transfusion and quality; to replace or improve blood products through new therapies or technologies.

ELIGIBILITY:
The principal investigator must be affiliated with a Canadian academic program as a faculty member. The project team must include at least two investigators, including the principal investigator. All investigators must have a defined role in the project, and their expertise must be clearly required to adequately address the project goals. All investigators must be affiliated with a Canadian academic program as faculty members.

Proposals must be aligned with one or more of the research priorities identified. Proposals that are not relevant to any of these priorities will not be considered for funding.

GEOG. RESTRICTIONS: Canada.

FINANCIAL DATA:
Amount of support per award: Up to $200,000 per year.
Total amount of support: $1,200,000 for the year 2020.

NO. AWARDS: Up to 3 for the year 2020.

APPLICATION INFO:
Candidate must complete the Canadian Blood Services Intramural Research Grant Registration Form as per the instructions. Registration Form must be submitted to the Centre for Innovation at the e-mail address listed above. After administrative review, Canadian Blood Services will contact all registrants and provide the full application form to those who meet the basic eligibility criteria. No feedback on the proposed project will be provided to the registrants.

Unsolicited applications will not be accepted.
Duration: Two years.
Deadline: Registration: February 26. Application: April 23.

ADDRESS INQUIRIES TO:
Centre for Innovation
(See telephone and e-mail address above.)

*SPECIAL STIPULATIONS:
Awards must be held in Canada.

CANADIAN BLOOD SERVICES [2020]
1800 Alta Vista Drive
Ottawa ON K1G 4J5 Canada
(613) 739-2496
Fax: (613) 739-2201
E-mail: centreforinnovation@blood.ca
Web Site: blood.ca

AREAS OF INTEREST:
Research in transfusion science.

NAME(S) OF PROGRAMS:
● **Kenneth J. Fyke Award**

TYPE:
Project/program grants; Research grants. In order to honor the contributions of Kenneth J. Fyke to Canada's health care system, the Kenneth J. Fyke Award was established in his name. This competition supports one health services or policy research project for a period of one year. The competition is held on a biennial basis.

PURPOSE:
To support health services and policy research in order to promote the development of evidence-based Canadian practices and policies in blood transfusion, blood stem cell transplantation, and organ and tissue donation and transplantation for the benefit of Canadian patients.

ELIGIBILITY:
Applicants must be Canadian researchers affiliated with a Canadian academic program related to health services or health policy, or transfusion medicine, stem cell transplantation, or organ/tissue donation and transplantation medicine. Priority will be given to applicants that are not employees of or contracted to Canadian Blood Services at the time of application. Priority will also be given to projects that are collaborative in nature and, when relevant, include team members from different disciplines.

GEOG. RESTRICTIONS: Canada.

FINANCIAL DATA:
Amount of support per award: Up to $100,000.

Total amount of support: Up to $100,000.

NO. AWARDS: 1.

APPLICATION INFO:
Application form and supporting documents must be submitted to the Centre for Innovation at the e-mail address listed above.
Duration: One year.
Deadline: March 19.

ADDRESS INQUIRIES TO:
Centre for Innovation
(See telephone and e-mail address above.)

*SPECIAL STIPULATIONS:
Awards must be held in Canada.

CANADIAN BLOOD SERVICES [2021]
1800 Alta Vista Drive
Ottawa ON K1G 4J5 Canada
(613) 739-2496
Fax: (613) 739-2201
E-mail: centreforinnovation@blood.ca
Web Site: blood.ca

AREAS OF INTEREST:
Research in transfusion science.

NAME(S) OF PROGRAMS:
● **James Kreppner Award**

TYPE:
Project/program grants; Research grants. In order to honor the contributions of James Kreppner to Canada's blood system, the James Kreppner Award was established in his name. The competition supports one legal research project for a period of one year. Research priorities include the legal and regulatory aspects of donation, collection, storage, and use of blood, blood products, and hematopoietic stem cells, and organ and tissue donation and transplantation.

PURPOSE:
To support legal and/or bioethical research relevant to Canadian Blood Services' priorities.

ELIGIBILITY:
Applicant must be a Canadian legal or bioethics researcher affiliated with a Canadian academic program as a faculty member. There is no restriction on the number of team members. However, all team members must have a defined role in the project, and their expertise must be clearly required to adequately address the project goals. The project must have a clear plan with defined goals and deliverables that will be completed within the term of the award and that are aligned with the research priorities. Priority will be given to projects that are collaborative in nature and, when relevant, include team members from different disciplines.

GEOG. RESTRICTIONS: Canada.

FINANCIAL DATA:
Amount of support per award: Up to $50,000.

Total amount of support: Up to $50,000.

NO. AWARDS: 1.

APPLICATION INFO:
Application form and supporting documents must be submitted to the Centre for Innovation at the e-mail address listed above.
Duration: One year.
Deadline: Winter.

ADDRESS INQUIRIES TO:
Centre for Innovation
Tel: (613) 739-2564
(See e-mail address above.)

*SPECIAL STIPULATIONS:
Awards must be held in Canada.

CANADIAN BLOOD SERVICES [2022]
1800 Alta Vista Drive
Ottawa ON K1G 4J5 Canada
(613) 739-2496
Fax: (613) 739-2201
E-mail: centreforinnovation@blood.ca
Web Site: blood.ca

AREAS OF INTEREST:
Research in transfusion science.

NAME(S) OF PROGRAMS:
- **BloodTechNet Award Program**

TYPE:
Project/program grants.

PURPOSE:
To support the development of innovative educational projects that network the transfusion, cellular therapy and transplantation communities in Canada.

ELIGIBILITY:
The primary applicant must be a health professional belonging to the transfusion, cellular therapy and/or transplantation communities in Canada. This program is targeted towards medical lab technologists, nurses and physicians. There is no restriction on the number of team members. However, all team members must have a defined role in the project, and their expertise must be clearly required to adequately address the project goals. The project must have a clear plan with defined educational goals and deliverables that will be completed within the term of the award. Priority will be given to projects that are collaborative in nature and, when relevant, include team members from a variety of health care professions, departments, organizations and/or jurisdictions.

GEOG. RESTRICTIONS: Canada.

FINANCIAL DATA:
Amount of support per award: Up to $50,000.
Total amount of support: $50,000 for the year 2020.

NO. AWARDS: Varies depending on the requested budgets.

APPLICATION INFO:
Application package must be submitted to the Centre for Innovation at the e-mail address listed above.
Duration: One year.
Deadline: Fall 2021.

ADDRESS INQUIRIES TO:
Centre for Innovation
Tel: (613) 739-2564
(See e-mail address above.)

*SPECIAL STIPULATIONS:
Awards must be held in Canada.

CANADIAN LIVER FOUNDATION
3100 Steeles Avenue East
Suite 801
Markham ON L3R 8T3 Canada
(416) 491-3353
(800) 563-5483 (within Canada and U.S.)
Fax: (905) 752-1540
E-mail: clf@liver.ca
Web Site: www.liver.ca

TYPE:
Scholarships. One graduate studentship may be awarded to a student in Alberta whose research project is related to hepatobiliary research and two graduate studentships may be awarded to students in Canada whose research projects are related to hepatitis B.

See entry 2164 for full listing.

CANADIAN LIVER FOUNDATION [2023]
3100 Steeles Avenue East
Suite 801
Markham ON L3R 8T3 Canada
(416) 491-3353
(800) 563-5483 (within Canada and U.S.)
Fax: (905) 752-1540
E-mail: clf@liver.ca
Web Site: www.liver.ca

FOUNDED: 1969

AREAS OF INTEREST:
Research and education into the causes, diagnosis, prevention and treatment of diseases of the liver.

NAME(S) OF PROGRAMS:
- **Summer Studentships**

TYPE:
Scholarships. One summer studentship grant may be awarded to a student in Canada whose research project is related to hepatobiliary research. Two summer studentship grants may be awarded to students in Canada whose research projects are related to liver cancer. One Raj Bhargava Memorial Summer Studentship may be awarded to a student enrolled at the University of Alberta whose research project is related to radiology of liver disease.

PURPOSE:
To provide an opportunity for a limited number of well-motivated students with records of strong academic performance to participate in liver-related research in Canada.

LEGAL BASIS:
Registered Canadian charity.

ELIGIBILITY:
Applicants must be registered at a Canadian institution in an undergraduate degree program.

Canadian citizens, landed immigrants, and permanent residents will receive first consideration.

GEOG. RESTRICTIONS: Canada.

FINANCIAL DATA:
Amount of support per award: $3,500 stipend plus $500 for supplies.

NO. AWARDS: 4 for the year 2020.

APPLICATION INFO:
A single PDF file of the entire grant application, one reference letter from someone other than the applicant's supervisor, and a scanned copy of the applicant's academic transcript must be submitted by e-mail to researchgrants@liver.ca by the deadline.
Duration: Any three summer months (May to August).
Deadline: February 24, for awards to become tenable the following June 1.

PUBLICATIONS:
Program description and guidelines.

STAFF:
Nem Maksimovic, Manager, National Health Promotion and Education

ADDRESS INQUIRIES TO:
Nem Maksimovic, Manager
National Health Promotion and Education
(See address above.)

*SPECIAL STIPULATIONS:
At the conclusion of the award period, a written report of approximately 1,000 words must be submitted to the CLF National Office giving an overview of the summer's work, including methods used, an evaluation of the results with a discussion of their significance, and an evaluation of the experience gained.

CANADIAN LIVER FOUNDATION
3100 Steeles Avenue East
Suite 801
Markham ON L3R 8T3 Canada
(416) 491-3353
(800) 563-5483 (within Canada and U.S.)
Fax: (905) 752-1540
E-mail: clf@liver.ca
Web Site: www.liver.ca

TYPE:
Research grants. Operating grants may be offered to one researcher in Canada whose research project is related to hepatobiliary research, one researcher in Canada whose research project is related to hepatitis B, and one researcher in Canada whose research project is related to liver cancer.

See entry 2163 for full listing.

CHINESE AMERICAN MEDICAL SOCIETY [2024]
11 East Broadway, Suite 4-C
New York, NY 10038
(212) 334-4760
Fax: (646) 304-6373
E-mail: jlove@camsociety.org
Web Site: www.camsociety.org

FOUNDED: 1963

AREAS OF INTEREST:
Medicine.

NAME(S) OF PROGRAMS:
- **CAMS Scholarship Program**
- **Medical Student Summer Research Fellowship**

TYPE:
Fellowships; Scholarships.

YEAR PROGRAM STARTED: 1973

PURPOSE:
To promote the scientific association of medical professionals of Chinese descent; to advance medical knowledge and scientific research with emphasis on aspects unique to the Chinese; to establish scholarships to medical and dental students and to provide

endowments to medical schools and hospitals of good standing; to promote the health status of Chinese Americans.

LEGAL BASIS:
A nonprofit, charitable, educational, and scientific society.

ELIGIBILITY:
Candidates must currently be in their first, second or third year of medical or dental school in a U.S.-accredited medical or dental school when applying. Candidates must reside in the U.S. at the time of application either as an alien student or citizen of the U.S. Students who have just been accepted into medical or dental school at the time of application are not eligible.

FINANCIAL DATA:
Amount of support per award: Scholarships: $5,000; Research Fellowships: Maximum $5,000.
Total amount of support: Varies.

NO. AWARDS: Scholarships: 3 to 5; Research Fellowships: Up to 4.

APPLICATION INFO:
Details and application form are available online.
Duration: One-time award.
Deadline: Research Fellowships: March 2; Scholarship: March 31.

STAFF:
Ms. Jamie Love, Administrator

ADDRESS INQUIRIES TO:
Warren W. Chin, M.D.
Executive Director
(See address above.)

COLLEGE OF PHYSICIANS OF PHILADELPHIA
Francis Clark Wood Institute
for the History of Medicine
19 South 22nd Street
Philadelphia, PA 19103-3097
(215) 399-2301
Fax: (215) 569-0356
E-mail: travelgrants@collegeofphysicians.org
Web Site: www.collegeofphysicians.
org/library/wood-institute

TYPE:
Travel grants; Visiting scholars. This program allows scholars to conduct short-term research in the College's Library and/or Mutter Museum.
See entry 532 for full listing.

CUREPSP, INC.
1216 Broadway, Second Floor
New York, NY 10001
(347) 294-2871
Fax: (410) 785-7009
E-mail: info@curepsp.org
Web Site: www.curepsp.org

TYPE:
Research grants.
See entry 2208 for full listing.

THE DANA FOUNDATION   [2025]
505 Fifth Avenue, Sixth Floor
New York, NY 10017
(212) 223-4040
Fax: (212) 317-8721
E-mail: danainfo@dana.org
grantsinfo@dana.org
Web Site: www.dana.org

FOUNDED: 1950

AREAS OF INTEREST:
Science, health and education, with a current focus on neuroscience research.

TYPE:
Awards/prizes; Research grants.

YEAR PROGRAM STARTED: 1950

PURPOSE:
To strengthen and improve the quality of science, health and education.

LEGAL BASIS:
Private, independent philanthropic foundation.

ELIGIBILITY:
The Foundation, in general, makes its grants in accordance with the following policies: (1) it supports programs in science, health and education; carefully defined objectives in each field guide its grantmaking; (2) in many cases, it requires grantee institutions to share the cost of a project; (3) it makes no grants directly to individuals; (4) it does not support annual operating budgets of organizations, deficit reduction, capital campaigns or individual sabbaticals and; (5) it does not schedule meetings with applicants, other than by specific invitation initiated by the Foundation.

GEOG. RESTRICTIONS: United States.

FINANCIAL DATA:
Total amount of support: Varies by program.

NO. AWARDS: Varies.

APPLICATION INFO:
Application details can be found on the web site.
Duration: Up to three years. Renewals are rare.

PUBLICATIONS:
Annual report; *Dana Report*, newsletter; application guidelines.

IRS I.D.: 06-6036761

BOARD OF DIRECTORS:
Steven E. Hyman, M.D., Chairman
Edward Bleier
Wallace L. Cook
Charles A. Dana, III
Hildegarde E. Mahoney
Ann McLaughlin-Korologos
Peter A. Nadosy
Herbert J. Siegel

ADMINISTRATION:
Caroline Montojo, Ph.D., President
Barbara E. Gill, Executive Vice President, Assistant Treasurer and Assistant Secretary
Burton M. Mirsky, Treasurer

ADDRESS INQUIRIES TO:
Celina Sooksatan, Grants Associate
(See address above.)

DERMATOLOGY FOUNDATION   [2026]
1560 Sherman Avenue
Suite 500
Evanston, IL 60201-4808
(847) 328-2256
Fax: (847) 328-0509
E-mail: dfgen@dermatologyfoundation.org
Web Site: www.dermatologyfoundation.org

FOUNDED: 1964

AREAS OF INTEREST:
Cancer and other diseases of the skin, hair and nails.

TYPE:
Fellowships; Research grants. Research funding in the form of career development grants, dermatologist investigator research and fellowships, project grants, and patient-directed investigator and research grants for academic investigators in their early to midcareer.

There are 12 research award categories. Career development awards include Physician Scientist, Dermatologic Surgery, Public Health, Medical Dermatology, Science of Human Appearance, Dermatopathology Research, Pediatric Research, Basic Research, and Women's Health.

YEAR PROGRAM STARTED: 1964

PURPOSE:
To advance the research careers of young individuals in dermatology and cutaneous biology, with the emphasis on research benefiting the dermatology community at large.

LEGAL BASIS:
Nonprofit charitable organization.

GEOG. RESTRICTIONS: United States.

FINANCIAL DATA:
Amount of support per award: Career development awards: $55,000; Fellowships: $30,000; Grants: $20,000; Sun Pharma Research Award: $100,000.
Total amount of support: $2,710,000 in research funding for the year 2020.

NO. AWARDS: 60 for the year 2020.

APPLICATION INFO:
Forms are available only on the Foundation web site.
Duration: Most awards are for one to three years. Renewal possibilities vary.
Deadline: October 15. Announcement midwinter at the annual meeting of the American Academy of Dermatology.

PUBLICATIONS:
Annual report; *Dermatology Focus*, scientific publication.

IRS I.D.: 04-6115524

OFFICERS:
Elizabeth I. McBurney, M.D., Chairman, Board of Trustees
Janet A. Fairley, M.D., President
Sewon Kang, M.D., Vice President
Renee J.. Mathur, M.D., Secretary/Treasurer

ADDRESS INQUIRIES TO:
John E. Bournas, Executive Director
(See address above.)

EMERGENCY MEDICINE FOUNDATION   [2027]
4950 West Royal Lane
Irving, TX 75063-2524
(469) 499-0297
(800) 798-1822 ext. 3217
Fax: (972) 580-2816
E-mail: csingh@acep.org
Web Site: www.emfoundation.org

FOUNDED: 1972

AREAS OF INTEREST:
Emergency medicine research.

NAME(S) OF PROGRAMS:
• **Emergency Medicine Research**

TYPE:
Research grants; Technical assistance.
Policy-based research awards in emergency medicine.

YEAR PROGRAM STARTED: 1972

PURPOSE:
To promote education and research in emergency medicine.

LEGAL BASIS:
501(c)(3) nonprofit.

ELIGIBILITY:
Must be an emergency medicine researcher.

GEOG. RESTRICTIONS: United States.

FINANCIAL DATA:
Amount of support per award: $5,000 to $250,000.
Total amount of support: Varies.

NO. AWARDS: 28 for the year 2020-21.

APPLICATION INFO:
Contact the Foundation.
Deadline: Varies.

IRS I.D.: 75-2331221

STAFF:
Peggy Brock, Executive Director
Cynthia Singh, Deputy Executive Director

ADDRESS INQUIRIES TO:
Cynthia Singh
Deputy Executive Director
(See address above.)

FOUNDATION FOR ANESTHESIA EDUCATION AND RESEARCH [2028]
1061 American Lane
Schaumburg, IL 60173-4973
(630) 912-2554
Fax: (847) 825-2085
E-mail: FAER@faer.org
Web Site: www.asahq.org/faer

AREAS OF INTEREST:
Anesthesiology, critical care, pain, and all areas of perioperative medicine.

NAME(S) OF PROGRAMS:
• **FAER Mentored Research Training Grant**
• **FAER Research Fellowship Grant**
• **FAER Research in Education Grant**
• **FAER Transition to Independence Grant**

TYPE:
Fellowships; Research grants; Training grants. These grants are designed to create opportunities for physicians to excel in an exceedingly competitive environment and to eventually acquire NIH funding.

PURPOSE:
To provide research grant funding for promising investigators to train in clinical, basic science and translational anesthesiology research.

ELIGIBILITY:
FAER Mentored Research Training Grant: Applicants must be instructors or assistant professors who are within 10 years of their initial appointment.

FAER Research Fellowship Grant: Open to anesthesiology residents after CA-1 training and six months of clinical scientist track.

FAER Research in Education Grant: Open to anesthesiology residents or faculty.

A 20-member committee consisting of both clinical and basic science anesthesiologists reviews proposals. Clinical and outcomes projects are encouraged.

GEOG. RESTRICTIONS: United States.

FINANCIAL DATA:
Amount of support per award: $75,000 to $250,000.
Total amount of support: $3,100,000 annually.

NO. MOST RECENT APPLICANTS: 63.

NO. AWARDS: Average 15 per year.

APPLICATION INFO:
Contact the Foundation.
Duration: One to two years.
Deadline: February 15 and August 15.

IRS I.D.: 52-1494164

ADDRESS INQUIRIES TO:
Maggie Voves, Coordinator
(See address above.)

THE FOUNDATION OF THE AMERICAN SOCIETY OF NEURORADIOLOGY [2029]
800 Enterprise Drive, Suite 205
Oak Brook, IL 60523
(630) 574-0220
Fax: (630) 574-0661
E-mail: rbhala@asnr.org
Web Site: foundation.asnr.org

FOUNDED: 1995

AREAS OF INTEREST:
Neuroradiology.

TYPE:
Research grants.

PURPOSE:
To promote education and research in the field of neuroradiology and the development of new ideas for clinical practice.

ELIGIBILITY:
Applicant must be a member in good standing of the American Society of Neuroradiology with an M.D., D.O. or Ph.D. degree and must be board-certified or board-eligible in radiology by the American Board of Radiology or the Royal College of Physicians and Surgeons of Canada.

FINANCIAL DATA:
Amount of support per award: Up to $75,000.
Total amount of support: Approximately $300,000 in grants annually.

NO. AWARDS: Varies.

APPLICATION INFO:
Award prospectus and information on applying is posted on the Foundation web site in October. Applicants must submit a letter of intent and a one-page abstract of the research proposal. Those selected will receive a follow-up e-mail invitation.
Duration: One year. Some renewals.
Deadline: Varies.

PUBLICATIONS:
American Journal of Neuroradiology.

ADDRESS INQUIRIES TO:
Theresa Espinosa, Manager of Development
E-mail: tespinosa@asnr.org

THE MICHAEL J. FOX FOUNDATION FOR PARKINSON'S RESEARCH [2030]
Grand Central Station
P.O. Box 4777
New York, NY 10163-4777
(212) 509-0995
(800) 708-7644
Fax: (212) 509-2390
E-mail: grants@michaeljfox.org
Web Site: www.michaeljfox.org

FOUNDED: 2000

AREAS OF INTEREST:
Medical research and Parkinson's disease.

TYPE:
Conferences/seminars; Research grants.

YEAR PROGRAM STARTED: 2000

PURPOSE:
To find a cure for Parkinson's disease through an aggressively funded research agenda; to ensure the development of improved therapies for those living with Parkinson's today.

LEGAL BASIS:
501(c)(3).

ELIGIBILITY:
Varies depending on research program.

FINANCIAL DATA:
Amount of support per award: Varies.
Total amount of support: Varies.

APPLICATION INFO:
The Foundation has implemented an electronic grant submission and review system that will enable research to be funded quickly and efficiently. Applicants should consult the Foundation web site for information.
Duration: Varies.
Deadline: Varies.

PUBLICATIONS:
The Fox Focus, newsletter; annual report; progress report.

IRS I.D.: 13-4141945

STAFF:
Deborah W. Brooks, Co-Founder and Chief Executive Officer
Todd Sherer, Ph.D., Executive Vice President Research Strategy
Sohini Chowdhuri, Deputy Chief Executive Officer
Brian Fiske, Chief Science Officer Research Programs
Mark Frasier, Chief Science Officer Research Programs

ADDRESS INQUIRIES TO:
Brian Fiske, Chief Science Officer
Research Programs
(See address above.)

THE PARKER B. FRANCIS FELLOWSHIP PROGRAM [2031]
UVMMC, 111 Colchester Avenue
Fletcher 311
Burlington, VT 05401
(802) 847-2550
Fax: (802) 847-5368
E-mail: polly.parsons@uvmhealth.org
Web Site: www.francisfellowships.org

FOUNDED: 1951

AREAS OF INTEREST:
Research related to lung biology, critical illness and control of breathing.

TYPE:
Fellowships. Awarded to scientists embarking on careers in clinical, laboratory or translational science in pulmonary, critical care and sleep medicine.

YEAR PROGRAM STARTED: 1975

PURPOSE:
To exert a favorable and lasting influence on the field of pulmonary medicine by providing the means to support promising young physicians and scientists for a period of training in research.

LEGAL BASIS:
Private foundation.

ELIGIBILITY:
Evaluation criteria and eligibility requirements can be found on the Foundation's web site.

GEOG. RESTRICTIONS: United States and Canada.

FINANCIAL DATA:
Funds to be used for stipends and fringe benefits, with up to $2,000 per year as a travel allowance.
Amount of support per award: $225,000 over three years.

NO. AWARDS: 10 to 14.

APPLICATION INFO:
Contact the Program.
Duration: Three years.
Deadline: October of each year.

STAFF:
Laurie St. Gelais, PBF Fellowship Program Administrator

ADDRESS INQUIRIES TO:
Laurie St. Gelais
PBF Fellowship Program Administrator
E-mail: pbf@thoracic.org

FRAXA RESEARCH FOUNDATION   [2032]
10 Prince Place
Suite 203
Newburyport, MA 01950
(978) 462-1866
E-mail: info@fraxa.org
Web Site: www.fraxa.org

FOUNDED: 1994

AREAS OF INTEREST:
Medical research aimed at the treatment of Fragile X Syndrome.

NAME(S) OF PROGRAMS:
● **FRAXA Grants and Fellowships**

TYPE:
Fellowships; Research grants; Research contracts.

YEAR PROGRAM STARTED: 1994

PURPOSE:
To promote research aimed at finding a specific treatment for Fragile X Syndrome; to provide funds for postdoctoral fellowships and investigator-initiated grants.

FINANCIAL DATA:
Amount of support per award: Up to $45,000 per year for fellowships. No limit on grants.

APPLICATION INFO:
Application form, plus a one-page initial inquiry letter.
Duration: Fellowships: Up to two years. Second year contingent upon successful progress and timely submission of renewal application.

Deadline: Fellowships: February 1.

PUBLICATIONS:
Newsletter; e-mail updates.

IRS I.D.: 04-3222167

OFFICER:
Katherine Clapp, President

ADDRESS INQUIRIES TO:
Michael Tranfaglia, Chief Scientific Officer
E-mail: mtranfaglia@fraxa.org and
Katherine Clapp, President
E-mail: kclapp@fraxa.org

FSHD SOCIETY, INC.   [2033]
75 North Main Street
Suite 1073
Randolph, MA 02368
(781) 301-6060
E-mail: grants@fshdsociety.org
Web Site: www.fshdsociety.org

FOUNDED: 1991

AREAS OF INTEREST:
Facioscapulohumeral Muscular Dystrophy.

TYPE:
Conferences/seminars; Project/program grants; Research grants.

YEAR PROGRAM STARTED: 1998

PURPOSE:
To promote research on and disperse information on Facioscapulohumeral Muscular Dystrophy.

LEGAL BASIS:
501(c)(3) organization.

ELIGIBILITY:
Preference will be given to postdoctoral trainees, clinical fellows and younger faculty establishing their first independent laboratory (less than five years). More established researchers should allow their postdoctoral trainees and fellows apply for these awards directly, while providing mentorship and guidance for a successful outcome to the proposal.

FINANCIAL DATA:
Amount of support per award: $5,000 to $100,000 per year.
Total amount of support: $332,906 for the year 2019.

NO. MOST RECENT APPLICANTS: 6 for the year 2019.

NO. AWARDS: 3 for the year 2019.

APPLICATION INFO:
Contact the Society.
Duration: Up to two years.
Deadline: February 28 and August 31.

PUBLICATIONS:
FSH Watch Newsletter; patient information on FSHD (English and Spanish).

IRS I.D.: 52-1762747

STAFF:
Mark A. Stone, Chief Executive Officer
June Kinoshita, Director of Research and Patient Engagement
Daniel Paul Perez, Co-Founder

ADDRESS INQUIRIES TO:
Daniel Paul Perez, Co-Founder
(See address above.)

GLAUCOMA RESEARCH FOUNDATION
251 Post Street, Suite 600
San Francisco, CA 94108
(415) 986-3162
Fax: (415) 986-3763
E-mail: research@glaucoma.org
Web Site: www.glaucoma.org/research

TYPE:
Research grants.
See entry 2270 for full listing.

THE GRAYSON-JOCKEY CLUB RESEARCH FOUNDATION [2034]
821 Corporate Drive
Lexington, KY 40503
(859) 224-2850
Fax: (859) 224-2853
E-mail: jhaydon@jockeyclub.com
Web Site: www.grayson-jockeyclub.org

FOUNDED: 1940

AREAS OF INTEREST:
Race horses, veterinary medicine and research for all horses.

TYPE:
Fellowships; Project/program grants; Research grants. Supports research relevant to equine health and performance.

YEAR PROGRAM STARTED: 1940

PURPOSE:
To promote research in veterinary medicine and in the breeding, raising and handling of horses.

LEGAL BASIS:
Nonprofit foundation.

ELIGIBILITY:
The principal investigator should have some professional rank and salary from the institution involved, or hold some grade of Research Professorship with salary from the institution. Research interest must be relevant to the equine, particularly in regard to, but not limited to, cardiopulmonary disorders, infectious diseases, musculoskeletal disorders, and reproduction.

FINANCIAL DATA:
Amount of support per award: Average $75,000.
Total amount of support: Approximately $1,000,000 annually.

NO. MOST RECENT APPLICANTS: Approximately 55.

NO. AWARDS: 24 research grants and 2 fellowships for the year 2020.

APPLICATION INFO:
The Foundation will only accept the online application. Complete information is available on the Foundation web site.
Duration: One or two years.
Deadline: October 1. Announcement April 1.

PUBLICATIONS:
Application; guidelines; *Research Today,* newsletter.

IRS I.D.: 61-6031750

OFFICERS:
Dell Hancock, Chairman
Kevin Lavin, D.V.M., Vice Chairman
Jamie Haydon, President
Laura Barillaro, Treasurer
Resia Ayres, Secretary

STAFF:
Holly E. White, Director of Development
Shannon Kelly, Development Manager

Resia Ayres, Operations Manager
Dr. Johnny Mac Smith, Veterinary Consultant

HEALTH RESOURCES AND SERVICES ADMINISTRATION   [2035]
Bureau of Health Workforce
Division of Medicine and Dentistry
5600 Fishers Lane, Room 9A-27
Rockville, MD 20857
(301) 443-8437
E-mail: aanyanwu@hrsa.gov
Web Site: bhw.hrsa.gov/grants/medicine

NAME(S) OF PROGRAMS:
- **Primary Care Training and Enhancement (PCTE)**

TYPE:
Residencies; Training grants. Grants to strengthen the primary care workforce by supporting enhanced training for future primary care clinicians, teachers, and researchers and promoting primary care practice in rural and underserved areas. This grant focuses on producing primary care providers who will be well prepared to practice in and lead transforming health care systems aimed at improving access, quality of care, and cost effectiveness.

YEAR PROGRAM STARTED: 1972

PURPOSE:
To improve and expand access to quality health care for all.

LEGAL BASIS:
Section 747(a) of the PHS Act, as amended by the Health Professions Education Extension Amendments of 1992, Public Law 102-408.

ELIGIBILITY:
Applicants for the PCTE program must focus on training for transforming health care systems, particularly enhancing the clinical training experience of trainees.

Eligible applicants are accredited health professions schools and programs, including schools of allopathic or osteopathic medicine, academically affiliated physician assistant training programs, accredited public or nonprofit private hospitals, and public or nonprofit private entity capable of carrying out the grant.

GEOG. RESTRICTIONS: United States.

NO. AWARDS: Varies.

APPLICATION INFO:
Applicants are required to apply for this funding opportunity electronically through www.grants.gov.

All applications are competitively reviewed and evaluated.

Duration: Five years.

THE LARRY L. HILLBLOM FOUNDATION, INC.   [2036]
755 Baywood Drive, Suite 180
Petaluma, CA 94954
(707) 762-6691
Fax: (707) 762-6694
E-mail: petaluma@llhf.org
Web Site: www.llhf.org

FOUNDED: 1996

AREAS OF INTEREST:
Medical research on diabetes mellitus and diseases associated with aging.

NAME(S) OF PROGRAMS:
- **Fellowship Research Grants**
- **Network Grants**
- **Start-Up Research Grants**

TYPE:
Assistantships; Block grants; Endowments; Fellowships. Fellowship Research Grants are intended to enable qualified institutions to provide postdoctoral research fellowship training to qualified applicants in one of the two areas of stated interest to the Foundation.

Network Grants facilitate interaction between a network of researchers. It is anticipated these investigators will be independently funded and have demonstrated productivity in their own field.

Start-Up Research Grants are offered to qualified institutions to enable them to select and assist qualified researchers to initiate independent research careers.

YEAR PROGRAM STARTED: 2000

PURPOSE:
To provide philanthropic support exclusively for charitable, religious, scientific, literary and educational purposes.

ELIGIBILITY:
Eligible organizations must have 501(c)(3) status.

GEOG. RESTRICTIONS: Primarily, California.

FINANCIAL DATA:
Amount of support per award: Fellowship Grants: Up to $65,000 per year; Network Grants: $300,000 per year; Start-Up Grants: $70,000 per year.

Total amount of support: Varies.

NO. MOST RECENT APPLICANTS: Varies.

NO. AWARDS: Varies.

APPLICATION INFO:
All grant applications must be submitted electronically through the Foundation's online grant management system. Hard copies will not be accepted.

Duration: Fellowship Grants and Start-Up Grants: Up to three years; Network Grants: Four years.

Deadline: Fellowship Grants and Start-Up Grants: January. Notification by June. Network Grants: January 29 for Letters of Inquiry; August 27 for full application.

HIMSS FOUNDATION   [2037]
33 West Monroe Street, Suite 1700
Chicago, IL 60603-5616
(312) 915-9289
Fax: (312) 664-6143
E-mail: scholarships@himss.org
Web Site: www.himss.org/health-it.education/scholarships

FOUNDED: 1961

AREAS OF INTEREST:
Health care information and management systems.

NAME(S) OF PROGRAMS:
- **HIMSS Foundation Scholarship Program**

TYPE:
Awards/prizes; Conferences/seminars; Fellowships; Internships; Research grants; Scholarships.

YEAR PROGRAM STARTED: 1986

PURPOSE:
To recognize students who have the potential to be future leaders in the health care information management systems industry.

ELIGIBILITY:
For scholarship consideration, nominees must meet the following criteria:
(1) The primary occupation of the applicant at the time the scholarship is awarded must be that of student in an accredited undergraduate, graduate, or doctoral program related to the health information or management systems field. The specific degree program is not a critical factor, although it is expected that programs similar to those in industrial engineering, operations research, bioinformatics, health informatics, computer science and information systems, mathematics, and quantitative programs in business administration, clinical disciplines, and health administration will predominate;
(2) Undergraduate applicants must be at least a first-term junior when the scholarship is awarded;
(3) Current member in good standing of HIMSS;
(4) Not currently serving on one of HIMSS boards (HIMSS NA, HIMSS Analytics, PCHAlliance) and;
(5) Cannot be currently employed by HIMSS, nor engaged in a consulting contract with any component of HIMSS.

Award judges and previous Foundation Scholarship recipients are ineligible.

FINANCIAL DATA:
An all-expense-paid trip to the HIMSS global conference is awarded in addition to grant.
Amount of support per award: $5,000 and $200 honorarium.

Total amount of support: Varies.

NO. MOST RECENT APPLICANTS: 125.

NO. AWARDS: 8 for the year 2018.

APPLICATION INFO:
Application may be requested by e-mail and is also posted on the Foundation web site in early August.
Duration: One year.
Deadline: September 23.

ADDRESS INQUIRIES TO:
See e-mail address above.

THE MAXIMILIAN E. & MARION O. HOFFMAN FOUNDATION, INC.   [2038]
970 Farmington Avenue, Suite 203
West Hartford, CT 06107
(860) 521-2949
Fax: (860) 561-5082

AREAS OF INTEREST:
Education, medicine and the arts.

TYPE:
Project/program grants.

PURPOSE:
To provide funding to 501(c)(3) nonprofits conducting projects in education, medicine, and the arts.

LEGAL BASIS:
Nonprofit private foundation.

ELIGIBILITY:
Applicants must be 501(c)(3). No grants to individuals.

GEOG. RESTRICTIONS: United States, with preference to Connecticut.

FINANCIAL DATA:
Amount of support per award: Varies depending on needs and nature of the request.

APPLICATION INFO:
Submit Letter of Inquiry with copy of 501(c)(3).
Duration: One year. Some multiyear grants. Renewal possible by reapplication.
Deadline: The Board of Directors meets four to six times a year to consider requests.

PUBLICATIONS:
Application form.

IRS I.D.: 22-2648036

ADDRESS INQUIRIES TO:
Marion Barrak, President
(See address above.)

INTERNATIONAL ANESTHESIA RESEARCH SOCIETY (IARS)   [2039]
90 New Montgomery Street
Suite 412
San Francisco, CA 94105
(415) 296-6905
Fax: (415) 296-6901
E-mail: awards@iars.org
Web Site: www.iars.org

FOUNDED: 1922

AREAS OF INTEREST:
Anesthesia.

NAME(S) OF PROGRAMS:
● **Frontiers in Anesthesia Research Award**
● **IARS Mentored Research Awards**

TYPE:
Research grants. Education awards.

YEAR PROGRAM STARTED: 1983

ELIGIBILITY:
Applicant must be a member of the IARS.

FINANCIAL DATA:
Amount of support per award: Frontiers in Anesthesia Research Award: $750,000, in three annual installments; IARS Mentored Research Awards: $175,000.

NO. MOST RECENT APPLICANTS: Frontiers in Anesthesia Research Award: 30; IARS Mentored Research Awards: Average 30.

NO. AWARDS: Frontiers in Anesthesia Research Award: 1 triennially; IARS Mentored Research Awards: 4 annually.

APPLICATION INFO:
Interested applicants should visit the IARS web site. Applications can be submitted online.
Duration: Frontiers in Anesthesia Research Award: Three years; IARS Mentored Research Awards: Two years.
Deadline: Contact IARS for exact date.

PUBLICATIONS:
Anesthesia & Analgesia, journal; *Anesthesia & Analgesia Case Reports,* online journal.

ADDRESS INQUIRIES TO:
See e-mail address above.

INTERNATIONAL COLLEGE OF SURGEONS (ICS)   [2040]
1524 North Lakeshore Drive
Chicago, IL 60610-1694
(312) 560-5006
E-mail: max@icsglobal.org
Web Site: www.icsglobal.org

AREAS OF INTEREST:
Health care, including humanitarian surgery.

NAME(S) OF PROGRAMS:
● **ICS Scholarship**

TYPE:
Scholarships. ICS makes grants available to surgeons who wish to enhance their surgical skills through postgraduate training.

PURPOSE:
To support education.

ELIGIBILITY:
Open to surgeons around the world traveling to developing countries to further their education.

FINANCIAL DATA:
Amount of support per award: Varies.
Total amount of support: Varies.

NO. MOST RECENT APPLICANTS: Varies.

NO. AWARDS: Varies.

APPLICATION INFO:
Send request to ICS.
Duration: Varies.

ADDRESS INQUIRIES TO:
Max C. Downham, Executive Director
(See address above.)

INTERNATIONAL MYELOMA FOUNDATION (IMF)   [2041]
12650 Riverside Drive, Suite 206
North Hollywood, CA 91607-3421
(818) 487-7455
Fax: (818) 487-7454
E-mail: theimf@myeloma.org
Web Site: www.myeloma.org

FOUNDED: 1990

AREAS OF INTEREST:
Myeloma.

NAME(S) OF PROGRAMS:
● **Brian D. Novis Research Grants**

TYPE:
Internships; Research grants; Travel grants.

YEAR PROGRAM STARTED: 1995

PURPOSE:
To promote research into better treatments, management, prevention and a cure for myeloma.

LEGAL BASIS:
Nonprofit organization.

ELIGIBILITY:
Open to junior researchers or senior researchers working in the field of multiple myeloma. Junior researchers must have completed postdoctoral studies or clinical fellowships no later than August 1 of the application year and must have the ability to devote a minimum of 50% of his or her time to research during the award year. Also, must provide a completed application with evidence of a meritorious research project.

FINANCIAL DATA:
Amount of support per award: Junior researchers: $50,000; Senior researchers: $80,000.
Total amount of support: Varies each year.

APPLICATION INFO:
Applications can be downloaded from the Foundation's web site.
Duration: One year. Renewable upon reapplication.

Deadline: August 1 (postmarked) for the following year's program.

PUBLICATIONS:
Myeloma Today, newsletter.

IRS I.D.: 95-4296919

STAFF:
Susie Durie, President and Chief Executive Officer
Lisa Paik, Senior Vice President of Clinical Education and Research Initiatives

ADDRESS INQUIRIES TO:
Lisa Paik, Senior Vice President of Clinical Education and Research Initiatives or
Amirah Limayo
Senior Research Project Coordinator
(See address above.)

ROBERT WOOD JOHNSON FOUNDATION   [2042]
50 College Road East
Princeton, NJ 08540
(877) 843-7953
Fax: (609) 627-6436
E-mail: aliebling@rwjf.org
Web Site: www.rwjf.org

FOUNDED: 1972

AREAS OF INTEREST:
Health leadership, healthy children and families, healthy communities, and transforming health/healthcare systems.

TYPE:
Research grants. Program contracts; Evaluations.

YEAR PROGRAM STARTED: 1972

PURPOSE:
To build a national culture of health; to raise the health of everyone in the U.S. to the level a great nation deserves by placing well-being at the center of every aspect of life.

LEGAL BASIS:
Private foundation.

ELIGIBILITY:
Preference is given to tax-exempt, public agencies under Section 501(c)(3). The Foundation does not fund basic biomedical research, drug therapies or devices research, direct support of individuals, or lobbying of any kind.

Additionally, the Foundation rarely makes grants for conferences, unless they relate clearly to the Foundation's goals, or for publications and media projects, except those that grow out of one of the Foundation's grant programs.

GEOG. RESTRICTIONS: United States.

FINANCIAL DATA:
Amount of support per award: Most grants average $634,044 for the year 2020.
Total amount of support: $693,643,885 for the year 2020.
Matching fund requirements: Varies; only a limited number of awards include matching fund requirements.

NO. MOST RECENT APPLICANTS: 8,198 for the year 2020.

NO. AWARDS: 1,094 for the year 2020.

APPLICATION INFO:
Funding is awarded through targeted calls for proposals. The Foundation will accept brief proposals for funding of new and creative approaches to building a culture of health.

Duration: Varies.

Deadline: Varies.

STAFF:
Richard E. Besser, President and Chief
Executive Officer
Katherine Hatton, J.D., Vice President,
General Counsel and Secretary
William Roell, B.S., C.P.A., Interim Chief
Financial Officer and Treasurer
Brian S. O'Neil, MBA, C.F.A., Chief
Investment Officer
Shannan Gonzalez, MHRM, Interim Director,
Human Resources Operations and Systems

ADDRESS INQUIRIES TO:
Adam Liebling
Director, Grants Management
(See address above.)

THE JACOB AND VALERIA LANGELOTH FOUNDATION [2043]

275 Madison Avenue
Suite 2102
New York, NY 10016
(212) 687-1133
E-mail: info@langeloth.org
Web Site: www.langeloth.org

AREAS OF INTEREST:
Justice reform, safe and healthy communities,
racial equity, social justice, and health care
policy.

NAME(S) OF PROGRAMS:
● **Justice Reform**
● **Safe and Healthy Communities**

TYPE:
Demonstration grants; Project/program
grants; Research grants.

PURPOSE:
To promote and support effective and creative
programs, practices and policies related to
healing from illness, accident, physical,
social or emotional trauma; to extend the
availability of programs that promote healing
to underserved populations.

ELIGIBILITY:
Grants are made to organizations that have
tax-exempt status under Section 501(c)(3) of
the Internal Revenue Code and that are
health care providers, academic research
institutions or community-based
organizations. Grants are made nationwide,
with a specific interest in New York state.

GEOG. RESTRICTIONS: Primarily New York state.

FINANCIAL DATA:
$98,080,429 in assets (unaudited) for fiscal
year ended December 31, 2019.
Amount of support per award: Varies.
Total amount of support: Approximately
$7,400,000 for the year 2019.

NO. AWARDS: 19.

APPLICATION INFO:
Letter of intent and proposal submissions are
by invitation only. Interested organizations
must first register their project for review.
Duration: Up to three years.
Deadline: June and December.

STAFF:
Scott Moyer, President
Andrea Fionda, Director of Programs
Melissa Houston, Grants and Office
Administrator

*SPECIAL STIPULATIONS:
Foundation does not accept unsolicited
proposals.

LEUKEMIA RESEARCH FOUNDATION

191 Waukegan Road
Suite 105
Northfield, IL 60093
(847) 424-0600
Fax: (847) 424-0606
E-mail: grants@lrfmail.org
Web Site: www.allbloodcancers.org

TYPE:
Research grants. The goal of the grant
program is to support new investigators. It
funds scientists and physicians around the
world.

See entry 2192 for full listing.

LOWE SYNDROME ASSOCIATION [2044]

7025 County Road 46A, Box 434
Suite 1071
Lake Mary, FL 32746-4753
(216) 630-7723
E-mail: info@lowesyndrome.org
jgkubicki@gmail.com
Web Site: www.lowesyndrome.org

FOUNDED: 1982

AREAS OF INTEREST:
Medical research pertaining to Lowe
Syndrome.

NAME(S) OF PROGRAMS:
● **The Leland McSpadden Memorial
Fund for Medical and Scientific
Research**

TYPE:
Research grants. Supports research leading to
a better understanding of the metabolic basis
of Lowe Syndrome, to better treatments of
the major complications of Lowe Syndrome,
to the prevention of Lowe Syndrome, and/or
to a cure for Lowe Syndrome.

YEAR PROGRAM STARTED: 1983

PURPOSE:
To improve the lives of persons with Lowe
Syndrome and their families through
fostering communication, providing education
and supporting research so that individuals
can attain their highest potential.

ELIGIBILITY:
Researchers of all types are invited to send
applications, including but not limited to,
universities, hospitals, and other nonprofit
organizations with interest in research in
areas specified by the Association.

FINANCIAL DATA:
Amount of support per award: Varies.
Total amount of support: Varies.

NO. MOST RECENT APPLICANTS: Varies.

NO. AWARDS: Varies.

APPLICATION INFO:
Contact the Association.
Duration: One year.
Deadline: Varies.

ADDRESS INQUIRIES TO:
Lisa Waldbaum, President
(See address above.)

LUPUS FOUNDATION OF AMERICA, INC. [2045]

2121 K Street, N.W., Suite 200
Washington, DC 20037
(202) 349-1150 ext. 150
(800) 875-2562 (customer support)
Fax: (202) 349-1156
E-mail: marion@lupus.org
Web Site: www.lupus.org/finzifellowships

FOUNDED: 1977

AREAS OF INTEREST:
Lupus research.

NAME(S) OF PROGRAMS:
● **Gina M. Finzi Memorial Student
Summer Fellowship Program**

TYPE:
Summer Fellowship. The Gina M. Finzi
Memorial Student Summer Fellowship
Program proposes to foster an interest among
students in the areas of basic, clinical,
translational, epidemiological or behavioral
research relevant to lupus under the
sponsorship and supervision of an
established, tenure-track Principal
Investigator who directs a laboratory
dedicated at least in part to the investigation
of lupus at a U.S. or Canadian academic,
medical or research institution.

YEAR PROGRAM STARTED: 1984

PURPOSE:
To cultivate an interest in lupus research
among young scientists.

ELIGIBILITY:
Institution must be in the U.S., Canada, or
Mexico.

FINANCIAL DATA:
The Finzi Student Summer Fellowship
provides financial support for a summer
research project, opportunities for
professional training, enrichment and
mentorship, lifetime professional association
with LFA network, and access to LFA
professional resources.
Amount of support per award: $4,000.

NO. MOST RECENT APPLICANTS: 17.

NO. AWARDS: 6.

APPLICATION INFO:
Applications must be submitted through the
Fluxx online grants management system.
Applicants must first complete an eligibility
quiz and registration form. Hard copies of
applications will not be accepted.
Duration: One summer.
Deadline: April 17.

ADDRESS INQUIRIES TO:
Ashley Marion, Research and
Grants Senior Coordinator
(See e-mail address above.)

JOSIAH MACY JR. FOUNDATION [2046]

44 East 64th Street
New York, NY 10065
(212) 486-2424
Fax: (212) 644-0765
E-mail: info@macyfoundation.org
Web Site: www.macyfoundation.org

FOUNDED: 1930

AREAS OF INTEREST:
Health care, health professions and medical
education.

NAME(S) OF PROGRAMS:
- **Board Grants**
- **Macy Faculty Scholars**
- **President's Grants**

TYPE:
Conferences/seminars; Demonstration grants; Development grants; Matching gifts; Project/program grants. Major interest in education for careers in medicine or medical science. Special programs on preparation of minority groups for health professions and teamwork among and between health professions.

YEAR PROGRAM STARTED: 1930

PURPOSE:
To promote diversity, equity and belonging; to increase collaboration among future health professionals; to prepare future health professionals to navigate ethical dilemmas.

LEGAL BASIS:
Private foundation.

ELIGIBILITY:
Applicants must be qualified not-for-profit institutions with appropriate interests. No grants are made directly to individuals, nor for building, annual fund appeals or medical research.

GEOG. RESTRICTIONS: United States.

FINANCIAL DATA:
Amount of support per award: Board Grants: Varies based on need; Macy Faculty Scholars: Up to $100,000 per year; President's Grants: Up to $25,000, including overhead.
Total amount of support: Varies.
Matching fund requirements: Foundation matches gifts from full-time employees, directors and officers only to charitable organizations.

NO. AWARDS: Up to 40 annually.

APPLICATION INFO:
Complete application information can be found on the Foundation web site.
Duration: Board Grants: One to three years. Macy Faculty Scholars: Two years. President's Grants: Up to one year.

PUBLICATIONS:
Annual report; conference proceedings.

STAFF:
Holly J. Humphrey, M.D., M.A.C.P., President
Peter Goodwin, MBA, Chief Operating Officer and Treasurer
Karen Butler, Assistant Treasurer
Yasmine R. Legendre, MPA, Program Associate
Heather Snijdewind, Program Assistant, Macy Faculty Scholars Program
Stephen C. Schoenbaum, M.D., M.P.H., Special Advisor to the President

BOARD OF DIRECTORS:
William H. Wright, II, Chairman
Holly J. Humphrey, M.D., M.A.C.P., President
David Blumenthal, M.D., M.P.P.
Francisco G. Cigarroa, M.D.
Terry Fulmer, Ph.D., R.N.
Meredith B. Jenkins
Howard K. Koh, M.D., M.P.H.
Valerie Montgomery Rice, M.D.
Steven M. Safyer, M.D.
Mary K. Wakefield
Gregory H. Warner, MBA

ADDRESS INQUIRIES TO:
See e-mail address above.

MARCH OF DIMES [2047]
1550 Crystal Drive, Suite 1300
Arlington, VA 22202
(571) 257-1044
E-mail: researchgrantssupport@marchofdimes.org
Web Site: www.marchofdimes.org
modresearchgrants.aibs-scores.org (online application system)

FOUNDED: 1938

AREAS OF INTEREST:
Prevention of premature birth and pregnancy-related disorders, infant morbidity and mortality, severe morbidity and mortality, and the health disparities that persist across these.

NAME(S) OF PROGRAMS:
- **Basil O'Connor Starter Scholar Research Award**

TYPE:
Research grants. Basil O'Connor Starter Scholar Research Awards (BOC) support young physicians/scientists committed to the mission of the March of Dimes. March of Dimes leads the fight for the health of all moms and babies.

YEAR PROGRAM STARTED: 1973

PURPOSE:
To support young scientists just embarking on their independent research careers.

LEGAL BASIS:
Tax-exempt 501(c)(3) organization.

ELIGIBILITY:
The Basil O'Connor Starter Scholar Research Award is intended to be an early career grant to young investigators who are just embarking on an independent research career. M.D. or M.D./Ph.D. applicants should be four to nine years past their last year of clinical training required for medical specialty board certification, must hold a full-time tenure-track faculty position (or equivalent) at their current U.S. based institution and must have received their first tenure-track appointment no more than four years prior to the submission deadline.

For Ph.D. scientists, the same timelines apply, but the four- to nine-year window begins upon completion of the terminal degree. Scientists must have either primary or secondary appointments in clinical departments related to maternal or child health.

Applicants who have transition faculty-mentored awards (e.g., K99/R00) are welcome if they still have one year of the mentored portion. If not, application should be deferred. K12 and K08 applicants are encouraged.

Candidates may not simultaneously hold a grant for any other March of Dimes research program. Applicants may not have total grant support exceeding $200,000 per year before the award start date. Those who have previously submitted an application to this program are ordinarily not eligible for resubmission; however, exceptions will be considered on an individual basis.

March of Dimes takes into account the purpose of the research program and plan submitted, qualifications, experience and abilities of the persons who are to supervise and participate in the proposed program and the facilities available.

FINANCIAL DATA:
The budget covers salary support for technical help and a portion of the Principal Investigator's salary, which may not exceed 10% of the NIH salary cap.
Amount of support per award: $75,000 per year for two years.

NO. MOST RECENT APPLICANTS: 27 for the year 2020.

NO. AWARDS: 3 for the year 2020.

REPRESENTATIVE AWARDS:
$150,000 to Ripla Arora, Ph.D., Michigan State University, for "Non-Steroidal Anti-Inflammatory Drugs Influence Uterine 3D Patterning and Pregnancy Outcomes;" $150,000 to Corina Lesseur, M.D., Ph.D., Icahn School of Medicine at Mount Sinai, for "Characterizing the Effects of Genetics and Gestational Diabetes on the Placental DNA Methylome of Pacific Islanders;" $150,000 to Jamie Lo, M.D., MCR, Oregon Health and Science University, for "The Effect of Chronic Prenatal and Postnatal Marijuana Exposure on Infant Neurodevelopment."

APPLICATION INFO:
The entire process must be completed online via the March of Dimes online application system.

The following information is required from the candidate:
(1) Application (template provided) for the proposed research. Application must include, in exact order, contact information, project information, academic appointment details, animal/human subject use and assurance information, payee information and references. Attachments, to be received in the following order, include candidate's biographical sketch, current financial support, pending financial support, professional personnel, consent form (if applicable), budget, budget justification, research plan, and research plan citations;
(2) Letter of nomination. Deans, chairs of departments or directors of institutes/centers may submit nominations for this award. Nominator's name, academic appointment, mailing address, telephone and e-mail address should be included. The nomination letter should be submitted via the online system, and should vouch for a candidate's having an unrestricted faculty position and dedicated lab/clinical research space. Information provided should explicitly include details concerning the candidate's faculty appointment, independence, laboratory space (assigned to the candidate), startup package and access to core facilities. This information will be scrutinized closely and;
(3) Two letters of recommendation, one from a postdoctoral mentor and another of the applicant's choosing.
Duration: Awards are approved for two years.
Deadline: Nominations: July 9. Reviewed through September for October 1 funding cycle.

PUBLICATIONS:
Program announcement and grants list.

ADDRESS INQUIRIES TO:
Rachel Hauser
Research Grants Administrator
E-mail: rhauser@marchofdimes.org

*PLEASE NOTE:
The Foundation does not accept applications dealing with infertility.

*SPECIAL STIPULATIONS:
Basil O'Connor applicants may not be recipients of a major grant (e.g., an R01, or other grant exceeding $200,000 a year) at the time of the application. If an application for such other grant is under review, eligibility for Basil O'Connor remains so long as it has not been awarded at the time of March of Dimes review. Applicants who have transition faculty-mentored awards (e.g., K99/R00) are welcome, if they have completed the mentored portion. If not, application should be deferred. Candidates may not simultaneously submit an application for any other March of Dimes research program. Those who have previously submitted an application to the March of Dimes are not eligible for a Basil O'Connor Award unless permission has been explicitly given; however, application for a regular research grant is welcomed.

MARCH OF DIMES   [2048]
1550 Crystal Drive, Suite 1300
Arlington, VA 22202
(571) 257-1044
E-mail: researchgrants@marchofdimes.org
Web Site: www.marchofdimes.org
modresearchgrants.aibs-scores.org (online application system)

FOUNDED: 1938

AREAS OF INTEREST:
Prevention of premature birth and pregnancy-related disorders, infant morbidity and mortality, severe morbidity and mortality, and the health disparities that persist across these.

NAME(S) OF PROGRAMS:
• **Research Grants Program**

TYPE:
Research grants. March of Dimes is committed to advancing the health of all moms and babies, and that involves seeking answers through a diverse research portfolio. Applicants are sought for research grant funding that involves translational and actionable science that will lead directly to interventions or preventions. The goal is to turn observations in the laboratory, clinic, and community into interventions, therapeutics, and devices that improve the health of moms and babies. The March of Dimes is committed to learning about differences in populations integrated into key research areas. The proposed research should focus on one of these priority areas: Pregnancy-related disorders: Prevention and treatment of diseases in either mom or baby that lead to spontaneous or medically indicated premature birth. This may include studies related to inflammation and immune signaling, placental or cervical health, and hypertensive disorders of pregnancy. Investigations addressing all pregnancy-related disorders must have the potential to improve clinical care to prevent adverse maternal and child outcomes. Developmental origins of infant health: Research on the role of the placenta and the maternal-fetal interface on pregnancy outcomes, and immediate and long-term health outcomes for the infant. Studies must lead to clinical impact in the areas of prevention and treatment of developmental disorders, and have the direct potential to improve the quality of life of those affected. Maternal morbidity and mortality: Studies addressing the leading contributors to the

rising rates of severe morbidity and maternal mortality, such as preeclampsia, cardiovascular and metabolic health, and environmental factors including the effect of stress. This may include investigations regarding during pregnancy, intrapartum and up to one year postpartum, specifically impacting maternal health outcomes. Studies must have the potential to improve clinical care to decrease the rate of maternal morbidity.

YEAR PROGRAM STARTED: 1974

PURPOSE:
To support programs designed to gain new knowledge about the mechanisms that cause birth defects and to find ways of controlling or preventing them.

LEGAL BASIS:
Tax-exempt 501(c)(3) organization.

ELIGIBILITY:
The March of Dimes invites submissions from health professionals, health researchers, epidemiologists and social scientists with doctoral degrees and either a faculty appointment or equivalent at academic universities, hospital and research institutions; or employees of small businesses, startup companies, nonprofit organizations or pharmaceutical companies committed to research in the area of maternal and child health.

These applications are not limited to U.S. citizens and are open to global applicants.

Applicants may not hold any other concurrent March of Dimes grants when applying.

FINANCIAL DATA:
The budget covers salary support for technical help and a portion of the Principal Investigator's salary, which may not exceed 10% of the NIH salary cap.
Amount of support per award: $200,000 to $300,000 over 24 to 36 months.

NO. MOST RECENT APPLICANTS: 63 for the year 2019.

NO. AWARDS: 14 for the year 2019.

REPRESENTATIVE AWARDS:
Rupsa Boelig, M.D., Thomas Jefferson University, for "Aspirin Prevention of Preeclampsia: Individual Determinants of Platelet Response and Pregnancy Outcomes;" Jennifer Condon, Ph.D., Wayne State University, for "A Novel Uterine Secretome Generated by Gestational Preconditioning Acts to Mitigate Preterm Birth;" Dean Carson, Ph.D., Katana Pharmaceuticals, for "Development of a preservative free oxytocin formulation and pediatric nasal delivery device for the treatment of neonatal abstinence syndrome."

APPLICATION INFO:
The entire process must be completed online via the March of Dimes online application system. Applicants may only submit one application, listed as a principal investigator or co-principal investigator. Application for the proposed research must include:
(1) title and abstract of proposed project;
(2) statement of objective and hypothesis;
(3) preliminary data and background studies;
(4) research approach and intended deliverables;
(5) budget and budget justification;
(6) candidate's biographical sketch and;
(7) facilities available.

Applicant must also submit a list of current and pending financial support for the conduct of this research.
Duration: 24 to 36 months, with a set of deliverables to be met for each year before the next year's support can be distributed.
Deadline: September 1. Notification by December 13, for funding to be initiated on January 1.

PUBLICATIONS:
Program announcement; grants list.

ADDRESS INQUIRIES TO:
Rachel Hauser
Research Grants Administrator
E-mail: rhauser@marchofdimes.org

*PLEASE NOTE:
The Foundation does not accept applications dealing with infertility.

Please adhere to the instructions precisely. Any letter that does not follow this precise format will not be included in the review process.

MAYO CLINIC   [2049]
Mayo School of Graduate Medical Education
200 First Street, S.W.
Rochester, MN 55905
(507) 538-6453
Fax: (507) 538-3267
E-mail: pathologyeducation@mayo.edu
Web Site: www.mayo.edu/msgme

AREAS OF INTEREST:
Surgical and medical pathology, including bone and soft tissue pathology, cardiovascular pathology, cytopathology, GI/liver pathology, breast pathology, and renal pathology.

NAME(S) OF PROGRAMS:
• **Surgical Pathology Fellowships**

TYPE:
Fellowships. Available subspecialty fellowships include bone and soft tissue pathology, breast pathology, cardiovascular pathology, cytopathology, gastrointestinal pathology, hematopathology, molecular genetic pathology, neuropathology, pulmonary pathology, renal pathology, special coagulation, and surgical pathology. Each fellowship will give ample opportunity to diagnose and work with a large diverse volume of tissue specimens. Fellows will assist Mayo's staff consultants with projects and will be encouraged to initiate and participate in clinical pathology and basic research studies for publication and presentation at national meetings. Fellows will also develop and present studies at conferences and seminars and may assist in teaching pathology residents, medical students and fellows from other departments. Each specialty fellowship consists of a one-year program except neuropathology, which is a two-year appointment. Combined fellowships are also possible.

PURPOSE:
To promote the belief that physicians need to work together, teach and learn from others and conduct research to provide sustained, excellent patient care.

LEGAL BASIS:
Hospital.

ELIGIBILITY:
Applicants must have a medical degree with U.S. or Canadian specialty training in anatomic pathology for all specialty fellowships.

FINANCIAL DATA:
Fellows will be permitted 15 days each year for vacation. Fellows will also receive a stipend and benefits package including a comprehensive medical care plan, short-term disability insurance, voluntary family life insurance, dental assistance plan, professional liability coverage and excess personal liability insurance.
Amount of support per award: Varies depending on experience and fellowship.

NO. AWARDS: 1 in each specialty except for surgical pathology, which has 9 fellows.

APPLICATION INFO:
Applications are to be submitted through the Apply Yourself application service. Completed online application must include: (1) three letters of recommendation (one must be from applicant's current program director or supervisor); (2) curriculum vitae; (3) personal statement of professional goals; (4) copy of graduate school and/or medical school diploma; (5) dean's letter; (6) official final transcripts; (7) official test transcripts for all applicable examinations (USMLE, LMCC, COMLEX, NBOME, FMGEMS, FLEX, NBME); (8) valid ECFMG certificate (if applicable) and; (9) copy of completion certification from each of applicant's prior residency and/or fellowship training programs.

There is a $15 application fee.

If an applicant is considered for an appointment, they will be asked to visit Mayo Clinic Rochester for an interview with the program director and selected faculty. Interviews are conducted September and October of each year.
Duration: One year.
Deadline: July 1 of the year preceding appointment.

BENJAMIN AND MARY SIDDONS MEASEY FOUNDATION   [2050]
P.O. Box 258
Media, PA 19063
(610) 566-5800
Fax: (610) 566-8197
E-mail: admin@measeyfoundation.org
Web Site: measeyfoundation.org

FOUNDED: 1958

AREAS OF INTEREST:
Medical education in Philadelphia area processed through Philadelphia medical schools only.

NAME(S) OF PROGRAMS:
● **Medical Education Grants**

TYPE:
Challenge/matching grants; Fellowships; Grants-in-aid.

YEAR PROGRAM STARTED: 1958

PURPOSE:
To advance medical education of physicians.

LEGAL BASIS:
1958 Trust Document.

ELIGIBILITY:
Grants are made through accredited medical schools in the immediate Philadelphia, PA area. Individual applications are not accepted by the Foundation; institutions only.

GEOG. RESTRICTIONS: Philadelphia, Pennsylvania area.

FINANCIAL DATA:
Amount of support per award: $7,500 to $500,000.
Total amount of support: $2,000,000.

NO. MOST RECENT APPLICANTS: 10.

APPLICATION INFO:
Application is by letter. Organizations must provide 501(c)(3) tax-exempt information.
Duration: One year. Nonrenewable.
Deadline: One month prior to quarterly meetings held in March, June, September and December.

IRS I.D.: 23-6298781

STAFF:
James C. Brennan, Esq., Manager
M.S. Donaldson, Esq., Secretary

ADDRESS INQUIRIES TO:
James C. Brennan, Esq., Manager and Counsel
(See address above.)

*SPECIAL STIPULATIONS:
No applications to Foundation directly.

MEDICAL LIBRARY ASSOCIATION
225 West Wacker Drive
Suite 650
Chicago, IL 60606
(312) 419-9094
E-mail: awards@mail.mlahq.org
Web Site: www.mlanet.org

TYPE:
Fellowships; Scholarships. Awarded for study and doctoral work in health sciences librarianship.

See entry 673 for full listing.

NATIONAL ALOPECIA AREATA FOUNDATION
65 Mitchell Boulevard
Suite 200-B
San Rafael, CA 94903
(415) 472-3780
Fax: (415) 480-1800
E-mail: info@naaf.org
abby@naaf.org
Web Site: www.naaf.org

TYPE:
Internships; Research grants. Bridge Grants are intended to support researchers who have submitted highly meritorious but unfunded K-type (career development) and R-type applications to the National Institutes of Health with a focus on alopecia areata. This grant is intended to provide a critical year of additional support to near-miss applicants whose projects were well-scored by the NIH, but not funded so that they can collect data that strengthens a future application.

Mentored Investigator Awards are intended to support postdoctoral researchers training to conduct alopecia areata research independently. The goal is to put recipients in a position to compete for larger grants in the future and to establish successful long-term careers with an enduring focus on research relevant to alopecia areata.

Pilot and Feasibility Grants are intended to support studies that explore preliminary ideas and conduct proof-of-concept experiments.

The goal is to stimulate the development of new research programs in the field of alopecia areata capable of competing for long-term funding from the NIH or similar agencies in the future. Proposals must be hypothesis-driven and reflect innovative approaches to address critical questions in alopecia areata research.

Research Grants are intended to support studies focused on understanding the mechanisms behind disease pathophysiology, translational application of basic discoveries, or provide insight into new therapies using translational, clinical, or epidemiologic approaches. Proposals must be hypothesis-driven and provide sufficient preliminary data to justify NAAF support.

Student Internship Awards are intended to support students, residents and fellows conducting short-term research projects focused on alopecia areata under the supervision of experienced investigators in the field. The goal is to enable promising young scientists and physicians to acquire skills that will further their careers in research relevant to alopecia areata.

See entry 1945 for full listing.

NATIONAL HEART, LUNG AND BLOOD INSTITUTE (NHLBI)
Division of Extramural Research
Two Rockledge Center, Suite 7100
6701 Rockledge Drive, MSC 7902
Bethesda, MD 20892-7902
(301) 435-0166
Fax: (301) 451-5462
E-mail: lombardr@nhlbi.nih.gov
Web Site: www.nhlbi.nih.gov

TYPE:
Conferences/seminars; Fellowships; Project/program grants; Research grants; Training grants; Loan forgiveness programs. Career awards and other grant mechanisms to foster research on heart, vascular and lung diseases, and to develop scientists in these areas. Also, small business grants. Loan forgiveness programs are for research.

See entry 2143 for full listing.

THE NATIONAL HEMOPHILIA FOUNDATION   [2051]
7 Penn Plaza
370 Seventh Avenue, Suite 1204
New York, NY 10001
(212) 328-3700
(800) 424-2634
Fax: (212) 328-3777
E-mail: mwitkop@hemophilia.org
Web Site: www.hemophilia.org/Researchers-Healthcare-Providers/Research-Grant-Programs

FOUNDED: 1948

AREAS OF INTEREST:
Biochemistry, genetics, hematology, microbiology, orthopedics, psychiatry and other disciplines related to hemophilia and other bleeding disorders.

NAME(S) OF PROGRAMS:
● **Bridge Award**
● **Excellence Fellowships for Nursing, Physical Therapy and Social Work**
● **Innovative Investigator Award**
● **Jeanne Maria Lusher Diversity Fellowship**

- **NHF Career Development Award**
- **Judith Graham Pool Postdoctoral Research Fellowships in Bleeding Disorders**

TYPE:
Development grants; Fellowships; Research grants. Support for research in clinical and/or basic sciences in areas relating to problems in hemophilia and other bleeding disorders.

Bridge Award assists hematology investigators to continue their critical research into inherited bleeding disorders.

Excellence Fellowships for Nursing, Physical Therapy and Social Work supports nursing, physical therapy and social work research and clinical projects focused on bleeding disorders care.

Innovative Investigator Award and NHF Career Development Award fund innovative projects that promote the development of novel technologies and/or therapies to advance the field of bleeding disorder research.

Jeanne Maria Lusher Diversity Fellowship aims to increase diversity among benign hematologists by fostering a career-long interest in inherited bleeding disorders.

Judith Graham Pool Postdoctoral Research Fellowships are designed to support research studies of high scientific merit and relevance to bleeding disorders. They are awarded through professional and graduate schools, or research institutions.

YEAR PROGRAM STARTED: 1972

PURPOSE:
To encourage and support hemophilia-related and other bleeding disorders research.

LEGAL BASIS:
Voluntary, nonprofit health organization.

ELIGIBILITY:
Applicants must have completed doctoral training and must enter the fellowship program from a doctoral, postdoctoral, internship or residency training program.

Individuals with more than six years of experience since completing doctoral training are not eligible to apply. Established investigators or faculty members are also not eligible.

Bridge Award seeks applications from hematology investigators who have submitted to the NIH an R01 or R01-equivalent application within the past 18 months that was scored but not funded. Applicant must be the principal investigator on the submission.

Excellence Fellowships for Nursing, Physical Therapy and Social Work provides support for a registered nurse, physical therapist or social worker currently employed or interested in hemophilia care to conduct research or clinical projects. Endorsement by a federally funded hemophilia treatment center is recommended. Only providers from an appropriately accredited school practicing hemophilia care may apply. Collaboration with multidisciplinary care providers and/or between two or more hemophilia centers is accepted and encouraged.

Innovative Investigator Award seeks research grant applications from any multidisciplinary team member within the federally funded Hemophilia Treatment Center (HTC) network for innovative-investigator research (IIR) projects that demonstrate a commitment to the bleeding disorders community.

Jeanne Maria Lusher Diversity Fellowship candidates must be enrolled in a doctoral program in a biomedical research field relevant to blood disorders. Fellowship candidates will be BIPOC or individuals from gender, racial and ethnic groups underrepresented in the hematologic field and enrolled in a doctoral program (M.D./Ph.D.) or a fellowship program (M.D. or M.D./Ph.D.) in a biomedical research field relevant to bleeding disorders. M.D./Ph.D. candidate students may apply in their second year of the Ph.D. portion of their program or beyond. M.D. or M.D./Ph.D. hematology fellows may apply in their first year of fellowship if actively engaged in a bleeding disorders related research project. Established investigators or faculty members are ineligible.

NHF Career Development Award seeks research grant applications from established investigators, preferably at the assistant professor level or above, who have demonstrated a commitment to bleeding disorders research.

GEOG. RESTRICTIONS: United States.

FINANCIAL DATA:
Amount of support per award: Bridge Award: Up to $125,000; Excellence Fellowships for Nursing, Physical Therapy and Social Work: $15,000; Innovative Investigator Award: Up to $60,000; Jeanne Maria Lusher Diversity Fellowship: Up to $52,000 per year; NHF Career Development Award: Up to $70,000; Judith Graham Pool Postdoctoral Research Fellowship: Up to $52,000 per year.

Total amount of support: Varies.

NO. MOST RECENT APPLICANTS: Over 30.

NO. AWARDS: Varies.

APPLICATION INFO:
For the Career Development Awards, Excellence Fellowships, Lusher Fellowship and Pool Fellowships, interested candidates must submit a Letter of Intent. This should be a brief letter identifying the researcher, their mentor, institution, and a description of the proposed research project. Letters of Intent should include an NIH-style curriculum vitae or biosketch for both candidate and mentor. After review, candidates may be invited to submit a full application.

Duration: Bridge Award: One year; Excellence Fellowships: 12 to 18 months; Innovative Investigator Award: 12 to 18 months. Continuation for second year is based upon progress report and continuation application; Lusher Diversity Fellowship: Up to three years; NHF Career Development Award: Up to three years. Continuation for second and third year is based upon progress report and continuation application; Judith Graham Pool Postdoctoral Research Fellowships: Up to two years. Continuation for second year is based upon progress report and continuation application.

Deadline: Varies. Check web site frequently for updates.

ADDRESS INQUIRIES TO:
Michelle Witkop, DNP
Head of Research
(See e-mail address above.)

NATIONAL INSTITUTE OF ENVIRONMENTAL HEALTH SCIENCES

Division of Extramural Research and Training
MD K3-05
111 T.W. Alexander Drive
Research Triangle Park, NC 27709
(984) 287-3285
E-mail: mastin@niehs.nih.gov
Web Site: www.niehs.nih.gov

TYPE:
Conferences/seminars; Demonstration grants; Development grants; Fellowships; Project/program grants; Research grants; Training grants. NIEHS pursues its mission by supporting basic and applied research on the consequences of the exposure of humans to potentially toxic or harmful agents in the environment.

Research of interest encompasses studies that relate to the biological effects of environmental chemicals and physical factors including such agents as hazardous gases, suspended particles, aerosols, industrial by-products and intermediates, heavy metals, trace elements, food additives, adulterants and pesticides.

Research Training Programs support individuals at both the predoctoral and postdoctoral levels in the areas of environmental toxicology, environmental pathology, environmental mutagenesis and environmental epidemiology.

See entry 1976 for full listing.

NATIONAL INSTITUTE OF GENERAL MEDICAL SCIENCES [2052]

National Institutes of Health
45 Center Drive, MSC 6200
Bethesda, MD 20892-6200
(301) 496-7301
Fax: (301) 402-0224
E-mail: info@nigms.nih.gov
Web Site: www.nigms.nih.gov

FOUNDED: 1962

AREAS OF INTEREST:
Basic biomedical research and research training.

TYPE:
Fellowships; Research grants; Training grants; Research contracts. Capacity building. The National Institute of General Medical Sciences (NIGMS) supports basic research that increases understanding of biological processes and lays the foundation for advances in disease diagnosis, treatment and prevention. NIGMS-funded scientists investigate how living systems work at a range of levels, from molecules and cells to tissues, whole organisms and populations. The Institute also supports research in certain clinical areas, primarily those that affect multiple organ systems. To assure the vitality and continued productivity of research enterprise, NIGMS provides leadership in training the next generation of scientists, in enhancing the diversity of scientific workforce, and in developing research capacities throughout the country.

YEAR PROGRAM STARTED: 1962

PURPOSE:
To support basic biomedical research that lays the foundation for advances in disease

diagnosis, treatment, and prevention; to help provide the most critical element of good research: well-prepared scientists.

LEGAL BASIS:
Part of a government agency under the PHS Act, various sections, and various public laws.

ELIGIBILITY:
For Research Grants, applicants must be academic institutions, teaching hospitals, public agencies, nonprofit organizations and for-profit corporations.

National Research Service Awards for the above areas may be made to individuals for postdoctoral training or nonprofit institutions for the training of individuals at the predoctoral and postdoctoral level.

For Small Business Innovative Research Program, applicants must be qualified small businesses to stimulate technological innovation in areas of interest to the Institute.

FINANCIAL DATA:
Amount of support per award: Varies by program.
Total amount of support: $2.937 billion for fiscal year 2020.

NO. AWARDS: 5,450 NIGMS-funded research grants for fiscal year 2020.

APPLICATION INFO:
Instructions vary by program. Application materials are available on the NIMH web site.
Duration: Varies.
Deadline: Varies by program.

STAFF:
Stephanie Older, Chief, Office of Communications and Public Liaison

ADDRESS INQUIRIES TO:
Office of Communications and Public Liaison
(See address above.)

NATIONAL INSTITUTE OF GENERAL MEDICAL SCIENCES   [2053]
Center for Research Capacity Building
45 Center Drive, MSC 6200
Bethesda, MD 20892-6200
(301) 594-3900
Fax: (301) 480-2753
E-mail: irina.krasnova@nih.gov
Web Site: www.nigms.nih.gov

FOUNDED: 1972

AREAS OF INTEREST:
Public health.

NAME(S) OF PROGRAMS:
● **Support of Competitive Research Awards**

TYPE:
Development grants; Research grants. Grants to assist eligible institutions to strengthen the institutions' biomedical research capabilities and provide opportunities to students to engage in biomedical or behavioral research and other activities in preparation for Ph.D. training in these areas.

YEAR PROGRAM STARTED: 1972

PURPOSE:
To increase the number of faculty, students, and investigators who are members of groups underrepresented in the biomedical and behavioral sciences who are engaged in research in these fields.

LEGAL BASIS:
Public Health Service Act of 1944 as amended, Section 301(c); U.S.C. 241.d.

ELIGIBILITY:
Applicant must be located in a state, the District of Columbia or a U.S. territory, and be a public or private university, four-year college or other institution offering undergraduate, graduate or health professional degrees with more than 50% minority enrollment, a public or private nonprofit four-year college or other institution offering undergraduate, graduate or health professional degrees, with a significant enrollment (but not necessarily more than 50%) derived from ethnic minorities, if the secretary of DHHS determines that the institution is committed to encouragement and assistance to ethnic minority faculty, students and investigators, or an Indian tribe with a recognized governing body which performs substantial government functions or an Alaska Regional Corporation (ARC) as defined in the Alaska Native Claims Settlement Act and located in a state, the District of Columbia, Puerto Rico, the Virgin Islands, the Canal Zone, Guam, American Samoa or the Trust Territory of the Pacific Islands.

GEOG. RESTRICTIONS: United States and its territories.

FINANCIAL DATA:
Amount of support per award: $75,000 to $250,000 direct costs.

CO-OP FUNDING PROGRAMS: Co-funding with other NIH Institutes.

APPLICATION INFO:
Detailed information is available from the Branch Chief.
Duration: Typically three to four years.

ADDRESS INQUIRIES TO:
Dr. Irina N. Krasnova, Program Director
(See address above.)

NATIONAL INSTITUTE OF GENERAL MEDICAL SCIENCES   [2054]
Natcher Building, MSC 6200
45 Center Drive, 2AS-13C
Bethesda, MD 20892-6200
(301) 594-0943
Fax: (301) 480-2004
E-mail: stefan.maas@nih.gov
Web Site: www.nigms.nih.gov

AREAS OF INTEREST:
Basic biomedical research.

NAME(S) OF PROGRAMS:
● **Medical Scientist Training Program**

TYPE:
Grants-in-aid; Training grants. The goal of this program is to prepare its graduates to function independently in both clinical practice and scientific research. MSTP has 50 participating programs.

YEAR PROGRAM STARTED: 1964

PURPOSE:
To support research training leading to the combined M.D.-Ph.D. degree.

ELIGIBILITY:
Applicants must be U.S. domestic institutions.

GEOG. RESTRICTIONS: United States.

FINANCIAL DATA:
Many institutions supplement the basic stipend provided by the MSTP grant. Trainees incur no payback obligation.
Amount of support per award: $24,816 stipend, plus tuition allowance of up to $21,000, travel allowance of $300, and $4,200 for equipment, supplies and health care for the year 2019.
Total amount of support: Varies.

NO. AWARDS: Approximately 970.

APPLICATION INFO:
Individuals who wish to enter the program should contact the program office at the participating institution(s) of their choice directly for curriculum information and admission requirements. Interested institutions should contact the NIGMS program director. Institutions should include the standard Form 424.

Applications guidelines are available online.
Duration: Up to five years, although the course of study for the combined degree may take longer. Continued support conditional upon annual review and availability of funds to the institution.
Deadline: January 25, May 25 and September 25. Grant awarded only once per year.

NATIONAL INSTITUTES OF HEALTH   [2055]
6705 Rockledge 1
Bethesda, MD 20817
(301) 945-7573
TTY: (301) 451-5936
E-mail: grantsinfo@nih.gov
oer@od.nih.gov
Web Site: grants.nih.gov/grants/oer.htm

FOUNDED: 1930

AREAS OF INTEREST:
Biomedical research and improvement of human health.

NAME(S) OF PROGRAMS:
● **Ruth L. Kirschstein National Research Service Awards (NRSA) for Individual Postdoctoral Fellows (Parent F32)**

TYPE:
Fellowships; Research grants; Training grants. This individual postdoctoral research training fellowship is to enhance training of promising postdoctoral candidates who have the potential to become productive, independent investigators in scientific health-related research fields relevant to the missions of the participating NIH Institutes and Centers.

PURPOSE:
To help ensure that a diverse pool of highly trained scientists is available in appropriate scientific disciplines to address the nation's biomedical, behavioral and clinical research needs.

ELIGIBILITY:
Eligible organizations: Higher education institutions, nonprofits other than institutions of higher education, for-profit organizations, governments and other (non-U.S.) entities.

Eligible Individuals: Applicant - Project Director/Principal Investigator (PD/PI) - must be a citizen or a permanent resident of the U.S. and must have received a research doctoral degree from an accredited domestic or foreign institution.

Before the award can be activated, the candidate must have received a Ph.D., M.D., D.O., D.C., D.D.S., D.V.M., O.D., D.P.M., Sc.D., Eng.D., Dr.P.H., DNSc., N.D., Pharm.D., D.S.W., Psy.D., or equivalent doctoral degree from an accredited domestic or foreign institution.

GEOG. RESTRICTIONS: United States and its territories.

FINANCIAL DATA:
Award budgets are composed of stipends, tuition and fees, and institutional allowance. NIH does not separately reimburse indirect costs (also known as Facilities and Administrative - or F and A - Costs) for fellowships. Costs for administering fellowships are part of institutional allowance.

NO. AWARDS: Varies.

APPLICATION INFO:
Guidelines and detailed information are available on the NIH web site. Applicants are encouraged to apply early to allow adequate time to make any corrections to errors found in the application during the submission process by the due date. Paper applications will not be accepted.

Applicants are strongly urged to check the NIH web site for the most up-to-date information.
Duration: Varies; up to three years for individuals.

*SPECIAL STIPULATIONS:
Conformance to all requirements (both in the Application Guide and the Funding Opportunity Announcement (FOA)) is required and strictly enforced.

At the time of award, individuals are required to pursue their research training on a full-time basis, normally defined as 40 hours per week or as specified by the sponsoring institution in accordance with its own policies.

NATIONAL INSTITUTES OF
HEALTH   [2056]
6705 Rockledge 1
Bethesda, MD 20817
(301) 945-7573
TTY: (301) 451-5936
E-mail: grantsinfo@nih.gov
oer@od.nih.gov
Web Site: grants.nih.gov/grants/oer.htm

FOUNDED: 1887

AREAS OF INTEREST:
Biomedical and behavioral research and improvement of human health.

NAME(S) OF PROGRAMS:
● **Mentored Clinical Scientist Research Career Development Award (Parent K08)**

TYPE:
Research grants. This program prepares qualified individuals for careers that have a significant impact on the health-related research needs of the nation.

PURPOSE:
To help ensure that a diverse pool of highly trained scientists is available in appropriate scientific disciplines to address the nation's biomedical, behavioral and clinical research needs.

LEGAL BASIS:
Public Health Service Act, Section 301(c).

ELIGIBILITY:
Eligible organizations include higher education institutions, nonprofits other than institutions of higher education, for-profit organizations, different domestic levels of government, Native American tribal organizations and faith-based or community-based organizations.

Eligible individuals (program director/principal investigator) must be a citizen or a noncitizen national of the U.S. or have been lawfully admitted for permanent residence. They must have a clinical doctoral degree (e.g., M.D., D.D.S., D.M.D., D.O., D.C., O.D., N.D., D.V.M., Pharm.D., or, in certain clinical disciplines, Ph.D.). The K08 award may be used by candidates with different levels of prior research training and at different stages in their mentored career development.

GEOG. RESTRICTIONS: United States.

NO. AWARDS: Varies.

APPLICATION INFO:
Applications must be submitted electronically. Paper applications will not be accepted.

Applicants are strongly urged to check the NIH web site for the most up-to-date information.
Duration: Up to five years.

NATIONAL INSTITUTES OF
HEALTH   [2057]
6705 Rockledge 1
Bethesda, MD 20817
(301) 945-7573
TTY: (301) 451-5936
E-mail: grantsinfo@nih.gov
oer@od.nih.gov
Web Site: grants.nih.gov/grants/oer.htm

FOUNDED: 1930

AREAS OF INTEREST:
Biomedical research and improvement of human health.

NAME(S) OF PROGRAMS:
● **Ruth L. Kirschstein National Research Service Awards (NRSA) for Individual Senior Fellows (Parent F33)**

TYPE:
Fellowships. This program awards senior individual research training fellowships to experienced scientists who wish to make major changes in the direction of their research careers or who wish to broaden their scientific background by acquiring new research capabilities as independent investigators in research fields relevant to the missions of the participating NIH Institutes and Centers.

PURPOSE:
To help ensure that a diverse pool of highly trained scientists is available in appropriate scientific disciplines to address the nation's biomedical, behavioral and clinical research needs.

LEGAL BASIS:
An agency of the U.S. Public Health Service.

ELIGIBILITY:
Eligible organizations include higher education institutions, nonprofits other than institutions of higher education, for-profit organizations, governments and other (non-U.S.) entities.

The Project Director/Principal Investigator must have had at least seven subsequent years of relevant research or professional experience and will have established an independent research career. By the time of the award, that individual must be a citizen or permanent resident of the U.S.

GEOG. RESTRICTIONS: United States.

FINANCIAL DATA:
Award budgets are composed of stipends, tuition and fees, and institutional allowance. NIH does not separately reimburse indirect costs (also known as Facilities and Administrative - or F and A - Costs) for fellowships. Costs for administering fellowships are part of institutional allowance.

NO. AWARDS: Varies.

APPLICATION INFO:
Guidelines and detailed information are available on the NIH web site. Applicants are encouraged to apply early to allow adequate time to make any corrections to errors found in the application during the submission process by the due date. Paper applications will not be accepted.

Applicants are strongly urged to check the NIH web site for the most up-to-date information.
Duration: Typically, up to two years.

*SPECIAL STIPULATIONS:
Conformance to all requirements (both in the Application Guide and the Funding Opportunity Announcement (FOA)) is required and strictly enforced.

At the time of award, individuals are required to pursue their research training on a full-time basis, normally defined as 40 hours per week or as specified by the sponsoring institution in accordance with its own policies.

NATIONAL INSTITUTES OF
HEALTH   [2058]
Office of Research Infrastructure Programs
One Democracy Plaza, Room 966
6701 Democracy Boulevard, MSC 4877
Bethesda, MD 20892-4877
(301) 435-0772
Fax: (301) 480-3819
E-mail: sig@mail.nih.gov
Web Site: orip.nih.gov/construction-and-instruments

FOUNDED: 1930

AREAS OF INTEREST:
Biomedical research and improvement of human health.

NAME(S) OF PROGRAMS:
● **Shared Instrumentation Grant Program**

TYPE:
Project/program grants.

YEAR PROGRAM STARTED: 1982

PURPOSE:
To provide research institutions the opportunity to obtain expensive (over $50,000 per item) commercially available instruments to be shared by groups of NIH-funded investigators.

LEGAL BASIS:
An agency of the U.S. Public Health Service.

ELIGIBILITY:
Federal agencies, foreign institutions and for-profit institutions are not eligible.

GEOG. RESTRICTIONS: United States.

FINANCIAL DATA:
Amount of support per award: Maximum award is $600,000.
Total amount of support: $35,000,000 for fiscal year 2020.

NO. AWARDS: Approximately 75.

APPLICATION INFO:
Contact the National Institutes of Health.
Duration: One year. No renewals.
Deadline: May 31.

ADDRESS INQUIRIES TO:
Shared Instrumentation Grant Program
(See address above.)

NATIONAL INSTITUTES OF HEALTH [2059]
6705 Rockledge 1
Bethesda, MD 20817
(301) 945-7573
E-mail: grantsinfo@nih.gov
oer@od.nih.gov
Web Site: grants.nih.gov/grants/oer.htm

NAME(S) OF PROGRAMS:
● **Research Project Grant Program (R01)**

TYPE:
Project/program grants; Research grants. Research Project Grant (R01) is an award made to support a discrete, specified, circumscribed project to be performed by the named investigator(s) in an area representing the investigator's specific interest and competencies, based on the mission of the NIH. The Research Project Grant (R01) is the original and historically oldest grant mechanism used by NIH. The R01 provides support for health-related research and development based on the mission of the NIH.

PURPOSE:
To provide support for health-related research and development.

LEGAL BASIS:
Government agency.

FINANCIAL DATA:
The following are allowable costs:
(1) salary and fringe benefits for Principal Investigator, key personnel and other essential personnel;
(2) equipment and supplies;
(3) consultant costs;
(4) alterations and renovations;
(5) publications and miscellaneous costs;
(6) contract services;
(7) consortium costs;
(8) facilities and administrative costs (indirect costs) and;
(9) travel expenses.
Amount of support per award: Varies.

NO. AWARDS: Contingent upon appropriations and submission of a sufficient number of meritorious applications.

APPLICATION INFO:
Applicants may find it helpful to seek advice from an experienced investigator and to contact the Institute or Center most likely to fund their application.

Applicants are strongly urged to check the NIH web site for the most up-to-date information.
Duration: Generally three to five years.
Deadline: Varies.

NATIONAL INSTITUTES OF HEALTH [2060]
6705 Rockledge 1
Bethesda, MD 20817
(301) 945-7573
E-mail: grantsinfo@nih.gov
oer@od.nih.gov
Web Site: grants.nih.gov/grants/oer.htm

NAME(S) OF PROGRAMS:
● **Small Research Grant Program (Parent R03)**

TYPE:
Research grants. This program supports different types of projects including pilot and feasibility studies; secondary analysis of existing data; small, self-contained research projects; development of research methodology; and development of new research technology.

PURPOSE:
To support small research projects that can be carried out in a short period of time with limited resources.

ELIGIBILITY:
The Small Research Grant Program supports discrete, well-defined projects that realistically can be completed in two years and that require limited levels of funding.

Higher education institutions, other nonprofits, for-profit organizations, governments, other institutions, and foreign institutions are eligible to apply.

Any individual(s) with the skills, knowledge and resources necessary to carry out the proposed research as the Program Director(s)/Principal Investigator(s) (PD(s)/PI(s)) is invited to work with his or her organization to develop an application for support. Individuals from underrepresented racial and ethnic groups as well as individuals with disabilities are always encouraged to apply for NIH support.

FINANCIAL DATA:
This grant support mechanism provides money, property or both to an eligible entity to carry out an approved project or activity.
Amount of support per award: Up to $50,000 in direct costs per year.

NO. AWARDS: Varies depending on NIH appropriations and the submission of a sufficient number of meritorious applications.

APPLICATION INFO:
Policies and procedures that apply to this grant mechanism can be found at PA-19-052.
Duration: Up to two years.

ADDRESS INQUIRIES TO:
See e-mail addresses above.

NATIONAL INSTITUTES OF HEALTH [2061]
Office of Research Infrastructure Programs
One Democracy Plaza, Suite 902
6701 Democracy Boulevard, MSC 4877
Bethesda, MD 20892-4877
(301) 435-0772
Fax: (301) 480-3819
E-mail: hei@mail.nih.gov
Web Site: dpcpsi.nih.gov/orip/diic/shared_instrumentation

FOUNDED: 1930

AREAS OF INTEREST:
Biomedical research and improvement of human health.

NAME(S) OF PROGRAMS:
● **High-End Instrumentation (HEI) Grant Program**

TYPE:
Project/program grants.

YEAR PROGRAM STARTED: 1982

PURPOSE:
To provide research institutions the opportunity to obtain expensive (over $600,001 per item) commercially available instruments to be shared by groups of NIH-funded investigators.

LEGAL BASIS:
An agency of the U.S. Public Health Service.

ELIGIBILITY:
High-End Instrumentation Grant Program encourages applications from groups of NIH-supported investigators to purchase or upgrade a single item of expensive, specialized, commercially available instruments or integrated systems. Types of instruments supported include, but are not limited to, X-ray diffraction systems, nuclear magnetic resonance (NMR) and mass spectrometers, DNA and protein sequencers, biosensors, electron and confocal microscopes, cell-sorters, and biomedical imagers.

GEOG. RESTRICTIONS: United States.

FINANCIAL DATA:
Amount of support per award: $600,001 to $2,000,000.
Total amount of support: Approximately $30,000,000 for fiscal year 2020.

NO. AWARDS: Varies.

APPLICATION INFO:
Contact the National Institutes of Health.
Duration: One year. No renewals.
Deadline: June 1.

ADDRESS INQUIRIES TO:
Shared Instrumentation Grant Program
(See address above.)

NATIONAL MEDICAL FELLOWSHIPS, INC. [2062]
P.O. Box 3875
New York, NY 10163
(212) 483-8880
Fax: (212) 483-8897
E-mail: scholarships@nmfonline.org
Web Site: www.nmfonline.org

FOUNDED: 1946

AREAS OF INTEREST:
Underrepresented minority students in medicine and the health professions and the health care of low-income and minority communities.

NAME(S) OF PROGRAMS:
● **Alliant Health Solutions/NMF Alzheimer's or Related Dementia Care Scholarship**
● **Anarcha, Betsy, and Lucy Memorial Scholarship**
● **Hugh J. Andersen Memorial Scholarship**
● **The Aspiring Future Physicians Scholarship in Memory of Dr. Tamara O'Neal**
● **The Aspiring Physicians Endowed Scholarship**
● **Association of American Medical Colleges (AAMC)/Darrell G. Kirch, M.D. Scholarship**

- **Wayne Anthony Butts Scholarship**
- **William and Charlotte Cadbury Award**
- **Carl H. and Thelma C. Caison, Sr. Scholarship**
- **Mary Ball Carrera Scholarship**
- **Dr. Randolph Chase Memorial Scholarship**
- **Colgate-Palmolive/NMF Dental Leadership Program**
- **Drs. Ludlow & Ruth Creary Family Foundation Scholarship**
- **Dr. James Curtis Scholarship**
- **Dr. Darrell L. Edwards Scholarship**
- **Empire State Medical Association Scholarship Award**
- **Genentech/NMF Diversity Innovation Fellowship Program**
- **Dr. Herman and Shirley Gray Family Scholarship**
- **Dr. Joe L. Hargrove Scholarship Award**
- **Johnson & Johnson/NMF Future Leaders Scholarship Program**
- **Genita Evangelista Johnson Endowed Scholarship**
- **Henrietta Lacks Memorial Scholarship**
- **Dr. Daniel Denis Laroche, Sr. Scholarship**
- **Don Levin Trust Scholarship**
- **Josiah Macy Jr. Foundation Scholarship**
- **Manhattan Central Medical Society Scholarship**
- **Dr. David Kearney McDonogh Scholarship in Ophthalmology/ENT**
- **Franklin C. McLean Award**
- **Michigan Scholarship Fund**
- **Dr. Theodore Quincy Miller Scholarship**
- **New York Community Trust/NMF Medical Research Scholarships**
- **NMA Emerging Scholars Awards**
- **NMA Emerging Scholars Infectious Diseases Research Awards**
- **NMF Fitzbutler-James Alumni Society of the University of Michigan Scholarship Fund**
- **NMF National Alumni Council Scholarship Program**
- **NMF Primary Care Leadership Program**
- **Dr. Fred D. Parrott's The Real Men Cook Foundation Academic Scholarship of Excellence and Endowment Challenge Fund**
- **Dr. Muriel Petioni Scholarship**
- **Andrea Pinnock Scholarship**
- **Victor Grifols Roura Scholarship**
- **Dr. James McCune Smith Medical Student Award**
- **Dr. Prentiss Taylor Scholarship**
- **United Health Foundation/NMF Diverse Medical Scholars Program**
- **Dr. Richard Zapanta Scholarship**
- **Zimmer Biomet/NMF Orthopaedic Scholarship**

TYPE:
Awards/prizes; Project/program grants; Scholarships. Service learning. NMF supports underrepresented minority medical students and health professions students enrolled in U.S. accredited programs as they matriculate. Awards are available to students M1 to M4/5. In addition to financial support, NMF provides opportunities for aspiring doctors to take their learning into the community.

YEAR PROGRAM STARTED: 1946

PURPOSE:
To improve the health of low-income and minority communities by increasing the number of minority physicians and addressing the special needs of these communities.

LEGAL BASIS:
Nonprofit corporation.

ELIGIBILITY:
Varies by program. Scholarship applicants must be U.S. citizens or have Deferred Action for Childhood Arrivals (DACA) approval.

FINANCIAL DATA:
Amount of support per award: Varies.
Total amount of support: Varies.

NO. MOST RECENT APPLICANTS: Varies.

NO. AWARDS: Varies.

APPLICATION INFO:
Guidelines and official application materials are available on the organization web site.
Duration: Varies by program.
Deadline: Varies by program.

BOARD OF DIRECTORS AND OFFICERS:
Sandra B. Nichols, M.D., FAAFP, Chairman
Stephen N. Keith, M.D., M.S.P.H., Treasurer and Secretary
Rahn K. Bailey, M.D.
Neal Ball
Bryan P. Baugh, M.D.
Lloyd C. Bishop
Cedric M. Bright, M.D., FACP
Larry J. Harrison, M.P.H., MBA
Emil Hill
Darrell G. Kirch, M.D.
Pamela T. Miller, Esq.
Denise Powell, M.D.
Jennifer Schlener
Efrain Talamantes, M.D., MBA
Carmen Sachiko Villar
Calvin Wheeler, M.D.

ADDRESS INQUIRIES TO:
Dr. Joy L. Jones
Chief Program Officer or
Ali Gemma
Director, Scholarships and Programs
(See address above.)

THE NATIONAL ORGANIZATION FOR RARE DISORDERS (NORD)   [2063]
55 Kenosia Avenue
Danbury, CT 06810
(203) 744-0100
Fax: (203) 263-9938
E-mail: research@rarediseases.org
Web Site: www.rarediseases.org

FOUNDED: 1983

AREAS OF INTEREST:
Rare "orphan" disease.

NAME(S) OF PROGRAMS:
- **Rare Disease Research Grant Program**

TYPE:
Research grants; Seed money grants. The Rare Disease Research Grant Program provides seed money grants to academic scientists and clinicians for translational or clinical studies related to development of potential new diagnostics or treatments for rare disease.

YEAR PROGRAM STARTED: 1989

PURPOSE:
To provide small seed grants to scientists and clinicians performing basic translational sciences, studying new treatments, or developing diagnostic tests for rare diseases.

ELIGIBILITY:
For each grant, the principal investigator must have sufficient education and experience to demonstrate subject matter expertise. Strong preference is given to researchers holding a faculty-level appointment or senior scientific position at an academic or nonprofit institution or foundation. Grants are available to researchers both within the U.S. and internationally.

FINANCIAL DATA:
Overhead and indirect costs are not awarded.
Amount of support per award: Minimum $35,000.
Total amount of support: Varies.

NO. MOST RECENT APPLICANTS: Approximately 40.

NO. AWARDS: Varies.

APPLICATION INFO:
Submit a letter of intent, curriculum vitae, one-page abstract, and a brief budget. Full proposals by invitation only. Requests for proposals announcements typically posted online.
Duration: One to two years.
Deadline: Varies.

ADDRESS INQUIRIES TO:
Research Program Administrator
(See address above.)

*SPECIAL STIPULATIONS:
Reports and communication must be written in English and adhere to the most recent guidelines set forth by the National Institutes of Health.

NATIONAL SOCIETY DAUGHTERS OF THE AMERICAN REVOLUTION [2064]
1776 D Street, N.W.
Washington, DC 20006-5303
(202) 879-3263
E-mail: scholarships@nsdar.org
Web Site: www.dar.org

FOUNDED: 1895

AREAS OF INTEREST:
Medicine and psychiatric nursing.

NAME(S) OF PROGRAMS:
- **Irene and Daisy MacGregor Memorial Scholarship**

TYPE:
Scholarships.

YEAR PROGRAM STARTED: 1991

PURPOSE:
To provide ways and means to aid students in attaining higher education.

LEGAL BASIS:
Incorporated historical society.

ELIGIBILITY:
Scholarships are awarded without regard to race, religion, sex or national origin. All four-year scholarships must be for consecutive years and are renewable only upon review and approval of annual transcript. Candidates must be U.S. citizens and must attend or plan to attend an accredited college or university in the U.S. No affiliation or relationship to DAR is required for qualification. Awards are judged on the basis of academic excellence, commitment to field of study, as required, and financial need.

The MacGregor Memorial Scholarship is awarded to students of high scholastic standing and character who have been accepted into or are pursuing an approved course of study to become a medical doctor (not pre-med) at an approved, accredited medical school.

This MacGregor Memorial Scholarship is also available to students who have been accepted into or who are pursuing an approved course of study in the field of psychiatric nursing, graduate level, at medical schools, colleges or universities. There is a preference to females "if equally qualified."

GEOG. RESTRICTIONS: United States.

FINANCIAL DATA:
Amount of support per award: $5,000 annually.

NO. AWARDS: 2.

APPLICATION INFO:
Applicants must use the DAR Scholarship Committee's online submission process found on the DAR public web site. Once applicants have set up their scholarship profile, they will be able to complete the application. If necessary, applicants will be able to provide access to individuals wishing to submit confidential letters of recommendations or school transcripts.
Duration: Up to four consecutive years possible, depending upon availability of funds. Annual transcript review required for renewal and award.
Deadline: January 31.

PUBLICATIONS:
American Spirit, magazine.

ADDRESS INQUIRIES TO:
National Vice Chairman
E-mail: macgregorscholarship@nsdar.org

NORTH AMERICAN SPINE SOCIETY (NASS)   [2065]
7075 Veterans Boulevard
Burr Ridge, IL 60527
(630) 230-3691
Fax: (630) 230-3791
E-mail: kjames@spine.org
Web Site: www.spine.org

FOUNDED: 1985

AREAS OF INTEREST:
Disorders and functions of the human spine.

NAME(S) OF PROGRAMS:
● **Clinical Traveling Fellowship**
● **Research Grant**
● **Research Traveling Fellowship**
● **Young Investigator Grants**

TYPE:
Awards/prizes; Fellowships; Research grants. Clinical Traveling Fellowship: At least one month to be spent in three to five different medical centers studying spine techniques.

Research Traveling Fellowship: At least five months at one medical center, other than the one in which the applicants currently practice. This Fellowship primarily covers the cost of travel and housing.

Research Grant: This grant is for investigative, basic, clinical and translational research on the spine.

Young Investigator Grant: This grant is for projects in basic science, clinical or translational.

YEAR PROGRAM STARTED: 1989

PURPOSE:
To advance quality spine care through education, research and advocacy; to encourage and support basic and clinical science that is performed with integrity and with a goal towards improving quality spine care for patients and understanding underlying disorders.

ELIGIBILITY:
Qualified investigators are eligible to apply. Grant applicants must be NASS members.

FINANCIAL DATA:
Amount of support per award: $20,000 to $40,000.
Total amount of support: Varies.

NO. MOST RECENT APPLICANTS: 82.

NO. AWARDS: Varies.

APPLICATION INFO:
Contact the Organization for application procedures. Budget restrictions are available when requesting an application.
Duration: Two years.
Deadline: Letters of Proposals for Grants: Second week in February. Invited Grants and Fellowships: Second week in May.

ADDRESS INQUIRIES TO:
Karen James
Senior Manager of Research
(See address above.)

ORTHOPAEDIC RESEARCH AND EDUCATION FOUNDATION   [2066]
9400 West Higgins Road
Suite 215
Rosemont, IL 60018-4975
(847) 698-9980
Fax: (847) 698-7806
E-mail: grants@oref.org
Web Site: www.oref.org

FOUNDED: 1955

AREAS OF INTEREST:
Orthopaedic research.

NAME(S) OF PROGRAMS:
● **Career Development Grant Award**

TYPE:
Research grants. Grants for scientific research in orthopaedic surgery.

YEAR PROGRAM STARTED: 1984

PURPOSE:
To encourage a commitment to scientific research in orthopaedic surgery.

LEGAL BASIS:
501(c)(3) special-interest foundation.

ELIGIBILITY:
Candidates must have completed residency in orthopaedic surgery and have demonstrated a sustained interest in research, as well as excellence in clinical training. Letters of nomination and support must offer convincing evidence of the candidate's potential to develop as an investigator.

GEOG. RESTRICTIONS: United States.

FINANCIAL DATA:
Amount of support per award: $225,000.
Total amount of support: $225.000.

NO. AWARDS: 1.

APPLICATION INFO:
Contact the Foundation.
Duration: Up to three years, conditional upon annual review.

Deadline: Letter of Intent: October 4.

PUBLICATIONS:
Annual report; application guidelines.

ADDRESS INQUIRIES TO:
See e-mail address above.

*SPECIAL STIPULATIONS:
Applicant must be working in the U.S. only.

ORTHOPAEDIC RESEARCH AND EDUCATION FOUNDATION   [2067]
9400 West Higgins Road
Suite 215
Rosemont, IL 60018-4975
(847) 698-9980
Fax: (847) 698-7806
E-mail: grants@oref.org
Web Site: www.oref.org

FOUNDED: 1955

AREAS OF INTEREST:
Orthopaedic surgery research.

NAME(S) OF PROGRAMS:
● **Resident Clinician Scientist Training Grant**

TYPE:
Research grants. Grants to prepare residents for a career with research as a major component.

YEAR PROGRAM STARTED: 1961

PURPOSE:
To encourage the research interests and meritorious projects of residents and fellows in approved orthopaedic programs.

LEGAL BASIS:
501(c)(3) special-interest foundation.

ELIGIBILITY:
Candidates must be residents or fellows in approved orthopaedic programs.

GEOG. RESTRICTIONS: United States.

FINANCIAL DATA:
Grants provide funds for supplies and expenses, but not for resident salary or travel.
Amount of support per award: $20,000.
Total amount of support: Varies.

APPLICATION INFO:
Applications are available on the web site.
Duration: One year.

PUBLICATIONS:
Annual report; application guidelines.

ADDRESS INQUIRIES TO:
See e-mail address above.

*SPECIAL STIPULATIONS:
Resident must be working in the U.S.

ORTHOPAEDIC RESEARCH AND EDUCATION FOUNDATION   [2068]
9400 West Higgins Road
Suite 215
Rosemont, IL 60018-4975
(847) 430-5109
Fax: (847) 698-7806
E-mail: grants@oref.org
Web Site: www.oref.org

FOUNDED: 1955

AREAS OF INTEREST:
Musculoskeletal research.

NAME(S) OF PROGRAMS:
- **OREF Clinical Research Award**

TYPE:
Awards/prizes.

YEAR PROGRAM STARTED: 1996

PURPOSE:
To award outstanding research related to clinical musculoskeletal disease or injury.

LEGAL BASIS:
Special-interest foundation, 501(c)(3).

ELIGIBILITY:
Individual applicants must be members of the AAOS, ORS, Canadian Orthopaedic Association, Canadian ORS or sponsored by a member.

FINANCIAL DATA:
Amount of support per award: $20,000.
Total amount of support: $20,000.

NO. AWARDS: 1.

APPLICATION INFO:
Submission guidelines are available on the web site.
Duration: One-time award.
Deadline: July 1.

PUBLICATIONS:
Annual report; application guidelines.

ADDRESS INQUIRIES TO:
See e-mail address above.

OSTEOGENESIS IMPERFECTA FOUNDATION   [2069]
804 West Diamond Avenue
Suite 210
Gaithersburg, MD 20878
(301) 947-0083
(844) 889-7579
Fax: (301) 947-0456
E-mail: bonelink@oif.org
Web Site: www.oif.org

FOUNDED: 1970

AREAS OF INTEREST:
Osteogenesis imperfecta medical research.

NAME(S) OF PROGRAMS:
- **Michael Geisman Fellowships**

TYPE:
Fellowships.

YEAR PROGRAM STARTED: 1970

PURPOSE:
To expand understanding and identify improved treatments for osteogenesis imperfecta.

LEGAL BASIS:
Nonprofit organization.

ELIGIBILITY:
Applicants for the fellowship must be postdoctoral fellows in academic institutions and the work must be done under the supervision of a mentor with appropriate training and experience in osteogenesis imperfect (OI) or related field.

FINANCIAL DATA:
Amount of support per award: Up to $50,000 per year ($35,000 toward the investigator's salary and up to $15,000 per year for supplies).

APPLICATION INFO:
Applicants should submit an original application with 10 copies. The application should include an abstract for a lay audience, budget, education, previous research experience, professional training, publications and a research plan. Electronic submissions are accepted.
Duration: One year with possible renewal.
Deadline: December 1.

PUBLICATIONS:
Annual report; application guidelines; bimonthly newsletter.

IRS I.D.: 23-7076021

ADDRESS INQUIRIES TO:
OIF Research Department
(See address above.)

OXALOSIS AND HYPEROXALURIA FOUNDATION   [2070]
579 Albany Post Road
New Paltz, NY 12561
(212) 777-0470
(800) 643-8699
Fax: (212) 777-0471
E-mail: info@ohf.org
kimh@ohf.org
Web Site: www.ohf.org

FOUNDED: 1989

AREAS OF INTEREST:
Hyperoxaluria and oxalosis.

NAME(S) OF PROGRAMS:
- **OHF Research Grant**

TYPE:
Research grants. The Research Grant program assists investigators, new or established, who have research projects for which they need support.

PURPOSE:
To support research that will ultimately lead to new diagnostics, treatments and a cure for primary hyperoxaluria and related hyperoxaluria conditions.

ELIGIBILITY:
Applicants must hold an M.D., Ph.D. or equivalent degree by the start of the funding period and have an appointment at an academic institution. Compliance with local and federal statutes and regulations of the country of origin must be met.

FINANCIAL DATA:
Funds may be used for salaries for the investigators, technical assistance, special equipment, animals, supplies and travel.
Amount of support per award: Up to $200,000.
Total amount of support: Varies.

APPLICATION INFO:
All completed applications must be submitted electronically to grantapp@ohf.org in Word or PDF format. Late applications will not be accepted. Applications must be typed, single-spaced, 11-point Times New Roman with at least one-inch margins. A short paragraph should be included in the General Objectives and Rationale section describing the relevance of the proposed research to the goals of the OHF.
Duration: Up to two years.
Deadline: December 15.

ADDRESS INQUIRIES TO:
Kim Hollander, Executive Director
(See address above.)

OXNARD FOUNDATION   [2071]
5 Royal St. George Road
Newport Beach, CA 92660
(949) 644-4160
Fax: (949) 644-4171
E-mail: covlineage@gmail.com

AREAS OF INTEREST:
General medical research.

TYPE:
Matching gifts; Research grants.

PURPOSE:
To help continue medical research in the areas of concern for the Foundation.

ELIGIBILITY:
IRS 501(c)(3) tax-exempt organizations, schools and hospitals.

GEOG. RESTRICTIONS: California, Florida, New Mexico and Tennessee.

FINANCIAL DATA:
Amount of support per award: $35,000 to $50,000.
Total amount of support: Varies.

APPLICATION INFO:
Applicants should first send a letter and include a copy of the IRS tax determination letter.
Duration: One to three years.
Deadline: Applications are reviewed at Board meetings in February, June and November.

IRS I.D.: 23-7323007

ADDRESS INQUIRIES TO:
Christopher Veitch, President
(See address above.)

PHARMACEUTICAL RESEARCH AND MANUFACTURERS OF AMERICA FOUNDATION, INC.   [2072]
950 F Street, N.W.
Suite 300
Washington, DC 20004
(202) 572-7756
E-mail: foundation@phrma.org
Web Site: www.phrmafoundation.org

FOUNDED: 1965

AREAS OF INTEREST:
Biology, biomedical engineering, biotechnology, clinical outcomes assessment, drug delivery, drug discovery, genetics, health outcomes, medical research, pharmaceutical biotechnology, pharmaceutics, pharmacology and toxicology.

NAME(S) OF PROGRAMS:
- **Postdoctoral Fellowship in Drug Delivery**
- **Postdoctoral Fellowship in Drug Discovery**
- **Postdoctoral Fellowship in Health Outcomes Research**
- **Postdoctoral Fellowship in Translational Medicine**

TYPE:
Fellowships. This program provides stipend to well-trained graduates from Pharm.D., M.D., and Ph.D. programs who seek to further develop and refine research skills through formal postdoctoral training.

PURPOSE:
To encourage graduates from Ph.D. programs in drug delivery, drug discovery and translational medicine to continue their research skills through formal postdoctoral training.

LEGAL BASIS:
501(c)(3) organization.

ELIGIBILITY:
Applicant must live in the U.S. and attend a university or research institution in the U.S.

Postdoctoral Fellowship in Drug Delivery and Drug Discovery applicants must have a firm commitment from a sponsor/mentor at an accredited U.S. university. The award supports candidates proposing to gain new skills in drug delivery or drug discovery research. Ideal applicants will be within their first two years of postdoctoral study. Applicants must hold a Ph.D. or appropriate terminal research doctoral in a field related to the proposed postdoctoral activities or expect to receive such a degree before activating the award.

Postdoctoral Fellowship in Health Outcomes Research applicants must be attending schools of medicine, pharmacy, public health, nursing or dentistry. Applicants must hold a Ph.D. degree or appropriate terminal research doctoral in a field of study logically or functionally related to the proposed postdoctoral activities or expect to receive the Ph.D. before activating the award.

Eligible candidates for the Postdoctoral Fellowship in Translational Medicine will have doctoral degrees, e.g., Ph.D., D.Sc., D.Eng., M.D., before award activation and seek to further develop and refine their skills and understanding of translational medicine through postdoctoral training.

GEOG. RESTRICTIONS: United States.

FINANCIAL DATA:
Stipend support only. Funds may not be used for travel, tuition, indirect costs or fringe benefits. The award is made to the university on behalf of the fellow and provides a stipend, payable quarterly. This award is intended solely as a stipend and may not be used otherwise. If necessary, the institution may supplement the award to a level that is consistent with other postdoctoral fellowships it offers. An individual may not simultaneously hold or interrupt any other fellowship providing stipend support while the PhRMA Foundation Fellowship is active. These funds are nontransferable. Unspent funds will be returned to the PhRMA Foundation upon the fellowship's conclusion.
Amount of support per award: Drug Delivery and Drug Discovery: $50,000 stipend per year; Health Outcomes: $55,000 stipend per year; Translational Medicine: $60,000 stipend per year.
Total amount of support: Varies.

NO. MOST RECENT APPLICANTS: Varies.

NO. AWARDS: Varies.

APPLICATION INFO:
Applications should be submitted on the Foundation web site.
Duration: Two years. Funding beyond the first year is contingent upon a ten-month progress report approved by the PhRMA Foundation and a first year financial report.
Deadline: Drug Delivery and Drug Discovery: Letter of Intent due May 15. Selected submissions will be notified by July 1 to submit a full application. Health Outcomes and Translational Medicine: February 1. Announcement April 15.

PUBLICATIONS:
Brochure.

IRS I.D.: 52-6063009

ADDRESS INQUIRIES TO:
See e-mail address above.

*SPECIAL STIPULATIONS:
Funds are not to be used for fringe benefits, indirect costs to the institution, travel or tuition.

PHARMACEUTICAL RESEARCH AND MANUFACTURERS OF AMERICA FOUNDATION, INC.
950 F Street, N.W.
Suite 300
Washington, DC 20004
(202) 572-7756
E-mail: foundation@phrma.org
Web Site: www.phrmafoundation.org

TYPE:
Project/program grants; Research grants; Seed money grants. Starter grants to support research in the fields of biology, biomedical engineering, biopharmaceutics, clinical outcomes assessment, disease modeling, drug delivery, drug discovery, genetics, health outcomes, molecular epidemiology, pharmaceutics, pharmaceutical biotechnology, pharmaceutical engineering, pharmacology and toxicology. The grants offer financial support to individuals beginning independent research careers at the faculty level.

See entry 2292 for full listing.

PHARMACEUTICAL RESEARCH AND MANUFACTURERS OF AMERICA FOUNDATION, INC.   [2073]
950 F Street, N.W.
Suite 300
Washington, DC 20004
(202) 572-7756
E-mail: foundation@phrma.org
Web Site: www.phrmafoundation.org

FOUNDED: 1965

AREAS OF INTEREST:
Biology, biomedical engineering, biopharmaceutics, chemistry, drug delivery, drug discovery, health outcomes research, medical research, pharmaceutical biotechnology, pharmaceutics, pharmacology and toxicology.

NAME(S) OF PROGRAMS:
● **Predoctoral Fellowship in Drug Delivery**
● **Predoctoral Fellowship in Drug Discovery**
● **Predoctoral Fellowship in Health Outcomes Research**

TYPE:
Fellowships. Stipend support for full-time students in the areas of drug delivery, drug discovery and health outcomes research during their thesis research.

PURPOSE:
To support promising students during their advanced stages of training and thesis research.

LEGAL BASIS:
501(c)(3) organization.

ELIGIBILITY:
Applicant must live in the U.S. and attend a university or research institution in the U.S.

In the areas of drug delivery and drug discovery, applicant must hold a B.S., M.S. or Pharm.D. degree from an accredited

school in pharmacy or a related area. Applicants must expect to complete the requirements for a Ph.D. in two years or less from the time the fellowship begins.

In the area of health outcomes research, applicants must be attending schools of medicine, pharmacy, public health, nursing or dentistry. This program supports full-time, in-residence students who will have completed most of their pre-thesis requirements (at least two years of study) and be engaged in thesis research as Ph.D. candidates by the time the award is active.

GEOG. RESTRICTIONS: United States.

FINANCIAL DATA:
Award is made to the university on behalf of the fellow. Annual stipend payable quarterly, which includes $1,000 per year for incidentals directly associated with thesis research preparation.
Amount of support per award: Maximum $50,000 ($25,000 per year).
Total amount of support: Varies.

NO. MOST RECENT APPLICANTS: Varies.

NO. AWARDS: Varies.

APPLICATION INFO:
Applications should be submitted on the Foundation web site.
Duration: 12, 18 or 24 months. Funding beyond the first 12 months is contingent upon a ten-month progress report approved by the PhRMA Foundation and a first year financial report.
Deadline: Drug Delivery and Drug Discovery: Letter of Intent due May 15. Selected submissions will be notified by July 1 to submit a full application. Health Outcomes Research: February 1. Announcement April 15.

PUBLICATIONS:
Brochure.

IRS I.D.: 52-6063009

STAFF:
Eileen Cannon, President
Joanne Westphal, Director of Development

BOARD OF DIRECTORS:
Alfred Sandrock, M.D., Ph.D., Chairman
Andrew Plump, M.D., Ph.D., Treasurer
Mikael Dolsten, M.D., Ph.D.
Iris Loew-Friedrich, M.D.
Aran Maree, M.B., B.Ch.
Joseph P. Miletich, M.D., Ph.D.
Richard Moscicki, M.D.
John C. Reed, M.D., Ph.D.
Daniel Skovronsky, M.D., Ph.D.
Rupert Vessey, FRCP, D.Phil.

ADVISORY COMMITTEE:
Terry L. Bowlin, Ph.D.
Michael J. Hageman, Ph.D.
Michael N. Liebman, Ph.D.
Bryan R. Luce, Ph.D., MBA
Richard Moscicki, M.D.
Nancy C. Santanello, M.D., M.S.

ADDRESS INQUIRIES TO:
See e-mail address above.

*SPECIAL STIPULATIONS:
Funds are not to be used for fringe benefits, indirect costs to the institution, travel or tuition.

PHARMACEUTICAL RESEARCH AND MANUFACTURERS OF AMERICA FOUNDATION, INC. [2074]

950 F Street, N.W.
Suite 300
Washington, DC 20004
(202) 572-7756
E-mail: foundation@phrma.org
Web Site: www.phrmafoundation.org

FOUNDED: 1965

AREAS OF INTEREST:
Clinical sciences, health care evaluation, health economics, outcomes research and value assessment.

NAME(S) OF PROGRAMS:
● **Value Assessment Challenge Awards**
● **Value Assessment Research Award**

TYPE:
Awards/prizes; Project/program grants. The PhRMA Foundation, through the Value Assessment Challenge Awards, seeks papers that describe solutions to a pressing question related to value assessment in health care. Each year the question is updated.

The PhRMA Foundation, through the Value Assessment Research Award, seeks transformative, multi-stakeholder driven solutions to address challenges in assessing the value of medicines and health care services to improve patient outcomes and reduce inefficiency.

PURPOSE:
To address challenges in assessing the value of medicines and health care services to improve patient outcomes and reduce inefficiency.

LEGAL BASIS:
501(c)(3) organization.

ELIGIBILITY:
Award opportunities are open to all individuals and organizations with training in health economics, outcomes research, clinical sciences or health care evaluation. Eligible applicants should have an advanced degree in a field of study logically or functionally related to the proposed activities, such as a Ph.D. or equivalent. Interdisciplinary collaboration is highly encouraged.

For the Value Assessment Research Award, at least one collaborator must also have a firm commitment from an accredited U.S. university or research organization.

FINANCIAL DATA:
Value Assessment Research Award: Level of funding will depend on the scope of proposed activities. A maximum of 20% of the award may be used for indirect institutional costs and/or fringe benefits. Funding may not be used for tuition assistance.

Amount of support per award: Value Assessment Challenge Awards: $50,000 for first place, $25,000 for second place, $5,000 for third and fourth place; Value Assessment Research Award: Up to $100,000.

NO. MOST RECENT APPLICANTS: Varies.

NO. AWARDS: Value Assessment Challenge Awards: 4 budgeted; Value Assessment Research Award: 3 budgeted.

APPLICATION INFO:
Applications should be submitted on the Foundation web site.

Duration: Value Assessment Challenge Awards: One-time award; Value Assessment Research Award: One year.

Deadline: Letter of Intent: July 15. Selected submissions will be notified by August 10 to submit a full application.

PUBLICATIONS:
Brochure.

IRS I.D.: 52-6063009

ADDRESS INQUIRIES TO:
See e-mail address above.

*PLEASE NOTE:
Value Assessment Research Award recipient must submit a final progress report and financial report upon the conclusion of the grant.

DR. AND MRS. ARTHUR WILLIAM PHILLIPS CHARITABLE TRUST [2075]

P.O. Box 316
Oil City, PA 16301-0316
(814) 676-2736
Fax: (814) 676-2736
E-mail: bwinters_pct@comcast.net
Web Site: phillipscharitabletrust.
communityforce.com

FOUNDED: 1979

AREAS OF INTEREST:
Primarily medical centers, research and education.

TYPE:
Project/program grants; Scholarships.

PURPOSE:
To support many varied projects.

ELIGIBILITY:
Organizations must be:
(1) IRS 501(c)(3) tax-exempt;
(2) located in northwestern Pennsylvania;
(3) able to raise the balance of necessary funding from other sources and;
(4) able to show evidence of financial responsibility that will insure the completion and success of the project.

GEOG. RESTRICTIONS: Northwestern Pennsylvania.

FINANCIAL DATA:
Amount of support per award: Varies.
Total amount of support: Approximately $652,000.

NO. MOST RECENT APPLICANTS: 37.

NO. AWARDS: 28.

APPLICATION INFO:
Applicants must follow directions and file electronically at phillipscharitabletrust.communityforce.com.
Duration: Typically one year.
Deadline: March 15 for spring meeting; July 31 for fall meeting.

IRS I.D.: 25-6201015

TRUSTEES:
Larry S. Adams
Robert W. McFate
Trenton E. Moulin

ADDRESS INQUIRIES TO:
Robert W. McFate, Trustee
(See address above.)

PLASTIC SURGERY FOUNDATION (PSF) [2076]

ASPS/PSF
444 East Algonquin Road
Arlington Heights, IL 60005
(847) 228-9900
E-mail: research@plasticsurgery.org
Web Site: www.thepsf.org/research/grants-program

AREAS OF INTEREST:
Basic/translational research, clinical, or health services research.

NAME(S) OF PROGRAMS:
● **ASE/PSF Combined Research Grant**
● **Combined Pilot Research Grants**
● **Innovation in Wound Care Research and Academic Development Fellowship**
● **National Endowment for Plastic Surgery**
● **Pilot Research Grants**
● **PSF Directed Research Grant - Breast Implant Safety**
● **The PSF Translational and Innovation Research Grant**
● **The PSF/MTF Biologics Allograft Tissue Research Grant**
● **Research Fellowships**
● **Scott Spear Innovation in Breast Reconstruction Research Fellowship**

TYPE:
Awards/prizes. ASE/PSF Combined Research Grant: The PSF and the Association for Surgical Education (ASE) recognize the importance of fostering the development of surgeon scientists that yield improvements in patient care in surgery. The ASE/PSF Combined Research Grant is intended to fund a research project that will advance the scientific knowledge and aims to develop and validate new methods of surgical care.

Combined Pilot Research Grants: The PSF, along with the AHS, AAPPS, AAPS, ACAPS, ASMS, ASPN, ASRM and PSRC, recognizes the importance of promoting innovative research in hand surgery, academic plastic surgery related to research, peripheral nerve research, microsurgery and stimulating fundamental research in plastic surgery. Together, these subspecialty organizations are dedicated to fostering the development of surgeon scientists and are committed to increasing the amount of research dollars, in order to fund pilot research studies that set the stage for investigators to apply to larger funding agencies.

Innovation in Wound Care Research and Academic Development Fellowship: This grant is to promote and support the career development of junior surgeon-scientists who are focused on advancing wound healing patient care through research and are interested in building a competitive research lab.

National Endowment for Plastic Surgery: This grant is intended to support research projects which translate clinical or basic science research findings into clinically relevant advancements or tools with a high likelihood of impacting daily practice and patient care within the next few years.

Pilot Research Grants are intended to support residents and junior faculty in their efforts to address focused research questions, obtain preliminary data to support larger grant proposals in the future, and develop a line of research that can be carried forward into an academic career. This grant supports the preliminary or pilot phase of these research projects.

PSF Directed Research Grant: Studies designed to assess breast implant safety, including local and systemic complications and illnesses related to breast implants, will be considered. Proposals that examine implant surveillance techniques and imaging are also invited. Basic, translational and clinical research studies are all within scope.

The PSF Translational and Innovation Research Grant aims to accelerate the translation of scientific discoveries and technical developments into practical solutions that improve human health through innovative funding, and to encourage collaborative, transdisciplinary work to accelerate the translation of medical discoveries into improved health. These seed grants will be awarded in the areas of medical technology, therapeutics, diagnostics, population health sciences and community engagement.

The PSF/MTF Biologics Allograft Tissue Research Grant: The PSF and MTF Biologics offer research grants to investigators studying allograft tissue transplantation in plastic and reconstructive surgery. These grants are intended to provide support for research projects focused on biologic reconstruction with a strong clinical translation component that utilize dermal, adipose, placental or other allograft transplant technologies. Grants are offered to projects with a high likelihood of impact on scientific discipline and/or on patient care. Both clinical and basic science research projects will be considered.

Research Fellowships support investigators from the beginning of their careers, during residence and as they advance to becoming experienced and well-established plastic surgeons. The purpose is to encourage research and academic career development in plastic surgery. This grant is for salary support only for a resident or fellow to obtain training and experience in research, under the guidance of an experienced mentor.

The Scott Spear Innovation in Breast Reconstruction Research Fellowship aims to nurture and grow the training and expertise of young academicians considering a career in breast reconstruction and patient care. The fellowship provides salary support to residents and fellows to undertake a research project under the guidance of an experienced mentor. The research project must be focused on breast cancer or breast reconstruction.

ELIGIBILITY:
ASE/PSF Combined Research Grant: Applicants must be M.D., D.O. or Ph.D. and hold a full-time clinical or research position in a U.S. or Canadian institution where the research will be conducted. Applicants must be an active or candidate member of ASPS or obtain sponsorship from an active ASPS member at one's institution. Additional eligibility criteria may apply.

Combined Pilot Research and Pilot Research Grants: Applicants must be M.D., D.O. or Ph.D. and hold a full-time clinical or research position in a U.S. or Canadian institution where the research will be conducted. Applicants must be an active or candidate member of ASPS or obtain sponsorship from an active ASPS member at

one's institution. Additional eligibility criteria may apply for the Combined Pilot Research Grant.

Innovation in Wound Care Research and Academic Development Fellowship: Eligible applicants must be plastic surgeons within the first five years of entering practice and interested in establishing an academic research career with a clinical focus in wound care. Competitive applications must describe a multiyear structured research plan that includes conduct of basic and/or clinical research with emphasis on biochemical and molecular biologic mechanisms of wound healing and/or clinical innovation.

National Endowment for Plastic Surgery: Applicants must be M.D., D.O. or Ph.D. and hold a full-time clinical or research position in a U.S. or Canadian institution where the research will be conducted. Applicants must be an active or candidate member of ASPS or obtain sponsorship from an active ASPS member at one's institution.

The PSF/MTF Allograft Tissue Research Grant: Applicants must be an M.D., D.O. or Ph.D. and hold a full-time clinical or research position in a U.S. or Canadian institution where the research will be conducted. Applicants must be an active or candidate member of ASPS or obtain sponsorship from an active ASPS member at one's institution.

Research Fellowship: Applicants must be an M.D. or D.O. and hold a full-time clinical or research position in a U.S. or Canadian institution where the research will be conducted. Applicants must be a resident or within five years of an initial faculty appointment and must be an active or candidate member of ASPS or obtain sponsorship from an active ASPS member at one's institution.

FINANCIAL DATA:
Amount of support per award: ASE/PSF Combined Research Grant: Up to $15,000; Combined Pilot Research Grants and Pilot Research Grants: Up to $10,000; Innovation in Wound Care Research and Academic Development Fellowship: Up to $150,000; National Endowment for Plastic Surgery Grant, PSF Directed Research Grant, The PSF Translational and Innovation Research Grant and Research Fellowship: Up to $50,000; PSF/MTF Biologics Allograft Tissue Research Grant: Up to $100,000; Scott Spear Innovation in Breast Reconstruction Research Fellowship: Up to $72,500 for one-year projects ($50,000 salary support and $22,500 for research).

Total amount of support: The Foundation awarded $891,274 in grant funding in 2019.

NO. MOST RECENT APPLICANTS: 146 for the 2018 cycle.

NO. AWARDS: 33 research grants for the 2019 cycle.

APPLICATION INFO:
Application instructions can be found on the Foundation web site.

Duration: One to two years.

Deadline: Approximately December 1.

ADDRESS INQUIRIES TO:
Mary Ruth Arway
Research Grants Project Manager
E-mail: rarway@plasticsurgery.org

POST-POLIO HEALTH INTERNATIONAL [2077]
50 Crestwood Executive Center
Suite 440
St. Louis, MO 63126
(314) 534-0475
Fax: (314) 534-5070
E-mail: director@post-polio.org
Web Site: www.post-polio.org

FOUNDED: 1995

AREAS OF INTEREST:
Neuromuscular respiratory diseases and post-poliomyelitis.

NAME(S) OF PROGRAMS:
● **The Research Fund**

TYPE:
Research grants; Seed money grants. The Research Fund supports the work of researchers investigating the late effects of poliomyelitis and/or neuromuscular respiratory disease through one of two grants:

The Thomas Wallace Rogers Memorial Respiratory Research Grant: To study the cause(s) and treatment of neuromuscular respiratory insufficiency and the effects of long-term home mechanical ventilation.

The Post-Poliomyelitis Research Grant: This grant is to study the cause(s), treatment and management of the problem of the late effects of polio.

YEAR PROGRAM STARTED: 2000

PURPOSE:
To help support researchers, scientists, and clinicians worldwide to investigate the cause, treatment, and management of post-poliomyelitis and neuromuscular respiratory disease; to seek scientific information leading to eventual amelioration of the consequences of poliomyelitis and/or neuromuscular respiratory diseases.

LEGAL BASIS:
Not-for-profit organization.

ELIGIBILITY:
Applicants must be affiliated with an institution or organization. Citizens of all countries may apply. Applications, however, must be in English. Proposals will not be accepted via fax. The research may be quantitative and/or qualitative and follow sound and appropriate research standards relevant to the subject matter. The research findings must relate to improving the quality of life for people with disabilities. Preference will be given to innovative or original research.

FINANCIAL DATA:
Amount of support per award: $50,000 per year; maximum $100,000.

NO. MOST RECENT APPLICANTS: 11.

NO. AWARDS: 1.

APPLICATION INFO:
Contact the organization.

Duration: Up to two years.

IRS I.D.: 34-0961952

ADDRESS INQUIRIES TO:
Brian Tiburzi, Executive Director
(See address above.)

PULMONARY FIBROSIS FOUNDATION [2078]

230 East Ohio Street
Suite 500
Chicago, IL 60611
(888) 733-6741
Fax: (866) 587-9158
E-mail: grants@pulmonaryfibrosis.org
Web Site: www.pulmonaryfibrosis.org

AREAS OF INTEREST:
Research of and treatment for pulmonary fibrosis.

NAME(S) OF PROGRAMS:
● **PFF Scholars Program**

TYPE:
Matching gifts; Research grants. Supports early career investigators in their emerging research in the field of pulmonary fibrosis.

YEAR PROGRAM STARTED: 2000

PURPOSE:
To support projects that offer a high likelihood of improving the understanding of pulmonary fibrosis in the areas of basic science, translational research, clinical medicine and research, social sciences, and quality of life.

ELIGIBILITY:
Junior investigators who are within five years of formal training are eligible to apply. Established investigators who are over five years beyond their formal training may also apply.

FINANCIAL DATA:
Amount of support per award: $50,000 over a two-year period.
Total amount of support: Varies.

NO. AWARDS: 6 for the year 2019.

APPLICATION INFO:
Letter of Intent must be submitted between October and the November deadline. Full proposals are by invitation only.
Duration: Two years, with six-month and annual deliverables.
Deadline: Letter of Intent: November. Full proposal: February or March. Notification in May or June.

IRS I.D.: 84-1558631

ADDRESS INQUIRIES TO:
Zoe Dirks Bubany, Vice President of Board and External Relations
(See address above.)

RADIOLOGICAL SOCIETY OF NORTH AMERICA RESEARCH AND EDUCATION FOUNDATION [2079]

820 Jorie Boulevard, Suite 200
Oak Brook, IL 60523-2251
(630) 571-7816
E-mail: kosley@rsna.org
Web Site: www.rsna.org/re-foundation

FOUNDED: 1984

AREAS OF INTEREST:
Radiology.

NAME(S) OF PROGRAMS:
● **Research Seed Grant**

TYPE:
Seed money grants. Research Seed Grant support is available for any area of research related to the radiologic sciences.

PURPOSE:
To enable investigators to gain experience in defining objectives and testing hypotheses in preparation for major grant applications to corporations, foundations and governmental agencies.

ELIGIBILITY:
Applications are accepted from individuals throughout the world. Applicants must be RSNA members at the time of application. Contact the Foundation for full details.

FINANCIAL DATA:
Research Seed Grant is to support the preliminary or pilot phase of scientific projects, not to supplement major funding already secured. No salary support for the principal investigator will be provided.
Amount of support per award: Up to $40,000.
Total amount of support: Varies.

NO. MOST RECENT APPLICANTS: Foundation generally funds approximately 25% of the applications received.

NO. AWARDS: 12 for the year 2020.

APPLICATION INFO:
Applications are completed using the online Grant Application System.
Duration: One year.
Deadline: January 15.

ADDRESS INQUIRIES TO:
Keshia Osley
Assistant Director, Grant Administration
(See address above.)

RADIOLOGICAL SOCIETY OF NORTH AMERICA RESEARCH AND EDUCATION FOUNDATION [2080]

820 Jorie Boulevard, Suite 200
Oak Brook, IL 60523-2251
(630) 571-7816
E-mail: kosley@rsna.org
Web Site: www.rsna.org/re-foundation

FOUNDED: 1984

AREAS OF INTEREST:
Radiology.

NAME(S) OF PROGRAMS:
● **Research Medical Student Grant**

TYPE:
Research grants. Research Medical Student Grant is for any area of research related to the radiologic sciences.

PURPOSE:
To make radiology research opportunities possible for medical students and to encourage them, early in their medical careers, to consider academic radiology as an important option for their future.

ELIGIBILITY:
Applicants must be RSNA members at the time of application and be full-time medical students at an accredited North American medical school. The scientific advisor or one of the co-investigators must also be a dues-paying RSNA member. Contact the Foundation for full details.

FINANCIAL DATA:
Funds are intended to secure protected time for the recipient and may not be used for nonpersonnel research expenses.
Amount of support per award: $3,000 stipend.
Total amount of support: Approximately $75,000.
Matching fund requirements: $3,000 to be matched by the sponsoring department ($6,000 total) as a stipend for the medical student.

NO. AWARDS: 26 for the year 2020.

APPLICATION INFO:
Applications are completed using the online Grant Application System.
Duration: 10 weeks full-time (or equivalent).
Deadline: February 3.

ADDRESS INQUIRIES TO:
Keshia Osley
Assistant Director, Grant Administration
(See address above.)

RADIOLOGICAL SOCIETY OF NORTH AMERICA RESEARCH AND EDUCATION FOUNDATION [2081]

820 Jorie Boulevard, Suite 200
Oak Brook, IL 60523-2251
(630) 571-7816
E-mail: kosley@rsna.org
Web Site: www.rsna.org/re-foundation

FOUNDED: 1984

AREAS OF INTEREST:
Radiology.

NAME(S) OF PROGRAMS:
● **Education Scholar Grant**

TYPE:
Training grants. Any area of education related to the radiologic sciences.

PURPOSE:
To fund individuals in radiology or related disciplines who are seeking an opportunity to develop their expertise in radiologic education; to develop teachers in radiology who can share their knowledge with the radiology community.

ELIGIBILITY:
Applications are accepted from individuals throughout the world. Applicants must be RSNA members (at any level) at the time of application. Contact the Foundation for full details.

FINANCIAL DATA:
Education Scholar Grant to be used for salary support and/or other project costs.
Amount of support per award: Up to $75,000.

NO. MOST RECENT APPLICANTS: Foundation generally funds approximately 25% of the applications received.

NO. AWARDS: 1 for the year 2020.

APPLICATION INFO:
Applications are completed using the online Grant Application System.
Duration: Up to three years.
Deadline: January 11.

ADDRESS INQUIRIES TO:
Keshia Osley
Assistant Director, Grant Administration
(See address above.)

RADIOLOGICAL SOCIETY OF NORTH AMERICA RESEARCH AND EDUCATION FOUNDATION [2082]

820 Jorie Boulevard, Suite 200
Oak Brook, IL 60523-2251
(630) 571-7816
E-mail: kosley@rsna.org
Web Site: www.rsna.org/re-foundation

FOUNDED: 1984

AREAS OF INTEREST:
Radiology.

NAME(S) OF PROGRAMS:
● **RSNA/AUR/APDR/SCARD Radiology Education Research Development Grant**

TYPE:
Research grants.

PURPOSE:
To encourage innovation and improvement in health sciences education by providing research opportunities to individuals in pursuit of advancing the science of radiology education; to help in building a critical mass of radiology education researchers and promote the careers of persons advancing the science of radiology education.

ELIGIBILITY:
Applications are accepted from individuals throughout the world. Grants are awarded to any person, at any level of career development, who have a primary appointment in a radiology department. Applicants must be members of one or more of the sponsoring organizations. Contact the Foundation for full details.

FINANCIAL DATA:
Grants can be used to help cover the costs of research materials, research assistant support and limited primary investigator salary support (no more than half of grant award).
Amount of support per award: Up to $10,000.
Total amount of support: Varies.

CO-OP FUNDING PROGRAMS: Co-sponsored by the Radiological Society of North America (RSNA), Association of University Radiologists (AUR), Association of Program Directors in Radiology (APDR), and Society of Chairmen of Academic Radiology Departments (SCARD).

NO. MOST RECENT APPLICANTS: Foundation generally funds approximately 25% of the applications received.

NO. AWARDS: 1 for the year 2020.

APPLICATION INFO:
Applications must be submitted online.
Duration: One year.
Deadline: January 11.

ADDRESS INQUIRIES TO:
Keshia Osley
Assistant Director, Grant Administration
(See address above.)

RADIOLOGICAL SOCIETY OF NORTH AMERICA RESEARCH AND EDUCATION FOUNDATION [2083]

820 Jorie Boulevard, Suite 200
Oak Brook, IL 60523-2251
(630) 571-7816
E-mail: kosley@rsna.org
Web Site: www.rsna.org/re-foundation

FOUNDED: 1984

AREAS OF INTEREST:
Radiology.

NAME(S) OF PROGRAMS:
● **RSNA Research Scholar Grant**

TYPE:
Research grants.

PURPOSE:
To support junior faculty members who have completed the conventional resident/fellowship training programs but have not yet been recognized as independent investigators.

ELIGIBILITY:
Any area of research related to the radiologic sciences is eligible for Research Scholar Grant support. Applicants must be nominated by their department chair (one new application per department per year). Contact the Foundation for full details.

GEOG. RESTRICTIONS: North America.

FINANCIAL DATA:
Amount of support per award: $150,000 ($75,000 per year).
Total amount of support: Varies.

NO. MOST RECENT APPLICANTS: Foundation generally funds approximately 25% of the applications received.

NO. AWARDS: 9 for the year 2020.

APPLICATION INFO:
Applications must be submitted online.
Duration: Two years.
Deadline: January 15.

ADDRESS INQUIRIES TO:
Keshia Osley
Assistant Director, Grant Administration
(See address above.)

*SPECIAL STIPULATIONS:
Applicant must commit to devoting 40% of time to granted project.

RADIOLOGICAL SOCIETY OF NORTH AMERICA RESEARCH AND EDUCATION FOUNDATION [2084]

820 Jorie Boulevard, Suite 200
Oak Brook, IL 60523-2251
(630) 571-7816
E-mail: kosley@rsna.org
Web Site: www.rsna.org/re-foundation

FOUNDED: 1984

AREAS OF INTEREST:
Radiology.

NAME(S) OF PROGRAMS:
● **Research Resident/Fellow Grant**

TYPE:
Research grants. Grants will be awarded for diverse types of projects in the radiologic sciences including basic science and clinical research studies. This program is not intended to fund Ph.D. postdoctoral projects, nor to support those whose primary aim is to obtain practical experience in clinical radiology.

PURPOSE:
To provide young investigators not yet professionally established in the radiologic sciences an opportunity to gain further insight into scientific investigation and to develop competence in research techniques and methods.

ELIGIBILITY:
At the time of application, the applicant must:
(1) be an RSNA member (at any level);
(2) be (if an applicant within North American educational institutions) a resident or fellow in a department of radiology, radiation oncology or nuclear medicine; applicants from outside North America must already be accepted into a one- or two-year Fellowship position at a North American education institution at the time of the grant application;
(3) have completed the internship year (PGY-1) and at least six months of specialty training in the radiologic sciences (PGY-2) for the resident grant, or be in the last year of, or have completed, the prescribed residency training for the fellow grant. (If awarded the latter, recipient must be in a fellowship position during the period of grant support);
(4) be certified by the American Board of Radiology, or on track for certification;
(5) not have been principal investigator on external/extramural grant/contract amounts totaling more than $60,000 in a single calendar year (includes support from single or combined grants or contracts from any source including government, private or industrial/commercial sources);
(6) not be agent(s) of any for-profit, commercial company in the radiologic sciences (applies to applicant/co-principal investigator);
(7) not submit more than one research or education grant application to the RSNA Research and Education Foundation per year;
(8) not have concurrent RSNA grants and;
(9) devote at least 50% of applicant's time to granted project under the guidance of a scientific advisor/mentor.

Supplementation of funding from other grant sources must be approved by Foundation staff if not described in the original research plan. Awards from other sources may be approved by Foundation staff if the investigator submits a satisfactory plan to address any budgetary overlap.

Contact the Foundation for full details.

FINANCIAL DATA:
Funds may be used for salary and/or nonpersonnel research expenses.
Amount of support per award: $50,000 salary support for one-year Research Fellow project or $30,000 salary support for one-year Research Resident project.
Total amount of support: Varies.

NO. MOST RECENT APPLICANTS: Foundation generally funds approximately 25% of the applications received.

NO. AWARDS: 23 for the year 2020.

APPLICATION INFO:
Applications are completed online using the Online Grant Application System.
Duration: One year; however, residents may opt for a six-month, full-time research project.
Deadline: January 15.

ADDRESS INQUIRIES TO:
Keshia Osley
Assistant Director, Grant Administration
(See address above.)

SAVOY FOUNDATION [2085]
230 Foch Street
St.-Jean-sur-Richelieu QC J3B 2B2 Canada
(450) 358-9779
Fax: (450) 346-1045
E-mail: epilepsy@savoy-foundation.ca
Web Site: savoy-foundation.ca

FOUNDED: 1971

AREAS OF INTEREST:
Epilepsy and medical research.

TYPE:
Fellowships; Research grants; Scholarships.

PURPOSE:
To promote research on epilepsy.

ELIGIBILITY:
Studentships will be awarded to meritorious applicants wishing to acquire training and pursue research in a biomedical discipline, the health sciences or social sciences related to epilepsy. To be eligible, the candidate must have a good university record (B.Sc., M.D. or equivalent diploma) and have ensured that a qualified researcher affiliated to a university and/or hospital will supervise his or her work. Concomitant registration in a graduate program (M.Sc. or Ph.D.) is encouraged.

Post-Doctoral and Clinical Research Fellowships will be awarded to scientists or medical specialists (Ph.D. or M.D.) wishing to carry out a full-time research project in the field of epilepsy.

Research Grants are available to clinicians and/or established scientists working on epilepsy or related subjects.

Studentships, fellowships, and grants are available to Canadian researchers, to foreign nationals or for projects conducted in Canada.

FINANCIAL DATA:
Amount of support per award: Studentships: $17,000 (CAN) per year. Postdoctoral and Clinical Research Fellowships: $35,000. Research Grants: Up to $25,000.

Total amount of support: More than $320,000 (CAN) per year.

NO. MOST RECENT APPLICANTS: 63 for the year 2019-20.

NO. AWARDS: 15 for the year 2019-20.

APPLICATION INFO:
Application information is available on the web site.

Duration: Studentships: One year. Renewable for a maximum duration of four years; Post-Doctoral, Clinical Research Fellowships and Research Grants: One year. Nonrenewable.

Deadline: January 31 (postmark). If January 31 falls on a weekend or holiday, the Foundation will consider the next working day as the deadline.

EXECUTIVE COMMITTEE:
George M. Savoy, President
Caroline Savoy, Vice President/Secretary
Alain Barbeau, Secretary and Treasurer

ADDRESS INQUIRIES TO:
Caroline Savoy, Secretary
(See address above.)

SCLERODERMA FOUNDATION [2086]
300 Rosewood Drive, Suite 105
Danvers, MA 01923
(978) 463-5843
(800) 722-4673
Fax: (978) 777-1313
E-mail: research@scleroderma.org
Web Site: www.scleroderma.org

FOUNDED: 1998

AREAS OF INTEREST:
Scleroderma and systemic sclerosis (SSc).

NAME(S) OF PROGRAMS:
● **Scleroderma Foundation Research Grants**

TYPE:
Research grants.

YEAR PROGRAM STARTED: 1998

PURPOSE:
To support research in the area of scleroderma.

ELIGIBILITY:
Applicants must be principal investigators.

GEOG. RESTRICTIONS: United States for new and established investigators; international for established investigators only.

FINANCIAL DATA:
Amount of support per award: $150,000.
Total amount of support: Average $1,000,000 annually.

NO. AWARDS: Average 7 annually.

APPLICATION INFO:
Applicants must use the application form following NIH guidelines which is available, along with other pertinent information, on the Foundation's web site.

Duration: Established investigators: Two years; New investigators: Three years.
Deadline: September 15 annually. Deadline is subject to change. Call or visit the web site to verify deadline date.

PUBLICATIONS:
Quarterly magazine; literature.

IRS I.D.: 52-1375827

ADDRESS INQUIRIES TO:
Research Department
(See e-mail address above.)

SMITH FAMILY AWARDS PROGRAM FOR EXCELLENCE IN BIOMEDICAL RESEARCH [2087]
2 Boylston Street, 4th Floor
Boston, MA 02116
E-mail: lcarver@hria.org
Web Site: hria.org/tmf/smith

FOUNDED: 1991

AREAS OF INTEREST:
Basic biomedical science including physics, chemistry and engineering with a focus on biomedical research.

TYPE:
Research grants.

YEAR PROGRAM STARTED: 1991

PURPOSE:
To provide research grants for newly independent junior faculty.

ELIGIBILITY:
Detailed information is available on the web site.

GEOG. RESTRICTIONS: Massachusetts, Yale University and Brown University.

FINANCIAL DATA:
Amount of support per award: $300,000 over three years.
Total amount of support: $1,800,000 in new awards for the year 2019.

CO-OP FUNDING PROGRAMS: Funding provided by the Richard and Susan Smith Family Foundation.

NO. MOST RECENT APPLICANTS: 67 initial stage applicants for the year 2021.

NO. AWARDS: 6 for the funding cycle 2021-24.

REPRESENTATIVE AWARDS:
"Maintenance of Genome Stability by the Hippo Tumor Suppressor Pathway;" "Neuro-molecular Mechanisms Underlying Alcoholism;" "Micro-Environmental Regulation of Network State and Drug Sensitivity in Triple-Negative Breast Cancer."

APPLICATION INFO:
Information and forms are available on the web site.
Duration: Three years. Nonrenewable.
Deadline: Initial stage: August. Full application (by invitation only): December.

PUBLICATIONS:
Application guidelines; directory of grant recipients (online); summaries of current and previous funded projects.

ADDRESS INQUIRIES TO:
Grants Officer
(See address above.)

THE SOCIETY FOR INVESTIGATIVE DERMATOLOGY [2088]
526 Superior Avenue East
Suite 340
Cleveland, OH 44114-1999
(216) 579-9300
Fax: (216) 579-9333
E-mail: sid@sidnet.org
Web Site: www.sidnet.org

FOUNDED: 1938

AREAS OF INTEREST:
Skin biology, skin disease, and publication and results of skin research.

CONSULTING OR VOLUNTEER SERVICES:
Advocacy for biomedical research.

NAME(S) OF PROGRAMS:
● **Albert M. Kligman Fellowship Fund Award**

TYPE:
Awards/prizes; Conferences/seminars; Fellowships; Research grants; Travel grants. Awards will be used to support resident, fellow and medical student travel to the Society's annual meetings to present their scientific work.

YEAR PROGRAM STARTED: 1973

PURPOSE:
To encourage trainees to become skin scientists; to encourage the best and brightest young scholars to become members of the research community in dermatology and to participate in the activities of the Society; to advance and promote the sciences relevant to skin health and diseases through education, advocacy and scholarly exchange of scientific information.

LEGAL BASIS:
Tax-exempt.

ELIGIBILITY:
Applicants must hold the M.D. or Ph.D.
Project must be skin-/skin disease-related.
Preceptor is required. One year of work
minimum.

FINANCIAL DATA:
No indirect costs.
Amount of support per award: $25,000.

NO. AWARDS: Approximately 20.

APPLICATION INFO:
Information on application can be obtained
from the address above.
Duration: One year.
Deadline: Contact the Society for exact
dates.

IRS I.D.: 23-1361165

OFFICERS:
Janet Fairley, M.D., President
Andrew Kowalczyk, Ph.D., Vice President

SOCIETY OF CARDIOVASCULAR ANESTHESIOLOGISTS
1061 East Main Street
Suite 300
East Dundee, IL 60118
(855) 658-2828
Fax: (847) 375-6323
E-mail: info@scahq.org
Web Site: www.scahq.org

TYPE:
Research grants.

See entry 2147 for full listing.

SOCIETY OF CRITICAL CARE MEDICINE   [2089]
500 Midway Drive
Mount Prospect, IL 60056
(847) 827-6888
Fax: (847) 439-7226
E-mail: vkumar@sccm.org
Web Site: www.sccm.org

AREAS OF INTEREST:
Critical care medicine.

NAME(S) OF PROGRAMS:
● **SCCM-Weil Research Grant**

TYPE:
Research grants. Recipients receive financial
rewards, prestige and recognition within the
field of critical care medicine.

PURPOSE:
To promote excellence in critical care
teaching and research for the improved care
of the critically ill and injured.

ELIGIBILITY:
SCCM membership is required for research
grants. Entries are judged by a committee
with expertise in the field.

FINANCIAL DATA:
Amount of support per award: $50,000.
Total amount of support: $100,000.

NO. AWARDS: 2.

APPLICATION INFO:
Contact the Society for guidelines.

ADDRESS INQUIRIES TO:
Vishakha Kumar, Senior Manager, Research
(See e-mail address above.)

TASTE AND SMELL CLINIC   [2090]
Center for Molecular Nutrition and Sensory
Disorders
5125 MacArthur Boulevard, N.W., Suite 20
Washington, DC 20016
(202) 364-4180
Fax: (202) 364-9727
E-mail: doc@tasteandsmell.com
Web Site: www.tasteandsmell.com

FOUNDED: 1969

AREAS OF INTEREST:
Taste and smell, clinical treatment of patients
with taste and smell disorders, growth factors
in relationship to stem cell maturation and
development, saliva, salivary diagnostics,
salivary proteins, functional magnetic
imaging of the brain, transcranial magnetic
stimulation of the brain, nasal mucus
physiology and pathology, and nasal mucus
diagnostics.

CONSULTING OR VOLUNTEER SERVICES:
The Taste and Smell Dysfunction Foundation.

NAME(S) OF PROGRAMS:
● **Taste and Smell Disorders Internship
Program**

TYPE:
Internships; Training grants. The Taste and
Smell Disorders Internship Program is
offered to provide internships and programs
to evaluate and treat patients with taste and
smell dysfunctions.

YEAR PROGRAM STARTED: 1975

PURPOSE:
To provide internships and other programs to
evaluate and treat patients with taste and
smell dysfunctions; to study salivary and
nasal mucus proteins; to support biochemists
and physicians interested in cognitive
neurology who want to come work with the
clinic.

LEGAL BASIS:
Private organization.

ELIGIBILITY:
Preference to individuals from the
Washington, DC metropolitan area.

GEOG. RESTRICTIONS: Washington, DC region.

FINANCIAL DATA:
Stipend commensurate with best academic
and/or clinical achievement.
Amount of support per award: Varies
depending on need and tasks required.
Total amount of support: $20,000 to $60,000
per year.

CO-OP FUNDING PROGRAMS: Taste and Smell
Dysfunction Foundation.

NO. MOST RECENT APPLICANTS: 3.

NO. AWARDS: 1.

APPLICATION INFO:
Resume and three letters of recommendation
from scientific mentors are required.
Duration: One year. Renewable for second
and third year.
Deadline: June 30.

STAFF:
R.I. Henkin, Director
S. Holen, Staff Scientist
S.J. Potolicchio, Senior Scientist in
Neurology

ADDRESS INQUIRIES TO:
R.I. Henkin, Director
(See address above.)

*SPECIAL STIPULATIONS:
Work limited to Washington, DC region.

U.S. DEPARTMENT OF THE NAVY   [2091]
Navy Bureau of Medicine and Surgery
NM Accessions Department
8955 Wood Road, Room 13132
Bethesda, MD 20889-5628
(301) 319-4059
(301) 295-9950
E-mail: usn.ohstudent@mail.mil
Web Site: www.med.navy.
mil/Accessions/Pages/default.aspx

FOUNDED: 1972

AREAS OF INTEREST:
Medicine, dentistry, optometry, and clinical
psychology.

CONSULTING OR VOLUNTEER SERVICES:
Navy Recruiting Command.

NAME(S) OF PROGRAMS:
● **Navy Health Professions Scholarship
Program (HPSP)**

TYPE:
Scholarships. This is an educational support
program for individuals pursuing graduate
degrees in professional medical programs and
who have a desire to serve in the U.S. Navy
following graduation.

YEAR PROGRAM STARTED: 1972

PURPOSE:
To provide officers for the Navy who are
trained in these disciplines.

LEGAL BASIS:
Authorized by Public Law 92-426.

ELIGIBILITY:
Applicants must be:
(1) U.S. citizens (dual citizenship not
permitted);
(2) physically qualified for a commission as a
U.S. Navy officer and;
(3) accepted into or enrolled in an AMA or
AOA school of medicine, an ADA school of
dentistry, an accredited optometry or
physician assistant Masters' program, or in
the first year of didactic education for a
Ph.D. or Psy.D. in clinical psychology from
an APA accredited school. School must be
located in the U.S. or Puerto Rico.

Applicant must not have reached the age of
42 at the time of entry into active duty
following completion of their education.

GEOG. RESTRICTIONS: United States and Puerto
Rico.

FINANCIAL DATA:
Amount of support per award: Scholarship
includes full tuition (no upper limit) and
allowable fees, reimbursement for all
required books, supplies and equipment
(some limits apply), $20,000 signing bonus
(medicine and dentistry only), monthly
stipend of $2,330 (taxable), full pay and
allowances of an ensign (O-1) for 45 days
per year (about $4,500), and reimbursement
for student's health insurance if required by
school.
Total amount of support: Over $125,000,000
in tuition and stipends. Part of annual
Congressional appropriation.

NO. MOST RECENT APPLICANTS: 500 for
medical; 200 for dental.

NO. AWARDS: 330.

APPLICATION INFO:
Must apply through Navy Recruiting Command.

Duration: Two to four years, according to year level upon entry. Acceptance of the program requires continuous participation until graduation. Dental scholarships are the same as medical scholarships.

Deadline: Rolling acceptance for medical, dental and optometry. Clinical psychology applications: January.

ADDRESS INQUIRIES TO:
See e-mail address above.

*SPECIAL STIPULATIONS:
For Scholarship awardees, one year of active duty (not in training) is required for each year of the Scholarship, with a three-year minimum.

THE UNIVERSITY OF CALGARY

Faculty of Graduate Studies
Earth Sciences Building, Room 1010
2500 University Drive, N.W.
Calgary AB T2N 1N4 Canada
(403) 220-4938
Fax: (403) 289-7635
E-mail: gsaward@ucalgary.ca
Web Site: grad.ucalgary.ca/awards

TYPE:
Awards/prizes; Scholarships. Awards for study in the medical sciences. Tenable at The University of Calgary. Award endowed through a bequest of the late William H. Davies.

See entry 1596 for full listing.

THE UNIVERSITY OF SYDNEY [2092]

Scholarships Office
Level 4, Jane Foss Russell Building G02
The University of Sydney N.S.W. 2006
Australia
61 (02) 8627 1444
E-mail: scholarships.officer@sydney.edu.au
Web Site: www.sydney.edu.au/scholarships

FOUNDED: 1850

AREAS OF INTEREST:
Medicine.

NAME(S) OF PROGRAMS:
● **Sydney Medical School Postgraduate Research Scholarships**

TYPE:
Scholarships. For research leading to a higher degree. Tenable in the Sydney Medical School at the University of Sydney.

PURPOSE:
To promote and encourage research in the medical sciences at the University of Sydney.

LEGAL BASIS:
University.

ELIGIBILITY:
Available to full-time research candidates, normally Ph.D., in any department or research unit associated with the Sydney Medical School at the University of Sydney. Applicants must be either Australian or New Zealand citizens or permanent residents of Australia.

Scholarships are awarded on the basis of academic merit and any other criteria stipulated for individual scholarships.

FINANCIAL DATA:
Amount of support per award: Varies.

NO. AWARDS: Varies according to availability of funds.

APPLICATION INFO:
Contact the University for guidelines.

Duration: Varies.

ADDRESS INQUIRIES TO:
Scholarships Officer
Sydney Medical School
Edward Ford Building (A27)
Fisher Road
The University of Sydney
N.S.W. 2006 Australia
(See e-mail address above.)

*PLEASE NOTE:
Very few awards are available and competition for them is extremely keen. They are awarded strictly on academic merit and only graduates with First Class Honours or equivalent qualifications (e.g., graduation magna cum laude) will be considered.

THE VALLEY FOUNDATION [2093]

999 West Taylor Street
Suite A
San Jose, CA 95126
Web Site: www.valley.org

FOUNDED: 1984

AREAS OF INTEREST:
Medical services and health care for lower-income households, the arts, senior citizens, education and research.

TYPE:
Project/program grants.

YEAR PROGRAM STARTED: 1984

PURPOSE:
To provide funding for nonprofit organizations, with an emphasis in the medical field.

LEGAL BASIS:
Nonprofit foundation.

ELIGIBILITY:
Qualified 501(c)(3) charitable organizations. No individuals or political organizations.

GEOG. RESTRICTIONS: United States.

FINANCIAL DATA:
The Foundation prefers to avoid grants which provide more than one-half of an organization's total budget in a 12-month period, usually expecting community and applicant commitment to a project through local cost sharing.

Amount of support per award: $2,500 to $1,000,000.

APPLICATION INFO:
Guidelines are available on the Foundation web site.

Duration: Varies, but multiple-year requests are discouraged. Organizations which have received funding must wait at least one full year before submitting another application. Organizations that did not make it to the full LOI full proposal cycle can reapply on the anniversary of their first LOI submission.

Deadline: February 20, May 20, August 20 and November 20.

PUBLICATIONS:
Application guidelines.

IRS I.D.: 94-1584547

ADDRESS INQUIRIES TO:
See e-mail address above.

Allergy, immunology, infectious diseases

AMERICAN ACADEMY OF ALLERGY ASTHMA & IMMUNOLOGY [2094]

555 East Wells Street, Suite 1100
Milwaukee, WI 53202-3823
(414) 272-6071
Fax: (414) 272-6070
E-mail: info@aaaai.org
Web Site: www.aaaai.org

FOUNDED: 1943

AREAS OF INTEREST:
Allergy and immunology.

NAME(S) OF PROGRAMS:
● **Domestic Fellow-In-Training Travel Scholarship**

TYPE:
Travel grants. Travel scholarships to attend the AAAAI Annual Meeting.

PURPOSE:
To advance the knowledge and practice of allergy by discussion at meetings, by fostering the education of students and the public, by encouraging union and cooperation among those engaged in this field and by promoting and stimulating research and study in allergy.

LEGAL BASIS:
Nonprofit.

ELIGIBILITY:
Travel grants for the annual meeting are awarded to member fellows-in-training in the field of allergy and immunology. The grants will be awarded on the basis of merit as judged by the committee. Individuals with a faculty appointment will not be considered.

GEOG. RESTRICTIONS: United States and Canada.

FINANCIAL DATA:
Amount of support per award: Maximum of $800 for first- or second-year Fellow-In-Training who apply for a travel scholarship without an accepted abstract or case report for presentation; Maximum of $650 for third-, fourth- or fifth-year Fellow-In-Training who apply for a travel scholarship without an accepted abstract for presentation; Maximum of $1,100 to Fellow-In-Training who applies for a travel scholarship and is the first author of an accepted abstract for presentation or is the first author Fellow-In-Training with a Case Report (candidate must present their abstract or case report at the Annual Meeting in order to be eligible).

Total amount of support: Varies.

NO. MOST RECENT APPLICANTS: 232.

NO. AWARDS: 231.

APPLICATION INFO:
Application information is available online.

Deadline: November 2021.

See entry 426 for full listing.

ADDRESS INQUIRIES TO:
Mari Duran, Program Manager
E-mail: mduran@aaaai.org

ARTHRITIS NATIONAL RESEARCH FOUNDATION (ANRF)

19200 Von Karman Avenue
Suite 350
Irvine, CA 92612
(800) 588-2873
(562) 437-6808
E-mail: grants@curearthritis.org
Web Site: www.curearthritis.org

TYPE:
Research grants; Travel grants. ANRF Arthritis Research Grants are intended to support basic and clinical research focusing on rheumatic and related autoimmune diseases, such as osteoarthritis and rheumatoid arthritis.

See entry 2012 for full listing.

CANCER RESEARCH INSTITUTE

29 Broadway, 4th Floor
New York, NY 10006
(212) 688-7515
(800) 992-2623
Fax: (212) 832-9376
E-mail: grants@cancerresearch.org
Web Site: www.cancerresearch.org

TYPE:
Research grants. The CRI Lloyd J. Old STAR Program - Scientists Taking Risks - provides long-term funding to midcareer scientists, giving them the freedom and flexibility to pursue high-risk, high-reward research at the forefront of discovery and innovation in cancer immunotherapy.

See entry 2184 for full listing.

CANCER RESEARCH INSTITUTE

29 Broadway, 4th Floor
New York, NY 10006
(212) 688-7515
(800) 992-2623
Fax: (212) 832-9376
E-mail: grants@cancerresearch.org
Web Site: www.cancerresearch.org

TYPE:
Seed money grants. The Cancer Research Institute Technology Impact Award provides seed funding to address the gap between technology development and clinical application of cancer immunotherapies. These grants aim to encourage collaboration between technology developers and clinical cancer immunologists and to generate a proof-of-principle of a novel platform technology in bioinformatics, ex vivo or in silico modeling systems, immunological or tumor profiling instrumentation, methods, reagents and assays, or other relevant technologies that can enable clinical scientists to generate deeper insights into the mechanisms of action of effective or ineffective cancer immunotherapies.

See entry 2185 for full listing.

CANCER RESEARCH INSTITUTE

29 Broadway, 4th Floor
New York, NY 10006
(212) 688-7515
(800) 992-2623
Fax: (212) 832-9376
E-mail: grants@cancerresearch.org
Web Site: www.cancerresearch.org

TYPE:
Fellowships; Research grants; Training grants.

See entry 2182 for full listing.

DYSTROPHIC EPIDERMOLYSIS BULLOSA RESEARCH ASSOCIATION OF AMERICA, INC. (DEBRA)   [2095]

75 Broad Street
Suite 300
New York, NY 10004
(212) 868-1573 ext. 110
Fax: (212) 868-9296
E-mail: staff@debra.org
Web Site: www.debra.org

FOUNDED: 1980

AREAS OF INTEREST:
Research into the causes, treatment and cure of EB and other genetic disorders of the skin.

NAME(S) OF PROGRAMS:
- **debra International Research Grants**

TYPE:
Research grants. Financial aid for EB families in crisis.

YEAR PROGRAM STARTED: 1980

PURPOSE:
To provide opportunity to advance research into the effects, causes, treatments and cure for epidermolysis bullosa.

ELIGIBILITY:
Peer-reviewed grants made to full-time or part-time researchers.

FINANCIAL DATA:
Amount of support per award: Varies.
Total amount of support: Varies.

APPLICATION INFO:
Guidelines may be obtained from the organization at the address above.
Duration: One to three years.

IRS I.D.: 11-2519726

ADDRESS INQUIRIES TO:
Brett Kopelan, Executive Director
(See address above.)

MAGIC JOHNSON FOUNDATION

9100 Wilshire Boulevard
Suite 700, East Tower
Beverly Hills, CA 90212
(310) 246-4400
Fax: (310) 786-8796
Web Site: magicjohnson.org

TYPE:
Project/program grants; Technical assistance.

See entry 151 for full listing.

ROBERT MAPPLETHORPE FOUNDATION, INC.

477 Madison Avenue, 15th Floor
New York, NY 10022-5835
(212) 755-3025
Fax: (212) 941-4764
E-mail: joree@mapplethorpe.org
info@mapplethorpe.org
Web Site: www.mapplethorpe.org

TYPE:
Project/program grants. Funds medical research in the fight against AIDS and HIV infection and supports the promotion of photography as a fine art, embracing exhibitions, acquisitions, and publications.

See entry 426 for full listing.

Dentistry

AMERICAN ACADEMY OF IMPLANT DENTISTRY (AAID) FOUNDATION   [2096]

211 East Chicago Avenue
Suite 1100
Chicago, IL 60611
(312) 335-1550
Fax: (312) 335-9090
E-mail: barb@aaid.com
Web Site: www.aaid.com

FOUNDED: 1979

AREAS OF INTEREST:
Dental implant research.

NAME(S) OF PROGRAMS:
- **Humanitarian Project Support**
- **Research Award**
- **Student Research Grant**
- **Wish a Smile**

TYPE:
Awards/prizes; Project/program grants; Research grants. Research Award provides limited support for meritorious dental implant research projects which determine the feasibility of a larger research project. This may be described as the conduct of pilot studies or venture research to develop and test new techniques and procedures, to carry out a small clinical or animal research project and to analyze existing data.

Student Research Grant is available for all graduate dental students. Research must be related to dental implant.

Wish a Smile, a partnership between the AAID Foundation, Dental Lifeline Network, Implant and Bone Grafting corporate sponsors and volunteer dentists, aims to provide free dental service to patients who have congenitally missing teeth and are financially disadvantaged, disabled veterans with congenitally missing teeth, and disabled veterans with no teeth remaining requiring implants to retain a denture. The AAIDF and DLN would seek to get all needed restorative supplies and services donated in addition to implant.

YEAR PROGRAM STARTED: 1981

PURPOSE:
To provide limited support for meritorious dental implant research projects; to provide a humanitarian service to the public; to increase public awareness of the AAID Foundation, AAID, AAID's members and Dental Lifeline Network.

LEGAL BASIS:
Research foundation.

ELIGIBILITY:
Investigators from any scientific discipline and at any stage of their career may apply for a Research Award. These awards are appropriated for new investigators and those changing areas of research or resuming research careers.

Student Research Grant is available to postgraduate dental students for implant-related research studies.

Wish a Smile requires applicants to meet the following criteria:
(1) be 17 years of age or older at the time of application;
(2) be congenitally missing one to three teeth with no more than three teeth requiring replacement;
(3) be medically healthy and a nonsmoker and;
(4) have a patient or family gross income (if patient is a dependent minor) that is low or displays significant need.

FINANCIAL DATA:
Grants may be used for supplies, small items of equipment and salary for technical and support personnel.
Amount of support per award: Humanitarian Project Support: Varies; Small Research Award: Up to $25,000 (total project costs); Student Research Grant: Up to $2,500 per year.
Total amount of support: $100,000.

NO. MOST RECENT APPLICANTS: 36.

NO. AWARDS: Research Award: 4; Student Research Grant: Up to 8.

APPLICATION INFO:
Required documentation includes abstract of research plan, budget estimate, explanation of the project, including its specific aims, significance, experimental design and methods, sequence of events and time schedule and a complete bibliography, curriculum vitae and a list of all co-investigators and consultants.
Duration: Student Research Grant: Up to two years. Nonrenewable.
Deadline: Research Award: August 1. Student Research Grant: June 15.

PUBLICATIONS:
Guidelines.

OFFICERS:
James L. Bush, Chairman
Richard Mercurio, D.D.S., Vice Chairman

ADDRESS INQUIRIES TO:
E-mail: foundation@aaid.com

AMERICAN ASSOCIATION FOR DENTAL RESEARCH   [2097]
1619 Duke Street
Alexandria, VA 22314-3406
(703) 548-0066
Fax: (703) 548-1883
E-mail: ajones@iadr.org
Web Site: www.aadr.org

AREAS OF INTEREST:
Dental research.

NAME(S) OF PROGRAMS:
● **AADR Hatton Competition**

TYPE:
Awards/prizes. For junior investigators (junior, senior and postdoctoral) who exhibit potential for a productive career in dental research.

PURPOSE:
To advance research and increase knowledge for the improvement of oral health; to support and represent the oral health research community; to facilitate the communication and application of research findings.

ELIGIBILITY:
Applicants must be U.S. citizens or noncitizen nationals of the U.S. (or who have been lawfully admitted for permanent residence at the time of submission of the abstract - those with a "green card") or persons of other nationalities whose research is performed in the U.S. Must be an AADR member. There is no age limit for entrants in the AADR competition.

FINANCIAL DATA:
Amount of support per award: First prize: $1,000; Second prize: $500.
Total amount of support: $4,500.

NO. MOST RECENT APPLICANTS: Over 100.

NO. AWARDS: 3 First Prizes and 3 Second Prizes.

APPLICATION INFO:
Details of the abstract to be submitted are available on the web site.
Deadline: March 12.

ADDRESS INQUIRIES TO:
Anthony Jones, Awards Coordinator
(See address above.)

AMERICAN ASSOCIATION FOR DENTAL RESEARCH   [2098]
1619 Duke Street
Alexandria, VA 22314-3406
(703) 548-0066
Fax: (703) 548-1883
E-mail: ajones@iadr.org
Web Site: www.aadr.org

AREAS OF INTEREST:
Basic and clinical research related to oral health.

NAME(S) OF PROGRAMS:
● **Student Research Fellowships**

PURPOSE:
To advance research and increase knowledge for the improvement of oral health; to support and represent the oral health research community; to facilitate the communication and application of research findings.

ELIGIBILITY:
Applicant must be enrolled in an accredited D.D.S./D.M.D. or hygiene program in a dental institution and must be sponsored by a faculty member. Students should not have received their degree, nor should they in the year of award. Applicant may have an advanced degree in a basic science subject. Must be an AADR member.

GEOG. RESTRICTIONS: United States.

FINANCIAL DATA:
Amount of support per award: $2,700.
Total amount of support: Varies.

NO. MOST RECENT APPLICANTS: 60.

NO. AWARDS: 16 for the year 2021.

APPLICATION INFO:
Proposals will follow the general format of the Public Health Service Grant Application

Form PHS 398, which is to be used only as a guideline. Each proposal must include the following:
(1) objectives, describing what the research is intended to accomplish and the hypothesis to be tested;
(2) research strategy, including significance, innovation and approach;
(3) facilities and equipment to be used for the research project;
(4) other support for applicant and sponsor and;
(5) for those projects involving Recombinant DNA/Recombinant DNA Molecules, an indication that the project adheres to the current NIH Guidelines for Research Involving Recombinant DNA Molecules.

The following documents must also be included:
(1) cover letter from the applicant's sponsor, indicating the dental school's and the sponsor's support of the proposed research;
(2) cover letter from the applicant explaining student's motivations and reasons to have the Fellowship experience and what plans are after completion of this phase of their education;
(3) curriculum vitae, not to exceed two pages, outlining the student's career up to the time of application;
(4) sponsor's biographical sketch in NIH format, not to exceed two pages;
(5) literature cited and;
(6) documentation that the project has been approved by the Institutional Review Board for projects involving human subjects or vertebrate animals.

Proposals longer than four pages (PDF) and/or 1,400 words will not be considered.
Deadline: April 2.

ADDRESS INQUIRIES TO:
Anthony Jones, Awards Coordinator
(See address above.)

AMERICAN ASSOCIATION FOR DENTAL RESEARCH   [2099]
1619 Duke Street
Alexandria, VA 22314-3406
(703) 548-0066
Fax: (703) 548-1883
E-mail: ajones@iadr.org
Web Site: www.aadr.org

AREAS OF INTEREST:
Clinical research in periodontology.

NAME(S) OF PROGRAMS:
● **William B. Clark Fellowship in Clinical Research**

TYPE:
Fellowships.

PURPOSE:
To advance research and increase knowledge for the improvement of oral health; to support and represent the oral health research community; to facilitate the communication and application of research findings.

ELIGIBILITY:
Applicant must have completed first professional degree, should be appointed at an accredited dental school or academic research center in U.S., and must be a member of AADR.

GEOG. RESTRICTIONS: United States.

FINANCIAL DATA:
Amount of support per award: $5,000.
Total amount of support: $5,000.

NO. MOST RECENT APPLICANTS: 1.

NO. AWARDS: 1.

APPLICATION INFO:
Applicants must submit the following:
(1) letter stating their interest in applying for the award;
(2) curriculum vitae;
(3) three- to four-page (double-spaced) overview of their proposed areas of training, including how the experience will affect future research to be conducted by the applicant;
(4) brief description of the facility which will provide the training and;
(5) letter of support from the proposed mentor.
Deadline: January 21.

ADDRESS INQUIRIES TO:
Anthony Jones, Awards Coordinator
(See address above.)

AMERICAN ASSOCIATION FOR DENTAL RESEARCH [2100]
1619 Duke Street
Alexandria, VA 22314-3406
(703) 548-0066
Fax: (703) 548-1883
E-mail: ajones@iadr.org
Web Site: www.aadr.org

AREAS OF INTEREST:
Dental research.

NAME(S) OF PROGRAMS:
● **William J. Gies Award**

TYPE:
Awards/prizes. For the best paper published in the *Journal of Dental Research* during the preceding year.

PURPOSE:
To advance research and increase knowledge for the improvement of oral health; to support and represent the oral health research community; to facilitate the communication and application of research findings.

FINANCIAL DATA:
Amount of support per award: $1,000.
Total amount of support: $3,000.

NO. MOST RECENT APPLICANTS: More than 10 nominations.

NO. AWARDS: 3.

APPLICATION INFO:
Information on the nomination process is available on the web site.
Deadline: January 15.

ADDRESS INQUIRIES TO:
Anthony Jones, Awards Coordinator
(See address above.)

AMERICAN ASSOCIATION OF WOMEN DENTISTS [2101]
7794 Grow Drive
Pensacola, FL 32514
(850) 484-9987
(800) 920-2293
Fax: (850) 484-8762
E-mail: info@aawd.org
Web Site: www.aawd.org

FOUNDED: 1921

AREAS OF INTEREST:
Dentistry.

NAME(S) OF PROGRAMS:
● **Eleanor Bushee Award**
● **Lucy Hobbs Taylor Award**

TYPE:
Awards/prizes; Scholarships. The Eleanor Bushee Award honors senior dental students who have achieved academic excellence and have demonstrated outstanding leadership.
Lucy Hobbs Taylor Award is presented to a woman dentist who has made outstanding individual achievements in civic, cultural, academic and professional areas and exhibits role model qualities that positively reflect the image of women dentists and commitment to the profession.

PURPOSE:
To encourage women dental students who contribute to the school, to dentistry or dental health who are in need of financial assistance.

ELIGIBILITY:
Applicants must be dentists or junior/senior dental students. Lucy Hobbs Taylor Award applicant must be an AAWD member in good standing.

FINANCIAL DATA:
Amount of support per award: Varies.
Total amount of support: Varies.

APPLICATION INFO:
Detailed guidelines are posted on the Association web site.
Duration: One year.
Deadline: Varies.

PUBLICATIONS:
Chronicle; Women's Dental Journal.

AMERICAN DENTAL ASSISTANTS ASSOCIATION [2102]
180 Admiral Cochrane Drive
Suite 370
Annapolis, MD 21401
(630) 994-4247
Fax: (630) 351-8490
E-mail: jaykasper@adaausa.org
Web Site: www.adaausa.org

FOUNDED: 1924

AREAS OF INTEREST:
Dental assisting.

NAME(S) OF PROGRAMS:
● **Juliette A. Southard Scholarship Program**

TYPE:
Scholarships. Tuition scholarships awarded to dental professional students interested in furthering their education.

YEAR PROGRAM STARTED: 1924

PURPOSE:
To provide financial assistance for highly qualified applicants pursuing dental professional education.

LEGAL BASIS:
Nonprofit professional organization.

ELIGIBILITY:
Applicants must be high school graduates or equivalent and enrolled in a dental professional program. Candidates will be considered on the basis of academic achievement, ability, interest in dentistry and personal attributes. Must be a member of the ADAA.

GEOG. RESTRICTIONS: United States.

FINANCIAL DATA:
Amount of support per award: Up to $750, a congratulatory letter and one year active membership with the ADAA.

NO. MOST RECENT APPLICANTS: 11 for the year 2020.

NO. AWARDS: 3 for the year 2020.

APPLICATION INFO:
Applicants must submit academic transcripts (high school and/or college), proof of acceptance into an accredited program and a letter of intent to pursue a long-range career in dental profession. Two letters of reference are also required.
Duration: One year.
Deadline: March 15.

STAFF:
Jay Kasper, Executive Director

ADDRESS INQUIRIES TO:
Scholarship Committee
(See address above.)

AMERICAN DENTAL HYGIENISTS' ASSOCIATION INSTITUTE FOR ORAL HEALTH [2103]
444 North Michigan Avenue
Suite 400
Chicago, IL 60611
(312) 440-8900 ext. 244
E-mail: institute@adha.net
Web Site: www.adha.org/institute-for-oral-health

FOUNDED: 1927

AREAS OF INTEREST:
Dental hygiene.

NAME(S) OF PROGRAMS:
● **ADHA Institute for Oral Health Dental Hygiene Scholarships**

TYPE:
Scholarships. ADHA Institute for Oral Health (IOH) Scholarship Program supports dental hygiene professionals by offering academic financial assistance to dental hygiene students and dental hygienists at all levels of their education who demonstrate a commitment to the discipline of dental hygiene.

YEAR PROGRAM STARTED: 1986

PURPOSE:
To invest in the future careers of dental hygiene students by ensuring that they will be of exceptional quality and dedication.

LEGAL BASIS:
501(c)(3) public charity, as described in Sections 509(1)(1)-170(b)(1)(A)(vi) of the Internal Revenue Code.

ELIGIBILITY:
Applicant must be an active member of the American Dental Hygienists' Association and be an undergraduate or graduate student in an accredited dental hygiene program in the U.S and an active member of the American Dental Hygienists' Association.

GEOG. RESTRICTIONS: United States.

FINANCIAL DATA:
Amount of support per award: Varies.
Total amount of support: Varies.

NO. MOST RECENT APPLICANTS: Varies.

NO. AWARDS: Varies.

APPLICATION INFO:
Scholarship opportunities offered by IOH are posted on the ADHA web site.
Duration: Scholarships are awarded for a period of one academic year.

PUBLICATIONS:
Annual report.

ADDRESS INQUIRIES TO:
Shanna Young
IOH Development Coordinator
(See e-mail address above.)

HISPANIC DENTAL ASSOCIATION FOUNDATION   [2104]

17225 El Camino Real
Houston, TX 77058
(317) 714-0037
E-mail: hdafoundationscholarships@gmail.com
Web Site: hdassoc.org

FOUNDED: 1990

AREAS OF INTEREST:
Oral health careers.

NAME(S) OF PROGRAMS:
● **A-dec Scholarship**
● **Colgate-Palmolive Dental Residency or Specialty Program Scholarship**
● **Colgate-Palmolive Scholarship for Dental Students and Dental Hygiene Students**
● **Procter & Gamble Scholarship**
● **Dr. Esperanza Rodriguez Scholarship**
● **Dr. Juan D. Villarreal Scholarship**

TYPE:
Awards/prizes; Conferences/seminars; Internships; Product donations; Scholarships.

YEAR PROGRAM STARTED: 1990

PURPOSE:
To encourage entry of Hispanics into oral health careers.

ELIGIBILITY:
Students must have permanent resident status in the U.S., be current student members of the Hispanic Dental Association, and attending U.S. dental schools.

A-dec Scholarship is open to third- or fourth-year dental students.

Colgate-Palmolive Dental Residency or Specialty Program Scholarships are open to student members of the Association who have been accepted into or are currently enrolled in an accredited residency program in a dentistry-related field. Students must have an undergraduate or graduate degree in an oral health-related field (dental hygienist, dentistry, etc.) from the U.S. or abroad.

Colgate-Palmolive Scholarship for Dental Students and Dental Hygiene Students are awarded to students enrolled in an accredited dental or dental hygiene program.

Procter & Gamble Scholarship is open to first- to fourth-year dental students and first- and second-year dental hygiene and dental assisting students.

Dr. Esperanza Rodriguez Scholarship is open to first-, second- or third-year dental students.

Dr. Juan D. Villarreal Scholarships are open to student members of the Association who have been accepted into or are currently enrolled in an accredited dental school or dental hygiene program in the state of Texas. The student may be at any stage of the undergraduate program, first through fourth years.

GEOG. RESTRICTIONS: Dr. Juan D. Villareal Scholarship: Texas; United States for all others.

FINANCIAL DATA:
Amount of support per award: A-dec Scholarship: $4,000; Colgate-Palmolive Dental Residency or Specialty Program Scholarship: $5,000; Colgate-Palmolive Scholarship for Dental Students and Dental Hygiene Students: $4,000 for Dental students and $2,000 for Dental Hygiene students; Procter & Gamble Scholarships: $2,000 to $4,000; Dr. Esperanza Rodriguez Scholarship and Dr. Juan D. Villarreal Scholarship: $2,000.

Total amount of support: Varies.

NO. MOST RECENT APPLICANTS: Approximately 90.

NO. AWARDS: A-dec Scholarship: 2; Colgate-Palmolive Scholarships: 4 Resident, 6 Dental students and 2 Hygiene students; Procter & Gamble Scholarships: 9; Dr. Esperanza Rodriguez Scholarships: 1; Dr. Juan D. Villarreal Scholarships: 2 for Dental students and 1 for Dental Hygiene student.

APPLICATION INFO:
Application can be downloaded from the web site.
Duration: One year. Renewal possible by reapplication.
Deadline: July 1.

STAFF:
Jen Blake, Director

ADDRESS INQUIRIES TO:
See e-mail address above.

INTERNATIONAL ASSOCIATION FOR DENTAL RESEARCH (IADR)   [2105]

1619 Duke Street
Alexandria, VA 22314-3406
(703) 548-0066
Fax: (703) 548-1883
E-mail: ajones@iadr.org
Web Site: www.iadr.org

AREAS OF INTEREST:
Original research in the area of oral health, basic, clinical and applied studies.

NAME(S) OF PROGRAMS:
● **IADR Colgate Research in Prevention Travel Awards**

TYPE:
Awards/prizes; Travel grants. These Awards are for young investigators who have submitted an abstract which has a preventive component for a travel award to support their attendance at the IADR General Session.

Contact IADR for the full range of awards.

PURPOSE:
To advance research and increase knowledge for the improvement of oral health; to support and represent the oral health research community; to facilitate the communication and applications of research findings.

ELIGIBILITY:
Applicants must be IADR members. Young investigators (up to five years postgraduation from dental, dental hygiene, specialty training or pre-Ph.D.) are eligible to apply for a travel award. (No persons who have already obtained a Ph.D. are eligible to apply.) Entrants must provide a verification letter of their educational status and can only receive this Award once.

FINANCIAL DATA:
Amount of support per award: $2,000.

Total amount of support: $2,000.

NO. MOST RECENT APPLICANTS: 16.

NO. AWARDS: At least 1 for North America (Canada, U.S. and Mexico). There are also Awards for other geographic regions.

APPLICATION INFO:
In applying for this Award, candidates must submit their abstract as well as a separate and more detailed overview of their projects (two pages, double-spaced). This overview must include brief details of their material and methods, the results of the research including details of statistical analysis and a brief discussion including how the research will affect the prevention of the condition stated.
Deadline: March 12.

ADDRESS INQUIRIES TO:
Anthony Jones, Awards, Fellowships and Grants Coordinator
(See e-mail address above.)

NATIONAL INSTITUTE OF DENTAL AND CRANIOFACIAL RESEARCH (NIDCR)   [2106]

National Institutes of Health
6701 Democracy Boulevard, Room 688
Bethesda, MD 20892
(301) 496-4263
E-mail: leslie.frieden@nih.gov
Web Site: www.nidcr.nih.gov

FOUNDED: 1948

AREAS OF INTEREST:
Dental, craniofacial health and research.

NAME(S) OF PROGRAMS:
● **Individual NRSA Postdoctoral Fellowships (F-32)**

TYPE:
Fellowships. Provides up to three years of support for trainees at academic institutions to broaden their scientific background or extend their potential for research in health-related areas.

YEAR PROGRAM STARTED: 1974

PURPOSE:
To develop individuals for careers in oral health research.

LEGAL BASIS:
Public Health Service Act as amended, Section 301c; 42 CFR 61; 42 U.S.C. 288a.

ELIGIBILITY:
Applicants must be citizens, non-citizen nationals or permanent residents of the U.S. at the time of the award and have a Ph.D., M.D., D.D.S., D.O., D.V.M. or equivalent degree prior to the beginning date of the proposed fellowship.

GEOG. RESTRICTIONS: United States.

FINANCIAL DATA:
Stipend level is based on number of years of postdoctoral experience and at NRSA level. Additional funds are available for other training-related expenses.
Total amount of support: Varies.

APPLICATION INFO:
Detailed information can be obtained from the Institute.
Duration: One, two or three years.
Deadline: April 8, August 8 and December 8.

ADDRESS INQUIRIES TO:
Leslie Frieden
Extramural Training Officer
(See address above.)

NATIONAL INSTITUTE OF DENTAL AND CRANIOFACIAL RESEARCH (NIDCR)   [2107]

National Institutes of Health
31 Center Drive, Room 5B-55
MSC 2190
Bethesda, MD 20892-2190
(301) 496-4261
E-mail: nidcrinfo@mail.nih.gov
Web Site: www.nidcr.nih.gov

FOUNDED: 1948

AREAS OF INTEREST:
Multiple areas of research with the goal of improving dental, oral and craniofacial health.

NAME(S) OF PROGRAMS:
- **Behavioral & Social Science Research**
- **Clinical Research & Epidemiology**
- **Clinical Technologies Research**
- **Clinical Trials**
- **Clinical Trials & Practice-Based Research**
- **Data Science, Computational Biology & Bioinformatics**
- **Dental Materials & Biomaterials**
- **Developmental Biology & Genetics**
- **HIV/AIDS & Oral Health**
- **Microbiology**
- **Mineralized Tissue Physiology**
- **Neuroscience of Orofacial Pain & Temporomandibular Disorders**
- **Oral & Salivary Cancer Biology**
- **Oral Health Disparities & Inequities**
- **Research Training & Career Development**
- **Salivary Biology & Immunology**
- **Small Business Innovation/Small Business Technology Transfer (SBIR/STTR)**
- **Tissue Engineering and Regenerative Medicine**
- **Translational Genetics & Genomics**

TYPE:
Conferences/seminars; Project/program grants; Research grants; Research contracts. Grants for the support of basic and clinical research.

YEAR PROGRAM STARTED: 1948

PURPOSE:
To develop methods for preventing and treating oral diseases and conditions through research related to oral and craniofacial health.

LEGAL BASIS:
Public Health Service Act as amended, Section 301c; 42 CFR 61; 42 U.S.C. 288a.

ELIGIBILITY:
Open to scientists at universities, hospitals, laboratories and other public, nonprofit or profit institutions. Applications are competitively rated on the basis of scientific merit and grants must be approved by the National Advisory Dental and Craniofacial Research Council.

FINANCIAL DATA:
Amount of support per award: Varies.

APPLICATION INFO:
Varies by program. Visit the NIDCR web site above for detailed information.
Duration: Varies.

NATIONAL INSTITUTE OF DENTAL AND CRANIOFACIAL RESEARCH (NIDCR)   [2108]

National Institutes of Health
6701 Democracy Boulevard, Room 688
Bethesda, MD 20892
(301) 496-4263
E-mail: leslie.frieden@nih.gov
Web Site: www.nidcr.nih.gov

FOUNDED: 1948

AREAS OF INTEREST:
Biomedical and behavioral research.

NAME(S) OF PROGRAMS:
- **Individual NRSA Senior Fellowship Award (F-33)**

TYPE:
Fellowships. Provides health research training for experienced scientists, enabling them to update their skills or make changes in the direction of their career.

YEAR PROGRAM STARTED: 1979

PURPOSE:
To provide opportunities for experienced scientists to make major changes in the direction of their research careers, to enlarge their scientific background, to acquire new research capabilities, or to enlarge their command of an allied research field.

LEGAL BASIS:
Section 472 of the Public Health Service Act as amended (42 U.S.C. 2981-1).

ELIGIBILITY:
Applicants must be citizens, non-citizen nationals or permanent residents of the U.S. at the time of the award. Applicants must be at least seven years beyond the qualifying doctoral degree and have a sponsoring institution and mentor.

GEOG. RESTRICTIONS: United States.

FINANCIAL DATA:
A stipend is provided. Additional funds are available for other training-related expenses.
Amount of support per award: Varies based on experience.
Total amount of support: Varies.

APPLICATION INFO:
Detailed information can be obtained from the Institute.
Duration: Up to two years.
Deadline: April 8, August 8 and December 8.

ADDRESS INQUIRIES TO:
Leslie Frieden
Extramural Training Officer
(See address above.)

Internal medicine

AMERICAN SOCIETY OF HEMATOLOGY   [2109]

2021 L Street, N.W.
Suite 900
Washington, DC 20036
(202) 776-0544
E-mail: awards@hematology.org
Web Site: www.hematology.org

AREAS OF INTEREST:
Scientific abstracts.

NAME(S) OF PROGRAMS:
- **Abstract Achievement Award**
- **Outstanding Abstract Achievement Award**

TYPE:
Awards/prizes; Travel grants.

PURPOSE:
To offer need- and merit-based awards to select individuals in order to help defray annual meeting travel expenses.

ELIGIBILITY:
Abstract Achievement Award: Applicants must be undergraduate students, medical students, graduate students, resident physicians, and postdoctoral fellows who are both first author and presenter of an abstract.

Outstanding Abstract Achievement Award: Awards are offered to the first authors/presenters of abstracts that receive the highest score in the categories of undergraduate student, medical student, graduate student, resident physician, and postdoctoral fellow (M.D. or Ph.D.).

FINANCIAL DATA:
Amount of support per award: Abstract Achievement Award: $500; Outstanding Abstract Achievement Award: $2,000.
Total amount of support: Varies.

APPLICATION INFO:
Contact the Society for application procedures.
Duration: One-time award.
Deadline: Early August.

ADDRESS INQUIRIES TO:
Vonnie Calemine
Awards Program Specialist
(See address above.)

AMERICAN SOCIETY OF NEPHROLOGY   [2110]

1401 H Street, N.W.
Suite 900
Washington, DC 20005
(202) 640-4660
Fax: (202) 637-9793
E-mail: grants@asn-online.org
Web Site: www.asn-online.org

AREAS OF INTEREST:
Nephrology.

NAME(S) OF PROGRAMS:
- **William and Sandra Bennett Clinical Scholars Program**
- **OHF - ASN Foundation for Kidney Research Grant**

TYPE:
Project/program grants; Research grants. William and Sandra Bennett Clinical Scholars Program supports aspiring nephrology educators to conduct a project to advance all facets of nephrology education and teaching.

OHF - ASN Foundation for Kidney Research Grant supports research on topics relevant to oxalosis, primary hyperoxaluria and related stone diseases.

PURPOSE:
To enhance and assist the study and practice of nephrology; to provide a forum for the promulgation of research; to meet the professional and continuing education needs of its members.

FINANCIAL DATA:
Amount of support per award: William and Sandra Bennett Clinical Scholars Program: $50,000 annually; OHF - ASN Foundation for Kidney Research Grant: $100,000 annually.

NO. AWARDS: 1 of each award annually.

APPLICATION INFO:
Only online applications will be accepted.
Duration: Two years.
Deadline: Mid-December.

ADDRESS INQUIRIES TO:
E-mail: grants@asn-online.org

AMERICAN SOCIETY OF NEPHROLOGY [2111]
1401 H Street, N.W.
Suite 900
Washington, DC 20005
(202) 640-4660
Fax: (202) 637-9793
E-mail: grants@asn-online.org
Web Site: www.asn-online.org

AREAS OF INTEREST:
Nephrology.

NAME(S) OF PROGRAMS:
- **Carl W. Gottschalk Research Scholar Grant**
- **John Merrill Grant in Transplantation**
- **Norman Siegel Research Scholar Grant**

TYPE:
Research grants. The Gottschalk, Merrill and Siegel Grants are part of the Transition to Independent Grants program.

PURPOSE:
To enhance and assist the study and practice of nephrology; to provide a forum for the promulgation of research; to meet the professional and continuing education needs of its members; to foster the independent careers of young investigators in biomedical research related to nephrology and transplantation.

ELIGIBILITY:
Merrill and Gottschalk Grants: Applicants must be active ASN members and hold an M.D., Ph.D., or equivalent degree. At the time of submission, the applicant's membership must be current and their dues paid. Appointment to full-time faculty must be confirmed in writing by the department chair, indicating the date of first full-time faculty appointment, and providing assurance that the department will provide needed resources for conducting independent research. Additionally, applicants will be considered ineligible should they submit more than one ASN grant application during any particular grants cycle.

GEOG. RESTRICTIONS: North America.

FINANCIAL DATA:
Amount of support per award: $100,000 per year.

APPLICATION INFO:
Only online applications will be accepted.
Duration: Two years.
Deadline: Mid-December.

ADDRESS INQUIRIES TO:
See e-mail address above.

AMERICAN SOCIETY OF NEPHROLOGY [2112]
1401 H Street, N.W.
Suite 900
Washington, DC 20005
(202) 640-4660
Fax: (202) 637-9793
E-mail: grants@asn-online.org
Web Site: www.asn-online.org

AREAS OF INTEREST:
Nephrology.

NAME(S) OF PROGRAMS:
- **ASN Research Fellowships**

TYPE:
Fellowships. ASN Research Fellowships: The Society especially encourages applications from women and members of underrepresented minorities.

PURPOSE:
To fund fellows to conduct original, meritorious research projects, fostering, under the direction of a sponsor, the training of fellows who are highly motivated to make contributions to the understanding of kidney biology and disease.

ELIGIBILITY:
To apply for an ASN Research Fellowship, a candidate:
(1) must hold an M.D., D.O., Ph.D. or the equivalent degree;
(2) may not have completed more than three years of research training after the completion of the M.D. or D.O. degree or equivalent, or one year of postdoctoral research training after the Ph.D. degree (at the time of the activation of the award);
(3) cannot have or have had at any time a faculty position at any academic institution;
(4) must complete research under the direction and mentorship of a sponsor;
(5) must be a member of ASN at the time of the fellowship application; the sponsor of the candidate must also be an ASN member at the time of the fellowship application;
(6) cannot hold another full fellowship award such as another foundation fellowship or grant or a postdoctoral research fellowship from the National Institutes of Health; however, a candidate's institutions may supplement the support provided by ASN;
(7) must be working in North or Central America during the fellowship period and;
(8) must commit a minimum of 75% time to research during the fellowship period.

GEOG. RESTRICTIONS: North America.

FINANCIAL DATA:
Funds must be used for salary support (including fringe benefits) and cannot be used for project costs, travel expenses or overhead costs.
Amount of support per award: $50,000 per year for up to two years.
Total amount of support: Varies.

NO. AWARDS: Approximately 10.

APPLICATION INFO:
Only online applications will be accepted.
Duration: Up to two years. Second-year funding is contingent on a satisfactory progress report.
Deadline: Mid-December.

ADDRESS INQUIRIES TO:
See e-mail address above.

ASPEN RHOADS RESEARCH FOUNDATION
8401 Colesville Road
Suite 510
Silver Spring, MD 20910
(301) 587-6315
Fax: (301) 587-2365
E-mail: foundation@nutritioncare.org
Web Site: www.nutritioncare.org/foundation

TYPE:
Research grants. Annual support for nutritional research.
See entry 2162 for full listing.

CANCER FEDERATION, INC. [2113]
711 West Ramsey Street
Banning, CA 92220
(951) 849-4325
E-mail: info@cancerfed.org
Web Site: cancerfed.org

FOUNDED: 1977

AREAS OF INTEREST:
Cancer.

TYPE:
Awards/prizes; Research grants; Scholarships; Seed money grants.

YEAR PROGRAM STARTED: 1977

PURPOSE:
To fund research in cancer immunology and scholarships.

LEGAL BASIS:
501(c)(3) tax-exempt.

ELIGIBILITY:
Candidates must major in biology, microbiology, oncology, hematology, psychiatry, psychology or natural sciences.

FINANCIAL DATA:
Total amount of support: Varies.

NO. AWARDS: Varies.

APPLICATION INFO:
Scholar is chosen by institution.
Duration: One year. Renewal possible by reapplication. Scholarships are one-time only.
Deadline: Varies according to sponsoring institution.

PUBLICATIONS:
Challenge, magazine; *CF Newsletter*; *Four Women Against Cancer*; and several others.

IRS I.D.: 95-3133568

ADDRESS INQUIRIES TO:
Lya Cole, Executive Director
P.O. Box 1298
Banning, CA 92220

CHILDREN'S TUMOR FOUNDATION [2114]
405 Lexington Avenue
New York, NY 10174
(212) 344-6633
Fax: (212) 747-0004
E-mail: slarosa@ctf.org
Web Site: www.ctf.org

AREAS OF INTEREST:
Neurofibromatosis research.

NAME(S) OF PROGRAMS:
- **Clinical Research Awards**
- **Drug Discovery Initiative Registered Reports (DDI-RR)**
- **NF Clinic Network (CTF-NFCN)**
- **Young Investigator Awards**

TYPE:

Conferences/seminars; Research grants; Seed money grants; Travel grants; Research contracts. Clinic support grants.

PURPOSE:

To improve the health and well-being of individuals and families affected by neurofibromatosis.

ELIGIBILITY:

Clinical Research Award: Preclinical/clinical collaborative studies, pilot clinical trials, and clinical enabling studies are considered for support.

Drug Discovery Initiative Registered Reports: Applicants should have an M.D., Ph.D., or equivalent degree and access to all resources needed. Applicants from academia and the private sector are welcome, and partnerships between the two are encouraged. Applications are welcomed from all qualified individuals worldwide.

NF Clinic Network: Any clinic in the U.S. that sees NF patients may apply to be a CTF-NFCN Affiliate Clinic.

Young Investigator Award: Open to graduate students, postdoctoral fellows and young investigators no more than seven years past completion of their M.D./Ph.D. training. The Investigator can be a graduate student or postdoctoral fellow associated with the laboratory of a more senior researcher, who acts as the research sponsor.

FINANCIAL DATA:

Amount of support per award: Clinical Research Award: Up to $150,000; Drug Discovery Initiative Registered Reports: Up to $85,000 for in vivo studies and up to $40,000 for in vitro studies; NF Clinic Network: Up to $6,000 per year; Young Investigator Award: $64,000 to $174,000, commensurate with experience.

Total amount of support: Varies.

NO. MOST RECENT APPLICANTS: Clinical Research Award: 10; Drug Discovery Initiative Registered Reports: 10 to 15; NF Clinic Network: Approximately 50 annually; Young Investigator Award: Approximately 25.

NO. AWARDS: Clinical Research Award: 2; Drug Discovery Initiative Registered Reports: 3; Young Investigator Award: 8.

APPLICATION INFO:

Application information is available on the web site. Applications may be submitted online.

Clinical Research Award: Letter of Inquiry required. Based on review, applicant may be invited to submit full application.

Duration: Clinical Research Award: 18 to 24 months; Drug Discovery Initiative and NF Clinic Network: One year; Young Investigator Award: Up to two years.

Deadline: Clinical Research Award: September 13 for Letter of Intent and October 25 for full application. Drug Discovery Initiative Registered Reports: May 17 for Letter of Intent and July 5 for full proposal. NF Clinic Network: October. Young Investigator Award: January 3 for Letter of Intent and March 5 for full application.

IRS I.D.: 13-2298956

STAFF:

Vidya Browder, Basic Science Senior Manager

ADDRESS INQUIRIES TO:

Salvatore La Rosa
Chief Scientific Officer
(See address above.)

HISTIOCYTOSIS ASSOCIATION [2115]

332 North Broadway
Pitman, NJ 08071
(856) 589-6606
Fax: (856) 589-6614
E-mail: grants@histio.org
Web Site: www.histio.org

FOUNDED: 1986

AREAS OF INTEREST:

Histiocytosis, hemophagocytic lymphohistiocytosis, Langerhans cell histiocytosis, and histiocytic disorders.

NAME(S) OF PROGRAMS:

- **Research Grant Program**

TYPE:

Project/program grants; Research grants; Seed money grants.

YEAR PROGRAM STARTED: 1989

PURPOSE:

To fund worthy scientific research projects; to educate physicians and scientists; to encourage and support symposia into histiocytic disorders; to directly participate in research projects; to encourage publication of scientific information.

ELIGIBILITY:

Applicants must be full-time faculty members at an academic institution.

FINANCIAL DATA:

Amount of support per award: Up to $50,000 for one-year grants.

Total amount of support: Varies.

NO. MOST RECENT APPLICANTS: 25.

NO. AWARDS: 6.

APPLICATION INFO:

Application must be submitted online.

Duration: Up to one year.

Deadline: July 1.

IRS I.D.: 22-2827069

EXECUTIVE DIRECTOR:

Deanna Fournier

ADDRESS INQUIRIES TO:

Heather Fullerton
Research Grants Director
(See address above.)

THE LEUKEMIA & LYMPHOMA SOCIETY [2116]

3 International Drive
Suite 200
Rye Brook, NY 10573
(914) 821-8301
(914) 949-5213
E-mail: researchprograms@lls.org
Web Site: www.lls.org

AREAS OF INTEREST:

Leukemia, lymphoma and myeloma.

NAME(S) OF PROGRAMS:

- **Career Development Program**

TYPE:

Fellowships; Research grants; Scholarships. The Career Development Program provides awards intended to meet the specific needs of investigators at different stages of their

research careers. The five awards, Fellow, Scholar, Scholar in Clinical Research, Special Fellow and Special Fellow in Clinical Research, provide stipends to investigators, allowing them to devote themselves to researching questions of direct relevance to hematological malignancies and/or relevant pre-malignant conditions.

YEAR PROGRAM STARTED: 1949

PURPOSE:

To cure leukemia, lymphoma, Hodgkin's disease and myeloma; to improve the quality of life of patients and their families; to support individuals pursuing careers in basic or clinical research in leukemia, lymphoma and myeloma.

ELIGIBILITY:

Qualified investigators affiliated with appropriate institutions are eligible to apply. Applicants must have the approval of the institution and recommendation of the department head where the research training will be conducted. Ph.D. or M.D. status is required.

FINANCIAL DATA:

Amount of support per award: Fellows: $60,000 per year; Scholars: $120,000; Scholars in Clinical Research: $125,000 per year; Special Fellows and Special Fellows in Clinical Research: $67,000 per year.

APPLICATION INFO:

The Society uses its own research portal for preliminary and full application submission. First-time users must register by sending an e-mail to the address listed above.

Duration: Renewable for up to five years at the level of Scholar and three years at the level of Special Fellow and Fellow.

Deadline: Eligibility: September 1. Abstracts: September 13. Reference Letters and Full Application: September 27.

ADDRESS INQUIRIES TO:

Senior Director of Research Administration
(See address above.)

THE LEUKEMIA & LYMPHOMA SOCIETY [2117]

3 International Drive
Suite 200
Rye Brook, NY 10573
(914) 821-8301
(914) 949-5213
E-mail: researchprograms@lls.org
Web Site: www.lls.org

AREAS OF INTEREST:

Leukemia, lymphoma and myeloma.

NAME(S) OF PROGRAMS:

- **Translational Research Program**

TYPE:

Research grants. Translational Research Program is intended to encourage and provide support for new and novel clinical research. The goal of the program is to accelerate transfer of findings from the laboratory to clinical application.

YEAR PROGRAM STARTED: 1996

PURPOSE:

To encourage and provide early-stage support for clinical research in leukemia, lymphoma, and myeloma, with the intention of developing innovative approaches to treatment, diagnosis or prevention; to support projects that translate laboratory findings to clinical application.

ELIGIBILITY:
Ph.D., M.D., or D.V.M. status is required. Candidates must be affiliated with a nonfederal public or private nonprofit institution engaged in cancer-related research.

FINANCIAL DATA:
Amount of support per award: Maximum $216,666.66 annually.

APPLICATION INFO:
Guidelines are available on the web site.

Duration: Three years. In special cases these may be renewed for two years.

Deadline: Letter of intent: August 31. Full application: October 31.

ADDRESS INQUIRIES TO:
See e-mail address above.

THE LEUKEMIA & LYMPHOMA SOCIETY   [2118]
3 International Drive
Suite 200
Rye Brook, NY 10573
(914) 821-8301
(914) 949-5213
E-mail: researchprograms@lls.org
Web Site: www.lls.org

AREAS OF INTEREST:
Leukemia, lymphoma, Hodgkin's disease and myeloma.

NAME(S) OF PROGRAMS:
● **Specialized Center of Research Program**

TYPE:
Research grants. The core program intends to bring together established investigators from one or several institutions to develop a focused research program, foster new interactions and cooperation, and enhance disciplinary research among the participants to understand the causes of hematological malignancies and ultimately develop effective treatments for cancer patients.

PURPOSE:
To support research programs that are focused on any aspect of leukemia, lymphoma, Hodgkin's disease and myeloma in order to foster interactions, cooperation, and to enhance interdisciplinary research among the participants.

ELIGIBILITY:
Applications may be submitted by individuals holding an M.D., Ph.D., D.V.M.or equivalent degree, working in domestic or foreign nonprofit organizations, such as universities, colleges, hospitals or laboratories. Applications may be multi-institutional in nature. Applicants need not be U.S. citizens, and there are no restrictions on applicant age, race, gender or creed.

FINANCIAL DATA:
Expenses for administrative staff (including secretarial) costs cannot exceed one full-time equivalent for the Center per year. The aggregate of office supplies and telephone costs cannot exceed $6,000 per year for the Center.
Amount of support per award: Up to $1,000,000 annually.
Total amount of support: $2,000,000.

NO. MOST RECENT APPLICANTS: 10.

NO. AWARDS: 2.

APPLICATION INFO:
Guidelines are available on the web site.

Duration: Five years.
Deadline: Letter of Intent: October 1. Notification sent to those selected for full application submission by December 31. Application: March 30.

ADDRESS INQUIRIES TO:
See e-mail address above.

LYMPHOMA RESEARCH FOUNDATION   [2119]
Wall Street Plaza
88 Pine Street, Suite 2400
New York, NY 10005
(212) 349-2910
Fax: (212) 349-2886
E-mail: researchgrants@lymphoma.org
Web Site: lymphoma.org/grants

FOUNDED: 2001

AREAS OF INTEREST:
Lymphoma and chronic lymphocytic leukemia research.

CONSULTING OR VOLUNTEER SERVICES:
The LRF Ambassador program is comprised of individuals from around the country, each with a personal lymphoma story. The ambassadors represent several subtypes and treatment options for the disease. The group includes current patients, caregivers of patients and survivors. Ambassadors are able to share their individual stories and experiences navigating this diagnosis.

The LRF Advocacy Program offers volunteers a variety of opportunities, including attending in-person meetings with members of Congress and submitting letters to the editor and op-eds which cover issues important to the lymphoma community.

NAME(S) OF PROGRAMS:
● **Clinical Investigator Career Development Awards (CDA)**
● **Disease Focus Area Grants for Senior Investigators**
● **LRF Scientific Research Mentoring Program (LSRMP)**
● **Jamie Peykoff Follicular Lymphoma Research Initiative**
● **Postdoctoral Fellowship Grants**

TYPE:
Fellowships; Research grants; Training grants.

YEAR PROGRAM STARTED: 1992

PURPOSE:
To support innovative lymphoma research in keeping with the Foundation's mission to eradicate lymphoma and serve those touched by this disease.

LEGAL BASIS:
Nonprofit organization.

ELIGIBILITY:
CDA: Advanced fellows or junior faculty with at least two years fellow/postdoctoral experience and no more than five years beyond completion of fellowship/postdoctoral; 35 to 50% protected time for research; must be licensed physicians at a nonprofit clinical research institution.

Disease Focus Area Grants (including Peykoff Follicular Lymphoma Initiative Grants): Open to licensed senior researchers (usually Assistant, Associate or Full Professor or their equivalent) at accredited, nonprofit research institutions; other restrictions vary by individual RFP.

LSRMP Clinical Track: Applicant must hold an M.D. or equivalent degree within at least the second year of the fellowship or no more than four years in their first faculty position. LSRMP Translational Track: Applicant must hold a Ph.D. or equivalent degree with no more than seven years of postdoctoral work or no more than four years in faculty level position, or M.D. or equivalent in at least the second year of clinical fellowship or no more than four years in instructor level position.

Postdoctoral Fellowship Grants: Advanced clinical fellows or those with postdoctoral experience (with no more than five years fellow/postdoctoral experience). M.D. applicants must have completed at least two years of clinical fellowship work. Faculty are not eligible for this grant.

CDA, LSRMP and Postdoctoral Fellowship Grants are limited to applicants based at institutions in the U.S. or Canada for the duration of the grant. Citizenship is not required. For other programs, refer to RFP.

FINANCIAL DATA:
Amount of support per award: CDA: $225,000 total over three years, salary support and professional development expenses; Disease Focus Area Grants: Research expenses (personnel and nonpersonnel) vary by RFP; LSRMP: $10,000 total professional development expenses over two years plus travel to LSRMP workshops; Peykoff Initiative Grant: $750,000 over three years; Postdoctoral Fellowship Grants: $105,000 total over two years, salary support and professional development expenses.
Total amount of support: Varies.

NO. MOST RECENT APPLICANTS: 75.

NO. AWARDS: 29 grants in fiscal year 2021.

REPRESENTATIVE AWARDS:
$225,000 CDA to Anita Kumar, M.D., Memorial Sloan Kettering Cancer Center for "A Multicenter Phase I Study of Ibrutinib in Relapsed and Refractory T-cell Lymphoma;" $105,000 Fellowship to Andrea Rabellino, Ph.D., University of Texas - Southwestern Medical Center for "Role of PIAS1 in c-MYC-driven lymphomagenesis;" $100,000 Disease Focus Area Grant (in Adolescent/Young Adult Lymphoma Correlative Studies) to David Scott, M.D., MBChB of British Columbia Cancer Agency for "Biomarkers predicting early treatment response in advanced stage classical Hodgkin lymphoma."

APPLICATION INFO:
Application information is available online.
Duration: CDA: Three years. Disease Focus Area Grants: Varies by RFP (usually two to three years). LSRMP and Postdoctoral Fellowship Grants: Two years.
Deadline: CDA, Postdoctoral Fellowship Grants and LSRMP generally opens early June and closes early September. Disease Focus Area Grants: Varies by RFP. Peykoff Initiative Grant opens for Letters of Inquiry in March.

IRS I.D.: 95-4335088

BOARD OF DIRECTORS:
Steven Eichberg, Chairman
Jeff Block, Vice Chairman and Treasurer
Kim Metcalf, Vice Chairman
Leigh Olson, Secretary
Morton Coleman, M.D., Chairman, Medical Affiliates Board

Andrew D. Zelenetz, M.D., Chairman,
Scientific Advisory Board
Michael Akinyele
Kevin Fennessey
Michael Froy
Tom Goldstone
Keith Hoogland
Bob McAuley
John A. Nelson
Scott Pansky
Diane Parks

ADDRESS INQUIRIES TO:
Whitney Steen
(See e-mail address above.)

NATIONAL HEADACHE FOUNDATION [2120]

820 North Orleans, Suite 201
Chicago, IL 60610-3132
(312) 274-2650
(888) 643-5552
Fax: (312) 640-9049
E-mail: info@headaches.org
Web Site: www.headaches.org

FOUNDED: 1970

AREAS OF INTEREST:
Headache and pain.

TYPE:
Research grants. Support for research in the field of headache and pain.

YEAR PROGRAM STARTED: 1970

PURPOSE:
To enhance the health care of individuals with headache; to provide a source of help to families, physicians and allied health care professionals who treat them, and to the public; to provide educational and informational resources, supporting headache research, and advocating for the understanding of headache as a legitimate neurobiological disease.

LEGAL BASIS:
Nonprofit organization.

ELIGIBILITY:
Investigators from departments of neurology and pharmacology are invited to apply. Submissions from other departments and individual investigators are also welcome. No funding for overhead, salaries, rent or indirect expenses. Grants may be used for data analysis, interpretation, reading of results, etc.

GEOG. RESTRICTIONS: United States.

FINANCIAL DATA:
Full or partial funding may be granted.
Amount of support per award: Varies depending on project.

NO. MOST RECENT APPLICANTS: Approximately 9.

NO. AWARDS: Approximately 2 when funding available.

APPLICATION INFO:
Applicants must submit abstract of research proposal on Foundation form as well as protocol and proposed budget. Proposed projects will be evaluated at the winter board meeting of the NHF.
Duration: One year.
Deadline: Varies.

PUBLICATIONS:
Program announcement.

ADDRESS INQUIRIES TO:
Mary A. Franklin, Executive Director
(See address above.)

NATIONAL HEART, LUNG AND BLOOD INSTITUTE (NHLBI) [2121]

One Rockledge Center, Suite 408-R
6705 Rockledge Drive, MSC 7950
Bethesda, MD 20892-7950
(301) 435-0080
Fax: (301) 480-0867
E-mail: hootswk@mail.nih.gov
Web Site: www.nhlbi.nih.gov

FOUNDED: 1948

AREAS OF INTEREST:
Research on the causes, prevention, and treatment of nonmalignant blood diseases, including anemias, sickle cell disease, and thalassemia; premalignant processes such as myelodysplasia and myeloproliferative disorders; hemophilia and other abnormalities of hemostasis and thrombosis; and immune dysfunction.

NAME(S) OF PROGRAMS:
• **Blood Diseases and Resources Research**

TYPE:
Conferences/seminars; Demonstration grants; Fellowships; Grants-in-aid; Project/program grants; Training grants; Research contracts. Funding encompasses a broad spectrum of research ranging from basic biology to medical management of blood diseases.

YEAR PROGRAM STARTED: 1972

PURPOSE:
To develop programs that will reduce the morbidity and mortality caused by blood diseases, lead to the primary prevention of these diseases and ensure the availability of adequate supplies of safe and efficacious blood products.

LEGAL BASIS:
Public Health Service Act, Section 301(e) and Section 412; Public Law 78-410, as amended; 42 U.S.C. 241; 42 U.S.C. 287a; Public Health Service Act, Section 472; Public Law 78-410, as amended; 42 U.S.C. 289 1-1.

ELIGIBILITY:
Any nonprofit organization engaged in biomedical research and institutions (or companies) organized for profit may apply for grants with the exception of National Research Service Awards. Only citizens and noncitizen nationals are eligible for support by research training and career development programs. Other mechanisms are not restricted.

FINANCIAL DATA:
Grants may support salaries, equipment, supplies, travel and patient hospitalization as required to perform the research effort.
Amount of support per award: Varies by the type of grant.

APPLICATION INFO:
Application information is available on the web site.
Duration: One to five years. Renewable through reapplication.
Deadline: Varies.

PUBLICATIONS:
Annual report.

DIRECTORS:
W. Keith Hoots, M.D., Director

RESEARCH STAFF:
Simone Glynn, M.D., M.Sc., M.P.H., Branch Chief, Blood Epidemiology and Clinical Therapeutics Branch
Traci Mondoro, Ph.D., Branch Chief, Translational Blood Science and Resources Branch
Yu-Chung Yang, Ph.D., Branch Chief, Molecular, Cellular and Systems Blood Science Branch

ADDRESS INQUIRIES TO:
Division of Blood Diseases and Resources
(See address above.)

Cardiovascular and pulmonary

AMERICAN COLLEGE OF CARDIOLOGY [2122]

2400 N Street, N.W.
Washington, DC 20037
(202) 375-6000 ext. 6390
Fax: (202) 375-6842
E-mail: kroberts@acc.org
Web Site: www.acc.org

AREAS OF INTEREST:
Cardiology.

NAME(S) OF PROGRAMS:
• **ACC Young Investigators Awards Competition**

TYPE:
Awards/prizes. Awarded in three categories:
(1) Clinical Investigations;
(2) Basic and Translational Sciences and;
(3) Outcomes Research.

PURPOSE:
To encourage and recognize young scientific investigators of promise.

ELIGIBILITY:
Physicians, scientists, medical students and other health care providers currently in residency or fellowship training programs or who have been in such programs within the past three years are eligible to apply.

FINANCIAL DATA:
Each candidate receives up to $1,500 reimbursement for travel to attend the annual meeting.
Amount of support per award: First Place: $2,000; Second Place: $1,000; Honorable Mention: $500.

NO. MOST RECENT APPLICANTS: 150.

NO. AWARDS: 18 awards; 6 awards per category.

APPLICATION INFO:
Guidelines and application form are available online.
Deadline: September.

ADDRESS INQUIRIES TO:
Kristin Robertson, Director
(See address above.)

AMERICAN HEART ASSOCIATION [2123]

AHA National Center
7272 Greenville Avenue
Dallas, TX 75231-4596
(214) 360-6107
E-mail: apply@heart.org
Web Site: professional.heart.org

FOUNDED: 1948

AREAS OF INTEREST:
Research broadly related to cardiovascular function and disease and stroke, or to related clinical, translational, population, basic science, bioengineering or biotechnology, and public health problems, including multidisciplinary efforts.

NAME(S) OF PROGRAMS:
● **Institutional Award for Undergraduate Student Training**

TYPE:
Fellowships. This is an institutional award, made to qualified research institutions that can offer a meaningful research experience that supports the mission of the American Heart Association to undergraduate college students. The institution must demonstrate the ability to provide a meaningful research experience to students during the allotted 10-week fellowship experience.

PURPOSE:
To encourage students from all disciplines to consider research careers.

LEGAL BASIS:
Research association.

ELIGIBILITY:
Research awards are limited to U.S.-based nonprofit institutions, including medical, osteopathic and dental schools, veterinary schools, schools of public health, pharmacy schools, nursing schools, universities and colleges, public and voluntary hospitals and other institutions that can demonstrate the ability to conduct the proposed research. Applications proposed by federal institutions or employees will not be accepted, except from Veterans Administrations employees.

The program director is the applicant for this award. At the time of application, the program director must:
(1) possess a demonstrated track record of providing mentoring to student researchers;
(2) be a full-time faculty member at the level of assistant professor or equivalent, or above and;
(3) be a U.S. citizen, permanent resident, pending permanent resident, or hold an E-3, H-1B, J-1, O-1, TN, or G-4 visa. Program director must maintain one of these designations throughout the duration of the award.

FINANCIAL DATA:
Amount of support per award: $6,000 per student for the 10-week research experience.

APPLICATION INFO:
Guidelines and application form are available on the web site.
Duration: Three years.
Deadline: Typically July.

ADDRESS INQUIRIES TO:
See e-mail address above.

AMERICAN HEART ASSOCIATION   [2124]
AHA National Center
7272 Greenville Avenue
Dallas, TX 75231-4596
(214) 360-6107
E-mail: apply@heart.org
Web Site: professional.heart.org

FOUNDED: 1948

AREAS OF INTEREST:
Research broadly related to cardiovascular function and disease and stroke, or to related

clinical, translational, population or basic science, bioengineering or biotechnology, and public health problems, including multidisciplinary efforts.

NAME(S) OF PROGRAMS:
● **AHA Institutional Research Enhancement Award (AIREA)**

TYPE:
Research grants. AIREA award supports any part of the full range of research and development from very basic to clinical. The goals of the program are to support meritorious research, expose students to research, and strengthen the research environment of the institution.

PURPOSE:
To support small-scale research projects related to cardiovascular diseases and stroke at educational institutions that provide Baccalaureate or advanced degrees but that have not been major recipients of NIH support.

LEGAL BASIS:
Research association.

ELIGIBILITY:
AHA awards are open to the array of academic and health professionals. Clinical, translational, population, and basic scientists are encouraged to apply. AHA strongly encourages applications by women, underrepresented minorities in the sciences, and those who have experienced varied and nontraditional career trajectories.

Institution must be a domestic accredited public or nonprofit institution of higher education. Federal government institutions are not eligible. The institution must grant Baccalaureate or advanced degrees in the biomedical or behavioral sciences. Institution may not have received more than $6,000,000 per year in NIH support in each of four of the last seven years.

Principal Investigator must have a primary appointment at an AREA-eligible institution. While no minimum percent effort is specified, the principal investigator must demonstrate that adequate time will be devoted to ensuring the successful completion of the proposed project. At the time of application, the principal investigator must be a U.S. citizen, permanent resident, pending permanent resident, or hold an E-3, H1-B, J-1, O-1, TN or G-4 visa. Awardee must maintain one of these designations throughout the duration of the award.

FINANCIAL DATA:
Amount of support per award: $77,000 per year (including up to 10% indirect costs).

APPLICATION INFO:
Guidelines and application form are available on the web site.
Duration: Two years.
Deadline: Typically July.

ADDRESS INQUIRIES TO:
See e-mail address above.

AMERICAN HEART ASSOCIATION   [2125]
AHA National Center
7272 Greenville Avenue
Dallas, TX 75231-4596
(214) 360-6107
E-mail: apply@heart.org
Web Site: professional.heart.org

FOUNDED: 1948

AREAS OF INTEREST:
Research broadly related to cardiovascular function and disease and stroke, or to related clinical, basic science, bioengineering or biotechnology, and public health problems, including multidisciplinary efforts.

NAME(S) OF PROGRAMS:
● **Merit Award**

TYPE:
Research grants. Merit Award supports individual scientists with a trajectory of success, who propose novel approaches to major research challenges in the areas of cardiovascular disease and stroke that have the potential to produce unusually high impact. This competition will enable AHA to further develop and strengthen the community of cardiovascular and stroke researchers and bring innovative approaches to basic, clinical, population and translational studies through funding a variety of disciplines.

PURPOSE:
To fund highly promising investigators with stellar track records of accomplishment who have the potential to move a field of science forward with creative approaches that are aligned with the mission of the American Heart Association.

LEGAL BASIS:
Research association.

ELIGIBILITY:
Applicant must be an AHA Professional Member. Applications are encouraged from all basic disciplines as well as epidemiological, behavioral, community and clinical investigations that bear on cardiovascular and stroke problems, and must describe the capacity of the investigator's work to transform public health policy. This award will be given to applicants with the following or equivalent credentials:
(1) have a Ph.D., M.D., or the equivalent;
(2) hold a tenured or tenure-track position as associate professor or higher academic rank at an eligible nonprofit U.S. institution or, if at an eligible institution that has no tenure track, hold an appointment that reflects a significant institutional commitment at the time of the application deadline and;
(3) be the principal investigator on multiple active, national peer-reviewed research awards of at least three years' duration. Mentored awards, career development and training grants do not qualify.

Federal government employees are not eligible.

At the time of application, the principal investigator must be a U.S. citizen, permanent resident, pending permanent resident, or hold a H1-B, J-1, O-1, G-4, TN or E-3 visa. Awardee must meet AHA citizenship criteria throughout the duration of the award.

FINANCIAL DATA:
Amount of support per award: $200,000 per year.

NO. AWARDS: 2 for the year 2019.

APPLICATION INFO:
A Letter of Intent (LOI), limited to three pages, will be required. AHA will contact applicants with the highest-rated LOIs and invite them to submit a full application.
Duration: Five years.
Deadline: Letter of Intent: Typically July.

ADDRESS INQUIRIES TO:
See e-mail address above.

AMERICAN HEART ASSOCIATION [2126]

AHA National Center
7272 Greenville Avenue
Dallas, TX 75231-4596
(214) 360-6107
E-mail: apply@heart.org
Web Site: professional.heart.org

FOUNDED: 1948

AREAS OF INTEREST:
Research broadly related to cardiovascular function, cardiovascular disease and stroke, or to related clinical, basic science, bioengineering, biotechnology, or public health problems.

NAME(S) OF PROGRAMS:
● **Collaborative Sciences Award**

TYPE:
Research grants. Award is intended to foster collaboration between established and early- or midcareer investigators.

PURPOSE:
To foster innovative collaborative approaches to research projects that propose novel pairing of investigators from at least two broadly disparate disciplines.

LEGAL BASIS:
Research association.

ELIGIBILITY:
Each applicant must be an AHA Professional Member. Proposal must focus on the collaborative relationship, such that the scientific objectives could not be achieved without the efforts of at least two co-principal investigators and their respective disciplines. The combination and integration of studies may be inclusive of basic, clinical, population, behavioral, and/or translational research. Project must include at least one co-principal investigator from a field outside cardiovascular disease and stroke. Applications by existing collaborators are permitted, provided that the proposal is for a new and novel idea or approach that has not been funded before.

While no minimum percent effort is specified, the co-principal investigators must demonstrate that adequate time will be devoted to ensuring successful completion of the proposed project.

At the time of application, each co-principal investigator must be a U.S. citizen, permanent resident, pending permanent resident, or hold an E-3, H1-B, F-1, J-1, O-1, TN or G-4 visa. Awardee must meet AHA citizenship criteria throughout the duration of the award.

Sponsoring institution must be a U.S.-based nonprofit institution, including medical, osteopathic and dental schools, veterinary schools, schools of public health, pharmacy schools, nursing schools, universities and colleges, public and voluntary hospitals and others that can demonstrate the ability to conduct the proposed research. Applications will not be accepted for work with funding to be administered through any federal institution or work to be performed by a federal employee, except for Veterans Administration employees.

FINANCIAL DATA:
Amount of support per award: $250,000 per year (including 10% institutional indirect costs).

NO. AWARDS: Up to 6 for the year 2018.

APPLICATION INFO:
A Letter of Intent (three-page limit) is required to ensure responsiveness to the novel, collaborative nature of this program. Only those applicants who submit a Letter of Intent and are invited to apply may submit a full application.
Duration: Three years.
Deadline: Key dates will be announced four months prior to the Letter of Intent deadline.

ADDRESS INQUIRIES TO:
See e-mail address above.

AMERICAN HEART ASSOCIATION [2127]

AHA National Center
7272 Greenville Avenue
Dallas, TX 75231-4596
(214) 360-6107
E-mail: apply@heart.org
Web Site: professional.heart.org

FOUNDED: 1948

AREAS OF INTEREST:
Research broadly related to cardiovascular function and disease and stroke, or to related clinical, translational, behavioral, population or basic science, bioengineering or biotechnology, and public health problems, including multidisciplinary efforts.

NAME(S) OF PROGRAMS:
● **Career Development Award**

TYPE:
Awards/prizes; Development grants; Research grants. Career Development Award is intended to develop the research skills to support and greatly enhance the awardee's chances to obtain and retain a high quality cardiovascular and/or stroke career position.

YEAR PROGRAM STARTED: 1997

PURPOSE:
To support promising health care and academic professionals in the early years of their first professional appointment; to explore innovative questions or pilot studies that will provide preliminary data and training necessary to ensure future success as a research scientist in the field of cardiovascular and stroke research.

LEGAL BASIS:
Research association.

ELIGIBILITY:
Applicant must be an AHA Professional Member and a U.S. citizen or permanent resident. At the time of application, the applicant must hold an M.D., Ph.D., D.O., D.V.M., D.D.S., or equivalent post-Baccalaureate doctoral degree.

At the time of award activation, candidate must hold a faculty/staff position up to and including the rank of assistant professor (or equivalent). No more than four years may have elapsed since the first faculty/staff appointment at the assistant professor level or equivalent. Applications may be submitted for review in the final year of a postdoctoral research fellowship or in the initial years of the first faculty/staff appointment. While no minimum percent effort is required, the

applicant must demonstrate that adequate time will be devoted to ensuring successful completion of the project.

GEOG. RESTRICTIONS: United States.

FINANCIAL DATA:
Amount of support per award: $77,000 per year, including 10% institutional indirect costs.

APPLICATION INFO:
Guidelines and application form are available on the web site.
Duration: Three years. Nonrenewable.
Deadline: Typically October.

ADDRESS INQUIRIES TO:
See e-mail address above.

AMERICAN HEART ASSOCIATION [2128]

AHA National Center
7272 Greenville Avenue
Dallas, TX 75231-4596
(214) 360-6107
E-mail: apply@heart.org
Web Site: professional.heart.org

FOUNDED: 1948

AREAS OF INTEREST:
All basic, clinical, translational, behavioral and population research broadly related to cardiovascular function and disease and stroke, or to related clinical, behavioral, basic science, bioengineering or biotechnology, and public health problems.

NAME(S) OF PROGRAMS:
● **Postdoctoral Fellowship**

TYPE:
Fellowships. Recognizing the unique challenges that clinicians, in particular, experience in balancing research and clinical activity, this award aims to be as flexible as possible to enable applicants to develop academic careers in research alongside fulfilling clinical service commitments.

PURPOSE:
To enhance the integrated research and clinical training of postdoctoral applicants who are not yet independent.

LEGAL BASIS:
Research association.

ELIGIBILITY:
Applicant must be an AHA Professional Member. Awards are open to the array of academic and health professionals. This includes, but is not limited to, all academic disciplines (biology, chemistry, mathematics, technology, physics, etc.) and all health-related professions (physicians, nurses, nurse practitioners, pharmacists, dentists, physical and occupational therapists, statisticians, nutritionists, etc.). Clinical, translational, population, and basic scientists are encouraged to apply.

AHA strongly encourages applications by women, underrepresented minorities in the sciences, and those who have experienced varied and nontraditional career trajectories.

At the time of award activation the candidate must:
(1) be a U.S. citizen, permanent resident, pending permanent resident, or have an E-3, F-1, H1-B, J-1, O-1, TN or G-4 visa;
(2) hold a post-Baccalaureate Ph.D degree or equivalant;
(3) have no more than five years of

postdoctoral research training or experience and;

(4) not be pursuing a doctoral degree.

A postdoctoral fellowship applicant who is outside the U.S. at the time of application must provide visa documentation prior to award activation. Funding is prohibited for awards at non-U.S. institutions.

GEOG. RESTRICTIONS: United States.

FINANCIAL DATA:
Amount of support per award: Varies per initiative for each geographical area and years of experience.

APPLICATION INFO:
Guidelines and application form are available on the web site.
Duration: One or two years. May apply for second two-year award.
Deadline: Typically July.

ADDRESS INQUIRIES TO:
See e-mail address above.

AMERICAN HEART ASSOCIATION   [2129]
AHA National Center
7272 Greenville Avenue
Dallas, TX 75231-4596
(214) 360-6107
E-mail: apply@heart.org
Web Site: professional.heart.org

FOUNDED: 1948

AREAS OF INTEREST:
Research broadly related to cardiovascular function and disease and stroke, or to related clinical, basic science, bioengineering or biotechnology, and public health problems, including multidisciplinary efforts.

NAME(S) OF PROGRAMS:
● **Predoctoral Fellowship**

TYPE:
Fellowships.

PURPOSE:
To enhance the integrated research and clinical training of promising students who are matriculated in predoctoral or clinical health professional degree training programs and who intend careers as scientists, physicians-scientists or other clinician-scientists, or related careers aimed at improving global cardiovascular health.

LEGAL BASIS:
Research association.

ELIGIBILITY:
Applicant must be an AHA Professional Member. Proposals are encouraged from all basic, behavioral, epidemiological, and community and clinical investigations that bear on cardiovascular and stroke problems. Applicants must meet the following criteria:
(1) be a U.S. citizen, permanent resident, pending permanent resident, or have an E-3, F-1, H1-B, J-1, O-1, TN or G-4 visa;
(2) be post-Baccalaureate, predoctoral M.D., Ph.D., D.O., D.V.M. (or equivalent) student seeking research training with a sponsor/mentor prior to embarking on a research career and;
(3) be a full-time student working toward their degree.

GEOG. RESTRICTIONS: United States.

FINANCIAL DATA:
Amount of support per award: Stipend of $25,320, plus $4,200 per year for health insurance and project support.

APPLICATION INFO:
Guidelines and application form are available on the web site.
Duration: One or two years.
Deadline: Typically July.

ADDRESS INQUIRIES TO:
See e-mail address above.

AMERICAN HEART ASSOCIATION   [2130]
AHA National Center
7272 Greenville Avenue
Dallas, TX 75231-4596
(214) 360-6107
E-mail: apply@heart.org
Web Site: professional.heart.org

FOUNDED: 1948

AREAS OF INTEREST:
Research broadly related to cardiovascular function and disease and stroke, or to related clinical, basic science, bioengineering or biotechnology, and public health problems, including multidisciplinary efforts.

NAME(S) OF PROGRAMS:
● **Transformational Project Award**

TYPE:
Awards/prizes; Project/program grants.

PURPOSE:
To support independent investigators with innovative and advanced projects related to cardiovascular disease and stroke.

LEGAL BASIS:
Research association.

ELIGIBILITY:
Applicant must be an AHA Professional Member. Proposals are encouraged from all basic disciplines, as well as epidemiological, behavioral, community and clinical investigations that bear on cardiovascular and stroke problems.

At the time of application, the applicant must be a U.S. citizen, permanent resident, pending permanent resident or hold these visas: E-3, H1-B, J-1, O-1, TN or G-4.

At the time of activation, the candidate must hold a post-baccalaureate Ph.D. degree or equivalent, or a doctoral-level clinical degree, such as M.D., D.O., D.V.M., Pharm.D., or Ph.D. in nursing, public health, or other clinical health science.

No limit is placed on eligibility based on career state, academic rank or discipline. Evidence of employment at a qualified institution is required.

While no minimum percent effort is specified, the principal investigator must demonstrate that adequate time will be devoted to ensuring successful completion of the proposed project.

GEOG. RESTRICTIONS: United States.

FINANCIAL DATA:
Amount of support per award: $100,000 (including 10% indirect costs) per year.

APPLICATION INFO:
Guidelines and application form are available on the web site.
Duration: Three years.
Deadline: To be announced approximately four months prior to application deadline.

ADDRESS INQUIRIES TO:
See e-mail address above.

AMERICAN HEART ASSOCIATION   [2131]
AHA National Center
7272 Greenville Avenue
Dallas, TX 75231-4596
(214) 360-6107
E-mail: apply@heart.org
Web Site: professional.heart.org

FOUNDED: 1948

AREAS OF INTEREST:
Research broadly related to cardiovascular function and disease and stroke, or to related clinical, basic science, bioengineering or biotechnology, and public health problems, including multidisciplinary efforts.

NAME(S) OF PROGRAMS:
● **Innovative Project Award**

TYPE:
Research grants. Program funds ideas that may introduce new paradigms, challenge current paradigms, look at existing problems from new perspectives, or exhibit other uniquely creative qualities.

PURPOSE:
To support highly innovative, high-impact research that could ultimately lead to critical discoveries or major advancements that will accelerate the field of cardiovascular and stroke research.

LEGAL BASIS:
Research association.

ELIGIBILITY:
Applicant must be an AHA Professional Member. Proposals are encouraged from all basic, behavioral, epidemiological, and community and clinical investigations that bear on cardiovascular and stroke problems. At the time of application, the applicant must:
(1) hold a post-Baccalaureate Ph.D. degree or equivalent, or a doctoral-level clinical degree, such as M.D., D.O., D.V.M., Pharm.D., or Ph.D. in nursing, public health, or clinical health science and;
(2) be a U.S. citizen, permanent resident, pending permanent resident, or have one of the following visas: E-3, H-1B, J-1, O-1, TN or G-4.

There is no limit on eligibility based on career stage, academic rank or discipline.

While no minimum percent effort is specified, the principal investigator must demonstrate that adequate time will be devoted to ensuring successful completion of the proposed project.

FINANCIAL DATA:
Amount of support per award: $100,000 per year (including 10% indirect costs).

APPLICATION INFO:
Proposal is limited to five pages.
Duration: Two years.
Deadline: October.

ADDRESS INQUIRIES TO:
See e-mail address above.

AMERICAN HEART ASSOCIATION   [2132]
AHA National Center
7272 Greenville Avenue
Dallas, TX 75231-4596
(214) 360-6107
E-mail: apply@heart.org
Web Site: professional.heart.org

FOUNDED: 1948

AREAS OF INTEREST:
Research broadly related to cardiovascular function and disease and stroke, or to related clinical, translational, population or basic science, bioengineering or biotechnology, and public health problems, including multidisciplinary efforts.

NAME(S) OF PROGRAMS:
● **Established Investigator Award**

TYPE:
Research grants. Candidates for this award have a demonstrated commitment to cardiovascular or cerebrovascular science as indicated by prior publication history and scientific accomplishments. A candidate's career is expected to be in a rapid growth phase.

PURPOSE:
To support midcareer investigators with unusual promise and an established record of accomplishments.

LEGAL BASIS:
Research association.

ELIGIBILITY:
Applicant must be an AHA Professional Member. Proposals are encouraged from all basic disciplines as well as epidemiological, behavioral, community and clinical investigations that bear on cardiovascular and stroke problems.

At the time of application, the applicant must:
(1) have an M.D., Ph.D., D.O. or equivalent doctoral degree;
(2) be a faculty/staff member;
(3) have current national-level funding as a principal investigator (or co-PI) on an R01 grant or its equivalent and;
(4) be a U.S. citizen, permanent resident, pending permanent resident, or have an H1-B, J-1, O-1, TN or E3 visa.

At the time of award activation, the applicant must be at the level of associate professor/staff scientist or equivalent.

FINANCIAL DATA:
Amount of support per award: $80,000 per year (including up to 10% indirect costs).

APPLICATION INFO:
Applicant must submit a Letter of Intent no more than two pages. AHA will contact applicants with the highest-rated LOIs and invite them to submit a full application. The LOI should briefly address the investigator's competitiveness in terms of:
(1) demonstrated commitment to cardiovascular or cerebrovascular diseases, and scientific innovation;
(2) independence as assessed by publications, research funding, and impact of scientific work as a principal investigator and;
(3) how the award will enhance the investigator's rapid growth phase.

In addition to the Letter of Intent, applicant must identify and list their 15 best papers (limited to two pages) and submit a biosketch (limited to five pages).

No reference letters are to be supplied with the initial LOI. Three references will be required from those selected to submit a full application.
Duration: Five years. No renewals.
Deadline: To be announced.

ADDRESS INQUIRIES TO:
See e-mail address above.

AMERICAN LUNG ASSOCIATION [2133]
55 West Wacker Drive
Suite 1150
Chicago, IL 60601
E-mail: research@lung.org
Web Site: www.lung.org/research

FOUNDED: 1904

AREAS OF INTEREST:
Research and education for the prevention and control of lung disease.

NAME(S) OF PROGRAMS:
● **Lung Cancer Discovery Awards**

TYPE:
Research grants. The objective of these awards is to support independent investigators conducting clinical, laboratory, epidemiological or any groundbreaking project aimed at revolutionizing our current understanding of lung cancer and improving diagnostic, clinical and treatment methods.

PURPOSE:
To support research to find better methods of detection, treatment and cures for all lung diseases.

LEGAL BASIS:
Nonprofit foundation.

ELIGIBILITY:
At the time of application, candidates must be U.S. citizens or foreign nationals holding a green card, J-1, H-1B, TN, E-3 or O-1 visa status. Applicant must be employed by a U.S. institution at the time of application and throughout the award period.

Applicant must hold a doctoral degree, have a faculty appointment at an academic institution (including research institutions not formally associated with a university), and have completed a training fellowship. Applicants may be at any level of research experience.

Applicants must be independent, self-directed researchers for whom their institution must provide space and other resources customary for independent investigators. The application must convey the commitment of the institution to the applicant and the proposed research activities.

GEOG. RESTRICTIONS: United States.

FINANCIAL DATA:
Grant funds may be used for the salary and fringe benefit costs of personnel other than the applicant. No more than 75% of the requested budget may be used for an awardee's salary and/or fringe benefits and no more than 30% of the total award budget may go to fund the purchase of permanent equipment.
Amount of support per award: $100,000 per year.

NO. MOST RECENT APPLICANTS: 46.

NO. AWARDS: 5.

APPLICATION INFO:
A Letter of Intent is required and must be submitted through proposalCENTRAL. Outcome notifications of the first stage of the application process will be e-mailed to applicants. Those applicants selected to go forward will be asked to submit a full proposal.
Duration: Up to two years.
Deadline: Letter of Intent: October 3. Application: January 23. Announcement in June.

PUBLICATIONS:
Program announcement.

ADDRESS INQUIRIES TO:
See e-mail address above.

AMERICAN LUNG ASSOCIATION [2134]
55 West Wacker Drive
Suite 1150
Chicago, IL 60601
E-mail: research@lung.org
Web Site: www.lung.org/research

FOUNDED: 1904

AREAS OF INTEREST:
Research and education for the prevention and control of lung disease.

NAME(S) OF PROGRAMS:
● **Dalsemer Research Grant**

TYPE:
Seed money grants. This mentored award provides seed money to junior investigators for researching the mechanisms and biology of interstitial lung disease.

PURPOSE:
To support research in interstitial lung disease.

LEGAL BASIS:
Nonprofit.

ELIGIBILITY:
At the time of application, applicant must:
(1) hold a doctoral degree and be assured of a faculty appointment or equivalent with demonstrated institutional commitment (salary support, research space) by the start of the award;
(2) have completed two years of postdoctoral research training;
(3) be U.S. citizens or foreign nationals holding one of the following visa immigration statuses: permanent resident (Green Card), exchange visitor (J-1), temporary worker in a specialty occupation (H-1, H-1B), Canadian or Mexican citizen engaging in professional activities (TC or TN), or temporary worker with extraordinary abilities in the sciences (O-1). Non-citizens must submit a notarized copy of proof of visa immigration status and;
(4) be employed by a U.S. institution.

Grantee organizations must be recognized academic or other nonprofit research entities.

Medical residents, those presently enrolled in a degree program (e.g., graduate students), and established investigators are not eligible to apply.

FINANCIAL DATA:
No more than 75% of the requested budget may be used for the awardee's salary and/or fringe benefits. No more than 30% of the total award budget may be used to fund the purchase of permanent equipment. Grant funds may be used for the salary and fringe benefit costs of personnel other than the applicant.
Amount of support per award: $50,000 per year.

NO. AWARDS: 1 to 2.

APPLICATION INFO:
Applications are accepted through proposalCENTRAL.
Duration: Up to two years.

Deadline: December 12. Announcement in June.

PUBLICATIONS:
Program announcement.

ADDRESS INQUIRIES TO:
See e-mail address above.

AMERICAN LUNG ASSOCIATION   [2135]

55 West Wacker Drive
Suite 1150
Chicago, IL 60601
E-mail: research@lung.org
Web Site: www.lung.org/research

FOUNDED: 1904

AREAS OF INTEREST:
Research and education for the prevention and control of lung disease.

NAME(S) OF PROGRAMS:
- **Allergic Respiratory Diseases Research Award**

TYPE:
Research grants. The American Lung Association and the American Academy of Allergy, Asthma & Immunology Allergic Respiratory Diseases Research Award represents a joint effort to encourage and support early-stage investigators with a primary faculty appointment in an allergy/immunology division or section conducting research into advancing the understanding of allergic respiratory disease. One of the goals of this collaboration is to fund researchers at important crossroads of their careers.

PURPOSE:
To encourage and support research into advancing the understanding of allergic respiratory disease.

LEGAL BASIS:
Nonprofit organization.

ELIGIBILITY:
At the time of application, candidates must be U.S. citizens or foreign nationals holding a green card, J-1, H-1B, TN, E-3 or O-1 visa immigration status. At the time of application and throughout the award, an applicant must be employed by a U.S. institution.

Applicant must hold a doctoral degree and have a primary faculty appointment in a Clinical Allergy and Immunology division or section of an academic institution. Applicants from outside of an Allergy and Immunology Division will not be considered.

Applicant must be undertaking a project related to allergic respiratory disease, have completed training, and be an independent and self-directed researcher for whom their institution must provide space and other resources customary for independent investigators. Applicant may be at any level of research experience, but priority will be given to applicants below the rank of associate professor who have not received more than one R award.

GEOG. RESTRICTIONS: United States.

FINANCIAL DATA:
No more than 75% of the requested budget may be used for an awardee's salary and/or fringe benefits. No more than 30% of the total award budget may be used to fund the purchase of permanent equipment. Grant

funds may be used for the salary and fringe benefit costs of personnel other than the applicant.
Amount of support per award: $75,000 per year.

NO. MOST RECENT APPLICANTS: 15.

NO. AWARDS: 1.

APPLICATION INFO:
Application information is available on the web site.
Duration: Up to two years.
Deadline: December 12. Notification in June.

ADDRESS INQUIRIES TO:
See e-mail address above.

AMERICAN LUNG ASSOCIATION   [2136]

55 West Wacker Drive
Suite 1150
Chicago, IL 60601
E-mail: research@lung.org
Web Site: www.lung.org/research

FOUNDED: 1904

AREAS OF INTEREST:
Adult pulmonary medicine, lung biology, pediatric pulmonary medicine, and research and education for the prevention and control of lung disease.

NAME(S) OF PROGRAMS:
- **Catalyst Award**

TYPE:
Training grants. American Lung Association Catalyst Award is a mentored award meant to support outstanding investigators on the path to independence for research into the mechanisms of lung disease and general lung biology.

YEAR PROGRAM STARTED: 1948

PURPOSE:
To prevent lung disease and promote lung health through research, education and advocacy.

LEGAL BASIS:
Nonprofit foundation.

ELIGIBILITY:
At the time of application, candidates must be U.S. citizens or foreign nationals holding green card, J-1, H-1B, TN, E-3 or O-1 visa immigration status. At the time of application and throughout the award, an applicant must be employed by a U.S. institution.

Applicant must hold a doctoral degree and have a faculty appointment or equivalent with demonstrated institutional commitment (salary support and research space) in a recognized academic or other not-for-profit institution.

Preference is given to projects that are novel, innovative in design and approach, utilize modern technologies, and incorporate a multidisciplinary collaborative training plan.

Medical residents, those presently enrolled in a degree program, and established investigators are not eligible to apply.

GEOG. RESTRICTIONS: United States.

FINANCIAL DATA:
Amount of support per award: $50,000 per year.

APPLICATION INFO:
Application information is available on the web site.

Duration: Up to two years.
Deadline: December 12. Notification in June.

PUBLICATIONS:
Program announcement.

ADDRESS INQUIRIES TO:
See e-mail address above.

AMERICAN LUNG ASSOCIATION   [2137]

55 West Wacker Drive
Suite 1150
Chicago, IL 60601
E-mail: research@lung.org
Web Site: www.lung.org/research

FOUNDED: 1904

AREAS OF INTEREST:
Research and education for the prevention and control of lung disease.

NAME(S) OF PROGRAMS:
- **Innovation Award**

TYPE:
Seed money grants. The aim of this award is to support promising independent investigators who are leveraging their existing body of work to conduct basic science, behavioral, clinical, or translational research for lung health.

YEAR PROGRAM STARTED: 1921

PURPOSE:
To prevent lung disease and promote lung health through research, education and advocacy.

LEGAL BASIS:
Nonprofit foundation.

ELIGIBILITY:
Intended for junior investigators researching the mechanisms of lung disease and general lung biology. At the time of application, candidates must:
(1) be U.S. citizens or foreign nationals;
(2) be employed by a U.S. institution;
(3) hold a doctoral degree;
(4) have a faculty appointment or equivalent with demonstrated institutional commitment in a recognized academic or other not-for-profit research institute and;
(5) have held a K or R level grant in the three years prior to the application.

FINANCIAL DATA:
Amount of support per award: $75,000 per year.

APPLICATION INFO:
Application information is available on the web site.
Duration: Up to two years.
Deadline: December 12. Announcement in June.

PUBLICATIONS:
Program announcement.

ADDRESS INQUIRIES TO:
See e-mail address above.

AMERICAN LUNG ASSOCIATION   [2138]

55 West Wacker Drive
Suite 1150
Chicago, IL 60601
E-mail: research@lung.org
Web Site: www.lung.org/research

FOUNDED: 1904

AREAS OF INTEREST:
Research and education for the prevention and control of lung disease.

NAME(S) OF PROGRAMS:
- **Public Policy Research Award**

TYPE:
Research grants. Public Policy Research Award is intended to support research on and evaluation of existing public policy and programs, as well as pilot and demonstration projects that inject innovative ideas and provide evidence for the development of new public policies impacting lung health.

PURPOSE:
To help stimulate and inform important public policy debates around healthy air and lung disease; to support research on and evaluation of existing public policy and programs, as well as projects that inject innovative ideas into public policies impacting lung health.

LEGAL BASIS:
Nonprofit foundation.

ELIGIBILITY:
At the time of application, candidates must be U.S. citizens or foreign nationals holding a green card, J-1, H-1B, TN, E-3 or O-1 visa status. Applicant must be employed by a U.S. institution at the time of application and throughout the award period.

Applicant must hold a doctoral degree or relevant terminal professional degree such as an M.P.H. and have a faculty appointment or equivalent with demonstrated institutional commitment in a recognized academic institution or established not-for-profit research entity.

Applicants should be on-track to pursue a career in public policy research. The application is open to researchers in public policy, economics, political science, sociology, law, and related disciplines.

GEOG. RESTRICTIONS: United States.

FINANCIAL DATA:
No more than 50% of the requested budget may be used for an awardee's salary and/or fringe benefits. No more than 30% of the total award budget may be used to fund the purchase of permanent equipment. Grant funds may be used for the salary and fringe benefit costs of personnel other than the applicant.
Amount of support per award: $50,000 per year.

APPLICATION INFO:
Proposal should include the following information:
(1) lay summary;
(2) curriculum vitae for the Principal Investigator and team;
(3) information on the project;
(4) study design and methods, including statistical analysis;
(5) plan for dissemination and translation;
(6) itemized project budget and;
(7) references.

The application must include a letter from the applicant's chair or institutional equivalent that conveys the commitment of the institution to the applicant and the proposed research activities.
Duration: Up to two years. Second year of funding is based on demonstrating satisfactory progress and availability of funding.
Deadline: December 12. Notification in June.

PUBLICATIONS:
Program announcement.

ADDRESS INQUIRIES TO:
See e-mail address above.

THE CANADIAN LUNG ASSOCIATION (CLA) [2139]
885 Meadowlands Drive
Suite 502
Ottawa ON K2C 3N2 Canada
(613) 569-6411 ext. 262
(888) 566-5864 (within Canada)
Fax: (613) 569-8860
E-mail: research@lung.ca
Web Site: www.lung.ca

FOUNDED: 1959

AREAS OF INTEREST:
Prevention and control of lung disease including asthma, emphysema, chronic bronchitis, tuberculosis and lung cancer; air pollution and smoking.

NAME(S) OF PROGRAMS:
- **Breathing as One: Research Fellowships and Studentships**

TYPE:
Fellowships. The Lung Association - National Office - offers two types of research trainee awards to the medical and scientific community: postdoctoral fellowships and Ph.D. graduate studentships.

YEAR PROGRAM STARTED: 1959

PURPOSE:
To build Canadian research capacity that contributes to the field of respiratory health in Canada.

LEGAL BASIS:
Not-for-profit, incorporated.

ELIGIBILITY:
Open to members and non-members of CTS and CRHP who are conducting lung research that aligns with the Lung Association mandate. To be eligible for a Breathing as One Fellowship or Studentship Award the following criteria apply:
(1) Studentship applicants should be enrolled or accepted in a graduate (thesis-based) program at the doctoral level at a Canadian academic institution. Individuals who have applied to a graduate program but have not received acceptance may apply for a Studentship award. The award, however, will be conditional on acceptance into the program;
(2) Fellowship applicants should be working under supervision of a faculty member at an accredited Canadian academic institution. Under special circumstances, an applicant may pursue a fellowship in another country; however, the applicant must justify why they could not find the same kind of training in Canada and must have plans to pursue a career in research in Canada;
(3) Awardee may not be in receipt of another major award at the same time as holding a Fellowship or Studentship Award from the Lung Association - National Office and;
(4) Applicant must be pursuing a research study with respiratory health as the major focus.

FINANCIAL DATA:
Amount of support per award: Fellowships: $45,000 to $55,000 (CAN) per year; Studentships: $21,000 (CAN) per year.
Total amount of support: Varies.

CO-OP FUNDING PROGRAMS: Partnerships include CIHR and the pharmaceutical industry (peer review only).

NO. AWARDS: Approximately 6 each year.

APPLICATION INFO:
Forms may be downloaded from the Lung Association web site. Applicant must upload one copy of the completed application and all relevant documents.
Duration: One to two years. Competitive renewal.
Deadline: July 17.

PUBLICATIONS:
Canadian Respiratory Journal.

ADDRESS INQUIRIES TO:
Fatima Kazoun, Manager
National Research Programs
(See address above.)

THE CANADIAN LUNG ASSOCIATION (CLA)
885 Meadowlands Drive
Suite 502
Ottawa ON K2C 3N2 Canada
(613) 569-6411 ext. 262
(888) 566-5864 (within Canada)
Fax: (613) 569-8860
E-mail: research@lung.ca
Web Site: www.lung.ca

TYPE:
Fellowships; Research grants. Fellowships are offered to registered nurses pursuing postgraduate education with a major component of the program involving respiratory nursing practice, physiotherapists pursuing postgraduate training with respiratory research as the major component, and respiratory therapists pursuing postgraduate education with a major component of the program involving respiratory therapy practice.

Grants for research and feasibility studies are offered to registered nurses undertaking research investigations related to nursing management of patients with respiratory disease and symptoms. Grants are also offered to physiotherapists undertaking investigations related to management of patients with respiratory disease. Respiratory therapists undertaking research investigations related to the management of patients with respiratory disease and symptoms may also qualify.

See entry 2237 for full listing.

GREENBURG-MAY FOUNDATION
280 Park Avenue, 41st Floor
New York, NY 10017
(212) 451-3200
E-mail: pmay@trianpartners.com

TYPE:
Development grants; Research grants. Social services.

See entry 2190 for full listing.

HEART AND STROKE FOUNDATION OF CANADA [2140]
1525 Carling Avenue
Suite 110
Ottawa ON K1Z 8R9 Canada
(613) 691-4045
Fax: (613) 727-1895
E-mail: research@heartandstroke.ca
Web Site: www.heartandstroke.ca/research

FOUNDED: 1956

AREAS OF INTEREST:
Cardiovascular/cerebrovascular research.

NAME(S) OF PROGRAMS:
- **Grant-in-Aid**

TYPE:
Grants-in-aid. Grant-in-Aid program provides operating funds to support important, pertinent, novel research in the areas of heart disease and stroke. Funding promotes research discovery, exploration and innovation across all health research themes. Knowledge gained from scientific findings contributes to the cardiovascular and cerebrovascular health of Canadians through prevention, treatment and recovery.

YEAR PROGRAM STARTED: 1958

PURPOSE:
To reduce the morbidity and mortality from cardiovascular/cerebrovascular disease in Canada.

LEGAL BASIS:
Nonprofit.

ELIGIBILITY:
Researchers at all career stages are encouraged to apply. Principal Investigators must have a full-time academic or faculty appointment in Canada at the time of application.

GEOG. RESTRICTIONS: Canada.

FINANCIAL DATA:
Amount of support per award: Varies, depending upon the needs and nature of the request.

APPLICATION INFO:
Applications will be completed online using Heart and Stroke's online system, CIRCUlink. A scanned copy of the original signature and electronic signatures will be accepted. Applicants need not send an original copy of the signature page to the Foundation.

Due to conflict of interest, letters of support from the Foundation are not permitted as part of any application to any Heart and Stroke research competition.

Applicants are required to attach a detailed research proposal, which must include:
(1) hypothesis to be tested;
(2) knowledge to date;
(3) methods to be used;
(4) anticipated results and conclusions;
(5) possible problems and;
(6) pertinent references.
Research proposal should be predominantly text and is limited to 10 pages.

Duration: One to three years.

Deadline: Applications must be submitted online by the submission deadline (listed online) for funding to become effective on July 1 of the following year.

ADDRESS INQUIRIES TO:
Research Department
(See e-mail address above.)

HEART AND STROKE FOUNDATION OF CANADA   [2141]

1525 Carling Avenue
Suite 110
Ottawa ON K1Z 8R9 Canada
(613) 691-4045
Fax: (613) 727-1895
E-mail: research@heartandstroke.ca
Web Site: www.heartandstroke.ca/research

FOUNDED: 1956

AREAS OF INTEREST:
Cardiovascular and cerebrovascular research.

NAME(S) OF PROGRAMS:
- **National New Investigator**

TYPE:
Awards/prizes; Scholarships. National New Investigator program is a salary award to support new investigators who have demonstrated excellence in their doctoral and postdoctoral training and wish to establish their own independent research career. Salary support opportunities of this kind provide an added incentive for researchers to continue or begin their program of research within Canada.

YEAR PROGRAM STARTED: 1958

PURPOSE:
To reduce the morbidity and mortality from cardiovascular disease in Canada.

LEGAL BASIS:
Nonprofit.

ELIGIBILITY:
At the time of submission, applicant must have a full-time appointment at the assistant professor level or above in Canada. The candidate should clearly demonstrate the potential to become an independent investigator. No more than five years may have passed since the date of the first faculty appointment.

Applicant must have an M.D., Ph.D. or equivalent degree.

Applications for this award must be supported by the university or institution at which the applicant will conduct the proposed research program. The university or institution is expected to guarantee the applicant appropriate academic rank and to provide adequate space and facilities for the investigator's research, commensurate with the status of the individual's experience and level of support by the Heart and Stroke Foundation.

GEOG. RESTRICTIONS: Canada.

FINANCIAL DATA:
Amount of support per award: $60,000 (CAN) including employer's portion of fringe benefits.

APPLICATION INFO:
Complete application must include:
(1) a six-page detailed description of the proposed research program, which includes identification of the applicant's role and how the execution of the research plan contributes to the applicant's development as an independent researcher;
(2) an institutional statement completed by the Dean and Department Head (or institutional equivalents) confirming that the applicant will have 75% of their time allocated to the proposed research program;
(3) three letters of recommendation in sealed envelopes with the signature of the referee across the seal;
(4) an executive summary of the proposed research;
(5) sex and gender considerations;
(6) a complete structured lay summary with a clear explanation of how the proposed research is directly relevant to heart disease and/or stroke and what is the impact of the proposed research to heart disease and/or stroke;
(7) a completed copy of the applicant's common curriculum vitae (HSFC version

only) and;
(8) original signatures, a scanned copy of the original signatures, or electronic signatures.

Duration: Maximum three years.

Deadline: September 4, to become tenable July 1 of the following year.

ADDRESS INQUIRIES TO:
Research Department
(See e-mail address above.)

NATIONAL BLOOD FOUNDATION, A PROGRAM OF AABB   [2142]

4550 Montgomery Avenue
Suite 700, North Tower
Bethesda, MD 20814-2749
(301) 215-6552
Fax: (301) 686-7865
E-mail: nbf@aabb.org
Web Site: www.aabb.org/nbf

FOUNDED: 1983

AREAS OF INTEREST:
Blood banking, blood safety, transfusion medicine, tissue transplantation, cellular therapy, and patient blood management.

NAME(S) OF PROGRAMS:
- **Early-Career Scientific Research Grants Program**

TYPE:
Awards/prizes; Development grants; Research grants; Seed money grants. Basic medical research grants.

The focus of the NBF's Scientific Research Grants Program is to support early career researchers in the field of transfusion medicine, to include aspects of immunology, hematology, tissue and transplantation medicine, cellular therapies, emerging infectious disease, immunohematology, donor health and recruitment and retention, implementation of technological advances, and patient blood management. Priority is given to early-stage investigators and innovative new projects with the potential to have a practical impact on patients and donors in transfusion medicine and biotherapies.

YEAR PROGRAM STARTED: 1985

PURPOSE:
To actively support the leadership role of the AABB in establishing and promoting the highest standards of care for patients and donors by funding basic and applied scientific research, administrative research/projects, professional education in all aspects of blood banking, transfusion medicine, cellular therapies and patient blood management.

LEGAL BASIS:
Nonprofit association.

ELIGIBILITY:
An applicant must be a doctor (M.D or Ph.D.), medical technologist, transfusion medicine or cellular therapies professional. All applicants will be considered regardless of age, race, gender, national origin or religion.

The NBF accepts national and international early-career applicants. The NBF intends to fund researchers on a path towards independence. No candidate is eligible to receive more than one NBF grant over the course of their career. No particular project can be funded more than once. Applications for research into innovative and new projects are a priority.

Awards will not be made to increase the funding available for currently funded research projects. NBF grants are intended to provide "seed" funding that allows the principal investigator to enhance preliminary data. This data may be useful in applying for larger grants.

FINANCIAL DATA:
Grant awards may not cover indirect costs. Equipment expenditures cannot exceed $8,000 per grant.
Amount of support per award: Up to $75,000.
Total amount of support: $450,000.

NO. MOST RECENT APPLICANTS: 32.

NO. AWARDS: 6.

APPLICATION INFO:
Required application forms are available from the Foundation and must be submitted electronically. Application fee of $160 if applicant is not an AABB Individual Healthcare Professional or Physician in Residency member.
Duration: One to two years.
Deadline: December 1. Announcement in June for funds to be distributed in July.

PUBLICATIONS:
Application; program announcement.

IRS I.D.: 36-2384118

ADDRESS INQUIRIES TO:
Amy Quiggins, Director
(See address above.)

NATIONAL HEART, LUNG AND BLOOD INSTITUTE (NHLBI) [2143]
Division of Extramural Research
Two Rockledge Center, Suite 7100
6701 Rockledge Drive, MSC 7902
Bethesda, MD 20892-7902
(301) 435-0166
Fax: (301) 451-5462
E-mail: lombardr@nhlbi.nih.gov
Web Site: www.nhlbi.nih.gov

FOUNDED: 1948

AREAS OF INTEREST:
Diseases of the heart, blood vessels, lung and blood, sleep disorders, clinical use of blood and blood resources, and transfusion medicine.

TYPE:
Conferences/seminars; Fellowships; Project/program grants; Research grants; Training grants; Loan forgiveness programs. Career awards and other grant mechanisms to foster research on heart, vascular and lung diseases, and to develop scientists in these areas. Also, small business grants. Loan forgiveness programs are for research.

YEAR PROGRAM STARTED: 1948

PURPOSE:
To support research into the causes, improved diagnosis, treatment and prevention of cardiovascular diseases in arteriosclerosis, hypertension, cardiovascular disease, coronary heart disease, peripheral vascular disease, arrhythmias, heart failure and shock,

congenital and rheumatic heart disease, cardiomyopathies and infections of the heart, circulatory assistance and AIDS.

LEGAL BASIS:
Public Health Service Act, Sections 301(c), 412 and 472.

ELIGIBILITY:
Any nonprofit or for-profit organization engaged in biomedical research may apply. An individual may apply for a fellowship award. Some restrictions may apply to foreign grantee institutions.

FINANCIAL DATA:
Amount of support per award: Varies by type of award.

APPLICATION INFO:
Application information is available on the web site.
Duration: Varies.
Deadline: Varies.

PUBLICATIONS:
NHLBI Fact Book; Annual Report of Director, NHLBI.

OFFICER:
Ryan Lombardi, Director, Office of Grants Management

ADDRESS INQUIRIES TO:
Ryan Lombardi, Director
Office of Grants Management
(See address above.)

NATIONAL HEART, LUNG AND BLOOD INSTITUTE (NHLBI) [2144]
Two Rockledge Center, Suite 10042
6701 Rockledge Drive, MSC 7952
Bethesda, MD 20892-7952
(301) 435-0233
Fax: (301) 480-3547
E-mail: nhlbiinfo@nhlbi.nih.gov
Web Site: www.nhlbi.nih.gov

FOUNDED: 1948

AREAS OF INTEREST:
Pulmonary research, prevention, education and training programs in pulmonary diseases.

NAME(S) OF PROGRAMS:
● **Lung Diseases Research**

TYPE:
Project/program grants. Cooperative agreements.

YEAR PROGRAM STARTED: 1970

PURPOSE:
To use available knowledge and technology to solve specific disease problems of the lungs; to promote further studies on the structure and function of the lung; to achieve improvement in the prevention and treatment of lung diseases.

LEGAL BASIS:
Public Health Service Act, Section 301, 422 and 487, as amended, Public Laws 78-410 and 99-158, 42 U.S.C. 241, 42 U.S.C. 285, and 42 U.S.C. 288, as amended.

ELIGIBILITY:
Any nonprofit or for-profit organization engaged in biomedical research may apply for grants with the exception of NRSAs. An individual may apply for an NRSA or, in some cases, may qualify for a research grant if adequate facilities in which to perform the research are available.

Some grants are available to U.S. citizens or institutions only.

FINANCIAL DATA:
Grants may support salaries, equipment, supplies, travel, and patient hospitalization as required to perform the research effort.

APPLICATION INFO:
Funding opportunities and award policies are posted online.
Duration: One to five years. Renewable.

PUBLICATIONS:
Annual Program Report.

STAFF:
James P. Kiley, Ph.D., Director, Division of Lung Diseases
Gail Weinmann, M.D., Deputy Director

ADDRESS INQUIRIES TO:
James P. Kiley, Ph.D., Director
Division of Lung Diseases
(See address above.)

THE POTTS MEMORIAL FOUNDATION [2145]
P.O. Box 1015
Hudson, NY 12534
(518) 851-2292
E-mail: pottsfoundation@outlook.com

FOUNDED: 1922

AREAS OF INTEREST:
Tuberculosis.

TYPE:
Fellowships; Grants-in-aid; Research grants; Seed money grants. At present, the program allows the Foundation to provide for the care, treatment and rehabilitation of persons afflicted with tuberculosis by methods selected by the trustees. This may include maintenance, operation of hospitals, research, vocational counseling and guidance, scholarships, subsidies for education and training, job placement, grants to hospitals and charitable institutions and the operation of sheltered workshops.

YEAR PROGRAM STARTED: 1922

PURPOSE:
To help people who are battling tuberculosis.

LEGAL BASIS:
Nonprofit corporation.

FINANCIAL DATA:
Amount of support per award: $1,000 to $50,000.

NO. MOST RECENT APPLICANTS: Under 50.

NO. AWARDS: 10 to 15.

APPLICATION INFO:
A letter of request and proposal should be furnished in as much detail as possible, including a detailed budget, to the Foundation. Eight (8) copies would be appreciated.
Duration: One year.
Deadline: 30 days prior to May 15 and October 15.

IRS I.D.: 14-1347714

OFFICERS:
Kathleen A. McDonough, Ph.D., President
John Chan, M.D., Vice President
Sidney D. Richter, Treasurer
Donna D. Klose, Secretary

TRUSTEES:
Richard Gullot, M.D.
Anthony Malanga, M.D.

Donna O'Hare, M.D.
Martin S. Pavelka, Jr., Ph.D.
Ananthakrishnan Ramani, M.D.

ADDRESS INQUIRIES TO:
Donna D. Klose, Secretary
(See address above.)

SALON NATIONAL LA BOUTIQUE

P.O. Box 1108
Lake Dallas, TX 75065-1108
(940) 230-0919
E-mail: lasecretaire@8and40.org
Web Site: www.8and40.org

TYPE:
Scholarships. Grants for registered nurses.

See entry 2245 for full listing.

THE SARNOFF CARDIOVASCULAR RESEARCH FOUNDATION   [2146]

731 Walker Road
Suite G2
Great Falls, VA 22066
(703) 759-7600
E-mail: dboyd@sarnofffoundation.org
Web Site: www.sarnofffoundation.org

FOUNDED: 1981

AREAS OF INTEREST:
Cardiovascular research.

NAME(S) OF PROGRAMS:
- **Sarnoff Fellowship Program**
- **Sarnoff Scholar Award**

TYPE:
Awards/prizes; Fellowships. Research Fellowship and Award.

PURPOSE:
To give medical students the opportunity to spend a year conducting intensive work in a biomedical research laboratory; to provide financial support to former Sarnoff Fellows committed to pursuing a career in cardiovascular research.

ELIGIBILITY:
Sarnoff Fellowship Program is for medical students enrolled in any accredited medical school in the U.S. Applications are encouraged from second- and third-year medical students. Fourth-year medical students are required to submit an official letter from their medical schools granting graduation deferment. There are no citizenship requirements for application, but those who are not U.S. citizens must have and maintain an appropriate visa. Applicants enrolled in an M.D./Ph.D. program are ineligible. The Foundation strongly encourages applicants from members of underrepresented or historically disadvantaged backgrounds.

Sarnoff Scholar Award applicant must be a former Sarnoff Fellow pursuing a career in cardiovascular research. Applicants may apply during the second half of their post-residency training/fellowship program and/or overlapping with the first two junior faculty years.

FINANCIAL DATA:
Amount of support per award: Fellowship: $35,000 stipend and up to $8,000 allowance for moving expenses, health insurance, financial support to attend the Sarnoff Annual Scientific Meeting and American Heart

Association Scientific Sessions, and travel to present a paper, based on Fellowship research, at two national conferences.

Scholar: $90,000 stipend; up to $12,000 for laboratory supplies and professional journal subscriptions; up to $1,500 annually to defray the cost of health insurance; travel funds up to $1,500 to enable the Scholar to present a paper at a national conference; and maximum of 10% indirect costs paid to the institution for handling the award.

NO. AWARDS: Fellowship: Up to 18 annually; Scholar: 1 to 2 annually.

APPLICATION INFO:
Applicants to the Fellowship Program must submit the following:
(1) one-page personal statement describing scholarly interests and career plans;
(2) three-page essay on the applicant's cardiovascular topic of interest;
(3) completed application form and signed statement of confidentiality;
(4) official medical school transcript;
(5) curriculum vitae;
(6) recommendation from the applicant's sponsor;
(7) two additional recommendations and;
(8) any other material that the applicant determines is appropriate to support the application.

Duration: Fellowship: One year; Scholar: Two years.

Deadline: January 12.

ADDRESS INQUIRIES TO:
Dana Quinn Boyd, Executive Director
(See address above.)

SOCIETY OF CARDIOVASCULAR ANESTHESIOLOGISTS   [2147]

1061 East Main Street
Suite 300
East Dundee, IL 60118
(855) 658-2828
Fax: (847) 375-6323
E-mail: info@scahq.org
Web Site: www.scahq.org

AREAS OF INTEREST:
Cardiothoracic and vascular anesthesia.

NAME(S) OF PROGRAMS:
- **SCA/IARS Mid-Career Grant**
- **SCA/IARS Starter Grants**

TYPE:
Research grants.

PURPOSE:
To promote excellence in patient care through education and research in perioperative care for patients undergoing cardiothoracic and vascular procedures.

ELIGIBILITY:
Grant applicants must be a member of Society of Cardiovascular Anesthesiologists and hold an M.D. or Ph.D. degree.

No part of the grant may be used for salary support of the principal investigator (or fellows or residents), travel or tuition expenses of the principal investigator, patient costs (except to pay for pertinent laboratory studies), consultant costs, alterations or renovations.

FINANCIAL DATA:
Amount of support per award: Mid-Career Grant: Up to $50,000 per year; Starter Grant: Up to $25,000 per year.

Total amount of support: Up to $100,000 per recipient, depending on which grant is applied for.

NO. MOST RECENT APPLICANTS: 21.

NO. AWARDS: Maximum of 5 each year.

APPLICATION INFO:
Application information is available on the web site.
Duration: Up to two years.
Deadline: Varies.

IRS I.D.: 72-0863580

ADDRESS INQUIRIES TO:
See e-mail address above.

Metabolism, gastroenterology, nephrology

AMERICAN DIABETES ASSOCIATION   [2148]

2451 Crystal Drive
Suite 900
Arlington, VA 22202
(703) 549-1500 ext. 5532
Fax: (703) 621-3759
E-mail: grantquestions@diabetes.org
Web Site: www.professional.diabetes.org/grants

FOUNDED: 1940

AREAS OF INTEREST:
Programs serving the needs of people with diabetes, their families, researchers, clinicians and health care professionals.

CONSULTING OR VOLUNTEER SERVICES:
Various support and education programs carried out at affiliate level. Research program on national level.

NAME(S) OF PROGRAMS:
- **Innovative Basic Science Award (IBS)**
- **Innovative Clinical or Translational Science Award (ICTS)**
- **Junior Faculty Development Award (JFD)**
- **Minority Junior Faculty Development Award (JDFM)**
- **Minority Postdoctoral Fellowship**
- **Minority Undergraduate Internship (MUI)**
- **Postdoctoral Fellowship (PDF)**

TYPE:
Fellowships; Research grants; Training grants.

YEAR PROGRAM STARTED: 1952

PURPOSE:
To aid in the search for a cure and prevention of diabetes; to help those with diabetes complications.

LEGAL BASIS:
Nonprofit voluntary health organization.

ELIGIBILITY:
Applicants must have a Ph.D., M.D., Pharm.D., D.O. or D.P.M. degree or appropriate health or science-related degrees and must hold full-time faculty position or the equivalent at university-affiliated institutions within the U.S. or its possessions. Postdoctoral Fellowship applicants must hold a full-time postdoctoral fellowship or the equivalent.

All investigators must be legally authorized to work in the U.S. Institutional certification of work permission will be required for all funded awards.

For the Junior Faculty Development Award, applicants can have any level of faculty appointment up to and including Assistant Professor and have no more than 10 years of research experience following receipt of their terminal degree.

For the Minority Junior Faculty Development and the Minority Postdoctoral Awards, underrepresented minorities are defined as the minority groups that are underrepresented in the area of biomedical and behavioral research: African American or Black, Hispanic/Spanish/Latino, American Indian/Alaskan Native, and Native Hawaiian or other Pacific Islander descent.

GEOG. RESTRICTIONS: United States.

FINANCIAL DATA:
Amount of support per award: Innovative Basic Science Award: Up to $115,000 per year; Innovative Clinical or Translational Science Award: Up to $200,000 per year; Junior Faculty Development Award and Minority Junior Faculty Development Award: $138,000 per year, plus optional student loan repayment of $10,000 per year; Minority Postdoctoral Fellowship and Postdoctoral Fellowship: $47,484 to $55,581 per year salary, plus $5,000 per year research and $5,000 per year fringe allowances; Minority Undergraduate Internship: $3,000 stipend.

NO. MOST RECENT APPLICANTS: 1,000.

APPLICATION INFO:
Applicants for all grants must submit application forms, a nontechnical description of the research project of less than 200 words and a scientific abstract of the proposal of no more than 200 words.
Duration: Innovative Basic Science Award, Innovative Clinical or Translational Science Award, Minority Postdoctoral Fellowship and Postdoctoral Fellowship: Up to three years; Junior Faculty Development Award and Minority Junior Faculty Development Award: Two to four years, dependent on previous career development funding; Minority Undergraduate Internship: Up to one year.
Deadline: July 15.

PUBLICATIONS:
Annual reports.

ADDRESS INQUIRIES TO:
Magda Galindo, Director Research and Community Programs
(See address above.)

AMERICAN GASTROENTEROLOGICAL ASSOCIATION (AGA) [2149]

4930 Del Ray Avenue
Bethesda, MD 20814
(301) 654-2055
Fax: (301) 654-5920
E-mail: awards@gastro.org
Web Site: www.gastro.org/research-and-awards

FOUNDED: 1990

AREAS OF INTEREST:
Gastroenterology and related fields.

NAME(S) OF PROGRAMS:
● **AGA-R. Robert and Sally D. Funderburg Research Award in Gastric Cancer**

TYPE:
Research grants. Research award supporting an established investigator in the field of gastric cancer research working to enhance our fundamental understanding of gastric cancer pathobiology or approaches to prevent, treat or cure gastric cancer.

YEAR PROGRAM STARTED: 1990

PURPOSE:
To support an established investigator in the field of gastric biology which enhances our fundamental understanding of gastric cancer pathobiology in order to prevent or develop a cure for the disease.

LEGAL BASIS:
Nonprofit foundation.

ELIGIBILITY:
Applicants must hold faculty positions at an institution in North America and be established as an independent investigator in the field of gastric biology. AGA membership is required. Female or from racial/ethnic groups underrepresented in biomedical research are strongly encouraged to apply.

The recipient will be selected based on significance, investigator, innovation, approach, environment, evidence of institutional commitment, and relevance to AGA's mission. Preference will be given to novel approaches.

GEOG. RESTRICTIONS: North America.

FINANCIAL DATA:
Amount of support per award: $100,000 ($50,000 per year).

NO. AWARDS: 1.

APPLICATION INFO:
Application information is available online.
Duration: Two years.
Deadline: July 21.

PUBLICATIONS:
Announcements.

ADDRESS INQUIRIES TO:
See e-mail address above.

AMERICAN GASTROENTEROLOGICAL ASSOCIATION (AGA) [2150]

4930 Del Ray Avenue
Bethesda, MD 20814
(301) 654-2055
Fax: (301) 654-5920
E-mail: awards@gastro.org
Web Site: www.gastro.org/research-and-awards

FOUNDED: 1990

AREAS OF INTEREST:
Gastroenterology and related fields.

NAME(S) OF PROGRAMS:
● **AGA-Takeda Pharmaceuticals Research Scholar Award in Inflammatory Bowel Disease**

TYPE:
Research grants. Research award for early career faculty working toward independent careers in inflammatory bowel disease research.

YEAR PROGRAM STARTED: 1990

PURPOSE:
To support early-career investigators working toward independent and productive research careers in inflammatory bowel disease.

LEGAL BASIS:
Nonprofit foundation.

ELIGIBILITY:
Applicants must hold an M.D., Ph.D. or equivalent degrees (e.g., M.B.B.S., D.O.), and a full-time faculty or equivalent position at an institution in North America by the start of this award. AGA membership is required. The award is intended for early-career faculty who have demonstrated exceptional promise and have some record of accomplishment in research. Physician-scientists, female or from racial/ethnic groups underrepresented in biomedical research are strongly encouraged to apply. Applicants working in a nonprofit institution in North America are eligible for this award (U.S. citizenship is not required).

For M.D. applicants, no more than seven years shall have elapsed following the completion of clinical training (GI fellowship or its equivalent) at the start date of the award. For Ph.D. applicants, no more than seven years shall have elapsed following the conferment of the Ph.D. and the start date of the award. Appropriately documented medical or parental leaves of absence will not be counted toward the seven-year eligibility criteria if approved by AGA before application submission. Other exceptional circumstances may be considered.

Applicants cannot hold, or have held, an R01, R29, K-series award, Veterans Affairs Career Development Award or any award with similar objectives from non-federal sources prior to receiving the first payment of this award.

GEOG. RESTRICTIONS: North America.

FINANCIAL DATA:
Amount of support per award: $300,000 ($100,000 per year).

NO. AWARDS: 1.

APPLICATION INFO:
Applications must be submitted through the AGA Grants Management System. Application materials will not be accepted via mail, fax or e-mail.
Duration: Three years.
Deadline: November 10.

ADDRESS INQUIRIES TO:
See e-mail address above.

AMERICAN GASTROENTEROLOGICAL ASSOCIATION (AGA) [2151]

4930 Del Ray Avenue
Bethesda, MD 20814
(301) 654-2055
Fax: (301) 654-5920
E-mail: awards@gastro.org
Web Site: www.gastro.org/research-and-awards

AREAS OF INTEREST:
Gastroenterology and related fields.

NAME(S) OF PROGRAMS:
● **AGA Student Abstract Award**

TYPE:
Awards/prizes; Travel grants. Awards for graduate students, medical students and residents presenting an abstract chosen by AGA for presentation during Digestive Disease Week (DDW).

PURPOSE:
To stimulate interest in gastroenterology/hepatology research careers through competition and recognition.

LEGAL BASIS:
Nonprofit foundation.

ELIGIBILITY:
Applicants must be graduate or medical students or medical residents (up to and including postgraduate year three) who have performed original research related to diseases, structure or functioning of the digestive system. The applicant's sponsor must be a member of AGA. Applicants may only submit one abstract for consideration and must be the designated presenter. Awardees will be selected based on novelty, significance of the proposal, clarity of the abstract and contribution of the student.

Postdoctoral fellows, technicians, visiting scientists and M.D. research fellows are not eligible.

GEOG. RESTRICTIONS: North America.

FINANCIAL DATA:
Amount of support per award: Travel Award: $500; Student Abstract of the Year: $1,000.

NO. AWARDS: 16.

APPLICATION INFO:
Applications must be submitted through the AGA Grants Management System. Application materials will not be accepted by mail, fax or e-mail.
Deadline: February 16, 2022.

ADDRESS INQUIRIES TO:
See e-mail address above.

AMERICAN GASTROENTEROLOGICAL ASSOCIATION (AGA)   [2152]
4930 Del Ray Avenue
Bethesda, MD 20814
(301) 654-2055
Fax: (301) 654-5920
E-mail: awards@gastro.org
Web Site: www.gastro.org/research-and-awards

AREAS OF INTEREST:
Gastroenterology and related fields.

NAME(S) OF PROGRAMS:
• **AGA-Moti L. and Kamla Rustgi International Travel Awards**

TYPE:
Awards/prizes; Travel grants. Awards for young basic, translational and clinical investigators residing outside North America to offset travel expenses to attend Digestive Disease Week (DDW).

PURPOSE:
To enable young investigators outside of North America to attend DDW and encourage them to maintain a commitment to digestive disease research.

LEGAL BASIS:
Nonprofit foundation.

ELIGIBILITY:
The applicant must hold an M.D. or Ph.D. degree or a non-U.S. equivalent degree, be 35 years of age or younger at the time of DDW and be fluent in English. The applicant must be an AGA member, who is sponsored by an international AGA member. The applicant must be a presenting author of an abstract accepted by the AGA for presentation at DDW and provide evidence of abstract acceptance. Applicants may only submit one abstract for consideration.

Awardees will be selected based on the applicant's credentials and achievements as documented in their application.

FINANCIAL DATA:
Amount of support per award: $750.

NO. AWARDS: 2.

APPLICATION INFO:
Applications must be submitted through the AGA Grants Management System. Application materials will not be accepted by mail, fax or e-mail.
Deadline: February 16, 2022.

ADDRESS INQUIRIES TO:
See e-mail address above.

AMERICAN GASTROENTEROLOGICAL ASSOCIATION (AGA)   [2153]
4930 Del Ray Avenue
Bethesda, MD 20814
(301) 654-2055
Fax: (301) 654-5920
E-mail: awards@gastro.org
Web Site: www.gastro.org/research-and-awards

AREAS OF INTEREST:
Gastroenterology and related fields.

NAME(S) OF PROGRAMS:
• **AGA Fellow Abstract Award**

TYPE:
Awards/prizes; Travel grants. Awards to support recipients who are M.D., Ph.D. or equivalent fellows giving abstract-based oral or poster presentations at Digestive Disease Week (DDW).

PURPOSE:
To stimulate interest in gastroenterology and hepatology research careers.

LEGAL BASIS:
Nonprofit foundation.

ELIGIBILITY:
Applicants must be clinical postdoctoral fellows with an M.D. and/or Ph.D. degree who are active AGA members, and must be sponsored by a member of AGA. Applicants must be a presenting author of an abstract accepted by AGA for oral or poster presentation, and must provide confirmation of AGA abstract acceptance.

GEOG. RESTRICTIONS: North America.

FINANCIAL DATA:
Amount of support per award: Travel Award: $500; Fellow Abstract of the Year: $1,000.

NO. AWARDS: 16.

APPLICATION INFO:
Applications must be submitted through the AGA Grants Management System. Application materials will not be accepted by mail, fax or e-mail.
Deadline: February 16, 2022.

ADDRESS INQUIRIES TO:
See e-mail address above.

AMERICAN GASTROENTEROLOGICAL ASSOCIATION (AGA)   [2154]
4930 Del Ray Avenue
Bethesda, MD 20814
(301) 654-2055
Fax: (301) 654-5920
E-mail: awards@gastro.org
Web Site: www.gastro.org/research-and-awards

AREAS OF INTEREST:
Gastroenterology and related fields.

NAME(S) OF PROGRAMS:
• **AGA-Caroline Craig Augustyn and Damian Augustyn Award in Digestive Cancer**

TYPE:
Research grants. Award for an early career investigator who currently holds a federal or non-federal career development award devoted to conducting research related to digestive cancer.

PURPOSE:
To support early career investigators conducting research relevant to the pathogenesis, prevention, diagnosis, or treatment of digestive cancer by supplementing existing career development funding.

LEGAL BASIS:
Nonprofit foundation.

ELIGIBILITY:
Applicants must hold an M.D., Ph.D. or equivalent degree and a full-time faculty or equivalent position at an institution in North America. AGA membership is required of all applicants. Applicants must hold an NIH K series or other federal or non-federal career development award of at least four years duration. There must be at least one remaining year on the award by the start date of this award. Applicants who are physician-scientists, female or from racial/ethnic groups underrepresented in biomedical research are strongly encouraged to apply. Awardees are selected based on qualifications of the candidate, the novelty, feasibility and significance of their research and the potential for a future independent research career.

For M.D. applicants, no more than seven years shall have elapsed following the completion of clinical training (GI fellowship or its equivalent) and the start date of this award. For Ph.D. applicants, no more than seven years shall have elapsed following the conferment of the Ph.D. and the start date of this award. Appropriately documented medical or parental leaves of absence will not be counted toward the seven-year eligibility criteria if approved by AGA before submission. Other exceptional circumstances may also be considered.

Applicants may not hold an R01 or equivalent, such as a VA Merit award; therefore, established investigators will not be considered for this award.

FINANCIAL DATA:
Amount of support per award: $40,000.

NO. AWARDS: 1.

APPLICATION INFO:
Applications must be submitted through the AGA Grants Management System. Application materials will not be accepted by mail, fax or e-mail.

Duration: One year.

Deadline: July 21.

ADDRESS INQUIRIES TO:
See e-mail address above.

AMERICAN GASTROENTEROLOGICAL ASSOCIATION (AGA)   [2155]

4930 Del Ray Avenue
Bethesda, MD 20814
(301) 654-2055
Fax: (301) 654-5920
E-mail: awards@gastro.org
Web Site: www.gastro.org/research-and-awards

AREAS OF INTEREST:
Gastroenterology and related fields.

NAME(S) OF PROGRAMS:
- **AGA-Gastric Cancer Foundation Ben Feinstein Memorial Research Scholar Award in Gastric Cancer**

TYPE:
Awards/prizes. Scholar award offered every third year for early career faculty working toward an independent career in gastric cancer research.

PURPOSE:
To support young gastroenterologists working toward independent and productive research careers in digestive diseases.

LEGAL BASIS:
Nonprofit foundation.

ELIGIBILITY:
Candidate must hold an M.D., Ph.D. or equivalent degree and a full-time faculty position at a North American institution by the start date of the award. Proposals spanning the research spectrum, from basic to clinical science, are eligible.

Candidate must be an AGA member in good standing at the time of application submission.

Women, minorities and physician-scientist investigators are strongly encouraged to apply.

GEOG. RESTRICTIONS: North America.

FINANCIAL DATA:
Amount of support per award: $100,000.
Total amount of support: $300,000.

NO. AWARDS: 1.

APPLICATION INFO:
Applications must be submitted through the AGA Grants Management System. Materials will not be accepted via mail, fax or e-mail.
Duration: Three years.
Deadline: Fall 2022.

ADDRESS INQUIRIES TO:
Nick Tomeo, Manager, Research Affairs (See address above.)

*SPECIAL STIPULATIONS:
AGA membership must be maintained throughout the three-year duration of the award.

AMERICAN GASTROENTEROLOGICAL ASSOCIATION (AGA)   [2156]

4930 Del Ray Avenue
Bethesda, MD 20814
(301) 654-2055
Fax: (301) 654-5920
E-mail: awards@gastro.org
Web Site: www.gastro.org/research-and-awards

FOUNDED: 1990

AREAS OF INTEREST:
Gastroenterology and related fields.

NAME(S) OF PROGRAMS:
- **AGA Research Scholar Award**

TYPE:
Research grants. Research Scholar Award provides funding to early career faculty working toward an independent career in digestive disease research.

PURPOSE:
To support early-career investigators working toward independent and productive research careers in digestive diseases by ensuring that a major proportion of their time is protected for research.

LEGAL BASIS:
Nonprofit foundation.

ELIGIBILITY:
Applicants must hold an M.D., Ph.D. or equivalent degrees and a full-time faculty or equivalent position at an institution in North America by the start of the award. AGA membership is required at the time of application. Proposals spanning the research spectrum, from basic to clinical science, are eligible. Applicants who are physician-scientists, female or from racial/ethnic groups underrepresented in biomedical research are strongly encouraged to apply.

For M.D. applicants, no more than seven years shall have elapsed following the completion of clinical training (GI fellowship or its equivalent) and the start date of this award. For Ph.D. applicants, no more than seven years shall have passed following the conferment of the Ph.D. and the start date of this award. Appropriately documented medical or parental leaves of absence will not be counted toward the seven-year eligibility criteria if approved by AGA before application submission. Other exceptional circumstances may also be considered.

At the time of application submission, candidate may not hold, or have held, an NIH K01, K08, K23, K99, R00, R01, R21, R29, Veterans Affairs Career Development Award or any award with similar objectives from non-federal sources.

GEOG. RESTRICTIONS: North America.

FINANCIAL DATA:
Amount of support per award: $300,000 ($100,000 per year).

NO. AWARDS: 5.

APPLICATION INFO:
Applications must be submitted through the AGA Grants Management System. Application materials will not be accepted via mail, fax or e-mail.
Duration: Three years.
Deadline: November 10.

PUBLICATIONS:
Announcements.

ADDRESS INQUIRIES TO:
See e-mail address above.

AMERICAN GASTROENTEROLOGICAL ASSOCIATION (AGA)   [2157]

4930 Del Ray Avenue
Bethesda, MD 20814
(301) 654-2055
Fax: (301) 654-5920
E-mail: awards@gastro.org
Web Site: www.gastro.org/research-and-awards

FOUNDED: 1990

AREAS OF INTEREST:
Gastroenterology and related fields.

NAME(S) OF PROGRAMS:
- **AGA-Takeda Pharmaceuticals Research Scholar Awards in Celiac Disease**

TYPE:
Research grants. Research award for early career faculty working toward independent careers in celiac disease research.

PURPOSE:
To support early career investigators working toward independent and productive research careers in digestive diseases.

LEGAL BASIS:
Nonprofit foundation.

ELIGIBILITY:
Applicants must hold an M.D., Ph.D. or equivalent degrees and a full-time faculty or equivalent position at an institution in North America by the start of the award. AGA membership is required at the time of application. Proposals spanning the research spectrum, from basic to clinical science, are eligible. Applicants who are physician-scientists, female or from racial/ethnic groups underrepresented in biomedical research are strongly encouraged to apply.

For M.D. applicants, no more than seven years shall have elapsed following the completing of clinical training (GI fellowship or its equivalent) and the start date of this award. For Ph.D. applicants, no more than seven years shall have elapsed following the conferment of the Ph.D. and the start date of this award. Appropriately documented medical or parental leaves of absence will not be counted toward the seven-year eligibility criteria if approved by AGA before application submission. Other exceptional circumstances may also be considered.

At the time of application submission, candidate may not hold, or have held, an NIH K01, KI08, K23, K99, R00, R01, R21, R29, Veterans Affairs Career Development Award or any award with similar objectives from non-federal sources. Applicants with active KL2 or K12 may apply in the final years of KL2/K12 support.

GEOG. RESTRICTIONS: North America.

FINANCIAL DATA:
Amount of support per award: $300,000 ($100,000 per year).

NO. AWARDS: 1.

APPLICATION INFO:
Applications must be submitted through the AGA Grants Management System. Application materials will not be accepted via mail, fax or e-mail.
Duration: Three years.
Deadline: November 10.

ADDRESS INQUIRIES TO:
See e-mail address above.

AMERICAN GASTROENTEROLOGICAL ASSOCIATION (AGA)   [2158]

4930 Del Ray Avenue
Bethesda, MD 20814
(301) 654-2055
Fax: (301) 654-5920
E-mail: awards@gastro.org
Web Site: www.gastro.org/research-and-awards

FOUNDED: 1990

AREAS OF INTEREST:
Gastroenterological and related fields.

NAME(S) OF PROGRAMS:
- **AGA-Medtronic Pilot Research Award in Technology Innovation**

TYPE:
Research grants. Research award for independent investigators at any career stage to support the research and development of novel devices or technologies that will potentially impact the diagnosis or treatment of digestive disease.

PURPOSE:
To provide funds to early career investigators to help establish their research careers or to support projects that represent new research directions for established investigators.

LEGAL BASIS:
Nonprofit foundation.

ELIGIBILITY:
Applicants must hold an M.D., Ph.D. or equivalent degree and a full-time faculty or equivalent position at an institution in North America. AGA membership is required at the time of application submission.

Applicants performing any type of research relevant to digestive disorders are eligible to apply. Projects must focus on designing and/or testing improvements to existing technology, developing a new device, diagnostic, research method technology, and/or investigating the application of nanotechnology or methodologies such as computational biology to gastroenterology- or hepatology-related areas.

Applicants who are physician-scientists, female, or from racial/ethnic groups underrepresented in biomedical research are strongly encouraged to apply.

GEOG. RESTRICTIONS: North America.

FINANCIAL DATA:
Amount of support per award: $30,000.

NO. AWARDS: 1.

APPLICATION INFO:
Applications must be submitted through the AGA Grants Management System. Application materials will not be accepted via mail, fax or e-mail.
Duration: One year.
Deadline: August 23.

ADDRESS INQUIRIES TO:
See e-mail address above.

AMERICAN GASTROENTEROLOGICAL ASSOCIATION (AGA)   [2159]
4930 Del Ray Avenue
Bethesda, MD 20814
(301) 654-2055
Fax: (301) 654-5920
E-mail: awards@gastro.org
Web Site: www.gastro.org/research-and-awards

FOUNDED: 1990

AREAS OF INTEREST:
Gastroenterology and related fields.

NAME(S) OF PROGRAMS:
- **AGA-Pfizer Pilot Research Award in Inflammatory Bowel Disease**

TYPE:
Research grants. Research award for independent investigators at any career stage

to support research focused on improving the diagnosis and treatment of inflammatory bowel disease.

PURPOSE:
To provide funds for early career investigators to help establish their careers or to support projects that represent new research directions for established investigators.

LEGAL BASIS:
Nonprofit foundation.

ELIGIBILITY:
Applicants must hold an M.D., Ph.D. or equivalent degree and a full-time faculty position or equivalent at an institution in North America. AGA membership is required at the time of application submission.

Applicants performing any type of research relevant to digestive disorders are eligible to apply. Projects must focus on new research areas that could improve the diagnosis and treatment of inflammatory bowel disease (IBD).

Applicants who are physician-scientists, female or from racial/ethnic groups underrepresented in biomedical research are strongly encouraged to apply.

GEOG. RESTRICTIONS: North America.

FINANCIAL DATA:
Amount of support per award: $30,000.

NO. AWARDS: 1.

APPLICATION INFO:
Applications must be submitted through the AGA Grants Management System. Application materials will not be accepted via mail, fax or e-mail.
Duration: One year.
Deadline: August 23.

ADDRESS INQUIRIES TO:
See e-mail address above.

AMERICAN GASTROENTEROLOGICAL ASSOCIATION (AGA)   [2160]
4930 Del Ray Avenue
Bethesda, MD 20814
(301) 654-2055
Fax: (301) 654-5920
E-mail: awards@gastro.org
Web Site: www.gastro.org/research-and-awards

FOUNDED: 1990

AREAS OF INTEREST:
Gastroenterology and related fields.

NAME(S) OF PROGRAMS:
- **AGA-Bern Schwartz Family Fund Research Scholar Award in Pancreatic Cancer**

TYPE:
Research grants. Research Scholar Award provides funding to early career faculty working toward an independent career in digestive disease research.

PURPOSE:
To support early-career investigators working toward independent and productive research careers in digestive diseases by ensuring that a major portion of their time is protected for research.

LEGAL BASIS:
Nonprofit foundation.

ELIGIBILITY:
Applicants must hold an M.D., Ph.D. or equivalent degree(s) and a full-time faculty or equivalent position at an institution in North America by the start of the award. AGA membership is required at the time of application. Proposals spanning the research spectrum, from basic to clinical science, are eligible. Applicants who are physician-scientists, female or from racial/ethnic groups underrepresented in biomedical research are strongly encouraged to apply.

For M.D. applicants, no more than seven years shall have elapsed following the completion of clinical training (GI fellowship or its equivalent) and the start date of this award. For Ph.D. applicants, no more than seven years shall have elapsed following the conferment of the Ph.D. and the start date of this award. Appropriately documented medical or parental leaves of absence will not be counted toward the seven-year eligibility criteria if approved by AGA before application submission. Other exceptional circumstances may also be considered.

At the time of application submission, candidates may not hold, or have held, an NIH K01, K08, K23, K99, R00, R01, R21, R29, Veterans Affairs Career Development Award or any award with similar objectives from non-federal sources. Applicants with an active KL2 or K12 may apply in the final year of KL2/K12 support.

GEOG. RESTRICTIONS: North America.

FINANCIAL DATA:
Amount of support per award: $300,000 ($100,000 per year).

NO. AWARDS: 1.

APPLICATION INFO:
Applications must be submitted through the AGA Grants Management System. Application materials will not be accepted via mail, fax or e-mail.
Duration: Three years.
Deadline: November 10.

ADDRESS INQUIRIES TO:
See e-mail address above.

AMERICAN GASTROENTEROLOGICAL ASSOCIATION (AGA)   [2161]
4930 Del Ray Avenue
Bethesda, MD 20814
(301) 654-2055
Fax: (301) 654-5920
E-mail: awards@gastro.org
Web Site: www.gastro.org/research-and-awards

FOUNDED: 1990

AREAS OF INTEREST:
Gastroenterology and related fields.

NAME(S) OF PROGRAMS:
- **Pilot Research Award in Health Disparities**

TYPE:
Research grants. Research award for independent investigators at any career stage to support research focused on health and health care disparities in digestive diseases. Projects must be related to understanding the causes of or testing interventions intended to eliminate such disparities. They may focus on the pathophysiology, epidemiology, prevention, diagnosis, patient access to or

quality of care, treatment or patient outcomes of a digestive disease or disorder associated with a health difference that is closely linked with economic, social or environmental disadvantage.

PURPOSE:
To provide funds to advance research on health and health care disparities related to digestive diseases.

LEGAL BASIS:
Nonprofit foundation.

ELIGIBILITY:
Applicants must hold an M.D., Ph.D. or equivalent degree and a full-time faculty position or equivalent at an institution in North America. AGA membership is required at the time of application submission.

Applicants performing any type of research relevant to digestive disorders are eligible to apply. Projects must focus on new research areas that could improve the diagnosis and treatment of inflammatory bowel disease (IBD).

Applicants who are physician-scientists, female or from racial/ethnic groups underrepresented in biomedical research are strongly encouraged to apply.

GEOG. RESTRICTIONS: North America.

FINANCIAL DATA:
Amount of support per award: $30,000.

NO. AWARDS: 5.

APPLICATION INFO:
Applications must be submitted through the AGA Grants Management System. Application materials will not be accepted via mail, fax or e-mail.
Duration: One year.
Deadline: August 23.

ADDRESS INQUIRIES TO:
See e-mail address above.

ASPEN RHOADS RESEARCH FOUNDATION [2162]
8401 Colesville Road
Suite 510
Silver Spring, MD 20910
(301) 587-6315
Fax: (301) 587-2365
E-mail: foundation@nutritioncare.org
Web Site: www.nutritioncare.org/foundation

FOUNDED: 1975

AREAS OF INTEREST:
Metabolic issues and nutrition support therapy.

TYPE:
Research grants. Annual support for nutritional research.

YEAR PROGRAM STARTED: 1992

PURPOSE:
To support the personal and professional development of nutrition researchers throughout their careers.

LEGAL BASIS:
Nonprofit foundation.

ELIGIBILITY:
Applicants are encouraged from the fields of medicine, dietetics, nursing and pharmacy. Grants are only given to individuals. There are no citizenship requirements. Preference is given to individuals who are active in developing a career in nutritional research. ASPEN membership is required.

FINANCIAL DATA:
Amount of support per award: Up to $25,000.
Total amount of support: Up to $120,000 annually.

NO. AWARDS: Up to 4 at $25,000; 2 at $10,000.

APPLICATION INFO:
Application form required. Contact the Foundation for additional information.
Duration: One year. Renewal possible up to two years.

PUBLICATIONS:
Application guidelines.

ADDRESS INQUIRIES TO:
Michelle Spangenburg
Director, Education and Research
(See address above.)

CANADIAN LIVER FOUNDATION [2163]
3100 Steeles Avenue East
Suite 801
Markham ON L3R 8T3 Canada
(416) 491-3353
(800) 563-5483 (within Canada and U.S.)
Fax: (905) 752-1540
E-mail: clf@liver.ca
Web Site: www.liver.ca

FOUNDED: 1969

AREAS OF INTEREST:
Research and education into the causes, diagnosis, prevention and treatment of diseases of the liver.

NAME(S) OF PROGRAMS:
● **Canadian Liver Foundation Operating Grant**

TYPE:
Research grants. Operating grants may be offered to one researcher in Canada whose research project is related to hepatobiliary research, one researcher in Canada whose research project is related to hepatitis B, and one researcher in Canada whose research project is related to liver cancer.

YEAR PROGRAM STARTED: 1970

PURPOSE:
To support research projects directed towards a defined objective, conducted by an investigator working alone or in collaboration with others.

LEGAL BASIS:
Registered Canadian charity.

ELIGIBILITY:
Investigators with primary research interest in liver disease who hold an academic appointment in a Canadian university or affiliated institution are eligible to apply. Clinical investigators and basic scientists will be considered. Applicants for operating grants must be members of the Canadian Association for the Study of the Liver.

Canadian citizens, landed immigrants, and permanent residents will receive first consideration.

GEOG. RESTRICTIONS: Canada.

FINANCIAL DATA:
Amount of support per award: $60,000 (CAN) per year.
Total amount of support: Varies depending on the number of suitable candidates and the funds available.

NO. AWARDS: 3 for the year 2020.

APPLICATION INFO:
A single PDF of the entire grant application, including curriculum vitae and other attachments, should be sent by e-mail to researchgrants@liver.ca by the deadline.
Duration: Two years.
Deadline: March 31, for awards to become tenable the following September 1.

PUBLICATIONS:
Program description and guidelines.

STAFF:
Nem Maksimovic, Research Grants Administrator

ADDRESS INQUIRIES TO:
Nem Maksimovic
Research Grants Administrator
(See address above.)

CANADIAN LIVER FOUNDATION [2164]
3100 Steeles Avenue East
Suite 801
Markham ON L3R 8T3 Canada
(416) 491-3353
(800) 563-5483 (within Canada and U.S.)
Fax: (905) 752-1540
E-mail: clf@liver.ca
Web Site: www.liver.ca

FOUNDED: 1969

AREAS OF INTEREST:
Research and education into the causes, diagnosis, prevention and treatment of diseases of the liver.

NAME(S) OF PROGRAMS:
● **Graduate Studentships**

TYPE:
Scholarships. One graduate studentship may be awarded to a student in Alberta whose research project is related to hepatobiliary research and two graduate studentships may be awarded to students in Canada whose research projects are related to hepatitis B.

PURPOSE:
To enable academically superior students to undertake full-time studies in a Canadian university in a discipline relevant to the objectives of the Foundation.

LEGAL BASIS:
Registered Canadian charity.

ELIGIBILITY:
Applicants must be accepted into a full-time university graduate science program in a medically-related discipline related to a Master's or doctoral degree and hold a record of superior academic performance in studies relevant to the proposed training.

Canadian citizens, landed immigrants, and permanent residents will receive first consideration.

Applicants must be sponsored by a faculty supervisor with a record of productive medical research and sufficient competitively acquired research funding to ensure the satisfactory conduct of the student's research during the term of the award. The supervisor's publication record should indicate significant contribution to liver related studies. The supervisor must agree to provide personal, direct and continuing supervision of the student and must be a member of the Canadian Association for the Study of the Liver.

GEOG. RESTRICTIONS: Canada.

FINANCIAL DATA:
Amount of support per award: $20,000 (CAN) per year paid in quarterly installments.

NO. AWARDS: 3 for the year 2020.

APPLICATION INFO:
A single PDF file of the entire grant application, a Referee's Assessment Form completed by three referees, and a scanned copy of the official transcript must be submitted by e-mail to researchgrants@liver.ca by the deadline.
Duration: Two years.
Deadline: March 31.

PUBLICATIONS:
Program description and guidelines.

STAFF:
Nem Maksimovic, Manager, National Health Promotion and Education

ADDRESS INQUIRIES TO:
Nem Maksimovic, Manager
National Health Promotion
and Education
(See address above.)

CANADIAN LIVER FOUNDATION

3100 Steeles Avenue East
Suite 801
Markham ON L3R 8T3 Canada
(416) 491-3353
(800) 563-5483 (within Canada and U.S.)
Fax: (905) 752-1540
E-mail: clf@liver.ca
Web Site: www.liver.ca

TYPE:
Scholarships. One summer studentship grant may be awarded to a student in Canada whose research project is related to hepatobiliary research. Two summer studentship grants may be awarded to students in Canada whose research projects are related to liver cancer. One Raj Bhargava Memorial Summer Studentship may be awarded to a student enrolled at the University of Alberta whose research project is related to radiology of liver disease.

See entry 2023 for full listing.

COOLEY'S ANEMIA FOUNDATION, INC. [2165]

330 7th Avenue
Suite 200
New York, NY 10001-5264
(212) 279-8090 ext. 201
Fax: (212) 279-5999
E-mail: info@thalassemia.org
Web Site: www.thalassemia.org

FOUNDED: 1954

AREAS OF INTEREST:
Cooley's anemia and all thalassemias.

TYPE:
Fellowships; Research grants. Clinical grants. Research, public and professional education, patient care and public information. Basic and clinical research and fellowships.

YEAR PROGRAM STARTED: 1954

PURPOSE:
To provide impetus to benefit the advancement of knowledge and the quality of care in Cooley's anemia and other thalassemias.

LEGAL BASIS:
Federal tax-exempt, nonprofit, voluntary health agency.

ELIGIBILITY:
Medical researchers who are interested in initiating a thalassemia related project or who have an existing project that requires additional funding may apply.

FINANCIAL DATA:
Amount of support per award: Fellowships: $50,000; Clinical grants: Up to $50,000.
Total amount of support: $250,000 for the year 2020.

NO. MOST RECENT APPLICANTS: 30.

APPLICATION INFO:
Applications are available on the Foundation web site.
Duration: One year. Possibility for renewal for second year.
Deadline: First Monday in February.

PUBLICATIONS:
Lifeline Newsletter; screening material; educational pamphlets.

IRS I.D.: 11-1971539

OFFICERS:
Peter Chieco, President

ADDRESS INQUIRIES TO:
Craig Butler, National Executive Director
(See address above.)

CROHN'S AND COLITIS FOUNDATION [2166]

733 Third Avenue, Suite 510
New York, NY 10017
(646) 943-7505
(800) 932-2423
E-mail: grant@crohnscolitisfoundation.org
Web Site: www.crohnscolitisfoundation.org

FOUNDED: 1967

AREAS OF INTEREST:
Research and education in inflammatory bowel disease (Crohn's disease and ulcerative colitis).

CONSULTING OR VOLUNTEER SERVICES:
Medical committees (consisting of physician volunteers) provide services in the areas of patient and professional education, research development, grants review, etc.

NAME(S) OF PROGRAMS:
• **Career Development Award**
• **Research Fellowship Award**
• **Research Initiative**
• **Senior Research Award**
• **Student Research Fellowship Awards**

TYPE:
Awards/prizes; Conferences/seminars; Fellowships; Project/program grants; Research grants; Scholarships; Training grants; Visiting scholars. Career Development Awards prepare potential basic/translational researchers to transition to a career of independent investigation and research.

Research Fellowship Awards support postdoctoral individuals in developing skills related to basic and/or clinical investigation into IBD.

Research Initiative program provides support for cutting-edge translational studies focused on the priority areas to address unmet clinical needs in IBD.

Senior Research Award provides funding for established basic/translational researchers so they are able to generate enough preliminary data to be competitive for additional funding.

Student Research Fellowship Awards are available for undergraduate, graduate, and medical students to support their IBD-related research.

YEAR PROGRAM STARTED: 1967

PURPOSE:
To fund research leading to understanding of and ultimate cure for Crohn's disease and ulcerative colitis.

LEGAL BASIS:
Nonprofit, special-interest foundation.

ELIGIBILITY:
For Career Development Awards, candidates must have at least five years of relevant postdoctoral experience prior to the beginning date of the awards and not in excess of 10 years beyond the attainment of their Doctorate degrees.

For Research Fellowship Awards, candidates must have two years of relevant postdoctoral experience prior to the beginning date of the award.

For Research Training Awards, candidates must be sponsored by a public or private nonprofit institution or a government institution engaged in health care and health-related research within the U.S. and its possessions. Individuals who already are well established in the field are not considered eligible for these awards. Applicants must hold M.D. or Ph.D. degrees and be employed within the U.S. at the time of submission. Eligibility is not restricted by citizenship.

For Senior Research Awards, applicants must be established researchers in the field of inflammatory bowel disease.

FINANCIAL DATA:
Amount of support per award: Career Development Award: $90,000 per year; Research Fellowship Award: $58,250 per year; Senior Research Award: $115,830 per year; Student Research Fellowship Award: Up to $2,500.
Total amount of support: Approximately $28,000,000 annually.

CO-OP FUNDING PROGRAMS:
NASPGHAN/CDHNF.

NO. MOST RECENT APPLICANTS: 500 to 600.

NO. AWARDS: 200.

APPLICATION INFO:
Before submitting a Letter of Intent or Full Proposal, applicants are urged to view the online policies and instructions. After the Letter of Intent is submitted and approved, Research Grants Administration will send an e-mail to the applicant with a link to complete and submit a Full Proposal.
Duration: Career Development Award, Research Fellowship Award and Senior Research Award: One to three years.
Deadline: Career Development Award, Research Fellowship Award and Senior Research Award: Letter of Intent due November 8 for Spring/Summer and May 5 for Fall/Winter. Online Application due January 28 for Spring/Summer and July 20 for Fall/Winter. Decision June and December, respectively; Student Research Fellowship Awards: March 31. Awards begin on or about June 15.

PUBLICATIONS:
Annual report; *Inflammatory Bowel Diseases*; *Foundation Focus*; brochures.

IRS I.D.: 13-6193105

STAFF:
Michael Osso, President and Chief Executive Officer

FOUNDERS:
Henry D. Janowitz, M.D.
William D. Modell
Irwin M. Rosenthal

ADDRESS INQUIRIES TO:
Orlando Green, Senior Manager
(See address above.)

CYSTIC FIBROSIS FOUNDATION [2167]

4550 Montgomery Avenue
Suite 1100 N
Bethesda, MD 20814
(301) 841-2614
(800) 344-4823
E-mail: grants@cff.org
Web Site: www.cff.org

FOUNDED: 1955

AREAS OF INTEREST:
Research, care and education programs to benefit patients with cystic fibrosis.

NAME(S) OF PROGRAMS:
- **CFF/NIH Unfunded Grants**
- **Clinical Fellowship Awards**
- **Clinical Pilot and Feasibility Awards**
- **Clinical Research Awards**
- **Leroy Matthews Physician/Scientist Award**
- **Pilot and Feasibility Awards**
- **Postdoc-to-Faculty Transition Awards**
- **Postdoctoral Research Fellowship Award**
- **Research Grants**
- **Harry Shwachman Clinical Investigator Award**

TYPE:
Fellowships; Research grants; Training grants. CFF/NIH Unfunded Grants support excellent cystic fibrosis-related research projects that have been submitted to and approved by the National Institute of Health, but cannot be supported by available NIH funds.

Clinical Fellowship Awards encourage specialized training early in a physicians career and prepare candidates for careers in academic medicine.

Clinical Pilot and Feasibility Awards are intended to support projects involving human subjects or samples that will develop and test new hypotheses and/or new methods in research areas relevant to cystic fibrosis.

Clinical Research Awards provide support for generating clinical data that will make future award applications competitive upon submission to the NIH. Projects may address diagnostic or therapeutic methods related to cystic fibrosis or the pathophysiology of CF, and applicants must demonstrate access to a sufficient number of CF patients from CF Foundation-accredited care.

The Leroy Matthews Physician-Scientist Award encourages outstanding newly trained pediatricians and internists to enhance clinical proficiency in cystic fibrosis-related subspecialties and to develop the necessary research capabilities.

Pilot and Feasibility Awards are intended to support basic science research studies focused on developing and testing new hypothesis in areas relevant to cystic fibrosis.

The Postdoc-to-Faculty Transition Awards are designed to support postdoctoral research fellows during their cystic fibrosis fellowship and aid in their transition to an independent research faculty position.

Postdoctoral Research Fellowship Awards are offered to M.D.s, Ph.Ds, and M.D./Ph.D.s who are interested in conducting basic or clinical research related to cystic fibrosis.

Research Grants are intended to encourage the development of new information that contributes to the understanding of the basic etiology and pathogenesis of cystic fibrosis.

The Harry Shwachman Clinical Investigator Award provides the opportunity for clinically-trained physicians to develop into independent biomedical research investigators who are actively involved in cystic fibrosis-related areas. .

YEAR PROGRAM STARTED: 1955

PURPOSE:
To encourage clinical research into the cause, care and treatment of cystic fibrosis; to train specialists for careers in academic medicine.

LEGAL BASIS:
501(c)(3) organization, incorporated as a nonprofit, tax-exempt organization.

ELIGIBILITY:
Contact the Foundation for specific eligibility details for the various grant programs.

FINANCIAL DATA:
Amount of support per award: CFF/NIH Unfunded Grants: Up to $125,000 per year; Clinical Fellowship Awards: Up to $80,000 stipend and $20,000 for research cost; Clinical Pilot and Feasibility Awards: $80,000 annually; Clinical Research Awards: Up to $150,000 per year (single-center) and up to $350,000 per year (multicenter); Leroy Matthews Physician/Scientist Award: $70,000 for year one to $130,000 for year six; Pilot Feasibility Awards: $50,000 per year; Postdoc-to-Faculty Transition Awards: $58,850 to $70,500 stipend, plus $10,000 research support, based on years of postdoctoral experience; Postdoctoral Research Fellowship Award: $58,850 salary and fringe, plus $1,500 travel and $3,000 research support for year one, $61,200 salary and fringe, plus $1,500 travel and $3,000 research support for year two; Research Grants: $125,000 per year; Harry Shwachman Clinical Investigator Award: $100,000 per year, plus $30,000 for supplies.

APPLICATION INFO:
Detailed information can be obtained from the CFF Grants and Contracts Office.
Duration: CFF/NIH Unfunded Grants, Clinical Pilot and Feasibility Awards, Pilot and Feasibility Awards and Research Grants: Up to two years; Clinical Fellowship Awards: Three to five years; Clinical Research Awards: Three years maximum; Leroy Matthews Physician/Scientist Award: Up to six years; Postdoc-to-Faculty Transition Awards: Up to five years; Postdoctoral Research Fellowship Award: Two years; Harry Shwachman Clinical Investigator Award: Three years.
Deadline: Varies. Consult web site for exact dates.

PUBLICATIONS:
Annual report; application form; guidelines.

IRS I.D.: 13-1930701

STAFF:
Michael P. Boyle, M.D., President and Chief Executive Officer
Marc S. Ginsky, Executive Vice President and Chief Operating Officer
Irina Barisic, Executive Vice President and Chief Financial Officer
William Skach, M.D., Executive Vice President and Chief Scientific Officer
Marybeth McMahon, Ph.D., Chief of Staff

ADDRESS INQUIRIES TO:
Grants and Contracts Manager
(See address above.)

DIABETES CANADA [2168]

522 University Avenue
Suite 1300
Toronto ON M5G 2R5 Canada
(416) 363-3373
Fax: (416) 363-7465
E-mail: research@diabetes.ca
Web Site: www.diabetes.ca

FOUNDED: 1953

AREAS OF INTEREST:
Research supporting the prevention, treatment and management of diabetes.

NAME(S) OF PROGRAMS:
- **Charles H. Best Research Fund**

TYPE:
Fellowships; General operating grants; Research grants; Training grants. Scholar awards. Support for new and ongoing research into better ways to prevent, treat, and manage diabetes and to ultimately find a cure.

YEAR PROGRAM STARTED: 1975

PURPOSE:
To promote the health of Canadians through diabetes research, education, service, and advocacy.

LEGAL BASIS:
Nonprofit.

ELIGIBILITY:
Individuals and groups may apply for research programs in Canada only.

GEOG. RESTRICTIONS: Canada.

FINANCIAL DATA:
Total amount of support: Varies.

NO. MOST RECENT APPLICANTS: 200.

APPLICATION INFO:
Guidelines and application form are available on the web site.
Duration: One to five years, depending on the type of grant/award.

ADDRESS INQUIRIES TO:
Research and Education
(See e-mail address above.)

JDRF INTERNATIONAL [2169]

200 Vesey Street
28th Floor
New York, NY 10281
(212) 785-9500
(800) 533-2873
Fax: (212) 785-9595
E-mail: info@jdrf.org
preawardsupport@jdrf.org
Web Site: www.jdrf.org

FOUNDED: 1970

AREAS OF INTEREST:
To support research into the causes, treatment, prevention and cure of diabetes and its complications.

NAME(S) OF PROGRAMS:
- **Strategic Research Agreements: Project Concept Call**

TYPE:
Project/program grants; Research grants; Training grants. Support for a variety of needs, such as salaries for technical assistance, special equipment, animals and supplies for scientific investigations related to diabetes.

YEAR PROGRAM STARTED: 1973

PURPOSE:
To support scientific investigations of diabetes.

LEGAL BASIS:
Incorporated not-for-profit voluntary health agency.

ELIGIBILITY:
Applicants must hold an M.D., D.M.D., D.V.M., Ph.D., or equivalent and have a faculty position or equivalent at a college, university, medical school, company, or other research facility. Applications may be submitted by domestic and foreign nonprofit organizations, public and private, such as colleges, universities, hospitals, laboratories, units of state and local governments, and eligible agencies of the federal government. Ordinarily, for-profit organizations will not be considered, except under special circumstances.

There are no citizenship requirements for this program. To assure continued excellence and diversity among applicants and awardees, JDRF welcomes applications from all qualified individuals and encourages applications from persons with disabilities, women, and members of minority groups underrepresented in the sciences.

Project Concepts are selected on the basis of programmatic fit and robustness of the concept. In addition, projects that hold a prospect for transformative breakthroughs that prevent, treat or cure Type 1 diabetes will be given top priority.

FINANCIAL DATA:
Salary support plus fringe benefits for the principal investigator may not exceed his or her percentage effort on the project multiplied by institutional base salary. Indirect costs (excluding equipment) may not exceed 10% of the total direct costs. Funds may be used for salaries for key project personnel, other costs, travel, supplies, equipment, and subcontract costs.

Amount of support per award: Varies.

Total amount of support: Varies.

APPLICATION INFO:
An investigator interested in pursuing a research opportunity with JDRF must submit a Project Concept through JDRF's Project Concept Call in RMS360 (jdrf.smartsimple.us). Applicants must submit an application that outlines the rationale for the request, a proposed budget, and the principal investigator's other support (current and pending) and curriculum vitae. Only those Project Concepts approved by JDRF will be asked to submit a full research application.

Duration: Up to three years.

Deadline: Project Concepts are due by 5 P.M. on February 4, August 1 and November 1. No extensions will be granted. Notification in March, September and December, respectively.

PUBLICATIONS:
Annual report; policy statement; research appropriations sheet; *Countdown Magazine.*

ADDRESS INQUIRIES TO:
Director, Operations and Administration (See address above.)

JDRF INTERNATIONAL [2170]

200 Vesey Street
28th Floor
New York, NY 10281
(212) 785-9500
(800) 533-2873
Fax: (212) 785-9595
E-mail: info@jdrf.org
Web Site: www.jdrf.org

FOUNDED: 1970

AREAS OF INTEREST:
To support research into the causes, treatment, prevention and cure of diabetes and its complications.

NAME(S) OF PROGRAMS:
- **Postdoctoral Fellowships**

TYPE:
Fellowships. Postdoctoral fellowships to attract qualified and promising scientists entering their professional career into fields of research in diabetes. The applicant is required to work with a sponsor who can provide a training environment most conducive to beginning a career in diabetes-relevant research. Fellowship research may be conducted at foreign and domestic, for-profit and nonprofit, public and private organizations such as universities, colleges, hospitals, laboratories, units of state and local governments, and eligible agencies of the federal government.

YEAR PROGRAM STARTED: 1973

PURPOSE:
To support advanced training in fields of research directly related to diabetes.

LEGAL BASIS:
Incorporated not-for-profit voluntary health agency.

ELIGIBILITY:
By the beginning of the period of support sought, the applicant must have a doctoral degree (M.D., D.M.D., D.V.M., Ph.D. or the equivalent) for no more than five years before the fellowship and may not have a faculty appointment. Each applicant must be sponsored by a scientist who is affiliated full-time with an accredited institution and who agrees to supervise that individual's training. JDRF welcomes applications from persons with disabilities, women and members of minority groups underrepresented in the sciences.

The applicant is responsible for selecting a research mentor and for making arrangements to work in this person's laboratory. The designated mentor must be the senior scientist who will directly supervise the proposed research.

FINANCIAL DATA:
The stipend is dependent on the number of years of relevant experience.

Amount of support per award: Varies.

APPLICATION INFO:
Application forms are available from the address above. Applicants must submit a signed original with 15 copies. The applicant must include three letters of reference assessing the scientific abilities and potential of the applicant and a statement of career goals with the relevance to diabetes-related research. The sponsor must outline a specific training program, confirm the space and facilities for the research project, provide information on all sources of grant support (current or pending, federal or nonfederal) and must include the title, amounts, funding periods and abstract pages of all current and pending support.

Duration: Three years.

Deadline: Contact JDRF for up-to-date details.

PUBLICATIONS:
Annual report; policy statement; research appropriations sheet; *Countdown Magazine.*

ADDRESS INQUIRIES TO:
E-mail: preawardsupport@jdrf.org

*SPECIAL STIPULATIONS:
Awardees will be required to produce a progress report at the end of each funding year. Awardees must spend at least 75% of time and effort on the research project during the period of the award.

JDRF INTERNATIONAL [2171]

200 Vesey Street
28th Floor
New York, NY 10281
(212) 785-9500
(800) 533-2873
Fax: (212) 785-9595
E-mail: info@jdrf.org
Web Site: www.jdrf.org

FOUNDED: 1970

AREAS OF INTEREST:
Prevention and treatment of type I diabetes and its complications.

NAME(S) OF PROGRAMS:
- **Career Development Awards**

TYPE:
Development grants; Research grants; Training grants. Grants are awarded to promising scientists entering their professional career in the diabetes research field. In the five-year term, awardees will focus their research efforts in a subject directly related to JDRF's research mission goals and position themselves to work at the leading edge of diabetes research.

YEAR PROGRAM STARTED: 1979

PURPOSE:
To attract qualified and promising scientists early in their faculty careers and to give them the opportunity to establish themselves in areas that reflect the JDRF research mission goals.

LEGAL BASIS:
Charitable foundation.

ELIGIBILITY:
The individuals must be in a relatively early stage of their career who have demonstrated superior scholarship and show the greatest promise for future achievement in research, including either clinically relevant research or basic research. Ordinarily, their first degree (M.D., Ph.D., D.M.D., D.V.M. or equivalent) will have been received at least three, but not more than seven, years before the award. The applicant must hold an academic faculty-level

position (including assistant professor or equivalent) at the time of the proposal, at a university, health science center or comparable institution with strong, well-established research and training programs for the chosen area of interest.

FINANCIAL DATA:
Indirect costs cannot exceed 10% of subtotal direct costs.
Amount of support per award: Up to $150,000 per year, including indirect costs; these funds may be used for a research allowance, which can include a technician, supplies, equipment and travel up to $2,000 per year. Salary for additional research personnel is permitted. Requests for equipment, in years other than the first year, must be strongly justified. Salary requests must be consistent with the established salary structure of the applicant's institution.

APPLICATION INFO:
Application forms are available from the address above. Applicants must submit a signed original with 15 copies and include three letters of reference assessing the candidate's scientific abilities, assurance from the university of an academic commitment to the applicant and the research project, all other sources of funding (current, federal and nonfederal), with the title, abstract, annual and total amount of support and inclusive funding periods of all current and pending grants.
Duration: Up to five years.
Deadline: Contact JDRF for up-to-date details.

PUBLICATIONS:
Annual report; policy statement; research appropriations sheet; *Countdown Magazine.*

ADDRESS INQUIRIES TO:
E-mail: preawardsupport@jdrf.org

THE KIDNEY FOUNDATION OF CANADA [2172]
5160 Decarie Boulevard, Suite 880
Montreal QC H3X 2H9 Canada
(514) 369-4806
(800) 361-7494
E-mail: christine.marquis@kidney.ca
Web Site: www.kidney.ca

FOUNDED: 1964

AREAS OF INTEREST:
Research that may further the current knowledge pertaining to the kidney and urinary tract or improve health in areas relevant to the vision and mission of the Foundation.

NAME(S) OF PROGRAMS:
● **Kidney Health Research Grants**

TYPE:
Research grants.

YEAR PROGRAM STARTED: 1972

PURPOSE:
To encourage and support research across the four pillars (biomedical, clinical, health systems, and population health) to improve treatments and quality of life for people with kidney disease; to fund the best kidney research across all research pillars conducted at Canadian universities or other recognized Canadian academic institutions.

LEGAL BASIS:
Corporation.

ELIGIBILITY:
A nominated principal applicant is a Canadian citizen or a permanent resident (e.g., a person who has been granted admission to Canada as an immigrant) who is an independent researcher. Applicants with the necessary educational qualifications who are neither Canadian citizens nor permanent residents may be nominated principal applicants if they are employed or can provide evidence that they will be employed by an eligible Canadian institution at the time the grant begins.

Grant applications for equipment only will not be considered.

GEOG. RESTRICTIONS: Canada.

FINANCIAL DATA:
Funds are allocated to assist in defraying the cost of research. This includes materials, supplies and equipment, and the payment of laboratory assistants. Salaries should conform to those of the institution in which the research is carried out and may include the employer's share of staff benefits for which such personnel may be eligible. Personnel employed under grants are employees of the institution concerned, not The Kidney Foundation.
Amount of support per award: Maximum $50,000 (CAN) per year.

NO. AWARDS: Varies depending on funding.

APPLICATION INFO:
All forms, policies and procedures can be found on the proposalCENTRAL web site.
Duration: Up to two years; three years if eligible as a New Investigator. Grants run from July 1 to June 30.

ADDRESS INQUIRIES TO:
Christine Marquis, Research Grants and Awards Manager
(See e-mail address above.)

THE KIDNEY FOUNDATION OF CANADA [2173]
5160 Decarie Boulevard, Suite 880
Montreal QC H3X 2H9 Canada
(514) 369-4806
(800) 361-7494
E-mail: christine.marquis@kidney.ca
Web Site: www.kidney.ca

FOUNDED: 1964

AREAS OF INTEREST:
Research that may further the current knowledge pertaining to the kidney or improve health in areas relevant to the vision and mission of The Kidney Foundation.

NAME(S) OF PROGRAMS:
● **Allied Health Kidney Research Grant**

TYPE:
Research grants.

YEAR PROGRAM STARTED: 1972

PURPOSE:
To encourage allied health professionals to pursue research relevant to the areas of nephrology and organ donation, including clinical, health services, social, cultural, environmental and population health research; to fund the best kidney research across all pillars conducted at Canadian universities or other recognized Canadian academic institutions.

LEGAL BASIS:
Corporation.

ELIGIBILITY:
A nominated principal applicant is a Canadian citizen or a permanent resident (e.g., a person who has been granted admission to Canada as an immigrant) who is an independent researcher. Applicants with the necessary educational qualifications who are neither Canadian citizens nor permanent residents may be nominated principal applicants if they are employed or can provide evidence that they will be employed by an eligible Canadian institution at the time the grant begins.

Funds are available for research conducted in Canada related to clinical practice in nephrology or organ donation and relevant to the mission of the Foundation. Principal applicant must be an allied health professional, including but not limited to, nurses, psychologists, social workers, technicians, biomedical engineers, dietitians, physiotherapists, pharmacists and occupational therapists.

Grant applications for equipment only will not be considered.

GEOG. RESTRICTIONS: Canada.

FINANCIAL DATA:
Grant funds are allocated to assist in defraying the cost of research. This includes materials, supplies and equipment, and the payment of laboratory assistants. Salaries should conform to those of the institution in which the research is carried out and may include the employer's share of staff benefits for which such personnel may be eligible. Personnel employed under grants are employees of the institution concerned, not The Kidney Foundation.
Amount of support per award: Up to $50,000 (CAN) per year.

NO. AWARDS: Varies depending on funding.

APPLICATION INFO:
All forms, policies and procedures can be found on the proposalCENTRAL web site.
Duration: Up to two years. Grants run from July 1 to June 30.

ADDRESS INQUIRIES TO:
Christine Marquis, Research Grants and Awards Manager
(See e-mail address above.)

THE KIDNEY FOUNDATION OF CANADA [2174]
5160 Decarie Boulevard, Suite 880
Montreal QC H3X 2H9 Canada
(514) 369-4806
(800) 361-7494
E-mail: christine.marquis@kidney.ca
Web Site: www.kidney.ca/krescent

FOUNDED: 1964

AREAS OF INTEREST:
All disciplines relevant to kidney disease (i.e., biomedical, clinical, health services and population health).

NAME(S) OF PROGRAMS:
● **KRESCENT: Kidney Research Scientist Core Education and National Training Program**

TYPE:
Awards/prizes. Salary support. The KRESCENT program is comprised of the following categories:
(1) Allied Health Kidney Doctoral Award;
(2) New Investigator Awards and;
(3) Post-doctoral Fellowships.

The objectives of the KRESCENT program are to enhance kidney research capacity by training increased numbers of highly skilled scientists, across multiple disciplines, focused on the prevention of end-stage renal disease and improving the health of Canadians with kidney disease, to engage kidney researchers in the development of transdisciplinary kidney research networks, and to create sustainable momentum in supporting research careers of kidney scientists.

YEAR PROGRAM STARTED: 2005

PURPOSE:
To encourage and support early career kidney research scientists and trainees in multiple disciplines, who will reinvent the future of kidney health research in Canada.

LEGAL BASIS:
Corporation.

ELIGIBILITY:
Applicants must be Canadian citizens or permanent residents at the time of submission of their application.

For the Allied Health Doctoral Fellowship Award, through the KRESCENT program, the Kidney Foundation offers a limited number of fellowships that fund full-time academic study and preparation for research at the doctoral level. The objective of this program is to promote and enhance the development of allied health professionals in Canada in the field of nephrology and/or organ donation.

For New Investigator Awards, applicants must apply through a university department or affiliated institution offering the faculty appointment.

For Post-doctoral Fellowships, applicants must apply through a university department or affiliated institution that has been accepted as suitable for research training by the KRESCENT program. Institutions eligible to host a KRESCENT Fellow include Canadian and foreign universities, affiliated research hospitals, and colleges with a strong research mandate and capacity.

FINANCIAL DATA:
Amount of support per award: Allied Health Kidney Doctoral Award: Maximum $31,000 per year; New Investigator Awards: $65,000 to $70,000 per year, plus match up to $25,000 of infrastructure support (lab start-up costs and staff); Post-doctoral Fellowships: $55,000 to $65,000 per year.

APPLICATION INFO:
All forms, guidelines and procedures can be found on the proposalCENTRAL web site.
Duration: Two to three years.

PUBLICATIONS:
Guidelines; end of award report.

ADDRESS INQUIRIES TO:
Christine Marquis, Research Grants and Awards Manager
(See e-mail address above.)
Stephanie Lord-Fontaine
National Director of Research
(See address above.)

THE KIDNEY FOUNDATION OF CANADA   [2175]
5160 Decarie Boulevard, Suite 880
Montreal QC H3X 2H9 Canada
(514) 369-4806
(800) 361-7494
E-mail: christine.marquis@kidney.ca
Web Site: www.kidney.ca

AREAS OF INTEREST:
Research that may further the current knowledge pertaining to the kidney and urinary tract or improve health in areas relevant to the vision and mission of the Foundation.

NAME(S) OF PROGRAMS:
- **Allied Health Kidney Doctoral Fellowship**
- **Allied Health Kidney Scholarship**

TYPE:
Fellowships; Scholarships. Allied Health Kidney Fellowship program aims to promote and enhance the development of nephrology/organ donation allied health investigators in Canada. The Fellowship is designed to encourage new students to enter doctoral programs, as well as support students currently enrolled in a program.

Allied Health Kidney Scholarship award is to encourage students with a demonstrated interest in nephrology and/or organ donation to pursue education at the Master's level, and in turn to promote and enhance the development of allied health investigators in the nephrology field in Canada.

YEAR PROGRAM STARTED: 1991

PURPOSE:
To promote and enhance the development of nephrology/organ donation allied health investigators in Canada.

LEGAL BASIS:
Corporation.

ELIGIBILITY:
Allied Health Kidney Doctoral Fellowship: Preference will be given to applications submitted by allied health professionals, including but not limited to, nurses, psychologists, social workers, technicians, biomedical engineers, dietitians, pharmacists, physiotherapists and occupational therapists. Applicants must meet the following eligibility requirements:
(1) have Canadian citizenship or landed immigrant status;
(2) have a demonstrated commitment to the area of nephrology or organ donation, with a focus on increasing the number of kidneys available for transplantation, in either direct clinical practice or research experience. Preference will be given to applicants with a minimum of two years full-time equivalent experience;
(3) be accepted in proposed course of full-time study and;
(4) have the intention to return to Canada, if studies are outside the country.

Allied Health Kidney Scholarship: Applicants must meet the following eligibility requirements:
(1) serve as a nephrology nurse or technician, social worker, pharmacist, dietitian, transplant coordinator or other allied health professional;
(2) have a demonstrated commitment to the area of nephrology or organ donation with an interest in kidney research;
(3) have Canadian citizenship or landed immigrant status and;
(4) be accepted in proposed course of full-time or part-time study. Preference will be given to applicants with a minimum of two years full-time equivalent experience.

FINANCIAL DATA:
Amount of support per award: Allied Health Kidney Doctoral Fellowship: $25,000 to

$31,000 per year; Allied Health Kidney Scholarship: Up to $5,000 per year for full-time studies and $2,500 per year for part-time studies up to a maximum of $10,000 (CAN).

NO. AWARDS: Varies depending on funding.

APPLICATION INFO:
Allied Health Kidney Doctoral Fellowship: All forms, policies and procedures can be found on the proposalCENTRAL web site; Allied Health Kidney Scholarship: All applications must be submitted by e-mail.
Duration: Allied Health Kidney Doctoral Fellowship: Two years. Must reapply for third and fourth year of funding; Allied Health Kidney Scholarship: One year. Must reapply for second year of funding.

PUBLICATIONS:
Policies; application forms; end of award report.

ADDRESS INQUIRIES TO:
Christine Marquis, Research Grants and Awards Manager
(See e-mail address above.)

NATIONAL KIDNEY FOUNDATION   [2176]
30 East 33rd Street
New York, NY 10016
(212) 889-2210
(800) 622-9010
Fax: (212) 889-4287
E-mail: research@kidney.org
Web Site: www.kidney.
org/professionals/research/awards

AREAS OF INTEREST:
Improvement in the treatment and prevention of kidney disease.

NAME(S) OF PROGRAMS:
- **Young Investigator Grant Program**

TYPE:
Development grants; Project/program grants; Research grants; Seed money grants.

YEAR PROGRAM STARTED: 1987

PURPOSE:
To support research in the fields of nephrology, urology and related disciplines by individuals who have completed fellowship training and who hold junior faculty positions at university-affiliated medical centers in the U.S.

LEGAL BASIS:
Voluntary health agency.

ELIGIBILITY:
Applications will be considered from individuals who will have completed research training in nephrology or closely related fields prior to the start of the grant award and who intend to pursue research directly related to these areas. At the time funding begins (July 1), the applicant must hold a full-time appointment to a faculty position at a university or an equivalent position as a scientist on the staff of a research-oriented institution, e.g., National Institutes of Health (NIH) or other research organization, in the U.S. Customarily, the appropriate faculty rank is that of Assistant Professor. (In some institutions a title other than Assistant Professor, e.g., Instructor, is used to designate junior faculty status; individuals at that rank in such institutions are eligible to

apply for a Young Investigator Grant). Qualifications should be documented in the bio-sketch (maximum four pages).

Young Investigator Grants will be awarded to individuals no later than four years after initial appointment to a faculty (or equivalent) position or after appointment to a staff scientist (or equivalent) position in a research organization. It is the responsibility of the applicant to demonstrate that he or she satisfies the eligibility requirements for a Young Investigator Grant. Eligibility rules will be strictly enforced. Anyone who may not be certain as to his or her eligibility should request an advisory opinion from NKF staff before submitting an application.

Young Investigator Grants are primarily intended to support research by individuals holding M.D. or Ph.D. degrees who are commencing careers on the faculty of medical schools or research institutions. In all cases, the applicant's research and career goals must be directed to the study of normal or abnormal kidney function or of diseases of the kidney and urinary tract. Only one investigator in an institution will be supported in any funding cycle by a Young Investigator Grant. Since the NKF research support program is an integral part of the Foundation's overall scientific mission, it is expected that candidates for support pursuant to this funding mechanism participate as dues-paying professional members of the National Kidney Foundation, Inc.

GEOG. RESTRICTIONS: United States.

FINANCIAL DATA:
Amount of support per award: $35,000.

NO. MOST RECENT APPLICANTS: 15.

NO. AWARDS: 3 to 5.

APPLICATION INFO:
Application form, letter of commitment from the applicant's department and three letters of recommendation are required.
Duration: One year, with the opportunity to apply for a second year of funding.
Deadline: Second Monday in February.

PUBLICATIONS:
Program announcement.

STAFF:
Kerry Willis, Chief Scientific Officer
Jessica Joseph, Senior Vice President, Scientific Operations
Kiley Thornton, Director, Professional Membership

ADDRESS INQUIRIES TO:
Kiley Thornton
Director, Professional Membership
(See address above.)

Oncology

AMERICAN ASSOCIATION FOR CANCER RESEARCH [2177]
615 Chestnut Street, 17th Floor
Philadelphia, PA 19106
(215) 440-9300
Fax: (267) 825-9550
E-mail: grants@aacr.org
Web Site: www.aacr.org

FOUNDED: 1907

AREAS OF INTEREST:
Cancer.

NAME(S) OF PROGRAMS:
- **AACR Independent Investigator Grants**
- **AACR NextGen Grants for Transformative Cancer Research**
- **AACR Team Science Grants**
- **Career Development Awards**
- **Research Grants and Fellowships**
- **Scholar-in-Training Awards**

TYPE:
Awards/prizes; Fellowships; Research grants; Travel grants. AACR Independent Investigator Grants support research by junior and senior investigators. These grants provide funding for investigators to develop and study new ideas and innovative approaches to cancer research.

AACR NextGen Grants for Transformative Cancer Research support early-career scientists within the first three years of a tenure-eligible faculty appointment. These grants are intended to promote and support creative, paradigm-shifting cancer research that may not be funded through conventional channels.

AACR Team Science Grants provide support for multi-institutional teams conducting innovative, collaborative cancer research.

Career Development Awards in Cancer Research support research by junior investigators. These awards provide an important source of support for direct research expenses as researchers embark on their independent research careers.

Research Fellowships in Basic, Clinical and Translational Research foster cancer research throughout the world by scientists currently at the postdoctoral or clinical research fellow level.

Scholar-in-Training Awards enhance the education and training of graduate students, medical students and residents, clinical fellows or equivalent, and postdoctoral fellows by facilitating their attendance at the Annual Meeting and Special Conferences of the American Association for Cancer Research. These awards are presented to scientists in training who are presenters of abstracts that have been highly rated by AACR.

PURPOSE:
To facilitate communication and dissemination of knowledge among scientists and others dedicated to the cancer problem; to foster research in cancer and related biomedical sciences; to encourage presentation and discussion of new and important observations in the field; to foster public education, science education and training; to advance the understanding of cancer etiology, prevention, diagnosis and treatment throughout the world.

LEGAL BASIS:
Not-for-profit society.

ELIGIBILITY:
Grants are given to individuals. For some programs, applicants must be working at an academic institution in the U.S. No grants to religious organizations. Associate Members of AACR are eligible for awards.

Career Development Award candidates must be full-time, junior faculty at the time the grant term begins. Candidates must also have completed productive postdoctoral research

and demonstrated independent, investigator-initiated research. Employees of a national government and employees of private industry are not eligible. Candidates must be nominated by a member of AACR and must be an AACR member or apply for membership by the time the application is submitted. AACR Associate Members may not serve as nominators.

Fellowship candidates must have completed a Ph.D., M.D., or other doctoral degree. Candidates must be working as a postdoctoral or clinical research fellow at an academic facility, teaching hospital, or research institution, and must be in their second, third, or fourth year of a cancer research fellowship at the beginning of the award year. Academic faculty holding the rank of adjunct professor, associate professor, assistant professor, or higher, graduate or medical students, medical residents, permanent national government employees, and employees of private industry are not eligible. Candidates must be nominated by a member of AACR and must be an AACR member or apply for membership by the time the fellowship application is submitted. AACR Associate Members may not serve as nominators.

Independent Investigator Grant candidates must be full-time faculty at the time the grant term begins. These grants are open to faculty members at all career stages. Employees of a national government and employees of private industry are not eligible.

NextGen Grants for Transformative Cancer Research candidates must be in a full-time, tenure-eligible faculty position for no more than three years at the time the grant term begins. Candidates must also have completed productive postdoctoral research and demonstrated independent, investigator-initiated research. Employees of a national government and employees of private industry are not eligible. Candidates must be nominated by a member of AACR and must be an AACR member or apply for membership by the time the application is submitted. AACR Associate Members may not serve as nominators.

FINANCIAL DATA:
Amount of support per award: Career Development Awards: $75,000 to $100,000 per year; Fellowships: $50,000 to $100,000 salary support per year; Independent Investigators Grants: $100,000 to $200,000 per year; NextGen Grants: $150,000 per year; Team Science Grants: $300,000 to $500,000 per year.
Total amount of support: Varies.

NO. MOST RECENT APPLICANTS: Over 600.

NO. AWARDS: Scholar-in-Training: Approximately 250 per year; Awards and Fellowships: More than 70 per year.

APPLICATION INFO:
Application form is available online.
Duration: Career Development Awards and Independent Investigators Grants: Two to three years. Fellowships: One to three years; NextGen Grants and Team Science Grants: Three years; Scholar-in-Training Awards: One year.
Deadline: Scholar-in-Training: November of each year for Annual Meeting Awards, with notification the following February; Fellowships and Awards: Fall of each year, with notification the following February.

PUBLICATIONS:
Cancer Research, scientific journal; *Clinical Cancer Research*, journal; *Cell Growth and Differentiation*, journal; *Cancer Epidemiology, Biomarkers and Prevention*, journal.

ADDRESS INQUIRIES TO:
Scientific Review and
Grants Administration Department
(See e-mail address above.)

AMERICAN BRAIN TUMOR ASSOCIATION

8550 West Bryn Mawr Avenue
Suite 550
Chicago, IL 60631
(773) 577-8750
Fax: (773) 577-8738
E-mail: grants@abta.org
Web Site: www.abta.org/research

TYPE:
Fellowships; Seed money grants; Training grants. Medical Student Summer Fellowships support a 10- to 12-week summer laboratory experience.

See entry 2204 for full listing.

AMERICAN CANCER SOCIETY, INC. [2178]

250 Williams Street, N.W.
6th Floor
Atlanta, GA 30303-1002
(404) 329-7558
Fax: (404) 417-5974
E-mail: grants@cancer.org
Web Site: www.cancer.org/research

FOUNDED: 1946

AREAS OF INTEREST:
All forms of cancer and their cures.

NAME(S) OF PROGRAMS:
• **Postdoctoral Fellowship**

TYPE:
Fellowships.

YEAR PROGRAM STARTED: 1946

PURPOSE:
To speed the conquest of cancer by training and supporting personnel for cancer research.

LEGAL BASIS:
Nonprofit corporation.

ELIGIBILITY:
Applicants must be U.S. citizens or legal permanent residents. The latter must provide notarized evidence of their legal resident alien status. Applicants who hold doctoral degrees in appropriate disciplines are eligible to apply. Applicant shall have been awarded a doctoral degree prior to the activation of the grant.

GEOG. RESTRICTIONS: United States.

FINANCIAL DATA:
Amount of support per award: Award includes an annual stipend of $52,000 in the first year, $54,000 in the second and $56,000 in the third. Relocation travel expenses for fellow only and a fellowship allowance of up to $4,000 per year.

APPLICATION INFO:
Official application materials are available on the Society's web site.
Duration: Up to three years.

Deadline: For receipt of completed materials: April 1, for approved grants to be activated on or after January 1; and October 15, for approved grants to be activated on July 1.

ADDRESS INQUIRIES TO:
Shannon Pair
Operations Systems Manager
(See address above.)

AMERICAN CANCER SOCIETY, INC. [2179]

250 Williams Street, N.W.
6th Floor
Atlanta, GA 30303-1002
(404) 329-7558
Fax: (404) 417-5974
E-mail: grants@cancer.org
Web Site: www.cancer.org/research

FOUNDED: 1946

AREAS OF INTEREST:
Cancer and its cures.

NAME(S) OF PROGRAMS:
• **Institutional Research Grants**

TYPE:
Block grants. Grants for institutional cancer research projects. Support is available for integration of varied efforts in cancer research within the institution and preliminary testing of new and venturesome ideas for research on cancer by junior investigators without other national research support.

YEAR PROGRAM STARTED: 1957

PURPOSE:
To eliminate cancer as a major health problem by preventing cancer, saving lives and diminishing suffering from cancer through research, education, advocacy and service.

LEGAL BASIS:
Nonprofit corporation.

ELIGIBILITY:
Institutions of higher learning in the U.S. and its territories are eligible to apply for support of appropriate research to be conducted by qualified investigators.

GEOG. RESTRICTIONS: United States.

FINANCIAL DATA:
Amount of support per award: Average $120,000 per year.

APPLICATION INFO:
Grant application materials become available January 1 and are accessible on the Society's web site.
Duration: One to three years. Renewable upon reapplication.
Deadline: April 1.

ADDRESS INQUIRIES TO:
Shannon Pair
Operations Systems Manager
(See address above.)

AMERICAN GASTROENTEROLOGICAL ASSOCIATION (AGA)

4930 Del Ray Avenue
Bethesda, MD 20814
(301) 654-2055
Fax: (301) 654-5920
E-mail: awards@gastro.org
Web Site: www.gastro.org/research-and-awards

TYPE:
Research grants. Research award supporting an established investigator in the field of gastric cancer research working to enhance our fundamental understanding of gastric cancer pathobiology or approaches to prevent, treat or cure gastric cancer.

See entry 2149 for full listing.

AMERICAN INSTITUTE FOR CANCER RESEARCH [2180]

1560 Wilson Boulevard
Suite 1000
Arlington, VA 22209
(202) 600-3004
Fax: (703) 527-8264
E-mail: research@aicr.org
Web Site: www.aicr.org

FOUNDED: 1982

AREAS OF INTEREST:
Diet, nutrition, physical activity and the prevention and treatment of cancer; diet, nutrition, physical activity and cancer survivorship.

NAME(S) OF PROGRAMS:
• **Investigator Initiated Grants (IIG)**

TYPE:
Research grants. The Investigator Initiated Research Grant program is open to researchers at not-for-profit universities, hospitals or research centers. The Institute encourages new research on modifiable lifestyle factors (diet, body weight and physical activity) for preventing and treating cancer, or improving the lives of cancer patients and survivors.

YEAR PROGRAM STARTED: 1983

PURPOSE:
To fund research on cancer prevention, treatment and survival related to diet, nutrition, body composition and physical activity.

ELIGIBILITY:
Institutions: Research grants are awarded to nonprofit institutions in the Americas. Grant applications will not be accepted from agencies of the federal government or agencies supported entirely by the federal government of any country. Proof of nonprofit status of the institution must be submitted with the grant application.

Investigators: The Principal Investigator must have a Ph.D. or equivalent degree or M.D. degree and be a research staff or faculty member at a nonprofit academic or research institution at the minimum level of an assistant professor (or its equivalent) or higher. The Principal Investigator at an institution in the U.S. must be a citizen of the U.S. or foreign national with a permanent residence visa that is valid for the duration of the grant award. In other countries, the Principal Investigator must meet the requirements of that country for permanent residency and employment.

GEOG. RESTRICTIONS: North, Central and South America and the Caribbean.

FINANCIAL DATA:
Amount of support per award: Up to $75,000 per year, plus 10% direct and indirect costs.
Total amount of support: $165,000 to $247,500.

NO. MOST RECENT APPLICANTS: Letters of Intent: 125; Full Applications: 54.

NO. AWARDS: 7 to 10.

APPLICATION INFO:
Online application is required. There are two stages to the application process. Letter of Intent is required before full application invitation.

Duration: One to three years.

Deadline: Letter of Intent: Late January; Full Application: Mid-May.

PUBLICATIONS:
Grant application package; recipients list.

ADDRESS INQUIRIES TO:
Research Department
(See address above.)

CANADIAN CANCER SOCIETY [2181]

55 St. Clair Avenue West
Suite 300
Toronto ON M4V 2Y7 Canada
(416) 961-7223
Fax: (416) 961-4189
E-mail: research@cancer.ca
Web Site: www.cancer.ca/research

FOUNDED: 1947

AREAS OF INTEREST:
Cancer research.

TYPE:
General operating grants; Research grants; Travel grants. Innovation grants. Grants for support of clinical cancer research and basic research projects related to the problem of cancer.

PURPOSE:
To stimulate Canadian investigators in a very broad spectrum of cancer research, not limited to but including biological, chemical, physical, clinical and population health sciences.

LEGAL BASIS:
Registered charity.

ELIGIBILITY:
Applicants must be persons holding eligible appointments at Canadian universities or other recognized Canadian institutions. Basic equipment and research facilities and necessary administrative services must be available at the institution concerned.

GEOG. RESTRICTIONS: Canada.

FINANCIAL DATA:
Grants may be used for the purchase and maintenance of animals, for expendable supplies and minor items of equipment and for payment of graduate students, postdoctoral fellows and technical and professional assistants, but do not include personal support for the grantee.

Amount of support per award: Varies.

Total amount of support: Approximately $40,000,000 (CAN) for fiscal year ended January 2019.

NO. MOST RECENT APPLICANTS: Varies.

NO. AWARDS: Varies.

APPLICATION INFO:
Applications must be made via online application system available on Institute web site.

Duration: Up to five years.

Deadline: Varies.

PUBLICATIONS:
Research report/impact report.

BOARD OF DIRECTORS:
Robert Lawrie, Chairperson

ADDRESS INQUIRIES TO:
See e-mail address above.

CANCER RESEARCH INSTITUTE [2182]

29 Broadway, 4th Floor
New York, NY 10006
(212) 688-7515
(800) 992-2623
Fax: (212) 832-9376
E-mail: grants@cancerresearch.org
Web Site: www.cancerresearch.org

FOUNDED: 1953

AREAS OF INTEREST:
Tumor immunology.

NAME(S) OF PROGRAMS:
● **Cancer Research Institute Irvington Postdoctoral Fellowship**

TYPE:
Fellowships; Research grants; Training grants.

YEAR PROGRAM STARTED: 1971

PURPOSE:
To offer postdoctoral fellowships to qualified individuals in the formative stages of their career who wish to receive training in cancer immunology.

LEGAL BASIS:
Private, nonprofit organization.

ELIGIBILITY:
Applicants must have a doctoral degree and must conduct research under a sponsor who holds a formal appointment at the sponsoring institution. There are no nationality restrictions. Work may be carried out in the U.S. or abroad at nonprofit institutions and medical centers. Fellows with five or more years of postdoctoral experience are ineligible.

FINANCIAL DATA:
Amount of support per award: $55,000 stipend for the first year, $57,000 for the second year, and $59,000 for the third year. An institutional allowance of $1,500 is provided for the host institution to cover laboratory supplies, scientific travel and health insurance on behalf of the fellow.

Total amount of support: Approximately $5,265,000 for the year 2019.

NO. MOST RECENT APPLICANTS: Approximately 350 for the year 2019.

NO. AWARDS: Average 26 annually.

APPLICATION INFO:
Paper applications will not be accepted. Applicants must complete an electronic application form to be submitted with the following attachments:
(1) scanned copy of paper application form with signatures of certifying officers;
(2) brief description of the applicant's background;
(3) list of other funding sources to which applications have been submitted;
(4) applicant's curriculum vitae and bibliography;
(5) brief summary of project with description of how the proposed research is relevant to cancer immunology;
(6) abstract of research in nontechnical English;
(7) concise research proposal, not to exceed six pages;
(8) letter of introduction from sponsor;
(9) sponsor's curriculum vitae, bibliography

and current support and;
(10) letters of reference from two individuals acquainted with applicant's work.

Duration: Up to three years.

Deadline: April 1 and October 1. Notification eight to 10 weeks after the deadline.

PUBLICATIONS:
Annual report; application guidelines.

IRS I.D.: 13-1837442

STAFF:
Jill O'Donnell-Tormey, Chief Executive Officer and Director, Scientific Affairs
Lynne Harmer, Director of Grants Administration

ADDRESS INQUIRIES TO:
Ryan Godfrey, Grants Administrator
(See address above.)

CANCER RESEARCH INSTITUTE [2183]

29 Broadway, 4th Floor
New York, NY 10006
(212) 688-7515
Fax: (212) 832-9376
E-mail: grants@cancerresearch.org
Web Site: www.cancerresearch.org

FOUNDED: 1953

AREAS OF INTEREST:
Tumor immunology.

NAME(S) OF PROGRAMS:
● **Clinic and Laboratory Integration Program (CLIP)**

TYPE:
Awards/prizes; Research grants. This Program awards investigators at tenure-track assistant professor level or higher seeking to answer clinically relevant questions aimed at improving the effectiveness of cancer immunotherapies.

YEAR PROGRAM STARTED: 2011

PURPOSE:
To support qualified scientists who are working to explore clinically relevant questions aimed at improving the effectiveness of cancer immunotherapies; to support basic, preclinical and translational research, which will provide information that can be directly applied to optimizing cancer immunotherapy in the clinic.

ELIGIBILITY:
Investigators must be tenure-track assistant professors or higher when award activates. Eligible organizations must have IRS 501(c)(3) not-for-profit status. Grants are not made to religious organizations.

FINANCIAL DATA:
The award can be used at the recipient's discretion for salary, technical assistance, supplies and/or equipment.

Amount of support per award: Up to $100,000 per year for two years.

NO. MOST RECENT APPLICANTS: 200.

NO. AWARDS: 10.

APPLICATION INFO:
Letters of Intent are accepted November 1 annually. Candidates will be notified by December 15 whether or not they have been invited to submit a full grant proposal. An application form needs to be completed.

Duration: Up to two years. Grant is not renewable.

Deadline: Letters of Intent: November 1 annually. Full application: February 1.

ADDRESS INQUIRIES TO:
Ryan Godfrey, Grants Administrator
Cancer Research Institute
(See address above.)

CANCER RESEARCH INSTITUTE [2184]

29 Broadway, 4th Floor
New York, NY 10006
(212) 688-7515
(800) 992-2623
Fax: (212) 832-9376
E-mail: grants@cancerresearch.org
Web Site: www.cancerresearch.org

FOUNDED: 1953

AREAS OF INTEREST:
Tumor immunology.

NAME(S) OF PROGRAMS:
● **Lloyd J. Old STAR Program**

TYPE:
Research grants. The CRI Lloyd J. Old STAR Program - Scientists Taking Risks - provides long-term funding to midcareer scientists, giving them the freedom and flexibility to pursue high-risk, high-reward research at the forefront of discovery and innovation in cancer immunotherapy.

YEAR PROGRAM STARTED: 2019

PURPOSE:
To support world-class academic investigators who have made notable contributions to immunology and have the greatest potential to propel the field forward.

LEGAL BASIS:
Private, nonprofit organization.

ELIGIBILITY:
Candidates from both U.S. and non-U.S. institutions are eligible to apply, provided that the institution is a nonprofit entity.

Candidates must meet the following requirements:
(1) applicant must have an M.D., Ph.D. or M.D./Ph.D. (or equivalent) and;
(2) applicant must be a tenure-track assistant professor with a minimum of three years in this position appointed on or before July 1, 2018 or a tenure-track associate professor with a maximum of three years in this position appointed on or after July 1, 2018 as of July 1, 2021.

Adjunct or acting positions are not eligible.

FINANCIAL DATA:
Grant payments are issued quarterly to the host institution in U.S. currency.
Amount of support per award: Up to $250,000 per year.
Total amount of support: Varies.

NO. AWARDS: 5 for the year 2020.

APPLICATION INFO:
Applicant must complete the online application form and submit, in exact order, the following documents:
(1) a 300-word abstract which provides an overview of the research questions, goals and approaches of the applicant's lab. Contents should be written in non-technical English;
(2) a research summary (not to exceed four pages) of the ongoing and planned research, highlighting past work and plans for the next five years;
(3) a list of five peer-reviewed papers that

cover the applicant's most important scientific contributions. For each publication provide a citation followed by a 300-word or less summary of the publication's significance. Do not include copies of the publications;
(4) curriculum vitae and bibliography (limit bibliography to past five years and relevant publications) and;
(5) a list of current research support.

Only PDF documents will be accepted. All files must be combined into one document. Do not submit multiple attachments.

Duration: Up to five years.

Deadline: January 15. Notification in early March.

IRS I.D.: 13-1837442

STAFF:
Jill O'Donnell-Tormey, Chief Executive Officer and Director, Scientific Affairs
Lynne Harmer, Director of Grants Administration

ADDRESS INQUIRIES TO:
Ryan Godfrey, Grants Administrator
(See address above.)

*SPECIAL STIPULATIONS:
Applicants are expected to commit a minimum of 80% of their time to conducting research.

CANCER RESEARCH INSTITUTE [2185]

29 Broadway, 4th Floor
New York, NY 10006
(212) 688-7515
(800) 992-2623
Fax: (212) 832-9376
E-mail: grants@cancerresearch.org
Web Site: www.cancerresearch.org

FOUNDED: 1953

AREAS OF INTEREST:
Tumor immunology.

NAME(S) OF PROGRAMS:
● **Technology Impact Award**

TYPE:
Seed money grants. The Cancer Research Institute Technology Impact Award provides seed funding to address the gap between technology development and clinical application of cancer immunotherapies. These grants aim to encourage collaboration between technology developers and clinical cancer immunologists and to generate a proof-of-principle of a novel platform technology in bioinformatics, ex vivo or in silico modeling systems, immunological or tumor profiling instrumentation, methods, reagents and assays, or other relevant technologies that can enable clinical scientists to generate deeper insights into the mechanisms of action of effective or ineffective cancer immunotherapies.

PURPOSE:
To advance technologies that can speed efforts in developing immunotherapies that are effective for all cancer patients.

LEGAL BASIS:
Private, nonprofit organization.

ELIGIBILITY:
Candidates from both U.S. and non-U.S. institutions are eligible to apply, provided that the institution is a nonprofit entity.

Applicants must hold a faculty appointment as a tenure-track assistant professor or higher at the time of award activation. If not, documentation from their institution must accompany the Letter of Intent indicating they will hold the position of assistant professor or higher by the time of award activation.

The grant will be awarded to a scientist who describes an extraordinarily novel, yet practical research plan that is creative and technically sophisticated.

Joint submissions from collaborators will also be considered. The collaborators will share the award. Each collaborator must meet the eligibility criteria.

The most competitive applicants will address areas where technological innovation stands to benefit the field and cancer patients most and that will ultimately lead to effective next generation cancer immunotherapies.

FINANCIAL DATA:
Funds may be used for salary, technical assistance, supplies, capital equipment, or scientific travel. The Cancer Research Institute does not provide funds for indirect costs.

Grant payments are issued quarterly to the host institution in U.S. currency.
Amount of support per award: $100,000 per year.

APPLICATION INFO:
Letter of Intent must be submitted electronically. After completing all of the required fields on the online form, applicant must upload, in exact order, the following supporting documents:
(1) an abstract of research in non-technical English explaining the significance of the new technology platform and its impact on the field of cancer immunotherapy (not to exceed 250 words);
(2) an initial research concept not to exceed three pages;
(3) a brief description of applicant's recent research and;
(4) curriculum vitae and bibliography (bibliography limited to last five years or publications relevant to proposed research). If applicable, curriculum vitae for all group members, as well as a description of each member's research focus.

Duration: One to two years.

Deadline: Letter of Intent: November 15. Full proposal: March 15. Announcement on or about June 30.

IRS I.D.: 13-1837442

STAFF:
Jill O'Donnell-Tormey, Chief Executive Officer and Director, Scientific Affairs
Lynne Harmer, Director of Grants Administration

ADDRESS INQUIRIES TO:
Ryan Godfrey, Grants Administrator
(See address above.)

CANCER RESEARCH SOCIETY [2186]

625 President Kennedy Avenue
Suite 402
Montreal QC H3A 3S5 Canada
(514) 861-9227
E-mail: grants@src-crs.ca
Web Site: www.src-crs.ca

FOUNDED: 1945

AREAS OF INTEREST:
Cancer research.

NAME(S) OF PROGRAMS:
● **Scholarship for the Next Generation of Scientists**

TYPE:
Fellowships; Research grants. One year of salary award as a senior postdoctoral fellow and two-year operating grant available when the awardee secures an academic appointment in a Canadian accredited institution.

YEAR PROGRAM STARTED: 2013

PURPOSE:
To support the future generation of Canadian researchers in the field of cancer research.

LEGAL BASIS:
Nonprofit registered fund-raising corporation.

ELIGIBILITY:
Applicants must be Canadian citizens or permanent residents for the entire scholarship, and must be residing in Canada at the starting date of the operating grant part of the scholarship. Applicants must be holders of a Ph.D. or a professional diploma (M.D., D.M.V.) obtained within the last six years and undergoing an additional postdoctoral training since a minimum of two years, each one of these two years having been completed uninterrupted, with at least 75% of the time devoted to research.

In order to receive the operating grant attached to the award, the awardee must obtain an academic appointment in a Canadian university or accredited institution and must begin his or her functions with 18 months of the start of the fellowship award.

FINANCIAL DATA:
Amount of support per award: $50,000 for the first year (fellowship) and $60,000 for the second and third year (operating grant).

NO. MOST RECENT APPLICANTS: Approximately 30.

NO. AWARDS: 3 to 4.

APPLICATION INFO:
Application information is available on the web site.
Duration: Three years. No renewal possible.
Deadline: Late April.

ADDRESS INQUIRIES TO:
Dajan O'Donnell, Ph.D.
Director of Scientific Affairs and Partnerships
(See address above.)

CANCER RESEARCH SOCIETY   [2187]
625 President Kennedy Avenue
Suite 402
Montreal QC H3A 3S5 Canada
(514) 861-9227
E-mail: grants@src-crs.ca
Web Site: www.src-crs.ca

FOUNDED: 1945

AREAS OF INTEREST:
Cancer research.

NAME(S) OF PROGRAMS:
● **Grants for Cancer Research**

TYPE:
General operating grants.

YEAR PROGRAM STARTED: 1946

PURPOSE:
To find the cause, cure and prevention of cancer.

LEGAL BASIS:
Nonprofit registered fund-raising corporation.

ELIGIBILITY:
Any qualified researcher who is associated with a Canadian accredited institution may apply, provided the research is done in Canada.

GEOG. RESTRICTIONS: Canada.

FINANCIAL DATA:
Amount of support per award: $60,000 per year.
Total amount of support: $8,800,000 in grants budgeted for the year 2020.

CO-OP FUNDING PROGRAMS: Funding through different partnerships available for several of the operating grants.

NO. MOST RECENT APPLICANTS: Approximately 400.

NO. AWARDS: 60 to 70.

APPLICATION INFO:
Application information is available on the web site.
Duration: Two years. Renewal possible.
Deadline: Mid-February.

OFFICERS AND DIRECTORS:
Francois Painchaud, President
Heidi Lange, C.R.H.A., Vice President and Secretary
Marie Valcourt, C.P.A., Treasurer
Ghassan Deko
Benoit Durocher
Annie Lemieux
Peter McCarthy
Monique Mercier
Sean O'Brien
Christian Paupe
Joanna Wilson
George Zogopoulos, M.D., Ph.D.

ADDRESS INQUIRIES TO:
Dajan O'Donnell, Ph.D.
Director of Scientific Affairs and Partnerships
(See address above.)

CANCER RESEARCH UK   [2188]
Research Funding
2 Redman Place
London E20 1JQ England
(44) 020 7242 0200
(44) 020 3469 5452 (grants helpline)
Fax: (44) 020 3469 6400
E-mail: grants.helpline@cancer.org.uk
Web Site: www.cancerresearchuk.org/funding-for-researchers

FOUNDED: 2002

AREAS OF INTEREST:
Research into the causes, diagnosis, treatment and prevention of cancer.

TYPE:
Fellowships; Project/program grants; Research grants; Training grants; Travel grants. There are various grant programs for cancer research including clinical trials. Funding includes research groups, fellowships, programs and project grants.

YEAR PROGRAM STARTED: 2002

PURPOSE:
To carry out world-class research to improve understanding of cancer and find out how to prevent, diagnose and treat different kinds of cancer; to ensure that the findings are used to improve the lives of all cancer patients; to help people to understand cancer, the progress being made and the choices each person can make; to work in partnership with others to achieve the greatest impact in the fight against cancer.

LEGAL BASIS:
Charity (public-funded).

ELIGIBILITY:
Research should be conducted in the U.K. Awards are made to researchers in universities, medical schools and independent research organizations.

GEOG. RESTRICTIONS: United Kingdom.

FINANCIAL DATA:
Amount of support per award: Varies.
Matching fund requirements: Varies.

NO. MOST RECENT APPLICANTS: Over 800.

NO. AWARDS: Over 1,100 projects supported.

APPLICATION INFO:
Contact a member of Research Funding for a discussion prior to sending an application. Applications for funding must be made using the electronic Grants Management System (eGMS).
Duration: Two to six years (longer for clinical trials).
Deadline: Varies.

PUBLICATIONS:
Scientific Yearbook; Annual Review.

THE JANE COFFIN CHILDS MEMORIAL FUND FOR MEDICAL RESEARCH   [2189]
333 Cedar Street
New Haven, CT 06510
(203) 785-4612
Fax: (203) 785-3301
E-mail: jccfund@yale.edu
Web Site: www.jccfund.org

FOUNDED: 1937

AREAS OF INTEREST:
Cancer-related research.

TYPE:
Fellowships. Postdoctoral fellowships for studies in the medical and related sciences bearing on cancer.

YEAR PROGRAM STARTED: 1944

PURPOSE:
To further research into the causes, origins and treatment of cancer.

LEGAL BASIS:
Private foundation.

ELIGIBILITY:
Applicants must be U.S. or foreign citizens holding the M.D. or Ph.D. degree in the proposed field of study (or the equivalent in training and experience) and have no more than one year postdoctoral experience. The prior sponsorship of the laboratory at which they promise to work must be obtained.

Awards to foreign nationals will be made only for work in the U.S., whereas fellowships to American citizens are tenable in the U.S. or any foreign country.

FINANCIAL DATA:
Amount of support per award: $52,000 for year one, $54,000 for year two and $56,000 for year three. A grant of $2,000 per year to

be applied toward the cost of research is usually made available to the sponsoring laboratory each year.

Total amount of support: $4,000,000.

NO. MOST RECENT APPLICANTS: 434.

NO. AWARDS: 25 to 33.

APPLICATION INFO:
Official application materials are available online.

Duration: Three years.

Deadline: February 1 to be considered at late spring meetings.

IRS I.D.: 06-6034840

OFFICERS:
John D. Childs, Chairman
Bronwen Childs, Vice-Chairman and Treasurer

STAFF:
Bonnie Basler, Science Director
Kim Roberts, Executive Director

ADDRESS INQUIRIES TO:
Kim Roberts, Executive Director
(See address above.)

GREENBURG-MAY FOUNDATION [2190]

280 Park Avenue, 41st Floor
New York, NY 10017
(212) 451-3200
E-mail: pmay@trianpartners.com

FOUNDED: 1947

AREAS OF INTEREST:
Medical research, Parkinson's disease, with primary focus on research in cancer and heart disease, the aged, and Jewish institutions.

TYPE:
Development grants; Research grants. Social services.

PURPOSE:
To improve health conditions and expedite cures in many diseases through research.

ELIGIBILITY:
Eligible organizations must be IRS 501(c)(3) tax-exempt and be located in Florida or New York. No funding to individuals.

GEOG. RESTRICTIONS: Florida and New York.

FINANCIAL DATA:
Amount of support per award: Varies depending on project.

Total amount of support: Varies.

APPLICATION INFO:
Applicants must submit a copy of their tax-exempt determination letter. Contact the Foundation for further guidelines.

ADDRESS INQUIRIES TO:
Isabel May, President
(See address above.)

SUSAN G. KOMEN [2191]

5005 LBJ Freeway
Suite 526
Dallas, TX 75244
(972) 855-4390
(877) 465-6636
E-mail: helpdesk@komengrantsaccess.org
Web Site: www.komen.org

FOUNDED: 1982

AREAS OF INTEREST:
Breast cancer research.

CONSULTING OR VOLUNTEER SERVICES:
Through a Komen Affiliate; find a Komen Affiliate on the Organization's web site.

NAME(S) OF PROGRAMS:
- **Career Catalyst Research Grants (CCR)**
- **Global Grants**
- **Graduate Training in Disparities Research (GTDR)**
- **Investigator-Initiated Research (IIR)**
- **Komen Scholar Grants**
- **Postdoctoral Fellowship (PDF)**
- **Promise Grants**

TYPE:
Fellowships; Research grants; Training grants.

YEAR PROGRAM STARTED: 1982

PURPOSE:
To support breast cancer research and awareness.

LEGAL BASIS:
Texas nonprofit corporation.

ELIGIBILITY:
Varies with each award or grant.

FINANCIAL DATA:
Amount of support per award: CCR: Up to $150,000 per year: GTDR: $135,000 per year; IIR: Up to $1,000,000; PDF: $60,000 per year; Promise Grants: Up to $7,500,000.

Total amount of support: Varies per program.

APPLICATION INFO:
Application information is available on the web site.

Duration: CCR and PDF: Two or three years; GTDR: Up to three years; IIR: Three or four years; Promise Grants: Three to five years.

PUBLICATIONS:
Annual report.

IRS I.D.: 75-1835298

LEUKEMIA RESEARCH FOUNDATION [2192]

191 Waukegan Road
Suite 105
Northfield, IL 60093
(847) 424-0600
Fax: (847) 424-0606
E-mail: grants@lrfmail.org
Web Site: www.allbloodcancers.org

FOUNDED: 1946

AREAS OF INTEREST:
Curing all blood cancers.

NAME(S) OF PROGRAMS:
- **New Investigator Awards**

TYPE:
Research grants. The goal of the grant program is to support new investigators. It funds scientists and physicians around the world.

YEAR PROGRAM STARTED: 1946

PURPOSE:
To conquer all blood cancers by funding research into their causes and cures; to enrich the quality of life of those touched by these diseases.

ELIGIBILITY:
Preference will be given to applicants proposing new lines of investigation.

FINANCIAL DATA:
Amount of support per award: Up to $100,000.

Total amount of support: More than $1,000,000 annually.

NO. AWARDS: Varies.

APPLICATION INFO:
Guidelines are posted on the Foundation web site.

Duration: One year. Funding cycle begins July 1.

Deadline: Letter of Intent: Early February. Full application: Early April.

IRS I.D.: 36-6102182

ADDRESS INQUIRIES TO:
Carrie Callas, Research Grants Administrator
(See e-mail address above.)

ONCOLOGY NURSING FOUNDATION [2193]

125 Enterprise Drive
Pittsburgh, PA 15275-1214
(866) 257-4667 (option 4)
E-mail: grants@onfgivesback.org
Web Site: www.onfgivesback.org

FOUNDED: 1981

AREAS OF INTEREST:
Oncology nursing.

TYPE:
Awards/prizes; Research grants; Scholarships.

YEAR PROGRAM STARTED: 1984

PURPOSE:
To provide opportunity for oncology nurses through education, research and leadership to pursue their career goals.

LEGAL BASIS:
National public, nonprofit, charitable organization.

ELIGIBILITY:
Applicant must be a registered nurse actively pursuing a career in some aspect of cancer patient care, education or research, and be a Ph.D. student. Funding preference is given to projects that promote theoretically based oncology practice.

FINANCIAL DATA:
Amount of support per award: Varies.

Total amount of support: Over $700,000 for the year 2019.

NO. AWARDS: Varies.

APPLICATION INFO:
Letters of Intent and applications must be submitted online.

Duration: Research Grant: Up to two years.

Deadline: Varies.

PUBLICATIONS:
Program announcement; applications; guidelines; *Recognition of Achievement: Awards, Grants, Honors, Scholarships.*

THE ELSA U. PARDEE FOUNDATION [2194]

P.O. Box 2767
Midland, MI 48641-2767
(989) 832-3691
E-mail: kmcdonald@pardeefoundation.org
Web Site: www.pardeefoundation.org

FOUNDED: 1944

AREAS OF INTEREST:
Research for control and cure of cancer.

TYPE:

Research grants. Grants for research projects relating to the cure and control of cancer and for the treatment needs of cancer victims.

The Foundation supports activities in two major areas:
(1) innovative and new approaches to cancer research and;
(2) Pardee Cancer Treatment Funds in six counties in central Michigan and one Texas county. The Treatment Funds assist cancer patients, who are residents of those counties, with their treatment expenses.

PURPOSE:

To promote the control and cure of cancer.

LEGAL BASIS:

Private foundation.

ELIGIBILITY:

Grants are limited under the terms of the charter to the cure and control of cancer, and in general do not provide for building funds, equipment (except that used in a specific project), fellowships or fund-raising campaign contributions.

Priority is given to researchers at nonprofit institutions in the U.S. who are new to the field of cancer research, or to established research investigators examining new approaches to cancer cure.

FINANCIAL DATA:

The Foundation has provided more than $146,500,000 since 1944 to support its purpose. Generally, two-thirds of the Foundation's annual gift giving is directed toward research.

Amount of support per award: Grants vary in amount, depending upon the needs and nature of the request.

Total amount of support: $2,523,717 for the year 2019.

NO. MOST RECENT APPLICANTS: 298 for the year 2019.

NO. AWARDS: 17 for the year 2019.

REPRESENTATIVE AWARDS:

$138,939 to the University of Alabama, Birmingham for the study of targeting ncRNA as a curative therapy for metastatic breast cancer; $99,876 to Memorial Sloan Kettering Cancer Center for exercise therapy in lung cancer prevention and treatment; $152,174 to Northwestern University for novel targeted combination therapies based on PIM kinase inhibition.

APPLICATION INFO:

Grant applications are required to be submitted online at the Foundation web site.

Duration: Typically one year.

Deadline: Grant applications are reviewed by the Medical Committee in April, August and December, with final approval occurring at the Board of Trustees meetings in September, December and May, respectively.

PUBLICATIONS:

Annual report; application guidelines.

OFFICERS AND TRUSTEES:

Gail E. Lanphear, President
Lisa J. Gerstacker, Vice President and Assistant Treasurer
William C. Lauderbach, Treasurer
Laurie G. Bouwman, Secretary
W. James Allen, Trustee
Alan W. Ott, Trustee
Bill Schuette, Trustee
William G. Schuette, Trustee
Andreas Teich, Trustee

PREVENT CANCER FOUNDATION [2195]

1600 Duke Street, Suite 500
Alexandria, VA 22314
(703) 836-4412
Fax: (703) 836-4413
E-mail: ximena.marquez@preventcancer.org
Web Site: www.preventcancer.org

FOUNDED: 1985

AREAS OF INTEREST:

Cancer prevention and cancer early detection.

TYPE:

Fellowships; Research grants.
Grants/Fellowships are given for prevention and early detection of cancer through scientific research and education.

PURPOSE:

To support innovative projects in prevention and early detection of cancer through scientific research.

ELIGIBILITY:

Fellowships: Citizenship is unrestricted, but research must be conducted primarily in the U.S. Postdoctoral Fellows (graduate students who will have their doctoral degrees before the project start date) are eligible to apply. Individuals with academic or professional degrees (e.g., M.D., Phar.D., Ph.D.) who are conducting cancer prevention research under the guidance of a mentor are also eligible.

Grants: Citizenship is unrestricted, but research must be conducted primarily in the U.S. Researchers at the instructor or assistant professor level with relevant academic or professional degrees (e.g., M.D., Phar.D., Ph.D.) who are conducting cancer prevention research and researchers who are farther along in their careers and who are shifting their focus to cancer prevention are eligible to apply.

GEOG. RESTRICTIONS: United States.

FINANCIAL DATA:

Indirect costs will not be covered.

Amount of support per award: $50,000 per year.

Total amount of support: Varies.

NO. MOST RECENT APPLICANTS: 56.

APPLICATION INFO:

Application process begins on May 18. Applicants must submit proposals electronically through proposalcentral.altrum.com.

Duration: Two years.

Deadline: June 24.

ADDRESS INQUIRIES TO:

Ximena Marquez, Grants Manager
(See e-mail address above.)

DAMON RUNYON CANCER RESEARCH FOUNDATION [2196]

One Exchange Plaza
55 Broadway, Suite 302
New York, NY 10006
(212) 455-0520
E-mail: awards@damonrunyon.org
shannon.donovan@damonrunyon.org
Web Site: www.damonrunyon.org

FOUNDED: 1946

AREAS OF INTEREST:

All theoretical and experimental research that is relevant to the study of cancer and the search for cancer causes, mechanisms, therapies and prevention.

NAME(S) OF PROGRAMS:

- **Damon Runyon Clinical Investigator Award**
- **Damon Runyon Dale F. Frey Award for Breakthrough Scientists**
- **Damon Runyon Fellowship Award**
- **Damon Runyon Physician-Scientist Training Award**
- **Damon Runyon Quantitative Biology Fellowship Award**
- **Damon Runyon-Rachleff Innovation Award**
- **Damon Runyon-Sohn Pediatric Cancer Fellowship Award**

TYPE:

Fellowships; Project/program grants; Research grants; Training grants. The Damon Runyon Clinical Investigator Award supports early career physician-scientists conducting patient-oriented research. The goal of this innovative program is to increase the number of physicians capable of moving seamlessly between the laboratory and the patient's bedside in search of breakthrough treatments.

Damon Runyon Dale F. Frey Award for Breakthrough Scientists provides additional funding to scientists completing a Damon Runyon Fellowship who are most likely to make paradigm-shifting breakthroughs. This funding is to accelerate their path to independence and their impact on cancer.

The Damon Runyon Fellowship Award supports the training of the brightest postdoctoral scientists as they embark upon their research careers. This funding enables them to be trained by established investigators in leading research laboratories across the country.

The Damon Runyon Physician-Scientist Training Award is designed to encourage outstanding physicians to pursue cancer research careers by providing them with the opportunity for a protected research training experience under the mentorship of a highly qualified and gifted mentor.

The Damon Runyon-Rachleff Innovation Award supports the next generation of exceptionally creative thinkers with high-risk/high-reward ideas that have the potential to significantly impact our understanding of and/or approaches to the prevention, diagnosis or treatment of cancer, but lack sufficient preliminary data to obtain traditional funding.

The Damon Runyon-Sohn Pediatric Cancer Fellowship Award provides funding to basic scientists and clinicians who conduct research with the potential to significantly impact the prevention, diagnosis, or treatment of one or more pediatric cancers.

YEAR PROGRAM STARTED: 1947

PURPOSE:

To advance cancer research through supporting the development of the most promising young talent in cancer research.

LEGAL BASIS:

501(c)(3) organization, classified as a publicly supported organization and not as a private foundation under Section 509(a)(1) of the IRS, incorporated in New York.

ELIGIBILITY:

Clinical Investigator Award: Each applicant must be nominated by his or her institution. Applicants must be conducting independent research at a U.S. research institution and be within the first four years of his or her initial full faculty appointment.

For the Fellowship Award, applicants must have completed one or more of the following degrees or its equivalent: M.D., M.D./Ph.D., Ph.D., D.D.S., D.V.M.

Level I Funding is for basic and physician scientist applicants who must have received their degrees within the year prior to the FAC meeting at which their applications are to be considered.

Level II Funding is for physician scientists (M.D.) and clinical scientists (M.D., M.D./Ph.D., D.D.S., D.V.M. or the equivalent) who have completed their residencies and clinical fellowship training, are board-eligible, and have not yet been appointed Assistant Professor (or equivalent).

The proposed investigation must be conducted at a university, hospital, or research institution. Foreign candidates may only apply to do research in the U.S.

Only candidates who are beginning their first full-time postdoctoral research fellowship are eligible.

Frey Award: Damon Runyon Fellows are eligible to apply in the fourth year of their Fellowship.

Innovation Award: Institutional nominations are not required and there is no limit to the number of applications that can be received from a particular institution. Applicants (including non-U.S. citizens) must be conducting independent research at a U.S. research institution.

Physician-Scientist Training Award: Applicant must have an M.D. degree. Applicants must have completed their residencies and clinical training and be U.S. Specialty Board eligible at the time of application.

FINANCIAL DATA:
Awards are made to institutions for the support of the Damon Runyon scientist, pursuant to the requirements of the specific award. Awardees may be eligible to retire up to $100,000 of their medical school debt for the Clinical Investigator Award, Fellowship Award, Physician-Scientist Training Award, Quantitative Biology Fellowship Award and the Sohn Fellowship Award. A sum of $2,000 is awarded each year to the laboratory in which the Fellow is working, and can be used by the Fellow for their educational and scientific expenses for the Fellowship Award, Quantitative Biology Fellowship Award and Sohn Fellowship Award. Additionally, the Foundation provides a $1,000 Dependent Child Allowance per child per year for the Fellowship Award, Physician-Scientist Training Award, Quantitative Biology Fellowship Award and the Sohn Fellowship Award.

Amount of support per award: Clinical Investigator Award and Innovation Award: $200,000 per year; Dale F. Frey Award: $100,000; Fellowship Award and Sohn Fellowship Award: $223,000 over four years; Physician-Scientist Training Award: $460,000 over four years.

Total amount of support: Clinical Investigator Award: $2,400,000; Dale F. Frey Award: $600,000; Fellowship Award: $7,200,000; Innovation Award: $2,400,000; Physician-Scientist Training Award:

$2,300,000; Quantitative Biology Fellowship Award: $2,200,000; Sohn Fellowship Award: $462,000.

NO. MOST RECENT APPLICANTS: Clinical Investigator Awards: 60; Fellowship Awards: 297; Frey Awards: 19; Innovation Awards: 93; Physician-Scientist Awards: 19; Quantitative Biology Fellowship Award: 29; Sohn Fellowship Awards: 11.

NO. AWARDS: Clinical Investigator Awards: 4; Fellowship Awards: 31; Frey Awards: 6; Innovation Awards: 6; Physician-Scientist Awards: 5; Quantitative Biology Fellowship Award: 9; Sohn Fellowship Awards: 2.

REPRESENTATIVE AWARDS:
Damon Runyon Clinical Investigator Award: Carey K. Anders, M.D., "mTOR inhibition in the treatment of HER2-positive breast cancer brain metastases," with Lisa A. Carey, M.D., and Charles M. Peron, Ph.D., University of North Carolina, Chapel Hill, NC; Damon Runyon Postdoctoral Fellowship: Douglas H. Phanstiel, Ph.D., "Exploring the regulatory role of long-range chromatin interactions," with Michael P. Snyder, Ph.D., Stanford University School of Medicine, Stanford, CA.

APPLICATION INFO:
The following requirements apply:
(1) online At-a-Glance form; the information submitted here must match one's application; therefore, bookmark the "Edit your response" link in case one needs to make changes;
(2) application cover sheet; applicants must submit a hard copy of the cover sheet with all required signatures; signatures can be ink or electronic, or a mix of the two; electronic signatures are acceptable but not required for the USB copy; (if applying under the mentorship of two sponsors, one's second sponsor must fill out the co-sponsor cover sheet;)
(3) sponsor's biographical sketch in NIH format and a list of current funding; do not include sponsor's full bibliography; (if applying under the mentorship of two sponsors, co-Sponsor must also submit a biosketch;)
(4) sponsor's letter including: description of training plan for the candidate; and numerical percentage (_%) of proposal written by the candidate (if applying under the mentorship of two sponsors, the training plan for the candidate must be written jointly and each co-sponsor must submit his or her individual track record of mentorship with list of graduate and postdoctoral fellows trained;)
(5) sponsor's mentorship track record with names and current positions of graduate and postdoctoral trainees from the past 10 years;
(6) applicant's curriculum vitae, including a bibliography of all published works;
(7) applicant's letter of approximately two pages including: description of previous research and teaching experience; statement on the transformative impact he or she had on his or her field of research as a graduate student; if applicant is training at the same institution in which he or she received his or her degree, an explanation of the reasons(s) for remaining at the same institution (can be copied for page 2 of cover sheet);
(8) statement of applicant's long-term commitment to a career in cancer research; this statement should be no longer than one paragraph and indicate what applicant plans to do after completing his or her postdoctoral experience;
(9) research proposal, not to exceed five pages of single-spaced, 12-point type with at least 1/2-inch margins; in the proposal, the

applicant should: provide a summary of the research proposed (this is in addition to the required summary form); provide a brief background to the proposed research; state specific research objectives/aims; describe concisely the method of approach for the proposed research; explain the significance of the proposed research to the Foundation's goals: understanding the causes and mechanisms of cancer and developing more effective cancer therapies and prevention; demonstrate the relevance of his or her own background and the background and previous work of the Sponsor and any other investigators to the proposed research; list references including the full title of each work cited - references are not included in the five-page limit; figures or tables may be appended or incorporated into the text (not to exceed two extra pages); if the figures are incorporated into the text, the proposal may be up to seven pages;
(10) copy of the applicant's degree certificate; applicants who have not yet received their Ph.D. diploma but have successfully completed all Ph.D. requirements, including Ph.D. defense, may submit a letter from their graduate school explicitly stating such, with the dates of the Ph.D. defense and degree conferral;
(11) summary of Research Form, not to exceed one page - no attachments;
(12) if available, PDFs of up to three of applicant's published papers (no submitted manuscripts, no hard copies) and;
(13) if applicable, up to two letters from collaborators indicating their willingness to contribute equipment, materials or expertise (not reference letters).

Duration: Clinical Investigator Award: Three years. Awardees can apply for a two-year continuation grant. Damon Runyon-Sohn Pediatric Cancer Fellowship, Fellowship Award and Physician-Scientist Training Award: Four years. Frey Award: Up to two years. Innovation Award: Two years with the possibility of two years additional funding. Quantitative Biology Fellowship Award: Three years.

Deadline: Clinical Investigator Award: February 1; Damon Runyon-Sohn Pediatric Cancer Fellowship Award: March 15; Fellowship Award: March 15 and August 15; Frey Award: July 15; Innovation Award: July 1; Physician-Scientist Training Award and Quantitative Biology Fellowship Award: December 1.

PUBLICATIONS:
Annual report; award brochures.

ADDRESS INQUIRIES TO:
Clare M. Cahill, Chief Administrative Officer
(See address above.)

THE SKIN CANCER FOUNDATION   [2197]

205 Lexington Avenue, 11th Floor
New York, NY 10016
(212) 725-5176
Fax: (212) 725-5751
E-mail: research@skincancer.org
Web Site: www.skincare.org/about-us/research-grants

FOUNDED: 1979

AREAS OF INTEREST:
Basic and clinical studies that address improved methods of prevention, detection and treatment of skin cancer.

NAME(S) OF PROGRAMS:
● **Research Grants Program**

TYPE:
Awards/prizes; Research grants; Seed money grants.

YEAR PROGRAM STARTED: 1981

PURPOSE:
To reduce the incidence, morbidity, and mortality of skin cancer.

LEGAL BASIS:
Nonprofit foundation.

ELIGIBILITY:
Applications must be for research conducted by dermatology residents, fellows, or junior investigators (five to 10 years past first academic appointment) from institutions within the U.S. and Canada. Preference is given to projects that address, at the basic science and clinical level, improved methods of prevention, detection and treatment of skin cancers.

GEOG. RESTRICTIONS: United States.

FINANCIAL DATA:
Amount of support per award: $25,000 to $50,000.
Total amount of support: $125,000 annually.

NO. MOST RECENT APPLICANTS: 14.

NO. AWARDS: 3.

APPLICATION INFO:
Application information is available on the web site.
Duration: One year.
Deadline: Research Grant: Mid-October.

IRS I.D.: 13-2948778

ADDRESS INQUIRIES TO:
See e-mail address above.

*SPECIAL STIPULATIONS:
E-mail applications are not accepted. Because the amounts of the grants are small, the Foundation does not fund overhead or indirect costs.

LADY TATA MEMORIAL TRUST   [2198]

c/o Mr. F.H. Parekh
Tata Limited
18 Grosvenor Place
London SW1X 7HS England
(44) 020 7235 8281
Fax: (44) 020 7259 5996
E-mail: sonia@tata.co.uk
pam@tata.co.uk
Web Site: www.ladytatatrust.org

FOUNDED: 1933

AREAS OF INTEREST:
Leukemia research.

TYPE:
Fellowships. Studentships (Ph.D.). Annual awards for postgraduate scientists of any nationality to support programs of research likely to throw light on the nature of leukemia. One or more grants of a studentship for a student entering an M.Phil./Ph.D. program is available. The Trustees especially wish to encourage studies on the leukaemogenic agents and on the epidemiology, pathogenesis, immunology and genetic basis of leukemia. The work may be done in any country or in an institution where the candidate has been accepted.

YEAR PROGRAM STARTED: 1933

PURPOSE:
To support research in leukemia.

LEGAL BASIS:
Registered charity.

ELIGIBILITY:
Suitably qualified medical or science graduates of any nationality, who are accepted in the institution where the work is to be undertaken, may apply.

FINANCIAL DATA:
Stipends are paid in quarterly installments. Since amounts vary according to age, qualifications, experience and the scales appropriate to the institution where the applicant has been accepted, intending applicants should try to find out the range of salary that would be appropriate before they apply.
Amount of support per award: GBP 25,000 to 35,000 per annum.
Total amount of support: GBP 350,000 per year.

NO. MOST RECENT APPLICANTS: 40 to 50.

NO. AWARDS: 8 for the year 2020-21.

APPLICATION INFO:
Applications are only accepted online during the current year schedule.
Duration: All awards are tenable for one academic year, October to September. Awards for two years may be given if considered by the Trust to be in best interests of a particular project.
Deadline: March 15. Announcements June 18.

OFFICERS:
Prof. Brian Huntly, Chairperson, Scientific Advisory Board
Prof. Nicholas Cross, Secretary

ADDRESS INQUIRIES TO:
Professor Brian Huntly, Chairperson
c/o Mr. F.H. Parekh
(See address above.)

*SPECIAL STIPULATIONS:
Holders of awards are expected to submit yearly reports on their progress to the Scientific Advisory Committee and to acknowledge the support of the Trust in their publication.

UNION FOR INTERNATIONAL CANCER CONTROL (UICC)   [2199]

31-33 Avenue Giuseppe Motta
1202 Geneva Switzerland
(41) 22 809 1811
Fax: (41) 22 809 1810
E-mail: fellows@uicc.org
Web Site: www.uicc.org/what-we-do/capacity-building

FOUNDED: 1933

AREAS OF INTEREST:
Cancer research, clinical oncology, oncology nursing and voluntary cancer societies.

NAME(S) OF PROGRAMS:
● **Bourses pour L'Afrique Francophone (BAF)**
● **UICC Technical Fellowhips (UICC-TF)**
● **Yamagiwa-Yoshida Memorial International Study Grants (YY)**

TYPE:
Fellowships. The UICC Fellowships Programme provides long-, medium- and short-term fellowships abroad to qualified investigators, clinicians, and nurses, who are actively engaged in cancer research, clinical oncology, or oncology nursing. Short-term scheme offers nonmedical training opportunities in the Asia-Pacific region.

YEAR PROGRAM STARTED: 1933

PURPOSE:
To enable qualified cancer investigators, doctors, nurses, cancer society staff or accredited volunteers to carry out specific research and clinical projects, or to obtain training in cancer society work in appropriate organizations abroad.

ELIGIBILITY:
Candidates must:
(1) possess appropriate professional qualifications and experience according to the specific fellowship applied for;
(2) be currently engaged in cancer research, clinical oncology practice, oncology nursing, or cancer society work;
(3) be on the staff payroll of a university, research laboratory or institute, hospital,

oncology unit, or voluntary cancer society (or be accredited volunteers of such societies) to where they will return at the end of a fellowship and;
(4) have adequate fluency in a language that will permit effective communication at the host institute.
Candidates may submit application for only one fellowship scheme at a time. Applicants who have already obtained a UICC fellowship in the past may apply for further UICC awards only if they are members of the Association of UICC Fellows.

No distinction will be made among candidates on the basis of gender, ethnic origin, religious or political beliefs. Awards are made on the basis of scientific and expert evaluation of the application and the proposed work as set out by the candidate in the project description by reviewers of the highest international standing in their respective fields. Decisions are final and cannot be appealed.

Fellowships are conditional on Fellows returning to the home institutes at the end of the fellowship period. Awards are not granted for basic training courses, lectures, meetings, conferences, congresses or for visiting institutes. They cannot prolong or run concurrently with other awards and cannot be granted to candidates who are already physically present at the proposed host institute while their applications are under consideration.

FINANCIAL DATA:
Amount of support per award: BAF: $2,000 to $3,400; UICC-TF: Up to $3,400; YY: $10,000 average.

NO. AWARDS: BAF: 9 for the year 2018; UICC-TF: 50 to 60; YY: 6 to 8.

APPLICATION INFO:
Applications and all supporting documentation must be submitted in English. Applications may be submitted using the online grant system and will be acknowledged promptly. Candidates will be advised if items are missing. Those proposals that have undergone a review and selection process and were not approved for funding cannot be resubmitted. However, candidates are encouraged to submit new applications for new work programs.
Duration: BAF and UICC-TF: One month. YY: Three months.
Deadline: BAF and UICC-TF: Applications are accepted at any time; YY: October.

ADDRESS INQUIRIES TO:
UICC Fellowships Department
(See address above.)

*SPECIAL STIPULATIONS:
UICC requires an end-of-the-project report in English within one month of the end of the project.

Rheumatology

ARTHRITIS FOUNDATION [2200]
1355 Peachtree Street
Suite 600
Atlanta, GA 30309
(800) 283-7800
E-mail: AFScience@arthritis.org
Web Site: www.arthritis.org/science

FOUNDED: 1948

AREAS OF INTEREST:
Quality of care, juvenile arthritis, osteoarthritis and rheumatology.

TYPE:
Awards/prizes; Research contracts. Deliverable-based contracts.

YEAR PROGRAM STARTED: 1951

PURPOSE:
To support scientific projects that show promise to achieve a faster cure for types of arthritis.

LEGAL BASIS:
Nonprofit organization.

ELIGIBILITY:
The Foundation will post descriptions of opportunities and initiatives on the web site when actively seeking applicants.

FINANCIAL DATA:
Amount of support per award: Varies.
Total amount of support: Varies.

NO. AWARDS: Varies.

APPLICATION INFO:
Official application materials are available from the Foundation.
Duration: One to three years.
Deadline: Varies.

OFFICERS:
Frank Longobardi, Chairperson
Ann M. Palmer, President and Chief Executive Officer

ADDRESS INQUIRIES TO:
Science Department
(See address above.)

THE ARTHRITIS SOCIETY [2201]
393 University Avenue, Suite 1700
Toronto ON M5G 1E6 Canada
(416) 979-7228
Fax: (416) 979-1149
E-mail: research@arthritis.ca
Web Site: arthritis.ca

FOUNDED: 1948

AREAS OF INTEREST:
Arthritis medical and scientific research.

NAME(S) OF PROGRAMS:
- **CRA (CIORA) AS New Clinical Investigator Grant**
- **Graduate Ph.D. Award**
- **Postdoctoral Fellowship Award**
- **Stars Career Development Award**
- **Strategic Operating Grants**

TYPE:
General operating grants; Research grants; Scholarships. Salary awards.

PURPOSE:
To invest in cutting-edge research, proactive advocacy and innovative solutions that will deliver better health outcomes and an improved quality of life for people affected with arthritis.

LEGAL BASIS:
Registered charity.

ELIGIBILITY:
Applicants are restricted to Canadian citizens and permanent residents of Canada. Applicants for research grants must hold faculty appointments at Canadian medical schools. Specific requirements vary by program.

GEOG. RESTRICTIONS: Canada.

FINANCIAL DATA:
Amount of support per award: Varies.
Total amount of support: Varies.
Matching fund requirements: Graduate Student Awards and Postdoctoral Fellowship Awards require a 50:50 match per year.

NO. MOST RECENT APPLICANTS: 100.

NO. AWARDS: 23.

APPLICATION INFO:
Application to any program must be submitted through the Society's online grant management system.
Duration: Varies by program.
Deadline: Varies by program.

PUBLICATIONS:
Annual report; regulations.

BOARD MEMBERS:
Duncan Mathieson, Chairperson
Trish Barbato, President and Chief Executive Officer
Jennifer LaPlante, Treasurer and Chairperson, Audit and Finance Committee
Nancy Hopkins, Chairperson, Governance and Nominating Committee
Dr. Giovanni Di Battista, Director
Ingrid Gutzmann, Director
Thomas Jedrej, Director
Cathy McIntyre, Director
Neal Oswald, Director
Anne-Marie Renaud, Director
Dr. Evelyn Sutton, Director
Michele Walsh, Director
Stephen Weiss, Director

ADDRESS INQUIRIES TO:
The Research Department
(See e-mail address above.)

LUPUS FOUNDATION OF AMERICA, INC.
2121 K Street, N.W., Suite 200
Washington, DC 20037
(202) 349-1150 ext. 150
(800) 875-2562 (customer support)
Fax: (202) 349-1156
E-mail: marion@lupus.org
Web Site: www.lupus.org/finzifellowships

TYPE:
Summer Fellowship. The Gina M. Finzi Memorial Student Summer Fellowship Program proposes to foster an interest among students in the areas of basic, clinical, translational, epidemiological or behavioral research relevant to lupus under the sponsorship and supervision of an established, tenure-track Principal Investigator who directs a laboratory dedicated at least in part to the investigation of lupus at a U.S. or Canadian academic, medical or research institution.

See entry 2045 for full listing.

Neurology

THE ALS ASSOCIATION [2202]
National Headquarters
1300 Wilson Boulevard, Suite 600
Arlington, VA 22209
(202) 407-8580
E-mail: researchgrants@alsa-national.org
Web Site: www.alsa.org

FOUNDED: 1985

AREAS OF INTEREST:
Amyotrophic lateral sclerosis (ALS) programs include research grants, patient services, public education and awareness, local chapter development, and advocacy.

NAME(S) OF PROGRAMS:
- **Research Grant Program**

TYPE:
Awards/prizes; Conferences/seminars; Fellowships; Project/program grants; Research grants; Technical assistance; Research contracts. Grants, for a specified number of years, to neuroscientific researchers to pursue a project of relevance to Amyotrophic Lateral Sclerosis. Both basic and clinical research supported (including postdoctoral fellowships). The ALS Association forms partnerships on clinical trials.

YEAR PROGRAM STARTED: 1985

PURPOSE:
To direct, encourage, identify, fund and monitor relevant and cutting-edge research into the cause, treatment, prevention and cure for amyotrophic lateral sclerosis.

LEGAL BASIS:
Nonprofit voluntary health agency under IRS 501(c)(3).

ELIGIBILITY:
All nationalities are welcome to apply. Applicant should be a faculty member at a reputable scientific facility.

FINANCIAL DATA:
Amount of support per award: Drug development grants: Maximum $250,000 per year; Multiyear grants: Maximum $100,000 per year; Postdoctoral fellows: Maximum $50,000 per year; Starter grants: Maximum $50,000.
Total amount of support: Varies.

NO. MOST RECENT APPLICANTS: Over 100.

NO. AWARDS: Over 25.

REPRESENTATIVE AWARDS:
$50,000 to Thomas Gaj, Ph.D., Board of Trustees of the University of Illinois; $100,000 to Paul McKeever, B.Sc., Ph.D., The Governing Council of the University of Toronto; $300,000 to Meredith Jackrel, Ph.D., Washington University in St. Louis; $499,413 to Kuti Baruch, Ph.D., ImmunoBrain Checkpoint, Inc.; $200,000 to Dexter Ang, Pison Technology, Inc.

APPLICATION INFO:
Detailed information can be found on the Foundation web site.
Duration: Managing ALS and Postdoctoral fellows: Two years. Multiyear grants: Up to three years. Starter grants: One year.
Deadline: Information available upon request to the e-mail address above.

PUBLICATIONS:
Research ALS Today, newspaper; miscellaneous ALS information and patient care brochures; *ALS Journal News,* monthly.

IRS I.D.: 13-3271855

STAFF:
Kuldip Dave, Ph.D., Vice President, Research

ADDRESS INQUIRIES TO:
See e-mail address above.

ALZHEIMER'S ASSOCIATION [2203]
225 North Michigan Avenue, Floor 17
Chicago, IL 60601-7633
(312) 335-5747
E-mail: grantsapp@alz.org
Web Site: www.alz.org

FOUNDED: 1980

AREAS OF INTEREST:
Basic biology; clinical, adoptive technology, social/behavioral and cognitive/functional.

NAME(S) OF PROGRAMS:
- **Alzheimer's Association Clinician Scientist Fellowship (AACSF)**
- **Alzheimer's Association Clinician Scientist Fellowship to Promote Diversity (AACSF-D)**
- **Alzheimer's Association Research Fellowship (AARF)**
- **Alzheimer's Association Research Fellowship to Promote Diversity (AARF-D)**
- **Alzheimer's Association Research Grant (AARG)**
- **Alzheimer's Association Research Grant to Promote Diversity (AARG-D)**
- **Zenith Fellows Award (ZNTH)**

TYPE:
Fellowships; Research grants; Seed money grants. International Research Grant Program funds investigations that advance our understanding of Alzheimer's disease, help identify new treatment strategies, provide information to improve care for people with dementia, and further our knowledge of brain health and disease prevention. Awards support investigators at every professional stage and always include categories specifically designed to help talented young scientists establish careers in Alzheimer's research. The Association's entire grant portfolio is structured to meet the needs of the field and to nurture fresh ideas.

YEAR PROGRAM STARTED: 1982

PURPOSE:
To accelerate the global effort to eliminate Alzheimer's disease; to connect with scientific, academic, government and industry thought-leaders and key stakeholders worldwide; to become a catalyst toward the time when there will be disease-modifying treatments, preventive strategies and gold-standard care for all people affected by Alzheimer's disease.

LEGAL BASIS:
Voluntary health association, not-for-profit 501(c)(3).

ELIGIBILITY:
Each program has specific requirements. Therefore, contact the Association for additional information.

FINANCIAL DATA:
Amount of support per award: AACSF, AACSF-D, AARF, AARF-D, AARG and AARG-D: Maximum $155,000; ZNTH: $450,000.
Total amount of support: Approximately $37,000,000 for the year 2020.

NO. AWARDS: 139 for the year 2020.

APPLICATION INFO:
The first step in applying for any research grant is to submit a Letter of Intent (LOI) through the proposalCENTRAL online application system at proposalcentral.altum.com. Applications will not be accepted without an approved LOI.

The Association requires all applicants be registered as a reviewer with the Association to submit an LOI. Additionally, it is required that the applicant review at least one grant proposal within their area of expertise, outside the grant competition to which they are applying.

LOI and completed application must be submitted by a single Principal Investigator. A PI cannot submit an LOI that had been approved or rejected during a previous grant cycle. All LOIs must be approved or rejected in the current grant cycle.

Applicants are responsible for adhering to the space limitations, as outlined in the Program Announcement.

Hard copies of the LOI will not be accepted. LOIs will not be accepted after the deadline date.
Duration: Up to three years.
Deadline: Varies per grant cycle.

PUBLICATIONS:
Annual report; application guidelines.

ADDRESS INQUIRIES TO:
See e-mail address above.

AMERICAN BRAIN TUMOR ASSOCIATION [2204]
8550 West Bryn Mawr Avenue
Suite 550
Chicago, IL 60631
(773) 577-8750
Fax: (773) 577-8738
E-mail: grants@abta.org
Web Site: www.abta.org/research

AREAS OF INTEREST:
Brain tumor research.

NAME(S) OF PROGRAMS:
- **ABTA Research Collaboration Grant**
- **Basic Research Fellowship Awards**
- **Discovery Grants**
- **Medical Student Summer Fellowships**

TYPE:
Fellowships; Seed money grants; Training grants. Medical Student Summer Fellowships support a 10- to 12-week summer laboratory experience.

PURPOSE:
To encourage talented scientists early in their careers to enter, or remain in, the field of brain tumor research; to facilitate the development of potentially important research studies; to support innovative brain tumor research.

ELIGIBILITY:
Varies by grant mechanism.

GEOG. RESTRICTIONS: Medical Student Summer Fellowship: United States and Canada.

FINANCIAL DATA:
Amount of support per award: ABTA Research Collaboration Grant: $200,000; Discovery Grants: $50,000; Medical Student Summer Fellowships: $3,000; Research Fellowships: $100,000.

NO. MOST RECENT APPLICANTS: Varies by grant mechanism.

NO. AWARDS: Varies.

APPLICATION INFO:
Details are available on the Association web site.

Duration: ABTA Research Collaboration Grant and Research Fellowships: Two years; Discovery Grants: One year; Medical Student Summer Fellowships: 10 to 12 weeks over the summer.

Deadline: Current deadlines are posted on the Association web site.

ADDRESS INQUIRIES TO:
Research Grants Manager
(See e-mail address above.)

AMERICAN EPILEPSY SOCIETY (AES)   [2205]

135 South LaSalle Street
Suite 2850
Chicago, IL 60603
(312) 883-3800
Fax: (312) 896-5784
E-mail: info@aesnet.org
Web Site: www.aesnet.org

FOUNDED: 1936

AREAS OF INTEREST:
Study and acquisition, dissemination and application of knowledge concerning epilepsy in all its phases including biological, clinical and social.

NAME(S) OF PROGRAMS:
- **Junior Investigator Awards**
- **Postdoctoral Research Fellowship**
- **Predoctoral Research Fellowship**
- **Research and Training Workshops**
- **Seed Grants**
- **Susan S. Spencer Clinical Research Training Fellowship in Epilepsy**

TYPE:
Awards/prizes; Fellowships; Seed money grants. The American Epilepsy Society is one of the oldest neurological professional organizations in the U.S. The Society, in partnership with other organizations, funds Grants and Fellowships that are awarded to individuals with a professional degree whose research impacts an aspect of the study of, and work toward the cure for, epilepsy. Some funding programs are for Society members only.

Junior Investigator Awards support research by recently independent investigators with the intent to facilitate successful competition for subsequent longer-term support from the NIH or other sources. Proposals are welcome across the spectrum of basic, translational, and clinical epilepsy research, including studies of disease mechanisms or treatments, epidemiologic or behavioral studies, the development of new technologies, and health services and outcomes research.

Postdoctoral Research Fellowship: This one-year fellowship, administered by AES, is available to physicians or Ph.D. neuroscientists who desire postdoctoral research experience.

Predoctoral Research Fellowship: This one-year fellowship, administered by AES, is offered to graduate students matriculating in a full-time doctoral (Ph.D.) program with an academic career focus, with dissertation research related to epilepsy.

Research and Training Workshops: The Society, through the Research and Training Committee, provides funding for targeted workshops, intended for clinical or scientific audiences and on specific collaborative topics in neuroscience.

Seed Grants: This grant is to foster collaborative interactions between two or more established investigators to make future grants related to epilepsy more competitive for larger awards and to fuel multi-investigator projects.

Susan S. Spencer Clinical Research Training Fellowship in Epilepsy: A two-year fellowship, administered by the American Academy of Neurology, to support clinical research training in the field of epilepsy.

YEAR PROGRAM STARTED: 1970

PURPOSE:
To promote interdisciplinary communications, scientific investigation and exchange of clinical information about epilepsy; to improve the quality of life for people with epilepsy; to provide those engaged in research with information and assistance of potential benefit in advancing their work.

LEGAL BASIS:
501(c)(3) organization.

ELIGIBILITY:
Details for the different programs can be found online.

FINANCIAL DATA:
Amount of support per award: Varies by mechanism.
Total amount of support: Varies.

CO-OP FUNDING PROGRAMS: The Society has formed alliances with other organizations that provide research funding, including the Grass Foundation, Epilepsy Foundation and other funding sources.

Susan S. Spencer Clinical Research Training Fellowship in Epilepsy is supported by the AAN Foundation, the American Epilepsy Society and the Epilepsy Foundation.

NO. MOST RECENT APPLICANTS: Varies.

NO. AWARDS: Varies.

APPLICATION INFO:
Application information is available on the web site.
Duration: One to two years.
Deadline: Varies.

IRS I.D.: 04-6112600

AMERICAN PARKINSON DISEASE ASSOCIATION, INC.   [2206]

135 Parkinson Avenue
Staten Island, NY 10305
(718) 981-8491
(800) 223-2732
Fax: (718) 981-4399
E-mail: hgray@apdaparkinson.org
Web Site: www.apdaparkinson.org

FOUNDED: 1961

AREAS OF INTEREST:
Parkinson's disease, medical neurology and neuropathology.

NAME(S) OF PROGRAMS:
- **Post-Doctoral Research Fellowships**

TYPE:
Fellowships.

PURPOSE:
To support postdoctoral trainees at U.S. research institutions whose research training focuses on new insights into the pathophysiology, etiology, and/or treatment of Parkinson's disease.

LEGAL BASIS:
Not-for-profit organization.

ELIGIBILITY:
Applicants must have completed their M.D., Ph.D., M.D./Ph.D. or clinical residency program within two years of the onset of the proposed award.

Funding is not to be used for indirect costs, institutional overhead, travel expenses, publication costs higher than $1,000 or equipment costs higher than $8,000.

GEOG. RESTRICTIONS: United States.

FINANCIAL DATA:
Amount of support per award: Maximum $50,000.

APPLICATION INFO:
Completed application must be uploaded as one PDF document. Description of the research proposal should not exceed three pages and should consist of background, specific aims, research design, and a statement of significance for Parkinson's disease research. The applicant's NIH biosketch, the mentor's NIH biosketch, as well as a letter of reference from the mentor and any other key collaborators should be included. The applicant should list all current and pending support, including sponsoring agency, amount and dates for awards. The application should indicate how other sponsored research complements or supplements the present proposal.

The three page limit only applies to the length of the proposal, not the entire application.
Duration: One year. Nonrenewable.
Deadline: March 12. Notification in July.

PUBLICATIONS:
Program announcement; guidelines.

ADDRESS INQUIRIES TO:
Heather Gray, Programs and Research Manager
(See address above.)

BENIGN ESSENTIAL BLEPHAROSPASM RESEARCH FOUNDATION INC.

755 South 11th Street
Suite 211
Beaumont, TX 77701
(409) 832-0788
Fax: (409) 832-0890
E-mail: bebrf@blepharospasm.org
Web Site: www.blepharospasm.org

TYPE:
Project/program grants; Research grants; Seed money grants.

See entry 2263 for full listing.

BRIGHT FOCUS FOUNDATION   [2207]

22512 Gateway Center Drive
Clarksburg, MD 20871
(301) 948-3244
(800) 437-2423
Fax: (301) 948-4403
E-mail: researchgrants@brightfocus.org
Web Site: www.brightfocus.org

FOUNDED: 1973

AREAS OF INTEREST:
Alzheimer's disease research.

NAME(S) OF PROGRAMS:
- **Alzheimer's Disease Research**

TYPE:
Research grants. Awards for basic research into the causes and treatment of Alzheimer's.

YEAR PROGRAM STARTED: 1985

PURPOSE:
To develop treatments, preventions and cures for Alzheimer's disease.

LEGAL BASIS:
Nonprofit foundation.

ELIGIBILITY:
Grants are awarded on the basis of the proposal's scientific merit and its relevance to understanding the disease studied. No funds for large equipment, institutional overhead costs, construction or building expenses.

Fellowships are limited to researchers within five years of doctoral degree conferral.

FINANCIAL DATA:
Amount of support per award: $100,000 per year.
Total amount of support: Varies.

NO. MOST RECENT APPLICANTS: 390 for fiscal year 2020.

NO. AWARDS: 46 for fiscal year 2020.

APPLICATION INFO:
Applications are submitted through ProposalCentral.
Duration: Three-year projects and two-year research fellowships.
Deadline: November 1.

PUBLICATIONS:
Annual report; clinical brochures; newsletters.

ADDRESS INQUIRIES TO:
Kara Summers, Program Officer
(See e-mail address above.)

CUREPSP, INC.   [2208]
1216 Broadway, Second Floor
New York, NY 10001
(347) 294-2871
Fax: (410) 785-7009
E-mail: info@curepsp.org
Web Site: www.curepsp.org

FOUNDED: 1990

AREAS OF INTEREST:
Progressive supranuclear palsy, corticobasal degeneration, and related brain diseases.

TYPE:
Research grants.

YEAR PROGRAM STARTED: 1997

PURPOSE:
To provide support for basic and clinical research in progressive supranuclear palsy and corticobasal degeneration.

ELIGIBILITY:
Qualified investigators affiliated with appropriate institutions are eligible to apply. Applicants must have the approval of the institution where the research training will be conducted. Ph.D. or M.D. status is required.

FINANCIAL DATA:
Amount of support per award: Varies.
Total amount of support: $100,000.

NO. MOST RECENT APPLICANTS: 10 to 20 per round.

NO. AWARDS: 3 to 4 per round.

APPLICATION INFO:
Application information is available on the web site.

Duration: Two to three years with two possible no cost extensions.
Deadline: October and April.

ADDRESS INQUIRIES TO:
Nancy Caccappolo
E-mail: caccappolo@curepsp.org

DYSAUTONOMIA FOUNDATION, INC.   [2209]
315 West 39th Street
Suite 701
New York, NY 10018
(212) 279-1066
Fax: (212) 279-2066
E-mail: info@famdys.org
Web Site: www.familialdysautonomia.org

FOUNDED: 1951

AREAS OF INTEREST:
Familial dysautonomia.

CONSULTING OR VOLUNTEER SERVICES:
Dysautonomia Treatment and Evaluation Center at New York University Medical Center, 530 First Avenue, Suite 9Q, New York, NY 10016, under the direction of Felicia B. Axelrod, M.D.

NAME(S) OF PROGRAMS:
● **Dysautonomia Research Program**

TYPE:
Project/program grants; Research grants; Seed money grants. In addition to support for research and clinical study, the Foundation also provides financial support to the Dysautonomia Treatment and Evaluation Center at NYU and the Israeli FD Center in Tel Aviv.

YEAR PROGRAM STARTED: 1955

PURPOSE:
To fund research for treatment and/or cure for familial dysautonomia; to stimulate and promote medical research into familial dysautonomia (an inherited disease of the autonomic nervous system); to provide information to lay and medical public.

LEGAL BASIS:
Nonprofit, tax-exempt corporation.

ELIGIBILITY:
Researcher connected with a recognized medical and/or teaching institution may apply.

FINANCIAL DATA:
Amount of support per award: Varies, depending upon the needs and nature of the request.
Total amount of support: Varies.

APPLICATION INFO:
Application forms are supplied upon request. Researchers must check online to see if the Foundation is soliciting research application before submitting.
Duration: One year with option to apply for ongoing research and/or renewal. Renewal application (with progress report) is required each year.
Deadline: Contact the Foundation.

IRS I.D.: 13-6145280

EXECUTIVE DIRECTOR:
Lanie Etkind

DYSTONIA MEDICAL RESEARCH FOUNDATION [2210]
One East Wacker Drive
Suite 1730
Chicago, IL 60601-1980
(312) 755-0198
Fax: (312) 803-0138
E-mail: dystonia@dystonia-foundation.org
Web Site: www.dystonia-foundation.org

FOUNDED: 1976

AREAS OF INTEREST:
Dystonia.

NAME(S) OF PROGRAMS:
● **Research Grants**

TYPE:
Project/program grants; Research grants. Research Grants to be used for hypothesis-driven dystonia relevant research.

YEAR PROGRAM STARTED: 1976

PURPOSE:
To fund research into the cause of, treatments and a cure for, dystonia.

LEGAL BASIS:
Private foundation.

ELIGIBILITY:
For all programs, all nonprofit institutions or organizations within the U.S., Canada and those foreign countries where supervision of grant administration is possible are eligible. For all investigations involving humans, approval by the institution's human subject protection committee is necessary. No support for medical care of dystonia patients, construction or alterations. Investigators must have M.D. or Ph.D. degrees.

FINANCIAL DATA:
Support cannot be used for indirect costs, new construction or renovation of existing facilities, consultant fees or travel costs unless specified in the original grant application.
Amount of support per award: $65,000 to $85,000, depending upon the Request for Applications.
Total amount of support: Varies.

APPLICATION INFO:
Application form required for all programs.
Duration: Up to two years.
Deadline: Varies.

PUBLICATIONS:
Guidelines.

IRS I.D.: 95-3378526

ADDRESS INQUIRIES TO:
Jody Roosevelt, Grants Manager
E-mail: jroosevelt@dystonia-foundation.org

EPILEPSY FOUNDATION OF AMERICA   [2211]
8301 Professional Place, Suite 200
Landover, MD 20785-2353
(800) 332-1000
Fax: (301) 577-4941
E-mail: grants@efa.org
research.department@efa.org
Web Site: www.epilepsy.com

FOUNDED: 1968

AREAS OF INTEREST:
Epilepsy research and training.

NAME(S) OF PROGRAMS:
● **AES/EF Clinical Research and Training Fellowship Award**

- **AES/EF Junior Investigator Research Award**
- **Cannabinoids and Epilepsy**
- **My Seizure Gauge**
- **New Therapy Commercialization Grants**
- **Shark Tank Awards**
- **SUDEP Biomarker Challenge**

TYPE:
Fellowships; Research grants; Seed money grants. Commercialization grants; Innovation grants. Seed grants are awarded to clinical investigators or basic scientists for support of biological or behavioral research which will advance the understanding, treatment and prevention of epilepsy.

PURPOSE:
To provide funding for investigators in the early stages of their careers.

LEGAL BASIS:
Private foundation.

ELIGIBILITY:
Criteria varies per initiative.

GEOG. RESTRICTIONS: United States.

FINANCIAL DATA:
Amount of support per award: AES/EF Clinical Research and Training Fellowship Award, AES/EF Junior Investigator Research Award and Cannabinoids and Epilepsy: Up to $50,000; My Seizure Gauge: $1,000,000; New Therapy Commercialization Grants: Up to $200,000; Shark Tank Awards: Up to $150,000; SUDEP Biomarker Challenge: Up to $800,000 prize.

APPLICATION INFO:
Application forms and guidelines are available on the Foundation's web site.
Duration: One to two years.
Deadline: Varies.

ADDRESS INQUIRIES TO:
E-mail: grants@efa.org

THE GRASS FOUNDATION [2212]
P.O. Box 11342
Takoma Park, MD 20913
(310) 405-6915
Fax: (310) 986-2252
E-mail: info@grassfoundation.org
Web Site: www.grassfoundation.org

FOUNDED: 1955

AREAS OF INTEREST:
Research and education in neuroscience.

NAME(S) OF PROGRAMS:
- **Grass Fellowships in Neuroscience**

TYPE:
Fellowships; Research grants. Summer research support for independent research projects in neuroscience at the Marine Biological Laboratories, Woods Hole, MA.

YEAR PROGRAM STARTED: 1955

PURPOSE:
To encourage young investigators in the field of neuroscience.

LEGAL BASIS:
Private foundation.

ELIGIBILITY:
Applicants must be late predoctoral, postdoctoral, or early independent investigators. Fellow must be a U.S. citizen, permanent resident, or have proper visa.

FINANCIAL DATA:
The Grass Foundation pays traveling expenses, reasonable living expenses while at MBL and certain laboratory costs. There is a modest drawing account for personal expenses. Expenses of the spouse or domestic partner and dependent children are likewise paid.
Amount of support per award: Varies.
Total amount of support: Varies.

NO. AWARDS: 10 to 12.

APPLICATION INFO:
Application materials may be obtained from the Foundation's web site.
Duration: 14 weeks.
Deadline: December 5. Announcement in January.

TRUSTEES:
Catherine E. Carr, Ph.D.
Victor Chin, C.F.A.
Elva Diaz, Ph.D.
Kafui Dzirasa, M.D., Ph.D.
Andre Fenton, Ph.D.
Bernice Grafstein, Ph.D.
Henry J. Grass, M.D.
Joshua Grass, Ph.D.
Ronald R. Hoy, Ph.D
Kamran Khodakhah, Ph.D.
Michael Long, Ph.D.
Matt McFarlane, Ph.D, J.D.
Vanessa Ruta, Ph.D.
Felix E. Schweizer, Ph.D
Steven J. Zottoli, Ph.D

ADDRESS INQUIRIES TO:
Executive Assistant
(See address above.)

HUNTINGTON'S DISEASE SOCIETY OF AMERICA, INC. [2213]
505 Eighth Avenue, Suite 902
New York, NY 10018
(212) 242-1968
Fax: (212) 239-3430
E-mail: lfox@hdsa.org
Web Site: www.hdsa.org

FOUNDED: 1967

AREAS OF INTEREST:
Research into Huntington's disease.

NAME(S) OF PROGRAMS:
- **HD Human Biology Project**
- **HDSA Berman-Topper Family Huntington's Disease Career Development Fellowship**
- **Donald King Summer Research Fellowship**

TYPE:
Fellowships; Research grants.

YEAR PROGRAM STARTED: 1986

PURPOSE:
To support and stimulate research into the cause, prevention and treatment of Huntington's disease.

LEGAL BASIS:
Nonprofit, tax-exempt voluntary health agency.

FINANCIAL DATA:
Amount of support per award: HDSA Berman-Topper Fellowship: $80,000 per year; Human Biology Project: $75,000 per year; Summer Research Fellowship: $4,000.
Total amount of support: Varies.

NO. MOST RECENT APPLICANTS: HDSA Berman-Topper Family Fellowship: 8; Human Biology Project: 25; Summer Research Fellowship: 5.

NO. AWARDS: HDSA Berman-Topper Family Fellowship: 1; Human Biology Project: 5; Summer Research Fellowship: 5.

APPLICATION INFO:
Application information is available on the web site.
Duration: HDSA Berman-Topper Family Fellowship: Up to three years. Human Biology Project: One or two years. Nonrenewable. Summer Research Fellowship: 10 weeks.
Deadline: HDSA Berman-Topper Family Fellowship: March. Human Biology Project: Letter of Intent must be received by May; full application deadline is June. Summer Research Fellowship: March.

PUBLICATIONS:
Annual report; application guidelines; *Toward a Cure*; *The Marker*.

IRS I.D.: 13-3349872

TRUSTEES:
Victor Sung, M.D., Chairman
Teresa Srajer, Chairman Elect
Kamran Alam, Treasurer
Jenne Coler-Dark, Secretary
Dan Brennan
Mark Coe
Stacy Coen
Wendy Erier
Erin Furr-Stimming
Jay Hughes
Jonathan Klein
Kelsey Porter
Dominique Thomas
Leslie Thompson, Ph.D.
Vicki Wheelock, M.D.

ADDRESS INQUIRIES TO:
Leora Fox, Ph.D.
Assistant Director of Research
(See address above.)

THE MCKNIGHT ENDOWMENT FUND FOR NEUROSCIENCE [2214]
The McKnight Foundation
710 South Second Street, Suite 400
Minneapolis, MN 55401
(612) 333-4220
E-mail: info@mcknight.org
Web Site: www.mcknight.org

FOUNDED: 1986

AREAS OF INTEREST:
Neuroscience.

NAME(S) OF PROGRAMS:
- **McKnight Neuroscience Scholar Award**

TYPE:
Awards/prizes; Research grants.

PURPOSE:
To encourage neuroscientists in the early stages of their careers to focus on disorders of learning and memory.

LEGAL BASIS:
Nonprofit.

ELIGIBILITY:
Applicants must hold an M.D. and/or Ph.D. degree, have completed formal postdoctoral training and be in the early stages of an independent research career. Applicants

should show evidence of a commitment to a continuing career in neuroscience and be in a tenured or tenure-track position.

GEOG. RESTRICTIONS: United States.

FINANCIAL DATA:
Awards are made to the sponsoring institution.
Amount of support per award: $75,000 per year.

NO. MOST RECENT APPLICANTS: 55.

NO. AWARDS: Up to 6 annually.

APPLICATION INFO:
Application forms and guidelines are available in September.
Duration: Three years.
Deadline: Early January. Announcement by late May.

ADDRESS INQUIRIES TO:
Eileen Maler, Program Manager
(See address above.)

MULTIPLE SCLEROSIS SOCIETY OF CANADA   [2215]
250 Dundas Street West
Suite 500
Toronto ON M5T 2Z5 Canada
(416) 922-6065
(866) 922-6065
Fax: (416) 922-7538
E-mail: ms.grants@mssociety.ca
Web Site: mssociety.ca

FOUNDED: 1948

AREAS OF INTEREST:
Neurology, immunology, virology, pathology and biochemistry, fields of biomedical research, and clinical and population health research.

NAME(S) OF PROGRAMS:
● **endMS Doctoral Studentship Award**
● **endMS Master's Studentship Award**

TYPE:
Research grants. Studentships offered at the Master's and Ph.D. levels.

PURPOSE:
To find the cause and cure of multiple sclerosis.

LEGAL BASIS:
Charitable organization.

ELIGIBILITY:
Applicant must be a Canadian citizen, landed immigrant, or person holding a Canadian student visa who is going to school at a recognized Canadian research institute, or a Canadian citizen or landed immigrant who is going to school at a recognized foreign research institute.

FINANCIAL DATA:
Amount of support per award: Master's: $20,000 (CAN) per year; Ph.D.: $22,000 (CAN) per year; Ph.D. (who hold an M.D.): $50,500 (CAN) per year.
Total amount of support: Varies.

NO. AWARDS: 11 Master's Studentships and 23 Doctoral Studentships for the year 2018-19.

APPLICATION INFO:
Applications must be submitted through ProposalCentral.
Duration: endMS Master's Studentships: Up to two years. No renewals; endMS Doctoral Studentships: Up to four years. No renewals.

Deadline: December 15. Announcement the following June to begin July 1.

ADDRESS INQUIRIES TO:
Research Department
(See e-mail address above.)

MULTIPLE SCLEROSIS SOCIETY OF CANADA   [2216]
250 Dundas Street West
Suite 500
Toronto ON M5T 2Z5 Canada
(416) 922-6065
(866) 922-6065
Fax: (416) 922-7538
E-mail: msresearchgrants@mssociety.ca
Web Site: mssociety.ca

FOUNDED: 1948

AREAS OF INTEREST:
Neurology, immunology, virology, pathology and biochemistry.

NAME(S) OF PROGRAMS:
● **Discovery Research Grant Program**
● **Discovery Research Pilot Grant**

TYPE:
Research grants.

PURPOSE:
To find the cause and cure of multiple sclerosis.

LEGAL BASIS:
Charitable organization.

ELIGIBILITY:
Applicants must carry out research at a recognized Canadian research institute (e.g., university or hospital).

FINANCIAL DATA:
Amount of support per award: Discovery Research Grants: Up to $100,000 (CAN) per year; Discovery Research Pilot Grant: Approximately $50,000 for up to two years.
Total amount of support: Varies.

APPLICATION INFO:
The Society uses an online research grants and awards management system that enables researchers to submit and review applications on the Web. The system is called Easygrants and can be accessed through www.mscanadagrants.ca.
Duration: Discover Research Grant: One to three years; Discover Research Pilot Grant: One to two years.
Deadline: October 1, with announcement the following March.

ADDRESS INQUIRIES TO:
Research Department
(See e-mail address above.)

MULTIPLE SCLEROSIS SOCIETY OF CANADA   [2217]
250 Dundas Street West
Suite 500
Toronto ON M5T 2Z5 Canada
(416) 922-6065
(866) 922-6065
Fax: (416) 922-7538
E-mail: ms.grants@mssociety.ca
Web Site: mssociety.ca

FOUNDED: 1948

AREAS OF INTEREST:
Neurology, immunology, virology, pathology and biochemistry, fields of biomedical research, and clinical and population health research.

NAME(S) OF PROGRAMS:
● **endMS Postdoctoral Fellowship**

TYPE:
Fellowships. The program is intended to support research for training of postdoctoral fellows in studies related to MS.

PURPOSE:
To find the cause and cure of multiple sclerosis.

LEGAL BASIS:
Charitable organization.

ELIGIBILITY:
Applicant must be a Canadian citizen, landed immigrant or person holding a Canadian student visa who is working at a recognized Canadian research institute, or a Canadian citizen or landed immigrant who is working at a recognized foreign research institute. Applicant must have completed their doctoral degree within the last three years by the time of the competition deadline.

FINANCIAL DATA:
Amount of support per award: Postdoctoral Fellows: $41,000 (CAN) per year; Postdoctoral Fellows (for those who hold an M.D.): $50,500 (CAN) per year.
Total amount of support: Varies.

NO. AWARDS: 13 for the year 2018-19.

APPLICATION INFO:
Applications must be submitted through ProposalCentral.
Duration: Up to three years. No renewals.
Deadline: December 15. Announcement the following June to begin July 1.

ADDRESS INQUIRIES TO:
Research Department
(See e-mail address above.)

MUSCULAR DYSTROPHY ASSOCIATION   [2218]
161 North Clark Street
Suite 3550
Chicago, IL 60601
(312) 254-0632
E-mail: grants@mdausa.org
Web Site: www.mda.org

FOUNDED: 1950

AREAS OF INTEREST:
Research into diseases of the neuromuscular system.

NAME(S) OF PROGRAMS:
● **MDA Conference Grants**
● **MDA Development Grants**
● **MDA Idea Awards**
● **MDA Venture Philanthropy Program**

TYPE:
Conferences/seminars; Research grants; Training grants. Translational Research Grants. Basic scientific and clinical research grants are offered.

MDA Conference Grants support meetings and conferences focused on the muscular dystrophies and related diseases of the neuromuscular system. These are the muscular dystrophies (including Duchenne and Becker); motor neuron diseases (including ALS and SMA); the peripheral nerve disorders (CMT and Friedreich's ataxia); inflammatory myopathies; disorders of the neuromuscular junction; and metabolic diseases of muscle as well as other myopathies. Conference grants are awarded to encourage scientific meetings for researchers and/or clinicians to exchange ideas and to establish collaborations. Meetings focused on therapy development will be considered a priority.

MDA Development Grants aim to expand the number of scientists conducting meritorious research in the field of neuromuscular disease.

MDA Idea Awards support bold, innovative research ideas that can have an impact in the field of neuromuscular disease. The idea should be supported by a strong scientific premise and include a feasible experimental plan.

YEAR PROGRAM STARTED: 1950

PURPOSE:
To find the causes of, and treatments for, neuromuscular diseases.

LEGAL BASIS:
Nonprofit, voluntary health agency.

ELIGIBILITY:
An applicant must be a professional or faculty member at an appropriate educational, medical or research institution and be qualified to conduct and supervise a program of original research, have access to institutional resources necessary to conduct the proposed research project and hold a Doctor of Medicine, Doctor of Philosophy, Doctor of Science or equivalent degree.

Proposals from applicants outside the U.S. will be considered only for projects of highest priority to MDA and when, in addition to the applicant's having met the eligibility requirements noted above, one or more of the following conditions exist: the applicant's country of residence has inadequate sources of financial support for biomedical research, collaboration with an MDA-supported U.S. investigator is required to conduct the project, or an invitation to submit an application has been extended by MDA.

MDA Development Grants: Postdoctoral fellows working in the laboratory of a senior investigator under whose guidance the researcher will be given flexibility to work independently or as part of a collaborative effort are encouraged to apply.

FINANCIAL DATA:
Amount of support per award: MDA Development Grants: Up to $70,000 per year; MDA Idea Awards: $25,000.

Total amount of support: Over $8,000,000 for the year 2020.

NO. AWARDS: Approximately 250 research grants annually.

APPLICATION INFO:
Guidelines are available on the web site.

Duration: Varies.

Deadline: Varies.

STAFF:
Donald S. Wood, Ph.D., President and Chief Executive Officer
Michael J. Kennedy, MBA, C.P.A., Executive Vice President and Chief Financial Officer
Sharon Hesterlee, Ph.D., Executive Vice President and Chief Research Officer

ADDRESS INQUIRIES TO:
See e-mail address above.

MYASTHENIA GRAVIS FOUNDATION OF AMERICA, INC. [2219]
290 Turnpike Road
Suite 5-315
Westborough, MA 01581
(800) 541-5454
E-mail: mgfa@myasthenia.org
Web Site: www.myasthenia.org

FOUNDED: 1952

AREAS OF INTEREST:
Myasthenia gravis and related neuromuscular conditions.

CONSULTING OR VOLUNTEER SERVICES:
Nationwide Support Group Network.

NAME(S) OF PROGRAMS:
● **Nursing Research Grant**

TYPE:
Research grants. The Foundation supports research that will improve the lives of patients with myasthenia gravis and related neuromuscular junction disorders. There are five broad research priorities:
(1) Biomarkers: facilitate early diagnosis, predict clinical outcomes and immunosuppressive therapy response and utilize in clinical trials;
(2) Disease Mechanisms: understand basic mechanisms and self-tolerance loss throughout course of disease;
(3) Targeted Therapies: develop new therapeutic targets, prevent widespread immunosuppression and off-target side effects, optimize treatment strategies with existing therapies;
(4) Patient Outcomes: understand the full impact of disease on daily living and patient treatment priorities, understand collateral effects of disease, related medical conditions, side effects and financial impact and;
(5) Pediatric Treatment: identify strategies, safety conforms, and long-term outcomes.

YEAR PROGRAM STARTED: 1988

PURPOSE:
To support research that will improve the lives of patients with myasthenia gravis and related neuromuscular junction disorders.

LEGAL BASIS:
Nonprofit corporate foundation.

ELIGIBILITY:
High impact clinical research proposals should focus on patient outcome measurements or alteration in clinical or research practices that aid in present treatment paradigm. Scientific pilot projects will require a clear plan that will lead to new federal, pharmaceutical, or private foundation supported investigations. The proposal should be within the scope of the research agenda of the Foundation. A clear plan of how success will be assessed is mandatory.

FINANCIAL DATA:
Amount of support per award: Maximum direct cost of $50,000.
Total amount of support: Varies.

NO. AWARDS: 4 for the year 2019.

APPLICATION INFO:
Applicant must submit a Letter of Intent. Full proposal will be requested by invitation only.
Duration: Two years.
Deadline: March 25.

PUBLICATIONS:
Guidelines.

IRS I.D.: 13-5672224

ADDRESS INQUIRIES TO:
See e-mail address above.

NATIONAL ATAXIA FOUNDATION [2220]
600 Highway 169 South
Suite 1725
Minneapolis, MN 55426
(763) 553-0020
Fax: (763) 553-0167
E-mail: beth@ataxia.org
Web Site: www.ataxia.org

FOUNDED: 1957

AREAS OF INTEREST:
Cause and treatment of ataxia.

NAME(S) OF PROGRAMS:
● **National Ataxia Foundation Pioneer SCA3/MJD Translational Research Award**
● **National Ataxia Foundation Postdoctoral Fellowship Award**
● **National Ataxia Foundation Seed Money Research Grant**
● **National Ataxia Foundation Young Investigator Award**

TYPE:
Fellowships; Seed money grants. Young investigator award. Translation research awards.

YEAR PROGRAM STARTED: 1978

PURPOSE:
To support research into hereditary and sporadic ataxia, as well as treatment, services, and education of the disorder.

LEGAL BASIS:
Nonprofit 501(c)(3) organization.

ELIGIBILITY:
Individuals and organizations, including religious, can apply.

FINANCIAL DATA:
Amount of support per award: Pioneer SCA3/MJD Translational Research Award: $100,000; Postdoctoral Fellowship Award: Up to $35,000; Research Seed Money Grant and Young Investigator Award: Up to $50,000.

Total amount of support: Approximately $1,000,000 for the year 2020-21.

NO. MOST RECENT APPLICANTS: 66.

NO. AWARDS: 19 for the year 2021-22.

APPLICATION INFO:
Letter of Intent must be submitted one month prior to application deadlines.
Duration: Pioneer SCA3/MJD Translational Award and Young Investigator Award: One year. Seed Money Research Grant and Research Fellowship: One year. Renewals by reapplication each year for continuing support.
Deadline: Letters of Intent: September 21 for Seed Money Grant; September 28 for Young Investigator Award; October 5 for Pioneer SCA3/MJD Translational Award and Postdoctoral Fellowship Award. Full Proposals: October 19 for Seed Money Grant; October 26 for Young Investigator Award; November 2 for Pioneer SCA3/MJD Translation Award and Postdoctoral Fellowship Award.

PUBLICATIONS:
Annual report; application guidelines.

IRS I.D.: 41-0832903

ADDRESS INQUIRIES TO:
Beth Bowerman
Research Services Coordinator
(See address and e-mail above.)

NATIONAL HEADACHE FOUNDATION

820 North Orleans, Suite 201
Chicago, IL 60610-3132
(312) 274-2650
(888) 643-5552
Fax: (312) 640-9049
E-mail: info@headaches.org
Web Site: www.headaches.org

TYPE:
Research grants. Support for research in the field of headache and pain.

See entry 2120 for full listing.

NATIONAL INSTITUTE OF NEUROLOGICAL DISORDERS AND STROKE [2221]

Building 31, Room 8A34
31 Center Drive, MSC 2540
Bethesda, MD 20892
(301) 496-4927
E-mail: quynh.ly@nih.gov
Web Site: www.ninds.nih.gov

FOUNDED: 1950

AREAS OF INTEREST:
Neurological disorders, including multiple sclerosis and amyotrophic lateral sclerosis, movement disorders, such as the dystonias and Tourette's syndrome and degenerative and dementing disorders such as Parkinson's, Huntington's and Alzheimer's diseases, stroke, spinal cord injury, neural regeneration and plasticity, coma, chronic pain, head injury, traumatic brain injury, peripheral nerve injury, tumors of the nervous system, brain edema and manipulative therapy, and convulsive, developmental and neuromuscular disorders.

TYPE:
Assistantships; Conferences/seminars; Fellowships; Project/program grants; Research grants; Training grants; Research contracts. Support for research, including neurological science basic research, which explores the fundamental structure and function of the brain and the nervous system, research to understand the causes and origins of pathological conditions of the nervous system with the goal of prevention of these disorders, research on the natural course of neurological disorders, research training in the basic neurological sciences and mechanisms associated with stroke and other cerebrovascular disorders, effects of trauma to the nervous system, neuroplasticity and regeneration and tumors of neural and sensory tissues.
Research may include:
(1) improved methods of disease prevention;
(2) new methods of diagnosis and treatment;
(3) clinical trials;
(4) drug development;
(5) development of neural prostheses for stroke and paraplegia;
(6) epidemiological research and;
(7) research training in the clinical sciences.

PURPOSE:
To support research on neurological diseases and stroke.

LEGAL BASIS:
PHS Act, Section 301, Section 431 and Section 433; Public Law 78-410, as amended; (42 U.S.C. 241), (42 U.S.C. 289C). PHS Act, Section 472; Public Law 78-410, as amended; (42 U.S.C. 289L-1).

ELIGIBILITY:
Research grants are available to any public or private nonprofit university, college, hospital, laboratory, or other institution, including state and local units of government, or to any individual. National Research Service Awards for the above areas may be made to individuals or to nonfederal public and private nonprofit institutions for the training of individuals at the pre- and postdoctoral levels.

FINANCIAL DATA:
Grants may be used for any usual research expenses including salaries, equipment supplies, travel to scientific meetings, patient care, publications, etc.
Amount of support per award: Approximately $380,000.
Total amount of support: $2.2 billion appropriated for fiscal year 2019.

APPLICATION INFO:
Application forms may be requested from the Division of Research Grants, National Institutes of Health, Bethesda, MD 20892.
Duration: One to five years. Renewal applications may be submitted.
Deadline: November 1, March 1, and July 1. Awards are announced throughout the year.

ADDRESS INQUIRIES TO:
Director, Division of Extramural Activities
NINDS, NIH MSC 9531
6001 Executive Boulevard
Rockville, MD 20892

NATIONAL MULTIPLE SCLEROSIS SOCIETY [2222]

733 Third Avenue, 3rd Floor
New York, NY 10017-3288
(212) 476-0475
Fax: (212) 986-7981
E-mail: elisabeth.mari@nmss.org
Web Site: www.nationalmssociety.org

FOUNDED: 1946

AREAS OF INTEREST:
Multiple sclerosis.

NAME(S) OF PROGRAMS:
● **Postdoctoral Fellowships Program in Multiple Sclerosis Research**

TYPE:
Fellowships. Postdoctoral fellowships for training leading to an academic career involving clinical or basic research in multiple sclerosis.

YEAR PROGRAM STARTED: 1955

PURPOSE:
To support investigators for whom further assistance may be critical in obtaining the training required for a research or academic career, or for whom the additional training will increase research or teaching potential in areas related to multiple sclerosis.

LEGAL BASIS:
Voluntary health agency, tax status 501(c)(3).

ELIGIBILITY:
Qualified investigators holding a doctoral-level degree in medicine or appropriate biological fields are eligible to

apply. Candidates must select their own training institutions and make all necessary arrangements for the conduct of proposed training or study program. Awards are based upon the applicant's professional status, training and experience.

FINANCIAL DATA:
Candidates must request all funds required.
Amount of support per award: Varies.
Total amount of support: Varies.

NO. MOST RECENT APPLICANTS: Varies.

NO. AWARDS: Varies.

APPLICATION INFO:
Instructions for completing the pre-application and full application are available on the Society's web site.
Duration: Up to three years.
Deadline: Mid-August. Pre-application one week prior to full application deadline.

OFFICERS OF THE BOARD:
Peter A. Galligan, Chairman
Cynthia Zagieboylo, President and Chief Executive Officer
Peter Porrino, Treasurer
Linda J. McAleer, Secretary

ADDRESS INQUIRIES TO:
Elisabeth R. Mari, Ph.D.
Director of Biomedical Programs
(See telephone and e-mail address above.)

NATIONAL MULTIPLE SCLEROSIS SOCIETY [2223]

Research Programs
733 Third Avenue, 3rd Floor
New York, NY 10017-3288
(212) 476-0451
Fax: (212) 986-7981
E-mail: cathy.carlson@nmss.org
Web Site: www.nationalmssociety.org

FOUNDED: 1946

AREAS OF INTEREST:
Multiple sclerosis.

NAME(S) OF PROGRAMS:
● **National Multiple Sclerosis Society Research Grants Program**

TYPE:
Awards/prizes; Fellowships; Research grants; Research contracts. Pilot grants; Training/early career awards. Grants for fundamental or applied research in scientific areas pertinent to multiple sclerosis. Grants are available for clinical or nonclinical studies, providing they show relevance to the Society's research priorities.

YEAR PROGRAM STARTED: 1947

PURPOSE:
To support research into the cause, prevention, alleviation and cure of multiple sclerosis.

LEGAL BASIS:
Voluntary health agency, tax status 501(c)(3).

ELIGIBILITY:
Qualified investigators affiliated with appropriate institutions are eligible to apply. Institutions are the official recipients of grants. Some commercial partnerships supported.

FINANCIAL DATA:
The principal investigator and the grantee institution will be advised of the exact amount and duration of the grant award. Grant funds may be requested for

professional and nonprofessional personnel, consumable supplies, travel and other expenditures and indirect costs.

Amount of support per award: Varies.

Total amount of support: Varies.

NO. MOST RECENT APPLICANTS: 613 for the year 2019.

NO. AWARDS: 110 for the year 2019.

APPLICATION INFO:
Before submitting a proposal for research support, investigators must submit preapplication online to determine whether the research plan is appropriate and relevant to the Society's goals.

Duration: Maximum of five years.

Deadline: February and August for research grants. Usually January, May and September for pilot research grants. Specific dates are posted online.

OFFICERS OF THE BOARD:
Richard Knutson, Chairman
Cynthia Zagieboylo, President and Chief Executive Officer
Peter Porrino, Treasurer
Linda J. McAleer, Secretary

ADDRESS INQUIRIES TO:
See e-mail address above.

THE NEURO [2224]
3801 University Street
Room 636
Montreal QC H3A 2B4 Canada
(514) 398-1238
Fax: (514) 398-8248
E-mail: john.mccall@mcgill.ca
Web Site: mcgill.ca/neuro

FOUNDED: 1934

AREAS OF INTEREST:
Neurology, neurosurgery and neuroscience.

NAME(S) OF PROGRAMS:
• **Jeanne Timmins Costello Fellowships**
• **Molson Neuroengineering Fellowship**
• **Preston Robb Fellowship**

TYPE:
Exchange programs; Fellowships. Studentships; Travel awards. Awards for research and study in the fields of clinical and basic neurosciences.

PURPOSE:
To provide the recipient with the experience of going from laboratory bench to the patient's bedside by exploiting the strengths of the Institute in basic and clinical science.

LEGAL BASIS:
University, research institute.

ELIGIBILITY:
For the Costello Fellowship, candidates must have an M.D. or Ph.D. degree. Those candidates with M.D. degrees will ordinarily have completed clinical studies in neurology or neurosurgery. Research themes at the MNI include neuroanatomy, neurochemistry, neurogenetics, molecular genetics, neuroimaging, neuroimmunology, epilepsy, neuromuscular disease, neuro-oncology, molecular and cellular biology and neuropsychology.

For the Robb Fellowship, candidates must have an M.D. degree with clinical studies in neurology or neurosurgery.

For the Molson Fellowship, candidates must have an M.D. or Ph.D. degree and be interested in pursuing high-level work in neuroengineering.

FINANCIAL DATA:
Amount of support per award: Costello and Robb Fellowships: $40,000; Molson Fellowship: $50,000; Studentships: $1,500 to $25,000 depending upon award.

NO. AWARDS: Jeanne Timmins Costello Fellowships: 3; Molson Fellowship and Preston Robb Fellowship: 1 per fellowship.

APPLICATION INFO:
Application form and guidelines are available online from August 1 to October 31.

Duration: One year. Renewal possible for one additional year.

Deadline: October 31.

PUBLICATIONS:
Annual report.

ADDRESS INQUIRIES TO:
Fellowship Committee
E-mail: fellowships.mni@mcgill.ca

NEUROSURGERY RESEARCH AND EDUCATION FOUNDATION [2225]
5550 Meadowbrook Drive
Rolling Meadows, IL 60008-3852
(847) 378-0500
Fax: (847) 378-0600
E-mail: info@nref.org
Web Site: www.nref.org

FOUNDED: 1982

AREAS OF INTEREST:
Neurosurgery.

NAME(S) OF PROGRAMS:
• **Research Fellowships**
• **Young Clinician Investigator Award**

TYPE:
Awards/prizes; Fellowships; Research grants.

YEAR PROGRAM STARTED: 1983

PURPOSE:
To advance the neurosciences.

LEGAL BASIS:
Private foundation.

ELIGIBILITY:
Applicants for the Research Fellowship must be physicians who have been accepted into or who are in an approved residency training program in neurological surgery in North America.

Applicants for the Young Clinician Investigator Award must be neurosurgeons, no more than two years from having completed their neurosurgical residency training and/or clinical fellowship, who are full-time faculty in North American teaching institutions.

Those who accept grants from other sources for the same project are ineligible.

GEOG. RESTRICTIONS: North America.

FINANCIAL DATA:
Amount of support per award: Up to $50,000.

NO. AWARDS: 12 for the year 2019-20.

APPLICATION INFO:
Applications are only available online through the application portal on the NREF web site.

Duration: One year.

Deadline: November 1. Announcement no later than February 15.

ADDRESS INQUIRIES TO:
E-mail: grants@nref.org.

PARKINSON'S FOUNDATION [2226]
1359 Broadway, Suite 1509
New York, NY 10018
(212) 923-4700
(800) 457-6676
E-mail: bvernaleo@parkinson.org
grants@parkinson.org
Web Site: www.parkinson.org

FOUNDED: 1957

AREAS OF INTEREST:
Basic and clinical research toward finding the cause and cure for Parkinson's disease.

CONSULTING OR VOLUNTEER SERVICES:
Information and referral service to Parkinson's disease patients and caregivers; counseling.

NAME(S) OF PROGRAMS:
• **Conference Awards**

TYPE:
Conferences/seminars.

PURPOSE:
To support the gathering of experts in the field working to address unsolved clinical or basic science problems relevant to Parkinson's disease.

ELIGIBILITY:
Open to independent investigators, both nationally and internationally, possessing postdoctoral training or a medical degree (or the equivalent). The Award supports gatherings of experts in the field in order to address emerging clinical or basic science questions about Parkinson's. Award is not open to postdoctoral researchers or fellows.

FINANCIAL DATA:
Amount of support per award: Average award $10,000, with a maximum of $15,000.

NO. AWARDS: 3 to 4.

APPLICATION INFO:
All applications must be submitted online. Paper copies will not be accepted.

Duration: Up to one year.

Deadline: Applications will be accepted anytime, as long as they are submitted at least 90 days prior to proposed conference start date; award notification four to six weeks after application submission.

ADDRESS INQUIRIES TO:
Beth A. Vernaleo, Ph.D.
Senior Director of Research Programs or James Beck, Ph.D., Chief Scientific Officer
(See address above.)

PARKINSON'S FOUNDATION [2227]
1359 Broadway, Suite 1509
New York, NY 10018
(212) 923-4700
(800) 457-6676
E-mail: bvernaleo@parkinson.org
grants@parkinson.org
Web Site: www.parkinson.org

FOUNDED: 1957

AREAS OF INTEREST:
Basic and clinical research toward finding the cause and cure for Parkinson's disease.

NAME(S) OF PROGRAMS:
• **Stanley Fahn Faculty Scholar Award**

PURPOSE:
To seek the cause and cure of Parkinson's disease.

LEGAL BASIS:
Nonprofit organization.

ELIGIBILITY:
Any clinician-scientist licensed to care for patients regardless of nationality or location may apply. Physicians must have completed a residency in neurology or be able to justify the relevance of their training pathway is of benefit to people with pulmonary disease. Allied health professionals must hold an advanced research degree, typically a Ph.D. All applicants must demonstrate a significant research focus on pulmonary disease.

Preference will be given to early career scientists.

FINANCIAL DATA:
Amount of support per award: $200,000 in total costs. Indirect costs, not exceeding 10% of direct costs, may be deducted from the total. Applicant salary support is permitted up to 40% of total salary.
Total amount of support: $600,000.

NO. MOST RECENT APPLICANTS: 29 for the year 2019.

NO. AWARDS: 2 to 3.

APPLICATION INFO:
Application information is available on the web site.
Duration: Two years.
Deadline: Letter of Intent: January 21. Invited Full Application: April 10.

PUBLICATIONS:
Annual reports; research reports; application guidelines and forms.

ADDRESS INQUIRIES TO:
Beth A. Vernaleo, Ph.D.
Senior Director of Research Programs or
James Beck, Ph.D.
Chief Scientific Officer
(See address above.)

PARKINSON'S FOUNDATION [2231]
1359 Broadway, Suite 1509
New York, NY 10018
(212) 923-4700
(800) 457-6676
E-mail: bvernaleo@parkinson.org
grants@parkinson.org
Web Site: www.parkinson.org

FOUNDED: 1957

AREAS OF INTEREST:
Basic and clinical research toward finding the cause and cure for Parkinson's disease.

CONSULTING OR VOLUNTEER SERVICES:
Information and referral service to Parkinson's disease patients and caregivers.

NAME(S) OF PROGRAMS:
• **Postdoctoral Fellowship**

TYPE:
Fellowships. The Postdoctoral Fellowship program has two distinct components: (1) Postdoctoral Fellowship for Basic Scientists and (2) Postdoctoral Fellowship for Neurologists.

YEAR PROGRAM STARTED: 1990

PURPOSE:
To provide support and training for Parkinson's disease researchers at early stages in their careers.

LEGAL BASIS:
Nonprofit organization.

ELIGIBILITY:
Postdoctoral Fellowship for Basic Scientists: The applicant must be within five years of receiving his or her Ph.D., and must identify an individual who will serve as his or her mentor and supervisor of the research.

Postdoctoral Fellowship for Neurologists: Applicants seeking a Postdoctoral Fellowship for Neurologists must possess an M.D. or equivalent and be within three years of having completed a residency in neurology. Applicants may not have their own lab and must identify an individual who will serve as his or her mentor and supervisor of their research.

FINANCIAL DATA:
The Postdoctoral Fellowship does not pay indirect or overhead costs and requires the grant recipient to account for all expenditures. The second year's funding is dependent upon submission of a satisfactory report covering the first year's work.
Amount of support per award: Postdoctoral Fellowship for Basic Scientists: Up to $55,000, plus $5,000 research allowance. Postdoctoral Fellowship for Neurologists: Up to $65,000, plus $5,000 research allowance.
Total amount of support: $600,000.

NO. MOST RECENT APPLICANTS: 76.

NO. AWARDS: 5.

APPLICATION INFO:
Applications must be submitted online. Applicants for the Postdoctoral Fellowship must also submit the investigator's curriculum vitae, an outline of work to be undertaken and a detailed budget.
Duration: Two years.
Deadline: Letter of Intent: November 12. Invited Full Application: February 18. Award notification in late April.

PUBLICATIONS:
Annual reports; research reports; application guidelines.

ADDRESS INQUIRIES TO:
Research
(See address above.)

PARKINSON'S FOUNDATION [2232]
1359 Broadway, Suite 1509
New York, NY 10018
(212) 923-4700
(800) 457-6676
E-mail: bvernaleo@parkinson.org
grants@parkinson.org
Web Site: www.parkinson.org

FOUNDED: 1957

AREAS OF INTEREST:
Basic and clinical research toward finding the cause and cure for Parkinson's disease.

CONSULTING OR VOLUNTEER SERVICES:
Information and referral service to Parkinson's disease patients and caregivers; counseling.

NAME(S) OF PROGRAMS:
• **Parkinson's Foundation Summer Student Fellowship**

TYPE:
Fellowships. Supports medical students and undergraduates for study under the supervision of an established investigator.

YEAR PROGRAM STARTED: 2002

PURPOSE:
To seek the cause and cure of Parkinson's disease.

LEGAL BASIS:
Nonprofit organization.

ELIGIBILITY:
Undergraduate and medical students are eligible.

FINANCIAL DATA:
Amount of support per award: $4,000 stipend, plus up to $1,000 travel to a PD-related conference to present summer project data.
Total amount of support: $40,000.

NO. MOST RECENT APPLICANTS: 26.

NO. AWARDS: 8.

APPLICATION INFO:
Application information is available on the web site.
Duration: 10 weeks.
Deadline: December 2. Award notification by March 2.

PUBLICATIONS:
Annual reports; research reports; application guidelines and forms.

STAFF:
John L. Lehr, President and Chief Executive Officer
Veronica Todaro, Executive Vice President and Chief Operating Officer
James Beck, Ph.D., Senior Vice President and Chief Scientific Officer
Curt De Greff, Senior Vice President and Chief Financial Officer

ADDRESS INQUIRIES TO:
Beth A. Vernaleo, Ph.D.
Senior Director of Research Programs or
James Beck, Ph.D.
Chief Scientific Officer
(See address above.)

TOURETTE ASSOCIATION OF AMERICA, INC. [2233]
42-40 Bell Boulevard
Suite 205
Bayside, NY 11361-2820
(718) 224-2999
Fax: (718) 279-9596
E-mail: support@tourette.org
Web Site: www.tourette.org

FOUNDED: 1972

AREAS OF INTEREST:
Education, research and services relating to Tourette Syndrome and relevant scientific fields, such as biochemistry, neuroanatomy, neurophysiology, genetics, molecular biology, epidemiology, psychiatry, psychology, neuropsychology, neurology, neuroimaging, neuropathology, pharmacology and/or animal models.

NAME(S) OF PROGRAMS:
• **Young Investigator Program**

TYPE:
Fellowships; General operating grants; Research grants; Seed money grants; Technical assistance. Research grants available for Ph.D. and M.D. researchers in the following categories:
(1) proposals in basic neuroscience specifically relevant to Tourette Syndrome

and;
(2) clinical studies related to the etiology, pathophysiology and treatment of Tourette Syndrome.

Fellowships provide one-year postdoctoral training.

YEAR PROGRAM STARTED: 1984

PURPOSE:
To support significant basic and clinical research in Tourette Syndrome.

LEGAL BASIS:
Not-for-profit organization.

ELIGIBILITY:
Open to Ph.D. and M.D. investigators from all areas of science who can contribute to the understanding of the genetics, pathogenesis, pathophysiology and the treatment of Tourette Syndrome. Investigators already studying Tourette Syndrome and those currently working in areas of science that can be applied to the problems of Tourette Syndrome are invited to apply.

FINANCIAL DATA:
These designated award levels can include indirect costs no greater than 10%. However, the total grant award cannot exceed $80,000 for a one-year research grant or $160,000 for a two-year award.
Amount of support per award: $80,000 per year.
Total amount of support: Varies.

REPRESENTATIVE AWARDS:
$150,000 to Deanna Greene, Ph.D., Washington University School of Medicine, St. Louis, MO, for "Network Architecture of the Brain in Tourette Syndrome and in Phenotypic Sub-Groups;" $150,000 to Izhar Bar-Gad, Ilan University, Ramat-Gan, Israel, for "Interaction of the Dopaminergic and GABAergic Systems in the Formation of Tics."

APPLICATION INFO:
Application information is available on the web site.

For preliminary screening, a preproposal is required. The approximate project funding level should be included. Inquirers will be informed as to whether to proceed with a full application.
Duration: One or two years.
Deadline: Preproposals are due December 4 each year. Final proposals are due February 1. Awards are announced in July.

PUBLICATIONS:
Brochure.

ADDRESS INQUIRIES TO:
Leo Neuringer, Program Assistant
Research and Medical Programs
(See address above.)

*PLEASE NOTE:
The Scientific Advisory Board guides the Tourette Association of America in defining the strategic direction for grant funding. Ultimately, the Scientific Advisory Board makes recommendations for grant funding to the TAA's Board of Directors.

Nursing

AMERICAN ASSOCIATION FOR THE HISTORY OF NURSING, INC. [2234]
P.O. Box 7
Mullica Hill, NJ 08062
(609) 519-9689
E-mail: grants@aahn.org
Web Site: www.aahn.org

FOUNDED: 1978

AREAS OF INTEREST:
Nursing historical research.

NAME(S) OF PROGRAMS:
- **Competitive Student Research H-31 Predoctoral Grant**
- **H-15 Grant for Faculty Members or Independent Researchers**

TYPE:
Awards/prizes; Research grants. Research awards.

YEAR PROGRAM STARTED: 2008

PURPOSE:
To encourage and support research in nursing history.

ELIGIBILITY:
Competitive Student Research H-31 Predoctoral Grant: Student must be an AAHN member enrolled in an accredited Master's or doctoral program. Proposals must focus on a significant question in the history of nursing and the research advisor will be doctorally prepared with scholarly activity in the field of nursing history and prior experience in guidance of research training.

H-15 Grant: Applicant must be an AAHN member with a doctoral degree. Proposals must outline a historical research project and will be judged for scholarly merit and significance to the field of nursing history.

FINANCIAL DATA:
Amount of support per award: Competitive Student Research H-31 Predoctoral Grant: $2,000; H-15 Grant: $3,000, including eight percent indirect costs for facilities and administration fees.
Total amount of support: $5,000.

NO. MOST RECENT APPLICANTS: 8 to 12.

NO. AWARDS: 1 per award.

APPLICATION INFO:
Contact the Association.
Deadline: April 1.

ADDRESS INQUIRIES TO:
Brian Riggs, Executive Director
(See address above.)

AMERICAN NURSES FOUNDATION [2235]
8515 Georgia Avenue
Suite 400
Silver Spring, MD 20910
(301) 628-5227
Fax: (301) 628-5354
E-mail: givetonursing@ana.org
Web Site: www.nursingworld.org/foundation

FOUNDED: 1955

AREAS OF INTEREST:
Nursing research.

NAME(S) OF PROGRAMS:
- **Nursing Research Grants**

TYPE:
Research grants.

YEAR PROGRAM STARTED: 1955

PURPOSE:
To encourage the research career development of nurses.

LEGAL BASIS:
Not-for-profit corporation under Section 501(c)(3) of the Internal Revenue Code.

ELIGIBILITY:
Nurse researchers at all levels and expertise both in academia and in clinical settings are encouraged to apply. Funding is considered towards all studies that contribute to the advancement of nursing science and the enhancement of patient care.

FINANCIAL DATA:
Total funding is dependent, in part, on the participation of external sponsors.
Amount of support per award: Varies.
Total amount of support: Varies.

NO. MOST RECENT APPLICANTS: Varies.

NO. AWARDS: Varies.

APPLICATION INFO:
The application packet is available online beginning February 1.
Duration: One year.
Deadline: May 1. Award announcement: Fall.

PUBLICATIONS:
Annual report; newsletter; research publications.

BOARD OF TRUSTEES:
Timothy Porter-O'Grady, Chairperson
Joyce Fitzpatrick, Vice Chairperson

ADDRESS INQUIRIES TO:
Patrick Giblin, Development Associate
(See address above.)

*PLEASE NOTE:
Some of the grants are restricted to a particular field of study.

ASSOCIATION OF WOMEN'S HEALTH, OBSTETRIC AND NEONATAL NURSES (AWHONN) [2236]
1800 M Street, N.W.
Suite 740 South
Washington, DC 20036
(202) 261-2400
Fax: (202) 728-0575
E-mail: researchprograms@awhonn.org
Web Site: www.awhonn.org

FOUNDED: 1969

AREAS OF INTEREST:
Women's health, obstetrics, neonatal nursing, newborns, nursing profession, advocacy, research and clinical resources for nurses.

NAME(S) OF PROGRAMS:
- **AWHONN Research Grants Program**

TYPE:
Research grants.

YEAR PROGRAM STARTED: 1993

PURPOSE:
To promote the advancement of nursing research among members.

ELIGIBILITY:
Applicant must be a full member at the time of application and at time of selection and funding. Researchers who are currently principal investigators on a federally funded

grant, or who have received an AWHONN-funded research grant within the past five years are ineligible to apply.

GEOG. RESTRICTIONS: United States and its territories.

FINANCIAL DATA:
Amount of support per award: $5,000 to $15,000.
Total amount of support: $37,000 for the year 2020.

NO. AWARDS: 5 for the year 2020.

APPLICATION INFO:
Application information is available on the web site.
Duration: One year.
Deadline: December 13.

PUBLICATIONS:
Journal of Obstetric, Gynecologic and Neonatal Nursing; Nursing for Women's Health.

ADDRESS INQUIRIES TO:
Research Programs
(See e-mail address above.)

THE CANADIAN LUNG ASSOCIATION (CLA)   [2237]
885 Meadowlands Drive
Suite 502
Ottawa ON K2C 3N2 Canada
(613) 569-6411 ext. 262
(888) 566-5864 (within Canada)
Fax: (613) 569-8860
E-mail: research@lung.ca
Web Site: www.lung.ca

FOUNDED: 1959

AREAS OF INTEREST:
Respiratory health.

NAME(S) OF PROGRAMS:
● **Breathing as One: Allied Health Research Fellowships**
● **Breathing as One: Allied Health Research Grants**

TYPE:
Fellowships; Research grants. Fellowships are offered to registered nurses pursuing postgraduate education with a major component of the program involving respiratory nursing practice, physiotherapists pursuing postgraduate training with respiratory research as the major component, and respiratory therapists pursuing postgraduate education with a major component of the program involving respiratory therapy practice.

Grants for research and feasibility studies are offered to registered nurses undertaking research investigations related to nursing management of patients with respiratory disease and symptoms. Grants are also offered to physiotherapists undertaking investigations related to management of patients with respiratory disease. Respiratory therapists undertaking research investigations related to the management of patients with respiratory disease and symptoms may also qualify.

PURPOSE:
To promote research in areas that contribute to the field of respiratory health in Canada; to build research capacity within the respiratory health professional community; to support respiratory health professionals completing postgraduate studies in the completion of thesis-based programs.

LEGAL BASIS:
Not-for-profit, incorporated.

ELIGIBILITY:
To be eligible for a Breathing as One: Allied Health Fellowship Award the applicant must be:
(1) a Canadian citizen, Canadian resident or landed immigrant;
(2) a respiratory health professional from a recognized clinically based discipline (e.g., registered nurse, nurse practitioner, physiotherapist, respiratory therapist, pharmacist, cardiopulmonary technologist, polysomnographic technologist, kinesiologist, dietician, occupational therapist, social worker, or psychologist). M.Ds. are not eligible for support;
(3) enrolled in a graduate (thesis-based) program at the Master's or doctoral level during the funding period. Individuals who have applied to a graduate program but have not received acceptance may apply for a Fellowship. The award, however, will be conditional on acceptance into the program and;
(4) pursuing a research study with respiratory health as the major focus.

To be eligible for a Breathing as One: Allied Health Research Grant the principle applicant must be:
(1) a Canadian citizen, permanent Canadian resident or landed immigrant;
(2) a respiratory health professional from a recognized clinically based discipline (e.g., registered nurse, nurse practitioner, physiotherapist, respiratory therapist, pharmacist, cardiopulmonary technologist, polysomnographic technologist, kinesiologist, dietician, occupational therapist, social worker, or psychologist). M.Ds. are not eligible for support as a principal investigator;
(3) affiliated with a health care organization, an educational institution or any other Canadian institution that can manage funds in the approved way and;
(4) pursuing a research study with respiratory health as the major focus.

FINANCIAL DATA:
Amount of support per award: Research Fellowship: $10,000 maximum for full-time and $5,000 for part-time students; Research Grant: Up to $20,000.
Total amount of support: Varies.

NO. MOST RECENT APPLICANTS: Approximately 12.

NO. AWARDS: Approximately 8 each year.

APPLICATION INFO:
Forms may be downloaded from the Lung Association web site. Applicant must upload one copy of the completed application and all relevant documents.
Duration: One year.
Deadline: July 17.

PUBLICATIONS:
Brochure; newsletters.

ADDRESS INQUIRIES TO:
Fatima Kazoun, Manager
National Research Programs
(See address above.)

FOUNDATION FOR NEONATAL RESEARCH AND EDUCATION (FNRE)   [2238]
200 East Holly Avenue
Sewell, NJ 08080
(856) 256-2343
Fax: (856) 589-7463
E-mail: contact@ajj.com
Web Site: www2.ajj.com/fnre

FOUNDED: 1992

AREAS OF INTEREST:
Neonatal nursing.

TYPE:
Research grants; Scholarships.

YEAR PROGRAM STARTED: 1992

PURPOSE:
To support research and education in neonatal nursing; to promote the development of expertise in the neonatal profession; to raise awareness of the general public as consumers of neonatal services.

LEGAL BASIS:
Nonprofit.

ELIGIBILITY:
Members of the FNRE Research Review Committee and the FNRE Board members are not eligible to apply.

All grant applicants must be professionally active neonatal nurses. Applicant must be principal investigator of the project. If the principal investigator has limited research experience, it is expected that the application will reflect appropriate nursing research consultation.

Scholarship applicants must:
(1) be officially admitted to a college or school of higher education for Bachelor of Science in Nursing, Master in Science in Nursing for Advance Practice in Neonatal Nursing, Doctoral degree in Nursing, or Master's or Post-Master degree in Nursing Administration or Business Management;
(2) have a 3.0 grade point average or higher;
(3) be a professionally active neonatal nurse and;
(4) not have received a FNRE scholarship or grant in the past five years.

GEOG. RESTRICTIONS: United States.

FINANCIAL DATA:
Amount of support per award: Grants: Up to $5,000 per project.
Total amount of support: Varies.

NO. AWARDS: 1 to 2.

APPLICATION INFO:
Grant applicants must submit:
(1) a research plan addressing the problem or significance of the project, literature review (five-page maximum), methodology, data collection instruments, data analysis and completion schedule;
(2) Institutional Review Board approval;
(3) documentation verifying that research procedures meet federal guidelines for animal protection if animals are to be used;
(4) detailed budget;
(5) one-page curriculum vitae of each principal investigator, co-investigator and support person;
(6) a conflict of interest disclosure and;
(7) the signature of their major advisor or dissertation/thesis/project committee chairperson.
Duration: One year. Extensions requested in writing may be granted.

Deadline: May 1. Award notifications will be mailed by September.

FOUNDATION OF THE NATIONAL STUDENT NURSES' ASSOCIATION, INC.   [2239]

45 Main Street
Suite 606
Brooklyn, NY 11201-1075
(718) 210-0705
Fax: (718) 797-1186
E-mail: lauren@nsna.org
fnsna@forevernursing.org
Web Site: www.forevernursing.org

FOUNDED: 1969

AREAS OF INTEREST:
Nursing education.

TYPE:
Scholarships. General Scholarship Program awards funds based on a set of criteria established by the sponsor of the scholarship. These scholarships typically reflect a specific area of specialization within the nursing profession such as oncology, critical care, or emergency nursing or a certain population of the nursing profession that is often underrepresented.

PURPOSE:
To provide aid to nursing students.

LEGAL BASIS:
501(c)(3) charitable foundation.

ELIGIBILITY:
Applicants must be U.S. citizens or students with an Alien Registration number. They must also be currently enrolled in state-approved schools of nursing or pre-nursing in Associate degree, Baccalaureate, diploma, generic Doctorate, generic Master's and 16- to 18-month accelerated programs. Funds are not available for graduate study unless it is for a first degree in nursing. Graduating high school seniors are not eligible. Monies are awarded in the spring to be used in the next academic year and summer school. Monies can only be used for nursing or pre-nursing in one of the above-mentioned programs. No monies can be used for graduate education unless leading to a first degree in nursing. If applicant is matriculating into a nursing program, letter of acceptance must accompany this application. Proof of enrollment will be required at time of award. Current Association Board of Directors and Association Nominating and Elections Committee members are not eligible.

FINANCIAL DATA:
Amount of support per award: Scholarships: $1,000 to $7,500.
Total amount of support: Over $250,000 annually in the general scholarship program.

NO. AWARDS: 189 for the 2021-22 academic year.

APPLICATION INFO:
Applications can be completed online at the NSNA web site from September until the following January.

Applicants must submit a copy of their recent nursing school and college transcripts, or grade report. NSNA members must submit proof of their membership. Registered nurses in Baccalaureate programs and licensed practical/vocational nurses in programs leading to registered nurse licensure must submit a copy of their license to be considered for the Career Mobility Scholarships.

Duration: One year. Scholarships are awarded in the spring for use in the upcoming academic year.

Deadline: January.

ADDRESS INQUIRIES TO:
Lauren Sperle
Scholarship Program Committee
(See address above.)

*PLEASE NOTE:
The scholarships are based on academic achievement, financial need, and involvement in nursing student organizations and community activities related to health care. Additional criteria may be required by some sponsors.

MYASTHENIA GRAVIS FOUNDATION OF AMERICA, INC.

290 Turnpike Road
Suite 5-315
Westborough, MA 01581
(800) 541-5454
E-mail: mgfa@myasthenia.org
Web Site: www.myasthenia.org

TYPE:
Research grants. The Foundation supports research that will improve the lives of patients with myasthenia gravis and related neuromuscular junction disorders. There are five broad research priorities:
(1) Biomarkers: facilitate early diagnosis, predict clinical outcomes and immunosuppressive therapy response and utilize in clinical trials;
(2) Disease Mechanisms: understand basic mechanisms and self-tolerance loss throughout course of disease;
(3) Targeted Therapies: develop new therapeutic targets, prevent widespread immunosuppression and off-target side effects, optimize treatment strategies with existing therapies;
(4) Patient Outcomes: understand the full impact of disease on daily living and patient treatment priorities, understand collateral effects of disease, related medical conditions, side effects and financial impact and;
(5) Pediatric Treatment: identify strategies, safety conforms, and long-term outcomes.

See entry 2219 for full listing.

NATIONAL BLACK NURSES ASSOCIATION, INC.   [2240]

8630 Fenton Street
Suite 910
Silver Spring, MD 20910
(301) 589-3200
Fax: (301) 589-3223
E-mail: info@nbna.org
Web Site: www.nbna.org

AREAS OF INTEREST:
HIV/AIDS, cardiovascular disease, women and children's health, cancer, substance abuse, diabetes, obesity, and violence in African American communities.

NAME(S) OF PROGRAMS:
- **Dr. Martha A. Dawson Genesis Nurse Leader Scholarship**
- **Lynne Edwards Research Scholarship**
- **Dr. Millicent Gorham Scholarship**
- **George McGuire Memorial Scholarship**
- **NBNA Board of Directors Scholarship**
- **Margaret Pemberton Scholarship**
- **Dr. Lauranne Sams Scholarship**
- **VITAS Healthcare/Esther Colliflower Scholarship**
- **Dr. Eric J. Williams Scholarship**

TYPE:
Scholarships.

PURPOSE:
To advance nursing practice, improve health care for all Americans, particularly the unserved and the underserved, and shape health policy for the access and delivery of health care services.

LEGAL BASIS:
Nonprofit professional association.

ELIGIBILITY:
Awards are given primarily to African Americans enrolled at any level in a nursing program (AD, BSN or LPN/LVN). Applicant must be in good standing at the time of application and be a member of NBNA.

GEOG. RESTRICTIONS: United States.

FINANCIAL DATA:
Amount of support per award: $1,000 to $5,000.

NO. MOST RECENT APPLICANTS: 63.

NO. AWARDS: 25.

APPLICATION INFO:
Applicant must provide:
(1) official transcript from an accredited school of nursing;
(2) two-page written essay;
(3) two letters of recommendation (one from applicant's school of nursing and one from the local chapter, or a nurse in the area if a local chapter does not exist). Letters of recommendation and essay must be attached to the application and;
(4) a clean/clear professional headshot.

Additional items to accompany the application in support of the candidate's eligibility and desirability may include documented evidence of participation in student nurse activities and involvement in the African American community, i.e., letters, news clippings, awards, certificates, etc.

Completed application and all supporting documents are to be sent via e-mail to charold@nbna.org. Scholarship applications will not be accepted by mail.

Duration: One year. May reapply.

Deadline: April 15. Awards are presented at the July/August conference.

BOARD OF DIRECTORS:
Dr. Martha A. Dawson, President

ADDRESS INQUIRIES TO:
Scholarships Committee
(See address above.)

NATIONAL INSTITUTE OF NURSING RESEARCH   [2241]

Building 31, Room B1-B55
31 Center Drive
Bethesda, MD 20892-2178
(301) 496-0207
Fax: (301) 480-4969
E-mail: info@ninr.nih.gov
Web Site: www.ninr.nih.gov

FOUNDED: 1986

AREAS OF INTEREST:
Health of individuals, families, communities and populations.

CONSULTING OR VOLUNTEER SERVICES:
For potential principal investigators.

NAME(S) OF PROGRAMS:
- **Career Development Grants**
- **Research Grants**
- **Research Training Grants**
- **Small Business Innovation Research Grants**

TYPE:
Fellowships; Project/program grants; Research grants; Training grants. Funds may be used for salaries, consultation, equipment, travel and other usual costs, subject to federal regulations applicable to the grant. Fellowships are for postdoctoral research training; predoctoral support is also available.

YEAR PROGRAM STARTED: 1986

PURPOSE:
To support nursing research, research training at pre- and postdoctoral levels, and research related to patient care, the promotion of health, the prevention of disease and the mitigation of the effects of acute and chronic illnesses and disabilities.

LEGAL BASIS:
Public Health Service Act, Sections 301, 483, 484, and 487, as amended by Public Law 99-158.

ELIGIBILITY:
Applicant may be a for-profit organization, a nonprofit organization, a public or private institution such as a university, college, hospital and laboratory, a unit of state government, a unit of local government, an eligible agency of the federal government, a foreign institution, a domestic institution, a faith-based or community-based organization, an Indian/Native American tribal government (federally recognized), an Indian/Native American tribal government (other than federally recognized), or an Indian/Native American tribally designated organization.

FINANCIAL DATA:
Amount of support per award: Varies based on type of grant and duration.
Total amount of support: Varies.

CO-OP FUNDING PROGRAMS: Co-funding of research project grants with other NIH Institutes and Centers.

APPLICATION INFO:
With few exceptions, all types of grant applications are electronic. When determining which form to submit, applicants are encouraged to read the funding opportunity announcement.
Duration: Varies.
Deadline: Applications are accepted at any time for inclusion in one of the three annual review cycles (depending on the activity code).

PUBLICATIONS:
Investigators' publications.

ADDRESS INQUIRIES TO:
Jo-Ann Kriebel, Acting Chief, Office of Communications and Public Liaison (See address above.)

NATIONAL SOCIETY DAUGHTERS OF THE AMERICAN REVOLUTION [2242]
1776 D Street, N.W.
Washington, DC 20006-5303
(202) 879-3263
E-mail: scholarships@nsdar.org
Web Site: www.dar.org

FOUNDED: 1895

AREAS OF INTEREST:
Nursing.

NAME(S) OF PROGRAMS:
- **Madeline Pickett (Halbert) Cogswell Nursing Scholarship**
- **District of Columbia Nursing Scholarship**
- **Caroline E. Holt Nursing Scholarship**
- **Mildred Nutting Nursing Scholarship**

TYPE:
Scholarships. Awarded to students who are enrolled or currently attending an accredited school of nursing.

PURPOSE:
To provide ways and means to help students to attain higher education; to perpetuate the memory and spirit of men and women who achieved American Independence by acquisition and protection of historical spots and erection of monuments; to carry out injunction of Washington in his farewell address to the American people; to maintain institutions of American Freedom; to aid liberty.

LEGAL BASIS:
Incorporated historical society.

ELIGIBILITY:
Scholarships are awarded without regard to race, religion, sex or national origin. Candidates must be U.S. citizens and must attend an accredited college or university in the U.S. Awards are judged on the basis of academic excellence, commitment to field of study, as required, and financial need.

Applicants for the Cogswell Nursing Scholarship must be members, descendants of members or eligible for membership in NSDAR. DAR member number must be on the application.

The District of Columbia Nursing Scholarship is intended for minority students in need who are enrolled in or attending the University of the District of Columbia.

No affiliation or relationship to DAR is required for qualification for the Holt Nursing Scholarship.

GEOG. RESTRICTIONS: United States.

FINANCIAL DATA:
Amount of support per award: Nutting Scholarship: $2,000; All others: $2,500.
Total amount of support: Cogswell and District of Columbia Scholarships: $5,000; Holt Scholarship $7,500; Nutting Scholarship: $4,000.

NO. AWARDS: Cogswell, District of Columbia and Nutting Scholarships: 2; Holt Scholarship: 3.

APPLICATION INFO:
Applicants must use the DAR Scholarship Committee's online submission process found on the DAR public web site. Once applicants have set up their scholarship profile, they will be able to complete the application. If necessary, applicants will be able to provide access to individuals wishing to submit confidential letters of recommendations or school transcripts.
Duration: One academic year. Nonrenewable.
Deadline: January 31.

PUBLICATIONS:
American Spirit, magazine.

ADDRESS INQUIRIES TO:
National Vice Chairman
E-mail:

mphcogswellnursingscholarship@nsdar.org, dcscholarship@nsdar.org
carolineeholtscholarship@nsdar.org or mildrednuttingscholarship@nsdar.org

*PLEASE NOTE:
Awards are placed on deposit with the college or university. Any unused portion shall be returned to the National Society.

NATIONAL SOCIETY DAUGHTERS OF THE AMERICAN REVOLUTION
1776 D Street, N.W.
Washington, DC 20006-5303
(202) 879-3263
E-mail: scholarships@nsdar.org
Web Site: www.dar.org

TYPE:
Scholarships.

See entry 2064 for full listing.

NURSES EDUCATIONAL FUNDS, INC.   [2243]
137 Montague Street, Suite 144
Brooklyn, NY 11201
(917) 524-8051
E-mail: info@n-e-f.org
Web Site: n-e-f.org

FOUNDED: 1912

AREAS OF INTEREST:
Graduate nursing education.

TYPE:
Scholarships. Scholarships for registered nurses seeking Master's and Doctorate degrees in nursing.

YEAR PROGRAM STARTED: 1912

PURPOSE:
To increase the number of graduate prepared nurses in leadership positions in nursing education, research, clinical care, academic and health care administrative positions.

LEGAL BASIS:
Nonprofit organization; 501(c)(3) corporation.

ELIGIBILITY:
Registered nurses with proof of current citizenship or legal residence status, such as U.S. passport (biographic page), birth certificate, naturalization certificate from the USCIS, or permanent resident (Green Card) are eligible to apply if they are enrolled full- or part-time in a Master's or doctoral program that is a professionally accredited nursing program. Accredited Graduate Programs including, but not limited to, Accreditation Commission for Education in Nursing (ACEN), Commission on Collegiate Nursing Education (CCNE), Southern Association of Colleges and Schools Commission on Colleges (CACSCC), New England Commission of Higher Education (NECHE), or other recognized American Nursing College or School of Nursing accrediting bodies. Applicants must be able to present proof of membership in a national professional nursing association.

GEOG. RESTRICTIONS: United States.

FINANCIAL DATA:
Amount of support per award: Scholarships vary in amount, according to the funds available.

Total amount of support: Varies.

NO. MOST RECENT APPLICANTS: 200 to 700 annually.

NO. AWARDS: 23 to 29 annually.

APPLICATION INFO:
Applications are submitted online beginning October 1.

Duration: One academic year. Can reapply for additional years provided two semesters remain before graduation.

Deadline: February 1 annually.

IRS I.D.: 13-6122744

BOARD OF DIRECTORS:
Joan M. Marren, M.Ed., R.N., President
Cynthia Sculco, Ed.D., R.N., Vice President
Joan Arnold, Ph.D., R.N., Treasurer
Rebecca R. Eddy, MBA, PDDM, Secretary
Allison Adams, B.S., B.A.
Susan Bowar-Ferres, Ph.D., R.N.
Craig Donner
Sarah Garrity
Carl A. Kirton, D.N.P., R.N.
Mathy Mezey, Ed.D., R.N.
Rosanne Raso, M.S., R.N.
Thelma Schoor, B.S.N., R.N.
Lawrence J. Siegel, MBA, J.D.
Henry B. Spencer
Gerhard Stubi
Madeleine S. Sugimoto, M.Ed., R.N.
Edwidge Thomas, D.N.P.
Ann Vanderberg, MBA, R.N.
Judith Ann Vessey, Ph.D., R.N.
Victoria Weiss, MBA

ADDRESS INQUIRIES TO:
Jerelyn Weiss, Executive Director
(See e-mail address above.)

REHABILITATION NURSING FOUNDATION (RNF) [2244]

8735 West Higgins Road
Suite 300
Chicago, IL 60631
(800) 229-7530
Fax: (847) 375-6481
E-mail: info@rehabnurse.org
Web Site: www.rehabnurse.org

FOUNDED: 1976

AREAS OF INTEREST:
Rehabilitation nursing.

NAME(S) OF PROGRAMS:
● **ARN/RNF Grant**

TYPE:
Research grants. Quality improvement grants.

YEAR PROGRAM STARTED: 1988

PURPOSE:
To promote and advance professional rehabilitation nursing practice through education, advocacy, collaboration, and research to enhance the quality of life for those affected by disability and chronic illness.

ELIGIBILITY:
Quality Improvement Grants projects must be based on the best evidence and seek to improve rehabilitation outcomes for patients with disabilities and chronic illnesses. Projects must have the potential of changing systems of care within an organizational structure.

Research Grants fund research studies that seek to advance the science and practice of rehabilitation nursing. Proposals that have the potential for generating findings that will lead to further extramural funding and that have the potential of contributing to the larger body of rehabilitation and health care knowledge are preferred. Research Grants do not fund quality improvement projects, program evaluation, or other performance improvement projects.

Preference will be given to applicants who are members of the Association of Rehabilitation Nurses.

FINANCIAL DATA:
Amount of support per award: Quality Improvement Grants: $1,000 per recipient; Research Grant: $15,000.

NO. MOST RECENT APPLICANTS: Varies.

NO. AWARDS: Quality Improvement Grants: Up to 2; Research Grant: 1 for the year 2021.

APPLICATION INFO:
Details are provided on the RNF web site.

Duration: Two years.

Deadline: June 1.

ADDRESS INQUIRIES TO:
Melissa Bellows, Operations Manager
(See e-mail address above.)

SALON NATIONAL LA BOUTIQUE [2245]

P.O. Box 1108
Lake Dallas, TX 75065-1108
(940) 230-0919
E-mail: lasecretaire@8and40.org
Web Site: www.8and40.org

FOUNDED: 1919

NAME(S) OF PROGRAMS:
● **Eight and Forty Lung and Respiratory Disease Nursing Scholarship Fund**

TYPE:
Scholarships. Grants for registered nurses.

YEAR PROGRAM STARTED: 1957

PURPOSE:
To allow registered nurses to further their education at the graduate level in the area of pediatric lung and respiratory diseases.

ELIGIBILITY:
Applicant must be a registered nurse, in adequate health and a U.S. citizen. Applicant must also have freedom to pursue full-time employment, have qualities of leadership and be able to attend classes full- or part-time at an accredited school of nursing.

FINANCIAL DATA:
Amount of support per award: Up to $3,000.

NO. MOST RECENT APPLICANTS: 100.

APPLICATION INFO:
Application forms may be obtained from the address above on or after January 1.

Duration: One school year.

Deadline: May 15. Announcement July 1.

PUBLICATIONS:
Brochure.

ADDRESS INQUIRIES TO:
Eight and Forty Scholarships
(See address above.)

SIGMA THETA TAU INTERNATIONAL [2246]

Honor Society of Nursing
550 West North Street
Indianapolis, IN 46202
(317) 634-8171 (Local)
(888) 634-7575 (U.S./Canada)
Fax: (317) 634-8188
E-mail: research@sigmanursing.org
Web Site: sigmanursing.org

FOUNDED: 1922

AREAS OF INTEREST:
Nursing.

NAME(S) OF PROGRAMS:
● **Rosemary Berkel Crisp Research Award**
● **Doris Bloch Research Award**
● **Joan K. Stout, R.N., Research Grant**

TYPE:
Research grants.

YEAR PROGRAM STARTED: 1936

PURPOSE:
To encourage qualified nurses to contribute to the advancement of nursing through research.

LEGAL BASIS:
Incorporated.

ELIGIBILITY:
Applicants must meet the following requirements:
(1) be a registered nurse with a current license;
(2) hold a Master's or doctoral degree or be enrolled in a doctoral program;
(3) be ready to implement research project when funding is received and;
(4) complete the project within one year of funding.

For the Rosemary Berkel Crisp Research Award, applicant must be a member of Sigma Theta Tau International. Some preference will be given to applicants residing in Arkansas, Illinois, Kentucky, Missouri and Tennessee.

FINANCIAL DATA:
Amount of support per award: $5,000 maximum.

NO. AWARDS: 1 per award or grant.

APPLICATION INFO:
Application information is available on the web site.

Duration: For approved research time.

Deadline: Varies.

PUBLICATIONS:
Guidelines; applications.

ADDRESS INQUIRIES TO:
Grants Coordinator
(See address above.)

U.S. DEPARTMENT OF HEALTH AND HUMAN SERVICES [2247]

HRSA/BHW, Division of Nursing and Public Health
11N Parklawn Building, Room 9-89
5600 Fishers Lane
Rockville, MD 20857
(301) 443-0856
Fax: (301) 443-0791
E-mail: mmccalla@hrsa.gov
Web Site: bhw.hrsa.gov/grants/nursing

AREAS OF INTEREST:
Nursing education and practice.

TYPE:
Project/program grants; Training grants.

YEAR PROGRAM STARTED: 1965

PURPOSE:
To improve nursing practice and education through projects that increase the knowledge and skills of nursing personnel, enhance their effectiveness in primary care delivery, increase the number of qualified professional nurses and increase nursing workforce diversity.

LEGAL BASIS:
Amendment to Public Health Service Act, Title VIII, Section 820 by "The Health Professions Education Partnership Act of 1998" Public Law 105-392, Subtitle B.

ELIGIBILITY:
Eligible entities are schools of nursing, nursing centers, academic health centers, state or local governments, and other public or private nonprofit entities appropriate by the Secretary that submit an application in accordance with Section 802.

GEOG. RESTRICTIONS: United States.

FINANCIAL DATA:
Amount of support per award: Grants vary in amount, depending on the needs and nature of the project.
Total amount of support: Varies.

APPLICATION INFO:
Contact the U.S. Department of Health and Human Services.
Duration: Varies according to project.

ADDRESS INQUIRIES TO:
Division of Nursing and Public Health, BHW/HRSA
Nursing Education Practice Quality and Retention Branch
(See address above.)

VIRGINIA DEPARTMENT OF HEALTH [2248]
Office of Health Equity
109 Governor Street, Seventh Floor
Suite 714 West
Richmond, VA 23219
(804) 864-7435
Fax: (804) 864-7440
E-mail: incentiveprograms@vdh.virginia.gov
Web Site: www.vdh.virginia.gov/health-equity

NAME(S) OF PROGRAMS:
● **Commonwealth of Virginia Nurse Educator Scholarship Program**
● **Mary Marshall Nursing Scholarship/Practical Nurse Program**
● **Mary Marshall Nursing Scholarship/Registered Nurse Program**
● **Nurse Practitioner/Nurse Midwife Scholarship Program**

TYPE:
Awards/prizes; Challenge/matching grants; Scholarships; Technical assistance; Loan forgiveness programs. Awarded to eligible students enrolled in undergraduate or graduate nursing programs at schools of nursing approved by the Virginia State Board of Nursing to assist with their professional education.

Undergraduate nursing programs are defined as those leading to a licensed practical nurse, an Associate degree, diploma, or Baccalaureate degree in nursing.

YEAR PROGRAM STARTED: 1950

PURPOSE:
To provide the citizens of the state with more skilled and greater nursing care coverage.

LEGAL BASIS:
Funding is appropriated by the General Assembly of Virginia under code 23-35.9-23-35.13; code 32.1-122.6-01; and Title 32.1, Chapter 6, 32.1-122.6-02.

ELIGIBILITY:
Criteria vary for the different scholarships. Because of the strict nature of these criteria, it is vital that the applicant contact the Department for full particulars.

GEOG. RESTRICTIONS: Virginia.

FINANCIAL DATA:
Amount of scholarships varies, depending upon amount appropriated by the General Assembly, amount collected by the Board of Nursing and the number of qualified applicants. There are strict conditions attached to these scholarships. (They are not outright gifts; require service in the Commonwealth of Virginia.)
Amount of support per award: Varies each year.
Total amount of support: Varies each year.

NO. AWARDS: Varies each year.

APPLICATION INFO:
Applications are available online. Required data for application include most current transcript of grades (or last school attended if not currently enrolled), verification of need from the Financial Aid Officer and recommendation of the Director of the School of Nursing.
Duration: Each scholarship is awarded for a single year. Upon reapplication, scholarships may be awarded for succeeding years to a maximum of four years.
Deadline: June 30.

PUBLICATIONS:
Guidelines.

OFFICER:
Olivette Burroughs, Health Workforce Specialist

ADDRESS INQUIRIES TO:
Nursing Scholarships
(See address above.)

Obstetrics and gynecology

CENTRAL ASSOCIATION OF OBSTETRICIANS AND GYNECOLOGISTS [2249]
15 North Main
Minot, ND 58703
(701) 838-8323
Fax: (701) 852-8733
E-mail: rhickel@caog.org
Web Site: www.caog.org

FOUNDED: 1929

AREAS OF INTEREST:
Obstetrics and gynecology, including investigative and/or clinical work.

NAME(S) OF PROGRAMS:
● **Annual Central Prize Award**
● **Central Poster Award**
● **Community Hospital Award**
● **FAR Research Network Award**
● **President's Certificate of Merit Award**
● **Young Investigator's Award**

TYPE:
Awards/prizes. The Annual Central Prize Award, President's Certificate of Merit Award and Central Poster Awards are presented annually for manuscripts demonstrating outstanding investigative or clinical work in the field of obstetrics and gynecology.

The Community Hospital Award is presented annually for clinical study or research in the field of obstetrics and gynecology to members located in community hospitals who are not full-time faculty in medical schools. Preference for this award will be given to papers concerning gynecologic endoscopy or any other diagnostic or therapeutic procedures which enhance the quality of care of gynecologic or obstetric patients.

The Young Investigator's Award is presented annually for clinical study or research in the field of obstetrics and gynecology to residents, fellows, and clinicians residing in the geographic confines of the Central Association.

YEAR PROGRAM STARTED: 1929

PURPOSE:
To encourage original work in obstetrics and gynecology.

LEGAL BASIS:
Nonprofit medical organization.

ELIGIBILITY:
Those eligible to compete are accredited physicians, teachers, research workers and medical students whose work was done within the geographic area of the Association.

For the Community Hospital Award, at least one author must be a member of the Central Association. Manuscripts must be written expressly for this competition and they must be original, not having been previously presented or published. Manuscripts will be considered for both the general program and the award unless the author specifically requests otherwise in writing.

GEOG. RESTRICTIONS: Alabama, Arizona, Arkansas, Colorado, Idaho, Illinois, Indiana, Iowa, Kansas, Kentucky, Louisiana, Michigan, Minnesota, Mississippi, Missouri, Montana, Nebraska, Nevada, New Mexico, North Dakota, Ohio, Oklahoma, South Dakota, Tennessee, Texas, Utah, West Virginia, Wisconsin and Wyoming.

FINANCIAL DATA:
Amount of support per award: Annual Central Prize Award: $2,000; Central Poster Award: $500 each; Community Hospital Award and FAR Research Network Award: $1,000; President's Certificate of Merit Award: $1,500; Young Investigator's Award: $750.

NO. MOST RECENT APPLICANTS: 50.

NO. AWARDS: Annual Central Prize Award, Community Hospital Award, FAR Research Network Award, President's Certificate of Merit, and Young Investigator's Award: 1 of each annually. Central Poster Award: 2 annually.

APPLICATION INFO:
For consideration for these awards, an online abstract must be submitted. The abstract maximum length is 800 words.
Duration: One year. Nonrenewable.
Deadline: Late April. Award winners notified early May.

THE LALOR FOUNDATION, INC. [2250]

c/o GMA Foundations
2 Liberty Square, Suite 500
Boston, MA 02109
(617) 426-7080
(617) 391-3088
E-mail: gsullivan@gmafoundations.com
Web Site: lalorfound.org

FOUNDED: 1935

AREAS OF INTEREST:
Sexual and reproductive health, contraception and pregnancy termination.

NAME(S) OF PROGRAMS:
● **The Anna Lalor Burdick Program**

TYPE:
Project/program grants.

PURPOSE:
To empower young women through education about healthy reproduction in order to broaden and enhance their options in life.

LEGAL BASIS:
Tax-exempt philanthropic foundation.

ELIGIBILITY:
Applicants must be tax-exempt under Section 501(c)(3) of the Internal Revenue Code and defined as "not a private foundation" under Section 509(a). Projects may take place outside of the U.S., but organization must be based in the U.S.

Grants are not normally made to individuals, research projects and scholarships, requests for endowment or major capital support, or general operating support for ongoing programs.

FINANCIAL DATA:
Amount of support per award: $10,000 to $35,000.

Total amount of support: $193,255 for fiscal year 2019.

NO. AWARDS: 10 for the year 2019.

APPLICATION INFO:
Applicant must submit a Concept Paper online. Full application information is available on the web site.

Duration: One year.

Deadline: Varies. Check web site for up-to-date information.

IRS I.D.: 51-6000153

ADDRESS INQUIRIES TO:
Fellowship Manager
(See e-mail address above.)

REPRODUCTIVE SCIENTIST DEVELOPMENT PROGRAM (RSDP) [2251]

University of Missouri
Department of Obstetrics, Gynecology and Women's Health
500 North Keene, Suite 203
Columbia, MO 65201
(573) 817-3114
E-mail: heflina@missouri.edu
Web Site: www.rsdprogram.org

FOUNDED: 1986

AREAS OF INTEREST:
Obstetric-gynecologic academic investigative careers in fundamental biomedical science.

TYPE:
Research grants. National career development program grant for full-time basic research under the mentorship of internationally recognized senior scientists.

YEAR PROGRAM STARTED: 1988

PURPOSE:
To train obstetrician-gynecologists committed to academic investigative careers in fundamental biomedical science.

ELIGIBILITY:
Candidates must be seeking a career in academic obstetrics and gynecology research and meet the following criteria:
(1) possess M.D. or D.O. degree;
(2) be a U.S. citizen, noncitizen national, verification as a permanent citizen at time of award;
(3) have completed a four-year internship and residency in obstetrics-gynecology approved by the Accreditation Council for Graduate Medical Education or the Royal College of Physicians and Surgeons of Canada and;
(4) submit a research proposal as part of application.

GEOG. RESTRICTIONS: United States.

FINANCIAL DATA:
Amount of support per award: Up to $125,000 for salary plus fringes and up to $25,000 for research support may be provided from NICHD funds for Phase I scholars.

Up to $100,000 for salary plus fringes and up to $25,000 for research support may be provided from NICHD funds for Phase II scholars. Phase II Scholars are also eligible to receive support from program sponsors of the RSDP Program. Award amounts vary.

NO. MOST RECENT APPLICANTS: 6.

NO. AWARDS: Up to 2 new positions are available each year.

APPLICATION INFO:
Applicant must submit a Letter of Intent to the RSDP office indicating the name of the Department of Ob/Gyn sponsor, name and address of proposal scientific mentor, and a brief description of the research project. This will be reviewed by the Executive Committee for appropriateness, and feedback will be provided to potential applicants.

Duration: Two to four years of support is available.

Deadline: Letter of Intent: August 15. Application: October 1.

ADDRESS INQUIRIES TO:
Amanda Heflin, MBA
Program Administrator
Tel: (618) 977-8070
(See address above.)

U.S. DEPARTMENT OF HEALTH AND HUMAN SERVICES [2252]

Maternal and Child Health Bureau
Parklawn Building, Room 5C 26
5600 Fishers Lane
Rockville, MD 20857
(301) 443-2204
Fax: (301) 443-9354
E-mail: CallCenter@hrsa.gov (grants information)
Web Site: mchb.hrsa.gov

FOUNDED: 1936

AREAS OF INTEREST:
Health of mothers and children.

NAME(S) OF PROGRAMS:
● **Maternal and Child Health Services Block Grant**

TYPE:
Block grants. The Title V Block Grant Program has as a general purpose the improvement of the health of all mothers and children in the nation. The Block Grant Program has three components: Formula Block Grants to 59 states and other political jurisdictions, Special Projects of Regional and National Significance (SPRANS), and Community Integrated Service Systems (CISS) Grants.

PURPOSE:
To improve the health of all mothers and children; to create federal-state partnerships to develop service systems in U.S. communities that can meet the critical challenges facing maternal and child health.

LEGAL BASIS:
Title V, Section 501, of the Social Security Act, as amended by Public Law 101-239.

ELIGIBILITY:
State health agencies.

GEOG. RESTRICTIONS: United States and its territories.

FINANCIAL DATA:
Amount of support per award: Grants vary in amount, depending upon the number of children at the poverty level in the state.

Total amount of support: Varies.

Matching fund requirements: The Title V Block Grant Program requires that every four dollars of federal Title V money must be matched by at least three dollars of state and local money.

CO-OP FUNDING PROGRAMS: NICHD, CDC, Department of Education, ADAMHA and other inter-agency agreements.

NO. AWARDS: 59.

APPLICATION INFO:
Instructions available at grants.gov.

Duration: One to two years. Must reapply annually.

Deadline: July 15.

ADDRESS INQUIRIES TO:
Maternal and Child Health Bureau
(See address above.)

Ophthalmology and otolaryngology

THE ALCON FOUNDATION, INC.   [2253]
6201 South Freeway
Fort Worth, TX 76134-2099
(817) 293-0450
E-mail: alcon.foundation@alcon.com
Web Site: www.alcon.com

AREAS OF INTEREST:
Ophthalmology and vision care.

TYPE:
Project/program grants.

YEAR PROGRAM STARTED: 1962

PURPOSE:
To support programs that improve the quality of eye care services and patient access to care, as well as programs that promote the advancement of eye health education, training and skills-transfer; to support select cultural, humanitarian and community development programs that meaningfully enhance quality of life in the communities where Alcon has a U.S. facility.

LEGAL BASIS:
Corporate foundation.

ELIGIBILITY:
Eligible organizations must be 501(c)(3) nonprofit entities. The Foundation accepts charitable monetary donation applications from 501(c)(3) charities with high-quality programs and services, well-defined goals, a commitment to maximizing available resources, a reputation for meeting results, and the ability to report results.

GEOG. RESTRICTIONS: For cultural, humanitarian and community development programs: Irvine and Lake Forest, CA; Johns Creek, GA; Sinking Spring, PA; Fort Worth and Houston, TX; and Huntington, WV.

APPLICATION INFO:
Only online application will be accepted.

Duration: One year.

Deadline: July 31 for requests larger than $10,000.

ADDRESS INQUIRIES TO:
Melissa Thompson, President
(See address above.)

AMERICAN ACADEMY OF OPTOMETRY FOUNDATION   [2254]
622 East Washington Street
Suite 300
Orlando, FL 32801
(321) 319-4858
Fax: (407) 893-9890
E-mail: helenv@aaoptom.org
Web Site: www.aaopt.org/home/aaof/programs

FOUNDED: 1922

AREAS OF INTEREST:
Vision science and vision care.

NAME(S) OF PROGRAMS:
● **Julius F. Neumueller Award in Optics**

TYPE:
Awards/prizes.

YEAR PROGRAM STARTED: 1969

PURPOSE:
To advance optometric education in optics.

LEGAL BASIS:
Tax-exempt corporation.

ELIGIBILITY:
Applicant must be a student pursuing an O.D. degree in a school of optometry recognized by the AOA Council on Optometric Education.

GEOG. RESTRICTIONS: Primarily United States and Canada.

FINANCIAL DATA:
Amount of support per award: Approximately $750.

Total amount of support: Approximately $750 annually.

NO. MOST RECENT APPLICANTS: 2.

NO. AWARDS: 2.

APPLICATION INFO:
Applicant must submit a paper, not to exceed 3,000 words, on Geometrical Optics, Physical Optics, Ophthalmic Optics or Optics of the Eye. Each school may submit two papers each year to the Chairman of the Awards Committee, which are judged by selected members of the American Academy of Optometry.

Duration: One-time award.

Deadline: April 1. Award announcement July 1.

ADDRESS INQUIRIES TO:
Helen Viksnins
Senior Director of Programs
(See address above.)

AMERICAN ACADEMY OF OPTOMETRY FOUNDATION   [2255]
622 East Washington Street
Suite 300
Orlando, FL 32801
(321) 319-4870
Fax: (407) 893-9890
E-mail: aaoawards@aaoptom.org
Web Site: www.aaopt.org/home/aaof/programs

FOUNDED: 1947

AREAS OF INTEREST:
Optometric research and education.

NAME(S) OF PROGRAMS:
● **J. Pat Cummings Scholarships**
● **VSP and AAOF Canadian Practice Excellence Scholarships**
● **VSP and AAOF Practice Excellence Scholarships**

TYPE:
Scholarships; Travel grants. In collaboration with Johnson & Johnson Vision, the Pat Cummings Scholarships are bestowed annually to second- or third-year optometry students who best demonstrate the ideal eye care standards of practice, achievement in both academic performance and extracurricular activities, and participation with other professional pursuits such as involvement with patients through internships, community service, and other volunteer activities.

VSP and AAOF Canadian Practice Excellence Scholarships are awarded to optometry students at two schools of optometry in Canada. The travel grant will enable outstanding students to attend a premier education opportunity in primary eye care, as well as attend a reception co-hosted

by VSP and the AAOF to help foster networking opportunities and teach the importance of Academy Fellowship.

VSP and AAOF Practice Excellence Scholarships are awarded to optometry students at every school and college of optometry in the U.S. and Puerto Rico. The travel grant will enable outstanding students to attend a premier education opportunity in primary eye care, as well as attend a reception co-hosted by VSP Global and AAOF to help foster networking opportunities and teach the importance of Academy Fellowship.

YEAR PROGRAM STARTED: 1952

PURPOSE:
To encourage careers in optometry and to further vision research, both basic and clinical.

LEGAL BASIS:
IRS tax status 501(c)(3).

ELIGIBILITY:
Student must be a member of the American Academy of Optometry.

VSP and AAOF Canadian Practice Excellence Scholarship and VSP and AAOF Practice Excellence Scholarship Programs: Candidate must excel in primary eye care services to clinical patients and must have a grade point average that ranks in the top half of the class. Student should have a commitment to enter the practice of optometry. Participation in the private practice or practice management club on campus is recommended, with special consideration given to students who have served a leadership role.

GEOG. RESTRICTIONS: Canada, Puerto Rico and United States.

FINANCIAL DATA:
Amount of support per award: Cummings Scholarships: $875; VSP and AAOF Canadian Scholarships: $6,000 total among four students, plus $750 travel support to attend the AAO Annual Meeting; VSP and AAOF Scholarships: $4,000, including $750 travel support.

Total amount of support: Varies.

NO. AWARDS: Cummings Scholarships: 24; VSP and AAOF Canadian Scholarships: 4; VSP and AAOF Scholarships: 50.

APPLICATION INFO:
The J. Pat Cummings Nomination Form and a copy of the appropriate IRS tax form are provided directly to institution contacts via e-mail prior to the opening of the submission window. The appropriate award selection committee at each school or college of optometry will select the one student who meets the eligibility requirements and best demonstrates the detailed qualities. The AAOF will not accept applications directly from students. Interested students should relay their desire for consideration to the award chair or financial aid representative at their institution.

VSP and AAOF Canadian Practice Excellence Scholarships and VSP and AAOF Practice Excellence Scholarships: Each institution's Awards and Scholarship committee is tasked with selecting a pool of five business-minded students who meet the clinical and academic standards and then choose two scholarship recipients. The AAOF will not accept applications directly from students for this program. AAOF will notify institutional contacts that the submission window is open for nominations.

Duration: Fellowships are awarded for a period of one year.

Deadline: Cummings Scholarships: September 15; VSP and AAOF Canadian Scholarships and VSP and AAOF Scholarships: August 17.

PUBLICATIONS:
Application guidelines/criteria.

STAFF:
Peter Scott, C.A.E., MBA, Executive Director
Bob Gray, Development Director
Jennifer Rubin, Grants and Awards Manager

BOARD OF DIRECTORS AND OFFICERS:
Wendy Harrison, O.D., Ph.D., President
Dr. Rachel A. Coulter, O.D., M.S., President-Elect
Valerie L. Sharpe, O.D., Secretary-Treasurer
Jennifer L. Coyle, O.D., M.S.
Kerry Giedd, O.D., M.S.
April Jasper, O.D.
Peter Kollbaum, O.D., Ph.D.
A. Mika Moy, O.D.
Kathryn L. Richdale, O.D., Ph.D.
David G. Sattler
Loretta Szczotka-Flynn, O.D., Ph.D.
Danne Ventura
Suresh Viswanathan, M.S., Ph.D.

ADDRESS INQUIRIES TO:
Jennifer Rubin, Grants and Awards Manager (See e-mail address above.)

AMERICAN ACADEMY OF OPTOMETRY FOUNDATION [2256]

622 East Washington Street
Suite 300
Orlando, FL 32801
(321) 319-4870
Fax: (407) 893-9890
E-mail: aaoawards@aaoptom.org
Web Site: www.aaopt.org/home/aaof/programs

FOUNDED: 1947

AREAS OF INTEREST:
Vision science and vision education.

NAME(S) OF PROGRAMS:
- **Joe and Janet Barr Early Career Cornea and Contact Lens Research Award**

TYPE:
Awards/prizes; Seed money grants.

YEAR PROGRAM STARTED: 2012

PURPOSE:
To advance optometric education in cornea/ocular surface or contact lenses.

LEGAL BASIS:
Tax-exempt corporation.

ELIGIBILITY:
Applicant must be a student member of the American Academy of Optometry. Applicant must be an entering first- or second-year M.S. or Ph.D. vision science or physiological optics student attending a North American school or college of optometry. Applicant can be in a graduate program alone or combined with professional/residence program.

To receive this award, applicant must not have applied during the same application year nor previously received an Ezell Fellowship.

GEOG. RESTRICTIONS: Primarily United States and Canada.

FINANCIAL DATA:
Amount of support per award: $2,000, plus $750 travel funding to attend the AAO Annual Meeting.

NO. AWARDS: 1.

APPLICATION INFO:
The following documents must be submitted in PDF format to Jennifer Rubin, Grants and Awards Manager, at jenniferr@aaoptom.org:
(1) a copy of a current curriculum vitae or resume;
(2) a one-page statement describing past and present educational and research achievements, future educational objectives, and long-term career goals in the areas of cornea and contact lens research;
(3) an up to two-page summary of the proposed research project including a summary of the relevant background and hypotheses, purpose, methods and budget;
(4) up to three best representations of students submitted or published papers, if applicable;
(5) a letter from the Dean, Associate Dean for Research, or authorized official stating that the applicant has been accepted into or is currently enrolled in a Vision Science/Physiological Optics M.S. or Ph.D. program at a school or college of optometry and that any funds received from the AAOF will go only in support of the proposed project and not decrease any academic financial support and;
(6) a letter from a research supervisor or mentor describing their support of the described project and education advancement of the applicant during the award period.

Duration: One-time renewal possible.

Deadline: April 1.

ADDRESS INQUIRIES TO:
Jennifer Rubin, Grants and Awards Manager (See e-mail address above.)

*SPECIAL STIPULATIONS:
Recipient must attend the Annual Meeting of the American Academy of Optometry and attend the AAOF Celebration Luncheon to receive their award. The recipient is also required to perform volunteer service at the AAOF Booth.

AMERICAN ACADEMY OF OPTOMETRY FOUNDATION [2257]

622 East Washington Street
Suite 300
Orlando, FL 32801
(321) 319-4870
Fax: (407) 893-9890
E-mail: aaoawards@aaoptom.org
Web Site: www.aaopt.org/home/aaof/programs

FOUNDED: 1947

AREAS OF INTEREST:
Vision science and vision care.

NAME(S) OF PROGRAMS:
- **Bert C. and Lydia M. Corwin Contact Lens Residency Award**
- **Douglas W. Hopkins Primary Care Residency Award**
- **Alfred A. Rosenbloom, Jr. Low Vision Residency Award**
- **Sheldon Wechsler and George Mertz Contact Lens Residency Award**

TYPE:
Residencies; Training grants. The Bert C. and Lydia M. Corwin Contact Lens Residency Award is intended to promote the practice and development of the field of contact lenses by providing incentive and support to talented optometric residents who demonstrate a passion and commitment to practice, research and education.

The Douglas Hopkins Primary Care Residency Award is intended to promote the practice and development of the field of primary care optometry by providing incentive and support to talented optometric residents who demonstrate a passion and commitment to practice, research and education in primary care.

The Alfred A. Rosenbloom, Jr. Residency Award is intended to promote the practice and development of the field of low vision by providing incentive and support to sustain talented optometric residents who demonstrate a passion and commitment to practice, research, and education.

The Sheldon Wechsler and George Mertz Contact Lens Residency Programs, which are funded by Johnson & Johnson Vision, are intended to promote the practice and development of the field of contact lenses by providing incentive and support to sustain talented optometric residents who demonstrate a passion and commitment to practice, research and education.

PURPOSE:
To advance optometric education.

LEGAL BASIS:
Tax-exempt corporation.

ELIGIBILITY:
Applicant must be a student member of the American Academy of Optometry.

Corwin Contact Lens Residency Award: Any optometrist currently serving in a 2021-22 academic year calendar contact lens residency through a North American school or college of optometry is eligible to apply.

Hopkins Primary Care Residency Award: Any optometrist currently serving in a 2021-22 academic year calendar primary care/family practice residency through a North American school or college of optometry or veterans administration facility is eligible to apply.

Rosenbloom, Jr. Low Vision Residency Award: Any optometrist currently serving in a 2021-22 academic year calendar advanced practice low vision residency program through a North American school or college of optometry may apply.

Wechsler and Mertz Contact Lens Residency Award: Optometrists currently serving in a 2021-22 academic year calendar advanced practice contact lens residency program through a North American school or college of optometry may apply.

For all awards, anyone who has yet to begin a residency for the 2021-22 academic year calendar is ineligible.

GEOG. RESTRICTIONS: Primary United States and Canada.

FINANCIAL DATA:
Amount of support per award: $2,000, plus $750 travel fellowship to attend the AAO Annual Meeting.

NO. AWARDS: Corwin, Hopkins, and Rosenbloom, Jr. Residency Award: 1; Wechsler and Mertz Residency Award: 2.

APPLICATION INFO:
Applicant must be a member of the American Academy of Optometry, whether as a student, candidate or fellow at the time of acceptance of any award. Application must include:
(1) a cover page that lists the applicant's name, any degrees, residency facility, the residency's host optometric institution, current and permanent address information, e-mail and telephone contact information;
(2) applicant's education, clinical, research and teaching experience, typically in the form of a curriculum vitae;
(3) a brief description of the residency program and the names and e-mail addresses of the three people applicant has contacted to submit letters of recommendation;
(4) a one-page statement of career goals and;
(5) three letters of recommendation from persons qualified to comment on the applicant's educational qualifications, research abilities and potential. One must be from the Residency Director or Program Coordinator of the host optometric institution. These letters should be e-mailed separately by the recommender.

Applications and letters of recommendation must be submitted electronically to the Foundation at the e-mail address listed above. Include the residency name and applicant's last name in the subject line.

Duration: One-time award.

Deadline: June 1.

ADDRESS INQUIRIES TO:
Jennifer Rubin, Grants and Awards Manager (See e-mail address above.)

AMERICAN ACADEMY OF OPTOMETRY FOUNDATION   [2258]

622 East Washington Street
Suite 300
Orlando, FL 32801
(321) 319-4870
Fax: (407) 893-9890
E-mail: aaoawards@aaoptom.org
Web Site: www.aaopt.org/home/aaof/programs

FOUNDED: 1947

AREAS OF INTEREST:
Vision science and vision care.

NAME(S) OF PROGRAMS:
● **Beta Sigma Kappa (BSK) Student Travel Fellowship**
● **Elmer H. Eger Memorial Student Travel Fellowship**
● **N. Rex Ghormley Student Travel Fellowship**
● **Kirschen Family Student Travel Fellowship**

TYPE:
Fellowships; Travel grants. The BSK Student Travel Fellowship gives an optometry student the opportunity to engage in cutting edge learning, participate in hands on workshops, and experience an amazing exhibit hall at the annual Academy meeting.

The Eger Memorial Student Travel Fellowship is designed to support students whose professional goal is to be in private practice. It is also designed to encourage optometry students to attend key national meetings and exchange scientific ideas and research for use in an everyday clinical environment.

Ghormley Student Travel Fellowship is designed to encourage optometry students to attend key national meetings and exchange scientific ideas and research for use in an everyday clinical environment.

The Kirschen Family Student Travel Fellowship encourages optometry students to come to the annual meeting and become fellows in the Academy.

PURPOSE:
To advance optometric education.

LEGAL BASIS:
Tax-exempt corporation.

ELIGIBILITY:
Student must be a member of the American Academy of Optometry.

BSK Student Travel Fellowship: Optometry students who are currently enrolled full-time as second-, third- or fourth-year students may apply.

Eger Memorial Student Travel Fellowship: Schools will follow a rotation schedule which gives eight schools each year the opportunity to submit a nominee. Nominee must be pursuing a career in private practice and must be a third- or fourth-year student. Postdoctoral students and residents are not eligible.

The Ghormley Student Travel Fellowship: Optometry students who are currently enrolled full-time or have graduated within a year of the meeting are eligible to apply. Applicant must have had an abstract accepted as a first presenter/author of a paper or poster. Postdoctoral students and residents are not eligible. Fellowship will be awarded primarily for accomplishment and potential in optometric research and education. Academic abilities, including clinical abilities if relevant, are considered.

Kirschen Family Student Travel Fellowship is available to students currently in their third or fourth year of optometry school, who are in good academic standing and plan to pursue a career in private practice. Presentation of a paper or poster is desired, but not a requirement for this award.

GEOG. RESTRICTIONS: Primarily United States and Canada.

FINANCIAL DATA:
Amount of support per award: $750.

NO. AWARDS: 1 per award.

APPLICATION INFO:
BSK Student Travel Fellowship applicant must submit a short essay (300 to 500 words) on the subject "Why I want to attend the AAO meeting and how it will help me contribute to the professional in the future." Being a presenter of a paper or poster is desired, but not required. If applicable, submit a copy of the accepted paper or poster.

Eger Memorial Student Travel Fellowship: Student must submit a one-page statement describing why they want to pursue a career in private practice.

Ghormley Student Travel Fellowship: Student must submit a one-page statement which includes their commitment and interest in optometric research and/or education, their short- and long-term career goals, previous research training talks, papers and posters, summary of academic training (including honors), and demonstrated potential for self-motivation, independence and leadership.

Also include a copy of the abstract of paper or poster that has been accepted and a recommendation letter from faculty.

Kirschen Family Student Travel Fellowship: Applicant must submit a one-page statement about themselves and why they are choosing private practice. One letter of recommendation is required.

Duration: One-time award.

ADDRESS INQUIRIES TO:
Jennifer Rubin, Grants and Awards Manager (See e-mail address above.)

AMERICAN ACADEMY OF OPTOMETRY FOUNDATION   [2259]

622 East Washington Street
Suite 300
Orlando, FL 32801
(321) 319-4870
Fax: (407) 893-9890
E-mail: aaoawards@aaoptom.org
Web Site: www.aaopt.org/home/aaof/programs

FOUNDED: 1947

AREAS OF INTEREST:
Vision science and vision care.

NAME(S) OF PROGRAMS:
● **Allergan Foundation Research Grant**
● **Award of Excellence in Contact Lens Patient Care Grant**
● **Korb-Exford Dry Eye Career Development Grant**
● **Fredric Rosemore Low Vision Educational Grants**

TYPE:
Development grants; Project/program grants; Research grants. Allergan Foundation Research Grant supports talented optometry and vision science faculty and researchers in the area of glaucoma or the anterior segment.

Award of Excellence in Contact Lens Patient Care Grant, sponsored by Johnson & Johnson Vision, recognizes outstanding fourth-year student clinicians who have demonstrated excellence in contact lens patient care during their optometric education.

The Korb-Exford Dry Eye Career Development Grant is designed to support an individual to further their knowledge in the broad area of dry eye.

The Rosemore Low Vision Educational Grants are intended to increase and reward excellence in the field of low vision for faculty at North American schools and colleges of optometry.

PURPOSE:
To advance optometric education.

LEGAL BASIS:
Tax-exempt corporation.

ELIGIBILITY:
Allergan Foundation Research Grant is open to all faculty and researchers in optometry and vision science. Preference will be given to North American applicants. The Principal Investigator must be a member of the American Academy of Optometry. It is also encouraged that the co-investigator be a member.

Award of Excellence nominee must be a fourth-year student and a student member of the American Academy of Optometry. Nominee must represent outstanding clinical patient care as demonstrated by the student's overall knowledge in the contact lens field and skillful, considerate and professional care of their contact lens patients.

Korb-Exford Development Grant applicant must possess an O.D. or relevant graduate degree and must be a member of the American Academy of Optometry as a student, candidate or fellow at the time of applying for the award. The successful individual must have a demonstrable interest in either a clinical or basic science area of dry eye and may be a clinician, educator, researcher or student. Funds from this award may not be used to purchase major equipment for an institution for dry eye research.

Fredric Rosemore Educational Grants applicant must be a member of the American Academy of Optometry as a student, candidate or fellow at the time of acceptance of this award. Grant may be used to provide care, to support personnel, to provide equipment, or to fill any other need in the field of low vision as identified by the institution and consistent with the AAOF mission.

FINANCIAL DATA:
Amount of support per award: Allergan Grant: $60,000; Award of Excellence: $500; Korb-Exford Development Grant: $25,000; Rosemore Educational Grants: $1,000.

NO. AWARDS: Allergan Grant, Korb-Exford Development Grant and Rosemore Educational Grants: 1; Award for Excellence: 25 for the year 2021.

APPLICATION INFO:
Allergan Foundation Research Grant proposal must contain the following components:
(1) a cover page, including project title, institution and address, name and titles for principal investigator and a maximum of three co-investigators with contact information;
(2) an introduction including background and significance, specific aims, preliminary studies, and study design and methods (no more than five pages);
(3) references (maximum one page);
(4) budget and budget justification;
(5) biographical sketch of principal investigator and up to three co-investigators (maximum two pages for each investigator) and;
(6) a signed Letter of Assurance by the Dean or President indicating that the proposal has been reviewed and meets with the standards of the institution and, if warranted, observes all rules and regulations regarding compliance with research on human or animal subjects.

Award of Excellence: Institutions will be contacted directly via e-mail as to the opening of the submission window. The appropriate grant selection committee at each school or college of optometry will select the one student who best demonstrates the qualities outlined for this award.

The Korb-Exford Dry Eye Career Development Grant application must begin with a cover letter consisting of full contact information including how the applicant's degree should appear in reports and/or news items. The applicant must submit a two-page description of how the "Dry Eye Grant" will be used, the exceptional opportunity that it will provide, and the impact it will have on

the applicant's career. Curriculum vitae of no more than three pages should accompany the application.

Fredric Rosemore Low Vision Educational Grants application should include:
(1) a curriculum vitae with applicant's education, clinical, research and employment experience;
(2) a proposal and budget and;
(3) a letter of endorsement by the Dean, President or Director of the school or college (optional).
Duration: One year.
Deadline: Allergan Grant: July 15. Award of Excellence: April 1. Korb-Exford Development Grant: July 1. Rosemore Educational Grants: June 1.

ADDRESS INQUIRIES TO:
Jennifer Rubin, Grants and Awards Manager (See e-mail address above.)

AMERICAN ACADEMY OF OPTOMETRY FOUNDATION [2260]
622 East Washington Street
Suite 300
Orlando, FL 32801
(321) 319-4870
Fax: (407) 893-9890
E-mail: aaoawards@aaoptom.org
Web Site: www.aaopt.org/home/aaof/programs

FOUNDED: 1947

AREAS OF INTEREST:
Vision science and vision care.

NAME(S) OF PROGRAMS:
● **Beta Sigma Kappa Research Fellowships**
● **William C. Ezell Fellowship**
● **David and Diane Goss Optometry History Fellowship**

TYPE:
Fellowships. The Beta Sigma Kappa Research Fellowships support new optometric and vision science faculty research and optometric resident research. The funding is designed to benefit individuals early in their careers whose academic curiosity leads them to seek answers to a vast variety of professionally-based questions covering a wide area of vision science, clinical practice or eye-related public health.

William C. Ezell Fellowship aims to encourage talented persons to pursue full-time careers in optometric research and education in a school or college of optometry. These fellowships provide support to graduate students enrolled in a full-time program of study and training in vision-related research that leads to a Master's or Ph.D. degree.

The David and Diane Goss Optometry History Fellowship, awarded biennially, provides support to an individual pursuing research in optometric history. Researcher or student may use the funds to visit a library, archives or museum to conduct research.

PURPOSE:
To advance optometric education.

LEGAL BASIS:
Tax-exempt corporation.

ELIGIBILITY:
Applicant must be a member of the American Academy of Optometry.

Beta Sigma Kappa Research Fellowships: All optometric-related faculty, including adjunct faculty, within three years of faculty appointment, optometric residents, and Advanced Practice Fellows at any school or college of optometry, irrespective of membership in BSK, are eligible to apply.

William C. Ezell Fellowship focuses on specialized areas of research, such as glaucoma, cornea and contact lenses, and binocular vision and pediatrics. Preference will be given to first-time awardees. Previous Ezell fellows are eligible to apply, although the maximum number of years an individual can be awarded this fellowship is two years. Applicant must be a graduate student enrolled in a full-time program of study and training in vision-related research that leads to a Master's or Ph.D. degree. Completion of the degree program cannot be within the calendar years of the award competition.

David and Diane Goss Optometry History Fellowship applicants may be optometrists or optometry students, but may also be individuals outside the field of optometry, such as a historian or librarian, and may be at any career stage from student to retirement.

GEOG. RESTRICTIONS: Primarily United States and Canada.

FINANCIAL DATA:
Amount of support per award: Beta Sigma Kappa Research Fellowships: $4,000; Ezell Fellowship: $8,000; Goss Fellowship: $1,000.

NO. MOST RECENT APPLICANTS: Ezell Fellowship: Approximately 40.

NO. AWARDS: Beta Sigma Kappa Research Fellowships: 1; Ezell Fellowship: 9 to 11; Goss Fellowship: 1 biennially.

APPLICATION INFO:
Beta Sigma Kappa Research Fellowships: Applications should consist of six pages or less and contain the following:
(1) a cover page with project title, institution and address, name (including degrees) and title for faculty member with contact information;
(2) research plan;
(3) budget explanation;
(4) Helsinki Declaration (required only if human subjects are involved) and;
(5) letter of endorsement by Faculty Advisor, Dean or President/Director of the school or college that also indicates the proposal was reviewed and meets with the standards of the institution.

William C. Ezell Fellowship: Applicant must upload the "non-fellowship" NIH formatted bio sketch, their published works bibliography submitted as a URL link, and three letters of recommendation from persons qualified to comment on the applicant's educational qualifications, research abilities and potential, and future teaching capabilities and potential.

David and Diane Goss Optometry History Fellowship applicants must include the following:
(1) a cover letter consisting of full contact information including how the applicant's degree should appear in reports and/or news items;
(2) a two-page description of how the fellowship will be used, the opportunity that it will provide and the impact it will have on the applicant's career and;
(3) a curriculum vitae (no more than three pages).

Duration: Beta Sigma Kappa Research Fellowships: Up to one year; Ezell Fellowship: One year.

Deadline: Beta Sigma Kappa Research Fellowships and Goss Fellowship: August 2. Ezell Fellowship: February 1.

ADDRESS INQUIRIES TO:
Jennifer Rubin, Grants and Awards Manager (See e-mail address above.)

*SPECIAL STIPULATIONS:
One year after the award is made, the Goss Fellowship recipient must submit a progress report suitable for publication in *Hindsight,* the Optometric Historical Society's quarterly publication.

AMERICAN DIABETES ASSOCIATION
2451 Crystal Drive
Suite 900
Arlington, VA 22202
(703) 549-1500 ext. 5532
Fax: (703) 621-3759
E-mail: grantquestions@diabetes.org
Web Site: www.professional.diabetes.org/grants

TYPE:
Fellowships; Research grants; Training grants.

See entry 2148 for full listing.

AMERICAN OTOLOGICAL SOCIETY RESEARCH FOUNDATION [2261]
Administrative Office
5830 1st Street North
St. Petersburg, FL 33703
(217) 638-0801
Fax: (727) 800-9428
E-mail: administrator@
americanotologicalsociety.org
Web Site: www.americanotologicalsociety.org

FOUNDED: 1868

AREAS OF INTEREST:
Research related to any aspects of the ear, hearing and balance disorders.

NAME(S) OF PROGRAMS:
• **Clinical Investigations Grant**
• **Clinician-Scientist Award**
• **Fellowship Grant**
• **Research Grant**

TYPE:
Fellowships; Research grants. Clinical Investigations Grant: Intended to encourage and support academic research in sciences related to the ear.

Clinician-Scientist Award: For salary and research support of a new academic clinician-scientist, at the Assistant Professor level, in order to facilitate development into an independent otologic investigator. Department chair guarantees at least 50% time commitment in research.

Fellowship Grant: For clinical fellows, residents, medical students postdoctoral fellows and graduate students, to support full-time research conducted outside of residency training.

Research Grant: Research on any topic related to ear disorders.

YEAR PROGRAM STARTED: 1926

PURPOSE:
To encourage and support academic research in sciences related to the ear.

LEGAL BASIS:
Private foundation.

ELIGIBILITY:
Clinical Investigations Grant: Grant awards may involve research on any topic related to ear disorders. The research need not be directly on an otological disease but may explore normal functions of the cochlea, labyrinth or central auditory or vestibular systems. However, the applicant must describe how the proposed research will benefit the understanding, diagnosis or treatment of otological disorders. The Research Foundation Advisory Board will review applications that propose, as a central focus, a clinical trial or other "hands-on" patient clinical investigative study. Applicants should follow general guidelines for research proposals and also include information about the clinical study design and ethical requirements regarding human research subject participation. Grants are available to physician or doctoral-level investigators in the U.S. and Canada only.

For the Clinician-Scientist Award, the applicant must:
(1) hold or be approved for a full-time university faculty appointment at the rank of Assistant Professor in a department or division of Otolaryngology - Head and Neck Surgery;
(2) be citizens of the U.S., or have been lawfully admitted for permanent U.S. residency at the time of application;
(3) hold a Doctor of Medicine (M.D.) or equivalent degree from an accredited institution awarded within the last 10 years;
(4) have completed an ACGME-approved otolaryngology residency program and;
(5) have demonstrated the capacity or potential for a highly productive, independent research career with an emphasis in otology/neurotology.
Preference will be given to candidates who are currently enrolled in or have completed (within the preceding three years) a two-year otology/neurotology fellowship program.

Fellowship Grant: Research must be conducted in U.S. or Canadian institutions. Applicants must be medical students, residents or fellows (not nonmedical postgraduate researchers). Recipients must be relieved of all clinical duties during the fellowship period.

Research Grants are available to physician or doctoral-level investigators in the U.S. and Canada only.

FINANCIAL DATA:
Amount of support per award: Clinical Investigations Grant: Up to $66,000 per year, including indirect costs (overhead); indirect costs not to exceed 10% of direct costs; Clinician-Scientist Award: Up to $80,000 for salary and research support; Fellowship Grant: $44,000 stipend including $5,000 for supplies and $4,000 indirect costs; Research Grant: $55,000 maximum per year, including indirect costs.
Total amount of support: $350,000.

NO. MOST RECENT APPLICANTS: Approximately 35 applicants and 20 invitations.

NO. AWARDS: 6 to 8.

APPLICATION INFO:
Clinical Investigations Grant uses a simplied version of the NIDCD Early Career Research Award (R21) application. The Clinician-Scientist Award uses a simplified

version of the NIDCD Early Career Research Award (K08/K23) application. The Fellowship Grant uses a simplfied version of the NIH NRSA Individual Postdoctoral Fellowship (F32) application. The Research Grant uses a simplified version of the NIDCD Early Career Research Award (R21) application.

For all awards, there are no forms to fill out. All applications must be formatted using 11-point Arial font, with page margins set to be 0.5 inches circumferentially. The Principal Investigator's name must appear on each page. The completed application should be submitted in PDF format. Applications must meet the formatting rules to be considered.
Duration: Clinical Investigations Grant: One year. Clinician-Scientist Award: Up to three years. Renewable annually. Fellowship Grant and Research Grant: One year. Non-renewable.
Deadline: Letter of Intent: November 1. Invited applications: January 31.

STAFF:
John S. Oghalai, M.D., Executive Secretary

ADDRESS INQUIRIES TO:
Kristen Bordignon, Executive Administrator
American Otological Society
Research Foundation
(See e-mail address above.)

AMERICAN SPEECH-LANGUAGE-HEARING FOUNDATION [2262]
2200 Research Boulevard
Rockville, MD 20850-3289
(301) 296-8703
Fax: (301) 296-8567
E-mail: foundationprograms@asha.org
Web Site: www.ashfoundation.org

FOUNDED: 1946

AREAS OF INTEREST:
Communication sciences and disorders.

NAME(S) OF PROGRAMS:
• **Clinical Research Grant**
• **Louis M. DiCarlo Award for Recent Clinical Achievement**
• **Graduate Student Scholarship for International/Minority Students**
• **Graduate Student Scholarship for Minority Students**
• **Graduate Student Scholarship for NSSLHA Members**
• **Graduate Student Scholarship for Students with a Disability**
• **Graduate Student Scholarships**
• **Frank R. Kleffner Clinical Career Award**
• **New Century Scholars Doctoral Scholarship**
• **New Century Scholars Research Grant**
• **New Investigators Research Grant**
• **Speech Science Research Grant**
• **Student Research Grant in Audiology**
• **Student Research Grant in Early Childhood Language Development**
• **Rolland J. Van Hattum Award for Contribution in the Schools**

TYPE:
Research grants; Scholarships. Clinical achievement awards. Clinical Research Grants are awarded to researchers to advance knowledge of the efficacy of treatment and assessment practices in communication sciences and disorders.

Louis M. DiCarlo Award for Clinical Achievement recognizes individuals demonstrating outstanding achievement in the advancement of knowledge in clinical practice within the past three years.

Graduate Student Scholarships are available to students demonstrating outstanding academic achievement in communication sciences and disorders. These include general scholarships, scholarships for students with disabilities, scholarships for international and minority students, and scholarships for NSSLHA members.

Frank R. Kleffner Clinical Career Award recognizes outstanding lifetime achievement in clinical science and practice.

New Century Scholars Doctoral Scholarships are available to students enrolled in a research doctoral program (Ph.D. or equivalent) in communication sciences and disorders.

New Century Scholars Research Grants are awarded to individuals committed to teacher-investigator careers in the university or college environment or in external research institutes or laboratories.

New Investigators Research Grants are awarded to new scientists to pursue research in audiology or speech-language pathology.

Speech Science Research Grants are awarded to new investigators to encourage research activities in the area of speech science.

Student Research Grant in Audiology supports a proposed one-year study to conduct research in audiology.

Student Research Grant in Early Childhood Language supports a proposed one-year study to conduct research in early childhood language development.

Rolland J. Van Hattum Award for Contribution in the Schools recognizes professionals demonstrating significant contribution to the delivery of audiology and/or speech pathology services in the schools.

YEAR PROGRAM STARTED: 1979

PURPOSE:
To further education in speech, language and hearing through the provision of financial assistance; to recognize and support research and similar endeavors which contribute to the advancement of knowledge and improvement of practice in serving children and adults with speech, language, or hearing disorders; to identify and facilitate new directions in the field of communication sciences and disorders through support of such vehicles as conferences, publications and other activities.

LEGAL BASIS:
501(c)(3) association.

FINANCIAL DATA:
Amount of support per award: Research Grants: $2,000 to $75,000, depending on grant type; Scholarships: $5,000 to $10,000.
Total amount of support: Varies.

NO. MOST RECENT APPLICANTS: Approximately 300 for all programs.

NO. AWARDS: 82.

APPLICATION INFO:
Guidelines are available from the ASH Foundation web site. Required documentation for scholarships includes application form, academic documentation, faculty

recommendation committee report, and student essay. Research grant submissions require a research proposal.
Duration: One year. Nonrenewable.
Deadline: Usually April or May. Awards presented in November.

PUBLICATIONS:
Annual report; program and application guidelines; fact sheet.

IRS I.D.: 52-6055761

BOARD OF TRUSTEES:
Patricia A. Prelock, President

ADDRESS INQUIRIES TO:
Program Administrator
(See address above.)

BENIGN ESSENTIAL BLEPHAROSPASM RESEARCH FOUNDATION INC.   [2263]
755 South 11th Street
Suite 211
Beaumont, TX 77701
(409) 832-0788
Fax: (409) 832-0890
E-mail: bebrf@blepharospasm.org
Web Site: www.blepharospasm.org

FOUNDED: 1981

AREAS OF INTEREST:
Benign essential blepharospasm, Meige syndrome, hemifacial spasm and related disorders and infirmities of the facial musculature.

TYPE:
Project/program grants; Research grants; Seed money grants.

YEAR PROGRAM STARTED: 1985

PURPOSE:
To undertake, promote, develop and carry on the search for the cause and cure for benign essential blepharospasm and other related disorders and infirmities of the facial musculature.

LEGAL BASIS:
Foundation.

ELIGIBILITY:
Research proposals must relate specifically to benign essential blepharospasm and Meige to include new treatments, pathophysiology and genetics, photophobia and dry eye.

FINANCIAL DATA:
Amount of support per award: $10,000 to $50,000.
Total amount of support: $50,000 for the year 2021.

NO. MOST RECENT APPLICANTS: 1 for the year 2021.

APPLICATION INFO:
Application information is available on the web site or by sending an e-mail to the address above.
Duration: One to two years. Extensions have been granted.
Deadline: August 31.

PUBLICATIONS:
Program announcement; application guidelines; brochure.

IRS I.D.: 74-2193322

BOARD OF DIRECTORS:
Heidi Coggeshall, President and Treasurer
Tishana Cundiff, First Vice President
Peter Bakalor, Vice President of Development

Jane Boyd, M.D., Vice President of Physician Outreach
Charlene Hudgins, Executive Director and Secretary
Barbara Benton
Robert Campbell, Ph.D.
Cynthia Clark
Jonathan Healy, Esq.
Barbara Kimmel
Bryan Renehan

ADDRESS INQUIRIES TO:
Charlene Hudgins, Executive Director
E-mail: charlene@blepharospasm.org

BRIGHT FOCUS FOUNDATION
22512 Gateway Center Drive
Clarksburg, MD 20871
(301) 948-3244
(800) 437-2423
Fax: (301) 948-4403
E-mail: researchgrants@brightfocus.org
Web Site: www.brightfocus.org

TYPE:
Research grants.

See entry 1284 for full listing.

BRIGHT FOCUS FOUNDATION   [2264]
22512 Gateway Center Drive
Clarksburg, MD 20871
(301) 948-3244
(800) 437-2423
Fax: (301) 948-4403
E-mail: researchgrants@brightfocus.org
Web Site: www.brightfocus.org

FOUNDED: 1978

AREAS OF INTEREST:
Glaucoma research.

NAME(S) OF PROGRAMS:
● **National Glaucoma Research Program**

TYPE:
Research grants. Support for basic research into the causes and potential treatments of glaucoma.

YEAR PROGRAM STARTED: 1978

PURPOSE:
To develop treatments, preventions and cures for glaucoma.

LEGAL BASIS:
Nonprofit foundation.

ELIGIBILITY:
Grants are awarded on the basis of the proposal's scientific merit and its relevance to understanding the disease studied. No funds for large equipment, institutional overhead costs, construction or building expenses.

FINANCIAL DATA:
Amount of support per award: Postdoctoral Fellowship: $75,000 per year; Standard Award: $100,000 per year.
Total amount of support: Varies.

NO. MOST RECENT APPLICANTS: 87 for the year 2020.

NO. AWARDS: 17 for the year 2020.

APPLICATION INFO:
Applications are submitted through ProposalCentral.
Duration: Up to two years.
Deadline: October 26.

PUBLICATIONS:
Annual report; newsletters; clinical brochures.

ADDRESS INQUIRIES TO:
Kara Summers, Program Officer
(See e-mail address above.)

CANADIAN NATIONAL INSTITUTE FOR THE BLIND [2265]

1929 Bayview Avenue
Toronto ON M4G 3E8 Canada
(416) 486-2500
Fax: (416) 480-7700
E-mail: info@cnib.ca
Web Site: www.cnib.ca

FOUNDED: 1918

AREAS OF INTEREST:
Ophthalmic subspecialties, vision research and macular degeneration.

NAME(S) OF PROGRAMS:
● **CNIB Barbara Tuck MacPhee Award in Macular Degeneration**

TYPE:
Research grants. Award supports researchers in the field of macular degeneration.

YEAR PROGRAM STARTED: 1961

PURPOSE:
To conduct research focused on better serving and improving the quality of life for people with vision loss; to fund cutting-edge medical research aimed at improving our understanding of how to prevent, diagnose and treat eye disease.

LEGAL BASIS:
Registered charity.

ELIGIBILITY:
Applicants must be residents of Canada and research must be conducted primarily in Canada.

FINANCIAL DATA:
Amount of support per award: Up to $25,000.
Total amount of support: Varies.

NO. AWARDS: 1 per year.

APPLICATION INFO:
Applications must be submitted online.
Duration: One year.
Deadline: January 15. Decision by March 31.

PUBLICATIONS:
Guidelines.

ADDRESS INQUIRIES TO:
Grants Administrator
(See address above.)

EYE BANK ASSOCIATION OF AMERICA [2266]

1101 17th Street, N.W.
Suite 400
Washington, DC 20036
(202) 775-4999
Fax: (202) 429-6036
E-mail: info@restoresight.org
Web Site: www.restoresight.org

FOUNDED: 1961

AREAS OF INTEREST:
Restoration of sight through eye banks.

NAME(S) OF PROGRAMS:
● **EBAA Pilot Research Grant**
● **High Impact Research Grant**

TYPE:
Research grants; Travel grants.

PURPOSE:
To promote scientific research in the fields of eye banking and corneal transplantation; to promote innovation in eye banking and corneal transplantation.

ELIGIBILITY:
Pilot Research Grant applicant must be a physician, including corneal surgeon and other eye care specialist, basic scientist, including biomedical and social scientists, or eye-bank technician, nurse, fellow, ophthalmology fellow or medical student that is supervised by a physician.

FINANCIAL DATA:
Amount of support per award: EBAA Pilot Research Grant: Maximum $7,500; High Impact Research Grant: Maximum $50,000.
Total amount of support: Varies.

NO. AWARDS: EBAA Pilot Research Grant: 7 for the year 2020; High Impact Research Grant: 1 annually.

APPLICATION INFO:
Application information is available on the EBAA web site.
Duration: EBAA Pilot Research Grant: One year.
Deadline: EBAA Pilot Research Grant: March 22. High Impact Research Grant: July 12.

ADDRESS INQUIRIES TO:
Stacey Gardner, Director of Education
(See address above.)

FIGHT FOR SIGHT, INC. [2267]

381 Park Avenue South
Suite 1119
New York, NY 10016
(212) 679-6060
Fax: (212) 679-4466
E-mail: janice@fightforsight.org
Web Site: www.fightforsight.org

FOUNDED: 1946

AREAS OF INTEREST:
Ophthalmology and visual sciences.

NAME(S) OF PROGRAMS:
● **Research Awards Program**

TYPE:
Grants-in-aid; Research grants. Summer student fellowships. Fight for Sight supports new investigators at the beginning of their academic and research careers, provides pilot funding to generate preliminary data for applications to the NEI/NIH and other sources of major support, and provides summer student fellowships to undergraduate and graduate students, thereby encouraging individuals to consider careers in eye and vision research.

YEAR PROGRAM STARTED: 1946

PURPOSE:
To support and inspire eye and vision research by funding promising young scientists early in their careers.

LEGAL BASIS:
501(c)(3) corporation.

ELIGIBILITY:
Grants-in-Aid applicants should be within the first three years of an academic appointment and without major grant support.

Summer Student Fellowship applicants may be any undergraduate or graduate student pursuing degrees in the U.S. or Canada interested in pursuing eye-related clinical or basic research projects.

GEOG. RESTRICTIONS: United States and Canada.

FINANCIAL DATA:
Amount of support per award: Grants-in-Aid: $22,500; Summer Fellowship: $2,500.
Total amount of support: Varies.

NO. MOST RECENT APPLICANTS: 90.

NO. AWARDS: Grants-in-Aid: 2 to 4; Summer Student Fellowships: Up to 20.

APPLICATION INFO:
Application guidelines are available on the web site.
Duration: Grants-in-Aid: One year; Summer Fellowships: Typically eight to 12 weeks.
Deadline: Grants-in-Aid: November 15. Start date between July 1 and September 1. Summer Fellowship: February 15.

PUBLICATIONS:
Brochure.

IRS I.D.: 23-7085732

ADDRESS INQUIRIES TO:
Janice Benson, Associate Director
(See address above.)

FIGHT FOR SIGHT, INC. [2268]

381 Park Avenue South
Suite 1119
New York, NY 10016
(212) 679-6060
Fax: (212) 679-4466
E-mail: janice@fightforsight.org
Web Site: www.fightforsight.org

FOUNDED: 1946

AREAS OF INTEREST:
Ophthalmology and visual sciences.

NAME(S) OF PROGRAMS:
● **Fight for Sight Postdoctoral Award**

TYPE:
Fellowships. Grant to support postdoctoral scientists (e.g., Ph.D., M.D., O.D., D.V.M., or Dr.P.H.) with research projects related to ophthalmology, eye research or visual science.

YEAR PROGRAM STARTED: 1953

PURPOSE:
To advance our basic and clinical understanding of the underlying causes, treatment and prevention of eye diseases and/or visual impairment.

LEGAL BASIS:
501(c)(3) corporation.

ELIGIBILITY:
Any individual with a doctoral degree engaged in postdoctoral research under the supervision of a more senior scientist with interests in fundamental or clinical research in ophthalmology, vision or related sciences may apply. Doctoral degree candidates about to finish their degree program should submit a cover letter confirming that the Doctorate degree will be conferred prior to beginning the award.

FINANCIAL DATA:
Funds are to be used to defray costs of equipment, consumable supplies and/or salaries.
Amount of support per award: $22,500.

NO. MOST RECENT APPLICANTS: 50.

NO. AWARDS: 2 to 4.

APPLICATION INFO:
  Applications are available online. Completed applications should include:
  (1) application face pages and related information completed online and including information about the applicant, his or her education and training, institution and sponsor;
  (2) a research proposal of no more than eight single-spaced pages, not including references;
  (3) a letter of support from a sponsor or departmental chair. The letter should include an evaluation of the student, the role of the mentor in advising the applicant during the project, the training plan, any extracurricular training the student will receive and other information helpful to the committee in evaluating the mentor, the laboratory and the institutional resources in support of a FFS Postdoctoral Award. They should specifically address the suitability of the applicant's training, his or her academic achievements and, most importantly, his or her potential to develop into an independent eye and vision researcher and/or leader in academic ophthalmology;
  (4) curriculum vitae and NIH-style biosketch of the applicant and sponsor;
  (5) supplemental information, including relevant awards, previous research experience and academic or career goals and;
  (6) a cover letter.
  Duration: One year.
  Deadline: November 15. Start date is between July 1 and September 1.

PUBLICATIONS:
  Brochure.

IRS I.D.: 23-7085732

ADDRESS INQUIRIES TO:
  Janice Benson, Associate Director
  (See address above.)

THE GLAUCOMA FOUNDATION [2269]

80 Maiden Lane, Suite 700
New York, NY 10038-4778
(212) 285-0080
Fax: (212) 651-1888
E-mail: info@glaucomafoundation.org
Web Site: www.glaucomafoundation.org

FOUNDED: 1984

AREAS OF INTEREST:
  Glaucoma.

TYPE:
  Research grants.

PURPOSE:
  To fund research to determine the causes of glaucoma; to improve methods of treatment, and ultimately to develop cures for the various kinds of glaucoma.

ELIGIBILITY:
  Applicants must have a full-time faculty position or the equivalent. Applicant must also demonstrate the Principal Investigator's understanding of glaucoma or his or her collaboration with an investigator who has experience in glaucoma research. If collaboration is warranted, a letter of support from the glaucoma researcher must be included in the application.

FINANCIAL DATA:
  Amount of support per award: Up to $60,000.
  Total amount of support: Varies.

NO. MOST RECENT APPLICANTS: 20.

APPLICATION INFO:
  Grant application and instructions are posted on the Foundation web site.
  Duration: One year. Renewable.
  Deadline: Varies.

GLAUCOMA RESEARCH FOUNDATION [2270]

251 Post Street, Suite 600
San Francisco, CA 94108
(415) 986-3162
Fax: (415) 986-3763
E-mail: research@glaucoma.org
Web Site: www.glaucoma.org/research

FOUNDED: 1978

AREAS OF INTEREST:
  Research and education pertaining to glaucoma.

NAME(S) OF PROGRAMS:
  • **Shaffer Fund for Innovative Glaucoma Research**

TYPE:
  Research grants.

PURPOSE:
  To cure glaucoma and restore vision through innovative research.

ELIGIBILITY:
  Applicants must hold a graduate degree.

FINANCIAL DATA:
  Amount of support per award: $50,000.
  Total amount of support: Typically $450,000.

NO. MOST RECENT APPLICANTS: 55.

NO. AWARDS: 9.

APPLICATION INFO:
  Preliminary proposals are accepted annually between June 1 and July 15, when a link to the online application will be available on the GRF web site. A link to the full online grant application will be e-mailed to those whose preliminary proposals meet the required criteria.

  Applications received by mail will not be reviewed or returned.
  Duration: One year.
  Deadline: Preliminary proposals: June 1 to July 15. Full grant application: September 1 to September 30.

IRS I.D.: 94-2495035

ADDRESS INQUIRIES TO:
  Catalina San Agustin, Director of Operations
  (See e-mail address above.)

HEARING HEALTH FOUNDATION [2271]

575 Eighth Avenue
Suite 1201
New York, NY 10018
(212) 257-6140
Fax: (212) 257-6139
E-mail: info@hhf.org
grants@hhf.org
Web Site: hearinghealthfoundation.org

FOUNDED: 1958

AREAS OF INTEREST:
  Research concerning the causes, treatment and prevention of hearing loss and related ear and balance disorders.

NAME(S) OF PROGRAMS:
  • **Emerging Research Grants (ERG)**
  • **Hearing Restoration Project (HRP)**

TYPE:
  Research grants. Limited in amount and term, Emerging Research Grants are awarded as seed funding in support of projects directed by early career and senior investigators or for promising new studies in areas of demonstrable basic science or clinical importance.

  Specifically, applications will be considered for research directed to any aspect of the ear; that is, investigation of the function, physiology, biochemistry, genetics, anatomy or pathology. Basic and applied research is welcome.

  Through the Hearing Restoration Project (HRP), the Foundation is striving toward a cure for hearing loss and tinnitus, a promise that is very real. Underlying that promise is the discovery that chickens have the ability to spontaneously restore their hearing and the HRP is aiming to enable just that in humans.

YEAR PROGRAM STARTED: 1958

PURPOSE:
  To prevent and cure hearing loss through groundbreaking research.

LEGAL BASIS:
  Nonprofit public voluntary organization.

ELIGIBILITY:
  ERG Program: Applications are accepted from all U.S. institutions, including universities, hospitals and nonprofit tax-exempt institutions, public or private.

  The HHF's Scientific Review Committee will consider the subject of the research, the quality of its design, its potential for significant advance in basic knowledge or clinical application, the available facilities and personnel at the institution in which the research will be carried out and the qualifications of the investigators.

  In accepting a research grant, the institution and the principal investigator are responsible for using grant funds only for those purposes set forth in the application and approved in the HHF award letter.

GEOG. RESTRICTIONS: United States.

FINANCIAL DATA:
  Grant funds may be budgeted and used for direct costs of carrying out approved projects, including equipment purchases and supplies. Grant funds may not be used for the salary of principal investigator, travel, living expenses, printing costs, overhead costs exceeding 10% of project costs or public information/education programs.
  Amount of support per award: Grant amount is determined at the discretion of the Foundation. Regardless of the indirect amount, the HHF award will not exceed $50,000.
  Total amount of support: Varies.

NO. MOST RECENT APPLICANTS: 55 for the year 2021.

NO. AWARDS: ERG: 7 for the year 2020.

APPLICATION INFO:
  New project applications and renewal applications must be submitted using the current forms available on the web site.
  Duration: One calendar year, October 1 to September 30. Grants are eligible for renewal for an additional year.
  Deadline: ERG: Mid-February. Principal investigators are notified in late summer.

PUBLICATIONS:
Hearing Health Magazine.

IRS I.D.: 13-1882107

STAFF:
Timothy L. Higdon, Chief Executive Officer

ADDRESS INQUIRIES TO:
Christopher Geissler, Ph.D.
Director of Program and Research Support
(See address above.)

HEED OPHTHALMIC FOUNDATION   [2272]
655 Beach Street
San Francisco, CA 94109
(415) 447-0249
Fax: (415) 561-8531
E-mail: heed@aao.org
Web Site: www.heed.org

AREAS OF INTEREST:
Diseases and surgery of the eye or research in opthalmology.

NAME(S) OF PROGRAMS:
● **Heed Fellowship**

TYPE:
Fellowships.

YEAR PROGRAM STARTED: 1947

PURPOSE:
To provide assistance to ophthalmology residents and fellows who desire to further their education or to conduct research in ophthalmology.

ELIGIBILITY:
Graduates who are U.S. citizens from accredited medical schools, schools of osteopathic medicine, or hold an ECEMG certificate are eligible.

FINANCIAL DATA:
Amount of support per award: $10,000.
Total amount of support: $220,000 for the year 2021-22.

NO. MOST RECENT APPLICANTS: 105.

NO. AWARDS: 22 for the year 2021-22.

APPLICATION INFO:
Applicants are required to submit:
(1) a one-page statement setting forth the applicant's major ophthalmic interest, professional aims and objectives, and noting qualifications deserving of particular consideration;
(2) a letter of recommendation from the Chair of Ophthalmology who supervised residency training;
(3) a letter from the preceptor of the applicant's fellowship program describing the program, including a statement that a minimum of 20% of the fellowship will be spent in research;
(4) two additional letters of recommendation from physicians who have supervised the applicant;
(5) a letter of acceptance of the applicant at the institution where the fellowship is to be taken (this may be a copy of the applicant's match letter) and;
(6) a letter of recommendation from the Chairman of the department who has offered an academic appointment (optional).

Do not send curriculum vitae.
Duration: One year. Nonrenewable.
Deadline: March 1.

ADDRESS INQUIRIES TO:
Lisa Brown
Heed Administrator
(See e-mail address above.)

THE MARFAN FOUNDATION   [2273]
22 Manhasset Avenue
Port Washington, NY 11050
(516) 883-8712 ext. 117
Fax: (516) 883-8040
E-mail: research@marfan.org
Web Site: www.marfan.org

FOUNDED: 1981

AREAS OF INTEREST:
Research relating to Marfan syndrome and related disorders.

NAME(S) OF PROGRAMS:
● **Clinical Research Program**
● **Early Investigator Grant Program**
● **Faculty Grant Program**
● **Victor A. McKusick Fellowship Program**

TYPE:
Fellowships; Research grants. Basic, translational and clinical research related to the Marfan syndrome and related connective tissue conditions. Specific areas of specialty include genetics, cardiology, ophthalmology and orthopedic issues of the Marfan syndrome.

YEAR PROGRAM STARTED: 1986

PURPOSE:
To provide financial support for investigators, scientists and physicians studying any or all disciplines involved in Marfan syndrome research.

ELIGIBILITY:
The principal investigator must hold an M.D., D.O., Ph.D., Sc.D., D.D.S., D.V.M. or equivalent degree. The investigator must have proven ability to pursue independent research publications in peer-reviewed journals.

FINANCIAL DATA:
Amount of support per award: Clinical Research $25,000 to $50,000 per year; Early Investigator: $37,500; Faculty: $50,000; Fellowship: $50,000 to $75,000.
Total amount of support: Varies.

NO. MOST RECENT APPLICANTS: 25 for the year 2019.

NO. AWARDS: 3 Faculty, 2 Clinical Investigator and 2 Fellowship Awards for the year 2018.

APPLICATION INFO:
Application information is available on the web site.
Duration: Up to two years.
Deadline: Early Investigator and Fellowship: February; Clinical and Faculty: April.

ADDRESS INQUIRIES TO:
Josephine Grima, Ph.D.
Chief Science Officer
(See address above.)

NATIONAL EYE INSTITUTE   [2274]
National Institutes of Health
6700B Rockledge Drive, Suite 3400
Bethesda, MD 20817
(301) 451-2020
Fax: (301) 402-0528
E-mail: esl@nei.nih.gov
Web Site: www.nei.nih.gov

AREAS OF INTEREST:
Vision research, cooperative clinical trials for evaluation, diagnosis and therapy of ocular diseases, and epidemiologic and risk factor studies of ocular diseases.

NAME(S) OF PROGRAMS:
● **Center Core Grants**

TYPE:
Research grants.

PURPOSE:
To support centralized resources and facilities shared by investigators with existing NEI-funded research projects; to enrich the effectiveness of ongoing research; to promote new research directions.

FINANCIAL DATA:
Amount of support per award: Applicants may request up to $200,000 (over a five-year period) for less than 20 R01s or up to $2,500,000 for 20 or more R01s in direct costs.
Total amount of support: Varies depending on the indirect costs at the institution.
Matching fund requirements: Cost sharing is not required to be eligible for this program. However, it is strongly encouraged for applicant organizations to make appropriate and needed commitments to the Center in order to maximize the effectiveness and utility of the shared resources.

NO. AWARDS: Approximately 40.

APPLICATION INFO:
Contact NEI for details.
Duration: Maximum project period of five years.
Deadline: September 30.

ADDRESS INQUIRIES TO:
Ellen S. Liberman, Ph.D.
(See address above.)

NATIONAL EYE INSTITUTE   [2275]
National Institutes of Health
6700B Rockledge Drive, MSC 6914
Bethesda, MD 20817
(301) 451-2020
E-mail: paek.lee@nih.gov
Web Site: www.nei.nih.gov

FOUNDED: 1968

AREAS OF INTEREST:
Vision research, cooperative clinical trials for evaluation, diagnosis and therapy of ocular diseases, and epidemiologic and risk factor studies of ocular diseases.

NAME(S) OF PROGRAMS:
● **Cooperative Clinical Research Grants**
● **Small Business Innovation Research Awards**

TYPE:
Conferences/seminars; Fellowships; Research grants; Training grants. Research Project Grants support individual investigators whose work is aimed at discovering means of improving the prevention, diagnosis and treatment of blinding and disabling eye and vision disorders.

Small Business Innovation Research Awards aim to stimulate technological innovations, to use small business to meet federal research-development needs that may ultimately lead to commercial products or services and to foster and encourage participation by minority and disadvantaged persons in technological innovations.

Areas of study include vision research, retinal diseases, corneal diseases, cataract, glaucoma, low vision and blindness rehabilitation, visual impairment and its rehabilitation, strabismus, amblyopia and visual processing.

YEAR PROGRAM STARTED: 1968

PURPOSE:
To gain new knowledge about normal and abnormal functioning of the eye and visual system; to support research aimed at improving the prevention, diagnosis and treatment of eye disease and disorders of vision. These are essential for progress against the major causes of blindness and visual disability.

ELIGIBILITY:
Research grants are available to any public or private university, college, hospital, laboratory, or other institution, including state and local units of government and federal institutions; eligibility is no longer restricted to nonprofit organizations.

GEOG. RESTRICTIONS: Cooperative Clinical Research Grants: Primarily United States; Small Business Innovation Research Awards: United States.

FINANCIAL DATA:
Amount of support per award: Grants vary in amount, depending upon the needs and nature of the request and the limitations of the program.

APPLICATION INFO:
Those interested in applying are encouraged to contact the NEI staff prior to submitting applications.
Duration: Cooperative Clinical Research Grants: Up to five years; Small Business Innovation Research Award: Six months to two years.
Deadline: Varies according to award.

IRS I.D.: 52-0858115

STAFF:
Michael A. Steinmetz, Ph.D., Director

ADDRESS INQUIRIES TO:
PaekGyu Lee, Ph.D.
Program Director, Small Business
SBIR/STTR
(See address above.)

Osteopathy

AMERICAN OSTEOPATHIC FOUNDATION [2276]

142 East Ontario Street, Suite 1450
Chicago, IL 60611-2864
(312) 202-8235
Fax: (312) 202-8216
E-mail: info@aof.org
Web Site: www.aof.org

FOUNDED: 1949

AREAS OF INTEREST:
Osteopathic medical education, research and international humanitarian outreach.

TYPE:
Awards/prizes; Scholarships. Research, community service and international outreach grants.

PURPOSE:
To support programs and services that promote osteopathic medicine and enhance patient-centered care.

LEGAL BASIS:
Public charity.

ELIGIBILITY:
Specific requirements can be found on the Foundation web site.

FINANCIAL DATA:
Amount of support per award: $500 to $25,000.
Total amount of support: Varies.

NO. MOST RECENT APPLICANTS: More than 400.

NO. AWARDS: 130.

APPLICATION INFO:
Applications or nomination forms are available at various times throughout the year on the AOF web site.
Duration: Varies.
Deadline: Varies.

PUBLICATIONS:
Application; brochure.

IRS I.D.: 36-6056120

ADDRESS INQUIRIES TO:
Rita Forden, Chief Executive Offcer
(See address above.)

FOUNDATION FOR OSTEOPATHIC EMERGENCY MEDICINE [2277]

111 West Jackson Boulevard
Suite 1412
Chicago, IL 60604
(847) 686-2235
Fax: (312) 587-9951
E-mail: eburch@acoep.org
Web Site: www.foem.org

FOUNDED: 1998

AREAS OF INTEREST:
Osteopathic emergency medicine.

NAME(S) OF PROGRAMS:
• **Benjamin J. Field, D.O., FACOEP Medical Education Grant**
• **Investigator Research Grant**
• **David A. Kuchinski Memorial Research Grant**
• **Resident Research Grant**
• **Young Investigator Research Grant**

TYPE:
Awards/prizes; Research grants.

YEAR PROGRAM STARTED: 1998

PURPOSE:
To improve patient care through quality research and education in osteopathic emergency medicine.

LEGAL BASIS:
501(c)(3).

ELIGIBILITY:
Grants are made to individuals or organizations that have tax-exempt status under Section 501(c)(3) of the Internal Revenue Code.

GEOG. RESTRICTIONS: United States.

FINANCIAL DATA:
Amount of support per award: Investigator Grant and Young Investigator Grant: $1,000 to $3,000; Kuchinski Memorial Research Grant: Varies; Resident Research Grant: $500 to $2,000.

Total amount of support: Varies.

NO. AWARDS: 1 per award.

APPLICATION INFO:
Contact the Foundation for application procedures.
Duration: One-time grants.
Deadline: Postmarked by July 31. Reviewed in April, July and October.

PUBLICATIONS:
Research Beacon.

MAINE OSTEOPATHIC ASSOCIATION [2278]

29 Association Drive
Manchester, ME 04351
(207) 623-1101
Fax: (207) 623-4228
E-mail: info@mainedo.org
Web Site: www.mainedo.org

FOUNDED: 1912

AREAS OF INTEREST:
Osteopathic medicine.

NAME(S) OF PROGRAMS:
• **Maine Osteopathic Association Scholarship**

TYPE:
Scholarships. The program is a tuition subsidy for eligible students who enroll in a qualifying medical school program.

LEGAL BASIS:
Nonprofit physician membership organization.

ELIGIBILITY:
Any Maine resident who will enroll in a participating accredited college of osteopathic medicine. School does not have to be located in Maine.

FINANCIAL DATA:
Amount of support per award: $1,000.
Total amount of support: Varies.

NO. AWARDS: Varies.

APPLICATION INFO:
Application is available online or by contacting the Association directly.
Duration: One year.
Deadline: June 30.

ADDRESS INQUIRIES TO:
Amanda Richards, Executive Director
(See address above.)

NEW JERSEY OSTEOPATHIC EDUCATION FOUNDATION [2279]

666 Plainsboro Road
Suite 356
Plainsboro, NJ 08536
(732) 940-9000 ext. 303
Fax: (732) 940-8899
E-mail: info@njosteo.com
Web Site: www.njosteo.com

FOUNDED: 1901

AREAS OF INTEREST:
Osteopathic education.

TYPE:
Scholarships. For students pursuing osteopathic medical education. A first-year scholarship will be awarded to New Jersey residents accepted to the fall class of any approved college of osteopathic medicine.

YEAR PROGRAM STARTED: 1965

PURPOSE:
To provide the means to promote education in the field of osteopathic medicine.

LEGAL BASIS:
Not-for-profit corporation.

ELIGIBILITY:
Applicants must be residents of New Jersey having completed four years of pre-medical education and entering their first year in an osteopathic college. Applicants must have a 3.0 grade point average on a 4.0 scale or be in the upper 25% of his or her class. Selections are based on class standing, financial need, high motivation and professional promise. Students accepting scholarships must agree to become members of the New Jersey Association of Osteopathic Physicians and Surgeons and the American Osteopathic Association.

GEOG. RESTRICTIONS: New Jersey.

FINANCIAL DATA:
The scholarship sum will be paid directly to the college to cover part of the first year's tuition.
Amount of support per award: $4,000 to $7,000.
Total amount of support: $27,000.

NO. MOST RECENT APPLICANTS: 20.

NO. AWARDS: 10.

APPLICATION INFO:
To apply for a scholarship, qualified students must:
(1) submit a completed NJOEF scholarship application;
(2) provide four named references, at least one of whom is an osteopathic physician;
(3) provide four completed reference evaluation forms;
(4) supply MCAT scores with confirmation code;
(5) supply pre-med college transcripts directly from the college;
(6) supply copy of medical school acceptance letter;
(7) compose an essay sharing his or her desire to become an osteopathic physician (why osteopathic medicine?) and;
(8) supply the prior year's tax return or that of the parent/guardian, if the student is claimed as a dependent.
Duration: One year.
Deadline: June 14.

IRS I.D.: 22-6088562

ADDRESS INQUIRIES TO:
Scholarship Program
(See address above.)

Pediatrics

ACADEMIC PEDIATRIC ASSOCIATION (APA) [2280]
6728 Old McLean Village Drive
McLean, VA 22101
(703) 556-9222
Fax: (703) 556-8729
E-mail: info@academicpeds.org
Web Site: www.academicpeds.org

FOUNDED: 1960

AREAS OF INTEREST:
General pediatrics and pediatric hospitalist medicine.

NAME(S) OF PROGRAMS:
● **APA Young Investigator Awards Program**

TYPE:
Research grants.

YEAR PROGRAM STARTED: 1994

PURPOSE:
To assist pediatric clinician-educators and clinician-researches in developing themselves as fulfilled faculty members engaged in important and exciting research and to increase the quality and breadth of child health research.

ELIGIBILITY:
The principal investigator of any proposal submitted must be a member of the APA or have submitted an application for membership. Preference will be given to new investigators, including those in training. Preference will be given to proposals that have the potential of leading to projects of a larger or longer-term nature.

FINANCIAL DATA:
Amount of support per award: Up to $10,000.
Total amount of support: $60,000.

NO. MOST RECENT APPLICANTS: 32 for the year 2020.

NO. AWARDS: 6 for the year 2020.

APPLICATION INFO:
Applicants must submit a two-page proposal. Only electronic submissions as an e-mail attachment are accepted. The proposals should contain a brief overview of the project including purpose, methods, evaluation and estimated budget. A curriculum vitae for the principal investigator must also be included with the proposal. Budget requests should not include overhead or salary for the principal investigator if they are full-time faculty. The review panel will identify those that warrant further elaboration. Re-submitted proposals can be no more than 10 pages in length including tables and appendices. They must contain background, hypothesis, description of key personnel, detailed budget with justification and methods.
Duration: One year. Award recipients can request up to a 12-month no-cost extension.
Deadline: Fall.

ADDRESS INQUIRIES TO:
See address and e-mail above.

*SPECIAL STIPULATIONS:
The applicant must be a member of the APA or have submitted an application for membership.

AMERICAN ACADEMY OF PEDIATRICS [2281]
345 Park Boulevard
Itasca, IL 60143
(847) 434-4000
(800) 433-9016 ext. 6134
Fax: (847) 434-8000
E-mail: kvandenbrook@aap.org
Web Site: www.aap.org/sopt

FOUNDED: 1930

AREAS OF INTEREST:
Pediatric training.

NAME(S) OF PROGRAMS:
● **American Academy of Pediatrics Hardship Scholarship Program**

TYPE:
Residencies; Scholarships. Stipend for the support of pediatric residents and fellowship trainees.

YEAR PROGRAM STARTED: 1982

PURPOSE:
To enable young physicians to complete their pediatric training.

LEGAL BASIS:
Nonprofit organization.

ELIGIBILITY:
Applicant must have completed, or will have completed by July 1, a qualifying approved internship (PL-0) and have a definite commitment for a first-year pediatric residency (PL-1) accredited by the Residency Review Committee for Pediatrics. In addition, applicant must be a pediatric resident or chief resident (categorical pediatrics or combined-training program) in a training program and have made a definite commitment for another year of residency (not fellowship) in a U.S. or Canadian program accredited by the Residency Review Committee for Pediatrics, as well as have a substantial need for financial assistance.

GEOG. RESTRICTIONS: United States and Canada.

FINANCIAL DATA:
Amount of support per award: $1,000 to $5,000.
Total amount of support: Varies.

APPLICATION INFO:
Official application materials are available upon request in December. Applications must be supported by a form from the Department Head or the Chief of Service or the Residency Program Director addressing the financial need, commitment to pediatrics and performance in the program.
Duration: One year. Possible renewals.
Deadline: Last day in February.

ADDRESS INQUIRIES TO:
Kimberley VandenBrook
Member Engagement Specialist
(See address above.)

CHILDREN'S LEUKEMIA RESEARCH ASSOCIATION [2282]
585 Stewart Avenue
Suite 520
Garden City, NY 11530
(516) 222-1944
Fax: (516) 222-0457
E-mail: info@childrensleukemia.org
Web Site: www.childrensleukemia.org

FOUNDED: 1965

AREAS OF INTEREST:
Leukemia.

NAME(S) OF PROGRAMS:
● **Children's Leukemia Research Grants**

TYPE:
Research grants. Support for research efforts into the causes and cure of leukemia. Patient aid to families in need while meeting the expenses incurred in leukemia treatment.

YEAR PROGRAM STARTED: 1965

PURPOSE:
To work towards a cure for leukemia; to provide patient aid.

ELIGIBILITY:
Any doctor at the Ph.D. or M.D. level who is involved in research towards finding the causes and cure for leukemia may apply.

FINANCIAL DATA:
Amount of support per award: Up to $30,000 per year.

APPLICATION INFO:
Information is available on the Association's web site.
Duration: One year. Renewal for a second year is considered if other funding for promising projects has not been obtained.
Deadline: June 30.

ADDRESS INQUIRIES TO:
Anthony R. Pasqua, President
(See address above.)

DYSAUTONOMIA FOUNDATION, INC.
315 West 39th Street
Suite 701
New York, NY 10018
(212) 279-1066
Fax: (212) 279-2066
E-mail: info@famdys.org
Web Site: www.familialdysautonomia.org

TYPE:
Project/program grants; Research grants; Seed money grants. In addition to support for research and clinical study, the Foundation also provides financial support to the Dysautonomia Treatment and Evaluation Center at NYU and the Israeli FD Center in Tel Aviv.

See entry 2209 for full listing.

CHARLES H. HOOD FOUNDATION, INC. [2283]
2 Boylston Street, 4th Floor
Boston, MA 02116
(617) 695-9439
E-mail: cmancusi@hria.org
Web Site: charleshoodfoundation.org

FOUNDED: 1942

AREAS OF INTEREST:
Child health research.

NAME(S) OF PROGRAMS:
- **Child Health Research Awards Program**

TYPE:
Research grants. Medical research grants that are relevant to child health. Projects must be hypothesis-driven clinical, basic science, public health, health services research or epidemiology.

YEAR PROGRAM STARTED: 1942

PURPOSE:
To improve the health and quality of life for children through grant support of New England-based pediatric researchers.

LEGAL BASIS:
Private family foundation.

ELIGIBILITY:
Investigators working in tax-exempt academic, medical and research institutions in New England are eligible. Grants must have relevance to child health. Investigators must be within five (Ph.D. scientists) or seven (physician-scientists) years of their first faculty appointment. In addition to basic science research, grants are also given to researchers in public health, epidemiology, clinical research and health services research.

GEOG. RESTRICTIONS: New England.

FINANCIAL DATA:
Amount of support per award: $82,500 per year for two years (inclusive of 10% overhead).

NO. MOST RECENT APPLICANTS: 42 for the year 2019.

NO. AWARDS: 10 new grants for the year 2019.

APPLICATION INFO:
Application guidelines, instructions and forms are available on the web site.
Duration: Two years.
Deadline: Spring and Fall for Child Health Research Grants. Funding begins on July 1 and January 1. Deadlines and guidelines change each cycle.

PUBLICATIONS:
Application guidelines; alumni directory; summaries of current and previous funded projects.

IRS I.D.: 04-3507847

OFFICERS:
Neil Smiley, President and Treasurer
John Parker, Jr., Vice President and Clerk

TRUSTEES:
Robert Boutwell
Barbara Bula
Brendon Bula
Elizabeth Hood

ADDRESS INQUIRIES TO:
See e-mail address above.

HUMAN GROWTH FOUNDATION [2284]
997 Glen Cove Avenue, Suite 5
Glen Head, NY 11545
(516) 671-4041
(800) 451-6434
Fax: (516) 671-4055
E-mail: hgf1@hgfound.org
Web Site: www.hgfound.org

FOUNDED: 1965

AREAS OF INTEREST:
Growth disorders and pediatrics.

NAME(S) OF PROGRAMS:
- **Small Grants for Research in Field of Short Stature**

TYPE:
Research grants.

YEAR PROGRAM STARTED: 1965

PURPOSE:
To help medical science better understand the process of growth and to help individuals with growth-related disorders, their families and health care professionals through education, research and advocacy.

ELIGIBILITY:
Applicants must be involved in research of the human growth process. Special consideration will be given to young investigators and to projects dealing with psychological, social, and educational aspects of dwarfism and its treatment and to new approaches to diagnosis and management, as well as clinical and basic research in the mechanisms of statural growth disorders of children including chondrodystrophies, genetic, or psychological causes.

FINANCIAL DATA:
Amount of support per award: Maximum $10,000.

NO. MOST RECENT APPLICANTS: Over 40.

NO. AWARDS: Up to 3.

APPLICATION INFO:
Applicant must submit a biographical sketch and two-page Letter of Intent online.
Duration: One-time funding.
Deadline: Letter of Intent: July 5. Final application: December 1.

ADDRESS INQUIRIES TO:
Patricia D. Costa, Executive Director
(See address above.)

SICKKIDS FOUNDATION
525 University Avenue, Suite 835
Toronto ON M5G 2L3 Canada
(416) 813-8104
(800) 661-1083 ext. 2354
E-mail: national.grants@sickkidsfoundation.com
Web Site: www.sickkidsfoundation.com/about-us/grants

TYPE:
Awards/prizes; Conferences/seminars; Project/program grants; Research grants. Community Conference Grants program brings together families with researchers and clinicians for medical presentations and family-oriented discussions. It helps ensure knowledge exchange with families so that they are able to access the most up-to-date information about their children's health.

New Investigator Research Grants program focus is to ensure that there continues to be well-trained researchers across the country working to address the most pressing childhood diseases and conditions.

See entry 1319 for full listing.

SOCIETY FOR PEDIATRIC DERMATOLOGY [2285]
8365 Keystone Crossing, Suite 107
Indianapolis, IN 46240
(317) 202-0224
E-mail: info@pedsderm.net
Web Site: www.pedsderm.net/grants-awards

FOUNDED: 1975

AREAS OF INTEREST:
Pediatric dermatology.

NAME(S) OF PROGRAMS:
- **PeDRA Research Grants**
- **Weston Pediatric Dermatology Career Development Award (CDA)**

TYPE:
Research grants; Seed money grants. PeDRA Research Grants support early stage research projects where preliminary data may be lacking, and to establish infrastructure and foster collaborations that support larger-scale studies in the future.

Weston Career Development Award supports an early career investigator in the conduct of an innovative research study under the direction of a senior mentor.

PURPOSE:
To foster research in pediatric dermatology.

LEGAL BASIS:
Medical society.

ELIGIBILITY:
PeDRA Research Grants: Applications may be submitted by either a single investigator or multiple investigators at multiple institutions. Priority will be given to early-to-midcareer principal investigators collatorating with senior mentors, projects that address

high-priority patient-centered research questions, and projects that align with the focus of any of the PeDRA's working groups.

Weston Career Development Award: Applications may be submitted by pediatric dermatologists no more than seven years out of training.

FINANCIAL DATA:
Amount of support per award: PeDRA Research Grants: Up to $15,000. Weston Pediatric Dermatology Career Development Award: $40,000.
Total amount of support: Varies.

CO-OP FUNDING PROGRAMS: Pediatric Dermatology Research Alliance (PeDRA).

NO. AWARDS: PeDRA Research Grants: Varies. Weston Pediatric Dermatology Career Development Award: 1.

APPLICATION INFO:
PeDRA Research Grants: Applications are submitted through the PeDRA application portal located at pedraresearch.org.
Duration: PeDRA Research Grants: One year, with possibility to renew for a second year of funding. Weston Pediatric Dermatology Career Development Award: One year.
Deadline: PeDRA Research Grants: May 1 for first cycle. Notification in June. December 3 for second cycle. Notification no later than March 15. Weston Pediatric Dermatology Career Development Award: December 3.

ADDRESS INQUIRIES TO:
Katherine Devenport, Research Coordinator
E-mail: katherine.devenport@pedraresearch.org

*SPECIAL STIPULATIONS:
Research funds may not be used for investigator travel expenses to attend meetings or to present their work.

THRASHER RESEARCH FUND   [2286]
68 South Main Street, Suite 400
Salt Lake City, UT 84101
(801) 240-4753
Fax: (801) 240-1625
E-mail: martinezaf@thrasherresearch.org
Web Site: www.thrasherresearch.org

FOUNDED: 1977

AREAS OF INTEREST:
Pediatric medical research, with emphasis on clinical/translational research with potential findings that would be clinically applicable in a short period of time in the prevention, diagnosis and/or treatment of pediatric medical problems.

TYPE:
Research grants. Grants for support of research that addresses problems in children's health in areas of critical illnesses that have been insufficiently researched or investigated. The Fund assumes that significant solutions to children's health problems remain undiscovered and invites a broad array of applications designed to remedy these deficiencies.

YEAR PROGRAM STARTED: 1977

PURPOSE:
To provide grants for pediatric medical research that addresses problems in children's health that are significant in terms of either magnitude or severity.

LEGAL BASIS:
Private organization.

ELIGIBILITY:
The Fund supports medical research that seeks to prevent or cure children's critical illnesses, injuries and disabilities. Projects should:
(1) be scientifically sound and culturally appropriate;
(2) document methods and practices that have sustainable benefits;
(3) have specific aims and a well-designed methodology and;
(4) evaluate the significance of impact on children's health.

Funding is limited to research. The Fund does not award grants for general operations, construction or renovation of buildings or facilities, nor does the Fund award grants for general donations, loans, student aid, scholarships, educational programs or support of other funds or institutions.

The Fund excludes research using human fetal tissue, stem cell research, or behavioral science research.

FINANCIAL DATA:
Support may be provided for supplies, minor equipment and technical personnel assistance related to a specific Fund-sponsored project. Principal investigators in need of salary support for a specific project may apply for 20% support, based on federal guidelines.
Amount of support per award: $25,000 to $500,000. Typically $250,000 to $350,000.
Total amount of support: Varies.

NO. MOST RECENT APPLICANTS: 100.

NO. AWARDS: 25.

APPLICATION INFO:
Application guidelines are available on the Fund's web site. Potential applicants are encouraged to contact Fund staff prior to a formal submission to determine the potential fit of a project with current Fund interests.
Duration: Up to three years.

PUBLICATIONS:
Brochure; application information.

STAFF:
R. Justin Brown, M.P.H., President
Aaron V. Pontsler, M.S., MBA, Research Manager
Brittni Smith, Ph.D., Research Manager

U.S. DEPARTMENT OF HEALTH AND HUMAN SERVICES
Maternal and Child Health Bureau
Parklawn Building, Room 5C 26
5600 Fishers Lane
Rockville, MD 20857
(301) 443-2204
Fax: (301) 443-9354
E-mail: CallCenter@hrsa.gov (grants information)
Web Site: mchb.hrsa.gov

TYPE:
Block grants. The Title V Block Grant Program has as a general purpose the improvement of the health of all mothers and children in the nation. The Block Grant Program has three components: Formula Block Grants to 59 states and other political jurisdictions, Special Projects of Regional and National Significance (SPRANS), and Community Integrated Service Systems (CISS) Grants.

See entry 2252 for full listing.

Pharmacology

AMERICAN ASSOCIATION OF COLLEGES OF PHARMACY   [2287]
1400 Crystal Drive
Suite 300
Arlington, VA 22202
(703) 739-2330
Fax: (703) 836-8982
E-mail: nia@aacp.org
Web Site: www.aacp.org

FOUNDED: 1900

AREAS OF INTEREST:
Pharmaceutical education.

NAME(S) OF PROGRAMS:
● New Investigator Award

TYPE:
Research grants.

YEAR PROGRAM STARTED: 1985

PURPOSE:
To provide start-up funds for new faculty members to assist in establishing a research program; to assist new faculty in establishing themselves as independent investigators.

LEGAL BASIS:
Nonprofit foundation, tax-exempt under the IRS Code.

ELIGIBILITY:
Applicants must have earned terminal degrees in their disciplines (Pharm.D., Ph.D.), hold a regular full-time academic faculty appointment in a college or school of pharmacy, hold the rank of assistant professor, and be in the first to fifth year of their academic appointment. The applicant must be a current individual member of AACP. Only one application per investigator will be accepted for review.

A faculty member who has been a principle investigator on an AACP NIA or equivalent starter grant, on a professional (e.g., ACCP, ASHP, AAPS, PhRMA, etc.), organizational (e.g., American Heart or American Cancer) or federal grant (e.g., NIH, NSF, AHRQ, DOD, CDC, etc.) is not eligible to apply.

Intramural university or college/school start-up support may be used for supplementing the proposed research.

GEOG. RESTRICTIONS: United States.

FINANCIAL DATA:
No overhead allowed. In addition to grant monies, each award winner will receive $1,000 for required travel to the AACP Annual Meeting.
Amount of support per award: $10,000 maximum.

NO. MOST RECENT APPLICANTS: 138.

NO. AWARDS: Up to 16.

APPLICATION INFO:
Application specifics are available on the AACP web site.
Duration: One year.
Deadline: Letter of Intent: July 31. Full Proposal: September 18.

PUBLICATIONS:
Program announcement.

OFFICERS:
Lucinda Maine, Executive Vice President and Chief Executive Officer

ADDRESS INQUIRIES TO:
See e-mail address above.

AMERICAN FOUNDATION FOR PHARMACEUTICAL EDUCATION (AFPE) [2288]

11325 Random Hills Road
Suite 360A-105
Fairfax, VA 22030
(703) 875-3095
Fax: (703) 875-3098
E-mail: fuentes@afpepharm.org
Web Site: afpepharm.org

FOUNDED: 1942

AREAS OF INTEREST:
Pharmaceutical education.

NAME(S) OF PROGRAMS:
- **Phi Lambda Sigma-AFPE First Year Graduate Fellowship**
- **Rho Chi-AFPE First Year Graduate Fellowship**

TYPE:
Fellowships. Phi Lambda Sigma-AFPE First Year Graduate Fellowship encourages outstanding Phi Lambda Sigma members to pursue the Ph.D. in a college or school of pharmacy graduate program.

Rho Chi-AFPE First Year Graduate Fellowship encourages outstanding Rho Chi Honor Society members to pursue the Ph.D. in a college of pharmacy graduate program.

YEAR PROGRAM STARTED: 1985

PURPOSE:
To encourage outstanding Rho Chi and Phi Lambda Sigma members to continue their education in a graduate program for the Ph.D. in a college of pharmacy.

LEGAL BASIS:
Nonprofit foundation, tax-exempt under the IRS Code.

ELIGIBILITY:
Phi Lambda Sigma-AFPE Fellowship: Applicant must be a member of Phi Lambda Sigma and a pharmacy Pharm.D. degree student in the final year of professional studies who is planning to enroll full-time for the Ph.D. degree in the pharmaceutical sciences after graduation in a Ph.D. degree program at or affiliated with an accredited U.S. school/college of pharmacy or be a pharmacy Pharm.D. degree student in the final year of professional studies who is currently enrolled in a joint Pharm.D./Ph.D. degree program at or affiliated with an accredited U.S. school or college of pharmacy who will pursue full-time graduate study in the year the award is made. U.S. citizenship or permanent resident status is required.

Rho Chi-AFPE Fellowship: Applicants must be members of the Rho Chi Honor Society. Applicants must be a pharmacy student in the final year of professional studies or a professional pharmacy degree program graduate entering a pharmaceutical sciences (including social/administrative sciences) Ph.D. program in an accredited U.S. school or college of pharmacy as a full-time student. Pharmacy students who have initiated graduate work through a dual Pharm.D./Ph.D. degree pathway are eligible if they have completed their professional degree and will

be pursuing full-time graduate study in the year the award is made. Applicants must be a U.S. citizen or permanent resident.

GEOG. RESTRICTIONS: United States.

FINANCIAL DATA:
Phi Lambda Sigma-AFPE: The scholarship may be used for any purpose decided by the awardee and faculty sponsor that will enable the student to have a successful program, i.e., student stipend, laboratory supplies, books, materials, travel, etc., related to the program of graduate study. None of the funds shall be used for indirect costs by the institution.

Amount of support per award: $7,500.

Total amount of support: $15,000.

NO. MOST RECENT APPLICANTS: 12.

NO. AWARDS: 1 of each.

APPLICATION INFO:
For the Phi Lambda Sigma-AFPE Fellowship, the following information should be sent to exec_director@philambdasigma.org:
(1) letters of recommendation from two college faculty members who are acquainted with the student and his or her potential for graduate study;
(2) name of the graduate school the student plans to attend (if known);
(3) a one- to two-page statement by applicant elaborating reasons for wishing to attend graduate school;
(4) a list of special honors, awards and accomplishments in high school and college reflecting achievement and ability to succeed in graduate school and;
(5) an official transcript of all collegiate grades and copies of GRE, SAT and other national achievement test scores.

For the Rho Chi Fellowship, application forms are available from Rho Chi Faculty Advisors or the Secretary of Rho Chi. Required information should be sent to: The Rho Chi Society National Office, UNC Eshelman School of Pharmacy, 3210 Kerr Hall, CB No. 7569, Chapel Hill, NC 27599-7569; Tel: (919) 843-9001; E-mail: rhochi@unc.edu. The packet should include the following:
(1) a completed application form;
(2) a one-page description of present academic status including all previous scholarships and fellowships and memberships in professional, scientific, scholastic and honor societies;
(3) a one-page account of involvement in professional and extracurricular activities, list of proposed expenses for the year; if married, include spouse and family expenses; list all sources and amounts of income;
(4) name of university to be attended and planned field of study;
(5) graduate record examination scores;
(6) a one- to two-page statement describing career goals;
(7) official transcripts from all colleges or universities attended and;
(8) letters of reference from three individuals who are directly familiar with the applicant and can speak specifically to educational achievements and capacity for graduate study.

Duration: One academic year.

Deadline: Phi Lambda Sigma-AFPE Fellowship: May 15. Rho Chi Fellowship: May 1.

PUBLICATIONS:
Program announcement.

OFFICERS:
Ellen L. Woods, President and Secretary

AMERICAN FOUNDATION FOR PHARMACEUTICAL EDUCATION (AFPE) [2289]

11325 Random Hills Road
Suite 360A-105
Fairfax, VA 22030
(703) 875-3095
Fax: (703) 875-3098
E-mail: fuentes@afpepharm.org
Web Site: afpepharm.org

FOUNDED: 1942

AREAS OF INTEREST:
Pharmaceutical education.

NAME(S) OF PROGRAMS:
- **Kappa Epsilon-AFPE-Nellie Wakeman First Year Graduate Fellowship**

TYPE:
Fellowships.

PURPOSE:
To encourage an outstanding pharmacy school graduate to pursue an advanced degree in the pharmaceutical sciences.

ELIGIBILITY:
An applicant must be in the final year of the Pharm.D. program or have completed a pharmacy degree. Consideration is given to those who need financial assistance to further their education in pharmacy. At the time of application, the Kappa Epsilon member must be in good financial standing with the KE Fraternity and planning to pursue a Doctor of Philosophy (Ph.D.) degree, a Master's degree, or a combined Residency/Master's degree program at a U.S. college or school of pharmacy.

FINANCIAL DATA:
The funds may be used for any purpose decided by the awardee and faculty sponsor that will enable the student to have a successful program, e.g., student stipend, laboratory supplies, books, materials, travel related to the program of study. None of the funds shall be used for indirect costs by the institution.

Amount of support per award: $7,500.

Total amount of support: $7,500.

NO. AWARDS: 1.

APPLICATION INFO:
Applications can be downloaded from the web site. Applications must include:
(1) a completed application form (application and reference forms available from a Kappa Epsilon faculty advisor or the Kappa Epsilon Executive Office, Tel: (913) 262-2749);
(2) a letter of recommendation from the faculty advisor and one other faculty member familiar with the applicant (both faculty members are to complete a letter of reference form) and;
(3) official transcripts of all collegiate grades, undergraduate and graduate.
Applications should be sent to the Kappa Epsilon Executive Office: 7700 Shawnee Mission Parkway, Suite 201, Overland Park, KS 66202.

Duration: One year.

Deadline: All application materials must be received by February 1. Notification end of April.

AMERICAN INSTITUTE OF THE HISTORY OF PHARMACY [2290]

University of Wisconsin School of Pharmacy
Rennebohm Hall
777 Highland Avenue
Madison, WI 53705-2222
(608) 262-5378
E-mail: aihp@aihp.org
Web Site: www.aihp.org

FOUNDED: 1941

AREAS OF INTEREST:
History of pharmacy.

NAME(S) OF PROGRAMS:
● **AIHP Ph.D. Research Support Grant Program**

TYPE:
Grants-in-aid; Research grants.

PURPOSE:
To contribute to the understanding of the development of civilization by fostering the creation, preservation and dissemination of knowledge concerning the history and related humanistic aspects of the pharmaceutical field.

ELIGIBILITY:
Open to all Ph.D. students enrolled in a university based in the U.S., regardless of department or discipline. The student need not be an American citizen.

The research topic does not need to be in the field of American history. Research must be clearly and significantly related to the history of pharmacy or pharmaceuticals, broadly defined.

FINANCIAL DATA:
Grants only cover direct costs of research attributable to supplies and other expenses that cannot be reimbursed by the degree-granting institution itself. These can include computer time and programming, obtaining a photocopy or microform of essential sources, travel and maintenance at a site away from the home university. Ineligible expenses include routine typing of the manuscript, living expenses at the home university, publication of research results or routine illustrations for the manuscript.
Amount of support per award: Up to $2,000.

APPLICATION INFO:
Applicants should submit their application as a single PDF document of no more than four pages in length that includes:
(1) the applicant's name, address, e-mail address, telephone number, university affiliation, expected graduate degree, major area of specialization, and expected graduation date;
(2) a tentative title and short prospectus of the research project;
(3) a brief narrative explaining the significance of the research for the history of pharmacy or pharmaceuticals and describing the activities that will be supported by the grant and;
(4) an itemized and annotated estimate of expenses for which a grant is being sought. Include a brief statement of other financial support received or applied for to be used within the period for which the AIHP grant is sought.

In addition to the applications, applicants should also submit by e-mail a letter of support from a faculty member or supervisor.

E-mail complete application materials to grants@aihp.org.
Deadline: March 1.

ADDRESS INQUIRIES TO:
Beth D. Fisher
Director of Curatorial Affairs
(See address above.)

AMERICAN SOCIETY OF REGIONAL ANESTHESIA AND PAIN MEDICINE [2291]

3 Penn Center West
Suite 224
Pittsburgh, PA 15276
(412) 471-2718
Fax: (412) 471-7503
E-mail: asraassistant@asra.com
Web Site: www.asra.com

AREAS OF INTEREST:
Regional anesthesia and pain medicine.

NAME(S) OF PROGRAMS:
● **ASRA Carl Koller Memorial Research Grant**
● **ASRA Chronic Pain Research Grant**

TYPE:
Research grants.

PURPOSE:
To support research related to any aspect of regional anesthesia, acute and chronic pain medicine and their application to surgery, obstetrics and pain control; to encourage anesthesiologists and other researchers who are interested in the field.

ELIGIBILITY:
Applicant must be North American and a member of the ASRA.

FINANCIAL DATA:
Amount of support per award: $10,000 to $200,000.

Total amount of support: Up to $200,000 biennially.

NO. MOST RECENT APPLICANTS: 17.

NO. AWARDS: 1 every other year per award.

APPLICATION INFO:
The application, which must be written by the applicant, should be accompanied by a complete narrative research protocol. The research proposal must be concerned with an original idea or concept. The research must be carried out primarily by the applicant.
Deadline: Specific deadlines are posted on the ASRA web site.

ADDRESS INQUIRIES TO:
Angie Stengel, Executive Director
(See address above.)

AMERICAN SOCIETY OF REGIONAL ANESTHESIA AND PAIN MEDICINE

3 Penn Center West
Suite 224
Pittsburgh, PA 15276
(412) 471-2718
Fax: (412) 471-7503
E-mail: asraassistant@asra.com
Web Site: www.asra.com

TYPE:
Research grants.

See entry 2008 for full listing.

PHARMACEUTICAL RESEARCH AND MANUFACTURERS OF AMERICA FOUNDATION, INC. [2292]

950 F Street, N.W.
Suite 300
Washington, DC 20004
(202) 572-7756
E-mail: foundation@phrma.org
Web Site: www.phrmafoundation.org

FOUNDED: 1965

AREAS OF INTEREST:
Biology, biomedical engineering, biopharmaceutics, clinical outcomes assessment, disease modeling, drug delivery, drug discovery, genetics, health outcomes, molecular epidemiology, pharmaceutics, pharmaceutical biotechnology, pharmaceutical engineering, pharmacology and toxicology.

NAME(S) OF PROGRAMS:
● **Research Starter Grant in Drug Delivery**
● **Research Starter Grant in Drug Discovery**
● **Research Starter Grant in Health Outcomes Research**
● **Research Starter Grant in Translational Medicine**

TYPE:
Project/program grants; Research grants; Seed money grants. Starter grants to support research in the fields of biology, biomedical engineering, biopharmaceutics, clinical outcomes assessment, disease modeling, drug delivery, drug discovery, genetics, health outcomes, molecular epidemiology, pharmaceutics, pharmaceutical biotechnology, pharmaceutical engineering, pharmacology and toxicology. The grants offer financial support to individuals beginning independent research careers at the faculty level.

PURPOSE:
To help promising young scientists advance their research projects; to offer financial support to individuals beginning their independent research careers at the faculty level.

LEGAL BASIS:
501(c)(3) organization.

ELIGIBILITY:
Applicants must currently be in Ph.D. and/or M.S. degree granting institutions in the U.S. Those holding the academic rank of assistant professor (or research assistant professor) within a tenure track (or research track) appointment, or instructor, if eligible to apply for independent research funding by their institution, are eligible to apply for the Research Starter Grant in Drug Delivery or Research Starter Grant in Drug Discovery, providing their proposed research is neither directly nor indirectly already being subsidized to any significant degree by an extramural support mechanism. Individuals receiving only intramural funding or start-up funding from their institution may apply.

Applicants for the Research Starter Grant in Health Outcomes Research must be beginning independent research careers at the faculty level in schools of medicine, pharmacy, public health, nursing or dentistry. This program is not intended for individuals in postdoctoral training. However, those enrolled in postdoctoral training programs scheduled to conclude by July 1, who will hold an academic appointment by that time, may apply. Those holding academic rank of instructor or assistant professor, and investigators at the doctoral level with equivalent positions, are eligible to apply, provided the proposed research is neither directly nor indirectly subsidized to any significant degree by an extramural support mechanism.

Applicants for the Research Starter Grant in Translational Medicine must hold the academic rank of assistant professor (or research assistant professor) within a tenure track (or research track) appointment, or instructor, if eligible to apply for independent research funding by their institution, providing their proposed research is neither directly nor indirectly already being subsidized to any significant degree by an extramural support mechanism.

GEOG. RESTRICTIONS: United States.

FINANCIAL DATA:
Up to $1,500 may be used for travel to a scientific conference for the grantee. Funds may be budgeted for the hourly support of a technical assistant or graduate student. Funds may not be used for fringe benefits, indirect costs or tuition assistance. Up to 25% of the award may be used for the Research Starter Grant in Health Outcomes Research grantee's stipend.
Amount of support per award: $100,000 per award.
Total amount of support: Varies.

NO. MOST RECENT APPLICANTS: Varies.

NO. AWARDS: Varies.

APPLICATION INFO:
Applications should be submitted on the Foundation web site.
Duration: One year.
Deadline: Drug Delivery and Drug Discovery: Letter of Intent due May 15. Selected submissions will be notified by July 1 to submit a full application. Health Outcomes and Translational Medicine: February 1.

PUBLICATIONS:
Brochure.

IRS I.D.: 52-6063009

STAFF:
Eileen Cannon, President
Joanne Westphal, Director of Development

BOARD OF DIRECTORS:
Alfred Sandrock, M.D., Ph.D., Chairman
Andrew Plump, M.D., Ph.D., Treasurer
Mikael Dolsten, M.D., Ph.D.
Iris Loew-Friedrich, M.D.
Aran Maree, M.B., B.Ch.
Joseph P. Miletich, M.D., Ph.D.
Richard Moscicki, M.D.
John C. Reed, M.D., Ph.D.
Daniel Skovronsky, M.D., Ph.D.
Rupert Vessey, FRCP, D.Phil.

ADVISORY COMMITTEE:
Terry L. Bowlin, Ph.D.
Michael J. Hageman, Ph.D.
Michael N. Liebman, Ph.D.
Bryan R. Luce, Ph.D., MBA
Richard Moscicki, M.D.
Nancy C. Santanello, M.D., M.S.

ADDRESS INQUIRIES TO:
See e-mail address above.

*PLEASE NOTE:
A final progress report and financial report are due upon the conclusion of the grant.

*SPECIAL STIPULATIONS:
Funds may not be used for fringe benefits, indirect costs, or tuition.

Physical medicine and rehabilitation

AMERICAN BURN ASSOCIATION [2293]
311 South Wacker Drive
Suite 4150
Chicago, IL 60606-6671
(312) 642-9260
Fax: (312) 642-9130
E-mail: info@ameriburn.org
Web Site: ameriburn.org

AREAS OF INTEREST:
Thermal injury.

NAME(S) OF PROGRAMS:
● **Cheryl Jordan Scholarship Fund**

TYPE:
Exchange programs; Travel grants.

PURPOSE:
To support efforts that address the problems of burn injuries and burn victims; to provide care and rehabilitation to burn patients, conduct burn-related research, educate burn team members, develop and implement burn injury prevention programs, fight fires and address the psychosocial needs of burn victims.

ELIGIBILITY:
Applicant must be a non-physician burn team member.

GEOG. RESTRICTIONS: United States and Canada.

FINANCIAL DATA:
Amount of support per award: Varies.
Total amount of support: Varies.

NO. AWARDS: Varies.

APPLICATION INFO:
Application is submitted through the Association web site.

ADDRESS INQUIRIES TO:
Kimberly A. Hoarle, Executive Director
(See address above.)

AMERICAN GERIATRICS SOCIETY [2294]
40 Fulton Street, 18th Floor
New York, NY 10038
(212) 308-1414
Fax: (212) 832-8646
E-mail: info.amger@americangeriatrics.org
Web Site: www.americangeriatrics.org

AREAS OF INTEREST:
Problems of the aged.

NAME(S) OF PROGRAMS:
● **Clinical Student Research Award**
● **Clinician of the Year Award**
● **Health in Aging Foundation New Investigator Awards**
● **Edward Henderson Student Award**
● **Dennis W. Jahnigen Memorial Award**
● **Nascher/Manning Award**
● **Outstanding Junior Clinician Education Manuscript**
● **Outstanding Junior Clinician Educator of the Year**
● **Outstanding Junior Investigator of the Year**
● **Outstanding Junior Research Manuscript**
● **Outstanding Mid-Career Clinician Educator of the Year**
● **Scientist-in-Training Research Award**
● **Thomas and Catherine Yoshikawa Award for Outstanding Scientific Achievement in Clinical Investigation**

TYPE:
Awards/prizes. The AGS Student Research Award is presented to an undergraduate student in medicine, dentistry, nursing, social work, pharmacy, occupational therapy, or physical therapy for presenting at the AGS Annual Meeting.

Clinician of the Year Award was established to recognize the great contributions of practitioners for delivering quality health care for older people, as well as to showcase the importance of the geriatrics clinician in our health care system.

Health in Aging Foundation New Investigator Awards are presented to individuals whose original research, as presented in a submitted abstract, reflects new and relevant insights in geriatrics.

Edward Henderson Student Award is presented to a medical student interested in pursuing a career in geriatrics who has demonstrated excellence in the field.

Dennis W. Jahnigen Memorial Award is given annually to an AGS member who has provided leadership to train students in geriatrics and has contributed significantly to the progress of geriatrics education in health professions schools.

Nascher/Manning Award recognizes distinguished, lifelong achievement in clinical geriatrics, including medicine, psychiatry, and all other related disciplines.

Outstanding Junior Clinician Education Manuscript Award is given to a junior faculty member (Assistant Professor/Instructor) or an Associate Professor (having held the position for no more than three years) who has been first author on an important peer-reviewed clinical education article published in a scientific journal.

Outstanding Junior Clinician Educator of the Year Award is given to an outstanding clinician educator junior faculty member (Assistant Professor/Instructor) for an impressive body of work in geriatric education.

Outstanding Junior Investigator of the Year Award is given to an outstanding junior investigator for their body of work. The award takes into consideration independence of thought and originality in new and relevant research in geriatrics and gerontology.

Outstanding Junior Research Manuscript Award is given to a junior investigator (Assistant Professor/Instructor or equivalent) who has been first author on an important or interesting peer-reviewed geriatrics research article within the past year.

Outstanding Mid-Career Clinician Educator of the Year Award is given to an outstanding clinician educator midcareer faculty member (Associate Professor) for an impressive body of work in geriatric education.

Scientist-in-Training Research Award is presented to a predoctoral candidate from a range of disciplines, including psychology, gerontology, epidemiology, to celebrate the awardees promise as a geriatrics scientist.

Thomas and Catherine Yoshikawa Award for Outstanding Achievement in Clinical Investigation recognizes outstanding achievement in clinical research addressing health problems of older adults as evaluated by an investigator actively involved in direct patient care.

PURPOSE:
To encourage and promote the field of geriatrics and to stress the importance of medical research in the field of aging; to recognize individuals whose outstanding work in geriatrics education, research and clinical practice contribute to the delivery of high-quality care for older people.

FINANCIAL DATA:
Amount of support per award: Clinical Student Research Award and Scientist-in-Training Research Award: $500; Clinician of the Year and Thomas and Catherine Yoshikawa Award: $2,000; Health in Aging Foundation New Investigator Awards: $1,000; Dennis W. Jahnigen Memorial Award and Nascher/Manning Award: Travel expenses to attend the AGS meeting.
Total amount of support: Varies.

APPLICATION INFO:
Application is posted on the Society web site by mid-August.
Deadline: December 1.

ADDRESS INQUIRIES TO:
Dennise McAlpin, Assistant Director Professional Education and Special Projects (See address above.)

AMERICAN KINESIOTHERAPY ASSOCIATION, INC.   [2295]
P.O. Box 24822
Richmond, VA 23224
(800) 296-2582
E-mail: info@akta.org
Web Site: www.akta.org

FOUNDED: 1946

AREAS OF INTEREST:
Kinesiotherapy, including adaptive physical education.

NAME(S) OF PROGRAMS:
● **AKTA Lou Montalvano Memorial Scholarship**

TYPE:
Scholarships. Award for students in AKTA-accredited kinesiotherapy programs.

PURPOSE:
To recognize academic excellence and career planning through funding for educational needs.

LEGAL BASIS:
Incorporated, nonprofit organization.

ELIGIBILITY:
Candidate must be currently enrolled in an AKTA-accredited kinesiotherapy program in a university and have definite intentions to pursue certification and a career in kinesiotherapy. Candidate must be a current member of the AKTA. Past AKTA scholarship winners are ineligible to apply for further AKTA scholarships.

FINANCIAL DATA:
Amount of support per award: $500.
Total amount of support: $500.

NO. AWARDS: 1 annually.

APPLICATION INFO:
Application process includes college transcripts and three letters of recommendation. Further information is available from the Association.
Duration: One year.
Deadline: August 31.

ADDRESS INQUIRIES TO:
Kathy Camp, Executive Director
E-mail: executivedirector@akta.org

THE AMERICAN ORTHOPAEDIC SOCIETY FOR SPORTS MEDICINE (AOSSM)   [2296]
9400 West Higgins Road
Suite 300
Rosemont, IL 60018
(877) 321-3500 (IL only)
(847) 292-4900
Fax: (847) 292-4905
E-mail: kevin@aossm.org
Web Site: www.sportsmed.org/research

FOUNDED: 1972

AREAS OF INTEREST:
Sports medicine.

NAME(S) OF PROGRAMS:
● **Steven P. Arnoczky Young Investigator Grant**

TYPE:
Awards/prizes; Research grants. Grant is intended to encourage early career researchers.

PURPOSE:
To increase the knowledge of and improve the care of sports-related injuries and disease.

ELIGIBILITY:
Grants will be awarded to the principal investigators who fulfill the following criteria:
(1) has not received any peer-reviewed external funding nor any external funding greater than $25,000;
(2) must be an early career orthopedic surgeon or sports medicine fellow who has graduated from an approved residency program;
(3) must document and play the primary role in the proposed investigation and;
(4) must stay at the parent institution while completing the project.

FINANCIAL DATA:
Amount of support per award: Up to $40,000 over a 24-month period.

NO. MOST RECENT APPLICANTS: 10 to 15.

NO. AWARDS: 1.

APPLICATION INFO:
Online submission only.
Duration: Two years.
Deadline: Pre-review (required) and final deadlines are posted online.

ADDRESS INQUIRIES TO:
Kevin Boyer, M.P.H., Director of Research
(See address above.)

THE AMERICAN ORTHOPAEDIC SOCIETY FOR SPORTS MEDICINE (AOSSM)   [2297]
9400 West Higgins Road
Suite 300
Rosemont, IL 60018
(847) 292-4900
(877) 321-3500 (IL only)
Fax: (847) 292-4905
E-mail: kevin@aossm.org
Web Site: www.sportsmed.org/research

AREAS OF INTEREST:
Sports medicine.

NAME(S) OF PROGRAMS:
● **AOSSM Sandy Kirkley Clinical Outcome Research Grant**

TYPE:
Research grants. Research grant provides start-up seed or supplemental funding for an outcome research project or pilot study.

PURPOSE:
To support clinical outcome research that has the potential to inform evidence-based practice.

ELIGIBILITY:
Grants will be awarded to the principal investigators who fulfill the following criteria:
(1) must document and play the primary role in the proposed investigation and;
(2) must stay at the parent institution while completing the project.

FINANCIAL DATA:
Amount of support per award: Up to $20,000 over two years.

NO. MOST RECENT APPLICANTS: 8 to 10.

NO. AWARDS: 1.

APPLICATION INFO:
Online submission only.
Duration: Two years.
Deadline: Pre-review and final deadlines are posted online.

ADDRESS INQUIRIES TO:
Kevin Boyer, M.P.H.
Director of Research
(See address above.)

FOUNDATION FOR PHYSICAL THERAPY RESEARCH, INC.   [2298]
3030 Potomac Avenue
Suite 110
Alexandria, VA 22305-3085
(800) 875-1378
Fax: (703) 684-4083
E-mail: info@foundation4pt.org
Web Site: foundation4pt.org

FOUNDED: 1979

AREAS OF INTEREST:
Physical therapy research, investigative studies that add to or refine the body of clinical knowledge on which physical therapy practice is based, and intervention projects involving therapeutic procedures and modalities.

TYPE:
Research grants.

YEAR PROGRAM STARTED: 1998

PURPOSE:
To add to or refine the body of clinical knowledge on which physical therapy practice is based and to evaluate patient interventions.

LEGAL BASIS:
Foundation.

ELIGIBILITY:
Awards are made to qualified physical therapists and physical therapist assistants or groups of investigators. Must be a U.S. citizen or permanent resident. Projects must be sponsored by a U.S. institution or organization. No funds will be approved to finance cost overruns or deficits on existing projects or to finance projects already in progress.

GEOG. RESTRICTIONS: United States.

FINANCIAL DATA:
Amount of support per award: Maximum $40,000 to $360,000 depending upon grant.
Total amount of support: $1,063,000 for the year 2020.

NO. AWARDS: 30.

APPLICATION INFO:
Application guidelines and access to the online application system are available on the Foundation's web site.
Duration: One to two years.
Deadline: Proposals are due first week in August for most types of grants. Contact Foundation for details.

PUBLICATIONS:
Application guidelines.

IRS I.D.: 13-6161225

ADDRESS INQUIRIES TO:
Barbara Malm, Chief Executive Officer (See address above.)

*PLEASE NOTE:
Applicants can only apply to one grant mechanism per cycle.

FOUNDATION FOR PHYSICAL THERAPY RESEARCH, INC.   [2299]

3030 Potomac Avenue
Suite 110
Alexandria, VA 22305-3085
(800) 875-1378
Fax: (703) 684-4083
E-mail: info@foundation4pt.org
Web Site: foundation4pt.org

FOUNDED: 1979

AREAS OF INTEREST:
Physical therapy.

NAME(S) OF PROGRAMS:
● **New Investigator Fellowship Training Initiative (NIFTI)**
● **Promotion of Doctoral Studies Scholarships (PODS)**

TYPE:
Fellowships; Scholarships. Fellowships for postdoctoral physical therapy research. Scholarships for physical therapists who intend to pursue physical therapy research as a career.

YEAR PROGRAM STARTED: 1979

PURPOSE:
To provide scholarships that support physical therapists who wish to continue their doctoral coursework and enter the dissertation phase; to provide fellowships that support developing researchers and improve their competitiveness in securing external funding for future research.

LEGAL BASIS:
Foundation.

ELIGIBILITY:
Must be U.S. citizen or permanent resident. Scholarship applicants must be physical therapists or physical therapist assistants pursuing a doctoral degree in physical therapy or a related field with a research focus related to the clinical practice of physical therapy. Applicants must demonstrate a commitment to research.

Fellowship applicants must be physical therapists or physical therapist assistants who have completed Doctorate, or the professional education degree in physical therapy for those already holding a post-professional doctoral degree in the last five years.

One year of teaching is expected for each year of support.

FINANCIAL DATA:
Amount of support per award: PODS I: $7,500; PODS II: $15,000; Fellowship: $100,000.

NO. AWARDS: 20 to 25.

APPLICATION INFO:
Applicants must check the online eligibility guidelines, review the application instructions, then submit the online application.
Duration: Scholarships: One year. Must reapply. Fellowships: Two years.
Deadline: Mid-January.

IRS I.D.: 13-6161225

ADDRESS INQUIRIES TO:
Barbara Malm, Chief Executive Officer (See address above.)

INTERNATIONAL ORDER OF ALHAMBRA   [2300]

4200 Leeds Avenue
Baltimore, MD 21229-5496
(800) 478-2946
(410) 242-0660
Fax: (410) 536-5729
E-mail: salaam@orderofalhambra.org
Web Site: www.orderalhambra.org

FOUNDED: 1904

AREAS OF INTEREST:
Scholarships for those interested in teaching special education.

NAME(S) OF PROGRAMS:
● **Scholarship and Charity Fund**

TYPE:
Grants-in-aid; Scholarships.

YEAR PROGRAM STARTED: 1970

PURPOSE:
To further education in the field of the intellectually disabled.

LEGAL BASIS:
A nonprofit 501(c)(3) fraternal organization of Catholic men and women dedicated to assisting intellectually disabled persons.

ELIGIBILITY:
Applicant should be attending college or postgraduate study. Applicants must be majoring in special education, which involves the mentally, physically or emotionally handicapped person, and must be eligible to teach special education upon graduation.

GEOG. RESTRICTIONS: United States and Canada.

FINANCIAL DATA:
Amount of support per award: Varies depending on the level of education.

NO. AWARDS: Varies.

APPLICATION INFO:
Students may only apply for one semester per application. Call (800) 478-2946 for further information.
Duration: One semester. Renewable by reapplication.
Deadline: March 1.

*PLEASE NOTE:
Student is limited to two scholarships.

NATIONAL AMBUCS, INC. [2301]

4285 Regency Drive
Greensboro, NC 27410
(800) 838-1845
Fax: (336) 852-6830
E-mail: scholars@ambucs.org
Web Site: www.ambucs.org

FOUNDED: 1948

AREAS OF INTEREST:
Physical therapy, occupational therapy, speech-language pathology and hearing audiology.

NAME(S) OF PROGRAMS:
● **AMBUCS Scholars-Scholarships for Therapists**

TYPE:
Scholarships. AMBUCS Scholars is the largest private single source of educational grants for therapists in America. The goal of this program is to provide financial assistance to needy students studying therapy, which in return places trained individuals in the therapy community to help people with disabilities.

YEAR PROGRAM STARTED: 1955

PURPOSE:
To financially assist students studying for qualification in one of the therapy professions.

LEGAL BASIS:
Private nonprofit association.

ELIGIBILITY:
Applicant must be a citizen of the U.S., document financial need, document good scholastic standing and be accepted at the graduate level in an accredited program by the appropriate health therapy profession authority in occupational therapy, physical therapy, speech-language pathology or hearing audiology.

GEOG. RESTRICTIONS: United States.

FINANCIAL DATA:
Amount of support per award: Average $750, plus one two-year scholarship (awarded annually) of $3,000.
Total amount of support: Approximately $200,000 annually.

CO-OP FUNDING PROGRAMS: Funding for this scholarship program is provided entirely by individual AMBUCS chapters and private donations.

NO. MOST RECENT APPLICANTS: 1,400.

NO. AWARDS: 250.

APPLICATION INFO:
Applications must be submitted electronically. If the student is being sponsored by a local chapter, the student should give the local chapter a copy of the

completed application, along with the most current FAFSA SAR, a narrative statement, and enrollment certification.

Duration: One academic year.

Deadline: Applications accepted from early March to mid-May.

ADDRESS INQUIRIES TO:
AMBUCS Scholarship Coordinator
AMBUCS Resource Center
P.O. Box 5127
High Point, NC 27262
E-mail: ambucs@ambucs.org

NATIONAL ASSOCIATION OF HEALTH SERVICES EXECUTIVES (NAHSE)   [2302]

NAHSE National Office
1050 Connecticut Avenue, N.W.
Suite 500
Washington, DC 20036
(202) 772-1030
Fax: (202) 772-1072
E-mail: nahsehq@nahse.org
Web Site: www.nahse.org

FOUNDED: 1968

AREAS OF INTEREST:
Health care.

NAME(S) OF PROGRAMS:
- **The Ellis Bonner Award**
- **The Florence Gaynor Award**
- **The Haynes Rice Award**

TYPE:
Scholarships. The Ellis Bonner Award is a special scholarship to recognize the distinguished leadership and academic achievement among non-traditional graduate students who are striving to become future leaders in health care management and NAHSE.

The Florence Gaynor Award recognizes outstanding achievements among female graduate students who are striving to become future leaders in health care management and NAHSE.

The Haynes Rice Award is bestowed by NAHSE to outstanding graduate students who are striving to become future leaders in health care management and NAHSE.

PURPOSE:
To promote the advancement and development of Black health care leaders and elevate the quality of health care services rendered to minority and underserved communities.

ELIGIBILITY:
Applicant must:
(1) be either enrolled or accepted in an accredited college or university program, pursuing a B.S., M.S. or Doctorate degree, majoring in computer science, management of information technology or information management, or provide proof of intent to pursue a major in one of the above areas of study;
(2) be able to demonstrate financial need;
(3) be an active NAHSE member;
(4) have a minimum academic grade point average of 3.0 or above on a scale of 4.0 and;
(5) submit a position paper examining new information and technology trends and their effects on health care.

To retain the scholarship for the second year, the recipient must maintain a 3.0 grade point average and produce a position paper on new technologies and present the position paper to an FCG or NAHSE panel.

FINANCIAL DATA:
Amount of support per award: $5,000.
Total amount of support: $15,000.

NO. MOST RECENT APPLICANTS: 12.

NO. AWARDS: 3.

APPLICATION INFO:
Contact the Association for guidelines.
Duration: One year.
Deadline: June 30.

ADDRESS INQUIRIES TO:
Beverly Glover, Manager
(See address above.)

NATIONAL MULTIPLE SCLEROSIS SOCIETY

Research Programs
733 Third Avenue, 3rd Floor
New York, NY 10017-3288
(212) 476-0451
Fax: (212) 986-7981
E-mail: cathy.carlson@nmss.org
Web Site: www.nationalmssociety.org

TYPE:
Awards/prizes; Fellowships; Research grants; Research contracts. Pilot grants; Training/early career awards. Grants for fundamental or applied research in scientific areas pertinent to multiple sclerosis. Grants are available for clinical or nonclinical studies, providing they show relevance to the Society's research priorities.

See entry 2223 for full listing.

NATIONAL SOCIETY DAUGHTERS OF THE AMERICAN REVOLUTION [2303]

1776 D Street, N.W.
Washington, DC 20006-5303
(202) 879-3263
E-mail: scholarships@nsdar.org
Web Site: www.dar.org

FOUNDED: 1895

AREAS OF INTEREST:
Occupational and physical therapy.

NAME(S) OF PROGRAMS:
- **Occupational/Physical Therapy Scholarship**

TYPE:
Scholarships. Awarded to students who are in financial need and have been accepted or are attending an accredited school of occupational or physical therapy (including art, music, or physical therapy).

PURPOSE:
To provide ways and means to aid students in attaining higher education.

LEGAL BASIS:
Incorporated historical society.

ELIGIBILITY:
Scholarships are awarded without regard to race, religion, sex or national origin. Candidates must be U.S. citizens and must be enrolled in an accredited school of occupational or physical therapy in the U.S. No affiliation or relationship to DAR is required for qualification.

Candidate must be majoring in occupational therapy or physical therapy and must be in financial need.

Awards are judged on the basis of academic excellence, commitment to field of study, as required, and need.

GEOG. RESTRICTIONS: United States.

FINANCIAL DATA:
Amount of support per award: $2,000.
Total amount of support: $4,000.

NO. AWARDS: 2.

APPLICATION INFO:
Applicants must use the DAR Scholarship Committee's online submission process found on the DAR public web site. Once applicants have set up their scholarship profile, they will be able to complete the application. If necessary, applicants will be able to provide access to individuals wishing to submit confidential letters of recommendations or school transcripts.
Duration: One-time scholarship.
Deadline: January 31.

PUBLICATIONS:
American Spirit, magazine.

ADDRESS INQUIRIES TO:
National Vice Chairman
E-mail: occupationalphysicaltherapyscholarship@nsdar.org

PARALYZED VETERANS OF AMERICA RESEARCH AND EDUCATION FOUNDATIONS   [2304]

801 Eighteenth Street, N.W.
Washington, DC 20006
(202) 416-7611
E-mail: lindsayp@pva.org
Web Site: www.pva.org/research-foundation

FOUNDED: 1976

AREAS OF INTEREST:
Basic and applied research in spinal cord injury and diseases.

TYPE:
Development grants; Fellowships; Project/program grants; Research grants. The PVA Research Foundation aims to increase scientific knowledge leading to a cure for spinal cord injury. The Foundation also funds research that deals with applied medical, psychological and technological areas of importance to persons with spinal cord injury or disease.

YEAR PROGRAM STARTED: 1976

PURPOSE:
To support research projects designed to alleviate and eventually end the serious medical, rehabilitative, and psycho social consequences of spinal cord injury and/or disease.

LEGAL BASIS:
Tax-exempt corporation under Sections 170(c) and 501(c)(3) of the Internal Revenue Code. Incorporated in the District of Columbia as a nonprofit organization.

ELIGIBILITY:
All applications must be submitted by fiscally responsible organizational entities in the name of the Principal Investigator. Entities should be nonprofit academic institutions, health care providers, associations and/or organizations. Each

application must include appropriate endorsement of an official who is responsible for the administration of awarded funds (hereafter called the "Grant Administrator").

Grantee institutions must be located in the U.S. or Canada. However, investigators and fellows are not required to be U.S. or Canadian citizens. The Foundation does not fund undergraduate or predoctoral students. Postdoctoral students who received their Ph.D. or M.D. within four years or less should apply for a fellowship grant, and may not be proposed as a Principal Investigator if they have not held such a position under previous funding (from any source). However, if a postdoctoral student has completed a postdoctoral fellowship under any source (please document), they may apply as a Principal Investigator. The Foundation is concerned about any Principal Investigator committing 5% effort or less in a project, with project activities falling primarily on less experienced investigators. Foreign nationals who will serve as a grant's Project Director (PD), Principal Investigator (PI), Research Fellow (RF) or a Significant Project Staff member(s) (20% of time) must provide verification that their U.S. or Canadian visa is current and that the visa will allow sufficient in-country (U.S. or Canada) time to complete the approved and funded grant project or fellowship award. Visa verification can be accomplished by submitting a letter from the PDs, PIs, RFs or significant staff on the sponsoring institution's letterhead that identifies the individual's visa expiration date. The letter must bear the individual's signature and the signature of the institution's grant administrator. The PD, PI, RF or significant staff person may also submit a copy of his or her current visa that identifies the visa's expiration date.

GEOG. RESTRICTIONS: United States and Canada.

FINANCIAL DATA:
Fringe benefits limited to 40%. Indirect cost limited to eight percent.
Amount of support per award: Fellowships: Maximum $50,000 per year; Basic science, clinical, design development: Maximum $75,000 per year.
Total amount of support: Varies.

NO. MOST RECENT APPLICANTS: 79 for the year 2019.

NO. AWARDS: 6 for the year 2019.

APPLICATION INFO:
Before submitting a grant application, carefully read the Research Foundation's Policies and Procedures, as policies may change from year to year. Submission must be made through the link on the Foundation web site.
Duration: One or two years.
Deadline: July. Announcement in December.

PUBLICATIONS:
Annual report; application guidelines.

IRS I.D.: 52-1064398

EXECUTIVE COMMITTEE:
David Zurfluh, National President
Charles Brown, National Senior Vice President
Hack Albertson, National Vice President
Tammy Jones, National Vice President
Ken Ness, National Vice President
Robert Thomas, National Vice President
Tom Wheaton, National Treasurer
Marcus Murray, National Secretary
Carl Blake, Executive Director
Shaun Castle, Deputy Executive Director

ADDRESS INQUIRIES TO:
Rita Obi, Associate Director of Research and Education
(See address above.)

CHRISTOPHER & DANA REEVE FOUNDATION [2305]
636 Morris Turnpike, Suite 3A
Short Hills, NJ 07078
(973) 379-2690
(800) 225-0292
Fax: (973) 912-9433
E-mail: qol@christopherreeve.org
Web Site: www.christopherreeve.org

FOUNDED: 1982

AREAS OF INTEREST:
Improving the quality of life for individuals living with paralysis, as well as their families.

NAME(S) OF PROGRAMS:
• **Quality of Life Grants**

TYPE:
Project/program grants. Provides grants to nonprofit organizations whose projects and initiatives foster inclusion, involvement and community engagement, while promoting health and wellness for those affected by paralysis in the U.S. and U.S. territories.

YEAR PROGRAM STARTED: 1999

PURPOSE:
To support exemplary organizations that provide valuable services to individuals with paralysis and their quality of life and health.

LEGAL BASIS:
Not-for-profit organization.

ELIGIBILITY:
Quality of Life Grants are awarded to 501(c)(3) organizations, as well as community parks, schools, veterans hospitals, tribal entities, etc.

Funds cannot be used to support food, grants to individuals, research, rehabilitative therapy, or new construction (although facility modifications to improve accessibility in existing structures is allowed).

GEOG. RESTRICTIONS: United States.

FINANCIAL DATA:
Amount of support per award: Direct Effect (Tier 1): Up to $25,000; Expanded Impact: Up to $100,000; High Impact: $30,000 for Tier 2, $40,000 for Tier 3, and $50,000 for Tier 4. High Impact Assistive Technology Grants: Up to $75,000.
Total amount of support: $3,124,856 for the year 2020.
Matching fund requirements: Although matching funds are not required, it is beneficial to seek funding from additional sources.

CO-OP FUNDING PROGRAMS: Quality of Life Grants are currently funded through a cooperative agreement with the Administration for Community Living (ACL).

NO. MOST RECENT APPLICANTS: Approximately 800.

NO. AWARDS: 133 for the year 2020.

APPLICATION INFO:
Guidelines are available on the Foundation web site. Applications are submitted through the online portal.
Duration: Generally one year or less.
Deadline: Varies. Schedule is posted on the Foundation web site.

PUBLICATIONS:
Guidelines; application questions; final report form; People First Language Guide; A Quick Guide to Establishing Evaluation Indicators.

IRS I.D.: 22-2939536

ADDRESS INQUIRIES TO:
Mark Bogosian, Director
Quality of Life Grants Program
(See address above.)

*SPECIAL STIPULATIONS:
Prior grant recipients must wait two years following the close of their grant to reapply for funding.

U.S. DEPARTMENT OF HEALTH AND HUMAN SERVICES [2306]
Administration for Community Living
300 C Street, S.W., Room 1317B
Washington, DC 20201
(202) 795-7356
(202) 401-4634
E-mail: robert.groenendaal@acl.hhs.gov
Web Site: acl.gov

FOUNDED: 1978

AREAS OF INTEREST:
Priorities are established annually for certain programs.

NAME(S) OF PROGRAMS:
• **Assistive Technology Programs**

TYPE:
Project/program grants. Assistive Technology Program provides states with financial assistance that supports programs designed to maximize the ability of individuals with disabilities and their family members, guardians, advocates, and authorized representatives to obtain assistive technology devices and assistive technology services.

YEAR PROGRAM STARTED: 1978

PURPOSE:
To support state efforts to improve the provision of assistive technology devices and services to individuals with disabilities of all ages through comprehensive statewide programs of technology-related assistance.

LEGAL BASIS:
Assistive Technology Act of 1998, as amended by Public Law 108-364.

ELIGIBILITY:
Requirements vary according to program. Full information is available on the Administration for Community Living web site.

FINANCIAL DATA:
Amount of support per award: Grants vary in amount depending on type of program.

APPLICATION INFO:
Guidelines are available online.
Duration: Annual formula grant awards.
Deadline: Varies.

ADDRESS INQUIRIES TO:
Robert Groenendaal
Assistive Technology Programs Manager
(See e-mail address above.)

Psychiatry, psychology, mental health

AMERICAN ACADEMY OF CHILD AND ADOLESCENT PSYCHIATRY [2307]

3615 Wisconsin Avenue, N.W.
Washington, DC 20016-3007
(202) 966-7300 ext. 117
Fax: (202) 966-5894
E-mail: aarcher@aacap.org
Web Site: www.aacap.org

FOUNDED: 1953

AREAS OF INTEREST:
Child and adolescent psychiatry.

NAME(S) OF PROGRAMS:
- **Jeanne Spurlock Minority Medical Student Research Fellowship in Substance Abuse and Addiction**
- **Summer Medical Student Fellowship**

TYPE:
Awards/prizes; Conferences/seminars; Fellowships; Research grants; Travel grants. Jeanne Spurlock Minority Medical Student Research Fellowship in Substance Abuse and Addiction provides support for research training in substance abuse and addiction under a mentor with experience in the type of research that is being proposed, and whose work includes children and adolescents participants.

Summer Medical Student Fellowship provides clinical or research training under a child and adolescent psychiatrist mentor.

YEAR PROGRAM STARTED: 1994

PURPOSE:
To increase the number of minority child and adolescent psychiatrists trained in research.

LEGAL BASIS:
Nonprofit organization.

ELIGIBILITY:
Spurlock Minority Medical Student Research Fellowship: Applications are considered from African American, Native American, Alaskan Native, Mexican American, Hispanic, Asian and Pacific Islander students in accredited U.S. medical schools or students whose research will focus on minorities.

GEOG. RESTRICTIONS: United States.

FINANCIAL DATA:
Amount of support per award: Spurlock Fellowship: Up to $4,000, plus travel support for AACAP's Annual Meeting; Summer Fellowship: $3,500, plus travel support for AACAP's Annual Meeting.
Total amount of support: All awards contingent upon available funding.

NO. MOST RECENT APPLICANTS: Spurlock Fellowship: 2 for the year 2018.

NO. AWARDS: Spurlock Fellowship: 3 for the year 2017.

APPLICATION INFO:
E-mail training@aacap.org to receive application materials.
Duration: 12 weeks.
Deadline: March.

PUBLICATIONS:
Program announcement; *Research Notes*, newsletter.

ADDRESS INQUIRIES TO:
Research, Grants and Workforce Department
E-mail: training@aacap.org

AMERICAN ACADEMY OF CHILD AND ADOLESCENT PSYCHIATRY [2308]

3615 Wisconsin Avenue, N.W.
Washington, DC 20016-3007
(202) 966-7300 ext. 117
Fax: (202) 966-5894
E-mail: aarcher@aacap.org
Web Site: www.aacap.org

FOUNDED: 1953

AREAS OF INTEREST:
Child and adolescent psychiatry.

NAME(S) OF PROGRAMS:
- **Educational Outreach Program**
- **Paramjit Toor Joshi, M.D., International Scholar Awards**
- **Junior Investigator Award**
- **Life Members Mentorship Grant for Medical Students**
- **Pilot Awards**
- **Ülkü Ülgür, M.D., International Scholar Award**

TYPE:
Conferences/seminars; Fellowships; Research grants; Travel grants. Educational Outreach Program provides travel support for residents and CAP fellows to travel to the Annual Meeting and network with child and adolescent psychiatrists.

Joshi International Scholar Awards recognize midcareer international physicians who primarily work with children and adolescents providing mental health services outside the U.S.

Junior Investigator Award is offered for one child and adolescent psychiatry junior faculty to pursue innovative research. The research may be basic or clinical in nature but must be relevant to the understanding, treatment and prevention of child and adolescent mental health disorders. The award also includes the cost of attending AACAP's Annual Meeting for five days.

Life Members Mentorship Grant for Medical Students provides travel support for medical student recipients to receive a formal overview of child and adolescent psychiatry, establish mentor relationships with child and adolescent psychiatrists, and experience AACAP's Annual Meeting.

Pilot Awards are offered to members with a career interest in child and adolescent mental health research.

Ülgür International Scholar Award recognizes a child and adolescent psychiatrist or a physician in the international community who has made significant contributions to the enhancement of mental health services for children and adolescents.

PURPOSE:
To increase the number of minority child and adolescent psychiatrists trained in research.

LEGAL BASIS:
Nonprofit organization.

ELIGIBILITY:
Joshi International Scholar Awards: Qualified international physicians may include pediatricians, family medicine doctors, adult psychiatrists, child and adolescent psychiatrists and other physicians who primarily work with children and adolescents providing mental health services.

FINANCIAL DATA:
Amount of support per award: Educational Outreach Program and Life Members

Mentorship Grant for Medical Students: Up to $1,000; Junior Investigator Award: Up to $30,000 per year; Pilot Awards: Up to $15,000. All awards are contingent upon available funding.

NO. MOST RECENT APPLICANTS: Educational Outreach Program: 136; Life Members Mentorship Grant for Medical Students: 56.

NO. AWARDS: Educational Outreach Program: 64; Joshi International Scholar Awards: 2; Junior Investigator Award: 1; Life Members Mentorship Grant for Medical Students: 13; Pilot Awards: 1; Ülgür International Scholar Award: 1.

APPLICATION INFO:
E-mail training@aacap.org to receive application materials.
Duration: Educational Outreach Program, Joshi International Scholar Awards, Life Members Mentorship Grant for Medical Students and Ülgür International Scholar Award: One week. Junior Investigator Award: Two years. Pilot Awards: Up to two years.
Deadline: Educational Outreach Program and Life Members Mentorship Grant: July. Joshi International and Ülgür Scholar Awards: May. Junior Investigator Award: March. Pilot Awards: April.

PUBLICATIONS:
Program announcement; *Research Notes*, newsletter.

ADDRESS INQUIRIES TO:
Research, Grants and Workforce Department
E-mail: training@aacap.org

AMERICAN ACADEMY OF CHILD AND ADOLESCENT PSYCHIATRY [2309]

3615 Wisconsin Avenue, N.W.
Washington, DC 20016-3007
(202) 966-7300 ext. 117
Fax: (202) 966-5894
E-mail: aarcher@aacap.org
Web Site: www.aacap.org

FOUNDED: 1953

AREAS OF INTEREST:
Child and adolescent psychiatry.

NAME(S) OF PROGRAMS:
- **Marilyn B. Benoit, M.D., Child Maltreatment Mentorship Award**
- **Psychodynamic Faculty Training and Mentorship Initiative**

TYPE:
Project/program grants; Research grants; Travel grants. The Marilyn B. Benoit, M.D., Child Maltreatment Mentorship Award facilitates the completion of a project in which the applicant collaborates with a mentor specializing in the areas of child welfare, foster care, and/or children maltreatment prevention/intervention.

The Psychodynamic Faculty Training and Mentorship Initiative provides a reimbursable travel stipend to cover travel support for attending the required program events during AACAP's Annual Meeting.

PURPOSE:
To increase awareness and interest in the fields of child welfare, foster care, and/or child maltreatment prevention/intervention; to strengthen psychodynamic psychotherapy

training in child and adolescent psychiatry residency programs through faculty development.

LEGAL BASIS:
Nonprofit organization.

ELIGIBILITY:
For the Marilyn B. Benoit, M.D., Child Maltreatment Mentorship Award, applicant must:
(1) be a current AACAP member or have a pending membership application submitted;
(2) be either a child and adolescent psychiatry fellow or early career psychiatrist within seven years of graduating a fellowship program and;
(3) have a mentor who has had experience in key issues in the areas of child welfare, foster care and/or child maltreatment prevention/intervention. It is preferred that the mentor's work include children and adolescents.

For the Psychodynamic Faculty Training and Mentorship Initiative, candidate must:
(1) have an M.D., D.O. or equivalent degree;
(2) teach in a child psychiatry, triple board or post-pediatric portal training program;
(3) be affiliated with an ACGME accredited training program and;
(4) be an active AACP member or have a membership application pending at the time of submission.

GEOG. RESTRICTIONS: United States.

FINANCIAL DATA:
Amount of support per award: Marilyn B. Benoit, M.D., Child Maltreatment Mentorship Award: Up to $8,000; Psychodynamic Faculty Training and Mentorship Initiative: $350.
Total amount of support: All awards are contingent upon available funding.

NO. AWARDS: Marilyn B. Benoit, M.D., Child Maltreatment Mentorship Award: 1 or 2; Psychodynamic Faculty Training and Mentorship Initiative: Up to 6.

APPLICATION INFO:
Requirements and application forms are available online.
Duration: Marilyn B. Benoit, M.D., Child Maltreatment Mentorship Award: 12 to 16 weeks; Psychodynamic Faculty Training and Mentorship Initiative: One year.
Deadline: Marilyn B. Benoit, M.D., Child Maltreatment Mentorship Award: April 15; Psychodynamic Faculty Training and Mentorship Initiative: May 1.

PUBLICATIONS:
Program announcement; *Research Notes,* newsletter.

ADDRESS INQUIRIES TO:
Research, Grants and Workforce Department
E-mail: training@aacap.org

AMERICAN PSYCHIATRIC ASSOCIATION   [2310]
800 Maine Avenue, S.W.
Suite 900
Washington, DC 20024
(202) 559-3900
(800) 368-5777
Fax: (202) 403-3094
E-mail: lthompson@psych.org
Web Site: www.psychiatry.org

AREAS OF INTEREST:
Psychiatric research.

NAME(S) OF PROGRAMS:
● **Kempf Fund Award for Research Development in Psychobiological Psychiatry**

TYPE:
Awards/prizes; Research grants. The Award supports the research-career development of a young research psychiatrist working in a mentor-trainee relationship with the award winner on further research in the field of schizophrenia.

YEAR PROGRAM STARTED: 1988

PURPOSE:
To recognize a senior researcher who has made a significant contribution to research on the causes and treatment of schizophrenia as both a researcher and a mentor.

ELIGIBILITY:
Applicants must be psychiatrists, American Psychiatric Association members and citizens or permanent residents of the U.S. or Canada.

FINANCIAL DATA:
Amount of support per award: $1,500 award to the senior researcher and $20,000 for support of the research-career development of a young research psychiatrist working in a mentor-trainee relationship with the award winner on further research in this field.

APPLICATION INFO:
Applicants are required to submit their application to the e-mail address above with the subject of the e-mail entitled "Kempf Fund Award."
Duration: One year. Nonrenewable.
Deadline: August 15.

ADDRESS INQUIRIES TO:
Laura Thompson, M.S.
(See e-mail address above.)

AMERICAN PSYCHIATRIC ASSOCIATION   [2311]
800 Maine Avenue, Suite 900
Washington, DC 20024
(202) 559-3900
(202) 459-9872
Fax: (202) 403-3094
E-mail: fellowships@psych.org
Web Site: www.psychiatry.org/residents

AREAS OF INTEREST:
Psychiatric research and mental health disparities.

NAME(S) OF PROGRAMS:
● **APA Child & Adolescent Psychiatry Fellowship**
● **APA Public Psychiatry Fellowship**
● **APA SAMHSA Minority Fellowships**
● **APA/APAF Leadership Fellowship**

TYPE:
Fellowships. APA Child & Adolescent Psychiatry Fellowship: This fellowship is designed to promote interest among general psychiatry residents in pursuing careers in child and adolescent psychiatry. Fellows will learn about new clinical research, successful treatments for children and adolescents with mental disorders and many other issues associated with child and adolescent mental health.

APA Public Psychiatry Fellowship: This fellowship aims to create the next generation of leaders in public psychiatry. Fellows will participate in APA activities, plan workshops at IPS, and interact with thought leaders in the field of public psychiatry.

APA SAMHSA Minority Fellowships: These fellowships endeavor to eliminate racial and ethnic disparities in mental health and substance abuse care by providing specialized training to psychiatry residents and medical students interested in serving minority communities.

APA/APAF Leadership Fellowship: This two-year fellowship offers psychiatric residents, with exceptional leadership potential, many different experiences that prepare them for leadership roles. Only the Chair of the Department or the Director of the Training Program can nominate.

PURPOSE:
To promote psychiatric research.

ELIGIBILITY:
Applicant must be in a psychiatry residency training program. APA membership required.

FINANCIAL DATA:
Amount of support per award: APA SAMHSA Minority Fellowships: $25,000 to $28,000, based on postgraduate year.

NO. MOST RECENT APPLICANTS: 10 to 20 per fellowship.

NO. AWARDS: APA Child & Adolescent Psychiatry Fellowship, APA Public Psychiatric Fellowship and APA/APAF Leadership Fellowship: Up to 15, pending funding; APA SAMHSA Minority Fellowships: Up to 28, pending funding.

APPLICATION INFO:
Applications must be submitted online.
Duration: APA Child & Adolescent Psychiatry Fellowship, APA Public Psychiatry Fellowship and APA/APAF Leadership Fellowship: Two years. APA SAMHSA Minority Fellowships: One year. Optional second year with reapplication.
Deadline: January 31.

ADDRESS INQUIRIES TO:
APA Fellowship Programs
(See address above.)

AMERICAN PSYCHIATRIC ASSOCIATION   [2312]
800 Maine Avenue, Suite 900
Washington, DC 20024
(202) 559-3900
(202) 459-9782
Fax: (202) 403-3094
E-mail: fellowships@psych.org
Web Site: www.psychiatry.org/residents

AREAS OF INTEREST:
Psychiatric research.

NAME(S) OF PROGRAMS:
● **Psychiatric Research Fellowship**
● **Jeanne Spurlock, M.D. Congressional Fellowship**

TYPE:
Fellowships; Travel grants. Psychiatric Research Fellowship sponsors one postgraduate psychiatry trainee specifically to focus on research and personal scholarship.

Jeanne Spurlock, M.D. Congressional Fellowship provides a psychiatry resident or early career psychiatrist an opportunity to work in a congressional office on federal health policy, particularly policy related to child and/or minority issues.

ELIGIBILITY:
Applicant must be in a psychiatry residency training program or an early career psychiatrist. APA membership required.

FINANCIAL DATA:
Amount of support per award: Psychiatric Research Fellowship: Up to $45,000; Spurlock Fellowship: $85,000 stipend, plus $10,000 housing allowance, $5,000 towards insurance and up to $3,500 for moving expenses.

NO. AWARDS: Psychiatric Research Fellowship: 1; Spurlock Fellowship: 2.

APPLICATION INFO:
Applications must be submitted online.
Duration: Psychiatric Research Fellowship: Two years. Spurlock Fellowship: 10 months.
Deadline: January 31.

ADDRESS INQUIRIES TO:
APA Fellowship Programs
(See address above.)

AMERICAN PSYCHOLOGICAL ASSOCIATION   [2313]
Minority Fellowship Program/APA
750 First Street, N.E.
Washington, DC 20002-4242
(202) 336-6127
Fax: (202) 336-6012
E-mail: mfp@apa.org
Web Site: www.apa.org/pi/mfp

FOUNDED: 1892

AREAS OF INTEREST:
Psychology.

NAME(S) OF PROGRAMS:
● **MFP Services for Transition Age Youth**

TYPE:
Fellowships.

YEAR PROGRAM STARTED: 2014

PURPOSE:
To support training of Master's level practitioners in mental health services.

LEGAL BASIS:
Nonprofit.

ELIGIBILITY:
Applicant must:
(1) be U.S. citizens, noncitizen nationals, or permanent residents;
(2) have a strong commitment to a career in mental health services with ethnic minority transition age youth and their families;
(3) be enrolled full-time in a terminal Master's program in psychology;
(4) be on track to graduate and/or receive the specialist/certificate portion of their Master's Program at any time during 2022 for the 2021 deadline and;
(5) be prepared to enter the field as a mental health practitioner immediately upon graduation.

It is not required for applicants to identify as ethnic minorities; however, African-Americans, Alaska Natives, American Indians, Asian-Americans, Hispanics/Latinos, Native Hawaiians and Pacific Islanders are especially encouraged to apply.

FINANCIAL DATA:
Amount of support per award: Up to $10,000.

CO-OP FUNDING PROGRAMS: Funding for services training is made available through Substance Abuse and Mental Health Services Administration allocations.

NO. AWARDS: 23.

APPLICATION INFO:
Applications are available mid-October to January 15. Guidelines are available online.
Duration: One academic year, in last year of Master's Program.
Deadline: January 15. Announcement by April.

ADDRESS INQUIRIES TO:
Minority Fellowship Program
(See telephone and e-mail address above.)

AMERICAN PSYCHOLOGICAL ASSOCIATION   [2314]
Government Relations Office
Public Interest Directorate
750 First Street, N.E.
Washington, DC 20002-4242
(202) 336-6166
Fax: (202) 336-6063
E-mail: abishop@apa.org
Web Site: www.apa.org/about/awardes/congress-fellow

FOUNDED: 1892

AREAS OF INTEREST:
Professional organization to advance psychology as a science and profession and as a means of promoting health, education and human welfare.

NAME(S) OF PROGRAMS:
● **APA Congressional Fellowship Program**

TYPE:
Fellowships. Program provides trained scientists and practitioners an opportunity for enhanced understanding of and involvement in the federal policymaking process by serving as congressional staff in Washington, DC.

YEAR PROGRAM STARTED: 1974

PURPOSE:
To provide an opportunity for psychologists to participate in the policymaking process.

LEGAL BASIS:
Nonprofit professional organization.

ELIGIBILITY:
Doctoral degree in psychology and APA membership required. Two years of postdoctoral experience is preferred. Individuals with sabbatical funds are eligible. Must be U.S. citizen and willing to relocate to Washington, DC.

GEOG. RESTRICTIONS: United States.

FINANCIAL DATA:
Amount of support per award: For the year 2019-20: $75,000 to $90,000, depending on years of postdoctoral experience. Up to $3,750 is allocated per Fellow for relocation to the Washington, DC area and for travel expenses during the year.
Total amount of support: Varies.

CO-OP FUNDING PROGRAMS: Fellowship is sponsored by the APA in cooperation with the American Association for the Advancement of Science and with funds from the American Psychological Foundation Goldman Fellowship.

NO. AWARDS: Up to 2.

APPLICATION INFO:
Completed online application form, curriculum vitae, three letters of reference and a statement of interest are required.
Duration: September through August. Nonrenewable.

Deadline: Early January. Announcement in March.

STAFF:
Aaron Bishop, Program Director

ADDRESS INQUIRIES TO:
Aaron Bishop, Program Director
APA Congressional Fellowship Program
(See telephone and e-mail address above.)

AMERICAN PSYCHOLOGICAL ASSOCIATION   [2315]
Minority Fellowship Program/APA
750 First Street, N.E.
Washington, DC 20002-4242
(202) 336-6127
Fax: (202) 336-6012
E-mail: mfp@apa.org
Web Site: www.apa.org/pi/mfp

FOUNDED: 1892

AREAS OF INTEREST:
Psychology.

NAME(S) OF PROGRAMS:
● **MFP Mental Health and Substance Abuse Services Fellowship**

TYPE:
Fellowships. Fellowship is geared to those pursuing careers as practitioners specializing in the delivery of behavioral health services to ethnic minority populations. Students specializing in clinical, school and counseling psychology are encouraged to apply.

YEAR PROGRAM STARTED: 1974

PURPOSE:
To provide financial support, professional development activities, and guidance to promising doctoral students, postdoctoral trainees and early career professionals with the goals of promoting culturally competent behavioral health services and increasing the number of ethnic minority psychologists providing behavioral health services to and developing policy for ethnic minority populations.

LEGAL BASIS:
Nonprofit.

ELIGIBILITY:
Applicants must:
(1) be citizens, noncitizen nationals, or permanent residents of the U.S.;
(2) have a strong commitment to a career in ethnic minority behavioral health services or policy;
(3) be enrolled full-time in an APA-accredited doctoral program during the fall term immediately following the application deadline and;
(4) not be interns.

It is not required for applicants to identify as ethnic minorities; however, African-Americans, Alaska Natives, American Indians, Asian-Americans, Hispanics/Latinos, Native Hawaiians and Pacific Islanders are especially encouraged to apply.

FINANCIAL DATA:
Amount of support per award: Follows NRSA guidelines.

CO-OP FUNDING PROGRAMS: Funding for services training is made available through the Substance Abuse and Mental Health Services Administration allocations.

NO. MOST RECENT APPLICANTS: 145.

NO. AWARDS: Generally 5% to 7% acceptance rate.

APPLICATION INFO:
Applications are available mid-October to January 15. Guidelines are available online.

Duration: One academic year. Renewable for up to two additional years.

Deadline: January 15. Announcement by April.

ADDRESS INQUIRIES TO:
Minority Fellowship Program
(See telephone and e-mail address above.)

AMERICAN PSYCHOSOMATIC SOCIETY [2316]

6728 Old McLean Village Drive
McLean, VA 22101
(703) 556-9222
Fax: (703) 556-8729
E-mail: info@psychosomatic.org
Web Site: www.psychosomatic.org

FOUNDED: 1942

AREAS OF INTEREST:
Psychosomatic medicine.

NAME(S) OF PROGRAMS:
● **Patricia R. Barchas Award in Sociophysiology**

TYPE:
Awards/prizes.

YEAR PROGRAM STARTED: 1999

PURPOSE:
To further the field of sociophysiology, the study of the reciprocal relationships that could lead to long-term change both in social behavior and in physiology.

ELIGIBILITY:
Applicant must have accomplished interesting and exciting work to expand knowledge of the interface of the social and psychological worlds.

FINANCIAL DATA:
Amount of support per award: $1,500, complimentary meeting registration and a plaque, which is presented at the Annual Meeting.

NO. AWARDS: 1.

APPLICATION INFO:
Nominations should include a 500- to 1,000-word justification for the nomination and an updated curriculum vitae.

Duration: One-time award.

Deadline: November 1.

IRS I.D.: 11-1866747

ADDRESS INQUIRIES TO:
Awards Committee
(See address above.)

AMERICAN PSYCHOSOMATIC SOCIETY [2317]

6728 Old McLean Village Drive
McLean, VA 22101
(703) 556-9222
Fax: (703) 556-8729
E-mail: info@psychosomatic.org
Web Site: www.psychosomatic.org

FOUNDED: 1942

AREAS OF INTEREST:
Psychosomatic medicine.

NAME(S) OF PROGRAMS:
● **Distinguished Scientist Award**

TYPE:
Awards/prizes.

YEAR PROGRAM STARTED: 2012

PURPOSE:
To acknowledge senior scientists and physicians who have made an important and protracted contribution in the field of psychosomatic medicine.

ELIGIBILITY:
Recipients must be senior scientists and physicians who have made an important and protracted contribution in any research field within the Society's areas of interest. Nominees should be members of the Society and would be expected to have contributed substantially over the years to its aims and goals.

FINANCIAL DATA:
Amount of support per award: $1,500, a commemorative plaque and complimentary meeting registration.

NO. AWARDS: 1.

APPLICATION INFO:
Nominations should include a 500- to 1,000-word justification for the nomination and an updated curriculum vitae of the nominee.

Duration: One-time award.

Deadline: November 1.

ADDRESS INQUIRIES TO:
Award Committee
(See address above.)

AMERICAN PSYCHOSOMATIC SOCIETY [2318]

6728 Old McLean Village Drive
McLean, VA 22101
(703) 556-9222
Fax: (703) 556-8729
E-mail: info@psychosomatic.org
Web Site: www.psychosomatic.org

FOUNDED: 1942

AREAS OF INTEREST:
Psychosomatic medicine.

NAME(S) OF PROGRAMS:
● **Paul D. MacLean Award**

TYPE:
Awards/prizes. This award is intended to honor Dr. Paul D. MacLean and promote the line of research that he created on emotion, the brain and physical disease.

YEAR PROGRAM STARTED: 2010

PURPOSE:
To reward outstanding neuroscience research in psychosomatic medicine.

ELIGIBILITY:
Nominee must have performed outstanding neuroscientific research (human or animal) that advances knowledge directly related to Dr. MacLean's hypothesis regarding altered cortical-subcortical interactions affecting physical disease outcomes or mediating processes (e.g., autonomic, neuroendocrine, immune) that can be directly linked to disease outcomes.

Individuals may self-nominate.

FINANCIAL DATA:
Amount of support per award: Up to $1,000 in travel expenses, complimentary meeting registration, a plaque and the opportunity to give a talk at the APS Annual Meeting.

NO. AWARDS: 1.

APPLICATION INFO:
Nominations should include a 500- to 1,000-word supporting statement, the nominee's curriculum vitae and three representative reprints.

Deadline: November 1.

IRS I.D.: 11-1866747

ADDRESS INQUIRIES TO:
Award Committee
(See address above.)

AMERICAN PSYCHOSOMATIC SOCIETY [2319]

6728 Old McLean Village Drive
McLean, VA 22101
(703) 556-9222
Fax: (703) 556-8729
E-mail: info@psychosomatic.org
Web Site: www.psychosomatic.org

FOUNDED: 1942

AREAS OF INTEREST:
Psychosomatic medicine.

NAME(S) OF PROGRAMS:
● **Herbert Weiner Early Career Award for Contributions to Psychosomatic Society**

TYPE:
Awards/prizes.

YEAR PROGRAM STARTED: 1991

PURPOSE:
To support individuals who show substantial promise in continuing study in psychosomatic medicine.

LEGAL BASIS:
Not-for-profit organization.

ELIGIBILITY:
Nominees must be fewer than 10 years past their final academic degree and must be members of the American Psychosomatic Society.

FINANCIAL DATA:
Amount of support per award: $1,000, plaque, complimentary meeting registration and an opportunity to present the research for which the award was given during the annual meeting of the Society.

NO. MOST RECENT APPLICANTS: 5.

NO. AWARDS: 1.

APPLICATION INFO:
Nominations must include a 500- to 1,000-word justification for the nomination, an updated curriculum vitae and reprints of the two to six publications of the work for which the nomination is being made.

Duration: One-time award.

Deadline: November 1.

PUBLICATIONS:
Award announcement.

IRS I.D.: 11-1866747

ADDRESS INQUIRIES TO:
Award Committee
(See address above.)

ANNA-MONIKA-FOUNDATION [2320]

Kieshecker Weg 240
D-40468 Duesseldorf Germany
(49) 211 437187 13
Fax: (49) 211 437187 23
E-mail: m.bommers@gospax.com
Web Site: anna-monika-stiftung.de

FOUNDED: 1965

AREAS OF INTEREST:
Biochemistry, neurophysiology, neuropathology, psychopharmacology, psychiatry, depression and psychosomatic illnesses.

NAME(S) OF PROGRAMS:
● **The Anna-Monika-Foundation Prize**

TYPE:
Awards/prizes. Prizes for research papers investigating the biological substrate and functional disturbances of depression. Prize-winning lectures will be published in *Pharmacopsychiatry*.

YEAR PROGRAM STARTED: 1966

PURPOSE:
To support international pioneering research in the area of depression research.

LEGAL BASIS:
Private foundation, authorized by the state of Nordrhein-Westfalen, Germany.

ELIGIBILITY:
As far as possible, the papers describing the studies should feature information about the recent advances and the knowledge that should be helpful in promoting treatment and open new paths of scientific progress in depression. Papers published in the last two years in an international scientific peer-reviewed journal may be submitted. Papers should be written in English.

FINANCIAL DATA:
Total amount of support: EUR 25,000.

NO. AWARDS: Maximum of 3 biennially in odd-numbered years.

APPLICATION INFO:
A maximum of three publications (in sets of four copies) plus a short summary (approximately 600 words) emphasizing the relevance and importance of the research are required. A curriculum vitae and summary of achievements in the field should be added; hitherto unpublished studies or papers published in an international professional journal within the past two years may also be submitted. Papers may be written in English and should be submitted to the Chairman of the Jury by e-mail to Rainer.Rupprecht@medbo.de.
Deadline: February 28.

ADDRESS INQUIRIES TO:
Michael Bommers, Managing Director
(See address above.)

ASSOCIATION FOR BEHAVIORAL AND COGNITIVE THERAPIES   [2321]
305 Seventh Avenue
16th Floor
New York, NY 10001
(212) 647-1890
Fax: (212) 647-1865
E-mail: mjeimer@abct.org
Web Site: www.abct.org

AREAS OF INTEREST:
Behavior therapy and cognitive behavior therapy.

NAME(S) OF PROGRAMS:
● **Virginia Roswell Dissertation Award**

TYPE:
Awards/prizes.

PURPOSE:
To explore the application of behavioral and cognitive sciences to understanding human

behavior, developing interventions to enhance the human condition, and promoting the appropriate utilization of these interventions.

ELIGIBILITY:
Applicant must be an ABCT student member who has already had their dissertation proposal approved and be investigating an area of direct relevance to behavior therapy or cognitive behavior therapy.

FINANCIAL DATA:
Amount of support per award: $1,000.

NO. AWARDS: 1.

APPLICATION INFO:
All candidates must be nominated. Self-nominations are accepted. Contact the Organization for nomination procedures.
Deadline: March 1.

ADDRESS INQUIRIES TO:
M.J. Eimer, Executive Director
(See address above.)

ASSOCIATION FOR BEHAVIORAL AND COGNITIVE THERAPIES   [2322]
305 Seventh Avenue
16th Floor
New York, NY 10001
(212) 647-1890
Fax: (212) 647-1865
E-mail: mjeimer@abct.org
Web Site: www.abct.org

AREAS OF INTEREST:
Behavior therapy and cognitive sciences.

NAME(S) OF PROGRAMS:
● **President's New Researcher Award**

TYPE:
Awards/prizes.

PURPOSE:
To explore the application of behavioral and cognitive sciences to understanding human behavior, developing interventions to enhance the human condition, and promoting the appropriate utilization of these interventions.

ELIGIBILITY:
Must be authored by an ABCT member with five years or less posttraining experience and have been published in the last two years or currently in press.

FINANCIAL DATA:
Amount of support per award: $500.

NO. AWARDS: 1.

APPLICATION INFO:
Contact the Organization for application procedures.
Deadline: March.

ADDRESS INQUIRIES TO:
M.J. Eimer, Executive Director
(See address above.)

AUTISM SPEAKS INC.
1060 State Road, 2nd Floor
Princeton, NJ 08540
(609) 228-7313
E-mail: jnew@autismspeaks.org
Web Site: www.autismspeaks.org

TYPE:
Fellowships; Research grants. Autism Service Provider grants. Research grants that are in line with Autism Speaks research priorities.

See entry 2014 for full listing.

BRAIN & BEHAVIOR RESEARCH FOUNDATION [2323]
747 Third Avenue, 33rd Floor
New York, NY 10017
(800) 829-8289
Fax: (646) 681-4891
E-mail: grants@bbrfoundation.org
Web Site: www.bbrfoundation.org

FOUNDED: 1987

AREAS OF INTEREST:
Mental health, brain and behavior disorders.

NAME(S) OF PROGRAMS:
● **NARSAD Distinguished Investigator Grant**
● **NARSAD Independent Investigator Grant**
● **NARSAD Young Investigator Grant**

TYPE:
Research grants. Distinguished Investigator Grant supports senior investigators (professor or equivalent level) who maintain a laboratory and who propose an innovative and new direction in their research with a one-year grant to encourage pursuit of innovative projects in schizophrenia, affective disorders, or other serious mental illnesses.

Independent Investigator Grant is intended for the scientist at the academic level of associate professor or equivalent, who has won national competitive support as a principal investigator. Assistant professors who have NIH R01s and equivalent are also eligible. The program is intended to facilitate innovative research opportunities.

Young Investigator Grant enables promising investigators to either extend their research fellowship training or to begin careers as independent research faculty.

PURPOSE:
To raise and distribute funds for scientific research into the causes, cures, treatments and prevention of severe psychiatric brain disorders.

LEGAL BASIS:
Private, not-for-profit organization.

ELIGIBILITY:
Applicant must hold a doctoral-level degree and be affiliated with a university or research institution.

For the Distinguished Investigator Grant, applicant must be a full professor (or professional equivalent) who maintains a laboratory.

For the Independent Investigator Grant, applicant must be at associate professor level with national competitive support as a principal investigator. Assistant professors who have NIH R01s and equivalent are also eligible.

For the Young Investigator Grant, applicant must be advanced postdoctoral fellow through assistant professor (or equivalent) to either extend research fellowship training or to begin career as independent research faculty. Basic and/or clinical investigators are supported, but research must be relevant to schizophrenia, major affective disorders or other serious mental illnesses.

FINANCIAL DATA:
Amount of support per award: Distinguished Investigator: $100,000; Independent Investigator: $50,000 per year for two years; Young Investigator: Up to $35,000 per year for up to two years.

NO. MOST RECENT APPLICANTS: Young
Investigator: Over 1,000 for the year 2020.

NO. AWARDS: Distinguished Investigator: 15;
Independent Investigator: 40; Young
Investigator: 150 for the year 2020.

APPLICATION INFO:
Guidelines are available on the Foundation
web site.
Duration: Distinguished Investigator Grant:
One-year, one-time award; Independent
Investigator Grant: Two-year, one-time
award; Young Investigator Grant: One or two
years. May not apply more than twice for
initial grant and more than once for second
grant.
Deadline: Varies.

IRS I.D.: 31-1020010

STAFF:
Jeff Borenstein, President and Chief
Executive Officer
Lou Innamorato, Vice President, Finance and
Chief Financial Officer
Lauren Duran, Vice President,
Communications, Marketing and Public
Relations
Faith Rothblatt, Vice President of
Development
Sho Tin Chen, Director, Research Grants
Nieves Ortiz, Manager of Donor-based
Management
Grace Nagaur, Manager, Research Grants
John Bayat, Senior Accountant
Mike Kirsic, Senior Accountant

ADDRESS INQUIRIES TO:
Grants Management
(See address above.)

JAMES MCKEEN CATTELL
FUND   [2324]
Duke University
Genome Sciences Research Building II, 3rd
floor
572 Research Drive, Box 91050
Durham, NC 27708
(919) 660-5638
Fax: (919) 660-5726
E-mail: williams@psych.duke.edu
Web Site: www.cattell.duke.edu

FOUNDED: 1941

NAME(S) OF PROGRAMS:
● **James McKeen Cattell Fund Sabbatical
Fellowships for Psychologists**

TYPE:
Fellowships. The fellowship provides funds
to supplement the regular sabbatical
allowance provided by the recipients' home
institutions.

YEAR PROGRAM STARTED: 1942

PURPOSE:
To promote scientific research and the
dissemination of knowledge with the object
of obtaining results beneficial to the
development of the science of psychology.

LEGAL BASIS:
Tax-exempt foundation.

ELIGIBILITY:
The awards are available to psychologists
who are faculty members at colleges and
universities in the U.S. and Canada and are
eligible, according to the regulations of their
own institutions, for a sabbatical leave or its
equivalent.

GEOG. RESTRICTIONS: United States and
Canada.

FINANCIAL DATA:
Amount of support per award: Up to
$40,000.
Total amount of support: Varies.

NO. MOST RECENT APPLICANTS: 45 for the year
2019.

NO. AWARDS: 1 to 4 per year.

APPLICATION INFO:
Fellowship application is available at the
Fund web site.
Duration: One academic year.
Deadline: January 15.

TRUSTEES AND OFFICERS:
Peter A. Ornstein, Managing Trustee
Christina L. Williams, Secretary-Treasurer
Robert W. Levenson
Scott E. Maxwell
Sharon Thompson-Schill

ADDRESS INQUIRIES TO:
Dr. Christina L. Williams
Secretary-Treasurer
(See address above.)

COUNCIL ON SOCIAL WORK
EDUCATION
333 John Carlyle Street
Suite 400
Alexandria, VA 22314
(703) 683-8080
Fax: (703) 683-8099
E-mail: dnguyen@cswe.org
Web Site: www.cswe.org

TYPE:
Fellowships. Awards for doctoral-level
studies in social work, specializing in mental
health and substance abuse-related education,
research, policy and practice.

See entry 896 for full listing.

DEPARTMENT OF VETERANS
AFFAIRS   [2325]
Associated Health Education (14AA)
Office of Academic Affiliations
810 Vermont Avenue, N.W.
Washington, DC 20420
(202) 705-5209
E-mail: jeffrey.bates@va.gov
Web Site: www.psychologytraining.va.gov

FOUNDED: 1946

AREAS OF INTEREST:
Veterans' mental health.

NAME(S) OF PROGRAMS:
● **VA Psychology Training Program**

TYPE:
Fellowships; Internships. Stipends for
internship and postdoctoral training in
clinical or counseling psychology. Provides
one year of supervised training in the skills
and techniques of these specialty areas.
Participants have no obligation to remain
with the VA after completion of training.

YEAR PROGRAM STARTED: 1946

PURPOSE:
To provide a source of highly qualified
psychologists who are interested in the direct
delivery of professional services in federal,
state, and community facilities; to provide
internship training to students enrolled in
doctoral programs in clinical or counseling
psychology from those schools accredited by
the American Psychological Association
(APA), Canadian Psychological Association

(CPA), or Psychological Clinical Science
Accreditation System (PCSAS); to provide
postdoctoral fellowships to graduates of
clinical or counseling psychology doctoral
programs accredited by the APA, CPA, or
PCSAS and internships that are accredited by
APA or CPA.

LEGAL BASIS:
Federal agency.

ELIGIBILITY:
Applicant must be a U.S. citizen. Prospective
intern must be enrolled in an academic
graduate program leading to the doctoral
degree in clinical or counseling psychology
from an APA-, CPA-, or PCSAS-accredited
program. Prospective postdoctoral fellow
must have completed a doctoral program in
clinical or counseling psychology from an
APA-, CPA-, or PCSAS-accredited program
and an internship accredited by APA or CPA.

FINANCIAL DATA:
Amount of support per award: Stipend of
$26,735 to $32,079 for full-time interns and
$47,105 to $59,575 for full-time postdoctoral
fellows.
Total amount of support: Varies based on
locality adjustment.

NO. AWARDS: 711 intern positions at 131 sites
and 453 postdoctoral residency positions at
70 sites for academic year 2020-21.

APPLICATION INFO:
Interested persons should contact the Director
of Psychology Training at the VA Medical
Center they are interested in.
Duration: One year. Occasionally two years
for postdoctoral residencies.
Deadline: November.

ADDRESS INQUIRIES TO:
Chief of Psychology Service or
Director of Psychology Training
at a local VA Medical Center

ALBERT ELLIS
INSTITUTE   [2326]
145 East 32nd Street, 9th Floor
New York, NY 10016
(212) 535-0822
Fax: (212) 249-3582
E-mail: krisdoyle@albertellis.org
info@albertellis.org
Web Site: www.albertellis.org

FOUNDED: 1968

AREAS OF INTEREST:
Psychotherapy.

CONSULTING OR VOLUNTEER SERVICES:
Work-study positions offered.

NAME(S) OF PROGRAMS:
● **Postgraduate Clinical Fellowship
Training Program at the Albert Ellis
Institute**

TYPE:
Conferences/seminars; Fellowships;
Internships; Work-study programs.
Postdoctoral fellowships and internships in
cognitive behavior therapy for a
comprehensive program, featuring intensive
supervision of individual and group clients
seen at the Institute's clinic, seminars and
workshops.

YEAR PROGRAM STARTED: 1969

PURPOSE:
To train professionals in cognitive behavioral
and Rational Emotive Behavior Therapy.

LEGAL BASIS:
501(c)(3) nonprofit organization.

ELIGIBILITY:
Applicant must have a Ph.D. in psychology, M.D., M.S.W. or R.N.

NO. MOST RECENT APPLICANTS: 30.

NO. AWARDS: 6.

APPLICATION INFO:
Application form and information are available online.
Duration: One to two years.
Deadline: January 19.

ADDRESS INQUIRIES TO:
Dr. Kristene Doyle, Director
(See address above.)

*PLEASE NOTE:
Training takes place in New York City.

FONDATION DES ETATS-UNIS
15, boulevard Jourdan
75014 Paris France
(33) 1 53 80 68 80
Fax: (33) 1 53 80 68 99
E-mail: culture@fondationdesetatsunis.org
Web Site: fondationdesetatsunis.org/hhw-scholarship

TYPE:
Awards/prizes; Development grants; Scholarships. Bequeathed to the Fondation des Etats-Unis, Cite Internationale Universitaire de Paris in the early 1930s, the Harriet Hale Woolley Scholarship is awarded annually to a select number of exceptional American artists and musicians who plan to pursue their studies in Paris.

A scholarship is also available to French, Swiss and American medical postgraduates specializing in psychiatry with an internship in a Parisian hospital.

The scholarship is not intended for research in art history or musicology, nor for dance or theater.

See entry 704 for full listing.

FOUNDATION FOR EDUCATION AND RESEARCH IN BIOFEEDBACK AND RELATED SCIENCES (FERB)   [2327]
1230 South Federal Highway
Boynton Beach, FL 33435
(561) 742-7122
Fax: (561) 742-7452
E-mail: ferbfound@gmail.com
Web Site: www.aapb.org

FOUNDED: 1969

AREAS OF INTEREST:
Biofeedback and psychophysiology.

TYPE:
Travel grants.

PURPOSE:
To advance the development, dissemination and utilization of knowledge about applied psychophysiology and biofeedback to improve health and the quality of life through research, education and practice.

ELIGIBILITY:
Must be a full-time student pursuing a professional or doctoral degree in a health-related field.

FINANCIAL DATA:
Total amount of support: Varies.

NO. AWARDS: Varies.

APPLICATION INFO:
Contact the Organization for application procedures.
Deadline: February 20.

INTERNATIONAL OCD FOUNDATION   [2328]
55 Court Street, Suite 310
Boston, MA 02108
(617) 973-5801
Fax: (617) 973-5803
E-mail: info@iocdf.org
Web Site: iocdf.org

FOUNDED: 1986

AREAS OF INTEREST:
Obsessive-compulsive disorders and obsessive compulsive spectrum disorder.

NAME(S) OF PROGRAMS:
● **Annual Conference**
● **Behavior Therapy Training Institute (BTTI)**
● **Research Awards**

TYPE:
Awards/prizes; Conferences/seminars; Research grants. The International OCD Foundation is committed to finding and promoting the most effective treatment methods for OCD and related disorders. Research is vital to better understanding OCD and related disorders, and improving treatment. To help achieve these goals, each year the IOCDF awards research grants to promising studies thanks to generous donors from within the OCD community. The IOCDF awards grants to investigators whose research focuses on the nature, causes, and treatment of OCD and related disorders.

YEAR PROGRAM STARTED: 1986

PURPOSE:
To increase access to effective treatment; to end the stigma associated with mental health issues; to foster a community for those affected by OCD and the professionals who treat them.

ELIGIBILITY:
Research Awards: Investigators whose research focuses on the nature, causes and treatment of OCD and related disorders are eligible to apply. Junior investigators are encouraged to apply. Senior investigators may also ask for grant funding for projects that would provide pilot data for future larger-scale federal grant applications.

FINANCIAL DATA:
Awards do not cover indirect or travel costs.
Amount of support per award: Varies.
Total amount of support: Varies.

NO. MOST RECENT APPLICANTS: Research Awards: Approximately 50.

NO. AWARDS: Research Awards: 8 for the year 2019.

APPLICATION INFO:
Application information is available on the web site. Applicants can request application guidelines from the Foundation.
Duration: One to two years.
Deadline: January.

PUBLICATIONS:
OCD Newsletter.

IRS I.D.: 22-2894564

STAFF:
Jeff Szymanski, Ph.D., Executive Director
Lise Lawrence, Events Manager

ADDRESS INQUIRIES TO:
See e-mail address above.

THE KLINGENSTEIN THIRD GENERATION FOUNDATION   [2329]
80 8th Avenue
Suite 1400
New York, NY 10011
(332) 219-0601
E-mail: info@klingenstein.org
Web Site: www.ktgf.org

FOUNDED: 1993

AREAS OF INTEREST:
Child and adolescent depression and ADHD.

TYPE:
Fellowships; Research grants. The Foundation funds research and other programs related to childhood and adolescent ADHD and depression. All funding is directed towards three research fellowship programs (funding postdoctoral research in ADHD, depression and access to care) and the medical student training program. The Foundation does not accept general applications for project or research funding.

YEAR PROGRAM STARTED: 1993

PURPOSE:
To address the need for further research in pediatric ADHD and pediatric depression, and the need to cultivate more child and adolescent psychiatrists and psychologists.

LEGAL BASIS:
Family foundation.

ELIGIBILITY:
The Foundation makes fellowship grants to medical institutions that have nominated research projects led by outstanding postdoctoral candidates.

The Foundation is prohibited from making grants to political action groups and from lobbying the government, and makes no grants to individuals.

FINANCIAL DATA:
Amount of support per award: Fellowships: $30,000 per year.

NO. AWARDS: Fellowships: Up to 5.

APPLICATION INFO:
Applications must be submitted online.
Duration: Fellowships: Two years.
Deadline: Fellowship nominations: November 15.

ADDRESS INQUIRIES TO:
See e-mail address above.

*PLEASE NOTE:
The Foundation does not accept unsolicited applications.

DELLA MARTIN FOUNDATION   [2330]
333 South Hope Street
43rd Floor
Los Angeles, CA 90071
(213) 617-4143
Fax: (213) 620-1398
E-mail: lgould@sheppardmullin.com

FOUNDED: 1975

AREAS OF INTEREST:
Mental health research.

TYPE:
Endowments; Fellowships; Professorships. Foundation has endowed four university chairs for mental health research and seven postdoctoral mental health research fellowships.

YEAR PROGRAM STARTED: 1975

PURPOSE:
To promote research into causes of and cures for mental illness.

LEGAL BASIS:
Nonprofit foundation.

ELIGIBILITY:
For southern California tax-exempt organizations only. No grants are made to individuals.

GEOG. RESTRICTIONS: Southern California.

FINANCIAL DATA:
Amount of support per award: Varies.
Total amount of support: $450,000 annually.
Matching fund requirements: Generally 1:1.

NO. MOST RECENT APPLICANTS: 20.

NO. AWARDS: 1 annually.

REPRESENTATIVE AWARDS:
$450,000 to California Institute of Technology for endowment of postdoctoral research fellowships.

APPLICATION INFO:
Send brief letter to the Foundation describing grant request.

IRS I.D.: 23-7444954

TRUSTEES:
Laurence K. Gould, Jr.
Kelly Kinnon
James A. Lonergan
Allen W. Mathies, Jr., M.D.
Nancy B. Reimann
Eileen D. Sheppard
Philip A. Swan

ADDRESS INQUIRIES TO:
Laurence K. Gould, Jr., Chairperson
(See address above.)

NATIONAL INSTITUTE OF MENTAL HEALTH [2331]
6001 Executive Boulevard, Room 6146
Bethesda, MD 20892
(301) 443-1368
E-mail: jnoronha@mail.nih.gov
Web Site: www.nimh.nih.gov

FOUNDED: 1948

AREAS OF INTEREST:
Basic neuroscience, genetics, basic behavioral science aimed at understanding mental disorders, research training, resource and technology development and drug discovery; translational research on the mechanisms of adult psychopathology and the development of novel treatment approaches for adult mental disorders; integrated research and research training that translates knowledge from basic/behavioral science into a better understanding of pediatric psychopathology and the development of novel treatment and prevention strategies; research on mechanisms and interventions on the interrelationship of physical and mental health; mental health research on AIDS that includes studies that range from the molecular and cellular basis of HIV/AIDS

CNS infection to the domestic and international dissemination of effective preventative interventions; research that evaluates the effectiveness of treatment and preventive mental health interventions and mental health services research.

TYPE:
Development grants; Fellowships; Project/program grants; Research grants; Training grants; Research contracts.

YEAR PROGRAM STARTED: 1948

PURPOSE:
To support innovative science that will profoundly transform the diagnosis, treatment and prevention of mental disorders, paving the way for a cure; to reduce the burden of mental illness and behavioral disorders through research on mind, brain and behavior.

LEGAL BASIS:
Government agency.

ELIGIBILITY:
Public, private, profit or nonprofit agencies, including state and local government agencies, eligible Federal agencies, universities, colleges, hospitals, and academic or research institutions may apply for research grants. SBIR grants can be awarded only to domestic small businesses, and STTR grants can be awarded only to domestic small businesses which partner with a research institution in cooperative research and development.

An applicant for individual predoctoral fellowship support must be enrolled in a research doctoral degree program by the proposed activation date of the fellowship. A postdoctoral applicant must have received a Ph.D., Psy.D., M.D., D.D.S., Sc.D., D.N.S., D.O., D.S.W., or equivalent degree from an accredited institution to be eligible for an individual postdoctoral fellowship.

All research training awards are made to appropriate domestic research centers, medical schools, departments of psychiatry, nonmedical academic departments, psychiatric hospitals or hospitals with psychiatric services, community mental health centers, and biomedical research institutes on behalf of individuals who need the opportunity to realize research potential. Except for the NIH Pathway to Independence Award, the individuals must be citizens or nationals of the U.S. or have been lawfully admitted for permanent residence. NIH Pathway to Independence Award is open to both U.S. citizens and non-U.S. citizens. Individuals must qualify by scholastic degree and previous training and/or experience.

FINANCIAL DATA:
Amount of support per award: Grants and awards vary in amount, depending upon the program and type of funding mechanism.
Total amount of support: Varies.

APPLICATION INFO:
Application materials are available on NIMH web site. Prospective applicants should contact NIMH staff prior to submission to ensure the area of research that they investigate is within NIMH priorities.
Duration: Varies, with project periods ranging one to five years. Funding commitments are made annually.

ADDRESS INQUIRIES TO:
Dr. Jean Noronha, Director
Division of Extramural Activities
(See address above.)

NATIONAL INSTITUTE OF MENTAL HEALTH
Division of Translational Research (DTR)
6001 Executive Boulevard
Room 7111, MSC 9632
Bethesda, MD 20892-9632
(301) 443-9232
E-mail: ftuma@nih.gov
Web Site: www.nimh.nih.gov/about/organization/dtr

TYPE:
Fellowships; Project/program grants; Research grants; Technical assistance; Training grants.

See entry 1669 for full listing.

NATIONAL SCIENCE FOUNDATION [2332]
Directorate for Social Behavorial and Economic Sciences
2415 Eisenhower Avenue
Alexandria, VA 22314
(703) 292-8728
Fax: (703) 292-9083
E-mail: sbreckle@nsf.gov
Web Site: www.nsf.gov

FOUNDED: 1950

AREAS OF INTEREST:
Human social behavior, including cultural differences and development over the lifespan.

NAME(S) OF PROGRAMS:
● **Social Psychology Program**

TYPE:
Project/program grants; Research grants; Training grants; Travel grants; Visiting scholars.

YEAR PROGRAM STARTED: 1972

PURPOSE:
To initiate and support scientific research and programs to strengthen research potential.

LEGAL BASIS:
National Science Foundation Act of 1950.

ELIGIBILITY:
Applicants may be colleges and universities on behalf of their staff members, nonprofit, nonacademic research institutions, such as independent museums, observatories, research laboratories, stock centers and similar organizations, private profit organizations, in exceptional circumstances, rarely, foreign institutions utilizing U.S. currency and, under special circumstances, unaffiliated U.S. scientists.

GEOG. RESTRICTIONS: United States.

FINANCIAL DATA:
Support may cover salaries, research assistantships, staff benefits if a direct cost, permanent equipment, travel, publication costs, computer costs and certain other direct and indirect costs.
Amount of support per award: Average $100,000 to $500,000.

NO. MOST RECENT APPLICANTS: Varies.

NO. AWARDS: Varies.

APPLICATION INFO:
Proposals must be submitted via FastLane or Grants.gov.

Duration: Research grants may be awarded for periods of up to five years. Most grants are for two or three years.

Deadline: Target dates are January 15 and July 15.

ADDRESS INQUIRIES TO:
Program Director
(See address above.)

NATIONAL SCIENCE FOUNDATION   [2333]
Division of Behavioral and Cognitive Sciences
2415 Eisenhower Avenue
Alexandria, VA 22314
(703) 292-7238
Fax: (703) 292-9068
Web Site: www.nsf.gov

FOUNDED: 1950

AREAS OF INTEREST:
Human behavior.

NAME(S) OF PROGRAMS:
● **Perception, Action & Cognition Program**

TYPE:
Research grants. Supports research on perception, action and cognition. Emphasis is on research strongly grounded in theory. Research topics include vision, audition, haptics, attention, memory, reasoning, written and spoken discourse, motor control, and developmental issues in all topic areas. The program encompasses a wide range of theoretical perspectives such as symbolic computation, connectionism, ecological, nonlinear dynamics, complex systems, and a variety of methodologies including both experimental studies and modeling. Research involving acquired or developmental deficits is appropriate if the results speak to basic issues of cognition, perception or action.

YEAR PROGRAM STARTED: 1976

PURPOSE:
To initiate and support scientific research and programs to strengthen research potential.

LEGAL BASIS:
National Science Foundation Act of 1950.

ELIGIBILITY:
Requirements vary according to program. Applicants should consult web site for current programs.

GEOG. RESTRICTIONS: United States.

FINANCIAL DATA:
Amount of support per award: Approximately $120,000 per year.
Total amount of support: Varies.

APPLICATION INFO:
Application should be submitted by FastLane, research.gov or through the Foundation's web site. Standard grant proposal guidelines apply.
Duration: 12 to 60 months, depending on the scientific merit and requirements of the project, and the type of program.

STAFF:
Betty Tuller, Ph.D., Program Director

ADDRESS INQUIRIES TO:
Betty Tuller, Ph.D., Program Director
(See address above.)

PARAPSYCHOLOGY FOUNDATION, INC.   [2334]
P.O. Box 1562
New York, NY 10021-0043
(212) 628-1550
Fax: (212) 628-1559
E-mail: office@parapsychology.org
Web Site: parapsychology.org

AREAS OF INTEREST:
Parapsychology.

NAME(S) OF PROGRAMS:
● **Eileen J. Garrett Scholarship**

TYPE:
Scholarships. Assists students attending an accredited college or university in pursuing the academic study of the science of parapsychology.

PURPOSE:
To promote research in parapsychology.

ELIGIBILITY:
Open to nationals of any country.

FINANCIAL DATA:
Amount of support per award: $2,000.

NO. AWARDS: 1.

APPLICATION INFO:
Applicants must submit samples of writings on the subject with an application form from the Foundation. Letters of reference from three individuals who are familiar with the applicant's work and/or studies in parapsychology are required.
Duration: One year.
Deadline: July 1. Notification on August 1.

PARAPSYCHOLOGY FOUNDATION, INC.   [2335]
P.O. Box 1562
New York, NY 10021-0043
(212) 628-1550
Fax: (212) 628-1559
E-mail: office@parapsychology.org
Web Site: parapsychology.org

AREAS OF INTEREST:
Parapsychology and psychic phenomena.

NAME(S) OF PROGRAMS:
● **Frances P. Bolton Fellowship**

TYPE:
Fellowships.

PURPOSE:
To further write up and polish the data amassed during the preparation of a doctoral dissertation/thesis.

ELIGIBILITY:
Awarded to a person who obtained their Ph.D. on the basis of a dissertation/thesis which dealt with some aspect of parapsychological phenomena.

FINANCIAL DATA:
Amount of support per award: $2,000.

NO. AWARDS: 1.

APPLICATION INFO:
Applications must be accompanied by a copy of the doctoral dissertation/thesis, three references, and a description of how the Fellowship will be utilized.
Deadline: November 1. Award notification January 1.

ADDRESS INQUIRIES TO:
Lisette Coly, Executive Director
(See address above.)

PARAPSYCHOLOGY FOUNDATION, INC.   [2336]
P.O. Box 1562
New York, NY 10021-0043
(212) 628-1550
Fax: (212) 628-1559
E-mail: office@parapsychology.org
Web Site: parapsychology.org

AREAS OF INTEREST:
Parapsychology and psychic phenomena.

NAME(S) OF PROGRAMS:
● **Charles T. and Judith A. Tart Student Incentive Award**

TYPE:
Awards/prizes. Incentive award for research proposal.

YEAR PROGRAM STARTED: 2001

ELIGIBILITY:
Student must demonstrate a strong commitment to work within parapsychology. Open to undergraduate, graduate and postgraduate students who have in mind a specific research proposal which may be experimental, experiential, clinical, historical, survey- or questionnaire-based, archival, bibliographic, literary or any other type of investigation a student may propose.

FINANCIAL DATA:
Amount of support per award: $500.

APPLICATION INFO:
Application must be in English and should be accompanied by two letters of reference, a one- to two-page description of the project that includes purpose, method, materials and duration of the project, and a one-page budget.
Deadline: September 1. Award notification on or around October 1.

ADDRESS INQUIRIES TO:
Lisette Coly, Executive Director
(See address above.)

SCOTTISH RITE CHARITABLE FOUNDATION OF CANADA   [2337]
4 Queen Street South
Hamilton ON L8P 3R3 Canada
(905) 522-0033
Fax: (905) 522-3716
E-mail: grantsandawards@srcf.ca
info@srcf.ca
Web Site: www.srcf.ca

FOUNDED: 1970

AREAS OF INTEREST:
Biomedical research into intellectual impairment.

NAME(S) OF PROGRAMS:
● **Scottish Rite Charitable Foundation Major Research Grants**

TYPE:
Research grants. SRCFC grants support biomedical research into Solving the Puzzles of the Mind focused on the following:
(1) the causes of Puzzles of the Mind, such as dyslexia and autism, especially as it affects children;
(2) the causes and eventual cure of cognitive impairments such as Alzheimer's disease and other neurodegenerative diseases and;
(3) research into other Puzzles of the Mind may be considered.

The focus of the research should be on the causes and cure of the disease as opposed to the active treatment or palliative care.

YEAR PROGRAM STARTED: 1970

PURPOSE:
To provide financial support to researchers studying developmental disabilities.

LEGAL BASIS:
Nonprofit.

ELIGIBILITY:
Applications are limited to researchers who have no more than five years experience as an independent investigator. A researcher who is designated as the Principal Investigator on the research grant must be based in, or formally affiliated with, an eligible Canadian host institution such as a university, research institute or health care agency. The Foundation does not consider trainees, including postdoctoral fellows, research assistants or research associates, to be eligible to apply as the Principal Investigator.

Research projects must be endorsed by the Research Services Department or equivalent of the university, hospital or research institute.

GEOG. RESTRICTIONS: Canada.

FINANCIAL DATA:
Amount of support per award: Up to $40,000 per year.

NO. AWARDS: Approximately 12 new and renewals per year.

APPLICATION INFO:
Application package consists of the Research Grant Form and Application Guide. All applicants must refer to the Application Guide when completing an application.
Duration: One, two or three years. Renewal contingent on a progress report of the work and research results.
Deadline: April 30 each year.

OFFICERS:
Gareth R. Taylor, President
Brian W. Gilkinson, Vice President
James G. Vasko, Treasurer
Thomas E. Wills, Secretary

ADDRESS INQUIRIES TO:
The Awards Committee
(See address above.)

SOCIETY OF BIOLOGICAL PSYCHIATRY [2338]
5034A Thoroughbred Lane
Brentwood, TN 37027
(615) 432-0096
E-mail: sobp@sobp.org
Web Site: sobp.org

FOUNDED: 1945

AREAS OF INTEREST:
Biological psychiatry, neuropsychopharmacology and clinical neuroscience.

NAME(S) OF PROGRAMS:
● **A.E. Bennett Research Awards**

TYPE:
Awards/prizes. Awards for recent, unpublished research papers in the field of biological psychiatry.

YEAR PROGRAM STARTED: 1958

PURPOSE:
To promote research in biological psychiatry.

LEGAL BASIS:
Nonprofit foundation.

ELIGIBILITY:
Applicants must be qualified investigators with appropriate interests. Candidates shall either:
(1) have not passed their 45th birthday by January 1 for the year of the award or;
(2) have not been engaged in research for greater than 10 years following award of their terminal degree or the end of formal clinical/fellowship training, whichever is later.

Membership in the Society is not required. The prize will be awarded based on a body of work rather than a single paper.

FINANCIAL DATA:
Amount of support per award: $5,000 each for the best basic science paper and the best clinical/translational science paper submitted.

NO. AWARDS: 1 or 2 each year.

APPLICATION INFO:
Applications are submitted electronically.
Duration: One year.
Deadline: Nominations must be submitted online on or before September 30.

OFFICERS:
David Lewis, M.D., President
Trey Sunderland, Treasurer
Scott Rauch, M.D., Executive Secretary

SOCIETY OF BIOLOGICAL PSYCHIATRY [2339]
5034A Thoroughbred Lane
Brentwood, TN 37027
(615) 432-0096
E-mail: sobp@sobp.org
Web Site: sobp.org

FOUNDED: 1945

AREAS OF INTEREST:
Biological psychiatry, neuropsychopharmacology and clinical neuroscience.

NAME(S) OF PROGRAMS:
● **Ziskind-Somerfeld Research Award**

TYPE:
Awards/prizes. Award for recent, unsubmitted, unpublished research paper in the field of biological psychiatry.

YEAR PROGRAM STARTED: 1991

PURPOSE:
To stimulate investigations in biological psychiatry by senior investigators.

LEGAL BASIS:
Nonprofit.

ELIGIBILITY:
The award winner is the first author of the award paper. Special consideration is given to the originality of the approach and independence of thought in the archival report. The studies and the data must not have been published elsewhere.

FINANCIAL DATA:
Amount of support per award: $5,000.
Total amount of support: $5,000 annually.

NO. AWARDS: 1 each year.

APPLICATION INFO:
No application submission is required for the award. The Society provides a list of the top 15 articles to the Ziskind-Somerfeld Award Committee to review and make a final award selection.
Duration: One-time award.

Deadline: Announcement in May.

SUBSTANCE ABUSE AND MENTAL HEALTH SERVICES ADMINISTRATION, DISASTER TECHNICAL ASSISTANCE CENTER [2340]
5600 Fishers Lane
Rockville, MD 20857
(800) 308-3515
E-mail: dtac@samhsa.hhs.gov
Web Site: www.samhsa.gov/dtac

AREAS OF INTEREST:
Emergency mental health and crisis counseling.

NAME(S) OF PROGRAMS:
● **Crisis Counseling Assistance and Training Program**

TYPE:
Project/program grants. Grants to address the various dimensions of mental health crises affecting victims of presidentially declared major disasters. Support is available for development of training models and other psychological material for the delivery of crisis intervention services/outreach.

YEAR PROGRAM STARTED: 1974

PURPOSE:
To provide supplemental support to victims of major disasters and their families in emergency mental health and crisis intervention.

LEGAL BASIS:
Section 416 of The Robert T. Stafford Disaster Relief and Emergency Assistance Act (Public Law 100-707).

ELIGIBILITY:
Must be presidentially declared major disaster. U.S. territories and federally recognized tribes are also eligible.

FINANCIAL DATA:
Amount of support per award: Grants given according to justifiable need. Amounts vary in accordance with existing resources in stricken community.
Total amount of support: Varies.

CO-OP FUNDING PROGRAMS: Program funding is supplemental when existing programs are inadequate to meet the needs of the community.

NO. MOST RECENT APPLICANTS: 21 for the year 2017.

NO. AWARDS: 21 for the year 2017.

APPLICATION INFO:
Contact the organization for guidelines.
Duration: Nine months; renewal possible upon approval of CMHS and SAMHSA. Extension of grant possible in limited circumstances.
Deadline: 60 days following the disaster.

ADDRESS INQUIRIES TO:
Nikki Bellamy, Project Officer
SAMHSA/CMHS
(See address above.)

VAN AMERINGEN FOUNDATION, INC.   [2341]

c/o Fulton Vittoria LLP
One Rockefeller Plaza, Suite 301
New York, NY 10020-2002
(212) 758-6221
Fax: (212) 688-2105
E-mail: grants@vanamfound.org
Web Site: www.vanamfound.org

FOUNDED: 1950

AREAS OF INTEREST:
Mental illness and mental health.

TYPE:
Demonstration grants; Development grants;
General operating grants; Project/program
grants; Research grants; Seed money grants.
Grants for projects and activities in areas of
social welfare, with particular emphasis on
mental health.

YEAR PROGRAM STARTED: 1950

PURPOSE:
To promote mental health through preventive
medicine, research, treatment and
rehabilitation.

LEGAL BASIS:
Private foundation.

ELIGIBILITY:
Tax-exempt organizations with appropriate
interests are eligible. No grants are made to
individuals.

GEOG. RESTRICTIONS: Metropolitan New York
area and Philadelphia, Pennsylvania.

FINANCIAL DATA:
Amount of support per award: $25,000 to
$250,000, based on the needs and nature of
the project.
Total amount of support: Approximately
$8,000,000 for the year 2019.

NO. MOST RECENT APPLICANTS: Approximately
500.

NO. AWARDS: 40 for the year 2019.

APPLICATION INFO:
Applicants must first complete a brief
eligibility quiz. Those organizations that meet
the basic eligibility requirements will then be
able to register and submit a letter of inquiry
through the grants application portal.

Foundation staff will contact those
organizations selected to submit a full
proposal and schedule a site visit.

Duration: Up to three years.

Deadline: Varies.

PUBLICATIONS:
Annual report; guidelines.

DIRECTORS:
Kenneth A. Kind, President and Treasurer
Maurizio Morello, Vice President and
Secretary
Judith Beck
Alexandra Herzan
Christina K. Kind
Valerie Kind-Rubin
Andrew Kindfuller
Laura K. McKenna
Clarence Sundram

ADDRESS INQUIRIES TO:
Kenneth A. Kind, President
(See address above.)

TECHNOLOGY AND INDUSTRY

Technology and industry

AGC EDUCATION AND RESEARCH FOUNDATION
2300 Wilson Boulevard, Suite 300
Arlington, VA 22201
(703) 837-5356
E-mail: courtney.bishop@agc.org
Web Site: www.agcfoundation.org

TYPE:
Awards/prizes; Internships; Project/program grants; Scholarships. Allhands Essay Competition: Awarded to a student essay on a specific topic that is deemed to be beneficial to the advancement of technological, educational or vocational expertise in the construction industry.

Graduate Scholarship Program: Scholarships for students enrolled in ABET- or ACCE-accredited construction management or construction-related engineering programs.

Industry Case Studies: Commissioning case studies on industry scenarios.

Outstanding Educator Award: Awards to top competitors in essay competition for seniors and faculty nominated as outstanding educator.

Undergraduate Scholarship Program: Scholarships for students enrolled in ABET- or ACCE-accredited construction management or construction-related engineering programs.

Workforce Development Scholarship: Awarded for students entering craft training or technical programs.

See entry 2376 for full listing.

AIR & WASTE MANAGEMENT ASSOCIATION (A&WMA)   [2342]
Koppers Building
436 Seventh Avenue, Suite 2100
Pittsburgh, PA 15219
(412) 904-6006
Fax: (412) 232-3450
E-mail: sglyptis@awma.org
Web Site: www.awma.org

FOUNDED: 1907

AREAS OF INTEREST:
Air quality, waste management, environmental management/policy/law and sustainability research.

NAME(S) OF PROGRAMS:
● **Scholarship Endowment Trust Fund**

TYPE:
Scholarships.

PURPOSE:
To provide monies for students with interest in the area of air quality, waste management and/or environmental management/policy/law.

ELIGIBILITY:
Must be a full-time graduate student pursuing studies in the area of air quality, waste management and/or environmental management/policy/law.

FINANCIAL DATA:
Amount of support per award: Varies.
Total amount of support: Approximately $26,000 annually.

NO. MOST RECENT APPLICANTS: 50.

NO. AWARDS: Approximately 10.

APPLICATION INFO:
Applications must be completed online.
Duration: One year. Renewal possible by reapplying.
Deadline: January.

ADDRESS INQUIRIES TO:
Stephanie Glyptis, Executive Director
(See address above.)

AIR TRAFFIC CONTROL ASSOCIATION (ATCA)   [2343]
225 Reinekers Lane
Suite 400
Alexandria, VA 22314-2875
(703) 299-2430 ext. 300
E-mail: mindy.soranno@atca.org
Web Site: www.atca.org

FOUNDED: 1956

AREAS OF INTEREST:
Air traffic control and aviation.

TYPE:
Scholarships. Scholarships to promising young men and women enrolled in programs leading to careers in aviation or air traffic control and scholarships for dependents of air traffic controllers pursuing a degree.

PURPOSE:
To promote careers in air traffic control or aviation disciplines.

LEGAL BASIS:
Private, 501(c)(3) charity.

ELIGIBILITY:
Requirements vary per award category.

FINANCIAL DATA:
Amount of support per award: $2,000 to $10,000.
Total amount of support: Varies.

NO. MOST RECENT APPLICANTS: 300.

NO. AWARDS: 8 to 12.

APPLICATION INFO:
Application, with supporting documents, must be completed online.
Duration: One year.
Deadline: May 15.

ADDRESS INQUIRIES TO:
Mindy Soranno, Membership Manager
(See address above.)

AMERICAN GROUND WATER TRUST   [2344]
50 Pleasant Street, Suite 2
Concord, NH 03301-4073
(603) 228-5444
Fax: (603) 228-6557
E-mail: trustinfo@agwt.org
Web Site: www.agwt.org/content/scholarship-opportunities

FOUNDED: 1986

AREAS OF INTEREST:
Groundwater education, sustainable management and protection.

NAME(S) OF PROGRAMS:
● **Baroid Scholarship**
● **Flexcon Industries Scholarship**
● **Thomas M. Stetson Scholarship**

TYPE:
Awards/prizes; Scholarships.

YEAR PROGRAM STARTED: 1986

PURPOSE:
To provide education outreach to inform the public about the optimal utilization and protection of groundwater for the benefit of mankind.

LEGAL BASIS:
501(c)(3) nonprofit organization.

ELIGIBILITY:
Applicants must be U.S. citizens, apply during their senior year in high school, and be enrolled the following year in an undergraduate program relevant to the groundwater industry.

GEOG. RESTRICTIONS: United States.

FINANCIAL DATA:
Amount of support per award: $2,000.

NO. MOST RECENT APPLICANTS: Approximately 20.

NO. AWARDS: 3.

APPLICATION INFO:
Applicant must submit only one application to be considered for all scholarships. Completed application form must be accompanied by two letters of recommendation. A 500-word essay and a 300-word description of the applicant's high school groundwater project and/or practical environmental work experience must accompany the application. Documentary evidence of scholastic achievements and references will be requested from finalists.
Duration: One academic year.
Deadline: July 30. The Trust will write to all applicants (successful and unsuccessful) at the end of August.

IRS I.D.: 23-7244958

EXECUTIVE DIRECTOR:
Andrew W. Stone

ADDRESS INQUIRIES TO:
Andrew W. Stone, Executive Director or Cheryl Gosselin, Office Manager
(See address above.)

AMERICAN SOCIETY FOR ENOLOGY AND VITICULTURE
1724 Picasso Avenue, Suite E
Davis, CA 95618-0551
(530) 753-3142
Fax: (530) 753-3318
E-mail: info@asev.org
Web Site: www.asev.org

TYPE:
Scholarships. Awards for undergraduate or graduate students enrolled in enology or viticulture or in a curriculum which emphasizes a science basic to the wine and grape industry and who intend to pursue a career in research for the wine or grape industry after graduation from college or university.

See entry 1905 for full listing.

THE AMERICAN SOCIETY FOR NONDESTRUCTIVE TESTING, INC.   [2345]
1711 Arlingate Lane
Columbus, OH 43228-0518
(614) 274-6003
(800) 222-2768
Fax: (614) 274-6899
E-mail: james@asnt.org
Web Site: www.asnt.org

FOUNDED: 1941

AREAS OF INTEREST:
Nondestructive testing.

NAME(S) OF PROGRAMS:
● ASNT Fellowship Award

TYPE:
Fellowships. Nondestructive evaluation and testing (NDE/NDT) is the science of examining components and systems in a manner that does not impair their further usefulness. NDE/NDT is a complex, multidisciplinary field offering exciting career opportunities. Current areas for applying new and advanced nondestructive testing technology include power plant life extension, aging aircraft and deteriorating civil engineering structures.

YEAR PROGRAM STARTED: 1981

PURPOSE:
To provide assistance to university or college graduate students in defraying costs of their postgraduate research in NDT.

LEGAL BASIS:
Nonprofit organization.

ELIGIBILITY:
Academic institutions with graduate educational research in NDT related fields are eligible for this fellowship.

FINANCIAL DATA:
Amount of support per award: $20,000.
Total amount of support: Up to $100,000.

NO. AWARDS: Up to 5 per year.

APPLICATION INFO:
Guidelines and application are available online.
Duration: One year.
Deadline: October 15.

ADDRESS INQUIRIES TO:
Jessica Ames
ASNT Program Specialist
(See address above.)

AWS FOUNDATION, INC.   [2346]
8669 N.W. 36th Street
No. 130
Miami, FL 33166
(305) 443-9353 ext. 212
(800) 443-9353 ext. 212
E-mail: jdouglass@aws.org
Web Site: www.aws.org

FOUNDED: 1989

AREAS OF INTEREST:
Welding and materials joining.

NAME(S) OF PROGRAMS:
● AWS National, District and Section Scholarships

TYPE:
Scholarships.

YEAR PROGRAM STARTED: 1991

PURPOSE:
To promote education in the welding industry.

ELIGIBILITY:
Student must be enrolled or planning to enroll in a welding program or related field.

FINANCIAL DATA:
Amount of support per award: $500 to $6,500.
Total amount of support: $800,000.

NO. AWARDS: 675.

APPLICATION INFO:
Details are available on the Foundation web site.
Duration: One year.
Deadline: March 1.

ADDRESS INQUIRIES TO:
John Douglass, Associate Director
(See address above.)

AWS FOUNDATION, INC.   [2347]
8669 N.W. 36th Street
No. 130
Miami, FL 33166
(305) 443-9353 ext. 212
(800) 443-9353 ext. 212
E-mail: jdouglass@aws.org
Web Site: www.aws.org

FOUNDED: 1989

AREAS OF INTEREST:
Welding and materials joining.

NAME(S) OF PROGRAMS:
● Welding Workforce Grant

TYPE:
Training grants.

PURPOSE:
To improve and expand training programs and institutions to increase the number of welding graduates across the country.

ELIGIBILITY:
Schools or training institutions must be AWS Educational Institution members and SENSE registered.

FINANCIAL DATA:
Amount of support per award: Up to $25,000.
Total amount of support: Up to $300,000 annually.

NO. AWARDS: 10 to 14.

APPLICATION INFO:
Application must be submitted on the AWS web site.
Duration: One year.
Deadline: April 1 and October 1.

ADDRESS INQUIRIES TO:
John Douglass, Associate Director
(See e-mail address above.)

AWS FOUNDATION, INC.   [2348]
8669 N.W. 36th Street
No. 130
Miami, FL 33166
(305) 443-9353 ext. 212
(800) 443-9353 ext. 212
E-mail: jdouglass@aws.org
Web Site: www.aws.org

FOUNDED: 1989

AREAS OF INTEREST:
Welding and materials joining.

NAME(S) OF PROGRAMS:
● Graduate Research Fellowship

TYPE:
Fellowships.

PURPOSE:
To foster university research in joining; to recognize outstanding faculty and student talent.

ELIGIBILITY:
Fellowships are awarded to students for graduate research toward a Master's or Ph.D. degree under a sponsoring professor.

GEOG. RESTRICTIONS: North America.

FINANCIAL DATA:
Amount of support per award: Up to $30,000.
Total amount of support: $120,000.

NO. AWARDS: 4.

APPLICATION INFO:
Guidelines are available online.
Duration: One year. Renewal up to three years possible. Must reapply.
Deadline: August 15.

ADDRESS INQUIRIES TO:
John Douglass, Associate Director
(See address above.)

AWS FOUNDATION, INC.   [2349]
8669 N.W. 36th Street
No. 130
Miami, FL 33166
(305) 443-9353 ext. 212
(800) 443-9353 ext. 212
E-mail: jdouglass@aws.org
Web Site: www.aws.org

FOUNDED: 1989

AREAS OF INTEREST:
Welding and materials joining.

NAME(S) OF PROGRAMS:
● Welder Training Scholarship

TYPE:
Scholarships.

PURPOSE:
To encourage education pertaining to welding and materials joining.

ELIGIBILITY:
Applicant must be planning to attend a trade school, community college, or other facility providing welder training.

FINANCIAL DATA:
Amount of support per award: $1,000.
Total amount of support: $550,000.

NO. MOST RECENT APPLICANTS: 1,600.

NO. AWARDS: 550.

APPLICATION INFO:
Applications must be submitted online.
Duration: One year.
Deadline: Applications are accepted on an ongoing basis.

ADDRESS INQUIRIES TO:
John Douglass, Associate Director
(See address above.)

CHARLES BABBAGE INSTITUTE   [2350]
University of Minnesota
211 Elmer L. Anderson Library
222 21st Avenue South
Minneapolis, MN 55455
(612) 624-5050
E-mail: cbi@umn.edu
Web Site: www.cbi.umn.edu

FOUNDED: 1978

AREAS OF INTEREST:
History of computers and information technology.

NAME(S) OF PROGRAMS:
● The Adelle and Erwin Tomash Fellowship in the History of Information Technology

TYPE:
Fellowships.

YEAR PROGRAM STARTED: 1978

PURPOSE:
To advance the professional development of historians of information technology.

LEGAL BASIS:
University and research association.

ELIGIBILITY:
Open to graduate students whose dissertation addresses some aspect of the history of computers and information technology. Topics may be chosen from the technical history of hardware or software, economic or business aspects of the information technology industry or other topics in the social, institutional or legal history of computing. Theses that consider technical issues in their socio-economic context are especially encouraged.

Priority will be given to students who have completed all requirements for the doctoral degree except the research and writing of the dissertation.

The fellowship may be held at the home academic institution, the Babbage Institute or any other location where there are appropriate research facilities.

FINANCIAL DATA:
Amount of support per award: $14,000 stipend.
Total amount of support: $14,000.

NO. MOST RECENT APPLICANTS: 5.

NO. AWARDS: 1.

APPLICATION INFO:
Applicants must provide a curriculum vitae and a five-page (single-spaced) statement and justification of the research project including a discussion of methods, research materials, evidence of faculty support for the project, and bibliography (bibliography does not count toward page count). Applicants should arrange for three letters of reference and certified copies of graduate school transcripts to be sent directly to CBI.

Application materials should be sent to the e-mail address listed above.
Duration: One academic year.
Deadline: January 15.

PUBLICATIONS:
Newsletter.

ADDRESS INQUIRIES TO:
Jeffrey Yost, Director
Charles Babbage Institute
E-mail: yostx003@umn.edu
(See address above.)

COIN-OP CARES CHARITABLE AND EDUCATION FOUNDATION [2351]
c/o Amusement & Music Operators Association
380 Terra Cotta Road, Suite F
Crystal Lake, IL 60012
(800) 937-2662
Fax: (815) 893-6248
E-mail: laura@amoa.com
Web Site: www.amoa.com

FOUNDED: 1948

AREAS OF INTEREST:
Higher education.

NAME(S) OF PROGRAMS:
● **Wayne E. Hesch Memorial Scholarships**

TYPE:
Scholarships. Designed to provide financial support to students who are, or plan or hope to be, engaged in the profession.

YEAR PROGRAM STARTED: 1985

PURPOSE:
To provide leadership for the amusement, music, entertainment and vending industry; to protect and promote the industry interests.

ELIGIBILITY:
Open to individuals in need of financial assistance who are attending or plan to attend an institution of higher education and have a 3.0 grade point average on a 4.0 scale.

FINANCIAL DATA:
Amount of support per award: $1,000 each.

APPLICATION INFO:
Applicant must call AMOA office to receive the form.
Duration: One year.
Deadline: February 13.

ADDRESS INQUIRIES TO:
AMOA Executive Office
(See address above.)

EARLY AMERICAN INDUSTRIES ASSOCIATION, INC. [2352]
P.O. Box 524
Hebron, MD 21830-0524
(703) 967-9399
E-mail: executivedirector@eaiainfo.org
Web Site: www.eaiainfo.org

FOUNDED: 1933

AREAS OF INTEREST:
To encourage study and better understanding of early American industries in the home, shop, on the farm and the sea; to discover, identify, classify, preserve and exhibit obsolete tools, implements and mechanical devices used in early America, craft practices, and industrial technology.

NAME(S) OF PROGRAMS:
● **Research Grants Program**

TYPE:
Research grants. These are not scholarship or internship grants.

YEAR PROGRAM STARTED: 1977

PURPOSE:
To preserve and present historic trades, crafts and tools, and to interpret their impact on the present generation.

LEGAL BASIS:
Nonprofit corporation.

ELIGIBILITY:
Applicants may be sponsored by an institution or engaged in self-directed projects. Projects must relate to the purposes of the Association. Grants can supplement existing aid. These are not scholarship, fellowship or internship funds. A grant may not be used to pay for salaries, historical artifacts, software or equipment in whole or in part.

GEOG. RESTRICTIONS: United States.

FINANCIAL DATA:
Amount of support per award: Up to $3,000.

NO. MOST RECENT APPLICANTS: 7.

NO. AWARDS: 3.

APPLICATION INFO:
Application is available online, and must be completed and mailed to the above address.

Duration: One year. Nonrenewable.
Deadline: March 15 annually.
Announcements in April annually.

PUBLICATIONS:
The Chronicle, quarterly journal; *Shavings,* newsletter for members; application guidelines; E.A.I.A. brochure.

OFFICERS:
John H. Verrill, Executive Director

ADDRESS INQUIRIES TO:
John H. Verrill, Executive Director
(See address above.)

*PLEASE NOTE:
A project report, including a statement of expenditures, must be filed by recipients.

FEDERAL HIGHWAY ADMINISTRATION [2353]
Center of Transportation Workforce Development
1200 New Jersey Avenue, S.E.
Washington, DC 20590
(703) 235-0538
E-mail: transportationedu@dot.gov
Web Site: www.fhwa.dot.gov/ugp

AREAS OF INTEREST:
Transportation-related disciplines.

NAME(S) OF PROGRAMS:
● **Dwight David Eisenhower Transportation Fellowship Program**

TYPE:
Fellowships; Internships; Research grants. Dwight David Eisenhower Transportation Fellowship Program's objectives are to attract the nation's brightest minds to the field of transportation, to enhance the careers of transportation professionals by encouraging them to seek advanced degrees, and to retain top talent in the transportation industry of the U.S. This Program encompasses all areas of transportation. The Program has seven award categories:
(1) Eisenhower Graduate (GRAD) Fellowships enable students to pursue Master's degrees or Doctorates in transportation-related fields at the university of their choice;
(2) Eisenhower Grants for Research (GRF) Fellowships acquaint undergraduate and graduate students with transportation research, development and technology-transfer activities at the U.S. Department of Transportation facilities;
(3) Eisenhower Historically Black Colleges and Universities (HBCU) Fellowships provide HBCU students with additional opportunities to enter careers in transportation. The Fellowships also serve as a feeder for other Eisenhower fellowships;
(4) Eisenhower Hispanic Serving Institutions (HSI) Fellowships provide HSI students with additional opportunities to enter careers in transportation. The Fellowships also serve as a feeder for other Eisenhower fellowships;
(5) Eisenhower Tribal College and Universities Fellowships (TCU) provides students with additional opportunities to enter careers in transportation. The Fellowships also serve as a feeder for other Eisenhower fellowships;
(6) Eisenhower Intern Fellowships (EIF) provides students with opportunities to perform a wide range of transportation-related activities at public and private-sector transportation organizations and;
(7) Eisenhower Community College

Fellowships provide students at community colleges with opportunities to enter careers in transportation. The Fellowships also serve as a feeder for other Eisenhower fellowships.

YEAR PROGRAM STARTED: 1983

PURPOSE:
To attract the nation's brightest minds to the field of transportation; to enhance the careers of transportation professionals by encouraging them to seek advanced degrees; to retain top talent in the transportation industry of the U.S.

LEGAL BASIS:
Government agency.

ELIGIBILITY:
Applicants must be enrolled in transportation-related disciplines (e.g., engineering, computer science, physics, transportation planning) at accredited U.S. universities.

GEOG. RESTRICTIONS: United States.

FINANCIAL DATA:
Award may include an allowance for tuition, stipend and travel expenses for the student to attend the annual Transportation Research Board (TRB) conference held in Washington, DC every January.
Amount of support per award: $1,500 to $35,500.
Total amount of support: Varies.

NO. AWARDS: 150 to 200 annually.

APPLICATION INFO:
Undergraduate applicants must submit applications through their faculty advisors and be nominated for awards by their respective universities. Graduate applicants must apply to the Arlington, VA office. Further information is available from the Administration.
Duration: Minimum three months during the summer. Maximum three years of funding, with five years to complete the course.
Deadline: Annual notice of funding programs are published on www.grants.gov.

PUBLICATIONS:
Application guidelines; brochures.

ADDRESS INQUIRIES TO:
Ewa Flom, Program Manager
Universities and Grants Programs
(See address above.)

FOUNDATION FOR TECHNOLOGY AND ENGINEERING EDUCATION

1914 Association Drive
Suite 201
Reston, VA 20191-1539
(703) 860-2100
Fax: (703) 860-0353
E-mail: kdelapaz@iteea.org
Web Site: www.iteea.org

TYPE:
Scholarships. The scholarship is for an undergraduate student majoring in technology and engineering education teacher preparation.

See entry 1503 for full listing.

FOUNDATION FOR TECHNOLOGY AND ENGINEERING EDUCATION

1914 Association Drive
Suite 201
Reston, VA 20191-1539
(703) 860-2100
Fax: (703) 860-0353
E-mail: kdelapaz@iteea.org
Web Site: www.iteea.org

TYPE:
Scholarships.

See entry 1388 for full listing.

FOUNDATION FOR TECHNOLOGY AND ENGINEERING EDUCATION

1914 Association Drive
Suite 201
Reston, VA 20191-1539
(703) 860-2100
Fax: (703) 860-0353
E-mail: kdelapaz@iteea.org
Web Site: www.iteea.org

TYPE:
Scholarships.

See entry 1504 for full listing.

THE FOUNDATION OF FLEXOGRAPHIC TECHNICAL ASSOCIATION   [2354]

3920 Veterans Memorial Highway, Suite 9
Bohemia, NY 11716
(631) 737-6020
Fax: (631) 737-6813
E-mail: srubin@flexography.org
Web Site: www.flexography.org

FOUNDED: 1958

AREAS OF INTEREST:
Flexographic printing.

NAME(S) OF PROGRAMS:
● **Flexographic Technical Association Scholarship**

TYPE:
Scholarships.

PURPOSE:
To support education in the study of flexography.

ELIGIBILITY:
Must be enrolled in a qualified school offering a study of flexography. Must have grade point average of 3.0 or better.

FINANCIAL DATA:
Amount of support per award: $3,000 per year.
Total amount of support: Varies.

NO. AWARDS: Varies.

APPLICATION INFO:
Contact the Organization for application procedures.
Duration: One year. Renewable upon reapplication.
Deadline: Usually March of each year.

ADDRESS INQUIRIES TO:
Shelley Rubin
Manager, Educational Services
(See address above.)

GREAT MINDS IN STEM   [2355]

5211 East Washington Boulevard
Suite 2, No. 320
Los Angeles, CA 90040
(323) 262-0997
E-mail: scholars@greatmindsinstem.org
Web Site: www.greatmindsinstem.org
gmis-scholars.org

FOUNDED: 1989

AREAS OF INTEREST:
Science, technology, computer science, engineering and math.

NAME(S) OF PROGRAMS:
● **GMiS Scholars Program**

TYPE:
Scholarships.

YEAR PROGRAM STARTED: 2000

PURPOSE:
To provide undergraduate and graduate scholarships to students majoring in science, technology, computer science, engineering and math.

ELIGIBILITY:
Applicants must be of Hispanic origin and/or must significantly participate in and promote organizations and activities in the Hispanic community. Applicants must be enrolled in an undergraduate or graduate engineering or science program at a college or university and must be planning to pursue a career in either area. Selection is based on academic standing, career potential and character.

GEOG. RESTRICTIONS: United States and Puerto Rico.

FINANCIAL DATA:
Amount of support per award: $500 to $10,000.
Total amount of support: Varies.

NO. MOST RECENT APPLICANTS: Over 1,200.

NO. AWARDS: 104 for the year 2020.

APPLICATION INFO:
All applications must be completed and submitted electonically. Absolutely no faxes will be accepted.
Duration: One academic year. Renewal possible.
Deadline: April 30.

STAFF:
Sonia Martinez, Chief Academic Officer
Dr. Gary Cruz, Director of Academic Affairs

ADDRESS INQUIRIES TO:
GMiS Scholars Program
(See address above.)

HIMSS FOUNDATION

33 West Monroe Street, Suite 1700
Chicago, IL 60603-5616
(312) 915-9289
Fax: (312) 664-6143
E-mail: scholarships@himss.org
Web Site: www.himss.org/health-it.education/scholarships

TYPE:
Awards/prizes; Conferences/seminars; Fellowships; Internships; Research grants; Scholarships.

See entry 2037 for full listing.

IEEE HISTORY CENTER
445 Hoes Lane
Piscataway, NJ 08854
(732) 562-5468
Fax: (732) 562-6020
E-mail: ieee-history@ieee.org
Web Site: www.ieee.org/history_center

TYPE:
Fellowships; Internships. Fellowship in the
History of Electrical and Computing
Technology: Award for one year of full-time
doctoral or postdoctoral work in the history
of electrical engineering and technology at a
college or university of recognized standing.

The Elizabeth and Emerson Pugh Young
Scholar in Residence: Two-month internship
for graduate research.

See entry 549 for full listing.

INSTITUTE OF FOOD
TECHNOLOGISTS
FOUNDATION   [2356]
525 West Van Buren Street
Suite 1000
Chicago, IL 60607
(312) 782-8424
Fax: (312) 416-7919
E-mail: feedingtomorrow@ift.org
Web Site: www.ift.org

FOUNDED: 1939

AREAS OF INTEREST:
Food science and technology.

NAME(S) OF PROGRAMS:
● **Freshman Scholarships**
● **Graduate Scholarships**
● **Undergraduate Scholarships**

TYPE:
Scholarships. Freshman Scholarships and
Undergraduate Scholarships encourage
undergraduate enrollment in food science and
technology. Graduate Scholarships support
advanced study in the field of food science
and technology.

YEAR PROGRAM STARTED: 1950

PURPOSE:
To encourage and support outstanding
research in food science/technology including
such areas as food packaging, flavor
chemistry, new food ingredients and
products; to recognize scholastic
achievement.

LEGAL BASIS:
Nonprofit 501(c)(3) foundation.

ELIGIBILITY:
Freshman scholarships are awarded to high
school seniors entering college for the first
time. Applicant must be a current high
school senior and accepted into an
IFT-approved undergraduate food science
program, have at least a 3.0 cumulative grade
point average, and become an IFT student
member.

Graduate scholarships are awarded to
outstanding M.S. and Ph.D. students pursuing
research and education in the field of food
science and technology. Student applicants
must be pursuing a graduate with an
emphasis in food science and related
disciplines. They must be able to understand
and appreciate the impact of their research on
the global food supply. Research in such
disciplines as genetics, horticulture, nutrition,
microbiology, biochemistry, engineering,
chemistry, etc. are not eligible unless it is

directly related to the student's research
program in food science, except as otherwise
noted. The school of enrollment can be any
educational institution conducting
fundamental investigations for the
advancement of food science and food
technology, unless there are stated exceptions
of scholarship criteria for sponsored
scholarships. Applicant must be enrolled as a
full-time M.S. or Ph.D. student, have at least
a 3.0 cumulative grade point average, and be
a student member of IFT at the time of
application.

Undergraduate scholarships are awarded to
sophomore, junior, and senior students
enrolled as a full-time student pursuing an
undergraduate degree in an IFT-approved
undergraduate food science program, have at
least a 3.0 cumulative grade point average,
and be a student member of IFT at the time
of application.

FINANCIAL DATA:
Amount of support per award: $1,000 to
$5,000.
Total amount of support: Varies.

CO-OP FUNDING PROGRAMS: The scholarships
are sponsored by Feeding Tomorrow donors.

NO. MOST RECENT APPLICANTS: Approximately
300.

NO. AWARDS: Approximately 75.

APPLICATION INFO:
Applications are available on the Institute's
web site.
Duration: One year.
Deadline: Varies.

ADDRESS INQUIRIES TO:
Jaime Gutshall, Coordinator
(See address and e-mail above.)

THE INTERNATIONAL
EXECUTIVE HOUSEKEEPERS
ASSOCIATION   [2357]
1001 Eastwind Drive
Suite 302
Westerville, OH 43081-3361
(847) 982-3471
Fax: (614) 895-1248
E-mail: excel@ieha.org
Web Site: www.ieha.org

FOUNDED: 1930

AREAS OF INTEREST:
Directors, project managers, managers and
supervisors of environmental services or
housekeeping departments, facilities
management, and training.

NAME(S) OF PROGRAMS:
● **PECP Self Study Program**

TYPE:
Scholarships. The PECP Program is a
330-hour course.

YEAR PROGRAM STARTED: 1960

PURPOSE:
To provide a professional organization for
executive housekeepers, directors of
environmental services, managers within the
housekeeping or custodial activities, and
suppliers of custodial goods and services.

ELIGIBILITY:
Must be a member of IEHA and be working
towards any degree program at a university
or college, in a certification program or
engaged in self-study.

FINANCIAL DATA:
Amount of support per award: $1,000 to
$1,800 per year.
Total amount of support: Varies.

NO. MOST RECENT APPLICANTS: 5.

NO. AWARDS: Approximately 3.

APPLICATION INFO:
Application may be requested from the
e-mail address above.
Duration: One year.
Deadline: Must be postmarked by May 31.

ADDRESS INQUIRIES TO:
Michael Patterson, Executive Director
(See address above.)

INTERNATIONAL FOOD
SERVICE EXECUTIVES
ASSOCIATION, INC.
(IFSEA)   [2358]
9510 S.W. 70th Loop
Ocala, FL 34481
(855) 273-6379
E-mail: hq@ifsea.org
Web Site: www.ifsea.org

FOUNDED: 1901

AREAS OF INTEREST:
Food service field.

NAME(S) OF PROGRAMS:
● **Worthy Goal Scholarship**

TYPE:
Scholarships. Tuition scholarships.

YEAR PROGRAM STARTED: 1939

PURPOSE:
To give needed assistance to qualified young
people in furthering their careers in the food
service field.

LEGAL BASIS:
Nonprofit.

ELIGIBILITY:
Students must be enrolled as or accepted as a
full-time student in hospitality management
or a food service-related major at a two- or
four-year college/university.

GEOG. RESTRICTIONS: United States.

FINANCIAL DATA:
Amount of support per award: $500 to
$2,500.
Total amount of support: Approximately
$36,000.

NO. MOST RECENT APPLICANTS: 17.

NO. AWARDS: 17.

APPLICATION INFO:
Scholarship application is available at the
Association web site.
Duration: One year. Renewable.
Deadline: March 31. The scholarship is
awarded every spring for the following fall
semester.

ADDRESS INQUIRIES TO:
Dr. Ernest Boger
Worthy Goal Scholarship Chairperson
E-mail: epboger@umes.edu

PRINT AND GRAPHICS SCHOLARSHIP FOUNDATION [2359]

P.O. Box 787
Warrendale, PA 15095
(412) 259-1740
(866) 556-7473
E-mail: bernie.eckert@pgsf.org
Web Site: pgsf.org

FOUNDED: 1956

AREAS OF INTEREST:
Graphic communications, printing technology, printing management and publishing.

TYPE:
Fellowships. For advanced study relating to the printing, publishing and packaging industries. Support is provided for research and study in engineering, chemistry, physics, mathematics, industrial education or such business technology areas as systems analysis, operations research and marketing research, provided the area of study has potential application in the printing, publishing and packaging industries.

YEAR PROGRAM STARTED: 1956

PURPOSE:
To strengthen the print and graphics industry through scholarship assistance.

LEGAL BASIS:
Nonprofit organization.

ELIGIBILITY:
Applicants must be students who plan to major and have a career in graphic communications, printing technology, printing management or publishing. Must have and maintain a 3.0 grade point average.

FINANCIAL DATA:
Amount of support per award: $1,000 to $5,000.

NO. MOST RECENT APPLICANTS: 10 to 15.

NO. AWARDS: Varies.

APPLICATION INFO:
Fellowship application is not available online. Contact the Foundation.
Duration: One academic year. Renewable.
Deadline: April 1.

ADDRESS INQUIRIES TO:
Bernadine Eckert, Administrator
(See address above.)

PRINT AND GRAPHICS SCHOLARSHIP FOUNDATION [2360]

P.O. Box 787
Warrendale, PA 15095
(412) 259-1740
(866) 556-7473
E-mail: bernie.eckert@pgsf.org
Web Site: pgsf.org

FOUNDED: 1956

AREAS OF INTEREST:
Graphic communications and graphic arts; printing technology and management.

TYPE:
Scholarships. Awarded to students who plan to major and have a career in graphic communications, printing technology, printing management or publishing.

YEAR PROGRAM STARTED: 1956

PURPOSE:
To encourage eligible students to enter the field of graphic communications in the printing and publishing industries.

LEGAL BASIS:
Nonprofit foundation.

ELIGIBILITY:
Applicant must:
(1) be a high school senior or a high school graduate;
(2) be pursuing a career in print technology, printing management, publishing, or graphic communications;
(3) be a full-time student enrolled in a printing or graphics program at a technical school, college or university within the U.S. and;
(4) be able to maintain a grade point average of 3.0 or higher.

GEOG. RESTRICTIONS: United States.

FINANCIAL DATA:
Awards are paid directly to colleges for payment of tuition, fees and other charges.
Amount of support per award: $1,000 to $5,000.

NO. MOST RECENT APPLICANTS: 400.

NO. AWARDS: 200.

APPLICATION INFO:
Applications and letters of recommendation must be submitted online.
Duration: Renewable for up to four years (unless otherwise specified).
Deadline: April 1. Decisions are announced in July.

PUBLICATIONS:
Annual reports; newsletter; career brochures.

IRS I.D.: 25-1668339

ADDRESS INQUIRIES TO:
Bernadine Eckert
Scholarship Administrator
(See address above.)

*SPECIAL STIPULATIONS:
Candidates must be pursuing a career in graphic communications or printing and must maintain a 3.0 grade point average.

SME-EF (SOCIETY OF MANUFACTURING ENGINEERS EDUCATION FOUNDATION) [2361]

1000 Town Center
Suite 1910
Southfield, MI 48075
(313) 425-3300
Fax: (313) 425-3410
E-mail: foundation@sme.org
Web Site: www.smeef.org

FOUNDED: 1932

AREAS OF INTEREST:
Manufacturing and industrial engineering technology, machining technology, robotics, automated systems and technology.

NAME(S) OF PROGRAMS:
● **Connie and Robert T. Gunter Scholarship**
● **Clinton J. Helton Manufacturing Scholarship**
● **Kalamazoo Chapter No. 116-Roscoe Douglas Scholarship**
● **Lucille B. Kaufman Women's Scholarship**
● **E. Wayne Kay Scholarships**

● **St. Louis Chapter No. 17 Scholarship**
● **Myrtle and Earl Walker Scholarship**
● **William E. Weisel Scholarship**

TYPE:
Scholarships. Support for full- or part-time students seeking careers in manufacturing or industrial engineering technology or closely related fields.

YEAR PROGRAM STARTED: 1982

LEGAL BASIS:
Professional society.

ELIGIBILITY:
Applicants must reside in the U.S. or Canada, be a full- or part-time student pursuing a degree in manufacturing engineering, manufacturing engineering technology, or a closely related engineering field of study, and must attend an accredited institution in the U.S. or Canada. Applicants must have a minimum 2.5 grade point average.

GEOG. RESTRICTIONS: United States and Canada.

FINANCIAL DATA:
Amount of support per award: Varies according to scholarship.
Total amount of support: Over $650,000 awarded annually.

NO. MOST RECENT APPLICANTS: 1,094 for the academic year 2021-22.

NO. AWARDS: 317.

APPLICATION INFO:
Application must be completed online.
Duration: One year. Students may reapply.
Deadline: February 1. Announcements in May and June.

PUBLICATIONS:
Program announcement.

BOARD OF DIRECTORS:
Joe Kann, President
Frank Ervin, III, Vice President
John Miller, Secretary/Treasurer
Adam Clayton
Valerie Freeman
Wayne Frost, LSME, CMfgE
Kimberly Green
Andrew Jones
Robert Komljenovic
Art McClellan
Christopher Rake
Kyle Riegel
Joe Tate
Marion Wells
Meghan West

ADDRESS INQUIRIES TO:
Kathy Carter, Senior Scholarship Officer
(See address above.)

TRANSPORTATION ASSOCIATION OF CANADA FOUNDATION [2362]

401-1111 Prince of Wales Drive
Ottawa ON K2C 3T2 Canada
(613) 736-1350
Fax: (613) 736-1395
E-mail: foundation@tac-atc.ca
Web Site: tac-atc.ca/en/tac-foundation

FOUNDED: 2003

AREAS OF INTEREST:
Transportation.

NAME(S) OF PROGRAMS:
● **TAC Foundation Scholarships and Bursaries**

TYPE:
Scholarships. Awards are provided for the study of road and transportation sciences, such as highway engineering, transport economics and administration.

YEAR PROGRAM STARTED: 2004

PURPOSE:
To encourage studies by Canadians in the field of transportation.

LEGAL BASIS:
Foundation.

ELIGIBILITY:
Applicants must be Canadian citizens or permanent residents in Canada who are enrolled in a university or college pursuing studies full-time in some aspect of transportation. Student must have achieved an overall B average or equivalant in their previous academic year.

GEOG. RESTRICTIONS: Canada.

FINANCIAL DATA:
Amount of support per award: Scholarships: $2,500 to $6,000.
Total amount of support: $86,000 in scholarships for the year 2020.

NO. MOST RECENT APPLICANTS: Approximately 125.

NO. AWARDS: 20 for the year 2020.

APPLICATION INFO:
Full information is available on the Foundation web site.
Duration: One year. Applicants may apply at each level: college student, undergraduate and graduate.
Deadline: End of February.

ADDRESS INQUIRIES TO:
See e-mail address above.

THE UNIVERSITY OF CALGARY
Faculty of Graduate Studies
Earth Sciences Building, Room 1010
2500 University Drive, N.W.
Calgary AB T2N 1N4 Canada
(403) 220-4938
Fax: (403) 289-7635
E-mail: gsaward@ucalgary.ca
Web Site: grad.ucalgary.ca/awards

TYPE:
Awards/prizes; Scholarships. Graduate scholarship for study in all areas relevant to the petroleum industry. Tenable at The University of Calgary. Award endowed through a bequest of the late Corinne Patteson.

See entry 1595 for full listing.

Aeronautics and astronautics

AIRCRAFT ELECTRONICS ASSOCIATION (AEA)   [2363]
3570 N.E. Ralph Powell Road
Lee's Summit, MO 64064
(816) 347-8400
E-mail: info@aea.net
Web Site: www.aea.net/educationalfoundation/scholarships.asp

FOUNDED: 1957

AREAS OF INTEREST:
Avionics and aircraft electronics.

NAME(S) OF PROGRAMS:
- **David Arver Memorial Scholarship**
- **Dutch and Ginger Arver Scholarship**
- **Gene Baker Memorial Scholarship**
- **Jim Cook Honorary Scholarship**
- **Johnny Davis Memorial Scholarship**
- **Duncan Aviation Scholarship**
- **Field Aviation Company Scholarship**
- **Chuck Freeland Memorial Scholarship for Flight Training**
- **Garmin - Jerry Smith Memorial Scholarship**
- **Garmin Scholarship**
- **Gogo Business Aviation Scholarship**
- **Leon Harris/Les Nichols Memorial Scholarship**
- **Mid-Continent Instrument Scholarship**
- **Chuck Peacock Memorial Scholarship**
- **Sporty's Foundation Scholarship**
- **Stone Foundation Scholarship**
- **Lee Tarbox Memorial Scholarship**
- **Tom Taylor Memorial Scholarship**
- **Marshall Temple Memorial Scholarship**
- **Universal Avionics Systems Corporation Scholarship**

TYPE:
Scholarships.

PURPOSE:
To provide funding for students seeking higher education in the fields of avionics and aircraft electronics.

LEGAL BASIS:
Nonprofit.

ELIGIBILITY:
Applicants for the Arver Scholarship, Johnny Davis Memorial Scholarship, Duncan Aviation Scholarship, Field Aviation Scholarship, Garmin Scholarship, Garmin-Jerry Smith Scholarship, Gogo Business Aviation Scholarship, Mid-Continent Instruments Scholarship, Stone Foundation Scholarship, Lee Tarbox Memorial Scholarship, Chuck Peacock Memorial Scholarship, Marshall Temple Memorial Scholarship and Universal Avionics Systems Scholarship can be anyone who plans to or is enrolled in an avionics or aircraft maintenance program in an accredited U.S. or Canadian school at the time of the award.

Gene Baker Memorial Scholarship and Jim Cook Honorary Scholarship are available to AEA members, their children, grandchildren or dependents.

Leon Harris/Les Nichols Memorial Scholarship is awarded to an individual wanting to pursue an Associate degree in applied science in aviation electronics at the Spartan College of Aeronautics and Technology. The applicant cannot be enrolled currently in the avionics program at Spartan.

Tom Taylor Memorial Scholarship is awarded to an individual desiring to pursue an Associate degree in applied science or a diploma in aviation maintenance technology at the Spartan College of Aeronautics and Technology. The applicant cannot be enrolled currently in the AMT program at Spartan.

The Scholarships are not available to obtain pilot licenses.

GEOG. RESTRICTIONS: North America.

FINANCIAL DATA:
Amount of support per award: $1,000 to $35,000, depending on award.

Total amount of support: More than $100,000 in scholarships for the 2020-21 academic year.

NO. AWARDS: 22.

APPLICATION INFO:
Contact the Association.
Duration: One year.
Deadline: Approximately April 1.

ADDRESS INQUIRIES TO:
Educational Foundation
(See address above.)

THE AMERICAN HISTORICAL ASSOCIATION
400 A Street, S.E.
Washington, DC 20003
(202) 544-2422
E-mail: awards@historians.org
Web Site: www.historians.org

TYPE:
Fellowships. The Association annually funds at least one fellow for a period of six to nine months, to undertake a proposed research project related to aerospace history. The Fellowship is supported by the National Aeronautics and Space Administration (NASA).

See entry 528 for full listing.

AMERICAN INSTITUTE OF AERONAUTICS AND ASTRONAUTICS   [2364]
12700 Sunrise Valley Drive
Suite 200
Reston, VA 20191-5807
(800) 639-2422
E-mail: scholarships@aiaa.org
Web Site: www.aiaa.org/get-involved

FOUNDED: 1977

AREAS OF INTEREST:
Arts, sciences, and technology of aeronautics and astronautics.

NAME(S) OF PROGRAMS:
- **American Institute of Aeronautics and Astronautics Undergraduate Scholarship and Graduate Awards Program**

TYPE:
Scholarships. Graduate financial awards. Program presents yearly scholarships to college sophomores, college juniors and college seniors. Graduate awards are also offered.

YEAR PROGRAM STARTED: 1977

PURPOSE:
To encourage original research; to further dissemination of new knowledge; to foster the professional development of those engaged in scientific and engineering activities in the aerospace or mechanical engineering fields; to improve public understanding of the profession and its contributions; to foster education in engineering and science; to promote communication among engineers and scientists and with other professional groups; to stimulate outstanding professional accomplishments.

ELIGIBILITY:
Applicants must meet the following eligibility requirements:
(1) be a current AIAA student member in good standing;
(2) have completed at least one academic

semester of full-time college work;
(3) have a minimum cumulative grade point
average of 3.3 on a 4.0 scale and;
(4) be enrolled in an accredited college or
university within the U.S. or U.S. territories.

Applicant's education plan shall be such as to
provide entry into some field of science or
engineering encompassed by the technical
activities of AIAA.

Certain awards or scholarships are eligible
for international students.

FINANCIAL DATA:
Amount of support per award: Up to
$10,000.
Total amount of support: Varies.

NO. MOST RECENT APPLICANTS: 100.

NO. AWARDS: 23.

APPLICATION INFO:
Award applications must be submitted online.
Duration: One year.
Deadline: Applications must be received by
January 31.

ADDRESS INQUIRIES TO:
See e-mail address above.

AMERICAN METEOROLOGICAL
SOCIETY   [2365]
45 Beacon Street
Boston, MA 02108-3693
(617) 227-2426 ext. 3907
Fax: (617) 742-8718
E-mail: dfernandez@ametsoc.org
Web Site: www.ametsoc.org

FOUNDED: 1919

AREAS OF INTEREST:
Weather, water and climate.

NAME(S) OF PROGRAMS:
- **AMS Freshman Undergraduate
  Scholarship Program**
- **AMS Graduate Fellowship in the
  History of Science**
- **AMS Graduate Fellowships**
- **AMS Minority Scholarship**
- **AMS Senior Named Scholarships**
- **AMS Women in Science Scholarship**
- **The Father James B. Macelwane
  Annual Awards in Meteorology**

TYPE:
Fellowships; Scholarships. AMS Freshman
Undergraduate Scholarship Program awards
funding to high school seniors entering their
freshman year of undergraduate study in the
fall.

AMS Graduate Fellowship in the History of
Science is awarded to a student wishing to
complete a dissertation on the history of the
atmospheric and related oceanic or
hydrologic sciences.

AMS Graduate Fellowships are designed to
attract students entering their first year of
graduate study in the fall who wish to pursue
advanced degrees in the atmospheric and
related oceanic and hydrologic sciences.

AMS Minority Scholarship awards funding to
high school minority students entering
freshman year of undergraduate study in the
fall who have been traditionally
underrepresented in the sciences, especially
Hispanic, Native American and Black/African
American students.

AMS Senior Named Scholarships are
directed to students entering their final year
of undergraduate study in the fall.

The Father James B. Macelwane Annual
Awards in Meteorology is intended to
stimulate interest in meteorology among
college students through the submission of
original student papers concerned with some
phase of the atmospheric sciences. The
student must be enrolled as an undergraduate
at the time the paper was written.

YEAR PROGRAM STARTED: 1965

PURPOSE:
To stimulate interest in meteorology among
college students and to recognize academic
excellence and achievement; to stimulate
careers in atmospheric and related oceanic
and hydrologic sciences.

LEGAL BASIS:
Nonprofit organization.

ELIGIBILITY:
Candidates must be U.S. citizens or hold
permanent resident status.

AMS encourages applications from women,
minorities and disabled students who are
traditionally underrepresented in the
atmospheric and related oceanic and
hydrologic sciences.

AMS Freshman Undergraduate Scholarship
Program makes awards on the basis of
academic excellence.

AMS Graduate Fellowship in the History of
Science: Candidate must be a graduate
student in good standing who proposes to
complete a dissertation on the history of the
atmospheric, or related oceanic or hydrologic
sciences.

AMS Graduate Fellowships: Applicants must
be entering their first year of graduate study
in the fall pursuing an advanced degree in
the atmospheric and related oceanic and
hydrologic sciences. Prospective candidates
from the fields of chemistry, computer
sciences, engineering, environmental
sciences, mathematics or physics who intend
to pursue careers in the atmospheric or
related oceanic or hydrologic sciences are
also encouraged to apply.

AMS Minority Scholarship: Funding to high
school minority students who have been
traditionally underrepresented in the sciences,
especially Hispanic, Native American and
Black/African American students. Minority
students must be entering their freshman year
of undergraduate study in the fall at a
four-year U.S. accredited institution, and
must plan to pursue a career in the
atmospheric or related oceanic or hydrologic
sciences.

AMS Senior Named Scholarships: Candidates
must be entering their final undergraduate
year in the fall and majoring in the
atmospheric or related oceanic or hydrologic
sciences and/or must show clear intent to
make atmospheric or related sciences their
career.

Father James B. Macelwane Annual Awards
in Meteorology: Student must be enrolled as
an undergraduate at the time the paper is
written. No more than two students from any
one institution may enter papers in any one
contest.

GEOG. RESTRICTIONS: United States.

FINANCIAL DATA:
Amount of support per award: AMS
Freshman Undergraduate Scholarship
Program: $2,500 per year (freshman and
sophomore years); AMS Graduate Fellowship

in the History of Science: $20,000 stipend;
AMS Graduate Fellowships: Up to $25,000;
AMS Minority Scholarship: $3,000 per year
(freshman and sophomore years); AMS
Senior Named Scholarships: Up to $10,000;
AMS Women in Science Scholarship:
$10,000 for the senior year; Father James B.
Macelwane Annual Awards in Meteorology:
$1,000 stipend and partial travel support to
the AMS Annual Meeting.
Total amount of support: Varies.

NO. MOST RECENT APPLICANTS: 340.

NO. AWARDS: 55.

APPLICATION INFO:
Those interested should apply online at the
AMS web site. When writing for an
application package, specify which
application is being requested, and what year
of academic study applicant will be entering
in the fall. Submit a complete application
form, written letters of reference and official
transcripts.
Duration: AMS Freshman Undergraduate
Scholarship Program: Up to two years; AMS
Graduate History of Science Fellowship and
AMS Women in Science Scholarship: One
year; AMS Minority Scholarship: Two years;
AMS Graduate Fellowships: Nine months.
Deadline: AMS Senior Named Scholarship:
March. Graduate Fellowship: January.
Graduate Fellowship in the History of
Science: April. Father James B. Macelwane:
Mid-June. All other programs: February.

PUBLICATIONS:
Program announcement.

OFFICERS:
Dr. Keith L. Seitter, Executive Director

ADDRESS INQUIRIES TO:
Donna Fernandez, Development and
Student Programs Manager
Tel: (617) 227-2426 ext. 3907
E-mail: dfernandez@ametsoc.org or

Stephanie Armstrong
Associate Executive Director
Tel: (617) 227-2426 ext. 3906
E-mail: armstrong@ametsoc.org

*SPECIAL STIPULATIONS:
Applicants must review program
requirements before applying.

AVIATION DISTRIBUTORS AND
MANUFACTURERS
ASSOCIATION (ADMA)   [2366]
P.O. Box 3948
Parker, CO 80134
(720) 249-0999
Fax: (720) 496-4974
E-mail: info@adma.org
Web Site: www.adma.org

FOUNDED: 1943

AREAS OF INTEREST:
Aviation and pilot education, mechanics and
maintenance.

NAME(S) OF PROGRAMS:
- **ADMA Scholarship Programs**

TYPE:
Scholarships.

PURPOSE:
To provide assistance to youth aviation
students pursuing careers in the aviation
field.

ELIGIBILITY:

Applicant must be one of following:
(1) third- or fourth-year B.S. candidate with Aviation Management major, emphasis in General Aviation, Airway Science Management, Aviation Maintenance or Airway Science Maintenance Management;
(2) third- or fourth-year B.S. candidate with major in Professional Pilot with any of the following emphases: General Aviation, Flight Engineer, Airway Science A/C Systems Management or;
(3) second-year student in A/P education program (two-year accredited aviation technical school).

Applicant must also have 3.0 grade point average or higher.

GEOG. RESTRICTIONS: United States.

FINANCIAL DATA:

Amount of support per award: $1,500.

Total amount of support: $6,000 for the year 2019.

NO. MOST RECENT APPLICANTS: 25.

NO. AWARDS: 4 for the year 2019.

APPLICATION INFO:

Detailed information is available from the Association.

Duration: One year.

Deadline: May 21.

ADDRESS INQUIRIES TO:

Nicole Singleton, Executive Director
(See address above.)

AVIATION INSURANCE ASSOCIATION (AIA)   [2367]

2365 Harrodsburg Road
Suite A325
Lexington, KY 40504
(859) 219-3545
E-mail: info@aiaweb.org
Web Site: www.aiaweb.org

FOUNDED: 2005

AREAS OF INTEREST:

Aviation insurance.

NAME(S) OF PROGRAMS:

● **AIA Scholarship**

TYPE:

Scholarships.

PURPOSE:

To help students with an interest in aviation insurance to continue on to higher education.

LEGAL BASIS:

Nonprofit association.

ELIGIBILITY:

Applicants must:
(1) be currently enrolled in an accredited undergraduate or graduate degree program;
(2) currently be an intern or recently completed an internship program within a facet of the aviation insurance industry;
(3) have completed at least 45 college credits and;
(4) have a minimum 2.5 grade point average on a 4.0 scale.

FINANCIAL DATA:

Amount of support per award: $2,500.

NO. AWARDS: 4.

APPLICATION INFO:

Applicants must submit the following documents to be considered a scholarship candidate:

(1) completed AIA Scholarship application;
(2) letter describing activities, indicating leadership qualities, goals, rolls and reason for applying;
(3) at least one letter of recommendation from a supervisor during the internship program and;
(4) latest transcript(s) from all universities and colleges attended.

Duration: One-time award.

Deadline: February 28.

ADDRESS INQUIRIES TO:

Mary E. Gratzer, Executive Director
(See address above.)

NATIONAL BUSINESS AVIATION ASSOCIATION   [2368]

1200 G Street, N.W.
Suite 1100
Washington, DC 20005
(202) 783-9000
(202) 783-9353
E-mail: scholarships@nbaa.org
Web Site: www.nbaa.org/professional-development/scholarships

AREAS OF INTEREST:

Aviation.

NAME(S) OF PROGRAMS:

● **William M. Fanning Maintenance Scholarship**
● **Flight Attendants/Flight Technicians Scholarship**
● **International Operators Scholarship**

TYPE:

Scholarships. The William M. Fanning Maintenance Scholarship is for those who are pursuing careers as maintenance technicians.

The Flight Attendants/Flight Technicians Scholarship is dedicated to promoting education and training as a means to increase professionalism for business aviation flight attendants and flight technicians.

The International Operators Scholarship is dedicated to promoting education and training to increase safety and professionalism for business aviation professionals engaged in international operations.

PURPOSE:

To help students continue their education in aviation and advance in that field.

LEGAL BASIS:

Nonprofit association.

ELIGIBILITY:

Contact the Association for details.

GEOG. RESTRICTIONS: United States.

FINANCIAL DATA:

Amount of support per award: Fanning Maintenance Scholarship: $2,500; International Operators Scholarship: Up to $9,000.

Total amount of support: Varies.

NO. AWARDS: Fanning Maintenance Scholarship: 2.

APPLICATION INFO:

Applications are available at the Association web site.

Duration: One-time award.

Deadline: Fanning Maintenance Scholarship: July 31; Flight Attendants/Flight Technicians Scholarship: February 28; International Operators Scholarship: December 20.

STAFF:

Molly Hitch, Manager, Professional Development

ADDRESS INQUIRIES TO:

See e-mail address above.

*PLEASE NOTE:

Awards will be made to U.S. citizens without regard to sex, race, religion or national origin.

NATIONAL BUSINESS AVIATION ASSOCIATION   [2369]

1200 G Street, N.W.
Suite 1100
Washington, DC 20005
(202) 783-9000
(202) 783-9353
E-mail: scholarships@nbaa.org
Web Site: www.nbaa.org/scholarships

AREAS OF INTEREST:

Aviation and business aviation.

NAME(S) OF PROGRAMS:

● **Lawrence Ginocchio Scholarship**
● **Schedulers & Dispatchers Scholarship**
● **UAA Janice K. Barden Scholarship**

TYPE:

Scholarships. Janice K. Barden Scholarship is presented to undergraduates who are studying aviation-related curricula.

Lawrence Ginocchio Scholarship honors individuals whose strength of character inspired a high standard. Applicants must be students at NBAA/UAA Member programs.

PURPOSE:

To help students continue their education in aviation and advance in that field.

LEGAL BASIS:

Nonprofit association.

ELIGIBILITY:

Contact the Association for details.

FINANCIAL DATA:

Amount of support per award: Janice K. Barden Scholarship: Minimum $1,000; Lawrence Ginocchio Scholarship: $4,500; Schedulers & Dispatchers Scholarship: Up to $10,000.

Total amount of support: Janice K. Barden Scholarship: Minimum $5,000; Lawrence Ginocchio Scholarship: $22,500.

NO. AWARDS: Janice K. Barden and Lawrence Ginocchio Scholarships: 5 each.

APPLICATION INFO:

Contact the Association for guidelines.

Deadline: Varies.

STAFF:

Molly Hitch, Manager, Professional Development

ADDRESS INQUIRIES TO:

Molly Hitch, Manager, Professional Development
(See address above.)

NATIONAL BUSINESS AVIATION ASSOCIATION   [2370]

1200 G Street, N.W.
Suite 1100
Washington, DC 20005
(202) 783-9000
(202) 783-9353
E-mail: scholarships@nbaa.org
Web Site: www.nbaa.org/scholarships

AREAS OF INTEREST:

Aviation.

NAME(S) OF PROGRAMS:
- **Donald A. Baldwin Sr. Business
  Aviation Management Scholarship**

TYPE:
Scholarships. Promotes professional
development in business aviation.

YEAR PROGRAM STARTED: 2007

PURPOSE:
To benefit individuals seeking to become
NBAA-Certified Aviation Managers (CAMs).

ELIGIBILITY:
Applicants must be eligible within two years
of award date to take the CAM exam.

FINANCIAL DATA:
Amount of support per award: Up to $1,225
per recipient.

NO. AWARDS: 1.

APPLICATION INFO:
Applicants must submit their resume, a
250-word essay explaining their plans for a
career in business aviation, two letters of
recommendation in support, and meet
minimum qualifications to take the CAM
exam.
Duration: One year.
Deadline: November 30.

ADDRESS INQUIRIES TO:
Molly Hitch, Manager, Professional
Development
(See address above.)

RTCA   [2371]
1150 18th Street, N.W.
Suite 910
Washington, DC 20036
(202) 330-0680
Fax: (202) 833-9434
E-mail: khofmann@rtca.org
Web Site: www.rtca.org

FOUNDED: 1935

AREAS OF INTEREST:
Aviation electronics, telecommunications, and
other closely allied fields such as
determination of common operational
requirements, state-of-the-art developments
and applications, other problems associated
with air traffic control, navigation,
communications, and efficient utilization of
airports and airspace.

NAME(S) OF PROGRAMS:
- **The William E. Jackson Award**

TYPE:
Awards/prizes. Award for a paper by an
outstanding graduate student in aviation
electronics or telecommunications, in
memory of William E. Jackson, an
outstanding pioneer in the development and
implementation of the present airways, air
traffic control, and aviation communication
systems.

YEAR PROGRAM STARTED: 1975

PURPOSE:
To honor an outstanding graduate student in
aviation electronics or telecommunications.

LEGAL BASIS:
Nonprofit, 501(c)(3) organization.

ELIGIBILITY:
Open to any graduate student earning a
degree in the field of aviation electronics or
telecommunication systems. There are no
restrictions as to race, creed, color, religious

affiliation, national origin or citizenship. The
sole basis for selection will be the written
report, which must be in English.

FINANCIAL DATA:
The recipient will travel at the expense of
RTCA to the location of the award
presentation. Complimentary registration for
any RTCA business meeting taking place
concurrently is also awarded.
Amount of support per award: $5,000.

NO. MOST RECENT APPLICANTS: 3.

NO. AWARDS: 1.

APPLICATION INFO:
Submissions must be in the form of a thesis,
project report, or paper in a technical journal.
The work must have been completed no
earlier than three years before the submission
deadline and only those in English and
without publication restrictions will be
considered. Joint authors may submit if both
or all qualify as students and candidates for
undergraduate or graduate degrees in this
field. Joint authors would share the award.
Additionally, candidates must submit a one-
to two-page summary of the written material,
a biographical sketch of the candidate, and a
letter of endorsement from the candidate's
instructor, professor, or departmental head.

All materials must be submitted
electronically.
Deadline: December 4.

OFFICERS:
Karan Hofmann, Program Director

ADDRESS INQUIRIES TO:
William E. Jackson Award Committee
(See address above.)

SMITHSONIAN NATIONAL AIR
AND SPACE MUSEUM   [2372]
P.O. Box 37012, MRC 312
Washington, DC 20013-7012
(202) 633-2648
E-mail: nasm-fellowships@si.edu
Web Site: airandspace.si.edu

FOUNDED: 1946

AREAS OF INTEREST:
Aeronautics.

NAME(S) OF PROGRAMS:
- **Aviation Space Writers Foundation
  Award**
- **Guggenheim Fellowship**
- **Charles A. Lindbergh Chair in
  Aerospace History**
- **Postdoctoral Earth and Planetary
  Sciences Fellowship**
- **A. Verville Fellowship**

TYPE:
Fellowships; Research grants. Aviation Space
Writers Foundation Award, offered in
even-numbered years, is intended to support
research on aerospace topics.

The Guggenheim Fellowship is a competitive
three- to 12-month in-residence fellowship
for pre- or postdoctoral research in aviation
and space history.

The Charles A. Lindbergh Chair in
Aerospace History is a competitive 12-month
fellowship.

Postdoctoral Earth and Planetary Sciences
Fellowship supports scientific research in the
area of earth and planetary sciences.
Scientists in the Center for Earth and
Planetary Studies concentrate on geologic

and geophysical research of the earth and
other terrestrial planets, using remote sensing
data obtained from earth-orbiting and
interplanetary spacecraft. Research also
focuses on global environmental change.

The A. Verville Fellowship is a competitive
nine- to 12-month in-residence fellowship
intended for analysis of major trends,
developments, and accomplishments in the
history of aviation or space studies.

All candidates are encouraged to pursue
programs of research and writing that support
publication of works that are scholarly in
tone and substance, and/or addressed to an
audience with broad interests. Each fellow
will work closely with staff members who
share similar interests.

PURPOSE:
To promote research into, and writing about,
the history of aviation and space flight.

ELIGIBILITY:
All applicants must be able to write and
converse fluently in English. Additional
information is available online.

Aviation Space Writers Foundation Award:
The product created as a result of the grant
must be in any form suitable for potential
public dissemination in print, electronic,
broadcast or other visual medium, including,
but not limited to, a book manuscript, a
video, or film script or monograph.

Guggenheim Fellowship: Predoctoral
applicants should have completed preliminary
course work and examinations and be
engaged in dissertation research. Postdoctoral
applicants should have received their Ph.D.
within the past seven years.

Lindbergh Chair in Aerospace History: Open
to senior scholars with distinguished records
of publication who are at work on, or
anticipate being at work on, books in
aerospace history.

Verville Fellowship: Open to interested
candidates with demonstrated skills in
research and writing. Publishing experience
should demonstrate either a mid-level
academic record of accomplishment or
proven ability to engage in a reliable manner
broader audiences. An advanced degree in
history or a related field is preferred but not
a requirement.

FINANCIAL DATA:
Amount of support per award: Aviation
Space Writers Foundation Award: Grant of
$5,000; Guggenheim Fellowship: Annual
stipend of $30,000 for predoctoral candidates
and $45,000 for postdoctoral candidates;
Lindbergh Chair in Aerospace History:
Support is available for living expenses in the
Washington, DC area up to a maximum of
$100,000 a year; Postdoctoral Earth and
Planetary Sciences Fellowship: Stipends are
compatible with National Research Council
postdoctoral fellowships in the applicant's
field; Verville Fellowship: Annual stipend of
$55,000 (for a 12-month fellowship tenure),
with limited additional funds for travel and
miscellaneous expenses.

NO. AWARDS: 1 per award or fellowship.

APPLICATION INFO:
All applications must be submitted
electronically through the Smithsonian Online
Academic Appointment System (SOLAA).
Duration: Guggenheim Fellowship: Three to
12 months; Lindbergh Chair in Aerospace
History: Typically for an academic year

(September through August); Postdoctoral Earth and Planetary Sciences Fellowship: Appointments can be made for one or more years; Verville Fellowship: Nine to 12 months.

Deadline: Postdoctoral Earth and Planetary Sciences Fellowship: November 1. All others: Application due December 1; Recommendation letters due December 15; Award presented mid-March.

PUBLICATIONS:
Brochure; application package.

ADDRESS INQUIRIES TO:
Aviation Space Writers Foundation Award:
Dr. Dominick A. Pisano
Aeronautics Department
National Air and Space Museum
E-mail: pisanod@si.edu

Guggenheim, Lindbergh and Verville Fellowships:
Collette Williams, Administrative Program Specialist
(See e-mail address above.)

Postdoctoral Earth and Planetary Sciences Fellowship: Rosemary Aiello
Center for Earth and Planetary Studies
National Air and Space Museum
Washington, DC 20560
Tel: (202) 633-2480
E-mail: aiellor@si.edu

*PLEASE NOTE:
Applicants are restricted to applying for a single National Air and Space Museum fellowship grant at a time. Proposals must reflect that the research to be undertaken is intended for publication in peer-reviewed books and journals.

SMITHSONIAN NATIONAL AIR AND SPACE MUSEUM [2373]
601 Independence Avenue, S.W.
Room 3762, MRC 305
Washington, DC 20560
(202) 633-2214
Fax: (202) 633-1957
E-mail: staplesa@si.edu
Web Site: airandspace.si.edu/support/get-involved/internships

FOUNDED: 1946

AREAS OF INTEREST:
Aeronautics.

NAME(S) OF PROGRAMS:
● **Summer Internship Program**

TYPE:
Internships. Full-time interns work 40 hours per week from approximately the first week in June until the second week in August.

PURPOSE:
To give interns a firsthand opportunity to learn about the historic artifacts and archival materials housed in the Museum and to study the scientific and technological advances they represent.

ELIGIBILITY:
Applicant must be a high school graduate and be enrolled in, or recently graduated from, a degree-granting undergraduate or graduate program at an accredited college or university. Applicant is expected to have a strong academic record.

Applicants from outside the U.S. are welcome. International applicants must have the appropriate J-1 visa and are responsible for any other necessary official documents.

FINANCIAL DATA:
Interns are responsible for locating and securing lodging.
Amount of support per award: $5,500.

NO. MOST RECENT APPLICANTS: 350 for the year 2020.

NO. AWARDS: 36 paid internships in 2018.

APPLICATION INFO:
Application information is available on the web site. Visit the Smithsonian Online Academic Appointment System (SOLAA) web site, which opens January 15, to apply.
Duration: 10 weeks during the summer; schedule is flexible.
Deadline: Applications are accepted from January 15 to February 15 during the calendar year of the internship. Interns are notified of the status of their application on or before April 1.

ADDRESS INQUIRIES TO:
See e-mail address above.

*SPECIAL STIPULATIONS:
A commitment of 10 weeks during the summer is required.

VERTICAL FLIGHT FOUNDATION [2374]
2700 Prosperity Avenue, Suite 275
Fairfax, VA 22031
(703) 684-6777
Fax: (703) 739-9279
E-mail: bchen@vtol.org
Web Site: www.vtol.org/vff

FOUNDED: 1967

AREAS OF INTEREST:
Support of scientific and educational activities related to VTOL (Vertical Take-Off and Landing) flight.

NAME(S) OF PROGRAMS:
● **Vertical Flight Foundation Engineering Scholarships**

TYPE:
Awards/prizes; Scholarships. Annual scholarships to undergraduate senior, Master's or Ph.D. students interested in pursuing careers in some technical aspect of helicopter or vertical flight engineering.

YEAR PROGRAM STARTED: 1967

PURPOSE:
To acquire the best technical experts for the vertical flight industry.

LEGAL BASIS:
Independent, charitable trust.

ELIGIBILITY:
Applicants must be full-time college students at an accredited school in a technical program. Technical disciplines relevant to complex aeronautics/aeronautics engineering or aviation systems, even if not directly considered vertical lift engineering, will receive equal consideration.

FINANCIAL DATA:
Amount of support per award: $3,000 to $6,000.
Total amount of support: $100,000 for the year 2021.

NO. AWARDS: Varies based on size of endowment.

APPLICATION INFO:
Detailed instructions are available at the web site. Professor's recommendation letter and

transcripts must be submitted directly from the school. Submission by the student will not be accepted as valid documents.
Duration: One academic year.
Deadline: February 1, 2022. Postmark governs timeliness.

PUBLICATIONS:
Applications.

IRS I.D.: 13-1953506

ADDRESS INQUIRIES TO:
Betty Chen, Scholarship Coordinator
(See address above.)

Engineering

ADSC: THE INTERNATIONAL ASSOCIATION OF FOUNDATION DRILLING [2375]
950 East State Highway 114
Suite 160
Southlake, TX 76092
(469) 359-6000
Fax: (469) 359-6007
E-mail: adsc@adsc-iafd.com
Web Site: www.adsc-iafd.com

FOUNDED: 1972

AREAS OF INTEREST:
Civil, geotechnical and structural engineering.

TYPE:
Scholarships.

PURPOSE:
To promote the foundation drilling and anchored earth retention industry.

ELIGIBILITY:
Must be a graduate student studying civil engineering.

GEOG. RESTRICTIONS: United States or Canada.

FINANCIAL DATA:
Amount of support per award: Maximum $3,000.
Total amount of support: Approximately $42,000 annually.

NO. AWARDS: Minimum of 17 per year.

APPLICATION INFO:
Applicants must submit a brief letter outlining personal goals, two letters of recommendation and a copy of their transcript with application. Further information and application may be obtained from the Association.
Duration: One year.
Deadline: Contact the Association for deadline.

ADDRESS INQUIRIES TO:
Emily Matthews, Director of Operations
(See address above.)

AGC EDUCATION AND RESEARCH FOUNDATION [2376]
2300 Wilson Boulevard, Suite 300
Arlington, VA 22201
(703) 837-5356
E-mail: courtney.bishop@agc.org
Web Site: www.agcfoundation.org

FOUNDED: 1968

AREAS OF INTEREST:
Construction and civic interest in improving the quality of educational programs for

students specifically in the area of commercial construction and construction research.

NAME(S) OF PROGRAMS:
- **James L. Allhands Essay Competition**
- **Graduate Scholarship Program**
- **Industry Case Studies**
- **Outstanding Educator Award**
- **Undergraduate Scholarship Program**
- **Workforce Development Scholarship**

TYPE:
Awards/prizes; Internships; Project/program grants; Scholarships. Allhands Essay Competition: Awarded to a student essay on a specific topic that is deemed to be beneficial to the advancement of technological, educational or vocational expertise in the construction industry.

Graduate Scholarship Program: Scholarships for students enrolled in ABET- or ACCE-accredited construction management or construction-related engineering programs.

Industry Case Studies: Commissioning case studies on industry scenarios.

Outstanding Educator Award: Awards to top competitors in essay competition for seniors and faculty nominated as outstanding educator.

Undergraduate Scholarship Program: Scholarships for students enrolled in ABET- or ACCE-accredited construction management or construction-related engineering programs.

Workforce Development Scholarship: Awarded for students entering craft training or technical programs.

YEAR PROGRAM STARTED: 1968

PURPOSE:
To improve the science of construction through the funding of scholarships and construction research projects.

LEGAL BASIS:
501(c)(3).

ELIGIBILITY:
James L. Allhands Essay Competition is for seniors only in a four- or five-year ABET- or ACCE-accredited university construction management or construction-related engineering program.

Undergraduate scholarships are available to college sophomores and juniors enrolled or planning to enroll in a full-time, four- or five-year ABET- or ACCE-accredited construction or civil engineering program. High school seniors and college freshman are not eligible.

Graduate awards are available to college seniors enrolled in an undergraduate construction or civil engineering degree program, or others possessing an undergraduate degree in construction or civil engineering. The applicant must be enrolled, or planning to enroll, in a graduate-level construction or civil engineering degree program as a full-time student. All candidates must be U.S. citizens or permanent U.S. residents.

Workforce Development Scholarship is available to students already enrolled or planning to enroll in craft training or technical programs up to two years in length.

Contact the Foundation for details.

GEOG. RESTRICTIONS: United States.

FINANCIAL DATA:
Amount of support per award: Allhands Essay Competition: First Prize $1,000 and an expense-paid trip to the AGC Convention; Graduate Scholarships: Up to $7,500; Industry Case Studies: $9,000 grant; Outstanding Educator Award: $5,000 award and an expense-paid trip to the AGC Convention, plus two $2,500 scholarships for students of the educator; Undergraduate Scholarships: $2,500 per year renewable to a maximum of $7,500; Workforce Development Scholarship: $1,000 per year, renewable up to $2,000.

Total amount of support: $500,000 for all programs.

NO. AWARDS: First, second and third prizes awarded in Allhands Essay. Outstanding Educator: 1. Over 150 scholarships are awarded each year.

APPLICATION INFO:
Undergraduate and graduate applications are posted online after July 1. Online link: scholarship.agc.org. All other application links can be found at www.agcfoundation.org.

Duration: Varies.

Deadline: Allhands Essay Competition and Outstanding Educator Award: November 15; Graduate and Undergraduate Scholarships: Applications are accepted July 1 to November 1; Workforce Development Scholarship: Applications are accepted March 1 to June 1. Contact the Foundation for other deadlines.

IRS I.D.: 52-6083465

STAFF:
Courtney Bishop, Program Director

BOARD OF DIRECTORS:
Scott Holloway, President
Fran Madigan, III, Vice President
Phil Beck, Treasurer
Conor O'Brien, Secretary

ADDRESS INQUIRIES TO:
Courtney Bishop, Program Director
(See address above.)

AMERICAN CHEMICAL SOCIETY

1155 16th Street, N.W.
Washington, DC 20036-4801
(202) 872-4575
Fax: (202) 776-8008
E-mail: awards@acs.org
Web Site: www.acs.org/awards

TYPE:
Awards/prizes.

See entry 1850 for full listing.

AMERICAN INSTITUTE OF CHEMICAL ENGINEERS (AICHE)   [2377]

120 Wall Street, Floor 23
New York, NY 10005-4020
(800) 242-4363
Fax: (646) 495-1503
E-mail: awards@aiche.org
Web Site: www.aiche.org

FOUNDED: 1908

AREAS OF INTEREST:
Chemical engineering.

NAME(S) OF PROGRAMS:
- **Minority Scholarship Awards for College Students**

TYPE:
Scholarships.

YEAR PROGRAM STARTED: 1994

PURPOSE:
To encourage minority undergraduate study of chemical engineering.

LEGAL BASIS:
Nonprofit.

ELIGIBILITY:
Applicants shall be required to be undergraduates in chemical engineering during the current academic year and be members of a minority group that is under-represented in chemical engineering (African American, Hispanic, Native American, Alaskan Native and Pacific Islander).

FINANCIAL DATA:
Amount of support per award: $1,000.

NO. AWARDS: 15 for the year 2020.

APPLICATION INFO:
Contact the Institute.

Duration: One scholastic year. Renewable following year if student continues to meet eligibility requirements.

Deadline: Usually in summer.

PUBLICATIONS:
Awards nomination form.

ADDRESS INQUIRIES TO:
E-mail: felig@aiche.org

AMERICAN NUCLEAR SOCIETY (ANS)   [2378]

555 North Kensington Avenue
LaGrange Park, IL 60526
(708) 352-6611
Fax: (708) 352-0499
E-mail: scholarships@ans.org
Web Site: www.ans.org

FOUNDED: 1954

AREAS OF INTEREST:
Nuclear science, nuclear engineering or nuclear-related field.

NAME(S) OF PROGRAMS:
- **Delayed Education for Women Scholarship**
- **John and Muriel Landis Scholarships**

TYPE:
Scholarships. Delayed Education for Women Scholarship is designed for women in a nuclear-related field whose formal studies have been delayed or interrupted for at least one year.

Landis Scholarships are administered by the ANS NEED Committee, and are awarded to undergraduate and graduate students who have greater-than-average financial need.

PURPOSE:
To encourage mature women whose formal studies in the field of nuclear science, nuclear engineering, or a nuclear-related field have been delayed or interrupted for at least one year; to provide financial aid to students with greater-than-average need.

ELIGIBILITY:
Applicants must be ANS student members.

Delayed Education for Women Scholarship: Applicants must have experienced a minimum of a one-year delay or interruption of their undergraduate studies and must be entering a four-year curriculum. Those at graduate level of education can also apply. Applicants must also have proven academic ability as well as demonstrated financial need. An applicant must be a U.S. citizen or possess a permanent resident visa, be enrolled in a U.S. college or university, and must be sponsored by an ANS local section, division, student branch, committee or organization member. More than one applicant can be sponsored by any of these organizations. Those applying must be enrolled in a course of study relating to a degree in nuclear science or nuclear engineering in a U.S. institution. Applicants must be mature women whose undergraduate studies in nuclear science, nuclear engineering, or a nuclear-related field have been delayed.

Landis Scholarships: Applicants must be undergraduate or graduate students who have greater-than-average financial need. Consideration is given to conditions or experiences that render the student disadvantaged (poor high school/undergraduate preparation, etc.). Applicants should be planning a career in nuclear science, nuclear engineering, or a nuclear-related field and be enrolled or planning to enroll in a college or university located in the U.S. Applicants need not be U.S. citizens.

GEOG. RESTRICTIONS: United States.

FINANCIAL DATA:
Scholarship funds may be used by the student to defray any bona fide education costs including tuition, books, room and board.
Amount of support per award: $5,000.

CO-OP FUNDING PROGRAMS: Delayed Education for Women Scholarship: Sponsored jointly by the NEED and Professional Women in the ANS Committees.

NO. AWARDS: Delayed Education for Women Scholarship: 1; Landis Scholarships: Up to 5.

APPLICATION INFO:
Applications must be submitted online.
Duration: One year. Nonrenewable.
Deadline: February 1.

ADDRESS INQUIRIES TO:
Scholarship Coordinator
(See address above.)

*PLEASE NOTE:
Scholarships are only offered to ANS student members.

*SPECIAL STIPULATIONS:
Student may receive no more than three NEED scholarships over the course of their undergraduate and graduate studies.

AMERICAN NUCLEAR SOCIETY (ANS) [2379]
555 North Kensington Avenue
LaGrange Park, IL 60526
(708) 352-6611
Fax: (708) 352-0499
E-mail: scholarships@ans.org
Web Site: www.ans.org

FOUNDED: 1954

AREAS OF INTEREST:
Nuclear science, nuclear engineering or nuclear-related fields.

NAME(S) OF PROGRAMS:
● **Decommissioning and Environmental Sciences (DESD) Undergraduate Scholarship**

TYPE:
Scholarships. For an undergraduate student pursuing a degree in engineering or science major with emphasis on decommissioning/decontamination, management/characterization of radioactive waste, restoration of the environment, or nuclear engineering.

YEAR PROGRAM STARTED: 2013

ELIGIBILITY:
Applicant must be at junior or senior undergraduate level and must be a U.S. citizen or permanent resident. He or she must be enrolled in a course of study relating to a degree in nuclear science or nuclear engineering in a U.S. institution. Additional criteria to be met include:
(1) the student must be enrolled in a curriculum of engineering or science that is associated either with decommissioning/decontamination of nuclear facilities, management/characterization of nuclear waste, restoration of the environment, or nuclear engineering;
(2) the scholarship is limited to U.S. citizens who are enrolled in U.S. schools;
(3) the student will join the American Nuclear Society (ANS);
(4) the student will designate the ANS DDR Division as one of his or her professional divisions and;
(5) he or she will commit to provide student support to the ANS DDR Division at the next ANS meeting after receipt of the scholarship award. (DDR will provide funding for the student's travel to the ANS meeting, including student registration, reasonable transportation, food and lodging.)

FINANCIAL DATA:
Scholarship funds may be used by the student to defray any bona fide education costs including tuition, books, room and board.
Amount of support per award: $2,000.

NO. AWARDS: 1 annually.

APPLICATION INFO:
Applications must be submitted online.
Duration: One year. Nonrenewable.
Deadline: February 1.

ADDRESS INQUIRIES TO:
Scholarship Coordinator
(See address above.)

*PLEASE NOTE:
Scholarships are only offered to ANS student members.

AMERICAN NUCLEAR SOCIETY (ANS) [2380]
555 North Kensington Avenue
LaGrange Park, IL 60526
(708) 352-6611
Fax: (708) 352-0499
E-mail: scholarships@ans.org
Web Site: www.ans.org

FOUNDED: 1954

AREAS OF INTEREST:
Nuclear science, nuclear engineering or nuclear-related field.

NAME(S) OF PROGRAMS:
● **Raymond DiSalvo Memorial Scholarship**
● **Robert T. Liner Memorial Scholarship**
● **Operations and Power Division Scholarship**
● **Charles (Tommy) Thomas Memorial Scholarship**

TYPE:
Scholarships. Award for a full-time undergraduate student in a program leading to a degree in nuclear science or nuclear engineering at an accredited institution in the U.S.

ELIGIBILITY:
U.S. and non-U.S. applicants must be ANS student members enrolled in an accredited institution in the U.S. Applicant must be a U.S. citizen or possess a permanent resident visa.

Academic accomplishments must be substantiated by transcript. Applicants must be sponsored by an ANS local section, division, student branch, committee or organization member.

Operations and Power Division Scholarship: Applicants must have completed a minimum of two complete academic years in a four-year nuclear science or engineering program.

Charles (Tommy) Thomas Memorial Scholarship: Undergraduate of at least junior-year status pursuing a degree in a discipline preparing them for a career dealing with the environmental aspects of nuclear science or nuclear engineering.

GEOG. RESTRICTIONS: United States.

FINANCIAL DATA:
Scholarship funds may be used by the student to defray any bona fide education costs including tuition, fees, books, room and board.
Amount of support per award: Raymond DiSalvo and Robert T. Liner Scholarship: $2,000; Charles (Tommy) Thomas Memorial Scholarship: $3,000; Operations and Power Division Scholarship: $2,500.

NO. AWARDS: Operations and Power Division Scholarship: 2; All others: 1 each.

APPLICATION INFO:
Applications must be submitted online.
Duration: One year. Nonrenewable.
Deadline: February 1.

ADDRESS INQUIRIES TO:
Scholarship Coordinator
(See address above.)

*PLEASE NOTE:
Scholarships are only offered to ANS student members.

AMERICAN NUCLEAR SOCIETY (ANS)
555 North Kensington Avenue
LaGrange Park, IL 60526
(708) 352-6611
Fax: (708) 352-0499
E-mail: scholarships@ans.org
Web Site: www.ans.org

TYPE:
Scholarships. Scholarship award to recognize one outstanding undergraduate student or one graduate student pursuing a career in radioanalytical chemistry or analytical applications of nuclear science.

See entry 1851 for full listing.

AMERICAN NUCLEAR SOCIETY (ANS) [2381]

555 North Kensington Avenue
LaGrange Park, IL 60526
(708) 352-6611
Fax: (708) 352-0499
E-mail: scholarships@ans.org
Web Site: www.ans.org

FOUNDED: 1954

AREAS OF INTEREST:
Nuclear science, nuclear engineering or nuclear-related fields.

NAME(S) OF PROGRAMS:
- **ANS Undergraduate Scholarships**
- **Joseph R. Dietrich Memorial Scholarship**
- **Allan F. Henry/Paul A. Greebler Memorial Scholarship**
- **John R. Lamarsh Memorial Scholarship**

TYPE:
Scholarships.

ELIGIBILITY:
U.S. and non-U.S. applicants must be ANS student members enrolled in and attending an accredited institution in the U.S. Applicants must have completed a minimum of two complete academic years in a four-year nuclear engineering program and must be U.S. citizens or possess a permanent resident visa. Academic accomplishments must be substantiated by transcript. Applicant must be sponsored by an ANS local section, division, student branch, committee or organization member.

ANS Undergraduate Scholarships and Lamarsh Memorial Scholarship are open to full-time undergraduate students in a program leading to a degree in nuclear science or nuclear engineering at an accredited institution in the U.S.

Joseph R. Dietrich Scholarship is open to a full-time graduate student in a program leading to a degree in nuclear science or nuclear engineering at an accredited institution in the U.S.

Henry/Greebler Scholarship is open to a full-time graduate student of a North American university engaged in Master's or Ph.D. research in the area of nuclear reactor physics or radiation transport. Students of all nationalities are eligible.

FINANCIAL DATA:
Scholarship funds may be used by the student to defray any bona fide education costs including tuition, fees, room and board.
Amount of support per award: ANS Undergraduate, Joseph R. Dietrich Memorial and John R. Lamarsh Memorial Scholarships: $2,000; Alan F. Henry/Paul A. Greebler Memorial Scholarship: $3,500.

NO. AWARDS: ANS Undergraduate Scholarships: Up to 5; Dietrich, Greebler and Lamarsh Memorial Scholarships: 1 each.

APPLICATION INFO:
Applications must be submitted online.
Duration: One year. Nonrenewable.
Deadline: February 1.

ADDRESS INQUIRIES TO:
Scholarship Coordinator
(See address above.)

*PLEASE NOTE:
Scholarships are only offered to ANS student members.

AMERICAN NUCLEAR SOCIETY (ANS) [2382]

555 North Kensington Avenue
LaGrange Park, IL 60526
(708) 352-6611
Fax: (708) 352-0499
E-mail: scholarships@ans.org
Web Site: www.ans.org

FOUNDED: 1954

AREAS OF INTEREST:
Nuclear science, nuclear engineering or nuclear-related field.

NAME(S) OF PROGRAMS:
- **ANS Graduate Scholarships**
- **Everitt P. Blizard Memorial Scholarship**
- **Robert A. Dannels Memorial Scholarship**
- **James F. Schumar Scholarship**

TYPE:
Scholarships. Blizard Scholarship is for students pursuing graduate studies in the field of radiation protection and shielding.

Schumar Scholarship is for a student pursuing graduate studies in material science and technology for nuclear applications.

PURPOSE:
To support higher education in the field of nuclear science.

ELIGIBILITY:
U.S. and non-U.S. applicants must be ANS student members. Applicant must be a U.S. citizen or possess a permanent resident visa, be enrolled in a U.S. university and must be sponsored by an ANS local section, division, student branch, committee or organization member. More than one applicant can be sponsored by any of these organizations.

The Dannels Scholarship is for a graduate-level course of study leading toward a degree in mathematics and computation. Only U.S. citizens or persons possessing a permanent resident visa are eligible. Nomination of handicapped persons is encouraged.

GEOG. RESTRICTIONS: United States.

FINANCIAL DATA:
Scholarship funds may be used to defray any bona fide education costs including tuition, books, room and board.

Amount of support per award: ANS Graduate, Blizard and Schumar Scholarships: $3,000 each; Dannels Scholarship: $3,500.

NO. AWARDS: ANS Graduate Scholarships: Up to 5; Blizard, Dannels and Schumar Scholarships: 1 each.

APPLICATION INFO:
Applications must be submitted online.
Duration: One year. Nonrenewable.
Deadline: February 1.

ADDRESS INQUIRIES TO:
Scholarship Coordinator
(See address above.)

*PLEASE NOTE:
Scholarships are only offered to ANS student members.

AMERICAN NUCLEAR SOCIETY (ANS) [2383]

555 North Kensington Avenue
LaGrange Park, IL 60526
(708) 352-6611
Fax: (708) 352-0499
E-mail: scholarships@ans.org
Web Site: www.ans.org

FOUNDED: 1954

AREAS OF INTEREST:
Nuclear science, nuclear engineering and nuclear-related field.

NAME(S) OF PROGRAMS:
- **Pittsburgh Local Section Scholarship**

TYPE:
Scholarships. Two Pittsburgh Local Section Scholarships: one for a graduate student (studying nuclear science and technology) and one for an undergraduate student (studying nuclear science and technology) who either have some affiliation with western Pennsylvania or who attend school at a nearby university within the region.

PURPOSE:
To support higher education in nuclear science.

ELIGIBILITY:
Applicant must be a U.S. citizen or possess a permanent resident visa, be enrolled in a U.S. college or university, and must be sponsored by an ANS local section, division, student branch, committee or organization member. More than one applicant can be sponsored by any of these organizations.

GEOG. RESTRICTIONS: Western Pennsylvania.

FINANCIAL DATA:
Scholarship funds may be used to defray any bona fide education costs including tuition, books, room and board.
Amount of support per award:
Undergraduate: $2,000; Graduate: $3,500.

NO. AWARDS: Undergraduate and Graduate: 1 each.

APPLICATION INFO:
Applications must be submitted online.
Duration: One year. Nonrenewable.
Deadline: February 1.

ADDRESS INQUIRIES TO:
Scholarship Coordinator
(See address above.)

*PLEASE NOTE:
Scholarships are only offered to ANS student members.

AMERICAN PUBLIC POWER ASSOCIATION [2384]

2451 Crystal Drive
Suite 1000
Arlington, VA 22202
(202) 467-2900
(202) 467-2960
Fax: (202) 467-2910
E-mail: deed@publicpower.org
Web Site: www.publicpower.org/deed

FOUNDED: 1980

AREAS OF INTEREST:
Engineering, mathematics and computer science.

NAME(S) OF PROGRAMS:
- **DEED Interships**
- **Educational Scholarship**

- **Student Research Grant**
- **Technical Design Project**

TYPE:
Demonstration grants; Development grants; Internships; Project/program grants; Research grants; Scholarships.

YEAR PROGRAM STARTED: 1980

PURPOSE:
To promote the involvement of students studying in energy-related disciplines in the public power industry; to provide host utilities with technical assistance.

ELIGIBILITY:
Open to students conducting research on a project approved by the sponsoring utility who will then submit a final report on the project, describing the activities, cost, bibliography, achievements, problems, results and recommendations. Applicants will not be discriminated against on the basis of sex, race, religion, national origin or citizenship.

Student must be accepted or enrolled in an accredited technical/trade/vocational school, community college, or four-year university in the U.S.

FINANCIAL DATA:
Amount of support per award: DEED Internships and Student Research Grant: $4,000; Educational Scholarship: $2,000; Technical Design Project: $5,000.
Total amount of support: Varies.

NO. MOST RECENT APPLICANTS: 37.

NO. AWARDS: 33.

APPLICATION INFO:
Applications must be sent from a DEED member utility and must be dated on the last page by an authorized individual at the utility.
Deadline: Spring cycle: Applications accepted December 1 to February 15; Fall cycle: Applications accepted August 1 to October 15.

ADDRESS INQUIRIES TO:
DEED Team
(See address above.)

AMERICAN SOCIETY FOR ENGINEERING EDUCATION   [2385]
1818 N Street, N.W., Suite 600
Washington, DC 20036
(202) 350-5763
(202) 350-5757
Fax: (202) 463-1401
E-mail: postdocs@asee.org
Web Site: nrl.asee.org

FOUNDED: 1893

AREAS OF INTEREST:
Engineering education programs, scientific research in government, industry and the military.

NAME(S) OF PROGRAMS:
- **Naval Research Laboratory (NRL) Postdoctoral Fellowship Program**

TYPE:
Fellowships. Offered at Naval research and development centers and laboratories. NRL is charged with developing technologies that will support Naval Forces in meeting future operational needs. Scientists and fellows working at NRL pursue research on subjects including, but not limited to, processing, biomedicine, logistics, command control and intelligence, training and oceanography.

YEAR PROGRAM STARTED: 2002

PURPOSE:
To significantly increase the involvement of creative and highly trained scientists and engineers from academia and industry in scientific and technical areas of interest and relevance to the Navy.

LEGAL BASIS:
Special interest society.

ELIGIBILITY:
Applicants must be U.S. citizens and permanent residents and must be eligible for a Department of Defense security clearance of "Secret." In most cases, participants will be permitted to do research pending completion of the security clearance. All appointments are contingent upon fellows obtaining the appropriate level of security clearance. Prior to appointment, participants must present evidence of having received the Ph.D., Sc.D. or other earned research doctoral degree recognized in U.S. as equivalent to the Ph.D. within seven years of the date of application or must present acceptable evidence of having completed all formal academic requirements for one of these degrees. No support to applicants who received prior postdoctoral appointment under any program at the same Navy laboratory. No appointments or denials based on grounds of race, creed, color, national origin, age or sex.

GEOG. RESTRICTIONS: United States.

FINANCIAL DATA:
Awards include stipend, insurance, relocation expenses and travel.
Amount of support per award: Maximum stipend $81,548.
Total amount of support: Varies.

NO. AWARDS: Approximately 45 new appointments each year.

APPLICATION INFO:
Applicants should contact the research facility of interest to develop a suitable research proposal. Proposals developed closely with the proposed host facility stand the greatest chance of success in the selection process. A proposal should be no more than 10 pages, be concise, and address a problem of mutual interest to the applicant and Navy research facility.
Duration: One year. Renewable for a second and third year with satisfactory performance and availability of funds.

PUBLICATIONS:
Program announcement.

STAFF:
Shannon Becks, Program Director
Elisheba Wilson, Program Assistant

ADDRESS INQUIRIES TO:
NRL Postdoctoral Program
Contracts/Grants Office
(See address above.)

THE AMERICAN SOCIETY FOR NONDESTRUCTIVE TESTING, INC.
1711 Arlingate Lane
Columbus, OH 43228
(614) 274-6003
(800) 222-2768
Fax: (614) 274-6899
E-mail: james@asnt.org
Web Site: www.asnt.org

TYPE:
Scholarships.
See entry 1478 for full listing.

AMERICAN SOCIETY OF CIVIL ENGINEERS   [2386]
1801 Alexander Bell Drive
Reston, VA 20191-4400
(703) 295-6300 ext. 6382
(800) 548-2723
E-mail: awards@asce.org
Web Site: www.asce.org

FOUNDED: 1852

AREAS OF INTEREST:
Civil engineering.

NAME(S) OF PROGRAMS:
- **O.H. Ammann Research Fellowship in Structural Engineering**
- **CI Construction Engineering Scholarship and Student Prizes**
- **Lawrence W. and Francis W. Cox Scholarship**
- **Trent R. Dames and William W. Moore Fellowship**
- **Eugene C. Figg, Jr. Civil Engineering Scholarship**
- **Freeman Fellowship**
- **Jack E. Leisch Memorial National Graduate Fellowship**
- **John Lenard Civil Engineering Scholarship**
- **Robert B.B. and Josephine N. Moorman Scholarship**
- **J. Waldo Smith Hydraulic Fellowship**
- **Samuel Fletcher Tapman ASCE Student Chapter Scholarship**
- **B. Charles Tiney Memorial ASCE Student Chapter Scholarship**
- **Arthur S. Tuttle Memorial Fellowship**
- **Y.C. Yang Civil Engineering Scholarship**

TYPE:
Fellowships; Grants-in-aid; Research grants; Scholarships. Scholarships, fellowships and grants for research; undergraduate and graduate studies in civil engineering fields from ASCE endowments, operation or other funds.

Fellowships and scholarships are awarded annually.

YEAR PROGRAM STARTED: 1924

PURPOSE:
To aid and encourage education, research and studies in civil engineering.

LEGAL BASIS:
Nonprofit professional organization.

ELIGIBILITY:
Qualified engineers or engineering undergraduate or graduate students with appropriate interests are eligible to apply. Undergraduate students must be enrolled at an ABET-accredited university, be a member of an ASCE student chapter and also be a

national student member in good standing. (A list of schools that have student chapters is available from the address above.)

FINANCIAL DATA:
Amount of support per award: Varies.

APPLICATION INFO:
Application forms are available at www.asce.org/student_resources.
Duration: One year.
Deadline: Majority due close of business February 10. O.H. Ammann Research Fellowship: November 1.

PUBLICATIONS:
Scholarships/Fellowships brochure.

OFFICERS:
Thomas Smith, Executive Director

ADDRESS INQUIRIES TO:
See e-mail address above.

*SPECIAL STIPULATIONS:
Requires ASCE membership of some kind.

THE AMERICAN SOCIETY OF MECHANICAL ENGINEERS AUXILIARY, INC.   [2387]
2 Park Avenue, MS-RB
New York, NY 10016-5990
(212) 591-7650
E-mail: bigleyr@asme.org
Web Site: go.asme.org/scholarships

FOUNDED: 1923

AREAS OF INTEREST:
Mechanical engineering students.

NAME(S) OF PROGRAMS:
- **Allen J. Baldwin Scholarship**
- **Berna Lou Cartwright Scholarship**
- **Carolyn and James M. Chenoweth Scholarship**
- **Lucy and Charles W.E. Clarke Scholarship**
- **Sylvia W. Farny Scholarship**
- **Agnes Malakate Kezios Scholarship**
- **Elisabeth M. and Winchell M. Parsons Scholarship**
- **Marjorie Roy Rothermel Scholarship**
- **Charles B. Scharp Scholarship**
- **Student Loan Fund**
- **Myrna R. and Sam Y. Zamrik Scholarship**

TYPE:
Scholarships. Lucy and Charles W.E. Clarke Scholarship is for high school seniors participating on a FIRST team.

Baldwin, Cartwright, Chenoweth, Farny, Kezios, Scharp and Zamrik Scholarships are for undergraduate students in mechanical engineering.

Parsons and Rothermel Scholarships are for graduate students with a degree in mechanical engineering, to be used to pursue a Master's or Ph.D. degree in mechanical engineering.

Student Loan Fund is for juniors, seniors or graduate students enrolled as degree candidates in good standing.

YEAR PROGRAM STARTED: 1924

PURPOSE:
To give financial assistance to mechanical engineering students.

LEGAL BASIS:
Not-for-profit organization.

ELIGIBILITY:
Applicants must be U.S. citizens, enrolled in a degree program in a school with accredited mechanical engineering curriculum and members of the ASME for scholarships and student loans.

FINANCIAL DATA:
Amount of support per award: Lucy and Charles W.E. Clarke Scholarship: $7,000. All other Scholarships: $3,000; Student Loans: $10,000 maximum.
Total amount of support: Varies.

NO. MOST RECENT APPLICANTS: Undergraduate Scholarships: 15; Parsons and Rothermel: 10.

NO. AWARDS: Undergraduate Scholarships: 14; Parsons Scholarship: 2; Rothermel Scholarship: 4 for the academic year 2021-22.

APPLICATION INFO:
Applicants may contact the Society or review scholarship details online.
Duration: One year. Nonrenewable.
Deadline: Contact the Auxiliary for individual scholarship deadlines and notification dates.

PUBLICATIONS:
Application guidelines; scholarship forms; applications.

OFFICERS:
Ella Baldwin-Viereck, President
Ada Ezekoye, Executive Vice President
Stella Seiders, Treasurer
Ed Seiders, Student Loan Fund Treasurer
Vatsala Menon, Recording Secretary
Lynn Gerber, Corresponding Secretary

ADDRESS INQUIRIES TO:
RuthAnn Bigley
Manager, Governance Programs
(See address above.)

AMERICAN SOCIETY OF NAVAL ENGINEERS (ASNE)   [2388]
1423 Powhatan Street
Suite 1
Alexandria, VA 22314
(703) 836-6727
E-mail: scholarships@navalengineers.org
Web Site: www.navalengineers.org

FOUNDED: 1888

AREAS OF INTEREST:
Naval Engineering includes all arts and sciences as applied in the research, development, design, construction, operation, maintenance and logistic support of surface and sub-surface ships and marine craft, naval maritime auxiliaries, aviation and space systems, combat systems, command control, electronics and ordnance systems, ocean structures and associated shore facilities, which are used by naval and other military forces and civilian maritime organizations for the defense and well-being of the Nation.

CONSULTING OR VOLUNTEER SERVICES:
Volunteer Services.

NAME(S) OF PROGRAMS:
- **ASNE Scholarship Program**

TYPE:
Scholarships. Stipend for tuition, fees and expenses to follow a full-time or co-op program of study that applies to naval engineering, such as naval architecture, marine engineering, ocean engineering, mechanical engineering, structural engineering, electrical engineering, electronic

engineering and the physical sciences, as well as other programs leading to careers with civilian and military maritime organizations supporting and developing work and life at sea.

YEAR PROGRAM STARTED: 1979

PURPOSE:
To encourage college students to enter the field of naval engineering; to support naval engineers seeking advanced education in the field.

LEGAL BASIS:
Nonprofit professional society.

ELIGIBILITY:
Support will be limited to the last year of undergraduate education or one year of graduate education in an accredited college or university. Candidates must be U.S. citizens and must have demonstrated or expressed a genuine interest in a career in naval engineering. Graduate students must be members of ASNE or SNAME and may apply at time of application.

Selection criteria will be based on academic record, work history, professional promise and interest in naval engineering, extracurricular activities, recommendations of college faculty, employers and other character references. Demonstrated financial need is not a requirement, but it may be taken into consideration by the Scholarship Committee.

A scholarship will not be awarded to a doctoral candidate or to a person already having an advanced degree.

GEOG. RESTRICTIONS: United States.

FINANCIAL DATA:
The award will be in the form of a check for the first academic period payable jointly to the awardee and the college or university that the student will attend. Transcripts showing satisfactory performance constitute the basis for further awards for subsequent academic periods.
Amount of support per award: $4,000 per year.

NO. AWARDS: Varies.

APPLICATION INFO:
Application information is available on the Society's web site.
Duration: One year.
Deadline: February 28. Notification by early May.

PUBLICATIONS:
Naval Engineers Journal.

IRS I.D.: 53-0229465

EXECUTIVE DIRECTOR:
Dale Lumme

ADDRESS INQUIRIES TO:
ASNE Scholarship Committee
(See address above.)

AMERICAN SOCIETY OF SAFETY PROFESSIONALS [2389]
520 North Northwest Highway
Park Ridge, IL 60068
(847) 699-2929
Fax: (847) 296-9221
E-mail: copa@assp.org
Web Site: www.assp.org

FOUNDED: 1911

AREAS OF INTEREST:
Occupational safety and health.

NAME(S) OF PROGRAMS:
- **Safety Professional of the Year Award**

TYPE:
Awards/prizes. Cash honorarium to Society-selected award winners.

YEAR PROGRAM STARTED: 1980

PURPOSE:
To recognize exemplary achievements in Safety, Health and Environmental (SHE) Education.

LEGAL BASIS:
Not-for-profit professional society.

ELIGIBILITY:
Nominees must be active dues-paying professional members or members of the Society, domestic or international, and cannot have received this award within the past five years. The Society President is not eligible for the award until five years after he or she has left the Board of Directors. ASSE Fellows and members currently serving on the Society Technical and Professional Recognition Committee and/or the Board of Directors are ineligible.

FINANCIAL DATA:
Amount of support per award: $2,000 honorarium and an engraved statuette.

NO. MOST RECENT APPLICANTS: 9.

NO. AWARDS: 1 each year.

APPLICATION INFO:
Nominations must be submitted electronically. Individual members, chapters, regions, practice specialty, councils or the Society Board of Directors may submit them. Must be accompanied by a letter of endorsement from the nominating colleague (Chapter, Regional Operating Committees, Practice Specialty, Councils or the Society Board of Directors), as well as the immediate employment supervisor, a single-page resume, plus a petition listing the nominee's achievements.
Deadline: November 1. Award announcement in early May.

ADDRESS INQUIRIES TO:
Laura Clements
Director of External Affairs
(See address above.)

ASM MATERIALS EDUCATION FOUNDATION
9639 Kinsman Road
Materials Park, OH 44073-0002
(440) 338-5151
(800) 336-5152
Fax: (440) 338-4634
E-mail: jeane.deatherage@asminternational.org
Web Site: www.asmfoundation.org

TYPE:
Scholarships.

See entry 2420 for full listing.

CANADIAN SOCIETY FOR CHEMICAL ENGINEERING   [2390]
222 Queen Street
Suite 1009
Ottawa ON K1P 5V9 Canada
(613) 232-6252
Fax: (613) 232-5862
E-mail: awards@cheminst.ca
Web Site: www.cheminst.ca/awards

FOUNDED: 1945

AREAS OF INTEREST:
Chemical engineering.

NAME(S) OF PROGRAMS:
- **The CSChE Chemical Engineering Local Section Scholarships**
- **ZETON Plant Design Competition**

TYPE:
Scholarships. The CSChE Chemical Engineering Local Section Scholarships are offered to undergraduate students in chemical engineering about to enter the final year of studies at a Canadian university.

The ZETON Plant Design Competition is offered to students enrolled in undergraduate chemical engineering programs at Canadian universities.

PURPOSE:
To promote undergraduate study in chemical engineering and provide financial support for that study.

LEGAL BASIS:
Special interest society.

ELIGIBILITY:
Applicants for the CSChE Chemical Engineering Local Section Scholarships must be undergraduate students in chemical engineering entering their final year of studies at a Canadian university. The scholarship will look at academic performance, leadership qualities, and demonstrated contributions to the Society. Applicants must be paid undergraduate student members of the Canadian Society for Chemical Engineering.

Applicants for the ZETON Plant Design Competition must be individuals and groups of undergraduate students registered in chemical engineering programs in Canadian universities during the current academic year. Applicants must be student members of the CSChE. To minimize the number of projects to be judged, each chemical engineering department may submit no more than two entries.

GEOG. RESTRICTIONS: Canada.

FINANCIAL DATA:
Amount of support per award: Chemical Engineering Local Section: $2,000; ZETON Plant Design Competition: $1,000 for first place and $500 for second place. Each member of the top three teams will receive a certificate.

NO. AWARDS: Local Section Scholarships: 2; ZETON Plant Design Competition: 3.

APPLICATION INFO:
For the CSChE Chemical Engineering Local Section Scholarships, application letters should document contributions to the Society. Applicant must provide a transcript of academic performance and two letters of support, along with the application letter. Applications must be submitted electronically.

Entries for the ZETON Plant Design Competition must be submitted electronically and must include the following:
(1) a letter from the head of the department indicating that the information is not confidential;
(2) a list of students who performed the work along with their permanent addresses and e-mail addresses;
(3) an executive summary of the project, including a simplified flow sheet of the process;
(4) a copy of the final report submitted to the university at the end of the project and;
(5) names of any collaborating organization/engineers who assisted the students.
Deadline: Local Section Scholarships: April 30; ZETON Competition: July 31.

PUBLICATIONS:
Announcement.

ADDRESS INQUIRIES TO:
Awards Manager
(See address above.)

CHEMICAL INSTITUTE OF CANADA
222 Queen Street
Suite 1009
Ottawa ON K1P 5V9 Canada
(613) 232-6252
Fax: (613) 232-5862
E-mail: awards@cheminst.ca
Web Site: www.cheminst.ca/awards

TYPE:
Awards/prizes. The Environment Division Early Career Research Award recognizes an outstanding early career researcher who has made distinguished contributions in the fields of environmental chemistry or environmental chemical engineering, while working in any sector in Canada, e.g., academic, government, industry, for-profit, non-for-profit, private or public sector.

See entry 1857 for full listing.

GEORGE WASHINGTON UNIVERSITY   [2391]
Department of Electrical and Computer Engineering
Science and Engineering Hall
800 22nd Street N.W., Suite 5000
Washington, DC 20052
(202) 994-6083
Fax: (202) 994-0227
E-mail: ece@gwu.edu
Web Site: www.ece.seas.gwu.edu

FOUNDED: 1821

AREAS OF INTEREST:
Electrical engineering, computer engineering, and telecommunications.

NAME(S) OF PROGRAMS:
- **Graduate Teaching Assistantships**

TYPE:
Assistantships. Merit-based awards for graduate studies at George Washington University.

PURPOSE:
To attract high-quality graduate students.

LEGAL BASIS:
University.

ELIGIBILITY:
Usually for currently enrolled students. Some fellowships are limited to U.S. citizens. Must have a grade point average of 3.5 on a possible scale of 4.0 and have taken the Graduate Record Examination.

GEOG. RESTRICTIONS: United States.

FINANCIAL DATA:
Amount of support per award: Varies.
Total amount of support: Varies.

APPLICATION INFO:
Graduate students should submit an application for admission to the School of Engineering and Applied Science.
Duration: One academic year. Must reapply for additional funding.

OFFICERS:
Suresh Subramanian, Department Chair

ADDRESS INQUIRIES TO:
Robert Baden
Department Operations Manager
Tel: (202) 994-5905
E-mail: robbaden@gwu.edu

GREAT MINDS IN STEM
5211 East Washington Boulevard
Suite 2, No. 320
Los Angeles, CA 90040
(323) 262-0997
E-mail: scholars@greatmindsinstem.org
Web Site: www.greatmindsinstem.org
gmis-scholars.org

TYPE:
Scholarships.

See entry 2355 for full listing.

INSTITUTE OF INDUSTRIAL AND SYSTEMS ENGINEERS (IISE)   [2392]
3577 Parkway Lane
Building 5, Suite 200
Norcross, GA 30092
(770) 349-1102
Fax: (770) 441-3295
E-mail: bcameron@iise.org
Web Site: www.iise.org

FOUNDED: 1948

AREAS OF INTEREST:
Industrial engineering.

NAME(S) OF PROGRAMS:
- **CISE Undergraduate Scholarship**
- **John S.W. Fargher Scholarship**
- **C.B. Gambrell Undergraduate Scholarship**
- **Dwight D. Garden Scholarship**
- **Gilbreth Memorial Fellowship**
- **IISE Council of Fellows Undergraduate Scholarship**
- **IISE Fellows William Biles, Hamid Parsaei and Victor Zaloom Endowed Scholarship**
- **John L. Imhoff Scholarship**
- **Henry and Elisabeth Kroeze Memorial Scholarship**
- **Harold and Inge Marcus Scholarship**
- **Marvin Mundel Memorial Scholarship**
- **Presidents Scholarship**
- **A.O. Putnam Memorial Scholarship**
- **Vinod and Gail Sahney Scholarship**
- **E.J. Sierleja Memorial Fellowship**
- **Society for Health Systems Scholarship**
- **United Parcel Service Scholarship for Female Students**
- **United Parcel Service Scholarship for Minority Students**
- **Lisa Zaken Award of Excellence**

TYPE:
Fellowships; Scholarships. The Institute supports the advancement of engineering education and research through scholarships and fellowships to recognize and support these types of endeavors.

PURPOSE:
To recognize graduate and undergraduate industrial engineering students for academic excellence and campus leadership.

LEGAL BASIS:
Nonprofit, international professional membership society.

ELIGIBILITY:
Candidates must be active Institute members enrolled full-time in graduate or undergraduate industrial engineering programs. The nominee's scholastic ability, character, leadership, service, and financial need are all considered.

Membership is not required for the Imhoff Scholarship.

FINANCIAL DATA:
Amount of support per award: Varies per award.

NO. MOST RECENT APPLICANTS: 28.

NO. AWARDS: 18.

APPLICATION INFO:
Students may not apply directly for scholarships. They must be nominated by their department head or faculty advisor. Nominations must be mailed to the Institute. Call for nominations are sent out at the beginning of each school year in the fall.
Duration: One academic year.
Deadline: Vinod and Gail Sahney Scholarship: December 31. Society for Health Systems Scholarship: December 1. All others: November 15 (postmark).

STAFF:
Don Greene, Chief Executive Officer

ADDRESS INQUIRIES TO:
Bonnie Cameron
Headquarters Operations Administrator
(See address above.)

THE JAMES F. LINCOLN ARC WELDING FOUNDATION   [2393]
22801 St. Clair Avenue
Cleveland, OH 44117
(216) 481-8100
Fax: (216) 486-6476
E-mail: lori_hurley@lincolnelectric.com
Web Site: www.lincolnelectric.com
www.jflf.org

FOUNDED: 1936

AREAS OF INTEREST:
Engineering, welded design and fabrication.

NAME(S) OF PROGRAMS:
- **Awards for Achievement in Arc Welded Design, Engineering and Fabrication: College Division**

TYPE:
Awards/prizes. Awards to recognize and reward achievement by engineering and technology students (graduate and undergraduate) in solving design, engineering or fabricating problems involving the knowledge or application of arc welding.

YEAR PROGRAM STARTED: 1956

PURPOSE:
To recognize outstanding work in the welding design and fabrication field.

LEGAL BASIS:
Private corporate foundation.

ELIGIBILITY:
Graduate or undergraduate students enrolled in college or university programs leading to a

Bachelor's, Master's or doctoral degree may submit papers completed within a one-year period, ending June 30 of the year of the contest. Papers should represent students' work on design, engineering or fabrication problems relating to any type of building, bridge or other generally stationary structure, any type of machine, product or mechanical apparatus or arc welding research, testing, procedure or process development.

Students to participate in the Undergraduate Division must be enrolled in a four-year or longer curriculum leading to a Bachelor's degree. Students to participate in the Graduate Division must be enrolled in a graduate program leading to a Master's or Doctorate degree. Qualified students may apply individually or jointly in groups of not more than six. Undergraduate students compete for 17 awards, and graduate students compete for 12 awards.

GEOG. RESTRICTIONS: United States.

FINANCIAL DATA:
Amount of support per award: $50 to $1,000.
Total amount of support: Varies.

NO. AWARDS: Varies.

APPLICATION INFO:
Official application materials are available upon request to the Secretary. Any number of entries may be submitted from one school, but no student may participate in more than one entry.
Deadline: June 30.

EXECUTIVE STAFF:
Leslie Brown, President
Jason Scales, Executive Director
Lori Hurley, Secretary

ADDRESS INQUIRIES TO:
Lori Hurley, Secretary
(See address above.)

LOS ALAMOS NATIONAL LABORATORY
P.O. Box 1663
MS-P290
Los Alamos, NM 87545
(505) 665-6406
E-mail: hrstaffing-postdocs@lanl.gov
Web Site: www.lanl.gov/science/postdocs

TYPE:
Fellowships. The Distinguished Postdoctoral Fellowships provide the opportunity for the recipients to collaborate with LANL scientists and engineers on staff-initiated research. Candidates for these awards must display extraordinary ability in scientific research and show clear and definite promise of becoming outstanding leaders in the research they pursue.

See entry 1635 for full listing.

NATIONAL ACTION COUNCIL FOR MINORITIES IN ENGINEERING, INC. (NACME)   [2394]
1432 Duke Street
Alexandria, VA 22314
(914) 539-4010
Fax: (914) 539-4032
E-mail: scholarships@nacme.org
Web Site: www.nacme.org

FOUNDED: 1974

AREAS OF INTEREST:
Engineering.

CONSULTING OR VOLUNTEER SERVICES:
NACME communicates and cooperates with the precollege, college and industry communities that are involved in the minority engineering effort.

NAME(S) OF PROGRAMS:
● **NACME Bridge Scholarship**

TYPE:
Block grants; Scholarships. The NACME Bridge Scholarship program is designed to support students who have received and accepted freshman admission to an undergraduate engineering or computer science program at a NACME Partner Institution and have been invited to attend a residential academic program the summer prior to freshman matriculation. The scholarship covers the published cost of participation of the Bridge program.

PURPOSE:
To enhance awareness of the engineering profession among students, parents, teachers, and guidance counselors; to recognize high school graduating seniors who have achieved exemplary academic performance and have decided to pursue an engineering education.

LEGAL BASIS:
Nonprofit organization incorporated in New York.

ELIGIBILITY:
Student must be a high school senior applying to an engineering or computer science program at a NACME Partner Institution. U.S. citizenship or permanent residency is required. Student must have a cumulative grade point average of 2.8.

GEOG. RESTRICTIONS: United States.

FINANCIAL DATA:
Amount of support per award: $1,000.

NO. MOST RECENT APPLICANTS: Varies.

NO. AWARDS: Varies.

APPLICATION INFO:
To apply for any NACME scholarship, block grant, bridge, corporate named scholarship or special named scholarship, an updated NACME common application must be on file.
Duration: One-time award.
Deadline: January 15.

STAFF:
Michele Lezama, President and Chief Executive Officer
Aisha Lawrey, Senior Director, Programs and Scholarships
Kevin G. Smith, Program Manager, Professional Development
Felisha Britton, Program Manager, Scholarships

ADDRESS INQUIRIES TO:
Felisha Britton
Program Manager, Scholarships
E-mail: scholars@nacme.org

NATIONAL ACTION COUNCIL FOR MINORITIES IN ENGINEERING, INC. (NACME)   [2395]
1432 Duke Street
Alexandria, VA 22314
(914) 539-4010
Fax: (914) 539-4032
E-mail: scholarships@nacme.org
Web Site: www.nacme.org

FOUNDED: 1974

AREAS OF INTEREST:
Engineering and computer science.

CONSULTING OR VOLUNTEER SERVICES:
NACME communicates and cooperates with the precollege, college and industry communities that are involved in the minority engineering effort.

NAME(S) OF PROGRAMS:
● **Bechtel Engineering Scholarship**
● **Chevron/Diversity Association Scholarship Program**
● **Ford-HS Bridge Scholars**
● **Sidney and Katherine Friend Scholarship**
● **GE Foundation Engineering Scholarship**
● **William Randolph Hearst Endowment Scholarship**
● **Phillip D. Reed Undergraduate Endowment Fellowship**

TYPE:
Fellowships; Scholarships. Chevron/Diversity Association Scholarship Program awards current matriculating students in engineering, specifically mechanical, chemical, electrical, civil and petroleum as well as computer science (and qualifying information technology programs), who have the potential to excel as scholars, leaders and potential contributors to Chevron Corporation. Assessment will be based on academic merit and leadership potential.

Sidney and Katherine Friend Scholarship is a joint endowment established between NACME and New York University, Tandon School of Engineering.

William Randolph Hearst Endowment Scholarship is supported by the William Randolph Hearst Foundation.

Phillip D. Reed Undergraduate Endowment Fellowship is made possible through an endowment from the Phillip D. Reed Foundation.

PURPOSE:
To increase the representation of underrepresented minorities in engineering and computer science.

LEGAL BASIS:
Nonprofit organization incorporated in New York.

ELIGIBILITY:
To be eligible for any NACME administered scholarship, students must be either a high school senior applying to an engineering or computer science program at a NACME Partner Institution or be currently matriculating in an engineering or computer science program at a NACME Partner Institution, a U.S. citizen or permanent resident, and have a minimum high school cumulative grade point average of 3.0 (some named scholarships may have other grade point average requirements).

GEOG. RESTRICTIONS: United States.

FINANCIAL DATA:
Amount of support per award: Bechtel Engineering, Chevron/Diversity Association, GE Foundation Engineering and Reed: $5,000; Ford-HS Bridge Scholars, Friend and Hearst: $2,500.

NO. AWARDS: Varies.

APPLICATION INFO:
An updated NACME common application must be on file.

Duration: Bechtel Engineering, Chevron/Diversity Association and GE Foundation Engineering: One-time award. Friend: One year. Renewable up to five years. Ford-HS Bridge Scholars and Hearst: One year. Renewable up to four years. Reed: One year. Renewable up to three years.
Deadline: October 30.

STAFF:
Michele Lezama, President and Chief Executive Officer
Aisha Lawrey, Senior Director, Programs and Scholarships
Kevin G. Smith, Program Manager, Professional Development
Felisha Britton, Program Manager, Scholarships

ADDRESS INQUIRIES TO:
Felisha Britton
Program Manager, Scholarships
E-mail: scholars@nacme.org

THE NATIONAL GEM CONSORTIUM
1430 Duke Street
Alexandria, VA 22314
(703) 562-3646
Fax: (202) 207-3518
E-mail: info@gemfellowship.org
Web Site: www.gemfellowship.org

TYPE:
Fellowships; Internships; Travel grants. Future Faculty and Professionals (FFP) Symposium is a career development program for future faculty members and industry professionals. The goal is to provide graduate students with improved research and career competitiveness, tools and metrics for greater control in career planning, and to gain access to a powerful network of peers and mentors. Travel grants provide current GEM Fellow or non-Fellow graduate students the opportunity to take advantage of the program focused specifically on their needs, and support successful matriculation to completion of their graduate STEM degree.

G.E.M Fellowships provide all-expenses for graduate study (tuition and stipend) and paid summer work experience in a scientific or engineering environment.

See entry 911 for full listing.

NATIONAL RESEARCH COUNCIL OF CANADA
1200 Montreal Road, Building M-58
Room E-109
Ottawa ON K1A 0R6 Canada
(613) 993-9101
E-mail: info@nrc-cnrc.gc.ca
racoordinator.hrb@nrc-cnrc.gc.ca
Web Site: www.nrc-cnrc.gc.ca

TYPE:
Associateships. Research Associate Program provides promising scientists and engineers with the opportunity to work in a challenging research environment during the early stages of their career. Applicants will be selected competitively and must demonstrate the ability to perform original, high-quality research in their chosen field.

Research Associates will be offered appointments to the staff of the National Research Council on a term basis and will be offered salaries and benefits currently available to Research Officers.

See entry 1641 for full listing.

NATIONAL SCIENCE FOUNDATION [2396]

Directorate for Engineering
Office of Assistant Director
2415 Eisenhower Avenue
Arlington, VA 22314
(703) 292-8300
Fax: (703) 292-9467
Web Site: www.nsf.gov

FOUNDED: 1950

AREAS OF INTEREST:
Chemical, biochemical and thermal
engineering, mechanics, structures and
materials engineering, electrical,
communications and systems engineering,
design, manufacturing and computer
engineering, emerging engineering systems,
cross-disciplinary research, engineering
research centers, civil and environment
engineering, earthquake engineering and
small business innovation research.

NAME(S) OF PROGRAMS:
● **Directorate for Engineering Grants Program**

TYPE:
Project/program grants; Research grants.

YEAR PROGRAM STARTED: 1984

PURPOSE:
To strengthen U.S. engineering education and
research; to focus on areas relevant to
national problems by supporting research
across the entire range of engineering
disciplines and by identifying areas where
results are expected to have timely
applications.

LEGAL BASIS:
Government agency.

ELIGIBILITY:
Proposals may be submitted by colleges,
universities, profit and nonprofit organizations
and by state, local or regional governments.
Industry, state and local governments and
other organizations are eligible to participate.
Joint proposals are encouraged.

NSF does not make loans or grants to
develop or promote any business venture,
technical assistance, pilot plant efforts,
research requiring security classification, the
development of products for commercial
marketing or market research for a particular
product or invention.

GEOG. RESTRICTIONS: United States and its
territories.

FINANCIAL DATA:
Amount of support per award: $2,000 to
$5,000,000. Average $63,000.
Total amount of support: Varies.

APPLICATION INFO:
Informal inquiry to the Directorate for
Engineering may be made to determine
whether or not a potential project would
qualify for support.
Duration: One to five years. Average is
approximately 30 months.
Deadline: Varies. Approximately six to eight
months are required for consideration of
formal proposals.

PUBLICATIONS:
Grants for Research and Education in
Science and Engineering; Guide to Programs.

ADDRESS INQUIRIES TO:
Directorate for Engineering
(See address above.)

NATIONAL SOCIETY OF PROFESSIONAL SURVEYORS (NSPS) [2397]

5119 Pegasus Court
Suite Q
Frederick, MD 21704
(240) 439-4615 ext. 105
Fax: (240) 439-4952
E-mail: info@nsps.us.com
Web Site: www.nsps.us.com

FOUNDED: 1986

AREAS OF INTEREST:
Surveying and surveying technology.

NAME(S) OF PROGRAMS:
● **The Berntsen International Scholarship in Surveying Technology**

TYPE:
Scholarships. Berntsen International
Scholarship in Surveying Technology is for
students enrolled in two-year degree
programs in surveying technology.
Scholarship awarded in even years only.

PURPOSE:
To provide financial assistance to students
pursuing two- or four-year degree programs
in surveying, surveying technology or closely
related fields.

LEGAL BASIS:
Nonprofit, educational organization.

ELIGIBILITY:
Student applicants must be enrolled in
two-year degree programs in surveying
technology.

GEOG. RESTRICTIONS: United States.

FINANCIAL DATA:
Amount of support per award: $2,000.

CO-OP FUNDING PROGRAMS: Scholarships are
made possible by Berntsen International, Inc.,
of Madison, WI.

NO. MOST RECENT APPLICANTS: 20.

NO. AWARDS: 1 in even-numbered years.

APPLICATION INFO:
Required documentation includes:
(1) a completed application form;
(2) proof of student membership in NSPS
(this will be checked);
(3) a brief yet complete statement indicating
educational objectives, future plans of study
or research, professional activities and
financial need;
(4) three letters of recommendation (at least
two from faculty members familiar with the
student's work) and;
(5) a complete original official transcript
through the end of the school year prior to
when the award will be presented; in
addition, send unofficial transcripts for the
fall semester when available.

Do not send applications by fax or e-mail.
Mail all documents in one envelope.
Incomplete or improperly completed
applications will be discarded.

Duration: One academic year.

Deadline: February 15.

ADDRESS INQUIRIES TO:
Patricia Milburn, Office Manager
(See telephone and e-mail address above.)

NATIONAL SOCIETY OF PROFESSIONAL SURVEYORS (NSPS) [2398]

5119 Pegasus Court
Suite Q
Frederick, MD 21704
(240) 439-4615 ext. 105
Fax: (240) 439-4952
E-mail: info@nsps.us.com
Web Site: www.nsps.us.com

FOUNDED: 1986

AREAS OF INTEREST:
Surveying.

NAME(S) OF PROGRAMS:
● **The Schonstedt Scholarship in Surveying**

TYPE:
Scholarships. For students enrolled in
four-year degree programs in surveying or in
closely related degree programs such as
geomatics or surveying engineering.

PURPOSE:
To encourage and recognize students
committed to a career in surveying.

LEGAL BASIS:
Nonprofit educational organization.

ELIGIBILITY:
The Schonstedt Scholarship is for students
enrolled in four-year degree programs in
surveying or in closely related degree
programs such as geomatics or surveying
engineering. Preference will be given to
applicants with junior or senior standing.

GEOG. RESTRICTIONS: United States, Canada
and South America.

FINANCIAL DATA:
Amount of support per award: $2,000.

Total amount of support: $2,000 annually.

CO-OP FUNDING PROGRAMS: Scholarship is
made possible by a donation from the
Schonstedt Instrument Company of
Kearneysville, WV.

NO. MOST RECENT APPLICANTS: 32.

NO. AWARDS: 1 annually.

APPLICATION INFO:
Required documentation includes:
(1) a completed application form;
(2) proof of student membership in NSPS
(this will be checked);
(3) a brief yet complete statement indicating
educational objectives, future plans of study
or research, professional activities and
financial need;
(4) three letters of recommendation (at least
two from faculty members familiar with the
student's work) and;
(5) a complete original official transcript
through the end of the school year prior to
when the award will be presented; in
addition, send unofficial transcripts for the
fall semester when available.

Do not send applications by fax or e-mail.
Mail all documents in one envelope.
Incomplete or improperly completed
applications will be discarded.

Duration: One academic year.

Deadline: February 15.

ADDRESS INQUIRIES TO:
Patricia Milburn, Office Manager
(See telephone and e-mail address above.)

NATIONAL SOCIETY OF PROFESSIONAL SURVEYORS (NSPS) [2399]

5119 Pegasus Court
Suite Q
Frederick, MD 21704
(240) 439-4615 ext. 105
Fax: (240) 439-4952
E-mail: info@nsps.us.com
Web Site: www.nsps.us.com

FOUNDED: 1986

AREAS OF INTEREST:
Surveying.

NAME(S) OF PROGRAMS:
● **NSPS Board of Directors Scholarship**
● **The NSPS Scholarship**

TYPE:
Scholarships.

PURPOSE:
To recognize outstanding surveying students; to encourage qualified candidates to pursue an undergraduate degree in surveying.

LEGAL BASIS:
Nonprofit foundation.

ELIGIBILITY:
NSPS Board of Directors Scholarship applicants must be enrolled in studies in surveying or in closely related degree programs and entering their junior year of study in a four-year degree program of their choice (either full- or part-time) and must have maintained a minimum 3.0 grade point average.

The NSPS Scholarship is awarded in even-numbered years to students enrolled in four-year degree programs in surveying or in closely related degree programs such as geomatics or surveying engineering. The Scholarship is intended to recognize an outstanding student enrolled full-time in undergraduate surveying programs.

GEOG. RESTRICTIONS: United States.

FINANCIAL DATA:
Amount of support per award: $2,000 per scholarship.

NO. MOST RECENT APPLICANTS: 34.

NO. AWARDS: NSPS Board of Directors Scholarship: 1 (awarded in even-numbered years only); The NSPS Scholarship: 1.

APPLICATION INFO:
Applicants must submit (in the following order):
(1) a completed application form;
(2) proof of student membership in NSPS (this will be checked);
(3) a brief yet complete statement indicating educational objectives, future plans of study or research, professional activities and financial need;
(4) three letters of recommendation (at least two from faculty members familiar with the student's work) and;
(5) a complete original official transcript through the end of the school year prior to when the award will be presented; in addition, send unofficial transcripts for the fall semester when available.

Do not send applications by fax or e-mail. Mail all documents in one envelope. Incomplete or improperly completed applications will be discarded.
Duration: One academic year.
Deadline: February 15.

ADDRESS INQUIRIES TO:
Patricia Milburn, Office Manager
(See telephone and e-mail address above.)

NATIONAL SOCIETY OF PROFESSIONAL SURVEYORS (NSPS) AMERICAN ASSOCIATION FOR GEODETIC SURVEYING (AAGS) [2400]

5119 Pegasus Court
Suite Q
Frederick, MD 21704
(240) 439-4615 ext. 105
Fax: (240) 439-4952
E-mail: info@nsps.us.com
Web Site: www.aagsmo.org
www.nsps.us.com

FOUNDED: 1986

AREAS OF INTEREST:
Geodetic surveying.

NAME(S) OF PROGRAMS:
● **American Association for Geodetic Surveying (AAGS) Graduate Fellowship Award**

TYPE:
Fellowships. Annual fellowship award to support graduate study in a program with a significant focus on geodetic surveying or geodesy at a school of the recipient's choice.

PURPOSE:
To recognize outstanding graduate students committed to the pursuit of knowledge in geodetic surveying, thus enhancing the ability of the profession to better serve the needs of society.

LEGAL BASIS:
Nonprofit educational organization.

ELIGIBILITY:
Nominees must be members of the American Association for Geodetic Surveying (AAGS) and should be enrolled in or accepted by a graduate program in geodetic surveying or geodesy. Preference will be given to applicants having at least two years of employment experience in the surveying profession.

GEOG. RESTRICTIONS: United States, Canada and South America.

FINANCIAL DATA:
Amount of support per award: $2,000 and an appropriate citation to be presented at the annual meeting.
Total amount of support: $2,000 annually.

CO-OP FUNDING PROGRAMS: Provided by the American Association for Geodetic Surveying and administered by NSPS Foundation.

NO. MOST RECENT APPLICANTS: 4.

NO. AWARDS: 1 annually.

APPLICATION INFO:
Required documentation includes:
(1) a completed application form;
(2) proof of student membership in AAGS (this will be checked);
(3) a brief yet complete statement indicating educational objectives, future plans of study or research, professional activities and financial need;
(4) three letters of recommendation (at least two from faculty members familiar with the student's work) and;
(5) a complete original official transcript through the end of the school year prior to

when the award will be presented; in addition, send unofficial transcripts for the fall semester when available.

Do not send applications by fax or e-mail. Mail all documents in one envelope. Incomplete or improperly completed applications will be discarded.
Duration: One academic year.
Deadline: February 15.

PUBLICATIONS:
Surveying and Land Information Science Journal.

ADDRESS INQUIRIES TO:
Patricia Milburn, Office Manager
(See telephone and e-mail address above.)

NATIONAL SOCIETY OF PROFESSIONAL SURVEYORS (NSPS) AMERICAN ASSOCIATION FOR GEODETIC SURVEYING (AAGS) [2401]

5119 Pegasus Court
Suite Q
Frederick, MD 21704
(240) 439-4615 ext. 105
Fax: (240) 439-4952
E-mail: info@nsps.us.com
Web Site: www.aagsmo.org
www.nsps.us.com

FOUNDED: 1986

AREAS OF INTEREST:
Geodetic surveying.

NAME(S) OF PROGRAMS:
● **AAGS Joseph F. Dracup Scholarship Award**

TYPE:
Scholarships. The award is intended for students enrolled in four-year degree programs in surveying or in closely related degree programs.

PURPOSE:
To promote study in the surveying and mapping professions.

LEGAL BASIS:
Nonprofit educational organization.

ELIGIBILITY:
Nominees must be members of the National Society of Professional Surveyors. Student applicants must be enrolled in four-year degree programs in surveying or in closely related degree programs such as geomatics or surveying engineering. Preference will be given to applicants from programs with a significant focus on geodetic surveying.

GEOG. RESTRICTIONS: United States, Canada and South America.

FINANCIAL DATA:
Amount of support per award: $2,000 and an appropriate citation to be presented at the annual meeting.
Total amount of support: $2,000 annually.

CO-OP FUNDING PROGRAMS: Provided by the American Association for Geodetic Surveying and administered by NSPS.

NO. MOST RECENT APPLICANTS: 25.

NO. AWARDS: 1 annually.

APPLICATION INFO:
Required documentation includes:
(1) a completed application form;
(2) proof of student membership in AAGS (this will be checked);
(3) a brief yet complete statement indicating educational objectives, future plans of study

or research, professional activities and financial need;
(4) three letters of recommendation (at least two from faculty members familiar with the student's work) and;
(5) a complete original official transcript through the end of the school year prior to when the award will be presented; in addition, send unofficial transcripts for the fall semester when available.

Do not send applications by fax or e-mail. Mail all documents in one envelope. In addition, send unofficial transcripts for the fall semester when available. Incomplete or improperly completed applications will be discarded.

Duration: One academic year.

Deadline: February 15.

PUBLICATIONS:
Surveying and Land Information Science Journal.

ADDRESS INQUIRIES TO:
Patricia Milburn, Office Manager
(See telephone and e-mail address above.)

OAK RIDGE INSTITUTE FOR SCIENCE AND EDUCATION (ORISE)   [2402]
100 ORAU Way
Oak Ridge, TN 37830
(865) 576-3424
E-mail: science.education@orau.org
Web Site: orise.orau.gov

FOUNDED: 1946

AREAS OF INTEREST:
Energy-related disciplines and technologies.

TYPE:
Fellowships; Internships; Scholarships. ORISE administers a broad range of internships, scholarships, fellowships and research experiences. ORISE programs include research experiences at Department of Energy national laboratories as well as other federal agencies with research facilities located across the country as well as some positions outside the U.S.

YEAR PROGRAM STARTED: 1950

PURPOSE:
To provide hands-on research training for students seeking Associate, Baccalaureate, or graduate degrees in appropriate disciplines relating to science and engineering education, training and management systems, energy and environment systems.

LEGAL BASIS:
Government agency.

ELIGIBILITY:
ORISE programs are available to science and engineering students and educators at every academic level from K-12th grade, to college students and postdoctoral researchers, to university faculty members.

APPLICATION INFO:
Contact ORISE for general information and application guidelines.

PUBLICATIONS:
Program announcement; ORISE Resource Guide.

ADDRESS INQUIRIES TO:
Craig Layman
Director, Workforce Development
(See address above.)

PRECAST/PRESTRESSED CONCRETE INSTITUTE   [2403]
8770 West Bryn Mawr Avenue
Suite 1150
Chicago, IL 60631
(312) 786-0300
Fax: (312) 621-1114
E-mail: rbecker@pci.org
Web Site: www.pci.org

AREAS OF INTEREST:
Research, design and construction of buildings, bridges and other structures using precast/prestressed concrete.

NAME(S) OF PROGRAMS:
• **Daniel P. Jenny Research Fellowships**

TYPE:
Fellowships.

YEAR PROGRAM STARTED: 1972

PURPOSE:
To engage the interest of young engineering students in the precast concrete industry while providing a research experience of value to both the student and the Institute.

LEGAL BASIS:
Nonprofit trade association.

ELIGIBILITY:
Fellowship program is open to any university in North America with the facilities to conduct structural research. Students may be Ph.D. candidates, but Master's students are preferred.

GEOG. RESTRICTIONS: North America.

FINANCIAL DATA:
Amount of support per award: Varies.

NO. AWARDS: Varies.

APPLICATION INFO:
Application information is available online.
Duration: One to two years.
Deadline: January 14. Announcement by March 29.

ADDRESS INQUIRIES TO:
Roger Becker
Vice President Technical Services
(See address above.)

SNAME THE SOCIETY OF NAVAL ARCHITECTS AND MARINE ENGINEERS   [2404]
99 Canal Center Plaza, Suite 310
Alexandria, VA 22314
(703) 997-6701
E-mail: sname@sname.org
Web Site: www.sname.org

FOUNDED: 1893

AREAS OF INTEREST:
Naval architecture, marine engineering, ocean engineering and other maritime industry-related fields.

NAME(S) OF PROGRAMS:
• **Graduate Scholarships**
• **Undergraduate Scholarships**

TYPE:
Scholarships. SNAME annually offers competitive scholarships to undergraduate and graduate students of naval architecture, marine engineering, ocean engineering, or of other fields directly related to the maritime industry.

YEAR PROGRAM STARTED: 1933

PURPOSE:
To encourage young men and women to enter the fields of naval architecture, marine engineering, ocean engineering or marine industry-related fields as a career by aiding them to pursue courses of study in these specialties and to provide the incentive and attractions for such a career.

LEGAL BASIS:
Internationally recognized non-profit, professional society.

ELIGIBILITY:
SNAME scholarships are based solely on merit, not financial need. Selection is based upon Scholarships Committee recommendations and Executive Committee approval. Complete details are available online.

FINANCIAL DATA:
Amount of support per award: Graduate Scholarships: Up to $20,000 per year; Undergraduate Scholarships: Up to $6,000.
Total amount of support: Varies.

NO. AWARDS: Varies.

APPLICATION INFO:
Applications are available online. Supporting documents may be submitted along with the online application or e-mailed separately to scholarships@sname.org.
Duration: Graduate Scholarships: One year. No renewals. Undergraduate Scholarships: One year. Awardee may apply for a Graduate Scholarship.
Deadline: Graduate Scholarships: Application must be submitted prior to February 1; supporting documents by February 15. Selection made in April.

Undergraduate Scholarships: Application must be submitted prior to June 1; supporting documents by June 15. Selection made in July.

SCHOLARSHIP COMMITTEE:
David Chapman, Chairman

ADDRESS INQUIRIES TO:
E-mail: scholarships@sname.org

SOCIETY OF WOMEN ENGINEERS
130 East Randolph Street
Suite 3500
Chicago, IL 60601
(312) 596-5223
(877) 793-4636
Fax: (312) 312-9550
E-mail: scholarships@swe.org
Web Site: swe.org/scholarships

TYPE:
Awards/prizes; Conferences/seminars; Scholarships. Support for undergraduate and graduate engineering studies including women who have been out of the engineering job market and out of school for a minimum of two years and who will return to school for an engineering program.

See entry 989 for full listing.

SYSTEMS PLUS, INC.   [2405]
DoD NDSEG Fellowship Program Office
One Research Court, Suite 360
Rockville, MD 20850
(301) 948-4232
Fax: (301) 948-3918
E-mail: ndseg.pmo@sysplus.com
Web Site: ndseg.sysplus.com

FOUNDED: 1893

AREAS OF INTEREST:
STEM disciplines.

NAME(S) OF PROGRAMS:
- **Department of Defense National Defense Science and Engineering Graduate Fellowship Program (NDSEG)**

TYPE:
Fellowships.

YEAR PROGRAM STARTED: 1964

ELIGIBILITY:
For students at or near the beginning of their doctoral study in science or engineering. Field of study must fit under one of 15 supported STEM disciplines. Applicants must be citizens or nationals of the U.S.

FINANCIAL DATA:
Provides competitive stipend, full tuition and all mandatory fees, $5,000 travel budget, and up to $1,200 per year in health insurance.
Amount of support per award: Stipend of $38,400 per year.
Total amount of support: Varies.

NO. AWARDS: Up to 500.

APPLICATION INFO:
Application guidelines are available online.
Duration: Three years.
Deadline: Typically December. Applications open late summer/early fall.

ADDRESS INQUIRIES TO:
See e-mail address above.

SYSTEMS PLUS, INC. [2406]
One Research Court
Suite 360
Rockville, MD 20850
(301) 948-4232
E-mail: afsffp.pmo@sysplus.com
Web Site: afsffp.sysplus.com

AREAS OF INTEREST:
Science, engineering and mathematics.

NAME(S) OF PROGRAMS:
- **USAF Summer Faculty Fellowship Program**

TYPE:
Fellowships. Research fellowship.

PURPOSE:
To complement research efforts and build critical links between Air Force scientists and counterparts in the academic community.

ELIGIBILITY:
Applicants must be citizens of the U.S. Applicants must currently hold a full-time appointment at an accredited Baccalaureate-granting U.S. college, university or technical institution, and have earned a Ph.D. in science, mathematics or Air Force-relevant engineering discipline.

GEOG. RESTRICTIONS: United States.

FINANCIAL DATA:
Amount of support per award: Assistant Professor: $1,545 per week; Associate Professor: $1,751 per week; Full Professor: $1,957 per week.
Total amount of support: Varies.

NO. MOST RECENT APPLICANTS: 205.

NO. AWARDS: Up to 150.

APPLICATION INFO:
A complete application includes:
(1) a completed online application form, including citizenship, demographic, contact and employment information;
(2) an electronic copy of applicant's curriculum vitae uploaded in Adobe PDF format;
(3) complete contact information for three references, one of whom must be the applicant's department head or dean and;
(4) an electronic copy of the research proposal uploaded in Adobe PDF format. If the proposal includes using a graduate student in the research, their application must be included with the proposal.
Note: It is suggested that the applicant receive approval from the advisor of the program before uploading his or her proposal.
Duration: Eight to 12 weeks during the summer.
Deadline: Late November.

ADDRESS INQUIRIES TO:
AFSFFP Program Officer
(See address above.)

THE TAU BETA PI ASSOCIATION, INC. [2407]
508 Dougherty Engineering Building
1512 Middle Drive - UTK
Knoxville, TN 37996-2215
(865) 546-4578
E-mail: tbp@tbp.org
fellowships@tbp.org
Web Site: www.tbp.org

FOUNDED: 1885

AREAS OF INTEREST:
Engineering.

NAME(S) OF PROGRAMS:
- **Raymond A. and Ina C. Best Fellowship for MBA at Rensselaer Polytechnic Institute**
- **Graduate Fellowship in Engineering**
- **Tau Beta Pi Undergraduate Scholarship**

TYPE:
Fellowships; Scholarships. Fellowship awards are for one academic year of study in engineering for qualified graduate students.

Scholarships are awarded for senior year of full-time undergraduate study.

YEAR PROGRAM STARTED: 1928

PURPOSE:
To support the advancement of engineering education and the profession.

LEGAL BASIS:
Corporation.

ELIGIBILITY:
Candidate must be a member of Tau Beta Pi.

Scholarship applicants must be planning to return to school for at least one semester, one trimester, or two quarters of full-time undergraduate study in engineering on campus in the upcoming academic year.

FINANCIAL DATA:
Fellows having other graduate study financial aid that is in excess of tuition may be awarded Tau Beta Pi Fellowships without stipend. Persons supported by a salary from industry, government or other sources may not be entitled to the stipend.
Amount of support per award: Fellowships: $10,000. Scholarships: $2,000 for full year, $1,000 for one semester, one trimester or two quarters.
Total amount of support: $700,000 to $820,000 per year.

NO. AWARDS: 30 fellowships and at least 250 scholarships annually.

APPLICATION INFO:
Application forms are available November 1 for fellowships and January 15 for scholarships for the following academic year.
Duration: One academic year. Fellowships and scholarships are not renewable.
Deadline: Fellowships: February 1. Scholarships: April 1.

PUBLICATIONS:
The Bent of Tau Beta Pi, quarterly magazine.

IRS I.D.: 62-0479545

OFFICERS:
Curtis D. Gomulinski, Executive Director
Sally J. Steadman, Ph.D., Director of Fellowships

EXECUTIVE COUNCIL:
C. Craig Smith, President
George J. Morales, Ph.D., Vice President
Scott E. Fable, Treasurer
Rachel K. Alexander, Secretary
Stephen L. King-Monroe, Councillor
Michael L. Peterson, Councillor
Russ W. Pierce, Councillor
George Youssef, Councillor
Menna M. Youssef, Councillor

ADDRESS INQUIRIES TO:
Director of Fellowships
The Tau Beta Pi Association, Inc.
P.O. Box 2697
Knoxville, TN 37901-2697
E-mail: fellowships@tbp.org

U.S. DEPARTMENT OF ENERGY [2408]
3610 Collins Ferry Road
P.O. Box 880
Morgantown, WV 26507-0880
(304) 285-4764
Fax: (304) 285-4403
Web Site: www.netl.doe.gov

FOUNDED: 1979

AREAS OF INTEREST:
Materials development to support direct power extraction and low-cost distributed sensing of fossil energy power systems.

NAME(S) OF PROGRAMS:
- **University Coal Research Program**

TYPE:
Assistantships; Project/program grants; Research grants. Topics change annually. In general, the program areas could include high performance materials, sensors and controls, simulation-based engineering, and water management research and development.

YEAR PROGRAM STARTED: 1980

PURPOSE:
To foster the highest quality fundamental research on coal at the university level; to ensure the continued training of researchers in the areas of fossil energy.

LEGAL BASIS:
Government agency.

ELIGIBILITY:
Open to U.S. colleges, universities and university-affiliated research institutions. Projects selected for an award must have a teaching professor as Principal Investigator or a Co-Principal Investigator.

GEOG. RESTRICTIONS: United States.

FINANCIAL DATA:
Amount of support per award: Maximum
DOE funding for grant applications submitted
by a U.S. college or university is up to
$400,000 for a 36-month performance period.
Total amount of support: $3,825,000 for
fiscal year 2020.
Matching fund requirements: No matching
fund requirements; however, cost-sharing
and/or industrial collaboration is encouraged.

NO. AWARDS: 7 for the year 2019.

APPLICATION INFO:
Funding opportunities are posted on the web
site above.
Duration: Approximately 90 to 180 days. No
renewals.
Deadline: Varies and subject to change.
Check with contact person(s) listed on the
Funding Opportunity Announcement.

U.S. SOCIETY ON DAMS   [2409]
9975 Wadsworth Parkway
Suite K-2, 145
Westminster, CO 80021
(303) 792-8753
Fax: (303) 792-8782
E-mail: info@ussdams.org
Web Site: www.ussdams.org

AREAS OF INTEREST:
Dams and water resources.

NAME(S) OF PROGRAMS:
• **USSD Scholarship Award**

TYPE:
Awards/prizes; Scholarships.

PURPOSE:
To advance the technology of dam
engineering, construction, operation,
maintenance and dam safety; to foster
socially and environmentally responsible
water resources projects; to promote
awareness of the role of dams in the
beneficial and sustainable development of the
nation's water resources.

ELIGIBILITY:
Open to U.S. college or university graduate
students whose research studies have a
potential for developing practical solutions to
design and construction problems and other
dam-related issues. Applicants must be U.S.
citizens or permanent residents enrolled
full-time in U.S. academic institutions which
have programs related to dams.

GEOG. RESTRICTIONS: United States.

FINANCIAL DATA:
Amount of support per award: Varies.
Total amount of support: $20,000 for the
year 2019.

NO. MOST RECENT APPLICANTS: 7 for the year
2019.

NO. AWARDS: 4 for the year 2019.

APPLICATION INFO:
Applicants must submit a proposal describing
a specific research topic. The proposed
research work should be original and
innovative. The proposed research can be part
of an ongoing research project. Applicants
are encouraged to submit proposals in topics
that are related to their graduate research
work. The application package must include
the application form, a description of the
proposed research work, an official set of
academic transcripts and two letters of
recommendation, one of which must be from
the applicant's academic advisor.

Deadline: March 31.

ADDRESS INQUIRIES TO:
See e-mail address above.

THE UNIVERSITY OF SYDNEY
Scholarships Office
Level 4, Jane Foss Russell Building G02
The University of Sydney N.S.W. 2006
Australia
61 (02) 8627 1444
E-mail: scholarships.officer@sydney.edu.au
Web Site: www.sydney.edu.au/scholarships

TYPE:
Scholarships. Awarded for research leading to
a higher degree. Tenable at the University of
Sydney.

See entry 1927 for full listing.

Home economics and
nutrition

THE ACADEMY OF NUTRITION
AND DIETETICS
FOUNDATION   [2410]
120 South Riverside Plaza
Suite 2190
Chicago, IL 60606
(800) 877-1600
E-mail: ereichling@eatright.org
Web Site: www.eatrightfoundation.org

FOUNDED: 1966

AREAS OF INTEREST:
Food, nutrition, dietetics and food service
management.

TYPE:
Awards/prizes; Fellowships; Grants-in-aid;
Research grants; Scholarships. Continuing
education awards; Disaster relief;
International awards; Program development
awards; Recognition awards.

YEAR PROGRAM STARTED: 1966

PURPOSE:
To further progress in the educational and
scientific advancement of dietetics.

LEGAL BASIS:
Public, not-for-profit foundation.

ELIGIBILITY:
Applicant must be a member of the Academy
to qualify for its scholarships and (in general)
for its awards as well.

GEOG. RESTRICTIONS: Primarily United States.

FINANCIAL DATA:
Amount of support per award: Awards: $150
to $30,000; Grants: $1,000 to $20,000;
Scholarships: $500 to $10,000.
Total amount of support: Over $942,000.

CO-OP FUNDING PROGRAMS: Collaborative
Consumer Research Program.

NO. MOST RECENT APPLICANTS: Scholarships:
Over 1,000.

NO. AWARDS: Grants and Awards: 46;
Scholarships: 261.

APPLICATION INFO:
One common application form is used for all
scholarships. Scholarship applications are
available online to Academy members.

Awards applications are available online.

Deadline: Awards and Grants: February 1,
unless otherwise stated. Fellowships:
Opportunities are posted as they become
available. Scholarships: April 19.
Announcement in July.

PUBLICATIONS:
Annual report.

IRS I.D.: 36-6150906

ADDRESS INQUIRIES TO:
Elisha Reichling, Program Coordinator
(See address above.)

AMERICAN ASSOCIATION OF
FAMILY AND CONSUMER
SCIENCES (AAFCS)
107 South West Street
Suite 816
Alexandria, VA 22314
(703) 706-4600
(800) 424-8080
Fax: (703) 636-7648
E-mail: awards@aafcs.org
Web Site: www.aafcs.org/resources/recognition

TYPE:
Fellowships. AAFCS awards fellowships to
individuals who have exhibited the potential
to make contributions to the family and
consumer sciences profession.

See entry 870 for full listing.

AMERICAN ASSOCIATION OF
FAMILY AND CONSUMER
SCIENCES (AAFCS)   [2411]
107 South West Street
Suite 816
Alexandria, VA 22314
(703) 706-4600
(800) 424-8080
Fax: (703) 636-7648
E-mail: awards@aafcs.org
Web Site: www.aafcs.org/resources/recognition

FOUNDED: 1909

AREAS OF INTEREST:
Family and consumer sciences.

NAME(S) OF PROGRAMS:
• **National Teacher of the Year Award**

TYPE:
Awards/prizes. Recognizes exemplary
teachers who utilize cutting-edge methods,
techniques and activities to provide the
stimulus for and give visibility to family and
consumer sciences elementary and secondary
education.

YEAR PROGRAM STARTED: 1974

PURPOSE:
To provide leadership and support for
professionals whose work assists individuals,
families and communities in making
informed decisions about their well-being,
relationships and resources to achieve
optimal quality of life.

LEGAL BASIS:
501(c)(3) nonprofit charity.

ELIGIBILITY:
Requirements vary from year to year.

FINANCIAL DATA:
Amount of support per award: A
commemorative plaque and a $2,500 award,
plus up to $1,000 of support for one year of
AAFCS membership and participation in the
AAFCS Annual Conference & Expo.

NO. MOST RECENT APPLICANTS: 10.

NO. AWARDS: Up to 3 merit finalists, from whom 1 National Teacher of the Year is selected.

APPLICATION INFO:
Detailed guidelines and instructions are available from the Association.

Deadline: Second Monday in January.

ADDRESS INQUIRIES TO:
See e-mail address above.

CANADIAN FOUNDATION FOR DIETETIC RESEARCH (CFDR)   [2412]

c/o Dietitians of Canada
99 Yorkville Avenue, Second Floor
Toronto ON M5R 1C1 Canada
(416) 642-9309
Fax: (416) 596-0603
E-mail: info@cfdr.ca
Web Site: www.cfdr.ca

FOUNDED: 1991

AREAS OF INTEREST:
Applied research in food and nutrition/dietetic research.

NAME(S) OF PROGRAMS:
● **Research Grants in Dietetics**

TYPE:
Awards/prizes; Research grants.

YEAR PROGRAM STARTED: 1991

PURPOSE:
To promote and support dietetic research.

ELIGIBILITY:
For research awards, applicants must be practicing dietitians who are delivering direct/indirect client/patient public care or service. One of the investigators must be a member of the dietetic profession, as identified by membership in a professional association of dietitians and/or registration as a member of a Canadian dietetics regulatory body.

GEOG. RESTRICTIONS: Canada.

FINANCIAL DATA:
Amount of support per award: Maximum $20,000.

Total amount of support: $91,774 for the year 2020.

NO. AWARDS: 5 for the year 2020.

APPLICATION INFO:
Applicant must submit a Letter of Intent package. Full proposal by invitation only.

Duration: Up to two years.

Deadline: Research grant letters of intent: Mid-September. Full proposal: March 1. Announcement in June.

PUBLICATIONS:
Canadian Journal of Dietetic Practice and Research (*Revue Canadienne de la Pratique et de la Recherche en Dietetique*).

STAFF:
Janis Randall Simpson, Executive Director

ADDRESS INQUIRIES TO:
See e-mail address above.

CENTER FOR SCIENCE IN THE PUBLIC INTEREST   [2413]

1220 L Street, N.W.
Suite 300
Washington, DC 20005
(202) 332-9110
Fax: (202) 265-4954
E-mail: hr@cspinet.org
Web Site: www.cspinet.org

FOUNDED: 1971

AREAS OF INTEREST:
Consumer advocacy on nutrition, diet and health, and food safety.

NAME(S) OF PROGRAMS:
● **Public Interest Internships**

TYPE:
Internships. These unpaid internships allow interns to work on specific projects under the direction of a Project Director or the Executive Director.

YEAR PROGRAM STARTED: 1978

PURPOSE:
To provide interns with direct, practical experience; to provide the Center with extra assistance.

LEGAL BASIS:
501(c)(3).

ELIGIBILITY:
Students in undergraduate, graduate, law and medical schools are eligible to apply. Requirements vary depending on specific internship applied for.

Must work out of the Washington, DC office.

NO. MOST RECENT APPLICANTS: 250.

NO. AWARDS: Varies.

APPLICATION INFO:
Cover letter should indicate preferred dates. Application materials should include the following:
(1) cover letter indicating issues of interest, future plans, and the dates that applicant is available;
(2) resume (experience with advocacy groups is not required, but would be advantageous) and;
(3) writing sample (a popularly written piece is preferred over a technical report).

Duration: 10 weeks. Renewal possible.

Deadline: Applicants are advised to follow the application guidelines and apply as soon as possible. Applications are taken on a rolling basis until all positions have been filled.

PUBLICATIONS:
Status report; general brochure; publications list; *Nutrition Action Healthletter*.

OFFICERS:
Dr. Peter Lurie, President and Executive Director

ADDRESS INQUIRIES TO:
Colleen O'Day, Human Resources Director (See address above.)

DIETITIANS OF CANADA (DC)   [2414]

99 Yorkville Avenue
Second Floor
Toronto ON M5R 1C1 Canada
(416) 596-0857
Fax: (416) 596-0603
E-mail: contactus@dietitians.ca
Web Site: www.dietitians.ca

FOUNDED: 1935

AREAS OF INTEREST:
Dietetics and nutrition.

NAME(S) OF PROGRAMS:
● **Graduate Student Awards**
● **Undergraduate Student Awards**

TYPE:
Awards/prizes.

YEAR PROGRAM STARTED: 1966

PURPOSE:
To provide financial support to students in undergraduate and graduate levels of study.

LEGAL BASIS:
Incorporated under Canada Corporations Act.

ELIGIBILITY:
Applicants must be members of Dietitians of Canada and registered in a food and nutrition or related program.

GEOG. RESTRICTIONS: Canada.

FINANCIAL DATA:
Amount of support per award: $2,500 cash prize, plus $1,000 for travel support to attend the DC national conference.

NO. AWARDS: 2 for the year 2020.

APPLICATION INFO:
Completed online application, academic transcript, and names and contact information for two references are required.

Deadline: January 31.

ADDRESS INQUIRIES TO:
E-mail:centralinfo@dietitians.ca

FOOD AND DRUG LAW INSTITUTE (FDLI)

1155 15th Street, N.W., Suite 910
Washington, DC 20005-2706
(202) 371-1420
(800) 956-6293
E-mail: info@fdli.org
Web Site: www.fdli.
org/resources/career/austern-writing-competition

TYPE:
Awards/prizes. The subject matter of the competition is an in-depth analysis of a current issue relevant to the food and drug field, including a relevant case law, legislative history and other authorities, particularly where the U.S. Food and Drug Administration is involved.

See entry 1772 for full listing.

HANNAFORD CHARITABLE FOUNDATION

145 Pleasant Hill Road
Scarborough, ME 04074
E-mail: hannafordcharitablefoundation@hannaford.com
Web Site: www.hannaford.com

TYPE:
Capital grants; Project/program grants. Employee scholarships.

See entry 1391 for full listing.

ILLINOIS RESTAURANT ASSOCIATION EDUCATIONAL FOUNDATION

33 West Monroe, Suite 250
Chicago, IL 60603
(312) 787-4000
E-mail: khodges@illinoisrestaurants.org
Web Site: www.illinoisrestaurants.org

TYPE:
Product donations; Scholarships. Grants for impacted food service employees.

See entry 1511 for full listing.

INTERNATIONAL ASSOCIATION FOR FOOD PROTECTION [2415]
2900 100th Street
Suite 309
Des Moines, IA 50322-3855
(515) 276-3344
Fax: (515) 276-8655
E-mail: info@foodprotection.org
Web Site: www.foodprotection.org

FOUNDED: 1911

AREAS OF INTEREST:
Food science and research.

NAME(S) OF PROGRAMS:
• **Harold Barnum Industry Award**
• **Larry Beuchat Young Researcher Award**
• **Food Safety Award**
• **Food Safety Innovation Award**
• **Harry Haverland Citation Award**
• **International Leadership Award**
• **James M. Jay Diversity in Food Safety Award**
• **Elmer Marth Educator Award**
• **Sanitarian Award**
• **Student Travel Scholarship Award**
• **Ewen C.D. Todd Control of Foodborne Illness Award**
• **Travel Award for Food Safety Professionals in a Country with a Developing Economy**
• **Travel Award for State or Provincial Health or Agricultural Department Employees**
• **Maurice Weber Laboratorian Award**

TYPE:
Awards/prizes; Travel grants. Cash awards and plaques to outstanding members.

YEAR PROGRAM STARTED: 1973

PURPOSE:
To provide food safety professionals worldwide with a forum to exchange information on protecting the food supply; to recognize and reward outstanding member contributions in the specified award area.

LEGAL BASIS:
Nonprofit, incorporated professional association.

ELIGIBILITY:
Nominees must be members of the International Association for Food Protection.

FINANCIAL DATA:
Amount of support per award: $1,500 to $2,500 and plaque or travel expense paid.

NO. AWARDS: Generally, 1 of each award annually. Travel awards: Multiple.

APPLICATION INFO:
Varies by award. Details are available on the Association web site.
Deadline: Mid-February.

IRS I.D.: 35-0894354

OFFICERS:
Roger Cook, President
Ruth Petran, President-Elect
Michelle Danyluk, Vice President
Jose Emilio Esteban, Secretary

EXECUTIVE DIRECTOR:
David W. Tharp

ADDRESS INQUIRIES TO:
David W. Tharp, Executive Director
(See address above.)

KAPPA OMICRON NU HONOR SOCIETY [2416]
P.O. Box 798
Okemos, MI 48805-0798
(727) 940-2658 ext. 2003
E-mail: info@kon.org
Web Site: www.kon.org

FOUNDED: 1912

AREAS OF INTEREST:
Home economics, family and consumer sciences, and human sciences.

NAME(S) OF PROGRAMS:
• **Marjorie M. Brown Dissertation Fellowship**
• **Ruth E. Hawthorne Research Grant**
• **Eileen C. Maddex Fellowship**
• **National Alumni Chapter Fellowship**
• **National Alumni Chapter Grant**
• **New Initiatives Grant**
• **Omicron Nu Master's Fellowship**
• **Omicron Nu Research Fellowship**
• **Betty Jeanne Root Fellowship**
• **Undergraduate Research Award**

TYPE:
Fellowships; Project/program grants; Research grants; Scholarships. Awarded to members for graduate or postgraduate study and research in human sciences or one of its specializations at colleges or universities with strong research programs and supporting disciplines for the chosen major or topic.

YEAR PROGRAM STARTED: 1969

PURPOSE:
To promote research and graduate study in human sciences by recognizing and encouraging scholastic excellence.

LEGAL BASIS:
Nonprofit corporation, 501(c)(3) status.

ELIGIBILITY:
Fellowships/Grants: Applicant must be a member of Kappa Omicron Nu who has demonstrated scholarship, research and leadership potential.

FINANCIAL DATA:
Amount of support per award: $300 to $10,000 per year.
Total amount of support: Approximately $27,000 annually.

NO. MOST RECENT APPLICANTS: 11.

NO. AWARDS: Doctoral Fellowships: 2; Master's Fellowships: 3; Scholar Grants: Varies; Marjorie M. Brown Dissertation Fellowship, Ruth E. Hawthorne Research Grant, National Alumni Chapter Grant, New Initiatives Grant and Betty Jeanne Root Fellowship: 1 per award or fellowship.

APPLICATION INFO:
All submissions will be electronic and reviewed electronically on ProposalSpace.
Duration: One academic year. Nonrenewable.
Deadline: April 1. Notification by May 15.

PUBLICATIONS:
Brochure.

IRS I.D.: 38-1245233

STAFF:
Holly Roseski, Executive Director and Chief Executive Officer

BOARD OF DIRECTORS:
Dr. Amber Roth, Chairperson
Dr. Melinda Adams, Chairperson Elect
Dr. Doug Kyle, First Vice Chairperson
Ashley Williams, Second Vice Chairperson
Dr. Basem Boutros, Secretary

ADDRESS INQUIRIES TO:
Holly Roseski, Executive Director and Chief Executive Officer
(See address above.)

NATIONAL CATTLEMAN'S BEEF ASSOCIATION, A CONTRACTOR TO THE BEEF CHECKOFF [2417]
9110 East Nichols Avenue
Suite 300
Centennial, CO 80112-3450
(202) 879-9130
Fax: (303) 694-2851
E-mail: beefnutritionfp@beef.org
Web Site: www.beefresearch.org

FOUNDED: 1922

AREAS OF INTEREST:
Human nutrition, beef's role in optional human health and well-being and the prevention of chronic disease.

NAME(S) OF PROGRAMS:
• **Human Nutrition Research**

TYPE:
Grants-in-aid; Research grants; Research contracts. Research contracts and grants-in-aid for experimental projects in the areas of:
(1) beef as part of a balanced diet;
(2) parity studies;
(3) health benefits of beef lipids and;
(4) contribution of beef nutrients to total diet.

Proposals solicited via specific RFPs (request for proposals).

YEAR PROGRAM STARTED: 1923

PURPOSE:
To gain further knowledge of the value of beef in our diets; to develop research technology that can be applied to the areas noted above.

LEGAL BASIS:
Professional, nonprofit association.

ELIGIBILITY:
Open to qualified institutions (including universities, medical centers, nonprofit organizations and/or contract research laboratories) with appropriate interests.

GEOG. RESTRICTIONS: Primarily United States.

FINANCIAL DATA:
Amount of support per award: $20,000 to $50,000 for one year to $200,000 to $400,000 for multiyear awards. Most are $100,000 to $200,000.
Total amount of support: Varies.

CO-OP FUNDING PROGRAMS: Occasionally federally funded programs are under way that can be facilitated with other funds to expand the scope of the work.

NO. MOST RECENT APPLICANTS: 32.

NO. AWARDS: 7.

APPLICATION INFO:
Official application materials are available upon request to NCBA at the address above, after it has been established that the proposal would be of mutual interest.
Duration: Support is provided for one to three years depending upon the project.
Deadline: Varies for RFPs.

PUBLICATIONS:
Annual research report.

ADDRESS INQUIRIES TO:
Clara Lau, Ph.D.
Director, Human Nutrition Research
(See address above.)

NATIONAL DAIRY COUNCIL [2418]
10255 West Higgins Road
Suite 900
Rosemont, IL 60018-5616
(847) 803-2000
Fax: (847) 803-2077
E-mail: nutritionresearch@rosedmi.com
Web Site: researchsubmission.
nationaldairycouncil.org

FOUNDED: 1915

AREAS OF INTEREST:
Independent research to aid in the ongoing discovery of information about dairy foods' important role in a healthy lifestyle. This research provides insights to industry for new dairy product innovation.

NAME(S) OF PROGRAMS:
● **Nutrition Research Program**

TYPE:
Research contracts. The National Dairy Council is the nutrition research, education and communications arm of Dairy Management Inc. On behalf of U.S. dairy farmers, the National Dairy Council provides science-based nutrition information to, and in collaboration with, a variety of stakeholders committed to fostering a healthier society, including health professionals, educators, school nutrition directors, academia, industry, consumers and media. The National Dairy Council comprises a staff of nutrition science researchers, registered dietitians and communications experts dedicated to educating the public on the health benefits of consuming milk and milk products throughout a person's lifespan.

YEAR PROGRAM STARTED: 1915

PURPOSE:
To research and discover health benefits for dairy foods and ingredients and advance scientific understanding of these benefits; to increase demand for dairy.

LEGAL BASIS:
Nonprofit educational-scientific institution under IRS 501(c)(3).

ELIGIBILITY:
Qualified investigators associated with accredited institutions of higher learning are eligible for support. Applicants must hold a Ph.D., M.D., D.D.S., D.V.M. or other degree, with experience demonstrating ability to conduct the proposed research.

Funds are not available for alteration of facilities or purchase of permanent equipment.

FINANCIAL DATA:
Amount of support per award: Administered research contracts vary in amount, depending upon the needs and nature of the request.
Total amount of support: Varies.

CO-OP FUNDING PROGRAMS: If research interests of additional organizations coincide, cooperative projects are preferred to enhance efficiency of funds utilized and to benefit the researcher through a broader base of support.

NO. MOST RECENT APPLICANTS: Average 80 preproposals; approximately 16 selected for full proposal submission.

NO. AWARDS: Varies.

APPLICATION INFO:
The National Dairy Council invites submission of two-page preproposals in the beginning of each calendar year, typically early July. Applications which meet the needs of the research program, which are stated in the guidelines for preproposal submission, will be reviewed. Approximately two to three weeks following the submission deadline, all applicants will receive notice of the outcome of this screening process. Applicants whose preproposals generated interest will receive further information and materials for submission of a detailed full research application to the program. Full proposals will be due approximately six to eight weeks later. All full proposals will be peer-reviewed for scientific merit by the Nutrition Research Scientific Advisory Committee, which is comprised of expert scientists from academia, government and industry. For information on the research program and research topics of interest in the next solicitation, please send a letter requesting the information and a self-addressed label to the address above or contact the NDC research office.
Duration: Projects supported on a yearly basis for up to three years.
Deadline: Preproposal: Late July, with decision made early August; Full Proposal: Mid-September, with decision made October or November.

PUBLICATIONS:
Guidelines for application and administration.

THE NATIONAL RESTAURANT ASSOCIATION EDUCATIONAL FOUNDATION [2419]
2055 L Street, N.W.
Washington, DC 20036
(202) 973-3672
E-mail: scholars@nraef.org
Web Site: www.chooserestaurants.org/programs-and-scholarships

FOUNDED: 1987

AREAS OF INTEREST:
Foodservice education and training.

NAME(S) OF PROGRAMS:
● **National Restaurant Association Educational Foundation (NRAE) Scholarship Program**

TYPE:
Scholarships. Provides scholarships for students who are pursuing an education and career in the foodservice industry.

YEAR PROGRAM STARTED: 1987

PURPOSE:
To encourage and support students pursuing an education and career in the foodservice industry.

LEGAL BASIS:
Not-for-profit organization.

ELIGIBILITY:
All scholarship applicants must be:
(1) enrolled or accepted as a full-time or part-time undergraduate student at an accredited postsecondary institution, college, or university for the upcoming academic year;

(2) majoring in an undergraduate level restaurant, foodservice, or hospitality-related program;
(3) plan to be enrolled for at least two consecutive undergraduate terms or on track to complete an undergraduate degree within one term and;
(4) unrelated to any employees or family members of the National Restaurant Association, National Restaurant Association Educational Foundation, or any state restaurant association.

A limited number of scholarships are available for Canadian citizens attending school in Canada.

GEOG. RESTRICTIONS: United States and its territories.

FINANCIAL DATA:
Amount of support per award: Undergraduate Scholarships: $2,500 to $10,000.

NO. MOST RECENT APPLICANTS: 700.

NO. AWARDS: Approximately 300.

APPLICATION INFO:
Online application must be submitted through the CommunityForce application platform, which is located at nraef1.communityforce.com. All applicants need:
(1) a valid e-mail address;
(2) one letter of recommendation and;
(3) student transcripts that include a cumulative grade point average.

Additionally, applicant may need to supply their Student Aid Report (if FAFSA has been filed for the upcoming school year).
Duration: Varies depending upon the award.
Deadline: March 15.

PUBLICATIONS:
Awards brochure.

ADDRESS INQUIRIES TO:
Scholarships
(See address above.)

USDA FOOD AND NUTRITION SERVICE
Child Nutrition Service
1320 Braddock Place, 4th Floor
Alexandria, VA 22314
(703) 305-2054
Web Site: www.fns.usda.gov

TYPE:
Formula grants; Grants-in-aid; Project/program grants. Reimbursement for the support of food service in schools, child and adult care institutions to improve nutrition.

The Child and Adult Care Food Program helps child care facilities and institutions serve nutritious meals and snacks to preschool and school-age children. To participate, facilities and institutions must be licensed or approved to provide child care services. They must also meet certain other eligibility requirements. The program operates in nonresidential day care centers, settlement houses, outside-school-hours care centers, family day care homes, institutions providing day care for handicapped children and others. Participating facilities and institutions get cash assistance, USDA-donated foods and technical guidance. In child care centers, the amount of cash assistance varies according to the family size and income of children served. In day care homes, the amount of cash assistance is based on a food service payment rate.

Similar benefits are also now available to adult day care centers which serve functionally impaired adults or persons 60 years of age or older.

The Fresh Fruit and Vegetable Program introduces school children to a variety of produce that they otherwise might not have the opportunity to sample. The goal is to improve children's overall diet and create healthier eating habits to impact their present and future health.

The National School Lunch Program makes well-planned nutritious meals available to school children. Any public or nonprofit private schools of high school grade or under and licensed public or nonprofit private residential child care institutions are eligible to participate in the National School Lunch and School Breakfast Programs. Schools that participate are required to provide free and reduced-price meals to children unable to pay the full price. Eligibility is based on application information submitted by a parent or guardian. The household income limit for free lunches is set at or below 130% of the federal poverty level and for reduced price lunches household income must be above 130% or at or below 185% of the federal poverty level. Children from households not eligible for free or reduced-price meals must pay the school's full price charge for lunch. Cash and donated commodities are provided to participating schools and institutions according to the number of meals served.

The School Breakfast Program makes nutritious breakfasts available to school children under the same eligibility guidelines and general requirements as the National School Lunch Program.

The Special Milk Program makes it possible for all children attending a participating school or institution to purchase milk at a reduced price or receive it free, if they are eligible. Reimbursement is provided for each half-pint of milk served under the program. Schools and institutions that participate in other federal child nutrition programs authorized under the National School Lunch Act or the Child Nutrition Act of 1966 may not participate in the Special Milk Program, except for split-session kindergarten programs conducted in schools in which the children do not have access to the other meal program.

The Summer Food Service Program helps communities serve meals to needy children when school is not in session. The program is sponsored by public or private nonprofit school food authorities or local, municipal, county or state governments. Public or private nonprofit residential camps, other private nonprofit organizations, colleges and universities which participate in the National Youth Sports Program also may be sponsors. The program operates in areas in which at least 50% of the children meet the income criteria for free and reduced-price school meals. USDA reimburses sponsors for operating costs of food services up to a specified maximum rate for each meal served. In addition, sponsors receive some reimbursement for planning, operating and supervising expenses.

See entry 1041 for full listing.

Mining and metallurgy

ASM MATERIALS EDUCATION FOUNDATION [2420]
9639 Kinsman Road
Materials Park, OH 44073-0002
(440) 338-5151
(800) 336-5152
Fax: (440) 338-4634
E-mail: jeane.deatherage@asminternational.org
Web Site: www.asmfoundation.org

FOUNDED: 1913

AREAS OF INTEREST:
Materials science and engineering in related fields such as metallurgy, metallurgical engineering, polymeric engineering, ceramic engineering, advanced composites engineering and engineering of electronic materials.

NAME(S) OF PROGRAMS:
- **Acta Materialia Scholarships**
- **ASM Outstanding Scholars**
- **David J. Chellman Scholarship**
- **Edward J. Dulis Scholarship**
- **John M. Haniak Scholarship**
- **Ladish Co. Foundation Scholarships**
- **George A. Roberts Scholarship**
- **Lucille & Charles A. Wert Scholarship**
- **William Park Woodside Founder's Scholarship**

TYPE:
Scholarships.

YEAR PROGRAM STARTED: 1953

PURPOSE:
To encourage and support capable students with interest and potential in the field of metallurgy and materials science.

LEGAL BASIS:
501(c)(3) educational charity.

ELIGIBILITY:
Applicant must be a member of ASM International or Material Advantage student member. Additionally, the applicant must meet the following requirements:
(1) must have an intended or declared major in metallurgy or materials science engineering. Applicants majoring in related science or engineering disciplines will be considered if they demonstrate a strong academic emphasis and interest in materials science;
(2) must have completed at least one year of college and;
(3) must have junior or senior standing in the fall at a North American university. University must have an accredited science and engineering program leading to a Bachelor's degree.

All scholarships, except the ASM Outstanding Scholar Awards, are only awarded to students studying in North America who demonstrate financial need in addition to academic merit.

ASM Outstanding Scholar Awards are open to international students. Financial need is not considered.

GEOG. RESTRICTIONS: United States.

FINANCIAL DATA:
Most awards include a certificate of recognition and travel allowance for attendance to the awards ceremony.
Amount of support per award: Up to $10,000.

NO. AWARDS: Varies.

APPLICATION INFO:
To be considered, applicant must complete the online application and submit the following supporting papers by e-mail to ScholarshipsUG@asminternational.org:
(1) transcript;
(2) resume;
(3) photograph and;
(4) two letters of recommendation.

Applicant must forward the online Scholarships Recommendation Form to their references.
Duration: One academic year.
Deadline: Application and materials must be sent by May 1. Award winners will be notified by August 15.

IRS I.D.: 34-6541397

ADDRESS INQUIRIES TO:
ASM Foundation Undergraduate Scholarship Program
E-mail: foundation@asminternational.org

*SPECIAL STIPULATIONS:
Must have completed one year of undergraduate work.

INSTITUTE OF MATERIALS, MINERALS AND MINING [2421]
The Boilerhouse
Springfield Business Park
Caunt Road
Grantham Lincs NG31 7FZ England
(44) 01476 513886
Fax: (44) 01476 513899
E-mail: anita.horton@iom3.org
Web Site: www.iom3.org

FOUNDED: 1892

AREAS OF INTEREST:
Mining and metallurgy.

NAME(S) OF PROGRAMS:
- **Centenary Scholarship**
- **Stanley Elmore Fellowship Fund**
- **G. Vernon Hobson Bequest**
- **Mining Club Award**
- **Edgar Pam Fellowship**
- **The Tom Seaman Travelling Scholarship**
- **Bosworth Smith Trust Fund**

TYPE:
Awards/prizes; Fellowships; Research grants; Scholarships; Training grants; Travel grants. The Centenary Scholarship is restricted to first- or second-year undergraduates in student membership of the Institute and will be awarded for projects, visits, etc., in furtherance of applicants' career development.

Stanley Elmore Fellowship Fund offers fellowships (normally two for one year) applicable at a U.K. university for research into all branches of extractive metallurgy and mineral processing and, in special cases, for expenditure related to such research.

The G. Vernon Hobson Bequest awards are given for the advancement of teaching and practice of geology as applied to mining. One or more awards may be made for travel, research or other objects in accordance with the terms of the Bequest.

The Mining Club Award will be offered to British subjects 21 to 35 years of age who are actively engaged (in full- or part-time postgraduate study or in employment) in the minerals industry, as defined by the Institute, for travel purposes (for example, to study mineral industry operations in the U.K. or overseas, to present a paper at an international minerals industry conference or to assist the applicant in attending a full-time course of study related to the minerals industry outside the U.K.), or for any other similar purpose that may be regarded as being within the spirit of the award.

The Edgar Pam Fellowship is awarded for postgraduate study in subjects within the Institute's fields of interest, which range from exploration geology to extractive metallurgy. Those eligible for the award are young graduates, domiciled in Australia, Canada, New Zealand, South Africa and the U.K., who wish to undertake advanced study or research in the U.K.

The Tom Seaman Travelling Scholarship is awarded annually to a member, not older than 35 years of age, who is training or has been trained for a career in mining and/or related technologies. The scholarship shall be to assist the study for an aspect of engineering in the minerals industry, with the intention of advancing the associated standards or techniques.

The Bosworth Smith Trust Fund is given for the assistance of postgraduate research in metal mining, non-ferrous extraction metallurgy or mineral dressing. Applications will be considered for grants towards working expenses, the cost of visits to mines and plants in connection with such research, and purchase of apparatus.

ELIGIBILITY:
Applicants should note that, in general, preference will be given to members of the Institution (student membership is required for the Centenary Scholarship). Recipients of the awards will be required to submit summary reports of the ways in which such awards have been used for publication.

In judging the applications received for each award, the Institute will take into account academic excellence and scholarship. The application must, therefore, specify academic ability. Candidates merely seeking assistance for financial hardship will not be considered.

Applicants for awards must ensure that the particular fund from which support is being sought is relevant to their field(s) of interest. Applications not in accordance with the specified terms and conditions of the various funds, those which are received after the deadline, and those for which the appropriate letters of support have not been received by that date will not be submitted to the awards committee.

FINANCIAL DATA:
Amount of support per award: Centenary Scholarship: GBP 500; Stanley Elmore Fellowship Fund: Up to GBP 14,000 distributed between one or two awardees; G. Vernon Hobson Bequest: Up to GBP 1,300; Mining Club Award: Up to GBP 1,500; Edgar Pam Fellowship: Maximum GBP 2,000; Tom Seaman Travelling Scholarship: Up to GBP 5,500; Bosworth Smith Trust Fund: Approximately GBP 5,000 in grants.

APPLICATION INFO:
Application form required. Applications not in accordance with the specified terms and conditions of the various funds, those which are received after the closing date each year, and those for which the appropriate levels of support have not been received by that date, will not be accepted for consideration.
Duration: Stanley Elmore Fellowships and Edgar Pam Fellowship: One year.

Deadline: March 31.

PUBLICATIONS:
Guidelines.

ADDRESS INQUIRIES TO:
Cleo Williams
E-mail: cleo.williams@iom3.org

INTERNATIONAL CENTRE FOR DIFFRACTION DATA   [2422]
12 Campus Boulevard
Newtown Square, PA 19073-3273
(610) 325-9814
Fax: (610) 325-9823
E-mail: sjennings@icdd.com
Web Site: www.icdd.com

FOUNDED: 1991

AREAS OF INTEREST:
The science of crystallography.

NAME(S) OF PROGRAMS:
● **The Ludo Frevel Crystallography Scholarship Award**

TYPE:
Scholarships.

YEAR PROGRAM STARTED: 1991

PURPOSE:
To encourage promising graduate students to pursue crystallographically oriented research.

ELIGIBILITY:
Applicant should be a graduate student seeking a degree with major interest in crystallography, crystal structure analysis, crystal morphology, modulated structures, correlation of atomic structures with physical properties, systematic classification of crystal structures, phase identification and materials characterization. There are no restrictions on country, race, age or sex. Students with a graduation date prior to July 1 of the award year are not eligible.

Funds can be used for travel to conferences or for research-related purposes.

FINANCIAL DATA:
The scholarship stipend is to be used by the graduate student to help defray tuition and laboratory fees. A portion of the stipend may be applied to registration fees to accredited scientific meetings related to crystallography.
Amount of support per award: $2,000 to $2,500.

NO. MOST RECENT APPLICANTS: 54 for fiscal year 2020.

NO. AWARDS: 6 for fiscal year 2020.

APPLICATION INFO:
The following information must be prepared in advance of applying online:
(1) a description of the candidate's proposed research (limit two pages), including purpose and rationale for the research, proposed methodology to be used in the study, and references and/or descriptions of the scientific background for the proposed research and;
(2) a curriculum vitae, including educational preparation (institutions, dates, degrees obtained and in progress, and particularly pertinent coursework), awards/honors received, any research publications and/or presentations given, any work experience (dates, employers, positions), and professional activities and memberships.
Duration: One year. Renewals possible. Renewal applications will be considered on a competitive basis in conjunction with all applications that have been submitted up to the closing date.

Deadline: Mid-October. Contact Centre for exact date.

ADDRESS INQUIRIES TO:
Stephanie Jennings, Conference Coordinator (See address above.)

MINERALOGICAL ASSOCIATION OF CANADA   [2423]
490, rue de la Couronne
Quebec QC G1K 9A9 Canada
(418) 653-0333
Fax: (418) 654-2563
E-mail: office@mineralogicalassociation.ca
Web Site: mineralogicalassociation.ca

FOUNDED: 1955

AREAS OF INTEREST:
Mineralogy.

NAME(S) OF PROGRAMS:
● **Leonard G. Berry Medal**
● **Hawley Medal**
● **MAC Foundation Scholarship**
● **MAC Student Travel/Research Grants**
● **Peacock Medal**
● **Pinch Medal**
● **Undergraduate Awards**
● **Young Scientist Award**

TYPE:
Awards/prizes; Grants-in-aid; Research grants; Scholarships; Travel grants.

PURPOSE:
To promote and advance the knowledge of mineralogy and the allied disciplines of crystallography, petrology, geochemistry and mineral deposits.

LEGAL BASIS:
Nonprofit scientific and charitable organization.

ELIGIBILITY:
The Leonard G. Berry Medal is awarded for distinguished service to the Mineralogical Association of Canada.

The Hawley Medal is presented to the author(s) of what is judged to be the best paper published in the preceding year's volume of *The Canadian Mineralogist*.

The MAC Foundation Scholarship is awarded to a graduate student involved in an M.Sc. or Ph.D. thesis program in the fields of mineralogy, crystallography, petrology, geochemistry or mineral deposits.

The MAC Student Travel/Research Grants are given to assist honours undergraduate and graduate students in the mineral sciences.

The Peacock Medal is awarded annually for excellence in research to a scientist who has made outstanding contributions to the mineralogical sciences in Canada.

The Pinch Medal is awarded every other year to recognize major and sustained contributions to the advancement of mineralogy by members of the collector-dealer community.

Undergraduate Awards are given to university students in mineralogy. The Association presents a MAC publication to the top student in the introductory mineralogy course at each Canadian university.

The Young Scientist Award is given to a young scientist who has made a significant international research contribution in a promising start to a scientific career.

FINANCIAL DATA:
  Amount of support per award: Varies depending on award.
  Total amount of support: $25,000.

NO. MOST RECENT APPLICANTS: MAC Travel/Research Grants: 32 for the year 2020.

NO. AWARDS: Varies.

APPLICATION INFO:
  Contact the Association.
  Duration: Varies.
  Deadline: Varies.

PUBLICATIONS:
  The Canadian Mineralogist.

STAFF:
  Lee A. Groat, Editor

ADDRESS INQUIRIES TO:
  Johanne Caron, Business Manager (See address above.)

Indexes

Entry Listing by Chapter

MULTIPLE SPECIAL PURPOSE: 1-302

HUMANITIES (GENERAL): 303-365
Architecture: 366-383
Arts (multiple disciplines): 384-479
   Performing arts: 480-494
   Fine arts: 495-523
History: 524-597
Languages: 598-610
Literature: 611-654
Museums and libraries: 655-685
Music: 686-733
Religion and theology: 734-754

INTERNATIONAL AFFAIRS AND AREA STUDIES: 755-792
International studies and research abroad: 793-868
Programs for foreign scholars: 869-878
Technical assistance and cooperative research: 879-881

SPECIAL POPULATIONS: 882-928
African-American: 929-939
Native American: 940-961
Spanish-speaking: 962-966
Women: 967-998

URBAN AND REGIONAL AFFAIRS: 999-1363
Children and youth: 999-1042
Community development and services: 1043-1275
Crime prevention: 1276-1280
Public health: 1281-1328
Social welfare: 1329-1363

EDUCATION: 1364-1614
Educational projects and research (general): 1364-1427
Elementary and secondary education: 1428-1440
Higher education projects and research: 1441-1469
Scholar aid programs (all disciplines): 1470-1614

SCIENCES (MULTIPLE DISCIPLINES): 1615-1654

SOCIAL SCIENCES (GENERAL): 1655-1694
Business and economics: 1695-1722
Communications: 1723-1763
Labor: 1764-1767
Law: 1768-1781
Political science: 1782-1810
Sociology and anthropology: 1811-1818

PHYSICAL SCIENCES (GENERAL): 1819-1830
Astronomy and aerospace science: 1831-1846
Chemistry: 1847-1861
Earth sciences: 1862-1879
Mathematics: 1880-1887
Physics: 1888-1893

LIFE SCIENCES (GENERAL): 1894-1901
Agriculture, land resources, rural development: 1902-1929
Biology: 1930-1952
Environment: 1953-1993
Medicine (multiple disciplines): 1994-2093
Allergy, immunology, infectious diseases: 2094-2095
Dentistry: 2096-2108
Internal medicine: 2109-2121
   Cardiovascular and pulmonary: 2122-2147
   Metabolism, gastroenterology, nephrology: 2148-2176
   Oncology: 2177-2199
   Rheumatology: 2200-2201
Neurology: 2202-2233
Nursing: 2234-2248
Obstetrics and gynecology: 2249-2252
Ophthalmology and otolaryngology: 2253-2275
Osteopathy: 2276-2279
Pediatrics: 2280-2286
Pharmacology: 2287-2292
Physical medicine and rehabilitation: 2293-2306
Psychiatry, psychology, mental health: 2307-2341

TECHNOLOGY AND INDUSTRY: 2342-2362
Aeronautics and astronautics: 2363-2374
Engineering: 2375-2409
Home economics and nutrition: 2410-2419
Mining and metallurgy: 2420-2423

Subject Index

A

Academic Medicine. *See* Medicine, Academic

Accessibility: 2305

Accounting: 1369, 1449, 1485, 1540, 1695, 1696, 1697, 1698, 1699, 1704, 1705; *see also* Business; Financial Management

Acoustics: 1824; *see also* Noise

Acquired Immunodeficiency Syndrome (AIDS): 151, 278, 426, 915, 1155, 1292, 1337, 2087, 2121

Acting. *See* Theatre

Actuarial Science: 1880, 1881, 1882, 1887; *see also* Insurance

Administration. *See* Arts Administration; Business Administration; Educational Administration; Health Administration; Library Administration; Management; Museum Administration; Public Administration

Adolescence. *See* Child Welfare and Health; Youth Adoption; Children, Adoption and Foster Care

Adult Education. *See* Education, Adult

Advertising: 543, 900, 1711; *see also* Business; Public Relations

Aerodynamics: 2385

Aeronautics: 1652, 2363, 2364, 2366, 2367, 2368, 2369, 2371, 2372, 2374

Aerospace Sciences: 1823, 1824, 1843, 1845, 1846, 1963, 2363, 2366, 2367, 2368, 2369, 2371, 2372; *see also* Engineering; Sciences; Technology, Aerospace

Aerospace Sciences, History: 528, 1648, 2373

Africa: 157, 310, 364, 845, 846, 1383, 1816; *see also* History, African; Literature, African; also specific nations

African-American Studies. *See* Minority Studies; Race Relations; also any discipline that may be given African-American emphasis

African Americans: 353, 364, 553, 574, 922, 933, 936, 1120, 2240; *see also* America; Inner-City; Minority Studies; Race Relations; Urban Affairs; also any discipline that may be given African American emphasis or be of concern to African Americans

African Americans, Eligibility of: 883, 885, 886, 896, 900, 908, 911, 918, 924, 929, 930, 931, 934, 935, 938, 1169, 1386, 1443, 1541, 1701, 1783, 1880, 1934, 1941, 2062, 2313, 2315, 2353, 2394, 2395; *see also* Minority Group Members, Eligibility of

African Countries, Nationals of: 1774; *see also* Foreign Nationals, Eligibility of

Aged: 26, 29, 65, 83, 110, 121, 134, 136, 146, 150, 152, 170, 173, 178, 179, 195, 200, 216, 221, 234, 257, 267, 283, 905, 919, 1019, 1054, 1057, 1061, 1079, 1103, 1132, 1142, 1144, 1156, 1160, 1167, 1171, 1199, 1236, 1282, 1288, 1293, 1302, 1308, 1310, 1317, 1322, 1330, 1333, 1339, 1352, 1356, 1924, 1995, 1998, 1999, 2025, 2093, 2207, 2294; *see also* Geriatrics and Gerontology

Agricultural Cooperatives. *See* Cooperatives, Rural and Consumer

Agricultural Economics: 1908, 1916, 1919, 1921, 1988

Agricultural Sciences: 57, 70, 133, 136, 792, 1183, 1389, 1629, 1919, 1988, 2418; *see also* Animal Sciences; Food Technology; Nutrition

Agricultural Sciences, Education: 176, 524, 1087, 1744, 1903, 1905, 1909, 1910, 1911, 1912, 1913, 1914, 1915, 1919, 1920, 1929

Agricultural Sciences, Research and Study Abroad: 774, 1860, 1906, 1926

Agrodiversity: 57

Agroecology: 57

Air Pollution: 1294, 1963, 2342; *see also* Environmental Studies

Alabama: 205, 384, 655, 1122, 1143, 1470, 1471, 1472, 1616

Alaska: 213, 385, 915, 1955

Alaskan Natives. *See* American Indians and Alaskan Natives

Alcohol Abuse and Alcoholism: 1312, 1321; *see also* Behavioral Sciences; Medicine

Allergy: 2094; *see also* Immunology

Alpine Area: 1957

Alzheimer's Disease: 25, 1995, 2190, 2203, 2207, 2221, 2337

America: 700, 1752, 1803, 1880, 1904; *see also* Economics; History, American; Literature, American; Minority Studies; Political Science

American Indian and Alaskan Native Community Development: 947, 948, 952, 953, 955, 957, 1258, 1410; *see also* Minority Community and Institutional Development; Minority-Owned Businesses; Small Business Development

American Indians and Alaskan Natives: 347, 671, 672, 920, 922, 943, 949, 956, 960, 961, 1538, 1539; *see also* Minority Studies; Race Relations; also any discipline that may be given American Indian emphasis or be of concern to American Indians

American Indians and Alaskan Natives, Eligibility of: 349, 883, 885, 886, 896, 897, 908, 911, 924, 940, 941, 942, 944, 945, 946, 947, 948, 949, 950, 951, 952, 954, 957, 958, 959, 961, 1410, 1424, 1443, 1590, 1701, 1783, 1880, 1934, 1941, 2053, 2062, 2313, 2315, 2353, 2394, 2395; *see also* Minority-Group Members, Eligibility of

American Indians and Alaskan Natives, Employment: 946, 952, 1765; *see also* Equal Employment Opportunity; Labor

Amyotrophic Lateral Sclerosis (ALS): 2202, 2218, 2221

Anatomy: 2233

Anesthesiology: 2028, 2039, 2052

Animal Cruelty: 76, 173, 178, 212, 1248, 1254, 1633, 1898, 2010

Animal Sciences: 177, 1151, 1617, 1629, 1664, 1829, 1894, 1898, 1900, 1919, 1931, 1947, 2009, 2034; *see also* Veterinary Sciences

Animal Welfare: 15, 55, 141, 253, 259, 905, 920, 1102, 1109, 1110, 1146, 1191, 1971

Antarctica: 1644

Anthropology: 321, 340, 356, 363, 400, 590, 762, 792, 795, 814, 1612, 1613, 1619, 1620, 1648, 1661, 1662, 1811, 1812, 1814, 1815, 1816, 1817, 1818, 1932, 1936; *see also* Behavioral Sciences; History; Sociology

Applied Sciences: 3, 829, 1312

Appraisal: 1700

Apprenticeships. *See* In-Service Training Projects

Aquatic Ecology. *See* Ecology, Aquatic

Arboriculture: 1925; *see also* Forestry

Archaeology: 307, 309, 312, 316, 546, 579, 580, 792, 810, 816, 817, 986, 1612, 1625, 1626, 1811, 1813, 1817

Archaeology, Research and Study Abroad: 310, 311, 313, 315, 331, 389, 757, 794, 796, 807, 809, 811, 814, 815, 818, 826, 827, 1445, 1480

Architecture: 197, 328, 360, 365, 366, 368, 369, 370, 371, 372, 373, 375, 378, 379, 380, 381, 382, 395, 424, 428, 435, 442, 468, 522, 564, 571, 759, 853, 857, 968, 1612, 1613; *see also* Arts; Landscape Design; Urban and Regional Planning

Architecture, Research and Study Abroad: 303, 310, 369, 377, 378, 383, 522, 811

Arctic: 1446, 1645, 1957

Area Studies: 363, 594, 595, 607, 608, 609, 755, 759, 776, 778, 782, 783, 786, 787, 804, 838, 839, 852, 853, 854, 1464, 1525, 1661; *see also* Africa; America; Asia; Atlantic Community; Canada; Europe; Geography; Latin and South America; Mediterranean Area; Middle East; NATO Member Countries; Orient; Pacific Area; Slavic and East Europe; also specific states, U.S. regions, or nations

Argentina: 1514

Arizona: 17, 111, 115, 390, 499, 684, 942, 945, 1058

Arkansas: 68, 161, 429, 1059, 1157

Armaments: 2385; *see also* Defense Projects and Research; International Security; National Security

Armed Services Personnel and Dependents, Eligibility of: 1496, 1545; *see also* Veterans, Eligibility or; Veterans' Children and Dependents, Eligibility of

Arms Control: 51, 760, 781, 789

Art Galleries: 426, 433, 516; *see also* Exhibitions; Museums

Art History: 185, 303, 304, 307, 315, 326, 328, 330, 340, 356, 360, 362, 363, 365, 389, 400, 404, 433, 470, 496, 497, 503, 506, 508, 510, 521, 795, 811, 857, 863, 864, 865, 1607, 1612, 1648

Art Therapy: 2303

Arthritis. *See* Rheumatology and Rheumatic Diseases

Arts: 1, 2, 4, 5, 6, 9, 13, 14, 15, 16, 21, 27, 28, 29, 30, 34, 35, 36, 44, 45, 46, 47, 48, 52, 55, 57, 59, 64, 65, 66, 69, 73, 75, 76, 80, 81, 84, 87, 89, 95, 96, 103, 104, 105, 106, 108, 110, 111, 113, 116, 118, 125, 128, 130, 131, 132, 133, 138, 140, 141, 144, 145, 146, 150, 158, 164, 165, 167, 170, 173, 175, 179, 180, 186, 188, 194, 198, 201, 205, 206, 208, 209, 211, 213, 214, 216, 220, 225, 226, 229, 234, 235, 239, 248, 249, 253, 255, 259, 260, 261, 262, 266, 275, 277, 278, 280, 281, 285, 288, 290, 292, 296, 299, 300, 301, 302, 325, 334, 362, 375, 384, 385, 386, 388, 390, 391, 392, 393, 394, 396, 401, 402, 403, 405, 406, 408, 409, 412, 414, 415, 416, 417, 418, 419, 420, 421, 422, 424, 425, 426, 427, 428, 429, 430, 431, 432, 433, 434, 435, 436, 438, 439, 441, 442, 443, 444, 445, 446, 447, 448, 449, 451, 452, 453, 455, 456, 457, 458, 459, 460, 464, 466, 468, 469, 472, 473, 474, 478, 491, 513, 516, 523, 545, 591, 652, 667, 700, 759, 853, 856, 890, 893, 905, 979, 980, 987, 1004, 1011, 1044, 1046, 1048, 1049, 1050, 1057, 1060, 1063, 1065, 1078, 1081, 1082, 1085, 1089, 1091, 1094, 1098, 1100, 1101, 1102, 1103, 1105, 1106, 1108, 1109, 1110, 1115, 1116, 1117, 1118, 1119, 1122, 1123, 1124, 1125, 1126, 1127, 1129, 1131, 1132, 1136, 1138, 1139, 1140, 1142, 1145, 1146, 1147, 1150, 1151, 1153, 1154, 1155, 1156, 1158, 1159, 1164, 1165, 1166, 1167, 1168, 1169, 1171, 1172, 1173, 1174, 1175, 1177, 1178, 1181, 1182, 1186, 1187, 1189, 1190, 1193, 1196, 1197, 1198, 1204, 1207, 1215, 1216, 1219, 1222, 1223, 1224, 1225, 1228, 1229, 1233, 1236, 1237, 1240, 1241, 1242, 1243, 1245, 1248, 1251, 1252, 1255, 1258, 1260, 1268, 1270, 1274, 1292, 1346,

1347, 1352, 1357, 1376, 1381, 1391, 1400, 1402, 1421, 1438, 1453, 1460, 1646, 1794, 2038, 2305; *see also* Crafts; Creative Arts; Cultural Affairs; Cultural Events, Community; Fine Arts; Humanities; Performing Arts; also specific arts

Arts Administration: 445, 487, 488

Arts, Construction and Facilities Projects: 172, 433; *see also* Construction and Facilities Projects

Arts, Consulting Services: 384, 385, 390, 401, 403, 405, 409, 415, 416, 418, 420, 427, 428, 429, 435, 436, 443, 444, 447, 456, 458, 466, 472, 474, 720, 732

Arts, Education: 229, 276, 292, 390, 394, 402, 405, 407, 412, 416, 420, 423, 433, 434, 436, 439, 440, 442, 445, 448, 451, 454, 455, 458, 461, 464, 474, 476, 509, 522, 704, 830, 930, 1087, 1144, 1194, 1400; *see also* specific arts

Arts, In-Service Training Programs: 455, 510

Arts, Publication: 375, 404, 426; *see also* Publication Prizes, History and Humanities

Arts, Research and Study Abroad: 303, 496, 508, 517, 521, 522, 704, 807, 1517; *see also* specific arts

Arts, Workshops and Residencies: 362, 385, 390, 394, 399, 415, 427, 431, 434, 436, 443, 450, 455, 464, 465, 466, 475, 476, 477, 487, 489, 511, 515; *see also* specific art forms

Asia: 114, 391, 408, 768, 769, 833, 845, 846; *see also* History, Asian; Languages, Asian; Orient; Southeast Asia; also specific nations

Asian-Americans: 922, 925; *see also* Minority Studies; Race Relations; also any discipline that may be given Asian- American emphasis

Asian-Americans, Eligibility of: 613, 777, 886, 896, 924, 1482, 1483, 1484, 1783, 2313, 2315; *see also* Minority-Group Members, Eligibility of

Asian Nationals, Eligibility of: 1774

Asian Nations: 185; *see also* specific nations

Asian Nations, Research and Study in: 975

Asthma: 2139, 2237

Astronautics: 2364

Astronomy: 1624, 1642, 1827, 1831, 1832, 1833, 1834, 1835, 1836, 1837, 1838, 1841, 1842, 1843, 1844, 1845, 1888, 1896; *see also* Physical Sciences

Astrophysics: 1638, 1822, 1832, 1840, 1841, 1842, 1843, 1844, 1845, 1932, 2372, 2385

At-Risk Youth: 1037, 1227

Athletics: 997; *see also* Physical Education; Sports

Atmospheric Sciences: 881, 1638, 1644, 1645, 1823, 1826, 1872, 1963, 2365; *see also* Earth Sciences

Atomic Energy. *See* Nuclear Sciences

Audiology: 2262; *see also* Deafness and Hearing Impairments; Speech Impairments and Communicative Disorders

Australia: 314, 449, 642, 858, 878, 1514, 1860, 1927, 1991, 2092

Austria: 759, 852, 853, 1514

Austrian-American Relations: 759

Autism: 63, 2014

Aviation: 1793, 2343, 2363, 2366, 2367, 2368, 2369, 2370, 2371, 2372, 2373; *see also* Aerospace Sciences

B

Ballet. *See* Dance; Performing Arts

Bands: 689; *see also* Music

Bangladesh: 801

Basic, Clinical and Translational Biomedical Research 2045

Behavioral Sciences: 1418, 1658, 1714, 2031, 2307, 2308, 2309, 2322, 2331, 2333; *see also* Anthropology; Psychology; Social Sciences; Sociology

Behavioral Sciences, Education: 908, 1613, 2055, 2056

Behavioral Sciences, Research: 193, 879, 1310, 1311, 1312, 1442, 1460, 1644, 1659, 1663, 1669, 1694, 1812, 1813, 1950, 2055, 2056, 2108, 2211, 2324, 2330, 2332

Belgium: 725, 820

Bibliographic Research: 304, 339, 664; *see also* Libraries and Librarianship; Writers and Writing

Biochemical Engineering: 1938

Biochemistry: 867, 1598, 1634, 1824, 1852, 1853, 1854, 1858, 1937, 1946, 1963, 2031, 2051, 2167; *see also* Biological Sciences; Chemistry

Biodiversity: 7, 57, 1877

Bioethics: 1895; *see also* Medical Ethics

Biography: 533, 585, 630, 638

Biological Pollution: 1970

Biological Psychiatry: 2338, 2339

Biological Sciences: 3, 111, 193, 637, 856, 911, 969, 1616, 1625, 1626, 1629, 1637, 1644, 1645, 1648, 1651, 1669, 1820, 1824, 1853, 1931, 1932, 1936, 1937, 1938, 1939, 1942, 1946, 1947, 1976, 1983, 2052, 2072, 2073, 2086, 2292, 2338, 2339; *see also* Chemistry; Life Sciences; Medicine; Sciences; also specific biological sciences

Biological Sciences, Education: 908, 1598, 1612, 1613, 1624, 1900, 1934, 1939, 1948, 2113, 2284

Biological Sciences, Research and Study: 1372, 1615, 1635, 1847, 1849, 1896, 1930, 1932, 1938, 1940, 1941, 1942, 1950, 1983

Biological Sciences, Research and Study Abroad: 867, 1938

Biomedical Engineering: 881, 2072, 2073, 2292

Biomedical Sciences and Research: 246, 879, 912, 1310, 1311, 1442, 1460, 1612, 1613, 1634, 1646, 1653, 1820, 1901, 1931, 1934, 1938, 2016, 2052, 2053, 2055, 2056, 2058, 2061, 2086, 2087, 2108, 2121, 2172, 2189, 2207, 2211, 2215, 2217, 2251, 2274, 2275, 2286, 2337; *see also* Medical Research; Medicine

Biophysics: 1824, 1856, 1946, 2031; *see also* Biological Sciences; Physical Sciences

Biotechnology: 2107, 2385

Birth Control. *See* Family Planning; Population Studies

Birth Defects: 2014, 2044, 2047, 2048, 2284; *see also* Genetics; Handicapped; Mental Retardation

Black Community Development: 937, 1210; *see also* Minority Community and Institutional Development

Blacks. *See* African Americans

Blacksmithing: 413

Blind, Assistance for: 910, 999, 1019, 1474; *see also* Handicapped

Blindness. *See* Ophthalmology; Visual Disorders

Blood. *See* Hematology

Blood Banks: 2142

Botany: 1910, 1911, 1912, 1914, 1915, 1930, 1933, 1936, 1944, 1947, 1966, 1967, 1968; *see also* Ecology; Plant Physiology and Pathology

Broadcast Media: 909, 994, 1567, 1724, 1725, 1735, 1738, 1743, 1744, 1748, 1750, 1751, 1757; *see also* Communications; Radio and Television; Telecommunications

Building Projects. *See* Construction and Facilities Projects

Business: 509, 916, 1449, 1465, 1506, 1529, 1702, 1711, 1712, 1714, 1730, 1733, 1772; *see also* Accounting; Economics; Finance; Labor; Management; Small Business Development

Business Administration: 792, 916, 968, 1612, 1613, 1701, 1708, 1710, 1718, 1720, 2289; *see also* Management

Business Development Assistance: 1214, 1908; *see also* Small Business Development

Business, Education: 176, 240, 900, 937, 938, 945, 951, 1449, 1465, 1551, 1599, 1705, 1710, 1716, 1721, 1722

Business, History: 543, 553, 591

Business, International: 766, 825, 1719

Business, Internships: 1805

Business, Publication: 1742

Byzantine Studies: 326, 810, 813, 817; *see also* Archaeology; Classical Studies; History

C

California: 22, 56, 78, 95, 120, 133, 137, 145, 170, 218, 219, 224, 227, 228, 229, 230, 255, 259, 295, 394, 452, 453, 503, 583, 600, 601, 663, 905, 924, 942, 945, 967, 1008, 1028, 1061, 1079, 1147, 1161, 1182, 1186, 1227, 1242, 1243, 1247, 1264, 1285, 1286, 1299, 1306, 1313, 1336, 1352, 1389, 1455, 1487, 1488, 1499, 1510, 1519, 1608, 1721, 1785, 1974, 2071

Canada: 174, 398, 877, 974, 1175, 1316, 1319, 1328, 1446, 1450, 1489, 1527, 1595, 1596, 1597, 1598, 1599, 1600, 1601, 1602, 1603, 1604, 1641, 1646, 1718, 1737, 1762, 1770, 1781, 1965, 2017, 2018, 2019, 2020, 2021, 2022, 2172, 2173, 2186, 2187, 2216, 2337, 2356, 2361

Canadians, Eligibility of: 130, 311, 313, 315, 497, 525, 548, 621, 624, 657, 659, 685, 721, 737, 767, 805, 809, 821, 822, 857, 1183, 1450, 1489, 1516, 1527, 1592, 1593, 1594, 1597, 1600, 1641, 1656, 1675, 1676, 1677, 1678, 1679, 1728, 1730, 1737, 1762, 1769, 1854, 1855, 1856, 1857, 1935, 1944, 2023, 2139, 2140, 2141, 2163, 2164, 2168, 2174, 2175, 2181, 2201, 2215, 2217, 2219, 2224, 2237, 2324, 2362, 2363, 2390, 2404, 2420

Cancer: 2031, 2087, 2107, 2113, 2177, 2182, 2184, 2185, 2188, 2191, 2193, 2197, 2204

Cancer Research: 193, 267, 2026, 2113, 2116, 2117, 2118, 2149, 2154, 2160, 2177, 2179, 2180, 2181, 2182, 2183, 2184, 2185, 2186, 2187, 2188, 2189, 2190, 2191, 2192, 2193, 2194, 2195, 2196, 2197, 2198, 2199; *see also* Medical Research

Cancer Research Training: 293, 2177, 2178, 2191, 2195, 2196, 2199

Cancer Support Services: 63

Cancer Therapy and Treatment: 2177, 2189, 2194; *see also* Rehabilitation

Capacity Building: 295, 1086, 1160

Cardiology and Cardiovascular Diseases: 267, 2087, 2122, 2123, 2124, 2125, 2126, 2127, 2128, 2129, 2130, 2131, 2132, 2140, 2141, 2143, 2146, 2147, 2190, 2273; *see also* Stroke; Vascular Diseases

Cardiovascular Research Training: 2123, 2124, 2125, 2126, 2128, 2129, 2130, 2131, 2132, 2140, 2141, 2146, 2147, 2148

Career Counseling: 1764, 2143

Caribbean: 130, 157, 530, 780, 876

Cartography: 530, 1644

Cartoons: 356

Catholicism: 72, 287, 535, 536, 537, 538, 539, 579, 736, 737, 738, 745, 751, 752, 902, 1524

Cell Biology: 1938, 2031, 2274, 2275; *see also* Biological Sciences

Ceramics: 387, 413; *see also* Crafts; Creative Arts

Chemical Engineering: 1618, 1848, 1850, 1852, 1853, 1857, 2377, 2390, 2396

Chemistry: 3, 881, 1627, 1628, 1629, 1638, 1642, 1651, 1652, 1819, 1827, 1828, 1847, 1848, 1849, 1850, 1852, 1854, 1856, 1857, 1861, 1983, 2072, 2073, 2292, 2402; *see also* Biological Sciences; Physical Sciences; also specific chemical sciences

Chemistry, Education: 184, 1612, 1624, 1819, 1848, 1851, 1858, 1859

Chemistry, Research and Study: 1635, 1819, 1847, 1849, 1850, 1852, 1854, 1896, 1963, 2359

Chemistry, Research and Study Abroad: 867, 1860

Chicanos. *See* Spanish-Speaking Americans

Chicanos, Eligibility of: 896, 908, 1701; *see also* Minority-Group Members, Eligibility of

Child Abuse: 35, 93, 117, 178, 283, 1006, 1012, 1339

Child Care. *See* Preschool Education and Care

Child Development and Behavior: 70, 1016, 1020, 1029, 1037, 1038, 1077, 1308, 1350, 1378, 1460, 2309, 2329; *see also* Behavioral Sciences

Child Welfare and Health: 13, 34, 35, 45, 94, 97, 119, 149, 171, 212, 259, 267, 283, 301, 746, 1006, 1008, 1009, 1012, 1017, 1019, 1022, 1023, 1028, 1029, 1030, 1031, 1034, 1035, 1037, 1038, 1040, 1041, 1059, 1143, 1224, 1267, 1304, 1318, 1319, 1331, 1334, 1359, 1476, 2252, 2283, 2286, 2307, 2308; *see also* Pediatrics; Social Welfare

Childhood Obesity: 1337, 2042

Children: 19, 29, 35, 66, 105, 116, 132, 133, 136, 146, 164, 173, 179, 196, 206, 216, 224, 234, 235, 245, 257, 278, 292, 293, 295, 297, 301, 905, 927, 933, 987, 999, 1000, 1003, 1004, 1005, 1008, 1012, 1015, 1021, 1022, 1023, 1028, 1029, 1032, 1033, 1034, 1035, 1037, 1040, 1042, 1058, 1061, 1086, 1092, 1098, 1102, 1103, 1127, 1155, 1171, 1182, 1201, 1230, 1251, 1252, 1253, 1259, 1285, 1304, 1336, 1339, 1342, 1352, 1431, 1451, 1490, 2282, 2285; *see also* Child Welfare and Health; Education, Elementary; Education, Secondary; Preschool Education and Care; Social Welfare; Youth

Children, Adoption and Foster Care: 1026, 1035, 1040, 1056, 1092, 1387

Children, Handicapped. *See* Handicapped Children

Children's Literature: 618, 619, 631, 646, 650, 651; *see also* Writers and Writing

Chile: 1514

China: 496, 822, 1514, 1981

Choir: 702; *see also* Music

Choreography: 487, 488, 491; *see also* Dance; Performing Arts

Christianity: 79, 748, 1402; *see also* Catholicism; Protestantism; Religion

Church Facilities and Construction. *See* Construction and Facilities Projects; Religious Institutions

Church History. *See* Religion, History

Cinema. *See* Film

Citizen Action Legislation: 250, 1084

Citizenship: 167, 1476

City and Regional Planning. *See* Urban and Regional Planning

Civic Affairs: 6, 18, 23, 35, 40, 54, 56, 67, 72, 74, 88, 98, 100, 109, 113, 116, 126, 127, 150, 157, 167, 169, 184, 190, 198, 214, 217, 218, 222, 228, 232, 240, 241, 243, 257, 265, 278, 284, 289, 299, 301, 388, 414, 743, 933, 987, 1005, 1031, 1044, 1074, 1085, 1099, 1100, 1108, 1109, 1110, 1117, 1118, 1123, 1136, 1139, 1141, 1145, 1147, 1159, 1161, 1168, 1174, 1177, 1186, 1197, 1199, 1204, 1214, 1216, 1223, 1237, 1241, 1242, 1249, 1257, 1258, 1274, 1296, 1376, 1438, 1961; *see also* Community Development; Community Services; Urban Affairs

Civil Liberties: 1161, 1292, 1329, 1655, 1736; *see also* Human Rights

Classical Studies: 307, 316, 321, 327, 340, 363, 623, 817, 986, 1445; *see also* Archaeology; History; Humanities; Languages, Classical; Literature, Classical

Classical Studies, Overseas: 303, 310, 313, 315, 325, 331, 389, 809, 810, 811

Climatology: 7, 71, 81, 202, 1248, 1346, 1625, 1626, 1872, 1963, 1983; *see also* Atmospheric Sciences; Earth Sciences; Environmental Studies; Meteorology

Clinical Laboratory Science: 1621, 2202; *see also* Medical Technology

Clinical Medicine: 2039, 2074

Clinical Psychology: 2091; *see also* Psychology

Clinical Research: 2031, 2048, 2099, 2123, 2124, 2125, 2126, 2128, 2129, 2130, 2131, 2132, 2155, 2157, 2199, 2215, 2217, 2273

Clinics. *See* Health Care Facilities; Sciences, Equipment and Facilities

Coal: 1622, 1623, 2408; *see also* Mineral Sciences; Technology, Mining

Cognitive Processes. *See* Learning Process and Memory

Collective Bargaining. *See* Labor, Management Relations

College Teaching, Career Preparation: 591, 924, 1189, 1386, 1612, 1707; *see also* Education, Teacher Preparation

Colorado: 83, 100, 101, 141, 161, 218, 229, 396, 457, 499, 546, 942, 945, 1007, 1200, 1307, 1339, 1342, 1655, 1971

Commerce. *See* Business

Commercial Design: 373; *see also* Creative Arts; Design

Commercial Growth: 1860

Communications: 110, 160, 329, 423, 495, 766, 792, 1084, 1529, 1711, 1738, 1740, 1743, 1749, 1762, 1763, 1789, 1793, 1794, 1801, 1805, 2385, 2413; *see also* Broadcast Media; Educational Media; Film; Information Sciences; Journalism; Print Media; Publications; Radio and Television; Technology, Communications; Telecommunications

Communications Media, Internships: 1739

Communications Science: 1278, 1762, 2262

Communicative Disorders. *See* Speech Impairments and Communicative Disorders

Community Centers: 1179

Community Colleges. *See* Junior Colleges

Community Development: 1, 3, 5, 7, 10, 14, 15, 16, 17, 19, 24, 28, 29, 31, 36, 37, 41, 43, 53, 58, 59, 60, 62, 64, 65, 66, 67, 68, 69, 70, 73, 76, 86, 88, 96, 98, 103, 104, 105, 108, 119, 123, 124, 127, 129, 132, 145, 154, 157, 166, 169, 181, 186, 187, 189, 191, 202, 203, 204, 206, 207, 208, 214, 216, 217, 222, 232, 235, 251, 255, 262, 266, 268, 276, 277, 278, 282, 286, 290, 301, 371, 393, 396, 421, 774, 957, 960, 972, 985, 1043, 1045, 1048, 1049, 1050, 1053, 1055, 1057, 1060, 1062, 1063, 1066, 1068, 1070, 1071, 1072, 1074, 1086, 1088, 1091, 1093, 1094, 1098, 1099, 1100, 1101, 1102, 1105, 1106, 1108, 1110, 1111, 1112, 1113, 1115, 1121, 1122, 1125, 1126, 1127, 1128, 1132, 1133, 1134, 1136, 1138, 1141, 1142, 1148, 1149, 1150, 1155, 1157, 1162, 1164, 1165, 1166, 1167, 1168, 1169, 1170, 1172, 1173, 1176, 1177, 1179, 1181, 1182, 1195, 1196, 1197, 1198, 1199, 1201, 1203, 1205, 1208, 1211, 1214, 1219, 1220, 1221, 1222, 1223, 1225, 1226, 1227, 1228, 1231, 1232, 1234, 1236, 1237, 1238, 1239, 1242, 1247, 1248, 1251, 1253, 1255, 1258, 1260, 1262, 1265, 1266, 1269, 1271, 1274, 1275, 1296, 1338, 1343, 1346, 1352, 1371, 1378, 1379, 1381, 1417, 1438, 1458, 1655, 1717, 1908, 1921, 2042; *see also* Business; Civic Affairs; Cultural Events, Community; Environmental Studies; Housing; Inner-City; Poverty Programs; Small Business Development; Social Welfare; Urban Affairs; Urban and Regional Planning

Community Development, Consulting Services: 1223

Community Economic Development: 247

Community Education: 960, 1073, 1087, 1208

Community Funds: 80, 107, 113, 143, 223, 269, 1043, 1052, 1070, 1079, 1090, 1104, 1127, 1166, 1199, 1204, 1206, 1212, 1223, 1245, 1256, 1263, 1295; *see also* Relief Organizations

Community Government: 1092, 1786; *see also* Government

Community Health and Welfare. *See* Health; Health Care Facilities; Public Health; Social Welfare

Community Leadership: 111, 1045, 1208, 1235, 1242, 1274

Community Organization: 127, 671, 672, 972, 1097, 1107, 1329

Community Services: 33, 40, 44, 47, 49, 50, 67, 92, 97, 100, 109, 117, 121, 129, 132, 157, 158, 170, 174, 183, 200, 205, 211, 219, 228, 240, 241, 243, 256, 258, 260, 263, 282, 285, 289, 295, 744, 803, 957, 1028, 1043, 1047, 1059, 1060, 1067, 1069, 1071, 1077, 1079, 1086, 1095, 1099, 1100, 1112, 1113, 1114, 1121, 1129, 1132, 1137, 1149, 1151, 1152, 1154, 1155, 1162, 1165, 1167, 1170, 1174, 1176, 1196, 1199, 1208, 1209, 1218, 1223, 1224, 1225, 1243, 1244, 1245, 1247, 1252, 1259, 1268, 1269, 1274, 1299, 1339, 1417, 1506; *see also* specific services

Comparative Education. *See* Education, Comparative

Compensatory Education. *See* Equal Educational Opportunity

Composition. *See* Music, Composition.

Computer Analysis and Modeling: 2408

Computer Engineering: 2350, 2391

Computer Sciences: 3, 207, 862, 867, 899, 951, 968, 989, 993, 1277, 1489, 1622, 1623, 1635, 1642, 1694, 1705, 1824, 1828, 1885, 1896, 2355, 2371, 2384, 2396, 2402; *see also* Information Sciences; Mathematics; Operations Research

Concrete: 2403; *see also* Engineering; Technology

Conferences: 436, 1818, 1884, 1946, 1947, 2046, 2327; *see also* International Projects and Seminars; Seminars; Travel Grants, Seminar Attendance; Workshops; also specific disciplines

Conflict Resolution: 767; *see also* International Security

Connecticut: 5, 322, 402, 489, 665, 1064, 1101

Conservation: 1, 46, 55, 107, 117, 164, 172, 188, 202, 204, 210, 216, 220, 229, 231, 250, 288, 301, 473, 667, 1117, 1123, 1150, 1187, 1201, 1238, 1379, 1622, 1623, 1640, 1673, 1721, 1830, 1871, 1900, 1935, 1939, 1949, 1954, 1955, 1960, 1961, 1964, 1965, 1967, 1968, 1971, 1977, 1980, 1984, 1985, 1986, 1991, 1993, 2408; see also Ecology; Energy Resources and Utilization; Environmental Studies; Life Sciences

Conservation, Art Objects: 503, 506, 521, 667, 675, 864

Construction: 1179, 2376; see also Engineering

Construction and Facilities Projects: 55, 100, 172, 272, 1018, 1129, 1179, 1262, 1469, 2376, 2403; see also Equipment Grants; also specific fields of interest

Consulting Services: 418, 676, 874, 1360; see also Counseling and Guidance; Technical Assistance; also specific fields of interest

Consumer Action: 1772

Consumer Affairs: 1706, 2413

Consumer Information and Education: 1281; see also Business

Continuing Education. See Education, Continuing

Cooley's Anemia: 2165; see also Hematology

Cooperatives, Rural and Consumer: 176

Corrective Therapy: 2295; see also Rehabilitation

Cost Engineering. See Engineering; Finance

Counseling and Guidance: 1034, 1230; see also Career Counseling; Consulting Services; Education, Counseling and Guidance; Family Services; Mental and Emotional Health; Psychology; Social Work

Crafts: 397, 409, 413, 416, 428, 439, 440, 445, 469, 470, 980; see also Ceramics; Creative Arts; Folk Arts; Mosaics; Printmaking; Weaving

Crafts, Research and Study Abroad: 497

Creative Arts: 130, 305, 384, 386, 395, 396, 401, 402, 405, 409, 413, 448, 460, 467, 468, 513, 1437, 1601; see also Arts; Crafts; Fine Arts; Performing Arts; Visual Arts; Writers and Writing; also related disciplines

Creative Arts, Workshops and Residencies: 411, 450, 465

Crime Prevention: 26, 59, 206, 1167, 1276, 1277, 1354, 1669; see also Juvenile Delinquency; Law Enforcement

Criminal Justice: 1, 242, 1204, 1244, 1277, 1278, 1351, 1401, 1738, 1779; see also Justice

Criminal Rehabilitation: 1276

Criminology: 1264, 1276, 1661; see also Law Enforcement

Crippled. See Handicapped; Rehabilitation

Cross-Cultural Studies: 793; see also Cultural Affairs

Cross-Disciplinary Study. See Interdisciplinary Research and Study

Cubans, Eligibility of: 395, 896, 1701; see also Foreign Nationals, Eligibility of

Culinary Arts: 2358; see also Restaurant Management and Food Service

Cultural Affairs: 1, 6, 10, 14, 15, 20, 26, 27, 28, 29, 33, 42, 48, 50, 55, 56, 57, 60, 61, 64, 67, 70, 72, 76, 81, 89, 95, 98, 101, 103, 104, 105, 107, 109, 111, 112, 113, 124, 126, 139, 143, 144, 145, 150, 153, 161, 162, 166, 167, 168, 176, 184, 198, 201, 213, 214, 217, 219, 220, 228, 235, 240, 241, 243, 253, 255, 257, 268, 280, 282, 290, 294, 299, 301, 388, 392, 428, 433, 457, 542, 560, 591, 667, 766, 768, 769, 780, 854, 905, 933, 960, 1011, 1044, 1046, 1048, 1058, 1060, 1061, 1062, 1064, 1065, 1067, 1069, 1078, 1085, 1091, 1092, 1101, 1102, 1106, 1108, 1110, 1116, 1122, 1125, 1126, 1131, 1132, 1138, 1139, 1140, 1142, 1146, 1152, 1154, 1158, 1165, 1166, 1167, 1168, 1171, 1174, 1175, 1177, 1181, 1182, 1188, 1193, 1197, 1198, 1203, 1213, 1219, 1228, 1234, 1236, 1240, 1241, 1243, 1248, 1255, 1260, 1265, 1268, 1274, 1361, 1429, 1559; see also Fine Arts; International Relations and International Affairs; Performing Arts; also specific arts

Cultural Events, Community: 16, 40, 106, 116, 140, 153, 186, 209, 216, 230, 260, 265, 274, 299, 302, 384, 385, 393, 394, 398, 401, 402, 403, 405, 409, 412, 420, 425, 427, 429, 436, 438, 443, 444, 445, 446, 447, 448, 451, 454, 456, 458, 459, 466, 468, 472, 474, 743, 759, 960, 1004, 1034, 1063, 1073, 1093, 1095, 1099, 1101, 1110, 1120, 1160, 1169, 1186, 1187, 1215, 1223, 1233, 1272, 1404, 1438, 1907; see also Community Development

Cultural Exchange Programs: 391, 395, 773, 776, 777, 791, 793, 797, 801, 808, 819, 825, 832, 833, 837, 848, 1425, 1444, 1454; see also International Study and Research Programs

Cultural Studies: 618, 759, 853

Curriculum Development: 601, 773, 775, 789, 1393, 1464, 1719, 2046; see also Education and entries beginning with Education and Educational; Humanities; Curriculum Development; Instructional Materials; Sciences, Curriculum Development

Cystic Fibrosis: 2167; see also Metabolism and Metabolic Disorders

Cytology: 1946

D

Dairy Sciences. See Agricultural Sciences; Animal Sciences

Dance: 398, 402, 405, 409, 416, 419, 422, 423, 428, 434, 437, 439, 442, 443, 454, 469, 481, 482, 483, 485, 486, 487, 488, 491, 493, 714, 716, 869; see also Choreography; Performing Arts

Data Processing. See Computer Sciences; Information Sciences

Day Care Service. See Preschool Education and Care

Deaf, Educational Support for: 891; see also Education, Special

Deafness and Hearing Impairments: 891, 1019, 2261, 2271; see also Audiology; Handicapped; Otology; Rehabilitation; Speech Impairments and Communicative Disorders

Decorative Arts: 362, 367, 376, 404, 432, 512; see also Fine Arts

Defense Projects and Research: 2385; see also Military Sciences; National Security; Technology, Strategic and Tactical

Delaware: 401

Democracy: 24, 51, 137, 153, 191, 247, 1161

Demography. See Population Studies

Demonstration Projects. See specific disciplines

Denmark: 808; see also Scandinavia

Dental Administration. See Health Administration

Dental Assisting: 2102

Dental Education: 2101, 2103, 2104; see also Medical Education and Training

Dental Hygiene: 1019, 2097, 2098, 2099, 2100, 2103, 2105

Dental Research: 2096, 2097, 2098, 2099, 2100, 2105

Dentistry: 298, 2101, 2106, 2107

Dentistry, Education: 1489, 2091, 2101, 2104; see also Medical Education and Training

Dentistry, Preventive: 2106, 2107

Dermatology: 2026, 2086, 2088, 2095, 2197, 2285

Desert Research. See Environmental Studies

Design: 367, 395, 416, 422, 423, 434, 523, 2393; see also Commercial Design; Creative Arts; Decorative Arts; Fine Arts; Industrial Design; Interior Design; Landscape Design

Developing Nations: 774, 780, 1962; see also International Relations and International Affairs; also specific nations

Developing Nations, Economic Growth: 112, 774; see also Economics, International

Developing Nations, Education: 774

Developing Nations, Health and Nutrition: 774; see also Food Technology; Health; Nutrition

Developing Nations, Resource Development: 774, 1962; see also Resource Development and Management

Development Grants. See specific areas of interest

Developmental Biology 2048

Developmental Disabilities: 63, 216, 928, 1261

Diabetes: 2036, 2087, 2148, 2168, 2169, 2170, 2171, 2190; see also Metabolism and Metabolic Disorders

Diagnosis of Illness. See Medicine, Diagnostic

Dietetics: 2180, 2358, 2410, 2412, 2413, 2414; see also Nutrition

Digestive Diseases: 2149, 2150, 2152, 2153, 2154, 2155, 2156, 2157, 2158, 2159, 2160, 2161

Disabilities: 83, 97, 268, 2305

Disabled. See Handicapped

Disadvantaged: 90, 112, 116, 119, 131, 148, 152, 176, 216, 244, 245, 271, 905, 950, 1000, 1021, 1026, 1027, 1029, 1038, 1084, 1144, 1200, 1233, 1285, 1387, 1413, 1463, 1547, 2002, 2379; see also Equal Economic Opportunity; Equal Educational Opportunity; Equal Employment Opportunity; Inner-City; Minority-Group Members; Poverty Programs

Disaster. See Emergency Grants; Emergency Measures Research

District of Columbia: 47, 103, 161, 403, 958, 1000, 1013, 1777, 1804, 2090

Diversity: 62

Divorce. See Family Life

Domestic Violence: 97, 117, 1006, 1301, 1320, 1332, 1339, 1658, 1669, 2002; see also Behaviorial Sciences; Sexual Abuse

Drama: 360, 480, 628, 869, 1729; see also Playwrights; Theatre; Writers and Writing

Drama, Theatre: 482, 490, 494, 645; see also Playwrights; Theatre

Drop-Out Prevention: 1354

Drug Abuse: 1301, 1321, 1408; see also Narcotics; Rehabilitation

Drugs. See Pharmacy and Pharmacology

Dysautonomia: 2209

E

Early Childhood Education: 191, 414, 1000, 1033, 1036, 1042, 1079, 1354, 1429, 1439, 1606; *see also* Preschool Education and Care

Earth Sciences: 881, 1612, 1616, 1620, 1624, 1625, 1626, 1631, 1635, 1642, 1644, 1648, 1652, 1826, 1865, 1866, 1870, 1872, 1875, 1879, 1899, 1932, 1963; *see also* Atmospheric Sciences; Geology; Oceanography; Petroleum Sciences

Earthquake: 1963

East European Studies. *See* Slavic and East Europe

Eastern States: 294, 1510, 2025; *see also* states by name

Ecological Restoration: 1625, 1970

Ecology: 81, 829, 1616, 1624, 1625, 1626, 1645, 1900, 1939, 1941, 1947, 1950, 1953, 1959, 1962, 1969, 1972, 1975, 1980, 1983, 1988, 1989, 1990; *see also* Biological Sciences; Botany; Conservation; Environmental Studies

Ecology, Aquatic: 1409, 1640, 1645, 1873, 1874, 1935, 1947, 1965, 1975, 1978, 1992; *see also* Marine Biology

Economic Education: 1709

Economic Growth and Development: 17, 24, 27, 42, 49, 54, 66, 67, 69, 99, 108, 115, 119, 129, 131, 146, 153, 157, 182, 186, 203, 206, 286, 302, 388, 774, 780, 920, 937, 949, 960, 1046, 1058, 1074, 1084, 1089, 1093, 1100, 1101, 1109, 1116, 1122, 1129, 1132, 1134, 1151, 1166, 1174, 1181, 1182, 1187, 1193, 1199, 1201, 1204, 1205, 1210, 1224, 1243, 1249, 1258, 1260, 1331, 1343, 1354, 1554, 1712, 1736; *see also* Developing Nations, Economic Growth

Economic History: 543, 591, 1703, 1793

Economic Justice: 122, 914, 972, 1135, 1154, 1657

Economic Policy: 18, 1084, 1672, 1788; *see also* Policy Analysis

Economics: 264, 276, 528, 542, 762, 768, 780, 792, 795, 960, 1097, 1344, 1451, 1590, 1661, 1662, 1672, 1709, 1714, 1730, 1795, 1887, 1981; *see also* Appraisal; Business; Finance; Labor, Economics; Management; Social Sciences

Economics, Education: 1401, 1449, 1489, 1562, 1604, 1612, 1670, 1700, 1712, 1716

Economics, International: 766, 767, 776

Economics, Research: 856, 881, 1703, 1764, 1789

Ecuador: 1514

Education: 1, 2, 3, 4, 5, 6, 7, 9, 10, 15, 16, 19, 20, 21, 22, 23, 25, 26, 27, 28, 29, 30, 31, 33, 35, 36, 37, 39, 40, 41, 42, 43, 44, 45, 46, 47, 52, 53, 54, 55, 56, 58, 59, 60, 63, 64, 66, 67, 69, 72, 74, 75, 76, 78, 82, 83, 84, 86, 88, 90, 91, 92, 95, 96, 98, 99, 100, 101, 103, 104, 105, 107, 110, 111, 112, 115, 118, 119, 120, 121, 123, 124, 125, 127, 128, 131, 132, 133, 135, 136, 137, 138, 139, 140, 141, 142, 143, 145, 146, 149, 151, 153, 157, 158, 161, 164, 165, 166, 168, 169, 170, 179, 180, 181, 182, 186, 188, 189, 194, 195, 196, 197, 198, 204, 205, 208, 210, 211, 212, 213, 216, 217, 218, 219, 220, 221, 222, 224, 226, 229, 230, 235, 237, 238, 239, 240, 241, 243, 244, 246, 248, 249, 251, 253, 255, 256, 257, 258, 260, 262, 263, 265, 266, 269, 270, 271, 273, 275, 277, 278, 280, 284, 285, 286, 288, 299, 300, 301, 302, 328, 376, 388, 393, 397, 407, 421, 445, 493, 531, 603, 620, 656, 657, 682, 743, 756, 774, 780, 792, 893, 897, 901, 902, 905, 920, 921, 925, 933, 961, 1000, 1003, 1004, 1008, 1009, 1010, 1012, 1014, 1018, 1019, 1020, 1022, 1032, 1033, 1035, 1042, 1044, 1046, 1048, 1049, 1050, 1051, 1053, 1054, 1055, 1060, 1061, 1062, 1065, 1067, 1069, 1070, 1075, 1076, 1077, 1080, 1081, 1082, 1083, 1084, 1085, 1089, 1091, 1093, 1094, 1095, 1098, 1100, 1101, 1102, 1105, 1106, 1108, 1109, 1110, 1115, 1116, 1117, 1118, 1119, 1120, 1123, 1124, 1125, 1126, 1129, 1130, 1131, 1133, 1136, 1137, 1138, 1139, 1140, 1142, 1144, 1145, 1146, 1147, 1150, 1151, 1152, 1153, 1155, 1156, 1157, 1158, 1159, 1161, 1162, 1163, 1164, 1165, 1166, 1167, 1168, 1169, 1170, 1172, 1173, 1174, 1175, 1177, 1178, 1186, 1187, 1188, 1193, 1194, 1196, 1197, 1198, 1199, 1201, 1202, 1203, 1204, 1207, 1213, 1215, 1218, 1219, 1222, 1223, 1224, 1225, 1229, 1230, 1234, 1235, 1236, 1237, 1238, 1241, 1244, 1245, 1247, 1248, 1249, 1251, 1255, 1256, 1257, 1260, 1265, 1266, 1268, 1270, 1271, 1272, 1274, 1288, 1317, 1321, 1322, 1327, 1331, 1336, 1347, 1353, 1357, 1361, 1364, 1365, 1366, 1367, 1368, 1375, 1376, 1377, 1381, 1382, 1391, 1392, 1393, 1395, 1399, 1400, 1405, 1412, 1415, 1417, 1421, 1428, 1429, 1432, 1434, 1438, 1439, 1448, 1452, 1462, 1469, 1472, 1476, 1506, 1524, 1532, 1549, 1552, 1571, 1572, 1608, 1611, 1612, 1662, 1712, 1713, 1764, 1871, 1878, 1886, 1921, 1939, 1950, 1983, 2038, 2064, 2075, 2239, 2419; *see also* Consumer Information and Education; Curriculum Development; entries beginning with Education and Educational; Equal Educational Opportunity; Faculty, Study and Research Programs; Instructional Materials; International Study and Research Programs; Medical Education and Training; Nursing Education; Preschool Education and Care; Reading; Teaching, Outside U.S.; also specific professions and areas of study

Education, Adult: 1267, 1423, 1470, 1552, 1765; *see also* Education, Continuing

Education, Alternative Modes: 1468

Education, Comparative: 868

Education, Continuing: 978, 1436; *see also* Education, Adult

Education, Counseling and Guidance: 1463

Education, Developing Nations. *See* Developing Nations, Education

Education, Elementary: 292, 956, 1024, 1027, 1164, 1191, 1250, 1354, 1388, 1390, 1412, 1422, 1424, 1430, 1432, 1437, 1447, 1490, 1504

Education, Elementary and Secondary, Construction and Facilities Projects: 1273, 1632; *see also* Construction and Facilities Projects

Education, Government Policy and Legislation. *See* Education, Policy-Making

Education, Higher, Aid Programs for Undergraduate and Graduate Students in All Disciplines: 13, 169, 183, 267, 268, 364, 368, 376, 423, 600, 647, 683, 840, 842, 844, 858, 870, 876, 878, 884, 887, 891, 897, 898, 901, 903, 907, 910, 913, 916, 918, 926, 929, 932, 934, 938, 939, 940, 941, 942, 944, 950, 951, 959, 961, 964, 965, 966, 971, 973, 974, 976, 978, 991, 992, 1011, 1026, 1110, 1133, 1141, 1152, 1178, 1189, 1291, 1369, 1375, 1380, 1385, 1386, 1387, 1388, 1414, 1420, 1441, 1443, 1447, 1459, 1465, 1467, 1470, 1471, 1472, 1473, 1474, 1476, 1478, 1479, 1481, 1485, 1487, 1488, 1491, 1492, 1493, 1494, 1495, 1496, 1497, 1498, 1499, 1500, 1501, 1502, 1503, 1504, 1505, 1506, 1507, 1508, 1509, 1511, 1512, 1513, 1514, 1517, 1518, 1519, 1520, 1521, 1522, 1523, 1524, 1527, 1528, 1529, 1530, 1532, 1533, 1534, 1535, 1536, 1537, 1538, 1539, 1542, 1543, 1544, 1545, 1546, 1547, 1548, 1549, 1550, 1551, 1552, 1553, 1554, 1555, 1556, 1557, 1558, 1559, 1560, 1563, 1565, 1566, 1568, 1569, 1570, 1571, 1573, 1574, 1575, 1576, 1577, 1578, 1579, 1580, 1581, 1582, 1583, 1584, 1585, 1586, 1587, 1588, 1589, 1590, 1591, 1592, 1593, 1594, 1595, 1597, 1600, 1602, 1605, 1607, 1609, 1610, 1613, 1614, 1632, 1695, 1696, 1697, 1698, 1699, 1704, 1722, 1762, 1795, 1810, 1821, 1851, 1958, 1974, 1987, 2049, 2101, 2113, 2239, 2279, 2290, 2299, 2302, 2343, 2344, 2351, 2355, 2357, 2361, 2363, 2367, 2368, 2369, 2375, 2378, 2379, 2380, 2381, 2383, 2388, 2392, 2394, 2395, 2399; *see also* specific disciplines

Education, Higher, Aid Programs for Undergraduate and Graduate Students in Surveying and Geomatics: 2398

Education, Higher, Aid Programs for Undergraduate Students in All Disciplines of Surveying: 2397

Education, Higher, Construction and Facilities Projects: 100, 103, 172, 184, 231, 272, 1469; *see also* Construction and Facilities Projects

Education, Higher, Research, Project, and General Support: 8, 17, 38, 48, 50, 51, 60, 73, 79, 80, 85, 94, 109, 113, 126, 140, 150, 162, 181, 184, 190, 201, 214, 225, 228, 231, 232, 253, 259, 272, 274, 279, 281, 282, 290, 295, 324, 423, 591, 596, 597, 610, 692, 724, 754, 761, 787, 830, 897, 912, 935, 939, 970, 975, 1001, 1002, 1030, 1043, 1052, 1063, 1064, 1088, 1160, 1170, 1189, 1250, 1272, 1375, 1385, 1388, 1392, 1402, 1411, 1422, 1427, 1447, 1448, 1451, 1452, 1453, 1455, 1456, 1457, 1458, 1464, 1468, 1503, 1504, 1516, 1616, 1636, 1661, 1704, 1705, 1729, 1785, 1863, 2025, 2062, 2289, 2324, 2371, 2382, 2383, 2386

Education, Independent Schools: 939, 1246, 1416, 1433; *see also* Education, Secondary

Education, Learning Process. *See* Learning Process and Memory

Education, Legal. *See* Law, Education

Education, Loan Funds: 678, 681, 876, 1243, 1377, 1472, 1499, 1512, 1609, 2387

Education, Medical. *See* Medical Education and Training; Nursing Education

Education, Methods: 131, 1393, 1407, 1422, 1436, 1456; *see also* specific subjects of instruction

Education, Musical. *See* Music, Education

Education, Physical. *See* Physical Education

Education, Policy-Making: 4, 1393, 1422; *see also* Policy Analysis

Education, Preschool. *See* Preschool Education and Care

Education, Private Institutions: 48, 85, 257, 268, 739, 1256, 1491, 1576, 2025; *see also* Education, Higher, Research, Project, and General Support; Education, Secondary

Education, Professional. *See* specific professions

Education, Programs for Undergraduate and Graduate Students in the Field of Geodetic Surveying: 2400

Education, Publication. *See* Publication Prizes, Education

Education Reform: 51, 1170, 1456, 1788

Education, Religious. *See* Religious Education

Education, Secondary: 87, 92, 194, 292, 338, 951, 956, 1013, 1027, 1029, 1160, 1250, 1272, 1388, 1390, 1411, 1412, 1413, 1419, 1422, 1423, 1424, 1430, 1431, 1432, 1433, 1437, 1440, 1447, 1448, 1463, 1490, 1504, 1756; *see also* Education, Elementary and Secondary, Construction and Facilities Projects

Education, Special: 927, 1017, 1031, 1397, 1423, 1463, 1474, 1476, 1524, 2300; *see also* specific handicaps

Education, STEM 10, 185, 240, 241, 297, 1066, 1163, 1238, 1326, 1388, 1503, 1504

Education, Teacher Preparation: 461, 608, 791, 854, 945, 951, 1024, 1375, 1382, 1388, 1411, 1426, 1459, 1464, 1476, 1503, 1504, 1524, 1535, 1589, 1613, 1707; *see also* College Teaching, Career Preparation; Faculty, Study and Research Programs; Language Teachers, Study and Research Abroad

Education, Technical: 54, 848, 938, 1438, 1487, 1528, 1549, 1551, 2057, 2343, 2344, 2392, 2394, 2395

Education, Vocational: 10, 189, 848, 901, 946, 1170, 1375, 1396, 1403, 1423, 1438, 1487, 1519, 1528, 1569, 1785, 2346, 2347, 2348, 2349; *see also* Industrial Arts and Education; specific fields

Education, Work-Study: 911, 1587, 1610

Educational Administration: 1393, 1422, 1454

Educational Exchange Programs: 773, 793, 820, 832, 841, 848, 868, 1425, 1444, 1454, 1468; *see also* International Study and Research Programs

Educational Measurement: 1384

Educational Media: 658, 659, 677, 1436; *see also* Curriculum Development; Education, Methods; Instructional Materials

Educational Research: 131, 185, 369, 856, 1370, 1384, 1393, 1401, 1405, 1407, 1418, 1422, 1436, 1907, 2057, 2092, 2321

Egypt: 804; *see also* Africa; Middle East

Elderly. *See* Aged

Electrical Engineering: 2391

Electrochemistry: 1627, 1628

Electron Microscopy: 1637

Electronics: 1651, 2371; *see also* Engineering; Physical Sciences

Embryology: 1624; *see also* Biological Sciences; Life Sciences

Emergency Financial Assistance: 504, 629

Emergency Grants: 38, 1988, 2340

Emergency Measures Research: 2340

Emergency Medical Services. *See* Medical and Health Services

Emotional Health. *See* Mental and Emotional Health

Employment and Training. *See* Labor, Employment and Training

Endocrinology: 2148; *see also* Biological Sciences; Metabolism and Metabolic Disorders

Energy Resources and Utilization: 102, 202, 227, 881, 947, 948, 1068, 1238, 1417, 1823, 1961, 1963, 1964, 1973, 2378, 2379, 2380, 2381, 2382, 2402, 2408; *see also* Coal; Conservation; Engineering; Forest and Range Resources; Mineral Sciences; Petroleum Sciences; Resource Development and Management; Solar Energy and Solar Research; Technology; Water Resources

Engineering: 264, 825, 843, 969, 1452, 1506, 1639, 1641, 1646, 1651, 1652, 1705, 1824, 1846, 1850, 1886, 1963, 2355, 2364, 2371, 2376, 2377, 2384, 2385, 2386, 2388, 2389, 2390, 2392, 2393, 2396, 2403, 2405, 2406, 2420; *see also* Aerospace Sciences; Nuclear Sciences; Ocean Engineering; Sciences; Technology

Engineering, Education: 184, 232, 872, 899, 908, 911, 942, 945, 951, 968, 973, 989, 993, 1014, 1368, 1382, 1436, 1452, 1478, 1541, 1604, 1612, 1613, 1649, 2355, 2359, 2361, 2375, 2376, 2378, 2379, 2380, 2381, 2382, 2386, 2387, 2391, 2392, 2394, 2395, 2402, 2404, 2407, 2420

Engineering, Research and Development 843, 1622, 1623, 1635, 1963, 2350, 2385, 2390

Engineering, Research and Study: 924, 1316, 1896, 2402, 2406

Engineering, Research and Study Abroad: 823, 843

England: 365, 375, 651, 823, 842, 855, 856, 1514, 1966, 2188

England, Eligibility Limited to Residents of: 1860

English-American Relations: 356

English as a Second Language: 1384

Enology. *See* Viticulture and Enology

Entomology: 1619, 1916, 1932, 1936; *see also* Biological Sciences

Entrepreneurship: 63, 86, 1069, 1353, 1401, 1713

Environment: 7, 47, 50, 55, 57, 69, 82, 85, 89, 116, 135, 141, 154, 180, 187, 188, 189, 190, 216, 230, 247, 248, 252, 253, 291, 302, 397, 591, 905, 920, 1060, 1065, 1078, 1091, 1102, 1106, 1109, 1110, 1132, 1133, 1146, 1150, 1155, 1167, 1175, 1183, 1187, 1191, 1196, 1204, 1219, 1242, 1245, 1248, 1259, 1270, 1379, 1381, 1421, 1977, 1979

Environmental Conservation: 15, 75, 87, 93, 103, 114, 158, 186, 255, 768, 769, 1950; *see also* Conservation; Resource Development and Management

Environmental Design. *See* Design; Industrial Design; Landscape Design

Environmental Education: 1087, 1139, 1368

Environmental Engineering: 70, 1857, 1981, 1987

Environmental Health: 985, 1129, 1287, 1307, 1309, 1404, 1973, 1975

Environmental Law: 1605, 1771, 1992

Environmental Pollution: 1258, 1266, 1294, 1389, 1877, 1953, 1962, 1975, 1978, 1980, 1981, 1988, 1989, 1992; *see also* Air Pollution; Sanitation; Solid Waste Management; Wastewater Management; Water Pollution

Environmental Science: 70, 792, 814, 1646, 1896, 1939, 1941

Environmental Studies: 1, 6, 16, 44, 59, 73, 88, 131, 137, 140, 215, 227, 250, 276, 421, 768, 911, 987, 1048, 1083, 1101, 1138, 1147, 1151, 1155, 1161, 1164, 1171, 1207, 1238, 1243, 1249, 1255, 1336, 1590, 1640, 1645, 1651, 1652, 1726, 1788, 1873, 1874, 1876, 1877, 1904, 1947, 1953, 1957, 1963, 1965, 1969, 1971, 1972, 1975, 1976, 1983, 1987, 1988, 1992, 1993, 2342, 2344, 2402; *see also* Conservation; Ecology; Engineering; Resource Development and Management; Water Resources

Environmental Technology: 378, 881, 1622, 1623, 1877, 1975, 1989, 1992, 2396

Environmental Toxicology: 1953, 1992

Epidemiology: 2014, 2025, 2031, 2107, 2198

Epilepsy: 2085, 2205, 2211; *see also* Neuromuscular Disorders

Equal Economic Opportunity: 82, 983, 987, 1349, 1655; *see also* Social Welfare

Equal Educational Opportunity 40, 70, 82, 131, 264, 907, 942, 950, 952, 987, 1084, 1463, 1487; *see also* Education; Race Relations; Social Welfare

Equal Employment Opportunity: 82, 250, 1084, 1379, 1765; *see also* Labor

Equal Rights. *See* Human Rights

Equipment Grants: 55, 100, 172, 272, 1129, 1647, 1946, 2386; *see also* Construction and Facilities Projects; specific fields of interest

Equity: 62, 137, 207, 286, 1170, 1232, 1979

Essays: 636, 790; *see also* Nonfiction

Ethics: 20, 1513, 1643, 1752, 1895; *see also* Human Values; Legal Ethics; Medical Ethics

Ethnology: 304, 340, 363, 412, 925, 1989; *see also* Anthropology; Sociology

Eurasia and East Europe 778, 845, 846

Europe: 497, 833, 852; *see also* Area Studies; History, European; Languages; Literature; Slavic and East Europe; Social Sciences; also specific nations

European Integration: 762

Evolution: 1811, 1947

Exchange Programs. *See* Cultural Exchange Programs; Educational Exchange Programs; International Projects and Seminars; International Study and Research Programs; Scientific Exchange Programs

Exhibitions: 394, 406, 427, 458, 2352; *see also* Cultural Events, Community; Museums; also specific disciplines

Experimental and Pilot Programs. *See* specific disciplines

Exploration and Field Research: 252, 1625, 1626, 1631, 1644, 1870, 1871, 1899, 1950, 1957, 1978

F

Faculty Development: 775

Faculty, Study and Research Programs: 130, 335, 337, 338, 341, 342, 343, 345, 346, 347, 354, 598, 1426, 1433, 1453, 1710, 1711, 2149, 2150, 2151, 2152, 2154, 2156, 2157, 2287, 2324, 2405; *see also* Education, Teacher Preparation

Faculty, Study and Research Programs Abroad: 854, 1425; *see also* specific disciplines

Families in Crisis: 1029, 1040

Family Development: 4, 116, 133, 248, 933

Family Life: 4, 116, 117, 221, 224, 235, 892, 983, 1098, 1131, 1162, 1182, 1212, 1253, 1266, 1350, 1356, 2411, 2416

Family Planning: 144, 967, 1092, 1362, 1971, 2250; *see also* Genetics; Population Studies; Reproduction Research; Social Sciences; Social Welfare

Family Practice. *See* Medicine, Family Practice

Family Services: 45, 48, 71, 97, 132, 229, 1033, 1035, 1147, 1186, 1224, 1225, 1287, 1354, 1362; *see also* Social Services

Fashion: 400, 1585

Fats and Proteins. *See* Biological Sciences; Food Technology; Nutrition

Fiction: 611, 614, 620, 627, 628, 630, 631, 634, 635, 641, 647, 649, 982; *see also* Literature; Manuscript Prizes, Poetry and Fiction; Publication Prizes, Creative Writing; Writers and Writing

Field Research. *See* Exploration and Field Research

Film: 305, 374, 398, 409, 417, 419, 424, 434, 450, 453, 470, 495, 702, 869, 994, 1761; *see also* Creative Arts

Film, Directing: 417, 491, 994

Filmmaking: 478

Finance: 71, 766, 1713, 1714, 1717, 1721, 1742, 1801, 1887; *see also* Business; Economics

Financial Assistance. *See* Emergency Financial Assistance

Financial Counseling: 2413

Financial Management: 18, 241, 1695, 1699; *see also* Accounting

Fine Arts: 39, 106, 289, 375, 385, 390, 402, 425, 426, 427, 436, 444, 446, 448, 454, 457, 468, 474, 495, 499, 500, 501, 510, 513, 516, 523, 1191, 1336, 1612; *see also* Arts; Creative Arts; Decorative Arts; Design; Graphic Arts; Humanities; Painting; Photography; Sculpture

Fine Arts, Publication: 375, 404, 426; *see also* Publication Prizes, History and Humanities

Fine Arts, Research and Study: 321, 365, 452, 509, 511, 522, 1613

Fine Arts, Research and Study Abroad: 303, 331, 497, 517, 522, 704

Fine Arts, Workshops and Residencies: 502, 511

Finland: 808, 868; *see also* Scandinavia

Fire Control: 1825

Fire Department Administration: 1515

Fire Prevention and Research: 1515, 1825, 2293

Fish and Game Management: 1409, 1640, 1935, 1965, 1978; *see also* Animal Sciences; Conservation; Ecology, Aquatic; Marine Biology; Wildlife

Fitness. *See* Physical Fitness

Fitness: 245, 2305

Flemish Studies. *See* Arts; Europe; History, European

Floriculture: 1904, 1916; *see also* Botany; Horticulture

Florida: 45, 95, 206, 234, 405, 682, 919, 932, 964, 1027, 1109, 1296, 1300, 1315, 1437, 1501, 1502, 2190

Folk Arts: 394, 396, 405, 409, 415, 416, 422, 423, 436, 439, 442, 443, 445, 451, 454, 458, 469, 474, 479, 980; *see also* Crafts; Creative Arts

Folk Studies. *See* Ethnology

Food Service. *See* Restaurant Management and Food Service

Food Technology: 157, 171, 1618, 1629, 2162, 2356, 2415; *see also* Nutrition

Foreign Faculty Study Programs: 874; *see also* Foreign Nationals, Eligibility of; Travel Grants, Foreign Faculty and Researchers; also specific nations

Foreign Languages. *See* Languages

Foreign Nationals, Eligibility of: 11, 12, 308, 354, 361, 365, 408, 508, 530, 533, 686, 693, 709, 711, 719, 725, 726, 768, 769, 780, 788, 794, 796, 805, 818, 826, 827, 831, 857, 858, 869, 870, 871, 872, 874, 875, 876, 877, 878, 912, 978, 1276, 1525, 1634, 1648, 1673, 1737, 1775, 1776, 1817, 1824, 1831, 1845, 1940, 2189, 2196, 2198, 2268, 2387; *see also* Foreign Faculty Study Programs; Travel Grants, Foreign Faculty and Researchers; Travel Grants, Foreign Students; Women, Foreign Nationals, Eligibility of; also specific nations

Foreign Policy Studies: 18, 765, 1790

Forest and Range Resources: 1967, 1988; *see also* Conservation; Ecology; Environmental Studies; Resource Development and Management

Forestry: 197, 1185, 1258, 1925

Forestry, Education: 1922, 1923

France: 584, 704, 821, 829, 847, 1454, 1514

Franco-American Relations: 584

Fraternal Organizations, Eligibility Limited to Members of: 1509, 2407

Freedom: 1362, 1758, 1792

Freshwater: 1970

G

Gardens. *See* Horticulture; Landscape Design

Gas: 1865; *see also* Petroleum Sciences

Gastroenterology: 2149, 2150, 2151, 2152, 2153, 2154, 2155, 2156, 2157, 2158, 2159, 2160, 2161, 2166, 2167

Gay and Lesbian Issues: 97, 206, 888, 889, 890, 892, 895, 901, 915, 920, 983, 1155, 1258, 1292, 1343; *see also* Acquired Immunodeficiency Syndrome (AIDS); Minority Affairs

Genetics: 177, 1284, 1895, 1946, 1947, 2014, 2031, 2044, 2047, 2048, 2051, 2052, 2072, 2167, 2210, 2213, 2218, 2220, 2233, 2264, 2273, 2275, 2292, 2331; *see also* Biological Sciences; Birth Defects; Medical Research; Reproduction Research

Genocide Studies: 590

Geochemistry: 1875, 1983

Geodesy: 1875, 2401; *see also* Earth Sciences; Engineering; Mathematics

Geographic Information Systems/Land Information Systems 1821, 2401

Geography: 762, 768, 1631, 1652, 1667, 1862, 1863, 1864, 1963; *see also* Area Studies; Earth Sciences; Social Sciences

Geology: 3, 1604, 1644, 1645, 1819, 1865, 1866, 1867, 1870, 1875, 1876, 1936, 2279; *see also* Earth Sciences; Mineral Sciences

Geophysics: 1604, 1624, 1635, 1644, 1645, 1652, 1832, 1866, 1875, 1876, 1878, 1963; *see also* Earth Sciences; Physical Sciences; Physics

Georgia: 218, 288, 301, 409, 668, 1080, 1099, 1104, 1143

Geospatial Sciences: 1821

Geriatrics and Gerontology: 134, 1240, 1287, 1310, 1330, 1995, 1998, 1999, 2036, 2294; *see also* Aged

Germany: 542, 590, 797, 830, 831, 868, 1442, 1454, 1475, 1514

Gerontology. *See* Geriatrics and Gerontology

Glaciology: 1644, 1645; *see also* Earth Sciences; Geology

Government: 51, 112, 131, 160, 250, 766, 1033, 1092, 1670, 1672, 1750, 1785, 1788, 1789, 1790, 1792, 1797, 1801, 1803, 1808, 1809, 1810; *see also* Community Government; Political Science; Public Administration

Government, Internships: 931, 958, 962, 1782, 1786, 1796, 1799, 1800, 1802, 1804, 1805, 2314

Graphic Arts: 413, 509; *see also* Arts; Creative Arts; Design; Fine Arts; Visual Arts

Graphic Communications: 2359, 2360

Great Britain. *See* England; Ireland; Scotland

Greece: 310, 313, 315, 389, 809, 810, 811, 812, 813, 814, 815, 884, 898

Greece, Eligibility Limited to Descendants of: 884, 898, 976

Growth Factor Research: 2090

Guidance. *See* Counseling and Guidance

Gynecology. *See* Obstetrics and Gynecology

H

Haiti: 157

Handicapped: 136, 146, 173, 190, 221, 257, 278, 297, 899, 910, 999, 1019, 1107, 1151, 1177, 1200, 1261, 1291, 1342, 1373, 1435, 1552, 1974, 2145, 2304, 2305, 2306, 2382; *see also* Education, Special; Occupational Therapy; Rehabilitation; also specific handicapping conditions

Handicapped Children: 927, 1017, 1031, 1342, 1435, 2252

Hawaii: 53, 114, 412, 671, 672, 768, 769, 1177, 1429, 1974

Health: 5, 19, 20, 26, 27, 30, 31, 33, 43, 47, 50, 52, 55, 56, 60, 64, 67, 69, 72, 76, 84, 96, 101, 102, 104, 108, 125, 128, 129, 132, 133, 135, 138, 139, 140, 141, 143, 146, 149, 150, 158, 161, 164, 165, 171, 178, 188, 189, 192, 194, 198, 205, 208, 211, 214, 222, 234, 243, 245, 249, 252, 256, 277, 278, 279, 285, 290, 295, 299, 300, 301, 393, 591, 743, 746, 774, 905, 929, 987, 1005, 1009, 1015, 1019, 1020, 1046, 1049, 1066, 1067, 1068, 1073, 1075, 1079, 1084, 1091, 1093, 1101, 1105, 1108, 1109, 1118, 1119, 1120, 1123, 1126, 1129, 1130, 1151, 1152, 1153, 1159, 1161, 1171, 1172, 1190, 1192, 1193, 1196, 1197, 1203, 1211, 1218, 1223, 1235, 1236, 1241, 1248, 1250, 1255, 1271, 1273, 1284, 1289, 1290, 1292, 1293, 1294, 1295, 1296, 1300, 1301, 1306, 1308, 1309, 1314, 1315, 1318, 1320, 1325, 1326, 1334, 1354, 1359, 1363, 1415, 1451, 1452, 1458, 1611, 2002, 2025, 2038, 2063, 2106, 2173, 2292, 2413; *see also* Medicine; Public Health; Social Welfare; entries beginning with Health

Health Administration: 95, 134, 945, 1291, 1299, 2243, 2276

Health Agencies: 98, 140, 1058, 1458, 2035

Health Agencies, Construction and Facilities Projects: 100, 172; *see also* Construction and Facilities Projects; Health; Hospitals, Construction and Facilities Projects

Health and Human Services: 1, 6, 17, 27, 28, 39, 42, 43, 45, 46, 50, 59, 70, 75, 88, 98, 105, 124, 127, 131, 140, 145, 180, 182, 186, 206, 213, 216, 217, 232, 238, 253, 255, 265, 266, 275, 277, 388, 414, 421, 746, 753, 1008, 1013, 1028, 1064, 1069, 1083, 1085, 1102, 1110, 1116, 1117, 1123, 1125, 1131, 1136, 1138, 1139, 1142, 1146, 1155, 1164, 1165, 1168, 1173, 1174, 1175, 1187, 1189, 1191, 1197, 1215, 1229, 1237, 1242, 1243, 1268, 1274, 1288, 1327, 1336, 1339, 1347, 1357, 1376, 1381, 1417, 1421, 1429

Health and Medical Research. *See* Medical Research

Health and Well-Being: 10, 15, 49, 115, 157, 206, 221, 248, 914, 920, 933, 990, 1027, 1028, 1060, 1063, 1105, 1122, 1127, 1157, 1204, 1219, 1270, 1297, 1298, 1379, 2305

Health Care: 32, 48, 61, 65, 85, 97, 111, 113, 118, 124, 134, 144, 145, 151, 168, 179, 192, 195, 199, 200, 210, 216, 217, 228, 244, 253, 254, 259, 265, 278, 291, 293, 296, 297, 414, 421, 756, 893, 928, 967, 977, 981, 1008, 1028, 1032, 1044, 1048, 1054, 1057, 1061, 1070, 1079, 1081, 1089, 1098, 1107, 1124, 1186, 1188, 1194, 1212, 1222, 1224, 1257, 1282, 1283, 1285, 1286, 1289, 1290, 1292, 1296, 1299, 1300, 1301, 1302, 1306, 1313, 1314, 1315, 1317, 1320, 1322, 1325, 1334, 1335, 1337, 1355, 1359, 1363, 1421, 1461, 1590, 1611, 1895, 1907, 2013, 2037, 2040, 2042, 2043, 2046, 2074, 2089, 2161, 2234; *see also* Medical and Health Services

Health Care Facilities: 142, 172, 184, 244, 265, 301, 366, 1031, 1270, 1286, 1314, 1317, 1322, 1323, 1325

Health Care Practitioners. *See* Medical and Health Practitioners

Health Journalism. *See* Journalism, Medical and Health; Publication Prizes, Medical and Health Sciences

Health Policy Research: 1028, 1286, 2086

Health Sciences: 881, 1290, 1415, 1442, 1565, 1616, 1897, 1976, 2059

Health Sciences, Education: 199, 1021, 1316, 1328, 1394, 1551, 1576, 2046, 2057, 2139, 2237; *see also* Medical Education and Training

Health Services. *See* Medical and Health Services

Healthy Eating: 157, 953, 1391

Hearing Defects. *See* Deafness and Hearing Impairments

Heart Disease. *See* Cardiology and Cardiovascular Diseases

Hebrew Studies. *See* Judaism

Helicopter. *See* Aeronautics; Aviation

Hematology: 2005, 2006, 2007, 2017, 2018, 2019, 2020, 2021, 2022, 2051, 2109, 2121, 2142, 2165, 2198, 2282

Hemophilia: 2051

Hepatology: 2023, 2150, 2151, 2154, 2160, 2163, 2164

Herpetology: 1619

High School Seniors, Scholarships and Financial Aid: 386, 945, 1001, 1002, 1253, 1479, 1491, 1493, 1496, 1498, 1529, 1553, 1554, 1555, 1560, 1563, 1586, 1588, 1649; *see also* Education, Higher, Aid Programs for Undergraduate and Graduate Students in All Disciplines; Education, Loan Funds

Higher Education. *See* Education, Higher, Research, Project, and General Support

Hispanics: 885, 896, 900, 911, 916, 962, 963, 964, 965, 1169, 1265, 1386, 1701, 1778, 1880, 1934, 1941, 2104, 2313, 2315; *see also* Spanish-Speaking Americans

Histology: 2115

Historic Preservation and Restoration: 28, 55, 61, 77, 96, 156, 216, 233, 235, 268, 333, 367, 372, 376, 397, 546, 564, 566, 567, 571, 667, 743, 987, 1046, 1102, 1123, 1165, 1173, 1197, 1207

Historic Site Administration: 156, 566, 567, 591, 592; *see also* Museum Administration

History: 23, 50, 159, 160, 309, 312, 315, 327, 328, 356, 357, 360, 363, 402, 421, 526, 531, 532, 542, 548, 549, 556, 557, 558, 565, 566, 578, 580, 584, 593, 623, 762, 767, 790, 795, 943, 975, 1453, 1612, 1662, 1790, 2350; *see also* Area Studies, also area studies by name; Classical Studies; Ethnology; Humanities; Labor, History; Law, History; Medicine, History; Medieval Studies; Military History; Political History; Religion, History; Renaissance Studies; Sciences, History; Social History; Social Sciences; Technology, History; Theatre, History; also specific disciplines which lend themselves to an historical approach

History, African: 353, 526

History, American: 305, 328, 330, 345, 348, 524, 525, 526, 527, 533, 541, 542, 543, 544, 545, 552, 553, 554, 555, 561, 562, 563, 564, 566, 568, 569, 570, 580, 582, 583, 585, 586, 587, 591, 594, 595, 1648, 1670, 1787, 1789, 1790, 1791, 1808

History, American–Colonial: 304, 350, 530, 561, 573, 574, 575

History, American–Contemporary: 1797, 1809

History, Asian: 526

History, Canadian: 526, 584, 1646

History, English: 330, 351, 365, 432, 526

History, European: 351, 525, 526, 543, 574, 590, 759, 838, 839, 852, 853, 986

History, Latin American: 526, 530, 533

History, Publication: 404, 525, 526, 529, 533, 541, 544, 548, 551, 559, 561, 562, 576, 639, 1374, 2290; *see also* Publication Prizes, History and Humanities

History, Research and Study: 308, 316, 321, 326, 330, 340, 343, 345, 348, 350, 351, 353, 527, 528, 530, 532, 540, 543, 546, 568, 570, 572, 573, 574, 575, 577, 578, 580, 586, 589, 591, 592, 594, 986, 1562

History, Research and Study Abroad: 310, 331, 358, 359, 389, 550, 584, 590, 794, 807, 809, 811, 813, 817, 818, 857

History, Teaching Methods: 592

Home Economics: 870, 2411, 2416; *see also* Food Technology; Housing; Nutrition; Technology

Homelessness: 143, 170, 221, 295, 1019, 1027, 1079, 1107, 1179, 1339; *see also* Disadvantaged; Poverty Programs; Urban Affairs

Horticulture: 1510, 1902, 1904, 1909, 1912, 1913, 1914, 1915, 1917, 1918, 1925, 1929, 1933, 1966, 1968; *see also* Arboriculture; Botany; Floriculture

Hospice: 1293

Hospital Administration. *See* Health Administration

Hospitals: 80, 94, 195, 209, 234, 257, 270, 294, 1075, 1143, 1152, 1286, 2035, 2049; *see also* Health Care Facilities; Medical and Health Services; Medicine

Hospitals, Construction and Facilities Projects: 172, 266, 272, 1160; *see also* Construction and Facilities Projects

Hotel Management: 2357

Housing and Shelter: 69, 97, 104, 146, 204, 206, 221, 248, 571, 1011, 1073, 1079, 1084, 1120, 1135, 1166, 1171, 1179, 1180, 1202, 1205, 1214, 1230, 1238, 1260, 1262, 1271, 1317, 1322, 1340, 1417, 1736, 1924; *see also* Community Development; Homelessness; Poverty Programs; Social Welfare; Urban Affairs; Urban and Regional Planning

Human Rights: 57, 71, 112, 122, 147, 789, 857, 893, 934, 1084, 1329, 1362, 1401, 1736, 1788

Human Sciences: 2416

Human Values: 1393, 1513, 1643, 1674, 2332; *see also* Ethics

Humanities: 11, 12, 21, 47, 64, 100, 113, 128, 141, 146, 165, 192, 201, 211, 225, 251, 260, 266, 275, 323, 324, 327, 329, 333, 335, 336, 355, 360, 363, 397, 545, 590, 762, 829, 954, 1055, 1081, 1146, 1151, 1223, 1242, 1249, 1347, 1352, 1357, 1376, 1442, 1486, 1646, 1659, 1676, 1679, 1748, 1763, 1794, 1801; *see also* Arts; Social Sciences; specific disciplines

Humanities, Curriculum Development 322, 461

Humanities, International Cooperative Programs: 776

Humanities, Publication, Exhibition, and Public Information Projects: 322, 329, 332, 1250, 1656; *see also* Publication Prizes, History and Humanities

Humanities, Related to Other Disciplines: 306, 324, 361, 1643

Humanities, Research and Study: 304, 306, 317, 318, 319, 320, 321, 324, 330, 334, 335, 337, 338, 339, 340, 341, 342, 343, 344, 345, 346, 347, 348, 349, 350, 351, 352, 353, 354, 361, 362, 530, 572, 755, 782, 908, 954, 1316, 1486, 1513, 1603, 1613, 1675, 1676, 1677, 1678, 1679, 1763, 1814

Humanities, Research and Study Abroad 314, 325, 331, 783, 794, 796, 799, 805, 807, 818, 824, 826, 827, 850, 1450, 1489

Humanities, Workshops and Seminars: 307, 324, 338, 347

Humor: 624

Hunger: 170, 171, 176, 1061, 1106, 1192, 1196, 1344, 1345, 1358; *see also* Disadvantaged; Poverty Programs, Social Welfare

Huntington's Disease: 2213, 2221; *see also* Neuromuscular Disorders

Hydrology: 1875, 1972, 1983, 2365

I

Iberia: 600; *see also* Europe; specific nations

Iceland: 808

Ichthyology: 1619, 1936

Idaho: 143, 213, 415, 915, 1360, 1577, 1578, 1959

Illinois: 32, 63, 89, 103, 106, 118, 187, 218, 238, 283, 290, 744, 919, 1069, 1070, 1091, 1213, 1511, 1520, 1632, 1657, 1973

Illustration: 212, 462, 646, 650; *see also* Graphic Arts

Immigrant Resettlement: 188, 1079, 1154, 1247

Immigration: 255

Immigration Studies. *See* Ethnology

Immunology: 151, 903, 1824, 1946, 2086, 2094, 2107, 2182, 2183, 2184, 2185, 2198; *see also* Microbiology

In-Service Training Projects: 659, 780, 900, 1622, 1733, 1739, 1755, 1766, 2326, 2410; *see also* specific disciplines

India: 599, 802, 851, 1454, 1462

Indiana: 27, 181, 416, 670, 1138, 1263, 1512, 1657, 1909

Industrial Arts and Education: 2359, 2360, 2392; *see also* Education, Technical; Education, Vocational

Industrial Design: 1564

Industrial Development: 2352

Industry and Industrial Research: 1852, 1860; *see also* Technology, Industrial

Infectious Diseases: 2286; *see also* Immunology; Microbiology

Information Sciences: 207, 659, 660, 661, 662, 673, 677, 792, 1277, 1705, 2037, 2350; *see also* Communications; Computer Sciences; Educational Media; Libraries and Librarianship

Inner-City: 29, 118, 271, 1037, 1179, 1230; *see also* Community Development; Urban Affairs

Instructional Materials: 791, 1436; *see also* Communications; Curriculum Development; Education; Educational Media

Instrumentation, Biomedical: 2058, 2061

Insurance: 1707, 1880; *see also* Business; Finance

Interdisciplinary Research and Study: 320, 768, 769, 1643, 1890; *see also* Humanities, Related to Other Disciplines; Medicine, Related to Other Disciplines; Sciences, Related to Other Disciplines

Interior Design: 367, 432

Internal Medicine. *See* Medicine, Internal

International Development: 771, 780, 857, 1183, 1184, 1185, 1788; *see also* Developing Nations

International Education. *See* Education, Comparative

International Exchange. *See* Cultural Exchange Programs; Educational Exchange Programs; International Study and Research Programs

International Law. *See* Law, International

International Market. *See* Trade

International Projects and Seminars: 854, 1454, 1468, 1818; *see also* Humanities, International Cooperative Programs; Medicine, International Cooperative Programs; Scientific Research and Development, International Cooperative Programs; Social Sciences, International Cooperative Programs

International Relations and International Affairs: 51, 71, 112, 117, 147, 590, 607, 609, 758, 760, 763, 764, 765, 767, 768, 769, 770, 771, 772, 773, 776, 779, 780, 781, 784, 786, 787, 788, 789, 790, 792, 848, 852,

854, 857, 978, 1348, 1349, 1464, 1562, 1661, 1732, 1773, 1789, 1806, 1807; *see also* Area Studies; Economics, International: Environment, International; Law, International; Political Science, International; Social Sciences; also specific nations and disciplines of international concern

International Security: 51, 765, 1672

International Study and Research Programs: 303, 314, 361, 599, 762, 766, 771, 772, 775, 778, 780, 782, 783, 785, 787, 791, 793, 795, 798, 799, 800, 801, 802, 803, 804, 808, 809, 820, 821, 822, 823, 824, 825, 828, 830, 832, 833, 834, 835, 836, 838, 839, 840, 842, 844, 845, 846, 848, 849, 850, 851, 852, 853, 854, 855, 856, 857, 858, 859, 860, 861, 862, 863, 864, 865, 866, 867, 868, 881, 918, 978, 1183, 1184, 1185, 1433, 1450, 1468, 1489, 1514, 1526, 1769, 1770, 1831, 1860, 1899, 1956, 1966; *see also* specific disciplines, research and study abroad

International Travel: 780, 802, 854; *see also* Travel Grants, Foreign Faculty and Researchers

Internships. *See* In-Service Training Projects

Interracial Cooperation. *See* Race Relations

Inventory. *See* Materials Handling

Iowa: 418, 919, 1022, 1053, 1165

Ireland: 1514

Islam: 796; *see also* Religion

Israel: 170, 246, 753, 756, 794, 828, 867, 869, 881, 893, 904, 1013, 1186, 1450, 1926

Italian-American Relations: 525, 551, 921

Italy: 303, 310, 325, 508, 521, 525, 550, 686, 850, 859, 860, 861, 862, 863, 864, 865, 866, 921, 1514, 1536

Italy, Eligibility Limited to Descendants of: 921, 1536, 1559

J

Japan: 408, 775, 782, 834, 835, 843, 868, 879, 1454, 1514; *see also* Orient

Japanese-American Relations: 763, 776, 784, 791, 837, 1796

Japanese Studies: 763, 775, 837, 1517

Jazz: 434, 483, 487, 488, 702; *see also* Music

Jewish Life: 25, 81, 125, 179, 590, 594, 595, 596, 597, 749, 753, 803, 893, 904, 1013, 1096, 1161, 1232, 1302, 1520; *see also* Judaism

Job Preparedness: 86, 115, 182, 241, 253, 263, 283, 920, 1007, 1029, 1233, 1271, 1368, 1419; *see also* Labor, Employment and Training

Journalism: 91, 159, 160, 191, 197, 613, 625, 766, 1482, 1483, 1484, 1567, 1728, 1729, 1732, 1734, 1736, 1737, 1738, 1740, 1741, 1742, 1744, 1751, 1752, 1753, 1754, 1756, 1759, 1763, 1792, 1793, 1795; *see also* Communications; News Reporting: Public Relations; Publications; Writers and Writing

Journalism, Digital 1733, 1751

Journalism, Education: 167, 909, 1392, 1567, 1731, 1733, 1735, 1737, 1749, 1750, 1751, 1755, 1757, 1761, 1763

Journalism, Internships: 1730, 1733, 1739, 1755, 1782, 1801

Journalism, Medical and Health: 1739

Journalism, Religious: 923, 1760

Journalism, Scientific: 1723, 1731, 1745, 1746, 1747, 1888

Judaism: 25, 125, 170, 246, 594, 595, 621, 747, 749, 753, 836, 917, 1096, 1186, 1244, 1292, 1519; *see also* Religion

Judicial Administration: 1276

Judicial Reform: 1013, 1279

Justice: 106, 112, 122, 152, 153, 187, 191, 216, 1084, 1097, 1126, 1232, 1277, 1343, 1344, 2043; *see also* Criminal Justice; Judicial Reform; Juvenile Justice; Law; Law Enforcement

Juvenile Delinquency: 1279, 1280; *see also* Children; Youth

Juvenile Justice: 242, 1029, 1056, 1264, 1279, 1280, 1334, 1351, 1359

K

Kansas: 161, 429, 942, 945, 988, 1169, 1304, 1363, 1521

Kentucky: 420, 552, 919, 979, 1158, 1522, 1523, 1909, 1992

Korea: 821, 1454

L

Labor: 18, 23, 222, 1162, 1736, 1749, 1767; *see also* American Indians and Alaskan Natives, Employment; Business; Business Development Assistance; Economics; Equal Employment Opportunity; Industrial Development; Management; Women, Employment

Labor, Economics: 1219

Labor, Employment and Training: 4, 40, 97, 104, 118, 123, 153, 170, 203, 221, 271, 278, 283, 882, 1007, 1162, 1202, 1205, 1378, 1435, 1764, 1765, 1766, 1767

Labor, History: 543, 594, 1768

Labor, Management Relations: 1766

Labor, Manpower Research: 1767

Labor, Unemployment: 1095, 1767

Land Use Management: 229, 1168, 1247, 1673, 1908

Landmark Preservation. *See* Historic Preservation and Restoration

Landscape Design: 303, 326, 372, 1510, 1913, 1956, 1966, 1974; *see also* Architecture

Language Teachers, Study and Research Abroad: 601, 833, 841, 854; *see also* Faculty, Study and Research Programs Abroad; International Study and Research Programs

Languages: 363, 468, 531, 595, 603, 1424, 1719; *see also* Esperanto; Humanities; Linguistics; Translation

Languages, Asian: 599, 775, 776, 1612

Languages, Classical: 316, 598, 809, 986

Languages, Germanic: 603, 759, 830, 852, 1612

Languages, Latin and Romance: 521, 598, 601, 603, 986, 1770

Languages, Mid- and Near-Eastern: 806

Languages, Modern: 321, 606, 1612

Languages, Publication Projects: 602; *see also* Translation; Writers and Writing

Languages, Research and Study: 321, 595, 602, 604, 607, 609, 610, 845, 846, 986

Languages, Research and Study Abroad: 331, 599, 601, 608, 766, 806, 825, 833, 837, 838, 845, 846, 847, 852, 854, 857, 1526

Languages, Semitic: 23

Languages, Slavic: 603, 833

Laser Physics: 1822

Latin and South America: 157, 786, 845, 846, 854, 1737; *see also* Area Studies; History; Languages; Literature; also specific nations

Latin and South American Nationals, Eligibility of: 130, 526, 874, 876, 1728, 1737, 1774, 2062

Law: 340, 590, 792, 795, 856, 925, 1486, 1562, 1605, 1613, 1669, 1768, 1772, 1801, 1808; *see also* Citizen Action Legislation; Civic Affairs; Community Services; Crime Prevention; Environmental Law; Judicial Reform; Justice; Juvenile Delinquency; Maritime Law; Public Administration; Race Relations

Law, Criminal. *See* Criminal Justice

Law, Education: 656, 883, 934, 968, 1448, 1450, 1489, 1605, 1769, 1770, 1777, 1778, 1780, 1781

Law Enforcement: 1277, 1278

Law, History: 351, 526, 812, 1489

Law, International: 18, 766, 789, 1773, 1774, 1775, 1776

Law, Internships: 1777

Law Library: 656, 657, 1780; *see also* Library Science, Education; Library Services and Collection Utilization

Law, Preventive: 1772

Law, Publication: 1771

Leadership Development: 36, 106, 111, 157, 181, 264, 286, 503, 933, 990, 998, 1086, 1092, 1141, 1168, 1235, 1266, 1304, 1314, 1332, 1334, 1359, 1371, 1393, 1506, 1795, 1796, 2351; *see also* Community Leadership

Learning Disabilities: 1012, 1397, 1406; *see also* Education, Special

Learning Process and Memory: 193, 604, 1418, 1422, 2214, 2333; *see also* Behavioral Sciences; Education

Legal Ethics: 1769

Legal Research: 1768, 1769, 2021

Legal Services: 106, 144, 1264

Leukemia: 2192, 2198, 2282; *see also* Cancer; Hematology

Libraries and Librarianship: 55, 73, 159, 160, 173, 237, 259, 325, 332, 339, 532, 658, 660, 663, 672, 674, 677, 682, 1075; *see also* Art Galleries; Educational Media; Information Sciences; Law Library; Medical Library; Museums; Scientific Library

Libraries and Librarianship, Elementary and Secondary School: 658, 669

Library Acquisitions: 677, 775

Library Administration: 160, 591, 676; *see also* Management

Library Construction and Facilities: 8, 676, 1075; *see also* Construction and Facilities Projects

Library Science, Continuing Education: 662, 665, 676, 678

Library Science, Education: 531, 655, 656, 657, 659, 660, 661, 662, 663, 668, 669, 670, 673, 678, 679, 680, 681, 683, 684, 685, 792, 875, 906, 1443

Library Science, Research: 325, 660, 661, 662

Library Services and Collection Utilization: 672, 674, 676, 677, 682, 1075

Life Sciences: 334, 881, 911, 1642, 1651; *see also* Biological Sciences; Medicine; Sciences; also specific life sciences

Life Sciences, Research and Study: 1622, 1623, 1899

Lifelong Learning. *See* Education, Adult

Lighting Research: 1974

Linguistics: 604, 807, 943, 1384, 1817; *see also* Languages

Literacy: 19, 20, 45, 86, 91, 164, 259, 677, 1017, 1027, 1086, 1144, 1161, 1226, 1233, 1346, 1390, 1392, 1398, 1407, 1438

Literary Criticism: 618, 619, 643; *see also* Writers and Writing

Literature: 2, 23, 212, 357, 360, 363, 395, 396, 401, 402, 405, 409, 416, 419, 420, 422, 423, 428, 431, 432, 435, 439, 442, 443, 458, 468, 469, 530, 531, 579, 590, 602, 603, 606, 625, 630, 632, 633, 652, 695, 795, 1453, 1729; *see also* Languages; Publications; Reading; Writers and Writing

Literature, African: 630

Literature, American: 237, 304, 305, 328, 330, 617, 633

Literature, Asian: 630

Literature, Classical: 316, 623, 809, 986; *see also* Classical Studies

Literature, Comparative: 356, 1612

Literature, English: 237, 330, 365, 647, 1601

Literature, European: 759, 838, 839, 986

Literature, Publication Projects: 1093; *see also* Manuscript Prizes; Publication Prizes

Literature, Research and Study: 321, 330, 340, 616, 618, 619, 651, 986, 1497

Literature, Research and Study Abroad: 303, 331, 358, 359, 807, 847, 857

Liver: 2023, 2150, 2163, 2164; *see also* Metabolism and Metabolic Disorders

Loan Funds: 567; *see also* Education, Loan Funds

Logistics: 1708

Louisiana: 43, 157, 393, 422, 423, 544, 545, 1157, 1171, 1427

Lunar Science: 1839; *see also* Aerospace Sciences

Lung. *See* Respiratory and Pulmonary Diseases

Lutheranism: 746, 1373

M

Magazines: 1723, 1736, 1742, 1754; *see also* News Reporting; Publications

Maine: 44, 180, 212, 425, 1019, 1207, 1344, 2278

Mammalogy: 1619, 1936

Management: 264, 1604, 1708; *see also* Arts Administration; Business Administration; Educational Administration; Hotel Management; Labor; Library Administration; Museum Administration; Restaurant Management and Food Service

Management, Education: 916, 1465, 1599, 1701, 1702, 1705

Manpower. *See* Labor

Manuscript Completion: 646; *see also* Writers and Writing; specific disciplines

Manuscript Prizes, Medical and Health Sciences: 674, 2249, 2338, 2339

Manuscript Prizes, Nonfiction: 541, 551, 569, 578, 585, 587, 606, 628, 652, 661, 736, 738, 742, 790

Manuscript Prizes, Poetry and Fiction: 611, 614, 625, 626, 628, 644, 648, 649, 653

Manuscript Prizes, Sciences: 2338, 2339, 2371, 2393

Marine Biology: 1876, 1935, 1959, 1978, 1983

Marine Policy. *See* Ocean Management and Marine Policy

Marine Resource Conservation: 53

Marine Sciences: 1409, 1619, 1625, 1626, 1640, 1642, 1645, 1868, 1873, 1874, 1876, 1965, 1978, 2388; *see also* Oceanography; Sciences

Marketing: 900, 1702, 1711; *see also* Advertising; Business; Public Relations

Maryland: 29, 103, 168, 183, 392, 427, 648, 1000, 1004, 1111, 1162, 1194, 1233, 1530

Mass Communications. *See* Broadcast Media; Communications; Journalism; Print Media

Mass Spectrometry: 1820

Massachusetts: 33, 46, 61, 97, 102, 218, 233, 245, 271, 332, 377, 555, 556, 557, 558, 565, 972, 999, 1018, 1019, 1065, 1073, 1129, 1153, 1188, 1251, 1252, 1253, 1317, 1322, 1340, 1356, 1361, 1392, 1417, 1531, 1532, 2087

Materials Science: 881, 1624, 1635, 1642, 1652, 1848, 1855, 1896, 2408, 2420, 2421

Maternal Health Care: 149, 2252; *see also* Health; Medical and Health Services

Mathematics: 3, 264, 1014, 1415, 1639, 1642, 1651, 1652, 1824, 1828, 1883, 1884, 1885, 1886, 2355, 2384, 2406; *see also* Computer Sciences; Sciences; Statistics

Mathematics, Education: 908, 951, 968, 973, 1247, 1368, 1415, 1430, 1436, 1612, 1613, 1649, 1880, 1881, 1882, 1886, 1887, 2359

Mathematics, Research and Study: 924, 1622, 1623, 1635, 1881, 1896, 2406

Mathematics, Research and Study Abroad: 823, 867, 881

Measurement Sciences: 1822, 2408

Mechanical Arts. *See* Industrial Arts and Education

Media. *See* Communications; also specific media forms

Media Arts: 106, 396, 401, 405, 416, 417, 420, 423, 469, 484, 980, 1724, 1725, 1756, 1761; *see also* Arts

Medical Administration. *See* Health Administration

Medical and Health Practitioners: 32, 977, 1281, 2174, 2175, 2247, 2276; *see also* Medical and Health Services; Midwifery; Nursing

Medical and Health Services: 14, 44, 48, 52, 134, 151, 152, 229, 230, 237, 274, 920, 1110, 1132, 1246, 1281, 1283, 1306, 1318, 1319, 1323, 1324, 1325, 1328, 1335, 1359, 1363, 1515, 2001, 2042, 2086, 2241, 2286, 2302, 2331; *see also* Health Care Facilities; Hospitals

Medical Conference, Symposia, and Workshops: 1477, 2094

Medical Costs: 1281, 1283, 1324, 2042, 2282

Medical Education and Training: 149, 151, 257, 294, 945, 968, 977, 992, 1021, 1290, 1308, 1314, 1319, 1476, 1477, 1489, 1531, 1609, 1611, 1613, 1649, 1998, 1999, 2005, 2007, 2013, 2024, 2035, 2046, 2050, 2054, 2055, 2057, 2062, 2064, 2091, 2135, 2136, 2178, 2233, 2276, 2278, 2279, 2281, 2331; *see also* Midwifery; Nursing Education; specific diseases and areas of medicine by name

Medical Education and Training, Armed Services: 2091

Medical Education and Training, Outside of U.S.: 1402, 1596, 2023, 2092, 2164, 2199

Medical Ethics: 1895; *see also* Bioethics

Medical Facilities, Construction Grants 2093; *see also* Construction and Facilities Projects; Hospitals, Construction and Facilities Projects

Medical Journalism. *See* Journalism, Medical and Health

Medical Library: 673, 674, 875, 906; *see also* Library Science, Education; Library Services and Collection Utilization

Medical Research: 76, 84, 92, 93, 193, 222, 234, 256, 259, 262, 267, 293, 294, 532, 999, 1160, 1177, 1189, 1240, 1284, 1289, 1313, 1316, 1319, 1377, 1447, 1650, 1652, 1653, 1824, 1896, 1945, 1967, 1994, 1996, 1998, 1999, 2003, 2006, 2008, 2011, 2012, 2013, 2015, 2016, 2026, 2030, 2032, 2033, 2039, 2041, 2044, 2047, 2048, 2049, 2052, 2055, 2056, 2060, 2063, 2065, 2066, 2067, 2068, 2069, 2070, 2071, 2072, 2073, 2074, 2075, 2077, 2078, 2085, 2086, 2088, 2090, 2093, 2108, 2109, 2111, 2115, 2119, 2120, 2133, 2134, 2135, 2136, 2137, 2138, 2142, 2144, 2145, 2147, 2148, 2158, 2159, 2161, 2162, 2166, 2168, 2169, 2171, 2172, 2173, 2174, 2175, 2176, 2180, 2182, 2184, 2185, 2190, 2191, 2192, 2193, 2196, 2197, 2202, 2204, 2206, 2207, 2208, 2209, 2210, 2213, 2218, 2233, 2255, 2264, 2265, 2266, 2270, 2271, 2274, 2275, 2280, 2282, 2284, 2285, 2286, 2291, 2292, 2296, 2297, 2304, 2316, 2317, 2318, 2319, 2323; *see also* diseases and areas of medicine by name

Medical Research, Outside U.S.: 843, 856, 879, 1442, 1475, 2060, 2092, 2163, 2189

Medical Research, Supplies and Equipment: 2058, 2061, 2179, 2181, 2271; *see also* Sciences, Equipment and Facilities

Medical Technology: 739, 1281, 2158, 2280, 2286; *see also* Dental Laboratory Technology

Medicine: 4, 23, 80, 107, 111, 166, 219, 233, 266, 279, 298, 299, 704, 969, 1070, 1283, 1376, 1611, 2001, 2027, 2028, 2034, 2038, 2044, 2046, 2054, 2066, 2067, 2068, 2075, 2077, 2086, 2093, 2120, 2202, 2220, 2231, 2239, 2280, 2290, 2317, 2318, 2319; *see also* Biomedical Sciences and Research; Health; Hospitals; Surgery; also diseases and areas of medicine by name

Medicine, Academic: 1475, 1997, 2016, 2072, 2135, 2136, 2167, 2251

Medicine, Critical Care 2089

Medicine, Diagnostic: 2002, 2196

Medicine, Family Practice: 2035

Medicine, History: 532, 977, 2290; *see also* Sciences, History

Medicine, Internal: 2119, 2120, 2166

Medicine, International Cooperative Programs: 1442

Medicine, Organ Transplant: 2174

Medicine, Preventive: 151, 1998, 1999, 2030, 2180, 2196, 2286

Medicine, Public Information Projects: 151, 1281, 1319, 2093, 2286; *see also* Community Education

Medicine, Publication: 2054, 2318, 2319; *see also* Journalism, Medical and Health; Manuscript Prizes, Medical and Health Sciences; Publication Prizes, Medical and Health Sciences

Medicine, Related to Other Disciplines: 2093, 2296, 2297

Medieval Studies: 357, 559, 579; *see also* History; Humanities; Literature

Mediterranean Area: 311

Memory. *See* Learning Process and Memory

Mental and Emotional Health: 29, 198, 216, 293, 746, 896, 1058, 1172, 1196, 1243, 1257, 1287, 1341, 1669, 2307, 2308, 2309, 2310, 2311, 2312, 2320, 2323, 2328, 2329, 2330, 2331, 2341

Mental Health Services: 893, 1359, 2331, 2340, 2341; *see also* Medical and Health Services

Mental Retardation: 999, 1261, 2300, 2337

Metabolism and Metabolic Disorders: 1946, 2047, 2048, 2168, 2176

Metallurgy: 1627, 1628, 1651, 1652, 2420, 2421, 2422, 2423; *see also* Materials Sciences; Physical Sciences; Technology, Mining

Meteorology: 1644, 1645, 2365; *see also* Atmospheric Sciences; Climatology

Mexican-Americans. *See* Spanish-Speaking Americans

Mexicans, Eligibility of: 761, 883, 2420

Mexico: 122, 157, 761, 821, 1151, 2356

Michigan: 67, 129, 157, 194, 263, 285, 300, 334, 428, 902, 919, 981, 1047, 1048, 1081, 1105, 1133, 1172, 1178, 1181, 1187, 1203, 1222, 1395, 1579, 1580, 1909

Microbiology: 1598, 1824, 1934, 1941, 1942, 1983, 2031, 2051, 2107; *see also* Biological Sciences

Middle East: 758, 794, 796, 818, 826, 827, 845, 846; *see also* Area Studies; History; Languages; Literature; Social Sciences; also specific nations

Midwestern States: 153, 919, 2249; *see also* states by name

Military History: 526, 580, 588, 589; *see also* History

Military Sciences: 2385; *see also* Defense Projects and Research

Mineral Sciences: 1869, 2423; *see also* Geology; Materials Sciences; Sciences

Minimal Brain Dysfunction. *See* Learning Disabilities

Mining. *See* Technology, Mining

Minnesota: 10, 86, 176, 188, 200, 281, 293, 406, 419, 645, 676, 996, 1053, 1054, 1055, 1074, 1078, 1131, 1145, 1150, 1163, 1218, 1228, 1231, 1260, 1346

Minority Affairs: 131, 146, 294, 888, 889, 892, 1079, 1340, 1348, 1438, 1543, 2062, 2377; *see also* Equal Educational Opportunity; Equal Employment Opportunity; Poverty Programs; Race Relations; Social Welfare; Urban Affairs; also specific minority groups

Minority Community and Institutional Development: 106, 1266, 1312, 1383; *see also* Community Development

Minority-Group Members, Eligibility of: 368, 657, 659, 663, 692, 883, 885, 886, 891, 892, 896, 900, 906, 907, 908, 911, 912, 918, 923, 924, 926, 930, 932, 962, 963, 964, 1291, 1369, 1384, 1443, 1485, 1487, 1608, 1624, 1701, 1710, 1783, 1880, 1934, 1941, 1974, 2046, 2052, 2053, 2062, 2146, 2262, 2313, 2315, 2353, 2392, 2394, 2395; *see also* specific minority groups

Minority Studies: 347, 353, 364, 922, 925, 960, 975, 1383, 1657; *see also* American Indians and Alaskan Natives; Asian-Americans; Blacks; Spanish-Speaking Americans; specific minority groups

Mississippi: 43, 68, 157, 1157, 1393

Missouri: 48, 132, 161, 429, 919, 988, 1020, 1032, 1126, 1169, 1533, 1534

Molecular Biology: 193, 1598, 1941, 1946, 2031, 2202, 2204, 2274, 2275

Molecular Physics: 1822, 1844, 1890

Money and Banking. *See* Banking

Montana: 213, 915, 1206, 1268, 1360, 1959

Morocco: 1514

Morphology: 2290

Mortuary Education. *See* Funeral Service; Thanatology

Motion Pictures. *See* Film

Multidisciplinary Studies. *See* Interdisciplinary Research and Study

Multimedia Reporting 1735, 1751; *see also* Journalism

Multiple Sclerosis: 2215, 2216, 2217, 2221, 2222, 2223; *see also* Neuromuscular Disorders

Muscular Atrophy: 2279

Muscular Dystrophy: 2218

Museology: 309, 667

Museum Administration: 580, 591, 592; *see also* Historic Site Administration

Museum Education: 509, 512, 560, 590, 666

Museums: 73, 84, 89, 173, 230, 400, 402, 409, 426, 442, 454, 469, 503, 510, 590, 667, 671; *see also* Cultural Affairs; Historic Preservation and Restoration; Libraries and Librarianship

Museums, Acquisitions: 426

Museums, Collection Utilization and Maintenance: 426, 464, 506, 667, 671

Music: 2, 224, 360, 390, 398, 402, 405, 409, 416, 419, 422, 423, 428, 434, 437, 439, 442, 443, 454, 468, 469, 471, 483, 522, 700, 706, 712, 718, 722, 759, 830, 853, 869, 980, 1191, 1565; *see also* Choir; Opera; Performing Arts

Music, Competitions: 687, 688, 689, 690, 691, 693, 694, 699, 702, 707, 708, 709, 710, 711, 713, 714, 717, 718, 719, 721, 722, 723, 725, 727, 728, 729, 732, 733

Music, Composition: 303, 395, 424, 431, 437, 465, 478, 686, 687, 688, 689, 694, 696, 699, 700, 702, 705, 707, 713, 714, 715, 716, 720, 722, 723, 728, 1729

Music, Conducting: 686, 700, 702

Music, Education: 461, 686, 692, 695, 698, 701, 702, 707, 708, 714, 716, 718, 724, 725, 726, 731, 1497, 1612

Music, Festivals: 715

Music, History: 596, 597, 702, 706

Music, Instrumentalists: 686, 693, 695, 697, 698, 702, 703, 707, 708, 709, 711, 714, 719, 721, 725, 729, 732

Music, Lyricists and Vocalists: 686, 693, 700, 714, 717, 725, 727, 730; *see also* Choir; Opera

Music, Publication: 691

Music, Research and Study Abroad: 522, 686, 702, 704

Music, Therapy: 716, 2303

Music, Workshops and Residencies: 399, 431, 450, 465, 715, 718

Myasthenia Gravis: 2218, 2219

Mycology: 1944; *see also* Botany

N

National Security: 71, 845, 846, 993, 1672; *see also* Defense Projects and Research

Native American Art 437

Native Americans. *See* American Indians and Alaskan Natives

NATO Member Countries: 880

Natural Resources: 21, 70, 116, 147, 176, 1172, 1258, 1970, 1971, 1981, 1989, 2344; *see also* Conservation; Energy Resources and Utilization; Environmental Studies; Forest and Range Resources; Land Use Management; Mineral Sciences; Petroleum Studies; Resource Development and Management; Water Resources

Natural Sciences: 12, 57, 213, 824, 843, 1316, 1446, 1615, 1625, 1626, 1723, 1830, 1930, 1983; *see also* Physical Sciences; Sciences

Natural Sciences, Education: 945, 1896

Near East: 804, 836; *see also* Area Studies; History; Languages; Literature; Social Sciences; also specific nations

Nebraska: 75, 209, 223, 228, 429, 435, 1274, 1544

Neonatology: 2236

Nephrology: 2000, 2001, 2110, 2111, 2112, 2172, 2173, 2174, 2175, 2176

Netherlands: 1514

Neurobiology: 1941, 1951, 2107, 2213, 2323

Neurodegenerative Disorders: 2223

Neurological Research: 2087, 2114, 2203, 2205, 2206, 2210, 2213, 2216, 2219, 2220, 2221, 2224

Neurological Research Training: 2215, 2217, 2222, 2226, 2227, 2228, 2229, 2230, 2232

Neurology: 2014, 2090, 2120, 2202, 2204, 2207, 2208, 2209, 2210, 2231, 2233, 2263

Neuromuscular Disorders: 2211, 2213, 2218, 2219, 2220, 2221, 2223, 2226, 2227, 2228, 2229, 2230, 2231, 2232, 2233; *see also* specific diseases

Neurophysiology: 2226, 2227, 2228, 2229, 2230, 2232

Neuropsychiatry: 2339

Neurosciences: 193, 1310, 1346, 1828, 1995, 2025, 2029, 2031, 2087, 2090, 2204, 2205, 2206, 2208, 2210, 2212, 2213, 2214, 2220, 2231, 2274, 2275, 2323, 2331, 2339

Neurosurgery: 2040, 2204, 2224, 2225; *see also* Surgery

Nevada: 244, 436

New England States. *See* Eastern States; also states by name

New Hampshire: 438, 678, 1019, 1067

New Jersey: 4, 142, 149, 218, 235, 439, 489, 566, 567, 568, 569, 570, 679, 1033, 1037, 1053, 1225, 1266, 1507, 1508, 1545, 1546, 1547, 2279

New Mexico: 83, 157, 161, 440, 499, 680, 914, 920, 942, 945, 1151, 1212, 2071

New York: 4, 142, 152, 154, 216, 246, 254, 268, 329, 404, 419, 441, 442, 489, 498, 541, 571, 904, 1010, 1018, 1100, 1107, 1130, 1144, 1152, 1160, 1257, 1300, 1440, 1467, 1492, 1548, 1549, 1550, 1551, 1554, 1581, 1582, 1799, 1800, 1801, 1802, 1972, 1979, 2190

New Zealand: 1514

News Reporting: 1567, 1726, 1727, 1730, 1732, 1735, 1736, 1741, 1751, 1752, 1753, 1755, 1759; *see also* Journalism

Newspaper: 339, 1723, 1727, 1733, 1736, 1741, 1742, 1752, 1754, 1755; *see also* Communications; Journalism; Publications

Nonfiction: 612, 614, 617, 628, 643, 982, 1736; *see also* Journalism; Literature; Manuscript Prizes, Nonfiction; Publication Prizes; Writers and Writing; also specific disciplines

Nonprofit Organizations. *See* areas of interest to nonprofit organizations

North Carolina: 70, 94, 110, 156, 220, 253, 443, 681, 1024, 1114, 1355, 1378, 1415, 1421, 1428, 1459, 1553

North Dakota: 444, 1074

Norway: 808, 857, 1444; *see also* Scandinavia

Novel: 627; *see also* Publication Prizes, Creative Writing; Writers and Writing

Nuclear Proliferation: 765, 781; *see also* Arms Control

Nuclear Sciences: 1622, 1623, 1851, 1890, 2378, 2379, 2380, 2381, 2382; *see also* Energy Resources and Utilization; Engineering; Physical Sciences; Radiology and Radiation Sciences; Sciences

Numismatics: 307

Nurse-Midwifery. *See* Midwifery

Nursery Schools. *See* Preschool Education and Care

Nursing: 1394, 2193, 2199, 2234, 2238, 2239, 2240; *see also* Hospitals; Medicine

Nursing Education: 257, 1461, 1549, 1560, 2064, 2193, 2234, 2237, 2239, 2240, 2242, 2243, 2245, 2247, 2248; *see also* Medical Education and Training

Nursing Research: 2193, 2219, 2234, 2235, 2236, 2237, 2238, 2241, 2243, 2244, 2246

Nutrition: 157, 197, 221, 236, 774, 870, 1041, 1066, 1130, 1326, 1345, 1358, 1391, 1629, 1772, 2106, 2162, 2286, 2410, 2411, 2412, 2414, 2418; *see also* Agricultural Sciences; Dietetics; Food Technology; Home Economics; Medicine

Nutrition Research: 1015, 2162, 2180, 2413, 2417, 2418

O

OAS Member Countries: 780

Obstetrics and Gynecology: 2016, 2236, 2249, 2251

Occupational Safety and Health: 115, 126, 983, 1895, 2389; *see also* Health; Industry and Industrial Research

Occupational Therapy: 298, 2301, 2303; *see also* Handicapped; Health; Rehabilitation

Ocean Engineering: 1640, 1654, 1873, 1874, 2388, 2404

Ocean Management and Marine Policy: 1640, 1873, 1874; *see also* Environmental Studies

Oceanography: 881, 1638, 1640, 1644, 1652, 1654, 1823, 1828, 1873, 1874, 1876, 1978, 2365, 2385; *see also* Earth Sciences; Physical Sciences

Ohio: 62, 107, 109, 126, 131, 169, 184, 214, 218, 445, 1036, 1044, 1093, 1095, 1096, 1121, 1158, 1166, 1172, 1229, 1249, 1256, 1272, 1308, 1432, 1556, 1557, 1898, 1909

Oklahoma: 161, 256, 388, 429, 446, 499, 942, 945, 1216, 1458

Oncology. *See* Cancer

Opera: 439, 482, 702, 716, 717, 727, 730, 733; *see also* Music; Performing Arts

Ophthalmology: 1284, 2263, 2264, 2265, 2267, 2268, 2270, 2272, 2273, 2274, 2275; *see also* Visual Disorders

Optics: 1822, 2253, 2265

Optometry: 298, 2091, 2253, 2254, 2255, 2256, 2257, 2258, 2259, 2260, 2265, 2269, 2272

Oregon: 56, 64, 204, 213, 447, 915, 1071, 1082, 1219, 1348, 1360, 1959

Organ Transplant. *See* Medicine, Organ Transplant

Ornithology: 1619, 1936, 1949, 1952, 1967; *see also* Zoology

Orphanages. *See* Children, Adoption and Foster Care

Orthopaedics. *See* Podiatry and Orthopaedics

Osteopathic Medicine: 298, 2035, 2276, 2277, 2278, 2279

Otology: 2261

P

Pacific Area: 768, 769, 2199; *see also* Area Studies; History; Languages; Literature; also specific nations

Pacific Islanders, Eligibility of: 886, 908, 957, 1424, 1443, 1934

Pain: 2008, 2120, 2291; *see also* Neurology

Painting: 395, 424, 428, 449, 452, 460, 470, 497, 505, 509, 516, 520, 869; *see also* Arts; Creative Arts; Fine Arts

Painting, Workshops and Residencies: 303, 465, 478, 502, 518

Pakistan: 755

Paleobiology: 1648, 1947

Paleontology: 1619, 1620, 1811, 1875, 1932, 1936; *see also* Geology

Paralysis: 2305

Parapsychology: 2334, 2335, 2336

Parasitology: 1824, 1941

Parkinson's Disease: 2030, 2206, 2221, 2226, 2227, 2228, 2229, 2230, 2231, 2232

Parks and Recreation. *See* Recreation

Pathology: 2049, 2163; *see also* Cytopathology: related sciences

Pathology, Plant. *See* Plant Physiology and Pathology

Peace. *See* International Relations and International Affairs

Pediatric Nursing: 2245

Pediatrics: 1318, 2016, 2026, 2136, 2236, 2280, 2281, 2282, 2283, 2284, 2285; *see also* Child Welfare and Health

Pennsylvania: 90, 103, 108, 144, 166, 195, 235, 266, 267, 448, 927, 938, 1034, 1077, 1090, 1154, 1155, 1173, 1201, 1223, 1224, 1245, 1560, 1570, 1909, 2050, 2075, 2383

Penology. *See* Correctional Institutions and Procedures

Performing Arts: 80, 93, 137, 146, 224, 230, 254, 305, 325, 384, 385, 390, 391, 394, 396, 398, 401, 402, 405, 406, 409, 412, 420, 422, 423, 425, 427, 429, 434, 435, 436, 437, 438, 439, 440, 443, 444, 445, 446, 447, 448, 450, 454, 457, 458, 466, 468, 474, 479, 482, 483, 484, 493,

513, 690, 695, 697, 701, 702, 703, 704, 705, 710, 713, 717, 726, 729, 730, 733, 930, 980, 1068, 1191, 1481, 1506; *see also* Arts; Cultural Affairs; Dance; Music; Theatre

Performing Arts, Workshops and Residencies: 492

Periodontology: 2099, 2106

Petroleum Sciences: 1595, 1819, 1865, 1879, 1989; *see also* Earth Sciences

Pharmacy and Pharmacology: 298, 1995, 2001, 2031, 2052, 2072, 2073, 2233, 2287, 2290, 2292; *see also* Morphology

Pharmacy and Pharmacology, Education: 1441, 2008, 2288, 2289, 2291

Philanthropy: 116, 157, 166, 181, 223, 261, 581, 724, 756, 1019, 1059, 1094, 1097, 1099, 1106, 1122, 1143, 1156, 1158, 1214, 1239, 1248, 1395, 1421, 1559, 2010

Philology. *See* Linguistics

Philosophy: 279, 327, 360, 363, 579, 590, 623, 652, 1561, 1612, 1671, 1795; *see also* Humanities; Political Philosophy

Philosophy, Classical. *See* Classical Studies

Philosophy, Renaissance. *See* Renaissance Studies

Philosophy, Research and Study: 321, 340, 1497

Philosophy, Research and Study Abroad: 331

Photogrammetry: 1821; *see also* Photography; Surveying

Photography: 386, 409, 424, 426, 434, 452, 460, 465, 470, 478, 498, 507, 509, 518, 519, 521, 523, 1754; *see also* Creative Arts; Fine Arts; Visual Arts

Physical Education: 1305, 2295

Physical Fitness: 1305, 1326, 2180

Physical Sciences: 12, 264, 334, 637, 969, 1616, 1637, 1644, 1651, 1845, 1890, 2087, 2402; *see also* Chemistry; Materials Sciences; Natural Sciences; Nuclear Sciences; Physics; also specific physical sciences

Physical Sciences, Education: 908, 945, 993, 1613, 1624, 1889

Physical Sciences, Research and Study: 924, 1622, 1623, 1822, 1824, 1827, 1890

Physical Sciences, Research and Study Abroad: 867, 1442

Physical Therapy: 298, 2298, 2299, 2301, 2303; *see also* Rehabilitation

Physics: 867, 881, 1573, 1612, 1624, 1635, 1638, 1642, 1644, 1645, 1651, 1652, 1824, 1827, 1828, 1845, 1888, 1891, 1892, 1893, 1896, 1963, 1983, 2359, 2402; *see also* Mathematics; Nuclear Sciences; Physical Sciences

Physiology: 177, 1634, 1824, 1941, 1946, 1950, 2031, 2052, 2090, 2316; *see also* Biological Sciences; related sciences

Physiotherapy: 2237

Planetology: 1839, 1845

Plant Physiology and Pathology: 1624, 1916, 1941; *see also* Botany

Plastic Surgery: 2040, 2076

Playwrights: 424, 450, 453, 489, 490, 491, 492, 494, 645; *see also* Drama; Literature; Theatre; Writers and Writing

Podiatry and Orthopaedics: 298, 927, 2051, 2066, 2067, 2068, 2273, 2296, 2297

Poetry: 87, 432, 478, 614, 616, 620, 625, 626, 628, 630, 632, 633, 644, 647, 653, 654, 982; *see also* Literature; Manuscript Prizes, Poetry and Fiction; Publication Prizes, Creative Writing; Writers and Writing

Poetry, Publication Support: 625, 626

Poetry, Translation: 605, 611, 616, 632

Poland: 838, 839, 840, 841, 1526

Poland, Eligibility Limited to Descendants of: 1473, 1525

Police. *See* Law Enforcement

Policy Analysis: 791, 1384, 1661, 1672, 1674

Political History: 304, 542, 1787, 1790, 1791, 1793, 1809

Political Philosophy: 327, 340, 363, 1803; *see also* Political Science

Political Science: 3, 71, 135, 159, 174, 554, 590, 762, 767, 792, 795, 1232, 1661, 1662, 1750, 1783, 1784, 1788, 1790, 1792, 1793, 1798, 1807, 1808; *see also* Area Studies; Government; International Relations and International Affairs; Social Sciences

Political Science, Education: 984, 995, 1562, 1612, 1670, 1700, 1783, 1784

Political Science, International: 758, 766, 768, 770, 1790, 1798

Political Science, Internships: 931, 958, 962, 1782, 1785, 1794, 1796, 1801, 1802, 1804

Political Science, Research 582, 1784

Political Science, Research and Study Abroad: 857

Pollution. *See* Air Pollution; Environmental Pollution; Water Pollution

Population Planning: 71, 229, 774, 1895, 1971

Population Studies: 71, 137, 768, 769, 1895, 2016; *see also* Developing Nations, Population Studies; Family Planning; Social Sciences; Sociology

Portugal: 600, 601, 757; *see also* Iberia

Poverty Programs: 24, 112, 131, 153, 194, 200, 258, 756, 1009, 1019, 1034, 1061, 1083, 1084, 1086, 1093, 1135, 1179, 1200, 1230, 1235, 1317, 1320, 1322, 1338, 1340, 1348, 1358, 1657, 1765; *see also*

Community Development; Equal Educational Opportunity; Equal Employment Opportunity; Minority Affairs; Race Relations; Social Welfare

Pre-Collegiate Education: 247

Presbyterianism: 750, 1566

Preschool Education and Care: 1009, 1033, 1037, 1038, 1272, 1429; *see also* Child Welfare and Health

Press: 1751, 1758

Print Media: 423, 1729, 1743, 1751; *see also* Communications; Journalism; Magazines; Newspaper; Publications

Printing and Publishing Industry: 424, 1380, 2354, 2359, 2360

Printmaking: 395, 452, 470, 505, 516, 575, 2354; *see also* Crafts

Production Planning: 1988

Professional Development: 109, 479, 916, 1302, 1398, 1715

Prosthetics. *See* Orthotics and Prosthetics

Protestantism: 79, 740, 741, 742

Psychiatry: 704, 1070, 2064, 2233, 2307, 2308, 2309, 2310, 2311, 2312, 2320, 2323, 2328, 2330, 2331, 2338, 2339; *see also* Mental and Emotional Health; Psychology

Psychical Manifestations: 2335, 2336

Psychology: 3, 321, 356, 853, 881, 1070, 1350, 1384, 1642, 1661, 1682, 1685, 1686, 1687, 1689, 1690, 1691, 1692, 1693, 1807, 2031, 2233, 2314, 2317, 2318, 2319, 2321, 2322, 2323, 2324, 2327, 2328; *see also* Behavioral Sciences; Child Psychology; Mental and Emotional Health; Psychiatry; Social Psychology; Social Sciences

Psychology, Education: 1612, 2313, 2315, 2325

Psychology, Experimental: 1694

Psychology, Internships: 2325

Psychology, Organizational: 1694

Psychology, Research and Study: 1663, 1682, 1686, 1687, 1689, 1690, 1691, 1692, 1693

Psychotherapy: 2326

Public Administration: 24, 197, 995, 1793, 1800, 1801, 1804, 1808; *see also* Government; Law Enforcement; Political Science

Public Affairs: 6, 40, 87, 99, 165, 172, 203, 299, 766, 998, 1376, 1466, 1706, 1797, 1807; *see also* Civic Affairs

Public Art 437, 445

Public Assistance: 1348

Public Broadcasting: 85

Public Health: 197, 260, 581, 768, 774, 792, 925, 1142, 1152, 1182, 1200, 1285, 1287, 1300, 1304, 1306, 1308, 1309, 1314, 1391, 1477, 1972, 1989, 2053, 2123, 2124, 2125, 2126, 2128, 2129, 2130, 2131, 2132, 2293, 2327; *see also* Environmental Studies; Health; entries beginning with Medical and Medicine; Social Welfare

Public Information Programs: 40, 789, 1364, 1365, 1366, 1367, 1672, 1731; *see also* Communications; Community Education; Cultural Events, Community; Humanities, Publication, Exhibition, and Public Information Projects; Medicine, Public Information Projects; Sciences, Public Information and Citizen Involvement Projects; Publication Prizes, Public Information

Public Policy: 147, 255, 361, 581, 766, 963, 1033, 1068, 1082, 1225, 1275, 1308, 1338, 1590, 1660, 1684, 1686, 1687, 1788, 1806, 1807, 1808, 2314

Public Policy Research: 162, 770, 995, 1972

Public Relations: 1529; *see also* Advertising; Business

Public Service: 147, 296, 904, 934, 1136, 1796, 1810; *see also* Public Administration; Social Services

Public Welfare. *See* Social Welfare

Publication Assistance: 237, 541, 644, 775, 969, 1480, 1656, 2352; *see also* specific fields

Publication Prizes, Creative Writing: 620, 621, 622, 624, 625, 627, 631, 633, 634, 635, 636, 638, 639, 640, 642, 648, 654, 1729

Publication Prizes, Education: 1397

Publication Prizes, History and Humanities: 404, 408, 525, 526, 529, 533, 544, 547, 548, 559, 569, 576, 606, 612, 621, 622, 642, 643, 737, 1736, 1738, 1740, 1809, 1815

Publication Prizes, Medical and Health Sciences: 2318, 2319

Publication Prizes, Public Information: 1726, 1727, 1728, 1742

Publication Prizes, Sciences: 548, 637, 643, 1723, 1816, 1852, 1888

Publication Prizes, Social Sciences: 1815

Publications: 757, 1374, 1729, 1738; *see also* Fiction; Journalism; Literature; Magazines; Manuscript Completion; Manuscript Prizes; Newspaper; Novel; Playwrights; Poetry; Translation; Writers and Writing; also specific fields

Publishing Industry. *See* Printing and Publishing Industry

Puerto Rican Community Development. *See* Minority Community and Institutional Development; Minority-Owned Businesses; Small Business Development

Puerto Ricans. *See* Spanish-Speaking Americans; also any discipline that may be given Puerto Rican emphasis

Puerto Ricans, Eligibility of: 883, 896, 908, 1701; *see also* Minority-Group Members, Eligibility of

Pulmonary Diseases. *See* Respiratory and Pulmonary Diseases

R

Race Relations: 893, 985, 1100, 1166, 1349, 1657, 1979, 2377; *see also* Equal Educational Opportunity; Equal Employment Opportunity; Human Relations; Minority Affairs; Poverty Programs; Social Welfare

Racial Equity: 157, 260, 972, 987, 1014, 1033, 1154, 1182, 1275, 1296, 1340, 1343, 1413, 2043

Radio and Television: 409, 869, 1723, 1724, 1725, 1736, 1738, 1743, 1744, 1748, 1757; *see also* Broadcast Media; Communications; Educational Media; Social Sciences; Technology, Communications; Telecommunications

Radiology and Radiation Sciences: 2004, 2029, 2079, 2080, 2081, 2082, 2083, 2084; *see also* Medicine; Nuclear Sciences; Physical Sciences

Range Resources. *See* Forest and Range Resources

Rape. *See* Sexual Abuse

Reading: 322, 951, 1397, 1398, 2333; *see also* Education and entries beginning with Education or Educational

Real Estate: 1700; *see also* Appraisal; Business; Finance

Recreation: 27, 108, 110, 173, 259, 277, 933, 1020, 1025, 1060, 1117, 1120, 1161, 1168, 1175, 1187, 1190, 1200, 1211, 1243, 1255, 1305, 1331, 1404, 1971; *see also* Athletics; Community Development; Sports; Urban and Regional Planning

Regional Planning. *See* Urban and Regional Planning

Rehabilitation: 4, 1021, 2145, 2244, 2293, 2295, 2299, 2304, 2305; *see also* Corrective Therapy; Education, Special; Handicapped; Narcotics; Occupational Therapy; Physical Therapy; Vocational Rehabilitation

Relief Organizations: 756, 1052, 1079; *see also* Community Funds; Community Services; Emergency Grants

Religion: 2, 35, 41, 64, 74, 96, 110, 120, 135, 138, 141, 165, 181, 262, 279, 321, 340, 363, 397, 590, 734, 735, 739, 746, 751, 752, 753, 754, 917, 1005, 1080, 1096, 1127, 1146, 1152, 1225, 1290, 1421, 1481, 1513, 1537, 1794; *see also* Catholicism; Christianity; Islam; Journalism, Religious; Judaism; Lutheranism; Protestantism

Religion, History: 535, 536, 537, 538, 539, 736, 737, 738, 742, 747

Religion - Interfaith 85, 1107

Religion, Research and Study Abroad: 734, 836

Religious Denominations, Eligibility Limited to Members of: 741, 742, 743, 748, 750, 751, 753, 1096, 1565, 1566

Religious Education: 185, 287, 741, 746, 748, 750, 917, 1290, 1402, 1448, 1565

Religious Institutions: 94, 165, 287, 739, 751, 905; *see also* Construction and Facilities Projects

Remote Sensing: 1821, 1963

Renaissance Studies: 325, 342, 351, 357, 859, 860, 861, 862, 863, 864, 865, 866; *see also* Arts; History; Literature; Philosophy

Renal Diseases. *See* Nephrology

Reproduction Research: 1634, 2047, 2048, 2251; *see also* Biological Sciences; Family Planning; Genetics; Medicine; Population Studies

Research: 11, 113, 130, 335, 462, 581, 775, 824, 833, 895, 1294, 1441, 1710, 1811, 1845, 1852, 1862, 1872, 1925, 1995, 2014, 2027, 2047, 2048, 2059, 2063, 2087, 2093, 2142, 2273, 2345; *see also* Educational Research; Medical Research; Scientific Research and Development; Technological Research; also specific fields of interest

Research Training: 1426, 1675, 1677, 1678, 1822, 2139, 2170, 2174, 2175, 2310, 2311, 2312; *see also* specific disciplines

Residential Artist or Scholar Programs: 303, 304, 308, 317, 319, 326, 340, 344, 353, 361, 394, 399, 411, 415, 431, 450, 465, 511, 530, 573, 574, 794, 859, 866, 1648, 1814, 1956; *see also* specific disciplines

Resource Development and Management: 87, 100, 768, 786, 948, 1640, 1978, 1984, 1985, 1986; *see also* Developing Nations, Resource Development; Energy Resources and Utilization; Environmental Studies; also specific resources

Respiratory and Pulmonary Diseases: 1307, 2031, 2133, 2134, 2135, 2136, 2137, 2138, 2139, 2144, 2237

Respiratory and Pulmonary Diseases, Research Training: 2135, 2136, 2237, 2245

Restaurant Management and Food Service: 1041, 1511, 1715, 2358, 2410, 2419

Restoration. *See* Historic Preservation and Restoration

Rheumatology and Rheumatic Diseases: 293, 2012, 2086, 2200, 2201

Rhode Island: 55, 218, 248, 333, 451, 1805

Rockefeller Organizations: 581

Rural Development: 1212, 1250, 1264, 1543, 1673, 1924, 1928; *see also* Agricultural Sciences; Cooperatives, Rural and Consumer; Sociology; Urban and Regional Planning

Russia: 766, 778, 821, 833; *see also* other former republics of the U.S.S.R.
Russian Studies. *See* Slavic and East Europe

S

Sabbatical. *See* Faculty, Study and Research Programs
Safety. *See* Occupational Safety and Health; Social Welfare; Traffic Engineering and Safety
Safety: 113, 164, 289, 990, 1211, 2413
Salivary Research: 2090
Sanitation: 2415; *see also* Engineering; Environmental Pollution; Health; Solid Waste Management, Wastewater Management
Scandinavia: 497, 808; *see also* Europe; specific nations
Schools. *See* entries beginning with Education and Educational
Science, Communications: 1731, 1743
Science, Technology, Engineering and Mathematics Education: 109, 938, 1497, 1642
Sciences: 2, 6, 9, 23, 41, 43, 54, 64, 121, 199, 210, 211, 219, 226, 261, 279, 334, 421, 548, 759, 1014, 1107, 1187, 1312, 1376, 1415, 1460, 1618, 1634, 1636, 1639, 1641, 1646, 1872, 1886, 1896, 2405, 2406; *see also* specific sciences
Sciences, Conferences and Symposia: 1643, 1651, 1946, 1947
Sciences, Curriculum Development and Teaching Methods: 1436, 2046
Sciences, Education: 14, 212, 229, 232, 899, 942, 945, 951, 973, 1368, 1415, 1430, 1436, 1440, 1563, 1630, 1632, 1649, 1731, 1821, 1844, 1851, 1878, 1886, 1934, 2355, 2378, 2379, 2380, 2381, 2382; *see also* specific sciences
Sciences, Equipment and Facilities: 8, 1946, 1947, 2386; *see also* specific sciences
Sciences, Ethics: 1643; *see also* Bioethics; Medical Ethics
Sciences, History: 308, 330, 528, 547, 548, 1642, 1648, 2290, 2350, 2372
Sciences, In-Service Programs: 1626, 1654, 2314, 2405
Sciences, Public Information and Citizen Involvement Projects: 1436, 1743; *see also* Community Education
Sciences, Publication Projects: 1723, 1731, 1745, 1746, 1747, 1957; *see also* Journalism, Scientific; Manuscript Prizes, Sciences; Publication Prizes, Sciences
Sciences, Related to Other Disciplines: 1395, 1643, 1731, 1801
Sciences, Research and Study Abroad: 823, 831, 850, 856, 867, 881, 1489
Scientific Exchange Programs: 831, 1475, 1839, 1966
Scientific Research and Development: 11, 12, 26, 282, 706, 867, 902, 1158, 1303, 1311, 1316, 1409, 1441, 1447, 1616, 1621, 1629, 1631, 1633, 1634, 1635, 1638, 1641, 1643, 1644, 1646, 1647, 1650, 1651, 1652, 1684, 1820, 1821, 1823, 1828, 1839, 1842, 1843, 1873, 1874, 1905, 1946, 1990, 2052, 2172, 2173, 2186, 2187, 2233, 2337, 2396; *see also* specific scientific disciplines
Scientific Research and Development, International Cooperative Programs: 355, 879, 880, 881, 1831
Scotland: 331, 849, 1966
Scotland, Eligibility Limited to Descendants of: 849
Sculpture: 310, 395, 424, 428, 452, 460, 470, 478, 505, 509, 516, 869; *see also* Arts; Creative Arts; Fine Arts; Humanities
Sculpture, Workshops and Residencies: 303, 465, 502, 518
Secondary Education. *See* Education, Secondary
Seismology. *See* Earth Sciences
Semantics. *See* Linguistics
Seminars: 307, 385, 390, 1454, 1946, 1947; *see also* Conferences; International Projects and Seminars; Teacher Seminars and Workshops; Travel Grants, Seminar Attendance; Workshops; also specific disciplines
Sensory Function: 2090
Sex Role Stereotyping: 895, 1657; *see also* Family Life; Women's Rights
Sexual Abuse: 983, 1669
Skin Diseases. *See* Dermatology
Slavic and East Europe: 594, 595, 603, 778, 833, 845, 846; *see also* Area Studies; History; Languages; Literature; also specific nations
Small Business Development: 86, 1312, 1353, 2275; *see also* Business Development Assistance
Social Change and Development: 112, 125, 774, 892, 979, 985, 1074, 1084, 1134, 1196, 1321, 1329, 1338, 1344, 1348, 1349, 1360, 1655, 1907, 2332
Social History: 360, 362, 543, 553, 560, 590, 1648, 1809
Social Justice and Equity: 81, 97, 131, 154, 247, 273, 972, 1012, 1264, 1275, 1296, 1655, 2043
Social Psychology: 881, 1680, 1681, 1683, 1688, 2332; *see also* Behavioral Sciences
Social Sciences: 9, 11, 197, 306, 531, 581, 829, 862, 925, 995, 1070, 1446, 1486, 1565, 1616, 1638, 1643, 1657, 1658, 1659, 1660, 1661, 1676, 1679, 1682, 1685, 1686, 1687, 1689, 1690, 1691, 1692, 1693; *see also* social sciences by name

Social Sciences, Education: 908, 954, 1613, 1616, 1667, 1668
Social Sciences, Publication: 1656, 1682, 1693
Social Sciences, Research and Study: 355, 361, 755, 782, 788, 789, 883, 1016, 1310, 1311, 1316, 1350, 1486, 1513, 1613, 1646, 1663, 1665, 1666, 1667, 1668, 1674, 1675, 1676, 1677, 1678, 1679, 1680, 1681, 1682, 1683, 1686, 1687, 1688, 1689, 1690, 1691, 1692, 1693, 1694, 1768, 1817, 1895, 2211
Social Sciences, Research and Study Abroad: 783, 784, 786, 799, 805, 824, 852, 853, 856, 1185, 1489
Social Sciences, Teaching: 1665, 1666
Social Services: 4, 6, 14, 20, 22, 23, 26, 27, 28, 29, 30, 32, 35, 44, 45, 46, 52, 54, 55, 56, 61, 66, 67, 72, 84, 86, 90, 96, 97, 98, 103, 108, 110, 118, 126, 129, 142, 146, 150, 155, 163, 172, 175, 176, 182, 184, 192, 198, 200, 205, 207, 211, 220, 222, 228, 230, 235, 238, 249, 251, 260, 270, 278, 281, 282, 301, 328, 334, 591, 743, 746, 894, 905, 936, 1004, 1013, 1033, 1044, 1048, 1053, 1060, 1062, 1069, 1078, 1079, 1082, 1083, 1093, 1100, 1109, 1118, 1119, 1124, 1126, 1130, 1136, 1137, 1138, 1143, 1144, 1145, 1152, 1153, 1156, 1159, 1161, 1167, 1170, 1172, 1177, 1186, 1187, 1192, 1201, 1218, 1222, 1225, 1228, 1230, 1241, 1242, 1244, 1257, 1272, 1288, 1309, 1317, 1322, 1325, 1327, 1331, 1346, 1352, 1355, 1357, 1361, 1417, 1438, 1451, 1452, 1458, 1565, 1788; *see also* Community Funds; Community Services
Social Welfare: 9, 13, 14, 21, 59, 69, 70, 73, 74, 75, 83, 90, 100, 101, 102, 104, 107, 115, 117, 125, 128, 133, 135, 138, 139, 145, 158, 167, 168, 188, 194, 208, 209, 214, 216, 218, 221, 232, 233, 239, 243, 244, 249, 257, 258, 263, 267, 271, 277, 287, 290, 294, 296, 407, 744, 753, 936, 957, 1004, 1008, 1019, 1046, 1055, 1067, 1072, 1073, 1079, 1084, 1085, 1091, 1095, 1108, 1110, 1120, 1123, 1129, 1136, 1142, 1152, 1160, 1162, 1165, 1166, 1167, 1171, 1176, 1182, 1188, 1193, 1197, 1202, 1213, 1214, 1224, 1230, 1235, 1237, 1240, 1247, 1248, 1250, 1255, 1269, 1273, 1285, 1325, 1332, 1336, 1339, 1340, 1347, 1349, 1357, 1358, 1360, 1674, 1717, 1736, 1750, 2341; *see also* Aged; Child Welfare and Health; Health; Human Relations; Minority Affairs; Poverty Programs
Social Work: 197, 792, 1350, 2326; *see also* Social Services
Social Work, Education: 896, 1612, 1613
Sociology: 3, 321, 356, 590, 762, 792, 881, 1350, 1652, 1661, 1662, 1682, 1685, 1686, 1687, 1693, 2316; *see also* Behavioral Sciences; Social Sciences
Sociology, Education: 886, 1562
Solar Energy and Solar Research: 1840; *see also* Atmospheric Sciences; Energy Resources and Utilization; Physical Sciences
Solid State Sciences. *See* Physical Sciences; Sciences
South Africa: 1514
South Carolina: 89, 94, 455, 1094, 1246, 1575
South Dakota: 456
Southeast Asia: 185; *see also* Asia
Southern States: 186, 274; *see also* states by name
Space Sciences. *See* Aerospace Sciences
Spain: 865, 1514; *see also* Iberia
Spanish-Speaking Americans: 886, 908, 909, 922, 924, 962, 963, 964, 965, 966, 1783, 2395; *see also* Minority-Group Members, Eligibility of; Minority Studies; Race Relations; also any discipline that may be given Spanish-Speaking American emphasis or be of concern to Spanish-Speaking Americans
Special Education. *See* Education, Special
Speech Impairments and Communicative Disorders: 2262
Speech, Language and Hearing Therapy: 2262, 2301; *see also* Rehabilitation
Sports: 245, 868, 997, 1025, 1211, 1255, 1305, 2305; *see also* Recreation
Sri Lanka: 799, 800
Staffing Grants. *See* specific disciplines
State Agencies, Eligibility of. *See* areas of interest to state agencies
Statistics: 3, 1384, 1881, 1882, 1887; *see also* Actuarial Science; Insurance; Mathematics
Stroke: 2123, 2124, 2125, 2126, 2127, 2128, 2129, 2130, 2131, 2132, 2146, 2221; *see also* Cardiology and Cardiovascular Diseases
Student Aid Programs. *See* Education, Higher, Aid Programs for Undergraduate and Graduate Students in All Disciplines; also specific disciplines
Substance Abuse: 1, 83, 146, 216, 1217, 1259; *see also* Alcohol Abuse and Alcoholism
Suicide: 1364, 1365, 1366, 1367
Surgery: 2076, 2272; *see also* Neurosurgery; Plastic Surgery; also diseases and areas of medicine by name
Surveying: 1821, 2399; *see also* Engineering; Mathematics
Sustainability: 207, 247, 920, 1091, 1977, 2342
Sweden: 355, 785, 808, 819, 1444; *see also* Scandinavia
Switzerland: 771, 821

Systematic Biology: 1943
Systems Science: 1694, 2359, 2396; *see also* Computer Sciences; Mathematics

T

Taxonomy: 1943
Teacher Education. *See* Education, Teacher Preparation
Teacher Seminars and Workshops: 338, 789, 1425; *see also* Faculty, Study and Research Programs; specific disciplines
Teaching, Outside U.S.: 830, 831, 841, 1425; *see also* Language Teachers, Study and Research Abroad; also specific nations
Technical Assistance: 385, 390, 418, 444, 833, 1097, 1102, 1196; *see also* Consulting Services
Technical Education. *See* Education, Technical
Technological Research: 2345, 2353
Technology: 167, 252, 989, 1014, 1132, 1183, 1241, 1312, 1382, 1401, 1438, 1506, 1639, 1643, 1853, 1871, 2355, 2361, 2403; *see also* Dental Laboratory Technology; Engineering; Industrial Arts and Education; Medical Technology; Sciences
Technology, Aerospace: 2371, 2372
Technology, Communications: 1743, 1757
Technology, History: 308, 543, 549, 1648, 2352
Technology, Industrial: 1989, 2359, 2360, 2361, 2392; *see also* Industry and Industrial Research
Technology, Maritime: 2388
Technology, Mining: 2421, 2422, 2423
Teen Pregnancy: 1050, 1287, 1301; *see also* Family Life
Telecommunications: 1567, 2371; *see also* Broadcast Media; Communications; Radio and Television
Television. *See* Radio and Television
Tennessee: 20, 68, 186, 274, 458, 1112, 1113, 1159, 1583
Texas: 80, 139, 158, 161, 163, 184, 198, 249, 283, 284, 429, 459, 463, 499, 500, 501, 586, 587, 683, 1060, 1108, 1127, 1128, 1136, 1148, 1151, 1221, 1239, 1240, 1254, 1259, 1267, 1376, 1563, 1861, 1971, 2104
Textiles: 400, 980
Thanatology: 1895
Theatre: 360, 397, 398, 402, 405, 409, 416, 419, 422, 423, 424, 434, 437, 439, 442, 443, 454, 469, 483, 488, 491, 492, 493, 494, 687; *see also* Drama; Performing Arts; Playwrights
Theatre, Actors and Acting: 491
Theatre Arts, Education: 461, 487, 491
Theatre, Consulting Services: 645
Theatre, Criticism: 482
Theatre, History: 482
Theatrical Design: 491
Theology: 279, 623, 734, 735, 739, 740, 754, 813, 856; *see also* Religion
Therapy. *See* Corrective Therapy; Music Therapy; Occupational Therapy; Physical Therapy; Psychotherapy; Rehabilitation; Speech, Language, and Hearing Therapy
Tourism: 780
Toxicology: 1848, 1941, 1989, 1992, 2031, 2072, 2073, 2292
Trade: 780, 1719; *see also* International Market; International Relations and International Affairs
Traffic Engineering and Safety: 872, 1332, 2343, 2353, 2362; *see also* Transportation
Translation: 605, 611, 640; *see also* Languages; Poetry, Translation; Writers and Writing
Translational Medicine 2048, 2273
Transportation: 29, 206, 1247, 1332, 1964, 2343, 2353, 2362; *see also* Traffic Engineering and Safety
Travel Grants, Domestic: 462, 501, 535, 536, 537, 538, 650, 659, 997, 1097, 1616, 1754, 1790, 2094
Travel Grants, Foreign Students: 311
Travel Grants, Outside U.S.: 310, 501, 517, 777, 991, 1673, 1754
Travel Grants, Seminar Attendance: 1637; *see also* Seminars
Tropics: 1967
Tuberculosis: 1307, 2139, 2145, 2237
Turkey: 805, 806, 807

U

Ukraine: 358, 359
Underdeveloped Nations. *See* Developing Nations
Unemployment. *See* Labor, Unemployment
Union of Soviet Socialist Republics. *See* Baltics; Russia; Ukraine; other former republics of the U.S.S.R.
United Funds: 40, 98, 103, 126, 150, 176, 184, 200, 231

United Kingdom: 866, 873, 2188; *see also* England; Ireland; Scotland; Wales
United Nations: 780
Urban Affairs: 40, 112, 113, 246, 1160, 1172, 1195, 1262, 1340, 1417, 1657, 1786; *see also* Civic Affairs; Community Development; Community Services; Inner-City; Social Welfare
Urban Affairs, Research and Study Abroad: 1051
Urban and Regional Planning: 186, 202, 301, 372, 373, 792, 885, 1051, 1100, 1262, 1266, 1590, 1661, 1673, 1925, 1971; *see also* Architecture; Community Development; Environmental Studies; Rural Development
Urban History: 369
Urology: 2176
Utah: 83, 262, 464

V

Vacuum Science: 1889; *see also* Physical Sciences
Values. *See* Human Values
Vascular Diseases: 2143, 2146; *see also* Cardiology and Cardiovascular Diseases
Venereal Disease. *See* Infectious Diseases
Vermont: 114, 466, 1019, 1037, 1257, 1609
Veterans' Children and Dependents, Eligibility of: 894, 1476, 1479, 1546, 1549, 1556, 1572
Veterans, Eligibility of: 15, 191, 894, 1243, 1543, 1545
Veterinary Sciences: 298, 1894, 1898, 1927, 1931, 2009, 2010, 2034; *see also* Animal Sciences; Medicine
Video Arts: 374, 398, 419, 453, 519, 1723, 1761; *see also* Broadcast Media; Communications; Film; Radio and Television; Telecommunications
Violence. *See* Behavioral Sciences
Virgin Islands: 468
Virginia: 469, 470, 574, 1053, 1176, 1269, 1301, 1347, 1357, 1576, 1992, 2248
Virology: 2031; *see also* Biomedical Sciences and Research; Immunology; Microbiology
Vision Impaired, Eligibility of: 2265
Visual Arts: 230, 233, 303, 356, 384, 385, 390, 391, 394, 396, 397, 398, 401, 402, 405, 406, 409, 410, 416, 419, 420, 422, 423, 424, 425, 426, 427, 429, 434, 435, 436, 439, 442, 443, 446, 447, 448, 453, 458, 466, 468, 469, 470, 474, 479, 484, 498, 499, 500, 501, 503, 504, 505, 507, 514, 515, 517, 518, 521, 890, 930, 980, 982, 1506, 1564; *see also* Fine Arts
Visual Arts, Workshops and Residencies: 399, 431, 450, 465, 478, 502
Visual Disorders: 2253, 2255, 2263, 2265, 2267, 2268, 2270, 2272, 2273, 2274, 2275; *see also* Ophthalmology; Optometry
Viticulture and Enology: 1905; *see also* Agricultural Sciences
Vocational Education. *See* Education, Vocational
Vocational Rehabilitation: 882, 1474, 2306; *see also* Occupational Therapy; Rehabilitation
Volunteer Service: 4, 170, 841, 1076, 1135, 1333
Volunteerism: 998, 1332

W

War. *See* International Security
Washington: 56, 213, 217, 260, 901, 915, 1071, 1191, 1235, 1327, 1360, 1431, 1610, 1611, 1959, 1982
Wastewater Management: 236, 1928, 1988, 1989; *see also* Environmental Pollution; Sanitation
Water Pollution: 1346, 1963, 1988, 1992; *see also* Environmental Pollution
Water Resources: 176, 236, 1928, 1958, 1960, 1965, 1970, 1974, 1984, 1985, 1986, 1988, 1991, 2344, 2409; *see also* Environmental Studies; Resource Development and Management
Water Sports. *See* Sports
Weapons. *See* Armaments; Defense Projects and Research
Weather Modification: 1963; *see also* Climatology; Meteorology
Weaving: 413; *see also* Crafts; Creative Arts
Welfare. *See* Social Welfare
West Virginia: 472, 1158, 1614, 1909, 1992
Wildlife: 259, 1288, 1619, 1625, 1626, 1721, 1900, 1962, 1965, 1971, 1988; *see also* Conservation; Fish and Game Management
Wisconsin: 25, 218, 474, 593, 919, 1053, 1054, 1055, 1062, 1074, 1145, 1149, 1167, 1170, 1198, 1331, 1476
Women, Education of: 185, 346, 938, 954, 974, 977, 988, 990, 991, 992, 996, 1109, 1226, 1696, 1866, 2101, 2378

Women, Eligibility of: 346, 529, 534, 741, 898, 907, 910, 924, 954, 967, 968, 969, 970, 971, 972, 973, 975, 976, 977, 978, 980, 981, 982, 984, 985, 986, 989, 991, 992, 993, 994, 997, 998, 1496, 1572, 1613, 1624, 1630, 1646, 1722, 1832, 1846, 1866, 1974, 2002, 2101, 2392

Women, Employment: 250, 977, 981, 983, 988, 990, 996, 1765, 2002; *see also* Equal Employment Opportunity

Women, Foreign Nationals, Eligibility of: 871, 877, 978

Women's Health: 236, 245, 1161, 1410, 1971, 2236, 2250

Women's Issues: 84, 90, 105, 122, 146, 155, 164, 278, 967, 972, 979, 983, 985, 987, 990, 996, 998, 1105, 1132, 1155, 1161, 1226, 1258, 1265, 1287, 1362, 1410

Women's Rights: 122, 152, 250, 914, 967, 972, 983, 988, 998, 1079, 1379

Women's Studies: 346, 531, 534, 954, 975, 977

Work. *See* Labor

Workers' Rights: 242

Workforce Development 1, 7, 25, 42, 97, 253, 289, 1046, 1089, 1171, 1227, 1260, 1282, 1302, 1315, 1378

Workshops: 436, 1946, 1947; *see also* Conferences; International Projects and Seminars; Seminars; Teacher Seminars and Workshops; also any discipline that lends itself to a workshop approach

World Affairs. *See* Area Studies; International Relations and International Affairs

Writers and Writing: 120, 305, 386, 413, 424, 434, 453, 462, 478, 480, 484, 490, 584, 602, 612, 613, 614, 615, 620, 624, 625, 627, 628, 629, 630, 631, 632, 633, 634, 635, 636, 637, 638, 639, 640, 641, 642, 643, 647, 649, 650, 654, 736, 737, 738, 795, 980, 1460, 1723, 1730, 1731, 1735, 1740, 1741, 1745, 1746, 1747, 1792, 1864; *see also* Art Criticism; Biography; Children's Literature; Drama; Fiction; Journalism; Literary Criticism; Literature; Magazines; Manuscript Completion; Manuscript Prizes; News Reporting; Newspaper; Nonfiction; Novel; Playwrights; Poetry; Publication Prizes; Translation; also specific subjects

Writers and Writing, Publication Support: 631, 646, 1180, 1731, 2122; *see also* specific subjects

Writers and Writing, Subsistence Aid: 617

Writers and Writing, Workshops and Residencies: 399, 431, 450, 463, 465, 502, 615, 645

Wyoming: 83, 1360

Y

Youth: 25, 26, 27, 28, 29, 33, 40, 55, 56, 59, 64, 76, 84, 102, 107, 108, 132, 133, 136, 146, 148, 151, 152, 157, 170, 175, 181, 182, 216, 224, 229, 230, 234, 235, 278, 288, 292, 295, 301, 396, 438, 467, 753, 868, 892, 905, 933, 981, 1000, 1003, 1005, 1007, 1016, 1018, 1021, 1026, 1027, 1028, 1032, 1033, 1034, 1035, 1036, 1037, 1039, 1042, 1050, 1054, 1057, 1059, 1069, 1079, 1081, 1086, 1098, 1101, 1105, 1118, 1120, 1131, 1138, 1140, 1142, 1150, 1152, 1153, 1155, 1156, 1162, 1163, 1169, 1171, 1182, 1190, 1201, 1211, 1228, 1230, 1235, 1236, 1251, 1252, 1253, 1268, 1272, 1288, 1301, 1304, 1318, 1332, 1334, 1339, 1343, 1352, 1354, 1359, 1368, 1387, 1390, 1417, 1438, 1439, 1490; *see also* Children; Community Development; Social Welfare

Youth Agencies: 148, 150, 184, 209, 219, 231, 259, 294, 1010, 1018, 1023, 1035, 1037, 1039, 1058, 1160, 1362

Youth Development: 36, 46, 49, 66, 69, 83, 104, 106, 174, 195, 216, 221, 277, 283, 414, 933, 953, 987, 1009, 1011, 1013, 1014, 1016, 1020, 1029, 1053, 1063, 1102, 1106, 1107, 1127, 1132, 1133, 1147, 1163, 1167, 1191, 1196, 1200, 1233, 1240, 1258, 1266, 1417, 1419, 1437, 1447, 1554, 1655, 2307, 2308, 2309

Z

Zoology: 1620, 1930, 1931, 1936, 1939, 1983, 2031; *see also* Animal Sciences; Biological Sciences

Organization and Program Index

The Organization and Program Index alphabetically lists grant programs in upper-lower case and funding organizations in upper case. In addition, programs also are listed following the organizations which sponsor them.

A

A Place to Perform: 1099
A-T CHILDREN'S PROJECT
    A-T Postdoctoral Fellowship Award: 1994
    A-T Research Grant Program: 1994
A-T Postdoctoral Fellowship Award: 1994
A-T Research Grant Program: 1994
A-dec Scholarship: 2104
A.R.S. Lazarian Graduate Scholarship: 887
A.R.S. Undergraduate Scholarship: 887
AA&MDSIF Research Grant Program: 2011
AAAS Kavli Science Journalism Awards: 1723
AACR Independent Investigator Grants: 2177
AACR NextGen Grants for Transformative Cancer Research: 2177
AACR Team Science Grants: 2177
AADR Hatton Competition: 2097
AAG Dissertation Research Grants: 1863
AAG Globe Book Award for Public Understanding of Geography: 1864
AAG Meridian Book Award for the Outstanding Scholarly Work in Geography: 1864
AAG Research Grant: 1862
AAGS Joseph F. Dracup Scholarship Award: 2401
AAPG Foundation Grants-in-Aid: 1865
AAS American Society for Eighteenth Century Studies Fellowship: 304
AAS Fellowship for Creative and Performing Artists and Writers: 305
AAS National Endowment for the Humanities Fellowships: 304
AASL Collaborative School Library Award: 658
AASL Frances Henne Award: 658
AASL Innovative Reading Grant: 658
AASL National School Library of the Year Award: 658
AAUW Career Development Grants: 971
AAUW International Fellowships: 871
AAUW Selected Professions Fellowships: 968
ABC-CLIO Leadership Grant: 658
ABC Trust Community Grant: 6
Abe Fellowship for Journalists Program: 775
Abe Fellowship Program: 775, 784
ABEL FOUNDATION: 1043
ABELARD FOUNDATION-EAST (THE): 1329
ABELL FOUNDATION, INC. (THE): 1
ABF/ALI Doctoral Fellowship Program in Legal & Higher Education: 1768
ABLE TRUST (THE)
    Board Directed Initiative Grants: 882
    General Support for Employment Placement Programs: 882
    Strategic Employment Placement Initiatives: 882
ABNEY FOUNDATION (THE): 2
Abramowicz (The Dina) Emerging Scholar Fellowship: 597
Abrams (Charles) Scholarship Program: 1051
Abstract Achievement Award: 2109
ABTA Research Collaboration Grant: 2204
Academic Achievement Graduate Assistantships: 907
Academic Enrichment Grants: 1434
ACADEMIC PEDIATRIC ASSOCIATION (APA)
    APA Young Investigator Awards Program: 2280
Academic Studies: 780
ACADEMY FOUNDATION OF THE ACADEMY OF MOTION PICTURE ARTS AND SCIENCES
    Academy Nicholl Fellowships in Screenwriting (The): 480
    Student Academy Awards Competition: 495
Academy Nicholl Fellowships in Screenwriting (The): 480
ACADEMY OF NATURAL SCIENCES OF PHILADELPHIA (THE)
    Gallagher (John J. and Anna H.) Fellowship: 1615
    Jessup Fellowship: 1930
    McHenry Fellowship: 1930
ACADEMY OF NUTRITION AND DIETETICS FOUNDATION (THE): 2410
Acadia Graduate Scholarships/Acadia Graduate Teaching Assistantships: 3

ACADIA UNIVERSITY
    Acadia Graduate Scholarships/Acadia Graduate Teaching Assistantships: 3
ACC Young Investigators Awards Competition: 2122
ACCADEMIA MUSICALE CHIGIANA
    Scholarships for Summer Music Courses: 686
Access Camps: 129
Access Missouri Financial Assistance Program: 1534
Access Reimbursement Grants: 447
Access to Better Learning and Education Grant Program (ABLE): 1501
Access to College and Career Education (ACE) Program: 938
Access to Health Care-System Change and Advocacy: 1363
Accessibility Grant: 435
ACHELIS AND BODMAN FOUNDATION (THE): 4
Acheson (Edward Goodrich) Award: 1627
ACLS Fellowship: 306
ACOR-CAORC Fellowship: 796
ACOR-CAORC Postdoctoral Fellowships: 796
ACORN FOUNDATION: 1953
ACPC Scholarship, Summer Studies in Poland: 1473
ACS Scholars Program: 1848
ACS Training Award: 1543
Acta Materialia Scholarships: 2420
Action Grants: 329
Actuarial Diversity Scholarship: 1880
ACTUARIAL FOUNDATION (THE)
    Actuarial Diversity Scholarship: 1880
    Actuary of Tomorrow - Stuart A. Robertson Memorial Scholarship: 1881
    Huntington (Curtis E.) Memorial Scholarship: 1882
Actuary of Tomorrow - Stuart A. Robertson Memorial Scholarship: 1881
ADAMS (EMMA J.) MEMORIAL FUND, INC.: 1330
Adams (The Herbert Baxter) Prize: 526
ADDF/NIH: 1995
Addiction and Health Equity Program: 1217
ADHA Institute for Oral Health Dental Hygiene Scholarships: 2103
Adler Fellowships: 727
ADMA Scholarship Programs: 2366
ADSC: THE INTERNATIONAL ASSOCIATION OF FOUNDATION DRILLING: 2375
Advanced Fellowships: 811
Advanced Informal STEM Learning (AISL): 1436
Advanced Language Program in India: 599
Advanced Seminar Program: 1814
Advanced Studies Certificate: 486
Advanced Technological Education (ATE): 1436
Advancement of Music: 724
Advancing Medicare: 1335
Advancing Wellness Grants Program: 1287
Advocacy Program: 1223
Advocacy Unrestricted: 1223
AES/EF Clinical Research and Training Fellowship Award: 2211
AES/EF Junior Investigator Research Award: 2211
AETNA FOUNDATION, INC.
    Cultivating Healthy Communities: 5
    Healthiest Cities and Counties Challenge: 5
Affiliated Fellowships: 1592
Affiliated Writer Program: 645
AFPE Predoctoral Fellowships in the Pharmaceutical Sciences: 1441
Africa and South Asia: Child and Maternal Health: 1031
African-American and African Studies Fellowships: 364
African American Community Fund: 1120
African American Endowment Fund (The): 1057
African American Graduate Fellowship: 1582
African American Male Mentoring Initiative (AAMMI): 938
African American Unity Fund: 223
AFS Faces of America Diversity Scholarship Program: 793
AFS Global Prep: 793
AFS INTERCULTURAL PROGRAMS/USA
    AFS Faces of America Diversity Scholarship Program: 793
    AFS Global Prep: 793
    AFS Semester Program: 793
    AFS Summer Program: 793
    AFS Year Program: 793
    AFSNext: 793
    Congress-Bundestag Youth Exchange (CBX): 793
    Kennedy-Lugar Youth Exchange and Study Abroad (YES Abroad): 793
    National Securities Languages Initiative for Youth (NSLI-Y): 793
AFS Semester Program: 793
AFS Summer Program: 793

AFS Year Program: 793
AFSA National High School Essay Contest: 790
AFSNext: 793
After-School Programs: 1390
AGA-Bern Schwartz Family Fund Research Scholar Award in Pancreatic
    Cancer: 2160
AGA-Caroline Craig Augustyn and Damian Augustyn Award in Digestive
    Cancer: 2154
AGA Fellow Abstract Award: 2153
AGA-Gastric Cancer Foundation Ben Feinstein Memorial Research
    Scholar Award in Gastric Cancer: 2155
AGA-Medtronic Pilot Research Award in Technology Innovation: 2158
AGA-Moti L. and Kamla Rustgi International Travel Awards: 2152
AGA-Pfizer Pilot Research Award in Inflammatory Bowel Disease: 2159
AGA-R. Robert and Sally D. Funderburg Research Award in Gastric
    Cancer: 2149
AGA Research Scholar Award: 2156
AGA Student Abstract Award: 2151
AGA-Takeda Pharmaceuticals Research Scholar Award in Inflammatory
    Bowel Disease: 2150
AGA-Takeda Pharmaceuticals Research Scholar Awards in Celiac Disease:
    2157
Agan (Tessie) Award Competition: 1180
AGC EDUCATION AND RESEARCH FOUNDATION
    Allhands (James L.) Essay Competition: 2376
    Graduate Scholarship Program: 2376
    Industry Case Studies: 2376
    Outstanding Educator Award: 2376
    Undergraduate Scholarship Program: 2376
    Workforce Development Scholarship: 2376
AGENCY FOR HEALTHCARE RESEARCH AND QUALITY (AHRQ)
    AHRQ Research Grants: 1281
Aging Research: 1310
AGRICULTURAL HISTORY SOCIETY
    Edwards (Everett E.) Awards in Agricultural History: 524
    Fite (Gilbert C.) Dissertation Award: 524
    Rasmussen (Wayne D.) Award: 524
    Saloutos (Theodore) Book Award: 524
    Wallace (Henry A.) Award: 524
AHA Institutional Research Enhancement Award (AIREA): 2124
Ahmanson and Getty Postdoctoral Fellowships: 320
Ahmanson Research Fellowships for the Study of Medieval and
    Renaissance Books and Manuscripts: 357
AHRQ Research Grants: 1281
AIA Arthur N. Tuttle, Jr. Graduate Fellowship in Health Facility Planning
    and Design: 366
AIA Publication Subvention Program (The): 1480
AIA Scholarship: 2367
AICPA Fellowship for Minority Doctoral Students: 1485
AICPA Foundation Scholarship for Future CPAs: 1695
AICPA Foundation Two-Year Transfer Scholarship: 1698
AICPA Scholarship for Minority Accounting Students: 1369
AICPA/Robert Half Student Scholarships: 1697
AIHP Ph.D. Research Support Grant Program: 2290
AIIS Fellowships: 802
AINA Grants-in-Aid: 1446
AIPS Post Doctoral Fellowship: 755
AIPS Pre-Doctoral Fellowship: 755
AIR & WASTE MANAGEMENT ASSOCIATION (A&WMA)
    Scholarship Endowment Trust Fund: 2342
AIR TRAFFIC CONTROL ASSOCIATION (ATCA): 2343
AIRCRAFT ELECTRONICS ASSOCIATION (AEA)
    Arver (David) Memorial Scholarship: 2363
    Arver (Dutch and Ginger) Scholarship: 2363
    Baker (Gene) Memorial Scholarship: 2363
    Cook (Jim) Honorary Scholarship: 2363
    Davis (Johnny) Memorial Scholarship: 2363
    Duncan Aviation Scholarship: 2363
    Field Aviation Company Scholarship: 2363
    Freeland (Chuck) Memorial Scholarship for Flight Training: 2363
    Garmin - Jerry Smith Memorial Scholarship: 2363
    Garmin Scholarship: 2363
    Gogo Business Aviation Scholarship: 2363
    Harris (Leon)/Les Nichols Memorial Scholarship: 2363
    Mid-Continent Instrument Scholarship: 2363
    Peacock (Chuck) Memorial Scholarship: 2363
    Sporty's Foundation Scholarship: 2363
    Stone Foundation Scholarship: 2363
    Tarbox (Lee) Memorial Scholarship: 2363

    Taylor (Tom) Memorial Scholarship: 2363
    Temple (Marshall) Memorial Scholarship: 2363
    Universal Avionics Systems Corporation Scholarship: 2363
AISLS Dissertation Planning Grant: 800
AISLS Fellowship Program: 799
Akehurst (Carville M.) Memorial Scholarship: 1510
AKRON COMMUNITY FOUNDATION: 1044
AKTA Lou Montalvano Memorial Scholarship: 2295
ALA Awards: 659
ALA Spectrum Scholarship: 1443
ALA/Century Scholarship: 1443
ALABAMA ACADEMY OF SCIENCE, INC.
    Gorgas Scholarship: 1616
    Mason Science Teaching Fellowships: 1616
    Student Research Grants: 1616
    Student Travel Awards: 1616
ALABAMA COMMISSION ON HIGHER EDUCATION
    Alabama National Guard Educational Assistance Program: 1471
    Alabama Student Assistance Program: 1472
    Alabama Student Grant Program: 1472
    Senior Adult Scholarship Program: 1470
ALABAMA LIBRARY ASSOCIATION SCHOLARSHIP FUND, INC.
    Scholarships in Library Science: 655
Alabama National Guard Educational Assistance Program: 1471
ALABAMA POWER FOUNDATION
    ABC Trust Community Grant: 6
    Classroom Grant: 6
    Elevate Grant: 6
    Foundation Grants: 6
    Gateway Grant: 6
    Good Roots Grant: 6
    Power to Play Grant: 6
    Students to Stewards Program: 6
ALABAMA STATE COUNCIL ON THE ARTS
    Art and Cultural Facilities: 384
    Arts-in-Education: 384
    Community Arts Development: 384
    Folk Arts: 384
    Literary Art: 384
    Performing Arts: 384
    Visual Arts and Crafts: 384
Alabama Student Assistance Program: 1472
Alabama Student Grant Program: 1472
ALASKA CONSERVATION FOUNDATION
    Alaska Defense Fund: 1955
    Discovery Grants Program: 1955
    Rapid Response Grant: 1954
Alaska Defense Fund: 1955
ALASKA STATE COUNCIL ON THE ARTS: 385
ALBION COMMUNITY FOUNDATION: 1045
ALBRIGHT INSTITUTE OF ARCHAEOLOGICAL RESEARCH (AIAR)
    Fellowships at the Albright Institute of Archaeological Research in
    Jerusalem: 794
ALBUQUERQUE COMMUNITY FOUNDATION: 1046
ALCOA FOUNDATION: 7
ALCON FOUNDATION, INC. (THE): 2253
ALDEN (GEORGE I.) TRUST: 8
ALDEN (THE JOHN W.) TRUST: 999
Alessio (Maria and Paolo) Southern Italy Scholarship: 1591
ALEXANDER (JUDD S.) FOUNDATION: 1331
Alexander (Paula J.) Memorial Scholarship (Undergraduate): 976
Alfa Fellowship Program: 766
Alfoldi-Rosenbaum (Elizabeth) Fellowship: 315
ALGER REGIONAL COMMUNITY FOUNDATION: 1047
ALISE Research Awards: 660
ALISE/ProQuest Methodology Paper Competition: 661
All for NC: 247
All-In Cincinnati Racial Equity Coalition: 1166
Allaire (Yvan) Medal: 1646
ALLEGAN COUNTY COMMUNITY FOUNDATION: 1048
ALLEGHENY FOUNDATION: 9
Allen (Frances C.) Fellowship: 954
ALLENDE (THE ISABEL) FOUNDATION
    Esperanza Grants: 967
Allergan Foundation Research Grant: 2259
Allergic Respiratory Diseases Research Award: 2135
Allhands (James L.) Essay Competition: 2376
ALLIANCE FOR YOUNG ARTISTS & WRITERS (THE)
    Scholastic Art and Writing Awards (The): 386
Alliant Health Solutions/NMF Alzheimer's or Related Dementia Care
    Scholarship: 2062

Allied Health Kidney Doctoral Fellowship: 2175
Allied Health Kidney Research Grant: 2173
Allied Health Kidney Scholarship: 2175
Allport (Gordon) Intergroup Relations Prize: 1680
ALLSTATE FOUNDATION (THE): 1332
ALS ASSOCIATION (THE)
    Research Grant Program: 2202
ALSC/Bound-to-Stay-Bound Books Scholarship: 1443
ALSC/Frederic G. Melcher Scholarship: 1443
Altenhofen (Robert E.) Memorial Scholarship: 1821
ALTERNATIVES RESEARCH AND DEVELOPMENT FOUNDATION
    Annual Open Grant Program: 1617
    Cave (William and Eleanor) Award: 1617
ALTMAN FOUNDATION: 1049
ALZHEIMER'S ASSOCIATION
    Alzheimer's Association Clinician Scientist Fellowship (AACSF): 2203
    Alzheimer's Association Clinician Scientist Fellowship to Promote
    Diversity (AACSF-D): 2203
    Alzheimer's Association Research Fellowship (AARF): 2203
    Alzheimer's Association Research Fellowship to Promote Diversity
    (AARF-D): 2203
    Alzheimer's Association Research Grant (AARG): 2203
    Alzheimer's Association Research Grant to Promote Diversity
    (AARG-D): 2203
    Zenith Fellows Award (ZNTH): 2203
Alzheimer's Association Clinician Scientist Fellowship (AACSF): 2203
Alzheimer's Association Clinician Scientist Fellowship to Promote
    Diversity (AACSF-D): 2203
Alzheimer's Association Research Fellowship (AARF): 2203
Alzheimer's Association Research Fellowship to Promote Diversity
    (AARF-D): 2203
Alzheimer's Association Research Grant (AARG): 2203
Alzheimer's Association Research Grant to Promote Diversity (AARG-D):
    2203
Alzheimer's Disease Research: 2207
ALZHEIMER'S DRUG DISCOVERY FOUNDATION
    ADDF/NIH: 1995
    Biomarkers Development: 1995
    Drug Development: 1995
    Prevention Beyond the Pipeline: 1995
    Program to Accelerate Clinical Trials (PACT): 1995
AMARILLO AREA FOUNDATION: 1050
AMBUCS Scholars-Scholarships for Therapists: 2301
AMCOR CARES FOUNDATION
    Community Enrichment Grant Program: 10
    Community Support Grant Program: 10
    Nonprofit/Educational Gift Matching Program: 10
    United Way Program: 10
AMERICA-ISRAEL CULTURAL FOUNDATION: 869
AMERICAN ACADEMY IN BERLIN (THE)
    Berlin Prize Fellowship: 795
AMERICAN ACADEMY IN ROME
    Rome Prize Fellowship in Landscape Architecture (The): 1956
    Rome Prize Fellowships: 303
AMERICAN ACADEMY OF ALLERGY ASTHMA & IMMUNOLOGY
    Domestic Fellow-In-Training Travel Scholarship: 2094
AMERICAN ACADEMY OF ARTS AND LETTERS
    Rodgers (The Richard) Awards: 687
AMERICAN ACADEMY OF CHILD AND ADOLESCENT
    PSYCHIATRY
    Benoit (Marilyn B.), M.D., Child Maltreatment Mentorship Award:
    2309
    Educational Outreach Program: 2308
    Joshi (Paramjit Toor), M.D., International Scholar Awards: 2308
    Junior Investigator Award: 2308
    Life Members Mentorship Grant for Medical Students: 2308
    Pilot Awards: 2308
    Psychodynamic Faculty Training and Mentorship Initiative: 2309
    Spurlock (Jeanne) Minority Medical Student Research Fellowship in
    Substance Abuse and Addiction: 2307
    Summer Medical Student Fellowship: 2307
    Ülgür (Ülkü), M.D., International Scholar Award: 2308
AMERICAN ACADEMY OF IMPLANT DENTISTRY (AAID)
    FOUNDATION
    Humanitarian Project Support: 2096
    Research Award: 2096
    Student Research Grant: 2096
    Wish a Smile: 2096
AMERICAN ACADEMY OF OPTOMETRY FOUNDATION
    Allergan Foundation Research Grant: 2259
    Award of Excellence in Contact Lens Patient Care Grant: 2259

Barr (Joe and Janet) Early Career Cornea and Contact Lens Research
    Award: 2256
    Beta Sigma Kappa (BSK) Student Travel Fellowship: 2258
    Beta Sigma Kappa Research Fellowships: 2260
    Corwin (Bert C. and Lydia M.) Contact Lens Residency Award: 2257
    Cummings (J. Pat) Scholarships: 2255
    Eger (Elmer H.) Memorial Student Travel Fellowship: 2258
    Ezell (William C.) Fellowship: 2260
    Ghormley (N. Rex) Student Travel Fellowship: 2258
    Goss (David and Diane) Optometry History Fellowship: 2260
    Hopkins (Douglas W.) Primary Care Residency Award: 2257
    Kirschen Family Student Travel Fellowship: 2258
    Korb-Exford Dry Eye Career Development Grant: 2259
    Neumueller (Julius F.) Award in Optics: 2254
    Rosemore (Fredric) Low Vision Educational Grants: 2259
    Rosenbloom (Alfred A.), Jr. Low Vision Residency Award: 2257
    VSP and AAOF Canadian Practice Excellence Scholarships: 2255
    VSP and AAOF Practice Excellence Scholarships: 2255
    Wechsler (Sheldon) and George Mertz Contact Lens Residency Award:
    2257
AMERICAN ACADEMY OF PEDIATRICS
    American Academy of Pediatrics Hardship Scholarship Program: 2281
American Academy of Pediatrics Hardship Scholarship Program: 2281
AMERICAN ACADEMY OF RELIGION
    Collaborative Research Grants: 734
    Individual Research Grants: 734
    International Dissertation Research Grant: 734
    Regional Development Grants: 735
AMERICAN ACCORDION MUSICOLOGICAL SOCIETY
    Annual Symposium and Festival: 688
AMERICAN ALPINE CLUB
    Catalyst: Adventure Grants for Change: 1957
    Climbing Grief Grants: 1957
    Cornerstone Conservation Grant: 1957
    Cutting Edge Grant: 1957
    Jones Backcountry Adventure Grant: 1957
    Live Your Dream Grant: 1957
    Martin (Zack) Breaking Barriers Grant: 1957
    McNeill-Nott Award: 1957
    Mountaineering Fellowship Fund Grant: 1957
    Research Grants: 1957
    TINCUP Partner in Adventure: 1957
AMERICAN ANTIQUARIAN SOCIETY (AAS)
    AAS American Society for Eighteenth Century Studies Fellowship: 304
    AAS Fellowship for Creative and Performing Artists and Writers: 305
    AAS National Endowment for the Humanities Fellowships: 304
    American Historical Print Collectors Fellowship: 304
    Botein (Stephen) Fellowships: 304
    Drawn to Art Fellowship (The): 304
    Jaffee (David) Fellowship: 304
    Keller (Kate Van Winkle) Fellowship: 304
    Lapides (Linda F. and Julian L.) Fellowship: 304
    Last (Jay and Deborah) Fellowship: 304
    Legacy Fellowship (The): 304
    Morgan (Alstott) Fellowship: 304
    Packer (Barbara) Fellowship: 304
    Peterson (Kate B. and Hall J.) Fellowships: 304
    Reese Fellowship (The): 304
    Schiller (Justin G.) Fellowship: 304
    Tracy (Joyce A.) Fellowship: 304
American Art Program: 185
AMERICAN ASSOCIATION FOR CANCER RESEARCH
    AACR Independent Investigator Grants: 2177
    AACR NextGen Grants for Transformative Cancer Research: 2177
    AACR Team Science Grants: 2177
    Career Development Awards: 2177
    Research Grants and Fellowships: 2177
    Scholar-in-Training Awards: 2177
AMERICAN ASSOCIATION FOR DENTAL RESEARCH
    AADR Hatton Competition: 2097
    Clark (William B.) Fellowship in Clinical Research: 2099
    Gies (William J.) Award: 2100
    Student Research Fellowships: 2098
American Association for Geodetic Surveying (AAGS) Graduate
    Fellowship Award: 2400
AMERICAN ASSOCIATION FOR HAND SURGERY: 1996
AMERICAN ASSOCIATION FOR THE ADVANCEMENT OF
    SCIENCE
    AAAS Kavli Science Journalism Awards: 1723

AMERICAN ASSOCIATION FOR THE HISTORY OF NURSING, INC.
  Competitive Student Research H-31 Predoctoral Grant: 2234
  H-15 Grant for Faculty Members or Independent Researchers: 2234
AMERICAN ASSOCIATION OF COLLEGES OF PHARMACY
  New Investigator Award: 2287
AMERICAN ASSOCIATION OF FAMILY AND CONSUMER
  SCIENCES (AAFCS)
  National Fellowship: 870
  National Teacher of the Year Award: 2411
AMERICAN ASSOCIATION OF GEOGRAPHERS (THE)
  AAG Dissertation Research Grants: 1863
  AAG Globe Book Award for Public Understanding of Geography: 1864
  AAG Meridian Book Award for the Outstanding Scholarly Work in
    Geography: 1864
  AAG Research Grant: 1862
AMERICAN ASSOCIATION OF LAW LIBRARIES
  Library Degree for Law School Graduates: 656
  Library Degree for Non-Law School Graduates: 656
  Library School Graduates Attending Law School: 656
  Library School Graduates Seeking a Non-Law Degree: 656
  Strait (George A.) Minority Stipend Scholarship Endowment: 657
AMERICAN ASSOCIATION OF PETROLEUM GEOLOGISTS
  FOUNDATION
  AAPG Foundation Grants-in-Aid: 1865
AMERICAN ASSOCIATION OF SCHOOL LIBRARIANS
  AASL Collaborative School Library Award: 658
  AASL Frances Henne Award: 658
  AASL Innovative Reading Grant: 658
  AASL National School Library of the Year Award: 658
  ABC-CLIO Leadership Grant: 658
AMERICAN ASSOCIATION OF UNIVERSITY WOMEN
  AAUW Career Development Grants: 971
  AAUW International Fellowships: 871
  AAUW Selected Professions Fellowships: 968
  American Fellowships: 970
  Research Publication Grants in Engineering, Medicine and Science: 969
AMERICAN ASSOCIATION OF WOMEN DENTISTS
  Bushee (Eleanor) Award: 2101
  Taylor (Lucy Hobbs) Award: 2101
AMERICAN ASSOCIATION OF ZOO KEEPERS
  Bowling for Rhinos Conservation Resource Grant (BFR CRG): 1931
  Conservation, Preservation and Restoration (CPR) Grant: 1931
  Latin American Professional AAZK Travel Grant: 1931
  Professional Development Grants: 1931
  Research Grant: 1931
  Trees for You and Me (TFYM) Reforestation Grant: 1931
AMERICAN ASTRONOMICAL SOCIETY
  Chrétien International Research Grant: 1831
  Pierce (Newton Lacy) Prize in Astronomy: 1832
AMERICAN BANDMASTERS ASSOCIATION (THE)
  Sousa/ABA/Ostwald Award: 689
AMERICAN BAR FOUNDATION
  ABF/ALI Doctoral Fellowship Program in Legal & Higher Education:
    1768
  Summer Undergraduate Research Fellowships: 883
AMERICAN BRAIN TUMOR ASSOCIATION
  ABTA Research Collaboration Grant: 2204
  Basic Research Fellowship Awards: 2204
  Discovery Grants: 2204
  Medical Student Summer Fellowships: 2204
AMERICAN BURN ASSOCIATION
  Jordan (Cheryl) Scholarship Fund: 2293
AMERICAN CANCER SOCIETY, INC.
  Institutional Research Grants: 2179
  Postdoctoral Fellowship: 2178
AMERICAN CATHOLIC HISTORICAL ASSOCIATION
  Ellis (John Tracy) Dissertation Award: 738
  Guilday (The Peter) Prize: 736
  Marraro (The Howard R.) Prize: 525
  Presidential Graduate Travel Grant: 738
  Shea (The John Gilmary) Prize: 737
  Summer Research and Writing Grant: 738
AMERICAN CENTER OF RESEARCH (THE)
  ACOR-CAORC Fellowship: 796
  ACOR-CAORC Postdoctoral Fellowships: 796
  Bikai (Pierre and Patricia) Fellowship: 796
  de Vries (Bert and Sally) Fellowship: 796
  Geraty (Lawrence T.) Travel Scholarship: 796
  Groot (Jennifer C.) Fellowships in the Archaeology of Jordan: 796
  Harrell Family Fellowship: 796
  MacDonald/Sampson Fellowship: 796

National Endowment for the Humanities (NEH) Fellowship: 796
  Russell (Kenneth W.) Fellowship: 796
  Sauer (James A.) Fellowship: 796
AMERICAN CERAMIC SOCIETY (THE)
  Graduate Student Poster Contest: 387
  Student Speaking Contest: 387
  Undergraduate Student Poster Contest: 387
AMERICAN CHEMICAL SOCIETY
  ACS Scholars Program: 1848
  Murphree (E.V.) Award in Industrial and Engineering Chemistry: 1850
  Nakanishi Prize: 1849
  Petroleum Research Fund (The): 1819
  Sigal (Irving S.) Postdoctoral Fellowship: 1847
AMERICAN CHESTNUT FOUNDATION (THE): 1902
AMERICAN CLASSICAL LEAGUE (THE): 598
AMERICAN COLLEGE OF CARDIOLOGY
  ACC Young Investigators Awards Competition: 2122
AMERICAN COLLEGE OF LEGAL MEDICINE
  American College of Legal Medicine's Student Writing Competition in
    Law, Medicine and Bioethics: 1997
American College of Legal Medicine's Student Writing Competition in
  Law, Medicine and Bioethics: 1997
AMERICAN COUNCIL FOR POLISH CULTURE (ACPC)
  ACPC Scholarship, Summer Studies in Poland: 1473
  Polish Studies Scholarship: 1473
  Pulaski Scholarships for Advanced Studies: 1473
  Zachariasiewicz (Wladyslaw) Memorial Journalism Scholarship: 1473
AMERICAN COUNCIL OF LEARNED SOCIETIES
  ACLS Fellowship: 306
AMERICAN COUNCIL OF THE BLIND
  American Council of the Blind Scholarships: 1474
American Council of the Blind Scholarships: 1474
American Council of Young Political Leaders: 100
AMERICAN DANCE FESTIVAL
  Tuition Scholarships: 481
AMERICAN DENTAL ASSISTANTS ASSOCIATION
  Southard (Juliette A.) Scholarship Program: 2102
AMERICAN DENTAL HYGIENISTS' ASSOCIATION INSTITUTE FOR
  ORAL HEALTH
  ADHA Institute for Oral Health Dental Hygiene Scholarships: 2103
AMERICAN DIABETES ASSOCIATION
  Innovative Basic Science Award (IBS): 2148
  Innovative Clinical or Translational Science Award (ICTS): 2148
  Junior Faculty Development Award (JFD): 2148
  Minority Junior Faculty Development Award (JDFM): 2148
  Minority Postdoctoral Fellowship: 2148
  Minority Undergraduate Internship (MUI): 2148
  Postdoctoral Fellowship (PDF): 2148
AMERICAN EPILEPSY SOCIETY (AES)
  Junior Investigator Awards: 2205
  Postdoctoral Research Fellowship: 2205
  Predoctoral Research Fellowship: 2205
  Research and Training Workshops: 2205
  Seed Grants: 2205
  Spencer (Susan S.) Clinical Research Training Fellowship in Epilepsy:
    2205
AMERICAN FARM BUREAU FOUNDATION FOR AGRICULTURE
  White-Reinhardt Fund for Education: 1903
AMERICAN FEDERATION FOR AGING RESEARCH (AFAR)
  Beeson (Paul) Career Development Awards in Aging Research Program:
    1999
  Glenn Foundation for Medical Research and AFAR Grants for Junior
    Faculty: 1999
  Glenn Foundation for Medical Research Breakthroughs in Gerontology
    (BIG) Awards: 1999
  Glenn Foundation for Medical Research Postdoctoral Fellowships in
    Aging Research: 1998
  Kalman (Diana Jacobs)/AFAR Scholarships for Research in the Biology
    of Aging: 1999
  Medical Student Training in Aging Research Program (MSTAR): 1999
American Fellowships: 970
AMERICAN FIDELITY FOUNDATION: 388
AMERICAN FLORAL ENDOWMENT: 1904
AMERICAN FOUNDATION FOR PHARMACEUTICAL EDUCATION
  (AFPE)
  AFPE Predoctoral Fellowships in the Pharmaceutical Sciences: 1441
  Kappa Epsilon-AFPE-Nellie Wakeman First Year Graduate Fellowship:
    2289
  Phi Lambda Sigma-AFPE First Year Graduate Fellowship: 2288
  Rho Chi-AFPE First Year Graduate Fellowship: 2288

AMERICAN FOUNDATION FOR SUICIDE PREVENTION (THE)
Distinguished Investigator Innovation Grants: 1366
Pilot Innovation Grant: 1364
Postdoctoral Research Fellowship Innovation Grants: 1365
Standard Research Innovation Grants: 1367
Young Investigator Innovation Grants: 1367
AMERICAN FRIENDS OF THE ALEXANDER VON HUMBOLDT
FOUNDATION
German Chancellor Fellowship: 797
Humboldt Research Award Programme: 1475
Humboldt Research Fellowship for Experienced Researchers: 798
Humboldt Research Fellowship for Postdoctoral Researchers: 1442
AMERICAN GASTROENTEROLOGICAL ASSOCIATION (AGA)
AGA-Bern Schwartz Family Fund Research Scholar Award in
Pancreatic Cancer: 2160
AGA-Caroline Craig Augustyn and Damian Augustyn Award in
Digestive Cancer: 2154
AGA Fellow Abstract Award: 2153
AGA-Gastric Cancer Foundation Ben Feinstein Memorial Research
Scholar Award in Gastric Cancer: 2155
AGA-Medtronic Pilot Research Award in Technology Innovation: 2158
AGA-Moti L. and Kamla Rustgi International Travel Awards: 2152
AGA-Pfizer Pilot Research Award in Inflammatory Bowel Disease:
2159
AGA-R. Robert and Sally D. Funderburg Research Award in Gastric
Cancer: 2149
AGA Research Scholar Award: 2156
AGA Student Abstract Award: 2151
AGA-Takeda Pharmaceuticals Research Scholar Award in Inflammatory
Bowel Disease: 2150
AGA-Takeda Pharmaceuticals Research Scholar Awards in Celiac
Disease: 2157
Pilot Research Award in Health Disparities: 2161
AMERICAN GEOSCIENCES INSTITUTE (AGI) (THE)
Wallace (Harriet Evelyn) Scholarship: 1866
AMERICAN GERIATRICS SOCIETY
Clinical Student Research Award: 2294
Clinician of the Year Award: 2294
Health in Aging Foundation New Investigator Awards: 2294
Henderson (Edward) Student Award: 2294
Jahnigen (Dennis W.) Memorial Award: 2294
Nascher/Manning Award: 2294
Outstanding Junior Clinician Education Manuscript: 2294
Outstanding Junior Clinician Educator of the Year: 2294
Outstanding Junior Investigator of the Year: 2294
Outstanding Junior Research Manuscript: 2294
Outstanding Mid-Career Clinician Educator of the Year: 2294
Scientist-in-Training Research Award: 2294
Yoshikawa (Thomas and Catherine) Award for Outstanding Scientific
Achievement in Clinical Investigation: 2294
AMERICAN GROUND WATER TRUST
Baroid Scholarship: 2344
Flexcon Industries Scholarship: 2344
Stetson (Thomas M.) Scholarship: 2344
AMERICAN HEART ASSOCIATION
AHA Institutional Research Enhancement Award (AIREA): 2124
Career Development Award: 2127
Collaborative Sciences Award: 2126
Established Investigator Award: 2132
Innovative Project Award: 2131
Institutional Award for Undergraduate Student Training: 2123
Merit Award: 2125
Postdoctoral Fellowship: 2128
Predoctoral Fellowship: 2129
Transformational Project Award: 2130
AMERICAN HELLENIC EDUCATIONAL PROGRESSIVE
ASSOCIATION (THE): 884
AMERICAN HISTORICAL ASSOCIATION (THE)
Adams (The Herbert Baxter) Prize: 526
Beer (The George Louis) Prize: 526
Bentley (The Jerry) Prize: 526
Beveridge (The Albert J.) Award: 526
Beveridge (The Albert J.) Grant: 526
Breasted (The James Henry) Prize: 526
Dunning (The John H.) Prize in United States History: 526
Fairbank (The John K.) Prize in East Asian History: 526
Feis (The Herbert) Award: 526
Fellowship in Aerospace History: 528
Forkosch (The Morris D.) Prize: 526
Gershoy (The Leo) Award: 526
Haring (The Clarence H.) Prize: 526

Jameson (J. Franklin) Award: 526
Jameson (The J. Franklin) Fellowship: 527
Katz (The Friedrich) Prize: 526
Kelly (The Joan) Memorial Prize in Women's History: 526
Klein (Martin A.) Prize in African History: 526
Kraus (Michael) Research Grant: 526
Leland (The Waldo G.) Prize: 526
Littleton-Griswold Grant: 526
Littleton-Griswold Prize in American Law and Society (The): 526
Major (The J. Russell) Prize: 526
Marraro (The Helen and Howard R.) Prize in Italian History: 526
Mosse (The George L.) Prize: 526
O'Connor (The John E.) Film Award: 526
Rawley (The James A.) Prize in Atlantic History: 526
Richards (John F.) Prize in South Asian History: 526
Rosenberg (The Dorothy) Prize: 526
Schmitt (Bernadotte E.) Grant: 526
Wesley-Logan Prize (The): 526
American Historical Print Collectors Fellowship: 304
AMERICAN HONDA FOUNDATION: 1368
AMERICAN INDIAN COLLEGE FUND
Full Circle Scholarship Program: 940
TCU Scholarship Program: 940
American Indian Endowed Scholarship Program: 961
AMERICAN INDIAN GRADUATE CENTER
Fellowships for American Indians or Alaskan Natives: 941
American Indian Scholarship: 1538
AMERICAN INDIAN SCIENCE AND ENGINEERING SOCIETY
(AISES): 942
AMERICAN INSTITUTE FOR CANCER RESEARCH
Investigator Initiated Grants (IIG): 2180
AMERICAN INSTITUTE FOR SRI LANKAN STUDIES (AISLS)
AISLS Dissertation Planning Grant: 800
AISLS Fellowship Program: 799
AMERICAN INSTITUTE OF AERONAUTICS AND ASTRONAUTICS
American Institute of Aeronautics and Astronautics Undergraduate
Scholarship and Graduate Awards Program: 2364
American Institute of Aeronautics and Astronautics Undergraduate
Scholarship and Graduate Awards Program: 2364
AMERICAN INSTITUTE OF ARCHITECTS (THE)
AIA Arthur N. Tuttle, Jr. Graduate Fellowship in Health Facility
Planning and Design: 366
AMERICAN INSTITUTE OF BANGLADESH STUDIES
Junior Fellowship: 801
Pre-Dissertation Fellowships: 801
Seminar and Conference Support: 801
Senior Fellowship: 801
AMERICAN INSTITUTE OF CERTIFIED PUBLIC ACCOUNTANTS
(AICPA)
AICPA Foundation Scholarship for Future CPAs: 1695
AICPA Foundation Two-Year Transfer Scholarship: 1698
AICPA Scholarship for Minority Accounting Students: 1369
AICPA/Robert Half Student Scholarships: 1697
AWSCPA Scholarship Award: 1696
Carey (John L.) Scholarship: 1699
AMERICAN INSTITUTE OF CHEMICAL ENGINEERS (AICHE)
Food, Pharmaceutical and Bioengineering Division Award in Chemical
Engineering: 1618
Minority Scholarship Awards for College Students: 2377
AMERICAN INSTITUTE OF INDIAN STUDIES
Advanced Language Program in India: 599
AIIS Fellowships: 802
AMERICAN INSTITUTE OF PAKISTAN STUDIES
AIPS Post Doctoral Fellowship: 755
AIPS Pre-Doctoral Fellowship: 755
Community College Faculty Exchange: 755
Lecture Series: 755
Workshop Series: 755
AMERICAN INSTITUTE OF PHYSICS
American Institute of Physics Science Communication Awards: 1888
American Institute of Physics Science Communication Awards: 1888
AMERICAN INSTITUTE OF THE HISTORY OF PHARMACY
AIHP Ph.D. Research Support Grant Program: 2290
American Jewish Archives Fellowship Program (The): 747
AMERICAN JEWISH JOINT DISTRIBUTION COMMITTEE (THE)
Goldman (The Ralph I.) Fellowship: 803
AMERICAN KIDNEY FUND
Clinical Scientist in Nephrology (CSN): 2000
Patient Services Grants: Safety Net Grant Program: 2001
AMERICAN KINESIOTHERAPY ASSOCIATION, INC.
AKTA Lou Montalvano Memorial Scholarship: 2295

American Legion Auxiliary Badger Girls State Scholarships: 1476
AMERICAN LEGION AUXILIARY - DEPARTMENT OF WISCONSIN
    American Legion Auxiliary Badger Girls State Scholarships: 1476
    American Legion Auxiliary National Scholarships: 1476
    Child Welfare Scholarship: 1476
    Health Careers Scholarships: 1476
    Knox (Eileen) Memorial Scholarship: 1476
    Lewis (H.S. and Angeline) Scholarships: 1476
    Merit and Memorial Scholarships: 1476
    State President's Scholarships: 1476
    Van Deuren (Della) Scholarships: 1476
    Van Deuren Memorial Scholarship: 1476
American Legion Auxiliary National Scholarships: 1476
AMERICAN LIBRARY ASSOCIATION (ALA)
    ALA Awards: 659
    ALA Spectrum Scholarship: 1443
    ALA/Century Scholarship: 1443
    ALSC/Bound-to-Stay-Bound Books Scholarship: 1443
    ALSC/Frederic G. Melcher Scholarship: 1443
    Clift (David H.) Scholarship: 1443
    Drewes (Tom and Roberta) Scholarship: 1443
    Gaver (Mary V.) Scholarship: 1443
    Hornback (Miriam L.) Scholarship: 1443
    Hoy (Christopher J.)/ERT Scholarship: 1443
    Leisner (Tony B.) Scholarship: 1443
    LITA/Christian Larew Memorial Scholarship: 1443
    Lyman (Peter) Memorial/SAGE Scholarships: 1443
    Rozkuszka (W. David) Scholarship: 1443
AMERICAN LUNG ASSOCIATION
    Allergic Respiratory Diseases Research Award: 2135
    Catalyst Award: 2136
    Dalsemer Research Grant: 2134
    Innovation Award: 2137
    Lung Cancer Discovery Awards: 2133
    Public Policy Research Award: 2138
AMERICAN MATHEMATICAL SOCIETY
    American Mathematical Society Centennial Fellowship: 1883
American Mathematical Society Centennial Fellowship: 1883
AMERICAN MATTHAY ASSOCIATION FOR PIANO
    Wells (Clara) Fellowships: 690
AMERICAN MEDICAL ASSOCIATION FOUNDATION
    Excellence in Medicine Awards: 1477
    Giambalvo (Joan F.) Memorial Fund: 1477
    Leadership Development Institute: 1477
    LGBTQ+ Fellowship: 1477
    Physicians of Tomorrow Scholarship: 1477
AMERICAN MEDICAL WOMEN'S ASSOCIATION, INC.
    American Women's Hospitals Service (AWHS): 2002
AMERICAN METEOROLOGICAL SOCIETY
    AMS Freshman Undergraduate Scholarship Program: 2365
    AMS Graduate Fellowship in the History of Science: 2365
    AMS Graduate Fellowships: 2365
    AMS Minority Scholarship: 2365
    AMS Senior Named Scholarships: 2365
    AMS Women in Science Scholarship: 2365
    Macelwane (The Father James B.) Annual Awards in Meteorology:
        2365
AMERICAN MUSEUM OF NATURAL HISTORY (THE)
    Collection Study Grants: 1619
    Graduate Student Fellowship Program: 1932
    Lerner-Gray Grants for Marine Research: 1619
    Postdoctoral Research Fellowship Program: 1620
    Roosevelt (Theodore) Memorial Grants: 1619
AMERICAN MUSICOLOGICAL SOCIETY
    AMS Teaching Award: 691
    Brett (The Philip) Award: 691
    Brown (Howard Mayer) Fellowship: 692
    Cohen (The H. Robert)/RIPM Award: 691
    Early Music Award: 691
    Einstein (The Alfred) Award: 691
    Greenberg (Noah) Award: 691
    Hampson (Thomas) Award: 691
    Holmes/D'Accone Dissertation Fellowship in Opera Studies: 692
    Jackson (The Roland) Award: 691
    Johnson (Alvin H.) AMS 50 Dissertation Fellowships: 692
    Kinkeldey (The Otto) Award: 691
    Lockwood (Lewis) Award: 691
    Music in American Culture Award: 691
    Palisca (Claude V.) Award: 691
    Pisk (Paul A.) Prize: 691
    Slim (H. Colin) Award: 691

    Solie (Ruth A.) Award: 691
    Stevenson (Robert M.) Award: 691
    Tsou (Judy) Critical Race Studies Award: 691
AMERICAN NUCLEAR SOCIETY (ANS)
    ANS Graduate Scholarships: 2382
    ANS Undergraduate Scholarships: 2381
    Blizard (Everitt P.) Memorial Scholarship: 2382
    Dannels (Robert A.) Memorial Scholarship: 2382
    Decommissioning and Environmental Sciences (DESD) Undergraduate
        Scholarship: 2379
    Delayed Education for Women Scholarship: 2378
    Dietrich (Joseph R.) Memorial Scholarship: 2381
    DiSalvo (Raymond) Memorial Scholarship: 2380
    Henry (Allan F.)/Paul A. Greebler Memorial Scholarship: 2381
    Lamarsh (John R.) Memorial Scholarship: 2381
    Landis (John and Muriel) Scholarships: 2378
    Liner (Robert T.) Memorial Scholarship: 2380
    Operations and Power Division Scholarship: 2380
    Pittsburgh Local Section Scholarship: 2383
    Schumar (James F.) Scholarship: 2382
    Thomas (Charles Tommy) Memorial Scholarship: 2380
    Vogt (James R.) Radiochemistry Scholarship: 1851
AMERICAN NUMISMATIC SOCIETY (THE)
    Newman (The Eric P.) Graduate Summer Seminar: 307
AMERICAN NURSES FOUNDATION
    Nursing Research Grants: 2235
AMERICAN OIL CHEMISTS SOCIETY (AOCS)
    Bailey (Alton E.) Award: 1852
    Chang (Stephen S.) Award: 1852
    Corporate Achievement Award: 1852
    Schroepfer Medal: 1852
    Supelco AOCS Research Award: 1852
    Young Scientist Research Award: 1852
AMERICAN ORCHID SOCIETY
    American Orchid Society Grants for Orchid Research: 1933
American Orchid Society Grants for Orchid Research: 1933
AMERICAN ORIENTAL SOCIETY
    Hackney (Louise Wallace) Fellowship: 496
AMERICAN ORTHOPAEDIC SOCIETY FOR SPORTS MEDICINE
    (AOSSM) (THE)
    AOSSM Sandy Kirkley Clinical Outcome Research Grant: 2297
    Arnoczky (Steven P.) Young Investigator Grant: 2296
AMERICAN OSTEOPATHIC FOUNDATION: 2276
AMERICAN OTOLOGICAL SOCIETY RESEARCH FOUNDATION
    Clinical Investigations Grant: 2261
    Clinician-Scientist Award: 2261
    Fellowship Grant: 2261
    Research Grant: 2261
American Overseas Research Centers (AORC) Program: 787
AMERICAN PARKINSON DISEASE ASSOCIATION, INC.
    Post-Doctoral Research Fellowships: 2206
AMERICAN PHILOSOPHICAL SOCIETY
    Franklin Research Grants: 11
    Lewis and Clark Fund for Exploration and Field Research (The): 12
    Library Resident Research Fellowships (The): 308
    Phillips Fund for Native American Research: 943
AMERICAN PLANNING ASSOCIATION
    Abrams (Charles) Scholarship Program: 1051
    APA Foundation Scholarship: 885
AMERICAN POLITICAL SCIENCE ASSOCIATION
    APSA Minority Fellows Program: 1783
    Congressional Fellowship Program: 1782
    Small Research Grant Program: 1784
AMERICAN PORPHYRIA FOUNDATION (THE): 2003
AMERICAN PSYCHIATRIC ASSOCIATION
    APA Child & Adolescent Psychiatry Fellowship: 2311
    APA Public Psychiatry Fellowship: 2311
    APA SAMHSA Minority Fellowships: 2311
    APA/APAF Leadership Fellowship: 2311
    Kempf Fund Award for Research Development in Psychobiological
        Psychiatry: 2310
    Psychiatric Research Fellowship: 2312
    Spurlock (Jeanne), M.D. Congressional Fellowship: 2312
AMERICAN PSYCHOLOGICAL ASSOCIATION
    APA Congressional Fellowship Program: 2314
    MFP Mental Health and Substance Abuse Services Fellowship: 2315
    MFP Services for Transition Age Youth: 2313
AMERICAN PSYCHOSOMATIC SOCIETY
    Barchas (Patricia R.) Award in Sociophysiology: 2316
    Distinguished Scientist Award: 2317

MacLean (Paul D.) Award: 2318
Weiner (Herbert) Early Career Award for Contributions to
Psychosomatic Society: 2319
AMERICAN PUBLIC POWER ASSOCIATION
   DEED Interships: 2384
   Educational Scholarship: 2384
   Student Research Grant: 2384
   Technical Design Project: 2384
AMERICAN RESEARCH CENTER IN EGYPT, INC.
   Fellowships for Research in Egypt: 804
AMERICAN RESEARCH INSTITUTE IN TURKEY, INC.
   ARIT Fellowship Program: 805
   Bogazici University Summer Language Program for Intensive Advanced
   Turkish Language Study: 806
   NEH Fellowships for Research in Turkey: 807
AMERICAN ROENTGEN RAY SOCIETY
   ARRS Annual Scholarship Program: 2004
AMERICAN-SCANDINAVIAN FOUNDATION (THE)
   American-Scandinavian Foundation Translation Competition: 611
   ASF Awards for Study in Scandinavia: 808
   Visiting Lectureships: 1444
American-Scandinavian Foundation Translation Competition: 611
AMERICAN SCHLAFHORST FOUNDATION: 13
AMERICAN SCHOOL OF CLASSICAL STUDIES AT ATHENS
   Advanced Fellowships: 811
   Bikakis (The Harry) Fellowship: 812
   CAORC Multi-Country Research Fellowships: 389
   Cotsen Traveling Fellowship for Research in Greece: 813
   Frantz (M. Alison) Fellowship in Post-Classical Studies at the
   Gennadius Library: 810
   Hirsch (Jacob) Fellowship: 816
   National Endowment for the Humanities Fellowships: 809
   Regular Member Program Fellowships: 817
   Robinson (Henry S.) Corinth Research Fellowship: 815
   Wiener Laboratory Post-Doctoral Fellowship: 814
   Wiener Laboratory Pre-Doctoral Fellowship: 814
   Wiener Laboratory Programmatic Post-Doctoral Fellowship: 814
   Wiener Laboratory Research Associateships: 814
AMERICAN SCHOOLS OF ORIENTAL RESEARCH (ASOR)
   Dever (William G.) Fellowship for Biblical Scholars: 818
   Foundation for Biblical Archaeology Scholarships: 818
   Harris Grants: 818
   Heritage Fellowships: 818
   MacAllister (P.E.) Fellowships: 818
   Member Supported Fellowships: 818
   Mesopotamian Fellowship: 818
   Meyers (Eric and Carol) Fellowships: 818
   Meyers (Shirlee)/G. Ernest Wright Fellowships: 818
   Platt Fellowships: 818
   Sheeler (Harva L.) Excavation Fellowships: 818
   Strange/Midkiff Families Fellowships: 818
   Student Travel Grants: 818
   Study of Collections Fellowships: 818
American Society for Eighteenth-Century Studies (ASECS) Fellowships:
   572
AMERICAN SOCIETY FOR ENGINEERING EDUCATION
   Naval Research Laboratory (NRL) Postdoctoral Fellowship Program:
   2385
AMERICAN SOCIETY FOR ENOLOGY AND VITICULTURE: 1905
AMERICAN SOCIETY FOR MASS SPECTROMETRY
   ASMS Research Awards in Mass Spectrometry: 1820
AMERICAN SOCIETY FOR MICROBIOLOGY
   Research Capstone Fellowship: 1934
   Undergraduate Research Fellowship: 1934
AMERICAN SOCIETY FOR NONDESTRUCTIVE TESTING, INC.
   (THE)
   ASNT Faculty Grant Award: 1370
   ASNT Fellowship Award: 2345
   Engineering Undergraduate Award: 1478
   Oliver (Robert B.) Scholarship: 1478
AMERICAN SOCIETY FOR THEATRE RESEARCH (ASTR)
   ASTR Collaborative Research Award (The): 482
   ATHE-ASTR Award for Excellence in Digital Scholarship: 482
   Biennial Sally Banes Publication Prize: 482
   Brockett (Oscar G.) Essay Prize: 482
   Cambridge University Press Prize: 482
   Chinoy (Helen Krich) Dissertation Research Fellowships: 482
   Co-sponsored Events Awards: 482
   Cohen (Selma Jeanne) Conference Presentation Award: 482
   Distinguished Scholar Award: 482
   Grants for Researchers with Heavy Teaching Loads: 482

Hewitt (Barnard) Award: 482
Hill (Errol) Award: 482
Kahan (Gerald) Scholar's Prize: 482
Keller (David) Travel Grants: 482
Marshall (Thomas F.) Graduate Student Awards: 482
McNamara (Brooks) Publishing Subvention: 482
Research Fellowships: 482
Targeted Research Areas Grants: 482
AMERICAN SOCIETY OF CIVIL ENGINEERS
   Ammann (O.H.) Research Fellowship in Structural Engineering: 2386
   CI Construction Engineering Scholarship and Student Prizes: 2386
   Cox (Lawrence W. and Francis W.) Scholarship: 2386
   Dames (Trent R.) and William W. Moore Fellowship: 2386
   Figg (Eugene C., Jr.) Civil Engineering Scholarship: 2386
   Freeman Fellowship: 2386
   Leisch (Jack E.) Memorial National Graduate Fellowship: 2386
   Lenard (John) Civil Engineering Scholarship: 2386
   Moorman (Robert B.B. and Josephine N.) Scholarship: 2386
   Smith (J. Waldo) Hydraulic Fellowship: 2386
   Tapman (Samuel Fletcher) ASCE Student Chapter Scholarship: 2386
   Tiney (B. Charles) Memorial ASCE Student Chapter Scholarship: 2386
   Tuttle (Arthur S.) Memorial Fellowship: 2386
   Yang (Y.C.) Civil Engineering Scholarship: 2386
AMERICAN SOCIETY OF HEMATOLOGY
   Abstract Achievement Award: 2109
   Fellow Scholar Award: 2006
   Fellow to Faculty Scholar Award: 2006
   HONORS (Hematology Opportunities for the Next Generation of
   Research Scientists): 2007
   Junior Faculty Scholar Award: 2006
   Outstanding Abstract Achievement Award: 2109
   Physician-Scientist Career Development Award: 2005
   Research Training Award for Fellows: 2005
AMERICAN SOCIETY OF INTERIOR DESIGNERS EDUCATIONAL
   FOUNDATION, INC.
   ASID Foundation Legacy Scholarships for Graduate Students: 367
   ASID Foundation Legacy Scholarships for Undergraduates: 367
   ASID Foundation Transform Grant: 367
   Eno (Irene Winifred) Grant: 367
   Polsky (Joel) Academic Achievement Award: 367
   Polsky (Joel) Prize: 367
AMERICAN SOCIETY OF MECHANICAL ENGINEERS AUXILIARY,
   INC. (THE)
   Baldwin (Allen J.) Scholarship: 2387
   Cartwright (Berna Lou) Scholarship: 2387
   Chenoweth (Carolyn and James M.) Scholarship: 2387
   Clarke (Lucy and Charles W.E.) Scholarship: 2387
   Farny (Sylvia W.) Scholarship: 2387
   Kezios (Agnes Malakate) Scholarship: 2387
   Parsons (Elisabeth M. and Winchell M.) Scholarship: 2387
   Rothermel (Marjorie Roy) Scholarship: 2387
   Scharp (Charles B.) Scholarship: 2387
   Student Loan Fund: 2387
   Zamrik (Myrna R. and Sam Y.) Scholarship: 2387
AMERICAN SOCIETY OF NAVAL ENGINEERS (ASNE)
   ASNE Scholarship Program: 2388
AMERICAN SOCIETY OF NEPHROLOGY
   ASN Research Fellowships: 2112
   Bennett (William and Sandra) Clinical Scholars Program: 2110
   Gottschalk (Carl W.) Research Scholar Grant: 2111
   Merrill (John) Grant in Transplantation: 2111
   OHF - ASN Foundation for Kidney Research Grant: 2110
   Siegel (Norman) Research Scholar Grant: 2111
AMERICAN SOCIETY OF REGIONAL ANESTHESIA AND PAIN
   MEDICINE
   ASRA Carl Koller Memorial Research Grant: 2291
   ASRA Chronic Pain Research Grant: 2291
   ASRA Early-Career Investigator Award: 2008
   ASRA Graduate Student Award: 2008
AMERICAN SOCIETY OF SAFETY PROFESSIONALS
   Safety Professional of the Year Award: 2389
AMERICAN SOCIOLOGICAL ASSOCIATION
   Minority Fellowship Program: 886
AMERICAN SPEECH-LANGUAGE-HEARING FOUNDATION
   Clinical Research Grant: 2262
   DiCarlo (Louis M.) Award for Recent Clinical Achievement: 2262
   Graduate Student Scholarship for International/Minority Students: 2262
   Graduate Student Scholarship for Minority Students: 2262
   Graduate Student Scholarship for NSSLHA Members: 2262
   Graduate Student Scholarship for Students with a Disability: 2262
   Graduate Student Scholarships: 2262

Kleffner (Frank R.) Clinical Career Award: 2262
New Century Scholars Doctoral Scholarship: 2262
New Century Scholars Research Grant: 2262
New Investigators Research Grant: 2262
Speech Science Research Grant: 2262
Student Research Grant in Audiology: 2262
Student Research Grant in Early Childhood Language Development: 2262
Van Hattum (Rolland J.) Award for Contribution in the Schools: 2262
AMERICAN SWEDISH INSTITUTE (THE)
    Lorénzen (Lilly) Scholarship: 819
AMERICAN TINNITUS ASSOCIATION (ATA)
    ATA Student Research Grant Program: 1621
    ATA Tinnitus Research Grant Program: 1621
AMERICAN VACUUM SOCIETY (AVS)
    Graduate Research Awards: 1889
    Varian (Russell and Sigurd) Award: 1889
    Whetten (Nellie Yeoh) Award: 1889
AMERICAN VETERINARY MEDICAL ASSOCIATION
    AVMA Fellowship: 2009
AMERICAN WATER RESOURCES ASSOCIATION
    Herbert (Richard A.) Memorial Scholarship: 1958
American Women's Hospitals Service (AWHS): 2002
Americans Overseas Summer, Semester and Year Programs: 868
AMERICORPS
    Foster Grandparent Program: 1333
    Retired and Senior Volunteer Program (RSVP): 1333
    Senior Companion Program: 1333
AmeriCorps VISTA: 1135
AMES (THE KATHRYN) FOUNDATION: 756
AMGEN FOUNDATION, INC.: 14
Ammann (O.H.) Research Fellowship in Structural Engineering: 2386
AMPCO-PITTSBURGH CHARITABLE FOUNDATION: 1052
Amplifying Voices: 720
AMS Freshman Undergraduate Scholarship Program: 2365
AMS Graduate Fellowship in the History of Science: 2365
AMS Graduate Fellowships: 2365
AMS Minority Scholarship: 2365
AMS Senior Named Scholarships: 2365
AMS Teaching Award: 691
AMS Women in Science Scholarship: 2365
AMVETS
    AMVETS National Scholarship Program: Entering College Freshman Scholarship: 1479
    AMVETS National Scholarship Program: JROTC Scholarship: 1479
    AMVETS National Scholarship Program: Entering College Freshman Scholarship: 1479
    AMVETS National Scholarship Program: JROTC Scholarship: 1479
An Extra Wish: 1099
Anarcha, Betsy, and Lucy Memorial Scholarship: 2062
ANDERSEN CORPORATE FOUNDATION (THE): 1053
ANDERSEN (FRED C. AND KATHERINE B.) FOUNDATION: 1054
ANDERSEN (HUGH J.) FOUNDATION: 1055
Andersen (Hugh J.) Memorial Scholarship: 2062
ANDRUS FAMILY FUND
    Foster Care Program: 1056
    Juvenile Justice Program: 1056
ANIMAL ASSISTANCE FOUNDATION: 2010
Animal Protection Program: 1254
Animal Welfare Grants: 1110
Animating Infrastructure Grants: 466
ANN ARBOR AREA COMMUNITY FOUNDATION
    African American Endowment Fund (The): 1057
    Bach (The Anna Botsford) Fund: 1057
    Community Grantmaking: 1057
    Coordinated Funding: 1057
    Cultural Economic Development: 1057
    Youth Council: 1057
    Ypsilanti Area Community Fund (The): 1057
ANNA-MONIKA-FOUNDATION
    Anna-Monika-Foundation Prize (The): 2320
Anna-Monika-Foundation Prize (The): 2320
ANNENBERG FOUNDATION (THE): 15
Annenberg Graduate Fellowship Program: 1608
Annual Central Prize Award: 2249
Annual Competitive Grant Program: 1191
Annual Conference: 2328
Annual Loren L. Zachary National Vocal Competition for Young Opera Singers: 733
Annual Open Grant Program: 1617

Annual Responsive Grants: 1240
Annual Symposium and Festival: 688
ANRF Arthritis Research Grants: 2012
ANS Graduate Scholarships: 2382
ANS Undergraduate Scholarships: 2381
Anson (Abraham) Memorial Scholarship: 1821
AOSSM Sandy Kirkley Clinical Outcome Research Grant: 2297
APA Child & Adolescent Psychiatry Fellowship: 2311
APA Congressional Fellowship Program: 2314
APA Foundation Scholarship: 885
APA Public Psychiatry Fellowship: 2311
APA SAMHSA Minority Fellowships: 2311
APA Young Investigator Awards Program: 2280
APA/APAF Leadership Fellowship: 2311
APLASTIC ANEMIA AND MDS INTERNATIONAL FOUNDATION
    AA&MDSIF Research Grant Program: 2011
Appalachian Scholarship (The): 681
Applegate-Jackson-Parks Future Teacher Scholarship: 1535
Appleton (Bonnie) Memorial Scholarship: 1925
Applied Materials Corporate Philanthropy Program: 16
APPLIED MATERIALS, INC.
    Applied Materials Corporate Philanthropy Program: 16
Applied Social Issues Internship Program (The): 1689
Appraisal Institute Education and Relief Foundation Scholarship: 1700
APPRAISAL INSTITUTE OF PROFESSIONAL RESOURCES
    Appraisal Institute Education and Relief Foundation Scholarship: 1700
Apprenticeships: 438
APS CORPORATE GIVING PROGRAM: 17
APSA Minority Fellows Program: 1783
ARCA FOUNDATION (THE): 18
ARCHAEOLOGICAL INSTITUTE OF AMERICA
    AIA Publication Subvention Program (The): 1480
    Archaeology of Portugal Fellowship (The): 757
    Bartman (Elizabeth) Museum Internship: 309
    Colburn (Anna C. and Oliver C.) Fellowship: 313
    Coleman (John R.) Traveling Fellowship: 310
    James (Olivia) Traveling Fellowship: 310
    Kress (Samuel H.) Grants for Research and Publication in Classical Art and Architecture: 1480
    Pomerance (Harriet and Leon) Fellowship: 311
    Waldbaum (Jane C.) Archaeological Field School Scholarship: 312
    Woodruff (Helen M.) Fellowship of the AIA and the American Academy in Rome: 1445
Archaeology of Portugal Fellowship (The): 757
Archaeology Program: 1813
Archaeometry Program: 1813
ARCHITECTS FOUNDATION (THE)
    Architects Foundation Diversity Advancement Scholarship: 368
Architects Foundation Diversity Advancement Scholarship: 368
ARCHITECTURAL LEAGUE OF NEW YORK
    League Prize for Young Architects and Designers (The): 370
    Norden (Deborah J.) Fund: 369
ARCHSTONE FOUNDATION: 1282
ARCTIC INSTITUTE OF NORTH AMERICA
    AINA Grants-in-Aid: 1446
Arctic Research Program: 1645
ARD INTERNATIONAL MUSIC COMPETITION: 693
ARGONNE NATIONAL LABORATORY
    Graduate Research Program: 1623
    Science Undergraduate Laboratory Internships: 1622
ARIT Fellowship Program: 805
Arizona Center for Civic Leadership: 111
ARIZONA COMMISSION ON THE ARTS: 390
ARIZONA COMMUNITY FOUNDATION
    Communities for All Ages: 1058
ARIZONA STATE UNIVERSITY
    ASU Leadership Scholarship Program: 1371
Arkans (Rick) Eagle Scout Scholarship: 1537
ARKANSAS COMMUNITY FOUNDATION: 1059
ARMENIAN GENERAL BENEVOLENT UNION
    Heritage Scholar Grant: 1481
    International Scholarship: 1481
    Performing Arts Scholarship: 1481
    Religious Studies Scholarship: 1481
    U.S. Graduate Scholarship: 1481
ARMENIAN RELIEF SOCIETY OF EASTERN U.S.A., INC.
    A.R.S. Lazarian Graduate Scholarship: 887
    A.R.S. Undergraduate Scholarship: 887
ARN/RNF Grant: 2244
Arnoczky (Steven P.) Young Investigator Grant: 2296
ARRAS FOUNDATION: 19

ARRS Annual Scholarship Program: 2004
Art Administration Interns: 498
Art and Change Grant: 980
Art and Cultural Facilities: 384
Art Awards: 453
Art Bank Program: 403
Art History Fellowships in Florence: 508
Art-in-Education Artists' Book Residency Grant: 476
Art in State Buildings Program: 466
Art Meets Activism: 979
ARTHRITIS FOUNDATION: 2200
Arthritis Grants: 293
ARTHRITIS NATIONAL RESEARCH FOUNDATION (ANRF)
    ANRF Arthritis Research Grants: 2012
ARTHRITIS SOCIETY (THE)
    CRA (CIORA) AS New Clinical Investigator Grant: 2201
    Graduate Ph.D. Award: 2201
    Postdoctoral Fellowship Award: 2201
    Stars Career Development Award: 2201
    Strategic Operating Grants: 2201
Artist Career Development Grants: 456
Artist Collaboration Grants: 456
Artist Development Grants: 466
Artist Enrichment: 979
Artist Entrepreneurial Workshops: 438
Artist Fellowships: 443, 456
Artist in Residence: 438
Artist Initiated Skill Share: 451
Artist Laureates: 454
Artist Residencies: 399, 431
Artist Residency Program: 424
Artist Services: 438
Artist Services Program: 436
Artist Support Grants: 461
Artistic Innovations Grant Program: 429
Artists in Communities: 394
Artists-in-Education Residency Grant Program (AIE): 439
Artists in Residence: 444
Artists in Schools: 394
Artists in Schools & Communities (AISC) Grants: 456
Artists in Schools Grants: 466
Artists-in-Schools Grants Program: 461
Artists-in-Schools/Communities Grants: 435
Artists Open Studio Tours Grant (AOST): 451
Artists with Disabilities Access: 445
Artists' Book Residency Grants: 475
Artists' Fellowships: 441
Arts: 1346
Arts Access: 445
Arts Access Grant (AAG): 451
Arts Access Project Grants: 479
Arts and Accessibility: 394
Arts and Culture: 228, 1154
Arts & Culture Grants: 1517
Arts and Entertainment Districts General Operating Support: 427
Arts and Entertainment Districts Technical Assistance: 427
Arts and Humanities Education Projects: 403
Arts and Humanities Fellowship Program: 403
Arts and Humanities Grants: 425
Arts and Public Media: 394
Arts Build Communities: 447
Arts Challenge Grants: 456
Arts Education: 455
Arts Education Exposure: 394
Arts Education Program Grants: 409
Arts Education Projects: 415
Arts Education Special Initiatives (AESI): 439
Arts First Aid: 420
Arts Impact Grants: 466
Arts-in-Education: 384
Arts in Education: 401, 427, 438
Arts in Education Collaboration Grant (AIEC): 444
Arts in Education Grants: 428, 443
Arts in Health Project Grants: 438
Arts in Society: 396
Arts Integration Training: 394
Arts Learning: 425
Arts Learning Grants: 447
Arts Learning Program: 436
Arts Learning Projects: 435

Arts Learning: Artist Express: 445
Arts Learning: Arts Partnership: 445
Arts Learning: TeachArtsOhio: 445
ARTS MIDWEST
    Arts Midwest Conference: 483
    GIG Fund: 483
Arts Midwest Conference: 483
Arts Organization Grants: 448
Arts Organizations Grants: 401
Arts Partnership Grants: 466
Arts Program: 93, 167
Arts Project Grants: 435
Arts Project Support (APS): 439
Arts Resources and Artists Programs: 418
Arts, Culture and Humanities: 1229
ArtsCONNECT: 430
ArtsEverywhere Fund: 1120
ArtsNEXT: 445
ArtStars Awards: 88
ArtSTART: 445
Arver (David) Memorial Scholarship: 2363
Arver (Dutch and Ginger) Scholarship: 2363
ASCAP FOUNDATION (THE)
    ASCAP Foundation Deems Taylor/Virgil Thomson Awards (The): 612
    ASCAP Foundation Morton Gould Young Composer Awards (The): 694
ASCAP Foundation Deems Taylor/Virgil Thomson Awards (The): 612
ASCAP Foundation Morton Gould Young Composer Awards (The): 694
ASCP: 2013
ASE/PSF Combined Research Grant: 2076
ASECS/Clark Library Fellowships: 319
ASF Awards for Study in Scandinavia: 808
ASHBURN INSTITUTE INC.
    Frank Educational Fund: 758
Asia Pacific Leadership Program: 769
Asia Program: 185
ASIAN AMERICAN JOURNALISTS ASSOCIATION
    Chen (Stanford) Internship Grant: 1482
    Chin (Vincent) Memorial Scholarship: 1483
    CIC/Anna Chennault Scholarship: 1483
    Eng (Dinah) Leadership Fellowship: 1484
    Ing (Mary Quon Moy) Memorial Scholarship: 1483
    Kim (Michael) Broadcast Fellowship: 1484
    LaCuesta (Lloyd) Internship Grant: 1482
    Lin (Sam Chu) Internship Grant: 1482
    Sports Task Force/Al Young Sports Journalism Scholarship: 1483
    Woo (William) Print & Online News Internship Grant: 1482
    Yee (Jimmie & Suey Fong) Scholarship: 1483
ASIAN AMERICAN WRITERS' WORKSHOP
    Margins Fellowship (The): 613
    Open City Fellowship: 613
ASIAN CULTURAL COUNCIL
    Graduate Scholarship: 391
    Individual Fellowship Program: 391
    New York Fellowship Program: 391
    Organization and Project Grant: 391
    Travel Grant: 391
ASID Foundation Legacy Scholarships for Graduate Students: 367
ASID Foundation Legacy Scholarships for Undergraduates: 367
ASID Foundation Transform Grant: 367
ASLA Council of Fellows Scholarship: 1974
ASLA Florida Chapter Career Discovery Scholarships: 1974
ASLA-NY Designing in the Public Realm Scholarship: 1974
ASM MATERIALS EDUCATION FOUNDATION
    Acta Materialia Scholarships: 2420
    ASM Outstanding Scholars: 2420
    Chellman (David J.) Scholarship: 2420
    Dulis (Edward J.) Scholarship: 2420
    Haniak (John M.) Scholarship: 2420
    Ladish Co. Foundation Scholarships: 2420
    Roberts (George A.) Scholarship: 2420
    Wert (Lucille & Charles A.) Scholarship: 2420
    Woodside (William Park) Founder's Scholarship: 2420
ASM Outstanding Scholars: 2420
ASMS Research Awards in Mass Spectrometry: 1820
ASN Research Fellowships: 2112
ASNE Scholarship Program: 2388
ASNT Faculty Grant Award: 1370
ASNT Fellowship Award: 2345
ASPEN RHOADS RESEARCH FOUNDATION: 2162
Aspiring Future Physicians Scholarship in Memory of Dr. Tamara O'Neal
    (The): 2062

Aspiring Physicians Endowed Scholarship (The): 2062
ASPRS - THE IMAGING AND GEOSPATIAL INFORMATION
  SOCIETY
   Altenhofen (Robert E.) Memorial Scholarship: 1821
   Anson (Abraham) Memorial Scholarship: 1821
   Behrens (John O.) Institute for Land Information (ILI) Memorial
   Scholarship: 1821
   Colwell (Robert N.) Memorial Fellowship: 1821
   Fischer (William A.) Memorial Scholarship: 1821
   Liang (Ta) Memorial Award: 1821
   Moffitt (Francis H.) Memorial Scholarship: 1821
   Osborn (The Kenneth J.) Memorial Scholarship: 1821
   Wolf (Paul R.) Memorial Scholarship: 1821
ASRA Carl Koller Memorial Research Grant: 2291
ASRA Chronic Pain Research Grant: 2291
ASRA Early-Career Investigator Award: 2008
ASRA Graduate Student Award: 2008
Assembly Session Internships: 1799
ASSISI FOUNDATION OF MEMPHIS INC.: 20
Assistance to Worthy Music Teachers: 724
Assistive Technology Programs: 2306
ASSOCIATION FOR BEHAVIORAL AND COGNITIVE THERAPIES
   President's New Researcher Award: 2322
   Roswell (Virginia) Dissertation Award: 2321
ASSOCIATION FOR LIBRARY AND INFORMATION SCIENCE
  EDUCATION (ALISE)
   ALISE Research Awards: 660
   ALISE/ProQuest Methodology Paper Competition: 661
   Garfield (The Eugene)/ALISE Doctoral Dissertation Competition: 661
   Wynar (Bohdan S.) Research Paper Competition: 661
Association of American Medical Colleges (AAMC)/Darrell G. Kirch,
   M.D. Scholarship: 2062
ASSOCIATION OF INTERNATIONAL CERTIFIED PROFESSIONAL
  ACCOUNTANTS (THE ASSOCIATION)
   AICPA Fellowship for Minority Doctoral Students: 1485
ASSOCIATION OF WOMEN'S HEALTH, OBSTETRIC AND
  NEONATAL NURSES (AWHONN)
   AWHONN Research Grants Program: 2236
ASSOCIATION OF WRITERS & WRITING PROGRAMS (THE)
   AWP Award Series in the Novel: 614
   Hall (Donald) Prize for Poetry: 614
   Paley (Grace) Prize for Short Fiction: 614
   Silverman (Sue William) Prize for Creative Nonfiction: 614
ASSOCIATION ON AMERICAN INDIAN AFFAIRS
   Association on American Indian Affairs Scholarship Program: 944
Association on American Indian Affairs Scholarship Program: 944
Asthma Mitigation Project: 1334
ASTR Collaborative Research Award (The): 482
ASTRAEA LESBIAN FOUNDATION FOR JUSTICE
   Global Arts Fund: 890
   International Fund: 888
   U.S. General Fund: 889
ASTRONOMICAL SOCIETY OF THE PACIFIC
   Brennan (Thomas J.) Award: 1835
   Emmons (Richard H.) Award: 1838
   Klumpke-Roberts Award: 1834
   Las Cumbres Amateur Outreach Award: 1836
   Muhlmann (Maria and Eric) Award: 1833
   Myers (The Gordon) Amateur Achievement Award: 1836
   Walker (Arthur B.C. II) Award: 1837
Astronomy and Astrophysics Research Grants: 1842
ASU Leadership Scholarship Program: 1371
ATA Student Research Grant Program: 1621
ATA Tinnitus Research Grant Program: 1621
ATHE-ASTR Award for Excellence in Digital Scholarship: 482
ATHWIN FOUNDATION: 21
ATKINSON FOUNDATION
   Community: 22
   Education and Youth Development: 22
Atkinson Scholarship Program (The): 1253
Atlanta AIDS Fund: 1099
ATLANTIC SALMON FEDERATION
   Olin Fellowships: 1935
ATRAN FOUNDATION, INC.: 23
Austern (H. Thomas) Writing Competition: 1772
AUSTIN COMMUNITY FOUNDATION (THE)
   Community Grant Program: 1060
AUSTRALIAN NATIONAL UNIVERSITY (THE)
   Visiting Fellows Program: 314
AUSTRO-AMERICAN ASSOCIATION OF BOSTON: 759
AUTISM SPEAKS INC.: 2014

AUTRY FOUNDATION: 1061
AVIATION DISTRIBUTORS AND MANUFACTURERS ASSOCIATION
  (ADMA)
   ADMA Scholarship Programs: 2366
AVIATION INSURANCE ASSOCIATION (AIA)
   AIA Scholarship: 2367
Aviation Space Writers Foundation Award: 2372
AVMA Fellowship: 2009
Award for Global Understanding in Honor of James M. Becker: 1668
Award for Research Excellence in Materials Chemistry: 1855
Award of Excellence in Contact Lens Patient Care Grant: 2259
Award Program for Summer Music Festivals and Music Centers: 715
Awards: 187
Awards for Achievement in Arc Welded Design, Engineering and
   Fabrication: College Division: 2393
Awards for Excellence: 100
Awards for Outstanding Teaching and Mentoring: 1682
Awards for Teaching Excellence: 1411
Awards to Scholarly Publications Program: 1656
AWHONN Research Grants Program: 2236
AWP Award Series in the Novel: 614
AWS FOUNDATION, INC.
   AWS National, District and Section Scholarships: 2346
   Graduate Research Fellowship: 2348
   Welder Training Scholarship: 2349
   Welding Workforce Grant: 2347
AWS National, District and Section Scholarships: 2346
AWSCPA Scholarship Award: 1696

B

B.A.E.F. Fellowships for Study in Belgium: 820
BABBAGE (CHARLES) INSTITUTE
   Tomash (The Adelle and Erwin) Fellowship in the History of
   Information Technology: 2350
BABCOCK (MARY REYNOLDS) FOUNDATION
   Moving People and Places Out of Poverty: 24
Bach (The Anna Botsford) Fund: 1057
Bachelor of Music: 701
Backus Award: 1944
BADER PHILANTHROPIES, INC.: 25
BADGER METER FOUNDATION, INC.: 1062
Bahlsen (Bettina) Memorial Graduate Scholarship: 1598
Bailey (Alton E.) Award: 1852
Bailey (Carolyn) and Dominick Argento Vocal Competition: 717
BAINUM FAMILY FOUNDATION: 1000
Baker Artist Portfolios: 392
Baker (Gene) Memorial Scholarship: 2363
BAKER (R.C.) FOUNDATION: 26
BAKER (THE WILLIAM G., JR.) MEMORIAL FUND
   Baker Artist Portfolios: 392
Bakken (Gordon Morris) Scholarship in Western History: 577
Baldwin (Allen J.) Scholarship: 2387
Baldwin (Birgit) Fellowship: 559
Baldwin (Donald A. Sr.) Business Aviation Management Scholarship:
   2370
BALL BROTHERS FOUNDATION: 27
BALL (GEORGE AND FRANCES) FOUNDATION: 28
BALTIMORE COMMUNITY FOUNDATION: 29
Bancroft Award (The): 1646
Bancroft Prizes: 533
BANFF CENTRE (THE): 484
Banting Postdoctoral Fellowships: 1679
BARAGA COUNTY COMMUNITY FOUNDATION: 1063
Barborinas Family Fund Grant: 1925
Barchas (Patricia R.) Award in Sociophysiology: 2316
Bard (Allen J.) Award: 1627
BARNES GROUP FOUNDATION: 1064
Barnum (Harold) Industry Award: 2415
Baroid Scholarship: 2344
BARR FOUNDATION: 1065
Barr (Joe and Janet) Early Career Cornea and Contact Lens Research
   Award: 2256
BARRA FOUNDATION: 30
Barrett (Anne Louise) Fellowship: 991
Bartman (Elizabeth) Museum Internship: 309
Bartnicki-Garcia (Salomon) Award: 1944
Basic Research Fellowship Awards: 2204
Basic Support Grants: 435

Basilone (Sargeant John) Memorial Graduate Scholarship: 1591
BAT CONSERVATION INTERNATIONAL
  BCI Student Research Scholarships: 1372
BATON ROUGE AREA FOUNDATION: 393
Batten Disease Research Grant: 2015
BATTEN DISEASE SUPPORT AND RESEARCH ASSOCIATION
  Batten Disease Research Grant: 2015
BATTLE CREEK COMMUNITY FOUNDATION: 31
BAXTER INTERNATIONAL FOUNDATION (THE): 32
BAYER FUND: 1066
Bayliss (John) Scholarship Award: 1724
BAYRD (ADELAIDE BREED) FOUNDATION: 33
BCC Training Award: 1543
BCI Student Research Scholarships: 1372
BEA Founders Award: 1724
BEAN (NORWIN S. AND ELIZABETH N.) FOUNDATION: 1067
Beard Scholarship: 668
Beattie (Catherine H.) Fellowship for Conservation Horticulture: 1906
Bechtel Engineering Scholarship: 2395
Beer (The George Louis) Prize: 526
Beeson (Paul) Career Development Awards in Aging Research Program: 1999
Begun Scholarship: 663
Behavior Therapy Training Institute (BTTI): 2328
Behavioral & Social Science Research: 2107
Behrens (John O.) Institute for Land Information (ILI) Memorial Scholarship: 1821
Beldecos (Helen J.), Past Grand President, Scholarship (Undergraduate): 976
BELGIAN AMERICAN EDUCATIONAL FOUNDATION, INC.
  B.A.E.F. Fellowships for Study in Belgium: 820
BELK FOUNDATION (THE): 1428
BELL (ALEXANDER GRAHAM) ASSOCIATION FOR THE DEAF AND HARD OF HEARING
  Bell (Alexander Graham) College Scholarship Awards: 891
Bell (Alexander Graham) College Scholarship Awards: 891
BEN & JERRY'S FOUNDATION: 892
BENIGN ESSENTIAL BLEPHAROSPASM RESEARCH FOUNDATION INC.: 2263
Bennett (A.E.) Research Awards: 2338
Bennett (William and Sandra) Clinical Scholars Program: 2110
Benoit (Marilyn B.), M.D., Child Maltreatment Mentorship Award: 2309
Bentley (The Jerry) Prize: 526
Berardo (Felix) Mentoring Award: 1350
Berenson Fellowship: 861
BERGER (H.N. AND FRANCES C.) FOUNDATION: 34
Berger (Mike) Award: 1727
Berkel Crisp (Rosemary) Research Award: 2246
BERKS COUNTY COMMUNITY FOUNDATION: 1068
BERKSHIRE CONFERENCE OF WOMEN HISTORIANS: 529
Berlin Prize Fellowship: 795
BERNSEN (THE GRACE AND FRANKLIN) FOUNDATION: 35
Berntsen International Scholarship in Surveying Technology (The): 2397
BERRIEN COMMUNITY FOUNDATION: 36
Berry (Leonard G.) Medal: 2423
Berryman (Clifford K. and James T.) Award for Editorial Cartoons: 1750
BERWIND CORPORATION: 37
Best (Charles H.) Research Fund: 2168
Best (Raymond A. and Ina C.) Fellowship for MBA at Rensselaer Polytechnic Institute: 2407
BETA PHI MU
  Garfield (Eugene) Doctoral Dissertation Fellowship: 662
  Lancour (Harold) Foreign Research Fellowship: 662
  Reed (Sarah Rebecca) Scholarship: 662
  Sessa (Frank B.) Scholarship for Continuing Professional Education of Beta Phi Mu Members: 662
  Woolls (Blanche E.) Scholarship for School Library Media Service: 662
Beta Sigma Kappa (BSK) Student Travel Fellowship: 2258
Beta Sigma Kappa Research Fellowships: 2260
BETHESDA LUTHERAN COMMUNITIES
  Intellectual and Developmental Disabilities Scholastic Achievement Scholarships: 1373
Bethune (Mary McLeod) Scholarship Program (MMB): 1501
Beuchat (Larry) Young Researcher Award: 2415
Beveridge (The Albert J.) Award: 526
Beveridge (The Albert J.) Grant: 526
BFWG Marjorie Shaw Fellowship: 978
Bhaskaran (The Varun) (WAS) Scholarship Program of IDF: 903
BIBLIOGRAPHICAL SOCIETY OF AMERICA
  BSA Fellowship Program: 1374

Biennial Dissertation Competition: 717
Biennial Sally Banes Publication Prize: 482
Biennium Grants Program: 412
Biestock (N.S.) Fellowship: 1757
Big Bets: 187
Big Five Graduate Scholarship (The): 976
Big Yellow School Bus: 445, 451
Bigelow (Timothy) and Palmer W. Bigelow, Jr. Scholarship: 1510
Biggane (James L.) Fellowship in Finance: 1801
Bikai (Pierre and Patricia) Fellowship: 796
Bikakis (The Harry) Fellowship: 812
BINC FOUNDATION
  Emergency Financial Assistance Grants: 38
  Professional Development Scholarships: 38
BINGHAM (THE WILLIAM) FOUNDATION: 39
Bingham (Worth) Prize for Investigative Journalism: 1753
Binnie (Ruth) Fellowship: 974
Biomarkers Development: 1995
Bistline (The F.M., Anne G., and Beverly B.) Foundation Fund: 143
BLAIR (WILLIAM) AND COMPANY FOUNDATION: 1069
Blanchan/Doubleday Fellowships: 479
BLAUSTEIN (JACOB AND HILDA) FOUNDATION: 893
Blinder (Richard L.) Award: 372
Blizard (Everitt P.) Memorial Scholarship: 2382
Bloch (Doris) Research Award: 2246
Block (Jeanne Humphrey) Dissertation Award: 1663
Blood Diseases and Resources Research: 2121
Blood Efficiency Accelerator Program: 2018
BloodTechNet Award Program: 2022
BLOWITZ-RIDGEWAY FOUNDATION: 1070
BLUE MOUNTAIN COMMUNITY FOUNDATION: 1071
Bluefin Tuna Research Program Grants: 1873
BLUESCOPE FOUNDATION NORTH AMERICA (THE): 40
Blum (Stella) Research Grant: 400
BNSF RAILWAY FOUNDATION
  Native American Scholarship Program: 945
BNY MELLON FOUNDATION OF SOUTHWESTERN PENNSYLVANIA (THE): 1072
Board Directed Initiative Grants: 882
Board Grants: 2046
Bogazici University Summer Language Program for Intensive Advanced Turkish Language Study: 806
Bolton (Frances P.) Fellowship: 2335
Bombardier (Joseph-Armand) Canada Graduate Scholarships Program - Master's Scholarships: 1677
Bonner County Fund for Arts Enhancement: 143
Bonner County Human Rights Task Force Fund: 143
Bonner (The Ellis) Award: 2302
Bonner Scholarship: 1141
BONNEVILLE ENVIRONMENTAL FOUNDATION
  Model Watershed Program: 1959
  Renewable Energy Program: 1959
Bonwich (Joe) Media Scholarship: 1567
Book Award: 762
BOOTH-BRICKER FUND (THE): 41
Boren and Gilman Scholarship Support Grants: 1514
Boren Fellowships: 846
Boren Scholarships: 845
BOSTON FOUNDATION (THE): 1073
BOSTON WOMEN'S FUND: 972
Botein (Stephen) Fellowships: 304
Boulton (Maxwell) Q.C. Fellowship: 1780
Bourses pour L'Afrique Francophone (BAF): 2199
Bowers (Margaret Freeman) Fellowship: 991
Bowling for Rhinos Conservation Resource Grant (BFR CRG): 1931
BOY SCOUTS OF AMERICA, NATIONAL EAGLE SCOUT ASSOCIATION (THE)
  Cooke (Mabel and Lawrence S.) Scholarship: 1002
  Hall/McElwain Merit Scholarships: 1001
  National Eagle Scout Scholarship Fund: 1002
  Palmer (Robert and Rebeca) Scholarship: 1001
Bradlee (Benjamin C.) Editor of the Year Award: 1750
Bradley (Ed) Scholarship: 1757
Bradley Fellowship Program: 1486
BRADLEY (THE LYNDE AND HARRY) FOUNDATION, INC.
  Bradley Fellowship Program: 1486
BRAIN & BEHAVIOR RESEARCH FOUNDATION
  NARSAD Distinguished Investigator Grant: 2323
  NARSAD Independent Investigator Grant: 2323
  NARSAD Young Investigator Grant: 2323
BRANDON UNIVERSITY: 695

Brandt (John) Memorial Scholarship Fund: 177
Bray (Jeanne E.) Memorial Scholarship: 1555
BREAD LOAF WRITERS' CONFERENCE
    Fellowship and Scholarship Program for Writers: 615
Breasted (The James Henry) Prize: 526
Breathing as One: Allied Health Research Fellowships: 2237
Breathing as One: Allied Health Research Grants: 2237
Breathing as One: Research Fellowships and Studentships: 2139
BREMER (OTTO) TRUST: 1074
Brennan (Thomas J.) Award: 1835
BRETT FAMILY FOUNDATION
    Nonprofit Media Grant Program: 1655
    Social Justice Grant Program: 1655
Brett (The Philip) Award: 691
Bridge Award: 2051
Bridge Grant: 409
Bridge Grants: 1945
BRIGHAM AND WOMEN'S HOSPITAL
    Deland Fellowship Program in Health Care and Society: 1283
BRIGHT FOCUS FOUNDATION
    Alzheimer's Disease Research: 2207
    Macular Degeneration Research Program: 1284
    National Glaucoma Research Program: 2264
Bright (Norman and Marion) Memorial Award: 1853
British Marshall Scholarships: 856
BROADCAST EDUCATION ASSOCIATION
    Bayliss (John) Scholarship Award: 1724
    BEA Founders Award: 1724
    Eaton (Richard) Foundation Award: 1724
    Fritts (Edward O.) Award: 1724
    Library of American Broadcasting Foundation Award: 1724
    Orlik (Peter B.) Award: 1724
    PILOT Media Technology and Innovation Scholarships: 1725
    Voron (Abe) Award: 1724
    Wasilewski (Vincent T.) Award: 1724
Brockett (Oscar G.) Essay Prize: 482
Brodman (Estelle) Award for the Academic Medical Librarian of the Year: 674
BROOKHAVEN WOMEN IN SCIENCE
    Chasman (Renate W.) Scholarship for Women: 973
BROOKS (GLADYS) FOUNDATION: 1075
BROWARD EDUCATION FOUNDATION
    Broward Education Foundation School Supply Center: 1375
    Innovative Teacher Grants: 1375
    Student Scholarships: 1375
Broward Education Foundation School Supply Center: 1375
BROWN FOUNDATION, INC. (THE): 1376
Brown (Howard Mayer) Fellowship: 692
BROWN (JAMES GRAHAM) FOUNDATION, INC.: 42
BROWN (THE JOE W. AND DOROTHY DORSETT) FOUNDATION: 43
BROWN (JOHN CARTER) LIBRARY
    Brown (The John Carter) Library Research Fellowships: 530
Brown (The John Carter) Library Research Fellowships: 530
Brown (John Nicholas) Prize: 559
Brown (Marjorie M.) Dissertation Fellowship: 2416
Bruce (W.B.) European Fine Art Travel Scholarship: 497
BRUCEBO FINE ART SCHOLARSHIP FOUNDATION
    Bruce (W.B.) European Fine Art Travel Scholarship: 497
    Brucebo Fine Art Summer Residency Scholarship: 497
Brucebo Fine Art Summer Residency Scholarship: 497
Brunswick Employee Sons and Daughters Scholarship: 1076
BRUNSWICK FOUNDATION, INC.
    Brunswick Employee Sons and Daughters Scholarship: 1076
    Dollars for Doers Volunteer Program: 1076
BRUNSWICK PUBLIC FOUNDATION: 1960
BSA Fellowship Program: 1374
BUHL FOUNDATION (THE): 1077
Building Community: 116
Building Cultural Diversity: 445
Building Healthy Communities: 1334
Building Healthy Communities Initiative: 1285
Building Voice and Power: 122
Buildings Program: 1964
BULLITT FOUNDATION (THE)
    Deep Green Buildings: 1961
    Energy, Climate and Materials: 1961
    Regional Ecosystem Health: 1961
    Resilient Cities, Healthy Communities: 1961
Bullock (Dorothy Dann) Music Therapy Award: 716

BUREAU OF INDIAN AFFAIRS
    Energy and Mineral Development Program (EMDP) Grant: 948
    Indian Employment Assistance: 946
    Native American Business Development Institute (NABDI): 949
    Public Law 102-477: 946
    Tribal Energy Development Capacity (TEDC) Grant: 947
BUREAU OF INDIAN EDUCATION
    Higher Education Grant Program for American Indians and Alaska Natives: 950
BURNHAM (THE MARGARET E.) CHARITABLE TRUST: 44
BURNS (FRITZ B.) FOUNDATION: 1377
Burris (Donald R.) Journalism Scholarship: 1567
BURROUGHS WELLCOME FUND
    Career Awards at the Scientific Interface: 2016
    Career Awards for Medical Scientists: 2016
    Investigators in the Pathogenesis of Infectious Disease: 2016
    Preterm Birth Initiative: 2016
BUSH (EDYTH) CHARITABLE FOUNDATION, INC.: 45
Bush (Laura) 21st Century Librarian Program: 672
Bushee (Eleanor) Award: 2101
Business of Art and Design (MPS): 509
BUTLER (PATRICK AND AIMEE) FAMILY FOUNDATION: 1078
Butts (Wayne Anthony) Scholarship: 2062
BYNNER (THE WITTER) FOUNDATION FOR POETRY, INC.: 616

C

CAARI/CAORC Research Fellowships: 827
Cabell (Harry H.) Scholarship Program: 1570
CABOT FAMILY CHARITABLE TRUST: 46
Cabot (Maria Moors) Prizes: 1728
Cadbury (William and Charlotte) Award: 2062
Cadogan (Edwin Anthony and Adelaide Boudreaux) Scholarships: 452
CAFRITZ (THE MORRIS AND GWENDOLYN) FOUNDATION: 47
Cairns (The A.T.J.) Memorial Scholarship: 1601
Caison (Carl H. and Thelma C., Sr.) Scholarship: 2062
Cal Grants A, B and C: 1487
CALDER (THE LOUIS) FOUNDATION: 1003
CALERES CARES CHARITABLE TRUST: 48
CALIFORNIA ACADEMY OF SCIENCES
    Summer Systematics Institute: 1936
CALIFORNIA ARTS COUNCIL
    Artists in Communities: 394
    Artists in Schools: 394
    Arts and Accessibility: 394
    Arts and Public Media: 394
    Arts Education Exposure: 394
    Arts Integration Training: 394
    Creative California Communities: 394
    Cultural Pathways: 394
    JUMP StArts: 394
    Local Impact: 394
    Organizational Development: 394
    Professional Development: 394
    Reentry Through the Arts: 394
    Research in the Arts: 394
    State-Local Partners: 394
    Statewide and Regional Networks: 394
    Veterans in the Arts: 394
    Youth Arts Action: 394
CALIFORNIA COMMUNITY FOUNDATION
    Education: 1079
    Health: 1079
    Housing: 1079
    Immigration: 1079
CALIFORNIA ENDOWMENT (THE)
    Building Healthy Communities Initiative: 1285
California Funders for Boys and Men of Color: 1334
California Funders for Boys and Men of Color (CFBMOC): 1343
CALIFORNIA HEALTHCARE FOUNDATION
    Health Innovation Fund: 1286
    Improving Access: 1286
    People-Centered Care: 1286
CALIFORNIA LIBRARY ASSOCIATION
    Begun Scholarship: 663
    CLA Scholarship for Minority Students in Memory of Edna Yelland: 663
California Regions Grant Program: 176

CALIFORNIA STUDENT AID COMMISSION
Cal Grants A, B and C: 1487
Law Enforcement Personnel Dependents' Grant Program (LEPD): 1488
CALIFORNIA WELLNESS FOUNDATION (THE)
Advancing Wellness Grants Program: 1287
Calinescu (Matei) Prize: 603
CALLAWAY FOUNDATION, INC.: 1080
CAMBRIDGE UNIVERSITY LIBRARY
Munby Fellowship in Bibliography (The): 664
Cambridge University Press Prize: 482
Camp Scholarships: 1019
CAMPBELL FOUNDATION, INC.: 1004
CAMPBELL SOUP FOUNDATION
Dollars for Doers Fund: 49
Matching Gift Program: 49
United Way Match Program: 49
CAMS Scholarship Program: 2024
Camuy (Jonathan) Scholarship: 909
Canada-China Scholars' Exchange Program: 822
CANADIAN BAR ASSOCIATION (THE)
Viscount Bennett Fellowship: 1769
CANADIAN BLOOD SERVICES
Blood Efficiency Accelerator Program: 2018
BloodTechNet Award Program: 2022
Canadian Blood Services Graduate Fellowship Program: 2017
Canadian Blood Services Postdoctoral Fellowship Program: 2017
Fyke (Kenneth J.) Award: 2020
Intramural Research Grant Program: 2019
Kreppner (James) Award: 2021
Canadian Blood Services Graduate Fellowship Program: 2017
Canadian Blood Services Postdoctoral Fellowship Program: 2017
CANADIAN BUREAU FOR INTERNATIONAL EDUCATION (CBIE)
Canada-China Scholars' Exchange Program: 822
Foreign Government Awards Program: 821
CANADIAN CANCER SOCIETY: 2181
CANADIAN FEDERATION FOR THE HUMANITIES AND SOCIAL
SCIENCES
Awards to Scholarly Publications Program: 1656
CANADIAN FEDERATION OF UNIVERSITY WOMEN
Binnie (Ruth) Fellowship: 974
Canadian Home Economics Association (CHEA) Fellowship: 974
CFUW Aboriginal Women's Award (AWA): 974
CFUW Bourse Georgette Lemoyne: 974
CFUW Dr. Alice E. Wilson Awards: 974
CFUW Dr. Margaret McWilliams Pre-Doctoral Fellowship: 974
CFUW Elizabeth and Rachel Massey Award: 974
CFUW Linda Souter Humanities Award: 974
CFUW Memorial Fellowship: 974
CFUW 1989 Ecole Polytechnique Commemorative Awards: 974
CFUW 100th Anniversary Legacy Fellowship: 974
CANADIAN FOUNDATION FOR DIETETIC RESEARCH (CFDR)
Research Grants in Dietetics: 2412
CANADIAN FRIENDS OF THE HEBREW UNIVERSITY: 1489
Canadian Home Economics Association (CHEA) Fellowship: 974
CANADIAN INSTITUTE FOR ADVANCED LEGAL STUDIES
French Language Scholarship: 1770
Martin (The Right Honourable Paul Sr.) Scholarship: 1770
CANADIAN INSTITUTE IN GREECE/L'INSTITUT CANADIEN EN
GRECE
Alfoldi-Rosenbaum (Elizabeth) Fellowship: 315
Leipen (Neda and Franz) Fellowship: 315
Thompson (Homer and Dorothy) Fellowship: 315
Winter (Frederick E. and Joan) Student Travel Bursary: 315
CANADIAN INSTITUTE OF UKRAINIAN STUDIES
Darcovich (The Helen) Memorial Doctoral Fellowship: 531
Neporany Doctoral Fellowship: 531
Research Grants: 531
CANADIAN LIVER FOUNDATION
Canadian Liver Foundation Operating Grant: 2163
Graduate Studentships: 2164
Summer Studentships: 2023
Canadian Liver Foundation Operating Grant: 2163
CANADIAN LUNG ASSOCIATION (CLA) (THE)
Breathing as One: Allied Health Research Fellowships: 2237
Breathing as One: Allied Health Research Grants: 2237
Breathing as One: Research Fellowships and Studentships: 2139
CANADIAN NATIONAL INSTITUTE FOR THE BLIND
CNIB Barbara Tuck MacPhee Award in Macular Degeneration: 2265
Canadian Natural Resources Limited Graduate Scholarship: 1604

CANADIAN SOCIETY FOR CHEMICAL ENGINEERING
CSChE Chemical Engineering Local Section Scholarships (The): 2390
ZETON Plant Design Competition: 2390
CANADIAN SOCIETY FOR CHEMICAL TECHNOLOGY
Bright (Norman and Marion) Memorial Award: 1853
CANADIAN SOCIETY FOR CHEMISTRY
Award for Research Excellence in Materials Chemistry: 1855
CCUCC Chemistry Doctoral Award: 1854
IntelliSyn Pharma Research Excellence Award: 1856
CANCER FEDERATION, INC.: 2113
Cancer Grants: 293
CANCER RESEARCH INSTITUTE
Cancer Research Institute Irvington Postdoctoral Fellowship: 2182
Clinic and Laboratory Integration Program (CLIP): 2183
Old (Lloyd J.) STAR Program: 2184
Technology Impact Award: 2185
Cancer Research Institute Irvington Postdoctoral Fellowship: 2182
CANCER RESEARCH SOCIETY
Grants for Cancer Research: 2187
Scholarship for the Next Generation of Scientists: 2186
CANCER RESEARCH UK: 2188
Cannabinoids and Epilepsy: 2211
CANNON FOUNDATION, INC. (THE): 50
CAORC Multi-Country Research Fellowships: 389
Capacity Building: 445
Capacity-Building Grant Initiative: 1107
Capacity Building Grants: 251, 1132, 1348
Capezio Dance Award: 485
CAPEZIO/BALLET MAKERS DANCE FOUNDATION, INC.
Capezio Dance Award: 485
Grants Program: 485
Capital Grants: 1186
Capital Improvement Grants: 428
CAPITAL REGION COMMUNITY FOUNDATION: 1081
Capital Support: 724
Capitol Art Travel Subsidies: 446
Career Awards at the Scientific Interface: 2016
Career Awards for Medical Scientists: 2016
Career Catalyst Research Grants (CCR): 2191
Career Development Award: 2127, 2166
Career Development Awards: 2171, 2177
Career Development Grant Award: 2066
Career Development Grants: 2241
Career Development Program: 2116
Career Enhancement Award for Stem Cell Research (K18): 1311
Career Opportunity Grants: 447
Carey (John L.) Scholarship: 1699
Caring for Community: 73
CARING FOR MILITARY FAMILIES: THE ELIZABETH DOLE
FOUNDATION
Hidden Heroes Fund: 894
CARNEGIE CORPORATION OF NEW YORK: 51
CARNEGIE FUND FOR AUTHORS: 617
CARNEGIE INSTITUTION FOR SCIENCE
Predoctoral and Postdoctoral Fellowships at the Carnegie Institution:
1624
CARPENTER FOUNDATION (THE): 1082
Carrera (Mary Ball) Scholarship: 2062
CARSON SCHOLARS FUND, INC. (THE)
Carson Scholarship Program: 1490
Carson Scholarship Program: 1490
CARTER (AMON G.) FOUNDATION: 52
Cartwright (Berna Lou) Scholarship: 2387
CARVEL (THOMAS AND AGNES) FOUNDATION: 1005
CARVER (ROY J.) CHARITABLE TRUST: 1447
Cash Grants: 1296
CASTLE (HAROLD K.L.) FOUNDATION: 53
CASTLE (SAMUEL N. AND MARY) FOUNDATION: 1429
Catalyst Award: 2136
Catalyst Initiative: 1204
Catalyst: Adventure Grants for Change: 1957
CATCHING THE DREAM
Math and Science Teaching (MAST): 951
MESBEC (Math, Engineering, Science, Business, Education and
Computers) Program: 951
Native American Leadership in Education (NALE) Program: 951
Reading Award Program (RAP): 951
Tribal Business Management (TBM) Program: 951
CATERPILLAR FOUNDATION: 1083

CATHOLIC CAMPAIGN FOR HUMAN DEVELOPMENT
    Community Development Grant: 1084
    Economic Development Grant: 1084
CATTELL (JAMES MCKEEN) FUND
    Cattell (James McKeen) Fund Sabbatical Fellowships for Psychologists:
    2324
    Cattell (James McKeen) Fund Sabbatical Fellowships for Psychologists:
    2324
Cave (William and Eleanor) Award: 1617
CBC Spouses Education Scholarship: 929
CBC Spouses Performing Arts Scholarship: 930
CBC Spouses Visual Arts Scholarship: 930
CBCF Congressional Fellows Program (The): 931
CBCF Congressional Internship Program (The): 931
CCE Professional Development Award: 1543
CCUCC Chemistry Doctoral Award: 1854
CCWH/Berkshire Conference of Women Historians Graduate Student
    Fellowship: 534
CEMALA FOUNDATION (THE): 1378
Census 2020 Outreach: 1334
Centenary Scholarship: 2421
CENTER AT SIERRA HEALTH FOUNDATION (THE)
    Asthma Mitigation Project: 1334
    Building Healthy Communities: 1334
    California Funders for Boys and Men of Color: 1334
    Census 2020 Outreach: 1334
    Elevate Youth California: 1334
    Leadership Development for Racial Equity: 1334
    Medi-Cal Health Navigator Project: 1334
    Medication Assisted Treatment Access Points Project: 1334
    My Brother's Keeper Sacramento Collaborative: 1334
    Oak Park Project: 1334
    Positive Youth Justice Initiative: 1334
    San Joaquin Valley Health Fund: 1334
    San Joaquin Valley Impact Investment Fund: 1334
    Steering Committee on Reducation of African American Child Deaths:
    1334
    Youth and Community PopUps: 1334
Center Core Grants: 2274
CENTER FOR CALIFORNIA STUDIES, CAPITAL FELLOWS
    PROGRAMS
    Executive Fellowship Program: 1785
    Judicial Fellowship Program: 1785
    Senate Fellowship Program: 1785
    Unruh (Jesse M.) Assembly Fellowship Program: 1785
Center for Community Partnerships: 260
CENTER FOR HELLENIC STUDIES: 316
CENTER FOR INTERNATIONAL SECURITY AND COOPERATION
    (CISAC)
    Cybersecurity and International Security Fellowship: 760
    Human-Centered Artificial Intelligence (HAI): 760
    MacArthur Foundation Nuclear Security Fellowship (The): 760
    Natural Sciences or Engineering International Security Fellowship: 760
    Social Sciences or Humanities International Security Fellowship: 760
    Stanford International Observatory Research Fellowship: 760
    Stanton Nuclear Security Fellowship (The): 760
CENTER FOR LGBTQ STUDIES (THE)
    Duberman-Zal Fellowship (The): 895
CENTER FOR PHOTOGRAPHY AT WOODSTOCK (THE)
    Art Administration Interns: 498
    Woodstock A-I-R: 498
CENTER FOR PLANT CONSERVATION
    Beattie (Catherine H.) Fellowship for Conservation Horticulture: 1906
CENTER FOR SCIENCE IN THE PUBLIC INTEREST
    Public Interest Internships: 2413
CENTER FOR 17TH AND 18TH CENTURY STUDIES
    Ahmanson and Getty Postdoctoral Fellowships: 320
    ASECS/Clark Library Fellowships: 319
    Clark Predoctoral Fellowships: 318
    Short-Term Research Fellowships: 317
CENTER FOR THE HUMANITIES
    Mellon (Andrew W.) Postdoctoral Fellowship: 321
CENTER FOR U.S.-MEXICAN STUDIES, UNIVERSITY OF
    CALIFORNIA, SAN DIEGO
    USMEX Visiting Fellows Program: 761
Center Stage: 437
Centers for International Business Education Program: 1719
CENTRAL ASSOCIATION OF OBSTETRICIANS AND
    GYNECOLOGISTS
    Annual Central Prize Award: 2249
    Central Poster Award: 2249

    Community Hospital Award: 2249
    FAR Research Network Award: 2249
    President's Certificate of Merit Award: 2249
    Young Investigator's Award: 2249
CENTRAL INDIANA COMMUNITY FOUNDATION: 1085
CENTRAL MAINE POWER COMPANY
    Central Maine Power Company Corporate Contributions Program: 54
Central Maine Power Company Corporate Contributions Program: 54
CENTRAL NEW YORK COMMUNITY FOUNDATION: 1086
Central Poster Award: 2249
Centre for Studies and Research in International Law and International
    Relations: 1773
CES Small Event Grants: 762
CFF/NIH Unfunded Grants: 2167
CFI Matching Funds: 1316
CFT for Business: 65
CFUW Aboriginal Women's Award (AWA): 974
CFUW Bourse Georgette Lemoyne: 974
CFUW Dr. Alice E. Wilson Awards: 974
CFUW Dr. Margaret McWilliams Pre-Doctoral Fellowship: 974
CFUW Elizabeth and Rachel Massey Award: 974
CFUW Linda Souter Humanities Award: 974
CFUW Memorial Fellowship: 974
CFUW 1989 Ecole Polytechnique Commemorative Awards: 974
CFUW 100th Anniversary Legacy Fellowship: 974
CGP Grant Program - Discretionary Grants: 775
CGP Grant Program - Education Grants: 775
CGP Grant Program - Grassroots Program: 775
CGP Grant Program - Intellectual Exchange: 775
CH FOUNDATION (THE): 1907
Chairman's Citation: 1750
Chall (Jeanne S.) Research Fellowship: 1397
Challenge America: 433
Challenge Grants Program: 336
CHAMBER MUSIC AMERICA
    Chamber Music America Classical Commissioning Program: 696
Chamber Music America Classical Commissioning Program: 696
Chamber Opera Competition: 717
Champion (Bryan A.) Memorial Scholarship: 1510
CHAMPLIN FOUNDATION (THE): 55
Chancellor's Graduate Fellowship Program at Washington University in
    St. Louis (The): 1612
Chang (Stephen S.) Award: 1852
CHAPIN (HARRY) FOUNDATION: 1087
Chapin (Jim) Memorial Teacher Scholarship: 722
Charitable Giving Program: 241
CHARLESTON AREA CHARITABLE FOUNDATION: 1088
Chase (Dr. Randolph) Memorial Scholarship: 2062
Chasman (Renate W.) Scholarship for Women: 973
Chateaubriand Humanities & Social Sciences (HSS) Fellowship Program:
    829
CHATHAM UNIVERSITY
    Chatham University Merit Scholarship Programs (The): 1491
Chatham University Merit Scholarship Programs (The): 1491
CHATLOS FOUNDATION, INC. (THE): 739
Chaudhuri (Nupur) First Article Prize: 534
CHAUTAUQUA REGION COMMUNITY FOUNDATION (THE): 1089
Chauveau (The Pierre) Medal: 1646
CHCI Congressional Internship: 962
CHCI Graduate Fellowship Program: 963
CHCI Public Policy Fellowship: 963
Chellman (David J.) Scholarship: 2420
CHEMICAL INSTITUTE OF CANADA
    Environment Division Early Career Research Award: 1857
Chen (Stanford) Internship Grant: 1482
CHENEY (BEN B.) FOUNDATION: 56
Chenoweth (Carolyn and James M.) Scholarship: 2387
CHEROKEE NATION
    College Resource Center: 952
Chesapeake Bay Fisheries Research Program: 1409
CHESTER COUNTY COMMUNITY FOUNDATION: 1090
Chevron/Diversity Association Scholarship Program: 2395
CHICAGO BOARD OF TRADE FOUNDATION: 1288
CHICAGO COMMUNITY TRUST (THE): 1091
Child Abuse Prevention and Treatment Act (CAPTA) Discretionary
    Grants: 1006
Child and Adult Care Food Program (The): 1041
Child Development and Behavior Branch (CDBB): 1318
Child Health Recognition Awards: 1415
Child Health Research Awards Program: 2283

Child Language Doctoral Program: 1606
Child Welfare Scholarship: 1476
Child Welfare Waiver Demonstration Projects: 1040
Child Well-being Program: 93
Children and Families: 116
Children of Veterans Tuition Grant (CVTG): 1579
CHILDREN'S BUREAU
    Child Abuse Prevention and Treatment Act (CAPTA) Discretionary
    Grants: 1006
CHILDREN'S LEUKEMIA RESEARCH ASSOCIATION
    Children's Leukemia Research Grants: 2282
Children's Leukemia Research Grants: 2282
CHILDREN'S LITERATURE ASSOCIATION
    ChLA Beiter Graduate Student Research Grants: 619
    ChLA Diversity Research Grant: 618
    ChLA Faculty Research Grants: 619
Children's Medical Health Grants: 293
CHILDREN'S TUMOR FOUNDATION
    Clinical Research Awards: 2114
    Drug Discovery Initiative Registered Reports (DDI-RR): 2114
    NF Clinic Network (CTF-NFCN): 2114
    Young Investigator Awards: 2114
Children, Early Care and Education Grants: 1243
Children, Families and Communities: 229
Children, Youth and Families Program: 1253
CHILDS (THE JANE COFFIN) MEMORIAL FUND FOR MEDICAL
    RESEARCH: 2189
Chin (Vincent) Memorial Scholarship: 1483
Chinard (The Gilbert) Prize: 584
CHINESE AMERICAN MEDICAL SOCIETY
    CAMS Scholarship Program: 2024
    Medical Student Summer Research Fellowship: 2024
Chinoy (Helen Krich) Dissertation Research Fellowships: 482
ChLA Beiter Graduate Student Research Grants: 619
ChLA Diversity Research Grant: 618
ChLA Faculty Research Grants: 619
CHOPIN FOUNDATION OF THE U.S.
    Scholarship Program for Young Pianists: 697
Chopin Piano Competition: 708
Chrétien International Research Grant: 1831
CHRISTENSEN FUND (THE)
    Kenya/East Africa: 57
    Mexico/Latin America: 57
Churchill Scholarship: 823
CHURCHILL (WINSTON) FOUNDATION OF THE UNITED STATES
    Churchill Scholarship: 823
CI Construction Engineering Scholarship and Student Prizes: 2386
CIC/Anna Chennault Scholarship: 1483
Cintas Fellowships in the Arts: 395
CINTAS FOUNDATION
    Cintas Fellowships in the Arts: 395
CIRES Visiting Fellowship Program in Environmental Sciences: 1963
CISE Undergraduate Scholarship: 2392
Cities and States Program: 112
CITY OF NEW YORK
    New York City Urban Fellows Program: 1786
Civic Engagement and Government Program: 112
Civic Engagement Fund: 1099
Civic Orchestra Lesson Scholarship Stipends: 698
CIVIC ORCHESTRA OF CHICAGO
    Civic Orchestra Lesson Scholarship Stipends: 698
Civic, Community, and Environment: 228
CLA Scholarship for Minority Students in Memory of Edna Yelland: 663
CLAIBORNE (LIZ) ART ORTENBERG FOUNDATION: 1962
Clark (Evert)/Seth Payne Award for Young Science Journalists: 1731
CLARK FOUNDATION (THE)
    Clark Foundation Scholarship Program: 1492
Clark Foundation Scholarship Program: 1492
Clark (Michele) Fellowship: 1757
Clark Predoctoral Fellowships: 318
CLARK (ROBERT STERLING) FOUNDATION: 1092
Clark (Septima) Book Awards: 1665
Clark (William B.) Fellowship in Clinical Research: 2099
Clarke (Lucy and Charles W.E.) Scholarship: 2387
Classroom and Community Grants: 1385
Classroom Grant: 6
Clay Postdoctoral Fellowship: 1844
CLEVELAND-CLIFFS FOUNDATION (THE): 58
CLEVELAND FOUNDATION (THE): 1093
Cleven (The Nels Andrew) Founder's Paper Prize Awards: 578

Clift (David H.) Scholarship: 1443
Climate Crisis Activism: 1993
Climate Program: 1872, 1964
Climbing Grief Grants: 1957
Clinic and Laboratory Integration Program (CLIP): 2183
Clinical Fellowship Awards: 2167
Clinical Investigations Grant: 2261
Clinical Investigator Career Development Awards (CDA): 2119
Clinical Pilot and Feasibility Awards: 2167
Clinical Research & Epidemiology: 2107
Clinical Research Award: 2230
Clinical Research Awards: 2114, 2167
Clinical Research Grant: 2262
Clinical Research Program: 2273
Clinical Scientist in Nephrology (CSN): 2000
Clinical Student Research Award: 2294
Clinical Technologies Research: 2107
Clinical Traveling Fellowship: 2065
Clinical Trials: 2107
Clinical Trials & Practice-Based Research: 2107
Clinician of the Year Award: 2294
Clinician-Scientist Award: 2261
CMRS Conference Travel Grants: 357
CMRS Dissertation Research Fellowship: 357
CMRS Research and Study Travel Grants: 357
CNIB Barbara Tuck MacPhee Award in Macular Degeneration: 2265
Co-sponsored Events Awards: 482
COASTAL BEND COMMUNITY FOUNDATION: 59
COASTAL COMMUNITY FOUNDATION OF SOUTH CAROLINA
    Regional Grants: 1094
    Specialized Grants: 1094
Coastal Conservation Research Program: 1950
COCA-COLA FOUNDATION, INC. (THE): 1379
COCA-COLA SCHOLARS FOUNDATION
    Coca-Cola Scholars Program: 1493
Coca-Cola Scholars Program: 1493
COCKRELL FOUNDATION (THE): 60
CODMAN (THE OGDEN) TRUST: 61
CODRINGTON (THE GEORGE W.) CHARITABLE FOUNDATION: 62
Cogeco Inc. Graduate Scholarship: 1762
Cogswell (Madeline Pickett) (Halbert) Nursing Scholarship: 2242
Cohee (Melvin H.) Student Leader Conservation Scholarship: 1985
Cohen (The H. Robert)/RIPM Award: 691
Cohen (Morton N.) Award for a Distinguished Edition of Letters: 602
Cohen (Selma Jeanne) Conference Presentation Award: 482
Cohn (The Victor) Prize for Excellence in Medical Science Reporting:
    1731
COIN-OP CARES CHARITABLE AND EDUCATION FOUNDATION
    Hesch (Wayne E.) Memorial Scholarships: 2351
Colaianni (Lois Ann) Award for Excellence and Achievement in Hospital
    Librarianship: 674
Colburn (Anna C. and Oliver C.) Fellowship: 313
Cole (Arthur H.) Grants-in-Aid: 1703
COLEMAN FOUNDATION, INC. (THE): 63
Coleman (John R.) Traveling Fellowship: 310
Colgate-Palmolive Dental Residency or Specialty Program Scholarship:
    2104
Colgate-Palmolive Scholarship for Dental Students and Dental Hygiene
    Students: 2104
Colgate-Palmolive/NMF Dental Leadership Program: 2062
Collaborative Research Grants: 734
Collaborative Sciences Award: 2126
Collection Study Grants: 1619
Collections Assessment for Preservation (CAP): 667
College Access Program (CAP): 1522
College and University Scholarships: 1114
COLLEGE OF PHYSICIANS OF PHILADELPHIA
    Wood Institute Travel Grants: 532
College Resource Center: 952
College Scholarship Fund: 680
College Scholarship Program: 1495
College Scholarships: 267
Collegiate ECHO Marketing Challenge: 1711
Collegiate Inventors Competition: 1639
Collegiate Opera Scenes Competition: 717
Collegiate Summit: 1711
COLLINS FOUNDATION (THE): 64
Colorado Creates: 396

COLORADO CREATIVE INDUSTRIES
Arts in Society: 396
Colorado Creates: 396
Creative Career Advancement Grant: 396
COLUMBIA JOURNALISM SCHOOL
Berger (Mike) Award: 1727
Cabot (Maria Moors) Prizes: 1728
Oakes (John B.) Award: 1726
COLUMBIA UNIVERSITY
Bancroft Prizes: 533
Horwitz (The Louisa Gross) Prize: 1937
Knight-Bagehot Fellowship in Economics and Business Journalism: 1730
Pulitzer Fellowships: 1729
Pulitzer Prizes: 1729
COLUMBUS FOUNDATION (THE)
Fund for Capital Improvements: 1095
Fund for Financial Innovation: 1095
Fund for Innovative Operations: 1095
Fund for Targeted Needs: 1095
COLUMBUS JEWISH FOUNDATION: 1096
Colwell (Robert N.) Memorial Fellowship: 1821
Combined Pilot Research Grants: 2076
COMMON COUNSEL FOUNDATION: 1097
COMMONWEALTH FUND (THE)
Advancing Medicare: 1335
Controlling Health Care Costs: 1335
Federal and State Health Policy: 1335
Health Care Coverage and Access: 1335
Health Care Delivery System Reform: 1335
International Health Policy and Practice Innovations: 1335
Tracking Health System Performance: 1335
Commonwealth of Virginia Nurse Educator Scholarship Program: 2248
Communities for All Ages: 1058
COMMUNITIES FOUNDATION OF TEXAS, INC.
CFT for Business: 65
Community Impact Grants: 65
Donor-Advised Grants: 65
Educate Texas: 65
Communities Program: 167, 191
Community: 22
Community and Business Project Grants: 1706
Community Arts: 116
Community Arts Access: 444
Community Arts Development: 384, 427, 436
Community Based Organizations Grants: 401
Community College Faculty Exchange: 755
Community Conference Grants Program: 1319
Community Connection Employee Volunteer Gift Program: 184
Community Conservation Program: 1992
Community Conversations Program: 329
Community Development: 1157
Community Development Block Grant Program: Entitlement Program: 1262
Community Development Grant: 1084
Community Disaster Relief Fund: 1243
Community Education: 200
Community Enrichment Grant Program: 10
COMMUNITY FOUNDATION FOR A GREATER RICHMOND: 66
Jenkins Foundation: Improving the Health of Greater Richmond (The): 1098
R.E.B. Awards for Teaching Excellence: 1098
Sheltering Arms Fund: 1098
COMMUNITY FOUNDATION FOR GREATER ATLANTA, INC.
A Place to Perform: 1099
An Extra Wish: 1099
Atlanta AIDS Fund: 1099
Civic Engagement Fund: 1099
Metropolitan Atlanta Arts Fund: 1099
Neighborhood Fund: 1099
Newton Fund: 1099
Nonprofit Toolbox: 1099
Strategic Restructuring Fund: 1099
COMMUNITY FOUNDATION FOR GREATER BUFFALO: 1100
COMMUNITY FOUNDATION FOR GREATER NEW HAVEN (THE): 1101
COMMUNITY FOUNDATION FOR MONTEREY COUNTY
Community Impact Grants Program: 1102
Neighborhood Grants Program: 1102
Opportunity Grants: 1102
Organizational Development Grants: 1102

COMMUNITY FOUNDATION FOR NORTHEAST FLORIDA (THE): 1103
COMMUNITY FOUNDATION FOR NORTHEAST GEORGIA: 1104
COMMUNITY FOUNDATION FOR NORTHEAST MICHIGAN: 1105
COMMUNITY FOUNDATION FOR PALM BEACH AND MARTIN COUNTIES: 1106
COMMUNITY FOUNDATION FOR SOUTHEAST MICHIGAN: 67
COMMUNITY FOUNDATION FOR THE GREATER CAPITAL REGION (THE): 1380
Capacity-Building Grant Initiative: 1107
Regular Competitive Grants: 1107
COMMUNITY FOUNDATION OF ABILENE: 1108
COMMUNITY FOUNDATION OF COLLIER COUNTY: 1109
COMMUNITY FOUNDATION OF EASTERN CONNECTICUT
Animal Welfare Grants: 1110
Community Foundation Scholarships: 1110
Environmental Grants: 1110
Northeast Area Women and Girls Fund: 1110
Norwich Area Women and Girls Fund: 1110
Norwich Youth Grants: 1110
Southeast Area Women and Girls Fund: 1110
Southeastern General Grants: 1110
Windham Area Women and Girls Fund: 1110
COMMUNITY FOUNDATION OF FREDERICK COUNTY, MD, INC. (THE): 1111
COMMUNITY FOUNDATION OF GREATER CHATTANOOGA, INC. (THE): 1112, 1113
COMMUNITY FOUNDATION OF GREATER GREENSBORO
College and University Scholarships: 1114
Community Grants Program: 1114
Pre-College Scholarships: 1114
COMMUNITY FOUNDATION OF GREATER MEMPHIS
Nonprofit Capacity Building Grants: 68
Scholarship Funds: 68
COMMUNITY FOUNDATION OF GREATER ROCHESTER: 1115
COMMUNITY FOUNDATION OF HERKIMER & ONEIDA COUNTIES, INC. (THE): 1116
COMMUNITY FOUNDATION OF JACKSON HOLE: 1117
COMMUNITY FOUNDATION OF LORAIN COUNTY (THE): 1118
COMMUNITY FOUNDATION OF LOUISVILLE, INC. (THE): 397
COMMUNITY FOUNDATION OF NORTH CENTRAL WISCONSIN: 1119
COMMUNITY FOUNDATION OF SAINT JOSEPH COUNTY
African American Community Fund: 1120
ArtsEverywhere Fund: 1120
Leighton Award for Nonprofit Excellence: 1120
Senior Living Initiative: 1120
Special Project Challenge Grant: 1120
COMMUNITY FOUNDATION OF SHELBY COUNTY (THE): 1121
COMMUNITY FOUNDATION OF SOUTH ALABAMA (THE): 1122
COMMUNITY FOUNDATION OF THE EASTERN SHORE
Community Needs Grants: 1123
Education Grants Program: 1123
Henson (Richard A.) Award of Excellence: 1123
Mini Grants: 1123
Morris (Frank H.) Humanitarian Award: 1123
Nonprofit Support Program: 1123
Women's Fund Grants: 1123
Workforce Development Grants: 1123
COMMUNITY FOUNDATION OF THE FOX RIVER VALLEY: 1124
COMMUNITY FOUNDATION OF THE HOLLAND/ZEELAND AREA (THE): 69
COMMUNITY FOUNDATION OF THE LOWCOUNTRY, INC.: 1381
COMMUNITY FOUNDATION OF THE NORTH STATE
McConnell Fund (The): 1125
Redding Rancheria Community Fund: 1125
COMMUNITY FOUNDATION OF THE OZARKS: 1126
COMMUNITY FOUNDATION OF THE TEXAS HILL COUNTRY: 1127
COMMUNITY FOUNDATION OF THE VERDUGOS: 1336
COMMUNITY FOUNDATION OF WEST TEXAS
Mini Grant for Teachers Program: 1128
COMMUNITY FOUNDATION OF WESTERN MASSACHUSETTS (CFWM): 1129
COMMUNITY FOUNDATION OF WESTERN NORTH CAROLINA (THE): 70
Community Foundation Scholarships: 1110
COMMUNITY FOUNDATIONS OF THE HUDSON VALLEY
Community Response Grants: 1130
Farm Fresh Food Initiatives: 1130
Fund for Excellence in Education Grants: 1130

Community Fund: 1263
Community Grant Program: 1060
Community Grantmaking: 1057
Community Grants: 97, 1017, 1297
Community Grants Program: 113, 176, 206, 1114, 1219
Community Hospital Award: 2249
Community Impact Awards: 88
Community Impact Grants: 65
Community Impact Grants Program: 1102, 1179
Community Justice Initiative: 191
Community Leadership Awards: 1242
Community Leadership Fund: 920
Community Needs Grants: 1123
Community Organizations Grants/Programs: 455
Community Possible: 1260
Community Response Fund: 996
Community Response Grant: 1182
Community Response Grants: 1130
Community Support Grant Program: 10
Community Support Grants: 479
Community-Wide Affordable Housing Strategy: 1166
COMMUNITYGIVING: 1131
Competition for Orchestral Compositions: 699
Competitive Advantage: 1701
Competitive Grantmaking Program: 104
Competitive Student Research H-31 Predoctoral Grant: 2234
COMPTON FOUNDATION, INC.: 71
Conant (Roger) Grants in Herpetology: 1829
Concerto Competition "Theodor Leschetizky" for Gifted Young Pianists: 710
CONCORDIA UNIVERSITY
    Concordia University Graduate Fellowships: 1494
Concordia University Graduate Fellowships: 1494
Conference and Education Center: 1359
Conference and Workshop Grants: 1818
Conference Awards: 2226
CONFERENCE BOARD OF THE MATHEMATICAL SCIENCES
    NSF-CBMS Regional Conferences in the Mathematical Sciences: 1884
Conference Grants: 1418
Conference Travel Grants: 762
Conferences/Seminars: 413
Congress-Bundestag Youth Exchange (CBX): 793
Congress-Bundestag Youth Exchange for Young Professionals: 825
Congress-Bundestag Youth Exchange Program: 868
CONGRESSIONAL BLACK CAUCUS FOUNDATION, INC.
    CBC Spouses Education Scholarship: 929
    CBC Spouses Performing Arts Scholarship: 930
    CBC Spouses Visual Arts Scholarship: 930
    CBCF Congressional Fellows Program (The): 931
    CBCF Congressional Internship Program (The): 931
Congressional Fellowship Program: 1782
Congressional Fellowships on Women and Public Policy: 995
CONGRESSIONAL HISPANIC CAUCUS INSTITUTE
    CHCI Congressional Internship: 962
    CHCI Graduate Fellowship Program: 963
    CHCI Public Policy Fellowship: 963
Congressional Internships: 958
Congressional Research Grants: 1787
Conklin (Edwin G.) Medal: 1948
CONNECTICUT COMMUNITY FOUNDATION
    Capacity Building Grants: 1132
    Nonprofit Assistance Initiative: 1132
    Program Grants: 1132
    Scholarships: 1132
    Training Programs: 1132
CONNECTICUT HUMANITIES
    Connecticut Humanities Fund: 322
Connecticut Humanities Fund: 322
CONNECTICUT LIBRARY ASSOCIATION
    Proficiency Enhancement Grants (PEG): 665
CONNELLY FOUNDATION (THE): 72
CONSEIL DES ARTS DE MONTREAL
    Programme de tournees: 398
    Programme General: 398
Conservation and Science: 229
Conservation and Scientific Research Fellowships: 675
Conservation Fellowships: 506
Conservation Grant Program: 506
Conservation, Preservation and Restoration (CPR) Grant: 1931
Conserving Ecologically Valuable Land: 202

CONSORTIUM FOR GRADUATE STUDY IN MANAGEMENT (THE)
    Competitive Advantage: 1701
    Fellowships for Under-Represented Minorities in Management: 1701
CONSUMERS ENERGY FOUNDATION
    Caring for Community: 73
    Volunteer Investment Program: 73
Consumption: 1993
CONTEMPORARY MUSIC FESTIVAL
    Competition for Orchestral Compositions: 699
Continuing Education Grants: 680
Contraception Research Branch (CRB): 1318
Controlling Health Care Costs: 1335
COOK FAMILY FOUNDATION: 1133
Cook (Jim) Honorary Scholarship: 2363
COOKE (JACK KENT) FOUNDATION
    College Scholarship Program: 1495
    Undergraduate Transfer Scholarship: 1495
    Young Scholars Program: 1495
Cooke (Mabel and Lawrence S.) Scholarship: 1002
COOKE (V.V.) FOUNDATION: 74
COOLEY'S ANEMIA FOUNDATION, INC.: 2165
Cooper (Alan) Leadership in the Arts Award: 430
COOPER FOUNDATION: 75
Cooperative Clinical Research Grants: 2275
COOPERATIVE DEVELOPMENT FOUNDATION: 1134
COOPERATIVE INSTITUTE FOR RESEARCH IN ENVIRONMENTAL SCIENCES (CIRES)
    CIRES Visiting Fellowship Program in Environmental Sciences: 1963
Cooperative Research Program Grants: 1873
COOPERSTOWN GRADUATE PROGRAM: 666
Coordinated Funding: 1057
COORDINATING COUNCIL FOR WOMEN IN HISTORY, INC. (THE)
    CCWH/Berkshire Conference of Women Historians Graduate Student Fellowship: 534
    Chaudhuri (Nupur) First Article Prize: 534
    Gold (Carol) Best Article Award: 534
    Prelinger (Catherine) Award: 975
    Wells (Ida B.) Graduate Student Fellowship: 534
COORS (ADOLPH) FOUNDATION: 1007
COPLAND (AARON) FUND FOR MUSIC, INC.
    Performance Program: 700
    Recording Program: 700
    Supplemental Program: 700
CORBIN (THE MARY S. AND DAVID C.) FOUNDATION: 76
Core Apprentice Program: 645
Core Writer Program: 645
CORNELL UNIVERSITY
    Mellon Postdoctoral Fellowships: 323
    Society for the Humanities Fellowships: 324
Cornerstone Conservation Grant: 1957
Corporate Achievement Award: 1852
Corporate and Political Accountability: 81
Corporate Contributions Program: 99
Corporate Giving Program: 103
Corporate Scholarship Program: 868
CORPORATION FOR NATIONAL AND COMMUNITY SERVICE (AMERICORPS)
    AmeriCorps VISTA: 1135
CORPORATION OF YADDO (THE)
    Artist Residencies: 399
Corwin (Bert C. and Lydia M.) Contact Lens Residency Award: 2257
Corwin Literacy Leader Award: 1397
Costello (Jeanne Timmins) Fellowships: 2224
COSTUME SOCIETY OF AMERICA
    Blum (Stella) Research Grant: 400
    CSA Travel Research Grant: 400
    Filene (Adele) Student Presenter Grant: 400
Cotsen Traveling Fellowship for Research in Greece: 813
Cottone Postgraduate Scholarship (Medical Only): 1591
Cottrell Scholar Awards: 1827
COUNCIL FOR EUROPEAN STUDIES AT COLUMBIA UNIVERSITY
    Book Award: 762
    CES Small Event Grants: 762
    Conference Travel Grants: 762
    First Article Prize in Humanities and Social Sciences: 762
    Mellon-CES Dissertation Completion Fellowship in European Studies: 762
    SAE-CES Pre-Dissertation Research Fellowships: 762
COUNCIL FOR THE ADVANCEMENT OF SCIENCE WRITING, INC.
    Clark (Evert)/Seth Payne Award for Young Science Journalists: 1731
    Cohn (The Victor) Prize for Excellence in Medical Science Reporting:

1731
  Taylor (Rennie)/Alton Blakeslee Fellowships for Graduate Study in
    Science Writing: 1731
COUNCIL OF AMERICAN OVERSEAS RESEARCH CENTERS
  (CAORC)
  Multi-Country Research Fellowship Program: 824
COUNCIL ON FOREIGN RELATIONS
  International Affairs Fellowship (IAF): 764
  International Affairs Fellowship in Japan (IAF-J): 763
  Murrow (Edward R.) Press Fellowship: 1732
  Stanton Nuclear Security Fellowship Program (SNSF): 765
COUNCIL ON SOCIAL WORK EDUCATION
  Mental Health and Substance Abuse Fellowship Program (The): 896
COUNCIL ON TECHNOLOGY AND ENGINEERING TEACHER
  EDUCATION (CTETE)
  Outstanding Research Award: 1382
COVID-19 Relief Grants: 88
COVID-19 Response: 1166
COVINGTON (MARION STEDMAN) FOUNDATION: 77
COWELL (S.H.) FOUNDATION: 78
Cowen (Walker) Memorial Prize: 652
Cox (The Eugene L.) Fellowship: 991
Cox (Lawrence W. and Francis W.) Scholarship: 2386
Cox (William J.) Memorial Fund Scholarship: 1922
CRA (CIORA) AS New Clinical Investigator Grant: 2201
Craigie (Peter C.) Memorial Scholarship: 1603
CRAIL-JOHNSON FOUNDATION (THE): 1008
Crawford (William A.) Minority Teacher Scholarship: 1512
Creary (Drs. Ludlow & Ruth) Family Foundation Scholarship: 2062
Creation and Presentation: 474
Creation Grants: 466
Creative Aging Grant: 425
Creative California Communities: 394
Creative Career Advancement Grant: 396
Creative City Boston: 437
Creative Communities: 235, 474
Creative Writing Fellowships: 433
Creativity and Free Expression Program: 112
Creativity Grant Program: 427
Criminal and Juvenile Justice Program: 1351
Criminal Justice: 242
Crisis Counseling Assistance and Training Program: 2340
Critical Response Grants: 1348
CROHN'S AND COLITIS FOUNDATION
  Career Development Award: 2166
  Research Fellowship Award: 2166
  Research Initiative: 2166
  Senior Research Award: 2166
  Student Research Fellowship Awards: 2166
Cross-Disciplinary Fellowships: 1938
CROSSROADS FUND: 1657
CROWELL (HENRY P. AND SUSAN C.) TRUST: 79
CSA Travel Research Grant: 400
CSChE Chemical Engineering Local Section Scholarships (The): 2390
CULLEN FOUNDATION (THE): 80
CULLEN TRUST FOR HEALTH CARE (THE): 1289
Cultivating Healthy Communities: 5
Cultural Anthropology Program: 1812
Cultural Conservation: 438
Cultural Economic Development: 1057
Cultural Facilities Grant: 409
Cultural Facilities Grants: 466
Cultural Facilities Program: 405
Cultural Pathways: 394
Cultural Planning Grant: 425
CULTURAL VISTAS
  Alfa Fellowship Program: 766
  Congress-Bundestag Youth Exchange for Young Professionals: 825
Cummings (J. Pat) Scholarships: 2255
CUMMINGS (THE NATHAN) FOUNDATION, INC.
  Corporate and Political Accountability: 81
  Inclusive Clean Economy: 81
  Racial and Economic Justice: 81
  Voice, Creativity and Culture: 81
CUMMINS FOUNDATION, INC. (THE): 82
Cunningham Memorial International Fellowship: 875
Curatorial Grant Program: 403
CUREPSP, INC.: 2208
Curtis (Dr. James) Scholarship: 2062

CURTIS INSTITUTE OF MUSIC
  Bachelor of Music: 701
  Diploma: 701
  Master of Music: 701
  Post-Baccalaureate Diploma: 701
  Professional Studies Certificate: 701
CUSHWA CENTER FOR THE STUDY OF AMERICAN
  CATHOLICISM
  D'Agostino (Peter R.) Research Travel Grant: 537
  Davis (The Cyprian), O.S.B., Prize: 539
  Guerin (Mother Theodore) Research Travel Grant: 538
  Hibernian Research Award: 535
  Research Travel Grants: 536
Cutting Edge Grant: 1957
Cutting Edge Grants: 1186
Cybersecurity and International Security Fellowship: 760
CYPRUS AMERICAN ARCHAEOLOGICAL RESEARCH INSTITUTE
  CAARI/CAORC Research Fellowships: 827
  O'Donovan (The Anita Cecil) Fellowship: 826
  Parks (The Danielle) Memorial Fellowship: 826
  Peltenburg (Edgar J.) Postdoctoral Research Fellowship in Cypriot
    Prehistory: 827
  Swiny (The Helena Wylde) and Stuart Swiny Fellowship: 826
CYSTIC FIBROSIS FOUNDATION
  CFF/NIH Unfunded Grants: 2167
  Clinical Fellowship Awards: 2167
  Clinical Pilot and Feasibility Awards: 2167
  Clinical Research Awards: 2167
  Matthews (Leroy) Physician/Scientist Award: 2167
  Pilot and Feasibility Awards: 2167
  Postdoc-to-Faculty Transition Awards: 2167
  Postdoctoral Research Fellowship Award: 2167
  Research Grants: 2167
  Shwachman (Harry) Clinical Investigator Award: 2167
Czaplewski Fellowship Award: 1350

D

D'Agostino (Peter R.) Research Travel Grant: 537
DAAD Emigre Memorial German Internship Program
  (EMGIP-Bundestag): 830
DAAD German Studies Research Grant: 830
DAAD Research Grant: 830
DAAD Research Internships in Science and Engineering (RISE): 830
DAAD Research Stays for University Academics and Scientists: 830
DAAD RISE Professional: 830
DAAD Study Scholarship: 830
DAAD University Summer Course Grant: 830
DAAD Visiting Professorship: 830
Dafoe Book Prize: 767
DAFOE (J.W.) FOUNDATION
  Dafoe Book Prize: 767
  Dafoe (John W.) Graduate Fellowship: 767
Dafoe (John W.) Graduate Fellowship: 767
DALLAS FOUNDATION (THE): 1136
DALLAS MUSEUM OF ART
  DeGolyer (Clare Hart) Memorial Fund: 499
  Dozier (Otis and Velma Davis) Travel Grant: 501
  Kimbrough (Arch and Anne Giles) Fund: 500
Dalsemer Research Grant: 2134
Dames (Joan Foster) Women's Journalism Scholarship: 1567
Dames (Trent R.) and William W. Moore Fellowship: 2386
DANA FOUNDATION (THE): 2025
DANIELS FUND
  Daniels Fund Ethics Initiative: 83
  Daniels Fund Grants Program: 83
  Daniels Fund Scholarship Program: 83
Daniels Fund Ethics Initiative: 83
Daniels Fund Grants Program: 83
Daniels Fund Scholarship Program: 83
Daniels (Mitch) Early Graduation Scholarship: 1512
Dannels (Robert A.) Memorial Scholarship: 2382
DAR Centennial Scholarship: 376
Darbaker (Leasure K.) Prize in Botany: 1990
Darcovich (The Helen) Memorial Doctoral Fellowship: 531
DARLING (HUGH AND HAZEL) FOUNDATION: 1448
Darling (Louise) Medal for Distinguished Achievement in Collection
  Development in the Health Sciences: 674
DARRIN (MARGARET A.) CHARITABLE TRUST: 84

DARTMOUTH COLLEGE
  Eastman/Marshall Dissertation Fellowships: 897
Data Science, Computational Biology & Bioinformatics: 2107
DAUGHTERS OF PENELOPE FOUNDATION, INC.
  Alexander (Paula J.) Memorial Scholarship (Undergraduate): 976
  Beldecos (Helen J.), Past Grand President, Scholarship (Undergraduate): 976
  Big Five Graduate Scholarship (The): 976
  Daughters of Penelope National Scholarship Awards: 898
  Daughters of Penelope Past Grand Presidents Memorial Scholarship (Undergraduate): 976
  Daughters of Penelope Past Grand Presidents Undergraduate Scholarship: 976
  Daughters of Penelope - St. Basil's Academy: 976
  Eos #1 Mother Lodge Chapter Scholarship (Undergraduate): 976
  Hologgitas (Joanne V.), Ph.D., Past Grand President, Scholarship (Undergraduate): 976
  Hopewell Agave Chapter #224 Scholarship (Undergraduate): 976
  Kandaras (Mary) Memorial Scholarship (Undergraduate): 976
  Kottis Family Scholarship (Undergraduate): 976
  Payne (Clara R.) Memorial Scholarship: 976
  Quincey (Dorothy Lillian) Memorial Graduate Scholarship: 976
  Sonenfeld (Alexandra Apostolides) Memorial Undergraduate Scholarship: 976
  Stefanadis (Sonja B.) Graduate Student Scholarship: 976
  Thorndyke (Barbara Edith Quincey) Memorial Undergraduate Scholarship: 976
  Verges (Mary M.), Past Grand President, Scholarship (Undergraduate): 976
  Zervoulias (The Sotiri) & Lea Soupata Scholarship (St. Basil's Academy): 976
Daughters of Penelope National Scholarship Awards: 898
Daughters of Penelope Past Grand Presidents Memorial Scholarship (Undergraduate): 976
Daughters of Penelope Past Grand Presidents Undergraduate Scholarship: 976
Daughters of Penelope - St. Basil's Academy: 976
DAUGHTERS OF THE CINCINNATI
  Daughters of the Cincinnati Scholarship Program: 1496
Daughters of the Cincinnati Scholarship Program: 1496
Davidson Fellows: 1497
DAVIDSON INSTITUTE
  Davidson Fellows: 1497
Davies (William H.) Medical Research Scholarships: 1596
Davini (William C.) Scholarship: 1591
DAVIS (THE ARTHUR VINING) FOUNDATIONS: 85
Davis (The Cyprian), O.S.B., Prize: 539
DAVIS (IRENE E. AND GEORGE A.) FOUNDATION: 1137
Davis (Johnny) Memorial Scholarship: 2363
DAVIS (THE LADY) FELLOWSHIP TRUST
  Postdoctoral Researchers Fellowship: 828
  Visiting Professorships Fellowship: 828
Davis (Natalie Zemon) Graduate Student Award: 584
DAVIS (SHELBY CULLOM) CENTER FOR HISTORICAL STUDIES: 540
Davis (Watson) and Helen Miles Davis Prize: 548
Dawson (Dr. Martha A.) Genesis Nurse Leader Scholarship: 2240
Dawson (The Sir John William) Medal: 1646
de Nora (Vittorio) Award: 1627
de Vries (Bert and Sally) Fellowship: 796
DEARBORN COMMUNITY FOUNDATION, INC.: 1138
debra International Research Grants: 2095
DECA INC.: 1702
Decommissioning and Environmental Sciences (DESD) Undergraduate Scholarship: 2379
DEED Interships: 2384
Deep Green Buildings: 1961
DeGolyer (Clare Hart) Memorial Fund: 499
Deland Fellowship Program in Health Care and Society: 1283
DELAWARE COUNTY FOUNDATION
  Designated Funds: 1139
  Donor Advised Funds: 1139
  Field of Interest Funds: 1139
  Organizational Endowment Funds: 1139
  Scholarship Funds: 1139
  Special Project Funds: 1139
  Unrestricted Funds: 1139
DELAWARE DIVISION OF THE ARTS
  Arts in Education: 401
  Arts Organizations Grants: 401
  Community Based Organizations Grants: 401
  Gallery Program: 401
  Individual Artist Fellowships: 401
  Opportunity Grants: 401
Delayed Education for Women Scholarship: 2378
DELL (CHIEF JUSTICE ROGER L.) AND AGNES C. DELL CHARITABLE TRUST: 1140
DELL (MICHAEL AND SUSAN) FOUNDATION: 1009
  Dell Scholars Program: 1498
Dell Scholars Program: 1498
DELMAS (GLADYS KRIEBLE) FOUNDATION
  Humanities Program: 325
  Performing Arts Program: 325
  Research Library Program: 325
  Venetian Research Program: 325
DELOITTE FOUNDATION: 1449
DELUXE CORPORATION FOUNDATION: 86
Democracy Program: 191
Dent (Albert W.) Graduate Student Scholarship: 1291
Dental Health: 1019
Dental Materials & Biomaterials: 2107
Department of Defense National Defense Science and Engineering Graduate Fellowship Program (NDSEG): 2405
DEPARTMENT OF ECONOMIC AND COMMUNITY DEVELOPMENT/CONNECTICUT OFFICE OF THE ARTS: 402
DEPARTMENT OF VETERANS AFFAIRS
  VA Psychology Training Program: 2325
Departmental Grants: 1861
DEPAUW UNIVERSITY INTERNATIONAL BONNER SCHOLARSHIP
  Bonner Scholarship: 1141
Dependent Children Scholarship Program: 1583
DERMATOLOGY FOUNDATION: 2026
Designated Funds: 1139
Developmental Biology & Genetics: 2107
Developmental Biology and Structural Variation Branch (DBSVB): 1318
Developmental Biology-SDB Lifetime Achievement Award: 1948
Dever (William G.) Fellowship for Biblical Scholars: 818
DIABETES CANADA
  Best (Charles H.) Research Fund: 2168
DiCarlo (Louis M.) Award for Recent Clinical Achievement: 2262
DICKINSON AREA COMMUNITY FOUNDATION: 1142
DIETITIANS OF CANADA (DC)
  Graduate Student Awards: 2414
  Undergraduate Student Awards: 2414
Dietrich (Joseph R.) Memorial Scholarship: 2381
Digital Art History Grant Program: 506
DiMattio Celli Undergraduate Study Abroad Program: 1591
Dingman (The Archibald Waynne) Memorial Graduate Scholarship: 1595
Diploma: 701
Direct Grants Program: 1238
Direct Operating Grants: 1339
Direct Service: 1223
Directorate for Engineering Grants Program: 2396
Directory of Teaching Artists: 415
DIRKSEN CONGRESSIONAL CENTER (THE)
  Congressional Research Grants: 1787
Dirksen (Everett McKinley) Award for Distinguished Reporting of Congress: 1750
Disability Grants: 1514
DiSalvo (Raymond) Memorial Scholarship: 2380
Disaster Relief Program: 1179
Discover New Jersey History License Plate Fund for Heritage Tourism: 566
Discovery Grants: 2204
Discovery Grants Program: 1955
Discovery Research Grant Program: 2216
Discovery Research Pilot Grant: 2216
Discovery Research PreK-12 (DR K12): 1436
Discretionary Grant Programs: 1040
Discretionary Grants: 154
Discussion Grants: 332
Disease Focus Area Grants for Senior Investigators: 2119
Dissertation Fellowships: 362
Dissertation Year Fellowships: 588, 1809
Distinguished Investigator Innovation Grants: 1366
Distinguished Scholar Award: 482
Distinguished Scientist Award: 2317
DISTRICT OF COLUMBIA COMMISSION ON THE ARTS AND HUMANITIES
  Art Bank Program: 403
  Arts and Humanities Education Projects: 403

Arts and Humanities Fellowship Program: 403
Curatorial Grant Program: 403
East of the River Program: 403
Facilities and Buildings: 403
General Operating Support: 403
LiftOff: 403
Projects, Events and Festivals: 403
Public Art Building Communities: 403
Sister Cities Grant: 403
UPSTART Program: 403
District of Columbia Nursing Scholarship: 2242
Diversity Scholarships: 1514
Division of Arts Programs: 458
Division of Communications, Information & Technology: 458
Division of Environmental Biology: 1947
Division of Molecular and Cellular Biosciences Programs: 1946
DIXON FOUNDATION (THE): 1143
DJ & T FOUNDATION: 1894
Dobie Paisano Fellowship Program (The): 463
Doctor (John) Best Education Award: 1948
Doctoral and Postdoctoral Fellowships: 542
Doctoral Awards: 1675
Doctoral Minority Fellowship: 1543
Doctoral Program in Chemistry: 1858
Doctoral Scholarships in International Law: 1775
DODGE (THE CLEVELAND H.) FOUNDATION, INC.: 1010
DODGE (GERALDINE R.) FOUNDATION: 87
Doe (Janet) Lectureship: 674
Dollars for Doers Fund: 49
Dollars for Doers Grants: 88
Dollars for Doers Program: 176
Dollars for Doers Volunteer Program: 1076
Dollars 4 Schools: 920
Domestic Biodiversity: 1993
Domestic Fellow-In-Training Travel Scholarship: 2094
Domestic Public Policy Program: 1672
DOMINION ENERGY CHARITABLE FOUNDATION
    ArtStars Awards: 88
    Community Impact Awards: 88
    COVID-19 Relief Grants: 88
    Dollars for Doers Grants: 88
    Environmental Education and Stewardship Grants: 88
    Solar for Students Program: 88
DONNELLEY (GAYLORD AND DOROTHY) FOUNDATION: 89
DONNER CANADIAN FOUNDATION: 1788
Donor Advised Funds: 1139
Donor-Advised Grants: 65
Donor Funded Scholarships: 1514
Dorroh (Marion) Memorial Scholarship: 680
DOUGLASS (FREDERICK) INSTITUTE FOR AFRICAN AND
    AFRICAN-AMERICAN STUDIES
    FDI Postdoctoral Fellowship: 1383
DOUTY FOUNDATION (THE): 90
DOW JONES FOUNDATION: 91
DOW JONES NEWS FUND (THE)
    Multimedia Training Academies: 1733
    Summer High School Journalism Workshops: 1733
    Summer Journalism Intern Programs: 1733
Dozier (Otis and Velma Davis) Travel Grant: 501
Drawn to Art Fellowship (The): 304
Drewes (Tom and Roberta) Scholarship: 1443
DREXEL UNIVERSITY COLLEGE OF MEDICINE
    Gloeckner (M. Louise), M.D., Summer Research Fellowship: 977
DREYFUS (THE JEAN AND LOUIS) FOUNDATION, INC.: 1144
Driscoll (Alfred E.) Dissertation Prize: 569
DROWN (JOSEPH) FOUNDATION: 92
Drug Development: 1995
Drug Discovery Initiative Registered Reports (DDI-RR): 2114
du Pont (Henry Belin) Dissertation Fellowship in Business, Technology,
    and Society: 543
du Pont (Henry Belin) Research Grants: 543
Dual Enrollment: 1579
Duberman-Zal Fellowship (The): 895
DUKE (DORIS) CHARITABLE FOUNDATION
    Arts Program: 93
    Child Well-being Program: 93
    Environment Program: 93
    Medical Research Program: 93
DUKE ENDOWMENT (THE): 94
Duling (John) Grant: 1925

Dulis (Edward J.) Scholarship: 2420
DULUTH SUPERIOR AREA COMMUNITY FOUNDATION: 1145
DUMBARTON OAKS
    Fellowships and Project Grants in Byzantine Studies, Pre-Columbian
        Studies and Garden and Landscape Studies: 326
Duncan Aviation Scholarship: 2363
DUNCAN (THE JOHN G.) TRUST: 1146
Dunlap (Joseph R.) Memorial Fellowship: 432
Dunning (The John H.) Prize in United States History: 526
DUNSPAUGH DALTON FOUNDATION: 95
DUPONT (JESSIE BALL) FUND: 96
Duquesne University Graduate Assistantship: 327
DUQUESNE UNIVERSITY, DEPARTMENT OF PHILOSOPHY
    Duquesne University Graduate Assistantship: 327
Dynamic Language Infrastructure-Doctoral Dissertation Research
    Improvement Grants (DLI-DDRI): 604
DYSAUTONOMIA FOUNDATION, INC.
    Dysautonomia Research Program: 2209
Dysautonomia Research Program: 2209
DYSTONIA MEDICAL RESEARCH FOUNDATION
    Research Grants: 2210
DYSTROPHIC EPIDERMOLYSIS BULLOSA RESEARCH
    ASSOCIATION OF AMERICA, INC. (DEBRA)
    debra International Research Grants: 2095

E

Earhart (Amelia) Fellowship: 1846
EARLY AMERICAN INDUSTRIES ASSOCIATION, INC.
    Research Grants Program: 2352
Early-Career Artist Project Grant: 406
Early-Career Artist Research and Development Grant: 406
Early Career Research Awards: 1767
Early Career Research Grants: 1938
Early-Career Scientific Research Grants Program: 2142
Early Childhood Development: 1363
Early Childhood Development Program (The): 1024
Early Investigator Grant Program: 2273
Early Music Award: 691
Early Postdoctoral Research Fellowship Program in Biomedical Sciences:
    1653
EARN Indiana (State Work Study): 1512
Earthwatch Educator Program: 1626
Earthwatch Funding for Field Research: 1625
EARTHWATCH INSTITUTE
    Earthwatch Educator Program: 1626
    Earthwatch Funding for Field Research: 1625
    Earthwatch Teach Earth USA Program: 1626
Earthwatch Teach Earth USA Program: 1626
EAST BAY COMMUNITY FOUNDATION (THE): 1147
East of the River Program: 403
EAST TENNESSEE FOUNDATION: 1011
EAST TEXAS COMMUNITIES FOUNDATION: 1148
EAST-WEST CENTER (THE)
    Asia Pacific Leadership Program: 769
    East-West Center Graduate Degree Fellowship: 768
East-West Center Graduate Degree Fellowship: 768
EASTERN BANK CHARITABLE FOUNDATION
    Community Grants: 97
Eastman School of Music Graduate Awards: 702
EASTMAN SCHOOL OF MUSIC OF THE UNIVERSITY OF
    ROCHESTER
    Eastman School of Music Graduate Awards: 702
Eastman/Marshall Dissertation Fellowships: 897
EATON CHARITABLE FUND: 98
Eaton (Richard) Foundation Award: 1724
EAU CLAIRE COMMUNITY FOUNDATION: 1149
EBAA Pilot Research Grant: 2266
EBELL OF LOS ANGELES (THE)
    Ebell/Flint Scholarship: 1499
Ebell/Flint Scholarship: 1499
ECF Fellowship Partners Program: 740
ECOLAB FOUNDATION: 1150
Economic Development Grant: 1084
ECONOMIC HISTORY ASSOCIATION
    Cole (Arthur H.) Grants-in-Aid: 1703
Economic Justice: 983
Economic Justice for Women: 250
ECS Summer Fellowships: 1628

EDISON INTERNATIONAL
Corporate Contributions Program: 99
Edison Scholars Program: 99
Employee Matching Gifts Program: 99
Volunteer Program: 99
Edison Scholars Program: 99
EDSA Minority Scholarship: 1974
Educate Texas: 65
Education: 137, 228, 1019, 1035, 1079, 1157, 1229, 1346
Education and Leadership: 1212
Education and Youth Development: 22
Education Grants Program: 1123
Education Opportunity Fellowship: 907
Education Program: 191
Education Research: 1422
Education Scholar Grant: 2081
Educational and Scholastic Advancement Programs: 1716
Educational Environments: 754
EDUCATIONAL FOUNDATION FOR WOMEN IN ACCOUNTING
(THE)
Laurels Fund: 1704
McDonald (Michelle L.) Scholarship: 1704
Moss Adams LLP Scholarship: 1704
O'Leary (Rhonda J.) Scholarship: 1704
Women in Need Scholarship: 1704
Women in Transition Scholarship: 1704
Educational Grant Program: 601
Educational Loans and Grants Program: 1519
Educational Outreach Program: 2308
Educational Programme Grants: 375
Educational Scholarship: 2384
EDUCATIONAL TESTING SERVICE
Summer Internship Program for Graduate Students: 1384
Edwards (Dr. Darrell L.) Scholarship: 2062
Edwards (Everett E.) Awards in Agricultural History: 524
Edwards (Lynne) Research Scholarship: 2240
Effective Access to Student Education (EASE): 1501
Eger (Elmer H.) Memorial Student Travel Fellowship: 2258
Eight and Forty Lung and Respiratory Disease Nursing Scholarship Fund:
2245
Einstein (The Alfred) Award: 691
Eisenhower (Dwight David) Transportation Fellowship Program: 2353
EISENHOWER FOUNDATION (THE)
Travel Grants: 1789
EISENHOWER INSTITUTE AT GETTYSBURG COLLEGE (THE)
Eisenhower Institute Scholarship Programs: 770
Eisenhower Institute Scholarship Programs: 770
EISNER FOUNDATION (THE): 1012
EL PASO COMMUNITY FOUNDATION: 1151
El Pomar Fellowship: 100
EL POMAR FOUNDATION
American Council of Young Political Leaders: 100
Awards for Excellence: 100
El Pomar Fellowship: 100
El Pomar Internship: 100
Emerging Leaders Development: 100
Empty Stocking Fund: 100
Forum for Civic Advancement: 100
Grants Program: 100
Military Affairs: 100
Nonprofit Executive Leadership Program: 100
Penrose House Conference Center: 100
Pikes Peak Heritage Series: 100
Regional Partnerships: 100
El Pomar Internship: 100
ELECTROCHEMICAL SOCIETY (THE)
Acheson (Edward Goodrich) Award: 1627
Bard (Allen J.) Award: 1627
de Nora (Vittorio) Award: 1627
ECS Summer Fellowships: 1628
Linford (Henry B.) Award for Distinguished Teaching: 1627
Moore (Gordon E.) Medal for Outstanding Achievement in Solid State
Science and Technology: 1627
Olin Palladium Award: 1627
Tobias (Charles W.) Young Investigator Award: 1627
Wagner (Carl) Memorial Award: 1627
Elevate Grant: 6
Elevate Youth California: 1334
Eliot (Ida and George) Prize: 674
Elliott (Van Courtlandt) Prize: 559

ELLIS (ALBERT) INSTITUTE
Postgraduate Clinical Fellowship Training Program at the Albert Ellis
Institute: 2326
Ellis (John Tracy) Dissertation Award: 738
Elmore (Stanley) Fellowship Fund: 2421
EMBASSY OF FRANCE IN THE U.S., SCAC
Chateaubriand Humanities & Social Sciences (HSS) Fellowship
Program: 829
France on Campus Award: 829
Teaching Assistant Program in France: 829
Transatlantic Mobility Program: 829
Emergency Conservation Program (ECP): 1988
Emergency Financial Assistance Grants: 38
Emergency Fund: 1153
Emergency Grant Program: 504
Emergency Grants: 1212
Emergency Loans: 567
EMERGENCY MEDICINE FOUNDATION
Emergency Medicine Research: 2027
Emergency Medicine Research: 2027
Emerging Artist Award: 420
Emerging Leaders Development: 100
Emerging Research Grants (ERG): 2271
EMERSON (FRED L.) FOUNDATION, INC.: 1152
Emmons (Richard H.) Award: 1838
Empire State Medical Association Scholarship Award: 2062
Employee Giving and Volunteer Programs: 207
Employee Matching Gifts Program: 99
emPOWER: 1343
Empty Stocking Fund: 100
endMS Doctoral Studentship Award: 2215
endMS Master's Studentship Award: 2215
endMS Postdoctoral Fellowship: 2217
Endowment Challenge Fund: 1165
Endowment Funds of Southwest Iowa: 223
Enduring Commitments: 187
Energy and Mineral Development Program (EMDP) Grant: 948
Energy Fellowship Program: 1823
ENERGY FOUNDATION (THE)
Buildings Program: 1964
Climate Program: 1964
Energy Foundation China: 1964
Power Program: 1964
Public Engagement Program: 1964
Transportation Program: 1964
Energy Foundation China: 1964
Energy Program: 1973
Energy, Climate and Materials: 1961
Eng (Dinah) Leadership Fellowship: 1484
Engineering Undergraduate Award: 1478
ENGLAND (LOIS AND RICHARD) FAMILY FOUNDATION: 1013
Engle (The Corliss Knapp) Scholarship in Horticulture: 1914
Eno (Irene Winifred) Grant: 367
ENTERPRISE COMMUNITY PARTNERS
Enterprise Rose Fellowship: 371
Enterprise Rose Fellowship: 371
Entry Track: 415
Environment: 116, 137, 250
Environment Division Early Career Research Award: 1857
Environment Program: 93
Environment Program Grant: 154
Environmental and Natural Resources Management Program: 147
Environmental Education and Stewardship Grants: 88
Environmental Education Fund: 1982
Environmental Education Internship: 1950
Environmental Grant Program: 1980
Environmental Grants: 1110
Environmental Health Sciences Research and Training Grants: 1976
ENVIRONMENTAL LAW INSTITUTE: 1771
Environmental Regulatory Enhancement: 957
Envision Fund: 920
Eos #1 Mother Lodge Chapter Scholarship (Undergraduate): 976
EPILEPSY FOUNDATION OF AMERICA
AES/EF Clinical Research and Training Fellowship Award: 2211
AES/EF Junior Investigator Research Award: 2211
Cannabinoids and Epilepsy: 2211
My Seizure Gauge: 2211
New Therapy Commercialization Grants: 2211
Shark Tank Awards: 2211
SUDEP Biomarker Challenge: 2211

EPISCOPAL CHURCH FOUNDATION
    ECF Fellowship Partners Program: 740
Equality Fund for LGBTQIA: 223
ERION FOUNDATION: 101
ERNST & YOUNG FOUNDATION: 1705
Escue (Walter H.) Memorial Scholarship: 683
Esperanza Grants: 967
ESSEX COUNTY COMMUNITY FOUNDATION
    Emergency Fund: 1153
    Essex County Land and Environment Initiative: 1153
    First Jobs Fund: 1153
    Fund for Excellence in Essex County: 1153
    Greater Lawrence Community Fund: 1153
    Greater Lawrence Summer Fund: 1153
    Greater Newburyport Fund for the Blind: 1153
    Institute for Trustees: 1153
    Merrimack Valley Municipal Business Development and Recovery
        Fund: 1153
    North Shore Community Health Network: 1153
    Webster (Dee & King) Memorial Fund for Greater Lawrence: 1153
    Women's Fund of Essex County (The): 1153
Essex County Land and Environment Initiative: 1153
Established Investigator Award: 2132
Ethnic Studies Fellowships: 925
Everest (D.C.) Fellowship: 593
EVERSOURCE ENERGY FOUNDATION: 102
Excellence Fellowships for Nursing, Physical Therapy and Social Work:
    2051
Excellence in Institutional Writing Awards: 1747
Excellence in Medicine Awards: 1477
Executive Fellowship Program: 1785
EXELON CORPORATION
    Corporate Giving Program: 103
Exemplary Research in Social Studies: 1665
Exhibitions: 413
Exhibitions Abroad Support Program: 775
Expanding Opportunities for Participation in the Arts: 468
Exploring Program: 1403
External Faculty Fellowships: 354
External Programme: 1774
Extra Innings Fellowship Program (EIF): 918
EYE BANK ASSOCIATION OF AMERICA
    EBAA Pilot Research Grant: 2266
    High Impact Research Grant: 2266
Ezell (William C.) Fellowship: 2260

F

FACES Grant: 407
Facilities and Buildings: 403
Faculty Grant Program: 2273
Faculty of Law Graduate Scholarship: 1605
Faculty Practices and Vocation: 754
FAER Mentored Research Training Grant: 2028
FAER Research Fellowship Grant: 2028
FAER Research in Education Grant: 2028
FAER Transition to Independence Grant: 2028
Fahn (Stanley) Faculty Scholar Award: 2227
Fairbank (The John K.) Prize in East Asian History: 526
FAIRFIELD COUNTY'S COMMUNITY FOUNDATION
    Competitive Grantmaking Program: 104
Fall/Spring/Summer Study Abroad: 521
Fanning (William M.) Maintenance Scholarship: 2368
FAR Research Network Award: 2249
Fargher (John S.W.) Scholarship: 2392
FARGO-MOORHEAD AREA FOUNDATION: 105
FARM AID: 1908
Farm and Local Food Program: 1253
Farm Fresh Food Initiatives: 1130
Farm Kids for College Scholarships: 1920
Farny (Sylvia W.) Scholarship: 2387
Farrar (Marjorie M. and Lancelot L.) Memorial Awards: 584
FATS AND PROTEINS RESEARCH FOUNDATION, INC.: 1629
FCS Scholarship Fund: 1387
FDI Postdoctoral Fellowship: 1383
Feddie Reporting Award (The): 1750
Federal and State Health Policy: 1335
FEDERAL HIGHWAY ADMINISTRATION
    Eisenhower (Dwight David) Transportation Fellowship Program: 2353

Federal Supplemental Educational Opportunity Grant (FSEOG): 1588
Federal Work-Study: 1587
FEDERATION OF AMERICAN CONSUMERS AND TRAVELERS
    Classroom and Community Grants: 1385
    Community and Business Project Grants: 1706
    Scholarship Program: 1385
Federico II Scholarship: 550
FEEA SCHOLARSHIP PROGRAM: 1500
Feis (The Herbert) Award: 526
Felix (Robert) Memorial Scholarship: 1925
Fellow Scholar Award: 2006
Fellow to Faculty Scholar Award: 2006
Fellowship and Scholarship Program for Writers: 615
Fellowship Grant: 2261
Fellowship in Aerospace History: 528
Fellowship in American Jewish Studies: 594
Fellowship in Baltic Jewish Studies: 596
Fellowship in East European Arts, Music, and Theater: 595
Fellowship in East European Jewish Literature: 595
Fellowship in East European Jewish Studies: 596
Fellowship in Polish Jewish Studies: 596
Fellowship in the Digital Humanities: 862
Fellowship Program: 843
Fellowship Program at the Woodrow Wilson International Center for
    Scholars: 361
Fellowship Program for Journalists: 1754
Fellowship Research Grants: 2036
Fellowships: 337, 415, 451
Fellowships and Project Grants in Byzantine Studies, Pre-Columbian
    Studies and Garden and Landscape Studies: 326
Fellowships at the Albright Institute of Archaeological Research in
    Jerusalem: 794
Fellowships for American Indians or Alaskan Natives: 941
Fellowships for Research in Egypt: 804
Fellowships for Under-Represented Minorities in Management: 1701
FELS (SAMUEL S.) FUND
    Arts and Culture: 1154
    Focused Populations: 1154
    Social, Racial and Economic Justice: 1154
FENIMORE ART MUSEUM
    Fox (The Dixon Ryan) Manuscript Prize of the Fenimore Art Museum:
        541
    Moe (Henry Allen) Prize: 404
Fertility and Infertility (FI) Branch: 1318
Feynman (Richard P.) Postdoctoral Fellowship in Theory and Computing:
    1635
FfWG Crosby Hall Fellowship: 978
Field Aviation Company Scholarship: 2363
Field (Benjamin J.), D.O., FACOEP Medical Education Grant: 2277
FIELD FOUNDATION OF ILLINOIS: 106
Field Grants: 1211
Field of Interest Funds: 1139
Field Support: 187
Fielding (Carole) Student Grants: 1761
Figg (Eugene C., Jr.) Civil Engineering Scholarship: 2386
Fight for Sight Postdoctoral Award: 2268
FIGHT FOR SIGHT, INC.
    Fight for Sight Postdoctoral Award: 2268
    Research Awards Program: 2267
Filene (Adele) Student Presenter Grant: 400
Filmmaking (MFA): 509
Financial Aid for Study at The Graduate Institute of International and
    Development Studies: 771
Financial Grants of Support: 1163
FINE ARTS WORK CENTER IN PROVINCETOWN
    Visual Arts Fellowship: 502
    Writing Fellowship: 502
Finzi (Gina M.) Memorial Student Summer Fellowship Program: 2045
Fire Research Grants Program: 1825
FIRMAN FUND: 107
First Article Prize in Humanities and Social Sciences: 762
FIRST COMMUNITY FOUNDATION PARTNERSHIP OF
    PENNSYLVANIA: 108
First Generation Matching Grant Program (FGMG): 1501
First Jobs Fund: 1153
FIRST NATIONS DEVELOPMENT INSTITUTE: 953
FIRSTENERGY FOUNDATION: 109
    STEM Grants Program: 1430
Fischer (William A.) Memorial Scholarship: 1821
FISHAMERICA FOUNDATION
    Fisheries Conservation and Research Projects: 1965

Fishbein (Morris) Fellowship in Medical Editing: 1739
FISHER (AVERY) ARTIST PROGRAM
    Fisher (The Avery) Career Grants: 703
    Fisher (The Avery) Prize: 703
Fisher (The Avery) Career Grants: 703
Fisher (The Avery) Prize: 703
Fisher (Professor Elizabeth F.) Fellowship: 991
Fisheries Conservation and Research Projects: 1965
FITCH (THE JAMES MARSTON) CHARITABLE FOUNDATION
    Blinder (Richard L.) Award: 372
    Mid-Career Fellowship: 372
Fite (Gilbert C.) Dissertation Award: 524
Flavelle Medal (The): 1646
Fleming (Charlie) Scholarship: 913
Fleming (Patricia) Visiting Fellowship in Bibliography and Book History: 685
FLETCHER (A.J.) FOUNDATION: 110
Flexcon Industries Scholarship: 2344
Flexit: 355
Flexographic Technical Association Scholarship: 2354
Flight Attendants/Flight Technicians Scholarship: 2368
FLINN FOUNDATION (THE)
    Arizona Center for Civic Leadership: 111
    Flinn Scholars Program: 111
Flinn Scholars Program: 111
Florida Bright Futures Scholarship Program: 1502
Florida Cultural Endowment Program: 405
FLORIDA DEPARTMENT OF EDUCATION
    Access to Better Learning and Education Grant Program (ABLE): 1501
    Bethune (Mary McLeod) Scholarship Program (MMB): 1501
    Effective Access to Student Education (EASE): 1501
    First Generation Matching Grant Program (FGMG): 1501
    Florida Bright Futures Scholarship Program: 1502
    Florida Farmworker Student Scholarship Program: 1501
    Florida Student Assistance Grant Program (FSAG): 1501
    Florida Work Experience Program (FWEP): 1501
    Marti (Jose) Scholarship Challenge Grant Fund: 964
    Rosewood Family Scholarship Program: 932
    Scholarships for Children and Spouses of Deceased or Disabled Veterans (CSDDV): 1501
FLORIDA DEPARTMENT OF STATE, DIVISION OF CULTURAL AFFAIRS
    Cultural Facilities Program: 405
    Florida Cultural Endowment Program: 405
    General Program Support Grants Program: 405
    Specific Cultural Projects Grants Program: 405
FLORIDA EDUCATION FUND
    McKnight Doctoral Fellowship: 1386
Florida Farmworker Student Scholarship Program: 1501
Florida Student Assistance Grant Program (FSAG): 1501
Florida Work Experience Program (FWEP): 1501
Focused Populations: 1154
Folk and Traditional Arts Apprenticeship: 420
Folk & Traditional Arts Mentoring Project Grants: 479
Folk and Traditional Arts Touring Network: 430
Folk Arts: 384
Folk Arts Apprenticeship Program: 474
Folk Arts Apprenticeships and Fellowships: 451
Folk Arts Apprenticeships (FAA): 439
Folk Arts Grants: 464
Folklife Program: 436
FONDATION DES ETATS-UNIS
    Woolley (Harriet Hale) Scholarship: 704
FOOD AND DRUG LAW INSTITUTE (FDLI)
    Austern (H. Thomas) Writing Competition: 1772
Food Banks: 1019
Food Safety Award: 2415
Food Safety Innovation Award: 2415
Food, Clothing and Shelter: 267
Food, Pharmaceutical and Bioengineering Division Award in Chemical Engineering: 1618
Ford (Anne) Scholarship: 1406
FORD FOUNDATION (THE)
    Cities and States Program: 112
    Civic Engagement and Government Program: 112
    Creativity and Free Expression Program: 112
    Future of Work(ers) Program: 112
    Gender, Racial and Ethnic Justice Program: 112
    Natural Resources and Climate Change Program: 112
    Technology and Society Program: 112

Ford Foundation Fellowship Programs: 908
FORD (GERALD R.) PRESIDENTIAL LIBRARY
    Ford (Gerald R.) Scholar Award (Dissertation Award) in Honor of Robert M. Teeter: 1791
    Research Travel Grant Program: 1790
Ford (Gerald R.) Scholar Award (Dissertation Award) in Honor of Robert M. Teeter: 1791
Ford-HS Bridge Scholars: 2395
FORD MOTOR COMPANY FUND AND COMMUNITY SERVICES
    Community Grants Program: 113
FORECAST PUBLIC ART
    Early-Career Artist Project Grant: 406
    Early-Career Artist Research and Development Grant: 406
    Mid-Career Professional Development Grant: 406
    Mid-Career Project Grant: 406
Foreign Government Awards Program: 821
Foreign Language and Area Studies Fellowships: 607
Foreman (George) Tribute to Lyndon B. Johnson: 1757
Forest Fungal Ecology Awards: 1944
Forever Idaho Regional Grant Program: 143
Forkosch (The Morris D.) Prize: 526
Forum for Civic Advancement: 100
Foster Care Program: 1056
FOSTER CARE TO SUCCESS
    FCS Scholarship Fund: 1387
Foster Grandparent Program: 1333
Fostering Economic Self-Sufficiency: 1205
Fostering Futures Scholarship: 1579
FOUNDATION FOR ADVANCEMENT IN CONSERVATION (FAIC) (THE)
    Collections Assessment for Preservation (CAP): 667
FOUNDATION FOR ANESTHESIA EDUCATION AND RESEARCH
    FAER Mentored Research Training Grant: 2028
    FAER Research Fellowship Grant: 2028
    FAER Research in Education Grant: 2028
    FAER Transition to Independence Grant: 2028
Foundation for Biblical Archaeology Scholarships: 818
FOUNDATION FOR EDUCATION AND RESEARCH IN BIOFEEDBACK AND RELATED SCIENCES (FERB): 2327
FOUNDATION FOR ENHANCING COMMUNITIES (THE): 1155
FOUNDATION FOR NEONATAL RESEARCH AND EDUCATION (FNRE): 2238
FOUNDATION FOR OSTEOPATHIC EMERGENCY MEDICINE
    Field (Benjamin J.), D.O., FACOEP Medical Education Grant: 2277
    Investigator Research Grant: 2277
    Kuchinski (David A.) Memorial Research Grant: 2277
    Resident Research Grant: 2277
    Young Investigator Research Grant: 2277
FOUNDATION FOR PHYSICAL THERAPY RESEARCH, INC.: 2298
    New Investigator Fellowship Training Initiative (NIFTI): 2299
    Promotion of Doctoral Studies Scholarships (PODS): 2299
FOUNDATION FOR SCIENCE AND DISABILITY: 899
FOUNDATION FOR SPIRITUALITY AND MEDICINE (THE): 1290
FOUNDATION FOR TECHNOLOGY AND ENGINEERING EDUCATION
    FTEE Undergraduate Scholarship: 1503
    Litherland/FTEE Scholarship Undergraduate Major in Technology and Engineering Education: 1504
    Maley/FTEE Scholarship Technology and Engineering Teacher Professional Development: 1388
FOUNDATION FOR THE CAROLINAS: 1156
FOUNDATION FOR THE MID SOUTH
    Community Development: 1157
    Education: 1157
    Health & Wellness: 1157
    Wealth Building: 1157
FOUNDATION FOR THE TRI-STATE COMMUNITY, INC.
    21st Century Endowment Fund: 1158
Foundation Grants: 6
Foundation Initiative Grants: 258
FOUNDATION OF FLEXOGRAPHIC TECHNICAL ASSOCIATION (THE)
    Flexographic Technical Association Scholarship: 2354
FOUNDATION OF THE AMERICAN COLLEGE OF HEALTHCARE EXECUTIVES (THE)
    Dent (Albert W.) Graduate Student Scholarship: 1291
    McGaw (Foster G.) Graduate Student Scholarship: 1291
FOUNDATION OF THE AMERICAN SOCIETY OF NEURORADIOLOGY (THE): 2029
FOUNDATION OF THE NATIONAL STUDENT NURSES' ASSOCIATION, INC.: 2239

Four Year Doctoral Fellowships: 1594
4A'S
    Multicultural Advertising Intern Program (MAIP): 900
Fourth Estate Scholarships: 1567
Fourth Generation: 1204
Fox (The Dixon Ryan) Manuscript Prize of the Fenimore Art Museum:
    541
FOX (THE MICHAEL J.) FOUNDATION FOR PARKINSON'S
    RESEARCH: 2030
France on Campus Award: 829
FRANCIS (THE PARKER B.) FELLOWSHIP PROGRAM: 2031
Frank Educational Fund: 758
Franklin (Miles) Literary Award: 642
Franklin Research Grants: 11
Franklin (Ursula) Award in Gender Studies: 1646
Frantz (M. Alison) Fellowship in Post-Classical Studies at the Gennadius
    Library: 810
FRAXA Grants and Fellowships: 2032
FRAXA RESEARCH FOUNDATION
    FRAXA Grants and Fellowships: 2032
FREEDOM ALLIANCE
    Freedom Alliance Scholarship Fund: 1505
Freedom Alliance Scholarship Fund: 1505
Freeland (Chuck) Memorial Scholarship for Flight Training: 2363
FREEMAN (CARL M.) FOUNDATION
    FACES Grant: 407
Freeman (Don) Memorial Grant-in-Aid: 646
Freeman Fellowship: 2386
FREEMAN FOUNDATION: 114
FREEPORT-MCMORAN FOUNDATION
    Matching Gifts Program: 115
    Social Investment Program: 115
FREER GALLERY OF ART AND ARTHUR M. SACKLER GALLERY
    Lee (The J.S.) Memorial Fellowship: 408
    Smithsonian Institution Fellowship: 408
    van Biema (Anne) Fellowship: 408
French Language Scholarship: 1770
Fresh Fruit and Vegetable Program (The): 1041
Freshman Scholarships: 2356
Frevel (The Ludo) Crystallography Scholarship Award: 2422
FREY FOUNDATION
    Building Community: 116
    Children and Families: 116
    Community Arts: 116
    Environment: 116
Friend (Sidney and Katherine) Scholarship: 2395
FRIST FOUNDATION (THE)
    Frist Foundation Awards of Achievement (The): 1159
    Frist Foundation Technology Grants Program (The): 1159
Frist Foundation Awards of Achievement (The): 1159
Frist Foundation Technology Grants Program (The): 1159
Fritts (Edward O.) Award: 1724
FROMM MUSIC FOUNDATION AT HARVARD: 705
Frontiers in Anesthesia Research Award: 2039
FROST FOUNDATION, LTD. (THE): 117
FRY (LLOYD A.) FOUNDATION: 118
FSHD SOCIETY, INC.: 2033
FTEE Undergraduate Scholarship: 1503
Fuertes (Louis Agassiz) Grant: 1952
Fulbright-Hays Doctoral Dissertation Research Abroad: 608
Fulbright-Hays Group Projects Abroad Program: 854
Fulbright International Education Administrators Program: 1454
Fulbright Scholar-in-Residence Program: 773
Fulbright Specialist Program: 792
Fulbright Teacher Exchanges: 1425
Fulbright U.S. Student Program: 832
Fulbright - University of Manchester Award: 856
Full Circle Scholarship Program: 940
FULLER (H.B.) COMPANY FOUNDATION
    Leadership Development for Youth: 1014
    Racial Equity: 1014
    STEM Education: 1014
FUND FOR AMERICAN STUDIES (THE)
    Novak (Robert) Journalism Fellowship Program: 1792
Fund for Capital Improvements: 1095
Fund for Change (FFC): 1343
Fund for Excellence in Education Grants: 1130
Fund for Excellence in Essex County: 1153
Fund for Financial Innovation: 1095
Fund for Innovative Operations: 1095

FUND FOR INVESTIGATIVE JOURNALISM: 1734
Fund for Omaha: 223
Fund for Targeted Needs: 1095
Fund for the Arts: 437
Funding and Arts in Education Programs: 418
Funds for One: 1339
Furthermore Grant: 154
Future Faces of Physics Awards: 1892
Future Faculty and Professionals (FFP) Travel Grant: 911
Future Latino Leaders Summer Law Institute: 1778
Future NEED Scholars: 938
Future of Work(ers) Program: 112
Futuro Latino Fund: 223
Fyke (Kenneth J.) Award: 2020

G

Gallagher (John J. and Anna H.) Fellowship: 1615
Gallery Program: 401
GAMBLE FOUNDATION (THE): 1389
Gambrell (C.B.) Undergraduate Scholarship: 2392
GANNETT FOUNDATION: 119
GARDEN CLUB OF AMERICA (THE)
    Engle (The Corliss Knapp) Scholarship in Horticulture: 1914
    Garden Club of America Award in Coastal Wetland Studies (The): 1968
    Garden Club of America Hope Goddard Iselin Fellowship in Public
        Horticulture (The): 1909
    Garden Club of America Internship in Garden History and Design
        (The): 1913
    Garden Club of America Motine M. Freeman Scholarship in Native
        Plants (The): 1915
    Garden Club of America Summer Scholarship in Field Botany (The):
        1910
    GCA and The Royal Horticultural Society Interchange Fellowships
        (The): 1966
    GCA Awards for Summer Environmental Studies: 1969
    Hunt (The Joan K.) and Rachel M. Hunt Summer Scholarship in Field
        Botany: 1912
    Peacock (The Frances M.) Scholarship for Native Bird Habitat: 1967
    Zeller Summer Scholarship in Medicinal Botany (The): 1911
Garden Club of America Award in Coastal Wetland Studies (The): 1968
Garden Club of America Hope Goddard Iselin Fellowship in Public
    Horticulture (The): 1909
Garden Club of America Internship in Garden History and Design (The):
    1913
Garden Club of America Motine M. Freeman Scholarship in Native Plants
    (The): 1915
Garden Club of America Summer Scholarship in Field Botany (The):
    1910
Garden (Dwight D.) Scholarship: 2392
Garfield (Eugene) Doctoral Dissertation Fellowship: 662
Garfield (The Eugene)/ALISE Doctoral Dissertation Competition: 661
Garmin - Jerry Smith Memorial Scholarship: 2363
Garmin Scholarship: 2363
Garnier (Junior) and Bud Ashford Military Veterans Fund: 143
Garrett (Eileen J.) Scholarship: 2334
Gateway Grant: 6
Gaul (Harvey) Music Composition Contest: 723
Gaver (Mary V.) Scholarship: 1443
Gaynor (The Florence) Award: 2302
GCA and The Royal Horticultural Society Interchange Fellowships (The):
    1966
GCA Awards for Summer Environmental Studies: 1969
GCDF Scholarship: 1543
GE Foundation Engineering Scholarship: 2395
GE-Reagan Foundation Scholarship Program: 1568
Geach (Portia) Memorial Award: 449
GEFFEN (THE DAVID) FOUNDATION: 1292
Geiger Memorial Internship: 583
Geisman (Michael) Fellowships: 2069
GELLERT (CARL) AND CELIA BERTA GELLERT FOUNDATION
    (THE): 120
GELLERT (THE FRED) FAMILY FOUNDATION: 121
GEM M.S. Engineering Fellowship (The): 911
GEM Ph.D. Engineering Fellowship (The): 911
GEM Ph.D. Science Fellowship (The): 911
Gender Equity and Governance: 137
Gender, Racial and Ethnic Justice Program: 112
Genentech/NMF Diversity Innovation Fellowship Program: 2062

GENERAL BOARD OF HIGHER EDUCATION AND MINISTRY, THE UNITED METHODIST CHURCH
  Harkness (Georgia) Scholarships: 741
General College Scholarship Program: 965
GENERAL COMMISSION ON ARCHIVES AND HISTORY OF THE UNITED METHODIST CHURCH
  Ness (John Harrison) Memorial Award: 742
General Community Grants: 1186
General Fund Grants: 1348
General Operating Support: 403
General Operating Support for Arts, Museums and Local Arts Agencies: 464
General Operating Support (GOS): 439
General Operating Support Grants: 568
General Program Support (GPS): 439
General Program Support Grants Program: 405
General Project Grants: 438
GENERAL SERVICE FOUNDATION
  Building Voice and Power: 122
General Support for Employment Placement Programs: 882
Gentile (Major Don S.) Scholarship: 1591
GEOLOGICAL SOCIETY OF AMERICA, INC. (THE)
  GSA Research Grants: 1867
GEORGE WASHINGTON UNIVERSITY
  Graduate Teaching Assistantships: 2391
GEORGETOWN UNIVERSITY
  Doctoral Program in Chemistry: 1858
GEORGIA COUNCIL FOR THE ARTS
  Arts Education Program Grants: 409
  Bridge Grant: 409
  Cultural Facilities Grant: 409
  Partner Grants: 409
  Project Grants: 409
  Vibrant Communities Grants: 409
GEORGIA LIBRARY ASSOCIATION
  Beard Scholarship: 668
  Hubbard Scholarship: 668
GEORGIA-PACIFIC FOUNDATION: 123
Georgian Papers Programme Fellowships: 574
Geraty (Lawrence T.) Travel Scholarship: 796
GERBER FOUNDATION (THE): 1015
GERMAN ACADEMIC EXCHANGE SERVICE
  DAAD Emigre Memorial German Internship Program (EMGIP-Bundestag): 830
  DAAD German Studies Research Grant: 830
  DAAD Research Grant: 830
  DAAD Research Internships in Science and Engineering (RISE): 830
  DAAD Research Stays for University Academics and Scientists: 830
  DAAD RISE Professional: 830
  DAAD Study Scholarship: 830
  DAAD University Summer Course Grant: 830
  DAAD Visiting Professorship: 830
German Chancellor Fellowship: 797
GERMAN HISTORICAL INSTITUTE
  Doctoral and Postdoctoral Fellowships: 542
Gershoy (The Leo) Award: 526
Get Together Grant Program: 1243
Getty Images Inclusion Scholarship: 909
GETTY (J. PAUL) TRUST, GETTY FOUNDATION: 503
GHEENS FOUNDATION, INC. (THE): 124
Ghormley (N. Rex) Student Travel Fellowship: 2258
Giambalvo (Joan F.) Memorial Fund: 1477
Gies (William J.) Award: 2100
GIFFORD FOUNDATION (THE): 1160
GIG Fund: 483
Gilbreth Memorial Fellowship: 2392
Gill Family Foundation Dissertation Research Fellowship: 381
Ginocchio (Lawrence) Scholarship: 2369
girlsBEST Fund: 996
GLAUCOMA FOUNDATION (THE): 2269
GLAUCOMA RESEARCH FOUNDATION
  Shaffer Fund for Innovative Glaucoma Research: 2270
Glenn Foundation for Medical Research and AFAR Grants for Junior Faculty: 1999
Glenn Foundation for Medical Research Breakthroughs in Gerontology (BIG) Awards: 1999
Glenn Foundation for Medical Research Postdoctoral Fellowships in Aging Research: 1998
Global Arts Fund: 890
Global Grants: 2191

Global Issues: 355
Global Ph.D. Fellowship: 1608
GLOECKNER (THE FRED C.) FOUNDATION, INC.: 1916
Gloeckner (M. Louise), M.D., Summer Research Fellowship: 977
GMiS Scholars Program: 2355
Gogo Business Aviation Scholarship: 2363
Gold (Carol) Best Article Award: 534
Golden Key Graduate Scholarship Award (The): 1506
Golden Key Humanitarian/Service Response Award: 1506
GOLDEN KEY INTERNATIONAL HONOUR SOCIETY, INC.
  Golden Key Graduate Scholarship Award (The): 1506
  Golden Key Humanitarian/Service Response Award: 1506
  Golden Key Outstanding Member Award: 1506
  Golden Key Professional Development Grant: 1506
  Nelson (Joan) Study Abroad Scholarship: 1506
  Undergraduate Achievement Scholarship: 1506
Golden Key Outstanding Member Award: 1506
Golden Key Professional Development Grant: 1506
GOLDMAN (HERMAN) FOUNDATION: 125
GOLDMAN (LISA AND DOUGLAS) FUND: 1161
Goldman (The Ralph I.) Fellowship: 803
Goldmark (Ruth Ingersoll) Fellowship: 991
GOLDSEKER FOUNDATION: 1162
Gomez (Luis) Scholarship: 909
Good Roots Grant: 6
GOODYEAR TIRE & RUBBER COMPANY (THE): 126
Gorgas Scholarship: 1616
Gorham (Dr. Millicent) Scholarship: 2240
Goss (David and Diane) Optometry History Fellowship: 2260
GOTTLIEB (ADOLPH AND ESTHER) FOUNDATION, INC.
  Emergency Grant Program: 504
  Individual Support Program: 504
Gottschalk (Carl W.) Research Scholar Grant: 2111
GRACO FOUNDATION (THE)
  Financial Grants of Support: 1163
GRAD Lab: 911
Graduate Faculty Council Scholarship: 1602
Graduate Fellowship in Engineering: 2407
Graduate Fellowship Program for Alternatives to the Use of Animals in Science: 1633
GRADUATE INSTITUTE OF INTERNATIONAL AND DEVELOPMENT STUDIES
  Financial Aid for Study at The Graduate Institute of International and Development Studies: 771
Graduate Nursing Loan-Forgiveness Program: 1583
Graduate Ph.D. Award: 2201
Graduate Program in Creative Writing: 647
Graduate Research Awards: 1889
Graduate Research Fellowship: 2348
Graduate Research Program: 1623
Graduate Scholar Internship: 1800
Graduate Scholarship: 391
Graduate Scholarship Program: 2376
Graduate Scholarships: 2356, 2404
Graduate School Scholarships for Study in Italy: 850
Graduate Student Awards: 2414
Graduate Student Creative Writing Award: 606
Graduate Student Essay Prize: 606
Graduate Student Fellowship Program: 1926, 1932
Graduate Student Poster Contest: 387
Graduate Student Scholarship for International/Minority Students: 2262
Graduate Student Scholarship for Minority Students: 2262
Graduate Student Scholarship for NSSLHA Members: 2262
Graduate Student Scholarship for Students with a Disability: 2262
Graduate Student Scholarships: 2262
Graduate Studentships: 2164
Graduate Support Initiative: 1593
Graduate Teaching Assistantships: 2391
Graduate Training in Disparities Research (GTDR): 2191
GRADUATE WOMEN IN SCIENCE
  GWIS Fellowships Program: 1630
GRADUATE WOMEN INTERNATIONAL (GWI)
  BFWG Marjorie Shaw Fellowship: 978
  FfWG Crosby Hall Fellowship: 978
  NZFGW Daphne Purves Grant: 978
  Spurgeon (Caroline) Centenary Fellowship: 978
GRAHAM FOUNDATION FOR ADVANCED STUDIES IN THE FINE ARTS
  Manny (Carter) Award: 373
  Production and Presentation Grants: 373
  Research and Development Grants: 373

GRAHAM HOLDINGS COMPANY: 127
GRAHAM (MARTHA) SCHOOL OF CONTEMPORARY DANCE, INC.
    Advanced Studies Certificate: 486
    Graham 2 Company: 486
    Independent Program: 486
    Summer Intensive: 486
    Teacher Training Program: 486
    Teens@Graham Young Artists Program: 486
    Two-Year Certificate Program: 486
    Winter Intensive: 486
GRAHAM (PHILIP L.) FUND: 128
Graham 2 Company: 486
Grambs (Jean Dresden) Distinguished Career in Social Studies: 1665
GRAMMY MUSEUM (THE): 706
GRAND HAVEN AREA COMMUNITY FOUNDATION: 1164
GRAND RAPIDS COMMUNITY FOUNDATION
    Access Camps: 129
Grant for the Enhancement of Geographic Literacy in Honor of James F.
    Marren: 1667
Grant-in-Aid: 2140
Grant (Kenneth E.) Research Scholarship: 1984
Grant Program: 243
GRANT (THE WILLIAM T.) FOUNDATION
    Grant (William T.) Scholars Program: 1016
    Institutional Challenge Grant: 1016
    Research Grants Program: 1016
    Youth Service Improvement Grants Program: 1016
Grant (William T.) Scholars Program: 1016
Grants: 791
Grants for Art Projects: 433
Grants for Cancer Research: 2187
Grants for Change: 1344
Grants for Organizations: 427
Grants for Researchers with Heavy Teaching Loads: 482
Grants in Aid of Research: 1647
Grants-in-Aid Project: 1650
Grants Program: 100, 436, 485, 1416
Grants-to-Educators Program: 1432
Grants to State Library Administrative Agencies: 672
Grass Fellowships in Neuroscience: 2212
GRASS FOUNDATION (THE)
    Grass Fellowships in Neuroscience: 2212
Grasso (Ella) Literary Scholarship: 1591
Grassroots Arts Program: 443
GRAVES (NANCY) FOUNDATION
    Graves (Nancy) Grant for Visual Artists: 410
Graves (Nancy) Grant for Visual Artists: 410
Gray (Charles Montgomery) Fellowship: 351
Gray (Dr. Herman and Shirley) Family Scholarship: 2062
GRAYSON-JOCKEY CLUB RESEARCH FOUNDATION (THE): 2034
GREAT LAKES COLLEGES ASSOCIATION NEW WRITERS
    AWARDS
    New Writers Awards: 620
GREAT LAKES PROTECTION FUND: 1970
Great Learning: 235
GREAT MINDS IN STEM
    GMiS Scholars Program: 2355
GREATER CEDAR RAPIDS COMMUNITY FOUNDATION (THE)
    Endowment Challenge Fund: 1165
    Linn County Fund: 1165
    Nonprofit Network: 1165
    Organization Support Fund: 1165
    President's Fund: 1165
    Program Support Fund: 1165
GREATER CINCINNATI FOUNDATION
    All-In Cincinnati Racial Equity Coalition: 1166
    Community-Wide Affordable Housing Strategy: 1166
    COVID-19 Response: 1166
    Racial Equity Matters: 1166
    Women's Fund of Greater Cincinnati Foundation: 1166
GREATER GREEN BAY COMMUNITY FOUNDATION: 1167
GREATER KANAWHA VALLEY FOUNDATION (THE): 1168
GREATER KANSAS CITY COMMUNITY FOUNDATION: 1169
Greater Lawrence Community Fund: 1153
Greater Lawrence Summer Fund: 1153
GREATER MILWAUKEE FOUNDATION: 1170
GREATER NEW ORLEANS FOUNDATION (THE): 1171
Greater Newburyport Fund for the Blind: 1153
GREATER TOLEDO COMMUNITY FOUNDATION: 1172
Greco (Bishop Charles P.) Graduate Fellowships: 1524

Greenberg (Noah) Award: 691
GREENBURG-MAY FOUNDATION: 2190
Greenfield (Albert M.) Foundation Dissertation Fellowships: 553
Greenfield (Vivian) Education Award: 683
GREENSHIELDS (THE ELIZABETH) FOUNDATION
    Greenshields (The Elizabeth) Foundation Grant: 505
Greenshields (The Elizabeth) Foundation Grant: 505
Grimes (John E.) Timpani Scholarship: 722
Griswold (Enid Hall) Memorial Scholarship: 1670
Gritton (Henry Bertie and Florence Mabel) Postgraduate Research
    Scholarships: 1860
Groot (Jennifer C.) Fellowships in the Archaeology of Jordan: 796
Gruber (Freddie) Scholarship: 722
GRUNDY FOUNDATION (THE): 1173
GSA Research Grants: 1867
GSBA SCHOLARSHIP FUND: 901
Guerin (Mother Theodore) Research Travel Grant: 538
Guggenheim Fellowship: 2372
Guggenheim Fellowships: 130
GUGGENHEIM (THE HARRY FRANK) FOUNDATION
    Guggenheim (The Harry Frank) Foundation Distinguished Scholar
    Award: 1659
    Guggenheim (The Harry Frank) Foundation Emerging Scholars Award:
    1658
Guggenheim (The Harry Frank) Foundation Distinguished Scholar Award:
    1659
Guggenheim (The Harry Frank) Foundation Emerging Scholars Award:
    1658
GUGGENHEIM (JOHN SIMON) MEMORIAL FOUNDATION
    Guggenheim Fellowships: 130
Guilday (The Peter) Prize: 736
GUITAR FOUNDATION OF AMERICA
    International Concert Artists Competition: 707
    International Youth Competition: 707
    Regional Events: 707
GULF COAST COMMUNITY FOUNDATION: 1174
GUND (THE GEORGE) FOUNDATION: 131
Gunter (Connie and Robert T.) Scholarship: 2361
GWATHMEY MEMORIAL TRUST (THE): 328
GWIS Fellowships Program: 1630
Gynecologic Health and Disease Branch (GHDB): 1318

H

H-15 Grant for Faculty Members or Independent Researchers: 2234
Hackney (Louise Wallace) Fellowship: 496
Hagley Exploratory Research Grant: 543
HAGLEY MUSEUM AND LIBRARY
    du Pont (Henry Belin) Dissertation Fellowship in Business, Technology,
    and Society: 543
    du Pont (Henry Belin) Research Grants: 543
    Hagley Exploratory Research Grant: 543
HAGUE ACADEMY OF INTERNATIONAL LAW (THE)
    Centre for Studies and Research in International Law and International
    Relations: 1773
    Doctoral Scholarships in International Law: 1775
    External Programme: 1774
    Hague Academy of International Law Summer Courses: 1776
Hague Academy of International Law Summer Courses: 1776
Hague (The George) Memorial Travel Award: 1859
HALBERT CENTRE FOR CANADIAN STUDIES
    Halbert Centre for Canadian Studies Visiting Professors Program: 1450
Halbert Centre for Canadian Studies Visiting Professors Program: 1450
Hall (Donald) Prize for Poetry: 614
HALL FAMILY FOUNDATION: 132
Hall (George A.)/Harold F. Mayfield Grant: 1952
Hall/McElwain Merit Scholarships: 1001
HALLETT CHARITABLE TRUSTS (THE): 1451
HALLIBURTON FOUNDATION, INC.: 1452
HAMBIDGE
    Hambidge Residency Program Fellowships: 411
Hambidge Residency Program Fellowships: 411
Hamburger (Viktor) Outstanding Educator Prize: 1948
HAMILTON COMMUNITY FOUNDATION: 1175
HAMILTON FAMILY CHARITABLE TRUST
    After-School Programs: 1390
    In-School Programs: 1390
    Summer Programs: 1390
Hammond (Dr. George P.) Paper Prize: 578
Hampson (Thomas) Award: 691

HAMPTON ROADS COMMUNITY FOUNDATION (THE): 1176
Haniak (John M.) Scholarship: 2420
HANNAFORD CHARITABLE FOUNDATION: 1391
Hannah (The Jason A.) Medal: 1646
HARBUS FOUNDATION: 1392
HARDEN FOUNDATION: 133
HARDIN (THE PHIL) FOUNDATION: 1393
Hargrove (Dr. Joe L.) Scholarship Award: 2062
Haring (The Clarence H.) Prize: 526
Harkness (Georgia) Scholarships: 741
Harper Fund Award: 606
Harrell Family Fellowship: 796
Harris Grants: 818
Harris (Leon)/Les Nichols Memorial Scholarship: 2363
HARTFORD (THE JOHN A.) FOUNDATION, INC.: 134
HARTFORD PUBLIC LIBRARY
    Hewins (The Caroline M.) Scholarship: 669
HARVARD TRAVELLERS CLUB, PERMANENT FUND: 1631
HASBRO CHILDREN'S FUND
    Community Grants: 1017
HASTINGS CENTER (THE)
    Visiting Scholars Program: 1895
Haverland (Harry) Citation Award: 2415
Hawaii Chapter ASLA/David T. Woolsey Scholarship: 1974
HAWAII COMMUNITY FOUNDATION: 1177
HAWAII STATE FOUNDATION ON CULTURE AND THE ARTS
    Biennium Grants Program: 412
Hawley Medal: 2423
Hawthorne (Ruth E.) Research Grant: 2416
Hay (Elizabeth D.) New Investigator Award: 1948
HAYDEN (CHARLES) FOUNDATION: 1018
HAYNES (THE JOHN RANDOLPH) AND DORA HAYNES
    FOUNDATION: 1660
HAYSTACK MOUNTAIN SCHOOL OF CRAFTS
    Conferences/Seminars: 413
    Exhibitions: 413
    Maine Programs: 413
    Open Studio Residency: 413
    Summer Conference: 413
    Summer Workshops: 413
Hazen (Joseph H.) Education Prize: 548
HBA-DC Foundation Fellowship (The): 1777
HCR MANORCARE FOUNDATION: 1293
HD Human Biology Project: 2213
HDSA Berman-Topper Family Huntington's Disease Career Development
    Fellowship: 2213
Head Start: 1038
Head Start Arts Integration Program: 466
Health: 1079
Health and Human Services: 228
Health and Welfare: 1019
Health & Wellness: 1157
Health and Wellness Grant: 1237
Health Care Coverage and Access: 1335
Health Care Delivery System Reform: 1335
Health Care Improvement Grant Program: 1325
Health Careers Scholarships: 1476
Health Center Program (The): 1323
HEALTH EFFECTS INSTITUTE (HEI)
    Health Effects of Air Pollution: 1294
    Rosenblith (Walter A.) New Investigator Award: 1294
Health Effects of Air Pollution: 1294
HEALTH FOUNDATION OF GREATER INDIANAPOLIS, INC. (THE):
    1337
    Indiana AIDS Fund: 1295
HEALTH FOUNDATION OF SOUTH FLORIDA
    Cash Grants: 1296
    Mission Related Investments Contracts: 1296
    Officers and Trustees Discretionary Grants: 1296
Health Improvement in North Carolina: 1355
Health in Aging Foundation New Investigator Awards: 2294
Health Innovation Fund: 1286
Health Leadership Program: 1359
Health Partnership Grants: 1298
HEALTH RESOURCES AND SERVICES ADMINISTRATION
    Primary Care Training and Enhancement (PCTE): 2035
    Scholarships for Disadvantaged Students: 1394
HEALTH TRUST (THE)
    Community Grants: 1297
    Health Partnership Grants: 1298

HEALTHCARE FOUNDATION FOR ORANGE COUNTY (THE)
    Partnership for a Healthy Orange County: 1299
Healthiest Cities and Counties Challenge: 5
HealthRise: 200
Healthy Aging Program: 254
Healthy Congregations Program: 1363
Healthy Sacramento Coalition: 1359
HEARING HEALTH FOUNDATION
    Emerging Research Grants (ERG): 2271
    Hearing Restoration Project (HRP): 2271
Hearing Restoration Project (HRP): 2271
Hearst Journalism Awards Program: 1735
Hearst (William Randolph) Endowment Scholarship: 2395
HEARST (WILLIAM RANDOLPH) FOUNDATION
    Hearst Journalism Awards Program: 1735
    Hearst (William Randolph) Foundation Fellowship: 560
Heart and Mind: 933
HEART AND STROKE FOUNDATION OF CANADA
    Grant-in-Aid: 2140
    National New Investigator: 2141
HeartRescue: 200
Heed Fellowship: 2272
HEED OPHTHALMIC FOUNDATION
    Heed Fellowship: 2272
HEINRICH HERTZ-STIFTUNG: 831
Heinz (Elgin) Outstanding Teacher Award: 791
Heinz (Karl) and Doris Finzel Photojournalism Scholarship: 1567
Helton (Clinton J.) Manufacturing Scholarship: 2361
Henderson (Edward) Student Award: 2294
HENDERSON FOUNDATION: 135
Henry (Allan F.)/Paul A. Greebler Memorial Scholarship: 2381
Henson (Richard A.) Award of Excellence: 1123
HERB SOCIETY OF AMERICA, INC. (THE)
    HSA Research Grant: 1917
Herbert (Richard A.) Memorial Scholarship: 1958
Heritage Conservation Grant: 154
Heritage Fellowships: 818
Heritage Scholar Grant: 1481
HERSHEY (THE JACOB AND TERESE) FOUNDATION: 1971
Hesch (Wayne E.) Memorial Scholarships: 2351
HESS (MYRTLE E. AND WILLIAM G.) CHARITABLE TRUST: 902
HESS (WILLIAM G. AND MYRTLE E.) CHARITABLE TRUST: 1395
HEUERMANN (B. KEITH & NORMA F.) FOUNDATION: 136
Hewins (The Caroline M.) Scholarship: 669
Hewitt (Barnard) Award: 482
HEWLETT (THE WILLIAM AND FLORA) FOUNDATION
    Education: 137
    Environment: 137
    Gender Equity and Governance: 137
    Performing Arts: 137
    Philanthropy: 137
Hibernian Research Award: 535
Hidden Heroes Fund: 894
Hidden Talent Grants: 933
High-End Instrumentation (HEI) Grant Program: 2061
High Impact Research Grant: 2266
High School Journalism Scholarship: 1567
Higher Education Grant Program for American Indians and Alaska
    Natives: 950
Higher Education Program: 185
HIGHER EDUCATION STUDENT ASSISTANCE AUTHORITY (THE)
    Law Enforcement Officer Memorial Scholarship: 1507
    New Jersey Governor's Industry Vocations Scholarship for Women and
        Minorities (NJ-GIVS): 1507
    New Jersey Student Tuition Assistance Reward Scholarship (NJ
        STARS): 1507
    New Jersey Student Tuition Assistance Reward Scholarship II (NJ
        STARS II): 1507
    New Jersey World Trade Center Scholarship: 1507
    NJBEST Scholarship: 1507
    Survivor Tuition Benefits Program: 1507
    Tuition Aid Grant (TAG): 1508
Hill (Errol) Award: 482
HILLBLOM (THE LARRY L.) FOUNDATION, INC.
    Fellowship Research Grants: 2036
    Network Grants: 2036
    Start-Up Research Grants: 2036
Hillman Prizes for Journalism: 1736
HILLMAN (THE SIDNEY) FOUNDATION, INC.
    Hillman Prizes for Journalism: 1736
    Sidney Awards: 1736

HILLSDALE COUNTY COMMUNITY FOUNDATION: 1178
HILLSDALE FUND, INC.: 138
HIMSS FOUNDATION
    HIMSS Foundation Scholarship Program: 2037
HIMSS Foundation Scholarship Program: 2037
Hinrich Foundation Award for Distinguished Reporting on Trade: 1750
Hirsch (Jacob) Fellowship: 816
HISPANIC BAR ASSOCIATION OF D.C. FOUNDATION (THE)
    HBA-DC Foundation Fellowship (The): 1777
HISPANIC DENTAL ASSOCIATION FOUNDATION
    A-dec Scholarship: 2104
    Colgate-Palmolive Dental Residency or Specialty Program Scholarship:
        2104
    Colgate-Palmolive Scholarship for Dental Students and Dental Hygiene
        Students: 2104
    Procter & Gamble Scholarship: 2104
    Rodriguez (Dr. Esperanza) Scholarship: 2104
    Villarreal (Dr. Juan D.) Scholarship: 2104
HISPANIC NATIONAL BAR FOUNDATION (THE)
    Future Latino Leaders Summer Law Institute: 1778
HISPANIC SCHOLARSHIP FUND
    General College Scholarship Program: 965
HISTIOCYTOSIS ASSOCIATION
    Research Grant Program: 2115
HISTORIC NEW ORLEANS COLLECTION (THE)
    Williams (Kemper and Leila) Prize in Louisiana History: 544
    Woest (The Dianne) Fellowship in the Arts and Humanities: 545
Historic Properties Fund: 571
HISTORY COLORADO STATE HISTORICAL FUND: 546
History of Art and Visual Culture Fellowships: 511
History of Art Grant Program: 506
History of Art: Institutional Fellowships: 506
HISTORY OF SCIENCE SOCIETY
    Davis (Watson) and Helen Miles Davis Prize: 548
    Hazen (Joseph H.) Education Prize: 548
    Levinson (Suzanne J.) Prize: 548
    Pauly (Philip J.) Prize: 548
    Pfizer Prize: 548
    Price (Derek)/Rod Webster Prize: 547
    Rainger (Ronald) Prize: 548
    Reingold (Nathan) Prize: 548
    Rossiter (Margaret W.) History of Women in Science Prize: 548
HIV/AIDS & Oral Health: 2107
HOBLITZELLE FOUNDATION: 139
Hobson (G. Vernon) Bequest: 2421
Hoffberger (LeRoy E.) School of Painting (MFA): 509
HOFFMAN (THE MAXIMILIAN E. & MARION O.) FOUNDATION,
    INC.: 2038
Holiday Funding Program: 1182
Hollinshead (Marilyn) Fellowship: 462
Holmes/D'Accone Dissertation Fellowship in Opera Studies: 692
Hologgitas (Joanne V.), Ph.D., Past Grand President, Scholarship
    (Undergraduate): 976
Holt (Caroline E.) Nursing Scholarship: 2242
HOME DEPOT FOUNDATION (THE)
    Community Impact Grants Program: 1179
    Disaster Relief Program: 1179
    National Partner Grants Program: 1179
    Team Depot: 1179
    Veteran Housing Grants Program: 1179
Homeless Shelters: 1019
HONIG (VICTOR AND LORRAINE) FUND: 1338
HONOR SOCIETY OF PHI KAPPA PHI (THE)
    Phi Kappa Phi Fellowship (The): 1509
HONORS (Hematology Opportunities for the Next Generation of
    Research Scientists): 2007
HOOD (CHARLES H.) FOUNDATION, INC.
    Child Health Research Awards Program: 2283
Hoover (Herbert) Presidential Travel Grant Program: 1793
HOOVER PRESIDENTIAL FOUNDATION
    Hoover (Herbert) Presidential Travel Grant Program: 1793
Hopewell Agave Chapter #224 Scholarship (Undergraduate): 976
Hopkins (Douglas W.) Primary Care Residency Award: 2257
Hopscotch House Artist Retreat and Residency Center: 979
Horizons Foundation Scholarship Program: 993
Hornback (Miriam L.) Scholarship: 1443
Horner (Bob) Scholarship: 1757
HOROWITZ FOUNDATION FOR SOCIAL POLICY (THE): 1661
HORTICULTURAL RESEARCH INSTITUTE, INC.
    Akehurst (Carville M.) Memorial Scholarship: 1510
    Bigelow (Timothy) and Palmer W. Bigelow, Jr. Scholarship: 1510

Champion (Bryan A.) Memorial Scholarship: 1510
    HRI Competitive Research Grant Program: 1918
    Muggets Scholarship: 1510
    Spring Meadow Nursery Scholarship: 1510
    Usrey Family Scholarship: 1510
    Usrey (Susie and Bruce) Education Scholarship: 1510
Horton Fellowship: 512
Horton-Hallowell Fellowship: 991
Horwitz (The Louisa Gross) Prize: 1937
Horwitz (Tony) Prize: 585
Housing: 1079
HOUSING EDUCATION AND RESEARCH ASSOCIATION (HERA)
    Agan (Tessie) Award Competition: 1180
HOUSTON ENDOWMENT INC.: 140
HOWARD (THE GEORGE A. AND ELIZA GARDNER)
    FOUNDATION: 1453
Howard (Peggy) Fellowship in Economics: 991
Hoy (Christopher J.)/ERT Scholarship: 1443
HRI Competitive Research Grant Program: 1918
HSA Research Grant: 1917
Hubbard Scholarship: 668
HUDSON RIVER FOUNDATION (THE)
    Hudson River Fund: 1972
    Hudson River Improvement Fund: 1972
    New York City Environmental Fund: 1972
    New York-New Jersey Harbor & Estuary Program: 1972
Hudson River Fund: 1972
Hudson River Improvement Fund: 1972
HUDSON-WEBBER FOUNDATION: 1181
HUEBNER (THE S.S.) FOUNDATION FOR INSURANCE
    EDUCATION: 1707
HUGHES (MABEL Y.) CHARITABLE TRUST: 141
HUGOTON FOUNDATION: 1300
Human-Centered Artificial Intelligence (HAI): 760
HUMAN FRONTIER SCIENCE PROGRAM ORGANIZATION
    Cross-Disciplinary Fellowships: 1938
    Early Career Research Grants: 1938
    Long-Term Fellowships: 1938
    Program Grants: 1938
HUMAN GROWTH FOUNDATION
    Small Grants for Research in Field of Short Stature: 2284
Human Nutrition Research: 2417
Human Rights Program: 147
Human Service: 1229
Humane Studies Fellowships: 1794
Humanitarian Project Support: 2096
HUMANITIES NEW YORK
    Action Grants: 329
    Community Conversations Program: 329
    Quick Grants: 329
    Reading and Discussion Program: 329
    Vision Grants: 329
Humanities Program: 325
HUMBOLDT AREA FOUNDATION
    Community Response Grant: 1182
    Holiday Funding Program: 1182
    Jacoby (Victor Thomas) Award: 1182
    Lochtie (Robert) Memorial Fund: 1182
    Native Cultures Fund: 1182
    School Enrichment Grant Program: 1182
    Senior Citizens Grant: 1182
    Summer Youth Program: 1182
    Youth Leadership Fund: 1182
Humboldt Research Award Programme: 1475
Humboldt Research Fellowship for Experienced Researchers: 798
Humboldt Research Fellowship for Postdoctoral Researchers: 1442
Hunt (The Joan K.) and Rachel M. Hunt Summer Scholarship in Field
    Botany: 1912
HUNTER (A.V.) TRUST, INC.
    Direct Operating Grants: 1339
    Funds for One: 1339
Hunter (Amy Louise) Fellowship: 593
Huntington (Curtis E.) Memorial Scholarship: 1882
HUNTINGTON LIBRARY, ART MUSEUM AND BOTANICAL
    GARDENS
    Research Awards at the Huntington Library, Art Museum and Botanical
    Gardens: 330

HUNTINGTON'S DISEASE SOCIETY OF AMERICA, INC.
  HD Human Biology Project: 2213
  HDSA Berman-Topper Family Huntington's Disease Career
  Development Fellowship: 2213
  King (Donald) Summer Research Fellowship: 2213
HURI Research Fellowships in Ukrainian Studies (The): 359
HUSTON (THE STEWART) CHARITABLE TRUST: 743
HUTCHINSON COMMUNITY FOUNDATION: 414
HWF Academic Scholarship Program: 478
HWF Artist Residency Program: 478
HYAMS FOUNDATION, INC. (THE): 1340
HYDE AND WATSON FOUNDATION (THE): 142

I

I Tatti Fellowship: 859
I Tatti/Museo Nacional del Prado Joint Fellowship: 865
IADR Colgate Research in Prevention Travel Awards: 2105
IAICDV Annual Scholarship: 1396
IAPA Scholarship Fund: 1737
IARS Mentored Research Awards: 2039
IASA Memorial Fellowship: 551
IBM Herman Goldstine Memorial Postdoctoral Fellowship for Research in
  Mathematical and Computer Sciences: 1885
IBM THOMAS J. WATSON RESEARCH CENTER
  IBM Herman Goldstine Memorial Postdoctoral Fellowship for Research
  in Mathematical and Computer Sciences: 1885
ICS Scholarship: 2040
IDA Documentary Awards: 417
IDA/David L. Wolper Student Documentary Achievement Award: 417
IDAHO COMMISSION ON THE ARTS
  Arts Education Projects: 415
  Directory of Teaching Artists: 415
  Entry Track: 415
  Fellowships: 415
  Public Programs in the Arts: 415
  Quick Funds: 415
  Traditional Arts Apprenticeship Program: 415
  Writer-in-Residence Program: 415
IDAHO COMMUNITY FOUNDATION
  Bistline (The F.M., Anne G., and Beverly B.) Foundation Fund: 143
  Bonner County Fund for Arts Enhancement: 143
  Bonner County Human Rights Task Force Fund: 143
  Forever Idaho Regional Grant Program: 143
  Garnier (Junior) and Bud Ashford Military Veterans Fund: 143
  Idaho Future Fund: 143
  lfft Foundation Fund: 143
  Shelton (Perc H.) and Gladys A. Pospisil Shelton Foundation Advised
  Fund: 143
Idaho Future Fund: 143
Idaho Governor's Cup Scholarship: 1578
Idaho Opportunity Scholarship: 1577
IDRC Doctoral Research Awards (IDRA): 1183
IDRC John G. Bene Research Fellowship in Developing Countries: 1185
IDRC Research Awards: 1184
IEEE Fellowship in the History of Electrical and Computing Technology:
  549
IEEE HISTORY CENTER
  IEEE Fellowship in the History of Electrical and Computing
  Technology: 549
  Pugh (The Elizabeth and Emerson Young) Scholar in Residence at the
  IEEE History Center: 549
IISE Council of Fellows Undergraduate Scholarship: 2392
IISE Fellows William Biles, Hamid Parsaei and Victor Zaloom Endowed
  Scholarship: 2392
ILLINOIS CLEAN ENERGY COMMUNITY FOUNDATION
  Energy Program: 1973
  Natural Areas Program: 1973
ILLINOIS RESTAURANT ASSOCIATION EDUCATIONAL
  FOUNDATION
  IRA Educational Foundation Scholarship Program: 1511
  IRAEFF Restaurant Employee Relief Fund: 1511
ILLINOIS STATE ACADEMY OF SCIENCE
  Scientific Research Grants/Proposal Writing Contest: 1632
Imagine America Adult Skills Education Program (ASEP): 1764
IMAGINE AMERICA FOUNDATION
  Imagine America Adult Skills Education Program (ASEP): 1764
  Imagine America High School Scholarship Program: 1764
  Imagine America Military Award Program (MAP): 1764
Imagine America High School Scholarship Program: 1764

Imagine America Military Award Program (MAP): 1764
Imhoff (John L.) Scholarship: 2392
IMMANUEL BIBLE FOUNDATION: 744
Immigration: 1079
IMMUNE DEFICIENCY FOUNDATION
  Bhaskaran (The Varun) (WAS) Scholarship Program of IDF: 903
Impact Capacity Grant: 1304
Impact Grant: 1223
Importation of Musicians Grants: 456
Improving Access: 1286
In-School Programs: 1390
Inclusive Clean Economy: 81
Inclusive Economies (The): 276
INDEPENDENCE FOUNDATION
  Individual Artists Fellowship/Performing and Visual Arts: 144
  New Theater Works Initiative: 144
  Public Interest Law Fellowships: 144
Independent Program: 486
Independent Scientist Awards (K02): 1311
Indian Education-Formula Grants to Local Education Agencies (LEAs):
  956
Indian Employment Assistance: 946
Indiana AIDS Fund: 1295
INDIANA ARTS COMMISSION: 416
INDIANA COMMISSION FOR HIGHER EDUCATION, DIVISION OF
  STUDENT FINANCIAL AID
  Crawford (William A.) Minority Teacher Scholarship: 1512
  Daniels (Mitch) Early Graduation Scholarship: 1512
  EARN Indiana (State Work Study): 1512
  National Guard Supplemental Grant: 1512
  Next Generation Hoosier Educators Scholarship: 1512
  O'Bannon (The Frank) Grant: 1512
  Rogers (Earline S.) Student Teaching Stipend for Minorities: 1512
  Student Teaching Stipend for High-Needs Fields: 1512
  21st Century Scholars Program: 1512
INDIANA LIBRARY FEDERATION
  Schlundt (The Esther) Memorial Fund: 670
  Weller (The Sue Marsh) Fund: 670
Individual Artist Awards: 427
Individual Artist Fellowship Awards (IAFA): 439
Individual Artist Fellowships: 401, 435
Individual Artist Grants and Services: Traditional Arts Apprenticeships:
  445
Individual Artist Grants/Programs: 455
Individual Artist Support Grants: 982
Individual Artists Fellowship Grants: 447
Individual Artists Fellowship/Performing and Visual Arts: 144
Individual Artists Fellowships: 444
Individual Fellowship Program: 391
Individual NRSA Postdoctoral Fellowships (F-32): 2106
Individual NRSA Senior Fellowship Award (F-33): 2108
Individual Research Grants: 734, 1817
Individual Support Program: 504
Industry Case Studies: 2376
Ing (Mary Quon Moy) Memorial Scholarship: 1483
Innis-Gérin Medal (The): 1646
Innovation Award: 2137
Innovation in Wound Care Research and Academic Development
  Fellowship: 2076
Innovative Basic Science Award (IBS): 2148
Innovative Clinical or Translational Science Award (ICTS): 2148
Innovative Investigator Award: 2051
Innovative Project Award: 2131
Innovative Proof-of-Concept Grants: 1316
Innovative Storytelling Award: 1750
Innovative Teacher Grants: 1375
Innovative Teaching Award: 1681
Innovative Technology Experiences for Students and Teachers (ITEST):
  1436
Inserra Scholarships: 1591
Inspire! Grants for Small Museums: 671
Institut Francais d'America Fund Research Fellowships (The): 584
INSTITUTE FOR ADVANCED STUDIES IN THE HUMANITIES
  (THE)
  Visiting Research Fellowships: 331
INSTITUTE FOR ADVANCED STUDY
  School of Social Science Fellowships: 1662
INSTITUTE FOR CITIZENS & SCHOLARS
  Newcombe (Charlotte W.) Doctoral Dissertation Fellowships: 1513
INSTITUTE FOR HUMANE STUDIES (IHS)
  Humane Studies Fellowships: 1794

INSTITUTE FOR QUANTITATIVE SOCIAL SCIENCE, HARVARD
    UNIVERSITY
    Block (Jeanne Humphrey) Dissertation Award: 1663
INSTITUTE FOR SUPPLY MANAGEMENT
    Richter (R. Gene) Scholarship Program: 1708
INSTITUTE FOR THE INTERNATIONAL EDUCATION OF
    STUDENTS (IES)
    Boren and Gilman Scholarship Support Grants: 1514
    Disability Grants: 1514
    Diversity Scholarships: 1514
    Donor Funded Scholarships: 1514
    Need Based Aid: 1514
    Partner University Scholarships: 1514
    Public University Grants: 1514
Institute for Trustees: 1153
Institute of American Cultures Grant: 960
Institute of American Cultures Visiting Research Scholar Fellowship
    Program in Ethnic Studies: 922
Institute of American Cultures Visiting Research Scholar Program in
    Ethnic Studies: 966
INSTITUTE OF CURRENT WORLD AFFAIRS: 772
INSTITUTE OF FOOD TECHNOLOGISTS FOUNDATION
    Freshman Scholarships: 2356
    Graduate Scholarships: 2356
    Undergraduate Scholarships: 2356
INSTITUTE OF INDUSTRIAL AND SYSTEMS ENGINEERS (IISE)
    CISE Undergraduate Scholarship: 2392
    Fargher (John S.W.) Scholarship: 2392
    Gambrell (C.B.) Undergraduate Scholarship: 2392
    Garden (Dwight D.) Scholarship: 2392
    Gilbreth Memorial Fellowship: 2392
    IISE Council of Fellows Undergraduate Scholarship: 2392
    IISE Fellows William Biles, Hamid Parsaei and Victor Zaloom
      Endowed Scholarship: 2392
    Imhoff (John L.) Scholarship: 2392
    Kroeze (Henry and Elisabeth) Memorial Scholarship: 2392
    Marcus (Harold and Inge) Scholarship: 2392
    Mundel (Marvin) Memorial Scholarship: 2392
    Presidents Scholarship: 2392
    Putnam (A.O.) Memorial Scholarship: 2392
    Sahney (Vinod and Gail) Scholarship: 2392
    Sierleja (E.J.) Memorial Fellowship: 2392
    Society for Health Systems Scholarship: 2392
    United Parcel Service Scholarship for Female Students: 2392
    United Parcel Service Scholarship for Minority Students: 2392
    Zaken (Lisa) Award of Excellence: 2392
INSTITUTE OF INTERNATIONAL EDUCATION
    Fulbright Scholar-in-Residence Program: 773
    Fulbright U.S. Student Program: 832
INSTITUTE OF INTERNATIONAL EDUCATION/COUNCIL FOR
    INTERNATIONAL EXCHANGE OF SCHOLARS
    Fulbright International Education Administrators Program: 1454
INSTITUTE OF MATERIALS, MINERALS AND MINING
    Centenary Scholarship: 2421
    Elmore (Stanley) Fellowship Fund: 2421
    Hobson (G. Vernon) Bequest: 2421
    Mining Club Award: 2421
    Pam (Edgar) Fellowship: 2421
    Seaman (The Tom) Travelling Scholarship: 2421
    Smith (Bosworth) Trust Fund: 2421
INSTITUTE OF MUSEUM AND LIBRARY SERVICES
    Bush (Laura) 21st Century Librarian Program: 672
    Grants to State Library Administrative Agencies: 672
    Inspire! Grants for Small Museums: 671
    Museum Assessment Program: 671
    Museum Grants for African American History and Culture: 671
    Museums Empowered: Professional Development Opportunities for
      Museum Staff: 671
    Museums for America: 671
    National Leadership Grants for Libraries: 672
    National Leadership Grants for Museums: 671
    National Medal for Museum and Library Service: 671, 672
    Native American Library Services: Basic Grants and Enhancement
      Grants: 672
    Native American/Native Hawaiian Museum Services Program: 671
    Native Hawaiian Library Services Grant: 672
Institutional Accountability and Individual Liberty: 250
Institutional Award for Undergraduate Student Training: 2123
Institutional Challenge Grant: 1016
Institutional Grants: 786
Institutional Project Support Grant Program for Japanese Studies: 775

Institutional Project Support Small Grant Program for Japanese Studies:
    775
Institutional Research Grants: 2179
Institutional Support: 444
Intellectual and Developmental Disabilities Branch (IDDB): 1318
Intellectual and Developmental Disabilities Scholastic Achievement
    Scholarships: 1373
IntelliSyn Pharma Research Excellence Award: 1856
Inter-American Music Awards: 728
INTER AMERICAN PRESS ASSOCIATION (IAPA)
    IAPA Scholarship Fund: 1737
INTERCOLLEGIATE STUDIES INSTITUTE (THE)
    Weaver (Richard M.) Graduate Fellowship: 1795
Intern Program at Jacob's Pillow (The): 488
International: 1346
International Affairs Education Program: 147
International Affairs Fellowship (IAF): 764
International Affairs Fellowship in Japan (IAF-J): 763
INTERNATIONAL ANESTHESIA RESEARCH SOCIETY (IARS)
    Frontiers in Anesthesia Research Award: 2039
    IARS Mentored Research Awards: 2039
INTERNATIONAL ASSOCIATION FOR DENTAL RESEARCH (IADR)
    IADR Colgate Research in Prevention Travel Awards: 2105
INTERNATIONAL ASSOCIATION FOR FOOD PROTECTION
    Barnum (Harold) Industry Award: 2415
    Beuchat (Larry) Young Researcher Award: 2415
    Food Safety Award: 2415
    Food Safety Innovation Award: 2415
    Haverland (Harry) Citation Award: 2415
    International Leadership Award: 2415
    Jay (James M.) Diversity in Food Safety Award: 2415
    Marth (Elmer) Educator Award: 2415
    Sanitarian Award: 2415
    Student Travel Scholarship Award: 2415
    Todd (Ewen C.D.) Control of Foodborne Illness Award: 2415
    Travel Award for Food Safety Professionals in a Country with a
      Developing Economy: 2415
    Travel Award for State or Provincial Health or Agricultural Department
      Employees: 2415
    Weber (Maurice) Laboratorian Award: 2415
International Association of Fire Chiefs Foundation Scholarship Program:
    1515
INTERNATIONAL ASSOCIATION OF FIRE CHIEFS FOUNDATION,
    INC.
    International Association of Fire Chiefs Foundation Scholarship
      Program: 1515
INTERNATIONAL ASSOCIATION OF ICE CREAM DISTRIBUTORS
    AND VENDORS (IAICDV)
    IAICDV Annual Scholarship: 1396
International Biodiversity: 1993
INTERNATIONAL CENTRE FOR COMPARATIVE CRIMINOLOGY
    Research Fieldwork: 1276
INTERNATIONAL CENTRE FOR DIFFRACTION DATA
    Frevel (The Ludo) Crystallography Scholarship Award: 2422
INTERNATIONAL COLLEGE OF SURGEONS (ICS)
    ICS Scholarship: 2040
International Concert Artists Competition: 707
INTERNATIONAL CRANE FOUNDATION, INC.: 1939
INTERNATIONAL DEVELOPMENT RESEARCH CENTRE (IDRC)
    IDRC Doctoral Research Awards (IDRA): 1183
    IDRC John G. Bene Research Fellowship in Developing Countries:
      1185
    IDRC Research Awards: 1184
International Dissertation Research Fellowship Program (IDRF): 783
International Dissertation Research Grant: 734
International Doctoral Scholarship for Studies Specializing in Jewish
    Fields: 749
INTERNATIONAL DOCUMENTARY ASSOCIATION
    IDA Documentary Awards: 417
    IDA/David L. Wolper Student Documentary Achievement Award: 417
    Lorentz (Pare) Award: 417
    Lorentz (Pare) Documentary Fund: 417
    Los Angeles County Arts Commission Internships: 417
INTERNATIONAL EXECUTIVE HOUSEKEEPERS ASSOCIATION
    (THE)
    PECP Self Study Program: 2357
International Fellowship in Jewish Studies and Jewish Culture: 749
INTERNATIONAL FOOD SERVICE EXECUTIVES ASSOCIATION,
    INC. (IFSEA)
    Worthy Goal Scholarship: 2358
INTERNATIONAL FOUNDATION (THE): 774

INTERNATIONAL FOUNDATION FOR ETHICAL RESEARCH, INC. (IFER)
  Graduate Fellowship Program for Alternatives to the Use of Animals in Science: 1633
International Fund: 888
International Health Policy and Practice Innovations: 1335
International Leadership Award: 2415
INTERNATIONAL LITERACY ASSOCIATION (ILA)
  Chall (Jeanne S.) Research Fellowship: 1397
  Corwin Literacy Leader Award: 1397
  Johns (Jerry) Outstanding Teacher Educator in Reading Award: 1398
  Leaders Inspiring Readers Award: 1397
  Shanahan (Timothy and Cynthia) Outstanding Dissertation Award: 1397
  Stahl (Steven A.) Research Grant: 1397
INTERNATIONAL MYELOMA FOUNDATION (IMF)
  Novis (Brian D.) Research Grants: 2041
INTERNATIONAL OCD FOUNDATION
  Annual Conference: 2328
  Behavior Therapy Training Institute (BTTI): 2328
  Research Awards: 2328
International Operators Scholarship: 2368
INTERNATIONAL ORDER OF ALHAMBRA
  Scholarship and Charity Fund: 2300
INTERNATIONAL RESEARCH & EXCHANGES BOARD (IREX): 833
INTERNATIONAL ROAD FEDERATION
  IRF Fellowship Program: 872
International Scholarship: 1481
International Security and Foreign Policy Program: 1672
International Semester and Year Programs: 868
International Travel Awards: 1944
INTERNATIONAL WOMEN'S FISHING ASSOCIATION SCHOLARSHIP TRUST
  IWFA Scholarship Trust: 1868
International Youth Competition: 707
Internship Program: 722
Interpretive Fellowships at Art Museums: 506
Intramural Research Grant Program: 2019
INVESTED
  InvestED School Partnership/Funding Program: 1431
InvestED School Partnership/Funding Program: 1431
INVESTIGATIVE REPORTERS AND EDITORS
  Investigative Reporters and Editors Contest: 1738
Investigative Reporters and Editors Contest: 1738
Investigator Initiated Grants (IIG): 2180
Investigator-Initiated Research (IIR): 2191
Investigator-Initiated Research Projects: 1890
Investigator Research Grant: 2277
Investigators in the Pathogenesis of Infectious Disease: 2016
Investments in Arts and Culture (IAC): 451
IODE
  War Memorial Scholarships: 1516
IOWA ARTS COUNCIL
  Arts Resources and Artists Programs: 418
  Funding and Arts in Education Programs: 418
  Technical Assistance and Community Development Programs: 418
Iowa Short Fiction Award (The): 649
IRA Educational Foundation Scholarship Program: 1511
IRAEFF Restaurant Employee Relief Fund: 1511
IRF Fellowship Program: 872
Israel Grants: 1186
ISTITUTO ITALIANO PER GLI STUDI STORICI
  Federico II Scholarship: 550
  Istituto italiano per gli studi storici Scholarships for Graduate Students and Young Postdocs: 550
Istituto italiano per gli studi storici Scholarships for Graduate Students and Young Postdocs: 550
ITALIAN AMERICAN STUDIES ASSOCIATION
  IASA Memorial Fellowship: 551
ITTLESON FOUNDATION, INC.: 1341
IWFA Scholarship Trust: 1868

J

J-LEAP: 1517
J.M.K. Innovation Prize (The): 154
JACK AND JILL OF AMERICA FOUNDATION (THE)
  Heart and Mind: 933
  Hidden Talent Grants: 933

  Our Village: 933
  Reading Corner Literacy Grant: 933
  Teen Community Service Award: 933
JACKSON (ANN) FAMILY FOUNDATION: 145
JACKSON FOUNDATION (THE): 146
JACKSON (HENRY M.) FOUNDATION
  Environmental and Natural Resources Management Program: 147
  Human Rights Program: 147
  International Affairs Education Program: 147
  Public Service Program: 147
Jackson (The Roland) Award: 691
Jackson (The William E.) Award: 2371
JACKSONVILLE JAGUARS FOUNDATION: 148
JACL Kakehashi Program: 777
JACL National Scholarship and Awards Program: 1518
JACOB'S PILLOW, INC.
  Intern Program at Jacob's Pillow (The): 488
  School at Jacob's Pillow (The): 487
Jacoby (Victor Thomas) Award: 1182
Jacques (Harry and Laura) Graduate Scholarship: 1879
Jacyk (Petro) Distinguished Fellowship in Ukrainian Studies: 358
Jaffee (David) Fellowship: 304
Jahnigen (Dennis W.) Memorial Award: 2294
James (Olivia) Traveling Fellowship: 310
James River Water Quality Improvement Program: 1992
Jameson (J. Franklin) Award: 526
Jameson (The J. Franklin) Fellowship: 527
Jamestown Rediscovery-Omohundro Institute (JR-OI) Short-Term Visiting Fellowship: 574
Jane's Fellowship Program: 1235
Janeway (Ray C.) Scholarship: 683
Jansky Fellowships at the NRAO: 1841
JAPAN FOUNDATION, LOS ANGELES (THE)
  Arts & Culture Grants: 1517
  J-LEAP: 1517
  Japanese Language Grants: 1517
JAPAN FOUNDATION, NEW YORK (THE)
  Abe Fellowship for Journalists Program: 775
  Abe Fellowship Program: 775
  CGP Grant Program - Discretionary Grants: 775
  CGP Grant Program - Education Grants: 775
  CGP Grant Program - Grassroots Program: 775
  CGP Grant Program - Intellectual Exchange: 775
  Exhibitions Abroad Support Program: 775
  Institutional Project Support Grant Program for Japanese Studies: 775
  Institutional Project Support Small Grant Program for Japanese Studies: 775
  Japanese Studies Fellowship Program: 775
  JFNY Grant for Japanese Studies: 775
  JFNY Grant Program - Arts and Culture: 775
  Performing Arts Japan Program: 775
  Support Program for Translation and Publication on Japan: 775
  U.S.-Southeast Asia-Japan Collaboration and Exchange Initiative: 775
JAPAN INFORMATION CENTER
  Japanese Government (Monbukagakusho) Scholarships for Japanese Studies: 834
  Japanese Government (Monbukagakusho) Scholarships for Research Students: 835
Japan Society for the Promotion of Science Postdoctoral Research Fellowships (Extramural): 879
JAPAN-U.S. FRIENDSHIP COMMISSION: 776
Japan-U.S. Senate Youth Exchange Program: 868
JAPANESE AMERICAN CITIZENS LEAGUE (JACL) (THE)
  JACL Kakehashi Program: 777
  JACL National Scholarship and Awards Program: 1518
  Masaoka (Mike M.) Fellowship Fund Congressional Program: 1796
Japanese Government (Monbukagakusho) Scholarships for Japanese Studies: 834
Japanese Government (Monbukagakusho) Scholarships for Research Students: 835
Japanese Language Grants: 1517
Japanese Studies Fellowship Program: 775
Jay (James M.) Diversity in Food Safety Award: 2415
Jazz Touring Network: 430
JDRF INTERNATIONAL
  Career Development Awards: 2171
  Postdoctoral Fellowships: 2170
  Strategic Research Agreements: Project Concept Call: 2169
JEFFRESS (THOMAS F. AND KATE MILLER) MEMORIAL TRUST
  Jeffress Trust Awards Program in Interdisciplinary Research: 1896
Jeffress Trust Awards Program in Interdisciplinary Research: 1896

JELLISON BENEVOLENT SOCIETY: 1399
JENKINS FOUNDATION (THE): 1301
Jenkins Foundation: Improving the Health of Greater Richmond (The): 1098
JENNINGS (MARTHA HOLDEN) FOUNDATION
  Grants-to-Educators Program: 1432
  Open Grants: 1432
Jenny (Daniel P.) Research Fellowships: 2403
Jensen (The Walter J.) Fellowship for French Language, Literature and Culture: 847
Jerome Fellowships: 645
JEROME FOUNDATION, INC.: 419
Jessup Fellowship: 1930
JEWISH BOOK COUNCIL
  National Jewish Book Award-American Jewish Studies: 621
  National Jewish Book Award-Anthologies and Collections: 621
  National Jewish Book Award-Autobiography and Memoir: 621
  National Jewish Book Award-Biography: 621
  National Jewish Book Award-Book Club: 621
  National Jewish Book Award-Children's Literature: 621
  National Jewish Book Award-Contemporary Jewish Life and Practice: 621
  National Jewish Book Award-Debut Fiction: 621
  National Jewish Book Award-Education and Jewish Identity: 621
  National Jewish Book Award-Fiction: 621
  National Jewish Book Award-Food Writing and Cookbooks: 621
  National Jewish Book Award-History: 621
  National Jewish Book Award-Holocaust: 621
  National Jewish Book Award-Modern Jewish Thought and Experience: 621
  National Jewish Book Award-Poetry: 621
  National Jewish Book Award-Scholarship: 621
  National Jewish Book Award-Sephardic Culture: 621
  National Jewish Book Award-Visual Arts: 621
  National Jewish Book Award-Women's Studies: 621
  National Jewish Book Award-Writing Based on Archival Material: 621
  National Jewish Book Award-Young Adult Literature: 621
JEWISH COMMUNITY FOUNDATION OF LOS ANGELES
  Capital Grants: 1186
  Cutting Edge Grants: 1186
  General Community Grants: 1186
  Israel Grants: 1186
  Next Stage Grants: 1186
  Reimagine Grants: 1186
JEWISH FAMILY AND CHILDREN'S SERVICES
  Educational Loans and Grants Program: 1519
JEWISH FEDERATION OF METROPOLITAN CHICAGO ACADEMIC SCHOLARSHIP PROGRAM: 1520
JEWISH HEALTHCARE FOUNDATION OF PITTSBURGH (THE): 1302
Jewson (Ruth) Award: 1350
JFNY Grant for Japanese Studies: 775
JFNY Grant Program - Arts and Culture: 775
JILA
  Postdoctoral Research Associateships: 1822
  Visiting Fellowships: 1822
JOHNS HOPKINS CENTER FOR ALTERNATIVES TO ANIMAL TESTING (THE): 1303
Johns (Hyland) Grant: 1925
Johns (Jerry) Outstanding Teacher Educator in Reading Award: 1398
JOHNSON & JOHNSON FAMILY OF COMPANIES: 149
Johnson & Johnson/NMF Future Leaders Scholarship Program: 2062
JOHNSON CONTROLS FOUNDATION: 150
Johnson (Genita Evangelista) Endowed Scholarship: 2062
Johnson (Lyndon B.) School of Public Affairs: 1466
JOHNSON (THE LYNDON BAINES) FOUNDATION
  Middleton Fellowship in Presidential Studies: 1797
  Moody Research Grants: 1797
JOHNSON (MAGIC) FOUNDATION
  Johnson (Magic) Foundation HIV/AIDS Grant: 151
  Johnson (Magic) Foundation HIV/AIDS Grant: 151
JOHNSON (ROBERT WOOD) FOUNDATION: 2042
Jones Backcountry Adventure Grant: 1957
JONES (DAISY MARQUIS) FOUNDATION: 152
JONES (THE FLETCHER) FOUNDATION: 1455
Jordan (Cheryl) Scholarship Fund: 2293
Joshi (Paramjit Toor), M.D., International Scholar Awards: 2308
JOSLYN (THE CARL W. AND CARRIE MAE) CHARITABLE TRUST: 1342

JOURNAL OF THE AMERICAN MEDICAL ASSOCIATION
  Fishbein (Morris) Fellowship in Medical Editing: 1739
Journalism Foundation Scholarships: 1567
Journalism Program: 167
JOYCE FOUNDATION (THE): 153
Judaic and Related Studies Postdoctoral Fellowships: 836
Judicial Fellowship Program: 1785
JUMP StArts: 394
Junior Faculty Development Award (JFD): 2148
Junior Faculty Scholar Award: 2006
Junior Fellowship: 801
Junior Fellowships: 375
Junior Investigator Award: 2308
Junior Investigator Awards: 2205
Justice Reform: 2043
Juvenile Justice and Delinquency Prevention Allocation to States: 1280
Juvenile Justice and Delinquency Prevention Program: 1279
Juvenile Justice Program: 1056

K

Kabis (Dorothy) Internship: 984
Kahan (Gerald) Scholar's Prize: 482
Kalamazoo Chapter No. 116-Roscoe Douglas Scholarship: 2361
Kalman (Diana Jacobs)/AFAR Scholarships for Research in the Biology of Aging: 1999
Kanawha and Ohio River Valleys Program: 1992
Kandaras (Mary) Memorial Scholarship (Undergraduate): 976
KANSAS BOARD OF REGENTS
  Kansas Comprehensive Grant: 1521
Kansas Comprehensive Grant: 1521
KANSAS HEALTH FOUNDATION
  Impact Capacity Grant: 1304
KANTZLER FOUNDATION (THE): 1187
Kaplan-Goodkind Memorial Scholarship Fund: 731
KAPLAN (THE J.M.) FUND, INC.
  Discretionary Grants: 154
  Environment Program Grant: 154
  Furthermore Grant: 154
  Heritage Conservation Grant: 154
  J.M.K. Innovation Prize (The): 154
  Social Justice Grant: 154
Kappa Epsilon-AFPE-Nellie Wakeman First Year Graduate Fellowship: 2289
KAPPA OMICRON NU HONOR SOCIETY
  Brown (Marjorie M.) Dissertation Fellowship: 2416
  Hawthorne (Ruth E.) Research Grant: 2416
  Maddex (Eileen C.) Fellowship: 2416
  National Alumni Chapter Fellowship: 2416
  National Alumni Chapter Grant: 2416
  New Initiatives Grant: 2416
  Omicron Nu Master's Fellowship: 2416
  Omicron Nu Research Fellowship: 2416
  Root (Betty Jeanne) Fellowship: 2416
  Undergraduate Research Award: 2416
KAPPA TAU ALPHA
  Mott (Frank Luther) KTA Research/Book Award: 1740
Kass Teacher Fellowships at MHS: 556
KATE SPADE NEW YORK FOUNDATION: 155
Katz (The Friedrich) Prize: 526
KATZ (HERBERT D.) CENTER FOR ADVANCED JUDAIC STUDIES
  Judaic and Related Studies Postdoctoral Fellowships: 836
Kaufman (Lucille B.) Women's Scholarship: 2361
Kay (E. Wayne) Scholarships: 2361
KAZANJIAN (THE CALVIN K.) ECONOMICS FOUNDATION, INC.: 1709
KCC-JEE High School Essay Contest (The): 837
Keats (Ezra Jack)/Janina Domanska Children's Literature Research Fellowship: 651
Keats (The Ezra Jack)/Kerlan Memorial Fellowship: 650
KELLENBERGER (MAY GORDON LATHAM) HISTORICAL FOUNDATION: 156
Keller (David) Travel Grants: 482
Keller (Kate Van Winkle) Fellowship: 304
KELLEY (EDWARD BANGS) & ELZA KELLEY FOUNDATION, INC.: 1188
KELLOGG (W.K.) FOUNDATION: 157
Kelly (Barbara Mandigo) Peace Poetry Awards: 779
Kelly (The Joan) Memorial Prize in Women's History: 526

Kempf Fund Award for Research Development in Psychobiological
  Psychiatry: 2310
KEMPNER (HARRIS AND ELIZA) FUND
  Matching Gifts Program: 158
  Primary Grant Program: 158
  Program Related Investments: 158
KENAN (WILLIAM R., JR.) CHARITABLE TRUST: 1400
KENNEDY (JOHN F.) LIBRARY FOUNDATION
  Kovler (Marjorie) Fellowship: 159
  Schlesinger (Arthur M., Jr.) Fellowship: 159
  Schwartz (Abba T.) Fellowship: 159
  Sorensen (Theodore C.) Fellowship: 159
KENNEDY (JOHN F.) PRESIDENTIAL LIBRARY
  Kennedy Library Archival Internships: 160
Kennedy Library Archival Internships: 160
Kennedy-Lugar Youth Exchange and Study Abroad (YES Abroad): 793
KENNEDY MEMORIAL TRUST (THE)
  Kennedy Scholarships: 873
KENNEDY (ROBERT F.) HUMAN RIGHTS
  RFK Book Award: 622
  RFK Journalism Awards: 622
Kennedy Scholarships: 873
KENTUCKY ARTS COUNCIL
  Arts First Aid: 420
  Emerging Artist Award: 420
  Folk and Traditional Arts Apprenticeship: 420
  Kentucky Arts Partnerships: 420
  Kentucky Peer Advisory Network: 420
  Poetry Out Loud: 420
  Showcasing the Arts: 420
  Smith (Al) Individual Artist Fellowships: 420
  Teaching Art Together: 420
  TranspARTation: 420
Kentucky Arts Partnerships: 420
Kentucky Educational Excellence Scholarship (KEES): 1522
KENTUCKY FOUNDATION FOR WOMEN
  Art Meets Activism: 979
  Artist Enrichment: 979
  Hopscotch House Artist Retreat and Residency Center: 979
KENTUCKY HIGHER EDUCATION ASSISTANCE AUTHORITY
  (KHEAA)
  College Access Program (CAP): 1522
  Kentucky Educational Excellence Scholarship (KEES): 1522
  Kentucky National Guard Tuition Award Program: 1523
  Kentucky Tuition Grant (KTG): 1522
KENTUCKY HISTORICAL SOCIETY
  Scholarly Research Fellowship Program: 552
Kentucky National Guard Tuition Award Program: 1523
Kentucky Peer Advisory Network: 420
Kentucky Tuition Grant (KTG): 1522
Kenya/East Africa: 57
KERR FOUNDATION, INC. (THE): 161
KERR (GRAYCE B.) FUND, INC.: 162
Kestnbaum (Robert) Research Program: 1711
KETTERING FUND (THE): 1189
KEWEENAW COMMUNITY FOUNDATION: 1190
Kezios (Agnes Malakate) Scholarship: 2387
Kidder (The Louise) Early Career Award: 1692
KIDNEY FOUNDATION OF CANADA (THE)
  Allied Health Kidney Doctoral Fellowship: 2175
  Allied Health Kidney Research Grant: 2173
  Allied Health Kidney Scholarship: 2175
  Kidney Health Research Grants: 2172
  KRESCENT: Kidney Research Scientist Core Education and National
    Training Program: 2174
Kidney Health Research Grants: 2172
Killam (Izaak Walton) Doctoral Scholarships: 1597
Kim (Michael) Broadcast Fellowship: 1484
KIMBERLY-CLARK FOUNDATION, INC.: 163
Kimbrough (Arch and Anne Giles) Fund: 500
Kimmel (Jack) International Grant: 1925
King (Donald) Summer Research Fellowship: 2213
KING (STEPHEN AND TABITHA) FOUNDATION: 164
King (Steven G.) Play Environments Scholarship: 1974
Kinkeldey (The Otto) Award: 691
Kinley (Kate Neal) Memorial Fellowship: 522
Kiplinger (W.M.) Distinguished Contributions to Journalism Award: 1750
KIRBY (F.M.) FOUNDATION, INC.: 165
Kirschen Family Student Travel Fellowship: 2258
Kirschstein (Ruth L.) National Research Service Awards (NRSA) for
  Individual Postdoctoral Fellows (Parent F32): 2055

Kirschstein (Ruth L.) National Research Service Awards (NRSA) for
  Individual Senior Fellows (Parent F33): 2057
KITSAP COMMUNITY FOUNDATION
  Annual Competitive Grant Program: 1191
Klausman (Jane M.) Women in Business Scholarships: 1722
Kleffner (Frank R.) Clinical Career Award: 2262
Klein (Martin A.) Prize in African History: 526
Kligman (Albert M.) Fellowship Fund Award: 2088
Kline Foundation Grants: 166
KLINE (JOSIAH W. AND BESSIE H.) FOUNDATION, INC.
  Kline Foundation Grants: 166
Klineberg (Otto) Intercultural and International Relations Award: 1807
KLINGENSTEIN CENTER FOR INDEPENDENT SCHOOL
  LEADERSHIP
  Klingenstein Heads of Schools Program: 1433
  Klingenstein Summer Institute for Early Career Teachers: 1433
  Master's Degree in Private School Leadership: 1433
Klingenstein Heads of Schools Program: 1433
Klingenstein Summer Institute for Early Career Teachers: 1433
KLINGENSTEIN THIRD GENERATION FOUNDATION (THE): 2329
Klumpke-Roberts Award: 1834
Knight-Bagehot Fellowship in Economics and Business Journalism: 1730
KNIGHT (JOHN S. AND JAMES L.) FOUNDATION
  Arts Program: 167
  Communities Program: 167
  Journalism Program: 167
  Learning and Impact Program: 167
Knight Science Journalism Fellowship: 1743
Knight-Wallace Fellowships for Journalists: 1763
KNIGHTS OF COLUMBUS
  Greco (Bishop Charles P.) Graduate Fellowships: 1524
  McDevitt (John W.) Fourth Degree Scholarships: 1524
  Pro Deo and Pro Patria Scholarships: 1524
KNIGHTS OF COLUMBUS VATICAN FILM LIBRARY AT ST. LOUIS
  UNIVERSITY
  Vatican Film Library Mellon Fellowship: 623
KNOTT (MARION I. AND HENRY J.) FOUNDATION, INC.: 168
KNOX COUNTY FOUNDATION: 169
Knox (Eileen) Memorial Scholarship: 1476
KOBE COLLEGE CORPORATION-JAPAN EDUCATION EXCHANGE
  KCC-JEE High School Essay Contest (The): 837
KOCH (CHARLES G.) CHARITABLE FOUNDATION: 1401
KOCH FOUNDATION, INC.: 745
Komen Scholar Grants: 2191
KOMEN (SUSAN G.)
  Career Catalyst Research Grants (CCR): 2191
  Global Grants: 2191
  Graduate Training in Disparities Research (GTDR): 2191
  Investigator-Initiated Research (IIR): 2191
  Komen Scholar Grants: 2191
  Postdoctoral Fellowship (PDF): 2191
  Promise Grants: 2191
Korb-Exford Dry Eye Career Development Grant: 2259
Koren (The William, Jr.) Prize: 584
KORET FOUNDATION: 170
Kosciuszko Foundation Graduate Studies and Research in Poland (The):
  840
Kosciuszko Foundation Tuition Scholarship (The): 1525
Kosciuszko Foundation Year Abroad Program (The): 839
KOSCIUSZKO FOUNDATION, INC. (THE)
  Chopin Piano Competition: 708
  Kosciuszko Foundation Graduate Studies and Research in Poland (The):
    840
  Kosciuszko Foundation Tuition Scholarship (The): 1525
  Kosciuszko Foundation Year Abroad Program (The): 839
  Summer Study Abroad Programs: 838
  Teaching English in Poland: 841
  Wisconsin Study in Poland (WSIP): 1526
Koshland Young Leader Awards: 255
Kottis Family Scholarship (Undergraduate): 976
Kovacs (Katherine Singer) Prize: 603
Kovler (Marjorie) Fellowship: 159
KPMG FOUNDATION: 1710
KRAFT HEINZ COMPANY FOUNDATION (THE): 171
Kraus (Michael) Research Grant: 526
Kreppner (James) Award: 2021
KRESCENT: Kidney Research Scientist Core Education and National
  Training Program: 2174
KRESGE FOUNDATION (THE): 172

KRESS (SAMUEL H.) FOUNDATION
  Conservation Fellowships: 506
  Conservation Grant Program: 506
  Digital Art History Grant Program: 506
  History of Art Grant Program: 506
  History of Art: Institutional Fellowships: 506
  Interpretive Fellowships at Art Museums: 506
Kress (Samuel H.) Grants for Research and Publication in Classical Art
  and Architecture: 1480
Kroeze (Henry and Elisabeth) Memorial Scholarship: 2392
KROGER COMPANY FOUNDATION (THE): 1192
KRONKOSKY (ALBERT AND BESSIE MAE) CHARITABLE
  FOUNDATION: 173
Kuchinski (David A.) Memorial Research Grant: 2277
Kummerow (Glenn) Memorial Scholarship: 1744
Kun Scholarship Fund: 731
KVAMME (THE JEAN AND E. FLOYD) FOUNDATION: 1402

L

Labatt (John) Limited Scholarship: 1599
Lacks (Henrietta) Memorial Scholarship: 2062
LaCuesta (Lloyd) Internship Grant: 1482
Ladish Co. Foundation Scholarships: 2420
LA84 FOUNDATION: 1305
LAF Honor Scholarship for Inclusive Community Design: 1974
LAF Honor Scholarship in Memory of Joe Lalli, FASLA: 1974
LAIDLAW FOUNDATION
  Youth Action Fund: 174
Lalor Burdick (The Anna) Program: 2250
Lalor Foundation Postdoctoral Fellowship Program (The): 1634
LALOR FOUNDATION, INC. (THE)
  Lalor Burdick (The Anna) Program: 2250
  Lalor Foundation Postdoctoral Fellowship Program (The): 1634
Lamarsh (John R.) Memorial Scholarship: 2381
LAMB FOUNDATION: 175
Lancour (Harold) Foreign Research Fellowship: 662
LAND O'LAKES FOUNDATION
  Brandt (John) Memorial Scholarship Fund: 177
  California Regions Grant Program: 176
  Community Grants Program: 176
  Dollars for Doers Program: 176
  Matching Gifts to Education Program: 176
  Member Co-op Match Program: 176
  Mid-Atlantic Grant Program: 176
Landis (John and Muriel) Scholarships: 2378
LANDSCAPE ARCHITECTURE FOUNDATION
  ASLA Council of Fellows Scholarship: 1974
  ASLA Florida Chapter Career Discovery Scholarships: 1974
  ASLA-NY Designing in the Public Realm Scholarship: 1974
  EDSA Minority Scholarship: 1974
  Hawaii Chapter ASLA/David T. Woolsey Scholarship: 1974
  King (Steven G.) Play Environments Scholarship: 1974
  LAF Honor Scholarship for Inclusive Community Design: 1974
  LAF Honor Scholarship in Memory of Joe Lalli, FASLA: 1974
  Landscape Forms Scholarship in Memory of Peter Schaudt, FASLA:
    1974
  Paul (Courtland) Scholarship: 1974
  Peridian International Inc./Rae L. Price, FASLA Scholarship: 1974
  Rain Bird Intelligent Use of Water Scholarship: 1974
  Thomas (Douglas Dockery) Fellowship in Garden History and Design:
    1974
Landscape Forms Scholarship in Memory of Peter Schaudt, FASLA: 1974
LANGELOTH (THE JACOB AND VALERIA) FOUNDATION
  Justice Reform: 2043
  Safe and Healthy Communities: 2043
Language Resource Centers Program: 610
Lapides (Linda F. and Julian L.) Fellowship: 304
Lapidus-OI Fellowship: 575
Large Research Grants: 1418
Laroche (Dr. Daniel Denis, Sr.) Scholarship: 2062
Las Cumbres Amateur Outreach Award: 1836
LASPAU, INC.: 874
Last (Jay and Deborah) Fellowship: 304
Latin American Professional AAZK Travel Grant: 1931
LATKIN (HERBERT AND GERTRUDE) CHARITABLE
  FOUNDATION: 178
Laurels Fund: 1704
LAURIE (THE BLANCHE AND IRVING) FOUNDATION: 179
Law Enforcement Officer Memorial Scholarship: 1507

Law Enforcement Personnel Dependents' Grant Program (LEPD): 1488
LAWRENCE COUNTY COMMUNITY FOUNDATION: 1193
Layser (Pattie) Greater Yellowstone Creative Writing & Journalism
  Fellowship: 479
LDF Earl Warren Legal Training Program: 934
LDF Herbert Lehman Education Fund Scholarship Program: 934
LEACOCK (STEPHEN) ASSOCIATES
  Leacock (Stephen) Memorial Medal for Humour: 624
Leacock (Stephen) Memorial Medal for Humour: 624
Leaders Inspiring Readers Award: 1397
Leadership Development for Racial Equity: 1334
Leadership Development for Youth: 1014
Leadership Development Institute: 1477
Leadership Grant: 1223
League Prize for Young Architects and Designers (The): 370
Leakey Foundation Grants: 1811
LEAKEY (L.S.B.) FOUNDATION
  Leakey Foundation Grants: 1811
Learning and Impact Program: 167
LEARNING FOR LIFE
  Exploring Program: 1403
Lebowitz (Dr. Martin R.) and Eve Lewellis Lebowitz Prize for
  Philosophical Achievement and Contribution (The): 1671
Lecture Series: 755
Lee (The J.S.) Memorial Fellowship: 408
LEEDS INTERNATIONAL PIANO COMPETITION (THE): 709
LEEWAY FOUNDATION (THE)
  Art and Change Grant: 980
  Leeway Transformation Award: 980
Leeway Transformation Award: 980
LEF FOUNDATION (THE)
  Moving Image Fund: 374
Legacy Fellowship (The): 304
LEHIGH VALLEY COMMUNITY FOUNDATION: 421
LEIDY (THE JOHN J.) FOUNDATION: 1194
Leighton Award for Nonprofit Excellence: 1120
Leipen (Neda and Franz) Fellowship: 315
Leisch (Jack E.) Memorial National Graduate Fellowship: 2386
Leisner (Tony B.) Scholarship: 1443
Leland (The Waldo G.) Prize: 526
Lenard (John) Civil Engineering Scholarship: 2386
Lerner-Gray Grants for Marine Research: 1619
LESCHETIZKY ASSOCIATION, INC. (THE)
  Concerto Competition "Theodor Leschetizky" for Gifted Young
    Pianists: 710
LEUKEMIA & LYMPHOMA SOCIETY (THE)
  Career Development Program: 2116
  Specialized Center of Research Program: 2118
  Translational Research Program: 2117
LEUKEMIA RESEARCH FOUNDATION
  New Investigator Awards: 2192
Leviant (Fenia and Yaakov) Memorial Prize in Yiddish Studies: 603
Levin (Don) Trust Scholarship: 2062
Levinson (Suzanne J.) Prize: 548
Lewis and Clark Fund for Exploration and Field Research (The): 12
Lewis (H.S. and Angeline) Scholarships: 1476
Lewis (Lloyd) Fellowships in American History: 345
lfft Foundation Fund: 143
LGBTQ Community Fund: 206
LGBTQ+ Fellowship: 1477
Liang (Ta) Memorial Award: 1821
LIBERTY HILL FOUNDATION
  California Funders for Boys and Men of Color (CFBMOC): 1343
  emPOWER: 1343
  Fund for Change (FFC): 1343
  Marks (Wally) Leadership Institute for Change: 1343
  Ready to Rise: 1343
  Stay Housed LA: 1343
LIBRA FOUNDATION: 180
LIBRARY COMPANY OF PHILADELPHIA
  Greenfield (Albert M.) Foundation Dissertation Fellowships: 553
  NEH Postdoctoral Fellowships: 553
  Program in African-American History: 553
  Program in Early American Economy and Society: 553
  Research Fellowships in American History and Culture: 553
Library Construction Grants: 676
Library Degree for Law School Graduates: 656
Library Degree for Non-Law School Graduates: 656
Library of American Broadcasting Foundation Award: 1724
Library Resident Research Fellowships (The): 308
Library School Graduates Attending Law School: 656

Library School Graduates Seeking a Non-Law Degree: 656
Library Services and Technology Act: 682
Library Services and Technology Act Competitive Grants: 676
Life Members Mentorship Grant for Medical Students: 2308
LIFE SCIENCES RESEARCH FOUNDATION (LSRF)
    Three-Year Postdoctoral Fellowships: 1940
LiftOff: 403
LIGHT WORK
    Light Work Artist-in-Residence Program: 507
    Light Work Grants in Photography: 507
Light Work Artist-in-Residence Program: 507
Light Work Grants in Photography: 507
LILLY ENDOWMENT INC.: 181
Lin (Sam Chu) Internship Grant: 1482
LINCOLN FINANCIAL FOUNDATION: 182
LINCOLN (THE JAMES F.) ARC WELDING FOUNDATION
    Awards for Achievement in Arc Welded Design, Engineering and
    Fabrication: College Division: 2393
Lindbergh (Charles A.) Chair in Aerospace History: 2372
LINDSAY (THE AGNES M.) TRUST
    Camp Scholarships: 1019
    Dental Health: 1019
    Education: 1019
    Food Banks: 1019
    Health and Welfare: 1019
    Homeless Shelters: 1019
Liner (Robert T.) Memorial Scholarship: 2380
Linford (Henry B.) Award for Distinguished Teaching: 1627
Linguistics Program: 604
Linguistics Program-Doctoral Dissertation Research Improvement Grants
    (Ling-DDRI): 604
LINK FOUNDATION
    Energy Fellowship Program: 1823
    Oceanography Engineering Fellowship Program: 1823
    Simulation Fellowship Program: 1823
Linn County Fund: 1165
Lipman (David S.) Scholarship: 1567
LITA/Christian Larew Memorial Scholarship: 1443
Literacy Interventions PreK-3rd Grades: 1024
Literary Art: 384
Literary Arts Fellowships: 479
Litherland/FTEE Scholarship Undergraduate Major in Technology and
    Engineering Education: 1504
LITTAUER (THE LUCIUS N.) FOUNDATION, INC.: 904
Littleton-Griswold Grant: 526
Littleton-Griswold Prize in American Law and Society (The): 526
Live Your Dream Grant: 1957
Living Legacy Jazz Award: 430
LIVINGSTON AWARDS
    Livingston Awards for Young Journalists: 1741
Livingston Awards for Young Journalists: 1741
LIVINGSTON MEMORIAL FOUNDATION
    Operational Program Grants: 1306
    Special Project Grants: 1306
LLOYD (JOHN M.) FOUNDATION: 1779
LOATS FOUNDATION, INC. (THE): 183
Local- and State-Level Policy Work Grants: 1686
Local Arts Grants: 454
Local Grantmaking Program: 229
Local History Grants: 332
Local Impact: 394
Local Impact in Forsyth County: 1355
Local Impact Investing Initiative: 920
LOCAL INITIATIVES SUPPORT CORPORATION: 1195
Lochtie (Robert) Memorial Fund: 1182
Lockwood (Lewis) Award: 691
LOEB (THE GERALD) AWARDS: 1742
Logan (The George) Scholarship: 1744
Londin (Larrie) Memorial Scholarship: 722
LONG ISLAND COMMUNITY FOUNDATION: 1196
Long-Term Fellowships: 1938
Long-Term Research Fellowship: 558
LONG-THIBAUD-CRESPIN COMPETITION: 711
LONGHI (THE ROBERTO) FOUNDATION FOR THE STUDY OF THE
    HISTORY OF ART
    Art History Fellowships in Florence: 508
Loran Awards: 1527
LORAN SCHOLARS FOUNDATION
    Loran Awards: 1527
Lorentz (Pare) Award: 417

Lorentz (Pare) Documentary Fund: 417
Lorénzen (Lilly) Scholarship: 819
Loring (Suzanne and Caleb) Fellowship: 555
LOS ALAMOS NATIONAL LABORATORY
    Feynman (Richard P.) Postdoctoral Fellowship in Theory and
    Computing: 1635
    Oppenheimer (J. Robert) Postdoctoral Fellowship: 1635
    Reines (Frederick) Postdoctoral Fellowship in Experimental Sciences:
    1635
Los Angeles County Arts Commission Internships: 417
LOS ANGELES RAMS FOUNDATION: 1020
LOUISIANA DIVISION OF THE ARTS, DEPARTMENT OF
    CULTURE, RECREATION AND TOURISM: 423
    Louisiana Project Grants: 422
Louisiana Project Grants: 422
LOWE SYNDROME ASSOCIATION
    McSpadden (The Leland) Memorial Fund for Medical and Scientific
    Research: 2044
Lowell (James Russell) Prize: 603
Loxton (F.H.) Postgraduate Studentships: 1927
LPI Summer Intern Program in Planetary Science: 1839
LRF Scientific Research Mentoring Program (LSRMP): 2119
LUBRIZOL FOUNDATION (THE)
    Community Connection Employee Volunteer Gift Program: 184
    Matching Gift Program: 184
Luce (Clare Boothe) Program: 185
Luce Foundation Religion and Theology Program: 185
LUCE (THE HENRY) FOUNDATION, INC.
    American Art Program: 185
    Asia Program: 185
    Higher Education Program: 185
    Luce (Clare Boothe) Program: 185
    Luce Foundation Religion and Theology Program: 185
    Luce Scholars Program: 185
    Public Policy Program: 185
Luce Scholars Program: 185
LUMINA FOUNDATION: 1456
Lumsden-Kouvel (The Audrey) Fellowship: 342
LUNAR AND PLANETARY INSTITUTE
    LPI Summer Intern Program in Planetary Science: 1839
Lung Cancer Discovery Awards: 2133
Lung Diseases Research: 2144
LUPUS FOUNDATION OF AMERICA, INC.
    Finzi (Gina M.) Memorial Student Summer Fellowship Program: 2045
Lusher (Jeanne Maria) Diversity Fellowship: 2051
LUSO-AMERICAN EDUCATION FOUNDATION
    Educational Grant Program: 601
    Luso-American Education Foundation Scholarships: 600
Luso-American Education Foundation Scholarships: 600
LUTHERAN FOUNDATION OF ST. LOUIS: 746
Lyman (Peter) Memorial/SAGE Scholarships: 1443
LYMPHOMA RESEARCH FOUNDATION
    Clinical Investigator Career Development Awards (CDA): 2119
    Disease Focus Area Grants for Senior Investigators: 2119
    LRF Scientific Research Mentoring Program (LSRMP): 2119
    Peykoff (Jamie) Follicular Lymphoma Research Initiative: 2119
    Postdoctoral Fellowship Grants: 2119
LYNDHURST FOUNDATION: 186

M

M & M AREA COMMUNITY FOUNDATION: 1197
MA Graphic Design: 509
MA Illustration: 509
MA in Art History: 521
MA Social Design: 509
MAC College Money Program: 1267
MAC Foundation Scholarship: 2423
MAC Student Travel/Research Grants: 2423
MacAllister (P.E.) Fellowships: 818
MacArthur Foundation Nuclear Security Fellowship (The): 760
MACARTHUR (JOHN D. AND CATHERINE T.) FOUNDATION
    Awards: 187
    Big Bets: 187
    Enduring Commitments: 187
    Field Support: 187
MACDONALD (THE DR. JOHN T.) FOUNDATION, INC.: 1021
MacDonald/Sampson Fellowship: 796
MACDOWELL
    Artist Residency Program: 424

Macelwane (The Father James B.) Annual Awards in Meteorology: 2365
MacGregor (Irene and Daisy) Memorial Scholarship: 2064
MacLean (Paul D.) Award: 2318
Macomber Travel Grant: 523
Macular Degeneration Research Program: 1284
Macy Faculty Scholars: 2046
MACY (JOSIAH JR.) FOUNDATION
    Board Grants: 2046
    Macy Faculty Scholars: 2046
    President's Grants: 2046
Macy (Josiah Jr.) Foundation Scholarship: 2062
Maddex (Eileen C.) Fellowship: 2416
MADDIE'S FUND: 1664
MADISON COMMUNITY FOUNDATION: 1198
Madison (James) Fellowship Program: 554
MADISON (JAMES) MEMORIAL FELLOWSHIP FOUNDATION
    Madison (James) Fellowship Program: 554
Maguire (Richard C.) Scholarship: 580
Mahoney (Matthew J.) Artist-in-Residence Program: 516
Maine Artist Fellowship: 425
MAINE ARTS COMMISSION
    Arts and Humanities Grants: 425
    Arts Learning: 425
    Creative Aging Grant: 425
    Cultural Planning Grant: 425
    Maine Artist Fellowship: 425
    Morrison (Jane) Film Fund: 425
    Organizational Development: 425
    Partnership Grant: 425
    Project Grant for Artists: 425
    Project Grant for Organizations: 425
    Springboard Artist Grant: 425
    Traditional Arts Apprenticeship: 425
MAINE INITIATIVES
    Grants for Change: 1344
MAINE OSTEOPATHIC ASSOCIATION
    Maine Osteopathic Association Scholarship: 2278
Maine Osteopathic Association Scholarship: 2278
Maine Programs: 413
Major Grant Support: 446
Major (The J. Russell) Prize: 526
Maker-Creator Fellowships: 362
Maley/FTEE Scholarship Technology and Engineering Teacher
    Professional Development: 1388
Manhattan Central Medical Society Scholarship: 2062
Mankin (Richard Claude) Scholarship: 1991
Manny (Carter) Award: 373
Many Voices Fellowships: 645
Many Voices Mentorships: 645
MAPPLETHORPE (ROBERT) FOUNDATION, INC.
    Photography Program: 426
MARBROOK FOUNDATION: 188
MARCH OF DIMES
    O'Connor (Basil) Starter Scholar Research Award: 2047
    Research Grants Program: 2048
Marconi (Guglielmo) Engineering Scholarship: 1591
Marcus (Harold and Inge) Scholarship: 2392
MARCUS (JACOB RADER) CENTER OF THE AMERICAN JEWISH
    ARCHIVES
    American Jewish Archives Fellowship Program (The): 747
MARFAN FOUNDATION (THE)
    Clinical Research Program: 2273
    Early Investigator Grant Program: 2273
    Faculty Grant Program: 2273
    McKusick (Victor A.) Fellowship Program: 2273
Margins Fellowship (The): 613
MARIETTA COMMUNITY FOUNDATION: 1199
MARIN COMMUNITY FOUNDATION: 189
MARINE BIOLOGICAL LABORATORY
    Marine Biological Laboratory Research Awards: 1941
Marine Biological Laboratory Research Awards: 1941
MARINE CORPS SCHOLARSHIP FOUNDATION, INC.: 1528
Marine Fisheries Initiative Grants: 1873
Maritime Education: 267
MARKETING EDGE
    Collegiate ECHO Marketing Challenge: 1711
    Collegiate Summit: 1711
    Kestnbaum (Robert) Research Program: 1711
    Marketing EDGE Scholarship Program: 1711
    Professor's Institute: 1711

    Shankar-Spiegel Award for the Best Dissertation Proposal in
        Direct/Interactive Marketing: 1711
    Student Career Forums: 1711
Marketing EDGE Scholarship Program: 1711
Marks (Wally) Leadership Institute for Change: 1343
Marraro (The Helen and Howard R.) Prize in Italian History: 526
Marraro (The Howard R.) Prize: 525
Marraro (Howard R.) Prize: 603
MARRIOTT INTERNATIONAL, INC.: 190
MARSHALL AID COMMEMORATION COMMISSION
    Marshall Scholarships: 842
MARSHALL COMMUNITY FOUNDATION: 1404
Marshall (Mary) Nursing Scholarship/Practical Nurse Program: 2248
Marshall (Mary) Nursing Scholarship/Registered Nurse Program: 2248
Marshall Scholarships: 842
Marshall (Thomas F.) Graduate Student Awards: 482
MARSHALL (THURGOOD) COLLEGE FUND (TMCF)
    TMCF Scholarships: 1529
Marth (Elmer) Educator Award: 2415
Marti (Jose) Scholarship Challenge Grant Fund: 964
Martin-Baker Research Awards: 1944
MARTIN (DELLA) FOUNDATION: 2330
Martin (The Right Honourable Paul Sr.) Scholarship: 1770
Martin (Zack) Breaking Barriers Grant: 1957
Marvin (Frances Crawford) American Indian Scholarship: 1539
MARYLAND HIGHER EDUCATION COMMISSION
    Maryland State Scholarships: 1530
MARYLAND INSTITUTE COLLEGE OF ART
    Business of Art and Design (MPS): 509
    Filmmaking (MFA): 509
    Hoffberger (LeRoy E.) School of Painting (MFA): 509
    MA Graphic Design: 509
    MA Illustration: 509
    MA Social Design: 509
    Master of Arts in Teaching: 509
    MBA/MA in Design Leadership: 509
    MFA Community Arts: 509
    MFA Curatorial Practice: 509
    MFA Illustration Practice: 509
    MFA in Graphic Design: 509
    Mt. Royal School of Art (MFA): 509
    MPS in Information Visualization: 509
    Photographic and Electronic Media (MFA): 509
    Rinehart School of Sculpture (MFA): 509
    Studio Art (Low-residency MFA): 509
    UX Design (MPS): 509
MARYLAND STATE ARTS COUNCIL
    Arts and Entertainment Districts General Operating Support: 427
    Arts and Entertainment Districts Technical Assistance: 427
    Arts in Education: 427
    Community Arts Development: 427
    Creativity Grant Program: 427
    Grants for Organizations: 427
    Individual Artist Awards: 427
    Maryland Traditions: 427
    Professional Development Program: 427
    Public Art Program: 427
Maryland State Scholarships: 1530
Maryland Traditions: 427
Masaoka (Mike M.) Fellowship Fund Congressional Program: 1796
Mason Science Teaching Fellowships: 1616
MASS HUMANITIES
    Discussion Grants: 332
    Local History Grants: 332
    Project Grants: 332
Massachusetts Cash Grant: 1532
Massachusetts Gilbert Matching Student Grant Program: 1532
MASSACHUSETTS HISTORICAL SOCIETY (THE)
    Kass Teacher Fellowships at MHS: 556
    Long-Term Research Fellowship: 558
    Loring (Suzanne and Caleb) Fellowship: 555
    Short-Term Research Fellowship: 557
    Swensrud Teacher Fellowships at MHS: 556
MASSACHUSETTS INSTITUTE OF TECHNOLOGY
    Knight Science Journalism Fellowship: 1743
Massachusetts Medical Society International Health Studies Grant
    Program: 1531
MASSACHUSETTS MEDICAL SOCIETY (MMS)
    Massachusetts Medical Society International Health Studies Grant
        Program: 1531

Massachusetts Medical Society (MMS) Annual Scholars Program: 1531
MMS Medical Information Technology Awards: 1531
MMS Student Section Community Service Grants: 1531
Massachusetts Medical Society (MMS) Annual Scholars Program: 1531
MASSACHUSETTS OFFICE OF STUDENT FINANCIAL ASSISTANCE
Massachusetts Cash Grant: 1532
Massachusetts Gilbert Matching Student Grant Program: 1532
MASSGrants: 1532
MASSERINI (MAURICE J.) TRUST: 905
MASSGrants: 1532
Master of Arts in Teaching: 509
Master of Music: 701
Master's Awards: 1677
Master's Degree in Private School Leadership: 1433
Master's Youth Addictions Minority Fellowship: 1543
Master's Youth Minority Fellowship: 1543
Matching Gift Program: 49, 184, 243
Matching Gifts Program: 115, 158
Matching Gifts to Education Program: 176
Maternal and Child Health Services Block Grant: 2252
Maternal and Pediatric Infectious Disease Branch (MPIDB): 1318
Math and Science Teaching (MAST): 951
MATSUMAE INTERNATIONAL FOUNDATION (THE)
Fellowship Program: 843
Matthews (Leroy) Physician/Scientist Award: 2167
Mattingly (Carolyn C.) Award for Mental Health Reporting: 1750
Mayo (Clara) Grants: 1690
MAYO CLINIC
Surgical Pathology Fellowships: 2049
Mayr (Ernst) Grants in Animal Systematics: 1943
MAYTAG (FREDA)-GRACE CRAWFORD TRUST: 1307
MAZON: A JEWISH RESPONSE TO HUNGER
Quick Reaction Fund (QRF): 1345
Mazza (Theodore) Scholarship: 1591
MBA/MA in Design Leadership: 509
McAuliffe (Christa) Reach for the Stars Award: 1666
MCBEAN (ALLETTA MORRIS) CHARITABLE TRUST: 333
MCCARTHEY DRESSMAN EDUCATION FOUNDATION
Academic Enrichment Grants: 1434
Student Teaching Scholarship: 1434
Teacher Development Grants: 1434
MCCAULEY (LUTHER T.) CHARITABLE TRUST: 1200
McConnell Fund (The): 1125
McCormick (Richard P.) Prize for Scholarly Publication: 569
MCCORMICK (ROBERT R.) FOUNDATION
Communities Program: 191
Community Justice Initiative: 191
Democracy Program: 191
Education Program: 191
Veterans Program: 191
McDermid (The Honourable N.D.) Graduate Scholarships in Law: 1781
McDevitt (John W.) Fourth Degree Scholarships: 1524
MCDONALD (J.M.) FOUNDATION, INC.: 192
McDonald (Michelle L.) Scholarship: 1704
MCDONNELL (JAMES S.) FOUNDATION
Special Initiatives: 193
Understanding Dynamic and Multi-Scale Systems: 193
Understanding Human Cognition: 193
McDonogh (Dr. David Kearney) Scholarship in Ophthalmology/ENT: 2062
MCDOWELL (VERNE CATT) CORPORATION
McDowell (Verne Catt) Scholarship: 748
McDowell (Verne Catt) Scholarship: 748
MCELROY (R.J.) TRUST: 1022
McGaw (Foster G.) Graduate Student Scholarship: 1291
MCGILL UNIVERSITY
Boulton (Maxwell) Q.C. Fellowship: 1780
MCGREGOR FUND: 194
McGuire (George) Memorial Scholarship: 2240
McHenry Fellowship: 1930
MCJ AMELIOR FOUNDATION (THE): 1023
McKinley Research Fund: 1990
McKnight Doctoral Fellowship: 1386
MCKNIGHT ENDOWMENT FUND FOR NEUROSCIENCE (THE)
McKnight Neuroscience Scholar Award: 2214
McKnight Fellowships in Playwriting: 645
MCKNIGHT FOUNDATION (THE)
Arts: 1346
Education: 1346

International: 1346
Midwest Climate and Energy: 1346
Neuroscience: 1346
McKnight National Residency and Commission: 645
McKnight Neuroscience Scholar Award: 2214
McKnight Theater Artist Fellowships: 645
McKusick (Victor A.) Fellowship Program: 2273
McLaughlin Medal (The): 1646
MCLEAN CONTRIBUTIONSHIP (THE): 195
McLean (Franklin C.) Award: 2062
MCMICKING (THE JOSEPH AND MERCEDES) FOUNDATION: 196
McNamara (Brooks) Publishing Subvention: 482
MCNAMARA (THE MARGARET) EDUCATION GRANTS (MMEG): 197
McNeill-Nott Award: 1957
McSpadden (The Leland) Memorial Fund for Medical and Scientific Research: 2044
McWherter (Ned) Scholars Program: 1583
MDA Conference Grants: 2218
MDA Development Grants: 2218
MDA Idea Awards: 2218
MDA Venture Philanthropy Program: 2218
MEADOWS FOUNDATION, INC.: 198
MEASEY (BENJAMIN AND MARY SIDDONS) FOUNDATION
Medical Education Grants: 2050
MEBANE CHARITABLE FOUNDATION, INC.
Early Childhood Development Program (The): 1024
Literacy Interventions PreK-3rd Grades: 1024
Teacher Training and Professional Development Program (The): 1024
Medi-Cal Health Navigator Project: 1334
Medicaid: 1324
Medical Education Grants: 2050
MEDICAL LIBRARY ASSOCIATION
Brodman (Estelle) Award for the Academic Medical Librarian of the Year: 674
Colaianni (Lois Ann) Award for Excellence and Achievement in Hospital Librarianship: 674
Cunningham Memorial International Fellowship: 875
Darling (Louise) Medal for Distinguished Achievement in Collection Development in the Health Sciences: 674
Doe (Janet) Lectureship: 674
Eliot (Ida and George) Prize: 674
Meyerhoff (Erich) Prize: 674
MLA Continuing Education Grants: 199
MLA Doctoral Fellowship: 673
MLA Scholarship: 673
MLA Scholarship for Underrepresented Students: 906
Noyes (Marcia C.) Award: 674
Rittenhouse Award: 674
Rogers (Frank Bradway) Information Advancement Award: 674
Medical Research: 267
Medical Research Program: 93
Medical Scientist Training Program: 2054
Medical Student Summer Fellowships: 2204
Medical Student Summer Research Fellowship: 2024
Medical Student Training in Aging Research Program (MSTAR): 1999
Medication Assisted Treatment Access Points Project: 1334
Medieval Academy Dissertation Grants: 559
MEDIEVAL ACADEMY OF AMERICA (THE)
Baldwin (Birgit) Fellowship: 559
Brown (John Nicholas) Prize: 559
Elliott (Van Courtlandt) Prize: 559
Medieval Academy Dissertation Grants: 559
Schallek Awards: 559
Schallek Fellowship: 559
MEDTRONIC FOUNDATION
Community Education: 200
HealthRise: 200
HeartRescue: 200
Strengthening Health Systems: 200
MELLON (THE ANDREW W.) FOUNDATION: 201
Mellon (Andrew W.) Foundation Fellowships: 352
Mellon (Andrew W.) Postdoctoral Fellowship: 321
Mellon (Andrew W.) Postdoctoral Fellowships in the Humanities: 363
Mellon-CES Dissertation Completion Fellowship in European Studies: 762
MELLON (THE PAUL) CENTRE FOR STUDIES IN BRITISH ART
Educational Programme Grants: 375
Junior Fellowships: 375
Mellon (Paul) Centre Rome Fellowship: 375
Mid-Career Fellowships: 375

Postdoctoral Fellowships: 375
Research Support Grants: 375
Senior Fellowships: 375
Mellon (Paul) Centre Rome Fellowship: 375
Mellon Postdoctoral Fellowships: 323, 579
MELLON (RICHARD KING) FOUNDATION: 1201
Member Co-op Match Program: 176
Member Supported Fellowships: 818
Member's Best First Book Award: 576
Member's Best Subsequent Book Award: 576
MEMORIAL FOUNDATION FOR JEWISH CULTURE
International Doctoral Scholarship for Studies Specializing in Jewish Fields: 749
International Fellowship in Jewish Studies and Jewish Culture: 749
Mental Health and Substance Abuse Fellowship Program (The): 896
Mentor Student Travel Awards: 1944
Mentored Clinical Scientist Research Career Development Award (Parent K08): 2056
Mentored Investigator Awards: 1945
Mentored Patient-Oriented Research Career Development Award (K23): 1311
Mentored Quantitative Research Career Development Award (K25): 1311
Mentoring and Leadership Program: 918
MERCK FAMILY FUND
Conserving Ecologically Valuable Land: 202
Promoting a Price on Carbon: 202
Promoting Energy Efficiency: 202
Promoting Sustainable Paper Production: 202
Urban Agriculture and Youth Leadership: 202
Merit and Memorial Scholarships: 1476
Merit Award: 2125
Merola Opera Program: 727
Merrill (John) Grant in Transplantation: 2111
Merrimack Valley Municipal Business Development and Recovery Fund: 1153
MESBEC (Math, Engineering, Science, Business, Education and Computers) Program: 951
Mesopotamian Fellowship: 818
Metcalf (The Larry) Exemplary Dissertation Award: 1665
METLIFE FOUNDATION: 203
Metropolitan Atlanta Arts Fund: 1099
METROPOLITAN MUSEUM OF ART (THE): 510
Conservation and Scientific Research Fellowships: 675
History of Art and Visual Culture Fellowships: 511
Mexico/Latin America: 57
MEYER (EUGENE AND AGNES E.) FOUNDATION: 1202
MEYER MEMORIAL TRUST: 204
MEYER (ROBERT R.) FOUNDATION: 205
Meyerhoff (Erich) Prize: 674
Meyers (Eric and Carol) Fellowships: 818
Meyers (Shirlee)/G. Ernest Wright Fellowships: 818
MFA Community Arts: 509
MFA Curatorial Practice: 509
MFA Illustration Practice: 509
MFA in Graphic Design: 509
MFA in Studio Art: 521
MFP Mental Health and Substance Abuse Services Fellowship: 2315
MFP Services for Transition Age Youth: 2313
MIAMI FOUNDATION (THE)
Community Grants Program: 206
LGBTQ Community Fund: 206
Moon (Denise) Memorial Fund: 206
Michigan Competitive Scholarship (MCS): 1579
MICHIGAN COUNCIL FOR ARTS AND CULTURAL AFFAIRS
Arts in Education Grants: 428
Capital Improvement Grants: 428
Operational Support Grants: 428
Project Support Grants: 428
MICHIGAN GATEWAY COMMUNITY FOUNDATION: 1203
Michigan Gear Up: 1579
Michigan Scholarship Fund: 2062
MICHIGAN SOCIETY OF FELLOWS
Postdoctoral Fellowships in the Humanities and the Arts, Sciences and Professions: 334
MICHIGAN STATE UNIVERSITY
MSU Education Abroad Scholarships: 844
MICHIGAN STATE UNIVERSITY, THE GRADUATE SCHOOL
Academic Achievement Graduate Assistantships: 907
Education Opportunity Fellowship: 907
University Distinguished Fellowships: 907
University Enrichment Fellowships: 907

Michigan Tuition Grant (MTG): 1580
MICHIGAN WOMEN FORWARD
Young Women for Change: 981
Microbiology: 2107
MICRON TECHNOLOGY FOUNDATION, INC.: 1886
Microscopy & Microanalysis (M & M) Student Award: 1637
MICROSCOPY SOCIETY OF AMERICA
Microscopy & Microanalysis (M & M) Student Award: 1637
MSA Professional Technical Staff Awards: 1942
Undergraduate Research Scholarship Program: 1636
MICROSOFT PHILANTHROPIES
Employee Giving and Volunteer Programs: 207
Product Donations Program: 207
MID-AMERICA ARTS ALLIANCE
Artistic Innovations Grant Program: 429
Regional Touring Program: 429
Touring Exhibits through ExhibitsUSA: 429
MID ATLANTIC ARTS
ArtsCONNECT: 430
Cooper (Alan) Leadership in the Arts Award: 430
Folk and Traditional Arts Touring Network: 430
Jazz Touring Network: 430
Living Legacy Jazz Award: 430
Mid Atlantic Creative Fellowships: 430
Mid Atlantic Tours: 430
Performing Arts Global Exchange: 430
Special Presenter Initiatives: 430
USArtists International: 430
Mid Atlantic Creative Fellowships: 430
Mid-Atlantic Grant Program: 176
Mid Atlantic Tours: 430
Mid-Career Fellowship: 372
Mid-Career Fellowships: 375
Mid-Career Professional Development Grant: 406
Mid-Career Project Grant: 406
Mid-Continent Instrument Scholarship: 2363
MID-NEBRASKA COMMUNITY FOUNDATION, INC.: 208
Midcareer Investigator Award in Patient-Oriented Research (K24): 1311
Middleton Fellowship in Presidential Studies: 1797
Midwest Climate and Energy: 1346
Miele (Alphonse A.) Scholarship: 1591
Mihaychuk (Jaroslaw and Nadia) Research Fellowships in Ukrainian Studies (The): 359
Mildenberger (Kenneth W.) Prize: 602
Military Affairs: 100
Military and Veteran Healing Arts Grants: 443
Military Enhanced Recognition Incentive and Tribute (MERIT): 1549
MILLARD (ADAH K.) CHARITABLE TRUST: 209
MILLAY COLONY FOR THE ARTS, INC. (THE)
Artist Residencies: 431
Miller (Dr. Theodore Quincy) Scholarship: 2062
Miller (Sarah Bryan) Scholarship: 1567
Miller (Willet G.) Medal: 1646
MILLIPORESIGMA: 210
Mineralized Tissue Physiology: 2107
MINERALOGICAL ASSOCIATION OF CANADA
Berry (Leonard G.) Medal: 2423
Hawley Medal: 2423
MAC Foundation Scholarship: 2423
MAC Student Travel/Research Grants: 2423
Peacock Medal: 2423
Pinch Medal: 2423
Undergraduate Awards: 2423
Young Scientist Award: 2423
MINERALOGICAL SOCIETY OF AMERICA (THE)
Research Grant in Crystallography, Mineral Physics or Chemistry and Mineralogy: 1869
Student Research Grant in Mineralogy and Petrology: 1869
Mini Grant for Teachers Program: 1128
Mini Grants: 435, 1123
Mining Club Award: 2421
MINNEAPOLIS FOUNDATION (THE)
Catalyst Initiative: 1204
Fourth Generation: 1204
Racial and Economic Justice: 1204
Reimagine Education: 1204
MINNESOTA DEPARTMENT OF EDUCATION
Library Construction Grants: 676
Library Services and Technology Act Competitive Grants: 676

Multi-Type Library Cooperation Aid: 676
Regional Library Telecommunications Aid: 676
Regional Public Libraries Systems Support: 676
Minnotte (Jacque I.) Fellowship: 1757
Minority Fellowship Program: 886
Minority Health and Health Disparities Research Training Program (MHRT): 912
Minority Junior Faculty Development Award (JDFM): 2148
Minority Postdoctoral Fellowship: 2148
Minority Scholarship Awards for College Students: 2377
Minority Teaching Fellows Program: 1583
Minority Undergraduate Internship (MUI): 2148
Mission Related Investments Contracts: 1296
MISSOURI DEPARTMENT OF HIGHER EDUCATION AND WORKFORCE DEVELOPMENT
Access Missouri Financial Assistance Program: 1534
Missouri Higher Education Academic Scholarship Program ("Bright Flight"): 1533
Missouri Higher Education Academic Scholarship Program ("Bright Flight"): 1533
MITSUBISHI ELECTRIC AMERICA FOUNDATION: 1435
Mizuho Community Involvement Grants Program: 1205
Mizuho Matching Gifts Program: 1205
MIZUHO USA FOUNDATION, INC.
Fostering Economic Self-Sufficiency: 1205
Mizuho Community Involvement Grants Program: 1205
Mizuho Matching Gifts Program: 1205
Promoting Economic Development: 1205
Strengthening Affordable Housing: 1205
MLA Continuing Education Grants: 199
MLA Doctoral Fellowship: 673
MLA Prize for a First Book: 603
MLA Prize for an Edited Collection: 603
MLA Prize for Collaborative, Bibliographical or Archival Scholarship: 603
MLA Prize in United States Latina and Latino and Chicana and Chicano Literary and Cultural Studies: 603
MLA Scholarship: 673
MLA Scholarship for Underrepresented Students: 906
MLB-MLBPA YOUTH DEVELOPMENT FOUNDATION: 1025
MMS Medical Information Technology Awards: 1531
MMS Student Section Community Service Grants: 1531
Model Watershed Program: 1959
MODERN LANGUAGE ASSOCIATION OF AMERICA
Calinescu (Matei) Prize: 603
Cohen (Morton N.) Award for a Distinguished Edition of Letters: 602
Kovacs (Katherine Singer) Prize: 603
Leviant (Fenia and Yaakov) Memorial Prize in Yiddish Studies: 603
Lowell (James Russell) Prize: 603
Marraro (Howard R.) Prize: 603
Mildenberger (Kenneth W.) Prize: 602
MLA Prize for a First Book: 603
MLA Prize for an Edited Collection: 603
MLA Prize for Collaborative, Bibliographical or Archival Scholarship: 603
MLA Prize in United States Latina and Latino and Chicana and Chicano Literary and Cultural Studies: 603
Modern Language Association Prize for a Scholarly Edition: 602
Modern Language Association Prize for Independent Scholars: 602
Roth (Lois) Award for a Translation of a Literary Work: 603
Scaglione (Aldo and Jeanne) Prize for a Translation of a Literary Work: 603
Scaglione (Aldo and Jeanne) Prize for a Translation of a Scholarly Study of Literature: 603
Scaglione (Aldo and Jeanne) Prize for Comparative Literary Studies: 603
Scaglione (Aldo and Jeanne) Prize for French and Francophone Studies: 603
Scaglione (Aldo and Jeanne) Prize for Italian Studies: 603
Scaglione (Aldo and Jeanne) Prize for Studies in Germanic Languages and Literatures: 603
Scaglione (Aldo and Jeanne) Prize for Studies in Slavic Languages and Literatures: 603
Scaglione (Aldo and Jeanne) Publication Award for a Manuscript in Italian Literary Studies: 603
Scarborough (William Sanders) Prize: 603
Shaughnessy (Mina P.) Prize: 602
Modern Language Association Prize for a Scholarly Edition: 602
Modern Language Association Prize for Independent Scholars: 602
Moe (Henry Allen) Prize: 404
Moffett (Edna V.) Fellowship: 991

Moffitt (Francis H.) Memorial Scholarship: 1821
MoGro: 920
Molson Neuroengineering Fellowship: 2224
MONEY FOR WOMEN/BARBARA DEMING MEMORIAL FUND, INC.
Individual Artist Support Grants: 982
MONTANA COMMUNITY FOUNDATION
Women's Foundation of Montana: 1206
Monticello College Foundation Fellowship for Women: 346
MOODY FOUNDATION (THE): 211
Moody Research Grants: 1797
Moon (Bill and Carolyn) Scholarships: 1542
Moon (Denise) Memorial Fund: 206
Moore (Gordon E.) Medal for Outstanding Achievement in Solid State Science and Technology: 1627
Moorman (Robert B.B. and Josephine N.) Scholarship: 2386
Morgan (Alstott) Fellowship: 304
MORGAN (THE BURTON D.) FOUNDATION: 1712
MORGAN (MARIETTA MCNEILL) AND SAMUEL TATE MORGAN, JR. TRUST: 1347
Morgan (Thomas S.) Memorial Scholarship: 577
Morris (Frank H.) Humanitarian Award: 1123
MORRIS (WILLIAM) SOCIETY IN THE U.S.
Dunlap (Joseph R.) Memorial Fellowship: 432
Morrison (Jane) Film Fund: 425
Morrow (Mary)/Edna Richards Scholarship Fund: 1459
MORTON-KELLY CHARITABLE TRUST (THE): 1207
Moss Adams LLP Scholarship: 1704
Mosse (The George L.) Prize: 526
MOTT (CHARLES STEWART) FOUNDATION: 1208
Mott (Frank Luther) KTA Research/Book Award: 1740
Mt. Royal School of Art (MFA): 509
MT. SINAI HEALTH CARE FOUNDATION: 1308
MOUNT VERNON HOTEL MUSEUM & GARDEN
Hearst (William Randolph) Foundation Fellowship: 560
Mountaineering Fellowship Fund Grant: 1957
Moving Image Fund: 374
Moving People and Places Out of Poverty: 24
MPS in Information Visualization: 509
MRG FOUNDATION
Capacity Building Grants: 1348
Critical Response Grants: 1348
General Fund Grants: 1348
Travel Grants: 1348
MS. FOUNDATION FOR WOMEN
Economic Justice: 983
Women's Health: 983
Women's Safety: 983
MSA Graduate Fellowship: 1944
MSA Professional Technical Staff Awards: 1942
MSU Education Abroad Scholarships: 844
Muggets Scholarship: 1510
Muhlmann (Maria and Eric) Award: 1833
MULFORD (THE CLARENCE E.) TRUST: 212
Multi-Country Research Fellowship Program: 824
Multi-Type Library Cooperation Aid: 676
Multicultural Academic Opportunity Graduate Student Scholars Program: 926
Multicultural Advertising Intern Program (MAIP): 900
Multimedia Training Academies: 1733
MULTIPLE SCLEROSIS SOCIETY OF CANADA
Discovery Research Grant Program: 2216
Discovery Research Pilot Grant: 2216
endMS Doctoral Studentship Award: 2215
endMS Master's Studentship Award: 2215
endMS Postdoctoral Fellowship: 2217
Munby Fellowship in Bibliography (The): 664
Mundel (Marvin) Memorial Scholarship: 2392
MURDOCK (M.J.) CHARITABLE TRUST: 213
Murphree (E.V.) Award in Industrial and Engineering Chemistry: 1850
Murphy (Jack K. and Gertrude) Fellowships: 452
Murrow (Edward R.) Press Fellowship: 1732
MUSCULAR DYSTROPHY ASSOCIATION
MDA Conference Grants: 2218
MDA Development Grants: 2218
MDA Idea Awards: 2218
MDA Venture Philanthropy Program: 2218
Museum Assessment Program: 671
Museum Grants for African American History and Culture: 671

MUSEUM OF COMPARATIVE ZOOLOGY
  Mayr (Ernst) Grants in Animal Systematics: 1943
MUSEUM OF EARLY SOUTHERN DECORATIVE ARTS (MESDA)
  Horton Fellowship: 512
Museums Empowered: Professional Development Opportunities for
  Museum Staff: 671
Museums for America: 671
Music Education Grant: 1237
Music in American Culture Award: 691
MUSKINGUM COUNTY COMMUNITY FOUNDATION
  Scholarship Central: 1209
MUSTE (A.J.) MEMORIAL INSTITUTE: 1349
My Brother's Keeper Sacramento Collaborative: 1334
My Seizure Gauge: 2211
MYASTHENIA GRAVIS FOUNDATION OF AMERICA, INC.
  Nursing Research Grant: 2219
MYCOLOGICAL SOCIETY OF AMERICA
  Backus Award: 1944
  Bartnicki-Garcia (Salomon) Award: 1944
  Forest Fungal Ecology Awards: 1944
  International Travel Awards: 1944
  Martin-Baker Research Awards: 1944
  Mentor Student Travel Awards: 1944
  MSA Graduate Fellowship: 1944
  NAMA Memorial Fellowship: 1944
  Rippon (John W.) Research Award: 1944
  Rogerson (Clark T.) Research Award: 1944
  Smith (Alexander H. and Helen V.) Research Fund: 1944
  Undergraduate Research Award: 1944
Myers (The Gordon) Amateur Achievement Award: 1836

N

NAACP LEGAL DEFENSE AND EDUCATIONAL FUND, INC. (THE)
  LDF Earl Warren Legal Training Program: 934
  LDF Herbert Lehman Education Fund Scholarship Program: 934
NACB Internship Program: 1410
NACME Bridge Scholarship: 2394
NAFEO Internship Program: 935
NAHJ Ana Real Scholarship: 909
NAHJ Cecilia Alvear Scholarship: 909
NAHJ Facebook Journalism Project Scholarship: 909
NAHJ General Scholarships (Ruben Salazar Fund): 909
NAHJ Maria Elena Salinas Scholarship: 909
NAHJ/NBC News Summer Fellows Program: 909
NAKAMICHI (E.) FOUNDATION: 712
Nakanishi Prize: 1849
NAMA Memorial Fellowship: 1944
NANTUCKET HISTORICAL ASSOCIATION
  Verney (E. Geoffrey and Elizabeth Thayer) Fellowship: 561
NARSAD Distinguished Investigator Grant: 2323
NARSAD Independent Investigator Grant: 2323
NARSAD Young Investigator Grant: 2323
NASA Hubble Fellowship Program: 1845
Nascher/Manning Award: 2294
NASDAQ FOUNDATION: 1713
NASW Idea Grants: 1746
NATIONAL ACADEMIES OF SCIENCES, ENGINEERING, AND
  MEDICINE (THE)
  Ford Foundation Fellowship Programs: 908
  NRC Research Associateship Programs: 1824
NATIONAL ACADEMY OF EDUCATION (THE)
  National Academy of Education/Spencer Dissertation Fellowship: 1405
  National Academy of Education/Spencer Postdoctoral Fellowship: 1405
National Academy of Education/Spencer Dissertation Fellowship: 1405
National Academy of Education/Spencer Postdoctoral Fellowship: 1405
NATIONAL ACTION COUNCIL FOR MINORITIES IN
  ENGINEERING, INC. (NACME)
  Bechtel Engineering Scholarship: 2395
  Chevron/Diversity Association Scholarship Program: 2395
  Ford-HS Bridge Scholars: 2395
  Friend (Sidney and Katherine) Scholarship: 2395
  GE Foundation Engineering Scholarship: 2395
  Hearst (William Randolph) Endowment Scholarship: 2395
  NACME Bridge Scholarship: 2394
  Reed (Phillip D.) Undergraduate Endowment Fellowship: 2395
NATIONAL ALOPECIA AREATA FOUNDATION
  Bridge Grants: 1945
  Mentored Investigator Awards: 1945

  Pilot and Feasibility Grants: 1945
  Research Grants: 1945
  Student Internship Awards: 1945
National Alumni Chapter Fellowship: 2416
National Alumni Chapter Grant: 2416
NATIONAL AMBUCS, INC.
  AMBUCS Scholars-Scholarships for Therapists: 2301
National Apprenticeship System: 1766
NATIONAL ASSOCIATION FOR EQUAL OPPORTUNITY IN HIGHER
  EDUCATION (NAFEO)
  NAFEO Internship Program: 935
NATIONAL ASSOCIATION OF BLACK SOCIAL WORKERS, INC.
  (THE)
  Office of Student Affairs Community Leadership Tuition Scholarship:
  936
  Williams (Cenie Jomo) Tuition Scholarship: 936
NATIONAL ASSOCIATION OF COMPOSERS, USA (NACUSA)
  Young Composers' Competition: 713
NATIONAL ASSOCIATION OF FARM BROADCASTERS
  FOUNDATION
  Kummerow (Glenn) Memorial Scholarship: 1744
  Logan (The George) Scholarship: 1744
  Samuelson (Orion) Scholarship: 1744
NATIONAL ASSOCIATION OF GEOSCIENCE TEACHERS
  Scholarships for Field Study: 1870
  Stout (Dottie) Professional Development Grants: 1870
NATIONAL ASSOCIATION OF HEALTH SERVICES EXECUTIVES
  (NAHSE)
  Bonner (The Ellis) Award: 2302
  Gaynor (The Florence) Award: 2302
  Rice (The Haynes) Award: 2302
NATIONAL ASSOCIATION OF HISPANIC JOURNALISTS
  Camuy (Jonathan) Scholarship: 909
  Getty Images Inclusion Scholarship: 909
  Gomez (Luis) Scholarship: 909
  NAHJ Ana Real Scholarship: 909
  NAHJ Cecilia Alvear Scholarship: 909
  NAHJ Facebook Journalism Project Scholarship: 909
  NAHJ General Scholarships (Ruben Salazar Fund): 909
  NAHJ Maria Elena Salinas Scholarship: 909
  NAHJ/NBC News Summer Fellows Program: 909
NATIONAL ASSOCIATION OF SCHOLARS
  Shaw (The Peter) Memorial Award: 1457
NATIONAL ASSOCIATION OF SCIENCE WRITERS, INC.
  Excellence in Institutional Writing Awards: 1747
  NASW Idea Grants: 1746
  Science in Society Awards: 1745
NATIONAL ATAXIA FOUNDATION
  National Ataxia Foundation Pioneer SCA3/MJD Translational Research
  Award: 2220
  National Ataxia Foundation Postdoctoral Fellowship Award: 2220
  National Ataxia Foundation Seed Money Research Grant: 2220
  National Ataxia Foundation Young Investigator Award: 2220
National Ataxia Foundation Pioneer SCA3/MJD Translational Research
  Award: 2220
National Ataxia Foundation Postdoctoral Fellowship Award: 2220
National Ataxia Foundation Seed Money Research Grant: 2220
National Ataxia Foundation Young Investigator Award: 2220
NATIONAL BLACK MBA ASSOCIATION
  NBMBAA Graduate Scholarship Program: 1210
  NBMBAA Undergraduate Scholarship Program: 937
NATIONAL BLACK NURSES ASSOCIATION, INC.
  Dawson (Dr. Martha A.) Genesis Nurse Leader Scholarship: 2240
  Edwards (Lynne) Research Scholarship: 2240
  Gorham (Dr. Millicent) Scholarship: 2240
  McGuire (George) Memorial Scholarship: 2240
  NBNA Board of Directors Scholarship: 2240
  Pemberton (Margaret) Scholarship: 2240
  Sams (Dr. Lauranne) Scholarship: 2240
  VITAS Healthcare/Esther Colliflower Scholarship: 2240
  Williams (Dr. Eric J.) Scholarship: 2240
NATIONAL BLOOD FOUNDATION, A PROGRAM OF AABB
  Early-Career Scientific Research Grants Program: 2142
National Book Fund (NBF): 1226
NATIONAL BUSINESS AVIATION ASSOCIATION
  Baldwin (Donald A. Sr.) Business Aviation Management Scholarship:
  2370
  Fanning (William M.) Maintenance Scholarship: 2368
  Flight Attendants/Flight Technicians Scholarship: 2368
  Ginocchio (Lawrence) Scholarship: 2369

International Operators Scholarship: 2368
Schedulers & Dispatchers Scholarship: 2369
UAA Janice K. Barden Scholarship: 2369
NATIONAL CATTLEMAN'S BEEF ASSOCIATION, A CONTRACTOR TO THE BEEF CHECKOFF
Human Nutrition Research: 2417
NATIONAL CENTER FOR ATMOSPHERIC RESEARCH
Newkirk Graduate Research Fellowship: 1840
Postdoctoral Fellowships at NCAR: 1638
NATIONAL CENTER FOR LEARNING DISABILITIES
Ford (Anne) Scholarship: 1406
Thomas (Allegra Ford) Scholarship: 1406
NATIONAL COUNCIL FOR EURASIAN AND EAST EUROPEAN RESEARCH (THE): 778
NATIONAL COUNCIL FOR THE SOCIAL STUDIES
Award for Global Understanding in Honor of James M. Becker: 1668
Clark (Septima) Book Awards: 1665
Exemplary Research in Social Studies: 1665
Grambs (Jean Dresden) Distinguished Career in Social Studies: 1665
Grant for the Enhancement of Geographic Literacy in Honor of James F. Marren: 1667
McAuliffe (Christa) Reach for the Stars Award: 1666
Metcalf (The Larry) Exemplary Dissertation Award: 1665
Outstanding Social Studies Teacher of the Year Awards (Elementary, Middle and Secondary Levels): 1665
Woodson (Carter G.) Book Awards: 1665
NATIONAL COUNCIL OF TEACHERS OF ENGLISH RESEARCH FOUNDATION: 1407
NATIONAL COUNCIL ON FAMILY RELATIONS
Berardo (Felix) Mentoring Award: 1350
Czaplewski Fellowship Award: 1350
Jewson (Ruth) Award: 1350
NCFR Student Award: 1350
Winter (Cindy) Scholarship Award: 1350
NATIONAL DAIRY COUNCIL
Nutrition Research Program: 2418
NATIONAL DAIRY SHRINE
National Dairy Shrine Student Recognition Program: 1919
NDS/DMI Education and Communication Scholarship: 1919
NDS/DMI Milk Marketing Scholarships: 1919
NDS/Iager Scholarship: 1919
NDS/Kildee Scholarships: 1919
NDS/Lancaster Sophomore Scholarship: 1919
NDS/Maurice E. Core Scholarship: 1919
NDS/McCullough Scholarships: 1919
NDS/Sowerby Junior Merit Scholarship: 1919
National Dairy Shrine Student Recognition Program: 1919
National Dance Project: 437
National Eagle Scout Scholarship Fund: 1002
NATIONAL ENDOWMENT FOR DEMOCRACY
National Endowment for Democracy Grants: 1798
National Endowment for Democracy Grants: 1798
NATIONAL ENDOWMENT FOR FINANCIAL EDUCATION (NEFE)
NEFE Research Funding Program: 1714
National Endowment for Plastic Surgery: 2076
NATIONAL ENDOWMENT FOR THE ARTS
Challenge America: 433
Creative Writing Fellowships: 433
Grants for Art Projects: 433
Our Town: 433
Partnership Agreements: 433
Research Grants in the Arts: 433
Translation Projects: 433
NATIONAL ENDOWMENT FOR THE HUMANITIES
Challenge Grants Program: 336
Fellowships: 337
Preservation and Access: 339
Public Humanities Projects: 1748
Research Program: 335
Seminars and Institutes Program: 338
Summer Stipends: 337
National Endowment for the Humanities Fellowships: 809
National Endowment for the Humanities (NEH) Fellowship: 796
National Endowment for the Humanities (NEH) Fellowships: 343
NATIONAL EYE INSTITUTE
Center Core Grants: 2274
Cooperative Clinical Research Grants: 2275
Small Business Innovation Research Awards: 2275
NATIONAL FARMER'S ORGANIZATION
Farm Kids for College Scholarships: 1920

NATIONAL FEDERATION OF MUSIC CLUBS
Award Program for Summer Music Festivals and Music Centers: 715
Bullock (Dorothy Dann) Music Therapy Award: 716
NFMC Competitions and Awards: 714
NATIONAL FEDERATION OF REPUBLICAN WOMEN
Kabis (Dorothy) Internship: 984
National Pathfinder's Scholarship: 984
Rendel (Betty) Scholarship: 984
NATIONAL FEDERATION OF STATE POETRY SOCIETIES, INC.
NFSPS College Undergraduate Poetry (CUP) Competition: 625
NATIONAL FEDERATION OF THE BLIND
National Federation of the Blind Scholarship Program: 910
National Federation of the Blind Scholarship Program: 910
National Fellowship: 870
NATIONAL FISH AND WILDLIFE FOUNDATION (NFWF): 1975
NATIONAL FOOTBALL LEAGUE FOUNDATION
Field Grants: 1211
Player Foundation Grants: 1211
Pro Bowl Grants: 1211
Youth Football Grants: 1211
NATIONAL FOSTER PARENT ASSOCIATION
NFPA Youth Scholarship: 1026
Walk Me Home Program: 1026
NATIONAL GEM CONSORTIUM (THE)
Future Faculty and Professionals (FFP) Travel Grant: 911
GEM M.S. Engineering Fellowship (The): 911
GEM Ph.D. Engineering Fellowship (The): 911
GEM Ph.D. Science Fellowship (The): 911
GRAD Lab: 911
NATIONAL GEOGRAPHIC SOCIETY
National Geographic Society Committee for Research and Exploration: 1871
National Geographic Society Committee for Research and Exploration: 1871
National Glaucoma Research Program: 2264
National Guard Supplemental Grant: 1512
NATIONAL HEADACHE FOUNDATION: 2120
NATIONAL HEALTH SERVICE CORPS (NHSC)
National Health Service Corps Scholarship Program: 1309
National Health Service Corps Scholarship Program: 1309
NATIONAL HEART, LUNG AND BLOOD INSTITUTE (NHLBI): 2143
Blood Diseases and Resources Research: 2121
Lung Diseases Research: 2144
NATIONAL HEMOPHILIA FOUNDATION (THE)
Bridge Award: 2051
Excellence Fellowships for Nursing, Physical Therapy and Social Work: 2051
Innovative Investigator Award: 2051
Lusher (Jeanne Maria) Diversity Fellowship: 2051
NHF Career Development Award: 2051
Pool (Judith Graham) Postdoctoral Research Fellowships in Bleeding Disorders: 2051
NATIONAL HISTORICAL PUBLICATIONS AND RECORDS COMMISSION: 562
NATIONAL HOME LIBRARY FOUNDATION: 677
NATIONAL HUMANITIES CENTER
National Humanities Center Fellowships: 340
National Humanities Center Fellowships: 340
NATIONAL INSTITUTE FOR LABOR RELATIONS RESEARCH
Applegate-Jackson-Parks Future Teacher Scholarship: 1535
Ruggles (The William B.) Journalist Scholarship: 1749
NATIONAL INSTITUTE OF DENTAL AND CRANIOFACIAL RESEARCH (NIDCR)
Behavioral & Social Science Research: 2107
Clinical Research & Epidemiology: 2107
Clinical Technologies Research: 2107
Clinical Trials: 2107
Clinical Trials & Practice-Based Research: 2107
Data Science, Computational Biology & Bioinformatics: 2107
Dental Materials & Biomaterials: 2107
Developmental Biology & Genetics: 2107
HIV/AIDS & Oral Health: 2107
Individual NRSA Postdoctoral Fellowships (F-32): 2106
Individual NRSA Senior Fellowship Award (F-33): 2108
Microbiology: 2107
Mineralized Tissue Physiology: 2107
Neuroscience of Orofacial Pain & Temporomandibular Disorders: 2107
Oral & Salivary Cancer Biology: 2107
Oral Health Disparities & Inequities: 2107
Research Training & Career Development: 2107
Salivary Biology & Immunology: 2107

Small Business Innovation/Small Business Technology Transfer (SBIR/STTR): 2107
   Tissue Engineering and Regenerative Medicine: 2107
   Translational Genetics & Genomics: 2107
NATIONAL INSTITUTE OF ENVIRONMENTAL HEALTH SCIENCES
   Environmental Health Sciences Research and Training Grants: 1976
NATIONAL INSTITUTE OF GENERAL MEDICAL SCIENCES: 2052
   Medical Scientist Training Program: 2054
   Support of Competitive Research Awards: 2053
NATIONAL INSTITUTE OF JUSTICE, U.S. DEPARTMENT OF JUSTICE
   Research Grants: 1277
NATIONAL INSTITUTE OF MENTAL HEALTH: 2331
   Traumatic Stress Research Program: 1669
NATIONAL INSTITUTE OF NEUROLOGICAL DISORDERS AND STROKE: 2221
NATIONAL INSTITUTE OF NURSING RESEARCH
   Career Development Grants: 2241
   Research Grants: 2241
   Research Training Grants: 2241
   Small Business Innovation Research Grants: 2241
NATIONAL INSTITUTE OF STANDARDS AND TECHNOLOGY, FIRE RESEARCH DIVISION
   Fire Research Grants Program: 1825
NATIONAL INSTITUTE ON AGING
   Aging Research: 1310
NATIONAL INSTITUTE ON ALCOHOL ABUSE AND ALCOHOLISM
   Career Enhancement Award for Stem Cell Research (K18): 1311
   Independent Scientist Awards (K02): 1311
   Mentored Patient-Oriented Research Career Development Award (K23): 1311
   Mentored Quantitative Research Career Development Award (K25): 1311
   Midcareer Investigator Award in Patient-Oriented Research (K24): 1311
   NIH Pathway to Independence Award (K99/R00): 1311
   Scientist Development Awards for Mentored Clinical (K08): 1311
   Scientist Development Awards for Mentored Research (K01): 1311
   Small Business Innovation Research Program: 1312
NATIONAL INSTITUTE ON DRUG ABUSE: 1408
NATIONAL INSTITUTE ON MINORITY HEALTH AND HEALTH DISPARITIES
   Minority Health and Health Disparities Research Training Program (MHRT): 912
NATIONAL INSTITUTES OF HEALTH
   High-End Instrumentation (HEI) Grant Program: 2061
   Japan Society for the Promotion of Science Postdoctoral Research Fellowships (Extramural): 879
   Kirschstein (Ruth L.) National Research Service Awards (NRSA) for Individual Postdoctoral Fellows (Parent F32): 2055
   Kirschstein (Ruth L.) National Research Service Awards (NRSA) for Individual Senior Fellows (Parent F33): 2057
   Mentored Clinical Scientist Research Career Development Award (Parent K08): 2056
   Research Project Grant Program (R01): 2059
   Shared Instrumentation Grant Program: 2058
   Small Research Grant Program (Parent R03): 2060
NATIONAL INVENTORS HALL OF FAME
   Collegiate Inventors Competition: 1639
NATIONAL ITALIAN AMERICAN FOUNDATION (THE)
   NIAF Scholarship Program: 1536
National Jewish Book Award-American Jewish Studies: 621
National Jewish Book Award-Anthologies and Collections: 621
National Jewish Book Award-Autobiography and Memoir: 621
National Jewish Book Award-Biography: 621
National Jewish Book Award-Book Club: 621
National Jewish Book Award-Children's Literature: 621
National Jewish Book Award-Contemporary Jewish Life and Practice: 621
National Jewish Book Award-Debut Fiction: 621
National Jewish Book Award-Education and Jewish Identity: 621
National Jewish Book Award-Fiction: 621
National Jewish Book Award-Food Writing and Cookbooks: 621
National Jewish Book Award-History: 621
National Jewish Book Award-Holocaust: 621
National Jewish Book Award-Modern Jewish Thought and Experience: 621
National Jewish Book Award-Poetry: 621
National Jewish Book Award-Scholarship: 621
National Jewish Book Award-Sephardic Culture: 621
National Jewish Book Award-Visual Arts: 621
National Jewish Book Award-Women's Studies: 621
National Jewish Book Award-Writing Based on Archival Material: 621

National Jewish Book Award-Young Adult Literature: 621
NATIONAL JEWISH COMMITTEE ON SCOUTING
   Arkans (Rick) Eagle Scout Scholarship: 1537
   Vernon (Chester M.) Memorial Eagle Scout Scholarship: 1537
   Weil (Frank L.) Memorial Eagle Scout Scholarship: 1537
NATIONAL KIDNEY FOUNDATION
   Young Investigator Grant Program: 2176
National Leadership Grant Competition: 921
National Leadership Grants for Libraries: 672
National Leadership Grants for Museums: 671
National Medal for Museum and Library Service: 671, 672
NATIONAL MEDICAL FELLOWSHIPS, INC.
   Alliant Health Solutions/NMF Alzheimer's or Related Dementia Care Scholarship: 2062
   Anarcha, Betsy, and Lucy Memorial Scholarship: 2062
   Andersen (Hugh J.) Memorial Scholarship: 2062
   Aspiring Future Physicians Scholarship in Memory of Dr. Tamara O'Neal (The): 2062
   Aspiring Physicians Endowed Scholarship (The): 2062
   Association of American Medical Colleges (AAMC)/Darrell G. Kirch, M.D. Scholarship: 2062
   Butts (Wayne Anthony) Scholarship: 2062
   Cadbury (William and Charlotte) Award: 2062
   Caison (Carl H. and Thelma C., Sr.) Scholarship: 2062
   Carrera (Mary Ball) Scholarship: 2062
   Chase (Dr. Randolph) Memorial Scholarship: 2062
   Colgate-Palmolive/NMF Dental Leadership Program: 2062
   Creary (Drs. Ludlow & Ruth) Family Foundation Scholarship: 2062
   Curtis (Dr. James) Scholarship: 2062
   Edwards (Dr. Darrell L.) Scholarship: 2062
   Empire State Medical Association Scholarship Award: 2062
   Genentech/NMF Diversity Innovation Fellowship Program: 2062
   Gray (Dr. Herman and Shirley) Family Scholarship: 2062
   Hargrove (Dr. Joe L.) Scholarship Award: 2062
   Johnson & Johnson/NMF Future Leaders Scholarship Program: 2062
   Johnson (Genita Evangelista) Endowed Scholarship: 2062
   Lacks (Henrietta) Memorial Scholarship: 2062
   Laroche (Dr. Daniel Denis, Sr.) Scholarship: 2062
   Levin (Don) Trust Scholarship: 2062
   Macy (Josiah Jr.) Foundation Scholarship: 2062
   Manhattan Central Medical Society Scholarship: 2062
   McDonogh (Dr. David Kearney) Scholarship in Ophthalmology/ENT: 2062
   McLean (Franklin C.) Award: 2062
   Michigan Scholarship Fund: 2062
   Miller (Dr. Theodore Quincy) Scholarship: 2062
   New York Community Trust/NMF Medical Research Scholarships: 2062
   NMA Emerging Scholars Awards: 2062
   NMA Emerging Scholars Infectious Diseases Research Awards: 2062
   NMF Fitzbutler-James Alumni Society of the University of Michigan Scholarship Fund: 2062
   NMF National Alumni Council Scholarship Program: 2062
   NMF Primary Care Leadership Program: 2062
   Parrott's (Dr. Fred D.) The Real Men Cook Foundation Academic Scholarship of Excellence and Endowment Challenge Fund: 2062
   Petioni (Dr. Muriel) Scholarship: 2062
   Pinnock (Andrea) Scholarship: 2062
   Roura (Victor Grifols) Scholarship: 2062
   Smith (Dr. James McCune) Medical Student Award: 2062
   Taylor (Dr. Prentiss) Scholarship: 2062
   United Health Foundation/NMF Diverse Medical Scholars Program: 2062
   Zapanta (Dr. Richard) Scholarship: 2062
   Zimmer Biomet/NMF Orthopaedic Scholarship: 2062
NATIONAL MOLE DAY FOUNDATION
   Hague (The George) Memorial Travel Award: 1859
   National Mole of the Year Award (MOTY): 1859
National Mole of the Year Award (MOTY): 1859
NATIONAL MULTIPLE SCLEROSIS SOCIETY
   National Multiple Sclerosis Society Research Grants Program: 2223
   Postdoctoral Fellowships Program in Multiple Sclerosis Research: 2222
National Multiple Sclerosis Society Research Grants Program: 2223
National New Investigator: 2141
NATIONAL OCEANIC AND ATMOSPHERIC ADMINISTRATION
   Bluefin Tuna Research Program Grants: 1873
   Chesapeake Bay Fisheries Research Program: 1409
   Climate Program: 1872
   Cooperative Research Program Grants: 1873

Marine Fisheries Initiative Grants: 1873
National Sea Grant College Program: 1640
Ocean Exploration and Research Program: 1874
NATIONAL OPERA ASSOCIATION, INC.
Bailey (Carolyn) and Dominick Argento Vocal Competition: 717
Biennial Dissertation Competition: 717
Chamber Opera Competition: 717
Collegiate Opera Scenes Competition: 717
Opera Production Competition: 717
Scholarly Paper Competition: 717
NATIONAL ORCHESTRAL INSTITUTE: 718
NATIONAL ORGANIZATION FOR RARE DISORDERS (NORD)
(THE)
Rare Disease Research Grant Program: 2063
National Partner Grants Program: 1179
National Pathfinder's Scholarship: 984
NATIONAL POETRY SERIES (THE)
National Poetry Series Open Competition: 626
National Poetry Series Open Competition: 626
NATIONAL PRESS FOUNDATION
Berryman (Clifford K. and James T.) Award for Editorial Cartoons:
1750
Bradlee (Benjamin C.) Editor of the Year Award: 1750
Chairman's Citation: 1750
Dirksen (Everett McKinley) Award for Distinguished Reporting of
Congress: 1750
Feddie Reporting Award (The): 1750
Hinrich Foundation Award for Distinguished Reporting on Trade: 1750
Innovative Storytelling Award: 1750
Kiplinger (W.M.) Distinguished Contributions to Journalism Award:
1750
Mattingly (Carolyn C.) Award for Mental Health Reporting: 1750
Taishoff (Sol) Award for Excellence in Broadcast Journalism: 1750
Technology in Journalism Award: 1750
National Professional Development Program: 1424
NATIONAL RADIO ASTRONOMY OBSERVATORY
Jansky Fellowships at the NRAO: 1841
NATIONAL RESEARCH COUNCIL OF CANADA
National Research Council Research Associate Program: 1641
National Research Council Research Associate Program: 1641
National Resource Centers (NRC) Program: 609
NATIONAL RESTAURANT ASSOCIATION EDUCATIONAL
FOUNDATION (THE)
National Restaurant Association Educational Foundation (NRAE)
Scholarship Program: 2419
Professional Development Grants for Educators: 1715
National Restaurant Association Educational Foundation (NRAE)
Scholarship Program: 2419
National School Lunch Program (The): 1041
NATIONAL SCIENCE FOUNDATION: 1826, 1875
Advanced Informal STEM Learning (AISL): 1436
Advanced Technological Education (ATE): 1436
Archaeology Program: 1813
Archaeometry Program: 1813
Arctic Research Program: 1645
Astronomy and Astrophysics Research Grants: 1842
Cultural Anthropology Program: 1812
Directorate for Engineering Grants Program: 2396
Discovery Research PreK-12 (DR K12): 1436
Division of Environmental Biology: 1947
Division of Molecular and Cellular Biosciences Programs: 1946
Dynamic Language Infrastructure-Doctoral Dissertation Research
Improvement Grants (DLI-DDRI): 604
Innovative Technology Experiences for Students and Teachers (ITEST):
1436
Investigator-Initiated Research Projects: 1890
Linguistics Program: 604
Linguistics Program-Doctoral Dissertation Research Improvement
Grants (Ling-DDRI): 604
NSF Dynamic Language Infrastructure-NEH Documenting Endangered
Languages (DLI-DEL): 604
NSF Graduate Research Fellowship Program: 1642
Ocean Section: 1876
Perception, Action & Cognition Program: 2333
Science and Technology Studies: 1643
Social Psychology Program: 2332
U.S. Antarctic Research Program: 1644
National Sea Grant College Program: 1640
National Securities Languages Initiative for Youth (NSLI-Y): 793

NATIONAL SECURITY EDUCATION PROGRAM
Boren Fellowships: 846
Boren Scholarships: 845
NATIONAL SOCIETY DAUGHTERS OF THE AMERICAN
REVOLUTION
American Indian Scholarship: 1538
Cogswell (Madeline Pickett) (Halbert) Nursing Scholarship: 2242
DAR Centennial Scholarship: 376
District of Columbia Nursing Scholarship: 2242
Griswold (Enid Hall) Memorial Scholarship: 1670
Holt (Caroline E.) Nursing Scholarship: 2242
MacGregor (Irene and Daisy) Memorial Scholarship: 2064
Marvin (Frances Crawford) American Indian Scholarship: 1539
Nutting (Mildred) Nursing Scholarship: 2242
Occupational/Physical Therapy Scholarship: 2303
Pittenger (Dr. Aura-Lee A. and James Hobbs) American History
Scholarship: 563
NATIONAL SOCIETY OF ACCOUNTANTS SCHOLARSHIP
FOUNDATION
NSA Scholarships: 1540
Stearman (The Stanley H.) Award: 1540
NATIONAL SOCIETY OF BLACK ENGINEERS: 1541
NATIONAL SOCIETY OF PROFESSIONAL SURVEYORS (NSPS)
Berntsen International Scholarship in Surveying Technology (The):
2397
NSPS Board of Directors Scholarship: 2399
NSPS Scholarship (The): 2399
Schonstedt Scholarship in Surveying (The): 2398
NATIONAL SOCIETY OF PROFESSIONAL SURVEYORS (NSPS)
AMERICAN ASSOCIATION FOR GEODETIC SURVEYING (AAGS)
AAGS Joseph F. Dracup Scholarship Award: 2401
American Association for Geodetic Surveying (AAGS) Graduate
Fellowship Award: 2400
NATIONAL TAXIDERMISTS ASSOCIATION
Fleming (Charlie) Scholarship: 913
National Teacher of the Year Award: 2411
National Theater Project: 437
NATIONAL TRUST FOR HISTORIC PRESERVATION
National Trust Preservation Funds (NTPF): 564
National Trust Preservation Funds (NTPF): 564
NATIONAL WILDLIFE FEDERATION
NWF EcoLeaders Fellowships: 1977
NATIONAL YOUNGARTS FOUNDATION
National YoungArts Week: 434
U.S. Presidential Scholars in the Arts: 434
YoungArts Los Angeles: 434
YoungArts Miami: 434
YoungArts New York: 434
National YoungArts Week: 434
NATIONWIDE FOUNDATION: 214
Native American Advised Fund: 920
Native American and Alaska Native Children in School Program: 1424
Native American Business Development Institute (NABDI): 949
NATIVE AMERICAN COMMUNITY BOARD (NACB)
NACB Internship Program: 1410
Native American Leadership in Education (NALE) Program: 951
Native American Library Services: Basic Grants and Enhancement Grants:
672
Native American Scholarship Program: 945
Native American/Native Hawaiian Museum Services Program: 671
Native Art Fellowship: 479
Native Cultures Fund: 1182
Native Hawaiian Library Services Grant: 672
Native Languages: 957
NATSO FOUNDATION
Moon (Bill and Carolyn) Scholarships: 1542
Natural Areas Program: 1973
Natural Resources and Climate Change Program: 112
Natural Sciences or Engineering International Security Fellowship: 760
NAUMBURG (THE WALTER W.) FOUNDATION, INC.: 719
Naval Research Laboratory (NRL) Postdoctoral Fellowship Program: 2385
Navy Health Professions Scholarship Program (HPSP): 2091
NBCC Foundation Military Scholarship: 1543
NBCC Foundation Rural Scholarship: 1543
NBCC FOUNDATION, INC.
ACS Training Award: 1543
BCC Training Award: 1543
CCE Professional Development Award: 1543
Doctoral Minority Fellowship: 1543
GCDF Scholarship: 1543
Master's Youth Addictions Minority Fellowship: 1543

Master's Youth Minority Fellowship: 1543
NBCC Foundation Military Scholarship: 1543
NBCC Foundation Rural Scholarship: 1543
NBMBAA Graduate Scholarship Program: 1210
NBMBAA Undergraduate Scholarship Program: 937
NBNA Board of Directors Scholarship: 2240
NCFR Student Award: 1350
NDS/DMI Education and Communication Scholarship: 1919
NDS/DMI Milk Marketing Scholarships: 1919
NDS/Iager Scholarship: 1919
NDS/Kildee Scholarships: 1919
NDS/Lancaster Sophomore Scholarship: 1919
NDS/Maurice E. Core Scholarship: 1919
NDS/McCullough Scholarships: 1919
NDS/Sowerby Junior Merit Scholarship: 1919
NEA FOUNDATION (THE)
    Awards for Teaching Excellence: 1411
    NEA Foundation Learning and Leadership Grants: 1412
    NEA Foundation Student Success Grants: 1412
NEA Foundation Learning and Leadership Grants: 1412
NEA Foundation Student Success Grants: 1412
NEBRASKA ARTS COUNCIL
    Accessibility Grant: 435
    Artists-in-Schools/Communities Grants: 435
    Arts Learning Projects: 435
    Arts Project Grants: 435
    Basic Support Grants: 435
    Individual Artist Fellowships: 435
    Mini Grants: 435
    Nebraska Touring Program: 435
    School Bus for the Arts Grants: 435
Nebraska Opportunity Grant: 1544
Nebraska Touring Program: 435
NEBRASKA'S COORDINATING COMMISSION FOR
POSTSECONDARY EDUCATION
    Nebraska Opportunity Grant: 1544
NEED
    Access to College and Career Education (ACE) Program: 938
    African American Male Mentoring Initiative (AAMMI): 938
    Future NEED Scholars: 938
    NEED HBCU (Historically Black Colleges and Universities)
    Educational Tour (The): 938
    Science, Technology, Engineering, Art and Math (STEAM) Female
    Mentoring Program: 938
    Unmet NEED Grants and Scholarships: 938
Need Based Aid: 1514
NEED HBCU (Historically Black Colleges and Universities) Educational
Tour (The): 938
NEFE Research Funding Program: 1714
NEH Fellowships for Research in Turkey: 807
NEH Postdoctoral Fellowship: 362
NEH Postdoctoral Fellowships: 553
Neighborhood Fund: 1099
Neighborhood Grants Program: 1102
NELA Annual Scholarship Contest: 1923
NELLIE MAE EDUCATION FOUNDATION: 1413
Nelson (Joan) Study Abroad Scholarship: 1506
Neporany Doctoral Fellowship: 531
Ness (John Harrison) Memorial Award: 742
Network Grants: 2036
Neumueller (Julius F.) Award in Optics: 2254
NEURO (THE)
    Costello (Jeanne Timmins) Fellowships: 2224
    Molson Neuroengineering Fellowship: 2224
    Robb (Preston) Fellowship: 2224
Neuroscience: 1346
Neuroscience of Orofacial Pain & Temporomandibular Disorders: 2107
NEUROSURGERY RESEARCH AND EDUCATION FOUNDATION
    Research Fellowships: 2225
    Young Clinician Investigator Award: 2225
NEVADA ARTS COUNCIL
    Artist Services Program: 436
    Arts Learning Program: 436
    Community Arts Development: 436
    Folklife Program: 436
    Grants Program: 436
Nevins (Allan) Dissertation Prize: 585
New Century Scholars Doctoral Scholarship: 2262
New Century Scholars Research Grant: 2262
NEW DRAMATISTS: 489

NEW ENGLAND BIOLABS FOUNDATION: 215
New England Dance Fund: 437
NEW ENGLAND FOUNDATION FOR THE ARTS
    Center Stage: 437
    Creative City Boston: 437
    Fund for the Arts: 437
    National Dance Project: 437
    National Theater Project: 437
    New England Dance Fund: 437
    New England Presenter Travel Fund: 437
    New England States Touring Program: 437
    New Work New England: 437
    Public Art Learning Fund: 437
New England Presenter Travel Fund: 437
NEW ENGLAND REGIONAL FELLOWSHIP CONSORTIUM: 565
New England States Touring Program: 437
NEW HAMPSHIRE LIBRARY ASSOCIATION
    Norris (Rosalie) Scholarship: 678
    Winchell (F. Mabel) Loan Fund: 678
NEW HAMPSHIRE STATE COUNCIL ON THE ARTS
    Apprenticeships: 438
    Artist Entrepreneurial Workshops: 438
    Artist in Residence: 438
    Artist Services: 438
    Arts in Education: 438
    Arts in Health Project Grants: 438
    Cultural Conservation: 438
    General Project Grants: 438
    Operating Grants: 438
    Percent for Art: 438
    Public Value Partnerships: 438
    Traditional Arts Apprenticeship: 438
    Youth Arts Project Grants: 438
New Initiatives Grant: 2416
New Investigator Award: 2287
New Investigator Awards: 2192
New Investigator Fellowship Training Initiative (NIFTI): 2299
New Investigator Operating Grants: 1316
New Investigator Research Grants: 1319
New Investigators Research Grant: 2262
NEW JERSEY DEPARTMENT OF MILITARY AND VETERANS
AFFAIRS
    Prisoner of War/Missing in Action (POW/MIA) Program: 1546
    Veterans Tuition Credit Program (VTCP): 1545
New Jersey Educational Opportunity Fund (EOF) Program (The): 1547
New Jersey Governor's Industry Vocations Scholarship for Women and
    Minorities (NJ-GIVS): 1507
NEW JERSEY HISTORIC TRUST
    Discover New Jersey History License Plate Fund for Heritage Tourism:
    566
    Emergency Loans: 567
    Preserve New Jersey Historic Preservation Fund for Capital Projects:
    567
    Preserve New Jersey Historic Preservation Fund for Planning Grants:
    566
NEW JERSEY HISTORICAL COMMISSION
    Driscoll (Alfred E.) Dissertation Prize: 569
    General Operating Support Grants: 568
    McCormick (Richard P.) Prize for Scholarly Publication: 569
    Project Grants: 570
NEW JERSEY LIBRARY ASSOCIATION
    Scholarships: 679
NEW JERSEY OFFICE OF THE SECRETARY OF HIGHER
EDUCATION (OSHE)
    New Jersey Educational Opportunity Fund (EOF) Program (The): 1547
NEW JERSEY OSTEOPATHIC EDUCATION FOUNDATION: 2279
NEW JERSEY STATE COUNCIL ON THE ARTS
    Artists-in-Education Residency Grant Program (AIE): 439
    Arts Education Special Initiatives (AESI): 439
    Arts Project Support (APS): 439
    Folk Arts Apprenticeships (FAA): 439
    General Operating Support (GOS): 439
    General Program Support (GPS): 439
    Individual Artist Fellowship Awards (IAFA): 439
New Jersey Student Tuition Assistance Reward Scholarship (NJ STARS):
    1507
New Jersey Student Tuition Assistance Reward Scholarship II (NJ STARS
    II): 1507
New Jersey World Trade Center Scholarship: 1507
NEW MEXICO ARTS: 440

NEW MEXICO FOUNDATION
　　Education and Leadership: 1212
　　Emergency Grants: 1212
NEW MEXICO LIBRARY ASSOCIATION
　　College Scholarship Fund: 680
　　Continuing Education Grants: 680
　　Dorroh (Marion) Memorial Scholarship: 680
New Music Capacity Building Program: 720
New Music Creator Development Fund: 720
NEW MUSIC USA
　　Amplifying Voices: 720
　　New Music Capacity Building Program: 720
　　New Music Creator Development Fund: 720
　　Organizational Development Fund: 720
　　Reel Change: The Fund for Diversity in Film Scoring: 720
New Plays on Campus: 645
New Theater Works Initiative: 144
New Therapy Commercialization Grants: 2211
New Work New England: 437
New Writers Awards: 620
New York City Environmental Fund: 1972
New York City Urban Fellows Program: 1786
NEW YORK COMMUNITY TRUST (THE): 216
New York Community Trust/NMF Medical Research Scholarships: 2062
New York Fellowship Program: 391
NEW YORK FOUNDATION FOR THE ARTS
　　Artists' Fellowships: 441
NEW YORK LANDMARKS CONSERVANCY
　　Historic Properties Fund: 571
　　Non-Profit Technical Assistance Grants Program: 571
　　Sacred Sites Program: 571
　　Technical Services Program: 571
New York-New Jersey Harbor & Estuary Program: 1972
NEW YORK SEA GRANT: 1978
NEW YORK STATE ASSEMBLY INTERN COMMITTEE
　　Assembly Session Internships: 1799
　　Graduate Scholar Internship: 1800
NEW YORK STATE COUNCIL ON THE ARTS: 442
NEW YORK STATE EDUCATION DEPARTMENT
　　Regents Physician Loan Forgiveness Award Program: 1548
　　Scholarships for Academic Excellence: 1548
NEW YORK STATE HIGHER EDUCATION SERVICES
　　CORPORATION
　　Military Enhanced Recognition Incentive and Tribute (MERIT): 1549
　　New York State Tuition Assistance Program (TAP): 1551
　　NYS Aid for Part-Time Study (APTS): 1550
　　NYS Memorial Scholarships: 1549
NEW YORK STATE SENATE
　　Biggane (James L.) Fellowship in Finance: 1801
　　New York State Senate Legislative Fellows Program: 1801
　　Roth (Richard J.) Journalism Fellowship: 1801
　　Undergraduate Session Assistants Program: 1802
　　Wiebe (Richard A.) Public Service Fellowship: 1801
New York State Senate Legislative Fellows Program: 1801
New York State Tuition Assistance Program (TAP): 1551
Newberry Consortium of American Indian and Indigenous Studies
　　(NCAIS) Faculty Fellowship: 347
NEWBERRY LIBRARY (THE)
　　Allen (Frances C.) Fellowship: 954
　　American Society for Eighteenth-Century Studies (ASECS)
　　Fellowships: 572
　　Gray (Charles Montgomery) Fellowship: 351
　　Lewis (Lloyd) Fellowships in American History: 345
　　Lumsden-Kouvel (The Audrey) Fellowship: 342
　　Mellon (Andrew W.) Foundation Fellowships: 352
　　Monticello College Foundation Fellowship for Women: 346
　　National Endowment for the Humanities (NEH) Fellowships: 343
　　Newberry Consortium of American Indian and Indigenous Studies
　　(NCAIS) Faculty Fellowship: 347
　　Newberry Library - Jack Miller Center Fellowships: 348
　　Newberry Short-Term Resident Fellowships for Individual Research:
　　341
　　Power (Susan Kelly) and Helen Hornbeck Tanner Fellowship: 349
　　Society of Mayflower Descendants in the State of Illinois Fellowship:
　　350
　　Weinberg (Arthur and Lila) Fellowship for Independent Scholars and
　　Researchers: 344
Newberry Library - Jack Miller Center Fellowships: 348
Newberry Short-Term Resident Fellowships for Individual Research: 341
Newcombe (Charlotte W.) Doctoral Dissertation Fellowships: 1513

NEWCOMBE (THE CHARLOTTE W.) FOUNDATION
　　Newcombe Fellowships: 1552
　　Newcombe Scholarships for Mature Students: 1552
　　Newcombe Scholarships for Students with Disabilities: 1552
　　Special Scholarship Endowment Grants: 1552
Newcombe Fellowships: 1552
Newcombe Scholarships for Mature Students: 1552
Newcombe Scholarships for Students with Disabilities: 1552
Newkirk Graduate Research Fellowship: 1840
Newman (The Eric P.) Graduate Summer Seminar: 307
NEWMEXICOWOMEN.ORG: 914
Newton Fund: 1099
Next Generation Hoosier Educators Scholarship: 1512
Next Stage Grants: 1186
NF Clinic Network (CTF-NFCN): 2114
NFMC Competitions and Awards: 714
NFPA Youth Scholarship: 1026
NFSPS College Undergraduate Poetry (CUP) Competition: 625
NHF Career Development Award: 2051
NIAF Scholarship Program: 1536
NICSA
　　NICSA/William T. Blackwell Scholarship Fund (The): 1414
NICSA/William T. Blackwell Scholarship Fund (The): 1414
Nieman Fellowships in Journalism: 1751
NIEMAN FOUNDATION FOR JOURNALISM AT HARVARD
　　Bingham (Worth) Prize for Investigative Journalism: 1753
　　Nieman Fellowships in Journalism: 1751
　　Taylor Family Award for Fairness in Journalism: 1752
Nigogosian (Aram and Rose) Fund: 731
NIH Pathway to Independence Award (K99/R00): 1311
NJBEST Scholarship: 1507
NM Health Equity Partnership: 920
NMA Emerging Scholars Awards: 2062
NMA Emerging Scholars Infectious Diseases Research Awards: 2062
NMF Fitzbutler-James Alumni Society of the University of Michigan
　　Scholarship Fund: 2062
NMF National Alumni Council Scholarship Program: 2062
NMF Primary Care Leadership Program: 2062
No Kid Hungry: 1358
NOBLE (THE SAMUEL ROBERTS) FOUNDATION: 1458
Non-Profit Technical Assistance Grants Program: 571
Nonprofit Assistance Initiative: 1132
Nonprofit Capacity Building Grants: 68
Nonprofit Event Sponsorships: 1359
Nonprofit Executive Leadership Program: 100
Nonprofit Media Grant Program: 1655
Nonprofit Network: 1165
Nonprofit Support Program: 1123
Nonprofit Toolbox: 1099
Nonprofit/Educational Gift Matching Program: 10
NORCLIFFE FOUNDATION (THE): 217
Norden (Deborah J.) Fund: 369
NORDSON CORPORATION FOUNDATION (THE)
　　Time and Talent: 218
NORRIS (KENNETH T. AND EILEEN L.) FOUNDATION: 219
Norris (Rosalie) Scholarship: 678
North American Foundation Awards: 856
NORTH AMERICAN SPINE SOCIETY (NASS)
　　Clinical Traveling Fellowship: 2065
　　Research Grant: 2065
　　Research Traveling Fellowship: 2065
　　Young Investigator Grants: 2065
NORTH ATLANTIC TREATY ORGANIZATION
　　Science for Peace and Security (SPS) Programme: 880
NORTH CAROLINA ARTS COUNCIL
　　Artist Fellowships: 443
　　Arts in Education Grants: 443
　　Grassroots Arts Program: 443
　　Military and Veteran Healing Arts Grants: 443
　　Organizational Development: 443
　　Program Support: 443
　　Regional Artist Project Grants: 443
　　SmART Initiative: 443
　　State Arts Resources: 443
　　Statewide Service Organizations: 443
NORTH CAROLINA ASSOCIATION OF EDUCATORS
　　Morrow (Mary)/Edna Richards Scholarship Fund: 1459
NORTH CAROLINA COMMUNITY FOUNDATION: 220

NORTH CAROLINA GLAXOSMITHKLINE FOUNDATION
  Child Health Recognition Awards: 1415
  Ribbon of Hope: 1415
  Traditional Grants: 1415
  Women in Science Scholars Program: 1415
NORTH CAROLINA LIBRARY ASSOCIATION
  Appalachian Scholarship (The): 681
  North Carolina Library Association Memorial Scholarship (The): 681
  Query-Long Scholarship (The): 681
North Carolina Library Association Memorial Scholarship (The): 681
NORTH CAROLINA STATE EDUCATION ASSISTANCE
  AUTHORITY/COLLEGE FOUNDATION OF NORTH CAROLINA:
  1553
NORTH DAKOTA COUNCIL ON THE ARTS
  Artists in Residence: 444
  Arts in Education Collaboration Grant (AIEC): 444
  Community Arts Access: 444
  Individual Artists Fellowships: 444
  Institutional Support: 444
  Professional Development: 444
  Special Projects: 444
  Traditional Arts Apprenticeships: 444
North Shore Community Health Network: 1153
NORTHEAST AGRICULTURAL EDUCATION FOUNDATION: 1921
Northeast Area Women and Girls Fund: 1110
NORTHEASTERN LOGGERS' ASSOCIATION, INC.
  Cox (William J.) Memorial Fund Scholarship: 1922
  NELA Annual Scholarship Contest: 1923
NORTHERN CHAUTAUQUA COMMUNITY FOUNDATION: 1554
Northern Trust Company Charitable Trust (The): 1213
NORTHERN TRUST CORPORATION
  Northern Trust Company Charitable Trust (The): 1213
  Northern Trust Matching Gift Program (The): 1213
  Volunteer Grants Program: 1213
Northern Trust Matching Gift Program (The): 1213
NORTHWEST MINNESOTA FOUNDATION (THE): 1214
NORTHWESTERN MUTUAL FOUNDATION (THE): 1215
Norwich Area Women and Girls Fund: 1110
Norwich Youth Grants: 1110
Novak (Robert) Journalism Fellowship Program: 1792
Novis (Brian D.) Research Grants: 2041
NOYES (JESSIE SMITH) FOUNDATION: 1979
Noyes (Marcia C.) Award: 674
NRA (THE)
  Bray (Jeanne E.) Memorial Scholarship: 1555
NRC Research Associateship Programs: 1824
NSA Scholarships: 1540
NSERC Alliance-RM ACT Grant: 1316
NSF-CBMS Regional Conferences in the Mathematical Sciences: 1884
NSF Dynamic Language Infrastructure-NEH Documenting Endangered
  Languages (DLI-DEL): 604
NSF Graduate Research Fellowship Program: 1642
NSPS Board of Directors Scholarship: 2399
NSPS Scholarship (The): 2399
NUCLEAR AGE PEACE FOUNDATION
  Kelly (Barbara Mandigo) Peace Poetry Awards: 779
Nurse Practitioner/Nurse Midwife Scholarship Program: 2248
NURSES EDUCATIONAL FUNDS, INC.: 2243
Nursing Research Grant: 2219
Nursing Research Grants: 2235
Nutrition Research Program: 2418
Nutting (Mildred) Nursing Scholarship: 2242
NWF EcoLeaders Fellowships: 1977
NYS Aid for Part-Time Study (APTS): 1550
NYS Memorial Scholarships: 1549
NZFGW Daphne Purves Grant: 978

O

O'Bannon (The Frank) Grant: 1512
O'Connor (Basil) Starter Scholar Research Award: 2047
O'Connor (The John E.) Film Award: 526
O'Donovan (The Anita Cecil) Fellowship: 826
O'Leary (Rhonda J.) Scholarship: 1704
O'NEILL (WILLIAM J. AND DOROTHY K.) FOUNDATION: 221
OAK GROVE SCHOOL FOUNDATION
  Grants Program: 1416
  Tuition Assistance: 1416
Oak Park Project: 1334

OAK RIDGE INSTITUTE FOR SCIENCE AND EDUCATION (ORISE):
  2402
Oakes (John B.) Award: 1726
Obstetric and Pediatric Pharmacology and Therapeutics Branch (OPPTB):
  1318
Occupational/Physical Therapy Scholarship: 2303
Ocean Exploration and Research Program: 1874
Ocean Section: 1876
Oceanography Engineering Fellowship Program: 1823
Office of Student Affairs Community Leadership Tuition Scholarship: 936
Officers and Trustees Discretionary Grants: 1296
OHF - ASN Foundation for Kidney Research Grant: 2110
OHF Research Grant: 2070
Ohio Artists on Tour: 445
OHIO ARTS COUNCIL
  Artists with Disabilities Access: 445
  Arts Access: 445
  Arts Learning: Artist Express: 445
  Arts Learning: Arts Partnership: 445
  Arts Learning: TeachArtsOhio: 445
  ArtsNEXT: 445
  ArtSTART: 445
  Big Yellow School Bus: 445
  Building Cultural Diversity: 445
  Capacity Building: 445
  Individual Artist Grants and Services: Traditional Arts Apprenticeships:
  445
  Ohio Artists on Tour: 445
  Ohio Heritage Fellowship Awards: 445
  Sustainability: 445
Ohio Chapter ISA Education Grant: 1925
Ohio College Opportunity Grant Program (OCOG): 1557
OHIO DEPARTMENT OF HIGHER EDUCATION
  Ohio College Opportunity Grant Program (OCOG): 1557
  Ohio War Orphan and Severely Disabled Veterans' Children
  Scholarships: 1556
Ohio Heritage Fellowship Awards: 445
OHIO NATIONAL GUARD SCHOLARSHIP PROGRAM: 1558
Ohio War Orphan and Severely Disabled Veterans' Children Scholarships:
  1556
OISHEI (THE JOHN R.) FOUNDATION: 222
OKLAHOMA ARTS COUNCIL
  Capitol Art Travel Subsidies: 446
  Major Grant Support: 446
  Organizational Support: 446
  Small Grant Support: 446
  Small Grant Support for Schools: 446
OKLAHOMA CITY COMMUNITY FOUNDATION, INC.: 1216
Old (Lloyd J.) STAR Program: 2184
Oldfield (Vada and Barney) Fellowship for National Security Reporting:
  1757
Olin Fellowships: 1935
Olin Palladium Award: 1627
Olin (Spencer T. and Ann W.) Fellowship for Women in Graduate Study:
  1613
Oliver (Robert B.) Scholarship: 1478
OMAHA COMMUNITY FOUNDATION
  African American Unity Fund: 223
  Endowment Funds of Southwest Iowa: 223
  Equality Fund for LGBTQIA: 223
  Fund for Omaha: 223
  Futuro Latino Fund: 223
  Omaha Neighborhood Grants Program: 223
Omaha Neighborhood Grants Program: 223
Omicron Nu Master's Fellowship: 2416
Omicron Nu Research Fellowship: 2416
Omohundro Institute-NEH Postdoctoral Fellowship: 573
OMOHUNDRO INSTITUTE OF EARLY AMERICAN HISTORY AND
  CULTURE
  Georgian Papers Programme Fellowships: 574
  Jamestown Rediscovery-Omohundro Institute (JR-OI) Short-Term
  Visiting Fellowship: 574
  Lapidus-OI Fellowship: 575
  Omohundro Institute-NEH Postdoctoral Fellowship: 573
ONCOLOGY NURSING FOUNDATION: 2193
Open City Fellowship: 613
Open Grants: 1432
OPEN MEADOWS FOUNDATION: 985
OPEN SOCIETY INSTITUTE - BALTIMORE
  Addiction and Health Equity Program: 1217
  Criminal and Juvenile Justice Program: 1351

Open Studio Residency: 413
Opera Production Competition: 717
Operating Funds: 251
Operating Grants: 438
Operating Support Grants: 447
Operational Program Grants: 1306
Operational Support Grants: 428
Operations and Power Division Scholarship: 2380
Oppenheimer (J. Robert) Postdoctoral Fellowship: 1635
Opportunity Grants: 401, 1102
Oral & Salivary Cancer Biology: 2107
Oral Health Disparities & Inequities: 2107
ORANGE COUNTY COMMUNITY FOUNDATION: 224
ORCHESTRE SYMPHONIQUE DE MONTREAL (OSM)
  OSM Competition: 721
ORDEAN FOUNDATION (THE): 1218
ORDER SONS OF ITALY IN AMERICA, GRAND LODGE OF
  FLORIDA: 1559
OREF Clinical Research Award: 2068
OREGON ARTS COMMISSION
  Access Reimbursement Grants: 447
  Arts Build Communities: 447
  Arts Learning Grants: 447
  Career Opportunity Grants: 447
  Individual Artists Fellowship Grants: 447
  Operating Support Grants: 447
  Oregon Media Arts Fellowship: 447
  Small Operating Grants: 447
OREGON COMMUNITY FOUNDATION (THE)
  Community Grants Program: 1219
Oregon Media Arts Fellowship: 447
Organization and Project Grant: 391
ORGANIZATION OF AMERICAN STATES
  Academic Studies: 780
  Professional Development: 780
  Rowe (The Leo S.) Pan American Fund: 876
Organization Support Fund: 1165
Organizational Capacity Building: 919
Organizational Development: 394, 425, 443
Organizational Development Fund: 720
Organizational Development Grants: 1102
Organizational Endowment Funds: 1139
Organizational Support: 446
ORLANDO MAGIC YOUTH FOUNDATION: 1027
Orlik (Peter B.) Award: 1724
ORTHOPAEDIC RESEARCH AND EDUCATION FOUNDATION
  Career Development Grant Award: 2066
  OREF Clinical Research Award: 2068
  Resident Clinician Scientist Training Grant: 2067
Osborn (The Kenneth J.) Memorial Scholarship: 1821
OSHER (THE BERNARD) FOUNDATION: 225
OSM Competition: 721
OSTEOGENESIS IMPERFECTA FOUNDATION
  Geisman (Michael) Fellowships: 2069
Our Town: 433
Our Village: 933
OUTER BANKS COMMUNITY FOUNDATION: 1220
Outstanding Abstract Achievement Award: 2109
Outstanding Educator Award: 2376
Outstanding Junior Clinician Education Manuscript: 2294
Outstanding Junior Clinician Educator of the Year: 2294
Outstanding Junior Investigator of the Year: 2294
Outstanding Junior Research Manuscript: 2294
Outstanding Mid-Career Clinician Educator of the Year: 2294
Outstanding Research Award: 1382
Outstanding Social Studies Teacher of the Year Awards (Elementary,
  Middle and Secondary Levels): 1665
OXALOSIS AND HYPEROXALURIA FOUNDATION
  OHF Research Grant: 2070
OXNARD FOUNDATION: 2071

P

P.E.O. International Peace Scholarship: 877
P.E.O. SISTERHOOD
  P.E.O. International Peace Scholarship: 877
PACCAR FOUNDATION: 226
PACIFIC GAS AND ELECTRIC COMPANY: 227

PACIFIC LIFE FOUNDATION
  Arts and Culture: 228
  Civic, Community, and Environment: 228
  Education: 228
  Health and Human Services: 228
PACKARD (THE DAVID AND LUCILE) FOUNDATION
  Children, Families and Communities: 229
  Conservation and Science: 229
  Local Grantmaking Program: 229
  Reproductive Health: 229
PACKARD (LUCILE) FOUNDATION FOR CHILDREN'S HEALTH:
  1028
Packer (Barbara) Fellowship: 304
Paley (Grace) Prize for Short Fiction: 614
Palisca (Claude V.) Award: 691
Palmer (Alice Freeman) Fellowship: 991
Palmer (Robert and Rebeca) Scholarship: 1001
Pam (Edgar) Fellowship: 2421
Panowski (Mildred and Albert) Playwriting Award: 492
Pape Research Fund: 1990
PARALYZED VETERANS OF AMERICA RESEARCH AND
  EDUCATION FOUNDATIONS: 2304
PARAPSYCHOLOGY FOUNDATION, INC.
  Bolton (Frances P.) Fellowship: 2335
  Garrett (Eileen J.) Scholarship: 2334
  Tart (Charles T. and Judith A.) Student Incentive Award: 2336
PARDEE (THE ELSA U.) FOUNDATION: 2194
PARKER FOUNDATION (THE): 230
PARKER HANNIFIN FOUNDATION: 231
PARKINSON'S FOUNDATION
  Clinical Research Award: 2230
  Conference Awards: 2226
  Fahn (Stanley) Faculty Scholar Award: 2227
  Parkinson's Foundation-PSG Mentored Clinical Research Award: 2229
  Parkinson's Foundation Summer Student Fellowship: 2232
  Postdoctoral Fellowship: 2231
  Visiting Scholar Award: 2228
Parkinson's Foundation-PSG Mentored Clinical Research Award: 2229
Parkinson's Foundation Summer Student Fellowship: 2232
Parkman (Francis) Prize: 585
Parks (The Danielle) Memorial Fellowship: 826
Parrish (William E.) Scholarship: 577
Parrott's (Dr. Fred D.) The Real Men Cook Foundation Academic
  Scholarship of Excellence and Endowment Challenge Fund: 2062
Parsons (Elisabeth M. and Winchell M.) Scholarship: 2387
PARSONS (THE RALPH M.) FOUNDATION: 232
Partner Grants: 409
Partner University Scholarships: 1514
Partnership Agreements: 433
Partnership for a Healthy Orange County: 1299
Partnership Grant: 425
PAS/Armand Zildjian Percussion Scholarship: 722
PAS/Remo, Inc. Fred Hoey Memorial Scholarship: 722
PASADENA COMMUNITY FOUNDATION: 1352
PASIC International Scholarship: 722
PASIC Scholarships: 722
PATAGONIA INC.
  Environmental Grant Program: 1980
Patient Services Grants: Safety Net Grant Program: 2001
Patriots Connection (The): 1227
PATRON SAINTS FOUNDATION (THE): 1313
PATTERSON (THE ALICIA) FOUNDATION
  Fellowship Program for Journalists: 1754
Paul (Courtland) Scholarship: 1974
Pauly (Philip J.) Prize: 548
Payne (Clara R.) Memorial Scholarship: 976
PEABODY (AMELIA) CHARITABLE FUND: 233
Peacock (Chuck) Memorial Scholarship: 2363
PEACOCK FOUNDATION, INC.: 234
Peacock (The Frances M.) Scholarship for Native Bird Habitat: 1967
Peacock Medal: 2423
PECP Self Study Program: 2357
Pediatric Growth and Nutrition Branch (PGNB): 1318
Pediatric Trauma and Critical Illness Branch (PTCIB): 1318
PeDRA Research Grants: 2285
Pell Grant: 1586
Peltenburg (Edgar J.) Postdoctoral Research Fellowship in Cypriot
  Prehistory: 827
Pemberton (Margaret) Scholarship: 2240

PEN AMERICA
  PEN America Writers' Emergency Fund: 629
  PEN Award for Poetry in Translation: 632
  PEN Open Book Award: 630
  PEN Prison Writing Program: 628
  PEN Translation Prize: 605
  PEN/Diamonstein-Spielvogel Award for the Art of the Essay: 636
  PEN/E.O. Wilson Prize for Literary Science Writing: 637
  PEN/Heim Translation Fund Grant: 640
  PEN/Hemingway Award for a Debut Novel: 627
  PEN/Jacqueline Bograd Weld Award for Biography: 638
  PEN/Jean Stein Grant for Literary Oral History: 639
  PEN/Laura Pels International Foundation for Theater Award -
    Mid-Career Playwright: 490
  PEN/Phyllis Naylor Grant for Children's and Young Adult Novelists:
    631
  PEN/Robert J. Dau Short Story Prize for Emerging Writers: 635
  PEN/Robert W. Bingham Prize for Debut Short Story Collection: 634
  PEN/Voelcker Award for Poetry Collection: 633
PEN America Writers' Emergency Fund: 629
PEN Award for Poetry in Translation: 632
PEN Open Book Award: 630
PEN Prison Writing Program: 628
PEN Translation Prize: 605
PEN/Diamonstein-Spielvogel Award for the Art of the Essay: 636
PEN/E.O. Wilson Prize for Literary Science Writing: 637
PEN/Faulkner Award for Fiction: 641
PEN/FAULKNER FOUNDATION
  PEN/Faulkner Award for Fiction: 641
PEN/Heim Translation Fund Grant: 640
PEN/Hemingway Award for a Debut Novel: 627
PEN/Jacqueline Bograd Weld Award for Biography: 638
PEN/Jean Stein Grant for Literary Oral History: 639
PEN/Laura Pels International Foundation for Theater Award - Mid-Career
    Playwright: 490
PEN/Phyllis Naylor Grant for Children's and Young Adult Novelists: 631
PEN/Robert J. Dau Short Story Prize for Emerging Writers: 635
PEN/Robert W. Bingham Prize for Debut Short Story Collection: 634
PEN/Voelcker Award for Poetry Collection: 633
PENN (THE WILLIAM) FOUNDATION
  Creative Communities: 235
  Great Learning: 235
  Watershed Protection: 235
PENNSYLVANIA COUNCIL ON THE ARTS
  Arts Organization Grants: 448
PENNSYLVANIA HIGHER EDUCATION ASSISTANCE AGENCY
  Pennsylvania State Grant Program: 1560
Pennsylvania State Grant Program: 1560
Penrose House Conference Center: 100
People-Centered Care: 1286
Pepler (George) International Award: 1673
PEPSICO FOUNDATION: 236
Percent for Art: 438
Perception, Action & Cognition Program: 2333
Percussion Composition Contest: 722
PERCUSSIVE ARTS SOCIETY
  Chapin (Jim) Memorial Teacher Scholarship: 722
  Grimes (John E.) Timpani Scholarship: 722
  Gruber (Freddie) Scholarship: 722
  Internship Program: 722
  Londin (Larrie) Memorial Scholarship: 722
  PAS/Armand Zildjian Percussion Scholarship: 722
  PAS/Remo, Inc. Fred Hoey Memorial Scholarship: 722
  PASIC International Scholarship: 722
  PASIC Scholarships: 722
  Percussion Composition Contest: 722
  Zildjian Family Opportunity Fund: 722
Performance Program: 700
Performance Scholarships in Music for Students in Bachelor and Master
    of Music Programs: 726
Performing Arts: 137, 254, 384
Performing Arts Fellowships: 479
Performing Arts Global Exchange: 430
Performing Arts Japan Program: 775
Performing Arts Program: 325
Performing Arts Scholarship: 1481
Peridian International Inc./Rae L. Price, FASLA Scholarship: 1974
PERMIAN BASIN AREA FOUNDATION: 1221
PERPETUAL TRUSTEE COMPANY LTD.
  Franklin (Miles) Literary Award: 642
  Geach (Portia) Memorial Award: 449

Perryman (The Leonard M.) Communications Scholarship for Ethnic
    Minority Students: 923
Peterson (Charles E.) Fellowship of the Buildings of the U.S. and the
    Athenaeum of Philadelphia: 382
Peterson (Kate B. and Hall J.) Fellowships: 304
Petioni (Dr. Muriel) Scholarship: 2062
PETOSKEY-HARBOR SPRINGS AREA COMMUNITY FOUNDATION:
    1222
Petroleum Research Fund (The): 1819
PEW FELLOWSHIPS AT THE PEW CENTER FOR ARTS &
    HERITAGE: 513
Peykoff (Jamie) Follicular Lymphoma Research Initiative: 2119
PFD RESEARCH FOUNDATION
  PFD Research Foundation Grants Program: 1897
PFD Research Foundation Grants Program: 1897
PFF Scholars Program: 2078
Pfizer Prize: 548
PFORZHEIMER (THE CARL AND LILY) FOUNDATION, INC.: 237
PHARMACEUTICAL RESEARCH AND MANUFACTURERS OF
    AMERICA FOUNDATION, INC.
  Postdoctoral Fellowship in Drug Delivery: 2072
  Postdoctoral Fellowship in Drug Discovery: 2072
  Postdoctoral Fellowship in Health Outcomes Research: 2072
  Postdoctoral Fellowship in Translational Medicine: 2072
  Predoctoral Fellowship in Drug Delivery: 2073
  Predoctoral Fellowship in Drug Discovery: 2073
  Predoctoral Fellowship in Health Outcomes Research: 2073
  Research Starter Grant in Drug Delivery: 2292
  Research Starter Grant in Drug Discovery: 2292
  Research Starter Grant in Health Outcomes Research: 2292
  Research Starter Grant in Translational Medicine: 2292
  Value Assessment Challenge Awards: 2074
  Value Assessment Research Award: 2074
PHI ALPHA THETA HISTORY HONOR SOCIETY
  Bakken (Gordon Morris) Scholarship in Western History: 577
  Cleven (The Nels Andrew) Founder's Paper Prize Awards: 578
  Hammond (Dr. George P.) Paper Prize: 578
  Member's Best First Book Award: 576
  Member's Best Subsequent Book Award: 576
  Morgan (Thomas S.) Memorial Scholarship: 577
  Parrish (William E.) Scholarship: 577
  Tunstall (Graydon A.) Undergraduate Student Scholarship: 577
  Turner (Dr. Lynn W.) Paper Prize: 578
  Zimmerman (A.F.) Scholarship: 577
Phi Beta Kappa Book Awards (The): 643
PHI BETA KAPPA SOCIETY (THE)
  Jensen (The Walter J.) Fellowship for French Language, Literature and
    Culture: 847
  Lebowitz (Dr. Martin R.) and Eve Lewellis Lebowitz Prize for
    Philosophical Achievement and Contribution (The): 1671
  Phi Beta Kappa Book Awards (The): 643
  Romanell-Phi Beta Kappa Professorship in Philosophy (The): 1561
  Sibley (Mary Isabel) Fellowship: 986
PHI CHI THETA EDUCATIONAL FOUNDATION
  Educational and Scholastic Advancement Programs: 1716
Phi Kappa Phi Fellowship: 1509
Phi Lambda Sigma-AFPE First Year Graduate Fellowship: 2288
PHILADELPHIA FOUNDATION (THE)
  Advocacy Program: 1223
  Advocacy Unrestricted: 1223
  Direct Service: 1223
  Impact Grant: 1223
  Leadership Grant: 1223
Philanthropy: 137
PHILLIPS (DR. AND MRS. ARTHUR WILLIAM) CHARITABLE
    TRUST: 2075
Phillips Fund for Native American Research: 943
PHILLIPS (JAY AND ROSE) FAMILY FOUNDATION OF
    MINNESOTA: 1353
Photographic and Electronic Media (MFA): 509
Photography Program: 426
Physician-Scientist Career Development Award: 2005
Physicians of Tomorrow Scholarship: 1477
Pi Gamma Mu Scholarships: 1562
PI GAMMA MU, INTERNATIONAL HONOR SOCIETY IN SOCIAL
    SCIENCE
  Pi Gamma Mu Scholarships: 1562
PICK (THE ALBERT, JR.) FUND: 238
Pierce (The Lorne) Medal: 1646
Pierce (Newton Lacy) Prize in Astronomy: 1832
Pikes Peak Heritage Series: 100

Pilot and Feasibility Awards: 2167
Pilot and Feasibility Grants: 1945
Pilot Awards: 2308
Pilot Innovation Grant: 1364
PILOT Media Technology and Innovation Scholarships: 1725
Pilot Research Award in Health Disparities: 2161
Pilot Research Grants: 2076
Pinch Medal: 2423
PINKERTON FOUNDATION (THE): 1029
Pinkney (The David H.) Prize: 584
Pinnock (Andrea) Scholarship: 2062
PIPER FUND: 1803
PIPER (MINNIE STEVENS) FOUNDATION
    Piper Professor Program: 1563
    Piper Scholar Program: 1563
    Student Loan Program: 1563
Piper Professor Program: 1563
Piper Scholar Program: 1563
Pisk (Paul A.) Prize: 691
PITT POETRY SERIES
    Starrett (Agnes Lynch) Poetry Prize: 644
Pittenger (Dr. Aura-Lee A. and James Hobbs) American History
    Scholarship: 563
PITTSBURGH FOUNDATION (THE): 1224
Pittsburgh Local Section Scholarship: 2383
PITTSBURGH NEW MUSIC ENSEMBLE, INC. (THE)
    Gaul (Harvey) Music Composition Contest: 723
Pizzigati (Antonio) Prize for Software in the Public Interest: 1258
PLANNING AND VISUAL EDUCATION PARTNERSHIP (THE): 1564
PLASTIC SURGERY FOUNDATION (PSF)
    ASE/PSF Combined Research Grant: 2076
    Combined Pilot Research Grants: 2076
    Innovation in Wound Care Research and Academic Development
    Fellowship: 2076
    National Endowment for Plastic Surgery: 2076
    Pilot Research Grants: 2076
    PSF Directed Research Grant - Breast Implant Safety: 2076
    PSF Translational and Innovation Research Grant (The): 2076
    PSF/MTF Biologics Allograft Tissue Research Grant (The): 2076
    Research Fellowships: 2076
    Spear (Scott) Innovation in Breast Reconstruction Research Fellowship:
    2076
Platt Fellowships: 818
Player Foundation Grants: 1211
PLAYWRIGHTS' CENTER (THE)
    Affiliated Writer Program: 645
    Core Apprentice Program: 645
    Core Writer Program: 645
    Jerome Fellowships: 645
    Many Voices Fellowships: 645
    Many Voices Mentorships: 645
    McKnight Fellowships in Playwriting: 645
    McKnight National Residency and Commission: 645
    McKnight Theater Artist Fellowships: 645
    New Plays on Campus: 645
PLOUGH FOUNDATION: 1354
Poetry Out Loud: 420
Police Officer's and Fire Fighter's Survivor Tuition Grant (STG): 1580
Polish Studies Scholarship: 1473
POLLOCK-KRASNER FOUNDATION, INC. (THE): 514
Polsky (Joel) Academic Achievement Award: 367
Polsky (Joel) Prize: 367
Pomerance (Harriet and Leon) Fellowship: 311
PONTIFICAL INSTITUTE OF MEDIAEVAL STUDIES
    Mellon Postdoctoral Fellowships: 579
POOL (THE DOROTHY RIDER) HEALTH CARE TRUST: 1314
Pool (Judith Graham) Postdoctoral Research Fellowships in Bleeding
    Disorders: 2051
Population Dynamics Branch (PDB): 1318
PORTER (IRWIN ANDREW) FOUNDATION: 239
Positive Youth Justice Initiative: 1334
Post Baccalaureate Certificate Program in Conservation: 521
Post-Baccalaureate Diploma: 701
Post-Doctoral Research Fellowships: 2206
POST-POLIO HEALTH INTERNATIONAL
    Research Fund (The): 2077
Postdoc-to-Faculty Transition Awards: 2167
Postdoctoral Earth and Planetary Sciences Fellowship: 2372
Postdoctoral Fellowship: 362, 2128, 2178, 2231
Postdoctoral Fellowship Award: 2201

Postdoctoral Fellowship Grants: 2119
Postdoctoral Fellowship in Drug Delivery: 2072
Postdoctoral Fellowship in Drug Discovery: 2072
Postdoctoral Fellowship in Health Outcomes Research: 2072
Postdoctoral Fellowship in Translational Medicine: 2072
Postdoctoral Fellowship (PDF): 2148, 2191
Postdoctoral Fellowships: 375, 2170
Postdoctoral Fellowships at NCAR: 1638
Postdoctoral Fellowships in the Humanities and the Arts, Sciences and
    Professions: 334
Postdoctoral Fellowships Program at the Weizmann Institute of Science:
    867
Postdoctoral Fellowships Program in Multiple Sclerosis Research: 2222
Postdoctoral Research Associateships: 1822
Postdoctoral Research Fellowship: 2205
Postdoctoral Research Fellowship Award: 2167
Postdoctoral Research Fellowship Innovation Grants: 1365
Postdoctoral Research Fellowship Program: 1620
Postdoctoral Researchers Fellowship: 828
Postgraduate Clinical Fellowship Training Program at the Albert Ellis
    Institute: 2326
Postgraduate Research Scholarships: 855
POTTS MEMORIAL FOUNDATION (THE): 2145
Power Program: 1964
Power (Susan Kelly) and Helen Hornbeck Tanner Fellowship: 349
Power to Play Grant: 6
PPG INDUSTRIES FOUNDATION: 240
Prato (Lou and Carole) Sports Reporting Scholarship: 1757
Pre-College Scholarships: 1114
Pre-Dissertation Fellowships: 801
PRECAST/PRESTRESSED CONCRETE INSTITUTE
    Jenny (Daniel P.) Research Fellowships: 2403
Predoctoral and Postdoctoral Fellowships at the Carnegie Institution: 1624
Predoctoral Fellowship: 2129
Predoctoral Fellowship in Drug Delivery: 2073
Predoctoral Fellowship in Drug Discovery: 2073
Predoctoral Fellowship in Health Outcomes Research: 2073
Predoctoral Research Fellowship: 2205
Predoctoral Research Fellowships: 1843
Pregnancy and Perinatology Branch (PPB): 1318
Prelinger (Catherine) Award: 975
PRESBYTERIAN CHURCH (U.S.A.)
    Presbyterian Study Grants: 750
    Robinson (Samuel) Award: 1566
    Student Opportunity Scholarship: 1565
Presbyterian Study Grants: 750
Preservation and Access: 339
Preserve New Jersey Historic Preservation Fund for Capital Projects: 567
Preserve New Jersey Historic Preservation Fund for Planning Grants: 566
President's Certificate of Merit Award: 2249
PRESIDENT'S COMMISSION ON WHITE HOUSE FELLOWSHIPS
    White House Fellowships: 1804
President's Doctoral Scholar Award: 856
President's Fund: 1165
President's Grants: 2046
President's New Researcher Award: 2322
President's Scholarships (The): 1757
Presidential Graduate Travel Grant: 738
Presidents Scholarship: 2392
Presidio La Bahia Award: 586
Press Club and St. Louis Post-Dispatch Ronald Wade Journalism
    Scholarship: 1567
Press Club Internship Scholarships: 1567
Press Club Journalism Scholarship: 1567
Press Club Media Summer Internship Scholarships: 1567
Press Club Neiman Marcus Media Scholarship: 1567
PRESS CLUB OF ST. LOUIS CHARITABLE FUND - ST. LOUIS
    PRESS CLUB (THE)
    Bonwich (Joe) Media Scholarship: 1567
    Burris (Donald R.) Journalism Scholarship: 1567
    Dames (Joan Foster) Women's Journalism Scholarship: 1567
    Fourth Estate Scholarships: 1567
    Heinz (Karl) and Doris Finzel Photojournalism Scholarship: 1567
    High School Journalism Scholarship: 1567
    Journalism Foundation Scholarships: 1567
    Lipman (David S.) Scholarship: 1567
    Miller (Sarah Bryan) Scholarship: 1567
    Press Club and St. Louis Post-Dispatch Ronald Wade Journalism
    Scholarship: 1567
    Press Club Internship Scholarships: 1567

Press Club Journalism Scholarship: 1567
Press Club Media Summer Internship Scholarships: 1567
Press Club Neiman Marcus Media Scholarship: 1567
PRESSER FOUNDATION
    Advancement of Music: 724
    Assistance to Worthy Music Teachers: 724
    Capital Support: 724
    Presser Foundation Graduate Music Award (The): 724
    Presser Foundation Undergraduate Scholar Award (The): 724
    Special Projects: 724
Presser Foundation Graduate Music Award (The): 724
Presser Foundation Undergraduate Scholar Award (The): 724
Preterm Birth Initiative: 2016
PREVENT CANCER FOUNDATION: 2195
Prevention Beyond the Pipeline: 1995
Preyer (Kathryn Conway) Fellowship: 991
Price (Derek)/Rod Webster Prize: 547
PRIDE FOUNDATION: 915
Primary Care Training and Enhancement (PCTE): 2035
Primary Grant Program: 158
Princess Grace Awards: 491
PRINCESS GRACE FOUNDATION-USA
    Princess Grace Awards: 491
PRINCETON AREA COMMUNITY FOUNDATION: 1225
PRINCIPAL FINANCIAL GROUP FOUNDATION INC.
    Charitable Giving Program: 241
PRINT AND GRAPHICS SCHOLARSHIP FOUNDATION: 2359, 2360
Prisoner of War/Missing in Action (POW/MIA) Program: 1546
PRITCHETT TRUST: 1030
Pro Bowl Grants: 1211
Pro Deo and Pro Patria Scholarships: 1524
Pro Futura: 355
Procter & Gamble Scholarship: 2104
Product Donations Program: 207
Production and Presentation Grants: 373
Professional Development: 394, 444, 780
Professional Development Grants: 1931
Professional Development Grants for Educators: 1715
Professional Development Program: 427
Professional Development Scholarships: 38
Professional Development/Career Advancement Grants: 479
Professional Fellowship Program: 470
Professional Student Exchange Program (PSEP): 298
Professional Studies Certificate: 701
Professional Training: 1983
Professor's Institute: 1711
Proficiency Enhancement Grants (PEG): 665
Program Grants: 1132, 1938
Program in African-American History: 553
Program in Early American Economy and Society: 553
Program Related Investments: 158
Program Support: 443
Program Support Fund: 1165
Program Support Grants: 461
Program to Accelerate Clinical Trials (PACT): 1995
Program/Project Support: 251
Programme de tournees: 398
Programme General: 398
Project Grant for Artists: 425
Project Grant for Organizations: 425
Project Grants: 332, 409, 456, 464, 570
Project Grants for Education (PGE and PGA): 451
Project Grants for Individuals (PGI): 451
Project Grants in Healthcare: 451
Project Support Grants: 428
Projects of National Significance for Persons with Developmental
    Disabilities: 1261
Projects, Events and Festivals: 403
PROLITERACY WORLDWIDE
    National Book Fund (NBF): 1226
Promise Grants: 2191
Promoting a Price on Carbon: 202
Promoting Economic Development: 1205
Promoting Energy Efficiency: 202
Promoting Sustainable Paper Production: 202
Promotion of Doctoral Studies Scholarships (PODS): 2299
PROSPANICA
    Prospanica Scholarship Program: 916
Prospanica Scholarship Program: 916
Provost's Ph.D. Fellowship Program: 1608

PSF Directed Research Grant - Breast Implant Safety: 2076
PSF Translational and Innovation Research Grant (The): 2076
PSF/MTF Biologics Allograft Tissue Research Grant (The): 2076
Psychiatric Research Fellowship: 2312
Psychodynamic Faculty Training and Mentorship Initiative: 2309
Public Art Building Communities: 403
Public Art Learning Fund: 437
Public Art Program: 427
Public Engagement Program: 1964
Public Humanities Projects: 1748
Public Interest Internships: 2413
Public Interest Law Fellowships: 144
Public Law 102-477: 946
Public Policy Program: 185
Public Policy Research Award: 2138
Public Programs in the Arts: 415
Public Service Program: 147
Public University Grants: 1514
Public Value Partnerships: 438
PUBLIC WELFARE FOUNDATION, INC.
    Criminal Justice: 242
    Special Opportunities: 242
    Youth Justice: 242
Pugh (The Elizabeth and Emerson Young) Scholar in Residence at the
    IEEE History Center: 549
Pulaski Scholarships for Advanced Studies: 1473
Pulitzer Fellowships: 1729
Pulitzer Prizes: 1729
PULLIAM JOURNALISM FELLOWSHIP: 1755
PULMONARY FIBROSIS FOUNDATION
    PFF Scholars Program: 2078
Putnam (A.O.) Memorial Scholarship: 2392

Q

QUAKER CHEMICAL FOUNDATION (THE)
    Grant Program: 243
    Matching Gift Program: 243
    Scholarship Program: 243
Quality of Life Grants: 2305
QUANTUM FOUNDATION: 1315
QUEEN ELISABETH INTERNATIONAL MUSIC COMPETITION OF
    BELGIUM (THE): 725
Query-Long Scholarship (The): 681
Quick Funds: 415
Quick Grants: 329
Quick Reaction Fund (QRF): 1345
QUILL AND SCROLL FOUNDATION: 1756
Quincey (Dorothy Lillian) Memorial Graduate Scholarship: 976

R

R.E.B. Awards for Teaching Excellence: 1098
Racial and Economic Justice: 81, 1204
Racial Equity: 1014
Racial Equity Matters: 1166
Radcliffe Institute Fellowship Program: 1460
RADCLIFFE INSTITUTE FOR ADVANCED STUDY, HARVARD
    UNIVERSITY
    Radcliffe Institute Fellowship Program: 1460
Radiant Peace Education Awards: 1437
RADIANT PEACE FOUNDATION INTERNATIONAL, INC. (THE)
    Radiant Peace Education Awards: 1437
RADIO TELEVISION DIGITAL NEWS ASSOCIATION FOUNDATION
    Biestock (N.S.) Fellowship: 1757
    Bradley (Ed) Scholarship: 1757
    Clark (Michele) Fellowship: 1757
    Foreman (George) Tribute to Lyndon B. Johnson: 1757
    Horner (Bob) Scholarship: 1757
    Minnotte (Jacque I.) Fellowship: 1757
    Oldfield (Vada and Barney) Fellowship for National Security Reporting:
    1757
    Prato (Lou and Carole) Sports Reporting Scholarship: 1757
    President's Scholarships (The): 1757
    Reynolds (Mike) Journalism Scholarship: 1757
    Simpson (Carole) Scholarship: 1757
    Thornton (Lee) Scholarship: 1757
    Wilson (Pete) Scholarship: 1757

RADIOLOGICAL SOCIETY OF NORTH AMERICA RESEARCH AND
    EDUCATION FOUNDATION
    Education Scholar Grant: 2081
    Research Medical Student Grant: 2080
    Research Resident/Fellow Grant: 2084
    Research Seed Grant: 2079
    RSNA Research Scholar Grant: 2083
    RSNA/AUR/APDR/SCARD Radiology Education Research
        Development Grant: 2082
RAGDALE FOUNDATION
    Residencies at Ragdale Foundation: 450
Rain Bird Intelligent Use of Water Scholarship: 1974
Rainger (Ronald) Prize: 548
RANCHO SANTA FE FOUNDATION
    Patriots Connection (The): 1227
    Rancho Santa Fe Women's Fund: 1227
Rancho Santa Fe Women's Fund: 1227
Randolph (Jennings) Senior Fellowship Programs for International Peace:
    788
Rapid Response Grant: 1954
Rare Disease Research Grant Program: 2063
RASKOB FOUNDATION FOR CATHOLIC ACTIVITIES: 751
RASMUSSEN (V. KANN) FOUNDATION: 1877
Rasmussen (Wayne D.) Award: 524
Rawley (The James A.) Prize in Atlantic History: 526
RBC Emerging Artists Project: 1228
RBC FOUNDATION - U.S.A.
    RBC Emerging Artists Project: 1228
    RBC Youth Mental Well-being Project: 1228
RBC Youth Mental Well-being Project: 1228
Reading and Discussion Program: 329
Reading Award Program (RAP): 951
Reading Corner Literacy Grant: 933
Ready to Rise: 1343
REAGAN (RONALD) PRESIDENTIAL FOUNDATION AND
    INSTITUTE
    GE-Reagan Foundation Scholarship Program: 1568
Recording Program: 700
Redding Rancheria Community Fund: 1125
REDFIELD (THE NELL J.) FOUNDATION: 244
REEBOK FOUNDATION (THE): 245
Reed (Phillip D.) Undergraduate Endowment Fellowship: 2395
Reed (Sarah Rebecca) Scholarship: 662
Reel Change: The Fund for Diversity in Film Scoring: 720
Reentry Through the Arts: 394
Reese Fellowship (The): 304
REEVE (CHRISTOPHER & DANA) FOUNDATION
    Quality of Life Grants: 2305
Regeneron Science Talent Search: 1649
Regents Physician Loan Forgiveness Award Program: 1548
Regional Artist Project Grants: 443
Regional Development Grants: 735
Regional Ecosystem Health: 1961
Regional Events: 707
Regional Grants: 1094
Regional Library Telecommunications Aid: 676
Regional Partnerships: 100
Regional Public Libraries Systems Support: 676
Regional Touring Program: 429
Regular Competitive Grants: 1107
Regular Member Program Fellowships: 817
REHABILITATION NURSING FOUNDATION (RNF)
    ARN/RNF Grant: 2244
Reimagine Education: 1204
Reimagine Grants: 1186
REINBERGER FOUNDATION (THE)
    Arts, Culture and Humanities: 1229
    Education: 1229
    Human Service: 1229
Reines (Frederick) Postdoctoral Fellowship in Experimental Sciences:
    1635
Reingold (Nathan) Prize: 548
Religious Studies Scholarship: 1481
Rendel (Betty) Scholarship: 984
Renewable Energy Program: 1959
REPLOGLE (LUTHER I.) FOUNDATION: 1230
REPORTERS COMMITTEE FOR FREEDOM OF THE PRESS
    Reporters Committee Legal Fellowships (The): 1758
Reporters Committee Legal Fellowships (The): 1758
Reproductive Health: 229

REPRODUCTIVE SCIENTIST DEVELOPMENT PROGRAM (RSDP):
    2251
Research and Development Grants: 373
Research and Training Workshops: 2205
Research Award: 2096
Research Awards: 2328
Research Awards at the Huntington Library, Art Museum and Botanical
    Gardens: 330
Research Awards Program: 2267
Research Capstone Fellowship: 1934
RESEARCH CORPORATION FOR SCIENCE ADVANCEMENT
    Cottrell Scholar Awards: 1827
    Scialog Awards: 1827
Research Fellowship Award: 2166
Research Fellowships: 482, 2076, 2225
Research Fellowships in American History and Culture: 553
Research Fieldwork: 1276
Research Fund (The): 2077
Research Grant: 1809, 1931, 2065, 2261
Research Grant in Crystallography, Mineral Physics or Chemistry and
    Mineralogy: 1869
Research Grant Program: 2115, 2202
Research Grants: 355, 531, 1277, 1861, 1945, 1952, 1957, 2167, 2210,
    2241
Research Grants and Fellowships: 2177
Research Grants in Dietetics: 2412
Research Grants in the Arts: 433
Research Grants Program: 1016, 2048, 2197, 2352
Research in the Arts: 394
Research Initiative: 2166
Research Library Program: 325
RESEARCH MANITOBA
    CFI Matching Funds: 1316
    Innovative Proof-of-Concept Grants: 1316
    New Investigator Operating Grants: 1316
    NSERC Alliance-RM ACT Grant: 1316
    Strategic Partnership Program: 1316
    Trainee Awards: 1316
Research Medical Student Grant: 2080
Research-Practice Partnershp Grants: 1418
Research Program: 335
Research Project Grant Program (R01): 2059
Research Publication Grants in Engineering, Medicine and Science: 969
Research Resident/Fellow Grant: 2084
Research Seed Grant: 2079
Research Starter Grant in Drug Delivery: 2292
Research Starter Grant in Drug Discovery: 2292
Research Starter Grant in Health Outcomes Research: 2292
Research Starter Grant in Translational Medicine: 2292
Research Stipend Program at the Rockefeller Archive Center: 581
Research Support Grants: 375
Research Training & Career Development: 2107
Research Training Award for Fellows: 2005
Research Training Grants: 2241
Research Training Program (RTP): 858
Research Travel Award: 584
Research Travel Grant Program: 1790
Research Travel Grants: 536
Research Traveling Fellowship: 2065
Residencies at Ragdale Foundation: 450
Resident Clinician Scientist Training Grant: 2067
Resident Research Grant: 2277
Resident Scholar Fellowships: 1814
Resilient Cities, Healthy Communities: 1961
RESOURCES FOR THE FUTURE
    Summer Research Internship: 1981
Responsive Grants: 919
Responsive Grants Program: 1359
Retired and Senior Volunteer Program (RSVP): 1333
REVSON (THE CHARLES H.) FOUNDATION: 246
REYNOLDS (KATE B.) CHARITABLE TRUST
    Health Improvement in North Carolina: 1355
    Local Impact in Forsyth County: 1355
Reynolds (Mike) Journalism Scholarship: 1757
REYNOLDS (Z. SMITH) FOUNDATION, INC.
    All for NC: 247
RFK Book Award: 622
RFK Journalism Awards: 622
Rho Chi-AFPE First Year Graduate Fellowship: 2288
RHODE ISLAND FOUNDATION/RHODE ISLAND COMMUNITY
    FOUNDATION (THE): 248

RHODE ISLAND STATE COUNCIL ON THE ARTS
  Artist Initiated Skill Share: 451
  Artists Open Studio Tours Grant (AOST): 451
  Arts Access Grant (AAG): 451
  Big Yellow School Bus: 451
  Fellowships: 451
  Folk Arts Apprenticeships and Fellowships: 451
  Investments in Arts and Culture (IAC): 451
  Project Grants for Education (PGE and PGA): 451
  Project Grants for Individuals (PGI): 451
  Project Grants in Healthcare: 451
RHODE ISLAND STATE GOVERNMENT INTERNSHIP PROGRAM
  Rhode Island State Government Internship Program: 1805
Rhode Island State Government Internship Program: 1805
RIBA Research Fund: 378
Ribbon of Hope: 1415
Rice (The Haynes) Award: 2302
Richards (John F.) Prize in South Asian History: 526
RICHARDSON (SID) MEMORIAL FUND: 1569
RICHARDSON (SID W.) FOUNDATION: 249
RICHARDSON (SMITH) FOUNDATION, INC.
  Domestic Public Policy Program: 1672
  International Security and Foreign Policy Program: 1672
Richter (R. Gene) Scholarship Program: 1708
Ridgway (General and Mrs. Matthew B.) Military History Research Grant:
  589
RIGHTEOUS PERSONS FOUNDATION: 917
RILEY (THE MABEL LOUISE) FOUNDATION: 1417
Rinehart School of Sculpture (MFA): 509
Ripley Memorial Foundation: 996
Rippon (John W.) Research Award: 1944
Rittenhouse Award: 674
Robb (Preston) Fellowship: 2224
ROBERTS (FOREST) THEATRE
  Panowski (Mildred and Albert) Playwriting Award: 492
Roberts (George A.) Scholarship: 2420
Roberts (Summerfield G.) Award: 587
Robinson (Henry S.) Corinth Research Fellowship: 815
ROBINSON (JACKIE) FOUNDATION (JRF)
  Extra Innings Fellowship Program (EIF): 918
  Mentoring and Leadership Program: 918
  Robinson (Rachel) International Fellowship Program (RRIF): 918
Robinson (Rachel) International Fellowship Program (RRIF): 918
Robinson (Samuel) Award: 1566
ROCHESTER AREA COMMUNITY FOUNDATION: 987
ROCHESTER AREA FOUNDATION: 1231
ROCK ISLAND ARSENAL MUSEUM
  Maguire (Richard C.) Scholarship: 580
ROCKEFELLER ARCHIVE CENTER
  Research Stipend Program at the Rockefeller Archive Center: 581
ROCKEFELLER FAMILY FUND
  Economic Justice for Women: 250
  Environment: 250
  Institutional Accountability and Individual Liberty: 250
ROCKWELL FUND, INC.
  Capacity Building Grants: 251
  Operating Funds: 251
  Program/Project Support: 251
Rodgers (The Richard) Awards: 687
Rodriguez (Dr. Esperanza) Scholarship: 2104
Rogers (Earline S.) Student Teaching Stipend for Minorities: 1512
Rogers (Frank Bradway) Information Advancement Award: 674
Rogerson (Clark T.) Research Award: 1944
Rolex Awards for Enterprise Program: 252
ROLEX SA
  Rolex Awards for Enterprise Program: 252
Romanell-Phi Beta Kappa Professorship in Philosophy (The): 1561
Romani (The George T. and Margaret W.) Fellowship: 357
Romanowski (The Miroslaw) Medal: 1646
Rome Prize Fellowship in Landscape Architecture (The): 1956
Rome Prize Fellowships: 303
RONALD MCDONALD HOUSE CHARITIES
  Africa and South Asia: Child and Maternal Health: 1031
  U.S. Grants: Children's Oral Health Care: 1031
ROOSEVELT (FRANKLIN D.) LIBRARY AND MUSEUM
  Roosevelt Institute Research Grants: 582
Roosevelt Institute Research Grants: 582
Roosevelt (Theodore) Memorial Grants: 1619
Root (Betty Jeanne) Fellowship: 2416
ROSE COMMUNITY FOUNDATION: 1232

Rose Hills Ph.D. Fellowship: 1608
Rosemore (Fredric) Low Vision Educational Grants: 2259
Rosenberg (The Dorothy) Prize: 526
ROSENBERG (HENRY AND RUTH BLAUSTEIN) FOUNDATION:
  1233
Rosenblith (Walter A.) New Investigator Award: 1294
Rosenbloom (Alfred A.), Jr. Low Vision Residency Award: 2257
Rosewood Family Scholarship Program: 932
ROSS FOUNDATION: 1234
Rossiter (Margaret W.) History of Women in Science Prize: 548
ROSWELL ARTIST-IN-RESIDENCE PROGRAM: 515
Roswell (Virginia) Dissertation Award: 2321
ROTARY CLUB OF BRYN MAWR (THE)
  Cabell (Harry H.) Scholarship Program: 1570
ROTARY FOUNDATION OF ROTARY INTERNATIONAL (THE)
  Rotary Peace Fellowships: 848
Rotary Peace Fellowships: 848
Rotch Travelling Scholarship: 377
ROTCH TRAVELLING SCHOLARSHIP IN ARCHITECTURE
  Rotch Travelling Scholarship: 377
Roth (Lois) Award for a Translation of a Literary Work: 603
Roth (Richard J.) Journalism Fellowship: 1801
Rothermel (Marjorie Roy) Scholarship: 2387
Roura (Victor Grifols) Scholarship: 2062
Rowe (The Leo S.) Pan American Fund: 876
ROYAL INSTITUTE OF BRITISH ARCHITECTS
  RIBA Research Fund: 378
ROYAL SOCIETY OF CANADA (THE)
  Allaire (Yvan) Medal: 1646
  Bancroft Award (The): 1646
  Chauveau (The Pierre) Medal: 1646
  Dawson (The Sir John William) Medal: 1646
  Flavelle Medal (The): 1646
  Franklin (Ursula) Award in Gender Studies: 1646
  Hannah (The Jason A.) Medal: 1646
  Innis-Gérin Medal (The): 1646
  McLaughlin Medal (The): 1646
  Miller (Willet G.) Medal: 1646
  Pierce (The Lorne) Medal: 1646
  Romanowski (The Miroslaw) Medal: 1646
  Rutherford Memorial Medals (The): 1646
  Synge (The John L.) Award: 1646
  Tory (The Henry Marshall) Medal: 1646
  Tyrrell (The J.B.) Historical Medal: 1646
ROYAL TOWN PLANNING INSTITUTE (THE)
  Pepler (George) International Award: 1673
Rozkuszka (W. David) Scholarship: 1443
RRF FOUNDATION FOR AGING
  Organizational Capacity Building: 919
  Responsive Grants: 919
RSNA Research Scholar Grant: 2083
RSNA/AUR/APDR/SCARD Radiology Education Research Development
  Grant: 2082
RTCA
  Jackson (The William E.) Award: 2371
Ruggles (The William B.) Journalist Scholarship: 1749
Runaway and Homeless Youth (RHY) Programs: 1039
RUNNING STRONG FOR AMERICAN INDIAN YOUTH: 955
RUNYON (DAMON) CANCER RESEARCH FOUNDATION
  Runyon (Damon) Clinical Investigator Award: 2196
  Runyon (Damon) Dale F. Frey Award for Breakthrough Scientists: 2196
  Runyon (Damon) Fellowship Award: 2196
  Runyon (Damon) Physician-Scientist Training Award: 2196
  Runyon (Damon) Quantitative Biology Fellowship Award: 2196
  Runyon (Damon)-Rachleff Innovation Award: 2196
  Runyon (Damon)-Sohn Pediatric Cancer Fellowship Award: 2196
Runyon (Damon) Clinical Investigator Award: 2196
Runyon (Damon) Dale F. Frey Award for Breakthrough Scientists: 2196
Runyon (Damon) Fellowship Award: 2196
Runyon (Damon) Physician-Scientist Training Award: 2196
Runyon (Damon) Quantitative Biology Fellowship Award: 2196
Runyon (Damon)-Rachleff Innovation Award: 2196
Runyon (Damon)-Sohn Pediatric Cancer Fellowship Award: 2196
Rural Housing Grants (Section 504): 1924
RURAL HOUSING SERVICE
  Rural Housing Grants (Section 504): 1924
RUSSELL FAMILY FOUNDATION (THE)
  Environmental Education Fund: 1982
  Jane's Fellowship Program: 1235
RUSSELL (JOSEPHINE G.) TRUST: 1317

Russell (Kenneth W.) Fellowship: 796
Rutherford Memorial Medals (The): 1646

S

Sacred Sites Program: 571
SAE-CES Pre-Dissertation Research Fellowships: 762
Safe and Healthy Communities: 2043
Safe Arborist Techniques Fund Grant: 1925
Safety Professional of the Year Award: 2389
SAGE (RUSSELL) FOUNDATION: 1674
SAGES Program (The): 1691
SAGINAW COMMUNITY FOUNDATION: 1236
SAH Prize for Historical Fiction: 585
Sahney (Vinod and Gail) Scholarship: 2392
SAIGH FOUNDATION (THE): 1032
SAILORS' SNUG HARBOR OF BOSTON: 1356
ST. ANDREW'S SOCIETY OF THE STATE OF NEW YORK
    Scholarship Program for Graduate Study in Scotland: 849
ST. CROIX VALLEY FOUNDATION
    Health and Wellness Grant: 1237
    Music Education Grant: 1237
    Valley Arts Initiative Grant: 1237
SAINT-GOBAIN CORPORATION FOUNDATION
    Direct Grants Program: 1238
St. Louis Chapter No. 17 Scholarship: 2361
SALISBURY-ROWAN COMMUNITY FOUNDATION: 253
Salivary Biology & Immunology: 2107
SALON NATIONAL LA BOUTIQUE
    Eight and Forty Lung and Respiratory Disease Nursing Scholarship
    Fund: 2245
Saloutos (Theodore) Book Award: 524
SAMLA Studies Award: 606
Sams (Dr. Lauranne) Scholarship: 2240
SAMUELS (THE FAN FOX AND LESLIE R.) FOUNDATION, INC.
    Healthy Aging Program: 254
    Performing Arts: 254
Samuelson (Orion) Scholarship: 1744
SAN ANGELO AREA FOUNDATION: 1239
San Antonio Area African-American Community Fund: 1240
SAN ANTONIO AREA FOUNDATION
    Annual Responsive Grants: 1240
    San Antonio Area African-American Community Fund: 1240
    Special and Urgent Needs: 1240
    Women and Girls Development Fund: 1240
SAN DIEGO ART INSTITUTE
    Mahoney (Matthew J.) Artist-in-Residence Program: 516
SAN DIEGO FOUNDATION (THE): 1241
SAN FRANCISCO CONSERVATORY OF MUSIC
    Performance Scholarships in Music for Students in Bachelor and Master
    of Music Programs: 726
SAN FRANCISCO FOUNDATION
    Art Awards: 453
    Cadogan (Edwin Anthony and Adelaide Boudreaux) Scholarships: 452
    Community Leadership Awards: 1242
    Koshland Young Leader Awards: 255
    Murphy (Jack K. and Gertrude) Fellowships: 452
SAN FRANCISCO OPERA CENTER
    Adler Fellowships: 727
    Merola Opera Program: 727
San Joaquin Valley Health Fund: 1334
San Joaquin Valley Impact Investment Fund: 1334
Sanitarian Award: 2415
SANTA BARBARA FOUNDATION
    Children, Early Care and Education Grants: 1243
    Community Disaster Relief Fund: 1243
    Get Together Grant Program: 1243
    Small Impact Building Grants: 1243
SANTA BARBARA MISSION ARCHIVE-LIBRARY
    Geiger Memorial Internship: 583
Santa Fe Baby Fund: 920
SANTA FE COMMUNITY FOUNDATION
    Community Leadership Fund: 920
    Dollars 4 Schools: 920
    Envision Fund: 920
    Local Impact Investing Initiative: 920
    MoGro: 920
    Native American Advised Fund: 920
    NM Health Equity Partnership: 920
    Santa Fe Baby Fund: 920

SAR Prize: 606
SARKEYS FOUNDATION: 256
SARNOFF CARDIOVASCULAR RESEARCH FOUNDATION (THE)
    Sarnoff Fellowship Program: 2146
    Sarnoff Scholar Award: 2146
Sarnoff Fellowship Program: 2146
Sarnoff Scholar Award: 2146
Sauer (James A.) Fellowship: 796
SAVOY FOUNDATION: 2085
SCA/IARS Mid-Career Grant: 2147
SCA/IARS Starter Grants: 2147
Scaglione (Aldo and Jeanne) Prize for a Translation of a Literary Work:
    603
Scaglione (Aldo and Jeanne) Prize for a Translation of a Scholarly Study
    of Literature: 603
Scaglione (Aldo and Jeanne) Prize for Comparative Literary Studies: 603
Scaglione (Aldo and Jeanne) Prize for French and Francophone Studies:
    603
Scaglione (Aldo and Jeanne) Prize for Italian Studies: 603
Scaglione (Aldo and Jeanne) Prize for Studies in Germanic Languages
    and Literatures: 603
Scaglione (Aldo and Jeanne) Prize for Studies in Slavic Languages and
    Literatures: 603
Scaglione (Aldo and Jeanne) Publication Award for a Manuscript in
    Italian Literary Studies: 603
SCAIFE (SARAH) FOUNDATION, INC.: 1806
Scarborough (William Sanders) Prize: 603
SCCM-Weil Research Grant: 2089
Schallek Awards: 559
Schallek Fellowship: 559
Scharp (Charles B.) Scholarship: 2387
Schedulers & Dispatchers Scholarship: 2369
Schiller (Justin G.) Fellowship: 304
Schimke (Mary McEwen) Scholarship: 992
Schizophrenia Grants: 293
Schlesinger (Arthur M., Jr.) Fellowship: 159
Schlundt (The Esther) Memorial Fund: 670
Schmitt (Bernadotte E.) Grant: 526
Scholar-in-Training Awards: 2177
Scholar's Award: 1809
Scholarly Paper Competition: 717
Scholarly Research Fellowship Program: 552
Scholarship and Charity Fund: 2300
Scholarship Central: 1209
Scholarship Endowment Trust Fund: 2342
Scholarship for the Next Generation of Scientists: 2186
Scholarship Funds: 68, 1139
Scholarship Program: 243, 1385
Scholarship Program for Graduate Study in Scotland: 849
Scholarship Program for Young Pianists: 697
Scholarships: 679, 1132
Scholarships for Academic Excellence: 1548
Scholarships for Children and Spouses of Deceased or Disabled Veterans
    (CSDDV): 1501
Scholarships for Disadvantaged Students: 1394
Scholarships for Field Study: 1870
Scholarships for Summer Music Courses: 686
Scholarships in Library Science: 655
Scholastic Art and Writing Awards (The): 386
SCHOLL (DR.) FOUNDATION: 257
SCHOMBURG CENTER FOR RESEARCH IN BLACK CULTURE,
    NEW YORK PUBLIC LIBRARY (THE)
    Schomburg Scholars-in-Residence: 353
Schomburg Scholars-in-Residence: 353
Schonstedt Scholarship in Surveying (The): 2398
School at Jacob's Pillow (The): 487
School Breakfast Program (The): 1041
School Bus for the Arts Grants: 435
School Enrichment Grant Program: 1182
SCHOOL FOR ADVANCED RESEARCH
    Advanced Seminar Program: 1814
    Resident Scholar Fellowships: 1814
    Staley (J.I.) Prize: 1815
School of Social Science Fellowships: 1662
SCHOOL OF THE MUSEUM OF FINE ARTS AT TUFTS
    UNIVERSITY, BOSTON
    Traveling Fellowship Award: 517
Schork (Kurt) Awards in International Journalism: 1759
SCHORK (KURT) MEMORIAL FUND
    Schork (Kurt) Awards in International Journalism: 1759

Schroepfer Medal: 1852
SCHUMANN FUND FOR NEW JERSEY (THE): 1033
Schumar (James F.) Scholarship: 2382
SCHUSTERMAN (CHARLES AND LYNN) FAMILY
    PHILANTHROPIES: 1244
SCHWAB (CHARLES AND HELEN) FOUNDATION
    Foundation Initiative Grants: 258
SCHWAB (CHARLES) FOUNDATION
    Schwab Moneywise: 1717
Schwab Moneywise: 1717
Schwartz (Abba T.) Fellowship: 159
Scialog Awards: 1827
Science and Technology Studies: 1643
Science for Peace and Security (SPS) Programme: 880
Science in Society Awards: 1745
Science Undergraduate Laboratory Internships: 1622
Science, Technology, Engineering, Art and Math (STEAM) Female
    Mentoring Program: 938
Scientific Research Grants/Proposal Writing Contest: 1632
Scientist Development Awards for Mentored Clinical (K08): 1311
Scientist Development Awards for Mentored Research (K01): 1311
Scientist-in-Training Research Award: 2294
SCLERODERMA FOUNDATION
    Scleroderma Foundation Research Grants: 2086
Scleroderma Foundation Research Grants: 2086
ScotiaMcLeod Scholarship: 1599
SCOTT (KENNETH A.) CHARITABLE TRUST: 1898
Scottish Rite Charitable Foundation Major Research Grants: 2337
SCOTTISH RITE CHARITABLE FOUNDATION OF CANADA
    Scottish Rite Charitable Foundation Major Research Grants: 2337
SCOVILLE (HERBERT, JR.) PEACE FELLOWSHIP: 781
SCRANTON AREA COMMUNITY FOUNDATION: 1245
SCRIPPS (THE ELLEN BROWNING) FOUNDATION: 259
Scudder (Vida Dutton) Fellowship: 991
SCUOLA NORMALE SUPERIORE
    Graduate School Scholarships for Study in Italy: 850
SDB Boot Camp for New Faculty: 1948
SDB Education Activities Grant: 1948
SDB Emerging Models Grant: 1948
SDB Innovation Grant: 1948
SDB International Scholarships: 1948
SDB Meeting Grants: 1948
SDB Trainee Science Communication Award: 1948
SDB Travel Awards: 1948
Seaman (The Tom) Travelling Scholarship: 2421
SEATTLE FOUNDATION
    Center for Community Partnerships: 260
SEAVER INSTITUTE (THE): 261
SEAY (GEORGE J. AND EFFIE L.) MEMORIAL TRUST: 1357
Seed Grants: 2205
SEG Scholarship Program: 1878
SELF FAMILY FOUNDATION (THE): 1246
Seminar and Conference Support: 801
Seminars and Institutes Program: 338
Senate Fellowship Program: 1785
Senior Adult Scholarship Program: 1470
Senior Citizens Grant: 1182
Senior Companion Program: 1333
Senior Fellowship: 801
Senior Fellowships: 375
Senior Living Initiative: 1120
Senior Research Award: 2166
Senior Research Fellowship Program: 1926
Sessa (Frank B.) Scholarship for Continuing Professional Education of
    Beta Phi Mu Members: 662
SEYBERT FOUNDATION (THE): 1034
SFU Graduate Fellowships: 1718
Shackford (M.A. Cartland) Medical Fellowship: 992
Shaffer Fund for Innovative Glaucoma Research: 2270
Shanahan (Timothy and Cynthia) Outstanding Dissertation Award: 1397
Shankar-Spiegel Award for the Best Dissertation Proposal in
    Direct/Interactive Marketing: 1711
SHARE OUR STRENGTH
    No Kid Hungry: 1358
Shared Instrumentation Grant Program: 2058
Shark Tank Awards: 2211
SHASTRI INDO-CANADIAN INSTITUTE (SICI): 851
Shaughnessy (Mina P.) Prize: 602
Shaw (Harriet A.) Fellowship: 991
Shaw (The Peter) Memorial Award: 1457

Shea (The John Gilmary) Prize: 737
Sheeler (Harva L.) Excavation Fellowships: 818
Sheltering Arms Fund: 1098
Shelton (Perc H.) and Gladys A. Pospisil Shelton Foundation Advised
    Fund: 143
Short-term Fellowship: 362
Short-Term Research Fellowship: 557
Short-Term Research Fellowships: 317
Showcasing the Arts: 420
SHRIVER (EUNICE KENNEDY) NATIONAL INSTITUTE OF CHILD
    HEALTH AND HUMAN DEVELOPMENT
    Child Development and Behavior Branch (CDBB): 1318
    Contraception Research Branch (CRB): 1318
    Developmental Biology and Structural Variation Branch (DBSVB):
        1318
    Fertility and Infertility (FI) Branch: 1318
    Gynecologic Health and Disease Branch (GHDB): 1318
    Intellectual and Developmental Disabilities Branch (IDDB): 1318
    Maternal and Pediatric Infectious Disease Branch (MPIDB): 1318
    Obstetric and Pediatric Pharmacology and Therapeutics Branch
        (OPPTB): 1318
    Pediatric Growth and Nutrition Branch (PGNB): 1318
    Pediatric Trauma and Critical Illness Branch (PTCIB): 1318
    Population Dynamics Branch (PDB): 1318
    Pregnancy and Perinatology Branch (PPB): 1318
SHUBERT FOUNDATION, INC. (THE): 493
Shwachman (Harry) Clinical Investigator Award: 2167
Sibley (Mary Isabel) Fellowship: 986
SICKKIDS FOUNDATION
    Community Conference Grants Program: 1319
    New Investigator Research Grants: 1319
Sidney Awards: 1736
Siegel (Norman) Research Scholar Grant: 2111
Sierleja (E.J.) Memorial Fellowship: 2392
SIERRA HEALTH FOUNDATION
    Conference and Education Center: 1359
    Health Leadership Program: 1359
    Healthy Sacramento Coalition: 1359
    Nonprofit Event Sponsorships: 1359
    Responsive Grants Program: 1359
Sigal (Irving S.) Postdoctoral Fellowship: 1847
SIGMA ALPHA IOTA PHILANTHROPIES, INC.
    Inter-American Music Awards: 728
SIGMA THETA TAU INTERNATIONAL
    Berkel Crisp (Rosemary) Research Award: 2246
    Bloch (Doris) Research Award: 2246
    Stout (Joan K.), R.N., Research Grant: 2246
SIGMA XI: THE SCIENTIFIC RESEARCH HONOR SOCIETY
    Grants in Aid of Research: 1647
SILICON VALLEY COMMUNITY FOUNDATION: 1247
SILICON VALLEY CREATES
    Artist Laureates: 454
    Local Arts Grants: 454
Silverman (Sue William) Prize for Creative Nonfiction: 614
SIMMONS FAMILY FOUNDATION: 262
Simmons (The John) Short Fiction Award: 649
SIMON FRASER UNIVERSITY
    SFU Graduate Fellowships: 1718
Simpson (Carole) Scholarship: 1757
Simulation Fellowship Program: 1823
Sister Cities Grant: 403
SISTERS OF ST. JOSEPH HEALTHCARE FOUNDATION: 1320
SKELLY (GERTRUDE E.) CHARITABLE FOUNDATION: 1461
Skiera (Bob) Memorial Fund Building Bridges Initiative Grant: 1925
SKILLBUILDERS FUND: 988
SKILLMAN FOUNDATION (THE): 263
SKIN CANCER FOUNDATION (THE)
    Research Grants Program: 2197
SKOWHEGAN SCHOOL OF PAINTING AND SCULPTURE: 518
SLADEN (THE PERCY) MEMORIAL FUND
    Sladen (Percy) Memorial Fund Grants: 1899
Sladen (Percy) Memorial Fund Grants: 1899
Slim (H. Colin) Award: 691
SLOAN (ALFRED P.) FOUNDATION: 264
    Sloan Research Fellowships: 1828
Sloan Research Fellowships: 1828
Small Business Innovation Research Awards: 2275
Small Business Innovation Research Grants: 2241
Small Business Innovation Research Program: 1312
Small Business Innovation/Small Business Technology Transfer
    (SBIR/STTR): 2107

Small Grant Support: 446
Small Grant Support for Schools: 446
Small Grants for Research in Field of Short Stature: 2284
Small Impact Building Grants: 1243
Small Operating Grants: 447
Small Research Grant Program: 1784
Small Research Grant Program (Parent R03): 2060
Small Research Grants: 1418
Small-Scale Events Advancing SPSSI (SEAS) Grants: 1685
SmART Initiative: 443
SME-EF (SOCIETY OF MANUFACTURING ENGINEERS
    EDUCATION FOUNDATION)
    Gunter (Connie and Robert T.) Scholarship: 2361
    Helton (Clinton J.) Manufacturing Scholarship: 2361
    Kalamazoo Chapter No. 116-Roscoe Douglas Scholarship: 2361
    Kaufman (Lucille B.) Women's Scholarship: 2361
    Kay (E. Wayne) Scholarships: 2361
    St. Louis Chapter No. 17 Scholarship: 2361
    Walker (Myrtle and Earl) Scholarship: 2361
    Weisel (William E.) Scholarship: 2361
SMITH (A.O.) FOUNDATION: 265
Smith (Al) Individual Artist Fellowships: 420
Smith (Alexander H. and Helen V.) Research Fund: 1944
Smith (Alice E.) Fellowship: 593
Smith (Bosworth) Trust Fund: 2421
Smith (Dr. James McCune) Medical Student Award: 2062
SMITH (THE ETHEL SERGEANT CLARK) MEMORIAL FUND: 266
SMITH FAMILY AWARDS PROGRAM FOR EXCELLENCE IN
    BIOMEDICAL RESEARCH: 2087
SMITH (HORACE) FUND: 1571
Smith (J. Waldo) Hydraulic Fellowship: 2386
Smith (W. Eugene) Grant in Humanistic Photography: 519
SMITH (W. EUGENE) MEMORIAL FUND
    Smith (W. Eugene) Grant in Humanistic Photography: 519
SMITH (THE W.W.) CHARITABLE TRUST
    College Scholarships: 267
    Food, Clothing and Shelter: 267
    Maritime Education: 267
    Medical Research: 267
SMITHERS (THE CHRISTOPHER D.) FOUNDATION, INC.: 1321
SMITHSONIAN ASTROPHYSICAL OBSERVATORY
    Clay Postdoctoral Fellowship: 1844
    Predoctoral Research Fellowships: 1843
SMITHSONIAN ENVIRONMENTAL RESEARCH CENTER (SERC)
    Professional Training: 1983
Smithsonian Graduate Student Fellowships: 1648
SMITHSONIAN INSTITUTION
    Smithsonian Graduate Student Fellowships: 1648
    Smithsonian Postdoctoral Fellowships: 1648
    Smithsonian Predoctoral Fellowships: 1648
    Smithsonian Senior Fellowships: 1648
Smithsonian Institution Fellowship: 408
SMITHSONIAN NATIONAL AIR AND SPACE MUSEUM
    Aviation Space Writers Foundation Award: 2372
    Guggenheim Fellowship: 2372
    Lindbergh (Charles A.) Chair in Aerospace History: 2372
    Postdoctoral Earth and Planetary Sciences Fellowship: 2372
    Summer Internship Program: 2373
    Verville (A.) Fellowship: 2372
Smithsonian Postdoctoral Fellowships: 1648
Smithsonian Predoctoral Fellowships: 1648
Smithsonian Senior Fellowships: 1648
Smyth (Craig Hugh) Fellowship: 864
SNAME THE SOCIETY OF NAVAL ARCHITECTS AND MARINE
    ENGINEERS
    Graduate Scholarships: 2404
    Undergraduate Scholarships: 2404
SNOW (THE JOHN BEN) FOUNDATION, INC.: 268
Social and Economic Development Strategies (SEDS) for Native
    Americans: 957
Social Investment Program: 115
Social Issues Dissertation Award (The): 1693
SOCIAL JUSTICE FUND NORTHWEST: 1360
Social Justice Grant: 154
Social Justice Grant Program: 1655
Social Psychology Program: 2332
SOCIAL SCIENCE RESEARCH COUNCIL
    Abe Fellowship Program: 784
    International Dissertation Research Fellowship Program (IDRF): 783
    SSRC/JSPS Long-Term Fellowship: 782
    SSRC/JSPS Short-Term Fellowship: 782

SOCIAL SCIENCES AND HUMANITIES RESEARCH COUNCIL OF
    CANADA
    Banting Postdoctoral Fellowships: 1679
    Bombardier (Joseph-Armand) Canada Graduate Scholarships Program -
        Master's Scholarships: 1677
    Doctoral Awards: 1675
    Master's Awards: 1677
    SSHRC Postdoctoral Fellowships: 1676
    Vanier Canada Graduate Scholarships (CGS): 1678
Social Sciences or Humanities International Security Fellowship: 760
Social, Racial and Economic Justice: 1154
SOCIETY FOR DEVELOPMENTAL BIOLOGY
    Conklin (Edwin G.) Medal: 1948
    Developmental Biology-SDB Lifetime Achievement Award: 1948
    Doctor (John) Best Education Award: 1948
    Hamburger (Viktor) Outstanding Educator Prize: 1948
    Hay (Elizabeth D.) New Investigator Award: 1948
    SDB Boot Camp for New Faculty: 1948
    SDB Education Activities Grant: 1948
    SDB Emerging Models Grant: 1948
    SDB Innovation Grant: 1948
    SDB International Scholarships: 1948
    SDB Meeting Grants: 1948
    SDB Trainee Science Communication Award: 1948
    SDB Travel Awards: 1948
    Teaching and Junior Faculty Travel Grants: 1948
SOCIETY FOR FRENCH HISTORICAL STUDIES
    Chinard (The Gilbert) Prize: 584
    Davis (Natalie Zemon) Graduate Student Award: 584
    Farrar (Marjorie M. and Lancelot L.) Memorial Awards: 584
    Institut Francais d'America Fund Research Fellowships (The): 584
    Koren (The William, Jr.) Prize: 584
    Pinkney (The David H.) Prize: 584
    Research Travel Award: 584
Society for Health Systems Scholarship: 2392
SOCIETY FOR INVESTIGATIVE DERMATOLOGY (THE)
    Kligman (Albert M.) Fellowship Fund Award: 2088
SOCIETY FOR PEDIATRIC DERMATOLOGY
    PeDRA Research Grants: 2285
    Weston Pediatric Dermatology Career Development Award (CDA):
        2285
SOCIETY FOR SCIENCE AND THE PUBLIC
    Regeneron Science Talent Search: 1649
Society for the Humanities Fellowships: 324
SOCIETY FOR THE PSYCHOLOGICAL STUDY OF SOCIAL ISSUES
    (SPSSI) (THE)
    Allport (Gordon) Intergroup Relations Prize: 1680
    Applied Social Issues Internship Program (The): 1689
    Awards for Outstanding Teaching and Mentoring: 1682
    Innovative Teaching Award: 1681
    Kidder (The Louise) Early Career Award: 1692
    Klineberg (Otto) Intercultural and International Relations Award: 1807
    Local- and State-Level Policy Work Grants: 1686
    Mayo (Clara) Grants: 1690
    SAGES Program (The): 1691
    Small-Scale Events Advancing SPSSI (SEAS) Grants: 1685
    Social Issues Dissertation Award (The): 1693
    SPSSI Action Teaching Grants: 1683
    SPSSI Grants-in-Aid: 1688
    SPSSI James Marshall Fellowship in Public Policy: 1684
    Taylor (Dalmas A.) Memorial Summer Minority Policy Fellowship:
        1687
SOCIETY FOR THE SCIENTIFIC STUDY OF SEXUALITY (THE)
    Grants-in-Aid Project: 1650
    Student Research Grants: 1650
SOCIETY FOR THE STUDY OF AMPHIBIANS AND REPTILES
    Conant (Roger) Grants in Herpetology: 1829
SOCIETY OF ACTUARIES (SOA)
    Society of Actuaries' James C. Hickman Scholar Doctoral Stipend
        Program: 1887
Society of Actuaries' James C. Hickman Scholar Doctoral Stipend
    Program: 1887
SOCIETY OF AMERICAN HISTORIANS (THE)
    Horwitz (Tony) Prize: 585
    Nevins (Allan) Dissertation Prize: 585
    Parkman (Francis) Prize: 585
    SAH Prize for Historical Fiction: 585
SOCIETY OF ARCHITECTURAL HISTORIANS
    Gill Family Foundation Dissertation Research Fellowship: 381
    Peterson (Charles E.) Fellowship of the Buildings of the U.S. and the

Athenaeum of Philadelphia: 382
Study Program Fellowships: 380
Tompkins (Sally Kress) Fellowship: 379
SOCIETY OF BIOLOGICAL PSYCHIATRY
Bennett (A.E.) Research Awards: 2338
Ziskind-Somerfeld Research Award: 2339
SOCIETY OF CARDIOVASCULAR ANESTHESIOLOGISTS
SCA/IARS Mid-Career Grant: 2147
SCA/IARS Starter Grants: 2147
SOCIETY OF CHILDREN'S BOOK WRITERS AND ILLUSTRATORS
Freeman (Don) Memorial Grant-in-Aid: 646
Work-In-Progress Grants: 646
SOCIETY OF CRITICAL CARE MEDICINE
SCCM-Weil Research Grant: 2089
SOCIETY OF DAUGHTERS OF THE U.S. ARMY
Society of Daughters of the United States Army Scholarships: 1572
Society of Daughters of the United States Army Scholarships: 1572
SOCIETY OF EXPLORATION GEOPHYSICISTS
SEG Scholarship Program: 1878
Society of Mayflower Descendants in the State of Illinois Fellowship: 350
SOCIETY OF PHYSICS STUDENTS
Future Faces of Physics Awards: 1892
Society of Physics Students Leadership Scholarship: 1573
SPS Award for Outstanding Undergraduate Research: 1891
White (Marsh W.) Awards: 1893
Society of Physics Students Leadership Scholarship: 1573
SOCIETY OF WOMEN ENGINEERS
Society of Women Engineers Scholarship Program: 989
Society of Women Engineers Scholarship Program: 989
SOIL AND WATER CONSERVATION SOCIETY
Cohee (Melvin H.) Student Leader Conservation Scholarship: 1985
Grant (Kenneth E.) Research Scholarship: 1984
Williams (Donald A.) Soil Conservation Scholarship: 1986
Solar for Students Program: 88
Solie (Ruth A.) Award: 691
SOMMERHOCHSCHULE - UNIVERSITY OF VIENNA
univie: summer school for International and European Studies: 852
univie: winter school for Cultural Historical Studies: 853
Sonenfeld (Alexandra Apostolides) Memorial Undergraduate Scholarship: 976
SONS OF ITALY FOUNDATION
National Leadership Grant Competition: 921
SONS OF THE REPUBLIC OF TEXAS (THE)
Presidio La Bahia Award: 586
Roberts (Summerfield G.) Award: 587
SONY CORPORATION OF AMERICA: 1438
Sorensen (Theodore C.) Fellowship: 159
SOROS (THE PAUL & DAISY) FELLOWSHIPS FOR NEW AMERICANS: 1574
Sousa/ABA/Ostwald Award: 689
SOUTH ATLANTIC MODERN LANGUAGE ASSOCIATION
Graduate Student Creative Writing Award: 606
Graduate Student Essay Prize: 606
Harper Fund Award: 606
SAMLA Studies Award: 606
SAR Prize: 606
Undergraduate Essay Award: 606
SOUTH CAROLINA ARTS COMMISSION
Arts Education: 455
Community Organizations Grants/Programs: 455
Individual Artist Grants/Programs: 455
SOUTH CAROLINA HIGHER EDUCATION TUITION GRANTS COMMISSION
South Carolina Tuition Grants Program: 1575
South Carolina Tuition Grants Program: 1575
SOUTH DAKOTA ARTS COUNCIL
Artist Career Development Grants: 456
Artist Collaboration Grants: 456
Artist Fellowships: 456
Artists in Schools & Communities (AISC) Grants: 456
Arts Challenge Grants: 456
Importation of Musicians Grants: 456
Project Grants: 456
Statewide Services Grants: 456
Touring Arts: 456
Traditional Arts Apprenticeship Grants: 456
Southard (Juliette A.) Scholarship Program: 2102
Southeast Area Women and Girls Fund: 1110
Southeastern General Grants: 1110
SOUTHWEST FLORIDA COMMUNITY FOUNDATION: 1248
SOWERS CLUB OF NEBRASKA FOUNDATION: 269

SPACE TELESCOPE SCIENCE INSTITUTE
NASA Hubble Fellowship Program: 1845
Spear (Scott) Innovation in Breast Reconstruction Research Fellowship: 2076
Special and Urgent Needs: 1240
Special Initiatives: 193
Special Milk Program (The): 1041
Special Opportunities: 242
Special Presenter Initiatives: 430
Special Project Challenge Grant: 1120
Special Project Funds: 1139
Special Project Grants: 1306
Special Projects: 444, 724
Special Scholarship Endowment Grants: 1552
Specialized Center of Research Program: 2118
Specialized Grants: 1094
Specific Cultural Projects Grants Program: 405
Speech Science Research Grant: 2262
SPENCER FOUNDATION
Conference Grants: 1418
Large Research Grants: 1418
Research-Practice Partnershp Grants: 1418
Small Research Grants: 1418
Spencer (Lyle) Research Awards: 1418
Spencer (Lyle) Research Awards: 1418
Spencer (Susan S.) Clinical Research Training Fellowship in Epilepsy: 2205
Sports Task Force/Al Young Sports Journalism Scholarship: 1483
Sporty's Foundation Scholarship: 2363
SPRAGUE (SETH) EDUCATIONAL AND CHARITABLE FOUNDATION: 270
Spring Meadow Nursery Scholarship: 1510
Springboard Artist Grant: 425
SPS Award for Outstanding Undergraduate Research: 1891
SPSSI Action Teaching Grants: 1683
SPSSI Grants-in-Aid: 1688
SPSSI James Marshall Fellowship in Public Policy: 1684
Spurgeon (Caroline) Centenary Fellowship: 978
Spurlock (Jeanne) Minority Medical Student Research Fellowship in Substance Abuse and Addiction: 2307
Spurlock (Jeanne), M.D. Congressional Fellowship: 2312
SSHRC Postdoctoral Fellowships: 1676
SSRC/JSPS Long-Term Fellowship: 782
SSRC/JSPS Short-Term Fellowship: 782
STACEY (THE JOHN F. AND ANNA LEE) SCHOLARSHIP FUND: 520
Stahl (Steven A.) Research Grant: 1397
Staley (J.I.) Prize: 1815
Standard Research Innovation Grants: 1367
Stanfield and D'Orlando Art Scholarships: 460
STANFORD HUMANITIES CENTER
External Faculty Fellowships: 354
Stanford International Observatory Research Fellowship: 760
Stanley Drama Award: 494
Stanton Nuclear Security Fellowship (The): 760
Stanton Nuclear Security Fellowship Program (SNSF): 765
STARK COMMUNITY FOUNDATION: 1249
Starrett (Agnes Lynch) Poetry Prize: 644
Stars Career Development Award: 2201
Start-Up Research Grants: 2036
State & Tribal Grant Programs: 1040
State Arts Resources: 443
STATE COUNCIL OF HIGHER EDUCATION FOR VIRGINIA
Virginia Tuition Assistance Grant Program (VTAG): 1576
State Family Assistance Grants: 1765
State Justice Statistics for Statistical Analysis Centers: 1278
STATE LIBRARY AND ARCHIVES OF FLORIDA
Library Services and Technology Act: 682
State-Local Partners: 394
STATE OF IDAHO BOARD OF EDUCATION
Idaho Governor's Cup Scholarship: 1578
Idaho Opportunity Scholarship: 1577
STATE OF MICHIGAN DEPARTMENT OF TREASURY
Children of Veterans Tuition Grant (CVTG): 1579
Dual Enrollment: 1579
Fostering Futures Scholarship: 1579
Michigan Competitive Scholarship (MCS): 1579
Michigan Gear Up: 1579

Michigan Tuition Grant (MTG): 1580
Police Officer's and Fire Fighter's Survivor Tuition Grant (STG): 1580
Tuition Incentive Program (TIP): 1580
State President's Scholarships: 1476
STATE STREET FOUNDATION
Strategic Grantmaking Program: 271
Statewide and Regional Networks: 394
Statewide Service Organizations: 443
Statewide Services Grants: 456
STAUFFER (JOHN) CHARITABLE TRUST: 272
Stay Housed LA: 1343
Stearman (The Stanley H.) Award: 1540
STEARNS (ARTEMAS W.) TRUST: 1322
Steedman (James Harrison) Memorial Fellowship in Architecture: 383
STEELCASE FOUNDATION: 273
STEELE-REESE FOUNDATION (THE): 1250
Steering Committee on Reducation of African American Child Deaths: 1334
Stefanadis (Sonja B.) Graduate Student Scholarship: 976
STEM Doctoral Fellowships: 1582
STEM Education: 1014
STEM Grants Program: 1430
Stetson (Thomas M.) Scholarship: 2344
STEVENS (THE ABBOT AND DOROTHY H.) FOUNDATION: 1251
Stevens (Mary Elvira) Traveling Fellowship: 991
STEVENS (THE NATHANIEL AND ELIZABETH P.) FOUNDATION: 1252
Stevenson (Robert M.) Award: 691
Stewart (E. Lyman) Fellowship and Assistantship: 592
Stewart (Paul A.) Grants: 1952
STIFTELSEN RIKSBANKENS JUBILEUMSFOND
Flexit: 355
Global Issues: 355
Pro Futura: 355
Research Grants: 355
STODDARD CHARITABLE TRUST (THE): 1361
STOKELY (THE WILLIAM B., JR.) FOUNDATION: 274
Stone Foundation Scholarship: 2363
STONE (H. CHASE) TRUST: 457
STONE (W. CLEMENT & JESSIE V.) FOUNDATION: 1439
Stoody-West Fellowship (The): 1760
Stout (Dottie) Professional Development Grants: 1870
Stout (Joan K.), R.N., Research Grant: 2246
Strait (George A.) Minority Stipend Scholarship Endowment: 657
Strange/Midkiff Families Fellowships: 818
Strategic Employment Placement Initiatives: 882
Strategic Grantmaking Program: 271
Strategic Operating Grants: 2201
Strategic Partnership Program: 1316
Strategic Research Agreements: Project Concept Call: 2169
Strategic Restructuring Fund: 1099
Strengthening Affordable Housing: 1205
Strengthening Health Systems: 200
Strong (Walter Mersh) Scholarship: 878
STUART FOUNDATION
Education: 1035
Student Academy Awards Competition: 495
Student Career Forums: 1711
Student Fellowship Program: 470
Student Internship Awards: 1945
Student Loan Fund: 2387
Student Loan Program: 1563
Student Opportunity Scholarship: 1565
Student Research Fellowship Awards: 2166
Student Research Fellowships: 2098
Student Research Grant: 2096, 2384
Student Research Grant in Audiology: 2262
Student Research Grant in Early Childhood Language Development: 2262
Student Research Grant in Mineralogy and Petrology: 1869
Student Research Grants: 1616, 1650
Student Scholarships: 1375
Student Speaking Contest: 387
Student Teaching Scholarship: 1434
Student Teaching Stipend for High-Needs Fields: 1512
Student Travel Awards: 1616, 1952
Student Travel Grants: 818
Student Travel Scholarship Award: 2415
Students to Stewards Program: 6
Studio Art (Low-residency MFA): 509

STUDIO ARTS COLLEGE INTERNATIONAL (SACI)
Fall/Spring/Summer Study Abroad: 521
MA in Art History: 521
MFA in Studio Art: 521
Post Baccalaureate Certificate Program in Conservation: 521
Studio Residency Grant: 477
Study of Collections Fellowships: 818
Study Program Fellowships: 380
STURGIS (ROY AND CHRISTINE) CHARITABLE AND EDUCATIONAL TRUST: 275
SUBARU OF AMERICA FOUNDATION, INC.: 1419
SUBCOMMITTEE ON CATHOLIC HOME MISSIONS: 752
SUBSTANCE ABUSE AND MENTAL HEALTH SERVICES ADMINISTRATION, DISASTER TECHNICAL ASSISTANCE CENTER
Crisis Counseling Assistance and Training Program: 2340
SUDBURY FOUNDATION
Atkinson Scholarship Program (The): 1253
Children, Youth and Families Program: 1253
Farm and Local Food Program: 1253
Sudbury Program (The): 1253
Sudbury Program (The): 1253
SUDEP Biomarker Challenge: 2211
Summer Conference: 413
Summer Food Service Program (The): 1041
Summer High School Journalism Workshops: 1733
Summer Intensive: 486
Summer Internship Program: 2373
Summer Internship Program for Graduate Students: 1384
Summer Journalism Intern Programs: 1733
Summer Medical Student Fellowship: 2307
Summer Programs: 1390
Summer Research and Writing Grant: 738
Summer Research Internship: 1981
Summer Stipends: 337
Summer Student Fellowship Program in Oceanography: 1654
Summer Studentships: 2023
Summer Study Abroad Programs: 838
Summer Systematics Institute: 1936
Summer Undergraduate Research Fellowships: 883
Summer Workshops: 413
Summer Youth Program: 1182
SUMMERLEE FOUNDATION (THE)
Animal Protection Program: 1254
Texas History: 1254
SUMMIT FOUNDATION (THE): 1255
SUMNERS (HATTON W.) FOUNDATION: 1808
SUNNEN FOUNDATION: 1362
Supelco AOCS Research Award: 1852
Superfund State and Indian Tribe Core Program Cooperative Agreements: 1989
Superfund State, Political Subdivision, and Indian Tribe Site-Specific Cooperative Agreements: 1989
Supplemental Program: 700
Support of Competitive Research Awards: 2053
Support Program for Translation and Publication on Japan: 775
SURDNA FOUNDATION INC.
Inclusive Economies (The): 276
Sustainable Environments: 276
Thriving Cultures: 276
Surgical Pathology Fellowships: 2049
Survivor Tuition Benefits Program: 1507
Sustainability: 445
Sustainable Environments: 276
Swann Foundation Fellowship: 356
SWANN FOUNDATION FOR CARICATURE AND CARTOON
Swann Foundation Fellowship: 356
SWEA Scholarship in Literature, Language and Area Studies: 785
SWEDISH WOMEN'S EDUCATIONAL ASSOCIATION INC.
SWEA Scholarship in Literature, Language and Area Studies: 785
Swensrud Teacher Fellowships at MHS: 556
Swiny (The Helena Wylde) and Stuart Swiny Fellowship: 826
Switzer Environmental Fellowship Program: 1987
SWITZER (THE ROBERT & PATRICIA) FOUNDATION
Switzer Environmental Fellowship Program: 1987
Sydney Medical School Postgraduate Research Scholarships: 2092
SYMPHONY OF THE MOUNTAINS
Vaughn (Elizabeth Harper) Concerto Competition: 729
Synge (The John L.) Award: 1646
SYNTHOMER/OMNOVA SOLUTIONS FOUNDATION: 1256

References in index are to entry numbers.

SYRACUSE UNIVERSITY
   African American Graduate Fellowship: 1582
   Graduate Program in Creative Writing: 647
   STEM Doctoral Fellowships: 1582
   Syracuse University Fellowship: 1582
   Syracuse University Graduate Assistantships: 1581
Syracuse University Fellowship: 1582
Syracuse University Graduate Assistantships: 1581
SYSTEMS PLUS, INC.
   Department of Defense National Defense Science and Engineering
   Graduate Fellowship Program (NDSEG): 2405
   USAF Summer Faculty Fellowship Program: 2406

T

TAC Foundation Scholarships and Bursaries: 2362
TAHOE TRUCKEE COMMUNITY FOUNDATION: 277
TAILHOOK EDUCATIONAL FOUNDATION
   Tailhook Educational Foundation Scholarship Award: 1420
Tailhook Educational Foundation Scholarship Award: 1420
Taishoff (Sol) Award for Excellence in Broadcast Journalism: 1750
TAIT (THE FRANK M.) FOUNDATION: 1036
TALBOT (THE AMAURY) FUND
   Talbot (Amaury) Prize for African Anthropology: 1816
Talbot (Amaury) Prize for African Anthropology: 1816
TAPER (S. MARK) FOUNDATION: 278
Tapman (Samuel Fletcher) ASCE Student Chapter Scholarship: 2386
TARAKNATH DAS FOUNDATION: 1462
Tarbox (Lee) Memorial Scholarship: 2363
Targeted Research Areas Grants: 482
Tart (Charles T. and Judith A.) Student Incentive Award: 2336
Tarte (Robert J.) Scholarship for Italian Studies: 1591
TASTE AND SMELL CLINIC
   Taste and Smell Disorders Internship Program: 2090
Taste and Smell Disorders Internship Program: 2090
TATA (LADY) MEMORIAL TRUST: 2198
TAU BETA PI ASSOCIATION, INC. (THE)
   Best (Raymond A. and Ina C.) Fellowship for MBA at Rensselaer
   Polytechnic Institute: 2407
   Graduate Fellowship in Engineering: 2407
   Tau Beta Pi Undergraduate Scholarship: 2407
Tau Beta Pi Undergraduate Scholarship: 2407
Taylor (Dalmas A.) Memorial Summer Minority Policy Fellowship: 1687
Taylor (Dr. Prentiss) Scholarship: 2062
Taylor Family Award for Fairness in Journalism: 1752
Taylor (Lucy Hobbs) Award: 2101
Taylor (Rennie)/Alton Blakeslee Fellowships for Graduate Study in
   Science Writing: 1731
Taylor (Tom) Memorial Scholarship: 2363
TCA Grant Programs: 459
TCU Scholarship Program: 940
Teacher Development Grants: 1434
Teacher Education Assistance for College and Higher Education (TEACH)
   Grant: 1589
Teacher Training and Professional Development Program (The): 1024
Teacher Training Program: 486
Teaching and Junior Faculty Travel Grants: 1948
Teaching Art Together: 420
Teaching Assistant Program in France: 829
Teaching English in Poland: 841
Team Depot: 1179
Technical Assistance and Community Development Programs: 418
Technical Design Project: 2384
Technical Services Program: 571
Technology and Society Program: 112
Technology Impact Award: 2185
Technology in Journalism Award: 1750
Teen Community Service Award: 933
Teens@Graham Young Artists Program: 486
Temple (Marshall) Memorial Scholarship: 2363
TEMPLETON (JOHN) FOUNDATION: 279
Temporary Assistance for Needy Families (TANF): 1765
TENNESSEE ARTS COMMISSION
   Division of Arts Programs: 458
   Division of Communications, Information & Technology: 458
Tennessee Education Lottery Scholarship Program: 1583
Tennessee Math & Science Teachers Loan Forgiveness Program: 1583
Tennessee Promise: 1583
Tennessee Reconnect: 1583

Tennessee Student Assistance Award: 1583
TENNESSEE STUDENT ASSISTANCE CORPORATION
   Dependent Children Scholarship Program: 1583
   Graduate Nursing Loan-Forgiveness Program: 1583
   McWherter (Ned) Scholars Program: 1583
   Minority Teaching Fellows Program: 1583
   Tennessee Education Lottery Scholarship Program: 1583
   Tennessee Math & Science Teachers Loan Forgiveness Program: 1583
   Tennessee Promise: 1583
   Tennessee Reconnect: 1583
   Tennessee Student Assistance Award: 1583
   Tennessee Teaching Scholars Program: 1583
Tennessee Teaching Scholars Program: 1583
Tenth Gate Prize: 654
TEXAS COMMISSION ON THE ARTS
   TCA Grant Programs: 459
Texas History: 1254
TEXAS INSTRUMENTS FOUNDATION: 280
TEXAS LIBRARY ASSOCIATION
   Escue (Walter H.) Memorial Scholarship: 683
   Greenfield (Vivian) Education Award: 683
   Janeway (Ray C.) Scholarship: 683
   TLA Summer School Scholarship: 683
   Van Dusen-Tobin-Kaiser Scholarship: 683
TEXAS WOMEN'S FOUNDATION: 990
Thomas (Allegra Ford) Scholarship: 1406
Thomas (Charles Tommy) Memorial Scholarship: 2380
Thomas (Douglas Dockery) Fellowship in Garden History and Design:
   1974
Thompson (Homer and Dorothy) Fellowship: 315
THOMPSON (THOMAS) TRUST: 1257
Thorndyke (Barbara Edith Quincey) Memorial Undergraduate Scholarship:
   976
Thornton (Lee) Scholarship: 1757
THRASHER RESEARCH FUND: 2286
Three-Year Postdoctoral Fellowships: 1940
3M FOUNDATION, INC.: 281
Thriving Cultures: 276
TIDES FOUNDATION
   Pizzigati (Antonio) Prize for Software in the Public Interest: 1258
Time and Talent: 218
TINCUP Partner in Adventure: 1957
Tiney (B. Charles) Memorial ASCE Student Chapter Scholarship: 2386
Tinker Field Research Grants: 786
TINKER FOUNDATION INC.
   Institutional Grants: 786
   Tinker Field Research Grants: 786
   Tinker Visiting Professor: 786
Tinker Visiting Professor: 786
Tissue Engineering and Regenerative Medicine: 2107
TLA Summer School Scholarship: 683
TMCF Scholarships: 1529
Tobey (David and Julie) Fellowship: 863
Tobias (Charles W.) Young Investigator Award: 1627
Todd (Ewen C.D.) Control of Foodborne Illness Award: 2415
Tomash (The Adelle and Erwin) Fellowship in the History of Information
   Technology: 2350
TOMFOHRDE (JOHN H. AND H. NAOMI) FOUNDATION: 282
Tompkins (Sally Kress) Fellowship: 379
TOPFER FAMILY FOUNDATION: 283
Torraco (Bernard and Carolyn) Nursing Scholarships: 1591
Torraco (Louise) Memorial Scholarship for Science: 1591
Torraco (Ralph J.) Fine Arts Scholarship: 1591
Torraco (Ralph J.) Scholarship: 1591
Torraco (Ralph J.) Scholarship for Special Education: 1591
Torraco (Ralph J.) Scholarship for Therapy Sciences: 1591
Tory (The Henry Marshall) Medal: 1646
TOSHIBA AMERICA FOUNDATION: 1440
TOTAL USA FOUNDATION: 284
TOURETTE ASSOCIATION OF AMERICA, INC.
   Young Investigator Program: 2233
Touring Arts: 456
Touring Exhibits through ExhibitsUSA: 429
TOWSLEY (THE HARRY A. AND MARGARET D.) FOUNDATION:
   285
TOWSON UNIVERSITY
   Towson University Prize for Literature: 648
Towson University Prize for Literature: 648
Tracking Health System Performance: 1335
Tracy (Joyce A.) Fellowship: 304
Traditional Arts Apprenticeship: 425, 438

Traditional Arts Apprenticeship Grants: 456
Traditional Arts Apprenticeship Program: 415
Traditional Arts Apprenticeships: 444
Traditional Grants: 1415
Trainee Awards: 1316
Training Programs: 1132
Transatlantic Mobility Program: 829
Transformational Project Award: 2130
Translation Projects: 433
Translational Genetics & Genomics: 2107
Translational Research Program: 2117
TranspARTation: 420
TRANSPORTATION ASSOCIATION OF CANADA FOUNDATION
    TAC Foundation Scholarships and Bursaries: 2362
Transportation Program: 1964
Traumatic Stress Research Program: 1669
Travel & Training Fund: 997
Travel Award for Food Safety Professionals in a Country with a
    Developing Economy: 2415
Travel Award for State or Provincial Health or Agricultural Department
    Employees: 2415
Travel Grant: 391
Travel Grants: 1348, 1789
Traveling Fellowship Award: 517
Tree and Soil Research Fund Grant: 1925
TREE RESEARCH & EDUCATION ENDOWMENT FUND (TREE
    FUND)
    Appleton (Bonnie) Memorial Scholarship: 1925
    Barborinas Family Fund Grant: 1925
    Duling (John) Grant: 1925
    Felix (Robert) Memorial Scholarship: 1925
    Johns (Hyland) Grant: 1925
    Kimmel (Jack) International Grant: 1925
    Ohio Chapter ISA Education Grant: 1925
    Safe Arborist Techniques Fund Grant: 1925
    Skiera (Bob) Memorial Fund Building Bridges Initiative Grant: 1925
    Tree and Soil Research Fund Grant: 1925
    Utility Arborist Research Fund Grant Program: 1925
    Ward (Fran) Women in Arboriculture Scholarship: 1925
    Wright (John) Memorial Scholarship: 1925
Trees for You and Me (TFYM) Reforestation Grant: 1931
TRIANGLE COMMUNITY FOUNDATION: 1421
Tribal Business Management (TBM) Program: 951
Tribal Energy Development Capacity (TEDC) Grant: 947
TRUIST FOUNDATION: 286
TRULL FOUNDATION (THE): 1259
Truman (Harry S.) Book Award: 1809
TRUMAN (HARRY S.) LIBRARY INSTITUTE
    Dissertation Year Fellowships: 1809
    Research Grant: 1809
    Scholar's Award: 1809
    Truman (Harry S.) Book Award: 1809
TRUMAN (THE HARRY S.) SCHOLARSHIP FOUNDATION
    Truman (Harry S.) Scholarship Program: 1810
Truman (Harry S.) Scholarship Program: 1810
TRUST FUNDS INCORPORATED: 287
Tsou (Judy) Critical Race Studies Award: 691
Tucker (Richard) Award: 730
Tucker (Richard) Career Grants: 730
TUCKER (THE RICHARD) MUSIC FOUNDATION, INC.
    Tucker (Richard) Award: 730
    Tucker (Richard) Career Grants: 730
    Tucker (Sara) Study Grants: 730
Tucker (Sara) Study Grants: 730
Tuition Aid Grant (TAG): 1508
Tuition Assistance: 1416
Tuition Incentive Program (TIP): 1580
Tuition Scholarships: 481
TULL CHARITABLE FOUNDATION, INC.: 288
Tunstall (Graydon A.) Undergraduate Student Scholarship: 577
Turner (Dr. Lynn W.) Paper Prize: 578
TURRELL FUND: 1037
Tuttle (Arthur S.) Memorial Fellowship: 2386
21st Century Endowment Fund: 1158
21st Century Scholars Program: 1512
TWO TEN FOOTWEAR FOUNDATION
    Two Ten Footwear Foundation Design Scholarship Program: 1585
    Two Ten Footwear Foundation Scholarship Program: 1584
Two Ten Footwear Foundation Design Scholarship Program: 1585
Two Ten Footwear Foundation Scholarship Program: 1584

Two-Year Certificate Program: 486
Tyler (Maria Opasnov) '52 Scholarship: 991
Tyrrell (The J.B.) Historical Medal: 1646
Tyson (Sarah Bradley) Memorial Fellowship: 1929

U

U.S. Antarctic Research Program: 1644
U.S. ARMY CENTER OF MILITARY HISTORY
    Dissertation Year Fellowships: 588
U.S. ARMY HERITAGE AND EDUCATION CENTER
    Ridgway (General and Mrs. Matthew B.) Military History Research
    Grant: 589
U.S. ARMY RESEARCH INSTITUTE FOR BEHAVIORAL AND
    SOCIAL SCIENCES: 1694
U.S. ARMY RESEARCH OFFICE: 1651
U.S. BANCORP FOUNDATION
    Community Possible: 1260
U.S. DEPARTMENT OF AGRICULTURE
    Emergency Conservation Program (ECP): 1988
U.S. DEPARTMENT OF EDUCATION: 1423
    American Overseas Research Centers (AORC) Program: 787
    Centers for International Business Education Program: 1719
    Education Research: 1422
    Federal Supplemental Educational Opportunity Grant (FSEOG): 1588
    Federal Work-Study: 1587
    Foreign Language and Area Studies Fellowships: 607
    Fulbright-Hays Doctoral Dissertation Research Abroad: 608
    Fulbright-Hays Group Projects Abroad Program: 854
    Indian Education-Formula Grants to Local Education Agencies (LEAs):
    956
    Language Resource Centers Program: 610
    National Professional Development Program: 1424
    National Resource Centers (NRC) Program: 609
    Native American and Alaska Native Children in School Program: 1424
    Pell Grant: 1586
    Teacher Education Assistance for College and Higher Education
    (TEACH) Grant: 1589
    Undergraduate International Studies and Foreign Language Program:
    1464
    Upward Bound: 1463
U.S. DEPARTMENT OF ENERGY
    University Coal Research Program: 2408
U.S. DEPARTMENT OF HEALTH AND HUMAN SERVICES: 2247
    Assistive Technology Programs: 2306
    Child Welfare Waiver Demonstration Projects: 1040
    Discretionary Grant Programs: 1040
    Environmental Regulatory Enhancement: 957
    Head Start: 1038
    Health Center Program (The): 1323
    Maternal and Child Health Services Block Grant: 2252
    Medicaid: 1324
    Native Languages: 957
    Projects of National Significance for Persons with Developmental
    Disabilities: 1261
    Runaway and Homeless Youth (RHY) Programs: 1039
    Social and Economic Development Strategies (SEDS) for Native
    Americans: 957
    State & Tribal Grant Programs: 1040
U.S. DEPARTMENT OF HEALTH AND HUMAN
    SERVICES/ADMINISTRATION FOR CHILDREN AND
    FAMILIES/OFFICE OF FAMILY ASSISTANCE
    State Family Assistance Grants: 1765
    Temporary Assistance for Needy Families (TANF): 1765
U.S. DEPARTMENT OF HOUSING AND URBAN DEVELOPMENT
    Community Development Block Grant Program: Entitlement Program:
    1262
U.S. DEPARTMENT OF JUSTICE
    Juvenile Justice and Delinquency Prevention Allocation to States: 1280
    Juvenile Justice and Delinquency Prevention Program: 1279
    State Justice Statistics for Statistical Analysis Centers: 1278
U.S. DEPARTMENT OF LABOR
    National Apprenticeship System: 1766
U.S. DEPARTMENT OF STATE, FULBRIGHT TEACHER
    EXCHANGES
    Fulbright Teacher Exchanges: 1425
U.S. DEPARTMENT OF THE NAVY
    Navy Health Professions Scholarship Program (HPSP): 2091
    University Research Initiative: 1652
    Young Investigator Program: 1652

References in index are to entry numbers.

U.S. ENVIRONMENTAL PROTECTION AGENCY
  Superfund State and Indian Tribe Core Program Cooperative
  Agreements: 1989
  Superfund State, Political Subdivision, and Indian Tribe Site-Specific
  Cooperative Agreements: 1989
U.S. General Fund: 889
U.S. Graduate Scholarship: 1481
U.S. Grants: Children's Oral Health Care: 1031
U.S. INSTITUTE OF PEACE
  AFSA National High School Essay Contest: 790
  Randolph (Jennings) Senior Fellowship Programs for International
  Peace: 788
  U.S. Institute of Peace Grants & Fellows Program: 789
  USIP Peace Scholar Dissertation Fellowship: 788
U.S. Institute of Peace Grants & Fellows Program: 789
U.S.-ISRAEL BINATIONAL AGRICULTURE RESEARCH AND
  DEVELOPMENT FUND (BARD)
  Graduate Student Fellowship Program: 1926
  Senior Research Fellowship Program: 1926
  Vaadia-BARD Postdoctoral Fellowship Program: 1926
U.S.-ISRAEL BINATIONAL SCIENCE FOUNDATION (BSF): 881
U.S.-Japan Leadership Program: 791
U.S. Presidential Scholars in the Arts: 434
U.S. SOCIETY ON DAMS
  USSD Scholarship Award: 2409
U.S.-Southeast Asia-Japan Collaboration and Exchange Initiative: 775
UAA Janice K. Barden Scholarship: 2369
UCLA CENTER FOR MEDIEVAL AND RENAISSANCE STUDIES
  Ahmanson Research Fellowships for the Study of Medieval and
  Renaissance Books and Manuscripts: 357
  CMRS Conference Travel Grants: 357
  CMRS Dissertation Research Fellowship: 357
  CMRS Research and Study Travel Grants: 357
  Romani (The George T. and Margaret W.) Fellowship: 357
  White (Lynn and Maude) Fellowship: 357
UCLA CHICANO STUDIES RESEARCH CENTER
  Institute of American Cultures Visiting Research Scholar Program in
  Ethnic Studies: 966
UCLA INSTITUTE OF AMERICAN CULTURES (IAC)
  Institute of American Cultures Visiting Research Scholar Fellowship
  Program in Ethnic Studies: 922
UDALL (THE MORRIS K.) AND STEWART L. UDALL
  FOUNDATION
  Congressional Internships: 958
  Udall Scholarship: 1590
Udall Scholarship: 1590
UICC Technical Fellowhips (UICC-TF): 2199
UKRAINIAN RESEARCH INSTITUTE AT HARVARD UNIVERSITY
  HURI Research Fellowships in Ukrainian Studies (The): 359
  Jacyk (Petro) Distinguished Fellowship in Ukrainian Studies: 358
  Mihaychuk (Jaroslaw and Nadia) Research Fellowships in Ukrainian
  Studies (The): 359
Ülgür (Ülkü), M.D., International Scholar Award: 2308
Undergraduate Achievement Scholarship: 1506
Undergraduate Awards: 2423
Undergraduate Essay Award: 606
Undergraduate International Studies and Foreign Language Program: 1464
Undergraduate Research Award: 1944, 2416
Undergraduate Research Fellowship: 1934
Undergraduate Research Scholarship Program: 1636
Undergraduate Scholarship Program: 2376
Undergraduate Scholarships: 2356, 2404
Undergraduate Session Assistants Program: 1802
Undergraduate Student Awards: 2414
Undergraduate Student Poster Contest: 387
Undergraduate Transfer Scholarship: 1495
Understanding Dynamic and Multi-Scale Systems: 193
Understanding Human Cognition: 193
UNICO NATIONAL, INC.
  Alessio (Maria and Paolo) Southern Italy Scholarship: 1591
  Basilone (Sargeant John) Memorial Graduate Scholarship: 1591
  Cottone Postgraduate Scholarship (Medical Only): 1591
  Davini (William C.) Scholarship: 1591
  DiMattio Celli Undergraduate Study Abroad Program: 1591
  Gentile (Major Don S.) Scholarship: 1591
  Grasso (Ella) Literary Scholarship: 1591
  Inserra Scholarships: 1591
  Marconi (Guglielmo) Engineering Scholarship: 1591
  Mazza (Theodore) Scholarship: 1591
  Miele (Alphonse A.) Scholarship: 1591
  Tarte (Robert J.) Scholarship for Italian Studies: 1591

Torraco (Bernard and Carolyn) Nursing Scholarships: 1591
Torraco (Louise) Memorial Scholarship for Science: 1591
Torraco (Ralph J.) Fine Arts Scholarship: 1591
Torraco (Ralph J.) Scholarship: 1591
Torraco (Ralph J.) Scholarship for Special Education: 1591
Torraco (Ralph J.) Scholarship for Therapy Sciences: 1591
UNION FOR INTERNATIONAL CANCER CONTROL (UICC)
  Bourses pour L'Afrique Francophone (BAF): 2199
  UICC Technical Fellowhips (UICC-TF): 2199
  Yamagiwa-Yoshida Memorial International Study Grants (YY): 2199
UNION PACIFIC FOUNDATION: 289
UNITARIAN UNIVERSALIST ASSOCIATION OF CONGREGATIONS
  Stanfield and D'Orlando Art Scholarships: 460
UNITED ARTS COUNCIL OF RALEIGH AND WAKE COUNTY, INC.
  Artist Support Grants: 461
  Artists-in-Schools Grants Program: 461
  Program Support Grants: 461
United Health Foundation/NMF Diverse Medical Scholars Program: 2062
UNITED HOSPITAL FUND OF NEW YORK
  Health Care Improvement Grant Program: 1325
UNITED JEWISH APPEAL-FEDERATION OF JEWISH
  PHILANTHROPIES OF NEW YORK: 753
UNITED METHODIST COMMUNICATIONS
  Perryman (The Leonard M.) Communications Scholarship for Ethnic
  Minority Students: 923
  Stoody-West Fellowship (The): 1760
UNITED METHODIST HEALTH MINISTRY FUND
  Access to Health Care-System Change and Advocacy: 1363
  Early Childhood Development: 1363
  Healthy Congregations Program: 1363
UNITED NEGRO COLLEGE FUND (UNCF): 939
United Parcel Service Scholarship for Female Students: 2392
United Parcel Service Scholarship for Minority Students: 2392
UNITED SOUTH AND EASTERN TRIBES, INC.: 959
UNITED STATES HOLOCAUST MEMORIAL MUSEUM - JACK,
  JOSEPH AND MORTON MANDEL CENTER FOR ADVANCED
  HOLOCAUST STUDIES
  Visiting Scholars Program: 590
UNITED STATES-JAPAN FOUNDATION
  Grants: 791
  Heinz (Elgin) Outstanding Teacher Award: 791
  U.S.-Japan Leadership Program: 791
United Way Match Program: 49
United Way Program: 10
UNITY FOUNDATION OF LAPORTE COUNTY (THE)
  Community Fund: 1263
Universal Avionics Systems Corporation Scholarship: 2363
University Coal Research Program: 2408
University Distinguished Fellowships: 907
University Enrichment Fellowships: 907
UNIVERSITY FILM AND VIDEO ASSOCIATION
  Fielding (Carole) Student Grants: 1761
UNIVERSITY OF ARIZONA SCHOOL OF INFORMATION: 684
UNIVERSITY OF BRISTOL
  Postgraduate Research Scholarships: 855
UNIVERSITY OF BRITISH COLUMBIA (THE)
  Affiliated Fellowships: 1592
  Four Year Doctoral Fellowships: 1594
  Graduate Support Initiative: 1593
UNIVERSITY OF CALGARY (THE)
  Bahlsen (Bettina) Memorial Graduate Scholarship: 1598
  Cairns (The A.T.J.) Memorial Scholarship: 1601
  Canadian Natural Resources Limited Graduate Scholarship: 1604
  Cogeco Inc. Graduate Scholarship: 1762
  Craigie (Peter C.) Memorial Scholarship: 1603
  Davies (William H.) Medical Research Scholarships: 1596
  Dingman (The Archibald Waynne) Memorial Graduate Scholarship:
  1595
  Faculty of Law Graduate Scholarship: 1605
  Graduate Faculty Council Scholarship: 1602
  Jacques (Harry and Laura) Graduate Scholarship: 1879
  Killam (Izaak Walton) Doctoral Scholarships: 1597
  Labatt (John) Limited Scholarship: 1599
  McDermid (The Honourable N.D.) Graduate Scholarships in Law: 1781
  ScotiaMcLeod Scholarship: 1599
  University of Calgary Silver Anniversary Graduate Fellowships (The):
  1600
  Willson (Robert A.) Doctoral Management Scholarship: 1465
University of Calgary Silver Anniversary Graduate Fellowships (The):
  1600

UNIVERSITY OF CALIFORNIA
  University of California President's Postdoctoral Fellowship Program: 924
University of California President's Postdoctoral Fellowship Program: 924
UNIVERSITY OF CALIFORNIA, LOS ANGELES
  Ethnic Studies Fellowships: 925
  Institute of American Cultures Grant: 960
UNIVERSITY OF DELAWARE-HAGLEY GRADUATE PROGRAM (THE): 591
UNIVERSITY OF DELAWARE, DEPARTMENT OF HISTORY
  Stewart (E. Lyman) Fellowship and Assistantship: 592
UNIVERSITY OF ILLINOIS AT URBANA-CHAMPAIGN
  Kinley (Kate Neal) Memorial Fellowship: 522
UNIVERSITY OF IOWA (THE)
  Iowa Short Fiction Award (The): 649
  Simmons (The John) Short Fiction Award: 649
UNIVERSITY OF KANSAS CHILD LANGUAGE DOCTORAL PROGRAM
  Child Language Doctoral Program: 1606
UNIVERSITY OF MANCHESTER (THE)
  British Marshall Scholarships: 856
  Fulbright - University of Manchester Award: 856
  North American Foundation Awards: 856
  President's Doctoral Scholar Award: 856
UNIVERSITY OF MANITOBA
  University of Manitoba Graduate Fellowships: 1426
University of Manitoba Graduate Fellowships: 1426
UNIVERSITY OF MICHIGAN
  Knight-Wallace Fellowships for Journalists: 1763
UNIVERSITY OF MINNESOTA
  Hollinshead (Marilyn) Fellowship: 462
  Keats (The Ezra Jack)/Kerlan Memorial Fellowship: 650
UNIVERSITY OF NEBRASKA AT OMAHA
  UNO Graduate Assistantships: 1720
UNIVERSITY OF OSLO INTERNATIONAL SUMMER SCHOOL: 857
UNIVERSITY OF PITTSBURGH
  Darbaker (Leasure K.) Prize in Botany: 1990
  McKinley Research Fund: 1990
  Pape Research Fund: 1990
UNIVERSITY OF SOUTHERN CALIFORNIA: 1607
  Annenberg Graduate Fellowship Program: 1608
  Global Ph.D. Fellowship: 1608
  Provost's Ph.D. Fellowship Program: 1608
  Rose Hills Ph.D. Fellowship: 1608
UNIVERSITY OF SOUTHERN CALIFORNIA, GAYLE GARNER ROSKI SCHOOL OF ART AND DESIGN
  Macomber Travel Grant: 523
UNIVERSITY OF SOUTHERN MISSISSIPPI (THE)
  Keats (Ezra Jack)/Janina Domanska Children's Literature Research Fellowship: 651
UNIVERSITY OF SYDNEY (THE)
  Gritton (Henry Bertie and Florence Mabel) Postgraduate Research Scholarships: 1860
  Loxton (F.H.) Postgraduate Studentships: 1927
  Mankin (Richard Claude) Scholarship: 1991
  Research Training Program (RTP): 858
  Strong (Walter Mersh) Scholarship: 878
  Sydney Medical School Postgraduate Research Scholarships: 2092
UNIVERSITY OF TEXAS AT AUSTIN (THE)
  Dobie Paisano Fellowship Program (The): 463
  Johnson (Lyndon B.) School of Public Affairs: 1466
UNIVERSITY OF TORONTO
  Fleming (Patricia) Visiting Fellowship in Bibliography and Book History: 685
UNIVERSITY OF VIRGINIA PRESS
  Cowen (Walker) Memorial Prize: 652
University Research Initiative: 1652
univie: summer school for International and European Studies: 852
univie: winter school for Cultural Historical Studies: 853
Unmet NEED Grants and Scholarships: 938
UNO Graduate Assistantships: 1720
Unrestricted Funds: 1139
Unruh (Jesse M.) Assembly Fellowship Program: 1785
UPJOHN (W.E.) INSTITUTE FOR EMPLOYMENT RESEARCH
  Early Career Research Awards: 1767
UPSTART Program: 403
Upward Bound: 1463
Urban Agriculture and Youth Leadership: 202
US COMMUNITY PARTNERSHIPS: 1326
USAF Summer Faculty Fellowship Program: 2406
USArtists International: 430

USDA FOOD AND NUTRITION SERVICE
  Child and Adult Care Food Program (The): 1041
  Fresh Fruit and Vegetable Program (The): 1041
  National School Lunch Program (The): 1041
  School Breakfast Program (The): 1041
  Special Milk Program (The): 1041
  Summer Food Service Program (The): 1041
USDA - RURAL UTILITIES SERVICE
  Water and Waste Disposal Systems for Rural Communities: 1928
USG FOUNDATION, INC.: 290
USIP Peace Scholar Dissertation Fellowship: 788
USMEX Visiting Fellows Program: 761
Usrey Family Scholarship: 1510
Usrey (Susie and Bruce) Education Scholarship: 1510
USSD Scholarship Award: 2409
UTAH DIVISION OF ARTS & MUSEUMS
  Folk Arts Grants: 464
  General Operating Support for Arts, Museums and Local Arts Agencies: 464
  Project Grants: 464
Utility Arborist Research Fund Grant Program: 1925
UX Design (MPS): 509

V

VA Psychology Training Program: 2325
Vaadia-BARD Postdoctoral Fellowship Program: 1926
Valley Arts Initiative Grant: 1237
VALLEY FOUNDATION (THE): 2093
Value Assessment Challenge Awards: 2074
Value Assessment Research Award: 2074
VAN AMERINGEN FOUNDATION, INC.: 2341
van Biema (Anne) Fellowship: 408
Van Deuren (Della) Scholarships: 1476
Van Deuren Memorial Scholarship: 1476
Van Dusen-Tobin-Kaiser Scholarship: 683
Van Hattum (Rolland J.) Award for Contribution in the Schools: 2262
VAN LOBEN SELS/REMBEROCK FOUNDATION: 1264
Vanier Canada Graduate Scholarships (CGS): 1678
Varian (Russell and Sigurd) Award: 1889
Vatican Film Library Mellon Fellowship: 623
Vaughn (Elizabeth Harper) Concerto Competition: 729
VCCA (VIRGINIA CENTER FOR THE CREATIVE ARTS): 465
Venetian Research Program: 325
VENTURA COUNTY COMMUNITY FOUNDATION: 1265
Verges (Mary M.), Past Grand President, Scholarship (Undergraduate): 976
VERIZON FOUNDATION: 291
VERMONT ARTS COUNCIL
  Animating Infrastructure Grants: 466
  Art in State Buildings Program: 466
  Artist Development Grants: 466
  Artists in Schools Grants: 466
  Arts Impact Grants: 466
  Arts Partnership Grants: 466
  Creation Grants: 466
  Cultural Facilities Grants: 466
  Head Start Arts Integration Program: 466
Vermont Incentive Grants and Scholarships: 1609
Vermont Outreach Programs: 1609
VERMONT STUDENT ASSISTANCE CORPORATION
  Vermont Incentive Grants and Scholarships: 1609
  Vermont Outreach Programs: 1609
Verney (E. Geoffrey and Elizabeth Thayer) Fellowship: 561
Vernon (Chester M.) Memorial Eagle Scout Scholarship: 1537
VERTICAL FLIGHT FOUNDATION
  Vertical Flight Foundation Engineering Scholarships: 2374
Vertical Flight Foundation Engineering Scholarships: 2374
Verville (A.) Fellowship: 2372
Veteran Housing Grants Program: 1179
Veterans in the Arts: 394
VETERANS OF FOREIGN WARS AUXILIARY
  Young American Creative Patriotic Art Awards: 467
Veterans Program: 191
Veterans Tuition Credit Program (VTCP): 1545
Vibrant Communities Grants: 409
VICTORIA FOUNDATION, INC.: 1266
VILLA I TATTI: THE HARVARD UNIVERSITY CENTER FOR ITALIAN RENAISSANCE STUDIES
  Berenson Fellowship: 861

Fellowship in the Digital Humanities: 862
I Tatti Fellowship: 859
I Tatti/Museo Nacional del Prado Joint Fellowship: 865
Smyth (Craig Hugh) Fellowship: 864
Tobey (David and Julie) Fellowship: 863
Wallace Fellowship: 860
Warburg/I Tatti Joint Fellowship: 866
Villarreal (Dr. Juan D.) Scholarship: 2104
VIOLIN SOCIETY OF AMERICA (THE)
Kaplan-Goodkind Memorial Scholarship Fund: 731
Kun Scholarship Fund: 731
Nigogosian (Aram and Rose) Fund: 731
VIRGIN ISLANDS COUNCIL ON THE ARTS
Expanding Opportunities for Participation in the Arts: 468
VIRGINIA COMMISSION FOR THE ARTS: 469
VIRGINIA DEPARTMENT OF HEALTH
Commonwealth of Virginia Nurse Educator Scholarship Program: 2248
Marshall (Mary) Nursing Scholarship/Practical Nurse Program: 2248
Marshall (Mary) Nursing Scholarship/Registered Nurse Program: 2248
Nurse Practitioner/Nurse Midwife Scholarship Program: 2248
VIRGINIA ENVIRONMENTAL ENDOWMENT
Community Conservation Program: 1992
James River Water Quality Improvement Program: 1992
Kanawha and Ohio River Valleys Program: 1992
Virginia Program: 1992
VIRGINIA MUSEUM OF FINE ARTS
Professional Fellowship Program: 470
Student Fellowship Program: 470
VIRGINIA POLYTECHNIC INSTITUTE AND STATE UNIVERSITY
Multicultural Academic Opportunity Graduate Student Scholars
Program: 926
Virginia Program: 1992
VIRGINIA SOCIETY OF ORNITHOLOGY
VSO Conservation Fund: 1949
Virginia Tuition Assistance Grant Program (VTAG): 1576
Viscount Bennett Fellowship: 1769
Vision Grants: 329
Visiting Fellows Program: 314
Visiting Fellowships: 1822
Visiting Lectureships: 1444
Visiting Professorships Fellowship: 828
Visiting Research Fellowship Program: 360
Visiting Research Fellowships: 331
Visiting Scholar Award: 2228
Visiting Scholar Awards: 365
Visiting Scholars Program: 590, 1895
Visual Arts and Crafts: 384
Visual Arts Fellowship: 502
Visual Arts Fellowships: 479
VITAS Healthcare/Esther Colliflower Scholarship: 2240
Vogt (James R.) Radiochemistry Scholarship: 1851
Voice, Creativity and Culture: 81
Volunteer Grants Program: 1213
Volunteer Investment Program: 73
Volunteer Program: 99
Voron (Abe) Award: 1724
VSO Conservation Fund: 1949
VSP and AAOF Canadian Practice Excellence Scholarships: 2255
VSP and AAOF Practice Excellence Scholarships: 2255

W

WABASH CENTER FOR TEACHING AND LEARNING IN
THEOLOGY AND RELIGION (THE)
Educational Environments: 754
Faculty Practices and Vocation: 754
WACO FOUNDATION (THE)
MAC College Money Program: 1267
Wagner (Carl) Memorial Award: 1627
WAGNER COLLEGE
Stanley Drama Award: 494
Waldbaum (Jane C.) Archaeological Field School Scholarship: 312
Walk Me Home Program: 1026
Walker (Arthur B.C. II) Award: 1837
Walker (Myrtle and Earl) Scholarship: 2361
Wallace Fellowship: 860
WALLACE FOUNDATION (THE): 292
Wallace (Harriet Evelyn) Scholarship: 1866
Wallace (Henry A.) Award: 524

WALPOLE (LEWIS) LIBRARY
Visiting Research Fellowship Program: 360
War Memorial Scholarships: 1516
Warburg/I Tatti Joint Fellowship: 866
Ward (Fran) Women in Arboriculture Scholarship: 1925
WASHINGTON (DENNIS & PHYLLIS) FOUNDATION: 1268
WASHINGTON FORREST FOUNDATION: 1269
Washington Health Corps: 1611
Washington Prize (The): 653
Washington State Need Grant Program: 1610
Washington State Work-Study Program: 1610
WASHINGTON STUDENT ACHIEVEMENT COUNCIL
American Indian Endowed Scholarship Program: 961
Washington Health Corps: 1611
Washington State Need Grant Program: 1610
Washington State Work-Study Program: 1610
WASHINGTON UNIVERSITY IN ST. LOUIS
Chancellor's Graduate Fellowship Program at Washington University in
St. Louis (The): 1612
Olin (Spencer T. and Ann W.) Fellowship for Women in Graduate
Study: 1613
Steedman (James Harrison) Memorial Fellowship in Architecture: 383
WASIE FOUNDATION (THE)
Arthritis Grants: 293
Cancer Grants: 293
Children's Medical Health Grants: 293
Schizophrenia Grants: 293
Wasilewski (Vincent T.) Award: 1724
Water and Waste Disposal Systems for Rural Communities: 1928
Watershed Protection: 235
WATSON (JEANNETTE K.) FELLOWSHIP: 1467
WATSON (THOMAS J.) FELLOWSHIP PROGRAM: 1468
Wealth Building: 1157
Weaver (Richard M.) Graduate Fellowship: 1795
Weber (Maurice) Laboratorian Award: 2415
Webster (Dee & King) Memorial Fund for Greater Lawrence: 1153
WEBSTER (EDWIN S.) FOUNDATION: 294
Wechsler (Sheldon) and George Mertz Contact Lens Residency Award:
2257
WEEDEN FOUNDATION
Climate Crisis Activism: 1993
Consumption: 1993
Domestic Biodiversity: 1993
International Biodiversity: 1993
WEGE FOUNDATION: 1270
WEHR (TODD) FOUNDATION: 1469
Weil (Frank L.) Memorial Eagle Scout Scholarship: 1537
WEILL (KURT) FOUNDATION FOR MUSIC: 471
Weinberg (Arthur and Lila) Fellowship for Independent Scholars and
Researchers: 344
WEINBERG (THE HARRY AND JEANETTE) FOUNDATION, INC.:
1271
Weiner (Herbert) Early Career Award for Contributions to Psychosomatic
Society: 2319
WEINGART FOUNDATION: 295
Weisel (William E.) Scholarship: 2361
WEIZMANN INSTITUTE OF SCIENCE
Postdoctoral Fellowships Program at the Weizmann Institute of Science:
867
WELCH (THE ROBERT A.) FOUNDATION
Departmental Grants: 1861
Research Grants: 1861
Welch Summer Scholar Program: 1861
Welch Summer Scholar Program: 1861
WELDER (ROB AND BESSIE) WILDLIFE FOUNDATION: 1900
Welder Training Scholarship: 2349
Welding Workforce Grant: 2347
Weller (The Sue Marsh) Fund: 670
WELLESLEY COLLEGE
Barrett (Anne Louise) Fellowship: 991
Bowers (Margaret Freeman) Fellowship: 991
Cox (The Eugene L.) Fellowship: 991
Fisher (Professor Elizabeth F.) Fellowship: 991
Goldmark (Ruth Ingersoll) Fellowship: 991
Horton-Hallowell Fellowship: 991
Howard (Peggy) Fellowship in Economics: 991
Moffett (Edna V.) Fellowship: 991
Palmer (Alice Freeman) Fellowship: 991
Preyer (Kathryn Conway) Fellowship: 991
Schimke (Mary McEwen) Scholarship: 992
Scudder (Vida Dutton) Fellowship: 991

Shackford (M.A. Cartland) Medical Fellowship: 992
Shaw (Harriet A.) Fellowship: 991
Stevens (Mary Elvira) Traveling Fellowship: 991
Tyler (Maria Opasnov) '52 Scholarship: 991
Wood (Sarah Perry) Medical Fellowship: 991
Workman (Fanny Bullock) Fellowship: 991
Wells (Clara) Fellowships: 690
Wells (Ida B.) Graduate Student Fellowship: 534
WENNER-GREN FOUNDATION FOR ANTHROPOLOGICAL
RESEARCH, INC.
Conference and Workshop Grants: 1818
Individual Research Grants: 1817
Wenner-Gren Symposium Program: 1818
Wenner-Gren Symposium Program: 1818
Wert (Lucille & Charles A.) Scholarship: 2420
Wesley-Logan Prize (The): 526
WEST (HERMAN O.) FOUNDATION: 296
WEST PHARMACEUTICAL SERVICES, INC.: 297
WEST VIRGINIA DEPARTMENT OF ARTS, CULTURE AND
HISTORY: 472
West Virginia Higher Education Grant Program: 1614
WEST VIRGINIA HIGHER EDUCATION POLICY COMMISSION
West Virginia Higher Education Grant Program: 1614
WESTERN INTERSTATE COMMISSION FOR HIGHER EDUCATION
Professional Student Exchange Program (PSEP): 298
Weston Pediatric Dermatology Career Development Award (CDA): 2285
WETLANDS INSTITUTE (THE)
Coastal Conservation Research Program: 1950
Environmental Education Internship: 1950
WFMN Fund for Safety: 996
WHARTON (WILLIAM P.) TRUST: 1830
Whetten (Nellie Yeoh) Award: 1889
WHITAKER FOUNDATION: 473
White House Fellowships: 1804
White (Lynn and Maude) Fellowship: 357
White (Marsh W.) Awards: 1893
White-Reinhardt Fund for Education: 1903
WHITE (THOMAS H.) FOUNDATION: 1272
WHITEHALL FOUNDATION, INC.: 1951
WHITEHEAD (JOSEPH B.) FOUNDATION: 1042
WHITEHORSE FOUNDATION (THE): 1327
WHITNEY (THE HELEN HAY) FOUNDATION
Early Postdoctoral Research Fellowship Program in Biomedical
Sciences: 1653
WICHITA COMMUNITY FOUNDATION: 1273
WIDENER MEMORIAL FOUNDATION IN AID OF HANDICAPPED
CHILDREN: 927
Wiebe (Richard A.) Public Service Fellowship: 1801
WIEGAND (E. L.) FOUNDATION: 299
Wiener Laboratory Post-Doctoral Fellowship: 814
Wiener Laboratory Pre-Doctoral Fellowship: 814
Wiener Laboratory Programmatic Post-Doctoral Fellowship: 814
Wiener Laboratory Research Associateships: 814
WILEY FOUNDATION, INC. (THE)
Wiley Prize in Biomedical Sciences: 1901
Wiley Prize in Biomedical Sciences: 1901
Williams (Cenie Jomo) Tuition Scholarship: 936
Williams (Donald A.) Soil Conservation Scholarship: 1986
Williams (Dr. Eric J.) Scholarship: 2240
Williams (Kemper and Leila) Prize in Louisiana History: 544
Willson (Robert A.) Doctoral Management Scholarship: 1465
Wilson (Alexander) Prize: 1952
WILSON (MATILDA R.) FUND: 300
WILSON ORNITHOLOGICAL SOCIETY
Fuertes (Louis Agassiz) Grant: 1952
Hall (George A.)/Harold F. Mayfield Grant: 1952
Research Grants: 1952
Stewart (Paul A.) Grants: 1952
Student Travel Awards: 1952
Wilson (Alexander) Prize: 1952
Wilson (Pete) Scholarship: 1757
WILSON (WOODROW) INTERNATIONAL CENTER FOR SCHOLARS
Fellowship Program at the Woodrow Wilson International Center for
Scholars: 361
Winchell (F. Mabel) Loan Fund: 678
Windham Area Women and Girls Fund: 1110
Winter (Cindy) Scholarship Award: 1350
Winter (Frederick E. and Joan) Student Travel Bursary: 315
Winter Intensive: 486

WINTERTHUR MUSEUM, GARDEN & LIBRARY
Dissertation Fellowships: 362
Maker-Creator Fellowships: 362
NEH Postdoctoral Fellowship: 362
Postdoctoral Fellowship: 362
Short-term Fellowship: 362
WISCONSIN ARTS BOARD
Creation and Presentation: 474
Creative Communities: 474
Folk Arts Apprenticeship Program: 474
Wisconsin Regranting Program: 474
WISCONSIN HISTORICAL SOCIETY PRESS
Everest (D.C.) Fellowship: 593
Hunter (Amy Louise) Fellowship: 593
Smith (Alice E.) Fellowship: 593
Wisconsin Regranting Program: 474
Wisconsin Study in Poland (WSIP): 1526
Wish a Smile: 2096
WITH FOUNDATION: 928
WITTER (THE DEAN) FOUNDATION: 1721
Woest (The Dianne) Fellowship in the Arts and Humanities: 545
WOLF HUMANITIES CENTER
Mellon (Andrew W.) Postdoctoral Fellowships in the Humanities: 363
Wolf (Paul R.) Memorial Scholarship: 1821
WOMAN'S NATIONAL FARM & GARDEN ASSOCIATION, INC.
Tyson (Sarah Bradley) Memorial Fellowship: 1929
Women and Girls Development Fund: 1240
WOMEN IN DEFENSE
Horizons Foundation Scholarship Program: 993
WOMEN IN FILM
Women in Film Finishing Fund: 994
Women in Film Finishing Fund: 994
Women in Need Scholarship: 1704
Women in Science Scholars Program: 1415
Women in Transition Scholarship: 1704
WOMEN'S CONGRESSIONAL POLICY INSTITUTE (WCPI)
Congressional Fellowships on Women and Public Policy: 995
WOMEN'S FOUNDATION OF MINNESOTA
Community Response Fund: 996
girlsBEST Fund: 996
Ripley Memorial Foundation: 996
WFMN Fund for Safety: 996
Young Women's Initiative: 996
Women's Foundation of Montana: 1206
Women's Fund Grants: 1123
Women's Fund of Essex County (The): 1153
Women's Fund of Greater Cincinnati Foundation: 1166
Women's Health: 983
Women's Safety: 983
WOMEN'S SPORTS FOUNDATION
Travel & Training Fund: 997
WOMEN'S STUDIO WORKSHOP (WSW)
Art-in-Education Artists' Book Residency Grant: 476
Artists' Book Residency Grants: 475
Studio Residency Grant: 477
Woo (William) Print & Online News Internship Grant: 1482
Wood Institute Travel Grants: 532
Wood (Sarah Perry) Medical Fellowship: 991
Woodruff (Helen M.) Fellowship of the AIA and the American Academy
in Rome: 1445
WOODRUFF (THE ROBERT W.) FOUNDATION: 301
WOODS CHARITABLE FUND, INC.: 1274
WOODS FUND CHICAGO: 1275
WOODS HOLE OCEANOGRAPHIC INSTITUTION
Summer Student Fellowship Program in Oceanography: 1654
Woodside (William Park) Founder's Scholarship: 2420
Woodson (Carter G.) Book Awards: 1665
WOODSON (CARTER G.) INSTITUTE FOR AFRICAN-AMERICAN
AND AFRICAN STUDIES
African-American and African Studies Fellowships: 364
Woodstock A-I-R: 498
WOODWARD'S (MR. AND MRS. P.A.) FOUNDATION: 1328
Woolley (Harriet Hale) Scholarship: 704
Woolls (Blanche E.) Scholarship for School Library Media Service: 662
WORD WORKS, INC. (THE)
Tenth Gate Prize: 654
Washington Prize (The): 653
Work-In-Progress Grants: 646
Workforce Development Grants: 1123
Workforce Development Scholarship: 2376

References in index are to entry numbers.

Workman (Fanny Bullock) Fellowship: 991
Workmen's Circle (The)/Dr. Emanuel Patt Visiting Professorship: 597
Workshop Series: 755
WORLD LEARNING INC.
   Fulbright Specialist Program: 792
Worthy Goal Scholarship: 2358
Wright (John) Memorial Scholarship: 1925
Writer-in-Residence Program: 415
Writing Fellowship: 502
WURLITZER (THE HELENE) FOUNDATION OF NEW MEXICO
   HWF Academic Scholarship Program: 478
   HWF Artist Residency Program: 478
Wynar (Bohdan S.) Research Paper Competition: 661
WYOMING ARTS COUNCIL
   Arts Access Project Grants: 479
   Blanchan/Doubleday Fellowships: 479
   Community Support Grants: 479
   Folk & Traditional Arts Mentoring Project Grants: 479
   Layser (Pattie) Greater Yellowstone Creative Writing & Journalism
   Fellowship: 479
   Literary Arts Fellowships: 479
   Native Art Fellowship: 479
   Performing Arts Fellowships: 479
   Professional Development/Career Advancement Grants: 479
   Visual Arts Fellowships: 479

X

XCEL ENERGY FOUNDATION: 302

Y

YALE CENTER FOR BRITISH ART
   Visiting Scholar Awards: 365
Yamagiwa-Yoshida Memorial International Study Grants (YY): 2199
Yang (Y.C.) Civil Engineering Scholarship: 2386
Yee (Jimmie & Suey Fong) Scholarship: 1483
YIVO INSTITUTE FOR JEWISH RESEARCH
   Abramowicz (The Dina) Emerging Scholar Fellowship: 597
   Fellowship in American Jewish Studies: 594
   Fellowship in Baltic Jewish Studies: 596
   Fellowship in East European Arts, Music, and Theater: 595
   Fellowship in East European Jewish Literature: 595
   Fellowship in East European Jewish Studies: 596
   Fellowship in Polish Jewish Studies: 596
   Workmen's Circle (The)/Dr. Emanuel Patt Visiting Professorship: 597
Yoshikawa (Thomas and Catherine) Award for Outstanding Scientific
   Achievement in Clinical Investigation: 2294
Young American Creative Patriotic Art Awards: 467
Young Clinician Investigator Award: 2225
Young Composers' Competition: 713
Young Concert Artists International Auditions: 732
YOUNG CONCERT ARTISTS, INC.
   Young Concert Artists International Auditions: 732
Young Investigator Awards: 2114

Young Investigator Grant Program: 2176
Young Investigator Grants: 2065
Young Investigator Innovation Grants: 1367
Young Investigator Program: 1652, 2233
Young Investigator Research Grant: 2277
Young Investigator's Award: 2249
Young Scholars Program: 1495
Young Scientist Award: 2423
Young Scientist Research Award: 1852
Young Women for Change: 981
Young Women in Public Affairs Awards: 998
Young Women's Initiative: 996
YoungArts Los Angeles: 434
YoungArts Miami: 434
YoungArts New York: 434
Youth Action Fund: 174
Youth and Community PopUps: 1334
Youth Arts Action: 394
Youth Arts Project Grants: 438
Youth Council: 1057
Youth Football Grants: 1211
YOUTH FOR UNDERSTANDING USA
   Americans Overseas Summer, Semester and Year Programs: 868
   Congress-Bundestag Youth Exchange Program: 868
   Corporate Scholarship Program: 868
   International Semester and Year Programs: 868
   Japan-U.S. Senate Youth Exchange Program: 868
Youth Justice: 242
Youth Leadership Fund: 1182
Youth Service Improvement Grants Program: 1016
Ypsilanti Area Community Fund (The): 1057

Z

Zachariasiewicz (Wladyslaw) Memorial Journalism Scholarship: 1473
ZACHARY (THE LOREN L.) SOCIETY FOR THE PERFORMING
   ARTS
   Annual Loren L. Zachary National Vocal Competition for Young Opera
   Singers: 733
Zaken (Lisa) Award of Excellence: 2392
Zamrik (Myrna R. and Sam Y.) Scholarship: 2387
Zapanta (Dr. Richard) Scholarship: 2062
Zeller Summer Scholarship in Medicinal Botany (The): 1911
Zenith Fellows Award (ZNTH): 2203
Zervoulias (The Sotiri) & Lea Soupata Scholarship (St. Basil's Academy):
   976
ZETON Plant Design Competition: 2390
ZIGLER (FRED B. AND RUTH B.) FOUNDATION: 1427
Zildjian Family Opportunity Fund: 722
Zimmer Biomet/NMF Orthopaedic Scholarship: 2062
Zimmerman (A.F.) Scholarship: 577
Ziskind-Somerfeld Research Award: 2339
ZONTA FOUNDATION FOR WOMEN
   Earhart (Amelia) Fellowship: 1846
   Klausman (Jane M.) Women in Business Scholarships: 1722
   Young Women in Public Affairs Awards: 998

Geographical Index

UNITED STATES

Alabama

Alabama Academy of Science, Inc.: 1616
Alabama Commission on Higher Education: 1470, 1471, 1472
Alabama Library Association Scholarship Fund, Inc.: 655
Alabama Power Foundation: 6
Alabama State Council on the Arts: 384
Community Foundation of South Alabama (The): 1122
Dixon Foundation (The): 1143
Meyer (Robert R.) Foundation: 205

Alaska

Alaska Conservation Foundation: 1954, 1955
Alaska State Council on the Arts: 385

Arizona

American Association of Zoo Keepers: 1931
APS Corporate Giving Program: 17
Arizona Commission on the Arts: 390
Arizona Community Foundation: 1058
Arizona State University: 1371
Flinn Foundation (The): 111
Freeport-McMoRan Foundation: 115
Institute for Supply Management: 1708
Research Corporation for Science Advancement: 1827
Udall (The Morris K.) and Stewart L. Udall Foundation: 1590, 958
University of Arizona School of Information: 684

Arkansas

Arkansas Community Foundation: 1059
Ross Foundation: 1234

California

Academy Foundation of the Academy of Motion Picture Arts and
    Sciences: 480, 495
Acorn Foundation: 1953
Allende (The Isabel) Foundation: 967
American Honda Foundation: 1368
American Society for Enology and Viticulture: 1905
American Society for Theatre Research (ASTR): 482
Amgen Foundation, Inc.: 14
Annenberg Foundation (The): 15
Applied Materials, Inc.: 16
Archstone Foundation: 1282
Arthritis National Research Foundation (ANRF): 2012
Astronomical Society of the Pacific: 1833, 1834, 1835, 1836, 1837, 1838
Atkinson Foundation: 22
Autry Foundation: 1061
Baker (R.C.) Foundation: 26
Berger (H.N. and Frances C.) Foundation: 34
Burns (Fritz B.) Foundation: 1377
California Academy of Sciences: 1936
California Arts Council: 394
California Community Foundation: 1079
California Endowment (The): 1285
California Healthcare Foundation: 1286
California Library Association: 663
California Student Aid Commission: 1487, 1488
California Wellness Foundation (The): 1287
Cancer Federation, Inc.: 2113
Center at Sierra Health Foundation (The): 1334
Center for California Studies, Capital Fellows Programs: 1785
Center for International Security and Cooperation (CISAC): 760
Center for Plant Conservation: 1906
Center for 17th and 18th Century Studies: 317, 318, 319, 320
Center for U.S.-Mexican Studies, University of California, San Diego: 761
Christensen Fund (The): 57
Common Counsel Foundation: 1097
Community Foundation for Monterey County: 1102
Community Foundation of the North State: 1125
Community Foundation of the Verdugos: 1336

Compton Foundation, Inc.: 71
Cowell (S.H.) Foundation: 78
Crail-Johnson Foundation (The): 1008
Darling (Hugh and Hazel) Foundation: 1448
DJ & T Foundation: 1894
Drown (Joseph) Foundation: 92
East Bay Community Foundation (The): 1147
Ebell of Los Angeles (The): 1499
Edison International: 99
Eisner Foundation (The): 1012
Energy Foundation (The): 1964
Gamble Foundation (The): 1389
Geffen (The David) Foundation: 1292
Gellert (Carl) and Celia Berta Gellert Foundation (The): 120
Gellert (The Fred) Family Foundation: 121
General Service Foundation: 122
Getty (J. Paul) Trust, Getty Foundation: 503
Glaucoma Research Foundation: 2270
Goldman (Lisa and Douglas) Fund: 1161
GRAMMY Museum (The): 706
Great Minds in STEM: 2355
Guitar Foundation of America: 707
Harden Foundation: 133
Haynes (The John Randolph) and Dora Haynes Foundation: 1660
Health Trust (The): 1297, 1298
HealthCare Foundation for Orange County (The): 1299
Hearst (William Randolph) Foundation: 1735
Heed Ophthalmic Foundation: 2272
Hewlett (The William and Flora) Foundation: 137
Hillblom (The Larry L.) Foundation, Inc.: 2036
Hispanic Scholarship Fund: 965
Honig (Victor and Lorraine) Fund: 1338
Humboldt Area Foundation: 1182
Huntington Library, Art Museum and Botanical Gardens: 330
International Anesthesia Research Society (IARS): 2039
International Documentary Association: 417
International Myeloma Foundation (IMF): 2041
Jackson (Ann) Family Foundation: 145
Japan Foundation, Los Angeles (The): 1517
Jewish Community Foundation of Los Angeles: 1186
Jewish Family and Children's Services: 1519
Johnson (Magic) Foundation: 151
Jones (The Fletcher) Foundation: 1455
Koret Foundation: 170
Kvamme (The Jean and E. Floyd) Foundation: 1402
LA84 Foundation: 1305
Latkin (Herbert and Gertrude) Charitable Foundation: 178
Leakey (L.S.B.) Foundation: 1811
Liberty Hill Foundation: 1343
Livingston Memorial Foundation: 1306
Lloyd (John M.) Foundation: 1779
Loeb (The Gerald) Awards: 1742
Los Angeles Rams Foundation: 1020
Luso-American Education Foundation: 600, 601
Maddie's Fund: 1664
Marin Community Foundation: 189
Martin (Della) Foundation: 2330
Masserini (Maurice J.) Trust: 905
MAZON: A Jewish Response to Hunger: 1345
McBean (Alletta Morris) Charitable Trust: 333
McMicking (The Joseph and Mercedes) Foundation: 196
Nakamichi (E.) Foundation: 712
National Alopecia Areata Foundation: 1945
National Association of Science Writers, Inc.: 1745, 1746, 1747
Norris (Kenneth T. and Eileen L.) Foundation: 219
Nuclear Age Peace Foundation: 779
Orange County Community Foundation: 224
Osher (The Bernard) Foundation: 225
Oxnard Foundation: 2071
Pacific Gas and Electric Company: 227
Pacific Life Foundation: 228
Packard (The David and Lucile) Foundation: 229
Packard (Lucile) Foundation for Children's Health: 1028
Parker Foundation (The): 230
Parsons (The Ralph M.) Foundation: 232
Pasadena Community Foundation: 1352
Patagonia Inc.: 1980
Patron Saints Foundation (The): 1313
Rancho Santa Fe Foundation: 1227
Reagan (Ronald) Presidential Foundation and Institute: 1568

Righteous Persons Foundation: 917
San Diego Art Institute: 516
San Diego Foundation (The): 1241
San Francisco Conservatory of Music: 726
San Francisco Foundation: 1242, 255, 452, 453
San Francisco Opera Center: 727
Santa Barbara Foundation: 1243
Santa Barbara Mission Archive-Library: 583
Schwab (Charles and Helen) Foundation: 258
Schwab (Charles) Foundation: 1717
Scripps (The Ellen Browning) Foundation: 259
Seaver Institute (The): 261
Sierra Health Foundation: 1359
Silicon Valley Community Foundation: 1247
Silicon Valley Creates: 454
Sisters of St. Joseph Healthcare Foundation: 1320
Society of Children's Book Writers and Illustrators: 646
Stanford Humanities Center: 354
Stauffer (John) Charitable Trust: 272
Stuart Foundation: 1035
Tahoe Truckee Community Foundation: 277
Tailhook Educational Foundation: 1420
Taper (S. Mark) Foundation: 278
Tides Foundation: 1258
Trust Funds Incorporated: 287
UCLA Center for Medieval and Renaissance Studies: 357
UCLA Chicano Studies Research Center: 966
UCLA Institute of American Cultures (IAC): 922
University of California: 924
University of California, Los Angeles: 925, 960
University of Southern California: 1607, 1608
University of Southern California, Gayle Garner Roski School of Art and
    Design: 523
Valley Foundation (The): 2093
van Loben Sels/RembeRock Foundation: 1264
Ventura County Community Foundation: 1265
Weingart Foundation: 295
WITH Foundation: 928
Witter (The Dean) Foundation: 1721
Women In Film: 994
Zachary (The Loren L.) Society for the Performing Arts: 733

Colorado

American Alpine Club: 1957
American Indian College Fund: 940
American Indian Science and Engineering Society (AISES): 942
Animal Assistance Foundation: 2010
Aviation Distributors and Manufacturers Association (ADMA): 2366
Brett Family Foundation: 1655
Bureau of Indian Affairs: 947, 948
Calder (The Louis) Foundation: 1003
Colorado Creative Industries: 396
Cooperative Institute for Research in Environmental Sciences (CIRES):
    1963
Coors (Adolph) Foundation: 1007
Crowell (Henry P. and Susan C.) Trust: 79
Daniels Fund: 83
El Pomar Foundation: 100
Erion Foundation: 101
First Nations Development Institute: 953
Geological Society of America, Inc. (The): 1867
History Colorado State Historical Fund: 546
Hunter (A.V.) Trust, Inc.: 1339
JILA: 1822
McCauley (Luther T.) Charitable Trust: 1200
McDonald (J.M.) Foundation, Inc.: 192
National Cattleman's Beef Association, a contractor to the Beef Checkoff:
    2417
National Center for Atmospheric Research: 1638, 1840
National Endowment for Financial Education (NEFE): 1714
Rose Community Foundation: 1232
Society for French Historical Studies: 584
Stone (H. Chase) Trust: 457
Summit Foundation (The): 1255
U.S. Society on Dams: 2409
Western Interstate Commission For Higher Education: 298

Connecticut

Aetna Foundation, Inc.: 5
Barnes Group Foundation: 1064
Belgian American Educational Foundation, Inc.: 820
Center for the Humanities: 321
Childs (The Jane Coffin) Memorial Fund for Medical Research: 2189
Community Foundation for Greater New Haven (The): 1101
Community Foundation of Eastern Connecticut: 1110
Connecticut Community Foundation: 1132
Connecticut Humanities: 322
Deloitte Foundation: 1449
Department of Economic and Community Development/Connecticut
    Office of the Arts: 402
Eversource Energy Foundation: 102
Fairfield County's Community Foundation: 104
Hartford Public Library: 669
Hoffman (The Maximilian E. & Marion O.) Foundation, Inc.: 2038
Knights of Columbus: 1524
National Organization for Rare Disorders (NORD) (The): 2063
Richardson (Smith) Foundation, Inc.: 1672
Walpole (Lewis) Library: 360
Yale Center for British Art: 365

Delaware

Delaware Division of the Arts: 401
Freeman (Carl M.) Foundation: 407
Hagley Museum and Library: 543
Intercollegiate Studies Institute (The): 1795
International Literacy Association (ILA): 1397, 1398
Raskob Foundation for Catholic Activities: 751
University of Delaware-Hagley Graduate Program (The): 591
University of Delaware, Department of History: 592
Winterthur Museum, Garden & Library: 362

District of Columbia

American Academy of Child and Adolescent Psychiatry: 2307, 2308,
    2309
American Association for the Advancement of Science: 1723
American Association of Geographers (The): 1862, 1863, 1864
American Association of University Women: 871, 968, 969, 970, 971
American Astronomical Society: 1831, 1832
American Chemical Society: 1819, 1847, 1848, 1849, 1850
American College of Cardiology: 2122
American Farm Bureau Foundation for Agriculture: 1903
American Friends of the Alexander von Humboldt Foundation: 1442,
    1475, 797, 798
American Hellenic Educational Progressive Association (The): 884
American Historical Association (The): 526, 527, 528
American Institute of Architects (The): 366
American Institute of Bangladesh Studies: 801
American Political Science Association: 1782, 1783, 1784
American Psychiatric Association: 2310, 2311, 2312
American Psychological Association: 2313, 2314, 2315
American Society for Engineering Education: 2385
American Society for Microbiology: 1934
American Society of Hematology: 2005, 2006, 2007, 2109
American Society of Interior Designers Educational Foundation, Inc.: 367
American Society of Nephrology: 2110, 2111, 2112
American Sociological Association: 886
American Veterinary Medical Association: 2009
AmeriCorps: 1333
Arca Foundation (The): 18
Architects Foundation (The): 368
Asian American Journalists Association: 1482, 1483, 1484
Association of Women's Health, Obstetric and Neonatal Nurses
    (AWHONN): 2236
Bell (Alexander Graham) Association for the Deaf and Hard of Hearing:
    891
Broadcast Education Association: 1724, 1725
Bureau of Indian Affairs: 946, 949
Cafritz (The Morris and Gwendolyn) Foundation: 47
Caring for Military Families: The Elizabeth Dole Foundation: 894
Carnegie Institution for Science: 1624
Catholic Campaign for Human Development: 1084
Center for Hellenic Studies: 316
Center for Science in the Public Interest: 2413
Children's Bureau: 1006
Congressional Black Caucus Foundation, Inc.: 929, 930, 931

Congressional Hispanic Caucus Institute: 962, 963
Cooperative Development Foundation: 1134
Corporation for National and Community Service (AmeriCorps): 1135
Council of American Overseas Research Centers (CAORC): 824
Cultural Vistas: 766, 825
Daughters of Penelope Foundation, Inc.: 898, 976
Department of Veterans Affairs: 2325
District of Columbia Commission on the Arts and Humanities: 403
Dumbarton Oaks: 326
Eisenhower Institute at Gettysburg College (The): 770
Embassy of France in the U.S., SCAC: 829
Environmental Law Institute: 1771
Eye Bank Association of America: 2266
Federal Highway Administration: 2353
Food and Drug Law Institute (FDLI): 1772
Foundation for Advancement in Conservation (FAIC) (The): 667
Freer Gallery of Art and Arthur M. Sackler Gallery: 408
Fund for American Studies (The): 1792
Fund for Investigative Journalism: 1734
George Washington University: 2391
Georgetown University: 1858
German Historical Institute: 542
Gwathmey Memorial Trust (The): 328
Hispanic Bar Association of D.C. Foundation (The): 1777
Hispanic National Bar Foundation (The): 1778
Institute of Current World Affairs: 772
Institute of International Education: 773
Institute of International Education/Council for International Exchange of Scholars: 1454
Institute of Museum and Library Services: 671, 672
International Research & Exchanges Board (IREX): 833
Jack and Jill of America Foundation (The): 933
Japan-U.S. Friendship Commission: 776
Japanese American Citizens League (JACL) (The): 1518, 1796, 777
Jeffress (Thomas F. and Kate Miller) Memorial Trust: 1896
Kennedy (Robert F.) Human Rights: 622
Landscape Architecture Foundation: 1974
Lupus Foundation of America, Inc.: 2045
Marshall (Thurgood) College Fund (TMCF): 1529
McNamara (The Margaret) Education Grants (MMEG): 197
Meyer (Eugene and Agnes E.) Foundation: 1202
Morgan (Marietta McNeill) and Samuel Tate Morgan, Jr. Trust: 1347
Morris (William) Society in the U.S.: 432
National Academies of Sciences, Engineering, and Medicine (The): 1824, 908
National Academy of Education (The): 1405
National Association for Equal Opportunity in Higher Education (NAFEO): 935
National Association of Black Social Workers, Inc. (The): 936
National Association of Health Services Executives (NAHSE): 2302
National Association of Hispanic Journalists: 909
National Business Aviation Association: 2368, 2369, 2370
National Center for Learning Disabilities: 1406
National Council for Eurasian and East European Research (The): 778
National Endowment for Democracy: 1798
National Endowment for the Arts: 433
National Endowment for the Humanities: 1748, 335, 336, 337, 338, 339
National Fish and Wildlife Foundation (NFWF): 1975
National Geographic Society: 1871
National Historical Publications and Records Commission: 562
National Institute of Justice, U.S. Department of Justice: 1277
National Italian American Foundation (The): 1536
National Press Foundation: 1750
National Restaurant Association Educational Foundation (The): 1715, 2419
National Security Education Program: 845, 846
National Society Daughters of the American Revolution: 1538, 1539, 1670, 2064, 2242, 2303, 376, 563
National Trust for Historic Preservation: 564
NEA Foundation (The): 1411, 1412
Organization of American States: 780, 876
Paralyzed Veterans of America Research and Education Foundations: 2304
Patterson (The Alicia) Foundation: 1754
PEN/Faulkner Foundation: 641
Pharmaceutical Research and Manufacturers of America Foundation, Inc.: 2072, 2073, 2074, 2292
Phi Beta Kappa Society (The): 1561, 1671, 643, 847, 986
President's Commission on White House Fellowships: 1804
Public Welfare Foundation, Inc.: 242
Radio Television Digital News Association Foundation: 1757

Replogle (Luther I.) Foundation: 1230
Reporters Committee for Freedom of the Press: 1758
Resources for the Future: 1981
RTCA: 2371
Rural Housing Service: 1924
Schork (Kurt) Memorial Fund: 1759
Scoville (Herbert, Jr.) Peace Fellowship: 781
Share Our Strength: 1358
Smithsonian Institution: 1648
Smithsonian National Air and Space Museum: 2372, 2373
Society for Science and the Public: 1649
Society for the Psychological Study of Social Issues (SPSSI) (The): 1680, 1681, 1682, 1683, 1684, 1685, 1686, 1687, 1688, 1689, 1690, 1691, 1692, 1693, 1807
Sons of Italy Foundation: 921
Subcommittee on Catholic Home Missions: 752
Swann Foundation for Caricature and Cartoon: 356
Taste and Smell Clinic: 2090
Truman (The Harry S.) Scholarship Foundation: 1810
U.S. Army Center of Military History: 588
U.S. Department of Agriculture: 1988
U.S. Department of Education: 1422, 1423, 1424, 1463, 1464, 1586, 1587, 1588, 1589, 1719, 607, 608, 609, 610, 787, 854, 956
U.S. Department of Health and Human Services: 1038, 1039, 1040, 1261, 2306, 957
U.S. Department of Health and Human Services/Administration for Children and Families/Office of Family Assistance: 1765
U.S. Department of Housing and Urban Development: 1262
U.S. Department of Justice: 1278, 1279, 1280
U.S. Department of Labor: 1766
U.S. Department of State, Fulbright Teacher Exchanges: 1425
U.S. Environmental Protection Agency: 1989
U.S. Institute of Peace: 788, 789, 790
United Negro College Fund (UNCF): 939
United States Holocaust Memorial Museum - Jack, Joseph and Morton Mandel Center for Advanced Holocaust Studies: 590
USDA - Rural Utilities Service: 1928
Wilson (Woodrow) International Center for Scholars: 361
Women's Congressional Policy Institute (WCPI): 995
Word Works, Inc. (The): 653, 654
World Learning Inc.: 792
Youth For Understanding USA: 868

Florida

A-T Children's Project: 1994
Able Trust (The): 882
American Academy of Optometry Foundation: 2254, 2255, 2256, 2257, 2258, 2259, 2260
American Association of Women Dentists: 2101
American Orchid Society: 1933
American Otological Society Research Foundation: 2261
AWS Foundation, Inc.: 2346, 2347, 2348, 2349
Broward Education Foundation: 1375
Bush (Edyth) Charitable Foundation, Inc.: 45
Chatlos Foundation, Inc. (The): 739
Chopin Foundation of the U.S.: 697
Cintas Foundation: 395
Community Foundation for Northeast Florida (The): 1103
Community Foundation for Palm Beach and Martin Counties: 1106
Community Foundation of Collier County: 1109
Davis (The Arthur Vining) Foundations: 85
Dunspaugh Dalton Foundation: 95
duPont (Jessie Ball) Fund: 96
Florida Department of Education: 1501, 1502, 932, 964
Florida Department of State, Division of Cultural Affairs: 405
Florida Education Fund: 1386
Foundation for Education and Research in Biofeedback and Related Sciences (FERB): 2327
Foundation for Science and Disability: 899
Gulf Coast Community Foundation: 1174
Health Foundation of South Florida: 1296
Inter American Press Association (IAPA): 1737
International Food Service Executives Association, Inc. (IFSEA): 2358
International Women's Fishing Association Scholarship Trust: 1868
Jacksonville Jaguars Foundation: 148
Knight (John S. and James L.) Foundation: 167
Koch Foundation, Inc.: 745
Lowe Syndrome Association: 2044
Macdonald (The Dr. John T.) Foundation, Inc.: 1021
Miami Foundation (The): 206

National Oceanic and Atmospheric Administration: 1873
National YoungArts Foundation: 434
Order Sons of Italy in America, Grand Lodge of Florida: 1559
Orlando Magic Youth Foundation: 1027
Peacock Foundation, Inc.: 234
Phi Alpha Theta History Honor Society: 576, 577, 578
Planning and Visual Education Partnership (The): 1564
Quantum Foundation: 1315
Radiant Peace Foundation International, Inc. (The): 1437
Skelly (Gertrude E.) Charitable Foundation: 1461
Southwest Florida Community Foundation: 1248
State Library and Archives of Florida: 682
Swedish Women's Educational Association Inc.: 785
Whitehall Foundation, Inc.: 1951

Georgia

American Academy of Religion: 734, 735
American Cancer Society, Inc.: 2178, 2179
Arthritis Foundation: 2200
Callaway Foundation, Inc.: 1080
Children's Literature Association: 618, 619
Coca-Cola Foundation, Inc. (The): 1379
Coca-Cola Scholars Foundation: 1493
Community Foundation for Greater Atlanta, Inc.: 1099
Community Foundation for Northeast Georgia: 1104
Costume Society of America: 400
Georgia Council for the Arts: 409
Georgia Library Association: 668
Georgia-Pacific Foundation: 123
Golden Key International Honour Society, Inc.: 1506
Hambidge: 411
Home Depot Foundation (The): 1179
Huebner (The S.S.) Foundation for Insurance Education: 1707
Institute of Industrial and Systems Engineers (IISE): 2392
National Black MBA Association: 1210, 937
South Atlantic Modern Language Association: 606
Tull Charitable Foundation, Inc.: 288
Whitehead (Joseph B.) Foundation: 1042
Woodruff (The Robert W.) Foundation: 301

Hawaii

Castle (Harold K.L.) Foundation: 53
Castle (Samuel N. and Mary) Foundation: 1429
East-West Center (The): 768, 769
Hawaii Community Foundation: 1177
Hawaii State Foundation on Culture and the Arts: 412

Idaho

Idaho Commission on the Arts: 415
Idaho Community Foundation: 143
Micron Technology Foundation, Inc.: 1886
State of Idaho Board of Education: 1577, 1578

Illinois

Academy of Nutrition and Dietetics Foundation (The): 2410
Actuarial Foundation (The): 1880, 1881, 1882
Allstate Foundation (The): 1332
Alzheimer's Association: 2203
American Academy of Implant Dentistry (AAID) Foundation: 2096
American Academy of Pediatrics: 2281
American Association of Law Libraries: 656, 657
American Association of School Librarians: 658
American Bandmasters Association (The): 689
American Bar Foundation: 1768, 883
American Brain Tumor Association: 2204
American Burn Association: 2293
American College of Legal Medicine: 1997
American Dental Hygienists' Association Institute for Oral Health: 2103
American Epilepsy Society (AES): 2205
American Institute of Indian Studies: 599, 802
American Library Association (ALA): 1443, 659
American Lung Association: 2133, 2134, 2135, 2136, 2137, 2138
American Medical Association Foundation: 1477
American Medical Women's Association, Inc.: 2002
American Nuclear Society (ANS): 1851, 2378, 2379, 2380, 2381, 2382, 2383
American Oil Chemists Society (AOCS): 1852

American Orthopaedic Society for Sports Medicine (AOSSM) (The): 2296, 2297
American Osteopathic Foundation: 2276
American Planning Association: 1051, 885
American Society of Safety Professionals: 2389
Appraisal Institute of Professional Resources: 1700
Argonne National Laboratory: 1622, 1623
ASCP: 2013
Baxter International Foundation (The): 32
Blair (William) and Company Foundation: 1069
Blowitz-Ridgeway Foundation: 1070
Brunswick Foundation, Inc.: 1076
Brunswick Public Foundation: 1960
Caterpillar Foundation: 1083
Charleston Area Charitable Foundation: 1088
Chicago Board of Trade Foundation: 1288
Chicago Community Trust (The): 1091
Civic Orchestra of Chicago: 698
Coin-Op Cares Charitable and Education Foundation: 2351
Coleman Foundation, Inc. (The): 63
Community Foundation of the Fox River Valley: 1124
Crossroads Fund: 1657
Dermatology Foundation: 2026
Dirksen Congressional Center (The): 1787
Donnelley (Gaylord and Dorothy) Foundation: 89
Dystonia Medical Research Foundation: 2210
Exelon Corporation: 103
Federation of American Consumers and Travelers: 1385, 1706
Field Foundation of Illinois: 106
Foundation for Anesthesia Education and Research: 2028
Foundation for Osteopathic Emergency Medicine: 2277
Foundation of the American College of Healthcare Executives (The): 1291
Foundation of the American Society of Neuroradiology (The): 2029
Fry (Lloyd A.) Foundation: 118
Graham Foundation for Advanced Studies in the Fine Arts: 373
Great Lakes Protection Fund: 1970
HIMSS Foundation: 2037
Illinois Clean Energy Community Foundation: 1973
Illinois Restaurant Association Educational Foundation: 1511
Illinois State Academy of Science: 1632
Immanuel Bible Foundation: 744
Institute for the International Education of Students (IES): 1514
Institute of Food Technologists Foundation: 2356
International College of Surgeons (ICS): 2040
International Foundation for Ethical Research, Inc. (IFER): 1633
Jewish Federation of Metropolitan Chicago Academic Scholarship Program: 1520
Journal of the American Medical Association: 1739
Joyce Foundation (The): 153
Kobe College Corporation-Japan Education Exchange: 837
Kraft Heinz Company Foundation (The): 171
Leukemia Research Foundation: 2192
MacArthur (John D. and Catherine T.) Foundation: 187
McCormick (Robert R.) Foundation: 191
Medical Library Association: 199, 673, 674, 875, 906
Millard (Adah K.) Charitable Trust: 209
Muscular Dystrophy Association: 2218
National Council of Teachers of English Research Foundation: 1407
National Dairy Council: 2418
National Headache Foundation: 2120
Neurosurgery Research and Education Foundation: 2225
Newberry Library (The): 341, 342, 343, 344, 345, 346, 347, 348, 349, 350, 351, 352, 572, 954
North American Spine Society (NASS): 2065
Northern Trust Corporation: 1213
Orthopaedic Research and Education Foundation: 2066, 2067, 2068
Pick (The Albert, Jr.) Fund: 238
Plastic Surgery Foundation (PSF): 2076
Precast/Prestressed Concrete Institute: 2403
Pulmonary Fibrosis Foundation: 2078
Radiological Society of North America Research and Education Foundation: 2079, 2080, 2081, 2082, 2083, 2084
Ragdale Foundation: 450
Rehabilitation Nursing Foundation (RNF): 2244
Rock Island Arsenal Museum: 580
Ronald McDonald House Charities: 1031
Rotary Foundation of Rotary International (The): 848
RRF Foundation for Aging: 919
Scholl (Dr.) Foundation: 257
Society of Actuaries (SOA): 1887

Society of Architectural Historians: 379, 380, 381, 382
Society of Cardiovascular Anesthesiologists: 2147
Society of Critical Care Medicine: 2089
Society of Women Engineers: 989
Spencer Foundation: 1418
Stone (W. Clement & Jessie V.) Foundation: 1439
Tree Research & Education Endowment Fund (TREE Fund): 1925
University of Illinois at Urbana-Champaign: 522
USG Foundation, Inc.: 290
Woods Fund Chicago: 1275
Zonta Foundation for Women: 1722, 1846, 998

Indiana

Ball Brothers Foundation: 27
Ball (George and Frances) Foundation: 28
Central Indiana Community Foundation: 1085
Community Foundation of Saint Joseph County: 1120
Contemporary Music Festival: 699
Cummins Foundation, Inc. (The): 82
Cushwa Center for the Study of American Catholicism: 535, 536, 537, 538, 539
Dearborn Community Foundation, Inc.: 1138
DePauw University International Bonner Scholarship: 1141
Health Foundation of Greater Indianapolis, Inc. (The): 1295, 1337
History of Science Society: 547, 548
Indiana Arts Commission: 416
Indiana Commission for Higher Education, Division of Student Financial Aid: 1512
Indiana Library Federation: 670
Lawrence County Community Foundation: 1193
Lilly Endowment Inc.: 181
Lincoln Financial Foundation: 182
Lumina Foundation: 1456
National Federation of Music Clubs: 714, 715, 716
Percussive Arts Society: 722
Pulliam Journalism Fellowship: 1755
Sigma Theta Tau International: 2246
Society for Pediatric Dermatology: 2285
Unity Foundation of LaPorte County (The): 1263
Wabash Center for Teaching and Learning in Theology and Religion (The): 754

Iowa

Carver (Roy J.) Charitable Trust: 1447
Greater Cedar Rapids Community Foundation (The): 1165
Hoover Presidential Foundation: 1793
International Association for Food Protection: 2415
Iowa Arts Council: 418
McElroy (R.J.) Trust: 1022
National Farmer's Organization: 1920
P.E.O. Sisterhood: 877
Principal Financial Group Foundation Inc.: 241
Quill and Scroll Foundation: 1756
Soil and Water Conservation Society: 1984, 1985, 1986
University of Iowa (The): 649

Kansas

Eisenhower Foundation (The): 1789
Hutchinson Community Foundation: 414
Jellison Benevolent Society: 1399
Kansas Board of Regents: 1521
Kansas Health Foundation: 1304
Pi Gamma Mu, International Honor Society in Social Science: 1562
SkillBuilders Fund: 988
United Methodist Health Ministry Fund: 1363
University of Kansas Child Language Doctoral Program: 1606
Wichita Community Foundation: 1273

Kentucky

Aviation Insurance Association (AIA): 2367
Brown (James Graham) Foundation, Inc.: 42
Community Foundation of Louisville, Inc. (The): 397
Cooke (V.V.) Foundation: 74
Foundation for the Tri-State Community, Inc.: 1158
Gheens Foundation, Inc. (The): 124
Grayson-Jockey Club Research Foundation (The): 2034
Kentucky Arts Council: 420

Kentucky Foundation for Women: 979
Kentucky Higher Education Assistance Authority (KHEAA): 1522, 1523
Kentucky Historical Society: 552
Presbyterian Church (U.S.A.): 1565, 1566, 750

Louisiana

ASPRS - The Imaging and Geospatial Information Society: 1821
Baton Rouge Area Foundation: 393
Booth-Bricker Fund (The): 41
Brown (The Joe W. and Dorothy Dorsett) Foundation: 43
Greater New Orleans Foundation (The): 1171
Historic New Orleans Collection (The): 544, 545
Honor Society of Phi Kappa Phi (The): 1509
Louisiana Division of the Arts, Department of Culture, Recreation and Tourism: 422, 423
Zigler (Fred B. and Ruth B.) Foundation: 1427

Maine

Burnham (The Margaret E.) Charitable Trust: 44
Central Maine Power Company: 54
Hannaford Charitable Foundation: 1391
Haystack Mountain School of Crafts: 413
King (Stephen and Tabitha) Foundation: 164
Libra Foundation: 180
Maine Arts Commission: 425
Maine Initiatives: 1344
Maine Osteopathic Association: 2278
Morton-Kelly Charitable Trust (The): 1207
Mulford (The Clarence E.) Trust: 212
Oak Grove School Foundation: 1416
Switzer (The Robert & Patricia) Foundation: 1987

Maryland

Abell Foundation, Inc. (The): 1
Agency for Healthcare Research and Quality (AHRQ): 1281
American Catholic Historical Association: 525, 736, 737, 738
American Dental Assistants Association: 2102
American Gastroenterological Association (AGA): 2149, 2150, 2151, 2152, 2153, 2154, 2155, 2156, 2157, 2158, 2159, 2160, 2161
American Institute of Physics: 1888
American Kidney Fund: 2000, 2001
American Nurses Foundation: 2235
American Porphyria Foundation (The): 2003
American Speech-Language-Hearing Foundation: 2262
Ames (The Kathryn) Foundation: 756
AMVETS: 1479
Aplastic Anemia and MDS International Foundation: 2011
ASPEN Rhoads Research Foundation: 2162
Association of Writers & Writing Programs (The): 614
Association on American Indian Affairs: 944
Bainum Family Foundation: 1000
Baker (The William G., Jr.) Memorial Fund: 392
Baltimore Community Foundation: 29
Blaustein (Jacob and Hilda) Foundation: 893
Bright Focus Foundation: 1284, 2207, 2264
Campbell Foundation, Inc.: 1004
Carson Scholars Fund, Inc. (The): 1490
Community Foundation of Frederick County, MD, Inc. (The): 1111
Community Foundation of the Eastern Shore: 1123
Cystic Fibrosis Foundation: 2167
Early American Industries Association, Inc.: 2352
England (Lois and Richard) Family Foundation: 1013
Epilepsy Foundation of America: 2211
Foundation for Spirituality and Medicine (The): 1290
Goldseker Foundation: 1162
Grass Foundation (The): 2212
Health Resources and Services Administration: 1394, 2035
Immune Deficiency Foundation: 903
International Association of Ice Cream Distributors and Vendors (IAICDV): 1396
International Order of Alhambra: 2300
Johns Hopkins Center for Alternatives to Animal Testing (The): 1303
Kerr (Grayce B.) Fund, Inc.: 162
Knott (Marion I. and Henry J.) Foundation, Inc.: 168
Leidy (The John J.) Foundation: 1194
Life Sciences Research Foundation (LSRF): 1940
Loats Foundation, Inc. (The): 183
Marriott International, Inc.: 190

Maryland Higher Education Commission: 1530
Maryland Institute College of Art: 509
Maryland State Arts Council: 427
Mid Atlantic Arts: 430
Nasdaq Foundation: 1713
National Black Nurses Association, Inc.: 2240
National Blood Foundation, A Program of AABB: 2142
National Council for the Social Studies: 1665, 1666, 1667, 1668
National Eye Institute: 2274, 2275
National Federation of the Blind: 910
National Health Service Corps (NHSC): 1309
National Heart, Lung and Blood Institute (NHLBI): 2121, 2143, 2144
National Home Library Foundation: 677
National Institute of Dental and Craniofacial Research (NIDCR): 2106, 2107, 2108
National Institute of General Medical Sciences: 2052, 2053, 2054
National Institute of Mental Health: 1669, 2331
National Institute of Neurological Disorders and Stroke: 2221
National Institute of Nursing Research: 2241
National Institute of Standards and Technology, Fire Research Division: 1825
National Institute on Aging: 1310
National Institute on Alcohol Abuse and Alcoholism: 1311, 1312
National Institute on Drug Abuse: 1408
National Institute on Minority Health and Health Disparities: 912
National Institutes of Health: 2055, 2056, 2057, 2058, 2059, 2060, 2061, 879
National Oceanic and Atmospheric Administration: 1409, 1640, 1872, 1874
National Orchestral Institute: 718
National Society of Professional Surveyors (NSPS): 2397, 2398, 2399
National Society of Professional Surveyors (NSPS) American Association for Geodetic Surveying (AAGS): 2400, 2401
Open Society Institute - Baltimore: 1217, 1351
Osteogenesis Imperfecta Foundation: 2069
PFD Research Foundation: 1897
Rosenberg (Henry and Ruth Blaustein) Foundation: 1233
Shriver (Eunice Kennedy) National Institute of Child Health and Human Development: 1318
Smithsonian Environmental Research Center (SERC): 1983
Society for Developmental Biology: 1948
Society of Physics Students: 1573, 1891, 1892, 1893
Space Telescope Science Institute: 1845
Substance Abuse and Mental Health Services Administration, Disaster Technical Assistance Center: 2340
Systems Plus, Inc.: 2405, 2406
Towson University: 648
U.S. Department of Health and Human Services: 1323, 1324, 2247, 2252
U.S. Department of the Navy: 2091
Weinberg (The Harry and Jeanette) Foundation, Inc.: 1271

Massachusetts

Abelard Foundation-East (The): 1329
Alden (George I.) Trust: 8
Alden (The John W.) Trust: 999
American Antiquarian Society (AAS): 304, 305
American Association for Hand Surgery: 1996
American Institute for Sri Lankan Studies (AISLS): 799, 800
American Meteorological Society: 2365
Archaeological Institute of America: 1445, 1480, 309, 310, 311, 312, 313, 757
Armenian Relief Society of Eastern U.S.A., Inc.: 887
Association for Library and Information Science Education (ALISE): 660, 661
Austro-American Association of Boston: 759
Barr Foundation: 1065
Bayrd (Adelaide Breed) Foundation: 33
Boston Foundation (The): 1073
Boston Women's Fund: 972
Brigham and Women's Hospital: 1283
Cabot Family Charitable Trust: 46
Codman (The Ogden) Trust: 61
Community Foundation of Western Massachusetts (CFWM): 1129
Connecticut Library Association: 665
Davis (Irene E. and George A.) Foundation: 1137
Earthwatch Institute: 1625, 1626
Eastern Bank Charitable Foundation: 97
Enterprise Community Partners: 371
Essex County Community Foundation: 1153

Farm Aid: 1908
Fine Arts Work Center in Provincetown: 502
FRAXA Research Foundation: 2032
Fromm Music Foundation at Harvard: 705
FSHD Society, Inc.: 2033
Harbus Foundation: 1392
Harvard Travellers Club, Permanent Fund: 1631
Health Effects Institute (HEI): 1294
Henderson Foundation: 135
Hood (Charles H.) Foundation, Inc.: 2283
Hyams Foundation, Inc. (The): 1340
Institute for Quantitative Social Science, Harvard University: 1663
International OCD Foundation: 2328
Jacob's Pillow, Inc.: 487, 488
Kelley (Edward Bangs) & Elza Kelley Foundation, Inc.: 1188
Kennedy (John F.) Library Foundation: 159
Kennedy (John F.) Presidential Library: 160
Lalor Foundation, Inc. (The): 1634, 2250
Laspau, Inc.: 874
LEF Foundation (The): 374
Lindsay (The Agnes M.) Trust: 1019
Marine Biological Laboratory: 1941
Mass Humanities: 332
Massachusetts Historical Society (The): 555, 556, 557, 558
Massachusetts Institute of Technology: 1743
Massachusetts Medical Society (MMS): 1531
Massachusetts Office of Student Financial Assistance: 1532
Medieval Academy of America (The): 559
Merck Family Fund: 202
MilliporeSigma: 210
Museum of Comparative Zoology: 1943
Myasthenia Gravis Foundation of America, Inc.: 2219
Nantucket Historical Association: 561
Nellie Mae Education Foundation: 1413
New England Biolabs Foundation: 215
New England Foundation for the Arts: 437
New England Regional Fellowship Consortium: 565
NICSA: 1414
Nieman Foundation for Journalism at Harvard: 1751, 1752, 1753
Peabody (Amelia) Charitable Fund: 233
Piper Fund: 1803
Radcliffe Institute for Advanced Study, Harvard University: 1460
Reebok Foundation (The): 245
Riley (The Mabel Louise) Foundation: 1417
Rotch Travelling Scholarship in Architecture: 377
Russell (Josephine G.) Trust: 1317
Sailors' Snug Harbor of Boston: 1356
School of the Museum of Fine Arts at Tufts University, Boston: 517
Scleroderma Foundation: 2086
Smith Family Awards Program for Excellence in Biomedical Research: 2087
Smith (Horace) Fund: 1571
Smithsonian Astrophysical Observatory: 1843, 1844
State Street Foundation: 271
Stearns (Artemas W.) Trust: 1322
Stevens (The Abbot and Dorothy H.) Foundation: 1251
Stevens (The Nathaniel and Elizabeth P.) Foundation: 1252
Stoddard Charitable Trust (The): 1361
Sudbury Foundation: 1253
Thompson (Thomas) Trust: 1257
Tomfohrde (John H. and H. Naomi) Foundation: 282
Two Ten Footwear Foundation: 1584, 1585
Ukrainian Research Institute at Harvard University: 358, 359
Unitarian Universalist Association of Congregations: 460
University Film and Video Association: 1761
Webster (Edwin S.) Foundation: 294
Wellesley College: 991, 992
Wharton (William P.) Trust: 1830
Woods Hole Oceanographic Institution: 1654

Michigan

Albion Community Foundation: 1045
Alger Regional Community Foundation: 1047
Allegan County Community Foundation: 1048
American Matthay Association for Piano: 690
American Oriental Society: 496
Ann Arbor Area Community Foundation: 1057
Baraga County Community Foundation: 1063
Battle Creek Community Foundation: 31
Berrien Community Foundation: 36

Binc Foundation: 38
Capital Region Community Foundation: 1081
Community Foundation for Northeast Michigan: 1105
Community Foundation for Southeast Michigan: 67
Community Foundation of Greater Rochester: 1115
Community Foundation of the Holland/Zeeland Area (The): 69
Consumers Energy Foundation: 73
Cook Family Foundation: 1133
Dickinson Area Community Foundation: 1142
Ford (Gerald R.) Presidential Library: 1790, 1791
Ford Motor Company Fund and Community Services: 113
Frey Foundation: 116
Gerber Foundation (The): 1015
Grand Haven Area Community Foundation: 1164
Grand Rapids Community Foundation: 129
Great Lakes Colleges Association New Writers Awards: 620
Hess (Myrtle E. and William G.) Charitable Trust: 902
Hess (William G. and Myrtle E.) Charitable Trust: 1395
Hillsdale County Community Foundation: 1178
Hudson-Webber Foundation: 1181
Kantzler Foundation (The): 1187
Kappa Omicron Nu Honor Society: 2416
Kellogg (W.K.) Foundation: 157
Keweenaw Community Foundation: 1190
Kresge Foundation (The): 172
Livingston Awards: 1741
M & M Area Community Foundation: 1197
Marshall Community Foundation: 1404
McGregor Fund: 194
Michigan Council for Arts and Cultural Affairs: 428
Michigan Gateway Community Foundation: 1203
Michigan Society of Fellows: 334
Michigan State University: 844
Michigan State University, The Graduate School: 907
Michigan Women Forward: 981
Mott (Charles Stewart) Foundation: 1208
National Mole Day Foundation: 1859
National Opera Association, Inc.: 717
Pardee (The Elsa U.) Foundation: 2194
Petoskey-Harbor Springs Area Community Foundation: 1222
Roberts (Forest) Theatre: 492
Saginaw Community Foundation: 1236
Skillman Foundation (The): 263
SME-EF (Society of Manufacturing Engineers Education Foundation): 2361
State of Michigan Department of Treasury: 1579, 1580
Steelcase Foundation: 273
Towsley (The Harry A. and Margaret D.) Foundation: 285
University of Michigan: 1763
Upjohn (W.E.) Institute for Employment Research: 1767
Wege Foundation: 1270
Wilson (Matilda R.) Fund: 300
Wilson Ornithological Society: 1952
Woman's National Farm & Garden Association, Inc.: 1929

Minnesota

American Swedish Institute (The): 819
Andersen Corporate Foundation (The): 1053
Andersen (Fred C. and Katherine B.) Foundation: 1054
Andersen (Hugh J.) Foundation: 1055
Arts Midwest: 483
Athwin Foundation: 21
Babbage (Charles) Institute: 2350
Bremer (Otto) Trust: 1074
Butler (Patrick and Aimee) Family Foundation: 1078
CommunityGiving: 1131
Conference Board of the Mathematical Sciences: 1884
Dell (Chief Justice Roger L.) and Agnes C. Dell Charitable Trust: 1140
Deluxe Corporation Foundation: 86
Duluth Superior Area Community Foundation: 1145
Ecolab Foundation: 1150
Forecast Public Art: 406
Fuller (H.B.) Company Foundation: 1014
Graco Foundation (The): 1163
Hallett Charitable Trusts (The): 1451
Jerome Foundation, Inc.: 419
Land O'Lakes Foundation: 176, 177
Marbrook Foundation: 188
Mayo Clinic: 2049

McKnight Endowment Fund for Neuroscience (The): 2214
McKnight Foundation (The): 1346
Medtronic Foundation: 200
Minneapolis Foundation (The): 1204
Minnesota Department of Education: 676
National Association of Geoscience Teachers: 1870
National Ataxia Foundation: 2220
National Council on Family Relations: 1350
Northwest Minnesota Foundation (The): 1214
Ordean Foundation (The): 1218
Phillips (Jay and Rose) Family Foundation of Minnesota: 1353
Playwrights' Center (The): 645
Porter (Irwin Andrew) Foundation: 239
RBC Foundation - U.S.A.: 1228
Rochester Area Foundation: 1231
3M Foundation, Inc.: 281
U.S. Bancorp Foundation: 1260
University of Minnesota: 462, 650
University of Oslo International Summer School: 857
Wasie Foundation (The): 293
Women's Foundation of Minnesota: 996
Xcel Energy Foundation: 302

Mississippi

Foundation for the Mid South: 1157
Hardin (The Phil) Foundation: 1393
University of Southern Mississippi (The): 651

Missouri

Aircraft Electronics Association (AEA): 2363
Bayer Fund: 1066
BlueScope Foundation North America (The): 40
Caleres Cares Charitable Trust: 48
Community Foundation of the Ozarks: 1126
Consortium for Graduate Study in Management (The): 1701
Greater Kansas City Community Foundation: 1169
Hall Family Foundation: 132
Investigative Reporters and Editors: 1738
Kappa Tau Alpha: 1740
Knights of Columbus Vatican Film Library at St. Louis University: 623
Lutheran Foundation of St. Louis: 746
McDonnell (James S.) Foundation: 193
Mid-America Arts Alliance: 429
Missouri Department of Higher Education and Workforce Development: 1533, 1534
National Association of Farm Broadcasters Foundation: 1744
Post-Polio Health International: 2077
Press Club of St. Louis Charitable Fund - St. Louis Press Club (The): 1567
Reproductive Scientist Development Program (RSDP): 2251
Saigh Foundation (The): 1032
Sunnen Foundation: 1362
Truman (Harry S.) Library Institute: 1809
Veterans of Foreign Wars Auxiliary: 467
Washington University in St. Louis: 1612, 1613, 383
Whitaker Foundation: 473

Montana

Housing Education and Research Association (HERA): 1180
Montana Community Foundation: 1206
National Taxidermists Association: 913
Washington (Dennis & Phyllis) Foundation: 1268

Nebraska

Abel Foundation: 1043
Cooper Foundation: 75
Heuermann (B. Keith & Norma F.) Foundation: 136
Mid-Nebraska Community Foundation, Inc.: 208
Nebraska Arts Council: 435
Nebraska's Coordinating Commission for Postsecondary Education: 1544
Omaha Community Foundation: 223
Sowers Club of Nebraska Foundation: 269
Union Pacific Foundation: 289
University of Nebraska at Omaha: 1720
Woods Charitable Fund, Inc.: 1274

Nevada

Davidson Institute: 1497
Nevada Arts Council: 436
Redfield (The Nell J.) Foundation: 244
Wiegand (E. L.) Foundation: 299

New Hampshire

American Ground Water Trust: 2344
Bean (Norwin S. and Elizabeth N.) Foundation: 1067
Dartmouth College: 897
MacDowell: 424
New Hampshire Library Association: 678
New Hampshire State Council on the Arts: 438

New Jersey

American Accordion Musicological Society: 688
American Association for the History of Nursing, Inc.: 2234
American School of Classical Studies at Athens: 389, 809, 810, 811, 812, 813, 814, 815, 816, 817
Atran Foundation, Inc.: 23
Autism Speaks Inc.: 2014
Campbell Soup Foundation: 49
Capezio/Ballet Makers Dance Foundation, Inc.: 485
Darrin (Margaret A.) Charitable Trust: 84
Davis (Shelby Cullom) Center for Historical Studies: 540
Dodge (Geraldine R.) Foundation: 87
Dow Jones News Fund (The): 1733
Educational Testing Service: 1384
Electrochemical Society (The): 1627, 1628
Ernst & Young Foundation: 1705
Foundation for Neonatal Research and Education (FNRE): 2238
General Commission on Archives and History of The United Methodist Church: 742
Graduate Women in Science: 1630
Higher Education Student Assistance Authority (The): 1507, 1508
Histiocytosis Association: 2115
Horowitz Foundation for Social Policy (The): 1661
Hyde and Watson Foundation (The): 142
IEEE History Center: 549
Institute for Advanced Study: 1662
Institute for Citizens & Scholars: 1513
International Foundation (The): 774
Johnson & Johnson Family of Companies: 149
Johnson (Robert Wood) Foundation: 2042
Kirby (F.M.) Foundation, Inc.: 165
KPMG Foundation: 1710
Laurie (The Blanche and Irving) Foundation: 179
MCJ Amelior Foundation (The): 1023
National Poetry Series (The): 626
New Jersey Department of Military and Veterans Affairs: 1545, 1546
New Jersey Historic Trust: 566, 567
New Jersey Historical Commission: 568, 569, 570
New Jersey Library Association: 679
New Jersey Office of the Secretary of Higher Education (OSHE): 1547
New Jersey Osteopathic Education Foundation: 2279
New Jersey State Council on the Arts: 439
Newcombe (The Charlotte W.) Foundation: 1552
Princeton Area Community Foundation: 1225
Reeve (Christopher & Dana) Foundation: 2305
Schumann Fund for New Jersey (The): 1033
Seay (George J. and Effie L.) Memorial Trust: 1357
Sprague (Seth) Educational and Charitable Foundation: 270
Subaru of America Foundation, Inc.: 1419
Turrell Fund: 1037
UNICO National, Inc.: 1591
Verizon Foundation: 291
Victoria Foundation, Inc.: 1266
Wetlands Institute (The): 1950
Wiley Foundation, Inc. (The): 1901

New Mexico

Albuquerque Community Foundation: 1046
American Indian Graduate Center: 941
American Society for Mass Spectrometry: 1820
Bynner (The Witter) Foundation for Poetry, Inc.: 616
Catching the Dream: 951
Frost Foundation, Ltd. (The): 117

Los Alamos National Laboratory: 1635
New Mexico Arts: 440
New Mexico Foundation: 1212
New Mexico Library Association: 680
NewMexicoWomen.org: 914
Roswell Artist-in-Residence Program: 515
Santa Fe Community Foundation: 920
School for Advanced Research: 1814, 1815
Wurlitzer (The Helene) Foundation of New Mexico: 478

New York

Achelis and Bodman Foundation (The): 4
Adams (Emma J.) Memorial Fund, Inc.: 1330
AFS Intercultural Programs/USA: 793
Alliance for Young Artists & Writers (The): 386
Altman Foundation: 1049
Alzheimer's Drug Discovery Foundation: 1995
America-Israel Cultural Foundation: 869
American Academy in Rome: 1956, 303
American Academy of Arts and Letters: 687
American Council of Learned Societies: 306
American Federation for Aging Research (AFAR): 1998, 1999
American Foundation for Suicide Prevention (The): 1364, 1365, 1366, 1367
American Geriatrics Society: 2294
American Institute of Chemical Engineers (AIChE): 1618, 2377
American Jewish Joint Distribution Committee (The): 803
American Museum of Natural History (The): 1619, 1620, 1932
American Musicological Society: 691, 692
American Numismatic Society (The): 307
American Parkinson Disease Association, Inc.: 2206
American-Scandinavian Foundation (The): 1444, 611, 808
American Society of Mechanical Engineers Auxiliary, Inc. (The): 2387
American Vacuum Society (AVS): 1889
Andrus Family Fund: 1056
Architectural League of New York: 369, 370
Armenian General Benevolent Union: 1481
ASCAP Foundation (The): 612, 694
Asian American Writers' Workshop: 613
Asian Cultural Council: 391
Association for Behavioral and Cognitive Therapies: 2321, 2322
Astraea Lesbian Foundation for Justice: 888, 889, 890
Bibliographical Society of America: 1374
Brain & Behavior Research Foundation: 2323
Brookhaven Women in Science: 973
Brooks (Gladys) Foundation: 1075
Cancer Research Institute: 2182, 2183, 2184, 2185
Carnegie Corporation of New York: 51
Carnegie Fund for Authors: 617
Carvel (Thomas and Agnes) Foundation: 1005
Center for LGBTQ Studies (The): 895
Center for Photography at Woodstock (The): 498
Central New York Community Foundation: 1086
Chamber Music America: 696
Chapin (Harry) Foundation: 1087
Chautauqua Region Community Foundation (The): 1089
Children's Leukemia Research Association: 2282
Children's Tumor Foundation: 2114
Chinese American Medical Society: 2024
Churchill (Winston) Foundation of the United States: 823
City of New York: 1786
Claiborne (Liz) Art Ortenberg Foundation: 1962
Clark Foundation (The): 1492
Clark (Robert Sterling) Foundation: 1092
Columbia Journalism School: 1726, 1727, 1728
Columbia University: 1729, 1730, 1937, 533
Commonwealth Fund (The): 1335
Community Foundation for Greater Buffalo: 1100
Community Foundation for the Greater Capital Region (The): 1107, 1380
Community Foundation of Herkimer & Oneida Counties, Inc. (The): 1116
Community Foundations of the Hudson Valley: 1130
Cooley's Anemia Foundation, Inc.: 2165
Cooperstown Graduate Program: 666
Copland (Aaron) Fund for Music, Inc.: 700
Cornell University: 323, 324
Corporation of Yaddo (The): 399
Council for European Studies at Columbia University: 762
Council on Foreign Relations: 1732, 763, 764, 765
Crohn's and Colitis Foundation: 2166
Cummings (The Nathan) Foundation, Inc.: 81

CurePSP, Inc.: 2208
Dana Foundation (The): 2025
Daughters of the Cincinnati: 1496
Delmas (Gladys Krieble) Foundation: 325
Dodge (The Cleveland H.) Foundation, Inc.: 1010
Douglass (Frederick) Institute for African and African-American Studies: 1383
Dow Jones Foundation: 91
Dreyfus (The Jean and Louis) Foundation, Inc.: 1144
Duke (Doris) Charitable Foundation: 93
Dysautonomia Foundation, Inc.: 2209
Dystrophic Epidermolysis Bullosa Research Association of America, Inc. (debra): 2095
Eastman School of Music of the University of Rochester: 702
Ellis (Albert) Institute: 2326
Emerson (Fred L.) Foundation, Inc.: 1152
Episcopal Church Foundation: 740
Fenimore Art Museum: 404, 541
Fight For Sight, Inc.: 2267, 2268
Fisher (Avery) Artist Program: 703
Fitch (The James Marston) Charitable Foundation: 372
Ford Foundation (The): 112
Foundation of Flexographic Technical Association (The): 2354
Foundation of the National Student Nurses' Association, Inc.: 2239
4A's: 900
Fox (The Michael J.) Foundation for Parkinson's Research: 2030
Freeman Foundation: 114
Garden Club of America (The): 1909, 1910, 1911, 1912, 1913, 1914, 1915, 1966, 1967, 1968, 1969
German Academic Exchange Service: 830
Gifford Foundation (The): 1160
Glaucoma Foundation (The): 2269
Gloeckner (The Fred C.) Foundation, Inc.: 1916
Goldman (Herman) Foundation: 125
Gottlieb (Adolph and Esther) Foundation, Inc.: 504
Graham (Martha) School of Contemporary Dance, Inc.: 486
Grant (The William T.) Foundation: 1016
Graves (Nancy) Foundation: 410
Greenburg-May Foundation: 2190
Guggenheim (The Harry Frank) Foundation: 1658, 1659
Guggenheim (John Simon) Memorial Foundation: 130
Hartford (The John A.) Foundation, Inc.: 134
Hastings Center (The): 1895
Hayden (Charles) Foundation: 1018
Hearing Health Foundation: 2271
Hillman (The Sidney) Foundation, Inc.: 1736
Hudson River Foundation (The): 1972
Hugoton Foundation: 1300
Human Growth Foundation: 2284
Humanities New York: 329
Huntington's Disease Society of America, Inc.: 2213
IBM Thomas J. Watson Research Center: 1885
Institute of International Education: 832
Italian American Studies Association: 551
Ittleson Foundation, Inc.: 1341
Japan Foundation, New York (The): 775
Japan Information Center: 834, 835
JDRF International: 2169, 2170, 2171
Jewish Book Council: 621
Jones (Daisy Marquis) Foundation: 152
Kaplan (The J.M.) Fund, Inc.: 154
Kate Spade New York Foundation: 155
Klingenstein Center for Independent School Leadership: 1433
Klingenstein Third Generation Foundation (The): 2329
Kosciuszko Foundation, Inc. (The): 1525, 1526, 708, 838, 839, 840, 841
Kress (Samuel H.) Foundation: 506
Langeloth (The Jacob and Valeria) Foundation: 2043
Leschetizky Association, Inc. (The): 710
Leukemia & Lymphoma Society (The): 2116, 2117, 2118
Light Work: 507
Link Foundation: 1823
Littauer (The Lucius N.) Foundation, Inc.: 904
Local Initiatives Support Corporation: 1195
Long Island Community Foundation: 1196
Luce (The Henry) Foundation, Inc.: 185
Lymphoma Research Foundation: 2119
Macy (Josiah Jr.) Foundation: 2046
Mapplethorpe (Robert) Foundation, Inc.: 426
Marfan Foundation (The): 2273
Marketing EDGE: 1711

Mellon (The Andrew W.) Foundation: 201
Memorial Foundation for Jewish Culture: 749
MetLife Foundation: 203
Metropolitan Museum of Art (The): 510, 511, 675
Millay Colony for the Arts, Inc. (The): 431
Mizuho USA Foundation, Inc.: 1205
MLB-MLBPA Youth Development Foundation: 1025
Modern Language Association of America: 602, 603
Money for Women/Barbara Deming Memorial Fund, Inc.: 982
Mount Vernon Hotel Museum & Garden: 560
Ms. Foundation for Women: 983
Muste (A.J.) Memorial Institute: 1349
NAACP Legal Defense and Educational Fund, Inc. (The): 934
National Association of Scholars: 1457
National Football League Foundation: 1211
National Hemophilia Foundation (The): 2051
National Kidney Foundation: 2176
National Medical Fellowships, Inc.: 2062
National Multiple Sclerosis Society: 2222, 2223
Naumburg (The Walter W.) Foundation, Inc.: 719
New Dramatists: 489
New Music USA: 720
New York Community Trust (The): 216
New York Foundation for the Arts: 441
New York Landmarks Conservancy: 571
New York Sea Grant: 1978
New York State Assembly Intern Committee: 1799, 1800
New York State Council on the Arts: 442
New York State Education Department: 1548
New York State Higher Education Services Corporation: 1549, 1550, 1551
New York State Senate: 1801, 1802
Northeast Agricultural Education Foundation: 1921
Northeastern Loggers' Association, Inc.: 1922, 1923
Northern Chautauqua Community Foundation: 1554
Noyes (Jessie Smith) Foundation: 1979
Nurses Educational Funds, Inc.: 2243
Oishei (The John R.) Foundation: 222
Open Meadows Foundation: 985
Oxalosis and Hyperoxaluria Foundation: 2070
Parapsychology Foundation, Inc.: 2334, 2335, 2336
Parkinson's Foundation: 2226, 2227, 2228, 2229, 2230, 2231, 2232
PEN America: 490, 605, 627, 628, 629, 630, 631, 632, 633, 634, 635, 636, 637, 638, 639, 640
PepsiCo Foundation: 236
Pforzheimer (The Carl and Lily) Foundation, Inc.: 237
Pinkerton Foundation (The): 1029
Pollock-Krasner Foundation, Inc. (The): 514
Potts Memorial Foundation (The): 2145
Princess Grace Foundation-USA: 491
ProLiteracy Worldwide: 1226
Rasmussen (V. Kann) Foundation: 1877
Revson (The Charles H.) Foundation: 246
Robinson (Jackie) Foundation (JRF): 918
Rochester Area Community Foundation: 987
Rockefeller Archive Center: 581
Rockefeller Family Fund: 250
Roosevelt (Franklin D.) Library and Museum: 582
Runyon (Damon) Cancer Research Foundation: 2196
Sage (Russell) Foundation: 1674
St. Andrew's Society of the State of New York: 849
Samuels (The Fan Fox and Leslie R.) Foundation, Inc.: 254
Schomburg Center for Research in Black Culture, New York Public Library (The): 353
Shubert Foundation, Inc. (The): 493
Skin Cancer Foundation (The): 2197
Skowhegan School of Painting and Sculpture: 518
Sloan (Alfred P.) Foundation: 1828, 264
Smith (W. Eugene) Memorial Fund: 519
Smithers (The Christopher D.) Foundation, Inc.: 1321
Snow (The John Ben) Foundation, Inc.: 268
Social Science Research Council: 782, 783, 784
Society of American Historians (The): 585
Sony Corporation of America: 1438
Soros (The Paul & Daisy) Fellowships for New Americans: 1574
Steele-Reese Foundation (The): 1250
Surdna Foundation Inc.: 276
Syracuse University: 1581, 1582, 647
Taraknath DAS Foundation: 1462
Tinker Foundation Inc.: 786
Toshiba America Foundation: 1440
Tourette Association of America, Inc.: 2233

Tucker (The Richard) Music Foundation, Inc.: 730
United Hospital Fund of New York: 1325
United Jewish Appeal-Federation of Jewish Philanthropies of New York: 753
United States-Japan Foundation: 791
van Ameringen Foundation, Inc.: 2341
Wagner College: 494
Wallace Foundation (The): 292
Watson (Jeannette K.) Fellowship: 1467
Watson (Thomas J.) Fellowship Program: 1468
Weeden Foundation: 1993
Weill (Kurt) Foundation for Music: 471
Wenner-Gren Foundation for Anthropological Research, Inc.: 1817, 1818
Whitney (The Helen Hay) Foundation: 1653
Women's Sports Foundation: 997
Women's Studio Workshop (WSW): 475, 476, 477
YIVO Institute for Jewish Research: 594, 595, 596, 597
Young Concert Artists, Inc.: 732

North Carolina

Albright Institute of Archaeological Research (AIAR): 794
American Chestnut Foundation (The): 1902
American Dance Festival: 481
American Institute of Certified Public Accountants (AICPA): 1369, 1695, 1696, 1697, 1698, 1699
American Schlafhorst Foundation: 13
Association of International Certified Professional Accountants (The Association): 1485
Babcock (Mary Reynolds) Foundation: 24
Belk Foundation (The): 1428
Burroughs Wellcome Fund: 2016
Cannon Foundation, Inc. (The): 50
Cattell (James McKeen) Fund: 2324
Cemala Foundation (The): 1378
Community Foundation of Greater Greensboro: 1114
Community Foundation of Western North Carolina (The): 70
Coordinating Council for Women in History, Inc. (The): 534, 975
Covington (Marion Stedman) Foundation: 77
Duke Endowment (The): 94
Duncan (The John G.) Trust: 1146
Fletcher (A.J.) Foundation: 110
Foundation for the Carolinas: 1156
Hillsdale Fund, Inc.: 138
Hughes (Mabel Y.) Charitable Trust: 141
Kellenberger (May Gordon Latham) Historical Foundation: 156
Kenan (William R., Jr.) Charitable Trust: 1400
Mebane Charitable Foundation, Inc.: 1024
Museum of Early Southern Decorative Arts (MESDA): 512
National AMBUCS, Inc.: 2301
National Humanities Center: 340
National Institute of Environmental Health Sciences: 1976
NBCC Foundation, Inc.: 1543
North Carolina Arts Council: 443
North Carolina Association of Educators: 1459
North Carolina Community Foundation: 220
North Carolina GlaxoSmithKline Foundation: 1415
North Carolina Library Association: 681
North Carolina State Education Assistance Authority/College Foundation of North Carolina: 1553
Outer Banks Community Foundation: 1220
Reynolds (Kate B.) Charitable Trust: 1355
Reynolds (Z. Smith) Foundation, Inc.: 247
Salisbury-Rowan Community Foundation: 253
Sigma Alpha Iota Philanthropies, Inc.: 728
Sigma Xi: The Scientific Research Honor Society: 1647
Triangle Community Foundation: 1421
Truist Foundation: 286
U.S. Army Research Office: 1651
United Arts Council of Raleigh and Wake County, Inc.: 461
US Community Partnerships: 1326

North Dakota

Central Association of Obstetricians and Gynecologists: 2249
Fargo-Moorhead Area Foundation: 105
North Dakota Council on the Arts: 444

Ohio

Akron Community Foundation: 1044
American Ceramic Society (The): 387
American Classical League (The): 598
American Society for Nondestructive Testing, Inc. (The): 1370, 1478, 2345
ASM Materials Education Foundation: 2420
Batten Disease Support and Research Association: 2015
Bingham (The William) Foundation: 39
Cleveland-Cliffs Foundation (The): 58
Cleveland Foundation (The): 1093
Codrington (The George W.) Charitable Foundation: 62
Columbus Foundation (The): 1095
Columbus Jewish Foundation: 1096
Community Foundation of Lorain County (The): 1118
Community Foundation of Shelby County (The): 1121
Corbin (The Mary S. and David C.) Foundation: 76
Delaware County Foundation: 1139
Eaton Charitable Fund: 98
Educational Foundation for Women in Accounting (The): 1704
Firman Fund: 107
FirstEnergy Foundation: 109, 1430
Foster Care to Success: 1387
Goodyear Tire & Rubber Company (The): 126
Greater Cincinnati Foundation: 1166
Greater Toledo Community Foundation: 1172
Gund (The George) Foundation: 131
HCR ManorCare Foundation: 1293
Herb Society of America, Inc. (The): 1917
Horticultural Research Institute, Inc.: 1510, 1918
International Executive Housekeepers Association (The): 2357
Jennings (Martha Holden) Foundation: 1432
Kettering Fund (The): 1189
Knox County Foundation: 169
Kroger Company Foundation (The): 1192
Lincoln (The James F.) Arc Welding Foundation: 2393
Lubrizol Foundation (The): 184
Marcus (Jacob Rader) Center of the American Jewish Archives: 747
Marietta Community Foundation: 1199
Morgan (The Burton D.) Foundation: 1712
Mt. Sinai Health Care Foundation: 1308
Muskingum County Community Foundation: 1209
National Inventors Hall of Fame: 1639
Nationwide Foundation: 214
Nordson Corporation Foundation (The): 218
O'Neill (William J. and Dorothy K.) Foundation: 221
Ohio Arts Council: 445
Ohio Department of Higher Education: 1556, 1557
Ohio National Guard Scholarship Program: 1558
Parker Hannifin Foundation: 231
Reinberger Foundation (The): 1229
Scott (Kenneth A.) Charitable Trust: 1898
Society for Investigative Dermatology (The): 2088
Stark Community Foundation: 1249
Synthomer/OMNOVA Solutions Foundation: 1256
Tait (The Frank M.) Foundation: 1036
White (Thomas H.) Foundation: 1272

Oklahoma

American Association of Petroleum Geologists Foundation: 1865
American Fidelity Foundation: 388
Bernsen (The Grace and Franklin) Foundation: 35
Cherokee Nation: 952
Kerr Foundation, Inc. (The): 161
Noble (The Samuel Roberts) Foundation: 1458
Oklahoma Arts Council: 446
Oklahoma City Community Foundation, Inc.: 1216
Sarkeys Foundation: 256
Schusterman (Charles and Lynn) Family Philanthropies: 1244
Society of Exploration Geophysicists: 1878
Stacey (The John F. and Anna Lee) Scholarship Fund: 520

Oregon

Bonneville Environmental Foundation: 1959
Carpenter Foundation (The): 1082
Collins Foundation (The): 64
Jackson Foundation (The): 146
Lamb Foundation: 175

McDowell (Verne Catt) Corporation: 748
Meyer Memorial Trust: 204
MRG Foundation: 1348
National Association of Composers, USA (NACUSA): 713
Oregon Arts Commission: 447
Oregon Community Foundation (The): 1219

Pennsylvania

Academy of Natural Sciences of Philadelphia (The): 1615, 1930
Air & Waste Management Association (A&WMA): 2342
Alcoa Foundation: 7
Allegheny Foundation: 9
Alternatives Research and Development Foundation: 1617
American Association for Cancer Research: 2177
American Philosophical Society: 11, 12, 308, 943
American Research Institute in Turkey, Inc.: 805, 806, 807
American Society of Regional Anesthesia and Pain Medicine: 2008, 2291
Ampco-Pittsburgh Charitable Foundation: 1052
Barra Foundation: 30
Berks County Community Foundation: 1068
Berkshire Conference of Women Historians: 529
Berwind Corporation: 37
Beta Phi Mu: 662
BNY Mellon Foundation of Southwestern Pennsylvania (The): 1072
Buhl Foundation (The): 1077
Chatham University: 1491
Chester County Community Foundation: 1090
College of Physicians of Philadelphia: 532
Connelly Foundation (The): 72
Curtis Institute of Music: 701
Douty Foundation (The): 90
Drexel University College of Medicine: 977
Duquesne University, Department of Philosophy: 327
Fels (Samuel S.) Fund: 1154
First Community Foundation Partnership of Pennsylvania: 108
Foundation for Enhancing Communities (The): 1155
Grundy Foundation (The): 1173
Hamilton Family Charitable Trust: 1390
Huston (The Stewart) Charitable Trust: 743
Independence Foundation: 144
International Centre for Diffraction Data: 2422
Jewish Healthcare Foundation of Pittsburgh (The): 1302
Katz (Herbert D.) Center for Advanced Judaic Studies: 836
Kazanjian (The Calvin K.) Economics Foundation, Inc.: 1709
Kline (Josiah W. and Bessie H.) Foundation, Inc.: 166
Leeway Foundation (The): 980
Lehigh Valley Community Foundation: 421
Library Company of Philadelphia: 553
McLean Contributionship (The): 195
Measey (Benjamin and Mary Siddons) Foundation: 2050
Mellon (Richard King) Foundation: 1201
National Federation of State Poetry Societies, Inc.: 625
NEED: 938
Oncology Nursing Foundation: 2193
Penn (The William) Foundation: 235
Pennsylvania Council on the Arts: 448
Pennsylvania Higher Education Assistance Agency: 1560
Pew Fellowships at the Pew Center for Arts & Heritage: 513
Philadelphia Foundation (The): 1223
Phillips (Dr. and Mrs. Arthur William) Charitable Trust: 2075
Pitt Poetry Series: 644
Pittsburgh Foundation (The): 1224
Pittsburgh New Music Ensemble, Inc. (The): 723
Pool (The Dorothy Rider) Health Care Trust: 1314
PPG Industries Foundation: 240
Presser Foundation: 724
Print and Graphics Scholarship Foundation: 2359, 2360
Quaker Chemical Foundation (The): 243
Rotary Club of Bryn Mawr (The): 1570
Saint-Gobain Corporation Foundation: 1238
Scaife (Sarah) Foundation, Inc.: 1806
Scranton Area Community Foundation: 1245
Seybert Foundation (The): 1034
Smith (The Ethel Sergeant Clark) Memorial Fund: 266
Smith (The W.W.) Charitable Trust: 267
Society for the Scientific Study of Sexuality (The): 1650
Templeton (John) Foundation: 279
U.S. Army Heritage and Education Center: 589
University of Pittsburgh: 1990

West (Herman O.) Foundation: 296
West Pharmaceutical Services, Inc.: 297
Widener Memorial Foundation in Aid of Handicapped Children: 927
Wolf Humanities Center: 363

Rhode Island

American Mathematical Society: 1883
Brown (John Carter) Library: 530
Champlin Foundation (The): 55
Council on Technology and Engineering Teacher Education (CTETE): 1382
Hasbro Children's Fund: 1017
Howard (The George A. and Eliza Gardner) Foundation: 1453
Rhode Island Foundation/Rhode Island Community Foundation (The): 248
Rhode Island State Council on the Arts: 451
Rhode Island State Government Internship Program: 1805

South Carolina

Abney Foundation (The): 2
Arras Foundation: 19
Ashburn Institute Inc.: 758
Coastal Community Foundation of South Carolina: 1094
Community Foundation of the Lowcountry, Inc.: 1381
Self Family Foundation (The): 1246
South Carolina Arts Commission: 455
South Carolina Higher Education Tuition Grants Commission: 1575

South Dakota

Native American Community Board (NACB): 1410
South Dakota Arts Council: 456

Tennessee

Assisi Foundation of Memphis Inc.: 20
Community Foundation of Greater Chattanooga, Inc. (The): 1112, 1113
Community Foundation of Greater Memphis: 68
East Tennessee Foundation: 1011
Frist Foundation (The): 1159
General Board of Higher Education and Ministry, The United Methodist Church: 741
Lyndhurst Foundation: 186
Oak Ridge Institute for Science and Education (ORISE): 2402
Plough Foundation: 1354
Society of Biological Psychiatry: 2338, 2339
Stokely (The William B., Jr.) Foundation: 274
Symphony of the Mountains: 729
Tau Beta Pi Association, Inc. (The): 2407
Tennessee Arts Commission: 458
Tennessee Student Assistance Corporation: 1583
United Methodist Communications: 1760, 923
United South and Eastern Tribes, Inc.: 959

Texas

ADSC: The International Association of Foundation Drilling: 2375
Alcon Foundation, Inc. (The): 2253
Amarillo Area Foundation: 1050
American Heart Association: 2123, 2124, 2125, 2126, 2127, 2128, 2129, 2130, 2131, 2132
Austin Community Foundation (The): 1060
Bat Conservation International: 1372
Benign Essential Blepharospasm Research Foundation Inc.: 2263
BNSF Railway Foundation: 945
Boy Scouts of America, National Eagle Scout Association (The): 1001, 1002
Brown Foundation, Inc. (The): 1376
Carter (Amon G.) Foundation: 52
CH Foundation (The): 1907
Coastal Bend Community Foundation: 59
Cockrell Foundation (The): 60
Communities Foundation of Texas, Inc.: 65
Community Foundation of Abilene: 1108
Community Foundation of the Texas Hill Country: 1127
Community Foundation of West Texas: 1128
Cullen Foundation (The): 80
Cullen Trust for Health Care (The): 1289
Dallas Foundation (The): 1136
Dallas Museum of Art: 499, 500, 501
Dell (Michael and Susan) Foundation: 1009, 1498

East Texas Communities Foundation: 1148
El Paso Community Foundation: 1151
Emergency Medicine Foundation: 2027
Halliburton Foundation, Inc.: 1452
Hershey (The Jacob and Terese) Foundation: 1971
Hispanic Dental Association Foundation: 2104
Hoblitzelle Foundation: 139
Houston Endowment Inc.: 140
Johnson (The Lyndon Baines) Foundation: 1797
Joslyn (The Carl W. and Carrie Mae) Charitable Trust: 1342
Kempner (Harris and Eliza) Fund: 158
Kimberly-Clark Foundation, Inc.: 163
Komen (Susan G.): 2191
Kronkosky (Albert and Bessie Mae) Charitable Foundation: 173
Learning for Life: 1403
Lunar and Planetary Institute: 1839
Maytag (Freda)-Grace Crawford Trust: 1307
Meadows Foundation, Inc.: 198
Moody Foundation (The): 211
National Foster Parent Association: 1026
National Jewish Committee on Scouting: 1537
Permian Basin Area Foundation: 1221
Phi Chi Theta Educational Foundation: 1716
Piper (Minnie Stevens) Foundation: 1563
Prospanica: 916
Richardson (Sid) Memorial Fund: 1569
Richardson (Sid W.) Foundation: 249
Rockwell Fund, Inc.: 251
Salon National La Boutique: 2245
San Angelo Area Foundation: 1239
San Antonio Area Foundation: 1240
Sons of the Republic of Texas (The): 586, 587
Sturgis (Roy and Christine) Charitable and Educational Trust: 275
Summerlee Foundation (The): 1254
Sumners (Hatton W.) Foundation: 1808
Texas Commission on the Arts: 459
Texas Instruments Foundation: 280
Texas Library Association: 683
Texas Women's Foundation: 990
Topfer Family Foundation: 283
Total USA Foundation: 284
Trull Foundation (The): 1259
University of Texas at Austin (The): 1466, 463
Violin Society of America (The): 731
Waco Foundation (The): 1267
Welch (The Robert A.) Foundation: 1861
Welder (Rob and Bessie) Wildlife Foundation: 1900

Utah

McCarthey Dressman Education Foundation: 1434
Simmons Family Foundation: 262
Thrasher Research Fund: 2286
Utah Division of Arts & Museums: 464

Vermont

Ben & Jerry's Foundation: 892
Bread Loaf Writers' Conference: 615
Francis (The Parker B.) Fellowship Program: 2031
Vermont Arts Council: 466
Vermont Student Assistance Corporation: 1609

Virgin Islands

Virgin Islands Council on the Arts: 468

Virginia

Academic Pediatric Association (APA): 2280
AGC Education and Research Foundation: 2376
Air Traffic Control Association (ATCA): 2343
ALS Association (The): 2202
American Association for Dental Research: 2097, 2098, 2099, 2100
American Association of Colleges of Pharmacy: 2287
American Association of Family and Consumer Sciences (AAFCS): 2411, 870
American Center of Research (The): 796
American Council for Polish Culture (ACPC): 1473
American Council of the Blind: 1474
American Diabetes Association: 2148

American Floral Endowment: 1904
American Foundation for Pharmaceutical Education (AFPE): 1441, 2288, 2289
American Geosciences Institute (AGI) (The): 1866
American Institute for Cancer Research: 2180
American Institute of Aeronautics and Astronautics: 2364
American Kinesiotherapy Association, Inc.: 2295
American Psychosomatic Society: 2316, 2317, 2318, 2319
American Public Power Association: 2384
American Research Center in Egypt, Inc.: 804
American Roentgen Ray Society: 2004
American Schools of Oriental Research (ASOR): 818
American Society of Civil Engineers: 2386
American Society of Naval Engineers (ASNE): 2388
American Tinnitus Association (ATA): 1621
American Water Resources Association: 1958
Bureau of Indian Education: 950
Community Foundation for a greater Richmond: 1098, 66
Cooke (Jack Kent) Foundation: 1495
Council on Social Work Education: 896
Cyprus American Archaeological Research Institute: 826, 827
DECA Inc.: 1702
Dominion Energy Charitable Foundation: 88
Fats and Proteins Research Foundation, Inc.: 1629
FEEA Scholarship Program: 1500
FishAmerica Foundation: 1965
Foundation for Physical Therapy Research, Inc.: 2298, 2299
Foundation for Technology and Engineering Education: 1388, 1503, 1504
Freedom Alliance: 1505
Gannett Foundation: 119
Graham Holdings Company: 127
Graham (Philip L.) Fund: 128
Hampton Roads Community Foundation (The): 1176
Imagine America Foundation: 1764
Institute for Humane Studies (IHS): 1794
International Association for Dental Research (IADR): 2105
International Association of Fire Chiefs Foundation, Inc.: 1515
International Road Federation: 872
Jenkins Foundation (The): 1301
Koch (Charles G.) Charitable Foundation: 1401
Madison (James) Memorial Fellowship Foundation: 554
March of Dimes: 2047, 2048
Marine Corps Scholarship Foundation, Inc.: 1528
Microscopy Society of America: 1636, 1637, 1942
Mineralogical Society of America (The): 1869
Mitsubishi Electric America Foundation: 1435
National Action Council for Minorities in Engineering, Inc. (NACME): 2394, 2395
National Federation of Republican Women: 984
National GEM Consortium (The): 911
National Institute for Labor Relations Research: 1535, 1749
National Radio Astronomy Observatory: 1841
National Science Foundation: 1436, 1642, 1643, 1644, 1645, 1812, 1813, 1826, 1842, 1875, 1876, 1890, 1946, 1947, 2332, 2333, 2396, 604
National Society of Accountants Scholarship Foundation: 1540
National Society of Black Engineers: 1541
National Wildlife Federation: 1977
NATSO Foundation: 1542
NRA (The): 1555
Omohundro Institute of Early American History and Culture: 573, 574, 575
Prevent Cancer Foundation: 2195
Running Strong for American Indian Youth: 955
Sarnoff Cardiovascular Research Foundation (The): 2146
SNAME The Society of Naval Architects and Marine Engineers: 2404
Society of Daughters of the U.S. Army: 1572
State Council of Higher Education for Virginia: 1576
U.S. Army Research Institute for Behavioral and Social Sciences: 1694
U.S. Department of the Navy: 1652
University of Virginia Press: 652
USDA Food and Nutrition Service: 1041
VCCA (Virginia Center for the Creative Arts): 465
Vertical Flight Foundation: 2374
Virginia Commission for the Arts: 469
Virginia Department of Health: 2248
Virginia Environmental Endowment: 1992
Virginia Museum of Fine Arts: 470
Virginia Polytechnic Institute and State University: 926
Virginia Society of Ornithology: 1949
Washington Forrest Foundation: 1269

Women In Defense: 993
Woodson (Carter G.) Institute for African-American and African Studies: 364

Washington

Blue Mountain Community Foundation: 1071
Bullitt Foundation (The): 1961
Cheney (Ben B.) Foundation: 56
Council for the Advancement of Science Writing, Inc.: 1731
GSBA Scholarship Fund: 901
InvestED: 1431
Jackson (Henry M.) Foundation: 147
Kitsap Community Foundation: 1191
Microsoft Philanthropies: 207
Murdock (M.J.) Charitable Trust: 213
Norcliffe Foundation (The): 217
PACCAR Foundation: 226
Pride Foundation: 915
Russell Family Foundation (The): 1235, 1982
Seattle Foundation: 260
Social Justice Fund Northwest: 1360
Washington Student Achievement Council: 1610, 1611, 961
Whitehorse Foundation (The): 1327

West Virginia

Greater Kanawha Valley Foundation (The): 1168
U.S. Department of Energy: 2408
West Virginia Department of Arts, Culture and History: 472
West Virginia Higher Education Policy Commission: 1614

Wisconsin

Alexander (Judd S.) Foundation: 1331
Amcor Cares Foundation: 10
American Academy of Allergy Asthma & Immunology: 2094
American Institute of Pakistan Studies: 755
American Institute of the History of Pharmacy: 2290
American Legion Auxiliary - Department of Wisconsin: 1476
Bader Philanthropies, Inc.: 25
Badger Meter Foundation, Inc.: 1062
Bethesda Lutheran Communities: 1373
Bradley (The Lynde and Harry) Foundation, Inc.: 1486
Community Foundation of North Central Wisconsin: 1119
Eau Claire Community Foundation: 1149
Economic History Association: 1703
Greater Green Bay Community Foundation: 1167
Greater Milwaukee Foundation: 1170
International Crane Foundation, Inc.: 1939
Johnson Controls Foundation: 150
Madison Community Foundation: 1198
Mycological Society of America: 1944
National Dairy Shrine: 1919
Northwestern Mutual Foundation (The): 1215
Pritchett Trust: 1030
St. Croix Valley Foundation: 1237
Smith (A.O.) Foundation: 265
Society for the Study of Amphibians and Reptiles: 1829
Wehr (Todd) Foundation: 1469
Wisconsin Arts Board: 474
Wisconsin Historical Society Press: 593

Wyoming

Community Foundation of Jackson Hole: 1117
Wyoming Arts Council: 479

FOREIGN COUNTRIES

Australia

Australian National University (The): 314
Perpetual Trustee Company Ltd.: 449, 642
University of Sydney (The): 1860, 1927, 1991, 2092, 858, 878

Austria

Sommerhochschule - University of Vienna: 852, 853

Belgium

North Atlantic Treaty Organization: 880
Queen Elisabeth International Music Competition of Belgium (The): 725

Canada

Acadia University: 3
Agricultural History Society: 524
Arctic Institute of North America: 1446
Arthritis Society (The): 2201
Atlantic Salmon Federation: 1935
Banff Centre (The): 484
Brandon University: 695
Brucebo Fine Art Scholarship Foundation: 497
Canadian Bar Association (The): 1769
Canadian Blood Services: 2017, 2018, 2019, 2020, 2021, 2022
Canadian Bureau for International Education (CBIE): 821, 822
Canadian Cancer Society: 2181
Canadian Federation for the Humanities and Social Sciences: 1656
Canadian Federation of University Women: 974
Canadian Foundation for Dietetic Research (CFDR): 2412
Canadian Friends of the Hebrew University: 1489
Canadian Institute for Advanced Legal Studies: 1770
Canadian Institute in Greece/L'Institut Canadien en Grèce: 315
Canadian Institute of Ukrainian Studies: 531
Canadian Liver Foundation: 2023, 2163, 2164
Canadian Lung Association (CLA) (The): 2139, 2237
Canadian National Institute for the Blind: 2265
Canadian Society for Chemical Engineering: 2390
Canadian Society for Chemical Technology: 1853
Canadian Society for Chemistry: 1854, 1855, 1856
Cancer Research Society: 2186, 2187
Chemical Institute of Canada: 1857
Concordia University: 1494
Conseil des Arts de Montreal: 398
Dafoe (J.W.) Foundation: 767
Diabetes Canada: 2168
Dietitians of Canada (DC): 2414
Donner Canadian Foundation: 1788
Greenshields (The Elizabeth) Foundation: 505
Hamilton Community Foundation: 1175
Heart and Stroke Foundation of Canada: 2140, 2141
International Centre for Comparative Criminology: 1276
International Development Research Centre (IDRC): 1183, 1184, 1185
IODE: 1516
Kidney Foundation of Canada (The): 2172, 2173, 2174, 2175
Laidlaw Foundation: 174
Leacock (Stephen) Associates: 624
Loran Scholars Foundation: 1527
McGill University: 1780
Mineralogical Association of Canada: 2423
Multiple Sclerosis Society of Canada: 2215, 2216, 2217
National Research Council of Canada: 1641
Neuro (The): 2224
Orchestre symphonique de Montréal (OSM): 721
Pontifical Institute of Mediaeval Studies: 579
Research Manitoba: 1316
Royal Society of Canada (The): 1646
Savoy Foundation: 2085
Scottish Rite Charitable Foundation of Canada: 2337
Shastri Indo-Canadian Institute (SICI): 851
SickKids Foundation: 1319
Simon Fraser University: 1718
Social Sciences and Humanities Research Council of Canada: 1675, 1676, 1677, 1678, 1679
Transportation Association of Canada Foundation: 2362
University of British Columbia (The): 1592, 1593, 1594
University of Calgary (The): 1465, 1595, 1596, 1597, 1598, 1599, 1600, 1601, 1602, 1603, 1604, 1605, 1762, 1781, 1879
University of Manitoba: 1426
University of Toronto: 685
Woodward's (Mr. and Mrs. P.A.) Foundation: 1328

England

Cambridge University Library: 664
Cancer Research UK: 2188
Institute of Materials, Minerals and Mining: 2421
Kennedy Memorial Trust (The): 873
Leeds International Piano Competition (The): 709

Marshall Aid Commemoration Commission: 842
Mellon (The Paul) Centre for Studies in British Art: 375
Royal Institute of British Architects: 378
Royal Town Planning Institute (The): 1673
Sladen (The Percy) Memorial Fund: 1899
Talbot (The Amaury) Fund: 1816
Tata (Lady) Memorial Trust: 2198
University of Bristol: 855
University of Manchester (The): 856

France

Fondation des Etats-Unis: 704
Human Frontier Science Program Organization: 1938
Long-Thibaud-Crespin Competition: 711

Germany

American Academy in Berlin (The): 795
Anna-Monika-Foundation: 2320
ARD International Music Competition: 693
Heinrich Hertz-Stiftung: 831

Israel

Davis (The Lady) Fellowship Trust: 828
Halbert Centre for Canadian Studies: 1450
U.S.-Israel Binational Agriculture Research and Development Fund
(BARD): 1926
U.S.-Israel Binational Science Foundation (BSF): 881
Weizmann Institute of Science: 867

Italy

Accademia Musicale Chigiana: 686
Istituto Italiano per gli Studi Storici: 550
Longhi (The Roberto) Foundation for the Study of the History of Art: 508
Scuola Normale Superiore: 850
Studio Arts College International (SACI): 521
Villa I Tatti: The Harvard University Center for Italian Renaissance
Studies: 859, 860, 861, 862, 863, 864, 865, 866

Japan

Matsumae International Foundation (The): 843

The Netherlands

Hague Academy of International Law (The): 1773, 1774, 1775, 1776

Scotland

Institute for Advanced Studies in the Humanities (The): 331

Sweden

Stiftelsen Riksbankens Jubileumsfond: 355

Switzerland

Graduate Institute of International and Development Studies: 771
Graduate Women International (GWI): 978
Rolex SA: 252
Union for International Cancer Control (UICC): 2199

Personnel Index

A

Aas, Kathleen: 302
Aase, Craig: 242
Abascal, Manuel A.: 232
Abbott, David T.: 131
Abbott, Judy A.: 1434
Abbott, Lisa: 416
Abregu, Martin: 112
Abstein, Teri: 405
Ackermann, Daniel: 512
Acosta, Daniel J.: 965
Acuff, A. Marshall, Jr.: 1208
Adams, Aileen: 295
Adams, Allan B.: 1339
Adams, Allison, B.S., B.A.: 2243
Adams, Christopher, Dr.: 767
Adams, Jeanna: 1528
Adams, Larry S.: 2075
Adams, Matthew J., Dr.: 794
Adams, Melinda, Dr.: 2416
Adams, Rukaiyah: 204
Adamson, Peter: 1079
Addams, Cynthia G.: 64
Addison, Garrik: 211
Aditya, Shoma: 46
Adkins, Denice: 660, 661
Adkinson, Kimberly M.: 924
Adolphe, Marie: 1711
Advaithi, Revathi: 98
Adwan, Teresa B.: 256
Agger, David: 225
Aguado, Lynn: 844
Ahlgrim, Judy A.: 251
Ahmed, Manan: 613
Ahmed, Rashid, Dr.: 1316
Ahumada, Lorena E.: 235
Aidenbaum, Ashley: 263
Ainsworth, Maryan: 820
Aja, Melissa: 1943
Akin, Bruce: 1965
Akincigil, Ayse: 1661
Akinyele, Michael: 2119
Akman, Jonathan: 1013
Akman, Nonie: 1013
Akpovi, Teri: 1401
Alam, Kamran: 2213
Alberding, Ellen S.: 153
Alberti, Janet: 330
Albertson, Hack: 2304
Alcocer, Rudyard: 606
Alcock, Charles R.: 1843, 1844
Alden, A.F. Drew: 1101
Alder, Laurel Cannon: 464
Alenier, Karren L.: 653
Alesson, Tami: 486
Alexander, Bruce K.: 1339
Alexander, Elizabeth: 201, 1729
Alexander, Jeff: 698
Alexander, Rachel K.: 2407
Alexander, W. Robert: 1339
Alexander, W.R.: 141
Alfonso-Jones, Sol Marie: 1196
Allan, Karen C.: 1082
Allen, John H.: 134
Allen, LaRue: 486
Allen, W. James: 2194
Allen, William C.: 295
Alley, Kendall: 253, 1156
Allio, Michael K.: 248
Allred, Steve: 415
Allworth, Jim: 1328
Alonso, Andres A.: 1016
Alonso, Leticia Perez: 606
Alpers, Ann: 78

Alsace, Tamara O., Ph.D.: 1100
Alstad, Jennifer: 996
Alvarado, Gil: 1334, 1359
Alvarez, Frank: 1266
Alvarez, Jose B.: 153
Amonette, Rex A., M.D.: 2197
Amorin, Jim: 1700
Amoroso, Henry: 1266
Amundson, Dana: 192
Anand, Supreet: 1424
Anchia, Raphael M.: 139
Anders, Jessica Eiland: 263
Anderson, Andrea: 263
Anderson, C.T.: 1428
Anderson, Cindy: 1164
Anderson, Dana: 1346
Anderson, David: 804
Anderson, Debbie: 1227
Anderson, Eve: 934
Anderson, Gerard M.: 194
Anderson, Greg: 911
Anderson, Johanna: 1428
Anderson, Maggie: 451
Anderson, Melanie K.: 1254
Anderson, R. Lanier: 354
Anderson, Sally: 1961
Anderson, Tammy: 917
Andrews, Robert: 1018
Angeles, Fatima: 1287
Angelica, Robert E.: 1037
Anglin, Dale Robinson: 1552
Anstine, Mary K.: 1339
Antonine, Deborah, Dr.: 997
Antov, Nikolay: 805, 806, 807
Apap Heller, Mary Ann: 459
Aparicio Clark, Amy: 5
Apodaca, Patricia: 1046
Applewhite, Hunter A.: 88
Aragon, Andrea: 100
Aranda, Peter: 1701
Arb, Sheryl G.: 67
Ardillo, Eileen: 1554
Ardisana, Lizabeth: 263, 1208
Arellano, Hilda: 774
Arenas, Zamawa: 1073
Argento, Carol: 1018
Arias, Nicole: 1751
Armiento, Angelo: 686
Armor, David J.: 1661
Armstrong, Sherrie: 66, 1098
Arnason, Freyja: 1316
Arning, Robert F.: 1710
Arnold, Isaac, III: 80
Arnold, Joan, Ph.D., R.N.: 2243
Arnott, Andrew: 1073
Arredondo, Jaime: 64
Arrington, Christine: 901
Arriola, Elvia R.: 982
Artis, Rosalyn Clark, Dr.: 1575
Artis, Sharnnia, Ph.D.: 911
Asam, Claire L., Dr.: 53
Aschwanden, Christie: 1731
Asher, James: 1735
Aso, Kazuko: 391
Ata, Athar, Dr.: 1316
Ataiyero, Kayce: 153
Atkins, William: 354
Atran, Harris: 23
Au, Carlton K.C.: 53
Auchincloss, Andrew: 1341
Audette, Melanie: 1964
Auerbach, Elise: 599, 802
Auger-Dominguez, Daisy: 1092
Auh, Jin: 613
Aupperle, Tammy B.: 171
Austen, Christopher M.: 167
Austin, Dannyelle: 1154
Austin, Kenneth W.: 292
Ax, Emanuel: 703
Aybar, Rosanna: 1016

Ayres, James: 1129
Ayres, Resia: 2034

B

Baba, Gwen: 1079
Bacharach, Samuel B., Ph.D.: 1321
Backus, Lisa, Dr.: 78
Bader, Daniel J.: 25
Bader, David M.: 25
Bader, Linda C.: 25
Bader, Michelle Berrong: 25
Bagley, Nancy R.: 18, 247
Bagley, Nicole: 18
Baheti, Arun: 1287
Bahl, Judi: 1316
Bailey, Jen, Rev.: 96
Bailey, Kacey: 1393
Bailey, Rahn K., M.D.: 2062
Bakalor, Peter: 2263
Baker, Chanda Smith: 153
Baker, Chris: 1139
Baker, Dru: 363
Baker, Patrick: 456
Baker, Tracy: 1015
Balbach, Jennifer Chalmers: 1100
Baldwin, Kittredge A., Dr.: 53, 1429
Baldwin-Viereck, Ella: 2387
Bales, John F.: 195
Baliles, Robin D.: 1992
Ball, Charles: 27
Ball, Korri: 1227
Ball, Neal: 2062
Ball, Ramsay: 1059
Balson, Annissa: 1735
Bame, Tracy: 115
Bamford, Holly, Ph.D.: 1975
Banchero, Stephanie: 153
Bancroft, Bob: 81
Bane, Scott: 134
Banerjee, Rini: 1979
Banks, Cynthia D.: 1282
Bannon, Brian: 89
Baptista, Ana: 1266
Barbato, Trish: 2201
Barbeau, Alain: 2085
Barber, Michael: 1954, 1955
Bardes, Judith L.: 90
Barillaro, Laura: 2034
Barisic, Irina: 2167
Barker, Alberta: 416
Barker, Deborah J.: 142
Barker, Peter K.: 1455
Barlow, Toby: 1181
Barnes, Dale: 1965
Barnes, Nancy: 1729
Barnet, William, III: 94
Barnhart, Cynthia: 264
Barnholt, Ned: 229
Baron, Martin: 167
Barr, Gwin: 253
Barr, Kate: 419
Barreiro, Mark: 134
Barrett, David: 1735
Barrios, Jarrett Tomas: 1079
Barron, Laura: 179
Barry, Nicole: 1316
Barth, Andrew F.: 330
Bartlett, Terri L.: 1711
Bartter, Kate: 1970
Base, Elizabeth: 256
Basler, Bonnie: 2189
Bass, Edward P.: 249
Bass, Lee M.: 249
Bass, Sid R.: 249
Bassler, Bonnie: 264
Batliner, Payton: 947, 948
Battle, LaVeeda: 24
Bauer, Douglas: 1492
Bauer, Verena: 852, 853

Baugh, Bryan P., M.D.: 2062
Baugh, Jim: 1960
Baum, Patricia P.: 29
Baumann, Marsha: 1259
Baumgardner, Cindy: 218
Baumgart, Melissa: 1100
Bayat, John: 2323
Baynes, Yen: 1360
Baza, Larry: 394
Beall, James, Dr.: 653
Bean, Andrew: 21
Bean, Bruce W.: 21
Bean, Glen: 21
Bean, Mary F.: 21
Bean, Rachael: 21
Beard, Felicia: 1100
Beaujean, Oswald: 693
Becher, Amy: 1491
Becht, Colleen: 1100
Beck, James, Ph.D.: 2232
Beck, Judith: 2341
Beck, Phil: 2376
Becks, Shannon: 2385
Beeson, Joel T.: 1355
Beinecke, Candace K.: 292
Beirne, David M.: 2196
Bekavac, Nancy: 261
Belali, Austin: 18
Belfonte, Winell: 1202
Belk, Judy: 1287
Bell, Frank: 1099
Bell, Hilton S.: 544
Bell, John, Dr.: 256
Bell, Judy: 100
Bell, Kandice: 1059
Bell, R. Terry: 251
Bell, Samuel P.: 1455
Bell, Sue: 677
Bell-Rose, Stephanie: 167, 242
Bellamy, Sarah: 419
Benavidez, Britt: 1428
Benden, Dana M., M.D.: 2249
Bender, Michael J.: 965
Bendicksen, Beverly R.: 1046
Benedict, James: 26
Benjamin, Marilyn: 96
Bennack, Frank A., Jr.: 1735
Bennett, Mary Frey: 116
Bennett, Samantha: 723
Bennett-Scott, Sandi, Ed.D.: 1431
Benton, Barbara: 2263
Benton-Johnson, Felicia, Ed.D.: 911
Berenbom, Merilyn K.: 1809
Berg, Peter S., Rabbi: 1099
Bergeron, Corinne C.: 1159
Bergman, Marilyn: 694
Berlin, Charles: 904
Berliner, James E.: 1079
Berman, Amy J., R.N.: 134
Berman, Francine: 264
Bernard, Andre: 130
Bernhardt, Robert K., Rev.: 746
Bernstein, Charles: 694
Bernstein, Margaret: 131
Bernstein, Richard: 264
Berry, Chad: 24
Berry, Thomas W.: 142
Berson, Jena: 1122
Bertolini, Mark T.: 5
Bertrand, Alexia: 820
Beschloss, Afsaneh: 93
Bessant, Cathy: 253, 1156
Besser, Richard E.: 2042
Bethlehem, Marlene: 749
Beveridge, Piper Neal: 247
Beyerstein, Lindsay: 1736
Bhagat, Vandna Wendy: 677
Bien-Gund, Susanna: 131
Biga, Eric: 868
Bildsten, Lars, Ph.D.: 1827

Billings-Burford, Diahann: 1092
Billiter, Mary: 479
Bilowith, Karen: 143
Bilski, Mark A.: 904
Biltekoff, James: 1100
Binger, Anne: 1346
Binger, Erika: 1346
Bingham, Bethany: 1931
Birckmayer, Ann: 154
Bird, Jeff: 27
Bird, Peter F., Jr.: 1159
Birdzell, Flora Hewlett: 137
Biscoll, Gary: 49
Bishop, Aaron: 2314
Bishop, Courtney: 2376
Bishop, Gregg: 1092
Bishop, Lloyd C.: 2062
Bisognano, Maureen: 1335
Bitterman, Mary G.F.: 225
Black, Caroline: 514
Black, Janice: 1155
Black, Paul M.: 1809
Blackburn, Sharon L., Judge: 205
Blackwell, Angela Glover: 983
Blair, Angela: 211
Blair, Michael: 1672
Blake, Carl: 2304
Blake, Jen: 2104
Blake, Pier A.H.: 933
Blake, Sarah: 414
Blandford, David: 901
Blank, Edward: 594, 595
Blankenship, Terry, Ph.D.: 1900
Blankley, John H.: 849
Blanton, Ben W.: 181
Blau, Robert: 1729
Blausey, Bill: 98
Blazevich, David: 225
Bleier, Edward: 2025
Blischke, Karl: 448
Block, Jeff: 2119
Bloodworth, Carolyn A.: 73
Bloom, Kenneth: 486
Blount, Sally: 153
Blount, TiAnda: 938
Blum, Deborah: 1731
Blumenstein, Penny B.: 67
Blumenthal, Amy: 486
Blumenthal, David, M.D.: 1335
Blumenthal, David, M.D., M.P.P.: 2046
Blutt, Mitchell J., M.D.: 1335
Blymier, Michael: 1155
Bobby, Ted: 171
Bobo, Lawrence D.: 130
Bodzin, Zelma: 710
Boehmer, Hans Martin: 1661
Bohorquez, Fernando, Jr.: 216
Bohra, Lindsey G.: 1552
Boivin, M. Remi: 1276
Bolin, Daniel, Dr.: 689
Bolin, Melissa: 1716
Bollinger, Lee C.: 1729
Bolser, Chad: 416
Bomberger, Carolyn L.: 745
Bomberger, Matthew A.: 745
Bomberger, Michelle H.: 745
Bomberger, Rachel A.: 745
Bomberger, William A.: 745
Bonde-Henricksen, Nils: 1631
Bonner, Robert C., III: 95
Bonta, Diana M.: 1282
Boo, Katherine: 1729
Bookbinder, Alan: 842
Booker, Matthew: 340
Bookstein, Emily: 1360
Borda, Deborah: 703
Borenstein, Jeff: 2323
Borges, Francisco L.: 167
Borish, Michael: 1434
Bornick, Sue: 1149

Boswell, Donald K.: 222
Bosworth, Wendy Reed: 1170
Botti, Romayne: 911
Bottoms, Robert G.: 153
Boucher, Jeffrey L.: 169
Boufford, Jo Ivey, M.D.: 1325
Bouler, Chantay: 253, 1156
Boulpaep, Emile L., Dr.: 820
Bouman, John: 919
Boumtje, Martine: 606
Boutros, Basem, Dr.: 2416
Boutwell, Robert: 2283
Bouwman, Laurie G.: 2194
Bowar-Ferres, Susan, Ph.D., R.N.: 2243
Bower, Laura: 221
Bowlin, John R.: 1552
Bowlin, Terry L., Ph.D.: 2073, 2292
Bowman, Jim: 1096
Bowman, Noor: 1034
Boyce, Phillip R.: 2093
Boyd, Bonnie: 544
Boyd, Charlotte: 1163
Boyd, Jane, M.D.: 2263
Boyer, Jeff: 901
Boyer, Tamara: 1011
Boyette, Kirstie: 1134
Boykin, Jerry, USA (Ret.), Lt Gen: 1505
Boyle, Alan: 1731
Boyle, Michael P., M.D.: 2167
Boyle, Robert A.: 746
Boyles, Brian: 332
Bozzuto, Thomas S.: 29
Brabander, Cynthia: 98
Bracken, Elizabeth: 27
Bracken, Will: 28
Bracken, William: 27
Bradach, Mary: 1100
Bradford, Carol: 1079
Bradford-White, Alison: 1059
Bradley, Frank: 46
Bradley, James, Dr.: 1616
Brady, Maureen: 982
Bragg, Brian: 118
Bralove, Susan Haas: 413
Brandenburger, Paul: 1931
Brannen, Elizabeth: 1401
Brasel, Susan S.: 1362
Brassey, Mike: 1578
Bray, Emily: 158
Brazell, Torryn: 1621
Brelsford, Jonathan: 1224
Brennan, Dan: 2213
Brennan, James C., Esq.: 2050
Breslauer, Gerald: 917
Breul, Jonathan D.: 1661
Brewer, E. Thomas: 232
Brewer, Michael F.: 47, 153
Brewster, Sharon: 1016
Bricker, Diane R.: 266
Brickner, Lynne: 261
Briggs, Taylor: 901
Bright, Cedric M., M.D., FACP: 2062
Brinkmeyer, William A.: 746
Brinson, Bree: 782, 784
Brisson, Katie G.: 67
Britt, Deirdre: 25
Britton, Felisha: 2394, 2395
Brock, Dale W.: 459
Brock, Peggy: 2027
Brockenbrough, Austin, IV: 66, 1098
Brodhead, Richard H.: 201
Broemer, Lisa: 1190
Bronars, Edward J., USMC, Lt Gen: 1505
Brooke, Sandra: 330
Brooks, Deborah W.: 2030
Brooks, Edward: 188
Brooks, Katherine Werner: 188
Brooks, Minna K.: 188
Brossoit, Jean-Francois: 73
Brothers, M. Elizabeth: 1321
Brotherton, Angie: 1431

Brotherton, Dawn: 1155
Broughton, Bruce: 694
Brouwer-Ancher, Alexis: 797, 798, 1442, 1475
Browder, Vidya: 2114
Brown, Andrea: 419
Brown, Andrew: 1202
Brown, Ben: 1112
Brown, Charles: 2304
Brown, Denise: 980
Brown, Emery: 130
Brown, Francis K., II: 33
Brown, Jessica: 263
Brown, Julia: 645
Brown, Leslie: 2393
Brown, Matthew: 1401
Brown, Meghan Binger: 1346
Brown, Michael, Dr.: 1814, 1815
Brown, Neil: 1729
Brown, R. Justin, M.P.H.: 2286
Brown, Robert W., M.D.: 52
Brown, Shana L.: 167
Brown, Steven D.: 1431
Brown-Graham, Anita: 247
Browne, Jeff: 1756
Browne, Robert: 1514
Browne, Susan: 412
Brun, Nalani: 412
Bruno, Timothy: 1970
Bruseth, Jim, Ph.D.: 1254
Bryan, Betsy: 804
Bryant, Angela R.: 247
Brynteson, Susan: 399
Bryson, Louise Henry: 1079
Bucco, Diana A.: 1077
Buchanan, Judith, Prof.: 842
Buchanan, Leslie W.: 95
Buck, Terrence: 911
Buckland, Elke: 1032
Buckley, Linda M.: 1806
Buckmaster, Raleigh D., Dr.: 1022
Buckner, Ellen B., Dr.: 1616
Buek, Peter A.: 181
Buell, Mark: 189
Buford, Calvin: 1166
Buhr-Gund, Charlotte: 131
Bula, Barbara: 2283
Bula, Brendon: 2283
Bullitt, Harriett: 1961
Bullock, Otis, Jr.: 195
Bullock, Quintin B.: 1077
Bunting, LaSharah S.: 1733
Burakoff, Steven J., M.D.: 2196
Burchinal, Margaret R.: 1016
Burdick, Amy: 901
Burgess, Karen E.: 357
Burke, Jenny: 1202
Burke, Keelin: 341, 342, 343, 344, 345, 348, 349, 350, 351, 352, 572, 954
Burke, Sheila P., R.N.: 1335
Burnes, Brian, Dr.: 1616
Burnett, Jason K.: 229
Burnett, Marc: 458
Burnett, Nancy Packard: 229
Burnham, Patricia R.: 1354
Burns, Fran: 72
Burns, Jennifer, Dr.: 1491
Burns, Richard R., Jr.: 33
Burns, Ursula: 112
Burroughs, Melissa: 1378
Burroughs, Olivette: 2248
Burrows, David D.: 823
Burt, Thomas: 849
Burton, Angus M.: 268
Burton, Darren H.: 1710
Busansky, Alex: 983
Bush, Chad: 1164
Bush, James L.: 2096
Bush, Keith: 86
Buskey, Raeann: 1155
Bussman-Wise, Jenna: 983

Bustos, Camila: 1967
Buthman, Mark A.: 296
Butler, Brian M.: 45
Butler, Catherine C.: 1078
Butler, Dixon M.: 1992
Butler, John K.: 1078
Butler, Karen: 2046
Butler, Letitia K.: 774
Butler, Maddie: 1078
Butler, Patrick, Jr.: 1078
Butler, Paul S.: 1078
Byerly, Stacy S.: 274
Byers, William: 1096
Bynum, Richard: 128
Byrne, Rebecca: 1122

C

Cabral, Anna Escobedo: 96
Cafritz, Anthony W.: 47
Cafritz, Calvin: 47
Cafritz, Elliot S.: 47
Cafritz, Jane Lipton: 47
Cahillane, Mary: 1514
Cahn, Tita: 694
Cain, Jonathan: 1925
Cairo, Anu: 78
Calder, M. Alexander: 1003
Calder, Peter D.: 1003
Calderon-Patino, Elena: 451
Calderon-Rosado, Vanessa, Ph.D.: 1073
Caldwell, Joseph: 478
Caldwell, Stacy: 277
Callahan, Eugene J.: 1354
Calvocoressi, Gabrielle: 982
Camarena, Gene: 965
Cameron, Ben: 419
Campbell, Dennis M., Ph.D.: 94
Campbell, Johnny: 1569
Campbell, Lebrena Fulp: 2
Campbell, Mary Schmidt: 93
Campbell, Natasha: 470
Campbell, Ray: 1474
Campbell, Robert, Ph.D.: 2263
Campbell, Ryan O.: 1339
Campos, Laura: 81
Campos, Luis: 548
Campoverdi, Alejandra: 1079
Camunez, Michael C.: 229
Canedy, Dana: 1729
Cannon, Eileen: 2073, 2292
Cannon, William C.: 156
Capers, Garry, Jr.: 86
Carabine, Angela D.: 154
Cardinale, Ruth: 1362
Carey, Ashley: 1942
Carlile, Jack: 154
Carlson, Maria: 778
Carlson, Richard, Dr.: 1624
Carlson, Trevor: 1431
Carmichael, Daniel P.: 181
Carmody, Jane: 134
Caro, Robert A.: 130
Carpenter, Matt: 100
Carpenter, Robert J., Jr., M.D.: 2249
Carpenter, Suzanne: 714, 715, 716
Carr, Catherine E., Ph.D.: 2212
Carrasco, Rudy: 213
Carrera, Jackie: 1243
Carrigan, Laura C.: 46
Carroll, Andrew D.: 186
Carroll, David: 1186
Carroll, Maureen McMeel: 1809
Carroll, Nicole: 1729
Carson, Carrie: 901
Carson, Jadee: 415
Carswell, Shirley: 1733
Carter, Christopher: 1270
Carter, Ed: 1965

Carter, Edward: 1740
Carter, Lynn: 808
Carter, Prudence L.: 1016
Case, Lucia Gill: 250
Case, Peter Gill: 250
Casey, Joan: 1254
Casey, William: 1756
Cassidy, Bill: 1740
Castaneda, Xochitl: 1287
Castle, Alfred L.: 1429
Castle, Shaun: 2304
Castles, John W.: 213
Catani, Deanene: 1011
Catania, Michael: 1266
Cathers, Christopher: 420
Cecil, John F.A.V.: 94
Certo, Matthew W.: 45
Cervantes, Pablo: 1274
Ceserani, Giovanna: 354
Cetnar, Cindy: 243
Chadwick, Douglas: 1962
Chaffin, Betsy: 89
Chahim, Leda: 901
Chamberlin, Katie: 202
Chamberlin, Nat: 202
Chamberlin, Patience: 202
Champer, Jeanne M.: 193
Chan, John, M.D.: 2145
Chan, Rebecca: 1360
Chan, Stephen: 1073
Chandler, Patricia, C.P.A.: 29
Chandrasoma, Nishka: 112
Chang, Lan Samantha: 649
Chang, Theresa W.: 459
Chanin, Anthony: 1186
Chapman, David: 2404
Chapman, Joey: 901
Chapman, Laura: 80
Chapman, Max C., Jr.: 1975
Chapoton, John E.: 47
Charnock, Emily, Dr.: 873
Chase, Allison: 882
Chasin, Alexandra: 250
Chatfield-Taylor, Adele: 130
Chatlos, Janet A.: 739
Chatlos, William J.: 739
Chatlos, William J., III: 739
Chatman, Robin F., M.D.: 1166
Chavers, Dean, Dr.: 951
Chavez, Carlos: 901
Chemi, Louis: 1965
Chen, Ida K.: 1154
Chen, Milton: 157
Chen, Sho Tin: 2323
Cheng, Eva: 134
Chernin, Louise: 901
Chernin, Rachel: 901
Cherry, Elyse: 1073
Cherry, Kevin, Dr.: 156
Chieco, Peter: 2165
Chigbrow, Cordell: 1578
Child, Desmond: 694
Childs, Bronwen: 2189
Childs, John D.: 2189
Chiloyan, Vart: 887
Chin, Victor, C.F.A.: 2212
Chiu, Libby: 416
Chlebeck, Eliza: 1053
Choate, Millard: 1099
Choi, Cathy: 1012
Choi, William C.: 1079
Chowdhuri, Sohini: 2030
Christ, Donald C.: 333
Christensen, Dale C., Jr.: 1325
Christian, Ronald C., Esq.: 1166
Christiano, Katherine: 235
Christie, Elizabeth W.: 1037
Christophersen, Eric: 1215
Chrysler, Josh: 479
Chu, Benjamin K., M.D.: 1335

Chubb, Sally: 1266
Chumley, Brenda: 1169
Chun, Brandon: 901
Church, Ramah: 1556
Cicatello, Anthony: 1033
Cigarroa, Francisco G., M.D.: 112, 2046
Ciociola, Christina M.: 1101
Cisar, Elizabeth: 153
Cisneros, Adriana: 167
Cisneros, Mary Ann: 1931
Clapp, Katherine: 2032
Clark, Andrew M., Dr.: 1823
Clark, Benic M., III: 186
Clark, Bert: 1099
Clark, Bob: 581
Clark, Celeste: 157
Clark, Chelsea: 206
Clark, Cynthia: 2263
Clark, David G., Dr.: 1916
Clark, Jane Forbes: 1492
Clark, John: 1112
Clark, Kristen: 171
Clark, Kristin Kennedy: 354
Clark, Marian Steele: 253, 1156
Clark, Melanca D.: 1181
Clark, Sierra: 229
Classen, Julia: 996
Claxton, Jose: 1018
Clayton, Adam: 2361
Clayton-Johnson, Mark-Anthony: 1779
Cleary, Jennifer: 1316
Cleaver, Mikayla: 1573, 1891, 1892, 1893
Clement, Jane: 412
Clemons, G. Scott: 1827
Cliatt, Cass: 1817
Clifford, Erin: 165
Clifford, Linda France: 221
Clifford, Matt: 873
Clifton, Rachel: 479
Cline, J. Michael: 1975
Clodfelter, Daniel G.: 247
Cloeter, Jeffrey P., Rev.: 746
Clore, Dale Ann: 1399
Cloyd, Brian: 273
Co, Eric: 53
Cobb, Steven J.: 1079
Coble, Christopher L.: 181
Cochems, Beth: 514
Cochran, Scott: 1575
Cockrell, David A.: 60
Cockrell, Ernest D.: 60
Cockrell, Ernest H.: 60
Cockrell, Janet S.: 60
Coe, Mark: 2213
Coen, Stacy: 2213
Coffin, Levi: 901
Coffman, Mia: 1431
Coggeshall, Heidi: 2263
Coggins, Christa: 920
Cohen, Barbara: 486
Cohen, Carl: 1418
Cohen, Jeremy: 645
Cohen, Mary B.: 157
Cohen, Mitch: 189
Colburn, Michael: 689
Cole, Holly: 1164
Cole, Steve: 1970
Coleman, Barbara Bell: 1033
Coleman, Christopher: 1431
Coleman, Deborah J.: 2196
Coleman, Jennifer: 131
Coleman, Leonard S., Jr.: 1033
Coleman, Morton, M.D.: 2119
Coler-Dark, Jenne: 2213
Coles, Robyn: 2196
Coll, Steve: 1729
Collard, Yvette: 1133
Collins, Donna S.: 445
Collins, Gail: 1729
Collins, J. Barclay, II: 1325

Collins, James E.: 8
Collins, Melony: 186
Collins, Truman W., Jr.: 64
Colon, Pedro: 1170
Colvin, Gail, (Ret.), Col.: 100
Colvin, Theresa M.: 430
Companik, Rich: 502
Compton, Ian: 71
Compton, Wilson M.: 165
Comstock, Ross: 157
Conarroe, Joel: 130
Conner, Stephanie B.: 458
Connolly, Harriet Cann: 743
Connolly-Keesler, Eileen: 1109
Connors, Michael P.: 1075
Conomikes, John G.: 1735
Conrad, Cecilia A., Dr.: 1514
Conrad, Jay: 1274
Considine, Jill: 1205
Considine, William H.: 167
Constantine, Betsy: 1100
Conway, Brian: 1073
Conway, William: 1962
Cook, Jaclyn: 1611
Cook, Kathleen D.: 1067
Cook, Phyllis: 225
Cook, Roger: 2415
Cook, Wallace L.: 2025
Cooke, Julian Cossman: 731
Cooke, Terry: 1175
Coolidge, Calvin: 1505
Cooper, Timothy: 86
Cooper-Basch, Irene: 1266
Cooper-Lewter, Stephanie: 1355
Cooperman, Leon G.: 2196
Corbin, Hunter W.: 142
Corbo, Mike: 1435
Cordero, Arellana: 1046
Cordle, Chris, Ph.D.: 169
Cords, Danny: 901
Coriz, Lakota: 941
Cornali, Racquel: 464
Corrado, Mark A., C.P.A.: 2197
Cortes, Emilie: 71
Costa, Flavio: 163
Cota, Irma: 1287
Cote, Frederic: 398
Cote, James: 85
Cotter, Jeffrey: 86
Cotter, Mary Carole: 1164
Coudreaut Curiel, Terese: 167
Coulon, Robbin M., Esq.: 1058
Coulter, Ann: 186
Coulter, Rachel A., O.D., M.S., Dr.: 2255
Courts, Richard W., IV: 1099
Cowling, Ruth Ann: 416
Coy, Oona: 202
Coyle, Jennifer L., O.D., M.S.: 2255
Craft, Brian: 797, 798, 1442, 1475
Craig, Richard, Dr.: 1916
Craig, Taylor: 479
Crain, John W.: 1254
Cramer, Kary L.: 1339
Crane, Christopher M.: 103
Crane, Clarence: 181
Crane, Robert: 1964
Crary, Horace I., Jr.: 4
Cravins, Don, Jr.: 1964
Crawford, James: 1514
Crawford, Milly Ritzen: 198
Creighton, Peter: 1631
Cremieux, Anne, Dr.: 704
Cresci, Andrew A.: 120
Crier, Rondell: 1112
Crisafulli, Shawn: 568, 570
Criswell, Pamela: 192
Crochet, Marcel: 820
Crocker, Katrina M.: 1086
Croft, Thomas: 1166
Cron, Marie-Michele: 398

Cronin, Dennis: 26
Crosby, Gary: 1100
Cross, Nicholas, Prof.: 2198
Crothers, Chris: 96
Crotty, Margaret: 1325
Crum, Guenevere: 882
Crum, Valerie: 206
Cruse, Rebecca: 456
Cruz, Gary, Dr.: 2355
Cruz, Serena: 64
Cude, Tracy: 1059
Cuellar, Mariano-Florentino: 137
Cullar, Catherine: 1998, 1999
Cullen, Matthew P.: 1181
Cullen, Meredith T.: 80
Culpepper, Bruce: 1975
Cummings, Kathleen Sprows: 535, 536, 537, 538, 539
Cummins, Tom: 326
Cundiff, Tishana: 2263
Cunyus, Ingrid: 1127
Cuprill-Comas, April: 204
Curbelo, Carlos: 1964
Cureton, Jesse: 253, 1156
Cureton, Sara R.: 569
Curley, Jason: 958, 1590
Curran, Richard B.: 60
Currica, Michelle: 1154
Curry, Ravenel B., III: 94
Curtis, Cynthia: 19
Curtis Horowitz, Mary E.: 1661
Curtiss, David: 1865
Cushing, Margaret J.: 786
Cusic, Anne, Dr.: 1616
Cutler, Wendy: 791

D

D'Arcy, Stephen R.: 1181
D'Olier, H. Mitchell: 53
Dackerman, Susan: 354
Daggett, Christopher J.: 1033
Daily, Ed: 1505
Dallas, Stephanie: 901
Daly, James J.: 1075
Daly, Tim: 153
Dammrich, Thomas: 1965
Dana, Charles A., III: 2025
Dana, Danielle: 1827
Dando, Kathryn: 1362
Dane, John, III: 1975
Daniel, Clifton Truman: 1809
Daniel, Leah Angel: 1100
Daniel, Samuel J., M.D.: 1325
Daniels, Jyarland: 868
Daniels, Kathy: 169
Daniels, Lamond: 5
Daniszewski, John: 1729
Dankers, Paul: 1205
Dannhaeuser, Cherlyn: 739
Dant, William: 868
Danyluk, Michelle: 2415
Danziger, Sheldon: 1674
Dapolito, Matthew: 486
Dardess, Margaret B.: 1415
Daucher, Lynn, Hon.: 1282
Daudet, Yves, Prof.: 1773, 1774, 1776
Daugherty, Barbara: 1993
Daugherty, Margery: 1916
Daughtry, Deborah K.: 71
Dave, Kuldip, Ph.D.: 2202
Davenport, Vanessa: 71
Davidson, Betsy: 154
Davidson, Bradford: 154
Davidson, Gwen: 392
Davidson, J. Matthew: 154
Davidson, Marty: 1393
Davidson, Peter W.: 154
Davies, Andrea: 354

Davies, Ben: 149
Davies, Pamela: 94
Davis, Carol Bunch, Ph.D.: 158
Davis, Carrie L.: 153
Davis, Chastity: 1213
Davis, Christopher V.: 85
Davis, Danae: 1170
Davis, Diana Champ: 1099
Davis, Jonathan P.: 85
Davis, Leigh Evans: 1176
Davis, Sarah H.: 85
Davis, Shelly A.: 238
Davis, Tamara A.: 85
Davis, Wade: 983
Davis, Willma H.: 1340
Davison, H.: 1341
Dawson, Martha A., Dr.: 2240
Day, Kevin: 752
Day, Martha: 1033
Dayton, John W.: 139
De Greff, Curt: 2232
de Hoyos, Debora: 1514
De La Cruz-Viesca, Melany: 925
De La Garza, Lisa: 990
De La Rosa, Gabriel: 1710
De Maio, Stephen: 733
de Molina, Al: 253, 1156
De Naut, James: 1827
Dean, Jennie: 261
Dean, Kyle: 261
Dean, Nathan: 261
Dean, Tamara: 52
Dean, Victoria Seaver: 261
Deary, Jack: 1631
deBuys, William: 1962
DeCardy, Chris: 229
Decatur, Sean, Ph.D.: 169
DeCoudreaux, Alecia A.: 137
Dedecker, Clotilde Perez-Bode: 1100
Deen, R.B., Jr.: 1393
Dehne, Tanuja: 87
Dekker, Christopher: 1076
Dekker, Hans: 142
Deko, Ghassan: 2187
Delaney, Michael: 1067
DeLano, Mike: 1435
Delgado, Oscar: 1305
DeLoach, Harris E., Jr.: 94
DeLucia, Michael S.: 1019
DeMain, John: 733
DeMaio, Jeannie: 1196
DeMarchi, Vita: 1970
Demond, Avery H., Ph.D.: 911
Demyan, Kirk: 1155
Dendas, Ronald C., M.S.: 1314
Denton, Tricia: 1016
Denyer, Mary C.: 842
DePass, Michelle: 204
DePillis, Mark S., Esq.: 927
Depp, Sheri: 911
Dernoncourt, Nicolas: 725
Desai, Vishakha N.: 93
DeSantis, Paul: 1256
DeShazo, Nikki, Hon.: 1254
DeShields, Tom: 1545, 1546
Deutschman, Kathleen F.: 1306
DeVenny, Susan W.: 19
Devonish, Carrolle Perry: 90
DeVore, Nealon: 81
Dey, Ken: 1578
Di Battista, Giovanni, Dr.: 2201
Di Martino, David: 134
Dial, Beth: 626
Diaz, Elva, Ph.D.: 2212
Diaz, Monica: 49
Dick, Stacy: 246
Dickinson, Molly: 451
Dickler, Susan: 983
Dickson, Austin: 1127
Dicovitsky, Gary: 774

DiCristofaro, David: 1710
DiCroce, Deborah M.: 1176
Dien, Laurie: 1029
DiLello-Morton, Linda: 901
Dill, Joanne So Young: 1970
Dillan, John: 1935
Dinkel, John F., Jr.: 1067
Dinneen, Anne: 292
Dinovitz, Dino: 1735
Dinstel, Ray: 228
Dion, Ernest E.: 1019
Dionne, Shelley D., Dr.: 1823
DiPaola, Paul: 1046
Dishman, J. Dallas, Ph.D.: 1292
Disla, Janet: 81
Diver, Colin: 242
Divola, Julie: 1264
Dixon, Edith R.: 927
Dixon, George W.: 927
Dizon, Gabby: 1979
Doane, Ken: 78
Dodson, David: 242
Dodson, Richard: 731
Dolan, Paul: 1092
Dolhare, Walter: 965
Dolsten, Mikael, M.D., Ph.D.: 2073, 2292
Domaschko, John: 1166
Donahey, David: 221
Donahey, Robert W.: 221
Donaldson, M.S., Esq.: 2050
Donaldson, Phil: 1053
Donley, Shannon: 1970
Donnelley, Laura: 89
Donnelley, Shawn M.: 89
Donnelly, Edward J., III, M.D.: 1224
Donnelly, Inanna: 89
Donner, Craig: 2243
Donner, Fred: 354
Donohue, William: 134
Donovan, Thomas J.: 1067
Doppstadt, Eric W.: 112
Dorcas, Todd: 1168
Dorhout, Peter K., Ph.D.: 1827
Dorn, Holbrook F.: 1376
Doss, Anna: 1046
Doughty, Heather: 448
Douthwright, Toby: 206
Dowd, Jacqueline: 181
Dowd, Patrick, Ph.D.: 1224
Doyle, Jennifer: 1155
Doyle, Timothy: 1624
Dragan, Christine: 1012
Drake, Jamie: 216
Drake, Michael V., M.D.: 1335
Dreff, Ashley Boggan: 742
Dreibelbis, Jennifer: 435
Drell, Persis S.: 137
Dressman, Mark: 1434
Droth, Martina: 365
Drury, David J.: 1170
du Monceau, Diego: 820
Dubester, Ilana: 247
Duckmann, Stephanie: 27
Duff, Stephen M.: 404
Duggan, Ervin S.: 677
Duke, Barbara: 1925
Dukes, Charlene M.: 1202
Dumont, Michael: 458
Dunbar, Wendell: 285
Dunbar, William: 1202
Duncan, Greg: 1016
Dunlap, Jamie: 448
Dunlop, Karen: 1316
Dunlop, Lorin: 213
Dunn, John M.: 1767
Dunn, Kathryn: 1170
Dunn, Peter A.: 1086
Dunn, Robert P.: 1809
Dunsworth, Holly: 1059
Duran, Lauren: 2323

Durand, Bonnie R., Ph.D.: 1100
Durand, Christophe: 1325
Durie, Susie: 2041
Durocher, Benoit: 2187
Duronio, Carolyn: 1077
Durso-Finley, Gianna, Dr.: 1552
Durst, Lisa: 98
Dvorak, Elizabeth: 45
Dyck, Richard E.: 791
Dykstra, Craig R.: 181
Dziak, Alicia: 1100
Dziko, Trish Millines: 1431
Dzirasa, Kafui, M.D., Ph.D.: 2212

E

Earle, Linda: 419
Earnest, Josh: 1809
Easter, Colette R.: 1159
Easterling, Melissa P.: 35
Ebie, Bill: 478
Eckartsberg, Lauren von: 264
Eckenrode, Beth: 171
Ecker, Robert: 1660
Eckert, Ross J.: 1100
Eckmann, Pam: 1119
Eddinger, Pam Y., Ph.D.: 1073
Eddy, Rebecca R., MBA, PDDM: 2243
Eder, Tim: 1970
Edgar, J.A.: 184
Edison, Roz: 901
Edlen, Mark: 1961
Edwards, Brent: 353
Edwards, Carl T.: 2
Edwards, Richard: 1661
Effron, Cheryl Cohen: 246
Efron, Sonni: 1750
Egbert, Marcia: 131
Ehrler, Audrey: 1929
Eichberg, Steven: 2119
Eilber, Janet: 486
Eisenberg, D.D.: 1354
Eisenson, Michael R.: 1073
El-Gabalawy, Hani, Dr.: 1316
Ela, Susan: 1170
Elam, Emily A.: 746
Elbaz, Elyssa: 1079
Elcan, Chuck: 1159
Elcan, Lauren: 1159
Elcan, Patricia Frist: 1159
Elderidge, Rev. Joseph: 18
Eliadis, Pearl: 1661
Elledge, Amy: 1970
Elliott, Jane: 86
Ellsworth, Laura: 1224
Ellwein, Charles E.: 78
Elmes, Faith: 1155
Elston, Jan: 1011
Embrey, Lauren: 983
Embry, Robert C., Jr.: 1
Emerson, Bill: 263
Emig, Tiffani: 667
Eng, Torbjorn, Dr.: 355
Engel, William V.: 142
Engelberg, Stephen: 1729
Engfer, Patricia: 45
England, Rick: 1013
Englander, Peter, Dr.: 873
Engleman, Thomas E.: 1733
Enright, William G.: 181
Enriquez, Mary Schneider: 46
Ensign, Katie: 96
Erickson, Ceil: 260, 1327
Erier, Wendy: 2213
Erjavec, Steve: 1106
Erlbaum, Gary E.: 2196
Ernst, Joshua T.: 746
Erskine, Edward: 1202
Ervin, Frank, III: 2361

Escaler, Ernest de Leon: 391
Escobar, Luis: 1316
Escobeda, Efrain: 1079
Escobedo, Marcus R., M.P.A.: 134
Esmail, Reena: 720
Esposito, Orlando C.: 1223
Essex, Kate: 1162
Esteban, Jose Emilio: 2415
Esterline, Bruce H.: 198
Estrada, Erik: 100
Estrin, Eliot: 122, 1779
Estrin, Jesse: 122, 1779
Estrin, Mary Lloyd: 122
Estrin, Robert L.: 1779
Etkind, Lanie: 2209
Evans, Jodie: 394
Evans, Linda Perryman: 198
Evans, Scott: 1016
Evans, Stephen O.: 1058
Evans, Susie S.: 1809
Eveillard, Elizabeth: 506
Evelyn, Douglas E.: 404, 541
Everett, Joe: 1218
Evers-Willox, Maureen: 1710
Eversley, Alan C.: 5
Eyle, Maximilian: 1160
Ezeigbo, Chibuzo: 153
Ezekoye, Ada: 2387

F

Fabiano, Michael: 733
Fable, Scott E.: 2407
Fahey, Thomas J., Jr., M.D.: 2196
Fain, Jonathan D.: 248
Fainzilber, Michael, Prof.: 867
Fair, Deb: 49
Fairley, Janet A., M.D.: 2026
Fairley, Janet, M.D.: 2088
Faison, Michael: 415
Falahee, William P.: 154
Falayi, Tokunbo: 1975
Falcone, Marylou: 703
Falk, Adam F.: 264, 1828
Falls, Amy C.: 112
Fanton, Jonathan: 391
Faraci, John V., Jr.: 1975
Farber, Jeffrey A.: 170
Farkas, Charles M.: 134
Farley, Katherine: 201
Farr, Olivia: 202
Farren, David: 89
Farzan, Dorienne: 333
Fauci, Anthony S.: 93
Faulkner, Ermalene M.: 28
Fauquher, Ronald K.: 28
Faust, James D.: 296
Favorite, Annette: 296
Faye, Sira: 1100
Fedor, Ashley: 687
Feinman, Abby: 1186
Feinstein, Karen Wolk, Ph.D.: 1302
Feldman, Noah, Dr.: 1817
Feliz, Carrie Bridges: 248
Fennessey, Kevin: 2119
Fenton, Andre, Ph.D.: 2212
Ferguson, R.S.: 289
Ferrell, Lynne J.: 116
Ferrell, Nora: 1355
Ferris, Dan: 1965
Fey, Grace: 1417
Fick, Leslie: 1155
Fick, Toya: 204
Fiddler, Josh E.: 29
Field, Jemma, Dr.: 365
Fields, Curtland E.: 1037
Fiene, Michael: 269
Finch, Steve: 1100
Fincher, Malia: 1616

Finckel, David: 703
Findlen, Paula: 354
Fink, Jill: 1034
Finn, Hayley: 645
Fionda, Andrea: 2043
Fioramonti, Marie: 1514
Firestone-Teeter, Naomi: 621
Firman, Stephanie: 107
Fischer, Allison: 23
Fish, Lawrence K.: 791
Fish, Marion Hancock: 268
Fisher, James A.: 27
Fiske, Brian: 2030
FitzGerald, Karen: 1202
Fitzgerald, Laurie: 228
Fitzgerald, Melody: 1202
Fitzpatrick, Deborah: 198
Fitzpatrick, Jack: 120
Fitzpatrick, James A., Jr.: 823
Fitzpatrick, Joyce: 2235
Fitzpatrick, Susan, Dr.: 193
Flanagan, Kathleen: 404, 541
Flanagan, Mollie: 451
Flanders, Stephanie: 873
Fleming, Kim Tillotson: 1077, 1224
Fleming, Nancy: 515
Fletcher, Allen W.: 1361
Fletcher, Justin L.: 1361
Fletcher, Megan: 1227, 1361
Fletcher, Warner S.: 8, 1361
Flick, Robert: 261
Flood, Eugene, Jr., Ph.D.: 1827
Flores-New, Fernando: 1015
Florsheim, Thomas W., Jr.: 1170
Flumenbaum, Martin: 594, 595
Flynn, Bob: 269
Flynn, Guy E.: 29
Flynn, Kathy: 1022
Flynn, Kevin: 120
Fogel, Henry: 703
Fogg, Anthony: 703
Foley, Dia: 445
Foley, Peter: 1965
Foliart, Dan: 694
Folson, James: 330
Fonalledas, Blas: 1975
Fong, Pauline: 213
Fonseca, Caio: 154
Fonseca, Isabel: 154
Fonseca, Quina: 154
Foote-Hudson, Marilyn E.: 1415
Foran, Julianne: 1076
Ford, Cynthia N.: 194
Ford, Henry, III: 112
Foreman, Robin: 1176
Forster, Meret: 693
Fortunato, Kim: 49
Foster, Carlie: 1578
Foster, Lee B., II: 1224
Foster, Margaret: 25
Fotias, Natalie: 263
Foucher, Monica: 1360
Foulkes, Anne M.: 240
Fournier, Deanna: 2115
Foutty, Janet: 1449
Fowler, Wyche, Jr.: 493
Fox, Regina, S.S.N.D., Sister: 1320
Foxley, Griff: 122, 1779
Foxley, Zoe L.: 122
Foxley, Zoe Lloyd: 1779
Francis, Alexandra: 254
Francis, Beth: 1153
Francis, Bobby R.: 689
Francis-Sharma, Lauren: 615
Francisco, Betty: 1073
Franco, Lawrence C.: 1100
Frank, Elizabeth T.: 1552
Frank, Karla W.: 1672
Frank, Pamela: 703
Frankel, Lisa B.: 747

Frankel, Merrie S.: 486
Franklin, John: 213
Franklin, Carmela Vircillo: 506
Franklin, Melissa: 513
Franklin, Tilly: 873
Fraschillo, Thomas V.: 689
Frasier, Mark: 2030
Frederickson, Kari: 1809
Frederickson, Michelle: 1089
Fredrickson, Michelle: 857
Freeman, Ashley Horton: 165
Freeman, Graeme: 114
Freeman, Valerie: 2361
Freitag, Amy L.: 154
French, Buck: 2196
French, Janel: 1163
Frey, Allison: 1721
Frey, Campbell W.: 116
Frey, David J., Jr.: 116
Frey, Edward J., Jr.: 116
Frey, Katrine E.: 116
Frey, Laura D.: 116
Frey, Sarah: 116
Friberg, Susan: 820
Friedman, Ellen: 71
Friedman, Jeni S.: 749
Friedman, Joshua S.: 201
Friedman, Yamit: 1155
Friend, Robert: 225
Frieser, Hannah: 498
Frist, Jennifer: 1159
Frist, Julie D.: 1159
Frist, Thomas F., III: 1159
Frist, William R.: 1159
Fritthum, George, Dr.: 733
Fritz, L.M.: 289
Frost, Robert D.: 904
Frost, Wayne, LSME, CMfgE: 2361
Froy, Michael: 2119
Frumkin, Howard: 1961
Frye, Irene: 919
Frye, Jocelyn: 983
Fuchs, Elaine V., Ph.D.: 2196
Fuller, Tricia: 284
Fulmer, Terry, Ph.D., R.N.: 134, 2046
Fulp, John R., III: 2
Fulp, John R., Jr.: 2
Fulton, Scott: 1771
Furr-Stimming, Erin: 2213
Furth, Rebecca: 246
Furtivo, Benay: 357

G

Gabbard, Marveline Vallo: 941
Gabriel, Claire: 1674
Gabriel, James: 243
Gabriel, Regina M.: 1314
Gabriele, Amy: 448
Gadkaree, Sameer: 153
Gaines, Charles C.: 459
Galaida, Laura: 413
Galan, Nely: 965
Gale, Tom: 198
Gallagher, Daniel: 168
Gallagher, David: 168
Gallagher, Dottie: 1100
Gallagher, Edward P.: 611, 808
Gallagher, Linda: 1100
Gallagher, Mary Lindsay: 168
Gallagher, Matthew D.: 1162
Gallagher, Michael: 168
Gallegos, Kathleen: 394
Galli, Jaime: 394
Galligan, Peter A.: 2222
Galliher, Michael B.: 28
Gallo, John: 225
Galvez, Melida: 134
Galvin, Chris: 1053

Galvin, Robert S., M.D.: 1325
Gamble, Laura L.: 392
Gamoran, Adam: 1016
Gandhi, Rutuma M.: 134
Gann, Pamela Brooks, Dr.: 1514
Gannett, Craig: 147
Gannon, Paul C.: 1073
Gannon, William S., Rev.: 1037
Garcetti, Gil: 1660
Garcia, Gloria: 868
Garcia, Maria: 1297
Garcia, Marlene L.: 1488
Garcia Ortega, Rigo: 901
Gardere, Ashleigh: 24
Gardiner, Earl: 1316
Gardner, Liz: 302
Gardner, Michael R.: 677
Gardner, Roger L.: 152
Garen, Wendy: 232
Garfunkel, Ben: 1710
Gargan, Denise M.: 1314
Garrison, Debbie: 1155
Garrity, Sarah: 2243
Garthwait, Bob: 1505
Gary, Holland P.: 139
Gates, Laura: 89
Gatti, Stanlee R.: 394
Gaw, Mali Sananikone: 216
Gayle, Helene D.: 1091
Gaynor, Richard B., M.D.: 2196
Geffen, Jeremy: 703
Gelb, Leah: 1013
Gellerstedt, Lawrence L., III: 301, 1042
Gellert, Annette: 121
Gellert, Fred, Jr.: 121
Gellert, Julia: 121
Gellert, Landon: 121
Generett, William, Jr.: 1224
Genna, Lenny: 1823
George, Terrence R.: 53
Georgopoulou, Maria, Dr.: 813
Gephart, Jay: 689
Gerald, Laura: 1355
Gerber, Ann Rogers: 117
Gerber, Lynn: 2387
Gerber, Selwyn: 1186
Gerber, Ted: 778
Gerdes, Chris: 1435
Geren, Pete: 1569
Gerken, Heather: 201
Gerschel, Patrick A.: 823
Gerstacker, Lisa J.: 2194
Geurtsen, Juta: 415
Ghubril, Saleem H.: 1077
Gibbs, Gary, Dr.: 459
Gibson, Anna: 188
Gibson, Mila: 459
Gideon, Cheryl: 233
Giedd, Kerry, O.D., M.S.: 2255
Giemza, Bryan: 606
Gilbert, Erin: 258
Gilbert, Percy, Ph.D.: 911
Gilfillan, Christine C.: 1023
Gilkinson, Brian W.: 2337
Gill, Barbara E.: 2025
Gill, Patrick M.: 1965
Gill, Sam: 93
Gillespie, Charlotte A.: 1339
Gillespie, Eric: 225
Gilligan, Ellen M.: 1170
Gillinson, Clive: 93
Gillis, Gladys: 901
Gillum, Roderick: 157
Gilmer, Micah: 24
Gimon, Eric: 137
Ginsberg, William W.: 1101
Ginsky, Marc S.: 2167
Gioia, Robert D.: 222
Giordano, Roberto: 550
Gipson, Nellie: 404, 541

Gisel, William G., Jr.: 222
Givens, Joseph: 733
Glasper, Rufus: 1058
Glasscock, Selma, Ph.D.: 1900
Glawe, Laura Porfilio: 1170
Gleba, Michael W.: 1806
Glembocki, Raymond: 1473
Glenn, Lavastian: 81
Glenn, Micah A., Rev.: 746
Glover, Charles: 198
Glynn, Simone, M.D., M.Sc., M.P.H.: 2121
Goff, Phyllis: 1346
Golay, Inga M.: 486
Goldbach, Justin: 154
Goldberg, Leonard H., M.D.: 2197
Golden, Charles E.: 181
Golden, Rebecca: 892
Golden, Thelma: 201
Goldman, Dorothy Tapper: 130
Goldman, Ruth: 202
Goldseker, Ana: 1162
Goldseker, Deby: 1162
Goldseker, Sharna: 1162
Goldseker, Sheldon: 1162
Goldseker, Shelley: 1162
Goldsmith, Shane: 1343
Goldsmith, Virginia Self: 1246
Goldstone, Tom: 2119
Golinski, Jan: 548
Goll, Edward: 1453
Golub, Todd R., M.D.: 2196
Gomez, Erin: 1961
Gomez, Iris: 1340
Gomulinski, Curtis D.: 2407
Gonzales, Aminda Marques: 1729
Gonzales, Carmen: 1434
Gonzales, Peter, Esq.: 90
Gonzales-Chavez, Lilia: 394
Gonzalez, Henry: 1817
Gonzalez, Jerry: 24
Gonzalez, Shannan, MHRM: 2042
Gonzalez, Will: 1154
Good, Lynn: 253
Good, Theresa, Dr.: 1946
Goodman, Jean R., M.D.: 2249
Goodpasture, Philip H.: 66
Goodpasture, Philip M.: 1098
Goodridge, Julie: 1340
Goodwin, Peter, MBA: 2046
Gordon, David W.: 1334, 1359
Gordon, Mariko: 613
Gordon, Michael L.: 2196
Gore, Cecelia: 1170
Goren, Nicky: 1202
Gorman, Paul: 243
Gosney, Timothy J., Esq.: 272
Goulart, Steven: 203
Gould, Laurence K., Jr.: 2330
Gourley, Eve: 901
Gove, Peter: 1970
Grace, Oliver: 4
Grafstein, Bernice, Ph.D.: 2212
Graham, Alan, Q.C.: 1935
Graham, Christopher: 242
Graham, Garth N., M.D., M.P.H.: 5
Graham, Lowell: 689
Graham, Margaret: 977
Graham, Shelley: 404, 541
Grande, Matthew A.: 1034
Grandy-Mock, Jada: 1156
Grant, Bruce: 778
Grant, Charisse: 206
Grant, Susan: 1099
Grass, Henry J., M.D.: 2212
Grass, Joshua, Ph.D.: 2212
Grassilli, Robert J., Jr.: 120
Graumlich, Lisa: 1961
Gravano, Alan J.: 551
Graves, Milton T.: 60
Gray, Bob: 2255

Gray, Constance F.: 94
Gray, Katie: 1169
Grayson, Glenn, Rev.: 1224
Green, Emma: 999
Green, Joanne: 996
Green, Johney B., Jr., Ph.D.: 911
Green, Kimberly: 2361
Green, Mark, Ambassador: 361
Green, Maurice O.: 247
Green, Miriam: 1926
Greenawald, Sheri: 727
Greenberger, Sharon: 246
Greene, Don: 2392
Greene, Michael A.: 911
Greene, Roland: 354
Greenham, David: 425
Greenland, Don: 1059
Greenspan, Peter B., D.O.: 2249
Greenstein, Scott: 2196
Greer, Adrian: 842
Greer, Emily: 211
Greer, Patrice: 1099
Gregori, Mina: 508
Greif, Mark: 354
Greig, Sabrina: 118
Greiner-Lott, Gretchen: 47
Grieman, Pam: 960
Griesser, Carrie: 49
Griffin, Gail: 1733
Griffin, Jennifer: 714, 715, 716
Grimm, Kimberly: 739
Grindber, Tony: 302
Grinstein-Weiss, Michal: 1661
Groat, Lee A.: 2423
Grobman, Linda, Ed.D.: 927
Grodzki, Kevin: 1960
Groner, Lewis: 1186
Gross, Brian: 1082
Gross, Doreen A.: 85
Grossman, James R.: 526, 527, 528
Grossman, Pamela: 1418
Grotz, Jennifer: 615
Grove, E.A.: 184
Grub, James S.: 325
Grubb, Jeffrey T.: 213
Gruber, Nina: 852, 853
Grum, Allen (Pete): 1100
Guerra, Adrian: 459
Guerra, Lucas H.: 1340
Guerra, Rebecca: 1247
Guertin, Shawn: 5
Guess, Avery: 979
Guiler, Thomas A., Ph.D.: 362
Gullot, Richard, M.D.: 2145
Gund, Catherine: 131
Gund, Lara: 131
Gund, Zachary: 131
Gunderman, Kara: 1155
Gunderson, Greg, Ph.D.: 1809
Guon, Jane M.: 228
Gusbeth, Tiffany: 940
Gustafson, Daniel E., Jr.: 1983
Gustafson, Robert, Dr.: 1575
Guth, Peter: 733
Guthrie, Carlton L.: 153
Guttersen, Chandler: 158
Gutzmann, Ingrid: 2201
Guzelimian, Ara: 703
Guzzo, Dorothy: 566, 567

H

Haaga, Paul G., Jr.: 232
Haas, Andrew: 235
Haas, Christina: 235
Haas, Janet, M.D.: 235
Haas, Leonard C.: 235
Haas, Peter: 235
Haas, Sarah: 235

Haas, Thomas: 235
Haber, Thomas R.: 1415
Haberman, Phyllis: 1514
Hackett, Nickol: 153
Haden, Patrick C.: 1455
Haegel, Nancy, Ph.D.: 1827
Haeri, Niloofar: 354
Haerizadeh, Yasi: 1735
Hageman, Michael J., Ph.D.: 2073, 2292
Hagen, Erin: 1256
Hager, Kristen: 66, 1098
Hagerman, Lisa: 1735
Hahn, Hannah: 47
Hahn, Harald: 478
Hahn, Steven: 1729
Haire-Sievers, Noëmi: 704
Haist, Dave: 416
Hajra, Neel: 1057
Hakuta, Kenji: 1016
Halby, Peter: 122
Halby, Will: 122
Hale, Elizabeth K., M.D.: 2197
Haley, John: 205
Hall, Cindy: 995
Hall, Dale: 1975
Hall, Debra: 1355
Hall, Kathryn A.: 201
Hall, Nechie: 100
Hall, Rahsaan D.: 1340
Hall, Ronald, Jr.: 263
Hall, Serena Davis: 85
Hall-Witt, Jennifer: 332
Hallner, AnnaLena: 355
Halpern, Allan C., M.D.: 2197
Halpern, Daniel: 626
Hamada, Janet: 204
Hamburg, Margaret A., M.D.: 1335
Hamill, Deirdre: 1658, 1659
Hamilton, Amy Hodges: 606
Hamilton, Arthur: 694
Hamilton, Peter: 189
Hamilton, Rachel: 158
Hamm, Harold: 1975
Hammer, Daniel: 544
Hammer, Paul Allen, Dr.: 1916
Hammett, Elyse: 1099
Hammond, Aubrey: 1100
Hammond, Laura: 755
Hammond, William H.: 1037
Hampe, Michael: 733
Hamren, Robert, Dr.: 355
Hamrick, Miles, Sr.: 1700
Han, Wu: 703
Hancock, Dell: 2034
Hanft, Robert S.: 404, 541
Hang, Kaying: 1334, 1359
Hanger, Christina: 157
Hanifin, Michael: 84
Hanke, C. William, M.D.: 2197
Hannum, Diane E.: 1554
Hansen, Greta S.: 1247
Hansen, Lisa D.: 219
Hanson, Johanna: 71
Hanssen, Emily: 168
Hantman, Julie: 1032
Hapka, Markell: 188
Happ, Cambria, MPA, CAE: 660, 661
Harbert, Raymond J., Jr.: 205
Harcourt, Susan: 868
Hardcastle, Elizabeth: 734
Hardin, P. Russell: 301, 1042
Harding, Jenny: 901
Hardwick, Lisa: 1809
Hargrove-Young, Delores: 1166
Haring, Rachel, Dr.: 881
Harmer, Lynne: 2182, 2184, 2185
Harmes, Debbie: 1046
Harmon, John C., Esq.: 1224
Harper, Shelly: 81
Harper, Stephen: 1964

Harrington, Ann-Marie: 248
Harrington, Brendan: 1100
Harrington, David: 1202
Harrington, Kelsey: 28
Harrington, Rebecca: 1046
Harris, Alex: 53
Harris, Ashley: 990
Harris, Donn K.: 394
Harris, E.B.: 168
Harris, Henry U., III: 294
Harris, Kelly L.: 168
Harris, Richard: 1731
Harris, Sandra: 486
Harris, Thomas: 168
Harrison, Caroline: 842
Harrison, J. Kline, Dr.: 1514
Harrison, James: 384
Harrison, Larry J., M.P.H., MBA: 2062
Harrison, Wendy, O.D., Ph.D.: 2255
Hart, Heather: 330
Hart, Nailah: 47
Hartman, Sid: 189
Hartnett, Cathy: 983
Hartwig, Charles, Dr.: 1562
Harvey, Jill: 1330
Harvey, Thomas B., Esq.: 90
Hashemi Magura, Pari: 1154
Hashim, Carlisle: 168
Hashim, Marion: 168
Hashmall, Sarah: 47
Haslanger, Kathryn D.: 1335
Hastings, David R., III: 212
Hastings, Ken: 226
Hastings, Peter G.: 212
Hatch, Eliza: 202
Hatch, Susannah: 202
Hatcher, Steven: 415
Hathaway, Jean M.: 1507
Hatton, Katherine, J.D.: 2042
Hauptfuhrer, Barnes: 253, 1156
Havens, Louise A.: 267
Hawkins, Lauren: 263
Hawkins, Shannon: 1315
Hawley, Philip M.: 1660
Hayashida, Jennifer: 613
Hayden, Steve: 2196
Haydon, Jamie: 2034
Hayes, Denis: 1961
Hayes, Reiji P.: 73
Haynes, Julian A.: 1202
Healy, James T.: 287
Healy, Jonathan, Esq.: 2263
Hearst, George R., Jr.: 1735
Hearst, William R., III: 1735
Heaton, Robert: 1067
Heck, C. Laurence, Dr.: 1562
Hedin, Marika: 355
Hedrick, Virginia: 1287
Heery, Brian: 1435
Hegadorn, Tina: 788, 789
Heidel, Mark: 689
Heisner, Charles F.: 746
Heitkamp, Scott G.: 1095
Held, Andrew: 901
Helmreich, Anne: 503
Helms, Lila: 1975
Hemphill, Ross F.: 1672
Hempstead, David M.: 67
Henderson, Barclay G.: 135
Henderson, Frederick: 264
Henderson, Roberta: 135
Henderson, Stephen: 1181
Hendrian, Catherine A.: 73
Henkin, R.I.: 2090
Heraghty, Patrick: 1105
Herd-Barber, Jacqueline: 1170
Herda, Sarah: 373
Herlin, Cara P.: 1259
Herling, Marta, Dr.: 550
Herman, Dana, Dr.: 747

Herman, Hattie: 1998, 1999
Herman, Tammy: 439
Hermocillo, Jose: 1334, 1359
Hernandez, Antonia: 1079
Hernandez, Daisy: 982
Hernandez, Enrique, Jr.: 1660
Hernandez, Erica: 1756
Hernandez, Maria: 1360
Herrera, Irma: 1264
Herring, Paula: 198
Herzan, Alexandra: 2341
Hess, Gregory D., Dr.: 1514
Hesterlee, Sharon, Ph.D.: 2218
Hewitt, Chet P.: 1334, 1359
Hewlett, Billy: 137
Heyda, Patty: 383
Hiam, Alexander: 294
Higdon, Nichol: 1346
Higdon, Timothy L.: 2271
Higgins, William: 506
Higueras, Charles A.: 78
Hiles, Clay: 1972
Hill, Emil: 2062
Hill, Hilary: 261
Hill, Jennett M.: 181
Hill, Jennifer: 243
Hill, Michael: 624
Hill Scott, Karen: 232
Himberg, Philip: 424
Hindle, Steve: 330
Hines, Anson H.: 1983
Hines, Janel: 1170
Hing, James: 901
Hirokane, Jeanie: 225
Hirsch, Edward: 130
Hirsch, Sanford: 504
Hirsh, Sandy: 660, 661
Hitch, Molly: 2368, 2369
Ho, Eva: 1079
Ho, John: 1073
Hocker, Julie: 1261
Hockin-Mix, Sarah J.: 116
Hodgin, Laura L.: 33
Hoerauf, Matthew: 263
Hoffman, Michael D.: 1170
Hofmann, Karan: 2371
Hofmeister, Brandon J.: 73
Hojaboom, Carolyn: 901
Holcombe, Paul A., Jr.: 1415
Holefelder, Jack: 266
Holen, S.: 2090
Holender, Ioan: 733
Holland, Sonni: 1018
Holliman, Vonda: 1401
Hollis, Sally: 1022
Holloway, Jonathan: 201
Holloway, Scott: 2376
Holman, John W., III: 142
Holman, John W., Jr.: 142
Holmes, Daisey: 1072
Holmes, Lisette: 1109
Holmes, Robert: 1266
Holmes, Robert W., Jr.: 1417
Holt, Stephen: 195
Holton, Lindsay: 1647
Hong, Elisabeth: 355
Honwana, Nyeleti: 1658, 1659
Hood, Elizabeth: 2283
Hoogland, Keith: 2119
Hooker, Doug: 1099
Hooks, Brian: 1401
Hoone, Jeff: 507
Hooper, Dawn: 990
Hooper, Kristen: 1316
Hoots, W. Keith, M.D.: 2121
Hoover, Deborah D.: 1712
Hoover, Jewell: 253
Hoover, Jewell D.: 1156
Hoover, Margaret: 820
Hoover, Susan: 1168
Hopkins, Bryana: 116

References in index are to entry numbers.

Hopkins, David: 425
Hopkins, Nancy: 2201
Hopkins, Ronnie, Dr.: 1575
Horie, Ayumi: 413
Horii, Akinari: 791
Horne, Marilyn: 733
Hornecker, Mitch: 204
Horowitz, Roger: 543
Horowitz, Teri: 904
Horton, Alice K.: 165
Horvit, Beverly: 1740
Houck, Gayle L.: 222
Houk, Alice: 2011
House, Patricia A.: 137
Houston, Julia A.: 1099
Houston, Melissa: 2043
Hovland, Jeannie: 957
Howard, Doris: 726
Howard, Garry D.: 1733
Howell, Amelia Reid: 117
Howell, Philip B.: 117
Howell, Philip Carter: 117
Howell, Victoria: 1554
Howitt, Robert: 1018
Howse, Jennifer L., Ph.D.: 1325
Hoy, Ronald R., Ph.D: 2212
Hrabowski, Freeman A., III: 264
Hsu, Douglas Tong: 391
Hsu, Hua: 613
Hsu, Tonia: 391
Hu, Ji Hee: 1079
Huang, Mikiko, Dr.: 78
Hubbard, Jim: 1960, 1965
Huber, Marie Oh: 1247
Hubner, Peter: 733
Hudgins, Charlene: 2263
Hudiburg, Richard, Dr.: 1616
Hudler, Mary: 287
Hudson, Gilbert: 1181
Hudson, Joseph L., IV: 1181
Huff, Clair: 1393
Huff, Kim: 1256
Hughes, Jay: 2213
Hughes, John: 624
Hughes, Martha Ellen: 982
Hughes, Meghan, Ph.D: 248
Huh, Elmer: 213
Hui, Alexandria: 548
Hull, Greg: 416
Hulme, David: 733
Humenik, John: 1756
Humphrey, Holly J., M.D., M.A.C.P.: 2046
Humphries, Sarah: 1960
Hunt, Joe M., III: 156
Hunt, Kathleen S., M.D.: 186
Hunt, Margaret: 396
Hunter, Christina: 410
Hunting, Mary Anne: 273
Huntly, Brian, Prof.: 2198
Hurlburt, Bradley: 1106
Hurley, Lori: 2393
Hurley, Maureen: 222
Hurlock, Matthew H.: 774
Hussein, Hussein: 1401
Huston, Charles L., III: 743
Hutcheson, Mary Ellen, CPA: 45
Hutchinson, Eric: 1059
Huyghebaert, Baron Jan: 725
Hwee, Koh Boon: 137
Hybben, Robert: 1078
Hybl, Kyle H.: 100
Hybl, William J.: 100
Hybl, William J., Jr.: 100
Hylant, Richard: 1970
Hyman, Steven E., M.D.: 246, 2025
Hyre, Stephanie: 1168
Hystead, Marsha: 1218
Hyun, Phillip: 965

I

Ibarguen, Alberto: 167
Iguchi, Debra: 175
Ilitch, Denise: 263
Im, Katherine: 1562
Imani, Jakada: 71
Imboden, Connie E.: 392
Immens, Kirk: 1965
Ingram, Robert A.: 1415
Innamorato, Lou: 2323
Ions, Sharon R.: 5
Iquina-Perez, Andrea: 1155
Ireland, Jay W.: 2196
Irgang, Tory L.: 1089
Irti, Natalino, Prof.: 550
Irwin, John N., III: 4
Isaacs, Eric D.: 1624
Ishii, Anne: 613
Isley, Maria: 1218
Israel, Alex: 394
Ittleson, H. Anthony: 1341
Ittleson, H. Philip: 1341
Ittleson, Stephanie: 1341
Ivens, Barbara J.: 1015
Ivers, Mary: 285
Iverson, Brent L., Ph.D.: 1827
Iwano, Amy: 720

J

Jackson, Anthony: 911
Jackson, Cade: 1246
Jackson, David D., Hon.: 1254
Jackson, Debbie: 1610
Jackson, Glenn: 222
Jackson, John L., Jr.: 1154
Jackson, Major: 502
Jackson, Phillip A., Rev.: 246
Jackson, Shirley A.: 746
Jackson, Tandra C.: 1710
Jacobs, Alice, J.D.: 1100
Jacobs, Luke T.: 222
Jacobs, Neil, Dr.: 1975
Jacobson, Nelson: 1164
Jacoby, Charles H., Jr. (Ret.), Gen.: 100
James, Holly M.: 193
James, Juanita T.: 104
Jamison, Nelle Woods: 1274
Jamison, Stephanie W.: 496
Jankowski, Cheryl A.: 1100
Janowitz, Henry D., M.D.: 2166
Janssen, Daniel: 820
Jaquay, Robert B.: 131
Jardine, Drew: 544
Jasanoff, Maya, Prof.: 873
Jasper, April, O.D.: 2255
Jaxtimer, Joannie: 1417
Jayas, Digvir, Dr.: 1316
Jebsen, Hans Michael: 391
Jedlicka, Jill: 1970
Jedrej, Thomas: 2201
Jeffery, Dana: 892
Jelinek, Josef E.: 404, 541
Jemison, Steven: 1166
Jenereaux, Joyce: 194
Jenkins, Kristen: 1611
Jenkins, Meredith: 1817, 1818
Jenkins, Meredith B.: 2046
Jennings, J. Webb, III: 60
Jernigan, Charles: 228
Jester, Denise: 1733
Jethrow, K.L.: 184
Joh, Erik Edward: 1461
Johns, Richard P.: 1756
Johnson, Alan C.: 1008
Johnson, Alex M.: 1287
Johnson, Craig C.: 1008
Johnson, Douglas R.: 1823
Johnson, Erik S.: 301, 1042

Johnson, Holly A.: 116
Johnson, Jacqueline: 653
Johnson, Kate L.: 52
Johnson, Kierra: 122
Johnson, Louise U.: 1552
Johnson, Mark L.: 52
Johnson, Norah: 448
Johnson, Patrick: 1756
Johnson, Robert L., M.D.: 1266
Johnson, Ruth Sieber: 728
Johnson, Sarah: 1458
Johnson, Shayne: 1916
Johnson, Sheila B.: 52
Johnson, Stacy: 1112
Johnson, Sydney McNiff: 1975
Johnston, Stacy: 1218
Johnstone, Lori: 228
Jojola-Talburt, Winter: 947, 948
Jones, Andrew: 2361
Jones, Anne-Marie: 1305
Jones, Brian: 267
Jones, Daniel Alexander: 419
Jones, Eddie E., Jr., Rev.: 96
Jones, Edrea: 1213
Jones, Elizabeth: 1089
Jones, J. Trent: 94
Jones, Jacqueline: 526, 527, 528
Jones, John P., III: 1314
Jones, Landon, Esq.: 1034
Jones, Marcus: 1218
Jones, Meaghan: 1112
Jones, Paul J.: 1170
Jones, Tammy: 2304
Jones, William: 1569
Jonson-Reid, Melissa: 1661
Jordan, David: 1363
Jordan, Maria Woodruff: 263
Jordan, Rhonda: 1514
Joseph, Dallas: 1112
Joseph, Jessica: 2176
Joseph, Mark: 131
Jovan-Embiricos, Morana, Ph.D: 2196
Joyce, William: 1100
Junker, Jeanne: 1053
Juranek, Nicole: 1274

K

Kabat, Joanna: 1343
Kachinsky, Christine M.: 1710
Kaelin, William G., Jr., M.D.: 2196
Kaiser, Miranda: 250
Kalama, Corbett A.K.: 53
Kallaus, Kurt J.: 1362
Kallenborn, John: 544
Kallin, Anne: 624
Kallon, Abdul, Judge: 205
Kalra, Sarah A.: 142
Kandarian, Steven A.: 2196
Kang, Emil: 486
Kang, Sewon, M.D.: 2026
Kann, Joe: 2361
Kaplan, Harvey L.: 1809
Kaplan, Robert: 23
Kapoor, Nita: 857
Kapulnik, Yoram: 1926
Karanth, Ullas: 1962
Karet, Laura Shapira: 1224
Karlin, Trish Devine: 1779
Karp, Marcie: 511, 675
Kasabach, Chris: 1467
Kasama, Hiroyuki: 1205
Kasper, Jay: 2102
Kassa, Amaha: 18
Katcher, Katherine: 1287
Katona, Dan: 445
Katterhagen, Kelly: 1156
Katz, Ellen: 1166
Katz, Roberta: 354
Katzenberg, Susan B.: 1162

References in index are to entry numbers.

Kauffman, Richard L.: 292
Kawamoto, Yuko: 791
Kay, Dean: 694
Kay, Gwen: 548
Kayafas, Peter: 399
Keane, James: 273
Kearney, Catherine B.: 153
Kearney, William: 1731
Kearns, Nadine Duplessy: 1202
Keating, Mike: 1166
Kee, Dorothy Davis: 85
Kee, William Given: 85
Keenan, Daniel J., Dr.: 1432
Keenan, Frances M.: 1
Keene, Margaret: 261
Keilin, Eugene: 1325
Keilty, Nancy B.: 27
Keiser, Kim: 1037
Keith, Stephen N., M.D., M.S.P.H.: 2062
Kelch, Tasida: 468
Keleher, John: 927
Kelley, Joseph: 218
Kelley, Liz: 287
Kellogg, Daniel: 732
Kelly, Brian: 1514
Kelly, Carolyn T.: 373
Kelly, Gina: 1176
Kelly, Katharine L.: 996
Kelly, Shannon: 2034
Kelly, Thomas F., Dr.: 1823
Kelly, William P.: 130
Kelmar, Steven B.: 5
Kelso, Karen E.: 1438
Kemper, Charlotte L.: 1809
Kempner, Jack: 158
Kempner, Randall: 158
Kempner, Thomas L., Jr.: 112
Kenan, Thomas S., III: 94
Kendall, Bethany B.: 233
Kendall, Tyler: 604
Kendrick, James M.: 694
Kennedy, Caroline: 791
Kennedy, Jack: 1756
Kennedy, James O.: 186
Kennedy, Martha H.: 356
Kennedy, Michael J., MBA, C.P.A.: 2218
Kennedy, Parker S.: 1455
Kennedy, Peggy: 1993
Kennedy-Rogers, Carmen: 263
Kennon, Nora: 1100
Kenny, Maugha: 1817, 1818
Kent, Dale: 1170
Keohane, Nannerl O.: 93
Kern, Hardy: 1931
Kerr, Anne B., Ph.D.: 45
Kerr, Cody T.: 161
Kerr, Laura D.: 161
Kerr, Robert S., Jr., Mrs.: 161
Kerr, Steven: 161
Key, Cheryl: 1112
Kezer, C. Henry: 33
Khalaf, Michel: 203
Khan, Fariha: 1154
Khan, Obaid Z.: 216
Khimm, Mia: 153
Khodakhah, Kamran, Ph.D.: 2212
Kiczek, Justin J.: 165
Kidd, Elizabeth: 69
Kieler, Charles B.: 404, 541
Kiepura, Marjan: 733
Kilbride, Mary: 458
Kiley, James P., Ph.D.: 2144
Kilgannon, Thomas: 1505
Kilgore, Joe D.: 458
Kilmurry, Simon: 417
Kim, Anne-Marie: 142
Kim, Byung: 1008
Kim, Jeffrey S.: 1287
Kim, Kirby: 613
Kim, Leezie, Esq.: 1058

Kimball, Kristi: 258
Kimball, Robert: 694
Kimelman, Don: 235
Kimmel, Barbara: 2263
Kind, Christina K.: 2341
Kind, Kenneth A.: 2341
Kind-Rubin, Valerie: 2341
Kindfuller, Andrew: 2341
King, Bill: 188
King, Judith S.: 1361
King, Kelly: 253, 1156
King, Martha: 246
King, Mary E.: 18
King, Michael J.: 120
King, Russell: 1925
King, W. Winburne, III: 1672
King-Monroe, Stephen L.: 2407
Kinghorn, Thomas J.: 28
Kingston, Robert, Dr.: 246
Kinloch, Soloman: 263
Kinnon, Kelly: 2330
Kinoshita, June: 2033
Kinsella, Susan, Dr.: 1562
Kirby, Jefferson W.: 165
Kirby, Lonny: 1558
Kirby, Nancy J.: 90
Kirby, S. Dillard: 165
Kirch, Darrell G., M.D.: 2062
Kirkpatrick, Frederick S.: 1208
Kirsic, Mike: 2323
Kirton, Carl A., D.N.P., R.N.: 2243
Kiss, Elizabeth: 96
Kistler, Brian: 1431
Klag, Michael J.: 229
Klein, Jonathan: 2213
Klein, Leigh Kirby: 165
Klein, Linda Dorn: 1779
Kleiner, Charlene C.: 333
Kleinhaus, Emil: 594, 595
Kleinmann, Rami: 1489
Klesa, J. Michael: 1916
Klevan, Rebecca: 996
Klose, Donna D.: 2145
Kloth, Ronni: 181
Kluttz, Susan: 1156
Knabe, Walter: 416
Knapp, Andy: 1431
Knauf, Noah: 2196
Knight, Jeff: 264
Knight, Michael: 478
Knight, Nicholas: 478
Knight, Phaidra: 997
Knight, R.M., Jr.: 289
Knobloch, Carla: 80
Knott, Erin: 168
Knott, Marion I.: 168
Knott, Martin G., Jr.: 168
Knott, Martin G., Sr.: 168
Knott, Owen M.: 168
Knott, Teresa A.: 168
Knowles, Marie: 261
Knox, Allison G.S.: 1562
Knutson, Richard: 2223
Kochard, Lawrence: 1992
Koerth, Maggie: 1731
Koh, Howard K., M.D., M.P.H.: 2046
Kohn, Julie Ann: 391
Kollbaum, Peter, O.D., Ph.D.: 2255
Kollerstrom, Hanna: 355
Kolodgy, Kathleen: 919
Komljenovic, Robert: 2361
Konarska, Keith: 1164
Kongsgaard, Martha: 1961
Korf, Gene R., Esq.: 179
Korf, Scott: 179
Korn, Meredith: 246
Kortenhaus, Lynne: 502
Kortjohn, Martin D.: 1916
Kosinski, Dorothy: 47
Kostas, Diana L.: 165

Kotagal, Uma R., M.D.: 1166
Kotik, Charlotta: 504
Kovner, Victor: 1962
Kowalczyk, Andrew, Ph.D.: 2088
Kozik, Elisabeth: 693
Kraiem, Elizabeth Leiman: 246
Krainz, Anja: 693
Kramer, Larry: 137, 1247
Kramer, Mary L.: 263
Kramer, Robin: 1660
Krarup, Irene: 1877
Krava, Jen: 406
Kravet, Cary A.: 1325
Krecke, Kathryn: 157
Kreider, Matthew S.: 1362
Kreizenbeck, Jason: 1578
Krell, Candace: 1168
Kress, Cathann: 157
Kridler, Douglas F.: 1095
Krieger, John B.: 4
Kronick, Susan D.: 167
Kronley, Caroline B.: 786
Kroska, Andrea: 86
Kruger, Mary: 778
Kruse, William F., Esq.: 272
Kuczmarski, Thomas D.: 919
Kuda, Kim: 1883
Kuehnast, Kathleen: 788, 789
Kundert, David J.: 1170
Kuntz, Mark: 1435
Kunzel, Regina: 354
Kupchik, Andrew: 49
Kuraishi, Mari: 96
Kuriloff, Josh N.: 1325
Kurose, G. Alan, MD., MBA, FACP: 248
Kuykendall, Mary: 1569
Kvamme, Jean: 1402
Kwon, Julie Miraglia: 1247
Kyle, Doug, Dr.: 2416

L

Laffont, Ingrid C.: 41
Lambert, John D.: 169
Lambert, Michael: 250
Lambert, Rebecca: 250
Lamp, Kathryn: 1158
Lampert, Alan G.: 1019
Lampland, Martha: 778
Lampo, Nicholas: 731
Lanahan, Marty: 96
Lance, Ryan: 1975
Landenberger, Brett: 357
Landers, Matt: 901
Landers, Richard: 49
Landes, Andrea: 1335
Landesman, Debby: 1346
Lane, Alexina H.: 95
Lane, Christina: 1761
Lane, Karren: 1287
Lang, William P.: 1046
Lange, Heidi, C.R.H.A.: 2187
Lange, Michael: 479
Langenburg, Dianna: 157
Langley, Paul: 1328
Langston, Christopher A., Ph.D.: 1282
Lanham, Philip: 1166
Lanphear, Gail E.: 2194
Lapeyre, Charles: 544
Lapin, Chava, Dr.: 594, 595
LaPlante, Jennifer: 2201
Lara, Alicia: 983
Large, Barry: 1112
Larkin, Heather: 1059
Larsen, John: 188
Larsen, Nicole: 232
Larsen, Sara: 111
Larson-Cody, Jennifer: 213
LaRue, Sharon: 979

References in index are to entry numbers.

Lashley, Elinor: 743
Lassiter, Zachary: 24
Lauder, Laura: 225
Lauderbach, William C.: 2194
Laurence, Anna Marie: 147
Laurich, Jackie: 1256
Lavery, Kathy: 1672
Lavigne, Cat: 1034
Lavin, Kevin, D.V.M.: 2034
Lavine, Matthew: 548
Lavine, Steven: 130
Lawley, Thomas J., M.D.: 301
Lawrence, Karen: 330
Lawrence, Lise: 2328
Lawrence, Myra: 1100
Lawrey, Aisha: 2394, 2395
Lawrie, Robert: 2181
Lawson, Mark A., Ph.D.: 924
Layton, Gabrielle, Ph.D: 2196
Layton, Thomas C.: 1264
Lazarof, Janice Taper: 278
Le Du, Helen: 49
Leach, Kenneth C.: 1046
Lechleiter, John C.: 181
LeCompte, Celeste: 1731
Lederman, Stephanie: 1998, 1999
Lee, Andrew: 1916
Lee, Ashley: 129
Lee, Dwight E.: 130
Lee, Esther: 203
Lee, Janice Y.K.: 399
Lee, Jennifer 8.: 613
Lee, Ken: 506
Lee, Moses: 213
Lee, Nancy P.: 1334, 1359
Lee, Paul W.: 1073
Lee, Robert, C.P.A.: 2093
Lee, Vivian S., M.D.: 1335
Lefer Kuhn, Anna: 18
LeFevour, Kathleen: 1078
LeFevour, Suzanne A.: 1078
Legary, Andrea: 1316
Legendre, Yasmine R., MPA: 2046
Lehman, John F., Hon.: 491
Lehr, John L.: 2232
Leibold, Peter M., Esq.: 1314
Leibowitz, Nicholas: 1993
Leis, Jorge, Ph.D.: 911
Leith, Jennifer: 90
Lemieux, Annie: 2187
Lemke, Jill: 213
Lenart, Brian R.: 1224
Lenehan, Thomas: 292, 1817
Lenkowsky, Leslie: 4
Leon, Mercedes: 216
Leon, Tania: 694
Leonard, Patrick: 1431
Leonard, Stephanie: 164
Leong, Amye L., MBA: 1282
Leppanen, Karen L.: 67
Lerchbacher, K.A.: 184
Lerner, Suzanne: 983
Lescaze, Alexandra: 1736
Lesko, John, Ph.D: 911
Leslie, Leigh A.: 1350
Leung, Yin Ling: 983
Leutenachlager, David: 228
Levenson, Robert W.: 2324
Leventhal, Alan M.: 2196
Leversage, Jill: 1328
Levin, Rachel: 917
Levine, Richard J.: 1733
Levine, Ruth: 594, 595
Levit, Nicole: 782, 784
Levy, Reynold: 246
Levy, Sarah: 904
Lewis, Alison M., Ph.D.: 662
Lewis, Anne: 1077, 1224
Lewis, David, M.D.: 2338
Lewis, George: 705

Lewis, Jenny: 163
Lewis, Mark, D.P.M., Dr.: 1431
Lewis, Mary Ellen: 1716
Lewis, Michelle: 694
Lezama, Michele: 2394, 2395
Li, Junlei: 1037
Li, Philip: 1092
Li, Simon K.C.: 330
Liebman, Michael N., Ph.D.: 2073, 2292
Liederman, Carl: 1965
Liefer, Diana McLean: 195
Lien, Tyson: 188
Lightman, Bernard: 548
Lilly, Eli, II: 181
Lim, Serena: 121
Lin, Ba Zin: 1100
Lin, Leisle: 264, 1828
Lin, Tan: 613
Lin, Thomas: 1731
Lincoln, Edward, Dr.: 776
Lincoln, Kate: 5
Lind, Linda: 714, 715, 716
Lindenberg, Debbi: 47
Lindholm, Gerald: 1505
Lindo, Nashormeh: 394
Lindsey, Melvin D.: 1079
Lindsey, Rachel: 238
Lindvall, Bruce, Ph.D.: 911
Ling, Con Way: 486
Linker, Adam: 1355
Lintott, James W.: 791
Linz, Susan: 778
Linzer, Daniel, Ph.D.: 1827
Linzer, Lindsey: 206
Lippert, Martin: 203
Lipschutz, Neal: 1733
Lipscomb, Kristine: 1827
Lipsey, Rebecca Fishman: 206
Lisher, Mary K.: 181
Litterman, Robert: 264
Little, Dan: 256
Littlewolf, Nevada: 996
Liverett, Deborah: 1213
Livingston, David M., M.D.: 2196
Llewellyn, David: 96
Lloyd, Heidi Mage: 1779
Lloyd, Robin: 1731
Lockhart, Stephen H., Dr.: 229
Lockman, Carol Ressler: 543
Loeb, John L., Jr.: 823
Loew-Friedrich, Iris, M.D.: 2073, 2292
Loft, Richard M., M.D.: 1306
Loftis, Heather: 1059
Logan, Matt, M.D.: 1246
Loh, Penn S.: 1340
Lohrey, Ilona: 901
Lomax, Claire: 235
Lomax, Michael L., Ph.D: 939
Lombardi, Ryan: 2143
London, George, Mrs.: 733
Lonergan, James A.: 2330
Long, Ken E.: 116
Long, Michael, Ph.D.: 2212
Longman, Laura J., MBA: 1225
Longobardi, Frank: 2200
Loo, Wade W.: 1247
Loper, Robert B.: 506
Lopez, Lourdes: 112
Lopez, Maria: 199, 673, 674, 875, 906
Lord Wood of Anfield: 842
Loring, Robert S.: 1361
Loring, Valerie S.: 1361
Louis, Errol: 246
Loum, Cyril D.: 746
Lovass, Stephen: 218
Love, Jamie, Ms.: 2024
Lovelace, Robert: 1079
Lovett, Tiffany W.: 1208
Lowe, Elizabeth: 232
Lowe, Rick: 89

Lowry, Glenn D.: 201
Lozada, Carlos: 1729
Lozano, Monica C.: 295
Lubchenco, Jane: 229
Lucas, Charles C., III: 94
Lucas, Wonya: 1099
Luce, Bryan R., Ph.D., MBA: 2073, 2292
Lucio, Josh: 941
Ludwick, Adriane, Dr.: 1616
Luedeke, J. Barton: 1552
Lui, Earl: 1287
Lujan, James: 951
Lumarda, Joseph M.: 1287
Lumme, Dale: 2388
Lummis, Isabel: 1376
Lund, Jay: 1053
Lundmark, Fredrik, Dr.: 355
Lungren, Daniel E.: 1455
Lupi, Ginnie: 438
Luria, Isaac: 81
Luria, Ryan: 64
Lurie, Peter, Dr.: 2413
Lux, Mike: 18
Lynch, Elizabeth M.: 46
Lynton, Lily: 130
Lyskin, Zander: 1431
Lytle, Travis: 1112

M

Ma, Yo-Yo: 703
Mabry, Rhett N.: 94
Mabuchi, Kanako: 775
MacCowatt, Thomas H.: 142
MacDonald, John A.: 1809
MacFie, Valerie: 268
Mach, John R., Jr., M.D.: 134
Mack, Robert, Ed.D.: 927
Maclachlan, Patricia, Dr.: 776
MacLeod, Hazel: 1516
Macpherson, Fiona, Prof.: 873
Macrae, Jim: 1323
MacRae, Patti: 5
Madigan, Fran, III: 2376
Madison, Scott: 1578
Madole, Haley Davis: 85
Maestas, Steve: 1046
Magallenez, Marisa: 1046
Maguire, James: 202
Mahler, Heather: 1123
Mahoney, Hildegarde E.: 2025
Mailer, Dee Jay: 53
Mailloux, Kari: 414
Maine, Lucinda: 2287
Mainprize, Daphne: 624
Majeed, Yasmin Adele: 613
Makary, Tamer: 1154
Makkar, Lamia: 1034
Maksimovic, Nem: 2023, 2163, 2164
Malanga, Anthony, M.D.: 2145
Malesardi, Doris Fischer: 404, 541
Malik, Tariq: 1731
Mallett, Veronica, M.D.: 2249
Malloy, Amanda: 368
Maloney, Timothy J.: 1166
Manapat-Sims, Maria Cristina: 791
Mancini, Ginny: 694
Mand, Martin: 1205
Mandala, Anil: 1164
Mandes, Vinny: 368
Manfredi, Tony: 436
Mangold, Robert: 504
Mani, Meera, M.D., Ph.D.: 1325
Mankoff, Marcia Weiner: 1186
Manocherian, Jeffrey: 730
Mansfield, Todd: 253
Mansur, Susan C.: 33
Mantz, Jeffrey: 1812
Manus, Mara: 442

Manydeeds, Stephen: 947, 948
Manyika, James: 137
Manz, Beatrice: 805, 806, 807
Mao, Yi Ling: 391
Maple, Ted: 181
Mapp, Karen L.: 1340
Marcum, Deanna, Dr.: 776
Marcus, Gregory S.: 1170
Maree, Aran, M.B., B.Ch.: 2073, 2292
Marin Luna, Sergio: 1340
Marino, Theresa J.: 1282
Marion, Ken, Dr.: 1616
Mark, Jason: 1964
Mark, Peter: 733
Mark, Reuben: 1975
Markanda, Tina: 50
Markel, Kate Levin: 194
Markham, Leah: 1205
Marmor, Max: 506
Maroney, Mary P.: 1572
Maroon, Joseph: 1992
Marotta, Kim: 1970
Marquez, Enrique: 705
Marren, Joan M., M.Ed., R.N.: 2243
Marron, Catie: 93
Marshall, David G.: 2196
Marshall, Megan: 585
Marston, Carolyn: 1122
Martahus, Craig R., Esq.: 62
Martey, Katy Easterly: 1067
Martin, Courtney J.: 365
Martin, George: 996
Martin, James R.: 219
Martin, Jim: 1155
Martin, Kay: 1809
Martin, Kevin: 543
Martin, Stacy J.: 292
Martin, Valerie: 72
Martin, Wayne: 443
Martin, Webb F.: 1208
Martineau, Sylviane: 398
Martinez, Alexis: 1202
Martinez, Elaine: 100
Martinez, Jorge: 167
Martinez, Juan: 167
Martinez, Lizzie: 1348
Martinez, Paul: 157
Martinez, Sonia: 2355
Martinez-Helfman, Sarah: 1154
Martins, Tatiana R.: 786
Marx, Robert: 254
Marx, Robert O.: 491
Masiello, Kate: 1100
Maskin, Eric S.: 130
Mason, Betsy: 1731
Mason, Chelsea: 1012
Mason, Linda: 1073
Mason, Linda A.: 229
Masor, Harold: 1186
Matchett, Terri: 27
Mathies, Allen W., Jr., M.D.: 2330
Mathieson, Duncan: 2201
Mathieson, Peter F.: 1077
Mathis, William N.: 1376
Mathison, Dani: 293
Mathur, Renee J., M.D.: 2026
Mathur, Sourabh: 1431
Matsukado, Ann: 53
Matsumoto, Kenji: 775
Matsuura, Shuji: 1205
Matteson, C. John: 152
Matthews, Allan: 211
Maurer, Gilbert C.: 1735
Mavis, Richard K.: 169
Maxwell, Marcie: 1431
Maxwell, Scott E.: 2324
May, Jeremy O.: 1339
Mayer, Charles B.: 41
Mayer, Cheryl: 1316
Mayer, Christine Amer: 167

Mayer, Theodore V. H.: 506
Mayes, Kris: 1964
Mayfield, Pinkie: 128
Maynard, Olivia P.: 1208
Mazmanian, Daniel A., Dr.: 1660
McAdams, Ernest F., Jr., Esq.: 1166
McAleer, Linda J.: 2222, 2223
McAllister, Megan: 1049
McAuley, Bob: 2119
McAvoy, Laura K., Esq.: 1306
McBride, James: 694
McBurney, Elizabeth I., M.D.: 2026
McCabe, George: 4
McCaffrey, Eileen: 1387
McCall, Carol: 1516
McCandless, Bridget, M.D.: 1809
McCaney, Shawn: 235
McCann, Allison: 357
McCarter, Fred: 1138
McCarthey, Sarah: 1434
McCarthy, Barry: 86
McCarthy, Gina: 1964
McCarthy, Kerry: 216
McCarthy, Peter: 2187
McCarthy, Suzanne: 842
McCarty, Kathleen: 1799, 1800
McClamroch, Michael: 1011
McClellan, Art: 2361
McCloud, Elizabeth: 1560
McClung, Lindsay: 1160
McConn, Margaret E., C.P.A.: 251
McConn, Phyllis: 277
McConnell, Vicki: 1867
McCormack, Kristen J.: 1018
McCoy, Michael K.: 198
McCracken, Kris: 1067
McCutcheon, Maureen T.: 142
McDonald, Brian: 168
McDonald, Christina: 606
McDonald, Heidi: 1569
McDonald, Meghan: 168
McDonald, Patty: 1164
McDonnell, Alicia S.: 193
McDonnell, James S., III: 193
McDonnell, Jeffrey M.: 193
McDonnell, John F.: 193
McDonough, Colleen: 694
McDonough, Kathleen A., Ph.D.: 2145
McDowell, Deborah E.: 364
McElroy, Bridget E.: 1078
McElwaine, Andrew: 1970
McFarland, JoAnne: 653
McFarlane, Matt, Ph.D, J.D.: 2212
McFate, Robert W.: 2075
McGaffey, Jere D.: 25
McGarry, Michael H.: 240
McGee, Vincent: 1092
McGhee, David: 263
McGill, Anthony: 703
McGill, Carroll: 168
McGill, Peter: 168
McGillvary, Tracy B.: 641
McGinley, John R., Jr.: 1224
McGinnis, Jim: 1393
McGovern, Dawn: 1213
McGrath, Don J.: 1975
McGruder, Depelsha: 112
McGuire, Kent: 292
McGuire, Patricia: 47
McHenry, Stacy: 27
McIntosh, James C.: 53
McIntosh, James H.: 53
McIntyre, Cathy: 2201
McJunkin, Donald R.: 192
McKay, Mary: 1661
McKenna, Deborah J.: 267
McKenna, Laura K.: 2341
McKenzie, Debra: 1334, 1359
McKenzie, Jill: 543
McKenzie, Megan: 1022

McKeown, Jean: 1100
McKinney-James, Rose: 1964
McKinstry, Gregory J.D.: 1328
McKissick, Anne: 264
McKnight, Shawn, Bishop: 752
McKnight, Tacoma: 2249
McLain, Quincy, C.P.A.: 1325
McLaughlin-Korologos, Ann: 2025
McLean, Helen: 1788
McLean, Julianne N.: 134
McLean, Sandra L.: 195
McLean, Wendy: 195
McMahon, John: 415
McMahon, Kristan: 868
McMahon, Marybeth, Ph.D.: 2167
McNally, Jan: 458
McNally, Shanlee: 1022
McNamara, James: 965
McNiff, Audrey A.: 134
McNulty, Roger: 694
McPheeters, Paul C., Rev.: 33
McQuade, Barbara: 1181
McReynolds, Erna Morgan: 404, 541
McRobbie, Laurie Burns: 416
McWherter, Lisa C., Dr.: 2
Mead, Leslie: 1134
Meador, David E.: 1181
Meadows, Eric: 198
Meadows, John: 198
Meadows, Mark A.: 198
Meadows, Robert A.: 198
Meaney, Susan: 137
Meares, Tracey L.: 153
Meehan, Edward F., M.P.H.: 1314
Meehan, John T., Dr.: 2
Meere, Wyman: 506
Megan, Chris: 1965
Megonigal, Patrick: 1983
Mehrotra, Gita: 1360
Mehrotra, Priti: 1281
Meier, Linda R.: 354
Meisel, Joseph: 1453
Meissel, Franz-Stefan, Dr.: 852, 853
Meissner, Rose: 1120
Mekaru, Linda: 53
Mekemson, Kristen: 1170
Melamed, Carol: 128
Melamed, Leo: 594, 595
Melmed, Matthew E.: 1037
Mendez, Nancy: 131
Mendez, Tony: 248
Mendillo, Jane L.: 201
Mendoza, Lorie: 218
Menkiti, Bo: 1202
Menon, Vatsala: 2387
Mercier, Monique: 2187
Merck, Friedrike: 202
Merck, Wil: 202
Mercurio, Richard, D.D.S.: 2096
Merin, Kenneth D.: 1018
Merk, Greg: 218
Merkel, Joel C.: 147
Merklin, Karen: 479
Merritt, Sarah: 448
Meserve, Lauren: 1817, 1818
Metcalf, Kim: 2119
Metras, Claire: 398
Metzger, William L.: 1076
Meurs, Mieke: 778
Meyer, E. Nicole: 606
Meyers, Howard: 235
Meyers, Jack: 581
Meyers, Marissa: 1034
Meystre, Douglas Q.: 8
Mezey, Mathy, Ed.D., R.N.: 2243
Michalak, Anna, Dr.: 1624
Michel, Timothy: 85
Michioka, Ronald: 412
Miletich, Joseph P., M.D., Ph.D.: 2073, 2292
Miliniski, Sarah: 363
Millard, Jayne: 486

Miller, Ann T.: 92
Miller, Dana L.: 213
Miller, Edith D.: 927
Miller, Edmund: 153
Miller, John: 2361
Miller, Joy: 1577
Miller, Julia A., Dr.: 1037
Miller, Marcus: 694
Miller, Mark: 1735
Miller, Mick: 1431
Miller, Pamela T., Esq.: 2062
Miller, Shawn: 303, 1956
Miller, Terry, M.S.W.: 1224
Miller, Toraya: 901
Miller, Will: 292
Miller-Rehfeldt, Jennifer: 118
Milling, R. King: 1975
Milnes, Sherrill: 730
Milstein, Howard P.: 1325
Mims, Adrienne D., M.D.: 919
Mims, Marcus, C.P.A.: 1046
Mindich, Eric: 201
Minor, Judy: 1247
Minor-Ragan, Yvonne, Ph.D.: 222
Minter-Jordan, Myechia, Dr.: 1073
Miranda, Marie Lynn: 93
Mirsky, Burton M.: 2025
Mitchell, James: 24
Mitchell, John P., Rev. Dr.: 1037
Mitchell, Joseph: 254
Mitchell, Joseph C.: 325
Mitchell, Kate: 1247
Mitchell-Thomas, Kamilah: 1733
Mitsu Klos, Diana: 1733
Mitterholzer, John: 131
Mitzel, Mikayla: 1578
Mixon, Arrington: 253, 1156
Modell, William D.: 2166
Moeller, Max: 543
Moen, Linda L.: 746
Moen, Zachary: 731
Moerman, Filip: 820
Moffett, Mardell: 47
Moffett, Thomas: 225
Moler, Kathryn: 354
Molina, Gloria, Hon.: 1079
Moll, Jon H.: 28
Moloney, Michael H.: 1888
Monahan, Michael T.: 67
Monahan, Susan T.: 61, 282, 999, 1257
Moncrief, Kit: 1975
Mondoro, Traci, Ph.D.: 2121
Monhollon, Rusty, Dr.: 1575
Monson, Ingrid: 705
Montante, Alex: 1100
Montgomery Tabron, La June: 157
Montojo, Caroline, Ph.D.: 2025
Montoya, Consuelo: 394
Moodie, Danielle: 983
Moody, Elizabeth: 211
Moody, Libbie Shearn: 211
Moody, Ross R.: 211
Moody, W.L., Jr.: 211
Moody, William S.: 820
Moody-Dahlberg, Frances Anne: 211
Mooney, Katie: 901
Moore, J. Steven: 689
Moore, Jeremy: 788, 789
Moore, Johnny B., Jr.: 1354
Moore, Kevin S.: 1492
Moore, Marshall: 1256
Moore, Michele: 112
Moore, S.D.: 289
Moore, Steven G.W.: 213
Moore, Summer: 1079
Moore, Taylor F.: 117
Moore, Theresa: 248
Moorhouse, Linda: 689
Morales, Angel Luis: 965
Morales, Elizabeth: 263

Morales, George J., Ph.D.: 2407
Morales, Susana R., M.D.: 1325
Morales, Vince: 240
Morehead, Shawn: 216
Morel, Miguel: 1034
Morella, Constance A., The Hon.: 47
Morello, Maurizio: 2341
Moreno, Paula: 112
Morgado, Javier: 486
Morgan, Charles O., Jr.: 739
Morhouse, Sanford W., Esq.: 2196
Moriarty, Brunilda: 142
Moriearty, Perry: 1346
Morin, Darryl D.: 1170
Morley, Ashlee: 1155
Morning, John: 1037, 1208
Morowitz, Jacob: 594, 595
Morris, James T.: 228
Morris, Joseph W.: 256
Morris, Kimberly: 198
Morris, Martha: 195
Morris, Thomas Q., M.D.: 1075
Morris, Traci: 1218
Morse, Michael: 823
Morse, Samuel C., Dr.: 776
Mortazavi, Seena: 868
Moscicki, Richard, M.D.: 2073, 2292
Moscone, Jonathan: 394
Moses, Ansley: 1112
Mosher, Scott: 254
Mosley, Daniel L.: 1029
Mosqueda, Teresa: 1079
Mostue, Emily C.: 1082
Motley, J. Keith, Ph.D.: 1073
Mott, Maryanne: 1208
Moulds, Donald: 1335
Moulin, Trenton E.: 2075
Mountcastle, Holt: 24
Mountcastle, Kara: 24
Mountcastle, Kathy: 24
Mountcastle, Ken: 24
Mountcastle, Mary: 24, 247
Moy, A. Mika, O.D.: 2255
Moy, David: 1340
Moy, Ronald L., M.D.: 2197
Moyer, Scott: 2043
Mucci, Gary L.: 1100
Muir, Jeffrey S.: 1099
Mulcahy, Mary: 47
Mulchaey, John, Dr.: 1624
Mulkeen, Maria: 1340
Mullen, Michael: 171
Mullen, Stephanie: 30
Mulligan, Alisa E.: 229
Mulligan, Terence: 1287
Mullin, Ann K.: 131
Mullins, Donald C., Jr.: 142
Munger, Wendy: 330
Munoz, Cecilia: 153
Munroe, Anna Warburton: 247
Muraco, Julie: 1092
Murase, Satoru: 791
Murdy-Michael, Heidi: 1710
Murguía, Ramón: 157
Muria, Vaughn R.: 1325
Murnane, Richard: 1418
Murphy, Catherine J., Ph.D.: 1827
Murphy, David M.: 849
Murphy, Leah: 49
Murphy, Leslie A.: 194
Murphy, Maura E., Esq.: 61, 282, 1257
Murphy, Michael S.: 746
Murphy, Pamela: 107
Murphy, Stacia: 1321
Murray, Marcus: 2304
Murray, Michael J., Ph.D.: 85
Murray, Tim: 1154
Muscarolas, Miriam: 295
Musgrave, Thea: 733
Musolino, Sheila: 1031

Musser, Marcie J.: 122
Musser, Robert W.: 122
Mwanza, Angela K.: 93
Myers, John H.: 2196

N

Nadosy, Peter A.: 2025
Nagarajan, Sundaram: 218
Nagaur, Grace: 2323
Nagy, Gregory: 316
Nakasone, Michael: 689
Nakatomi, Debra: 1287
Nash, Bonnie: 2
Nash, Creshelle, M.D.: 1059
Nash, Shannon: 1247
Nasir, Na'ilah Suad: 1418
Natarajan, Jyothi: 613
Nathanail, Janet: 391
Natori, Josie Cruz: 391
Naumes, Sue: 1082
Naylor, Mary D., Ph.D., FAAN: 1314
Neal, Ann: 446
Neal, David L.: 247
Neal, Stephen C.: 137
Neas, Kiele: 1817
Nedd, Khan: 157
Needham, John A.D.: 849
Negron, Jennifer: 1029
Neils, Jenifer: 389, 809, 810, 811, 812, 816
Nelms, Charlie: 1208
Nelson, Alondra: 201
Nelson, Anna Spangler: 167
Nelson, Arvid R., Ph.D.: 1672
Nelson, David, Dr.: 1616
Nelson, Frances: 714, 715, 716
Nelson, John A.: 2119
Nelson, Jon: 1218
Nelson, Mary Goodwillie: 1270
Nelson, Peggy: 478
Nelson, Sue: 1119
Ness, Don: 1218, 1970
Ness, Ken: 2304
Nessen, Peter: 1073
Nettles, Cory L.: 1170
Neuhaus, Jennifer Mull: 1975
New, Eliza: 594, 595
Newbold, N. Carter, IV: 186
Newbury, Mary V., Hon. Madam Justice: 1328
Newkirk, Pamela: 493
Newman, David Wheeler: 1079
Newman, Kim: 213
Newman, Robert: 340
Newman, Stacy: 1458
Newsome, Clarence G.: 94
Ney, Alison: 1460
Neyman, Craig: 229
Nguyen, Tram: 1202
Nicholls, Katherine A.: 442
Nichols, Martin: 868
Nichols, Sandra B., M.D., FAAFP: 2062
Nicholson, James B.: 67
Nicholson, Mamie: 1246
Nicholson, Paul: 1082
Nickelson, Donald E.: 1455
Nielsen, Cara: 143
Nielsen, Christina: 330
Niemann, Craig: 273
Niepoky, Eli: 1042
Nieto, Ida: 965
Nieto, Kristina: 81
Nigam, Kamal: 1224
Niinami, Takeshi: 791
Niland, Bridget: 1100
Nipper, Steve: 1059
Nissen, Steven A.: 232
Nix-Hines, Crystal: 1079
Nixon, Kelly: 791
Nixon, Ronald T.: 60

References in index are to entry numbers.

Noak, MaDonna: 535, 536, 537, 538, 539
Noe, Kevin: 723
Noe'Rourke, Catherine: 723
Noland, Mariam C.: 67
Nolte, Kathleen: 186
Norcia, Jerry: 263
Nordberg, E. Wayne: 130
Norich, Samuel: 23
Noriega, Chon A.: 966
Norris, Bradley K.: 219
Norris, Brooks B.: 219
North, Oliver L., USMC (Ret.), Lt Col: 1505
Norton, Sylvia: 658
Nottberg, Leigh: 1809
Novakov, Lydia H.: 139
Novasio, Mike: 901
Nozaki, Koji: 775
Nutter, James B., Jr.: 1809

O

O'Brien, Bridget A.: 1078
O'Brien, Conor: 2376
O'Brien, Marie L.: 1170
O'Brien, Sean: 2187
O'Bryan, Michael: 1154
O'Connell, Michael F., Esq.: 61, 282, 1257
O'Connor, Lisa: 660, 661
O'Donnell, Kevin J.: 84
O'Donnell, Laurence G.: 1733
O'Donnell-Tormey, Jill: 2182, 2184, 2185
O'Hanley, Ron: 1073
O'Hare, Donna, M.D.: 2145
O'Hearn, Brian: 287
O'Hern, Veronica: 418
O'Keefe, Valerie: 367
O'Mara, Collin: 1977
O'Neil, Brian S., MBA, C.F.A.: 2042
O'Neil, Shannon K.: 786
O'Neil-McElrath, Tori: 1202
O'Neill, Timothy M.: 221
O'Neill, Wendy: 391
O'Quinn, Dustin: 901
O'Reilly, Richard J., M.D.: 2196
O'Shaughnessy, Laura: 128
Oakman, Jake: 416
Oberland, Greg: 1170
Ocen, Pricilla: 1779
Ochester, Ed: 644
Odahowski, David A.: 45
Oden, Vivian: 1176
Odmark, Erick: 1418
Odom, Cindy: 1100
Odum, Marvin E.: 80
Oetinger, Judy: 27
Oghalai, John S., M.D.: 2261
Ogle, Laura Kerr: 161
Ogles, Marisa: 1112
Oh, Alex: 901
Okorn, David: 1196
Okoroafer, Michael: 171
Older, Anne G.: 404, 541
Older, Stephanie: 2052
Oler, Lorraine: 486
Olfers, Kristan: 1259
Olfers, Sarah H.: 1259
Olivarez, Juan: 1270
Oliver, Lin: 646
Oliver-Farrow, Elizabeth: 965
Oliveros, Gumersindo: 242
Olson, Beverly Knight: 167
Olson, Leigh: 2119
Olsson, Bjorn: 355
Ono, Moto: 775
Oosterveen, Robin L.: 300
Opperman, Mike: 1919
Oravillo, Aaron: 1360
Orcutt, Cynthia: 425
Ormond, Karen: 19

Ornstein, Peter A.: 2324
Orr, David: 229
Orr, Katherine: 229
Orr, Susan Packard: 229
Ortez, Tim: 295
Orth, Cornelia Laemmli: 729
Ortiz, Christine, Ph.D.: 911
Ortiz, Nieves: 2323
Ortiz, Nolan: 1305
Osborn, David, C.F.A.: 1166
Osborne, Joe: 1431
Osborne, Robert C., Jr.: 1325
Osher, Barbro: 225
Osher, Bernard: 225
Osman, Johanna: 1270
Osso, Michael: 2166
Ostrow, David N.: 1328
Oswald, Neal: 2201
Otero, Maria: 242
Ott, Alan W.: 2194
Ottensmeyer, Patrick J.: 1809
Otter, Kari Den: 1202
Otting, Monika: 1925
Oubre, Linda: 295
Ouellette, Charles: 1190
Overlock, Trina: 1975
Owen, Sarah: 1248
Owens, Lisa: 1340
Owens, Melissa: 520
Owens, Reginald, Dr.: 1733
Oya, Nasahiro: 1435
Oyebode, Gbenga: 112
Oyler, Tennyson S.: 228

P

Pace, Nicholas A., M.D.: 1321
Pack, Karen: 1809
Packard, Julie E.: 229
Packer, Ed: 269
Padron, Eduardo: 1418
Paige, Katie Schwab: 258
Paik, Lisa: 2041
Painchaud, Francois: 2187
Painter, Nell: 424
Palandjian, Tracy: 1073
Palenchar, David J.: 100
Paley, Mark: 1340
Palfrey, John: 167
Palmer, Ann M.: 2200
Palmer, Elizabeth A.: 134
Palmer, Jodie: 951
Palmer, Lesley H.: 1205
Palmer, Nancy J.: 192
Palmer, Scott: 192
Panion, Henry, III, Dr.: 384
Pankam, R. Shani: 1340
Pansky, Scott: 2119
Pappano, Joseph E., Jr., Dr.: 266
Pappous, Perry: 1435
Paradee, Jennifer: 1361
Pardi, Lita Ugarte: 1099
Parfet, Donald R.: 1767
Parfet, Sydney: 1767
Parikh, Sudip, Dr.: 1723
Parke, Jennifer Hudson: 1181
Parke, Joseph R.: 1181
Parker, Amy Fenton: 2015
Parker, Darrell, Dr.: 1575
Parker, Deanie: 458
Parker, Franklin E., IV: 1266
Parker, Grant: 1962
Parker, Gray S.: 41
Parker, Jason C., Ph.D.: 1809
Parker, John F.: 1266
Parker, John, Jr.: 2283
Parker, Katie: 2010
Parker, Linda H.: 1046
Parker, Margaret H.: 1266

Parker, Mary Kay: 41
Parkes, Adam: 606
Parks, Diane: 2119
Parks, Terrence: 946
Parrella, Nicholas J.: 1802
Parrish, Susan Scott: 334
Partee, Karen: 459
Partin, Kelli: 1509
Partlow, Glenda: 1567
Partridge-Hix, Paige: 1059
Pass, Gregory A., Ph.D.: 623
Patazkis, Michele: 733
Patillo, Mary: 1016
Patiño, Douglas X.: 1208
Patrick, Cindy M.: 198
Patrick, Janice: 253, 1156
Patt, Richard A.: 179
Patten, Jennifer: 486
Pattenaude, Damien, Dr.: 1431
Patterson, Aubrey A.: 414
Patterson, Jane S.: 247
Pauli, Eric: 302
Paupe, Christian: 2187
Pavelka, Martin S., Jr., Ph.D.: 2145
Pavlovsky, Lilia: 660, 661
Payne, Dana: 448
Payne, Hal D.: 1100
Paz, Harold, M.D., M.S.: 5
Paz, Pedro: 1243
Peaper, Kelsey: 416
Pearlman, Mary O'Brien: 1514
Peasnall, Brian: 805, 806, 807
Pecht, Thomas P.: 1306
Peeler, Andy: 1059
Peet, Shelly: 218
Pell, Tripler: 134
Peltekian, Elizabeth M.: 47
Peltier, Valerie: 216
Pelton, M. Lee: 1073
Pembroke, Jeff: 218
Pena, Allison J.: 142
Pena, Rob: 1961
Pena, Saul: 189
Pendolino, Lisa: 892
Pennington, Hilary: 112
Pennoyer, Russell P.: 4, 1016
Penoyer, Darren: 1100
Pensiero, Karen Miller: 1733
Pepo, Nicole: 1931
Pereira, Mark: 1164
Perez, Bea: 965
Perez, Betsy: 694
Perez, Brittany: 479
Perez, Daniel: 1247
Perez, Daniel Paul: 2033
Perez, Gilad, Prof.: 867
Perez, Maritza, M.D.: 2197
Perkins, Arnold X.C.: 1287
Perkins, Nicole: 486
Perkovic, Sara, Ph.D.: 911
Perkul, Leslie: 221
Perlman, Noah B.: 904
Perreault, Jacques Y., Prof.: 315
Perry, Anthony J., M.D.: 919
Perry, Dana B.: 186
Peters, JoAnne: 1078
Peters, Robert, Dr.: 1429
Peters, Thomas, Ph.D.: 189
Petersen, Robert, C.P.A.: 1334, 1359
Peterson, Dawn Culbertson: 198
Peterson, Jeff: 1227
Peterson, Julie: 1029
Peterson, Michael L.: 2407
Peterson, Stephen: 689
Peterson, Steven D.: 1528
Peterson, Temple: 1078
Peterson-Mangum, Cicely, Esq.: 1034
Petito, Donne: 1662
Petran, Ruth: 2415
Petrone, Joseph C., Mrs.: 135

Petrozelli, Erika Riddle: 421
Petterson, Jay: 901
Pettit, Peter: 1354
Pettit, Steve: 1575
Pettker, John D.: 1455
Petts, John A.: 730
Petty, Frank B.: 27
Pew, Cary: 273
Pew, Robert C., III: 273
Peyton, Sean: 459
Pfeifer, Drew: 1970
Pfeiffer, Dave J.: 1965
Pfister, Thomas: 261
Philipp, Alicia: 1099
Phillips, Arielle: 47
Phillips, Diana: 493
Phillips, Larry Bob: 515
Phillips, Nathaniel P., III: 41
Phillips, Nathaniel P., Jr.: 41
Phillips, Peter R.: 248
Phillips, Tamara S.: 27
Phillips, Tamara S., C.P.A.: 28
Philpott, Lily: 613
Piccolomini, Angelica Lippi: 686
Pienczykowski, Angelina: 786
Pierce, Russ W.: 2407
Piereson, James: 1029
Pierson, Anne Straton: 391
Pierson, Clare M.: 250
Pierson, Phebe: 250
Pierson, Robert L.: 1194
Pierson, T. Charles: 1808
Pieschala, Gregory A.: 330
Pieski, Mary Kay, Ph.D.: 841
Pieterelle, J. Coffy, M.D.: 2249
Pike, Chad: 1975
Pike, James: 373
Pileggi, Dominic F., Hon.: 266
Pillsbury, Marnie S.: 1029
Pine, Rachael N., J.D.: 1049
Pineda, Gladys: 1112
Pines, Darryll, Ph.D.: 911
Pinneo, Jeff: 213
Piper, Jeremy: 1208
Piper, William H.: 1208
Pipoli, Katherine: 193
Pisano, Jane G., Dr.: 1660
Pisca, Jeremy: 1578
Pitts, J. Bryan: 184
Pitts, Shawn, Dr.: 458
Platt, Allen C., III: 416
Pleasants, Sheila Gulley: 465
Pletka, Irena: 594, 595
Plikuhn, Mari, Dr.: 1562
Pliner, Barbara Bing: 1099
Plocher, Jessica: 47
Plump, Andrew, M.D., Ph.D.: 2073, 2292
Poccia, Richard J.: 493
Podlogar, Susan: 203
Podolsky, Daniel K., M.D.: 139
Pohotsky, Tatiana: 216
Poindexter, Dashinika: 1363
Poler, Dwight: 1073
Poling, Kristi: 30
Polis, Jared: 396
Polivka, Karen Tiller: 412
Polley-Nordhaus, Gail: 996
Pollock, Robert: 628
Polomski, Stanley: 49
Polzin, David: 383
Pomeroy, Claire, Dr.: 1334, 1359
Ponchner, Debbie: 1731
Ponting, Wendy: 1170
Pontsler, Aaron V., M.S., MBA: 2286
Poo, Ai-jen: 112
Poplin, Chris: 253, 1156
Poppe, Patricia K.: 73
Porrino, Peter: 2222, 2223
Porter, David L.: 168
Porter, Joanna O.: 168

Porter, Kelsey: 2213
Porter, Laurel: 168
Porter, Martin: 168
Porter, Richard: 849
Porter-O'Grady, Timothy: 2235
Porzecanski, Arturo C.: 786
Posie, Stacie: 18
Post, Anton, Prof.: 881
Post, Janis: 1970
Poterba, James: 264
Potolicchio, S.J.: 2090
Pourier, Lori: 419
Pouschine, Tatiana: 4
Powell, Denise, M.D.: 2062
Powell, James: 1710
Powell, Jeffrey: 1610
Powell, Nena: 186
Prager, Merril: 118
Pratt, Marcel: 235
Pratt, Roger: 1033
Pray, Barbara H.: 35
Pray, Donald E.: 35
Preble, Jan: 293
Predmore, Jeane: 1155
Preisser, Brenna: 1076
Prelock, Patricia A.: 2262
Prendergast, S. Lawrence: 1037
Prescott, Elizabeth, Dr.: 1824
Presley, Kimberley D.: 219
Pressman, Jeffrey H., M.D.: 404, 541
Price, Michael: 694
Price, Terry: 302
Price-Letscher, Jennifer: 232
Printz-Platnick, Tobi: 47
Pritzker, John: 225
Prizel, Ilya: 594, 595
Prochaska, Alice, Dr.: 842
Prochnow, Jennifer: 302
Prohaska, Thomas R., Ph.D.: 919
Przewrocki, Shelley S.: 274
Pulver, Laurie Self, M.D.: 1246
Purugganan, Michael: 264
Putnam, Thomas O.: 404, 541

Q

Quam, Lois: 1335
Quigley, Eliza: 158
Quinn, Terrence M.: 1876
Quinn, Whayne: 47
Quinonez, Sonia: 1202
Quisenberry, Cynthia: 1429

R

Rachleff, Andrew S.: 2196
Radcliff, Derron: 1393
Ragin, Luther, Jr.: 1346
Rahe, Maribeth: 1166
Raindre, Elizabeth S.: 41
Raine, John: 842
Raj, Kumar: 263
Rajani, Rakesh: 137
Rake, Christopher: 2361
Ralstrom, Fran: 1929
Ramani, Ananthakrishnan, M.D.: 2145
Ramanujam, Nandini: 1661
Ramey, Samuel: 730
Ramirez, Steven: 1031
Ramme, Leslie: 1087
Ramos, Pedro A., Esq.: 1223
Ramous, Olga: 1672
Ramsey, Evan: 1959
Ramshaw, Emily: 1729
Rand, Bryan: 1099
Randall, Gail T.: 8
Randle, Kathryn A.: 739
Randolph, Nina: 1992

Random, Cindee: 739
Randt, Virginia: 1735
Ranelle, Shanda: 1569
Rangel, Carlos: 157
Rankin, J. David: 1970
Ranville, Andrew: 1190
Rao, Serena: 354
Rao, Venkat Dhenuvakonda: 73
Rapaport, Brooke: 504
Rappa, Gail: 436
Rasmussen, Elisa: 302
Raso, Rosanne, M.S., R.N.: 2243
Rassler, Bridget I.: 1314
Rattray, Carol: 391
Rau, Erik: 543
Rauch, Scott, M.D.: 2338
Raulet, Marie-Anne: 398
Raveis, William, Jr.: 2196
Rawles, Nancy: 1888
Rawlinson, Rex: 1377
Ray, Gilbert T.: 1660
Raynolds, Will: 154
Reade, Colby: 213
Rector, Amy: 1127
Redd, Kimberly: 1443
Redmond, Chuck: 96
Redrob, Karen: 363
Reed, John C., M.D., Ph.D.: 2073, 2292
Reed, Marci: 368
Reed, Walter G.D.: 333
Reeve, Todd: 1959
Reeves, Mamiko: 868
Reeves, Marsha Y.: 29
Regan, Kathleen: 1335
Regulska, Joanna: 778
Reich, Rob: 1418
Reid, Esthanette: 47
Reid, John C.: 1099
Reid, Rosalind: 1731
Reid-Smith, Randall: 472
Reimann, Nancy B.: 2330
Reinhackel, Sherrie J.: 60
Reis, Judson: 1016
Reisberg, Darren: 153
Reisdorf, Jackie: 222
Rembe, Toni: 1264
Remnick, David: 1729
Renaud, Anne-Marie: 2201
Render, Cecilia: 218
Renehan, Bryan: 2263
Rennie, Missie: 391
Repplinger, William M.: 122
Resnick, David: 246
Reuss, Mark: 263
Revoyr, Nina: 232
Revson, Charles H., Jr.: 246
Reyes, Susana, Dr.: 1431
Reyna, Diane: 478
Reynolds, Catherine: 73
Reynolds, Jan: 169
Reynolds, Robert J.: 189
Reynolds, W. Noah: 247
Reynoldson, Mike: 1578
Rhodes, Amy: 458
Ribeiro, Richard A.: 1037
Rice, Linda: 1176
Rice, Mabel L., Dr.: 1606
Rice, Valerie Montgomery, M.D.: 2046
Rich, Brian F.: 73
Rich, Harvey: 179
Rich, Linda: 30
Rich, Marsha E.: 1317, 1322
Richard, Alison: 1962
Richard, Karen: 1053
Richards, Cecile: 112
Richards, Jeff: 1431
Richards, Roxanne: 189
Richardson, Elaina: 399
Richardson, John: 1672
Richardson, Nico: 1672
Richardson, Peter L.: 1672

Richardson, Tanyelle: 1464
Richardson, Tyler B.: 1672
Richdale, Kathryn L., O.D., Ph.D.: 2255
Richert, Mark: 1474
Richland, Scott: 1186
Richman, Avi: 786
Richman, Estelle B.: 1016
Richmond, John: 594, 595
Richter, James: 778
Richter, Sidney D.: 2145
Ridzi, Frank M.: 1086
Riegel, Kyle: 2361
Riehl, John H., IV: 168
Riehl, Margie: 168
Riehl, Michael: 168
Riley, Bettina: 1616
Riley, Emily C.: 72
Riley, John A.: 45
Riley, Melissa: 1741
Riley, Thomas A.: 72
Rine, James D.: 1809
Rinehart, Marsha K.: 169
Riney, Robert G.: 1181
Rios-Aguilar, Cecilia: 1418
Rist, Ray C.: 1661
Ritzen, George: 198
Rivera-Torres, Nancy: 1016
Roach, Michele C.: 739
Robb, Lynda J.: 677
Robbins, Chuck: 112
Robbins, Katie H.: 139
Robbins, Mark: 1956
Robbins, N. Clay: 181
Roberson, Chantelle: 1112
Roberts, Kim: 2189
Roberts, Marci: 459
Robertson, Jocelyn: 415
Robertson, Kenneth: 1170
Robertson, Wilhelmina E.: 80
Robins, Elizabeth, Esq.: 2197
Robins, Harlan W.: 1096
Robins, Perry, M.D.: 2197
Robinson, Chase F.: 408
Robinson, Irwin Z.: 694
Robinson, Janet: 248
Robinson, John H.: 52
Robinson, Robby: 269
Robinson, Stephen C.: 216
Robinson, Theresa G.: 751
Rocha, Adriana: 1092
Roche, Carrie: 118
Roche, Kevin: 253
Rochow, Garrick J.: 73
Rockefeller, Charles: 391
Rockefeller, David, Jr.: 391
Rockefeller, Susan: 391
Rockefeller, Tara: 250
Rockenbach, Barbara: 1817
Rodgers, Brooke: 168
Rodgers, Denise: 1266
Rodgers, Fran: 250
Rodgers, Jonathan: 496
Rodgers, Mary Anne: 229
Rodgers, Patrick: 168
Rodgers, William: 1661
Rodriguez, Adam: 965
Rodriguez, Edwin R., Jr.: 1975
Rodriguez, Gina: 965
Rodriguez, Ray: 167
Roell, William, B.S., C.P.A.: 2042
Rogers, Karen H.: 94
Rogers, Margot M.: 153
Rogers, Nancy N.: 1992
Rogers, Richard L.: 194
Rogers, Sally J.: 1325
Rogers, Victoria: 167
Rohrbach, Sharon: 746
Rojas, Carmen: 122
Roller, Shamus: 1359
Rolston, Bradley P., Esq.: 91

Romo, Erin: 357
Ronco, Silvia, Ph.D.: 1827
Ronk, Jayson: 1578
Rooks, Steve: 486
Roole, Barbara: 96
Roper, Mitchell: 1569
Rosales, Alex: 206
Rose, C. Brian: 805, 806, 807
Rose, Catherine: 139
Rose, Kim: 169
Rose, T.J.: 1073
Rosen, Ellen: 1186
Rosen, Mark: 901
Rosenbaum, Randall: 451
Rosenberg, Dianne M.: 1166
Rosenberg, Mark A.: 238
Rosenthal, Irwin M.: 2166
Rosenzweig, David C.: 489
Roseski, Holly: 2416
Ross, George E.: 1208
Ross, Robert K., Dr.: 295
Rossi, Carlo: 686
Rosson, Chris: 1809
Rostov, David: 147
Roth, Amber, Dr.: 2416
Rothblatt, Daniel M.: 1186
Rothblatt, Faith: 2323
Rothschild, Loren R.: 330
Rottunda, Sara: 1078
Roux, Malcolm: 1993
Rowe, Betsy: 1330
Rowen, Mary Anne Rothberg: 354
Royal, Pamela J., M.D.: 66, 1098
Royce, Michael L.: 441
Royster, Randy: 1046
Royzman, Natella: 1186
Rubin, Jennifer: 2255
Rubin, Judith O.: 216
Rubin, Laura: 1970
Rubio, Luis: 786
Ruch, Joshua: 340
Rudd, Jason: 458
Rudner, Diane: 1354
Rueda, Juanita Galvis: 5
Ruiz de Velasco, Jorge: 292
Rullman, Stan, Dr.: 1625
Rumelhart, Judith D.: 285
Ruschak, Blane: 1710
Rush, W. Omari: 428
Russell, Cristine: 1731
Russell, Jenny: 202
Ruta, Vanessa, Ph.D.: 2212
Rutherford, Danilyn, Dr.: 1817, 1818
Ryan, Ray: 1112
Rybak, R.T.: 1204
Rybolt, Ryan: 1166
Ryer, Paul: 1814, 1815

S

Sabedra, Jessica: 243
Sachs, Adam P.: 1809
Sadowski, Kim: 1086
Saenz, Thomas A.: 1079
Safrit, Lynne Scott: 253
Safyer, Steven M., M.D.: 2046
Sagawa, Shirley: 242
Sakamoto, Clyde M., Dr.: 412
Salami, Seun: 1325
Salas, Angelica: 1287
Salcido, Anthony: 965
Salinas, Maria Elena: 965
Salmon, Jane E., M.D.: 216
Salmon, Marla, Dr.: 1514
Samolczyk, Mark: 1249
Samper, Cristian: 153
Sampson, Elbert: 90
Samson, Earl A., III: 134
Samuels, Diane: 112

Samuels, Richard J., Dr.: 791
Sanchez, Emilio: 1737
Sanders, Carolanne: 1360
Sandison, James: 1316
Sandorf, Julie: 246
Sandoval, Lester, Dr.: 951
Sandrock, Alfred, M.D., Ph.D.: 2073, 2292
Sandy, Heather Moulaison: 660, 661
Sani, Nicola: 686
Sankey, C. Patrick: 872
Sant, Vickie A.: 169
Santana, Miguel A.: 295, 1079
Santanello, Nancy C., M.D., M.S.: 2073, 2292
Santino, Alyssa: 92
Santora, Kenneth, Ph.D.: 1310
Santucci, Marryn D.: 228
Sanzio, Anthony: 49
Sapon, Anne: 1046
Saran, Sally: 1330
Sardone, Frank J.: 1767
Sargeant, Geoffrey: 694
Sarnoff, Deborah S., M.D.: 2197
Sarofim, Louisa: 1376
Sattler, David G.: 2255
Sauls, Shanaysha M.: 29
Sauvayre, Sara Chubb: 1266
Savage, Barbara D.: 1817
Savage, Eleanor: 419
Saville, Bei: 1266
Savoy, Caroline: 2085
Savoy, George M.: 2085
Sawyer, Raymond T., Esq.: 62
Sayer, Doug: 1578
Sayre, Teresa: 1082
Scace, Barbara: 235
Scalan, Jenna Skinner: 983
Scales, Jason: 2393
Scales, Suzanne: 1606
Scanlon, Erin: 1449
Scarola, Albert: 1205
Schakelford, Marcia: 1225
Schatz, Edward: 778
Scheid, Randy: 1315
Scherago, Nina: 506
Scherer, Carol: 795
Scherer, Thomas: 340
Scherzer, Mitchell: 1735
Schieber-Acker, Traude: 759
Schiff, Stacy: 130
Schisler, Kurt E.: 169
Schlack, Marilyn: 1767
Schlener, Jennifer: 2062
Schlessinger, Evan: 1186
Schlonsky, Michael: 1096
Schmid, Kate: 129
Schmidt, Cade: 901
Schmidt, Oscar: 203
Schmidt, Paul: 1733
Schnabel, Rockwell, Hon.: 1455
Schnarr, Laura: 1567
Schneider, Eric C., M.D.: 1335
Schneider-Salomon, Susanne: 831
Schnur, Eric R.: 184
Schoeler, Martina: 831
Schoenbaum, Stephen C., M.D., M.P.H.: 2046
Schoenhoff, Katie: 1363
Schoenmann, Charlotte: 1046
Scholl, Barry A.: 1335
Scholl, Pamela: 257
Scholnick, Lynn Okon, Ms.: 951
Schooley, Susan, M.D.: 194
Schoor, Thelma, B.S.N., R.N.: 2243
Schoppa, Leonard J., Jr., Dr.: 776
Schotland, Marvin I.: 1186
Schramling, Shaine: 1191
Schroeder, Lisa: 1224
Schubach, Carolyn: 1434
Schuckman, Karen: 1821
Schuette, Bill: 2194
Schuette, William G.: 2194

Schultz, Jonathan D.: 746
Schumann, Barbra: 450
Schwamborn, Laura: 1100
Schwark, Mary: 1929
Schwartz, Alan: 1514
Schwartz, Eric: 130
Schwartz, Mark: 1186
Schwartz, Mike: 47
Schwartz, Stephen: 694
Schwartz, Susan: 1378
Schweizer, Felix E., Ph.D: 2212
Schwenn, Carolyn: 1011
Schwer, Paul: 1961
Schwister, Ann: 1166
Sconiers, Rose H., Hon.: 1100
Scott, Elizabeth H.J.: 1330
Scott, F. Laurence, Jr.: 26
Scott, Frank L.: 26
Scott, Joshua: 228
Scott, Lauren E.: 158
Scott, Patrick: 1434
Scott, Peter, C.A.E., MBA: 2255
Scott, Rick: 419
Scott, Rita: 1505
Sculco, Cynthia, Ed.D., R.N.: 2243
Sealey, Michelle: 251
Seals, Carol E.: 28
Searles, Simonne: 263
Sears, Suzanne Harte: 294
Seaver, Martha: 261
Sedgley, Anna: 1733
Sedmak, Rich: 1034
Sedonaen, Maureen: 189
Seelbach, William R.: 62
Segal, Susan: 996
Segal, Susan L.: 786
Segarra, Tere: 228
Seiden, Michael V., M.D., Ph.D.: 2196
Seiders, Ed: 2387
Seiders, Stella: 2387
Seidler, Lee J.: 493
Seitter, Keith L., Dr.: 2365
Seitz, Karen D.: 2196
Self, Furman C.: 1246
Self, J.C., III: 1246
Self, Sally E., M.D.: 1246
Self, W.M., Jr.: 1246
Sells, Marcia Lynn: 246
Semelsberger, Ken: 98
Sen, Rinku: 983
Senchak, Andrew: 424
Sevillano, Lina M.: 876
Seymour, Peter: 354
Shabot, S. Benjamin: 158
Shafer, Kevin: 1970
Shah, Nirav R.: 134
Shaheen, Tim N.: 228
Shane, David N.: 181
Shang, Ruby: 391
Shank, Suzanne: 263
Shanley, Frank E.: 1003
Shannon, Kathleen T.: 1313
Shapira, Edith L., M.D.: 1224
Shapiro, Adina: 25
Shapiro, Alex: 694
Sharma, Prakash, Dr.: 1616
Sharpe, Dan A.: 1095
Sharpe, Valerie L., O.D.: 2255
Sharples, Amber: 446
Shaughnessy, Sandy: 405
Shaw, Kathleen: 1103
Shaw, Minor M.: 94
Shaw, Ruth: 253, 1156
Shearer, Chad: 1325
Sheehan, Mary: 1100
Sheely, Jay: 1916
Shelby, Tommy: 1729
Shelden, William W., Jr.: 194
Shelley-Tremblay, John: 1616
Sheng, Kimberlee Pierce: 64

Shenk, Janet: 18
Sheppard, Eileen D.: 2330
Sherer, Todd, Ph.D.: 2030
Sheriff, Edd: 2
Sherman, Cindy: 130
Sherman, Cynthia: 614
Sherman, Marny: 1809
Sherman, Sandra Brown: 165
Sherry, Andrew: 167
Shibukawa, Atsushi: 1205
Shih, Anthony, M.D., M.P.H.: 1325
Shockley, Scott E.: 27
Shore, Debra: 1970
Shorris, Anthony: 1325
Shrut, Arlene: 733
Shubinski, Barbara: 581
Shuford, Alex: 89
Shuford, Karen L.: 139
Shulman, Randy: 330
Sidell, Sydney: 118
Siegel, Herbert J.: 2025
Siegel, Lawrence J., MBA, J.D.: 2243
Sieger, Diana R.: 129
Sieghart, Mary Ann: 873
Siegler, Julie A.: 181
Sieracki, John: 332
Sieracki, Michael: 1876
Sierra, Horacio: 606
Sieve, Richard, M.D.: 2093
Sifferlin, Elena Brito: 996
Silvers, Sam: 1449
Simbeck, Mauricio: 1247
Simmelink, Laura: 1109
Simmons, Janelle, Dr.: 1647
Simmons, Omar: 1340
Simms-Mackey, Pamela J., Dr.: 1287
Simon, John D., Dr.: 1514
Simon, Renee B., M.S., M.L.S., Hon.: 1282
Simoncini, Matthew: 1181
Simonds, Joshua: 722
Simone, Joseph A.: 1916
Simonian, Nancy, M.D.: 2196
Simons, John C.: 1325
Simpkins, Jesse: 1965
Simpson, Janis Randall: 2412
Simpson, Judy: 1431
Simpson, Megan: 1168
Simpson, Valerie: 694
Simril, Renata: 1305
Singh, Cynthia: 2027
Singh, Sarah: 137
Singleton, Candi Castleberry: 983
Singleton, Gregory: 911
Sion, L. Gilles: 820
Sirmans, Franklin: 504
Siruno, April: 1482
Sit, Roger: 1346
Sittler, Hana: 759
Sjoquist, Gregg D.: 293
Skach, William, M.D.: 2167
Skaff, Daniel: 189
Skipwith, Aurelia: 1975
Skovronsky, Daniel, M.D., Ph.D.: 2073, 2292
Skrzesz, Ken: 427
Skulimowski, Marek: 708, 838, 839, 840, 1525, 1526
Slaughter, Sara: 1439
Slick, Duane: 502
Sloan, Cliff: 242
Sloan, Robert: 47
Sluder, Greenfield: 46
Sluder, Hendrika: 46
Slutsky, Lorie A.: 216
Small, Clara, Dr.: 1562
Smart, Ashley: 1731
Smiley, Neil: 2283
Smiley, Vance: 1059
Smith, Adam, Prof.: 842
Smith, Andy: 280
Smith, Bradford K.: 786

Smith, Brittni, Ph.D.: 2286
Smith, C. Craig: 2407
Smith, Chad: 703
Smith, Cherida Collins: 64
Smith, Christina Ittleson: 1341
Smith, Cindy: 157
Smith, Gary N.: 1254
Smith, Gerald: 211
Smith, James Allen: 1092
Smith, Johnny Mac, Dr.: 2034
Smith, Kathy: 198
Smith, Kathy Steinauer: 1274
Smith, Kevin G.: 2394, 2395
Smith, Lorenzo: 1018
Smith, Marie: 1196
Smith, Mark D., M.D.: 1335
Smith, Richard M.: 1029
Smith, Rob: 181
Smith, Robert B., Jr.: 1992
Smith, Robert, Jr.: 1022
Smith, Robert W.: 689
Smith, Sheila, Dr.: 776
Smith, Steven M: 28
Smith, Stewart R.: 1455
Smith, Tara: 49
Smith, Thomas: 2386
Smith, Virgil L.: 247
Smith, Walter H., Jr., Ph.D.: 1224
Smith-Baker, Chanda: 996
Smithers, Adele C.: 1321
Smithers, Brinkley: 1321
Smithers, Nikki: 1321
Smits, Steve: 1965
Smyers, Robyn Minter: 62
Smyth, Geralynn D.: 168
Smyth, John: 168
Sneider, David: 776
Snidow, Robin: 122
Snijdewind, Heather: 2046
Snoddy, Candis: 317, 318, 319, 320
Snow, David H.: 268
Snow, Elizabeth: 268
Snow, Jonathan L.: 268
Snow, Keegan: 268
Soboroff, Steven L.: 295
Soderman, Ludy: 90
Soler, Mark: 1016
Solomon, Geula R.: 904
Solomon, Peter J.: 904
Solomon, Sheena: 1160
Somers, John F.: 1100
Sommersell, Necole: 1316
Song, Allan: 1672
Song, Unmi: 118
Sosland, Meyer J.: 1809
Soto-Harmon, Lidia: 1202
Southall, Roderic: 996
Souto, Sofia: 416
Spacinsky, Charlotte L.: 745
Spalding, Pamela: 247
Sparks, Candace: 79
Spartz, Maggi: 1263
Spaulding, Jean G., M.D.: 94
Speed, Shannon: 960
Spellman, Mary: 1455
Spencer, David: 228
Spencer, Henry B.: 2243
Spencer, Tracy Toon: 250
Spencer, Valerie: 996
Spero, Suzanne: 1023
Spielberg, Steven: 917
Spoone, Dan: 1474
Sprigle, Karen: 1227
Sprong, Bradley N.: 1710
Squillace, Scott E., Esq.: 1073
Srajer, Teresa: 2213
St. Gelais, Laurie: 2031
Stack, David: 114
Stack, Richard L.: 1448
Stafford, E. Alexandra: 544
Staggers, Leroy, Dr.: 1575

Stahuljak, Zrinka: 357
Stallings, Janine C.: 228
Stam, Deirdre C.: 325
Stamp, Trent: 1012
Stamps, Sheila A.: 1514
Stanek, Mary Ellen: 1170
Stanton, Janet E.: 192
Stanwick, Paul: 804
Starr, G. Gabrielle: 130
Starshak, Michael J.: 919
Staryk, Noa: 1346
Staryk, Ted: 1346
Stasa, Marta: 759
Staton, Sara: 748
Steadman, Sally J., Ph.D.: 2407
Steeger, Dean H.: 1018
Steele, Bill: 1931
Steeley, James H.: 1560
Stein, Eugene: 1186
Stein, Todd: 429
Steinberg, Neil D.: 248
Steinmetz, Michael A., Ph.D.: 2275
Steinmeyer, Mark: 1672
Stemer, Yolanda: 416
Stenskold, Eva, Dr.: 355
Stenson, Diane M.: 181
Stephan, Allan J.: 733
Stephens, Louise: 229
Stern, David, Dr.: 904
Stern, Walter E.: 1046
Sterritt, Lisa: 901
Stetson, E. William, III: 1672
Stevens, Jerry: 1246
Stevens, Katherine: 332
Stevens, Marcella M.: 193
Stevens, Simon: 1335
Stevenson, Bryan: 112
Stevenson, Dick: 269
Stewart, Carter: 153
Stewart, Marise M.M.: 1208
Stiner-Jones, La'Tonia, Ph.D.: 911
Stockert, Dave: 1099
Stockert, David P.: 301
Stodd, Jamie: 168
Stoga, Alan: 786
Stokely, Clayton F.: 274
Stokely, Kay H.: 274
Stokely, William B., III: 274
Stokely, William B., IV: 274
Stolle, Joan: 1274
Stone, Amy: 1439
Stone, Andrew W.: 2344
Stone, Barbara: 1439
Stone, David: 1439
Stone, Debbie: 1439
Stone, Jeffrey: 1439
Stone, Jennifer: 1439
Stone, Mark A.: 2033
Stone, Michael A.: 1439
Stone, Samantha: 1797
Stone, Sandra: 1439
Stone, Sara: 1439
Stone, Steven M.: 1439
Stoquart, Vincent: 284
Stowe, Julie: 1112
Stowers, Ryan: 1401
Strain, John: 287
Strandjord, Jeannine: 1809
Strange, John: 1218
Streb, Elizabeth: 419
Streng, Hadley: 1164
Strickland, Annette: 1033
Strickland, William: 1224
Strine, Alice, Esq.: 266
Strmecki, Marin J., Ph.D.: 1672
Strongin, Naomi: 1186
Stuart, Dwight L., Jr.: 1035
Stubbe, Federico: 1975
Stubi, Gerhard: 2243
Stuller, David: 169

Suares, Rocky, C.F.P.: 1282
Suarez, Michelle: 1274
Subotnick, Stuart: 493
Subramaniam, Mega: 660, 661
Subramanian, Sneha: 1468
Subramanian, Suresh: 2391
Sudbeck, Carol R.: 228
Sugimoto, Madeleine S., M.Ed., R.N.: 2243
Suilebhan, Gwydion: 641
Sukys, Susan: 169
Sullivan, Heike, Esq.: 927
Sullivan, Michael, Dr.: 169
Sullivan, Pat: 1578
Sullivan-Marx, Eileen M., Ph.D.: 1325
Sulzberger, Cynthia: 2196
Sulzberger, Gabrielle: 112
Sumida, Susan: 53
Summerville, Scott: 1435
Sunderland, Trey: 2338
Sundman, Peter E.: 1514
Sundram, Clarence: 2341
Sung, Victor, M.D.: 2213
Supplee, Lauren: 1016
Suro, Roberto: 1660
Sustic, Mark: 1037
Suttles, Rebecca: 1112
Sutton, Alexis: 1213
Sutton, Evelyn, Dr.: 2201
Suzuki, Marcia: 1305
Swain, David: 1164
Swan, Philip A.: 2330
Swanson, Judy C.: 2196
Swanson, Scott: 49
Swanson, Zack: 1965
Swartz, Gigi: 1888
Swartz, Steven: 1735
Swayze, Carolyn: 1330
Swearer, Dell Marie Shanahan: 414
Swedlund, Searle: 444
Sweeney, Brian: 221
Sweetland, Theresa: 406
Swift, Dan: 391
Synder, Rani E., M.P.A.: 134
Syrmis, Pamela: 1341
Systrom, Nicole: 1964
Szapary, Gladys V.: 333
Szczepanik, Joan: 218
Szczotka-Flynn, Loretta, O.D., Ph.D.: 2255
Szmagala, Taras, Jr.: 98
Szutu, Peter C., M.P.H.: 1282
Szymanska, Gosia: 839
Szymanski, Jeff, Ph.D.: 2328

T

Tabankin, Margery: 18
Tagore, Sundaram: 391
Talamantes, Efrain, M.D., MBA: 2062
Talbot, Victor, M.D.: 1341
Talty, John: 93
Tambascio, Michelle: 1089
Tan, Lydia: 78
Tanaka, Akihiko, Dr.: 791
Tanaka, Shelly: 1700
Tani, Daniel, Dr.: 791
Tappan, Philip: 1059
Tarnopolsky, Matias: 703, 720
Tate, Joe: 2361
Tate, Lloyd P., Jr.: 247
Tate, Richard: 1287
Tavlin, Michael J.: 1274
Taylor, Benjamin: 130
Taylor, Bill: 1935
Taylor, Gareth R.: 2337
Taylor, Heather: 1733
Taylor, Helen: 1208
Taylor, Kerry: 689
Taylor, Nicole: 1247
Taylor, Peter J.: 232

Taylor, Scott: 201
Taylor-Thompson, Kim: 242
Tehan, Jean: 1119
Teich, Andreas: 2194
Tellez, Kip: 1434
Templeton, Alice: 982
Templeton, Mark: 89
Tennant, Brad, Dr.: 1562
Tenny, Barron: 216
Tepper, Michelle: 1828
Testa, Barbara Ann: 733
Thao, Pheng: 996
Tharp, David W.: 2415
Thomas, Alison, Dr.: 710
Thomas, Carl M.: 74
Thomas, Chris: 86
Thomas, Dominique: 2213
Thomas, Edwidge, D.N.P.: 2243
Thomas, Hughes C.: 1900
Thomas, James A.: 232
Thomas, Janice: 1202
Thomas, Robert: 2304
Thomas, Sarah E.: 201
Thompson, Carla: 157
Thompson, Chapel: 247
Thompson, Jere W., Jr.: 139
Thompson, Jessica: 118
Thompson, Kim: 78
Thompson, Leslie, Ph.D.: 2213
Thompson, Margaret E., M.D.: 285
Thompson, Robert: 1059
Thompson, Roslyn Dawson: 990
Thompson-Schill, Sharon: 2324
Thornbury, Kimberly: 213
Thorndike, Dan: 1082
Thorne, Daniel K.: 158
Thornton, Kiley: 2176
Thouvenin, Jean-Marc: 1773, 1774, 1776
Thurman, Punita Dani: 263
Tiedens, Lara, Dr.: 1514
Tielsch, Erin: 168
Tienda, Marta: 264
Tierney, Sue: 1964
Tillapaugh, Ellen: 404, 541
Timmerman, Stacy: 69
Timms, Henry: 703
Tingley, Chad: 1439
Titcombe, Don A., M.S.S.W.: 251
Tivey, Margaret K.: 1654
Todaro, Veronica: 2232
Todd, Russell G., Dr.: 1733
Tohtsoni, John, Jr.: 951
Toledano, Macon C.: 186
Tome, Ramon: 1099
Tomke, John A.: 1975
Tomlinson, Jonathan E., Dr.: 315
Toone, Brian, Dr.: 1616
Torabi, Masoud: 901
Torchia, Sandra B.: 1710
Torgerson, William T.: 746
Torgow, Gary: 263
Torma, Anna: 1578
Torregrossa, Bernice C.: 211
Torres, Nahir: 1340
Torres-Springer, Maria: 112
Tortorelli, Joseph J.: 228
Tourigny, Cheryl A.: 5
Tovar, Erica: 211
Towles, Amor H.: 292
Towne, Andrew: 868
Townsend, Margaret W.: 186
Traggio, Anna: 131
Trandahl, Jeff: 1975
Travland, Heather A.: 41
Trebour, Todd: 451
Tresnan, Steven: 720
Trevett, Kenneth P.: 1731
Tribe, Mark: 419
Triebwasser, Shayna Rose: 917
Trinchero, Brisa: 491

Triplett, Timothy W.: 1809
Trotti, Ricardo: 1737
Trouveroy, Olivier: 820
Trowbridge, Carrie: 216
True, Mike: 213
Trull, R. Scott: 1259
Tsandikos, George: 114
Tseng, Vivian: 1016
Tsoumas, Richard: 157
Tsujita, Aya: 791
Tsutsui, William M., Dr.: 776
Tucher, Andie: 585
Tucker, Barry: 730
Tucker, Robert S.: 730
Tucker, Therese: 1079
Tuller, Betty, Ph.D.: 2333
Tully, Mary Beth C.: 1325
Tunheim, Kathy: 1346
Tunstall, Wendy M.: 576, 577, 578
Turnage, Jennifer: 71
Turner, Laura Jennings: 60
Turner, Matt: 1614
Turner, Nat: 2196
Turner, Peggy: 965
Turner, Reginald M.: 67, 1181
Turner-Lowe, Susan: 330
Tutt, R. Thayer, Jr.: 100
Tyler, Ron, Ph.D.: 1254
Tyre, Peg: 1018
Tyree, John D'A.: 774
Tyree, Stephanie: 24
Tyus, Derek L.: 1170
Tzougros, George: 474

U

Ubarry, Grizel: 1266
Uchinaga, Yukako: 791
Uddin, Jafreen: 613
Ueshima, Takeshi: 791
Ulak, James T., Dr.: 791
Ulishney, Bryan: 235
Underwood, Danielle: 111
Underwood, Katie: 503
Unebasami, Lloyd: 412
Unterberg, Ann: 216
Upton, Cody: 687
Urbanski, Allie: 1100
Urbina, Julio: 254
Urbina, Ricardo M.: 677
Urrutia, Luz: 1247
Ushioda, Yoichiro: 391

V

Vachher, Monica: 1514
Vaessen, Jos: 1661
Vagnone, Mary: 1320
Valadez, Mary: 990
Valcourt, Marie, C.P.A.: 2187
Valentine, Anne Penny: 416
Vallance, Alan: 378
Vallely, Mark J.: 1975
Valliant, John R.: 162
Van Alfen, Peter, Dr.: 307
Van Camp, Peter: 2196
van Daele, Frans: 820
van der Horst, Ellen: 1166
van der Willik, Odette: 1998, 1999
Van Dusen, Amanda: 1181, 1767
Van Hook, James W., M.D.: 2249
Van Horn, Scott: 1059
Van Nostrand, Abbie: 489
Van Putten, Mark: 1270
Van Ranst, Alfred F., Jr.: 1073
Van Veckhoven, Michael: 1393
Vance, Alix: 1888
Vance, Derek: 1168

Vance, Kathleen M.: 677
Vandel, Kate: 456
Vander Ploeg, Mark: 1418
Vander Roest, Stan: 129
Vanderberg, Ann, MBA, R.N.: 2243
VanderRoest, Stan: 1015
Vanderwerken, Mark: 1100
VanHeest, Barb: 1164
Vanison, Richard C.: 404, 541
Varey, Downey R.: 919
Vargas, Cesar: 965
Vargas, Fidel A.: 965
Vargas, Sandy: 996
Varney, Sara: 363
Vasko, James G.: 2337
Vasquez, Francisco M., Ph.D.: 222, 1100
Vasset, Sophie, Dr.: 704
Vaughn, Andrew G., Ph.D.: 818
Vaughn, Gregory J., Dr.: 1099
Vaughn, Isaac: 1247
Vaughn, Mark, Ph.D.: 911
Vaz, Sara: 218
Vedder, Tim: 1578
Vega, Jeffrey M.: 1225
Vega, Susan: 786
Velazquez, Deborah T.: 1049
Ventura, Danne: 2255
VerDuin, Pat: 1164
Vergani, Ezio: 1514
Vergano, Dan: 1731
Verrill, John H.: 2352
Vessey, Judith Ann, Ph.D., R.N.: 2243
Vessey, Rupert, FRCP, D.Phil.: 2073, 2292
Vest, Lee Diane Collins: 64
Victor, Robert: 235
Viguier, Salome: 398
Villar, Carmen Sachiko: 2062
Villatoro, Ranfis Giannettino: 1360
Vincent, George H., Esq.: 1166
Vinik, Nina: 153
Vinjamuri, Leslie, Dr.: 842
Vinson, Ben, III: 340
Viramontes, Jose: 1046
Visbal, J. Malcolm: 120
Visher, Melva D.: 222
Viswanathan, Suresh, M.S., Ph.D.: 2255
Vives, Julie: 206
Vizanko, Jim: 1218
Voelkel, Emmett: 168
Voelkel, Ryan: 168
Volcansek, Mary, Ph.D.: 1254
Volker, Bernard: 711
Von Beschwitz, Bastian: 868
Von Drehle, David: 1809
Vorhees, Marianne: 28
Vossekuil, Ellen: 1931
Vosshall, Leslie, Dr.: 1817
Vraney, Inge L.: 745
Vraney, Jeffrey: 745
Vraney, Lawrence E., Jr.: 745
Vraney, Lori: 745
Vraney, Maura J.: 745

W

Wachenfeld, William: 1018
Wachtell, Wendy: 92
Wagner, Andrew F., M.D.: 2249
Wagner, Barbara: 261
Wagner, Harry: 594, 595
Wahl, Kristina L.: 30
Wakefield, Cathy: 1259
Wakefield, Mary K.: 2046
Waldorf, Emily: 49
Waldron, Kathleen: 786
Waletzky, Naomi: 250
Wali, Alaka: 89
Walker, Darren: 112
Walker, Douglas P.: 774

Walker, Joseph: 720
Walker, K. Todd: 94
Walker, Laura, MBA: 1335
Walker, Mark: 96
Walker, Sheria: 1160
Walker, Terry L.: 27
Walker, Trenholm: 89
Walker-Smith, Marrea D.: 195
Wall, Mary Brooks: 248
Wallace, Dawn: 111
Wallace, Moira: 873
Wallask, Robert M.: 33
Wallen, Kamilah: 206
Walley, Noah: 1016
Wallin, Marilyn: 731
Walling, Kevin: 240
Wallis, Craig: 1259
Wallman, Joel: 1658, 1659
Walport, Mark, FRS, Prof. Sir: 873
Walsh, Edward F., Jr.: 222
Walsh, John N., III: 1100
Walsh, K.C.: 1975
Walsh, Michele: 2201
Walsh, Phil: 1344
Walsh, Richard J.: 45
Walt, Chuck: 1218
Walter, Michael, Dr.: 1624
Walters, John R., M.D.: 1306
Walters, Joyce: 1431
Walton, Ronnie L.: 1393
Wands, Scott: 322
Wang, Liam: 250
Wang, Zhi-yong, Dr.: 1624
Wankel, Robert E.: 493
Ward, Jane: 1202
Ward, John A.J.: 156
Ward, Kari: 436
Ward, Robert: 1393
Ward, William R.: 100
Warmack, Dwaun, Dr.: 1575
Warman, Michele S.: 201
Warner, Alexandra: 1100
Warner, Gregory H., MBA: 2046
Warner, Sherman: 412
Warren, Robert: 1959
Warshawsky, Carol: 502
Washburne, Nina: 78
Washington, Alandra: 157
Washington, Alesha: 131
Washington, Eric: 242
Washington, Lara E.: 1077
Wasserman, Gail: 983
Wasserstein, Pam: 246
Watanabe, Tomoyuki: 791
Waterbury, James B.: 1022
Waters, Richard C., Dr.: 1435
Watkins, Ruth Ann: 919
Watson, Alison: 428
Watson, Elizabeth: 1328
Watson, Ian C.: 169
Watson, Tom: 983
Watten, Jan C.: 1735
Watts, Stephen, Dr.: 1616
Wauters, Dirk: 820
Wawrzaszek, Karen: 1202
Wayne, Valerie Rockefeller: 391
Webb, Aaron D., Esq.: 186
Webb, C.A.: 1073
Webb, Janet: 478
Webb, Karim: 1079
Weber, Christopher: 1256
Webster, Robert C., III: 107
Weeden, Alan: 1993
Weeden, Bob: 1993
Weeden, Donald A.: 1993
Weeden, John D.: 1993
Weeden, Leslie: 1993
Weeden, Norm, Ph.D.: 1993
Weeden, William: 1993
Weeks, Kenneth D., Jr., M.D.: 94

Wege, Caitlin: 1270
Wege, Christopher: 1270
Wege, Diana: 1270
Wege, Jonathan: 1270
Wege, Laura: 1270
Wei, Lily: 504
Weil, H.C.: 1900
Weil, Lisa: 384
Weiner, Bennet, Esq.: 2197
Weinert, Daryl: 868
Weingart, Brian: 1614
Weingart, Georgiana: 1384
Weinmann, Gail, M.D.: 2144
Weinstein, Joan: 503
Weir, Candace: 399
Weir, Eileen, Hon.: 1809
Weiser, Mary M.: 67
Weiser, Stuart: 415
Weiss, Carolyn M., C.P.A.: 216
Weiss, Daniel G.: 1079
Weiss, Daniel H.: 292, 506
Weiss, Howard M.: 1162
Weiss, Stephen: 2201
Weiss, Victoria, MBA: 2243
Welch, Alan G.: 1355
Welch, Elizabeth: 273
Welder, John J., V: 1900
Wells, James A., Ph.D.: 2196
Wells, Marion: 2361
Welsh, Suzanne: 235
Welvaert, Frank: 149
Wendel, Clyde F.: 1809
Wenner, Jennifer: 1870
Werbinski, Janice, M.D.: 2002
Wertman, Adlai: 1186
Wesley, Gregory M.: 1170
Wesson, Andre: 1431
West, James R.: 949
West, Mary Beth: 292
West, Meghan: 2361
West, Terry W.: 256
Westermann, Mariet: 201
Western, David: 1962
Westheimer, Sally: 1166
Westphal, Joanne: 2073, 2292
Wetherby, Debra: 189
Wexler, Nancy: 134
Weymouth, Katharine: 128
Whalen, Michael R., Esq.: 272
Wheaton, Tom: 2304
Wheeler, Calvin, M.D.: 2062
Wheeler, Johnnie: 458
Wheeler, Mimi: 89
Wheelock, Pamela: 1346
Wheelock, Vicki, M.D.: 2213
Whelan, Christine: 120
White, A. Dennis: 203
White, Andrea: 274
White, B. Joseph: 1767
White, Benjamin T.: 1099
White, H. Hunter, Jr.: 41
White, Holly E.: 2034
White, Jeremy: 213
White, Kathryn: 486
White, Lauren: 1791
White, Lynn T.: 285
White, Megan: 442
White, Nancy: 653
White, Ridgway H.: 1208
White, Stacy L.: 60
White, Thomas: 1569
Whited, E.F.: 289
Whited-Howell, Mary Amelia: 117
Whiteside, Carol: 1334
Whitfield, Fred: 253, 1156
Whitfield, Terry: 263
Whitridge, Morgan: 202
Whitten, Anthony: 1756
Whittier, Dorothy: 33
Whittington, Kinion E., D.O.: 2249

Whittington, Mary Andrews Self: 1246
Whittle, Andrew, Prof.: 873
Wickett, Xenia: 842
Wickwire, Susan: 147
Wiener, Richard, Ph.D.: 1827
Wiese, Ted: 28
Wigmore, Bill: 1259
Wijnberg, Sandra: 130
Wilcove, David S.: 93
Wilder, Phil: 1434
Wilen, Glenn: 1701
Wilgis, Linda Mason: 147
Wilhelm, Daniel: 1658, 1659
Wilhoite, Charles: 204
Wilkerson, Deborah L.: 1169
Wilkinson, Jerry: 1099
Willard, Thomas R.: 1809
Wille, Leslie: 1554
Willems, Jacques: 820
Willett, Greg: 1112
Williams, Amanda A.: 1325
Williams, Ashley: 2416
Williams, Cheryl: 995
Williams, Christina L.: 2324
Williams, Crystal: 982
Williams, Elizabeth: 1112
Williams, Emelie M.: 268
Williams, Irene: 1016
Williams, Jamie: 211
Williams, Joel T., III: 198
Williams, M. Nancy: 60
Williams, Mike: 1418
Williams, Nick: 1046
Williams, Paul: 694
Williams, Quintin: 153
Williams, Susan E.: 1399
Williamson, Donald: 157
Williamson, W. Bland: 35
Willis, Kerry: 2176
Wills, Thomas E.: 2337
Willson, Janet: 1339
Wilsey, Matt: 258
Wilson, Andrew: 198
Wilson, Barb: 901
Wilson, Christina P.: 1227
Wilson, Dave: 1431
Wilson, Elisheba: 2385
Wilson, Ernest J., III: 1287
Wilson, Gayle: 232
Wilson, George C.: 1073
Wilson, Joanna: 2187
Wilson, Lisa H.: 544
Wilson, Michelle: 332
Wilson, Roxanne: 261
Wilson, Sharon: 1059
Wilson-Oyelaran, Eileen, Dr.: 1767
Wilson-Taylor, Martella: 1340
Wiltsek, Nancy: 1264
Wimes, Ed: 1274
Winbush, Blair: 1992
Wingate, Ashton J.: 677
Wingens, Gary M.: 1266
Wingo, Nancy: 1390
Wiora, Lynne: 153
Wischmeyer, William: 383
Wise, Scott W.: 80
Wiseman, Mary Witten: 1158
Wishnia, Steven: 1354
Wisniewski, Jessica: 1628
Witharana, Rochelle: 1287
Witmer, Jean Hudson: 1181
Witt, John R.: 391
Witter, Brooke: 1721
Witter, Dean, III: 1721
Witter, Inger K.: 486
Witter, Malcolm G.: 1721
Wohlers, Laurence, Ambassador: 868
Wolfe, Jennifer: 458
Wolff, Elizabeth Barthelmes: 154
Wolff, Frances: 25

Wolff, Margaret L.: 134
Wolters, Kate Pew: 273
Wong, Allison: 412
Wong, Brian: 1264
Wong, Ryan Lee: 419
Wood, Anthony C.: 1341
Wood, Donald S., Ph.D.: 2218
Wood, Doug: 694
Wood, E. Jenner, III: 301, 1042
Wood, Elizabeth: 330, 778
Wood, Nadine M.: 748
Woodard, Joan B., Ph.D.: 1827
Woodruff, Judy: 94
Woodruff, Shirley: 1164
Woods, Ellen L.: 2288
Woods, Hank: 1274
Woods, Tom: 1274
Woodward, Christopher C.: 1328
Woodward, Will: 1166
Woolfolk, Brian T.: 228
Woolley-Wilson, Jessie: 1961
Woolliscroft, James O., M.D.: 1314
Worth, Alexi: 399
Worthy, Jo: 1434
Wortman, Suk: 1274
Wright, Doug: 399
Wright, James: 248
Wright, Jason H.: 216
Wright, William H., II: 93, 2046
Wu, Christina: 228
Wu, Shannon: 391
Wulf, Karin A.: 573, 575

Y

Yadav, Uday: 98
Yamauchi, Starla C.: 228
Yamba, A. Zachery: 1266
Yang, Yu-Chung, Ph.D.: 2121
Yang-Johnson, Geri: 1287
Yarberry, Sally: 1520
Yarce, Beto: 901
Yastine, Barbara A.: 1325
Yeaman, Eric K.: 53
Yearley, Steve, Prof.: 331
Yellen, John E., Dr.: 1813
Yelverton, Catherine: 983
Yi, Chen: 705
Yoshida, Takeshi: 775
Youn, Monica: 613
Young, Abigail: 442
Young, Heather M., Ph.D., R.N.: 1282
Young, Jessica: 1756
Young, Mike: 1022
Young, Rick: 1022
Young, Ryan: 1202
Young, Studie: 1099
Youssef, George: 2407
Youssef, Menna M.: 2407
Yu, Karen: 246
Yuknat, David A.: 162
Yuknat, Marcy Kerr: 162
Yun, William Y.: 1335
Yung, Tony: 1218

Z

Zachary, Nedra: 733
Zack, Marilyn: 129
Zafran, Alan: 1247
Zagel, Ellie Frey: 116
Zagieboylo, Cynthia: 2222, 2223
Zagoren, Robert M.: 179
Zajicek, Roger: 269
Zanino, Walter J.: 219
Zaragoza, Jason: 1750
Zarcone, Michael: 203
Zaremby, Justin: 1817

References in index are to entry numbers.

Zavalia de Miguens, Magdalena: 4
Zelenetz, Andrew D., M.D.: 2119
Zell, Helen: 698
Zell, John: 1103
Zheng, Jenny Yu: 391
Zheng, Yixian, Dr.: 1624
Zheng, Yuxing: 1756
Zhuang, Gabrielle: 1779
Ziegler, Melisa: 1611

Ziger, Steven G.: 392
Zimmerman, Kortney: 28
Zinkham, Helena: 356
Zionts, Nancy D., MBA: 1302
Zirkel, Jayne: 1127
Zobel, Katie Allan: 1129
Zobel, Mercedes: 391
Zogopoulos, George, M.D., Ph.D.: 2187
Zohn, Judy: 759

Zola, Gary P., Dr.: 747
Zottoli, Steven J., Ph.D: 2212
Zunick, Robert: 1059
Zuniga, Diana: 1779
Zur, Dafna: 354
Zurfluh, David: 2304
Zwilich, Ellen Taaffe: 130